For my Father and my Mother

*

Preface

This volume describes and comments upon the ways in which American lawyers go about their vital work.

The subject of legal ethics is sometimes understood to be rather narrowly circumscribed by the content of lawyer codes such as two codes written fourteen years apart by the American Bar Association—the 1969 Model Code of Professional Responsibility and the 1983 Model Rules of Professional Conduct. A decade ago or more, lawyer codes also defined the limits that many scholars imposed on their writing in the field and that teachers imposed on their students. With others, I consider those limits to be gratuitously and dangerously narrow. Lawyers do not spin in their own tight orbit. The lawyer codes are not written, do not operate, and cannot be fully understood, without attending to the broader legal, social, political, economic, and intellectual implications of lawyering.

Revolutions are over-reported occurrences in law. Mere twitches of the judicial or legislative pen have sometimes sent specialized legal commentators to their inkwells and word processors to report still another conflagration. Let me not say then that the field of legal ethics has experienced a revolution in the past decade. It certainly has been active. Anyone who has paid the slightest attention to the work of the Kutak Commission must have been struck by the wide and deep controversy that surrounded the Commission's work of drafting rules to guide lawyers.

I should say a word about the use of the phrase "legal ethics" as part of the title to what is written here. The phrase describes the so-called self-regulatory system out of which the legal profession's codes emerge, and the term was so used by Henry Drinker in his 1953 book of that name. It is also employed in the quite different sense of applied moral philosophy in the field of legal service. I use it here in those and possibly other ways, although the potentially ambiguous meaning will, I hope, emerge from the particular context. Although the phrase is both ambiguous and timeworn, its use should be preserved, and expanded. I use it here both for its familiar and traditional descriptions as well as for topics that are beyond the ken of writers of an earlier age. My purpose in resorting to such an imperfect vessel is to attempt to reshape it. I hope to contribute something to the ongoing effort of shifting the agenda of discussion about lawyers away from the confining traditions of the etiquette and pettiness of law practice to a much broader and more socially and morally important plane.

No one knows better than a scholar that most thought is derivative, the best of it only selectively so. My own debts and gratitude are great. This book began at the suggestion of my much-missed friend and colleague, the late Professor J. Morris Clark, and then became a joint undertaking with him. Many hours of talk and collaboration with him provided the basic orientation and much of the detailed conception of the moral and professional responsibility of lawyers that underlies my present views. Drafts and a wealth of research materials that his family found in Morris's files and kindly made available to me have been invaluable at many points, particularly in the sections on group legal services, legal services to the poor, advertising, lawyer competence, legal education, and the sociology of the legal profession. I have incorporated here much valuable work from early drafts that Morris was working on at the time of his death.

Many other scholars in the burgeoning field of legal ethics and professional responsibility have also aided me greatly with their work and in many cases with conversation, manuscripts of work in progress, and reprints. Numerous practicing lawyers and judges have served a similar function as critics and commentators, as well as supplying role examples of how to practice and administer law as a profession to serve the public. None supplied a more powerful and humane vision, and more selflessly, than the late Robert J. Kutak.

Deans and faculty at three law schools—the Cornell Law School, the University of Minnesota Law School, and the University of Southern California Law Center—have contributed lavish measures of encouragement and thought. My colleague and friend, Dean Peter W. Martin, has sustained my efforts in the past several years with great wisdom, interest, and generosity. Librarians at each of those institutions responded to many requests with dispatch, skill, and good cheer. Students in courses and seminars have been willing contributors and helpful critics for many tentative ideas. To many research assistants I owe profound gratitude—particularly to Harris Lindenfeld, Toni Sutliff, Richard Braman, Patrice Halbach, Wendy Legge, Mark Saunders, Karl Slifer, Dennis Slivinski, David Williams, and Richard Wilson. In the last months, the editing assistance of Martha J. Crowe has been indispensable. They along with many others can justly claim credit for much of what is useful and true here. The errors, of course, are mine. None of those, I will vouch, can be attributed to Marybeth M. Bloomquist, Jylanda M. Diles, Valerie W. King, and Carolyn Lynn, who diligently, accurately, and patiently performed the repetitive tasks of reducing vagrant thoughts, and second thoughts, to clear typescript.

Most importantly, I express to my family—Nancy, Catherine, and Peter—my love and gratitude for what they bore with patience and understanding.

Table of Contents

CHAPTER THREE. PROFESSIONAL DISCIPLINE OF LAWYERS

PART TWO. LAWYERS AND CLIENTS

CHAPTER FOUR. THE CLIENT-LAWYER RELATIONSHIP

CHAPTER FIVE. LAWYER COMPETENCE

CHAPTER SIX. LAWYERS AS CLIENT CONFIDANTS

CHAPTER SEVEN. CONFLICT OF INTEREST

CHAPTER EIGHT. SPECIAL CONFLICTS OF INTEREST TOPICS

CHAPTER NINE. CLIENT–LAWYER CONTRACTS

PART THREE. THE ROLE OF LAWYERS

CHAPTER TEN. THE ADVERSARY SYSTEM

CHAPTER ELEVEN. LAWYERS AS ADVOCATES

CHAPTER TWELVE. LAWYER FORENSICS

CHAPTER THIRTEEN. LAWYERS AS COUNSELORS

PART FOUR. DELIVERY OF LEGAL SERVICES

CHAPTER FOURTEEN. THE NEED FOR A LAWYER

CHAPTER FIFTEEN. THE RIGHT TO PRACTICE LAW

CHAPTER SIXTEEN. FORMS AND FUNDING OF LAW PRACTICE

MODERN LEGAL ETHICS

*

Part One
LAWYERS AND THE LEGAL PROFESSION

Chapter One
THE WORLD OF LAWYERS

Table of Sections

---

§ 1.1 LAWYERS

Lawyers as Viewed by Themselves and Others

Lawyers, more than the members of any other profession, enjoy power, prestige, income, and the genuine affection of both clients and nonclients. But, also probably more than any other profession, lawyers are the target of some of the most cutting, wide-sweeping, and relentless criticism. Lawyers in fact occupy a place of ambivalence in public life. Their work makes them indispensable to many; what they do at work makes them loathed by many others. Many persons who speak ill of lawyers [1] would be delighted if a son or daughter were admitted to law school.[2] In part, social ambivalence about lawyers reflects the variety, and contradictory nature, of the work that different lawyers do. In part, it reflects the reality that, on lawyers' own terms, there are both good and bad lawyers. And, in part, it also reflects genuine public misinformation, misunderstanding, and confusion about lawyers' roles. Many lawyers themselves are not free of ambivalence and confusion about their own roles and work.

The Role of Lawyers in Society

Why should a well-ordered society have lawyers? If a system of justice were being designed for the United States, from the ground up, should it include anything nearly resembling the present legal profession? Sev-

[1] On public-opinion polls on the legal profession, see infra at n.9.

[2] See Wall St.J., Feb. 15, 1977, at 1, col.4 (Roper poll of parents' preferences for children's future careers rank medicine, teaching, and law as first three); 64 ABA J. 34 (1978)(report of social science researcher's survey of prestige of professions, finding only university professors and physicians ahead of lawyers).

eral reasons can be advanced for the proposition that lawyers as America knows them are necessary. First, knowledge about the law and legal procedures is, to some extent, arcane and inaccessible for many of those subject to it. Whether justifiably or not, much of modern-day life is subject to extensive government regulation whose sheer volume requires extensive training by education and practice to permit efficient answers to questions about regulation. Persons skilled and trained in deciphering the law are necessary in order that legal rules are not applied arbitrarily, randomly, or unfairly. They are economically useful to the extent that the service that is provided is available at a price and quality that are superior to the services of possible competitors. Second, even if persons involved in a legal process could be knowledgeable about law, their self-interest and emotional commitment might prevent them from regarding their legal position with sufficient detachment to permit effective functioning within the legal system and, perhaps, to acquire understanding about the acceptability of personal impositions by the system.

Those justifications doubtless have force, but they are relatively culture-bound. Redesign of a legal system might have as one of its objectives the simplification of law in order to make it commonly intelligible. And professional detachment indeed is desirable in the present American adversarial system, but perhaps more because of its problematically contentious nature than because of any necessary order of things (§ 10.1). If those assessments are accurate, then one may wonder whether continuation of the status of lawyers depends to a great extent upon continuation of the present system of esoteric and extensive regulation and contentious representation in the adversary system.

Hero/Villain Myths

Writing by and about lawyers portrays them in two unrecognizably conflicting guises. On the one hand, lawyers are portrayed as helping, self-sacrificial individuals who heroically protect clients against otherwise overwhelming adversaries or social forces, often at great personal sacrifice.[3] Alternatively, but still in the same helping mode, lawyers are portrayed as wise and considerate counselors to troubled clients in need of advice that ranges widely across the landscape of human misery. Yet lawyers are also portrayed as little more than the accomplices of gangsters and the facilitators of the projects of sinister and evil clients. The extreme sentiment, which is by no means confined to Shakespearean butchers, is to abolish lawyers.[4] Terms such as "hired gun," "mouthpiece," and worse from the argot of thieves can also be found in the mouths of respectable citizens when referring to at least some lawyers. Neither image bears much correspondence to the social realities that are represented by studies of lawyers at work. Each mythologizes lawyers through partial and distorted versions of that social reality.

The Hero Mythology[5]

Too much writing about the legal profession—almost all of the genre coming from the

3 While the image is overblown, it suggests a lawyer self-perception that law work is both rewarding and pleasant. See Wall St.J., Sept. 29, 1982, at 35, col.4 (Gallup survey of self-reported stress in occupations showed lawyers almost as low as insurance executives in degree to which they thought work involved "great deal" of stress).

4 Henry VI, Pt. II, act iv, scene 2 (1590) ("The first thing we do, let's kill all the lawyers."). The abolition of the legal profession is a core concept of much utopian thinking. See M.Frankel, Partisan Justice 4 (1980); Auerbach, A Plague of Lawyers, Harper's Magazine at 37 (Oct.1977). The utopian ideal of a lawyerless society found expression in America's early history. The trustees of the colony of Georgia founded it in 1732 without lawyers because they planned "a happy, flourishing colony . . . free from that pest and scourge of mankind called lawyers." (Georgia Dep't of Human Resources v. Sistrunk, 249 Ga. 543, 291 S.E.2d 524, 531 (1982)(dissenting opinion of Smith, J.)(quoting Coulter, Georgia—A Short History 74 (1947)). See also, e.g., T.More, Utopia 114 (E.Surtz ed.1964)(More, himself a reknowned lawyer and judge of the sixteenth century, envisioned total banishment of lawyers, "who cleverly manipulate cases and cunningly argue legal points"); H. Melville, Typee 151 (Library of America ed.1982).

5 See Mindes & Aycock, Trickster, Hero, Helper: A Report on the Lawyer Image, 1982 Am.B.Found. Research J. 177.

pens of lawyers—attempts to perpetuate a larger-than-life image. Typical is the following description of "the lawyer" in American history:

> At times he has been called upon to render services above and beyond the call of purely selfish duty. He provided leadership in the American Revolution. He drew the constitutions of the Federal and State governments. He helped to write and to interpret the basic documents of government. He has the exclusive right to practice law. This means that he has an obligation to implement such constitutional guarantees as the "equal protection of the law." But above all this he has spiritual obligations which may be more difficult to define but are none the less compelling in their applications.
>
> Lawyers Are Very Remarkable People [6]

Those sentiments present overall a distorted view of the role of lawyers in America. They are one-sided because they neglect to add several counter-observations that also might be made. Probably a majority of lawyers at the time of the American Revolution were royalists who were openly sympathetic to England. Federal and state constitutions were drafted only in part by lawyers and often as self-interested attempts to protect client or other interest-group prerogatives. The basic laws that lawyers drafted were often seen by those subject to them (slave laws, peonage laws, laws that prevented injured workers from recovering from their employers) as twisted and unjust. The exclusive right to practice law is sometimes abused by lawyers as a self-arrogated privilege invoked to stifle desirable competition. Equal protection of the laws has certainly seen far more lawyers make far more money in legal fees resisting claims of its violation than ever vindicated the rights of the oppressed. And the great mass of lawyers spend a predominant amount of their time making money from fee-generating clients, and do little else. Like many other groups in a dynamic society, lawyers have a fascinating history, even fascinating to nonlawyers. The notion that lawyers are a little more like gods than men, however, is Law Day puffery designed primarily for lawyer self-consumption.

Lawyers and the Public

Tangible indications are not lacking that public esteem for the legal profession is quite low,[7] a matter that has hardly escaped the attention of lawyers.[8] A 1978 Harris poll of public attitudes toward sixteen public institutions found lawyers ranked very near the bottom with advertising agencies, labor unions, and Congress.[9] The public distrust of lawyers, as with other facts about them, should not be viewed in isolation. Similar polls of the public mood about other institutions show a striking decline in the positive feelings that Americans once had toward many institutions such as government, business, labor unions, and most other important

[6] AALS, Selected Readings on the Legal Profession 4-5 (1962).

[7] Antilawyer sentiment among the public is also well documented at earlier periods in history. E.g., M.Bloomfield, American Lawyers in a Changing Society, 1776-1876, at 39-40 (1976)(quoting speech to students by president Dwight of Yale); R.Ellis, The Jeffersonian Crisis 161-64 (1971)(various attacks by radical groups on legal profession, judges, and existing common-law distribution of property); C.Warren, A History of the American Bar 112-13 (1911)(antilawyer riots by debtors in the colonies during the economic crisis of 1769-1770); Ala. Code of Ethics, § 9, 118 Ala. xxiii, xxvi (1898)(on assumption that prejudice against lawyers was widespread, warns lawyers against pandering to "unjust" popular sentiment against lawyers).

[8] Hensley, Why People Don't Like Lawyers, and What You Can Do about It, 70 ABA J. 90 (1984); LawPoll: Lawyers Concerned about their Image and Credibility, 69 ABA J. 440 (1983); LawPoll: What Bothers Lawyers, 67 ABA J. 1450, 1451 (1981); Cribbett, Professional at Bay, 12 Forum 318 (1976); Waltz, Unpopularity of Lawyers in America, 25 Cleve.St.L.Rev. 143 (1976); Waltz, Some Thoughts on the Legal Profession Public Image, 23 DePaul L.Rev. 651 (1974); Thomason, What the Public Thinks of Lawyers, 46 N.Y.S.B.J. 151 (1974); Hertzberg, Watergate: Has the Image of the Lawyer Been Diminished?, 79 Comm.L.J. 73 (1974).

[9] Time, Apr.10, 1978, at 56. See also, N.Y.Times, Aug. 22, 1976, at 32, col.4 (Gallop poll showed only 25 percent of American public rated honesty and ethical standards of lawyers as "high," which put credibility of lawyers behind doctors, engineers, college teachers, and journalists (55, 48, 44, and 33 percent), and ahead of building contractors, business executives, senators, congressmen, labor union leaders, and advertising executives (22, 19, 19, 14, 13, and 11 percent)). Gallup polls in 1983 and 1981 showed similar results. See Wall St.J., Nov.2, 1983, at 33, col.5; Wall St.J., Sept. 20, 1981, at 36, col.1.

segments of American life.[10] While events such as the extensive involvement of lawyers in Watergate crimes, which distressed lawyers and aroused the public, are events about the legal profession, they are also symptomatic of failures of structure and will that extend far beyond the legal profession.

It must also be reckoned that, as with smoke and the probable presence of fire, the persistence and volume of public criticism of the legal profession are indications of some truth. At the same time, however, "there is ample sociological evidence of distortion in the other direction. There are many reasons why the legal profession is a convenient scapegoat for a variety of groups in society." [11] Among the reasons are the following. First, some lawyers are bad people and, because of the power that lawyers can wield, have the power to spread their evil far. Second, many lawyers deal with people in desperate trouble but, unlike ministers or social workers, the work of lawyers is not to give solace to a troubled soul's innermost being, but to deal with a limited range of external events. And as has become standard to observe, half of the lawyers in litigated cases will represent losing litigants. Third, as mentioned, law is and always will be complex. Complexity is not always the result of lawyers' work, but lawyers are able to manipulate results because of their skill in using complexity to a client's advantage. All of this typically transpires in ways that baffle and confuse nonlawyers who must deal with the legal system. Fourth, the practice of law in the United States is very much a free-market service in which the highest bidders are typically the wealthy and dominant powers. Lawyers thus emerge in the eyes of some members of the public as the lackeys of financial and industrial interests. Fifth, by their roles, many lawyers are forced into public performances that may appear unsavory. The most obvious illustration is the criminal defense lawyer. It is probably accurate, if controversial, to say that defense of persons accused of crime has led to more public antipathy toward the legal profession than any other cause. Yet, of course, it is both indispensable and honorable that lawyers continue in that and other difficult roles.

Language of Lawyers

A curious dualism afflicts the words used to describe members of the legal profession. *Lawyers*, who are called that by nearly everyone who isn't one, sometimes prefer to call themselves *attorneys*. Cribbing definitional lines might be erected here, perhaps between *lawyers* as the generic term for anyone graduated from law school and *attorneys* as those who actually represent clients or, more narrowly, who represent clients in court.[12] *Attorney* at common law described a person who served as a pleading drafter, but now the usage applies to all lawyerly roles. Since neither is particularly invidious and *lawyer* is shorter and strikes this ear as more elegant, and possibly a trifle less pompous, it will be used here throughout.

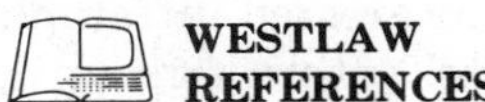
WESTLAW REFERENCES

topic(45) & opinion attitude critic! /3 public society social /s lawyer attorney counsel** (law legal /2 profession practice)

di attorney

§ 1.2 LAWYERS IN OTHER COUNTRIES

General

Lawyers practice in most of the civilizations of the world.[13] But the practices and philosophies of lawyers practicing in other legal cultures very often bear little resemblance to those of lawyers in the United States. Even in England, lawyers function in significantly

[10] S.Lipset & W.Schneider, The Confidence Gap: Business, Labor, and Government in the Public Mind (1983).

[11] T.Parsons, Essays in Sociological Theory 372 (1954).

[12] For a discussion of these and other variations, see Safire, On Language: We Wuz Robbed, N.Y. Times Magazine, Jan.31, 1982, at 13-14.

[13] Societies exist, however, in which all court proceedings go forward without lawyers of any kind. See M.Gluckman, The Judicial Process among the Barotse of Northern Rhodesia 15 (2d ed.1967).

different ways despite the fact that the English barrister and solicitor are derived from the same historial roots as the American lawyer. In other countries as well, whose governments operate under concepts of democracy similar to those held in the United States, the differences in the operating styles and attitude of lawyers may be great.[14] Needless to say, the role of lawyers is often profoundly different in legal systems with assumptions and objectives that are very different from those of the United States.[15]

Socialist Societies [16]

Lawyers in some socialist societies tend to reject the individualism that is characteristic of American lawyers. Instead, their guiding philosophy is that a lawyer, like all workers, is devoted to the collective good of society. No duty to a client that is inconsistent with the collective good can transcend that higher duty.[17] Those attitudes seem to typify the actual work of lawyers in socialist countries. At least in theory, significant differences could exist, however, in the extent to which the collective good might contemplate vigorous advocacy, for example, of a person accused of crime, in order to further collective goals of a just society.[18]

Western Europe [19]

Lawyers practicing in most of the countries of Western Europe function within inquisitorial judicial systems and under laws that are largely codified. As with American lawyers, all of those legal systems require rigorous

[14] See generally: *Japan.* Takao, The Urbanization of Lawyers and Its Functional Significance: Expansion in the Range of Work Activities and Change in Social Role, 13 L.Japan 20 (1980); Henderson, Japanese Lawyers: Types and Roles in th4e Legal Profession, 3 L.& Soc'y Rev. 411 (1968–69); Hattori, The Legal Profession in Japan: Its Historical Development and Present State, in Law in Japan: The Legal Order in a Changing Society (A.Von Mehren ed.1963).

India. Kidder, Formal Litigation and Professional Insecurity: Legal Entrepreneurship in South India, 9 L.& Soc'y Rev. 11 (1974); Galanter, Introduction: The Study of the Indian Legal Profession, 3 L.& Soc'y Rev. 201 (1968–69); Von Mehren, Law and Legal Education in India: Some Observations, 78 Harv.L.Rev. 1180 (1965).

[15] E.g., Lawyers in the Third World: Comparative and Developmental Perspectives (C.Dias, R.Luckham, D.Lynch & J.Paul eds.1981).

[16] See generally:

USSR and Eastern Bloc Countries. L.Shelley, Lawyers in Soviet Work Life (1984); G.Cameron, The Soviet Lawyer and His System: A Historical and Bibliographic Study (1978); R.Wortman, The Development of a Russian Legal Consciousness, ch. 1 (1976); H.Berman, Justice in the U.S.S.R. 68, 81 (rev.ed.1963); S.Klucherov, Courts, Lawyers, and Trials under the Last Three Tsars (1953); Harper, A Rare Look into Soviet Courts, 69 ABA J. 1492 (1983); Butler, Foreign Impression of Russian Law to 1800: Some Reflections, in Russian Law: History and Political Perspectives 64-92 (W.Butler ed.1977); Zile, Soviet Advocatura Twenty-five Years after Stalin, in Soviet Law after Stalin 207-37 (D.Barry, F.Feldbrugge, G.Ginsburg & P.Maggs eds.1979); Barry & Berman, The Soviet Legal Profession, 82 Harv.L.Rev. 1 (1968); Friedman & Zile, Soviet Legal Profession: Recent Developments in Law and Practice, 1964 Wisc.L.Rev. 32; Razi, Legal Education and the Role of the Lawyer in the Soviet Union and the Countries of Eastern Europe, 48 Calif.L. Rev. 776 (1960).

People's Republic of China. V.Li, Law Without Lawyers (1977); Symposium: The Developing Role of Law and Lawyers in China, 46 Alb.L.Rev. 687 (1982); Jones, Reflections on the Modern Chinese Legal System, 59 Wash.U.L.Rev. 1221 (1982); Gayle, Law and Lawyers in China, 64 ABA J. 348 (1978); Epstein, An American in Peking: Adapting to Anti-legal Rituals, 3 Distr.Law. 10 (June/July 1979); Cohen, Reflections on the Criminal Process in China, 68 J.Crim.L. & Criminology 323 (1977).

Other. Garlicki, Legal Profession in Poland, 24 St. Louis L.J. 486 (1980).

[17] That is particularly true in the area of the economy, requiring lawyers for state enterprises to assure their clients' observance of "socialist reality." Markovitz, Socialist vs. Bourgeois Rights—An East-West Comparison, 45 U.Chi.L.Rev. 612, 629 (1978).

[18] That possibility seems to be ignored in rough sketches such as, e.g., D'Amato & Eberle, Three Models of Legal Ethics, 27 St.Louis L.J. 761, 770-72 (1983).

[19] See generally Lawyers in Their Social Setting (D.MacCormick ed.1976)(France, West Germany, Italy, Norway, Scotland):

France. Trai Le, The French Legal Profession: A Prisoner of Its Glorious Past?, 15 Cornell Int'l L.J. 63 (1982); LePaulle, Law Practice in France, 50 Colum.L. Rev. 945 (1950); Renfield Corp. v. E.Remy Martin & Co., 98 F.R.D. 442, 444 (D.Del.1982)(description of categories of practice within French legal profession).

Germany. D.Rueschemeyer, Lawyers and Their Society (1973)(comparative examination of functions of German and American lawyers); Luban, The Sources of Legal Ethics: A German-American Comparison, in Rabels Zeitschrift für Ausländisches unter internationales Privatrecht (1983); Koitz, The Role and Functions of the Legal Professions in the Federal Republic of Germany, 11 Internationales Kongress für Rechtsvergleichung 69 (1982); Willig, The Bar in the Third Reich, 20 Am.J. Leg.Hist. 1 (1976); W.Weyrauch, The Personality of Lawyers: A Comparative Study of Subjective Factors in Law education and examinations and limit practice to admitted lawyers. As a very general characteristic, the inquisitorial system tends to deemphasize the role of the lawyer in litigation. Lawyers also function extensively outside the courtroom, dealing in a wide variety of property and contractual arrangements. Often the ranks of lawyers are rigidly divided among courtroom practitioners and office advisers and may include others, not regarded as lawyers in their own culture, who perform work very much like in-house counsel in the United States.[20] On the whole, however, lawyers are less extensively involved with business clients. For whatever reasons, it seems that lawyers in Europe are thought of by the public in derogatory ways that strongly resemble some segments of public opinion in the United States.[21]

British Commonwealth

One of the remarkable vestiges of English colonialism is the extent to which English law and legal institutions took firm root in many former colonies.[22] Particularly in countries such as Australia [23] and Canada,[24] in which the process of political separation has been gradual and on the whole peaceful, the forms of English legal practice are carried out, in some instances, with fidelity that approaches mimicry. The process of imitation, which is also common in newly independent former colonies in Africa, is part of the lingering prestige still associated with the formerly dominant colonial power.

A salient feature of legal practice in England and Wales is the divided bar of barristers and solicitors.[25] Barristers alone are admitted to practice before the trial courts of general jurisdiction and the appellate courts.[26] The more numerous branch, solicitors, perform primarily an office practice and may try cases before the inferior trial courts.[27] Continuation of the barrister-solicitor differentiation might be strongly influenced by class instincts. Through a system of class differentiation that most Americans find bewilderingly complex, English social regard still probably

(1964)(based on interviews with German lawyers); Cohn, The German Attorney—Experiences with a Unified Profession, 10 Int'l & Comp.L.Q. 103 (1961).

Italy. M.Cappelletti, J.Merryman & J.Perillo, The Italian Legal System 86-110 (1967); M.Cappelletti & J.Perillo, Italian Civil Procedure chs. 2 & 3 (1965).

[20] Renfield Corp. v. E.Remy Martin & Co., 98 F.R.D. 442, 444 (D.Del.1982)(divisions of French profession into *avocat* (courtroom and advice to clients), *conseil juridique* (independently practicing legal advisers), and employees of corporations and other businesses that give legal advice).

[21] Trai Le, The French Legal Profession: A Prisoner of Its Glorious Past?, 15 Cornell Int'l L.J. 63, 63-64 (1982) (reporting French television poll that indicated that 48 percent of French public thought that *avocats* were "money suckers;" 14 percent, that they had no conscience; 14 percent, that their wrongful acts were protected by the French bar).

[22] See generally F.Phillips, The Evolving Legal Profession in the Commonwealth (1978). On Commonwealth countries other than Australia and Canada, see, e.g., E.Lewis, Legal Ethics: A Guide to Professional Conduct for South African Attorneys (1982).

[23] See generally M.Sexton, The Legal Mystique: The Role of Lawyers in Australian Society (1982); Professional Practice Handbook (K.Andrews, P.Hamilton & G.Mann eds.1982); R.Tomasic, Lawyers and Their Work in New South Wales (1978); J.Disney, Lawyers (1977); Australian Lawyers and Social Change (A.Hambly & J.Goldring eds.1976).

[24] See generally Law Society of Upper Canada, Professional Conduct Handbook (1978)(applicable to all of Canada, except Quebec, which has a civil law system); Canadian Bar Association, Code of Professional Conduct (1975). See also, e.g., MacFarlane, The Legal Profession in Canada: A Research Perspective and Prospectus, 28 Chitty's L.J. 50 (1980).

[25] See generally B.Abel-Smith & R.Stevens, Lawyers and the Courts (1967). See also, e.g., P.Atiyah, Law and Modern Society (1983); M.Zander, The State of Knowledge about the English Legal Profession (1980); D.Podmore, Solicitors and the Wider Community (1980); A.Manchester, Modern Legal History of England and Wales (1980); H.Cecil, The English Judge 12-26 (1970); Webster, The Bar of England and Wales: Past, Present and Future, in Legal Institutions Today: English and American Approaches Compared 84-108 (J.Jones ed.1977). The English legal profession was subjected to a thorough review by a commission headed by Sir Henry Benson, an accountant. See Royal Commission on Legal Services, Final Report (1979).

[26] See generally W.Boulton, Conduct and Etiquette at the Bar (6th ed.1975). See also, e.g., Monopolies and Mergers Commission, Barrister's Services: A Report on the Supply by Her Majesty's Counsel Alone of their Services (1976); T.Daniel, The Lawyers: The Inns of Court: The Home of the Common Law (1976); W.Richardson, A History of the Inns of Court (1975); W.Prest, The Inns of Court (1972).

[27] See generally Law Society, A Guide to the Professional Conduct of Solicitors (1974); T.Lund, Guide to the Professional Conduct of Solicitors (1960). See also

holds that barristers are gentlefolk and solicitors are in trade.[28] Part of the commonality of solicitors is reflected in the nature of the practice, dealing extensively with actual clients and their immediate problems unlike barristers who are normally "briefed" on a new matter by a solicitor and thus rarely deal directly with clients.[29]

WESTLAW REFERENCES

di barrister

di solicitor

§ 1.3 HISTORY OF THE LEGAL PROFESSION

State of Legal History about the Legal Profession

If not the oldest profession, the practice of law is certainly ancient.[30] Yet an adequate history of the legal profession remains to be written, although the attention of serious legal historians is beginning to be directed toward the legal profession.[31] Some have been attempted, but have foundered seriously on erroneous assumptions or starting points. Too often those histories have been mere celebrations of elite lawyers and their bar organizations without much critical relief.[32] Some histories fail to resist the assumption that lawyers and their work have always been comparable to present, known conditions,[33] or the equally mistaken notion that lawyers in some distant age were better loved, more respected.[34]

Also to be resisted is the temptation to mark the history of lawyers by the history of their bar associations or other organizational structures. At one time, for example, histories of the legal profession written by lawyers who were not historians popularized the ideas that lawyers in America enjoyed a "golden age" in the early decades of the nineteenth

G.Graham-Green, Cordery's Law Relating to Solicitors (1981); H.Kirk, Portrait of a Profession: A History of the Solicitor's Profession, 1100 to the Present Day (1977); Monopolies and Mergers Commission, Services of Solicitors in England and Wales: A Report on the Supply of Services of Solicitors in England and Wales in Relation to Restrictions on Advertising (1976); C.Wickenden, The Modern Family Solicitor (1975); M.Birks, Gentlemen of the Law (1960); Murch, The Role of Solicitors in Divorce Proceedings, 40 Mod.L.Rev. 625 (1977); Note, Professional Discipline of Solicitors in England, 75 Mich.L.Rev. 1732 (1977); Leach, The New Look in Disciplinary Enforcement in England, 61 ABA J. 212 (1975).

28 B.Bledstein, The Culture of Professionalism 6 (1976); K.Charlton, The Education of the Professions in the Sixteenth Century, in Education and the Professions 21 (T.Cook ed.1973).

29 On the "cab-rank" rule and the role of the barrister's clerk, see § 10.2.2.

30 For a tracing of the English legal profession from before the end of the thirteenth century into the fourteenth, see 1 F.Pollock & F.Maitland, The History of English Law Before the Time of Edward I, at 211-220 (1923). On lawyers in colonial America, in addition to other works cited here, see A.Roeber, Faithful Magistrates and Republican Lawyers: Creators of Virginia Legal Culture, 1680-1810 (1981); G.Gawalt, The Promise of Power: The Emergence of the Legal Profession in Massachusetts, 1760-1840 (1978); R.Boden, The Colonial Bar and the American Revolution (1976); J.Main, The Social Structure of Revolutionary America 203-206 (1965); Klein, From Community to Status: The Development of the Legal Profession in Colonial New York, 60 N.Y.Hist. 136 (1979); Detweiler, Ben Franklin's "Dirty Pettifoggers," 59 ABA J. 1165 (1973). On more recent American history, e.g., J.Johnson, American Legal Culture, 1908-1940 (1981); J.Auerbach, Unequal Justice: Lawyers and Social Change in Modern America (1976); L.Friedman, A History of American Law, chs. xi-xii (1973).

31 See, e.g., The New High Priests: Lawyers in Post-Civil War America (G.Gawalt ed.1984); G.Gawalt, The Promise of Power: The Emergence of the Legal Profession in Massachusetts, 1760-1840 (1979); M.Bloomfield, American Lawyers in a Changing Society, 1776-1876 (1976); J.Auerbach, Unequal Justice: Lawyers and Social Change in Modern America (1976); Hurst, The Legal Profession, 1966 Wisc.L.Rev. 967.

32 See generally the critical introduction in Lawyers in Early Modern Europe and America (W.Prest ed.1981), at 11-14. The entire history of American lawyers can hardly be met with accolades. Most obviously, the entire legal structure created to maintain the institution of black slavery in the United States was the work of lawyers. See Wiecek, Latimer: Lawyers, Abolitionists, and the Problem of Unjust Laws, in Antislavery Reconsidered: New Perspectives on the Abolitionists 219 (L.Perry & M.Fellman eds.1979).

33 For an example of a more critical stance, see, e.g., Langbein, The Criminal Trial Before Lawyers, 45 U.Chi. L.Rev. 263 (1978)(on the very recent appearance of lawyers for both prosecution and defense in the trial of criminal cases).

34 B.Tuchman, A Distant Mirror: The Calamitous 14th Century 53-54 (1978)(in 1340 France, doctors were admired, lawyers universally hated and mistrusted); id. 373-74 (peasant rioters during June 1381 Peasants Revolt in England concentrated on lawyers and judges as their principal oppressors).

century and then entered an "era of decadence" during the Jacksonian era in the middle third of that century, primarily by paying attention to admission standards and the status of bar associations.[35]

Another common, and equally erroneous, assumption is that lawyers have a history divorced from the social, political, and intellectual history of their times. It has, for example, only recently come to be appreciated that the organization of lawyers into bar associations, the creation of educational and other admission barriers to law practice, the beginnings of a concept of unauthorized practice, and similar "guild" aspects of lawyer organizations were not unique to lawyers. During the same period—roughly 1860 to 1890—that those events were unfolding in the American legal profession, many other professional and working groups experienced parallel development.[36] Indeed, the similarities in the history of lawyers, doctors, educators, and other professional groups are much more striking than their differences. And there are interesting parallels between lawyers and such nonprofessional groups as farmers and manual workers.[37]

WESTLAW REFERENCES

history colonial (13th 14th 15th 16th 17th 18th 19th +1 century) /6 law legal /2 profession practice

§ 1.4 LAWYER DEMOGRAPHY

§ 1.4.1 *Statistical Profile of Lawyers*[38]

Growth of the American Legal Profession

The number of lawyers in the United States far exceeds, by absolute number or ratio, the number in any other legal culture. As of 1978, two-thirds of the lawyers in the world practiced law in the United States.[39] Since 1870 the ratio of lawyers in the United States to the general population has fallen from one lawyer for every 970 persons to one lawyer for every 376 persons in 1984.[40] As the following table shows, the increasing number of lawyers has not been steady but has been concentrated in two periods. One followed the Civil War and saw the number of lawyers more than double between 1870 and 1890. The rate of growth in lawyers' numbers then slowed considerably. The ratio generally rose

35 A prominent figure in the creation of that history was Roscoe Pound. See R.Pound, The Lawyer from Antiquity to Modern Times (1953), derived in part from Pound's earlier articles and other short pieces. See also C.Warren, A History of the American Bar (1911); 2 A.-H.Chroust, The Rise of the Legal Profession in America 283-87 (1965). Cf. J.Hurst, The Growth of American Law: The Law Makers 366 (1950)(description of post-Revolutionary "golden era" of political influence of lawyers but no corresponding maligning of Jacksonian era).

For studies disputing the idea of the "golden age" of law in the early nineteenth century, see, e.g., M.Bloomfield, American Lawyers in a Changing Society, 1776-1876, at 136 ff. (1976); Teachout, Book Review, 2 Vt. L.Rev. 229, 239-49 (1977). The social status and prestige of lawyers reportedly has remained constant over much of American history. See Tyree & Smith, Occupational Hierarchy in the United States: 1789-1969, 56 Soc. Forces 881 (1976).

36 B.Bledstein, The Culture of Professionalism 184-190 (1976)(social history of American lawyers in the context of cross-professional comparison).

37 See G. Gawalt, The Promise of Power: The Emergence of the Legal Profession in Massachusetts, 1760-1840, at 4 (1979).

38 Two general sources of statistics on lawyers are available; unfortunately, their figures disagree. One is the information collected on "lawyers and judges" by the Census Bureau, primarily from census poller reports. Census Bureau data appears in such publications as the bureau's Statistical Abstract. The other source is data gathered by the American Bar Association, primarily from listings in various lawyer directories, principally Martindale-Hubbell. The major difference is that the ABA figures list any lawyer admitted to practice, whether or not the person continues to practice. The Census Bureau data excludes nonpractitioners—retired, unemployed, and second-career lawyers who, although admitted to practice, do not do so. Unless otherwise noted, information in this section is based on Census Bureau material.

A new demographic profile of the legal profession is being prepared by the American Bar Foundation under the direction of researcher Barbara A. Curran. Results will appear in a series of monographs on groups within the profession.

39 P.Stern, Lawyers on Trial xvi (1980).

40 Assuming a lawyer population of 622,000 in 1983 (69 ABA J. 1367 (1983)) and a general population of 234,000,000 (Statistical Abstract of the United States table 6 (1984)).

again until a second increase in the number of lawyers began in the 1960s. Significant growth in lawyer numbers occurred in the 1950s, 1960s, and 1970s. Since the 1970s, the lawyer growth rate has been much greater than at any other period during the last century.

LAWYER-GENERAL POPULATION RATIO—1870-1980 [41]

	Lawyers (thousands)	Population (millions)	Ratio
1870	41	39.8	1:970
1880	64	50.2	1:784
1890	90	63.0	1:700
1900	108	76.0	1:704
1910	115	92.0	1:800
1920	123	105.7	1:859
1930	161	122.8	1:763
1940	182	131.7	1:724
1950	184	150.7	1:819
1960	218	179.3	1:822
1970	274	203.2	1:742
1980	530	226.6	1:428

Most of the large increase in the number of lawyers has occurred since the mid-1960s. In fact, the number of lawyers admitted to practice in 1966 was still virtually the same as the number admitted during each of the postwar boom years of 1949-1951.[42] The number of newly admitted lawyers annually was approximately 10,000 for well over a decade.[43] The number of lawyers increased from 322,000 in 1972 to 630,000 ten years later.[44] The American Bar Foundation estimates that the number of lawyers will reach one million by the year 2000.[45]

One of the distractions of large numbers in a time series is that they are sometimes viewed in isolation. For example, many lawyers who have become aware of the impressive figures indicating absolute growth in the size of the legal profession in the last fifteen years have been alarmed that the profession has become seriously overcrowded.[46] When considered in comparison to other personal service industries, however, the law profession can be seen to be only the last of them to have expanded to match a new technological and managerial way of running business and government. Moreover, the expansion of the numbers of lawyers in a time of a rapidly growing American economy since the Second World War matches periods of rapid growth of professions in similar periods of rapid economic expansion, such as after the Civil War.[47] The incomes of lawyers have also risen sharply in recent years along with their numbers. Census Bureau figures indicate that lawyer gross receipts grew from $17 billion in 1977 to $34 billion in 1982.[48] The new lawyers have not surged into a particular segment of law practice; recent graduates have found employment in virtually the same ratios as did lawyers of a decade earlier.[49]

§ 1.4.2 *Minorities in Law*

Historical and Continuing Underrepresentation

The small number of minority lawyers in the United States is a problem that has proved much more resistant than the historical underrepresentation of women. The increase in the number of black and other minority lawyers in the United States in the past decade has been significant.[50] The percentage of nonwhite lawyers rose from 1.9 percent of 320,000 lawyers in 1972 to 4.2

[41] U.S. Bureau of the Census, Historical Statistics of the United States: Colonial Time to 1970 (1976); id., Statistical Abstract of the United States (1984)(figures for 1980); id., microfilm materials (lawyer populations 1870, 1880, 1890).

[42] See ABA Statistical Report, table 8 (1971).

[43] Id.

[44] Statistical Abstract of the U.S. 419 (1984).

[45] See 69 ABA J. 1367 (1983).

[46] See LawPoll, 68 ABA J. 1080 (1982)(58 percent of surveyed lawyers thought there were too many lawyers).

[47] B.Bledstein, The Culture of Professionalism 39 (1976). See generally Pashigan, The Number and Growth of Lawyers: Some Recent Findings, 1978 Am.B. Found. Research J. 54; York & Hale, Too Many Lawyers? The Legal Services Industry: Its Structure and Outlook, 26 J.Leg.Educ. 1 (1973).

[48] Nat'l L.J., July 2, 1984, at 2, col.4 (reporting on Census Bureau figures).

[49] See N.B., Student Lawyer at 4 (Mar.1984).

[50] Some statistics on black, Hispanic, and American Indian lawyer populations are given in Knauss, Develop-

percent of 547,000 lawyers in 1980.[51] But the increase has been much more modest than the increase in women law students and lawyers (§ 1.5.3). Today, while black and Hispanic people represent over twenty-three percent of the nation's population, they represent less than ten percent of the nation's law students,[52] six percent of its lawyers,[53] and 5.6 percent of its law professors.[54] Minority lawyers are heavily underrepresented in law firms,[55] in law teaching,[56] in corporate practice,[57] and in leadership positions in bar associations.

The first nonwhite lawyer in the U.S. was a black man, Macon B. Allen, who was admitted to the Maine bar in 1844. Blacks in 1870 were 12 percent of the population but included very few admitted lawyers.[58] Progress has been slow in the intervening century. The 1910 census counted only 798 black lawyers; in 1940, three years before the American Bar Association officially admitted blacks to membership, there were 1,925, and in 1960, only 2,004 black lawyers.[59] Until the mid-1930s, almost all black lawyers were educated at black law schools.[60] Recruitment of minorities to law schools did not begin in earnest until the late 1960s under the pressure of federal affirmative action programs.[61] After some success, the decision of the Supreme Court in the *Bakke* case[62] and a changing political and economic climate has slowed the growth in the percentage increase in minorities in law school.[63] While entry has been difficult, exit from the legal profession is apparently on equal terms as courts have rejected arguments that professional discipline should be administered less severely against

ing a Representative Legal Profession, 62 ABA J. 591, 592 (1976).

51 U.S.Dep't of Commerce Bureau of the Census, Statistical Abstract of the United States 402 (1981).

52 Census Bureau figures put black law students at 7.5 percent of law student population in 1982. Statistical Abstract of the U.S. 162 (1984). Minority law school enrollment actually declined from 7 to 6 percent in the Midwest from 1975 to 1980. See 68 ABA J. 409 (1982).

53 The 1980 census results showed that 4.5 percent of lawyers and judges were black or Hispanic. All nonwhite lawyers and judges comprised just over 6 percent of the total. Statistical Abstract of the U.S. 416 (1984).

54 N.Y.Times, Feb.16, 1985, at 15, col.6 (testimony during hearings conducted by special ABA committee on minorities in the legal profession).

55 Nat'l L.J., Apr. 21, 1984, at 1, col.3 (number of black lawyers in nation's largest firms dropped to 1.5 percent from previous year's 2.9 percent); Nat'l L.J., Dec. 20, 1982, at 1, col.1 (2.9 percent of lawyers in largest firms were black, up from 1.4 percent previous year; Hispanics, .61 percent, up from .5 percent). See generally Rust, Why More Black Lawyers Aren't Recruited, 12 Stud.Law. 18 (April 1984).

56 Higginbotham, Foreword in G.Segal, Blacks in the Law xv (1984)("If I were to note that area of the law in which, from my view, there has been the greatest rigidity, and perhaps the least racial progress, it would not be the law firms, the corporations, the judiciary, or the government. I submit that the greatest rigidity in the legal field has been within the teaching profession."). See also, e.g., Jones, Employment Discrimination, Minority Faculty and the Predominantly White Law School—Some Observations, 4 Black L.J. 488 (1974); Richardson, Black Law Professors and the Integrity of American Legal Education, id. at 495.

57 Baker, Black Lawyers and Corporate and Commercial Practice: The Unfinished Business of the Civil Rights Movement, 18 How.L.J. 685 (1975).

58 Baker, supra 18 How.L.J. at 692–93.

59 Hurley, A Profession Divided: Are Black Law Schools Obsolete?, 12 Stud.Law. 12, 14 (Mar.1984).

60 A book focusing primarily on the biographies of pre-1960 black lawyers, with statistics on present black lawyer populations in several metropolitan areas, is G.Segal, Blacks in the Law (1983).

61 Penderhughes, Increasing Minority Group Students in Law Schools: The Rationale and the Critical Issues, 20 Buff.L.Rev. 447 (1971); Gellhorn, The Law Schools and the Negro, 1968 Duke L.J. 1069 (1968). Recruitment of minorities to law schools was aided by the founding in 1968 of the Council on Legal Education Opportunity (CLEO). G.Segal, Blacks in the Law 5 (1984). In 1980, the ABA House of Delegates adopted an amendment to its Standards for the Approval of Law Schools (Standard 212) that urged law schools to demonstrate and maintain "by concrete action, a commitment to providing full opportunities for the study of law and entry into the profession by qualified members of groups (notably racial and ethnic minorities) which have been victims of discrimination." Id. at 8.

62 Regents of University of California v. Bakke, 438 U.S. 265, 98 S.Ct. 2733, 57 L.Ed.2d 750 (1978)(state unconstitutionally discriminated against respondent, white male medical school applicant, by using minimum quota system to fill percentage of seats in entering medical school class with minority applicants with numerically lesser credentials than respondent's). See generally Symposium, 67 Calif.L.Rev. 1 (1979).

63 In 1969-70, 2,128 black students attended the nation's law schools. Only two years later (1972-73), the number had more than doubled, to 4,423. But in 1981-82 there were 5,789 black law students. G.Segal, Blacks in the Law 7 (1984).

minority lawyers because of their small number.[64]

Present Situation of Black and Other Minority Lawyers

The low figures on minority attendance at law school and membership in the bar are a reflection of the significant barriers that deny equal opportunity for blacks and other minorities in the legal profession. At that, those figures even overstate the degree of social integration of minority and white lawyers. A large percentage of black law students attend primarily black law schools,[65] and many blacks practice alone, in primarily black law firms,[66] or for government agencies.[67]

The barriers that exist are social and economic and are the direct consequences of historical patterns of racial discrimination. Blacks in law school often have the disadvantage of an inferior preparatory education and significantly different cultural experiences.[68] Black and other minority law students must contend with acute financial problems because of much lower family incomes.[69] Blacks experience much higher failure rates on bar examinations.[70] Blacks and other minorities that do gain positions in white law firms must often contend with an otherwise segregated society that is reluctant or unwilling to deal with minority lawyers on the same terms as white lawyers.[71] Black lawyers have difficulty attracting white clients because of social segregation yet have no monopoly of black clientele, particularly of wealthy black clients, because of a perception among some prospective black clients that they are better off represented by white lawyers.

Future for Minority Lawyers

As with probably no other social problem,[72] formal and active racial segregation in the United States, following centuries of slavery, has left a legacy of crippling barriers. They can hardly be legislated away by the removal of formal restraints. The change in underlying social and economic conditions has occurred only at an excruciatingly slow pace. That pace shows little sign of increasing and portends decades of continuing struggle before minority lawyers will stand on an equal footing. Clearly, however, movement is occurring, and minority law students and lawyers have some reason to think that the struggle will end within the careers of the younger of them.

§ 1.4.3 Women in Law

History of Barriers to Admission to Practice

The struggle of women to be admitted to practice in the last quarter of the nineteenth century only slowly broke down the barriers of admission to what had been until that time an all-male bar. At common law women were ineligible to practice law. In 1872 the United States Supreme Court declared that Illinois did not violate the federal Constitution by excluding women from its bar.[73]

64 Office of Disciplinary Counsel v. Grigsby, 493 Pa. 194, 425 A.2d 730, 733 (1981).

65 Hurley, A Profession Divided: Are Black Law Schools Obsolete?, 12 Stud.Law. 12 (Mar.1984).

66 M.Goldman, A Portrait of the Black Attorney in Chicago (1972).

67 Nat'l L.J., Apr. 21, 1984, at 1, col.3 (National Bar Association survey indicates that 22 percent of black lawyers work at lower pay for government agencies compared with national average of 5 percent of all lawyers).

68 Tollette, Making It Together, 53 Judicature 366, 369 (1970).

69 G.Segal, Blacks in the Law 9 (1984).

70 G.Segal, Blacks in the Law 10-16, 264-65 (1984); P.Stern, Lawyers on Trial 182-84 (1980).

71 In August 1983, the ABA House of Delegates voted to support an amendment to the federal civil rights laws to ban discrimination against women and members of minority groups in private business clubs. N.Y.Times, Aug. 3, 1983, at B7, col.5.

72 On the gains of disabled lawyers, see, e.g., N.Y. Times, July 18, 1983, at A1, col.3. In August 1983, the ABA House of Delegates narrowly defeated a resolution that called for an end to discrimination within the legal profession against homosexual lawyers. See LawScope: Gay Rights, 69 ABA J. 1370 (1983). On the difficulties of law schools with employers, primarily governmental organizations, that discriminate against homosexual lawyers, see Nat'l L.J., Aug. 2, 1982, at 1, col.1.

73 Bradwell v. Illinois, 83 U.S. (16 Wall.) 130 (1872). The majority opinion in *Bradwell* relied upon the narrow interpretation of the privileges and immunities clause

Among the first women admitted to practice was the petitioner in *In re Goodell*,[74] who forced her way into the Wisconsin courts with a special statute in 1879.[75] Several other state courts held, however, that women could not be admitted in the absence of a state constitutional provision or statute because women were not competent to be admitted to practice at common law.[76] In each case, however, legislation quickly overturned the decisions, and by 1891 the Colorado court believed that this legislative pattern together with changes in the status of women in other areas of the law in the preceding fifty years warranted departing from the common law.[77] It was not until 1920 that the final state to exclude women capitulated.[78]

The elimination of formal barriers did little, however, to affect underlying social and economic structures. The number of women in law schools rose during the last quarter of the nineteenth century,[79] until by 1901 over two hundred women were enrolled in sixty-four of the nation's one hundred and four law schools and over three hundred women had been admitted to practice.[80] Thereafter, the number of women in law schools and practice remained at relatively constant and low levels. A brief interlude occurred during the Second World War, when some law schools admitted greater numbers of women to fill seats left vacant by the military draft. Several law schools had enrollments of from 25 percent (Yale) to 40 percent (Columbia) women, until returning male veterans were permitted to retake almost all the seats again.[81]

In 1970 less than three percent of all lawyers admitted to practice were women.[82] Although roughly equal percentages of men and women lawyers were judges, only 1.77 percent of all judges were women.[83] Women were more likely than men to be in solo practice and much less likely to be partners in law firms.[84] The number of women law students remained at a relatively constant three to four percent from the postwar years until 1968.

that had been adopted by the Court the same day in the Slaughterhouse Cases, 83 U.S. (16 Wall.) 36 (1872). A concurring opinion by Justice Bradley went to great lengths to place decision on the broader ground that "the civil law, as well as nature herself, has always recognized a wide difference in the respective spheres and destinies of man and woman." 83 U.S. (16 Wall.) at 141. Chief Justice Chase dissented alone and without opinion.

The Illinois court, in In re Bradwell, 55 Ill. 535 (1872), had relied on the historical fact that no woman had ever been known to have been admitted to the bar of either England or Illinois. Within three months of the Supreme Court opinion, the Illinois legislature enacted a statute that prohibited exclusion of any person from "any profession" on the ground of sex. See Schuchardt v. People, 99 Ill. 501, 505 (1881).

74 48 Wis. 693, 81 N.W. 551 (1879) (admission pursuant to statute). See also In re Goodell, 39 Wis. 232 (1875) (admission denied in absence of statutory authorization).

75 The first woman admitted to practice in any state was Belle A. Mansfield, of Mount Pleasant, Iowa, who was first denied admission but admitted on June 18, 1869, pursuant to a corrective statute. See Jones, 1969—Centennial Celebration of Admission of First Woman to U.S. Bar, Cornell L.F. at 1 (Spring 1969). The first black woman admitted was Charlotte E. Ray, the next year (1870) in the District of Columbia. See Nat'l L.J., Aug. 24, 1981, at 11, col.4.

76 In re Robinson, 131 Mass. 376, 41 A.Rep. 239 (1881); In re Bradwell, 55 Ill. 535 (1869); In re Leonard, 12 Or. 93, 6 P. 426 (1885). The Supreme Court had also denied admission to a woman on the same ground. In re Lockwood, 9 Nott. & Hop. 346 (U.S.S.Ct.1877)(cited in In re Thomas, 16 Colo. 441, 27 P. 707, 707 (1891)). See also Davis, Belva Ann Lockwood: Remover of Mountains, 65 ABA J. 924, 927 (1979)(Lockwood admitted to Supreme Court in 1879 pursuant to Act of Congress); In re Lockwood, 154 U.S. 116, 116 (1894)("Mrs. Lockwood has been for many years a member of the bar of this court and of the Supreme Court of the District of Columbia, and also, she avers, of the bars of several States of the Union.").

77 In re Thomas, 16 Colo. 441, 27 P. 707 (1891). See also, e.g., In re Leach, 134 Ind. 665, 34 N.E. 641 (1893).

78 J. Angel, Careers for Women in the Legal Profession 7 (1961).

79 Some women had apparently attended law school without any intention of practicing in court, but intended to engage in an office practice as legal clerks. At that time apparently only court appearance required bar admission.

80 Rogers, Is Law a Field for Woman's Work?, 24 ABA Rep. 548, 548 (1901).

81 Stevens, Two Cheers for 1870: The American Law School, in Law in American History (D.Fleming & B.Bailyn eds.1971), at 504 n.146. Harvard refused to admit women under any circumstances until 1950. Id.

82 Am.B.Found., Women Lawyers: Supplementary Data to the 1971 Lawyer Statistical Report 5 (M.Grossblat & B.Sikes eds.1973).

83 Id. at 8.

84 Id. at 12.

Dramatic Increase in Women Law Students and Lawyers

In 1968 began one of the most dramatic and profound changes in the history of the American law profession. In that year the percentage of women law students began a steep rise from its historically low figures.[85] In 1982 it stood at over forty-three percent;[86] in the same year over fifteen percent of lawyers and judges were women.[87] At current rates of enrollment, women will comprise approximately a third of the nation's lawyers by the end of the twentieth century.[88] The pheonomenal surge of women into law schools beginning in the late 1960s was by no means limited to the United States. Other countries, such as the USSR [89] and Brazil,[90] whose social and political systems are as different from each other as each is from the United States, also experienced sudden large increases in the number of women law students.

Three barriers have blocked women from full participation in legal careers. First is admission to law schools, which now seems assured on a gender-neutral basis in most law schools. Second is admission to the bar which, after the struggle of the late nineteenth century, seems assured on at least the same proportional basis as men. The final and far more subtle set of barriers are those that block many career paths within the legal profession.[91] In general, women have roughly equal access to judgeships,[92] to associate positions in large firms,[93] and to government service and public interest positions.[94] But significant barriers still exist to obtaining high status positions in the profession—in firm partnerships,[95] law teaching,[96] appellate judgeships, general counsel in corporations and government, arguing cases in the Supreme Court,[97] and leadership positions in state and national bar associations.

Economic differences remain great: women lawyers in 1984, according to one study, earned only eighty percent of the salaries of males with comparable years of experience.[98] The Supreme Court's decision in *Hishon v.*

[85] Id. at 13.

[86] Statistical Abstract of the United States 162 (1984). For a sociological comparison of the attitudes and careers of women who had entered law before and after the upsurge in the numbers of women lawyers, see C.Epstein, Women in Law (1981).

[87] Statistical Abstract of the U.S. 416 (1984).

[88] See 68 ABA J. 251 (1982)(report of remarks of associate direction of American Bar Foundation).

[89] See Krol, From Russia with Law, Student Lawyer, Feb. 1984, at 21 (increase in women law students since 1974 from 25% to over 50%).

[90] See Barroso & Mello, O Accesso de Mulher ao Ensino Superior Brasileiro, 15 Cadernos de Pesquisa 47, 51 (Dec. 1975)(number of women law students increased from 12 percent in 1956 to 25 percent in 1971). See Lewin, Educacao e Forca de Trabalho Feminina no Brasil, 32 Cadernos de Pesquisa 45, 55 (Feb.1980)(in 1973, percentage grew to 48 percent, remaining in mid-40s through 1977).

[91] See E.Hughes, Sex Discrimination in America's Legal Profession 130-77 (dissertation 1979); Ginsburg, Women at the Bar—A Generation of Change, 2 U. Puget Sound L.Rev. 1 (1978); Wald, Women in the Law: Stage Two, 52 U.Mo.K.C.L.Rev. 46 (1983). On the recent and traditional career barriers against women in law, see White, Women in the Law, 65 Mich.L.Rev. 1051 (1967).

[92] Women Judges, 16 The Third Branch at 7 (June 1984)(Census Bureau report shows number of women judges in state and federal courts increased from 6.1 percent in 1970 to 17.1 percent in 1980). On the variability of access to the federal bench, see Slotnick, The Paths to the Federal Bench: Gender, Race and Judicial Recruitment Variation, 67 Judicature 370 (1984).

[93] Nat'l L.J., Apr. 21, 1984, at 1, col.3 (percentage of female associates in larges firms in 1983, 30.4 percent, almost same as percentage of female graduates in 1981, 32.4 percent); Nat'l L.J., Dec. 20, 1982, at 1, col.1 (survey of largest firms shows almost 17 percent women, almost all associates).

[94] Nat'l L.J., Feb. 5, 1979, at 1, col.1 (reporting National Association for Law Placement survey of class of 1977, showing that 22 percent of women are in government service compared to 15.5 percent men; 9.8 percent women in public interest and legal aid, compared to 4.3 percent men).

[95] Nat'l L.J., Apr. 21, 1984, at 1, col.3 (in nation's large firms, 30.4 percent of associates but only 5 percent of partners are women).

[96] Fossum, Women Law Professors, 1980 Am.B.Found. Research J. 903; Weisberg, Women in Law School Teaching: Problems and Progress, 30 J.Leg.Educ. 226 (1979).

[97] LawScope, 68 ABA J. 905 (1982)(during 1981-82 Term, 7 percent of lawyers who argued were women). On the treatment of women lawyers in court, see Gilsinan, Obernyer & Gilsinan, Women Attorneys and the Judiciary, 52 Denver L.J. 881 (1975).

[98] See Women Lawyers: Survey Spotlights Disparities, 70 ABA J. 33 (1984)(women who graduated between 1975 and 1981 earned average of $26,810, compared to $33,410

King & Spaulding[99] held that a law firm was liable under the federal civil rights laws for making a partnership decision with respect to a woman associate on different criteria than were applied to men. The effect of the *Hishon* decision on partnership decisions at small firms and on the hiring, compensation, and promotion practices of all law firms is uncertain.[1] Within many firms, the problems of work assignments, mentors and proteges, informal education, client resistance, social opportunities for business getting and within the firm structure, partnership decisions,[2] and maternity leave and other policies affecting the private lives of women lawyers[3] still require attention.

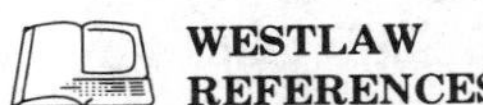

WESTLAW REFERENCES

discriminat*** exclu! /8 rac*** minority black negro /p law legal /2 profession practice school education

discriminat*** exclu! /8 woman gender sex! female /p law legal /2 profession practice school education /p admit*** admission

§ 1.5 LAW AS A PROFESSION

Culturally Contained Professions

Law is typically classified, by those disposed to do so, as one of the professions,[4] indeed one of the three learned professions, together with medicine and the ministry. Professions are said to share certain common and differentiating characteristics.[5] Not all delineations agree and some would include elements other than the quite elastically constructed list that appears below.[6] But most enterprises that have been able to enjoy both self-description as professional and a common cultural agreement with that description share the following characteristics:

(1) The professions are learned in the sense that one must undergo an extended period of education, training, or apprenticeship before being permitted to engage in the profession. The content and extent of the education might be controversial, but few would deny its importance because of assumptions about special information and mental skills that are

---

for male graduates during same period). See also, e.g., Winter, Survey: Women Lawyers Work Harder, Are Paid Less, but They're Happy, 69 ABA J. 1384 (1983).

99 467 U.S. 69, 104 S.Ct. 2229, 81 L.Ed.2d 59 (1984).

1 Zarefsky, How the Hishon Decision Will Affect Your Firm, 70 ABA J. 58 (1984).

2 On percentages of partners in various sized firms by gender, see, e.g., Study Shows Best Cities for Women Lawyers, 8 Distr.Law. 13 (July/Aug.1984).

3 Note, Law Firms and Lawyers with Children: An Empirical Analysis of Family/Work Conflict, 34 Stan.L. Rev. 1263 (1982). For an account of the nature of barriers to women professionals within a law practice, see, e.g., Epstein, Encountering the Male Establishment: Sex Status Limits on Women's Careers in Professions, 75 Am. J.Soc. 965 (1970).

4 There are different senses in which *professional* is also used. Sometimes is it used in opposition to *amateur.* (It is a strange usage, because logically it suggests that there might be a group of "amateur persons.") *Professional* in one common usage is a circumlocution to indicate that some persons do their work (doctors or lawyers) or play their game (tennis players or pool players) for pay. Lawyers certainly are professional in that different sense as well. Wasserstrom, Lawyers as Professionals: Some Moral Issues, 5 Human Rights 1, 1–2 n. 1 (1975).

5 P.Elliott, The Sociology of the Professions, 94 (1972); E.Schein & D.Kommers, Professional Education: Some New Directions 7–14 (1972); L.Patterson & E.Cheatham, Profession of Law 40 (1970); Greenwood, Attributes of a Profession, 2 Soc.Work 45 (July 1957); 5 R.Pound, Jurisprudence 676 (1959); R.Pound, The Lawyer from Antiquity to Modern Times 5 (1953) ("The term refers to a group of men pursuing a learned art as a common calling in the spirit of a public service—no less a public service because it may be a means of livelihood."); T.Parson, Essays in Sociological Theory 372 (rev.ed.1954); Kissam, Antitrust Law and Professional Behavior, 62 Tex.L.Rev. 1 (1983); Wasserstrom, Lawyers as Professionals: Some Moral Issues, 5 Human Rights 1, 1–2 n. 1 (1975); Wilensky, The Professionalization of Everyone, 70 Am.J.Soc. 137 (1965); Cogan, Toward a Definition of Profession, 23 Harv.Educ.Rev. 33 (Winter 1933).

6 Some would add, for example, that a profession is a *calling.* Cf., e.g., Pound, supra; Professional Responsibility: Report of the Joint Conference, 44 ABA J. 1159, 1159 (1958). The same notion is reflected in argruments that the professions (etymologically, what one declares oneself to be) should more appropriately be called *vocations* (what one is called or chosen to be). See J.Pike, Beyond the Law 18 (1962). The concept of calling is applied by some religions to refer to the process of selecting priests and ministers. But few today believe that persons become members of particular professions as the result of any significant calling different from the process described in the list in the text. But cf., e.g., Ellis v. Frawley, 165 Wis. 381, 161 N.W. 364, 366 (1917) (practice of lawyer is "not a trade, but a ministry").

required in at least some of the tasks undertaken by professionals.

(2) Not everyone can hold themselves out as a professional of a particular kind. First a person must be subjected to a process of testing by persons who already hold the rank and must be certified as minimally competent to function effectively as a professional.

(3) A person who is a professional enjoys, by that fact alone, an important advantage in social prestige. Part of the prestige attaches to high income (factor 4), part to assumed wisdom (factor 1), and part to the desirable nature of the work. Typically the work involves the mind much more than one's hands and back and is thus neither physically exhausting or dirty. The high prestige associated with professions makes occupational groups eager to assume that status and makes definitions of the concept controversial unless they are broadly inclusive.

(4) Professionals make more money than the average worker and often surprisingly more money than persons who do very similar work but are not certified professionals. High income is correlated with prestige (factor 3) but is likely causally related at least in part to self-regulation (factor 5).

(5) Professionals typically enjoy a significant amount of autonomy as a group, which is often referred to as professional independence. The independence is said to be a natural consequence of the fact that only other members of the same profession have the intense special learning of the profession (factor 1). It is also said to be required in order to assure that the professional's efforts are directed only to the welfare of users of the professional service.

(6) Organized groups of members of the profession attempt to exercise relatively rigid control over other group members. Often the control is exerted in the form of a code of ethics. Relative isolation from the surrounding community and intense self-regulation lend the profession a sharply defined membership, purpose, and reason for being. Regulatory control almost always extends to creating and enforcing standards of admission and exclusion and defining the qualifications of competence and character required of a professional in good standing. Either the professional group or the political organization in the surrounding society exercises a complementary power to preclude anyone who is not a licensed professional from performing similar or competing work. The complementary governmental activity often takes the form of enforcing the profession's code of ethics, or parts of it, with governmental authority. The profession thus enjoys a more or less monopolistic control over its own affairs and income but with a measure of state support for some of its important professional projects.[7]

(7) Professionals deal with needs that are vital to persons who use their services, yet the need is common to many people. The vital needs affect a person's health, freedom, spiritual state, economic well-being, and possibly other concerns. Because users of a professional's services usually have or are threatened with a deficit in one of those vital needs, the user tends to be anxious and vulnerable when seeking the professional's assistance.

(8) Professionals assume intensely personal relationships with and responsibilities toward users of their services and, in their ideals at least, aspire to a holistic servicing of all relevant needs of users. The special relationship is signified by special names such as *patient* or *client*.

(9) Professions often refer to an element of "public service," either in the work that is performed for individual users or in a claim that professionals or professional organizations undertake functions that transcend the narrow interests of the user or of the profession but serve the nonuser public in a way relevant to the profession's special competence. Thus doctors and lawyers may claim a

[7] In that sense, George Bernard Shaw referred to all professions as "conspiracies against the laity." G.Shaw, Doctor's Dilemma (preface).

special role in providing relevant services to potential users who are unable to pay normal fees or to deal with many matters of social policy affecting the service.[8] Sometimes the claim is made in the extreme form that the primary motivation of members of the profession is professional service rather than individual satisfactions. Professions are, or were, frequently contrasted with the money-getting "trades" in that respect.[9]

Cultural Relativity of Professional Status

Much professional self-examination of the self-congratulatory kind assumes a givenness to definitions of a profession that seems difficult to square with either history or comparative glances at other cultures. An esteemed profession at one time is a despised craft at another; one culture's titans of public service are another's horde of petty officials. Law, for example, did not acquire at least some of the traits of a profession until rather recently. Occupational groups called professions enjoy a certain status at the moment. It is not clear that anything intrinsic to the work of members of the group leads to its classification as a profession. The above list should be considered, accordingly, only descriptive and quite culture-bound to the United States.

Agendas of Professional Groups

Many occupational groups claim the title of "profession" for reasons that have more to do with economic, political, social, and legal issues than with any philosophically defensible content of the term. In examining each of the major occupational groups in the United States and England during at least the last century and a half, one is struck by the similarity of issues and movements that have gripped professional organizations and their members. In each can be found quite serious, and often quite insular, professional attention to these common themes: social status, technical knowledge, education, technical examinations, practitioner hierarchies, codes of conduct, standardization of work and the products of work, worker autonomy, collegial control, intimacy of relationship with clients, specialization, minimum fees or wages, legal protection against unauthorized practice, career placement, a claimed responsibility for the societal impacts of the work of the profession, and professional societies or associations to give common, and parochial, voice to all of these concerns.[10] Concentration on each of those issues can also, of course, be found in the distant and recent past of the legal profession.

Diminution of the Legal Profession's Elitist Status in Courts

Within the legal profession itself, the concept of profession has lost some of its luster. The Supreme Court itself in uncommonly straightforward language reminded the organized bars that "lawyers earn their livelihood at the bar." [11] The Court went on in a similar vein:

> We all know that law offices are big businesses, that they may have billion-dollar or million-dollar clients, they're run with computers, and all the rest. And so the argument may be made

[8] Cf. W.Hurst, Growth of American Law: The Law Makers 329 (1950).

[9] E.g., Canon 12 of 1908 Canons of Ethics ("the profession is a branch of the administration of justice and not a mere money-getting trade"); Wigmore, Introduction, to O.Carter, Ethics of the Legal Profession xxiii (1915) (too many young lawyers of the day regard law, not as a profession, but as a "trade, an occupation, a business—like any other worthy means of livelihood"). See F.Bennion, Professional Ethics: The Consultant Professions and Their Code 7–10 (1969) (historical survey of disdainful use of *trade* or *commerce* by those who consider themselves professionals).

[10] See, for example, the history of the several professions described in A.Carr-Saunders & P.Wilson, The Professions (Oxford, 1933), which unself-consciously traces those elements through each of the described occupational groups as if they were purposeful themes. For a perceptive examination of many of those themes, see Hughes, "Professions" in The Professions in America (K.Lynn ed. 1965) at 1–14. See also Layton, The Engineer and Business, in Engineering Professionalism and Ethics (J.Schaub & K.Pavlovic eds. 1983) at 38–54; E.Hughes, Men and Their Work (1958).

[11] Bates v. Arizona State Bar, 433 U.S. 350, 368, 97 S.Ct. 2691, 53 L.Ed.2d 810 (1977).

that to term them noncommercial is sanctimonious humbug.[12]

Subjecting lawyers to the state's deceptive trade practices act, a Texas appellate court noted that "the lawyer sells legal services and the client purchases them." [13] While other courts have persisted in giving special meaning to the attribution of "profession," most seem content, at least in the case of lawyers, to let actual actions and everyday practices speak louder than after-dinner speeches.

WESTLAW REFERENCES

di profession

§ 1.6 OFFICER OF THE COURT

General

Judges and other lawyers have often asserted that lawyers are officers of the court.[14] Sometimes the designation implies a title bestowing special privileges upon lawyers, but much more often it appears in the context of insisting that lawyers labor under special obligations. For the most part, the phrase is merely suggestive of the close working relationship between judges and traditional courtroom practitioners and today lacks much definitive significance in the law.[15]

Limited Significance of "Officer of the Court"

The origins of the "officer of the court" title are obscure. Historically, it may derive from the practice sometimes found in the older English courts that required a litigant to appear in court in company with an official court retainer. For example, the practice in English equity, which survived until the beginning of the last century, required every suitor to hire one of sixty equity clerks appointed by the court, in addition to a privately retained equity solicitor.[16] Aside from such isolated survivals, however, practicing lawyers in both law and equity courts had long since been freed from all but the limited court control exercised through admission to practice and disbarment.[17]

It is difficult to point to many respects today in which lawyers enjoy advantages over nonlawyers because of any presumed court officership, aside from the exclusive license to represent clients before courts. Lawyers are sometimes exempted from statutory obligations that apply to citizens generally, but this is usually accomplished in opinions relying on the inherent and exclusive power of courts to regulate lawyers.[18] Lawyers are typically excused from jury service in many jurisdictions,

[12] Bates v. Arizona State Bar, supra, 433 U.S. at 368 n. 19, 97 S.Ct. at 2701 n. 19.

[13] DeBakey v. Staggs, 605 S.W.2d 631, 633 (Tex.Civ. App.1980), affirmed per curiam 612 S.W.2d 924 (Tex.1981).

[14] Holt v. Virginia, 381 U.S. 131, 136, 85 S.Ct. 1375, 1377, 14 L.Ed.2d 290 (1965); Blankenbaker v. State, 201 Ind. 142, 166 N.E. 265 (1929); People ex rel. Karlin v. Culkin, 248 N.Y. 465, 470–71, 162 N.E. 487, 489, 60 A.L.R. 851 (1928). See generally Hurst, The Legal Profession, 1966 Wisc.L.Rev. 967, 976.

[15] For example, in Polk County v. Dodson, 454 U.S. 312, 319, 102 S.Ct. 445, 450, 70 L.Ed.2d 509 (1981), the Court held that "a lawyer representing a client is not, by virtue of being an officer of the court, a state actor 'under color of state law' " within the meaning of the civil rights act. See also, e.g., In re Griffiths, 413 U.S. 717, 729, 93 S.Ct. 2851, 37 L.Ed.2d 910 (1973) (although lawyers are licensed by the states, "they are not officials of the government by virtue of being lawyers"); Cammer v. United States, 350 U.S. 399, 405, 76 S.Ct. 456, 100 L.Ed. 474 (1956) (lawyer is not the kind of officer of court who can be summarily tried for contempt regardless of other circumstances); Powell v. Alabama, 287 U.S. 45, 73, 53 S.Ct. 55, 77 L.Ed. 158 (1932); Ex parte Garland, 71 U.S. (4 Wall.) 333, 378, 18 L.Ed. 366 (1867). But see, e.g., In re Florida Bd. of Bar Examiners, 350 So.2d 1072 (Fla.1977) (conviction in another state that deprives one of civil rights bars applicant from admission to practice as officer of court).

Special, if minor, official responsibilities may occasionally devolve upon lawyers in some jurisdictions. In Connecticut, for example, admitted lawyers are empowered to issue writs and subpoenas, administer oaths, and take depositions and acknowledgements of deeds. In re Griffiths, supra, 413 U.S. at 723. See also, e.g., Save Way Oil Co. v. 284 Eastern Parkway Corp., 115 Misc.2d 141, 453 N.Y.S.2d 554 (N.Y.Cty.Ct.1982), appeal dismissed 125 Misc.2d 26, 480 N.Y.S.2d 718 (1984) (limited statutory power of lawyers to issue restraining orders against debtors' bank accounts).

[16] See 9 W.Holdsworth, A History of English Law 369–70 (1926). The equity clerks' role seems to have been limited largely to that of collecting their fees.

[17] Id. 369 (equity); 3 id. 652–653 (law).

[18] In re Florida Bar, 316 So.2d 45 (Fla.1975) (financial disclosure statute inapplicable to lawyers functioning in

but this is probably due as much to the fact that they would routinely be stricken from a jury panel by peremptory challenge of trial lawyers, who would fear their domination of the jury.[19]

To an extent, it is true that lawyers labor under occasional special burdens because of their occupational status. Judges have sometimes imposed particularly harsh sentences on lawyers convicted of crime because of their obligation to conduct themselves according to high standards of honor and integrity.[20] Courts have insisted that lawyers who are also litigants owe a higher duty to the legal system than that owed by laymen.[21] At the very least, lawyer-litigants are to be accorded no special privileges.[22] Lawyers as a group are not considered more trustworthy as witnesses under oath.[23] The maxim that ignorance of the law is no excuse is applied with greater rigor to lawyers because of their presumed greater knowledge of the law and because of their duty to become fully conversant with the law.[24] Occasionally the concept of "officer of the court" is invoked to hold a lawyer to special obligations to treat judges with particular respect,[25] to speak to judges with candor,[26] or to uphold particular public policies.[27]

Lawyers as "Ministers of the Law"

The officer-of-the-court sobriquet should not be taken to limit a lawyer's public responsibilities to courts alone. The 1908 Canons spoke

their historical capacity as officers of the court); State ex rel. McCamic v. McCoy, ___ W.Va. ___, 276 S.E.2d 534 (1981) (prison regulation requiring all visitors to submit to personal search inapplicable to lawyers and their briefcases when lawyers visit inmates on legal business). On the judicial use of the inherent powers doctrine to invalidate legislation, see § 2.3.

19 See generally Note, The questionable Validity of the Automatic Exemption of Attorneys from Jury Service, 14 U.Rich.L.Rev. 837 (1980).

20 United States v. Blitstein, 626 F.2d 774 (10th Cir.1980), certiorari denied 449 U.S. 1102, 101 S.Ct. 898, 66 L.Ed.2d 828 (1981); United States v. Beecroft, 608 F.2d 753, 761 (9th Cir.1979); Webb v. State, 580 P.2d 295, 304 (Alaska 1978); In re Bricker, 90 N.J. 6, 446 A.2d 1195 (1982). But lawyers are not subject to a special criminal law containing standards of conduct different from those applicable to the general populace. E.g., Marcus v. State, 249 Ga. 345, 290 S.E.2d 470, 472 (1982) (grave equal-protection problems would be raised by application of different criminal conduct standards to lawyers); cf. United States v. Berry, 627 F.2d 193 (9th Cir.1980), certiorari denied 449 U.S. 1113, 101 S.Ct. 925, 66 L.Ed.2d 843 (1981). But cf. United States v. DeLucca, 630 F.2d 294, 301 (5th Cir.1980), certiorari denied 450 U.S. 983, 101 S.Ct. 1520, 67 L.Ed.2d 819 (1981) (lawyer whose clients hatched illegal cocaine importation conspiracy in his presence also guilty of conspiracy because, among other things, he violated duty as lawyer to report conspiracy to authorities).

21 Chira v. Lockheed Aircraft Corp., 634 F.2d 664, 667 (2d Cir.1980) (litigant was "clearly chargeable" with his lawyer's procedural defaults because the litigant was himself a lawyer); United States v. Baer, 575 F.2d 1295, 1300 (10th Cir.1978) (government lawyer who engaged in legal gamesmanship in attempt to resist $5 parking ticket). See also, e.g., Hudak v. Curators of University of Missouri, 586 F.2d 105 (8th Cir.1978), certiorari denied 440 U.S. 985, 99 S.Ct. 1799, 60 L.Ed.2d 247 (1979) (lawyer-litigant is less attractive claimant for in forma pauperis treatment in a civil case); United States v. Gates, 557 F.2d 1086 (5th Cir.1977), certiorari denied 434 U.S. 1017, 98 S.Ct. 737, 54 L.Ed.2d 763 (1978) (lawyer who had expertise in narcotics trials could clearly defend self at trial on narcotics charges); Spilker v. Hankin, 188 F.2d 35 (D.C.Cir.1951) (lawyer not benefited by customary rules of collateral estoppel in successive suits against former client on notes); Anderson v. Pryor, 537 F.Supp. 890, 895–96 (W.D.Mo.1982) (lawyers as clients are assumed to have level of sophistication exceeding that of ordinary clients; conflict of interest rules are for "the protection of the lambs, not the wolves", quoting Acorn Printing Co. v. Brown, 385 S.W.2d 812, 819 (Mo.App.1964)).

22 Hutchinson v. Gertsch, 97 Cal.App.3d 605, 159 Cal.Rptr. 40 (1979) (error for trial judge to admit lawyer-litigant "as a member of the bar" to chambers conferences with lawyers for both sides while excluding nonlawyer adverse party).

23 See Faulkner Radio, Inc. v. FCC, 557 F.2d 866 (D.C.Cir.1977) (administrative law judge erred in creating presumption that disputed testimony of lawyers was more credible than testimony of nonlawyers).

24 State ex rel. Nebraska Bar Ass'n v. Hollstein, 202 Neb. 40, 274 N.W.2d 508, 517 (1979); Estate of Douglas, 104 Misc.2d 430, 428 N.Y.S.2d 558 (N.Y.Surr.1980).

25 People v. Selby, 198 Colo. 386, 606 P.2d 45, 47 (1979) (lawyer disbarred for, among other offenses, secretly recording chambers conference with judge).

26 Holloway v. Arkansas, 435 U.S. 475, 98 S.Ct. 1173, 55 L.Ed.2d 426 (1978).

27 For an extreme example, see In re Backes, 16 N.J. 430, 109 A.2d 273 (1954) (lawyer suspended for year for groundless denial of client's adultery in divorce action; public policy of divorce law imposes special obligations on lawyers). See also, e.g., Minority Policy Officers Ass'n v. City of South Bend, 721 F.2d 197, 199 (7th Cir.1983) (lawyers as officers of court must assist federal courts in policing limits on subject matter jurisdiction even if contrary to client interests).

in Canon 32 of a lawyer's broader responsibilities by referring to "disloyalty to the law whose ministers we are." For the most part, the responsibilities of lawyers can be understood only in that broader context.

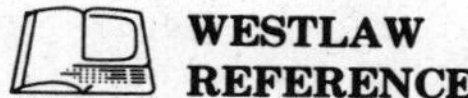

WESTLAW REFERENCES

topic(45) +p officer-of-the-court

Chapter Two

REGULATION OF LAWYERS AND THE LEGAL PROFESSION

Table of Sections

§ 2.1 THE FORMS OF LAWYER REGULATION

Formal Regulation: Admission and Discipline

The profession of law throughout its existence has been regulated in a variety of ways, in recent centuries chiefly through courts allied with bar associations. That system, which lawyers often call self-regulation, has functioned through processes that admit lawyers to practice subject to conditions (§ 14.4—admission) and hold open the threat of discipline through suspension or disbarment (Chapter Three). In this century, the form of discipline has been tightened by bar associations through the promulgation of codes of ethics (§ 2.6). In recent decades codes have increased greatly in regulatory importance because they have been given the force of law by courts and legislatures.

The Claim for Self-Regulation

Lawyer self-regulation has been defended both as traditional and as necessary for effective service to the public. The primary argument is that lawyers, like physicians and others in the specialized professions (§ 1.13—professions), practice in a highly technical and esoteric area. Moreover, nonlawyers should trust lawyers to exercise broad perspective and a public spirit when engaged in self-regulation. Because lawyers themselves are uniquely qualified to bring their specialized knowledge to bear in diagnosing professional problems and applying effective cures, any attempt by outsiders to share in professional regulation dooms the public service of lawyers to arbitrary and probably hurtful regulation.[1]

The argument for lawyer self-regulation is thus based on three claims. First, regulation

[1] For sympathetic versions of the argument, see, e.g., ABA Spec. Comm. on Evaluation of Disciplinary Enforcement, Problems and Recommendations in Disciplinary Enforcement (Clark Report), at 136-37 (1970); Arkin, Self-Regulation and Approaches to Maintaining Standards of Professional Integrity, 30 U.Miami L.Rev. 803, 825 (1976);

of lawyers involves too many legal complexities to be adequately understood by nonlawyers. Second, lawyers commonly engaged in regulation of the profession do indeed possess the necessary technical skill to achieve effective regulation. And, third, the history of lawyer self-regulation should give confidence to nonlawyers that lawyers have regularly kept the public interest foremost.

Those arguments are transparently debatable. It is doubtless true that some law practice issues involve legal complexity, but the further claims that those complexities are common and that only lawyers can and will comprehend them is highly dubious.[2] Sociologists have identified a process of "mystification" by which professional groups such as lawyers have attempted to immunize themselves against effective external control by asserting that their professional operations are so specialized and complex that outsiders cannot comprehend them.[3] But doubts about the soundness of those claims and the possibility of educating nonlawyers in the necessary complexities [4] probably leaves present-day unspecialized regulators as confident of success in regulating the legal profession as they are in areas of modern scientific or other complexity.

The claims that lawyer-regulators are technically equipped to deal with complexity and that lawyer self-regulation has been largely in the public interest are differently debatable. Lawyer self-regulation is a complex process, but at critical points it is controlled by lawyers or by lawyer-judges who are probably chosen, at least in part, because of their legal acumen. But lawyers who regulate, and to a lesser extent judges, are selected through screening processes that are controlled for the most part by organizations of lawyers. Those organizations have demonstrated a proclivity, which is not surprising, to take a self-protective stance when lawyer self-interest collides with other interests.[5] Few persons who are not lawyers would judge the resulting history of regulation to be one in which the public interest has regularly been vindicated. In sum, as in other areas in which occupations and professions are licensed and credentialed,[6] it seems clear that the claim of the legal profession for special and total exemption from external, nonlawyer control faces a skeptical public and an uncertain future.

Indirect, Formal Regulation

Lawyer admission and discipline are two of the chief levers by which the legal profession is regulated, and they remain largely under the effective control of lawyers functioning through bar associations and courts. But they are no longer the only important regulatory processes. At least three other types of formal control mechanisms exist. They are critical to an understanding of lawyer regulation and are important because in each the usual processes of lawyer self-regulation are absent or diminished in influence.

One is the application of sanctions against lawyers through damage awards in legal malpractice and similar suits (§ 5.7). Although the legal malpractice damage system is administered by the same courts that admit and disbar lawyers, the presence of jury trial, the

Bierig, Whatever Happened to Professional Self-Regulation, 69 ABAJ 616 (1983); Wade, Public Responsibility of the Learned Professions, 21 La.L.Rev. 130 (1960); Weckstein, Training for Professionalism, 4 Conn.L.Rev. 409, 414-15 (1972). The argument is much more likely to be made by lawyers than by others.

[2] See generally Wolfram, Barriers to Effective Public Participation in Regulation of the Legal Profession, 62 Minn.L.Rev. 619 (1978).

[3] T.Johnson, Professions and Their Power 42-43 (1972); Daniels, How Free Should Professions Be?, in The Professions and Their Prospects 40-42 (E.Freidson ed.1973); cf. C.Warren, A History of the American Bar 223-24 (1911) (discussing popular belief of post-Revolutionary War public that law was kept purposefully obscure by lawyers in order to protect their monopoly).

[4] Note, The Legal Profession's Attempt to Discipline Its Members: A Critique of the Clark Report, 1970 Utah L.Rev. 611, 617.

[5] See generally Morgan, The Evolving Concept of Professional Responsibility, 90 Harv.L.Rev. 702 (1977).

[6] See generally, e.g., Symposium: Professional Regulation, 7 Law & Hum.Behav. 99 (1983); B.Shimberg, B.Esser & D.Kruger, Occupational Licensing Practice and Policies (1972); Gellhorn, The Abuse of Occupational Licensing, 44 U.Chi.L.Rev. 6 (1976); Rose, Occupational Licensing: A Framework for Analysis, 1979 Ariz.St.L.J. 189.

absence of bar associations as directly interested parties, and the insistent presence of nonlawyer plaintiffs as litigants may mean that some courts more eagerly regulate lawyer conduct in those suits.

A second form of additional regulation by courts is effected through contempt sanctions (§ 12.1.3) and fee awards (§ 16.6.2; § 11.2.2 (harassment—sanctions)) in individual litigated cases. Courts also administer a kind of ad hoc and indirect discipline through granting motions to disqualify lawyers in particular cases because of conflict of interest rules (§ 7.1.7).

Third, courts have recently limited the freedom of action of bar associations through the expansive application of legal constraints. Most important of those are recent Supreme Court decisions that have extended the reach of the federal antitrust laws (§ 2.4) and First Amendment protections (§ 14.2.3) to the legal profession. Those laws have operated primarily as a negative control over the ability of bar associations and some passively compliant state courts to enforce professional rules to favor the economic interests of lawyers at the expense of the consumers of legal services.

Informal Regulation

The most widely effective form of regulation of lawyers, however, remains the system that is most properly called *self-regulation*—the network of informal sanctions that are brought to bear against lawyers who offend accepted norms of professional behavior. A lawyer who seriously offends against widely held professional norms faces unofficial but nonetheless powerful interdictions. Those include sanctions such as negative publicity and other expressions of peer disapproval, the cut-off of valuable practice opportunities (firm membership or referral business), denial of access to centers of power and prestige (bar association committee membership and officership), and preclusion from judicial posts. Those informal sanctions, of course, have not necessarily been employed to enforce norms that agree with the norms enforced by public agencies. The conspiracy of silence that traditionally has proved to be a practical limitation on the availability of the legal malpractice damage sanction is one illustration (§ 5.6.2).

WESTLAW REFERENCES

law*** attorney /p self-regulat*** /p profession** occupation practice

§ 2.2 INHERENT POWERS OF COURTS TO REGULATE LAWYERS

§ 2.2.1 The Inherent Powers of Courts

The Scope of Inherent Powers

For most of the past two centuries and increasingly in recent decades, courts have claimed the power to regulate various areas of the law even in the absence of specific language authorizing the exercise of power in either the state constitution or statutes. The regulatory power finds its source in a theory, usually referred to as the "inherent powers" doctrine, that is actually several different doctrines resembling each other only superficially.[8] The doctrines find expression in judicial claims of powers to devise particular remedies and procedures that are necessary to deal with cases that are unprovided for [9] and matters of judicial housekeeping;[10] to promulgate

[8] See generally J.Cratsley, Inherent Powers of the Courts (National Judicial College 1973).

[9] United States v. New York Tel. Co., 434 U.S. 159, 98 S.Ct. 364, 54 L.Ed.2d 376 (1977)(federal courts' inherent power to order telephone company to render technical assistance in gathering evidence and to order compensation paid to the company); Garfein v. McInnis, 248 N.Y. 261, 162 N.E. 73 (1928)(inherent power of court of equity to effect transfer of title to forum land in action for specific performance). See also C.D.M. v. Alaska, 627 P.2d 607 (Alaska 1981)(inherent power of court to order sterilization of mental incompetents); Severns v. Wilmington Medical Center, Inc., 421 A.2d 1334 (Del.1980) (inherent power to order termination of comatose patient's life-supporting system).

[10] Owen v. City Court of Tucson, 123 Ariz. 267, 599 P.2d 223 (1979) (inherent power of court of general jurisdiction to punish for contempt); Mosk v. Superior Court, 25 Cal. 3d 474, 159 Cal.Rptr. 494, 601 P.2d 1030 (1979) (inherent power of state supreme court chief justice to assign ran-

general procedural rules;[11] to deal, according to a few courts, with matters of court budgeting;[12] and, according to almost all American courts, to regulate the practice of law.[13]

Some judicial exercises of the inherent powers doctrine can be understood as simply particular instances of common-law adjudication in the context of a narrow question presented by a traditional case or controversy.[14] The court's assertion of a power to regulate in such cases is interstitial and incremental and is very similar to the normal workings of a traditional common-law court. But other invocations of the inherent powers doctrine cannot be explained in that way. The traditional common-law court claimed no legislative-like power to promulgate regulations outside the context of a case or controversy when no facts or justiciable issues were presented. And the traditional reaction of American courts is to defer to legislative expressions of will. Nonetheless, the majority of American courts have claimed unusual and sometimes sweeping regulatory powers when dealing with the legal profession. One uncomfortable consequence is that the same body that promulgates comprehensive sets of rules regulating the conduct of lawyers must also sit as the body that determines their validity if later attacked.[15]

Exclusive Judicial Power?

If the inherent powers doctrine went no further than to authorize courts to regulate lawyers in the absence of legislative action, it could be explained as an arguably necessary effort by courts to fill a regulatory void in a matter of considerable interest to the operation of the courts. But, as will be seen, most courts go much farther and assert a negative aspect of the doctrine. The negative inherent powers doctrine asserts that only the courts, and not the legislative or executive branches of government, may regulate the practice of law. Any attempt by a coordinate branch of government to trench on that prerogative of the judicial branch is unconstitutional.

The doctrinal moves of the courts here are cumulatively powerful. The affirmative aspect of the doctrine begins as a doctrine of tradition or necessity. It then turns by degrees into a doctrine that prohibits any other constitutional body, legislative or executive, from participating in the regulation of lawyers (§ 2.2.3 (negative)). Most jurisdictions

domly selected judges of intermediate appellate court as temporary supreme court justices to decide issues involving regular members of supreme court who were required to recuse themselves); Roberts v. Alprin, ___ R.I. ___, 443 A.2d 433 (1982) (inherent power to regulate admission of spectators to courtroom); O'Connor v. Matzdorff, 76 Wn. 2d 589, 458 P.2d 154 (1969) (judicial power to waive court's own requirement for payment of fees in order to consider case presented by impecunious litigant).

11 Iowa Civil Liberties Union v. Critelli, 244 N.W.2d 564 (1976); State v. Leonardis, 73 N.J. 360, 375 A.2d 607 (1977); Hudson v. State, 89 N.M. 759, 557 P.2d 1108 (1976), certiorari denied 431 U.S. 924, 97 S.Ct. 2198, 53 L.Ed.2d 238 (1977). See generally J.Parness & C.Korbakes, A Study of the Procedural Rule-Making Power in the United States (1973); Levin & Amsterdam, Legislative Control over Judicial Rule-Making: A Problem in Constitutional Revision, 107 U.Pa.L.Rev. 1 (1963).

12 C.Baar, Separate but Subservient: Court Budgeting in the American States (1975); Note, Judicial Financial Autonomy and Inherent Power, 57 Cornell L.Rev. 975 (1972); Comment, State Court Assertion of Power to Determine and Demand Its Own Budget, 120 U.Pa.L.Rev. 1187 (1972). The most extreme case in the area is Commonwealth ex rel. Carroll v. Tate, 442 Pa. 45, 274 A.2d 193 (1971), certiorari denied 402 U.S. 974, 91 S.Ct. 1665, 29 L.Ed.2d 138 (1971)(courts have inherent powers to compel legislature to accept courts' budget estimate and appropriate sufficient revenues to fund it).

13 See generally O.Carter, Ethics of the Legal Profession 80 (1915); H.Drinker, Legal Ethics 41-42 (1953); L.Patterson & E.Cheatham, The Profession of Law 33-36 (1971); Note, The Inherent Power of the Judiciary to Regulate the Practice of Law—A Proposed Delineation, 60 Minn.L.Rev. 783 (1976); Note, Admission to the Bar and the Separation of Powers, 7 Utah L.Rev. 82 (1960); Comment, Separation of Powers: Who Should Control the Bar?, 47 J.Urb.L. 715 (1969).

14 Hoffert v. General Motors Corp., 656 F.2d 161, 164 (5th Cir.1981), certiorari denied 456 U.S. 961, 102 S.Ct. 2037, 72 L.Ed.2d 485 (1982)(despite limitation in Fed.R. Civ.P. 17(c) that court may appoint guardian for minor when minor is incompetent or is "not otherwise represented" in action, court has inherent power to appoint when minor and general representative may have conflict of interest); M.S. v. Wermers, 557 F.2d 170, 175 (8th Cir.1977). See generally C.Wright & A.Miller, Federal Practice and Procedure § 1570, at 774-76 (1975).

15 See Board of Overseers of the Bar v. Lee, 422 A.2d 998, 1001 (Me.1980), appeal dismissed 450 U.S. 1036, 101 S.Ct. 1751, 68 L.Ed.2d 233 (1981); Berberian v. Kane, ___ R.I. ___, 425 A.2d 527 (1981).

also assert that only the state's supreme court, and not any lower court, may exercise the power (§ 2.2.4 (trial courts)). Courts have even occasionally invoked the doctrine as a warrant to suspend normally applicable and valid law.[16] Carried to that extreme, the doctrine asserts that a court is not subject to rules in this area.

The doctrine, an unwarranted exercise of which can be arrested only by amendment of a state's constitution, carries obvious risks of judicial abuse and maladministration. In some of its manifestations it bears the marks of a nakedly political grasp for unbridled power.[17] Of transcendant political importance is the fact that the negative aspect of the doctrine leaves lawyers subject to regulation primarily by courts. Courts, then, must inevitably bear the major political responsibility for the good or poor health of the legal profession.

§ 2.2.2 Traditional Powers of Courts

Affirmative Inherent Power over Lawyers

American courts, for most of the period of their existence, have asserted the affirmative power to regulate the legal profession.[18] The breadth of the doctrine covers every aspect of the practice of law, "starting with admission, ending with disbarment, and covering everything in between." [19] Courts employing the doctrine have claimed the power to promulgate an official lawyer's code;[20] to admit lawyers to practice under specified conditions [21] and to disbar or otherwise discipline admitted lawyers;[22] to define the unauthorized practice of law and to fashion remedies to banish nonlawyers from the defined realms of exclusive lawyer practice,[23] even when the assertedly unauthorized practice has nothing to do with court proceedings;[24] to construct an integrated bar of which all lawyers must be members in good standing in order to continue practicing law;[25] to levy an assessment that every lawyer must pay toward support of the

16 Sullivan v. Alaska Bar Ass'n, 551 P.2d 531 (Alaska 1976)(inherent power to depart from court's own rules on admission to practice); In re Loring, 73 N.J. 282, 374 A.2d 466 (1977)(exclusive jurisdiction of highest state court over bar regulation implies power to initiate disciplinary proceedings on its own motion as well as to review disciplinary proceedings as provided by law).

17 When speaking with each other, judges may refer to the question of inherent powers as an issue of "judicial clout." See J.Cratsley, Inherent Powers of the Courts v (National Judicial College 1973). The perhaps cynical view has been expressed that judges that hold that the regulation of disbarment is strictly within the judicial prerogatives may be motivated by collegial instincts of protectiveness that judges feel for other members of the legal profession. See Brown, Administrative Commissions and the Judicial Power, 19 Minn.L.Rev. 261, 288 (1935).

18 Ex parte Burr, 22 U.S. (9 Wheat.) 529, 6 L.Ed. 152 (1824).

19 In re LiVolsi, 85 N.J. 576, 428 A.2d 1268, 1272, 17 A.L.R.4th 972 (1981).

20 But cf. Supreme Court of Virginia v. Consumers Union, 446 U.S. 719, 100 S.Ct. 1967, 64 L.Ed.2d 641 (1980) (state supreme court was exercising legislative power in promulgating Code of Professional Responsibility and thus enjoyed absolute judicial immunity from either damages or award of attorney fees).

21 In re Opinion of the Justices, 279 Mass. 607, 180 N.E. 725, 81 A.L.R. 1059 (1932). See generally Dowling, The Inherent Power of the Judiciary, 21 ABAJ 635 (1935); Green, The Courts' Power over Admission and Disbarment, 4 Texas L.Rev. 1 (1925); Lee, The Constitutional Power of the Courts over Admission to the Bar, 13 Harv. L.Rev. 233 (1899).

22 Ex parte Bradley, 74 U.S. (7 Wall.) 364, 367, 19 L.Ed. 214 (1868); Stratmore v. State Bar, 14 Cal.3d 887, 123 Cal.Rptr. 101, 538 P.2d 229, 92 A.L.R.3d 803 (1975); Wallace v. Wallace, 225 Ga. 102, 166 S.E.2d 718, 723-24 (1969), cert. denied 396 U.S. 939, 90 S.Ct. 369, 24 L.Ed.2d 240 (1969).

23 State v. Cline, 170 Mont. 520, 555 P.2d 724, 731 (1976), and authorities cited; Richmond Ass'n of Credit Men v. Bar Ass'n of City of Richmond, 167 Va. 327, 189 S.E. 153 (1937). See generally Comment, Control of the Unauthorized Practice of Law: Scope of Inherent Judicial Powers, 28 U.Chi.L.Rev. 162 (1960).

24 Florida Bar v. Larkin, 298 So.2d 371 (Fla.1974)(retired Illinois lawyer giving advice on wills); Lukas v. Bar Ass'n, 35 Md.App. 442, 371 A.2d 669 (1977)(representation of employees before County Personnel Board and Workman's Compensation Commission and drafting of agreements).

25 In re Integration of the Bar, 216 Minn. 195, 12 N.W.2d 515, 518 (1943); In re Integration of Nebraska State Bar Ass'n, 133 Neb. 283, 275 N.W. 265, 114 A.L.R. 151 (1937).

court's activities in regulating the legal profession;[26] and to regulate the conduct of judges and to issue and enforce compliance with the Canons of Judicial Ethics.[27]

It has also been claimed that the doctrine permits a court, in any of its inherent powers exercises, to employ powers normally denied to it. Thus courts have claimed the power to exercise original jurisdiction without state constitutional or statutory warrant in a bar discipline matter[28] or in an original action challenging the court's own fee arbitration rule.[29] And courts can waive customary rules of standing in order to entertain a challenge to a nonlawyer's alleged unauthorized practice of law.[30]

While most American courts have recognized something like the affirmative inherent powers doctrine, probably a majority of them do not demonstrate a uniformly exuberant approach to its application. New York courts, for a prominent and perhaps extreme example, have resisted exercising broad supervisory powers over lawyers beyond those conferred by legislation.[31] A more modest approach than the doctrine might warrant seems particularly to be followed in most states if exercise of a claimed inherent power would have substantial budgetary effects.[32]

Origins of the Doctrine

The precise origin of the affirmative inherent powers doctrine with respect to lawyers is not entirely clear, although it almost certainly is a large tree grown only recently from the sapling of admission and disbarment. The English judicial tradition of regulating lawyers has sometimes been thought to support the American doctrine.[33] Chief Justice Taney spoke in 1856 with confidence of the "practice of common-law courts" in determining the required qualifications for admission to practice and the grounds for removal, although he cited no authority.[34] The English legal tradition supports Taney's view, to an extent, for English judges indeed actively supervised and regulated lawyers. The origins of their power

[26] Board of Overseers v. Lee, 422 A.2d 998 (Me.1980), appeal dismissed 450 U.S. 1036, 101 S.Ct. 1751, 68 L.Ed. 2d 233 (1981).

[27] Judicial Qualifications Comm'n v. Lowenstein, 252 Ga. 432, 314 S.E.2d 107 (1984); In re Code of Judicial Ethics, 36 Wis.2d 252, 155 N.W.2d 565 (1968). See generally Martineau, The Authority of a State Supreme Court to Regulate Judicial Ethics, 15 St.Louis U.L.J. 237 (1970).

[28] In re Loring, 73 N.J. 282, 374 A.2d 466 (1977).

[29] In re LiVolsi, 85 N.J. 576, 428 A.2d 1268, 17 A.L.R.4th 972 (1981).

[30] In re Estate of Margow, 77 N.J. 316, 390 A.2d 591 (1978).

[31] E.g., Greene v. Grievance Committee, 54 N.Y.2d 118, 444 N.Y.S.2d 883, 886, 429 N.E.2d 390 (1981), cert. denied 455 U.S. 1035, 102 S.Ct. 1738, 72 L.Ed.2d 153 (1982) (advertising provisions of Code do not supplant or limit statutes); Feinstein v. Attorney General, 36 N.Y.2d 199, 366 N.Y.S.2d 613, 326 N.E.2d 288 (1975) (lower court exceeded its powers in withholding approval of group legal service plans; "if regulation or supervision beyond the limited powers of the Appellate Division are required, its provision lies with the Legislature."); Gair v. Peck, 6 N.Y.2d 97, 188 N.Y.S.2d 491, 160 N.E.2d 43, 77 A.L.R.2d 390 (1959), dismissed and cert. denied 361 U.S. 374, 80 S.Ct. 401, 4 L.Ed.2d 380 (1960) (maximum fee schedule would not be valid if substantive law, but schedule under attack construed to be procedural in nature and thus within power of court to promulgate); People ex rel. Karlin v. Culkin, 248 N.Y. 465, 162 N.E. 487, 60 A.L.R. 851 (1928) (dicta) (court content to follow legislative arrangement for discipline of lawyers; statute is "declaratory of a jurisdiction that would have been implied"). For a review of the New York doctrine, see Mildner v. Gulotta, 405 F.Supp. 182, 207-09 (S.D.N.Y.1975)(three-judge court) (Weinstein, J., dissenting), affirmed, 425 U.S. 901, 96 S.Ct. 1489, 47 L.Ed.2d 751 (1976). Compare, e.g., First Nat'l Bank of East Islip v. Brower, 42 N.Y.2d 471, 398 N.Y.S.2d 875, 368 N.E.2d 1240 (1977) (inherent power to supervise charging of legal fees); In re H., 87 N.Y. 521, 524 (1882) (trial court had legal authority to determine validity of lawyer's asserted lien even if no specific statute so provided). California at one time also took a cautious approach to its inherent powers to regulate the bar. See Brydonjack v. State Bar, 208 Cal. 439, 281 1018, 66 A.L.R. 1507 (1929); but see Katz v. Workers' Compensation Appeals Bd., 30 Cal.3d 353, 178 Cal.Rptr. 815, 636 P.2d 1153 (1981) (statute purporting to confer power on state administrative agency to discipline lawyers appearing before it unconstitutional).

[32] E.g., Dade County v. Goldstein, 384 So.2d 183 (Fla. App.1980) (trial court clearly had inherent power to appoint second lawyer as cocounsel but lacked either statutory or inherent power to provide compensation).

[33] See generally State ex rel. Frieson v. Isner, ___ W.Va. ___, 285 S.E.2d 641, 648 n.1 (1981).

[34] Ex parte Secombe, 60 U.S. (19 How.) 9, 15 L.Ed. 565 (1856). See also Barker v. Cadie, 6 Ves.Jun. 681, 688, 31 Eng.Rep. 1256, 1259 (Ch.1802)(jurisdiction of equity "to compel its officers to do justice with each other" authorizes suit by chancery lawyer's clerk for work performed in chancery despite adequacy of remedy at law).

are found in ancient statutes.[35] Yet despite the remote statutory origins, regulation of the legal profession indeed has been the traditional practice of Anglo-American courts for at least the last several centuries.[36] In the United States, however, that tradition has frequently been interrupted by legislative regulation of the legal profession, some of the most important and most controversial of which has not been declared unconstitutional by a state court. That is most notably true of legislation in several states during the nineteenth century that declared that any citizen was entitled to practice law.

History nonetheless is a suitable foundation for the affirmative form of the inherent powers doctrine. History demonstrates that regulation of the legal profession is fittingly defined to be within the "judicial power" that is commonly conferred on a state's courts [37] by state constitutional provisions.[38] In a few states the matter is beyond question because the state constitution explicitly provides that the state's supreme court is empowered to regulate the practice of law.[39] On occasion, however, the interpretative feats performed by courts in order to find explicit authorization in the state constitution are striking.[40]

Aside from claims based on tradition or constitutional text, necessity is a third basis claimed to support the affirmative exercise. Courts have occasionally argued that implying a judicial power to regulate lawyers is necessary for the proper functioning of the courts.[41] In fact, two different arguments are harbored here. One argument is that courts need to control the functioning of important court operatives—lawyers—who otherwise could frustrate and corrupt the processes of the court.[42] A second, and much broader, claim is that courts need the protection of a captive constituency in order to maintain their independence from the other branches of government.[43] The former claim purports

35 2 W.Holdsworth, A History of English Law 313 n.11, 314 n.8, 315, 317 (4th ed.1936); B.Lyon, A Constitutional and Legal History of Medieval England 439 (1960); T.Plucknett, A Concise History of the Common Law 217-19 (5th ed.1956); F.Pollock & F.Maitland, The History of English Law 211 n.6, 213 n.2, 215-16 (2d ed.1923). See generally Degman, Admission to the Bar and the Separation of Powers, 7 Utah L.Rev. 82 (1961); Lee, The Courts and Admission to the Bar, 13 Harv.L.Rev. 233 (1899); Note, Admission to the Bar and the Separation of Powers, 7 Utah L.Rev. 82, 83-84 (1960); Note, Legislative or Judicial Control of Attorneys, 8 Fordham L.Rev.103 (1939).

36 Attorney Grievance Comm'n v. Kerpelman, 288 Md. 341, 375, 420 A.2d 940 (1980), cert. denied 450 U.S. 970, 101 S.Ct. 1492, 67 L.Ed.2d 621 (1981); Ex parte Steinman, 95 Pa. 220, 40 Am.Rep. 637 (1880)(Sharswood, J.).

37 In the District of Columbia, a 1970 reorganization of the courts by Congress was held to confer on the local, nonfederal courts the same power as state courts to promulgate and enforce standards of professional conduct for lawyers. See District of Columbia Court Reform and Criminal Procedure Act of 1970, Pub.L.No. 91-358, 84 Stat. 521 (1970); D.C.Code 1981, §§ 2501-03; Financial Bankshares, Inc. v. Metzger, 680 F.2d 768, 777 (D.C.Cir. 1982).

38 In Re Cooper, 22 N.Y. 67, 90 (1860)(legislature may properly entrust appointment of lawyers to courts, as this is an appropriate judicial function). The argument of counsel reprinted in the *Cooper* report, 22 N.Y. at 71 ff., contains an interesting advocate's view of English legal history. Columbia law school dean Theodore W. Dwight argued in behalf of the admission of his Columbia graduates to the New York bar that English law reflected a uniform history of statutory control over the admission of lawyers to practice. Dean Dwight's views are contested in Lee, The Constitutional Power of the Courts over Admission to the Bar, 13 Harv.L.Rev. 233, 253-55 (1899).

39 E.g., Ark.Const. Amend. XXVIII; West's F.S.A. Const. Art. 5, § 23; Ky.Const. § 116 (as amended in 1975); Mont.Const. Art. VII, § 2(3), construed in In re Senate Bill No. 630, 164 Mont. 366, 523 P.2d 484 (1974). Occasionally an inherent judicial power will be explicitly recognized by statute. E.g., Miss.Code Ann. § 73-3-301 (1978 supp.).

40 Pushinsky v. West Virginia Bd. of Law Examiners, ___ W.Va. ___, 266 S.E.2d 444, 451 (1980)(power to prescribe qualifications for admission to bar was "expressly conferred" by constitutional grant to supreme court of power "to promulgate rules . . . for all of the courts of the State relating to writs, warrants, process, practice and proceduce").

41 Petition of Florida St. Bar Ass'n, 40 So.2d 902, 905-06 (Fla.1949); Board of Overseers v. Lee, 422 A.2d 998, 1002 (Me.1980), appeal dismissed 450 U.S. 1036, 101 S.Ct. 1751, 68 L.Ed.2d 233 (1981); State ex rel. Frieson v. Isner, ___ W.Va. ___, 285 S.E.2d 641, 648 n.1 (1981).

42 Ex parte Burr, 22 U.S. (9 Wheat.) 529, 531, 6 L.Ed. 152 (1824)(power to discipline lawyers "is necessary for the preservation of decorum, and for the respectability of the profession").

43 The argument is not usually put that baldly. Most courts that make the argument are content simply to state that the inherent powers doctrine is necessary in order to maintain the independence of courts, without specifying how that independence is threatened and how broadly regulating lawyers assures judicial independence.

to be factual and could be tested by asking whether particular instances of lawyer activity (arguing cases in court, for example, compared with giving advice on a contract matter in an office or arguing a case before an administrative agency) affects the courts very directly. The second claim, that courts need a supporting constituency, is political and is hardly testable at all.

§ 2.2.3 *Negative Inherent Powers*

Scope of the Doctrine[44]

The inherent powers doctrine to this point merely affirms a power of courts to act without further legislative direction. But beyond the affirmative inherent powers notion lies another doctrine, allied to the political rationale for affirmative powers, that attempts to warn the legislature entirely off at least most of the judicial turf thus defined. The negative aspect of the inherent powers doctrine will first be described and some of its implications traced. We will then return to critique it.

If a state legislature were to reenact laws that were found in several states during the nineteenth century admitting all citizens to law practice without any examination or other prerequisites (see § 14.1), would the courts again permit the statutes to go into effect? Unlike most nineteenth-century courts,[45] many of today's courts are armed with a doctrine to prohibit any branch of government except the state's supreme court from regulating lawyers and the practice of law. That negative aspect of the inherent powers doctrine is assertedly based on the state constitutional law doctrine of separation of powers.

The separation of powers argument runs as follows. Each of the three branches of government—executive, legislative, and judicial—is separately empowered to act by the state's constitution and is supreme within its assigned sphere. Moreover, no branch may attempt to exercise a power devolved upon a coordinate branch. Regulation of the practice of law is part of the judicial function, as history shows. Therefore, at least in the radical statement of the doctrine, *any* attempt by either the legislative or executive branch to entrench on that exclusively judicial power is an unconstitutional usurpation.

That radical form of the negative inherent powers doctrine is followed by a large number, perhaps a majority, of American jurisdictions. Some courts are more restrained. They assert the less jealous doctrine that the courts will share the power to regulate lawyers with other branches of government so long as this poses no threat to the continued vitality of the judicial branch.[46]

Cases striking down legislation under the negative inherent powers doctrine range widely over situations affecting lawyers and vary in the extent to which they deal with activities affecting courts. Some applications of the doctrine seem straightforward, given its premises. For example, a statute that purports to impose a two-year statute of limita-

[44] Only cases dealing with regulation of the legal profession will be considered here. It is important to note, however, that the negative aspect of the inherent powers doctrine has other applications. E.g., Chadha v. Immigration & Naturalizaton Serv., 462 U.S. 919, 103 S.Ct. 2764, 77 L.Ed.2d 317 (1983)(federal Immigration and Naturalization Act provision permitting "one-house veto" of decision of executive branch to suspend deportation of aliens violates federal separation of powers doctrine); Deskins v. Waldt, 81 Wn.2d 1, 499 P.2d 206, 208 (1972) (power of court of general jurisdiction to punish for contempt is inherent power that cannot be taken away or abridged by legislature).

[45] Commonly cited as the first American decision to assert the negative aspect of the inherent powers doctrine is In re Mosness, 39 Wis. 509, 20 Am.Rep. 55 (1876). The court's concern about possible legislative corruption of the bar may have stemmed from a decision, reported in the same volume of reports, in which a woman had applied for admission. The court strongly intimated that it would refuse to follow a statute that required the court to admit a person whom it considered unqualified. See In re Goodell, 39 Wis. 232, 239, 20 Am.Rep. 42 (1875).

[46] Heslin v. Connecticut Law Clinic of Trantolo & Trantolo, 190 Conn. 510, 461 A.2d 938 (1983) (per Peters, J.); Ratterman v. Stapleton, 371 S.W.2d 939, 941 (Ky. 1963); Clark v. Austin, 340 Mo. 467, 101 S.W.2d 977, 986-96 (1937) (concurring opinion); North Carolina State Bar v. Frazier, 62 N.C.App. 172, 302 S.E.2d 648 (1983), review denied 308 N.C. 677, 303 S.E.2d 546 (1983); State ex rel. Robeson v. Oregon State Bar, 291 Or. 505, 632 P.2d 1255 (1981). See generally Note, The Inherent Power of the Judiciary to Regulate the Practice of Law—A Proposed Delineation, 60 Minn.L.Rev. 783, 799-803 (1976).

tions on acts for which a lawyer might be disbarred clearly impinges on the function of bar discipline and accordingly is invalid.[47] Statutes met a similar fate if, for example, they directed the court to reinstate a lawyer whom the court had previously suspended,[48] purported to limit the reexamination rights of bar applicants,[49] or required bar members to maintain a residence or office in the state as a condition of the right to practice law.[50]

But other decisions seem more farfetched. Consider, for example, decisions invalidating statutes that permitted real estate brokers to draft conveyances,[51] that permitted nonlawyers to represent clients before administrative agencies,[52] that empowered an administrative agency to discipline lawyers by suspension from practicing before the agency,[53] or that applied a business license fee to lawyers.[54] While those statutes related to the practice of law, the areas of statutory impact seem entirely remote from the operation of courts and, thus, far removed from relevant separation of powers concerns.

Comity with the Legislature

The negative inherent powers doctrine would produce an ironic result if applied to invalidate legislation with whose objectives the court is in sympathy. Courts conducting a constitutional scrutiny of legislation normally insist that their sole concern is with the constitutionality and not the wisdom of enactments. Under that view, even legislation that is fully compatible with the court's own goals for regulation of the legal profession would be susceptible to invalidation. Often, however, a state supreme court will stop short of declaring invalid a statute or regulation with the announcement that the court finds the legislative intent congenial and the regulation will be permitted to exist as valid.[55] That "comity" or "harmony" approach can be found in the earliest decisions asserting the negative doctrine.[56] A variation of the comity notion goes somewhat further and admits that legislation may provide a guiding influence on bar regulatory policy matters, apparently to the extent of moving the court in directions it would not otherwise take.[57] Under either view of comity, statutes in virtually every state can be found that affect law practice in some direct way, such as by regulating an attorney's lien, authorizing lawyers to practice in professional corporations, regulating the fees of lawyers, and prohibiting judges from practicing law.

Critique of the Negative Doctrine

More than likely, the negative aspect of the inherent powers doctrine, as tempered by the

[47] In re Tracy, 197 Minn. 35, 266 N.W. 88 (1936), modified on rehearing 197 Minn. 47, 267 N.W. 142 (1936).

[48] State v. Cannon, 206 Wis. 374, 240 N.W. 441 (1932).

[49] E.g., Board of Comm'rs of Ala. State Bar v. State ex rel. Baxley, 295 Ala. 100, 324 So.2d 256 (1975).

[50] Archer v. Ogden, 600 P.2d 1223 (Okl.1979).

[51] E.g., State Bar v. Arizona Land Title & Trust Co., 90 Ariz. 76, 366 P.2d 1 (1961); Cowern v. Nelson, 207 Minn. 642, 290 N.W. 795 (1940); Bennion, Van Camp, Hagen & Ruhl v. Kassler Escrow, Inc., 96 Wn.2d 443, 635 P.2d 730 (1981).

[52] Idaho State Bar Ass'n v. Idaho Pub. Utilities Comm'n, 102 Idaho 672, 637 P.2d 1168 (1981). But see, e.g., Florida Bar v. Moses, 380 So.2d 412 (Fla.1980).

[53] Hustedt v. Workers' Compensation Appeals Bd., 30 Cal.3d 329, 178 Cal.Rptr. 801, 636 P.2d 1139 (1981).

[54] Harlen v. City of Helena, ___ Mont. ___, 676 P.2d 191 (1984).

[55] In re Feingold, 296 A.2d 492, 496 (Me.1972)(statute allowing appeal of denial of admission to practice honored as matter of comity but without surrender of judicial powers); In re Opinion of the Justices, 279 Mass. 607, 180 N.E. 725, 81 A.L.R. 1059 (1932)(legislation establishing state board of bar examiners imposed no limit on court and thus was constitutional); State ex rel. Robeson v. Oregon State Bar, 291 Or. 505, 632 P.2d 1255 (1981) (statute authorizing suspension of lawyer for failure to pay assessed contributions to professional liability fund does not unduly burden or substantially interfere with judiciary); In re Senate Bill 287 (1979), in Vernon's Ann. Tex. Civ. Stat art. 320a-1 (West Supp.1984)(order of state supreme court accepting and supplementing statute, passed by large margin in legislature, to integrate bar); State ex rel. Reynolds v. Dinger, 14 Wis.2d 193, 109 N.W.2d 685 (1961)(acceptance of state agency definition of scope of unauthorized practice of law in real estate area).

[56] In re Splane, 123 Pa. 527, 539, 16 A. 481, 483 (1889) (prior willingness of court to apply predecessor statutes dealing with admission to practice explained on basis that the law was "merely declaratory" of what the court itself would have decreed).

[57] H.Rottschaeffer, Handbook of American Constitutional Law 57 (1939); Dowling, The Inherent Power of the Judiciary, 21 ABAJ 635, 638 (1935).

comity notion, serves the limited function of invalidating only an occasional statute that the court feels to be a serious compromise of its freedom of action in regulating the bar or that the court feels is an egregiously bad law on policy grounds. As a permanent fixture of a state's jurisprudence, the doctrine both limits legislative ambitions to usurp the judiciary's turf and limits the possibilities for reform of the legal profession.

Surely there is force to the argument made by state courts that the concept of separation of powers precludes coordinate branches from usurpation of the powers of other branches. At an extreme, if legislation provided that all persons must appear in court pro se without professional assistance, the statute would have an objectionably direct and deleterious impact on the operation of courts, even apart from the fact that it would seriously impair the ability of litigants to assert their rights. The impact of the statute would strike so deeply into court functioning that the court's act of invalidating it plainly could be supported on the ground of separation of powers.[58] In general, any attempted regulation by a sister branch that impinges directly and significantly on the core functions of the judicial branch offends the separation principle because it threatens the ability of the courts to function in even a minimal sense.

But the negative inherent powers doctrine has been carried much farther to invalidate indirect or insubstantial threats to judicial functions. Courts have invalidated legislation and administrative regulations that deal in any way with the practice of law. Courts have struck down statutes regardless of their specific effect on the operation of the courts as such, aside from the claimed, appended judicial function of bar regulation. Those decisions deal with objects at least equally of concern to the other branches. For example, decisions in several jurisdictions have invalidated administrative regulations that permitted nonlawyers to appear as advocates before an administrative agency.[59] Obviously, the quality of advocacy before other branches of government is a concern only for those branches and not for courts. Other decisions have invalidated legislation dealing with the prerogatives of lawyer members of a state legislative body[60] or prohibiting conflicts of interest on the part of a former state legislator in the interest of preserving the integrity of state administrative agencies.[61] The decisions invalidating those statutes have inflexibly asserted that anything touching the practice of law, regardless of its relationship to judicial business, is within the exclusive realm of the courts. The logic of strict separation could just as easily have led to the conclusion that a matter affecting the executive or legislative branch is of no legitimate concern of courts. At the very least, further reflection on the fact that most of the statutes sampled above have impacts on both branches of government suggests that such a court-centered approach is insupportable.

A closer look at the reasoning of judges in some of the more uninhibited cases that apply the negative aspect of the inherent powers doctrine reveals that the major defect is in visualizing the universe of coordinate branches as one containing only two dimensions with clear lines dividing them. The broad judicial holding that no part of any judicial function may be exercised by any other branch means that the judicial function of regulating lawyers must not be trifled with in any particular by another branch. That same conceptualization is not, however, extended to the

[58] Cf., e.g., People ex rel. Conn v. Randolph, 35 Ill.2d 24, 219 N.E.2d 337, 18 A.L.R.3d 1065 (1966)(state ordered to compensate court-appointed lawyer beyond statutory limits for extraordinary and ruinous expenses necessarily incurred in providing criminal defense mandated by Constitution).

[59] Idaho St. Bar Ass'n v. Idaho Pub. Utilities Comm'n, 102 Idaho 672, 637 P.2d 1168 (1981)(regulatory commission's order permitting nonprofit organizations and small businesses to be represented in hearings by nonlawyers invalid). But see Florida Bar v. Moses, 380 So.2d 412 (Fla.1980)(legislature has constitutional power to oust court of responsibility to define unauthorized practice before administrative agencies).

[60] Williams v. Bordons, Inc., 274 S.C. 275, 262 S.E.2d 881 (1980).

[61] Kury v. Commonwealth, 62 Pa.Cmwlth. 174, 435 A.2d 940 (1981).

other branches, such as by recognizing that a court intrudes into the executive branch's own operations when the court insists that only lawyers represent parties appearing before administrative agencies. The doctrine is thus both two-dimensional and one-way.

To a large extent, the judicial discussion of inherent powers assumes that sharp lines divide judicial from legislative and executive functions. But those spheres of activity as a general matter are not so much sharply segregated spheres as they are significantly melded universes with primary areas of essential responsibility.[62] It simply claims too much to assert that courts must enjoy total control over regulation of the legal profession. At the very least, some "officers of the court"—prosecutors—are incontrovertibly members of the executive branch of government.[63] Under the sharp-lines approach, it would be just as logical to claim that the conduct of prosecutors may be regulated solely by the executive branch and not by the judiciary. (It is, of course, regulated by both.)

Separation of powers cannot sensibly be a doctrine of two-dimensional, single-directional lines. The three branches of government necessarily interact with each other in a multitude of ways. Clearly the regulation of lawyers strongly involves the traditional legislative concerns with the peace, safety, and welfare of citizens and can involve matters of constitutionally legitimate concern to the executive branch as well. Much, but hardly all, of what lawyers do is also of proper interest to courts. It should not always be assumed that the other branch must yield in an interbranch struggle of wills over a matter of otherwise nonconstitutional policy.

It is also unavailing to argue, as some courts have, that English legal history demonstrates that regulation of the legal profession is a matter solely for courts. The argument, at best, lends only tarnished historical support for the separation of powers point because the English courts acted as they did pursuant to statutory authorization.[64] In any event, the English arrangement is not an apt historical precedent for American constitutional law issues. The unwritten constitution of England posits that Parliament and the crown possess all sovereignty and thus by their acts can retract as well as expand the powers bestowed on the courts.[65] Under American constitutional law, of course, the legislature is more limited in its powers and, to whatever extent, is subject to restraint because of the state constitutional doctrine of separation of powers. Thus, the analogy to the English division of functions between legislative and judicial branches does nothing to aid our understanding of the constitutionally proper relationship between American courts, legislature, and executive. The most that can be said in comparison with the English practice is that it is at least congruent with the result sought by the separation of powers argument.

Finally, one occasionally encounters arguments of a legal process kind in support of the negative inherent powers doctrine. Those arguments assert that legislatures lack the political invulnerability, expertise, and time to deal competently with matters of regulation of the legal profession.[66] The arguments seem forced, given the traditional reluctance of courts to draft lawyer rules independently of bar associations (see § 2.3—bar organizations) and given the intensely political way in

[62] See generally Nixon v. Administrator of General Services, 433 U.S. 425, 442, 97 S.Ct. 2777, 2789, 53 L.Ed. 2d 867 (1977).

[63] See ABA Prosecution Function § 1.1(a)(1982).

[64] See n.35 supra.

[65] The point is made in State ex rel. Frieson v. Isner, ___ W.Va. ___, 285 S.E.2d 641, 648 n.1 (1981); State v. Cannon, 206 Wis. 374, 240 N.W. 441, 445 (1932).

[66] Gray & Harrison, Standards for Lawyer Discipline and Disability Proceedings and the Evaluation of Lawyer Discipline Systems, 11 Capital U.L.Rev. 529, 536 (1982). See also ABA Spec. Comm. on Evaluation of Disciplinary Enforcement, Problems and Recommendations in Disciplinary Enforcement 12 (1970)(Clark Committee Report) (logrolling among legislators and work of lobbyists interested in low disciplinary norms would result in much less ambitious lawyer rules if produced in legislatures instead of in courts).

which lawyer codes are drafted and compromised under the inherent powers system (see § 2.6.4 (Model Rules)). The courts have shown themselves at least as vulnerable to the influence of lawyer groups lobbying for favorable treatment in lawyer rules as legislatures might be.

In American democratic theory, popularly elected legislatures are the primary source of lawmaking, whether judges enjoy their secondary lawmaking role or not. Legislatures are specifically the constitutionally preferred source of initiatives for altering the modes of regulating occupations such as the legal profession.[67] As stated earlier, the judiciary should insist upon its own conceptions of how to regulate the legal profession only in instances in which yielding to another branch would directly and substantially impair the ability of the courts to adjudicate cases and conduct other business necessarily and properly before them.[68] Any lesser impingement might be deeply regretted but should not for that reason be held unconstitutional.

§ 2.2.4 Regulation by Trial Courts

Almost without exception,[69] state supreme courts today refuse to permit lower trial or intermediate appellate courts[70] to exercise the inherent power to admit or discipline lawyers.[71] As with the negative aspect of the inherent powers doctrine, the prohibition against trial court regulation is both recent and contrary to the pattern of lawyer regulation that obtained in many states into the early part of this century.[72] The theory on which claims of exclusive supreme court power are based is not frequently discussed. If, as claimed, lawyer regulation is an aspect of judicial power, one would imagine it to be an aspect of the powers of trial courts as well. The reason for the limitation is probably that most state supreme courts exercise regulatory power over lawyers through rule making and through bar disciplinary and bar admission agencies appointed directly by the supreme court. It is those rule-making and administrative arrangements, and not any apparent constitutional doctrine, that would be upset by exercise of the same powers by trial courts.

[67] See Roadway Express, Inc. v. Piper, 447 U.S. 752, 764, 100 S.Ct. 2455, 2463, 65 L.Ed.2d 488 (1980), quoting Cooke v. United States, 267 U.S. 517, 539, 45 S.Ct. 390, 69 L.Ed. 767 (1925). It is occasionally argued in support of the negative aspect that legislatures lack the expertise required to regulate the legal profession. E.g., Todd, The Role of the State Appellate Court in the Professional Disciplinary Process, 11 Cap.U.L.Rev. 577, 578 (1982). In fact, the "mystification" argument has even been advanced, unsuccessfully, as a reason why the bar itself, and not courts, should be left free of interference to deal with claimed constitutional rights of lawyers. See Bates v. Arizona State Bar, 433 U.S. 350, 402-04, 97 S.Ct. 2691, 2718-19, 53 L.Ed.2d 810 (1977) (Powell, J., dissenting in part). Regulation of the legal profession, however, is a matter of no more impenetrable complexity than many other matters on the legislative agenda and is trifling compared with some areas of technological difficulty.

[68] See also Wolfram, Barriers to Effective Public Participation in Regulation of the Legal Profession, 62 Minn.L. Rev. 619, 636-39 (1978).

[69] But cf. State v. Tedesco, 175 Conn. 279, 294, 397 A.2d 1352, 1359 (1978) (in state in which trial courts still disbar lawyers, trial courts authorized to punish lawyer misconduct occurring in their presence by summary disbarment).

[70] In New York intermediate appellate courts exercise most regulatory power over lawyers. There, the doctrine prohibits lawyer regulation by trial courts. E.g., In re Hyatt Legal Services, 97 A.D.2d 983, 468 N.Y.S.2d 778 (1983).

[71] Grahan v. State, 427 So.2d 998 (Ala.Cr.App.1983) (trial court lacked power to punish lawyer's contempt by suspension from practice before it); Esch v. Superior Court, 577 P.2d 1039 (Alaska 1978)(trial court lacked inherent power to suspend lawyer from practice before it for failure to file brief in accordance with court's briefing schedule); People v. Belfor, 200 Colo. 44, 611 P.2d 979 (1980)(lawyer suspended from practice could not be empowered by trial court to appeal and dismiss complaint in divorce action); Burns v. Huffstetler, 433 So.2d 964 (Fla. 1983); In re Hague, 412 Mich. 532, 315 N.W.2d 524 (1982); In re LiVolsi, 85 N.J. 576, 428 A.2d 1268, 1278 (1981); Brown v. Oregon State Bar, 293 Or. 446, 648 P.2d 1289 (1982); Laffey v. Court of Common Pleas, 503 Pa. 103, 468 A.2d 1084 (1983); State ex rel. Askin v. Dostert, ___ W.Va. ___, 295 S.E.2d 271 (1982). Conversely, an appellate court may be limited by statute or rule from barring a lawyer from appearing in lower courts. In re Snyder, ___ U.S. ___, ___, n.3, 105 S.Ct. 2874, 2880, 86 L.Ed.2d 504 (1985) (under Federal Rules of Appellate Procedure, courts of appeal are without power to suspend lawyer from practicing in all federal courts in circuit).

[72] E.g., Ex parte Auditor of Public Accounts, 609 S.W.2d 682, 683-84 (Ky.1980)(history of transfer of bar regulation from trial to supreme court). See also n.69 supra.

The limitation on trial courts relates only to admission and discipline. Other inherent judicial powers remain unimpaired, such as the inherent power to punish for contempt unruly persons who appear before the court, including lawyers. And most courts hold that it is consistent with the inherent powers doctrine for trial and intermediate appellate courts to disqualify a lawyer because of a serious conflict of interest.[73] Unlike questions that might typically arise in the admission or discipline of a lawyer, a motion to disqualify for a conflict of interest raises an issue in pending litigation that an adversary party has standing to raise and that must be decided if that party's interests are not to be ignored.

§ 2.2.5 Federal Judicial and Legislative Regulation

Federal courts traditionally have claimed and exercised some forms of the affirmative aspect of inherent judicial power.[74] But on questions of lawyer admission and discipline, federal courts have never been required to rely on inherent powers;[75] from the time they were established by statute in 1789, the lower federal courts have been empowered by statute to regulate lawyers who appear before them.[76] Several decisions have opined that even in the absence of such a statute, the federal courts would have the traditional power of courts to regulate the admission and discipline of lawyers appearing before them.[77] And occasionally federal courts have invoked the inherent powers doctrine in order to determine the reasonableness of a fee charged by a lawyer in federal litigation,[78] to impose fee sanctions on errant lawyers practicing before the court,[79] and to disqualify a lawyer appearing in a case because of an impermissible conflict of interests.[80]

But no unreversed federal decision has sustained anything approaching the radical version of the negative aspect of the doctrine.[81] To the contrary, in 1866 the Supreme Court stated in *Ex Parte Garland* that "the legislature may undoubtedly prescribe qualifications for the office" of lawyer.[82] Perhaps because the constitutional grant of life tenure for fed-

[73] E.g., Pantori, Inc. v. Stephenson, 384 So.2d 1357 (Fla. App.1980). But see In re Appeal of a Juvenile, 61 Ohio App.2d 235, 401 N.E.2d 937 (1978)(inherent powers doctrine vests exclusive power to discipline lawyers in state supreme court; as result, lower courts lack authority to consider motion to disqualify defense lawyer for a conflict of interest).

[74] Link v. Wabash R.R., 370 U.S. 626, 629-33, 82 S.Ct. 1386, 1388-90, 8 L.Ed.2d 734 (1962) (inherent power of trial court to dismiss on own motion for want of prosecution); In re Peterson, 253 U.S. 300, 310, 40 S.Ct. 543, 546, 64 L.Ed. 919 (1920) (inherent power to appoint auditor to simplify issues for jury and to impose costs of auditor on parties); Anderson v. Dunn, 19 U.S. (6 Wheat.) 204, 227-28, 5 L.Ed. 242 (1821)(dictum)(inherent power of court to punish for contempt).

[75] Since the District of Columbia courts were defederalized by Act of Congress in 1970, those courts have been acknowledged to possess the same authority as state courts with respect to regulating the legal profession. E.g., District of Columbia Court of Appeals v. Feldman, 460 U.S. 462, 103 S.Ct. 1303, 75 L.Ed.2d 206 (1983); Doe v. Board on Professional Responsibility, 717 F.2d 1424, 1428 n.5 (D.C.Cir.1983). But, because of the statutory basis of the District courts' powers, local courts have no power to declare unconstitutional Acts of Congress that regulate the legal profession. See In re Kerr, 424 A.2d 94 (D.C.App.1980).

[76] Judiciary Act of 1789, ch. 20, § 35, 1 Stat. 73 (current version at 28 U.S.C.A. § 1654).

[77] See Ex parte Burr, 22 U.S. (9 Wheat.) 529, 531, 6 L.Ed. 152 (1824) ("The power is one . . . which is, we think, incidental to all Courts, and is necessary for the preservation of decorum, and for the respectability of the profession."). See also In re Snyder, ___ U.S. ___, ___, 105 S.Ct. 2874, 2880, 86 L.Ed.2d 504 (1985) ("Courts have long recognized an inherent authority to suspend or disbar lawyers. . . . This inherent power derives from the lawyer's role as an officer of the court which granted admission.").

[78] Esser v. A.H.Robins Co., 537 F.Supp. 197 (D.Minn. 1982).

[79] Roadway Express, Inc. v. Piper, 447 U.S. 752, 766-67, 100 S.Ct. 2455, 2464, 65 L.Ed.2d 488 (1980).

[80] Schloetter v. Railoc of Indiana, Inc., 546 F.2d 706, 710 (7th Cir.1976).

[81] Cf. Ex parte Garland, 71 U.S. (4 Wall.) 333, 379-80, 18 L.Ed. 366 (1866)(acceptance of statutory regulation of practice of law); United States v. Howard, 440 F.Supp. 1106, 1109-13 (D.Md.1977)(federal speedy trial statute unconstitutionally infringes upon judiciary's power in violations of separation of powers doctrine), reversed 590 F.2d 564 (4th Cir.1979). The difference between the federal and state courts might inhere in the fact that the federal Constitution grants Congress the express power (art. III, § 2; art. 1, § 8) to create the lower federal courts and thus Congress may not be constrained to the same extent by the separation of powers notion when vesting judicial authority. See In re Kerr, 424 A.2d 94 (D.C.App.1980).

[82] 71 U.S. (4 Wall.) 333, 379-80, 18 L.Ed. 366 (1866).

eral judges[83] immunizes them more against political pressures, including pressure from the bar, the federal courts have willingly accepted a number of congressional regulations of lawyers without questioning the competence of the legislative branch to act.[84] Thus it seems safe to say that the Supreme Court would not invalidate an act of Congress regulating the legal profession on a separation-of-powers ground,[85] except in the highly unlikely event that an act were passed that attempted to interfere directly with judicial functions, such as by severely restricting the right to counsel, an interference that would more likely be struck down on right-to-counsel[86] or similar grounds relating to the rights of litigants.[87]

Separation of powers doctrines of state and federal consitutional law, in general terms, do not directly affect each other. Thus no federal constitutional principle requires the states to follow, or restricts the states from adopting, any particular conception of separation of powers among the branches of state government.[88] Reciprocally, state conceptions of separation of powers cannot be employed by a state to interfere with the legislative powers of Congress as defined by the federal Constitution and interpreted by federal courts.[89] An act of Congress would not be invalid simply because it regulated all lawyers in a way that would be unconstitutional under the state's constitution if the same regulation were attempted by the state legislature.[90]

WESTLAW REFERENCES

inherent** /6 power authority /p disciplin***
regulat** sanction /p law*** attorney /p judge
judici*** court

exclusiv*** sole /6 power authority /p disciplin***
regulat*** sanction /p law*** attorney /p judge
judici*** court

prohibit*** limit! exclusiv*** lack*** (inherent** /5 power
empower***) /s (trial lower intermediate) (supreme
high***) +1 court /p regulat*** disciplin***
sanction /p attorney lawyer (law legal /3
profession practice)

§ 2.3 BAR ORGANIZATIONS

Bar Organizations as Bar Regulators

One whose reading about the legal profession was confined to appellate court reports might be led to believe that state supreme courts exercise both power and initiative in its regulation. In fact, courts serve as the largely passive sounding boards and official approvers or disapprovers of initiatives that are taken by lawyers operating through bar

83 U.S.Const. art. 3, § 1.

84 Goldfarb v. Virginia State Bar, 421 U.S. 773, 95 S.Ct. 2004, 44 L.Ed.2d 572 (1975) (federal antitrust statutes apply to legal profession); Sperry v. Florida ex rel. Fla. Bar, 373 U.S. 379, 403-04, 83 S.Ct. 1322, 1335, 10 L.Ed.2d 428 (1963) (Congress may regulate practice of law by permitting nonlawyers to appear in adversary proceedings in the Patent Office). Compare, e.g., In re Estate of Freeman, 34 N.Y.2d 1, 355 N.Y.S.2d 336, 311 N.E.2d 480, 484 (1974)(in view of history of nearly exclusive judicial regulation of practice of law, court would construe state antitrust statute not to apply to practice of law).

85 Legislation is occasionally introduced in Congress to establish a federal bar for the federal courts or to enhance the discipline of lawyers. Such bills are uniformly opposed by the ABA on separation-of-powers arguments. E.g., 1972 Midyear Meetings, Summary of Action Taken by the House of Delegates to the ABA, pp. 9, 26 (1972); Jaworski, Association Confronts Challenges of the 70's, 58 ABA J. 920, 922 (1972); 1975 Annual Meeting, Summary of Action Taken by the House of Delegates of the ABA, pp. 25-26 (1975). Cf. Wilkey, Proposal for a United States Bar, 58 ABA J. 355 (1972).

86 See generally §§ 14.3, 14.5—right to counsel, criminal and civil.

87 But cf., e.g., ABA Formal Op. 152 (1936)(lawyer advertising unethical despite any attempt by Congress to permit lawyers to publicize a specialty in patent law); 101 Ann.Rep.ABA 335 (1976)(ABA resolution opposing on negative inherent powers ground a proposed Act of Congress to establish professional discipline system for federal courts).

88 Cf., Sweezy v. New Hampshire, 354 U.S. 234, 77 S.Ct. 1203, 1 L.Ed.2d 1311 (1957); Dreyer v. Illinois, 187 U.S. 71, 23 S.Ct. 28, 47 L.Ed. 79 (1902); Attwell v. Nichols, 608 F.2d 228 (5th Cir.1979), cert.denied, 446 U.S. 955, 100 S.Ct. 2924, 64 L.Ed.2d 813 (1980); May v. Supreme Court of Colorado, 508 F.2d 136 (10th Cir.1974), cert.denied 422 U.S. 1008, 95 S.Ct. 2631, 45 L.Ed.2d 671 (1975).

89 See Central Fla. Legal Services, Inc. v. Eastmoore, 517 F.Supp. 497 (M.D.Fla.1981); Mid-Missouri Legal Services Corp. v. Kinder, 656 S.W.2d 309 (Mo.App.1983)(state courts have no power to appoint state-licensed lawyers who are funded by federal Legal Services Corporation to represent indigent defendants in state court when such representations conflict with regulations of federal agency).

90 See generally Frank, Federal Roles in Lawyer Reform, 27 Stan.L.Rev. 333 (1975).

associations. Bar associations set and execute the agenda of business of the organized bar. Their power can be much the same regardless of the particular form or official status of the bar association. Formal and, to an extent, functional differences do exist between unofficial bar associations and those, called "integrated" or mandatory bars, that every lawyer must join as a condition of being eligible to practice law. At the end of the day, however, bar associations exercise pervasive influence over bar admission and discipline, whatever the form of their organization.

Bar Associations

Bar associations arose in the American colonies as eating clubs or similar social gatherings of lawyers.[91] Lawyer business was also their object, and early rules setting uniform fees and regulating the admission of lawyers to practice came from the bar associations. Bar associations fell into decline and ceased to exist during the early part of the nineteenth century. Little formal organization characterized the American bar until after the Civil War, although the groups of lawyers that accompanied judges on circuit undoubtedly had some cohesion and exercised some collective power.

The American Bar Association

Among the earliest groups of lawyers to band together in the orgy of occupational organization that swept the industrial world in the last third of the nineteenth century was the American Bar Association.[92] The ABA was organized in the late summer of 1878 in Saratoga Springs, New York, a popular summering spot for the well-to-do. Its membership was hardly representative of the average lawyer, nor did it then have any such ambition. The purpose of the ABA was, and for most of its life has remained, that of raising the economic and social status of lawyers and particularly of its members.[93] It does that primarily through political action, broadly defined. The ABA started, and continues, as a private organization that controls its own membership and other affairs and is accountable to no public body for action it might take on organizational or policy matters.[94]

The ABA can advance several reasons in support of a claim that it speaks for the entire legal profession. The ABA is the only national organization with significant lawyer membership from all areas of practice. It operates primarily through sections that are devoted to many fields of law or law practice. Committees of the ABA, which are called sections and operate primarily through their officers, are active in developing policy positions on a wide range of emerging legal problems, in proposing legislation, and in taking public positions on legal and some political issues. The ABA holds national meetings twice annually, publishes the *American Bar Association Journal*, and supports social science research on the law and the legal profession through the American Bar Foundation. Its membership in recent decades has averaged 45 to 55 per-

[91] Among histories of bar associations, see, e.g., R.Pound, The Lawyer from Antiquity to Modern Times (1953); C.Warren, A History of the American Bar (2d ed. 1966). Pound and, to an extent, Warren give laudatory, and largely uncritical, acceptance to the notion that the most highly organized and powerful forms of bar associations are the best.

[92] Accounts of the founding of the ABA are given in E.Sunderland, History of the American Bar Association and Its Work (1953); C.Goetsch, Essays on Simeon E. Baldwin (1981). See generally Brockman, The History of the American Bar Association: A Bibliographic Essay, 6 Am.J.Leg.Hist. 269 (1962).

[93] It is the thesis of J.Auerbach, Unequal Justice: Lawyers and Social Change in Modern America (1975), that the work of the ABA in this century has centered on preserving the economic and social prerogatives of establishment lawyers against the onslaught of competing claims for power and influence of lawyers from recent immigrant groups. It has also been speculated that the ABA was founded in order to influence more effectively appointments to the federal courts in view of then recent decisions of the Supreme Court intimating that state regulation of industry was permissible in an expanded number of situations. See J.Goulden, The Benchwarmers 60-61 (1974).

[94] Suits proceeding on a theory that the ABA is a public entity or exercises governmental power have uniformly failed. E.g., Jackson v. ABA, 538 F.2d 829 (9th Cir.1976); Shaw v. ABA, 63 Ill.App.3d 219, 20 Ill.Dec. 55, 379 N.E.2d 888 (1978).

cent of the nation's licensed lawyers.[95] The ABA House of Delegates, its chief legislative arm, consists in large part of lawyers appointed from several sections or other parts of the ABA or elected from state and local bar associations that, in turn, exercise varying degrees of control over local lawyers.[96] Historically, the leadership of the ABA and officials of both national and state governments have worked in harmony on a variety of projects, including many in the area of lawyer regulation.

Nonetheless, the ABA is not operated as a democratic organization. Its House of Delegates for several years has been criticized as overly representative of nonurban lawyers and malapportioned because of the division of delegate seats among constituent groups, including life memberships held by some ABA ex-officers.[97] The ABA is probably also more attuned to the interests of older, male, and large-firm lawyers than to those of lawyers who are young, women, or minority members or who work in small firms or in solo practices. Most obviously missing from any influence within the ABA, or in any other bar association, is the great mass of the nonlawyer public. Only in the very recent past have efforts begun to give nonlawyers any voice in the business of bar associations. (§ 2.5).[98]

Other Bar Associations

The ABA has several fellow and sister bar associations, but none compares in size or power. Most state and local bar associations are aligned with the ABA but some have no connection. Most other bar associations are devoted to the interests of lawyer specialists or to a particular issue, cause, or ethnic group. For example, the Federal Bar Association consists primarily of lawyers employed by the federal government. Lawyers are eligible for membership in the Association of Trial Lawyers of America (ATLA) only if they represent claimants in personal injury, products liability, or worker compensation claims. Lawyers who belong to the American College of Trial Lawyers, by contrast, predominantly defend large businesses and insurance companies. The National Bar Association is an organization of black lawyers. The National Lawyers Guild is primarily an organization of leftist lawyers interested in civil rights, civil liberties, and poverty issues. The Association of the Customs Bar consists largely of lawyers practicing in the area of federal customs law. Both in membership and in power, all other special-interest bar associations taken together cannot equal the power of the ABA.

Local Bar Associations

State and local bar associations historically have operated much as the ABA—as autonomous, private organizations of largely like-minded lawyers within a state, county, city, judicial district, or other geographical area. Rarely have rival geographical bar associations existed for long, although the Chicago Bar Council and the Chicago Bar Association have competitively coexisted since 1969.[99] Even as purely private organizations, state and local bar associations gained considerable power in the early decades of this century. With growing influence they began to lead more ambitious campaigns to influence the education and admission of lawyers, to restrict nonlawyer competition through the creation of unauthorized-practice barriers, and to deal with disfavored practices such as solicita-

[95] In 1910, two years after the ABA Canons of Ethics were promulgated, the 3,690 lawyers who held membership in the ABA represented about 3 percent of the lawyers in the United States. See W.Hurst, The Growth of American Law: The Lawmakers 289 (1950).

[96] A dated account of the organization of the ABA is G.Winters, Bar Association Organization and Activities (1954).

[97] Barnard, A Proposal to Reorganize the House of Delegates, 64 ABA J. 8 (1978).

[98] See Wolfram, Barriers to Effective Public Participation in Regulation of the Legal Profession, 62 Minn.L. Rev. 619 (1978). On the conflict that developed in California between lawyer and nonlawyer members of the state bar's board of governors, see Schneyer, The Incoherence of the Unified Bar Concept: Generalizing from the Wisconsin Experience, 1983 Am.B.Found. Research J. 1, 68-72.

[99] See Powell, Anatomy of a Counter-Bar Association: The Chicago Council of Lawyers, 1979 Am.B.Found. Research J. 501.

tion and advertising by small-firm lawyers.[1] Their power on those and other professional issues was exerted through public and private pressure on courts and legislatures to cede a wider regulatory role to bar associations.[2]

The Operation of Bar Associations

While bar associations retained the formal status of private clubs, their legal powers widened increasingly as they came to gain political power over the profession. In recent decades, bar associations have turned to explicitly political activity such as legislative and administrative lobbying, public relations efforts, and the support of positions on issues.[3] Some of those efforts relate to law reform, some relate to more controversial political issues, and much does not relate directly to the economic or professional status of bar members. Bar associations do not, however, overtly support candidates for political office, aside from the practice of some associations of expressing approval or regret concerning candidates for judicial offices.

As is true of other professional organizations, the majority of the members of bar associations are inactive on most organizational projects. Most lawyers maintain bar membership as a credential and for such fringe benefits as life and disability insurance. Most members are precluded from actively participating in bar matters by apathy and the distractions of practice and other demands. Motivated and well-situated members of the organization thus may wield influence entirely disproportionate to their number or their ability accurately to reflect the interests of the general membership.[4] Most bar association business is conducted in private meetings of committees or boards. The general membership becomes simply the ratifier of predetermined menus of issues and proposals for their resolution. Of course, the general membership must remain content enough not to resign or to vote out a leadership that has struck off too far on its own. Such membership revolts are known among bar associations and serve to instill conservativism and timidity in bar leaders and executives.[5]

Mandatory Bars

The striving by local bars for more effective control of the legal profession resulted in an effort beginning in the early 1920s[6] to "integrate"[7] the bars of the various states. The term does not refer to racial or gender diversity, which, at that time, was rejected by most bar associations and their members. Instead, integration referred to an organized bar effort to enact court rules or statutes to require every lawyer who actively practiced law to belong to the state bar association. Among other things, making bar membership mandatory would permit the bar association

1 The interest of many local bar associations in solicitation and advertising issues has been almost compulsive. Some of the impetus, no doubt, was supplied by lawyers who attempted to employ the prestige of bar associations in behalf of clients such as railroads in efforts to control lawyers asserting injured workers' injury claims. See the list of cases cited in In re Ruffalo, 249 F.Supp. 432, 437 (N.D.Ohio 1965).

2 Cf., e.g., Dacey v. Connecticut Bar Ass'n, 170 Conn. 520, 368 A.2d 125 (1976) (because all judges on state supreme court were members of defendant state bar association, none was required to be recused from suit attacking unauthorized-practice policies of bar association).

3 Pike, Pushing the Law's Agenda, Nat'l L.J., Nov. 14, 1983, p.1, col.1.

4 See Halliday & Cappell, Indicators of Democracy in Professional Associations: Elite Recruitment, Turnover, and Decision Making in a Metropolitan Bar Association, 1979 Am.B.Found.Research J. 699 (study concludes that divergences between members and leadership on several important indicia have narrowed in 1950s and 1960s).

5 The widely held lawyer belief is that bar associations tend to be conservative groups heavily dominated by large-firm lawyers unsympathetic to social change. A sociologist has argued, however, that the history of the positions taken by various bar groups on controversial social and political issues since the Second World War suggests that liberal as well as conservative causes are often espoused. Halliday, The Idiom of Legalism in Bar Politics: Lawyers, McCarthyism, and the Civil Rights Era, 1982 Am.B.Found.Research J. 913.

6 North Dakota's was the first bar integrated, by legislation, in 1921. See N.D. Laws of 1921, ch. 25; D.McKean, The Integrated Bar 40-44 (1963).

7 Mandatory bars were originally referred to as "integrated" bars and are now more commonly called "unified." The term "mandatory" is less euphemistic and more descriptive of their salient characteristic.

to exercise greater control over the admission and particularly the discipline of lawyers.

Typically the bar was made mandatory by an order issued by the state supreme court under its inherent power to regulate the practice of law,[8] although several mandatory bars have been created by statute.[9] Courts have uniformly upheld the power of the courts themselves or of bar associations to exact mandatory bar fees from lawyers and threaten suspension from practice as a penalty for a lawyer who, without excuse, does not pay.[10] In 1961 a divided Supreme Court in *Lathrop v. Donohue*[11] rejected federal constitutional attacks on mandatory lawyer membership in state bars. By the early 1980s thirty-three states and the District of Columbia had mandatory bars.[12]

The relationship between the unified bar and the court that has often created it is sometimes that of unruly offspring and compliant parent. Courts have shown little inclination to resist strongly and widely held membership views.[13] Because courts lack the time, staff, funds, or means of information gathering, they probably are not intimately aware of the actual operation of mandatory bars and supervise them only in a passive and reactive capacity by passing upon initiatives that are generated and shaped in detail elsewhere.[14] Despite the public status and role of mandatory bars, courts have experienced difficulty in deciding whether to treat them as public agencies, compulsory-membership organizations, or nonpublic voluntary associations.[15]

Although mandatory bars have existed since 1921, they continue to generate controversy.[16] The concept of mandatory bar associations has been resisted for a number of reasons by many lawyers, primarily those in solo practice or small firms. Opponents have feared that annual dues would become too high[17] and that funds taken from members' dues would be used to support projects opposed by a majority of members or to support political causes.[18] The free speech and free association arguments advanced in *Lathrop v.*

[8] In re Integration of Nebraska State Bar Ass'n, 133 Neb. 283, 275 N.W. 265, 114 A.L.R. 151 (1937); In re Unification of New Hampshire Bar, 109 N.H. 260, 248 A.2d 709 (1968); State ex rel. Armstrong v. Board of Governors, 86 Wis.2d 746, 273 N.W.2d 356 (1979)(per curiam). On the courts' inherent powers, see § 2.2.1.

[9] Sullivan v. Alaska Bar Association, 551 P.2d 531 (Alaska 1976); Greene v. Zank, 158 Cal.App.3d 497, 204 Cal.Rptr. 770 (1984). The power of a legislature to integrate a state bar has been denied by some courts under the negative aspect of the inherent powers doctrine. E.g., Integration of Bar Case, 244 Wis. 8, 11 N.W.2d 604, 151 A.L.R. 586 (1943). Some legislatively created mandatory bars have been transformed into creatures of the state's supreme court by court order. E.g., In re Integration and Governance of Utah State Bar, 632 P.2d 845 (Utah 1981).

[10] Petition of Florida State Bar Ass'n, 40 So.2d 902 (Fla. 1949); In re Unification of New Hampshire Bar, 109 N.H. 260, 248 A.2d 709 (1968); Petition of Rhode Island Bar Ass'n, 118 R.I. 489, 374 A.2d 802 (1977). The Ninth Circuit has held that a state dental association rule that conditioned membership on membership in the national American Dental Association may violate the Sherman antitrust statute. Arizona St. Dental Ass'n v. Boddicker, 549 F.2d 626 (9th Cir.), cert.denied 434 U.S. 825, 98 S.Ct. 73, 54 L.Ed.2d 83 (1977).

[11] 367 U.S. 820, 81 S.Ct. 1826, 6 L.Ed.2d 1191 (1961). See also Cuyahoga Cty. Bar Ass'n v. Supreme Court of Ohio, 430 U.S. 901, 97 S.Ct. 1167, 51 L.Ed.2d 577 (1977) (summary affirmance of three-judge court ruling on constitutionality of annual license fee to support state mandatory bar and disciplinary system).

[12] See Nat'l L.J., July 14, 1980, p. 25. col. 1.

[13] In re Petition to Amend Rule 1, 431 A.2d 521 (D.C. App.1981)(majority of court that created mandatory bar association holds that court is virtually bound by result of membership referendum).

[14] A court may insist upon retaining some formal role in important matters of organizational change or discipline. E.g., Berberian v. Rhode Island Bar Ass'n, ___ R.I. ___, 424 A.2d 1072 (1981) (only court can order suspension of lawyer for nonpayment of mandatory bar dues).

[15] E.g., Horowitz v. Alaska Bar Association, 609 P.2d 39 (Alaska 1980)(3-2 decision holding that February meeting of mandatory bar's board of governors in Hawaii was not legally objectionable; bar was exempt from state's open meeting statute), disavowed in State v. Alex, 646 P.2d 203 (Alaska 1982). See generally Schneyer, The Incoherence of the Unified Bar Concept: Generalizing from the Wisconsin Experience, 1983 Am.B.Found. Research J. 1.

[16] See generally Schneyer, supra n.15. Professor Schneyer concludes that the contraditions inherent in the concept of a mandatory bar association should lead to their demise, with their functions taken over by voluntary bar associations or, if necessary, by special-purpose agencies for bar discipline and the like that are financed by court assessment of dues on all lawyers.

[17] See Douglas v. State Bar, 183 Mont. 155, 598 P.2d 1080 (1979).

[18] In re Petition to Amend Rule 1, 431 A.2d 521 (D.C. App.1981)(effect of membership revolt, stimulated by leadership proposal to increase mandatory dues, in reducing mandatory bar's expenditures for citizens advisory

Donohue against a mandatory bar were not rejected by the prevailing opinion but instead found to require additional facts before they could be considered. The Supreme Court has never heard the issue anew in the specific context of mandatory bars.[19] But lower court decisions have held that the "compelling state interest" test that the Supreme Court has adopted in related First Amendment cases requires that any lobbying for which mandatory dues are used, if permissible at all, must bear directly on bar-organization matters.[20]

Registration

Several states that do not have mandatory state bars have nonetheless achieved centralized funding and control over lawyer discipline through registration systems. Those typically require that all lawyers in a state register annually with the state's supreme court and pay a registration fee. Proceeds from the registration fee support the registration system and, more importantly, provide funds for operation of a lawyer discipline agency appointed by the state supreme court. While the system holds the promise of greater independence from the state bar, in operation most courts in registration states give the state bar association a strong role in selection of the members for disciplinary agencies, in proposing procedural rules, and, most importantly, in proposing lawyer codes of conduct.

WESTLAW REFERENCES

committee section /4 "american bar association" a.b.a. /s policy legislat*** promot*** recommend!

integrated unified mandatory +1 bar /p attorney lawyer counsel** (law legal /3 profession practice)

§ 2.4 BAR REGULATION AND NATIONAL ANTITRUST POLICY

§ 2.4.1 *Application of Federal Antitrust Laws*

General

Until 1975 the comforting assumption of the bar was that its regulation was almost exclusively in the hands of bar associations and courts. The tradition of self-regulation (§ 2.1) and wide acceptance of the negative version of the inherent powers doctrine (§ 2.2.3) kept most legislative regulation from the bar's door. That relaxed atmosphere was destroyed, however, when the Supreme Court held, in 1975, in *Goldfarb v. Virginia State Bar*[21] that the federal antitrust laws applied to anticompetitive activities of bar associa-

board, amicus curiae briefs, continuing legal education, lawyer referral, and bimonthly magazine); Falk v. State Bar, 411 Mich. 63, 305 N.W.2d 201 (1981)(remand for consideration of merits of continuing bar support for young lawyers section, lawyers wives' section, lawyer placement service, commercial sale of bar's mailing list, and lobbying activities); Reynolds v. State Bar, ___ Mont. ___, 660 P.2d 581 (1983)(successful suit to restrain mandatory bar from using compulsory dues for lobbying purposes); State ex rel. Armstrong v. Board of Governors, 86 Wis.2d 746, 273 N.W.2d 356, 357 (1979)(unsuccessful suit to return bar to nonmandatory status based in part on belief that lawyers were "forced, by the sovereign power of the state, to support the lobbying, political, social and other non-governmental activities of the State Bar"); In re Discontinuance of State Bar, 93 Wis.2d 385, 286 N.W.2d 601 (1980)(dissident lawyers' petition to disintegrate mandatory state bar denied, but governors of state bar directed to discontinue control over political-action committee); Work, California Bar Nears Split over Issue, Nat'l L.J., Feb. 12, 1979, p.7. col.l (survey of controversies in several states); 64 ABAJ 1488 (1978)(possible effect of state "sunset" legislation on mandatory bars); Pike, Reformers Challenge State Bars, Nat'l L.J., Jan.5, 1981, p.1, col.4.

19 The Court has held, however, in Abood v. Detroit Bd. of Educ., 431 U.S. 209, 97 S.Ct. 1782, 52 L.Ed.2d 261 (1977), that under the First Amendment mandatory dues paid to a labor union could be spent only for "collective bargaining activities" and not for "ideological activities unrelated to collective bargaining activities."

20 Arrow v. Dow, 636 F.2d 287 (10th Cir.1980); Schneider v. Colegio de Abagados, 565 F.Supp. 963 (D.P.R.1983), vacated 742 F.2d 32 (1st Cir.1984); Falk v. State Bar, 411 Mich. 63, 305 N.W.2d 201 (1981). Some states have provided for rebating a portion of the fees of members who oppose the bar's position on legislation. E.g., Report of Comm. to Review the State Bar, ___ Wis.2d ___, 334 N.W.2d 544 (1983). But cf. Ellis v. Brotherhood of Railway Clerks, 466 U.S. 435, 104 S.Ct. 1883, 80 L.Ed.2d 428 (1984). One commentator has concluded that mandatory bars as they now exist cannot survive the approach in the *Abood* decision, supra note 19. Sorenson, The Integrated Bar and the Freedom of Nonassociation—The Continuing Saga, 63 Neb.L.Rev. 30 (1984). See also Note, First Amendment Proscriptions on the Integrated Bar: Lathrop v. Donohue Reexamined, 22 Ariz.L.Rev. 939 (1980).

21 421 U.S. 773, 95 S.Ct. 2004, 44 L.Ed.2d 572 (1975).

tions. *Goldfarb* strongly implies that other federal regulatory laws may also apply to the legal profession. Several doctrines may, however, impinge to an extent upon the reach of federal antitrust laws.

The Antitrust Void in Bar Regulation

For almost a century after the federal antitrust laws were first enacted, it was widely assumed that lawyers were exempt from their reach. More traditional business enterprises such as business corporations engaged in industry and commerce were subjected to those laws that generally restricted such practices as price-fixing, the creation of barriers to entry of potential competitors, division of markets, and similar artificial constraints on the operation of a free competitive economy. Anyone adventuresome enough to speculate about the matter would probably have been unable to convince many lawyers that the Supreme Court would apply the antitrust laws to them. A successful suit would require demonstrating that the legal service or activity involved was "commerce" within the meaning of the act and, conversely, that the status of law as a "learned profession" did not afford lawyers a special exempt status.[22] It would also have to be shown that the challenged bar regulation was anticompetitive; that the regulation affected interstate commerce sufficiently to invoke the federal law; and that the antitrust laws applied despite state involvement through the state's supreme court.

The inapplicability of the antitrust laws, however, clearly could not have been based on a belief that competition was free and unencumbered in the legal profession. Whatever the underlying motivation, it is clear that much of the professional regulation of lawyers has had anticompetitive effects. Minimum fee schedules have kept fees high, unauthorized practice rules and bar admission standards have limited entry, restrictions on advertising and solicitation have reduced competition and the development of new markets for legal services, and limitations on nonlawyer ownership of law firms has reduced capital flow into legal services markets. The resulting losses in economic efficiency have traditionally been defended by bar associations on the ground that the restrictive rules prevent more harmful effects on clients and society. Economists, on the other hand, tend to believe that market efficiency is a net benefit to clients and society and probably to lawyers as a group.[23]

The Goldfarb Decision

The Supreme Court's decision in *Goldfarb v. Virginia State Bar*[24] has created shifts in economic forces within the profession. A surprisingly unanimous Supreme Court held that a mandatory bar association's enforcement of a minimum fee schedule that provided a price floor for legal fees for title searches for residential property sales violated the Sherman Act and entitled the plaintiff client to antitrust damages.[25]

Several aspects of *Goldfarb* bear emphasis. First, the Court held that the minimum fee schedule was an illegal price-fixing mecha-

[22] The Supreme Court had observed in Semler v. Oregon St. Bd. of Dental Examiners, 294 U.S. 608, 612, 55 S.Ct. 570, 572, 79 L.Ed. 1086 (1935), that what "is generally called the 'ethics' of the profession is but the consensus of expert opinion of the necessity of such standards."

[23] Evans, Professionals and the Production Function: Can Competition Policy Improve Efficiency in the Licensed Professions?, in Occupational Licensure and Regulation 225, 250-59 (S.Rottenberg ed.1980).

[24] 421 U.S. 773, 95 S.Ct. 2004, 44 L.Ed.2d 572 (1975) (per Burger, C.J.). The Justice Department had successfully resisted a summary judgment motion on many of the same issues decided in its favor in *Goldfarb* in earlier litigation over a minimum fee schedule against the Oregon State Bar. See United States v. Oregon St. Bar, 385 F.Supp. 507 (D.Or.1974). See also United States v. Oregon St. Bar, 405 F.Supp. 1102 (D.Or.1975) (price-fixing action against state bar mooted by bar's voluntary withdrawal of suggested-fee schedule).

[25] Among the articles examining *Goldfarb*, see Branca & Steinberg, Attorney Fee Schedules and Legal Advertising: The Implications of *Goldfarb*, 24 UCLA L.Rev. 475 (1977); Francis & Johnson, The Emperor's Old Clothes: Piercing the Bar's Ethical Veil, 13 Willamette L.J. 221 (1975); Rigler, Professional Codes of Conduct after *Goldfarb*: A Proposed Method of Antitrust Analysis, 29 Ark.L. Rev. 185 (1975); Tyler, *Goldfarb v. Virginia State Bar*: The Professions Are Subject to the Sherman Act, 41 Mo. L.Rev. 1 (1976).

nism despite the fact that it was called advisory. The Court pointed to the fact that ethics opinions had stated that a lawyer who persistently violated a bar association minimum fee schedule was subject to professional discipline. The Court noted that adherence to the schedule was motivated by the implicit assurance that other lawyers would not compete by underpricing.[26] The Court described the arrangement as "a classic illustration of price fixing." [27] Second, without intimating that all legal services had a sufficient effect on interstate commerce,[28] the Court was generous in its view of the facts that linked fees for title searches to interstate financing in residential real estate transactions. The fact that the anticompetitive activity was a classic price-fixing scheme leaves open the possibility that the Court might determine, in future cases involving bar regulations with anticompetitive features that are less recognizably classical, that the necessary connection with interstate commerce must be somewhat more direct than it was in *Goldfarb*.

The Effects of The Goldfarb Decision

A bar association assessing means of restructuring an anticompetitive practice in a way that assures immunity from the antitrust laws will find little solace in decisions following *Goldfarb*.[29] The Court has held that activities undertaken by individual members of a professional organization may nonetheless be attributed to the organization itself.[30] The Court also soon held that the "rule of reason" that the Court had occasionally permitted to show a special justification for an anticompetitive practice did not apply to a canon of ethics of a professional association that outlawed direct competitive bidding between professionals.[31] The American Bar Association was itself named defendant in a suit, filed by the Justice Department in 1976, challenging the ABA's restrictive rules on lawyer advertising.[32] After first condemning the suit and professing to foresee complete victory,[33] the ABA settled with the Justice Department after liberalizing its rules on advertising and changing the name of the Code of Professional Responsibility to Model Code of Professional Responsibility.[34] Immediate repercussions

26 This aspect of *Goldfarb* is consistent with the Court's tendency to "construe professional solidarity that is evidenced solely by relatively uniform behavior as a 'contract, combination or conspiracy' under the Sherman Act." Kissman, Antitrust Law and Professional Behavior, 62 Tex.L.Rev. 1, 23 (1983). But cf., e.g., Guzik v. State Bar of Texas, 659 F.2d 528 (5th Cir.1981)(provision by state bar of standard form of note containing clause providing for legal fees of 10 percent of unpaid amount of note did not sufficiently involve state bar to constitute combination or conspiracy).

27 421 U.S., at 783. See also Arizona v. Maricopa Cty. Med. Soc'y, 457 U.S. 332, 102 S.Ct. 2466, 73 L.Ed.2d 48 (1982)(setting of *maximum* fees by member doctors of nonprofit medical care foundation was per se violation of Sherman Act despite claim of benefit to public in lower prices because of effects of limiting entry by new providers and innovation in market).

28 See 421 U.S., at 785, 95 S.Ct., at 2012 ("There may be legal services that have no nexus with interstate commerce and thus are beyond the reach of the Sherman Act.").

29 The litigational aftermath of the decision in *Goldfarb* itself counsels caution for bar associations. The suit had been filed as a class action in behalf of 2,000 purchasers of residences in a county. After remand to the district court, it was settled for $200,000, which was paid by the Virginia State Bar and its codefendant, the Fairfax County Bar Association, through an assessment upon members. See ABA Bar Leader at 11 (January/February 1977).

30 American Soc'y of Mechanical Engineers v. Hydrolevel Corp., 456 U.S. 556, 102 S.Ct. 1935, 72 L.Ed.2d 330 (1982).

31 National Soc'y of Professional Engineers v. United States, 435 U.S. 679, 98 S.Ct. 1355, 55 L.Ed.2d 637 (1978). See generally Note, The Professionals and Noncommercial Purposes: Applicability of Per Se Rules under the Sherman Act, 11 U.Mich.J.L.Ref. 387 (1978). See also, e.g., Mardirosian v. American Institute of Architects, 474 F.Supp. 628 (D.D.C.1979)(professional canon prohibiting architect from negotiating for or accepting job for which another architect had been selected was unreasonable restraint on trade when architect was disciplined for accepting employment in job from which government had terminated another architect under contract terminable at will).

32 The text of the complaint appears in 62 ABA J. 979 (1976) and the answer in 62 ABA J. 1179 (1976).

33 Opinion and Comment: That Antitrust Suit, 62 ABA J. 1181 (1976). Aside from denials, the ABA's chief defense was the First Amendment right of expression and right to lobby.

34 See Justice Department Dismisses Antitrust Suit against ABA, 64 ABA J. 1538 (1978).

were felt in several other areas, among them the field of unauthorized practice. The ABA undertook to repeal several interprofessional treaties on unauthorized practice that had been negotiated over decades with several other professional associations.[35] A private antitrust suit by a surety company in a federal court in Virginia explored the antitrust implications of bar association attempts to regulate the unauthorized practice of the law.[36]

The applicability of the federal antitrust laws has had an obvious impact on the form and scope of bar regulation. *Goldfarb* has not meant that all ABA activities that lead to restrictions on the legal profession will be subject to antitrust attack.[37] For example, a divided lower court approved the ABA's restrictive rules on law lists, now repealed, which effectively limited directories to only one of much significance—the Martindale-Hubbell directory.[38] The ABA guidelines and accreditation program for paralegal schools have also withstood antitrust attack.[39] Taken together, however, the success of antitrust plaintiffs in *Goldfarb* and the Justice Department's action in filing suit against the ABA and several local and state bar associations[40] demonstrated that the federal antitrust laws would be applied to bar association restrictive trade practices that at one time were unassailable as the regulation of "legal ethics." Those developments also intimated that a measure of political support existed for executive branch policy making and oversight[41] with respect to the legal profession.

[35] 952 Antitrust & Trade Reg.Rptr. A-30 (Feb. 21, 1980) (ABA House of Delegates vote to repeal "joint statements" with four other professional organizations). See generally Statements of Principles: Are They on Their Way Out?, 66 ABA J. 129 (1980).

[36] See Surety Title Insur. Agency, Inc. v. Virginia State Bar, 431 F.Supp. 298 (E.D.Va.1977) (bar's opinion letter process for unauthorized practice enforcement, coupled with threat of disciplinary action against lawyers who ignored opinion letter, violated Sherman Act), vacated and remanded 571 F.2d 205 (4th Cir. 1978) (remanded for determination of applicability of state action defense because of possible role of state's supreme court in opinion process and for abstention pending outcome of suit raising similar issues in state courts), cert.denied 436 U.S. 941, 98 S.Ct. 2838, 56 L.Ed.2d 781 (1979). The Virginia Supreme Court promptly issued revised bar rules that required review by it before any bar association opinion could become effective if it advised that conduct was unauthorized practice. See Amendment of Rules for Integration of Virginia State Bar, 219 Va. 367 (1978). See also, e.g., United States v. New York County Lawyers Ass'n, 50 U.S.L.Wk. 2074 (S.D.N.Y.1981) (settlement of antitrust suit challenging bar's attempts to restrict trust and estate services provided by corporate banks and other institutions acting as trustees or executors of estates). See generally Little & Rush, Resolving the Conflict between Professional Ethics Opinions and Antitrust Laws, 15 Ga.L.Rev. 341 (1981).

[37] Some early appraisals of the possible reach of *Goldfarb* probably overstated its effects. E.g., Rigler, Professional Codes of Conduct After Goldfarb: A Proposed Method of Antitrust Analysis, 29 Ark.L.Rev. 185 (1975).

[38] Hester v. Martindale-Hubbell, Inc., 659 F.2d 433 (4th Cir.1981), cert. denied 455 U.S. 981, 102 S.Ct. 1489, 71 L.Ed.2d 691 (1982). By the end of 1978, however, the ABA had ceased to certify law lists because of antitrust implications. See Hester v. Martindale-Hubbell, Inc., supra at 434; Justice Department Dismisses Antitrust Suit Against ABA, 64 ABA J. 1538, 1541 (1978); § 14.2.1—law lists.

[39] See Paralegal Institute, Inc. v. ABA, 475 F.Supp. 1123 (E.D.N.Y.1979), affirmed 622 F.2d 575 (2d Cir.1980).

[40] The interest of the Justice Department has remained relatively unabated to the present day. E.g., Taylor, ABA's Rules on Fees and Clients Receive Antitrust Warning, Wall Street J., Sept. 25, 1984, at 10, col.3 (critique by chief of antitrust division of ABA Model Rules on fee size and solicitation in letter to highest courts in 40 states considering adoption of Model Rules).

[41] In addition to actions of the Justice Department, the Federal Trade Commission has indicated a regulatory interest in the legal profession, chiefly through surveys of the trade practices of lawyers and bar associations. E.g., M.Pertschuk, Revolt against Regulation (1982); Calvani, An FTC Commissioner's View of Regulating Lawyers, 70 ABA J. 70 (1984); FTC Survey to Probe Lawyers Ad Practices, 67 ABA J. 1435 (1981); Battle Shaping on Inquiry into the Legal Profession, N.Y.Times, Feb.6, 1981, p.7, col.5; FTC Opens Industrywide Probe of Restrictions on Legal Services, 844 Antitrust & Trade Reg.Rptr. A-14 (Dec. 22, 1977). See also XYZ Law Firm v. FTC, 525 F.Supp. 1235 (N.D.Ga.1981) ("mere possession of a license to practice law" does not exempt law firm from FTC scrutiny of its debt collection practices allegedly in violation of FTC requirements). The ABA has supported legislation to limit the regulatory jurisdiction of the FTC over the legal profession. E.g., 52 U.S.L.Wk. 2078 (August 9, 1983) (resolution of ABA House of Delegates supporting legislationto limit FTC jurisdiction over legal profession); 52 U.S.L.Wk. 2317 (Dec. 6, 1983) (Federal Bar Association leadership opposes legislation to restrict FTC). See also American Medical Ass'n v. FTC, 638 F.2d 443 (2d Cir.1980), affirmed by equally divided court, 455 U.S. 676, 102 S.Ct. 1744, 71 L.Ed.2d 546 (1982)(FTC properly issued order to AMA to cease promulgating or enforcing rules restricting physician advertising).

§ 2.4.2 State Action and State Autonomy

Supreme Court cases holding that the federal antitrust laws apply to bar associations do not mean that all instances in which the bar regulates with anticompetitive effect must be able to pass inspection under those laws. Several doctrines, principally the so-called state action doctrine, limit the reach of the antitrust laws in ways that create opportunities for continuation of some bar regulations that restrict trade practices among lawyers and prevent free competition between lawyers and nonlawyers. In order to conform to the state action doctrine, however, the bar's regulatory conduct must be so closely directed and supervised by the state supreme court that the opportunities for anticompetitive behavior are effectively limited.

State Action

At an intuitive level, one of the most difficult of antitrust doctrines to understand is the rule of Parker v. Brown [42] that anticompetitive action taken at the direction of the state is exempt from the federal antitrust laws. The exemption suggests that states are free to carve out exceptions to the reach of an important federal law, a suggestion that runs counter to the supremacy clause.[43] The rationale that the doctrine is based on considerations of "comity and federalism" merely restates the puzzle without answering it. Nonetheless, in two recent decisions [44] the Supreme Court has held that arguably anticompetitive behavior of the legal profession is exempt from federal scrutiny so long as the regulation bears the heavy stamp of direct and active involvement of the state's supreme court.

It seems certain under the state action doctrine of *Parker v. Brown* that bar regulation that has an anticompetitive effect but that is undertaken directly by a state supreme court will, at least for the purposes of liability under the antitrust laws,[45] be immune from federal regulation. What remains debatable is the required degree of actual state supreme court involvement that the Court will require, at a minimum, to invoke the doctrine. Other Supreme Court decisions in arguably analogous areas strongly suggest that the range of delegation is limited, possibly strictly limited. Most dramatically, a state cannot delegate its *Parker v. Brown* immunity, even to another state agency, such as a municipal corporation.[46] For the legal profession, the overriding issue is the extent to which a state court may delegate its state action immunity to bar associations, lawyer admissions and disciplinary committees, and other bar regulatory bodies composed entirely or dominantly of lawyers.

The first of the state action decisions, Bates v. Arizona State Bar,[47] seems straightforward, given the premises of the defense. In effect, the Court held that persons or organizations that performed anticompetitive acts at the direction and under the immediate control of the state's highest court were entitled to claim the state action immunity. The antiadvertising rule that the disciplined lawyers attacked had been directly adopted by the Arizona supreme court. That court had also authorized the defendant state bar to enforce it in a disciplinary system in which the same court retained extensive powers of review be-

[42] 317 U.S. 341, 63 S.Ct. 307, 87 L.Ed.2d 315 (1943).

[43] The only apparent limit on the state's power is that the statute or regulation, when considered in the abstract, must mandate or authorize some conduct that does not amount to a per se violation of the federal antitrust laws. See Rice v. Norman Williams Co., 458 U.S. 654, 102 S.Ct. 3294, 73 L.Ed.2d 1042 (1982).

[44] Bates v. State Bar of Arizona, 433 U.S. 350, 97 S.Ct. 2691, 53 L.Ed.2d 810 (1977); Ronwin v. Hocver, 466 U.S. 558, 104 S.Ct. 1989, 80 L.Ed.2d 590 (1984).

[45] The regulation may, of course, be assailable on other grounds. For example, in Bates v. State Bar of Arizona, supra, the Court went on to hold that the challenged state supreme court rules restricting advertising were invalid as an unconstitutional infringement of the First Amendment right of free expression. See generally § 14.2.3—advertising; constitutional law issues.

[46] See Community Communications Co. v. City of Boulder, 455 U.S. 40, 102 S.Ct. 835, 70 L.Ed.2d 810 (1982) (city's allegedly anticompetitive restrictions on cable television distribution not protected by state action doctrine).

[47] 433 U.S. 350, 97 S.Ct. 2691, 53 L.Ed.2d 810 (1977). See also § 14.2—advertising.

fore any formal disciplinary sanctions could become final. The court had approved the enforcement of the antiadvertising rule against the plaintiff lawyers in the very case before the Court. The Supreme Court held that the facts illustrated the paradigm of immune state action.

The second case to consider the state action issue in the specific context of the legal profession—Ronwin v. Hoover [48]—involved an arguably less immune arrangement. A state bar admissions committee denied admission to an applicant, using a grading formula that, according to the plaintiff, assigned unwarranted low grades to his and other bar examinations in order to limit the number of lawyers who would compete with lawyers who were already admitted. From the record it appeared that the state court had merely given perfunctory approval to the action of the bar committee with respect to all applicants and there was no indication that the state court had been aware of the allegedly anticompetitive conduct of the agency. Nonetheless, the Court held that the state action defense was available.

If the approach in the *Ronwin* decision is followed, antitrust immunity possibly can be achieved merely through pro forma state supreme court approval of bar association practices that are anticompetitive. If the challenged action is not that of the state's highest court (or other principal holder of either legislative or executive power), other decisions of the Court suggest that a holder of delegated regulatory power, such as a bar association, will enjoy state action immunity only if the party exercising that power can demonstrate (1) that the anticompetitive action is the result of "clearly articulated and affirmatively expressed state policy" and (2) that the policy is "actively supervised" by the state acting in its sovereign capacity.[49] An example of such expressed state policy actively supervised by the state is the role typically played by bar associations in bar discipline. Bar association discipline committees often serve as the tribunal of first instance for bar discipline under rules directly issued by a state supreme court or legislature, and, typically, further review is available in the state's highest court.[50] The fact that a bar association is integrated and thus is an official agency of the state does not suffice to assure applicability of the state action immunity in the absence of the essential factor of active involvement of the highest court or legislature in the very activity alleged to constitute a restrictive trade practice.[51]

The Court's apparently generous interpretation of the state action doctrine may finally put to rest the remnants of the "learned profession" doctrine that were left lying about in *Goldfarb*. The Court there intimated that the "public service aspect" of the legal profes-

[48] 466 U.S. 558, 104 S.Ct. 1989, 80 L.Ed.2d 590 (1984). Plaintiff in *Ronwin* sued for millions of dollars in antitrust damages because of an alleged conspiracy among the several defendants who included the members of the bar admissions committee that had administered the bar examination and recommended the list of passing examinees to the state supreme court.

Professor Kennedy, in Of Lawyers, Lightbulbs, and Raisins: An Analysis of the State Action Doctrine under the Antitrust Laws, 74 Nw.U.L.Rev. 31 (1979), observes that state action cases have typically granted an immunity from damage liability on the part of state functionaries or those operating with state action immunity, but that the Court has never held that non-damage remedies such as the injunction may not be available on state action grounds.

[49] Community Communications Co. v. City of Boulder, 455 U.S. 40, 51, 102 S.Ct. 835, 840, 70 L.Ed.2d 810 (1982); California Retail Liquor Dealers Ass'n v. Midcal Aluminum, Inc., 445 U.S. 97, 105, 100 S.Ct. 937, 943, 63 L.Ed.2d 233 (1980); City of Lafayette v. Louisiana Power & Light Co., 435 U.S. 389, 410, 98 S.Ct. 1123, 1135, 53 L.Ed.2d 364 (1978). The Court held in Town of Hallie v. City of Eau Claire, ___ U.S. ___, 105 S.Ct. 1713, 85 L.Ed.2d 24 (1985), that anticompetitive activities were immune if they were authorized by state law, even if neither compelled nor actively supervised by the state.

[50] Bates v. Arizona St. Bar, 433 U.S. 350, 97 S.Ct. 2691, 53 L.Ed.2d 810 (1977) (state action doctrine affords antitrust immunity to state bar enforcement of rule promulgated by state's supreme court in disciplinary process in which the state's supreme court was the ultimate trier of law and fact with respect to discipline); Foley v. Alabama St. Bar, 648 F.2d 355, 359 (5th Cir.1981).

[51] Goldfarb v. Virginia St. Bar, 421 U.S. 773, 95 S.Ct. 2004, 44 L.Ed.2d 572 (1975). See also Community Communications Co. v. City of Boulder, 455 U.S. 40, 102 S.Ct. 835, 70 L.Ed.2d 810 (1982)(city not automatically entitled to state action immunity despite fact that city was agency of state as regulator of cable television industry).

sion might justify an antitrust exemption.[52] To the extent that a bar agency cannot point to explicit state supreme court involvement in the anticompetitive activity, however, arguments about the public service nature of the bar's activity are rightly suspect. To the extent that such explicit and active involvement is involved, the state action doctrine supplies all of the immunity that seems warranted.

The Noerr-Pennington Doctrine

An unresolved issue is the extent to which a bar association can claim a First Amendment freedom from regulation, including freedom from application of the federal antitrust laws, for attempts to influence the political or legal process, including the process by which the bar itself is regulated. The Supreme Court in the *Noerr-Pennington* cases [53] came close to recognizing [54] such a constitutional right to employ the procedures of state and federal courts and agencies without incurring liability under the federal antitrust laws, even if the intent or effect of the activity is anticompetitive. But a bar association that actively engages in anticompetitive regulation not covered by the state action doctrine should be immune under *Noerr-Pennington*, however, only if the action involves the exercise of a First Amendment right, such as efforts before a state's supreme court to obtain promulgation of restrictive professional rules. If the First Amendment is extended to more than the lobbying or litigation activities themselves, then it would begin to cover some of the ground purposefully left exposed to antitrust scrutiny by the state action doctrine.[55]

State Autonomy

Some have argued that various interpretations of the Tenth Amendment to the federal Constitution shield state regulation of the legal profession from federal judicial review or from being supplanted by an act of Congress.[56] The view probably confuses accidental features of history with causal relationship or at least seeks to resurrect an argument that has been rejected for half a century. While it is true that the states were free of federal judicial or legislative competition in regulating the legal profession until the twentieth centu-

[52] 421 U.S. at 788-89 n.17, 95 S.Ct. at 2013-2014 n.17. See also, e.g., United States v. Oregon St. Bar, 385 F.Supp. 507, 516 (D.Or.1974) (dictum) (bar's regulation of solicitation and advertising might survive antitrust scrutiny "if the public benefit from those ethical canons outweighs the competitive harm").

[53] Eastern R.R. Presidents Conference v. Noerr Motor Freight, Inc., 365 U.S. 127, 81 S.Ct. 523, 5 L.Ed.2d 464 (1961); United Mine Workers v. Pennington, 381 U.S. 657, 85 S.Ct. 1585, 14 L.Ed.2d 626 (1965); Otter Tail Power Co. v. United States, 410 U.S. 366, 93 S.Ct. 1022, 35 L.Ed.2d 359 (1973); California Motor Transp. Co. v. Trucking Unlimited, 404 U.S. 508, 92 S.Ct. 609, 30 L.Ed. 2d 642 (1972). Courts have applied the *Noerr-Pennington* doctrine to litigation. E.g., Coastal States Marketing, Inc. v. Hunt, 694 F.2d 1358 (5th Cir.1983) (foreign country litigation alleged to violate federal antitrust laws immune under *Noerr-Pennington*).

[54] The question whether the *Noerr-Pennington* doctrine is constitutionally mandated is still open because the opinions relied ultimately upon statutory construction to find the antitrust exemption. See Suburban Restoration Co. v. ACMAT Corp., 700 F.2d 98 (2d Cir.1983).

[55] If, however, another federal agency should compel a bar association to take steps that otherwise might violate the antitrust laws, the activity may nonetheless be lawful, or at least may not create damage liability, under a doctrine that seeks to accommodate the possibly clashing impact of two or more federal programs. Cf., e.g., National Gerimedical Hospital v. Blue Cross, 452 U.S. 378, 393 n.18, 101 S.Ct. 2415, 2424 n.18, 69 L.Ed.2d 89 (1981); Hospital Bldg. Co. v. Trustees of Rex Hospital, 691 F.2d 678 (4th Cir.1982), cert.denied 464 U.S. 890, 104 S.Ct. 231, 78 L.Ed.2d 224 (1983). Moreover, to the extent that certain of a bar association's activities involve the state-regulated business of insurance, federal law provides an explicit antitrust exemption. Cf., e.g., Union Labor Life Ins. Co. v. Pireno, 458 U.S. 119, 102 S.Ct. 3002, 73 L.Ed.2d 647 (1982); Group Life & Health Ins. Co. v. Royal Drug Co., 440 U.S. 205, 99 S.Ct. 1067, 59 L.Ed.2d 261 (1979).

[56] Cf., e.g., In re Griffiths, 413 U.S. 717, 730, 733, 93 S.Ct. 2851, 2859, 2860, 37 L.Ed.2d 910 (1973) (Burger, C.J., dissenting) ("The fundamental factor . . . is that the States reserved, among other powers, that of regulating the practice of professions within their own borders. If that concept has less validity now than in the 18th century when it was made part of the 'bargain' to create a federal union, it is nonetheless part of that compact. . . . [T]he Court now strikes down a power of the States [to regulate the bar by excluding all resident aliens from practice] accepted as fundamental since 1787."). But cf., e.g., United Mine Workers v. Illinois Bar Ass'n, 389 U.S. 217, 234 n.17, 88 S.Ct. 353, 362 n.17, 19 L.Ed.2d 426 (1967) (Harlan, J., dissenting) ("[A]ll else failing, the Congress undoubtedly has the power to implement federal programs by establishing overriding rules governing legal representation in connection therewith.").

ry,[57] that merely reflected the general legal situation, in which the federal courts and Congress rarely intervened in state or local actions. That pattern weakened until it collapsed at the time of the substantive development of the Bill of Rights and Fourteenth Amendment protections in the third decade of the present century.

At one time, support for the argument could have been based on the "integral operations" doctrine of National League of Cities v. Usery.[58] Whatever the continuing vitality of the *Usery* doctrine in other areas,[59] it is clear that regulation of the legal profession is subject to no general Tenth Amendment barrier against federal court review (see § 2.5). And *Goldfarb*[60] itself stands for the proposition that the Tenth Amendment does not bar Congress from legislating in a way that blocks inconsistent regulation by the states by force of the Supremacy Clause.[61] Moreover, Goldfarb must also stand for the proposition that the historic role of the state courts in regulating the legal profession is no basis for exempting the legal profession from federal regulation.[62]

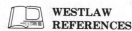

WESTLAW REFERENCES

topic(45 & 265)

state +1 action involvement /p (fee +1 schedule arrangement) pricing /p anti-trust anti-competitive /p attorney lawyer counsel** (law legal /2 profession** practice) (bar /2 state association)

"state action" /p raisin lightbulb /p attorney lawyer counsel** (law legal /2 profession practice) (bar /2 association state)

§ 2.5 EXTERNAL REVIEW OF BAR REGULATION

General

The impact of antitrust law has been the most dramatic, but not the only inroad upon a province that historically has been entirely controlled by lawyers and bar associations. Two other changes in the way that lawyers are regulated have also had an effect—the movement to appoint nonlawyers to lawyer regulatory bodies and the emergence of a limited federal court jurisdiction to review constitutional and statutory challenges to bar rules and other actions taken by bar associations and similar bar regulatory bodies.

[57] Martineau, The Supreme Court and State Regulation of the Legal Profession, 8 Hast.Const.L.Q. 199 (1981).

[58] 426 U.S. 833, 849, 96 S.Ct. 2465, 2473, 49 L.Ed.2d 245 (1976). For an *Usery*-inspired argument, see Steinberg & Koneck, Federalism, the Tenth Amendment and the Legal Profession, 56 Neb.L.Rev. 783 (1977). See also, e.g., In re Griffiths, 413 U.S. 717, 730-31, 93 S.Ct. 2851, 2859, 37 L.Ed.2d 910 (1973) (Burger, C.J., dissenting); United States v. Pastore, 537 F.2d 675, 684 (2d Cir.1976) (Lumbard, J., concurring).

[59] A series of decisions progressively narrowed and then questioned the underpinnings of *Usery*. Recently, the decision was explicitly overruled in Garcia v. San Antonio Metropolitan Transit Authority, ___ U.S. ___, 105 S.Ct. 1005, 83 L.Ed.2d 1016 (1985) (5–4 decision). In one of the prior decisions that had narrowed *Usery*, EEOC v. Wyoming, 460 U.S. 226, 239, 103 S.Ct. 1054, 1062, 75 L.Ed.2d 18 (1983), the doctrine was described as one whose purpose was only to "protect states from Federal intrusions that might threaten their 'separate and independent existence.'" Given the very attenuated sense in which lawyers perform any real public function, at least for the great mass of their work that is performed outside of state courts, federal regulation of lawyers would seem clearly not to be the sort of sapping of the vital strength of states that alone seems to be the energizing concern of the Court.

[60] Goldfarb v. Virginia St. Bar, 421 U.S. 773, 95 S.Ct. 2004, 44 L.Ed.2d 572 (1975).

[61] See also, e.g., Sperry v. Florida, 373 U.S. 379, 403, 83 S.Ct. 1332, 1335, 10 L.Ed.2d 428 (1963) (tenth amendment argument that Congress was powerless to set aside Florida Supreme Court restrictions on practice of law by nonlawyer before federal Patent Office is "singularly without merit").

[62] A year before *Goldfarb* was decided, a state court had held that the tradition of court regulation was a basis for interpreting the state's antitrust laws not to apply to regulation of the legal profession. See Lincoln Trust Co. v. Freeman, 34 N.Y.2d 1, 355 N.Y.S.2d 336, 311 N.E.2d 480 (1974).

For an examination of the implications of the tenth amendment in the context of the authors' proposal for federal legislation regulating interstate law practice, see Comisky & Patterson, The Case for a Federally Created National Bar by Rule or by Legislation, 55 Temp.L.Q. 945, 967-72 (1982).

Nonlawyer Participation in Bar Regulation [63]

Following the decision of the Supreme Court that the federal antitrust laws applied to bar regulation (§ 2.4.1), several bar associations moved, or were forced to move, toward opening positions on bar regulatory bodies to nonlawyers. Some critics would, of course, have gone much further and, for example, replaced the present system of bar regulation with regulation by a public agency whose membership was only or largely comprised of nonlawyers.[64]

Steps actually taken have ranged from legislation in California that required that a minority of the governing body of the mandatory state bar be nonlawyers to moves initiated by bars to appoint nonlawyers to bar disciplinary agencies, fee arbitration panels, bar governing boards, and similar agencies in many states.[65] About half the states now have nonlawyers as members of disciplinary hearing panels. In each instance, the number of nonlawyers has been a minority of the membership. As a result, the effect of the presence of nonlawyers has been confined primarily to occasional assertions of nonlawyer points of view. Sometimes the nonlawyer members have created voting blocs with a minority of lawyers that create results opposed by the majority of lawyers. The presence of nonlawyers on disciplinary hearing boards, however, does not necessarily alter the legal character of the board. For example, the board is not thereby limited to fact-finding and can pass upon legal questions, including constitutional questions.[66]

Federal Court Review[67]

Because bar regulation is largely the action of an agency of the state, it can be challenged under various federal constitutional provisions and under provisions of the federal civil rights statutes. In general, the Supreme Court and the lower federal courts have permitted some kinds of federal court challenges. But the jurisdiction of each set of courts has been limited in a roughly symmetrical fashion that, at least theoretically, provides a federal forum for all constitutional or federal statutory challenges but places a high premium on choosing the right federal court. The basic line of division is between attacks on rule-making functions relating to bar regulation and attacks on the application of rules in individual cases. The review doctrines are discussed at a later point (§ 3.4.5). In addition, through doctrines of immunity, the federal courts have restricted suits that seek to impose damages liability on bar regulators.

Judicial and Legislative Immunity

A lawyer properly invoking the jurisdiction of a lower federal court to challenge a state supreme court's rule on advertising, for example, is limited in the type of relief that may be requested. Because of a doctrine of legislative immunity, state judges enjoy absolute immunity from damage liability for actions of a legislative nature such as the promulgation of a mandatory rule.[68] Even if the state supreme court's action could be characterized as

63 See generally Wolfram, Barriers to Effective Public Participation in Regulation of the Legal Profession, 62 Minn.L.Rev. 619 (1978).

64 E.g., J. Lieberman, Crisis at the Bar 218 (1978); P.Stern, Lawyers on Trial 209 (1980); Garbus & Seligman, Sanctions and Disbarments in Verdicts on Lawyers at 50, 58 (R.Nader & M.Green eds.1976).

65 The ABA has endorsed the concept of nonlawyers in such traditionally lawyer-dominated bodies as advisory committees supervising lawyer referral services (see 64 ABA J. 323 (1978)) and specialization committees (id.).

66 See Middlesex Cty. Ethics Comm. v. Garden St. Bar Ass'n, 457 U.S. 423, 102 S.Ct. 2515, 2523, 73 L.Ed.2d 116 (1982).

67 See generally Martineau, The Supreme Court and State Regulation of the Legal Profession, 8 Hast.Const. L.Q. 199 (1981).

68 Supreme Court of Virginia v. Consumers Union, 446 U.S. 719, 100 S.Ct. 1967, 1975-76, 64 L.Ed.2d 641 (1980). The immunity probably also extends to agents of a mandatory state bar acting as an arm of the state supreme court in disciplining lawyers or assisting in promulgating mandatory rules to govern them. E.g., Levanti v. Tippen, 585 F.Supp. 499, 504-05 (S.D.Cal.1984), and authorities cited.

judicial rather than legislative, a barrier created by the defense of absolute judicial immunity from damage liability would similarly preclude that remedy.[69] But remedies are available, including damage remedies in appropriate cases. Most federal decisions hold that injunctive and declaratory relief is available in federal courts even against state judges and even when they are acting in their legislative capacity in regulating the bar.[70] And, as the Supreme Court's decision in *Goldfarb* itself illustrated, a bar association can incur nonimmunized liability for damages under the federal antitrust laws (§ 2.4.1).

Because the Supreme Court's powers are limited to review of judicial decisions of state courts, as opposed to legislative, administrative, or ministerial orders of those courts, review in the Supreme Court is precluded if what a petitioner seeks is review of a state court order that is essentially the administrative or legislative action of the state court in promulgating a bar regulation or rule.[71] But a lawyer's attack on a state court's application of a general rule or its refusal to waive a general rule in favor of the petitioner is a judicial act that, assuming that other jurisdictional requirements are met, can be reviewed in the Supreme Court.[72]

Conversely, suit in the lower federal courts is available only for the limited purpose of making generalized, systemic attacks upon state bar regulations that are generated by processes, including the rulemaking processes of a state's highest court, that are nonjudicial in nature.[73] A federal judicial doctrine generally precludes lower federal court interference with ongoing state administrative or judicial proceedings. That doctrine applies to state disciplinary proceedings, judicial in nature,[74] brought against a lawyer so long as they were not brought in bad faith or under flagrantly and patently unconstitutional regulations.[75] State proceedings of that kind involving the application of general rules to an individual lawyer, for example, in a discipline case, or to an individual bar applicant, such as in passing on the qualifications of the applicant to be admitted to practice, will not be interfered with by a lower federal court.[76] Final state court decisions in such cases can be reviewed only in the Supreme Court. Once the state court action has become final, it cannot be challenged in a lower federal court for reasons of both federalism and res judicata.[77]

[69] See Stump v. Sparkman, 435 U.S. 349, 98 S.Ct. 1099, 55 L.Ed.2d 331 (1978); Pierson v. Ray, 386 U.S. 547, 87 S.Ct. 1213, 18 L.Ed.2d 288 (1967).

[70] Person v. Association of Bar of City of New York, 554 F.2d 534, 537 (2d Cir.1977), cert.denied 434 U.S. 924, 98 S.Ct. 403, 54 L.Ed.2d 282 (1977); Rapp v. Committee on Professional Ethics, 504 F.Supp. 1092 (S.D.Ia.1980).

[71] E.g., In re Summers, 325 U.S. 561, 566, 65 S.Ct. 1307, 1310, 89 L.Ed.2d 1795 (1945). The question whether a state court's proceedings are judicial, and thus reviewable in the Supreme Court, or a nonreviewable legislative, administrative, or ministerial act is a question of federal law. In re Summers, 325 U.S. at 566, 65 S.Ct. at 1310; District of Columbia Ct. of Apps. v. Feldman, 460 U.S. 462, 476 n.13, 103 S.Ct. 1303, 1311 n.13, 75 L.Ed.2d 206 (1983).

[72] District of Columbia Ct. of Apps. v. Feldman, 460 U.S. 462, 103 S.Ct. 1313, 75 L.Ed.2d 206 (1983); In re Summers, 325 U.S. 561, 65 S.Ct. 1307, 89 L.Ed. 1795 (1945).

[73] E.g., Zimmerman v. Grievance Committee of Fifth Jud. Distr., 726 F.2d 85 (2d Cir.), cert.denied ___ U.S. ___, 104 S.Ct. 2681, 81 L.Ed.2d 876 (1984); Doe v. Pringle, 550 F.2d 596 (10th Cir.1976), cert.denied 431 U.S. 916, 97 S.Ct. 2179, 53 L.Ed.2d 227 (1977), cited and approved in District of Columbia Ct. of Apps. v. Feldman, 103 S.Ct. at 1316.

[74] A state ethics committee sanction, such as a private letter of admonition, that is not subject to judicial review in a state's courts, is administrative in nature and may be challenged in a lower federal court. See Miller v. Washington St. Bar Ass'n, 679 F.2d 1313 (9th Cir.1982).

[75] See Middlesex Cty. Ethics Comm. v. Garden St. Bar Ass'n, 457 U.S. 423, 102 S.Ct. 2515, 73 L.Ed.2d 116 (1982); Mildner v. Gulotta, 405 F.Supp. 182, 196-99 (E.D.N.Y. 1975)(three-judge court), affirmed, 425 U.S. 901, 96 S.Ct. 1489, 47 L.Ed.2d 751 (1976); American Civil Liberties Union v. Bozardt, 539 F.2d 340 (4th Cir.), cert.denied 429 U.S. 1022, 97 S.Ct. 639, 50 L.Ed.2d 623 (1976).

[76] District of Columbia Ct. of Apps. v. Feldman, 460 U.S. 462, 103 S.Ct. 1303, 75 L.Ed.2d 206 (1983); Brown v. Board of Bar Examiners, 623 F.2d 605, 609 (9th Cir.1980); Feldman v. State Bd. of Law Examiners, 438 F.2d 699, 704 (8th Cir.1971).

[77] See District of Columbia Ct. of Apps. v. Feldman, supra, 103 S.Ct. 1303, 1315-17. *Feldman* indicates that jurisdiction was erroneously exercised in cases such as Ktsanes v. Underwood, 552 F.2d 740 (7th Cir.1977), cert.denied 435 U.S. 933, 98 S.Ct. 1508, 55 L.Ed.2d 530 (1978)(Illinois Supreme Court's denial of lawyer's petition

WESTLAW REFERENCES

attorney lawyer counsel** (bar /2 state association) /4 regulat*** /p judicial judge legislat*** /5 immun***

§ 2.6 THE LAWYER CODES

§ 2.6.1 The Purpose and Function of Lawyer Codes

Professional Codes of Occupational Groups

The legal profession for most of the twentieth century has had a lawyer's code of conduct in place. Law was among the last of the professions to adopt a common code of behavior. Many other professions, medicine for example, had adopted codes of ethics even half a century earlier.[78] Today a code of ethics is required regalia for an occupational group that aspires to professional status. Codes can be found among such disparate occupations as lawyers, physicians,[79] psychologists,[80] accountants,[81] and landscape architects.[82]

There are several reasons why an occupational group might decide to agree upon a code of member conduct. Most of the reasons have to do with education, reinforcement, and deterrence.[83] New members of the profession or those who practice in isolated settings might have only sporadic contact with colleagues. A code of rules that is clear and fair can serve an important educational role by instructing receptive readers on what is considered right and wrong.[84] Even initially resistant members of the profession may alter their behavior, not only from fear of enforcement, but from a broader realization of the implications of their actions.[85] The existence of a code may also serve to affect behavior by reinforcing preexisting inclinations. Thus, a member of the regulated group can use the code as a public justification for engaging in conduct that is preferred for other reasons.[86] Most obviously, codes can be the source of prescriptive rules that are sanctioned in formal or informal ways, such as by peer disapproval, by expulsion or suspension from an unofficial professional group, or, as with lawyers, by suspension from the legal privilege of practicing the regulated profession.

Drafters of professional codes may be motivated by a wide array of objectives, including an altruistic concern with the public importance of the actions of the profession's members. On the other hand, for those disposed to hold such views of reality and social psychology, professional codes might be the products of grasping and selfish motivations, based on anticompetitive or class-based animus.[87]

for exemption from admission rule is administrative action that can be challenged in federal district court); and Dasher v. Supreme Ct. of Texas, 658 F.2d 1045 (5th Cir. 1981)(federal district court has jurisdiction over constitutional claims not raised in state judicial proceeding to obtain admission to state court).

[78] B.Bledstein, The Culture of Professionalism 107-08 (1976).

[79] N.Y. Times, July 23, 1980, p.A12, col.1 (new AMA principles of medical ethics).

[80] N.Y. Times, May 5, 1981, p.16, col.5 (American Psychological Association revises code of ethics, among other things, to permit giving psychological advice in nontraditional ways, such as through media and books).

[81] Am. Instit. Certified Public Accountants, Professional Standards—Ethics, Bylaws, Quality Control (1978).

[82] Am. Soc'y of Landscape Architects, Members Handbook 316 (1979).

[83] Schwartz, The Professionalism and Accountability of Lawyers, 66 Calif.L.Rev. 669, 682 (1978).

[84] R.Pavalko, Sociology of Occupations and Professions 101 (1971); E.Zimring & J.Hawkins, Deterrence 77-83 (1973).

[85] Kerhaghan, Codes of Ethics and Administrative Responsibility, 17 Can.Pub.Ad. 527, 533–34 (1974).

[86] E.g., Swaine, Impact of Big Business on the Profession, 35 ABA J. 89, 170 (1949)(lawyers who serve on boards of directors of corporate clients would probably favor ethical rule forbidding the practice as justification for resigning).

[87] Abel, Why Does the ABA Promulgate Ethical Rules?, 59 Tex.L.Rev. 639 (1981)(designed functions of lawyer ethics rules are, secondarily, market control and, principally, legitimation of role of elite lawyers); Rhode, Why the ABA Bothers: A Functional Perspective on Professional Codes, id. 689 (principal functions of lawyer codes are to protect members' economic and psychological stake in public esteem, to minimize both internal and external economic competition, and to reconcile client, colleague, and institutional interests in order to enhance perception that justice is accomplished in adversarial system). See generally M.Larson, The Rise of Professionalism: A Sociological Analysis (1977)(concept of professionalism as

But ethics codes are not drafted on a clean and uncluttered slate. Code drafters confront finite limits on the educative or enforcement effects of codes. Drafting is inherently a process of finding the lowest common denominator. A realist drafting a lawyer code must be reluctant to draft strong or radical provisions for fear that a powerful segment of lawyers will find them too odious or unprofitable to obey. Once a number of lawyers defy a code rule (or are believed by other lawyers to have taken a negative stance), the rule will be widely ignored because of competitive pressures and a sense of unfairness.[88] In that view of professional sociology, the area left for regulation is a relatively narrow range that falls between marginally enforceable rules and insubstantial ones.

Rationale of a Professional Code

For what good reasons should a profession such as law wish to write a code for practitioners? Should the code do more than, redundantly, tell practitioners to obey the law? On what basis should code drafters arrogate to themselves the power to mandate anything else? Should a code even concern itself with all law that might apply to a person who is a practitioner? For example, should a lawyer's code tell lawyers not to double park? If, as with courts, the code promulgator is itself a source of law, putting new legal rules into the form of a code may have the advantages of clarity and breadth of statement. But that hardly tells us what, substantively, should be included in the code.

One perusing the 1969 Code and the 1983 Model Rules will discover that, in the last analysis, little is required of lawyers that is not already required by other law—the law of crimes, torts, contracts, property, agency, evidence. That does not mean that the lawyers' code are otiose. At the very least the codes contain some additional requirements, serve an educational function, and, very importantly, form the basis for imposing an entirely new sanction for violation of other law, through professional discipline.

What, then, should be included in lawyer codes? The answer depends very much on the drafter's desires to reshape or preserve the legal profession, and the reasons for the drafter's wishes.[89] One incentive might be economic. Many theorists and policymakers today have a strong belief in the freedom of markets. A code drafter accordingly might wish to draft the code to maximize every lawyer's free access to clients and, within representations, every lawyer's autonomy to contract with clients and to assist clients in competing in the marketplace and in the adversarial system. The free market model, of course, implies very little regulation but does require a belief in its claims and in the justice of the economic and adversarial systems. A conflicting model holds that lawyers should be regulated as an industry, not only because lawyers have a significant impact upon society and a monopoly within a part of it, but because lawyers are important features of the system by which society claims an ability to deliver justice. That theory has only weak implications for such matters as client-lawyer relationships but strongly implies the desirability of expanding legal services and assigning societal resources to them through such reforms as legal services for the poor and the tax deductibility of legal expenses. A third model notices the respective positions of lawyer and client and concludes that vulnerable clients need consumer protection against lawyers who would otherwise overreach them. That theory concerns itself mainly with the nature of the client-lawyer relationship and

strategy to enhance an occupational group's autonomy, prestige, and economic position); B.Bledstein, The Culture of Professionalism (1976); G.Gilb, Hidden Hierarchies: The Professions and Government (1966); I.Illich, Disabling Professions (1977); Barber, Control and Responsibility in the Powerful Professions, 93 Pol.Sci.Q. 599 (1978-79); Green, The ABA as Trade Association, in Verdicts on Lawyers (R.Nader & M.Green eds.1976).

88 Luban, Calming the Hearse Horse: A Philosophical Research Program for Lawyers' Ethics, 40 Md.L.Rev. 451, 460-61 (1981).

89 An excellent analysis of many of these same issues from a slightly different perspective is Leubsdorf, Three Models of Professional Reform, 67 Corn.L.Rev. 1021 (1982).

has little to say about such things as the delivery of legal services.

An examination of the lawyer codes reveals that no one of those or other models of lawyer regulation has dominated the codes. Instead, the typical lawyer code is an eclectic collection of provisions that can be defended on one theory or another but hardly on all.

State Uniformity or State Balkanization

For a brief period it appeared likely that the dominance of the American Bar Association in regulating the legal profession would result in a uniform set of standards for all lawyers, regardless of the state in which they were admitted. A semblance of uniformity did exist for several decades because of the virtually unchallenged universality of the 1908 ABA Canons of Ethics. But the realm of the Canons was lilliputian; the Canons were widely ignored or superfluous for many regulatory purposes. When the 1969 Code of Professional Responsibility appeared, lawyer regulation began to have a more decided bite and the prospect loomed of greatly expanded enforcement of the lawyer rules in a form that was nationally uniform.

But as lawyer regulation has become more meaningful, it has also become more disparate. A conjunction of political, social, and legal forces has reversed the trend toward uniformity since the middle 1970s. Wrenching debates within the ABA over such issues as the amendment of the 1969 Code rules on delivery of legal services and advertising were greatly enlarged to include many other core professional issues during the ABA's contentious process of generating what became the 1983 Model Rules of Professional Conduct. Those debates reflect deep divisions within the legal profession itself. The great variety of state regulations of lawyer advertising that were produced by the Supreme Court decisions that liberalized lawyer advertising (see § 14.2.3) attests both to the diminished influence of the ABA over the shape of local regulation [90] and to the way that the strength of various segments of the bar fluctuates among different states. Different states also distribute power over the profession between state supreme court or legislature and bar assocation in different ways. That promises to contribute an additional measure of variation in the shape of local adoptions of the ABA's recommended codes of professional conduct.

Emerging Choice of Law Issues

As with other legal areas in which the applicable law varies from one jurisdiction to another, an issue of a lawyer's responsibilities may also entail the question of which jurisdiction's law should apply. The choice may be critical if a lawyer is confronted with professional rules that are in conflict and each of the jurisdictions can claim that its law should apply. The safe course is for a lawyer, if possible, to conform to the stricter standard of those that might be applicable.[91] But a lawyer may not be able to conform to both laws because they compel conflicting conduct, or the lawyer may have other good reasons for wishing to follow the professional rule that is more beneficial to the lawyer's client. For example, one jurisdiction may compel a lawyer to disclose a client's intention to commit a crime, while another arguably interested jurisdiction compels silence.

In instances of genuine and inescapable conflicts, the courts are confronted with the necessity of choice, which should be made in accordance with normal conflict of interest rules.[92] In the process, courts should particu-

[90] The Antitrust Division of the Justice Department in 1978 applauded the "refreshing independence in decision making and local variety in regulation" that characterized the process of liberalizing local advertising rules. See Justice Department Dismisses Antitrust Suit against ABA, 64 ABA J. 1538, 1540 (1978).

[91] Gwirtzman, The International Lawyer: Extra-Territorial Application of Professional Responsibility Standards, in Lawyers' Ethics: Contemporary Dilemmas at 251 (A.Gerson ed.1980).

[92] Elder v. Metropolitan Freight Carriers, Inc., 543 F.2d 513 (3d Cir.1976)(New York lawyer admitted pro hac vice in New Jersey personal injury diversity action is bound by New Jersey maximum limits on contingent fee). See generally Restatement (Second) of Conflicts § 6 (1971); Note, Attorneys: Interstate and Federal Practice, 80

larly avoid extravagant and chauvinistic attempts to apply local law regardless of the relevance of the law of other jurisdictions.[93] Moreover, discipline cases should not hold lawyers to unusual powers of clairvoyance in attempting in advance to determine how a court might resolve an open-ended choice-of-law issue.[94] On the other hand, if the question is whether a lawyer who, for example, has committed a serious crime in a foreign state or country can be disciplined in a jurisdiction, there is no reason to suppose that transjurisdictional character traits should be ignored.[95]

Relevance of Codes beyond Lawyer Discipline [96]

Modern lawyer codes plainly are adopted by courts and legislatures for the purpose of authoritatively measuring a lawyer's liability to professional discipline. But does that exhaust their legal utility? May they also be legitimately employed as a measure of a lawyer's liability for damages in a civil action, for example? Courts in civil litigation employ standards developed elsewhere in two familiar settings. Courts in every jurisdiction look to criminal statutes to see if they appropriately measure a law violator's civil duty of care. If not inconsistent with the statutory scheme, the court's use of the statutory standard furthers the fundamental policy choices of the legislature in proscribing the conduct in the first place.[97] Again, courts frequently employ custom, work practices, and work rules as a measure of liability. Judicial deference to such standards is fully defensible on grounds of fairness, efficiency, and legitimate deference to group practices.[98]

To be sure, both the 1969 Code [99] and the 1983 Model Rules [1] state that a lawyer's violation of a mandatory rule should not, by itself, be a basis for the imposition of civil liability.

Harv.L.Rev. 1711 (1967)(problems of determining which unauthorized practice rules apply to out-of-state lawyers).

93 One of the very few decisions involving an analogous choice-of-law issue may be open to criticism on that score. See Norris v. Kunes, 160 Ga.App. 686, 305 S.E.2d 426 (1983) (contingent fee contract made in Georgia to obtain compensation award from Maine commission valid despite Maine law prohibiting contingent fees in such cases).

MR 8.5 provides that a lawyer admitted in jurisdiction X "is subject to the disciplinary authority of this jurisdiction although engaged in practice elsewhere." The rule should be read as a rule of personal jurisdiction and not as a choice-of-law rule. As its comment makes clear, MR 8.5 merely acknowledges the existence of possible choice-of-law problems without offering any rules or guides to their solution other than a general reference to "principles of conflict of laws." (MR 8.5 comment (second paragraph)).

94 See also, e.g., § 15.4.2 (admission—multistate); § 3.4.6 (reciprocal discipline).

95 Office of Disciplinary Counsel v. Cashman, 63 Haw. 382, 629 P.2d 105 (1981)(conversion of client's funds in California as basis for discipline in Hawaii); In re Scallen, 269 N.W.2d 834 (Minn.1978)(lawyer's commission of fraud offense in Canada as basis for domestic discipline).

96 See generally Wolfram, The Code of Professional Responsibility as a Measure of Attorney Liability in Civil Litigation, 30 S.C.L.Rev. 281 (1979).

97 2 F.Harper & F.James, The Law of Torts § 17.6 (1st ed. 1956): R.Keeton, Venturing to Do Justice 94 (1969); Morris, The Relation of Criminal Statutes to Tort Liability, 46 Harv.L.Rev. 453 (1933); Thayer, Public Wrong and Private Action, 27 Harv.L.Rev. 317, 322 (1913).

For discussions in the specific context of the lawyer codes, see, e.g., Dodge, The Code of Professional Responsibility as an Independent Basis for Legal Malpractice Liability, 1984 Det.C.L.Rev. 135; Dahlquist, The Code of Professional Responsibility and Civil Damage Actions against Attorneys, 9 Ohio No.U.L.Rev. 1 (1982); Morgan, Conflicts of Interests and the Former Client in the Model Rules of Professional Conduct, 1980 Am.B.Found.Research J. 993, 1001-02; Schneyer, The Model Rules and Problems of Code Interpretation and Enforcement, 1980 Am.B.Found.Research J. 939, 946-47; Wolfram, The Code of Professional Responsibility as a Measure of Attorney Liability in Civil Litigation, 30 S.C.L.Rev. 281 (1979); Comment, Violation of the Code of Professional Responsibility as Stating a Cause of Action in Legal Malpractice, 6 Ohio No.U.L.Rev. 692 (1979).

98 See generally 2 F.Harper & F.James, supra, § 17.3 at 977; 2 J.Wigmore, Evidence § 461 (3d ed.1940); James & Sigerson, Particularizing Standards of Conduct in Negligence Trials, 5 Vand.L.Rev. 697, 709-10 (1952); Morris, Custom and Negligence, 42 Colum.L.Rev. 1147 (1942).

99 Preliminary Statement (Code does not "undertake to define standards for civil liability of lawyers for professional conduct").

1 Scope (paragraph 6): "Violation of a Rule should not give rise to a cause of action nor should it create any presumption that a legal duty has been breached. The Rules are designed to provide guidance to lawyers and to provide a structure for regulating conduct through disciplinary agencies. They are not designed to be a basis for civil liability . . . . Accordingly, nothing in the Rules should be deemed to augment any substantive legal duty of lawyers or the extra-disciplinary consequences of violating such a duty."

In other words, the codes should not be read as if they are inevitably to be followed as measures of civil liability. But nothing in either code suggests that it would be inappropriate for a court to examine the code as a possible source of guidance in a civil case. Particularly in jurisdictions in which the lawyer codes are adopted by courts, there is clearly no principle of deference to a coordinate branch of government that requires that a broad reading be given to the lawyer code disclaimers.

Judicial Application of the Lawyer Codes beyond Lawyer Discipline

Despite the lawyer code disclaimers, courts have applied both mandatory and recommended provisions of the codes in many civil contexts. Courts have looked to the codes for guidance on questions such as determining whether a lawyer's trial court behavior was contemptuous,[2] whether a lawyer had been properly appointed a client's executor,[3] whether a fee-splitting agreement was enforceable in a contract action,[4] whether a lawyer hired by an insurance company must inform a client-insured of the insurance company's intent to settle,[5] whether an impermissible conflict of interest or other code violation caused actionable harm for purposes of a legal malpractice suit,[6] whether a published statement that a lawyer acted in a way contrary to the lawyer code is libelous per se,[7] whether a lawyer's claim for fees should be reduced or denied because of code violations,[8] or whether ambiguities in a contingent fee contract should burden the lawyer drafter.[9] The most common nondisciplinary uses of the Code, recognized by all courts that have passed upon the issues, are as a basis for determining whether an impermissible conflict of interest requires a court to disqualify a lawyer from continuing with an appearance in litigation [10] and for determining the proper size of a court-awarded or court-reviewed fee.[11]

Typically, however, courts do not automatically and infinitely extend remedies to every lawyer code violation that an injured party might be able to prove.[12] They refuse to provide a claimed remedy if it is inappropriate to the nature of the violation [13] or if ex-

[2] Davis v. Superior Court, 580 P.2d 1176, 1179 (Alaska 1978).

[3] In re Estate of Weinstock, 40 N.Y.2d 1, 386 N.Y.S.2d 1, 351 N.E.2d 647, 649 (1976)(lawyers' violation of EC 5-6 by influencing client to name them as coexecutors as basis for removal of lawyers from that position and denial of double executor fees).

[4] Hofreiter v. Leigh, 124 Ill.App.3d 1052, 80 Ill.Dec. 319, 465 N.E.2d 110, 111-13 (1984); Fleming v. Campbell, 537 S.W.2d 118 (Tex.Civ.App.1976).

[5] Rogers v. Robson, Masters, Ryan, Brumund & Belom, 81 Ill.2d 201, 40 Ill.Dec. 816, 407 N.E.2d 47 (1980).

[6] Woodruff v. Tomlin, 616 F.2d 924, 936 (6th Cir.), cert.denied 449 U.S. 888, 101 S.Ct. 246, 66 L.Ed.2d 114 (1980) (Code's rules on conflicts of interest constitute "some evidence" of required conduct in legal malpractice case); Lipton v. Boesky, 110 Mich.App. 589, 313 N.W.2d 163, 166-67 (1981) (violation of Code constitutes rebuttable evidence of legal malpractice).

[7] Handelman v. Hustler Magazine, Inc., 469 F.Supp. 1048, 1051 (S.D.N.Y.1978) (New York law).

[8] Ross v. Scannell, 97 Wn.2d 598, 647 P.2d 1004, 1010-11 (1982).

[9] Cardenas v. Ramsey County, 322 N.W.2d 191, 193, 31 A.L.R.4th 89 (Minn.1982)(lawyer's failure to abide by EC 2-19 direction to reach "clear agreement" with client on matter of basis for fee is sufficient reason for construing ambiguous fee contract against lawyer).

[10] Unified Sewerage Agency v. Jelco, Inc., 646 F.2d 1339, 1342, n.1 (9th Cir.1981). See generally § 7.1.7 (conflict remedies).

[11] Nolan v. Foreman, 665 F.2d 738, 741 (5th Cir.1982) (use of Code to determine whether lawyer's fee charge was reasonable); Hull v. Douglas, 271 So.2d 1, 3-4, 6 (Fla. 1972)(lawyer may not share in any portion of fee for services rendered after lawyer learned he was subject to advocate-witness rule of DR 5-102); In re Estate of Kingseed, ___ Ind.App. ___, 413 N.E.2d 917 (1980)(trial court in exercising discretion to set fees for lawyer for decedent's estate properly considered "quality of services" under Code and, in that inquiry, properly took into account lawyer's defaults and neglect in providing services). See generally § 9.3.1 (fair fees).

[12] Some decisions denying relief suggest, overbroadly, that an ethical violation is irrelevant to the question of liability. E.g., Sullivan v. Birmingham, 11 Mass.App. 359, 416 N.E.2d 528, 534 (1981); Ayyildiz v. Kidd, 220 Va. 1080, 266 S.E.2d 108, 112 (1980).

[13] E.g., W.T. Grant Co. v. Haines, 531 F.2d 671 (2d Cir. 1976)(lawyers' violation of prohibition against giving legal advice to unrepresented party insufficient basis to dismiss client's subsequent lawsuit or disqualify law firm); People v. Green, 405 Mich. 273, 274 N.W.2d 448, 454 (1979) (prosecutor's violation of Code rule on contact with represented party not sufficient basis for exclusion of incriminatory statements in criminal trial of client); Brainard v. Brown, 91 A.D.2d 287, 458 N.Y.S.2d 735

isting bases of liability are considered sufficient to provide appropriate levels of deterrence and compensation.[14] For similarly justifiable reasons, courts have generally refused to employ the Code as a measure of criminal responsibility.[15] Courts are also wary about applying lawyer code provisions in civil litigation if the code provision in question provides the lawyer with a claimed immunity in derogation of other rules of liability.[16]

§ 2.6.2 The 1908 ABA Canons of Ethics [17]

Background and Adoption of Canons

The last century has witnessed a great expansion in the extent to which the organized legal profession has exercised disciplinary power over lawyers. Around 1870, disciplinary control was dispersed among local courts and exercised only sporadically, taking the form of very occasional disbarment proceedings against lawyers who had committed outrageous depredations.[18] The few existing bar associations apparently exercised little power and played little part in lawyer discipline in any organized way. When the American Bar Association was organized in 1878, no attention was paid to the matter of devising a uniform set of standards to govern lawyer conduct.[19] Lawyers and judges, and committees of these, had written various codes of ethics formulating a lawyer's responsibilities, but those codes were generally intended for edification rather than enforcement and had only the authority of their individual authors behind them.[20]

(1983)(in view of explicit statute of limitations on legal malpractice, former client could not cite Code violation as basis for breach of contract action).

[14] That is a common ground of decision in the many cases that have refused to create a new tort, parallel to but extending beyond the torts of malicious prosecution or abuse of process, against lawyers who file frivolous or otherwise unfounded litigation. E.g., Bob Godfrey Pontiac, Inc. v. Roloff, 291 Or. 318, 630 P.2d 840 (1981)(malicious prosecution tort sufficiently satisfies state interest in suppressing frivolous litigation, precluding creation of new tort for violation of obligation under lawyer code), and authorities cited.

[15] E.g., People v. Stein, 94 Cal.App.3d 235, 156 Cal.Rptr. 299, 302 (1979). See also State v. Douglas, 217 Neb. 199, 349 N.W.2d 870 (1984)(Code violations, by themselves, are not adequate ground for impeachment of state attorney general). But cf., e.g., United States v. DeLucca, 630 F.2d 294, 301 (5th Cir.1980), cert.denied 450 U.S. 983, 101 S.Ct. 1520, 67 L.Ed.2d 819 (1981)(Code appropriately considered in determining lawyer's willing participation in conspiracy to sell cocaine); People v. Keefe, 50 N.Y.2d 149, 428 N.Y.S.2d 446, 405 N.E.2d 1012, 1016-17 (1980)(dictum).

[16] First Bank & Trust Co. v. Zagoria, 250 Ga. 844, 302 S.E.2d 674 (1983) (EC 6-6 statement approving limitation of liability of members of professional corporation no bar to court's announcement of common-law rule of vicarious liability); Coon v. Landry, 400 So.2d 1144, 1146 (La.App.), affirmed 408 So.2d 262 (La.1981) (Code rule that client must ultimately be liable for expenses of litigation advanced by lawyer do not void lawyer's contract with client to bear those expenses); cf. Lott v. Ayres, 611 S.W.2d 473, 476 (Tex.Civ.App.1980)(on rehearing 1981) (lawyer did not breach contract with client when lawyer entitled, perhaps required, to withdraw under lawyer code). But cf. Jackson v. Jackson, 20 N.C.App. 406, 201 S.E.2d 722, 70 A.L.R.3d 1294 (1974) (law partner not vicariously liable for malicious prosecution, because tortfeasor partner prohibited from bad faith litigation by DR 7-102(A) and thus not acting within scope of partnership business).

[17] The Canons are cited in this treatise as "1908 Canons."

[18] See R.Pound, The Lawyer from Antiquity to Modern Times 184-85, 242, 248 (1953).

[19] The documents recording the beginnings of the ABA suggest that substantive law reform and social conviviality in Saratoga Springs, the site of all of the early ABA meetings, were the uppermost projects in mind. See Proceedings of the Conference Called for the Purpose of Organizing a National Bar Association and of the First Annual Meeting of the American Bar Association, 1 ABA Rep. 5, 16-19, 24 (1878). The ABA's committee on grievances scarcely functioned at all during the years 1878-1902. See E.Sunderland, History of the ABA 22 (1953).

[20] Hoffman, Professional Deportment, in A Course of Legal Study 324-34 (1817); Hoffman, Professional Deportment, in 11 A Course of Legal Study 720-75 (2d ed.1836); T.Walker, Introduction to American Law, Designed as a First Book for Students (1837); Report of the Commissioners on Practice and Pleadings, Code of Civil Procedure 204-09 (1850)(the "Field Code"); G.Sharswood, An Essay on Professional Ethics (1854) (republished in 32 ABA Rep. 1 (1907)); Alabama Code of Ethics, 118 Ala. xxiii (1899—first adopted by the Alabama State Bar Association in 1887); G.Warvelle, Essays in Legal Ethics (1902). A look at most of the earlier lawyer codes suggests that the authors often had other axes to grind. Sharswood, for example, republished his Essay on Professional Ethics in a second edition (1860) that begins with an "Introduction" consisting of a forty-five page diatribe on the duty of all lawyers to persuade legislators of the importance of private property rights. See Bloomfield, David Hoffman and the Shaping of a Republican Legal Culture, 38 Md.L.Rev. 673 (1979).

Nineteenth century English materials include: A. & W.Vuckland, Letters to an Attorney's Clerk, Containing

It was not until 1908 that the ABA was moved to devise a common statement of professional norms that presumably would reflect the values of most lawyers. The 1908 Canons originally consisted of thirty-two hortatory statements that insisted that a lawyer pursue the high road in every endeavor mentioned.[21] They did not attract a great deal of meaningful professional or public attention at the time.[22] The Canons were not orginally adopted in order to serve as a regulatory blueprint for enforcement through disbarment and suspension actions. Instead, they seem to have been a statement of professional solidarity—an assertion by elite lawyers in the ABA [23] of the legitimacy of their claim to professional stature. The fact that the Code was copied from much earlier documents, and in verbiage and conceptualization that even in 1908 must have appeared terribly dated,[24] was hardly objectionable in a document whose drafters intended primarily to celebrate the ancient lineage of the bar's professional stature.

Critiques of the Canons

One reading the Canons today [25] is struck by narrowness of vision. They speak of a kind of law practice that was carried on almost entirely in the courtroom.[26] The dominant points of reference are relationships between lawyer and client and lawyer and lawyer. Professor James Willard Hurst has described the Canons as imbued with the heavily individualistic flavor of honorable relations between individuals, paying little attention to larger issues of how lawyers relate to each other and to the bar and the general society.[27] The Canons assume that all lawyers are sufficiently homogenous to conform to common standards, an assumption that was probably unfounded in 1908 and certainly proved false as members of an increasingly stratified bar confronted a variety of contrasting practice settings in an increasingly indus-

Directions for His Studies and General Conduct (London 1824); S.Warren, the Moral, Social and Professional Duties of Attorneys and Solicitors (London 1848).

21 The 1908 Canons were not designed to break new ground. They were largely copied from the 1887 Code of Ethics of the Alabama State Bar Association. Supra n.20. Bar associations in ten states had adopted codes of ethics after 1887, borrowing heavily from the Alabama Code. The committee that drafted the ABA Code set about its task with the idea of using the existing eleven state codes as models. See 31 Ann.Rep. ABA 676, 680 (1907). The committee also noted that the Alabama Code was drawn, sometimes using the same words, from Sharswood's Essay on Professional Ethics. Id. 678. The committee that actually drafted the 1908 Code reported that it had followed those models closely. See 33 Ann.Rep. ABA 56-57 (1908). On the adoption of the 1908 Canons, see generally H.Drinker, Legal Ethics 23-25 (1953); J.Hurst, The Growth of American Law—The Law Makers 329-30 (1950); E.Sunderland, History of the American Bar Association and Its Work 110-12 (1953); Jones, Canons of Professional Ethics, Their Genesis and History, 7 Notre Dame Law. 483 (1932).

22 Works inspired by the ABA Canons include G.Archer, Ethical Obligations of the Lawyer (1910); O.Carter, The Ethics of the Legal Profession (1915); E.Thornton, A Treatise on Attorneys at Law (2 vols.1914); W.Vincent, The Lawyer in His Several Relations (1910). By 1914, thirty-one state bar associations had adopted the 1908 ABA Canons as their own. See H.Drinker, Legal Ethics 25 (1953); 39 Ann.Rep. ABA 559, 560-61 (1914).

23 Some 3,690 lawyers belonged to the ABA in 1908. J.Hurst, Growth of American Law: The Lawmakers 289 (1950). That number represented only 3 percent of the approximately 123,000 lawyers in the United States at that time.

24 A familiar critique of the Canons is A.Hays, City Lawyer 32 (1942) ("the sort of pontifical pap that is fed to intelligent and secretly bored youngsters just starting their professional lives. . . . Equipped with these virtues, a man could sit for years in an empty office, starving with quiet dignity."). Hays' "pap" remarks were a quotation from an article by then federal judge Manton. In context, it is clear that Hays' complaint is not against virtue, but against the idea that "good character, honesty, and loyalty" are all that a young lawyer needs to succeed in law practice.

25 The Canons, with their amendments (through 1954), can be found in ABA Opinions on Professional Ethics (1967).

26 The Canons' focus upon litigation is ironic. The importance of the lawyer's counselling function was already well recognized and controversial. The chairman of the committee that drafted the Canons was Henry St. George Tucker of Virginia. Tucker, while previously president of the ABA, had prominently noted at the 1905 ABA annual meeting that President Theodore Roosevelt a year earlier had criticized the "most influential and most highly remunerated members of the Bar" for their advice to wealthy clients on how best "to evade the laws which are made to regulate in the public interest the use of great wealth." 28 Ann.Rep.ABA 299, 383 (1905).

27 J.Hurst, The Growth of American Law: The Law Makers 329-30 (1950).

trialized and urbanized world.[28] Even if the ethical stance and scope of the Canons is accepted, their wording is too vague and general to afford guidance.[29] The most magisterial criticism was that of Justice Harlan Fiske Stone, of the Supreme Court, who in 1934 urged the bar to reappraise the lawyer's relationship to public, clients, and professional peers:

> That appraisal must pass beyond the petty details of form and manners which have been so largely the subject of our Code of Ethics, to more fundamental consideration of the way in which our professional activities affect the welfare of society as a whole. Our Canons of Ethics for the most part are generalizations designed for an earlier era. However undesirable the practices condemned, they do not profoundly affect the social order outside our own group.[30]

Although offered in a spirit of comradeship, Justice Stone's comments made the cruelest charge: the Canons were irrelevant.

Authoritative Effect of the Canons

The Canons were probably not intended to have any direct legal effect,[31] but it is clear that the ABA leadership contemplated that they would be influential in lawyer discipline proceedings in courts.[32] As bar associations became more active in enforcing professional standards through disbarment and suspension procedures of courts, the Canons came to be widely regarded as "wholesome standards of professional action" [33] or as "guidelines," [34] which lawyers could ignore only at their peril.[35] In some states the Canons were adopted by the state's bar association and were then enforced by the jurisdiction's courts in opinions dealing with questions of lawyer discipline.[36] Other states adopted the Canons

28 J.Carlin, Lawyers on Their Own (1962); id., Lawyers Ethics (1966)(Canon's approach ignores fact that "unethical" lawyer behavior is almost inevitably a consequence of pressures at bar's marginal levels and is probably beyond the reach of uniform standards). See also, e.g., J.Auerbach, Unequal Justice 204-05 (1976).

29 Bowman, Standards of Conduct for Prosecution and Defense Personnel: An Attorney's Viewpoint, 5 Am. Crim.L.Q. 28 (Fall 1966) ("[T]he Canons of Ethics are so vague, so ambiguous, and so contradictory that they are of little or no help in resolving these problems. . . . [A]lmost any position, on a given issue, can reasonably be defended with support from the Canons. . . ."); Starrs, Professional Responsibility: Three Basic Propositions, 5 Crim.L.Q. 17, 20 (Fall 1966)("glittering generalities which, as someone has said, lack a 'body to kick and a soul to condemn'."); A.Amsterdam (quoted in Time Magazine, May 13, 1966, p. 81, from a letter to Washington, D.C., grievance committee) ("vaporous platitudes called canons of ethics which have somewhat less usefulness as guides to lawyers in the predicaments of the real world than do valentine cards as guides to heart surgeons in the operating room"). A particularly embarrassing moment came in State v. Zwillman, 112 N.J.Super. 6, 270 A.2d 284, 288-89 (1970), when the court was compelled to hold that a trial court's verbatim quoting from the Canons in instructing a jury in a criminal case constituted reversible error, because the jury was entitled to an understandable instruction.

30 Stone, The Public Influence of the Bar, 48 Harv.L. Rev. 1, 10 (1934).

31 At a later date, the ABA ethics committee made extravagant and insupportable claims for the effectiveness of the Canons. In ABA Formal Op. 142 (1935), for example, the committee opined that a canon overrode contrary state statutes. See also, e.g., ABA Formal Op. 152 (1936)(Canons override federal statutes permitting advertising of patent specialty); ABA Formal Ops. 203 (1940); id. 164 (1936); id. 42 (1931)(Canons override judicial acquiesence in conduct that violates Canons); id. 6 (1925); id. 4 (1924).

32 Baldwin, The New American Code of Legal Ethics, 8 Col.L.Rev. 541, 546 (1908)("The courts will hesitate less in enforcing the discipline of the bar, since professional misconduct will be, more than ever before, a sinning against the light.").

33 In re Cohen, 261 Mass. 484, 159 N.E. 495, 496, 55 A.L.R. 1309 (1928).

34 Hunter v. Troup, 315 Ill. 293, 146 N.E. 321, 324 (1925); In re Kuzman, 335 N.E.2d 210, 212 (Ind.1975) (Canons, which governed pre-Code offenses, "do not have the authority of statutes or case law, but they evidence proper standards of conduct for the legal profession").

35 Some jurisdictions, at least at a time, rejected the argument that failure to abide by one of the Canons was a sufficient ground for disbarment. E.g., In re Clifton, 33 Idaho 614, 196 P. 670, 19 A.L.R. 931 (1921); Ringen v. Ranes, 263 Ill. 11, 104 N.E. 1023, 1025 (1914). But see, e.g., Hunter v. Troup, 315 Ill. 293, 146 N.E. 321, 324 (1925) (lawyer may be disciplined for not observing Canons).

36 In re Heirich, 10 Ill.2d 357, 140 N.E.2d 825, 67 A.L.R.2d 827 (1956), cert.denied 355 U.S. 805, 78 S.Ct. 22, 2 L.Ed.2d 49 (1957); In re Kuzman, 355 N.E.2d 210, 214 (Ind.1975); In re Connelly, 18 A.D.2d 466, 240 N.Y.S.2d 126 (1963). Most of the federal courts gave a similar effect to the Canons. E.g., T.C. Theatres Corp. v. Warner Bros. Pictures, Inc., 113 F.Supp. 265, 268 n.4 (S.D.N.Y. 1953).

more formally as court rules [37] or, in some few states, as legislation.[38] The significance of the Canons, aside from their historical importance as an episode in bar regulation, is that they served as the forerunner to the 1969 Code and the 1983 Model Rules. That pedigree is stressed at various other points in this treatise.

§ 2.6.3 1969 ABA Code of Professional Responsibility [39]

Drafting and Adoption of the 1969 Code

Persistent complaints about the outdated and vague [40] Canons led the ABA president and later Justice of the Supreme Court, Lewis F. Powell, Jr., to appoint an ABA committee in 1964 to study the Canons and prepare suggested amendments to them.[41] The committee, chaired by practitioner Edward L. Wright and known as the Wright Committee, eventually decided to begin anew with a new format and a new approach. Its product was presented in the form of a preliminary draft of January 1969.[42] Some revisions were made, [43] and the Code was finally adopted by the ABA House of Delegates at its midyear meeting in August 1969.[44] The Code was to become effective on January 1, 1970, but presumably it would bind only lawyers who were ABA members until adopted by local jurisdictions.

The Code acquired the force of law when it was adopted in a jurisdiction by state authority, typically the state's highest court. When the Code was adopted in 1969, the ABA appointed a special adoption committee and launched a highly organized campaign to persuade the states to adopt the Code as the official local set of standards for lawyers. In contrast to the 1908 Canons which were only slowly adopted in some states, the 1969 Code was an impressive and quick success. Not all states adopted all the parts of the Code. Several states omitted the Ethical Considerations. Counting adoptions by state bar associations, by 1972 the adoption committee could report that every jurisdiction had taken steps to adopt the Code except three states, including California.[45] Two of those states

[37] Comm. on Professional Ethics v. Mershon, 316 N.W.2d 895, 898 (Iowa 1982)(Iowa lawyers subject to ABA Canons (with one exception) by force of court rule); Ky. Sup.Ct.Rules, Rule 3.170 (1946)("accepts the principles embodied in" the Canons "as a sound statement of the standard of professional conduct required of members of the . . . Bar, and the Court regards these Canons as persuasive authority in all disciplinary proceedings against members of the Bar."); Minnesota Supreme Court Order of May 2, 1955, 241 Minn. xvii (1955); In re Schofield, 362 Pa. 201, 209, 66 A.2d 675, 679 (1949) (ABA Canons, adopted by reference in rules of procedure, have the force of statutory rules of conduct for lawyers).

[38] Bates v. Arizona State Bar, 433 U.S. 350, 362, n.15, 97 S.Ct. 2691, 53 L.Ed.2d 810 (1977) (enactment of Canons by Arizona legislature in 1919); In re Galton, 289 Or. 565, 615 P.2d 317, 326 (1980) (Canons adopted in 1935 by state bar association and given binding effect by statute); In re Arctander, 110 Wash. 296, 188 P. 380 (1920).

[39] The Code is cited in this treatise as "1969 Code."

[40] According to the draftsman of the 1969 Code, the imprecision of the Canons was the principal reason for redrafting them. See 1969 Code, Preface; Sutton, Introduction to Symposium—The American Bar Association Code of Professional Responsibility, 48 Tex.L.Rev. 255 (1970).

[41] For description of the process of adopting the 1969 Code, see, e.g., Sutton, supra.

[42] See ABA Spec. Comm. on Evaluation of Ethical Standards, Code of Professional Responsibility (Preliminary Draft, Jan. 15, 1969).

[43] The complete drafting history of the 1969 Code is traced in a very useful volume, ABF Annotated Code of Professional Responsibility (O.Maru ed.1979). Fascinating critique of the Code by its reporter appears at various points in Sutton, Commentary on the Texas Code of Professional Responsibility, in Texas Lawyers' Professional Ethics, at 6-2 (State Bar of Texas 1979). See also, e.g., Armstrong, The ABA Code of Professional Responsibility: Some Personal Reflections, 23 Baylor L.Rev. 679 (1972); Sutton, The American Bar Association Code of Professional Responsibility: An Introduction, 48 Tex.L.Rev. 255 (1970); Sutton, How Vulnerable Is the Code of Professional Responsibility, 57 N.C.L.Rev. 497 (1979)("largely as a consequence of the influence upon the Code of the political adoption process, the ABA Code at the outset contained several flaws obvious to many commentators").

[44] ABA Spec. Comm. on Eval. of Ethical Stands., Code of Professional Responsibility (Final Draft, July 1, 1969).

[45] Report of Spec. Comm. to Secure Adoption of the Code of Prof. Resp., 97 Ann.Rep. ABA 268 (1972). The committee listed several states as "adopting" the Code even if it had received only unofficial state bar approval. Official versions of a revised Code were not adopted in Illinois and Maine, for example, until 1980.

The official state version of the Code can be found typically in the state's compiled statutes (often among the adopted the Code soon thereafter,[46] and it has had a strong influence in California as well (§ 2.6.5).

But once adopted the 1969 Code proved to be much more controversial and less stable than were the 1908 Canons. The ABA was moved to adopt amendments to the Code every year between 1974 and 1980, when a first draft of the Model Rules, which would eventually replace the Code in the ABA's eyes, had already been published. In contrast to the rather uniform reception of the text of the original code,[47] some of the important Code amendments have been rejected by a large majority of states or many states adopted amendments that differed materially from the version recommended by the ABA. In part, the controversy that surrounded the Code's amendments attested to the increasing influence of the Code in shaping the outcomes of lawyer regulation. One of the last amendments to the Code was the addition, in 1978, of the limiting phrase "Model" to its title as part of a negotiated settlement of Justice Department antitrust charges that the ABA was attempting to act authoritatively in regulating competitive activities of lawyers.[48]

Legal Effect of the Code

Adoption of the Code raised a number of difficult legal issues, not all of which have been satisfactorily resolved. The same questions will recur if and when a state adopts the ABA's 1983 Model Rules. Among other questions raised are these. To what extent is the Code authoritative within a state? How are conflicts between the Code and state statutes or other law to be resolved? Is the Code relevant only for purposes of lawyer discipline, or can it be regarded as a legitimate source of legal doctrine for other purposes, such as procedural motions or in legal malpractice actions? How are codal provisions to be interpreted—as statutes? And if so, what kind of statute, and what are the appropriate judicial attitudes toward the task of interpretation? Are normal notions of prescriptive legality applicable to the Code, such as general principles that refuse to apply punitive sanctions retroactively or by means of expansive readings? The latter questions relate to the Code's impact in lawyer discipline cases (see § 3.3.1); the former raise issues about the basic legal standing of the Code.

In most states the Code was adopted as law and not merely as an approximation of law or the like. The Code was adopted in the great majority of states by the supreme court under the court's inherent and exclusive power to regulate the legal profession (§ 2.2.1). Thus the Code presumably prevails over everything other than federal law or state constitutional law.[49] State statutory or administrative law in conflict with a provision of the Code would be ineffective because of the negative aspect of the inherent powers doctrine (see § 2.2.3). In a few states, however, the view has been that the Code cannot amend or limit a legislative enactment.[50] In jurisdictions in which the Code was adopted by a bar association, and adopted by the state supreme court mere-

rules of court) or in a preface to a volume of the state's official reports. Many state bar associations publish annual "deskbooks" for practitioners that contain the Code and other material.

[46] At the time of the ABA adoption committee report, supra, only Alabama, North Carolina, and California were listed as nonadopting states. Alabama adopted the Code in late 1974. See In re McDonald, 292 Ala. 426, 296 So.2d 141, 142 (1974). The North Carolina bar adopted the Code, and the North Carolina Supreme Court approved it, in 1973. See 283 N.C. 848 (1973).

[47] The state variations in the code can be seen in ABF Code of Professional Responsibility by State (looseleaf 1980).

[48] See Justice Dept. Memorandum in Support of Motion to Dismiss, reprinted in 64 ABA J. 1538 (1978).

[49] The extreme form of the doctrine is that courts themselves have no power to depart from the Code. E.g., General Mill Supply Co. v. SCA Services, Inc., 697 F.2d 704, 711 (6th Cir.1982) (dictum) (disqualification of advocate-witness). Contra, e.g., J.P. Foley & Co. v. Vanderbilt, 523 F.2d 1357, 1359 (2d Cir.1975) (Gurfein, J., concurring).

[50] See Greene v. Grievance Committee, 54 N.Y.2d 118, 444 N.Y.S.2d 883, 886, 429 N.E.2d 390, 393 (1981), cert.denied 455 U.S. 1035, 102 S.Ct. 1738, 72 L.Ed.2d 153 (1982) (despite fact that Code has been incorporated by reference in court rule defining professional misconduct, "The Code of Professional Responsibility is, however, an enactment of the New York State Bar Association rather than the Legislature or any court. . . . [T]he code cannot, either directly or through incorporation in a court rule, amend or limit a statute adopted by the

ly as a guideline, the Code does not have the force of positive law.[51] And some judges continue to refer to the Code as merely "ethical" with an indeterminately lesser effect than "law."[52] The Code has also been widely adopted by the federal courts by a local rule or by decision. The federal courts almost invariably incorporate the same version of the Code that applies in the state in which the federal court sits or, as is the case with courts of appeals, if the federal court's jurisdictions covers more than one state, the version of the Code in force in the lawyer's state.[53]

Anatomy of the Code

The Code contains more than simply the verbiage necessary to provide mandatory rules for lawyers. Consequently the Code's drafters attempted to delineate the prescriptive and the nonprescriptive parts of the Code, but with only partial success. Because of the threatened confusion, several jurisdictions adopted only the Disciplinary Rules, the parts of the Code that were clearly intended to be employed in lawyer discipline proceedings.[54]

The Code consists of the following major parts. A *Preamble* states a desire to preserve "a free and democratic society" through a new lawyers' code. The *Preliminary Statement* contains important definitions of other portions of the Code and notes that the Code "does not undertake to define standards for civil liability of lawyers for professional conduct." The bulk of the Code consists of four kinds of provisions: Canons, Disciplinary Rules, Ethical Considerations, and a concluding set of Definitions.[55]

The *Canons* are defined in the Preliminary Statement as "axiomatic norms" that embody the general concepts from which the Disciplinary Rules and Ethical Considerations derive.

Legislature"); New York Criminal & Civil Cts. Bar Ass'n v. Jacoby, 61 N.Y.2d 130, 472 N.Y.S.2d 890, 460 N.E.2d 1325, 1327 (1984) ("the provisions of the Code . . . are not entitled in all instances to be accorded the status of statute or case law"). The attitude of New York courts is that "the courts should not denigrate [the provisions of the unofficially adopted Code] by indifference". In re Weinstock, 40 N.Y.2d 1, 386 N.Y.S.2d 1, 351 N.E.2d 647, 649 (1976).

[51] In re Friedman, 76 Ill.2d 392, 30 Ill.Dec. 288, 392 N.E.2d 1333, 1335, 16 A.L.R.4th 589 (1979)("Although this court has not formally approved the Code . . . it frequently serves as a guide for standards of professional conduct."); In re Dineen, 380 A.2d 603, 604 (Me.1977) (because voluntary bar's Code does not have force of law, court rejects respondent lawyer's attack on lawyer discipline on ground that court was enforcing rules of private organization).

[52] In re Corrugated Container Antitrust Litigation, 659 F.2d 1341, 1348 (5th Cir.1981)(Code nonetheless governs decision on motion to disqualify lawyer because of conflict of interest).

[53] Sixth Cir. R. of Discipl. Enforcement, Rule 4(B)(Code "adopted by this Court is deemed to be the Code . . . adopted by the highest court of a state in which the respondent-attorney is admitted to practice."); Paul E. Iacono Structural Engineer, Inc. v. Humphrey, 722 F.2d 435, 438-39 (9th Cir.1983), cert. denied 464 U.S. 851, 104 S.Ct. 162, 78 L.Ed.2d 148 (1983) (adoption by reference to California rules by California federal district courts); Pantry Pride, Inc. v. Finley, Kumble, Wagner, Heine, Underberg & Casey, 697 F.2d 524, 529 (3d Cir.1982) (federal district courts in circuit have adopted version of Code adopted by bar authority of the state in which the court sits). The common deference of federal courts to the adoption process in the states has been defended on the grounds of the state courts' superior expertise and access to information about local practice and of avoiding dual and possibly conflicting standards. E.g., United States v. Miller, 624 F.2d 1198, 1200–01 (3d Cir.1980); Dodson v. Floyd, 529 F.Supp. 1056, 1065 n.1 (N.D.Ga. 1981); Gould v. Lumonics Research Ltd., 495 F.Supp. 294, 298 (N.D.Ill.1980).

The Code has also been adopted by various federal agencies. E.g., 42 U.S.C.A. § 2996f(a)(10) (Code applicable to lawyers employed by the federal Legal Services Corporation or by contractors with it); Dep't of Navy Manual of Judge Advocate General § 1903, 32 CFR § 727.3 (Code governs conduct of all legal assistance officers on active duty).

[54] Ill. Code of Prof. Resp., added to Ill. R.771 June 3, 1980, eff. July 1, 1980; Mass.Sup.Jud.Ct.R. 307; In re Tonkon, 292 Or. 660, 642 P.2d 660, 661–62 (1982); Tex. Code of Prof. Resp., Tex. Bar R. art. XII(B)(8), 1A Tex.Civ. Code Ann. § 14 app. (Vernon 1982, pocket part). Commentators have judged that the Code's attempt to draw distinctions between DRs and ECs has been unsuccessful. See A.Kaufman, Problems in Professional Responsibility 30–31 (1976); Kaufman, A Professional Agenda, 6 Hofstra L.Rev. 619, 622 (1978). See also Kutak, Evaluating the Proposed Model Rules of Professional Conduct, 1980 Am.B.Found. Research J. 1016, 1017–18.

[55] An arguably additional part are *Footnotes* written by the Code's reporter. The first footnote modestly defines them as merely an attempt to relate provisions of the Code to some other authority but without any attempt at complete annotation. The Code footnotes have, however, sometimes played a significant role in its interpretation. E.g., Cartin v. Continental Homes, 134 Vt. 362, 360 A.2d 96, 99 (1976) (citation to footnote 10 of EC 5-10 for rule that trial lawyer who testifies may not argue the credibility of his or her own testimony).

Most of the Canons are little more than innocuous chapter headings under which the operative provisions have been grouped. An exception is Canon 9's injunction to lawyers to avoid creating the "appearance of impropriety." [56]

The *Disciplinary Rules*, which are referred to herein as *DRs*, are directly prescriptive. They are said by the Preliminary Statement to be rules that are "mandatory in nature" and that "state the minimum level of conduct below which no lawyer can fall without being subject to disciplinary action."

The Code's *Ethical Considerations*, called *ECs* herein, are defined in the Preliminary Statement in a manner clearly intended to contrast with the Disciplinary Rules. The ECs are "aspirational in character and represent the objectives toward which every member of the profession should strive." The Statement also suggests that the Ethical Considerations may provide "interpretive guidance" for a court or agency that is attempting to ascertain the meaning of an unclear Disciplinary Rule.[57] Clearly, "aspirational" as used in the Code means "recommended but not required," rather than "do your best under the circumstances." [58] Most jurisdictions have used the ECs in that nonbinding way.[59] But some jurisdictions, most notably Iowa, have insisted that the Ethical Considerations are as binding as any other part of the Code.[60] And some commentators would have all lawyer codes stated in nonbinding aspirational terms.[61]

Standards for Criminal Justice

The dominance of the ABA Code was impinged upon almost from the time it was first adopted by the ABA. Specialized groups promulgated their owns ethics codes, although the usual claim was that the specialized code was entirely compatible with the ABA Code.[62] During the same time that the

[56] For instances of occasional judicial misuses of Canon 9 in the described fashion, see § 7.1.4. Cf. also, e.g., Committee on Professional Ethics v. Durham, 279 N.W.2d 280 (Iowa 1979)(Canon 9 as basis for discipline); In re Cipriano, 68 N.J. 398, 346 A.2d 393 (1975)(same); In re Galton, 289 Or. 565, 615 P.2d 317 (1980)(dictum)(Canons may serve as independent basis for lawyer discipline).

[57] In re Rabideau, 102 Wis.2d 16, 306 N.W.2d 1, 7 n.7, appeal dismissed 454 U.S. 1025, 102 S.Ct. 559, 70 L.Ed.2d 469 (1981).

[58] The law sometimes employs "aspirational" standards in the latter, binding sense. E.g., Henderson & Pearson, Implementing Federal Environmental Policies: The Limits of Aspirational Commands, 78 Colum.L.Rev. 1429 (1978). The contents of the ECs make it clear that the nonbinding meaning was intended. Many of the ECs plainly are specific enough to serve as rules, and thus one must assume that lack of precision was not the reason for their nonbinding character. Presumably that reason had to do with their wisdom or with the perception that they were too strict to be fairly enforced in all likely situations.

[59] Kizer v. Davis, 174 Ind.App. 559, 369 N.E.2d 439 (1977)(EC 2–23 on fee-collection suits). One jurisdiction in which the Preliminary Statement was not officially adopted nonetheless recognizes the limited, unenforceable status of the ECs. See In re Sedor, 73 Wis.2d 629, 245 N.W.2d 895, 901-02 (1976).

[60] Committee on Professional Ethics v. Behnke, 276 N.W.2d 838 (Iowa 1979), appeal dismissed 444 U.S. 805, 100 S.Ct. 27, 62 L.Ed.2d 19 (1979); In re Frerichs, 238 N.W.2d 764, 766, 768–69 (Iowa 1976). See also, e.g., In re January 1976 Grand Jury, 534 F.2d 719, 729 (7th Cir. 1976)(concurring opinion)(prohibition in EC 7–27 against suppression of evidence by lawyer); In re Nulle, 127 Ariz. 299, 620 P.2d 214, 215 (1980)(lawyer's conduct was "in direct conflict" with EC 5–3, which prohibits lawyer from seeking to persuade client to permit lawyer to invest in client's undertaking); People v. Berge, 620 P.2d 23, 27 (Colo.1980) (EC 5–5 "makes explicit some long-accepted standards of legal ethics"); Kentucky Bar Ass'n v. DeCamillis, 547 S.W.2d 446, 447-48 (Ky.1977); In re Estate of Weinstock, 40 N.Y.2d 1, 386 N.Y.S.2d 1, 351 N.E.2d 647, 649 (1976) (EC 5–6, prohibiting lawyer from influencing client to name lawyer as executor in will is appropriate standard of conduct in proceeding to remove executor); Lake Cty. Bar Ass'n v. Needham, 66 Ohio St.2d 116, 419 N.E.2d 1104, 1107 (1981); In re Theodosen, 303 N.W.2d 104, 107 (S.D.1981) ("Such conduct gives rise, at the very least, to an appearance of impropriety under Canon 5, EC 5–6."). See generally D.Rosenthal, Lawyer and Client: Who's in Charge? 114–15 (1974).

[61] Teshner, Lawyer Morality, 38 Geo.Wash.L.Rev. 789 (1970); Freedman, Panel Discussion—Professional Responsibility in the Practice of Criminal Law, in Professional Responsibility of the Lawyer: The Murky Divide between Right and Wrong at 58 (1976); Uviller, id. at 59.

[62] Code of Trial Conduct of the American College of Trial Lawyers (1972); Operative Resolutions of the Commercial Law League of America Pertaining to the Relationship of the Forwarder and Receiver, in Commercial Bar: An International Directory (1974); Code of Professional Responsibility for Matrimonial Lawyers, 16 Fam.L. Newsletter 5 (1975); Poirier, The Federal Government Lawyer and Professional Ethics, 60 ABA J. 1541 (1974) (expanded ethical considerations for government lawyers adopted by Federal Bar Association).

Wright Committee was drafting what became the 1969 Code, another ABA group, under the chairmanship of then Circuit Judge Warren Burger, later Chief Justice of the United States, was drafting Standards for Criminal Justice. Included were standards for the Prosecution Function and the Defense Function. Those two standards were first approved by the ABA in 1971 [63] and amended in 1979.[64]

Unfortunately, the Standards did not clearly articulate their relationship with the Code. Some passages suggest that the Standards were merely offering possible interpretations of unclear provisions of the Code.[65] But other passages suggest that the commission felt free to manufacture new rules whose violation would result in professional discipline.[66] The Standards have functioned in courts and bar disciplinary agencies much as does a treatise—persuasively, if that, but not authoritatively.

§ 2.6.4 1983 ABA Model Rules of Professional Conduct

Background: Critiques of the 1969 Code

The Code of Professional Responsibility came under attack even before its adoption in 1969. Its critics started from different and sometimes conflicting positions. One group of reform-minded lawyers contended that the Code had been corrupted by revisions made during its drafting process and that opportunities had been missed to make the Code clearer and more responsive to modern practice realities, for example, by easing advertising and solicitation rules and restrictions on delivery of legal services.[67] Although the Code had aspired to deal more realistically with nonlitigation practice, that effort had been minimal.[68] Other critics claimed that the Code was deficient because it failed to provide relevant and helpful guidance on many problems actually faced by practitioners, particularly by solo practitioners in economically marginal practices.[69] Defects in the Code were sufficiently serious that the ABA's leadership began to call for thoroughgoing review of it within a matter of years after it was adopted.[70] One of the principal factors that motivated the ABA leadership to appoint a committee in 1977 to redraft the

[63] ABA Project on Standards of Criminal Justice, Standards Relating to The Administration of Criminal Justice 73 (1974) (The Prosecution Function—approved by ABA House of Delegates, Feb. 1971); id. 103 (The Defense Function).

[64] ABA Standards for Criminal Justice p.3.1 (2d ed. 1982)(The Prosecution Function—approved by ABA House of Delegates, Feb. 1979); id. p.4.1 (The Defense Function).

[65] Defense Function Standard 7.7(c), commentary, at 275-76 (approved draft 1971)(DR 7-102(B)(1) is "construed" not to apply to criminal defense lawyers).

[66] Standards Relating to the Prosecution Function § 2.9, commentary, at 6 (recommended amendments, March 1971)(change in earlier suggested draft "reflects the view that the standard would be too difficult to enforce as a disciplinary rule" and that the proposed disciplinary rule was preferable).

[67] J.Lieberman, Crisis at the Bar (1978); Verdicts on Lawyers (R.Nader & M.Green eds. 1976); Morgan, The Evolving Concept of Professional Responsibility, 90 Harv. L.Rev. 702 (1977); Frankel, Book Review [of 1969 Code], 43 U.Chi.L.Rev. 874 (1976); Joost, Professional Responsibility: The Missing Dimension, Trial at 20 (June/July 1969). See also writings of the Code's Reporter cited in n. 43, supra.

[68] Schwartz, The Professionalism and Accountability of Lawyers, 66 Calif.L.Rev. 669, 670 (1978); Rubin, Causerie on Lawyers' Ethics in Negotiation, 35 La.L.Rev. 577 (1975). The 1908 Canons had been criticized for their lack of attention to office counseling and similar nonlitigation practice settings. E.g., Thode, The Ethical Standard for the Advocate, 39 Tex.L.Rev. 575, 578-79 (1961). But while the importance of the matter was acknowledged by the Code's draftsman (see EC 7-3 n.9), the Code did not significantly improve on the 1908 Canons in that respect.

[69] J.Auerbach, Unequal Justice (1976); M.Freedman, Lawyers' Ethics in an Adversary System (1975); Schnapper, The Myth of Legal Ethics, 64 ABA J. 202 (1978); Burbank & Duboff, Ethics and the Legal Profession: A Survey of Boston Lawyers, 9 Suffolk L.Rev. 66, 68 (1974); Weinstein, On the Teaching of Legal Ethics, 72 Colum.L. Rev. 452, 463-66 (1972); Note, Legal Ethics and Professionalism, 79 Yale L.J. 1179 (1970).

[70] Spann, The Legal Profession Needs a New Code of Ethics, ABA Bar Leader (Nov./Dec.1977) (ABA president); Levy, Time to Review the Code, 62 ABA J. 225 (1976).

1969 Code was that continuing antitrust attacks were threatened.[71]

Kutak Commission (1977–1983)

The committee appointed to study the Code, called the Kutak Commission, after its chairman,[72] worked in relative obscurity until a first draft of what became the 1983 Model Rules of Professional Conduct [73] was leaked to the legal press during the ABA meeting in August 1979.[74] The Commission's early work showed that it intended a bold reworking of the Code. Included in the early draft were stark new rules limiting client confidentiality; requiring pro bono work by every lawyer; limiting the kinds of cases that a lawyer could accept by broad standards of good faith and competence; providing extensive new regulations on conflicts of interests, including the revolving door problem of former government lawyers; requiring full disclosure and fairness in trials and negotiations, including disclosure of client perjury and misrepresentation; and significantly expanding the permissible limits on advertising and solicitation.

Opposition to the Kutak Commission Proposals

The early drafts circulated by the Kutak Commission created turmoil and controversy within the ABA and to some extent outside it. The struggle for control of the Commission's product did not abate until a vastly revised set of rules was finally adopted in August 1983. In the intervening time of almost four years during which the Commission's work was publicly debated, the Commission offered successively milder drafts that gradually abandoned or compromised its early enthusiasms.[75] The Commission's process consisted of issuing drafts for public comments that were sometimes heard at formal hearings, revising the drafts, and eventually submitting reworked drafts to the ABA House of Delegates for approval. The Commission's work was elaborately documented, defended, and explained in numerous speeches and law review and bar journal articles by Commission members and others.[76] Increasingly elaborate and extensive research background notes were appended to succeeding early drafts.[77]

71 Justice Department Dismisses Antitrust Suit against ABA, 64 ABA J. 1538, 1541 (1978).

72 Robert J. Kutak of Omaha, Nebraska, was appointed chairman of the Special Commission on Professional Standards, named in August 1977 by ABA President Williams B. Spann, Jr. Its membership was dominated by reformist lawyers and legal educators. The commission's membership did not reflect the sentiments of large groups within the legal profession. Mr. Kutak died in late January 1983, just before the ABA meeting that approved the text of the Rules portion of the Model Rules. The reporters to the Commission were Professor Geoffrey C. Hazard, Jr., of the Yale Law School during the time when all of the published drafts of the Commission were issued and, during the first stages of the commission's work, Dean L. Ray Patterson of Emory University Law School. The original nine-member commission included two nonlawyer members. Their apparent impact was limited to advocacy for a provision requiring that fee contracts be written, a requirement that was eliminated by the ABA House of Delegates in August 1982.

73 Provisions of the Model Rules are generally cited herein as "MR." Its comments are cited, e.g., "MR 1.6 comment" with a notation to divisions and paragraphs of longer comments where necessary.

The title "Code of Professional Responsibility" was abandoned, according to the drafter of the Model Rules, because it was thought "a little pretentious." Hazard, The Legal and Ethical Position of the Code of Professional Responsibility, in 5 Social Responsibility: Journalism, Law, Medicine 5, 10 (L.Hodges ed. 1979).

74 The Record: Text of Initial Draft of Ethics Code Rewrite Committee, Legal Times of Washington, Aug. 27, 1979, at 26, col. 1; BNA Daily Report to Executives, Special Suppl. to Release No. 46 (Aug. 21, 1979).

75 The most noteworthy were: (1) ABA Comm'n on Evaluation of Professional Standards, Model Rules of Professional Conduct (Discussion Draft, Jan. 30, 1980); (2) id., (Proposed Final Draft, May 30, 1981); (3) id. (Final Draft, Oct., 1981); id. (Final Draft, Nov. 1982); and the completed and approved draft of August 1983 (variously published; see, e.g., 52 U.S.L.Wk. 1 (Aug. 16, 1983). Numerous other drafts were given limited circulation at various stages of the Commission's work.

76 Symposium, 1980 Am.B.Found. Research J. 921-1023; Symposium, 29 Emory L.J. 887-1027 (1980); Symposium, 35 U.Miami L.Rev. 639-813 (1981); Symposium, 26 Vill.L. Rev. 1121-1219 (1981); Symposium, 59 Tex.L.Rev. 639-786 (1981).

77 Compare Model Rules (Discussion Draft, Jan. 30, 1980)("references" after most comments) with Model Rules (Proposed Final Draft, May 30, 1981)(extensive "Code Comparison" and "Legal Background" notes after each rule and comment). The Legal Background notes were helpful but partisan and contained several statements that were difficult to reconcile with the proposed

Those, however, threatened controversy of their own and were suppressed in anticipation of formal ABA consideration of the Model Rules.[78]

Disagreement with the work of the Kutak Commission took a variety of forms. One criticism was that the Commission was unwisely abandoning the DR and EC format of the 1969 Code for a Rule-and-Comment approach as used in the ALI Restatements and in the ABA's recent Code of Judicial Conduct.[79] The deeper objection was that the Commission would abandon the concept that minimal standards did not necessarily describe the kind of lawyering toward which the profession aspired. A frontal assault was mounted by the Association of Trial Lawyers of America, an organization of lawyers devoted primarily to plaintiff personal injury and criminal defense practice. It sponsored a conference[80] and generated drafts of a self-described counterproposal to the Kutak Commission-ABA drafts, which was called the American Lawyer's Code of Conduct.[81] The major point of departure of the ATLA draft was that it vastly expanded the concept of client confidentiality, requiring, for example, that a lawyer participate in presenting a client's perjured testimony in both civil and criminal trials if necessary to avoid impairing a client confidence.[82] Opposition to the Kutak Commission's positions also came from many state and local bar associations, sections within the ABA, the American College of Trial Lawyers, the National Organization of Bar Counsel, and the Securities Exchange Commission.[83]

Adoption of the Model Rules

The ABA House of Delegates slowly worked its way through the Kutak Commission proposal in meetings in August 1982 and February and August 1983. The entire process was widely reported by the legal and nonlegal press.[84] Between meetings the Commission met informally with bar groups that opposed major provisions and attempted to negotiate compromise language. The process was completed in August 1983, when the ABA House of Delegates approved amendments to the Rule's comments and then, by a divided vote, the entire set of Rules and Comments.

It is clear that the Model Rules will not be accepted in the states in the same uniform way that the Code of Professional Responsibil-

Rule or Comment, and sometimes with authority that they cited.

78 Model Rules (Proposed Final Draft as Revised through June 30, 1982). The adopted version of the Model Rules (see "Scope" (last paragraph)) states that the "research notes" prepared for earlier drafts of the Model Rules "have not been adopted, do not constitute part of the Model Rules, and are not intended to affect the application or interpretation of the Rules and Comments." The reference apparently was only to the Legal Background notes because the Code Comparison notes were, with only slight editorial changes, republished along with the official ABA version of the finally adopted Model Rules. This treatise typically refers to the Legal Background and Code Comparison notes published in the Proposed Final Draft of May 30, 1981 and denominates them the "suppressed" notes. The Legal Background notes may be the more suppressed of the two.

79 Unkovic, The Current Format of the Code of Professional Responsibility Should Be Amended, Not Abandoned, 26 Vill.L.Rev. 1191 (1981).

80 Roscoe Pound-American Trial Lawyers Foundation, Ethics and Advocacy (1978).

81 Koskoff, Introduction in Commission on Professional Responsibility, Roscoe Pound-American Trial Lawyers Foundation, The American Lawyer's Code of Conduct ii (Public Discussion Draft, June 1980). The draft was authored by Professor Monroe H. Freedman and was said to reflect extensive comments by members of the ATLA Commission but was not approved by it. Id., at copyright page; Birnbaum, Preface, in id. at 1.

82 See generally Wolfram, Client Perjury: The Kutak Commission and the Association of Trial Lawyers on Lawyers, Lying Clients, and the Adversary System, 1980 Am.B.Found. Research J. 964; Hodes, The Code of Professional Responsibility, the Kutak Rules, and the Trial Lawyer's Code: Surprisingly, Three Peas in a Pod, 35 U.Miami L.Rev. 739 (1981).

83 Proposed Ethics Rules: A Try for Balance, 66 ABA J. 277 (1980); 49 U.S.L.Wk. 2125, 2126-28 (Aug.19, 1980); 48 U.S.L.Wk. 2288 (Oct. 23, 1979) (speech of SEC chairman Williams criticizing Kutak Commission for not requiring corporate counsel to investigate actively into questionable company practices); Carley, Battling Barristers: Lawyers Squabble about a New Code of Ethics, Wall St.J., Feb. 6, 1981, p. 36, col.1; Pike & Granelli, Ethics Code Keeps Inching Along, Nat'l L.J., Aug. 24, 1981; Carley, Proposed New Code of Legal Ethics Stirs Bitter Fight among Lawyers, Wall St.J., July 23, 1982, p. 19, col. 4.

84 Wiermiel, Negative Verdict: Lawyers' Public Image Is Dreadful, Spurring Concern by Attorneys, Wall St.J., Oct. 11, 1983, p.1, col.1.

ity was accepted fifteen years earlier.[85] The ABA's lobbying effort of 1970-72 in behalf of the Code was replaced with a much more modest informational service.[86] The first states that have completed review of the Model Rules have accepted significant portions of the Model Rules but have rejected important recommendations, primarily those restricting disclosure of client wrongdoing.[87] The bar remains deeply divided on the wisdom of replacing the Code, at least if the Model Rules approved by the ABA is the successor document. It seems apparent, after three-quarters of a century, that the ABA no longer has the capacity to generate a single set of standards of lawyer conduct that lawyers will generally accept.

Taxonomy of the Model Rules

The Model Rules are organized in a way different from either the 1908 Canons or the 1969 Code. The Model Rules begin with a *Preamble* that attempts to capture the underlying philosophy and spirit of the Model Rules, alludes to the necessity that a lawyer consider moral and other considerations in making discretionary professional decisions, and argues that an independent legal profession is essential in a democracy. The *Scope* attempts to place the Model Rules within the larger, surrounding context of other law, notes the significance of the rules for lawyer discipline, cautions that the rules were not drafted for automatic use in such other contexts as legal malpractice or motions to disqualify in litigated cases, and gives its own taxonomic interpretation. A *Terminology* section defines ten critical terms that are employed throughout the Rules and Comments.

The bulk of the Model Rules is taken up with fifty-two *Rules*, each of which is followed by an explanatory *Comment*. The Rules are of different kinds. Some, as described in the Scope note, impose an obligation or prohibition whose violation can lead to professional discipline.[88] Other Rules describe areas of professional discretion and allude to factors, rarely exhaustively, that a lawyer should consider in exercising discretion. While those Rules are obviously not enforceable in a disciplinary case, they are extremely relevant for disciplinary purposes because, in effect, they delineate areas of conduct in which any action taken by a lawyer is not subject to disciplinary scrutiny.[89] A third type of Rule simply describes aspects of the lawyer's professional role, although sometimes in terms that suggest that they are other than descriptive.[90]

A Comment, according to the Scope note, does not add obligations to the Rules, even if mandatory language such as "should" is employed in a Comment. Instead, the Comments are to "provide guidance for practicing in compliance with the Rules." [91] The Comments were also doubtless designed and will be employed by courts and other disciplinary officials as an authoritative and illustrative guide to interpretation of language in the Rules. Because several of the Comments add specific illustrations of mandatory lawyer conduct, they clearly cannot be ignored.

85 Just as the ABA was approving the final version of the Model Rules, the Virginia Supreme Court adopted an amended Code of Professional Responsibility that repudiated many of the changes in the Model Rules and accepted many of the proposals that the ABA had spurned. See Va.Code Prof.Resp., Va.Sup.Ct.Rules, Rule II.

86 See Status Report on Model Rules, 1 ABA/BNA Lawyers' Manual on Prof. Conduct, Current Repts. at 93 (1984).

87 By the end of 1984, only two states had acted finally and officially on the Model Rules. Both New Jersey, first, and then Arizona adopted them, but in each case with significant amendments. In both states the amendments to the confidentiality rules (MR 1.6) significantly broaden the discretion of lawyers to reveal client wrongdoing and require lawyer disclosure of intended client wrongdoing that threatens death or serious bodily injury or, in New Jersey, serious financial loss. See generally 1 ABA/BNA Lawyers' Manual on Professional Conduct 334 (New Jersey); id. at 445 (Arizona)(1984). The United States Claims Court adopted the Model Rule verbatim. Id. at 240.

88 MR Scope (first and fifth paragraphs).

89 See MR Scope (first paragraph).

90 MR 6.1 (lawyer "should" render pro bono legal service). Cf. MR Scope (first paragraph)(imperatives in Rules are cast in terms of "shall" and "shall not"; "should" when used in a Comment does not add obligations to the Rules).

91 MR Scope (first paragraph).

§ 2.6.5 *California Rules of Professional Conduct*

On matters of professional codes, California has shown an independence fairly unique among the states. A state statute authorizes the mandatory bar's Board of Governors to promulgate "rules of professional conduct for lawyers" with the approval of the supreme court.[92] The Rules of Professional Conduct have the force of statutory law in California once approved by the state's supreme court.[93] The supreme court has assigned itself an almost entirely passive role in the process.[94] California courts also occasionally rely upon a broad provision of the State Bar Act prescribing other "dut[ies] of an attorney." [95] The provisions of the State Bar Act are pivotal because the Rules lack, for example, any provision on client confidentiality. Instead, the confidentiality rule is stated in the State Bar Act itself.[96]

Both the 1928 [97] and the 1975 versions of the California Rules demonstrate an awareness of the 1908 Canons and 1969 Code, some of which are quoted or paraphrased. The 1975 California Rules differ significantly from the ABA Code adopted in 1969.[98] Nonetheless, the ABA Code remains independently authoritative within the state. Many local bar associations have adopted the ABA Code as part of their bylaws. Opinions of both California courts and bar ethics committees freely refer to the ABA Code for guidance when the California Rules are silent or obscure.[99] A kind of open-ended receptiveness toward restrictions on lawyer conduct by other sources is suggested in the California Rules themselves.[1] Similar catholicity is shown by the federal courts in California.[2]

Prominent voices within California have complained about the the state's confusing and vague provisions governing lawyer conduct.[3] Whether California will depart from its historical position of doing its own thing in lawyer regulation and adopt the 1983 ABA Model Rules seems doubtful in view of the

92 West's Ann.Cal.Bus. & Prof.Code § 6076.

93 West's Ann.Cal.Bus. & Prof.Code § 6077.

94 Maxwell v. Superior Court, 30 Cal.3d 606, 180 Cal. Rptr. 177, 639 P.2d 248, 255, n.9, 18 A.L.R.4th 333 (1982). A subordinate, if not passive, role is suggested by West's Ann.Cal.Bus. & Prof.Code § 6076 ("With the approval of the Supreme Court, the Board of Governors may formulate and enforce rules of professional conduct for all members of the bar in the State.").

95 State Bar Act, West's Ann.Cal.Bus. & Prof.Code § 6068.

96 West's Ann.Cal.Bus. & Prof.Code § 6068(d).

97 For the text of the 1928 Rules, see West's Ann.Cal. Bus. & Prof.Code § 6076 at 364-407 (1974 ed.).

98 The 1975 revision of the California Rules incorporated only selected provisions of the 1969 ABA Code, leaving most of the provisions uniquely Californian. See Janofsky, President's Message: After 45 Years—New Rules of Professional Conduct, 48 Cal.St.B.J. 224, 225 (1973). Most notably, the California Rules do not contain any of the ABA Code's Ethical Considerations. But cf. n.99, infra.

99 E.g., City of Los Angeles v. Decker, 18 Cal.3d 860, 135 Cal.Rptr. 647, 558 P.2d 545, 551 (1977)(lawyer misconduct at trial and EC 7-14); L.A.Cty.B. Ethics Comm.Ops., No. 360, reprinted in 52 L.A.B.J. 234 (1976) (DR 2–106 on fees; EC 2–17, 2–18, 2–26). The California Rules prior to January 1, 1975, explicitly incorporated by reference the 1969 ABA Code as an additional source of guidance for California lawyers. See West's Ann.Cal.Bus. & Prof.Code § 6076, app. (Rule 1) (1974 ed.). The reference was removed in the 1975 Rules. Nonetheless, the California courts continued to refer to the ABA Code. E.g., Paul E.Iacono Structural Engineer, Inc. v. Humphrey, 722 F.2d 435, 439–40 (9th Cir.1983), cert.denied 464 U.S. 851, 104 S.Ct. 162, 78 L.Ed.2d 148 (1983), and cases cited; City of Los Angeles v. Decker, supra. See generally Calif.Comm. on Prof.Resp. Formal Op. 1983–71, in 1 BNA Lawyers' Manual on Prof. Conduct 401 (1984).

1 Calif.R. 1-100 ("The prohibition of certain conduct in these rules is not to be interpreted as an approval of conduct not specifically mentioned."). Compare also Calif.Prof. Conduct Rule 1 ("The specification in these rules of certain conduct as unprofessional is not to be interpreted as an approval of conduct not specifically mentioned."); 1908 ABA Canons, Preamble ("The following canons of ethics are . . . a general guide, yet the enumeration of particular duties should not be construed as a denial of the existence of others equally imperative, though not specifically mentioned.").

2 For example, the local rules of the federal district court for the Central District of California adopt by reference both the State Bar Act and the Rules of Professional Conduct as well as the 1969 ABA Code. Rule 1.3(d).

3 Jeffrey v. Pounds, 67 Cal.App.3d 6, 136 Cal.Rptr. 373, 377 (1977) (Friedman, J.) ("As an educational instrumentality the California Rules of Professional Conduct are singularly uninspiring. They intermix fundamental tenets of ethical obligation with a turgid mass of superficial do's and don'ts, comparably to strewing the Ten Commandments among the interstices of the Internal Revenue Code.").

Board of Governors' strong opposition to early Kutak Commission drafts.[4]

§ 2.6.6 Ethics Committees and Opinions

Changing Significance of Ethics Opinions

At one time relatively significant disciplinary control over lawyers was exerted by local, state, and national bar associations through the promulgation of "opinions" by so-called ethics committees. Those opinions typically have answered questions on professional conduct posed to the ethics committee by lawyers. Ethics committee opinions sponsored the impression that a lawyer who disregarded their advice could be professionally disciplined. During periods when judicial discipline of lawyers has been lax, ethics opinions have at least publicized the bar's official positions on appropriate lawyer conduct and have provided a rallying point for peer disapproval of wayward lawyers. Ethics opinions are also a means by which the bar establishment can affirm its conception of the appropriate roles and attitudes of lawyers. Most ethics opinions are quickly dated for that reason, reflecting an order of bar leadership priorities that is no longer accepted. By a count taken in 1968, over half the ethics opinions issued by the ABA were devoted to advertising and solicitation issues.[5]

Both the sorts of issues that ethics opinions address and their influence have changed. One measure of the diminished importance of ethics committee opinions can be derived from comparing current scholarship in professional responsibility, which gives ethics opinions only minor mention, with two of the best-known works on lawyers' ethics in the last half century.[6] Both were written by longtime members of ethics committees, and both extensively cited and discussed ethics opinions. The circular citation was functional because writings in the legal ethics field were then noticed mainly in later ethics committee opinions and very rarely in judicial opinions.

Ethics opinions continue to be rarely cited and relied upon in judicial decisions.[7] In recent years, the production of ethics opinions has also been slowed by the threat of antitrust enforcement.[8] In the aftermath of the settlement of the 1976-78 government antitrust suit against the ABA, its ethics committee issued an opinion in 1978 declaring that its opinions were not binding on lawyers.[9] The pendency of proposals for sweeping amendments to the 1969 Code also doubtless slowed the production of opinions recently. Ethics opinions retain potential educational value through publication in bar journals and other lawyer periodicals. But their precedential value has proved to be limited in the Darwinian world of stare decisis and persuasive authority.

Work Product of Ethics Committees

Typical of the best, as well as the worst, ethics committee opinions is the substantial body of literature produced by the American Bar Association committee, now called the Committee on Ethics and Professional Responsibility.[10] The collected Formal Opinions

[4] 55 Calif.St.B.J. 395, 478 (1980) (opposition of State Bar Board of Governors to original proposals of Kutak Commission). The State Bar Ethics Committee, however, has indicated that the ABA Model Rules, to the extent persuasive, could be relevant in answering a question not authoritatively covered by the California Rules, State Bar Act, or other statutes. See Calif.Comm. on Prof.Resp. Formal Op. 1983–71, in 1 BNA Lawyers' Manual on Prof. Conduct 401, 402 (1984).

[5] Schuchman, Ethics and Legal Ethics: The Propriety of the Canons as a Group Moral Code, 37 Geo.Wash.L. Rev. 244, 255-56 (1968). See also J.Hurst, The Growth of American Law: The Law Makers 331 (1950)(of ABA ethics opinions between 1924 and 1936, about half "dealt simply with the business aspect of the profession").

[6] See H.Drinker, Legal Ethics (1953); R.Wise, Legal Ethics (2d ed.1970).

[7] One market measure of the influence of the ABA opinions is not encouraging. As of December 1981, the LEXIS "ABA" database did not include informal ABA opinions issued after 1974, because of low user demand.

[8] Justice Department Dismisses Antitrust Suit against American Bar Association, 64 ABA J. 1538, 1540-41 (1978); Little & Rush, Resolving the Conflict between Professional Ethics Opinions and Antitrust Laws, 15 Ga. L.Rev. 341 (1981).

[9] ABA Inf.Op. 1420 (1978).

[10] A sketch of the work of the predecessor ABA ethics committees is given in E.Sutherland, History of the

and Informal Opinions[11] of the ABA's ethics committees fill several volumes.[12] Many state and local bar association ethics committees also issue and publish ethics opinions.[13] The quality of ABA ethics opinions has been uneven, reflecting the talents and interests of volunteer members.[14] Many opinions are very dogmatic in their answers, without recognizing apparent areas of doubt or ambiguity. While clarity is always welcomed, too many opinions achieve this through strong statement rather than flawless reasoning. Ethics opinions seem written on the assumption that the provisions of the lawyer codes are self-evident to all but vicious or morally insensitive lawyers. Characteristically, they suggest only one solution to professional problems.[15] Certainty and dogmatism characterize even opinions overruling another opinion.[16] The righteousness of opinions often results in clarion calls for the profession as a whole to rally and eradicate perceived evils.[17] The strength of the committee's convictions is not always matched by strength of analysis, and its conclusions are often difficult to reconcile with other, often uncited opinions or to trace to specific provisions of the relevant lawyer codes.

Structural Limitations

Part of the explanation for the persistently narrow frame of reference in ethics committee opinions is structural: neither the inquiries nor the responses are likely to deal with major areas of concern. Most committees accept inquiries by lawyers only about their own future conduct, and not about past conduct (so as not to interfere with the work of bar disciplinary agencies) or about the conduct of other lawyers, including opposing lawyers.[18] As a result, most inquiries tend to be niggling and peripheral questions of a kind that might safely be raised about one's con-

American Bar Association and Its Work 189 (1953). See also ABA Opinions of the Committee on Professional Ethics 1-3 (1967); 1 ABA Informal Ethics Opinions, at 1-2 (1975).

11 The distinction between formal and informal opinions reflects the ABA ethics committee's estimate of their relative importance and general interest. Informal opinions are direct responses to specific and often narrow questions; formal opinions originate in somewhat the same fashion but tend to be more elaborately worked out advice on more important topics. See ABA Opinions of the Committee on Professional Ethics 6 (1976 ed.). A formal opinion trumps either formal or informal opinions with which it is in conflict, whether mentioned in the later opinion or not. See ABA Formal Op. 317 (1967). An informal opinion, on the other hand, overrides any earlier informal opinion with which it conflicts but never a formal opinion. Id; ABA Standing Committee on Ethics and Prof. Resp., Rules of Proc., rules 3 & 4, in 1 ABA Informal Ethics Opinions at 5 (1975).

12 The ABA committee was first authorized to publish formal opinions in 1922. The opinions are collected in ABA Opinions of the Committee on Professional Ethics (1967 ed.), together with abstracts of informal opinions. Informal opinions can be found in Informal Ethics Opinions (1975), volumes 1 and 2. Supplements and several unofficial reporting services carry more recent opinions. All ABA opinions are first published in the *ABA Journal*.

13 Those are typically published in local bar journals. They are also available in abstracted form in a series of publications of the American Bar Foundation. See ABF Digest of Bar Association Ethics Opinions (O.Maru & R.Clough eds.1970), with supplementary volumes. In larger states, collections of ethics opinions are sometimes published under the aegis of the bar assocation.

14 Two academics have given low marks to the ethics opinions of the ABA, finding them riddled with "serious flaws." Finman & Schneyer, The Role of Bar Association Ethics Opinions in Regulating Lawyer Conduct, 29 UCLA L.Rev. 67, 72 (1981)(analysis of 21 opinions issued since adoption of 1969 Code).

15 Exceptions might best demonstrate the point. Contrast the tentativeness of, e.g., Formal Op. 182 (1938), with opinions immediately preceding and following it.

16 ABA Formal Op. 271 (1946); ABA Formal Op. 186 (1938). Certainty is exuded in an even later opinion that is announced to be "not in conflict" with a prior opinion with which it seems hopelessly in conflict. Compare ABA Formal Op. 155 (1936)(lawyer must reveal whereabouts of fugitive client even if known as result of confidential communication) with ABA Formal Op. 23 (1930) (lawyer must not reveal whereabouts of fugitive client if known as result of confidential communication). The membership of the ethics committee had been entirely changed between 1930 and 1936. See "Membership of the Committee" in ABA Opinions of the Comm. on Prof. Ethics 4 (1967). ABA Formal Opinion 155, supra, was recently explicitly overruled in ABA Formal Op. 84-349 (1984).

17 ABA Formal Op. 135 (1935)(solicitation of automobile accident cases by part-time prosecutor whose duties included investigating accidents).

18 Rules of Proc. of Standing Comm. on Ethics and Prof. Resp., rule 2, in ABA Informal Ethics Opinions 5 (1975); Op. 80-94 of Comm. on Prof. & Jud. Ethics, 36 Rec.A.B. City N.Y. 507-08 (1981).

duct on a lawyer's own letterhead. For similar reasons, the responding opinions tend to err on the side of advising against contemplated conduct if any doubt might be raised about its legitimacy.

Much is told about the tenor of ethics committee opinions by a second common limitation: committees will not issue opinions about questions of "law." [19] The implicit assumption of the committees is that a distinction can fittingly be drawn between "law," on the one hand, and, on the other, "ethics" or whatever other term is used to describe the lawyer regulation that comes from a lawyer code.[20] The assumptions underlying the dichotomy are debatable. One possible, yet startling, assumption might be that what is discussed in ethics opinions is not "law." But the enforcement of the provisions of lawyer codes in lawyer discipline and other proceedings demonstrates clearly that the codes are legal prescriptions in every conventional sense. A more focused reason for hesitation on the part of a national bar association such as the ABA might be that the "law" of professional ethics often varies from one state to another and therefore that lack of uniformity in the law precludes the committee from issuing a definite opinion. Yet that assumption is not carried forward with respect to the lawyer codes themselves, which are, of course, discussed in ethics opinions but which increasingly vary from one jurisdiction to another.

Ethics Opinions in the Courts

Bar ethics opinions have not played a large role in the discipline of lawyers or in judicial rulings on such matters as the disqualification of a lawyer for a conflict of interest. The lawyers codes are frequently cited [21] but ethics opinions rarely so. Courts obviously do not feel bound to follow advice issued by ethics committees, whose members are largely if not exclusively practicing lawyers. When a court does notice ethics opinions that are contrary to the court's view, it generally seems not overly concerned about offering special justifications for rejecting the opinion.[22] In some jurisdictions, a lawyer can attack a published ethics opinion by petition to the state's supreme court, resulting in a judicial opinion that will have the respect normally accorded to judicial decisions.[23] Most jurisdictions at least seem to defer to ethics opinions to the extent that a lawyer who has acted in accordance with a recent ethics committee recommendation is ordinarily given the benefit of the doubt in disciplinary proceedings. Some ethics committees claim that their opinions are in some way binding on lawyers.[24] That is probably accurate only in the very rare instance in which the opinion might be relied upon by a bar association membership committee to remove an individual lawyer from membership in a voluntary bar association.

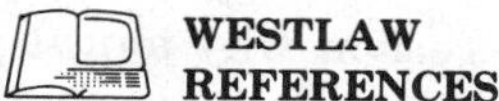

WESTLAW REFERENCES

attorney lawyer (law legal /2 profession practice) bar "professional responsibility" /5 code "model rule" /5 purpose rationale function policy

"preliminary statement" /p attorney lawyer (law legal /2 profession practice) bar "professional responsibility" /5 code

[19] ABA Standing Comm. on Ethics and Prof.Resp. R. of Proc. 9, in 1 ABA Informal Ethics Opinions 6 (1975)("The Committee will not issue opinions on questions of law, or pertaining to conduct which is the subject of pending litigation."); N.Y.Cty.Op. 645, N.Y.L.J., June 5, 1975, p.5, col. 1 ("This Committee does not pass on questions of law.").

[20] ABA Formal Op. 202 (1940)(attorney-client privilege as question of law); ABA Informal Op. 1233 (1972)(whether a particular conflict of interest results in a "procedural disqualification" is question of law).

[21] Wolfram, The Code of Professional Responsibility as a Measure of Attorney Liability in Civil Litigation, 30 S.C.L.Rev. 281 (1979).

[22] Corti v. Fleisher, 93 Ill.App.3d 517, 49 Ill.Dec. 74, 417 N.E.2d 764 (1981) (rejecting as erroneously reasoned ABA Informal Op. 870 (1965), which held that lawyer who made unethical fee-splitting agreement should not thereafter refuse to carry it out on ground of its illegality).

[23] In re Advisory Opinion of Kentucky Bar Ass'n, 613 S.W.2d 416 (1981).

[24] Digest of Bar Ass'n Ethics Ops. 2 (O.Maru & R.Clough eds.1970); Kurland, Result of Professional Ethics Questionnaire Conducted by Connecticut Bar Association, 5 Nat'l Am.B.Exec. News 1, 2 (1966).

§ 2.7 ETHICS AND MORAL PHILOSOPHY

§ 2.7.1 *The Place of Ethics*

Legal Ethics in Law Schools and Law Practice

Many of the issues discussed in this book involve the morality of a lawyer's actions. Yet lawyers, law professors, and students who have progressed very far into their first year of law school do not always feel comfortable talking about the morality or ethics of lawyers' conduct. There are several reasons why we feel that way, mainly psychological and sociological reasons. But none is a sufficient reason for concluding that ethics and moral philosophy should be particularly irrelevant in law practice or law schools.[25] The rules of ethics are normative, and talk about the ethics of lawyers strikes very close to one's sense of self worth; it is not easy to be self-critical of one's chosen role. Moreover, ethics is not very hard-edged. A professorial put-down sometimes heard in law school classrooms is that law has nothing to do with justice or with morality. Holmes groused that whenever he heard fellow judges talk about justice he knew they were not very good lawyers.

Part of the reason why moral philosophy is neglected in law schools is that it has been neglected in most university departments, including philosophy departments, for most of this century. In a university setting thoroughly embued with post-Enlightenment rationalism, it was congenial for law professors to believe that law was either science or sociology or perhaps only what courts said it was. In any event, law was simply a datum and lacked independent moral significance. Very little scholarship has been devoted to the ethics of law practice.[26] Most of what is called "legal ethics" is really discourse on the law of professional regulation or self-congratulatory encomia on professional solidarity and tradition.[27] Recently, however, both moral philosophers and law professors have increasingly taken an interest in the relevance of moral philosophy to law practice.[28]

A lawyer in practice might persist and assert that, whatever has been happening on university campuses, he or she does not feel the need to think of ethics in law practice. That kind of lawyer may assert, for example, that "it's every lawyer for himself or herself" or that "my only job is to do whatever is legal and in the best interests of protecting my client's legal rights"—and that these are not assertions about ethics. But, of course, such assertions state profoundly ethical norms. They may not be defensible norms, but they clearly are morally prescriptive because the lawyer making the assertion means to tell us that any other position would be wrongful in some strong sense.

Law as Morality

Lawyers sometimes assume that whatever is legal is moral. In part, the instinct might derive from the fact that law is itself often heavily normative. It can command, allow, condemn, forgive. In addition, lawyers in modern industrial societies are purveyors and explainers of legal restraints that run into almost every aspect of life. A lawyer thus might come to understand that law dictates most of the important choices that people make in life.

25 See generally Wolfram, The "Ethics" of Lawyers, 11 Corn.L.Forum 10 (June 1984); Shaffer, Moral Theology in Legal Ethics, 12 Cap.U.L.Rev. 179 (1982).

26 Some relevant discussion can be found in, e.g., F.Cohen, Ethical Systems and Legal Ideals (1933); J.Pike, Beyond the Law (1963); E.Rostow, The Ideal in Law 143 et seq. (1978); C.Wyzanski, Whereas—A Judge's Premises (1965). See also W.Taft, Ethics in Service 19-36 (1969 reissue of 1915 pub.).

27 Justice Frankfurter once referred to "the self-adulatory bombast of after-dinner speeches . . . that all the interests of man that are comprised under the constitutional guarantees given to 'life, liberty and property' are in the professional keeping of lawyers." Schware v. Board of Bar Examiners, 353 U.S. 232, 247, 77 S.Ct. 752, 760, 1 L.Ed.2d 796 (1957) (concurring opinion).

28 S.Bok, Lying: Moral Choice in Public and Private Life 146-52, 158–64 (1978); C.Fried, Right and Wrong 167–194 (1978); A.Goldman, The Moral Foundations of Professional Ethics (1980); The Good Lawyer (D.Luban ed.1984); T.Shaffer, On Being a Christian and a Lawyer (1981); Hazard, Conscience and Circumstance in Legal Ethics, 1 Social Responsibility: Journalism, Law, Medicine 36 (1975).

But law plainly does not exhaust the concept of morality. Most philosophical systems conceive of immoral laws that need not be obeyed. For example, many persons, whether philosophers or not, think that people who oppressed others in obedience to some of the laws of Hitler's Germany or other repressive totalitarian regimes acted immorally. Much more commonly, we confront in our everyday life innumerable situations in which interactions with other individuals are not governed by law. Then we are forced to make decisions about our conduct without any legal constraint or guidance. The same is true of law practice. Clearly, most lawyer decisions are open-ended and discretionary in the sense that a lawyer can choose between a variety of tactics or outcomes with no fear of violating any legal rule. In making those decisions, lawyers rely on some innate sense of proper behavior. One lawyer's sense might be the result of a very well thought out and consciously followed system of moral values. Another lawyer's sense might be nothing more complicated than an instinct that a lawyer may engage in any conduct that leads to a higher fee. Both lawyers are making moral decisions about the rightness or wrongness of conduct.

Moral philosophy may also be relevant to a lawyer's personal confrontation with the requirements of professional rules. For example, because of a failure of proof or an ambiguity in a professional norm courts may occasionally refuse to find that a lawyer has committed a disciplinary violation.[29] Should a lawyer, knowing that a court will take that approach and consequently that the lawyer's conduct will not be sanctioned, take action that the lawyer knows is contrary of the professional rule? In other words, might it be that what a lawyer can conscientiously extract from the meaning of a professional rule should guide a lawyer's personal conduct although, as a legal technician, the lawyer might advise another lawyer that the conduct would probably not in fact result in a court imposing a sanction? That is an illustration of the ways personal morality may diverge from the dictates of formally sanctioned norms. There are reasons why courts sometimes refuse to apply formal rules precisely, or according to their spirit, or to situations where the facts are not proved sufficiently. But actors in those same situations may have none of those reasons as justifications, in their own minds, for their personal conduct. In such instances, the command of the norm is moral and not, in the last analysis, legal.

Ethics in the Lawyer Codes

Until the appearance of the 1969 ABA Code, it was not clear to what extent the regulation of law practice concerned ethics. To be sure, the 1908 Canons were "of Ethics," but they were soon used to disbar lawyers—an unfamiliar use of purely ethical prescriptions. Many lawyers also thought that the Canons were applied selectively and often in the economic and social self-interest of lawyers rather than for any worthier reason. What else would explain the traditional preoccupation of ethics committees with lawyer advertising and solicitation? That suggested that "ethics" was perhaps only deceptive packaging for a political, social, economic, or organizational agenda of bar associations. Some lawyers suspected that the same might be true of other ethical claims as well.

For the first time, in the 1969 Code, an effort was made to separate out matters of regulation from matters of ethics.[30] The Disciplinary Rules were declared to be mandatory statements of minimally acceptable conduct, while the aspirational Ethical Considerations would point the way to morally praiseworthy conduct (see § 2.6.3). The Code's distinction mirrors a common philosophical distinction between moral duties and

[29] More commonly, however, courts give rather broad readings to professional rules. See § 3.3.1.

[30] See Frankel, Book Review of Code of Professional Responsibility, 43 U.Chi.L.Rev. 874, 877 (1976); Sutton, The American Bar Association Code of Professional Responsibilty: An Introduction, 48 Tex.L.Rev. 255, 258 (1970).

moral ideals.[31] The 1983 Model Rules differ sharply from the Code in that respect. Aside from occasional remarks in the Comments, the Rules make no effort to define or explore the moral dimensions of law practice. Those dimensions, however, the Model Rules do not deny. Instead, the Scope to the Rules states that:

> The Rules do not . . . exhaust the moral and ethical considerations that should inform a lawyer, for no worthwhile human activity can be completely defined by legal rules. The Rules simply provide a framework for the ethical practice of law.

The general omission of any discussion of ethical considerations in the Rules might reflect a judgment on the part of those who drafted the Rules that matters of morality are too indeterminate to permit a group as large, diverse, and unwieldy as the American Bar Association to make collective statements about them.[32] Yet the absence of consensus on moral matters clearly does not mean that issues of morality are unimportant. To the contrary, the refusal of the drafters of the Model Rules to engage in a drafting process in which some lawyers would be required to yield to the views of others on matters of personal morality implies that matters of conscience are too important to be logrolled in the process of arriving at compromised statements of professional morality. The Model Rules, instead, are limited to those prescriptions necessary and appropriate for effective regulation of the legal profession in the interest of protecting clients and third parties against the most harmful lawyer excesses. But it is a mistake to conclude that because a social order cannot legislate or form a consensus upon moral issues, it is not meaningful for the individual members of that social order to consider the morality of law or of personal choice.[33]

§ 2.7.2 An Outline of Theories of Ethics[34]

A compete description of moral philosophy for lawyers would be better written by others, at leisure, and not as a brief catalog. Moral philosophy is an ancient and continuous pursuit that has attracted great minds in every era and has developed a rich written tradition. There are, of course, a great many competing schools of thought in moral philosophy, and a sketch cannot begin to discuss them adequately. Each has subtleties that make general classification hazardous and, to an extent, misleading. Moreover, there are many similarities and enormous stretches of commonly held ground between competing ethical theories that can be obscured when one becomes preoccupied with sharply delineating their differences. But, with those important limitations in mind, at least the main elements of commonly discussed ethical theories can be briefly traced.

31 E.Cahn, The Moral Decision 39 (1956); L.Fuller, The Morality of Law 3–32 (rev.ed.1969) (distinction between a "morality of duty" and a "morality of aspiration"); Honoré, Law, Morals and Rescue, in The Good Samaritan and the Law (J.Ratcliffe ed.1966), at 225, 229:

> Broadly speaking, moral ideals concern patterns of conduct which are admired but not required. To live up to them is praiseworthy but not exigible. Moral duties, on the other hand, concern conduct which is required but not admired. With an important exception, to which I shall come, merely to do one's duty evokes no comment. Moral duties are pitched at a point where the conformity of the ordinary man can reasonably be expected. As a corollary, while it is tolerable, if deplorable, to fall short of the highest ideals, it is not permissible to neglect one's duties.

32 In that vein it has been suggested that special-function bar associations devoted to specific areas of law practice would be in a better position to draft their own sets of aspirational statements. See Schwartz, The Death and Regeneration of Ethics, 1980 Am.B.Found. Research J. 953. Those would probably be able to rise above the lowest-common-denominator quality so often encountered in the ECs of the 1969 Code but may reflect the particular political and social agenda of the special-function bar that drafts them.

33 That error apparently is made in Leff, Unspeakable Ethics, Unnatural Law, 1979 Duke L.J. 1229, 1239-40. From the fact that no "unchallengeable" (incontrovertable, universally agreed upon) ethical system exists, Professor Leff concluded that morality was not relevant to law. At the very least, Leff here confused legislating about morality and making individual moral decisions.

34 For other brief descriptions of ethics and moral philosophy, see, e.g., T.Beauchamp & J.Childress, Principles of Biomedical Ethics ch.1 (2d ed.1983); T.Beauchamp & L.Walters, Contemporary Issues in Bioethics ch.1 (2d ed. 1982). For a description in the specific context of legal ethics, see T.Morgan & R.Rotunda, Problems and Materials on Professional Responsibility 10-18 (1984).

The Nature of Ethical Choice

Many people are impatient with moral philosophy because it does not deliver the goods—clear answers that we can act upon with complete confidence. But, unfortunately, moral choice is often inherently dilemmatic and moral philosophy does not deal with realms as contained as those of the physical sciences. There is no clearly right course to choose, because of either the ambiguity of facts or the ambiguity of our values, no matter how sincerely we attempt to think about them. If, for example, a lawyer reveals secrets of a client in order to remedy the harm done by a client's lie, the lawyer inflicts harm on his or her client in the process. If, on the other hand, the lawyer does not disclose, in order to protect the client, harm is done to another person. Neither solution is clearly and intuitively correct, and both solutions cause harm. Too much of the popular and professional discourse about morality is bombastic triumphalism—a kind of self-congratulatory, one-dimensional moralizing. Missing is much sensitivity for the intractability of moral dilemma: moments of crisis when, viewed honestly, the paths of right and wrong conduct do not clearly stretch out from one's feet. It would be comforting, although perhaps in a merely escapist sort of way, if moral quandaries were merely legislative interpretation problems requiring only a carefully worded rule to resolve them. They are not.

Moral Skepticism or Relativism [35]

There are moral systems, however, that deny that a person can improve a moral decision by thinking about it or by talking with others about the rightness or wrongness of conduct.[36] Many of those systems share the common understanding that what we conceive of as autonomous moral judgments are overwhelmingly and involuntarily forced upon us by our cultural, social, psychological, or developmental environment. They claim that when we are confronted with the need to choose between alternative courses of action, we do not make a particular moral decision on the basis of reasoning. Instead, they believe, we are conditioned to make a choice by forces beyond our control.

There are several problems with such theories. If applied consistently, many versions of them would have to be applied, self-destructively, to their own premises because they create disabling skepticism about all knowledge, including knowledge concerning their own validity. That result follows because there is no reason to think that general philosophical thought is any less susceptible to deterministic forces than moral thought. Many deteriministic or relativistic theories also do not explain why morality is intellectually uninteresting, why we shouldn't try to reason about morality. They stop when they insist that knowing things about morality won't change the way people behave.

Cultural relativism also experiences great difficulty explaining the common problem of the person who functions in two cultures. A lawyer who practices law for a large corporation during the day and functions in a nonlegal culture the rest of the time may find sharply conflicting cultural values about corporate responsibility in the two environments. Does the theory mean that such a lawyer has two, conflicting value systems? Finally, cultural relativism assumes that culture speaks with only one voice on many important matters of moral choice. But there are plainly many important moral issues on which many members of any culture will disagree.

Individual Relativism

Another relativist theory of morality believes that every person's conception of correct conduct is as valid as any other's. One problem with such a theory is that it can say

[35] This and the following section rely heavily on D.Lyons, Ethics and the Rule of Law (1984).

[36] Doubts such as those lie at the root of commonly held beliefs that courses in legal ethics are feckless if they mean to teach persons otherwise not so disposed how to practice law according to new moral insights.

nothing about how lawyers, for example, should act if as few as two lawyers report different conceptions of correct conduct. More importantly, the theory also has nothing to say about a person who believes that it is correct conduct to harm third parties without justification. The theory's initial appeal because of its generosity appears, on further reflection, to be intuitively objectionable because it poses the risk of validating monstrous narcissism.

A theory somewhat similar to ethical relativism is ethical egoism. That theory holds that whatever is in the best interest of the actor is moral to do. Some people speak of their values as if they lived their lives in that way, looking out only for the interests of number one. But ethical egoism runs into some of the same kinds of problems as does individual relativism. What, if not combat and chaos, is proper conduct when two self-regarding actors come into conflict? How could a social or political system conceivably be ordered on egoistic grounds, aside perhaps from some elements of its foreign policy?

Being serious about the utility of moral philosophy requires two things. First, we must be able to think that a person who reflects seriously on the rightness and wrongness of acts can learn something useful from the exercise. Second, we must be able to think that what is learned can sometimes make a difference in the reflective person's choice of conduct. But we should also be alert to the reality that forms the basis for theories of moral skepticism based on the influence of culture and theories of individual relativism. It does seem to be true that persons from the same culture behave and think with great consistency and members of one culture tend to differ significantly from members of another culture on important matters of conduct. It is also true that respect for individuals and their personal choice is important, even if the exercise of personal choice is not as conclusive an argument for determining the morality of an action as individual relativists believe. Realizing both of those things should make us less dogmatic about our own moral beliefs. It should also induce us to be willing to assess and if necessary to criticize conventional moral views that we encounter in the culture and in the social groupings, such as professions, in which we find ourselves.

Teleological and Deontological Theories

Moral philosophers usually conceive of two main types of moral arguments, or two kinds of systems of moral philosophy. One kind regards the outcomes of conduct as pivotal; the other judges behavior by preexisting principles of right and wrong. The first kind of system, called *teleological*,[37] includes several theories, but the best known is *utilitarianism*. Utilitarian theories judge right and wrong by the impact of conduct upon the pleasure, happiness, or welfare of the actor and others. In that sense, the theory is result-oriented. A common form of the utilitarian theory asks whether conduct in question advances the greatest good of the greatest number.[38] The second grouping of theories is termed *deontological* and is represented most popularly by Kantian theories,[39] which assess conduct by first principles. For example, a commonly discussed modern theory of the deontological kind holds that conduct is to be judged moral only if it protects the autonomy of individuals.[40]

It is a mistake to insist too rigidly on the teleological-deontological division. Many

[37] Utilitarian theories are sometimes also called consequentialist.

[38] The foremost exponents of utilitarianism are the nineteenth-century English philosophers Jeremy Bentham and John Stuart Mill. See J.Bentham, An Introduction to the Principles of Morals and Legislation (1789) (J.Burns & H.Hart eds.1970); J.Mill, Utilitarianism (S.Gorovitz ed.1971). Among contemporaries, see, e.g., Smart, An Outline of a System of Utilitarian Ethics, in J.Smart & B.Williams, Utilitarianism: For and Against 3 (1973).

[39] See I.Kant, Groundwork of the Metaphysics of Morals (1785)(H.Paton transl.1961); I.Kant, Critique of Practical Reason (1788)(L.Beck transl.1956).

[40] Some modern exponents take as starting points starkly individualistic and absolute versions of autonomy. E.g., C.Fried, Right and Wrong (1978); R.Nozick, Anarchy, State, and Utopia (1974).

modern theories, for example, start by accepting some of the basic welfare assumptions of utilitarianism but then develop conceptions of rights that seem deontological and operate as limitations on utilitarian conceptions. Nonetheless, the division is a useful one for the limited purpose of general orientation in an otherwise complex area of thought. Both teleological and deontological theories have some general features and interrelationships that should usefully be kept in mind.

Teleology

A theory such as utilitarianism which looks only to the consequences of actions, holds that the usefulness of the results of action is the only valid test of moral rightness and wrongness. No action has intrinsic worth until we can assess all of its relevant impacts, both upon all other parties and upon the actor. Those acts are moral that, all such things considered, produce the highest net level of intrinsic good, such as health, happiness, pleasure, and knowledge. A person who saves a life performs a moral act, while another person who avoids ruining a new pair of shoes in order to step into shallow water to save a drowning child acts wrongfully. The future life of a child is more useful than a pair of shoes. A utilitarian holds that we should make a calculation of utilities for each action we think of taking or foregoing. We do this as best we can with available information. We should then always choose that course of action that will produce the most welfare (that will net the most usefulness or the least inutility if all courses open to us will produce harm).

Utilitarian theories have three principal difficulties.[41] Exponents of utilitarian theories have attempted to answer those difficulties or to place them in perspective by comparing them with the difficulties of competing theories. The first difficulty is the task of defining what "intrinsic goods" are to be pursued in working out the utilitarian calculus. It seems that people's actual preferences should play a major part, but then a utilitarian must in some way discount perverse or otherwise unacceptable preferences, such as a preference to discriminate on the basis of race, to rape, or to engage in self-destructive conduct. To what extent should social goods—such as community peace and orderliness—be recognized as intrinsic goods?

The second difficulty that utilitarians encounter is that of quantification. Even if we could develop a defensible list of one or more intrinsic goods, how much weight should each have? Lawyers are familiar with the problems of measuring "pain and suffering" in personal injury litigation. Yet something very much like assigning quantifiable values to pain, suffering, health, love, pleasure, tranquility, and the like must also be worked out in the utilitarian calculus. Moreover, unlike the relative leisure of a formal trial with its period of preparation, one must often make moral decisions under pressure of time. Utilitarians respond that many decisions in life are made under pressure of time or circumstances and that we learn from experiences with moral crisis how to respond in future dilemmas.

A third difficulty is that the utility of an act can turn on strange or unacceptable features. Consider two cases. First, suppose a lawyer is administering an elderly client's property in a trust. The client, who is without heirs and is in a coma near death, has left a will in which all of the client's property will be given to a charity to care for homeless cockroaches. The lawyer embezzles a substantial portion of the client's funds, leaving more than enough money to pay all debts of the client's estate. No one detects the embezzlement, and the lawyer and the lawyer's family enjoy great material satisfaction from their new wealth. Second, suppose another lawyer is in exactly the same position but has worse luck. That lawyer's theft is detected, and the lawyer is sent to jail and disbarred.

[41] See generally D.Lyons, Forms and Limits of Utilitarianism (1965); and Bernard Williams in Utilitarianism—For and Against (J.Smart & B.Williams eds.1973).

The lawyer and the lawyer's family suffer consequent lifelong humiliation and lost resources. Examining the situations of the two lawyers, a utilitarian may seem to be committed to the troublesome conclusion that the first lawyer has done no wrong, or at least not much, but the second clearly has done great wrong when measured by the consequences of that lawyer's identical acts. Yet embezzlement seems equally wrong in both instances. To judge the second act as more worthy of moral blame because of the unpleasantness that flowed from its accidental detection seems to have nothing legitimately to do with right and wrong. Possibly, utilitarians can suppress the unacceptable results problem by appealing to social goods such as an ideal of utility that excludes acts that frustrate the preferences of others.

"Rule" versus "Act" Utilitarianism

To contend with some of the problems of unacceptable intrinsic goods, quantifying goods, and unacceptably "right" acts, some utilitarians hold that the utility of acts is to be judged not on the particular facts of each instance of conduct but as a rule. Because a lawyer who takes entrusted funds without legal right would, as a rule, cause substantial harm, all lawyers who embezzle client funds act wrongfully. Moral blame will be assigned in all cases of generally inutile wrongdoing, including those occasions when a lawyer escapes detection by accident or cleverness and is able to elude harmful consequences. The only admissible exception would be an individual instance in which, for example, stealing a client's funds could be justified because it would clearly produce greater utility. That would be true, conceivably, if the lawyer embezzled the funds of a cockroach benefactor to feed starving people. One could then argue that in that instance the lawyer's act of saving lives was more useful, net, than the normally pernicious consequences of breaking rules and stealing. To take a perhaps less controversial example, many rule utilitarians would have no difficulty making the following statements. First, as a general rule it is wrongful to kill a person unless the person is another combatant in war. But, second, a civilian physician who was able to kill Hitler in 1943 would have acted correctly, even if Hitler could be considered a noncombatant.

Deontological First Principles

Deontological theories, with their concern for rights and duties that do not always hinge on consequences, face two central tasks. First is the choice and defense of first principles that define rights and duties. Second is the definition of a principle that holds persons to those rights or duties. What distinguishes deontological theories from teleological theories is that under deontological theories a first principle may take some account of consequences of actions, but not invariably so.

First principles, unless they are simply asserted without defense, are among the most difficult of concepts to defend convincingly. As with all philosophical concepts, they must be universalizable—global in their application to all similar acts and defensible on a basis that can rationally appeal to others. One can attempt to define first principles in terms of either *rights* or *duties*, although in modern times the emphasis is decidedly upon the former.[42]

The first principles selected by many deontologists strike many individuals, who judge on the basis of their own thinking and life experiences, as implausibly overstated or as very problematical in application. A familiar example is Kant's argument that the duty of truthfulness required a person never to speak untruthfully even if that meant telling a menacing fiend where to find an innocent victim. Lies to fiends strike most people as a lesser and even necessary evil, compared to facilitating the fiend's threatened harm to the innocent victim.

[42] B.Ackerman, Private Property and the Constitution (1977); R.Dworkin, Taking Rights Seriously (1977); C.Fried, Right and Wrong (1978); R.Nozick, Anarchy, State and Utopia (1974); R.Unger, Knowledge and Politics (1975).

Some persons find suppport for their deontological first principles in religious belief, in God-given first principles whose content need not be, or indeed is not supposed to be, analyzed rationally. Many other persons, including persons of religious conviction, find it difficult to accept assertedly God-given first principles without rational scrutiny.[43] Whether an asserted first principle is of that sort is one issue that the latter type of religious thinkers wants to investigate. They also conclude, however, that the origin of the first principle is some sort of divine command or other generative act.

Deontologists have tried several nontheistic approaches to the task of selecting rationally defensible first principles. Some find justification for first principles in natural law—an order of things that is intrinsic to the nature of man and to which conformity is by definition right conduct. Kant's ultimate principle was that persons must always be treated as ends in themselves and not as means to ends. One influential scholar has attempted to demonstrate that respect for every person as a rational creature is the core first principle.[44] A scholar very influential in law schools and elsewhere, John Rawls,[45] argues that first principles can be derived from a process of reasoning in a certain way. For Rawls the moral reasoning process assumes a "veil of ignorance" that blinds the rational person to all information about his or her own talents, wealth, and other advantages or preferences. He then asks the rational person to make disinterested choices of values.

The second major problem for a deontologist is to produce the glue that binds persons to each other or to certain kinds of conduct. To put the issue one way, if divine reward or retribution is not in the offing, why should a person behave morally? Some deontologists base the command or imperative of moral rules on variations of Kant's moral imperative—the notion that a person is only free when he or she knowingly acts according to correctly understood moral duties. For others, the imperative is based on a bond of love or friendship between humans. Still others might appeal to a notion of social utility. Rawls, for example, argues that only moral and social chaos is imaginable in the absence of agreement among persons and that the bonds of mutual agreement are the beginnings of individual and social order.

Moral Character[46]

Most ethical theories hold that actors in specific instances can influence their own decisions toward what are perceived to be moral instead of immoral actions. Is it also true that persons can develop habits or traits that solidify and make more instinctual their inclination toward moral acts? Does it make sense to speak of excellences—or deficits—of character? Those questions are not only psychological ones; they also involve moral philosophy. At the very least, many ethical theories hold that a good person can be identified as one who routinely uses appropriate moral considerations in judging rightness and wrongness of the person's own conduct.

Many ethical thinkers go further and assert that the moral life is not one for ethical dabblers or for ethical schizophrenics. Leading a moral life requires the development of attitudes, strengths, and inclinations that

[43] T.Shaffer, On Being a Christian and a Lawyer (1981); Shaffer, Christian Theories of Professional Responsibility, 48 So.Cal.L.Rev. 721 (1975).

[44] A.Donagan, The Theory of Morality (1977). Perhaps a similar concept underlies M.Freedman, Lawyers' Ethics in an Adversary System (1975), or so some have thought. See Donagan, Justifying Legal Practice in the Adversary System, in The Good Lawyer (D.Luban ed.1984), at 147 n. 6.

[45] J.Rawls, A Theory of Justice (1971).

[46] See generally, by Bernard Williams, Problems of the Self (1973) and Politics and Moral Character, in Public and Private Morality (S.Hampshire ed.1978). On the problem of character in lawyers' professional roles, see Williams, Professional Morality and Its Dispositions, in The Good Lawyer (D.Luban ed.1984), at 259; Eshete, Does a Lawyer's Character Matter? in id. at 270; and Postema, Self-Image, Integrity, and Professional Responsibility, in id. at 286. For the view that a lawyer's role in the adversary system does not call for any loss of integrity, see Held, The Division of Moral Labor and the Role of the Lawyer, in id. at 60.

serve to help the moral person to recognize ethical issues, to decide ethical issues in a consistent and satisfying way, to take moral action more often, and to act morally in the face of challenge, ridicule, material disadvantage, or other risks. Conversely, making wrong ethical decisions leads to an underdeveloped or perverse moral character. Acting against one's moral beliefs leads to a loss of integrity, to a sense of being at war with oneself.

§ 2.7.3 *Morality in Social Systems: Lawyer Role Morality*

Lawyers' Professional Role [47]

To the extent that conclusions about the interconnection between conduct and character are philosophically sound and psychologically accurate, they raise troubling issues. They suggest that lawyers might be self-deluded if they believe that they are capable of regularly acting in morally appropriate ways in both professional and nonprofessional life if they make moral judgments in radically different ways in those roles. For example, one view of integrity holds that it is not true that a lawyer who regularly lies for clients will find it as easy to act truthfully in nonlawyer situations. On the assumption that lawyers regularly engage in lying, bullying, and other forms of dissimulation and coercion in their practices, many nonlawyers, and some lawyers, contend that "legal ethics" is an oxymoron—one cannot be both a good lawyer and a good person.

Other philosophers disagree and contend that, within limits, a person can perform acts within one role that would be morally objectionable if performed in another. A familiar example is a person who is performing the role of parent. A parent may inflict discipline and in other ways act paternalistically toward his or her child. But a person who happened to be a parent and who disciplined adult friends in the same way would be considered strange, because the role of adult friend does not explain or justify paternalistic conduct.[48] Charles Fried has attempted to argue that the role of lawyers can usefully be analogized to that of a friend. Because we permit friends to show special favoritism toward their friends and their interests, similar client-favoring behavior is also permissible for lawyers.[49]

The lawyer-as-friend analogy, however, has serious difficulties. We do not ordinarily think that persons who are not prostitutes are in the business of playing the role of friend for a fee. Nor do we ordinarily expect that total strangers will work out within an initial consultation that might take only a half hour the emotional and personal basis on which the former strangers can build a true commit-

47 Important discussions include A.Goldman, The Moral Foundations of Professional Ethics 1-8, 90-155 (1980); Wasserstrom, Roles and Morality, in The Good Lawyer 25 (D.Luban ed.1984).

48 On paternalism, see generally Luban, Paternalism and the Legal Profession, 1981 Wisc.L.Rev. 455; Dworkin, Paternalism, in Morality and the Law 107 (R.Wasserstrom ed. 1971).

49 See Fried, The Lawyer as Friend: The Moral Foundations of the Lawyer-Client Relationship, 85 Yale L.J. 85 (1976). A later version is C.Fried, Right and Wrong ch.7 (1978). See also, e.g., Curtis, The Ethics of Advocacy, 4 Stan.L.Rev. 3 (1953).

Socrates seems to have originated the notion that friendship might be useful as an analogy to explain just and unjust social bonds. See Plato, The Republic, Book I, in The Dialogues of Plato 295, 297 (Great Books ed.1952). In the *Dialogues*, Socrates demonstrates to Polemarchus and more recent students of philosophy that the analogy of friendship, once underway, may prove difficult to keep under rein:

> [Socrates] Then after all the just man has turned out to be a thief. And this is a lesson which I suspect you must have learnt out of Homer; for he, speaking of Autolycus, the maternal grandfather of Odysseus, who is a favourite of his, affirms that *He was excellent above all men in theft and perjury*. And so, you and Homer and Simonides are agreed that justice is an art of theft; to be practiced however "for the good of friends and for the harm of enemies"—that was what you were saying?
>
> [Polemarchus] No certainly not that, though I do not know what I did say; but I will stand by the latter words.

(Emphasis in original.)

A sometimes telling but uncomfortably savage critique of Fried is Dauer & Leff, Correspondence: The Lawyer as Friend, 86 Yale L.J. 573 (1977). See also, e.g., D'Amato & Eberle, Three Models of Legal Ethics, 27 St.Louis L.J. 761 (1983).

ment of friendship. Nor that the friends will part without expectation of further relationship at the end of an episode of friendly help. Nor that only one of the parties will be burdened with the special responsibilities of friendly loyalty. In short, the analogy seems ill-fitted. Moreover, the analogy assumes a certain amount of given-ness in the role of lawyer; lawyers are taken to be loyal and committed to clients in a personal way. But professional roles are terribly contingent on history, culture, and circumstance, and that is certainly true of lawyers' roles. Finally, even if the fit were perfect, the force of the analogy would only be as strong as the arguments for the proposition that a person may depart from ordinary moral rules when helping a friend. In other words, the entire weight of the argument depends on whether we agree, first, that a person acting as a friend acts in a special moral role and, second, that a person who acts in such a special role, by virtue of the role alone, acts under special moral rules.

Nonetheless, pursued as exemplar and not as analogy, the lawyer-as-friend concept points in an interesting direction. It suggests that a special relationship may exist between lawyer and client that permits, and in some extreme settings may even compel, the lawyer to act professionally in ways that in nonlawyer roles the same person could not act with moral impunity. We could attempt to justify the lawyer's role at the personal level at which Professor Fried examines it. Or, differently, it has been argued that there are compelling reasons of social justice to concede that lawyers rightly occupy special moral roles. We could argue that a society that relies on law for the distribution of rights should have functioning within it specially trained persons (lawyers) whose task it is to maximize the legal entitlements of members of society (clients) who seek their assistance. One can attempt to defend that argument on the deontological grounds that every person is entitled to respect by the law and that proper respect entails legal assistance for any purpose allowed by the law.[50] A different defense would be based on the utilitarian ground that justice is more likely achieved in a representational system in which lawyers have special duties to act single-mindedly in a client's interests.[51]

Attention to a lawyer's role is important for another reason. Any discussion of ethics can bog down in unreal assumptions about human behavior. Sometimes the problem is that the discussion has roamed too far from real world entanglements and constraints that lawyers in fact encounter. Lawyers are not totally free agents that interact randomly with clients and third parties. They are members of a profession and probably of bar associations. They often are members of law firms and in almost all cases have secretaries, paralegals, junior lawyers, and others who are economically dependent on the lawyer to keep a steady flow of business coming through the office. Firms generate relationships between senior lawyers and junior lawyers, between lawyers who bring in the clients and lawyers who do the legal work. Lawyers have families and consequent economic and moral responsibilities. Issues of legal ethics, like ethical problems generally, come upon a lawyer suddenly and unlabeled for easy analysis. They also do not come to lawyers in their sleep; they arise in a practice and in an ethical environment in which lawyers will already have acquired a case orientation. Those and similar constraints impose real limits on the natural range of choice of lawyers.[52] They are good to keep in mind, although they are hardly determinative, in most discussions of a lawyer's ethical responsibilities. Moreover, the constraints of a lawyer's role are an important reason for believing that legal ethics can be well learned by law students in clinical settings in which stu-

50 Donogan, Justifying Legal Practice in the Adversary System, in The Good Lawyer (D.Luban ed.1984), at 123; Martin, Rights and the Meta-Ethics of Professional Morality, 91 Ethics 619 (1981).

51 Schwartz, The Zeal of the Civil Advocate, in The Good Lawyer (D.Luban ed.1984), at 150.

52 Greenebaum, Attorneys' Problems in Making Ethical Decisions, 52 Ind.L.J. 627 (1977).

dents represent clients with real human needs.[53]

WESTLAW REFERENCES

ethical moral +1 value evaluation norm

di ethics

utilitarian*** (greatest /3 good happiness pleasure utility) /p ethic** moral*** philosoph!

kant /p moral*** ethic** deontolog! "catagorical imperative"

rawls /p theory /3 justice

[53] Frank, Why Not a Clinical Lawyer-School?, 81 U.Pa. L.Rev. 907, 922 (1933).

Chapter Three
PROFESSIONAL DISCIPLINE OF LAWYERS

Table of Sections

---

§ 3.1 THE PHILOSOPHY OF LAWYER DISCIPLINE

General

The history of the regulation of the legal profession in the United States and England is primarily that of supervision by courts. By tradition and force of doctrine in many American jurisdictions (§ 2.2.3), courts alone are authorized to discipline lawyers. And normally that power is reserved to the state's supreme court which typically delegates its exercise to a lawyer disciplinary agency (§ 3.2). The disciplinary agencies take the place of bar associations and an occasional prosecutor that formerly brought disciplinary actions against offending lawyers.

Courts assert that the underlying purpose of disciplining lawyers is a broadly social one. The purpose is not to punish offending lawyers but to protect the public, the bar, and legal institutions against lawyers who have demonstrated an unwillingness to comply with minimal professional standards. There is reason to think, however, that a strong motivation for lawyer discipline is to reassure a doubtful public that notorious instances of lawyer depredation are being handled appropriately. That motivation is reflected in the often largely reactive way in which lawyer misconduct is detected, in the types of cases that are selected for the most severe lawyer discipline (§ 3.5.2), and in the general level of unconcern of lawyers with most problems of lawyer discipline that do not arise to notoriously intolerable levels.

Lawyer Deviance and Bar Response

As with measuring crime, measuring how frequently lawyers violate mandatory norms is also controversial. Some researchers report that lawyer violation of many norms is endemic in at least some kinds of law practice.[1] Statistics on lawyer discipline are an

[1] Wood, Professional Ethics among Criminal Lawyers, in Social Problems, at 70 (1959)(assertion that dishonesty is common among solo practitioners doing criminal defense work, such as feesplitting, thefts from clients, influence peddling, "fixing" charges, questionable use of fa-

unreliable measure of lawyer deviance for two reasons. First, there are ample reasons to believe that discipline is selective, episodic, subject to constraints of fluctuating budgets and personnel ability, influenced by political instability, and subject to like influences that grossly distort the extent to which lawyer discipline reflects levels of deviance and compliance among lawyers. Second, discipline statistics are quite incomplete. Statistics on disciplinary activity in the states are difficult to obtain on a national basis because record keeping of disciplinary actions is either localized or nonexistent.[2]

Recurring impressionistic accounts claim that the state of lawyer discipline demands urgent attention.[3] The best-known report was made in 1970 by an ABA committee headed by retired Justice Tom Clark. The Clark Report urged that lawyer discipline was a "scandalous situation"[4] which was generating political pressures for intrusions by alien regulators such as legislatures.[5] For the period between 1965 and 1973 fewer than 0.1 percent of American lawyers received professional discipline[6] during a time when the Clark Report found that a "substantial number of malefactors" continued to practice law.[7] In 1976 the ABA announced that nationally during 1975, 693 cases resulted in some form of public discipline of lawyers. That included 129 disbarments and 133 resignations from the bar in the face of disciplinary charges. Those statistics were based on 33,007 complaints of lawyer misconduct, or 47.6 complaints per instance of public discipline.[8] Whether more recent experience shows a significant increase in the level of enforcement of discipline is controverted.[9]

Objectives of Lawyer Discipline

Courts discipline lawyers to incapacitate the offending lawyer, to deter that and all other lawyers from repeated violations of professional regulations, and to protect the image of the bar. The classic statement of the purposes of judicial discipline of lawyers is that of Lord Mansfield in *Ex Parte Brounsall*:[10]

> [T]he question is, Whether, after the conduct of this man, it is proper that he should continue a member of a profession which should stand free from all suspicion. . . . It is not by way of

vors and gifts to obtain clients or to influence court officers).

[2] ABA Spec.Comm. on Eval. of Disciplinary Enforcement, Problems and Recommendations 77 (1970)(hereafter, the "Clark Report"); Mark & Cathcart, Discipline Within the Legal Profession: Is It Self-Regulation?, 1974 U.Ill.L.Forum 193, 208. The official ABA position is that record keeping is an important function of local disciplinary agencies to facilitate comparisons with the statistics of other jurisdictions. See ABA Joint Comm., Standards for Lawyer Disciplinary and Disability Proceedings 19-20 (1979). The ABA established a National Discipline Data Bank for discipline statistics under the aegis of its National Center for Professional Responsibility in 1968. The system relies on voluntary state reporting and is subject to the vagaries of state-by-state variations in reporting categories. See Flaherty, Statistics on Discipline Are Elusive, Nat'l L.J., July 12, 1982, p.22, col.2.

[3] Marks & Cathcart, Discipline Within the Legal Profession: Is It Self-Regulation?, 1974 U.Ill.L.Forum 193, 228 (when disciplinary process is considered as a whole, it appears that legal profession is creating the appearance of self-regulation without in fact engaging in the act of self-regulation).

[4] See the often-quoted words of the Clark Report (1970), at 1. Four years after his commission's report, Justice Clark reportedly said that "no progress has been made to amount to anything." Steele & Nimmer, Lawyers, Clients, and Professional Regulation, 1976 Am.B.Found. Research J. 919, 942 n.38. See also Manning, If Lawyers Were Angels: A Sermon on One Canon, 60 ABA J. 821, 822 (1974)(the impact of the Clark Report has "been that of a feather dropped into a well").

[5] Clark Report, at 2. For recent arguments along the same lines, see Burger, Annual State of the Judiciary Address to ABA, 52 U.S.L.Wk. 2471 (Feb.28, 1984).

[6] Burbank & Duboff, Ethics and the Legal Profession: A Survey of Boston Lawyers, 9 Suffolk U.L.Rev. 66, 70 (1974).

[7] Clark Committee Report, at 3.

[8] Tighter Discipline Shown by Statistics, 63 ABA J. 24 (1977).

[9] Compare, Burger, Address to ABA Midyear Meeting (Feb.1984), in McPike & Harrison, The True Story on Lawyer Discipline, 70 ABA J. 92, 94 (1984)(the Clark Report "stimulated action by some state bar associations, but any fair-minded examination of the whole picture today will reveal that what we have done falls far short of what is needed."); Miller, Why Crooked Lawyers go Free, Reader's Digest, Sept.1979, at 47 (only miniscule proportion of lawyer violations are effectively disciplined), with, McPike & Harrison, supra, 70 ABA J. 92 (1984)(state disciplinary systems, financing, and lawyer consciousness have all been vastly improved; 73% increase in sanctions from 1978 to 1982).

[10] 2 Cowp. 829, 98 Eng. Rep. 1385, 1385 (1778).

> punishment; but the court on such cases, exercise their discretion, whether a man whom they have formerly admitted, is a proper person to be continued on the roll or not.

Mansfield's protestation that lawyer discipline is not intended to punish the offending lawyer but to protect the public has been endlessly repeated by modern courts.[11]

A lawyer who continues to hold a license to practice law is probably viewed by the public as carrying a continuing judicial endorsement that the lawyer is trustworthy and competent.[12] Misconduct by a licensed lawyer suggests that unless discipline is imposed, the lawyer might use the shield of the license to induce trust in prospective clients, courts, and other lawyers and thereby gain the opportunity to harm members of the public. The indicated remedy is to incapacitate the lawyer, temporarily or permanently, by taking away the credential that permits the lawyer to continue to practice for as long as that danger exists. The sanction, obviously, should not be imposed lightly. From the lawyer's point of view, disbarment or suspension, while it lasts, deprives a lawyer of the substantial asset of a professional license gained through long and costly education and experience and throws a lawyer back into the search for employment officially stamped with disgrace and dishonor.[13]

Discipline, if effective and sufficiently publicized, may also serve to deter other lawyers from breaching professional obligations.[14] One of the working assumptions of courts that avowedly pursue a deterrence policy must be that formal lawyer discipline in fact significantly affects the behavior and attitudes of lawyers. But it is probable that the threat of discipline has traditionally been so minimal that, until recently, the existence of a disciplinary structure has exerted very little influence on the conduct of many lawyers.[15] There are signs, however, that a new consciousness is growing among lawyers that professional norms are important sources of conduct control and that disciplinary action for violations of professional rules is a real prospect. Effective deterrence, of course, requires adequate means by which lawyers will learn of discipline of other lawyers.

A different purpose for discipline is to protect the bar or the public image of the bar.[16] Some courts insist that that is an independent basis for discipline even if there is no danger that the lawyer involved in the particular case will repeat the misconduct.[17] Courts may seek to protect the reputation of the bar through lawyer discipline for reasons of respectability,[18] which hardly recommends itself, or for more appealing reasons. The defaults of a lawyer may cause the lawyer's

[11] In re Echeles, 430 F.2d 347, 349 (7th Cir.1970); In re Kastensmith, 101 Ariz. 291, 419 P.2d 75, 78 (1966); Maryland St. Bar Ass'n v. Agnew, 271 Md. 543, 318 A.2d 811, 814 (1974); Attorney Grievance Comm'n v. Lockhart, 285 Md. 586, 403 A.2d 1241, 1247 (1979); In re Nardi, 122 N.H. 277, 444 A.2d 512, 513 (1982); Jackson v. State, 21 Tex. 668, 673 (1858).

[12] In re Leopold, 469 Pa. 384, 366 A.2d 227, 230-31 (1976).

[13] Cohen v. Hurley, 366 U.S. 117, 147, 81 S.Ct. 954, 971, 6 L.Ed.2d 156 (1961) (Black, J., dissenting).

[14] In re Peterson, 108 Ariz. 255, 495 P.2d 851, 853 (1972)(purpose of discipline includes deterrence of "other lawyers from the temptation to violate their ethics"); In re Klepak, 250 Ga. 892, 302 S.E.2d 356, 358 (1983); Louisiana St. Bar Ass'n v. Schoemann, 444 So.2d 608, 610 (La.1984); In re Grimes, 414 Mich. 483, 326 N.W.2d 380, 382-83 (1982); Attorney Grievance Comm'n v. Marano, 299 Md. 633, 474 A.2d 1332, 1337-38 (1984)(disciplinary sanction "protects the public for the period of suspension, not only from being further victimized by the attorney's neglect but also by demonstrating the type of misconduct which the Court and legal profession will not tolerate.").

[15] J.Carlin, Lawyers Ethics: A Survey of the New York Bar 160-61 (1966)(deterrent effect of bar discipline is "minimal"); J.Handler, The Lawyer and His Community (1967); O.Maru, Research on the Legal Profession 29-32 (1972); Burbank & Duboff, Ethics and the Legal Profession: A Survey of Boston Lawyers, 9 Suffolk L.Rev. 66 (1974).

[16] In re Greenberg, 80 N.J. 503, 404 A.2d 308 (1979) (lawyer's conduct "was calculated to demean the bar and bring it into disrepute"); In re Bosch, 175 N.W.2d 11, 13-14 (N.D.1970)(acts which bring reproach upon the legal profession).

[17] In re Rohan, 21 Cal.3d 195, 145 Cal.Rptr. 855, 578 P.2d 102, 106 (1978)(discipline of lawyer convicted of federal tax offense required because failure to discipline "will not only demean the integrity of the profession but will encourage disrespect for and further violations of the law"); In re Walton, 251 N.W.2d 762, 764 (N.D.1977).

[18] Cf. Ex parte Burr, 22 U.S. (9 Wheat.) 529, 530-31, 6 L.Ed. 152 (1824)("The power is one which ought to be exercised with great caution, but which is, we think, incidental to all Courts, and is necessary for the preserva-

clients and the public to distrust the lawyer's competence or character. But the effect can be much wider. Members of the public may reasonably conclude, if the lawyer's conduct is unchecked, that lack of competence or character typifies lawyers generally.[19] Unless discipline is effectively imposed, the policy of protection of the bar will be distorted into a practice of protecting offending members of the bar against the embarrassment and inconvenience of professional discipline and of protecting the bar itself against the harmful effects of publicity about lawyer misconduct by attempting to minimize the publicity.[20]

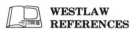

WESTLAW REFERENCES

(legal law /2 profession**) (lawyer attorney counsel** /s misconduct malfeasance disciplin*** /p deterren** deter /s purpose policy objective

§ 3.2 DISCIPLINARY AGENCIES AND STRUCTURE

Role of the Courts

Whether for sound reasons or otherwise, it is now settled in most jurisdictions that the melancholy business [21] of disciplining lawyers is reserved to the courts of the state.[22] Typically, only the supreme court of the state may exercise that power, to the exclusion of courts of lesser jurisdiction.[23] Following the recommendations of the ABA, most states have now adopted systems in which lawyer discipline is investigated, prosecuted, and administratively adjudicated in a single agency with jurisdiction-wide authority.[24] Centralization of disciplinary power in that fashion has the virtue of assuring uniform discipline throughout the state, to an extent removes the judges and administrators who provide the impetus for the design and working of the disciplinary system from the political pressure of local lawyers who may wish to diminish the reach of discipline, and permits cost savings and professionalism of enforcement personnel.

Separation of Prosecution and Adjudication

For reasons of due process, the Supreme Court has insisted that due process requires that a person exercising an adjudicatory function must be impartial and disinterested in the outcome of a particular matter.[25] For that reason the same person should not exer-

tion of decorum, and for the respectability of the profession.") (Marshall, C.J.).

[19] Louisiana St. Bar Ass'n v. Summers, 379 So.2d 1065, 1069 (La.1980).

[20] Marks & Cathcart, Discipline Within the Legal Profession: Is It Self-Regulation?, 1974 U.Ill.L. Forum 193.

[21] In re Gold, 77 Ill.2d 224, 32 Ill.Dec. 912, 914, 396 N.E.2d 25, 27 (1979).

[22] § 2.2. See also, e.g., ABA Spec.Comm. on Evaluation of Disciplinary Enforcement, Problems and Recommendations in Disciplinary Enforcement 10-18 (1970) (Clark Commission Report); ABA Joint Comm. on Prof. Discipline, Standards for Lawyer Disciplinary and Disability Proceedings 4-5 (approved 1979); People ex rel. Karlin v. Culkin, 248 N.Y. 465, 162 N.E. 487, 493, 60 A.L.R. 851 (1928)("if the house is to be cleaned, it is for those who occupy and govern it, rather than for strangers, to do the noisome work.").

[23] Weaver v. Superior Court, 572 P.2d 425 (Alaska 1977)(trial court has no power to suspend lawyer from practice in exercise of contempt powers); Jacobs v. State Bar, 20 Cal.3d 191, 141 Cal.Rptr. 812, 814, 570 P.2d 1230, 1231 (1977)(discussion of 1951 statute that excluded other courts from jurisdiction to discipline lawyers); McQueen v. State, 272 Ind. 229, 396 N.E.2d 903 (1979) (trial court has no power to suspend lawyer for contempt, even if limited to particular court imposing sanction); Kirven v. Bd. of Commissioners on Grievances and Discipline, 271 S.C. 194, 246 S.E.2d 857 (1978)(trial court has no jurisdiction to enjoin disciplinary proceedings). An extreme holding is Hahn v. Boeing Co., 95 Wn.2d 28, 621 P.2d 1263, 20 A.L.R.4th 846 (1980)(unauthorized solicitation of client whom lawyer sought to represent pro hac vice is not material question for trial court in view of exclusive jurisdiction of supreme court over questions of lawyer discipline). But cf. State v. Tedesco, 175 Conn. 279, 397 A.2d 1352 (1978)(before change by legislation, trial courts empowered to disbar summarily lawyer who committed acts constituting grounds for disbarment in presence of court); In re Hunoval, 294 N.C. 740, 247 S.E.2d 230 (1977) (power of trial court to discipline in summary judicial proceeding). See generally § 2.2.4.

[24] ABA Lawyer Disciplinary Standards at 6.

[25] Tumey v. Ohio, 273 U.S. 510, 47 S.Ct. 437, 71 L.Ed. 749 (1927)(mayor whose salary and whose village's financial requirements were met in significant part out of fees and costs levied in adjudicatory proceedings could not render decisions that comported with due process); Ward v. Village of Monroeville, 409 U.S. 57, 93 S.Ct. 80, 34 L.Ed.2d 267 (1972); Gibson v. Berryhill, 411 U.S. 564, 93 S.Ct. 1689, 36 L.Ed.2d 488 (1973)(application of *Tumey v. Ohio* to administrative agency); Stitt v. State Bar, 21 Cal. 3d 616, 146 Cal.Rptr. 878, 580 P.2d 293 (1978)(state bar hearing officer disqualified because of involvement of officer's partner and responding lawyer on different sides

cise both prosecutorial and adjudicatory powers in the same proceeding.[26] An impermissible merging of those functions is not caused merely because the judges hearing a lawyer disciplinary proceeding are members of the bar association that prosecutes it.[27] But is the principle of the impartial adjudicator offended if members of a bar disciplinary agency both conduct the investigation of complaints against a lawyer and adjudicate the resulting charges? The Supreme Court has upheld a medical discipline panel against constitutional attack on very similar facts in Withrow v. Larkin.[28] The Court was prepared to assume that the panel's exposure to inadmissible, or unadmitted, evidence during its investigation would properly be disregarded by the body in reaching its ultimate decision.[29]

The *Withrow v. Larkin* doctrine does not mean, however, that the person who actually prosecutes a charge against a lawyer can also sit in judgment. First, the person who exercises a prosecution function in bar discipline should be disinterested because the discretionary power to prosecute should not be influenced by the personal biases of the prosecutor.[30] Secondly, the prosecutor and hearing board members must be separated in their functions so that prosecutorial bias does not affect the ultimate deliberations and decision of the hearing body.[31]

The *Withrow* decision came down as disciplinary systems in many states were being reexamined in response to criticisms in the 1970 Clark Commission Report. Several states have adopted the system recommended by the 1979 ABA Standards for Lawyer Disciplinary and Disability Proceedings.[32] They now provide for separated functions of hearing panels and a bar counsel operating under the general supervision of a board appointed by the state's supreme court to oversee the operation of the disciplinary system.

Jurisdiction-Wide Regulation

During the early history of bar regulation in the United States, admission and discipline were administered by each local court. Thus a lawyer who had been disbarred by one district court in a state often remained free to practice in any other district court to which

in pending litigation); In re Ross, 99 Nev. 1, 656 P.2d 832 (1983), (due process precluded decision by board of bar governors, 20 percent of whose annual budget was represented by costs levied on lawyer it found guilty of professional misconduct).

26 Withrow v. Larkin, 421 U.S. 35, 95 S.Ct. 1456, 43 L.Ed.2d 712 (1975).

27 Ex parte Alabama St. Bar Ass'n, 92 Ala. 113, 8 So. 768 (1891); State v. Rhodes, 177 Neb. 650, 131 N.W.2d 118 (1964).

28 421 U.S. 35, 95 S.Ct. 1456, 43 L.Ed.2d 712 (1975). See also, e.g., In re Davis, 129 Ariz. 1, 628 P.2d 38 (1981) (participation in disciplinary agency deliberations of chairman of local hearing board that found probable cause to press charges conforms with *Withrow v. Larkin* standards); State v. Turner, 217 Kan. 574, 538 P.2d 966 (1975); In re Smeekens, 396 Mich. 719, 242 N.W.2d 391 (1976), cert. denied 429 U.S. 1032, 97 S.Ct. 723, 50 L.Ed.2d 743 (1977). In light of *Withrow*, consider the dubious holding in Tweedy v. Oklahoma Bar Ass'n, 624 P.2d 1049 (Okl.1981), that due process would be offended if the same state supreme court that would sit in final adjudicatory review of a recommendation to impose lawyer discipline ordered the disciplinary agency to conduct an investigation of a particular lawyer's conduct.

29 421 U.S. at 55, 95 S.Ct. at 1468.

30 Compare In re Robeson, 293 Or. 610, 652 P.2d 336 (1982)(bar counsel's former representation of complaining client in unrelated matter not shown to be prejudicial); In re Farris, 229 Or. 209, 367 P.2d 387 (1961)(better practice to appoint lawyer none of whose clients are interested in matters before the disciplinary agency, but no prejudice on facts here).

31 The ex parte presence of disciplinary counsel during the deliberations of the hearing panel on the merits of a submitted case offends due process. E.g., In re Beck, 400 Mich. 40, 252 N.W.2d 795 (1977); Mendicino v. Whitchurch, 565 P.2d 460 (Wyo.1977). Contra Walker v. Supreme Court Comm. on Prof. Conduct, 275 Ark. 158, 628 S.W.2d 552 (1982)(no fatal defect in absence of showing of prejudice from mere presence of executive secretary during hearing panel's deliberations but should not occur again); In re Logan, 71 N.J. 583, 367 A.2d 419 (1976) (same).

The necessary separation of adjudicatory and prosecution functions within the unitary discipline agency recommended by ABA Disciplinary Functions (at 7-8) is accomplished mainly by providing that the investigative and prosecutorial functions be performed by different persons with no interdependence between them. Id. §§ 3.4, 3.8.

32 See ABA Joint Comm. on Prof. Discipl., Standards for Lawyer Disciplinary and Disability Proceedings (approved 1979).

the lawyer might be admitted in the same state.

Most states today operate unified statewide lawyer disciplinary systems.[33] An exception is New York, which still retains an eighteenth-century system of dividing regulation among the four geographically defined "departments" of the intermediate appellate court.[34] The state's highest court, the Court of Appeals, has taken the position that the definition of professional misconduct and the determination of the appropriate sanction for misconduct is solely for the interested appellate department and is not subject to revision in the Court of Appeals [35] except on matters of constitutional law.[36] The arrangement seriously impinges on the power of any one appellate department to regulate lawyers in a way that is clearly different from the other departments because of a doctrine that "substantive" regulation of the profession must be uniform throughout the state.[37] In fact, however, there are wide variations from one appellate department to another in the extent to which the Code is enforced and in the sanctions that are imposed for apparently similar violations.[38]

General Structural Issues

Succeeding sections discuss important issues of the disciplinary process, including some that are structural in nature. In addition, general structural problems of financing, staffing, and publicity deserve attention. Typically, the financing of the disciplinary system is supported by levies upon admitted lawyers, often through a lawyer registration system that serves both to keep a current list of lawyers subject to discipline and to provide a method of annual assessments. The jurisdictions vary enormously in the per capita lawyer expenditure for discipline. In many jurisdictions, low budgets relegate bar counsel staffs to essential, triage cases, leaving both investigation and relatively less serious cases without attention.[39]

Traditionally, bar discipline has been the exclusive province of judges and lawyers. The 1979 ABA Disciplinary Standards recommended, however, that a third of the members of hearing panels in discipline cases be nonlawyers.[40] The concept has been adopted in a large number of states.[41] Another significant change from the traditional system of discipline is the increasingly professional

[33] For descriptions of the disciplinary systems in various states, see, e.g., Brill, The Arkansas Supreme Court Committee on Professional Conduct 1969-1979: A Call for Reform, 33 Ark.L.Rev. 571 (1980); Dubin & Schwartz, Survey and Analysis of Michigan's Disciplinary System for Lawyers, 61 U.Det.J.Urb.L. 1 (1983); Gardner, Report on Disciplinary Enforcement in New Hampshire, 15 N.H. B.J. 199 (1974); Machen, The Law of Disbarment and Reinstatement in Maryland, 36 Md.L.Rev. 703 (1977); Murphy, A Short History of Disciplinary Procedures in Illinois, 60 Ill.B.J. 528 (1972); Samad, Ohio Revised Rules for the Government of the Judiciary and the Bar: A Critique, 13 Cap.U.L.Rev. 25 (1983); Note, Enforcement of Legal Ethics in New Jersey, 28 Rutgers L.Rev. 707 (1975). For England, see, e.g., Leach, The New Look in Disciplinary Enforcement in England, 61 ABA J. 212 (1975).

[34] N.Y.—McKinney's Jud. Law § 90(2). For the history of the New York predecessor statutes and constitutional provisions, see People ex rel. Karlin v. Culkin, 248 N.Y. 465, 162 N.E. 487, 492, 60 A.L.R. 851 (1928). See also, e.g., Mildner v. Gulotta, 405 F.Supp. 182 (E.D.N.Y.1975) (three-judge court), affirmed 425 U.S. 901, 96 S.Ct. 1489, 47 L.Ed.2d 751 (1976)(rejecting broad attack on constitutionality of New York system); Note, Disbarment in the United States: Who Shall Do the Noisome Work?, 12 Colum.J. Law & Soc.Probs. 1, 15-16 (1975) (findings of Christ committee report on state of lawyer discipline in New York).

[35] Erie County Water Authority v. Western N.Y. Water Co., 304 N.Y. 342, 107 N.E.2d 479 (1952), cert.denied 344 U.S. 892, 73 S.Ct. 211, 97 L.Ed. 690 (1952).

[36] Greene v. Grievance Committee, 54 N.Y.2d 118, 444 N.Y.S.2d 883, 429 N.E.2d 390 (1981), cert. denied 455 U.S. 1035, 102 S.Ct. 1738, 72 L.Ed.2d 153 (1982)(constitutionality of statute and DR 2-103(A) proscribing solicitation as applied to direct mail contacts).

[37] Gair v. Peck, 6 N.Y.2d 97, 188 N.Y.S.2d 491, 160 N.E.2d 43, 77 A.L.R.2d 390 (1959), cert. denied 361 U.S. 374, 80 S.Ct. 401, 4 L.Ed.2d 380 (1960).

[38] 69 ABA J. 278 (1983)(reporting similar conclusions of ABA Standing Committee on Professional Discipline review committee); N.Y.Times, Jan. 6, 1983, p. B1, col.1.

[39] Granelli, Calif. Bar Disciplinarian Quits, Nat'l L.J., Feb.28, 1983, p. 3, col.1. See generally § 2.3 (lawyer registration).

[40] ABA Standards for Lawyer Disciplinary and Disability Proceedings § 3.4 (approved 1979). The Commentary stated that a third of the states already provided for nonlawyer representation in the disciplinary structure.

[41] See generally § 2.5 (nonlawyers).

prosecution of charges by bar counsel. Again following a central recommendation of the 1979 Disciplinary Standards[42] and the 1970 Clark Committee Report,[43] one or more full-time lawyers serve as bar counsel in many states. Many states, however, continue to rely on volunteer lawyers for much or all of the professional staff work necessary to investigate and prosecute lawyer misconduct. In some states the volunteer lawyers serve as members of local bar association investigating committees that are given responsibility for investigating and recommending a disposition of complaints to the statewide agency. The variation in ability, commitment, time, expertise, and philosophy of discipline of lawyer volunteers is, naturally, great.

Much of the information about lawyer discipline available to lawyers and researchers can be found only in bar journals and in reported appellate decisions. In a few states those serve as useful sources of information both about the court's views on the type of conduct that is permissible and impermissible and about the important characteristics of the disciplinary process. In other states, however, the brevity and lack of detail in opinions makes them little more than announcements of results in discipline cases and useless as guides for lawyers or as a basis to assess the proper treatment of future discipline cases.[44]

Even if appellate decisions were much more complete, they would not record the great majority of lawyer discipline. In a typical jurisdiction, resignation pending charges, the imposition of any sanction less than a substantial period of suspension or disbarment, and various "private" reprimands and warning letters are issued without public report. A lawyer investigated by another lawyer in a matter that is later dismissed may be significantly deterred in the future from ethical violations by the embarrassment and disruption of the investigation itself, even if no further steps are taken. The appellate decisions leave the impression that only conviction for a felony results in discipline. Impressions gained from within a disciplinary agency may be quite different. Because of rules of confidentiality that many jurisdictions apply (§ 3.4.4—secrecy), it is often not possible to calibrate the extent of the "hidden discipline" that occurs.

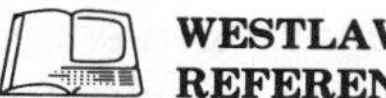
WESTLAW REFERENCES

jurisdiction power empower*** authority /s enjoin! suspen! disbar! disciplin*** /5 lawyer attorney (legal law /2 profession**) /s lesser trial +1 court

"due process" /p impartial*** disinterest** /p prosecutor*** adjudicat*** /p withrow

§ 3.3 GROUNDS FOR DISCIPLINE

§ 3.3.1 Standards of Discipline

Background

Nowhere does the uncertainty of the philosophy behind lawyer discipline manifest itself more than in the standards used by the lawyer codes and courts to define the grounds for which professional discipline should be imposed. One set of standards attempts to predict the likelihood that a lawyer in the future will violate important norms. But another set of standards merely holds lawyers who have engaged in questioned conduct in the past to very high standards with little effort to assess the lawyer's ability to perform professional functions. A similar ambiguity characterizes the judicial approach to the question whether a lawyer should be held to an expansive or merely to a narrow reading of the lawyer codes.

The Judicial Approach to Interpretation

A century ago courts disciplined lawyers only for egregious, or notorious, misconduct, which was nowhere defined with any preci-

42 ABA Standards for Lawyer Disciplinary and Disability Proceedings § 3.8.

43 Clark Committee Report 48-56 (1970).

44 ABA St. Comm. on Prof. Discipline, The Judicial Response to Lawyer Misconduct at VIII.4 to VIII.7 (1984); Gaetke & Casey, Professional Responsibility, 70 Ky.L.J. 325, 326 (1981).

sion. Today the grounds of discipline are spelled out in the lawyer codes. But most courts do not regard the codes as confining their discretion as statutes or administrative regulations might. Many courts ignore interpretative difficulties in the lawyer codes almost as a matter of policy. References to lawyer code provisions in many judicial opinions are offhand and open-ended. Thus in most jurisdictions bar disciplinary agencies may operate with as much functional freedom of maneuver as did nineteenth century courts.

Courts generally do not strictly construe the provisions of the lawyer codes. Two elements explain that approach. First, most courts probably conceive of their disciplinary role as one of discretion and creativity. The norms to be imposed are dynamic and flexible, as is true generally of exercising discretion in the common law. For many courts, that is much the same attitude found when they resort to the common-law inherent powers to adopt and enforce the lawyer codes (see § 2.2.2). Second, courts have been impatient with arguments by lawyers that Code language failed to give them fair notice of a forbidden practice. The prevailing, although not uniform,[45] judicial attitude has been that lawyers should be aware from an innate sense that certain conduct is wrongful.[46] A different reason has to do with the intended force of the lawyer rules: the lawyer codes are not to be strictly construed as are criminal codes, because a lawyer is held to knowledge of the lawyer code and should steer the widest possible course around arguably proscribed conduct.[47] For similar reasons, most attacks upon Code provisions charging that they are void for vagueness in violation of the due process clause have been unavailing.[48]

45 In re Tonkon, 292 Or. 660, 642 P.2d 660, 662 (1982) (discipline can be based on violation of a judicial rule only if the judicial rule "can be based on one of the code's disciplinary rules"). Occasionally a court will resort to prospective application of the lawyer codes and refuse to impose discipline for conduct on the ground that the code had not formerly been authoritatively interpreted to proscribe the questioned conduct. E.g., In re Nicholson, 243 Ga. 803, 257 S.E.2d 195 (1979)(conviction of repeated, willful failure to file federal tax returns as "moral turpitude" crime applicable prospectively only); In re Malloy, 248 N.W.2d 43, 47 (N.D. 1976)(prospective condemnation of failure to deal properly with client's perjury and to turn over promised documents to opposing counsel).

46 According to Justice White in In re Ruffalo, 390 U.S. 544, 555, 88 S.Ct. 1222, 1227, 20 L.Ed.2d 117 (1968)(concurring opinion):

> [M]embers of a bar can be assumed to know that certain kinds of conduct, generally condemned by responsible men, will be grounds for disbarment. This class of conduct certainly includes the criminal offenses traditionally known as *malum in se*. It also includes conduct which all responsible attorneys would recognize as improper for a member of the profession.

There are two different notions at work here. One is that goodness is innate and can divine the path of correct conduct in certain limited instances of particularly egregious conduct. The other is that a lawyer, as a specialist who is exposed to peer views on correct behavior, has less need for precise guidelines. E.g., In re Bithoney, 486 F.2d 319, 324 (1st Cir.1973); Committee on Professional Ethics v. Durham, 279 N.W.2d 280, 284 (Iowa 1979); In re Cipriano, 68 N.J. 398, 346 A.2d 393, 395 (1975). Sometimes the ideas are lumped into the sentiment that all lawyers should be aware that certain conduct is improper without being told. E.g., People v. Berge, 620 P.2d 23, 27 (Colo.1980); Kentucky Bar Ass'n v. Graves, 556 S.W.2d 890, 892 (Ky.1977)(lawyer with 40 percent contingent fee who also required client to pay office overhead items "needed no disciplinary regulation to tell him right from wrong").

Similar judicial attitudes are found in decisions holding that the lawyer code applies retroactively to conduct that occurred before the code was promulgated, on the ground that any lawyer should know that conduct of the kind in evidence should be avoided. E.g., State v. Martindale, 215 Kan. 667, 527 P.2d 703 (1974); Louisiana State Bar Ass'n v. Ponder, 340 So.2d 134 (1976), appeal dismissed 431 U.S. 934, 97 S.Ct. 2643, 53 L.Ed.2d 251 (1977).

47 General Motors Corp. v. City of New York, 501 F.2d 639, 649 (2d Cir.1974)("[T]he Code of Professional Responsibility is not designed for Holmes' proverbial 'bad man' who wants to know just how many corners he may cut, how close to the line he may play, without running into trouble with the law."); In re Scallen, 269 N.W.2d 834, 839-40, 98 A.L.R.3d 343 (Minn.1978).

48 In re Keiler, 380 A.2d 119, 126 (D.C.App.1977); In re Kesler, 272 Ind. 161, 397 N.E.2d 574 (1979), cert.denied 449 U.S. 829, 101 S.Ct. 96, 66 L.Ed.2d 34 (1980); State v. Nelson, 210 Kan. 637, 504 P.2d 211 (1972); In re Rook, 276 Or. 695, 556 P.2d 1351, 1357 (1976)(attack on DR 1-102(A)(1) and (A)(5) rejected because "as standards of professional conduct they are sufficiently definite for the purpose of a professional discipline proceeding."); Howell v. State, 559 S.W.2d 432 (Tex.Civ.App.1977), error refused n.r.e. ("conduct prejudicial to the administration of justice" standard of DR 1-102(A)(5) not impermissibly vague). A favored supporting citation is of the Supreme Court's decision upholding a vague "conduct unbecoming" standard in a military justice context. See Parker v. Levy, 417 U.S. 733, 756, 94 S.Ct. 2547, 2561, 41 L.Ed.2d 439 (1974). See generally Note, Lawyer Disciplinary Standards: Broad v. Narrow Interpretation, 65 Iowa L.Rev. 1386 (1980); Comment, ABA Code of Professional

Vagueness in the Lawyer Codes

Yet if anything is clear, it is that many provisions of the lawyer codes are plainly imprecise. Indeed, imprecision has probably been purposefully drafted into each of the lawyer codes. The 1908 Canons, in typically lofty phrases, argued that vagueness was a desired quality in drafting method because of the myriad and unpredictable ways in which questions of proper conduct might arise:

> No code or set of rules can be framed, which will particularize all the duties of the lawyer in the varying phases of litigation or in all the relations of professional life. The following canons of ethics are adopted . . . as a general guide, yet the enumeration of particular duties should not be construed as a denial of the existence of others equally imperative, though not specifically mentioned.[49]

The 1969 Code might be thought to have departed from that general philosophy because its mandatory norms are confined to a limited number of Disciplinary Rules that are alone to serve as the basis for discipline (§ 2.6.3). But the Code's attempted precision, to the extent that it might otherwise have successfully eliminated confusion, was thwarted when several broad and vague provisions were added to DR 1-101 with the purpose of providing catchall coverage for possibly unforeseen lawyer misconduct.[50] Thus courts have felt warranted in employing the catchall provisions as a means of assuring that the Code is broad enough to cover lawyer misconduct that was apparently unanticipated when other, more precise portions of the Code were drafted.[51] A similar fate befell the 1983 Model Rules [52] with the late addition of several of the "conduct unbecoming" provisions to MR 8.4.

Unnecessary breadth is to be regretted in professional rules that can be used to deprive a person of his or her means of livelihood through sanctions that are universally regarded as stigmatizing. Vague mandatory rules for lawyers create several difficulties. Plainly, they can be applied corruptly or for reasons of impermissible bias. For example, vague rules have fed charges, whether true or not, that the lawyer codes are used selectively against lawyers who defend unpopular causes or clients.[53] Vague phrases are also objectionable because they substantially dilute the procedural protections that otherwise narrow the area within which agencies could act arbitrarily or mistakenly.[54]

"Conduct Unbecoming" Offenses

Both the Code and the Model Rules nonetheless contain vague provisions that might govern an enormous range of doubtful lawyer behavior. The Code, among other broad provisions, provides in DR 1-102(A)(4) that a lawyer should not "engage in conduct involving dishonesty, fraud, deceit, or misrepresenta-

Responsibility: Void for Vagueness?, 57 N.C.L.Rev. 671 (1979).

[49] 1908 Canon, Preamble. The same sentiment that specific enumeration of grounds of duty does not exhaust the realm of mandatory duties has been repeated in many recent decisions. E.g., Board of Overseers of the Bar v. Rodway, 461 A.2d 1062, 1064 (Me.1983).

[50] Sutton, Commentary on the Texas Code of Professional Responsibility, in Texas Lawyers' Professional Ethics 6-2, at 6-5 (1979)(reporter for 1969 Code indicates that intention of drafting committee to write specific rules that would give fair notice "collapsed" when broad provisions of DR 1-102(A)(5) and (6) and DR 7-106(C)(6) were added, apparently out of apprehension that "Mother Hubbard" clauses were needed to guard against an unexpected but glaring omission from Code); id. at n.37 (DR 1-102(A)(5) and (6) and Canon 9 are "garbage cans of the Code . . . into which anything can be tossed."). Cf. Annotated Code of Professional Responsibility 12 (O.Maru ed.1979). Some deny that the Code lacks clarity. E.g., In re Arkansas Supreme Court Committee on Advisory Ethical Opinions, 611 S.W.2d 761, 762 (1981)(bar members' petition to create advisory committee rejected as unnecessary).

[51] Committee on Professional Ethics v. Durham, 279 N.W.2d 280, 284 (Iowa 1979).

[52] Even before the final round of amendments, the Model Rules were criticized for their lack of attainable precision. See Schneyer, The Model Rules and Problems of Code Interpretation and Enforcement, 1980 Am.B. Found. Research J. 939.

[53] Pollitt, Counsel for the Unpopular Cause: The "Hazard of Being Undone," 43 N.C.L.Rev. 9 (1964); Comment, Controlling Lawyers by Bar Associations and Courts, 5 Harv.C.R.-C.L.L.Rev. 301, 312-14 (1970).

[54] E.Freund, Administrative Powers over Persons and Property 120-25 (1928).

tion."[55] The same language was inserted into the Model Rules as MR 8.4(c) in the February 1983 amendments to the Kutak Commission proposals. Next, DR 1-102(A)(5) states that a lawyer shall not "engage in conduct that is prejudicial to the administration of justice."[56] The 1983 amendments added the same language to the Model Rules as MR 8.4(d). And DR 1-102(A)(6) states that a lawyer shall not "engage in any other conduct that adversely reflects on his fitness to practice law."[57] No similar catchall language is to be found in the Model Rules. Ultimate breadth is achieved in Rule 46(c) of the Federal Rules of Appellate Procedure, which provide for discipline in a federal appeals court for "conduct unbecoming a member of the bar" or failure to comply with any rule of court. And a few courts have used a charge that a lawyer failed to avoid the appearance of impropriety.[58] Under such broad provisions, the bar is not required to produce specific evidence of prejudice to the administration of justice or of adverse impact on fitness to practice.[59] Indeed, some courts take the position that a lawyer who violates any of the specific provisions of the code also violates one or more of the general provisions.[60]

Mens Rea

In general a violation of the lawyer codes sufficient to warrant discipline is made out by

[55] Some cases plainly involve fraud or misrepresentation. E.g., District of Columbia Bar v. Kleindienst, 345 A.2d 146 (D.C.App.1975)(direct and repeated misrepresentations in answering Congressional inquiries); In re LeMaster, 433 N.E.2d 787 (Ind.1982)(violation of SEC Rule 10 B-5 as corporate officer and director); In re Raskin, 307 Minn. 233, 239 N.W.2d 459 (1976)(false representations to clients, among others, to induce payment for stock that was never received, to make loans never repaid, and to perform services for which lawyer never paid); State v. Green, 210 Neb. 878, 317 N.W.2d 97 (1982) (reporter of supreme court opinions solicited payoffs in return for his assurance to printing company of continuation of contract to print opinions); In re Lavery, 90 Wn. 2d 463, 587 P.2d 157 (1978)(lawyer suspended for forging law school transcript and letters of recommendation in job search). Courts are brusk in rejecting technical legal arguments that dishonest acts were not fraudulent. E.g., In re Miller, 99 Wn.2d 695, 663 P.2d 1342, 1345-46 (1983) (scheme to defraud gambling casino not made less fraudulent by theory of unenforceability of gambling debts).

[56] Such conduct ranges over most imaginable contacts with the legal process. E.g., People v. Unruh, 621 P.2d 948 (Colo.1980)(while serving as deputy district attorney, agreeing to hide fugitive); In re Masters, 91 Ill.2d 413, 63 Ill.Dec. 449, 455, 438 N.E.2d 187, 193 (1982)(cooperation with extortion plot against client); In re Payne, ___ Ind. ___, 459 N.E.2d 718 (1984)(disclosure to target of wiretap application seen in public view on desk of assistant U.S. attorney); Dayton Bar Ass'n v. Atkins, 58 Ohio St.2d 194, 389 N.E.2d 506 (1979)(refusing to refund unearned portion of fee, thus preventing client from hiring another lawyer in bankruptcy matter). But see, e.g., Florida Bar v. Pettie, 424 So.2d 734 (Fla.1982)(involvement in illegal drug importation conspiracy not conduct prejudicial to administration of law, although in violation of other provisions of Code); In re Rochat, 295 Or. 533, 668 P.2d 376 (1983)(entering grand jury room and reading newspaper at desk of grand juror when jury not in session, while bizarre and ill-advised, was not prejudicial to administration of justice).

[57] The reference to "other" conduct in DR 1-102(A)(6) suggests that matters falling under one of the preceding subdivisions are not covered by it. But courts have employed the subdivision as a catchall to cover conduct that plainly was covered, if at all, under a more specific standard. E.g., In re Huffman, 289 Or. 515, 614 P.2d 586 (1980)(DR 1-102(A)(6) sufficiently charges lawyer with conduct that would better have been charged under DR 7-102(A)(1) or (2)(harassment or asserting unwarranted claim)).

[58] In re Jones, 294 N.W.2d 651 (S.D.1980)(appearance of impropriety rule in heading of DR 9-101); Gillock v. Board of Professional Responsibility, 656 S.W.2d 365 (Tenn.1983)(six-month suspension for violation of "Canon 9" by inadvertently permitting legislative and legal affairs to become commingled). The reporter for the 1969 Code, however, has asserted that the "appearances" provisions in Canon 9 were placed last in the Code to indicate their relative unimportance and were inserted merely as a guide to lawyers confronting doubtful situations rather than as a mandatory rule. Sutton, Commentary on the Texas Code of Professional Responsibility, in Texas Lawyers' Professional Ethics, at 6-6 (1980). For a critique of the "appearances of impropriety" rationale, see § 7.1.4.

[59] Kentucky Bar Ass'n v. Kramer, 555 S.W.2d 245, 246 (Ky.1977); In re Logan, 71 N.J. 583, 367 A.2d 419, 421 (1976). Occasionally, however, a court will buttress a resort to a vague phrase with a more precise legal standard derived from sources outside the lawyer codes. E.g., In re Rook, 276 Or. 695, 556 P.2d 1351 (1976) (DR 1-102(A) (5) charge substantiated by reference to state statute that proscribed lawyer's conduct).

[60] People v. Yoakum, 191 Colo. 269, 552 P.2d 291, 297 (1976)(lawyer charged with three offenses found to have violated thirteen sections of 1969 Code, including multiple violations of general provisions of DR 1-102(A)); Attorney Grievance Comm'n v. Willcher, 287 Md. 74, 411 A.2d 83 (1980)(violation of any provision of 1969 Code apparently also amounts to violation of DR 1-102(A)(1) and (6)). It is not apparent what independent force, if any, such "multiple" violations have on the level of sanction imposed.

a showing that the lawyer knowingly and without coercion[61] committed the acts[62] charged. The prosecution does not also have to show that the lawyer had the specific intent to violate a known code provision[63] or other law[64] or that the lawyer was impelled by improper motives.[65] The issue was decided by a narrow majority in In re Friedman,[66] which held that praiseworthy motives were no defense when a prosecutor suborned perjury in order to ensnare and assure the convictions of two defense lawyers who had offered bribes to witnesses. Courts have uniformly rejected arguments that a lawyer was entrapped into committing a disciplinary violation.[67] Lawyers much more than nonlawyers should be aware of the limits of the law and able to resist importunings that they violate those limits.[68]

The absence of a requirement to show specific intent is generally sound. Courts have commonly concluded in other areas of the law as well that evidence about subjective states of mind is almost always inaccessible or unverifiable.[69] Yet fairness and efficiency require that code enforcers at times recognize the relevance of state-of-mind issues in discipline cases. It is relevant that a lawyer was under a reasonable misapprehension about facts.[70] And some provisions of the lawyer codes are cast in terms that compel, or at least invite, an interpretation that makes critical the lawyer's subjective belief.[71] Other provisions make critical, not the lawyer's belief, but the belief that a hypothetical reasonable lawyer would entertain under the circumstances.[72] Courts have also not been immune to the appeal of fairness when a lawyer has, apparently sincerely, faced an unclear rule in a situation in which a choice had to be made. Following the advice of another on a question of legal ethics is persuasive of the lack of a guilty mind.[73] Arguably, it is also relevant that the lawyer's choice

[61] Cf. Trammell v. Disciplinary Board, 431 So.2d 1168, 1170-71 (Ala.1983)(apparently assuming that duress, if established, would be complete defense); Montag v. State Bar, 32 Cal.3d 721, 186 Cal.Rptr. 894, 652 P.2d 1370 (1982)(same).

[62] The act alone, and not its effects, is critical. The fact that a lawyer's offense did not in fact cause injury to a client or another person does not provide a defense. E.g., Allen v. State Bar, 20 Cal.3d 172, 141 Cal.Rptr. 808, 812, 570 P.2d 1226, 1230 (1977); Departmental Disciplinary Committee v. Norwood, 80 A.D.2d 278, 438 N.Y.S.2d 788 (1981); In re Robeson, 293 Or. 610, 652 P.2d 336 (1982); In re Srenaski, 105 Wis.2d 597, 314 N.W.2d 359, 361 (1982).

[63] Gassman v. State Bar, 18 Cal.3d 125, 132 Cal.Rptr. 675, 678, 553 P.2d 1147, 1150 (1976); Abeles v. State Bar, 9 Cal.3d 603, 108 Cal.Rptr. 359, 363-64, 510 P.2d 719, 723-24 (1973); In re Eisenberg, 75 N.J. 454, 383 A.2d 426, 427 n.1 (1978). Cf. People v. Stein, 94 Cal.App.3d 235, 156 Cal.Rptr. 299 (1979)(prosecution in criminal case could not show specific intent required in embezzlement case by showing violation of lawyer rules).

[64] In re Wines, 135 Ariz. 203, 660 P.2d 454, 457 (1983) (rejecting plea of ignorance of income-reporting requirements of federal tax laws). It is irrelevant in a discipline case that the same conduct, if charged as a crime, would have to be proved to have been committed with specific intent. E.g., McInnis v. State, 618 S.W.2d 389, 395 (Tex. Civ.App.1981), cert. denied 456 U.S. 976, 102 S.Ct. 2242, 72 L.Ed.2d 851 (1982).

[65] In re Clayter, 78 Ill.2d 276, 35 Ill.Dec. 790, 399 N.E.2d 1318 (1980); In re Sedor, 73 Wis.2d 629, 245 N.W.2d 895, 902 (1976).

[66] 76 Ill.2d 392, 30 Ill.Dec. 288, 392 N.E.2d 1333 (1979).

[67] Robinson v. Grievance Committee, 70 A.D.2d 209, 420 N.Y.S.2d 430 (1979), cert.denied 449 U.S. 830, 101 S.Ct. 97, 66 L.Ed.2d 34 (1980)(federal prosecutor caught in "sting" operation giving information on prospective targets of investigation to person whom he thought was underworld figure). See also McInnis v. State, 618 S.W.2d 389, 393-94 (Tex.Civ.App.1981), cert. denied 456 U.S. 976, 102 S.Ct. 2242, 72 L.Ed.2d 851 (1982)(entrapment defense not available in lawyer discipline cases).

[68] In re Porcelli, 77 Ill.2d 473, 34 Ill.Dec. 158, 160, 397 N.E.2d 830, 832 (1979)(because of special knowledge and role of lawyers, difficult to imagine circumstances in which defense of entrapment would be available).

[69] See generally W.Prosser & W.Keeton, Torts 176-79 (5th ed.1984); Seavey, Negligence—Subjective or Objective?, 41 Harv.L.Rev. 1 (1927); 3 A.Corbin, Contracts § 538 (rev.ed.1960); Restatement (Second), Contracts § 2 (1979); W.LaFave & A.Scott, Criminal Law § 27 (1972).

[70] Hicks v. State, 422 S.W.2d 539 (Tex.Civ.App.1967) (error in judgment not sanctionable if lawyer acted in good faith).

[71] DR 7-102(B)(2); DR 7-106(C)(1); DR 7-106(C)(2). Most in point in the Code, perhaps, are provisions such as DR 7-102(A)(7) and DR 7-102(A)(8), which limit their prohibitions to instances in which the lawyer "knows" that the client's behavior is illegal, fraudulent, or in violation of a Disciplinary Rule.

[72] DR 7-102(A)(1)("knows or it is obvious" that client's action would serve merely to harass or maliciously injure another); DR 7-103(A)(public prosecutor may not charge crime when "he knows or it is obvious" that the charges are not supported by probable cause).

[73] Cf. In re Ainsworth, 289 Or. 479, 614 P.2d 1127, 1133 (1980)(following advice of chairman of local ethics com-

of conduct in the face of an unclear rule was that which was customary among other lawyers in the community.[74]

§ 3.3.2 *Lawyer Crimes*

General

An impression gained from reading appellate decisions is that courts most often impose significant disciplinary sanctions on lawyers who have already been tried and convicted in a separate criminal proceeding. Certainly, once a lawyer is convicted of a crime, legitimate questions can often be raised about the lawyer's fitness to practice because of character defects that might be predictable from the course of criminal activity. It is often true as well that public pressure on the bar to "do something" will be strong following a lawyer's conviction of a crime, particularly if it is notorious.

Relevance of Criminal Proceedings

Procedurally, in a disciplinary proceeding, proof of a lawyer's conviction in a criminal proceeding suffices to prove the facts on which the conviction was based. Those facts may not be relitigated in the disciplinary proceeding.[75] The rule applies to guilty verdicts, guilty pleas, and pleas of no contest.[76] Courts give the same effect to a conviction handed down in another jurisdiction.[77] Courts thus refuse to permit the lawyer to offer, as a complete defense, evidence that the offense was less serious than appears from the fact of conviction or was excusable for some reason; but courts do permit evidence to be offered in mitigation of the sanction to be imposed so long as it is not inconsistent with the essential elements that must have been proved or confessed in order to support the conviction.[78]

In the case of serious crimes, many jurisdictions provide for the interim suspension [79] of a lawyer convicted after a trial, even while an

mittee on reference from counsel of state ethics committee does not provide defense to disciplinary violations, but no discipline should be imposed here). A plea of advice of counsel will, however, fall on deaf judicial ears if the advice was palpably erroneous. E.g., In re Davidson, 15 A.D.2d 327, 223 N.Y.S.2d 579 (1962)(lawyer disbarred for perjury at own disciplinary hearing, despite claim that this was by advice of counsel).

74 Walls v. Mississippi State Bar, 437 So.2d 30, 33 (Miss. 1983)(practice of many firms in holding open houses informs court's view whether to enforce bar ethics committee's view that such amounted to violation of antisolicitation rules). But a custom, even if said to be universal, of ignoring a clear prohibition in a lawyer code is no defense. E.g., Hansen v. Wightman, 14 Wn.App. 78, 538 P.2d 1238, 1244 (1975)(jury instruction was incorrect, as matter of law, that universal practice of referring lawyers was to retain one-third referral fee).

75 The conclusive effect given to the conviction comports with due process because the lawyer has already had an opportunity to litigate all of the essential facts in the criminal prosecution. Moreover, the standard of proof beyond a reasonable doubt employed in all criminal prosecutions is higher than that required in most lawyer discipline proceedings. See § 3.4.4 (burden of proof). See also ABA Disciplinary Standards § 9.4 and commentary (1979).

76 In re Gross, 33 Cal.3d 561, 189 Cal.Rptr. 848, 659 P.2d 1137 (1983); In re Hopfl, 48 N.Y.2d 859, 424 N.Y.S.2d 350, 400 N.E.2d 292 (1979); In re Rish, 273 S.C. 365, 256 S.E.2d 540 (1979). Contra, e.g., North Carolina St. Bar v. Hall, 293 N.C. 539, 238 S.E.2d 521 (1977); cf. Fed.Rules Evid.R. 803 (22)(judgment based on no contest plea not proof of underlying facts in subsequent proceedings).

77 Mississippi St. Bar v. Phillips, 385 So.2d 943, 945 (Miss.1980)(recognition of federal court conviction required by Full Faith and Credit clause of federal Constitution); In re Howard, 75 A.D.2d 933, 427 N.Y.S.2d 540 (1980); In re Scallen, 269 N.W.2d 834, 98 A.L.R.3d 343 (Minn.1978)(conviction in Canada). Cf. ABA Disciplinary Standards § 10.2 (1979)(findings against lawyer in disciplinary action in another jurisdiction conclusive in reciprocal proceeding in other jurisdictions in which admitted).

78 Louisiana St. Bar Ass'n v. Porobil, 444 So.2d 613, 615 (La.1984); In re Grimes, 414 Mich. 483, 326 N.W.2d 380, 383 (1982)(rejecting argument that jury in criminal case was more likely to convict because defendant was lawyer); In re Mirabelli, 79 N.J. 597, 401 A.2d 1090 (1979); In re Levy, 37 N.Y.2d 279, 372 N.Y.S.2d 41, 333 N.E.2d 350 (1975); In re Eisenberg, 81 Wis.2d 175, 259 N.W.2d 745, 747 (1977), cert. denied 436 U.S. 946, 98 S.Ct. 2850, 56 L.Ed.2d 788 (1978) (evidence that lawyer did not willfully commit offense of which convicted was admitted erroneously when such evidence is necessarily inconsistent with elements of offenses for which convicted). See also State ex rel. Oklahoma Bar Ass'n v. Jones, 566 P.2d 130, 132 (Okl.1977)(lawyer may show that violation was not willful because willfulness is not essential element of federal offense of violating campaign contributions law). See generally ABA Standards for Lawyer Disciplinary and Disability Proceedings § 9.4 and commentary (1978).

79 The absence of provisions for interim suspension in most jurisdictions was criticized in the Clark Report. See ABA Spec. Comm. on Evaluation of Disciplinary Enforce-

appeal is pending[80] or even before a conviction if compelling justification is shown.[81] If a lawyer's conviction is reversed on appeal or set aside on collateral review, the lawyer's suspension or disbarment that was based on the conviction will be lifted subject to further possible disciplinary action involving the underlying conduct.[82] If criminal charges are pending, the question arises whether disciplinary proceedings should be stayed until the termination of the criminal case. It has been argued that a stay should be granted in order to avoid the prospect of inconsistent outcomes, because of the danger of impairing the lawyer's defense in the criminal proceeding, and because the lawyer's defense of the disciplinary charges would be impeded by the fear of self-incrimination.[83] Courts generally treat the question of stays on a case-by-case basis because of the inevitable delay involved.[84] Another solution is to stay the disciplinary proceedings after entry of an order suspending the lawyer on an interim basis (see § 3.5.4—interim suspension).

A lawyer may be disciplined for acts that also constitute a crime, even if no prosecution was brought or if the lawyer was acquitted or the criminal charges dismissed.[85] The prosecutor's failure to file charge may be attributable to many factors that do not suggest innocence.[86] An acquittal is also legally irrelevant, because a failure to persuade a jury of guilt beyond a reasonable doubt does not imply that a lawyer cannot be found guilty of a professional offense for the same conduct under the lesser standards of proof employed in disciplinary proceedings.[87] Moreover, a court reviewing conduct that resulted in a conviction is not limited only to the elements of the offense charged but may

ment, Problems and Recommendations in Disciplinary Enforcement 122-30 (1970).

80 United States v. Jennings, 724 F.2d 436 (5th Cir.), cert. denied ___ U.S. ___, 104 S.Ct. 2682, 81 L.Ed.2d 877 (1984); In re Malvin, 466 A.2d 1220 (D.C.App.1983)(interim suspension and denial of access to client funds); Florida Bar v. Prior, 330 So.2d 697 (Fla.1976); Attorney Grievance Comm'n v. Reamer, 281 Md. 323, 379 A.2d 171 (1977); Mitchell v. Ass'n of Bar of City of N.Y., 40 N.Y.2d 153, 386 N.Y.S.2d 95, 351 N.E.2d 743 (1976)(summary disbarment of former attorney general of the United States following federal felony conviction). Contra In re Ming, 469 F.2d 1352 (7th Cir.1972)(questionably analogizing lawyer discipline cases to deportation cases in which irremediable effect of deportation requires exhaustion of appeal); Louisiana State Bar Ass'n v. Ehmig, 277 So.2d 137 (La.1973)(felony conviction of fraud and false statements presents no public interest justification for interim suspension). See generally ABA Disciplinary Standards §§ 9.1, 9.2 (1978).

81 In re Monteiro, ___ Nev. ___, 684 P.2d 506 (1984) (interim suspension if bar counsel affidavit shows "exigent circumstances"). Interim suspension can be obtained even if no criminal charges are filed. See § 3.5.4 (suspension—interim).

82 In re Campbell, 251 Ga. 850, 311 S.E.2d 167 (1984); Florida Bar v. Tifford, 373 So.2d 919 (Fla.1979); In re Ginsberg, 1 N.Y.2d 144, 151 N.Y.S.2d 361, 134 N.E.2d 193 (1956).

83 Clark Committee Report, at 82-85 (1970). The report would apply the same rule to copending civil litigation. See id. 82, 85. Courts have disagreed. E.g., Committee on Legal Ethics v. Pence, 161 W.Va. 240, 240 S.E.2d 668, 674, 93 A.L.R.3d 1046 (1977).

84 Compare, e.g., Committee on Legal Ethics v. Pence, 161 W.Va. 240, 240 S.E.2d 668, 674, 93 A.L.R.3d 1046 (1977)(case-by-case disposition but preference generally for staying disciplinary proceeding), with, e.g., McInnis v. State, 618 S.W.2d 389, 392-93 (Tex.Civ.App.1981), cert.denied 456 U.S. 976, 102 S.Ct. 2242, 72 L.Ed.2d 851 (1982)(in light of need to protect public before possibly drawn-out conclusion of criminal proceedings, trial court did not abuse discretion in refusing to stay disciplinary action).

85 Ex parte Wall, 107 U.S. 265, 2 S.Ct. 569, 27 L.Ed. 552 (1883); Harary v. Blumenthal, 555 F.2d 1113 (2d Cir. 1977)(disbarment of accountant before Treasury Department); Louisiana St. Bar v. Batson, 359 So.2d 70 (La. 1978); Robinson v. Grievance Committee, 70 A.D.2d 209, 420 N.Y.S.2d 430 (1979), cert. denied 449 U.S. 830, 101 S.Ct. 97, 66 L.Ed.2d 34 (1980); In re O'Brien, 95 Vt. 167, 113 A. 527, 14 A.L.R. 859 (1921); Annot., 76 A.L.R.3d 1028 (1977). See also United States v. One Assortment of 89 Firearms, 465 U.S. 354, 104 S.Ct. 1099, 79 L.Ed.2d 361 (1984)(in rem action against firearms can be maintained after acquittal of owner of charges of selling firearms without license). But cf. In re Florida Bd. of Bar Examiners re L.K.D., 397 So.2d 673, 676 (Fla.1981)(jury's finding of acquittal bars disciplinary charge that lawyer committed perjury in criminal trial by claiming innocence).

86 In re Hanratty, 277 N.W.2d 373 (Minn.1979). As a standard practice, prosecutors may decline to prosecute lawyers specifically because of the possibility of professional discipline. E.g., U.S. Dep't of Justice, Principles of Federal Prosecution 13 (1980).

87 In re Hurwitz, 17 Cal.3d 562, 131 Cal.Rptr. 402, 551 P.2d 1234 (1976); Maryland St. Bar Ass'n v. Frank, 272 Md. 528, 325 A.2d 718 (1974). Cf. Smolka v. Second Distr. Comm., 224 Va. 161, 295 S.E.2d 267, 269 (1982)(discipline after acquittal justified on argument that purpose of discipline is not to punish but to protect public).

review the lawyer's entire course of conduct.[88] The expunging of conviction records and pardons is typically ignored by courts because it does not remove the factual basis for the original conviction.[89] Similarly, a grant of immunity from criminal prosecution given to a lawyer in order to obtain his or her testimony in a criminal case does not bar the use of the lawyer's testimony in a disciplinary proceeding.[90]

Illegal Conduct Involving "Moral Turpitude"

At least on the surface, the codes do not make all criminal conduct the basis for discipline. The Code and the Model Rules differ significantly, however, in the way in which each delineates the kinds of criminal conduct that are covered. The Code, in DR 1-102(A)(3), invokes a traditional standard that a lawyer shall not "engage in illegal conduct involving moral turpitude." [91] Obviously, not all illegal conduct is covered, although the problem of possible overlap between the language of the several subdivisions of DR 1-102(A) once again is problematical.[92] The Code refers to "illegal conduct" so that even some simple misdemeanors are covered.[93] While the reference to "illegal" seems to encompass conduct that is not a crime, the criminal law is the virtually exclusive referent in the decisions.

The critical problem has been that of defining "moral turpitude." Constitutional attacks based on vagueness arguments have been uniformly rejected,[94] yet the range of views about what constitutes moral turpitude is hopelessly wide. It has been both asserted [95] and denied [96] that popular prevailing notions of morality should inform the court's judgment. At one extreme of hardy tolerance, ethics committee chairman Henry

88 In re Kristovich, 18 Cal.3d 468, 134 Cal.Rptr. 409, 411, 556 P.2d 771 (1976).

89 In re Couser, 122 Ariz. 500, 596 P.2d 26 (1979) (expunging); In re Patt, 81 Ill.2d 447, 43 Ill.Dec. 737, 410 N.E.2d 870 (1980)(expungement following discharge from probation); Hankamer v. Templin, 143 Tex. 572, 187 S.W.2d 549 (1945)(pardon).

90 Arnett v. State, 304 S.W.2d 386 (Tex.Civ.App.1957); Olitt v. Ass'n of Bar of City of N.Y., 61 A.D.2d 416, 402 N.Y.S.2d 410 (1978), cert.denied 439 U.S. 866, 99 S.Ct. 190, 58 L.Ed.2d 176 (1978).

91 The "moral turpitude" concept is found in various other areas of the law. It was probably taken from state statutes describing the grounds of disbarment. See generally Note, Disbarment: Non-Professional Conduct Demonstrating Unfitness to Practice, 43 Corn.L.Q. 489 (1958), cited in DR 1-102(A)(3) n.13.

92 Cf., e.g., Akron Bar Ass'n v. Murty, 62 Ohio St.2d 301, 405 N.E.2d 300 (1980)(notwithstanding defense that misrepresenting purpose for home improvement loan was minor offense without moral turpitude, DR 1-102(A)(4) on misrepresentation provides basis for finding of violation); In re Gillis, 402 Mich. 286, 262 N.W.2d 646 (1978)(although no moral turpitude involved, conviction of failure to file tax returns requires discipline to maintain integrity of legal profession); Attorney Grievance Comm'n v. Walman, 280 Md. 453, 374 A.2d 354, 361 (1977)(conviction of failure to file federal tax return does not per se involve moral turpitude but does involve conduct prejudicial to administration of justice).

93 State ex rel. Oklahoma v. Denton, 598 P.2d 663 (Okl. 1979)(quilty plea to misdemeanor charge of possession of marijuana; suspension for remainder of term of sentence of unsupervised probation); In re Mahr, 276 Or. 939, 556 P.2d 1359 (1976)(misdemeanor conviction for shoplifting).

94 Freedson v. State, 600 S.W.2d 349, 351 (Tex.Civ.App. 1980). See also Jordan v. DeGeorge, 341 U.S. 223, 71 S.Ct. 703, 95 L.Ed. 886 (1951) (term "moral turpitude" used in deportation statute has sufficiently definite meaning when applied to crimes in which fraud is an element).

95 In re Fahey, 8 Cal.3d 842, 106 Cal.Rptr. 313, 505 P.2d 1369, 1372 (1973)("the concept of moral turpitude depends upon the state of public morals, and may vary according to the community or the times"); State ex rel. Oklahoma v. Denton, 598 P.2d 663, 665 (Okl.1979). Sometimes the population whose moral views count is a small segment of the community. E.g., Bartos v. District Court, 19 F.2d 722, 732 (8th Cir.1927)(legal profession should not have lower standard on manufacture and sale of intoxicating liquor than do Masons, Odd Fellows, and Knights of Pythias); Searcy v. State Bar, 604 S.W.2d 256, 258 (Tex.Civ.App.1980)("immoral conduct is that which is wilful, flagrant, or shameless and which shows a moral indifference to the opinion of the good and respectable members of the community"). Cf. In re Colson, 412 A.2d 1160 (D.C.App.1979)(crime involving moral turpitude is one that "offends the generally accepted moral code of mankind"); In re Rabideau, 102 Wis.2d 16, 306 N.W.2d 1, 5, appeal dismissed 454 U.S. 1025, 102 S.Ct. 559, 70 L.Ed. 2d 469 (1981)(in defining moral turpitude by quotation from prior decision: " 'in our society moral standards are derived in large part from Christian teaching and are reflected more or less accurately in what is termed "public opinion," which is the consensual judgment of the general public.' ").

96 In re Fahey, 8 Cal.3d 842, 106 Cal.Rptr. 313, 505 P.2d 1369, 1376 (1973)("Our standard of moral turpitude depends not on popular impressions but on the violator's own motivation as it relates to his moral fitness to practice law"); State ex rel. Nebraska State Bar Ass'n v.

Drinker doubted whether participation in a Florida lynching involved the necessary degree of baseness.[97] At the opposite extreme of punctiliousness are holdings that moral turpitude could be found for conduct that was at the time politically unpopular, such as being a proclaimed conscientious objector during a popular war.[98] Moral turpitude has been found when a state legislator was convicted of bribery [99] but not when a federal senator was convicted of accepting a gratuity.[1] A core of agreement does cluster around convictions for fraud offenses by lawyers, such as convictions for obtaining money under false pretenses.[2] But that use of DR 1-102(A)(3) is superfluous, because DR 1-102(A)(4) already covers fraud and other dishonest acts, and without a limitation to moral turpitude.[3] The decisions are in conflict over whether, and to what extent, a conviction for willful failure to file a tax return involves moral turpitude.[4] There is general agreement, however, that convictions for sex,[5] drug,[6] and gambling [7] offenses are for acts sufficiently depraved to merit inclusion. In a jurisdiction that employs moral turpitude as an independent standard without regard to criminality of a lawyer's acts, the standard has been found to be violated even by gross negligence in representing a client.[8] Crimes of violence should be regarded as involving moral turpitude only when they involve premeditation and malicious intent to cause substantial injury.[9]

Addison, 198 Neb. 61, 251 N.W.2d 717, 719 (1977). See also, e.g., Cincinnati Bar Ass'n v. Shott, 10 Ohio St.2d 117, 226 N.E.2d 724, 733 (1967)(lawyer, because of training and position of trust, held to higher standard than layman).

97 H.Drinker, Legal Ethics 43 (1953).

98 Cf. In re Pontarelli, 393 Ill. 310, 66 N.E.2d 83 (1946) (in the actual case, the court was able to rest decision on the fact that the disciplined lawyer, although a conscientious objector, had not asserted that in the legally required way prior to refusing to be inducted). Popular feelings might also explain In re Welansky, 319 Mass. 205, 65 N.E.2d 202 (1946), in which the lawyer who owned a Boston night club that burned with the loss of many lives was disbarred after his conviction for involuntary manslaughter.

99 In re Connaghan, 613 S.W.2d 626, 632 (Mo.1981).

1 See Attorney Grievance Comm'n v. Brewster, 280 Md. 473, 374 A.2d 602 (1977).

2 In re Willcher, 447 A.2d 1198, 1200 (D.C.App.1982); Maryland State Bar Ass'n v. Agnew, 271 Md. 543, 318 A.2d 811, 817 (1974); State Bar of Texas v. Heard, 603 S.W.2d 829 (Tex.1980). The antifraud sentiment has extended to such relatively minor fraud offenses as misdemeanor convictions for shoplifting. E.g., Committee on Professional Ethics v. Toomey, 236 N.W.2d 39 (Iowa 1975); Columbus Bar Ass'n v. Tarmey, 4 Ohio St.3d 81, 446 N.E.2d 1120 (1983); In re Mahr, 276 Or. 939, 556 P.2d 1359 (1976).

3 See Weckstein, Maintaining the Integrity and Competence of the Legal Profession, 48 Tex.L.Rev. 267, 278 (1970).

4 Compare, e.g., In re Fahey, 8 Cal.3d 842, 106 Cal.Rptr. 313, 505 P.2d 1369 (1973)(willful failure to file does not constitute moral turpitude per se); Attorney Grievance Comm'n v. Walman, 280 Md. 453, 374 A.2d 354 (1977) (because intent to defraud is not element of federal conviction of failure to file tax returns, crime does not per se involve moral turpitude unless surrounding facts demonstrate this), with, e.g., Grievance Comm'n v. Pohlman, 248 N.W.2d 833, 835 (N.D.1976)(willful failure to file federal income tax return is crime involving moral turpitude); Columbus Bar Ass'n v. Wolfe, 70 Ohio St.2d 55, 434 N.E.2d 1096 (1982)(rule is that conviction of willful failure to file income tax returns results in indefinite suspension). See generally Annot., 63 A.L.R.3d 476 (1978). Distinguishable are convictions for tax offenses that involve fraud or misrepresentation as an essential element, such as willfully falsifying a tax return. E.g., Attorney Grievance Comm'n v. Deutsch, 294 Md. 353, 450 A.2d 1265 (1982)(falsifying law partnership tax returns by failing to report any case income warrants disbarment).

5 In re Kamin, 262 N.W.2d 162 (Minn.1978)(sexual offenses with children of client); In re Howard, 297 Or. 174, 681 P.2d 775 (1984)(conviction of prostitution following lawyer's engaging in sex with prostitute in payment for legal services). Among older cases, compare, e.g., Grievance Comm. v. Broder, 112 Conn. 263, 269, 152 A. 292 (1930)(adultery as offense involving moral turpitude), with, e.g., Ex parte Isojoki, 222 F. 151 (N.D.Cal.1915) (fornication does not involve moral turpitude).

6 Compare, e.g., Muniz v. State, 575 S.W.2d 408, 99 A.L.R.3d 277 (Tex.Civ.App.1978)(federal conviction of conspiracy to import and distribute marijuana), with In re Higbie, 6 Cal.3d 562, 99 Cal.Rptr. 865, 493 P.2d 97 (1972) (under current standards of morality, conviction of failure to pay marijuana transfer tax does not constitute moral turpitude per se). See generally Annot., 99 A.L.R. 3d 288 (1978).

7 In re Calaway, 20 Cal.3d 165, 141 Cal.Rptr. 805, 570 P.2d 1223 (1977); State ex rel. Oklahoma Bar Ass'n v. Grayson, 560 P.2d 566 (Okl.1977).

8 Gassman v. State Bar, 18 Cal.3d 125, 132 Cal.Rptr. 675, 553 P.2d 1147 (1976)(gross negligence that fell short of willfulness may nonetheless involve moral turpitude under standard not requiring conviction).

9 In re Johnson, 106 Ariz. 73, 471 P.2d 269 (1970) (isolated, relatively trivial instance of simple assault); In re Kuvara, 97 Wn.2d 743, 649 P.2d 834 (1982)(isolated instance of thoughtless violence in fistfight not ground

Many of the offenses swept within the definition of moral turpitude undoubtedly strongly suggest that the lawyers involved have deficits in their powers of self-control and social attitudes so profound as to raise serious doubts about their fitness to practice law. But the breadth of the concept plainly invites judges to intrude into privacy and to impose in a heavy-handed way personal viewpoint in matters of life-style that do not relate to law practice.[10] Some courts also seem to employ professional discipline as an additional societal sanction against lawyers for violating the criminal laws[11]—an exercise that may be needlessly repetitious and possibly unfair after the lawyer has been convicted in the criminal process. Some jurisdictions avoid the difficulties that inhere in attempts to classify offenses by their relative moral repugnance by using bright-line standards such as that in New York, under which any felony conviction is automatic grounds for disbarment.[12] Others candidly note that most felonies will be classified as crimes involving moral turpitude.[13]

Model Rule 8.4(b)

The Model Rules, in MR 8.4(b), depart from the Code by limiting crimes for which a lawyer may be disciplined to those "that reflect adversely on the lawyer's honesty, trustworthiness or fitness as a lawyer in other respects." The fitness-to-practice standard does not appear in the other subdivisions of MR 8.4, perhaps on the rationale that the other offenses listed necessarily point to defects in a lawyer's fitness to practice. The comment to MR 8.4 specifically rejects the concept of "moral turpitude" because it does not necessarily relate to characteristics relevant to fitness to practice.[14] Under MR 8.4(b) even minor offenses, if repeated, can be the basis for sanctions.[15] And illegal acts in some roles may be particularly indicative of a lack of trustworthiness—for example, offenses committed by lawyers who hold public office or positions of private trust, such as fiduciary, trustee, or officer of a corporation.[16] But MR 8.4(b) merely implies, rather than defines, a conception of the minimally law-abiding lawyer.

Instinctively, one might imagine that a lawyer who willfully commits any violation of the criminal law demonstrates unfitness to perform effectively, because the lawyer's role involves counselling others about complying with the law. But if the offense is relatively minor and unrepeated, a court may be warranted in concluding that it represents simply an isolated instance of uncharacteristically bad judgment rather than an indication of a settled disposition to break the law.

for discipline). See generally Annot., 21 A.L.R.3d 887 (1968).

10 Selinger & Schoen, "To Purify the Bar:" A Constitutional Approach to Non-Professional Misconduct, 5 Nat. Resources J. 299, 337-38 (1965); Weckstein, Maintaining the Integrity and Competence of the Legal Profession, 48 Tex.L.Rev. 267, 276-77 (1970).

11 State ex rel. Oklahoma v. Denton, 598 P.2d 663, 665 (Okl.1979)(suspension of lawyer convicted of misdemeanor charge of marijuana possession "serve[s] to deter respondent from committing similar acts in the future and it further acts as a restraining influence on other attorneys." (footnote omitted)).

12 The New York legislation refers to "serious" offenses, which roughly correspond to common-law felonies. See New York—McKinney's Judiciary Law § 90(4). E.g., Cahn v. Joint Bar Ass'n Grievance Comm., 52 N.Y.2d 479, 438 N.Y.S.2d 753, 420 N.E.2d 945 (1981). The same rule applies to convictions in a jurisdiction other than New York. E.g., In re Rosenbaum, 72 A.D.2d 251, 424 N.Y.S. 2d 435 (1980). A conviction of a felony under a federal law will be regarded as a sufficiently serious conviction in New York, even if the federal offense has no analogue under state law. E.g., In re Thies, 45 N.Y.2d 865, 410 N.Y.S.2d 575, 382 N.E.2d 1351 (1978), appeal dismissed 441 U.S. 939, 99 S.Ct. 2154, 60 L.Ed.2d 1041 (1979).

See also, e.g., U.S.Ct.Apps. Sixth Circ. Rs. of Discipl. Enforcement rule 1(B)(conviction of defined "serious crime" results in automatic suspension).

13 In re Krogh, 85 Wn.2d 462, 475, 536 P.2d 578, 585 (1975).

14 MR 8.4 comment (first paragraph)("That concept can be construed to include offenses concerning some matters of personal morality, such as adultery and comparable offenses, that have no specific connection to fitness for the practice of law.").

15 Ibid.

16 Id. (third paragraph).

§ 3.3.3 Noncriminal Acts

General

While many reported lawyer discipline cases involve crimes, lawyers might be subjected to professional discipline for much that is not criminal. Both the Code (DR 1-102(A)(1)) and the Model Rules (MR 8.4(a)) prohibit a lawyer from violating any mandatory provision.[17] As is discussed at other points in this book, many of those violations are not also criminal. The same is true of much of the conduct proscribed under the provisions on fraud and misrepresentation [18] and conduct prejudicial to the administration of justice.[19] The Code (DR 1-102(A)(6)), but not the Model Rules, also contains a final catchall provision prohibiting a lawyer from engaging in conduct that adversely reflects on the lawyer's fitness to practice. In light of the breadth of other catchall provisions in the Model Rules, the confinement of the fitness-to-practice concept in MR 8.4(b) to crimes should neither make that concept irrelevant in considering whether another section covers borderline conduct, nor suggest that other Model Rule catchall provisions are narrower than their Code predecessors.

Lawyer Disability

Until relatively recently, little attention had been given to the problem of lawyers who were disabled by alcoholism or similar drug dependency or by mental illness.[20] Substance dependency and mental illness disabilities raise at least three questions. First, should they provide a defense to a charge that a lawyer violated a provision of the lawyer codes? Second, should a serious disability at the time of the hearing lead to a deferral of the proceedings, as would occur in criminal trials? Third, should a disability at the time of the disciplinary hearing lead to any different disposition or sanction?

Alcoholism or Mental Illness as a Defense

The decisions are virtually unanimous in holding that a lawyer's alcoholism [21] or mental illness [22] at the time of misconduct is not a complete defense in the sense of exonerating the lawyer from any further disciplinary involvement. But courts are generally, and increasingly, willing to recognize those problems as the illnesses that they are and to deal with them in ways that attempt to provide an opportunity for the lawyer to achieve rehabilitation if that appears likely.[23] Because the courts uniformly act to protect possible future clients against the effects of the lawyer's disability, in any case in which a lawyer is incompetent to respond to disciplinary charges, the court doubtless should suspend the lawyer, at least during the continua-

[17] MR 8.4(a) goes further than DR 1-102(A)(1) in explicitly prohibiting an attempt to violate a rule, knowingly assisting or inducing another person to do so, or violating a rule through the act of another person. In addition, MR 8.4(f) prohibits a lawyer from assisting a judicial officer in conduct that is in violation of the code of judicial conduct or other law. Both offenses would probably be covered under one or the other of the Code's catchall provisions.

[18] DR 1-102(A)(4); MR 8.4(c).

[19] DR 1-102(A)(5); MR 8.4(d).

[20] See generally Stevens, The Lawyer's Mental Health and Discipline, 48 ABA J. 140 (1962). The extent of those problems, particularly alcoholism, among lawyers is probably higher than that in the general population. E.g., Flaherty, Drugs: Crisis for the Bar?, Nat'l L.J., Aug.8, 1983, p.1, col.1; Tenner v. State Bar, 28 Cal.3d 202, 168 Cal.Rptr. 333, 617 P.2d 486, 488 (1980)("[W]e are not insensitive to the personal and professional problems that frequently besiege the practitioner, including the all too frequent devastating impact of alcohol abuse.").

[21] Finch v. State Bar, 28 Cal.3d 659, 170 Cal.Rptr. 629, 621 P.2d 253 (1981); State ex rel. Nebraska St. Bar Ass'n v. Erickson, 204 Neb. 692, 285 N.W.2d 105, 109 (1979) (alcoholism is "the result of voluntary action on the part of respondent and affords no justification for his conduct"; lawyer suspended for one year with suspension to continue unless lawyer can demonstrate control of alcoholism).

[22] In re Crisel, 101 Ill.2d 332, 78 Ill.Dec. 160, 461 N.E.2d 994, 999 (1984)(depressive neurosis not defense, but mitigation); In re Lang, 641 S.W.2d 77, 79 (Mo.1982)(mental illness producing major depressive reaction); In re Cohn, 103 A.D.2d 856, 477 N.Y.S.2d 238, 239 (1984)(extended period of extreme emotional distress). But cf., e.g., In re Couser, 122 Ariz. 500, 596 P.2d 26, 28 (1979)(dicta)(lawyer's insanity under *M'Naghten* test will bar discipline).

[23] Attorney Grievance Comm'n v. Lockhart, 285 Md. 586, 403 A.2d 1241, 1247 (1979). See generally Comment, Mental or Physical Incapacity as a Bar to the Practice of Law, 4 J.Leg.Prof. 219 (1979); Annot., 26 A.L.R.4th 995 (1983)(mental problems).

tion of the disability.[24] Similarly, a disabling condition that appears to be permanent and incurable compels that the lawyer's license to practice be suspended or annulled.[25]

Disability as a Mitigating Factor

The present challenge for courts is to devise methods of dealing with alcoholism and mental illness that effectively prevent future harm to clients or the public yet provide an opportunity for a fully rehabilitated lawyer to become a useful and productive member of the profession. Courts have employed several techniques. Several courts have employed variations on the concept of probation by staying a sanction of suspension on condition that the lawyer attempt to deal with an alcoholism problem, for example, by abstaining from alcohol use, by seeking professional help, by practicing under supervision, or by applying some combination of these and other measures.[26] A suspended lawyer may obtain reinstatement by demonstrating effective control over a former disabling problem of alcohol abuse or mental illness.[27] In a growing number of jurisdictions, alcoholic lawyers can be helped by organizations of recovering alcoholic lawyers.[28] A lawyer may not, however, escape all sanctions by a general assurance that the cause of a former problem is now under control.[29] Nor can a lawyer obtain the relatively milder treatment provided for rehabilitation of disabled lawyers by generally alleging an alcohol or emotional problem that is not shown to be acute and causative. The courts attempt to distinguish between offenses that were substantially caused by alcoholism or mental illness and those that were simply accompanied by heavy drinking or emotional upset.[30] Necessarily controversial are claims of "burnout" or similarly vague assertions that disciplinary violations were produced by personality or life-adjustment problems.[31]

24 In re Lesser, 101 A.D.2d 349, 475 N.Y.S.2d 402 (1984).

25 In re Holmes, 226 Kan. 579, 612 P.2d 148 (1979) (transfer to disability status for elderly lawyer under care of physician for cardiovascular disease and memory impairment); In re Mentrup, 665 S.W.2d 324, 325 (Mo.1984) (structural brain defect requiring lifelong supervision); In re Ryan, 97 Wn.2d 284, 644 P.2d 675 (1982)(mental incompetency). Cf., In re Hansen, 318 N.W.2d 856 (Minn. 1982)(eighty-eight-year-old lawyer whose age caused offenses placed on inactive status with practice limited to family members). In California, termination of a disciplinary proceeding is proper only if a lawyer's mental illness renders him or her unable to form the intent that is an element of the charged offense, in which case the lawyer is dealt with in a disability proceeding. See Ballard v. State Bar, 35 Cal.3d 274, 197 Cal.Rptr. 556, 673 P.2d 226, 234 (1983).

26 In re Ackermann, 99 Ill.2d 56, 75 Ill.Dec. 415, 457 N.E.2d 409, 414 (1983)(new Illinois procedure for alcoholism probation); In re Corbett, 87 A.D.2d 140, 450 N.Y.S.2d 802 (1982)(supervision by members of bar association committee on alcoholism); In re Maragos, 285 N.W.2d 541, 547 (N.D.1979)(supervision by individual lawyer); In re Heath, 296 Or. 683, 678 P.2d 736 (1984) (supervisory lawyer in another jurisdiction where lawyer now lives); In re Walker, 254 N.W.2d 452, 457 (S.D.1977). See also, e.g., In re Gavic, 116 Wis.2d 374, 342 N.W.2d 244 (1984)(violating conditions of reinstatement by use of alcohol leads to period of suspension).

27 Florida Bar v. Larkin, 420 So.2d 1080 (Fla.1982); In re O'Hara, 330 N.W.2d 863, 865 (Minn.1983); In re Rochlin, 100 A.D.2d 263, 474 N.Y.S.2d 14 (1984); In re Livesey, 94 Wn.2d 251, 615 P.2d 1294 (1980); In re Rabideau, 102 Wis.2d 16, 306 N.W.2d 1, 10-11 (1981), appeal dismissed 454 U.S. 1025, 102 S.Ct. 559, 70 L.Ed.2d 469 (1981).

28 Macrory & Patton, Alcohol and the Lawyer: The Bar Responds, 6 District Lawyer at 50 (Sept./Oct.1981)(assistance groups in twenty-six state bars and thirty-seven local bars).

29 Committee on Professional Ethics v. Ryan, 341 N.W.2d 755, 757 (Iowa 1983).

30 Attorney Grievance Comm'n v. Burka, 292 Md. 221, 438 A.2d 514 (1981); In re Jacob, 95 N.J. 132, 469 A.2d 498 (1984); In re Noble, 100 Wn.2d 88, 667 P.2d 608, 618 (1983); In re Glasschroeder, 113 Wis.2d 672, 335 N.W.2d 621, 624 (1983). See also In re Johnson, 322 N.W.2d 616, 618-19 (Minn.1982)(five-factor test for alcoholic causation, including requirement that lawyer prove causation by clear and convincing evidence).

31 Compare, e.g., Snyder v. State Bar, 18 Cal.3d 286, 133 Cal.Rptr. 864, 555 P.2d 1104, 1107-08 (1976)(manic-depressive emotional disorder not defense or mitigation under circumstances); Attorney Grievance Comm'n v. Demyan, 299 Md. 652, 474 A.2d 1342 (1984)(lawyer alleging memory difficulties and loss of confidence in ability to practice law placed on inactive status); In re Haggerty, 661 S.W.2d 8, 10 (1983)("stress of trial practice" not defense or mitigation); In re McManus, 75 N.J. 238, 381 A.2d 352, 354, n. 1 (1978) (concern at tendency of lawyers to seek psychiatric help after charges filed and then assert mental disorder as cause of offense); In re Pinello, 100 A.D.2d 64, 473 N.Y.S.2d 7, 8-9, appeal dismissed 62 N.Y. 2d 940, 479 N.Y.S.2d 214, 468 N.E.2d 52 (1984)(suffering from extreme emotional, psychological, and physical distress due to mother's terminal illness, hepatitis, traumatic end of love affair, and felony charges that were dis-

§ 3.3.4 *Lawyers in Nonlawyer Roles*

A traditional view is that a lawyer is subject to professional discipline for conduct that the lawyer engaged in outside his or her role as a lawyer.[32] That view is generally sound under most conceptions of the purposes of professional discipline, but under some can lead to intrusive and unwarranted prying into irrelevant parts of a lawyer's nonpractice life. Clearly, conduct that suggests that a lawyer is presently incapable of practicing law in an honest and competent manner must be examined. Included are acts that stem directly from the practice of law, such as taking advantage of former clients or of the special privileges accorded to lawyers.[33] Also included by most modern decisions are acts that are remote from law practice, such as nonlegal business activities,[34] political activities,[35] civic activities,[36] activities in a foreign country,[37] or personal activities,[38] to the extent that they furnish proof of seriously deficient qualities of relevance to law practice. So also, a lawyer's conduct while under suspension,[39] or while subject to the regulatory power of another jurisdiction [40] or engaged in before the lawyer became a member of the bar,[41] may suffice to lead to disbarment. It is presumably under that theory that criminal acts not involving law practice can be sanctioned. For example, serious violent crimes by a lawyer, although they may not reflect dishonesty, may suggest fundamentally inappropriate attitudes toward an ordered system of conduct and the peaceful

missed cannot prevent disbarment), with, e.g., Florida Bar v. Ullensvang, 400 So.2d 969, 973 (Fla.1981)("not enjoying practice of law" and alcoholism as mitigating factors); Louisiana St. Bar Ass'n v. Heymann, 405 So.2d 826 (La.1981)(compulsive gambling leading to successive fraud felonies as mitigation); In re Kimmel, 322 N.W.2d 224, 227 (Minn.1982)("sexual dysfunction" analogous to chemical dependency); In re Loew, 292 Or. 806, 642 P.2d 1171, 26 A.L.R.4th 987 (1982)("burnt out syndrome" as mitigation).

32 Ex parte Wall, 107 U.S. 265, 2 S.Ct. 569, 27 L.Ed. 552 (1883)(participation in lynching); State v. Roggensack, 19 Wis.2d 38, 119 N.W.2d 412 (1963)(overruling prior cases). Contra, e.g., Lotto v. State, 208 S.W. 563 (Tex.Civ.App. 1919)(dishonorable conduct, in order to be grounds for disbarment, must be within scope of lawyer's conduct as such and not merely as a person). See generally ABA Formal Op. 336 (1974)(post-Watergate reaffirmation of principle that lawyer must comply with Code whether or not acting in professional capacity).

33 People v. McGonigle, 198 Colo. 315, 600 P.2d 61 (1979)(lawyer gained access to penitentiary in that role and engaged in sale of heroin inside prison); In re Lambert, 79 N.J. 74, 397 A.2d 1086, 1087 (1979)(failing to turn over funds belonging to business colleague who was former client).

34 In re Waleen, 190 Minn. 13, 18, 250 N.W. 798, 800 (1933); State ex rel. Nebraska St. Bar Ass'n v. Leonard, 212 Neb. 379, 322 N.W.2d 794, 796 (1982)(kickback scheme in making student loans); In re Franklin, 71 N.J. 425, 365 A.2d 1361 (1976)(former corporate president fired for extensive padding of expense account suspended one year for dishonesty); In re Briedman, 102 A.D.2d 427, 105 A.D.2d 631, 477 N.Y.S.2d 144 (1984)(cheating utility company as owner of rental property); Bar Ass'n of Greater Cleveland v. Bogomolny, 10 Ohio St.3d 110, 461 N.E.2d 1294 (1984)(antitrust violation by engaging in conspiracy to fix prices while chief executive officer of supermarket company).

35 Russell v. Kansas, 227 Kan. 897, 610 P.2d 1122, (1980), cert. denied 449 U.S. 983, 101 S.Ct. 400, 66 L.Ed.2d 245 (1980)(lawyer's dishonest acts in running for public office that did not require candidate to have license to practice); Attorney Grievance Comm'n v. Green, 278 Md. 412, 365 A.2d 39 (1976)(acting as county attorney).

36 Attorney Grievance Comm'n v. Silk, 279 Md. 345, 369 A.2d 70 (1977)(embezzlement from social organization); In re Stodd, 279 Or. 565, 568 P.2d 665 (1977) (president of nonprofit organization sponsoring youth football program).

37 In re Scallen, 269 N.W.2d 834, 98 A.L.R.3d 343 (Minn.1978)(conviction of felony in Canadian court for illegal business activities there).

38 In re Crisel, 101 Ill.2d 332, 78 Ill.Dec. 160, 461 N.E.2d 994, 998-99 (1984)(dishonesty and misrepresentation in covering up failed attempt to commit suicide); In re Norwood, 273 S.C. 780, 260 S.E.2d 177 (1979)(violating order of divorce court).

39 Kirven v. Bd. on Grievances and Discipline, 271 S.C. 194, 246 S.E.2d 857 (1978). A fortiori, disciplinary violations as a lawyer in another jurisdiction are sanctionable in either. See § 3.4.6.

40 Office of Disciplinary Counsel v. Cashman, 63 Haw. 382, 629 P.2d 105, 108-09 (1981)(discipline for engaging in unauthorized practice in another jurisdiction after suspension there); In re Davis, 264 N.W.2d 371 (Minn.1978) (while state has no jurisdiction to prohibit lawyer from practicing before federal Patent Office, misconduct as patent lawyer may be basis for disbarment from state's bar).

41 Stratmore v. State Bar, 14 Cal.3d 887, 123 Cal.Rptr. 101, 538 P.2d 229, 92 A.L.R.3d 803 (1975); In re Lamberis, 93 Ill.2d 222, 66 Ill.Dec. 623, 443 N.E.2d 549 (1982) (plagiarism while law student); In re Howe, 257 N.W.2d 420 (N.D.1977)(deceit in bar application); In re Elliott, 268 S.C. 522, 235 S.E.2d 111 (1977)(same).

resolution of disputes.[42] It is, of course, too narrow a focus to observe simply that such acts do not have an impact directly on law practice;[43] they might well reflect attitudes or a character that would be dangerous in law practice.

Some nonlawyer roles share many common characteristics with law practice, such as acting as a nonlawyer fiduciary,[44] and many such activities are also commonly engaged in by lawyers because they have legal ability. Wrongdoing in those capacities is particularly susceptible to strong disciplinary measures because of its strongly suggestive quality.[45] But wrongfulness should take its meaning from those other roles. There is, for example, no reason to think that the special restrictions that uniquely bind lawyers should normally be borne by lawyers when carrying on activities entirely separated from law practice.[46] An obvious instance are the rules on advertising. A lawyer who runs an entirely separate business should not be restricted to lawyerlike advertising rules so that promoting that other business is at the risk of professional discipline.

One also does not have to approve of or defend deviant social behavior in order to maintain that engaging in it may have no bearing on a lawyer's fitness to practice law. Thus, objectionable sexual practices that are not shown to have an impact on a lawyer's ability to practice should be irrelevant, or at least their relevance should not be magnified.[47] And peccadilloes in everyday life that do not speak strongly of character defects of a kind that threaten a repeat of the misconduct in the more somber realm of law practice should not be a ground for discipline.[48]

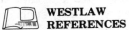

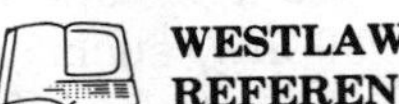

WESTLAW REFERENCES

"conduct unbecoming" /s attorney lawyer counsel** (legal law /2 professional)

"mens rea" inten! motive /p lawyer attorney

d.r. "disciplinary rule" /5 7-102 7-103 7-106

d.r. m.r. (disciplinary model +1 rule) /5 1-102(a)(1) 8.4(a)

alcoholi** (mental psychological** emotional** +1 ill****) "mitigating factor" /p attorney client lawyer /p disciplin***

---

42 Gaetke & Casey, Professional Responsibility, 70 Ky. L.J. 325, 336 (1981). Cf., e.g., In re Kuvara, 97 Wn.2d 743, 649 P.2d 834 (1982)(isolated instance of engaging in fistfight not appropriate cause for discipline).

43 But cf., e.g., In re Towles, 98 Ill.2d 179, 74 Ill.Dec. 625, 456 N.E.2d 127, 130 (1983)(lawyer's federal tax violations involve primarily interests of federal government in protecting its tax revenues).

44 In re Bailey, 30 Ariz. 407, 248 P. 29 (1926)(acting as personal representative of decedent's estate, although not the lawyer for the personal representative); Florida Bar v. Rhodes, 355 So.2d 774 (Fla.1978); Committee on Prof. Ethics v. Gross, 322 N.W.2d 82, 83 (Iowa 1982)(breaches of fiduciary duty as corporate officer and promoter); Kentucky Bar Ass'n v. Berry, 626 S.W.2d 632 (Ky.App.1981) (executor of large estate). But see, e.g., Attorney v. Mississippi St. Bar, 420 So.2d 1367 (Miss.1982)(lawyer who acted only as administrator of estate and not as its lawyer not subject to discipline for wrongful acts as administrator).

45 Lewis v. State Bar, 9 Cal.3d 704, 108 Cal.Rptr. 821, 511 P.2d 1173 (1973); Kentucky Bar Ass'n v. Berry, 626 S.W.2d 632 (Ky.App.1981); In re Gallop, 85 N.J. 317, 426 A.2d 509 (1981).

46 Rubin, A Causerie on Lawyers' Ethics in Negotiation, 35 La.L.Rev. 577, 577 (1975)(lawyers' special professional responsibilities come into play only when they are "practicing their profession as attorneys-at-law").

47 In re Kimmel, 322 N.W.2d 224 (Minn.1982)(two felony offenses of nonconsensual contact with members of same sex warrants discipline but not disbarment); Committee on Professional Ethics v. Durham, 279 N.W.2d 280 (Iowa 1979)(caressing and fondling between lawyer and client during lawyer's professional visits to inmate in penitentiary that were not illegal or inherently wrong warrants reprimand because of impact on professional role). But see, e.g., Florida Bar v. Turner, 369 So.2d 581 (Fla.1979)(engaging in unspecified "lewd and lascivious act" in isolated area at 3:00 a.m. observed by police officer as ground for forty-five-day suspension from practice); In re Titus, 66 Hun. 632, 21 N.Y.S. 724 (1892) (disbarment warranted where lawyer, sued for alienation of affections, was guilty of adultery with plaintiff's wife). See generally, Comment, Disciplining Attorneys for Nonprofessional Conduct Involving Alcohol and Sex, 1975 Ariz.St.L.J. 411.

48 In re Steffen, 279 Or. 313, 567 P.2d 544 (1977)(lawyer, who lied to police officer about current nature of identification when stopped for traffic offense, not subject to discipline).

§ 3.4 DISCIPLINARY PROCEDURE

§ 3.4.1 *The Formalization of Disciplinary Procedures*

From Trials to Administrative Hearings

Within the past fifteen years, the procedures employed in lawyer discipline cases have been substantially improved and regularized. They have moved from informal hearings before bar association committees to hearings that are more formal and regulated and are held before panels that are neutral. Lawyer discipline in its origins was a judicial proceeding held before a judge. Its modern replacement more resembles an adversarial administrative proceeding.

Systems of Lawyer Discipline

The states follow several different variations, but a commonly employed model [49] begins with an informal administrative proceeding to determine whether the matter should be dismissed or disposed of with a nondisciplinary admonition or, instead, whether there is reason to conclude that a serious violation, requiring a full hearing, has probably occurred. Any hearing is conducted before an administrative panel with the lawyer having a right to a rehearing before the full administrative board and a final right to review on the record in an appellate court. Some states replace the rehearing before the full board with a hearing before a referee. Texas still retains the fully judicial model.[50] Because of a state constitutional guaranty of jury trial, lawyer discipline proceedings are commenced by filing a complaint in court [51] and the action proceeds as a civil action tried before a jury.[52] No states other than Texas and Georgia afford a jury trial in discipline cases.[53]

The Legal Status of Disciplinary Proceedings

Courts uniformly insist that discipline is not a "criminal" proceeding, to which the stricter requirements of due process apply. The asserted reasons have to do with the absence of criminal-type sanctions.[54] Thus there is no right to a jury trial, to remain silent, or to indictment. But the proceedings are also not governed by state administrative procedure acts [55] or, unless the court so provides, by civil rules of procedure and evi-

[49] The following is based generally on ABA Joint Comm. on Prof. Discipline, Standards for Lawyer Disciplinary and Disability Proceedings (1979)(hereinafter "ABA Disciplinary Standards (1979)"). The Standards have been widely adopted in the states.

[50] Cf. also, e.g., Patrick v. State, 238 Ga. 497, 233 S.E.2d 757 (1977)(Georgia practice of ordering name stricken from role of lawyers for failure to perfect appeal originally docketed in criminal case).

[51] The complaint follows hearings before a grievance committee that are in the nature of probable-cause hearings. See Wilson v. State, 582 S.W.2d 484 (Tex.Civ.App. 1979). The committee may also make a final determination if the lawyer consents. 582 S.W.2d at 486.

[52] Discipline in Texas can be imposed on a motion for summary judgment at the close of the evidence. E.g., Searcy v. State Bar, 604 S.W.2d 256 (Tex.Civ.App.1980). And jury findings can be ignored if they involve questions of law. E.g., Howell v. State, 559 S.W.2d 432 (Tex.Civ. App.1977)(jury's finding that lawyer refused to answer question despite judge's order permits trial court in discipline case to find as matter of law that lawyer's conduct was prejudicial to administration of justice, despite jury's contrary finding on latter point). The question of the appropriate discipline is also one of "law." E.g., State v. Baker, 559 S.W.2d 145 (Tex.Civ.App.1977). A motion for reinstatement of a suspended or disbarred lawyer is also heard by a judge sitting without a jury. E.g., Steere v. State Bar, 512 S.W.2d 362 (Tex.Civ.App.1974).

[53] E.g., Attorney Grievance Comm'n v. Kerpelman, 288 Md. 341, 420 A.2d 940, 947-48 (1980), cert. denied 450 U.S. 970, 101 S.Ct. 1492, 67 L.Ed.2d 621 (1981); North Carolina St. Bar v. DuMont, 304 N.C. 627, 286 S.E.2d 89 (1982) (noting repeal of jury right in disciplinary proceedings); Mendicino v. Whitchurch, 565 P.2d 460, 464, n.9 (Wyo.1977)(same). The denial of jury trial grows out of the doctrine, now partially repudiated, that there is no jury trial right in summary punishment cases. See Ex parte Wall, 107 U.S. 265, 2 S.Ct. 569, 27 L.Ed. 552 (1883). Under that doctrine, two remedies, discipline and contempt, were thought to be aspects of the inherent power of a court to proceed in a summary way to protect its processes through regulation of its officers.

[54] In re Hanratty, 277 N.W.2d 373, 376 (Minn.1979) (charge of criminal conduct in discipline case does not result in application of criminal sanctions despite imposition of substantial fine and censure).

[55] Green v. State, 589 S.W.2d 160, 164 (Tex.Civ.App. 1979); Mendicino v. Whitchurch, 565 P.2d 460, 475 (Wyo. 1977).

dence.[56] Instead, discipline is a hybrid proceeding with a legal complexion of its own.[57] Some older cases go further and insist that discipline is not even an adversary hearing, but simply a judicial inquiry into the conduct of a court officer.[58] But the view of the Supreme Court on the scope of due process rights in professional disciplinary proceedings implies that several adversary-type features should be present.[59] The predominant view is that a discipline proceeding must at least provide the responding lawyer with notice of the charges, the right to a hearing, the right to be present, the right to confront and cross-examine all witnesses and to examine all other evidence that will be considered, the right to testify, the right to offer counterevidence, and the right to be represented by counsel of the respondent's choice.[60]

§ 3.4.2 Initiating Discipline

The Complaints Process

The great bulk of the work of lawyer disciplinary agencies is initiated by externally generated complaints, primarily from lawyer's clients or adversaries.[61] That largely reactive role is dictated by limitations on finances and by fear of intruding into lawyers' affairs.[62] Disciplinary agencies receive additional information about possible lawyer violations by the exchange of information with criminal prosecutors and review of newspapers and other public sources of information. Statutes, court rules, and common law in a growing number of states afford an absolute immunity to all persons associated with the lawyer discipline system, including individual complainants, from liability for damages for filing even maliciously false complaints or taking other actions within the disciplinary system.[63] A lawyer who sues a complainant

[56] Giddens v. State Bar, 28 Cal.3d 730, 170 Cal.Rptr. 812, 621 P.2d 851, 854 (1981).

[57] In re Ruffalo, 390 U.S. 544, 551, 88 S.Ct. 1222, 1226, 20 L.Ed.2d 117 (1968) ("quasi-criminal"); In re Roberts, 442 N.E.2d 986, 988 (Ind.1982)("unique character of such proceedings"); In re Rerat, 224 Minn. 124, 28 N.W.2d 168, 172 (1947)("sui generis"); Carter v. Folcarelli, 121 R.I. 667, 402 A.2d 1175, 1177 (1979)(" 'quasi-judicial administrative hearings' "). See generally ABA Disciplinary Standards 2-3 (1979).

[58] Mendicino v. Whitchurch, 565 P.2d 460, 464 (Wyo. 1977), and authorities cited.

[59] In re Ruffalo, 390 U.S. 544, 88 S.Ct. 1222, 20 L.Ed.2d 117 (1968); Withrow v. Larkin, 421 U.S. 35, 95 S.Ct. 1456, 43 L.Ed.2d 712 (1975).

[60] In re Jones, 506 F.2d 527 (8th Cir.1974); Giddens v. State Bar, 28 Cal.3d 730, 170 Cal.Rptr. 812, 621 P.2d 851 (1981); Netterville v. Mississippi St. Bar, 397 So.2d 878, 883-844 (Miss.1981). Some courts have denied, however, that there is a due process right to counsel (e.g., In re Peters, 332 N.W.2d 10, 16-17 (Minn.1983); Committee on Legal Ethics v. Pence, 161 W.Va. 240, 240 S.E.2d 668, 673, 93 A.L.R.3d 1046 (1977)).

[61] Marks & Cathcart, Discipline within the Legal Profession: Is It Self Regulation?, 1974 U.Ill.L.Forum 193, 206-07. One of the central features of many areas of American law—from criminal law to tort and contract law—is that it does not move unless impelled by a citizen complaint. See L.Friedman, The Legal System: A Social Science Perspective 110 (1975).

[62] Agencies are not, of course, limited by standing or jurisdictional notions to client complaints as a condition to initiating discipline proceedings. E.g., In re Stewart, 121 Ariz. 243, 589 P.2d 886 (1979); State v. Freeman, 229 Kan. 639, 629 P.2d 716, 718-19 (1981); State ex rel. Oklahoma Bar Ass'n v. Raskin, 642 P.2d 262, 265 (Okl. 1982); In re Norlin, 104 Wis.2d 117, 310 N.W.2d 789, 791 (1981).

[63] Absolute immunity: Simons v. Bellinger, 643 F.2d 774 (D.C.Cir.1980); Chen v. Fleming, 147 Cal.App.3d 36, 194 Cal.Rptr. 913 (1983); Netterville v. Lear, Siegler, Inc., 397 So.2d 1109 (Miss.1981); In re Hearing on Immunity for Ethics Complainants, 96 N.J. 669, 477 A.2d 339 (1984); Weiner v. Weintraub, 22 N.Y.2d 330, 292 N.Y.S.2d 667, 239 N.E.2d 540 (1968); Ramstead v. Morgan, 219 Or. 383, 347 P.2d 594, 77 A.L.R.2d 481 (1959); McAfee v. Feller, 452 S.W.2d 56 (Tex.Civ.App.1970); ABA Spec. Comm. on Evaluation of Discipl. Enforcement, Problems and Recommendations in Disciplinary Enforcement 74 (1970)(Clark Report). See also Rolle v. Nolan, 119 Misc.2d 1050, 464 N.Y.S.2d 930 (N.Y.Civ.Ct.1983)(absolute immunity of judge reporting lawyer's asserted misconduct under privilege for judicial acts).

Qualified immunity: Allen v. Ali, 105 Ill.App.3d 887, 61 Ill.Dec. 678, 435 N.E.2d 167 (1982); In re Proposed Rules Relating to Grievance Procedures, 115 N.H. 310, 341 A.2d 272, 274, 276 (1975)(immunity applies only to statements made "in good faith"; incorrectly citing Clark Report as favoring only qualified immunity).

Some jurisdictions have drawn a distinction between defamation and malicious prosecution, holding that an absolute immunity attaches to the former but requiring good faith, and thus extending only a qualified privilege, with respect to the latter. See generally Friedland v. Podhoretz, 174 N.J.Super. 73, 415 A.2d 381 (1980). The ABA Disciplinary Standards (1979) recommend absolute immunity both for all persons serving within the agency (§ 3.10) and for all complainants, but only for disclosures to the agency and not for disclosures of the information despite the existence of a clearly applicable immunity may violate the antiharassment rules.[64] Harassment by lawyers in other forms, such as attempted personal intimidation, has also been translated into additional disciplinary charges.[65]

The central role of complaints in bringing possible lawyer misconduct to light does not mean that, once exposed, a complaint about a lawyer should be able to be withdrawn by the complainant.[66] Lawyer discipline is not a substitute for civil proceedings for the settlement of interpersonal disputes. It involves the question whether charged misconduct is of a kind that requires discipline of a lawyer in order to protect future clients and the public.[67] Similarly, a complainant's malicious personal motivations against a lawyer do not affect the legitimacy of proceeding upon them, although they may affect the credibility of the complainant as a witness.[68]

Screening and Prosecutorial Discretion

The filing of a complaint should not inevitably lead to a full-blown hearing. Complaints can be illfounded in fact, and complainants might misapprehend the duties of lawyers. For those reasons it is important that a discretionary function should be vested in a public official to screen complaints, informally consult with complainants to obtain additional information or to inform them about lawyers' duties, and possibly to settle minor complaints.[69] Discretion, of course, can be abused, such as by routinely permitting a lawyer's denial of charges to serve as a basis for finding no probable cause.[70] Most jurisdictions today rely on a full-time bar counsel to handle screening and to make decisions about prosecuting complaints.[71] In some states that function is complemented by bar association committees that initially screen cases and, in some, must find probable cause before a hearing will proceed.[72] In others, prosecution has been handled by the state's attorney general.[73]

Stale Complaints

Most civil and criminal liability claims are subject to limitation or extinction because a long period of time has passed. Courts have generally resisted efforts to impose limitations on the time within which a complainant

to anyone else (§ 8.3), without distinguishing between kinds of tort actions. See generally Annot., 4 A.L.R.4th 807, 817-24 (1981); Annot., 9 A.L.R.4th 494 (1981).

64 In re Edwards, 279 S.C. 89, 302 S.E.2d 339 (1983), cert. denied 464 U.S. 935, 104 S.Ct. 342, 78 L.Ed.2d 310 (1983). See also In re Gonyo, 73 Wis.2d 624, 245 N.W.2d 893 (1976)(discipline of lawyer for filing criminal charges against complainant).

65 In re Friedland, 92 N.J. 107, 455 A.2d 1098 (1983). See also In re Jerome, 31 Ill.2d 284, 201 N.E.2d 440 (1964) (lawyer disciplined for settlement of civil suit conditioned on former client's dismissal of disciplinary complaint); In re Leibowitz, 88 A.D.2d 646, 442 N.Y.S.2d 802 (1981) (discipline of lawyer for making payment to client to withdraw complaint).

66 In re Woldman, 98 Ill.2d 248, 74 Ill.Dec. 533, 456 N.E.2d 35, 37 (1983); State v. Scott, 230 Kan. 564, 639 P.2d 1131, 1133 (1982); In re McWhorter, 407 Mich. 278, 284 N.W.2d 472, vacating 405 Mich. 563, 275 N.W.2d 259 (1979)(expressed wish of complainant to have proceedings against lawyer discontinued does not bind disciplinary counsel); State ex rel. Oklahoma Bar Ass'n v. Braswell, 663 P.2d 1228, 1230 (Okl.1983).

67 Similar considerations make victim condonation irrelevant in criminal prosecutions. See generally W.LaFave & A.Scott, Criminal Law 410-13 (1972).

68 Dixon v. State Bar, 32 Cal.3d 728, 187 Cal.Rptr. 30, 653 P.2d 321, 326-27 (1982).

69 Ramos Colon v. United States Attorney, 576 F.2d 1 (1st Cir.1978)(private citizen cannot prosecute lawyer disciplinary action); In re Phillips, 510 F.2d 126 (2d Cir. 1975); State ex rel. Chandler v. Dancer, 391 S.W.2d 504 (Tex.Civ.App.1965); ABA Disciplinary Standards § 8.4 (1979).

70 Krainz v. Attorney Grievance Comm'n, 413 Mich. 1106, 320 N.W.2d 54 (1982)(mandamus to require commission to investigate complaint that could not be dismissed on record containing only contradictory, unsworn statements of complainant and lawyer).

71 See ABA Disciplinary Standards §§ 3.8, 3.9 (1979).

72 In re Anonymous Member of St. Bar, 128 Ariz. 238, 624 P.2d 1286 (1981); Florida Bar v. G.B.T., 399 So.2d 357 (Fla.1981); Smith v. Grievance Committee, 475 S.W.2d 396 (Tex.Civ.App.1972).

73 People v. Yoakum, 191 Colo. 269, 552 P.2d 291 (1976); Mendicino v. Whitchurch, 565 P.2d 460 (Wyo.1977). See also In re Stroh, 97 Wn.2d 289, 644 P.2d 1161 (1982), cert. denied 459 U.S. 1202, 103 S.Ct. 1187, 75 L.Ed.2d 434 (1983)(prosecuting attorney has standing to petition for review of agency's dismissal of complaint).

must assert a complaint,[74] a lawyer must be notified of charges,[75] or the hearing process must be completed.[76] The question of the lawyer's capacity to function effectively as a lawyer often requires a determination of whether the lawyer's misconduct is an isolated instance or, much more seriously, part of a long-standing pattern of violations.[77]

Questions of timeliness implicate two sets of interests. First, a responding lawyer can sympathetically assert an interest in being able to defend against charges before so much time passes that gathering evidence to defend against or explain charges becomes prejudicially difficult. A lawyer can also reasonably claim an interest in being relieved of the further psychological drain of pending charges. Second, there is a public interest in goading an overly slow bar disciplinary agency into more-prompt action in the future in order to make the enforcement of the lawyer codes more effective. Those interests need not all be protected in the same way. If a lawyer claims that the passage of time has prejudiced a defense, it is fair to require the lawyer to demonstrate specifically the way in which that has occurred.[78] The lawyer's interest in a prompt hearing for reasons of repose is rarely articulately protected, but decisions mitigating the severity of sanctions on that basis are perhaps motivated by the notion that the ordeal of delay is itself a sanction.[79] An overly bureaucratic or inattentive bar disciplinary agency can be goaded by stern condemnation in published opinions [80] or, more acutely, by financial measures, such as the denial of costs.[81]

Notice of Charges

Fundamental to the concept of due process is notice to the subject of a contemplated judicial action that proceedings are to take place. The concept applies to lawyer discipline with several amplifications. A reasonable effort must be made to locate the lawyer in order to convey information about the intended hearing.[82] The notice must inform the lawyer of the nature of the charges against him or her in sufficient detail to permit the lawyer to prepare a defense.[83] The notice-pleading concept resembles modern pleading rules and requires notice only of the course of conduct to be examined. Notice is not required of such specific information as the precise rule in the lawyer code that was alleg-

[74] But see, e.g., In re Abagis, 386 Mass. 1001, 435 N.E.2d 1042, 1043 (1982)(six-year limitation period subject to exceptions for "good cause").

[75] Anne Arundel Bar Ass'n v. Collins, 272 Md. 578, 325 A.2d 724, 727 (1974)(courts uniformly refuse to apply general statutes of limitation to initiating disciplinary hearings). In In re Tracy, 197 Minn. 35, 266 N.W. 88 (1936), the court held that the negative inherent powers doctrine (§ 2.2.3) invalidated a statute that purported to impose a time limitation within which charges must be brought against a lawyer.

[76] In re Posler, 393 Mich. 38, 222 N.W.2d 511, 513 (1974)(rule requiring issuance of bar's opinion within thirty days of end of hearing is directory rather than jurisdictional). See generally Annot., 93 A.L.R.3d 1057 (1979).

[77] State ex rel. Oklahoma Bar Ass'n v. Warzyn, 624 P.2d 1068, 1071 (Okl.1981).

[78] In re Bossov, 60 Ill.2d 439, 328 N.E.2d 309 (1975), cert.denied 423 U.S. 928, 96 S.Ct. 275, 46 L.Ed.2d 256 (1975); Attorney Grievance Comm'n v. Engerman, 289 Md. 330, 424 A.2d 362, 370 (1981)(prejudice not made out by claim that earlier proceedings would have alerted lawyer to his responsibilities, thus preventing subsequent violations); State ex rel. Oklahoma Bar Ass'n v. Lowe, 640 P.2d 1361, 1362 (Okl.1982); In re Weinstein, 254 Or. 392, 459 P.2d 548 (1969), cert.denied 398 U.S. 903, 90 S.Ct. 1689, 26 L.Ed.2d 61 (1970). See In re Phillips, 510 F.2d 126, 127 (2d Cir.1975)(refusal to impose discipline for relatively minor offense in view of passage of time).

[79] Florida Bar v. Randolph, 238 So.2d 635, 638-39 (Fla. 1970)("During this unduly long period of investigation and prosecution, the accused lawyer is left roaming through the fields of Limbo where dwelt what Dante called 'the praiseless and the blameless dead.' "); Louisiana Bar Ass'n v. Edwards, 387 So.2d 1137, 1139-40 (La. 1980).

[80] In re Carroll, 124 Ariz. 80, 602 P.2d 461, 467-68 (1979)(concurring opinion of Cameron, C.J.).

[81] In re Gant, 293 Or. 359, 647 P.2d 933 (1982), modifying 293 Or. 130, 645 P.2d 23 (1982).

[82] Giddens v. State Bar, 28 Cal.3d 730, 170 Cal.Rptr. 812, 621 P.2d 851 (1981)(lawyer imprisoned in another state); Columbus Bar Ass'n v. Gross, 2 Ohio St.3d 5, 441 N.E.2d 570 (1982)(constructive service permissible when all efforts to reach lawyer at address he gave to post office failed).

[83] Randall v. Brigham, 74 U.S. (7 Wall.) 523, 540, 19 L.Ed. 285 (1868); Ex parte Robinson, 86 U.S. (19 Wall.) 505, 22 L.Ed. 205 (1873).

edly violated[84] or the precise sanction that will be sought if the charges are sustained.[85] Once effective notice has been given, it is the lawyer's responsibility to keep informed of reasonably announced steps in the proceeding and to keep the agency informed of means of being contacted.[86]

The notice given to the lawyer serves thereafter as a kind of due process limitation on the scope of the proceeding. According to the Supreme Court, in In re Ruffalo,[87] under the due process clause a disciplinary agency may not base a finding on evidence introduced at the hearing if the prior notice of charges to the accused lawyer did not indicate that such a charge would be considered. But new matters raised by the evidence can be the subject of an additional charge, either by consent of the accused lawyer or if the prosecutor files an amended statement of charges and the hearing agency grants a continuance to permit the lawyer to prepare additional defenses.[88]

§ 3.4.3 Responding to Disciplinary Charges

Mandatory Nature of Response

As in civil cases, and unlike in cases of criminal charges, a lawyer who has been properly notified of charges must deny them at the risk of having them taken as admitted and of effectively defaulting on the properly pleaded charges of misconduct.[89] As in the criminal process, many jurisdictions now permit a kind of plea bargaining in which the final agreement between the disciplinary counsel and the lawyer is embodied in a no contest plea.[90]

84 Phelps v. Kansas Supreme Court, 662 F.2d 649, 650-51 (10th Cir.1981), cert. denied 456 U.S. 944, 102 S.Ct. 2009, 72 L.Ed.2d 466 (1982); In re James, 452 A.2d 163 (D.C.App.1982), cert. denied 460 U.S. 1038, 103 S.Ct. 1429, 75 L.Ed.2d 789 (1983); State v. Regier, 228 Kan. 746, 621 P.2d 431, 435 (1980), cert. denied 460 U.S. 1038, 103 S.Ct. 1429, 75 L.Ed.2d 789 (1983); Board of Bar Overseers v. Rodway, 461 A.2d 1062, 1064 (Me.1983). Contra Attorney Grievance Comm'n v. Brewster, 280 Md. 473, 374 A.2d 602 (1977)(statement in notice of charges that conviction violated one provision of Code limited theory of prosecution to that provision and to no other subdivision of same DR).

85 Dixon v. State Bar, 32 Cal.3d 728, 187 Cal.Rptr. 30, 653 P.2d 321, 326 (1982).

86 People v. Hilgers, 200 Colo. 211, 612 P.2d 1134 (1980); Office of Disciplinary Counsel v. Johnson, 62 Haw. 95, 611 P.2d 993 (1980); Committee on Professional Ethics v. Toomey, 253 N.W.2d 573, 574 (Iowa 1977).

87 390 U.S. 544, 88 S.Ct. 1222, 20 L.Ed.2d 117 (1968). See also, e.g., In re Thorup, 432 A.2d 1221 (D.C.App.1981); People v. Emeson, 638 P.2d 293 (Colo.1981); Committee on Professional Ethics v. Crary, 245 N.W.2d 298, 304 (Iowa 1976). The rationale of *Ruffalo* has caused confusion. Ruffalo was originally charged with soliciting railroad injury clients through Orlando, a railroad employee. He and Orlando both testified at his disciplinary hearing that Orlando investigated cases against his employer but did not solicit. The disciplinary agency, after the hearings ended, then found that Ruffalo should be suspended indefinitely because of his employment of Orlando in a conflict of interest situation, a charge not previously made and that was based entirely on the testimony of the two men. Justice Douglas's opinion held that the procedure violated due process because the conflict of interest charge was not "known before the proceedings commence[d]," although he also suggested that the vice was in the "trap" of changing the charge after the men had testified, giving Ruffalo "no opportunity to expunge the earlier statements and start afresh." 390 U.S. at 551, 88 S.Ct. at 1226. It would be consistent with the former theory (prior notice) to amend the charge and begin the proceeding anew. But the latter theory (testimonial gamesmanship) would presumably not permit recharging. What the latter theory has to do with due process has never been clear.

88 In re Klein, 407 F.Supp. 570 (S.D.N.Y.1976); In re Smith, 403 A.2d 296 (D.C.App.1979); Mendicino v. Whitchurch, 565 P.2d 460 (Wyo.1977). Contra, e.g., In re Roberts, ___ Ind. ___, 442 N.E.2d 986, 988 (1982)(*In re Ruffalo* precludes bringing new charges against lawyer based on his testimony in original hearing, which revealed uncharged offenses); Attorney Grievance Comm'n v. Walman, 280 Md. 453, 374 A.2d 354, 360-61 (1977) (same).

89 Office of Disciplinary Counsel v. Johnson, 62 Haw. 95, 611 P.2d 993 (1980); Board of Bar Overseers v. Ingeneri, 440 A.2d 1039 (Me.1982); In re Larson, 324 N.W.2d 656, 658 (Minn.1982); In re Kane, 82 A.D.2d 970, 440 N.Y.S.2d 88 (1981); In re Marine, 82 Wis.2d 612, 264 N.W.2d 290, 291 (1979). Contra In re Williams, 464 A.2d 115 (D.C.App.1983)(because discipline cases are quasi-criminal, sanction may not be imposed in absence of factual record establishing charges by clear and convincing evidence). See also, e.g., In re Evans, 661 P.2d 171, 175 (Alaska 1983)(failure to respond is itself ground for discipline).

90 In re Heath, 292 Or. 562, 640 P.2d 617 (1982).

Self-Incrimination and Spevack v. Klein

To an extent that is quite unclear, criminal law concepts also determine the question whether a lawyer can respond to disciplinary charges by invoking a constitutional immunity against self-incrimination.[91] The answer to that question requires an examination of the Spevack v. Klein [92] doctrine. Spevack, a lawyer in private practice, was subpoenaed to produce financial records and to testify at a disciplinary hearing. He refused to honor the subpoenas on the ground that compliance might tend to incriminate him. A sharply divided Supreme Court held that he could not be disbarred solely on the ground that he had invoked the privilege.[93] How far beyond that narrow holding *Spevack* extends is unclear. The decision conflicts with the popular judicial notion that a lawyer is an officer of the court and must cooperate in examinations into the qualifications of its officers, and it has proved quite unpopular with bar officials and judges.[94]

Spevack v. Klein appears in the law of lawyer discipline as an exception to the otherwise prevailing principle that a lawyer must fully cooperate with the investigation of charges. The decision does not require that disciplinary proceedings be stayed pending the completion of a criminal prosecution involving the same matter; the lawyer must risk losing the disciplinary case or testifying and impairing a defense in the criminal case.[95] *Spevack* also does not preclude a disciplinary agency from finding that an invocation of the self-incrimination protection is admissible evidence that, together with other evidence, can substantiate a charge of other misconduct.[96] The *Spevack* rule does not apply if the lawyer actually testifies; any false answers may themselves be an asserted ground of discipline.[97] Lawyers have been sanctioned for discourtesy and lack of cooperation with bar investigators [98] and hearing agencies,[99] even if the court even-

[91] The assertion of the privilege by a lawyer is almost as old as American constitutional law. Chief Justice Marshall permitted Attorney General Levi Lincoln to assert the privilege as justification for refusing to answer questions that "would criminate" him in Marbury v. Madison, 5 U.S. (1 Cranch) 137, 144, 2 L.Ed. 60 (1803). See Cohen v. Hurley, 366 U.S. 117, 150, 81 S.Ct. 954, 972, 6 L.Ed.2d 156 (1961)(Douglas, J., dissenting).

[92] 385 U.S. 511, 87 S.Ct. 625, 17 L.Ed.2d 574 (1967). See generally Underwood, The Fifth Amendment and the Lawyer, 62 Nw.U.L.Rev. 129 (1967).

[93] The plurality opinion by Justice Douglas overruled Cohen v. Hurley, 366 U.S. 117, 81 S.Ct. 954, 6 L.Ed.2d 156 (1961) (5-4 decision), which had held squarely opposite, and relied on the broad ground that a disciplinary proceeding exacted a penalty for the lawyer's silence that could not be exacted consistent with the Fifth Amendment. Because the New York courts had not relied on the doctrine, the plurality found it not necessary to reach the issue whether the "required records" doctrine applied. Justice Fortas concurred, if only to write an opinion that was somewhat less enthusiastic about the result and intimated continuing support for the required-records doctrine. Four justices dissented.

A lawyer asserting a self-incrimination right under *Spevack* must establish that the threat of incrimination is well-founded and may not make a blanket objection to an entire line of inquiry. See, e.g., In re Zisook, 88 Ill.2d 321, 58 Ill.Dec. 786, 430 N.E.2d 1037 (1981), cert.denied 457 U.S. 1134, 102 S.Ct. 2962, 73 L.Ed.2d 1352 (1982); Mississippi St. Bar v. Attorney-Respondent, 367 So.2d 179 (Miss.1979).

[94] Franck, The Myth of Spevack v. Klein, 54 ABA J. 970 (1968); Friendly, The Fifth Amendment Tomorrow: The Case for Constitutional Change, 37 U.Cinn.L.Rev. 648, 708 (1968); Niles & Kaye, Spevack v. Klein: Milestone or Millstone in Bar Discipline?, 53 ABA J. 1121 (1967). See generally Comment, The Privilege against Self-Incrimination in Bar Disciplinary Proceedings: Whatever Happened to *Spevack*?, 23 Vill.L.Rev. 127 (1978).

[95] DeVita v. Sills, 422 F.2d 1172 (3d Cir.1970); Sternberg v. State Bar, 384 Mich. 588, 185 N.W.2d 395 (1971).

[96] McInnis v. State, 618 S.W.2d 389, 392 (Tex.Civ.App. 1981), cert. denied 456 U.S. 976, 102 S.Ct. 2242, 72 L.Ed. 2d 851 (1982). Cf. Brink's, Inc. v. City of New York, 717 F.2d 700 (2d Cir.1983)(invocation of Fifth Amendment in civil action is admissible as evidence in same action). See generally Baxter v. Palmigiano, 425 U.S. 308, 96 S.Ct. 1551, 1556-59, 47 L.Ed.2d 810 (1976) (inmate's silence at prison disciplinary proceeding may properly be taken as adverse inference of guilt of charged offense).

[97] Olquin v. State Bar, 28 Cal.3d 195, 167 Cal.Rptr. 876, 616 P.2d 858, 861 (1980); Florida Bar v. Doe, 384 So.2d 30 (Fla.1980); Galindo v. State, 535 S.W.2d 923 (Tex.Civ. App.1976).

[98] In re Cartwright, 282 N.W.2d 548 (Minn.1979)(six-month suspension for refusal to cooperate); In re Grinchis, 75 N.J. 495, 384 A.2d 137 (1978); In re Picciano, 81 A.D.2d 1000, 439 N.Y.S.2d 221 (1981); In re Kintz, 315 N.W.2d 328, 331 (S.D.1982); In re Norlin, 104 Wis.2d 117, 310 N.W.2d 789, 795 (1981).

[99] Louisiana St. Bar Ass'n v. Martin, 451 So.2d 561, 565 (La.1984)(lack of cooperation is taken to indicate intent

tually determines that the underlying charges were groundless,[1] while other courts have taken noncooperation into account as an aggravating factor in determining an appropriate sanction for other misconduct.[2] The practical effect of the *Spevack* case is further limited by narrow immunity devices and doctrines. A lawyer can be compelled to give incriminatory testimony in another proceeding under a grant of immunity that is sufficiently broad to assure that the lawyer will not be subjected to "self-incrimination," that is, compulsory testimony that can be used in that or a future criminal proceeding. But that protection will not preclude subsequent use of the incriminating testimony in a discipline case brought against the same lawyer, because discipline cases are not regarded as "criminal" in nature.[3] Apparently, however, the subsequent use must consist of a reading of the original immunized transcript. Unless a further immunity is granted, the lawyer may not be asked to repeat prior immunized testimony given before another tribunal.[4]

Required Records

Under the required-records doctrine, records that a lawyer is required by law to keep and to produce on demand of bar officials can be obtained by subpoena despite a self-incrimination plea.[5] As elucidated by the Supreme Court, that doctrine applies to records (1) sought in an essentially regulatory hearing, (2) in which the information sought is of the type the regulated party has customarily kept, and (3) that necessarily have "public aspects" that make them analogous to public documents.[6] Those criteria are satisfied for records that lawyers are required to keep regarding client funds and client fee agreements and possibly for other records.[7] The source of the obligation might be found either in an applicable provision of the lawyers code or in other law. Moreover, records of a law firm will often be subject to subpoena without regard to either the *Spevack* rule, immunity, or the required-records doctrine. The protection against self-incrimination is a personal right that cannot be asserted by corporations, unincorporated associations, part-

not to reform conduct and warrants severe discipline). Contra In re Geurts, 290 Or. 241, 620 P.2d 1373, 1376 (1980)(no disciplinary rule clearly condemns failure to respond to inquiries by bar); Committee on Legal Ethics v. Mullins, 159 W.Va. 647, 226 S.E.2d 427, 431 (1976) (lawyer has fundamental right to protect self against charges by refusing to cooperate, which may not be used as cause for discipline).

1 State v. Savaiano, 234 Kan. 268, 670 P.2d 1359 (1983); In re Clark, 99 Wn.2d 702, 663 P.2d 1339, 1342 (1983).

2 In re Larson, 324 N.W.2d 656, 659 (Minn.1982).

3 In re Daley, 549 F.2d 469 (7th Cir.), cert.denied 434 U.S. 829, 98 S.Ct. 110, 54 L.Ed.2d 89 (1977)(neither imperatives of Fifth Amendment nor authority of federal prosecutor warrants federal grant of immunity against state disciplinary use of testimony lawyer is compelled to give in federal prosecution); Segretti v. State Bar, 15 Cal.3d 878, 126 Cal.Rptr. 793, 544 P.2d 929, 933 (1976)(immunized congressional testimony in Watergate hearings); In re Connaghan, 613 S.W.2d 626, 629-31 (Mo.1981)(immunized testimony in federal criminal prosecution of another lawyer); Anonymous Attorneys v. Bar Ass'n, 41 N.Y.2d 506, 393 N.Y.S.2d 961, 362 N.E.2d 592 (1977) (immunized grand jury testimony). Cf. State Bar v. Superior Court, 113 Ariz. 440, 556 P.2d 315 (1976)(when complaining party had been one of parties to stipulation in civil action that in-chambers testimony in divorce action would be sealed, fairness required that holding that such agreements could not preclude use of testimony in lawyer discipline action be applied prospectively only). See generally Annot., 62 A.L.R.3d 1145 (1975).

4 Pillsbury Co. v. Conboy, 459 U.S. 248, 103 S.Ct. 608, 74 L.Ed.2d 430 (1983).

5 See generally Andresen v. Bar Ass'n, 269 Md. 313, 305 A.2d 845, 851-55, cert.denied 414 U.S. 1065, 94 S.Ct. 572, 38 L.Ed.2d 470 (1973)(mandatory audit of lawyer's real estate records that by statute must be maintained and opened to inspection); Andresen v. State, 24 Md.App. 128, 331 A.2d 78, 110-13 (1975), affirmed 427 U.S. 463, 96 S.Ct. 2737, 49 L.Ed.2d 627 (1976)(search warrant to seize office records).

6 Grosso v. United States, 390 U.S. 62, 68, 88 S.Ct. 709, 713, 19 L.Ed.2d 906 (1968). The "required records" doctrine was given its present form in Shapiro v. United States, 335 U.S. 1, 68 S.Ct. 1375, 92 L.Ed. 1787 (1948). The doctrine was treated as an open question in the plurality and concurring opinions in Spevack v. Klein, 385 U.S. 511, 87 S.Ct. 625, 17 L.Ed.2d 574 (1967), but it was reaffirmed in *Grosso*.

7 United States v. Silverman, 449 F.2d 1341, 1345 (2d Cir.1971), cert. denied 405 U.S. 918, 92 S.Ct. 943, 30 L.Ed. 2d 788 (1972)(lawyer's closing statements in contingent fee cases); In re Kennedy, 442 A.2d 79, 88-89 (Del.1982) (dicta)(spot check of all books and records relating to client funds); Florida Bar v. White, 384 So.2d 1266 (Fla. 1980)(trust account records); In re Hamm, 79 Wis.2d 1, 255 N.W.2d 308 (1977)(trust account records).

nerships, or similar entities, including law firms.[8] To the extent that the required-records doctrine does not apply, the personal records of a solo practitioner and the entirely personal and private files of a member of a firm may still be subject to an effective Fifth Amendment claim.[9]

§ 3.4.4 *The Hearing Process*

Discovery

The information available to an investigator in a disciplinary matter is quite extensive. Depending on local law, an investigator may deploy a wide array of compulsory methods, such as mandatory conferences, spot check of records, subpoenas to the lawyer or to third parties such as banks that hold relevant records, search warrants, and depositions. Cooperation with state and federal prosecutors may also bear evidentiary fruit.[10] The methods of discovery available to the responding lawyer may be more modest but may also be less needful because of much readier access to some facts.[11] States commonly make available in discipline proceedings the discovery rules that are employed in civil suits.[12]

Significant scrutiny of a lawyer's work often creates a threat to the principle of client confidentiality (§ 6.7.1). A straightforward method of dealing with the problem is to extend the protection and strictures of the attorney-client privilege to bar investigators.[13] Law office searches are particularly susceptible to difficulties, because the search may reveal information about many clients, including some whose affairs have nothing to do with the investigation.[14] Certainly, any disclosure of a client's confidential information in the course of an investigation or hearing should not result in waiver of the client's right to assert the privilege. Even in the disciplinary hearing itself, protection of the client's privilege has been held to be paramount over the public interest in enforcing rules of lawyer conduct. Remarkably, many published judicial opinions show little sensitivity to the interests of clients in privacy and their legal privilege by making needless disclosures and identifications.

Hearings

The hearing at which live testimony is heard and other evidence received must satisfy the minimum requirements of due process discussed above (§ 3.4.1). The accused lawyer has an obvious right to attend; indeed, lawyers are generally required to attend their own disciplinary hearings.[15]

8 See generally Bellis v. United States, 417 U.S. 85, 94 S.Ct. 2179, 40 L.Ed.2d 678 (1974)(grand jury subpoena for records of dissolved law firm partnership in hands of former partner not subject to self-incrimination plea because records were retained in custodian's representative, not personal, capacity). E.g., In re Zisook, 88 Ill.2d 321, 58 Ill.Dec. 786, 430 N.E.2d 1037 (1981), cert. denied 457 U.S. 1134, 102 S.Ct. 2962, 73 L.Ed.2d 1352 (1982)(Fifth Amendment protects records of solo practitioner but not single lawyer practicing as professional corporation). Cf. Doyle v. State Bar, 32 Cal.3d 12, 184 Cal.Rptr. 720, 723-25, 648 P.2d 942, 944-47 (1982)(privacy interest protected by state constitution not invaded by subpoena, based on good cause, to examine client fund records; better practice requires prior notice to affected clients).

9 See generally Bellis v. United States, 417 U.S. 85, 87-88, 92, 94 S.Ct. 2179, 2182, 2185, 40 L.Ed.2d 678 (1974).

10 A state disciplinary agency may obtain relevant federal grand jury records on a demonstration of "compelling necessity." E.g., United States v. Sobotka, 623 F.2d 764 (2d Cir.1980).

11 Courts have rejected arguments that due process requires that a responding lawyer be able to engage in discovery as in a civil suit. E.g., State v. Phelps, 226 Kan. 371, 598 P.2d 180 (1979), cert. denied 444 U.S. 1045, 100 S.Ct. 732, 62 L.Ed.2d 731 (1980); In re Murray, 266 Ind. 221, 362 N.E.2d 128 (1977), appeal dismissed 434 U.S. 1029, 98 S.Ct. 758, 54 L.Ed.2d 777 (1978).

12 West's Ann.Cal.Bus. & Prof.Code § 6085; Minn.Rs. on Lawyers Prof.Resp., Rule 9(c), (d)(request for admission and deposition); Texas St. Bar Rules, art. 12, sec. 21 (1973)(rules of civil discovery apply except where in conflict with specific provisions of Bar Rules). The ABA Disciplinary Standards § 8.29 (1979) apparently contemplate only a limited discovery consisting of the exchange of information between the disciplinary counsel and the responding lawyer, but no mention is made of discovery from third parties.

13 Ore.Rev.Stats. 9.750.

14 On the procedures that have been developed to limit law office searches, see § 14.6.4.

15 ABA Disciplinary Standards § 8.32 (1979). Cf. In re Jones, 119 Wis.2d 891, 350 N.W.2d 139 (1984)(state rule gives lawyer, in effect, option of attending or of being disciplined for nonattendance).

Secrecy of Disciplinary Proceedings

Traditionally, the disciplinary process has been conducted in secrecy. In order to protect the reputation of innocent lawyers unjustly accused,[16] all participants have been obliged not to reveal information except when specific exceptions are made to the confidentiality rule.[17] But the public has an interest in systems that purport to be operated in order to protect the public,[18] and some courts have recently opened up the disciplinary process.[19] The Oregon supreme court has held that the state's public-records statute applies to all stages of the disciplinary process from the time of filing a complaint.[20] Other courts have permitted a lawyer to waive the requirement of confidentiality even if the prosecuting counsel does not agree to the waiver.[21] A third set, following the recommendation of the ABA Disciplinary Standards, opens up hearings from the time of the filing of formal charges against a lawyer.[22] Still another group permits a court to order disclosure at its discretion, such as in a request by a legal malpractice litigant seeking evidence developed at a disciplinary hearing on related charges.[23]

[16] Peterson v. Sheran, 474 F.Supp. 1215, 1221 (D.Minn. 1979)("wholesale disclosure of every accusation leveled against attorneys can be a muckraker's holiday, but could serve no useful public purpose."), affirmed in part & vacated in part, 635 F.2d 1335 (8th Cir.1980); People ex rel. Karlin v. Culkin, 248 N.Y. 465, 478-79, 162 N.E. 487, 492 (1928). Confidentiality has also been defended on the ground that the proceedings of a grievance committee investigating a complaint, as with grand jury proceedings, require secrecy in order to protect complainants and witnesses against harassment by lawyers who are the targets of the investigation. See People v. Pacheco, 199 Colo. 470, 618 P.2d 1102, 1103-04 (1980); Florida Bar v. Simon, 171 So.2d 372, 374 (Fla.1964); McLaughlin v. Philadelphia Newspapers, Inc., 465 Pa. 104, 348 A.2d 376, 382-83, 83 A.L.R.3d 727 (1975). On that and related grounds, the National Organization of Bar Counsel has urged retention of broad confidentiality rules. See NOBC, Standards for Dissemination of Disciplinary Information (1980).

[17] McLaughlin v. Philadelphia Newspapers, Inc., 465 Pa. 104, 348 A.2d 376, 83 A.L.R.3d 727 (1975)(no First Amendment right of access to disciplinary hearings); Philadelphia Newspapers, Inc. v. Disciplinary Board, 468 Pa. 382, 363 A.2d 779 (1976)(board had authority to issue rule barring public from disciplinary proceedings, including reinstatement hearing); In re Ross, 99 Nev. 657, 668 P.2d 1089, 1091-92 (1983)(dismissal of charges with direction not to file new charges because extensive breaches of confidentiality have subjected responding lawyers to almost decade of "extra-legal torment"). For an argument that the First Amendment requires some public access to disciplinary hearings, see Erickson, First Amendment Limitations on the Confidentiality of Lawyer Disciplinary and Disability Proceedings, 67 Ky.L.J. 823 (1979).

A departure from a confidentiality rule by giving information about a lawyer's purported crimes to a prosecutor does not lead to suppression of the prosecution or of evidence in it. E.g., State v. Merski, 121 N.H. 901, 437 A.2d 710 (1981), cert.denied 455 U.S. 943, 102 S.Ct. 1439, 71 L.Ed.2d 655 (1982). Many states have made narrow provision for release of information about lawyer crimes to a prosecutor. E.g., State v. Pacheco, 199 Colo. 470, 618 P.2d 1102 (1980)(exception to secrecy rule for disclosure when ordered by court permits response to carefully tailored prosecutor's request for information about complaining parties not known to prosecutor); New Jersey v. Stroger, 97 N.J. 391, 478 A.2d 1175 (1984), cert.denied ___ U.S. ___, 105 S.Ct. 971, 83 L.Ed.2d 974 (1985) (regulation permitting release of information about crimes to prosecutor not inconsistent with general rule on confidentiality); ABA Disciplinary Standards § 3.15 (1979).

[18] Dep't of Air Force v. Rose, 425 U.S. 352, 96 S.Ct. 1592, 48 L.Ed.2d 11 (1976)(substantial public interest in operation of military academy honor codes requires disclosure under Freedom of Information Act of summaries of disciplinary proceedings).

[19] In re Arkansas Bar Ass'n, 666 S.W.2d (Advance Sheets) lix (1984)(rejecting bar proposal to return to closed hearings; majority of judges believe that open hearings lend credibility and improperly accused lawyers will receive public vindication).

[20] Sadler v. Oregon State Bar, 275 Or. 279, 550 P.2d 1218, 83 A.L.R.3d 762 (1976). Contra, e.g., Attorney Grievance Comm'n v. A.S.Abell Co., 294 Md. 680, 452 A.2d 656 (1982)(state's public information act providing access to "public records" inapplicable to disposition of complaints filed against lawyers).

[21] Capoccia v. Committee on Professional Standards, 59 N.Y.2d 549, 466 N.Y.S.2d 268, 453 N.E.2d 497 (1983) (if lawyer waives confidentiality in writing, hearings shall be open unless closure ordered for good cause).

[22] The ABA Disciplinary Standards §§ 8.24, 8.25 (1979), recommend confidentiality as a general rule until formal charges are filed, unless the proceedings are based upon conviction of a crime or upon allegations that have become generally known or unless the responding lawyer waives confidentiality. Once formal charges are filed, the proceeding (except for deliberations of the hearing panel) are to be open unless a protective order is issued.

[23] Attorney Grievance Comm'n v. Strathen, 287 Md. 111, 411 A.2d 102 (1980)(trial court could authorize disclosure of testimony of complainant before disciplinary hearing panel for use by lawyer in cross-examining complainant who had filed legal malpractice suit based on same occurrence); Porter v. Doe (Mass.1983); Axler v. An Attorney, (Mass.1983)(neither reported; cited in 69 ABA J. 569 (1983))(disclosure to legal malpractice plaintiff).

Secrecy rules also implicate the provisions of the lawyer codes dealing with extrajudicial comment (see § 12.2.2). The provisions of DR 7-107(A)-(E), restricting public commentary on criminal trials, are made expressly applicable to lawyer disciplinary proceedings by DR 7-107(F). Model Rule 3.6, on trial publicity, contains no similar provision or comment except the general rule (MR 3.6(a)) prohibiting "extrajudicial" statements that "have a substantial likelihood of materially prejudicing an adjudicative proceeding." [24]

Rules of Evidence

Disciplinary hearings are conducted much in the manner of administrative proceedings tried before a hearing officer.[25] Strict rules such as those followed in jury-tried cases are not enforced.[26] The rules of evidence are flexible, and because members of the hearing body are typically trained in the law and ultimate review is typically de novo before an appellate court, it is unlikely that a prejudicial error can be committed by admitting irrelevant or prejudicial evidence. Because the proceedings are not criminal in nature, courts have generally refused to apply exclusionary rules and, for example, have refused to suppress evidence seized in violation of the lawyer's constitutional rights.[27]

Burden of Proof

The burden of proving a violation is on the disciplinary prosecutor, who must offer proof from which the hearing panel can find misconduct if it is persuaded to the degree required by the standard of proof prevailing in the jurisdiction.[28] In general the lawyer need explain nothing. For example, the burden of proof does not shift to the lawyer to explain suspicious circumstances [29] or questionable advertising that is not shown to have violated any rule.[30] Because the hearing typically concerns itself with all issues, including any evidence of mitigation that a lawyer might wish to offer, a lawyer may as a practical matter be limited in offering explanatory information because it might be regarded as corroborating or implicitly admitting the charges.[31]

Courts, although they employ different catchwords, speak of three different standards

24 For a critique of strictures on lawyer comment on pending disciplinary charges, with a suggested rule providing for preclearance of public statements with the disciplinary agency, see Erickson, First Amendment Limitations on the Confidentiality of Lawyer Disciplinary and Disability Proceedings, 67 Ky.L.J. 823 (1979).

25 The ABA Disciplinary Standards § 8.31 (1979) recommends following the rules of evidence for nonjury civil trials employed in the jurisdiction. Those probably differ little from administrative agency rules of evidence in most jurisdictions.

26 In re Wilson, 76 Ariz. 49, 258 P.2d 433 (1953); Attorney Grievance Comm'n v. Kerpelman, 288 Md. 341, 420 A.2d 940, 949 (1980), cert. denied 450 U.S. 970, 101 S.Ct. 1492, 67 L.Ed.2d 621 (1981); In re Goldman, 179 Mont. 526, 588 P.2d 964, 977-78 (1978); North Carolina St. Bar v. Talman, 62 N.C.App. 355, 303 S.E.2d 175 (1983), review denied 309 N.C. 192, 305 S.E.2d 189 (1983).

27 Emslie v. State Bar, 11 Cal.3d 210, 113 Cal.Rptr. 175, 520 P.2d 991 (1974)(police officer making illegal arrest of unknown person would clearly not have been deterred by knowledge that lawyer disciplinary board would exclude evidence); People v. Harfmann, 638 P.2d 745, 20 A.L.R.4th 539 (Colo.1981)(evidence that clearly and unequivocally establishes misconduct, even if excluded from lawyer's criminal trial, can be introduced in disciplinary proceedings so long as official misconduct in obtaining the evidence does not shock the judicial conduct and was not obtained in bad faith); Florida Bar v. Lancaster, 448 So.2d 1019 (Fla.1984)(transcript of conversation between lawyer and roommate recorded in lawyer's home by warrantless electronic surveillance admissible); McInnis v. State, 618 S.W.2d 389 (Tex.Civ.App.1981), cert.denied 456 U.S. 976, 102 S.Ct. 2242, 72 L.Ed.2d 851 (1982)(tape recording of conversation between lawyer and client not suppressible even if government's conduct was "outrageous"). Cf. I.N.S. v. Lopez-Mendoza, ___ U.S. ___, 104 S.Ct. 3479, 82 L.Ed.2d 778 (1984) (evidence derived from illegal arrest can be employed in civil deportation hearing). Contra In re Langley, 230 Or. 319, 370 P.2d 228 (1962).

28 ABA Disciplinary Standards § 8.37 (1979).

29 In re Thorup, 432 A.2d 1221 (D.C.App.1981)(mere introduction of docket sheet showing lawyer's failure to file motion and grant of motion by successor lawyer does not shift burden of explaining actions to lawyer); In re Holman, 297 Or. 36, 682 P.2d 243, 260 (1984)(suspicious bookkeeping practices insufficient to require respondent to disprove specific intent).

30 In re Marcus, 107 Wis.2d 560, 320 N.W.2d 806, 815 (1982).

31 Cf., In re Smith, 75 Ill.2d 134, 25 Ill.Dec. 660, 387 N.E.2d 316 (1979), cert.denied 444 U.S. 841, 100 S.Ct. 81, 63 L.Ed.2d 53 (1979)(lawyer not denied due process by being required to present mitigation evidence prior to panel's finding of misconduct).

by which the fact finder is to assess the persuasive power of the proof against a lawyer. By far the most commonly employed standard is the "clear and convincing" formulation:[32] the evidence must demonstrate misconduct in a way that is both clear and convincing.[33] The words, as is apparent, mean little by themselves. It is somewhat more helpful to know that the clear-and-convincing formulation stands at a metaphorical midpoint between the other two formulations.[34] Those include the "preponderance of the evidence" standard,[35] the one commonly employed in civil trials, and the "beyond a reasonable doubt" standard,[36] which constitutionally must be applied [37] in criminal cases.

The three standards, at least theoretically, mark points along a continuum that ranges (1) from evidence that is just barely more persuasive of the facts needed to prove misconduct than unsatisfactory for that purpose [38] (2) through evidence that leaves the fact finder in a more contentedly convinced state of mind (3) to the ultimate state of vigorous and indubitable conviction free of any plausible explanation other than guilt of the charges. The assumption is that a jurisdiction that adopts the "preponderance" standard will more likely find a lawyer guilty, while such a finding becomes progressively less likely in jurisdictions that apply the "clear and convincing" and "beyond a reasonable doubt" standards. Accepting that assumption, or at least persuaded by its symbolic importance, the Supreme Court has insisted that the "clear and convincing" formula must be applied in civil cases in which a fundamental "liberty" interest, as opposed to a mere "property," interest is at stake.[39] Most courts that have addressed the issue, however, have regarded a lawyer disciplinary action as one in which only a property interest is at stake.[40]

[32] That is the standard recommended by the ABA Disciplinary Standards § 8.39 (1979), although no reason is given for selecting it.

[33] In re Morford, 46 Del. 144, 80 A.2d 429, 432 (1951) (convincing preponderance); Committee on Professional Ethics v. Kraschel, 260 Ia. 187, 148 N.W.2d 621, 625 (1967)(convincing preponderance); Disciplinary Bd. of Hawaii Supreme Court v. Kim, 59 Haw. 449, 583 P.2d 333, 335 (1978)(clear and convincing); In re Melnick, 383 Ill. 200, 48 N.E.2d 935 (1943)(clear and convincing); State v. Phelps, 226 Kan. 371, 598 P.2d 180 (1979), cert. denied 444 U.S. 1045, 100 S.Ct. 732, 62 L.Ed.2d 731 (1980)(substantial, clear, convincing, and satisfactory evidence); Louisiana St. Bar Ass'n v. Mitchell, 375 So.2d 1350, 1352 (La.1979)(clear and convincing); State ex rel. Nebraska St. Bar Ass'n v. Hollstein, 202 Neb. 40, 274 N.W.2d 508, 515 (1979)(clear preponderance); In re Sears, 71 N.J. 175, 364 A.2d 777, 788-89 (1976)(clear and convincing); In re Palmer, 296 N.C. 638, 252 S.E.2d 784, 789-90 (1979)(exhaustive collection of authorities); In re Maragos, 285 N.W.2d 541, 545-46 (N.D.1979)(clear and convincing); Carter v. Folcarelli, 121 R.I. 667, 402 A.2d 1175, 1177 (1979)(clear and convincing); Committee on Legal Ethics v. Pence, 161 W.Va. 240, 240 S.E.2d 668, 671, 93 A.L.R.3d 1046 (1977)(full, clear, and preponderating); State v. Preston, 38 Wis.2d 582, 588, 157 N.W.2d 615, 159 N.W.2d 684, cert.denied 393 U.S. 981, 89 S.Ct. 452, 21 L.Ed.2d 442 (1968)(clear and satisfactory, the middle burden of proof).

[34] Committee on Professional Ethics v. Bitter, 279 N.W.2d 521 (Iowa 1979)(clear-and-convincing standard requires more satisfying evidence than in normal civil case and less than required in criminal case).

[35] In re Walton, 676 P.2d 1078 (Alaska 1983), appeal dismissed ___ U.S. ___, 105 S.Ct. 54, 83 L.Ed.2d 6 (1984); Me.Bar Rules, rule 6(C)(amended 1980); In re Weiner, 547 S.W.2d 459, 461 (Mo.1977); In re Capoccia, 59 N.Y.2d 549, 466 N.Y.S.2d 268, 453 N.E.2d 497 (1983); State ex rel. Oklahoma Bar Ass'n v. Haworth, 593 P.2d 765 (Okl. 1979); In re Berlant, 458 Pa. 439, 328 A.2d 471 (1974), cert.denied 421 U.S. 964, 95 S.Ct. 1953, 44 L.Ed.2d 451 (1975); McInnis v. State, 618 S.W.2d 389, 397 (Tex.Civ. App.1981), cert. denied 456 U.S. 976, 102 S.Ct. 2242, 72 L.Ed.2d 851 (1982).

[36] Rules & Regulations of the St. Bar of Georgia, rule 4-221(e), 241 Ga. 643, 760 (1978).

[37] In re Winship, 397 U.S. 358, 90 S.Ct. 1068, 25 L.Ed.2d 368 (1970).

[38] An even less demanding standard was once applied by an administrative agency in suspending a lawyer, if an appellate court's report is to be credited. In Charlton v. FTC, 543 F.2d 903 (D.C.Cir.1976), the court reversed an agency's discipline of its own lawyer that was based on "substantial evidence" of a violation that was reportedly not the preponderance but "something less than the weight of the evidence."

[39] Addington v. Texas, 441 U.S. 418, 99 S.Ct. 1804, 60 L.Ed.2d 323 (1979) (civil commitment for mental incompetence or dangerousness); Fedorenko v. United States, 449 U.S. 490, 101 S.Ct. 737, 66 L.Ed.2d 686 (1981)(denaturalization proceeding); Santosky v. Kramer, 455 U.S. 745, 102 S.Ct. 1388, 71 L.Ed.2d 599 (1982)(termination of parental rights).

[40] In re Walton, 676 P.2d 1078 (Alaska 1983), appeal dismissed ___ U.S. ___, 105 S.Ct. 54, 83 L.Ed.2d 6 (1984); In re Moore, 453 N.E.2d 971 (Ind.1983)(fundamental liberty interest not at stake in lawyer discipline, but clear and convincing test adopted nonetheless); In re Capoccia, 59 N.Y.2d 549, 466 N.Y.S.2d 268, 453 N.E.2d 497, 499 (1983). Cf. Steadman v. SEC, 450 U.S. 91, 101 S.Ct. 999, 67 L.Ed. 2d 69 (1981)(SEC appropriately applied preponderance

Therefore the clear and convincing standard is not constitutionally required.

Despite their connection to constitutional values, it is clear that application of the standards is not susceptible to measurement in individual cases because the operation to which the standards relate is a largely subjective mental task applied to a matrix of indeterminate data. In each instance, the evidence is subjected to the scrutiny of assessors whose competence and stomach for the task probably varies greatly. The assessment depends upon unarticulated assumptions, values, and biases of panel members and reviewing courts. Each standard must be applied to evidence that is often conflicting and subject to differing inferences. Thus it must probably remain entirely a matter of speculation whether the fact that a jurisdiction follows one standard or another, or shifts from one standard to another, produces any discernible difference in the kinds of cases that are prosecuted or the percentage of prosecuted cases that result in various kinds of findings and sanctions.

Courts, however, have another reason than quantifiably verifiable differences in outcome for applying one standard instead of another. The bare-preponderance test, at least verbally, states only a minimal societal interest in reaching a result that is not erroneous.[41] In a case in which a lawyer's investment in a career is at stake and in which the social interest in avoiding erroneous sanctions is correspondingly high, the clear-and-convincing standard better marks the nature of the impact of a disciplinary decree upon the accused lawyer. Yet adoption of that standard implies that there is a low social interest in assuring that lawyers who pose a serious threat to future clients and to the legal system are detected and disciplined. When strong social interests in correct outcomes can be asserted on both sides, a court well might be disposed to resort to the preponderance standard.[42] Resort is dictated, not by the low social importance of the outcome, but by the strong, yet conflicting, social interests in results. It seems clear, however, that the realm of proof beyond a reasonable doubt speaks with the special awe that has been reserved for the impositions of the criminal law, when a relatively higher risk of nonconviction is tolerated.[43] The stigma of disbarment is, in the society's order of values, less than that of adjudication of criminal guilt, and thus there is no need to resort to the criminal standard of proof.

There is no requirement that the charge be made out, and the applicable burden satisfied, with any specific kind of evidence, so long as the evidence is properly produced before the hearing agency. Proof may come directly from an eyewitness or be established circumstantially. The testimony of a client or other person is sufficient, if believed, to establish a charge, even if it is denied by the lawyer.[44] But a finding that a lawyer has violated a rule cannot rest entirely upon "obverse inference"—the hearing panel's conviction that the lawyer's denials are false and in fact demonstrate the contrary.[45] Evidence that is sharply in conflict may nonetheless properly be taken to demonstrate a violation by clear and convincing evidence.[46]

standard in disciplinary action against investment adviser).

41 Addington v. Texas, 441 U.S. 418, 423, 99 S.Ct. 1804, 1807, 60 L.Ed.2d 323 (1979).

42 In re Walton, 676 P.2d 1078, 1085 (Alaska 1983), appeal dismissed ___ U.S. ___, 105 S.Ct. 54, 83 L.Ed.2d 6 (1984).

43 In re Winship, 397 U.S. 358, 370, 90 S.Ct. 1068, 1075, 25 L.Ed.2d 368 (1970)(Harlan, J., concurring).

44 In re James, 452 A.2d 163, 166-67 (D.C.App.1982), cert. denied 460 U.S. 1038, 103 S.Ct. 1429, 75 L.Ed.2d 789 (1983); Attorney Grievance Comm'n v. Kerpelman, 292 Md. 228, 438 A.2d 501, 507 (1981), cert. denied 450 U.S. 970, 101 S.Ct. 1492, 67 L.Ed.2d 621 (1981).

45 Edmondson v. State Bar, 29 Cal.3d 339, 172 Cal.Rptr. 899, 625 P.2d 812 (1981).

46 In re Weiner, 120 Ariz. 349, 586 P.2d 194, 198 (1978); Attorney Grievance Comm'n v. Kerpelman, 288 Md. 341, 420 A.2d 940, 949 (1980), cert. denied 450 U.S. 970, 101 S.Ct. 1492, 67 L.Ed.2d 621 (1981). But cf. In re Horton, 100 N.M. 13, 665 P.2d 275, 276 (1983)(dictum) (greater evidentiary demands of clear-and-convincing standard require that testimony of single witness denied under oath by lawyer must be corroborated).

Findings

The hearing panel prepares findings of fact and recommendations for a sanction if a violation is found. The findings are important as the basis for judicial review, although, as will be seen, courts typically insist that they review the record itself and without deference to ultimate findings of the panel.[47] The findings must be based on evidence properly before the agency, not on evidence gathered firsthand by members of the agency and thus not subjected to the winnowing process of the hearing or evidence heard but rejected at the hearing.[48]

§ 3.4.5 Review

General

Once a hearing panel has made findings and recommended a disposition, review can be had by either the disciplinary prosecutor or the accused lawyer. Some jurisdictions provide for review by the agency of which the hearing panel is a part.[49] Others permit the hearing body to impose mild sanctions without further review but require judicial imposition of sanctions that are more substantial.

Judicial Review

Modern procedures[50] in most jurisdictions provide for review by the highest court of recommendations made by disciplinary agencies.[51] The higher court will normally accept the findings and recommendations of the hearing body. But most courts refuse to be bound in all cases by findings of fact or suggestions for discipline and sometimes make their own findings or impose their own conception of appropriate discipline.[52] The articulated standards under which the states' supreme courts exercise their review function vary. Three standards of review are commonly encountered, the first of them much more often than the others. (1) De novo review permits the reviewing court to substitute its own judgment on matters of credibility and inference and freely to reach conclusions different from those of the hearing panel.[53] (2)

[47] See infra at n. 52.

[48] In re Thorup, 432 A.2d 1221, 1226 (D.C.App.1981).

[49] See ABA Disciplinary Standards 65-66 (1979). The procedure apparently assumes a large docket of discipline cases in which routine review of findings and recommendations of hearing panels is desirable.

[50] Nineteenth-century courts dispensed lawyer discipline in the setting of a lawsuit, without hearing panels or other administrative trappings. E.g., In re Cooper, 22 N.Y. 67 (1860)(because discipline is a judicial act, decision by lower court to impose sanctions is reviewable according to normal rules of appeal).

[51] Failure to comply with procedural requirements may prevent a party from obtaining judicial review. E.g., In re Ojala, 289 N.W.2d 108 (Minn.1979)(findings of referee become conclusive unless either party orders transcript of hearing within five days of filing of referee's findings and conclusions).

In systems that provide for an initial hearing before a hearing panel and appellate review before an administrative agency of which the panel is a part, standards of review governing the reviewing agency must also be propounded. E.g., In re Daggs, 411 Mich. 304, 307 N.W.2d 66, 71 (1981)(reviewing board must articulate reasons for rejecting findings or conclusions of hearing officer or panel); In re Kennedy, 97 Wn.2d 719, 649 P.2d 110, 111 (1982)(same). Cf. ABA Disciplinary Standards 65-66 (1979).

[52] Suggested sanctions rejected as too lenient: E.g., Cain v. State Bar, 25 Cal.3d 956, 160 Cal.Rptr. 362, 603 P.2d 464 (1979)(disbarment, rather than probation after suspension, for repeated misappropriations of client funds); Committee on Professional Ethics v. Crary, 245 N.W.2d 298, 302-03 (Iowa 1976)(disbarment rather than reprimand after court ordered further proceedings on own motion); In re Stroh, 97 Wn.2d 289, 644 P.2d 1161 (1982), cert. denied 459 U.S. 1202, 103 S.Ct. 1187, 75 L.Ed. 2d 434 (1983)(court sua sponte raised issue of increase in sanction and ordered disbarment); In re Sedor, 73 Wis.2d 629, 245 N.W.2d 895 (1976).

[53] Davidson v. State Bar, 17 Cal.3d 570, 131 Cal.Rptr. 379, 551 P.2d 1211 (1976)(court reweighs evidence and passes upon its sufficiency); Kentucky Bar Ass'n v. Cohen, 625 S.W.2d 573, 574 (Ky.1981), cert. denied 456 U.S. 1007, 102 S.Ct. 2298, 73 L.Ed.2d 1301 (1982)(recommendation of bar is advisory only; court must judge factual as well as legal issues); Attorney Grievance Comm'n v. Stewart, 285 Md. 251, 401 A.2d 1026, cert. denied 444 U.S. 845, 100 S.Ct. 89, 62 L.Ed.2d 58 (1979) ("independent review" standard); Levi v. Mississippi St. Bar, 436 So.2d 781, 782 (Miss.1983)("We are the triers of fact."); State ex rel. Oklahoma Bar Ass'n v. Raskin, 642 P.2d 262, 266 (Okl.1982)(court must pass on sufficiency and weight of evidence); Burns v. Clayton, 237 S.C. 316, 117 S.E.2d 300 (1960)(findings of disciplinary board advisory only, and court not in any way bound to accept findings or recommendations). Some courts insist that they are not bound by stipulations as to the level of discipline that are entered into by both the lawyer and the disciplinary prosecutor. E.g., In re Lee, 283 N.W.2d 179, 181 (N.D. 1979).

Under the "substantial evidence on the whole record" test, the court will normally accept factual determinations but will override them in compelling instances and in most cases will more freely draw its own conclusions on matters of inference.[54] And (3) under the "any competent evidence" standard, findings and conclusions will be accepted if they have any evidentiary support in the record made before the hearing panel.[55] The second and third standards obviously place at an intended disadvantage a lawyer or bar counsel who attempts to overturn an adverse finding; such a party bears the burden of demonstrating error.[56]

Choice of the standard involves a balance of fairness and consistency in rule application on the one hand and efficiency and similar considerations of judicial administration on the other. Practicalities also play a part and are at the base of the common attitude that findings of a disciplinary body based on conflicting testimony will normally not be disturbed because of the hearing panel's more advantageous position from which to determine the accuracy and veracity of testimony.[57] That superiority follows from the fact that whatever the standard of review, the appellate procedures in all states are similar and consist of review of the record made before the hearing panel without the reviewing court's hearing any live testimony on its own.[58]

Federal Court Review [59]

The federal courts have a limited power to review state court decisions dealing with the legal profession and a similarly limited power to review the validity of state court rule making with respect to the legal profession. The view is sometimes asserted that "since the founding of the Republic, the licensing and regulation of lawyers has been left exclusively to the States and the District of Columbia within their respective jurisdictions." [60] That is accurate only in the limited sense that during most of the years since 1789 the regulation of the legal profession has primarily, but not exclusively, been carried out by the states. Yet, at a minimum, the federal courts have always regulated lawyers appearing in federal courts (see § 2.2.5). And in many

A variation is for the court to announce a de novo review standard but indicate that customarily the court will defer to the agency's findings and recommendations because of its expertise. E.g., In re Simpson, 645 P.2d 1223, 1226 (Alaska 1982); State ex rel. Oklahoma Bar Ass'n v. Haworth, 593 P.2d 765, 767 (Okl.1979)(although court reviews weight of evidence, it will not reverse trial authority's fact-findings unless against clear weight of evidence); In re Judd, 629 P.2d 435, 437-38 (Utah 1981).

54 Walker v. Supreme Court Comm. on Professional Conduct, 275 Ark. 158, 628 S.W.2d 552, 555 (1982)(findings must not be contrary to weight of evidence); In re Dwyer, 399 A.2d 1, 11 (D.C.App.1979)(substantial-evidence standard); North Carolina St. Bar v. DuMont, 304 N.C. 627, 286 S.E.2d 89, 98-99 (1982)(whole-record standard).

55 Attorney Grievance Comm'n v. Kerpelman, 288 Md. 341, 420 A.2d 940, 946-47 (1980), cert. denied 450 U.S. 970, 101 S.Ct. 1492, 67 L.Ed.2d 621 (1981); Blue v. Seventh District Committee, 220 Va. 1056, 265 S.E.2d 753, 757 (1980)(lawyer complained against has choice of trial by jury or by bar discipline board; jury findings given finality under strict review standard, but board findings will be rejected if not "justified by a reasonable view of the evidence").

56 In re Haggard, 123 Ariz. 27, 597 P.2d 180, 181 (1979); Baranowski v. State Bar, 24 Cal.3d 153, 154 Cal.Rptr. 752, 593 P.2d 613, 617 (1979); State ex rel. Oklahoma St. Bar Ass'n v. Raskin, 642 P.2d 262, 265 (Okl.1982).

57 Himmel v. State Bar, 4 Cal.3d 786, 794, 94 Cal.Rptr. 825, 484 P.2d 993, (1971); In re Miller, 95 Wn.2d 453, 625 P.2d 701, 703 (1981).

58 Due process does not require that the court making the final and binding factual determinations hear the witnesses' testimony. See Mildner v. Gulotta, 405 F.Supp. 182 (E.D.N.Y.1975)(three-judge court), affirmed 406 U.S. 901, 96 S.Ct. 1489, 47 L.Ed.2d 751 (1976)(per curiam); Razatos v. Colorado Supreme Court, 549 F.Supp. 798 (D.Colo.1982), affirmed 746 F.2d 1429 (10th Cir.1984).

59 See generally Martineau, The Supreme Court and State Regulation of the Legal Profession, 8 Hast.Const. L.Q. 199 (1981).

60 Leis v. Flynt, 439 U.S. 438, 442, 99 S.Ct. 698, 700, 58 L.Ed.2d 717 (1979) (per curiam). See also In re Griffiths, 413 U.S. 717, 730-31, 93 S.Ct. 2851, 2859, 37 L.Ed.2d 910 (1973) (Burger, C.J., dissenting)("[T]he States reserved, among other powers, that of regulating the practice of professions within their own borders. . . . [T]hat concept . . . was made part of the 'bargain' to create a federal union . . . . [T]he Court now strikes down a power of the States [to regulate the bar by excluding resident aliens from law practice] accepted as fundamental since 1787. . . .). But see, e.g., Sperry v. Florida, 373 U.S. 379, 403, 83 S.Ct. 1322, 1335, 10 L.Ed.2d 428 (1963) (Tenth Amendment argument against power of Congress to set aside Florida Supreme Court's restrictions against nonlawyer practice before federal Patent Office is "singularly without merit.").

cases the Supreme Court itself has reviewed judicial action of the state courts that regulated lawyers.[61] A tradition nonetheless exists, founded on considerations of federalism, under which lower federal courts exercise only a limited power of review over state admission and discipline decisions.

The federalism doctrine divides review of state court action of a judicial, administrative, or legislative nature that has an impact upon the legal profession basically in the following way. The lower federal courts ordinarily[62] have no jurisdiction to review state court exercises of judicial powers, as opposed to state court exercises of legislative or administrative powers. Thus state adjudications dealing with such matters as the discipline of an individual lawyer cannot be reviewed in the lower federal courts.[63] A lawyer-litigant who seeks federal court review of a judicial act of a state court applying or refusing to waive a rule on a matter of bar discipline or admission can ordinarily obtain review only in the United States Supreme Court, assuming that other jurisdictional requirements have also been met.[64] On the other hand, state court action of a legislative or administrative nature can be challenged on federal statutory or constitutional grounds in the lower federal courts.[65] Continuing according to the largely reciprocal rules, a petitioner cannot obtain review in the Supreme Court of a state court order that is essentially the administrative or legislative act of the state court in promulgating a bar regulation; that follows from the doctrine that the Supreme Court's powers are limited to review of judicial decisions of state courts, as opposed to legislative, administrative, or ministerial orders.[66]

Pivotal to the difference between the jurisdictions of the Supreme Court and the lower federal courts is the distinction between adjudication on the one hand and legislation and administrative action on the other. There is at least a rough correspondence here between the general and the particular. An attack on the particular application of a state disciplinary or other rule to an individual lawyer typically involves an adjudicative act of a state court, which will not be interfered with by a lower federal court.[67] Once state court action of that kind has become final, it cannot

[61] In District of Columbia Ct. Apps. v. Feldman, 460 U.S. 462, 476 n.15, 103 S.Ct. 1303, 1314 n.15, 75 L.Ed.2d 206 (1983), the Supreme Court cited eight decisions in the period between 1957 and 1982 in which it had "review[ed] state court decisions on bar-related matters."

[62] The Supreme Court has stated, however, that a lawyer may be able to obtain lower federal court review of disciplinary or similar actions taken in bad faith or under flagrantly and patently unconstitutional regulations. Middlesex Cty. Ethics Comm. v. Garden St. Bar Ass'n, 457 U.S. 423, 102 S.Ct. 2515, 73 L.Ed.2d 116 (1982). See also Mildner v. Gulotta, 405 F.Supp. 182, 196-99 (E.D.N.Y. 1975)(three-judge court), affirmed 425 U.S. 901, 96 S.Ct. 1489, 47 L.Ed.2d 751 (1976); American Civil Liberties Union v. Bozardt, 539 F.2d 340 (4th Cir.1976), cert.denied 429 U.S. 1022, 97 S.Ct. 639, 50 L.Ed.2d 623 (1976).

[63] Theard v. United States, 354 U.S. 278, 282, 77 S.Ct. 1274, 1276, 1 L.Ed.2d 1342 (1957); Selling v. Radford, 243 U.S. 46, 50, 37 S.Ct. 377, 61 L.Ed. 585 (1917); Silverton v. Dep't of Treasury, 644 F.2d 1341 (9th Cir.), cert. denied 454 U.S. 895, 102 S.Ct. 393, 70 L.Ed.2d 210 (1981); Phelps v. Kansas Supreme Court, 662 F.2d 649 (10th Cir.1981), cert.denied 456 U.S. 944, 102 S.Ct. 2009, 72 L.Ed.2d 466 (1982).

[64] District of Columbia Ct. Apps. v. Feldman, 460 U.S. 462, 103 S.Ct. 1303, 75 L.Ed.2d 206 (1983); In re Summers, 325 U.S. 561, 65 S.Ct. 1307, 89 L.Ed. 1795 (1945). Sometimes the denial of jurisdiction of the lower federal courts to review discipline or admission decisions in adjudicated cases has been put on the ground that a litigant cannot circumvent the obligation to seek direct review in the Supreme Court. E.g., Martinez Rivera v. Trias Monge, 587 F.2d 539 (lst Cir.1978).

[65] Zimmerman v. Grievance Committee of Fifth Jud. Distr., 726 F.2d 85 (2d Cir.), cert. denied ___ U.S. ___, 104 S.Ct. 2681, 81 L.Ed.2d 876 (1984); Doe v. Pringle, 550 F.2d 596 (10th Cir.1976), cert.denied 431 U.S. 916, 97 S.Ct. 2179, 53 L.Ed.2d 227 (1977), cited and approved in District of Columbia Ct. Apps. v. Feldman, 103 S.Ct. at 1316. A state ethics committee sanction, such as a private letter of admonition, which is not subject to judicial review in a state's courts, is administrative in nature and may be challenged in a lower federal court. See Miller v. Washington St. Bar Ass'n, 679 F.2d 1313 (9th Cir.1982).

[66] In re Summers, 325 U.S. 561, 566, 65 S.Ct. 1307, 1310, 89 L.Ed. 1795 (1945). The question whether a state court's proceedings are judicial, and thus reviewable in the Supreme Court, or a nonreviewable legislative, administrative, or ministerial act is a question of federal law. In re Summers, 325 U.S. at 566, 65 S.Ct. at 1310; District of Columbia Ct. Apps. v. Feldman, 460 U.S. 462, 476 n.13, 103 S.Ct. 1303, 1311 n.13, 75 L.Ed.2d 206 (1983).

[67] District of Columbia Ct. Apps. v. Feldman, 460 U.S. 462, 103 S.Ct. 1303, 75 L.Ed.2d 206 (1983); Brown v. Board of Bar Examiners, 623 F.2d 605, 609 (9th Cir.1980); Feldman v. State Bd. of Law Examiners, 438 F.2d 699, 704 (8th Cir.1971).

be challenged in a lower federal court for reasons of both federalism and res judicata.[68] In contrast, a federal court attack upon a state rule in general, without regard to the facts of its particular application, tends to be regarded as an attack upon a legislative or administrative action that can be launched first in the lower federal courts.[69]

The restriction on federal court review of nonadjudicative state action involving the legal profession was most recently explored in District of Columbia Court of Appeals v. Feldman.[70] The Court there embraced the distinction between an attack on a general rule and an attack on a specific application of a general rule to a lawyer. Feldman's attack in the lower federal courts relied on federal grounds in seeking to demonstrate that his petition to the District of Columbia court was improperly denied. His petition had sought admission to the bar of the District of Columbia without satisfaction of the requirement of education in an ABA-accredited law school because, he asserted, his unique circumstances demonstrated that he had obtained the functional equivalent of such an education. The Court concluded that that attack merely challenged the application of a general rule to a specific applicant (through the local court's denial of his petition). Accordingly the Court held that the lower federal courts should not have reviewed the state action.[71] To an extent, the *Feldman* approach makes the question of federal court jurisdiction depend upon the nature of the action requested by the complaining lawyer in the state court, the nature of the proceedings employed by the state court in response, and the types of attacks that the dissatisfied lawyer chooses to make in the subsequent federal court action.[72]

Bar Discipline and Res Judicata

A decree of a disciplinary agency or court sanctioning a lawyer or dismissing charges may have ramifications for the future. As will be seen, a finding of misconduct may result in a variety of forms of discipline (§ 3.5), may form the basis for reciprocal discipline in other jurisdictions (§ 3.4.5), and may be used to enhance the sanction received in a subsequent disciplinary proceeding (§ 3.5.2—repetition of misconduct).[73] Disciplinary agencies, on the common sense notion that smoke suggests fire, also tend to pay attention even to former charges that were dismissed, despite the obviously differentiating fact that dismissed charges indicate that the complaint might have been illfounded.[74] A finding of misconduct in a disciplinary case will also

68 District of Columbia Ct. Apps. v. Feldman, 460 U.S. 462, 103 S.Ct. 1303, 1315-17, 75 L.Ed.2d 206 (1983). *Feldman* indicates that jurisdiction was erroneously exercised in cases such as Ktsanes v. Underwood, 552 F.2d 740 (7th Cir.1977), cert.denied 435 U.S. 933, 98 S.Ct. 1508, 55 L.Ed. 2d 530 (1978)(Illinois Supreme Court's denial of lawyer's petition for exemption from admission rule is administrative action that can be challenged in federal district court); and Dasher v. Supreme Ct. of Texas, 658 F.2d 1045 (5th Cir.1981)(federal district court has jurisdiction over constitutional claims not raised in state judicial proceeding to obtain admission to state court).

69 The distinctions become blurred when courts use such concepts as that of "ministerial" acts, which are regarded as nonadjudicative and thus as subject to lower federal court review. E.g., Ktsanes v. Underwood, 552 F.2d 740, 743 (7th Cir.1977), cert.denied 435 U.S. 933, 98 S.Ct. 1508, 55 L.Ed.2d 530 (1978). A related fallacy is to judge whether or not a state court determination is adjudicative by examining the nature of the issues that the state court petitioner has chosen to present for decision. Ibid. The former distinction suggests that some state court determinations of individual petitions are administrative-adjudicative, while others are judicial-adjudicative. The latter distinction ignores the operation of the doctrine of res judicata, under which a litigant is normally required to submit all grounds of attack in a single judicial petition.

70 460 U.S. 462, 103 S.Ct. 1303, 75 L.Ed.2d 206 (1983).

71 460 U.S. at 484, 103 S.Ct. at 1316 (discussing with approval Doe v. Pringle, 550 F.2d 596 (10th Cir.1976)), cert. denied 431 U.S. 916, 97 S.Ct. 2179, 53 L.Ed.2d 227 (1977).

72 Lowrie v. Goldenhersh, 716 F.2d 401, 405-08 (7th Cir. 1983).

73 See also, e.g., Disciplinary Board v. Banks, 641 S.W.2d 501, 504-05 (Tenn.1982)(federal court reprimand for private use of trust funds admissible in later state court disciplinary action in order to demonstrate awareness of impropriety of such conduct).

74 In order to cure problems with the lingering ill effects of dismissed charges, the ABA in 1982 voted to amend the ABA Disciplinary Standards to provide for expunging of the records of dismissed charges. See 51 U.S.L.Wk. 2123 (1982). See also, e.g., Berke v. Chattanooga Bar Ass'n, 58 Tenn.App. 636, 436 S.W.2d 296, 309 (1968).

preclude the lawyer from asserting claims in the future inconsistent with the facts necessarily supporting that finding.[75]

Courts have been reluctant to find that prior adjudications in civil or administrative actions have res judicata effects in a pending disciplinary action. A final resolution of prior charges in another disciplinary action will preclude new charges only if the same occurrence is alleged[76] and the same relief is sought.[77] An investigating committee's dismissal of charges will ordinarily be considered to be without prejudice unless the contrary is indicated in the dismissal.[78] And because of the importance of preserving the supreme court's role as the fact finder and final arbiter of lawyer conduct, a finding or other result in civil litigation does not preclude either party from relitigating the same issue in a disciplinary action.[79] As already discussed (§ 3.3.2), a lawyer's acquittal in a criminal case does not bar disciplinary charges based on the same alleged misconduct, but a lawyer's conviction of a crime will operate as res judicata.[80]

§ 3.4.6 Reciprocal Discipline

General

A century ago it was apparently not uncommon for a lawyer disbarred by one court to travel to another community, become admitted to the local bar, and continue to practice law. Without adequate records and communications, reciprocal discipline was a matter of chance. As late as 1970 the Clark Committee found that such evasions of effective sanctions were still common in major metropolitan areas situated in two states, between state and federal courts in the same community, and within states that admitted lawyers on a county-by-county basis.[81]

75 Coogan v. Cincinnati Bar Ass'n, 431 F.2d 1209 (6th Cir.1970), cited with approval in Preiser v. Rodriquez, 411 U.S. 475, 497, 93 S.Ct. 1827, 1840, 36 L.Ed.2d 439 (1973); and Allen v. McCurry, 449 U.S. 90, 97 n.9, 101 S.Ct. 411, 416 n.9, 66 L.Ed.2d 308 (1980).

76 Florida Bar v. Gentry, 447 So.2d 1342 (Fla.1984) (preclusion by merger with prior discipline for misuse of trust funds did not apply to subsequent charge of separate, additional, and continuing misuse of trust funds). See also People v. Forsyth, 191 Colo. 378, 553 P.2d 392 (1976)(several incidents that predated hearing that resulted in suspension relied on, in addition to suspension itself, as grounds for order of disbarment).

77 In re Jafree, 93 Ill.2d 450, 67 Ill.Dec. 104, 444 N.E.2d 143, 147 (1983)(dismissal of petition to transfer lawyer to inactive status because of mental disorder no bar to disciplinary action).

78 State v. Russell, 227 Kan. 897, 610 P.2d 1122, 1130, cert. denied 449 U.S. 893, 101 S.Ct. 400, 66 L.Ed.2d 245 (1980); State Bar v. Woll, 401 Mich. 155, 257 N.W.2d 650 (1977); State v. Sewell, 487 S.W.2d 716 (1972). Some courts have declared more broadly that the double jeopardy rule precluding multiple criminal prosecutions for the same alleged misconduct does not apply to lawyer discipline. E.g., Urbano v. State Bar, 19 Cal.3d 16, 136 Cal.Rptr. 572, 574, 560 P.2d 1 (1977); In re Kesler, 272 Ind. 161, 397 N.E.2d 574, 576 (1979), cert. denied 449 U.S. 829, 101 S.Ct. 96, 66 L.Ed.2d 34 (1980).

79 In re Strong, 616 P.2d 583 (Utah 1980)(disciplinary committee erroneously accepted as evidence findings of federal judge in legal malpractice action against lawyer); In re Kesler, 272 Ind. 161, 397 N.E.2d 574 (1979), cert. denied 449 U.S. 829, 101 S.Ct. 96, 66 L.Ed.2d 34 (1980) (trial court finding that lawyer's conduct complied with applicable rules cannot oust supreme court of its exclusive jurisdiction over issues of lawyer discipline); Levi v. Mississippi St. Bar, 436 So.2d 781, 787 n.1 (Miss.1983) (finding of fraud in civil action based only on preponderance plus inconsistency with court's role as fact finder in discipline cases); Office of Disciplinary Counsel v. Walker, 469 Pa. 432, 366 A.2d 563, 567-68 (1976)(favorable action by trial court in approving fiduciary account no bar to discipline); In re Strong, 616 P.2d 583 (Utah 1980) (federal court's finding of common-law fraud in civil action not binding against lawyer in disciplinary action because such a result would deprive supreme court of its proper function of reviewing all facts de novo). But cf., e.g., In re Burrows, 291 Or. 135, 629 P.2d 820, 826 (1981) (finding of probable cause by committing magistrate necessarily precludes finding that prosecutor lacked probable cause to charge under DR 7-103(A)). In re Jordan, 295 Or. 142, 665 P.2d 341 (1983), raised, but did not answer, the question whether a judge found guilty of misconduct in a judicial disciplinary proceeding is collaterally estopped to deny the same incident of misconduct when made the subject of a lawyer disciplinary charge.

80 Plainly, a finding in a criminal case that a defendant's lawyer had committed misconduct does not bind, and is not even relevant, in a subsequent disciplinary action against the lawyer. E.g., Office of Disciplinary Counsel v. McKinney, 668 S.W.2d 293, 296-97 (Tenn. 1984). Indeed, admission of the results of litigation to which the lawyer was not a party seems offensive to due process.

81 ABA Spec. Comm. on Eval. of Discipl. Enforcement, Problems and Recommendations in Disciplinary Enforcement 116-121, 156-60 (1970).

Courts now function with much more adequate information,[82] and their general rule is that discipline imposed in another jurisdiction can form the basis for local discipline.[83] There is some authority that the original judicial finding of misconduct must be accepted by other states because of the Full Faith and Credit Clause of the federal Constitution.[84] More typically, the second court will adopt the findings of the first court under a modified rule of res judicata.[85] Under it, the second court reserves the prerogative, very rarely exercised,[86] of rejecting the first state's findings if the lawyer can satisfactorily demonstrate that the original findings were seriously defective.[87]

That permits a breadth of inquiry that courts are normally denied by the doctrine of res judicata. The refusal of the second state to apply either Full Faith and Credit or res judicata in a stricter form is justifiable on the view that the question before each state's court is different. The question is whether clients, adversaries, other lawyers, and public institutions in that particular state should be required to deal with a lawyer who has engaged in the proven misconduct. To an extent, the tradition of local control over lawyers also supports the weaker doctrine of reciprocity. Finally, the Supreme Court would be hard put to explain why states are subject to the full vigor of the Full Faith and Credit Clause in lawyer discipline matters when the Court has insisted, as the next section reveals, that federal courts give a degree of deference to state court discipline that is even less respectful than that which modern state reciprocity notions accord to each other and to federal disciplinary decrees.

Most courts extend the reciprocity doctrine to include a practice of imposing a disciplinary sanction that normally will be the same in operative length and severity as that imposed in the first jurisdiction.[88] An inappropriately lenient or severe sanction, however, will not be copied.[89] Reinstatement in the second ju-

82 The Clark Committee could report (id., at 160) that its interim report to the ABA, recommending the establishment of a National Discipline Data Bank to keep all jurisdictions informed of disciplinary action taken against all lawyers, had been acted upon and the data bank established.

83 West Ann.Cal.Bus. & Prof. Code §§ 6049.1, 6049.2 (West 1982)(decree of any court or lawyer disciplinary agency against same lawyer in any state, territory, or federal court is "prima facie" evidence of findings in it; transcript of proceedings in such action or of testimony of witness in any civil proceeding to which charged lawyer was party also admissible); Florida Bar v. Abrams, 402 So.2d 1150 (Fla.1981)(reciprocal discipline based in part on discipline proceeding in Appellate Division of High Court for the Trust Territory of the Pacific Islands (Micronesia)); In re Anschell, 53 A.D.2d 297, 385 N.Y.S.2d 771 (1976)(discipline based on findings of Canadian bar association).

84 See Committee on Professional Ethics v. Sturek, 209 N.W.2d 899 (Iowa 1973). See also, e.g., In re Van Bever, 55 Ariz. 268, 101 P.2d 790 (1940); In re Leverson, 195 Minn. 42, 261 N.W. 480 (1935).

85 In re Witte, 99 Ill.2d 301, 76 Ill.Dec. 84, 458 N.E.2d 484, 487-88 (1984)(under specific Illinois rule); In re Weaver, 272 Ind. 491, 399 N.E.2d 748 (1980)(under Indiana rule making other state's disbarment or suspension "sufficient grounds" for disbarment or suspension in Indiana); In re Kaufman, 81 N.J. 300, 406 A.2d 972, 973 (1979)(under New Jersey rule).

86 But see In re Weiner, 530 S.W.2d 222, 81 A.L.R.3d 1272 (Mo.1975)(newly discovered evidence rejected by first state as ground for setting aside discipline suggests infirmity in finding that precludes second state from adopting findings of first state).

87 N.Y.Ct.Rules (First Dept.) § 603.3(c)(McKinney 1984); In re Witte, 99 Ill.2d 301, 76 Ill.Dec. 84, 458 N.E.2d 484, 486-87 (1983)(first state's findings based on proceedings that comported with procedural due process); In re Nulle, 87 A.D.2d 657, 447 N.Y.S.2d 540 (1982); In re Zimmerman, 277 S.C. 342, 287 S.E.2d 474 (1982)(under court rule). A rule to carry out such an approach was recommended by the Clark Report 121 (1970).

88 In re Goldberg, 460 A.2d 982 (D.C.App.1983)(suspension generally coterminous with first state's, but with possible decrease in term if lawyer voluntarily refrains from local practice and possible increase if lawyer delays unreasonably in notifying second jurisdiction of fact of discipline in first); In re Witte, 91 Ill.2d 301, 76 Ill.Dec. 84, 458 N.E.2d 484, 487 (1983)(suspension coterminous with first state's, and reinstatement in second state conditioned on prior reinstatement in first state unless first state refuses to reinstate within stated period); Attorney Grievance Comm'n v. James, 300 Md. 297, 477 A.2d 1185, 1189 (1984)(similar length of suspension, with reinstatement conditioned on being first reinstated by first jurisdiction); In re Kaufman, 81 N.J. 300, 406 A.2d 972 (1979); In re Nulle, 87 A.D.2d 657, 447 N.Y.S.2d. 540 (1982) (suspension to expire on expiration date of first state's suspension order).

89 Florida Bar v. Abrams, 402 So.2d 1150, 1152-53 (Fla. 1981)(rule that discipline in foreign jurisdiction is conclusive proof of misconduct does not preclude finding additional misconduct and imposing more severe sanction); In re Tumini, 95 N.J. 18, 468 A.2d 707 (1983)(although disbarment in first state permits lawyer to apply for

risdiction is also typically made contingent on satisfactory compliance with the sanctions imposed by the first.[90]

Reciprocity in Federal Courts

Federal courts proceed under a standard that is even less preclusive than the rule followed by most state courts.[91] Although admission to practice in the federal courts is almost entirely derivative from prior admission to practice in a state court, it does not follow that disbarment or suspension in a state court will automatically disbar or suspend the lawyer from practice in the federal court. In Theard v. United States[92] the Supreme Court held that although a disciplinary decree of a state court "brings title deeds of high respect," a federal court considering discipline against a lawyer could not give the judgment conclusive effect. The federal court must permit the disciplined lawyer to show that the federal court should not impose a similar sanction.[93] The Court in *Theard* held that questions raised about the lawyer's mental condition at the time of a forgery committed eighteen years before, which had been the basis for his disbarment in the Louisiana Supreme Court, were sufficiently grave to require a hearing in the lower federal court to determine whether the lawyer's underlying conduct warranted discipline.[94] In general, federal courts seem disposed to accept the findings of state courts and to seek parity between the terms of sanctions.[95]

WESTLAW REFERENCES

45K47

§ 3.5 DISCIPLINARY SANCTIONS

§ 3.5.1 The Process of Determining Sanctions

The Range of Sanctions

At least in theory, a disciplinary agency or court that finds a lawyer in violation of a

reinstatement after five years, when acts of misconduct found in first state would result in permanent disbarment in second, second state will permanently disbar); In re Neff, 83 Ill.2d 20, 46 Ill.Dec. 169, 413 N.E.2d 1282 (1980)(first state's requirement of continuing legal education not required when lawyer asserts that she does not intend to petition for reinstatement in jurisdiction with that requirement and second state does not require continuing legal education).

90 In re Neff, 83 Ill.2d 20, 46 Ill.Dec. 169, 413 N.E.2d 1282 (1980)(when lawyer suspended in Wisconsin did not intend to apply for reinstatement there, she would be reinstated in Illinois only after paying accrued court costs imposed by Wisconsin court).

91 Most federal courts participate in the ABA National Discipline Data Bank, reporting all instances of lawyer discipline and receiving quarterly reports of names of disciplined lawyers to match against the court's own register of admitted lawyers. See Burger, State of the Judiciary Address, in Third Branch, p.2, col.3 (Mar.1979).

92 354 U.S. 278, 282, 77 S.Ct. 1274, 1276, 1 L.Ed.2d 1342 (1957). See also In re Ruffalo, 390 U.S. 544, 547, 88 S.Ct. 1222, 1224, 20 L.Ed.2d 117 (1968).

93 Selling v. Radford, 243 U.S. 46, 50-51, 37 S.Ct. 377, 379, 61 L.Ed. 585 (1917)(federal courts should recognize the judgment of state court unless disciplined lawyer demonstrates (1) that state proceedings offended due process; (2) that "an infirmity of proof as to facts" infected the state court's conclusions; or (3) that acceptance of the state proceedings would be offensive to "principles of right and justice"); In re Randall, 640 F.2d 898, 902 (8th Cir.), cert. denied 454 U.S. 880, 102 S.Ct. 361, 70 L.Ed.2d 189 (1981)(lawyer's civil rights action for damages arising out of state disbarment barred by res judicata as to acts of misconduct; lawyer's resistance to federal court discipline based on state court findings unavailing where federal court's review of record in state court disciplinary hearing finds substantial support for finding of misconduct); In re Thies, 662 F.2d 771 (D.C.Cir.1980)(state disbarment of lawyer convicted of felony, without affording lawyer opportunity for hearing, offended due process and could not form exclusive basis for discipline in U.S. Tax Court); S.Ct.R. 8 (disbarment or suspension in any court of record results in suspension of lawyer as member of bar of Supreme Court, with automatic order to show cause why lawyer should not be disbarred).

94 See also Selling v. Radford, 243 U.S. 46, 37 S.Ct. 377, 60 L.Ed. 585 (1917); In re Ruffalo, 390 U.S. 544, 549-52, 88 S.Ct. 1222, 1225-26, 20 L.Ed.2d 117 (1968) (federal courts' acceptance of conclusions of state disciplinary agency erroneous when state hearing procedures denied due process).

95 Rules of App. Proc. (Second Circuit), rule 46(f)(1) (amended effective January 1978)(lawyer suspended or disbarred in state court shall be disciplined in Second Circuit "upon terms and conditions comparable to those set forth by the other court"); In re Abrams, 521 F.2d 1094 (3d Cir.1975), cert.denied 423 U.S. 1038, 96 S.Ct. 574, 46 L.Ed.2d 413 (1975). But cf. In re Strickland, 453 U.S. 907, 101 S.Ct. 3138, 69 L.Ed.2d 991 (1981)(dissenting opinion of Burger, C.J.)(five-year suspension in New Jersey should be a "per se basis for disbarment by this Court"); In re Sears, 425 F.Supp. 1190 (D.N.J.1977)(dissenting opinion).

mandatory rule will then determine an appropriate sanction. In practice, findings of violation and sanction are almost certainly interdependent in a number of ways. Certain violations call for severe sanctions, while others call for very light sanctions. Human elements doubtless intrude at many points. Under modern disciplinary systems, several scaled sanctions are available, ranging from the least severe sanction of a private informal admonition through private reprimand, public reprimand or censure, and suspension and concluding with the most severe sanction, disbarment.[96] The practical effect of those sanctions varies considerably, however, depending on their terms, as is seen in the sections discussing each of them. Their utility in carrying out the goals of lawyer discipline (§ 3.1) depends upon the will of the court and enforcing agency.

Reservation of Ultimate Determination to Supreme Courts

Generally, state supreme courts claim a power to select for themselves the appropriate sanction to be imposed. Recommendations of disciplinary panels or boards are taken into account.[97] Such deference is particularly appropriate if the disciplinary agency typically deals with the entire array of discipline cases, the court only deals with serious offenses, and the case at issue is on the margins.[98] But on the matter of sanctions, stipulations between the offending lawyer and disciplinary counsel do not bind the court.[99] In the end the court will exercise its own judgment on the basis of its view of the facts and of the seriousness of the offenses (see § 3.4.5). Exercise of that power may entail imposing a sanction more severe than that recommended by the disciplinary board,[1] or one more lenient.[2] The court's determination, no matter how circumscribed with verbal attempts to cabin it, is in the end recognized almost everywhere as discretionary.[3] Moreover, because appellate courts are collegial, resolution of the question of an appropriate sanction depends upon the configuration of the most lenient or most severe alignment of judges and can result in deep divisions within the court.[4]

96 Office of Disciplinary Counsel v. Walker, 469 Pa. 432, 366 A.2d 563, 568 n.7 (1976). See generally ABA Disciplinary Standards 33-43 (1979).

97 In re Haupt, 422 A.2d 768, 771 (D.C.App.1980); In re Hall, 95 Ill.2d 371, 69 Ill.Dec. 370, 447 N.E.2d 805, 806-07 (1983)(deference given to recommendation of bar counsel for appropriate sanction in case where hearing panel rejected and imposed more severe sanction); In re Alter, 389 Mass. 153, 448 N.E.2d 1262 (1983); In re Daffer, 344 N.W.2d 382, 386 (Minn.1984). Even more clearly, the fact that a judge has been lenient with a lawyer after a conviction in a criminal case is no reason for disciplinary lenience. E.g., In re Allen, 52 Cal.2d 762, 767-68, 344 P.2d 609 (1959). Contra Louisiana St. Bar Ass'n v. Porobil, 444 So.2d 613, 615 (La.1984)(fact that federal judge did not sentence federal offender to penitentiary indicates belief that lawyer's conviction did not warrant harsh sanction). On the other hand, courts may be influenced by the fact that a lawyer convicted of a crime is still under a sentence of imprisonment or probation from a criminal court. E.g., In re Griffin, 101 N.M. 1, 677 P.2d 614 (1983); In re Richter, 93 A.D.2d 505, 462 N.Y.S.2d 222, 223 (1983).

98 In re Noble, 100 Wn.2d 88, 667 P.2d 608, 612 (1983).

99 Finch v. State Bar, 28 Cal.3d 659, 170 Cal.Rptr. 629, 621 P.2d 253 (1981); Giovanazzi v. State Bar, 28 Cal.3d 465, 169 Cal.Rptr. 581, 619 P.2d 1005, 1008-09 (1980)(in view of clearly settled rule that court, and not disciplinary board, sets sanction, lawyer is held to knowledge that stipulation for discipline between him and bar counsel did not bind court); In re Green, 470 Pa. 164, 368 A.2d 245, 248-49 (1977)(stipulation on maximum sanction was "nullity" and bound neither disciplinary board nor court).

1 In re Steward, 96 Ariz. 49, 391 P.2d 911 (1964); Heavey v. State Bar, 17 Cal.3d 553, 131 Cal.Rptr. 406, 551 P.2d 1238 (1976).

2 At one time an ABA president claimed that courts tended to reduce the sanctions imposed by bar disciplinary agencies. See Maxwell, The Public View of the Legal Profession, in The Presidents Speak: Annual Addresses of the Presidents of the ABA 1910-1961, at 104 (J.Holton ed.1961)(speech in 1957). If true then, certainly the statement does not reflect the practice of courts today, as indicated by reported cases.

3 Steere v. State Bar, 464 S.W.2d 732 (Tex.Civ.App. 1971)(rule recognizing discretion of trial judge to select kind and length of sanction not unconstitutional). A notable exception is Georgia, which attempts to prescribe maximum penalties—most often a public reprimand—as the last sentence of every disciplinary rule. See Ga. St. Bar Rules and Regulations, Ga.Code, Title 9, appendix (1973), 241 Ga. at 651.

4 In re Davis, 276 S.C. 532, 280 S.E.2d 644 (1981)(3-2 decision)(public reprimand preferred by bare majority of court over recommendation of indefinite suspension by dissent).

§ 3.5.2 *Disciplinary Sanctions*

The Absence of Standards

The ABA, during the history of its regulation of lawyer conduct, has always separated issues of standards of conduct from issues of sanctions and has contributed little to the question of appropriate sanctions. The 1969 Code was purposefully designed to say nothing about sanctions.[5] The 1983 Model Rules, as finally adopted, simply note that the appropriate sanction will depend on the circumstances.[6] Even the ABA 1979 Standards for Lawyer Disciplinary and Disability Proceedings do not venture beyond generalities in describing the nonprocedural differences between the various sanctions that are described.[7]

Outline of Factors Actually Employed

Courts have emphasized a myriad of individuating factors in attempting to verbalize the proper sanction for a lawyer's proven misconduct. Some factors are ameliorating and mitigate the sanction, while others are aggravating and enhance it. In general, the factors relate to (1) the extent to which the lawyer's misconduct caused injury to others; (2) the blameworthiness of the lawyer under the circumstances; (3) the lawyer's general character; (4) the lawyer's prior disciplinary history or other indications of whether the conduct was isolated or part of a pattern of repeated behavior; (5) the lawyer's demeanor during, and reaction to, the disciplinary process; (6) the likely need to deter lawyers generally or the offending lawyer in particular from similar conduct in the future; (7) the desirability of parity among similar cases; and (8) the justness of the sanction for other reasons.[8] Listing factors obviously does not rank order them, nor does it suggest that factors in a discipline case can be quantified or that courts uniformly and consistently accord weight to them.[9] It should also not obscure the fact that many of the factors are interdependent. Most importantly, each factor and evidence adduced in support of it should be considered in light of the driving theories that justify maintaining a system of discipline at all (see § 3.1).

Scope of Injury

The extent to which a lawyer's misconduct has caused injury to others is important for a number of reasons. It suggests the extent to which the lawyer is capable of making careful and restrained use of the powers and special privileges with which lawyers are entrusted;[10] it indicates the extent to which the lawyer respects the legal and moral rights of others; it also serves as a barometer of what public

[5] 1969 Code, Preliminary Statement ("The Code makes no attempt to prescribe either disciplinary procedures or penalties for violation of a Disciplinary Rule . . . ."). Footnote 11 to this statement quotes a student note for the proposition that disciplinary measures are discretionary with courts, a condition that, apparently, the Code framers despaired of changing. See Note, Disbarment: Non-Professional Conduct Demonstrating Unfitness to Practice, 43 Corn.L.Q. 489, 495 (1958).

[6] 1983 Model Rules, Preamble: Scope ("[T]he Rules presuppose that whether or not discipline should be imposed for a violation, and the severity of a sanction, depend on all the circumstances, such as the willfulness and seriousness of the violation, extenuating factors and whether there have been previous violations.").

[7] ABA Joint Comm. on Prof. Discipl., Standards for Lawyer Disciplinary and Disability Proceedings 32-43 (1979). A single section and its commentary attempt to outline some of the factors relevant to selection of sanctions. Id. § 7.1, at 44-45. Noting the wide national disparity in sanctions, the same joint ABA committee that drafted the 1979 Standards is drafting new standards to provide uniformity. See 69 ABA J. 1810 (1983).

[8] See also, e.g., State ex rel. Nebraska St. Bar Ass'n v. Erickson, 204 Neb. 692, 285 N.W.2d 105, 109 (1979)("In making this determination we must consider the nature of the offense, the need for deterrence of others, maintenance of the reputation of the bar as a whole, protection of the public, the attitude of the offender generally, and his present or future fitness to continue in the practice of law."); In re Cary, 90 Wn.2d 762, 585 P.2d 1161, 1163 (1978)("In determining the measure of discipline, we should consider (a) the seriousness and circumstances of the offense, (b) avoidance of repetition, (c) deterrent effect upon others, (d) maintenance of respect for the honor and dignity of the legal profession, and (e) assurance that those who seek legal services will be insulated from unprofessional conduct.").

[9] For one portrayal of inconsistency in the cases in one jurisdiction, see In re Grant, 89 Ill.2d 247, 60 Ill.Dec. 462, 433 N.E.2d 259, 263 (dissenting opinion of Moran, J.), cert. denied 459 U.S. 838, 103 S.Ct. 84, 74 L.Ed.2d 80 (1982).

[10] Cf., e.g., In re Whipple, 296 Or. 105, 673 P.2d 172, 177 (1983)(vulnerability of client-victim of lawyer's misconduct requires enhanced discipline).

hue and cry might be expected if the lawyer were not deterred from future depredations of a similar kind.[11] Most of those factors, other than the last, suggest that it is only the natural and predictable consequences of the lawyer's conduct that should be taken into account.[12] The last factor also suggests that injury to clients should be treated as a more serious transgression than injuries to other lawyers or judges.[13] Some have also suggested that misconduct may be so trivial in nature that it should result in no discipline.[14]

Lawyer's Blameworthiness

Lawyer discipline, as is true also of the criminal law, should select for punishment persons who are prone to commit offenses and whose punishment would deter others from committing offenses in the future. But more is required. The process should also insist that the person punished be personally blameworthy.[15] So also in professional discipline: the relative degree of a lawyer's blameworthiness for misconduct may be relevant to the question of sanctions. The necessary degree of culpability is normally defined in terms that attempt to portray the "guilty mind" involved in the doctrine of mens rea (§ 3.3.1—mens rea). Relevant here is a showing of alcoholism or other substance addiction in mitigation of a sanction (see § 3.3.3—alcoholism).

A lawyer's culpability may be more or less, depending on the extent to which the lawyer must, or should, have known that mandatory norms prohibited the conduct. Courts and agencies are less likely to impose a significant sanction if the applicable standards were unclear when the lawyer acted, for example, if a split of authority existed in other jurisdictions and no local authority spoke clearly [16] or if the climate of practice suddenly changed, making previously tolerated behavior unacceptable.[17] Circumstances may also suggest that the standards were particularly clear and thus that misconduct was particularly objectionable. For example, the lawyer may have been completely aware that it was illegal [18] or may have been warned about the misconduct.[19]

The state of mind of the lawyer at the time of the misconduct may also be important if a court can infer that the conduct was either premeditated or impulsive. A seriously injurious course of conduct that consists of a program of wrongful acts extending over a considerable period of time strongly suggests blameworthiness.[20] Courts will normally react less severely to misconduct that grows out of a single incident or that involves less blameworthy states of mind, such as negligence, dilatoriness, or incompetence.[21] A violation that appears to be the product of an unusual conjunction of personal circum-

11 Cf., e.g., Louisiana St. Bar Ass'n v. Mundy, 423 So.2d 1126, 1129 (La.1982)(client forgiveness as mitigating factor).

12 But cf., e.g., Kentucky Bar Ass'n v. Berry, 626 S.W.2d 632, 633 (Ky.1981)(lawyer's interest-free loans to himself and friends from estate results only in suspension because, among other things, the estate had increased in value under his management; fact that increase had occurred during time of sharply rising investment values ignored).

13 Ohio St. Bar Ass'n v. Talbott, 59 Ohio St.2d 76, 391 N.E.2d 1028, 1030 (1979).

14 Di Sabatino v. State Bar, 27 Cal.3d 159, 162 Cal.Rptr. 458, 461, 606 P.2d 765, 768 (1980)(dissenting opinions) (conduct variously described as "trivial incident" and "pecadillo" should not result in discipline).

15 H.Packer, The Limits of the Criminal Sanction 62 (1968).

16 In re Evans, 113 Ariz. 458, 556 P.2d 792 (1976); Arden v. State Bar, 52 Cal.2d 310, 341 P.2d 6, 11 (1959); In re Malloy, 248 N.W.2d 43, 45 (N.D.1976); In re Two Anonymous Members of the Bar, 278 S.C. 477, 298 S.E.2d 450, 452 (1982).

17 In re Sears, 71 N.J. 175, 364 A.2d 777, 789-90 (1976) (in imposing sanctions, court must beware overreaction to post-Watergate perspectives from which acts of public officials are being newly viewed).

18 In re Thomas, 420 N.E.2d 1237, 1239 (Ind.1981).

19 In re Lehet, 95 N.J. 466, 472 A.2d 127, 129 (1984) (lawyer continued to commingle and use client funds after warning from disciplinary agency auditor).

20 Attorney Grievance Comm'n v. Deutsch, 294 Md. 353, 450 A.2d 1265, 1273 (1982); State ex rel. Neb. St. Bar Ass'n v. Frank, 214 Neb. 825, 336 N.W.2d 557, 560 (1983).

21 Inniss v. State Bar, 20 Cal.3d 552, 143 Cal.Rptr. 408, 573 P.2d 852 (1978); Attorney Grievance Comm'n v. Willcher, 287 Md. 74, 411 A.2d 83 (1980); In re Daffer, 344 N.W.2d 382, 385 (Minn.1984); In re Hansen, 584 P.2d 805, 807 (Utah 1978).

stances not likely to recur may also be treated more with compassion than with strictness.[22] Misconduct is also sometimes judged less harshly if it was not engaged in for the lawyer's own advantage or enrichment.[23] Misconduct that is not related to the practice of law may also not require discipline as severe as that reserved for violation of the special rules of the legal profession.[24] But if the nonlegal misconduct is of a kind (misappropriation of funds, for example) that bears direct relationship to a lawyer's normal responsibilties, it may be fully relevant.[25] While misconduct cannot be excused because of ignorance of the rules,[26] youth or inexperience may suggest that misconduct, particularly of a professionally technical kind, should not be the occasion for normally more substantial discipline.[27]

A Lawyer's General Character

The touch-stone for which all disciplinary alchemists search is a magic element that will provide a true guide for character that enables the disciplinary agency to assess the extent to which a miscreant lawyer is truly evil. As with attempts to command magic that can turn base metals into gold, however, so in lawyer discipline the search for a method of providing glittering evidence of character so far has resulted much more in false hopes and sham tests than in real progress in wisdom. The search for character has centered around testimonials of lawyers, judges,[28] and other notables attesting to their high opinion of the fine character of a lawyer accused of misconduct.

Few courts seem interested in examining testimonial evidence reflecting on the lawyer's general character with respect to the essentially factual question whether a lawyer has committed a sanctionable act.[29] But many courts purport to take it into account in determining an appropriate level of discipline.[30] Some courts are more careful and reject such opinion evidence if it was written or given in ignorance of the fact that the lawyer in fact committed the acts charged. Other courts wisely reject such evidence as valueless in all events because it is often given for reasons of human appeal but without sufficient regard for the needs of lawyer discipline.[31] Still other opinions applaud the motives of the persons giving testimonials but

22 In re Barron, 246 Ga. 327, 271 S.E.2d 474 (1980) (single-parent lawyer, who was sole support of children, under extreme financial strain, had recently undergone major surgery requiring three months' absence from office, was unable to borrow funds, and made restitution of client's funds by selling home and family heirlooms).

23 In re Swartz, 129 Ariz. 288, 630 P.2d 1020 (1981); In re Hopp, 291 Or. 697, 634 P.2d 238, 240 (1981).

24 In re Wines, 135 Ariz. 203, 660 P.2d 454, 458-59 (1983).

25 In re Daffer, 344 N.W.2d 382, 385 n.3 (Minn.1984).

26 In re Castello, 273 Ind. 136, 402 N.E.2d 970, 972-73 (1980)(if anything, ignorance of DRs illustrates lawyer's unfitness).

27 In re Stern, 92 N.J. 611, 458 A.2d 1279 (1983). Cf. In re Petty, 29 Cal.3d 356, 173 Cal.Rptr. 461, 627 P.2d 191 (1981)(youth and inexperience no mitigation; most lawyers are young and inexperienced at the outset of their careers but do not defraud insurance companies). Compare In re Haggard, 123 Ariz. 27, 597 P.2d 180, 182-83 (1979)(recent admission to bar mitigates neglect and similar offenses but not misrepresentation to disciplinary agency).

28 A judge's voluntary submission of letters of commendation or of unsubpoenaed testimony violates Judicial Canon 2(B)("[A judge] should not testify voluntarily as a character witness."). See generally E.Thode, Reporter's Notes to Code of Judicial Conduct 49 (1973); Florida Bar v. Prior, 330 So.2d 697, 703-04 (Fla.1976).

29 But see Kivitz v. SEC, 475 F.2d 956, 960-61 (D.C.Cir. 1973).

30 In re Sedor, 73 Wis.2d 629, 245 N.W.2d 895 (1976). Often the court's reception of the evidence of excellent community reputation indicates that it is only its absence that would be remarkable. E.g., In re Alter, 389 Mass. 153, 448 N.E.2d 1262, 1264 (1983). Sometimes, however, courts invite it. E.g., Cain v. State Bar, 25 Cal.3d 956, 160 Cal.Rptr. 362, 603 P.2d 464, 467 (1979); State v. Scott, 230 Kan. 564, 639 P.2d 1131, 1137 (1982).

31 In re Harris, 88 N.J.L. 18, 95 A. 761, 763 (1915): "Personally solicited letters or mere signatures obtained to a petition, while plenary evidence of the unwillingness of such signers to deny a personal favor, [are] very far from being cogent evidence of any particular state of facts, especially if it relates to the moral character of the person who obtains the letters or circulates the petition." See also, e.g., In re Hanley, 13 Cal.3d 448, 119 Cal.Rptr. 5, 530 P.2d 1381 (1975); Committee on Professional Ethics v. Wilson, 290 N.W.2d 17, 23-24 (Iowa 1980)(citing and quoting from the *Harris* case supra).

disregard their import.[32] Approaches that heavily discount or entirely reject the evidence are sound. Character testimonials are often the result of personal friendship, bar politics, antipathy to bar discipline, or ignorance of the facts. Their acceptance in evidence simply invites turning the proceeding from a deliberative process into a bench and bar plebiscite. Related to opinion testimonials are résumé items sometimes offered and sometimes deemed by courts to be mitigating. Included are such facts as the lawyer's service in the military,[33] government,[34] public causes,[35] or some other capacity.[36] The relevance of the lawyer's former, reflected glory to the question of sanctions is never pursued and is hardly obvious.

Yet certain facts do suggest a strong or a weak character in a way relevant to future law practice. Altered attitudes are suggested when a lawyer voluntarily reveals misconduct to authorities, acknowledges wrongdoing, demonstrates genuine remorse, and voluntarily undertakes to repair damage by making amends to injured persons and by restructuring a law practice to minimize the risk of recurring problems. With altered attitudes goes the possibility, the court may rightly hope, for altered conduct in the future.[37] The opposite of remorse does not invariably suggest the contrary.[38]

Isolation or Repetition of Misconduct

Our customary belief is that behavior reflects traits of character that are relatively persistent. Thus the fact that particular conduct has occurred only once in the course of a legal career [39] may imply that it will not likely be repeated, particularly if the conduct is explicable by unusually provocative circumstances.[40] The relevance of the fact that a lawyer possesses an unblemished record, of course, depends upon one's confidence that significant violations of lawyer norms are routinely and reliably detected, prosecuted, and made a matter of record. Known repetition clearly implies incorrigibility. Repeated misconduct after receiving the warning of a sanc-

32 In re Kesler, 272 Ind. 161, 397 N.E.2d 574, 579 (1979), cert. denied 449 U.S. 829, 101 S.Ct. 96, 66 L.Ed.2d 34 (1980).

33 In re Sorkin, 80 A.D.2d 31, 437 N.Y.S.2d 338 (1981); In re Perkins, 69 A.D.2d 160, 419 N.Y.S.2d 1 (1979).

34 Office of Disciplinary Counsel v. Eilberg, 497 Pa. 388, 441 A.2d 1193, 1197 (1982)(lawyer who as member of Congress received illegal payments suspended rather than disbarred because of significant contributions to constituents while in office); Carter v. Walsh, 122 R.I. 349, 406 A.2d 263, 266 (1979)(employment as legal officer over decade previously in city nationally recognized as an "All-American City").

35 Martin v. State Bar, 20 Cal.3d 717, 144 Cal.Rptr. 214, 575 P.2d 757, 759 (1978)(many years spent volunteering legal work for public causes, although praiseworthy, does not bear on conduct or sanction, which must be increased); Committee on Professional Ethics v. Kelly, 250 N.W.2d 388 (Iowa 1976)(services to indigent persons commendable, but not valid excuse for failing to file income tax returns).

36 Perloff v. Disciplinary Board, 424 So.2d 1305, 1307 (Ala.1982)(work on bar association projects mitigates offense concerning payments to city councilmen during tenure as city attorney).

37 Finch v. State Bar, 28 Cal.3d 659, 170 Cal.Rptr. 629, 633, 621 P.2d 253 (1981); Florida Bar v. Pettie, 424 So.2d 734 (Fla.1982); In re Nadler, 91 Ill.2d 326, 63 Ill.Dec. 460, 438 N.E.2d 198, 202 (1982); Attorney Grievance Comm'n v. Freedman, 285 Md. 298, 402 A.2d 75 (1979)(voluntarily reporting former associate's illegal activities to police); In re Brown, 97 Wn.2d 273, 644 P.2d 669 (1982). But cooperation that is solely self-protective and after-the-fact is without significance. E.g., In re Schwartz, 31 Cal.3d 395, 182 Cal.Rptr. 640, 643, 644 P.2d 833, 26 A.L.R.4th 1077 (1982)(cooperation with police given only after prosecutor agreed to drop twenty-three counts of pending indictment).

38 In re Hedlund, 293 N.W.2d 63, 65-66 (Minn.1980) (court refuses to consider as aggravating circumstance fact that convicted lawyer refused to admit guilt), citing and following In re Hiss, 368 Mass. 447, 333 N.E.2d 429 (1975)(refusal of person convicted of crime to admit guilt in application for reinstatement many years later does not bar reinstatement). See § 3.5.5.

39 In re Francovich, 94 Nev. 104, 575 P.2d 931 (1978); State ex rel. Okla. Bar Ass'n v. Hensley, 560 P.2d 567, 569 (Okl.1977). But misconduct very early in a legal career is not mitigated significantly by the lack of any prior disciplinary convictions. E.g., Finch v. State Bar, 28 Cal.3d 659, 170 Cal.Rptr. 629, 633, 621 P.2d 253, 257, (1981); Florida Bar v. Wilson, 425 So.2d 2, 3 (Fla.1983) (lawyer admitted for six months before arrest for cocaine trafficking).

40 Louisiana St. Bar Ass'n v. Marcal, 430 So.2d 47 (La. 1983)(conviction of bribery mitigated to some extent by fact that it was one blemish in otherwise public-spirited record). But see, e.g., Bar Ass'n of Baltimore City v. Siegel, 275 Md. 521, 340 A.2d 710, 714 (1975)(unblemished record of forty years not relevant to question of sanctions).

tion short of disbarment can confidently be regarded as an ill omen for compliance in the future.[41] The lawyer appears unable to profit from the warning, suggesting the need for sterner measures. Recidivism most strongly suggests a more severe sanction if the prior discipline was for misconduct that closely resembles the misconduct found in the pending case.[42] Also, if the lawyer has no prior disciplinary history but the charges are multiple, the sanction should reflect a more serious concern with the lawyer's attitude toward professional regulations or legality.[43] Similarly, the number and type of violations found might suggest a cumulatively serious case, even though the individual offenses, separately considered, appear minor.[44] Some courts have also relied upon uncharged misconduct, not as a basis for imposing discipline, but as a basis for enhancing the penalty for other misconduct.[45]

Disciplinary agencies, like the police, sometimes operate on the assumption that a pattern of complaints that do not result in discipline, like arrests that do not lead to convictions, nonetheless suggests a propensity for wrongdoing. Most courts rightly exclude evidence of such unfounded complaints in determining the appropriate discipline.[46]

Reactions to the Disciplinary Process

Courts place significant weight on the demeanor of the accused lawyer when confronted with disciplinary charges. A lawyer's refusal to cooperate with an agency by answering inquiries and supplying needed information will likely count against leniency.[47] A clear case is giving false testimony or presenting false evidence before a disciplinary hearing panel, actions that courts treat with gravity in setting a sanction.[48] It is not al-

41 Greene v. Grievance Committee, 54 N.Y.2d 118, 444 N.Y.S.2d 883, 429 N.E.2d 390, 392 (1981), cert. denied 455 U.S. 1035, 102 S.Ct. 1738, 72 L.Ed.2d 153 (1982)(case not moot, though no sanction imposed, because finding of violation itself can be considered in enhancement of other pending charges); Stark County Bar Ass'n v. Ergazos, 2 Ohio St.3d 59, 442 N.E.2d 1286, 1288 n.3 (1982)(local rule requiring sanction of indefinite suspension as minimum sanction for second offense); In re Mazza, 117 Wis.2d 770, 345 N.W.2d 492, 493 (1984). The fact that the prior disciplinary action was taken by an agency in another state is irrelevant. E.g., In re Wines, 135 Ariz. 203, 660 P.2d 454, 458 (1983). But a second finding of violations should not be treated as cumulative in the sense being discussed if the conduct occurred prior to the original proceeding. E.g., Florida Bar v. Carter, 429 So.2d 3, 4 (Fla.1983).

42 In re Perrello, 271 Ind. 560, 394 N.E.2d 127 (1979) (multiple instances of solicitation following first discipline for same offense); Florida Bar v. Bern, 425 So.2d 526 (Fla.1982); In re Florsheim, 77 A.D.2d 9, 432 N.Y.S. 2d 9 (1980), appeal denied 53 N.Y.2d 734, 439 N.Y.S.2d 356, 421 N.E.2d 848, appeal dismissed in part, denied in part 53 N.Y.2d 603, 439 N.Y.S.2d 1027, 421 N.E.2d 854 (1981).

43 In re Trebilcock, 30 Cal.3d 312, 178 Cal.Rptr. 630, 636 P.2d 594, 595 (1981)(robberies of six savings and loan associations over period of two and one-half months); Cain v. State Bar, 21 Cal.3d 523, 146 Cal.Rptr. 737, 579 P.2d 1053 (1978)(misconduct occurring during period of other acts for which lawyer was already under suspension, but not included with earlier charges because of client's delay in reporting misconduct, as basis for extending earlier suspension); In re DesBrisay, 288 Or. 625, 606 P.2d 1148, 1151 (1980)(for most of years of practice, lawyer filed no income tax returns or they were inexcusably late).

44 Florida Bar v. Greenspahn, 396 So.2d 182 (Fla.1981).

45 In re Roberts, 442 N.E.2d 986, 988 (Ind.1983)(uncharged misconduct cannot result in finding of violation on which discipline can be based; but proven uncharged misconduct relevant to question of sanction); State ex rel. Nebraska St. Bar Ass'n v. Erickson, 204 Neb. 692, 285 N.W.2d 105, 109 (1979); O'Dowd v. State, 304 S.W.2d 241 (Tex.Civ.App.1957), reversed on other grounds 158 Tex. 348, 312 S.W.2d 217 (1958)(evidence of alleged misconduct occurring when time-barred as basis for finding of sanctionable offense). On the due process requirement of basing findings of violations only on previously charged occurrences, see § 3.4.2 (notice of charges).

46 Blair v. State Bar, 27 Cal.3d 407, 165 Cal.Rptr. 834, 612 P.2d 924 (1980); Berke v. Chattanooga Bar Ass'n, 58 Tenn.App. 636, 436 S.W.2d 296, 309 (1968). See also 51 U.S.L.Wk. 2123 (1982)(amendment to ABA Disciplinary Standards to provide for expunging records of dismissed charges). Using dismissed charges as a prosecutorial matter may be different. A prosecutor who is personally convinced that a lawyer committed a violation that could not be proved by clear and convincing evidence should, it seems, be able to employ that information in deciding whether to press later charges and in making a decision about the type of sanction to press for.

47 In re Rudie, 294 Or. 740, 662 P.2d 321, 324 (1983) (lawyer's failure to answer disciplinary charges or to appear at hearing, although not a violation of any disciplinary rule, "demonstrates lack of an important element of professionalism"); In re Sifly, 279 S.C. 113, 302 S.E.2d 858, 859 (1983).

48 In re Haggard, 123 Ariz. 27, 597 P.2d 180, 182 (1979); Doyle v. State Bar, 32 Cal.3d 12, 184 Cal.Rptr. 720, 648 P.2d 942, 948 (1982); Carter v. Walsh, 122 R.I. 349, 406 A.2d 263 (1979) (inconsistent and incredible mitigation testimony).

ways clear whether a court is merely treating a lawyer's refusal to cooperate or a lawyer's false testimony as evidence of incorrigibility or is condemning it as a separate offense.[49] A similarly negative factor that requires enhancing the sanction is the lawyer's continuation on a challenged course of misconduct despite the filing of misconduct charges.[50] The extent to which a lawyer's failure to make restitution is relevant is considered at a separate point (§ 3.5.6).

Deterrence

The traditions of the practice of law and the decent instincts of most lawyers doubtless supply most of the motivating force behind lawyer observance of mandatory, minimal norms. But a powerful additional incentive to learn and to abide by the spirit of professional rules might be the threat of formal sanctions. If a lawyer's conduct is blatant and seems to defy the efficacy of a mandatory rule, emphatic discipline may be required in order to reassert the authority of the very notion of professional rules.[51] The need for deterrence might be particularly strong if a lawyer insists that misconduct is necessary in a practice [52] or was justified under the circumstances for reasons that suggest that similar validating grounds would also be claimed in the future.[53] On the other hand, a significant sanction may not be required if the lawyer's present and future circumstances suggest that the situation that gave rise to the misconduct will not likely recur.[54]

Much more debatable than the use of severe sanctions to goad a reluctant lawyer into compliance is the use of severe sanctions against a lawyer to give warning to other lawyers. Making an example of the lawyer who happens to have been first prosecuted may appear to be disturbingly undeserved. Nonetheless, courts in bar discipline and other contexts have upheld the general lawfulness of calibrating punishment by the social need to disseminate information that the law will be enforced.[55] Occasionally, courts will issue warnings to the bar that an apparent increase in a type of misconduct will result in

[49] In most such cases, enhancement of the sanction on the basis of a finding that the lawyer committed perjury during the hearing is not constitutionally objectionable. See § 12.5.1 at n.42. The constitutional requirement of notice of charges would, however, require that a lawyer accused of perjury during a disciplinary hearing be notified of those charges before being punished for perjury as a separate instance of misconduct. See § 3.4.2 (notice of charges).

[50] Gordon v. State Bar, 31 Cal.3d 748, 183 Cal.Rptr. 861, 866, 647 P.2d 137 (1982). See also State ex rel. Nebraska St. Bar v. Michaelis, 210 Neb. 545, 316 N.W.2d 46, 56, 26 A.L.R.4th 154, cert. denied 459 U.S. 804, 103 S.Ct. 27, 74 L.Ed.2d 42 (1982) (at hearing on charges of making unfounded charges against judges, lawyer continued such attacks, including attack on deciding court shortly before its decision).

[51] In re Carroll, 124 Ariz. 80, 602 P.2d 461, 467 (1979).

[52] Louisiana St. Bar Ass'n v. Jones, 372 So.2d 1186 (La. 1979), cert. denied 444 U.S. 1073, 100 S.Ct. 1017, 62 L.Ed. 2d 754 (1980)(lawyer testified that he didn't see how he could continue practicing without some commingling of client and personal funds).

[53] State v. Freeman, 229 Kan. 629, 629 P.2d 716, 720 (1981); State ex rel. Nebraska St. Bar Ass'n v. Erickson, 204 Neb. 692, 285 N.W.2d 105 (1979)(lawyer attempted to justify abandoning client because client's failure to pay fee on demand justified leaving client at courthouse without counsel); In re Denend, 98 Wn.2d 699, 657 P.2d 1379, 1382-83 (1983).

[54] Florida Bar v. Reese, 421 So.2d 495, 497 (Fla.1982) (suspension, instead of disbarment, when lawyer seeks to leave law practice and gain employment with federal government); In re Barron, 246 Ga. 327, 271 S.E.2d 474, 475 (1980)(lawyer under great personal and financial strain who invaded client's trust funds and who is no longer practicing law); State v. Hohman, 233 Kan. 183, 660 P.2d 567, 568 (1983)(lawyer censured for commingling of client funds on his representation that he was now retired from law practice); In re Heffernan, 351 N.W.2d 13, 15 (Minn.1984)(lawyer who committed trust fund violations now associated with law firm with established bookkeeping procedures); In re Mattice, 73 N.J. 103, 372 A.2d 1104, 1105 (1977)(lawyer's advanced age). Courts are hostile, however, to suggestions that some present positions are sanctuaries into which disciplinary sanctions should not reach. E.g., In re Castello, 273 Ind. 136, 402 N.E.2d 970, 973 (1980)(administrative hearing officer); In re Hennings, 283 N.W.2d 896 (Minn.1979)(dedication of life to ministry after conviction for theft does not prevent disbarment). The fact that a lawyer has left a jurisdiction and does not intend to return seems an unduly chauvinistic reason for imposing a lenient sanction. But cf., e.g., In re Feit, 81 A.D.2d 432, 440 N.Y.S.2d 725, 726 (1981); In re Harper, 69 A.D.2d 236, 418 N.Y.S.2d 470, 471 (1979).

[55] See generally, e.g., Day v. Woodworth, 54 U.S. (13 How.) 363, 370-71, 14 L.Ed. 181 (1851)(use of punitive damages in civil suits to deter others from similar tortious conduct).

penalties in the future that are more severe.[56] Equally debatable is an opposite practice. Decisions occasionally treat as mitigating a factor that seems to have nothing to do with the lawyer's ability to practice law according to rules, such as when they reduce disbarment to a mild suspension in order to reward a lawyer who cooperated with undercover investigators in breaking up a large drug operation in which the lawyer had been a willing participant.[57]

Parity or Proportionality of Sanctions

If all else were equal, imposing equal sanctions would also uphold one of the most central moral instincts of the law—treating likes alike. And some courts have gone to significant lengths to calibrate a sanction by comparison with sanctions mandated in assertedly comparable cases.[58] Consistency can, however, unacceptably freeze a disciplinary system into a level of sanctions that is either too severe or too lenient. A consistent level of sanctions in past discipline cases might prove to have been ineffective for a variety of reasons: because it did not suffice to stem a resistant kind of violation among lawyers generally; because it overlooked changing mores and practices that legitimately cast new light on a formerly denounced activity (such as advertising); or because it failed to take into account one or more of the other compelling bases for imposing differentiating levels of discipline that have already been discussed. Moreover, arguments for parity assume that ways can readily be found of isolating and quantifying all relevant factors that legitimately influence discretion. But each case must be determined carefully on its own circumstances and merits.[59] Something as evanescent as the strength of a judge's conviction that a lawyer in one case is a good risk for reformation is difficult to translate into a quantifiable reason for imposing a similar sanction in another case that is similar in all respects, except for the fact that the judge lacks such a compelling conviction. Moreover, great variations in disciplinary sanctions from one jurisdiction to another may reflect either relatively lax or overly strict enforcement, as is commonly suspected,[60] or may reflect very different local conditions.

Courts should seek to assure that sanctions, if not in parity, are proportional to the offense committed, reflect real needs for specific and general deterrence, and take account of the specific characteristics of the individual lawyer. If a court consistently pursues those goals, any resulting disparity in length or severity of sanctions should be fully explicable on the ground that the cases and lawyers involved were indeed different.

Other Factors

Judges have occasionally arrayed novel arguments for enhancing or, more typically of these cases, for mitigating the sanction. A lawyer's human condition will sometimes be emphasized as a reason for mercy, such as the fact that a lawyer is confined to a wheelchair.[61] As compelling as compassion is, it seems misplaced if it has nothing to do with the reasons that might explain the offense or the likelihood of its repetition. Possibly such factors are considered relevant because depriving such a lawyer of the income of a law practice would cause special hardship that is thought not to be warranted, despite the fact

[56] In re Boyer, 295 Or. 624, 630, 669 P.2d 326, 329 (1983).

[57] Florida Bar v. Pettie, 424 So.2d 734, 737 (Fla.1982).

[58] Georgia, for example, mandates the severity of sanctions in an addendum to each of most of its disciplinary rules. See supra, at note 3. The ABA Disciplinary Standards § 7.1 commentary (1979) advises against mandated dispositions for certain kinds of misconduct. On the struggles of members of a court to agree on a consistent sanctioning policy, see, e.g., In re Sheehy, 454 A.2d 1360 (D.C.App.1983); In re Johnson, 93 Ill.2d 441, 67 Ill. Dec. 114, 444 N.E.2d 153 (1983).

[59] In re Knox, 441 A.2d 265, 268 (D.C.App.1982); In re Grimes, 414 Mich. 483, 326 N.W.2d 380, 382 (1982); In re Noble, 100 Wn.2d 88, 667 P.2d 608, 612 (1983).

[60] Discipline Chaos, 69 ABA J. 1810 (1983)(great state-by-state disparities in sanctions as rationale for ABA committee effort to write national sanctioning code).

[61] In re Lacey, 283 N.W.2d 250 (S.D.1979). See also, e.g., In re Lukashok, 94 A.D.2d 10, 463 N.Y.S.2d 199, 200 (1983)(disciplinary proceedings have had adverse consequences on lawyer's professional and personal life).

that a lesser sanction creates a risk of nondeterrence.[62] Isolated invocation of such excepting circumstances probably does little harm, but their frequent recitation in discipline cases, which seems to be the practice in some jurisdictions, suggests that few lawyers are forced to face meaningful sanctions.

Another human element, most often reserved for the mighty who have fallen, is the "suffered enough" argument: a lawyer of prominence is subjected to great humiliation in a disciplinary proceeding, and this should mitigate the disciplinary sanction.[63] The argument is problematical because it suggests that lawyers of wealth, prominence, or success in practice operate with special, judicially approved advantages.[64] It ignores the consideration that those who have the benefits of advantages or who have accepted the responsibilities of high position are rightly held, if anything, to a higher standard of conduct.[65] The argument also ignores the deterrent value of such cases: significant sanctions in cases involving prominent lawyers are much more likely to attract the notice of a watching profession. The argument that the humiliating effect of the disciplinary process is itself a scourge is sometimes generalized to all lawyer respondents regardless of their prominence. It is found, for example, in arguments that a sanction should be minimal because a lawyer has suffered through publicity attending the disciplinary hearings or through strongly negative reactions from professional or personal friends. Or courts have cited a long period of delay, during which the stress of pending charges has taken a toll.[66]

Many things could be said in "mitigation" of the sanction in the great majority of discipline cases. Almost every lawyer can claim that his or her misconduct was to an extent caused by the pressure of circumstances, that some clients and practitioners hold the lawyer in high esteem, that the pain of the accusatory publicity and the threat to one's license to practice attending a disciplinary hearing has been psychologically excruciating, that both the lawyer and the lawyer's family depend upon the lawyer's income from law practice, that the lawyer has performed good works, and that the lawyer's record was hitherto unblemished. Because those and similar elements characterize almost every case, it is difficult to see how they can be particularly relevant as mitigating factors in any.[67]

§ 3.5.3 Reprimand

Private Reprimands and Admonitions

The mildest disciplinary sanction provided in the typical state system is a private reprimand.[68] Even milder in some jurisdictions, although it is claimed not to amount to discipline, is a private warning or admonition that

[62] See also, e.g., In re Tapper, 102 A.D.2d 332, 477 N.Y.S.2d 16, 17 (1984)(lawyer as sole source of support for dependent adult son). But cf., e.g., In re Hedlund, 293 N.W.2d 63, 67 (Minn.1980)(danger to public and law administration warrants disbarment despite impact on lawyer's family and financial situation).

[63] In re Sears, 71 N.J. 175, 364 A.2d 777, 789 (1976) (major figure in state and national politics); In re Perkins, 69 A.D.2d 160, 419 N.Y.S.2d 1 (1979)(lawyer suffered imprisonment and resignation from partnership in major law firm); In re Hansen, 584 P.2d 805, 807 (Utah 1978) (state attorney general). On similar logic lawyers have argued, unsuccessfully, that they should not be subjected to the indignity of severe punishment such as imprisonment as the penalty for a crime because of the likelihood that they will suffer professional discipline, e.g., Webb v. State, 580 P.2d 295, 304 (Alaska 1978)(dissenting opinion), and that they should be spared the indignity of severe professional discipline because of the suffering inflicted by a criminal conviction. Inconsistency also characterizes the same court's explanations. Compare, e.g., In re Sears, supra (public service as mitigating factor), with, e.g., In re Friedland, 95 N.J. 170, 470 A.2d 3, 5 (1984) (distinguishing *Sears*, fact of public service here called for enhancement of sanction because misconduct was violation of public trust).

[64] An obvious alternative reading is that courts are more assured that those with the privilege of position take more care to retain it by avoiding violations of enforceable rules.

[65] In re Moore, 453 N.E.2d 971, 974–75 (Ind.1983).

[66] Newman v. Committee on Professional Standards, 73 A.D.2d 1029, 424 N.Y.S.2d 529 (1980). See generally § 3.4.2 (stale complaints).

[67] In re Houchin, 290 Or. 433, 622 P.2d 723, 726 (1981).

[68] A court searching for the ultimate in non-onerous sanctions when a disciplinary violation has been found might wish to consider a "discharge" of the respondent rather than a dismissal of the complaint. See In re Friedman, 76 Ill.2d 392, 80 Ill.Dec. 288, 392 N.E.2d 1333, 10 A.L.R.4th 589 (1979).

officially denotes areas of problematical conduct or perceived misconduct of a relatively minor sort and suggests ways of avoiding the problem in the future.[69] A private reprimand exacts no immediate sanction but can enhance a sanction if the lawyer is again found to have violated the lawyer code.[70]

Public Reprimand

Because of its comparative mildness, a public reprimand is usually employed for relatively innocuous, technical, or isolated violations that suggest an unusual or minor lapse of judgment rather than a more derelict state of mind.[71] A public reprimand derives its sanctional power from humiliation. It exposes to public view the fact of the lawyer's misconduct and its condemnation by the disciplinary agency or court.[72] A court's purpose in requiring public rather than private reprimand may also be to assure that the deterrent value of the discipline is maximized. Public reprimands that are not appealed are usually published in the jurisdiction's bar journal. In some places they are delivered in open court.[73] Those appealed to the supreme court, or initiated there, are published both in the bar journal and in the official and unofficial reports of the decisions of the court.[74] A private reprimand can readily be transformed into a public one by the reviewing court's order.[75]

A different form of sanction by humiliating exposure occasionally employed by courts is punishment by publication. It resembles a public reprimand in that a court uses its power to publish judicial decisions in order to excoriate a lawyer for assertedly unprofessional conduct in the course of representing a client in a case decided by the decision.[76] Sometimes the printed opinion will include a statement that the matter is being referred to the lawyer disciplinary agency. The practice of publicly denouncing lawyers in that way is dubious. While one trained as a lawyer should be able to mark the difference between accusing and finding guilt, the special weight accorded to an accusation made by a judge and made in a permanent and public place seems to caution against thus impugning the

69 According to ABA Disciplinary Standards § 6.10 (1979), a nondisciplinary admonition can be issued by disciplinary counsel without a hearing. Admonitions are to be used for "certain kinds of minor misconduct." (Id. commentary.) Admonitions may be taken into account to enhance the sanction in a subsequent disciplinary hearing. (E.g., id.; In re Pravda, 101 A.D.2d 80, 474 N.Y.S.2d 509 (1984).) In order for a lawyer to avoid future enhancing use, the lawyer must refuse the admonition, which has the effect of setting the matter for a hearing. (Id. commentary.) The ABA's conception of an "admonition" resembles the "private reprimand" used in other jurisdictions in every respect except that it is not attended by notice and hearing. See Board of Overseers of the Bar v. Rodway, 461 A.2d 1062 (Me.1983), judgment vacated and information dismissd on other grounds 470 A.2d 790 (Me. 1984)("admonition" is discipline and not merely warning, thus entitling lawyer to full procedural rights of notice and hearing).

70 Florida Bar v. Leopold, 399 So.2d 978, 979 (Fla.1981).

71 Florida Bar v. Welty, 382 So.2d 1220 (Fla.1980); In re Rudie, 294 Or. 740, 662 P.2d 321, 324 (1983).

72 A reprimand may also contain conditions, making it similiar to probation. Violation of a condition of a reprimand can lead to additional sanctions. E.g., In re Solberg, 106 Wis.2d 242, 316 N.W.2d 347 (1982)(suspension ordered for failure to close estates within stipulated time and take other steps to reform practice).

73 In re Bronson, 246 Ga. 136, 269 S.E.2d 27 (1980).

74 Ferrer v. State, 434 So.2d 15, 16, 17 (Fla.App.1983) (publication of report to reprimand lawyer for failure to properly pursue appeal).

75 In re Burgess, 177 Mont. 493, 582 P.2d 356 (1978). Occasionally, a court transforms a reprimand from private to public apparently as a penalty for the lawyer's appeal of the private reprimand. E.g., Walker v. Supreme Court Committee on Professional Conduct, 275 Ark. 158, 628 S.W.2d 552, 555 (1982); In re Lauer, 108 Wis.2d 746, 324 N.W.2d 432, 439 (1982). An appeal can, of course, be decided and reported without identification of the lawyer involved, thus preserving the privacy of the reprimand. Surely the most feckless example of a public-private reprimand is a case such as In re Szymanski, 400 Mich. 469, 255 N.W.2d 601 (1977), in which a majority, after a full discussion of the facts and identification of the respondent, refuse to impose the recommended sanction of a private reprimand. All that is missing is judicial disapproval; the adverse publicity has already occurred.

76 United States v. Lespier, 558 F.2d 624, 627 (lst Cir. 1977); Lowenschuss v. Kane, 367 F.Supp. 911, 913 n.1 (S.D.N.Y.1973), reversed on other grounds 520 F.2d 255 (2d Cir.1975). Some instances are, by the court's own account, indistinguishable from disciplinary proceedings in which public censure is the sanction imposed—without notice or hearing. See Brookhaven Landscape & Grading Co. v. J.F. Barton Contracting Co., 681 F.2d 734, 735 (11th Cir.1982)(opinion denying joint motion of appellee and appellant to delete references in prior opinion to lawyer's failure to comply with rules of court or, alternatively, to dismiss the appeal).

professional reputations of lawyers.[77] The lawyer's conduct will at best have been dealt with peripherally in the hearing, and the lawyer's role there will typically have been to protect the interests of a client, and not the individual interests of the lawyer. In an extreme case, a petition to a higher court for an order requiring a lower court judge to expunge the offending remarks may be in order.[78]

§ 3.5.4 *Suspension or Disbarment*

Variations in Suspension Practices

The sanctions that carry the most emphatic impact upon a lawyer and that correspondingly assert most strongly that a jurisdiction condemns the misconduct are suspension and disbarment. Of those, disbarment conveys the strongest stigma and generally has the most serious consequences on the disciplined lawyer's future. The length of the term of suspension is variable in most jurisdictions. On a national basis, the terms "suspension" and "disbarment" [79] have no agreed-upon content. Much depends on the duration of the sanction and the ease with which a lawyer can be reinstated. An alternative to suspension or disbarment is resignation from the bar under conditions making it their functional equivalent.

Suspension versus Disbarment

Generally, in the same jurisdiction suspension is less severe than disbarment. But interjurisdictional variations are enormous. A lawyer disbarred in some jurisdictions, at least for some offenses, may never be reinstated.[80] In others, a disbarred lawyer may apply for reinstatement, although typically the lawyer must wait for a longer time than is required for a suspended lawyer.[81] A suspended lawyer in some states is automatically reinstated at the conclusion of the term of suspension. Even if a suspended lawyer must apply for reinstatement, the requirements are less stringent than those for a disbarred lawyer.[82] Suspension for a stated duration carries the implicit assumption that time will cure the perceived problem. Disbarment, on the other hand, bears the appearance of a certificate of professional death, indicating in an extreme case that the lawyer is unlikely ever to be able to persuade the court that reinstatement is justified.[83]

In some jurisdictions, however, or at least in different decisions, there may be little functional difference between suspension and disbarment. Suspension beyond a certain period, such as for two years or more, means in some jurisdictions that the lawyer will not be readmitted until the lawyer has successfully completed a readmission process that resembles the process required of disbarred lawyers.[84] In some jurisdictions a suspension may last as long as a decade. In others, by contrast, disbarment is not permanent and reinstatement can be gained within a relatively short time.[85]

[77] Presumably for reasons such as those, it is typically required that complaints to disciplinary boards be kept confidential. See Lowenschuss v. West Pub. Co., 542 F.2d 180, 182 n.1 (3d Cir.1976).

[78] In re Goldchip Funding Co., No. 75-1674 (3d Cir. 1975), cited in Lowenschuss v. West Pub. Co., supra, 542 F.2d at 183.

[79] One of the enduring myths of lawyering is that the origin of "disbarment" is to be found in an English court practice of having an unworthy lawyer physically cast over the courtroom "bar" that divided the judge and lawyers from the public. E.g., A.Pulling, The Order of the Coif 187-88 (1897), citing Byrchley's Case, 145 Eng. Rep. 187 (Ex.1584). No eyewitness accounts attesting to such debarments seem to have survived.

[80] See infra at § 3.5.5, n.19.

[81] Cf. In re Kali, 124 Ariz. 592, 606 P.2d 808, 811 (1980).

[82] Florida Bar v. Perri, 435 So.2d 827, 829-30 (Fla.1983) (concurring opinion of Ehrlich, J.)(lawyer suspended in state for three years has burden of demonstrating rehabilitation, but if disbarred would have burden of proving character and fitness, including passing all parts of bar examination).

[83] People v. Susman, 196 Colo. 458, 587 P.2d 782, 785 (1978).

[84] Ky.Sup.Ct.Rules, Rule 3.510(1)(suspension), Rule 3.520(1)(disbarment); In re Hersch, 108 Wis.2d 450, 321 N.W.2d 927 (1982).

[85] Compare, e.g., Schutrum v. Grievance Comm., 70 A.D.2d 143, 420 N.Y.S.2d 429 (1979)(two-year suspension for lawyer who failed to deliver client's funds promptly), with, e.g., In re Chesler, 70 A.D. 141, 420 N.Y.S.2d 429 (1979)(reinstatement of lawyer, automatically disbarred following grand larceny conviction).

Disbarment

Disbarment, naturally, is reserved for the most deliberate, flagrant, and usually unlawful acts. In most usages, disbarment means that the lawyer is indefinitely suspended [86] from practice, and it often carries the connotation that the disciplined lawyer's career as such is ended, at least for an extended period of time. Some jurisdictions make disbarment automatic for conviction of certain offenses, such as a serious crime.[87] If the lawyer's offense was committed in connection with applying for a license to practice law, a common sanction is to rescind the license, which has the same effect as disbarment, although it might also entail repassing the bar examination and the other elaborate ceremonies of admission.[88]

Suspension

Suspension invariably has the effect of preventing the lawyer from practicing law during its term. The suspension order may also require other conditions before the court is persuaded that a suspended lawyer has been rehabilitated.[89] If the suspension is for a short period, the order may simply require the lawyer not to practice during that time and the lawyer will be automatically readmitted without further ceremony. If the suspension endures for a long time, the lawyer ordinarily must apply and satisfy the requirements for reinstatement.[90]

On the whole, courts have rejected arguments that lawyers who are guilty of serious misconduct can be rapidly rehabilitated. Courts commonly require a period of actual suspension for such serious cases and are unwilling to accept arguments that rehabilitation has been successfully achieved in the period between the misconduct and the time of imposing the disciplinary sanction. Rather than accept avowals of good intentions, courts prefer to test resolve by suspending the lawyer for a period, at the end of which the lawyer can attempt to demonstrate that the intention has borne fruit.[91]

Duration of Suspension

Suspension orders can be found that run for a matter of days [92] or that are themselves suspended,[93] to those that are indefinite [94] or that run for a stated period of time that may be as long as ten years.[95] At a point, suspension for a long period of time should give way to disbarment. Suspension for an extended period is presumably imposed for very serious

[86] But cf., e.g., Florida Bar v. Nagel, 440 So.2d 1287 (Fla.1983)("disbarment" without eligibility for reinstatement for ten years).

[87] Mitchell v. Ass'n of Bar of City of N.Y., 40 N.Y.2d 153, 386 N.Y.S.2d 95, 351 N.E.2d 743 (1976).

[88] People v. Culpepper, 645 P.2d 5 (Colo.1982).

[89] People v. Luxford, 626 P.2d 675, 677 (Colo.1981) (abstaining from alcohol and making restitution). Suspension subject to conditions can be employed as a tool of discovery in the disciplinary proceeding itself, such as an order suspending a lawyer from practice until the lawyer produces documents sought in a disciplinary hearing. See In re Pierce, 71 A.D.2d 1036, 420 N.Y.S.2d 49 (1979).

[90] ABA Disciplinary Standards § 6.4 (1979)(suggesting six months as dividing line between automatic-reinstatement suspensions and those that require application).

[91] In re Schwartz, 31 Cal.3d 395, 182 Cal.Rptr. 640, 644 P.2d 833, 836-37 (1982); Florida Bar v. Routh, 414 So.2d 1023 (Fla.1982).

[92] Florida Bar v. Lund, 410 So.2d 922 (Fla.1982)(ten-day suspension for untruthful testimony before grievance committee involving other charges). Some suspension orders merely order a suspension for "time served"—the time that a lawyer has voluntarily ceased practice or during which the lawyer was under an interim suspension. E.g., In re Lindgren, 25 Cal.3d 65, 157 Cal.Rptr. 518, 598 P.2d 488 (1979); Florida Bar v. Seidler, 375 So.2d 849 (Fla.1979); In re Feldshuh, 84 A.D.2d 284, 445 N.Y.S. 2d 974 (1982).

[93] The practice of "suspending" some or all of a period of suspension has become routine in California. E.g., Alberta v. State Bar, 37 Cal.3d 1, 206 Cal.Rptr. 373, 686 P.2d 1177 (1984) cert.denied ___ U.S. ___, 105 S.Ct. 1366, ___ L.Ed.2d ___ (1985) (failing to deposit client's restitution funds warrants suspension for five years, with execution stayed conditioned on probation, which includes actual suspension for first year).

[94] Attorney Grievance Comm'n v. Willcher, 287 Md. 74, 411 A.2d 83 (1980). But see ABA Disciplinary Standards § 6.3 commentary (1979)(recommending against indefinite suspension).

[95] People v. Hilgers, 200 Colo. 211, 612 P.2d 1134 (1980) (misappropriating funds of clients requires ten-year suspension before lawyer may apply for readmission); Troughton v. Magagna, 590 P.2d 1332 (Wyo.1979)(four-year suspension for procrastination in closing estates). A long period of suspension may also accrue because of successive disciplinary hearings adding longer duration. E.g., Florida Bar v. Page, 419 So.2d 332 (Fla.1982).

conduct, yet its duration makes it unlikely that the lawyer will possess the knowledge and skills minimally necessary for law practice when the period is over.[96] The ABA accordingly recommends that no suspension should exceed three years.[97]

Interim Suspension

In extreme circumstances most courts are empowered to suspend a lawyer from practice before the completion of the hearing on the full disciplinary charges. That is done in cases when the lawyer has appealed from a conviction for a serious crime[98] or when the lawyer has failed entirely to respond to the notice of disciplinary proceedings involving serious charges.[99]

Effect of Suspension

Most jurisdictions spell out in some detail what a lawyer must do, or refrain from doing, under a suspension order. Common features include notifying all clients,[1] coparties and their lawyers, opposing lawyers and parties, and judges in docketed cases of the fact that the lawyer has been suspended; filing motions to withdraw in cases where this is necessary; returning all papers and other property to clients or other persons entitled to them and notifying them, if relevant, of their need to retain another lawyer; refunding any unearned portion of fees paid in advance; removing signs, telephone listings, stationery, or other public indications that the lawyer practices law; closing the lawyer's law office; and ceasing to engage in any way in the practice of law or to hold oneself out as a lawyer.[2]

Rules commonly require a suspended lawyer to certify to the court or agency that those and any other required steps have been taken. Failure of a lawyer to take necessary steps and to cease practicing law may result in further discipline.[3] Because the suspension order is a direct judicial order and because unauthorized practice is a crime in most jurisdictions, contempt and criminal sanctions

96 People v. Susman, 196 Colo. 458, 587 P.2d 782, 785 (1978); In re Yates, 90 Wn.2d 767, 585 P.2d 1164, 1166 (1978). In People v. Hilgers, supra, 200 Colo. at 213, 612 P.2d at 1135, the court required that once the lawyer carried the heavy burden of demonstrating fitness to practice after a minimum ten-year suspension, he would also be required to retake the bar examination successfully.

97 ABA Disciplinary Standards § 6.3 (1979).

98 United States v. Friedland, 502 F.Supp. 611 (D.N.J.1980), affirmed 672 F.2d 905 (3rd Cir.1981); Florida Bar v. Prior, 330 So.2d 697 (Fla.1976); In re Evans, 229 Kan. 182, 621 P.2d 991 (1981); Mitchell v. Ass'n of Bar of City of N.Y., 40 N.Y.2d 153, 386 N.Y.S.2d 95, 351 N.E.2d 743 (1976); Carter v. Romano, ___ R.I. ___, 426 A.2d 255 (1981). See generally ABA Disciplinary Standards § 6.5 (1979)(urging interim suspension following conviction of serious crime); ABA Spec. Comm. on Eval. of Discipl. Enforcement, Problems and Recommendations in Disciplinary Enforcement 122-28 (1970)(Clark Report) (same). But see, e.g., Bar Ass'n of Greater Cleveland v. Steele, 65 Ohio St.2d 1, 417 N.E.2d 104 (1981)(Ohio rule prohibiting discipline prior to completion of appeal from criminal conviction).

99 In re Mandel, 94 A.D.2d 278, 464 N.Y.S.2d 168 (1983); In re Staller, 94 A.D.2d 119, 463 N.Y.S.2d 459 (1983).

1 Cf. Gasbarini v. Medical Center of Beaver Cty., Inc., 487 Pa. 266, 409 A.2d 343 (1979)(widow allowed to proceed with wrongful death action despite running of statute of limitations period when her lawyer, in disregard of obligation following suspension, failed to notify her of suspension).

2 See generally ABA Disciplinary Standards § 6.11 (1979). Some or all of those requirements are listed in, e.g., Cal.Rules of Court, Rule 955; Colo. Rules Civ.Proc., Rule 255; Iowa Sup. Ct. Rules, Rule 118.18; In re Kennedy, 472 A.2d 1317, 1334-35 (Del.), cert. denied ___ U.S. ___, 104 S.Ct. 2388, 81 L.Ed.2d 346 (1984); In re Cummings, 471 A.2d 254 (D.C.App.1984); In re Kraus, 295 Or. 743, 670 P.2d 1012, 1016-17 (1983); In re Gonyo, 73 Wis. 2d 624, 245 N.W.2d 893, 895 (1976).

3 Athearn v. State Bar, 32 Cal.3d 38, 184 Cal.Rptr. 728, 648 P.2d 950 (1982)(six months' suspension for failure to notify clients); People v. Forsyth, 191 Colo. 378, 553 P.2d 392 (1976)(disbarment); In re McDonald, 70 A.D.2d 919, 417 N.Y.S.2d 746 (1979)(disbarment); In re Christianson, 215 N.W.2d 920 (N.D.1974)(denial of reinstatement); In re Kraus, 295 Or. 743, 670 P.2d 1012, 1017 (1983)(additional period of suspension); Office of Disciplinary Counsel v. Herman, 493 Pa. 267, 426 A.2d 101 (1981)(disbarment); In re Yamagiwa, 97 Wn.2d 773, 650 P.2d 203 (1982)(disbarment for failing to notify clients and continuing to practice law while under suspension for failure to comply with mandatory continuing legal education rule). A lawyer's reinstatement does not retroactively validate unauthorized practice during a period of suspension. See Florida Bar v. Bratton, 413 So.2d 754, 755 (Fla.1982). An obdurate suspended lawyer's failure to notify clients can be dealt with by the appointment of a lawyer as receiver of the suspended lawyer's client files in order to notify clients. E.g., In re Gittleman, 101 A.D.2d 88, 474 N.Y.S.2d 796, 798 (1984).

may also be imposed for violation of a suspension order.[4]

The states differ in the extent to which they require suspended lawyers to remove themselves entirely from law practice.[5] In all states, a suspended lawyer may not represent clients and is typically given a stated period within which to wind up a practice and within which the lawyer is not to accept new matters.[6] For some matters, a state court's discretion to preclude further practice is limited by its power. For example, a state court cannot order a lawyer not to practice in another state or before a federal court or agency.[7] All states seem to prohibit both actual practice as well as holding oneself out as a lawyer.[8] Some states permit lawyers to act as law clerks in other lawyers' offices during suspension.[9] But other states prohibit it, regarding the arrangement as a temptation to engage in surreptitious practice.[10] A lawyer who does engage in unauthorized practice while suspended probably forfeits any claim to a fee.[11] Fees earned to the point of disbarment should be recovered only on the basis of quantum meruit in any representation in which the lawyer has not completed the services.[12]

Resignation

Most states provide for resignation as an alternative to disbarment or indefinite suspension.[13] A lawyer who faces serious charges of misconduct may prefer to resign in order to avoid the stigma and collateral consequences of imposed discipline.[14] Unlike that of a private club or an unintegrated bar association,[15] however, membership in a bar cannot always be voluntarily resigned. Two methods have evolved to deal with attempted resignations in the face of disciplinary charges. In one, courts refuse to accept an attempted resignation if flagrant violations have been found or serious charges have been filed.[16] Under the second method, a standing

4 Florida Bar v. Hartnett, 398 So.2d 1352 (Fla.1981) (disbarment and contempt); In re Crumpacker, ___ Ind. ___, 431 N.E.2d 91, appeal dismissed 459 U.S. 803, 103 S.Ct. 25, 74 L.Ed.2d 41 (1982)(ninety days imprisonment without reduction for good time served and fine of $500); State v. Bucci, ___ R.I. ___, 430 A.2d 746 (1981)(imprisonment for six months); In re Hines, 275 S.C. 411, 272 S.E.2d 169 (1980)(imprisonment for thirty days).

5 See generally Annot., 87 A.L.R.3d 279 (1978).

6 See generally ABA Disciplinary Standards § 6.15 and commentary (1979).

7 Florida Bar v. Penn, 421 So.2d 497, 500-01 (Fla.1982) (court cannot order suspended lawyer not to practice in federal bankruptcy proceedings unless lawyer is also not member of federal court bar). But cf. In re Yamagiwa, 97 Wn.2d 773, 650 P.2d 203, 206 (1982)(lawyer's obligation to notify clients of suspension included clients with immigration and naturalization matters). On reciprocal discipline, see § 3.4.6.

8 Farnham v. State Bar, 17 Cal.3d 605, 131 Cal.Rptr. 661, 552 P.2d 445, 449 (1976); In re Peterson, 274 N.W.2d 922, 926 (Minn.1979).

9 Florida Bar v. Thomson, 310 So.2d 300, 87 A.L.R.3d 272 (Fla.1975), noted 4 Fla.L.Rev. 296 (1951); In re Stoldt, 37 N.J. 364, 181 A.2d 364 (1962); In re Easler, 275 S.C. 400, 272 S.E.2d 32 (1980). Sometimes this is put on the unduly narrow rationale that, for unauthorized law purposes, a nonlawyer can work for a lawyer. Violation of a suspension order can then be made out only on a showing that the lawyer in fact was not under the supervision of another lawyer. E.g., Grievance Administrator v. Chappell, 418 Mich. 1202, 344 N.W.2d 1 (1984); State ex rel. Oregon St. Bar v. Lenske, 284 Or. 23, 584 P.2d 759 (1978).

10 Committee on Professional Ethics v. Glenn, 259 N.W.2d 867, 868 (Iowa 1977). A lawyer who permits a suspended or disbarred lawyer to practice law in his or her office violates the prohibition against aiding unauthorized practice. E.g., Crawford v. State Bar, 54 Cal.2d 659, 7 Cal.Rptr. 746, 355 P.2d 490 (1960); In re Kuta, 86 Ill.2d 154, 56 Ill.Dec. 56, 427 N.E.2d 136 (1981); In re Lacy, 234 Mo.App. 71, 112 S.W.2d 594 (1937).

11 Fletcher v. Krise, 120 F.2d 809 (D.C.Cir.), cert.denied 314 U.S. 608, 62 S.Ct. 88, 86 L.Ed. 489 (1941); In re Estate of Giddings, 96 Misc.2d 824, 410 N.Y.S.2d 16 (N.Y.Sur.Ct. 1978).

12 In re Estate of Giddings, 96 Misc.2d 824, 410 N.Y.S.2d 16 (N.Y.Sur.Ct.1978)(quoting court rule).

13 Resignation, of course, is also available for non-disciplinary reasons, as when a lawyer has moved from a jurisdiction and petitions to resign in order to avoid paying an annual membership fee. E.g., In re Jenkins, 280 S.C. 190, 312 S.E.2d 6 (1984).

14 See In re Phillips, 452 A.2d 345, 347 (D.C.App.1982). But cf. In re Alfieri, 428 So.2d 662 (Fla.1983)(over bar's objection, lawyer convicted of two felony charges permitted to resign because both disbarred lawyers and those who resign may apply for readmission after three years).

15 Cf. In re Fodiman, 87 A.D.2d 267, 453 N.Y.S.2d 307, 308 (1982)(three year suspension ordered for lawyer who gave sentencing judge false impression that resignation from unintegrated state bar association would terminate right to practice).

16 In re Phillips, supra (disbarment following conviction for rape and sodomy); In re Hetland, 275 N.W.2d 582 (Minn.1978); In re Ditri, 71 N.J. 173, 364 A.2d 545 (1976);

rule treats resignations as admissions of any charges against the lawyer and the act of the court in accepting the petition to resign is equivalent to disbarring the lawyer.[17] Reinstatement following resignation is treated in the same fashion as if the charges had been fully established by evidence.

Disability Proceedings[18]

Many jurisdictions provide for various grades of bar membership, including some that can be employed for lawyers who are physically or mentally disabled. Moreover, many integrated bars provide for an inactive or retired status that may serve some of those same purposes. Involuntary transfer to a disabled or inactive status typically follows a hearing in which a lawyer's inability to practice law in light of senility, alcoholism or other drug dependency, or mental illness is determined.

§ 3.5.5 Reinstatement

Rehabilitation and Present Competence

Most jurisdictions recognize that even a disbarred lawyer might be able to persuade a court that the court should relent and readmit the lawyer to practice.[19] Reinstatement of a lawyer following suspension or disbarment is hardly comparable to admission of a new lawyer. In original admissions there is normally no reason to place a high burden of proof on the applicant. But when a suspended lawyer applies to be reinstated, the incontrovertible fact of adjudicated misconduct clearly gives sufficient reason to doubt whether the lawyer has become qualified to practice law.[20] Most jurisdictions accordingly require the petitioning lawyer to demonstrate by clear and convincing evidence that he or she should be readmitted.[21] The readmission is begun by the lawyer's petitioning the same disciplinary agency that adjudicates discipline cases, seeking a hearing on the lawyer's asserted grounds for readmission.

A petition for reinstatement raises two general issues. First, because of the conduct that constituted the original offense, is the lawyer rehabilitated from the conditions, habits, or attitudes that caused the offenses for which the lawyer was disciplined?[22] Second, because of the passage of time during the suspension or disbarment, is the lawyer now

Office of Disciplinary Counsel v. Herrmann, 475 Pa. 560, 381 A.2d 138 (1977); In re Nixon, 53 A.D.2d 178, 385 N.Y.S.2d 305 (1975). In an unusual twist on the court's discretion, the court in Carter v. Walsh, 122 R.I. 349, 406 A.2d 263 (1979), censured a lawyer-educator for deceit and neglect and ordered him to submit his resignation. See also, e.g., In re Wackerbarth, 287 N.W.2d 651 (Minn. 1979)(lawyer's attempt to transfer to retirement status denied and lawyer disbarred).

17 Florida Bar v. Jaffe, 428 So.2d 252 (Fla.1983)(resignation of lawyer convicted of violation of travel act accepted without leave to apply for reinstatement permanently); In re Tew, 249 Ga. 587, 292 S.E.2d 721 (1982); In re Gunderson, 75 A.D.2d 934, 428 N.Y.S.2d 63 (1980).

18 See generally ABA Disciplinary Standards 77-81 (1979).

19 In re Gordon, 385 Mass. 48, 429 N.E.2d 1150, 1154 (1982)("no offense is so grave as to preclude automatically a disbarred attorney from seeking reinstatement on adequate proof"); cf. In re Barton, 291 Md. 61, 432 A.2d 1335, 1338 (1981)("disbarment does not necessarily operate as a permanent disability"). The ABA Disciplinary Standards do not prescribe a sanction more permanent than disbarment for a minimum of five years. See Id. § 6.2. Contra, e.g., In re Kerr, 424 A.2d 94 (D.C.1980) (under local statute, disbarment for conviction of crime involving moral turpitude is permanent); In re Sugarman, 64 A.D.2d 166, 409 N.Y.S.2d 224 (1978)(absent reversal or pardon, court has no power to reinstate lawyer disbarred for conviction of serious crime); Dayton Bar Ass'n v. Prear, 68 Ohio St.2d 42, 428 N.E.2d 404, 405 (1981)(local rule mandates permanent disbarment of lawyer reinstated following indefinite suspension).

20 Roth v. State Bar, 40 Cal.2d 307, 313, 253 P.2d 969, 973 (1953).

21 Peterson v. Sheran, 474 F.Supp. 1215, 1224 (D.Minn. 1979), affirmed, vacated in part on other grounds 635 F.2d 1335 (8th Cir.1980); Bonner v. Disciplinary Board, 401 So.2d 734, 737 (Ala.1981); In re Henritze, 247 Ga. 620, 278 S.E.2d 383 (1981); In re Barton, 291 Md. 61, 432 A.2d 1335, 1338 (1981). Despite the difficult standard purportedly required by most courts, a reading of appellate decisions reveals that courts differ quite widely in the nature of evidence that is required and the evaluative strictness of the reviewing court. Compare, e.g., the majority and dissenting opinions in In re Persky, 92 A.D.2d 372, 460 N.Y.S.2d 316 (1983). The force of the clear and convincing requirement seems often offset by human sympathy and heartfelt judicial hopes for reform. E.g., In re McKeon, 201 Mont. 515, 656 P.2d 179, 182, 184 (1982). It has been opined by a disciplinary counsel that reinstatement has become increasingly frequent. See 51 U.S.L.Wk. 2761 (1983).

22 Jurisdictions that provide for permanent disbarment presumably proceed on the assumption that the underlying offense is so serious that successful rehabilitation is

minimally competent to practice law? Courts that also insist that a third factor must be taken into account—the public's probable reaction to an order of reinstatement—simply invite confusion and arbitrary decisions.[23]

Rehabilitation

A court must pursue two areas of inquiry in order to determine whether a lawyer is presently fit to be trusted with the responsibilities of law practice.[24] The court must first examine the original offense and assess the extent to which the lawyer might now be able to resist similar temptations.[25] The court, second, must examine, as well as it can, the lawyer's present attitudes and character, as illustrated by his or her activities during the period of suspension, in order to determine whether the emotional, attitudinal, economic, social, familial, or other causes of the original misconduct have been sufficiently ameliorated. The extent to which a court will insist upon a particularized and compelling showing of rehabilitation may vary, depending upon whether the original suspension was automatic or the result of the exercise of the court's considered judgment.[26] Because of the importance of examining the suspended lawyer's conduct during a considerable period of time after suspension, reinstatement petitions must sometimes be dismissed as premature,[27] particularly if the petitioner's original misconduct itself continued over a course of years.[28] Substantial waiting periods are commonly required following disbarment, for both evaluative and deterrent purposes.[29]

What should count as proof of rehabilitation, or of nonrehabilitation? A suspended lawyer's conduct during the period of suspension should be judged by a higher standard than simply the criminal law and similar constraints applicable to all citizens. The question before the court is whether, despite past failures, the lawyer can practice under

doubtful in most cases or on the principle that considerations other than the lawyer's character and abilities are relevant on the question of reinstatement. Punishment or concern with public opinion might be such considerations. See § 3.1.

[23] Compare e.g., In re Hiss, 368 Mass. 447, 333 N.E.2d 429 (1975)(unrepentant lawyer convicted of perjury twenty-five years earlier in nationally notorious case that still generated controversy readmitted), with, e.g., In re Gordon, 385 Mass. 48, 429 N.E.2d 1150, 1155-57 (1982) (repentant lawyer involved as judge in notorious local political corruption scandal sixteen years earlier denied readmission because of feared lessening of public respect for legal system). For a general critique of the concept of "appearance of impropriety," see § 7.1.4.

[24] Cf. ABA Disciplinary Standards § 6.4 (1979): "The lawyer . . . should not be reinstated unless he can show by clear and convincing evidence: rehabilitation, compliance with all applicable discipline or disability orders and rules, fitness to practice and competence." See also, e.g., In re Kuta, 86 Ill.2d 154, 56 Ill.Dec. 56, 427 N.E.2d 136, 138 (1981)(six-factor rule); In re Braverman, 271 Md. 196, 316 A.2d 246, 247 (1974)(factors on reinstatement petition are (1) nature and circumstances of original misconduct; (2) lawyer's subsequent conduct and reformation; (3) lawyer's present character; (4) lawyer's present qualifications and competence); In re Trombly, 398 Mich. 377, 247 N.W.2d 873, 875 (1976)(quoting and applying criteria listed in Michigan bar rule); In re Eddleman, 77 Wn.2d 42, 459 P.2d 387, 388 (1969)(eight factors).

[25] Probably the nature of the original offense as much as any single factor has led courts to reject reinstatement petitions. E.g., State v. Russo, 230 Kan. 5, 630 P.2d 711 (1981)(federal conviction for bribing police to protect client's prostitution operation); In re Raimondi, 285 Md. 607, 403 A.2d 1234 (1979), cert. denied 444 U.S. 1033, 100 S.Ct. 705, 62 L.Ed.2d 669 (1980)(conviction of bribery of public official).

[26] Cf., e.g, Florida Bar v. Steinbach, 427 So.2d 733 (Fla. 1983)(without amendment to rule, court would not require showing of competence on part of lawyer automatically suspended over thirty years previously for failure to pay bar dues); In re Chesler, 70 A.D.2d 141, 420 N.Y.S.2d 429 (1979)(reinstatement less than two years after automatic disbarment for conviction of crime of grand larceny; rehabilitation demonstrated by fact that disciplinary agency had not filed any new charges of misconduct against lawyer).

[27] In re Reed, 248 Ga. 748, 285 S.E.2d 726 (1982)(gravity of original offense can be taken into account in determining whether sufficient time for rehabilitation has passed).

[28] Bonner v. Disciplinary Board, 401 So.2d 734, 739 (Ala.1981)("We agree that although courts are slow to disbar, they are slower to reinstate. . . . The petitioner here has been disbarred for a little over three years. It is common knowledge that virtues do not come about more quickly than vices.").

[29] Florida Bar v. Drizin, 435 So.2d 796 (Fla.1983)(under rule providing for three-year minimum, court has discretion to impose disbarment without right to reapply for five years); Phillips v. Mississippi St. Bar, 427 So.2d 1380 (Miss.1983)(statutory minimum of three years). Occasionally the waiting period imposed may be the functional equivalent of permanent disbarment. E.g., Florida Bar v. Cooper, 429 So.2d 1 (Fla.1983)(disbarment without right to reapply for twenty years for involvement in several fraudulent schemes).

the stricter requirements of the lawyer codes.[30] Thus occurrences during suspension, such as the lawyer's violation of the lawyer codes[31] or other conduct that is not clearly illegal,[32] are negatively relevant. Some courts seem even more impressed with general character testimony when considering a lawyer's reinstatement than in original disciplinary proceedings, possibly because each testifying character witness can be cross-examined[33] about his or her knowledge of the lawyer's activities throughout the period of suspension.[34] Even more than in the case of original discipline, however, courts should appreciate that many fewer lawyers will be willing to testify against a lawyer's readmission than other lawyers will be willing, at least from compassion, to testify for it.[35] The better practice probably significantly discounts general character testimony.[36] A lawyer convicted of a crime and not restored to his or her civil rights has been held ineligible for reinstatement.[37] Courts have also considered most of the elements that were previously examined in connection with imposing discipline initially (§ 3.5.2). Restitution as a factor in reinstatement is considered below (§ 3.5.6).

If the lawyer's original difficulties involved conduct in violation of the lawyer code and were possibly due in part to ignorance of its requirements, a court may require the lawyer to repair that failing. The California Supreme Court routinely requires that, during the period of suspension, a lawyer pass the state's version of the multistate bar examination on professional responsibility.[38] Courts will also require proof of rehabilitation for an alcoholism or other drug problem.[39]

The question of a lawyer's present attitudes and character can naturally raise difficult issues of personal autonomy and privacy.[40] Following the lead of the Massachusetts Supreme Court in In re Hiss,[41] most courts agree that no inference of unfitness to practice should be drawn because the lawyer refuses to admit the facts underlying the original discipline.[42] Different, however, would be a lawyer's insistence that the rule under which he or she was disciplined need not be obeyed or that the lawyer's misconduct was justified.[43] And when the original reason for disbarment involved shockingly aberrant and calculating misconduct, a court will naturally be slow to agree that the petitioner has made

30 In re Peterson, 274 N.W.2d 922, 926 (Minn.1979).

31 Tardiff v. State Bar, 27 Cal.3d 395, 165 Cal.Rptr. 829, 612 P.2d 919 (1980)(lawyer permissibly clerking for another lawyer during suspension held to lawyer code standards in negotiating loan from other lawyer's client).

32 Gannon v. Board of Professional Responsibility, 671 S.W.2d 835 (Tenn.1984)(failing to make child-support payments and termination from employment after discovery of shortages, which were then paid).

33 Some courts purport to rely heavily upon character references given in the form of affidavits, which, of course, are not subject to cross-examination. E.g., In re Thomas, 76 Ill.2d 185, 28 Ill.Dec. 531, 390 N.E.2d 890, 893 (1979). Their value seems very limited, even if they are brought forward in great volume and even if their wording differs, which only suggests that the affidavits have not been prepared by the accused lawyer.

34 In re Johnson, 244 Ga. 109, 259 S.E.2d 57, 59-60 (1979); In re Wigoda, 77 Ill.2d 154, 32 Ill.Dec. 341, 395 N.E.2d 571, 575 (1979).

35 In re Harrington, 134 Vt. 549, 367 A.2d 161, 167 (1976).

36 Committee on Legal Ethics v. Pence, ___ W.Va. ___, 297 S.E.2d 843, 848 (1982).

37 Florida Bar v. Clark, 359 So.2d 863 (Fla.1978).

38 The requirement is known as the "*Segretti* requirement," from its origin in Segretti v. State Bar, 15 Cal.3d 878, 126 Cal.Rptr. 793, 544 P.2d 929 (1976). See also, e.g., In re Barket, 424 So.2d 751 (Fla.1982).

39 See generally § 3.3.3 (alcoholism; mental illness).

40 Notorious is the examination of a Marxist-Leninist in testimony before a multimember district court and denial of reinstatement for perceived dissembling in discussions about the meaning of communist writings. See In re Braverman, 399 F.Supp. 801 (D.Md.1975), reversed by divided panel 549 F.2d 913 (4th Cir.1976). For problematical reinstatement conditions, see, e.g., In re Sax, 321 N.W.2d 902, 904 (Minn.1982)(endorsement, without other details, of referee's requirement that lawyer first control "his problem of procrastination and recalcitrance in adapting to requirements of authority within his profession").

41 368 Mass. 447, 333 N.E.2d 429, 436-37 (1975).

42 In re Mitchell, 249 Ga. 280, 290 S.E.2d 426 (1982); In re Albert, 403 Mich. 346, 269 N.W.2d 173 (1978). A somewhat less liberal view is that continued protestation of innocence of the original offense is not itself a sufficient ground on which to deny reinstatement. E.g., In re Mandell, 89 Ill.2d 14, 59 Ill.Dec. 97, 431 N.E.2d 382, 385 (1982).

43 See § 3.5.2 at notes 52 & 53.

the enormous shift in character necessary to demonstrate rehabilitation.[44]

Competence

Reinstatement of a lawyer after an extended period of suspension raises concerns about the competence of the lawyer, and reinstatement may be denied for that reason.[45] Courts sometimes have accepted vague reassurances from lawyers that they have kept up on legal matters by reading.[46] A more careful approach is to require that the applicant at least show minimal competence by passing the state's bar examination.[47] Because of the burdens imposed by the examination requirement, it is ordinarily employed when the period of inactivity has been substantial [48] and the court is not otherwise persuaded that the lawyer has kept current on law and legal developments.[49] In one case, when the lawyer's only interest was in clearing his name after a period of suspension that extended into old age, one court permitted readmission to an inactive status that did not permit law practice.[50]

Status of Reinstated Lawyer

In most respects, a lawyer reinstated to practice enjoys all of the privileges and advantages of a newly admitted lawyer. In one respect, however, a reinstated lawyer practices under a special disability. If a reinstated lawyer is again found guilty of misconduct, the sanction is likely to be grave.[51]

§ 3.5.6 Restitution

Rationale for Restitution as a Disciplinary Factor

The fact that a lawyer makes restitution to an aggrieved client or other creditor, or fails to make restitution, might be relevant to a disciplinary proceeding in a number of ways. A court may consider the presence or absence of restitution in mitigation or enhancement of a sanction or when a suspended or disbarred lawyer petitions for readmission. Or a court may directly order restitution as a disciplinary sanction. With only occasional hesitation, courts have generally assumed that those remedial treatments of restitution are valid. So long as the remedy is applied with circumspection, it seems fully supportable by the traditional claims of courts that they are empowered to oversee lawyers. Moreover, restitution can serve important disciplinary purposes of deterring and rehabilitating lawyers.

Restitution as Mitigation or Enhancement

A lawyer's repayment of wrongfully appropriated funds may be considered strongly relevant in a discipline case.[52] It may indicate that the lawyer commendably feels remorse, desires to assume responsibility for misconduct, and is inclined to right wrongs. To put

[44] In re Mandell, 89 Ill.2d 14, 59 Ill.Dec. 97, 431 N.E.2d 382 (1982).

[45] In re Atkins, 2 Ohio St.3d 32, 442 N.E.2d 754 (1982).

[46] In re McKeon, 201 Mont. 515, 656 P.2d 179 (1982) (and see dissenting opinion of Haswell, C.J.).

[47] In re Kimball, 425 So.2d 531, 534 (Fla.1982); In re Christianson, 253 N.W.2d 410 (N.D.1977); In re Johnson, 92 Wn.2d 349, 597 P.2d 113, 114 (1979)(under state rule). See also, e.g., People v. Davis, 620 P.2d 725, 727 (Colo. 1980)(lawyer disbarred for minimum period of eight years must pass bar examination as condition to readmission).

[48] In re Livesey, 94 Wn.2d 251, 615 P.2d 1294 (1980) (reexamination not required when lawyer was suspended for one year and showed strong evidence of rehabilitation; sufficient showing of competence could be achieved by taking forty-five hours of continuing legal education).

[49] Compare e.g., In re Barket, 424 So.2d 751 (Fla.1982) (six years' suspension, during which time petitioner was home improvement contractor); In re Christianson, 253 N.W.2d 410 (N.D.1977); State v. Brodson, 11 Wis.2d 124, 103 N.W.2d 912 (1960), with, e.g., In re Barton, 291 Md. 61, 432 A.2d 1335 (1981)(fourteen years since disbarment does not require retaking bar examination when petitioner has been actively involved in law-related activities during much of period).

[50] In re Lindquist, 310 Minn. 558, 246 N.W.2d 35 (1976) (readmission to inactive status of seventy-one-year-old lawyer disbarred for failure to report for induction in 1943).

[51] Dayton Bar Ass'n v. Herzog, 70 Ohio St.2d 261, 436 N.E.2d 1037, cert. denied 459 U.S. 1016, 103 S.Ct. 377, 74 L.Ed.2d 510 (1982)(Ohio rule requiring permanent disbarment).

[52] See generally Annot., 95 A.L.R.3d 724 (1979).

an extreme instance, a lawyer who restores funds to a client, under circumstances in which the client would not have been aware that they had been converted, at least portrays residual honesty and contriteness. To take an opposite extreme, a lawyer evidences a serious character defect relevant to law practice if he or she refuses to restore a client's funds when the lawyer plainly has no claim to them, and is readily able to repay and the client is in great need. Restitution is also relevant to the deterrence purposes of discipline because it removes the economic incentive to engage in misconduct. Moreover, restitution obviously serves the interests of the injured party and avoids the necessity of that party's resort to expensive and time-consuming collection processes.

In order to encourage it, most courts routinely treat restitution as a mitigating element,[53] such as the fact that a lawyer has repaid funds wrongfully taken from a client.[54] But courts have not been persuaded to treat restitution as a complete defense or as conclusive evidence that the original transaction represented a "loan" to the lawyer.[55]

Despite its possible value as evidence of rehabilitation, however, restitution may be entirely prudential, made by the lawyer solely to contrive helpful evidence in a discipline case. Then restitution measures only a lawyer's wealth, borrowing ability, or good luck rather than any personal quality that suggests either that the original misconduct was out of character or that the lawyer has changed course and is not likely in the future to cause harm.[56] Deterrence is achieved, but only in a marginal way over the situation that obtains in any event because of the court's power to order restitution. Accordingly, some courts properly insist that the fact that a lawyer restores ill-gotten funds be taken to demonstrate a favorable change of character only if the lawyer does so voluntarily and not under the shadow of a disciplinary or similar charge.[57] To count as mitigation, of course, the restitution should come from the lawyer and not from a collateral, source such as a legal malpractice insurer, or involuntarily, such as when the creditor executes a judgment obtained against the lawyer.[58]

Reinstatement and Restitution

When considering reinstatement petitions, courts credit favorably a lawyer who has attempted promptly and voluntarily to make restitution to persons whom the lawyer has harmed [59] or to a client security fund that has compensated victims of the lawyer's misconduct.[60] Courts will note restitution with particular approval if the suspended lawyer had no legal obligation to repay the funds.[61]

[53] That position is endorsed in ABA Disciplinary Standards § 7.1 commentary (1979).

[54] See generally Annot., 95 A.L.R.3d 724 (1979).

[55] People v. McCamant, 193 Colo. 22, 561 P.2d 1255 (1977); In re Cary, 90 Wn.2d 762, 585 P.2d 1161, 1163 (1978).

[56] In re Wilson, 81 N.J. 451, 409 A.2d 1153, 1156 (1979) ("In the context of professional discipline, restitution suggests an 'honesty of compulsion,' proving mostly that the lawyer is anxious to become a lawyer again and that he is able somehow to raise the money. Practically every lawyer facing such charges *wants* to remain a lawyer, but not every lawyer is able to raise the money."). See also, e.g., State v. Raskin, 642 P.2d 262, 267-68 (Okla.1982); In re Albright, 274 Or. 815, 549 P.2d 527, 529 (1976).

[57] Finch v. State Bar, 28 Cal.3d 659, 170 Cal.Rptr. 629, 633, 621 P.2d 253 (1981)(restitution under pressure of law partners and state bar entitled to little weight); Bradpiece v. State Bar, 10 Cal.3d 742, 111 Cal.Rptr. 905, 518 P.2d 337 (1974); Committee on Professional Ethics v. Freed, 341 N.W.2d 757, 759 (Iowa 1983); In re Bartlett, 283 Or. 487, 584 P.2d 296, 302 (1978).

[58] Scales v. State Bd. of Law Examiners, 282 Ark. 578, 669 S.W.2d 895 (1984)(bonding company); Louisiana St. Bar Ass'n v. Summers, 379 So.2d 1065 (La.1980); In re Primus, 283 N.W.2d 519, 520 (Minn.1979).

[59] In re Bowden, 99 Wn.2d 684, 663 P.2d 1349, 1351 (1983). But see, e.g., In re McKeon, 201 Mont. 515, 656 P.2d 179, 183 (1982).

[60] In re Beckmann, 79 N.J. 402, 400 A.2d 792, 793 (1979).

[61] In re Leali, 320 N.W.2d 413, 414 (Minn.1982). Many lawyer debts involved in disciplinary cases will not be dischargeable in bankruptcy because the statute specifically precludes discharge of a debt involving fraud or defalcation by a fiduciary. See 11 U.S.C.A. § 523(a)(4). A decision of the Supreme Court dealing with automatic suspension of drivers' licenses for unpaid automobile judgments (Perez v. Campbell, 402 U.S. 637, 91 S.Ct. 1704, 29 L.Ed.2d 233 (1971)) has been read to preclude a state from imposing a postdischarge condition of restitution if the lawyer's debt is another kind and is discharged. See In re Batali, 98 Wn.2d 610, 657 P.2d 775 (1983). Whether the *Perez* decision precludes a court

Sometimes an order suspending a lawyer will expressly condition readmission on restitution.[62] Even if restitution is not stated as an express condition, courts will refuse to reinstate a suspended lawyer if he or she, although able, fails to make restitution,[63] only makes restitution at discounted figures,[64] or only makes efforts at restitution on the eve of the reinstatement hearing.[65] A lawyer who is valiantly and steadily paying off amassed debts, and who shows every indication of continuing to do so, will not be denied reinstatement solely because complete restitution has not yet been made.[66]

Disciplinary Order to Make Restitution

Courts have gone further than conditioning suspension or reinstatement on restitution and have directly ordered a lawyer to make restitution as a separate and unconditional sanction, including cases in which the lawyer's disbarment is also ordered.[67] Restitution has also been urged by the ABA.[68] Courts have ordered offending lawyers to make restitution of converted funds or funds wrongly obtained through receipt of a bribe,[69] of interest lost on such funds,[70] of fees wrongly charged [71] or received for work never done,[72] and of converted property [73] or property otherwise wrongly obtained.[74] Courts have, however, generally refused to order dis-

from taking restitution, or its absence, into account in determining the lawyer's fitness to practice despite bankruptcy is an open question. See also § 15.3.2 at n.55.

[62] Yokezeki v. State Bar, 11 Cal.3d 436, 113 Cal.Rptr. 602, 521 P.2d 858, cert. denied 419 U.S. 900, 95 S.Ct. 183, 42 L.Ed.2d 145 (1974)(rejecting state bar's argument that lawyer should be disbarred, ruled that lawyer who converted client's interest in apartment building and note for $65,000 suspended, but can achieve full reinstatement at any time full restitution is made); People v. Harthun, 197 Colo. 1, 593 P.2d 324, 326 (1979); In re Dawson, 131 So.2d 472 (Fla.1961). A Mississippi disciplinary rule requires a lawyer who applies for reinstatement to list all persons who suffered pecuniary loss from the lawyer's misconduct and show that full restitution has been made. See Burgin v. Mississippi State Bar, 453 So.2d 689 (Miss. 1984). In In re Rabideau, 102 Wis.2d 16, 306 N.W.2d 1, 11, appeal dismissed 454 U.S. 1025, 102 S.Ct. 559, 70 L.Ed.2d 469 (1981), the court held it improper for a referee to impose as a condition to reinstatement the requirement that the lawyer pay fines and costs assessed in a criminal case; but the court did state that nonpayment "may well be relevant" to an application for reinstatement.

[63] In re Shannon, 274 Ark. 106, 621 S.W.2d 853 (1981); In re Clark, 406 A.2d 28 (Del.1979); In re Berkley, 96 Ill. 2d 404, 71 Ill.Dec. 694, 451 N.E.2d 848 (1983)(restitution will always be required, except in rare instances in which lawyer can demonstrate that it is impossible); Louisiana Bar Ass'n v. Mundy, 423 So.2d 1126, 1129 (La.1982).

[64] In re Garrison, 44 N.C.App. 158, 260 S.E.2d 445, 447-48 (1979), appeal dismissed 299 N.C. 545, 265 S.E.2d 404 (1980)(disbarred lawyer, who made restitution only if creditors agreed to compromise and who renounced funds that would have enabled him to help satisfy judgments, denied reinstatement).

[65] In re Freedman, 406 Mich. 256, 277 N.W.2d 635, 638 (1979)(although earning significant income, lawyer made no effort until morning of reinstatement hearing to arrange to pay fine imposed in criminal case that led to suspension).

[66] In re Zahn, 82 Ill.2d 489, 45 Ill.Dec. 943, 413 N.E.2d 421, 424 (1980).

[67] In re Reno, 187 Mont. 262, 609 P.2d 704 (1980); In re Millard, 98 Wis.2d 114, 295 N.W.2d 352 (1980).

[68] ABA Disciplinary Standards § 6.12 commentary (1979)("Whenever possible, the disciplinary process should facilitate restitution to the victims of the respondent's misconduct, without requiring victims to institute separate proceedings at their own expense.").

[69] In re Kuta, 86 Ill.2d 154, 56 Ill.Dec. 56, 427 N.E.2d 136 (1981)(reinstatement denied unless amount of bribe paid to lawyer while city alderman was paid over to city).

[70] In re Couser, 122 Ariz. 500, 596 P.2d 26 (1979).

[71] Florida Bar v. Budish, 421 So.2d 501 (Fla.1982)(lawyer ordered to return fee charged that was greater than fee advertised); In re Hershberger, 288 Or. 559, 606 P.2d 623, 627 (1980)(lawyer who represented two clients in impermissibly conflicting representation required to pay for legal services rendered by substitute counsel); In re Hansen, 586 P.2d 413 (Utah 1978)(lawyer who received fees from client for conflict-ridden representation ordered to return fees paid or face indefinite suspension).

[72] People v. McCleary, 181 Colo. 261, 508 P.2d 783 (1973)(public reprimand and order to return fees for title abstract and divorce work never done for two clients); In re Roundtree, 467 A.2d 143, 148 (D.C.App.1983)(when lawyer's neglect led to dismissal of client's case, lawyer required to return full amount of fee paid, despite fact that lawyer did not retain full sum); In re Jaynes, 267 N.W.2d 782 (N.D.1978)(under court rule, lawyer publicly reprimanded for failing to complete probate work also ordered to refund all money paid for handling estate).

[73] In re Ojala, 289 N.W.2d 108 (Minn.1979)(reinstatement conditioned on return of files and property stolen from opposing lawyers).

[74] In re Pyatt, 280 S.C. 302, 312 S.E.2d 553 (1984) (lawyer reprimanded for impermissible business dealings with client and ordered to reconvey real property obtained in dealings).

ciplined lawyers to make payments that are nonrestitutionary and, thus, more in the nature of fines.[75]

One court [76] has balked at ordering restitution in any case because it converts a professional body concerned with protection of the public into a collection agency;[77] it deprives the lawyer of the constitutional right to jury trial in a civil claim for allegedly wrongfully withheld funds;[78] it deprives the lawyer of the opportunity to assert personal defenses against the claimant and to assert other rights, such as setoff; there is no necessary connection between a lawyer's ability to make restitution and the lawyer's qualifications to practice law; and courts lack the authority to order restitution. But an apparent majority of courts have, in effect, responded that the courts and disciplinary agencies are fully empowered to control the proceeding to prevent the issue of restitution from deflecting the inquiry from the central question of the lawyer's character and ability to practice law;[79] a lawyer has no right of jury trial in a disciplinary action with respect to any matter and courts have powers, traceable to nonjury proceedings in equity, to require a faithless fiduciary lawyer to account for and disgorge ill-gained property; lawyers' other procedural rights can be fully protected by making the restitutionary order conditional or by omitting it in cases in which defenses or setoff rights are asserted in apparent good faith;[80] thus controlled and limited, the court's order to make restitution is fully consistent with deterrent and rehabilitative objectives of lawyer discipline;[81] and a restitutionary order is fully within the inherent powers that a court possesses to devise sanctions less than disbarment in order to carry out the purposes of discipline.[82]

75 Florida Bar v. Rogowski, 399 So.2d 1390, 1391 (Fla. 1981)(court lacks authority to require lawyer to make payments to client security fund when no funds were paid out of that fund with respect to lawyer's defaults). See also § 3.5.7 at notes 4–6.

76 In re Ackerman, 263 Ind. 309, 330 N.E.2d 322, 323-24, 75 A.L.R.3d 302 (1975), overruling In re Case, 262 Ind. 118, 311 N.E.2d 797 (1974).

77 In re McKeon, 201 Mont. 515, 656 P.2d 179, 183 (1982)(reinstated lawyer's "duty of restitution is contractual, and is a matter between him and the other parties to the contract."); State ex rel. Foot v. Hughes, 92 Mont. 53, 10 P.2d 584, 585 (1932)(referee's recommendation to require lawyer to pay off note given to cover misappropriated funds rejected because "that smacks too much like making this court a collecting agency."). The "collection agency" objection is sound if limited to the practice, in some jurisdictions, of dismissing a complaint of misconduct against a lawyer if restitution is made. The mildly deterrent value of such remedies raises serious questions whether effective regulation of the offending lawyer has been achieved. E.g., ABA Spec. Comm. on Eval. of Discipl. Enforcement, Problems and Recommendations 98 (1970); Steele & Nimmer, Lawyers, Clients, and Professional Regulation, 1976 Am.B.Found. Research J. 917, 996. The use of avowedly coercive and public-oriented systems for settlement of individual disputes has occurred in other areas, such as in the use of criminal courts for bad-check collection. See Steele, Fraud, Dispute, and the Consumer: Responding to Consumer Complaints, 123 U.Pa.L.Rev. 1107 (1975); Zemans, Coercion to Restitution: Criminal Processing of Civil Disputes, 2 L.& Policy Q. 81 (1980). Courts must also guard against a lawyer's use of restitution to obtain the silence or other cooperation of a complaining party. E.g., In re Madera, 39 A.D.2d 202, 333 N.Y.S.2d 329 (1972), cert. denied 414 U.S. 865, 94 S.Ct. 120, 38 L.Ed.2d 85 (1973).

78 Compare also United States v. Brown, 587 F.Supp. 1005 (E.D.Pa.1984)(portions of federal Victim and Witness Protection Act that require federal court to order restitution to victims of some federal crimes do not unconstitutionally deprive defendant of civil jury trial right), with United States v. Welden, 568 F.Supp. 516 (N.D.Ala.1983) (contra), reversed sub nom. United States v. Satterfield, 743 F.2d 827 (11th Cir.1984).

79 Cf., e.g., In re Kunin, 252 Ga. 310, 313 S.E.2d 697 (1984)(lawyer's reinstatement conditioned on resolution of all fee disputes with clients through fee arbitration).

80 E.g., In re Cornelius, 521 P.2d 497, 499 (Alaska 1974) (because of lack of information about persons owed funds and amount of lawyer's obligation, restitution can be adequately handled by considering it when lawyer applies for reinstatement); In re Rinzel, 107 Wis.2d 549, 319 N.W.2d 873, 875 (1982)(in view of lawyer's asserted right to setoff claim for fees, restitution not directly ordered but reinstatement conditioned on resolution of claim and setoff).

81 The problem of a lawyer's inability to make full financial restitution, for example, can be handled by taking that factor into account in imposing discipline or in passing on a petition for reinstatement. E.g., In re Andreani, 14 Cal.2d 736, 97 P.2d 456, 462-63 (1939).

82 In re Harris, 88 N.J.L. 18, 95 A. 761 (1915). See also Florida Bar v. Winn, 208 So.2d 809, cert. denied 393 U.S. 914, 89 S.Ct. 236, 21 L.Ed.2d 199 (1968)(restitution of converted client funds specifically authorized by statute). If, as is the typical case, a court's order directs restitution to the lawyer's client, the proceedings closely resemble the traditional summary proceeding by a client to obtain relief from misconduct by a lawyer. E.g., Peoples Savings Bank v. Chesley, 138 Me. 353, 26 A.2d 632 (1942).

§ 3.5.7 Other Sanctions

General

Courts have imposed a wide variety of miscellaneous sanctions in discipline cases. Some sanctions, such as mandatory apologies,[83] seem to be spontaneous reactions to particular settings rather than applications of a well thought-out policy of sanctions. Other sanctions, however, such as conservatorship, probation, supervised practice, recertification, and the imposition of costs and other monetary sanctions, seem designed to carry out specific objectives of discipline. In addition, once discipline has been imposed, many collateral consequences can follow.[84]

Conservatorship

In extreme circumstances, a lawyer's disappearance, death, disability, or refusal to cooperate with a disciplinary agency may indicate that client files and interests are in jeopardy. Some jurisdictions accordingly provide for the appointment of a lawyer in such cases to serve as the confidential conservator or trustee of the lawyer's client files.[85] If circumstances indicate that the lawyer is engaged in widespread misuse or misaccounting of client funds, the court can order an audit of the lawyer's accounts and records.[86]

Probation and Supervised Practice

A lawyer may appear to a disciplinary agency or court to be sufficiently rehabilitated not to require a sanction more serious than a reprimand, but the circumstances might suggest that allowing the lawyer to practice without any restriction might entail substantial risks. Courts, in such cases, have employed one of several variations on the idea of conditional practice. One form is probation: the lawyer is permitted to practice, but under the threat, in effect, that any further departures from the lawyer code or the terms of probation will result in suspension or other serious discipline that is simultaneously imposed along with the probation but expressly made conditional on the lawyer's failure to abide by the terms of the probation.[87] The parallel to the model of probation in criminal practice is only a rough one. The chief miss-

[83] In re Lee, 283 N.W.2d 179 (N.D.1979)(letter of apology to client whose funds lawyer had commingled, resulting in check returned for insufficient funds and loss to client of $16.38 in interest); In re Pohlman, 248 N.W.2d 833, 837 (N.D.1976)(letters of apology required to members of disciplinary agency denounced in lawyer's strongly worded letter).

[84] United States v. Blitstein, 626 F.2d 774 (10th Cir. 1980), cert. denied 449 U.S. 1102, 101 S.Ct. 898, 66 L.Ed. 2d 828 (1981)(fact of discipline admissible against lawyer testifying as witness in subsequent case if lawyer's status as such is put into issue); In re Woodworth, 85 F.2d 50 (2d Cir.1936)(disbarred lawyer loses retaining lien); In re State ex rel. Wootan, 364 So.2d 1079 (La.App.1978)(Louisiana statute automatically removes power of suspended or disbarred lawyer to continue to act as notary public); McInerney v. Lally, 384 Mass. 810, 427 N.E.2d 1164 (1981)(suspended lawyer not automatically ineligible to be executor of will written while actively practicing, but trial court should consider its relevance); Peterson v. Knutson, 305 Minn. 53, 233 N.W.2d 716 (1975)(disbarred lawyer is not "learned in the law" as required by state constitution for electoral candidate for supreme court); Phagan v. State ex rel. Eyssen, 510 S.W.2d 655 (Tex.Civ. App.1974)(disbarment of incumbent district attorney renders him ineligible to hold that office); McBrayer v. Cravens, Dargan & Roberts, 265 S.W. 694 (Tex.Com.App. 1924)(statutory exemption from execution for lawyer's professional property continues during five-year suspension).

[85] In re Peck, 302 N.W.2d 356 (Minn.1981); In re Loomos, 90 Wn.2d 98, 579 P.2d 350 (1978); Haw. S.Ct. R. 16.20(a); N.Y.Ct. Rules (First Dept.) § 603.13(g). See generally ABA Disciplinary Standards § 13.1 (1979). The ABA recommends that, if necessary, the cost of the trusteeship be paid out of fees earned by the lawyer whose files are inventoried. See id. commentary. See also, e.g., Office of Disciplinary Counsel v. DeMello, 61 Haw. 223, 601 P.2d 1087, 1088 (1979)(costs of lawyer appointed by court to inventory files must be paid by disbarred lawyer prior to reinstatement); In re Peck, 302 N.W.2d 356, 360-61 (Minn.1981)(lawyer indefinitely suspended and ordered to pay costs of lawyer chosen by disciplinary counsel to act as trustee to protect respondent's clients). The trustee operates under an extension of the attorney-client privilege and, according to the ABA, is not to represent clients, but to report to the appointing judge what disposition should be made of client files. ABA Disciplinary Standards § 13.2 and commentary.

[86] ABA Disciplinary Standards § 13.3 (1979).

[87] Florida Bar v. Rogowski, 399 So.2d 1390, 1391 (Fla. 1981)(sixty-day suspension followed by one year probation with required quarterly reports by certified public accountant of status of trust accounts); Florida Bar v. Larkin, 370 So.2d 371 (Fla.1979)(in neglect case, lawyer publicly reprimanded and placed on probation for two years, with requirement of quarterly reports on cases assumed and disposed of).

ing ingredient is effective supervision;[88] lawyer disciplinary agencies are generally too thinly staffed to provide meaningful review.[89]

A possible solution to the objection of lack of supervision while the lawyer is on probation is supervised practice: a lawyer in good standing is appointed in behalf of the court to act as a supervisor over the practice of the disciplined lawyer, particularly with respect to matters or practices that gave rise to the initial difficulties.[90] Occasionally the order will be accompanied by a restriction prohibiting the lawyer, for a stated period, from practicing in the area of law that gave rise to difficulties[91] or requiring the lawyer to take continuing legal-education courses.[92] If probation or supervision fails, the lawyer may be subjected to much more severe sanctions.[93]

Retraining

Although rarely employed, a requirement that a lawyer acquire additional legal knowledge or skills training has much to commend it. If the lawyer demonstrates rank incompetence resulting in misconduct of a kind that further study and preparation might correct, a requirement of passing a bar examination may be the necessary stimulus to such study.[94] Short of that rather extreme step, a court might require that a lawyer with educational shortcomings in a particular area receive further education in it.[95] Similarly, a lawyer who demonstrates through misconduct that a specialty certification was unwarranted can be subjected to withdrawal of the certification.[96] California courts have developed a rather routine practice of requiring that a disciplined lawyer pass the state's profession-

[88] California employed probation in many suspension cases for thirty years before hiring staff to monitor lawyers on probation. See 51 U.S.L.Wk. 2761 (1983).

[89] In re Scannell, 289 Or. 699, 617 P.2d 256, 258 (1980).

[90] In re Fling, 316 N.W.2d 556, 559 (Minn.1982)(public reprimand, order of restitution, costs, and order to have lawyer experienced in law office management set up bookkeeping system in lawyer's office, audit system, and file reports for two years certifying compliance with rules on office books and trust accounts); In re Morgan, 95 N.M. 653, 625 P.2d 582 (1981)(practice restrictions plus supervision by lawyer, who must report compliance with restrictions); McKinnon v. Disciplinary Bd., 264 N.W.2d 448, 452 (N.D.1978)(before being reinstated, lawyer must secure supervising lawyer who will certify willingness to supervise and make regular reports to disciplinary agency). In some cases, the appointed lawyer's role is much more that of first-chair proctor in all matters. E.g., Attorney Grievance Comm'n v. Bailey, 286 Md. 630, 408 A.2d 1330, 1335 (1979). In Illinois the favored arrangement is a delegation of the details of supervision and reporting to the disciplinary agency. E.g., In re Chapman, 95 Ill.2d 484, 69 Ill.Dec. 940, 448 N.E.2d 852, 856 (1983)(discipline of two years' suspension stayed on condition that respondent serve two-year probationary period and report to, and follow supervision of, disciplinary agency).

[91] Florida Bar v. Hawkins, 444 So.2d 961, 962 (Fla.1984) (public reprimand plus two years probation during which lawyer may not practice criminal law, must take designated hours of continuing legal education in criminal law, and, once eligible to practice criminal law, must associate competent cocounsel in first five criminal cases undertaken); In re Scannell, 289 Or. 699, 617 P.2d 256, 258 (1980)(lawyer suspended for sixty days, then placed on two years' probation during which he cannot engage in representation of private clients in view of government employment). But see In re Sabath, 662 S.W.2d 511, 512 (Mo.1984)(request to resume practice under condition of associating with another lawyer in all matters rejected, for "there is no provision for a special or limited law license"); State Bar v. Edwards, 646 S.W.2d 543, 544 (Tex.App.1982)(trial court exceeded statutory power in permitting lawyer to practice, except before trial courts, for period of one year).

[92] In re Furuseth, 274 N.W.2d 122 (Minn.1978).

[93] In re Peck, 302 N.W.2d 356, 360 (Minn.1981)(lawyer twice placed under voluntary supervision, who continued to generate client complaints, indefinitely suspended); State ex rel. Oregon St. Bar v. Hollingsworth, 286 Or. 477, 595 P.2d 484 (1979)(lawyer who violated terms of probation suspended for one year).

[94] Florida Bar v. Glick, 397 So.2d 1140 (Fla.1981)(lawyer suspended for three months and thereafter until lawyer certifies success on bar examination in light of similarity between present offenses and offenses that led to earlier discipline).

[95] Florida Bar v. Byron, 424 So.2d 748 (Fla.1982)(lawyer who failed to keep proper trust account records required to complete accredited course in bookkeeping); In re Greene, 276 Or. 1117, 557 P.2d 644, 647 (1976)(lawyer who acted incompetently in probate matter placed on probation on condition that he complete courses in approved law school in legal ethics and probate, with grade of at least B). But cf. In re Bartlett, 283 Or. 487, 584 P.2d 296, 297, n.1 (1978)(questioning appropriateness of requiring successful completion of course in legal ethics at accredited law school).

[96] Cf. Florida Bar v. Fassett, 384 So.2d 1288 (Fla.1980) (without discussing nature of offenses, court suspends lawyer's designation as specialist in wills, estates, and estate planning).

al responsibility examination.[97] Several other states have followed that practice.[98]

Costs, Fines, and Other Monetary Sanctions

Courts commonly operate under rules that call for routinely imposing on lawyer-respondents the costs of the proceeding if a violation is found.[99] A few jurisdictions have occasionally imposed a further requirement that the lawyer pay the fees of the disciplinary counsel,[1] and at least one imposes the requirement as a matter of course.[2] But neither those nor other courts will award fees in favor of a prevailing lawyer.[3] The ABA Disciplinary Standards urge that fines not be employed as sanctions, because that would suggest that the trappings of criminal trials are appropriate.[4] Fines have occasionally been imposed by American courts,[5] however, and are a common feature in the discipline of solicitors in England.[6]

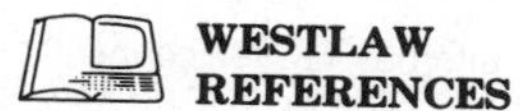
WESTLAW REFERENCES

45k58

attorney lawyer counsel** /s disciplin*** /5 sanction /p (private public +4 reprimand admoni!) disbar! suspen! censure*

factor standard /p disciplin*** /5 sanction /p attorney lawyer counsel**

attorney lawyer counsel** /s disciplin*** /s deterren**

digest(private +1 reprimand warning admonition)

digest("public reprimand")

digest(attorney lawyer counsel** /p suspen! /p disciplin*** punish! /p day)

digest(attorney lawyer counsel** /p suspen! /p disciplin*** punish! /p month)

digest(attorney lawyer counsel** /p suspen! /p disciplin*** punish! /p year)

interim /5 suspen! /p attorney lawyer counsel** /p punish! disciplin***

resign! /p attorney lawyer counsel** /p punish! disciplin***

45k61

[97] Segretti v. State Bar, 15 Cal.3d 878, 126 Cal.Rptr. 793, 544 P.2d 929, 936, n.8 (1976).

[98] In re Allen, 262 N.W.2d 25 (N.D.1978); N.H.S.Ct. R. 37, ¶(13), ¶(3)(c)(as amended Mar.1980).

[99] In re Greene, 277 Or. 737, 562 P.2d 539 (1977)(costs "and disbursements" entitle bar to recover for some items not recoverable in civil actions); In re Hetzel, 118 Wis.2d 257, 346 N.W.2d 782, 787, cert. denied ___ U.S. ___, 105 S.Ct. 186, 83 L.Ed.2d 120 (1984)(costs of $18,532.80 assessed); cf. State ex rel. Okl. Bar Ass'n v. Moss, 682 P.2d 205, 207 (Okl.1983)(disbarred lawyer spared costs in light of hearing panel recommendation and of lawyer's recantation before panel). On apportioning costs, compare, e.g., Florida Bar v. Davis, 419 So.2d 325, 328 (Fla.1982)(apportionment in court's discretion in light of fact that lawyer was acquitted on some charges), with, e.g., In re Wheeler, 108 Wis.2d 573, 322 N.W.2d 885, 886 (1982)(costs assessable against lawyer without being apportioned according to sustained and nonsustained charges).

See generally ABA Disciplinary Standards § 6.13 (1979). The ABA's commentary reasons, in appalling fashion, that a lawyer exonerated of all charges should not be awarded costs, because such a practice may cast doubt on other cases, against other lawyers, in which the charges are sustained! The result in the other cases would assertedly be suspect because it might appear that the charges were sustained there only to award costs to the agency. Id. commentary. Notice that the perceived problem could be resolved either as proposed or by denying costs in all cases. Some jurisdictions apparently follow the rule proposed by the ABA, although possibly for other reasons. E.g., In re Kelly, 109 Wis.2d 348, 325 N.W.2d 729, 735 (1982). Several jurisdictions follow the rule, common in civil cases, that the prevailing party recovers costs. E.g., Netterville v. Mississippi St. Bar, 404 So.2d 1026, 1029 (Miss.1981); In re Banks, 284 Or. 691, 588 P.2d 34, 35 (1978).

[1] In re Pohlman, 248 N.W.2d 833, 837 (N.D.1976). Contra, e.g., In re Banks, 284 Or. 691, 588 P.2d 34, 35 (1978); In re Swetz, 103 Wis.2d 301, 307 N.W.2d 654, 655 (1981). See also In re Brown, 94 Wn.2d 750, 620 P.2d 101, 103 (1980) (lawyer ordered to pay disciplinary counsel's legal fees caused by lawyer's delay in responding to charges).

[2] In re Kelly, 109 Wis.2d 348, 325 N.W.2d 729, 735 (1982).

[3] In re Marcus, 107 Wis.2d 560, 320 N.W.2d 806, 816 (1982)(lawyers who prevailed on advertising charges not entitled to recover legal fees). See also, e.g., Netterville v. Mississippi St. Bar, 404 So.2d 1026 (Miss.1981)(prevailing lawyer may not recover out-of-pocket expenses or legal fees). See generally § 16.6.1.

[4] ABA Disciplinary Standards § 6.14 commentary (1979). Accord, e.g., In re Laubenheimer, 113 Wis.2d 680, 335 N.W.2d 624, 626 (1983).

[5] In re Reed, 369 A.2d 686 (Del.1977)($5000 fine ordered paid to client security fund); In re Hanratty, 277 N.W.2d 373 (Minn.1979)(censure and $5000 fine for false affidavit to title insurance company that, in reliance on affidavit, released funds to client out of which lawyer was paid substantial fee).

[6] Perusal of the *Law Society Gazette*, the weekly newspaper of English solicitors, indicates that fines are a typical sanction for any violation not deemed sufficiently serious to require disbarment. The fines are substantial, amounting often to 750 pounds for each substantiated violation.

competen** /p attorney lawyer counsel** /p reinstate!

restitution /s attorney lawyer counsel** /s disciplin*** punishment

45k58 /p apology conservatorship probation supervis*** re-certif!

§ 3.6 DISCIPLINE IN OTHER FORUMS

§ 3.6.1 Federal Court Discipline [7]

Inherent Disciplinary Power of Federal Courts

Although federal courts have occasionally expressed reservations about their power to discipline lawyers appearing before them,[8] the clear weight of long-standing precedent has established the power beyond serious doubt. From an early time the Supreme Court has been content to recognize a power in the lower federal courts to discipline lawyers as an aspect of the inherent powers of those courts.[9] In modern times the statutes conferring rule-making power may provide additional authority.[10] Subject matter jurisdiction to discipline a lawyer appearing before a federal court has been exercised without question, in most cases presumably under the court's ancillary jurisdiction.[11] Unlike state courts, the federal district courts have always had their own bars separate from those of the courts of appeals, the specialized federal courts, and the Supreme Court, each of which has its own bar as well. The federal appellate courts do not exercise close supervisory power over the lower federal courts in matters of discipline. Those courts do, however, have the power to review individual cases on appeal for abuse of discretion.[12] Discipline in one federal court does not automatically result in discipline in any other of the federal courts. And the vigor with which lawyer compliance with rules is pursued through discipline varies significantly from one federal court to another.[13]

Grounds for Discipline

The federal courts basically regard discipline cases as regulated under the court's common-law powers.[14] The lawyer codes are referred to, sometimes with attention to details if the court's rules have formally adopted the code outright or have incorporated the version of the lawyer code in force in the state within which the federal court sits, as is common.[15] Appellate courts have urged that the lower federal courts respect the primary responsibility of the state courts to discipline

[7] See generally Note, Disbarment in the Federal Courts, 85 Yale L.J. 975 (1976).

[8] Board of Educ. v. Nyquist, 590 F.2d 1241, 1245-46 (2d Cir.1979)("[C]uriously, the power of the federal courts to disqualify attorneys in litigation pending before them has long been assumed without discussion . . . .").

[9] Ex parte Burr, 22 U.S. (9 Wheat.) 529, 531, 6 L.Ed. 152 (1824) ("The power is one which ought to be exercised with great caution, but which is, we think, incidental to all Courts, and is necessary for the preservation of decorum, and for the respectability of the profession.").

[10] 28 U.S.C.A. § 2071 (general rulemaking power). E.g., Fed.R.App.Proc. Rule 46 (c)(brief provision for "any appropriate disciplinary action against any attorney" who practices before a court of appeals). See In re Abrams, 521 F.2d 1094 (3d Cir.), cert. denied 423 U.S. 1038, 96 S.Ct. 574, 46 L.Ed.2d 413 (1975).

[11] As a jurisdictional matter, the federal district courts, in nonancillary disciplinary proceedings, may also look to the general "federal question" jurisdiction (28 U.S.C.A. § 1331(a)) on the notion that a disciplinary proceeding involves an exercise of substantive federal law powers. All federal courts may also be jurisdictionally warranted to discipline by the All Writs statute (28 U.S.C.A. § 1651).

[12] Selling v. Radford, 243 U.S. 46, 51, 37 S.Ct. 377, 379, 61 L.Ed. 585 (1917); In re Collis, 556 F.2d 804 (6th Cir. 1977); Hull v. Celanese Corp., 513 F.2d 568, 571 (2d Cir. 1975). Cf. In re Abrams, 521 F.2d 1094 (3d Cir.), cert. denied 423 U.S. 1038, 96 S.Ct. 574, 46 L.Ed.2d 413 (1975) (in absence of additional evidence, district court could not impose disciplinary sanction more severe than that imposed by state court when relying entirely on state court record).

[13] The Ninth Circuit Court of Appeals seems to have a zeal for discipline far exceeding that of the rest of the circuits combined. See generally J.Moore, Federal Practice ¶ 246.02[3] (2d ed.1983).

[14] In re Abrams, 521 F.2d 1094, 1100-01 (3d Cir.), cert. denied 423 U.S. 1038, 96 S.Ct. 574, 46 L.Ed.2d 413 (1975).

[15] One court has insisted that federal courts should be stricter with discipline because they are courts of limited jurisdiction; because federal disbarment has less impact on the ability of a lawyer to earn a living; and because federal judges, more than state judges, must be able to trust all federal court lawyers. See In re Mattox, 567 F.Supp. 415 (D.Colo.1983)(despite readmission by highest court of sitting state, applicant not readmitted to federal court because hearing demonstrated that lawyer "is incapable of candor").

lawyers.[16] But other courts have struck farther afield.[17] And some federal courts have insisted that higher standards of conduct are required of federal practitioners.[18]

A common reason why a federal court disciplines a lawyer is to achieve parity with discipline imposed by a state court or system.[19] Indeed, in some federal courts, such as in the United States Supreme Court, discipline is entirely derived from action taken by other courts, primarily by state courts.[20] Discipline in the state court does not automatically result in discipline in the federal court.[21] As discussed elsewhere (§ 3.4.5—reciprocity—federal courts), the lawyer disciplined in the state court must be given an opportunity to demonstrate a convincing reason why the state court's action should not be followed. Some federal courts have also resorted to the disciplinary process as a means of controlling lawyer behavior that has an immediate impact upon the operation of the court, such as inordinate delay in perfecting an appeal.[22]

Procedures

Probably because the power is exercised so infrequently that special procedures are unwarranted, the procedures in federal disbarment cases are starkly simple.[23] Federal court discipline, as with state court discipline, must comply with the notice and hearing requirements of due process.[24] The procedure in all federal courts is initiated by filing a motion for a rule to show cause, directing a lawyer to respond to charges. Under ABA guidelines approved by the federal Judicial Conference, a lawyer who is a member of a federal court's bar must inform it promptly of either a criminal conviction or discipline administered by any court.

§ 3.6.2 Discipline in Administrative Agencies[25]

The Question of Power

Federal courts and many state courts have diverged sharply over the question of the power of administrative agencies to admit and

16 In re Abrams, 521 F.2d 1094 (3d Cir.), cert. denied 423 U.S. 1038, 96 S.Ct. 574, 46 L.Ed.2d 413 (1975).

17 United States v. Chapel, 480 F.Supp. 591 (D.P.R.1979)(disbarment from federal court for contumacious failure to appear and other matters connected with lawyer's political beliefs and activities).

18 In re Mattox, 567 F.Supp. 415 (D.Colo.1983)(lawyer "incapable of candor" not readmitted, although readmitted in state courts; the only purpose of admission to federal courts, which are courts of limited jurisdiction, is to practice before its judges and magistrates, who must be able to rely on trustworthiness and honor of its bar).

19 In re Randall, 640 F.2d 898 (8th Cir.), cert. denied 454 U.S. 880, 102 S.Ct. 361, 70 L.Ed.2d 189 (1981)(affirming district court disbarment of former ABA president based on state court disbarment, affirming dismissal of lawyer's civil rights action against justices of state supreme court, and disbarring lawyer from court of appeals); In re Dawson, 609 F.2d 1139 (5th Cir.1980)(discipline based on state court disbarment for advancing funds to clients); Wrighten v. United States, 550 F.2d 990 (4th Cir.1977)(disbarment prompted by state court discipline).

20 Tucker, Disbarment and the Supreme Court of the United States, 35 Fed.B.J. 37 (1978). Chief Justice Burger, occasionally with one other Justice, has complained in several cases of the failure of the Supreme Court to spend more time in policing its own bar. E.g., In re Strickland, 453 U.S. 907, 101 S.Ct. 3138, 69 L.Ed.2d 991 (1981).

21 Theard v. United States, 354 U.S. 278, 282, 77 S.Ct. 1274, 1276, 1 L.Ed.2d 1342 (1957); In re Ruffalo, 390 U.S. 544, 88 S.Ct. 1222, 20 L.Ed.2d 117 (1968); In re Wilkes, 494 F.2d 472 (5th Cir.1974).

22 In re Hanson, 572 F.2d 192 (9th Cir.1977); In re Margolin, 518 F.2d 551 (9th Cir.1975); United States v. Farmer, 476 F.2d 996 (9th Cir.1973), cert. denied 419 U.S. 848, 95 S.Ct. 85, 42 L.Ed.2d 77 (1974).

23 According to the only apparent authority, the Federal Rules of Civil Procedure are inapplicable. Coughlan v. United States, 16 Alaska 407, 236 F.2d 927 (9th Cir.1956). In the wake of Watergate, proposals were made in Congress to provide by federal statute for a system of disciplining federally admitted lawyers. See ABA News at 5 (Mar.1976). As a preemptive move, the ABA promulgated a recommended set of Suggested Guidelines for Uniform Federal Rules of Disciplinary Enforcement in 1978. See 46 U.S.L.Wk. 2443 (1978). Versions of the ABA Guidelines have been adopted in several federal courts.

24 In re Ruffalo, 390 U.S. 544, 88 S.Ct. 1222, 20 L.Ed.2d 117 (1968); Bradley v. Fisher, 80 U.S. (13 Wall.) 335, 354-55, 20 L.Ed. 646 (1871); In re Thies, 662 F.2d 771 (D.C. Cir.1980); In re Los Angeles Cty. Pioneer Soc'y, 217 F.2d 190 (9th Cir.1954).

25 See generally Cox, Regulation of Attorneys Practicing before Federal Agencies, 34 Case W.Res.L.Rev. 173 (1983); Best, Shortcomings of Administrative Agency Discipline, 31 Emory L.J. 535 (1982).

discipline lawyers and other practitioners before them. The federal view, stated in the *Goldsmith* decision in 1926,[26] is that a federal administrative agency with legislative power to prescribe its rules of procedure has general authority to determine who may practice before it.[27] The American Bar Association has attacked the efforts of federal administrative agencies to regulate lawyer behavior,[28] primarily on grounds that ignore the *Goldsmith* decision or that argue as a matter of policy a preference for the preeminence of state court regulation of lawyers under all circumstances.[29]

Some states may take a view diametrically opposed to that expressed in the *Goldsmith* decision. California's supreme court, for example, has held unconstitutional a statute that attempted to confer power on an administrative agency to discipline lawyers who appeared before it.[30] The court's analysis proceeded under the negative aspect of the inherent powers doctrine (§ 2.2.3) and under the extreme view that only the court could regulate the practice of law, notwithstanding that the agency practice involved courts in no discernible way.

26 Goldsmith v. United States Bd. of Tax Appeals, 270 U.S. 117, 46 S.Ct. 215, 70 L.Ed. 494 (1926).

27 The legislative empowerment is not strictly limited to enacting rules of procedure. E.g., Koden v. Dep't of Justice, 564 F.2d 228 (7th Cir.1977)(Immigration and Naturalization Service under statute empowering attorney general to "establish such regulations . . . as he deems necessary for carrying out his authority"); Herman v. Dulles, 205 F.2d 715 (D.C.Cir.1953)(International Claims Commission under power given by Department of State "to prescribe such rules and regulations as may be necessary to enable it to carry out its functions").

28 The literature is immense. An uncommonly dispassionate view is Kaplan, Some Ruminations on the Role of Counsel for a Corporation, 56 Notre Dame Law. 873, 878-82 (1981). Partisan views are reported in, e.g., Editorial Opinion, 68 ABA J. 8 (1982); Ranii, ABA Opposes Securities Lawyers' Code, Nat'l L.J. p.5, col.1, Dec. 7, 1981. The Administrative Conference of the United States has refused to recommend either legislation or a uniform federal standard on agency regulation of practitioners. See 69 ABA J. 580 (1983).

29 See also § 2.2.5.

30 Hustedt v. Workers' Compensation Appeals Bd., 30 Cal.3d 329, 178 Cal.Rptr. 801, 636 P.2d. 1139 (1981).

Part Two
LAWYERS AND CLIENTS

Chapter Four
THE CLIENT–LAWYER RELATIONSHIP

Table of Sections

---

§ 4.1 LOYALTY: LAWYERS AS FIDUCIARY AGENTS

General

This chapter examines the nature of the client-lawyer[1] relationship. Too often the subject is left to inference and assumption, both in general discussions and in the individual work of lawyers with clients. In fact, the nature of the relationship is not at all apparent and involves many difficult and important issues of legal doctrine and legal theory. Considered here are issues that range from the basic question of what it means to say that a lawyer works "for a client" to technical questions concerning the safekeeping of client property. Other chapters deal with issues that also concern the client-lawyer relationship, such as the nature of the contract and its obligations (chapter nine), the lawyer's adversary role as representative of the client (chapter ten), and malpractice issues (chapter five).

Clients' Reasons for Seeking Legal Help

Why should a society saddle itself with the expense and possibly other inconveniences of lawyers? Why do clients go to lawyers? The answers are self-evident to lawyers, although less so to visionaries. Lawyers have special skills and knowledge not generally shared by

[1] By far the version of the phrase more commonly employed by lawyers is the "lawyer-client" relationship. Following the Model Rules, the reference here will be reversed in order to give textual primacy to the person in the relationship whose interests are primarily to be furthered. See the heading preceding MR 1.1 ("Client-Lawyer Relationship").

people and which it would be uneconomic for most people who are not themselves lawyers to attempt to acquire. People go to lawyers when they want to know what the law provides and, generally, when they desire to assert legal rights and avoid legal liability (§ 14.1—legal needs). On occasion, clients must go to lawyers because the law will not allow any other specialist to assist them (§ 15.1). Many of those occasions are ones in which the absence of a lawyer will almost certainly expose the client to a high risk of losing legal rights. The loss is threatened both because of the technically abstruse nature of the proceeding or of the definition of legal rights themselves and because of the fact that self-represented parties are accorded no more consideration in legal proceedings than those who have highly skilled legal assistance (§ 14.4).

The Expectation of Loyalty

Whatever may be the models that obtain in other legal cultures (§ 1.2), the client-lawyer relationship in the United States is founded on the lawyer's virtually total loyalty to the client and the client's interests (§ 10.3). The notion of loyalty here has both negative and affirmative aspects. On the negative side, a lawyer is not to accept a representation, or continue with it, if the lawyer discovers that another interest of the lawyer, either personal or professional, might compromise the lawyer's dedication to vindicating the client's legal position. That feature lies at the root of much of the law of conflicts of interest (see § 7.1.3—loyalty principle) and of other doctrines. Second, on the affirmative side, the lawyer must be willing to make in the client's behalf significant expenditures of the lawyer's intellectual, emotional, and professional resources in order to further the client's interests. That aspect of loyalty finds expression both in the principle of confidentiality (§ 6.7.1.) and in the principle of competence, which in turn is realized in the law of malpractice (§ 5.7), in the law of effective assistance of counsel (§ 14.6), and in the other rules defining specific steps that a lawyer must take in a client's behalf.

The Fiducial Relationship

The entrenched lawyerly conception is that the client-lawyer relationship is the embodiment of centuries of established and stable tradition. Lawyers probably also widely assume that the relationship is unique in its fiduciary responsibilities. Such beliefs are fed by rhetoric such as the following, from Stockton v. Ford: [2]

> There are few of the business relations of life involving a higher trust and confidence than that of attorney and client, or, generally speaking, one more honorably and faithfully discharged; few more anxiously guarded by the law, or governed by sterner principles of morality and justice; and it is the duty of the court to administer them in a corresponding spirit, and to be watchful and industrious, to see that confidence thus reposed shall not be used to the detriment or prejudice of the rights of the party bestowing it.

Whatever the antiquity of the present version of the client-lawyer relationship in Anglo-American law,[3] it is a relationship that is not unique. In legal contemplation, the designation of "fiduciary," which surely attaches to the relationship, also attaches to any relationship of principal and agent.[4] Thus one vital but nonexclusive basis of the client-lawyer relationship is the law of agency.[5]

Nature of the Lawyer's Professional Undertaking

The law of contract defines the client-lawyer relationship for many, but hardly for all purposes. At the least, any duty that a lawyer has under the law of contract is owed to

[2] 52 U.S. (11 How.) 232, 247, 13 L.Ed. 676 (1850).

[3] To the extent that legally enforceable aspects of the client-lawyer relationship revolve around principles of agency law, they cannot be very old, because the law of agency itself arose relatively late in the development of the common law. See 1 F.Pollock & F.Maitland, The History of English Law 211 (2d ed.1923).

[4] Restatement (Second) of Agency § 1(1-3)(1958).

[5] Patterson, Legal Ethics and the Lawyer's Duty of Loyalty, 29 Emory L.J. 909 (1980).

the client.[6] But because the relationship is a fiduciary one, a lawyer may incur legal responsibilities that have no parallel in the law of contract. It is best, then, to speak of the lawyer's professional undertaking rather than the lawyer's contractual duties. For example, a lawyer who spends a half hour speaking to a client in order to determine whether or not to represent the client, and who decides not to, still incurs significant professional and legal duties. Most prominently, the lawyer incurs a duty of confidentiality, despite the fact that contract law would declare that only preliminary negotiations toward a contract took place and that no contract was ever formed. Again, if a lawyer agrees to handle a matter for a client, the fact that they agreed that the client need not pay a fee does not mean that, because the relationship lacks consideration and thus no binding contract was formed, the lawyer incurs no duty to handle the matter competently and subject to all of the other rules controlling the client-lawyer relationship.[7]

Theoretical Basis of the Fiduciary Obligation

The theory on which a lawyer incurs obligations more onerous than those dictated by contract law is rarely spelled out. Some situations can be explained on the ground of special rules to protect persons unable to protect themselves. The notion would be that the client is relatively vulnerable because of inferior legal information and skills and because of the pressure of legal difficulties. But although many business and corporate clients could hardly be described in that way, yet the law extends the full measure of a lawyer's professional obligations to clients largely without regard to their vulnerability.[8] An alternative theory is trust: whatever their resources, clients have a right to assume that a lawyer who undertakes to listen to them and to render legal assistance can be trusted with information and with the responsibility of handling the client's matter in the client's best interest. The trust concept is reflected in the phrase, which courts often repeat, to the effect that the relationship between lawyer and client is one of "trust and confidence." [9] Related is the doctrine that the client-lawyer relationship is an intensely personal one, so that a client who refuses to proceed with a hired lawyer as counsel does not commit a breach of contract.[10] Efficiency notions might also play a part: the legal system operates with least cost if clients can trust their lawyers more than is warranted by the protection of other law.

Variability of the Client-Lawyer Relationship

Lawyers and judges use the term *client* in a specialized and unitary way. The mental image is that of an individual person who has come to the lawyer for a particular bit of legal advice or assistance about a discrete legal problem. The client is freestanding and autonomous and, even if in trouble with the law,

[6] It is controversial whether contracting parties in ordinary business relationships are held to their undertakings because of a desire to compensate a person who reasonably relied on a promise, because of a desire to promote future exchange relationships or economic efficiency, or because of a moral perception that persons incur obligations freely by invoking each other's trust. See generally C. Fried, Contract as Promise: A Theory of Contractual Obligation (1981)(espousing a Kantian moral position). In fiduciary settings such as lawyer and client, each of those theories has special force.

[7] Westinghouse Elec. Corp. v. Kerr-McGee Corp., 580 F.2d 1311 (7th Cir.1978), cert. denied 439 U.S. 955, 99 S.Ct. 353, 58 L.Ed.2d 346 (1978), reversing 448 F.Supp. 1284 (N.D.Ill.1978). See also, e.g., Farnham v. State Bar, 17 Cal.3d 605, 131 Cal.Rptr. 661, 552 P.2d 445, 449 (1976) ("No formal contract or arrangement or attorney fee is necessary to create the relationship of attorney and client. It is the fact of the relationship which is important."); Adger v. State, 584 P.2d 1056, 1060 (Wyo.1978) (payment of fee not essential to obligate lawyer to anticipate need to move for continuance because of proximity of trial).

[8] Cf. In re Sliz, 246 Ga. 797, 273 S.E.2d 177, 181 (1980) (lawyer's fiduciary obligations are not lessened by fact that client is friend).

[9] Clancy v. State Bar, 71 Cal.2d 140, 77 Cal.Rptr. 657, 664, 454 P.2d 329, 336 (1969).

[10] See § 9.5.2; Conway v. Parker, 250 N.W.2d 266 (N.D.1977)(personal nature of client-lawyer relationship requires that question of power of one personal representative of estate to force counsel upon the other be decided on case-by-case basis).

is capable of making informed and self-regarding decisions. While the relationship between client and lawyer is confidential and protective, the client remains effectively in control of the representation. If the client concurs, the lawyer will take steps to bring the matter to a conclusion that will end the relationship unless the client happens to return to the lawyer with another legal matter at a future time.

The image is antique.[11] It brings to mind the relationship that is thought to have existed between solo practitioners and individual adult clients in the middle and upper class in the period before the Civil War. It survives in some present-day representations. But to a large extent, the model ignores the great diversity of clients, lawyers, and work settings in which lawyers function and by which they are constrained. Corporate clients, the poor, clients with disabilities, those accused of serious crime, government agencies, and other clients are as much unlike the model as they are unlike each other. Great gulfs yawn between a storefront general practitioner and a Wall Street lawyer or a lawyer working full-time for a corporate client. Little of significant similarity can be found in the work of a public defender in a large city, a will-drafting lawyer in a small county seat, and a purveyor of moneyed political influence sitting in on a drafting session of a congressional committee. Each may have a "client" in some sense, but only in a weakly similar sense.

Following sections consider some of the ways in which courts and the framers of professional rules have recogized or ignored those differences between kinds of clients and kinds of lawyers in defining the client-lawyer relationship. Other sections examine some specific relationships more closely.[12]

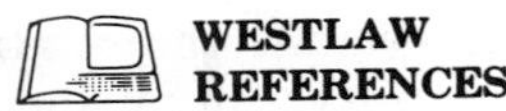

WESTLAW REFERENCES

General

45k106

lawyer attorney counsel** /2 client /s relationship /s defin! nature

Clients' Reason for Seeking Legal Help

di pro se

The Expectation of Loyalty

attorney lawyer counsel** /s loyal** /s client

The Fiducial Relationship

topic(45) /p fiducia**

Nature of the Lawyer's Professional Undertaking

duty /4 confinden! /p lawyer attorney counsel** /2 client

Theoretical Basis of the Fiduciary Obligation

digest,synopsis(lawyer attorney counsel** /2 client /s confiden! /s trust)

Variability of the Client-Lawyer Relationship

di client

§ 4.2 A LAWYER'S AUTHORITY

General

Once the client-lawyer relationship has been formed and the lawyer has begun to represent the client, questions may arise about the authority of the lawyer to proceed or the liability of the client for the consequences of actions taken by the lawyer. For the most part, courts have been content to trust that lawyers have obtained from their clients the necessary authority to act. When testing the reach of the authority of a lawyer to act, and thus the liability of a client because of a lawyer's acts, courts generally have held that the lawyer's powers are quite extensive, although not without limit.

[11] G.Hazard, Ethics in the Practice of Law 140 (1978); Cohen, Confronting Myth in the American Legal Profession: A Territorial Perspective, 22 Ala.L.Rev. 513 (1970). The model portrayed here may be one that is generally invoked in several other professions in addition to law. See Hughes, Professions, 92 Daedalus 655, 664 (1963) ("Professional ideology prefers a two-party arrangement: the professional and his client. It prefers the client who can speak for himself and pay for himself. This is not the prevailing arrangement, nor is it likely to be.").

[12] § 8.4 (insurance practice conflicts); § 10.5.3 (defense function); § 13.7 (corporate practice); § 13.8 (lawyers and the political process); § 13.9 (government lawyers); § 13.10 (prosecutors); § 16.9 (pro bono practice).

Scope of Lawyer's Authority

Many acts that lawyers perform as a matter of course would be utterly wrongful except for the fact that the acts are in behalf of a client. Without client authorization, an act as customary for lawyers as filing a suit against a defendant may be wrongful and subject the lawyer to a damage action for malicious prosecution [13] or to professional discipline.[14] Similarly, a stranger is entitled to assume on appropriate occasions that a lawyer acts for a client and thus may give notice to the client by giving notice to the lawyer.[15] A lawyer gains the necessary authority to act in behalf of a client when the client expressly or by implication consents to the representation [16] (so long as the client is empowered to act through that particular agent) [17] or if the client later ratifies the lawyer's action [18] after the client has knowledge of all material facts.[19] A court may also possess the power to appoint a lawyer to act in behalf of persons who suffer under a disability.[20] Under the doctrine of apparent authority, a client who hires a lawyer is held to have authorized the lawyer to act in ways that are conventional for lawyers in the jurisdiction, even if the client can honestly claim at a later time that the client never intended the lawyer to take certain action.

If a lawyer is indeed authorized to act in behalf of a client, the lawyer's powers to affect the client's interests produce results that are both beneficial and harmful. Acts that the law requires a person to perform may generally be performed by a lawyer acting in the person's behalf.[21] The lawyer can bind the client to many consequences, even if the client did not consciously consider those consequences or did not wish the lawyer to take the fatal steps that incurred them,[22] so long as the lawyer was acting with apparent authority and the client's reservations or restrictions on the lawyer's authority were not communicated to the others who acted in reasonable

[13] Huene v. Carnes, 121 Cal.App.3d 432, 175 Cal.Rptr. 374, 377 (1981)(absence of express or implied authorization of client to file suit would amount "prima facie" to filing suit without probable cause and with malice; crimes of champerty, maintenance, embracery, and barratry may also be thus committed; "sudden showers. . . may drench an attorney when he ventures out as a principal without the protective umbrella of his client.").

[14] In re Rosenzweig, 259 N.W.2d 252 (Minn.1977)(involving client in litigation without client's knowledge or authority).

[15] Harper v. Burgess, 701 F.2d 29 (4th Cir.1983). Distinguishable are situations in which the lawyer has no authority to act for the client. Thus a client's lawyer is normally not an appropriate person to serve with process in initiating a lawsuit. E.g., In re Wisconsin Elec. Power Co., 110 Wis.2d 649, 329 N.W.2d 186, 190 (1983). Procedural rules typically provide, however, that once an action is properly commenced, notice to a party may be served on the party's lawyer who has entered an appearance in the action. See infra note 41.

[16] Lohse v. Paulsel Lumber Co., 614 S.W.2d 899 (Tex. Civ.App.1981). A lawyer for a client has no general implied power to retain an unrelated lawyer to act for the client. E.g., Automobile Club Ins. Co. v. Lainhart, 609 S.W.2d 692, 695 (Ky.1980).

[17] State v. Abbott, 273 S.C. 170, 255 S.E.2d 673 (1979) (fact that defense lawyer appeared at trial for person accused of crime did not excuse failure of defendant to appear, thus forfeit of appearance bond warranted). In some circumstances, questions may arise over the power of a client to retain a lawyer. A court can, for example, override a corporate fiduciary's decision to hire a lawyer who drafted a document naming the corporation to that office if objecting parties show that the lawyer would not protect the best interests of the estate that the fiduciary is to administer. E.g., In re Estate of Effron, 117 Cal. App.3d 915, 173 Cal.Rptr. 93, 102 (1981), appeal dismissed 454 U.S. 1070, 102 S.Ct. 622, 70 L.Ed.2d 606 (1981). On the power of a corporate officer to retain a lawyer to represent the corporation, see, e.g., Valley Int'l Properties, Inc. v. Brownsville Sav. & Loan Ass'n, 581 S.W.2d 222, 226-27 (Tex.Civ.App.1979).

[18] United States v. Franklin, 598 F.2d 954 (5th Cir.), cert. denied 444 U.S. 870, 100 S.Ct. 147, 62 L.Ed.2d 95 (1979).

[19] Perkins v. Philbrick, 443 A.2d 73, 75 (Me.1982)(client who did not know of purported settlement did not by implication ratify it by receipt of proceeds of draft, made out to client, that lawyer had forged).

[20] See generally Mullane v. Central Hanover Bank & Trust Co., 339 U.S. 306, 70 S.Ct. 652, 94 L.Ed. 865 (1950). Cf. United States v. Weinstein, 511 F.2d 622 (2d Cir.), cert. denied 422 U.S. 1042, 95 S.Ct. 2655, 45 L.Ed.2d 693 (1975)(trial court had no authority to appoint lawyer to act in behalf of fugitives, who had neither authorized nor consented to representation).

[21] City of Des Moines v. Civil Serv. Comm'n, 334 N.W.2d 133 (Iowa 1983). Cf. n. 15, supra.

[22] Terry v. Kemper Ins. Co., 390 Mass. 450, 456 N.E.2d 465 (1983)(insurer not liable to client for amount of draft made out to client and sent to office of client's lawyer who, without client's consent, forged endorsement on draft and retained proceeds).

reliance on the lawyer's full authority to act.[23] For example, there are many circumstances, under the rules of evidence, in which a lawyer's statements can bind a client.[24] And a client who holds out a lawyer as the client's representative at the time of a real estate closing is bound by the lawyer's later agreement to extend the time for performance.[25]

The representational notion by which clients are bound by the acts of their lawyers is, of course, merely an application of the law of agency.[26] The effect of representation is sometimes referred to through the Latin metaphor that a lawyer is the *alter ego* of the client.[27] The law does not carry the notion to all of its possible extremes, however, and recognizes limits on the apparent authority of lawyers (§ 4.6). For example, while a lawyer's authority to act is normally of indefinite duration, until the client notifies others otherwise,[28] this authority normally ceases with the death of the client.[29] A lawyer who receives notice of a client's death is required to notify the court and opposing parties of the lawyer's lack of authority to proceed further.[30]

No coherent theory seems likely to explain the results of all cases that have raised the question of the scope of a lawyer's authority to act for a client. A theory that comes close, however, would focus upon the following elements: (1) the extent to which the dispute over the lawyer's authority implicates the interests of third parties who may have relied on the lawyer's actions; (2) the extent to which the lawyer's actions conformed to accepted patterns of lawyer behavior in the legal community; (3) the good faith of the lawyer in taking the challenged step; (4) the extent to which requiring specific client authorization or ratification would seriously diminish the efficiency of trials or other public processes or of important institutions such as contracting; and (5) whether the client has lost a just claim or defense as a result of the lawyer's action.

Establishing the Lawyer's Authority

A lawyer who purports to act in behalf of a client normally need only claim that status, and courts and other public bodies will accept the representation at face value.[31] By the mere act of entering an appearance in behalf of a client, for example, a lawyer is presumed to possess the power to act fully in the client's behalf, despite the fact that nothing other than the lawyer's possibly self-serving statement of authority attests it as the client's will.[32] The lawyer's power is remarkable but is explicable because of the control that courts

23 Gregory v. White, 604 S.W.2d 402 (Tex.Civ.App.1980), cert. denied 452 U.S. 939, 101 S.Ct. 3081, 69 L.Ed.2d 953 (1981).

24 Fed.R.Evid. 801(d)(2); United States v. Flores, 679 F.2d 173 (9th Cir.1982), cert. denied 459 U.S. 1148, 103 S.Ct. 791, 74 L.Ed.2d 996 (1983)(lawyer's demand that city return guns asserted to belong to client establish client's ownership of guns that were illegal to possess); Valley Title Co. v. Superior Court, 124 Cal.App.3d 867, 177 Cal. Rptr. 643 (1981); Wilkerson v. Williams, 667 S.W.2d 72, 78 (Tenn.Ct.Apps.1983).

25 Three S. Devel. Co. v. Santore, 193 Conn. 174, 474 A.2d 795, 797 (1984).

26 Davis v. United Fruit Co., 402 F.2d 328 (2d Cir.1968), cert. denied 393 U.S. 1085, 89 S.Ct. 869, 21 L.Ed.2d 778 (1969); Stricker v. Frauendienst, 669 P.2d 520 (Wyo. 1983).

27 Myrtle Beach Lumber Co. v. Globe Int'l Corp., 281 S.C. 290, 315 S.E.2d 142, 143 (1984).

28 Hodges v. Doctors Hospital, 150 Ga.App. 77, 256 S.E.2d 625 (1979); Hamlin v. Hamlin, 302 N.C. 478, 276 S.E.2d 381, 385 (1981).

29 Rogers v. Concrete Sciences, Inc., 394 So.2d 212 (Fla. App.1981); Bagalay v. Lahaina Restoration Found., 60 Hawaii 125, 588 P.2d 416, 423 (1978); Hemphill v. Rock, 87 A.D.2d 836, 449 N.Y.S.2d 267 (1982); In re Pratt, 99 Wn.2d 905, 665 P.2d 400, 402 (1983). As to the effect of the death of a lawyer on the client's responsibility to be aware of that fact and to substitute other counsel, see, e.g., N.Y.—McKinney's Civ.Prac.Law & R. 321(c) (1972). See generally Note, 4 J.Leg.Prof. 243 (1979).

30 Virzi v. Grand Trunk Warehouse & Cold Storage Co., 571 F.Supp. 507 (E.D.Mich.1983); Brown v. Wheeler, 437 So.2d 521 (Ala.1983).

31 Warren v. Bureau of Land Management, 724 F.2d 776 (9th Cir.1984); McDaniel v. Israel, 540 F.Supp. 404 (W.D.Va.1982). But if more than one lawyer claims the power to control a matter in behalf of the same client, any lawyer other than a lawyer of record will be accorded only "of counsel" status until that lawyer can demonstrate that the client has discharged the lawyer who formerly appeared. E.g., Oroshnik v. Schweiker, 569 F.Supp. 399 (D.N.J.1983).

32 Osborn v. Bank, 22 U.S. (9 Wheat) 738, 829-30, 6 L.Ed. 204 (1824); Pender v. McKee, 266 Ark. 18, 582

can exercise over all lawyers and their consequent power to discipline a lawyer who falsely claims to act for a client.[33] The burden is on the party, whether purported client or third party, who challenges the lawyer's authority to disprove that it existed.[34] The same rule applies whether the client whom the lawyer assertedly represented is an individual, a corporation, an unincorporated association,[35] or a governmental entity.[36]

Imputed Knowledge [37]

One of the chief applications of the agency doctrine is in the rule that information supplied to a party's lawyer is deemed to have been supplied to the party.[38] Proof that the lawyer in fact failed to transfer the information to the client is irrelevant.[39] As the courts say, the client has imputed knowledge of what the lawyer knows. That is true even when it is impossible. Thus a client is deemed to know the meaning of technical words of art or jargon in a document given to the client's lawyer so long as they are words whose meaning is commonly understood by lawyers.[40] The imputed-knowledge doctrine is the basis for the many statutes and rules that provide that notice to a party's lawyer is notice to the party.[41]

S.W.2d 929, 938 (1979); Lovering v. Lovering, 38 Md.App. 360, 380 A.2d 668, 670 (1977). But cf., e.g., NRK Management Corp. v. Donahue, 109 Misc.2d 601, 440 N.Y.S.2d 524 (Cty.Ct.1981)(opposing party's challenge to lawyer's authority to act for party requires lawyer to produce proof of authority). The presumption is, however, a rebuttable one. E.g., Broyles v. Califano, 495 F.Supp. 4 (E.D.Tenn.1980)(client's proof that lawyer filed action without her authorization after she had discharged lawyer warrants setting aside adverse judgment).

[33] In some jurisdictions, a court also has discretionary power to require a lawyer to produce proof of authority. E.g., Custard v. South Bend, 423 N.E.2d 712, 716-17 (Ind.App.1981), cert. denied 456 U.S. 991, 102 S.Ct. 2272, 73 L.Ed.2d 1286 (1982).

[34] Sam Daily Realty, Inc. v. Western Pac. Corp., 671 P.2d 450, 453 (Hawaii App.1983)(party seeking to assert lack of personal jurisdiction has burden of proving that answer filed in person's behalf by lawyer was without authority); ILL Lounge, Inc. v. Gaines, 217 Neb. 466, 348 N.W.2d 903, 907 (1984).

[35] Brotherhood of Maintenance Employees v. Hash, 294 S.E.2d 96, 100-101 (W.Va.1982).

[36] City of Tulsa v. Oklahoma St. Pension & Ret. Bd., 674 P.2d 10 (Okl.1983); City of San Antonio v. Aguilar, 670 S.W.2d 681 (Tex.Civ.App.1984).

[37] See generally Restatement (Second) of Agency ch.8 (Liability of Principal to Third Persons; Notice through Agent)(1958); id. § 9(3)("A person has notice of a fact if his agent has knowledge of the fact, reason to know it or should know it, or has been given a notification of it, under circumstances coming within the rules applying to the liability of a principal because of notice to his agent.").

[38] Link v. Wabash R.R., 370 U.S. 626, 634, 82 S.Ct. 1386, 8 L.Ed.2d 734 (1962) ("each party is deemed bound by the acts of his lawyer-agent and is considered to have 'notice of all facts, notice of which can be charged upon the attorney.' ")(quoting Smity v. Ayer, 101 U.S. 320, 326, 25 L.Ed. 955 (1879)). See also, e.g., Kuska v. Folkes, 73 Ill.App.3d 540, 391 N.E.2d 1082 (1979)(lawyer's knowledge of septic system problem imputed to client purchaser of property); Prater v. Game Time, Inc., 134 Mich.App. 669, 351 N.W.2d 882 (1984), judgment reversed ___ Mich. ___, 362 N.W.2d 239 (1985) (worker compensation claim, after settlement, based on asserted newly discovered emphysema condition barred because worker's lawyer heard witness testify about emphysema diagnosis during earlier stage of proceeding); Canutillo Indep. School Distr. v. Kennedy, 673 S.W.2d 407 (Tex.Civ.App.1984)(notice to teacher's lawyer is compliance with statutory requirement of service of notice of termination on teacher).

[39] Flying Diamond Corp. v. Pennaluna & Co., 586 F.2d 707 (9th Cir.1978); McNally v. Stonehenge, Inc., 242 Ga. 258, 248 S.E.2d 653 (1978)(fact that lawyer did not inform client of trial date before withdrawing irrelevant); People v. Tarkowski, 106 Ill.App.3d 597, 62 Ill.Dec. 367, 372, 435 N.E.2d 1339, 1343 (1982). The presumption is, however, one that deals with conventionalized fact situations and thus cannot be employed to relieve the prosecution of its burden to prove facts beyond a reasonable doubt in a criminal case. See State v. Blackbird, 187 Mo. 270, 609 P.2d 708 (1980)(trial court erroneously instructed jury in bail-jumping prosecution that notice of trial date to defendant's lawyer was notice to defendant).

[40] In re Taff's Estate, 63 Cal.App.3d 319, 133 Cal.Rptr. 737, 741 (1976). Compare State ex rel. Nicodemus v. Industrial Comm'n, 5 Ohio St.3d 58, 448 N.E.2d 1360, 1362 (1983)(because actuarial firm representing party before industrial commission was neither authorized to practice law nor engaged in that practice, import of commission order was not imputable to firm's employer).

[41] Fed.R.Civ.Proc. Rule 5(b); F.R.App.Proc. Rules 25(c), 45(c); F.R.Crim.Proc. Rule 49(b); Administrative Procedure Act § 500(f). See also, e.g., NLRB v. Sequoia Council of Carpenters, 568 F.2d 628, 633 (9th Cir.1977)(service of order on lawyer was service on client sufficient to warrant punishment of client for contempt of order if client had actual knowledge of order); Munday v. Brown, 617 S.W.2d 897 (Tenn.App.1981)(in light of rule providing for service of all papers and motions on lawyer for party, defendant whose lawyer failed to notify her of progress of litigation not entitled to relief from default judgment). Cf., Lovato v. Santa Fe Int'l Corp., 151 Cal.App.3d 549, 198 Cal.Rptr. 838 (1984)(ordinary rule that service of papers on lawyer provides constructive notice to client inapplicable when lawyer was suspended from practice at

The imputed-knowledge doctrine is another example of the reasons why a party who is represented by a lawyer will find many risks imposed because of the lawyer's assumed competence in performing steps of legal significance and assumed loyalty in performing those steps diligently and in the client's best interests. Obviously, those considerations do not warrant imputing to a client all that a lawyer may learn during a lifetime of practice. They should not apply, for example, if the notice is received by the lawyer after the lawyer has ceased to function in the client's behalf [42] or if the notice concerns a matter that is beyond the scope of the matters for which the lawyer has the authority to act for the client.[43] If a lawyer learns information of concern to Client A while representing Client B, it is not always clear that the knowledge should be imputed to both clients.[44] If it would be in the interest of Client B for the lawyer not to reveal the information to Client A, for example, the presumption of shared knowledge with Client A should not be imposed.[45] Similarly, if the lawyer's information is received confidentially from Client B, there should be no presumption that the lawyer has shared it with any other client.[46]

Tort and Contract Liability Imputed to Client

Lawyers, as is true generally of agents, have a limited power to create tort and contract liability on the part of their clients toward third parties. A common illustration of the imputed-negligence rule is procedural forfeitures, where a lawyer's negligence will routinely be imputed to the lawyer's client.[47] A lawyer's action can create tort liability on the part of a client even for intentional torts such as malicious prosecution [48] or willful interference with property.[49]

time of service and thus lacked authority to act for any client).

The notice-imputation rule sometimes works in reverse as well. Thus it is the general rule that if a party is bound by an injunction, the same order also binds the party's lawyer, among others. See F.R.Civ.Proc.Rule 65(d).

42 Jarvis v. Jarvis, 664 S.W.2d 694, 696-97 (Tenn.App. 1983)(nature of relationship of lawyer and client at time of notice controls: if lawyer has had no contact with client for extended period and no means of notifying client, notice to lawyer is insufficient as notice to client). But cf., e.g., Loyd v. Loyd, 731 F.2d 393, 400 (7th Cir.1984) (although lawyer withdrew from representing client at beginning of hearing because of client's failure to cooperate, notice to lawyer during hearing was notice to client); Griffith v. Griffith, 38 N.C.App. 25, 247 S.E.2d 30 (1978), cert. denied 296 N.C. 106, 249 S.E.2d 804 (1978)(service of motion for judgment for unpaid child support properly made in 1976 on lawyer who had represented husband in 1962 divorce action and never entered notice of withdrawal). As the *Jarvis* decision points out, when a lawyer represents a client in a divorce action or a similar equity action, in which the decree can be reopened long after entry, the better practice is for a lawyer to file with the court, after entry of the decree, a statement that the lawyer's authority to represent the client has ended, so that service on the client cannot be made years later by service on the lawyer. See 664 S.W.2d at 697.

43 Dickman v. DeMoss, 660 P.2d 1 (Colo.App.1982)(service on lawyer for plaintiff in wrongful-death action, of notice of bankruptcy action involving wrongful-death defendant, ineffective as notice to plaintiff because lawyer had no authority to represent plaintiff in bankruptcy matters). Cf. Allen v. Nissley, 184 Conn. 539, 440 A.2d 231, 234 (1981)(client not chargeable with notice of frauds committed against client by lawyer).

44 Insurance Company of North America v. Northampton Nat'l Bank, 708 F.2d 13, 16 (lst Cir.1983).

45 Arlinghaus v. Ritenour, 622 F.2d 629 (2d Cir.1980), cert. denied 449 U.S. 1013, 101 S.Ct. 570, 66 L.Ed.2d 471 (1980); Bayne v. Jenkins, 593 S.W.2d 519, 533 (Mo.1980); C.B. & T. Co. v. Hefner, 98 N.M. 594, 651 P.2d 1029 (1982), cert. denied 98 N.M. 590, 651 P.2d 636 (1982); Restatement (Second) of Agency § 282 (1958).

46 Restatement (Second) Agency § 381 comment (e) (1958).

47 Mohawk Data Sciences Corp. v. Industrial Comm'n, 671 P.2d 1335 (Colo.App.1983)(whether corporate general counsel was officer-employee or employee, his negligence was imputable to corporation). See generally § 4.6.1.

48 Blanchette v. Cataldo, 734 F.2d 869, 875 (lst Cir.1984) (filing of unfounded lawsuits against plaintiff by lawyers for agent of defendant fell easily within scope of authority of agent to decide when and how to file claims); Hulcher v. Archer Daniels Midland Corp., 88 Ill.App.3d 1, 409 N.E.2d 412, 417 (1980)(presence of malice, necessary to support substantial recovery against client, consisted almost entirely of statements made by lawyer; lawyer's statements were properly imputed to client); Nyer v. Carter, 367 A.2d 1375 (Me.1977)(malicious prosecution of action by lawyer for defendant will require defendant to respond in damages if lawyer was acting within scope of retainer by defendant). But cf. Williams v. Burns, 463 F.Supp. 1278 (D.Colo.1979)(client is not liable for libelous statements made by lawyer in absence of proof that client authorized or ratified statements); Plant v. Trust Co., 168

49 See note 49 on page 153.

A similar rule applies with respect to contractual liability. A lawyer has authority to take steps for the client that are reasonably or customarily necessary and proper in carrying out the representation, and the lawyer's authority to bind the client may be expanded by explicit or implicit authorization of the client. The lawyer need not be explicitly authorized to incur the contractual liability if the contract is one that is routine in the kind of representation for which the lawyer was engaged.[50] Normally, a lawyer handling litigation for a client has apparent authority to contract for services incident to litigation and thus create liability on the part of the client to pay fees for witnesses, detectives, appraisers, stenographers, experts, and printers.[51] A client will be bound by many other types of promises made by the lawyer with the client's authorization.[52] The client can also claim the benefit of contracts entered into by the lawyer for the client, such as a contract with a title insurance company.[53]

The laws of tort and contract diverge, however, with respect to a lawyer's personal liability because of tort or contract obligations that may be imputed to the lawyer's client. For many tortious acts that created imputed liability in the client, a lawyer may also be held liable.[54] But the same is not generally true of contractual liability. For the most part, acts of the lawyer that create contractual liability in the client do not create similar liability in the lawyer.[55] That result is based on a general rule of agency law that, unless otherwise agreed,[56] an agent for a disclosed principal does not become a party to the contract.[57] Some courts have created an exception, however, for contracts entered into by a lawyer with contractors such as court stenographers and surveyors. Those service suppliers can look to the lawyer for payment of their fees unless the lawyer has made it ex-

Ga.App. 909, 310 S.E.2d 745 (1983)(lawyer given debt to collect by client bank was independent contractor, and thus bank was not answerable for claim of intentional infliction of emotional distress by lawyer's abusive debt-collection techniques).

49 Racoosin v. LeSchack & Grodensky, 103 Misc.2d 629, 426 N.Y.S.2d 707 (1980)(lawyer's liability for willful interference with property, by obtaining execution of judgment that lawyer knew was based on lack of jurisdiction, imputed to client).

50 Bucher & Willis Consulting Engineers v. Smith, 7 Kan.App.2d 467, 643 P.2d 1156 (1982)(surveying work done on property owned by estate, for which lawyer for estate contracted, is chargeable to estate because contract was within estate lawyer's apparent authority).

51 Crisp, Courtemanche, Meador & Assoc. v. Medler, 663 P.2d 388 (Okl.App.1983)(lawyer retained to prosecute appeal has apparent authority to order full transcript, for which client must pay in absence of evidence that transcript reporter had actual notice of limitation on lawyer-agent's apparent authority). See generally Annot., 15 A.L.R.3d 536 (1967).

52 N.L.R.B. v. Donkin's Inn, Inc., 532 F.2d 138 (9th Cir. 1976), cert. denied 429 U.S. 895, 97 S.Ct. 257, 50 L.Ed.2d 179 (1976)(lawyer for employer had apparent authority to enter into binding agreement with union); Monti v. Tangora, 99 Ill.App.3d 575, 425 N.E.2d 597, 601 (1981) (lawyer may be authorized by client to act as client's agent in land sale); Trustees of Exermont Subdivision v. LaDriere, 636 S.W.2d 90, 93 (Mo.App.1982)(while mere existence of client-lawyer relationship does not establish authority of lawyer to make contracts for client, evidence here sufficient to show authority); Bower v. Davis & Symonds Lumber Co., 119 N.H. 605, 406 A.2d 119 (1979) (client authorized lawyer to extend time for performance by other party by adopting lawyer's acts); Avendanio v. Marcantonio, 75 A.D.2d 796, 427 N.Y.S.2d 512 (1980) (lawyer empowered to extend land vendor's time for performance); Inleasing Corp. v. Jessup, 475 A.2d 989, 995 (R.I.1984); Rekhi v. Olason, 28 Wn.App. 751, 626 P.2d 513, 516 (1981)(oral authorization to sell client's land). But cf. Pontchartrain State Bank v. Poulson, 684 F.2d 704 (10th Cir.1982)(dictum)(lawyer who signed document at request of president of corporation could not bind corporation under UCC § 9-203, which requires that agreement be signed by the debtor). Under familiar principles, the authority of a lawyer representing a public body to make representations that estop the client are limited. E.g., City of Hutchinson v. Otto, 306 Minn. 136, 235 N.W.2d 604 (1975).

53 Lawyers Title Ins. Corp. v. Noland Co., 140 Ga.App. 114, 230 S.E.2d 102, 105 (1976).

54 § 5.6.5.

55 McCorkle v. Weinstein, 50 Ill.App.3d 661, 8 Ill.Dec. 567, 365 N.E.2d 953 (1977); Riddle v. Lacey & Jones, 135 Mich.App. 241, 351 N.W.2d 916 (1984); Adler v. Robson, Miller & Osserman, 121 Misc.2d 411, 467 N.Y.S.2d 810 (1983).

56 The agreement must be that of the agent, the lawyer here. A promise by a client that a lawyer will pay a debt does not create a personal obligation of the lawyer to do so. Rafiy v. Davis, 104 Misc.2d 93, 427 N.Y.S.2d 917 (1980) (client's authorization for lawyer to pay physician's fee does not, without lawyer's own undertaking, oblige lawyer to pay fee).

57 Restatement (Second) of Agency § 320 (1958).

plicit that the lawyer will not be personally liable for their charges.[58]

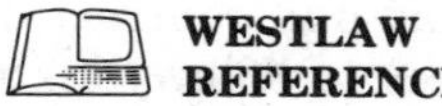
WESTLAW REFERENCES

General

topic(45) /p lawyer attorney counsel** /5 authori! /5 act

Scope of Lawyer's Authority

"apparent authority" /p client /p attorney lawyer counsel**

bind bound /10 client /s act statement agreement settlement /10 attorney lawyer counsel**

Establishing The Lawyer's Authority

proof prove /8 authori! /s lawyer attorney counsel** /p client

45k72

Imputed Knowledge

client /s input! /s knowledge /p lawyer attorney counsel**

Tort and Contract Liability Imputed to Client

negligen! neglect! /p imput! /p client /p lawyer attorney counsel**

228k143(10)

contract! /p "apparent authority" /p client /p attorney lawyer counsel**

45k81

---

§ 4.3 CLIENT–LAWYER AUTONOMY

General

There is no common agreement among lawyers and commentators on the legal profession on an ideal for client-lawyer relationships. In simplified terms, it is possible to think of the client-lawyer relationship in any of three different ways, and support for each as an operating model for law practice can also be found. First, the model that is suggested by the image of the lawyer as hired gun is the client-dominant model: the client directs and controls the lawyer. Second, and feared by many critics of the legal profession, is the lawyer-dominant model: whatever might be the client's wishes and directions, the lawyer either manipulates, browbeats, or ignores the client and pursues the lawyer's own interests in gaining maximum fee income and generally advances primarily the lawyer's own interests in the representation. A third and better model is one in which the lawyer and client cooperatively and with candor seek to work out a relationship that will create the maximum advantage for both of them.

Lawyers as Hired Guns

The concept that lawyers are to do the bidding of their clients is congenial to several ideas and practical needs. It fits the agency definition of the relationship, in which the client as principal authorizes and directs the lawyer to perform legal tasks (§ 4.2). It also serves to place distance between the lawyer's morality and the client's; the lawyer's role can be defined as carrying out the client's directions regardless of the immorality of the client's objectives or means (§ 2.7.3). To a large extent, it may also describe the way in which lawyers in practice indeed operate. At least it may describe the large segment of the bar that deals with corporate and business clients and clients of wealth.[59]

[58] Burt v. Gahan, 351 Mass. 340, 220 N.E.2d 817 (1966), 45 N.C.L.Rev. 690 (1967); Molezzo Reporters v. Patt, 94 Nev. 540, 579 P.2d 1243 (1978); Gaines Reporting Service v. Mack, 4 Ohio App.3d 234, 447 N.E.2d 1317 (1982). See also, e.g., Jones v. Schlender, 102 Idaho 776, 640 P.2d 1177 (1982)(lawyer personally liable to witness for usual witness fees when lawyer's secretary, who served subpoena without tendering witness fees, incorrectly told witness that failure to appear would result in contempt); Weeden Eng. Corp. v. Hale, 435 So.2d 1158 (La.App.1983), writ denied 441 So.2d 764 (1983)(under rule that agent may incur personal liability by express or implied pledge of own responsibility, payment of installment of fees from law firm's account and statement in original letter from lawyer that "I want to employ your company" created necessary responsibility). Cf., Portnow v. Berg, 593 S.W.2d 843 (Tex.Civ.App.1980)(jury question whether lawyer who retained psychiatrist to examine client in pending criminal case was liable for psychiatrist's compensation). Minnesota has created a rule of professional responsibility that a lawyer who orders services for a client must notify the service provider, in writing at the time of ordering the service, of the lawyer's intent not to assume personal responsibility if the lawyer wishes to assert nonresponsibility later. See In re Peters, 332 N.W.2d 10, 17 (Minn.1983).

[59] J.Heinz & E.Laumann, Chicago Lawyers: The Social Structure of the Bar (1982).

Lawyers as Master of the Ship

Many lawyers and judges have asserted that lawyers should control all of the important aspects of a representation.[60] Those assertions are made primarily in cases in which the client will not pay the fee, as in personal injury and other kinds of contingent fee representations;[61] fee-shifting cases, such as class actions for damages, and divorce litigation in which fees will be awarded by the court or taken out of marital property;[62] criminal cases;[63] and representations under poverty law programs.[64] Those are generally cases in which the economic and social position of the client does not permit much aggressiveness on the client's part.[65] The justification for strong lawyer control is usually based on assumptions about a lawyer's superior learning, training, and skill in legal matters—traits that a client could not duplicate in a reasonable period of time because of the client's emotional state and the mystifying complexity of law and legal institutions. A second argument, in particular instances, is that a lawyer is an officer of the court and in that role may not permit clients to direct the lawyer to perform in a way that the court would not approve.[66] To the extent that law does not in fact direct a lawyer to reject a client's wishes, however, the model rests ultimately upon no-

60 See generally Reed, The Lawyer-Client: A Managed Relationship?, 12 Acad. of Management J. 76 (March, 1969)(survey of practitioners indicates that most lawyers consider themselves to control all important decisions in a matter). A client perception that lawyers act toward them in a superior and indifferent manner may be one of the most common client complaints about lawyers. See Missouri Bar Prentice-Hall Survey: A Motivational Study of Public Attitudes and Law Office Management 66 (1963), cited and discussed in Mindes & Acock, Trickster, Hero, Helper: A Report on the Lawyer Image, 1982 Am. B.Found. Research J. 177, 215. Some sociologists have argued that lawyer control is socially benign because it permits lawyers to cajole clients with disparate and anti-social demands into accepting socially desirable norms. See views discussed in Heinz, The Power of Lawyers, 17 Ga.L.Rev. 891, 892-93 (1983).

61 D.Rosenthal, Attorney and Client: Who's in Charge? (1974).

62 People ex rel. Attorney General v. Beattie, 137 Ill. 553, 27 N.E. 1096, 1099 (1891)(in letter from lawyer (disbarred for suborning perjury) to divorce client: "If you are here on Saturday next, you will have your decree. If you are not here, it is no fault of mine. However, it may be as well to understand that I never suffer any scolding or dictation from my clients. I know better how to conduct their cases than they do, and I conduct my cases my own way.").

63 Contempt: Transcript of the Contempt Citations, Sentences and Responses of the Chicago Conspiracy 10, at 209 (1970)(assertion by Judge Julius Hoffman that a lawyer must exert control over client's courtroom behavior); Burger, Standards of Conduct for Prosecution and Defense Personnel, 5 Am.Crim.L.Q. 11, 51 (Fall, 1966) ("[T]he lawyer is a professional representative who must control the trial of a case just as the surgeon, not the patient, must control an operation."); Bress, Standards of Conduct of the Prosecution and Defense Function: An Attorney's Viewpoint, 5 Am.Crim.L.Q. 23, 26 (Fall, 1966) ("It is a cardinal principle that the lawyer should be in control of the defense of the case"); Nadjari, Panel Discussion: Professional Responsibility in the Practice of Criminal Law, in Professional Responsibility of the Lawyer: The Murky Divide between Right and Wrong 58 (1976)(in course of arguing that lawyer almost always decides whether client-accused should take the stand and that if client rejects the lawyer's advice, the client should be told to find another lawyer: "It's . . . self-evident to me that capable attorneys control their clients."). See generally Alschuler, The Defense Attorney's Role in Plea Bargaining, 84 Yale L.J. 1179, 1306 (1975)(interviews reveal that normal defense counsel attitude is that client-accused must accept bargain negotiated by defense lawyer or find new counsel); Blumberg, The Practice of Law as a Confidence Game: Organizational Co-optation of a Profession, 1 L. & Soc'y Rev. 15 (1967); Skolnick, Social Control in the Adversary System, 11 J.Conflict Resolution 52, 65 (1967)(in the client-lawyer relationship, the lawyer usually regards himself or herself as the "player").

64 See generally J.Katz, Poor People's Lawyers in Transition 32 (1982)(absence of fee payment makes poverty lawyers feel that client who ultimately decides not to obtain divorce has "stood up" the lawyer and "wasted" the lawyer's time); Hosticka, We Don't Care about What Happened, We Only Care about What Is Going to Happen: Lawyer-Client Negotiations of Reality, 26 Soc. Probls. 599 (1979).

65 One way for a beginning lawyer to understand feelings of a client is to read about dealing with lawyers from a client's point of view. A starting point would be a book such as J.McGinn, Lawyers: A Client's Manual (1979), which is largely successful in its attempt to portray in nontechnical language what a client wants to know about finding a lawyer, setting a fee, recognizing a legal problem, getting the most out of a lawyer, rights as a client, and the like. See also the Consumers Union suggestions in Guide to Consumer Services 185-203 (rev.ed.1979).

66 Cf., e.g., In re Katz, 90 N.J. 272, 447 A.2d 916, 921 (1982)(lawyer charged with dilatoriness in handling client's divorce could not be excused on ground that he delayed because of client's willingness to relinquish custody of child to other spouse, whom lawyer considered violent and dangerous with children; lawyer had option of withdrawal or moving court to obtain necessary protection for the child and for the lawyer).

tions of paternalism, if not manipulation, that raise serious moral questions.[67]

Cooperative Model

The model of client-lawyer relationships for which most legal scholars have argued,[68] and the model that is probably reflected in the lawyer codes,[69] is one in which lawyer and client assume joint responsibility for the representation. Variations exist among the theories as to the resolution of conflicts of viewpoint between client and lawyer and the extent to which a lawyer must counsel the client in order to assure that the client understands as much about the legal complexities as possible. As is true of the other models, the cooperation model must appreciate that coercion can be subtly different in different settings, depending on the peculiar vulnerabilities of client and lawyer.

Division of Responsibilities between Client and Lawyer

If a lawyer's representation of a client is a joint undertaking, it is also clear that each cannot have equal responsibility for each aspect of the representation. A client hires a lawyer for the lawyer's legal knowledge and skills, but not to direct a client whether or not to obtain a divorce, buy a home, sell a business, confess guilt, or build a new plant in India. The particular formulation that is used to describe the respective spheres of primary responsibility is probably not important.

The division of the realms of client and lawyer decision making has been variously phrased as ends-means, substance-procedure, strategy-tactics, or objectives-means. Each grouping probably refers to the same basic division between the goal toward which steps are taken and the steps themselves. Any one of the divisions has problems. One is that, at least at many points, the meaning of each concept will be blurred—is taking an appeal an objective or a means? It is also not clear that the resulting division, even if it could be made sharply and confidently, represents the way in which the division should be made from an institutional point of view. Moreover, it is not clear that clients or lawyers will always want to divide responsibilities in that way. Clients may prefer, for example, to rely on experts such as the lawyer to make decisions that should be made by the client personally [70]—a preference that lawyers must be aware of and guard against. More fundamentally, to attach great significance to the ultimate decision ignores the probably equal importance of the communications between lawyer and client that have preceded the decision, and the presence or absence of trust and mutual respect between lawyer and client.[71]

[67] Lehman, The Pursuit of a Client's Interests, 77 Mich. L.Rev. 1078 (1979); Wasserstrom, Lawyers as Professionals: Some Moral Issues, 5 Human Rights 1, 15 (1975).

[68] D.Rosenthal, Lawyer and Client: Who's in Charge? (1974); Basten, Control and the Lawyer-Client Relationship, 6 J.Leg.Prof. 7 (1981); Martyn, Informed Consent in the Practice of Law, 48 Geo.Wash.L.Rev. 307 (1980); Simon, The Ideology of Advocacy: Procedural Justice and Professional Ethics, 1978 Wisc.L.Rev. 29; Spiegel, The New Model Rules of Professional Conduct: Lawyer-Client Decision Making and the Role of Rules in Structuring the Lawyer-Client Dialogue, 1980 Am.B.Found. Research J. 1003; Spiegel, Lawyering and Client Decisionmaking: Informed Consent and the Legal Profession, 128 U.Pa.L. Rev. 41 (1979)(employing "interest" analysis, whenever lawyer's interest in taking important steps in representation could be in conflict with client's interests, client should decide unless informed consent of client has been given).

[69] Both the Model Rules and the Code are open to variant interpretations. One is the cooperative model, as suggested here. A different interpretation is that both documents accept both the hired-gun and the lawyer-dominant models but allocate decisions between client and lawyer depending on the nature of the matter to be decided.

Whatever the lawyer codes might provide, it is commonly believed that in many cases lawyers in fact make decisions that the professional codes reserve exclusively for clients. E.g., Blumberg, The Practice of Law as a Confidence Game: Organizational Cooptation of a Profession, 1 L.& Soc'y Rev. 15, 26 (June, 1967); Carrington, The Right to Zealous Counsel, 1979 Duke L.J. 1291, 1298.

[70] Katz, On Professional Responsibility, 80 Comm.L.J. 380, 382 (1975).

[71] See generally Burt, Conflict and Trust between Attorney and Client, 69 Geo.L.J. 1015 (1981); Lesnick, Comment in Becoming a Lawyer: A Humanistic Perspective on Legal Education and Professional Identity 216 (E.Dvorkin, J.Himmelstein & H.Lesnick eds.1980).

The Professional Codes

The client-lawyer relationship that is required by the Model Rules, and to an extent by the Code of Professional Responsibility, is one based on consultation, with ultimate decision-making power allocated to client or lawyer depending on the nature of the issue. In general, the breakdown in the Model Rules is between objectives and means—the former are decisions for the client, while the latter are matters on which the lawyer is to consult with the client but on which the lawyer retains the ultimate prerogative to act.[72] The client and lawyer can alter that relationship by agreement to the extent of agreeing that the representation will not include certain objectives or means,[73] but the lawyer should not agree to a representation that violates the Model Rules or other law.[74] The Model Rules rightly do not attempt to make too much of the objectives-means dichotomy and indicate that "in many cases" the relationship partakes of a joint undertaking.[75]

The 1969 Code essentially takes the position that the 1983 Model Rules restate. The only mandatory rule in point, DR 7-101(B)(1), states that a lawyer may waive or fail to assert a right of the client "where permissible" but does not indicate when that might be.[76] Additional guidance is supplied by the Ethical Considerations. A division is made in EC 7-7 between (a) the merits of the cause or matters that substantially affect the rights of the client, which are exclusively for decision by the client, and (b) other matters, on which the lawyer is entitled to make decisions without the client's concurrence.[77] The Code is unclear, however, whether the category of decisions to be made by the client is large or small.[78]

A Lawyer's Nonlegal Views

Lawyers are no more completely defined by their legal knowledge and skills than are clients adequately conceived of merely as embodiments of legal problems. Each is a whole person, with values and views that transcend law. Yet there are pressures to confine lawyers within narrow professional roles that exclude nonlegal considerations. "The proper

[72] MR 1.2(a)("A lawyer shall abide by a client's decisions concerning the objectives of representation, . . . and shall consult with the client as to the means by which they are to be pursued."); MR 1.2 comment (Scope of Representation; first paragraph)("[A] client also has a right to consult with the lawyer about the means to be used in pursuing those objectives. At the same time, a lawyer is not required to pursue objectives or employ means simply because a client may wish that the lawyer do so . . . . In questions of means, the lawyer should assume responsibility for technical and legal tactical issues, but should defer to the client regarding such questions as the expense to be incurred and concern for third persons who might be adversely affected."). For an examination of an earlier version of the Model Rules, see Spiegel, The New Model Rules of Professional Conduct: Lawyer-Client Decision Making and the Role of Rules in Structuring the Lawyer-Client Dialogue, 1980 Am.B. Found. Research J. 1003.

[73] MR 1.2 comment (Services Limited in Objectives or Means; first paragraph)("The terms upon which representation is undertaken may exclude specific objectives or means.").

[74] MR 1.2 comment (Services Limited in Objectives or Means; second paragraph). The comment specifically prohibits an agreement that would surrender the client's right to terminate the lawyer's services or to settle litigation without the lawyer's concurrence. Id.

[75] MR 1.2 comment (Scope of Representation; first paragraph).

[76] DR 7-101(A)(1) provides that "a lawyer shall not intentionally . . . fail to seek the lawful objectives of his client through reasonably available means permitted by law." That might be taken to imply that the client defines objectives. See, e.g., Davis v. State Bar, 33 Cal.3d 231, 188 Cal.Rptr. 441, 444, 655 P.2d 1276, 1279 (1983) (lawyer who attempted to justify neglect of client's claim on doubts (never communicated to client) that client's complaints of symptoms were genuine usurped client's right to decide whether to pursue claim); Wilder v. Third Distr. Comm., 219 Va. 175, 247 S.E.2d 355, 358 (1978) (decision whether to obtain judgment against defendant that lawyer thinks may be judgment-proof should be made by client, not by lawyer).

[77] A possible exception is suggested by other language in EC 7-7 distinguishing between lawyer decisions about nonmerits matters for tactical or strategic reasons (which are for the lawyer to decide) and lawyer decisions about nonmerits matters for nonlegal factors. The latter decision is ultimately for the client. A further exception is implied in EC 5-12, which states that if a client is represented by cocounsel who cannot agree "on a matter vital to the representation," they should submit the matter for resolution by the client.

[78] EC 7-7 is quite ambiguous and can be read either way. The last two sentences—illustrating client control over settlement and waiving affirmative defenses in civil cases, and over pleas and appeals in criminal cases—suggest that the area of client decision making might not be extensive.

role of a lawyer . . . does not include a self-appointed role as a paraclete, comforter, helper, or hand holder, under the guise of legal services and at a lawyer's compensation rate." [79] The sentiment is unexceptionable if it means that lawyers should not dupe ignorant, frightened, and legally harassed clients into accepting a lawyer's self-sponsored role as moral healer for large fees. But does it follow that a lawyer should never communicate to a client the lawyer's own values and views unless they are relevant in a narrowly legal sense?

The professional codes insist that a lawyer's role properly includes discussing nonlegal values with clients, but in the end a lawyer should make it clear to the client that decisions about legally available alternatives are for the client to make. If the lawyer believes that a course of action that the client insists upon is immoral or otherwise repugnant, the lawyer's only option is to withdraw.[80] The Code, in EC 7-8, urges lawyers to make sure that client decisions are based upon a broad understanding of the workings of legal institutions, as well as on a narrower understanding of the general import of legal rules. The same EC 7-8 alludes to other nonlegal matters, such as public relations impacts and similar "harsh consequences that might result from assertion of legally permissible positions." Moreover, "it is often desirable for a lawyer to point out those factors which may lead to a decision that is morally just as well as legally permissible." The Model Rules similarly endorse the concept that

> it is proper for a lawyer to refer to relevant moral and ethical considerations in giving advice. Although a lawyer is not a moral advisor as such, moral and ethical considerations impinge upon most legal questions and may decisively influence how the law will be applied.[81]

If a client indicates that only narrow legal assistance is sought, a lawyer should normally comply unless it appears that the client, because of inexperience with the nature of legal matters, misconceives the context of the legal question.[82]

The positions of the Code and the Model Rules are apparently identical in important features, and both comport with a view of morality that respects the autonomy of both client and lawyer. The client's autonomy is respected by the lawyer's offering both advice on the law (respecting the client's ability to assert legally enforceable rights) and by advice on other matters, such as public relations, economics, politics, and morality, because these are also important in many client decisions and the client might have overlooked either their relevance to a legal issue or their independent importance. To assume, without the client indicating this, that a client would not wish to have anything but the law discussed would dishonor the possible and morally healthy breadth of the client's interests.[83]

The lawyer's autonomy is respected because the codes recognize that a lawyer's work is more than narrowly technical in its conception and impact and that a lawyer is also capable of having values that cannot always be cabined by court decisions, statutes, and regulations. The lawyer is free to advise on moral values and to decline or to withdraw from a representation if the client's views remain fundamentally at odds with those of the lawyer. In the final analysis, the codes

[79] Stanley v. Board of Prof. Resp., 640 S.W.2d 210, 213 (Tenn.1982)(lawyer, in order to induce youth and parents to pay large fee, deceived them into thinking that youth would be prosecuted and arranged for youth, in asserted best interests of client, to enter halfway house for drug-dependent persons).

[80] See §§ 10.4.1, 13.3.10.

[81] MR 2.1 comment (Scope of Advice; second paragraph).

[82] MR 2.1 comment (Scope of Advice; third paragraph). The matter is obviously one that involves delicate interpersonal relations that can hardly be confined by a rule.

[83] Whether a client is willing to pay a lawyer for nonlegal advice is a separate issue. Normally, a lawyer's value as a counselor cannot neatly be cleaved into minutes of law, minutes of economics, and other minutes of morality. If a discussion has heavily concentrated upon matters that the client ultimately rejects as entirely nongermane, a lawyer should probably assume that the client does not want, and perhaps did not expect, to pay for that portion of the consultation. Rarely, however, will a lawyer's separable discussion about matters that are clearly irrelevant from a legal standpoint be so time-consuming that an issue of fair billing arises.

recognize that the client-lawyer relationship—whatever else it may also be—involves communications between two human beings whose common interests in matters include more than the legal, even if it is focused upon the law.

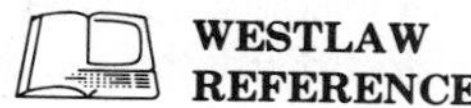

WESTLAW REFERENCES

General

digest,synopsis(model role /s lawyer attorney counsel** /s client)

45k106

Lawyers as Hired Guns

lawyer attorney counsel** /s client /s relationship /p principal

Lawyers as Master of The Ship

lawyer attorney counsel** /2 control! /s client

Cooperative Model

topic(45) /p "informed consent"

Division of Responsibilities between Client and Lawyer

digest,synopsis(lawyer attorney counsel** /s client /s conflict!)

The Professional Codes

d.r. +1 7–101(b)(1) 7–101(a)(1)

A Lawyer's Nonlegal Views

"professional responsibility" /p "e.c. 7–8"

§ 4.4 INCOMPETENT CLIENTS

Nature of the Relationship

The customary models that are used to work out the client-lawyer relationship assume that the client can understand important elements of the facts and law and make decisions. For some clients, however, those assumptions may be doubtful or plainly wrong. A lawyer may, for example, be appointed as guardian ad litem to represent the interests of an unconscious person, a very young child, or a profoundly retarded person.[84] In other cases, the capacity of a client to understand and to decide may be problematical, such as when a lawyer represents a person as a respondent in a proceeding to commit the client involuntarily to a mental institution,[85] an accused in a criminal case in which a plea of insanity or inability to stand trial might be made,[86] or a young person in a delinquency, custody, or neglected-child proceeding.[87] Or the person may be an adult of relatively normal capacities who is unable to decide on a course of action because the representation involves matters of unusual factual or legal complexity.

Some of the questions involved in representing clients who are unable to participate fully in making decisions are of little difficulty, but others are among the most perplexing that a lawyer confronts. Courts are understandably alert to any dealings between the lawyer and an incompetent client. The normal limitations on a lawyer's self-enrichment at the expense of a client are applied with enhanced strictness when the client is a child or otherwise not capable of making fully informed and voluntary decisions.[88]

By far the more difficult problem has been that of delineating a lawyer's responsibilities

[84] See generally S.Herr, The New Clients: Legal Services for Mentally Retarded Persons (1979); Mickenberg, The Silent Clients, 31 Stan.L.Rev. 625 (1979).

[85] See generally G.Dix, The Developing Role of the Defense Lawyer in Mental Health Litigation (1977); Schwartz, Fleischner, Schmidt, Gates, Costanzo & Winkelman, Protecting the Rights and Enhancing the Dignity of People with Mental Disabilities: Standards for Effective Legal Advocacy, 14 Rutgers L.Rev. 541 (1983); Hiday, The Attorney's Role in Involuntary Civil Commitment, 60 N.C.L.Rev. 1027 (1982); Elkins, Legal Representation of the Mentally Ill, 82 W.Va.L.Rev. 157 (1979); Galie, An Essay on the Civil Commitment Lawyer, 6 J.Psych. & L. 71 (Spring, 1978).

[86] See generally Chernoff & Schaffer, Defending the Mentally Ill: Ethical Quicksand, 10 Am.Crim.L.Rev. 505 (1972).

[87] See generally Guggenheim, The Right to Be Represented but Not Heard: Reflections on Legal Representation for Children, 59 NYU L.Rev. 76 (1984); Note, Lawyering for the Abused Child: "You Can't Go Home Again," 29 UCLA L.Rev. 1216 (1982).

[88] In re Crane, 96 Ill.2d 40, 70 Ill.Dec. 220, 449 N.E.2d 94 (1983)(discipline for obtaining additional fees from child-clients under suspicious circumstances); In re Witte, 615 S.W.2d 421, 422 (Mo.1981), cert. denied 454 U.S. 1025, 102 S.Ct. 559, 70 L.Ed.2d 469 (1981) ("For every degree that respondent by his testimony and evidence proved a less than normal mental and functional capacity on the part of his client, . . . he raised by an equivalent degree the standard of conduct which this Court must require of him in his dealings with his client."). Many of the cases involving client gifts to lawyers involve elderly clients. See generally § 8.12.

in decision making and advocacy. To what model of client-lawyer relationship should a lawyer adhere in those cases? To whom should the lawyer look for decisions of a kind that are normally made by a client? Complicating matters will often be the interests of parents, public agencies and officials, guardians, and the courts, which will create conflicting demands without the prospect of meaningful solution through client consent, which otherwise will permit a lawyer to proceed in many conflict-of-interest situations (§ 7.2.4).

The vehicle for the discussion that follows will be the representation of children. Most of the problems of incompetent clients are analytically the same whatever the source of the disability, although it is obvious that the nature of the disability can substantially affect the ability of the client to make or participate in decisions about the representation.

Lawyer for Parent or Guardian

Parents or guardians are often appointed or recognized as the representative of children in litigation. A lawyer for a parent or guardian may disagree with their decisions involving a child's interests, but the lawyer is ordinarily bound by their decisions in the same fashion as in any other client-lawyer relationship.[89] Because of the rules of client confidentiality, a lawyer is probably precluded in most cases from taking effective action if the parent or guardian is not adequately protecting the interests of the child and refuses to follow the lawyer's advice.[90] The only excepted cases recognized by the lawyer codes are situations in which the client intends to commit a crime or fraud against the child or when a lawyer is able to withdraw. The rules obviously provide little moral comfort to a lawyer who is aware from confidential client information that a child's legal representative proposes to take action that would not be in the interests of a child. For example, the representative may intend to recommend to the court that a child be placed in the custody of a parent-client who, the lawyer believes, would not be a proper custodial parent.[91]

Joint Representations Involving Children

If a lawyer represents simultaneously a child and an adult client in the same matter, serious conflicts of interest can arise. Suppose, for example, that a lawyer represents a parent and children in a wrongful death action that calls for a distribution of damages among the family members in an open-ended way. The difficulty of obtaining meaningful consent from a child and of protecting the child's interests while also protecting those of the parent are considerable. The law does not insist upon separate representation in every such case because of cost and inconvenience.[92] In addition, a lawyer in any but the clearest case would properly rely heavily upon a parent's wishes in determining the best interests of a child-client. The lawyer should proceed with the representation unless one of the parties objects to the representation or

[89] EC 7-12 ("Where an incompetent is acting through a guardian or other legal representative, a lawyer must look to such representative for those decisions which are normally the prerogative of the client."); MR 1.14 comment (third paragraph)("If a legal representative has already been appointed for the client, the lawyer should ordinarily look to the representative for decisions on behalf of the client."). E.g., Brode v. Brode, 278 S.C. 457, 298 S.E.2d 443 (1982)(lawyer could not take appeal after guardian ad litem had agreed with parents of mentally retarded handicapped child that sterilization was in best interests of child).

[90] The reference in MR 1.14 comment (fourth paragraph) to a lawyer's "obligation" to prevent or rectify a guardian's misconduct that would affect a ward's interests adversely cites MR 1.2(d), which merely prohibits a lawyer from engaging in a client's criminal or fraudulent course of conduct. See generally § 13.3.2.

[91] Cf. Michenberg, The Silent Clients, 31 Stan.L.Rev. 625 (1979)(lawyer for profoundly retarded person who disagrees with important decision of guardian should request appointment of new guardian or present conflict to court for resolution).

[92] Cf., e.g., Harhai, Ethical Considerations in the Representation of Children, ABA Nat'l Instit., Advocating for Children in the Courts 878-98 (2d ed.1980)(courts are often reluctant to add to expense and increased court time by appointing guardian in addition to lawyer for child, so lawyer should be prepared to assume both roles in order to further concept of separate legal representation for child).

insists upon action that is clearly inconsistent with vital interests of the child.[93]

Client Autonomy in Representing Children

If a lawyer represents only the child, the problems of conflict with others are removed and the lawyer must confront the question of making decisions in the representation. A lawyer in that context is still only a lawyer and not a full legal representative of the child.[94] For some legal steps, such as signing deeds, the lawyer cannot act for the client and a legal representative must be appointed.[95] In most instances, however, appointment of a legal representative is not required and may be too costly, inconvenient, or disturbing to the child.[96] The lawyer may then be forced to make decisions that would normally be made by a client.

The child-client may be incapable of making or participating in the decision, such as in the instance of a one-year-old client. The lawyer must make those decisions for the child to the extent that the law allows.[97] The lawyer should make those decisions as the child would if capable of making a fully informed and fully rational decision.[98]

It is not inevitable, of course, that a child-client will not be capable of participating to a large extent in making decisions in the representation simply because the client is a child.[99] At the very least, a child-client's views should be respected, and a lawyer should carefully discuss the representation with the child to the extent that the child is capable of receiving information and evaluating his or her own situation.[1] As with other client-lawyer conversations, those communi-

[93] Hurt v. Superior Court, 124 Ariz. 45, 601 P.2d 1329, 1334 (1979)(lawyer can represent both parent and child under wrongful-death statute that provided for distribution of damages between them "in proportion to their damages," but if "a party desires separate counsel, the right must be honored").

[94] Cf. Developmental Disabilities Advocacy Center, Inc. v. Melton, 521 F.Supp. 365 (D.N.H.1981)(lawyer purporting to represent mentally disabled persons could no more file suit without a client as party than other lawyers could do so in any other context).

[95] EC 7-12; MR 1.14 (third paragraph).

[96] MR 1.14 comment (third paragraph).

[97] EC 7-12 ("If a client under disability has no legal representative, his lawyer may be compelled in court proceedings to make decisions on behalf of the client."); MR 1.14 comment (second paragraph)("If the person has no guardian or legal representative, the lawyer often must act as de facto guardian."). But cf., e.g., U.S. Dep't of Justice Nat'l Advisory Comm. for Juvenile Justice and Delinquency Prevention, Standards for the Administration of Juvenile Justice 3.134 (Role of Counsel)(1980)(in any proceeding in which custody, detention, or treatment of juvenile is at issue and child is unable rationally to determine own legitimate interests, lawyer should request appointment of guardian ad litem); id. 3.169 (lawyer may also be appointed as guardian ad litem). But cf., e.g., Jones v. District Court, 617 P.2d 803 (Colo.1980) (regardless of advantage or disadvantage to client, lawyer who believes that client-defendant is mentally incompetent to stand trial must bring matter to attention of court).

[98] Nothing in the Code or Model Rules suggests how a lawyer, forced to do so, is to make decisions in behalf of an incompetent client. There is widespread agreement that such decisions are to be made from the client's viewpoint, even if that conflicts with institutional or other external interests. E.g., Instit. Jud. Admin. & ABA Joint Comm'n on Juvenile Justice Standards, Counsel for Private Parties 3.1 (1980); U.S. Dep't of Justice Nat'l Advisory Comm. for Juvenile Justice and Delinquency Prevention, Standards for the Admin. of Juv. Justice 3.169 (1980)(guardian is to "inquire thoroughly into all the circumstances that a careful and competent individual in the juvenile's position would in determining his/her interests in the proceedings").

[99] Cf., e.g., Frendak v. United States, 408 A.2d 364 (D.C. App.1979)(court may not force insanity defense on defendant who intelligently and voluntarily waives defense); People v. Brown, 111 Cal.App.3d 523, 168 Cal.Rptr. 806 (1980)(defense lawyer properly abided by decision of accused whether to press diminished-capacity defense); State v. Jones, 99 Wn.2d 735, 664 P.2d 1216 (1983)(trial court erroneously entered plea of not guilty by reason of insanity over objection of accused when no inquiry was made to determine whether defendant's waiver of right to plead insanity was intelligent and voluntary). Cf., People v. Bolden, 99 Cal.App.3d 375, 160 Cal.Rptr. 268 (1979) (accused not denied effective assistance of counsel when lawyer, over objection of accused, offered psychiatric testimony on basis of which accused was found incompetent to stand trial). See generally Singer, The Imposition of the Insanity Defense on an Unwilling Defendant, 41 Ohio St.L.J. 637 (1980). On the moral difficulties of deciding to replace a client's judgment with the lawyer's own, see Luban, Paternalism and the Legal Profession, 1981 Wisc. L.Rev. 454.

[1] EC 7-12 ("If the client is capable of understanding the matter in question or of contributing to the advancement of his interests, regardless of whether he is disqualified from performing certain acts, the lawyer should obtain from him all possible aid."). See also, e.g., George v. Caton, 93 N.M. 370, 600 P.2d 822, 827, cert. denied 93

cations should be kept in confidence.[2] Yet a client who is ten years old, for example, cannot be given all of the responsibility for decisions that an adult assumes. A child-client who is capable of participating to less than a full extent in decisions may want the lawyer to take a step in the representation that is irrational and not in the child's interests. The lawyer should refuse to cajole or coerce the child in other ways into agreeing with the lawyer's recommended course. Here, as in similar situations, withdrawal, even if permissible, only solves the lawyer's problem and may belittle the client's interests. A possibility alluded to by the comment to MR 1.14 is that a lawyer confronting an obdurate child-client may seek to have a legal representative appointed for the child.[3] As stated in MR 1.14(b), however, a lawyer should do that only when the lawyer reasonably believes that the client cannot act in the client's own interest.[4] If no legal representative is appointed and a lawyer is consequently acting alone, the lawyer must assume responsibility to make the decision in the child's best interests. The lawyer should take action that would be taken by a fully capable person if, after carefully considering the child's views, the lawyer is firmly of the view that the child's expressed preferences are not sound and the child lacks the capacity to make an autonomous decision.[5]

The final possibility is that a child-client, although under the law incapable of taking steps in his or her own behalf, is nonetheless fully capable of making particular decisions. The responsibility of a lawyer is clearly to follow those decisions of the child-client in the same way that a lawyer would in any other representation.[6]

Advocacy for Incompetent Clients: Children as Clients in Juvenile Delinquency Proceedings

Beyond the function of decision making, questions have frequently been raised about the proper role of a lawyer for a child in court proceedings. Should the lawyer assume a nonadversarial stance, such as the role of cooperative protector of the child[7] or adviser to the court, somewhat in the role of a true amicus curiae?[8] Or should the lawyer be a zealous advocate for the client's interests?[9] Those roles have been extensively debated in juvenile delinquency representations.[10] At a time when judges and society were enthusiastic about the benevolence of the juvenile-justice system, lawyers defending accused juveniles were under significant pressure to

N.M. 172, 598 P.2d 215 (1979)(lawyer representing Navajo-speaking client through interpreter had special duty to ascertain instructions of client; lawyer's liability in legal malpractice not diminished because of communication difficulties if lawyer did not take pains to communicate).

[2] Provencal v. Provencal, 122 N.H. 793, 451 A.2d 374 (1982)(lawyer as guardian ad litem in custody dispute following marriage dissolution).

[3] MR 1.14 comment (third paragraph)("If a legal representative has not been appointed, the lawyer should see to such an appointment where it would serve the client's best interests.").

[4] MR 1.14 comment (third paragraph) notes that appointment of a guardian may be expensive or traumatic for the client, and leaves the decision to the lawyer's professional judgment.

[5] Cf., e.g., People v. Bolden, 99 Cal.App.3d 375, 160 Cal. Rptr. 268 (1979)(lawyer properly refused to abide by client's wish not to plead incompetence to stand trial); State v. Aumann, 265 N.W.2d 316 (Iowa 1978)(trial lawyer properly filed appeal to contest constitutionality of statute placing burden of proving insanity on accused despite unwillingness of client to pursue appeal); People v. Baldi, 54 N.Y.2d 137, 444 N.Y.S.2d 893, 429 N.E.2d 400 (1981)(accused not denied effective assistance of counsel when court-appointed lawyer refused to follow defense of actual innocence and took stand to testify to defendant's confidential admissions of unusual behavior in support of ultimately unsuccessful plea of not guilty by reason of insanity).

[6] MR 1.14 comment (first paragraph). See also U.S. Dep't of Justice Nat'l Advisory Comm. for Juvenile Justice and Delinquency Prevention, supra n. 98, at 3.134.

[7] R.Gottesman, The Child and the Law 52 (1981)("It should be stressed that the role as guardian ad litem is not the role of an adversary. In fact, the parents and the state should not be considered as opponents").

[8] J.Costa & G.Nelson, Child Abuse and Neglect: Legislation, Reporting, and Prevention 42 (1978).

[9] It has also been argued that a lawyer should combine all of those roles, employing one or the other as the lawyer's professional judgment suggests is best. Isaacs, The Role of the Lawyer in Representing Minors in the New Family Court, 12 Buffalo L.Rev. 501, 506-07 (1963).

[10] See generally Long, When the Client Is a Child: Dilemmas in the Lawyer's Role, 21 J.Fam.L. 607 (1983).

act not as adversaries, but in a very neutral fashion that facilitated accurate fact-finding and sought the most suitable disposition of the child within the juvenile-justice system. Many juvenile-court judges severely criticized juvenile defenders who engaged in advocacy familiar to the adult criminal process, for example, by pressing exclusionary motions or conducting vigorous cross-examination of accusing witnesses thought by the lawyer to be telling the truth.

In recent years, however, the rehabilitative claims of the juvenile-justice system have been challenged.[11] Loss of confidence in the benevolence of the system has resulted in an increasing convergence of the models for criminal defense and juvenile defense attitudes and methods. A principle impetus was supplied by the decision of the Supreme Court in In re Gault,[12] holding that due process required that juvenile delinquency proceedings follow many of the adversarial system guarantees mandated for the criminal trial of adults, including the right to counsel. Not surprisingly, however, the Supreme Court has by no means extended all of the rights of adults to children.[13] For example, in Parham v. J.R. [14] the Court held that a child under eighteen could be civilly committed to a mental institution without an adversary hearing. Decisions following *Gault* have required juvenile-defense lawyers to follow the customary practices of lawyers in adversary proceedings.[15] The emerging solution is to expect advocacy from a juvenile-defense lawyer as if the child were an adult.[16] The lawyer's objective has become that of seeking to obtain the best result for the child, which is defined as the least entoilment with the juvenile-justice system.[17]

WESTLAW REFERENCES

Nature of Relationship

topic(45) /p represent! /4 child! juvenile minor incompetent

Lawyer for Parent or Guardian

digest,synopsis(attorney lawyer counsel** /5 represent! /s parent guardian /p child! juvenile minor incompetent)

Joint Representations Involving Children

lawyer attorney counsel** /s represent! /s both parent guardian /s child! juvenile minor incompetent

Client Autonomy in Representing Children

topic(211) /p lawyer attorney counsel** /p guardian /p child! juvenile minor

Advocacy for Incompetent Clients: Children as Clients in Juvenile Delinquency Proceedings

gault /p right /4 counsel** attorney lawyer /p child! juvenile minor

§ 4.5 COMMUNICATIONS WITH CLIENTS

Importance of Communications with Clients

Nothing lends more vitality to the client-lawyer relationship than effective communi-

[11] See generally Simpson, Rehabilitation as the Justification of a Separate Juvenile Justice System, 64 Calif.L. Rev. 984 (1976).

[12] 387 U.S. 1, 87 S.Ct. 1428, 18 L.Ed.2d 527 (1967).

[13] The tensions between universalistic claims of rights for children and the reality of the temporary conditions of youth are examined in F.Zimring, The Changing World of Adolescence (1982).

[14] 442 U.S. 584, 99 S.Ct. 2493, 61 L.Ed.2d 101 (1979).

[15] Jerome B. v. Cabell, 68 Cal.App.3d 395, 137 Cal.Rptr. 341, 348 (1977)(lawyer in juvenile delinquency proceeding who elicited harmful and patently hearsay testimony from police officers suffered from "an extraordinary misunderstanding of the nature of an adversary proceeding"). See also, e.g., State ex rel. Memmel v. Mundy, 75 Wis.2d 276, 249 N.W.2d 573 (1977)(lawyer in civil commitment case is to represent client with full independence and professional zeal).

[16] See generally U.S. Dep't of Justice Nat'l Advisory Comm. for Juvenile Justice and Delinquency Prevention, supra n. 98, at 3.134; Instit. of Jud. Admin.-ABA Jnt. Comm'n on Juv. Just. Standards, supra n. 98, at 3.1. Essentially the same standard has been insisted upon in other representations, such as a lawyer's representation of a child-client in a case involving custody questions. E.g., Veazey v. Veazey, 560 P.2d 382, 387 (Alaska 1977) (the result in *Veazey* has since been superceded by statute; see Deivert v. Oseira, 628 P.2d 575 (Alaska 1981)); DeMontigny v. DeMontigny, 70 Wis.2d 131, 233 N.W.2d 463, 468-69 (1975). See also, e.g., Note, The Role of Counsel in the Civil Commitment Process: A Theoretical Framework, 84 Yale L.J. 1540 (1975); Note, Developments—Civil Commitment of the Mentally Ill, 87 Harv.L. Rev. 1190, 1288-91 (1974).

[17] Instit. of Jud'l Admin.-ABA Standards, supra n. 98, at 3.1; ABA Informal Op. 1160 (1971).

cations between lawyer and client. Their importance is recognized in the extraordinary protection given to client and lawyer communications in the attorney-client privilege (§ 6.1.3). Clients must be able to communicate all of the facts concerning the matter. A client must also be able to communicate to a lawyer the client's wishes about the ends that the lawyer should seek to achieve and the client's wishes about compensating the lawyer. A client has an equal interest in receiving legal evaluations and advice from the lawyer and in being kept informed by the lawyer about important steps in the matter and, periodically, about whether progress is being made or not. Lawyer failure to maintain effective contact with clients may be one of the most serious complaints that clients have about lawyers. While most lapses in communication are probably caused by the fact that lawyers are unaware of the needs and wishes of clients for more and better information, it is clearly also the case that lawyers should not restrict the flow of information to clients in order to exercise control over clients or to manipulate client decisions [18] or because lawyers feel communication is relatively unimportant given the other demands on their time.

The Lawyer Codes

Client-lawyer communications is a matter that was neglected in the 1969 Code of Professional Responsibility but which is now dealt with in the 1983 Model Rules. The Code recognizes the importance of effective communication but in an almost offhand fashion in scattered references in Ethical Considerations.[19] Despite the lack of a specific Code provision, several courts have disciplined lawyers under the Code for failure to communicate with clients [20] or for misleading a client about the status of a matter.[21] Courts have also insisted upon effective communication as a part of the constitutionally required effective assistance of counsel to which an accused is entitled in a criminal case.[22] The Model Rules, in MR 1.4, explicitly require a lawyer to maintain communications with a client in two different ways that relate to reporting and consultation.

Reporting to Clients. First, MR 1.4(a) requires a lawyer to maintain contact with a client about the representation during its

[18] Cf. J.Katz, The Silent World of Doctor and Patient (1984)(unwillingness of physicians to communicate freely with patients may be traced to a need to retain authority over patients and generally to remain free of lay control).

[19] See EC 7-8 ("A lawyer should exert his best efforts to insure that decisions of his client are made only after the client has been informed of relevant considerations."); EC 9-2 ("In order to avoid misunderstandings and hence to maintain confidence, a lawyer should fully and promptly inform his client of material developments in the matters being handled for the client."). Cf. also DR 9-102(B)(1)(lawyer should "promptly notify" client of receipt of client's funds or property).

[20] McMorris v. State Bar, 35 Cal.3d 77, 196 Cal.Rptr. 841, 672 P.2d 431 (1983), cert. denied 466 U.S. 958, 104 S.Ct. 2170, 80 L.Ed.2d 553 (1984); In re Thorup, 461 A.2d 1018 (D.C.App.1983)(neglect under DR 6-101(A)(3)); Attorney Grievance Comm'n v. Montgomery, 296 Md. 113, 460 A.2d 597, 600 (1983)("In our view, lack of communication with one's client, for whatever reason, is a matter of continuing concern to the public."); State Bar v. Watkins, 98 Nev. 599, 655 P.2d 529 (1982)(under DR 1-102(A)(6) (conduct adversely reflecting on fitness to practice)); In re Ackerman, 95 N.J. 147, 469 A.2d 924 (1984); State ex rel. Oklahoma Bar Ass'n v. O'Brien, 611 P.2d 650 (Okl. 1980). Cf. In re Cassidy, 89 Ill.2d 145, 432 N.E.2d 274, 276 (1982)(lawyer's failure to communicate with client was "ungracious" but not serious neglect in light of client's constant repetition of request for same information). See generally Annot., 80 ALR3d 1240 (1977).

[21] In re Fuller, 284 Or. 273, 586 P.2d 1111 (1978) (whether lawyer misled client or permitted client to believe that he had taken steps that he had promised is irrelevant; either is deceitful in dealing with client). See also Mayo v. State Bar, 23 Cal.3d 72, 151 Cal.Rptr. 345, 587 P.2d 1158 (1978)(failing to inform client about nature of lawyer's own interest in matter); In re Deardorff, 426 N.E.2d 689 (Ind.1981)(misleading client about status of client's case); Kentucky Bar Ass'n v. Albert, 668 S.W.2d 62 (Ky.1984).

[22] Linton v. Perini, 656 F.2d 207, 212 (6th Cir.1981), cert. denied 454 U.S. 1162, 102 S.Ct. 1036, 71 L.Ed.2d 318 (1982). In Morris v. Slappy, 461 U.S. 1, 103 S.Ct. 1610, 75 L.Ed.2d 610 (1983), the majority dismissed an argument for a constitutionally mandated "meaningful relationship" between lawyer and client in a criminal case. The Court's concern there was to reject a claimed right of an accused to a continuance so the particular court-appointed lawyer that the accused wished could try the case. Neither the facts, result, nor the language of the opinion considered in context suggests that a failure of communication between defense counsel and client is never of constitutional dimension.

course. A lawyer must "keep a client reasonably informed about the status of the matter." The obligation of that part of the rule is not one that is triggered only by client requests, which are dealt with in a separate clause that requires a lawyer to comply with a client's reasonable requests for information. The reporting obligation of MR 1.4(a) is generated by the fact that sufficient time has passed since the lawyer's last contact with the client that a reasonable lawyer would know that the client would wish to be updated. That will be true whether or not progress is being made on the matter and whether or not the failure to make progress is the fault of the lawyer, another party, or circumstances. Even if a lawyer has recently given an updating report to a client, communication may also be necessary in order to keep a client reasonably informed about important developments in the matter.

Consultative Communications. Second, MR 1.4(b) requires a particular kind of lawyer communication: "a lawyer shall explain a matter to the extent reasonably necessary to permit the client to make informed decisions regarding the representation." As the comment points out, the purpose of the communication should be to facilitate the client's intelligent participation in decisions about both the objectives and means of the representation.[23]

The subjects covered in the consultative communication cannot be cataloged in advance. In part, the scope of the conversation depends on the existing state of knowledge and sophistication of the client, the stage of the representation at which the conversation occurs, the importance of the subject to the client's objectives in the case, the client's expressed wish for more or less information about a matter, the need to plan for foreseeable developments and contingencies, and similar considerations. An important example is a lawyer's conversation with a client about legal and professional restraints on a lawyer. Ordinarily, a lawyer would reasonably not feel it necessary to inform a client that perjury cannot be employed in trials or fraud in a business transaction. But the circumstance might arise in which it is apparent that the client misunderstands the nature of the assistance that a lawyer may give. In such circumstances, MR 1.2 (e) requires a lawyer to inform the client about the limits on the lawyer's assistance.

Offers of Settlement or Compromise

Offers of settlement from opposing parties must be promptly communicated to the lawyer's client.[24] The rule is strictly enforced with respect to criminal defense lawyers' obligation to communicate all plea bargain offers of a prosecutor.[25] If an offer more favorable than the eventual sentence is not communicated to the accused, the remedy is the grant of a new trial, because the defense lawyer's failure to communicate the offer is ineffective assistance of counsel. In the civil area, a lawyer's failure to communicate a settlement offer is a violation of professional standards that can result in discipline [26] or in a recovery

[23] MR 1.4 comment (first paragraph). The comment also notes exceptional circumstances in which the normally complete communication process may be either impracticable or unwanted: incapacitated clients; entity clients with multiple members or constituencies; routine matters handled on a perfunctory basis (minor collection matters, for example); or emergencies not of the lawyer's making. Id. (third paragraph).

[24] Under California Rules of Professional Conduct Rule 5-105, the requirement is limited to a "written offer of settlement" made by an opposing party.

[25] MR 1.2(a), 1.4 comment (first paragraph). E.g., United States ex rel. Caruso v. Zelinsky, 689 F.2d 435, 438 (3d Cir.1982); Harris v. State, 437 N.E.2d 44 (Ind.1982); People v. Whitfield, 40 Ill.2d 308, 239 N.E.2d 850 (1968); State v. Simmons, 65 N.C.App. 294, 309 S.E.2d 493 (1983). See generally ABA Defense Function Standards § 4-6.2(a) (2d ed.1982); Annot., 8 ALR4th 660 (1981). Moreover, the prosecutor's offer must be communicated accurately. E.g., McAleney v. United States, 539 F.2d 282 (lst Cir. 1976)(guilty plea could be withdrawn where based on lawyer's incompetent communication of lesser sentence than prosecutor agreed to and recommended).

[26] MR 1.4 comment (first paragraph)("A lawyer who receives from opposing counsel an offer of settlement in a civil controversy or a proffered plea bargain in a criminal case should promptly inform the client of its substance unless prior discussions with the client have left it clear that the proposal will be unacceptable."). See also § 4.6.2.

by the injured client against the client's lawyer.[27]

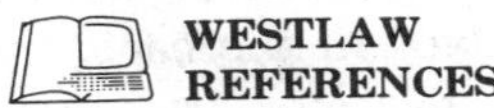

WESTLAW REFERENCES

Importance of Communications with Clients

di attorney-client privilege

The Lawyer Codes

fail! neglect! lack! /s communicat! /s lawyer attorney counsel** /s client

Reporting to Clients

digest,synopsis(lawyer attorney counsel** /s inform! /3 client)

Consultive Communications

consult! /s communicat! /s lawyer attorney counsel** /s client

Offers of Settlement or Compromise

communicat! /6 offer settlement /s lawyer attorney client

§ 4.6 SETTLEMENTS AND WAIVERS OF CLIENT RIGHTS

§ 4.6.1 *Procedural Forfeitures*

General

If the sole objective in a representation were to assure that a lawyer always followed a client's instructions, the law would have to provide that a client is bound by a lawyer's acts only when it is clear that the client directed the lawyer to act in the very way that the lawyer has acted or that the client approved the lawyer's act after the fact. But although client autonomy may be rigorously insisted upon in dealings between lawyer and client (§ 4.3), it is not obvious that it and the client's interest in obtaining a judicial determination of the client's claims or defenses on their merits should always override the interests of others. In litigation one must also consider the interests of opposing parties and coparties in a fair, evenhanded, and efficient hearing and the interest of judges in retaining the power "to manage their own affairs so as to achieve the orderly and expeditious disposition of cases." [28] Considerations such as those have led to a doctrine under which a client can inadvertently lose valuable rights because of a lawyer's carelessness.

Lawyers as Litigational Representatives of Their Clients

In order to accommodate the interests of other litigants and the judicial system, the general rule is that a client is bound by the acts of the client's lawyer in the course of the proceeding, whether the acts were deliberate or inadvertent, whether well- or ill-intentioned, whether done skillfully (if ultimately without success) or done clumsily.[29] In agency terms, a lawyer has apparent authority to bind the client to the ill effects of the lawyer's acts. The rule foists upon clients, instead of upon third parties or the courts, the procedural forfeitures incurred for clients by their lawyers.

Courts have offered several justifications for forcing clients to accept the results of procedural forfeitures. A justification commonly given is that it is necessary that a lawyer control the course of proceedings because legal actions are mysterious and technical matters that defy understanding by laypersons. A different justification is that the kinds of decisions that a lawyer controls are those that must be made without notice and thus without the opportunity to consult a client. A third rationale, hardly consistent with the preceding two, is that a client should determine the abilities of the client's chosen lawyer before the lawyer is hired or should detect the lawyer's derelictions, discharge the lawyer, and obtain more competent counsel.[30] Fourth, courts have argued their own interests in the smooth functioning of the judicial

27 Joos v. Auto-Owners Ins. Co., 94 Mich.App. 419, 288 N.W.2d 443, 445 (1979)(no need in legal malpractice case for expert testimony to establish duty of lawyer to inform client of settlement offer because duty is established as matter of law).

28 Link v. Wabash R.R., 370 U.S. 626, 630-31, 82 S.Ct. 1386, 1388-1389, 8 L.Ed.2d 734 (1962).

29 See generally Mazor, Power and Responsibility in the Attorney-Client Relation, 20 Stan.L.Rev. 1120 (1968).

30 Davis v. United Fruit Co., 402 F.2d 328, 331 (2d Cir. 1968), cert. denied 393 U.S. 1085, 89 S.Ct. 869, 21 L.Ed.2d 778 (1969)(client who "chose his attorney voluntarily . . . cannot be permitted to avoid the acts or omissions of his freely selected counsel."); North Carolina Nat'l

system and in the finality of judgments in the face of heavy caseloads and insufficient judicial resources.[31] A fifth rationale is that the client has an adequate remedy by a suit against the lawyer for malpractice [32] and, as between the client and a third party, the risks of incurring loss or additional expense because of the lawyer's default and because of any inadequacy in the malpractice remedy should fall upon the client.[33]

In general, those rationales, particularly the last two, have proved attractive to courts. In the landmark case of Link v. Wabash Railroad,[34] the Supreme Court itself approved dismissal of a plaintiff's complaint with prejudice when the plaintiff's lawyer was persistently remiss in fulfilling procedural responsibilities and, on the occasion of the penalty dismissal, had failed to attend a scheduled pretrial conference.[35] The language currently employed by the Court to describe the extreme cases in which penalty dismissals (or defaults) are justified is that the act or acts of the lawyer must indicate "flagrant bad faith" and a "callous disregard" of procedural responsibilities.[36] Lesser sanctions may be visited upon a party, or in some cases upon the party's lawyer, for virtually any violation of procedural rules.

Courts and rule framers in recent years have attempted to reach a better accommodation of conflicting interests through concentrating upon control over lawyers directly instead of visiting the consequences of procedural forfeitures always and only upon lawyers' clients. Imposing disciplinary sanctions on lawyers whose clients have suffered procedural forfeitures could be justified on the ground of assuring competence or of deterring lawyers from disrupting judicial proceedings.[37] The power to sanction lawyers directly, by fines that are imposed in lieu of sanctions directed only to the lawyers' clients, has grown through rule amendment and court decision in many jurisdictions, a development that commentators on the whole have applauded.[38] The future of doctrine in the area would seem to lie in the same direction of attempting to develop more effective measures of proportionality between the nature of the procedural offenses or defaults committed,[39] the effect of the offense or default upon

Bank v. Virginia Carolina Builders, Inc., 57 N.C.App. 628, 292 S.E.2d 135 (1982)(experienced businessman should have known he had to hire lawyer admitted to practice law in jurisdiction in which suit was pending), reversed 307 N.C. 563, 299 S.E.2d 629 (1983). A court can insist with more comfort that the client knowingly monitor the lawyer's actions if the client is also a lawyer. See Chira v. Lockheed Aircraft Corp., 634 F.2d 664 (2d Cir.1980). Occasionally a client will be required to prove diligent monitoring of the client's lawyer in order to demonstrate that "excusable neglect" caused the client's case to be dismissed. E.g., Bond v. Wilson, 398 A.2d 21 (D.C.App. 1979); Charolais Breeding Ranches Ltd. v. Wiegel, 92 Wis.2d 498, 285 N.W.2d 720 (1979).

31 Luis C. Forteza e Hijos, Inc. v. Mills, 534 F.2d 415, 418-19 (lst Cir.1976).

32 Brown v. E.W. Bliss Co., 72 F.R.D. 198, 200 (D.Md. 1976).

33 Link v. Wabash R.R., supra 370 U.S., at 634 n.10, 82 S.Ct., at 1390:

> [I]f an attorney's conduct falls substantially below what is reasonable under the circumstances, the client's remedy is against the attorney in a suit for malpractice. But keeping this suit alive merely because plaintiff should not be penalized for the omissions of his own attorney would be visiting the sins of plaintiff's lawyer upon the defendant.

See also, e.g., Inryco, Inc. v. Metropolitan Engineering Co., 708 F.2d 1225, 1234-35 (7th Cir.1983), cert. denied 104 S.Ct. 347, 78 L.Ed.2d 313 (1983); Village of Big Bend v. Anderson, 103 Wis.2d 403, 308 N.W.2d 887, 889 (1981).

34 Link v. Wabash R.R., supra.

35 But if the lawyer's sole default is failure to attend a pretrial conference, without a related history of dilatoriness as in *Link*, then it is an abuse of discretion for the trial court to impose a penalty dismissal instead of some lesser sanction more appropriately calibrated to the offense. See Tolbert v. Leighton, 623 F.2d 585 (9th Cir. 1980).

36 National Hockey League v. Metropolitan Hockey Club, Inc., 427 U.S. 639, 96 S.Ct. 2778, 2781, 49 L.Ed.2d 747 (1976). A penalty dismissal may be permissible for a single instance of misconduct that is particularly blatant. E.g., Cine Forty-Second St. Theatre Corp. v. Allied Artists, 602 F.2d 1062 (2d Cir.1979).

37 People v. Gottsegen, 623 P.2d 878, 879-80 (Colo.1981) (lawyer publicly censured for failing to respond to discovery request with result that client was required to pay legal fees of requesting party).

38 Mazor, Power and Responsibility in the Attorney-Client Relation, 20 Stan.L.Rev. 1120 (1968); Comment, An Attorney Fine: A Sanction to Assure Compliance with Court Calendar Orders, 30 U.Chi.L.Rev. 382 (1963); Note, The Emerging Deterrence Orientation in the Imposition of Discovery Sanctions, 91 Harv.L.Rev. 1033 (1978).

39 In the often-quoted opinion in Societe Internationale v. Rogers, 357 U.S. 197, 212, 78 S.Ct. 1087, 2 L.Ed.2d 1255

other parties and the judicial system,[40] and the level of sanction appropriate to remedy the wrong and to obtain desired levels of deterrence against similar departures from important rules in the present and in future cases.[41]

The procedural forfeiture concept is weakest in the area of criminal defense because of the constitutional right to the effective assistance of counsel (§ 14.6). In a broad sense, the responsibility of the state to supply competent counsel shifts some of the burden of serious mistakes by the lawyer from the client to the state. Nonetheless, there is by no means equivalence between the doctrines, and a defense lawyer can still incur substantial forfeitures to the harm of a client without violating the constitutional protection for competent counsel.[42]

Limitations on the Procedural Forfeiture Concept

In some few instances, however, courts have concluded that the interests at stake are too important to be waived by a lawyer's possibly unauthorized acts and have reserved those rights to the client. A prominent example is the rule in most jurisdictions that only a client may settle a lawsuit (§ 4.6.2). Another example is the decision whether to waive the attorney-client privilege.[43] There are few other such nondelegated areas in civil litigation. In criminal law, the list of rights for the client to determine is slightly longer (see § 4.6.3).

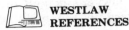

WESTLAW REFERENCES

45k109

Lawyers as Litigational Representatives of Their Clients

228k143(10)

link +4 wabash /p dismiss! default!

dismiss! /s lawyer attorney counsel** /6 neglect! negligen! omission

§ 4.6.2 Settlement Authority

General

Not all questions of a lawyer's authority are open-ended inquiries that depend upon minute examination of facts. Some situations permit relatively fixed rules because they arise frequently and because the absence of a fixed rule would inefficiently require extended factual hearings. An important example is the question whether a lawyer is empow-

(1958), the Court stressed the presence or absence of evidence that the "failure to comply has been due to . . . willfulness, bad faith, or any fault" of the forfeited party.

40 McCargo v. Hedrick, 545 F.2d 393 (4th Cir.1976)(lack of evidence of any prejudice to defendant because of delay caused by plaintiff's lawyer's failure to file pretrial conference document in timely fashion, among other factors, caused trial court's penalty dismissal to be abuse of discretion). A disquieting element with some procedural forfeiture cases and rules is that, as with the statutes of limitation, compliance is mechanically measured without regard to the presence or absence of prejudice in a particular case. Compare, e.g., Singelyn v. Superior Court, 62 Cal.App.3d 972, 133 Cal.Rptr. 486 (1976)(dismissal of action ordered under statute barring trial more than five years after action filed when trial date set one day after five-year limitation expired), with, e.g., Richards v. Swift, 241 Pa.Super. 359, 361 A.2d 688 (1976)(trial court did not abuse discretion in dismissing action that had lain dormant for nineteen years).

41 Roadway Express, Inc. v. Piper, 447 U.S. 752, 763-64, 100 S.Ct. 2455, 2462, 65 L.Ed.2d 488 (1980); Penthouse Int'l, Ltd. v. Playboy Enterprises, Inc., 663 F.2d 371 (2d Cir.1981) (dismissal within trial court's proper exercise of discretion following history of "prolonged and vexatious" obstruction of discovery and perjury by executives and lawyers with respect to existence of documents). The nondeterrable nature of the lawyer's conduct may be the basis for findings of courts that a lawyer's complete disappearance or mental incompetency may be an "extraordinary circumstance" relieving the lawyer's client from the normal procedural consequences of the lawyer's action or nonaction. E.g., United States v. Cirami, 563 F.2d 26 (2d Cir.1977); Vindigni v. Meyer, 441 F.2d 376 (2d Cir.1971).

42 See generally Wainwright v. Sykes, 433 U.S. 72, 97 S.Ct. 2497, 53 L.Ed.2d 594 (1977); Hill, The Forfeiture of Constitutional Rights in Criminal Cases, 78 Colum.L.Rev. 1050 (1978); Lawson, Presuming Lawyers Competent to Protect Fundamental Rights: Is It an Affordable Fiction?, 66 Ky.L.J. 459 (1978); Spritzer, Criminal Waiver, Procedural Default and the Burger Court, 126 U.Pa.L. Rev. 473 (1978); Tague, Federal Habeas Corpus and Ineffective Representation of Counsel: The Supreme Court Has Work to Do, 31 Stan.L.Rev. 1 (1978).

43 § 6.3.4. A client may delegate to the lawyer the power to decide whether to assert the privilege. E.g., In re Grand Jury Investigation of Ocean Transportation, 604 F.2d 672 (D.C.Cir.1979), cert. denied 444 U.S. 915, 100 S.Ct. 229, 62 L.Ed.2d 169 (1979).

ered to settle a client's lawsuit. Because settlement is often preferable to litigation, it may be a lawyer's responsibility to encourage a client to seek a settlement.[44] But the decision whether or not to settle is for the client to make. A lawyer who coerces a client to settle by misrepresentation or overreaching may incur liability to the client in damages[45] and, of course, is subject to discipline.[46] And courts have uniformly condemned contractual agreements under which clients agree not to settle a case without the concurrence of the client's lawyer.[47]

The great majority of civil suits are in fact settled. Settlements are relatively formal contracts that require the consent of all parties and are subject to the normal rules governing contract formation.[48] By their terms they typically contemplate that the parties will take official action to enter the agreed-upon judgment.[49] Under such circumstances it is both imperative and quite possible to enforce relatively straightforward rules governing the authority of lawyers in settlements.

Client Consent as Predicate

The rule that prevails in the great majority of jurisdictions is that the mere fact that a lawyer possesses the authority to represent a client gives the lawyer no implied authority to settle litigation.[50] Thus a local court rule requiring a lawyer to appear at a settlement conference with authority to settle requires a lawyer to appear with express authorization from the client to settle or with the client personally present.[51] Settlement authority must be expressly or implicitly conferred by the client, or the client must ratify the settlement. Parties who contract with a lawyer in the absence of one of those bases for validat-

[44] Clarion Corp. v. American Home Prods. Corp., 494 F.2d 860, 863-64 (7th Cir.), cert. denied 419 U.S. 870, 95 S.Ct. 128, 42 L.Ed.2d 108 (1974); 1908 Canon 8. Cf. EC 7-5. Abraham Lincoln's advice to a lawyer has often been quoted:

> Discourage litigation. Persuade your neighbors to compromise whenever you can. Point out to them how the nominal winner is often a real loser—in fees, expenses and waste of time. As a peacemaker, the lawyer has a superior opportunity of being a good man.

Abraham Lincoln, Notes for a Law Lecture, July 1, 1850, in II Complete Works of Abraham Lincoln 142 (1894). See generally Wachtler, Even if You Think Your Client Will Win, You May Have the Responsibility to Urge Settlement Anyway, 6 Hofstra L.Rev. 745 (1978).

[45] Swann v. Waldman, 465 A.2d 844 (D.C.App.1983).

[46] In re Stern, 81 N.J. 297, 406 A.2d 970 (1979).

[47] Olive v. Williams, 42 N.C.App. 380, 257 S.E.2d 90, 96 (1979); Dannenberg v. Dannenberg, 151 Kan. 600, 100 P.2d 667 (1940).

[48] Hall v. People to People Health Found., Inc., 493 F.2d 311 (2d Cir.1974)(accepting settlement offer after unreasonably long time ineffective); T.M. Cobb Co. v. Superior Court, 36 Cal.3d 273, 204 Cal.Rptr. 143, 682 P.2d 338 (1984)(settlement offer can be revoked prior to its acceptance); Norberg v. Fitzgerald, 122 N.H. 1080, 453 A.2d 1301 (1982)(fact that settlement involved realty did not require that it be in writing). Louisiana law normally requires that a settlement agreement be reduced to writing and signed before it is binding. E.g., Singleton v. Bunge Corp., 364 So.2d 1321 (La.App.1978).

[49] Unless a settlement contract so provides, however, no independent rule generally requires that a court approve a settlement or that a judgment be entered before the contract is effective. E.g., Davidson v. Davidson, 194 N.J.Super. 547, 477 A.2d 423 (1984)(client could not repudiate settlement contract after it was made but before court had entered judgment on it).

[50] United States v. Beebe, 180 U.S. 343, 21 S.Ct. 371, 45 L.Ed. 563 (1901); Hawk v. Biggio, 372 So.2d 303, 304 (Ala. 1979)(statute providing that lawyer has authority to bind client in any action by an agreement in relation thereto does not enlarge power of lawyer to settle without express consent of client); Linsk v. Linsk, 70 Cal.2d 272, 277-78, 74 Cal.Rptr. 544, 449 P.2d 760 (1969); Nehleber v. Anzalone, 345 So.2d 822, 822-23 (Fla.App.1977); Henderson v. Great Atl. & Pac. Tea Co., 374 Mich. 142, 147, 132 N.W.2d 75 (1965); Virginia Concrete Co. v. Board of Supervisors, 197 Va. 821, 91 S.E.2d 415, 56 A.L.R.2d 1283 (1956); In re J.H. & R.H., 144 Vt. 1, 470 A.2d 1182, 1184 (1983); cf. Klimas v. Mitrano, 17 Mass.App.Ct. 1004, 459 N.E.2d 1254, 1255 (1984)(trial court has discretion to relieve party of judgment entered on settlement entered into by lawyer without authority). Contra, e.g., Phoenix Properties, Inc. v. Umstead, 245 Ga. 172, 264 S.E.2d 8 (1980); Lord Jeff Knitting Co. v. Mills, 315 S.E.2d 377, 378-79 (S.C.App.1984)(lawyer has implied or apparent authority to settle when action is pending and lawyer is of record); cf. Rothman v. Fillette, 503 Pa. 259, 469 A.2d 543 (1983)(client who discovered five years later that lawyer had settled claim without authority and converted proceeds barred from reopening judgment and proceeding against original defendant who had settled in good faith). At least at one time, the English rule was also contrary: a barrister had the implied authority to consent to a verdict for the other side even in the absence of the client and without express authorization to do so. See Matthews v. Munster, 20 Q.B.D. 141 (1887).

[51] Continental Cas. Co. v. Chrysler Constr. Co., 80 Misc. 2d 552, 553-54, 363 N.Y.S.2d 258 (1975); Lodowski v. Roenick, 227 Pa.Super. 568, 307 A.2d 439, 441 (1973).

ing the settlement in effect generally assume the risk that the client will exercise his or her power to repudiate the agreement.

The client's consent [52] need not be expressed in any specific form. Whether the lawyer's authority is express,[53] implied,[54] or apparent [55] makes no difference with respect to the binding effect of the settlement vis-a-vis third parties. But a lawyer without express client authorization who enters into a settlement contract that detrimentally affects a client's interests because of the apparent-authority or implied-authority doctrines may be liable to the client for breach of contract.[56] A client may explicitly, but revocably, authorize a lawyer to settle a lawsuit at its outset.[57] But a clause of a client-lawyer contract purporting to give a lawyer power to veto a settlement that the client wants to accept is void.[58] Even if the client does not explicitly authorize a settlement, it may nonetheless be valid if the client, with full knowledge of the circumstances, ratifies the settlement by personally [59] taking action fatally inconsistent with denying it.[60]

If a settlement is entered into by a lawyer without authority, the client can have it set aside.[61] The client's power to repudiate is not cut off because of the fact that a court has entered a judgment or other order pursuant to the voidable settlement.[62] According to an Illinois decision, lawyers who were retained to

52 Consent by someone other than the client will bind the client only if, under agency rules, the actor has the derivative authority to convey the client's consent or to consent in behalf of the client. Compare, e.g., Dewitt v. Lutes, 581 S.W.2d 941 (Mo.App.1979)(evidence sufficiently demonstrated that wife had delegated authority to settle to spouse and to her lawyer), with, e.g., Kinkaid v. Cessna, 49 Md.App. 18, 430 A.2d 88 (1981)(consent of client's spouse ineffective in absence of evidence that client delegated settlement authority to spouse).

53 Sockolof v. Eden Pt. No. Condominium Ass'n, Inc., 421 So.2d 716 (Fla.App.1982)("Do the best you can under the circumstances."); Norberg v. Fitzgerald, 122 N.H. 1080, 453 A.2d 1301 (1982). Some decisions have recognized an "emergency" rule, under which a lawyer who agrees to a settlement, in circumstances preventing an opportunity to consult with the client, is deemed to have implied authority to settle. E.g., Bursten v. Green, 172 So.2d 472 (Fla.App.1965); Brumberg v. Chunghai Chan, 25 Misc.2d 312, 204 N.Y.S.2d 315, 319 (1959)(settlement enforced when defendant left country, trial had been twice delayed, and lawyer believed that trial would result in result less favorable than negotiated through settlement). A lawyer's misrepresentation to another negotiating party that the lawyer possesses express client authority to settle does not bind the client. E.g., Harrop v. Western Airlines, Inc., 550 F.2d 1143 (9th Cir.1977).

54 Szymkowski v. Szymkowski, 104 Ill.App.3d 630, 60 Ill.Dec. 310, 432 N.E.2d 1209 (1982)(client estopped to deny that lawyer had authority to settle when client sat silently while lawyer negotiated and concluded settlement in open court). An "implied" power to settle will not be found, however, if the opposing party was fully aware of the lawyer's lack of authority. E.g., Augustus v. John Williams & Assoc., Inc., 92 N.M. 437, 589 P.2d 1028, 1031 (1979).

55 Bergstrom v. Sears, Roebuck & Co., 532 F.Supp. 923, 933-34 (D.Minn.1982)(although lawyer initially lacked express authority to settle in client's behalf, client's acquiescence in conduct of lawyer that strongly indicated a power to settle created apparent authority in lawyer to settle).

56 Miotk v. Rudy, 4 Kan.App.2d 296, 605 P.2d 587, 589 (1980); Johnson v. Tesky, 57 Or.App. 133, 643 P.2d 1344, 1347 (Ore.App.1982).

57 Compare Hayes v. Eagle-Picher Indus., Inc., 513 F.2d 892 (10th Cir.1975)(agreement among several coclients to abide by majority vote in accepting settlement cannot bind clients who repudiated agreement and dissented from settlement); Rogers v. Robson, Masters, Ryan, Brumund & Belom, 81 Ill.2d 201, 40 Ill.Dec. 816, 407 N.E.2d 47, 49 (1980).

58 Mattioni, Mattioni & Mattioni v. Ecological Shipping Corp., 530 F.Supp. 910 (E.D.Pa.1981); Giles v. Russell, 222 Kan. 629, 567 P.2d 845, 850 (1977). Such a clause indeed may cause the entire client-lawyer contract to be voided to the lawyer's disadvantage. E.g., Mattioni, Mattioni & Mattioni v. Ecological Shipping Corp., supra; Olive v. Williams, 42 N.C.App. 380, 257 S.E.2d 90, 97 (1979). Courts have, however, quite generally upheld clauses in public liability insurance policies requiring that the insurer must consent to any settlement of a covered claim. See generally Annot., 18 ALR4th 249 (1982).

59 Actions of others, such as the client's lawyer, cannot serve as evidence of the client's ratification. E.g., Johnson v. Tesky, 57 Or.App. 133, 643 P.2d 1344 (1982).

60 Williams v. Int'l Ass'n of Machinists, 484 F.Supp. 917 (S.D.Fla.1978), affirmed 617 F.2d 44 (5th Cir.1980), cert. denied 449 U.S. 840, 101 S.Ct. 118 66 L.Ed.2d 47 (1980); Navrides v. Zurich Ins. Co., 5 Cal.3d 698, 97 Cal.Rptr. 309, 488 P.2d 637 (1971)(ratification by filing suit to enforce settlement agreement against insurance company); In re Hatfield, 231 Kan. 427, 646 P.2d 481 (1982); Petersen v. Petersen, 90 S.D. 666, 245 N.W.2d 285 (1976).

61 Odomes v. Nucare, Inc., 653 F.2d 246 (6th Cir.1981); Smith v. Widman Trucking & Excav., Inc., 627 F.2d 792, 796 (7th Cir.1980).

62 Coates v. Drake, 131 Mich.App. 687, 346 N.W.2d 858, 861 (1984).

represent the client by the client's insurer could be liable in damages to the client if the lawyers' failure to communicate a settlement offer to the client caused the client injury.[63]

Distinguishable Situations

The rule requiring client consent to settlements refers to the customary form of settlement, which must be distinguished from situations, discussed below,[64] in which lawyers possess a very comparable power to waive or to forfeit rights of a client, but in somewhat different settings. Also distinguishable is representative litigation such as a class action, in which the court has power to approve or disapprove settlements. There a lawyer for the class may accept or reject a settlement in behalf of the class, subject to court approval, even if the named representatives and all other members of the class have rejected it.[65] The lawyer must, of course, inform the court of the class's objections.[66] Similarly, a "no-client" lawyer for a governmental entity, such as a state's attorney general appearing in behalf of the state, may be empowered under applicable law to bind the state to a settlement.[67] On the other hand, a lawyer who represents a governmental agency or body may be required by local law to obtain the specific consent of the agency's highest authority before an effective settlement can be reached.[68]

The fact that a lawyer lacks implied authority to settle litigation does not mean that the lawyer's role and actions in the settlement are irrelevant. Representations by a lawyer, to the opposing party, of the meaning of certain terms in a proposed settlement agreement, for example, can bind the lawyer's client if dispute later arises.[69]

Professional Rules

The common-law rule that a lawyer is without implied authority to settle a client's lawsuit is enforced to some extent in the lawyer codes. All recognize that settlement authority rests in the client and not the lawyer.[70] Cases decided under the Code have held that a lawyer's attempt to settle a client's suit without the client's authority may subject the lawyer to discipline.[71] Model Rule 1.2(a) states that "a lawyer shall abide by a client's decision whether to accept an offer of settlement of a matter." The Model Rules also suggest that a lawyer may not alter that relationship by a term in a client-lawyer contract under which the client surrenders the right to control settlement decisions.[72] That suggested limitation should have no effect, however, upon the recognized right of a client

[63] Rogers v. Robson, Masters, Ryan, Brumund & Belom, 81 Ill.2d 201, 40 Ill.Dec. 816, 407 N.E.2d 47 (1980). The plaintiff, a physician, claimed damages from reputational and other harm that settlement of the medical malpractice action had caused. In order to recover the plaintiff would have to establish the amount of those harms. The court did not determine who had the burden of proof on the issue whether, in the absence of settlement, a result more favorable to the client's reputation would probably have been obtained. See also Joos v. Drillock, 127 Mich. App. 99, 338 N.W.2d 736 (1983).

[64] See § 4.6.3.

[65] Saylor v. Lindsley, 456 F.2d 896 (2d Cir.1972).

[66] Saylor v. Lindsley, supra, 456 F.2d at 900.

[67] State ex rel. Derryberry v. Kerr-McGee Corp., 516 P.2d 813 (Okl.1973).

[68] Presnell v. Board of Cty. Rd. Commissioners, 105 Mich.App. 362, 306 N.W.2d 516 (1981); Tice v. Dept. of Transportation, 67 N.C.App. 48, 312 S.E.2d 241 (1984).

[69] Victor Lalli Enterprises, Inc. v. Skippy Candle Corp., 578 F.Supp. 1384 (S.D.N.Y.1984); Hladek v. John A. Dalsin & Son, 310 Minn. 178, 245 N.W.2d 593, 596 (1976).

[70] EC 7-7 ("[I]n civil cases, it is for the client to decide whether he will accept a settlement offer . . . ."); MR 1.2(a) ("A lawyer shall abide by a client's decision whether to accept an offer of settlement of a matter.").

[71] In re Miller, 95 Wn.2d 453, 625 P.2d 701, 703 (1981) (lawyer disciplined for signing settlement contract stating that he had authority to settle, which he did not have: "Simply permitting the entry of such a judgment without disclosure to the Court [of the lawyer's lack of authority] is prejudicial to the administration of justice."). See also, e.g., Sampson v. State Bar, 12 Cal.3d 70, 115 Cal.Rptr. 43, 524 P.2d 139 (1974); In re Estes, 390 Mich. 585, 212 N.W.2d 903, 92 A.L.R.3d 275 (1973)(client who "virtually admitted" facts establishing liability did not thereby authorize lawyer to confess judgment against client for $30,654.53 without further notice to client); In re Zeitler, 85 N.J. 21, 424 A.2d 419, 420 (1980). Many of the discipline cases involve lawyers who have also wrongfully forged settlement checks and appropriated the proceeds. E.g., In re Dobbertin, 91 A.D.2d 264, 458 N.Y.S.2d 775 (1983).

[72] See MR 1.2 comment (Services Limited in Objectives or Means; second paragraph)("An agreement concerning the scope of representation must accord with the Rules of

expressly to authorize the client's lawyer, in a revocable way, to settle the client's claim.

Requirement to Communicate Offers of Settlement to Client

Pre-Code decisions have held that a lawyer must communicate an offer of settlement to a client.[73] The 1969 Code does not explicitly state such a requirement, although it is inferable from language stating that a decision whether to accept or reject a settlement offer is for the client to make.[74] The Model Rules are explicit in requiring a lawyer to communicate settlement offers unless the lawyer is aware from prior discussions with the client that the client would reject the offer.[75]

Courts have also held that it is part of the common-law duty of a lawyer to communicate settlement offers to a client so that the client may exercise the power to decide whether or not to accept.[76] But if a lawyer fails to communicate a settlement offer to a client, the offering party has no right to recover damages allegedly caused by the missed opportunity to settle for a figure lower than the eventual result.[77]

Settlements and Lawyers' Fee Interests

The only arguable reason, aside from paternalistic concerns with the client's own best interests, that a lawyer might have to attempt to prevent a client from settling a case is that the settlement does not provide for the lawyer's fee. But ordinarily a lawyer must be content with whatever protection is afforded by the existence of the lawyer's claim to a lien (§ 9.6.3). A lawyer may not, for example, provide a clause in the fee contract to the effect that the lawyer's consent is necessary before the client may accept a settlement.[78] Lawyers, of course, play an important role in settlements and the lawyer on neither side should attempt to endrun the other in achieving settlements. The professional rules against communicating directly with an opposing party represented by counsel (§ 11.6.2) require that all settlement negotiations be conducted between counsel or at least without avoiding counsel or otherwise violating those rules.[79] For the requirements with respect to settling related claims, see § 8.15.

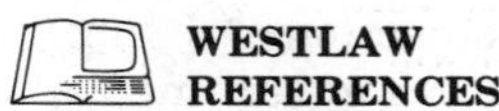

WESTLAW REFERENCES

General

authori! /s lawyer attorney counsel** /s settle! /s client

Client Consent as Predicate

authori! /s settle! /s express** imply implied** implicit** ratif!

Professional Conduct and other law. Thus, the client may not be asked . . . to surrender the right to terminate the lawyer's services or the right to settle litigation that the lawyer might wish to continue.").

[73] In re Brown, 104 Ariz. 387, 453 P.2d 958 (1969); Glenn v. State Bar, 14 Cal.2d 318, 94 P.2d 43 (1939).

[74] Such a requirement is, perhaps, inferable from EC 7-7 and from DR 7-101(A)(1) or (A)(2) on zealously representing a client. Cf. also EC 7-8; EC 9-2. E.g., In re Paauwe, 294 Or. 171, 654 P.2d 1117, 1118-19 (1982)(assuming, without deciding, that DR 1-102(A)(5) and DR 7-101(A)(3) create such a duty).

[75] See MR 1.4(a) and (b) and, expressly, MR 1.4 comment (first paragraph)("A lawyer who receives from opposing counsel an offer of settlement in a civil controversy, or a proffered plea bargain in a criminal case, should promptly inform the client of its substance unless prior discussions with the client have left it clear that the proposal will be unacceptable.").

[76] Rogers v. Robson, Masters, Ryan, Brumund & Belom, 81 Ill.2d 201, 40 Ill.Dec. 816, 818, 407 N.E.2d 47, 49 (1980); Joos v. Drillock, 127 Mich.App. 99, 338 N.W.2d 736 (1983).

[77] Parnell v. Smart, 66 Cal.App.3d 833, 136 Cal.Rptr. 246 (1977).

[78] See Lewis v. S.S. Baune, 534 F.2d 1115, 1122 (5th Cir. 1976); cf. Charal v. Andes, 81 F.R.D. 99 (E.D.Pa. 1979)(class action representatives bound by such a contract with their lawyer could not "adequately" represent a class). But see La.Rev.Stat.Ann. § 37:218 (Supp.1976) (permitting stipulation in client-lawyer contract that neither lawyer nor client may settle without written consent of the other); Mart v. Schlumberger, Ltd., 422 So. 2d 1205, 1207 (La.App.1982), writ denied 429 So.2d 128 (1983).

[79] Among other things, endrunning an opposing lawyer may expose the lawyer who negotiates a settlement directly with an opposing party to a suit for damages by the opposing lawyer on a theory of tortious interference with a prospective economic advantage if the settlement is in derogation of the opposing lawyer's lien interest. E.g., Pearlmutter v. Alexander, 97 Cal.App.3d Supp. 16, 158 Cal.Rptr. 762 (1979).

settle! /s client /s consent! consensual /s lawyer attorney counsel**

Distinguishable Situations

"class action" /s settlement /s approv! accept! disapprov! reject!

Professional Rules

"e.c. 7–7"

Requirement to Communicate Offers of Settlement to Client

d.r. +1 7–101(a)(1) 7–101(a)(2)

Settlements and Lawyers' Fee Interests

topic(45) /p settlement /p lawyer attorney counsel** /10 fee

§ 4.6.3 Waivers

General

Aside from indicating the role of the lawyer in settling a lawsuit, the cases are hardly consistent on the extent to which a lawyer has authority to control matters in the course of a representation. To an extent, answers to the question of lawyer control depend on whether the matter is in litigation or not, whether the case involves criminal or civil matters, whether providing for client control would seriously delay expeditious proceedings, and, whether the matter is normally of a kind, such as settlement, whose disposition will effectively dispose of a matter.

Criminal Representation

The extent of a lawyer's authority when a lawyer represents a person accused of crime has been comparatively well worked out, perhaps because the issues have so frequently been litigated. Courts generally agree that in fact the accused must explicitly consent to very few critical decisions on the part of the defendant's lawyer. Moreover, the courts do not generally draw distinctions between court-appointed defense lawyers and those personally retained by the accused. The four decisions to which client consent is required are those involving (1) the plea that will be entered; (2) whether to forego the right to jury trial; (3) whether the accused should testify;[80] and (4) whether to appeal.[81]

Civil Cases

Predictably, courts have been much more willing to permit lawyers to waive rights of a party in civil litigation. The central doctrinal problem is to determine which waivers are the functional equivalents of settlement agreements and, thus, are not permitted without explicit client consent. Most jurisdictions, for example, permit a defensive pleading to be signed by the lawyer for the defendant, and thus it is possible for a defendant to waive in the answer such important rights as the right to jury trial, and the right to assert otherwise available defenses. Beyond the pleading stage, a lawyer has the power to stipulate to certain procedures.[82]

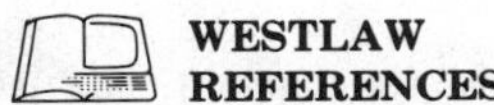

General

lawyer attorney counsel** /6 waiv! /5 right /p client /3 consent!

di waiver

Criminal Representation

client /5 consent! /s plea "jury trial" appeal!

Civil Cases

45k86

§ 4.7 ADVICE OF COUNSEL

Legal Advice and Legal Obligations

Probably most of the time of most lawyers is spent researching and conveying to clients advice about the requirements and permissions of the law. Clients must inevitably rely

[80] ABA Defense Function Standards § 4-5.2 (1980). Some jurisdictions have extended the list. E.g., State v. Sain, 34 Wn.App. 553, 663 P.2d 493 (1983)(right to be tried by elected judge rather than by judge pro tempore).

[81] ABA Defense Function Standards § 4-8.2(a)(1980).

[82] Hillman v. Commissioner, 687 F.2d 164 (6th Cir.1982) (taxpayers bound by stipulation of their lawyer that outcome of other cases being litigated by same lawyer would control their own). But see, e.g., Davis v. Black, 406 So.2d 408 (Ala.Civ.App.1981)(lawyer had no power to stipulate that case would be controlled by outcome of test case).

on lawyers to a greater or lesser extent and act in the expectation and hope that the advice has been well-founded. But what if it is not? Does the fact that a client has acted after receiving legal advice, and acted in a way that the lawyer advised was legally permissible, immunize the client from the toils of the law that would befall an actor otherwise similarly situated who had not acted on the advice of counsel? A general rule that all acts pursuant to the advice of counsel are exempt from the law would clearly be insupportable because lawyers would be substituted for lawfully constituted lawmakers and could not always be trusted to keep the public interest in mind. But it would also be intolerable always to ignore the fact that a client has acted with a lawyer's advice. Whenever evidence of a lawyer's advice is offered by a client and is relevant, the client implicitly waives any objection to the lawyer's testimony on the ground of attorney-client privilege.[83]

Relevance of Advice of Counsel to State of Mind and Similar Issues

No absolutely uniform rule on the relevance of advice of counsel emerges from the cases. Relatively clear cases of relevance involve issues of state of mind of the actor in which testimony about a lawyer's advice might demonstrate the actor's good faith. It is relatively well settled, for example, that a client is not liable in malicious prosecution if he or she relied in good faith on a lawyer's advice that there were good grounds to take the action of which the plaintiff now complains, even if the advice was erroneous.[84] The advice must be sought and given in good faith, with full disclosure from the client[85] and with nothing equivocal or suspicious about the lawyer's advice.[86] That is the general approach in other areas of the law in which malice must be shown[87] or, as in the criminal law, in which wilfullness is an issue.[88]

[83] § 6.3.7.

[84] Dawson v. Mead, 98 Idaho 1, 557 P.2d 595 (1976) (absent evidence to contrary, court assumes that lawyer controlled conduct of lawsuit, and thus continuation of lawsuit, after facts exonerating party sued became known, was not with malice because based on advice of counsel); St. Johnsbury & Lake Champlain RR. v. Hunt, 59 Vt. 294, 7 A. 277 (1886).

[85] To show good faith the client must prove "(1) that he sought counsel with an honest purpose of being informed as to the law, (2) that he made a full, correct, and honest disclosure to counsel of all material facts in his knowledge bearing on the plaintiff's guilt, or which should have been within his knowledge had he made a reasonably careful investigation bearing on such guilt and (3) that he was in good faith guided by the advice of counsel in causing the arrest of the plaintiff. . . .Whether such advice is thus sought and obtained is usually a question for the jury." Noell v. Angle, 217 Va. 656, 231 S.E.2d 330, 333 (1977)(facts conclusively showed reliance in good faith on advice of prosecuting attorney). See, e.g., Derby v. Jenkins, 32 Md.App. 386, 363 A.2d 967, 971 (1976)(client's failure to reveal all known facts to lawyer precludes defense). See also In re Kaufhold, 256 F.2d 181 (3d Cir. 1958)(district court improperly found lack of fraudulent intent in bankrupt who testified both that he had and that he had not made full disclosure to lawyer).

[86] Fogel v. Chestnutt, 533 F.2d 731 (2d Cir.1975), cert. denied 429 U.S. 824, 97 S.Ct. 77, 50 L.Ed.2d 86 (1976)(in suit claiming fund had been overcharged by investment adviser, defense of advice of counsel unavailing where, as other officers knew, lawyer owned 14 percent of stock in adviser company and advice was given in informal, unwritten way, which presumably suggested advice was provisional and not well considered by lawyer).

[87] Kirkland v. Nat'l Broadcasting Co., 425 F.Supp. 1111 (E.D.Pa.1976), affirmed 565 F.2d 152 (3d Cir.1977)(reliance on advice of counsel that work was in public domain relevant to demonstrate defendant's good faith and thus preclude author's recovery on theory of unfair competition); Porter v. Wilson, Walch, Fortner, Robinson & Beese, 384 So.2d 190 (Fla.App.1980), review denied 392 So.2d 1378 (1980)(no punitive damages when defendants acted in good-faith reliance on advice of counsel in breach-of-contract action); Rowland v. Lepire, 99 Nev. 308, 662 P.2d 1332, 1335 (1983)(evidence of reliance on advice of counsel tends to negative evidence of malice in slander-of-title action).

[88] See generally Williamson v. United States, 207 U.S. 425, 453, 28 S.Ct. 163, 52 L.Ed. 278 (1908)(in criminal action, accused can defend on ground of honest and good faith reliance on advice of counsel; "on the other hand, no man can willfully and knowingly violate the law, and excuse himself from the consequences thereof by pleading that he followed the advice of his counsel."). See also, e.g., United States v. Eisenstein, 731 F.2d 1540 (11th Cir. 1984)(testimony of defendant's lawyer of advice concerning currency-transaction reports relevant in prosecution for failing to file reports); United States v. Taglione, 546 F.2d 194, 200-01 (5th Cir.1977)(relevance in extortion prosecution of defendant's lawyer's proferred testimony that defendant received advice that insisting upon reward before return of property was legally proper); United States v. Hoopes, 545 F.2d 721 (10th Cir.1976), cert. denied 431 U.S. 954, 97 S.Ct. 2675, 53 L.Ed.2d 270 (1977) (advice-of-counsel defense properly kept from jury where

Irrelevance of Advice of Counsel in Strict Regulatory Areas

On the other hand, some legal obligations are imposed without regard to the state of mind of persons subject to the obligation. Advice of counsel is irrelevant to such obligations, even if the advice was sought and given in good faith.[89] In tax cases, the courts are divided at present on the issue whether a similar approach should determine a taxpayer's liability for penalities for late filing of a return when the taxpayer reasonably relied on a lawyer's undertaking to file the return or the lawyer's advice that a return was not required.[90] A lawyer who gives erroneous advice may, of course, be liable to the client for damages caused by the bad advice.[91]

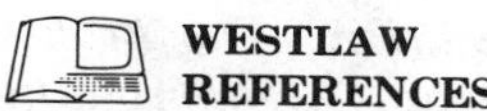

WESTLAW REFERENCES

Legal Advice and Legal Obligations

attorney /3 client /3 privilege /s advice

Relevance of Advice of Counsel to State of Mind and Similar Issues

lawyer counsel** attorney /5 advice /p "state of mind" "good faith" /p disclos!

Irrelevance of Advice of Counsel in Strict Regulatory Areas

erroneous** irrelevan** /7 advice /7 lawyer attorney counsel**

§ 4.8 CLIENT FUNDS AND PROPERTY

Safekeeping Client Funds and Property

On an average day, the seven hundred thousand lawyers in the United States probably have in their collective hands and bank accounts billions of dollars of the funds of others, primarily clients, and property or documents representing values several times that amount. A personal injury lawyer receives a check made out to the lawyer as the proceeds of a settlement. A probate lawyer has possession of a decedent's valuable coin collection in order to have it appraised, together with stocks, bonds, deeds, other property, and the proceeds of a life insurance policy. A general practitioner serves as the conservator of the estate of an elderly and incompetent client. The funds and property of others in the hands of a lawyer are totally unsecured because most lawyers are not bonded, nor are they required to be. In effect, the enormous wealth of clients and other persons over which lawyers have possessory and signatory power is secured only by the reputation of the profession to which the lawyer belongs, the honor of the individual lawyer-custodian and, to an extent, by malpractice insurance and rather limited client security funds in some jurisdictions. A client's remedies against a lawyer who violates the client's trust are otherwise limited to a complaint to a lawyer

only evidence showed that one lawyer advised that tax protestor's failure to file was precarious and defendant knew that advice from two disbarred lawyers who had been prosecuted for tax violations was shaky). Cf. Ketchum v. Ward, 422 F.Supp. 934 (W.D.N.Y.1976), affirmed 556 F.2d 557 (2d Cir.1977)(whether criminal statute is sufficiently specific to meet void-for-vagueness requirement of due process is determined by asking whether competent lawyer could determine from words of statute that it might be used as basis for prosecuting client). See also, e.g., Arthur Lipper Corp. v. SEC, 547 F.2d 171, 184 (2d Cir.1976), cert. denied 434 U.S. 1009, 98 S.Ct. 719, 54 L.Ed.2d 752 (1978)(relevance of reliance on advice of counsel in determining appropriate length of suspension of broker-dealer for violation of securities laws).

89 State v. Anderson, 306 Minn. 552, 236 N.W.2d 174 (1975)(advice of counsel irrelevant in action to rescind driver's license for failure to take chemical test).

90 Compare, e.g., United States v. Boyle, 710 F.2d 1251 (7th Cir.1983), judgment reversed ___ U.S. ___, 105 S.Ct. 687, 83 L.Ed.2d 622 (1985)(reliance on advice of counsel is "reasonable cause," excusing late-filing penalty), with, e.g., Estate of Lillehei v. Commissioner, 638 F.2d 65 (8th Cir.1981)(advice of counsel irrelevant when executor failed to file estate tax return on time); Millette & Assoc., Inc. v. Commissioner, 594 F.2d 121 (5th Cir.1979), cert. denied 444 U.S. 899, 100 S.Ct. 207, 62 L.Ed.2d 135 (1979).

91 Scherf v. Myers, 258 N.W.2d 831 (S.D.1977)(guardian, erroneously advised by lawyer that it was "legal" to use guardianship funds to pay bills of ward's relatives, could recover on indemnity theory from lawyer).

discipline agency or a claim in a court action against the lawyer.[92]

For the most part, lawyers have acquitted themselves honorably and skillfully in their role as the custodians and transferers of client property. They have done so under the anxious eyes of courts and lawyer disciplinary agencies, which have responded to reported instances of lawyer abuse of custodial powers with unusual vigor. The general law and the professional rules have attempted to protect client interests primarily by bookkeeping, notice, and safekeeping requirements. Their thrust is to require lawyers to deal with client property as fiduciaries, protecting the client's interests and ignoring the lawyer's own possible interest in using or acquiring the property. The 1983 Model Rules extend the same protections to the funds and property of any person, including clients.

The detailed requirements of the lawyer codes are not unique to lawyers, nor are they as stringent as some have urged. Many of the same requirements apply under the common law[93] or under statutes to other fiduciaries, such as escrow agents, accountants, banks, trust companies, and similar persons or entities that hold funds or property for others. The fiducial property rules in the lawyer codes are, by and large, applied without regard to the lawyer's good or bad faith. Thus claims of white-heart-but-empty-headed noncompliance because of a lawyer's innocent ignorance of the rules,[94] poor bookkeeping methods,[95] or the carelessness or ignorance of nonlawyer employees,[96] or because a lawyer had left the matter to be handled by others such as accountants,[97] are not usually successful. Courts in lawyer discipline cases seem particularly severe with a lawyer who converts client property[98] or who "commingles" client property with the lawyer's own.

Segregation: The Prohibition against Commingling

The lawyer codes explicitly require that when a lawyer receives[99] any client funds or property it must be segregated from the law-

92 In addition to common-law actions to recover converted or wrongfully withheld funds or property, some states afford clients a summary proceeding to order lawyers to account and make restitution. E.g., West v. Haupt, 163 Ga.App. 907, 296 S.E.2d 723 (1982); In re Hahn, 97 N.Y. 521 (1821).

93 In re Deschane, 84 Wn.2d 514, 527 P.2d 683, 684-85 (1974)(even if professional rules did not exist, lawyer would still be required as fiduciary to maintain current and accurate records of all client funds entrusted to lawyer).

94 In re Harrison, 461 A.2d 1034, 1036 (D.C.1983); In re Eisenberg, 75 N.J. 454, 383 A.2d 426, 427 n.1 (1978). An extreme case is Hamilton v. State Bar, 23 Cal.3d 868, 153 Cal.Rptr. 602, 591 P.2d 1254 (1979)(disbarment for, among other things, paying mandatory bar dues with check drawn on client trust account over prior protest of state bar that lawyer's actions were clearly improper).

95 In re Fling, 316 N.W.2d 556, 558 (Minn.1982); Iverson v. New York St. B. Ass'n, 51 A.D.2d 422, 381 N.Y.S.2d 711 (1976).

96 In re Mannis, 295 Or. 594, 668 P.2d 1224 (1983).

97 In re Rabb, 73 N.J. 272, 374 A.2d 461, 464 (1977).

98 Conversion of a client's funds has been called one of the least excusable acts for which a lawyer can be disciplined. In re Schwenn, 373 So.2d 1076 (Ala.1979)("Failure of an attorney to handle properly the funds of a client is one of the most frequent complaints made against attorneys."); Florida Bar v. Blalock, 325 So.2d 401, 404 (Fla.1976); Louisiana St. B. Ass'n v. Powell, 439 So.2d 415, 417 (La.1983)("The misuse of a client's funds by an attorney represents the gravest form of professional misconduct. It strikes at the heart of public confidence in the legal profession."); In re Walton, 251 N.W.2d 762, 763 (N.D.1977). A rule followed in many jurisdictions is that misappropriation of client funds or property requires disbarment in the absence of substantial mitigating circumstances. E.g., In re Couser, 122 Ariz. 500, 596 P.2d 26 (1979); Bradpiece v. State Bar, 10 Cal.3d 742, 746-47, 111 Cal.Rptr. 905, 518 P.2d 337, 341-342 (1974); Florida Bar v. Breed, 378 So.2d 783 (Fla.1979); In re Marks, 72 A.D.2d 399, 401, 424 N.Y.S.2d 229 (1980) (lawyer who converts entrusted funds presumptively unfit to be member of bar); Carter v. Ross, 461 A.2d 675, 676 (R.I.1983); In re Wilson, 81 N.J. 451, 409 A.2d 1153 (1979)(strict rule of disbarment in misappropriation cases); In re Pierson, 280 Or. 513, 571 P.2d 907, 908-09 (1977)("We hold that a single conversion by a lawyer to his own use of his client's funds will result in permanent disbarment."). Conversion of client property is not different because it was for the benefit of other clients and not for the lawyer's personal gain. Committee on Professional Ethics v. O'Connor, 329 N.W.2d 1, 5 (Iowa 1983).

99 Commingling can also occur if sums are left in a trust account for an extended period after the lawyer becomes entitled to withdraw them as fees. See In re Maran, 80 N.J. 160, 402 A.2d 924 (1979). Funds in a trust account that represent earned fees should ordinarily be withdrawn promptly.

yer's own funds and property.[1] The bland statement in EC 9-5, that commingling of a client's funds with those of a lawyer "should be avoided," seriously understates the grave concern with which most courts regard instances of commingling.[2] One reason for the prohibition against commingling is to assure that the lawyer does not mistakenly use a client's property for personal purposes. Use of a client's property for the lawyer's personal purposes is a serious offense, for example, the use of client funds to pay office, home, business, or other nonclient expenses,[3] no matter how temporarily the funds are "borrowed" for those purposes. Personal use of trust funds is typically dealt with as strictly as is a diversion of client funds into a personal account when they are first received.[4] Segregation is important for a second reason: it offers greater assurance under state debtor-creditor laws that creditors of the lawyer are not entitled to seize commingled property as if it were owned by the lawyer.[5] Thus it should normally be irrelevant that a client suffered no direct loss because of a lawyer's personal use of a trust account.[6]

[1] DR 9-102(A)(funds of clients to be kept in trust account in state of lawyer's office, "and no funds belonging to the lawyer or law firm shall be deposited therein" with limited exceptions); DR 9-102(B)(2)(identify and label securities and other property of client and place in safekeeping); MR 1.15(a)("A lawyer shall hold property of clients or third persons that is in a lawyer's possession in connection with a representation separate from the lawyer's own property.").

Commingling usually occurs when a lawyer withdraws client funds and deposits them to a lawyer's personal or office account or deposits a lawyer's personal or business funds into the lawyer's trust account. Commingling can also occur when a lawyer deposits personal or business funds into a client's account that the client has opened and over which the lawyer later is given signatory powers. E.g., Butler County Bar Ass'n v. Green, 1 Ohio St.3d 48, 438 N.E.2d 406 (1982). See Annot., 94 A.L.R.3d 846 (1979). Commingling can also occur if a lawyer deposits client funds into a trust account when the account has a negative balance. In re Haupt, 250 Ga. 422, 297 S.E.2d 284 (1982).

[2] Akron Bar Ass'n v. Hughes, 46 Ohio St.2d 369, 348 N.E.2d 712, 715 (1976)("[I]t has been the consistent practice of this court in recent years to impose a penalty of either indefinite suspension or disbarment in cases involving commingling of funds.")(footnotes omitted). Even single instances of commingling have been harshly condemned. E.g., Committee on Professional Ethics v. Toomey, 253 N.W.2d 573, 575 (Iowa 1977)("Commingling . . . warrants license revocation, not mere suspension."); In re Cohen, 98 Ill.2d 133, 74 Ill.Dec. 603, 456 N.E.2d 105, 107 (1983)("this court has repeatedly announced that commingling is an unacceptable practice regardless of why it occurred."). It has even been held that client consent to commingling does not abrogate the lawyer's responsibility to maintain separate accounts—an undoubtedly ill-considered holding if the court was indeed convinced that informed and voluntary client consent was given. See Archer v. State, 548 S.W.2d 71 (Tex.Civ.App.1977). See also State v. Pringle, 233 Kan. 726, 667 P.2d 283, 288 (1983)(lawyer's defense that he was following client's request by holding cash in office safe does not excuse intentional violation of rule requiring lawyer to hold funds in trust account).

[3] In re Rollins, 281 S.C. 467, 316 S.E.2d 670 (1984) (disbarment for investment of client funds in close corporation in which lawyer had business interest and borrowing funds for purchase of house).

[4] In re Cary, 90 Wn.2d 762, 585 P.2d 1161 (1978). Unauthorized use will often be assumed if the balance in a trust account falls below the total of trust deposits less authorized disbursements to clients. Giovanazzi v. State Bar, 28 Cal.3d 465, 169 Cal.Rptr. 581, 585, 619 P.2d 1005, 1009 (1980).

[5] See In re Clayter, 78 Ill.2d 276, 35 Ill.Dec. 790, 792, 399 N.E.2d 1318, 1320 (1980):

> The commingling of funds and depositing clients' funds or other money held by an attorney for another in an account standing in the attorney's name alone endangers the security of the interests of those to whom the money belongs. Commingling of funds has been the first step in a large number of cases which this court has considered involving wrongful conversion of funds by attorneys. Also, when funds belonging to another are deposited in an attorney's personal account, there is the danger of the conversion of these funds by operation of law; that is, in case of the death or insolvency of an attorney, these funds could well become assets of his estate, leaving the rightful owner with only a claim of a creditor against the attorney's estate. For these reasons, it is essential that such money be held in such a manner that there can be no doubt that the attorney is holding it only for another and that the money does not belong to him personally.

E.g., Black v. State Bar, 57 Cal.2d 219, 18 Cal.Rptr. 518, 522, 368 P.2d 118, 122 (1962); Trustees of Clients' Security Fund v. Beckmann, 143 N.J.Super. 548, 364 A.2d 15 (1976)(lawyer's divorced wife, security fund, and lawyer's client given equal footing to claim against lawyer under indictment for embezzling funds from clients).

[6] Fitzsimmons v. State Bar, 34 Cal.3d 327, 193 Cal.Rptr. 896, 667 P.2d 700, 702 (1983). But see Newman v. Bd. of Professional Responsibility, 73 A.D.2d 1029, 424 N.Y.S.2d 529 (1980)(covering personal check with trust account funds not improper where bank explicitly agreed to permit any resulting overcharge in trust account).

Funds Subject to the Fiduciary Requirements

Most funds can be readily identified as those of a client, a third party, or a lawyer. But ambiguities can arise because of the multiple roles that a lawyer may play or because the funds that a lawyer receives may be intended for a variety of different uses. Because the professional fiduciary rules apply generally, most courts have not been impressed with arguments that the requirements of the professional rules should be narrowly applied to client-lawyer relationships and have applied the rules even if the lawyer was technically functioning as a trustee,[7] guardian,[8] real estate broker,[9] or corporate officer [10] or was holding the funds as a correspondent for another lawyer [11] or holding funds of a third party who was not the lawyer's client.[12] The general rule of MR 1.15(a) limits the fiduciary rules to funds or property that comes into a lawyer's possession "in connection with a representation" but seems subject to an equally broad interpretation. Under both the Code and the Model Rules, the general prohibitions against dishonesty would also suffice to cover most instances of conversion of client or third party funds or property.[13]

Retainer Fees and Advance Fee Payments

Funds received from a client at the beginning of a representation are often intended to pay the lawyer.[14] One set of decisions treats most such funds as general office revenues that a lawyer can treat as personal or business funds and thus need not hold in a trust account.[15] Another group, however, requires that some advance fee payments, and perhaps even retainer fees, must be deposited into a trust account and withdrawn only as the lawyer earns the fee.[16] In jurisdictions in which it is permissible to treat a retainer fee as the

[7] In re Burton, 472 A.2d 831 (D.C.App.1984), cert. denied ___ U.S. ___, 105 S.Ct. 563, 83 L.Ed.2d 504 (1984) (court-appointed trustee); State v. Freeman, 229 Kan. 639, 629 P.2d 716 (1981); In re Gallop, 85 N.J. 317, 426 A.2d 509 (1981); In re Cary, 90 Wn.2d 762, 585 P.2d 1161 (1978)(misappropriation of funds by lawyer as trustee of family trust). Cf. also, e.g., Kentucky Bar Ass'n v. Ricketts, 599 S.W.2d 454 (Ky.1980)(lawyer who converted check known by him to have been mistakenly sent by insurance company disbarred).

[8] Clark v. State Bar, 39 Cal.2d 161, 246 P.2d 1 (1952).

[9] Simmons v. State Bar, 70 Cal.2d 361, 74 Cal.Rptr. 915, 450 P.2d 291 (1969). A lawyer's involvement in real estate transactions might in fact heighten fiduciary obligations. Cf. In re Feuerstein, 93 N.J. 441, 461 A.2d 750, 753 (1983)(real estate transactions mandate use of escrow account).

[10] Dresden v. Willock, 518 F.2d 281 (3d Cir.1975).

[11] In re Draper, 317 A.2d 106 (Del.1974); Oklahoma ex rel. Oklahoma Bar Ass'n v. Steger, 433 P.2d 225 (Okl. 1966). But cf. Louisiana St. B. Ass'n v. Causey, 440 So.2d 125 (La.1983)(willful failure to pay split fee to other lawyer for one month, while not to be condoned, does not constitute disciplinary violation); In re Rice, 99 Wn.2d 275, 661 P.2d 591 (1983)(charge that lawyer improperly drew funds from law firm account improperly seeks to turn law firm dispute into disciplinary proceeding).

[12] Johnstone v. State Bar, 64 Cal.2d 153, 49 Cal.Rptr. 97, 98, 410 P.2d 617, 618 (1966)("When an attorney receives money on behalf of a third party who is not his client, he nevertheless is a fiduciary as to such third party. Thus, the funds in his possession are impressed with a trust, and [the] conversion of such funds is a breach of the trust."); Louisiana St. B. Ass'n v. Orpys, 427 So.2d 842 (La.1983)(funds to be reimbursed to insurance company that had made payments to client); State ex rel. Oklahoma Bar Ass'n v. Smith, 615 P.2d 1014, 1017 (Okl.1980).

[13] In re Holman, 297 Or. 36, 682 P.2d 243, 255 (1984).

[14] Note, Attorney Misappropriation of Clients' Funds: A Study in Professional Responsibility, 10 U.Mich.J.L. Ref. 415, 436 (1977)(noting ambiguity in DR 9-102(A)(2)).

[15] In re Stern, 92 N.J. 611, 458 A.2d 1279, 1283-84 (1983)(pending study of provisions of 1983 Model Rules, "absent an explicit understanding that the retainer fee be separately maintained, a general retainer fee need not be deposited in an attorney's trust account"). Even if the lawyer is entitled to treat the fee payment as his or her own once it is received, however, if the lawyer is later required to repay the fee and fails to do so, one decision has held that the lawyer violates DR 9-102(B)(4). Office of Disciplinary Counsel v. Kagawa, 63 Hawaii 150, 622 P.2d 115, 120 (1981).

[16] In re Aronson, 352 N.W.2d 17 (Minn.1984); Proposed D.C. Ethics Opinion on Fees Advanced by Clients, 5 D.C. Lawyer 47 (July/August 1981)(proposed ruling that all fees paid in advance that are not retainer fees (to be kept by the lawyer regardless of number of hours or amount of work expended) are trust funds until earned). Cf. Baranowski v. State Bar, 24 Cal.3d 153, 154 Cal.Rptr. 752, 757 n.4, 593 P.2d 613, 618 (1979)(payment of fees in advance, as opposed to retainer fee, in future cases may be treated as trust funds until earned, but issue not reached here); In re Zderic, 92 Wn.2d 777, 600 P.2d 1297, 1302 (1979) (lawyer-respondent "does argue . . . that retainers need not be held in trust until services are actually rendered. We note the apparent confusion about the status of retainer fees. . . . Until the bar association clarifies its

lawyer's own, the retainer agreement should make it very clear that the client's payment to the lawyer will not be retained by the lawyer, but can be expended by the lawyer in the general course of business of the firm.

Client Advances for Costs and Expenses

A related area of possible ambiguity is the nature of client advances for payments by a lawyer to third parties. An exception from the segregation and trust account obligation is provided in DR 9-102(A) for client "advances for costs and expenses." Clearly the phrase does not refer to all payments by a client to a lawyer for payment to third parties at a later point.[17] For instance, a client's deposit with a lawyer of the purchase price of a real estate investment for a future closing, although possibly within the literal terms of the rule, must be kept in a trust account.[18] The exception should probably be interpreted narrowly to apply only to advances for incidental expenses of litigation, for which purpose convenience might urge that the lawyer retain the funds in the lawyer's office account.[19] No similar ambiguity arises under MR 1.15(a) and under the California rules—these treat all client and third party funds as equally subject to the trust account requirement.[20] Under that sort of rule, client prepayment of expenses must be treated as trust account funds until expended for their intended purpose.

Lawyer Power to Endorse Drafts Made out to Clients

The decisions also disagree over a lawyer's power to endorse an instrument, such as a settlement check, that is made out to the client or to the lawyer and the client jointly.[21] Obviously the only safe course is for the lawyer to obtain the client's signature, unless the law in the jurisdiction has clearly established that the lawyer's agency powers include that of endorsing the instrument for the client.

Bank Accounts

Both the Code (DR 9-102(A)) and the Model Rules (MR 1.15(a)) require that a lawyer who holds any client funds maintain a separate bank account for client funds in the state of the lawyer's home office.[22] Funds may not be held in other ways, such as in a lawyer's office safe.[23] The account must be identified as a client or trust account and cannot be the account maintained for a lawyer's law firm or

position regarding retainer fees which have not been earned in full, we will not consider the issue in a disciplinary proceeding.").

[17] State v. Hilton, 217 Kan. 694, 538 P.2d 977, 983 (1975)(payment to lawyer to be used for probation bond should be treated as trust funds); In re Lee, 283 N.W.2d 179, 182, n.6 (N.D.1979).

[18] Attorney Grievance Comm'n v. Bailey, 285 Md. 631, 403 A.2d 1261, 1267 (1979)(recording costs paid, by either client or other party to transaction, to lawyer must be treated as trust funds unless immediately expended for stated costs).

[19] State v. Hilton, 217 Kan. 694, 538 P.2d 977, 983 (1975). But cf. In re Kelly, 23 N.Y.2d 368, 382, 296 N.Y.S.2d 937, 244 N.E.2d. 456 (1968)(Code's fiduciary requirements apply only to funds to be paid to clients and not deposited with lawyer for payment to third parties).

[20] MR 1.15 comment (first paragraph). The California rules explicitly include advances for costs and expenses within the trust account requirements. Calif.Rule 8-101(A).

[21] Compare, e.g., Committee on Professional Ethics v. Kinion, 206 N.W.2d 726 (Iowa 1973)(cashing client's check without authority); Terry v. Kemper Ins. Co., 390 Mass. 450, 456 N.E.2d 465 (1983)(forgery for lawyer to sign client's name to settlement check made out jointly to client and lawyer), with, e.g., Hill v. State, 114 Ga.App. 527, 151 S.E.2d 818 (1966). Cf. Hafter v. Farkas, 498 F.2d 587 (2d Cir.1974)(trial court could order lawyer to accept settlement check made out to lawyer and client jointly in order to protect to some extent client's interest in prompt notification of receipt of funds). The need to negotiate the instrument promptly in order to protect against nonpayment argues for obtaining the client's signed permission to sign the client's name to the check as designated endorser. Prompt deposit of the endorsed check into a trust account fully complies with the funds-safekeeping requirement of DR 9-102.

[22] MR 1.15(a) alternatively permits the account to be maintained elsewhere with the consent of the client or third person whose funds are in question. That is increasingly necessary for interstate and international law practice. Calif. Rule 8-101(A) is similar, except that the client's permission must be in writing and there must be a "substantial relationship" between the client or the client's business and the other jurisdiction.

[23] State v. Pringle, 233 Kan. 726, 667 P.2d 283 (1983); Attorney Grievance Comm'n v. McIntire, 286 Md. 87, 405 A.2d 273 (1979).

other business purposes.[24] Because of the anticommingling rule, no personal, law firm, or other business funds of the lawyer may be deposited in that account,[25] even if the account contains no other funds.[26] In order to assure the integrity of the account, lawyers almost invariably employ a "trust account." Funds of all clients can generally be deposited in the same trust account, in which case adequate records must be maintained of each client's interest in the account.[27] Client trust account and similar financial information is confidential client information and should be kept confidential by a lawyer custodian (see § 6.7).[28]

Identification and Safekeeping

Client property other than funds [29] (such as stock certificates, deeds, jewels, or other valuables, and property left with a lawyer as an exhibit in litigation) that is received by a lawyer must be (a) labeled (DR 9-102(B)(2)) or identified as such (MR 1.15(a)) and (b) promptly safeguarded.[30] Typically, safeguarding requires maintenance of a separate safe-deposit box for client property. Client documents, of course, can be appropriately maintained in secure files in the lawyer's own office, as could property of relatively modest value or that a lawyer needs to have nearby for the purpose, for example, of conferring with the client or examining in order to prepare exhibits for trial.

Record Keeping

Both lawyer codes require that "complete records" of all client funds and other property be maintained.[31] Merely keeping checkbook

[24] Florida Bar v. Ragano, 403 So.2d 401 (Fla.1981).

[25] Jackson v. State Bar, 25 Cal.3d 398, 158 Cal.Rptr. 869, 872, 600 P.2d 1326, 1329 (1979); Florida Bar v. Borns, 428 So.2d 648 (Fla.1983)(use of trust account as depositary for lawyer's payroll tax money); Committee on Professional Ethics v. Gross, 326 N.W.2d 272, 273 (Iowa 1982)(deposit of personal funds in trust account to evade wife's attempt to satisfy judgment for past-due child-support payments). DR 9-102(A)("no funds belonging to the lawyer or law firm shall be deposited therein"); MR 1.15(a) and MR 1.15 comment (first paragraph). DR 9-102(A)(1) and (2) permit the lawyer to deposit law firm funds sufficient to pay bank charges and to deposit funds belonging partly to the lawyer and partly to the client, such as a check made out jointly to both. The same exceptions are plainly inferable from MR 1.15.

[26] Doyle v. State Bar, 32 Cal.3d 12, 184 Cal.Rptr. 720, 721, 648 P.2d 942, 947-48 (1982)(rule absolutely bars use of client trust account for personal purposes, even if no client funds are also on deposit and even if lawyer no longer intends to use account for trust purposes).

[27] MR 1.15 comment (first paragraph) notes that separate trust accounts may be desirable or necessary under court rules or statute when a lawyer administers estates. E.g., Attorney Grievance Comm'n v. Boehm, 293 Md. 476, 446 A.2d 52 (1982)(lawyer administering estate must maintain separate estate account clearly identified as account for single named estate only).

[28] Nonetheless, a subpoena or similar official command can compel disclosure of trust account records in a proper case. E.g., Gannet v. First Nat'l State Bank, 546 F.2d 1072 (3d Cir.1976), cert. denied 431 U.S. 954, 97 S.Ct. 2674, 53 L.Ed.2d 270 (1977); United States v. Bank of California, 424 F.Supp. 220 (N.D.Cal.1976). The attorney-client privilege may not apply in such cases because of the general rule that the client's identity and the fact and size of fee payment are not privileged. See § 6.3.5 (client identity). See also § 14.6.4 (law office searches).

[29] The "safekeeping" requirement of DR 9-102(B)(2) has been applied to client funds despite the fact that the obligation in the rule applies to "securities and property" of a client. In re McWhorter, 405 Mich. 563, 284 N.W.2d 472, 479 (1979). That interpretation is both strained and unnecessary because the requirement to deposit client funds in a trust account under DR 9-101(A) describes the method in which a lawyer is to provide safekeeping for client funds.

[30] DR 9-102(B)(2); MR 1.15(a). E.g., In re Grubb, 99 Wn.2d 690, 663 P.2d 1346 (1983)(client's ring). The safekeeping obligation applies as well to client documents in a lawyer's possession. See In re Kaleidoscope, Inc., 15, 232, 239 (Bankr.N.D.Ga.1981).

[31] DR 9-102(B)(3)(lawyer shall "maintain complete records of all funds, securities, and other properties of a client coming into the possession of the lawyer"); MR 1.15(a)("Complete records of such account funds and other property shall be kept by the lawyer and shall be preserved for a period of [five years] after termination of the representation."); Calif.R. 8-101(B)(3)(maintain records and accounts and "preserve such records for a period of no less than five years after final appropriate distribution of such funds or properties"). The California rule describing the event that begins the five-year record-retention period is preferable to that of the Model Rules in cases in which a lawyer defends against a charge of inappropriate nonpayment of funds by maintaining that the representation ended more than five years before the lawyer's records were destroyed.

While the Code does not prescribe a period for retaining records, an early demise of accounts and records should be treated as a highly suspicious circumstance or, if unreasonably prompt, as a violation of the record-keeping rule itself. See in re Marine, 82 Wis.2d 602, 264 N.W.2d 285 (1978)(destruction of client trust account records at end of each year violated trust account record requirement).

stubs for a trust account, for example, has been held not to comply with the record keeping requirement.[32] California courts require a lawyer who receives large funds from a client to obtain written directions from the client regarding their disposition and obtain a written receipt from third parties of client funds paid to them.[33] Another court requires individual client ledger sheets.[34] Some states' lawyer codes specify in some detail the types of ledgers and other accounting records that must be maintained and require complete books and records for all financial aspects of a law practice.[35] The record keeping rules are hardly to be sloughed over as tedium unworthy of great legal minds. Courts are quite insistent about their importance because of the danger of the loss of client funds if accurate, complete, and current records are not maintained.[36]

Accounting to a Client

Internal record keeping is not enough; a lawyer must also provide clients with information about their funds. The Code, in DR 9-102(B)(3), requires that "appropriate accounts" be rendered to each client.[37] MR 1.15(b) requires that a "complete accounting" be given to a client, but apparently only if requested by the client. Neither seems to require that accounts be rendered at any particular interval, such as quarterly or even annually. Good client relationships, of course, —and the lawyer codes in some jurisdictions—require periodic accounts.

Notification Requirement

Both DR 9-102(B)(1) and MR 1.15(b) require that a lawyer "promptly" notify a client of the lawyer's receipt of a client's funds or other property.[38] The obligation exists whether or not the lawyer was to turn over the property promptly to the client or was to hold it for any period or purpose.

Turnover Obligation

A lawyer is required by DR 9-102(B)(4) and MR 1.15(b) to deliver "promptly" to a client any funds or property [39] to which the client is entitled. The client, and not the lawyer, determines when and under what circumstances the lawyer should return funds or property.[40] Funds to which a client is entitled, such as the proceeds of a settlement, should normally be disbursed within a short time after they are received.[41] When a client so directs, a lawyer is obliged to turn over funds or proper-

The records that a lawyer is required to keep can be subject to compulsory process under the "required records" exception to the self-incrimination privilege. E.g., Florida Bar v. White, 384 So.2d 1266 (Fla.1980). Cf. Doyle v. State Bar, 32 Cal.3d 12, 184 Cal.Rptr. 720, 648 P.2d 942 (1982)(subpoena by state bar overrides client's privacy interests because of necessity to examine records to determine if lawyer has failed to comply with strict record keeping requirements).

32 In re Hennessy, 93 N.J. 358, 461 A.2d 156, 157 (1983).

33 Fitzsimmons v. State Bar, 34 Cal.3d 327, 193 Cal. Rptr. 896, 898, 667 P.2d 700, 702 (1983).

34 In re Koehler, 95 Wn.2d 606, 628 P.2d 461, 464 (1981).

35 Minn.Code DR 9-103 (as amended 1976)(every lawyer in private practice must maintain, on current basis, books and records sufficient to demonstrate income and expenses from practice, as well as books and records required by DR 9-102; lawyer must certify compliance with both record keeping requirements on annual registration statement); N.H.Rule 37, § 7 (trust accounting system with separate ledger page for each client, plus index to all trust accounts, including special interest-bearing trust accounts, probate accounts, custodial accounts, and client-agency accounts).

36 Fitzsimmons v. State Bar, 34 Cal.3d 327, 193 Cal. Rptr.896, 899, 667 P.2d 700, 703 (1983).

37 People v. Lanza, 660 P.2d 881 (Colo.1983)(refusing to provide accounting for money and jewelry of client); In re Dowdy, 247 Ga. 488, 277 S.E.2d 36, 39 (1981); In re Fling, 316 N.W.2d 556, 559 (Minn.1982)(failure to account to client despite repeated demands). But cf. Louisiana St. B. Ass'n v. Mitchell, 375 So.2d 1350, 1353 (La.1979)(lawyer, who never paid over amount of interest on judgment obtained in favor of clients, never billed them for fees, and never accounted to them for funds, committed, at most, only technical violations of DR 9-102).

38 Phillips v. State Bar, 14 Cal.3d 492, 121 Cal.Rptr. 605, 535 P.2d 733, 91 A.L.R.3d 966 (1975); Committee on Professional Ethics v. Toomey, 253 N.W.2d 573 (Iowa 1977); Oklahoma ex rel. Oklahoma Bar Ass'n v. Smith, 615 P.2d 1014, 1018 (Okl.1980). See also Calif.R. 8-101(B)(1).

39 The obligation extends to client papers. E.g., Hebisen v. State, 615 S.W.2d 866, 868 (Tex.Civ.App.1981).

40 Nolan v. Foreman, 665 F.2d 738, 742 (5th Cir.1982); State v. Pringle, 233 Kan. 726, 667 P.2d 283, 288 (1983); Hebisen v. State, 615 S.W.2d 866 (Tex.Civ.App.1981).

41 In re Boensch, 277 S.C. 148, 283 S.E.2d 442 (1981).

ty to a designated third party.[42] The codes are written, somewhat elliptically,[43] to assure that a lawyer may assert claims, such as the common-law and statutory attorneys' lien (§ 9.6.3), against a client's property that falls into the lawyer's hands.

Disputes over Funds or Property

A lawyer may withdraw from a trust account funds to which the lawyer is entitled as compensation.[44] But such a withdrawal should be made only when the lawyer and client have clearly agreed (1) that the lawyer has a right to withdraw the funds for that purpose; (2) that the amount proposed to be withdrawn is the correct amount; and (3) that the time for withdrawal is appropriate.[45] The Model Rules are somewhat more complete than the Code on what is to be done when the lawyer and client have a dispute over funds or property. The Code, in DR 9-102(A)(2), requires a lawyer to treat as trust funds any portion of client funds to which a lawyer claims entitlement as compensation but which the client claims is not due the lawyer.[46] Model Rule 1.15(c) requires that the portion of any property or funds over which the lawyer and any third person are in dispute should be kept "separate"[47] by the lawyer. The requirement presumably applies to client-lawyer disputes as well. Notice that, in the end, the lawyer's ability to protect his or her claimed interest in the property is protected by possession.

Audits of Client Accounts

Traditionally, lawyers have been the keepers and certifiers of their own books. Most states do not even require that an independent auditor certify that a lawyer's books and records are being kept in accordance with the requirements of the lawyer codes.[48] Increasingly, states find that some lawyers have failed to maintain required records. Audits are routinely conducted in all jurisdictions when probable cause is found to believe that the lawyer is violating the fiduciary rules,[49] or as a condition of probation following a finding of disciplinary violation.[50] Several states in

[42] Bonanza Motors, Inc. v. Webb, 104 Idaho 234, 657 P.2d 1102 (1983).

[43] DR 9-102(B)(4)(lawyer shall promptly turn over to client property or funds "which the client is entitled to receive"); MR 1.15(b)(lawyer shall promptly deliver funds and property to client "except as stated in this rule or otherwise permitted by law or by agreement with the client"). See also MR 1.15 comment (second paragraph) (as to funds received from third parties from which lawyer's fee is to be paid).

[44] DR 9-102(A)(2)("the portion belonging to the lawyer or law firm may be withdrawn when due"). There is no specifically comparable rule in the Model Rules, but presumably funds to which the lawyer is entitled are no longer the kinds of "property of clients or third persons" that are required to be kept separate under MR 1.15(a). Even if the lawyer is entitled to make the withdrawal, the court insisted in In re Rabb, 73 N.J. 272, 374 A.2d 461, 465 (1977), that the lawyer withdraw the funds from the client's trust account, to the lawyer's office account and deposit them and that a lawyer should not write checks directly on the trust account on the later explanation that the withdrawal was for fees earned.

[45] In re Marine, 82 Wis.2d 602, 264 N.W.2d 285, 288-89 (1978).

[46] In re Kramer, 92 Ill.2d 305, 65 Ill.Dec. 860, 861-862, 442 N.E.2d 171, 172-73 (1982); Attorney Grievance Comm'n v. McIntire, 286 Md. 87, 405 A.2d 273 (1979); In re Denend, 98 Wn.2d 699, 657 P.2d 1379 (1983). It has also been held that even if a client has not actually disputed the amount of a fee because of lack of information about the magnitude of the lawyer's claim, the lawyer's withdrawal of more than the agreed amount is conversion. Butler County Bar Ass'n v. Green, 1 Ohio St. 3d 48, 438 N.E.2d 406 (1982).

[47] MR 1.15 comment (paragraph two) says, as does DR 9-102(A)(2), in effect, that the disputed portion of funds is to be held "in trust." The lawyer should suggest means of resolving disputes over funds or property, such as arbitration. Id.

[48] In England a solicitor is required annually to obtain an auditor's certificate attesting to the proper handling of all client funds. Solicitors' Accounts Rules (1975), the Solicitors' Trust Account Rules (1975), The Accountant's Report Rules (1975), and the Solicitors' Accounts (Deposit Interest) Rules (1975). Favoring the English system, see Morgan, The Evolving Concept of Professional Responsibility, 90 Harv.L.Rev. 702, 731 (1977).

[49] Cf. ABA Jnt. Comm. on Prof. Discipline, Standards for Lawyer Disciplinary and Disability Proceedings § 13.3 (approved 1979). The only debate at the ABA meeting at which the Standards were approved concerned a defeated motion by the ABA Standing Committee on Professional Discipline that would have provided for "spot" audits by disciplinary counsel on a random basis without requiring probable cause. See 47 U.S.L.Wk. 2524 (1979).

[50] In re Fling, 316 N.W.2d 556, 559 (Minn.1982).

recent years have inaugurated systems of spot audits that do not require probable cause.[51]

Client Security Funds

In several jurisdictions, bar associations have established client security funds to provide a measure of reimbursement to clients, and possibly others, whose funds or property have been converted by a member of the state bar. Creation of the funds was stimulated by statistics indicating that the most frequent cause of lawyer discipline was lawyer conversion of client funds, yet the profession had done nothing to assure that victimized clients could recover anything.[52] Client security funds are supported by mandatory contributions or dues from lawyers.[53] Their protection, while doubtless welcomed by victims of lawyer dishonesty, is limited. Most systems require that all other methods of gaining restitution from the lawyer have been exhausted. In some systems, a claimant must present proof of an unsatisfied judgment against the lawyer. Elaborate proof requirements are typically imposed, and all funds limit, some quite severely, the size of individual claims and the cumulative claims against any one lawyer that will be compensated.[54]

Interest on Lawyers' Trust Accounts

Trust accounts are typically non-interest bearing, because no interest could be retained by the lawyer and it could not feasibly be distributed among the several clients with funds in the account because of the administrative burden of allocating interest earned among clients with different amounts of funds in the account for varying lengths of time. If the amount of the client's funds and the length of time that the lawyer must hold them warrants, they should be deposited into an interest-bearing trust account in order to protect the client's investment interest in them.[55] But that still leaves lawyers in every jurisdiction with client funds in non-interest-bearing accounts that are aggregately large but individually small. In order to take advantage of the large and untapped interest-producing potential that such trust accounts represent, a majority of jurisdictions have inaugurated IOLTA (interest on lawyers' trust

[51] Iowa Sup.Ct.R., Rule 121 (1970); Wash.Discipl.Rs. Attorneys Rule 13.1(a)(as amended 1977); Wisc.Stat.Ann. 256.293; In re Kennedy, 442 A.2d 79 (Del.1982)(attorney-client privilege and privacy challenges to spot-audit system rejected). See generally Lawyer Spot Audit Net Is Spreading, 67 ABA J. 1601 (1981); N.J. Attorneys Agreeing to Audits of Their Accounts, Nat'l L.J., Sept. 28, 1981, p. 2, col.4. California requires that a lawyer comply with an order for an audit of client fund accounts issued by the bar disciplinary authorities. Calif. Rule 8-101(A)(3).

[52] Amster, Clients' Security Funds: The New Jersey Story, 62 ABA J. 1610 (1976); Carpenter, The Negligent Attorney Embezzler: Delaware's Solution, 61 ABA J. 338 (1975); Standing Comm. on Clients' Security Funds, Report, 97 ABA Rep. 645, 646 (1972). See generally ABA Suggested Guidelines for Establishment and Operation of a Clients' Security Fund (1976).

[53] Hagopian v. Justices of the Supreme Judicial Court, 429 F.Supp. 367 (D.Mass.1977), affirmed 434 U.S. 802, 98 S.Ct. 34, 54 L.Ed.2d 63 (1977); In re Member of Bar, 257 A.2d 382 (Del.1969), appeal dismissed 396 U.S. 274, 90 S.Ct. 562, 24 L.Ed.2d 464 (1970); State ex rel. Robeson v. Oregon St. Bar, 291 Or. 505, 632 P.2d 1255 (1981)(statute creating mandatory client security fund contribution system does not infringe court's inherent regulatory powers over bar). Another method of funding is through fines levied on lawyers found to have violated the fiduciary rules. E.g., In re Reed, 369 A.2d 686 (Del.1977).

[54] Rules of Proc., Ark. Client Sec. Fund I 4(c)(as amended 1980)(losses payable limited to $5,000 per claimant, $10,000 per transaction, and $15,000 per lawyer or law firm).

[55] In re Petition of N.H.B. Ass'n, 122 N.H. 971, 453 A.2d 1258, 1261 (1982); In re Petition of Minn. St.B. Ass'n, 332 N.W.2d 151, 157 (Minn.1982)("[W]e believe that when larger sums of interest are involved that can more than cover administrative costs, bank fees and the like, such deposits should not lie idle but should draw interest for the benefit of the client."). Cf. Greenbaum v. State Bar, 15 Cal.3d 893, 126 Cal.Rptr. 785, 544 P.2d 921 (1976)(disbursal of client funds from trust account without authorization abused client's confidence and trust because it deprived clients of interest funds would have earned); In re Lee, 283 N.W.2d 179, 183 (N.D.1979)(fact that lawyer's mishandling of client funds caused only small loss of interest to client does not excuse mishandling); cf. A.Scott, Trusts §§ 180.3, 181 (3d ed.1967 and Supp.1981). The Arkansas Supreme Court refused to create a plan on public relations grounds, believing that without prior notice to and approval of each affected client (which it conceded made the plan impracticable), an IOLTA plan would diminish public confidence in the legal profession. See In re Interest on Lawyers' Trust Accounts, 279 Ark. 84, 648 S.W.2d 480 (1983). Public confidence is hardly enhanced, however, by knowing that vast aggregates of small individual accounts are earning income for no one but banks.

accounts) plans.[56] They are arrangements under which lawyers can or must maintain non-interest-bearing general trust accounts at banks that agree to pay over an amount of interest on the accounts' aggregate balances to a state bar fund, which uses the income for such purposes as providing legal services to the poor.[57]

WESTLAW REFERENCES

Safekeeping Client Funds and Property

commingl! /s client /s attorney lawyer counsel**
di commingle

Segregation: The Prohibition Against Commingling

"ec 9-5" /p commingl!
dr9-102 "dr 9-102" /p client /3 funds

Funds Subject to the Fiduciary Requirements

fiduciary /s client /s funds property /s lawyer attorney counsel**

Retainer Fees and Advance Fee Payments

advance retainer /8 fund fee /s trust /p attorney lawyer counsel**

Client Advances for Costs and Expenses

"dr 9-102(a)" dr9-102(a)

Lawyer Power to Endorse Drafts Made out to Clients

dr9-102 "dr 9-102" /p endors! deposit! /s check

Bank Accounts

"dr 9-102" /p trust bank /3 account

Identification and Safekeeping

client /5 document property security stock deed jewel! /s label! identif! safeguard!

Record Keeping

complete /3 record! /s client /5 fund document property

Accounting to a Client

"appropriate account" /s client

Notification Requirement

prompt** /6 notif! /p client /6 fund property

Turnover Obligation

deliver! return! turn-over /7 client /5 fund property

Disputes over Funds or Property

dr9-102 "dr 9-102" /p withdraw! /s money fund fee

Audits of Client Accounts

di audit

Client Security Funds

"client security fund"

Interest on Lawyers' Trust Accounts

interest /s lawyer counsel** attorney /s trust /3 account
45k120

---

56 In re Interest on Trust Accounts, 356 So.2d 799 (Fla. 1978); In re Petition of Minn. St.B. Ass'n, 332 N.W.2d 151 (Minn.1982). See generally England & Carlisle, History of Interest on Trust Accounts Program, 56 Fla.B.J. 101 (1982)(prior experience in Australian states and Canadian provinces); Note, Minnesota's New Interest on Lawyer Trust Account Program, 67 Minn.L.Rev. 1286 (1983); ABA Formal Op. 348 (1982)(nothing in Code prohibits lawyer from participating in state-authorized IOLTA plan).

57 The rapid rise in popularity of IOLTA plans was caused by curtailment of the funding of the national Legal Services Corporation and the financial success of the original IOLTA plan in Florida. See Nat'l L.J., April 4, 1983, p. 1, col.4 (Florida's plan raised nearly $1 million in first year of operation).

Chapter Five
LAWYER COMPETENCE

Table of Sections

§ 5.1 DEFINITION AND REGULATION OF COMPETENCE

The Principle of Lawyer Proficiency

Clients come to lawyers for help, yet lawyers as helpers to others are only as good as their knowledge, training, and attitudes toward their service function will allow. Clearly, the professional ideal of lawyers is one of great skill and technical proficiency in serving clients. But controversy has raged in recent decades over the extent to which lawyers in fact attain the ideal or even approach it, and, if there are deficiencies, how they may best be cured. Prominent voices, including many judicial voices,[1] have asserted that many lawyers who appear in court are seriously deficient in some essential feature of a good practitioner.[2] Surveys of client opinion have suggested that clients are dissatisfied

[1] Some of the judicial complaints might be well-intended judicial rhetoric. An empirical study of actual judicial reactions to the competence of lawyer performance in individual cases shows that 87 percent of individual trial performances are at least minimally competent. Maddi, Trial Advocacy Competence: The Judicial Perspective, 1978 Am.B.Found. Research J. 105. See also A.Partridge & G.Bermant, The Quality of Advocacy in the Federal Courts 5, 25–26 (1978)(study for Federal Judicial Center indicates that only 9 percent of lawyers' performances rated less than adequate by federal judges, with more-experienced judges reporting highest levels of approval). The other side of the judge-lawyer coin is the average lawyer's view of the competence of judges. According to one poll of lawyers, almost half of the nation's lawyers think that a significant proportion of judges are not qualified to preside over serious court cases. Lawpoll: Judges Qualified? Here's What Lawyers Think, 64 ABA J. 1659 (1978).

[2] The most famous critic has been Chief Justice Warren Burger. His most provocative and widely reported criticism was made in a speech published as Burger, The Special Skills of Advocacy: Are Specialized Training and Certification of Advocates Essential to Our System of Justice?, 42 Fordham L.Rev. 227 (1973). Its memorable charge was that between one-third and one-half of the nation's trial lawyers were incompetent. See 42 Fordham L.Rev. at 234. Six years earlier, the then Judge Burger's statistics showed 75 percent of trial lawyers deficient in basic skills. See Burger, A Sick Profession?, 5 Tulsa L.J. 1, 3 (1968). See also, e.g., Final Report of the Advisory Committee on Proposed Rules for Admission to Practice, 67 F.R.D. 159 (1975)(report of the Clare Committee); Report and Tentative Recommendations of the Committee to Consider Standards for Admission to Practice in the Federal Courts to the Judicial Conference of the United States, 79 F.R.D. 187 (1978); id. Final Report, 83 F.R.D. 215 (1980)(report of the Devitt Committee); Kaufman, The Court Needs a Friend in Court, 60 ABA J. 175 (1974); Bazelon, The Defective Assistance of Counsel, 42 U.Cin.L.Rev. 1 (1973). For a less alarmed view, see, e.g., Cramton, Lawyer Competence and the Law Schools, 4

with lawyer performance, although the reasons may have to do more with communication breakdowns than with the quality of the work that lawyers perform.[3] The means of assuring competence that have so far been attempted—legal education, bar examinations, legal malpractice recoveries, and professional discipline—have only enforced standards of minimal competence that are far below the professional ideal. Official efforts to raise the competence of the profession have generally relied heavily on professional education during lawyers' careers. One method whose proponents claim that it would raise levels of competence in many fields—specialization—has been restricted in almost every state by lawyer opposition and mistrust (§ 5.5).

The Elements of Competence

Competence is often defined from the perspective of the observer. Judges tend to regard prolonged or disrupted trials, missed assignments, improper objections, and the like as the clearest evidence of incompetence. Clients probably tend to think of competence more in terms of outcomes and communications. Both the judicial and the client outlooks focus upon actual performance by lawyers, although different aspects of performance. But lawyers themselves probably think of competence in terms of general technical proficiency, innate or trained elements that equip a lawyer to perform effectively.

A general definition that recognizes the different aspects of competence would include the following elements:[4]

Knowledge—a competent lawyer possesses sufficient information about law and legal institutions to be able to deal effectively with many common legal problems, to recognize legal problems that require additional research, and to assess the lawyer's own ability to deal with a legal problem.

Legal skills—a competent lawyer can effectively represent and sensitively communicate with a client in one or more of the common lawyer roles: analyzing a client's problem in the light of available facts and law, advising, negotiating, litigating, mediating, investigating, researching, and planning.

Office management—a competent lawyer has the intellectual, financial, and managerial ability to organize, equip, and staff an office system that permits a lawyer to use knowledge and legal skills efficiently and effectively for clients.

Character—a competent lawyer possesses strengths of character that lead the lawyer to be motivated to serve clients effectively, loyally, and without undue regard to the distractions of other commitments, demands, and interests.

Capability—a competent lawyer possesses physical and psychological well-being that permits a sustained level of effective practice.

Causes and Cures of Incompetence and Neglect

Some instances of lawyer incompetence are doubtless caused by serious deficiencies in an individual lawyer's mental power or formal training. But such thoroughly incompetent lawyers are probably quite rare.[5] Most instances of lawyer neglect are probably the

U.Ark. Little Rock L.J. 1 (1981); Frankel, Curing Lawyers' Incompetence: Primum Non Nocere, 10 Creighton L.Rev. 613 (1977); Ehrlich, A Critique of the Proposed New Admission Rule for District Courts in the Second Circuit, 61 ABA J. 1385 (1975); Sovern, A Better Prepared Bar—The Wrong Approach, 50 St. John's L.Rev. 473 (1976).

[3] D.Rosenthal, Lawyer and Client: Who's in Charge? 60–61 (1974)(one-third of clients dissatisfied, and panel of experts' evaluations of case files indicate that lawyers in 70 percent of surveyed personal injury plaintiffs' cases obtained inadequate results); A.Conard, Automobile Accident Costs and Payments 289 (1964)(40 percent of automobile plaintiffs dissatisfied).

[4] This listing draws heavily on Kelly, The Origin, Organization, and Purposes of the Houston Conference, in ALI-ABA Conference on Continuing Professional Education at xi-xii (1981).

[5] An opinion survey of judges found that the most frequently cited cause of incompetent trial performance was lack of adequate preparation. See Maddi, Trial Advocacy Competence: The Judicial Perspective, 1978 Am.B.Found. Research J. 105, 124–28. An earlier, admittedly rough, statistical survey is contained in Frankel,

result of motivational problems that cause a lawyer to give short shrift to the interests of some clients or to pay insufficient attention to the tiresome details of office management and client service. The causes of incompetent legal service are diverse; their cure usually involves little more than an elevation in a lawyer's self-conception as a professional helper.

A lawyer may become too busy with other, apparently more important or lucrative work and neglect particular clients. The appropriate remedy is for the overcommitted lawyer to ask the client to let another lawyer complete the matter.[6] The fact that a client's matter involves a small fee or no fee at all[7] or involves a matter being handled on the basis of friendship[8] does not excuse a lawyer who has accepted the representation from performing competently. Preferably a lawyer should be aware of the time demands of matters already undertaken and not accept new matters until the backlog has been reduced to more manageable proportions.[9] An office calendar system, or tickler system, as it is called, should be in place and operating to alert a lawyer to the proximity of important deadlines in all client matters.[10] Solo practitioners or members of small firms must be particularly alert to possibly great fluctuations in the time commitments demanded by matters pending in their offices.[11] Secretarial or other personnel problems must be recognized and dealt with before they cause serious inconvenience to clients.[12]

Competence requires a fair modicum of knowledge and skill. A lawyer must know at least the basic elements of the law involved in representing a client.[13] A lawyer should carefully investigate the facts and analyze the client's problem in light of applicable law.[14] A lawyer should not have an overdeveloped sense of his or her own competence or capacity for legal work. A lawyer should carefully assess whether a new matter will not require an inordinate time commitment or possibly a more knowledgeable lawyer because of its strangeness. No matter how carefully a lawyer attempts to work, an occasional misstep will bedevil the careers of all lawyers who are honest enough to be accurate self-reporters. When a misstep occurs, a lawyer should forthrightly confront its scope and consequences and should notify the client so that corrective action can be taken.[15]

An undertaking to represent a client is not merely an agreement to keep a client's matter on file or just out of a lawyer's reach in a busy practice. A lawyer should not accept a matter unless the lawyer can reasonably foresee that he or she is able to complete it in a fairly timely fashion.[16] Once a matter is undertaken, a lawyer is obliged to be properly diligent in moving the matter along. If the

Curing Lawyers' Incompetence: Primum Non Nocere, 10 Creighton L.Rev. 613, 619 (1977)(only small percentages of reported legal malpractice and ineffective assistance of counsel decisions that find incompetence deal with matters of technical proficiency as opposed to "more characterological than technical defaults, sins of sloth, indifference, and infidelity").

6 Committee on Professional Ethics v. Bitter, 279 N.W.2d 521, 524 (Iowa 1979).

7 In re Lieber, 442 A.2d 153 (D.C.App.1982)(discipline for neglecting court-appointed matter).

8 In re Sliz, 246 Ga. 797, 273 S.E.2d 177, 181 (1980).

9 Lopez v. Larson, 91 Cal.App.3d 383, 153 Cal.Rptr. 912, 922 (1979).

10 State ex rel. Oklahoma Bar Ass'n v. Braswell, 663 P.2d 1228, 1231–32 (Okl.1983).

11 Solo and small-firm practitioners are, however, generally held to the same standards for competence and dispatch as larger firms. E.g., Cortlett v. Gordon, 106 Cal.App.3d 1005, 165 Cal.Rptr. 524, 529 (1980).

12 Cf. McMorris v. State Bar, 29 Cal.3d 96, 171 Cal.Rptr. 829, 623 P.2d 781, 783 (1981)(secretarial problems no excuse for neglect of client matters and failure to respond to client inquiries).

13 In re Belser, 277 S.C. 250, 287 S.E.2d 139 (1982); Office of Disciplinary Counsel v. Henry, 664 S.W.2d 62 (Tenn.1983).

14 A lawyer does not competently represent clients by simply handing them standardized forms and instructions. See People v. Roehl, 655 P.2d 1381 (Colo.1983).

15 Codiga v. State Bar, 20 Cal.3d 788, 144 Cal.Rptr. 404, 406, 575 P.2d 1186, 1188, (1978)(when lawyer becomes aware of defect or ambiguity in wills prepared for clients, "the attorney-client relationship . . . demands no less than full and adequate notice of the defect to the attorney's clients. At the very least, his inaction constituted less than a faithful discharge of his obligations as well as a violation of his oath and duties as an attorney.").

16 Committee on Professional Conduct v. Bitter, 279 N.W.2d 521, 525 (Iowa 1979).

matter is a case pending in a court or agency or involves third parties to negotiations, a lawyer should take action to keep informed of the progress of the matter, or lack of progress, and to take necessary steps to expedite the matter.[17] When important events such as hearings or trials are scheduled, a lawyer should spend the time needed before the event to examine the matter, conduct any necessary research, prepare appropriate motions or requests for instructions, interview witnesses and review documents, and generally be prepared for the hearing.[18]

Competence in the Professional Regulations

The lawyer codes have moved tentatively from silence to a standard of reasonable competence in describing the required level of professional performance. Under the 1908 Canons of Ethics, it was apparently not unethical to be rankly incompetent. At least no provision of the Canons said anything about competence.[19] The 1969 Code of Professional Responsibility breaks new ground and devotes one of its nine canons, Canon 6, to the proposition that "a lawyer should represent a client competently." Aside from a disdainful glance at legal malpractice,[20] the Code announces that competence requires "the highest possible standards of integrity and competence,"[21] which are desirable because of a lawyer's "vital role in the legal process."[22]

The actual disciplinary standards in the Code are more modest. A lawyer is obliged by DR 6–101(A)(1) not to accept a representation that the lawyer "knows or should know that he is not competent to handle." But a lawyer could nonetheless accept such a case after "associating"[23] with a lawyer who is competent to handle it. Nowhere is *competent* defined or described. But whatever it is, EC 6–3 provides that it need not be a level of proficiency that has already been attained at the time the representation is accepted. Instead, so long as it would not cause unreasonable delay or expense to a client, a lawyer may accept a matter in which he or she is not presently competent to handle if "in good faith he expects to become qualified through study and investigation." From all that appears in the Code, that ambition for self-improvement permits any lawyer, no matter how junior or illprepared for practice, to accept any matter. A lawyer is required by the Code, then, to decline a representation because of present incompetence only if the lawyer does not intend to associate a competent lawyer or to become competent by self-study.[24]

The Code imposes only two performance standards once a lawyer has accepted a representation. Under DR 6–101(A)(2), a lawyer must engage in "preparation adequate in the circumstances," although the elements of adequate preparation are not otherwise defined.[25]

17 In re Appeal in Juvenile Action, 135 Ariz. 278, 660 P.2d 1205, 1206 (1982); Brent v. Board of Trustees of Davis & Elkins College, 311 S.E.2d 153, 160 (W.Va.1983).

18 Lamar v. American Finance System, Inc., 577 F.2d 953, 955 (5th Cir.1978); Shuber v. S.S.Kresge Co., 458 F.2d 1058 (3d Cir.1972)(failure to interview potential witness deprived client of favorable testimony at trial); In re Chambers, 292 Or. 670, 642 P.2d 286, 291 (1982).

19 R.Wise, Legal Ethics 83 (2d ed.1970); Gaudineer, Ethics and Malpractice, 26 Drake L.Rev. 88, 88 (1976); Thode, Canons Six and Seven: The Lawyer-Client Relationship, 48 Tex.L.Rev. 367, 374 (1970); Note, Neglect of a Legal Matter Entrusted to an Attorney under DR 6–101(A)(3), 4 J.Leg.Prof. 227, 227–31 (1979)(history of regulation of incompetence under pre-Code authority).

20 DR 6–102(A), discussed infra at § 5.6.7 (limiting liability). See also EC 6–5 ("A lawyer should have pride in his professional endeavors. His obligation to act competently calls for higher motivation than that arising from fear of civil liability or disciplinary penalty.").

21 EC 6–2.

22 EC 6–1.

23 EC 6–3 refers to obtaining the consent of the client to associate another lawyer. Because client consent is not needed to refer legal work within a law firm, the apparent assumption is that a lawyer would be associating with another lawyer for the purpose of the single representation. The corresponding assumption is that a lawyer in a firm may accept any case, so long as one other lawyer in the firm is competent in the matter. Cf. Calif.R. 6–101(1) (incompetent lawyer may accept representation if "he associates or, where appropriate, professionally consults another lawyer who he reasonably believes does possess the requisite learning and skill.").

24 Carter v. Walsh, 122 R.I. 349, 406 A.2d 263, 265 (1979).

25 In re Magar, 296 Or. 799, 681 P.2d 93, 96 (1984) (violation of DR 6–101(A)(2) for failure to interview client about dates when loans were incurred that client sought

And under DR 6–101(A)(3), a lawyer is not to "neglect" a matter "entrusted" to the lawyer. Occasional decisions have found other performance standards in other portions of the Code, such as a requirement of adequate legal research in the catchall provision in DR 1–102(A)(6) concerning fitness to practice law.[26]

As modest as it was, Canon 6 was apparently too troubling in its implications for many states, which have adopted standards that at least appear to be less stringent. California's Rule 6–101 threatens discipline only of a lawyer who "wilfully or habitually"[27] performs legal services in a deficient manner, and it urges the consideration of a lawyer's good faith "in determining whether acts done through ignorance or mistake warrant imposition of discipline."[28] The California rule improves on the Code, however, by offering a definition of competence. A lawyer must possess "the learning and skill ordinarily possessed by lawyers in good standing who perform, but do not specialize in, similar services practicing in the same or similar locality[29] and under similar circumstances."[30] Similarly, the performance standard of California Rule 6–101(2) is more illuminating. It provides that a lawyer shall not willfully or habitually "fail to use reasonable diligence and his best judgment in the exercise of his skill and in the application of his learning in an effort to accomplish, with reasonable speed, the purpose for which he is employed."

The 1983 Model Rules, in MR 1.1, flatly require "competent representation" of every client.[31] The competence standard is defined: "competent representation requires the legal knowledge, skill, thoroughness and preparation reasonably necessary for the representation." The comments to the rule acknowledge for the first time in a professional regulation that some matters may require the attention of a specialist and thus are beyond the competence of some, perhaps many, lawyers.[32] But the exceptions for competence through special preparation and through associating or consulting with a competent lawyer are retained in the comments.[33]

to discharge in bankruptcy, because dates were critical to discharge).

[26] In re Burns, 139 Ariz. 487, 679 P.2d 510, 514 (1984).

[27] Calif.R. 6–101. For a criticism of the drafting of the California rule, see Lewis v. State Bar, 28 Cal.3d 683, 170 Cal.Rptr. 634, 637–38, 621 P.2d 258, 261–62 (1981)(Bird, C.J., concurring). Cf., e.g., Texas Code Prof.Resp. DR 6–101(A)(3) (prohibits lawyer only from "willfully or intentionally" neglecting a legal matter). New Jersey's original version of the Code contained no standard for competence. One was added in 1978 that prohibits a lawyer from (1) handling a matter in such a manner that the lawyer's conduct constitutes gross negligence or (2) exhibiting a pattern of negligence or neglect in handling legal matters generally.

[28] California courts seem, however, to have ignored the limitation implicit in the disciplinary rule by reliance on a general standard in the lawyer's oath statute (Calif.Bus. & Prof.Code § 6103) requiring a lawyer to discharge his or her duties faithfully. E.g., Jackson v. State Bar, 23 Cal. 3d 509, 513, 153 Cal.Rptr. 24, 26, 591 P.2d 47, 50 (1979) ("Even if petitioner's conduct were not wilful and dishonest, gross carelessness and negligence constitute a violation of an attorney's oath faithfully to discharge his duties and involve moral turpitude."). In addition, incompetent representation will be found to be deliberate and willful if it is repeated. E.g., Inniss v. State Bar, 20 Cal.3d 552, 143 Cal.Rptr. 408, 410, 573 P.2d 852, 854 (1978)("[W]e have held that where a pattern of habitual offenses exists, even though the offenses may individually amount to no more than negligence or gross negligence, such consistent misconduct can only be regarded as deliberate and wilful.").

[29] No reported decision has made anything of the California rule's apparent allusion to standards that vary from one community to another within the state.

[30] Calif.R. 6–101(1) also contains the exception for accepting a matter in which the lawyer is not competent if the lawyer consults or associates with a lawyer reasonably believed to be competent in the matter. There is no mention in the California rules of an ambition-for-self-improvement exception corresponding to EC 6–3.

[31] The eventual language of MR 1.1 was taken from language recommended by a joint American Bar Association/American Law Institute Committee on Peer Group Review.

[32] MR 1.1 comment (Legal Knowledge and Skill; first paragraph)("Expertise in a particular field of law may be required in some circumstances.").

[33] MR 1.1 comment (Legal Knowledge and Skill; second paragraph)("A lawyer can provide adequate representation in a wholly novel field through necessary study. Competent representation can also be provided through the association of a lawyer of established competence in the field in question."). The sentiment on competence through study is repeated later. See id. (fourth paragraph)("A lawyer may accept representation where the requisite level of competence can be achieved by reasonable preparation.").

The Limited Enforcement of Competence

To date, the enforcement of competence standards has been generally limited to relatively exotic, blatant, or repeated cases of lawyer bungling.[34] Lawyers who make some showing of effort, and who do nothing other than perform badly, rarely appear in the appellate reports in discipline cases. The lawyers who are disciplined for incompetence have usually aggravated their situation. For example, several cases involve lawyers who, after their incompetent work, concocted elaborate schemes or lies to deceive a client whose case was mishandled.[35] Most decisions and official ABA policy insist that a single instance of "ordinary negligence" is usually not a disciplinary violation,[36] although some decisions hold a lawyer to a standard of ordinary care that is similar to that required in malpractice cases (§ 5.6.2)[37] or discipline a lawyer for a single instance of neglect.[38] Consistent with that position, courts will discipline lawyers when the neglect is accompanied by some other violation, as an impermissible conflict of interest,[39] or when the acts of negligence are repeated.[40]

The level of official enforcement efforts hardly assures a competent bar. The enforcement of competence in disciplinary cases has looked for proof of incompetence only to individual instances of charged neglect. Courts do not permit disciplinary agencies to engage in general appraisals of the qualifications of

[34] People ex rel. Goldberg v. Gordon, 607 P.2d 995 (Colo.1980)(discipline for, among other things, general incompetence to practice evidenced by mishandling attempt to obtain unnecessary probate of client's property); In re Williams, 221 Minn. 554, 560, 23 N.W.2d 4, 9 (1946) (setting up elaborate "trust" scheme, purportedly designed to permit client to avoid probate and death taxes, "constituting nothing less than gross negligence and sheer incompetence" because of the "wholly unlawyerlike and fantastic manner in which the estate was to be distributed"); In re Ozer, 93 A.D.2d 129, 461 N.Y.S.2d 40 (1983)(one-year suspension for neglect after five previous admonition letters for neglect over twenty-year period). See generally Annot., 96 ALR 2d 823 (1964). For suggestions on means of enhancing the ability of lawyer disciplinary agencies to enforce competence standards, see Martyn, Lawyer Competence and Lawyer Discipline: Beyond the Bar?, 69 Geo.L.J. 705 (1981).

[35] Olguin v. State Bar, 28 Cal.3d 195, 167 Cal.Rptr. 876, 616 P.2d 858 (1980)(false representations and supplying fabricated documents to bar investigator in procrastination case); Hansen v. State Bar, 23 Cal.3d 68, 151 Cal. Rptr. 343, 587 P.2d 1156 (1978)(misrepresentation and payment of hospital admission fee of client); Florida Bar v. Stockman, 370 So.2d 1146 (Fla.1979)(fabricating letters to client to persuade bar investigator that lawyer had been diligent); In re Levin, 101 Ill.2d 535, 79 Ill.Dec. 161, 537, 463 N.E.2d 715, 717 (1984), cert. denied ___ U.S. ___, 105 S.Ct. 331, 83 L.Ed.2d 267 (1984)(misrepresentations to clients and referring lawyers); Attorney Grievance Comm'n v. Bonnin, 294 Md. 507, 451 A.2d 326 (1982) (lawyer who had delayed in finalizing divorce advised client she was divorced and could remarry); In re Beck, 400 Mich. 40, 252 N.W.2d 795 (1977)(suspension for, among other things, lying to client about status of case that had previously been dismissed for failure of lawyer to proceed to trial); Akron Bar Ass'n v. Holt, 46 Ohio St. 2d 223, 348 N.E.2d 334 (1976)(misrepresenting that case had been filed in another state, with fabrication of complaint); In re Orton, 97 Wn.2d 243, 643 P.2d 448, 449 (1982)("Being overworked does not justify lying to a client.").

[36] Florida Bar v. Neale, 384 So.2d 1264, 1265 (Fla.1980) ("There is a fine line between simple negligence by an attorney and violation of Canon 6 that should lead to discipline. The rights of clients should be zealously guarded by the bar, but care should be taken to avoid the use of disciplinary action under Canon 6 as a substitute for what is essentially a malpractice action."); Committee on Legal Ethics v. Mullins, 226 S.E.2d 427 (W.Va.1976) (lawyer discipline bodies are not ordinarily to consider a lawyer's negligent malpractice as a ground for discipline); ABA Informal Op. 1273 (1973)(DR 6–101(A)(3), in its reference to "neglect a legal matter entrusted to him," does not refer to concept of "ordinary negligence"; "Neglect usually involves more than a single act or omission. Neglect cannot be found if the acts or omissions complained of were inadvertent or the result of an error of judgment made in good faith.").

[37] Walker v. Committee on Professional Conduct, 275 Ark. 158, 628 S.W.2d 552, 555 (1982)("Any neglectful conduct of a member of this bar regarding the interests of a client is, in fact, contemplated as answerable under the provisions of DR 6–101(A)(3). That is not to say, however, that citations incommensurate with the degree of neglect involved under this rule will never be subject to review by this court."); In re Chambers, 292 Or. 670, 642 P.2d 286, 291–92 (1982)(neglect under DR 6–101(A) for failure to prepare instruction in criminal case).

[38] In re Simpson, 645 P.2d 1223, 1227–28 (Alaska 1982) (grossly negligent filing of false interrogatory response); State v. Chartier, 234 Kan. 167, 670 P.2d 1335, 1336 (1983)(pattern of conduct involving single client here violates DR 6–101(A)(3)); In re Kitts, 278 S.C. 279, 294 S.E.2d 786 (1982)(defense lawyer in personal injury action who, despite notices from opposing counsel of expiration of time to answer, failed to file answer, with result that client suffered default).

[39] In re Greene, 276 Or. 1117, 557 P.2d 644 (1976).

[40] Grove v. State Bar, 66 Cal.2d 680, 58 Cal.Rptr. 564, 427 P.2d 164 (1967); In re Kennedy, 254 S.C. 463, 176 S.E.2d 125 (1970).

an admitted lawyer to continue to practice law.[41] As a result, only relatively blatant cases of incompetence are selected for disciplinary prosecution, and they often appear in isolation from the rest of the lawyer's practice, which may also be infected with incompetence, but of an unreported or milder variety. Lawyers whose incompetence in a single case has become notorious continue to practice law.[42] Despite the furor over incompetence created by speeches of judges, few judges report instances of incompetence that they encounter. Yet, beyond that function, trial judges probably have little power to deal with observed instances of incompetence because they are not normally empowered to decide whether a lawyer in a filed case is sufficiently competent to represent clients.[43]

Diligence and Dispatch versus Procrastination

Lack of diligence is a special and widespread variety of incompetence. It consists of incompetently failing to act when advancing or protecting a client's interests calls for action. The types of inactivity range from virtual abandonment of the client to procrastination. Some few lawyers in particular matters seem to be seized by a pathology of extreme inaction similar to abandoning a client. A pattern repeated in the cases is that a client will have an initial interview with such a lawyer, often an advance fee payment is made, and the lawyer undertakes the representation. Thereafter, the lawyer does little or nothing to advance the client's interests, retains the fee, and fails entirely to communicate with the client.[44] Sometimes inaction occurs at a particular sticking point. Representative are situations in which a lawyer apparently handles a matter with reasonable competence but then fails to take a critical step such as filing a pleading or appearing for a hearing.[45] Often procrastination cases are accompanied by a failure to consult with the lawyer's client,[46] failure to return client re-

41 In re Cope, 455 A.2d 1357, 1361 (D.C.App.1983); Office of Disciplinary Counsel v. Henry, 664 S.W.2d 62 (Tenn.1983). But cf., e.g., Dayton Bar Ass'n v. Timen, 62 Ohio St.2d 357, 405 N.E.2d 1038 (1980)(review of lawyer's representation in several cases, including testimony of federal judge describing his conclusions about lawyer's low state of preparation in criminal case, lead to finding of violation of DR 6–101(A)).

42 Professor Mazor has pointed out that the lawyer whose three years of neglect and procrastination produced the penalty dismissal of his client's claim in the leading case of Link v. Wabash R.R. Co., 370 U.S. 626, 82 S.Ct. 1386, 8 L.Ed.2d 734 (1962) (see § 4.6.1), continued to try cases and to fail to appear for hearings, which resulted in additional forfeitures in Esteva v. House of Segram, Inc., 314 F.2d 827 (7th Cir.1963), cert denied 375 U.S. 826, 84 S.Ct. 70, 11 L.Ed.2d 59 (1963). See Mazor, Power and Responsibility in the Attorney-Client Relation, 20 Stan.L. Rev. 1120, 1127 (1968).

43 An exception is class action litigation, in which a court may refuse to certify a class because of the incompetence of the lawyer that the class representative has chosen. E.g., Wetzel v. Liberty Mut. Insur. Co., 508 F.2d 239, 247 (3d Cir.1975), cert. denied 421 U.S. 1011, 95 S.Ct. 2415, 44 L.Ed.2d 679 (1975); Marquardt v. Fein, 25 Wn. App. 651, 612 P.2d 378 (1980)(two lawyers, with two and three years of experience, lacked necessary background to conduct complex defendant class action litigation).

44 Doyle v. State Bar, 15 Cal.3d 973, 126 Cal.Rptr. 801, 803, 544 P.2d 937, 939 (1976); Committee on Professional Ethics v. Freed, 341 N.W.2d 757, 759 (Iowa 1983)("We view respondent's retreat from the obligation he assumed as a serious matter, to be equated with the conduct of a surgeon who, without transferring responsibility, drops his scalpel and abandons his patient in the course of an operation."); In re Flinn, 243 Ga. 342, 253 S.E.2d 692 (1979); Kentucky Bar Ass'n v. Eubanks, 647 S.W.2d 789 (Ky.1983).

45 In re Chapman, 95 Ill.2d 484, 69 Ill.Dec. 940, 448 N.E.2d 852 (1983)(total abandonment of client not required for offense of neglect: failing to file appellate brief here constituted failure to pursue client matter with reasonable diligence); State v. Martin, 231 Kan. 481, 646 P.2d 459 (1982)(failure to appear for trial after judge's refusal to grant continuance requested on eve of trial).

46 In re Cassidy, 89 Ill.2d 145, 59 Ill.Dec. 690, 432 N.E.2d 274 (1982); State v. Fleming, 230 Kan. 260, 634 P.2d 444 (1981); In re Rosenthal, 90 N.J. 12, 446 A.2d 1198, 1200 (1982)(even if client tells lawyer that she no longer intends to pursue claim, lawyer should inform client of imminent dismissal; clients have right to be informed of progress of the case); In re Geurts, 290 Or. 241, 620 P.2d 1373, 1376 n.6 (1980)(lawyer's uncommunicated conclusion that client's claim lacked merit, and thus that it should not be pursued, does not excuse neglect of client's claim, because lawyer should then have promptly consulted with client and discussed that conclusion). A lawyer's failure to keep a client informed about a matter can form the basis for a later finding of fraudulent concealment, tolling the statute of limitations in the client's subsequent legal malpractice action against the lawyer. See United Fidelity Life Ins. Co. v. Best, Sharp, Thomas & Glas, 624 F.2d 145 (10th Cir.1980).

quests for information about the matter,[47] or misrepresentation of the status of the matter.[48] Variants of the procrastination problem seem to afflict some types of practitioners or areas of practice, such as probate work, more than others.[49] Procrastination may also be symptomatic of professional burnout,[50] alcoholism,[51] or mental problems.[52]

The Code provides a basis for discipline for those varieties of neglect in DR 6–101(A)(3), which provides that a lawyer shall not "neglect a legal matter entrusted to him," [53] and perhaps in the provisions of DR 7–101(A)(1)-(3), which prohibit a lawyer from "intentionally" [54] failing to seek the lawful objectives of a client, failing to carry out a contract of employment,[55] and prejudicing or damaging a client during a representation.[56] Some courts are insistent about lawyer diligence.[57] But many courts seem to treat the problem as a relatively minor client complaint, perhaps impelled by the belief that a legal malpractice recovery serves as an adequate sanction for the truly troublesome cases.[58] Some courts insist upon tangible prejudice to a client due to the lawyer's delay, such as dismissal of a case for failure to prosecute, before they will find a sanctionable offense.[59]

47 Spindell v. State Bar, 13 Cal.3d 253, 118 Cal.Rptr. 480, 530 P.2d 168 (1975); In re Maloney, 620 S.W.2d 362, 365 (Mo.1981); In re Palmieri, 75 N.J. 488, 383 A.2d 1142 (1978).

48 Florida Bar v. Gaskin, 403 So.2d 425, 426 (Fla.1981).

49 See generally Annot., 21 A.L.R.4th 75 (1983).

50 State ex rel. Nebraska St. B. Ass'n v. Doerr, 216 Neb. 504, 344 N.W.2d 464, 467–68 (1984); In re Loew, 292 Or. 806, 642 P.2d 1171, 1173–74 (1982); id., 642 P.2d at 1174–76 (concurring opinion of Peterson, J.).

51 State ex rel. Nebraska St. B. Ass'n v. Erickson, 204 Neb. 692, 285 N.W.2d 105 (1979).

52 In re Willcher, 404 A.2d 185 (D.C.App.1979); In re Hollis, 95 N.J. 253, 471 A.2d 10, 14–15 (1984).

53 In re Colson, 632 S.W.2d 470 (Mo.1982)(reprimand for delay of five years in filing suit, until last day of limitations period, and years of delay thereafter in pressing plaintiff-client's suit, which was finally tried successfully by new lawyers hired by the client).

54 Courts are divided over the state of mind required to make out a violation of DR 7–101(A). Compare, e.g., Haynes v. Alabama St. Bar, 447 So.2d 675, 677 (Ala.1984) ("wilful" neglect required under Alabama version of DR 6–101(A) and "intentionally" under DR 7–101(A) sufficiently made out on showing that lawyer undertook to handle matter and then took no action in client's behalf), with, e.g., In re Collier, 295 Or. 320, 667 P.2d 481, 484–85 (1983)(simply promising client repeatedly to handle matter but failing to do so was not shown to violate DR 7–101(A)(3), which requires "intentionally" failing to act and not merely negligently failing to act); In re Rudie, 294 Or. 740, 662 P.2d 321, 322–23 (1983)(discussing, without deciding, whether "intentionally" means being aware of an act and its consequences or, more narrowly, doing or failing to do something with the motive of causing harm). See also In re Haupt, 444 A.2d 317, 325 n.3 (D.C. App.1982)(collecting authorities). Even under the narrow view, a lawyer intentionally causes prejudice if, for example, the lawyer's failure to protect the client is pursuant to a threat to withhold legal services unless the client pays a fee charge. E.g., In re Boland, 288 Or. 133, 602 P.2d 1078 (1979).

55 A neglect violation may effect a lawyer's contractual right to collect a fee. If the lawyer's procrastination harms the client or is deliberate, the lawyer may be denied compensation even for properly performed services. In re Loomos, 90 Wn.2d 98, 579 P.2d 350, 353 (1978) (citing Restatement (Second) of Agency § 469 (1958)).

56 In re Davis, 429 N.E.2d 938, 942 (Ind.1982)(disbarment for course of neglect and delay that caused harmful consequences as "the product of a deliberate course of action"); In re Maloney, 620 S.W.2d 362 (Mo.1981). See also, e.g., In re Radigan, 660 S.W.2d 673 (Ky.1983), cert. denied ___ U.S. ___, 104 S.Ct. 2349, 80 L.Ed.2d 823 (1984) (contempt sanction imposed on public defender for failing to begin work on relatively simple appellate brief despite earlier show-cause order).

57 In re Koehler, 95 Wn.2d 606, 628 P.2d 461, 464 (1981) ("it is clear that moral turpitude is not a condition precedent to the sanction of suspension" in delay and neglect cases); Mendicino v. Magagna, 572 P.2d 21, 23 (Wyo.1977)(disbarment for extreme procrastination in closing estates: "we cannot tolerate this kind of negligent disregard of the public's business which has been entrusted to a member of this Bar. A member of the legal profession is never justified in delaying his or his client's business by reason of laziness, procrastination, or a cavalier approach to the client's interests.").

58 But see In re Jaynes, 267 N.W.2d 782, 784 (N.D.1978) (in case involving neglect of probate work, "the fact that an injured party may recover from a lawyer in a malpractice action is in itself not sufficient to maintain the necessary high standards.").

59 Compare, e.g., Attorney Grievance Comm'n v. Sherman, 295 Md. 229, 454 A.2d 359, 364 (1983)(no violation of DR 7–101(A)(3) because no prejudice or damage to client when lawyer abandoned criminal defendant who had been caught in commission of crime and who was ultimately represented by public defender and pled guilty); In re Walker, 293 Or. 297, 647 P.2d 468, 470(1982)(lawyer's nonexemplary delay in handling cases not subject to discipline where no prejudice to clients beyond their concern and upset), with, e.g., In re Maples, 249 Ga. 502, 291 S.E.2d 708, 709 (1982)("detriment" to client required by local bar standard sufficiently shown in case of procrastination by "worry and concern" that lawyer's delay caused client).

WESTLAW REFERENCES

The Principle of Lawyer Proficiency

lawyer attorney counsel** /5 competen** /s defin! means

The Elements of Competence

di competent

lawyer attorney counsel** /3 competen** /s skill!

Causes and Cures of Incompetence and Neglect

45k44(1) /p neglect! negligen!

Competence in the Professional Regulations

"dr 6–101(a)(1)" dr6–101(a)(1)

digest,synopsis(neglect! /s entrust /s lawyer attorney counsel**)

The Limited Enforcement of Competence

lawyer attorney counsel** /s competenc** incompetenc** /s negligen** neglect!

110k920

Diligence and Dispatch versus Procrastination

lack /5 diligen! /p competenc* incompeten** /s lawyer attorney counsel**

"dr 6–101(a)(3)" dr6–101(a)(3) /p neglect! negligen**

"dr 7–101(a)(3)" dr7–101(a)(3) /p intent!

§ 5.2 LEGAL EDUCATION

The Place of Legal Education in Law

It is very rare today, and impossible in most states, for a person to become a lawyer without passing through at least three years of legal education. What a student should be exposed to in law school, and in what state of preparedness for practice, has been extensively debated over the past several decades. Most will agree that every law student should leave legal studies with the abilities to engage in legal analysis—the method of identifying legal issues from complex and possibly incomplete factual patterns; to identify and research the areas of law that are specifically applicable; and to assess the probable resolution of the factual and legal issues involved by courts and administrative agencies. The areas of debate concern how best to teach those abilities and what other components legal education should stress.

Some, who regard education as a process of imparting data to persons who are unaware of the data—filling empty vessels or writing on blank tablets—assume that competent lawyer performance or lack of it can be traced directly to law school. Those commentators intuit that the prescription for the cure of deficient practitioner performance is to alter the content, structure, or methods of legal education. If substantive content were the only issue, there would be something to recommend that approach, although the implicit assumption that lawyers commonly recall a multitude of case holdings and other minutiae of substantive law years later in practice is, of course, dangerously fallacious. In any event, thoughtful critics have noted the extent to which deficient law practice reflects not substantive shortcomings but motivational deficiencies.

Legal Education in Professional Values

If the assigned role of legal education were to change students' values in a profound way, the task of education would be much more complex and difficult. Some critics of legal education have assumed that values can be taught like case holdings, with students receiving the information in law school and reliably retaining and acting on it in a forty-year legal career.[60] Commentators have extensively debated the extent to which it is possible to inculcate values of professionalism in the course of legal education.[61] That debate directly involves courses in legal ethics or professional responsibility, which were first required in American law schools in an

[60] Cf., e.g., ABA Spec. Comm. on Evaluation of Disciplinary Enforcement, Problems and Recommendations in Disciplinary Enforcement at xv (1970)(Clark Report)(call for further study of "the adequacy of law school courses designed to promote pride in the profession and to elevate ethical standards"); L.Lamborn, Legal Ethics and Professional Responsibility: A Survey of Current Methods of Instruction in American Law Schools 3 (1963).

[61] F.Zemans & V.Rosenblum, The Making of a Public Profession 187–96 (1981); Woody, Professional Responsibility Training in Law School and its Philosophical Background, 7 J.Leg.Prof. 119 (1982); Cramton, The Ordinary Religion of the Law School Classroom, 29 J.Leg.Educ. 247 (1978); Panel Discussion (Prof. Maurice Rosenberg, Hon. Martin B. Stecher, Hon. Jack B. Weinstein, Orison S. Marden), Law Schools Can Help Make Good Lawyers;

amendment to the accreditation standards in 1974.[62] Law students do not rank courses in professional responsibility very high.[63] Practitioners feel that they learned much more about high standards of professional responsibility from colleagues in their early practice than they did in law school.[64] Those phenomena, which may be connected, might reflect a socialization process in which amorality and value-free intellectualism are acquired in law school but weaken as newly admitted practitioners confront actual ethical problems and begin to deal with clients, other lawyers, and legal institutions in law practice. It may also reflect a failure of legal educators to come to grips with the appropriate content and approach to courses in professional responsibility.

History of Legal Education[65]

Legal education in the United States has a very short history. Prior to a period beginning shortly before the nineteenth century, formal legal education in this country was largely nonexistent.[66] Most lawyers were trained in one of two ways. Most lawyers clerked in the office of an established lawyer. Customarily the clerk paid a fee, which represented the value of the lawyer's forms that the clerk could copy and use in later practice and the value of the actual instruction that was sometimes given as well. The second, more formal method was to travel to the Inns of Court, in London, where many pre-Revolutionary leaders of the bar were trained. In 1784 the Litchfield Law School was founded in Connecticut as the first of a small number of private law schools that instructed students on the precepts of Blackstone and a few other writers. During the same time and extending well into the nineteenth century, various colleges and universities attempted to instruct in law, but most contented themselves with handing over such law schools as they had to practitioners and judges to run as schools to train lawyers in the rote of practice, primarily through lectures. The majority of lawyers continued to receive their training by appren-

Can Law Schools Help Makes Lawyers Good?, in Professional Responsibility of the Lawyer: The Murky Divide between Right and Wrong 149–170 (1976); Freund, The Moral Education of the Lawyer, 26 Emory L.J. 3 (1977); Weinstein, on the Teaching of Legal Ethics, 72 Colum.L. Rev. 452 (1972); Smith, Is Education for Professional Responsibility Possible?, 40 U.Colo.L.Rev. 509 (1968); Weckstein, Training for Professionalism, 4 Conn.L.Rev. 409 (1971); Carlin, What Law Schools Can Do about Professional Responsibility, 4 Conn.L.Rev. 459 (1971).

62 ABA Standards for the Approval of Law Schools standard 304(a)(iv)(as amended August 1974). The adoption of the amendment in late summer 1974 followed close on the heels of the involvement of many lawyers in the Watergate scandal. Pressure from within the ABA to make legal ethics a required course in all American law schools was constant from before the time the Canons of Ethics were adopted in 1908. See M.Kelly, Legal Ethics and Legal Education 9 (1980). The wording of the ABA standard was designed to allow ABA-accredited law schools to adopt the "pervasive" method of instruction instead of offering a specific course in professional responsibility. The pervasive method purportedly leavens all the rest of the courses in the curriculum with professional responsibility instruction. The distinct impression is that here, too, the meat of the matter is often difficult to detect. See M.Kelly, Legal Ethics and Legal Education 50–51 (1980).

63 Pipkin, Law School Instruction in Professional Responsibility: A Curricular Paradox, 1979 Am.B.Found. Research J. 247. Some of the possible reasons for student resistance to courses in professional responsibility are examined in, e.g., Watson, The Watergate Lawyer Syndrome: An Educational Deficiency Disease, 26 J.Leg. Educ. 441 (1974)(assertion by psychiatrist-law professor that much legal education develops analytic barriers to students' reliance on their personal moral reactions to situations); Schwartz, Moral Development, Ethics and the Professional Education of Lawyers, in Moral Development: Proceedings of the 1974 "ETS" Invitational Conference 32, 41 (1975). Part of student resistance might be the heavy reliance of professors upon documents such as the Code of Professional Responsibility, which provide an entirely inadequate standard for the evaluation of conduct. A.Goldman, The Moral Foundations of Professional Ethics 101 n.20 (1980). Another deficiency historically has been the underdeveloped state of legal scholarship in the area. See Stason, Foreword, in L.Lamborn, Legal Ethics and Professional Responsibility: A Survey of Current Methods of Instruction in American Law Schools at i (1963).

64 F.Zemans & V.Rosenblum, The Making of a Public Profession 173–87 (1981).

65 See generally R.Stevens, Law School: Legal Education in America from the 1850s to the 1980s (1983); A.Harno, Legal Education in the United States (1953); Stevens, Two Cheers for 1870: The American Law School, in Law in American History 405 (D.Fleming & B.Bailyn eds.1971).

66 Consalus, Legal Education during the Colonial Period, 1663–1776, 29 J.Leg.Educ. 295 (1978); McKirdy, The Lawyer as Apprentice: Legal Education in Eighteenth Century Massachusetts, 28 J.Leg.Educ. 124 (1977).

ticeships or reading law in the offices of established lawyers.

Historians have traced the beginnings of modern American legal education with remarkable unanimity to the appointment of Christopher Columbus Langdell as dean of the Harvard Law School in 1870.[67] During the twenty-four years of his deanship, Langdell established Harvard as the model for virtually every law school in the country, a role that it has occupied without serious challenge for over a century because of its large size and preeminence. He also instituted the case method of study, which has been adopted almost universally in American law schools. The essentials of the Harvard model were the study of law in large classes from collections of appellate case reports edited by law professors; the use of the so-called Socratic technique of teaching, which involved testing and expanding law students' understanding of the cases and principles that they were to master outside of class by intellectually rigorous professorial questioning during class; an emphasis, not upon mastering the welter of detail involved in the cases or in law generally, but in a process of critical and creative thinking that was thought to typify the work of the best lawyers; the requirement of obtaining a college degree before entering law school; and the largely mandatory prescription of a curriculum to run over three academic years.[68]

Like the lecture method of legal instruction that it succeeded, the Harvard model permitted inexpensive legal education because of the large student-faculty ratio that it could tolerate and that has always been tolerated at Harvard. From the resulting tuition income, law faculty could be induced to retire from law practice without the same degree of financial sacrifice that would be required if law schools were instead forced to offer them salaries that were as low as those in most other departments of academia. The ready supply of law teachers, the demand of applicants for access to the social and economic mobility of law practice, and the growth in the demand for legal services saw the number of law schools grow steadily, so that by 1984 there were 175 accredited [69] law schools and dozens of unaccredited law schools in the United States.[70]

The Curriculum of Law

It is much easier to describe the subjects that are taught in law school than to describe the underlying methodology of law teaching and thinking. Having progressed from an earlier concentration upon common-law subjects, modern American law schools offer a

67 Chase, The Birth of the Modern Law School, 23 Am. J.L.Hist. 329 (1979).

68 Suggestions for a two-year curriculum, with many variations, surfaced repeatedly during the period in which the three-year mandatory program became absolutely standard at full-time law schools. E.g., Rept. of Curriculum Study Project Comm. of Ass'n of American Law Schools, Training for the Public Professions of the Law (1971); Manning, Law Schools and Lawyer Schools—Two-Tier Legal Education, 26 J.Leg.Educ. 379 (1974).

69 In every jurisdiction but California, the accrediting agency for American legal education is the American Bar Association. ABA accreditation standards are subject to the legislative control of the ABA House of Delegates and provide a method of shaping legal education to some extent. See generally Fossum, Law School Education Standards and the Structure of American Legal Education, 1978 Am.B.Found. Research J. 515 (effect of ABA's accreditation activities on part-time and proprietary law schools). Operating through the ABA Section on Legal Education and Admissions to the Bar, volunteer members of inspection committees visit law schools at intervals of years, receive reports and conduct site examinations and interviews, and generally assess the extent to which the institution has complied with the written ABA accreditation standards. See ABA, Approval of Law Schools: ABA Standards and Rules of Procedure (as amended, 1983). For an antitrust analysis concluding that the ABA, and the American Association of Law Schools, is engaged in an unreasonable restraint of trade by discouraging new entries and innovation, see Frist, Competition in the Legal Education Industry (II): An Antitrust Analysis, 54 NYU L.Rev. 1049 (1979).

In California, bar applicants may demonstrate satisfaction of educational requirements by graduation from a school approved by the state bar, in addition to other means of obtaining a legal education. See West's Ann. Calif.Bus. & Prof. Code § 6060(e).

70 Most of the unaccredited law schools are in California, the only populous state that permits applicants to take a bar examination without satisfying the course of study at an accredited law school. The quality and status of California's approximately fifty unaccredited law schools are perennially debated. See Nat'l L.J., Oct.12, 1981, p. 31, col.4.

curriculum that is uniformly rich in course offerings from a wide variety of legal fields with a wide variety of types of law—common law, statutory, administrative, international—running through them. The curriculum concentrates upon areas of common interest to faculty and students, to faculty because of their practice experience and intellectual interests and to students because of their perceived vocational and intellectual needs. Law schools differ significantly in the extent to which their graduates find employment in various types of law practice, which has a significant impact upon the types of courses offered and upon the narrowness or breadth of focus of courses and course materials. Business law, administrative law, and complex litigation are emphasized, without regard to jurisdictional limitations, at prestigious schools whose graduates tend to find employment in larger firms, corporations, and government agencies in different parts of the country. Law schools whose graduates find employment as solo practitioners, members of small firms, and in such government positions as prosecutors tend to emphasize personal law subjects such as the law of injuries, crimes, and real estate and to focus upon the law of a particular jurisdiction.

One of the most remarkable features of legal education is its lack of any agreed-upon methodology or body of knowledge. In medicine, for example, all agree that science is the method of medical practice, even if medical practice also involves substantial elements of artlike intuition and creativity. But there is no equivalent "justice theory" that is widely accepted as the underlying methodology of legal thought and education. Law professors do not even share a well-thought-out philosophy of how courts decide cases, despite the devotion to the study of the common-law process that has characterized the past century of legal education. Various candidates have been put forward in place of a coherent legal theory—sociology and economics are prominent, philosophy and history are secondary. But no kindred discipline or uniquely legal theory has received wide recognition as the parent and vehicle for wisdom about law.

Critics of Legal Education

Legal education has not suffered a lack of critical attention. The critics have attacked from primarily three directions. The attack from the high road usually takes the same direction as the dictum of Thorsten Veblen that "law schools belong in the modern university no more than a school of fencing or dancing." [71] Veblen's sneer has not driven law schools from university campuses,[72] but thoughtful academics have wondered whether legal training can truly constitute a part of a university education or, instead, whether it is not simply vocational training of a kind only different in content from plumbing or fencing. The second attack is from a contrary direction. It charges that law schools are not banausic enough, that law professors are too concerned with theoretical and conceptual matters and not sufficiently concerned with seeing that their students receive a sound, practical education in the more mundane basics of law practice.[73] In fact, most university law schools attempt to take both the high

[71] T.Veblen, The Higher Learning in America 211 (1918).

[72] Veblen was neither alone nor a creature of his times. Nobel laureate and economist Paul Samuelson probably spoke for many nonlaw academics when he muttered more recently that "for better or worse the American law school has wormed its way into a corner of the university campus." Samuelson, The Convergence of the Law School and the University, 44 Am.Scholar 256, 257 (1975).

[73] A variation on the same outlook may also typify students and law faculties. See Kronman, Foreword: Legal Scholarship and Moral Education, 90 Yale L.J. 9555 (1981). Some law teachers have blamed part-time law student employment, among other factors, for the widely reported sense of student disengagement in the second and third years of law school. A study suggests, however, that such employment relates to neither disengagement nor to levels of examination performance. Pipkin, Moonlighting in Law School: A Multischool Study of Part-Time Employment of Full-Time Students, 1982 Am. B.Found. Research J. 1109. The disengagement has been with legal education for many decades. See Dunne, The Third Year Blahs: Felix Frankfurter after Fifty Years, 94 Harv.L.Rev. 1237 (1981). See also Carrington & Conleyu, The Alienation of Law Students, 75 Mich.L.Rev. 887 (1977).

and the low roads, which may or may not be schizophrenic.[74] The third attack charges that however well they do their assigned task, law schools are too much in the thrall of the existing social and economic orders and do little to prepare students for a career of public service and law reform.[75] More radical versions of that charge have been put forward by the proponents of the loosely allied schools of thought that collectively call themselves the Critical Legal Studies movement.[76]

Variations on those three themes have been repeated in several studies of American legal education in the twentieth century.[77] The only significant structural reform that has been inaugurated in this century—clinical legal education—in part responds to the concerns for practical training and, in some hands, to a desire to work for law reform and wealth redistribution. Clinical education attempts to provide skill training in those elements of law practice that cannot easily be taught in a classroom.[78] It does that through providing law students with the opportunity to work with actual cases involving clients, more or less under the direct supervision of an experienced practitioner-teacher. The concentration of clinical education upon law reform probably reflects the preferences of clinical teachers, who have been recruited primarily from organizations providing legal services to the poor, and the fact that competitive bar pressures have confined the clientele of most clinical programs to the poor, who would not otherwise receive legal services in return for fee payments.

Future of Legal Education

Whether or not with great consciousness of its motivating intellectual or practical strengths, legal education seems fit to survive the twentieth century with health that is at least as sound as that of other principal public institutions. Lawyers who reflect on their legal education have concluded that while it did not teach them everything that they wished to know before entering practice, on the whole, their legal education has been valuable.[79] Because of, or despite, its well-studied, but insufficiently understood, processes, legal education will probably remain relatively unchanged over the next few decades. Its denizens on the inside and practitioners outside are, if restively, probably content with

[74] McGowan, The University Law School and Practical Education, 65 ABA J. 374 (1979); Allen, The Causes of Popular Dissatisfaction with Legal Education, 62 ABA J. 447 (1976).

[75] Other primary attacks are that legal education fails to instill in students a sense of public service. J. Seligman, The High Citadel: The Influence of Harvard Law School (1978)(for a response, see Cox, Book Review, 92 Harv.L.Rev. 1170 (1979)); Auerbach, What Has the Teaching of Law to Do with Justice?, 53 NYU L.Rev. 457 (1978); Nader, Law Schools and Law Firms, New Republic (Oct.11, 1969), at 20.

[76] The Politics of Law: A Progressive Critique (D.Kairys ed.1983); Trilin, Harvard Law, The New Yorker (Mar.26, 1984), at 53; Shiffrin, Liberalism, Radicalism, and Legal Scholarship, 30 UCLA L.Rev. 1103 (1983); Unger, The Critical Legal Studies Movement, 96 Harv.L. Rev. 561 (1983); Note, 'Round and 'Round the Bramble Bush: From Legal Realism to Critical Legal Scholarship, 95 Harv.L.Rev. 1669 (1982).

[77] The first, and still the most famous, are the Reed reports. See A.Reed, Training for the Public Profession of the Law (1921); A.Reed, Present Day Law Schools in the United States (1928). See also, e.g., Bok, A Flawed System of Law Practice and Training, 33 J.Leg.Educ. 570 (1983); ABA Sect. of Leg. Educ. and Admission to the Bar, Report and Recommendations of the Task Force on Lawyer Competency: The Role of the Law Schools (1979) (Cramton Report); Boyer & Cramton, American Legal Education: An Agenda for Research and Reform, 59 Corn.L.Rev. 221 (1974); H.Packer & T.Ehrlich, New Directions in Legal Education (1972); Rept. of Curriculum Study Project Comm. of Ass'n of American Law Schools, Training for the Public Professions of the Law (1971) (Carrington Report); Symposium, Traditional Legal Education, 35 Mercer L.Rev. 751 (1984); Symposium, 40 Md. L.Rev. 203 (1981); Symposium, Legal Education, 59 Wash.U.L.Q. 591 (1981); Symposium: Clinical Legal Education and the Legal Profession, 29 Cleve.St.L.Rev. 345 (1980); Symposium on Legal Education, 53 NYU L.Rev. 291 (1978); Symposium, Legal Education, 1977 BYU L.Rev. 689; Symposium, Current Trends in Legal Education and the Legal Profession, 50 St.John's L.Rev. 434 (1976).

[78] It has been frequently observed, for example, that traditional legal education does not sufficiently expose students to the difficulties and techniques of fact investigation. E.g., J.Frank, Courts on Trial 225–46 (1949); G.Tullock, Trials on Trial: The Pure Theory of Civil Procedure 3 (1980).

[79] Zemans & Rosenblum, Preparation for the Practice of Law—the Views of the Practicing Bar, 1980 Am.B. Found. Research J. 1.

the essential soundness of the philosophy and general methods of legal education.[80]

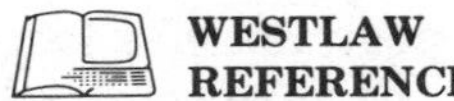

WESTLAW REFERENCES

The Place of Legal Education in Law

accredit! approv** /3 "law school"

Legal Education in Professional Values

law legal /3 education /s profession** /3 ethics values

History of Legal Education

legal law /3 education school /s unaccredited

The Curriculum of Law

legal law /3 education school /p curriculum

Critics of Legal Education

clinical /s law legal /3 education school

Future of Legal Education

[no queries]

§ 5.3 BAR EXAMINATIONS

Applicants who wish to practice law in most jurisdictions [81] must pass a written bar examination in order to demonstrate minimal competence to practice. Written bar examinations are much more recent than bar examinations themselves. Massachusetts was first with a standard written examination in 1855, but most jurisdictions had for many years required an oral examination. Some oral examinations were conducted by judges of the court to which the applicant sought to be admitted. Others, like that of Abraham Lincoln, were conducted by an admitted lawyer who would certify the competence of the oral examinee.

Bar examinations for admission to practice can today be taken only by persons who have completed a prescribed course of legal education.[82] Every jurisdiction publishes a list of subjects that the examination will, or might, cover. Those lists tend to influence students' election of courses in law school. The examination itself has traditionally consisted of essay-type questions that pose a factual situation and require students to analyze the legal issues involved, much as a usual law school examination. The essay answers are read and graded by teams of practicing lawyers under a variety of arrangements that seek to establish parity among the examiners' grading practices. Typically an examinee must obtain a passing average in the entire examination or retake the entire examination, which will be repeated once or twice a year. Most jurisdictions permit an examinee who fails an examination to retake a following bar examination a number of times.[83]

Essay examination questions have been supplemented in several states with multiple-choice examinations that have now been made national in scope through a multistate examination system.[84] California began requiring that all examinees obtain a passing

80 Brainerd Currie predicted a similarly steady-state future for legal education in Currie, Law and the Future: Legal Education, 51 Nw.U.L.Rev. 258, 263 (1956). He predicted that the second half of the twentieth century would see no dramatic changes in law school training, but "molecular" rather than sweeping institutional changes. With the sole possible exception of clinical legal education, Currie was clearly correct.

81 Excepted are those few jurisdictions that grant a "diploma privilege" admission to the bar for graduates of in-state law schools.

82 In California, persons who have completed the first year of education at an unaccredited law school must pass a "baby bar" examination in order to be eligible later to take the regular bar examination. The stated rationale is to permit students at such schools to assess their likelihood of passing the eventual bar examination. See Bib'le v. Committee of Bar Examiners, 26 Cal.3d 548, 162 Cal.Rptr. 426, 606 P.2d 733 (1980), cert. denied 449 U.S. 860, 101 S.Ct. 163, 66 L.Ed.2d 77 (1980).

83 Jones v. Board of Comm'rs of Alabama St. Bar, 737 F.2d 996 (11th Cir.1984)(constitutionality of state's rule prohibiting reexamination after applicant has failed five times); Younger v. Colorado St. Bd. of Law Examiners, 625 F.2d 372 (10th Cir.1980). Courts have suggested, in effect, that a privilege to retake the bar examination may be required by due process if the jurisdiction does not provide failing applicants with the right to obtain a review of their examination answers and an explanation of its grading. E.g., Lucero v. Ogden, 718 F.2d 355, 359 (10th Cir.1983), cert. denied 465 U.S. 1035, 104 S.Ct. 1308, 79 L.Ed.2d 706 (1984); Brewer v. Wegmann, 691 F.2d 216 (5th Cir.1982), cert. denied 461 U.S. 908, 103 S.Ct. 188, 76 L.Ed.2d 811 (1983); Whitfield v. Illinois Bd. of Law Examiners, 504 F.2d 474 (7th Cir.1974).

84 The multistate examination is described in, e.g., National Conf. of Bar Examiners v. Multistate Legal Studies, Inc., 692 F.2d 478 (7th Cir.1982), cert. denied 464 U.S. 814, 104 S.Ct. 69, 78 L.Ed.2d 83 (1983) (validity of copyright procedure by which multistate test can be registered for copyright protection without publication of con-

grade on a separate multiple-choice examination in professional responsibility in the early 1970s. A Multistate Professional Responsibility Examination has developed from it that is now offered nationally several times a year. As like California, most of the several states that require the examination require that it be separately passed and do not average its grade in with other components of the bar examination. A third type of examination recently introduced in California is a skills examination that has examinees write out an appellate brief or a solution to a legal problem by a legal memorandum to a senior lawyer.[85]

The extent to which bar examinations accurately and comprehensively test legal competence has been debated. The examination and grading process has been repeatedly attacked,[86] but upheld by courts against those attacks, as discriminatory against some minority groups,[87] arbitrary in its grading standards and practices,[88] and unrepresentative of the tasks that practitioners face. The pass rate on some states' examinations is quite low; well under half the examinees are successful. Some researchers have found in the data indications that the pass rate on bar examinations is inversely proportional to lawyers' income levels, suggesting that examiners limit entry to the legal profession as a means of maintaining the income levels of those who are already members of the bar.[89] Others have found no statistical evidence that bar examinations are being administered in an anticompetitive way.[90] Ultimately, the majority of graduates of most schools pass a bar examination,[91] and at many prestigious law schools the pass rate is comfortably high. For all examinees, the bar takes a toll of months of deferred income after law school while they study for the bar examination, take it, and await its results before being certified to practice. Many law graduates also spend several hundreds of dollars on bar review courses and materials in the weeks before the examination.

Bar examinations have been defended as a means of each jurisdiction's assuring itself that persons admitted to practice will possess the competence to perform basic lawyer functions.[92] They have also been defended as a point at which law students, possibly for the first time, have an occasion to integrate their learning from many different courses. Bar examinations also remove some pressure from

tents in order to assure reusability of examination contents).

85 Nat'l L.J., Jan.3, 1983, p. 24, col.1.

86 In Hoover v. Ronwin, 466 U.S. 558, 104 S.Ct. 1989, 80 L.Ed.2d 590 (1984), the Supreme Court held that Arizona's grading of bar examinations was conducted in such a way that the state-action immunity shielded the lawyer members of the examining committee from an antitrust damage action by a failing examinee.

87 Richardson v. McFadden, 563 F.2d 1130 (4th Cir. 1977)(en banc), cert. denied 435 U.S. 968, 98 S.Ct. 1606, 56 L.Ed.2d 59 (1978); Parish v. Board of Comm'rs of Alabama St. Bar, 533 F.2d 942 (5th Cir.1976); Delgado v., McTighe, 522 F.Supp. 886 (E.D.Pa.1981); Harper v. District of Columbia Comm. on Admissions, 375 A.2d 25 (D.C.App.1977).

88 Courts have uniformly held that subjective essay examination grading without a set of "objective" criteria is constitutional. E.g., Tyler v. Vickery, 517 F.2d 1089, 1102–03 (5th Cir.1975), cert. denied 426 U.S. 940, 96 S.Ct. 2660, 49 L.Ed.2d 393 (1976); Feldman v. State Bd. of Law Examiners, 438 F.2d 699, 705 (8th Cir.1971); Chaney v. State Bar of California, 386 F.2d 962 (9th Cir.1967), cert. denied 390 U.S. 1011, 88 S.Ct. 1262, 20 L.Ed.2d 162 (1968). See generally Schware v. Board of Bar Examiners, 353 U.S. 232, 77 S.Ct. 752, 1 L.Ed.2d 796 (1957).

89 Pashigian, Occupational Licensing and the Interstate Mobility of Professionals, 22 J.L. & Econ. 1 (1979); Maurizi, Occupational Licensing and the Public Interest, 82 J.Pol.Econ. 399 (1974); Holen, Effects of Professional Licensing Arrangements on Interstate Labor Mobility and Resource Allocation, 73 J.Pol.Econ. 492 (1965).

90 Getz, Siegfried & Calvani, Competition at the Bar: The Correlation between the Bar Examination Pass Rate and the Profitability of Practice, 67 Va.L.Rev. 863 (1981).

91 In recent years the national average for satisfactory examinations has varied within several percentage points of 67 percent, although the range among the states is from the vicinity of 45 percent to nearly complete passing rates in some small states. E.g., American Lawyer, p. 9, col.3 (Aug.1980). California has historically had one of the lowest pass rates. E.g., Nat'l L.J., June 8, 1981, p.3, col.1 (32.4 percent pass rate in February 1981 examination); In re Investigation of Conduct of Examination for Admission to Practice Law, 1 Cal.2d 61, 33 P.2d 829 (1934)(31 percent pass rate). The customary explanation for California is its liberality in permitting graduates of unaccredited law schools to sit for the examination despite their much higher failure rate.

92 See generally Griswold, In Praise of Bar Examinations, 60 ABA J. 91 (1974).

law schools to conform to bar association notions of proper legal education.

WESTLAW REFERENCES

"bar exam!" /p discriminat! arbitrar!

§ 5.4 POSTPROFESSIONAL EDUCATION, TRAINING, AND CERTIFICATION

The Need for Education after Bar Admission

Traditionally, bar membership has meant that an admitted lawyer has an entitlement like a life peerage—as long as the lawyer draws breath and has not been disbarred or suspended, the lawyer can continue to practice. Bar admission has also been general in the sense that an admitted lawyer could practice in any or all fields of the law and move from one specialty field to another, even late in a career, without any preparation. Sweeping changes in the law or in legal institutions do not require any alteration in a lawyer's privilege to continue to practice in that field even if a lawyer is not prepared to do so. Courts and bar leaders have been concerned that the traditional approach has caused harm to clients who have received incompetent legal service and has inadequately responded to the need of midcareer lawyers for retooling or for a new start in a strange field. As a result, attention has focused on one or more of several methods to enhance competence or to assure that a lawyer practicing in one or more specific fields has acquired and maintained special competence. Those methods include apprenticeship; continuing legal education; certification; reexamination and recertification; and specialization, which will be examined in the following section (§ 5.5).

Apprenticeships and Clerkships

A few states have attempted to bridge the gap between law school and the bar examination, on the one side, and the actual practice of law, on the other, by requiring a period of postgraduate legal training under the tutelage of an established, experienced practitioner. The systems, which have been inspired by, although they hardly copy, the English system of the articled clerk, are rudimentary in form and doubtful in their teaching effectiveness. Both teaching lawyer and learning pupil are often too engrossed in the demands of a busy practice, or the need to make a practice busy, to spend the early months of practice on rudimentary practice education. It has also been frequently charged that the systems are corrupted by too many tutoring lawyers who employ them as a source of cheap legal assistance for mundane and time-consuming tasks that have little true educational value.[93]

Continuing Legal Education

The notion that lawyers stop learning on graduating from law school is, of course, unsound. Lawyers have always taken professional pride in an ability to master new situations and new areas of law through self-directed study. A good legal education aims to instill habits and skills of self-learning among other appropriate traits for practice. Moreover, lawyers have always learned from each other. The figure of the senior lawyer who voluntarily advises and directs younger lawyers is a warm part of bar mythology. Some state bars have institutionalized the concept with "mentor" programs that make the advice of established lawyers available to newly admitted lawyers.[94] Lawyers in firms have helped educate each other for reasons of economics as well as altruism. In very large modern firms, formalized continuing-educa-

[93] Frankel, Curing Lawyers' Incompetence: Primum Non Nocere, 10 Creighton L.Rev. 613, 635 (1977).

[94] ALI-ABA Conf. on Continuing Professional Education 256 (1981). See also id. 255–63 (discussion of range of proposals and existing programs for voluntary and mandatory "peer review" of competence of practicing lawyers); ALI-ABA Comm. on Continuing Prof. Educ., A Model Peer Review System (discussion draft April 15, 1980); Martyn, Lawyer Competence and Lawyer Discipline: Beyond the Bar?, 69 Geo.L.J. 705, 726–29 (1981) (assessment of peer review proposals for marginal practitioners); Parker, Periodic Recertification of Lawyers: A Comparative Study of Programs for Maintaining Professional Competence, 1974 Utah L.Rev. 463, 466–73.

tion programs have been instituted both to assure that early career education takes place and to encourage senior lawyers to expand their horizons and to stay current on new developments.[95]

Bars in almost all states have assumed a jurisdiction-wide responsibility for postgraduate lawyer training through programs of continuing-legal education.[96] Some specialist programs contain continuing education provisions that are mandatory for certified specialists.[97] Political pressures to do something about incompetent lawyers have led some jurisdictions to make it mandatory that all admitted lawyers engage in a minimal amount of continuing legal education annually in order to retain their licenses to practice.[98] Most jurisdictions, however, have been unconvinced by the arguments that competent lawyers should be forced to undertake the unneeded and sometimes unrefreshing exposure to available formal courses and that incompetent lawyers will learn enough of what they need to be transformed into competent lawyers.[99]

Limitation by Certification

Various programs have proposed a system of certifying lawyers as competent in particular areas of the law. The programs differ in the extent to which they prohibit other lawyers from claiming similar competence or prohibit uncertified lawyers from practicing within the area of certification. The idea of a graded bar was in place in some of the more populous colonies prior to the American Revolution. Those generally required lawyers to demonstrate special competence in order to practice in appellate courts.[1] Two contemporary versions are the certification systems for specialists in California and Texas and the experimental federal litigation specialist plan. The California and Texas systems provide for certification of lawyers as

[95] Weinstein, A CLE Plan to Attract the Senior Practitioner, Nat'l L.J., July 26, 1982, p. 19, col. 3 (scholar-in-residence program at large law firm); Nat'l L.J., Sept.20, 1982, p. 2, col. 1 (manual for in-house training announced).

[96] Wolkin, On Improving the Quality of Lawyering, 50 St.John's L.Rev. 523 (1976); Friday, Continuing Legal Education: Historical Background, Recent Developments and the Future, 50 St.John's L.Rev. 502 (1976); Wolkin, A Better Way to Keep Lawyers Competent, 61 ABA J. 574 (1975); Comment, Once You're In: Maintaining Competence in the Bar, 56 Neb.L.Rev. 676 (1977). See generally ALI-ABA, A Model for Continuing Legal Education: Structure, Methods, Curriculum (1980).

[97] See generally Florida Bar in re Appeal from Decisions of Designation Appeals Committee, 374 So.2d 494 (Fla.1979).

[98] Mandatory continuing legal education began with Minnesota in 1975, among other reasons in order to forestall more onerous reforms that its proponents feared would be forced upon the bar by public consumer pressures. See Sheran & Harmon, Minnesota Plan: Mandatory Continuing Legal Education for Lawyers and Judges as a Condition for the Maintaining of Professional Licensing, 44 Fordham L.Rev. 1081, 1086–87, 1094 (1976). See also Byron, Mandatory Continuing Legal Education in Minnesota: The First Year, 50 St.John's L.Rev. 512 (1976); Harris, Minnesota CLE—The End of Licensing for Life?, Trial at 23 (July/Aug.1975); Parker, Periodic Recertification of Lawyers: A Comparative Study of Programs for Maintaining Professional Competence, 1974 Utah L.Rev. 463, 477–89 (favorable assessment of Minnesota plan on basis of experience with mandatory professional education programs in accounting and medical professions). On continuing education in other professions, see generally C.Houle, Continuing Learning in the Professions (1980).

The constitutionality of the mandatory feature of a similar program in Colorado was sustained in Verner v. Colorado, 716 F.2d 1352, 1353 (10th Cir.1983), cert. denied 466 U.S. 960, 104 S.Ct. 2175, 80 L.Ed.2d 558 (1984), on finding a " 'rational connection with the [attorney's] fitness or capacity to practice law.' " (quoting Schware v. Board of Bar Examiners, 353 U.S. 232, 239, 77 S.Ct. 752, 756, 1 L.Ed.2d 796 (1957)). See generally Massaro & O'Brien, Constitutional Limitations on State-Imposed Continuing Competency Requirements for Licensed Professionals, 25 Wm. & Mary L.Rev. 253 (1983).

By a 1980 amendment, lawyers newly admitted to practice in New Hampshire must within one year of their admission attend an unexamined course in "practical skills," to be offered by the state bar association. N.H.S. Ct. Rule 42, § 7.

[99] After study of the Minnesota and Iowa mandatory continuing legal education programs before they had begun operating, a National Conference on Continuing Legal Education concluded that the case for mandatory education could not be sustained in the absence of proof of the relationship between required education and the quality of legal services. See 62 ABA J. 210 (1976). See also, e.g., Frankel, Curing Lawyers' Incompetence: Primum Non Nocere, 10 Creighton L.Rev. 613, 627–32 (1977); Wolkin, More on a Better Way to Keep Lawyers Competent, 61 ABA J. 1064 (1975).

[1] A.Reed, Training for the Public Profession of the Law 39 (1921); Consalus, Legal Education during the Colonial Period, 1663–1776, 29 J.Leg.Educ. 295, 302–03 (1978).

specialists if they satisfy necessary prerequisites, which include concentrations in practice, continuing education, and initial and periodic reexaminations to assure continued specialist competence (§ 5.5). But a lawyer may practice law in any area in those states without being a certified specialist.

In contrast, the federal court plan for trial advocacy certification excludes all but certified lawyers from that area of law practice. The plan was endorsed in 1979 by the Judicial Conference of the United States on the recommendation of a report submitted earlier that year by the so-called Devitt Committee.[2] In the districts in which it has been adopted for a trial period,[3] the plan requires that lawyers who seek to be admitted to practice in federal courts must pass a special bar examination on federal practice, gain at least four trial-type experiences through a combination of supervised moot trials in an accredited institution and supervised actual trials,[4] and submit to peer review in the event that a committee of litigation specialists determines that there is reason to believe that the lawyer's performance as an advocate is deficient.

Reexamination and Recertification [5]

Why should lawyers who have successfully passed a bar examination be perpetually considered competent?[6] It might be argued that just as an initial bar examination purports to be able to identify prospective practitioners who are not minimally equipped to practice, a periodic examination of admitted practitioners should determine whether the initial assessment of minimal competence should be altered because of intervening bad habits or loss of contact with the content of law practice. While no state has seriously considered adopting such a plan,[7] it is possible to think of a requirement that all lawyers successfully pass periodic examinations, perhaps every three or five years, or be required to take remedial courses or possibly practice only under supervision if unable to pass. The concept, which is pleasing in theory, can probably not be reasonably administered in a fair and effective way that creates only an acceptable intrusion into ongoing legal careers.[8]

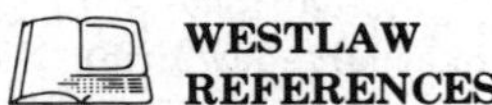
WESTLAW REFERENCES

Apprenticeship and Clerkship

di clerkship

[2] Devitt Committee Recommendations Accepted by Judicial Conference, in The Third Branch at 1 (Oct.1979); Committee to Consider Standards for Admission to Practice in the Federal Courts, Final Report to the Judicial Conference of the United States, 83 F.R.D. 215 (1979). The Devitt Committee's tentative report is published in 79 F.R.D. 187 (1978). For assessments, see, e.g., Meserve, Lynch & Daniel, The Devitt Report in Context: Public Responsibility of Lawyers in the 1980s, 11 U.Tol.L.Rev. 216, 223–25 (1980)(favoring); Bagg, What the Devitt Committee Recommends to Improve Advocacy in Federal Courts, 63 Judicature 309 (1980)(reviewing arguments); Greenberg, Devitt Report: New Hurdles for Minority Lawyers?, 65 ABA J. 561 (1979). For earlier, negative views, see, e.g., Cohen, Certification of Trial Lawyers—The Judicious Structuring of the American Legal Profession, 6 Hofstra L.Rev. 793 (1978)(trial bar certification as threat to desirable pluralism and generalism in American lawyers); Frankel, Curing Lawyers' Incompetence: Primum Non Nocere, 10 Creighton L.Rev. 613, 621–25 (1977)(criticizing earlier proposal for separate trial bar for Second Circuit).

[3] As of early 1984, thirteen of the ninety-one federal districts had adopted pilot admission plans. See Nat'l L.J., Mar.5, 1984, p. 4, col.3. A constitutional challenge to the plan was rejected in Brown v. McGarr, 583 F.Supp. 734 (N.D.Ill.1984).

[4] The trial-experience requirement is a kind of apprenticeship because the applicant must try a minimum of two actual trials in federal or state court under the supervision of an experienced litigator.

[5] O'Donnell, Perry & Abernathy, Compulsory Continuing Legal Education and Periodic Re-Examination and Re-Certification of Lawyers, 62 Women L.J. 20 (1976); Parker, Periodic Recertification of Lawyers: A Comparative Study of Programs for Maintaining Professional Competence, 1974 Utah L.Rev. 463.

[6] The concept of a limited duration to a license to practice law can be traced at least to 1932. See H.Arant, Cases and Other Materials on the American Bar and Its Ethics 85 (1933)(quoting letter to New York Times).

[7] Lawyers are reportedly strongly opposed to a relicensing requirement. See Lawpoll, 68 ABA J. 800 (1982)(68 percent of lawyers surveyed opposed in 1982; 59 percent opposed in 1977). See, e.g., Bar Board Abandons Plan for Relicensing Lawyers, Los Angeles Times, Apr. 16, 1977, p. 27, col.6. A subcommittee of the Devitt Committee considered the question of relicensing of lawyers, but the notion was not pursued.

[8] For critiques, see, e.g., Loeb & Loeb, Continuing Legal Education—Should It Be Compulsory?, 27 J.Leg.Educ. 110, 114 (1975); Parker, supra, 1974 Utah L.Rev. at 476–77.

Continuing Legal Education

"continuing legal education"

---

§ 5.5 SPECIALIZATION

The Specialization Conundrum

In actual practice, the majority of lawyers are de facto specialists and so regard themselves.[9] Some lawyers have been eager for the bar to inaugurate formal specialization programs,[10] but for more than a quarter century the organized bar has been unable to agree whether, and to what extent, lawyers should be permitted to hold themselves out to the public as specialists.[11] Specialization programs have nonetheless operated in some few states for several years, and Supreme Court decisions on the constitutional free speech rights of lawyers may imply that lawyers who are in fact specialists have a right to state that in advertising.

The Advantages and Disadvantages of Lawyer Specialization

From a public perspective, specialization may hold the promise of enhanced competence, as lawyers devote more time to post-professional education and training in order to qualify as specialists.[12] Specialist advertising may also be useful in enabling legal service consumers to find lawyers who are particularly well equipped to deal with some kinds of legal issues. Under one set of assumptions, specialization may lower legal costs to consumers as lawyers are able to become more efficient. From a narrower perspective, lawyer self-interest in regulating specialization probably involves both economic and social considerations. Economically, lawyers who are specialists may believe that their ability to attract new clients would be enhanced if they, but not unqualified lawyers, were able to hold themselves out as specialists. Lawyers who are specialists may also wish to separate themselves from the mass of lawyers in order to raise their image with the public [13] or, possibly, with other lawyers.[14]

9 Lawpoll, 68 ABA J. 800 (1982)(incidence of specialization increased among ABA members from 40 percent in 1977 to 55 percent in 1982); Comm. on Specialization, Preliminary Report: Results of Survey on Certification of Specialists, 44 Cal.St.B.J. 140 (1969)(two of three lawyers in California specialize, and in partnerships of more than ten lawyers, four of five lawyers do so); M.Altman & R.Weil, How to Manage Your Law Office § 2.08, at 2–30 (1976)(Maryland survey in 1968 indicates that more than two in five Baltimore private practitioners spent 75 percent or more of time working on matters falling within single field of law and 82 percent spent half or more of time). The statistics in each case are hardly conclusive because they rely on self-reporting and assume a unitary definition of "specialize."

10 The great majority of lawyers probably favor adopting some form of program to certify specialists and to permit advertising of specialization. See Lawpoll, 68 ABA J. 800 (1982)(73 percent of ABA lawyers favor).

11 Explicit recognition of the growing dimension of de facto specialization and of an asserted desirability for uniform regulation begins at least with Rept. of Spec. Comm. on Specialization and Specialized Legal Services, 79 ABA Rep. 582 (1954). A committee to consider liberalizing the Canons on the use of specialty designations on shingles and letterheads was first appointed in 1950. See E.Sunderland, History of the American Bar Association and Its Work 210 (1953); 75 ABA Rep. 44, 444 (1950). See also ABA Comm. on Specialization, Report, 93 ABA Rep. 261 (1969); ABA Comm. on Availability of Legal Services, Report on Specialization, 92 ABA Rep. 584 (1967); ABA Comm. on Recognition and Regulation of Specialization in Law Practice, Report, 87 ABA Rep. 361 (1962). See generally Comment, Legal Specialization: A Proposal for More Accessible and Higher Quality Legal Services, 40 Mont.L.Rev. 287, 292–93 (1979).

12 G.Greenwood & R.Fredrickson, Specialization in the Medical and Legal Professions 131–62 (1964); Brink, Let's Take Specialization Apart, 62 ABA J. 191 (1976); Cheatham, The Growing Need for Specialized Legal Services, 16 Vand.L.Rev. 497 (1963); Tweed, The Changing Practice of Law: The Question of Specialization, 48 ABA J. 423 (1962).

13 Mindes, Proliferation, Specialization, and Certification: The Splitting of the Bar, 11 U.Tol.L.Rev. 273 (1980); Laumann & Heinz, Specialization and Prestige in the Legal Profession: The Structure of Deference, 1977 Am. B.Found. Research J. 155. The objective of obtaining public recognition of a lawyer's sharply differentiated status may be unavailing because of a tendency of the public to regard all lawyers interchangeably. See Mindes & Acock, Trickster, Hero, Helper: A Report on the Lawyer Image, 1982 Am.B.Found. Research J. 177, 197.

14 Some lawyer specialists have developed vocabularies and procedures that may already make them as mysterious to other lawyers as they are to the nonlawyer public. See Hazard, Conscience and Circumstance in Legal Ethics, in Social Responsibility: Journalism, Law, Medicine at 36, 37 (L.Hodges ed.1975).

Lawyer specialization may be opposed from a consumeristic viewpoint for fear that it will drive up the cost of legal services, on the assumption that specialists would become monopolists; that it will draw away skilled general practitioners into narrow specialities that are relevant only to economic elites; that lawyers will lose their ability to deal with a broad range of legal problems and to solve apparently narrow legal problems with imaginative approaches; and that it will destroy the personal relationship between lawyers and clients.[15] Opposition to specialization within the legal profession may also reflect concern on the part of some lawyers that they will lose clients and prestige if specialization is permitted. General practitioners may fear that they will be unable to compete with the quality of service provided by specialists, or may be exposed to legal malpractice and disciplinary hazards if they do,[16] and that referrals of clients to specialists will be one-way.[17]

Types of Specialization Programs

Two basic systems of specialization—peer certification and self-designation—are found, sometimes in tandem, in the few states that formally permit lawyers to describe themselves as specialists.[18] The two systems are profoundly different in quality control measures. Certificated specialization was inaugurated in 1971 by California's experimental plan, still in operation,[19] to permit lawyers to submit to a relatively elaborate system of quality controls through examinations, education, peer reference, and commitment of a minimal percentage of their practice to the specialty.[20] California presently certifies lawyers in workers' compensation, criminal, tax, and family law.[21] Relatively rigorous quality

[15] Freund, The Moral Education of the Lawyer, 26 Emory L.J. 3, 9–10 (1977); Mindes, Lawyer Speciality Certification: The Monopoly Game, 61 ABA J. 42 (1975); Pedrick, Collapsible Specialists, 55 ABA J. 324 (1969); Teschner, Specialists, Experts, and Lawyers: On the Integrity of the Legal Profession, 41 U.Det.L.J. 483 (1964); Llewellyn, The Bar Specialized—With What Results?, 167 Annals 177 (1933).

[16] Horne v. Peckham, 97 Cal.App.3d 404, 158 Cal.Rptr. 714 (1979)(general practitioner should refer client to specialist if reasonably skillful practitioner would do so); Wright v. Williams, 47 Cal.App.3d 802, 121 Cal.Rptr. 194 (1975)(specialist held to specialist standard of care); Walker v. Bangs, 92 Wn.2d 854, 601 P.2d 1279 (1979) (lawyer who holds self out as specializing and possessing greater than ordinary knowledge and skill in particular field will be held to standard of performance of those who hold themselves out as specialists in that area); Lewis v. State Bar, 28 Cal.3d 683, 170 Cal.Rptr. 634, 621 P.2d 258 (1981)(discipline, under extreme facts, of lawyer who failed to consult experienced probate lawyer during administration of estate). See generally ABA Standing Comm. on Spec., Handbook on Specialization 26–27 (1983); Schnidman & Salzler, The Legal Malpractice Dilemma: Will New Standards of Care Place Professional Liability Insurance beyond the Reach of the Specialist, 45 U.Cin.L.Rev. 541 (1976); Note, Regulation of Legal Specialization: Neglect by the Organized Bar, 56 Notre Dame Law. 293, 297–301 (1980); Comment, Specialization: The Resulting Standard of Care and Duty to Consult, 30 Baylor L.Rev. 729 (1978).

[17] ALI-ABA Conference on Continuing Professional Education 343 (1981).

[18] For general descriptions of the state plans, see, e.g., ALI-ABA Conference on Continuing Professional Education 344–46 (1981); ABA Standing Comm. on Specialization, Interim Report, in 3 Alternatives: Legal Services and the Public 1 (1976); Nat'l L.J., May 10, 1982, p. 8, col. 1 (descriptions of plans in eight states); Comment, Legal Specialization: A Proposal for More Accessible and Higher Quality Legal Services, 40 Mont.L.Rev. 287, 295–300 (1979).

In 1979 the ABA House of Delegates approved a Model Plan of Specialization recommended by the ABA Standing Committee on Specialization. See ABA Standing Comm. on Spec., Handbook on Specialization A-3 (1983). Its basic features are recommending a dual system of self-designation and certification; requiring that any lawyer could practice within a specialty area and that specialists could practice outside their area; providing that a specialist who was referred a client could not perform legal services for the client beyond the lawyer's area of specialization; opposing grandfathering of existing de facto specialists who do not otherwise meet prescribed standards; recommending financing entirely from participant fees; providing for a mild form of peer review; and providing relatively minimal (ten hours per year) continuing legal education. The ABA recommendation, however, represented abandonment of the details of regulation of specialization to possibly disparate initiatives by the states.

[19] California's plan has been attended by much local controversy. E.g., 69 ABA J. 1622 (1983)(news report of conflict between state bar's board of governors and local bar associations and conference of delegates over making specialization program permanent).

[20] See generally R.Zehnle, Specialization in the Legal Profession 3–6 (1975).

[21] Weber, Why Formal Legal Specialization, 63 ABA J. 951 (1977). The Texas plan, which is very similar to that of California, offers specializations in civil trial, criminal, family, immigration, labor, personal injury, and estate and probate practice. See generally Wells, Certification

control is also exercised by a growing number of private specialty-certification organizations.[22]

Self-designation specialization is typified by the program in Florida.[23] The plan is basically an advertising plan and has little to do with the quality of legal services of designated specialists. Lawyers may designate themselves in any one of twenty-six common areas of law practice if they have been in practice for three years, if other lawyers are willing to attest to their "substantial experience" [24] in the designated fields, and if they have completed an average of ten hours of continuing legal education over the three-year period. It would be difficult to imagine why every lawyer with three years of practice would not be able to claim and advertise two or more Florida specialties. The plan thus appears to permit virtually unlimited advertising of specialization without offering assistance to prospective clients in differentiating between lawyers. Indeed, such plans may mislead some clients into thinking that the lawyer whom they think to be specialized is in fact especially qualified.[25]

Advertising Specializations

All existing plans for specialization permit lawyers to advertise some form of limited message identifying the lawyer as a specialist or as limiting his or her practice to a particular field. Few other states permit specialty advertising by explicit rule. Both the 1969 Code and the 1983 Model Rules limit allowable advertising of a specialty to patent and trademark practice and practice before the federal Patent Office.[26] Any other form of specialty advertising is referred to the state bar agency, if any, that deals with lawyer specialization.[27] Nonetheless, some courts may be receptive to an argument that the constitutional free speech protection recognized by the Supreme Court (§ 14.2.3) permits

in Texas: Increasing Lawyer Competence and Aiding the Public in Lawyer Selection, 30 Baylor L.Rev. 689 (1978).

22 See the description of the National Board of Trial Advocacy certification program in Johnson v. Director of Professional Responsibility, 341 N.W.2d 282 (Minn.1983).

23 See generally Davidson, The Florida Designation Plan: A Practical Approach to Legal Specialization, 30 Baylor L.Rev. 701 (1978). In 1978 Florida added a limited certification program to its self-designation plan. The program is limited to tax and civil trial specialists and exerts a modicum of quality control through a requirement of five years experience and passing an examination or twenty years experience without an examination.

24 In a variation on the experience criterion, under the Iowa specialization plan, lawyers must have devoted at least 20 percent of their time to the designated specialty in the two years before the self-designation.

25 In re Amendments to the Code of Professional Responsibility, 267 Ark. 1181, 590 S.W.2d 2 (1979)(court refuses to adopt specialization plan modeled on that of Florida because not convinced plan would assist public and in fact might mislead); (ALI-ABA Conference on Continuing Professional Education 345–46 (1981). The Arkansas court reversed itself, still with misgivings, less than three years later. In re Amendments to Code of Professional Responsibility, ___ Ark. ___, 637 S.W.2d 589 (1982). The reluctance of the Arkansas court was overcome by contrary bar opinion and the intervening decision in In re RMJ, 455 U.S. 191, 102 S.Ct. 929, 71 L.Ed.2d 64 (1982), limiting the states' powers to proscribe truthful advertising of areas of practice.

26 DR 2–105(A)(1)(patent practice); EC 2–14 (admiralty law); MR 7.4(a)(patent practice) and (b)(admiralty practice). As explained in MR 7.4 comment (second paragraph), the federal Patent and Trademark Office has long permitted its practitioners to advertise themselves as "patent attorney" or with a similar designation, and "designation of admiralty practice has a long historical tradition associated with maritime commerce and the federal courts." More than tradition and reliance on established practice is, of course, involved, at least in the case of patent practice. An attempt by a state to discipline a lawyer who relied on a federal authority to advertise would run afoul of the Supreme Court's ruling in Sperry v. Florida ex rel. Florida Bar, 373 U.S. 379, 83 S.Ct. 1322, 10 L.Ed.2d 428 (1963), holding that Florida could not discipline a lawyer for practicing federal patent law within the state under the authority of the federal patent office.

27 DR 2–105(A)(2) & (3); MR 7.4 (c). MR 7.4 draws a distinction, which is not alluded to in the 1969 Code, between self-advertising that a lawyer is a "specialist" and "communicat[ing] the fact that the lawyer does or does not practice in particular fields of law." The latter is unregulated, except by the false-or-misleading standard of MR 7.1. MR 7.4 comment (first paragraph), however, indicates that advertising that a lawyer's practice is "limited to" or "concentrated in" a particular field is prohibited because it is the equivalent of advertising a specialty. The allowable reference in advertising to "practicing in certain areas of law or . . . limiting [the lawyer's] practice" referred to in DR 5–105(A) is only permissible if made in accordance with rules developed within a jurisdiction. Nonetheless, some states have permitted references in advertising to areas of practice even if the state has not yet developed specialty advertising rules. E.g., N.Y.St.B.Ass'n Comm. on Prof. Ethics Op. No. 487 (1978).

a lawyer to make truthful statements about the lawyer's practice or credentials that may otherwise fall within the proscribed areas of specialization advertising.[28]

WESTLAW REFERENCES

The Specialization Conundrum

lawyer attorney counsel** /6 specialty specializ!

The Advantages and Disadvantages of Lawyer Specialization

specialty specializ! /s advertis! /p lawyer attorney counsel**

Types of Specialization Programs

specialty specializ! /s "workers compensation" tax! "family law" /s lawyer attorney counsel**

Advertising Specializations

"dr 2-105" /p specialty specializ!

§ 5.6 LEGAL MALPRACTICE AND OTHER PERFORMANCE–BASED LIABILITIES OF LAWYERS

§ 5.6.1 The Scope of Lawyer Liability to Clients

The Rationale of Legal Malpractice

Courts in the United States have recognized from a very early time a common-law right of a client to recover damages from a lawyer whose negligent performance has caused financial loss to the client.[29] A client may have other causes of action against a lawyer, such as for intentional torts,[30] but the legal malpractice action is by far the most important. The client's cause of action is closely akin, in general theory, to the cause of action for professional negligence,[31] which holds a person to a higher standard of care if the person has undertaken work that calls for special skill or knowledge. Malpractice is an important system for providing compensation to persons who have suffered loss because of the carelessness of lawyers. It is also a system that courts can employ to enhance the financial and reputational incentives for lawyers to perform competently. Although the basic doctrinal content of legal malpractice law has remained intact for decades, the number of successful legal malpractice actions has increased significantly within the past ten years.

Several socially undesirable consequences could result if courts expanded lawyer liability infinitely and heedlessly. One reaction of lawyers to heavy malpractice threats might be to practice a kind of self-protective law that would be uneconomic for many clients because marginally increased lawyer competence would have to be purchased at the price of greatly increased legal fees.[32] An adverse legal malpractice judgment imposes a negative professional stigma as well as financial burdens on a lawyer. Thus frequent malpractice awards based on scanty evidence of carelessness, or based on conduct that is common among reasonably careful lawyers, may give

[28] Compare Johnson v. Director of Professional Responsibility, 341 N.W.2d 282 (Minn.1983)(state could not constitutionally proscribe lawyer's truthful advertising that he had been certified by the National Board of Trial Advocacy), with In re Amendments to the Code of Professional Responsibility, ___ Ark. ___, 637 S.W.2d 589 (1982) (lawyers certified by National Board of Trial Advocacy could not advertise fact because not provided for under more limited specialization plan approved by court).

[29] The earliest American case is apparently Stephens v. White, 2 Va. (2 Wash.) 203 (1796).

[30] Barbara A. v. John G., 145 Cal.App.3d 369, 193 Cal. Rptr. 422 (1983)(client's counterclaim for battery and deceit, in lawyer's action for unpaid legal fees, that lawyer had falsely represented that he could not possibly get anyone pregnant).

[31] See generally Prosser and Keeton on the Law of Torts § 32, at 186 n.27 (W.Keeton ed.1984).

[32] A court long ago also argued that overly strict malpractice rules would lead lawyers to refuse to accept doubtful or difficult cases or might drive a lawyer from the profession. Goodman & Mitchell v. Walker, 30 Ala. 482, 495 (1857). Whether the court's prediction is feared or welcomed depends, obviously, on one's perception of the value of the rejected representations and departed lawyers. Another court once uttered the hope that strategically administered legal malpractice damage judgments might drive the incompetent from a harmful career of law practice. See Reilly v. Cavanaugh, 29 Ind. 435, 436 (1868)(stated in context of state constitutional provision that authorized every voter of good moral character to practice law). And legal malpractice or similar tort sanctions may be appropriate for a lawyer who brings groundless litigation. See § 5.6.5.

rise to a justifiable sense of unfairness. A second, theoretically possible kind of unfairness is that under some assumptions a malpractice plaintiff is better off because of the combined chances of recovering in an original action (despite the lawyer's alleged carelessness) and in the legal malpractice action.[33] Because most of the law of legal malpractice is common law, the task has fallen to courts to attempt to determine the points at which further expansion of the rights of clients, in the interest of compensating them for their losses because of the preventable carelessness of their lawyers, will lead to unfair and inefficient imposition of liability upon lawyers.

A lawyer who has not internalized the normal working conditions of the legal profession for the protection and advancement of client interests will still be strongly motivated to conform to those conditions because of the significantly increased threat of legal malpractice recovery. Talk about a "revolution" or "explosion" in legal malpractice perhaps puts the most theatrical garb on the situation,[34] but a steady rise in the number of claims against lawyers,[35] the number and size of legal malpractice insurance settlements and verdicts,[36] and a corresponding rise in the number of insured lawyers and in the size of their legal malpractice premiums all point to greatly increased levels of malpractice recovery for clients and of malpractice exposure for many lawyers.

The Limits of Legal Malpractice as a Remedy

Courts have reflected conflicting attitudes toward legal malpractice. On the one hand, the perhaps natural, if regrettable, favoritism that fellow and sister lawyers on the bench feel toward their colleagues when they are brought before the bar seems to have retarded the development of the tort action in some instances. That has sometimes produced surprising judicial rulings.[37] An action for legal malpractice has also been difficult for frustrated clients to bring because of what some have feared is a conspiracy of silence among most lawyers.[38] Some lawyers feel that it is against the interests and etiquette of the bar for lawyers to assist other lawyers' former clients to bring malpractice suits except in

33 The incremental increase in a plaintiff's chance of recovering may arise in some cases in which the malpractice occurred in litigation. Assume that a plaintiff lost a jury verdict in which the chances of prevailing were 60 percent, but in which the lawyer's carelessness reduced the plaintiff's chances to 40 percent. When the plaintiff's claim is relitigated, as is necessary, in a succeeding malpractice action, the chance of recovering on the original claim may still be 60 percent. Combined with the 40 percent chance of success that attended the first trial, the plaintiff's chance of success has been increased to 76 percent overall, which is intrinsically unwarranted. Nonetheless, because courts cannot ascertain whether such an advantage has accrued in a particular case, they have generally been willing to permit plaintiffs to proceed without examination of the point. See Note, Negligent Litigation and Relief from Judgments: The Case for a Second Chance, 50 So.Cal.L.Rev. 1207 (1977).

34 J.Goulden, The Million Dollar Lawyers 244 (1981); Time Magazine, Jan. 12, 1976, at 53; Scott, Lawyers Who Sue Lawyers, N.Y.Times Magazine, June 26, 1977, at 74 (doubling of malpractice suits in previous five years with large increases in malpractice insurance premiums). For example, the thesis has been advanced that the threat of legal malpractice liability may now be sufficiently great that lawyers will work to change needlessly intricate and anachronistic rules of law in order to remove a possible source of error by lawyers who are not experts in those intricacies. Dukeminier, Cleansing the Stables of Property: A River Found at Last, 65 Iowa L.Rev. 151 (1979).

35 See Nat'l L.J., Mar. 28, 1983, p. 1, col.4 (estimate by malpractice insurer that one in twenty lawyers would be sued for malpractice during coming year); id. at 8, col.1 (reports by malpractice insurers of malpractice insurance claims rising 40 percent in two years for one company, 49 percent higher in 1981 than in 1979 for another); id., Oct. 26, 1981, p. 3, col.1 (California study indicates that missing deadline or representing conflicting interests represent over half of malpractice claims and most of money paid out in settlement).

36 Nat'l L.J., Nov. 2, 1981, p. 2, col.3 (average size of verdict against personal injury lawyer during five-year period was $200,740).

37 Ziegler v. Cray, 148 Minn. 447, 450, 182 N.W. 616, 617 (1921)(in granting motion for directed verdict against client, court properly refused to consider client's testimony that lawyer had given certain advice that would have been erroneous, because lawyer had been too long at the bar and in active practice not to be perfectly familiar with the point).

38 J.Goulden, The Million Dollar Lawyers 243–44 (1981). The reticence of lawyers can lead to dilatory handling of a legal malpractice case that can itself give rise to a legal malpractice claim. E.g., Harvey v. Connor, 85 Ill.App.3d 1061, 41 Ill.Dec. 381, 383, 407 N.E.2d 879, 881 (1980).

the most extreme cases.[39] Such a custom would make it doubly difficult for a client to bring a legal malpractice case because, at a minimum in most cases, a client must be able to retain one lawyer to serve as advocate and another to serve as a necessary expert witness.[40] Moreover, there are many settings in which a legal malpractice remedy, no matter how sensitively administered, is not an apt remedy for a lawyer's incompetence. Many client injuries are not the sort that can be adequately compensated for by money damages, and many clients may be in no position to launch a legal malpractice suit.[41]

Despite the client's evident difficulty in achieving success in a legal malpractice action, courts have often relied on the existence of the legal malpractice remedy as a reason for not extending some other benefit or form of relief to clients. A commonly occurring illustration is in judicial decisions that explain why a lawyer's procedural forfeiture should preclude the client as well. Courts have reassured clients whipped out of the courthouse because of their lawyers' errors that the client can find solace in a malpractice action.[42] Some have argued that lawyers should not be subject to professional discipline because of alleged instances of incompetence for the reason that any injured client can resort to a legal malpractice suit.[43] It has been argued that the availability of legal malpractice protection justifies removing restrictions on quality claims in lawyer advertising.[44] All such claims for the efficacy of the legal malpractice remedy should be assessed in light of the difficulties of obtaining recovery in a malpractice action.

Preventing Legal Malpractice [45]

If legal malpractice claims by clients were always the result of lawyer performance that is technically incompetent, the obvious cure would be for a lawyer to obtain the necessary education or training to gain or restore technical competence. Sometimes technical shortcomings are at the root of incompetence, and in those cases methods of correction such as education in technical matters may solve them. But lawyer ignorance of technical legal information and lawyer blundering with techniques of practice may not be the only, or perhaps the most important, motivating sources of client claims. As are physicians, lawyers are discovering that client complaints frequently arise in part from inattention to client sensitivities during a representation. An example is a lawyer who treads close to

39 The existence of such a custom is obliquely suggested by constant official insistence that such a custom should not exist. E.g., EC 2–28; ABA Formal Op. 144 (1935) (lawyers should not respect custom of refusing to testify or proceed against other lawyers for malpractice or misconduct); Drinker, Canons 28 and 29—An Appraisal, 12 Vand.L.Rev. 779, 781 (1959). The Code is itself partly at fault for failure to clarify whether the rule against contact with a client represented by another lawyer applies to consultation with a client about the competence of the client's present lawyer. See § 11.6.2.

40 On the necessity for expert witness testimony to support the plaintiff's burden of proof in most cases, see § 5.6.2 (expert testimony). The same lawyer cannot serve as both advocate and expert witness because of the general prohibition against combining the advocate-witness roles. See § 7.5.

41 Clients in prison or deported because of a lawyer's negligence are unlikely to bring suit or to be compensated in a meaningful way if they do. A deceased client whose testamentary instructions were ignored or handled incompetently obviously can receive no benefit, and as will be seen, many American jurisdictions continue to prohibit malpractice recovery by frustrated beneficiaries against the negligent will-drafting lawyer. See § 5.6.4.

42 Link v. Wabash R.R.Co., 370 U.S. 626, 633 n.10, 82 S.Ct. 1386, 8 L.Ed.2d 734 (1962); Universal Film Exchanges, Inc. v. Lust, 479 F.2d 573, 577 (4th Cir.1973) (failure of lawyer, because of gross negligence, to assert defense no reason to set aside judgment, but clerk directed to send copy of opinion to negligent lawyer's client); Brown v. E.W. Bliss Co., 72 F.R.D. 198, 200 (D.Md.1976) ("Under the facts here, plaintiffs have a cause of action against their attorney for malpractice. All that plaintiffs need do for a full recovery is to sue their attorney, prove that they had a proper claim and are entitled to damages, and further allege and show that their failure to recover on their claim was due to the negligence of their attorney.").

43 The attitude was common in an earlier day. E.g., In re McKenna, 16 Cal.2d 610, 107 P.2d 258, 259–61 (1940) (Carter, J., dissenting); Note, The Profession of Attorney–Grounds for Suspension, 13 Rocky Mt.L.Rev. 352 (1940).

44 B.Christenson, Lawyers for People of Moderate Means 141 (1970)(laws against fraud and threat of civil liability provide substantial deterrents to false claims in lawyer advertising).

45 See generally J.Smith, Preventing Legal Malpractice (1981); Kindregan, Malpractice and the Lawyer 71–74 (rev.ed.1981).

the line in conflict of interest situations. The frustration and disappointment that a client will naturally feel over a disappointing outcome[46] can, because of a conflict of interest on the part of the lawyer, become client bitterness over perceived treachery. That can easily lead to the client's magnifying honest lawyer errors and mistakes into outright betrayal. Again, the general direction in EC 7–7, that the client should make all critical decisions except with regard to matters that do not substantially affect the merits of a representation, is sometimes ignored by lawyers who operate with supercilious attitudes about client incompetence. Communicating that attitude to clients or neglecting a client's case or failing to maintain effective communications with a client about the progress of a case can, if the outcome is unsatisfactory, lead to legal malpractice claims. The relatively mild injunction in EC 2–23, that lawyers should avoid suits against clients for fees, is underscored emphatically by the ease with which such a client can counterclaim for legal malpractice.

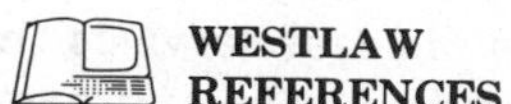
WESTLAW REFERENCES

The Rationale of Legal Malpractice

di malpractice

digest, synopsis ("legal malpractice" /p standard /3 care)

The Limits of Legal Malpractice

45k109 /p malpractice

Preventing Legal Malpractice

"ec 7–7"

§ 5.6.2 *Standards of Lawyer Liability for Malpractice*

General Outline of the Legal Malpractice Tort

The legal malpractice tort that is recognized in all American jurisdictions begins as a special application of the reasonable person standard for conduct liability. Lawyers may also occasionally be found liable to clients under such theories as fraud or breach of contract, but the tort theory is by far the most important theory of recovery. Malpractice law requires that a lawyer exercise in behalf of clients the care, skill, and diligence that is commonly exercised by lawyers practicing in similar situations.[47] If a lawyer fails to exercise the level of care that is commonly observed by other professionals, the lawyer can be required to compensate the injured client for all financial harm that has been proximately caused by the negligent omission or commission.[48] Legal malpractice law can thus be regarded as a special application to lawyers of the general fourfold negligence formula of duty, breach of duty, proximate causation, and damages.[49]

Predicating the Duty of Professional Care on the Client-Lawyer Relationship

In general, but not invariably,[50] the legal malpractice tort must be rested upon a finding of fact that a client-lawyer relationship existed between the plaintiff-client and the defendant-lawyer.[51] The relationship must have existed with respect to the matter that

---

[46] Clients' disappointment at losses in litigation and their psychic need to blame their lawyer rather than their weak case have often been cited by courts as a supposed stimulus to legal malpractice actions. E.g., Wooddy v. Mudd, 258 Md. 234, 265 A.2d 458, 466 (1970).

[47] Whether the situation should be confined to the locality in which the lawyer practices is examined below, as are the questions whether a "specialist" standard of care should apply and whether expert testimony is required.

[48] Restatement (Second) of Torts § 299A (1965). See generally Woodruff v. Tomlin, 593 F.2d 33, 43 (6th Cir. 1979), cert. denied 449 U.S. 888, 101 S.Ct. 246, 66 L.Ed.2d 114 (1980); Smith v. Lewis, 13 Cal.3d 349, 118 Cal.Rptr. 621, 530 P.2d 589 (1975); Kurtenbach v. TeKippe, 260 N.W.2d 53, 56 (Iowa 1977); Hutchinson v. Smith, 417 So. 2d 926, 928 (Miss.1982); Cook, Flanagan & Berst v. Clausing, 73 Wn.2d 393, 428 P.2d 865 (1968).

[49] A leading work on legal malpractice lists only three elements, conflating the last two elements listed here. R.Mallen & V.Levit, Legal Malpractice 206 (2d ed.1981).

[50] See infra §§ 5.6.4, 5.6.5.

[51] Ronningen v. Hertogs, 294 Minn. 7, 199 N.W.2d 420 (1972)(evidence insufficient to establish that lawyer, who was a complete stranger, had undertaken to provide legal services or advice to purported client).

the lawyer handled and at the time of the lawyer's alleged incompetence.[52] The basic relationship can be shown in a number of ways. First is the mine run of cases in which the relationship can be demonstrated from the terms of an express contract of professional employment. But, secondly, the relationship can also be implied.[53] The necessary relationship will be deemed to exist if the malpractice plaintiff sought legal advice or assistance from the lawyer in a serious and substantial matter,[54] the matter rested within the normal range of a lawyer's apparent competence, and the lawyer either gave or undertook to give the advice or assistance that the client sought.[55] The relationship might lack some of the features of an express contract—such as an explicit promise by the lawyer to perform the services that the client sought—but a contract to perform services can nonetheless be implied from their relationship. Third, the relationship can also be proved by the client's reasonable, detrimental reliance on the lawyer's undertaking to handle the matter and the lawyer's failing either to perform the service or to advise the client in a timely fashion that the matter would not be handled.[56] Fourth, a lawyer may assume the responsibility of due care through estoppel, as in the case of officious intermeddling. A lawyer who enters an appearance and incompetently defends against a claim purportedly in behalf of a person who did not hire the lawyer and was never served with process is liable to the "client" for the damages caused.[57]

In all instances, the presence or absence of a fee payment or a promise to pay a fee by the client is not critical. While a fee payment or promise is strong evidence of an express client-lawyer contract, malpractice can be maintained even when it is clear that the services were to be performed for free.[58] Similarly, the scope of the lawyer's duty to act can be expanded gratuitously by the lawyer, such as by undertaking to file a document for a client that originally the client was going to file.[59]

Defining the Duties of Lawyers

The lawyer's alleged breach of duty must be shown through proof by the malpractice plaintiff that the lawyer failed to exercise the skill, apply the knowledge, and exert the diligence that would be brought to bear in such a representation by a lawyer of ordinary competence and diligence. Malpractice is founded on protection of the reasonable expectations of consumers of legal services that their chosen lawyer will possess and exercise at least the competence, skills, and diligence that normally would be possessed and exercised by reasonably competent lawyers. The logic of that rationale requires that nonlawyers who

[52] Shelly v. Hansen, 244 Cal.App.2d 210, 53 Cal.Rptr. 20 (1966)(lawyer first hired to pursue claim, whom client had replaced with another lawyer for same purpose, was not responsible for running of limitation period on plaintiff's claim); Kurtenbach v. TeKippe, 260 N.W.2d 53, 56 (Iowa 1977), and authorities cited.

[53] Connelly v. Wolf, Block, Schorr & Solis-Cohen, 463 F.Supp. 914, 919 (E.D.Pa.1978).

[54] Courts have drawn a line of a sort between instances of casual, friendly, or social conversation, where no liability should arise, and more formal and serious occasions on which the lawyer could reasonably be understood to be applying or undertaking to apply the skills of a lawyer for the benefit of a client. See McGregor v. Wright, 117 Cal.App. 186, 3 P.2d 624 (1931); Blaustein, Liability of Attorney to Client in New York for Negligence, 19 Brooklyn L.Rev. 233, 243 (1953). If the client-lawyer relationship already exists at the time of the conversation, it is reasonable to assume that most communication with the client is formal and serious unless the lawyer takes pains to emphasize that the lawyer's words of advice are tentative and not to be relied on.

[55] Kurtenbach v. TeKippe, 260 N.W.2d 53, 56 (Iowa 1977); DeVaux v. American Home Assur. Co., 387 Mass. 814, 444 N.E.2d 355, 357 (1983); Togstad v. Vesely, Otto, Miller & Keefe, 291 N.W.2d 686 (Minn.1980); George v. Caton, 93 N.M. 370, 600 P.2d 822, 827 (Ct.App.), cert. quashed 93 N.M.172, 598 P.2d 215 (1979).

[56] Cases cited supra n. 55.

[57] In re Woodward v. Sonnesyn, 162 Minn. 397, 409, 203 N.W. 221 (1925). But cf. Zych v. Jones, 84 Ill.App.3d 647, 40 Ill.Dec. 369, 373, 406 N.E.2d 70, 74 (1980)(lawyer's unauthorized entry of appearance could not form basis for duty to continue to defend competently).

[58] Fort Myers Seafood Packers, Inc. v. Steptoe & Johnson, 127 App.D.C. 93, 381 F.2d 261, 262, 18 A.L.R.2d 974 (1967), cert.denied 390 U.S. 946, 88 S.Ct. 1033, 19 L.Ed. 1135 (1970); Glenn v. Haynes, 192 Va. 574, 66 S.E.2d 509 (1951). Early leading cases are Stephens v. White, 2 Va. (2 Wash.) 203 (1796); Donaldson v. Haldave, 7 Cl. & F. 762, 7 Eng.Rep. 1258 (H.L.1840). But cf. McGlone v. Lacy, 288 F.Supp. 662 (D.S.D.1968).

[59] Schwartz v. Greenfield, Stein and Weisinger, 90 Misc.2d 882, 396 N.Y.S.2d 582 (1977).

purport to perform legal services should be held to the same standard of care as lawyers, even if the nonlawyer is incapable of conforming to the commonly observed standards of lawyers.[60]

Necessity of Expert Testimony

The standard of care exacted from lawyers is not measured by the reasonable person standard of general negligence law. Courts instead employ variations on the more stringent reasonable lawyer standard, which is defined by the daily work of actual practitioners.[61] A jury will not be familiar with most of those practices. The plaintiff, therefore, must ordinarily present testimony from an expert witness who is familiar with lawyers' practices and can testify that the defendant-lawyer's performance departed from that of ordinarily competent practitioners.[62] Expert testimony is clearly not required when the undisputed facts establish the lawyer's negligence as a matter of law, as is commonly held when a lawyer fails to file a client's claim or take other required action within the period of the applicable statute of limitations[63] or when a lawyer examining a title overlooks a judgment entered of record against a property owner.[64] Expert testimony is also not required when the lawyer's lack of care, skill, or diligence is so clear that a jury could reasonably determine without the aid of expert testimony that the standard had not been met.[65]

Nature of the Standard of Care

In general, courts have elaborated lawyers' malpractice duties through the common-law process of deciding cases on the basis of the concrete facts of particular situations. Generalizations are rightly suspect, although the following general guide from the 1954 decision in *Hodges v. Carter*[66] has been frequently cited as a general measure of lawyer competence and diligence in both litigation and nonlitigation situations:

> Ordinarily when an attorney engages in the practice of the law and contracts to prosecute an action in behalf of his client, he impliedly repre-

[60] Wright v. Langdon, 274 Ark. 258, 623 S.W.2d 823, 826 (1981)(real estate broker drafting contract for parties to sale of real estate); Biakanja v. Irving, 49 Cal.2d 647, 320 P.2d 16 (1958)(notary public drafting will); Ford v. Guarantee Abstract & Title Co., 220 Kan. 244, 553 P.2d 254 (1976)(preparation of legal document by nonlawyer); Latson v. Eaton, 341 P.2d 247 (Okl.1959); Hecomovich v. Bielson, 10 Wn.App. 563, 518 P.2d 1081 (1974).

[61] Daugherty v. Runner, 581 S.W.2d 12, 18 (Ky.App. 1978).

[62] O'Neil v. Bergan, 452 A.2d 337, 341–42 (D.C.1982), and authorities cited. See generally Annot., 14 A.L.R.4th 170 (1982). At one time, most legal malpractice plaintiffs did not employ expert witnesses. One early case held that such testimony was downright inadmissible because it related to a question of law that was for the court alone. Gambert v. Hart, 44 Cal. 542 (1872). As recently as 1968, authority could be marshaled for the proposition that the majority of states did not require expert testimony. Note, Standard of Care in Legal Malpractice, 43 Ind. L.J. 771, 779 (1968). Today, however, there is little dissent from the propositions in the text about the general necessity of producing expert testimony. It is elementary, of course, that presenting expert testimony usually creates only a jury issue about the applicable standard. E.g., R. Mallen & V. Levit, Legal Malpractice §§ 667–68 (2d ed.1981). On the use of legal texts and articles, see Fall River Savings Bank v. Callahan, 18 Mass.App.Ct. 76, 463 N.E.2d 555, 560–61 (1984), review denied 392 Mass. 1103, 465 N.E.2d 262 (1984).

Quite distinguishable is expert testimony in the trial of lawyer discipline cases, which should not be admissible. E.g., In re Masters, 91 Ill.2d 413, 63 Ill.Dec. 449, 453–454, 438 N.E.2d 187, 191–92 (1982)(question of meaning of lawyer code is question of law on which court receives amicus briefs and opinions of qualified writers in law reviews, but not through expert testimony). But cf. Note, Expert Legal Testimony, 97 Harv.L.Rev. 797 (1984)(arguing for limited admissibility, although recognizing blackletter law excluding it).

[63] Kuehn v. Garcia, 608 F.2d 1143 (8th Cir.1979), cert. denied 445 U.S. 943, 100 S.Ct. 1340, 63 L.Ed.2d 777 (1980); George v. Caton, 93 N.M. 370, 600 P.2d 822, 829 (Ct.App.), certiorari denied 93 N.M. 172, 598 P.2d 215 (1979).

[64] Republic Oil Corp. v. Danziger, 9 Mass.App.Ct. 858, 400 N.E.2d 1315 (1980); St. Pius X House of Retreats v. Diocese of Camden, 88 N.J. 571, 442 A.2d 1052, 1061 (1982). See also, e.g., Lysick v. Walcom, 258 Cal.App.2d 136, 65 Cal.Rptr. 406 (1968)(liability as matter of law for clear conflict of interest representation obviated need for expert testimony).

[65] Joos v. Auto Owners Insur. Co., 94 Mich.App. 419, 288 N.W.2d 433 (1979)(breach of lawyer's duty to disclose good faith settlement offers to client); Hill v. Okay Constr. Co., 312 Minn. 324, 252 N.W.2d 107 (1977); McInnis v. Hyatt Legal Clinics, 10 Ohio St.3d 112, 461 N.E.2d 1295, 1297 (1984)(no need for expert testimony when lawyer disregards explicit instructions of client); Storrs v. Wills, 170 Ga.App. 179, 316 S.E.2d 758, 760 (1984)("except in clear and palpable cases, expert testimony is necessary").

[66] 239 N.C. 517, 80 S.E.2d 144, 145–46 (1954).

sents that (1) he possesses the requisite degree of learning, skill, and ability necessary to the practice of his profession and which others similarly situated ordinarily possess; (2) he will exert his best judgment in the prosecution of the litigation entrusted to him; and (3) he will exercise reasonable and ordinary care and diligence in the use of his skill and in the application of his knowledge to his client's cause.

The definition of the applicable standard of care has largely been a process of comparing the defendant's performance with the parallel performance of other lawyers in similar situations. Occasionally courts will impose absolute standards. If it were shown that most practitioners, and thus the practitioner of ordinary competence, acted unreasonably, no court should permit that to serve as the standard for malpractice. A court should exclude expert testimony if, for example, a lawyer attempted to defend on the ground that all practitioners customarily waited until the eve of trial to prepare or never communicated offers of settlement to their clients or commonly represented conflicting interests without client consent.

Noncomparative Standards

A lawyer's duties can be shaped by other noncomparative standards such as lawyer codes, statutes, and the content of the contract between lawyer and client or specific client instructions. Both the 1969 Code and the 1983 Model Rules are careful to assert that they do not automatically apply in malpractice suits. Courts have not hesitated, however, to apply the mandatory standards of the lawyer codes to lawyers as appropriate measures of required lawyer conduct in malpractice suits.[67] Statutes have also formed the basis for defining the required representational performance of a lawyer.[68] A lawyer may also assume special responsibilities by making explicit promises that go beyond the normally implied duties of a lawyer.[69] A lawyer who has been specifically instructed by a client to perform or not to perform a legal task in a particular and lawful way cannot unilaterally fail to follow that instruction to the client's detriment.[70] By the same token, a client who is fully informed can limit the scope of a lawyer's duties by explicit or implicit instructions.[71]

[67] See § 2.6.1 (judicial application). E.g., Woodruff v. Tomlin, 616 F.2d 924, 936 (6th Cir.) (en banc), cert. denied 449 U.S. 888, 101 S.Ct. 246, 66 L.Ed.2d 114 (1980) ("We recognize that the Code of Professional Responsibility 'does not undertake to define standards for civil liability of lawyers for professional conduct.' . . . Nonetheless, it certainly constitutes some evidence of the standards required of lawyers."); Kirsch v. Duryea, 21 Cal.3d 303, 146 Cal.Rptr. 218, 578 P.2d 935 (1978). See generally Wolfram, The Code of Professional Responsibility as a Measure of Attorney Liability in Civil Litigation, 30 S.C.L. Rev. 281 (1979).

[68] R.Mallen & V.Levit, Legal Malpractice § 110 (2d ed.1981); Brennan v. Reed, Smith, Shaw & McClay, 304 Pa.Super. 399, 450 A.2d 740, 747 (1982); Lucas v. Nesbitt, 653 S.W.2d 883, 886 (Tex.Civ.App.1983)(deceptive trade practices statute).

[69] Broyles v. Brown Engineering Co., 275 Ala. 35, 151 So.2d 767, 771 (1963). Courts are understandably reluctant to hold a lawyer to a glowing prediction of success in litigation, which has proved to be unfounded, as if it amounted to a contractual warranty of success. E.g., Corceller v. Brooks, 347 So.2d 274 (La.App.1977), writ denied 350 So.2d 1223 (La.1977).

[70] Coon v. Ginsberg, 509 P.2d 1293 (Colo.App.1973)(client hired lawyer to set aside judgment, but lawyer, at hearing on merits, entered into stipulation for new judgment); McWhorter, Ltd. v. Irvin, 154 Ga.App. 89, 267 S.E.2d 630, cert. dismissed 246 Ga. 224, 271 S.E.2d 216 (1980)(failing to draft deed with assumption-of-liability clause); Trustees of Schools of Township 42 North v. Schroeder, 2 Ill.App.3d 1009, 278 N.E.2d 431 (1971); Sjobeck v. Leach, 213 Minn. 360, 6 N.W.2d 819 (1942); Carroll v. Rountree, 34 N.C.App. 167, 237 S.E.2d 566 (1977), on rehearing 36 N.C.App. 156, 243 S.E.2d 821 (1978), cert. denied 295 N.C. 549, 248 S.E.2d 785 (1978) (disregard of agreement with client not to give checks to spouse until she had signed separation agreement and agreed to dismiss action against client); McInnis v. Hyatt Legal Clinics, 10 Ohio St.3d 112, 461 N.E.2d 1295 (1984) (publicizing information about pending divorce contrary to client's instructions); Olfe v. Gordon, 93 Wis.2d 173, 286 N.W.2d 573, 577 (1980). Liability in such cases is based on the duty generally imposed on agents either to accede to the material instructions of the principal, attempt to negotiate a change in the instructions with the principal, or withdraw from the relationship if permissible. See Restatement (Second) of Agency § 400 at 235–36 (1958).

[71] Kane, Kane & Kritzer, Inc. v. Altagen, 107 Cal.App. 3d 36, 165 Cal.Rptr. 534 (1980)(pattern of conduct in handling over fifty previous collection matters for client warranted lawyer in only sending demand letter and then awaiting client's further instructions before filing suit and in not warning client of impending bar of limitations); Boyd v. Brett-Major, 449 So.2d 952, 954 (Fla.App. 1984); cf. Southern California Funding, Inc. v. Hutto, 438 So.2d 426, 429 (Fla.App.1983), petition for review denied

Possible Geographic Limitations on the Basis for Comparative Practice Standards

A lawyer's duty under malpractice law is to conform to the commonly prevailing and reasonable standards of practice. A question that consequently must be addressed in legal malpractice law is whether the relevant practitioners with whose performance the fact finder is to compare the defendant-lawyer's are to be drawn from the profession at large,[72] only from the members of the profession practicing in the same jurisdiction,[73] or, most narrowly, only from the members of the profession practicing in the same or a similar community or locality.[74] While talk in cases supports each of those positions, a more satisfactory approach may be to reject a categorical position in favor of an assessment of the facts of various settings. Courts should be alert to the general desirability of uniform standards of practice and the undesirability of permitting backwaters of substandard practice to proliferate. Another factor arguing for uniform standards of practice is that the narrower the permissible frame of reference, the more likely that the plaintiff will be precluded from finding a lawyer who is both willing and competent to testify as the necessary expert witness. As the locale becomes smaller, there is a corresponding decrease in the likelihood that lawyers who interact professionally and socially will be willing to testify against a colleague. On the other hand, the special needs and constraints of practice in small communities with few research facilities and other possibly legitimate bases for different standards must not be ignored.

Mere Errors of Judgment—Lawyer Due Care in the Face of Uncertainty

A common expression in opinions denying that a lawyer's representation amounted to malpractice is that a lawyer is not liable for mere errors of judgment if the lawyer acted in the "good faith" belief that the lawyer's advice and other assistance was in the best interest of the client.[75] The same instinct has impelled English courts. As early as 1767 there were efforts by clients in the Court of King's Bench to hold lawyers liable in damages.[76] But the English courts rejected the notion that a lawyer was liable for anything other than "culpable negligence." Lord Mansfield in one of the first cases stated his concern:[77]

> But every man is liable to error: and I should be very sorry that it should be taken for granted, that an attorney is answerable for every error or mistake.

44 So.2d 265 (Fla.1984) (lawyer had no duty to secure survey of property that was security for client's loan when in over one hundred prior closings with various lawyers client had never obtained a survey).

[72] Storrs v. Wills, 170 Ga.App. 179, 316 S.E.2d 758, 760 (1984)(testimony limited to "Atlanta, Georgia area" not sufficient to create issue of fact). Cf. Walker v. Bangs, 92 Wn.2d 854, 601 P.2d 1279 (1979)(at least with respect to alleged negligence in federal court admiralty action, standard was national and thus lawyer unfamiliar with practice in the specific state in which alleged negligence occurred could testify).

[73] Cook, Flanagan & Berst v. Clausing, 73 Wn.2d 393, 438 P.2d 865, 866 (1968)(standards are same throughout state and do not differ in its various communities). Cf. Woodruff v. Tomlin, 593 F.2d 33, 43 n.10 (6th Cir.1979), on rehearing 616 F.2d 924 (6th Cir.1980), cert. denied 449 U.S. 888, 101 S.Ct. 246, 66 L.Ed.2d 114 (1980); Feil v. Wishek, 193 N.W.2d 218, 225 (N.D.1971).

[74] Newman v. Silver, 553 F.Supp. 485, 495 (S.D.N.Y. 1982), judgment affirmed in part, vacated and remanded in part 713 F.2d 14 (2d. Cir.1983); Ramp v. St. Paul Fire & Marine Ins. Co., 263 La. 774, 269 So.2d 239, 244 (1972); State v. Hawkman, 201 Neb. 605, 271 N.W.2d 46, 47 (1978); Hoyer v. Frazee, 323 Pa.Super. 421, 470 A.2d 990, 993 (1984). Cf. In re Cronin, 133 Vt. 234, 336 A.2d 164, 168 (1975)(customary skill and knowledge that normally prevail at the time and place).

[75] Savings Bank v. Ward, 100 U.S. 195, 198, 25 L.Ed. 621 (1879); Lucas v. Hamm, 56 Cal.2d 583, 591, 15 Cal. Rptr. 821, 825, 364 P.2d 685, 689 (1961); Glenna v. Sullivan, 310 Minn. 162, 245 N.W.2d 869, 872–73 (1976). The language of "good faith" may suggest to a casual reader that the courts are concerned in malpractice cases with lawyers' subjective states of mind and thus that well-intentioned blundering creates no liability. There is no solid indication of such a notion in the cases. Malpractice deals with objective manifestations of competence and due care. It does not seek to know the secrets of lawyers' hearts.

[76] Pitt v. Yalden, 4 Burr. 2060, 98 Eng.Rep. 74 (K.B.1767); Russell v. Palmer, 2 Wils., K.B. 325, 95 Eng. Rep. 837 (K.B.1767).

[77] Pitt v. Yalden, supra, 4 Burr. at 2061, 98 Eng.Rep. at 75. Lord Mansfield was also disposed to be lenient with the defendants, who were "country attornies" and may not have known the law.

Beyond sympathy for human fallibility, courts were also concerned about the complexity of the task that faced lawyers: "God forbid that it should be imagined that an attorney, or a counsel, or even a judge is bound to know all the law." [78]

Similar concerns have had a limited effect on the present shape of legal malpractice law in the United States. In explaining the limits of malpractice liability, courts are wont to say that a lawyer is not required to guarantee a favorable outcome [79]—a proposition that is evident from the formulation of the legal malpractice rule itself. The doctrines of liability without fault, which have been adopted in some areas in the last two decades in cases involving liability for defective products, have not been imported into contracts for services such as those performed by lawyers.[80] Several factors may impinge upon a lawyer. Time may be short and the facts and law both unclear, such as when a lawyer represents a client in an application for a preliminary injunction, and the standard of care must be applied with such constraints in mind.[81]

Forecasting the probable outcome of litigation that may stretch years into the future or stating how a court will decide an unsettled issue of law are the kinds of uncertainties with which a lawyer is often forced to work. But the presence of uncertainty should not create an immunity from malpractice liability. Clients reasonably expect that the lawyer's training and skill makes the lawyer a valuable source of information about probable outcomes in the legal system. A lawyer can act unreasonably in assessing the future just as well as a lawyer can act unreasonably in failing to file a client's claim within the statute of limitations. A client should be entitled to submit to the fact finder the question of malpractice that is raised, for example, by a lawyer's recommendation to accept a small settlement well below the defending party's limits of insurance in a case in which reasonable lawyers would agree that the range of probable recovery was a multiple of the amount received in settlement.[82] The question is one of degree—reasonable advice or other lawyer performance under the circumstances—and should not be treated as one of absolute categories.

Nonetheless, courts must sometimes draw lines between a lawyer's function as adviser about probable future consequences and the function of divinely inspired seer. Failing to measure up to the latter standard is not malpractice. Certainly, a lawyer should not always be held to be able to guess what the law is. A lawyer should be able to accept as a correct interpretation of the law the latest indication from the highest court of the jurisdiction so long as there are no clear indications that that interpretation might change.[83] If a lawyer in litigation is confronted with an adverse ruling by a trial court, the fact that an appellate court later disagrees with the trial court's determination normally should not demonstrate conclusively that the lawyer's decision (if it was a decision for the lawyer alone to make) to abide by the trial court's view of the law was unreasonable.[84] If the state of the law is uncertain, a lawyer's informed judgment about the probable resolu-

[78] Montriou v. Jeffreys, 2 Car. & P. 113, 116, 172 Eng. Rep. 51, 53 (Nisi Prius 1825).

[79] Savings Bank v. Ward, 100 U.S. 195, 198, 25 L.Ed. 621 (1879); Mazer v. Security Ins. Group, 507 F.2d 1338 (3d Cir.1975)(lawyer not liable for legal malpractice for failure to anticipate and take precautionary procedural steps to guard against subsequent ruling of appellate court that was both erroneous and surprising); Kirsch v. Duryea, 21 Cal.3d 303, 146 Cal.Rptr. 218, 222, 578 P.2d 935, 939 (1978); Dean v. Conn, 419 So.2d 148, 150 (Miss. 1982). On the interesting question of the extent of a lawyer's liability when the lawyer makes an explicit warranty of the accuracy of the lawyer's advice or other legal work, see Spivack, Shulman & Goldman v. Foremost Liquor Store, Inc., 124 Ill.App.3d 676, 80 Ill.Dec. 388, 465 N.E.2d 500 (1984).

[80] Blottner, Derrico, Weiss & Hoffman v. Fier, 101 Misc.2d 371, 420 N.Y.S.2d 999 (Civ.Ct.1979).

[81] Parkville Mobile Modular, Inc. v. Fabricant, 73 A.D.2d 595, 422 N.Y.S.2d 710 (1979).

[82] Stafford v. Garrett, 46 Or.App. 781, 613 P.2d 99 (1980).

[83] Martin v. Burns, 102 Ariz. 341, 429 P.2d 660 (1967); Denzer v. Rouse, 48 Wis.2d 528, 180 N.W.2d 521 (1970).

[84] Dillard Smith Constr. Co. v. Greene, 337 So.2d 841 (Fla.App.1976).

tion of relevant legal propositions should not be the basis for a claim of malpractice.[85]

A kind of legal uncertainty can be produced by a lawyer's ignorance of provisions that could be discovered by reasonable research. If the law is that of the lawyer's own jurisdiction, there is little to recommend any other standard of due care but one that requires that a lawyer resort to commonly employed research aids and collections of the law in order to ascertain the state of the law.[86] If such research is conducted or the lawyer is otherwise reasonably aware of the state of the law, a lawyer's advice based on an uncertain state of the law will normally be fully in compliance with the reasonable-practitioner standard.[87] Some decisions deal with a lawyer's obligation to conduct research when dealing with the law of a state in which the lawyer does not practice. Their dominant view is that a lawyer who undertakes legal work involving the law of another jurisdiction is required to conduct appropriate research into that other law.[88] If the lawyer's task is to understand the law of a foreign country's legal system, the possible necessity of obtaining legal assistance from an expert in that legal system must be considered.[89] If a lawyer recommends a specific foreign lawyer to the client to provide legal services under the laws of the other jurisdiction, the original lawyer's duty is limited to exercising due care in selecting the second lawyer,[90] unless the original lawyer also undertakes to supervise the work of the second lawyer.[91]

Preventing the Risk of Uncertainty by Planning

A final point about legal uncertainty is that it can often be avoided by commonly employed and less risky alternative arrangements.[92] While the mysteries of the rule against perpetuities confound the finest minds, there is rarely good reason for a client's transmission of property to fall afoul of the rule so long as a proper savings clause is drafted into the dispositive document.[93] Similarly, while the differences between a special and a general appearance may be legally

[85] Sprague v. Morgan, 185 Cal.App.2d 519, 523, 8 Cal. Rptr. 347 (1960); Meagher v. Kavli, 256 Minn. 54, 61, 97 N.W.2d 370 (1959).

[86] Smith v. Lewis, 13 Cal.3d 349, 360, 118 Cal.Rptr. 621, 530 P.2d 589 (1975)("Even as to doubtful matters, an attorney is expected to perform sufficient research to enable him to make an informed and intelligent judgment on behalf of his client"); Horne v. Peckham, 97 Cal. App.3d 404, 158 Cal.Rptr. 714, 721 (1979); Hill v. Mynatt, 59 S.W. 163, 167 (Tenn.Ch.App.1900). But see Herston v. Shitesell, 348 So.2d 1054 (Ala.1977)(jury question whether lawyer, who prepared document for client unaware of statute that clearly required signature under oath, had adhered to normal and customary role of lawyers in failing to conduct any research).

[87] Davis v. Damrell, 119 Cal.App.3d 883, 174 Cal.Rptr. 257, 259 (1981). Nonetheless, a question of fact may still exist whether a reasonable practitioner would assert a legal position in behalf of a client even if the position is legally doubtful. See Medrano v. Miller, 608 S.W.2d 781, 786 (Tex.Civ.App.1980)(concurring opinion).

[88] Degen v. Steinbrink, 202 App.Div. 477, 195 N.Y.S. 810 (1922), affirmed 236 N.Y. 669 (1923); In re Roel, 3 N.Y.2d 224, 165 N.Y.S.2d 31, 144 N.E.2d 24 (1957), appeal dismissed 355 U.S. 604, 78 S.Ct. 535, 2 L.Ed.2d 524 (1958); Rekeweg v. Federal Mut. Ins. Co., 27 F.R.D. 431 (N.D.Ind. 1961), affirmed 324 F.2d 150 (7th Cir.1963), cert. denied 376 U.S. 943, 84 S.Ct. 798, 11 L.Ed.2d 767 (1964). A nineteenth-century New Jersey court took the extreme, contrary position that a client is bound to know that a lawyer's work that relates to foreign law might well be defective and, in effect, assumes the risk of such defects. Fenaille & Despeaux v. Coudert, 44 N.J.L. 286 (1882).

[89] Janis, The Lawyer's Responsibility for Foreign Law and Foreign Lawyers, 16 Int'l Law. 693 (1982). Cf. EC 6–3.

[90] Wildermann v. Wachtell, 149 Misc. 623, 267 N.Y.S. 840 (1933).

[91] Tormo v. Yormack, 398 F.Supp. 1159 (D.N.J.1975) (dictum).

[92] Courts are occasionally too willing to exonerate a lawyer from malpractice because of legal uncertainty without noticing the fact—possibly because it was not argued—that, in many instances, preventive law approaches can satisfactorily avoid the problem about which the uncertainty has arisen. Thus, in Dillard Smith Construction Co. v. Greene, 337 So.2d 841 (Fla. App.1976), the court held that a lawyer could not be held liable for malpractice. The lawyer had erroneously construed a contractual provision that called for a "written" statement to include a prior exchange of correspondence. But it seems clear that if there was doubt that the exchange of correspondence was what the contract required, a prudent lawyer would insist upon a new writing that indisputably complied with the writing requirement in order to remove the doubt.

[93] But cf. Lucas v. Hamm, 56 Cal.2d 583, 15 Cal.Rptr. 821, 364 P.2d 685 (1961), cert.denied 368 U.S. 987, 82 S.Ct. 603, 7 L.Ed.2d 525 (1962)(particular perpetuities gaffe here, in will that lacked savings clause, was type that even competent lawyers could make).

doubtful, a plaintiff's lawyer who debates the point with an objecting defendant instead of serving the defendant with new and indisputably valid process within the statute of limitations, and thus removing the basis for the objection, commits malpractice.[94] In a planning setting, a lawyer should employ an approach whose legal efficaciousness is doubtful and unsettled only after thorough research and full consultation with a client about the risks involved and possible alternative courses of action that involve materially less risk.[95]

The Barrister Rule

Occasionally a few courts and commentators have attempted to reshape the mere-error-in-judgment point into a broad rule that a lawyer can never be held liable for negligent errors in litigation.[96] Such a rule is sometimes defended by noting the parallel protection for the barrister—the English trial lawyer—who, at least until recently, could not be held liable for malpractice, apparently without regard to the kind of negligence involved.[97] Some of the elements of the rationale that were thought to sustain the traditional Enlish rule are, however, entirely irrelevant in American law, and others are of insufficient strength to support an absolute immunity. The principal support for the immunity regards the inherent uncertainty of trials. Trial work may require split-second decisions in an atmosphere that is heavily charged with emotion, swift movement, and surprise. Many limits are imposed on a lawyer's advocacy to protect the courts and third parties.[98] It is argued that it would be unfair and unworkable to subject a lawyer thus constrained to the risk of an adverse malpractice judgment for mistakes in the midst of such a turbulent and largely uncontrollable scene. Moreover, to the extent that a lawyer can exercise a power of choice, advocacy often involves intuitive choices between tactics of uncertain value. Malpractice liability, it is argued, will deter daring or innovative approaches to the trial of cases.[99]

[94] O'Neill v. Gray, 30 F.2d 776, 780 (2d Cir.1929), cert.denied 279 U.S. 865, 49 S.Ct. 480, 73 L.Ed.2d 1003 (1929); Copeland Lumber Yards, Inc. v. Kincaid, 69 Or. App. 35, 684 P.2d 13, 15 (1984), review denied ___ Or. ___, 688 P.2d 845 (1984) (when adequate legal research would have revealed unsettled state of law on period within which to file foreclosure of client's lien, lawyer's "only exercise of an informed judgment would have been to seek a timely foreclosure."); Sheets v. Letnes, Marshall & Fiedler, 311 N.W.2d 175 (N.D.1981)(lawyer could have filed action within two-year period of limitations that arguably applied, but did not file, and case was lost because of new ruling that two-year statute and not six-year statute of limitations was applicable to wrongful death actions). But cf. Allred v. Rabon, 572 P.2d 979, 981 (Okl.1977)(lawyer's failure to file claim against decedent's estate, which resulted in dismissal of subsequent wrongful death action, not actionable as malpractice because of unsettled law on whether filing claim was necessary).

[95] Horne v. Peckham, 97 Cal.App.3d 404, 158 Cal.Rptr. 714, 721 (1979)("[A]n attorney has a duty to *avoid* involving his client in murky areas of the law if research reveals alternative courses of conduct. At least he should inform his client of uncertainties and let the client make the decision.")(emphasis in original). But cf. Quality Inns Int'l, Inc. v. Booth, Fish, Simpson, Harrison & Hall, 58 N.C.App. 1, 292 S.E.2d 755 (1982)(summary judgment for lawyers proper because nature of grantee's interests in "wrap-around" mortgage grew from uncertain and unsettled area of law).

[96] Stricklan v. Koella, 546 S.W.2d 810 (Tenn.App.1976); Nat'l L.J., Nov. 12, 1979, p. 22, col. 1.

[97] See generally Wade, The Attorney's Liability for Negligence, 12 Vand.L.Rev. 755–56 (1959). The barrister's immunity in England was exhaustively discussed and reaffirmed in Rondel v. Worsley, [1967] 1 All E.Rep. 467 (C.A.), [1967] 3 All E.Rep. 657, 993 (H.L.). Barristers do not deal directly with clients but only through a solicitor. Thus English courts had earlier rejected barrister malpractice liability because of the doctrine that required privity of contract between plaintiff and defendant as a basis for creating a duty of care. That traditional rationale was undercut in Hedley Byrne & Co. v. Heller & Partners, Ltd., [1964] A.C. 465, which held that privity was no longer required for liability in tort. In *Rondel*, the Lords relied instead on several forms of an argument that the English barrister is under a host of obligations toward the court that are inconsistent with a client's interests. Those obligations arguably make the immunity more defensible there. See Pugsley, The Advocate's Duty to the Court, in Fundamental Duties 119 (D.Lasok ed.1980). The *Rondel* rule has subsequently been narrowed. In Saif Ali v. Sidney Mitchell & Co., [1978] 3 Weekly L.Rep. 849 (H.L.)(3–2 decision), the Law Lords held that a barrister could be liable for negligence in giving pretrial advice on whom to sue among several potential defendants, intimating as well that the immunity recognized in *Rondel* was to be narrowly applied. Lord Diplock then claimed that talk about an absolute tort immunity for barristers was "legal folklore." [1978] 3 Weekly L.Rep. at 857.

[98] See generally Chapters Eleven and Twelve.

[99] Thomason, A Plea for Absolute Immunity for Errors in Trial Judgment, 3 Willamette L.J. 369 (1978); King,

But those are insufficient reasons to support a general rule exempting a lawyer from malpractice liability for all trial work regardless of the circumstances.[1] The pressures and special demands of trial practice are merely a circumstance, perhaps an important one in a particular case, for the fact finder to consider along with other evidence in determining whether a lawyer has acted reasonably. Perhaps the client's subsequent complaint can even be dismissed without a hearing if, for example, it only asserts that the lawyer should have chosen one available and commonly employed trial tactic instead of another, similar tactic.[2] The argument that the turbulence of trials makes advocacy errors unpreventable can readily be overblown. A lawyer's negligent failure to interview a known witness, and thus to discover readily available evidence needed to sustain a client's position, or a lawyer's negligent failure to object to clearly inadmissible evidence because of ignorance of generally known evidence rules, can hardly be explained away on the ground of swirling events and uncertain tactics.[3] Moreover, even to the extent that the argument is factually relevant to some claims of error, it is hardly a reason for categorical immunity. It is a reason for holding as a general matter that a lawyer is not responsible for errors of judgment that must be made under stress or for the failure of reasonably deployed tactics.[4]

Standard of Care for Legal Specialists

A lawyer who purports to specialize in an area of the law, or who practices in an area of the law that would be recognized by lawyers of ordinary prudence to require the skills and competence of a legal specialist, should be held to the higher standard of care to which legal specialists practicing in the same area would conform.[5]

WESTLAW REFERENCES

General Outline of the Legal Malpractice Tort

proximat** /3 caus! /p malpractice /3 legalawyer attorney counsel**

Predicating the Duty of Professional Care on the Client-Lawyer Relationship

lawyer attorney counsel** /3 client /10 relationship /p malpractice/4 law legal attorney lawyer

45k105 /p relationship

Necessity of Expert Testimony

45k107

law legal attorney lawyer /2 malpractice /p expert***

Nature of the Standard of Care

hodges /15 80 +5 144

Noncomparative Standards

malpractice /4 law legal lawyer attorney counsel** /p professional /3 responsibility

Possible Geographic Limitations on the Basis for Comparative Practice Standards

45k107 /p standard /p national state community jurisdiction locality

Mere Errors of Judgment—Lawyer Due Care in the Face of Uncertainty

topic(45) /p erro! mistak** /5 judgment /s attorney lawyer counsel**

Legal Malpractice: The Coming Storm, 50 Cal.St.B.J. 362 (1975).

1 See generally Woodruff v. Tomlin, 616 F.2d 924 (6th Cir.1980) (en banc), cert.denied 449 U.S. 888, 101 S.Ct. 246, 66 L.Ed.2d 114 (1980); Basic Food Industries, Inc. v. Grant, 107 Mich.App. 685, 310 N.W.2d 26 (1981).

2 Kirsch v. Duryea, 21 Cal.3d 303, 146 Cal.Rptr. 218, 222, 578 P.2d 935, 939 (1978).

3 Woodruff v. Tomlin, supra 616 F.2d at 934, 937 (failure to follow client's lead to favorable witness); Chockfoot v. Smith, 280 Or. 567, 571 P.2d 1255 (1977) (trial lawyer's failure to discover and present evidence and to appeal is actionable).

4 Woodruff v. Tomlin, 616 F.2d 924, 930 (6th Cir.1980) (en banc), cert.denied 449 U.S. 888, 101 S.Ct. 246, 66 L.Ed. 2d 114 (1980).

5 Weitzel v. Oil Chemical & Atomic Workers, 667 F.2d 785, 787 (9th Cir.1982); Neel v. Magana, 6 Cal.3d 176, 188, 98 Cal.Rptr. 837, 844, 491 P.2d 421, 428 (1971) (dicta) ("If he further specializes within the profession, he must meet the standards of knowledge and skill of such specialists."); Horne v. Peckham, 97 Cal.App.3d 404, 158 Cal. Rptr. 714 (1979) (duty of generalist to refer case to specialist); Rodriquez v. Horton, ___ N.M. ___, 622 P.2d 261 (Ct.App.1980) (worker compensation). See also Blegen v. Superior Court, 125 Cal.App.3d 959, 178 Cal.Rptr. 470 (1981) (lawyer who also possessed medical degree could be found liable, on standard that looks to lawyer's special medical knowledge, for urging client to forego necessary surgery in order to aggravate damages in lawsuit). See generally Schnidman & Salzler, The Legal Malpractice Dilemma: Will New Standards of Care Place Professional Liability Insurance beyond the Reach of the Specialist?, 45 U.Cin.L.Rev. 541 (1976).

Preventing the Risks of Uncertainty by Planning

erro! mistak** /5 judgment /s attorney lawyer counsel** /p uncertain** doubt! unsettl! (not /s settl!) /s law legal jurispruden!

The Barrister Rule

45k112 /p trial litigat! /6 conduct! tactic**

Standard of Care for Legal Specialists

topic(45) /p care skill knowledge standard /s specialist specializ! /s attorney lawyer counsel legal

§ 5.6.3 Proximate Causation and Damages in Legal Malpractice

Malpractice as the Factual and Legal Cause of Loss

A malpractice plaintiff, as is common in negligence actions, must demonstrate that the negligent act of the lawyer was the cause in fact of the plaintiff's loss. There is no requirement that the plaintiff demonstrate that the malpractice was the only cause, so long as there is competent proof that it was a cause that contributed significantly to the plaintiff's loss.[6] Few courts stumble at the preliminary point of recognizing the general requirement of proximate causation in legal malpractice cases. The complication arises in attempting to conceptualize how proximate causation must be proved. In general, the plaintiff must show that but for the lawyer's negligence, the representation would have resulted in a materially different, and more advantageous, outcome.[7] The ways in which clients have suffered losses are as various as the legal rights and defenses that clients have entrusted to their lawyers. Some common patterns do, however, stand out.

Suit-within-a-Suit: The Loss of a Recoverable Claim

Clients who were claimants in the prior suit must prove that they lost a recoverable claim in order to demonstrate proximate causation.[8] The amount of the claim, of course, relates to the quantum of damages. In order to show the loss of a recoverable claim, the malpractice plaintiff must show that if there had been a carefully handled presentation of the original claim, the plaintiff would have prevailed.[9] That requires that the merits of the first suit be tried as part of the second. The only alternative would be to provide for a telescoped assessment of the probable value of the lost claim, such as by means of the testimony of expert witnesses appraising the settlement value of the claim. Courts have not attempted to use such an approach and instead have insisted upon a full rehearsal of the original action, despite the fact that its procedural alignments, and certainly the parties, are sometimes quite different. The absence of the original defendant as a party, as a prominent example, will mean that the plaintiff-client's ability to obtain pretrial discovery

[6] Lysick v. Walcom, 258 Cal.App.2d 136, 65 Cal.Rptr. 406, 418 (1968); Lamb v. Barbour, 188 N.J.Super. 6, 455 A.2d 1122, 1125 (1982); Shealy v. Walters, 273 S.C. 330, 256 S.E.2d 739 (1979); Ward v. Arnold, 52 Wn.2d 581, 328 P.2d 164, 166 (1958); Restatement (Second) of Torts § 433B comment b (1965).

[7] M & S Bldg. Supplies, Inc. v. Keiler, 738 F.2d 467, 472–73 (D.C.Cir.1984)(client's loss not proximate cause as matter of law, where evidence clearly showed that client, of his own volition and without advice of lawyer, had already determined to take step that resulted in loss); Mayo v. Engel, 733 F.2d 807 (11th Cir.1984)(no proximate cause as matter of law where client fired lawyer knowing lawyer had not completed trademark search, and thus could not have relied on lawyer's allegedly negligent advice about status of trademark); Mylar v. Wilkinson, 435 So.2d 1237, 1239 (Ala.1983); Johnson v. Jones, 103 Idaho 702, 652 P.2d 650 (1982)(even if lawyer breached duty to client by failing to disclose conflict of interest in representing both buyer and seller, client cannot recover in absence of proof that disclosure of conflict would have altered course of representation).

[8] Occasionally it is asserted that the loss of a recoverable claim must be proved in addition to the normal elements of negligence. Webb v. Pomeroy, 8 Kan.App.2d 246, 655 P.2d 465, 467–68 (1982) (quoting from David J. Meiselman, Attorney Malpractice: Law and Procedure § 3.5, at 44 (1980)). But the proof that is required is better understood precisely as the required demonstration of proximate causation.

[9] The statement in Better Homes, Inc. v. Rodgers, 195 F.Supp. 93, 97 (N.D.W.Va.1961), that the client must prove that, as a matter of law, the plaintiff would have recovered in the original action, imposes a burden that most courts reject. The plaintiff's burden is simply to present sufficient evidence from which a reasonable fact finder could find that the client would have prevailed in the original action. See generally Note, The Standard of Proof of Causation in Legal Malpractice Cases, 63 Corn.L. Rev. 666, 668–70 (1978).

may be severely limited in the malpractice action.

The plaintiff's burden in proving causation is that of showing that the claim would have been established at the former proceeding.[10] There is no requirement that the plaintiff also carry the burden of disproving every affirmative defense that the original defendant might have asserted; that burden is rightly placed on the defendant-lawyer.[11] There is no sound reason to limit the malpractice tort to cases in which a client's claim was totally defeated. A claimant should also be able to demonstrate that the lawyer's neligence caused a material reduction in the amount that the claimant would have recovered.[12] If the plaintiff was an *appealing party* in the original action, the plaintiff must demonstrate that but for the defendant-lawyer's negligence, the plaintiff would have prevailed on appeal and consequently would have recovered a claim or would have been held harmless from a claim asserted against the plaintiff.[13]

The task facing a malpractice plaintiff, of reconstructing the facts and probable outcome of the underlying action, is often difficult and has often been made even more difficult because of the negligence of the lawyer.[14] Courts have occasionally lessened the client's burden of proof by means of presumptions and inferences. Occasionally courts have shifted to the lawyer the burden of demonstrating that the lawyer's negligence, if established, did not cause the client harm.[15] At least in cases in which the lawyer's negli-

[10] One court has wisely excluded as inadmissible testimony of the judge who presided at the original trial. The judge, as a witness, would have given a kind of firsthand speculation about how one would have decided the case if in fact the lawyer had not been negligent in presenting it. Helmbrecht v. St. Paul Ins. Co., 122 Wis.2d 94, 362 N.W.2d 118, 125 (1985).

[11] Romanian American Interests, Inc. v. Scher, 94 A.D.2d 549, 464 N.Y.S.2d 821, 822–24 (1983), and authorities cited. See also R.Mallen & V.Levit, Legal Malpractice § 657, at 817–18 (2d ed.1981). The cases disagree whether the plaintiff must prove that a favorable judgment against the original defendant would have been collectible and, if so, whether the burden includes raising as well as proving the matter. Compare, e.g., Floro v. Lawton, 187 Cal.App.2d 657, 10 Cal.Rptr. 98 (1960); Pickens, Barns & Abernathy v. Heasley, 328 N.W.2d 524, 526 (Iowa 1983), and cases cited (burden on client to prove collectibility), with, e.g., Wagner v. Tucker, 517 F.Supp. 1248, 1252 (S.D.N.Y.1981)(burden of producing evidence on noncollectibility on lawyer, with burden of persuasion on client). Cf., e.g., Wilder v. Third Distr. Committee of St. Bar, 219 Va. 175, 247 S.E.2d 355, 358 (1978)(lawyer, disciplined for gross neglect of tort client's case, could not successfully argue that he neglected case purposefully because judgment would have been uncollectible: "plaintiffs in damage suits frequently obtain judgment which they know cannot be immediately collected, but with the hope or expectation that at some time in the future their judgment debtor will accumulate or inherit property or otherwise become financially responsible"). The court in Hoppe v. Ranzini, 158 N.J.Super. 158, 385 A.2d 913, 919–20 (1978), called for a full consideration of a large number of factors relating to collectibility (insurance, expectations of plaintiff conveyed to lawyer, whether lawyer had expressed doubt about financial condition of original defendant, statutory life span of judgments, likelihood of discharge of judgment in bankruptcy, defendant's actual economic condition during reasonable period after date of trial, and other factors). The court held that those factors should be considered at a bifurcated proceeding on the question of collectibility that was to be held after, and if, the jury found for the plaintiff-client on other issues of liability.

[12] Winter v. Brown, 365 A.2d 381, 383 (D.C.1976); Schneider v. Richardson, 411 A.2d 656 (Me.1979). But see Schenkel v. Monheit, 266 Pa.Super. 396, 405 A.2d 493 (1979)(trial court properly granted summary judgment when former claimant claimed that lawyer, through negligence, failed to join as an additional defendant a corporate employer whose presence in the case assertedly would have caused a jury to award a much higher recovery). Similarly, there is no reason to require an injured client who was a defendant in the former proceeding to demonstrate that, absent the lawyer's negligence, the client's victory would have been complete. It should be enough if the client demonstates that the negligence caused some additional injury. E.g., Skinner v. Stone, Raskin & Israel, 724 F.2d 264 (2d Cir.1983) (lawyers' alleged negligence caused defendant-client to incur materially increased expenses in losing litigation).

[13] Pusey v. Reed, 258 A.2d 460 (Del.Super.1969); Nelson v. Appalachian Ins. Co., 399 So.2d 711 (La.App.1981) (whether appeal would have resulted in victory is question of law that can be decided by court as matter of law on basis of record in original proceeding); Hyduke v. Grant, 351 N.W.2d 675, 677 (Minn.App.1984); Jablonski v. Higgins, 6 Ohio Misc.2d 8, 453 N.E.2d 1296, 1298–99 (Common Pleas 1983); Bock v. Zittenfield, 66 Or.App. 97, 672 P.2d 1237, 1238 (1983), review denied 677 P.2d 702 (1984).

[14] See generally Note, The Standard of Proof of Causation in Legal Malpractice Cases, 63 Corn.L.Rev. 666 (1978).

[15] Smith v. Lewis, 13 Cal.3d 349, 118 Cal.Rptr. 621, 628–29, 530 P.2d 589, 596–97 n.9, (1975) (jury could infer proximate cause from lawyer's failure to assert element of claim because of lack of research); Jenkins v. St. Paul Fire & Marine Ins. Co., 422 So.2d 1109, 1110 (La.1982) (when lawyer has negligently failed to file suit within

gence has materially impaired the client's ability to demonstrate the loss of a recoverable claim, there is much to be said for shifting to the negligent lawyer the burden of proof on the issue of causation. Similarly, courts have normally not required the client to demonstrate that there is no longer any possible means of recovering from the original party if the lawyer's negligence has caused the loss of the most obvious and common method of pursuing the claim.[16]

The proof of causation is inevitably speculative, a fact that courts sometimes thoughtlessly place at the client's doorstep instead of the negligent lawyer's. Some courts, for example, have been too hasty in barring recovery because of a finding that the client was contributorily negligent if the client tolerated or did not recognize a lawyer's blundering handling of a case[17] or accepted a lawyer's erroneous interpretation of a document that the court was then prepared to call "unambiguous."[18] Yet some courts have curtly dismissed clients who have taken the initiative and attempted to take steps to prevent avoidable consequence on a finding that the effect of the original lawyer's negligence was impossible to identify.[19] The better-reasoned decisions, and apparently the majority of courts, have recognized the client's understandable difficulty in identifying and repairing a lawyer's carelessness. So long as the client-lawyer relationship apparently exists, clients should be able to rely on the good faith and loyalty of their lawyer without incurring the risk of being found contributorily negligent.[20] If the lawyer argues that superseding causes have displaced the lawyer's alleged malpractice, the preferable approach is to require the lawyer to demonstrate that the superseding cause

limitations period, lawyer carries burden of proving that client would not have recovered).

16 Orr v. Waldorf-Astoria Hotel Co., 291 F. 343, 349 (8th Cir.1923)(client could recover against lawyer who negligently failed to collect from maker of note without showing that endorser was not responsible); Winter v. Brown, 365 A.2d 381 (D.C.1976)(plaintiff not required to sue every conceivable codefendant after lawyer's negligence has removed most likely defendants from consideration; lawyer has burden of demonstrating residual value of still-available suit against suggested codefendant); Beeck v. Kapalis, 302 N.W.2d 90, 93–94 (Iowa 1981) (client is not required to file suit against original defendant in order to demonstrate that, in actual fact, original defendant would have asserted plainly available limitations defense). But see, e.g., Blue Ridge Sportcycle Co. v. Schroader, 60 N.C.App. 578, 299 S.E.2d 303 (1983)(malpractice action premature when client had not attempted to obtain cancellation of releases that defendant-lawyer had negligently advised client to sign). The decisions often raise difficult issues of the prematurity of the client's malpractice claim when the client is still attempting to repair the damage done by the lawyer in the original action. E.g., Birnhgolz v. Blake, 399 So.2d 375 (Fla.App.1981); Edelman v. Dowd, 648 S.W.2d 632 (Mo. App.1983)(client's action premature while original action still pending). One solution is to permit the client to file a single action against the original defendant and the allegedly negligent original lawyer. E.g., Commercial Truck & Trailer Sales, Inc. v. McCampbell, 580 S.W.2d 765, 770–71 (Tenn.1979).

17 In the leading case of Theobald v. Byers, 193 Cal. App.2d 147, 13 Cal.Rptr. 864 (1961), the trial court had denied recovery to a plaintiff whose loan turned out to be unsecured, when the lawyer negligently failed to file the security instrument, on the ground that the plaintiff should have asked the lawyer whether filing was necessary or discovered on his own that filing was necessary. The appellate court rejected the trial court's imposition on the client of a duty that the client had retained the lawyer to assume. But cf. Ishmael v. Millington, 241 Cal. App.2d 520, 50 Cal.Rptr. 592, 598 (1966)(jury could find that wife was contributorily negligent in failing independently to check values in husband's list of assets that wife's lawyer negligently failed to verify).

18 Berman v. Rubin, 138 Ga.App. 849, 227 S.E.2d 802 (1976); United Leasing Corp. v. Miller, 60 N.C.App. 40, 298 S.E.2d 409 (1982), review denied 308 N.C. 194, 302 S.E.2d 248 (1983).

19 Douglas v. Parks, 68 N.C.App. 496, 315 S.E.2d 84 (1984), review denied 311 N.C. 754, 321 S.E.2d 131 (1984) (client who accepted settlement of original action precluded by doctrine of election of remedies from maintaining malpractice action). A more sensible result is reached in cases such as Titsworth v. Mondo, 95 Misc.2d 233, 407 N.Y.S.2d 793 (1978)(plaintiff's settlement of original action and release of original tortfeasor no bar to malpractice action).

20 Cicorelli v. Capobianco, 89 A.D.2d 842, 453 N.Y.S.2d 21 (1982), order affirmed 59 N.Y.2d 626, 463 N.Y.S.2d 195, 449 N.E.2d 1273 (1983). See generally Note, Attorney Malpractice: Restricting the Availability of the Client Contributory Negligence Defense, 59 B.U.L.Rev. 950 (1979) (forceful argument for rule that contributory negligence defense should not be allowed if client's asserted negligence was within lawyer's areas of responsibility). Contributory negligence may still be relevant if, for example, the client clearly fails to follow the lawyer's advice or instructions. E.g., Ott v. Smith, 413 So.2d 1129, 1135 (Ala.1982). Client consent to, or ratification of, the lawyer's carelessness should be found only if the lawyer proves that the client's consent was based on full knowledge, a meaningful analysis and assessment of the proposed course of action, and voluntary acquiescence.

has completely and unforeseeably supplanted the lawyer's own negligence.[21]

Former-Suit Defending Parties

Malpractice on the part of the lawyer for a client who was a defending party in a prior suit is shown by demonstrating that the lawyer's unreasonably careless handling of the defense caused the client to lose or caused the judgment against the client to be larger than it would have been if the suit had been competently tried.[22] By the same token, a defendant who suffers an adverse result in a criminal prosecution because of the negligence of his or her defense lawyer is theoretically able to recover for consequential losses.[23] Some courts have followed a more liberal rule on causation, at least in civil cases in which the lawyer's negligence has caused a default judgment to be entered against the client. Once the plaintiff has demonstrated that the defense lawyer negligently failed to assert any defense, the burden shifts to the lawyer to demonstrate that the client would have lost in the underlying action, on the rationale that the client, as defendant in the original action, did not have the burden of proving entitlement to a judgment and should not be re-

[21] Cline v. Watkins, 66 Cal.App.3d 174, 135 Cal.Rptr. 838 (1977); DWL, Inc. v. Foster, 396 So.2d 726, 728 (Fla. App.), review denied 402 So.2d 609 (Fla.1981); Collins v. Greenstein, 61 Hawaii 26, 595 P.2d 275, 284–85 (1979) (sufficient evidence from which jury could find that negligence of second lawyer in attempting to cure problem created by first lawyer's negligence was foreseeable risk and thus not a superseding cause of client's loss); Cohen v. Lipsig, 92 A.D.2d 536, 459 N.Y.S.2d 98 (1983)(client's subsequent settlement of original action does not bar malpractice action where it was compelled because of mistakes of defendant-lawyer). On the question of possible claims by the original lawyer against a successor lawyer, including the client's present lawyer in the legal malpractice action, for contribution or indemnification, compare, e.g., Gibson, Dunn & Crutcher v. Superior Court, 94 Cal.App.3d 347, 156 Cal.Rptr. 326 (1979)(defendant-lawyer could not assert claim against client's legal malpractice lawyer for partial indemnity because of successor lawyer's alleged failure to limit loss); Hughes v. Housley, 599 P.2d 1250, 1254 (Utah 1979)(successor lawyer has no duty to preceding lawyer), with, e.g., Schauer v. Joyce, 54 N.Y.2d 1, 429 N.E.2d 83, 424 N.Y.S.2d 564 (1981)(malpractice defendant-lawyer can implead successor lawyer (who was not client's legal malpractice lawyer) for contribution). See generally Note, Liability among Attorneys in Legal Malpractice Actions, 34 S.C.L.Rev. 733 (1983). See also Vesely, Otto, Miller & Keefe v. Blake, 311 N.W.2d 3, 20 A.L.R.4th 332 (Minn.1981) (defendant-lawyer has no claim for contribution against original defendant against whom lawyer negligently failed to file proper action).

[22] Outboard Marine Corp. v. Liberty Mut. Ins. Co., 536 F.2d 730 (7th Cir.1976); Public Taxi Serv., Inc. v. Barrett, 44 Ill.App.3d 452, 2 Ill.Dec.789, 357 N.E.2d 1232 (1976); Basic Food Industries, Inc. v. Grant, 107 Mich.App. 685, 310 N.W.2d 26 (1981); Garguilo v. Schunk, 58 A.D.2d 683, 395 N.Y.S.2d 751, appeal denied 42 N.Y.2d 808, 398 N.Y.S.2d 1030, 368 N.E.2d 46 (1977). See generally Martin & Beane, Defending the Defender, 38 Ins.Couns.J. 422 (1971).

[23] Malloy v. Sullivan, 387 So.2d 169 (Ala.1980); Martin v. Hall, 20 Cal.App.3d 414, 97 Cal.Rptr. 730, 53 A.L.R.3d 719 (1971). The obstacles in the way of recovery are daunting. See generally Kaus & Mallen, The Misguiding Hand of Counsel—Reflections on "Criminal Malpractice," 21 UCLA L.Rev. 1191 (1974); Comment, Criminal Malpractice: Threshold Barriers to Recovery against Negligent Criminal Counsel, 1981 Duke L.J. 542. In theory the malpractice plaintiff should not have to prove innocence, but only that the outcome of the criminal case would have been materially more advantageous but for the defense lawyer's negligence. The cases rather uniformly disagree. E.g., Walker v. Kruse, 484 F.2d 802, 804 (7th Cir.1973); Bradshaw v. Pardee, 80 Cal.App.3d 1019, 144 Cal.Rptr. 296 (1978); Claudio v. Heller, 119 Misc.2d 432, 463 N.Y.S.2d 155 (1983)(must prove innocence of crime charged). Courts are prompt to hold that the malpractice suit is precluded by collateral estoppel if the lawyer's negligence was raised, unsuccessfully but presumably competently, as a ground for relief from the criminal conviction. E.g., Rastelli v. Sutter, Moffatt, Yannelli & Zerin, 87 A.D.2d 865, 449 N.Y.S.2d 305 (1982), appeal dismissed 57 N.Y.2d 773, 454 N.Y.S.2d 1034, 440 N.E.2d 1344 (1982). But cf. Myers v. Butler, 556 F.2d 398 (8th Cir.1977), cert.denied 434 U.S. 956, 98 S.Ct. 483, 54 L.Ed.2d 314 (1977) (defendant estopped by statements made at time of entry of guilty plea that his plea was not induced by representations of lawyer that client now asserts were negligently made); Hughes v. Malone, 146 Ga.App. 341, 247 S.E.2d 107, 112 (1978). In Ferri v. Ackerman, 444 U.S. 193, 100 S.Ct. 402, 62 L.Ed.2d 355 (1979), the Court held that federal law provided no absolute immunity to a suit against a court-appointed defender by a former criminal defense client. The states divide on the issue under state law. Compare, e.g., Spring v. Constantino, 168 Conn. 563, 362 A.2d 871 (1975), with, e.g., Ferri v. Rossetti, 483 Pa. 327, 396 A.2d 1193, judgment vacated 444 U.S. 987, 100 S.Ct. 516, 62 L.Ed.2d 417 (1979). But in Polk County v. Dodson, 454 U.S. 312, 102 S.Ct. 445, 70 L.Ed.2d 509 (1981), the Court held that a court-appointed lawyer's conduct was not "state action" for the purpose of a civil rights action by a former client, thus effectively closing the doors of the federal courts for most convicted persons, except those who can allege a conspiracy between the defense lawyer and a person, such as a judge or prosecutor, who is a state actor. See Tower v. Glover, 467 U.S. 914, 104 S.Ct. 2820, 81 L.Ed.2d 758 (1984).

quired to shoulder that burden because of the defendant-lawyer's negligence.[24]

Damages

In general, a malpractice plaintiff who succeeds in demonstrating that a lawyer's violation of a duty of care created an unreasonable risk of injury to the client that proximately caused loss is entitled to recover the damages that flowed directly and naturally from the loss.[25] If, for example, the client's tort claim against a defendant was lost because of the lawyer's negligent failure to file a suit on it within the limitations period, the measure of the client's loss is the amount that the client would have been awarded by a jury in the original action.[26] The client is also entitled to recover other economic losses, such as additional legal fees reasonably incurred because of the lawyer's negligence,[27] the amount of fines or similar penalties,[28] and the amount of business losses caused by the lawyer's negligence.[29] If the lawyer's malpractice caused the frustration of an economic benefit that the client sought to achieve by means of the representation, an appropriate measure of damages is either the value of the cost of replacing the expected benefit [30] or the reliance damages incurred by the client in reasonable expectation of receiving the benefit.[31] Recovery of general damages for such alleged injuries as mental distress, injury to reputation, and humiliation is generally permitted only on a showing that the lawyer's acts were willful or wanton.[32] Courts have been similarly reluctant to allow punitive damages unless the lawyer's malpractice was particularly outrageous.[33] Statutes in some jurisdictions

[24] Glidden v. Terranova, 12 Mass.App.Ct. 597, 427 N.E.2d 1169, 1171–72 (1981); Guiffria v. St. Paul Fire & Marine Ins. Co., 293 So.2d 518 (La.App.1974); Godefroy v. Jay, 7 Bing. 413, 131 Eng.Rep. 159 (1831)(Court of Common Pleas). See generally R.Mallen & V.Levit, Legal Malpractice § 657, at 815–16 (2d ed.1981).

[25] On the recovery of nominal damages, see, e.g., Fall River Sav. Bank v. Callahan, 18 Mass.App.Ct. 76, 463 N.E.2d 555, 560, review denied 392 Mass. 1103, 465 N.E.2d 262 (1984).

[26] See generally R.Mallen & V.Levit, Legal Malpractice ch. 11 (2d ed.1981). The plaintiff's recovery should not be reduced by the amount of the contingent fee that the plaintiff is "saved" because it need not be paid to the defendant, the apparent rationale in cases such as McGlone v. Lacey, 288 F.Supp. 662 (D.S.D.1968); and Sitton v. Clements, 257 F.Supp. 63 (E.D.Tenn.1966), affirmed 385 F.2d 869 (6th Cir.1967). The hypothetical saving is probably cancelled out in most cases because the client is required to pay a fee of at least as much to a legal malpractice lawyer. E.g., Duncan v. Lord, 409 F.Supp. 687, 691 (E.D.Pa.1976); Christy v. Saliterman, 288 Minn. 144, 179 N.W.2d 288, 307 (1970).

[27] Ramp v. St. Paul Fire & Marine Ins. Co., 263 La. 774, 269 So.2d 239 (1972); Hill v. Okay Construction Co., 252 N.W.2d 107, 121 (Minn.1977); Gustavson v. O'Brien, 87 Wis.2d 193, 274 N.W.2d 627, 632 (1979). Cf. Jenkins v. St. Paul Fire & Marine Ins. Co., 393 So.2d 851 (La.App. 1981), judgment affirmed 422 So.2d 1109 (1982)(malpractice plaintiff can recover $5000 fee, which plaintiff contracted to pay unconditionally to legal malpractice lawyer, from original, negligent lawyer despite fact that malpractice action was otherwise lost on finding that contributory negligence of client would have barred underlying action; but for lawyer's negligence in failing to file original action within limitations period, client's contingent fee with original lawyer would have permitted trial on merits of underlying claim without fee).

[28] Linck v. Barokas & Martin, 667 P.2d 171 (Alaska 1983)(gift taxes unnecessarily incurred because of allegedly defective tax advice); In re Remsen, 99 Misc.2d 92, 415 N.Y.S.2d 370 (1979)(interest and penalties for late filing of estate tax return).

[29] McInnis v. Hyatt Legal Clinics, 10 Ohio St.3d 112, 461 N.E.2d 1295 (1984)(loss of business customers because of adverse publicity caused by lawyer's unauthorized public release of information).

[30] Myerberg, Sawyer & Rue v. Agee, 51 Md.App. 711, 446 A.2d 69 (1982)(lawyer's negligent title search caused loan to be renegotiated at higher interest rates and caused increased construction costs, attorney fees in suit against adjoining landowner to establish access easement, and capital gains tax paid because client exceeded holding period for carryover of profit on sale of personal residence); Jennings v. Lake, 267 S.C. 677, 230 S.E.2d 903 (1976)(lawyer's negligence in preparing defective deed results in damages including price of strip of land negligently excluded from deed plus cost of survey for transfer of land).

[31] Wartzman v. Hightower Prods., Ltd., 53 Md.App. 656, 456 A.2d 82, 85–87 (1983)(lawyer's negligence in defectively forming corporation entitles client to recover cost of preparing stock offering for flagpole-sitting venture that had to be aborted).

[32] Garris v. Schwartz, 551 F.2d 156 (7th Cir.1977); Quezade v. Hart, 67 Cal.App.3d 754, 136 Cal.Rptr. 815 (1977); Hamilton v. Powell, Goldstein, Frazer & Murphy, 167 Ga.App. 411, 306 S.E.2d 340 (1983), judgment affirmed 252 Ga. 149, 311 S.E.2d 818 (1984). Cf. Betts v. Allstate Ins. Co., 154 Cal.App.3d 688, 201 Cal.Rptr. 528, 546 (1984)(recovery of substantial damages against lawyers hired by insurer for bad faith deception of client-insured, who suffered emotional distress and shock as result of lawyers' "host of ethical/legal improprieties").

[33] Bangert v. Harris, 553 F.Supp. 235, 239 (M.D.Pa. 1982); Bowman v. Doherty, 235 Kan. 870, 686 P.2d 112

provide for trebling damages in cases in which the lawyer's misconduct has been deceitful but are generally not frequently employed.[34]

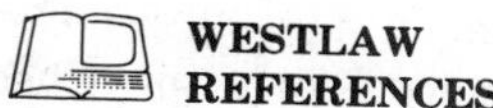

WESTLAW REFERENCES

Malpractice as the Factual and Legal Cause of Loss

proximate** /3 caus! /p lawyer legal attorney counsel** /s malpractice

Suit-within-a-Suit: The Loss of a Recoverable Claim

suit-within-a-suit & malpractice /4 legal law attorney lawyer counsel**

burden /3 proof prov! /p malpractice /4 lawyer attorney counsel** legal

caus! /3 proof prov! /p malpractice /3 lawyer attorney counsel** legal

Former-Suit Defending Parties

criminal prisoner convict! /s malpractice /3 lawyer attorney counsel** legal law

Damages

topic(45) /p malpractice negligen! /4 lawyer attorney counsel** legal law /p damage

45k129(4) /p malpractice negligen!

§ 5.6.4 Lawyer Liability to Nonclients for Negligence

The Loyalty Principle and Limits on Lawyer Liability

As will be seen (§ 5.6.5), lawyers may be liable to nonclients under a variety of theories that are unified by the common factor that the lawyer has acted purposefully in causing harm. Thus a lawyer may be liable to nonclients for fraud, collusion, or other malicious and intentional acts. But there is no general theory like legal malpractice itself under which a lawyer may be held liable for unintentional or merely negligent conduct that proximately causes injury to a nonclient. Under the traditional privity rule, courts have refused to recognize such an action for negligence. As in other areas in which the privity bar to tort recovery has been removed, so here there are indications that the absolute insistence on privity may yield to a more particularized inquiry.

The Traditional Requirement of Privity

A lawyer's common-law liability for negligent harm to a client also extends to those persons who, although not clients,[35] are "in privity" with the lawyer's client. Privity supplies a basis for a negligence claim when, for example, two lawyers make a valid contract to split fees and the forwarding lawyer later sues to recover damages because of the negligence of the second lawyer in failing to prosecute the claim.[36] Privity may also be the term used to describe the basis for liability for negligence when a lawyer voluntarily undertakes to perform legal services for a specific nonclient arising from work done for the lawyer's client.[37] But courts have traditionally not been expansive in defining privity and generally require some close relationship that factually brings the injured party very nearly into the status of a contracting party such as

(1984)(punitive damages properly awarded against lawyer for wanton disregard in failing to obtain continuance, as result of which client was jailed for several hours); Rodriquez v. Horton, 95 N.M. 356, 622 P.2d 261 (Ct.App.1980) (award upheld on facts); Fillion v. Troy, 656 S.W.2d 912 (Tex.Civ.App.1983)(same).

[34] Anderson v. Anderson, ___ Ind. ___, 399 N.E.2d 391, 402–03 (1979); Smith v. Chaffee, 181 Minn. 322, 232 N.W. 515 (1930); Graham v. Strom, ___ Misc. ___, 234 N.Y.S.2d 886 (1962).

[35] The existence of the client-lawyer contract may be express or implied. See §§ 4.2, 5.6.2. E.g., Ward v. Arnold, 52 Wn.2d 581, 328 P.2d 164 (1958)(wife who contacted lawyer to draw will for husband that would leave everything to wife was lawyer's client for purposes of later malpractice action alleging that will was negligently not executed).

[36] Vale v. Heitner, 90 Misc.2d 921, 396 N.Y.S.2d 602 (1977).

[37] Stewart v. Sbarro, 142 N.J.Super. 581, 362 A.2d 581 (1976), certification denied 72 N.J. 459, 371 A.2d 63 (1976); Schwartz v. Greenfield, Stein & Weisinger, 90 Misc.2d 882, 396 N.Y.S.2d 582 (1977)(borrower's lawyer liable to lender when at closing lawyer undertook to file security agreements necessary to create perfected security and failed to do so promptly before client-borrower became bankrupt); Lee v. Nash, 65 Or.App. 538, 671 P.2d 703, 707 (1983), review denied 296 Or. 253, 675 P.2d 491 (1984)(lawyer filed bankruptcy for plaintiff's estranged husband and, without her knowledge or authorization, for plaintiff with false and injurious statements).

a client.[38] Alternatively, there is authority for creating a duty of due care when a lawyer explicitly undertakes a special obligation to protect the interests of a nonclient.[39]

The privity doctrine was first connected to third-party legal malpractice cases by the Supreme Court's 1879 decision in *National Savings Bank v. Ward.*[40] The Court there held that a lawyer who negligently overlooked a prior conveyance in a title search for a client was not liable to a bank that had lent money on the strength of the lawyer's title opinion that the client had good title to the property as security for the loan.[41] The evidence clearly showed that the lawyer did not know the purpose for which his client had obtained his title opinion and that the lawyer was not engaged in any fraud or collusion.[42] Numerous decisions since have repeated the formula that a nonclient may not recover against a lawyer in the absence of privity.[43] Courts have been most insistent that no duty is owed to a nonclient when the plaintiff was an adversary to the lawyer's actual client, either in litigation [44] or in a contractual or negotiation setting.[45]

From Privity to Loyalty and Functional Concerns

In the century since *Ward*, the appeal of the privity rationale has lessened considerably in all areas of tort law. Contemporary decisions are more likely to refuse to impose liability on the grounds that recognizing a duty of care toward a nonclient is inconsistent with the duty of loyalty that a lawyer owes to his or her client and that it may create liability that is unlimited and unknown in its scope.[46] Moreover, third-party actions threaten confidentiality. As in a malpractice action, a third-party action may necessitate disclosure of confidential client information [47] by the defending lawyer. But unlike a client's malpractice action, there is now no warrant for believing that the client has impliedly consented to disclosure by bringing suit.[48]

Explicit exceptions to the privity doctrine began and have continued to be most frequent in the area of negligent will drafting. In the leading case, Biakanja v. Irving,[49] the court rejected the privity requirement and permitted an intended beneficiary of a testator's will to recover the amount of the lost bequest

[38] See generally Annot., 45 A.L.R.3d 1181 (1972).

[39] McEvoy v. Helikson, 277 Or. 781, 562 P.2d 540 (1977) (lawyer who undertook not to surrender passport to client until she had returned child to ex-spouse liable for negligent return of passport, which permitted client to take child to distant country).

[40] 100 U.S. 195, 25 L.Ed. 621 (1880).

[41] For modern cases to the same effect, see, e.g., Calamari v. Grace, 98 A.D.2d 74, 469 N.Y.S.2d 942 (1983); First Municipal Leasing Corp. v. Blankenship, Potts, Aikman, Hagin & Stewart, 648 S.W.2d 410 (Tex.Civ.App. 1983).

[42] 100 U.S. at 197 and 200.

[43] Franke v. Midwestern Okl. Devel. Authority, 428 F.Supp. 719, 726 (W.D.Okl.1976), judgment remanded 619 F.2d 856 (10th Cir.1980); Langeland v. Farmers St. Bank, 319 N.W.2d 26 (Minn.1982); Calamari v. Grace, 98 A.D.2d 74, 469 N.Y.S.2d 942, 945 (1983); Guy v. Liederbach, 501 Pa. 47, 459 A.2d 744 (1983). Courts have been most reluctant to recognize a negligence-based right of recovery when the lawyer's acts, if done intentionally, would not have been tortious. E.g., O'Toole v. Franklin, 279 Or. 513, 569 P.2d 561, 569 (1977)(where lawyer would not be liable for malicious prosecution in absence of "special injury" to client's adversary, claim based on lawyer's negligent maintenance of litigation fails a fortiori).

[44] Allied Fin. Services, Inc. v. Easley, 676 F.2d 422 (10th Cir.1982); Norton v. Hines, 49 Cal.App.3d 917, 123 Cal. Rptr. 237 (1975); Berlin v. Nathan, 64 Ill.App.3d 940, 21 Ill.Dec. 682, 381 N.E.2d 1367 (1978), cert.denied 444 U.S. 828, 100 S.Ct. 53, 62 L.Ed.2d 36 (1979); Strauch v. Gross, 10 Ohio App.3d 303, 462 N.E.2d 433 (1983).

[45] Chalpin v. Brennan, 114 Ariz. 124, 559 P.2d 680 (Ct. App.1976); Hughes v. Gibbs, 282 Ark. 488, 669 S.W.2d 451 (1984); Goodman v. Kennedy, 18 Cal.3d 335, 156 Cal. Rptr. 375, 556 P.2d 737 (1976)(lawyer for sellers of securities not liable to purchasers for alleged negligence in advising seller on validity of sale); Hoffman v. Franklin Cty. Mercantile Bank, 666 S.W.2d 446, 452 (Mo.App. 1984).

[46] Pelham v. Griesheimer, 92 Ill.2d 13, 64 Ill.Dec. 544, 440 N.E.2d 96 (1982); Friedman v. Dozorc, 412 Mich. 1, 312 N.W.2d 585 (1981). The classic statement of those concerns in nonprivity cases is Ultramares Corp. v. Touche, 255 N.Y. 170, 174 N.E. 441 (1931).

[47] Disclosure may be permissible under the self-defense exception to the general requirement of confidentiality. See generally § 6.7.8.

[48] Sullivan v. Chase Investment Services, Inc., 434 F.Supp. 171, 188–89 (N.D.Cal.1977).

[49] 49 Cal.2d 647, 320 P.2d 16 (1958). The California courts had previously applied the traditional privity rule, denying recovery to frustrated beneficiaries of defectively drafted wills. Buckley v. Gray, 110 Cal. 339, 42 P. 900 (1895).

when the will, prepared by the defendant notary public, was denied probate because it lacked the proper attestation. The California court's rationale has been frequently quoted:[50]

> [T]he determination whether in a specific case the defendant will be held liable to a third person not in privity is a matter of policy and involves the balancing of various factors, among which are the extent to which the transaction was intended to affect the plaintiff, the foreseeability of harm to him, the degree of certainty that the plaintiff suffered injury, the closeness of the connection between the defendant's conduct and the injury suffered, the moral blame attached to the defendant's conduct, and the policy of preventing future harm.

The *Biakanja* rationale was soon extended to lawyer will drafters in *Lucas v. Hamm* [51] and has been widely, although not unanimously, followed [52] and in some cases extended [53] in other jurisdictions.

The new concept is expressed in the primary-beneficiary doctrine, which is recognized in a growing minority of jurisdictions. Under it a negligent lawyer will be liable to nonclients if they are specific individuals or a recognized and limited group of individuals whom the client intended to be the primary beneficiary of the lawyer's work.[54] If the client's intent is clear,[55] there is no reason for concern about the compatibility of the lawyer's duty toward both the client and the injured nonclients. If

[50] 49 Cal.2d at 650. Quoted even more frequently is the paraphrase of the *Biakanja* rationale in Lucas v. Hamm, 56 Cal.2d 583, 15 Cal.Rptr. 821, 364 P.2d 685, 687 (1961), cert.denied 368 U.S. 987, 82 S.Ct. 603, 7 L.Ed.2d 525 (1962), which is the same except for the omission of any reference to moral blame.

[51] Supra.

[52] Stowe v. Smith, 184 Conn. 194, 441 A.2d 81 (1981); Needham v. Hamilton, 459 A.2d 1060 (D.C.1983); McAbee v. Edwards, 340 So.2d 1167 (Fla.App.1976); Woodfork v. Sanders, 248 So.2d 419, 425 (La.App.1971), cert.denied 259 La. 759, 252 So.2d 455 (1971). Contra, e.g., St. Mary's Church v. Tomek, 212 Neb. 728, 325 N.W.2d 164 (1982); Victor v. Goldman, 74 Misc.2d 685, 344 N.Y.S.2d 672 (1973), affirmed 43 A.D.2d 1021, 351 N.Y.S.2d 956 (1974); Auric v. Continental Cas. Co., 111 Wis.2d 507, 331 N.W.2d 325 (1983). In Guy v. Liederbach, 501 Pa. 47, 459 A.2d 744 (1983), a divided court rejected the *Bikanja-Lucas* rationale in favor of a purportedly narrower third-party beneficiary rationale based on Restatement (Second) of Contracts § 302 (1979). Kirgan v. Parks, 60 Md.App. 1, 478 A.2d 713 (1984), cert.denied 301 Md. 640, 484 A.2d 274 (1984), intimated that it might follow *Biakanja-Lucas*, but not in a case in which the will was valid and unambiguous on its face.

The California line of will cases was heavily relied on in an English decision that held a solicitor liable for negligent will drafting. Ross v. Caunters, 3 W.L.R. 605 (Chancery 1979). See Kaye, The Liability of Solicitor in Tort, 100 L.Q.Rev. 680 (1984).

[53] Wisdom v. Neal, 568 F.Supp. 4 (D.N.M.1982)(lawyer for estate liable to beneficiaries of estate for negligently making distribution per stirpes rather than per capita); Fickett v. Superior Court, 27 Ariz.App. 793, 558 P.2d 988 (1976)(lawyer for former guardian of incompetent's estate liable to conservator of incompetent for negligently failing to discover guardian's scheme and misappropriation); Ogle v. Fuiten, 102 Ill.2d 356, 80 Ill.Dec. 772, 466 N.E.2d 224 (1984)(lawyer liable for negligent will preparation, even though beneficiaries could not show from face of will that they were intended beneficiaries); Jenkins v. Wheeler, 69 N.C.App. 140, 316 S.E.2d 354 (1984), review denied 311 N.C.758, 321 S.E.2d (1984) (malpractice action maintainable against lawyer for decedent's estate by sole beneficiary for negligent failure to enlarge estate by bringing timely wrongful death action).

[54] Fickett v. Superior Court, 27 Ariz.App. 793, 558 P.2d 988 (1976); Biakanja v. Irving, 49 Cal.2d 647, 320 P.2d 16 (1958); Lucas v. Hamm, 56 Cal.2d 583, 15 Cal.Rptr. 821, 364 P.2d 685 (1961), cert.denied 368 U.S. 987, 82 S.Ct. 603, 7 L.Ed.2d 525 (1962); Licata v. Spector, 26 Conn.Sup. 378, 225 A.2d 28 (1966); Brody v. Ruby, 267 N.W.2d 902, 906 (Iowa 1978); Speedee Oil Change No. 2, Inc. v. National Union Fire Ins. Co., 444 So.2d 1304 (La.App.1984); Clagett v. Dacy, 47 Md.App. 23, 420 A.2d 1285 (1980); Marker v. Greenberg, 313 N.W.2d 4, 5 (Minn.1981); Stewart v. Sbarro, 142 N.J.Super. 581, 362 A.2d 581, 588 (1976), certification denied 72 N.J. 459, 371 A.2d 63 (1976); Insurance Co. v. Holt, 36 N.C.App. 284, 244 S.E.2d 177 (1978); cf. Baer v. Broder, 86 A.D.2d 881, 447 N.Y.S. 2d 538 (1982)(despite absence of privity, widow who had retained lawyer in her capacity as executrix could maintain negligence action against him for malpractice in wrongful death action because they had face-to-face relationship during action). Other decisions seem in transition away from exclusive reliance on privity toward a more functional approach. E.g., Scholler v. Scholler, 10 Ohio St.3d 98, 426 N.E.2d 158 (1984)(while asserting general requirement of privity, discusses importance of conflicting interests between client and nonclients asserting malpractice claim). See generally R.Mallen & R.Levit, Legal Malpractice § 80, at 156–59 (2d ed.1981); Note, Attorney's Liability to Third Parties for Malpractice: The Growing Acceptance of Liability in the Absence of Privity, 21 Washburn L.J. 48, 59 (1981); Comment, Liability of Lawyers to Third Parties for Professional Negligence in Oregon, 60 Ore.L.Rev. 375 (1981).

[55] A client may, of course, inform nonclients that a lawyer is representing the interests of the client and that nonclients should seek their own counsel, and that should have the effect of precluding later suit against the client's lawyer. See Page v. Frazier, 388 Mass. 55, 445 N.E.2d 148 (1983).

the client's intent is known to the lawyer, the lawyer is not subjected to an unknown risk of unlimited liability, but can always refuse to accept the scope of responsibility that the client's intent portends.[56]

The primary-beneficiary doctrine is not a large exception to the privity requirement. It remains true under it that a client involved in adversary proceedings normally does not intend to bestow the benefit of the lawyer's work on an adversary[57] and, depending on the facts, possibly on coparties or nonparties.[58] Despite its narrow breadth, however, the doctrine has been applied in areas that carry the potential for very substantial liability.[59]

Scope of Lawyer Liability in Negligence for Client Wrongdoing

If a lawyer does nothing to further or assist a client in a wrongful act that causes injury to a nonclient, may the nonclient recover from the lawyer on a theory that the lawyer's advice to the client was negligently erroneous or on a theory that the lawyer owed a duty to warn the nonclient of the client's intended injurious act? Traditionally, such cases would be dismissed because of the absence of privity. Today that result would continue to be reached in negligent-advice cases, at least if the lawyer's role was limited to advising and did not extend to active participation in the client's activities.[60] A duty to warn has been recognized with respect to a physician's or psychologist's knowledge that a patient clearly intends serious physical harm to an identified victim who is unaware of the danger.[61] It seems probable that a lawyer's duty to warn would extend no further and perhaps not that far.[62]

[56] See Probert & Hendricks, Lawyer Malpractice: Duty Relationships Beyond Contract, 55 Notre Dame Law. 708, 728 (1980).

[57] Commercial Standard Title Co. v. Superior Court, 92 Cal.App.3d 934, 155 Cal.Rptr. 393 (1979); Doyle v. Schlensky, 120 Ill.App.3d 807, 76 Ill.Dec. 466, 458 N.E.2d 1120 (1983); Page v. Frazier, 388 Mass. 55, 445 N.E.2d 148, 153 (1983). But cf. Silver v. George, 618 P.2d 1157 (Hawaii Ct.App.1980)(lawyer for maker who drew note with usurious rate of interest liable to payee for damages when note was voided because of usury).

[58] In Pelham v. Griesheimer, 92 Ill.2d 13, 64 Ill.Dec. 544, 440 N.E.2d 96, 101 (1982), the court held that in a contested divorce case children were not the intended third-party beneficiaries of their mother's lawyer's work because, on the facts of the case, there were conflicts of interest between the mother and children. See also, e.g., Travelers Ins. Co. v. Breese, 138 Ariz. 508, 675 P.2d 1327, 1332–33 (Ct.App.1983)(lawyer representing injured worker, in action against third party responsibile for injuries, not liable to worker's employer's compensation insurance carrier for alleged negligence in failing to bring third-party action within period of limitations); Marker v. Greenberg, 313 N.W.2d 4, 5 (Minn.1981)(client, father of plaintiff, did not intend son as primary beneficiary of lawyer's services in drafting deeds for father that, because of lawyer's alleged negligence, created taxable joint tenancy rather than tax-free tenancy in common); York v. Stiefel, 99 Ill.2d 312, 76 Ill.Dec. 88, 458 N.E.2d 488 (1983)(wives of corporate officer clients were at most secondary beneficiaries of lawyer's services in preparing documents so they could guarantee corporate debts).

[59] In Bradford Securities Processing Services, Inc. v. Plaza Bank & Trust Co., 653 P.2d 188 (Okl.1982), the court held that a bond counsel who negligently prepared an opinion that vouched for the validity and tax-exempt status of bonds could be liable to purchasers of the bonds who had suffered loss.

[60] Tillamook Cheese & Dairy Ass'n v. Tillamook Cty. Creamery Ass'n, 358 F.2d 115, 118 (9th Cir.1966)(lawyer for corporation not jointly liable for corporation's antitrust violations on theory of negligent advice to corporation that activites complied with law, unless lawyer also participated in making policy decisions for corporation); Invictus Records, Inc. v. American Broadcasting Co., 98 F.R.D. 419, 428 (E.D.Mich.1982). Cf. generally Restatement (Second) of Torts § 772 (1979)(immunity of honest advisers from liability for intentionally advising another not to perform contract or enter into prospective contract). If the lawyer becomes an active participant in an illegal scheme, the lawyer may be just as liable as nonlawyer actors. E.g., Tillamook Cheese & Dairy Ass'n v. Tillamook Cty. Creamery Ass'n, supra; Rowen v. Le Mars Mut. Ins. Co., 282 N.W.2d 639 (Iowa 1979)(lawyer's active participation in scheme by which majority ownership was sold for premium, for which he was rewarded by fees and seat on board of directors).

[61] Tarasoff v. Regents of University of California, 17 Cal.3d 425, 131 Cal.Rptr. 14, 551 P.2d 334 (1976); Hedlund v. Superior Court, 34 Cal.3d 695, 194 Cal.Rptr. 805, 669 P.2d 41 (1983); Durflinger v. Artiles, 234 Kan. 484, 673 P.2d 86 (1983), answer to certified question confirmed 727 F.2d 888 (10th Cir.1984). See generally Merton, Confidentiality and the "Dangerous" Patient: Implications of *Tarasoff* for Psychiatrists and Lawyers, 31 Emory L.J. 263 (1982); Annot., 83 A.L.R.3d 1201 (1978).

[62] Hawkins v. King County, 24 Wn.App. 338, 602 P.2d 361, 366 (1979)(common-law duty of lawyer to volunteer to court, considering pretrial release, information that

WESTLAW REFERENCES

The Loyalty Principle and Limits on Lawyer Liability

45k26

The Traditional Requirement of Privity

privity /s neglligen! malpractice /5 attorney lawyer counsel** legal law

ward /10 100 +4 195 /p malpractice negligen!

From Privity to Loyalty and Functional Concerns

biakanja /p malpractice negligen!

lucas +4 hamm /p malpractice negligen!

Scope of Lawyer Liability in Negligence for Client Wrongdoing

tarasoff /p "duty to warn"

§ 5.6.5 *Intentional Wrongs of Lawyers*

Lawyer Intentional Wrongs to Clients and Nonclients

A lawyer's duty of care toward a client readily translates into a duty not to inflict intentional harm on a client, a duty that is at least as extensive as the duty that tort law generally imposes on nonlawyers. Because of the special fiduciary relationship between lawyer and client, the scope of certain causes of action may in fact be broadened. The scope of the tort duty that lawyers owe to nonclients to avoid intentional infliction of harm is less, however, because of special doctrines of immunity that are designed to facilitate lawyer activity in behalf of clients even at the expense of incurring a greater risk of harm to nonclients. Despite the immunity, a lawyer can incur liability for participating in deliberate wrongs perpetrated by the lawyer or the lawyer's client against a nonclient.

Intentional Wrongs Injurious to Clients

The existence of a cause of action in tort by a client against a lawyer for intentional legal malpractice follows, as night the day, from the existence of a cause of action for negligent malpractice.[63] Thus lawyers (and their partners) have been held liable in damages for converting a client's funds,[64] fraudulently misrepresenting the size of the lawyer's fee,[65] fraudulently misrepresenting the size of a settlement offer in order to induce the client to accept it,[66] falsely representing that the lawyer was actively pursuing a claim,[67] or falsely representing that a small settlement had been achieved in order to disguise the fact that the lawyer negligently failed to file suit.[68]

Lawyer Conversion, Fraud, Misrepresentation [69]

A lawyer is liable in damages to a nonclient for *conversion* if the lawyer misappropriates the nonclient's property,[70] directs a client to

convinces lawyer that client intends to commit crime or inflict injury upon unknowing third party)(dictum).

63 Bangert v. Harris, 553 F.Supp. 235, 237 (M.D.Pa. 1982): "[N]egligent conduct is generally alleged by clients seeking redress for malpractice. It logically follows, however, that if a client alleges intentional actions by an attorney, which actions are not in the client's best interest and which the attorney knows or should know are not, the client may sue the wrongdoer. To argue that negligent conduct has a remedy but that intentional conduct does not is illogical and incorrect."

64 Husted v. McCloud, 450 N.E.2d 491 (Ind.1983). On the question of a lawyer's liability for fraudulent conversion when the lawyer was assertedly mentally incompetent to make a knowingly false representation, see Schumann v. Crofoot, 43 Or.App. 53, 602 P.2d 298 (1979).

65 Stinson v. Feminist Women's Health Center, Inc., 416 So.2d 1183 (Fla.App.1982).

66 Boynton v. Lopez, 473 A.2d 375 (D.C.1984)(intentional, but nonmalicious, misrepresentation).

67 McKinnon v. Tibbetts, 440 A.2d 1028 (Me.1982).

68 O'Callaghan v. Weitzman, 291 Pa.Super. 471, 436 A.2d 212 (1981)(fraudulently inducing client to believe that check received from malpractice insurer of forwardee-lawyer was proceeds of litigation of client's personal injury claim, which in fact had been barred by limitations).

69 For a description of doctrines of fraud and misrepresentation, see § 13.5.7.

70 Carricarte v. State, 384 So.2d 1261 (Fla.), cert.denied 449 U.S. 874, 101 S.Ct. 215, 66 L.Ed.2d 95 (1980)(lawyer's conviction for extortion upheld for threatening development company with stopping project unless hired as lawyer); Giuliani v. Chuck, 1 Hawaii App. 379, 620 P.2d 733, 738 (1980)(tort of intentional harm to property interest under Restatement (Second) of Torts § 871 (1979) by intentional and wrongful refusal to return property deposit); Husted v. McCloud, 450 N.E.2d 491 (Ind.1983)(conversion, by lawyer for estate, of check given him by executor for payment of estate taxes); Reiner v. Kelley, 8 Ohio App.3d 390, 457 N.E.2d 946, 950 (1983) (conversion of funds due real estate brokers).

do so and enjoys the benefit of the conversion,[71] or participates with the client in the conversion.[72] But a lawyer who advises a client about the legality of a course of action is not liable for a conversion [73] or other allegedly wrongful acts of the client [74] if the advice is incorrect so long as the lawyer acted honestly and the lawyer's activities did not pass beyond the "scope of honorable employment" of a lawyer.[75]

Similarly, a lawyer's involvement in *fraud* that injures a nonclient subjects the lawyer to a judgment for damages.[76] "[W]hile an attorney is privileged to give honest advice, even if erroneous, and generally is not responsible for the motives of his clients, admission to the bar does not create a license to act maliciously, fraudulently, or knowingly to tread upon the legal rights of others." [77] Thus a lawyer who knowingly prepares a title opinion that falsely states that the lawyer's client has good title is liable to a lender who relies on the title opinion to make a loan.[78] Fraud by a lawyer can take the form of a concealment of facts that the lawyer was under an obligation to reveal.[79] An obligation of fair dealing with nonclients may be enhanced when a nonclient reasonably reposes trust and confidence in the lawyer. Thus a 50 percent shareholder in a professional corporation was permitted to recover damages against a lawyer who represented the professional corporation and, unknown to the plaintiff, the other 50 percent shareholder.[80] Under the federal securities laws, a lawyer may be liable for knowing [81] involvement in fraudulent sale of stock in a corporation if the lawyer's role is that of

[71] Kahn v. Crames, 92 A.D.2d 634, 459 N.Y.S.2d 941 (1983).

[72] Promovoyage v. Bosco, 557 F.Supp. 1366, 1372 (S.D. N.Y.1983)(lawyer for escrow agent liable for fraud for assuming responsibilities under escrow agreement with no intent to perform and for assisting client-escrow agent to convert funds); Morales v. Field, DeGoff, Huppert & MacGowan, 99 Cal.App.3d 307, 160 Cal.Rptr. 239, 243–44 (1979)(liability to beneficiary of trust for fraudulent concealment of conflict of interest in role of lawyer for trustee); Andrews v. Tuttle-Smith Co., 191 Mass. 461, 78 N.E. 99, 101 (1906)(lawyer actively participated in fraudulent conversion).

[73] Cf. Shaffer v. Bond, 49 U.S.L.Wk. 3006 (Okl.App. 1979), cert.denied 449 U.S. 828, 101 S.Ct. 92, 66 L.Ed.2d 31 (1980)(lawyer who advised client that she would not violate law by taking child from custody of ex-husband, who had been awarded custody by decree subsequently declared void).

[74] Yoggerst v. Stewart, 623 F.2d 35, 38 (7th Cir. 1980)(lawyer not liable to nonclient injured by client's tortious act about which lawyer gave good faith legal advice); Worldwide Marine Trading Co. v. Marine Transp. Serv., Inc., 527 F.Supp. 581 (E.D.Pa.1981)(in order to be liable for malpractice, fraud, or other tortious acts of client, lawyer would have to be shown to have been active participant or stakeholder in conspiracy or in some other way to have gone beyond the role of adviser).

[75] Newburger, Loeb & Co. v. Gross, 563 F.2d 1057, 1080 (2d Cir.1977), cert.denied 434 U.S. 1035, 98 S.Ct. 769, 54 L.Ed.2d 782 (1978); Steinberg v. Guild, 22 A.D.2d 776, 254 N.Y.S.2d 7, 8–9 (1964).

[76] Newburger, Loeb & Co. v. Gross, 563 F.2d 1057 (2d Cir.1977), cert.denied 434 U.S. 1035, 98 S.Ct. 769, 54 L.Ed. 2d 782 (1978); Arnold v. Weck, 388 So.2d 269 (Fla.App. 1980), review denied 399 So.2d 1140 (1981)(lawyer's fraudulent misrepresentation of authority to settle action, which caused opposing party to dismiss pending action and take other steps in reliance on settlement that lawyer's client later repudiated because of lawyer's lack of authority); Steinberg v. Guild, 22 A.D.2d 776, 254 N.Y.S.2d 7 (1964); Singer v. Whitman & Ransom, 83 A.D.2d 862, 442 N.Y.S. 26 (1981)(allegations that lawyers for corporation wrongly and intentionally refused to issue opinion letter that would permit plaintiff to sell restricted stock); Cronin v. Scott, 78 A.D.2d 745, 432 N.Y.S.2d 656, 658 (1980), affirmed 52 N.Y.2d 999, 438 N.Y.S.2d 80, 419 N.E.2d 1079 (1981)(dictum). A lawyer may also be subject to criminal sanctions for fraud. United States v. Benjamin, 328 F.2d 854 (2d Cir.), cert.denied 377 U.S 953, 84 S.Ct. 1631, 12 L.Ed.2d 497 (1964).

[77] Newburger, Loeb & Co. v. Gross, supra, 563 F.2d at 1080.

[78] Capital Bank & Trust Co. v. Core, 343 So.2d 284 (La. App.1977), cert.denied 345 So.2d 504 (1977).

[79] Hennigan v. Harris County, 593 S.W.2d 380 (Tex.Civ. App.1979)(lawyer, who failed to disclose that his action against constable for refusing to execute judgment had become moot when judgment debtor paid full amount of judgment, committed fraudulent concealment, causing damages to constable measured by costs of defending lawyer's action).

[80] Fassihi v. Sommers, Schwartz, Silver, Schwartz & Tyler, 107 Mich.App. 509, 309 N.W.2d 645 (1981). See also Newburger, Loeb & Co. v. Gross, 563 F.2d 1057, 1079–80 (2d Cir.1977), cert.denied 434 U.S. 1035, 98 S.Ct. 769, 54 L.Ed.2d 782 (1978)(abusive treatment of client's partner); Rowen v. Le Mars Mut. Ins. Co., 282 N.W.2d 639, 654–56 (Iowa 1979)(participation with others in illegal sale of control in corporation to injury of minority shareholders).

[81] Stokes v. Lokken, 644 F.2d 779 (8th Cir.1981)(lawyer's liability can be established only by demonstrating scienter standard for statutory antifraud liability, which may consist of reckless reliance on information provided by client)(dictum).

advising on a stock offering,[82] acting as a principal in the transaction,[83] or serving as an officer or director.[84]

Misrepresentation is a species of fraud involving a knowingly false statement of material fact made to induce detrimental reliance in another. Thus a lawyer who misrepresents the terms of a contract to another contracting party is liable to that party.[85] A misrepresentation may be actionable if the lawyer makes a positive assertion recklessly, without any knowledge of its truth, and the statement is in fact false.[86] The caselaw, which is sparse, is divided on the question whether a nonclient may recover damages from a lawyer for negligent misrepresentation.[87]

Wrongful Interference with Contractual Advantages

In the nature of things, lawyers are always around deals. They represent either side as well as banks and other financing interests. They advise on contract, securities, tax, property, and the multiple other aspects of a commercial transaction. They are present at the creation and sometimes at the demise of consensual arrangements. Most American jurisdictions recognize an action for tortious interference with an advantageous contractual relationship.[88] But courts also hold that lawyers, in giving advice to their clients, may advise a client not to perform an agreement and that if the advice is not given for the purpose of maliciously injuring the promisee, it is not actionable.[89] The lawyer does not incur liability if the lawyer's client terminates a contract on the strength of the lawyer's erroneous opinion.[90] But if the lawyer intentionally procures the breach without justification[91] or for the purpose of causing harm,[92] the lawyer may be liable.

[82] Cronin v. Midwestern Okl. Development Authority, 619 F.2d 856 (10th Cir.1980); SEC v. National Student Marketing Corp., 360 F.Supp. 284 (D.D.C.1973); Hagert v. Glickman, 520 F.Supp. 1028 (D.Minn.1981)(although not liable as aiders and abettors, lawyers who participated in preparation of registration and prospectus containing materially false statements may be liable as principals).

[83] Junker v. Crory, 650 F.2d 1349 (5th Cir.1981)(lawyer functioned as seller of stock within meaning of securities laws through active participation in negotiations leading to sale); United States v. Rubinson, 543 F.2d 951 (2d Cir.), cert.denied 429 U.S. 850, 97 S.Ct. 139, 50 L.Ed.2d 124 (1976)(conviction of lawyer as principal for involvement in conspiracy with clients to violate securities laws). Cf. Croy v. Campbell, 624 F.2d 709 (5th Cir.1980)(lawyer not liable to stock purchasers as "seller" when lawyer's role limited to advising purchasers on tax consequences).

[84] Escott v. Barchris Construction Corp., 283 F.Supp. 643 (S.D.N.Y.1968). See generally Knepper, Liability of Lawyer-Directors, 40 Ohio St.L.J. 341 (1979).

[85] Wilbourn v. Mostek Corp., 537 F.Supp. 302 (D.Colo. 1982).

[86] Ames Bank v. Hahn, 205 Neb. 353, 287 N.W.2d 687, 689 (1980)(dictum).

[87] Compare Holland v. Lawless, 95 N.M. 490, 623 P.2d 1004 (Ct.App.1981)(lawyer for decedent's estate may be liable for negligent misrepresentation to purchaser of land from estate), with Bell v. Manning, 613 S.W.2d 335, 339 (Tex.Civ.App.1981)(negligent misrepresentation by lawyer to party with whom lawyer's client was dealing at arm's length not actionable because threat of liability would introduce undesirable self-protective reservations into lawyer's counseling role). Cf. Chalpin v. Brennan, 114 Ariz. 124, 559 P.2d 680 (Ct.App.1977)(lawyer who drafted contract containing misrepresentation of material fact could not be held liable in negligence to third-party purchaser); Goodman v. Kennedy, 18 Cal.3d 335, 134 Cal. Rptr. 375, 556 P.2d 737 (1976)(lawyer not liable in negligence for erroneous statement about exempt nature of sale of stock by client to plaintiff-nonclient); Portman v. George McDonald Law Corp., 99 Cal.App.3d 988, 160 Cal. Rptr. 505 (1979)(negligent representation that client (then insolvent) should not be required to file appeal bond because he was "sound as a dollar" not actionable because of absolute statutory privilege for statements made in course of judicial proceeding). See generally Restatement (Second) of Torts § 552 (1977); § 13.5.7.

[88] See generally Prosser and Keeton on Torts §§ 129 (contractual relations), 130 (prospective advantage)(1984).

[89] Kakadelis v. De Fabrities, 191 Conn. 276, 464 A.2d 57 (1983). See generally Restatement (Second) of Torts § 772 (1979)(immunity for truthful information or "honest advice within the scope of a request for the advice").

[90] Schott v. Glover, 109 Ill.App.3d 230, 64 Ill.Dec. 824, 827, 444 N.E.2d 376, 379 (1982); D & C Textile Corp. v. Rudin, 41 Misc.2d 916, 246 N.Y.S.2d 813 (1964).

[91] Furlev Sales & Assoc., Inc. v. North American Auto. Warehouse, Inc., 325 N.W.2d 20 (Minn.1982)(lawyer who advised client business owners to breach contract to sell business to key employees in order to purchase business himself). Cf. Livoti v. Elston, 52 A.D.2d 444, 384 N.Y.S.2d 484 (1976)(3–2 decision)(lawyer who induced client to repudiate contract to sell land, which was voidable because not in writing, not liable to intended vendee, although lawyer advised repudiation in order to purchase land himself).

[92] Arlington Heights Nat'l Bank v. Arlington Heights Fed. Savings & Loan Ass'n, 37 Ill.2d 546, 229 N.E.2d 514 (1967); Riverside Fin. Corp. v. Coniglio Builders, Inc., 73 A.D.2d 1039, 425 N.Y.S.2d 433 (1980).

Lawyer Defamation and the Representational Immunity

Lawyers in the course of representing clients must often deal with contentious, even combative, nonclients and with murky facts. If the law of defamation were strictly applied, much of the unpleasant statements about others that representation of a client involves would create such a high risk of liability for defamation damages that a lawyer's desirable advocacy for a client would be inappropriately chilled. Thus the social interest in encouraging zealous advocacy in a client's interest argues for a broad protection for statements made in that context.[93] But the privileged status of a lawyer's role should not provide a blanket authorization to hurl verbal assaults and inflict reputational harms without regard to the nature of the circumstances or the possible aid that the statement might lend to a client's cause. The tension between protecting the advocate's role, and deterring defamations and compensating the victims of those that do occur has been resolved in favor of doctrines that provide a special privilege for advocacy and participation in litigation.

Generally a lawyer may be protected by an immunity from liability for defamatory statements made in the course of a representation under one, or possibly both, of two privileges.[94] Lawyers—and all other participants in the process, such as judges, parties, and witnesses [95]—have an absolute privilege to utter defamatory statements in connection with judicial proceedings if the statements bear some relation to the proceedings.[96] Second, lawyers along with others similarly situated are protected by a conditional privilege to make statements that are intended to protect the interests of others. Being conditional, the interest-protection privilege can be established only on a showing that the statement was made with a reasonable belief that it was well founded.

Absolute Privilege for Judicial Proceedings. The absolute privilege consists of two elements: the statement must be made in the course of a judicial proceeding and the statement's utterance must bear some relationship to the proceeding. Courts have generally been generous, sometimes disturbingly so, in applying the immunity despite the fact that because the privilege is absolute,[97] it protects

93 The privilege against defamation is often placed on the ground of encouraging resort to litigation and zealous advocacy to protect clients' interests. E.g., McCarthy v. Yempuku, 678 P.2d 11, 14 (Hawaii App.1984); Restatement (Second) of Torts § 586 comment a (1977)("The privilege . . . is based upon a public policy of securing to attorneys as officers of the court the utmost freedom in their efforts to secure justice for their clients."). Some courts also invoke aphorisms that seem to embrace social Darwinism, or the lex talonis, in defense of the immunity. E.g., Star v. Simonelli, 76 A.D.2d 861, 428 N.Y.S.2d 617, 618 (1980) ("[W]e believe it would be pollyannaish to ignore that fact of life which was well put more than a century ago by Carlyle when he wrote: 'No man lives without jostling and being jostled; in all the ways he has to elbow himself through the world, giving and receiving offenses.' ").

94 The representational immunity is cousin to the doctrine, recognized in many jurisdictions, that a lawyer is immune from the service of process while attending court for a client. Lamb v. Schmitt, 285 U.S. 222, 52 S.Ct. 317, 76 L.Ed. 720 (1932). Illinois has gone a step further, providing by statute for an immunity from arrest in the case of a lawyer going to or coming from court. See People v. Holmes, 90 Ill.App.3d 606, 46 Ill.Dec. 106, 413 N.E.2d 546 (1980)(traffic citation).

95 Restatement (Second) of Torts §§ 585 (judges), 585 (parties in civil cases and both prosecuting witness and defendant in criminal cases), 588 (witnesses), 589 (jurors, but only with respect to statements about another juror) (1977).

96 See generally Restatement (Second) of Torts § 586 (1977).

97 The absolute nature of the privilege has to do with the fact that it applies despite the bad faith of the party it protects. The privilege is not properly called qualified simply because a claimant must qualify for the privilege by demonstrating that it applies. But see Chacharis v. Fadell, 438 N.E.2d 1032, 1033 (Ind.App.1982).

Louisiana recognizes only a qualified privilege, which can be defeated on a showing that the lawyer made the defamatory utterances without probable cause to believe they were true. E.g., Wattigny v. Lambert, 408 So.2d 1126 (La.App.), writ denied 410 So.2d 760 (La.1981), cert. denied 457 U.S. 1132, 102 S.Ct. 2957, 73 L.Ed.2d 1349 (1982). The privilege is qualified even with respect to statements made in documents submitted in the course of litigation. E.g., Freeman v. Cooper, 414 So.2d 355 (La. 1982). Georgia provides by statute that, except for statements made by a lawyer in pleadings to a court, the privilege is qualified and a lawyer can be held liable for defamatory statements made with malicious intent. Ga. Code Ann. § 105–710 (1968).

false and defamatory statements even if the lawyer made the statements maliciously, with knowledge of the falsity and with the intent to inflict harm,[98] or if they were made in the course of sham litigation.[99] The only remedies for false statements are to subject the lawyer to professional discipline and to strike scandalous material from the record.[1] Courts have even held, if with regret, that criminal utterances, such as forgeries [2] or perjury [3] and violations of a lawyer code,[4] are covered by the immunity.

In fact, in the hands of some courts, the privilege has been reshaped into something very much like a privilege for a lawyer to be bumptious and unrestrained in all matters vaguely related to litigation and regardless of whether the communication is calculated to advance or to retard justice or the proceeding. The statement need not even be in the client's interests, according to a dubious California decision that applied the absolute immunity to preclude a client from recovering reputational damages from his own lawyer.[5] Courts have employed the privilege beyond defamation and have held that suits are barred by the same immunity if they are based on negligent misrepresentation,[6] invasion of privacy,[7] or intentional infliction of emotional distress.[8]

The requirement that the statement be made in the course of a judicial proceeding has been applied loosely.[9] A communication may be immune even if it is made outside the courthouse and involves no function of the court or its officers.[10] In some modern cases the judicial-proceeding requirement means only that the statement be made while litigation is pending or contemplated [11] or while the speaker is reflecting upon it in its afterglow.[12] The audience must also be composed of persons more or less directly interested in the proceeding.[13] Courts have held that state-

[98] See Restatement (Second) of Torts § 586 comment a (1977).

[99] Nix v. Sawyer, 466 A.2d 407, 411 (Del.Super.1983). Cf. Restatement (Second) of Torts § 586 comment e (1977) (privilege applies to proposed judicial proceeding "only when the communication has some relation to a proceeding that is contemplated in good faith and under serious consideration. The bare possibility that the proceeding might be instituted is not to be used as a cloak to provide immunity for defamation when the possibility is not seriously considered.").

[1] McNeal v. Allen, 95 Wn.2d 265, 621 P.2d 1285, 1287 (1980).

[2] Pettitt v. Levy, 28 Cal.App.3d 484, 104 Cal.Rptr. 650 (1972).

[3] Kachig v. Boothe, 22 Cal.App.3d 626, 99 Cal.Rptr. 393 (1971); Eikelberger v. Tolotti, 96 Nev. 525, 611 P.2d 1086, 1090 (1980).

[4] O'Neil v. Cunningham, 118 Cal.App.3d 466, 173 Cal. Rptr. 422, 428 (1981).

[5] O'Neil v. Cunningham, 118 Cal.App.3d 466, 173 Cal. Rptr. 422 (1981)(defamatory letter by medical malpractice defendant's own lawyer (retained by malpractice insurer) commenting on lack of medical qualifications and sent to client's hospital that then refused to renew his contract). *O'Neil* and other California cases involve a state statute (West Ann.Cal.Civ.Code § 47, subd.2 (1982)) that is quite broad and perhaps extends further than the common-law privilege.

[6] Portman v. George McDonald Law Corp., 99 Cal.App. 3d 988, 160 Cal.Rptr. 505, 507 (1979).

[7] Lee v. Nash, 65 Or.App. 538, 671 P.2d 703, 706 (1983), review denied 296 Or. 253, 675 P.2d 491 (1984)("false light" claim).

[8] Anderson v. Rossman & Baumberger, 440 So.2d 591, 593 (Fla.App.1983), review denied 450 So.2d 485 (Fla.1984).

[9] A common expansion is to hold that complaints to, or other statements made in the course of a proceeding in a lawyer disciplinary agency are absolutely privileged. E.g., Allen v. Ali, 105 Ill.App.3d 887, 61 Ill.Dec. 678, 435 N.E.2d 167 (1982).

[10] Costa v. Superior Court, 157 Cal.App.3d 673, 204 Cal. Rptr 1, 3–4 (1984)(letter to members of interested fraternal organization explaining writer's position in other litigation and soliciting reactions).

[11] Jones v. RCA Music Service, 530 F.Supp. 767 (E.D. Pa.1982)(statement by creditor's lawyer to creditor, that debtor was in default, absolutely privileged because in connection with advice that creditor could sue debtor); Restatement (Second) of Torts § 586 (1977)(privilege applies to "a proposed judicial proceeding, or in the institution of, or during the course and as a part of a judicial proceeding").

[12] Cummings v. Kirby, 216 Neb. 314, 343 N.W.2d 747 (1984)(calling client's son "crook" in course of discussion whether to move for new trial in otherwise completed litigation).

[13] Asay v. Hallmark Cards, Inc., 594 F.2d 692 (8th Cir. 1979)(privilege does not extend to disseminating copy of complaint to news service); Sriberg v. Raymond, 544 F.2d 15 (1st Cir.1976)(no privilege for pretrial communication to party who, at most, would have been disinterested stakeholder in litigation with no interest in merits); Green Acres Trust v. London, 141 Ariz. 609, 688 P.2d 617 (1984)(no privilege for statements by lawyer made at press conference called to discuss proposed class action); Kennedy v. Cannon, 229 Md. 92, 182 A.2d 54, 58 (1962) (communication with newspaper).

ments are privileged if they are made in the course of attempts to negotiate a settlement of a judicial proceeding that the speaker contemplates or is threatening; [14] while the speaker is conducting pretrial factual investigation; [15] or when the speaker is interviewing a witness before trial.[16] But statements to a stranger to the litigation that are not related to fact gathering or the like are not covered.[17] Other jurisdictions put more careful limits on the privilege and do not, for example, apply it to pretrial statements out of court.[18]

The requirement of relationship to the proceedings is applied liberally. Courts have phrased the matter variously, but always broadly, and have held that a statement will qualify if it may possibly be pertinent [19] or is reasonably germane.[20] Most agree that all doubts are to be resolved in favor of relevancy.[21]

Conditional Privilege for Interest-Protecting Communications. Courts have recognized a conditional privilege that protects lawyers against liability for defamatory statements even in situations in which a lawyer does not enjoy an absolute privilege. A lawyer is protected by the conditional privilege if he or she makes a defamatory statement that the lawyer reasonably believes to be true, under circumstances in which the lawyer can reasonably believe that the statement is necessary to protect the interests of a client.[22] Because the privilege is only conditional, it is given a narrower and more technical application and can be defeated on a showing that the statement was made maliciously or without a reasonable ground for believing it to be true.[23]

Lawyer Liability for Wrongful Use of the Judicial Process

Most American courts narrowly confine the reach of liability rules that might provide damages to an injured party against a lawyer because of the lawyer's knowing involvement

14 Blanchette v. Cataldo, 734 F.2d 869, 877 (1st Cir. 1984); Hagendorf v. Brown, 699 F.2d 478 (9th Cir.), opinion amended 707 F.2d 1018 (9th Cir.1983); Penny v. Sherman, 101 N.M. 517, 684 P.2d 1182 (Ct.App.1984), cert.denied 101 N.M. 555, 685 P.2d 963 (1984); Zirn v. Cullom, 187 Misc. 241, 63 N.Y.S.2d 439, 440–41 (1946); Chard v. Galton, 277 Or. 109, 559 P.2d 1280 (1977).

15 Russell v. Clark, 620 S.W.2d 865 (Tex.Civ.App.1981).

16 Adams v. Peck, 43 Md.App. 168, 403 A.2d 840 (1979), affirmed 288 Md. 1, 415 A.2d 292 (1980).

17 Williams v. Burns, 540 F.Supp. 1243, 1248 (D.Colo. 1982)(statements made while negotiating contract under shadow of bankruptcy proceedings).

18 Pledger v. Burnup & Sims, Inc., 432 So.2d 1323, 1327 (Fla.App.1983), review denied 446 So.2d 99 (1984)(circulation of draft complaint as part of settlement negotiations subject only to qualified, not absolute, privilege); Converters Equipment Corp. v. Condes Corp., 80 Wis.2d 257, 258 N.W.2d 712 (1977)(letter written to customers of competitor, warning of possible patent infringements, related to matters in pending patent litigation but did not form integral part of a judicial proceeding). See generally Toker v. Pollak, 44 N.Y.2d 211, 219, 405 N.Y.S.2d 1, 376 N.E.2d 163 (1978)(absolute privilege is based on personal position or status of speaker and is limited to speaker's official participation in the processes of government).

19 Chard v. Galton, 277 Or. 109, 559 P.2d 1280, 1282–83 (1977)(false statement in offer of settlement to plaintiff's insurer, that plaintiff had been involved in previous fatal accident while in drunken stupor, need not concern matters directly admissible in evidence). The "possibly pertinent" phrase is usually attributed to a Cardozo opinion. Andrews v. Gardiner, 224 N.Y. 440, 121 N.E. 341, 343 (1918)(policy of immunity is not "strict or narrow test. Much must be left to the discretion of the advocate. The privilege embraces anything that may possibly be pertinent.").

20 Nix v. Sawyer, 466 A.2d 407, 411 (Del.Super.1983).

21 Russell v. Clark, 620 S.W.2d 865, 870, 23 A.L.R.4th 924 (Tex.Civ.App.1981).

22 Dano v. Royal Globe Ins. Co., 59 N.Y.2d 827, 464 N.Y.S.2d 741, 451 N.E.2d 488 (1983)(letter from lawyers for insurance company explaining to insured's lawyer circumstances that suggested that fire insurance policy was fraudulently procured); Kenny v. Cleary, 47 A.D.2d 531, 363 N.Y.S.2d 606 (1975)(statement made prior to commencement of judicial proceeding in effort to protect client's interests); cf. Petrus v. Smith, 91 A.D.2d 1190, 459 N.Y.S.2d 173, 174 (1983)(lawyer who called executor of estate, who had pocketed rent proceeds from estate property, liar and thief gratuitously and outside of probate accounting proceeding was protected by "qualified" privilege for matters in which parties have common interest); Restatement (Second) of Torts § 596 (1977)(conditional privilege for matters of common interest)). See generally Restatement (Second) of Torts § 595 comment f (1977)(conditional privilege "is applicable to persons in fiduciary relationships who act honestly and reasonably for the purpose of discharging the duties that arise from the relationships. It is applicable to . . . an attorney in making communications . . . to his . . . client, or to a third person, if the communication is made in a reasonable effort to protect the interest that is entrusted to him.").

23 See generally Restatement (Second) of Torts § 593 comment c (1977).

in wrongful use of the judicial process. The tort theories, which are variously called abuse of process or malicious prosecution, bristle with technical requirements that are technically applied. Calls by commentators for more generous causes of action against lawyers who file groundless suits[24] have been widely ignored. The restrictive approach of courts is justified on the reasoning that it is socially more useful to provide broad encouragement to prospective litigants to resort to court with their real or imagined grievances rather than to hedge access about with requirements of good faith.[25] Courts believe that good faith requirements might discourage parties from litigating and possibly encourage resort to socially undesirable measures of self-help.[26] Indeed, given the absolute privilege for defamatory statements, it is interesting that the access-to-court rationale has recognized only a qualified instead of an absolute protection to lawyers who participate in injurious litigation.[27]

The fact remains that lawyers occasionally, if rarely, can be held liable for participation in some forms of bad faith and malicious litigation of their clients.[28] The number of decisions holding a lawyer liable are far out-

[24] Thode, The Groundless Case—The Lawyer's Tort Duty to His Client and to the Adverse Party, 11 St. Mary's L.J. 59 (1979)(arguing for new tort of "reckless prosecution of civil proceeding" based on finding that no prudent lawyer would have decided to prosecute the suit); Wolfram, The Code of Professional Responsibility as a Measure of Attorney Liability in Civil Litigation, 30 S.C.L.Rev. 281, 310–14 (1979).

[25] Bickel v. Machie, 447 F.Supp. 1376 (N.D.Iowa 1978), affirmed 590 F.2d 341 (8th Cir.1978) ; Norton v. Hines, 49 Cal.App.3d 917, 123 Cal.Rptr. 237, 240 (1975); Morowitz v. Marvel, 423 A.2d 196, 197 (D.C.1980); Lyddon v. Shaw, 56 Ill.App.3d 815, 14 Ill.Dec. 489, 372 N.E.2d 685 (1978); Spencer v. Burglass, 337 So.2d 596 (La.App.1976), writ denied 340 So.2d 990 (1977); O'Toole v. Franklin, 279 Or. 513, 569 P.2d 561, 564–65 (1977).

The access-to-courts rationale finds expression in other areas of the law. By statute in many jurisdictions, a person who imposes a public or private penalty upon another person, because the other person filed a suit or testified in court, is made criminally or legally actionable. E.g., Kimble v. D.J. McDuffy, Inc., 623 F.2d 1060 (5th Cir.1980), rehearing granted 629 F.2d 1159 (5th Cir. 1980)(42 U.S.C.A. § 1985(2), making it illegal to prevent party from attending or testifying in United States court, provides damages remedy against company whose refusal to hire new employees was based on their previous filing of federal court damage actions against other companies in same industry).

[26] There is an inconsistency, although perhaps an explainable one, in encouraging access to court for all but those who are injured by litigation.

Sometimes the restrictions against malicious prosecution suits against other lawyers are justified on the ground that few more serious charges could be made against a lawyer or law firm and that the litigation will breed bitter feelings and unpleasantries between the lawyers. E.g., General Mill Supply Co. v. SCA Services, Inc., 505 F.Supp. 1093, 1098 (E.D.Mich.1981), affirmed and remanded 697 F.2d 704 (6th Cir.1982). The notion does not sit well that the sensitivities of lawyers to charges of professional impropriety are to be given greater recognition than, say, those of physicians.

[27] Woyczynski v. Wolf, 11 Ohio App.3d 226, 464 N.E.2d 612, 615 (1983). The customary explanation is that the rationale in favor of free access to the courts outweighs a policy of affording redress to parties injured by a malicious prosecution. E.g., Bird v. Rothman, 128 Ariz. 599, 627 P.2d 1097, 1099 (Ct.App.1981), cert.denied 454 U.S. 865, 102 S.Ct. 327, 70 L.Ed.2d 66 (1981); Albertson v. Roboff, 46 Cal.2d 375, 295 P.2d 405, 410 (1956); Brody v. Montalbano, 87 Cal.App.3d 725, 151 Cal.Rptr. 206, 213 (1978), cert.denied 444 U.S. 844, 100 S.Ct. 87, 62 L.Ed.2d 57 (1979); Beecy v. Pucciarelli, 387 Mass. 589, 441 N.E.2d 1035, 1038 n.7 (1982); R.Mallen & V.Levitt, Legal Malpractice § 48, at 100 (2d ed.1981).

[28] Sachs v. Levy, 216 F.Supp. 44, 46 (E.D.Pa.1963); Goucher v. Kineen, 471 A.2d 688 (Me.1984); Hoppe v. Klapperich, 224 Minn. 224, 28 N.W.2d 780 (1947); Bull v. McCuskey, 96 Nev. 706, 615 P.2d 957 (1980); Adelman v. Rosenbaum, 133 Pa.Super. 386, 3 A.2d 15 (1938). Cf. Nelson v. Miller, 227 Kan. 271, 607 P.2d 438 (1980) (remanding for trial under Rest. (Second) Torts § 674 comment d (1977)); Silbertstein v. Presbyterian Hospital, 96 A.D.2d 1096, 463 N.Y.S.2d 254 (1983)(allegations of wrongful issuance of process sufficient to support default judgment); Shaffer v. Stewart, 326 Pa.Super. 135, 473 A.2d 1017 (1984)(sufficient allegation of abuse of process in filing civil suit solely to extort settlement); Strid v. Converse, 111 Wis.2d 418, 331 N.W.2d 350 (1983)(pleadings sufficient to withstand motion to dismiss). See generally Annot., 27 A.L.R.3d 1113 (1969)(liability of lawyer for malicious prosecution or false imprisonment); Annot., 97 A.L.R.3d 688 (1980)(abuse of process); Annot., 84 A.L.R.3d 555 (1978)(physician countersuits).

Restatement (Second) of Torts § 674 comment d (1977):

> An attorney who initiates a civil proceeding on behalf of his client or one who takes any steps in the proceeding is not liable if he has probable cause for his action . . . ; and even if he has no probable cause and is convinced that his client's claim is unfounded, he is still not liable if he acts primarily for the purpose of aiding his client in obtaining a proper adjudication of his claim. . . . An attorney is not required or expected to prejudge his client's claim, and although he is fully aware that its chances of success are comparatively slight, it is his responsibility to present it to the court for adjudication if his client so insists after he has explained to the client the nature of the chances.

numbered by decisions, sometimes cast on very technical grounds, that deny recovery. The most difficult doctrinal requirements are the "one-two" punch of the requirement, in malicious prosecution actions, that the plaintiff show a special injury beyond those commonly associated with defending litigation[29] and the requirement, in abuse of process law, that the plaintiff show that the defendant had an ulterior motive in filing the action. Beyond the technical doctrines, courts have also stated broadly that the role of lawyers in the adversary system requires that they be given a large measure of discretion to press the apparent interests of their clients.[30] Courts do not allow the theories of recovery to stray into even closely related torts. For example, an action of fraud is not maintainable because, even if it is alleged that the lawyer acted dishonestly and maliciously, the common-law rule is that a losing litigant may not recover damages for the fraud of an opposing party in litigation or the party's lawyer because such a suit offends the principle opposed to repetitious litigation.[31] One court has held, dubiously, that the privilege for defamatory statements made during litigation means that allegedly defamatory remarks made by a lawyer during a trial are inadmissible later against the lawyer in a malicious prosecution suit that asserts that the original action was groundless.[32]

An arena in which the persistence and power of the access-to-court rationale has recently been played out concerns so-called physician countersuits. Doctors who claim reputational or other harm due to groundless medical malpractice suits have filed counterclaims or independent actions seeking damages against plaintiffs' lawyers. What at one time was thought to portend grave risks to careless lawyers who asserted groundless claims in medical malpractice cases has developed into a remedy only for the most extremely incompetent representations.[33] Courts have generally refused to base liability on negligence[34] or on a violation of the lawyer codes[35] but have insisted that the suing physician demonstrate that the technical requirements of abuse of process or malicious prosecution be

If, however, the attorney acts without probable cause for belief in the possibility that the claim will succeed, and for an improper purpose, as, for example, to put pressure upon the person proceeded against in order to compel payment of another claim of his own or solely to harass the person proceeded against by bringing a claim known to be invalid, he is subject to the same liability as any other person. . . . An attorney may also be subject to liability if he takes an active part in continuing a civil proceeding properly begun, for an improper purpose and without probable cause.

29 Ammerman v. Newman, 384 A.2d 637 (D.C.App. 1978); Berlin v. Nathan, 64 Ill.App.3d 940, 21 Ill.Dec. 682, 686, 381 N.E.2d 1367, 1381 (1978), cert. denied 444 U.S. 828, 100 S.Ct. 53, 62 L.Ed.2d 36 (1979); Brody v. Ruby, 267 N.W.2d 902, 904–05 (Iowa 1978); O'Toole v. Franklin, 279 Or. 513, 569 P.2d 561, 564 n.3 (1977); Moiel v. Sandlin, 571 S.W.2d 567, 570–71 (Tex.Civ.App.1978). The malicious prosecution plaintiff is also precluded from commencing the action until after successful termination of the original action in the plaintiff's favor. E.g., Babb v. Superior Court, 3 Cal.3d 841, 92 Cal.Rptr. 179, 479 P.2d 379 (1971); Gasis v. Schwartz, 80 Mich.App. 600, 264 N.W.2d 76 (1978).

30 Wong v. Tabor, 422 N.E.2d 1279, 1286 (Ind.App.1981).

31 Anderson v. Anderson, 399 N.E.2d 391, 399–400 (Ind. App.1979).

32 Bull v. McCuskey, 96 Nev. 706, 615 P.2d 957 (1980).

33 Illustrative of the extreme circumstances that must be established is one of the few physician countersuits that have been successful. In Peerman v. Sidicane, 605 S.W.2d 242 (Tenn.App.1980), the court upheld a jury verdict based on findings of abuse of process and malicious prosecution when the lawyer had pressed a medical malpractice action without consent or knowledge of his client, alleged in the complaint that the defendant physician had engaged in fee-splitting with a testing laboratory with no factual foundation whatever, made no effort to prove or support the allegation of fee-splitting, and did not consult any physician with respect to the applicable standard of care for the treatment of the malpractice plaintiff's condition.

34 Morowitz v. Marvel, 423 A.2d 196, 199 (D.C.1980); Hill v. Willmott, 561 S.W.2d 331 (Ky.App.1978); Lyddon v. Shaw, 56 Ill.App.3d 815, 14 Ill.Dec. 489, 372 N.E.2d 865 (1978); Drago v. Bounagurio, 46 N.Y.2d 778, 413 N.Y.S.2d 910, 386 N.E.2d 821 (1978); O'Toole v. Franklin, 279 Or. 513, 569 P.2d 561 (1977).

35 Berlin v. Nathan, 64 Ill.App.3d 940, 21 Ill.Dec. 682, 381 N.E.2d 1367 (1978), cert. denied 444 U.S. 828, 100 S.Ct. 53, 62 L.Ed.2d 36 (1979); Spencer v. Burglass, 337 So.2d 596 (La.App.1976), writ denied 340 So.2d 990 (1977); Friedman v. Dozorc, 83 Mich.App. 429, 268 N.W.2d 673, 674–75 (1978), affirmed in part, reversed in part 412 Mich. 1, 312 N.W.2d 585 (1981). See generally Bob Godfrey Pontiac, Inc. v. Roloff, 291 Or. 318, 630 P.2d 840, 847, 848 (1981)(collecting authorities from physician countersuit and other areas).

made out. At least one court has insisted, however, that in assessing whether the lawyer had the necessary probable cause to proceed with a client's action, the jury could consider not only the facts revealed to the lawyer by his or her client, but also those facts that could have been learned by diligent effort, and whether the lawyer, before filing the action, had made a demand on the defendant and called on him or her to respond with a different version of the facts.[36]

WESTLAW REFERENCES

Lawyer Intentional Wrongs to Clients and Nonclients

lawyer attorney counsel** /10 duty /s intent! /s client

Intentional Wrongs Injurious to Clients

lawyer attorney counsel** legal law /5 malpractice /p fraud! false* /3 misrepresent! represent!

Lawyer Conversion, Fraud, Misrepresentation

lawyer attorney counsel** legal law /5 malpractice /s malicious**

lawyer attorney counsel** legal law /5 malpractice /s fraud!

lawyer attorney counsel** legal law /5 malpractice /p misrepresent!

Wrongful Interference with Contractual Advantages

"tortious interference" /p lawyer attorney counsel**

Lawyer Defamation and the Representational Immunity

immunity privileg** /s defam! /p attorney counsel** lawyer

237k38(5)

Absolute Privilege for Judicial Proceedings

absolut! /2 privileg** immunity /s defam! /p attorney counsel** lawyer

relevan! /p attorney counsel** lawyer /p privileg** immunity /s defam!

Conditional Privilege for Interest-Protecting Communications

conditional** qualified /s privilege** immunity /s attorney counsel** lawyer /p defam!

Lawyer Liability for Wrongful Use of the Judicial Process

"abuse of process" /s lawyer attorney counsel**

313k168

di malicious prosecution

physician doctor surgeon /s lawyer counsel** attorney /s "abuse of process" "malicious prosecution"

§ 5.6.6 Vicarious Liability

Financial Liability for the Wrongs of Others

A lawyer practicing alone with no employees is a free-standing entity with respect to liability. But most lawyers practice in a partnership or professional corporation or have employees. The presence of such other persons complicates the question of the reach of liability toward clients and nonclients. In general a lawyer is financially responsible as a principal for the wrongful acts of employees and other agents within the scope of their agency responsibilities. A lawyer is generally regarded as the agent of his or her client, but the reverse is not true. Derelictions of a client are not, by the sole fact of their relationship, imputable to the lawyer.[37] A lawyer who is a member of a partnership will be jointly and severally liable with other firm members for their wrongs, with possible limitations for some intentional wrongs. A lawyer-member of a professional corporation may enjoy limited liability, but that result has been denied in several jurisdictions.

[36] Nelson v. Miller, 227 Kan. 271, 607 P.2d 438 (1980). See also, e.g., Metzger v. Silverman, 62 Cal.App.3d Supp. 30, 133 Cal.Rptr. 355, 360 (1976). But cf., e.g., Friedman v. Dozorc, 412 Mich. 1, 312 N.W.2d 585, 605 (1981)(normally, extent of lawyer's investigation should have no bearing on probable cause in malicious prosecution suit).

[37] Yoggerst v. Stewart, 623 F.2d 35, 38 (7th Cir.1980) (lawyer who had no supervisory powers over client in same government office not liable for torts of client, about which lawyer gave good faith legal advice); Harvey v. Pincus, 549 F.Supp. 332, 343 (E.D.Pa.1982), affirmed 716 F.2d 890 (3d Cir.), cert.denied 464 U.S. 918, 104 S.Ct. 284, 78 L.Ed.2d 262 (1983)(in absence of inducement or encouragement by lawyer, lawyer cannot be held liable for tortious conduct of his or her client); Zeavin v. Lee, 136 Cal.App.3d 766, 186 Cal.Rptr. 545, 548 (1982); Tool Research & Engineering Corp. v. Henigson, 46 Cal.App.3d 675, 682, 120 Cal.Rptr. 291 (1975).

Liability for the Wrongs of Employees and Agents

Various legal theories provide that a lawyer is liable for tortious or contractual wrongs committed by the lawyer's employees or agents. First, an agent with actual authority to act for the lawyer can bind the lawyer as principal.[38] Second, under the doctrine of apparent authority, a lawyer can cause a client or prospective client to believe reasonably that a nonlawyer employee has authority to perform acts that bind the lawyer. For example, in a Massachusetts case, the court held that the defendant lawyer had so arranged client intake procedures in his office that a former client reasonably believed that interviews with, and instructions from, the lawyer's secretary inaugurated the lawyer's legal services. Thus the lawyer was held liable for malpractice when the secretary misfiled the client's letter requesting legal advice and permitted the statute of limitations to run.[39] If the relationship between lawyer and nonlawyer is that of principal and independent contractor, however, the lawyer is not vicariously liable for wrongs of the independent contractor.[40] The lawyer would be liable only if the lawyer expressly directed or authorized those wrongs or if the lawyer knew the other person was an untrustworthy person and nonetheless delegated a task to the person that, under the known circumstances, created an unreasonable risk of harm to others.[41]

Vicarious Liability for Wrongs of Law Partners

Lawyers are subject to joint and several personal liability to others for the tortious acts that lawyers and nonlawyer employees of the partnership commit in the ordinary course of the partnership's law practice.[42] Wrongful acts that are either negligent or intentional [43] may be held to be within the course of the partnership business so long as

[38] Soberg v. Sanders, 243 Mich. 429, 220 N.W. 781 (1928).

[39] DeVaux v. American Home Assurance Co., 387 Mass. 814, 444 N.E.2d 355 (1983).

[40] Bockian v. Esanu, Katsky, Korins & Siger, 124 Misc. 2d 607, 476 N.Y.S.2d 1009 (1984)(lawyers not liable for "somewhat questionable" conduct of independent contractor process server in taping scurrilous sign stating that plaintiff suffered from venereal herpes to plaintiff's apartment building and assaulting plaintiff when she attempted to photograph him).

[41] Noble v. Sears, Roebuck & Co., 33 Cal.App.3d 654, 109 Cal.Rptr. 269 (1973)(law firm not liable for outrageous and intrusive activities of detective-employee of detective agency hired by law firm, in absence of proof that employee was known to be untrustworthy person, citing Restatement (Second) of Agency § 213(c)(1958)).

[42] Williams v. Burns, 463 F.Supp. 1278 (D.Colo.1979) (joint and several liability for libel under Uniform Partnership Act); Peterson v. Harville, 445 F.Supp. 16, 26–27 (D.Or.1977), affirmed 623 F.2d 611 (9th Cir.1980)(partners not vicariously liable for fraud of partner as member of board of directors of corporation where firm had never acted as counsel for corporation); Moore v. State Bar, 62 Cal.2d 74, 41 Cal.Rptr. 161, 165, 396 P.2d 577, 581 (1964); Husted v. McCloud, 450 N.E.2d 491 (Ind.1983)(partners liable for loss caused by partner's misrepresentation to client in course of informing client about outcome of settlement, despite fact that he acted entirely for own benefit, without knowledge of innocent partners, and without benefiting partnership); Wlodarek v. Thrift, 178 Md. 453, 13 A.2d 774, 778 (1940).

On the "course of partnership business point," compare, e.g., Zimmerman v. Hogg & Allen, 286 N.C. 24, 209 S.E.2d 795 (1974)(members of professional association, treated as partnership, jointly and severally liable for senior member's misappropriation of client's funds received for investment, because the investment service was to stimulate good will of client, and senior member had performed similar investment services for clients for number of years with knowledge of other members), with, e.g., Rouse v. Pollard, 130 N.J.Eq. 204, 21 A.2d 801 (1941) (other members of partnership not liable for conversion of funds left by client for investment because that was not part of law partnership business); Riley v. LaRocque, 163 Misc. 423, 297 N.Y.S. 756 (1937)(law partners not liable for partner's conversion of former client's funds when, following distribution of assets of estate that lawyer had handled, lawyer induced client to make investment through lawyer; investment was not part of partnership business).

[43] Blackmon v. Hale, 1 Cal.3d 548, 83 Cal.Rptr. 194, 463 P.2d 418 (1970)(partner liable for other partner's misappropriation of client's funds); Husted v. McCloud, 450 N.E.2d 491 (Ind.1983)(under Uniform Partnership Act, partners liable to client for funds wrongfully converted by partner despite fact that he acted wrongfully and they derived no benefit from the conversion); Myers v. Aragona, 21 Md.App. 45, 318 A.2d 263 (1974)(misappropriation). But see Jackson v. Jackson, 20 N.C.App. 406, 201 S.E.2d 722, 70 A.L.R.3d 1294 (1974)(law partners not vicariously liable for malicious prosecution of law partner because act was not within ordinary course of law partnership business in light of fact that DR 7–102(A) prohibits malicious prosecution). The court's analysis, of course, would undercut most areas of vicarious liability for law firms. The court's holding, immunizing law partners from personal liability for wrongs of partners that violate the lawyer code, seems erroneous as a matter of

they arise out of the practice of law. The members of the partnership are liable even if they did not participate in, ratify, or have knowledge of the wrongful conduct.[44] After the partnership comes to an end, the extent of liability depends upon the time at which the act occurred or the relationship creating liability existed. A partner who has left a partnership remains vicariously responsible for all tortious or contractual liability that is proved to have accrued during the partner's tenure.[45] Even after the dissolution of the partnership, all former partners remain liable to complete the unfinished business of clients of the firm at the time of dissolution.[46] An incoming partner is liable for all the obligations of the partnership at the time of admission, but the obligation can be satisfied only out of partnership property.[47]

Vicarious Liability and Professional Corporations

One of the important motivations for doing business in the corporate form is to gain the limited liability for participants in the corporation's activities that corporation law generally affords. But according to several decisions, the fact of professional incorporation need not ineluctably lead to limited liability.[48] Courts have refused to permit limited liability on the rationale that that result would deceive clients who, presumably, would deal with lawyer-members of the professional corporation in the mistaken belief that other members of the corporation were jointly and severally responsible for the representation.[49] Thus the shareholders of the professional corporation remain liable in those jurisdictions as if they were partners. The courts accomplished that result through the exercise of their inherent power to regulate the practice of law.[50]

Vicarious Liability of Cocounsel

A rule commonly encountered is that a lawyer from another jurisdiction must associate with local counsel when temporarily appearing in litigation in a state (§ 15.4.3).[51] In

general partnership law and poor policy as a matter of enforcing the lawyer code.

44 Uniform Partnership Act § 13 (1914).

45 Pettigrew & Bailey v. Pickle, 429 So.2d 340 (Fla.App. 1983); Greene v. Greene, 47 N.Y.2d 447, 418 N.Y.S.2d 379, 382, 391 N.E.2d 1355, 1358 (1979). But if a departed partner's personal conduct after departing causes that partner to be estopped to claim the protection of the statute of limitations against the injured party for an injury that occurred during the partnership's tenure, only that partner, and not other members of the former partnership, will remain subject to suit. Neel v. Magana, Olney, Levy, Cathcart, and Gelfand, 6 Cal.3d 176, 98 Cal. Rptr. 837, 491 P.2d 421 (1971). The cases disagree on the question of a former partner's liability for legal malpractice that occurs after the departure but with respect to a representation that had been undertaken by the firm prior to departure. Compare, e.g., Redman v. Walters, 88 Cal.App.3d 448, 152 Cal.Rptr. 42 (1979)(departing partner remains liable for malpractice of partner who accepted representation during partnership existence but failed to pursue it thereafter), with, e.g., Burnside v. McCrary, 384 So.2d 1292, 1293 (Fla.App.1980)(lawyer not responsible for former partner's malpractice because negligent acts occurred after lawyer became judge); Gibson v. Talley, 156 Ga.App. 593, 275 S.E.2d 154 (1980).

46 See generally § 16.2.3 (law partnership—dissolution). Cf. Burnside v. McCrary, 384 So.2d 1292 (Fla.App.1980) (partner of dissolved partnership not liable for occurrences after dissolution); Vollgraff v. Block, 117 Misc. 2d 489, 458 N.Y.S.2d 437, 440 (1982)(dictum)(in absence of notice to client of fact of dissolution of partnership and fact that dissolved partnership could no longer represent, and proof of retainer between client and new firm, mere dissolution of partnership ineffective in barring client's malpractice recovery against all firm members).

47 Uniform Partnership Act § 17 (1914).

48 First Bank & Trust Co. v. Zagoria, 250 Ga. 844, 302 S.E.2d 674 (1983); In re Petition of Bar Ass'n, 55 Hawaii 121, 516 P.2d 1267, 4 A.L.R.3d 375 (1973); In re Rhode Island Bar Ass'n, 106 R.I. 752, 263 A.2d 692 (1970); In re Florida Bar, 133 So.2d 554 (Fla.1961).

49 First Bank & Trust Co. v. Zagoria, 300 S.E.2d at 161: "When a client engages the services of a lawyer the client has the right to expect the fidelity of other members of the firm. It is inappropriate for the lawyer to be able to play hide-and-seek in the shadows and folds of the corporate veil and thus escape the responsibilities of professionalism."

50 The invocation of the inherent powers doctrine (see § 2.2.2 hints darkly that legislative attempts to alter the courts' decision by legislation might run afoul of the separation-of-powers doctrine. See § 2.2.3. E.g., First Bank & Trust Co. v. Zagoria, supra, 300 S.E.2d at 161.

51 The question of the degree of tort responsibility of local counsel for the malpractice of out-of-state associated lawyers and vice versa remains largely unresolved. See Misner, Local Associated Counsel in the Federal District Courts: A Call for Change, 67 Corn.L.Rev. 345, 369 (1982).

most such situations the designated local lawyer plays a largely passive role. Courts should therefore be reluctant to visit the local lawyer with vicarious liability.[52] But if the relationship is one of more nearly equal responsibility, authority, and profit sharing, it may fit the legal description of a joint venture, permitting an injured party to hold both foreign and local lawyer to joint and several liability.[53] If the lawyers are practicing together, there is more reason to apply the joint-venture rules. According to a California case, the only reported decision in point, a supervising lawyer may also recover from a subordinate lawyer for breach of fiduciary duty by negligent conduct in the course of the relationship.[54]

WESTLAW REFERENCES

Financial Liability for the Wrongs of Others

45k26 /p agency agent authority

Liability for the Wrongs of Employees and Agents

di apparent authority

Vicarious Liability for Wrongs of Law Partners

di vicarious liability

"uniform partnership act" /p joint** /3 several** /5 liable liability

Vicarious Liability and Professional Corporations

101k237

Vicarious Liability of CoCounsel

di joint venture

§ 5.6.7 *Limiting Liability*

A lawyer concerned about the extent of malpractice liability might consider entering into a contractual agreement with clients relieving the lawyer of liability. Aside from questions of informed consent, which would be raised if the lawyer attempted to defeat a malpractice suit on the basis of the agreement,[55] the professional rules also cast much doubt on the validity of such agreements. The Code, in DR 6–102(A), broadly prohibits a lawyer from "attempt[ing] to exonerate himself from or limit his liability to his client for his personal liability." [56] The rule clearly prohibits a consent in advance, but on one reading prohibits a lawyer from settling a client's malpractice claim against the lawyer. The prohibition against consent in advance also seems to apply both to total exonerations as well as to attempts to limit the representation because of time or fee payment constraints.

In fact, many of the reported disciplinary cases involve more egregious violations, such as surreptitious attempts to obtain releases from clients under false pretenses after the

52 Ortiz v. Barrett, 222 Va. 118, 278 S.E.2d 833 (1981) (summary judgment for local lawyer who, in the absence of a showing of joint venture, would only be liable for negligence in the performance of such tasks as lead counsel required of him).

53 Ortiz v. Barrett, supra, 278 S.E.2d at 840. Cf. Cottman v. Cottman, 56 Md.App. 413, 468 A.2d 131, 139 (1983)(doctrine of partnership by estoppel not basis for liability of associated lawyer in action for malicious use of process because of absence of reliance by victim of tortfeasor).

54 Pollak v. Lytle, 120 Cal.App.3d 931, 175 Cal.Rptr. 81 (1981). The court distinguished cases holding that a lawyer to whom a case is forwarded is not liable to the forwarding lawyer for negligent handling of the forwarded case on the ground that there it was desirable that the forwardee-lawyer function only in the best interests of the client. See, e.g., Gibson, Dunn & Crutcher v. Superior Court, 94 Cal.App.3d 347, 156 Cal.Rptr. 326 (1979); Christensen, O'Connor, Garrison & Havelka v. State, 97 Wn.2d 764, 649 P.2d 839 (1982)(referring law firms are not liable to their clients for malpractice of engaged law firm, nor can they recover from engaged law firm for such malpractice on that firm's part). In the principal-agent relationship, however, the associated lawyer is, by definition, subject to the direction of the principal lawyer.

55 See generally Cohen v. Surrey, Karasik & Morse, 427 F.Supp. 363 (D.D.C.1977)(release not invalid when clients, who were experienced in business and of whom one was lawyer, entered into agreement with full knowledge of facts).

56 The references in the DR to "his" liability suggest that a lawyer may negotiate to exonerate or limit the liability of partners of the lawyer. Similarly MR 1.8(h) applies only to agreements to limit "the lawyer's liability." No authority seems to have accepted or rejected such limited attempts to obtain a client release. Some courts have refused to permit limited liability under a professional corporation form of practice, but on the distinguishable ground that a client might be deceived. See § 16.2.4.

malpractice occurred[57] or routinely requiring clients to sign releases before the lawyer will release the client's files to them.[58] Some, however, may be instances in which a lawyer was disciplined for violation of the rule in attempting to settle an existing malpractice claim even though the lawyer did not engage in any aggravating deception or coercion.[59] Among those are cases that insist that a lawyer must inform a client of the existence of a possible malpractice claim against the lawyer, withdraw, and advise the client to seek independent legal advice before attempting to settle with the client.[60] The California rule, which explicitly permits a lawyer to settle or defend a malpractice action,[61] may also limit the circumstances in which a lawyer attempts to settle.[62]

The Model Rules, in MR 1.8(h), provide a more liberal rule. It permits a prospective limitation of liability only if (1) "permitted by law" and (2) if the client is independently represented in making the agreement. That portion of the rule obviously is limited to large and sophisticated undertakings. The rule also provides an enlargement of the power of a lawyer to settle claims after they have arisen. A lawyer may settle with an unrepresented client after advising the client in writing that "independent representation is appropriate in connection therewith."[63] The rather clear implication of the rule is that a lawyer is entirely free to negotiate and settle a malpractice claim with a client represented by another lawyer in the legal malpractice matter. Finally, MR 1.2(c) permits a lawyer to limit the "objectives" of a representation after consultation with a client. The rule plainly implies that it is permissible for a lawyer to agree with a client that a representation will be conducted in such a way as possibly to incur defined risks. For example, if a lawyer carefully describes to a client that, for the amount of fee that the client is willing to spend, the lawyer's research will be necessarily limited with described possible consequences, the lawyer should be able to proceed with the representation with client consent.

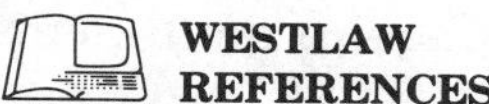

WESTLAW REFERENCES

"dr 6–102" dr6–102 /p limit! exonerat! releas! /p lawyer counsel! attorney /p malpractice

---

[57] People v. Good, 195 Colo. 177, 576 P.2d 1020 (1978) (typing restrictive endorsement on back of check issued to client which, if signed by client to whom check was issued to refund unearned fees, would have limited lawyer's malpractice liability to amount of repaid fee); In re Craven, 271 Ind. 67, 390 N.E.2d 163 (1979)(suspension for representing client in obtaining settlement from lawyer's own malpractice insurer under pretext of negotiating with insurer for original defendant, against whom lawyer had negligently failed to file timely action); In re Judd, 682 P.2d 302 (Utah 1984)(restrictive, exonerating endorsement on back of check to client). Cf. also, e.g., Spring v. Constantino, 168 Conn. 563, 362 A.2d 871, 878 n.7 (1975) (DR 6–102 as support for rejecting claim of public defender for judicial immunity from malpractice claim of client); Louisiana St. Bar Ass'n v. Summers, 379 So.2d 1065 (La.1980)(violation of DR 6–102 for lawyer to evade process servers and take other evasive action to prevent client recovering just debt owed by lawyer); Attorney Grievance Comm'n v. Stancil, 296 Md. 325, 463 A.2d 789, 791 (1983)(discipline under DR 1–102(A)(5) for paying client sum of money at least in part to induce client to withdraw complaint from disciplinary agency); In re Bengston, 116 Wis.2d 650, 342 N.W.2d 744 (1984)(suspension for making payments to client under false pretenses in order to lull client into not filing legal malpractice action against lawyer until statute of limitations had run).

[58] In re Clarke, 278 S.C. 627, 300 S.E.2d 595 (1983).

[59] Florida Bar v. Nemec, 390 So.2d 1190, 14 A.L.R.4th 204 (Fla.1980)(discipline for attempting to obtain client's signature on release form before paying client sum in settlement of client claim for lawyer's admitted negligence where lawyer failed to advise client to seek independent legal advice); In re Cissna, 444 N.E.2d 851 (Ind. 1983).

[60] In re Tallon, 86 A.D.2d 897, 447 N.Y.S.2d 50, 51 (1982).

[61] Calif. R. 6–102 ("A member of the State Bar shall not attempt to exonerate himself from or limit his liability to his client for his personal malpractice. This rule shall not prevent a member of the State Bar from settling or defending a malpractice claim.").

[62] Cf. Ambrose v. State Bar, 31 Cal.3d 184, 181 Cal. Rptr. 903, 904, 643 P.2d 486, 487 (1982)(apparently disapproving reference to attempt to exonerate self from legal malpractice claim of clients, although in context of fraudulent scheme to avoid paying on claim).

[63] The intrusion of legalese was resisted with a large measure of success by the Model Rule drafters. That the phrase "in connection therewith" should have crept into a rule describing the content of a client consultation is particularly regrettable. The rule presumably means that a lawyer must tell a client that the client ought to get legal advice about the proposed settlement from another lawyer.

§ 5.6.8 *Legal Malpractice Insurance*

Growing Importance of Legal Malpractice Insurance

Malpractice insurance for lawyers was unknown in the United States prior to the Second World War, except in a few firms that obtained insurance through Lloyd's of London.[64] Today it is unheard of for a firm of any size not to carry a substantial policy of legal malpractice insurance, and most lawyers in all forms of active practice now carry insurance against their own malpractice.[65] The growth of insurance may reflect the fiscal conservatism of lawyers, or it may reflect real growth in the number of claims filed against lawyers and in the size of recoveries.[66]

The argument has been made that all lawyers should be required to carry malpractice insurance in order to protect innocent clients against catastrophic losses at the hands of careless lawyers.[67] But it is not clear that many clients require the benefits of that protection or that most lawyers are unable to cover damage judgments with personal assets. From a social point of view, legal malpractice insurance is important for reasons of efficiency. The distributive effects of permitting clients to recover, and satisfy a judgment, for a malpractice award have impacts upon the costs of providing legal services and thus upon either legal fees charged or lawyers' profits or both. Another effect on efficiency is that lawyers, possibly required to do so by their insurance carriers as a condition of coverage, will take preventive steps to eliminate the most common causes of client claims. Mandatory insurance will necessarily add at least the administrative and profit costs of insurance to law office expenses. Preventive steps by lawyers will be efficient only if the cost of taking them is less than the amount of damage that is prevented. Beyond simple steps such as calendaring systems in law offices, it is not clear that mandatory standardized preventive measures will be efficient.

Coverage Questions

As with all insurance, questions of coverage under legal malpractice policies can be determined only on the basis of a construction of the particular policy involved and of the law of the jurisdiction.[68] The chief difficulties have been over the difference between "claims made" and "occurrences" coverage—the difference between coverage for all claims made during the effective period of a malpractice policy and coverage for all occurrences during that period, regardless of when the claim is filed.[69] Familiar doctrine prohibits,

[64] Dautch, Lawyers' Indemnity Insurance, 46 Com.L.J. 412, 412 (1941).

[65] A recent survey in one state indicated that 85 percent of lawyers in full-time practice, other than in government offices or legal departments of corporations, carried legal malpractice insurance. See Schneyer, Mandatory Malpractice Insurance for Lawyers in Wisconsin and Elsewhere, 1979 Wisc.L.Rev. 1019, 1030–31.

[66] On the elusiveness of hard data on the number and size of claims and on the incidence of legal malpractice generally, see Pfenningstorf, Types and Causes of Lawyers' Professional Liability Claims: The Search for Facts, 1980 Am.B.Found. Research J. 253.

[67] Boyer & Conner, Legal Malpractice and Compulsory Client Protection, 29 Hast.L.J. 835 (1978); Comment, Should Legal Malpractice Insurance Be Mandatory?, 1978 BYU L.Rev. 102. For a report of a study committee on the need for mandatory malpractice insurance, based on an empirical survey, see Schneyer, Mandatory Malpractice Insurance for Lawyers in Wisconsin and Elsewhere, 1979 Wisc.L.Rev. 1019. Interest in mandatory malpractice insurance was stimulated by the passage of legislation providing for this in Oregon in 1977. See Or. Rev.Stat. § 9.080 (Supp.1977–78).

[68] See generally Annot., 84 A.L.R.3d 187 (1978). On the question of the insurer's duty to defend under the policy, see, e.g., American Home Assurance Co. v. Miller, 717 F.2d 1310 (9th Cir.1983)(duty-to-defend clause requires insurer to defend against client's counterclaim for setoff due to lawyer's alleged malpractice in unrelated matter, which was asserted by client as defense to lawyer's action for fees); Jefferson-Pilot Fire Ins. Co. v. Boothe, Prichard & Dudley, 638 F.2d 670 (4th Cir.1980) (duty-to-defend clause broader than indemnity clause).

[69] The two types of coverage were considered in the context of an antitrust case involving a claim of an illegal combination of insurers to force policy purchasers to accept only one kind of coverage. The case involved medical malpractice insurance but is of interest to legal malpractice insurers and insureds. St. Paul Fire & Marine Ins. Co. v. Barry, 438 U.S. 531, 98 S.Ct. 2923, 57 L.Ed.2d 932 (1978). See also, e.g., St. Paul Fire & Marine Ins. Co. v. Parzen, 569 F.Supp. 753 (E.D.Mich.1983). See generally Stern, An Attorney's Guide for Purchasing Professional Liability Insurance and Practicing within the Coverages, 3 Am.J.Tr. Advocacy 13 (1979).

on public policy grounds, a potential tortfeasor from insuring against intentional and malicious acts because of the supposition that the insurance protection would encourage antisocial behavior on the part of insureds. The doctrine has led to a conflict over the question whether such torts as malicious prosecution and such remedies as punitive damages are covered by malpractice insurance and, if so, whether the coverage is legally permissible.[70]

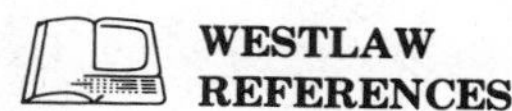

WESTLAW REFERENCES

Growing Importance of Legal Malpractice Insurance

legal law attorney lawyer counsel! /3 malpractice /7 insurance

Coverage Questions

"duty-to-defend clause"

[70] Perl v. St. Paul Fire & Marine Ins. Co., 345 N.W.2d 209 (Minn.1984)(malpractice insurance policy that covered lawyer's forfeiture of fee to client for breach of fiduciary duty void on public policy grounds; but coverage for vicarious liability of firm members permissible). See generally Note, Lawyers' Professional Liability Insurance: Coverage for Malicious Prosecution, Abuse of Process, Libel, and Slander, 33 S.C.L.Rev. 355 (1981).

Chapter Six
LAWYERS AS CLIENT CONFIDANTS

Table of Sections

---

§ 6.1 THE CONFIDENTIALITY PRINCIPLE

§ 6.1.1 Legal and Professional Protection of Confidentiality

By turns both sacred and controversial, the principle of the confidentiality of client information is well-embedded in the traditional notion of the Anglo-American client-lawyer relationship. Every state in the United States recognizes the attorney-client privilege (§ 6.3), the rule of evidence that precludes another party in litigation from asking either client or lawyer what either has exchanged in confidence. Modern decisions and procedural rules also recognize the "work product" protection—a client's privilege not to reveal information gathered by a lawyer from sources other than the client (§ 6.6). Agency law provides remedies for a disloyal lawyer's out-of-court misuse of a client's confidential information. The professional rules largely duplicate those doctrines enjoining a broad ethical duty not to divulge information about a client (§ 6.7.2). The matters covered only by the professional rules are referred to in the 1969 Code, and here, as "secrets" to distinguish them from matters privileged under the law of attorney-client privilege. The professional rules cover much more than the testimonial privilege and to some extent may extend beyond the agency rules.

WESTLAW REFERENCES

di confidential communication

---

§ 6.1.2 History of the Attorney-Client Privilege

The history of the attorney-client privilege is disputed. The conventional view is that attributed to Wigmore: the privilege, reflecting ideas at least as old as Roman Law,[1] was recognized in English law by the time of Elizabeth I and has been applied without serious question by both English and American

[1] Radin, The Privilege of Confidential Communication between Lawyer and Client, 16 Calif.L.Rev. 487 (1928).

courts since that time.[2] A familiar part of that history is the shift of its judicial rationale away from the early "gentleman's honor" notion that lawyers should not be embarrassed by being called upon to reveal unnice things about clients. The modern rationale is that the privilege serves the interests of clients in obtaining effective legal advice.[3] Professor Hazard has recently disputed Dean Wigmore's view and concludes that prior to the middle of the last century the scope of the privilege was constantly changing and in no predictable direction.[4] Whatever the merits of that debate, it seems clear that development of the privilege must have been influenced by other common-law evidentiary rules that strike us now as bizarre. One was the rule that a party was incompetent to testify in his or her own behalf (because of interest). The other was the rule that a party could claim a privilege of not being called to testify in behalf of an adversary (on the ground that it might be self-incriminatory or expose the witness to disgrace). In such a milieu, it would have been anomalous to require a party's lawyer to testify to damaging information.

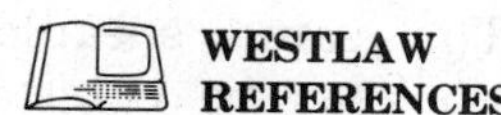
WESTLAW REFERENCES

wigmore /s 2290

§ 6.1.3 Policy behind the Privilege

In contemporary discussions the policy basis of the attorney-client privilege is said to rest upon a series of three assumptions—the first two of which are commonly acknowledged and the third of which is problematical. First, it is postulated that it is useful to a person to have the assistance of a legal advisor, certainly in litigation and just as surely (although for somewhat less popularly understood reasons) in nonlitigation situations. Second, it is assumed that the lawyer's legal advice and assistance must be based upon a firm grasp of the facts of the situation and information about the client's objectives gained from client disclosures.[5] Controversy begins with the third, linking assumption: in order for lawyers to obtain client disclosure, it is essential that lawyers be able to assure clients that their private conversations will always remain confidential.[6] The absence of data to support the third assumption has been noted.[7]

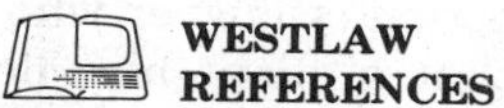
WESTLAW REFERENCES

reason /s attorney counsel** lawyer /2 client /s privilege*

§ 6.1.4 Critiques of the Privilege

Detraction from the Search for Truth

The assurance of confidentiality—the ultimate, and speculative, objective of the attorney-client privilege—is purchased only at the price of excluding from trials evidence from lawyers and clients about their conversations—a detraction from the search for truth

[2] 8 J.Wigmore, Evidence § 2290 (3d ed.1940). See also 9 W.Holdsworth, A History of English Law 198–203 (1926).

[3] Mounteney, B., in Annesley v. Earl of Anglesea, 17 How.St.Tr. 1139, 1225 (Ex.1743).

[4] Hazard, An Historical Perspective on the Attorney-Client Privilege, 66 Calif.L.Rev. 1061, 1087 n.120 (1978).

[5] Upjohn Co. v. United States, 449 U.S. 383, 389, 101 S.Ct. 677, 682, 66 L.Ed.2d 584 (1981)(quoting Trammel v. United States, 445 U.S. 40, 51, 100 S.Ct. 906, 913, 63 L.Ed. 2d 186 (1980))(the privilege assures that the "advocate and counselor [can] know all that relates to the client's reasons for seeking representation if the professional mission is to be carried out."); City & County of San Francisco v. Superior Court, 37 Cal.2d 227, 235, 231 P.2d 26 (1951)("[A]dequate legal representation in the ascertainment and enforcement of rights or the prosecution or defense of litigation compels a full disclosure of the facts by the client to his attorney.").

[6] E.g., Upjohn Co. v. United States, 449 U.S. 383, 389, 101 S.Ct. 677, 682, 66 L.Ed.2d 584 (1981); Fisher v. United States, 425 U.S. 391, 403, 96 S.Ct. 1569, 1577, 48 L.Ed.2d 39 (1976); Hunt v. Blackburn, 128 U.S. 464, 470, 9 S.Ct. 125, 127, 32 L.Ed. 488 (1888).

[7] Morgan, Foreword, ALI Model Code of Evidence at 28 (1942). The only study conducted of nonlawyer and lawyer perceptions of the privilege (Note, Functional Overlap between the Lawyers and Other Professionals: Its Implications for the Privileged Communication Doctrine, 71 Yale L.J. 1226, 1232 (1962)), concludes that lawyers in greater number than nonlawyers believe that the privilege encourages disclosures. Most nonlawyers are either unaware of the privilege or erroneously assume that it extends to other professional relationships as well.

that is "plain and concrete".[8] For that reason, the predominant judicial view is that the privilege is to be "strictly construed."[9]

The possibly deleterious impact of the exclusionary effect of the privilege upon the fact-finding process can be illustrated by its chief effect, that of keeping from the fact finder any testimony by the lawyer about confidential client communications about disputed issues of fact. Two situations are possible—either the client will be available to testify or he will not. If the client is unavailable as a witness or is available but claims amnesia or forgetfulness, then the lawyer becomes a unique source of information and a strong social policy supports disclosure in aid of accurate fact-finding. But the privilege frustrates that policy. For example, in one of its most extreme applications, the privilege can be invoked to bar from the witness stand, on the state's objection, a lawyer who could testify truthfully that a client now deceased had confessed in confidence that he had committed the capital offense for which an innocent person is on trial.[10] Assume, second, that the client is available to testify. It is well settled that the client can be made to testify to the facts that were communicated—or not—to the lawyer. All that is protected is the communication itself. If the client told his or her lawyer the truth and this is now repeated from the witness stand, then no apparent harm would come from disclosure of the client's communication to the lawyer. If, on the other hand, what is said from the witness stand differs from what was told to the lawyer, then the difference should be exposed and the client-witness forced to explain it.

Reducing Spurious Suits and Achieving Law Compliance

On another ground, it is sometimes argued that if clients were not encouraged by the privilege to supply information, lawyers would bring many actions that they would not bring if they possessed better information. But others have surmised that at least as many groundless suits are brought because of the shield provided by the privilege.[11] Client goes to Lawyer A and tells a truthful story and is told that a successful claim or defense is unavailable because of fact X. Client then goes to Lawyer B and says that the fact is non-X. Because of the privilege, neither Lawyer A nor Client can be compelled to testify. Client is deterred only by the not very realistic threat of a prosecution for perjury and can rest assured that in such a prosecution Lawyer A would probably be unable to testify over objection.[12] The same speculation and counterspeculation can be entertained over whether the privilege leads to more-effective law compliance advice by better-informed lawyers or to more-efficacious law evasion by clients who can more readily obtain advice about evading the reach of the law.

[8] See 8 J.Wigmore, Evidence § 2291, at 554 (J.McNaughton rev.ed.1961). See also C.McCormick, Evidence § 87, at 204–06 (E.Cleary 3d ed.1984).

[9] In re Horowitz, 482 F.2d 72, (2d Cir.), cert. denied 414 U.S. 867, 94 S.Ct. 64, 38 L.Ed.2d 87 (1973); Duplan Corp. v. Deering Milliken, Inc., 397 F.Supp. 1146 (D.S.C.1974); People ex rel. Dep't of Public Works v. Donovan, 57 Cal. 2d 346, 19 Cal.Rptr. 473, 476, 369 P.2d 1, 5 (1962); State v. Kociolek, 23 N.J. 400, 129 A.2d 417 (1957); Eloise Bauer & Associates, Inc. v. Electronic Realty Associates, Inc., 621 S.W.2d 200 (Tex.Civ.App.1981), error refused n.r.e. Contra, e.g., Lohman v. Superior Court, 81 Cal. App.3d 90, 146 Cal.Rptr. 171, 173 (1978); State v. Tensley, 249 N.W.2d 659 (Iowa 1977)(privilege should be given a liberal construction).

[10] Compare, e.g., State v. Macumber, 112 Ariz. 569, 544 P.2d 1084 (1976)(two lawyers, prepared to testify that their now-deceased client had confessed to murders for which present defendant was on trial, precluded from testifying by attorney-client objection raised by prosecutor); State v. Valdez, 95 N.M. 70, 618 P.2d 1234, 1237 (1980)(lawyer for third party could not be called to testify that his client had confessed to charge of armed robbery for which defendant here was convicted).

[11] C.McCormick, Evidence § 87, at 205 (E.Cleary 3d ed. 1984); Morgan, supra note 7, at 27; Radin, The Privilege of Confidential Communication between Lawyer and Client, 16 Calif.L.Rev. 489, 490 (1928).

[12] Under certain possible variations on the facts, Lawyer A's testimony could come in under the crime-fraud exception to the privilege. See § 6.4.10.

Preventing Disruption of the Client-Lawyer Relationship

Another argument is that if there were no privilege, lawyers would be forced into the undesirable role of being witnesses in suits that they were hired to try.[13] Relatedly, overzealous or lazy adversaries as a first resort would seek information from an opposing lawyer instead of pursuing it to its source. Those objections, however, do not support the privilege. They support only a rule of timing, and possibly of preference, under which a client communication would be conditionally privileged unless a special need is shown and certainly would be protected so long as other possible sources of information had not been exhausted. But if the party seeking the testimony can make a showing of sufficient need for the information, then a strong argument can be made for undertaking the special burdens of requiring a lawyer to step aside as trial counsel in order to be available as a witness. Such a limited-disclosure rule would serve the needs of accurate fact-finding while deterring opposing parties from gratuitous attempts to interfere with the normally confidential client-lawyer relationship.

Protecting Privacy Interests

It is also argued in behalf of the privilege that it protects an important societal interest in privacy by assuring that there will be some areas into which official prying cannot reach.[14] The argument is made in several forms. First, some argue that the privilege is necessary to protect the rights and dignity of individuals.[15] One of the rights of individuals is the right to counsel and to obtain what the law allows; an important condition for effective representation is that counsel know the facts. To force a client to make the choice between legal representation without effective communication and legal representation with all secrets revealed is to force the client to lose, in some cases, the right to counsel. Relatedly, the dignity of the individual is offensively restricted when, as the price for accepting the assistance of counsel, the client is forced to reveal hurtful secrets. The coerced exchange degrades the client's autonomy for the same reason that coerced self-incrimination offends the dignity of persons: it forces the individual to make the awful choice between truth and self-interest.[16] Third, from a moral point of view, confidentiality is also supportable on the grounds that a person should have some control over the spread of personal information and that others should respect relationships of confidentiality based on the bonds of shared information between lawyer and client.[17]

Weighing the Claims for Confidentiality

None of those privacy justifications, separately or together, justifies an unqualified privilege. They postulate only a presumptive claim for the moral value of confidentiality, for reasons may exist to override their moral force.[18] Moreover, if the moral claim of pro-

[13] See also the rule that normally requires an advocate to withdraw from a representation if it appears that the advocate must be a witness in the case. § 7.5.

[14] See testimony of Professor Charles L. Black in opposition to the Supreme Court's original proposals on evidentiary privileges, in Hearings on Proposed Rules of Evidence before the Special Subcomm. on Reform of Federal Criminal Laws of the House Comm. on the Judiciary, 93d Cong., lst Sess., Ser. 2, at 241 (1973). But cf., e.g., Krattenmaker, Testimonial Privileges in Federal Courts, 62 Geo.L.J. 61, 85 (1973)(perhaps a majority of evidence experts agree "that testimonial privileges are mere bothersome exclusionary rules, born of competing professional jealousies, that impede the accuracy of fact finding and serve no other important societal goals.").

[15] M.Freedman, Lawyers' Ethics in an Adversary System 4–5 (1975).

[16] L.Levy, Origins of the Fifth Amendment 331–32 (1968). See also S.Bok, Secrets 119–120 (1982). On the limits of the constitutional doctrines of self-incrimination as justification for the attorney-client privilege, see infra § 6.2.

[17] S.Bok, Secrets 119–120 (1982); Landesman, Confidentiality and the Lawyer-Client Relationship, 1980 Utah L.Rev. 765, 774–79. Because of the unfairness of misleading a client about confidentiality, in Bentham's world, in which clients have no privilege, he would have all lawyers warn their clients at the outset that the client's revelations could be forced from the lawyer later in testimony. See 7 Jeremy Bentham's Works 473–75 (J.Bowring ed.1843).

[18] S.Bok, Secrets 121 (1982).

fessionals that is based on the value of confidentiality is allowed to become ritualistic and universal, the claim can be overextended and result in a kind of moral blindness to the real issues of potential conflict and abuse that a broad and unqualified claim of confidentiality can mask.[19]

While the attorney-client privilege, the agency rule, and the professional regulations all admit several exceptions, they generally do not allow case-by-case balancing of the particular need for confidentiality against the particular need for disclosure. Such an approach has been advocated for the testimonial privilege by eminent writers[20] and has been accepted in such areas as the privilege of corporations in shareholder derivative actions[21] and of deceased clients in will contest cases.[22] But ordinarily the legal embodiments of the confidentiality principle fail to take specifically into account the inquiring party's need for the information, and the strengths and weaknesses of the claim for confidentiality being made by the client.[23] Custom and ease of application will probably result in continuation of a mechanical approach.

Bentham's Attack

The first systematic attack on the privilege was made by Jeremy Bentham, whose acidly worded arguments for legal reform rankled official England a century and a half ago.[24] His criticisms of the privilege have been refined by influential commentators over the years since.[25] Several of the shafts that Bentham loosed would fall harmlessly to earth today, at least in the United States. For example, he could argue 150 years ago that the law was incoherent because it both compelled an accused to testify against his interests and at the same time prohibited his lawyer from doing the same thing.[26] But in the United States the privilege against self-incrimination removes that inconsistency.[27]

Bentham's most telling argument is that the privilege is anti-utilitarian: it protects only the guilty, and the innocent have no need for the protection.[28] The modern-day response to that portion of the Bentham critique is to attempt to distinguish between three types of accused persons: the plainly guilty, the plainly innocent, and the innocent who are the victims of suspicious circumstances. Bentham's argument, it is asserted, addresses only the first two cases and not the third. The innocent person who is the victim of apparently damaging circumstances would be harmed both by the forcing of his or her lawyer to testify to damaging admissions and by being discouraged from obtaining assis-

19 Id. at 123.

20 Professor McCormick apparently was the first to call for modification of the attorney-client privilege so that its costs in individual classes of cases could be balanced against its benefits. See McCormick, The Scope of Privilege in the Law of Evidence, 16 Tex.L.Rev. 447, 469 (1938). See also C.McCormick, Evidence § 87 at 206 (E.Cleary 3d ed.1984); Note, The Attorney-Client Privilege: Fixed Rules, Balancing and Constitutional Entitlement, 91 Harv.L.Rev. 464 (1977); McGranahan v. Dahar, 119 N.H. 758, 408 A.2d 121, 125 (1979).

21 See § 6.5.5.

22 See infra § 6.3.4 (duration of the privilege).

23 Courts occasionally have attempted to take such additional criteria into account with other privileges. E.g., Black Panther Party v. Smith, 661 F.2d 1243 (D.C.Cir. 1981)(First Amendment claim of privilege against discovery is to be assessed by balancing threatened harm to rights of expression and association against relevance of information to requesting party's case and availability of information from alternative sources), vacated with directions to dismiss, 458 U.S. 1118, 102 S.Ct. 3505, 73 L.Ed.2d 1381 (1982).

24 7 Jeremy Bentham's Works 473–75 (J.Bowring ed. 1843).

25 M.Frankel, Partisan Justice 64–66 (1980); Morgan, Foreword, ALI Model Code of Evidence 26–28 (1942); Frankel, The Search for Truth Continued: More Disclosure, Less Privilege, 54 U.Colo.L.Rev. 51, 60–63 (1982); Hazard, An Historical Perspective on the Attorney-Client Privilege, 66 Calif.L.Rev. 1061 (1978); Radin, The Privilege of Confidential Communication between Lawyer and Client, 16 Calif.L.Rev. 487, 491–93 (1928).

26 7 Jeremy Bentham's Works 472 (J.Bowring ed.1843).

27 Similarly, Bentham's arguments about inconsistency based on the law of misprision of felony and accessory-after-the-fact are inapplicable today because of the disappearance or strict confinement of these crimes. See id. at 474–75.

28 Id. at 475.

tance from the lawyer in the first place.[29] Those defenders of the privilege do not argue against Bentham's utilitarian frame of argument; they respond in kind that the harm from the concealment of truth caused by the privilege is more than offset by the good of assisting the innocent victim of suspicious circumstances. On those terms, it is by no means clear whether Bentham or his utilitarian critics have the better of the empirical argument.

The Politics of the Privilege

From a political point of view, the vigor of the attorney-client privilege is palpably owed to the fact that lawyers make such laws and are benefited by them. The confidentiality principle reinforces the claim of lawyers as a group to professional status and strengthens their capacity to offer help to clients.[30] It has also advantaged lawyers in their competition against nonlawyers who seek to provide legal services. Because nonlawyers cannot offer the protection of confidential communications to potential clients, lawyers are able to sell a more valuable product.[31] The universality of the principle also means that lawyers need not, because they are prevented from doing so, defend publicly the reasons why they agree to represent repugnant clients.[32] When the principle rubs hard against lawyer self-interest, as in lawyers' attempts to collect fees from clients or in defenses against malpractice claims, exceptions are provided (§ 6.7.8).[33] In the end, the survival of broad and absolute forms of the privilege may be due only to the politically entrenched position of lawyers in courts and legislatures.[34]

One can confidently predict that if professors or members of another occupational group could convene a court or legislature of their kind to consider whether communications in their secret conclaves should be absolutely privileged, they too would solemnly decide to enact the privilege for compelling reasons. But courts are peopled only by lawyers, and no other occupational group has been benefited by an unqualified privilege recognized in all tribunals.[35]

A regrettable consequence of overstated claims for the confidentiality principle have caused it to come under suspicion. Too often judges and commentators treat the matter as if the only consideration worth discussing were the protection of client confidentiality.[36] The fact is that a conflict of values is present in most of the hard cases between claims of confidentiality and claims for disclosure in order to prevent greater harms.[37]

[29] 8 J.Wigmore, Evidence § 2291 at 552 (J.McNaughton rev.ed.1961).

[30] S.Bok, Secrets 116 (1982). It may also be that professional elitism causes established professional groups to resist claims by newly emerging professional groups to legal entitlement to confidentiality privileges. Id. 119.

[31] Morgan, The Evolving Concept of Professional Responsibility, 90 Harv.L.Rev. 702, 738 (1977).

[32] The positive aspect of this is that it encourages otherwise uncourageous lawyers to defend unpopular clients. Cf. Teitlebaum, The Advocate's Role in the Legal System, 6 N.M.L.Rev. 1, 27 (1975). Negatively, it provides cover for lawyers who willingly participate in sordid or illegal client enterprises.

[33] Morgan, supra note 29, at 738–39.

[34] Morgan, Foreword, Model Code of Evidence 28 (1942); Weissenberger, Toward Precision in the Application of the Attorney-Client Privilege for Corporations, 65 Iowa L.Rev. 899, 899 (1980).

[35] Couch v. United States, 409 U.S. 322, 93 S.Ct. 611, 34 L.Ed.2d 548 (1973)(no general federal accountant-client privilege); Gray v. Board of Higher Educ., 692 F.2d 901 (2d Cir.1982)(confidential academic personnel files must be disclosed).

[36] A remarkable example is the one-sided discussion in Upjohn Corp. v. United States, 449 U.S. 383, 101 S.Ct. 677, 66 L.Ed.2d 584 (1981), in which, from all that appears, there are only arguments in favor of confidentiality and no considerations opposed. See also M.Freeman, Lawyers' Ethics in an Adversary System, passim (1975). For contrasting views, see, e.g., Trammel v. United States, 445 U.S 40, 50–51, 100 S.Ct. 906, 912–13, 63 L.Ed. 2d 186 (1980)(cited and quoted in *Upjohn,* but not for this proposition)(privileges must be strictly construed because they contravene the fundamental principle that the public has a right to every man's evidence); Fisher v. United States, 425 U.S. 391, 403, 96 S.Ct. 1569, 1577, 48 L.Ed.2d 39 (1976); United States v. Nixon, 418 U.S. 683, 709, 94 S.Ct. 3090, 3108, 41 L.Ed.2d 1039 (1974).

[37] Alschuler, The Preservation of a Client's Confidences: One Value Among Many or a Categorical Imperative?, 52 U.Colo.L.Rev. 349 (1981).

WESTLAW REFERENCES

Detraction From the Search for Truth

(fact /3 find***) justice truth /p attorney counsel** lawyer /2 client /s privilege*

Reducing Spurious Suits and Achieving Law Compliance

bring brought file* groundless baseless spurious /3 suit action claim /s attorney counsel** lawyer /2 client /s privilege*

Preventing Disruption of the Client-Lawyer Relationship

corrupt*** disrupt*** /p testif! testimony witness /s attorney counsel** lawyer /2 client /s privilege*

Protecting Privacy Interests

privacy /s attorney counsel** lawyer /2 client /s privilege*

Weighing the Claims for Confidentiality

condition** moral qualif! unqualif! /s attorney counsel** lawyer /2 client /s privilege*

Bentham's Attack

bentham /p attorney counsel** lawyer /2 client /s privilege*

The Politics of the Privilege

politic** statut*** /s attorney counsel** lawyer /2 client /s privilege*

§ 6.2 CONFIDENTIALITY AND THE CONSTITUTION

§ 6.2.1 *Scope of the Claims for Constitutional Protection*

The extent to which the federal and state constitutions protect client communications to a lawyer is still unclear. Present authority suggests that such protection exists but that it is concerned primarily with intentional governmental intrusions into a confidential client-lawyer relationship. The protection is clearly in a process of evolution. It involves client claims of protection against self-incrimination under the Fifth Amendment, against unreasonable searches and seizures under the Fourth Amendment, and against deprivation of the right to counsel under the Sixth Amendment.

The attorney-client privilege developed historically without any relationship to constitutional rights.[38] For the most part, the privilege has been regarded as a creature of ordinary legislative enactment or common law. Statutes that restrict its reach are occasionally encountered and countenanced.[39] The fact that the privilege varies considerably among the states also suggests that there is no general recognition of a broad constitutional compulsion to the privilege. The ultimate question would probably be raised only by a legislative attempt to repeal the privilege in a significant way.[40] Large claims for a constitutionally protected zone of protection within the attorney-client privilege nonetheless have been argued for, but primarily in ways that stride in seven-league boots.[41] The case support is meager, and only some selectivity and strenuous interpretive ingenuity can find a path through a field of precedent that is in large part inhospitable.

WESTLAW REFERENCES

attorney counsel** lawyer /2 client /s privilege* /p constitution!

§ 6.2.2 *Fourth Amendment*

The constitutional guarantee against unreasonable searches and seizures and the requirement of a warrant finds expression, for pur-

[38] On the history of the privilege, see § 6.1.2.

[39] Attorney General v. Covington & Burling, 411 F.Supp. 371 (D.D.C.1976)(Federal Foreign Agents Registration Act).

[40] Bradt v. Smith, 634 F.2d 796, 800 (5th Cir.), cert. denied 454 U.S. 830, 102 S.Ct. 125, 70 L.Ed.2d 106 (1981) (state court's denial of attorney-client privilege claim of lawyer, even if incorrect as matter of state law, does not ordinarily give rise to claim of denial of federal constitutional right); Beckler v. Superior Court, 568 F.2d 661 (9th Cir.1978)(client's Fifth Amendment privilege against self-incrimination not violated by state court order to lawyer to turn over client documents in his possession to which state law does not extend attorney-client privilege); OKC Corp. v. Williams, 461 F.Supp. 540, 546 (N.D.Tex.1978) (attorney-client privilege claims are not ordinarily of constitutional dimension).

[41] Seidelson, The Attorney-Client Privilege and Client's Constitutional Rights, 6 Hofstra L.Rev. 693 (1978); Freedman, Book Review, 90 Yale L.J. 1496 (1981); Note, People v. Meredith: The Attorney-Client Privilege and the Criminal Defendant's Constitutional Rights, 70 Calif.L.Rev. 1048 (1982); Note, Extending the Attorney-Client Privilege: A Constitutional Mandate, 13 Pac.L.J. 437 (1982).

poses of the attorney-client privilege, principally in cases dealing with police searches of lawyers' offices (§ 14.6.4). The thrust of the cases in that area is that a search can be conducted so long as probable cause is certified by an independent judicial officer, although the better practice is also to afford a procedure where an independent law officer accompanies the search party to assure that client confidential information is not needlessly exposed to view. So long as those procedural requirements are satisfied, existing authority seems to permit such searches. A valid seizure does not inevitably mean that material seized may be used adversely against the searched lawyer's client; if the material is a protected confidential communication, its use against the client in a criminal prosecution may violate the Sixth Amendment right to counsel.[42]

WESTLAW REFERENCES

attorney counsel** lawyer /2 client /s privilege* /p "4th amendment" search*** seiz*** warrant

§ 6.2.3 Fifth Amendment

The privilege against self-incrimination can be implicated because of the possible criminality of the acts of either client or lawyer. The question of the client's rights was dealt with in the 1975 decision of the Supreme Court in Fisher v. United States.[43] In two separate cases the Internal Revenue Service had issued subpoenas to lawyers to obtain tax documents that accountants had prepared and returned to the clients. The clients had turned the tax documents over to their lawyers. The Supreme Court first held that seizure of the documents from the lawyers did not directly violate any Fifth Amendment right of the clients because the clients personally were compelled to do nothing.[44]

Second, the Court also suggested that documents that would be protected from compulsory seizure in the hands of the client under the Fifth Amendment would also be privileged in the hands of the client's lawyer if they were transferred to the lawyer for the purpose of obtaining legal advice.[45] But the protection of the Fifth Amendment for client-retained documents is limited. The fact that a document prepared by the client is incriminating is not independently important so long as its preparation was not compelled by the government.[46] The Court stopped short of saying that a court could order a compulsory production by an accused of papers where their authentication, existence, or possession by the accused was in issue. The act of the accused in producing papers identified in a summons could have testimonial value as the Court acknowledged.[47] If the governmental compulsion to produce documents takes the form of a

[42] Bishop v. Rose, 701 F.2d 1150 (6th Cir.1983).

[43] 425 U.S. 391, 96 S.Ct. 1569, 48 L.Ed.2d 39 (1976).

[44] 425 U.S. at 397, 96 S.Ct. at 1574. The Court had previously held in Couch v. United States, 409 U.S. 322, 93 S.Ct. 611, 34 L.Ed.2d 548 (1973), that a summons issued to a taxpayer's accountant under similar circumstances did not violate the Fifth Amendment.

[45] 425 U.S. at 404–05, 96 S.Ct. at 1577–78. See also § 6.3.5 (client documents).

[46] 425 U.S. at 410 n.11, 93 S.Ct. at 1580 n.11. In the same footnote, the Court noted that even oral incriminatory statements could be seized (citing wiretap cases) if the statements themselves were not made under governmental compulsion. In the text of the opinion immediately following the footnote, the Court stated: "The taxpayer cannot avoid compliance with the subpoena merely by asserting that the item of evidence which he is required to produce contains incriminatory writing, whether his own or that of someone else." See also, e.g., In re Grand Jury Empanelled February 14, 1978 (Markowitz), 603 F.2d 469, 476–77 (3d Cir.1979).

Compulsion can take the form of trickery. For example, in Estelle v. Smith, 451 U.S. 454, 101 S.Ct. 1866, 68 L.Ed.2d 359 (1981), the Court held that a court-ordered psychiatric examination of an accused with respect to his plea of incompetence to stand trial could not be used to produce testimony against the accused at the penalty phase of a murder trial. If trickery is lacking, then the testimony is admissible. E.g., Granviel v. Estelle, 655 F.2d 673, 682–83 (5th Cir.1981), cert. denied 455 U.S. 1003, 102 S.Ct. 1636, 71 L.Ed.2d 870 (1982)(if accused knows that his statements to a court-appointed psychiatrist can be used against him there is no right-to-counsel or self-incrimination requirement to keep the statements confidential).

[47] 425 U.S. at 410–13, 93 S.Ct. at 1580–82. The Court found, however, that the issue of the authenticity or accuracy of the accountants' papers was raised in the case, and thus the Court did not have to reach the issue of authentication-by-production. Full development of the question is pursued in C.McCormick, Evidence § 126 (E.Cleary 3d ed.1984); 8 J.Wigmore, Evidence § 2264 (J.McNaughton rev.1961).

search warrant, however, the element of compulsory identification is absent and does not preclude seizure. Under a valid search warrant, an accused can be coerced into standing aside and allowing a search conducted for incriminating evidence, including his or her own documents.[48] By extension, client documents in the hands of a lawyer should be at least equally accessible to compulsory reach because rarely will the lawyer's possession of them involve any compulsory testimonial element that can validly be called compulsory self-incrimination of the client. Different, of course, would be a case in which a lawyer asserts a personal self-incrimination privilege not to be compelled to testify or to perform testimonial acts because the testimony or response to the subpoena might implicate the lawyer (rather than the client) in wrongdoing.

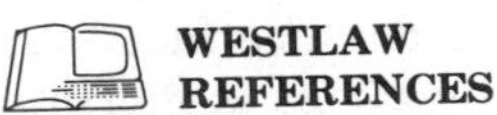
WESTLAW REFERENCES

attorney counsel** lawyer /2 client /s privilege* /p "5th amendment" incriminat***

§ 6.2.4 *Sixth Amendment*

The constitutional right to counsel guaranteed by the Sixth Amendment has been given a generous reading in recent decades in decisions establishing a right to court appointed counsel for indigent persons in criminal cases (§ 14.3.1), requiring that the competence of court-appointed counsel measure up to a minimal standard (§ 14.6), restricting law office searches and prohibiting other types of governmental intrusions into the lawyer-client relationship (§ 14.6.4). It is in the context of those doctrines that the strongest arguments for constitutional protection of the attorney-client privilege can be made.

In Bishop v. Rose,[49] for example, the Sixth Circuit held that the Sixth Amendment right to counsel of an accused person was violated when his confidential draft of a letter to his lawyer was seized from his cell during an otherwise lawful cell search and then used to impeach his trial testimony. The court distinguished cases under the Fourth Amendment that had held that illegally seized evidence could be used to impeach a defendant who elects to testify at trial,[50] because the evidence seized in those cases, unlike here, did not involve "a constitutional right which is at the heart of our adversary system of criminal justice."[51] The importance of such cases is that the court presumably reaches the conclusion that the breach of confidentiality offends the Constitution, notwithstanding state law to the contrary. The implications for a broader reach for constitutional protection of confidentiality are apparent.

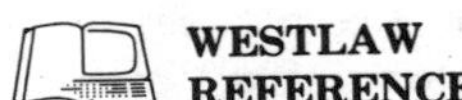
WESTLAW REFERENCES

attorney counsel** lawyer /2 client /s privilege* /p "right to counsel" "6th amendment"

§ 6.3 THE ATTORNEY–CLIENT PRIVILEGE

§ 6.3.1 *General*

The attorney-client privilege exists by virtue of statute, court rule, or common-law doctrine in every jurisdiction in the United States. Formulations and model statements of it abound.[52] Any general encapsulation

48 See Andresen v. Maryland, 427 U.S. 463, 96 S.Ct. 2737, 49 L.Ed.2d 627 (1976)(lawyer's law office and separate land development business office lawfully searched under warrant and business records properly admitted over his Fifth and Fourth Amendment objections).

49 701 F.2d 1150 (6th Cir.1983).

50 United States v. Havens, 446 U.S. 620, 100 S.Ct. 1912, 64 L.Ed.2d 559 (1980); Harris v. New York, 401 U.S. 222, 91 S.Ct. 643, 28 L.Ed.2d 1 (1971).

51 701 F.2d at 1157.

52 Probably the best known is Dean Wigmore's formula. 8 J.Wigmore, Evidence § 2292, at 554 (J.McNaughton rev.1961). See also, e.g., United States v. United Shoe Machinery Corp., 89 F.Supp. 357, 358–59 (D.Mass.1950) (Wysanski, J.); Unif.R.Evid. 501 (1974); id., Rule 26 (1953 ed.); Model Code of Evid. Rule 201 (1942). Rule 501 of the Supreme Court's proposed Evidence Rules (whose effectiveness was blocked by Congress) is still referred to as a standard. E.g., United States v. Mackey, 405 F.Supp. 854, 857–58 (E.D.N.Y.1975). For its text, see J.Weinstein & M.Berger, Weinstein's Evidence 503–1 to 503–2 (1982).

sacrifices completeness for brevity and overlooks important jurisdictional variations. In succeeding pages, the following Wigmorian conceptions will be developed: (1) a person (client) who seeks legal advice or assistance (2) from a lawyer acting in behalf of the client, (3) for an indefinite time may invoke, and the lawyer must invoke in the client's behalf, an unqualified privilege not to testify (4) concerning the contents of a client communication (5) that was made by the client or by the client's communicative agent (6) in confidence (7) to the lawyer or the lawyer's confidential agent, (8) unless the client expressly or by implication waives the privilege.

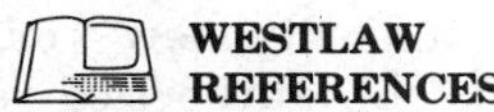
WESTLAW REFERENCES

topic(attorney /2 client /s privilege*)

§ 6.3.2 *Client Advice-Seeker*

The attorney-client privilege is not a rule protecting privacy per se, but only privacy in the context and for the purpose of encouraging full disclosure to a legal adviser by one seeking legal services. A person who seeks business advice,[53] preparation of a tax return,[54] or accounting services [55] or who speaks to a lawyer merely as a friend,[56] a depository or trustee,[57] a scrivener,[58] or a prospective employer [59] is not covered by the privilege or its purpose. A lawyer cannot be considered merely a friend, and not a lawyer, just because no fee is charged, and the cases consistently hold that the absence of a fee or formal fee contract is not critical.[60] What is essential is that the services sought be legal in nature. In the parlance of the industry, a lawyer serving as bagman is not serving as a lawyer. Thus a person who drops off a bundle of money for a lawyer to pay to conspirators in an extortion scheme does not seek legal advice, but only delivery services.[61]

Not everyone who speaks to a lawyer or pays the lawyer's fee is a "client." Nor is the designation of a person as client a matter solely of the lawyer's own later description. It must be shown that a person consulted the lawyer confidentially for the purposes of obtaining personal legal services.[62] A client need not actively seek out the lawyer, such as when a lawyer or guardian ad litem is appointed for a child or incompetent person.[63] Conversely, one who seeks legal advice or assistance is entitled to claim the privilege for confidences disclosed during the initial consultation even if the lawyer does not thereafter accept the representation.[64]

[53] United States v. Huberts, 637 F.2d 630, 640 (9th Cir. 1980), cert. denied 451 U.S. 975, 101 S.Ct. 2058, 68 L.Ed. 2d 356 (1981); SEC v. Gulf & Western Indus., Inc., 518 F.Supp. 675, 683 (D.D.C.1981); Kuiper v. District Court, ___ Mont. ___, 632 P.2d 694, 699 (1981).

[54] See generally Kenderdine, The Internal Revenue Service Summons to Produce Documents, 64 Minn.L.Rev. 73, 100–01 (1979). E.g., United States v. El Paso Co., 682 F.2d 530, 539 (5th Cir.1982), cert. denied ___ U.S. ___, 104 S.Ct. 1927, 80 L.Ed.2d 473 (1984). A conflict in the federal circuits exists over the question whether routine tax return preparation by a lawyer constitutes an activity covered by the attorney-client privilege. See In re Grand Jury Subpoena Duces Tecum (Dorokee Co.), 697 F.2d 277, 280 (10th Cir.1983), and cases cited.

[55] Brink v. DaLesio, 82 F.R.D. 664, 674 (D.Md.1979) (inactive member of Virginia bar who practiced only accounting in Maryland, where he was not licensed as lawyer, cannot invoke privilege for client for whom he performed accounting services).

[56] United States v. Stern, 511 F.2d 1364, 1367 (2d Cir. 1975), cert.denied 423 U.S. 829, 96 S.Ct. 47, 46 L.Ed.2d 46 (1975) (acquaintance of fellow indictee); Prichard v. United States, 181 F.2d 326, 330 (6th Cir.1950), affirmed for lack of quorum 339 U.S. 974, 70 S.Ct. 1029, 94 L.Ed. 1380 (1950)(lifelong friend and judge); In re Kinoy, 326 F.Supp. 400, 403–05 (S.D.N.Y.1970)(relative).

[57] Gold Coast Raceway, Inc. v. Ehrenfeld, 392 So.2d 1002, 1002–03 (Fla.App.1981).

[58] SEC v. Gulf & Western Indus., Inc., 518 F.Supp. 675, 683 (D.D.C.1981); Bloyea v. First Presbyterian Church, 196 N.W.2d 149 (N.D.1972).

[59] State v. Bissantz, 3 Ohio App.3d 108, 444 N.E.2d 92 (1982).

[60] 8 J.Wigmore, Evidence § 2303 (J.McNaughton rev. 1961).

[61] Hughes v. Meade, 453 S.W.2d 538 (Ky.1970)(lawyer retained to return stolen property); State v. Carter, 578 P.2d 1275, 1277 (Utah 1978).

[62] In re Bonanno, 344 F.2d 830, 833 (2d Cir.1965); Priest v. Hennessy, 51 N.Y.2d 62, 431 N.Y.S.2d 511, 515, 409 N.E.2d 983, 987 (1980).

[63] Provencal v. Provencal, 122 N.H. 793, 451 A.2d 374, 377 (1982)(guardian ad litem in child custody case).

[64] Commonwealth v. O'Brien, 377 Mass. 772, 388 N.E.2d 658, 661 (1979); Taylor v. Sheldon, 172 Ohio St. 118, 173 N.E.2d 892, 895 (1961).

While the privilege is typically asserted as a reason not to testify at a subsequent trial, there is no requirement that a client's initial consultation with a lawyer have been for the purpose of bringing or defending a lawsuit. A consultation that does not contemplate litigation at all, but that is concerned with obtaining legal advice or legal assistance on a nonlitigious matter such as drafting a contract, is equally covered.[65]

Even if the confidential relationship of lawyer and client is indisputably formed, it does not follow that every communication between them will be privileged. Some communications may have nothing to do with the lawyer's legal services, such as a side conversation about business. Yet if the client's legal matter concerns his or her business on an ongoing basis, client communications intended to keep the lawyer informed about the business in order to provide preventive legal advice should be privileged.[66] Some matters are conventionally not permitted to be considered part of the lawyer's work, such as communications about future crimes or frauds (§ 6.4.10). As will be seen, communications made for the purpose of supplying information to a lawyer in search of legal assistance must have other characteristics as well in order to qualify as privileged.

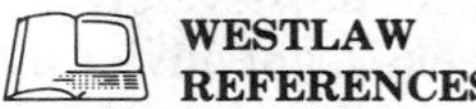
WESTLAW REFERENCES

attorney counsel** lawyer /2 client /s privilege* /p (advice advis*** assist! service /4 legal) fee friend scrivener

§ 6.3.3 Partisan Lawyer

The person from whom the client seeks legal advice must be a lawyer. Thus a law student will not do,[67] or a social service caseworker,[68] or a nonlawyer patent counsel according to the majority view [69] or, according to some authority, an authorized representative in welfare cases in an administrative fair hearing.[70] To be distinguished are situations in which a nonlawyer to whom a client or prospective client speaks is an authorized agent of a lawyer for receipt of confidential client information (§ 6.3.8). A difficult question is whether a client's good faith but mistaken belief that a legal adviser is an adequately credentialed lawyer should be sufficient for invoking the privilege.[71]

[65] Alexander v. United States, 138 U.S. 353, 357, 11 S.Ct. 350, 352, 34 L.Ed. 954 (1891); Foster v. Hall, 29 Mass. (12 Pick.) 89, 97 (1831); Wheeler v. Le Marchant, 17 Ch.D. 675, 682 (1881)(Jessel, M.R.). Contrast the work product protection which requires that the lawyer's work have been in contemplation of litigation. See § 6.6.2.

[66] Hercules, Inc. v. Exxon Corp., 434 F.Supp. 136, 144 (D.Del.1977). Courts occasionally say that the privilege only applies to client disclosures "necessary to obtain informed legal advice." E.g., Fisher v. United States, 425 U.S. 391, 403, 96 S.Ct. 1569, 1577, 48 L.Ed.2d 39 (1976). But no general doctrine requires that the client guess correctly that a contemplated disclosure indeed is "necessary" for the purpose. The cases indicate that the only requirement is that disclosures must be reasonably appropriate to obtaining legal advice.

[67] Dabney v. Investment Corp., 82 F.R.D. 464 (E.D.Pa. 1979); People v. Doe, 99 Misc.2d 411, 416 N.Y.S.2d 466, 469 (1979).

[68] E.g., In re T.D.S., 289 N.W.2d 137 (Minn.1980)(juvenile treatment program caseworker); L.J. v. J.B., 150 N.J.Super. 373, 375 A.2d 1202 (1977)(supervisor of county welfare board).

[69] Compare, e.g., Foseco Int'l Ltd. v. Fireline, Inc., 546 F.Supp. 22, 25 (N.D.Ohio 1982), and authorities cited (majority view), with, e.g., In re Ampicillin Antitrust Litig., 81 F.R.D. 377, 393–94 (D.D.C.1978), and authorities cited (privilege extended to patent counsel registered and subject to professional discipline of Patent Office in order to carry out holding of Sperry v. Florida, 373 U.S. 379, 83 S.Ct. 1322, 10 L.Ed.2d 428 (1963), that nonlawyer patent counsel can practice patent law in any state).

[70] Hunt v. Maricopa County Employees Merit System Comm'n, 127 Ariz. 259, 619 P.2d 1036, 1041 (1980). But cf. Welfare Rights Org. v. Crisan, 33 Cal.3d 766, 190 Cal. Rptr. 919, 922–23, 661 P.2d 1073, 1076–77, 31 A.L.R.4th 1214 (1983)(assumption that legislature intended to confer some kind of privilege on communication, but precise scope left open).

[71] See generally 8 J.Wigmore, Evidence § 2302 (J.McNaughton rev.1961)(supporting extension of privilege); United States v. Boffa, 513 F.Supp. 517, 523–25 (Del.1981)(on facts, improbable that lawyer-defendant reasonably believed that "jailhouse lawyer" was lawyer). Compare, e.g., Prichard v. United States, 181 F.2d 326 (6th Cir.1950), affirmed for lack of quorum 339 U.S. 974, 70 S.Ct. 1029, 94 L.Ed. 1380 (1950)(judge prohibited from practicing law had convened grand jury to investigate advice-seeker's activities in ballot box stuffing charge; lawyer who sought advice should have known of judge's disability to practice), with United States v. Ostrer, 422 F.Supp. 93, 97 (S.D.N.Y.1976)(client's good faith belief that friend-lawyer was functioning as counsel).

The fact that the person who receives a communication is clearly a lawyer does not suffice if the client-communicator has no reason to think that the lawyer is functioning as a partisan in the putative client's behalf. A call to a district attorney by a killer to arrange for a safe surrender is not a communication to such a partisan.[72] Nor is a call to one's former lawyer to make a threat against the lawyer's family and property.[73] In either case the "client" is plainly not encouraged by a confidential relationship to make a statement.

WESTLAW REFERENCES

attorney counsel** lawyer /2 client /s privilege* /s authori! card-carrying case-worker credential** (law legal /1 intern student) license*

§ 6.3.4 *Invoking the Privilege*

A client may, of course, invoke the privilege in any instance in which called as a witness, whether on direct or cross-examination and whether appearing only as witness or also as litigant. A lawyer also has responsibilities with respect to the client's testimonial privilege. An obligation of competence and loyalty requires that the lawyer advise the client about the availability of the privilege, so the client can decide whether to invoke it.[74]

The motives of the client in invoking the privilege must necessarily be irrelevant to the court's ruling.[75] Clients undoubtedly are often motivated, not by the public-spirited desire to vindicate the general sanctity of the lawyer's office, but by the partisan desire to avoid personal discomfort or, indeed, to obtain an unjust result in litigation by preventing the fact finder from learning the truth. The relevance of motives to morality is, of course, a separate matter.

A Lawyer's Duty to Invoke the Privilege

It is elementary that the privilege is not a rule about the general incompetence or immunity of lawyers as witnesses. A lawyer must comply with an order to appear as a witness.[76] But once on the witness stand, the lawyer must assert his or her client's privilege if the particular question asked cannot be responded to truthfully without its violation. The duty to invoke the privilege is one of professional responsibility and does not depend on the client's independent request to the lawyer to do so.[77] The duty is defined, however, by the client's own rights. If the client has made an effective waiver of the

[72] People v. O'Connor, 85 A.D.2d 92, 447 N.Y.S.2d 553, 557 (1982). See also, e.g., In re Grand Jury Subpoena Dated November 9, 1979, 484 F.Supp. 1099, 1106 (S.D. N.Y.1980)(Roe's communication to Doe's lawyer); In re Colocotronis Tanker Securities Litig., 449 F.Supp. 828 (S.D.N.Y.1978). To be distinguished are situations in which coclients make statements to a common lawyer. See § 6.4.8.

[73] Hopkinson v. State, 632 P.2d 79 (Wyo.1981), cert. denied 455 U.S. 922, 102 S.Ct. 1280, 71 L.Ed.2d 463 (1982).

[74] EC 4–4; Johnson v. Frontier Ford, Inc., 68 Ill.App.3d 315, 318–19, 24 Ill.Dec. 908, 911–12, 386 N.E.2d 112 (1979).

[75] United States v. Buckley, 586 F.2d 498, 502–03 (5th Cir.1978), cert. denied 440 U.S. 982, 99 S.Ct. 1792, 60 L.Ed.2d 242 (1979); De los Santos v. Superior Court, 27 Cal.3d 677, 166 Cal.Rptr. 172, 177, 613 P.2d 233, 238 (1980)(mother who was guardian ad litem asserted privilege to prevent testimony about minor's communication in order to protect her own claim for medical expenditures).

[76] In re Walsh, 623 F.2d 489 (7th Cir.); cert. denied 449 U.S. 994, 101 S.Ct. 531, 66 L.Ed.2d 291 (1980)(lawyer called to be interrogated by grand jury about matter in which client was involved cannot refuse to appear); Losavio v. District Court, 188 Colo. 127, 533 P.2d 32, 36 (1975); State v. Yates, 174 Conn. 16, 381 A.2d 536 (1977); In re Estate of Niemiec, 435 N.E.2d 570, 572 (Ind.App. 1982); McNulty v. McNulty, 81 A.D.2d 581, 437 N.Y.S.2d 438 (1981).

[77] EC 4–4; MR 1.6 comment (Disclosures Otherwise Required or Authorized); United States v. Hodgson, 492 F.2d 1175, 1177 (10th Cir.1974). Cf. Fisher v. United States, 425 U.S. 391, 402, n.8, 96 S.Ct. 1569, 1576, n.8, 49 L.Ed.2d 39 (1976)(privilege "may be raised by lawyer"). It has even been asserted that if an unrepresented witness fails to assert the privilege, a trial judge is under a mandatory duty to advise the witness of the right to assert it. People v. Flores, 71 Cal.App.3d 559, 139 Cal. Rptr. 546, 548 (1977). But see, e.g., Commonwealth v. Trolene, 263 Pa.Super. 263, 397 A.2d 1200, 1204 (1979) (third party implicated by client communication testified to by lawyer has no standing to assert privilege). The apparent implication in Warnaco, Inc. v. Freund, 94 F.R.D. 237, 238 (E.D.N.Y.1980), that a client must personally attend a hearing and direct his lawyer to assert the privilege, is plainly in error.

privilege, the lawyer has no power to revitalize it by subsequent objection.[78]

Once the privilege has been asserted, a lawyer-witness' remaining obligation to the client is determined by the ruling of the court.[79] A lawyer is entitled, but not required, to refuse to comply with a trial court order to testify if that is a recognized way of obtaining immediate appellate review of the order in the jurisdiction and the lawyer in good faith can argue on appeal that the order was erroneous.[80]

Proving the Privilege

The burden is on the person asserting the privilege to prove all of the elements necessary to demonstrate that it applies.[81] Such a showing, and rebuttal to it, may require a hearing to develop facts. At least when the judge is not sitting as fact finder in the trial or hearing at which the evidence will be offered, if admissible over the objection of privilege, close questions of applicability of the attorney-client privilege may be resolved by an in camera inspection of a challenged document or communication.[82] Once an objection on the ground of attorney-client privilege is made and sustained, no further attempt should be made by the inquiring party to insinuate to the jury that the document or communication is being kept from them. It would seriously undercut the purpose of the privilege to countenance repetition of the same question in a way designed to force the witness to reassert the privilege.[83]

Appellate Review

The majority rule is that an erroneous refusal of the trial court to sustain an objection grounded on the privilege does not automatically lead to appellate reversal. Under the harmless error rule, reversal is warranted only where the appellant demonstrates that it is likely that the fact finder was materially influenced in reaching the decision because of erroneous admission of the communication.[84] Even if prejudicial error is shown, it does not follow that an erroneous adverse ruling on the privilege will lead to the same appellate result in each instance. If the holder of the privilege is the party aggrieved by the ruling, and if the ruling is appealable, then, of course, the holder has standing to raise the issue on appeal. But suppose that the client is not a party or is not aggrieved by the final judgment. By a logic common to other privileges as well, the majority of jurisdictions sensibly hold that the nonholder lacks standing to appeal the erroneous refusal to respect the privilege.[85]

[78] Republic Gear Co. v. Borg-Warner Corp., 381 F.2d 551, 556 (2d Cir.1967). See § 6.4.

[79] The extravagant statement of two judges in People v. Kor, 129 Cal.App.2d 436, 447, 277 P.2d 94, 101 (1954), that a lawyer whose assertion of the privilege has been overruled by a trial judge is duty-bound to risk contempt and appeal to a higher court is simply judicial heavy breathing. Neither lawyers, trial courts, nor opposing litigants must regularly await the outcome of such needless gallantry. Certainly no lawyer code requires it. See DR 4–101(C)(2); cf. MR 1.6. Accord, e.g., Velsicol Chemical Corp. v. Parsons, 561 F.2d 671, 674 n.1 (7th Cir.1977), cert. denied 435 U.S. 942, 98 S.Ct. 1521, 55 L.Ed.2d 538 (1978).

[80] Maness v. Meyer, 419 U.S. 449, 458–59, 95 S.Ct. 584, 42 L.Ed.2d 574 (1975); In re Navarro, 93 Cal.App.3d 325, 155 Cal.Rptr. 522, 525 (1979). The matter is complex and a lawyer obviously proceeds here with caution. See generally § 12.1.3.

[81] In re Grand Jury Subpoena Duces Tecum (Dorokee Co.), 697 F.2d 277, 280 (10th Cir.1983); United States v. Osborn, 561 F.2d 1334, 1339 (9th Cir.1977); United States v. Kovel, 296 F.2d 918, 923 (2d Cir.1961). But cf. People v. Flores, 71 Cal.App.3d 559, 139 Cal.Rptr. 546, 548 (1977) (burden on inquiring party to establish that the communication was not confidential once lawyer-client communication is shown).

[82] E.g., United States v. Parker, 586 F.2d 422, 428 (5th Cir.1978), cert. denied 441 U.S. 962, 99 S.Ct. 2408, 60 L.Ed.2d 1067 (1979); O'Keeffe v. Bry, 456 F.Supp. 822, 826 (S.D.N.Y.1978). In camera review generally is prohibited in California. See Romo v. Southern Pac. Transp. Co., 71 Cal.App.3d 909, 922, 139 Cal.Rptr. 787, 795 (1977).

[83] Stanger v. Gordon, 309 Minn. 215, 244 N.W.2d 628, 631–32 (1976); 8 J.Wigmore, Evidence § 2322 (J.McNaughton rev.1961).

[84] People v. Watson, 46 Cal.2d 818, 836, 299 P.2d 243, 254 (1956). A different per se rule may apply, however, when in a criminal trial the communication takes the form of a confession by the accused of a crime. See People v. Gardner, 106 Cal.App.3d 882, 165 Cal.Rptr. 415, 419 (1980).

[85] C.McCormick, Evidence § 73, at 173–74 (E.Cleary 3d ed.1984).

The Privilege and Choice of Law

A variety of views has been expressed concerning the choice-of-law issues presented by an invocation of the privilege. A traditional view is to treat the matter as one of procedure, always to be decided by the law of the forum.[86] More recently, courts have indicated a disposition to apply the law of the jurisdiction in which the attorney-client relationship was centered.[87] In the federal courts, Federal Rule of Evidence, Rule 501 provides as a general matter that the matter of privilege is to be developed by case law. But in civil actions in which an element of a claim or defense is based on state law, state law determines whether a privilege applies.[88]

Extra-Judicial Applications

At one time it was debated whether the attorney-client privilege covered coerced testimony other than before a court. Did it cover, for example, a lawyer's testimony before an administrative agency or before a legislative committee, and did it apply to a lawyer's disclosures other than through testimony?[89] It is now generally accepted that most governmentally coerced revelations are covered by the privilege.[90] Even beyond coercion, at least in criminal cases, the government's intrusions into the attorney-client relationship can constitute constitutional violations (§ 6.2). Perhaps even a police-initiated but otherwise voluntary conversation with defendant's lawyer can violate a constitutional right.[91]

Duration of the Privilege

The termination of the attorney-client relationship does not end the privilege. The client's privilege continues, as does the lawyer's correlative obligation to assert it.[92] That application of the confidentiality principle is one of the cornerstones of former-client conflict law.[93] The privilege can also be invoked after the representation ends, even in later unrelated litigation.[94] The effect of the demise of a corporation on the privilege is differently treated. Some authorities hold that the privilege continues, possibly passing into the hands of receivers or others who succeed to the corporation's rights.[95] Other authority

86 Union Planters Nat'l Bank v. ABC Records, Inc., 82 F.R.D. 472, 473 (W.D.Tenn.1979)(applying Tennessee law in diversity case); Restatement of Conflicts § 596 (1934).

87 Restatement (Second), Conflicts §§ 138, 139 (1971); E.Scoles & P.Hay, Conflict of Laws 396–400 (1982); Reese & Leiwant, Testimonial Privileges and Conflict of Laws, 41 Law & Contemp. Probs. 85, 89 (1977); Sterk, Testimonial Privileges: An Analysis of Horizontal Choice of Law Problems, 61 Minn.L.Rev. 461 (1977). Cf. In re Grand Jury Proceedings (Bowe), 694 F.2d 1256, 1257–58 (11th Cir.1982)(in grand jury proceeding under U.S. law investigating records of U.S. citizens, claim of privilege by Bahamian lawyer could not rest on Bahamian law).

88 See generally 2 J.Weinstein & M.Berger, Weinstein's Evidence ¶501[02] (1982).

89 8 J.Wigmore, Evidence § 2300a (J.McNaughton rev. 1961); Comment, Congressional Investigations and the Privileges of Confidential Communications, 45 Calif.L. Rev. 347 (1957).

90 United States v. Calandra, 414 U.S. 338, 346, 94 S.Ct. 613, 619, 38 L.Ed.2d 561 (1974)(grand jury testimony); Wearly v. FTC, 462 F.Supp. 589 (D.N.J.1978), vacated as not ripe for judicial review 616 F.2d 662 (3d Cir.1980), cert.denied 449 U.S. 822, 101 S.Ct. 81, 66 L.Ed.2d 25 (1980)(administrative hearing); CAB v. Air Transp. Ass'n, 201 F.Supp. 318 (D.D.C.1961)(same); Welfare Rights Org. v. Crisan, 33 Cal.3d 766, 190 Cal.Rptr. 919, 922–23, 661 P.2d 1073, 1076–77, 31 A.L.R.4th 1214 (1983)(same); N.J.R. of Evid. N.J.Stat.Ann. § 84A–16, Rule 2(1)(privileges apply in "all proceedings, places and inquiries, whether formal, informal, public or private, as well as to all branches of government and by whomsoever the same may be conducted, and none of said provisions shall be subject to being relaxed."); N.Y.—McKinney's CPLR 4503(a); K.Davis, 3 Administrative Law Treatise § 16:10 (2d ed.1980).

91 Cf. United States v. Kleifgen, 557 F.2d 1293, 1297 (9th Cir.1977). Compare State v. Sandini, 395 So.2d 1178, 1180–81 (Fla.App.), review denied 408 So.2d 1095 (1981), cert. denied 456 U.S. 926, 102 S.Ct. 1971, 72 L.Ed.2d 440 (1982)(privileged material voluntarily disclosed by lawyer to police may be used to establish probable cause for search warrant).

92 E.g., United States v. Kleifgen, 557 F.2d 1293, 1297 (9th Cir.1977); Universal Athletic Sales Co. v. American Gym, Recreational & Athletic Equip. Corp., 546 F.2d 530, 539, n.22 (3d Cir.1976), cert.denied 430 U.S. 984, 97 S.Ct. 1681, 52 L.Ed.2d 378 (1977); Littlefield v. Superior Court (Buono), 136 Cal.App.3d 477, 186 Cal.Rptr. 368, 370 (1982). See EC 4–6.

93 See § 7.4. E.g., In re Nulle, 127 Ariz. 299, 620 P.2d 214, 218 (1980).

94 See Maryland Am. Gen. Ins. Co. v. Blackmon, 639 S.W.2d 455 (Tex.1982); LaRotunda v. Royal Globe Ins. Co., 87 Ill.App.3d 446, 42 Ill.Dec. 219, 228, 408 N.E.2d 928, 937 (1980).

95 Unif.R.Evid. 502; Commodity Futures Trading Comm'n v. Weintraub, ___ U.S. ___, 105 S.Ct. 1986, 85 L.Ed.2d 372 (1985)(trustee of corporation in bankruptcy

simply has the privilege expire with the enterprise.[96]

In general, courts hold that the death of the client does not end the privilege.[97] It does complicate matters, however, and in effect gives an expanded scope to the privilege. Most obviously, client consent can no longer waive the privilege. But it is commonly recognized that the privilege does not apply to testimony by a will-drafting lawyer after a client's death when the lawyer's testimony concerns the circumstances of the preparation and execution of the client's will and the litigation is between claimants under and against the will.[98] Professor McCormick argued that the law should go further and provide generally that death ends the privilege in all cases.[99] That is now provided only by the exception for postdeath litigation about the client's testamentary disposition, the one occasion above all others when a client is likely to be moved to silence in conversations with a lawyer if the client becomes aware that disclosures can be made after the client's death. It is less likely that client communication to lawyers will be chilled by mythic thoughts of such postdeath disclosures arising during consultations about nontestamentary matters. Nonetheless, the law continues the privilege in the latter case but generally not in the former.

Protective Remedies

Many remedies are available to protect the privilege. Invocation of the privilege normally takes place when the content of a privileged communication is sought by another party in litigation. The remedy there is to uphold a proper objection to the attempt to obtain the confidence. Other remedies are also available, although the authority is sparse. If a faithless lawyer secretly reveals the privileged communication to an opposing party, the fruits of the unauthorized revelation may be subject to a suppression order.[1] Suppression is justified because it deprives the opposing party of nothing to which he or she was entitled. Courts have occasionally issued an injunction against a lawyer's wrongful disclosure of client confidences.[2] The injunction might also extend to the party who has received an unauthorized disclosure from the lawyer.[3] Ultimately, a court in an extreme case may order dismissal of an action that is based entirely upon unauthorized disclosures of client information.[4] The faithless lawyer may also be exposed to the client's malpractice action for any damages that the

has power to waive corporation's attorney-client privilege with respect to pre-bankruptcy confidential communications, despite present objections of corporation's officers and directors); In re OPM Leasing Serv., Inc., 670 F.2d 383 (2d Cir.1982); Citibank, N.A. v. Andros, 666 F.2d 1192, 1195 (8th Cir.1981); United States v. DeLillo, 448 F.Supp. 840, 842 (E.D.N.Y.1978).

96 Model Code Evid.R. 209(c)(ii); Unif.R.Evid. 26(1).

97 Estate of Trotta, 99 Misc.2d 278, 416 N.Y.S.2d 179, 181 (Sur.Ct.1979); State v. Doster, 276 S.C. 647, 284 S.E.2d 218, cert.denied 454 U.S. 1030, 102 S.Ct. 566, 70 L.Ed.2d 473 (1981); C.McCormick, Evidence § 94 (E.Cleary 3d ed.1984); 8 J.Wigmore, Evidence § 2323 (J.McNaughton rev.1961).

98 United States v. Osborn, 561 F.2d 1334, 1340 (9th Cir.1977); Trustees of Baker Univ. v. Trustees of the Endowment Ass'n of Kansas State College, 222 Kan. 245, 564 P.2d 472 (1977); Mehus v. Thompson, 266 N.W.2d 920, 923 (N.D.1978); Tanner v. Farmer, 243 Or. 431, 414 P.2d 340 (1966); N.Y.—McKinney's CPLR 4503(b).

99 C.McCormick, Evidence § 94, at 229 (E.Cleary 3d ed. 1984).

1 Cf. SEC v. Gulf & Western Ind., Inc., 502 F.Supp. 343 (D.D.C.1980)(additional discovery required to determine extent to which possible suppression remedy should be considered), on rehearing 518 F.Supp. 675 (D.D.C.1981). If the opposing party did not initiate the violation of the attorney-client relationship, a weaker argument for suppression exists. Cf. United States v. Bonnell, 483 F.Supp. 1070 (D.Minn.1979)(lawyer's summary of confidential meeting with client copied without authorization by messenger and given to IRS; no suppression on facts here).

2 Doe v. A Corp., 330 F.Supp. 1352, 1356 (S.D.N.Y.1971), affirmed 453 F.2d 1375 (2d Cir.1972); United States v. Mahaney, 27 F.Supp. 463, 469 (N.D.Cal.1939); Slater v. Rimar, Inc., 462 Pa. 138, 338 A.2d 584, 589 (1975). Contra Murphy v. Riggs, 238 Mich. 151, 213 Mich. 110, 112 (1927)(former client's attempt to enjoin adverse use by lawyer of confidential information is beyond "province of equity").

3 United States v. Mahaney, 27 F.Supp. 463 (N.D.Cal. 1939).

4 Doe v. A Corp., 330 F.Supp. 1352, 1356 (S.D.N.Y.1971), affirmed 453 F.2d 1375 (2d Cir.1972).

unlawful disclosure proximately caused.[5] An unjustified revelation of client confidential information in violation of lawyer codes has also resulted in discipline.[6]

WESTLAW REFERENCES

attorney counsel** lawyer /s client /s privilege* /s inform*** tell told

A Lawyer's Duty to Invoke the Privilege

testif! testimony witness /s attorney counsel** lawyer /s client /s privilege*

Proving the Privilege

burden camera /s attorney counsel** lawyer /2 client /s privilege*

Appellate Review

attorney counsel** lawyer /2 client /s privilege* /s (appeal appellate /4 review***) erro! harmless prejudic***

The Privilege and Choice of Law

attorney counsel** lawyer /2 client /s privilege* /p choice conflict*** /5 forum jurisdiction** law

Extra-Judicial Applications

attorney counsel** lawyer /2 client /s privilege* /s administrat*** agency committee government police /s coerce* statement testif! testimony

Duration of the Privilege

attorney counsel** lawyer /2 client /s privilege* /s duration expir! terminat***

Protective Remedies

attorney counsel** lawyer /2 client /s privilege* /s dismiss*** enjoin*** injuncti** suppress***

§ 6.3.5 Client-Communicated Information

General

The attorney-client privilege aims at encouraging clients to divulge matters freely to their lawyers. One might imagine, therefore, that only the very things uttered by a client are privileged. In fact, coverage in most jurisdictions is broader and includes other communications, such as a lawyer's advice.

Client Communicative Acts

The content of any client communication to a lawyer lies within the privilege if it is relevant to the subject matter of the legal problem on which the client seeks legal assistance. The client's mode of expression is not critical and can take the form of either speech or writing. Nonverbal communication is also included, such as a client's acting out of a recalled scene, the use of signs or expressions, or any other form of communicative act.[7] At the other extreme, it is clear that a client (if otherwise a competent witness) can be required to testify about facts even if they have been shared with a lawyer.[8] What is protected is the specific content of the communication to the lawyer, not the facts themselves. Similarly, a lawyer's testimony about his or her own acts outside the presence of the client is plainly outside the privilege.[9] The difficult cases lie near the boundary between existential fact and client communication to a lawyer.

[5] State v. Sandini, 395 So.2d 1178, 1181 (Fla.App.1981), review denied 408 So.2d 1095 (1981), cert. denied 456 U.S. 926, 102 S.Ct. 1971, 72 L.Ed.2d 440 (1982)(dictum); ABA Formal Op. 341, at 3 n.6 (1975). Cf. Sands v. Weingrad, 99 Misc.2d 598, 416 N.Y.S.2d 969 (1979)(possibility of suit for damages under provisions of Internal Revenue Code prohibiting disclosure of tax returns).

[6] In re Conflenti, 29 Cal.3d 120, 172 Cal.Rptr. 203, 624 P.2d 253 (1981)(lawyer disbarred for directing burglars to homes of wealthy clients); Florida Bar v. Brennan, 377 So.2d 1181 (Fla.1979)(unwarranted report to court that lawyer suspected client was not candid in denying use of firearms in robbery); In re Rhame, 416 N.E.2d 823 (Ind. 1981)(misleading client that "associate" in lawyer's office during confidential lawyer-client conference was lawyer); Bar Ass'n of Greater Cleveland v. Watkins, 68 Ohio St.2d 11, 427 N.E.2d 516, 517 (1981); In re Strobel, 271 S.C. 61, 244 S.E.2d 537 (1978)(threat to reveal client confidences as leverage to collect claimed fee of $118). For older cases, see G.Warvelle, Legal Ethics 169 (2d ed.1920). See also In re Ojala, 289 N.W.2d 108 (Minn.1979)(discipline for publication of secrets stolen from client files of opposing lawyer). See generally § 6.7 (duties of lawyers under the confidentiality principle).

[7] People v. Glen Arms Estate, 230 Cal.App.2d 841, 41 Cal.Rptr. 303, 309 (1965)(dictum); Levitsky v. Prince George's Cty., 50 Md.App. 484, 439 A.2d 600, 605 n.3 (1982).

[8] Upjohn Co. v. United States, 449 U.S. 383, 395–96, 101 S.Ct. 677, 685–86, 66 L.Ed.2d 584 (1981); City of Philadelphia v. Westinghouse Elec. Corp., 205 F.Supp. 830, 831 (E.D.Pa.1962).

[9] Ole South Bldg. Supply Corp. v. Pilgrim, 425 So.2d 1086, 1087–88 (Ala.1983).

As the scene about which information is sought brings lawyer and client into closer proximity to each other, the lawyer can become a witness to ongoing events in which the client is involved. Generally, the lawyer in such settings is simply a witness to "facts" and can be made to testify about them even if the lawyer's client is an actor in the drama.[10] But what of such things as the state of mind of a client—is this an observed "fact" to which the lawyer must testify, or is it a composite of facts and communications covered by the privilege? The decisions are in disarray. Some of them hold that in criminal cases the question of the competence of the accused to stand trial is a factual matter about which the lawyer for the accused can be made to testify.[11] Similar holdings exist in the civil area.[12] That view seems dubious, given the purposes of encouraging client divulgence and the virtually inevitable mixture of communication and external observation that must form the basis for the lawyer's testimony about a client's state of mind.

Lawyer Communications

The courts have taken various approaches to the question of the applicability of the attorney-client privilege to evidence about the content of a lawyer's communications to a client. One approach is to treat all legal advice to a client as within the privilege, regardless of its specific content.[13] A middle approach is to determine the applicability of the privilege by inquiring whether the lawyer's communication reflects in turn any client communication upon which it is based or that it incorporates.[14] An extreme view is to regard no lawyer communication as privileged, regardless of its content.[15] The latter position has little to recommend it, in view of the policies of the privilege. The middle ap-

[10] United States v. Freeman, 619 F.2d 1112, 1119 (5th Cir.1980), cert.denied 450 U.S. 910, 101 S.Ct. 1348, 67 L.Ed.2d 334 (1981)(lawyer's testimony that he and client moved boxes of corporate records not disclosure of confidential communication); Sikes v. Segers, 266 Ark. 654, 587 S.W.2d 554, 559 (1979)(lawyer and client allegedly engaged in meritricious relationship: "[A]ny questions referring to *acts* of appellee and Mrs. Sikes, rather than communications between an attorney and his client, are not privileged."); Jones v. Jones, ___ Mont. ___, 620 P.2d 850, 852 (1980)(client's displays of temper toward and in presence of wife and children).

[11] Darrow v. Gunn, 594 F.2d 767, 774 (9th Cir.1979), cert.denied 444 U.S. 849, 100 S.Ct. 99, 62 L.Ed.2d 64 (1979)(competence of client to enter plea can be testified to by former lawyer); Malinauskas v. United States, 505 F.2d 649, 655 (5th Cir.1974)(lawyer could testify "from his observations and discussions with" client that client was not incompetent or under influence of drugs at time of entry of guilty plea); United States v. Kendrick, 331 F.2d 110, 114 (4th Cir.1964); People v. Bolden, 99 Cal.App.3d 375, 160 Cal.Rptr. 268 (1979)(under special Penal Code provision); People v. Baldi, 54 N.Y.2d 137, 444 N.Y.S.2d 893, 429 N.E.2d 400 (1981). But cf. Gunther v. United States, 230 F.2d 222, 223–24 (D.C.Cir.1956)(trial lawyer should not testify as to client's incompetency); State v. Adams, 277 S.C. 115, 283 S.E.2d 582, 585–86 (1981)(lawyer may not testify to observations about client regarding the voluntariness of his confession).

[12] Ange v. Ange, 54 N.C.App. 686, 284 S.E.2d 187 (1981) (deed grantor's mental capacity); DeFusco v. Giorgio, ___ R.I. ___, 440 A.2d 727, 731 (1982)(lack of duress on client in entering into consent judgment).

[13] In re LTV Securities Litig., 89 F.R.D. 595, 602–03 (N.D.Tex.1981); State ex rel. Great American Ins. Co. v. Smith, 574 S.W.2d 379, 384–85 (Mo.1978); West's Ann. Cal.Evid.Code § 952 ("'confidential communication between client and lawyer' . . . includes a legal opinion formed and the advice given by the lawyer"); Ind.Code 34–1–14–5.

[14] United States v. Amerada Hess Corp., 619 F.2d 980, 986 (3d Cir.1980)("Two reasons have been advanced in support of the two-way application of the privilege. The first is the necessity of preventing the use of an attorney's advice to support inferences as to the content of confidential communications by the client to the attorney . . . . The second is that, independent of the content of any client communication, legal advice given to the client should remain confidential."); Mead Data Cent., Inc. v. Department of Air Force, 566 F.2d 242, 254 (D.C. Cir.1977); United States v. United Shoe Mach. Corp., 89 F.Supp. 357, 359 (D.Mass.1950); 8 J.Wigmore, Evidence § 2320 (J.McNaughton rev.1961).

The leading case of City and County of San Francisco v. Superior Court, 37 Cal.2d 227, 231 P.2d 26 (1951), held that a physician's examination of a lawyer's client at the lawyer's request for the purpose of providing the lawyer with information by which he could evaluate the case was privileged. That result has been criticized, in part, on the ground that the doctor's examination would include both privileged communications from the client and the doctor's own observations and conclusions. Friedenthal, Discovery and Use of an Adverse Party's Expert Information, 14 Stan.L.Rev. 455, 463–64 (1962). The mixture of direct observation and client communication, however, does much to justify the California court's broad approach.

[15] Cf., e.g., Union Carbide Corp. v. Travelers Indem. Co., 61 F.R.D. 411, 414 (W.D.Pa.1973)(semble); C.McCormick, Evidence § 89, at 212 (E.Cleary 3d ed.1984)(noting argument).

proach does require some inquiry into the nature of the lawyer's communication and thus, at least in theory, poses some threat of unwanted divulgence. But it works well for certain types of lawyer communications to a client, such as that which is founded on public information.[16] By extension, a client cannot be asked to testify about a lawyer's advice if the lawyer's testimony about his or her own advice would be within the privilege.[17]

Lawyer as Conduit of Third-Party Information

A lawyer may serve as a conduit of information to a client from other sources. For example, a lawyer may secretly communicate what a nonclient witness has stated. For the most part such conduit communications are not privileged. A recurring example in bail-jumping cases is a lawyer's statement to a client about the time and place of a subsequent hearing in a criminal prosecution. Those are rather uniformly treated as a lawyer's conveyance of information from a third party and thus not privileged.[18] More generally, any lawyer communication that contains only information from third parties is unprivileged, regardless of how secretly the information was conveyed by the third party to the lawyer.[19]

Client Identity and Similar Matters

In most cases, a client's name and the fact that a client has retained a lawyer is not of much import, much less privileged. But particularly in criminal investigations, those details might be unknown and vital to an inquiring party. The general rule established by a large number of cases is that the identity of a lawyer's client is not privileged.[20] In the same vein, a lawyer can generally be required to testify whether a particular person retained the lawyer,[21] the details of the retainer,[22] the amount of the fee,[23] who paid the

[16] United States v. Silverman, 430 F.2d 106, modified 439 F.2d 1198 (2d Cir.1970), cert. denied 402 U.S. 953, 91 S.Ct. 1619, 29 L.Ed.2d 123 (1971)(information from public union minutes); Community Sav. & Loan Ass'n v. Federal Home Loan Bank Bd., 68 F.R.D. 378, 382 (E.D.Wis. 1975).

[17] Campbell v. State, 149 Ga.App. 299, 254 S.E.2d 389, 390 (1979), cert.denied 444 U.S. 933, 100 S.Ct. 279, 62 L.Ed.2d 191 (1979); People v. Glenn, 52 N.Y.2d 880, 437 N.Y.S.2d 298, 418 N.E.2d 1316 (1981).

[18] United States v. Hall, 346 F.2d 875, 882 (2d Cir.), cert.denied 382 U.S. 910, 86 S.Ct. 250, 15 L.Ed.2d 161 (1965). See also, e.g., United States v. Uptain, 552 F.2d 1108, 1109 (5th Cir.1977), cert. denied 434 U.S. 866, 98 S.Ct. 202, 54 L.Ed.2d 142 (1977); United States v. Freeman, 519 F.2d 67, 68 (9th Cir.1975); State v. Bilton, 36 Or.App. 513, 585 P.2d 50, 51–52 (1978).

[19] United States v. Osborn, 409 F.Supp. 406, 410–11 (D.Or.1975), affirmed in part, vacated in part, reversed in part on other grounds 561 F.2d 1334 (9th Cir.1977); 8 J.Wigmore, Evidence § 2317 at 619 (J.McNaughton rev. 1961). The lawyer work product protection, of course, covers material that a lawyer obtains from third parties. See § 6.6.2.

[20] Colton v. United States, 306 F.2d 633, 637 (2d Cir. 1962), cert.denied 371 U.S. 951, 83 S.Ct. 505, 9 L.Ed.2d 499 (1963); Liew v. Breen, 640 F.2d 1046 (9th Cir.1981) (applying California law); United States v. Lee, 107 F. 702, 704 (C.C.E.D.N.Y.1901); C.McCormick, Evidence § 90 (E.Cleary 3d ed.1984); 8 J.Wigmore, Evidence § 2311 (J.McNaughton rev.1961).

For that reason, it has been held that an ethics-in-government law requiring public officeholders to report publicly the names of all substantial fee-paying clients does not impinge on the attorney-client privilege. See Hays v. Wood, 25 Cal.3d 772, 160 Cal.Rptr. 102, 603 P.2d 19 (1979). In Pennsylvania a state ethics law that required candidates and officeholders to reveal the identities of clients paying fees in excess of $500 was overridden by a state supreme court amendment that added the words "including his identity" to Pennsylvania's DR 4–101(B)(1). See Order of Pennsylvania Supreme Court of September 21, 1979, 9 Pa.Admin.Bull. 3365; Nat'l L.J., October 22, 1979, p. 6, col. 1.

[21] United States v. Flores, 628 F.2d 521, 526 (9th Cir. 1980)(question regarding authority of lawyer to file claim in behalf of named person); Donnersbach v. State, 444 N.E.2d 1184 (Ind.1983)(confirmation that client was person referred to in public documents); State v. Conyers, 268 S.C. 276, 233 S.E.2d 95, 98 (1977)(client could not assert privilege with respect to fact that she had sought legal advice from lawyer). To be distinguished is testimony by the lawyer about the reasons why he was retained by his client; these are privileged matters. E.g., Chirac v. Reinicker, 24 U.S. (11 Wheat.) 280, 295, 6 L.Ed. 474 (1826) (Story, J.); In re Grand Jury Witness (Salas), 695 F.2d 359 (9th Cir.1982).

[22] United States v. Sherman, 627 F.2d 189, 192 (9th Cir. 1980); In re Michaelson, 511 F.2d 882 (9th Cir.1975), cert.denied 421 U.S. 978, 95 S.Ct. 1979, 44 L.Ed.2d 469 (1975).

[23] In re Semel, 411 F.2d 195, 197 (3d Cir.1969), cert.denied 396 U.S. 905, 90 S.Ct. 220, 24 L.Ed.2d 181 (1969); United States v. Jeffers, 532 F.2d 1101 (7th Cir. 1976), affirmed in part and vacated in part 432 U.S. 137, 97 S.Ct. 2207, 53 L.Ed.2d 168 (1977); Baskerville v. Baskerville, 246 Minn. 496, 75 N.W.2d 762 (1956).

fee,[24] and a client's whereabouts.[25] The same notion has also been applied to information about the dates, places, and times of meetings between a client and lawyer.[26] The rationale common to all such refusals to apply the privilege is that the subject to which the lawyer is forced to testify is not the content of a communication to the lawyer made for the purpose of securing legal assistance.[27]

For lawyers, whose partisan ardor is easily kindled by an instinct to protect a client's interests, those are hard sayings. Courts have not always resisted a vicarious temptation as former advocates to place limits on otherwise sound doctrine. That has produced at least two different reactions: a spurious "last-link" exception and a more sensible policy of preference for other means of obtaining evidence.

Baird v. Koerner's "Last Link" Rule

The last-link case of most fame is the Ninth Circuit decision in Baird v. Koerner.[28] The client there feared liability for fraud penalties because of a substantial underpayment of federal income taxes. The lawyer mailed a cashier's check to the Internal Revenue Service without disclosing the name of his client, stating in an accompanying letter the reason why the payment was being made anonymously. The government sought to compel the lawyer to give the name and address of the client, but *Baird* held that that information was privileged because "it may well be the link that could form a chain of testimony necessary to convict an individual of a federal crime."[29] What is apparent from the facts of *Baird* is that the link is self-created. It was only the lawyer's mailing of the check and the revela-

24 In re Grand Jury Proceeding (Pavlick), 680 F.2d 1026 (5th Cir.1982)(en banc)(third party who paid fees and supplied bond money for drug runners); In re Grand Jury Investigation (Tinari), 631 F.2d 17, 19 (3d Cir.1980), cert.denied 449 U.S. 1083, 101 S.Ct. 869, 66 L.Ed.2d 808 (1981)(third-party fee payer); Priest v. Hennessy, 51 N.Y.2d 62, 431 N.Y.S.2d 511, 409 N.E.2d 983 (1980)(identity of third-party fee payer for legal services for arrested prostitutes).

25 Communication about client's whereabouts not privileged: e.g., In re Walsh, 623 F.2d 489 (7th Cir.1980), cert.denied 449 U.S. 994, 101 S.Ct. 531, 66 L.Ed.2d 291 (1980); Burden v. Church of Scientology, 526 F.Supp. 44 (M.D.Fla.1981)(whereabouts for purpose of serving complaint); Sapp v. Wong, 62 Hawaii 34, 609 P.2d 137 (1980) (location of defendants whose testimony was sought in civil case); In re Jacqueline F., 47 N.Y.2d 215, 417 N.Y.S.2d 884, 391 N.E.2d 967 (1979)(location of client with unauthorized physical custody of child); In re Doe, 117 Misc.2d 197, 456 N.Y.S.2d 312 (Cty.Ct.1982)(whereabouts of alleged fugitive and his sister); Brennan v. Brennan, 281 Pa.Super. 362, 422 A.2d 510 (1980)(location of father client and child in custody dispute).

Client's whereabouts privileged: e.g., In re Grand Jury Subpoena (Field), 408 F.Supp. 1169 (S.D.N.Y.1976)(newly established address conveyed to lawyer in course of obtaining legal advice about relocating); Mercado v. Parent, 421 So.2d 740 (Fla.App.1982)(no compelling ground to require lawyer to reveal client's whereabouts in aid of execution); Potamkin Cadillac Corp. v. Karmgard, 100 Misc.2d 627, 420 N.Y.S.2d 104 (Civ.Ct.1979)(client's location sought in aid of execution of civil judgment from lawyer who had not represented client in unsuccessful prior litigation).

26 In re Grand Jury Proceedings (Twist), 689 F.2d 1351 (11th Cir.1982).

27 Donnersbach v. State, 444 N.E.2d 1184, 1185 (Ind.1983); People ex rel. Vogelstein v. Warden, 150 Misc. 714, 717–18, 270 N.Y.S. 362, 367, (1934), affirmed 242 App.Div. 611, 271 N.Y.S. 1059 (1934). Courts sometimes say that a lawyer's testimony about the identification of a client is not privileged because it is not "incriminating." E.g., In re Grand Jury Proceedings (Jones), 517 F.2d 666, 675 (5th Cir.1975)("inculpatory value" of testimony sought relevant to its privileged status); Brasfield v. State, 600 S.W.2d 288, 295 (Tex.Crim.App.1980). That something is incriminating, of course, has no bearing on whether it is or is not within the privilege. See, e.g., supra n. 10. On the other hand, the courts may be referring to the doctrine of Baird v. Koerner, 279 F.2d 623, 633 (9th Cir.1960), that, while identity is not normally within the privilege, it will be privileged against mandatory disclosure when the identity is sought in order to link the client to incriminating evidence. In such a case, the client's identity has independent significance, given the state of evidence. E.g., People v. Chapman, 36 Cal.3d 98, 201 Cal.Rptr. 628, 635, 679 P.2d 62, 69 (1984).

In some rare instances, a lawyer can personally assert a constitutional right not to testify to a client's identity on the ground that a coerced answer would violate the lawyer's personal right against self-incrimination protected by the Fifth Amendment. E.g., In re Grand Jury (Markowitz), 603 F.2d 469 (3d Cir.1979)(but immunity cured self-incrimination claim and attorney-client privilege did not protect client's identity).

28 279 F.2d 623 (9th Cir.1960). *Baird* purported to be applying California law. See 279 F.2d at 628–29. Subsequently, the Ninth Circuit has treated the *Baird* rule as "exceptional" when the issue is controlled by federal evidence law. United States v. Hodge & Zweig, 548 F.2d 1347, 1353–54 (9th Cir.1977).

29 279 F.2d at 633.

tion of its purpose in his letter that alerted the government to any of the links.

More fundamentally, asking a lawyer for a client's name asks for no essential communication from a client. No client needs to be assured of the protection of anonymity before he or she will be willing to say more to a lawyer. A name is an existential fact, like the fact that the client is bald or walks with a limp. Those are not themselves the contents of client communications, or at least if they are, they are redundantly so. A client may whisper to a lawyer that December 7, 1941, was the date of the attack on Pearl Harbor, but this does not make the date privileged if the lawyer is subsequently asked to testify to the date.

For those and like reasons, subsequent cases have treated *Baird* as invoking a "limited and rarely available" exception to be "narrowly applied." [30] On the basis of their facts, and to some extent of their language, some of the decisions protecting the client's identity can be understood as judicial impatience with lazy prosecutors or other litigants who have seized on the lawyer as a convenient source of information before exhausting alternative and available sources of information.[31] The privilege is not commonly employed as a tool for deferring questioning of a lawyer until other possible sources of information are exhausted, although perhaps those cases head in that wise direction.

Client Documents

Client communications to a lawyer in writing are clearly covered by the privilege.[32] It would be insensible to attempt by a contrary rule to distinguish between face-to-face conversation and more distant conversation carried on confidentially by mail or messenger. In order to fall within the privilege the communication must have come into existence simultaneously with or after the client's first consultation with the lawyer. Documents that substantially predate the relationship are quite unlikely to have been prepared for the purpose of seeking a lawyer's advice.[33]

Under the preexisting document rule, if a document in the hands of a client is not privileged, it does not become privileged because a lawyer later comes into possession of it, even if the client gave the document to the lawyer for the purpose of obtaining legal advice.[34] If a document could have been reached in the hands of the client by compul-

[30] In re Slaughter, 694 F.2d 1258, 1260 (11th Cir.1982) (limited and rarely available exception); In re Grand Jury Subpoenas Duces Tecum (Marger), 695 F.2d 363, 365 (9th Cir.1982)("narrowly applied"); In re Grand Jury Proceedings, 680 F.2d 1026, 1027 (5th Cir.1982)(en banc) ("limited and narrow exception"). For cases recognizing (usually in dicta) the exception in *Baird v. Koerner*, see authorities cited in In re Grand Jury Proceedings (Jones), 517 F.2d 666, 671 (5th Cir.1975). An occasional case carries *Baird* beyond its rationale. In re Kozlov, 79 N.J. 232, 393 A.2d 882 (1979), for example, held privileged a lawyer's identification of a client because the client possessed information about a corrupt juror that in no apparent way implicated the client personally in wrongdoing.

[31] In re Grand Jury Proceedings (Jones), 517 F.2d 666, 675 (5th Cir.1975)("peculiar facts" requiring exception to usual rule permitting inquiry into clients' identities included fact that large segment of city's criminal defense bar had been called before grand jury in broad attempt to canvass for information about local illicit drug industry); In re Stolar, 397 F.Supp. 520, 524–25 (S.D.N.Y.1975) ("knee-jerk" reaction of prosecutor to subpoena lawyer is abuse of grand jury processes); In re Kozlov, 79 N.J. 232, 398 A.2d 882 (1979)(information privileged when no attempt to secure information from less intrusive source); Stolowitz v. Stolowitz, 106 Misc.2d 853, 435 N.Y.S.2d 882, 885–86 (1980)(discovery sought of defendant-husband's clients' names and addresses denied in divorce action where alternative and less intrusive methods of verifying firm income available). See also, e.g., United States v. Hodge & Zweig, 548 F.2d 1347, 1353 (9th Cir.1977)(client identity must be disclosed by lawyer "where a party demonstrates that there is a legitimate need for a court to require disclosure").

[32] See generally C.McCormick, Evidence § 89, at 214 (E.Cleary 3d ed.1984); 8 J.Wigmore, Evidence § 2307 (J.McNaughton rev.1961). The same rule applies to client communications in the form of tape recordings. E.g., In re Vanderbilt (Rosner-Hickey), 57 N.Y.2d 66, 453 N.Y.S.2d 662, 439 N.E.2d 378 (1982).

[33] People v. Swearingen, 649 P.2d 1102, 1105 (Colo. 1982). It was held correctly in People v. Gardner, 106 Cal.App.3d 882, 165 Cal.Rptr. 415 (1980), that a letter written to a lawyer seeking legal assistance but intercepted by prison officials before the prisoner could dispatch it was nonetheless privileged.

[34] Fisher v. United States, 425 U.S. 391, 403–04, 96 S.Ct. 1569, 1577–78, 48 L.Ed.2d 39 (1976); Grant v. United States, 227 U.S. 74, 79–80, 33 S.Ct. 190, 192, 57 L.Ed. 423 (1913); Tober v. Sanchez, 417 So.2d 1053, 1055 (Fla. App.1982), review denied 426 So.2d 27 (Fla.1983).

sory process, a lawyer may not be used to insulate it from seizure.[35] Lawyers' offices otherwise would become documentary warehouses.

Suppose that a document in the hands of a client is arguably privileged—for example, because of the privilege against self-incrimination, or the spousal privilege, or on some other ground, but not because of the attorney-client privilege. If the client gives the document to a lawyer in confidence in order to obtain legal assistance, does the document then become covered by the attorney-client privilege even if, considered separately, the document seeks no legal assistance, was prepared prior to the inception of the client-lawyer relationship, or for some similar reason would not qualify for the attorney-client privilege? In Fisher v. United States,[36] the Supreme Court accepted the predominant judicial view that the attorney-client privilege would protect the document.[37] The court reasoned that the client would be reluctant to part with the privileged document unless, as with other client communications, the client would be assured that showing it to a lawyer would not create a greater risk that others could know its contents.[38] The *Fisher* approach requires a two-step analysis.[39] It first must be determined whether the document came to the lawyer under circumstances generally calling for application of the attorney-client privilege. Second, if so, it must then be determined whether the document in the hands of the client was privileged against mandatory disclosure.

Taking the *Fisher* result together with the normal rule that an unprivileged document gains no privileged status by transfer to a lawyer, it can be seen that a transitivity principle is at work. A document privileged in the client's hands remains privileged in the lawyer's but an unprivileged document gains no privilege by being communicated to a lawyer. The special question of the application of the attorney-client privilege to physical evidence other than documents is considered elsewhere.[40]

WESTLAW REFERENCES

General

di communication

Client Communicative Arts

attorney counsel** lawyer /2 client /s privilege* /s non-verbal speech verbal writ***

attorney counsel** lawyer /2 client /s privilege* /s communicat*** /s fact***

Lawyer Communications

legal +1 advice communication opinion /s attorney counsel** lawyer /2 client /s privilege*

Lawyer as Conduit of Third-Party Information

conduit "third party" /s attorney counsel** lawyer /2 client /s privilege*

Client Identity and Similar Matters

45k66

Baird v. Koerner's "Last Link" Rule

baird /15 279 +5 623

Client Documents

attorney counsel** lawyer /2 client /s privilege* /p already preexisting +2 document paper writing

§ 6.3.6 Client as the Communicative Source

General

In order to be privileged, a communication to a lawyer must find its source in a client. Communications from a nonclient, given with no matter what vows or other assurances of confidentiality, are outside the attorney-client privilege.[41] A lawyer's communications with a nonclient witness, for example, are not

35 United States v. Puckett, 692 F.2d 663, 670 (10th Cir. 1982), cert. denied 459 U.S. 1091, 103 S.Ct. 579, 74 L.Ed. 2d 939 (1982); In re Grand Jury Proceedings (McCoy), 601 F.2d 162, 171 n.7 (5th Cir.1979).

36 425 U.S. 391, 96 S.Ct. 1569, 48 L.Ed.2d 39 (1976).

37 See generally 8 J.Wigmore, Evidence § 2307, at 592–93 (J.McNaughton rev.1961).

38 425 U.S. at 404, 96 S.Ct. at 1577.

39 425 U.S. at 403–05, 96 S.Ct. at 1577–78. See also, e.g., United States v. Davis, 636 F.2d 1028, 1040 (5th Cir. 1981), cert. denied 454 U.S. 862, 102 S.Ct. 320, 70 L.Ed.2d 162 (1981); United States v. Osborn, 561 F.2d 1334, 1338 (9th Cir.1977).

40 See § 12.3.5.

41 Edgar v. Finley, 312 F.2d 533 (8th Cir.1963)(error for trial court to refuse to order disclosure of identity of

within the privilege.[42] In the case of corporate clients, the category of client can be quite expansive. The widely employed "subject matter" test for application of the privilege to corporations treats a wide circle of corporate functionaries as client-communicators.[43]

Lawyer-Generated Documents

Documents drafted or otherwise produced by a lawyer are generally not covered by the privilege. With a qualification to be noted, the following statement from Hickman v. Taylor [44] summarizes the law on the point:

> [T]he memoranda, statements and mental impresssions in issue in this case fall outside the scope of the attorney-client privilege.. . . [T]he protective cloak of this privilege does not extend to information which an attorney secures from a witness while acting for his client in anticipation of litigation. Nor does this privilege concern the memoranda, briefs, communications and other writings prepared by counsel for his own use in prosecuting his client's case; and it is equally unrelated to writings which reflect an attorney's mental impressions, conclusions, opinions or legal theories.

A necessary qualification to the breadth of that statement, although not relevant to any issue before the Court in *Hickman*, is that a lawyer's self-generated document is privileged if it reveals a client communication that itself is privileged.[45] In addition, a proposition for which the *Hickman* case is far better known is that much of material generated by a lawyer will be eligible for the qualified protection of the lawyer work-product doctrine (§ 6.6).

Facilitators of Client Communications

Under limited circumstances, a client's use of interpreters or similar agents to facilitate client communication with a lawyer can be privileged.[46] By extension, the translation can take the form of an expert's examination into a client's personal affairs or the like in order to evaluate and transmit that information to the client's lawyer in a manner of which the client is incapable because of the special scientific or technical nature of the information.[47] The less esoteric or otherwise inaccessible the data, the weaker the conduit argument becomes.[48] In addition, courts are

witness given to plaintiff's lawyer by another lawyer "in confidence"). See generally 8 J.Wigmore, Evidence § 2317 (J.McNaughton rev.1961).

42 FTC v. TRW, Inc., 479 F.Supp. 160, 163 (D.D.C.1979), affirmed 628 F.2d 207 (D.C.Cir.1980); United States v. United Shoe Mach. Corp., 89 F.Supp. 357, 359 (D.Mass. 1950); People v. Collie, 30 Cal.3d 43, 177 Cal. Rptr. 458, 634 P.2d 534 (1981).

43 See § 6.5.4.

44 329 U.S. 495, 508, 67 S.Ct. 385, 392, 91 L.Ed. 451 (1947).

45 Cf. In re Fischel, 557 F.2d 209, 211–12 (9th Cir.1977) (privilege unavailable where no link "irresistibly" leads from tax lawyer's "system accountings" summary of client's business transactions with third party to client communications to lawyer); Natta v. Zletz, 418 F.2d 633, 638 (7th Cir.1969).

46 *Interpreters*. E.g., United States v. Kovel, 296 F.2d 918, 921 (2d Cir.1961)(dictum), and authorities cited; People v. Doe, 99 Misc.2d 411, 416, 416 N.Y.S.2d 466, 469, (1979)(dictum).

Stenographers. E.g., Wolfle v. United States, 291 U.S. 7, 15, 54 S.Ct. 279, 289, 78 L.Ed. 617 (1933)(dictum); McCaffrey v. Estate of Brennan, 533 S.W.2d 264 (Mo.App.1976). See generally 8 J.Wigmore, Evidence § 2317 (J.McNaughton rev.1961).

Some states have stricter privileges. For example, Oklahoma confines the agency to persons authorized by the client to obtain legal services for the client and to no others. E.g., Naum v. State, 630 P.2d 785, 787–88 (Okl. Crim.App.1981), cert. denied 454 U.S. 1058, 102 S.Ct. 609, 70 L.Ed.2d 597 (1981)(client's statement to minister that he had committed crime and request to tell lawyer that client was turning himself in to police not covered by clergyman privilege because not confidential in that third-party (lawyer) was also intended to hear communication; attorney-client privilege inapplicable because clergyman had no authority to retain lawyer for client).

47 Pratt v. State, 39 Md.App. 442, 387 A.2d 779, 782–83 (1978), affirmed 284 Md. 516, 398 A.2d 421 (1979), and authorities cited (psychiatrist retained to evaluate client for purpose of advising lawyer on insanity defense); Utah Dep't of Transp. v. Rayco Corp., 599 P.2d 481, 491 (Utah 1979). Client communications to an expert, such as a psychiatrist, employed to treat the client rather than to evaluate and report to the client's lawyer is, however, not within the privilege. E.g., City & County of San Francisco v. Superior Court, 37 Cal.2d 227, 231 P.2d 26, 31–32 (1951).

48 On accountants, comparison of cases such as United States v. Brown, 478 F.2d 1038, 1040 (7th Cir.1973)(accountant retained by client generally not confidential conduit of this kind); with United States v. Kovel, 296 F.2d 918, 922 (2d Cir.1961)(lawyer-retained accountant's testimony can be protected by attorney-client privilege), suggests that courts may be more generous with the privilege when the expert is retained directly by the lawyer instead of by the client. See also § 6.3.8.

not always careful to determine whether the base information employed by the expert-conduit is itself confidential. If it is not, in some jurisdictions at least an expert retained to evaluate a party's case may be called by the opposing party and cannot be prevented from testifying by assertion of the attorney-client privilege.[49]

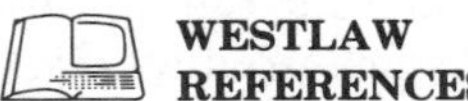

WESTLAW REFERENCES

General

attorney counsel** lawyer /s non-client /s privilege*

Lawyer-Generated Documents

attorney counsel** lawyer /2 client /s privilege* /s brief impression memo memorandum

Facilitators of Client Communications

attorney counsel** lawyer /2 client /s privilege* /p expert interpreter reporter stenographer

§ 6.3.7 Confidential Setting

The requirement that the client-lawyer communication be in nearly absolute secrecy stems directly from the purpose of the privilege. If the client is willing to speak to a crowd along with the lawyer, it is evident that no assurance of confidentiality played a part in eliciting the client's comments. The classic instance in which an aura of nonconfidentiality will be found is where a client communication is made in the presence and hearing of a third party whose presence is unnecessary to the communication.[50] Even if the third party who is present is a lawyer, if that person is not functioning as counsel for the client whose statements are sought, the client's statements are not in confidence.[51]

Courts have been willing to enlarge the rule prohibiting the presence of third parties and will tolerate the presence of persons who, as it is said, are necessary to protect the interests of the client. That might include a parent in the case of a young child who otherwise would be unwilling to confer with the lawyer.[52] But no matter how comforting, attendance of close friends and relatives at a client's conference with a lawyer prevents their meeting from being confidential if the presence of each third party is not necessary for the protection of the client's interests.[53] Authorized third parties might be present from the lawyer's own office or coterie of assistants. In fact, as will be seen (§ 6.3.8), a confidential client communication to an expert such as an accountant or psychiatrist retained by a lawyer to assess a client's matter may be protected by the privilege even in the absence of the lawyer.

Eavesdroppers

At one time, the common law permitted even surreptitious eavesdroppers to breach the intended confidentiality and thus destroy the privilege. The common-law approach was based on a mind-over-matter belief that if a lawyer and client really wanted to maintain

[49] Granger v. Wisner, 134 Ariz. 377, 656 P.2d 1238, 1240–41 (1982); Town of Thomaston v. Ives, 156 Conn. 166, 239 A.2d 515 (1968); People v. Speck, 41 Ill.2d 177, 242 N.E.2d 208, 221 (1968), judgment reversed in part on other grounds 403 U.S. 946, 91 S.Ct. 2279, 29 L.Ed.2d 855 (1971).

[50] United States v. Gordon-Nikkar, 518 F.2d 972, 975 (5th Cir.1975); Mobley v. State, 409 So.2d 1031, 1037–38 (Fla.1982)(statements in presence of cellmate with no attempt to assure confidentiality); State v. Burton, 163 W.Va. 40, 254 S.E.2d 129, 136 (1979)(banter with lawyer about offense in presence of several other jail inmates).

[51] United States v. Landof, 591 F.2d 36, 39 (9th Cir. 1978); In re Langswager, 392 F.Supp. 783, 787 (N.D.Ill. 1975). If the lawyers represent clients allied in interest in a common defense, however, the privilege commonly applies. See § 6.4.9.

[52] E.g., De los Santos v. Superior Court, 27 Cal.3d 677, 166 Cal.Rptr. 172, 613 P.2d 233 (1980)(mother and guardian ad litem of nine-year-old tort plaintiff); Bowers v. State, 29 Ohio St. 542, 546 (1876)(mother's presence during daughter's discussion of seduction case). Cf. United States v. Bigos, 459 F.2d 639 (1st Cir.1972), cert.denied 409 U.S. 847, 93 S.Ct. 53, 34 L.Ed.2d 88 (1972)(presence of young adult's father under facts here does not clearly indicate intent not to keep conversation confidential). Contra State v. Fingers, 564 S.W.2d 579, 582 (Mo.App. 1978)(presence of adult's father destroys privilege).

[53] Marshall v. Marshall, 140 Cal.App.2d 475, 295 P.2d 131 (1956)(client's son during preparation of deed); Kratzer v. Kratzer, 595 S.W.2d 453 (Mo.App.1980); State v. Murvin, 304 N.C. 523, 284 S.E.2d 289, 294 (1981). The California evidence rule is more relaxed and permits revelation of confidential information in the presence of family members, business associates, or agents when reasonably necessary to further the interests of the client. See Cooke v. Superior Court, 83 Cal.App.3d 582, 147 Cal. Rptr. 915, 919 (1978).

confidentiality they would find a way and prevent all possible leaks, even those that were inadvertent and involuntary.[54] Such insistence on rupture-proof secrecy was seriously questionable on fairness grounds a century and more ago. With the arrival of the mechanisms of modern surveillance, it is simply preposterous to maintain it any longer.[55]

The modern view is that the unknown presence of a third party is not fatal to the privilege if the client and lawyer have acted reasonably under the circumstances to assure that their conversation was private.[56] If a surreptitious eavesdropper has no right to overhear the communication, it is logical to exclude testimony by the eavesdropper as well as by the innocent participants.[57]

Intended or Past Broadcast

Aside from the presence of third parties, a client's intent not to keep a communication confidential can also be shown by the client's statements or understanding about future nonconfidential use of the communication or the client's previous treatment of the information. A client communication, even if made about the most dire matters and in the inner sanctum of the lawyer's office, is not made in confidence if the client directs or intends that the statement be made public.[58] Thus a client's intent that the lawyer inform a third party about a client communication indicates that the communication is not made in confidence.[59]

Similarly, a previously well-traveled and publicly repeated client communication is a poor candidate for subsequent confidential classification when it is repeated or shown to a lawyer. Because most documents that preexist the client-lawyer relationship will have already led an unprivileged life of their own, it will be difficult to argue that they are confidential when they reach the lawyer.[60] For example, a collection of the client's cancelled checks will have passed by many nonprivileged eyes and are not privileged when

[54] 8 J.Wigmore, Evidence § 2326 (J.McNaughton rev. 1961). Wigmore reports and defends the eavesdropper exception, although apparently (for reasons not given) he would extend it only as far as permitting testimony by the eavesdropper. Dean Wigmore was equally unforgiving of clients whose confidential documents were lost or were even stolen by a third party. Id. § 2325.

[55] Evidence codes at one time followed Wigmore's unrelenting rule on eavesdroppers. See Model Code Evid.R. 210 comment b. Modern codes take a contrary view. See Unif.R.Evid. 26; Fed.R.Evid., Rule 503(a)(4)(Supreme Court proposed rule); West's Ann. Cal.Evid.Code § 954; N.Y.—McKinney's CPLR § 4503.

[56] United States v. Bigos, 459 F.2d 639 (1st Cir.1972), cert. denied 409 U.S. 847, 93 S.Ct. 53, 34 L.Ed.2d 88 (1972); Blackmon v. State, 653 P.2d 669 (Alaska App. 1982); People v. Duarte, 79 Ill.App.3d 110, 34 Ill.Dec. 657, 668–69, 398 N.E.2d 332, 343–44 (1979). Cf., e.g., United States v. Lechoco, 542 F.2d 84, 85 (D.C.Cir.1976)(presence of client's kidnapping victim, whose presence was coerced by client at time of interview with lawyer, destroys confidentiality); Schwartz v. Wenger, 267 Minn. 40, 124 N.W.2d 489 (1963)(statement of nonsurreptitious eavesdropper occupying crowded courthouse hallway with lawyer and client admissible when no effort made by communicants to ensure secrecy); People v. Harris, 57 N.Y.2d 335, 456 N.Y.S.2d 694, 697, 442 N.E.2d 1205, 1208 (1982), cert. denied 460 U.S. 1047, 103 S.Ct. 1448, 75 L.Ed. 2d 803 (1983)(statement of client blurted out to lawyer on telephone before police officer who overheard it could complete his retreat from room).

[57] North v. Superior Court, 8 Cal.3d 301, 104 Cal.Rptr. 833, 838, 502 P.2d 1305, 1310 (1972).

[58] Colton v. United States, 306 F.2d 633, 638 (2d Cir. 1962), cert.denied 371 U.S. 951, 83 S.Ct. 505, 9 L.Ed.2d 499 (1963)(information supplied by client to lawyer for inclusion in client's tax return); Ex parte Griffith, 278 Ala. 344, 178 So.2d 169, 176 (1965), cert.denied 382 U.S. 988, 86 S.Ct. 548, 15 L.Ed.2d 475 (1966)(client statements intended to be alleged in pleadings); People v. Fentress, 103 Misc.2d 179, 425 N.Y.S.2d 485, 494 (Cty.Ct.1980) (client telephone call to lawyer and concurrence with lawyer's advice to call police with report that client had just killed someone). See also, e.g., Estate of Ragen, 79 Ill.App.3d 8, 34 Ill.Dec. 523, 528, 398 N.E.2d 198, 203 (1979)(letter to lawyer to institute proceeding for custody of illegitimate child); State v. Howell, 56 Or.App. 6, 641 P.2d 37, 39 (1982); State v. Driscoll, 116 R.I. 749, 360 A.2d 857, 860–61 (1976)(requesting lawyer to report client statements to others in order to launch public investigation); State v. Martin, 274 N.W.2d 893 (S.D.1979), cert.denied 444 U.S. 883, 100 S.Ct. 173, 62 L.Ed.2d 112 (1979).

[59] E.g., People v. Lambert, 40 Colo.App. 84, 572 P.2d 847 (Colo.App.1977)(client signed form applying for court determination of indigency); State v. Yates, 174 Conn. 16, 381 A.2d 536, 538 (1977); State v. Carlin, 7 Kan.App.2d 219, 640 P.2d 324, 328 (1982).

[60] It is also unlikely that such preexisting documents would have been prepared as communications to a lawyer seeking legal advice, as is independently required. See § 6.3.2.

they form part of a client's communication to a lawyer.[61]

In contrast, the fact that a client previously made an oral statement to a third party does not necessarily mean that the client's repetition of the same statement to a lawyer in confidence is unprivileged.[62] Unlike a document, an oral expression can be a new fact on each utterance and probably has subtle and perhaps even important variations from one utterance to another.[63] At some point, however, the client's repetition of the same statement on a number of nonconfidential occasions is persuasive that a similar statement to a lawyer is not intended to be confidential.[64] The prior statements to others, of course, are not themselves privileged in any event simply because they relate to, or even repeat exactly, the same matter that the client later communicates in confidence to the lawyer.[65]

A similar lack of confidentiality accompanies documents that a client has previously shown to others or left lying around for casual eyes to see. Documents left by a client in files readily accessible to and used by others who are not the client's communicative agents[66] or documents left by a client for a lawyer in a public hallway for several hours, where any passerby could read them,[67] are not part of a confidential communication. In that respect, the decision of the New York court in In re Vanderbilt (Rosner-Hickey)[68] is unsound. A married doctor suspected of attempting to bludgeon a woman friend to death made a tape recording, left it for colleagues in his medical office, and then unsuccessfully attempted suicide. The tape was found by his colleagues who, without listening to it, passed it to the man's wife. At the client's direction, the tape was given to his lawyer, still unheard. The court held that the fact that the client had intended the tape to be heard by third parties did not destroy its capacity of being a confidential communication at the time it was delivered.[69]

The considerations dealt with in this section have as their common ground the fact that confidentiality is compromised or destroyed before or during the client's conference with a lawyer. Even if confidentiality of the conference is not previously compromised and contemporaneous secrecy is assured so that the privilege arises, the client thereafter possesses the power to destroy the protection of the attorney-client privilege by waiver. One form of waiver, as will be seen (§ 6.4.4), is by unnecessary subsequent revelation to strangers to the privileged communication.

61 United States v. Werner, 442 F.Supp. 238 (S.D.N.Y. 1977); United States v. Hankins, 424 F.Supp. 606, 614 (N.D.Miss.1976), affirmed in part, reversed in part on other grounds 565 F.2d 1344 (5th Cir.1978), cert.denied 440 U.S. 909, 99 S.Ct. 1218, 59 L.Ed.2d 457 (1979)(document negotiated and signed with adversary party). Preexisting documents also cannot usually be considered communications made for the purpose of obtaining legal advice. See § 6.3.2.

62 Lohman v. Superior Court, 81 Cal.App.3d 90, 146 Cal. Rptr. 171, 175–76 (1978)(Feinberg, J.).

63 People v. Gardner, 106 Cal.App.3d 882, 165 Cal.Rptr. 415, 418 (1980)(client's statement to third parties that he had written a letter to his lawyer that "cleared" codefendants in undescribed manner is different from contents of letter to lawyer that explicitly confessed client's own guilt).

64 In re Langswager, 392 F.Supp. 783, 786 (N.D.Ill. 1975); Compton v. Compton, 101 Idaho 328, 612 P.2d 1175, 1185–86 (1980).

65 People v. Mitchell, 86 A.D.2d 976, 448 N.Y.S.2d 332, 333 (1982), affirmed 58 N.Y.2d 368, 461 N.Y.S.2d 267, 448 N.E.2d 121 (1983) (client's conversation with two secretaries and paralegal in waiting room shared by defendant with another lawyer while client awaited his first consultation with lawyer not privileged).

66 Jarvis, Inc. v. American Tel. & Tel. Co., 84 F.R.D. 286, 292 (D.Colo.1979); Hearn v. Rhay, 68 F.R.D. 574, 580 (E.D.Wash.1975), and authorities cited (documents left in files readily accessible to others).

67 In re Victor, 422 F.Supp. 475, 476 (S.D.N.Y.1976).

68 57 N.Y.2d 66, 453 N.Y.S.2d 662, 439 N.E.2d 378 (1982).

69 The majority's approach is also flawed because of the absence of any indication that the tape was made as part of the client's effort to obtain legal advice. As with many other kinds of preexisting documents, one is tempted to think that the highly incriminating nature of the tapes might have swayed the majority. But the privilege against self-incrimination was clearly lost once the tapes were given to the lawyer unless the attorney-client privilege then attached.

WESTLAW REFERENCES

General

attorney counsel** lawyer /2 client /s privilege* /s confidential** crowd** secre**

Eavesdroppers

attorney counsel** lawyer /2 client /s privilege* /p eavesdrop! surveillance

Intended or Past Broadcast

attorney counsel** lawyer /2 client /s privilege* /p publication repeat*** repetition

§ 6.3.8 Lawyer or Lawyer's Agent as Recipient

General

Confidential client communications for the purpose of obtaining legal advice are protected by the attorney-client privilege only if a lawyer is the client's intended recipient of the communication.[70] Almost of a metaphysical quality are decisions wrestling with the question whether a client's intended communication to a lawyer that misfires through no fault of client or lawyer is covered by the cloak of privilege.[71] Courts have also been required to deal with the problem of determining whether and to what extent a lawyer may authorize other persons to learn of a confidential client communication without causing loss of its privileged character.[72]

A modern law office is typically staffed by more than a single person, a lawyer practicing solo and unaided. Other lawyers, secretaries, clerks, paralegals, investigators, computer operators, accountants, and other specially trained personnel permanently or temporarily retained by a lawyer or law firm can be in a position to learn of confidential client information.[73] The least controversial extension of the privilege is its recognition for lawyer-to-lawyer intraoffice communications, as when two lawyers who have been hired by the same client as cocounsel in a matter discuss a client confidence conveyed to one of them.[74] It is a further small step to the common ground that a lawyer may permissibly discuss confidential information about a client with partners and associates in the lawyer's own firm, whether or not each of them has been separately retained by the client.[75] The accepted locution for that result is that a client retains the firm and not individual lawyers within it.

More expansively, modern cases hold that the privilege also attaches to client communications to paralegal personnel who learn of the communication either directly from a cli-

[70] On the general definition of a lawyer for the purpose of the privilege, see § 6.3.3.

[71] The position taken in People v. Gardner, 106 Cal. App.3d 882, 165 Cal.Rptr. 415, 417–18 (1980), that a letter written by a jail inmate to the public defender but seized by his jailer in a cell search prior to its dispatch was covered by the privilege, seems eminently correct.

[72] Some of the problems discussed here could equally well be analyzed as issues of subsequent waiver (see § 6.4.4) or as issues of nonconfidentiality (see § 6.3.7).

[73] Authority is surprisingly sparse, possibly because lawyers accept the thought so readily that it has not often been raised. Several states expressly provide for automatic extension of the privilege to "employees" of the lawyer by statute. E.g., Unif.R.Evid. 502; Minn.Stat. Ann. § 595.02; N.Y.—McKinney's CPLR § 4503(a). With respect to a lawyer's obligation to assure that employees are aware of the need to protect the privileged status of client information, see § 16.3.1.

[74] Joseph Schlitz Brewing Co. v. Muller & Phipps, Ltd., 85 F.R.D. 118 (W.D.Mo.1980).

[75] EC 4–2 ("Unless the client otherwise directs, a lawyer may disclose the affairs of his client to partners or associates of his firm."); MR 1.6 comment (Authorized Disclosure; second paragraph)("Lawyers in a firm may, in the course of the firm's practice, disclose to each other information relating to a client of the firm, unless the client has instructed that particular information be confined to specified lawyers."). The Code is arguably ambiguous concerning whether the consent of the client is necessary before an intrafirm discussion with "another lawyer" can occur "if there is a reasonable possibility that the identity of the client or his confidences or secrets" would be revealed (EC 4–2). Some would read such a limitation into the EC. R.Aronson & D.Weckstein, Professional Responsibility in a Nutshell 176 (1980). That reading would effectively emasculate the permission for intrafirm consultation previously mentioned in the EC, and for no discernible policy reason. More likely, the later reference in EC 4–2 to "another lawyer" to whom unconsented confidential disclosures were not authorized was intended to refer to lawyers who were outside the lawyer's own firm and who might be consulted on an occasional basis for information or a legal opinion. Even as to those lawyers, however, the proscription of EC 4–2 goes beyond the law of the evidentiary privilege.

ent or in the course of conducting research.[76] Similar treatment is given to confidential information encountered by investigators.[77] Consonant with that rationale, a majority of courts accord the protection of the privilege to communications by an insured to an insurer for the purpose of obtaining legal assistance in pending or imminent litigation.[78] A number of courts expand the privilege to include communications to and by specially trained experts retained by the lawyer for the purpose of studying and evaluating confidential client information to aid the lawyer in evaluating and presenting the client's case.[79] In some jurisdictions that expansion has been limited by statute,[80] while in others expansion has been resisted by decision.

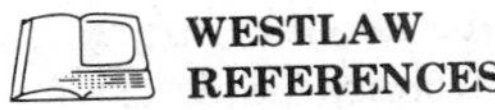
WESTLAW REFERENCES

General

attorney counsel** lawyer /2 client /s privilege* /60 accountant associate clerk investigator partner paralegal secretary

§ 6.4 CONFIDENTIALITY WAIVERS, EXCEPTIONS, AND EXTENSIONS

§ 6.4.1 *General*

Once the attorney-client privilege has struggled into existence, it lives a fragile life threatened by forces that can snuff it out. For the most part, those forces lie within the power of the client to control. The privilege can be extinguished by the consent of the client, client authorization of lawyer waivers, and similar situations.

§ 6.4.2 *Client Consent*

Actual Consent

Cases are rare in which a client actually consents to setting the privilege aside. Courts are willing enough to uphold consent freely given by a client under circumstances that suggest that the client's interests are protected.[81] Courts have been more reluctant to recognize consent given to a lawyer in advance as a ground to permit the lawyer's

76 People v. Canfield, 12 Cal.3d 699, 117 Cal.Rptr. 81, 84–86, 527 P.2d 633, 636–38 (1974)(paralegal representing public defender interviewing prospective client for purpose of filling out financial eligibility form).

77 E.g., Chapel v. Maryland Penitentiary Warden, 398 F.Supp. 1151 (D.Md.1975), affirmed 539 F.2d 705 (4th Cir. 1976); People v. Knippenberg, 66 Ill.2d 276, 6 Ill.Dec. 46, 362 N.E.2d 681 (1977).

78 People v. Ryan, 30 Ill.2d 456, 197 N.E.2d 15, 17 (1964); Asbury v. Beerbower, 589 S.W.2d 216 (Ky.1979). To be distinguished are communications with an insurer not in the context of a claim about which there is a substantial probability of imminent litigation. E.g., Kay Laboratories, Inc. v. District Court, 653 P.2d 721 (Colo. 1982).

79 *Physicians.* E.g., City and County of San Francisco v. Superior Court, 37 Cal.2d 227, 231 P.2d 26 (1951); Lindsay v. Lipson, 367 Mich. 1, 116 N.W.2d 60 (1962).

Psychiatrists. Compare, e.g., United States v. Alvarez, 519 F.2d 1036 (3d Cir.1975); People v. Lines, 13 Cal.3d 500, 119 Cal.Rptr. 225, 531 P.2d 793 (1975); State v. Pratt, 284 Md. 516, 398 A.2d 421 (1979)(extending attorney-client privilege to psychiatrists retained by lawyer to evaluate insanity defense after interview with client accused), with e.g., People v. Edney, 39 N.Y.2d 620, 385 N.Y.S.2d 23, 350 N.E.2d 400 (1976)(assertion of insanity defense is implied waiver by accused of attorney-client privilege with respect to statements of accused to lawyer-retained psychiatrist); State v. Carter, 641 S.W.2d 54, 57 (Mo.1982), cert. denied ___ U.S. ___, 103 S.Ct. 2096, 77 L.Ed.2d 305 (1983)(same); State v. Bonds, 98 Wn.2d 1, 653 P.2d 1024, 1035–36 (1982), cert. denied 464 U.S. 831, 104 S.Ct. 111, 78 L.Ed.2d 112 (1983) (same); Salzburg, Privileges and Professionals: Lawyers and Psychiatrists, 66 Va.L.Rev. 597 (1980)(favoring waiver position).

Accountants. Compare, e.g., Kovel v. United States, 296 F.2d 918 (2d Cir.1961)(communications to and from accountant retained to make financial information intelligible to lawyer privileged), with, e.g., In re J.K. Lasser & Co., 448 F.Supp. 103, 108 (E.D.N.Y.1978)(no privilege when lawyer's use of accountant did not involve highly technical accounting issues).

Appraisers. E.g, Levitsky v. Prince George's County, 50 Md.App. 484, 439 A.2d 600, 604–06 (1982)(majority view refuses to recognize privilege).

Polygraph Operators. Compare, e.g, People v. George, 104 Misc.2d 630, 428 N.Y.S.2d 825 (1980)(no privilege), with, e.g., People v. Marcy, 91 Mich.App. 399, 283 N.W.2d 754, 757 (1979)(privilege applies); State v. Melvins, 155 N.J.Super. 316, 382 A.2d 925, 929 (1978)(same).

80 People v. Sorna, 88 Mich.App. 351, 276 N.W.2d 892, 894–95 (1979)(by statute, defendant's statements to psychiatrist not privileged).

81 In re Grand Jury Proceedings, 73 F.R.D. 647, 652 (M.D.Fla.1977)(document signed by former client now under protective custody, whose voluntariness was corroborated by persons present at its signing, constituted prima facie proof of waiver of privilege).

subsequent representation of an adverse party in a substantially related matter.[82] The distinction is a wise one because of the difference in the nature of the fiduciary relationship between the parties to the consent in the two instances.

Implied Consent

As is common in the law, situations in which consent is freely given shade into more amorphous situations in which courts hold that consent is "implied." The usual reason that courts imply consent is that the client or the client's authorized agent has taken certain kinds of actions that are inconsistent with maintaining the protection of the privilege. Sometimes the resulting waiver can rightly be considered to be consistent with the client's subjective intent to make a formerly confidential matter public. On other occasions, however, the waiver in effect coerces disclosure as the price, exacted from the client for reasons of fairness or consistency, for taking the step that strips away the privilege, regardless of the subjective intent of the client and lawyer.[83]

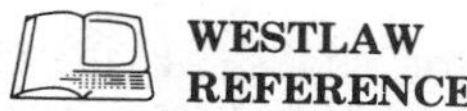

WESTLAW REFERENCES

Actual Consent

attorney counsel** lawyer /2 client /s privilege* /p consent*** waive* /4 actual** voluntar!

Implied Consent

attorney counsel** lawyer /2 client /s privilege* /p consent*** waive* /4 implied imply*** intend*** intent!

§ 6.4.3 Defective Assertion of the Privilege

Generally, a client must object to an offending inquiry into a privileged matter at the time the inquiry is attempted. Failure to raise the objection at trial plainly precludes arguing the point for reversal on appeal.[84] A defective objection also waives the privilege, such as when the client simply asserts a blanket objection that fails to specify the necessary facts establishing the privilege.[85] A corollary is that a failure to object to a question on the ground of the privilege removes privilege as a defense to a later charge that a client answered the question with a perjurious response.[86]

WESTLAW REFERENCES

attorney counsel** lawyer /2 client /s privilege* /p assert*** preserv! /5 error object*** trial

§ 6.4.4 Post-Communication Disclosure to Third Persons

A client may strip the communication of its privileged status by making a voluntary and unprivileged revelation of the communication or its content after the privilege attaches. Generally, courts apply this form of waiver liberally and hold that disclosure to a single nonprivileged person sets the privilege aside.

Partial Disclosure by Testimony

Disclosure to third parties sufficient to constitute a waiver can take the form of the client voluntarily testifying about the con-

[82] Westinghouse Elec. Corp. v. Gulf Oil Corp., 588 F.2d 221, 228 (7th Cir.1978). See § 7.2.2 at n.42.

[83] In re Davis, 38 Ohio St.2d 273, 313 N.E.2d 363, 365 (1974)(invocation of privilege by bar applicant with respect to his lawyer's information about a prior felony conviction is inconsistent with the obligation to make full and complete revelation of circumstances surrounding conviction); State v. von Bulow, ___ R.I. ___, 475 A.2d 995(1984), cert.denied, ___ U.S. ___, 105 S.Ct. 233, 83 L.Ed.2d 162 (1984)(actions of son of comatose mother and his lawyer in sharing client communications with police in order to assist prosecution of his mother's husband for attempted murder impliedly waived privilege so as to make other communications available to husband in attempted murder prosecution).

[84] United States v. Juarez, 573 F.2d 267, 276 (5th Cir.), cert. denied 439 U.S. 915, 99 S.Ct. 289, 58 L.Ed.2d 262 (1978); United States v. Gurtner, 474 F.2d 297, 299 (9th Cir.1973); Anderson v. State, 153 Ga.App. 401, 265 S.E.2d 299, 302–03 (1980).

[85] United States v. El Paso Co., 682 F.2d 530, 541 (5th Cir.1982), cert. denied ___ U.S. ___, 104 S.Ct. 1927, 80 L.Ed.2d 473(1984)(blanket objection); Bendele v. Tri-County Farmer's Co-op, 635 S.W.2d 459, 464 (Tex.App. 1982), judgment affirmed in part, vacated in part on other grounds 641 S.W.2d 208 (Tex.1982)(failure to object to discovery order until after turning over allegedly privileged materials).

[86] In re Malloy, 248 N.W.2d 43, 47 (N.D.1976); In re McCullough, 97 Utah 533, 95 P.2d 13, 24 (1939).

tents of the confidential communication, either in a prior proceeding,[87] at a deposition or other earlier hearing in the same proceeding,[88] or in the same proceeding.[89] Waiver similarly results if a client puts his or her lawyer on the witness stand to testify to privileged matters.[90] The theory of waiver here seems to be that the client cannot offer such testimony and consistently claim a need for confidentiality of undisclosed portions of the communication in view of the value of the assertedly privileged information to the ascertainment of truth. The client's own conduct demonstrates that the asserted fear of disclosure is either pretextual or at least mild enough to warrant further disclosures.

Nontestimonial Disclosure

The same rationale supports waiver of the privilege when a client makes an unprivileged disclosure of the content of otherwise protected client information to a third party. Courts have found waiver when the client has disclosed the contents to even one other person who is, in addition, the client's close associate or friend.[91] In order to count as a waiver of that kind, the client's disclosure must be voluntary and to a nonprivileged person, that is, a person not included within the limited kinds of client or lawyer agents who are recognized as auditors covered by the privilege (§§ 6.3.6, 6.3.8—authorized translators and auditors).[92]

The client's motivation in making the defective disclosure is irrelevant. Even if the disclosure was for an extremely worthy purpose, such as to aid in the arrest and conviction of a criminal, the disclosure is inconsistent with the extreme privacy that maintenance of the privileged status strictly requires.[93] Waiver by disclosure might be limited, however, by special considerations that arguably permit maintenance of the privilege despite disclosures to third parties. For example, encouraging voluntary disclosure to a government agency as part of a compliance program might be sufficient to warrant preservation of the privilege.[94]

At one time, reportedly, there was little authority on the issue of out-of-court disclosures to third parties.[95] Significant authority in recent years clearly demonstrates that waiver in those circumstances is readily rec-

87 In re Weiss, 596 F.2d 1185 (4th Cir.1979)(prior testimony in agency investigative hearing precludes assertion of privilege before grand jury); United States v. King, 536 F.Supp. 253, 263 (C.D.Cal.1982)(testimony at first trial waives privilege at second).

88 Goldman, Sachs & Co. v. Blondis, 412 F.Supp. 286, 288 (N.D.Ill.1976)(pretrial deposition); Gale v. United States, 391 A.2d 230, 234 (D.C.App.1978), cert. denied 439 U.S. 1133, 99 S.Ct. 1057, 59 L.Ed.2d 96 (1979)(pretrial hearing).

89 United States ex rel. Edney v. Smith, 425 F.Supp. 1038 (E.D.N.Y.1976), affirmed 556 F.2d 556 (2d Cir.1977), cert. denied 431 U.S. 958, 97 S.Ct. 2683, 53 L.Ed.2d 276 (1977)(waiver of privilege by own testimony about matter); Skelton v. Spencer, 98 Idaho 417, 565 P.2d 1374, 1377 (1977), cert.denied 434 U.S. 1014, 98 S.Ct. 730, 54 L.Ed.2d 758 (1978); Newton v. Meissner, 76 Ill.App.3d 479, 31 Ill.Dec. 864, 878, 394 N.E.2d 1241, 1255 (1979); State v. Tensley, 249 N.W.2d 659 (Iowa 1977)(waiver when lawyer's expert testified to confidential matters).

90 Aysseh v. Lawn, 186 N.J.Super. 218, 452 A.2d 213, 216–17 (1982), and authorities cited.

91 Herbert v. Lando, 73 F.R.D. 387, 400 (S.D.N.Y.1977) (publisher-client's waiver of privilege with respect to lawyer's letter questioning several passages in writer's text when letter sent to writer for his comments), remanded on other grounds 568 F.2d 974 (2d Cir.1977), reversed 441 U.S. 153, 99 S.Ct. 1635, 60 L.Ed.2d 115 (1979); Dutton v. State, 452 A.2d 127 (Del.1982)(close friend).

92 Church of Scientology v. Cooper, 90 F.R.D. 442 (S.D. N.Y.1981); SCM Corp. v. Xerox Corp., 70 F.R.D. 508, 514 (D.Conn.1976), appeal dismissed 534 F.2d 1031 (2d Cir. 1976).

93 State v. von Bulow, ___ R.I. ___, 475 A.2d 995, cert. denied ___ U.S. ___, 105 S.Ct. 233, 83 L.Ed.2d 162 (1984) (sharing of privileged information by client son of comatose mother and son's lawyer with police in furtherance of prosecution of mother's husband for attempted murder impliedly waived privilege when husband sought to call son and son's lawyer as witnesses for defense in criminal trial).

94 The varying approaches are canvassed in Schnell v. Schnall, 550 F.Supp. 650 (S.D.N.Y.1982). See generally Note, Limited Waiver of the Attorney-Client Privilege upon Voluntary Disclosure to the SEC, 50 Fordham L.Rev. 963 (1982); Note, Corporate Disclosure and Limited Waiver of the Attorney-Client Privilege, 50 Geo.Wash. L.Rev. 812 (1982); Note, Stuffing the Rabbit Back into the Hat: Limited Waiver of the Attorney-Client Privilege in an Administrative Agency Investigation, 130 U.Pa.L. Rev. 1198 (1982).

95 C.McCormick, Evidence § 93, at 227 (E.Cleary 3d ed. 1984).

ognized.[96] It has also been held that making materials protected by the privilege freely and indiscriminately available to nonprivileged third parties can waive it even if the third party did not actually examine the material.[97]

No case, however, has gone so far as to hold that every client repetition of information supplied to a lawyer constitutes waiver. Such a result would require that lawyers always instruct clients not to speak about the matter that formed the content of a client-lawyer communication to any unprivileged person. Besides needlessly stifling client attempts to obtain assistance on legal problems from others such as accountants and doctors, such a needlessly rigid rule would prevent opposing parties from obtaining voluntary or involuntary disclosures of information from a party. While not all of the cases can be reconciled, their general thrust is to find waiver in situations in which the disclosures to third parties have been identified in the course of those disclosures as repetitions of client-lawyer communications[98]

Lawyer Disclosures

Lawyers have it within their power to spread confidential client information about so broadly that its privileged status is destroyed by waiver. Occasionally lawyers speak too freely with other lawyers, proceeding as if the attorney-client privilege attached indiscriminately to all lawyers regardless of their relationship with a client. The protection of the privilege, of course, is much narrower. Indiscriminate disclosure of previously privileged information to lawyers who do not represent the client or with whom the client is not allied in interest within the meaning of the coclient rule (§ 6.4.8) or the pooled-information rule (§ 6.4.9) may result in waiver just as waiver results from disclosure to any other unprivileged third party.[99] Still protected, as discussed earlier (§ 6.3.8), are necessary lawyer communications with lawyers and other helpers from whom advice or assistance is sought to aid in representing the lawyer's client.

The law of agency determines the authority of a lawyer to waive the client's privilege by making a voluntary or inadvertent disclosure that is inconsistent with confidentiality. The question is one of the implied authority of the lawyer. Waiver will result if the lawyer's disclosure is within the course of the lawyer's work.[1] That a lawyer's disclosure was improvident and not in a client's best interests should not, of course, lead a court to conclude that the disclosure was not within the scope of a lawyer's authority.[2]

96 E.g., Weil v. Investment/Indicators, Research & Mgmt., Inc., 647 F.2d 18, 23–25 (9th Cir.1981); United States v. American Tel. & Tel. Co., 642 F.2d 1285, 1299 (D.C.Cir.1980); In re Horowitz, 482 F.2d 72, 81–82 (2d Cir.), cert.denied 414 U.S. 867, 94 S.Ct. 64, 38 L.Ed.2d 86 (1973); SEC v. Gulf & Western Indus., Inc., 518 F.Supp. 675, 683 (D.D.C.1981); Agnew v. State, 51 Md.App. 614, 446 A.2d 425, 444–45 (1982)(lawyer-client conversation detailed in nationally published book by former vice-president); People v. Fentress, 103 Misc.2d 179, 425 N.Y.S.2d 485, 495–96 (Cty.Ct.1980); Stark St. Properties, Inc. v. Teufel, 277 Or. 649, 562 P.2d 531, 536 (1977); State v. von Bulow, ___ R.I. ___, 475 A.2d 995 (1984), cert.denied ___ U.S. ___, 105 S.Ct. 233, 83 L.Ed.2d 162 (1984).

97 E.g., In re Horowitz, 482 F.2d 72, 81–82 (2d Cir.1973), cert.denied 414 U.S. 867, 94 S.Ct. 64, 38 L.Ed.2d 86 (1973); United States v. Kelsey-Hayes Wheel Co., 15 F.R.D. 461, 465 (E.D.Mich.1954).

98 The distinction drawn here is essentially the same as that drawn between facts and communications in delineating the kinds of testimony that can be elicited from a client or lawyer. See § 6.3.5.

99 See In re John Doe Corp., 675 F.2d 482, 488–89 (2d Cir.1982); Note, Waiver of Attorney-Client Privilege on Inter-Attorney Exchange of Information, 63 Yale L.J. 1030, 1035 (1954).

1 E.g., United States v. Franklin, 598 F.2d 954 (5th Cir. 1979), cert. denied 444 U.S. 870, 100 S.Ct. 147, 62 L.Ed.2d 95 (1979)(disclosure in course of unsuccessful plea bargaining); United States v. Mierzwicki, 500 F.Supp. 1331, 1334 (D.Md.1980); Klang v. Shell Oil Co., 17 Cal.App.3d 933, 95 Cal.Rptr. 265 (1971); Sprader v. Mueller, 265 Minn. 111, 121 N.W.2d 176, 180 (1963). Compare, e.g., Cruz v. State, 586 S.W.2d 861 (Tex.Crim.App.1979)(lawyer who brusquely took complete confession from client without informing him of his rights, took him to police station and assisted in duplicating confession had no authority to waive privilege).

2 See generally § 4.2 (tort and contract liability).

WESTLAW REFERENCES

Partial Disclosure by Testimony

attorney counsel** lawyer /2 client /s privilege* /p volunt! waive* /s disposition hearing testif! testimony

Nontestimonial Disclosure

attorney counsel** lawyer /2 client /s privilege* /p volunt! waive* /s friend neighbor (third +1 party person)

Lawyer Disclosures

attorney counsel** lawyer /2 client /s privilege* /p volunt! waive* /8 attorney counsel** lawyer % client /2 attorney counsel** lawyer /8 volunt! waive*

§ 6.4.5 *Inadvertent Disclosure*

Recent cases have grappled with the question whether inadvertent disclosure of privileged information destroys the privilege. The extremes of the possible positions have been staked out in decisions by federal courts in Chicago. One case takes the position that a client who disposes of a confidential document in the normal way of other trash waives the privilege.[3] Another swerves to the other side and holds that a mere assertion by a client that disclosure was inadvertent suffices to prevent waiver.[4] A position is needed that more fittingly accommodates the competing values of encouraging client divulgences to lawyers while keeping the privilege within reasonable bounds so as to provide access to facts by other parties.

Preferable is a standard that rejects client claims of purely subjective intent[5] and requires some showing that the inadvertent disclosure occurred despite the client's attempts in good faith to take reasonable measures to assure confidentiality.[6] In view of modern technology, clients and lawyers should be required to take reasonable steps to destroy the readability of client-lawyer communications before abandoning such material. Wigmore's strict view that the privilege is destroyed even by "disclosure" through theft of a confidential document[7] gives insufficient attention to the reasonableness of the client's attempts to protect confidentiality and, if widely followed, could result in lawless attempts to raid lawyer or client files. It is rejected in modern cases.[8] If a case arose in which a third party purloined a client communication and then published it, a difficult question would be presented whether a court should provide prophylactic protection for the privilege by treating the communication as still covered by the attorney-client privilege or deny the privilege on the practical ground that secrecy has already been irretrievably lost. A court's reasonable doubts about the necessity for the privilege (§ 6.1.3) could tip the scale. It would be preferable, here as with similar questions, to engage in a process of balancing the need for confidentiality against the specific need of the inquiring party for the information at the trial or hearing.

3 Suburban Sew 'N Sweep, Inc. v. Swiss-Bernina, Inc., 91 F.R.D. 254 (N.D.Ill.1981)(competitor's two-year search through client's trash dumpster that turned up handwritten notes to lawyer rewarded with waiver of privilege). The "dumpster" approach is reminiscent of Dean Wigmore' harsh rule that even theft of a confidential document from a client would destroy its confidential nature. See 8 J.Wigmore, Evidence § 2326, at 634 (J.McNaughton rev.1961).

4 Mendenhall v. Barber-Greene Co., 531 F.Supp. 951, 954–55 (N.D.Ill.1982).

5 Weil v. Investment/Indicators, Research & Mgmt., Inc., 647 F.2d 18, 25 (9th Cir.1981)("bare assertion that it did not subjectively intend to waive the privilege is insufficient to make out the necessary element of non-waiver").

6 In re Grand Jury Investigation of Ocean Transportation, 604 F.2d 672, 674–75 (D.C.Cir.1979), cert. denied 444 U.S. 915, 100 S.Ct. 229, 62 L.Ed.2d 169 (1979)(lawyer submitted two bundles of documents, one marked P, and insisted weeks later that this was not in error when adversary asked if privilege applied; waiver could not be resisted many months later, after documents had been extensively reviewed and digested by adversary); RCM Supply Co. v. Hunter Douglas, Inc., 510 F.Supp. 994 (D.Md.1981); United States v. Bonnell, 483 F.Supp. 1070, 1078 n. 10 (D.Minn.1979)(no waiver when work product document was sealed in envelope but opened and divulged to newspaper and IRS without authorization by employee of courier service who was aspiring journalist). Cf. Cities Service Helex, Inc. v. United States, 23 Fed.R.Serv.2d(Callaghan) 592 (Ct.Cl.1977)(no waiver when inadvertent disclosure made by lawyer who made mistake in following directions of superiors).

7 8 J.Wigmore, Evidence § 2325, at 633, 634 (J.McNaughton rev.1961).

8 In re Grand Jury Proceedings (Berkley & Co.), 466 F.Supp. 863, 869 (D.Minn.1979).

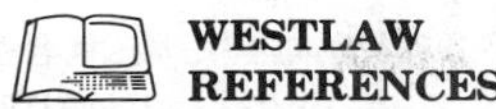

WESTLAW REFERENCES

attorney counsel** lawyer /2 client /s privilege* /p garbage (inadvert! mistake* unintention** /4 disclos***) trash waste

§ 6.4.6 *Partial Disclosure*

A client's disclosure of a part but not the whole of privileged information clearly results in waiver of the privilege with respect to the part but can also lead to a conclusion that more has also been waived. Part-whole waiver, however, is not inevitable and automatic. First, in order for partial disclosure to amount to waiver, the part disclosed must clearly compromise confidentiality; an insignificant or innocuous partial disclosure is not waiver of anything else.[9] Second, even a significant partial disclosure does not result in waiver of confidentiality for all privileged communications made by the client. For example, a court can find that disclosure of part of a privileged document results in waiver of the entire document, including relevant attachments to it, but not distinctively different documents or communications.[10] Similarly, if a client for tactical reasons reveals otherwise privileged information at trial, in fairness the opposing party is entitled to claim waiver of the privilege for additional materials that form the foundation for the waived information.[11]

At some point, a client's partial disclosures may become so random or thorough that a finding of complete waiver is warranted.[12] Even in such cases, however, the tendency is to limit the waiver to other privileged information about the same subject matter if there is more than one subject matter at issue.[13]

WESTLAW REFERENCES

attorney counsel** lawyer /2 client /s privilege* /p complete! compromis*** entir** incomplete! partial** some /6 disclos*** waive*

§ 6.4.7 *Putting Legal Assistance Into Issue*

A client-litigant can create situations in which a court will find waiver of the attorney-client privilege because of the nature of the litigant's attempted use of the communication. A familiar instance occurs when a convicted person attacks the judgment of conviction on the ground of denial of the effective assistance of counsel. The convicted person's lawyer can be made to testify to confidential communications if they are relevant and necessary to rebut the assertion of ineffectiveness.[14] Although that result is sometimes rested on a lawyer's interest in upholding his or her professional reputation,[15] a more ade-

[9] United States v. Layton, 90 F.R.D. 520, 525 (N.D.Cal. 1981); Champion Int'l Corp. v. International Paper Co., 486 F.Supp. 1328, 1333 (N.D.Ga.1980). See generally 2 J.Weinstein & M.Berger, Weinstein's Evidence ¶ 5511[02], at 511–7 to 511–8 (1982).

[10] In re Grand Jury Investigation of Ocean Transportation, 604 F.2d 672 (D.C. Cir.1979), cert.denied 444 U.S. 915, 100 S.Ct. 229, 62 L.Ed.2d 169 (1979); Great Atl. Ins. Co. v. Home Ins. Co., [1981] 1 W.L.R. 529, 536–37 (C.A.).

[11] International Paper Co. v. Fibreboard Corp., 63 F.R.D. 88, 92 (D.Del.1974); In re Penn Cent. Commercial Paper Litig., 61 F.R.D. 453, 464 (S.D.N.Y.1973).

[12] Edmund J. Flynn Co. v. LaVay, 431 A.2d 543, 550–51 (D.C.App.1981).

[13] Weil v. Investment/Indicators, Research & Mgmt., Inc., 647 F.2d 18, 25 (9th Cir.1981); Smith v. Alyeska Pipeline Serv. Co., 538 F.Supp. 977, 979 (D.Del.1982); In re Grand Jury Investigation of Ocean Transportation, 604 F.2d 672 (D.C.Cir.1979), cert.denied 444 U.S. 915, 100 S.Ct. 229, 62 L.Ed.2d 169 (1979); Herbert v. Lando, 73 F.R.D. 387, 400–01 (S.D.N.Y. 1977), reversed on other grounds 441 U.S. 153, 99 S.Ct. 1635, 60 L.Ed.2d 115 (1979). But cf. First Wisconsin Mortgage Trust v. First Wisconsin Corp., 86 F.R.D. 160, 173–74 (E.D.Wis.1980) (inadvertent disclosure of some privileged documents does not waive privilege as to others on same subject matter where no attempt to gain tactical advantage).

[14] Tasby v. United States, 504 F.2d 332 (8th Cir.1974), cert. denied 419 U.S. 1125, 95 S.Ct. 811, 42 L.Ed.2d 826 (1975); United States v. Woodall, 438 F.2d 1317, 1326 (5th Cir.1970)(en banc), cert.denied 403 U.S. 933, 91 S.Ct. 2262, 29 L.Ed.2d 712 (1971); State v. Moreno, 128 Ariz. 257, 625 P.2d 320, 323 (1981); In re Gray, 123 Cal.App.3d 614, 176 Cal.Rptr. 721 (1981); Roberts v. Greenway, 233 Ga. 473, 211 S.E.2d 764, 766–67 (1975); Lodermeier v. State, 292 N.W.2d 798 (S.D.1980).

[15] Cf. State v. Morris, 101 Idaho 120, 609 P.2d 652, 656 (1980); ABA Defense Function Standards § 4–8.6(c) (2d ed.1979)("A lawyer whose conduct of a criminal case is drawn into question is entitled to testify concerning the matters charged and is not precluded from disclosing the truth concerning the accusation, even though this in-

quate basis is that in fairness the privilege must yield to an interest in obtaining full exploration of the facts surrounding the lawyer's work for the convicted person.

Other sorts of client attacks on the work of a lawyer are handled similarly. A client's attack on a settlement on the ground that the client's lawyer wrongfully induced the client to agree to it constitutes implied waiver of the privilege.[16] A client who defends against a claim on the ground that the allegedly wrongful action was taken in good-faith reliance on advice of counsel also waives the privilege with respect to the lawyer's advice.[17] Although in most of those waiver cases the client has affirmatively and explicitly injected the issue of advice of counsel, that is not invariably so. A client who asserts that a statute of limitation did not apply when the client was ignorant of the existence of the cause of action waives the privilege with respect to discussions with a lawyer about the matter before the limitations period expired.[18]

A litigant does not put a lawyer's advice in issue simply by urging at trial a theory on which the lawyer might have given advice if the advice is not itself put into evidence.[19] When the lawyer's advice plays a direct part in shaping testimony for trial through refreshing a client's recollection, however, some courts find a waiver of the privilege.[20]

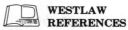

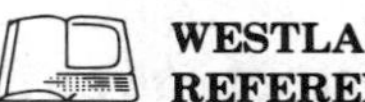

WESTLAW REFERENCES

attorney counsel** lawyer /2 client /s privilege* /p effective induce! ineffective wrongful** /5 advice counsel! legal

§ 6.4.8 *Coclient Rule*

If the same lawyer jointly represents two or more clients with respect to the same matter, the clients probably have no expectation that their communications to the lawyer with respect to the joint matter will be kept secret from each other. Thus those confidential client communications are not within the attorney-client privilege in subsequent litigation between the coclients[21] or in subsequent litigation in which the interests of the former

volves revealing matters which were given in confidence.").

16 Skelton v. Spencer, 98 Idaho 417, 565 P.2d 1374 (1977), cert.denied 434 U.S. 1014, 98 S.Ct. 730, 54 L.Ed.2d 758 (1978).

17 United States v. Miller, 600 F.2d 498, 502 (5th Cir. 1979), cert.denied 444 U.S. 955, 100 S.Ct. 434, 62 L.Ed.2d 327 (1979)(defense to charge of illegal transportation of securities); Handgards, Inc. v. Johnson & Johnson, 413 F. Supp. 926 (N.D.Cal.1976)(defense to plaintiff's claim of antitrust violation through harassment by bad faith patent infringement suits); Hearn v. Rhay, 68 F.R.D. 574, 581 (E.D.Wash.1975)(defense to claim of violation of civil rights with malice and knowledge of rights); Wender v. United Servs. Auto. Ass'n, 434 A.2d 1372 (D.C.App.1981) (defense by insurance company in suit by policyholder claiming bad faith refusal to settle).

18 Russell v. Curtin Matheson Scientific, Inc., 493 F.Supp. 456 (S.D.Tex.1980). Contra Miller v. Superior Court, 111 Cal.App.3d 390, 168 Cal.Rptr. 589 (1980).

19 Sedco Int'l, S.A. v. Cory, 683 F.2d 1201, 1206–07 (8th Cir.1982), cert. denied 459 U.S. 1017, 103 S.Ct. 379, 74 L.Ed.2d 512 (1982) (by pleading reliance on misrepresentations of fraudulent parties, client does not waive privilege with respect to lawyer's advice on legal and business aspects of transaction); People v. Lines, 13 Cal.3d 500, 119 Cal.Rptr. 225, 531 P.2d 793 (1975); Schlumberger, Ltd. v. Superior Court, 115 Cal.App.3d 386, 171 Cal.Rptr. 413, 417 (1981)(legal malpractice client does not put present lawyer's advice in issue by filing and pressing suit); Popelka, Allard, McCowan & Jones v. Superior Court, 107 Cal.App.3d 496, 165 Cal.Rptr. 748, 751 (1980)(defendant's lawyer in present malicious prosecution action can claim work product immunity for interoffice memoranda relating to action in which present defendant allegedly filed malicious action against present plaintiff). Contra, Franko v. State, 94 Nev. 610, 584 P.2d 678, 680 (1978)(testimony voluntarily given by accused that he had been beaten by police prior to confession waived right to object to question whether he had told his lawyer about the beatings).

20 The traditional view is that no waiver occurs where a client-witness uses privileged documents to refresh his or her recollection. E.g., Goldman v. United States, 316 U.S. 129, 62 S.Ct. 993, 86 L.Ed. 1322 (1942); Needelman v. United States, 261 F.2d 802 (5th Cir.1958), cert.dismissed 362 U.S. 600, 80 S.Ct. 960, 4 L.Ed.2d 980 (1960). But the new Federal Rules of Evidence (Rule 612) have been construed by some courts to provide that such pretestimonial review in effect creates a waiver so that the opposing party can ascertain the extent to which the privileged document shaped the ensuing testimony. E.g., James Julian, Inc. v. Raytheon, 93 F.R.D. 138, 144–46 (D.Del.1982); Wheeling-Pittsburgh Steel Corp. v. Underwriters Labs., Inc., 81 F.R.D. 8, 10 (N.D.Ill.1978); Berkey Photo, Inc. v. Eastman Kodak Co., 74 F.R.D. 613, 616 (S.D.N.Y.1977). Accord, E.R. Carpenter Co. v. ABC Carpet Co., 98 Misc.2d 1091, 415 N.Y.S.2d 351 (Civ.Ct.1979).

21 Black v. Missouri, 492 F.Supp. 848, 870–71 (W.D.Mo. 1980); Ex parte Taylor Coal Co., 401 So.2d 1, 8–9 (Ala.

coparties are adverse.[22] A case in which the rule is commonly applied is when an insured files suit against an insurer for bad faith refusal to settle a claim against the insured.[23] The privilege can be asserted, however, when a party who was not a coclient seeks to compel testimony about the communication.[24] As Wigmore points out, the confidentiality of the communication in that instance is not absolute; it is confidential as to the rest of the world, but not as to the coparties.[25]

The fact that either or both clients have brought other, unrelated legal business to the lawyer affords no reason to think that anything about that business is also open to the coclient. For example, a coclient who is represented mutually in a business dealing by the same lawyer who handles the client's separate personal legal matters does not surrender the attorney-client protection with respect to the personal matters.[26]

Courts have not carefully defined the theory on which they find no privilege in coclient situations. A straightforward explanation of most of the cases is that the communications are not confidential because the clients making them did not intend them to be kept from coclients and it would be incongruous to protect as confidential in litigation between them relevant information of which each was almost equally well informed.

Clear instances are those in which the coclients consult the same lawyer together and make the allegedly privileged statements in each other's presence. Here it is simple and accurate to conclude that, as a factual matter, confidentiality played no part in the tripartite communication.[27] For similar reasons, a communication made by one client in the absence of the other should not be privileged from the other if the client making the statement at that time had reason to know that the lawyer might share it with the other

1981); Estate of Torian v. Smith, 263 Ark. 304, 564 S.W.2d 521, (1978) cert.denied 439 U.S. 883, 99 S.Ct. 223, 58 L.Ed.2d 195 (1978); Croce v. Superior Court, 21 Cal. App.2d 18, 68 P.2d 369 (1937); Hamilton v. Hamilton Steel Corp., 409 So.2d 1111, 1113–14 (Fla.App.1982)(based on West's Fla.Stat.Ann. § 90.502(4)(e)); Dubias v. White, 240 N.C. 680, 685, 83 S.E.2d 785, 788 (1954). See generally C.McCormick, Evidence § 91, at 219–20 (E.Cleary 3d ed.1984); S.Ct. Standard 503(d)(5), in 2 J.Weinstein & M.Berger, Weinstein's Evidence ¶ 503–2 (1982); 8 J.Wigmore, Evidence § 2312 (J.McNaughton rev.1961); Note, 8 Colum.J.L. & Soc.Probs. 179 (1972).

The rule is one of long standing. E.g., Sherman v. Scott, 34 N.Y. (27 Hun.) 331 (N.Y.App.Div.1882); Gulick v. Gulick, 39 N.J.Eq. 516, 517 (1885); 1 E.Thornton, Attorneys at Law 183–84 (1914).

22 Cf. State v. Colton, 174 Conn. 135, 384 A.2d 343, 345–46 (1977)(statement of one coconspirator in presence of investigator for other should have been admitted to impeach his testimony as adverse witness for prosecution). For similar reasons, it has been held that the absence of the privilege applies to subsequent litigation between the coclients that does not relate to the former joint representation. See Grosberg v. Grosberg, 269 Wis. 165, 68 N.W.2d 725 (1955)(lawyer who represented both husband and wife in adoption proceedings and two damage suits could be called to testify in subsequent divorce action regarding wife's unfitness as mother).

23 Simpson v. Motorists Mut. Ins. Co., 494 F.2d 850, 855 (7th Cir.1974), cert. denied 419 U.S. 901, 95 S.Ct. 184, 42 L.Ed.2d 147 (1974); Truck Ins. Exch. v. St. Paul Fire & Marine Ins. Co., 66 F.R.D. 129, 132–33 (E.D.Pa.1975); Glacier Gen. Assurance Co. v. Superior Court, 95 Cal. App.3d 836, 157 Cal.Rptr. 435 (1979); Longo v. American Policyholders' Ins. Co., 181 N.J.Super. 87, 436 A.2d 577 (1981). But the coclient rule has no application when the insurance company refuses to defend the action. E.g., Houston Gen. Ins. Co. v. Superior Court, 108 Cal.App.3d 958, 166 Cal.Rptr. 904 (1980).

Some cases have concluded that a lawyer hired by an insurance company to defend an insured may freely convey to the insurance company confidential information gained from the insured-client, including information indicating that the event is not covered by the policy. E.g., Brasseaux v. Girouard, 214 So.2d 401, 408–10 (La.App. 1968), writ refused 253 La. 60, 216 So.2d 307 (1968). The conclusion is founded on the coclient rule and on the notion that the "cooperation" and similar clauses in the insurance contract warrant implying the insured's consent to disclosure by the attorney. A contrary view is that the lawyer may not report any statement made by the insured under circumstances indicating that the insured believed that the insurance company would not be informed. E.g., State Farm Mut. Auto. Ins. Co. v. Walker, 382 F.2d 548, 552 (7th Cir.1967), cert. denied 389 U.S. 1045, 88 S.Ct. 789, 19 L.Ed.2d 837 (1968); Moritz v. Medical Protective Co., 428 F.Supp. 865, 873 n.8 (W.D. Wis.1977). See generally Morris, Conflicts of Interest in Defending under Liability Insurance Policies, 1981 Utah L.Rev. 457, 480–83 (favoring latter view).

24 Houston Gen. Ins. Co. v. Superior Court, 108 Cal. App.3d 958, 166 Cal.Rptr. 904 (1980).

25 8 J.Wigmore, Evidence § 2312, at 603 (J.McNaughton rev.1961).

26 Bicas v. Superior Court, 116 Ariz. 69, 567 P.2d 1198, 1201 (App.1977); Glade v. Superior Court, 76 Cal.App.3d 738, 143 Cal.Rptr. 119 (1978).

27 Hellyer v. Hellyer, 129 Ariz. 453, 632 P.2d 263, 266 (Ct.App.1981).

coclient. Some cases arguably go beyond that, however, and in effect assume that one coclient will be aware that the lawyer would likely share information with coclients under circumstances in which the communication is made in the absence of the other coclients, conflicts with their best interests, and appears inherently not to have been intended to be shared with them.[28] In all instances, obviously, a lawyer should be careful to determine the probable reach of the privilege and to advise all affected coclients about the possible absence of confidentiality.

WESTLAW REFERENCES

attorney counsel** lawyer /2 client /s privilege* /s co-client co-conspira*** co-defendant co-party insured

§ 6.4.9 Pooled Information

Pooled Information and Coclient Doctrines

The "pooled information" or joint defense[29] doctrine is closely related to the coclient doctrine, but it is factually and doctrinally distinct from it. Both doctrines are exceptions to the general rule that disclosure to third parties waives the attorney-client privilege (§ 6.4.4). The pooled information exception is recognized for certain communications between parties who share a common interest in defending against or attacking a common litigational opponent but who are represented by separate lawyers.[30]

Scope of the Pooled Information Doctrine

What retains the privilege when coparties pool information is a perceived social need to facilitate interparty communications in confidence.[31] But those communications will be protected only if and so long as a community

[28] Garner v. Wolfinbarger, 430 F.2d 1093 (5th Cir.1970), cert. denied 401 U.S. 974, 91 S.Ct. 1191, 28 L.Ed.2d 323 (1971)(lawyer's advice to corporation not privileged against disclosure to dissident shareholders in shareholder derivative action); Valente v. Pepsico, Inc., 68 F.R.D. 361, 368 (D.Del.1975); Estate of Torian v. Smith, 263 Ark. 304, 564 S.W.2d 521, 526, cert.denied 439 U.S. 883, 99 S.Ct. 223, 58 L.Ed.2d 195 (1978)(lawyer's private statement to executor that contemplated distribution would unfairly benefit one set of beneficiaries held not to be privileged as between executor and all beneficiaries). The *Garner* line of cases is discussed in § 6.5.5. Instead of rather extravagant assumptions about the communicating client's state of mind, a better basis for those cases is the presence of a fiduciary-like duty on the part of the corporate counsel not to hold back information of importance to the benefitted party.

[29] The term *pooled information* better describes the doctrine than the more commonly employed *joint defense.* The latter misleadingly implies that the exception is limited to codefendants. Yet it is clear that it can extend as well to any coparties.

[30] Apparently the first case to recognize the exception was Chahoon v. Commonwealth, 62 Va. (21 Gratt.) 822, 841–42 (1871)(three defendants jointly indicted for same offense who met with two lawyers on common defense can invoke privilege). Case authority in the succeeding century has been surprisingly sparse. E.g., United States v. McPartlin, 595 F.2d 1321 (7th Cir.1979) cert. denied 444 U.S. 833, 100 S.Ct. 65, 62 L.Ed.2d 43 (1979); Hunydee v. United States, 355 F.2d 183 (9th Cir.1965); Continental Oil Co. v. United States, 330 F.2d 347, 350 (9th Cir.1964); In re Grand Jury Subpoena Duces Tecum Dated Nov. 16, 1974, 406 F.Supp. 381, 387–89 (S.D.N.Y.1975); State v. Emmanuel, 42 Wn.2d 799, 259 P.2d 845, 854–55 (1953). See generally Welles, A Survey of Attorney-Client Privilege in Joint Defense, 35 U.Miami L.Rev. 321 (1981); Note, The Attorney-Client Privilege in Multiple Party Situations, 8 Colum.J.L. & Soc.Probs. 179 (1972); Note, Waiver of Attorney-Client Privilege on Inter-Attorney Exchange of Information, 63 Yale L.J. 1031 (1954). The common defense rule would also have been recognized by the Supreme Court's proposed Rule 503(b)(3). See 2 J.Weinstein & M.Berger, Weinstein's Evidence ¶503–1 (1982).

The pooled information rationale has also been applied to protect Lawyer A's work product supplied to Lawyer B for the purpose of furthering a common cause. See United States v. American Tel. & Tel. Co., 642 F.2d 1285 (D.C.Cir.1980).

[31] An additional rationale is possibly alluded to in In re Grand Jury Subpoena Duces Tecum Dated Nov. 16, 1974, 406 F.Supp. 381, 386 (S.D.N.Y.1975), where the court stresses the intentions of the participants in the joint conference to have their communications remain confidential. But the intentions of parties, in all areas of the attorney-client privilege, are honored only if there is thought to be a strong social policy justifying the suppression of testimony to serve the end of encouraging the communication. All sorts of unprivileged information, from nonclient third parties, for example, might be given to a lawyer with the hope and intent that it go no further. But that subjective intent does not make it privileged.

of interest on one or more issues exists between the parties and only with respect to communications that serve the purpose of advancing the common interest.[32] Conversations between coparties are not covered by the doctrine unless it appears that they have agreed to cooperate on a matter of common interest. For example, if one coparty communicates with another for the purpose of developing either coparty's personal strategy or communications are made to a coparty with known hostile interests,[33] the exception is inapplicable.[34] A confession by one jointly charged codefendant that he or she alone committed a crime and that another codefendant was innocent, made for the purpose of exonerating the codefendant, advances no common purpose and is not within the exception.[35]

Few formal protocols for operation of the pooled information exception are required by the decisions. A communication directly by one coparty to the lawyer for another is protected if the other conditions for the exception are satisfied.[36] Yet it is obvious that the concept of common interest is ambiguous and its meaning can change as the representations develop new twists. A lawyer involved in such a pooled information situation, avowedly so or not, should carefully define the position of his or her own client with respect to confidentiality. Like the attorney-client privilege itself, the pooled information doctrine can apply even before litigation is filed or even if litigation has only been filed against one party if the other is a potential coparty.[37] It can also apply to a cooperating coparty who is not represented by counsel at the time of the communication.[38]

The pooled information doctrine shares another feature with the coclient doctrine: if litigation later develops between two or more of the cooperating coparties, any one of them may use a confidential communication shared among the group against the interests of any other.[39] Absent such adverse posture in subsequent litigation, the privilege cannot be

Independent support for the pooled information exception is that it facilitates the resolution of potential conflicts of interest among coparties by removing a possible privilege argument against separate representation. The parties can cooperate within the protection of the privilege just as effectively with separate counsel as with a single lawyer.

A narrow justification applicable only to some conspiracy cases is that the pooled information exception faciiitates access by a coconspirator to information about the unknown activities of others linked in the conspiracy. See Note, The Corporate Attorney-Client Privilege: Culpable Employees, Attorney Ethics, and Joint Defense Doctrine, 58 Tex.L.Rev. 809, 839–40 (1980). It has been speculated that the exception makes litigation more efficient by encouraging co-party cooperation. Note, 58 Tex. L.Rev. at 839. It is as likely that the exception causes inefficiency by keeping out evidence that must be duplicated in more elaborate ways.

32 United States v. McPartlin, 595 F.2d 1321, 1337 (7th Cir.1979), cert.denied 444 U.S. 833, 100 S.Ct. 65, 62 L.Ed. 2d 43 (1979); United States v. Friedman, 445 F.2d 1076, 1085 n.4 (9th Cir.1971), cert.denied 404 U.S. 958, 92 S.Ct. 326, 30 L.Ed.2d 275 (1971). In re Grand Jury Subpoena Duces Tecum Dated Nov. 16, 1974, 406 F.Supp. 381, 385 (S.D.N.Y.1975).

33 United States v. Cariello, 536 F.Supp. 698, 702 (D.N.J.1982); Williamson v. Superior Court, 21 Cal.3d 829, 148 Cal.Rptr. 39, 582 P.2d 126 (1978).

34 Cf., e.g., United States v. Melvin, 650 F.2d 641, 646 (5th Cir.1981)(undercover agent invited to meeting of codefendants under circumstances such that they should have known that he was not part of defense team); United States v. Gartner, 518 F.2d 633, 637–38 (2d Cir. 1975), cert.denied 423 U.S. 915, 96 S.Ct. 222, 46 L.Ed.2d 144 (1975)(conversation with codefendant known to be cooperating with prosecution). Those cases also rest on the related ground that the communications involved were not confidential.

35 Government of Virgin Islands v. Joseph, 685 F.2d 857, 862 (3d Cir. 1982).

36 United States v. McPartlin, 595 F.2d 1321, 1337 (7th Cir. 1979), cert.denied 444 U.S. 833, 100 S.Ct. 65, 62 L.Ed. 2d 43 (1979).

37 Hunydee v. United States, 355 F.2d 183 (9th Cir. 1965) (pre-indictment conference among potential co-indictees); Mason v. Village of Ravena, 114 Misc.2d 487, 451 N.Y.S.2d 994 (1982)(police chief consulted lawyer who shared communications with chief's employer, who was only party actually sued).

38 In re Grand Jury Subpoena Duces Tecum Dated Nov. 16, 1974, 406 F.Supp. 381, 391, 396 (S.D.N.Y.1975).

39 Ohio-Sealy Mattress Mfg. Co. v. Kaplan, 90 F.R.D. 21, 29, 32–33 (N.D.Ill.1980); In re Grand Jury Subpoena Duces Tecum Dated Nov. 16, 1974, 406 F.Supp. 381, 386 (S.D.N.Y.1975) (dictum). The court's actual holding in *Grand Jury* was that a subsequent falling out resulting in a civil action filed between former codefendant jointly cooperating with respect to administrative agency charges did not warrant breach of the pooled information privilege by testimony in a third proceeding, a grand jury criminal investigation. 406 F.Supp at 393–94. The point is obviously a debatable one.

waived without the consent of all parties to the cooperative exchange.[40]

Later Conflicts and Formerly Pooled Information

Pooled information cases will result in former-client conflict problems that should be viewed differently from the ordinary former-client case. Because of the limited nature of the confidential interchanges between the separately represented coparties, there is no reason for applying the strict irrebuttable presumption of shared confidential information. While it is legitimate to assume that a sharing of confidential information might have occurred that requires disqualification of all affected lawyers, this presumption should be rebuttable.[41] For example, if A, represented by X, and B, represented by Y, were coparties in litigation and they later find themselves opposing each other in substantially related litigation, the normal assumption in coclient cases is that the same lawyer cannot thereafter represent either client adversely to the other because of the loyalty and confidentiality principles. But in a pooled information situation, the loyalty principle is largely irrelevant because the clients have been separately represented. The confidentiality principle is relevant only to the extent that the party opposing the motion to disqualify can demonstrate that in fact confidential information relating to matters at issue in the subsequent litigation was not shared in the earlier representations.

Critique of the Pooled Information Doctrine

The pooled information doctrine rests on questionable support. It is correctly thought of as an extension of the attorney-client privilege allied to, but exceptionally compressing, the doctrine of implied waiver by subsequent publication (§ 6.4.4). It goes much farther than traditional doctrine in continuing to treat as confidential information that is shared, possibly very widely, among third parties. Rarely in coparty situations will the presence of the third party be at all necessary to facilitate communication between lawyer and client. More often it permits coconspirators to continue to conspire at a common defense, now with the privileged assistance of teams of lawyers. Much of what it covers would be covered independently by the lawyer work product doctrine (§ 6.6), with the difference that the pooled information doctrine supplies a prohibition against disclosure that a client (here a coparty) may invoke whatever the price exacted in less efficient and incomplete fact-finding.

Perhaps more than any other of the extensions of the attorney-client privilege, this furthest reach of it should be made subject to an exception for great need and substantial hardship that might be imposed on the party seeking the information if it were held to be privileged. That, concededly, would diminish the protection of the privilege in this area because it would be less certain. But the pooled information doctrine, along with the coclient privilege itself, is already uncertain because of the adverse-litigation exception to it. The additional uncertainty is a fair price to exact for the extraordinary protection that it affords, if in fact it is desirable to continue the exception at all.

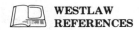

WESTLAW REFERENCES

Scope of the Pooled Information Doctrine

attorney counsel** lawyer /2 client /s privilege* /p "*joint* defense" (pool*** /3 information)

Later Conflicts and Formerly Pooled Information

attorney counsel** lawyer /2 client /s privilege* /p "joint defense" (pool*** /3 information) /s Confiden! loyal** subsequent**

[40] Ohio-Sealy Mattress Mfg. Co. v. Kaplan, 90 F.R.D. 21, 29 (N.D.Ill.1980).

[41] Wilson P. Abraham Const. Corp. v. Armco Steel Corp., 559 F.2d 250, 253 (5th Cir.1977); International Paper Co. v. Lloyd Mfg. Co., 555 F.Supp. 125, 133 (N.D.Ill. 1982).

§ 6.4.10 The Crime-Fraud Exception

Rationale for the Exception

American law, naturally, prohibits a lawyer from assisting a client in planning future crimes and other illegal acts. The prohibition translates readily into an exception to the attorney-client privilege for continuing and future client crimes and other wrongs, an exception that seems to be recognized everywhere.[42] Even in jurisdictions whose statutory formulations of the attorney-client privilege do not mention such an exception, courts construe their statutes to include the exception because of its solid acceptance at common law.[43]

Perhaps its rationale is too obvious to require extended judicial comment, but the decisions are remarkably obtuse about the justification for the crime-fraud exception. Some statements suggest that the exception is meant to punish wrongdoers or to prevent them from eluding the legal consequence of wrongdoing or to prevent lawyers from aiding wrongdoers.[44] But those hardly distinguish future crimes and frauds from those that are past and for which a client's communications clearly are protected by the privilege.

What divides communications about past crimes from those about future ones is that lawfully assisting a past wrongdoer to obtain an acquittal is an accepted contradiction built into the adversary system (§ 10.5.2). The risk of undeserved acquittals is accepted as the price for vigorous advocacy in an adversarial system. But a lawyer who acts as accessory before the fact in an ongoing or future client offense is not operating within that system. Denying the privilege when a client consults about a future wrongdoing incurs the cost of discouraging clients from seeking preventive legal advice and, possibly, means that some clients may not be dissuaded from an intended illegal course by an honorable lawyer. That cost, if it truly exists, is incurred in order to enhance the ability of society to gather information, primarily from lawyers, about illegal or fraudulent activities of clients. Denying the privilege here also denies unscrupulous lawyers the comfort of knowing that communications about future client wrongdoing will not be divulged. Because divulgence is possible, the lawyer must take into account the personal risks incurred of embarrassment or liability.

Privileged and Unprivileged Consultations

Despite some uncertainty at the peripheries, the crime-fraud exception clearly covers instances in which a lawyer is an active participant in planning the future crime with the client.[45] Conversely, the exception applies even if a lawyer is unaware of the client's intended crime or fraud.[46] The third possibility—that the privilege is also lost when the

[42] See generally 8 J.Wigmore, Evidence § 2298 (J.McNaughton rev.1961); C.McCormick, Evidence § 95 (E.Cleary 3d ed. 1984). A frequently cited Amercian case is Clark v. United States, 289 U.S. 1, 15–16, 53 S.Ct. 465, 469–70, 77 L.Ed. 993 (1933)(Cardozo, J.)(dictum).

[43] State ex rel. North Pac. Lumber Co. v. Unis, 282 Or. 457, 579 P.2d 1291, 1294–95 (1978)(in former employee's action for damages for tortious invasion of privacy, employer's consultation with lawyer about legality of eavesdropping by telephone operator on employee's calls on employer's premises not subject to crime-fraud exception because of lack of "general public awareness" of illegality of such eavesdropping.).

[44] Clark v. United States, 289 U.S. 1, 16, 53 S.Ct. 465, 470, 77 L.Ed. 993 (1933): "A privilege surviv[es] until the relation is abused and vanish[es] when abuse is shown." A common rationalization, which is more descriptive than explanatory, is that the privilege can be used as a shield of defense for crime already committed but cannot be used as a sword or weapon of offense to carry out contemplated crimes against society. E.g., In re Special Sept. 1978 Grand Jury (II), 640 F.2d 49, 59 (7th Cir.1980); Sullivan v. Chase Inv. Serv., Inc., 434 F.Supp. 171, 189 (N.D.Cal.1977); State v. Mullins, 26 Ohio App.2d 13, 268 N.E.2d 603, 606 (1971).

[45] Cogdill v. Commonwealth, 219 Va. 272, 247 S.E.2d 392 (1978)(lawyer attempted to procure client for purpose of prostitution). See also, e.g., United States v. Aldridge, 484 F.2d 655 (7th Cir.1973), cert.denied 415 U.S. 922, 94 S.Ct. 1423, 39 L.Ed.2d 477 (1974); United States v. Bob, 106 F.2d 37 (2d Cir.1939), cert.denied 308 U.S. 589, 60 S.Ct. 115, 84 L.Ed. 493 (1939); United States v. Amrep Corp., 418 F.Supp. 473 (S.D.N.Y.1976).

[46] In re Grand Jury Proceedings (Pavlick), 680 F.2d 1026, 1028–29 (5th Cir.1982)(en banc); In re Grand Jury Proceedings (Twist), 689 F.2d 1351, 1352 (11th Cir.1982); United States v. Loften, 518 F.Supp. 839, 848 (S.D.N.Y. 1981)(lawyer's alleged ignorance of client's investment of racketeering income in legitimate businesses); In re Westinghouse Elec. Corp., 76 F.R.D. 47, 57 (W.D.Pa.1977);

lawyer knows that the client's intended future act is illegal but the client does not—seems not to be accepted. Authority is sparse, but the better view is that the client's purpose must be more than the performance of acts that, as a court will later find, violate a criminal statute or are fraudulent. Matters whose legality is legitimately in doubt are precisely those that clients should be encouraged to bring to their lawyers for confidential guidance. Thus the exception should apply only if the client in bad faith seeks to harm the legally protected interests of another party or otherwise attempts to obtain legal assistance for a purpose reasonably known by the client to be against the law.[47]

Broader formulations have been suggested that would include much more client wrongdoing than crime and fraud. Some formulations include any "breach, by the lawyer or by the client, of a duty arising out of the lawyer-client relationship," [48] any "serious misconduct by a client," [49] or a "deliberate plan to defy the law and oust another person of his rights." [50] The original Uniform Rules of Evidence, in 1953, spoke of an exception for a consultation involving a "crime or a tort," [51] but the 1974 rewriting replaced *tort* with *fraud*.[52]

It is difficult to defend drawing a distinction between revelations about future crimes, even if the exception is limited (as seems appropriate) to crimes that pose serious risks of harm to the physical or economic interests of others,[53] and revelations about perhaps equally harmful and antisocial conduct that lacks the criminal stigma. Even more arbitrary would be a distinction between a client's frauds and other noncriminal yet wrongful acts. More likely, *fraud* in the catchword phrase used to describe the doctrine stands as synecdoche for all intentional wrongs involving a client acting with bad faith and intending, or purposefully oblivious to, serious harm to another.

Continuing Crimes and Frauds

All of the formulations include within the exception crimes [54] and frauds [55] that are

In re Grand Jury Subpoena Duces Tecum (Levy), 165 N.J. Super. 211, 397 A.2d 1132 (1978), affirmed 171 N.J.Super. 475, 410 A.2d 63 (1979)(documents that client used to obtain fraudulent assistance of public defender not privileged).

47 Ohio-Sealy Mattress Mfg. Co. v. Kaplan, 90 F.R.D. 21, 30 (N.D.Ill.1980)(lawyer's unsuccessful attempt to draft a restrictive trade document without violating federal antitrust laws does not establish lack of good faith); Glade v. Superior Court, 76 Cal.App.3d 738, 143 Cal.Rptr. 119, 124 (1978)(the exception "clearly requires an intention on the part of the client to abuse the attorney-client relationship, although the actual wrongdoing may be perpetrated by anyone. Accordingly, an attorney's misuse of confidential information to defraud others will not invoke the . . . exception if the client did not seek legal assistance to further this purpose and he was unaware of the attorney's contemplated wrongdoing."); State ex rel. North Pac. Lumber Co. v. Unis, 282 Or. 457, 579 P.2d 1291, 1296 (1978); Unif.R.Evid. 502(d)(1)("commit or plan to commit what the client knew or reasonably should have known to be a crime or fraud").

48 West's Ann. Cal.Evid.Code § 958. E.g., Jacobs v. State Bar, 67 Cal.App.3d 972, 136 Cal.Rptr. 920, 927 (1977)(exception removes privilege that would otherwise exist with respect to subpoena issued to physician by state bar investigating payments that he had made to various lawyers), opinion vacated 20 Cal.3d 191, 141 Cal. Rptr. 812, 570 P.2d 1230 (1977).

49 In re Sealed Case, 676 F.2d 793, 816 (D.C.Cir.1982) (Wright, J.). See also id. at 812 ("crime, fraud, or other type of misconduct fundamentally inconsistent with the basic premises of the adversary system").

50 Kahl v. Minnesota Wood Specialty, Inc., 277 N.W. 2d 395, 399 (Minn.1979)(dictum).

51 Unif.R.Evid. 26, 9A U.L.A. 613 (1965). That might have been the source for Judge Wyzanski's famous formulation of the privilege in United States v. United Shoe Mach. Corp., 89 F.Supp. 357, 358–59 (D.Mass.1950), which also excepted communications "for the purpose of committing a crime or tort."

52 Unif.R.Evid. 502(d), 13 U.L.A. 220 (1976).

53 Cf. Moody v. IRS, 654 F.2d 795, 801 (D.C.Cir.1981) ("No court should order disclosure . . . if the disclosure would traumatize the adversary process more than the underlying legal misbehavior.").

54 People v. Pic'l, 114 Cal.App.3d 824, 171 Cal.Rptr. 106, 141 (1981)(communication to lawyer about criminal plan of returning stolen property on payment of "reward" and promise of nonprosecution); Keller v. State, 651 P.2d 1339 (Okl.Crim.App.1982)(communication to lawyer about intent to commit murder not within privilege). The "aid" that a criminal conspirator seeks might be legal assistance that otherwise is entirely lawful. Thus an illegal drug enterprise's contacts with a lawyer to represent drug couriers against future criminal charges are within the crime-fraud exception. See United States v.

55 See note 55 on page 281.

planned for the future. The reasons for refusing to recognize a privilege for future crimes and frauds applies as well to crimes and frauds that are already underway at the time a client consults a lawyer.[56] Finding the balance point between the need to keep secrets and the need to prevent harms becomes more difficult if the client's continuing offense is a passive one, such as not reporting an offense or remaining a fugitive.[57]

Crime-Fraud and Work Product

The question whether the future crime and fraud exception applies to the work product immunity was not decided until relatively recently. Some of the first cases to confront the issue suggested that a greater immunity from required divulgence might be accorded to work product.[58] But it is now well established, at least in the federal courts, that the exception applies equally and under similar procedures to work product immunity claims.[59]

Applying the Exception

Procedurally, the crime-fraud doctrine comes into play only after the party seeking to resist disclosure has demonstrated the necessary elements of the attorney-client privilege. The party seeking disclosure then has the burden of making a so-called prima facie showing that the communication occurred in the course of a consultation about a continuing or future crime or fraud. The required prima facie showing resembles the quality of proof required to defeat a motion for directed verdict at the close of the proponent's case[60] or to establish a showing of probable cause.[61] It must amount to more than a mere allega-

Hodge & Zweig, 548 F.2d 1347, 1354–55 (9th Cir.1977); In re Grand Jury Subpoenas Dated Apr. 19, 1978, 451 F.Supp. 969 (E.D.N.Y.1978).

Clearly included within the exception as a future crime would be a conversation in a lawyer's office about plans to commit perjury. See United States v. Gordon-Nikkar, 518 F.2d 972, 975 (5th Cir.1975)("It would be a perversion of the privilege to extend it so as to protect communications designed to frustrate justice by committing other crimes to conceal past misdeeds."). See also In re Grand Jury Proceedings (Pavlick), 680 F.2d 1026 (5th Cir.1982) (en banc); United States v. King, 536 F.Supp. 253, 261–62 (C.D.Cal.1982); People v. Schultheis, 638 P.2d 8, 14 (Colo. 1981)(dictum); People v. Board, 656 P.2d 712, 714–15 (Colo.App.1982)(false affidavit); Gebhardt v. United Railways Co., 220 S.W. 667, 699 (Mo.1920)(client suing for personal injuries allegedly received in bus accident could not object on ground of privilege to testimony of her first lawyer that she had stated that she was not on the bus); State v. Phelps, 24 Or.App. 329, 545 P.2d 901 (1976).

55 United States Auto. Ass'n v. Werley, 526 P.2d 28 (Alaska 1974)(prima facie showing of insurer's bad faith failure to settle sets aside privilege with respect to insurer's confidential communications).

56 In re John Doe Corp., 675 F.2d 482, 491 (2d Cir.1982) ("It is indisputable that communications made in furtherance of an ongoing crime are not protected by the attorney-client privilege.").

57 Brazil, Unanticipated Client Perjury and the Collision of Ethics, Evidence and Constitutional Law, 44 Mo.L. Rev. 601, 620 (1979); Callan & David, Professional Responsibility and the Duty of Confidentiality: Disclosure of Client Misconduct in an Adversary System, 29 Rutgers L.Rev. 332, 363 (1976).

58 In re Murphy, 560 F.2d 326, 337–38 (8th Cir.1977); Duplan Corp. v. Deering Milliken, Inc., 540 F.2d 1215, 1220 (4th Cir.1976)(dictum).

59 In re Doe, 662 F.2d 1073, 1079–80 (4th Cir.1981), cert. denied 455 U.S. 1000, 102 S.Ct. 1632, 71 L.Ed.2d 867 (1982); In re Sealed Case, 676 F.2d 793, 812 (D.C.Cir.1982) (Wright, J.); In re Special September 1978 Grand Jury, 640 F.2d 49, 59 (7th Cir.1980); In re Grand Jury Proceedings (FMC Corp.), 604 F.2d 798 (3d Cir.1979). The few state cases in point also support waiver. E.g., Law Offices of Morley v. MacFarlane, 647 P.2d 1215, 1221 (Colo. 1982).

The Seventh Circuit has held, however, that "opinion" work product of an innocent lawyer would be immune from discovery even if the crime-fraud exception were established, unless the requesting party could demonstrate "extraordinary need" for access. See 1978 Grand Jury, supra, 640 F.2d at 52. See also In re John Doe Corp., 675 F.2d 482, 492–93 (2d Cir.1982). Why a lawyer's mental processes should be vaunted over other confidential materials and communications that are waived when employed in aid of a crime or fraud is not apparent.

The *Doe* decision by the Eighth Circuit found an "extraordinary circumstances" justification in the government's prima facie showing that a lawyer was attempting to use the work product doctrine to shield himself from prosecution for assisting a client and other witnesses to commit perjury in a prior case. See 662 F.2d at 1079–80.

60 United States v. Kahn, 366 F.2d 259 (2d Cir.1966), cert.denied 385 U.S. 948, 87 S.Ct. 321, 17 L.Ed.2d 226 (1966); United States v. King, 536 F.Supp. 253, 261 (C.D. Cal.1982); United States v. Amrep Corp., 418 F.Supp. 473, 474–75 (S.D.N.Y.1976).

61 In re John Doe Corp., 675 F.2d 482, 491 & n.7 (2d Cir. 1982).

tion of crime or fraud[62] and extend beyond the creation of a suspicion of illegality.[63] But the proof is not measured by the standard of proof beyond a reasonable doubt that applies in criminal trials.[64] Courts do not require a full evidentiary hearing, and the inquiring party can submit proof by affidavits.[65] The great preponderance of cases hold that the court can privately (in camera) examine the very document or other recording of assertedly privileged communication in question in order to determine whether the inquiring party has made out a prima facie case.[66]

Effect of the Exception upon Future Cases

Once the necessary prima facie showing of crime or fraud is made, the privilege is removed with respect to the tainted consultation for all future occasions on which the contents of the communications might be sought, including divulgence sought in litigation not related to the original client-lawyer consultation.[67] If the crime-fraud exception applies, the question arises whether the client loses the right to invoke the privilege with respect to all communications with his or her lawyer. Surely there should be a limit, and a fitting one is to hold the privilege inapplicable only to communications that appear to relate to the crime or fraud discussed.[68]

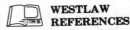

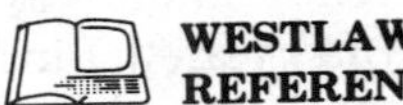
WESTLAW REFERENCES

Rationale for the Exception

attorney counsel** lawyer /2 client /s privilege* /p anticipat*** future /3 crime criminal fraud! illegal*** wrong-doing

Privileged and Unprivileged Consultations

attorney counsel** lawyer /2 client /s privilege* /p intend*** intent! purpose! /3 crime criminal fraud! illegal*** wrong-doing

Continuing Crimes and Frauds

attorney counsel** lawyer /2 client /s privilege* /p continu*** ongoing underway /3 crime criminal fraud! illegal*** wrong-doing

Crime-Fraud and Work Product

attorney counsel** lawyer /s work-product /s crime criminal fraud! illegal*** wrong-doing

Applying the Exception

attorney counsel** lawyer /2 client /s privilege* /p burden evidenc! "prima-facie" standard /p crime criminal fraud! illegal*** wrong-doing

Effect of the Exception Upon Future Cases

attorney counsel** lawyer /2 client /s privilege* /p concern*** relat*** relation! /s crime criminal fraud! illegal*** wrong-doing

---

62 In re Special Sept. 1978 Grand Jury, 640 F.2d 49, 60 (7th Cir.1980); Maryland Am. Gen. Ins. Co. v. Blackmon, 639 S.W.2d 455, 458 (Tex.1982)(semble). Prior authority holding that a mere allegation would suffice was repudiated in Clark v. United States, 289 U.S. 1, 15, 53 S.Ct. 465, 469, 77 L.Ed. 993 (1933).

63 Thus, if the government shows no more than that a third party has paid the legal fees for persons arrested while serving as drug couriers, this raises a suspicion of illegal involvement of the third party in the drug trade but does not make out a prima facie case of involvement. See In re Grand Jury Proceedings (Lawson), 600 F.2d 215, 218–19 (9th Cir.1979).

64 Wright, J., in In re Sealed Case, 676 F.2d 793, 814 (D.C.Cir. 1982); Duplan Corp. v. Deering Milliken, Inc., 540 F.2d 1215 (4th Cir.1976).

65 In re Sept. 1975 Grand Jury Term (Thompson), 532 F.2d 734, 737–38 (10th Cir.1976).

66 In re John Doe Corp., 675 F.2d 482, 489–90 (2d Cir. 1982); In re Berkley & Co., 629 F.2d 548, 553 (8th Cir. 1980). In re Special Sept. 1978 Grand Jury, 640 F.2d 49, 59–61 (7th Cir.1980). Contra United States v. Shewfelt, 455 F.2d 836, 840 (9th Cir.), cert.denied 406 U.S. 944, 92 S.Ct. 2042, 32 L.Ed.2d 331 (1972). The *Shewfelt* case has not been followed, even in the Ninth Circuit. See United States v. King, 536 F.Supp. 253, 262 (C.D.Cal.1982).

67 A troublesome dictum in Alexander v. United States, 138 U.S. 353, 11 S.Ct. 350, 34 L.Ed. 954 (1891), has haunted courts for nearly a century. The court stated that the crime-fraud exception was limited to a trial for the very crime or fraud in furtherance of which the consultation took place. The statement was irrelevant to any issue before the court, and, perhaps for this reason, the court did not cite, and probably could not have cited, any supporting authority or argument. No court has since followed *Alexander's* dictum. The rule has been widely criticized. E.g., 8 J.Wigmore, Evidence § 2298 at 571 n.1 (J.McNaughton rev.1961); C.McCormick, Evidence § 95, at 229 n.2 (E.Cleary 3d ed.1984). It has been expressly repudiated by at least two federal courts of appeal. In re Sawyer's Petition, 229 F.2d 805, 808–09 (7th Cir.), cert.denied 351 U.S. 966, 76 S.Ct. 1025, 100 L.Ed. 1486 (1956); In re Berkley & Co., 629 F.2d 548, 554–55 (8th Cir.1980). The exception would be senseless. It advances no discernible interest of confidentiality and limits access to relevant information that would be fully discoverable except for the use to which it would be put.

68 In re Special Sept. 1978 Grand Jury, 640 F.2d 49, 61 n.16 (7th Cir.1980); Ohio-Sealy Mattress Mfg. Co., 90 F.R.D. 21, 30 (N.D.Ill.1980).

§ 6.5 CORPORATE AND OTHER ENTITY CLIENTS

§ 6.5.1 General

The attorney-client privilege applies to clients who are not individual persons. It extends also to artificial entities such as corporations, governmental bodies, unincorporated associations, and partnerships. Application of the privilege in those areas has raised problems of great difficulty and controversy. Most aspects of the general standard for invocation of the privilege (§ 6.3) apply. A client may seek to protect only confidential communications made by the client or the client's agent to a lawyer functioning in that capacity. The problem has been to determine which persons speak for the entity client for purposes of invoking the privilege and waiving it.

§ 6.5.2 History of the Corporate Privilege

If the common law for the most part moves by small degrees, it is also true that it can occasionally move a great distance blithely, perhaps without appreciating that it is moving at all. Several federal cases over the last century applied the attorney-client privilege to corporations,[69] but the authority was sparse, and none analyzed why it was correct to assume that corporate clients were entitled to the same sort of privilege as were natural persons. Possible problems of implementing the privilege did not arise, because of a tendency to make the privilege very broad [70]—a treatment that was more in accord with the pre-1938 modes of litigation by secret and surprise and less in the spirit of modern trials, which are characterized by extensive pretrial discovery of an opponent's information. The arrival in 1938 of modern pleading and discovery rules, with their enlargement of the pretrial exchange of information in order to avoid surprise, did not have an immediate impact upon the privilege.

Upon that tranquil scene in 1962 burst the radical district court decision in Radiant Burners, Inc. v. American Gas Association.[71] After examining several possible reasons for extending the privilege to corporate clients, the court concluded that the privilege was a personal one. Corporations were no more able to claim the attorney-client privilege than they could claim the constitutional privilege against self-incrimination.[72] Although the district court was rebuffed and the extension of the privilege to corporations was quickly reaffirmed by the court of appeals on the basis of precedent, the *Radiant Burners* decision intensified interest in the rationale and scope of the corporate version of the privilege.

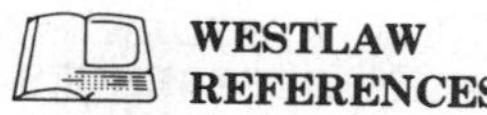

207 +5 771 /p privilege*

§ 6.5.3 Rationale of the Corporate Privilege

The general theories advanced to support the attorney-client privilege (§ 6.1.3) apply only with diminished strength or not at all to a corporate client. First, arguments based on human dignity are irrelevant.[73] The corpora-

69 Given the apparent importance of the question, the decisions have been suprisingly sparse. E.g., Cole v. Hughes Tool Co., 215 F.2d 924 (10th Cir.1954), cert.denied 348 U.S. 927, 75 S.Ct. 339, 99 L.Ed. 726 (1955); Belanger v. Alton Box Board Co., 180 F.2d 87 (7th Cir.1950); Western Union Tel. Co. v. Baltimore & Ohio Tel. Co., 26 F. 55 (C.C.S.D.N.Y.1885). An early decision of the Supreme Court assumed without discussion that the privilege applied to corporate clients. See United States v. Louisville & N. R.R., 236 U.S. 318, 336, 35 S.Ct. 363, 59 L.Ed. 598 (1915)(dictum).

70 United States v. United Shoe Mach. Corp., 89 F.Supp. 357, 359 (D.Mass.1950)(corporate attorney-client privilege covers any "information furnished by an officer or employee of the corporation in confidence and without the presence of third persons.").

71 207 F.Supp. 771 (N.D.Ill.1962)(per Campbell, C.J.), on rehearing 209 F.Supp. 321, reversed 320 F.2d 314 (7th Cir.1963), cert.denied 375 U.S. 929, 84 S.Ct. 330, 11 L.Ed. 2d 262 (1963).

72 207 F.Supp. at 773. The court also assumed that all communications to corporate counsel would be repeated to others within the corporation, thus "profaning" the communication and depriving it of its confidential nature.

73 Compare § 6.2. Analogously, the Supreme Court has held that the Fifth Amendment privilege against self-

tion as an entity has no legal or moral claims to dignity. The humans who act as the agents of the corporation are entitled to such dignity, but individually they are not the client and cannot claim the protection of the corporation's privilege for themselves if the corporation waives it.[74] Second, the force of arguments based on encouraging clients to resort to lawyers with their legal problems is diminished by the fact that business corporations are forced by circumstances and impelled by business necessity to resort to lawyers. Moreover, corporations are in a better position to calculate closely whether to accept the risk of lawyer disclosure or to keep a matter out of a lawyer's hands. The image of the befuddled and helpless innocent ill describes the corporate manager. Nonetheless, despite the absence of a compelling social reason for extending the privilege to corporations and similar bodies, every jurisdiction treats corporations as covered by it. The battleground that has mattered is the one on which the scope of the privilege has been worked out.

WESTLAW REFERENCES

attorney counsel** lawyer /s corporat*** /s privilege* /7 consideration purpose rationale reason

§ 6.5.4 Scope of the Corporate Privilege

Several competing tests have evolved for the corporate version of the privilege, but two have dominated. Each emphasizes one of the competing policies underlying the privilege. The *subject matter* test is broadly inclusive and gives full effect to the policy of encouraging full disclosure to the corporate lawyer. It provides that any communication to the corporate lawyer by a person associated with the corporation is privileged if made for the purpose of assisting the lawyer to render legal services to the corporation or to advise corporate personnel so long as the communicating person communicates about things that relate to the person's employment.[75] Judge Weinstein has proposed a "modified subject matter" test for the privilege.[76] His test adds two requirements: the request for legal services must originate with a superior officer of the corporation; and a "need to know" restriction must be enforced against further dissemination of the communication within the corporation.[77]

The *control group* test limits the privilege to those communications made to a corporate lawyer for the purpose of obtaining legal advice or assisting the lawyer in rendering legal services to the corporation only if the person making or receiving the communication was within the "control group" that had managerial responsibility for taking action in response to the lawyer's recommendation about a future course of action regarding the matter.[78] By the terms of the doctrine, the control group may be different for different legal problems. The resulting uncertainty in appli-

incrimination does not apply to corporations. See Bellis v. United States, 417 U.S. 85, 94 S.Ct. 2179, 40 L.Ed.2d 678 (1974). The point is examined in Luban, Corporate Counsel and Confidentiality, in Ethics in the Legal Profession (forthcoming)(F.Elliston ed.).

74 The decision in Upjohn Corp. v. United States, 449 U.S. 383, 101 S.Ct. 677, 66 L.Ed.2d 584 (1981), is not to the contrary. *Upjohn* held that the corporation's privilege extended broadly to communications to and from persons within the corporation. But it did not intimate that those persons could claim the privilege themselves if, for example, the corporation waived it.

75 The subject-matter test was first formulated in Harper & Row Publishers, Inc. v. Decker, 423 F.2d 487 (7th Cir.1970), affirmed per curiam by equally divided court 400 U.S. 348, 91 S.Ct. 479, 27 L.Ed.2d 433 (1971). It has enjoyed a modest following. E.g., Hasso v. Retail Credit Co., 58 F.R.D. 425 (E.D.Pa. 1973); Duplan Corp. v. Deering Milliken, Inc., 397 F.Supp. 1146 (D.S.C.1974)(in modified form).

76 2 J.Weinstein & M.Berger, Weinstein's Evidence ¶ 503(b)[04] (1975).

77 The test was enthusiastically adopted in the Eighth Circuit in Diversified Indus., Inc. v. Meredith, 572 F.2d 596 (8th Cir.1977)(en banc). Cf. Weissenberger, Toward Precision in the Application of the Attorney-Client Privilege for Corporations, 65 Iowa L.Rev. 899, 918 (1980) (proposes highly selective "but for" analysis producing modified subject-matter test, turning on whether "communication would not have existed *but for* the privilege . . .").

78 The first case to clearly articulate the control group test was City of Philadelphia v. Westinghouse Elec. Corp., 210 F.Supp. 483 (E.D.Pa.1962), mandamus denied sub nom. General Elec. Co. v. Kirkpatrick, 312 F.2d 742 (3d Cir.1962), cert.denied 372 U.S. 943, 83 S.Ct. 937, 9 L.Ed.2d

cation of the privilege is accepted in order to prevent a total blanket of silence being thrown over corporate affairs. At the same time, the shifting control group concept recognizes the fact that different persons within the corporation will have particular responsibilities that call for legal assistance and that no static designation, as of top corporate officers, would permit sufficiently broad consultation.

The Upjohn Decision

By 1981, when the Supreme Court finally addressed the existence and scope of the corporate privilege in Upjohn Co. v. United States,[79] the competing formulations and their rationale had been aired in decisions and in almost as many commentaries over a period of approximately thirty years.[80] The Court, unfortunately, issued an unilluminating opinion. The opinion discusses only some of the rationale supporting the privilege and little of that which opposes or limits it. The Court did reject the control group test on the ground of its lack of certainty.[81] Although it does not clearly adopt any other, the Court's language is plainly compatible with versions of the subject matter test.

On its facts, *Upjohn* demonstrates that the Court is willing to extend the privilege broadly to communications to a corporate lawyer by all employees of a corporate client.[82] Upjohn's management had been informed by an accountant of possible illegal payments abroad by its employees to officials of foreign countries, a matter that had United States tax and securities law implications. The corporation's general counsel and outside law firm conducted a highly confidential questionnaire survey of managers in many foreign countries, together with personal interviews with several of them. As a result, the corporation reported questionable payments to the Securities Exchange Commission. On the basis of that lead, the Internal Revenue Service attempted to enforce a summons to compel the corporation to turn over copies of the questionnaire returns and notes of the confidential interviews.

The Court held that the documents sought were privileged, stressing the need of lawyers to have a firm factual foundation for effective advice about matters involving client compliance with the law.[83] The Court noted that the information obtained by the corporation's lawyers was not available from upper-echelon employees and was needed in order to provide

969 (1963). Cases following the control group approach include In re Grand Jury Investigation, 599 F.2d 1224, 1237 (3d Cir.1979); Natta v. Hogan, 392 F.2d 686, 692 (10th Cir.1968). See generally Note, Attorney-Client Privilege for Corporate Clients: The Control Group Test, 84 Harv.L.Rev. 424 (1970).

79 449 U.S. 383, 101 S.Ct. 677, 66 L.Ed.2d 584 (1981). An excellent critique of the *Upjohn* decision is given in Sexton, A Post-*Upjohn* Consideration of the Corporate Attorney-Client Privilege, 57 NYU L.Rev. 443 (1982).

80 Among the most influential commentaries are Kobak, The Uneven Application of the Attorney-Client Privilege to Corporations in the Federal Courts, 6 Ga.L.Rev. 339 (1972); Gardner, A Personal Privilege for Communications of Corporate Clients—Paradox or Public Policy?, 40 U.Det.L.J. 299 (1963); Miller, The Challenges to the Attorney-Client Privilege, 49 Va.L.Rev. 262 (1963); Simon, The Attorney-Client Privilege as Applied to Corporations, 65 Yale L.J. 953 (1956); Note, Attorney-Client Privilege for Corporate Clients: The Control Group Test, 84 Harv.L.Rev. 424 (1970); Note, The Attorney-Client Privilege in the Corporate Setting: A Suggested Approach, 69 Mich.L.Rev. 360 (1970); Note, Privileged Communications—Inroads on the "Control Group" Test in the Corporate Area, 22 Syracuse L.Rev. 759 (1971); Note, The Privileged Few: The Attorney-Client Privilege as Applied to Corporations, 20 UCLA L.Rev. 288 (1972).

81 449 U.S. at 397, 101 S.Ct. at 686. Ironically, the Court's attempt to supply certainty falls far short. Among other things, the opinion cites Hickman v. Taylor, 329 U.S. 495, 67 S.Ct. 385, 91 L.Ed.2d 451 (1947), but fails to acknowledge that portion of *Hickman* that held that a company's attorney-client privilege does not protect witness' statements taken from company employees. See 329 U.S. at 508.

82 Chief Justice Burger, in a special concurrence, would have gone further and extended the privilege to all *former* employees of the corporation. See 449 U.S. at 403, 101 S.Ct. at 689. His concurrence urges adoption of a kind of "subject matter" test but does not identify which version.

A subsequent federal case extended *Upjohn* to former employees consulted about a matter of present concern to the corporation. In re Coordinated Pretrial Proceedings in Petroleum Prods. Antitrust Litig., 658 F.2d 1355, 1361 n.7 (9th Cir.1981), cert. denied 455 U.S. 990, 102 S.Ct. 1615, 71 L.Ed.2d 850 (1982).

83 449 U.S. at 392, 101 S.Ct. at 684.

a factual basis for advice about the law. The communications concerned the employees' duties for the corporation, and the employees spoke with the corporation's lawyers after learning of their employer's desire to obtain legal advice.

On first inspection, *Upjohn* appears to provide a very broad protection for communications between corporate lawyers and corporate employees. Unguarded language in the opinion invites the conclusion that the attorney-client privilege and the lawyer work product doctrine have been collapsed into an unqualified privilege for all corporate communications to a lawyer. There are several reasons for reading the decision more cautiously. First, the Court's refusal to adopt any general standard for the corporate privilege leaves the future course of adjudication uncertain. Second, the *Upjohn* decision is relevant only for federal question litigation in federal courts.[84] State courts remain free to follow or to reject *Upjohn*, and to date no state court has been persuaded to abandon a more restrictive test because of the reasoning of the *Upjohn* decision.[85] Thus a corporate lawyer can safely rely on the liberality of *Upjohn* only if the lawyer can confidently predict that the question of privilege will arise as to a federal question in federal court litigation. Third, *Upjohn* involved consultation about a completed act; consultation about ongoing or future payments to foreign officials would have introduced the uncertainties of the crime-fraud exception (§ 6.4.10). Fourth, fears that *Upjohn* will result in a corporate lawyer's office becoming a depository for important documents overlooks the requirement that the documents be kept confidential.[86] Wide circulation of documents within a corporation or showing them to others than the corporation's lawyers can result in implied waiver of the privilege (§ 6.4.4). And investigations of the kind involved in *Upjohn* will not be privileged unless extensive, and perhaps exclusive, lawyer involvement is directed by responsible corporate officers.[87] The expense and inaccessibility of lawyer-conducted corporate business as outlined in *Upjohn* suggests that it cannot be efficiently adapted for any but exceptional corporate operations. Fifth, *Upjohn* did not decide whether the privilege applies to interviews with nonemployees or to communica-

84 Fed. R.Evid., Rule 501:

Except as otherwise required by the Constitution of the United States or provided by Act of Congress or in rules prescribed by the Supreme Court pursuant to statutory authority, the privilege of a witness, person, government, State, or political subdivision thereof shall be governed by the principles of the common law as they may be interpreted by the courts of the United States in the light of reason and experience. However, in civil actions and proceedings, with respect to an element of a claim or defense as to which State law supplies the rule of decision, the privilege of a witness, person, government, State, or political subdivision thereof shall be determined in accordance with State law.

85 Consolidation Coal Co. v. Bucyrus-Erie Co., 89 Ill.2d 103, 59 Ill.Dec. 666, 432 N.E.2d 250 (1982)(*Upjohn*'s approach rejected in favor of control-group test because of its better accommodation of conflicting values between confidentiality and disclosure of truth in trials); Leer v. Chicago, M. St. P. & P. Ry., 308 N.W.2d 305, 309 (Minn. 1981), cert.denied 455 U.S. 939, 102 S.Ct. 1430, 71 L.Ed.2d 650 (1982) (*Upjohn* notwithstanding, employees who only witness occurrences do not report to company lawyers about matters within their employment).

86 In *Upjohn* itself, the Court stressed the fact that no corporate employee other than its lawyers had attended the interviews or seen copies of the questionnaires completed by corporate employees. See 449 U.S. at 395 n.5, 101 S.Ct. at 685 n. 5. Soon after *Upjohn* was decided, a district court held that attendance of noncontrol-group employees at a meeting of the board of directors where a prospective lawsuit was discussed with a corporate lawyer was not fatal to the privilege because the information of those employees was needed for informed discussion. Eglin Fed. Credit Union v. Cantor, Fitzgerald Sec. Corp., 91 F.R.D. 414, 418 (N.D.Ga.1981).

87 An investigation of the kind managed by lawyers in *Upjohn* could also have been conducted by nonlawyer employees of the client corporation, but in that case the results of the investigation would clearly not have been privileged. See In re Grand Jury Subpoena (General Counsel, John Doe, Inc.), 599 F.2d 504, 511 (2d Cir.1979). The superior corporate officer's direction to employees to communicate with the corporate lawyer, which was also stressed in *Upjohn*, has been dispensed with as a requirement in one subsequent case. In re International Sys. & Controls Corp. Sec. Litig., 91 F.R.D. 552, 556 (S.D.Tex. 1981), vacated on other grounds 693 F.2d 1235 (5th Cir. 1982). Some pre-*Upjohn* cases had stressed the need for formal direction by a high-level executive to outside lawyers to undertake investigations. E.g., In re Grand Jury Proceedings (Browning Arms Co.), 528 F.2d 1301, 1304 (8th Cir.1976).

tions with employees about matters not within the scope of their employment.[88]

Upjohn both overstates the need for certainty and does little to supply a significant measure of it. At the time of the decision most of the federal circuits had not yet decided which test to adopt for corporations and the pace of litigation of the issue was languid.[89] The course of lower court decisions since *Upjohn* seems not to have profited from such certainty as the decision thought it was bestowing. Plainly, many important issues concerning the scope of the corporate attorney-client privilege remain.

Corporate Control of the Privilege

Other problems of implementation of the privilege remain that are unaffected by the *Upjohn* decision. Under all of the tests, courts refuse to distinguish between house counsel and outside lawyers, applying the privilege in the same way with respect to communication to and from either kind of lawyer.[90] The general view is that an individual officer or employee of a corporation who has supplied confidential information to a corporate lawyer for the corporation's purposes may not later object to the corporation's use of the information. An officer or other person connected with the corporation cannot claim the privilege if the corporation has waived or failed to assert it.[91]

The suggestion has been made that *Upjohn* provides that waiver is effective only if both the corporation and the individual employee who made the privileged communication concur.[92] But the benefits of the privilege are solely for the advantage of the corporation. Its decision to forego those benefits—including the possible benefits of future employee willingness to reveal information to corporate lawyers—should not be subject to veto by an employee whose perspective might be quite personal. A related line of cases holds that a corporate lawyer who receives confidential information from a corporate officer is not disqualified from representing the corporation against the officer in litigation to which the confidential information relates.[93] But if the officer is independently a client of the same lawyer, then a privilege can be asserted, limited to the officer's own communications and legal affairs.[94]

Changes in corporate form can alter invocation of the privilege. In the case of a corporation that has entered bankruptcy, the preferable view is that the power to invoke or waive the privilege passes from the corporate officers to the trustee in bankruptcy.[95] If the corporate client has been acquired by another

[88] The reverse was decided, erroneously, in Baxter Travenol Laboratories, Inc. v. Lemay, 89 F.R.D. 410 (S.D. Ohio 1981). The court, attempting to follow *Upjohn,* held that a communication to a corporation's lawyer by a "litigation consultant" could not be discovered because of the privilege. The consultant was merely a witness to an event being litigated and his communication to his "employer" had nothing to do with events occurring during his employment as consultant. Equally surprisingly, one lower federal court has read *Upjohn* to protect as unqualifiedly privileged an ordinary accident statement taken from an occurrence witness who was a corporate employee. Royal Embassy of Saudi Arabia v. Steamship Mount Dirfys, 537 F.Supp. 55, 56 (E.D.N.C.1981).

[89] For example, in the Second Circuit, which handles as much corporate litigation as any other, the choice between tests had not been made at the time of *Upjohn.* See In re Grand Jury Subpoena (General Counsel, John Doe, Inc.), 599 F.2d 504, 509–10 (2d Cir.1979)(noting absence of Second Circuit resolution).

[90] Barr Marine Prods. Co. v. Borg-Warner Corp., 84 F.R.D. 631, 635–36 (E.D.Pa.1979), and authorities cited; Burlington Indus. v. Exxon Corp., 65 F.R.D. 26, 36 (D.Md. 1974); United States v. United Shoe Mach. Corp., 89 F.Supp. 357, 359 (D.Mass.1950); Kuiper v. District Court, ___ Mont. ___, 632 P.2d 694, 699 (1981).

[91] United States v. Demauro, 581 F.2d 50, 55 (2d Cir. 1978); United States v. Piccini, 412 F.2d 591, 593 (2d Cir. 1969), cert.denied 397 U.S. 917, 90 S.Ct. 923, 25 L.Ed.2d 98 (1970); In re Grand Jury Proceedings (Jackier), 434 F.Supp. 648, 649–50 (E.D.Mich.1977), affirmed 570 F.2d 562 (6th Cir.1978); In re Grand Jury Subpoena Duces Tecum, 391 F.Supp. 1029, 1034 (S.D.N.Y.1975).

[92] Sexton, A Post-*Upjohn* Consideration of the Corporate Attorney-Client Privilege, 57 NYU L. Rev. 443, 508–10 (1982).

[93] United States Indus. Inc. v. Goldman, 421 F.Supp. 7, 11 (S.D.N.Y.1976); Meehan v. Hopps, 144 Cal.App.2d 284, 301 P.2d 10, 15–16 (1956).

[94] Continental Oil Co. v. United States, 330 F.2d 347, 350 (9th Cir.1964); In re Grand Jury Subpoena Duces Tecum, 391 F.Supp. 1029, 1034 (S.D.N.Y.1975).

[95] Commodity Futures Trading Comm'n v. Weintraub, ___ U.S. ___, 105 S.Ct. 1986, 85 L.Ed.2d 372 (1985)(trustee of corporation in bankruptcy has power to waive corporation's attorney-client privilege with respect to pre-bankruptcy confidential communications, despite present ob-

entity and has ceased to exist, the acquiring entity becomes the holder of the privilege.[96] The board of directors of a corporation at the time the evidentiary issue arises controls exercise of the privilege.[97]

Other Artificial Entities

Artificial entities other than corporations are sometimes benefited by the privilege. The sparse authority that exists indicates that, for purposes of confidentiality, each member of an unincorporated association may be regarded as a client.[98] In each reported instance, however, the membership of the association was relatively small. At some point, the identification between individuals, on the one hand, and the entity and its management and direction, on the other, becomes so attenuated that analysis of the situation as if the entity were incorporated becomes appropriate. Certainly that should be the case when an association is an enormous organization such as a union or similar group with tens of thousands of members.

WESTLAW REFERENCES

attorney counsel** lawyer /s corporat*** /s privilege* /s subject-matter

attorney counsel** lawyer /s corporat*** /s privilege* /s control-group

The Upjohn Decision

449 +5 383 /p privilege*

Corporate Control of the Privilege

house outside retain*** /3 attorney counsel** lawyer /s corporat*** /s privilege*

attorney counsel** lawyer /s corporat*** /s privilege* /s employee officer trustee

Other Artificial Entities

attorney counsel** lawyer /s association unincorporat*** union /s privilege* % "bar association"

§ 6.5.5 Corporate Fiduciary Exception

One of the unanswered questions after *Upjohn* is the continuing vitality of the "good cause" exception for divulgence of otherwise privileged corporate communications in shareholder actions against a corporation and its officers. The exception gained currency following Garner v. Wolfinbarger.[99] The Fifth Circuit acknowledged that a corporate lawyer's advice to management about contemplated stock offerings was within the normal protection of the privilege. Nonetheless, the lower court could order disclosure of the content of the lawyer's advice for the use of shareholders in their suit against the corporation and its officers on the basis of alleged securities law violations. Production was warranted if the trial court's consideration of a nonexhaustive list of nine factors persuaded it that the privilege should be set aside under the facts of the particular case.[1] Those factors relate primarily to the apparent strength of the shareholders' factual and legal position in the litigation and the number of shareholders that will potentially be benefited by the suit.[2] The court analogized the corporation's management and its shareholders to dual clients whose communications to their common lawyer were not privileged from disclosure in subsequent litigation between themselves (see

jections of corporation's officers and directors); Citibank v. Andros, 666 F.2d 1192, 1195–96 (8th Cir.1981). Cf. In O.P.M. Leasing Serv. Inc., 670 F.2d 383 (2d Cir.1982).

96 Dickerson v. Superior Court, 135 Cal.App.3d 93, 185 Cal.Rptr. 97, 99 (1982).

97 United States v. De Lillo, 448 F.Supp. 840, 842 (E.D. N.Y.1978)(successor board, not board in power at time of confidential communications, has power to decide whether to waive privilege).

98 Westinghouse Elec. Corp. v. Kerr-McGee Corp., 580 F.2d 1311, 1318 n.11 (7th Cir.1978), cert.denied 439 U.S. 955, 99 S.Ct. 353, 58 L.Ed.2d 346 (1978); Benge v. Superior Court, 131 Cal.App.3d 336, 182 Cal.Rptr. 275, 281–82 (1982)(members of local union and union lawyers at closed union meeting engaged in client-lawyer conversation looking toward possible future legal employment by members on individual basis). Cf. Connelly v. Dun & Bradstreet, Inc., 96 F.R.D. 339 (D.Mass.1982)(privilege applies to communications between former customers of bankrupt and lawyer appointed by bankruptcy court to represent interests of former customers of bankrupt).

99 430 F.2d 1093 (5th Cir.1970), cert.denied 401 U.S. 974, 91 S.Ct. 1191, 28 L.Ed.2d 323 (1971).

1 430 F.2d at 1104.

2 The court also intimated that the fiduciary exception would apply beyond the context of shareholder derivative actions. See 430 F.2d at 1097 n.11.

§ 6.4.8).[3] Primarily, however, the court relied upon a balance of the benefits of disclosure to the shareholders against the possible costs of disclosure to the corporation,[4] in light of the fiduciary-like obligation that corporate managers have to shareholders to manage the corporation in the interests of the shareholders.

Garner v. Wolfinbarger has been followed by a number of courts in shareholder litigation.[5] Several lower federal courts have followed the *Garner* approach after the Supreme Court's decision in *Upjohn Co. v. United States.*[6] One line of cases has gone further and has refused to recognize the attorney-client privilege at all in analogous litigation. Thus courts do not require a showing of good cause as a condition of divulgence when a lawyer gives legal advice to a trustee of an express trust and the lawyer-trustee communication is sought by a trust beneficiary.[7]

The multifactored approach employed in *Garner* in deciding whether to set the privilege aside has concentrated on the fiduciary nature of the relationship between the corporate client and the party seeking otherwise privileged information. For that purpose, courts have examined that relationship both at the time of the alleged wrong and at the time suit is filed. Thus courts have held that *Garner* does not apply to an attempt by a shareholder of Corporation A to obtain from Corporation B materials relating to a lawyer's representation of Corporation A, even if the two corporations are related, so long as their separate corporate identities have been maintained.[8] It also has been held that *Garner* should not be applied to discover confidential information supplied to a lawyer retained to investigate and advise on the very matter in litigation, but should be limited to situations in which the lawyer's involvement, as in *Garner*, was contemporaneous with the acts being challenged.[9] The doctrine may also be inapplicable to suits in which a former shareholder attempts to recover damages from the corporation [10] or to suits in which management owed no fiduciary duty to the party seeking divulgence of the confidence.[11]

WESTLAW REFERENCES

attorney counsel** lawyer /s corporat*** /s privilege* /p fiduciary "good cause" s****holder

garner /p 430 +5 1093

§ 6.5.6 *Governmental Clients and the Privilege*

In general, the question of the applicability of the attorney-client privilege to governmental clients has not received extensive judicial or scholarly attention. The sparse authority is not in agreement on the basic question of the scope of the privilege for governmental clients.[12]

[3] 430 F.2d at 1103. As the court recognized, the fiduciary exception is more limited because disclosure is to be ordered only when good cause is shown.

[4] On remand, the district court ordered disclosure. See 56 F.R.D. 499 (S.D.Ala.1972).

[5] Cohen v. Uniroyal, Inc., 80 F.R.D. 480, 483–85 (E.D. Pa.1978); Valente v. Pepsico, Inc., 68 F.R.D. 361 (D.Del. 1975); Bailey v. Meister Brau, Inc., 55 F.R.D. 211 (N.D.Ill. 1972).

[6] See § 6.5.4 at n.79 supra. E.g., In re International Systems & Controls Corp. Securities Litig., 91 F.R.D. 552, 557 (S.D.Tex.1981), order vacated 693 F.2d 1235 (5th Cir. 1982); Donovan v. Fitzsimmons, 90 F.R.D. 583, 586 (N.D. Ill.1981); In re LTV Securities Litig., 89 F.R.D. 595, 606 (N.D.Tex.1981); SEC v. Gulf & Western Indus., Inc., 518 F.Supp. 675, 680 (D.D.C.1981).

[7] Washington-Baltimore Newspaper Guild v. Washington Star Co., 543 F.Supp. 906, 909 n.5 (D.D.C.1982)(employee-benefit trust); Riggs Nat'l Bank v. Zimmer, 355 A.2d 709 (Del.Ch.1976). Cf. Donovan v. Fitzsimmons, 90 F.R.D. 583, 586 (N.D.Ill.1981)(exception for good cause recognized for client-lawyer consultations in union-benefit trust).

[8] Valente v. Pepsico, Inc., 68 F.R.D. 361, 367–68 (D.Del. 1975).

[9] In re LTV Securities Litig., 89 F.R.D. 595, 607–08 (N.D.Tex.1981); Ohio-Sealy Mattress Mfg. Co. v. Kaplan, 90 F.R.D. 21, 31 (N.D.Ill.1980).

[10] Weil v. Investment/Indicators, Research & Mgmt., Inc., 647 F.2d 18, 23 (9th Cir.1981).

[11] In re Colocotronis Tanker Securities Litig., 449 F.Supp. 828 (S.D.N.Y.1978).

[12] Cf. EPA v. Mink, 410 U.S. 73, 86, 93 S.Ct. 827, 835, 35 L.Ed.2d 119 (1973)(drawing line between what government may withhold and what private litigants can obtain in many respects has "remained uncertain from the very beginning of the Republic.").

Open Government and the Privilege

One may wonder why, in a democracy, government clients should enjoy the iron-curtain protection of the privilege in any case. Freedom of information, government in the sunshine, and similar concepts have taken strong hold in both national and local government.[13] The basic concept of those laws is that few matters of democratic governance are legitimately kept from citizens. It thus might be argued that even when it is a matter of information confided by a government agent to a government lawyer, the public interest in the availability and free circulation of information possessed by government agents should restrict the reach of the attorney-client privilege, if indeed it applies at all to government agencies.

The broad appeal of open governement, however, has not meant the end of confidentiality in government. The statutory expressions of open-government policies contain exceptions for a variety of communications. One that finds common expression in the statutes covers confidential matter revealed to a government lawyer. For example, in NLRB v. Sears, Roebuck & Co.[14] the Supreme Court stated that the federal Freedom of Information Act exempted materials covered both by the attorney-client privilege and the work product doctrine. The general approach of state courts has been to read sunshine legislation narrowly so as to preserve room for confidential communications between government officials and their government lawyers, particularly with respect to matters in litigation.[15]

Scope of the Privilege for Governmental Clients

The decisions are quite nonspecific in spelling out the affirmative side of the issue—the applicability of the privilege to governmental clients. Some decisions assume that the privilege is applicable generally to communications in confidence between all governmental employees and government lawyers.[16] Another group applies something akin to the "control group" test for the corporate privilege and similarly limits the sources from which a government lawyer can acquire privileged information.[17] A third set of decisions express a preference for a governmental privilege that goes no further than the work product doctrine and that requires that the governmental client-lawyer communication take place in contemplation of litigation in order to be priv-

[13] 5 U.S.C.A. § 552 (Freedom of Information Act); 5 U.S.C.A. § 522B (Government in the Sunshine Act). See generally R.Berg & S.Klitzman, An Interpretive Guide to the Government in the Sunshine Act (1978); Litigation under the Amended Freedom of Information Act (C.Marwick 4th ed.1979).

[14] 421 U.S. 132, 154, 95 S.Ct. 1504, 1518, 44 L.Ed.2d 29 (1975). The fleeting reference in *Sears, Roebuck* alludes to a mention of the attorney-client privilege in a Senate report. Neither the opinion nor the Senate Report explores the scope of the privilege.

A related category of documents exempt from discovery under the federal Freedom of Information Act covers "pre-decisional" documents and other communications under the so-called deliberative-process exception to the act. See NLRB v. Sears, Roebuck & Co., 421 U.S. 132, 95 S.Ct. 1504, 44 L.Ed.2d 29 (1975); EPA v. Mink, 410 U.S. 73, 93 S.Ct. 827, 35 L.Ed.2d 119 (1973); Renegotiation Bd. v. Grumman Aircraft Engineering Corp., 421 U.S. 168, 95 S.Ct. 1491, 44 L.Ed.2d 57 (1975). The overlap between the attorney-client privilege and the deliberative-process exception to the act are discussed in Mead Data Cent., Inc. v. Department of Air Force, 566 F.2d 242, 254–55, n. 28 (D.C.Cir.1977).

[15] Mitchell v. School Bd. of Leon County, 335 So.2d 354 (Fla.Ct.App.1976); Minneapolis Star & Tribune Co. v. Housing & Redevelopment Authority, 310 Minn. 313, 251 N.W.2d 620 (1976); Oklahoma Ass'n of Municipal Attorneys v. State, 577 P.2d 1310 (Okl.1978); Port of Seattle v. Rio, 16 Wn.App. 718, 559 P.2d 18 (1977). But see Wait v. Florida Power & Light Co., 372 So.2d 420, 424 (Fla.1979) (if common-law attorney-client privilege is to be included within open-files statute, task is that of legislature and not courts); Lamar v. McCord, 245 Ark. 401, 432 S.W.2d 753 (1968)(same).

[16] E.g., Green v. IRS, 556 F.Supp. 79, 85 (N.D.Ind.1982), affirmed 734 F.2d 18 (7th Cir.1984)(the privilege "unquestionably is applicable to the relationship between Government attorneys and administrative personnel"); Hearn v. Rhay, 68 F.R.D. 574, 579 (E.D.Wash.1975); People v. Glen Arms Estate, Inc., 230 Cal.App.2d 841, 41 Cal.Rptr. 303 (1964); Booth Newspapers, Inc. v. Regents of the University of Michigan, 93 Mich.App. 100, 286 N.W.2d 55, 59 (1979); Rowley v. Ferguson, 48 N.E.2d 243 (Ohio App. 1942).

[17] Mead Data Cent., Inc. v. Department of Air Force, 566 F.2d 242, 253 n.24 (D.C.Cir.1977)(privilege extends to communications between government lawyers and all agents or employees of the organization who are authorized to act or speak for the organization in relation to the subject matter of the communication); Falcone v. IRS, 479 F.Supp. 985, 989 (E.D.Mich.1979).

ileged.[18] A fourth and even more restrictive approach is taken in the 1974 Uniform Rules of Evidence. Those provided that the privilege should not exist

> as to a communication between a public officer or agency and its lawyers unless the communication concerns a pending investigation, claim, or action and the court determines that disclosure will seriously impair the ability of the public officer or agency to process the claim or conduct a pending investigation litigation, or proceeding in the public interest.[19]

The lawyer codes take no independent position on the matter. The 1969 Code has nothing to say on it. Model Rule 1.11(e) defines confidential government information for the purpose of the former government lawyer conflict of interest rules as "information which, at the time this rule is applied, the government is prohibited by law from disclosing to the public or has a legal privilege not to disclose." But that approach merely incorporates, in part, the uncertain state of the law of privilege.

An enormous gulf divides an approach such as that in the Uniform Rules from, for example, the very expansive definition of the corporate privilege in a recent Supreme Court case.[20] The Uniform Rules obviously defer to the policy of open government with necessary and limited exceptions for such matters as client-lawyer conferences in a government agency concerning settlement of a condemnation action and similar situations in which the need for confidentiality is strong and specific. Presumably, a traditional and absolute version of the privilege would be preferred by courts that place predominant value on preserving confidentiality in order to assure free consultation between lawyer and client and that conclude that this opportunity should be as available to governmental clients as to private persons.[21] It is difficult to believe that governmental agencies that have functioned for decades, and in some cases centuries, with no sure guarantee of the attorney-client privilege could realistically claim a need for such protection. Its incompatibility with democratic precepts of state legitimacy also argues against a broad view.

The scanty authority that does exist on matters of detail is fairly consistent with a narrow reading of the privilege for governmental clients. The general approach is to confine the privilege at least as much as it is confined in nongovernmental settings. A communication by a government employee is not privileged if the employee is aware at the time that the information will be communicated to others, particularly if the employee is aware that it might be employed in considering disciplinary action against him or her.[22] A document assertedly privileged must be confined in its circulation to only those per-

[18] Niemeier v. Watergate Special Prosecution Force, 565 F.2d 967, 974 (7th Cir.1977)(memorandum to Watergate special prosecutor from his lawyer advising on the legality of continuing felony charges against former president after presidential pardon not within privilege); Falcone v. IRS, 479 F.Supp. 985, 990 (E.D.Mich.1979)(dictum). Decisions such as EEOC v. Georgia-Pacific Corp., 10 Empl.Prac.Dec. (CCH) ¶ 10,552 (D.Or.1975)(lawyer-client privilege bars discovery of communications from employee complaining of unlawful discrimination made to commission lawyers), can be understood as coming within that view or as founded on an exception for instances in which government lawyers, in effect, represent private citizens much as is done in private-practice representations.

[19] Unif.R.Evid. 502(d)(6). Few states have adopted the section. But see 12 Okl.St.Ann. § 2502(D)(6). Rule 502(d)(6) largely vitiates a broad inclusion of public officers and entities in the definition of client in Rule 502(a)(1). The Uniform Rule is apparently drawn from the narrow and limited privilege that has long been recognized for informal investigatory and trial preparation activities of governmental agencies. E.g., United States v. Morgan, 313 U.S. 409, 422, 61 S.Ct. 999, 1004, 85 L.Ed. 1429 (1941); 8 J. Wigmore, Evidence § 2378, at 805–808 (J.McNaughton rev.1961).

[20] Upjohn Co. v. United States, 449 U.S. 383, 101 S.Ct. 677, 66 L.Ed.2d 584 (1981). See § 6.5.4.

[21] Such a broad approach is favored in Note, The Applicability and Scope of the Attorney-Client Privilege in the Executive Branch of Government, 62 B.U.L.Rev. 1003 (1982), in order to encourage government policymakers to consult more frequently with lawyers. The assumption made is that government agents would consult less frequently if no privilege existed.

[22] See Gonzales v. Municipal Court, 67 Cal.App.3d 111, 136 Cal.Rptr. 475, 481 (1977). Cf. Ward v. Superior Court, 70 Cal.App.3d 23, 138 Cal.Rptr. 532, 539 (1977) (communication between county assessor and county counsel about internal operations of assessor's office could not be confidential as to governing body of county with oversight responsibility for that office).

sons within the agency who have a firm need to know of its contents if it is to remain privileged.[23]

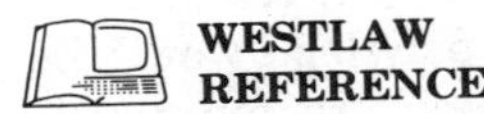
WESTLAW REFERENCES

Open Government and the Privilege

attorney counsel** lawyer /s govern! /s privilege* /p democra*** "freedom of information" f.o.i.a. open policy sun-shine

Scope of the Privilege for Governmental Clients

attorney counsel** lawyer /s govern! /s privilege* /s applicab! apply limit! reach*** "work product"

§ 6.6 LAWYER WORK PRODUCT[24]

§ 6.6.1 Background

Beginning in 1947, with the decision of the United States Supreme Court in Hickman v. Taylor,[25] the federal courts and the states[26] embraced a doctrine that qualifiedly immunizes from pretrial discovery materials prepared by an advocate in anticipation of litigation. This section will examine the history and general scope of the work product doctrine and contrast it with the attorney-client privilege with which it is sometimes confused. Attempts by an adversary to obtain information in the hands of an opposing lawyer were doomed to failure before the adoption of discovery rules modeled on those in the 1938 Federal Rules of Civil Procedure. Prior to that time discovery was generally unavailable in civil cases; to this day it remains generally unavailable to the accused in criminal cases. An attempt to obtain pretrial information with a subpoena or a search warrant would have been unsuccessful because of constitutional doctrines that then prohibited attempts to obtain "mere evidence"[27] or to obtain an individual's "private papers."[28]

The Federal Rules for the first time made generally available coercive mechanisms to obtain pretrial information from both opposing litigants and third parties. That created the need to address the extent to which lawyers for a litigant could be made to respond to such requests. The discovery rules themselves from the beginning prohibited attempts to discover privileged information,[29] and it was understood that this certainly included information protected by the attorney-client privilege.[30] But what about unprivileged information in the hands of a lawyer, such as statements taken from nonclient occurrence witnesses?

The Supreme Court addressed that general issue of unprivileged information in 1947 in Hickman v. Taylor.[31] The Court held that a lawyer's trial preparation materials must ordinarily be protected from discovery in order to enhance the proper preparation of a client's case for a trial. Only immunizing the product of a lawyer's work would assure a "certain degree of privacy" within which the lawyer could work free from unnecessary intrusion by opposing parties or their lawyers.[32] An absence of protection might mean that lawyers would be compelled to avoid reducing their thoughts to writing and might lead to

23 Coastal States Gas Corp. v. Department of Energy, 617 F.2d 854, 863–64 (D.C.Cir.1980); Coastal Corp. v. Duncan, 86 F.R.D. 514, 520–21 (D.Del.1980); State ex rel. Cartwright v. Oklahoma Indus. Authority, 629 P.2d 1244, 1250–51 (Okl.1981).

24 See generally Special Project: The Work Product Doctrine, 68 Cornell L.Rev. 760 (1983).

25 329 U.S. 495, 67 S.Ct. 385, 91 L.Ed. 451 (1947).

26 The work product doctrine has gained universal acceptance in the states. See C.Wright & A.Miller, Federal Practice and Procedure § 2022, at 189 n.98 (1970 and Supp.1983)(citations to state work product rules and statutes).

27 Gouled v. United States, 255 U.S. 298, 41 S.Ct. 261, 65 L.Ed. 647 (1921), overruled in Warden v. Hayden, 387 U.S. 294, 87 S.Ct. 1642, 18 L.Ed.2d 782 (1967).

28 Boyd v. United States, 116 U.S. 616, 6 S.Ct. 524, 29 L.Ed. 746 (1886), limited in Fisher v. United States, 425 U.S. 391, 409, 96 S.Ct. 1569, 1580, 48 L.Ed.2d 39 (1976); Andresen v. Maryland, 427 U.S. 463, 473–74, 96 S.Ct. 2737, 2744–45, 49 L.Ed.2d 627 (1976)(search warrant, but not subpoena, can reach incriminating personal papers).

29 Fed.R.Civ.P.Rule 26(b)(1): "Parties may obtain discovery regarding any matter, not privileged, which is relevant to the subject matter involved in the pending action . . . ."

30 Brockway Glass Co. v. Hartford-Empire Co., 36 F.Supp. 470 (W.D.N.Y.1941); Auer v. Hershey Creamery Co., 1 F.R.D. 14 (D.N.J.1939).

31 329 U.S. 495, 67 S.Ct. 385, 91 L.Ed. 451 (1947).

32 329 U.S. at 510–511, 67 S.Ct. at 393–94.

"inefficiency, unfairness and sharp practices" in trial preparation and client counseling. The resulting situation would be demoralizing to the legal profession and detrimental to the interests of clients and the system of justice.[33] Not mentioned by *Hickman* but possibly important is the fact that the work product protection permits a lawyer to record and file derogatory or otherwise indiscrete thoughts about clients without fear that they will ever, indirectly, reach a client's eyes or ears.[34]

The Court in *Hickman* identified two types of trial preparation materials. *Informational* work product such as substantially verbatim witness statements are protected from discovery, but an inquiring party nonetheless can obtain their exceptional disclosure by showing good cause—that the inquiring party lacks an effective substitute for the material sought and that the missing information is critically important to the inquiring party's case. *Mental impressions* work product, on the other hand, consists of the lawyer's own thoughts on strategy or legal theories and is immunized against discovery under a rule virtually as absolute as that of the attorney-client privilege itself.[35] The *Hickman* approach has undergone further doctrinal development in the decisions and has now been codified to an extent by a 1970 amendment to the Federal Rules of Civil Procedure.[36]

hickman /p 329 +5 495 /p "mental impression" "work product"

§ 6.6.2 Scope of Work Product

Under the federal rule and state rules modeled on it, the application of the lawyer work product doctrine covers much the same ground as first traversed in *Hickman* but with important additions. The doctrine operates as an exception to the normal broad sweep of the pretrial discovery rules: a party in litigation may not use the discovery devices to obtain from any other party materials prepared by the other party's lawyer or the lawyer's agent in anticipation of litigation. The privilege is qualified, however, in much the same way that *Hickman* was qualified: the inquiring party can gain access to some of those materials by demonstrating a substantial need for them and that their substantial equivalent cannot be obtained without undue hardship. The federal rules also recognize an unqualified right of any person to obtain a copy of the person's own substantially verbatim witness statement taken by a lawyer.[37] While comprehensive, the procedural rule both raises interpretative issues and has not precluded application of the *Hickman v. Taylor* doctrine to areas of civil discovery that are not covered by the literal language of the

[33] 329 U.S. at 511, 67 S.Ct. at 394. Justice Jackson, in a concurrence, added that discovery of a lawyer's own recollection of a witness' statement would often force the lawyer to the witness stand to explain an apparent inconsistency between the witness' trial testimony and the wording employed in the statement. 329 U.S. at 517.

[34] Cf. In re Sealed Case, 676 F.2d 793, 811 (D.C.Cir.1982) (no one listening in camera to cassette tape of in-house counsel's recounting of conversations with corporate executives "could imagine that [the lawyer] ever intended that it fall into the hands of his corporate superiors.").

[35] See generally Note, Protection of Opinion Work Product under the Federal Rules of Civil Procedure, 64 Va.L.Rev. 333 (1978). In Upjohn Co. v. United States, 449 U.S. 383, 101 S.Ct. 677, 687–88, 66 L.Ed.2d 584 (1981), the Supreme Court stressed that that kind of hard-core work product included the lawyer's recollection of statements made by witnesses because of the likelihood that the lawyer's recollections would be heavily influenced by the lawyer's own mental impressions and legal theories. The court stopped short of holding that the immunity from disclosure of hard-core work product was absolute. See 449 U.S. at 401, 101 S.Ct. at 688. Cf. Consolidation Coal Co. v. Bucyrus-Erie Co., 89 Ill.2d 103, 59 Ill.Dec. 666, 432 N.E.2d 250 (1982)(lawyer's nonverbatim notes and memoranda of witnesses' statements protected by hard-core work product concept unless inquiring party can demonstrate "absolute impossibility" of securing similar vital information from any other source).

[36] Fed.R.Civ.P.Rule 26(b)(3). On the scope of the work product rules, see generally 4 J.Moore, Federal Practice ¶ 26.63 (2d ed.1948); 8 C.Wright & A.Miller, Federal Practice and Procedure §§ 2021–28 (1970). An excellent examination of the underpinnings of *Hickman* and of the 1970 federal rule is Cooper, Work Product of the Rulesmakers, 53 Minn.L.Rev. 1269 (1969).

[37] Fed.R.Civ.P.Rule 26(b)(3)(second paragraph). See also Rule 26(b)(4)(privilege against disclosure of trial preparation materials of experts).

work product rule and to areas outside pretrial discovery in civil litigation.[38]

Several important problems are not directly resolved by the rule. A question raised by adapting new technology to law practice is the extent to which the work product privilege extends to materials in a computer system maintained by a law firm.[39] Generally, documents in such a system are themselves discoverable, but paraphrases of documents or a data base consisting of selectively inputted records may not be.[40] Three conflicting views have emerged to measure the life span of the work product protection once litigation has ended. A view at one extreme is that the protection is terminated by the ending of the litigation for which the material was prepared.[41] At the other extreme is the view that the protection is perpetual and trial preparation material cannot be discovered in subsequent litigation of any kind.[42] A preferable position is the third: work product that is significantly related to the terminated litigation remains immune in future litigation.[43]

As with other privileges, the work product immunity can be waived. Waiver can occur by the explicit agreement of the client-litigant. Or waiver may occur implicitly, such as by failure to assert the privilege in a timely fashion.[44] Disclosure of work product to a third party will result in waiver if the disclosure substantially increases the likelihood that potential adversaries can obtain the information.[45] Waiver does not normally result from disclosures to commonly interested third parties, however, so long as the protected information remains a secret from the opposing party.[46] Some cases take the position that work product is a personal protection for the lawyer's own work and thus that a decision to waive the protection should be the lawyer's alone.[47] But the protection is ultimately aimed at serving the client, and the view is emerging that, as with the attorney-client privilege, for most purposes the client must

38 Clermont, Surveying Work Product, 68 Cornell L.Rev. 755 (1983).

39 E.Kinney, Litigation Support Systems: An Attorney's Guide § 5.17 (1980); Note, Computer Discovery in Federal Litigation: Playing by the Rules, 60 Geo.L.J. 1465 (1981); Note, Computerized Litigation Support Systems and the Attorney Work Product Doctrine: The Need for Court Support against Discovery, 17 Val.U.L. Rev. 281 (1982).

40 Compare, e.g., In re IBM Peripheral EDP Devices Litig., 5 Computer Law Serv.Rep. 878 (N.D.Cal.1975)(discovery denied), with National Union Elec. Corp. v. Matsushita Elec. Indus. Co., 494 F.Supp. 1257 (E.D.Pa.1980) (discovery permitted; *IBM* case distinguished).

41 United States v. IBM Corp., 66 F.R.D. 154, 178 (S.D. N.Y.1974); Honeywell, Inc. v. Piper Aircraft Corp., 50 F.R.D. 117, 119 (M.D.Pa.1970).

42 In re Murphy, 560 F.2d 326, 334 (8th Cir.1977); Duplan Corp. v. Moulinage et Retorderie de Chavanoz, 487 F.2d 480, 483–84 (4th Cir.1973).

43 Grolier, Inc. v. FTC, 671 F.2d 553, 555–56 (D.C.Cir. 1982), reversed 462 U.S. 19, 103 S.Ct. 2209, 76 L.Ed.2d 387 (1983); Republic Gear Co. v. Borg-Warner Co., 381 F.2d 551, 557 (2d Cir.1967). This position is favored by commentators. See 4 J.Moore, Federal Practice ¶ 26.64[2], at 26–415 (2d ed. 1979); 8 C.Wright & A.Miller, Federal Practice and Procedure § 2024, at 201 (1970); Cooper, Work Product of the Rulesmakers, 53 Minn.L. Rev. 1269, 1299 n.100 (1969). In FTC v. Grolier, Inc., 462 U.S. 19, 103 S.Ct. 2209, 76 L.Ed.2d 387 (1983), the federal Freedom of Information Act was construed not to require disclosure of work product in terminated litigation without qualification. The Court, however, expressly left open the question of the life of the doctrine for the purpose of civil discovery. 103 S.Ct., at 2214.

44 United States v. Nobles, 422 U.S. 225, 239–40, 95 S.Ct. 2160, 2170–71, 45 L.Ed.2d 141 (1975)(waiver by putting investigator on witness stand); In re Sealed Case, 676 F.2d 793, 817–18 (D.C.Cir.1982)(implied waiver by voluntarily revealing to regulatory agency exculpatory documentary work product but suppressing inculpatory work product for which protection is now sought). Implicit waiver will not result, however, when disclosure is made under the direct force of an improper or otherwise erroneous judicial order. E.g., In re Grand Jury Investigation of Ocean Transp., 604 F.2d 672, 675 (D.C.Cir.1979), cert.denied 444 U.S. 915, 100 S.Ct. 229, 62 L.Ed.2d 169 (1979)(dictum); Transamerica Computer Co. v. IBM Corp., 573 F.2d 646, 651–52 (9th Cir.1978).

45 See generally C.Wright & A.Miller, Federal Practice and Procedure § 2024, at 210 (1970).

46 E.g., United States v. American Tel. & Tel. Co., 642 F.2d 1285, 1289–1302 (D.C.Cir.1980)(disclosure by private antitrust plaintiff of trial preparation materials to government to assist it in parallel government antitrust action against common defendant not waiver); GAF Corp. v. Eastman Kodak Co., 85 F.R.D. 46, 51–52 (S.D. N.Y.1979). Contra D'Ippolito v. Cities Service Co., 39 F.R.D. 610 (S.D.N.Y.1965). See generally Note, Waiver of the Work Product Immunity, 1981 U.Ill.L.F. 953. And see § 6.4.9.

47 See Hercules, Inc. v. Exxon Corp., 434 F.Supp. 136, 152 (D.Del.1977).

consent or act to create the waiver.[48] While no case seems to have confronted the issue, it seems clear that any part that a lawyer might play with respect to waiver must always be exercised in favor of protecting the client on the ground of either the loyalty or the confidentiality principle (§ 6.7.5).

The reach of the work product doctrine into criminal law has been mainly one-sided. The Supreme Court and many state courts agree that the doctrine protects the trial preparation materials of a defense lawyer.[49] The protection precludes discovery by the prosecution through grand jury questioning,[50] through subpoena or other coercive process,[51] or through attempted questioning at trial.[52] Work product protection for a prosecutor's trial preparation materials has been given less scope. The doctrine does preclude defense forays into the mental-impression work product of a prosecutor,[53] but some defense discovery of what otherwise would be protected informational work product is possible because of rules that require divulgence to the accused of certain witness statements or other unavailable evidence that may be helpful in supporting the case of the accused.[54] Aside from criminal cases, however, the Supreme Court has held that lawyers can generally claim for governmental clients a work product immunity for trial preparation materials as broad as that for private litigants.[55]

WESTLAW REFERENCES

fed.r.civ.p. fed.rules /s 26(b)(3) 26(b)(4)

attorney counsel** lawyer /s "work product" /s computer! hardship "mental impression" need verbatim

attorney counsel** lawyer /s "work product" /p litigation trial employ! /s complet*** end*** terminat***

attorney counsel** lawyer /s "work product" /s waive*

110k627.5(6)

§ 6.6.3 *Work Product and the Attorney-Client Privilege*

For the first time in a prominent way in American jurisprudence, *Hickman v. Taylor* attempted to differentiate sharply between the confusingly similar lawyer work product rule and the attorney-client testimonial privilege.[56] While closely related on some scores,

48 In re Grand Jury Proceedings (FMC Corp.), 604 F.2d 798, 801–02 (3d Cir.1979); United States v. Mitchell, 372 F.Supp. 1239, 1246 (S.D.N.Y.), appeal dismissed 485 F.2d 1290 (2d Cir.1973)(lawyer's consent to waiver not sufficient in absence of client's concurrence). In some instances, a waiver effective as to the client might not be effective as to the lawyer. E.g., In re Special Sept. 1978 Grand Jury, 640 F.2d 49, 63 (7th Cir.1980)(client's "waiver" of work product protection by fraud does not necessarily waive lawyer's independent objection); In re Grand Jury Investigation (Sturgis), 412 F.Supp. 943, 949 (E.D.Pa. 1976).

49 United States v. Nobles, 422 U.S. 225, 238, 95 S.Ct. 2160, 2170, 45 L.Ed.2d 141 (1975); Fed.R.Crim.P.Rule 16(b)(2). E.g., People v. Collie, 30 Cal.3d 43, 177 Cal.Rptr. 458, 634 P.2d 534 (1981); Richardson v. District Court, 632 P.2d 595, 598 n.3 (Colo.1981)(dictum); People v. Edney, 39 N.Y.2d 620, 385 N.Y.S.2d 23, 350 N.E.2d 400 (1976). See also Parks v. United States, 451 A.2d 591 (D.C.App.1982), cert. denied 461 U.S. 945, 103 S.Ct. 2123, 77 L.Ed.2d 1303 (1983)(work product immune from discovery by adverse codefendant).

50 In re Grand Jury Proceedings (Duffy), 473 F.2d 840, 842 (8th Cir.1973); In re Grand Jury Investigation (Sturgis), 412 F.Supp. 943, 947 (E.D.Pa.1976); In re Terkeltoub, 256 F.Supp. 683 (S.D.N.Y.1966).

51 In re Grand Jury Subpoena (John Doe, Inc.), 599 F.2d 504, 511–12 (2d Cir.1979); In re Grand Jury Proceedings (Duffy), 473 F.2d 840, 848 (8th Cir.1973). Cf. Upjohn Co. v. United States, 449 U.S. 383, 101 S.Ct. 677, 66 L.Ed.2d 584 (1981)(IRS summons enforcement action).

52 United States v. Nobles, 422 U.S. 225, 239, 95 S.Ct. 2160, 2170, 45 L.Ed.2d 141 (1975).

53 Fed.R.Crim.P.Rule 16(a)(2)(residual work product rule); State v. Bowen, 104 Ariz. 138, 449 P.2d 603, 607, cert. denied 396 U.S. 912, 90 S.Ct. 229, 24 L.Ed.2d 188 (1969)(prosecutor's notes of interview with prosecution witness).

54 Goldberg v. United States, 425 U.S. 94, 108, 96 S.Ct. 1338, 1347, 47 L.Ed.2d 603 (1976)(Jencks Act statements taken by prosecutor not immunized by work product doctrine). See generally § 13.10.5.

55 NLRB v. Sears, Roebuck & Co., 421 U.S. 132, 154, 95 S.Ct. 1504, 1518, 44 L.Ed.2d 29 (1975).

56 English law had long since hopelessly mixed the two. See generally 8 J.Wigmore, Evidence § 2318, at 621–24 n. 3 (J.McNaughton rev. 1961). E.g., Waugh v. British Railways Bd., [1979] 3 W.L.R. 150 (House of Lords 1979) (whether claim of privilege applies to accident reports taken by railway employees from other employees depends on whether "primary purpose" of reports was to assist solicitor in defending claims or was for purpose of railroad operation and safety). Some American jurisdictions had gone almost as far. E.g., Schmitt v. Emery, 211 Minn. 547, 2 N.W.2d 413 (1942)(witness statements taken

the rule and the privilege have at least these prominent differences:

(1) Work product protection extends to information prepared by a lawyer without regard to whether it was communicated to the lawyer in confidence and without regard to whether the lawyer's client or some other person was its source. In those senses, it is accurate to say that the work product immunity is broader in scope than the privilege.[57] For example, a lawyer's handwritten notes of a nonconfidential communication from a nonclient are not privileged but are covered by the work product immunity. The critical element for work product is possession of lawyer-generated information in the lawyer's mind or private files. The contrasting critical elements of the testimonial privilege are the sources of the information (only the client) and the setting in which it was communicated to the lawyer (in confidence).

(2) Work product is based on assumptions about the behavior of lawyers and how they would function in the absence of the protection. It aims to prevent parasitism, disruption, and harassment by an opposing party or lawyer, thus allowing a lawyer to work in an atmosphere of privacy. The attorney-client privilege assumes that its protection is necessary in order to overcome unfortunate secretiveness of clients in communicating with their lawyers. Both doctrines are presumably maintained in the ultimate interest of serving clients and, derivatively, the public interest.

(3) Work product provides a veil of secrecy against an opponent. That third parties other than an opponent possess the same information is thus irrelevant to the existence of the immunity. The attorney-client privilege, on the other hand, operates on assumptions that are destroyed by many kinds of disclosures to third parties.

(4) Work product protection is limited to information gathered in anticipation of litigation and, according to one view, can be freely discovered once that litigation has come to an end. The attorney-client privilege applies to all sorts of legal services, whether related to litigation or not, and the privilege in most of its applications is indefinite in duration.

(5) The informational work product immunity can be set aside on a showing of substantial need and undue hardship on the part of the inquiring party. The traditional attorney-client privilege in most of its applications purports to have no regard for individual needs of the inquiring party to pierce the secrecy of client-lawyer communications.

§ 6.7 DUTIES OF LAWYERS UNDER THE CONFIDENTIALITY PRINCIPLE

§ 6.7.1 The Confidentiality Principle

Lawyers in the United States operate under several legal rules that protect client information. The best known is the attorney-client privilege (§ 6.3). The lawyer work product doctrine further protects information prepared by a lawyer for a client in anticipation of litigation (§ 6.6). Agency law also protects clients against lawyer misuse of client information (§ 6.7.6). Extending a reach that includes all of those protections—and encompassing much of what they omit—is the professional regulation requiring a lawyer to keep a vast array of client information confidential and not to use it against the interests of the client. We will call that obligation the principle of confidentiality. It underlies a good part of several other areas of professional regulation, such as conflicts of interest (§ 7.1.3), client perjury (§ 12.5), supervision of nonlawyer employees (§ 16.3), and candor in negotiations (§ 13.5.8).

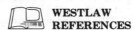

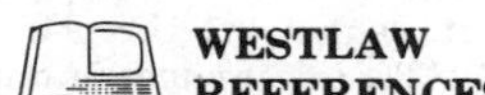
WESTLAW REFERENCES

attorney counsel** lawyer /s client /s confiden! /s principle regulat***

from employees by employer's claims agent are within attorney-client privilege), overruled in Leer v. Chicago, M.St.P. & P.Ry., 308 N.W.2d 305, 309 (Minn.1981), cert. denied 455 U.S. 939, 102 S.Ct. 1430, 71 L.Ed.2d 650 (1982).

57 United States v. Nobles, 422 U.S. 225, 238 n.11, 95 S.Ct. 2160, 2170 n.11, 45 L.Ed.2d 141 (1975); In re Grand Jury Proceedings (FMC Corp.), 604 F.2d 798, 801 (3d Cir. 1979).

§ 6.7.2 The Confidentiality Principle under the Lawyer Codes

The succeeding lawyer codes have progressed from passing reference to a lawyer's obligation of confidentiality to extensive and controversial involvement with it in recent years. The 1908 Canons were unclear about the extent of the rule. Canon 37, the main provision on confidentiality, simply posited a lawyer's obligation to protect the "confidences" of a client. Other provisions hinted at a broader duty. Canon 6, prohibiting conflicts of interest in successive representations, noted as one rationale for the rule the obligation of a lawyer to protect a client's "secrets or confidences." Nothing in the Canon further defined *secrets* as opposed to *confidences.*

Confidentiality under the 1969 Code

The 1969 Code takes several decisive steps in defining confidentiality. Borrowing the "secrets or confidences" phrase of the 1908 Canons, it elaborates a dual realm of confidentiality. First, *confidence* is defined in DR 4–101(A) to include communications protected by the attorney-client testimonial privilege.[58] Second, *secrets* is defined in the same DR to include a great deal of information not covered by the privilege: " 'secret' refers to other information gained in the professional relationship that the client has requested be held inviolate or the disclosure of which would be embarrassing or would be likely to be detrimental to the client." The term *secret*, when referring to client information, is employed in this treatise in that sense of a technical part of the professional regulations.[59]

The secrets rule of the Code is different from the protection of confidences in at least two important ways. First, its coverage is much broader. The confidence rule simply duplicates the coverage of the attorney-client testimonial privilege with its technical rules of coverage, exceptions, and waiver. The secrets protection, on the other hand, covers a great deal more. Indeed, under a straightforward reading of DR 4–101(A), secrets includes much that is excepted from the definition of confidences by one or the other of the exceptions contained in the rules of the testimonial privilege. Second, secrets have no necessary connection with the privacy of communication concept that underlies the protection of confidences. The definition of secrets stresses two elements, either of which can bring it into operation: a client explicitly requests that the lawyer not reveal the information or the nature of the information is such that its revelation is potentially embarrassing or detrimental to the client. Nothing in the Code requires that a client's insistence on secrecy be reasonable. Even irrational client fears about the consequences of disclosure require that the information be categorized as a secret. (Reasonability should, however, inform a decision about whether revelation of information would likely embarrass or be detrimental to a client when the client has not requested that it be kept confidential.)

The Code limits secrets to information "gained in the professional relationship." Thus, presumably, information obtained by a lawyer before the representation began or after it ended is not protected. A similar limitation applies under the laws of most jurisdictions to the coverage of the attorney-client privilege. But the reason for limiting the secret protection to information gained in the relationship is not apparent. By definition, the fact that the attorney-client privilege does not extend to information does not mean that

[58] "Confidence refers to information protected by the attorney-client privilege under applicable law." The reference to "applicable" law seems to acknowledge implicitly that the obligation may vary from one jurisdiction to another.

[59] The use of *secret* in association with *confidence* can be traced back at least as far as an oath for New York lawyers prescribed in the 1850 Field Code. See Report of the Commissioners on Practice and Pleadings, Code of Civil Procedure 205–06 (1850). The commissioners' notes claim that the language is a translation of a statutorily required oath of advocates in the Canton of Geneva. An oath similar to that drafted in 1850 can now be found in many states. E.g., West's Ann. Cal. Bus. & Prof. Code §§ 6067, 6068(e); Mo.Sup.Ct.R. 8.11; N.D.Cent.Code 27–13–01.

it should not be a secret. The secret protection applies, for example, to information even if it is also contained in public records (§ 6.7.4), information to which waiver under the attorney-client privilege would apply, information whose disclosure would cause no harm to the client, and the like. Given those expansions of the concept, the reason for the shortened duration for the time of gathering secrets is unclear.[60]

In contrast to limitations on the relevant period during which a lawyer receives information, once information has been received under circumstances and at a time such that it becomes secret, the information retains its confidential status indefinitely. The termination of representation of the client does not end the lawyer's duties of confidentiality.[61]

But other parts of DR 4–101 begin to chip away at its awesome structure, and other rules carry the prospect of significant further reduction. For example, DR 4–101(C)(2) provides that a lawyer "may" reveal confidential client information "when permitted under Disciplinary Rules or required by law or court order." Further, a lawyer is permitted under DR 4–101(C)(3) to reveal "the intention of his client to commit a crime and the information necessary to prevent the crime." And DR 4–101(C)(4) permits a lawyer to reveal any client information in order to collect a fee or to defend the lawyer or the lawyer's employees or associates against a charge of wrongdoing. Apparently revelation is permitted in those situations regardless of the source of the charge. Those provisions suggest the potential for inroad upon the initially broad protection of client information in the Code.

Confidentiality and the Model Rules

The 1983 Model Rules are even more expansive than the 1969 Code in the size of the initial zone of confidentiality that they create. The definition in MR 1.6 transcends the Code in three important respects: (1) it includes all information regardless of when it was learned by the lawyer; (2) it includes information without regard to whether disclosure would embarrass or work to the detriment of a client; and (3) it provides a more limited exception for future client wrongdoing.

Model Rule 1.6 states, flatly but globally, that a lawyer "shall not reveal information relating to representation of a client." As with secrets under DR 4–101(A), the information need not derive from a client communication. The comment to MR 1.6 notes that the definition applies "to all information relating to the representation, whatever its source." Information is confidential whether acquired by a lawyer before, during, or after the representation. Much could be made of the greater protection of client information supplied by that definition in the Model Rules, but the difference between the Code and the Model Rules in actual operation can readily be overstated. Rarely will a lawyer in fact acquire information about a client before or after the representation, although when that does occur the Model Rules sensibly treat the information as confidential. The Code, insensibly, does not.

Model Rule 1.6 makes information confidential without apparent regard to whether or not revealing it would embarrass or otherwise harm the interests of a client. The Code, by contrast, limits confidentiality to embarrassing or detrimental disclosures (DR 4–101(A)). A conflict of interest provision of the Model Rules, MR 1.8(b), does limit "use" of a client's information only to situations in which this is to the "disadvantage" of the client. But apparently MR 1.8(b) deals only with nonrevelatory uses and thus does not, by implication, impinge upon the breadth of statement of the confidentiality standard in MR 1.6.

60 Perhaps the words of the Code were intended to confine the secret protection simply because of a vague feeling that otherwise it would be too broad. Perhaps it was meant to reflect some kind of proprietary notion: the client does not pay for pre- or post-representation information gathering and thus is not entitled to protection. Obviously those are simply muddled considerations.

61 EC 4–6; MR 1.6 comment (Former Client). E.g., In re Nulle, 127 Ariz. 299, 620 P.2d 214, 218 (1980).

It is important to note that the exceptions to MR 1.6 do not include a broad exception like that in DR 4–101(C)(3) for information relating to a client's intention to commit a crime. The only surviving exceptions in the Model Rules that are similar to DR 4–101(C)(3) are two. First, MR 3.3(b) requires that a lawyer take remedial action with respect to client perjury even if doing this necessitates that the lawyer reveal confidential client information (see § 12.5.3). Second, MR 1.6(b)(1) permits, but does not require, a lawyer to reveal confidential information to the extent necessary to prevent a criminal act likely to result in imminent death or substantial bodily harm (see § 12.6.4). Model Rule 1.6 provides other exceptions, discussed elsewhere. Included is the exception in MR 1.6(a) for disclosures reasonably necessary to carry out the representation (§ 6.7.7). And MR 1.6(b)(2) recognizes additional exceptions for a lawyer's self-defense (§ 6.7.8).

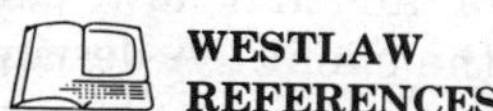
WESTLAW REFERENCES

canon /3 6 37 1908 /s confiden! conflict

Confidentiality Under the 1969 Code

disciplinary d.r. responsibility /5 4–101(a) 4–101(c)

confiden! /p secre** /p 4–101(a)

disciplinary d.r. responsibility /s 4–101(a) secre** /s except*** inclu! privacy reason! unreason!

Confidentiality and the Model Rules

"model rule" m.r. /s 1.6 confiden! information

§ 6.7.3 *The Rationale for "Secret" Protection*

The confidentiality principle, in its widest reach, is composed of (1) information within the attorney-client privilege and (2) information protected by the professional rules that prevent a lawyer from revealing confidential client information. Why do the lawyer codes protect information that the rules of evidence leave exposed to public view in testimony? Part of the answer requires that we broaden our focus beyond merely the law of evidence to include other bodies of law that also require confidentiality.

Several surviving references in both the 1969 Code and the 1983 Model Rules suggest that the attorney-client privilege is the only external legal source of the confidentiality principle.[62] But other bodies of law have for a long time enforced against lawyers a duty to avoid voluntary revelation or adverse use of a client's confidences and secrets. Most importantly, the general law of agency—to which lawyers have always been subject—imposes impressive duties of confidence-keeping upon all agents with respect to confidential information of their principals.[63] The confidentiality obligation is imposed on the lawyer by law and not by any express or implied term of the client-lawyer contract. Thus an agreement with a client under which a lawyer is to be paid for a promise not to disclose confidential information is illegal and unenforceable because the fiduciary obligation of the lawyer would require at least as much without any promise.[64] In a broad sense, all that is distinguishing, with respect to confidentiality,

[62] The suppressed Legal Background Note to what became MR 1.6 reflected an appreciation of the importance of agency law. See Model Rules at 42–43 (Proposed Final Draft, May 30, 1981). The official comment (then, as in the final version), however, refers only to "two related bodies of law, the attorney-client privilege in the law of evidence and the rule of confidentiality established in professional ethics." MR 1.6 comment (second paragraph). Cf. also EC 4–4.

[63] See generally Restatement (Second) of Agency §§ 395–96 (1958). The general obligation is stated in § 395: "an agent is subject to a duty to the principal not to use or to communicate information confidentially given him by the principal or acquired by him during the course of or on account of his agency." The rule, however, is subject to a power of the agent to reveal information when necessary to protect the superior interest of a third party. See id., § 395, comment (f); 2 F.Mechem, A Treatise on the Law of Agency § 2404 (1914).

[64] Restatement of Contracts § 557 (1932)("A bargain that has for its consideration the nondisclosure of discernible facts, or of facts that the promisee is under a fiduciary duty not to disclose, is illegal."); id., Illustration 3 ("A, in consultation with his lawyer, B, informs B of certain facts. Later, A promises B $500 if B will not disclose these facts. B accepts and does not disclose the facts. The bargain is illegal.").

about agents who are lawyers is that lawyers' work gets them much more commonly into the confidential information of their principals, clients. It is simply false professional posturing to pretend that self-regulation alone has resulted in lawyers assuming obligations of confidentiality toward their clients that external law does not already largely impose.

The ethical obligation of confidentiality is important nonetheless. It has heuristic value in addressing directly to lawyers the importance of keeping confidential client information from the rest of the world, and of not abusing it within the lawyer's own grasp. It provides additional and possibly more effective remedies through professional discipline. It also has interstitial value in placing beyond doubt the sanctionable responsibility of a lawyer to extend to clients the full protection of the attorney-client privilege and of agency law in instances in which confidentiality responsibilities might otherwise be a matter of doubt.

But recognizing the generating role of agency law does not supply as yet an adequate rationale for extending the area of mandatory confidentiality. A theoretical foundation for the broad protection of secrets that is commonly advanced is that of encouraging clients to provide their lawyers with information that would otherwise be kept from them.[65] It is not illogical to treat as secrets matters that result from attorney-client revelations but that are not covered by the attorney-client privilege—client revelations that are shared with a close circle of nonlawyer friends, for example. As mentioned, the secret rule assures that a lawyer will not mistakenly give too narrow an interpretation to the attorney-client privilege in doubtful cases and affords an additional assurance to a client revealing to a lawyer information that falls on the doubtful boundaries or entirely outside the privilege.[66]

For information derived from sources independent of client revelations, arguments for confidentiality cannot rest on the identity of the source except in rare instances in which a lawyer might owe an obligation of confidentiality to another person because of a special relationship or promise. The basic rationale for secrets must instead be sought in the effect that disclosure would have on the interests of the client. If, as indicated in DR 4-101(A), revealing the information would embarrass or be detrimental to the client, the harm that the client's lawyer causes is inconsistent with the undertaking of the lawyer. The essence of the client-lawyer relationship is that the lawyer stands ready to assist the client to obtain all that law and the legal system allows the client. A detrimental revelation of a client secret is inconsistent with that role and undertaking. The notion of loyalty exists independently of formal contract and certainly independently of a client's promise to pay a fee. Thus it is not necessarily embedded in arguments about a client's proprietary right, although proprietary claims may enchance the force of the client's position. Similarly, a client's direction to a lawyer to keep information secret should be respected by the lawyer, regardless of the source of the information, in order to assure the client's trust. Continuing the representation without reservations reasonably suggests to the client that the lawyer is undertaking to

[65] EC 4-1; MR 1.6 comment (first paragraph): "A fundamental principle in the client-lawyer relationship is that the lawyer maintain confidentiality of information relating to that representation. The client is thereby encouraged to communicate fully and frankly with the lawyer even as to embarrassing or legally damaging subject matter."

[66] It has been argued that the existence of the very extensive category of secrets that are protected against disclosure, even if they are not learned from the client, may disserve one of the most powerful arguments for the attorney-client privilege itself. Because the information is protected even if not disclosed by the client, the client is that much less encouraged to make full disclosure personally to the lawyer. A. Goldman, The Moral Foundations of Professional Ethics 100 (1980). That would only occur, however, if the client is distrustful of the lawyer, is unconvinced that revelation of the information will in fact be useful in advancing the client's interests, or believes that another source is preferable. It is doubtful that this speculative disincentive outweighs the advantages of protecting secrets, including the benefits of inducing most clients to disclose.

follow the client's wishes. So it is that DR 4–101(A) of the 1969 Code also treats as a secret the information that the client has requested the lawyer to keep confidential.

Because the lawyer learned the information in the course of performing services for another, the lawyer is not in a good position to argue that his or her personal autonomy is seriously compromised by the requirement of silence imposed by the broad confidentiality rule. The burden of silence is elective in some important senses. Prospective lawyers are aware early in their schooling of the professional requirement of silence. In practice, if they determine that particular representations ask too much of them by way of silence, lawyers are free to refuse to accept those cases or to ask to be relieved of them. That might partially explain why many lawyers avoid clients with particularly burdensome secrets such as are encountered in criminal defense and family law litigation.

Two limiting observations are in order. First, the normal expectation of lawyer loyalty to a client's interests is hardly an absolute. It does not purport to be a reason why a lawyer must always maintain silence regardless of the claims and interests of third persons. For example, a lawyer's dutiful silence about a client's intention to commit a serious crime might cause such a risk of harm to another person that the normal prohibition against voluntary disclosure should yield (§ 12.6) (client wrongdoing)). As another example, the law recognizes that matters that are secrets in respect to voluntary lawyer disclosure may nonetheless be required to be disclosed in pretrial discovery if they are not protected by the narrower attorney-client privilege or the work product doctrine.[67] Second, the expectation of confidentiality posited by the rationale of loyalty to client justifies prohibiting a lawyer from revealing information only if it poses a risk of harm to a client's interests. Yet MR 1.6 of the Model Rules, if read literally, goes much farther and prohibits a lawyer from revealing all client information, the good or neutral along with the potentially harmful. The only imaginable reason for such a universal prohibition is to provide prophylactic protection against lawyer misjudgments about which revelations are potentially harmful to a client's interests.[68] Yet it is hardly imaginable that MR 1.6 should be read literally to prohibit a lawyer from revealing absolutely any information about a client except in the limited exceptions explicitly provided in the rule. A statement to a lawyer's spouse that the lawyer must travel to a distant city overnight to argue a case for an identified client fits literally within the MR 1.6 prohibition. But to prohibit innocuous talk about a client would be senseless, would create morbid secretiveness among overscrupulous lawyers, and, by trivializing it, would detract from the soundness of the confidentiality principle. Instead, MR 1.6 should be read to prohibit those needless revelations of client information that incur some risk of harm to the client. Idle gossip, of course, should be prohibited because it incurs the risk of inadvertent disclosure of harmful client information and has no reason for utterance other than titillation or braggadocio.

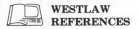

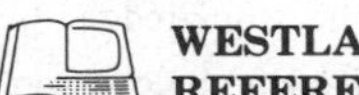

WESTLAW REFERENCES

agen** /7 attorney counsel** lawyer /s confiden! fiduciary

attorney counsel** lawyer /s secre** /56 assure! detriment** embarrass! loyal** trust***

§ 6.7.4 *Public Information as a Secret*

In light of their differing emphases on harmless or benign information about clients, the 1969 Code is surprisingly more protective

67 Edgar v. Finley, 312 F.2d 533, 535 (8th Cir.1963) (name of eyewitness given to lawyer in confidence by another lawyer not immune from discovery).

68 That rationale is suggested by the Code Comparison Note to ABA Model Rules at 41 (Proposed Final Draft, May 30, 1981): "[In contrast to DR 4–101, Rule 1.6] does not require the client to indicate information that is to be confidential or permit the lawyer to speculate whether particular information might be embarrassing or detrimental." The apparent assumption that this liberality in DR 4–101 had led to widespread undesirable consequences is merely implied, is not documented, and is probably unfounded.

of client confidentiality with respect to public information than are the 1983 Model Rules.[69] Under the Code no exception is provided for public information unless it could be said that if everyone knows client information, its further divulgence by the client's lawyer can no longer embarrass a client. Model Rule 1.9(b), on the other hand, specifically excepts from the prohibition against adverse use of a former client's information, information that "has become generally known." [70]

Some case authority supports the view that matters of public information are not within the attorney-client privilege. Cases have held that a lawyer's opinion based upon a publicly filed patent document is not within the privilege.[71] Other cases go farther and hold that information that can be gained from any public source is not within the protection of either the privilege [72] or the professional proscription.[73] The law of agency also permits a former agent to compete with a former principal if the agent employs only publicly available information.[74] On the other hand, 1908 Canon 37 prohibited a lawyer from using information obtained in a representation to the disadvantage of a former client "even though there are other available sources of such information." And some cases assert that information about a client available from public records nonetheless must be kept confidential.[75]

The stricter is the better view, particularly if the prohibition is confined (as in the Code) to a lawyer's adverse use of public information. A client communication that has become known is, of course, not within the attorney-client testimonial privilege because of the general requirement of continuing confidentiality (§ 6.3.7). But voluntary disclosure of a secret that has become generally known should be treated no differently than disclosure of any other client secret, unless it can be confidently said that the information has become so much a matter of public record that general knowledge of its content, its significance, and its public status is incontrovertible. Any lesser standard entails the risk that a lawyer might erroneously assume that any client information known by third persons is public and thus not subject to protection.

WESTLAW REFERENCES

attorney counsel** lawyer /s confiden! secre** /s common** general** public** /4 inform! kn*w! record source

---

[69] EC 4-4 (the protection of client secrets exists "without regard to the nature or source of information or the fact that others share the knowledge.").

[70] That provision is criticized below, see § 7.4.2(c). Note that MR 1.9(b) and MR 1.6 might be construed to apply to different matters. The former refers to a disadvantageous *use* of client information, while the latter refers to an obligation not to *reveal* client information.

[71] E.g., American Cyanamid Co. v. Hercules Power Co., 211 F.Supp. 85, 90 (D.Del.1962); United States v. United Shoe Mach. Corp., 89 F.Supp. 357, 359 (D.Mass.1950) ("[T]here is no privilege for so much of a lawyer's letter report or opinion as relates to a fact from . . . a public document such as a patent.").

[72] See Washington v. State, 441 N.E.2d 1355, 1358–59 (Ind.1982)(defendant's former lawyer properly testified in sentence enhancement proceeding about existence, nature, and date of prior convictions).

[73] City of Wichita v. Chapman, 214 Kan. 575, 521 P.2d 589, 596 (1971)(lawyer who knew of previous appraisal of same land by same real estate expert because of prior representation of City was not disqualified from representing another client adversely to the City in a substantially related matter in which the same expert would offer a different evaluation; his cross-examination related only to the prior appraisal, which was a matter of public record). The *City of Wichita* case has spawned confusion. In State v. Regier, 228 Kan. 746, 621 P.2d 431, 434 (1980), the same court held that a lawyer's knowledge that his client had a hairy chest but had shaved it before trial was neither a confidence nor a secret. The client was charged with a crime, proof of which would depend upon identification of the client as having a hairy chest. The court's distinction between secrets, on the one hand, and observable "physical characteristic[s]," on the other, is meaningless. If a lawyer uniquely knows certain information, even from observation of a client at two different times, the information still comes comfortably within the definition of *secret* in DR 4–101(A).

[74] See Restatement (Second) of Agency § 395 (1958); Vincent Horwitz Co. v. Cooper, 352 Pa. 7, 41 A.2d 870 (1945)(publicly available customer lists).

[75] NCK Org. Ltd. v. Bregman, 542 F.2d 128, 133 (2d Cir. 1976); Kaufman v. Kaufman, 63 A.D.2d 609, 405 N.Y.S.2d 79, 90 (1978)(information obtained by a lawyer from client was also available, but possibly in another form, from public records). That view is urged in Note, "Secrets" on the Public Record?, 6 J.Legal Prof. 357 (1981).

§ 6.7.5 *Lawyer Use or Revelation of Client Information*

The basic rule of the Code's DR 4–101(B)(1) and (2) and Model Rules 1.6(a) and 1.9(b) is that a lawyer must not reveal or make adverse use of a client's confidential information.[76] That general obligation gives rise to a number of duties that are examined at other points:

(1) A lawyer must see to it that the client's interest in full confidentiality of information is adequately protected. Conferences with clients should be arranged to avoid the presence of third parties that might prevent the privilege from attaching to a client's communications.[77] The lawyer's files should be confidentially maintained, and nonlawyer employees should be instructed, and periodically reminded of the need, to keep all office matters strictly confidential.[78]

(2) The confidentiality principle is also the source of a lawyer's obligation to invoke the attorney-client privilege and the work product immunity if the lawyer is called upon in litigation to give testimony or produce protected material.

(3) The client's desire to keep information from others can be manipulated by a lawyer to force the client to accede unwillingly to the lawyer's demands. The lawyer's use of the client's secrets in this way is obviously unfair and violates the lawyer codes.[79]

(4) The confidentiality principle is one of the two main supports for the extensive rules concerning conflicts of interest (§ 7.1.3). The confidentiality principle prohibits a lawyer from accepting a future representation under certain circumstances even if a secret rather than a confidence of a former client is threatened.[80]

(5) A lawyer might feel impelled to reveal confidential client information in order to prevent a client from committing a crime or other wrongful act directed towards a third person. The limited extent to which that is required or permitted is treated elsewhere (§ 12.6).

(6) Lawyers' needs to reveal client information for selfprotection create a limited exception. The lawyer codes generally recognize an exception permitting a lawyer to testify to information that is otherwise confidential if necessary to protect the lawyer against a claim of malpractice, to collect a fee from a client, and possibly for other purposes of self-protection (§ 6.7.8).

(7) A lawyer's use of a client's secret information can also violate law because of the unfair advantage that the lawyer's superior knowledge provides. A common example is the prohibition against insider trading of publicly traded shares of stock. A lawyer who uses secret information about a corporate client to gain a profit in the lawyer's trading in shares of the client's stock may also, of course, violate federal or state securities laws.[81]

76 Again, MR 1.9(b) excepts publicly known information from the prohibition against adverse use of a former client's confidential information. See § 6.7.4.

77 See generally EC 4–4. E.g., In re Agnew, 311 N.W.2d 869, 870 (Minn.1981)(discipline for introducing nonlawyer to client as "associate" and conducting otherwise confidential client discussion with nonlawyer present).

78 DR 4–101(D); EC 4–2; MR 5.3 comment. See also § 16.3.1.

79 In re Nelson, 327 N.W.2d 576, 578–79 (Minn.1982) (lawyer, following his discharge by client in dispute over size of fee, reported asserted but unfound tax violations to various governmental bodies); Bar Ass'n of Greater Cleveland v. Watkins, 68 Ohio St.2d 11, 427 N.E.2d 516 (1981)(lawyer suspended indefinitely for threatening client with report to police of assertedly illegal payments to client, learned from client in confidence, if client did not withdraw bar association complaint against lawyer); In re Strobel, 271 S.C. 61, 244 S.E.2d 537 (1978)(lawyer representing adoptive parents disciplined for threatening clients with revelation of their identity to natural mother unless they paid her hospital bill).

80 Osborn v. District Court, 619 P.2d 41 (Colo.1980) (assistant district attorney who took part in interview of rape victim, although not directly handling case, disqualified from later representing alleged rapist in private practice defense of same charge because of lawyer's possession of confidential information).

81 United States v. Hall, Sec.Reg.&L.Rep.(BNA) No.578, at A-6 (S.D.N.Y.1980)(lawyer guilty plea to criminal charge of insider trading in clients' corporate stock); SEC v. Hall, Sec.Reg.&L.Rep.(BNA) No.542, at A-5 (D.D.C.1980)(consent decree in civil suit involving same transactions as in United States v. Hall, supra); SEC v.

(8) Some insider trading may be a species of the traditional problem in agency and corporate law of agent self-dealing. A lawyer's use of client information to gain profits gives rise to issues both of agency law and of professional regulations (§ 6.7.6).

(9) Limits also exist on the extent to which a lawyer can invade the confidentiality of an opposing party. Members of a law firm who possess information concerning a former client of the firm are disqualified from using that information adversely under the former-client and imputed-disqualification rules (§ 7.4, § 7.6). Even with respect to opposing parties who were never clients, certain invasions of confidentiality are improper. At one extreme, theft of an opposing client's documents and publishing newspaper articles about them is prohibited.[82] A lawyer who comes into possession of normally protected client information concerning another lawyer's client, under circumstances such that the receiving lawyer should know that he or she receives it in violation of the other lawyer's duty of confidentiality, cannot employ the information for the lawyer's own profit.[83] But when a lawyer has done nothing to contribute to wrongful breach of the confidentiality of client information, obligations to the receiving lawyer's own client might dictate that the lawyer use the information to the advantage of his or her own client.[84]

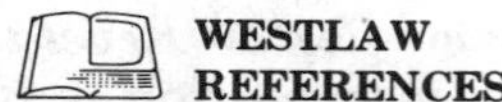

attorney counsel** lawyer /s confiden! secre** /s use* misuse*

disciplinary d.r. responsibility /5 4–101(b)

§ 6.7.6 *Lawyer Self-Dealing in Client Information*

Because of its business nature, much client information is commercially valuable. If the law did not prohibit it, a lawyer could take advantage of the client's secrets or confidences in order to turn a personal profit. In general, lawyer profiteering with client confidences is prohibited, whether the lawyer's dealing causes loss to the client or not. A classic illustration is a lawyer who knows of a client's intended purchase of valuable property. If the lawyer purchases the property before a client can obtain it, the lawyer clearly breaches a duty to the client.[85] Closely related and also prohibited is a lawyer's use of confidential information and aggressive persuasion to convince a client to permit the lawyer to obtain an equity interest in a client's enterprise.[86]

Suppose a lawyer knows from confidential information that a personal profit can be made without harming a client. Suppose the lawyer's client plans to develop a large shopping center. The lawyer knows that nearby land not within the development may also become quite valuable as a result. Assume further that the client had no intention of

Lerner, David, Littenberg & Samuel, Sec.Reg.&L. Rep.(BNA) No.548, at A-3 (D.D.C.1980)(consent decree in civil suit involving patent law firm).

[82] In re Ojala, 289 N.W.2d 108 (Minn.1979).

[83] Restatement (Second) of Agency § 312 comment (1958).

[84] Compare Cooke v. Superior Court, 83 Cal.App.3d 582, 147 Cal.Rptr. 915 (1978)(lawyer for wife in dissolution action not required to be disqualified because of receipt of confidential information about husband, including confidential communications between husband and his lawyer, purloined and passed to lawyer by husband's unfaithful agent), with ABA Formal Op. 41 (1931)(lawyer who learns, from opposing lawyer, client information detrimental to opposing party-client, in clear violation of duties of other lawyer, must resign from representation and not disclose information to lawyer's own client).

[85] City of Hastings v. Jerry Spady Pontiac-Cadillac, Inc., 212 Neb. 137, 322 N.W.2d 369 (1982)(lawyer holds property as constructive trustee for client); In re Nigohosian, 88 N.J. 308, 442 A.2d 1007, 1010–11 (1982)(discipline for lawyer's surreptitious purchase of property in which client was interested). If less classic, a more flagrant use of client information is to supply confidential and secret information about a client's possessions to a supposed gang of house burglars (actually, undercover police) in return for a 10% commission on all stolen articles. In re Conflenti, 29 Cal.3d 120, 172 Cal.Rptr. 203, 624 P.2d 253 (1981).

[86] In re Nulle, 127 Ariz. 299, 620 P.2d 214, 217 (1980). See generally § 8.11.

buying the adjoining land and the lawyer's ownership of it would not impair the value of the client's project. Can the lawyer employ the client's confidential information to make a personal purchase of the adjoining land? In that and similar situations, traditional agency law restricts an agent's freedom to realize a personal profit from the principal's business regardless of whether the agent's use of the principal's information harms the principal.[87] Anomalously, the professional rules do not track agency law in some particulars of the problem.

The broadest prohibition is in the 1969 Code. The Code's DR 4–101(B)(2) prohibits a lawyer from using a confidence or secret of a client to the client's disadvantage. Further, DR 4–101(B)(3) prohibits even a use that does not disadvantage a client, if the confidence or secret is used "for the advantage of [the lawyer] or of a third person." [88] Client consent, of course, permits use of the information.[89]

The 1983 Model Rules might be more permissive with lawyer use of client information. Rule 1.6 states generally and quite broadly that a lawyer must not reveal client information, without regard to whether revealing it would be adverse or benign. Client information may be revealed adversely only under limited circumstances.[90] And MR 1.8(b) provides that a lawyer shall not use a client's information "to the disadvantage of the client" unless the client gives informed consent.[91] What is missing from the Model Rules, apparently intentionally,[92] is any prohibition similar to that in DR 4–101(B)(3) against use of a client's information that is *nonadverse*. It is possible, of course, that most situations in which a lawyer makes unconsented use of a client's information—for example, to make a secret investment to capitalize on a client's unannounced commercial plans—would constitute adverse use because of the risk that the lawyer's own investment would alert others to the client's intentions. Absent such a risk, however, the Model Rules might permit such lawyer self-dealing with client information, although this is far from clear.[93]

If the Model Rules are intended to permit lawyers to speculate that a use or disclosure of client information will not be adverse, and thus that it would be permissible, they should be amended to conform to the broader prohibition that is implied by MR 1.6(a). At least for prophylactic purposes, a broad prohibition is sounder. Lawyer self-enrichment or other use of client information should be prohibited because of the special fiduciary obligation owed by a lawyer to every client to advance the client's interests without attention to the lawyer's own. The distractions of self-deal-

87 See generally Restatement (Second) of Agency § 388 comment (1958).

88 DR 4–101(B)(3), at this point, probably redundantly, provides an exception for client consent after full disclosure. The rule that immediately follows, DR 4–101(C)(1), provides that a lawyer may reveal confidences or secrets with the client's consent after full disclosure. If subrules (C)(1) and (B)(2) are read very restrictively, and in opposition to each other (*reveal* versus *use*), it could mean that subrule (B)(2), which unlike (B)(3) contains no consent language, imposes a non-consentable barrier to adverse use. There is no intelligible reason, however, for such a distinction to have been drawn by the Code drafters. Among other things, such an interpretation of DR 4–101(B)(2) would cast doubt on whether a lawyer could ever represent a subsequent client in a case that required adverse use of a former client's information, even if the former client freely consented.

89 DR 4–101(C)(1).

90 See §§ 12.5–12.10.

91 In an earlier draft of the Model Rules, a confusingly placed comment to MR 1.6 implied that the prohibition against disclosure was limited to situations in which the disclosure would be adverse to a client's interests. See MR 1.6 comment (Use of Information)(Proposed Final Draft, May 30, 1981)("A lawyer may not make use of information relating to the representation in a manner disadvantageous to the client."). The sentence was dropped from the final version of the Model Rules.

92 "Table of Related Sections in the ABA Model Code of Professional Responsibility" in the May 30, 1981, Proposed Final Draft of the Model Rules. The entry here for DR 4–101(B) lists only MR 1.6(a) and MR 1.8(b). Neither of those rules carries forward the DR 4–101(B)(3) restriction on a lawyer's use of nonadverse client information for the lawyer's own benefit. But compare the then confusing mention of DR 4–101(B)(3) in the Code Comparison Note to MR 1.8(b).

93 An entirely different question is whether a lawyer who makes an insider profit in a client's publicly traded stock on the basis of nonpublic client information is in violation of federal or state securities laws prohibiting insider trading. See § 6.7.6.

ings and the possibility that the lawyer will turn client information to his or her own advantage and possibly to the disadvantage of the client could impair the client-lawyer relationship and chill the willingness of clients to supply information to their lawyers.

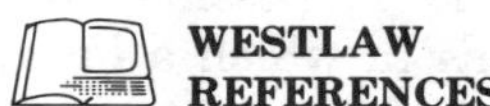

WESTLAW REFERENCES

attorney counsel** lawyer /7 advantage enrich! gain profit! /s confiden! secre**

§ 6.7.7 *Authorized Use of Client Information*

Discussion of a lawyer's responsibilites not to reveal confidential client information necessarily emphasizes the negative aspects—prohibitions against a lawyer's use or revelation. Yet there is a purpose for which lawyers come into possession of the information, and a lawyer's pursuit of the client's interests creates situations in which divulgence or use of confidential information must plainly be permissible.

Explicit client consent permits a lawyer to *reveal* client information, even if the revelation is not apparently in the client's interest.[94] The consent must be preceded by a full discussion with the client.[95] The discussion should sufficiently explore the fact that the client is not required to authorize the disclosure, review possible risks incurred in making the disclosure, and assure that the client's consent is knowing and intelligent. With respect to a lawyer's adverse *use* of client information, however, the Code, but not the Model Rules, draws a sharp distinction. Under DR 4–101(B)(2) a lawyer may not "use a confidence or secret of his client to the disadvantage of his client." Unlike the permission in the Code for a lawyer to reveal client information if the client consents, there is no similar exception for client consent to adverse use. Such adverse use is, however, permitted by 1983 Model Rule 1.9(b) which, through incorporation of the exception of MR 1.6, explicitly provides for client consent. The difference between the Code and the Model Rules on this point relates largely to the problem of conflicts of interest with a former client. The wording of MR 1.9(b) is analyzed at a later point (§ 7.4.2).

Revelation to Further the Client's Interests

Depending on breadth of definition, so much client information might be treated as confidential that it would be burdensome for a lawyer to represent a client with both fidelity and efficiency. The Code and Model Rules handle the problem in different ways, although both arrive at essentially the same point.

Under the Code there is no apparent provision for implied client consent to a lawyer's revelation of confidential information.[96] The definition of *secrets,* however, includes only information whose revelation would embarrass or be detrimental to the interests of the client. Revelation is permitted if it will advance the interests of the client. If, however, the information is a confidence or a secret whose revelation, while useful for strategic purposes, is nonetheless embarrassing to a client, the text of DR 4–101 requires client consent before disclosure.

Under the Model Rules, MR 1.6(a) starts with a global definition that includes all client information but then continues with a broad permission for "disclosures that are impliedly authorized in order to carry out the representation." The implied authorization exists unless the client instructs the lawyer not to disclose the information.[97]

94 DR 4–101(C)(1); EC 4–2; MR 1.6(a).

95 DR 4–101(C)(1)("full disclosure"); MR 1.6(a)("after consultation").

96 But cf. EC 4–2 (in addition to disclosure after client consent, a lawyer may reveal secrets or confidences "when necessary to perform his professional employment").

97 See MR 1.6 comment (Authorized Disclosure)("A lawyer is impliedly authorized to make disclosures about a client when appropriate in carrying out the representation, except to the extent that the client's instructions or special circumstances limit the authority. In litigation, for example, a lawyer may disclose information by admitting a fact that cannot properly be disputed, or in negoti-

To an extent, the law of evidence in some jurisdictions may expand the implied authority of a lawyer to reveal even apparently damaging client information during negotiation of a claim. Many jurisdictions recognize a doctrine that, in effect, provides a privilege for information contained in offers of compromise.[98] Some jurisdictions, but not all, extend the privilege as well to statements of facts made in the course of settlement discussions.[99] Sometimes a jurisdiction will make a statement inadmissible as evidence only if the person making it specifically invokes the privilege.[1] A traditional method of doing so, copied from the English practice that is still followed today,[2] is to preface any statement of fact with the obscure incantation "without prejudice" or a similar indication that statements are made only hypothetically or in confidence for the limited purpose of discussing settlement.

WESTLAW REFERENCES

attorney counsel** lawyer /s confiden! secre** /s consen! permi! /s complete full /3 disclos*** discuss***

Revelation to Further the Client's Interests

attorney counsel** lawyer /s confiden! secre** /p imply*** implied /4 authoriz! consent***

attorney counsel** lawyer /s confiden! secre** /s compromis*** prejudice negotiat! settle!

§ 6.7.8 Lawyer Self-Defense and Self-Interest

General

A lawyer may wish to employ confidential client information in order to defend against an adverse claim, to protect his or her reputation or to succeed in a fee dispute with a client. Despite the breadth and durability of antidisclosure rules in other contexts, both the 1969 Code and the 1983 Model Rules permit a lawyer to reveal otherwise confidential client information in those instances and, arguably, in others as well.[3] The cases and the evidence codes[4] agree, although the exception does not stand on very firm theoretical ground.

Litigation Involving Client Attacks

An exception to the attorney-client privilege for lawyer self-protection and self-interest is of recent origin.[5] Courts have recognized the exception in two types of suits. One is a suit by a client charging a lawyer with malpractice. A lawyer so charged can introduce otherwise privileged information in self-

ations by making a disclosure that facilitates a satisfactory conclusion.").

98 See generally 4 J.Wigmore, Evidence §§ 1061, 1062 (J.Chadbourn rev.1972); C.McCormick, Evidence § 274 (E.Cleary 3d ed.1984).

99 Fed.R.Evid. 408 (all statements made in settlement discussion inadmissible); Fed.R.Evid. 410 (same rule with respect to plea negotiations in criminal cases). Contra, e.g., Gagne v. New Haven Road Constr. Co., 87 N.H. 163, 175 A. 818 (1934).

1 C.McCormick, supra note 98 at 812.

2 Council of the Law Society, A Guide to the Professional Conduct of Solicitors 45 (P.Leach ed.1974); 15 Halsbury's Laws of England 406 (1977).

3 DR 4–101(C)(4)(lawyer "may reveal" "confidences or secrets necessary to establish or collect his fee or to defend himself against an accusation of wrongful conduct."); MR 1.6(b)(2)("A lawyer may reveal such [confidential] information to the extent the lawyer reasonably believes necessary . . . to establish a claim or defense on behalf of the lawyer in a controversy between the lawyer and the client, to establish a defense to a criminal charge or civil claim against the lawyer based upon conduct in which the client was involved, or to respond to the client's allegations in any legal proceeding concerning the lawyer's professional conduct for the client.").

The point of the broader language in the Model Rule is unclear. It was apparently intended to include lawyer claims against a client seeking the return of a lawyer's property (presumably an unusual situation), but may not be limited to those additional claims. See MR 1.6 code comparison note (sixth paragraph)("Rule 1.6(b)(3) enlarges the exception to include disclosure of information relating to claims by the lawyer other than for his fee; for example, recovery of property from the client.").

4 Model Code Evid.R. 213(2)(b); Unif.R.Evid. 26(2)(c); Unif.R.Evid. 502(d)(3). For the Supreme Court's standard 503(d)(3), virtually identical to Uniform Rule 502(d)(3), see 2 J.Weinstein & M.Berger, Weinstein's Evidence 503–2 (1982). Acceptance of the exception is by no means universal. England, for example, has no similar broad exception. See A.Cross, Evidence §§ 248–55 (4th ed. 1974).

5 One scholar found no case prior to an 1851 New York trial court decision, Rochester City Bank v. Suydam, 5 How.Pr. 254 (N.Y.Sup.Ct.1851). See Levine, Self-Interest or Self-Defense: Lawyer Disregard of the Attorney Client Privilege for Profit and Protection, 5 Hofstra L.Rev. 783, 788 (1977).

defense. Relatedly, courts also set aside the privilege when a convicted former client challenges the result of the criminal trial on the ground of ineffective assistance of counsel. A lawyer attacked by a client need not be a formal party to litigation in order to invoke the exception if the client attacks the lawyer's work in litigation with third persons.[6] In those instances, setting aside the privilege when it concerns a client who makes the charge is similar to what is done in other waiver situations (§ 6.4.7), in which a client is held to have abandoned the protection of the privilege by voluntarily placing the contents of privileged communications into issue. To permit the lawyer to respond fairly to the client's charges, the lawyer is authorized to breach the privilege defensively.

Fee-Collection Exception

The second commonly recognized exception is quite different because it permits a lawyer to employ client confidences offensively against the client's interests. The exception provides that a lawyer suing a client for an alleged wrongful failure to pay a fee may employ confidential information to establish the claim[7] and even to attach the former client's property.[8] No exception to the attorney-client privilege has done as much to draw it into question as the exception allowing lawyer self-protection.[9]

Justifications for the Lawyer Self-Interest Exceptions

Several justifications of exceptions founded on lawyer self-interest might be ventured. It could be argued that lawyers should be entitled to use privileged information to protect their economic interests. It has been argued, quite weakly, that since between client and lawyer there never was any confidentiality, disclosure in litigation between them must have been contemplated.[10] Or it could be argued that fairness should prevent a client from employing the privilege to the lawyer's disadvantage. The last argument has considerable force. But whatever might be said in favor of each of those arguments if they are viewed in isolation, the overriding consideration is that each one of them could also be made against many other applications of the attorney-client privilege. The privilege inflicts all sorts of harm on nonlawyers that has not been considered sufficient to set it aside. An exception addressed only to the special needs and fairness claims of lawyers naturally arouses strong suspicions of special pleading.

[6] Flood v. Commissioner, 468 F.2d 904, 905 (9th Cir. 1972)(taxpayer's former lawyer could permissibly testify against him that settlement of client's case was within power of attorney), cert.denied 411 U.S. 906, 93 S.Ct. 1529, 36 L.Ed.2d 195 (1973); Relf v. Cameron, 51 S.D. 554, 215 N.W. 881, 883 (1927).

[7] Cannon v. U.S. Acoustics Corp., 532 F.2d 1118, 1120 (7th Cir.1976); Carlson, Collins, Gordon & Bold v. Banducci, 257 Cal.App.2d 212, 64 Cal.Rptr. 915, 923 (1967); Sokol v. Mortimer, 81 Ill.App.2d 55, 225 N.E.2d 496 (1967); Weinshenk v. Sullivan, 100 S.W.2d 66 (Mo. App.1937); Mitchell v. Bromberger, 2 Nev. 345, 349 (1866).

[8] Nakasian v. Incontrade, Inc., 409 F.Supp. 1220, 1224 (S.D.N.Y.1976)(lawyer can employ former client's confidential information to attach client's property in suit for both unpaid fees and upaid compensation for nonlegal business assistance to client).

[9] The Code exception has been called "scandalously self-serving." A.Goldman, The Moral Foundations of Professional Ethics 101 (1980). The proposed code of the American Trial Lawyer's Association would delete it. See Roscoe Pound-American Trial Lawyer's Ass'n, The American Lawyer's Code of Conduct, Rule 1.4 (Discussion Draft, June 1980).

[10] One would be reluctant to trot out such a sway-backed nag, except that it is the chief argument that Wigmore employed to defend the exception. See 8 J.Wigmore, Evidence § 2312, at 607–08 (J.McNaughton rev.1961): "A communication by A to X as A's attorney, X afterwards becoming A's party opponent (as in a suit for fees or for negligence), is not privileged since there was no secrecy as between them at the time of the communication." See also C.McCormick, Evidence § 91, at 220–21 (E.Cleary 3d ed.1984)(Wigmore's rationale "offers a plausible reason" for the exception). The "since," of course, is no reason at all—unless it is also a reason to permit the lawyer to testify in all cases or, implausibly, unless the lawyer's subsequent fee litigation in some way could be held in complete secrecy. The plain fact is that the lawyer's public testimony to recover a contested fee chills client disclosures just as much as any other public divulgence of their private conversations. If the testimony is justifiable, it must be for some reason peculiar to fee suits, although none is apparent.

Two special considerations do lend some support to the fee-collection exception. A stricter rule of privilege that made fee-collection claims by lawyers impracticably difficult would likely compel lawyers to require more clients to prepay all fees or to exact security for them. That would increase the cost and decrease the availability of legal services for clients. And no other cause of action by any other group of persons would be so hobbled by the privilege as would a lawyer's action for fees. By their nature, most of the services performed to earn the fee involve privileged matters.

Even if exceptions for self-defense or fee collection are warranted, permitting a lawyer to determine whether to reveal confidential information, and how much, creates a risk that the lawyer will not carefully confine the disclosure to the minimum that may be required to accomplish the permitted exoneration or proof of a claim. Discipline cases have generally condemned, although only in extreme instances, lawyers who have made needless disclosure of client information in disputes with clients.[11] An arrangement that perhaps should be made mandatory is to provide a mechanism by which a neutral officer could pass on the need for disclosure before confidential information could be broadcast.[12]

Third-Party Litigation or Threats against a Lawyer

Whatever the force of arguments in support of setting the privilege aside in litigation between client and lawyer, at least the harm of disclosure can be prevented if the client capitulates to the lawyer's demands. But suppose that the lawyer is involved in litigation or other legal difficulties with third parties and can successfully defend only by revealing client confidential information. Both the lawyer codes and recent cases have applied the exception for lawyer self-interest in such instances. A lawyer can disclose confidential information to defend against charges of improper lawyer conduct made by third parties.

Both the 1969 Code and the 1983 Model Rules permit revelations of client confidential information in both testimonial and nontestimonial settings. The Code's DR 4–101(C)(4) explicitly exempts a lawyer from the confidentiality obligation if "necessary" to defend the lawyer or the lawyer's associates against "an accusation of wrongdoing" without regard to the source of the accusation. Model Rule 1.6(b)(2) accepts most of those provisions of the Code and the developments under them. The lawyer may reveal client information for permitted self-defense purposes "to the extent the lawyer reasonably believes necessary." [13]

In an Oregon case, In re Robeson,[14] a lawyer was reported to the bar disciplinary agency by the state's securities commission. An investigation suggested serious offenses involving conversion of a client's funds, but the affected client steadfastly refused to assist the investigation, to waive her attorney-client privilege, or, apparently, to testify at the disciplinary hearing. The lawyer objected to the finding of disciplinary violations, on the ground that he could not defend himself effectively because of the client's refusal to waive her privilege. The court held that the self-defense exception of DR 4–101(C)(4) was applicable

[11] Dixon v. State Bar, 32 Cal.3d 728, 187 Cal.Rptr. 30, 34, 653 P.2d 321 (1982); Florida Bar v. Ball, 406 So.2d 459 (Fla.1981)(suspension ordered for attempting to injure clients in adoption proceeding by informing adoption agency that clients might be financially unstable because of inability to pay lawyer's fee); In re Nelson, 327 N.W.2d 576 (Minn.1982)(lawyer reported former client's asserted tax violations after client discharged lawyer following fee dispute).

[12] After a perceptive review of the authorities, a scholar has suggested that if cases like *Meyerhofer* are generally accepted, the law should be recast to require judicial approval before client confidences may be revealed. Levine, Self-Interest or Self-Defense: Lawyer Disregard of the Attorney-Client Privilege for Profit and Protection, 5 Hofstra L.Rev. 783, 825–26 (1977).

[13] MR 1.6(b) and comment (Dispute Concerning Lawyer's Conduct). The comment expressly provides that a lawyer need not await the filing of formal charges so long as a serious assertion has been made. It also suggests that the lawyer notify the client of the charge by a third party and give the client an opportunity to respond. The comment concludes that "in any event, disclosure should be no greater than the lawyer reasonably believes is necessary to vindicate innocence."

[14] 293 Or. 610, 652 P.2d 336 (1982).

even though a third party, and not the client, was the complaining party.[15] With the exception provided by the Disciplinary Rule allowing disclosures in self-defense, the lawyer could not refuse to defend on the gound that confidentiality requirements prevented an effective defense.

A similar result was reached in Meyerhofer v. Empire Fire & Marine Insurance Company.[16] Goldberg, a young associate in a law firm involved in a public offering of Empire stock, objected to his superiors in the firm about an undisclosed finder's fee arrangement that the firm had with the issuer. The superiors were obdurate about not disclosing the finder's fee in the public offering documents, so he resigned from the firm and revealed extensive information about the stock offering to the Securities Exchange Commission. As a result of the ensuing investigation, the finder's fee matter became public and a shareholder derivative action for substantial damages was filed against Empire, the law firm, and former associate Goldberg. In order to extricate himself from the derivative action, Goldberg conferred with the plaintiffs' lawyer and gave him a copy of an affidavit that he had earlier furnished to the SEC.

The Second Circuit held that the information in the affidavit should not be suppressed in the action against the defendants who remained in the suit after Goldberg, following his disclosure, had been dismissed as a defendant. The court, in effect, held that the DR 4–101(C)(4) permission to reveal confidential client information in the lawyer's self-defense could be invoked when Goldberg was named a defendant in the third party's complaint.[17] It was probably critical in *Meyerhofer* that the lawyer involved did nothing to instigate the litigation from which he later sought to extricate himself by revealing client confidences.[18] A lawyer who did take an active part in supporting litigation against a former client would be in a much weaker position to argue a need for self-defense.[19]

Lawyer Use of Confidential Information against Third Parties

With increasing frequency, fee-shifting arrangements are becoming available that permit a lawyer to recover a fee from a third party (§§ 16.6.2, 16.6.3). One method of setting the fee that a defendant must pay to a lawyer for a prevailing party is to calculate the risk that the lawyer undertook in accepting the case. In showing the risk, may the lawyer show the factual weakness of the client's case, employing facts otherwise prohibited from disclosure under the confidentiality principle? Or should the fee-collection exception be limited to situations in which the lawyer seeks to recover a fee from a recalcitrant client?

The Code is open to the interpretation that the exception applies in both cases.[20] The

15 652 P.2d at 344–45. The court noted that if the client had made the complaint, "then there is a waiver of the privilege and it is simple to apply" the DR. 652 P.2d at 344. The court refused to pass on the question whether a statutory exception to the attorney-client privilege that displaced the privilege "as to a communication relevant to an issue of breach of duty by the lawyer to the client or by the client to the lawyer" was broader than DR 4–101(C)(4). 652 P.2d at 345–46.

16 497 F.2d 1190 (2d Cir.1974), cert.denied 419 U.S. 998, 95 S.Ct. 314, 42 L.Ed.2d 272 (1974). *Meyerhofer* can also be analyzed as a case in which the future crime-and-fraud exception set the privilege aside. See § 6.4.10.

17 497 F.2d at 1194–1195. See also In re Friend, 411 F.Supp. 776 (S.D.N.Y.1975)(in grand jury investigation of possible criminal activities of client and lawyer, lawyer entitled to turn over client confidences in self-defense); United States v. Amrep Corp., 418 F.Supp. 473, 474 (S.D. N.Y.1976)(lawyer Friend's disclosures notwithstanding, both he and his corporate client convicted of criminal charges; client cannot successfully object on attorney-client privilege grounds to lawyer's testimony to extricate himself from criminal charges). See generally McMonigle & Mallen, The Attorney's Dilemma in Defending Third Party Lawsuits: Disclosure of the Client's Confidences or Personal Liability?, 14 Willamette L.J. 35 (1978).

18 497 F.2d at 1194, 1195 (no evidence that lawyer Goldberg had caused instigation of the private suit; his role was not one of "intimacy with the prosecution of the litigation.").

19 Housler v. First Nat'l Bank of East Islip, 484 F.Supp. 1321 (E.D.N.Y.1980)(former general counsel of bank, who had supplied some information to shareholders in derivative action against bank, could not claim *Meyerhofer* self-defense exception when later named as third-party defendant by bank).

20 Cf. DR 4–101(C)(4).

Model Rules, on the other hand, more appropriately permit disclosure for fee purposes with respect only to a lawyer's controversies with a client.[21] Rarely will a lawyer necessarily suffer significant detriment if client secrets cannot be revealed in seeking payment of a fee from a third party. Most importantly, fairness between the lawyer and client does not require waiver of the confidentiality protections in a claim against a third party. In any event, client consent to make necessary revelations will almost always supply the lawyer with any necessary factual foundation for a fee claim against a third party.

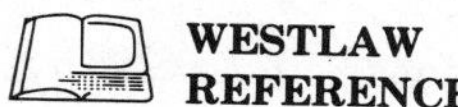

WESTLAW REFERENCES

General

disciplinary d.r. responsibility /5 4–101(c)(4)

[21] MR 1.6(b)(3)(disclosure permitted only "to establish a claim . . . on behalf of the lawyer in a controversy between the lawyer and the client").

Litigation Involving Client Attacks

attorney counsel** lawyer /s confiden! secre** /s accusation ineffective malpractice self-defense

Fee Collection Exception

attorney counsel** lawyer /s confiden! secre** /s attach! fee

Justifications for the Lawyer Self-Interest Exceptions

attorney counsel** lawyer /s confiden! secre** /s disbar! punish! reprimand*** suspen!

Third-Party Litigation or Threats Against a Lawyer

attorney counsel** lawyer /s confiden! secre** /s accusation defen! wrong-doing /s necess*** (third +1 party person)

Lawyer Use of Confidential Information Against Third Parties

attorney counsel** lawyer /s confiden! secre** /s fee /4 third +1 party person

Chapter Seven
CONFLICTS OF INTEREST

Table of Sections

---

§ 7.1 DIFFERING INTERESTS OF LAWYER AND CLIENT

§ 7.1.1 *Conflicts of Interest in Law Practice*

Multiple Masters and Multiple Roles

The regulation of conflicts of interest in the legal profession is of ancient origins [1] and has grown to great importance and complexity in recent years. Its importance, as well as its difficulty, is that conflicts of interest are part of the world around us, always have been, and inevitably must be. If it is true that no person can serve two masters,[2] it is also true that every person has many parts to play.[3] As in life, so in law an actor may not always be able to proceed single-mindedly without fear that actions will have impacts, or perceived motivations, that strike others in ways different from the actor's intent.

If lawyers were machines and could be programmed by a client to do only the client's bidding, there would be less reason to be concerned with conflicts of interest. The professional ideal of loyalty to a client, discretion in the possession of the client's confidences, and diligence in pursuit of the client's interests could then almost always be assured.[4] But lawyers are not machines. They are human beings of the same general sort as the rest of humanity, with their own interests, their own hopes and aspirations, their own bank accounts and investments, their own nagging pressures of personal belief and personal life. As such, lawyers are only imperfect agents for their clients, for their own interests sometimes make difficult the faithful, discrete, and diligent representation of clients' interests.

[1] H. Cohen, History of the English Bar 233–34 (1929), cites a provision of the London Ordinance of 1280, prohibiting lawyer conflicts of interest.

[2] Matthew 6:24 (King James).

[3] W. Shakespeare, As You Like It II, vii, 142.

[4] Even in a perfect world, at least the simultaneous representation of clients with conflicting interests would still create a problem for computers, or angels, much less lawyers.

The Pervasiveness of Conflicts in Law Practice

Conflict of interest problems are probably the most pervasively felt of all of the problems of professional responsibility that might haunt lawyers. They afflict lawyers both rich and poor, in large firms and in solo practice, in the most discrete private practice and the most public governmental position. The multiplicity of ways in which conflicts can arise are only imperfectly hinted at by the extensive treatment given in this chapter and Chapter Eight to several kinds of commonly encountered conflicts. In a sense, every representation begins with a lawyer-client conflict. If the representation is for a fee, the lawyer's economic interest will be to maximize the amount of the fee and the client's will be to minimize it. Even in pro bono representations, the ideological or altruistic motives that induce a lawyer to offer legal services in the first place can come into conflict with the client's interests. Lawyer self-interest can intrude at early as well as later points in the representation. A familiar point of conflict is over a proposed settlement out of which the lawyer might realize a large fee but which the client reasonably believes is not as favorable as might be obtained after a trial. Even after the representation is over, a future client's problems—and the lawyer's chance to earn a fee in solving them—might come into conflict with the lawyer's obligation not to betray the confidences or secrets of a former client.

Identifying Conflict of Interest Problems

Lawyers have not always acquitted themselves well in recognizing and resolving conflict problems. In part, serious conflict complications can arise because of inattention or a lawyer's failure to verbalize to all involved uncomfortable feelings about a representation, not least of all to the lawyer who harbors the thoughts. In part the problem is a tendency on the part of lawyers to accept fuzziness of arrangement and self-assurance of good faith in order to take on lucrative new law business or to protect the interests of an existing and substantial client. The problems that are thus created are among the potentially most embarrassing covered by professional rules.

Misperceptions about Conflicts of Interest

Lawyers sometimes feel, erroneously, that their profession is uniquely freighted with conflict of interest limitations. In fact, such limitations are hardly unique to lawyers. Every agent or fiduciary who acts as the representative of another is subject to special rules that seek to prevent an occasionally venal agent from exploiting the trust and confidence of the principal for the agent's own gain or for the gain of others.[5]

Because lawyer conflict rules are largely prophylactic, it is perhaps unfortunate that the subject is so commonly referred to as "conflict" of interests, which has a vaguely pejorative and motive-questioning ring. Much of what is circumscribed is only imperfectly described by that phrase. Better would be a phrase such as "additional interests," "compound interests," or the term "differing interests," which was employed by the 1969 Code. But "conflict of interest" is a term that is engrained too deeply into professional consciousness to permit the use of any other.

Professional Rules and Formal and Informal Sanctions

The basic thrust of the conflict of interest rules is to protect the reasonable expectations of clients with regard to the loyalty of the client's lawyer and the confidentiality of the work of a present or former lawyer. At the same time, the rules and courts, in interpreting them, have attempted to balance against

[5] See generally Restatement (Second) of Agency §§ 112, 394 (1958); Restatement (Second) of Trusts § 170 comment p, and § 206 comment l (1959); G. Bogert, Trusts & Trustees § 543(0), at 339–342 (2d ed. 1958); Abuse on Wall Street: Conflicts of Interest in the Securities Market (Report to the Twentieth Century Fund Steering Committee on Conflict of Interest in the Securities Markets) (1980).

clients' claims the interests of the public in the ready availability of legal services and the economic interests of lawyers. Unfortunately those interests and the manner in which they are to be accommodated emerges only murkily from the wording of the ABA Code. The new Model Rules substantially improve on clarity. Yet it remains true that, here perhaps more than in other areas, lawyers must carefully examine judicial doctrine for a working understanding of the complexities of conflicts law.

At times the clash between the interests of a lawyer and a client is so strong that the professional rules prohibit the lawyer from representing the client. Client consent may sometimes cure the conflict, and the client can accept a representation that is less than ideal, but in some cases the clash of interests might be so harsh that the lawyer may not proceed even with the client's consent.

The importance and pervasiveness of conflicts has led to several approaches for preventing and sanctioning them. An impermissible conflict can meet with professional discipline. Increasingly, courts permit opposing litigants to employ disqualification motions to remove an opposing lawyer from the case because of an impermissible conflict of interest. Other remedies include damage recoveries, restitution of client property, denial of class action certification, and denial of fees. A representation with conflicts can even constitute a criminal offense by the lawyer.[6] The presence of a perceived conflict of interest can be informally sanctioned because of the almost inevitable crimp that it places on effective and vigorous representation. For example, if a lawyer who is involved in multiparty negotiations with other lawyers apparently represents conflicting interests, the lawyer's effective role in the negotiations may be compromised because of the implicit threat by the other negotiating lawyers to make an issue of the conflict.[7]

WESTLAW REFERENCES

Multiple Masters and Multiple Roles

di conflict of interest

Professional Rules and Formal and Informal Sanctions

synopsis, digest(attorney counsel** lawyer /p conflict +2 interest /p "class action" (disqualif! /3 move motion))

§ 7.1.2 History of Conflict of Interest Rules

Conflicts of Interest in the 1908 ABA Canons of Ethics

The 1908 Canons of Ethics stated with beguiling simplicity in Canon 6 that it was "unprofessional to represent conflicting interests." A lawyer was under a duty to disclose to the client at the first opportunity any relationship the lawyer might have to the other parties or to the matter. Conflicting representations could be entered into only with "express consent of all concerned given after a full disclosure of the facts." Conflicting interests were defined operationally as occasions "when, in behalf of one client, it is his duty to contend for that which duty to another client requires him to oppose." The confidentiality principle was explicitly invoked as undergirding for the rule that forbade subsequent acceptance of a client in a matter adversely affecting any interest of a former client who had conveyed confidential information to the lawyer. The canonical, and unexplanatory, proscription of the representation of conflicting interests retains appeal, and much the same broadly proscriptive language can be found in the California rules.[8]

6 United States v. Bronston, 658 F.2d 920 (2d Cir.1981), cert. denied, 456 U.S. 915, 102 S.Ct. 1769, 72 L.Ed.2d 174 (1982)(conviction of lawyer upheld for fraudulent use of mails to further lawyer's own undisclosed interests that conflicted with those of client).

7 J. Stewart, The Partners 23 (1982).

8 Cal. Rule 4–101; id. Rule 5–102. See also, e.g., Treasury Dept. Rules of Practice, 31 C.F.R. § 10.29 (1982).

Obscurity of the 1969 Code Rules on Conflicts

The 1969 ABA Code is more roundabout but was designed to reach the same objectives as the Canons. The entire Canon 5 in the Code is given over to the proposition that "a lawyer should exercise independent professional judgment on behalf of a client." Lawyers are generally prohibited by DR 5–101(A) from accepting a case if the lawyer's own interests might affect representation of the client. And DR 5–101(A) prohibits representation when employment would likely adversely affect the lawyer's independent professional judgement or when it would involve the lawyer in representing "differing interests."[9] One must then repair to the "Definitions" at the end of the Code for the following critical, and inclusive, definition:

> (1) "Differing interests" include every interest that will adversely affect either the judgment or the loyalty of a lawyer to a client, whether it be a conflicting, inconsistent, diverse or other interest.[10]

The 1969 Code provisions in Canon 5 seem rather clearly to deal with two central situations—when a lawyer's personal interests clash with those of a client and when a lawyer repesents at the same time clients with differing interests. By 1969 several decades of decisions had also wrestled with a third kind of conflict problem—that created when a lawyer represents a second client against the interests of a former client. The former-client problem had been explicitly covered in Canon 6 of the 1908 Canons. But for unknown reasons, former-client conflicts problems were not specifically mentioned in any part of Canon 5 of the 1969 Code.[11] Another part of the Code, EC 4–5, does allude briefly to the former-client problem, but in an indirect way.

Despite the obscurity of reference, the confidentiality rules of Canon 4 are generally recognized as the source of most of the law under the 1969 Code concerning former-client conflicts. Many courts and ethics committees have also resorted for solace in former-client cases to the general language of Canon 9 of the ABA Code, whose magisterial words are that "a lawyer should avoid even the appearance of impropriety." The "appearances" rule has given rise to some of the most broad and uncertain rules under the Code (§ 7.1.4). Canon 9 has also played a prominent role in developing notions of imputed disqualification, the rule that disqualification of one lawyer in a firm requires disqualification of every lawyer in it.[12]

Elaboration of Conflicts Rules in the 1983 Model Rules

The framers of the 1983 Model Rules recognized the deficiencies of the Code treatment of conflict of interest problems and undertook to deal with the issues in a more straightforward and complete way. Six sections—Model Rules 1.7 through 1.12—deal explicitly with conflict of interest problems, and rule 1.13, on corporate representation, deals with it in

9 The 1969 version of the Code contained the "differing interest" definition, but the phrase was not employed in the Disciplinary Rules of Canon 5, to which it was apparently meant to refer. The omission was cured by amendment in 1974 to add to DR 5–105(A) and (B) the words "or it would be likely to involve him in representing differing interests." See ABF Annotated Code of Professional Responsibility 227 (O. Maru ed. 1979). Only twelve states had adopted the amended language by 1977. See ABA Code of Professional Responsibility by State, DR 5–105 at 16 (1977). But states the have not adopted the language seem to reach results in deciding conflicts issues under the Code's original language that are not perceptibly different from those in jurisdictions that have adopted the change.

10 The allusion in the definition to the lawyer's "judgment" is unclear but was probably intended to mean the same thing as the "independent professional judgment" in DR 5–105(A) and (B). See ABF Annotated Code of Professional Responsibility 226 (O. Maru ed. 1979). The definition of the term "differing interest" was designed by its drafters to broaden the scope of the 1908 Canon restrictions against representing conflicting interests. See Sutton, Commentary on the Texas Code of Professional Responsibility, in State Bar of Texas Young Lawyers Section, Texas Lawyers' Professional Ethics at 6–15 n.63 (1979).

11 Alabama added an additional section to its version of the 1969 Code to deal specifically with former-client conflicts. See Goldthwaite v. Disciplinary Board, 408 So. 2d 504, 508 (Ala.1982).

12 See also DR 5–105(D). See generally § 7.6.

part. The general approach of the Model Rules, with important exceptions, has been to follow, with clarifying and sharpening language, the judicial interpretations and glosses that have collected around the 1969 Code rules.

The most important Model Rule departures from the Code have been:

(1) the abandonment of the "appearances of impropriety" notion as a basis for disqualification (§ 7.1.4);

(2) a more explicit and complete requirement for consultation with a client before a lawyer seeks a client's consent to a conflict (§ 7.2.2);

(3) a "fair and reasonable" standard and a new writing requirement now control business dealings with a client (§ 8.11.2);

(4) a lawyer may advance court costs to a client and make the client's obligation to repay contingent on success in the lawsuit (§ 9.2.3);

(5) a new rule deals with conflicts between clients of lawyers who are spouses or who are related by blood (§ 7.6.6);

(6) an entire new rule is given over to former-client conflicts (§ 7.4.2);

(7) a new rule deals with imputed disqualification and provides both additional flexibility and an explicit provision for client consent (§ 7.6.2);

(8) a rule on conflict problems of a former government lawyer contains an exception for screening-and-notice and provides new rules on conflict of interest problems of present government lawyers (§§ 8.9, 8.10);

(9) the conflict problems of a former judge, law clerk, or arbitrator are addressed (§ 8.9.3); and

(10) a method is provided for identifying and dealing with conflicts of interest in the representation of a corporation, union, government agency, or other entity (§ 8.3).

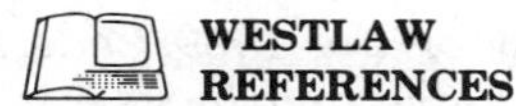

Conflicts of Interest in the 1908 ABA Canons of Ethics

attorney counsel** lawyer /s conflict*** +2 interest /s canon /4 1908 6

Obscurity of the 1969 Code Rules on Conflicts

1969 bar responsibility /4 code /p "differing interest" "independent professional"

Elaboration of Conflicts Rules in the 1983 Model Rules

"model rule" /s 1.7 1.8 1.9 1.10 1.11 1.12

§ 7.1.3 Conflict Principles and Competing Interests

Loyalty and Confidentiality

As other parts of this chapter reveal, conflict of interest problems are pervasive in law practice and can arise early, late, and at intermediate points throughout a representation in a bewildering variety of shapes and sizes. One should not, therefore, press too hard the question of general standards in a search for underlying ordering principles. Some general things can, however, be said. It is clear that there are two broad principles underlying all conflict rules for lawyers—the principle of loyalty and the principle of confidentiality. But treating these principles as single-value factors in resolving conflicts problems would cut sharply into important interests that argue for flexible rules. Also at a general level, the proper criterion for testing whether a conflict exists is that of a reasonable probability that one or both of these principles will be seriously impaired, rather than some lesser or higher standard.

Loyalty Principle

The principle of loyalty of lawyer to client is a basic tenet of the Anglo-American conception of the lawyer-client relationship. The 1969 Code states that the professional judgment of a lawyer should be exercised "solely for the benefit of his client and free of compromising influences and loyalties."[13] No

[13] EC 5-1.

other interest or consideration should be permitted to dilute the lawyer's "loyalty to his client." [14] The 1983 Model Rules concur: "loyalty is an essential element in the lawyer's relationship to a client." [15] Where choices have to be made between the interest of a client and any other person—whether the lawyer personally or another client, the lawyer must be in such a position that all options that might favor the client can be considered free from the likely impairment of any interest other than those of the client.[16] The principle of loyalty runs throughout conflicts thinking but is most prominent in the areas of simultaneous conflicts and conflicts involving the lawyer's personal interests.

The particular emotional commitment on the part of the lawyer that loyalty assumes is zeal.[17] Lawyers in this sense may be subjected to a greater requirement of zealousness than other agents, whose quality of work is less dependent upon the kind of emotional commitment to the principal's objectives that the agent brings to the job.[18] The lawyer should ideally be in a position to discuss freely with the client and vigorously assert on the client's behalf any lawful objective that the client might choose in the representation.[19] In consultation with the client, of course, the lawyer might recommend one objective instead of others that are also explained, and the recommendation might be based on legal as well as nonlegal considerations (§ 4.3). Once the client has made a decision to pursue a particular objective, however, the lawyer's emotional commitment to that objective should not be impaired by conflicting interests. The lawyer must be able to be fully open and candid with the client and forceful and single-minded in asserting the client's position with all other persons.

Confidentiality Principle

The second principle underlying many conflict of interest rules is the principle of confidentiality. As explained in the preceding chapter (§ 6.1.3), the assumption underlying the broad professional protection against disclosure or adverse use of a client's confidential information is that confidentiality encourages both individuals and the public at large to resort to legal services and to divulge all information that a fully informed lawyer would wish to have in order to assess the client's legal position and to give assistance. If clients feared that this protection could be used against them in favor of the lawyer personally or in favor of the lawyer's other clients, the spigot of client information might well be turned off, to the detriment of all clients. Any representation or other action of a lawyer that gives rise to a substantial threat that a current or former client's confidences may be revealed or employed against the interests of the client entails a potential threat to the principle of confidentiality and thus can raise a serious conflict of interest problem.

Principles supplementary to those of loyalty and confidentiality are sometimes asserted, but those two, at least, are unquestioned. Their realization under particular doctrines or in particular applications is, of course, often problematical. Another commonly asserted reason for finding a conflict of interest, the appearance of impropriety, is also found throughout the conflict area. Its potential for perniciousness is great, and it requires more extended discussion (§ 7.1.4).

14 Id.

15 MR 1.7 comment.

16 Id.

17 ABA Code, Canon 7.

18 EEOC v. Operating Engineers, Locals 14 and 15, 25 Empl.Prac.Dec. (CCH) ¶ 31,783 (S.D.N.Y. 1981)(expert witness not disqualified from testifying for EEOC despite fact that witness's partner in consulting firm had advised union now being sued by EEOC; experts, unlike lawyers, serve only as sources of information and not as advocates).

19 MR 1.7 comment (Loyalty to a Client): "Loyalty to a client is also impaired when a lawyer cannot consider, recommend or carry out an appropriate course of action for the client because of the lawyer's other responsibilities or interests. The conflict in effect forecloses alternatives that would otherwise be available to the client."

Countervailing Policy of Client Freedom of Choice of Counsel

If only protection of client loyalty and client confidentality were at stake, it would be a simple matter to devise conflict of interest rules that always required disqualification of the lawyer whenever the possibility of impairing these interests appeared. Even the slightest possibility of a conflict would suffice. But reasons of public importance can be claimed for both client freedom and lawyer freedom from unduly restrictive conflict rules.

Disqualification deprives the resulting unrepresented client of a free choice of counsel and will almost inevitably entail additional expense and delay.[20] Disqualification orders might be sought not to protect loyalty or confidentiality, but to gain strategic advantage in litigation by depriving an opponent of the services of an advocate known by experience to be particularly effective.[21]

Broad conflict rules create the danger that they will be manipulated by giant corporate clients to create conflicts of interest among all of the best available lawyers, thus blockading legal talent from potential adversaries.[22] Courts are mindful of the fact that, at least in metropolitan areas and for relatively routine legal matters, many other competent lawyers are available to handle the legal matters of a client when a conflict exists.[23] But conflict problems can also be persistent in a small community where a limited number of lawyers must serve the changing legal needs of often closely related persons and interests. Overly restrictive conflict rules might mean that only the most substantial of small community clients would have effective freedom in choosing counsel. Moreover, the possibilities for partnership and new professional associations might be so severely limited as to make small-town practice financially and professionally unattractive. A similar maldistribution of legal talent could result from overly strict conflict rules within an area of law practiced by only a small number of legal subspecialists.

Interests of Lawyers in Career Mobility

The interests of the legal profession are also implicated, if secondarily, in overly broad conflicts rules. These can limit the mobility of lawyers, particularly in a profession that is increasingly characterized by larger law firms and narrower specializations.[24] Under strict rules, an entire firm of hundreds of lawyers could inadvertently be blocked from further representation of a long-standing client by the hiring of a new junior associate. Policing conflict of interest problems has already become a notable cost in large firms, requiring computers, lawyer-staffed conflicts committees, paralegals, and delay in initiating emergency representations for new clients. Most importantly, if least appealingly, lawyer income is threatened by strict conflicts rules because a single lawyer is less able to add to a stable of substantial clients, diversify a practice, and accept new representation from former adversaries impressed with the skill of their former opponent.

20 Aetna Casualty & Sur. Co. v. United States, 570 F.2d 1197, 1202 (4th Cir.1978), cert. denied 439 U.S. 821, 99 S.Ct. 87, 58 L.Ed.2d 113 (1978); International Elec. Corp. v. Flanzer, 527 F.2d 1288, 1293 (2d Cir.1975).

21 Emle Industries, Inc. v. Patentex, Inc., 478 F.2d 562, 574 (2d Cir.1973). The motives of a prosecutor seeking, apparently altruistically, to obtain separate representation for grand jury targets, might be explicable on much less elegant grounds as an attempt to break apart a solid front in order to play one witness off against another. Cf., e.g., In re Special February 1975 Grand Jury, 406 F. Supp. 194, 197 (N.D.Ill.1975).

22 Weinstein, J., in Silver Chrysler Plymouth, Inc. v. Chrysler Motors Corp., 370 F.Supp. 581, 591 (E.D.N.Y. 1973), affirmed 518 F.2d 751 (2d Cir.1975). The Second Circuit disagreed, however, with Judge Weinstein's suggestion that vigorous enforcement of the anticonflict rules would itself raise possible federal antitrust implications. See 518 F.2d at 757 n.9.

23 Cord v. Smith, 338 F.2d 516, 525 (9th Cir.1964), mandate clarified 370 F.2d 418 (9th Cir.1966); Federal Sav. & Loan Ins. Corp. v. Fielding, 343 F.Supp. 543 n.1 (D. Nev.1972).

24 Silver Chrysler Plymouth, Inc. v. Chrysler Motors Corp., 518 F.2d 751, 757 (2d Cir.1975).

WESTLAW REFERENCES

Loyalty and Confidentiality

confiden! /s loyal** /s conflict***

attorney counsel** lawyer /s conflict*** /s probab!

Loyalty Principle

attorney counsel** lawyer /s loyal*** /s zeal!

Confidentiality Principle

attorney counsel** lawyer /s confiden! /s disclos*** divulg! reveal*** spigot /s client

Countervailing Policy of Client Freedom of Choice of Counsel

attorney counsel** lawyer /s client /3 choice choos*** select*** /p conflict*** disqualif!

---

§ 7.1.4 Appearances of Impropriety

The Allure of an Appearances Rationale

Conflict of interest problems can present some of the most complicated facts and some of the most difficult legal issues. A tantalizing way out is to seize upon a simple and soulful rubric that seems to make intuitive sense. Such has been the allure of the "appearance-of-impropriety" standard for resolving conflict of interest issues. Its charms, however, are only surface. Use of the phrase in decisions has both obscured the process by which courts formulate their decisions and, in some instances, has lead to seriously erroneous results.

The Illusory Content of the Appearances Rationale

Courts that invoke the appearances standard in conflicts cases typically cite Canon 9 of the 1969 Code, which states that "a lawyer should avoid even the appearance of impropriety." [25] Beyond the initial invocation of Canon 9, approaches vary. Some decisions describe the appearance that is to be avoided in terms of a violation of a more specific rule, such as the confidentiality rules of Canon 4 or the conflict of interest rules of Canon 5.[26] Still other courts purport to base disqualification solely on Canon 9, even if the court is not prepared to say that any specific mandatory rule [27] has been violated.[28] Representative of that extreme view is Renshaw v. Ravert,[29] in which the court first found that the substantial-relationship test (§ 7.4.3) did not require disqualification of the plaintiff's lawyer in a civil rights case against members of a police department. But the court nonetheless disqualified the lawyer because of his representation of one of the defendants almost ten years previously in an unrelated automobile accident claim. The sole basis for disqualifi-

[25] DR 9–101 contains a similar phrase as its catchline: "avoiding even the appearance of impropriety." But its three specific rules (on former-judge conflicts, former-government-lawyer conflicts, and boasts of influence-peddling prowess) are both more precise and much less inclusive of conflicts problems. In fact, only the first and second of the DRs deals with conflict of interest problems. The remainder of the DRs under Canon 9 deal only with client funds.

[26] In re Corrugated Container Antitrust Litigation, 659 F.2d 1341, 1345 and n. 4 (5th Cir.1981):

> "Our focus is on Canon 9 only. . . . In order to show this specific impropriety, we turn to . . . Canon 4, for it is clear that violations of other Canons may implicate Canon 9 as well. [At that point, in a footnote the opinion noted that 'there is some movement towards abandoning the amorphous standard of Canon 9 as a test for disqualification. . . . Our use of Canon 4 to inform our Canon 9 analysis avoids any possible harshness that might come from applying Canon 9 in the abstract.']"

See also Norton v. Tallahassee Memorial Hospital, 689 F.2d 938 (11th Cir.1982); Richardson v. Hamilton Int'l Corp., 469 F.2d 1382 (3d Cir.1972), cert. denied 411 U.S. 986, 93 S.Ct. 2271, 36 L.Ed.2d 964 (1973). The *Corrugated Container* approach was disavowed in Gibbs v. Paluk, 742 F.2d 181 (5th Cir.1984).

[27] Canon 9, because it is a "canon," is not such a mandatory rule. See 1969 Code Preliminary Statement; § 2.6.3. But cf. In re Petroleum Prods. Antitrust Litigation, 658 F.2d 1355, 1360 (9th Cir.1981), cert. denied 455 U.S. 990, 102 S.Ct. 1615, 71 L.Ed.2d 850 (1982)("If Canon 9 were not separately enforceable, it would be stripped of its meaning and significance. This suggests that it must be a sufficient ground for disqualification in itself.").

[28] Pantry Pride, Inc. v. Finley, Kumble, Wagner, Heine, Underberg & Casey, 697 F.2d 524 (3d Cir.1982); In re Petroleum Prods. Antitrust Litigation, 658 F.2d 1355 (9th Cir.1981), cert. denied 455 U.S. 990, 102 S.Ct. 1615, 71 L.Ed.2d 850 (1982); United States v. Trafficante, 328 F.2d 117, 120 (5th Cir.1964).

[29] 460 F.Supp. 1089 (E.D.Pa. 1978).

cation was Canon 9's appearance-of-impropriety standard.[30]

Another approach has been to take appearances of impropriety into account as one of several factors but at least implicitly to refuse to rest disqualification solely upon it.[31] The analysis in such cases is typically shifting and blurred, and the same court may take different positions in different decisions. The appearance that the line of cases creates in turn is one of ad hoc judgments based on subjective and undefended judicial impressions.

Methodological Weakness of the Appearances Standard

If carefully analyzed, the appearances standard in any of its incarnations quickly loses much strength. Its first problem is methodological. That weakness can be revealed by taking the standard seriously on its own terms. One prominent question that then arises is: Who are the observers to whom the relevant appearances present themselves? The most commonly recited observers are the faceless and unidentified members of "the public." [32] Sometimes the observers are identified as "the bar." [33] Perhaps more narrowly than the foregoing, some courts limit the relevant observers to "all reasonable persons." [34] In some former-client cases the observer might be identified as the former client.[35]

But if appearances to the general public, the bar, or all reasonable persons are critical, the judge's task of guessing at what those groups might hold in their minds will be extremely speculative. If the former client's views are pivotal, the best source of information can be expected to give self-serving reports on how things look from that vantage point. Moreover, to the extent that empirical research has been conducted on lay opinions about lawyers, one of the strongest conclusions is that lawyers as a group overestimate the extent to which the public distrusts and dislikes lawyers.[36] Some judges employing the appearances standard have been refreshingly frank about their lack of confidence that they can assess accurately the public's reaction to a particular challenged representation.[37]

Data about Appearances is either Irrelevant or Redundant

The second problem with the appearances rationale is doctrinal.[38] Assuming that it is somehow possible to gain an accurate perception of public reaction to a particular representation by a lawyer, what is to be done with the data? Is adverse public reaction generally a basis for decision? If it were generally accepted as an appropriate limit on lawyer representations, then lawyers should probably

30 460 F.Supp at 1093–94. The specific factor that the court found to be apparently improper was the lawyer's revocation of an earlier offer to withdraw in order to avoid any question of conflict. Id. at 1094.

31 Kessenich v. Commodity Futures Trading Comm'n, 684 F.2d 88, 97–98 (D.C.Cir.1982); Woods v. Covington County Bank, 537 F.2d 804, 813 (5th Cir.1976).

32 Arkansas v. Dean Foods Prods. Corp., 605 F.2d 380 (8th Cir.1979); Woods v. Covington County Bank, 537 F.2d 804, 813 n. 12 (5th Cir.1976). The Third Circuit approach is to inquire whether an "average layman" in the position of the objecting party would perceive an impropriety. See Pantry Pride, Inc. v. Finley, Kumble, Wagner, Heine, Underberg & Casey, 697 F.2d 524, 530 (3d Cir.1982).

33 Fred Weber, Inc. v. Shell Oil Co., 566 F.2d 602, 609 (8th Cir.1977), cert. denied 436 U.S. 905, 98 S.Ct. 2235, 56 L.Ed.2d 403 (1978)("Would a member of the public, or of the bar, see an 'impropriety' . . . ?").

34 In re Petroleum Prods. Antitrust Litigation, 658 F.2d 1355, 1361 (9th Cir.1981), cert. denied 455 U.S. 990, 102 S.Ct. 1615, 71 L.Ed.2d 850 (1982), and cases cited; Krebs v. Johns-Manville Corp., 496 F.Supp. 40, 44 (E.D. Pa.1980).

35 Cf. Rodriguez v. State, 129 Ariz. 67, 628 P.2d 950, 956–957 (1981)("persons charged with crime" observing operation of public defender office); Cardinale v. Golinello, 43 N.Y.2d 288, 401 N.Y.S.2d 191, 195, 372 N.E.2d 26, 30 (1977)("the first client is entitled to freedom from apprehension").

36 See Mindes & Acock, Trickster, Hero, Helper: A Report on the Lawyer Image, 1982 Am.B.Found. Research J. 177, 192–93.

37 United States v. Dorfman, 542 F.Supp. 402, 410 (N.D. Ill.1982)("[W]e do not profess the ability to divine the public's reaction.").

38 It stretches the matter to refer to a doctrinal content to the appearances notion. It appears in opinions more in an incantational, intuitive way, and its use is hardly ever defended. Abandoning it would deprive courts of no useful analytical tool and would fittingly narrow courts' range of umbridled discretion in passing on disqualification motions.

abandon criminal defense work and a fair amount of white-collar legal work as well. The 1969 Code itself warns against pusillanimous cowering before unreasonable public opinion.[39]

In response to such criticisms, an exponent of the appearances standard might be tempted to qualify it so that a conflict requires disqualification only when public opinion is well informed, carefully formulated, and reflective of all competing considerations.[40] While one cannot quarrel with the qualification, one is then entitled to ask what public opinion adds. Presumably the conflict of interest rules and standards themselves are informed, carefully formulated, and reflect the best accommodation of competing considerations. If not, they should be changed. If they are sound, they should be followed—possible, and ill-founded, adverse public opinion to the contrary notwithstanding.

Unfortunate Uses of the Appearances Standard

The appearance-of-impropriety standard can lead to untoward results, which is not surprising, given its doctrinal and operational deficiencies. An appearances basis for disqualification invites an appearances exception to disqualification rules that are otherwise applicable. One court has accepted the invitation with confusing results.[41] Another court has held that the bar imposed by Canon 9 is relevant principally when the alleged impropriety is one that the public is likely to discover. Thus, when the same lawyer, paid by one of the "target" witnesses before a grand jury, undertook to represent eight other witnesses, including some that were not themselves the targets of investigation, the court rejected an argument that Canon 9 required the lawyer's disqualification. The court observed, in its published opinion, that secrecy of grand jury proceedings made it unlikely that the public would learn of the conflicting representation.[42]

An additional misfortune that might attend reliance on the appearance-of-impropriety concept is that the court might feel warranted in imposing a merely apparent remedy to a conflicts problem instead of a more efficacious one. Thus the remedy imposed may be little more than a meaningless but costly public relations ceremony.[43] There is a fitness, but hardly a compelling need, to provide merely cosmetic solutions for appearance problems. But busy courts, litigants, and lawyers would do better to avoid the appearances exercise in the first place.

The Place of Appearances in the 1969 Code

The appearance-of-impropriety rubric is invoked much more commonly in cases dealing with the disqualification of lawyers from representing a party in litigation and less often in cases dealing with discipline of lawyers. The difference, of course, can readily be traced to the relatively more stigmatizing effect of discipline and the weakness of appearances as a reason for imposing the stigma. It is also more common in former-government-lawyer conflicts cases, perhaps because of the proximity of Canon 9's general language to the specific wording of DR 9–101(B) and its use as a heading to DR 9–101 as a whole. The prominent areas of application include imputed disqualification (§ 7.6) and former-

[39] EC 9–2: "While a lawyer should guard against otherwise proper conduct that has a tendency to diminish public confidence in the legal system or in the legal profession, his duty to clients or to the public should never be subordinate merely because the full discharge of his obligation may be misunderstood or may tend to subject him or the legal profession to criticism."

[40] Such a notion may be implicit in appeals to the segment of the public that is "reasonable" or to "the bar."

[41] Ex parte Taylor Coal Co., 401 So.2d 1, 8 (Ala.1981) (recognizing a "no public sense of impropriety" exception to former-client conflict rule); Goldthwaite v. Disciplinary Board, 408 So.2d 504, 509 (Ala.1982)(same exception employed to exonerate lawyer hired by bank to probate will who switched sides to assist will contestants by writing appellate brief challenging will).

[42] In re Special February 1975 Grand Jury, 406 F.Supp. 194, 198, 199 (N.D.Ill.1975).

[43] State v. Cline, 122 R.I. 297, 405 A.2d 1192, 1207 (1979)(criticizing proposed solution of disqualifying entire prosecution staff and appointing special prosecutor, who would then consult with disqualified lawyers to carry prosecution forward).

client conflicts (§ 7.4)—areas in which the Code provides the least helpful guidance on conflict problems.

The invocation of Canon 9's general language might not have been contrary to the intent of the framers of the 1969 Code. At a point distant from Canon 9, language can be found referring to it for a general-appearances concept.[44] Yet it also seems to be true that those references, in Canon 9 and elsewhere, are to the appearance of the violation of some specific rule and not a vague, general standard that exists independently of other rules.[45] In fact, in probably the majority of instances in which courts have relied solely upon Canon 9, the court justifiably could have relied upon a much more specific rule for the same result.

Appearances in the Final Analysis

For those and related reasons, many courts regard Canon 9 as "simply too slender a reed on which to rest a disqualification order except in the rarest of cases." [46] Academic commentators have denounced it.[47] The framers of the 1983 Model Rules plainly meant to abandon it as an independently operating standard.[48] As a general goal, gaining the confidence of the public and of clients in the legal profession, in the judicial system, and even in the conflict of interest rules is greatly to be encouraged. But courts lack both access to reliable facts and a workable method for thinking through, on a case-by-case basis, the question whether the particular result sought by one or the other of the parties will increase, decrease, or leave unaffected the general level of public or client confidence.

That is not to say that the public should be damned and the probable public perception of ethical doctrines ignored. It is to say that the public reaction should be relevant only to the extent that the court can confidently say how members of the public would react to a system of conflict rules and their implementation across the array of interrelated cases. So it is quite legitimate to provide the prophylactic substantial-relationship test for former-client conflicts in order to assure the public and future clients that lawyers will not misuse confidential information (§ 7.4.2). And it is defensible to disqualify a former government lawyer from handling, in private practice and even in a nonadverse representation, the same matter for which the lawyer had substantial responsibility in government practice in order to assure public confidence in the work of government lawyers (§ 8.10). But the standards and rules that are employed to apply those principles can be developed in ways that are focused, relatively precise, and much less likely to lead to ad hoc results than would a general-appearances test.

44 See EC 5–6, and id. n.5.

45 In re Ainsworth, 289 Or. 479, 614 P.2d 1127, 1134 n.4 (1980).

46 Board of Educ. v. Nyquist, 590 F.2d 1241, 1247 (2d Cir.1979). See also Fred Weber, Inc. v. Shell Oil Co., 566 F.2d 602, 609 (8th Cir.1977)(Canon 9 rejected because it constitutes an "eye of the beholder" test), cert. denied 436 U.S. 905, 98 S.Ct. 2235, 56 L.Ed.2d 403 (1978); International Elec. Corp. v. Flanzer, 527 F.2d 1288, 1295 (2d Cir. 1975); Silver Chrysler Plymouth, Inc. v. Chrysler Motors Corp., 518 F.2d 751 (2d Cir.1975); Sapienza v. Hayashi, 57 Haw. 289, 554 P.2d 1131, 1136 (1976); Higgins v. Committee on Professional Ethics, 73 N.J. 123, 373 A.2d 372, 375 (1977); In re Ainsworth, 289 Or. 479, 614 P.2d 1127 (1980). See generally ABF, Annotated Code of Professional Responsibility 400–03 (O. Maru ed.1979). ABA Formal Op. 342, at n.17 (1975), rejected Canon 9 as "too vague a phrase to be useful" and "perhaps the least helpful of the seven policy considerations" that were identified in the opinion's former-government-lawyer analysis. That apparently reverses, sub silentio, the position of ABA Formal Op. 337 (1974) that Canon 9 could be applied to a broad range of vaguely objectionable lawyer practices.

47 Kramer, The Appearance of Impropriety under Canon 9: A Study of the Federal Judicial Process Applied to Lawyers, 65 Minn. L. Rev. 243, 264–65 (1981); Liebmann, The Changing Law of Disqualification: The Role of Presumption and Policy, 73 Nw.U.L.Rev. 966 (1979); O'Toole, Canon 9 of the Code of Professional Responsibility: An Elusive Ethical Guideline, 62 Marq.L.Rev. 313 (1979). See also Note, Disqualification of Counsel for the Appearance of Professional Impropriety, 25 Cath. U.L.Rev. 343 (1976); Note, Appearance of Impropriety as the Sole Ground for Disqualification, 31 U. Miami L.Rev. 1516 (1977). Some commentators have, however, apparently urged its general adoption. E.g., Aronson, Conflict of Interest Problems of the Private Practitioner, in ABA, Professional Responsibility: A Guide for Attorneys 91, 92–93 (1978).

48 See MR 1.10 comment (Lawyers Moving between Firms; third paragraph); MR 1.7 Legal Background Note 52–54 (Proposed Final Draft May 30, 1981).

It is undoubtedly sound advice on the whole not to be seen bending down in someone else's melon patch, even if your shoe needs tying.[49] But as long as one keeps hands off the cantaloupes, either a serious need to tie a shoe or the unlikelihood of detection can be justification for ignoring the advice. Proponents of wholesale disqualifications of lawyers from situations that only look bad should not ignore the costs imposed by too worrisome a concern with public misunderstanding. Better to leave it as simply good advice to inform the exercise of wise professional discretion: even if no rule prohibits a representation, it is best to avoid creating an appearance of possible impropriety unless there is an overriding need to incur the risk.

WESTLAW REFERENCES

The Illusory Content of the Appearances Rationale

attorney counsel** lawyer /s "canon 9" conflict*** /s appearance +3 impropriety

Methodological Weakness of the Appearances Standard

"canon 9" conflict*** /49 appearance +3 impropriety /s "bar association" observ! public

Unfortunate Uses of the Appearances Standard

appearance +3 impropriety /s cosmetic! except*** lack

The Place of Appearances in the 1969 Code

appearance +3 impropriety /s discipline exclusive** rational! stigma!

§ 7.1.5 Standards for Conflict Identification

The Variant Standards in the 1969 Code

In light of the competing principles and interests that underlie conflicts rules, to what extent must it be evident that an impermissible conflict between clients exists? Expressions can be found in decisions under the 1969 Code that indicate that even a mere possibility[50] of a conflict is fatal. But most courts speak in weightier terms of a "substantial risk" of a conflict.[51] A provision of the Code states that a conflict exists if the lawyer's judgment "will be or reasonably may be affected."[52] "Reasonably" here seems to refer to the particular facts that confront the lawyer and to call for exercise of the judgment of a lawyer who is ordinarily cautious about the risks of conflicts. The basic and mandatory client-client conflict rules in the Code, DR 5-105(A) and (B), refer to the "likely" impairment of independent professional judgment or representation of differing interests. On the other hand, EC 5-15 gives the nonbinding advice that a lawyer confronted with "potentially differing interests . . . should resolve all doubts against the propriety of the representation."

The approach of the 1983 Model Rules is to define impermissible conflicts in terms of their impact upon the lawyer's representation of a client. A lawyer is prohibited from representating a client if it would be "directly adverse" to another client[53] or if the second representation would be "materially limited"

---

49 Wydick, Trial Counsel as Witness: The Code and the Model Rules, 15 U. Cal.-Davis L.Rev. 651, 665 (1982).

50 First Nat'l Bank v. Rapides Bank & Trust Co., 145 Ga.App. 514, 244 S.E.2d 51, 54 (1978)("possibilities"), and cases cited; Matter of Lantz, 442 N.E.2d 989, 990 (Ind.1982)("mere possibility"). Cf. R. Wise, Legal Ethics 273 (2d ed.1970)("slightest doubt" standard); In re Holmes, 290 Or. 173, 619 P.2d 1284, 1289 (1980)(same). But see, e.g., Realco Services, Inc. v. Holt, 479 F.Supp. 867, 872 n.4 (E.D.Pa.1979)("The . . . standard . . . serve[s] as a substitute for analysis rather than as a guide to it. It is easier to find a doubt than to resolve difficult questions of law and ethics. The disruption and prejudice that befall a client whose counsel is disqualified are reasons to avoid a hasty conclusion in favor of disqualification, based merely on a doubt about the propriety of the representation.")(cited and quoted in MR 1.9 Legal Background Note 67 (Proposed Final Draft, May 30, 1981)).

51 In re Tonkon, 292 Or. 660, 642 P.2d 660, 662 (1982).

52 DR 5-101(A). The words presumably mean "reasonably may *be expected to* be affected." See In re Tonkon, supra, 642 P.2d at 663 n.5. See also EC 5-2 ("reasonable possibility" of lawyer self-interest conflicting with interests of client).

53 MR 1.7(a) and comment.

by the lawyer's other interests or responsibilities.[54] The comment to MR 1.7 explains that

> a possible conflict does not itself preclude the representation. The critical questions are whether the conflict will eventuate and, if it does, whether it will materially interfere with the lawyer's independent professional judgment in considering alternatives or foreclose courses of action that reasonably should be pursued on behalf of the client. Consideration should be given to whether the client wishes to accommodate the other interest involved.[55]

Nonetheless, a lawyer may claim that personal possession of greater than ordinary fortitude guarantees independence of his or her judgment despite the powerful impingement of conflicting interests that might confound ordinary mortals. The most direct response provided by the Model Rules is in the comment directly concerned with client consent. Its reference to whether a "disinterested lawyer" [56] would conclude that the client should agree to the representation despite the conflict can also serve as a useful measure of whether a lawyer should conclude that a representation is directly adverse and whether its effect will be material.

Under both the Code and the Model Rules, conflict of interest problems should become ethical violations only at the point at which a reasonable probability of material impairment of loyalty or confidentiality exists. A stricter standard, such as an overly enthusiastic wielding of the appearance-of-impropriety notion (§ 7.1.4), or a looser standard, such as one that insists on a mathematically convincing demonstration of a conflict,[57] are both unsatisfactory. Most importantly, the general standard of reasonable probability of material impairment should be applied to the particular conflict of interest problem with keen attention to the discrete policy and other concerns that inform the rules on the particular subject.

WESTLAW REFERENCES

The Variant Standards in the 1969 Code

attorney counsel** lawyer /s conflict*** /s (affect*** impair! /s judgement judgment) (possib! potential** substantial** /s impair! risk)

§ 7.1.6 *Persons Burdened and Protected by Conflict Rules*

Burdened Lawyers and Similar Agents

Most cases of impermissible conflicts are those in which a person who was unquestionably a lawyer was disqualified because of the clear existence of a client-lawyer relationship. Even beyond the clear situations, courts have not hesitated to extend the burdens of the conflict of interest rules to a current lawyer who, at the time of the relationship with a former "client," was a nonlawyer patent agent [58] or a nonlawyer claims adjuster for an insurance company.[59] The critical element was that the actor's prior duties were those of a confidential agent.

Lawyers in Arguably Nonlawyer Roles

Not all the functions of a lawyer involve the kinds of loyalty and confidentiality that characterize most legal representations. A lawyer who serves on a citizen advisory board to a medical center is not disqualified from bringing a civil rights suit against it in behalf of patients.[60] In contrast, a lawyer who

54 MR 1.7(b).

55 MR 1.7 comment (Loyalty to a Client).

56 MR 1.7 comment (Consultation and Consent).

57 For example, the statement is surely wrong, in Norton v. Tallahassee Memorial Hospital, 689 F.2d 938, 941 (11th Cir.1982), that a conflicts test asks only whether specifically identifiable impropriety did in fact occur and not whether there is a reasonable likelihood that it will occur in the future. The statement might, however, be addressed to the remoteness of the likelihood of the future adverse impact and not to the fact that it has not yet occurred.

58 American Roller Co. v. Budinger, 513 F.2d 982 (3d Cir.1975)(nonlawyer patent agent while attending night school).

59 Hovel v. Minneapolis & St. L. R.R., 165 Minn. 449, 206 N.W. 710 (1926).

60 Ellen v. Rhodes, 507 F.Supp. 734 (S.D. Ohio 1981). See also Board of Educ. v. Nyquist, 590 F.2d 1241 (2d Cir. 1979)(lawyer hired by a teacher's association is not precluded from litigation in behalf of some members of the association against others, despite the fact that the opposing parties' dues, in a small part, paid his salary).

served as an elected city commissioner, with supervisory control over a city's lawyers, was disqualified from continuing litigation against an entity of the city.[61] Similarly, when a member of a law firm represented an employer's association in collective bargaining, another member of the firm could not file suit, in behalf of a terminated executive, against a division of a corporate member of the association when it plausibly appeared that the law firm might have come into possession of confidential information about the division's dealings with its executives as part of its representation in the collective bargaining case.[62] As a general matter, any person or entity that actually supplies material and confidential information to a lawyer who is functioning as such should be a good candidate to object to the third person's possibly adverse use of the information, unless it was clear to the supplier of the information that the lawyer was not protecting the interests of that person.

A particularly acute question of that kind was raised by ethics committee opinions barring a lawyer or a member of the lawyer's firm from representing a client involved in litigation with a person represented by a legal services organization if the lawyer was a member of the organization's board of directors.[63] The ensuing uproar was allayed in a contrary ruling of the ABA,[64] which held that the conflict could be waived by consent of all affected clients. A similar approach is mandated by Model Rule 6.3.

Lawyer Scriveners

Drawing on an exception sometimes recognized in the law of attorney-client privilege,[65] a lawyer might imagine that serving in the limited role of drafter of a document such as a contract or a will does not involve confidential client information and therefore does not fall under the conflict of interest rules. In that view, the lawyer-drafter would later be able to represent a party who seeks to invalidate the document. While the "scrivener" exception is debatably proper for the purposes of the testimonial privilege, it is inappropriate in the different setting of conflicts of interest.[66] Conflicts rules aim to protect against more than the misuse of information that falls within the narrow limits of the privilege (see § 7.1.3). Scriveners who are lawyers are also under an obligation of loyalty that should alone suffice to prevent them from attempting to upset their own work.

Lawyers as Litigants against Former Clients

Courts have not been impressed with arguments that a person who functioned as a lawyer in behalf of a former client was not in violation of conflict of interest rules if the lawyer appeared in a succeeding substantially

[61] Norton v. Tallahassee Memorial Hospital, 511 F.Supp 777 (N.D.Fla.1981), reversed 689 F.2d 938 (11th Cir.1982).

[62] Glueck v. Jonathan Logan, Inc., 653 F.2d 746 (2d Cir.1981). See also Whiting Corp. v. White Machinery Corp., 567 F.2d 713 (7th Cir.1977)(lawyer for plaintiff who had also represented corporation that owned 20 percent of shares of defendant corporation can continue representation only on condition that he not advise 20 percent share-owning client during litigation); Westinghouse Elec. Corp. v. Kerr-McGee Corp., 580 F.2d 1311 (7th Cir.), cert. denied 439 U.S. 955, 99 S.Ct. 353, 58 L.Ed.2d 346 (1978)(disqualification because of receipt of confidential information from client who was member of trade association); McCourt Co. v. FPC Properties, Inc., 386 Mass. 145, 434 N.E.2d 1234 (1982)(without client consent a lawyer could not sue his own client, defining client to include collectively both parent corporation and various wholly owned subsidiaries).

In Greene v. Greene, 47 N.Y.2d 447, 418 N.Y.S.2d 379, 391 N.E.2d 1355 (1979), two partners in Law Firm One left it and became partners in Law Firm Two. Other Firm Two lawyers then filed an action in behalf of the beneficiary of a trust against Firm One, alleging negligent mismanagement and other tortious conduct. Because of the fiduciary and confidential nature of the relationship between partners in the firm and because some of the tortious conduct allegedly occurred while the two partners were still with Firm One, the court ordered disqualification of Firm Two.

[63] ABA Informal Op. 1395 (1977); N.Y. St. B. Ass'n Op. 489 (1978).

[64] ABA Formal Op. 345 (1979).

[65] C. McCormick, Evidence § 88, at 209 (E.Cleary 3d ed. 1984).

[66] The scrivener exception has apparently been repudiated by the Model Rules. See MR 1.9 comment (first paragraph). See § 7.4.3.

related action against the former client as a party plaintiff in a shareholder derivative action.[67] The notion does not carry so far as to deprive the lawyer of any right to litigate a claim against a former client. That would be plainly inconsistent, for example, with the exception to the confidentiality and loyalty principles provided for a lawyer's suit against a client to recover a fee (§ 6.7.8). But, because of those principles, a lawyer will not be entitled to assume the additional position of representing others in a class action against a former client.

Parties Who Can Invoke Conflict Protections

Questions may also be raised whether a person claiming the benefit of the anticonflict rules is one of those intended to be protected by their policies. Here again the appropriate view is to give a generous hearing to the claims of a person asserting the status of a client if the person was in a position, during the relationship, in which it seems likely that the person imparted confidential information to the lawyer. Accordingly, it would clearly not matter that a person claiming to be a client paid no fee; a confidential client-lawyer relationship can be formed just as well when the lawyer charges no fee.[68] Even when the services performed by the lawyer for the client were more in the nature of business assistance than legal help, the lawyer should be disqualified from litigating against the client in a substantially related matter.[69] When a lawyer deals with another person as a business associate, the potential for overlapping and confusion of roles is great and the difficulties of satisfactorily proving the parties' understanding can be substantial. Applying the conflict rules generously to those relationships provides an assurance of protection to the confidentiality and loyalty principles.

Interested Parties as Virtual Clients

Some persons who deal with a lawyer should be aware that the lawyer does not extend loyalty or confidentiality to them. Suppose a lawyer represents one party to a contract and discusses its terms with the other, unrepresented party in a setting in which it would be unreasonable for the other party to believe that the lawyer was acting as that party's confidential legal adviser. If a dispute later arises about the transaction, the lawyer is entitled to bring suit against that party based on the contract.[70] The absence of any personal dealings or relationship between the lawyer and the person claiming the benefits of the conflict of interest rules might also be determinative. It has been held, for example, that a member of a large class in a class action who has had no relationship with the lawyer for the class might permissibly be sued by the same lawyer as part of another large class.[71]

But a closer relationship with a circle of persons might create conflicts. A lawyer will sometimes have extensive relationships with one member of a family who retains, pays, and generally directs the lawyer's work. If some of the lawyer's work is for the other members of the family—such as drafting wills or other legal documents for them—each becomes a client for the purpose of the conflict rules.[72] The same result follows when a law-

67 Doe v. A Corp., 330 F.Supp. 1352 (S.D.N.Y.1971), affirmed sub nom. Hall v. A Corp., 453 F.2d 1375 (2d Cir. 1972). See also Hull v. Celanese Corp., 513 F.2d 568, 572 (2d Cir.1975); Richardson v. Hamilton Int'l Corp., 469 F.2d 1382 (3d Cir.1972), cert. denied 411 U.S. 986, 93 S.Ct. 2271, 36 L.Ed.2d 964 (1973).

68 See generally 8 J. Wigmore, Evidence § 2303 (McNaughton rev.1961); § 6.3.2.

69 Cord v. Smith, 338 F.2d 516, 524 (9th Cir.1964), mandate clarified 370 F.2d 418 (9th Cir.1966).

70 Fielding v. Brebbia, 479 F.2d 195, 198 (D.C.Cir.1973); In re Brown, 49 N.J. 16, 19, 227 A.2d 506 (1976). See also Matter of Estate of Nuyen, 111 Ill.App.3d 216, 443 N.E.2d 1099, 1103 (1982)(no client-lawyer relationship, despite advice given to will beneficiary by lawyer for executor, because lawyer carefully told beneficiary that he was acting only as lawyer for executor).

71 The case of apparent first impression is Little Rock School Dist. v. Borden, Inc., 505 F.Supp. 77 (E.D.Ark. 1980)(on facts here, no risk to confidentiality or loyalty of lawyer for class to file unrelated action against another class one of whose members is also member of prior class).

72 Buntrock v. Buntrock, 419 So.2d 402 (Fla.App.1982) (father's lawyer drafted estate plan for daughter).

yer representing an organization such as a trade association performs legal work for the organization and invites and takes advantage of confidential communications from members of the organization in the process. It is not determinative that a classical client-lawyer relationship was not been formed with the members of the organization.[73]

Coclients

A lawyer involved in the representation of one of several coparties in a former representation is not disqualified from representing a client in a substantially related suit against another former coparty unless the coparty can show that the lawyer obtained confidential information from the coparty, in the prior representation, that could be employed against the interests of the coparty in the present case.[74]

Initial Consultation

One client question presents a dilemma. Suppose that a prospective client initially consults with a lawyer and gives the lawyer confidential information to enable the lawyer to determine whether to accept the case. Suppose that it comes out during the initial consultation that the lawyer already represents another client with adverse interests. It is clear at that point that the lawyer cannot represent the prospective client. But does it also follow that the lawyer, because he or she is now in possession of confidential information of the prospective client, must cease representing the *first* client?[75]

Under normal circumstances, disqualification should not result from an initial consultation alone, so long as the lawyer did not extend the consultation for too long a time or discuss items of confidential information irrelevant to determining whether a conflict existed. The lawyer must also have acted in good faith and may not, for example, use the initial consultation as a subterfuge to gain confidential information for the adverse use of an existing client. In order for sufficient information to be disclosed to permit a lawyer to know whether a conflict exists, there must often be some disclosure of information that is confidential. Without such disclosure, lawyers could not effectively police and prevent conflict problems. Although authority on the point seems not to exist, it must be clear that a lawyer who in good faith acquires the information needed to do a review of possible conflicts should not be barred from representing a present client adversely to the inquiring, prospective client.[76]

[73] Westinghouse Elec. Corp. v. Kerr-McGee Corp., 580 F.2d 1311, 1318–20 (7th Cir.), cert. denied, 439 U.S. 955, 99 S.Ct. 353, 58 L.Ed.2d 346 (1978); Bobbitt v. Victorian House, Inc., 545 F.Supp. 1124, 1126 (N.D.Ill.1982).

[74] Compare, e.g., Fred Weber, Inc. v. Shell Oil Co., 566 F.2d 602 (8th Cir.1977), cert. denied 436 U.S. 905, 98 S.Ct. 2235, 56 L.Ed.2d 403 (1978); Krebs v. Johns-Manville Corp., 496 F.Supp. 40 (E.D.Pa.1980)(lawyer not disqualified when, representing another building products defendant, he attended general coordinating meeting of committee of lawyers representing asbestos manufacturers, at which no confidential information was revealed); with Wilson P. Abraham Constr. Corp. v. Armco Steel Corp., 559 F.2d 250 (5th Cir.1977)(hearing required to determine whether confidential information shared); Nichols v. Village Voice, Inc., 99 Misc.2d 822, 417 N.Y.S.2d 415, 418 (1979)(reporter who, although separately represented, also consulted extensively with codefendant-publisher's lawyer had right to expect that publisher's lawyer would treat communications as confidential and thus was entitled to former-client conflict protection if otherwise applicable). On facts similar to those in *Nichols*, the court in International Paper Co. v. Lloyd Mfg. Co., 555 F.Supp. 125 (N.D.Ill.1982), employed the presumption-of-disqualification standard for former-client conflicts but permitted the lawyer to attempt to rebut the presumption).

[75] In Desbiens v. Ford Motor Company, 81 A.D.2d 707, 439 N.Y.S.2d 452 (1981), a lawyer forwarded a file so that law firm could decide whether to represent Estate B in a wrongful death action. After reviewing the file, and giving a tentative legal opinion, law firm responded that because of a possible conflict between Estate B and another client, Estate A, that had already approached it, law firm had decided to represent only Estate A. Ultimately neither estate was represented, but law firm represented the automobile manufacturer in defense of claims by the estates for product liability. The court ordered disqualification of law firm because of its prior examination of the plaintiff's file.

[76] Cf. Englishtown Sportswear, Ltd. v. Tuttle, 547 F. Supp. 700 (S.D.N.Y.1982)(lawyer's only contact was "de minimis," serving as translator in five-minute conference call in foreign country.)

WESTLAW REFERENCES

Burdened Lawyers and Similar Agents

adjuster (confidential patent +1 agent) /s conflict*** /4 interest

Lawyers in Arguably Nonlawyer Roles

attorney counsel** lawyer /s conflict*** /s advisory collective (elect*** /5 office) "legal services"

Lawyer Scriveners

attorney counsel** lawyer /s conflict*** /s draft! scrivener

Lawyers as Litigants against Former Clients

attorney counsel** lawyer /s former** +2 client /s "class action" litigant party sui**

Parties Who Can Invoke Conflict Protections

attorney counsel** lawyer /s conflict** /s benefi!

Interested Parties as Virtual Clients

attorney counsel** lawyer /s conflict*** /s circle dealing group member!

Initial Consultation

attorney counsel** lawyer /s conflict*** /p first initial** /2 consult!

§ 7.1.7 *Conflict Remedies and Procedures*

Various types of conflicts of interest have called forth different remedial and procedural responses from courts and lawyer disciplinary agencies, but enough is common to them to warrant collective consideration. The array of remedial responses to a detected conflict of interest is wide. Among the difficult procedural issues examined here are those involving judicial power and discretion in passing upon disqualification motions and the standing of parties to object to conflicts of interest in litigation.

Discipline of Lawyers for Impermissible Conflicts

Discipline of a lawyer for violation of the conflict of interest rules is not uncommon and seems to occur most often in instances of rather flagrant conflicts.[77] A question under the professional rules is whether, for disciplinary purposes, they prohibit conflicting representations as broadly and under the same standards as the common-law conflict rules, considered below, under which courts order disqualification of a lawyer in a pending case. The question might well be differently answered depending on whether the Code or the Model Rules is applicable.

Under the Code some conflict situations that could result in the grant of a motion to disqualify a lawyer in litigation would not necessarily result in a finding of a violation of the Disciplinary Rules. Disqualification opinions frequently mention that the lawyer had proceeded in good faith, if mistakenly, or that the court was ordering disqualification for prophylactic reasons and not because of any actual breach by the lawyer of confidentiality or loyalty rules.[78] For example, the Disciplinary Rule most obviously directed against side switching deals only with the case in which an attorney actually uses confidential information obtained in a prior representation.[79] Court decisions dealing with disqualification go far beyond that and, under the substantial-relationship standard, do not require that actual divulgence of client confidential information be shown (§ 7.4.2). The Model Rules, however, adopt the "substantially related" test as the standard for discipline as well, thus creating a mandatory rule of

[77] United States v. Costen, 38 F. 24 (C.C.D.Colo.1889) (lawyer disbarred when, after withdrawing from representation of complaining party, he offered to be secretly employed by the respondent and to supply confidential information). See also, e.g., United States v. Bronston, 658 F.2d 920 (2d Cir.1981), cert. denied 456 U.S. 915, 102 S.Ct. 1769, 72 L.Ed.2d 174 (1982)(affirming lawyer's conviction on mail fraud charge for undisclosed representation of conflicting interests); Codiga v. State Bar, 20 Cal.3d 788, 144 Cal.Rptr. 404, 575 P.2d 1186 (1978)(false concealment from clients of conflicting representation of adverse party related to lawyer as in-law); In re Banks, 283 Or. 459, 584 P.2d 284 (1978); In re Pahules, 334 So.2d 23 (Fla.1976). In re Donohoe, 90 Wn.2d 173, 580 P.2d 1093 (1978)(discipline for obtaining judgment against debtor and then representing the judgment debtor in bankruptcy proceeding).

[78] Cinema 5, Ltd. v. Cinerama, Inc., 528 F.2d 1384, 1387 (2d Cir.1976)(disqualification of lawyer and firm despite findings of entire good faith is "not intended as a criticism of the character and professional integrity" of lawyers; court is "sure that the dual representation came about inadvertently and unknowingly and . . . there has been no actual wrongdoing").

[79] DR 4–101(B)(2) & (3).

apparently equal dimensions for both disqualification motions and discipline.[80]

Judicial Disqualification Orders

The motion for a judicial order disqualifying a lawyer in pending litigation because of conflict is a traditional remedy that has come into prominence in recent years. After some initial enthusiasm, courts have become somewhat more wary of the problems of judicial administration and temptations for strategic manipulation that disqualification motions present.[81] The remedy is solidly entrenched, if with such reservations, and might reflect judicial awareness of the fact that conflicts rules are frequently violated by lawyers and yet are too rarely enforced in disciplinary proceedings. Courts fill the void.[82] Courts thus promote the policy of the lawyer rules that require withdrawal by a lawyer whose continued representation in a case would violate a mandatory rule.[83] Even if a lawyer is assertedly unaware of the existence of facts indicating a need to withdraw, the disqualification motion prevents the lawyer from blundering further when the conflict is apparent but uninvestigated.[84]

Other Judicially Administered Remedies

Beyond discipline of an offending lawyer lies an array of judicially administered sanctions to prevent violations of conflict rules or to remedy injuries caused by violations. The injury to a client threatened by the adverse use of confidential information or other disloyalty can be guarded against through an *injunction* against the disloyal lawyer's divulgence of the information.[85] A lawyer who causes injury to a client through a conflicting representation may suffer a *legal malpractice* judgment for damages in favor of the injured client.[86] A damage recovery is not the only—and perhaps not the most substantial—sanction available. Most courts will also impose a *fee forfeiture*. "Certainly by the beginning of the Seventeenth Century it had become a common-place that an attorney must not represent opposed interests; and the usual consequence has been that he is debarred from receiving any fee from either no matter how successful his labors. . . . [T]he prohibition is absolute and the consequence is a forfeiture of all pay." [87] Other courts will impose a forfeiture of only the portion of the fee attributable to legal services performed while the lawyer impermissibly represented conflicting interests.[88]

It might also be theoretically possible for a court to restore the imbalance that divulgence unfairly creates by *reciprocal disclosure*—requiring the faithless lawyer to reveal to the injured client confidential information that the benefited second client provided to the lawyer.[89] The suggestion, however, seems dif-

[80] MR 1.9(a).

[81] See infra at 332–335.

[82] Judd, Conflicts of Interest--A Trial Judge's Notes, 44 Fordham L.Rev. 1097 (1976).

[83] DR 1–110(B)(2); MR 1.16 (a)(1). Ultimately a lawyer's failure to abide by an order of disqualification because of a judicially detected conflict of interest can be sanctioned by an adjudication of contempt. E.g., United States v. Clarkson, 567 F.2d 270 (4th Cir.1977).

[84] Anderson v. Pryor, 537 F.Supp. 890, 899 (W.D.Mo. 1982).

[85] Cord v. Smith, 338 F.2d 516, 519 (9th Cir.1964), mandate clarified 370 F.2d 418 (9th Cir.1966); Handelman v. Weiss, 368 F.Supp. 258, 263 (S.D.N.Y.1973); Powers v. Board of Public Works, 216 Cal. 546, 15 P.2d 156 (1932)(temporary restraining order against conflicting representation).

[86] Hill v. Okay Constr. Co., 312 Minn. 324, 252 N.W.2d 107 (1977); Ishmael v. Millington, 241 Cal.App.2d 520, 50 Cal.Rptr. 592 (1966).

[87] Silbiger v. Prudence Bonds Corp., 180 F.2d 917, 920–21 (2d Cir.), cert. denied 340 U.S. 831, 71 S. Ct. 37, 95 L.Ed. 610 (1950). See also Woods v. City National Bank & Trust Co., 312 U.S. 262, 267–68, 61 S.Ct. 493, 496–97, 85 L.Ed. 820 (1941); Gesellschaft fur Drahtlose Telegraphie M.B.H. v. Brown, 78 F.2d 410 (D.C.Cir.), cert. denied 296 U.S. 618, 56 S.Ct. 139, 80 L.Ed. 439 (1935); Financial General Bankshares, Inc. v. Metzger, 523 F.Supp. 744, 773 (D.D.C.1981), reversed on other grounds, 680 F.2d 768 (D.C.Cir.1982); White v. Roundtree Transp., Inc., 386 So.2d 1287 (Fla.App.1980); Goldstein v. Lees, 46 Cal.App.3d 614, 120 Cal.Rptr. 253 (1975); Rolfstad, Winkjer, Suess, McKennett & Kaiser v. Hanson, 221 N.W.2d 734, 737 (N.D.1974).

[88] See § 9.6.1.

[89] Cf. National Texture Corp. v. Hymes, 282 N.W.2d 890 (Minn.1979). Inexplicably, the same decision sug-

ficult to square with the limits on recognized exceptions to the attorney-client privilege. The extreme remedy of a *penalty dismissal* of the complaint of a party whose lawyer engaged in an impermissible conflict of interests has been granted if the information upon which the suit was based was supplied entirely by the lawyer for the defendant who switched sides to represent the plaintiff.[90] In an independent proceeding, the court can *set aside a judgment* obtained through the treachery of a lawyer who furthers his or her own client's defeat in litigation because of a conflict of interest benefiting the prevailing party.[91] But if the prevailing party was not complicit and may not have benefited in fact from the lawyer's conflict, courts are understandably loath to impose a harsh dismissal or other forfeiture sanction.[92] If a direct benefit to the client can be shown, courts are not reluctant to require the client to disgorge the benefits unjustly conferred by a lawyer disloyal to another client. For example, a conflict of interest on the part of a lawyer who drafts for one client a will that benefits another can have the collateral effect of creating a strong presumption that the will was obtained by undue influence and thus is voidable.[93]

Rescinded Consent

Some disqualifications or withdrawals can present a further problem in the case of conflicts in simultaneous representations. Suppose that a lawyer, after appropriate consultation and with the consent of each, has performed substantial legal services for two clients with potentially conflicting interests.[94] At a later stage, however, one of the clients is unwilling to proceed with the joint representation because of increased concerns about the lawyer's loyalty. Can the lawyer, after dismissal by the concerned client or after the lawyer's own withdrawal from representing the objecting client, continue to represent the remaining client? An older view would hold that a question of etiquette was involved and that the lawyer should defer to the wishes of the client with whom the lawyer had maintained the longest relationship.[95] While such a primogeniture rule, if otherwise sensible, could be followed today if the conflict of interest appeared at the very outset of a proposed joint representation, it hardly meets a concerned client's objection to the lawyer's now adverse use of confidential information in the interests of the remaining client.

In such a situation it is apparent that in rescinded consent cases the lawyer should be required to withdraw from the representation of both clients.[96] For example, a lawyer hired

gests that the faithless lawyer's work product is to be protected at all costs. 282 N.W.2d at 896.

90 Doe v. A Corp., 330 F.Supp. 1352 (S.D.N.Y. 1971), affirmed per curiam sub nom. Hall v. A Corp., 453 F.2d 1375 (2d Cir.1972); Richardson v. Hamilton International Corp., 333 F.Supp. 1049 (E.D.Pa.1971)(dictum), affirmed 469 F.2d 1382 (3d Cir.1972), cert. denied 411 U.S. 986, 93 S.Ct. 2271, 36 L.Ed.2d 964 (1973); Slater v. Rimar, Inc., 462 Pa. 138, 338 A.2d 584, 590–91 (1975).

91 United States v. Throckmorton, 98 U.S. 61, 66, 25 L.Ed. 93 (1878); Bizzel v. Hemingway, 548 F.2d 505 (4th Cir.1977); Fiske v. Buder, 125 F.2d 841, 849 (8th Cir. 1942).

92 Fund of Funds, Ltd. v. Arthur Andersen & Co., 567 F. 2d 225, 236 (2d Cir.1977), and cases cited.

93 Haynes v. First Nat'l State Bank, 87 N.J. 163, 432 A. 2d 890, 899 (1981), and cases cited.

94 See § 7.2.1 (client consent). Similar issues are raised when a lawyer impermissibly represents clients with conflicting interests without consent and is later forced to withdraw or is disqualified.

95 Alabama Code of Ethics § 31, 118 Ala. xxiii, xxvii (1898).

96 United States v. Curcio, 680 F.2d 881, 890–91 nn.5 & 6 (2d Cir.1981); In re Grand Jury Proceedings at Lynchburg, Virginia, 432 F.Supp. 50, 54 (W.D.Va.1977); First Wis. Mortgage Trust v. First Wis. Corp., 422 F.Supp. 493 (E.D.Wis.1976), appeal dismissed 584 F.2d 201, 203 (7th Cir.1978)(en banc); In re Banks, 283 Or. 459, 584 P.2d 284, 1 A.L.R. 4th 1105 (1978); OpDyke v. Kent Liquor Market, Inc., 40 Del.Ch. 316, 181 A.2d 579 (1962). Cf. Clark v. Lomas & Nettleton Fin. Corp., 79 F.R.D. 658 (N.D.Tex.1978) (conflict created by joint representation of both corporation and individual officers and directors in shareholder derivative action cured by withdrawal as lawyers for corporation, although firm continued to represent the individuals when there was little real threat of divulgence of confidential information). Cases that seem to oppose the point seem to miss it as well. E.g., Neiman v. Local 144, 512 F.Supp. 187 (E.D.N.Y.1981)(former jointly represented client who knew all along that its labor lawyers also represented another party cannot reasonably have assumed that firm would keep its information secret from other clients); Watson v. District Court, 199

by an insurance company to defend an insured may receive confidential information from the insured indicating that the insured is not protected under the policy. It is not thereafter permissible for the lawyer to represent either the insured or the company in litigation between them concerning the scope of coverage.[97]

Simultaneous representation in the same matter that breaks down will almost always require the lawyer to discontinue representation of all parties involved, but there are possible exceptions. Readily distinguishable are situations in which a lawyer simultaneously represents clients with conflicting interests but in which there is no relationship between the matters that gives rise to a risk of later adverse use of confidential information. Disqualification or withdrawal from one representation in such a case leaves the lawyer free to continue to represent the other client.[98] Another possible exception might be recognized if a client consents in advance to the lawyer's continued representation of the other party if the joint representation later breaks down.[99] Withdrawal from both representations will also not be required if the conflict was discovered so early in the joint representation that the "released" client had not yet supplied material confidential information as a result of the client-lawyer relationship.[1]

Consultation with Successor Lawyer

A logical extension of the disqualification rule requires that a lawyer who cannot proceed with a representation because of a conflict that is disabling because of its threat to the confidentiality principle should not consult with a successor lawyer who is retained to carry the matter farther. If client confidences are not at the root of the disqualification order or would not be jeopardized by the consultation and if the lack of opportunity to consult with the disqualified lawyer about his or her work product would result in needless hardship to the client, limited consultation has been permitted.[2] In any event, the disqualified lawyer should consult with a successor lawyer only with court permission or consent of the affected clients. Among other things, surreptitious dealings with a successor lawyer can lead to a disqualification of the successor lawyer as well.[3]

Procedures in General

The procedures followed in employing a remedy for a conflict of interest depend upon the remedy sought. Discipline charges follow the course generally set out for those proceedings (§ 3.4). Disqualification motions in judicial proceedings have some characteristics and consequences that are quite different from those of discipline.[4]

Colo. 76, 604 P.2d 1165, 1168 (1980)(dictum)(defense lawyer disqualified in criminal case can elect which codefendant to represent).

97 H.Drinker, Legal Ethics 115 (1953).

98 Chateau de Ville Productions, Inc. v. Tams-Witmark Music Library, Inc., 474 F.Supp. 223 (S.D.N.Y.1979).

99 On consent in advance, see § 7.2.4(b) (timing of consent).

1 Lott v. Ayres, 611 S.W.2d 473 (Tex.Civ.App.1980); Lott v. Lott, 605 S.W.2d 665 (Tex.Civ.App.1980)(permissible for lawyer to withdraw from representing husband and continue to represent wife in action, originally brought to him by both spouses, for negligence against abortion service clinic). Such permitted representations against the interests of a former coclient should probably not extend much beyond what would be permissible under the rule governing initial consultation conflicts. See § 7.1.6 (initial consultation).

2 First Wis. Mortgage Trust v. First Wis. Corp., 584 F.2d 201 (7th Cir.1978)(en banc)(flexible approach to question indicates that if what is sought is laboriously gathered and expensive analysis of nonconfidential material, turnover of that portion of disqualified lawyer's work product should be ordered); IBM v. Levin, 579 F.2d 271, 283 (3d Cir.1978)(turnover of work product by disqualified firm to successor attorneys); Realco Serv., Inc. v. Holt, 479 F.Supp. 867, 880 (E.D.Pa.1979); Note, Attorney Disqualification and Access to Work Product: Toward a Principled Rule, 63 Cornell L.Rev. 1054 (1978); Comment, Access to the Disqualified Attorney's Work Product: A Plea for a Strict Prophylactic Rule, 52 U.Colo.L.Rev. 465 (1981); Comment, Access to the Work Product of a Disqualified Attorney, 1980 Wis.L.Rev. 105; Comment, Access to Work Product of Disqualified Counsel, 46 U.Chi.L. Rev. 443 (1979); Comment, Substitute Counsel's Access to Work Product of Disqualified Counsel, 21 Wm. & Mary L.Rev. 307 (1979); Comment, Attorney Disqualification and Work Product Availability: A Proposed Analysis, 47 Mo.L.Rev. 763 (1982).

3 Fund of Funds, Ltd. v. Arthur Andersen & Co., 567 F.2d 225 (2d Cir.1977).

4 In other ways discipline and motions to disqualify share attributes. For example, in each instance a state-

Judicial Power to Disqualify

A fundamental question that is presented by a motion by one party to disqualify the lawyer for another is whether the court has, and should exercise, the power to issue the order sought. Courts have traditionally claimed the power to disqualify as part of their inherent power to regulate the practice of law,[5] although in most other manifestations only the state's highest court can exercise the inherent power to regulate lawyers.[6] That does not explain, however, why a court should interrupt a proceeding between private parties to entertain a motion to disqualify the lawyer of one of them instead of simply reporting the matter to an appropriate lawyer disciplinary agency. More persuasive reasons have to do with the nature of the judicial function itself. When disqualification is based on the loyalty principle, a court might have legitimate concern with the vigor of the lawyer's representation and, thus, the existence of the proper conditions for the working of the adversarial system. When the confidentiality principle is invoked, the moving party draws in question both the policies implicit in the attorney-client privilege and, more broadly, an equity notion that neither litigant should have an unfair advantage over the other.[7]

But if no party moves to disqualify the lawyer, courts should be reluctant to issue advisory opinions and possibly interfere with the jurisdiction of lawyer disciplinary agencies to rule upon whether a lawyer's representation is proper.[8] If the party who would be expected to file a disqualification motion delays the filing for strategic purposes, courts properly hold that the objecting party waives the objection.[9] Granting a long-delayed motion to disqualify risks imposing on the now unrepresented party the financial burden and the uncertainty of finding another trusted lawyer, who must become educated in the matter while the proceeding is further delayed. In order to clear the air and to prevent manipulative delay by an opposing party, a lawyer with a concern about a possible conflict should be permitted to move early in a court proceeding for an order decreeing that the representation does not involve a conflict.[10]

Exercise of Discretion to Disqualify

The presence of judicial power to order disqualification does not, however, indicate that it is wise for a court to initiate an investigation into every situation that might reveal a violation of a mandatory rule and that thus might be an occasion for a lawyer disciplinary agency to consider imposing sanctions on a lawyer. Courts occasionally deny a motion to disqualify on a finding that the conflict was not sufficiently disabling. That does not necessarily suggest that the lawyer would be exonerated in a disciplinary proceeding.[11] It does indicate that courts are not oblivious to the possible strategic misuse of disqualification motions to achieve delay, impose expense, or attempt to embarrass. The possibility of strategic manipulation of conflict of interest rules fully justifies the requirement

ment made about a lawyer is absolutely privileged. E.g., Drummond v. Stahl, 127 Ariz. 122, 618 P.2d 616 (Ct.App. 1980), cert.denied 450 U.S. 967, 101 S.Ct. 1484, 67 L.Ed.2d 616 (1981).

5 General Motors Corp. v. City of New York, 501 F.2d 639, 643 n.11 (2d Cir.1974); State v. Jones, 180 Conn. 443, 429 A.2d 936, 939 (1980); Ennis v. Ennis, 88 Wis.2d 82, 276 N.W.2d 341, 348 (1979); People v. Superior Court, 19 Cal.3d 255, 261 n.4, 137 Cal.Rptr. 476, 561 P.2d 1164 (1977); Slater v. Rimer, Inc., 462 Pa. 138, 338 A.2d 584, 589 (1975), 37 U.Pitt.L.Rev. 577 (1976). See generally § 2.2.2.

6 See § 2.2.4.

7 Board of Educ. v. Nyquist, 590 F.2d 1241, 1246 (2d Cir. 1979).

8 In re Appeal of a Juvenile, 61 Ohio App.2d 235, 401 N.E.2d 937, 940 (1978).

9 Lewis v. Unigard Mut. Ins. Co., 83 A.D.2d 919, 442 N.Y.S.2d 522 (1981); Levitt v. Levitt, 9 Mass.App.Ct. 894, 403 N.E.2d 143 (1980); White v. Superior Court, 98 Cal. App.3d 51, 159 Cal.Rptr. 278 (1979).

10 Schloetter v. Railoc of Indiana, Inc., 546 F.2d 706 (7th Cir.1976); United States v. Standard Oil Co., 136 F.Supp. 345, 348 (S.D.N.Y.1955).

11 United States v. Curcio, 680 F.2d 881, 887 n.3 (2d Cir. 1982); Unified Sewerage Agency v. Jelco Inc., 646 F.2d 1339, 1350 n.15 (9th Cir.1981).

that a complaining party demonstrate some particular reason why judicial intervention is required instead of relying upon the workings of lawyer disciplinary agencies.[12] Nonetheless, a party could be unfairly burdened if forced to litigate against a lawyer with a conflict of interest substantially and adversely affecting that party.

In the Second Circuit, judicial weighing of these considerations has resulted in the standard that a conflicting representation will result in disqualification if the lawyer's continuation would likely "taint the trial," such as through the adverse use of confidential information.[13] Once the complaining party demonstrates standing and the necessary threat of unfairness, concern about possible manipulation of disqualification motions by other litigants should generate no lasting hostility toward the objecting party's own request for relief.

Standing to Move for Disqualification

A litigant's standing to raise an issue of conflict of interest is cognate to other kinds of standing problems. Here also, the general concern is to see that judicial and litigant resources are not needlessly expended in behalf of a litigant who, although able to show that an opposing party or lawyer has violated a rule, can point to no personal hurt or injury caused by the violation. Insistence on standing also assures that the appropriately contentious presentation of argument will occur, a normal condition for the effective functioning of the adversarial system (§ 10.1).

In order to raise an issue of conflict of interest the objecting party must be able to demonstrate that continued representation of the other party by his or her present lawyer would materially harm a cognizable interest of the objecting party.[14] That does not invariably mean that the complaining party must have been the client of the opposing lawyer. It suffices, for example, if the complaining party is a subsidiary of the lawyer's former client if there is a likelihood that the lawyer gained confidential information about the subsidiary during the prior representation.[15] But standing to raise an issue about a conflict of interest between other parties should not be recognized if the objecting party can not demonstrate any harmful impact upon that party's own interests from the asserted conflict.[16]

[12] MR "Scope" commentary; MR 1.7 comment (Conflict Charged by an Opposing Party); Morgan, Conflict of Interest and the Former Client in the Model Rules of Professional Conduct, 1980 Am.B.Found. Research J. 993, 1002 n.33. See generally Lindgren, Toward a New Standard of Attorney Disqualification, 1982 Am.B.Found. Research J. 419.

[13] The phrase originated in Lefrak v. Arabian American Oil Co., 527 F.2d 1136, 1141 (2d Cir.1975). See also In re IBM Corp., 687 F.2d 591, 596–97 (2d Cir.1982); W.T. Grant Co. v. Haines, 531 F.2d 671, 677 (2d Cir.1976). Cf., e.g., Pantori, Inc. v. Stephenson, 384 So.2d 1357, 1359 (Fla.App.1980)(purpose of disqualification hearing is not to determine whether lawyer should be disciplined but whether breach of conflict rules means that one party has "unfair advantage" that can only be eliminated by disqualification); Southern Valley Grain Dealers Ass'n v. Board of County Commrs., 257 N.W.2d 425, 432 (N.D.1977)(no reversal where no evidence that conflicted representation "played any part in the decision-making process").

[14] Hoidale v. Cooley, 143 Minn. 430, 433, 174 N.W. 413 (1919)(fact that same lawyer represented both defendant and intervening defendant does not concern plaintiff, who claims no relationship with lawyer). See also In re Yarn Processing Patent Validity Litigation, 530 F.2d 83, 88–90 (5th Cir.1976); Tadier v. American Photocopy Equipment Co., 531 F.Supp. 35 (S.D.N.Y.1981); Lowe v. Graves, 404 So.2d 652 (Ala.1981); Matter of Marine, 82 Wis.2d 602, 264 N.W.2d 285 (1978). But cf. Halperin v. Kissinger, 542 F.Supp. 829 (D.D.C.1982)(without discussion of standing, court undertakes to determine whether to grant plaintiffs' motion to disqualify some lawyers from representing codefendants on argument that joint representation hinders the plaintiffs' ability to conduct separate settlement negotiations with individual defendants). See also Aetna Casualty & Sur. Co. v. United States, 570 F.2d 1197 (4th Cir.), cert.denied 439 U.S. 821, 99 S.Ct. 87, 58 L.Ed.2d 113 (1978)(reversal of order disqualifying codefendants' lawyer on motion of plaintiffs without discussion of standing).

[15] Emle Industries, Inc. v. Patentex, Inc., 478 F.2d 562 (2d Cir.1973). See also McCourt Co. v. FPC Properties, Inc., 386 Mass. 145, 434 N.E.2d 1234 (1982). See generally § 7.1.6.

[16] In a leading case, however, the court without discussion assumed that a defendant who had lost verdicts to several plaintiffs had standing to seek a new trial on the ground that a conflict of interest among the plaintiffs existed, but without suggesting what deleterious impact the conflict might have had on any interest of the defendant in a fair trial. See Jedwabny v. Philadelphia Transp. Co., 390 Pa. 231, 135 A.2d 252 (1957), cert.denied 355 U.S. 966, 78 S.Ct. 557, 2 L.Ed.2d 541 (1958).

One argument for standing on the part of an adversary would be that if one of the jointly represented parties later withdrew consent or if the opposing single lawyer found it impossible to continue because of a deteriorating conflict problem, hardship would be imposed on all parties and the court because at least an extended recess would be required if substitute counsel then had to be retained.[17] That assumes that the court would in fact grant a recess. Another option for the court would be to deny the request for a recess on the ground that prior consent to the conflict binds both parties if detriment to the opposing party and the court would result from granting a recess. Any party injured by the actual conflict would be relegated to filing a malpractice action against his or her faithless lawyer. That course would incur the risk in an extreme case, of a charade of hopelessly contending "coparties" and create the possibility for jury misunderstanding. On the other hand, permitting an opposing party to raise the issue creates a clear danger of tactical use of the motion to disqualify and could impair the right of the jointly represented parties to choose their own counsel. Perhaps the best solution would be to defer resolution of the motion until a late point during discovery, when it might be more clearly determined whether a nonconsentable conflict in fact exists.[18]

Some courts have taken a different course despite the cogency and force of the reasons for limiting standing to file a disqualification motion to a party actually affected by an asserted conflict. Those courts have proclaimed a broad duty on the part of courts to police the legal profession, asserting a cognate duty on the part of all advocates to alert the court to any possible violation of professional rules on conflicts of interest regardless of the lack of injury to the advocate's client.[19] Often such statements are made in the face of facts clearly showing that the objecting party had standing. If standing is lacking, it is preferable to leave general policing of the profession to the disciplinary agencies, including the disciplinary arms of the very courts asked to entertain the motion, if only lawyer discipline and not some other public interest or need is at stake.

Prosecutor Standing in Criminal Cases

A controversial area of standing concerns the ability of a prosecutor to object to joint representation of codefendants or of grand jury witnesses.[20] The theory of courts that grant standing to the prosecutor is that the state has an interest in the proper administration of criminal justice and, possibly, in assuring that a criminal conviction will not be overturned because of an impermissible conflict of interest.[21] Other courts, however, have refused to apply an automatic rule to disqualify a lawyer from jointly representing codefendants in a criminal case [22] and have required a particularized showing of impairment of the grand jury or other criminal

[17] Shadid v. Jackson, 521 F.Supp. 87, 89 (E.D.Tex.1981); Cannon v. U.S. Acoustics Corp., 398 F.Supp. 209, 221 (N.D.Ill.1975), reversed in part on other grounds, 532 F.2d 1118 (7th Cir.1976).

[18] Cf. Richmond Hilton Assoc. v. City of Richmond, 690 F.2d 1086, 1089 (4th Cir.1982)(mere "potential conflict" not sufficient to require disqualification at early stages of case).

[19] Estates Theatres, Inc. v. Columbia Pictures Ind., Inc., 345 F.Supp. 93, 98 (S.D.N.Y.1972). See generally Black v. Missouri, 492 F.Supp. 848, 861–62 (W.D.Mo.1980), and authorities cited. The court in *Black* asserted a special need for careful policing of conflicts in school desegregation litigation because of the "interests of the public" in assuring that the proceedings were entirely valid. 492 F.Supp. at 861. That seems a more sympathetic reason for relaxed standing rules than an interest in policing the profession.

[20] The leading case holds that the prosecutor has standing. Pirillo v. Takiff, 462 Pa. 511, 341 A.2d 896, reaffirmed, 466 Pa. 187, 352 A.2d 11 (1975), cert.denied 423 U.S. 1083, 96 S.Ct. 873, 47 L.Ed.2d 94 (1976).

[21] In re Gopman, 531 F.2d 262 (5th Cir.1976)(prosecutor's standing stems from every lawyer's duty to bring ethical violations to attention of court; public interest in a properly functioning judicial system prevails over a client's Sixth Amendment right to counsel of choice); Pirillo v. Takiff, supra n.20 (right to counsel of choice and right of lawyers to practice law may be impaired or eliminated by overriding state interest, here grand jury secrecy and protection of investigative function for protection of society).

[22] In re Investigation before April 1975 Grand Jury, 531 F.2d 600 (D.C.Cir.1976); In re Taylor, 567 F.2d 1183 (2d Cir.1977); In re Investigation before Lynchburg Grand Jury, 563 F.2d 652 (4th Cir.1977). The entire

justice system function before ordering disqualification.[23]

Waiver of Objection

A frequently litigated issue concerns a claim by the lawyer who is in danger of being disqualified that the objection has been waived because of the objecting party's failure to raise the issue in a timely fashion. Some few decisions have announced a general rule that an objection to a conflicting representation is never waived.[24] But most courts seem indisposed to permit an objecting party who knows of the ground for an objection to wait until an opposing party's reliance upon the services of his or her lawyer has developed to a great extent before objecting to the lawyer's continued representation.[25] Arguably, delay in raising a disqualification objection might be excused on the ground that the parties were actively pursuing settlement negotiations.[26] A finding of waiver of the grounds for a disqualification motion in litigation should not inevitably lead to a conclusion in a disciplinary proceeding against the lawyer that no disciplinary violation has occurred. Foisting the consequences of a private litigant's delay upon the litigant is different from foisting the same waiver result upon the public, the courts, and the legal profession.

Hearings on Disqualification Motions

Generally courts are able to deal with disqualification motions without the need for extended evidentiary hearings. Often the issues can be adequately ventilated by affidavits, transcripts of prior proceedings, and oral statements of lawyers.[27] A factual hearing is necessary only if an important fact is disputed and its resolution is necessary to decision of the motion.[28] Trial judges should be required to state their reasons for a disqualification ruling to permit meaningful appellate review.[29] But more elaborate proceedings would only compound the problem of delay that disqualification motions entail, as well as risk a wasteful diversion of judicial resources into what might be a "distasteful, even obnox-

subject is extensively analyzed in Moore, Disqualification of an Attorney Representing Multiple Witnesses before a Grand Jury: Legal Ethics and the Stonewall Defense, 27 UCLA L.Rev. 1 (1979)(common lawyer for witnesses before grand jury should be disqualified only to protect witnesses against improvident or forced consent to conflict or to prevent perjury or other manifest corruptions of grand jury and not simply to avoid impairment of grand jury functions). For a contrary view, see Vaira & Huyett, Time for a Rule Certain: A Proposal to End Representation of Multiple Grand Jury Witnesses, 85 Dick.L.Rev. 381 (1981).

23 In re Special February 1977 Grand Jury, 581 F.2d 1262 (7th Cir.1978)(trial court within its discretion in refusing to find sufficient evidence of actual conflict of interest); In re Investigation before Lynchburg Grand Jury, 563 F.2d 652 (4th Cir.1977)(while simple multiple representation of codefendants does not disqualify if clients consent, when lawyer's cocounsel was also target of grand jury investigation, protection of secrecy and proper investigative function of grand jury required disqualification); In re Investigation before April 1975 Grand Jury, 531 F.2d 600, 606–07 n.11 (D.C.Cir.1976)(*Pirillo*, supra n.20, wrongly decided; multiple representation needn't necessarily harm grand jury proceedings, and no federal law prohibits grand jury witness from revealing contents of own testimony to others); In re Grand Jury Empaneled Jan. 21, 1975, 536 F.2d 1009 (3d Cir.1976); In re Special Investigation No. 231, 295 Md. 366, 455 A.2d 442 (1983).

24 Emle Indus., Inc. v. Patentex, Inc., 478 F.2d 562, 574 (2d Cir. 1973).

25 Trust Corp. v. Piper Aircraft Corp., 701 F.2d 85 (9th Cir.1983); Central Milk Producers Co-op v. Sentry Food Stores, Inc., 573 F.2d 988 (8th Cir.1978); Hall v. Hall, 421 So.2d 1270, 1271 (Ala.App.1982); Lau v. Valu-Bilt Homes, Ltd., 59 Haw. 283, 582 P.2d 195, 202–03 (1978).

26 Lee v. Todd, 555 F.Supp. 628, 632 (W.D.Tenn.1982).

27 General Mill Supply Co. v. SCA Services, Inc., 697 F.2d 704, 710–711 (6th Cir.1982); Bohack Corp. v. Gulf & Western Indus., Inc., 607 F.2d 258 (2d Cir.1979). The suggestion is advanced, without comment, in Kadish v. Commodity Futures Trading Comm'n, 553 F.Supp. 660, 663 (N.D.Ill.1982), that a firm's participation in a hearing on imputed disqualification could expose otherwise untainted firm members to confidential information from the opposing party that would independently require its disqualification. Surely evidence advanced at a hearing cannot be considered confidential for that purpose. In addition, courts employ presumptions that adequately avoid the need to divulge confidential information in the course of passing on conflict objections. See generally § 7.4.3 (substantial relationship standard for former-client conflicts), § 7.6.3 (imputed disqualification).

28 Melamed v. ITT Continental Baking Co., 534 F.2d 82 (6th Cir.1976); Fullmer v. Harper, 517 F.2d 20 (10th Cir. 1975).

29 Kreda v. Rush, 550 F.2d 888 (3d Cir.1977).

ious procedure" because of the high lawyer emotions that such motions often engender.[30]

In both discipline and disqualification cases the burden is on the party asserting an impermissible conflict to demonstrate a violation.[31] Although there is wide agreement on that, some courts confidently assert that disqualification must follow when there is the slightest doubt that a representation is permissible.[32] Such statements can usually be reconciled by taking the "slightest doubt" standard to describe, not who must present substantial and persuasive evidence of an impermissible conflict, but what action should be taken in cases where the evidence both in favor of and opposed to disqualification is equally balanced. In other words, the "slightest doubt" expression might relate more to a burden of persuasion.

Appellate Review

For reasons that are not entirely clear, the mid-seventies saw an exponential increase in the number of disqualification motions against opposing lawyers. The increase in motions raised the possibility that an allowance of an appeal from a lower court's order would deluge the appellate courts.[33] Moreover, the facts in many cases suggest that the motion is based not on a desire to protect legitimate client interests in confidentiality or loyalty but to harass an opponent and, possibly, to deprive him or her of the services of a lawyer known to be a worthy advocate.[34] In 1981 the Supreme Court quieted a dispute among lower federal courts over the appealability of an order *denying* disqualification, holding that such an order could not be appealed until there was a final judgment on the merits of the underlying action.[35] The Court has not yet decided, however, whether an order *granting* a motion to disqualify is appealable, although the general view of the courts of appeal is that an appeal will lie.[36]

The decisions are in a variegated state concerning the scope of appellate review of an otherwise appealable lower court determination on an issue of conflict of interest. A common view is that the lower court's rulings

30 General Mill Supply Co. v. SCA Services, Inc., 697 F.2d 704, 711 (6th Cir.1982).

31 Duncan v. Merrill Lynch, Pierce, Fenner & Smith, Inc., 646 F.2d 1020, 1028 (5th Cir.), cert.denied 454 U.S. 895, 102 S.Ct. 394, 70 L.Ed.2d 211 (1981)(former-client conflict); but cf. Westinghouse Elec. Corp. v. Gulf Oil Corp., 588 F.2d 221, 224 (7th Cir.1978)(former-client conflict).

32 The approach of the Code in debatable conflicts situations is that the attorney "should resolve all doubts against the propriety of the representation." EC 5–15. The same approach has been advocated for courts in passing upon motions to disqualify a lawyer in an arguable conflicts situation. E.g., International Business Machines Corp. v. Levin, 579 F.2d 271, 283 (3d Cir.1978); Coffelt v. Shell, 577 F.2d 30, 32 (8th Cir.1978); Reardon v. Marlayne, Inc., 83 N.J. 460, 416 A.2d 852, 858 (1980). See also § 7.1.5.

33 Community Broadcasting of Boston, Inc. v. FCC, 546 F.2d 1022, 1027 (D.C.Cir.1976): "Because of the fluidity of membership in large metropolitan law firms and the pattern of movement by lawyers between various employment positions, an appearance of conflict of interest can easily be alleged in many cases" leaving appellate courts "grappling with a deluge of interlocutory appeals that place the Court of Appeals in the role of overseer of the ethics of members of the legal profession." See Comment, The Ethics of Moving to Disqualify Opposing Counsel for Conflict of Interest, 1979 Duke L.J. 1310.

34 Melamed v. ITT Continental Banking Co., 592 F.2d 290, 295 (6th Cir.1979); Board of Educ. v. Nyquist, 590 F.2d 1241, 1246 (2d Cir.1979), and cases cited.

A patently frivolous motion to disqualify can perhaps be sanctioned, and similar motions thus discouraged, by the imposition of attorney fees and costs directly on the lawyer who filed the offending motion. See North American Foreign Trading Corp. v. Zale Corp., 83 F.R.D. 293 (S.D.N.Y.1979)(legal fees of $28,000 taxed against lawyers for defendant for filing patently frivolous motion to disqualify; facts showed that plaintiff's lawyers' former representation of defendant had no relationship to plaintiff's present claim).

35 Firestone Tire & Rubber Co., v. Risjord, 449 U.S. 368, 101 S.Ct. 669, 676, 66 L.Ed.2d 571 (1981).

36 United States v. Phillips, 699 F.2d 798 (6th Cir.1983); Freeman v. Chicago Musical Instrument Co., 689 F.2d 715 (7th Cir.1982); In re Petroleum Prods. Antitrust Litig., 658 F.2d 1355, 1356–58 (9th Cir.1981), certiorari denied 455 U.S. 990, 102 S.Ct. 1615, 71 L.Ed.2d 850 (1982); Board of Educ. v. Nyquist, 590 F.2d 1241, 1247 n.8 (2d Cir.1979). But see United States v. Greger, 657 F.2d 1109 (9th Cir. 1981), cert. denied 461 U.S. 913, 103 S.Ct. 1891, 77 L.Ed. 2d 281 (1983)(no appeal from order disqualifying privately retained lawyer in criminal case, because ability to obtain review of disqualification order after conviction is plainly adequate). The issue has since been put to rest in Richardson-Merrell, Inc. v. Koller, ___ U.S. ___, 105 S.Ct. 2757, 86 L.Ed.2d 340 (1985), which held that an order disqualifying a lawyer in a civil case was not a collateral order subject to immediate appeal.

are reviewable only for abuse of discretion, unless a purely legal issue is involved.[37] The familiar slipperiness of the law-fact distinction seems to have left appellate courts with few noticeable constraints in reviewing conflict of interest rulings.

WESTLAW REFERENCES

45k58 +p conflict***

Discipline of Lawyers for Impermissible Conflicts

attorney counsel** lawyer /s disqualif! /s disciplin***

Judicial Disqualification Orders

attorney counsel** lawyer /s motion move /3 disqualif! /s conflict***

Other Judicially Administered Remedies

attorney counsel** lawyer /s conflict*** +2 interest /p enjoin*** injuncti**

attorney counsel** lawyer /s conflict*** /p (dismiss*** fee malpractice /5 forfeit*** penalty sui**) (judgment judgement will /5 aside void!)

Rescinded Consent

attorney counsel** lawyer /s represent! /s joint simultaneous** /s consen!

Judicial Disqualification Orders

attorney counsel** lawyer /s motion move /3 disqualif! /s conflict***

Other Judicially Administered Remedies

attorney counsel** lawyer /s conflict*** +2 interest /p enjoin*** injuncti**

attorney counsel** lawyer /s conflict*** /p (dismiss*** fee malpractice /5 forfeit*** penalty sui**) (judgment judgement will /5 aside void!)

Rescinded Consent

attorney counsel** lawyer /s represent! /s joint simultaneous** /s consen!

Consultation with Successor Lawyer

topic(45) /p successor succeed*** /4 lawyer attorney counsel** "law firm" /p confiden! "work product"

Procedures in General

motion move* /3 disqualif! /p "conflict of interest" /p attorney lawyer counsel** "law firm"

Judicial Power to Disqualify

jurisdiction** power authority /3 court judge tribunal /s disqualif! /p "conflict of interest" /p attorney lawyer counsel** "law firm"

Exercise of Discretion to Disqualify

discretion*** /5 court judge tribunal exercis*** /s disqualif! /p "conflict of interest" /p attorney lawyer counsel** "law firm"

Standing to Move for Disqualification

motion move* /3 disqualif! /s standing /p "conflict of interest" /p attorney lawyer counsel** "law firm"

Waiver of Objection

waive* /s disqualif! & topic(45)

Hearings on Disqualification Motions

hearing /s disqualif! /5 motion move*

Appellate Review

(appeal! appellate /5 review) (discretion*** /3 abuse*) /s "conflict of interest"

§ 7.2 CLIENT CONSENT TO CONFLICTS

§ 7.2.1 General

The Limited Allowance for Conflicting Representations

Not every conflict of interest precludes a lawyer from undertaking a representation. In some conflict situations it is still possible for a lawyer to represent the client if effective client consent is given. Consent is relevant, it is important to note, only if the conflict would otherwise disqualify the lawyer from proceeding in its absence. The concept of consent in effect treats the right of the client to a conflict-free representation as one of those rights that a fully informed client should be able to relinquish.

The breadth of permissible consent might reflect a sense that the conflict of interest rules have sometimes gone further along the way of preventive legal rules than is necessary in every instance. Nonetheless, there is a strong element of client protectiveness in

[37] Pantry Pride, Inc. v. Finley, Kumble, Wagner, Heine, Underberg & Casey, 697 F.2d 524, 528 (3d Cir.1982); Richmond Hilton Assoc. v. City of Richmond, 690 F.2d 1086, 1088 (4th Cir.1982); Gas-A-Tron of Arizona v. Union Oil Co., 534 F.2d 1322, 1325 (9th Cir.), cert.denied 429 U.S. 861, 97 S.Ct. 164, 50 L.Ed.2d 139 (1976). Cf. Aetna Casualty & Sur. Co. v. United States, 570 F.2d 1197 (4th Cir.), cert.denied 439 U.S. 821, 99 S.Ct. 87, 58 L.Ed.2d 113 (1978); Woods v. Covington County Bank, 537 F.2d 804 (5th Cir.1976)(if facts not in dispute, district courts enjoy no advantage over appellate courts in formulation and application of ethical norms).

the consent rules themselves. That is recognizable in the rule that the burden is on the lawyer to initiate the question of consent; it is not the obligation of the client to recognize the problem and seek the lawyer's reaction to it. It is also recognizable in the rule that limits the occasions on which a lawyer may proceed with a representation even after the client consents, in effect recognizing a category of "nonconsentable" conflicts.

General Duty of Lawyer Representing Conflicting Interests with Adequate Consent

Consent is not a balm that, once it is given, heals all future lawyer wrongs in the representation. Even with a consent that is perfectly counseled and freely given, the lawyer representing conflicting interests remains responsible to render effective and competent assistance to all clients. A lawyer who fails to maintain neutrality, compromised no more than the consent allows, is liable to a malpractice recovery by a disadvantaged joint client.[38] The lawyer is also in violation of mandatory professional rules requiring zealous representation of a client.[39] Moreover, the lawyer has violated the mandatory rules on conflicts because the client's consent, once exceeded, is no longer a defense.

Consent Compared to Waiver, Estoppel, and Laches

Consent is not to be confused with other, related doctrines that excuse a lawyer's failure to obtain consent, at least for the purpose of judicial disqualification. The chief of those doctrines are waiver, estoppel, and laches. *Waiver* is the purposeful relinquishment of a known legal right—for example, a statement in a pleading that the party would not contest the right of an adversary's lawyer to appear despite an apparent conflict.[40] *Estoppel* is the general doctrine, equitable in origin, that a party who has induced another to take substantial steps constituting a change of position, in reliance on a condition created or contributed to by the estopped party, cannot later assert that the opposite party had no right to take those steps. As applied to conflicts, if a party who knowingly is entitled to object to a lawyer's conflicting representation of another party fails to do so until the point has been reached that removal of the lawyer would cause substantial hardship to the lawyer's client, the silent party is estopped.[41] *Laches* is the doctrine that relies entirely upon an inordinately long period of time to bar the party who otherwise would have been entitled to object, perhaps even in the absence of an estoppel.[42] It is important to note that those defensive doctrines are only reasons for

[38] Hill v. Okay Constr. Co., 312 Minn. 324, 252 N.W.2d 107, 117 (1977): "[lawyer who represented buyer and seller in same transaction] does not obligate himself to adhere to any higher duty or standard of care than if he endeavored to represent only one of those parties. On the other hand, he clearly owes no lesser duty to each of his clients, and he must protect the interests of each as zealously as if their interests were his sole responsibility."

[39] DR 7–101(A)(1)(fail to seek lawful objectives of client); DR 7–101(A)(2)(fail to carry out a contract of employment); MR 1.3 (act with reasonable diligence and promptness in representing client); MR 1.2 (abiding by client's decisions regarding the objectives of the representation).

[40] City of Cleveland v. Cleveland Elec. Illuminating Co., 440 F.Supp. 193, 205 (N.D.Ohio 1976), affirmed 573 F.2d 1310 (6th Cir.1977), cert.denied 435 U.S. 996, 98 S.Ct. 1648, 56 L.Ed.2d 85 (1978). Waiver of a conflict in one lawsuit does not relate to similar but distinct litigation. See In re Corrugated Container Antitrust Litigation, 659 F.2d 1341, 1348 (5th Cir.1981).

[41] Central Milk Producers Cooperative v. Sentry Food Stores, Inc., 573 F.2d 988 (8th Cir.1978)(defendant's lawyer expressly approved screening measures taken by opposing law firm and waited until two years into pretrial work before moving for disqualification); Idrissi v. Idrissi, 173 Conn. 295, 377 A.2d 330 (1977); Fugnitto v. Fugnitto, 113 Misc.2d 666, 452 N.Y.S.2d 976 (Sup.Ct.App.Term 1982); United Nuclear Corp. v. General Atomic Co., 96 N.M. 155, 629 P.2d 231, 320–321 (1980), cert.denied 451 U.S. 901, 101 S.Ct. 1966, 68 L.Ed.2d 289 (1981). But cf. Emle Industries, Inc. v. Patentex, Inc., 478 F.2d 562, 574 (2d Cir.1973); Kraus v. Davis, 6 Cal.App.3d 484, 85 Cal. Rptr. 846 (1970)(waiver will not generally be presumed from mere delay in raising objection).

[42] Redd v. Shell Oil Co., 518 F.2d 311 (10th Cir.1975); Marco v. Dulles, 169 F.Supp. 622, 632–33 (S.D.N.Y.), appeal dism'd, 268 F.2d 192 (2d Cir.1959). Occasionally courts take the unfounded view that laches is never a defense. E.g., Empire Linotype School, Inc. v. United States, 143 F.Supp. 627, 631 (S.D.N.Y.1956).

refusal of judicial disqualification of a lawyer from continuing with a representation already substantially undertaken. They do not necessarily have anything to do with the continuing power of a disciplinary agency to initiate proceedings.

WESTLAW REFERENCES

The Limited Allowance for Conflicting Representations

45k20

General Duty of Lawyer Representing Conflicting Interests with Adequate Consent

consen! /p "conflict of interest" /p attorney lawyer counsel** "law firm" client /p zeal! effective** competen**

Consent Compared to Waiver, Estoppel, and Laches

consen! /p "conflict of interest" /p attorney lawyer counsel** "law firm" client /p waive* estopp** laches

§ 7.2.2 Consentable Conflicts: Theory and the Rules

Contract and Autonomy Theories of Consent

Giving effect to a client's consent to a conflicting representation might rest either on the ground of contract freedom or on the related ground of personal autonomy of a client to choose whatever champion the client feels is best suited to vindicate the client's legal entitlements. As will be seen, professional rules and judicial decisions implement a balanced version of those theories by permitting a lawyer to proceed only in some conflict situations and then only after rather elaborate protective steps have been taken to assure that a client's consent is fully informed and voluntary. Many remaining situations will present conflicts that are not curable by consent.

Some extreme versions of either a contract or autonomy theory might reject limitations on client consent, viewing consent as a universal solvent that dissolves all conflicts. But such a view could only proceed on assumptions that are factually arbitrary and ignore substantial competing considerations. The freedom-to-contract theory must assume that the market for exchange of such consent bargains is a largely perfect one, in which buyers and sellers who are equally well informed predominate, or one in which it is efficient to preclude later client complaints even if the consent to the conflict was ill informed.

Such a theory assumes conditions that hardly characterize the market for legal services or the typical relationship between clients and their lawyers when a question of conflict arises. The lawyer possesses much more specialized knowledge of the probable strengths and weaknesses of the claims and position of each client and of the relative merits of joint or separate representations. That knowledge places lawyers in a position of bargaining superiority.[43] The lawyer has interests in maximizing an eventual fee by representing more clients and in minimizing costs of the representation by controlling more facets of it. The lawyer cannot therefore regularly be expected to be altruistic in giving advice to clients about conflicts. Most clients have no other competing legal "products" for which they can shop or forms of insurance that they can turn to as alternatives or as hedges against an improvident consent to a conflicting representation. And, because of continuing restrictions on lawyer advertising, a client's ability to know about the services of other lawyers is very limited.

Even if perfectly well informed clients can be assumed, it does not invariably follow that it should be one of freedom's proudest boasts that a client should be able to commit self-evisceration in the course of a legal representation. It is true that American constitutional liberties proceed on the highly individualistic theory that the "respect for the individual is the lifeblood of the law." [44] But respect for incompetent clients and those pressed into ill-

43 Cf. Anderson, Conflicts of Interest: Efficiency, Fairness and Corporate Structure, 25 UCLA L.Rev. 738 (1978).

44 Brennan, J., concurring, in Illinois v. Allen, 397 U.S. 337, 350–51, 90 S.Ct. 1057, 1064, 25 L.Ed.2d 353 (1970),

advised acquiescence by the force of economics or the influence of a disadvantageous bargaining environment does not require that asserted consents be universally honored. Nor do autonomy values always offset the claims of the generality of citizens that their systems of civil and criminal justice produce creditable results.[45] Taking account of other interests may require, not extreme paternalism,[46] but imposing some limits on client consent to take account of broader competing interests.

Consent in the 1969 Code

Both the 1969 Code and the 1983 Model Rules assert as a basic notion that client consent will not always cure a serious conflict of interest.[47] The approach taken by the Code was imperfectly expressed from the beginning. Perhaps because of a drafting oversight,[48] the provisions allowing client consent are contained only in the Disciplinary Rules dealing with impaired professional judgment,[49] business dealings with a client,[50] some of the other-client conflict rules,[51] settling related claims,[52] and third-party fee payment.[53] Client consent is also provided for without qualification in the confidentiality rules.[54] Conspicuously absent is any provision for client consent for either imputed-disqualification conflicts[55] or former-government-lawyer conflicts.[56] Courts have largely ignored the absence of an imputed-disqualification consent provision and with some resistance have also ignored the lack of provision for governmental-client consent. Most of the Code consent provisions recognize effective client consent only after disclosure.

The most general rule on consent, DR 5–105(C), contains a requirement of consentability in addition to client consent, a condition that has influenced the interpretation of other consent rules as well. It sets out a two-part test for determining whether a lawyer may represent multiple clients despite a conflict. First, it must be "obvious that [the lawyer] can adequately represent the interest of each client." Second, each client must freely consent to the compromised representation after a full disclosure.

Reasonably Consentable Conflicts in the 1983 Model Rules

Model Rule 1.7 provides an approach similar to the two-condition Code rule on client consent, although it is differently worded. Rule 1.7 broadly prohibits conflicting representations of several described kinds unless

quoted in Faretta v. California, 422 U.S. 806, 834, 95 S.Ct. 2525, 2540, 45 L.Ed.2d 562 (1975).

45 Maxwell v. Superior Court, 30 Cal.3d 606, 180 Cal. Rptr. 177 n.10, 639 P.2d 248, 256 n.10 (1982)(in holding that trial court cannot prevent fully informed defendant from freely consenting to representation by lawyer who negotiated publication-rights fee contract, "we do not deprive the trial court of power to act when an actual conflict materializes during the proceedings, producing an obviously deficient performance. Then the court's power and duty to ensure fairness and preserve the credibility of its judgments extends to recusal even when an informed defendant, for whatever reason, is cooperating in counsel's tactics.").

46 For example, either extreme paternalism or an utter disregard for client interests is often reflected in decisions that refuse to permit consent to cure conflicts under Code DR 5–101 and 5–102 (the advocate-witness rules). E.g., Supreme Beef Processors v. American Consumer Indus., 441 F.Supp. 1064 (N.D.Tex.1977). See generally § 7.5.2.

47 A scholar has recently criticized both the 1969 Code and the Model Rules for their failure to define the circumstances in which conflicts are nonconsentable. She proposes in their stead a standard under which client consent would always cure conflicts, no matter how apparently severe, so long as the client possessed the capacity to make an informed and free decision. Moore, Conflicts of Interest in the Simultaneous Representation of Multiple Clients: A Proposed Solution to the Current Confusion and Controversy, 61 Tex.L.Rev. 211 (1982).

48 See Morgan, The Evolving Concept of Professional Responsibility, 90 Harv.L.Rev. 702, 730 n.112 (1977).

49 DR 5–101(A).

50 DR 5–104(A).

51 DR 5–105(C).

52 DR 5–106(A).

53 DR 5–107(A).

54 DR 4–101(C)(a); see also DR 4–101(B)(3).

55 DR 5–105(D).

56 DR 9–101(B). Also omitted is any allowance for consent exceptions in the case of such other conflicts as advocate-witness conflicts (DR 5–101(B); DR 5–102), advancing nonlitigation expenses to a client (DR 5–103(B)), or publication-rights contracts (DR 5–104(B)). The absence of client consent for each of those otherwise forbidden activities has also been controversial. See §§ 7.5.2, 9.2.3, 9.3.3.

two conditions are met. First, the lawyer must "reasonably believe" that the representation will not be adversely affected because of the conflict.[57] Second, the client or clients involved must "consent after consultation." [58] Each element of the largely parallel, two-fold tests in the Code and the Model Rules gives rise to impressive difficulties of interpretation and application.

WESTLAW REFERENCES

Consent in the 1969 Code

consen! /p 5–101(a) 5–104(a) 5–105(c) 5–106(a) 5–107(a) 4–101(c) /p (impair! /5 judgment) (business /5 deal*** transaction) settle! third-party confiden!

Reasonably Consentable Conflicts in the 1983 Model Rules

"model rule" m.r. /8 1.7

§ 7.2.3 Consentable Conflicts: Reasonably Adequate Representation

Standard for Consentability under the Lawyer Codes

The "obviously adequate" test that is to be employed under the Code's DR 5–105(C) in determining whether a conflict may be consented to cannot be applied literally. Recall that the test is relevant only if under DR 5–105(A) the lawyer's professional judgment "will be or is likely to be" adversely affected by a conflict of interest. One might well ask how it could ever be "obvious" in such a situation that the representation, despite the conflict, can be adequate.[59] Moreover, the Code's language does not clearly indicate whether the standard of "obvious" adequacy is an objective or a subjective one. It seems both preferable and consistent to insist that a lawyer's necessarily self-interested feelings not play a pivotal role.[60] The only internally consistent reading of the Code's test is to regard it as simply an emphatic insistence that consent be relied upon only if it is objectively clear that the threat to the lawyer's independent judgment is minimal.

The Model Rules, in a comment, suggest a possibly less restrictive view than that of the Code, but in language that is hardly conclusive. According to the comment to MR 1.7, the test for determining whether it is proper for a lawyer to "reasonably believe" (MR 1.7(b)(1)) that the representation will not be adversely affected by the conflict is the judgment of "a disinterested lawyer." [61] Importantly, the comment does not require that either lawyer or client in fact consult with such a disinterested adviser. Instead, the lawyer burdened with the conflict is to assess in a dispassionate way whether to undertake the representation. Such a standard rather transparently supplies not much of a test at all and, as do the Code's formulations, simply stresses the importance of caution before a lawyer proceeds even with client consent. At the very least, the Model Rules approach, with its reference to "reasonable" belief and a "disinterested lawyer," does suggest that an objective standard is to be applied, whatever a lawyer's subjective intentions.

[57] The same phraseology is echoed in the parts of the general conflict rule dealing with two different kinds of conflicts. See MR 1.7(a)(1)(simultaneous conflict); MR 1.7(b)(1)(other conflicts).

[58] Id.

[59] The puzzle is presented and left unsolved in In re Porter, 283 Or. 517, 584 P.2d 744, 749 n.5 (1978). At least two states adopted revised versions of DR 5–105(C) that replaced the "obvious" language with "reasonably determines" (Alabama) or "believes" (New Jersey). See ABA Code of Professional Responsibility by State, DR 5–105, at 17–18 (1977).

[60] The debate over whether DR 5–105(C) sets forth an objective or subjective standard is traced in Annotated Code of Professional Responsibility 242–43 (O.Maru ed. 1979).

[61] The suppressed "Code Comparison" note of earlier drafts of the Model Rules stated that, independently of consent, the representation must "reasonably appear to be compatible with the best interests of the client." See MR 1.7 code comparison at 51 (May 30, 1981). The then accompanying Legal Background note made no mention of the problem of defining nonconsentable conflicts. Id. at 51–58.

To the extent that the Model Rules adopt an objective standard of assessing the advisability of a conflicting representation, its framers might have relied upon an early draft of DR 5–105(C) of the 1969 Code that would also have stated the "obvious" adequacy standard in terms of a "lawyer of ordinary prudence." See ABF Annotated Code of Professional Responsibility 242 (O.Maru ed.1979).

The Concept of Consentability in the Courts

Cases decided under the Code and earlier common-law decisions supply some insights into the meaning of the concept of a nonconsentable conflict. The category is an important one because client consent in a nonconsentable conflict case does not forestall either discipline [62] or disqualification.[63] The cases suggest the sensible idea that consentability has less to do with the ability of a lawyer to proceed "reasonably" after consent and more to do with the permissibility of accepting the consent of an impaired or less than fully informed client. In turn, courts detect impaired consent if it is objectively unreasonable for the client to have given consent.

Some decisions refer to "irreconcilable" conflicts, which are too severe for the cure of client consent.[64] Others speak of the need to avoid paternalism in the attempt to balance delicately an individual's right to a freely chosen lawyer with a lawyer's obligation to avoid a representation in which loyalty is realistically "impossible." [65] For example, in a California case the same lawyer represented both an employee accused of embezzlement and his employer, who was seeking to recover under a fidelity bond against an insurance company. The employer could recover on the indemnity bond only by convincing the court that the employee had intentionally embezzled funds; yet in other pending litigation the employee was attempting to deny such embezzlement in order to escape personal liability. The lawyer had been retained and was being paid by the employer. The court refused to permit the joint representation despite a claim that the employee had given fully informed consent.[66] Yet the court was unwilling to hold that the consent itself was defective. Instead, the court classified the conflict as nonconsentable. In an Arizona discipline case,[67] a lawyer had acted for a client in selling a business to a partnership in which the lawyer held a substantial interest. The lawyer-buyer and client-seller had different and irreconcilable objectives with respect to taxes, security for the price, financing, and other major goals. The court refused to permit the lawyer to function in a blatant conflict of interest situation despite the alleged fully informed and free consent of the client.[68]

The requirement that a lawyer be able to provide a reasonably adequate representation, even if the client explicitly consents, originated in decisions predating the 1969 Code.[69] The law of fiduciary relationships seeks to assure both that the ceremonial procedures of the relationship are properly observed and that the outcomes of the relationship are substantively fair to the client. The concept finds expression in such related conflict of interest doctrine as the common-law rules regulating business dealings between a lawyer and client (§ 8.11.3). Not only must a lawyer in such dealings with a client make full disclosure and obtain the client's fully informed consent, but the substantive aspects of the deal must be demonstrably fair enough that a court will later say that the presumption of fraud that normally attaches to such transactions has been overcome.[70]

[62] In re Mercer, 133 Ariz. 391, 652 P.2d 130 (1982); In re Holmes, 290 Or. 173, 619 P.2d 1284, 1289 (1980).

[63] United States v. Flanagan, 679 F.2d 1072 (3d Cir. 1982), reversed on other grounds 459 U.S. 1011, 103 S.Ct. 721, 74 L.Ed.2d 948 (1983); United States v. Dolan, 570 F.2d 1177 (3d Cir.1978); United States v. Agosto, 528 F.Supp. 1300, 1310 (D.Minn.1981), vacated and remanded for further fact-finding 675 F.2d 965, 976 (8th Cir.1982), on remand 538 F.Supp. 1149, 1150, n.1 (D.Minn.1982).

[64] In re Cohn, 46 N.J. 202, 216 A.2d 1 (1966); Greene v. Greene, 47 N.Y.2d 447, 418 N.Y.S.2d 379, 391 N.E.2d 1355, 1358 (1979).

[65] Unified Sewerage Agency v. Jelco Inc., 646 F.2d 1339, 1350 (9th Cir.1981).

[66] The court denounced consent to such a joint representation as " 'unthinkable,' " contrary to " 'common sense,' " and the result of a consent that must have been " 'neither intelligent nor informed.' " Valley Title Co. v. Superior Court, 124 Cal.App.3d 867, 177 Cal.Rptr. 643, 652 (1981), quoting from Klemm v. Superior Court, 75 Cal.App.3d 893, 898, 142 Cal.Rptr. 509 (1977).

[67] In re Mercer, 133 Ariz. 391, 652 P.2d 130 (1982).

[68] Cf. § 8.11 (business dealings with clients).

[69] Kelly v. Greason, 23 N.Y.2d 368, 296 N.Y.S.2d 937, 244 N.E.2d 456 (1968); ABA Informal Op. 967 (1966).

[70] § 8.11.3. A related doctrine, rooted in client-conflict concerns, creates a presumption of undue influence when a lawyer drafts a will for one client to the significant

A similar dual barrier confronts a lawyer thinking of seeking client consent to a conflict-ridden representation. The ceremonies of consent must be carefully attended to in the spirit of providing the affected client every opportunity and incentive to refuse to be represented because of the conflict. Yet compliance with the ceremony is not itself sufficient; it must also be apparent that a lawyer who proceeds with the conflicting representation is also able to represent fairly and honorably the interests of the client. Both requirements stem from concern about the potential for overreaching that is inherent in the client-lawyer relationship. Consent assures that competent clients are able to make decisions about accepting crippled representations; the requirement of a reasonably adequate representation assures that lawyer overreaching, and a possibly too perfunctory consent ceremony, will not expose the client to patently one-sided representations.

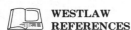

WESTLAW REFERENCES

Standard for Consentability Under the Lawyer Codes

(obvious! /4 adequa!) (reasonab! /4 determine* belie***) /p 5-105

The Concept of Consentability in the Courts

irreconcilab! non-reconcilab! (not no /5 reconcil!) paternalis*** /p consen! /p conflict*** multiple dual /4 interest represent!

§ 7.2.4 *Informed and Voluntary Consent*

Importance of the Circumstances of Consent

If a lawyer can perform an adequate job of representing the interests of the client in a conflict situation, a further barrier must be cleared: the client must consent after full disclosure. The fact that a conflict was consentable is not itself sufficient. It must also be clear that each affected client has been fully informed about the conflict and its dangers and, thereafter, has actually consented to the conflict.[71]

There are no definite rules about disclosure that, if faithfully followed, will invariably assure later judicial concurrence with the lawyer's decision to accept a conflicting representation. Courts tend to treat the adequacy of disclosure and consent as rather specific to the particular situation. The permissibility of proceeding after consent requires close examination of a number of interrelated variables: the nature and strength of the interests of each affected client; the nature of the legal services that the lawyer might perform for each client if no conflict existed as compared with the legal services in fact performed or contemplated in the conflicting relationship; the detail and intelligibility of the disclosures made by the lawyer; the capacity of the client to understand the conflict and consent to it; the timing of the disclosure and consent; and the apparent good faith of the lawyer. A court may find that relatively minimal compliance with the disclosure-and-consent requirement suffices if the threat of actual conflict was slight.[72] At the other extreme, as will be seen, even the most elaborate compliance with the disclosure-and-consent rules will not suffice to permit a lawyer to proceed with a seriously conflicting representation if the affected client is particularly susceptible to overreaching.

(a) *Full-Disclosure Consultation*

Each of the conflict rules that provides for consent states or assumes that client consent is effective only if given after full disclosure is made.[73] The disclosure and consent should

benefit of another. E.g., Haynes v. First Nat'l Bank, 87 N.J. 163, 432 A.2d 890 (1981).

[71] McCourt Co. v. FPC Properties, Inc., 386 Mass. 145, 434 N.E.2d 1234, 1235–36 (1982).

[72] Tadier v. American Photocopy Equip. Co., 531 F.Supp. 35 (S.D.N.Y.1981)(defense motion to disqualify plaintiffs' counsel in personal-injury action rejected on grounds of waiver based on lawyer's representation that clients were aware of it and consented; other strong grounds existed for rejecting standing of defendant, and claimed conflict seemed insubstantial).

[73] See Code and Model Rules provisions cited supra at nn. 47–58. See also 1908 Canon 6: "It is the duty of a lawyer at the time of retainer to disclose to the client all the circumstances of his relations to the parties, and any interest in or connection with the controversy, which might influence the client in the selection of counsel. It is unprofessional to represent conflicting interests, except

not be parts of a perfunctory ceremony.[74] A lawyer should not assume that a client is sufficiently aware of a conflict and its consequences from other sources, the client's own investigation, or general appearances. As Justice Story put it in 1824:[75]

> An attorney is bound to disclose to his client every adverse retainer, which may affect the discretion of the latter. No man can be supposed to be indifferent to the knowledge of facts, which work directly on his interests, or bear on the freedom of his choice of counsel. When a client employs an attorney, he has a right to presume, if the latter be silent on the point, that he has no engagements, which interfere, in any degree, with his exclusive devotion to the cause confided to him; that he has no interest, which may betray his judgment, or endanger his fidelity.

Normally a court will refuse to find that a client implied consent simply by virtue of the fact that the client failed to raise an objection with the lawyer, unless the remedy sought is disproportionate to the harm that would be caused by leaving the injured client to other remedies.[76]

Disclosure Contents under the Lawyer Codes

The setting, tone, and content of the consultation should be appropriate to the magnitude and complexity of the representation and the conflicts that are presented. The codes vary in the extent to which they supply detail on the content of required disclosures. The Code speaks of a "full disclosure of the possible effect of such representation on the exercise of [the lawyer's] independent professional judgment on behalf of each" client.[77] Model Rule 1.7(b)(2), on simultaneous representation, states that the required "consultation" with each of the multiple clients "shall include explanation of the implications of the common representation and the advantages and risks involved." [78] Other Model Rules require that particular kinds of client disclosures be made in writing.[79] Finally, the "Ter-

by express consent of all concerned given after a full disclosure of the facts."

74 But cf., e.g., In re Interest of H.W.E., 613 S.W.2d 71 (Tex.Civ.App.1981)(in involuntary termination of parental rights case, lawyer's unreported conversation with both parents during recess of hearing sufficiently supported finding of no conflict).

75 Williams v. Reed, 29 F.Cas. 1386, 1390 (C.C.Me.1824) (No. 17,733). See also, e.g., IBM Corp. v. Levin, 579 F.2d 271, 281–82 (3d Cir.1978); Financial General Bankshares, Inc. v. Metzger, 523 F.Supp. 744, 771 (D.D.C.1981), vacated and remanded, 680 F.2d 768 (D.C.Cir.1982).

76 Compare Turner v. Gilbreath, 3 Kan.App.2d 613, 599 P.2d 323 (1979)(no implied consent based on imagined acquaintanceship of lawyer's fourteen-year widow with Code of Professional Responsibility), with In re Estate of Seeger, 208 Kan. 151, 490 P.2d 407 (1971)(implied consent accepted where client had opportunity to object but did not.). See generally § 7.2.4.

77 DR 5–106(A), on the settlement of related claims, spells out in some detail that each client must be "advised of the existence and nature of all the claims involved in the proposed settlement, of the total amount of the settlement, and of the participation of each person in the settlement." Other conflict rules that provide for client consent simply refer to "full disclosure." See DR 5–101(A) (adverse effect on lawyer's independent judgment); DR 5–104(A) (business dealings with client); DR 5–107(A) (third-party influence).

78 It is not apparent why similar detail on the contents of the required "consultation" was not provided in other Model Rules that also require, without embellishment, "consultation." E.g., MR 1.7(a)(2); MR 1.8(b); MR 1.8(f)(1); MR 1.9(a); MR 1.9(b) (incorporating by reference MR 1.6(a)); MR 1.10(c) (incorporating MR 1.7); MR 1.11(a).

Three rules provide varying additional detail on the contents of the required consultation. (1) MR 1.8(a), on business transactions with a client, requires that the "transaction and terms" must be "fully disclosed" to the client in writing "in a manner which can be reasonably understood by the client." (2) MR 1.8(g), on aggregate settlements or guilty pleas, requires that the consultation include "disclosure of the existence and nature of all the claims or pleas involved and of the participation of each person in the settlement." (3) MR 1.8(i), on conflicts caused by the lawyer's personal relationships, requires "consultation regarding the relationship."

The Model Rules have been criticized for their failure to cure the 1969 Code defect of leaving the content of full disclosure almost entirely to speculation—and, it should be added, to case law. See Schneyer, The Model Rules and Problems of Code Interpretation and Enforcement, 1980 Am.B.Found. Research J. 939, 941–42.

79 See MR 1.8(a)(business dealings with clients); MR 1.8(h) (prospective limitation on malpractice liability); and MR 1.11 (former-government-lawyer conflict). The 1969 Code contains no writing requirement for any conflict of interest. By contrast, the California Rules require a writing for business dealings with a client (Cal.R.Prof. Cond.R. 5–101), as well as for conflicts that threaten confidential information (R. 4–101), conflicts arising out of the lawyer's personal interests (R. 5–102(A)), and conflicts arising from multiple representation (R. 5–102(B)).

minology" section of the Model Rules states that "consult" or "consultation" denotes "communication of information reasonably sufficient to permit the client to appreciate the significance of the matter in question." The definition underscores the requirement of reasonability and the focus on client understanding (rather than simply utterances by the lawyer) but obviously lacks specific content.

Items in a Full-Disclosure Consultation

A fuller description than the lawyer codes suggest can be given of the contents of a disclosure or consultation specifically addressed to conflicts problems. Generally the presence of an incipient conflict should require a lawyer to disclose to each affected client whatever a lawyer who was a stranger to the relationship [80] would consider appropriate in order to make each client's decision both intelligent and informed.[81] Specific explanations to a client would depend, naturally, on variables such as whether the conflict is detected and the consultation ensues at the beginning of the representation or whether the conflict could only have been discovered at a later stage; what kind of conflict has arisen; the extent to which the conflict affects the client's interests; the nature of the relationship between the individual lawyer and client; and, as will be discussed below, the capacity of the client to receive and act upon information of the kind involved in the consultation.

With those possible qualifications in mind, effective communication with a client about a conflict would usefully cover the following elements:[82]

(1) All important interests of the client being advised should be fully explained to that client, with particular attention to contingent, optional, and tactical considerations. As stressed in the Model Rules, the consultation should explore the alternative courses of action that would be foreclosed or made less readily available by the conflict.[83] The interests reviewed should include interests that the client might initially have considered abandoned or otherwise taken care of in prior discussions with others, particularly with other clients with whose interests the client's own interests conflict.

(2) The interests of the lawyer or other client that provoke the conflict should be fully and candidly explained. The conversation should contain sufficient detail and supporting analysis so that the client can comprehend the ways in which the interests of each are or may be in conflict.

(3) The lawyer should explain fully the nature of the representation that would result if all relevant parties consent.[84] In part, that explanation should candidly and fairly review any reservations that a disinterested lawyer might harbor if he or she were representing only the client being advised.[85]

(4) The lawyer should explain fully the consequences of a future withdrawal of consent by either client—particularly the probable consequence that the lawyer would have to withdraw from representing either client with

[80] The "stranger" formulation is borrowed here from the test commonly employed by courts in assessing the substantive fairness of business dealings between lawyer and client. See § 8.11.3.

[81] Spindle v. Chubb/Pacific Indemn. Group, 89 Cal.App. 3d 706, 713, 152 Cal.Rptr. 776 (1979), and cases cited.

[82] The list is a composite of several sources. See, e.g., Maine Bar Rule 3.4(a), in Maine Rules of Court Desk Book (West 1982)(as amended July 1, 1980); In re James, 452 A.2d 163, 167 (D.C.1982), cert. denied 460 U.S. 1038, 103 S.Ct. 1429, 75 L.Ed.2d 789 (1983); In re Lanza, 65 N.J. 347, 322 A.2d 445, 448 (1974); In re Boivin, 271 Or. 419, 424, 533 P.2d 171 (1975).

[83] MR 1.7 comment (Loyalty to a Client; third paragraph).

[84] Cf. Code EC 5–16 ("[B]efore a lawyer may represent multiple clients, he should explain fully to each client the implications of the common representation.").

[85] Courts have insisted that the client be able to understand from the content of the disclosure the reasons why it would be desirable to have representation by other counsel, whose independent exercise of judgment would not be compromised. In re Porter, 283 Or. 517, 584 P.2d 744, 748 (1978); In re Boivin, 271 Or. 419, 424, 533 P.2d 171, 174, (1975). Cf. MR 1.17 comment (Consultation and Consent).

resulting waste of time and legal fees for both.[86]

Advice to Seek Independent Counsel

The advice of an independent lawyer, one not connected with either the lawyer or any interested client, might be useful for a client considering a conflicting representation and in some situations is required. In simultaneous-representation conflicts, it is desirable to encourage both clients to seek independent legal advice if the importance of the matter and the severity of the potential conflict warrant it, but such independent consultation, and even advice by the common lawyer to seek it, is not required.[87] At the very least, if the clients involved obtain independent legal advice, it is more likely that a court will later find that consent was informed.[88]

Some conflicts are so potentially dangerous, however, that advice to a client to seek independent legal advice is explicitly required in the lawyer codes. The Model Rules and the California Rules require such advice in the case of business dealings between lawyer and client.[89] The mandatory portion of the Code on regulating business dealings (DR 5–104(A)) does not mention independent legal advice.[90] Nonetheless, courts interpreting the Code have frequently insisted that the disclosure to a client in a business-dealing setting must include the advice to obtain independent legal advice.[91]

(b) *Voluntary Client Consent*

Disclosure is the first step; client consent might follow, but only if the client is freely willing. Client consent should not be the result of the slightest pressure from the lawyer to continue the conflicting representation. Nor should it be accepted by the lawyer in the face of evidence of pressure by others—and most certainly when the pressuring party is the possessor of the conflicting interest. Client consent is most readily upheld if each client is fully capable of investigating the value of the conflicting representation and of taking steps to obtain alternative representation.[92]

Client consent must be explicit. It should rarely be implied from silence on the part of the client when faced with facts that, to the trained lawyer, might suggest adverse interests. The complexity of the law, and of many factual situations, may be such that the client reasonably relies heavily upon the lawyer's fidelity, diligence, and skill to avoid, among other hazards, conflict situations that are perilous to the client.[93] It is not enough that the lawyer indicate that he or she will proceed unless the client objects; the burden is on the lawyer to demonstrate that the client has sufficiently and affirmatively consented.[94] The concern that a client consent explicitly is dealt with by the requirement of the California rule that a client's consent is effective only if it is in writing.[95] Despite all of the necessary objective manifestations of consent,

[86] See infra at 348-49 (mandatory withdrawal when consent is retracted).

[87] United States v. Curcio, 694 F.2d 14, 27 (2d Cir.1982); Aetna Casualty & Sur. Co. v. United States, 570 F.2d 1197, 1201–02 (4th Cir.), cert.denied 439 U.S. 821, 99 S.Ct. 87, 58 L.Ed.2d 113 (1978).

[88] Aetna Casualty & Sur. Co. v. United States, supra, 570 F.2d at 1201–02; In re Estate of Rakestraw, 28 Wn. App. 585, 624 P.2d 1175, 1176 (1981).

[89] MR 1.8(a)(2); Cal.R. 5–101(2).

[90] Code EC 5–11 vaguely urges lawyers to be willing to accept "additional counsel" to represent a client if that is desirable in order to provide "proper representation." From its context, the allusion probably refers, not to conflict-of-interest situations, but to instances in which the lawyer is overworked or is beyond his or her accustomed depth in a complex matter and additional counsel is desirable for that reason.

[91] In re Bartlett, 283 Or. 487, 584 P.2d 296 (1978) (financial transaction with client).

[92] Unified Sewerage Agency v. Jelco Inc., 646 F.2d 1339 (9th Cir.1981)(prime contractor effectively consented to representation by lawyer who concurrently represented long-standing client, electrical subcontractor, in unrelated litigation against prime contractor); Melamed v. ITT Continental Baking Co., 592 F.2d 290 (6th Cir.1979)(lawyer-trustee in bankruptcy and other clients advised by independent counsel); Arcon Constr. Co. v. State, 314 N.W.2d 303 (S.D.1982)(construction company and surety on construction bond).

[93] Bryant v. Lewis, 27 S.W.2d 604, 607 (Tex.Civ.App. 1930).

[94] In re Hansen, 586 P.2d 413 (Utah 1978).

[95] Cal. R. of Professional Conduct, Rule 5–102(A): "A member of the State Bar who accepts employment under

courts have generally insisted that the lawyer be aware that the client's consent is voluntarily given—a factor that relates primarily to the capacity of a client to give free consent.

The Timing of Consent

The timing of a client's consent can raise concerns that it is not sufficiently voluntary. First, at the outset of a representation otherwise free of conflicts, a lawyer might indicate that, under the lawyer's standard arrangement, retained clients agree to the lawyer's later representation of clients with conflicts of interest. For example, the lawyer may practice in a narrow specialization in which conflicts between clients are frequent. Some authority exists for upholding such advanced consents, but in each instance the consenting client was a major entity with the actual assistance of independent legal advice.[96]

A related timing question can arise if the conflict of interest problem is raised at a late point, when a client's refusal to consent to a lawyer's joint representation of another client would require the first client to go to trouble and expense to find a new lawyer. Voluntary consent can be given under such circumstances, but the effectiveness of consent is enhanced if the lawyer was reasonably diligent in raising the conflict issue at the earliest possible time and if the client is relatively sophisticated in legal or business affairs.

Finally, the client should not be pressured to make a quick decision but should be allowed sufficient time to digest and contemplate the nature of the risks about to be undertaken.[97] Again, the relative sophistication of the client, the need for reasonable dispatch in resolving the conflict issue, the apparent magnitude of the clash of interests, and the magnitude of the interests at stake in the underlying matter are all relevant.

Client Capacity to Consent

Wise implementation of a concept of consent must pay attention to the intellectual and emotional capacities of the consenting client. That requires examination of the individual client's ability to receive and analyze information about the conflict and its consequences. It also requires examination of the particular client's ability to give consent voluntarily and not under the overriding influence of another person, including the lawyer. Sophisticated parties with extensive experience in business and in dealing with lawyers and the legal system are much more capable of giving effective consent than are more vulnerable clients such as children, incapacitated persons, persons who are naive about legal matters, or persons who are under emotional stress. A lawyer should also be alert if a client expresses unrealistic expectations about the nature of the legal services that the lawyer is to perform. Or, where contracting parties are of very different bargaining powers, it might not be possible for the same attorney to represent both adverse interests.[98]

A different kind of vulnerability to improvident consent might threaten entity clients such as corporations, unions, or governmental bodies. Courts have been understandably re-

this rule shall first obtain the client's written consent to such employment."

[96] Interstate Properties v. Pyramid Co., 547 F.Supp. 178 (S.D.N.Y.1982); City of Cleveland v. Cleveland Elec. Illuminating Co., 440 F.Supp. 193 (N.D.Ohio 1976), affirmed 573 F.2d 1310 (6th Cir.1977), cert.denied 435 U.S. 996, 98 S.Ct. 1648, 56 L.Ed.2d 85 (1978). The lines drawn in Note, Prospective Waiver of the Right to Disqualify Counsel for Conflicts of Interest, 79 Mich.L.Rev. 1074 (1981), are generally appealing. The author would have courts (1) reject consent, in advance (at the beginning of a representation), to adverse use of confidential information in a future, conflicting representation; (2) reject an attempt to use advance consent to justify a departure from the Canon 5 obligation of fidelity and independent judgment; but (3) uphold, after full disclosure and free consent, waiver of the imputed-disqualification rule and concerns with diluted loyalty. See also Westinghouse Elec. Corp. v. Gulf Oil Corp., 588 F.2d 221, 227–28 (7th Cir.1978) (drawing distinctions commended by above Comment). Because of the essentially paternalistic nature of the limitations on consent in advance, however, they should not sensibly apply to consent given by clients with large resources, extensive experience, and independent legal advice.

[97] United States v. Curcio, 680 F.2d 881, 889 (2d Cir. 1982).

[98] In re Sedor, 73 Wis.2d 629, 245 N.W.2d 895, 900 (1976)(loan by one client to another at exorbitant rate of interest in circumstances where borrowing client was in severe financial distress).

luctant to permit consent to cure a conflicting representation when the people who actually make the decision to consent are the same individuals whose interests are in conflict with the organization. Several shareholder-derivative cases have held that no consent would be availing in such a case.[99] The situation, it is said, requires that the entity be represented by separate counsel.[1] But it is not much more efficacious to have the allegedly manipulative controllers of the entity select the entity's succeeding lawyer and set the terms of his or her compensation and responsibilities in the representation. For that reason, a few cases have expressed a preference for judicial selection of the independent counsel if no mechanism exists within the corporation to make a disinterested choice.[2]

Doubt has been expressed whether the required knowing and voluntary consent can be given by a public officer or body, because of the dangers of corruption.[3] Such a flat rule threatens more harm than good unless it is limited to instances in which the potential for corruption is high because of the lawyer's relationship to the governmental body or to powerful political groups that might strongly influence decisions made in the body's behalf.[4]

Similarly, the extraordinary fiduciary responsibilities of persons functioning as trustees of an express trust and in analogous positions might make unacceptable a trustee's consent to the risk of a conflicting representation.[5]

Mandatory Withdrawal when Consent Is Retracted

Lawyers and clients in representations that require the consent of a client proceed with the continual threat that the consenting client will have a change of heart. As the matter progresses, the client might learn to regret the conflicting representation and, by retracting consent, cause it to come to an end. So in a joint representation, if either client later retracts consent, the lawyer must withdraw from all representation, because he or she will almost certainly be in possession of confidential information of both clients, whose use adversely to either client would be impermissible. The fact that the coclient exception to the attorney-client testimonial privilege would permit either client to call the lawyer as a witness in litigation with the other client (§ 6.4.8) does not mean that the lawyer would be released from all obligations of confidentiality and loyalty.[6] The client could possibly consent to a future adverse use

99 Messing v. FDI, Inc., 439 F.Supp. 776 (D.N.J.1977); Cannon v. United States Acoustics Corp., 398 F.Supp. 209, 216 (N.D.Ill.1975), modified 532 F.2d 1118 (7th Cir. 1976).

1 Id.

2 Rowen v. LeMars Mut. Ins. Co., 230 N.W.2d 905, 916 (Iowa 1975). Here, as with the approval of decisions about whether to support litigation against officers of the corporation, an acceptable mechanism might be the selection of independent counsel by a committee of "independent" directors of the corporation. See generally ALI Principles of Corporate Governance and Structure: Restatement and Recommendations § 7.03 (tent. draft no. 1, 1982). See also § 8.3.4.

3 City Council v. Sakai, 58 Haw. 390, 570 P.2d 565, 573 (1977)(dictum); In re A. and B., 44 N.J. 331, 209 A.2d 101, 102 (1965). Cf. Kesselhaut v. United States, 555 F.2d 791, 794 (Ct.Cl.1977)(consent by a governmental agency to a conflicting representation should not be accepted where the conflict is "flagrant").

4 City of Cleveland v. Cleveland Elec. Illuminating Co., 440 F.Supp. 193 (N.D. Ohio 1976), affirmed 573 F.2d 1310 (6th Cir.1977), cert.denied 435 U.S. 996, 98 S.Ct. 1648, 56 L.Ed.2d 85 (1978).

5 Shipman, Professional Responsibilities of the Corporations Lawyer, in Professional Responsibility: A Guide for Attorneys at 280 (1978); ABA Informal Op. 564 (1962).

6 Brennan's, Inc. v. Brennan's Restaurants, Inc., 590 F.2d 168 (5th Cir.1979); NCK Org., Ltd. v. Bregman, 542 F.2d 128 (2d Cir.1976); Oliver v. Kalamazoo Bd. of Educ., 346 F.Supp. 776 (W.D.Mich.1971), affirmed 448 F.2d 635 (6th Cir.1971); OpDyke v. Kent Liquor Mart, Inc., 40 Del. Ch. 316, 181 A.2d 579, 583 (1962). In *Brennan's*, supra, a lawyer represented individual members of the Brennan family and several of their corporations involved in the restaurant business in Louisiana, and in other states. One of his duties was to register a trademark. After disagreement arose over operation of the business, two contending family groups formed, each operating different restaurants. The lawyer chose to continue representing the defendant group, which the plaintiff group sued for trademark infringement. The defendants argued that it was understood that all would use the mark, although it was registered only in a plaintiff corporation and, alternatively, that the trademark was invalid. While recognizing that the coclient rule (§ 6.4.8) meant that there were likely few matters between the parties that would come under the attorney-client privilege, the court held that the common lawyer still owed a duty to every coclient to keep confidential, and not to use against

of confidential information,[7] but such consent should not be presumed.

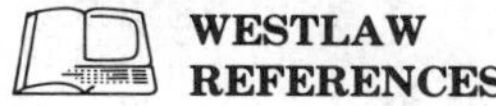

WESTLAW REFERENCES

Importance of the Circumstances of Consent

conflict*** multiple dual /4 interest represent! /p consen! /p disclos*** /p standard factor variable (nature /8 law legal perform*** /3 service practice matter)

(a) *Full-Disclosure Consultation*

impl*** /10 consent*** /p conflict*** multiple dual /4 interest represent!

Disclosure Contents Under the Lawyer Codes

disclos*** reveal*** /s possib! potential*** /s effect impact /s professional /s judgment judgement /p conflict*** multiple dual /4 interest represent!

Items in a Full-Disclosure Consultation

disclos*** reveal*** /s alternative option /p conflict*** multiple dual /4 interest represent!

digest(full* /3 disclos*** consult! /p attorney lawyer counsel** "law firm" client /p conflict*** multiple dual /4 interest represent!)

Advice to Seek Independent Counsel

advi*e* /s seek*** sought /s independent /s legal counsel** lawyer attorney /p conflict*** multiple dual /4 interest represent!

(b) *Voluntary Client Consent*

client /s consen! /4 imply implied explicit** implicit** actual** action inaction silence conduct /p conflict*** multiple dual /4 interest represent!

Client Capacity to Consent

consen! /p conflict*** multiple dual /4 interest represent! /p capacity incapacity voluntar! involuntar! coer! (undue overriding +1 influence) duress vulnerab! knowledge knowing** /8 client

any of them, their "secrets." That precluded him from representing any party in contentious litigation about a substantially related matter. The court also held, however, that a lawyer associated as cocounsel with the disqualified lawyer would not be disqualified, even if he heard some of those secrets, because the plaintiffs could not legitimately have assumed that they would be kept from the defendants themselves.

§ 7.3 CONFLICTS IN SIMULTANEOUS REPRESENTATIONS

§ 7.3.1 *Principles and Professional Rules*

Reasons for Restrictions, and for Consent

When one lawyer represents more than one client at the same time, the potential always exists for the lawyer to be tugged in different directions because of the differing interests of the clients. The values of both the loyalty principle and the confidentiality principle (§ 7.1.3) can be at stake. The lawyer might be tempted to sacrifice one client's interests in order to advance those of the other or to expose or use adversely one client's confidences to aid the other.

On the other hand, there are good reasons for clients to wish a lawyer to undertake a joint representation. The net fee charged to the clients can be less than for separate representations. Two or more clients may so trust or otherwise value the same lawyer that they are willing to overlook relatively minor differences in their positions. The clients might find it better for tactical reasons to band together behind a common champion rather than to hang separately. Among other things, clients may deliberately choose joint representation in order to minimize mutual recrimination.[8]

So long as the American legal system broadly permits parties to make individual or collective decisions to bypass entitlements that they otherwise might claim, it cannot be objectionable that jointly represented parties have foregone some available claims or defenses against each other in favor of what they regard as a more valuable position jointly asserted. In appreciation of the values of party autonomy, the law has generally permitted joint representation, even among par-

[7] On the problematical nature of consent in advance, see supra at n.96.

[8] Sartain v. SEC, 601 F.2d 1366, 1376 (9th Cir.1979) (Duniway, J.).

ties with differing interests, so long as their interests are not too antagonistic and so long as they properly consent.

Professional Regulations

All of the lawyer codes have extensively regulated simultaneous conflicts, or "concurrent" conflicts as they are sometimes called. In the 1969 code, DR 5–105 involves itself frontally with that problem,[9] as does Rule 5–102(B) of the California Rules[10] and Canon 6 of the 1908 Canons.

The 1983 Model Rules on simultaneous representation are MR 1.7(a) and MR 1.7(b). Each subdivision takes a different perspective, although in some instances both perspectives might be relevant. The perspective of MR 1.7(a) is the possible impact of a new representation upon existing clients. Referring to the new representation of Client Two being "adverse to another client" (Client One), MR 1.7(a) bars representation of Client Two, subject to an exception for knowing consent of both Clients One and Two that can be obtained if the lawyer "reasonably believes" that, despite the clients' adverse interests, the representation "will not adversely affect" the lawyer's representation of Client One. The perspective of MR 1.7(b) focuses upon Client Two and inquires whether the lawyer's ability to represent Client Two would be "materially limited" by the lawyer's responsibilities to Client One. None of that differs from the basic approach of the 1969 Code or the California Rules. The 1983 Model Rules simply spell out in more detail the two principal ways in which differing interests of two or more clients can have an impact on the lawyer's representation.[11]

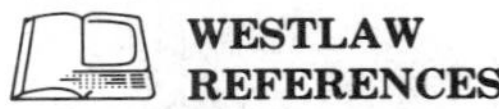

Reasons for Restrictions, and for Consent

sh 601f2d1366

Professional Regulations

simultaneous** concurrent** /6 conflict*** multiple dual joint** /4 interest represent!

---

§ 7.3.2 *Adverse Parties in Contemporaneous Litigation*

Something seems radically out of place if a lawyer sues one of the lawyer's own present clients in behalf of another client. Even if the representations have nothing to do with each other, so that no confidential information is apparently jeopardized, the client who is sued can obviously claim that the lawyer's sense of loyalty is askew. Lawyers advising themselves about potential conflicts of interest would in the great majority of instances never hesitate to decline to sue an existing client. But occasions can arise when it might be desirable or tempting to push the issue. The problem can arise in the context of both the same suit or different suits.

Adverse Representation in Simultaneous Litigation

Almost without exception, a lawyer may not represent adverse parties in the same litigation. Lawyers have done so and have been disciplined.[12] Some situations resemble Dr. Jekyll and Mr. Hyde played as a lawyering comedy, except for the serious consequences involved.[13] The insurmountable

[9] At least in a loose sense, an impermissible simultaneous representation may also be regarded as a violation of DR 5–107(A)(2), which prohibits the receipt by a lawyer of anything of value from a third party "related to [the lawyer's] representation of" a client. See In re Kali, 116 Ariz. 285, 569 P.2d 227, 229 (1977). The rule in DR 7–101 (A)(3) that a lawyer do nothing during the course of the representation to damage or prejudice a client, could also, superfluously, be invoked. See In re Smith, 292 Or. 84, 636 P.2d 923, 928–29 (1981).

[10] California Rule 5–102(B) prohibits a lawyer from representing "conflicting interests, except with the written consent of all parties concerned." The California writing requirement for consent differs from both the 1969 Code and the 1983 Model Rules. See supra n.79.

[11] See also MR 1.7 comment (Loyalty to a Client; paragraphs two and three).

[12] State v. Swoyer, 228 Kan. 799, 619 P.2d 1166 (1980) (lawyer filed suit for Client Two against Client One relating to demise of Client One's restaurant business, which had originally brought Client One to lawyer); In re Blatt, 42 N.J. 522, 201 A.2d 715 (1964).

[13] Lake County Bar Ass'n v. Gargiulo, 62 Ohio St.2d 239, 404 N.E.2d 1343 (1980)(lawyer and two clients involved in lending money to finance business of one of

problem is that the same lawyer cannot possibly scurry from one counsel table to another, changing from plaintiff's lawyer to defendant's in an instant in order to provide adequate representation to each of the adversaries.[14] Very rarely, a case might arise in which parties with congruent interests are named as apparent adversaries for purely tactical or formal reasons. It has been held that joint representation of the formal adversaries is then not impermissible.[15] The question whether that notion of merely apparent or formal adversariness can be extended to permit the same lawyer to represent both parties in obtaining an amicable divorce or dissolution has been debated and is the subject of conflicting decisions by courts (see § 8.6).

Impermissible adverse representation is not limited to same-suit conflicts, but can arise in different-suit representations as well. In some situations the conflict is less obviously direct. In a Louisiana case,[16] a lawyer had represented a corporation owned entirely by one man and was the lawyer of record in several pending suits brought by the corporation. The court held that he was disqualified to represent the owner's wife in her divorce action, since the largest portion of the disputed marital property consisted of stock in the corporation. Because division of the corporate stock along with other marital assets would require valuation of the stock, necessarily exposing confidential corporate information to view, the court properly disqualified the lawyer.[17]

Even if the different suits are about entirely unrelated matters, so that the risk of adverse use of confidential information is remote or entirely absent,[18] still there is the problem of loyalty. Concern with the loyalty principle motivated the Connecticut court in the leading case of Grievance Committee v. Rottner.[19] Lawyers in the firm had represented client Twible on a variety of minor matters and were still representing him as a plaintiff in a collection action when other firm lawyers filed an action against Twible in behalf of a second client, O'Brien, to recover substantial damages arising out of Twible's alleged assault on O'Brien. In the process, they attached Twible's house. The court affirmed an order that the lawyers in Twible's original lawyer's firm must withdraw from both representations with repayment of all retainers and without any liability of either client to pay fees for services rendered. The court found that the conduct represented a "reprehensible breach of loyalty." [20] So long as anything remained to be completed in the ongoing representations of Twible, the client was entitled to the complete loyalty of his retained lawyer. The lawyers could hardly have expected to fulfill faithfully their duties to Twible in the pending matters while pre-

them; eventual claims that the lawyer filed in the same action included claims in his own behalf against each client and by each client against the other).

[14] Morgan, The Evolving Concept of Professional Responsibility, 90 Harv.L.Rev. 702, 727 (1977).

[15] Brown & Williamson Tobacco Corp. v. Daniel Int'l Corp., 563 F.2d 671, 673–74 (5th Cir.1977)(permissible for same lawyer to represent both brother and sister corporations as nominally adversarial parties in essentially collusive suit).

[16] Teel v. Teel, 400 So.2d 357 (La.App.1981).

[17] See also Pennwalt Corp. v. Plough, Inc., 85 F.R.D. 264 (D.Del.1980)(simultaneous conflict created when adversary of one client acquired sister corporation of another client).

[18] The fact that the subject matters of the two litigations are entirely unrelated—for example, antitrust in one and an unrelated contract in the other—does not guarantee that confidentiality might not be threatened by the two adverse representations. In the example, the client's lawyer in the antitrust action, now appearing for the antitrust adversary, might be able to exploit information about the client's business practices in cross-examining the client. As another example, in the leading case of Grievance Committee v. Rottner, 152 Conn. 59, 203 A.2d 82 (1964), it is not unlikely that the seizure of the client's home in the second action filed against him for assault resulted from information about his ownership interest gained in prior representations of the client in otherwise unrelated matters.

[19] 152 Conn. 59, 203 A.2d 82 (1964). See also, e.g., IBM Corp. v. Levin, 579 F.2d 271 (3d Cir.1978); Fund of Funds, Ltd. v. Arthur Andersen & Co., 567 F.2d 225, 232–33 (2d Cir.1977); Jeffry v. Pounds, 67 Cal.App.3d 6, 136 Cal. Rptr. 373 (1977); People ex rel. Cortez v. Calvert, 617 P.2d 797, 800 (Colo.1980); In re Gillard, 271 N.W.2d 785 (Minn.1978); In re Cohn, 46 N.J. 202, 216 A.2d 1 (1966); United Nuclear Corp. v. General Atomic Co., 96 N.M. 155, 629 P.2d 231, 319–20 (1980), cert.denied 451 U.S. 901, 101 S.Ct. 1966, 68 L.Ed.2d 289 (1981); Kelley v. Greason, 23 N.Y.2d 368, 296 N.Y.S.2d 937, 244 N.E.2d 456 (1968); In re Hansen, 586 P.2d 413 (Utah 1978).

[20] 203 A.2d at 85. See also 203 A.2d at 84.

paring to cross-examine him about an assault in the other.

The possibility that a less strict rule might apply to unrelated adverse-litigation representations was suggested in Cinema 5, Ltd. v. Cinerama, Inc.,[21] but it seems doubtful that the exception was ever meant to be realized. The court stated that even when the relationship between the litigations is remote, the relevant test is one of "prima facie impropriety"[22] instead of the substantial-relationship test employed in former-client conflict cases (§ 7.4.3). The professional rule is that clients are entitled to rely upon a lawyer's "undivided allegiance and faithful, devoted service."[23] For a lawyer to sue a present client simply clashes too harshly with that requirement.

Loyalty, however, is for the client's benefit. The client is free to consent to a lawyer's adverse representation so long as the consent is fully informed and freely given and so long as the clash between the representations is not too extreme.[24] It is also conceivable that the need for loyalty is feigned. Concern has been expressed that a strict unrelated-suit conflict rule might permit a large corporate enterprise to spread its legal business among several of the best firms in a community and thus prevent any of them from suing the corporation. One response might be a rule that makes an exception for such anticipatory defensive behavior if it is shown.[25]

WESTLAW REFERENCES

Adverse Representation in Simultaneous Litigation

lawyer attorney counsel** "law firm" /4 sue* suing /4 client /p conflict*** multiple dual joint simultaneous** concurrent** adverse** /4 interest represent!

§ 7.3.3 *Coparties in Litigation*

Conflicts between Coparties

Conflicts of interest can beset coparties in litigation just as well as parties that are formally aligned as adversaries. A clear case is when coparties file cross-claims against each other; plainly the same lawyer cannot represent both.[26] A case that illustrates that, but in a disturbing procedural context, is the casebook chestnut Jedwabny v. Philadelphia Transportation Company.[27] A lawyer filed suit against a bus company in behalf of the driver-owner of a vehicle and his two automobile passengers. The claims arose out of a collision between the driver's vehicle and one of defendants' buses. Under the Pennsylvania practice at the time, the defendant

[21] 528 F.2d 1384, 1387 (2d Cir.1976).

[22] 528 F.2d at 1386 (propriety of conflicting representation must be measured not so much against concerns with confidentiality "as against the duty of undivided loyalty"). The *Cinema 5* "prima facie impropriety" test has been described as a "strict" standard that imposes "upon counsel who seeks to avoid disqualification a burden so heavy that it will rarely be met." Glueck v. Jonathan Logan, Inc., 653 F.2d 746, 749 (2d Cir.1981). See also United Nuclear Corp. v. General Atomic Co., 96 N.M. 155, 629 P.2d 231, 319–20 (1980), cert.denied 451 U.S. 901, 101 S.Ct. 1966, 68 L.Ed.2d 289 (1981).

[23] Von Moltke v. Gillies, 332 U.S. 708, 725, 68 S.Ct. 316, 324, 92 L.Ed.2d 309 (1948), quoted in Cinema 5, Ltd. v. Cinerama, Inc., 528 F.2d 1384, 1386 (2d Cir.1976). See also Williams v. Reed, 29 Fed.Cas. 1386 (C.C.D.Me.1824) (No. 17,733)(Story, J.).

[24] See § 7.2.4. The Model Code conception of a "consentable conflict" is a narrow one in simultaneous, unrelated adverse litigation. MR 1.7 comment (Conflicts in Litigation; second paragraph) cautiously intimates that it might be permissible in some instances for a lawyer who represents a corporate client with diverse operations to represent another client in unrelated litigation against the enterprise "if so doing will not adversely affect the lawyer's relationship with the enterprise or conduct of the suit and if both clients consent after consultation." Presumably the lawyer's relationship would be affected by such things as the need to cross-examine an officer or employee with whom the lawyer has dealt or will deal in the future. The comment also suggests that the same diverse-operations reasoning would permit a government lawyer, with the consent of both clients, to represent a government employee in a proceeding in which the opposing party is an agency of the same government. But it suggests that a suit charging fraud against an existing client, even if the charge is against another division of the enterprise, might be nonconsentable. Cf. § 7.2.2.

[25] McCourt Co. v. FPC Properties, Inc., 386 Mass. 145, 434 N.E.2d 1234, 1238 (1982).

[26] Lake County Bar Ass'n v. Gargiulo, 62 Ohio St.2d 239, 404 N.E.2d 1343 (1980).

[27] 390 Pa. 231, 135 A.2d 252 (1957), cert.denied 355 U.S. 966, 78 S.Ct. 557, 2 L.Ed.2d 541 (1958). A more straightforward case is Corvair Furniture Mfg. Co. v. Bull, 125 Ga.App. 141, 186 S.E.2d 559 (1971)(lawyer for several coplaintiffs in negligence case filed suit against several defendants, including one of the plaintiffs).

bus owner was permitted to plead against the driver-owner, not to obtain contribution or indemnification, but to add the driver-owner as an involuntary, additional defendant to the passengers' claims. The plaintiffs' lawyer proceeded to defend the driver-owner on that claim as well as press ahead with all plaintiffs' claims against the bus company. The jury returned a verdict against both the bus company and the driver-owner, for substantial damages. The bus company, but not the driver-owner appealed. The court held that the plaintiffs' lawyer was disqualified to function in all of the capacities that the Pennsylvania joinder rule permitted the defendant to manufacture.

What is doubly disturbing about the case (in addition to the rule permitting the bus company to realign a plaintiff as a defendant) is that the court chose to reverse the jury verdict and judgment because of the conflict, despite the fact that the conflict of interest point was argued only by the losing defendant and in the absence of any complaint by the prevailing plaintiffs or the losing driver-owner.[28] Almost obscured by that procedural morass is the possible soundness of the court's holding that, given the defendant's standing and the joinder rule, the lawyer's conflicting duties were insupportable if he was required to urge at the same time that two of his three plaintiff-clients could recover against his defendant-client but, then again (when defending the defendant-client), no, they couldn't.[29]

[28] § 7.1.7(2)(standing).

[29] It is not clear from the court's opinion whether that prospect could have materialized. There are suggestions in it that the passenger plaintiffs were taking the position that they were not interested in recovering from the driver-owner, even though the defendant's pleading had given them a procedural basis for doing so. If the passenger-plaintiffs had consented to abandon their claim against their coplaintiff even to the point of refusing to obtain execution on it (and whether their consent was freely given was no concern of the defendants), then there was no remaining, unconsented conflict of interest. If the coplaintiffs' consent was improvident or was coerced from them by their common lawyer, their remedy was against the lawyer for malpractice. In any event, their rights against their lawyer affords no basis for an award of new trial in favor of the defendant.

Unasserted Cross-Claims or Cross-Defenses

Procedural oddities, however, hardly tell the whole story. The conflict of interest problem of the lawyer in *Jedwabny* would not necessarily have been cured even if there had been no joinder device by which the defendant had been able to assert diversionary claims for his adversaries against one of their own number. Whether coparties have conflicts cannot, obviously, be determined conclusively from pleadings filed in their behalf by the lawyer whose disqualification is in question.[30] A lawyer who proposes to represent coparties in litigation is under an obligation of loyalty and competence to investigate the basis of apparent claims that each may have against the other. If such a claim appears plausible, the lawyer should proceed no further with the joint representation unless each client consents, if this is permissible, after disclosure.[31]

The widespread abandonment of guest-statute barriers to passengers' recoveries against their own drivers means, as a practical matter, that a passenger will almost always be well advised to assert claims against all other drivers, including the passenger's driver. The same lawyer's representing both passenger and driver incurs a substantial risk of a disqualifying conflict unless the facts plainly indicate no dispute about the absence of driver liability (as, for example, in a rear-end collision case, in which driver liability is remote).[32]

[30] Kerry Coal Co. v. UMW, 470 F.Supp. 1032 (W.D.Pa. 1979).

[31] See § 7.2.2.

[32] In re Thornton, 421 A.2d 1 (D.C.1980)(lawyer suspended, among other things, for representing both passenger and owner-operator); In re Morris, 72 N.J. 135, 367 A.2d 1172 (1977)(same). See also Fugnitto v. Fugnitto, 113 Misc.2d 666, 452 N.Y.S.2d 976, 978 (1982)("We emphatically disapprove the representation by counsel of both the driver and the passenger of a vehicle."); Holcomb v. Steele, 47 Tenn.App. 704, 342 S.W.2d 236 (1958)(lawyers who represented both passenger and driver guilty of conflict precluding right to fee).

Similar conflict of interest problems can arise in a lawyer's joint representation of codefendants, because of the possibility of cross-claims for indemnification or contribution or of defenses attempting to lay the entire blame on a codefendant. A recurring situation involves lawyers who jointly represent both a municipality and its employees in federal civil rights litigation. In many of those cases, the employees could shift liability to the city if they established that they acted in good faith pursuant to established city policy. The city, on the other hand, could seek exoneration by showing that the employees acted entirely outside the scope of their authority. Several decisions have required separate representation in such cases.[33]

Additional conflicts complexities can be introduced by indemnification agreements. For example, in Bell v. City of Milwaukee, [34] a city and several of its policemen were represented by the same lawyer in a federal civil rights action for wrongful death. The city had agreed to indemnify its officers, but only for acts in the course of their employment. At trial the jury was convinced by the evidence that one of the officers had engaged in a cover-up involving false reports and perjury at an inquest. The city argued that the finding exonerated it from its indemnification agreement. The court held that the cover-up and perjury were within the scope of employment, noting that if the officer were not covered by the city's indemnification, an impermissible conflict of interest existed.[35] But if the employer admits in its pleadings that the employee was within the scope of employment and if it has in effect a binding indemnification agreement, there is little prospect of a conflict, and joint representation is permissible.[36] Similar issues can arise if a lawyer in a shareholder derivative action represents both the corporation and directors accused of wrongdoing against it (see § 8.3.4). The issue of conflicts of interest in criminal defense representation is importantly different because of the special protections afforded by the right to counsel secured by the Constitution. Those issues are examined at a separate place (§ 8.2).

Most coparty-conflict problems can be cured by client consent. The lawyer must first fully inform all clients about the nature of their differing interests and about the risks of joint representation and can proceed only with the voluntary consent of all clients.[37] Even if the conflict is not so severe that the lawyer would be required to withdraw unless the clients consented, it is prudent for a lawyer to discuss even incipient, or all but entirely farfetched, conflicts of interest with all interested clients in order to clear the air and maintain complete trust and confidence through mutual lawyer and client agreement about how to proceed.

[33] Van Ooteghem v. Gray, 628 F.2d 488, 495 n.7 (5th Cir.1980), on rehearing 654 F.2d 304 (5th Cir.1981), cert. denied 455 U.S. 909, 102 S.Ct. 1255, 71 L.Ed.2d 447 (1982); Shadid v. Jackson, 521 F.Supp. 87 (E.D.Tex.1981)(nonconsentable conflict in such a case). Cf. Bell v. City of Milwaukee, 536 F.Supp. 462, 477 (E.D.Wis.1982), affirmed in part, vacated in part, reversed in part on other grounds 746 F.2d 1205 (7th Cir.1984) (conflict, but cured by result, which requires city to indemnify employees on facts found).

[34] 536 F.Supp. 462 (E.D.Wis.1982), affirmed in part, vacated in part, reversed in part on other grounds 746 F.2d 1205 (7th Cir.1984).

[35] 536 F.Supp. at 477.

[36] Aetna Casualty & Sur. Co. v. United States, 570 F.2d 1197, 1201 (4th Cir.), cert.denied 439 U.S. 821, 99 S.Ct. 87, 58 L.Ed.2d 113 (1978). Although the concern is hardly instinctive on the basis of the facts of the cases discussed in the text, a careful lawyer would take steps either to be certain that there was no basis for claims or defenses by one coclient at the expense of any other or, if in doubt, to withdraw from the representation unless the clients affected were freely willing to consent after consultation. See § 7.2.

[37] Compare, e.g., Altshul v. Paine Webber, Inc., 488 F.Supp. 858 (S.D.N.Y.1980)(client consent cured conflict when same lawyer represented coplaintiffs, one of whom had been counterclaimed against by defendant for indemnification), with e.g., Valley Title Co. v. Superior Court, 124 Cal.App.3d 867, 177 Cal.Rptr. 643, 652 (1981)(nonconsentable conflict when employee who claimed innocence was represented by same lawyer who also represented coparty employer, who sought to establish employee's embezzlement in order to recover on fidelity bond issued by insurance company despite pendency of other litigation in which employee was denying liability for same alleged embezzlement).

Determining Differing or Adverse Interests of Coparties

What constitutes a disabling differing or adverse interest in simultaneous representation in litigation will often be apparent but will sometimes require a careful analysis. The clearest cases are those discussed above, in which from the beginning one client's factual and legal position in the litigation, and thus that client's interests, diverge sharply from those of another corepresented party.

Differing interests in simultaneous representation can also arise at differing times and in more subtle ways. For example, suppose that a lawyer is retained to represent the administrator of an estate. May the lawyer also represent heirs in asserting their claims for a share of the estate? The absence of a clear demarcation in probate proceedings between plaintiffs and defendants does not always mean that all parties have congruent interests. If even one heir has an interest different from any other, the lawyer for the administrator, whose fees will be paid from the assets of the estate, should not represent any heir.[38]

Issue Conflicts

Differing interests can also arise when the same lawyer in a second suit contends for a legal result that, if accepted, would operate against the interests of another client in a pending suit. The problem of issue conflicts has only rarely been discussed in decided cases, although it has been pursued in the literature.[39] Issue-conflict disqualifications were given an overly zealous application in some discussions because of the breadth of the standard in Canon 6 of the 1908 Canons, which defined a conflict to include a situation "when, in behalf of one client, it is [the lawyer's] duty to contend for that which duty to another client requires him to oppose."

The classic case on issue conflicts, Estates Theatres, Inc. v. Columbia Pictures Industries, Inc.,[40] might reflect that influence. The court held that a lawyer was disqualified from representing a plaintiff in a newly filed antitrust case because success in that action would directly conflict with the legal position that another of his clients wished to establish in a prior pending action. As with all conflict of interest cases, the soundness of the result depends on a meticulous inspection of the facts. It suffices to say for present purposes that the court's analysis and conclusion are not beyond question. The problem is one that cannot be resolved categorically. Resolution should depend on the degree of probability that the issue would arise in each litigation and, if it would, the importance of the issue in each litigation and the likely impact of a decision upon the interests of the other client in the pending and undecided case.[41] Disqualification should be clear, unless both clients consent, if the issue would certainly be decided in each case and if its decision would adversely affect a material interest of the respective clients.

Procedural Conflicts

Conflicts of a similar kind—involving practical matters rather than legal issues—can occur even if the clients have substantive legal positions that are perfectly congruent.

[38] Richardson v. State Bar, 19 Cal.2d 707, 122 P.2d 889 (1942); Smith v. Jordan, 77 Conn. 469, 59 A.2d 507 (1904). See also Sullivan v. Committee on Admissions and Grievances, 395 F.2d 954 (D.C.Cir.1967)(joint representation of heir-finder service and heirs); Womble v. Womble, 228 Ga. 10, 183 S.E.2d 747 (1971)(lawyer for estate represented widow-administratrix as well as creditors who filed claims against estate).

[39] Legal Ethics Forum: Dealing with Conflicting Interests within a Firm, 67 ABA J. 1692 (1981).

[40] 345 F.Supp. 93 (S.D.N.Y.1972).

[41] MR 1.7 comment (Conflicts in Litigation), states that a lawyer may represent clients with antagonistic interests in a "legal question" in different cases, unless the interests of either client would be adversely affected. It then draws a distinction between such questions arising in different trial courts (permissible) as opposed to contemporaneous argument in appellate courts (impermissible). The distinction is apparently based on assumptions about operation of the rules of stare decisis, although the trial-versus-appellate-court scenarios carry this out only imperfectly. In many jurisdictions, such as the federal system, trial as well as appellate decisions are extensively reported and constitute persuasive authority in other courts of coordinate jurisdiction.

Consider, for example, two clients whose claims are of exactly the same kind and who have no conceivable conflicting relationship other than that they share the same lawyer. If two different courts press the lawyer to begin trial in both cases at conflicting times, to the potential detriment of both or either client, the lawyer has a conflict of interests and should obtain client consent to whatever arrangement is proposed.[42]

WESTLAW REFERENCES

Conflicts between Coparties

co-party /p conflict*** multiple joint dual /4 interest represent!

jedwabny

Unasserted Cross-Claims or Cross-Defenses

indemnif! cross-claim*** /p conflict*** multiple dual joint** /4 interest represent! /p attorney lawyer counsel** "law firm" client

Determining Differing or Adverse Interests of Coparties

synopsis,digest(differ*** advers*** /2 interest /s simultaneous** conflict*** multiple dual joint** /4 interest represent!)

Issue Conflicts

"estates theatres" /15 345 +5 93 /p conflict***

Procedural Conflicts

fi 606 p.2d 738

§ 7.3.4 Nonlitigation Simultaneous Representation

Greater Tolerability of Nonlitigation Conflicts

Courts demonstrate a somewhat more benign attitude as the scene of a conflict of interest moves away from litigation and into contract and other private-ordering transactions. Lawyers here, as a general matter, have more latitude to represent clients with arguably differing interests.[43] Two factors account for the greater freedom to represent. First, if a joint representation deteriorates at a late point in a transaction, it is generally less disruptive to stop the joint representation and continue with separate representations. On the other hand, trials can be seriously disrupted and delayed if an additional lawyer must be substituted in the case. Second, some transactions are so highly patterned and formulaic that a lawyer can know with much more certainty the possible dangers involved in joint representation. Residential real estate transactions, for example, unfold in much more predictable ways than does the typical multiparty litigation. That greater certainty may permit a lawyer who is asked to undertake a joint representation to determine with greater confidence whether or not it is appropriate to do so.

Identifying Simultaneous Conflicts

As with litigation conflicts, so in simultaneous representation in transactions, the existence of a conflict of interest is best determined on the basis of the facts of the particular case or recurring types of cases. The first step is to identify whether a conflict exists. The task generally consists of identifying at the outset of the representation the legal and other interests that the several clients have and that they may wish to assert or seriously consider as the transaction proceeds. With all those interests fully arrayed, the lawyer then examines each to see whether it diverges in a substantial way from any interest of another client. A conflict exists if any common material interest of different clients diverges in a significant way.

Some questions are readily answered: arranging for one client to lend another client money, to invest in another client's enterprise,[44] to post bond for another,[45] to sign a will leaving substantial property to another

42 People v. Johnson, 26 Cal.3d 557, 162 Cal.Rptr. 431, 606 P.2d 738 (1980).

43 In general, lawyers are given considerably greater latitude to represent clients with potentially differing interests in nonlitigation matters. E.g., EC 5-15; City Council v. Sakai, 58 Haw. 390, 570 P.2d 565, 573 (1977).

44 In re Kali, 116 Ariz. 285, 569 P.2d 227 (1977)(loan); People v. Kluver, 199 Colo. 511, 611 P.2d 971 (1980)(loan); Bar Ass'n of Greater Cleveland v. Shillman, 61 Ohio St.2d 364, 402 N.E.2d 514 (1980)(loan); In re Galton, 289 Or. 565, 615 P.2d 317 (1980)(investment).

45 See note 45 on page 375.

client[46] are all conflicting representations. In each of those instances the creditor or grantor client obviously wishes to minimize the risk and maximize the return on risk or capital. The borrower or recipient client's interests are quite the reverse. The paradigm of such a conflict is representing both the buyer and the seller of the same property (see § 8.5). Their diverging interests have serious legal implications because of the array of different options that each might wish to consider and insist upon or bargain for in formulating the terms of the transaction. Issues of much more complexity arise frequently in such contexts as that of corporate or other entity representation (see § 8.3) and in government law practice (§ 8.9).

The divergence of interests may be more subtle than it is in the case of buyer and seller in the same transaction, and, as a result, identification of the conflict may require some reflection. For example, suppose that the same lawyer is representing an impecunious inventor and a financier to set up an arrangement to market a new product. That much of their plainly differing interests is fully discussed, and each consents to the common representation. The lawyer wishes, however, not to discuss with each client the fee arrangements of the other. Suppose that the inventor is being represented on a contingent fee basis that contemplates future payment if the enterprise succeeds, and the financier on an hourly-charge basis with current billings. On close inspection, it appears that the financier is financing the legal services for the investor, at least to an extent. That conflict must also first be fully discussed and mutually agreed upon before the lawyer may proceed. A particular problem of that variety will be confronted by a lawyer representing clients with conflicting interests when only one of them is paying the fee or is a much more long-standing and substantial client. Those factors, of course, might tempt a lawyer to favor that client to the detriment of the other.[47]

A testing, and difficult, case is In re Ainsworth,[48] an Oregon decision holding that no conflict of interest existed when a lawyer represented Client Two in an entirely unrelated real estate matter at the same time that the lawyer was carrying on an extensive and sometimes heated negotiation with Client Two in behalf of Client One. The court concluded that it was not likely that the lawyer's independent professional judgment would be adversely affected in representing either client because of his work for the other.[49] Plainly, if both representations had involved litigation, the lawyer would have had a conflict of interest (§ 7.3.2). The difference between litigation and nonlitigation representations is in the different assumptions courts are prepared to make about the depth and extent of the emotional commitment that lawyers must make and in the flexibility or rigidity of the rituals of transaction representation as opposed to litigation representation. Categorical assumptions about such intangible feelings or rituals are not always convincing. In *Ainsworth* the question was discipline of the lawyer. If the question had been one of sound and reasonably cautious practice, no representation of Client Two should have been undertaken without the consent of all affected clients. While there was no clash between the parties on matters in which the same lawyer represented them—at least at the technical level of legal and factual issues—they were seriously at odds about the matter being negotiated. If either client had been unaware of the lawyer's representation of the other, that client could reasonably have doubted the loyalty of the lawyer.[50]

[45] In re Morris, 270 S.C. 308, 241 S.E.2d 911, cert.denied 439 U.S. 808, 99 S.Ct. 65, 58 L.Ed.2d 100 (1978).

[46] Haynes v. First Nat'l State Bank, 87 N.J. 163, 432 A.2d 890 (1981).

[47] Attorney Grievance Comm'n v. Lockhart, 285 Md. 586, 403 A.2d 1241, 1246 (1979). See generally § 8.8 (third-party control).

[48] 289 Or. 479, 614 P.2d 1127 (1980).

[49] 614 P.2d at 1131.

[50] Of the facts before it, the court in *Ainsworth* was likely influenced by the fact, which it did not discuss, that each client (certainly the complaining client, Client Two) was fully aware of the lawyer's representation of the other client. Moreover, Client Two had sought the

As a theoretical matter, a lawyer may represent multiple parties in a business or other nonlitigation transaction so long as the interests of all clients coincide.[51] That will not be common in ordinary business transactions. Most business transactions involve finite economic pies and parties with obviously differing interests in their share in the transaction. In such a case multiple representation may still be proper if the clients are fully aware of the circumstances under which their interests differ, if the lawyer can adequately represent the interests of each, and if the clients freely consent.[52] A hazard of joint representation, however, is that if the transaction breaks down and litigation ensues, the lawyer may not represent either party because of the confidentiality principle.[53]

WESTLAW REFERENCES

Greater Tolerability of Nonlitigation Conflicts

"ec 5–15" ec5–15

Identifying Simultaneous Conflicts

client /s (lend*** lent borrow*** /7 money fund capital) invest**** /p conflict*** dual joint** /4 interest represent! % 45k44(2)

§ 7.4 FORMER–CLIENT CONFLICTS OF INTEREST

§ 7.4.1 General

Former Clients and the Substantial-Relationship Standard

The problem of defining the circumstances under which a lawyer may file suit for, or take a position in behalf of, a present client against the interests of a former client has recently been a subject of frequent litigation and significant legal development. As with other conflict problems, an absolute rule prohibiting any such representation is unacceptable. Lawyer and client freedom to enter into new representations should be restricted only for weighty reasons.

Under the doctrine that has prevailed, any claim that a lawyer is disqualified because of a former-client representation must satisfy the two criteria of the substantial-relationship test. First, the former representation and the present one must be adverse in some material way. Second, the matters must be substantially related. Mere adverseness without substantial relationship is not disqualifying. Nothing should prohibit a lawyer from suing a former client on a matter entirely unrelated to the former representation.[54] Nor is mere substantial relationship disqualifying in the absence of adverseness. A lawyer who has successfully obtained a satisfied judgment for a passenger against a bus company in a vehicle negligence action is not disqualified from later representing a second passenger as a client in another suit against the bus company for damages arising out of the same accident.

Importance of the Distinction between Simultaneous and Former-Client Conflicts

The borderline between former-client conflicts and simultaneous-representation conflicts is critical because of the much stricter rule in simultaneous-representation cases

lawyer's assistance on the unrelated real estate matter at a time when the negotiations that the lawyer was conducting against Client Two were well under way. Although courts are quite reluctant to recognize a doctrine of "implicit" client consent in conflicts cases (see 7.2.4(b)), the decision suggests that conflicts of which clients are fully aware will be judged, at least for disciplinary purposes, less harshly than unknown or disguised conflicts.

51 Craft Builders, Inc. v. Ellis Taylor, Inc., 254 A.2d 233 (Del.1969).

52 McClendon v. Eubanks, 249 Ala. 170, 30 So.2d 261 (1947); Anglo-Pacific Oil & Gas, Ltd. v. Transcontinental Oil Corp., 34 Misc.2d 528, 224 N.Y.S.2d 122 (Sup.Ct.1961); In re Sedor, 73 Wis.2d 629, 245 N.W.2d 895 (1976). See generally § 7.2.

53 OpDyke v. Kent Liquor Mart, Inc., 40 Del.Ch. 316, 181 A.2d 579, 583 (1962). See generally § 7.2.2.

54 T.C. Theatres, Inc. v. Warner Bros. Circuit Management Corp., 216 F.2d 920 (2d Cir.1954); United States v. Standard Oil Co., 136 F.Supp. 345 (S.D.N.Y.1955); Finch v. Wallberg Dredging Co., 79 Idaho 521, 322 P.2d 701 (1958); Nichols v. Village Voice Inc., 99 Misc.2d 822, 417 N.Y.S.2d 415, 419 (Sup.Ct.1979). The point has not been universally recognized. For example, ABA Informal Op. 1233 (1972) ruled that lawyers for a legal services organization for the poor that first represented an Indian tribe in boundary litigation, which had been terminated, were later foreclosed from representing individual members of the tribe in unrelated litigation against the tribe. The opinion is wrong. Its conclusion serves no policy objective of the former-client conflict rules.

that litigation is generally and absolutely prohibited against a present client, regardless of the lack of relationship between the two matters (§ 7.3.2). For example, in Abbott Laboratories v. Centaur Chemical Company,[55] Abbott had retained a lawyer as an associated lawyer in a patent interference action handled primarily by in-house counsel. The matter had been submitted to the Patent Office, and a decision had been awaited for eleven months when the lawyer appeared[56] for Centaur in unrelated litigation against Abbott. Abbott moved to disqualify the lawyer. The court held that the dormancy of the patent action and the absence of any sure indication that the lawyer would be required to perform additional legal services on it meant that the less strict former-client conflict rule applied.[57] On the other hand, if a lawyer is on general retainer for a client, even if no active matters are being handled, the stricter simultaneous representation rules will generally apply.[58]

A strategem that might suggest itself to some is for the lawyer to withdraw from the less favored representation before a disqualification motion is filed in order to be able to enjoy the less restrictive former-client conflict rules. The strategem should be unavailing. Unless the concurrent representations were only momentary,[59] the loyalty principle would continue to bar an adverse representation, even in an unrelated matter.[60]

WESTLAW REFERENCES

Former Clients and the Substantial-Relationship Standard

"substantial relationship" /p client attorney lawyer counsel** "law firm" /p conflict*** dual multiple /4 interest represent!

Importance of the Distinction Between Simultaneous and Former-Client Conflicts

fi 497 f.supp 269

---

§ 7.4.2 Principles and Professional Rules

It is intuitively obvious that a lawyer who assists a wife in obtaining a contested divorce from her husband should be prohibited from later representing the ex-husband in seeking to set aside the divorce judgment in favor of the ex-wife.[61] The result seems almost as obvious as the rule disqualifying a lawyer who attempts simultaneously to represent both wife and husband in a contested divorce itself (§ 7.3.2).[62] The obvious case does not define the entire realm of former-client conflicts, but it can usefully serve as a specimen to examine in more detail. Objections can be raised to the lawyer's side switching on the grounds of both confidentiality and loyalty.

(a) *Former-Client Conflicts and the Confidentiality Principle*

First, under the confidentiality principle (§ 7.1.3), there are reasons to fear that things the former client told the lawyer in confidence during the prior representation might be used against the former client's present interests. The threat of the adverse use of

55 497 F.Supp. 269 (N.D.Ill.1980).

56 In fact, the lawyer who appeared in the *Centaur* litigation was not the same lawyer who handled the Patent Office matter, but was a partner in the same firm. Under imputed-disqualification rules (see § 7.6), the two lawyers are treated as one.

57 497 F.Supp. at 271–72.

58 IBM Corp. v. Levin, 579 F.2d 271, 281 (3d Cir.1978).

59 Pennwalt Corp. v. Plough, Inc., 85 F.R.D. 264 (D.Del. 1980).

60 Unified Sewerage Agency v. Jelco Inc., 646 F.2d 1339, 1345 n.4 (9th Cir.1981).

61 In an even more extreme case a lawyer switches sides in the midst of the same ongoing litigation. E.g., Weidekind v. Tuolumne County Water Co., 74 Cal. 386, 19 P. 173 (1887).

62 A logical third possibility might be to find an objectionable conflict between a present client and a *future* client. The result in Federal Trade Comm'n v. Exxon Corp., 636 F.2d 1336 (D.C.Cir.1980), could be analyzed in those terms. In that case of first impression, the court enjoined Exxon, the acquiring corporation, from maintaining a joint client-lawyer relationship through in-house or outside counsel with the "Drive Group" of Reliance Electric Corporation, which it had acquired, pending the completion of agency action that looked toward divestiture of the Drive Group. The court, in analyzing the need to invoke the equitable remedy, relied heavily upon the conflict that might exist in the future between Exxon and the Drive Group. The interests of the Drive Group were defined in terms of its possible future interests in the event that divestiture were ordered.

confidential client information could impair the willingness of all clients to confide in their lawyers for fear that the same lawyer would later use it against them. It would also seriously compromise such client prerogatives as the right to discharge a lawyer at any time (§ 9.5.2).

In individual cases, the actual threat of exposure of confidential information must be dealt with at an abstract level for several reasons. It would not do to accept the lawyer's representation that he or she in fact will not use confidential information, because violation of such an agreement might be inadvertent and would be difficult to detect in any case.[63] Moreover, it will normally not do to listen to elaborate explanations by the lawyer. A judge who first encountered the problem might have a momentary wish to hear the lawyer's explanation and the former client's attempt to disprove it, because it might be the case that the lawyer in fact did not acquire damaging information or acquired it from a nonconfidential source. And, if a full hearing were conducted, a court or disciplinary agency could more confidently determine whether in fact the succeeding representation really threatened client confidential information or merely presented the occasion for an illusory or contrived fear.

Yet it is clear that such an experiment might destroy the subject both upon which it must operate and which it is intended to protect. If the lawyer were permitted, and the former client thereby impelled, to lay bare in the succeeding representation details about the extent to which the client imparted confidential information, the former client would be confronted with the Hobson's choice of either revealing the confidential information, and thus robbing it of its confidential character, or remaining silent and risking adverse use of the information by the lawyer in favor of a current adversary. Either course seriously compromises confidentiality.[64]

For similar reasons, if the lawyer asserts that the only matters to be employed against the former client are not covered by the attorney-client evidentiary privilege, courts rightly insist that "secrets" as well must be protected.[65] There is a public interest in assuring every client that communications to a lawyer will not be used adversely in the lawyer's later work. Situations that create a realistic risk that that will occur are those in which the former-client conflict rules should require disqualification.

Courts sometimes speak in terms of the former client's being "entitled to freedom from apprehension" that confidences will be revealed in a succeeding representation.[66] The former client, to be sure, would probably feel the outrage of a violated trust. But the entitlement, to call it that, is not personal only to the former client and is not fully gauged only by seeking or imagining the reaction of the former client. For example, the fact that a client has died should not remove the protection of client confidentiality in the

[63] Emle Ind., Inc. v. Patentex, Inc., 478 F.2d 562, 570–71 (2d Cir.1973); Reardon v. Marlayne, Inc., 83 N.J. 460, 416 A.2d 852, 861 (1980).

[64] Government of India v. Cook, Indus., Inc., 569 F.2d 737, 740 (2d Cir.1978); In re Yarn Processing Patent Validity Litig., 530 F.2d 83, 89 (5th Cir.1976); T.C. Theatre Corp. v. Warner Bros. Pictures, 113 F.Supp. 265, 268 (S.D.N.Y.), reargument denied 125 F.Supp. 233 (S.D.N.Y. 1953). The extent to which that policy should be preserved against attempts to rebut the presumption of a confidentiality violation is considered in § 7.4.3.

[65] NCK Org. Ltd. v. Bregman, 542 F.2d 128 (2d Cir. 1976)(even if all information known to lawyer was independently known to present client, lawyer would still be disqualified from substantially related representation adverse to former client); Buntrock v. Buntrock, 419 So.2d 402 (Fla.App.1982)(former-client rule protects against disclosure of information even if it is discoverable from other sources). But cf. Anderson v. Pryor, 537 F.Supp. 890, 895 (W.D.Mo.1982)(former client who knew that information would be turned over to third party could not invoke substantial-relationship test to prevent former lawyer from representing third parties against former client in same matter); Moritz v. Medical Protective Co., 428 F.Supp. 865, 874–75 (W.D.Wis.1977)(same in case of coclients). For more on the coclient problem, see § 6.4.8.

[66] Cardinale v. Golinello, 43 N.Y.2d 288, 401 N.Y.S.2d 191, 195, 372 N.E.2d 26, 30 (1977); Desbiens v. Ford Motor Co., 81 A.D.2d 707, 439 N.Y.S.2d 452, 453 (1981). H. Drinker, Legal Ethics 115 (1953), is cited as a source for that view, but Drinker at that point refers to same-case side switching, in which disqualification would be automatic today. See § 7.3.

former-client rules.[67] The other important interest to be protected is the public interest of assuring all clients that lawyers can be trusted not to elicit their confidential information and then turn it against their interests. Only in that way can the assurance of confidentiality serve the objective of encouraging full client disclosure to a trusted lawyer (§ 6.1.1).

(b) *Loyalty Principle*

We have seen that the loyalty principle looms large in many conflict of interest situations (§ 7.1.3). It has been asserted that loyalty concerns play a smaller role in former-client conflict situations. By definition, the client-lawyer relationship is at an end, and it might be thought that there is no possibility that the lawyer will be tempted to act disloyally to either client, aside from the possibility of the lawyer's breaching the former client's confidences.[68] But in important respects, that is too cribbed a view.

Plausible motivations for lawyer disloyalty to either or both clients might exist in many former-client conflict cases. Which client—former or successor—a lawyer might be tempted to favor obviously cannot be stated without regard to the particular situation of the clients and the lawyer. A lawyer who expects to benefit from substantial future legal business and fees from the former client might favor the former client,[69] while a lawyer whose fee income would be enhanced by favoring the second client to the former client's disadvantage might incline in that direction. The ways in which economic and emotional pressures can work against the desired professional objectivity of a lawyer, and thwart the vigorous advocacy of every client's interests, are many and various.

Disloyalty to Former Client

Treachery to the former client can take at least three forms. The primary form of treachery has already been discussed—the adverse use of the former client's confidential information. A second form is treachery to the former client's misplaced continuing trust. It is implicated when, for example, a lawyer introduces a new client to a former client and recommends that the former client enter a business deal with the new client. Even if the lawyer does not explicitly vouch for the business acumen and trustworthiness of the new client, an implied vouching would probably be assumed by most former clients. At least in subsequent representations, then, that involve business or similar transactions, the former client is probably entitled to assume that his or her former lawyer remains a trustworthy protector and is not dealing at arm's length unless this is made clear.

A third form of treachery can also exist in many former-client situations. If it were permissible for a lawyer to resign from a representation and accept as a client a person with interests that are antagonistic to the first client's interests, we might be legitimately concerned that the lawyer would conduct the first representation in a way that would lay the basis for currying favor with, or obtaining advantages for the second, more favored client. An illustration is provided in E. F. Hutton & Company v. Brown.[70] A lawyer had formerly represented two clients, Brown and E. F. Hutton, under circumstances such that Brown had no confidences that it kept from E. F. Hutton. Later, the lawyer filed suit in behalf of E. F. Hutton against Brown in a related matter. The lawyer argued that be-

67 In re Williams, 57 Ill.2d 63, 309 N.E.2d 579 (1974) (lawyer hired by husband to remove wife as beneficiary of life insurance policy could not, after husband's death, represent wife in seeking proceeds of the policy).

68 2 M.Clark & C.Wolfram, Professional Responsibility: Issues for Minnesota Attorneys 571–72 (1976).

69 That concern underlies most of the "ethical" regulation of government lawyers and officials generally who enter government service from private practice. See § 8.9. It is hardly confined to present government lawyers, however.

70 305 F.Supp. 371 (S.D.Tex.1969). But cf. Renshaw v. Ravert, 460 F.Supp. 1089, 1092 (E.D.Pa.1978)(dictum)(concern of 1969 Code is for independent professional judgment for the protection of the second, not the first, client); Croce v. Superior Court, 21 Cal.App.2d 18, 68 P.2d 369 (1973)(lawyer is never disqualified from representing adverse party against former client if lawyer would not be disqualified from testifying about prior representation over objection of former client). The problem of former coclients, of which *E. F. Hutton* is illustrative, is discussed infra at 373–74.

cause there was no issue of confidential information, the former-client conflict rules should not preclude the subsequent representation. But the court asserted that more than confidentiality was protected by the former-client rule; it was also intended to protect justified client expectations of lawyer loyalty.[71]

The lawyer's loyalty to the first client might have been compromised in several ways. The client who later retained the lawyer's services was the more substantial client, and there is reason to wonder whether some lawyers' restricted and nonconfidential relationship with the less substantial client might have been influenced by their desire to leave the door open to future representations for the more substantial client. In other situations, the favored party need not be more substantial in terms of its absolute wealth; a lawyer's temptation might carefully take account of which client might be willing to pay a larger fee in the future. The danger in such a restricted representation is that the lawyer might not fully and zealously pursue the former client's interests during the earlier representation. The lawyer might also have overlooked purposefully (if the lawyer is venal) or unconsciously (if morally careless) important steps that could have been taken to protect the former client against legal risks such as that entailed in the subsequent, adverse representation. For reasons such as those, lawyers are generally prohibited from attacking their own work done for a former client, even if there is no threat to the first client's confidential information.[72]

Disloyalty to Second Client

The threat of treachery is directed not only at former clients. In many instances the most obvious threat of treachery or weakened advocacy is directed toward the succeeding client.[73] Most obviously, if a lawyer attempts to protect the confidentiality and loyalty interests of the former client, the second client will receive only a hobbled representation. An acute form of that would occur when the subsequent representation entailed litigation against a former client. For example, most lawyers of normal instincts would find it more difficult to cross-examine a former client than a stranger, a difficulty that could impair the vigor of the lawyer's advocacy for the second client.[74] Another case would occur when the former client was the judge before whom a lawyer was trying a case.[75] The judge's impartiality, obviously, would also be in question. But the judge's feelings of loyalty and gratitude to a former lawyer aside, the lawyer might feel unduly restrained in objecting to the former client judge's rulings in the case.[76]

(c) *The Lawyer Codes*

1908 ABA Canons of Ethics

The treatment of former-client conflicts in the lawyer codes has moved from vague generality toward additional precision. The 1908

[71] 305 F.Supp. at 394–95.

[72] NCK Org., Ltd. v. Bregman, 542 F.2d 128 (2d Cir. 1976); In re Evans, 113 Ariz. 458, 556 P.2d 792, 795 (1976) (DR 5–105 forbids lawyer to attack for Client Two the validity of an agreement that lawyer had prepared for Client One); In re Gant, 293 Or. 130, 645 P.2d 23, 26, modified on other grounds 293 Or. 359, 647 P.2d 933 (1982); In re Banks, 283 Or. 459, 584 P.2d 284 (1978).

[73] Note, however, that the Model Rules do not require the consent of the second client, but only of the former client, in former-client conflict situations. See MR 1.9(a).

[74] Trone v. Smith, 621 F.2d 994, 998–99 (9th Cir.1980); United States v. RMI Co., 467 F.Supp. 915, 923 (M.D.Pa. 1979). See also Yablonski v. UMW, 448 F.2d 1175 (D.C. Cir.1971)(lawyer who currently represents union in derivative action by dissident members against officers charged with corrupt union mismanagement disqualified because of representation of union president, one of current codefendants, in prior litigation charging related misconduct).

[75] Note that, in both hypothetical situations, the instinct to protect a former client might impair the lawyer's advocacy in favor of a succeeding client regardless of the presence or absence of any relationship between the matters in the first and second representations. While neither case should result in a career-long disqualification of the lawyer, at least a decent interval should transpire before the lawyer attempts to appear against the interests of the former client.

[76] Cf., e.g., N.Y.St. Bar Ethics Op. 511 (1979)(Canon 9 requires disqualification of former lawyer for judge). Compare also conflict of interest problems caused by the lawyer's financial or other relationships to other parties (§ 8.8).

Canons contained the following general rule as part of Canon 6:

> The obligation to represent the client with undivided fidelity and not to divulge his secrets or confidences forbids also the subsequent acceptance of retainers or employment from others in matters adversely affecting any interest of the client with respect to which confidence has been reposed.

In at least some possible readings of that language, all of the concerns previously discussed—both to protect the confidential information of the former client and to assure the lawyer's fidelity to the interests of both clients—are covered in Canon 6. A more likely reading is that the final clause ("interest of the client with respect to which confidence has been reposed") limits the scope of the Canon's prohibition to succeeding representations involving information that the former client has confided to the lawyer.

1969 ABA Code

The 1969 Code, in attempting to improve upon its coverage and possibly to broaden the scope of prohibited conflicts, inexplicably omitted any specific mention of the former-client conflict problem. There are indications that DR 5–105(A) was thought to cover the problem.[77] On the other hand, there are intimations in EC 4–5 that the former-client problem was thought to involve only problems of confidentiality.[78]

At least two serious potential defects inhere in the Code's unclear treatment of former-client conflicts. First, it is not clear that accepting a subsequent representation adverse to a former client on a substantially related matter is a violation of any mandatory rule in the Code. For example, suppose that a lawyer fully explained to the second client the possible risks to that client because of the lawyer's diligent efforts to avoid using any confidential information of the first client and the second client consented to such a hobbled representation. It may be that no Code violation has occurred. Unlike the common-law rules, which had already been developed and widely accepted in ruling on disqualification motions in litigation by the time it was drafted (§ 7.4.3(b)), the Code did not in clear terms forbid a lawyer to accept a representation in which there was a serious risk of compromising a former client's confidences or secrets so long as adverse use or revelation did not in fact occur.[79]

A second serious defect in the Code is that it seems to overlook entirely the loyalty principle in a former-client conflict situation.[80] Courts nonetheless have managed to find, sometimes with astonishing sleight-of-hand, the necessary Code basis by which to prohibit disloyalty to a former client in a substantially related matter, even in the absence of a misuse of confidences or secrets.[81] Indeed, cases imposing discipline on lawyers for successive

[77] See the references in the Code reporter's footnotes 35 and 36 to DR 5–105(A).

[78] EC 4–5: "Care should be exercised by a lawyer to prevent the disclosure of the confidences and secrets of one client to another, and no employment should be accepted that might require [sic] such disclosure." See also reporter's footnote 7 to EC 4–5. And see Slater v. Rimar, Inc., 462 Pa. 138, 338 A.2d 584, 587–88 (1975) (relevance of EC 4–6, the first sentence of which provides: "The obligation of a lawyer to preserve the confidences and secrets of his client continues after the termination of his employment.").

[79] Cf. ABA Formal Op. 342 (1975); ABA Informal Op. 1233 (1973). But cf., Buntrock v. Buntrock, 419 So.2d 402, 403 (Fla.App.1982)(necessary consequence of the substantial-relationship test for lawyer disqualification in litigation is that no actual evidence of impropriety need be shown). It is unclear whether the framers of the Code intended such permissiveness about former-client conflicts. It seems quite inconsistent with the Code's general effort to broaden conflict rules. Olvari Maru has suggested that the intent to make the substantial-relationship disqualification merely aspirational appears from the language of EC 4–5: "[N]o employment should be accepted that might require such disclosure [of confidences and secrets from one client to another]." See also nn. 7 & 8 to EC 4–5. See Annotated Code of Professional Responsibility 161 (O.Maru ed.1979). But it is not clear from EC 4–5 whether the quoted instruction is merely an aspirational statement or instead reiterates a mandatory rule as does, for example, the first sentence of the same EC and as commonly occurs in others.

[80] Renshaw v. Ravert, 460 F.Supp. 1089 (E.D.Pa.1978) (concerns of Canon 5 for lawyer's exercise of independent professional judgment on behalf of a client are for protection of second, not first, client).

[81] See cases cited supra note 72. See also E. F. Hutton & Co. v. Brown, 305 F.Supp. 371, 393 n.59 & 394 (S.D.Tex. 1969). For example, in In re Gant, 293 Or. 130, 645 P.2d 23, 26, modified on other grounds 293 Or. 359, 647 P.2d

representations in substantially related matters against a former client are not uncommon under the Code. No decision, however, has detailed the rationale for finding a violation of the Code in the absence of a finding of actual adverse use of the former client's confidences or secrets.

1983 Model Rules—Substantial Relationship

The Model Rules protect the interests of former clients more fully and clearly than did the Code. The wording of the Model Rules, however, might cause some confusion about the reach of the substantially-related test. It is also debatable whether it was wise to employ a prophylactic standard as a disciplinary rule as do the Model Rules.

Model Rule 1.9(a) explicitly prohibits a subsequent representation (1) if it is the same as, or substantially related to, that involved in the former client's representation and (2) if the second client's interests are "materially adverse" to an interest of the former client. The rule makes clear, as the Code did not, that a lawyer is prohibited from accepting a later representation, even if the former client cannot demonstrate that the lawyer will actually use the former client's confidential information. The substantial-relationship test covers all such possible instances of adverse use with a blanket rule that prohibits the lawyer from accepting the succeeding representation without the former client's consent. Rule 1.9(a) is a significant improvement over the 1969 Code with respect to the mine-run of former-client conflict problems. It breaks no new ground, and reflects the predominant view of modern courts that have grappled with former-client conflict problems in disqualification opinions.

Adverse "Use" Conflicts in the Model Rules

Even if the matter is not substantially related,[82] Rule 1.9(b) goes on to prohibit the lawyer's "use" of information relating to the former representation if the use will result in disadvantage to the former client. Two exceptions are provided—one for situations in which the information that will be adversely used "has become generally known,"[83] and the other for situations in which disclosure adverse to a client's interests is permitted under the confidential-information rule (MR 1.6).

Rule 1.9(b) raises serious, and curiously gratuitous, interpretative problems. It is doubtful that there is real need for it in the Model Rules. Its chief defect is its mysterious meaning. It is subject to misinterpretation by busy lawyers and judges, who hurriedly consult the Model Rules without paying careful attention to the background of former-client rules that courts have been developing for at least the last three decades and that are incorporated into Rule 1.9. Such a hasty reader first might notice the disjunctive "or" that connects Rules 1.9(a) and (b) and assume that subrule (b) covers a significant amount of terrain—and, by implication, that it excludes from its coverage a somewhat proportionate amount. With that hint to meaning in mind, the hasty reader would notice the substantial-relationship test alluded to in Rule 1.9(a) and assume that because Rule 1.9(b) deals with former-client confidential information, the substantial-relationship concept must be designed to deal with other problems. Re-

933 (1982), the court suspended a lawyer for such a disloyal representation against a former client on the reasoning that the lawyer had violated the obligation of DR 4–101(A) to maintain the former client's "confidence." The court consulted only a dictionary to determine that "confidence" included such subjective elements as "trust, state of feeling sure, state of mind characterized by reliance, state of trust." The court's dictionary-definition approach wrenches the word "confidence" entirely out of its obvious contextual reference to confidential information.

82 MR 1.9(a) and MR 1.9(b) are separated by the disjunctive "or."

83 MR 1.9 Code Comparison note (Proposed Final Draft, May 30, 1981) restated the exception as one for information "that is in the 'public domain.'" The source of the quotation was not given. It continues that "public domain" "use . . . is also not prohibited by the [1969] Code." No authority is cited, and it is doubtful that authority exists, under the Code or otherwise, for what is referred to here.

turning to subrule (b), the reader finds that only the *use* of confidential information is proscribed. Rule 1.9(b) seems to say that the acceptance of a representation in which a lawyer would have a strong motivation to use a client confidence violates no rule so long as the temptation is resisted. The lawyer might, therefore, be led to enter upon the representation resolved not to *use* the former client's confidential information.

The defect in the lawyer's reasoning is somewhat difficult to detect from the words employed in Rule 1.9. The words invite the thought, which is erroneous, that the substantial-relationship test does not regularly protect against disclosure of the former client's confidential information. But that is precisely its office, and the existence of Rule 1.9(b) only obscures that meaning. If the substantial-relationship test is given its intended scope—and both the comment to Rule 1.9 and its suppressed legal background note [84] make clear that that is intended—then there should be no doubt that a lawyer is disqualified from accepting or continuing with any case in which the adverse use of a former client's confidential information is a likely temptation.[85]

With every indication that the substantial-relationship test of Rule 1.9(a) was intended to be as fully protective of a former client's confidential information as are the common-law rules on the same subject, one is left to speculate about the intended function of Rule 1.9(b). Possibly it was meant to serve as a backstop to theoretically imaginable leaks that might develop in the substantial-relationship test. Unfortunately that intended use of Rule 1.9(b) is not obvious, and its presence might perversely invite those leaks to develop. Rule 1.9(b) seems to create more problems than it solves. Only an unduly restrictive application of the substantial-relationship test of Rule 1.9(a) would create conflict of interest situations in which a rule such as Rule 1.9(b) would be needed to prevent a lawyer's later adverse use of a former client's information. As Justice Frankfurter once complained about prior case authority that was ignored but not overruled, Rule 1.9(b) may float as a derelict upon the waters of the Model Rules, doing no good and bound to occasion collisions.[86] It, but not Rule 1.9(a), could be deleted from the Model Rules without any detectable adverse consequences.[87]

[84] MR 1.9 comment; MR 1.9 legal background note at 66–67 (Proposed Final Draft, May 30, 1981). In the same note (id. at 68) a short paragraph cited several authorities on adverse "use," none of which bears very directly on Rule 1.9(b). One—Restatement (Second) of Agency § 395 (1958)—does contain a "general knowledge" exception to a duty of confidentiality, but the duty is that of a general agent, which is a significantly weaker confidentiality rule than that which binds special fiduciaries such as lawyers.

[85] Rule 1.9(b) has other, similar interpretative problems. Its exceptions can be misleading. The exception for "generally known" former-client confidential information (in, note, a later representation that is not substantially related) invites dangerous speculation about how many others might now possess the information or its equivalent. The exceptions alluded to in MR 1.9(b) incorporate MR 1.6 by reference. But nothing in MR 1.6 is germane except for client consent.

Rule 1.9(b) is also defective because it implies (but compare MR 1.2 on client consultation and consent about the scope of the representation) that a lawyer could undertake a representation of the second client that was hobbled, in order to avoid "use" of a former client's confidential information without obtaining the consent of the second client.

Finally, as written, MR 1.9(b) is a virtual echo of MR 1.8(b). That presents the threat that a court might invoke the canon of construction that each part of a prescriptive text should be given a separate meaning, with potentially dangerous consequences.

[86] Dice v. Akron C. & Y. R.R., 342 U.S. 359, 368–69, 72 S.Ct. 312, 96 L.Ed. 398 (1952).

[87] A net improvement in the Model Rules would be achieved by recasting MR 1.9(b) as a part of MR 1.6 but expanding it to include the existing prohibition in the Code's DR 4–101(B)(2) and (B)(3) so as to prohibit *both* adverse as well as purportedly "benign" uses of the confidential information of either a former or a present client. See § 6.7.5 (benign use). Alternatively, the comment to MR 1.9 could be amended to make it clear that MR 1.9(b) deals only with relatively rare instances in which the later matter may, in some senses, be different from the matter involved in the former representation but in which the former client's information might nonetheless be adversely employed. An example is a situation in which a former client's prior scrapes with the law could be employed to impeach the client as a witness in a later suit that has nothing to do with the lawyer's former representation. That use of MR 1.9(b) is necessary only if the substantial-relationship test itself is too narrowly employed. See § 7.4.3(b).

Utility of Substantial Relationship as a Disciplinary Standard

A second major issue concerning Model Rule 1.9 is its adoption of the substantial-relationship standard as a disciplinary rule. The prophylactic approach of the test first found expression in decisions of courts on motions to disqualify an opposing lawyer. The primary purpose of MR 1.9(a) is to provide a mandatory rule for lawyers' behavior that is, if violated, a basis for the imposition of professional sanctions. Are the rationale of the substantial-relationship test and elements of its procedure also relevant and as justifiably applied in the context of discipline?

The question asks whether lawyers should be sanctioned for violation of prophylactic rules. The answer depends upon an assessment of the need to resort to prophylaxis rather than to insist upon a specific demonstrated impingement on underlying protected interests—here, confidentiality and loyalty. Other well-accepted mandatory rules are also plainly prophylactic, such as the rules requiring the maintenance of certain kinds of accounts for client funds (§ 4.8). In a sense, the rule protecting confidentiality might itself be argued to be prophylactic because it rests upon assumptions about client reactions that might not occur in particular instances.

The principal argument for a prophylactic, and thus broad, rule for former-client conflicts is twofold. First, as discussed above,[88] any other approach entails the need to disclose client information, although perhaps the ill effects of coerced disclosure could be limited in a lawyer discipline proceeding if the proceedings were nonpublic. Second, the rule would lose some of its self-regulatory force if lawyers were free to speculate that they might be able to manage a subsequent representation on a substantially related matter without violating either the rules against using a former client's confidential information or those requiring loyalty to both clients. The substantial-relationship test is perhaps over exclusive to some degree, although assuredly that extent is not large. Its cost is small payment for the protection that it supplies and the greater certainty of self-application that it allows.

WESTLAW REFERENCES

Former-Client Conflicts and the Confidentiality Principle

entitl! +2 freedom +2 apprehension

Disloyalty to Former Client

topic(45) & treachery

Disloyalty to Second Client

trone /15 621 +5 994 /p former succee! second /5 client representation

1969 ABA Code

date(aft 1968 & bef 1983) & "dr 5–105(a)" dr5–105(a) "ec 4–5" ec4–5

Utility of Substantial Relationship as a Disciplinary Standard

"model rule" /5 1.9 /p substantial** /3 relat!

§ 7.4.3 *Differing Interests and Substantial Relationships*

Lawyers are disqualified from accepting employment in a subsequent representation because of the representation of a former client if two conditions are satisfied: (1) the interests of the former client and the present client are adverse in some material respect and (2) the matters involved in the former and the current representations are the same or substantially related. The adverse-interest criterion has given little difficulty. The substantial-relationship standard is a matter of some complexity.

(a) *Adverse Interests*

In theory the differences in interests necessary to disqualify a lawyer in former-client cases are somewhat sharper and can be more substantial than those that disqualify in simultaneous representations (§ 7.3). In former-client cases the same lawyer is not handling the two clients' matters simultaneously, and thus there is less likelihood of confusion of roles and less threat that the lawyer might play off one set of interests against another.

[88] See text at notes 63–64 supra.

Temptations can exist, however, to make impermissible trade-offs between clients' interests and adverse use of confidential information (see § 7.4.2).

Probably no test can be devised that adequately describes all of the adverse interests that appropriately prevent the succeeding representation.[89] The test of the 1908 Canons [90]—a conflict exists when the lawyer is required in behalf of one client to contend for that which the lawyer is required to oppose for another—is both under- and overinclusive. The "differing interests" test of the Code is overinclusive unless reduced by a general and indeterminate qualification such as "material," which Model Rule 1.9(a) employs.

The comment to Model Rule 1.9 implies that the general conflict of interest standards of MR 1.7 should be used to determine whether interests of present and former clients are adverse.[91] The MR 1.9 comment itself gives two examples of adverse interests. One involves a lawyer who seeks in behalf of a new client to rescind a contract "drafted" [92] for a former client. The other example is a lawyer seeking to represent a person who claims damages from the government arising out of the same transaction for which the lawyer had earlier prosecuted the same person. Those examples are of client interests that are plainly in conflict. They lend little assistance in resolving two difficult problems of interpretation: situations involving alleged "ruse" client interests and situations in which the lawyer seeks for a second client to reap an advantage by use, allegedly in congruence with the former client's interests, of a former client's confidential information.

Real Interests versus Ruse Interests

The ruse question asks how to handle a claim by the complaining former client that his or her interests were asserted in the earlier representation in a particular way for tactical purposes only and that the "real" interests of the client are quite the reverse. Illustrative is In re Estate of Ragen.[93] Ragen hired a lawyer to represent him in a court in Taiwan to establish that he was the natural father of a child. After Ragen's death, the administrator of his estate denied his paternity of the child. The same lawyer was retained by the child to establish his claim as a natural heir to the estate of Ragen, the man declared to be his father by the court in Taiwan. The administrator claimed that other witnesses would testify that Ragen had asserted during his lifetime that the child was in fact not his and that his only reason for the paternity action was as a ruse to permit the child to be taken from an inadequate parent.

The Illinois court properly refused to disqualify the lawyer. If O. Henry twists on apparent client interests could be employed to make a prior matter seem the reverse of what the former client had made it appear, there would be little reason not to preclude all representations involving a substantially related matter, whether apparently adverse or not. Listening to a self-interested claim by a former client, or by others in his or her behalf, that matters in fact are 180 degrees from appearances would leave little room for any other choice.

Benign Conflicts

We have previously touched upon the problem presented by a claim that a lawyer's "benign" use of a former client's confidential information is permissible so long as the information will not be used adversely to the interests of the former client.[94] The lawyer's claim, while plausible, is not readily acceptable, because unless the former client consents, there can be no certainty that the use is not possibly adverse in ways that only the former client might reasonably appreciate. The lawyer might wish to take advantage of

89 See §§ 7.1.5, 7.3.3, 7.3.4.

90 1908 Canon 6.

91 MR 1.9 comment (first paragraph).

92 MR 1.9 comment (first paragraph). Query whether the comment implicitly rejects the so-called "scrivener" rule. See § 7.1.6.

93 79 Ill.App.3d 8, 34 Ill.Dec. 523, 398 N.E.2d 198 (1979).

94 See § 6.7.6.

information that a former client secretly plans to develop a large shopping center in order to benefit a second client by suggesting to the second client an investment in potentially valuable adjoining property. The lawyer might plausibly claim that the investment will not be adverse to the former client. Even if we assume as a certainty that the former client did not intend to buy the land in question, still the lawyer cannot be sure that the interest expressed by the new buyer will not alert others to the plans of the first client.

The question comes down to whether the lawyer rules should permit lawyers to speculate about the extent to which taking that kind of advantage of a former client's confidential information is benign or adverse. The Code seems to prohibit flatly any use of a client's confidential information;[95] the Model Rules do not clearly prohibit uses that are not obviously adverse.[96] Under the Model Rules, disciplinary agencies and courts are put into the difficult position of second-guessing what must, in most circumstances, be a speculative endeavor on the lawyer's part. The approach of the Code seems preferable.

(b) *Substantial Relationship*

In most instances it will be plain enough that client interests are, or are not, in conflict. What will typically be more difficult to determine is whether the substantial-relationship test is also satisfied. The test is now in general use as the standard by which to measure former-client conflicts of interest.[97] It is often traced to the 1953 decision by Judge Weinfeld in T.C. Theatre Corp. v. Warner Bros. Pictures, Inc.[98] In fact, the test is much older, as Judge Weinfeld himself demonstrated.[99] The opinion remains, however, the most eminently quotable of the genre:

> A lawyer's duty of absolute loyalty to his client's interest does not end with his retainer. He is enjoined for all time, except as he may be released by law, from disclosing matters revealed to him by reason of the confidential relationship. Related to this principle is the rule that where any substantial relationship can be shown between the subject matter of a former representation and that of a subsequent adverse representation, the latter will be prohibited. . . . [T]he former client need show no more than that the matters embraced within the pending suit wherein his former attorney appears on behalf of his adversary are substantially related to the matters or cause of action wherein the attorney previously represented him, the former client. The Court will assume that during the course of the former representation confidences were disclosed to the attorney bearing on the subject matter of the representation. It will not inquire into their nature and extent. Only in this manner can the lawyer's duty of absolute fidelity be enforced and the spirit of the rule relating to privileged communications be maintained.[1]

Although *T.C. Theatres* and the cases that have followed it primarily stress the objective of protecting the confidential information of the former client, the loyalty principle (§ 7.1.3) is not without significance as well, as the dual argument expressed in the last-quoted sentence of the opinion emphasizes.

The Presumption of Divulgence

The protection of confidential information is primarily responsible, however, for the procedural mechanism by which the substantial-relationship test is implemented. As discussed earlier,[2] if a client were required to

[95] DR 4–101(B)(3).

[96] Cf. MR 1.8(b).

[97] Ex parte Taylor Coal Co., 401 So.2d 1, 7 (Ala.1981) (rejecting former "confidentiality" rule, which required objecting party to show that former lawyer actually acquired confidential information); Aleut Corp. v. McGarvey, 573 P.2d 473, 474–75 (Alaska 1978); State v. Jones, 180 Conn. 443, 429 A.2d 936, 939 (1980); National Texture Corp. v. Hymes, 282 N.W.2d 890, 894 (Minn. 1979); Reardon v. Marlayne, Inc., 83 N.J. 460, 416 A.2d 852, 858 (1980); United Nuclear Corp. v. General Atomic Co., 96 N.M. 155, 629 P.2d 231, 319 (1980), cert. denied 451 U.S. 901, 101 S.Ct. 1966, 68 L.Ed.2d 289 (1981); Howard Hughes Medical Inst. v. Lummis, 596 S.W.2d 171, 174 (Tex.Civ.App.1980).

[98] 113 F.Supp. 265, 267 (S.D.N.Y.), reargument denied 125 F.Supp. 233 (S.D.N.Y.1953)

[99] See also, e.g., 113 F.Supp. at 268 n.3; Galbraith v. State Bar, 218 Cal. 329, 23 P.2d 291, 292 (1933); People v. Gerold, 265 Ill. 448, 477–78, 107 N.E. 165 (1914); Gillett v. Gillett, 269 Mich. 364, 257 N.W. 719, 720 (1934).

[1] 113 F.Supp. at 268–69.

[2] See text accompanying notes 63–64 supra.

offer evidence on the contents of confidential communications in order to have the client's former lawyer disqualified, the confidentiality of the information would be lost in the very process of attempting to protect it. That point has been appreciated both by courts, in the development of the common-law rules that disqualify a lawyer because of a former-client conflict, and by the framers of the 1983 Model Rules.

Courts have implemented the insight doctrinally by holding that once the former client shows the substantial relationship that is necessary to invoke the rule, a nonrebuttable presumption arises that the lawyer obtained in the former representation confidential information relating to each of its elements.[3] Because of the presumption, the lawyer is disqualified in a later representation if a risk exists that any of the presumed confidential information could be used against the interests of the former client.

A nonrebuttable presumption can, however, be a clumsy weapon unless the judges that wield it assess carefully the circumstances in which the presumption should be brought into play. Implementation of the presumption has raised two principal questions: (1) what are the appropriate comparatives—the elements in the current and the former representations that are to be compared to determine if they are substantially related, and (2) to what extent should the test take into account the nature and degree of the lawyer's involvement in the former representation?

Appropriate Comparatives

The substantial-relationship test should be implemented in a way that serves its intended function, but without undue restriction on the freedom of other clients to use the lawyer's legal services. It must be broad enough to give protection against adverse divulgence or use of the former client's confidential information, but not so sweeping that it includes many instances in which the threat to confidentiality or loyalty is either remote or illusory. Model Rule 1.9(a) asserts that what is being compared is the "matter" in each representation. Its comment states only that the scope of a "matter" "may depend on the facts of a particular situation or transaction."[4]

The substantial-relationship concept can be misused, or used analogously, for purposes different from those that directly underlie it. The misuse of judicial doctrine often stems from a too-hurried attempt to employ words talismanically, as if throwing the name of a doctrine at a complex problem would solve it. The analogous use of a doctrine is, of course, quite a different matter and can be legitimate or not, depending on the match between the purposes of the originial doctrine and the soundness of reasons given for borrowing it for other applications. For the present, each such use of the substantial-relationship test will be considered spurious. In that way, we can set to one side, as misleading or incomplete, instances in which courts have announced that the things being compared by the substantial-relationship test were such matters as (1) the lawyer's involvement in each representation (substantial involvement);[5] (2) the two or more lawyers who have been involved in both matters (substantial connection between lawyers);[6] (3) the extent to which the lawyer in fact was connected with the former-client confidential information (substantial risk of actual adverse use or disclosure); or (4) the extent to which the lawyer's representation of the former client was the result of a long-standing course of legal work for the same client (historically substantial period of representation).[7] None

[3] Westinghouse Elec. Corp. v. Gulf Oil Corp., 588 F.2d 221, 224 n.3 (7th Cir.1978); Emle Industries, Inc. v. Patentex, Inc., 478 F.2d 562, 571 (2d Cir.1973). More recently, the nonrebuttable nature of the presumption has been questioned. See infra at 368–69.

[4] See MR 1.9 comment (second paragraph).

[5] Cf. id.

[6] Fund of Funds, Ltd. v. Arthur Andersen & Co., 567 F.2d 225, 235 (2d Cir.1977)(substantial-relationship test borrowed to test triangular relationship between two firms and former client). Variations on the inquiry are seen in imputed-disqualification cases. See § 7.6.

[7] A long-standing relationship will naturally generate a significant array of matters that could create future substantial relationships. But the mere fact of a long-

of those adequately describes the things being compared in the substantial-relationship test. Some of them focus too narrowly on only some factors, but not all the important factors, that should be taken into account. As will be seen, some of them are objectionable because the inquiry they suggest would require an inspection of the actual confidential information.

Courts differ over the degree of generality or particularity that should be insisted upon in determining the scope of disqualifying similarities between matters. One set of decisions suggest a cause-of-action test: the cause of action in the second representation and that in the first are compared.[8] Other courts, a majority, insist upon a much more particularistic examination. The court conducts a three-stage examination of the former and the present representations. First, the court reconstructs the scope of the facts involved in the former representation and projects the scope of the facts that will be involved in the second representation. Second, the court assumes that the lawyer obtained confidential client information about all facts within the scope of the former representation. Third, the court then determines whether any factual matter in the former representation is so similar to any material factual matter in the latter representation that a lawyer would consider it useful in advancing the interests of the client in the latter representation.[9] That approach, while more painstaking than more general tests, is preferable.

It can be argued in favor of the cause-of-action or a similar approach, that it avoids the risk of exposing confidential information, because only a general examination of each representation is required. Moreover, unlike a more particularized examination of issues in the second case, the cause-of-action test conventionalizes the matters that will be involved in the second representation and thus permits final disposition of the issue of disqualification at the outset of the representation.[10] But conventionalizing in order to allow broad, generic treatment creates serious risk that the substantial-relationship test will be underinclusive.

Suppose, for example,[11] that a lawyer formerly represented a reporter in a libel action. Later the lawyer appeared for a plaintiff in a libel suit, against the reporter, based on an entirely separate publication. Was the second representation the same or a different cause of action? If the first case involved a newspaper article and the second involved a private letter— entirely separate transactions and factual settings—no threat of exposure of client confidential information was presented. Yet, if (as seems probable) it had been concluded under the cause-of-action test that there was no substantial relationship between

standing relationship is insufficient by itself to create a disqualification without an explicit showing of the necessary substantial relationship. E.g., In re Corrugated Container Antitrust Litigation, 659 F.2d 1341, 1346 (5th Cir.1981); Hydril Co. v. Multiflex, Inc., 553 F.Supp. 552 (S.D.Tex.1982).

8 Phillips v. Phillips, 242 Ga. 577, 250 S.E.2d 418 (1978) (lawyer's representation of grantee in suit to set aside series of deeds on ground of nonperformance of oral promises made contemporaneously was not "substantially related" to lawyer's serving as drafter of the deeds themselves for grantor). A broadbrush cause-of-action approach is suggested by the use of that phrase in the *T.C. Theatres* case itself. See 113 F.Supp. at 268.

9 The factual-reconstruction and comparable-issues approaches are suggested by Seventh Circuit cases. See Freeman v. Chicago Musical Instrument Co., 689 F.2d 715 722 n.10 (7th Cir.1982); Westinghouse Elec. Corp. v. Gulf Oil Corp., 588 F.2d 221, 225 (7th Cir.1978).

The statement in United States v. Standard Oil Co., 136 F.Supp. 345, 367 (S.D.N.Y.1955) has been frequently quoted: " [W]hen dealing with ethical principles, . . . we cannot paint with broad strokes. [T]he lines are fine and must be so marked. . . .The conclusion in a particular case can be reached only after a painstaking analysis of the facts and precise application of precedent." See also Duncan v. Merrill Lynch, Pierce, Fenner & Smith, Inc., 646 F.2d 1020, 1029 (5th Cir.) cert.denied 454 U.S. 895, 102 S.Ct. 394, 70 L.Ed.2d 211 (1981)("Only when the moving party delineates with specificity the subject matters, issues, and causes of action present in [the] former representation can the district court determine if the substantial relationship test has been met. Merely pointing to a superficial resemblance between the present and prior representations will not substitute for the careful comparison demanded.").

10 Cf. General Elec. Co. v. Valeron Corp., 608 F.2d 265 (6th Cir.1979), cert.denied 445 U.S. 930, 100 S.Ct. 1318, 63 L.Ed.2d 763 (1980).

11 Nichols v. Village Voice, Inc., 99 Misc.2d 822, 417 N.Y.S.2d 415 (Sup.Ct.1979).

the two matters, that might too hastily dismiss legitimate concerns of the former client. Suppose, for example, that in each case it was important to analyze the same facts relating to the work habits of the reporter in order to prove, or disprove, the reporter's good-faith basis for the allegedly libelous reports. The lawyer possessed confidential information concerning the common question of the former client's work habits, and that should have rather clearly required disqualification—a result that would follow only from a more particularized inquiry than the cause-of-action standard permits.[12] On the other hand, courts must be cautious not to presume too much through a more particularistic use of the substantial-relationship test. A particularized inquiry in some cases could produce such a vast array of facts that disqualification might be quite broad. That would be true, for example, if the prior representation involved a large business entity and related to such amorphous issues as the corporate structure of the client.[13] But to hold such information disqualifying would lead to the unacceptable result that most lawyers who represent large corporations would always be disqualified from representing any other client adversely to the interests of the corporation.

A particularized application of the substantial-relationship test, based on factual issues, must satisfy the competing policy objectives of the former-client conflict doctrine and, at the same time, should be administratively feasible. Such a test requires that the specific factual issues that were germane to the former representation, and not only those that were litigated or otherwise involved in it, be identified and compared. In litigation, the scope of review of the issues in the succeeding representation is primarily suggested by the pleadings and proceedings that have ensued at the time the motion is filed or the question otherwise arises, but is not necessarily confined to issues that are already articulated at the typically early stage in the litigation when the issue is raised. Issues that have not been placed in litigation at the pleading stage, but which it might be to the later advantage of the former or successor client to litigate, should also be taken into account.[14] The vantage point for viewing the future course of the succeeding representation should be one of maximum freedom for reasonably objective lawyers for both the former client and the successor client to develop and pursue alternative courses of action. A similar approach should be employed in determining whether a succeeding representation that does not involve litigation is substantially related to a former representation. In a sense the task of defining substantial relationship in cases not involving litigation is more amorphous because of the absence of pleadings to frame the issue. Yet many representations—will drafting, advising on a development project, applying for a license, and the like—will have rather readily predictable contours that permit confident scrutiny of factual issues.

12 In the actual case, the court analyzed the issues in each representation, concluded that the reporter's work habits were irrelevant in the second case, and therefore denied disqualification. Nichols v. Village Voice, Inc., 417 N.Y.S.2d at 419. See also, e.g., Avnet, Inc. v. OEC Corp., 498 F.Supp. 818 (N.D.Ga.1980)(lawyer disqualified when succeeding representation accused former client of illegal activities that involved industry, territory, and type of sales activity similar to those in former representation, in which lawyer had defended former client against similar charges).

13 Westinghouse Elec. Corp. v. Rio Algom, Ltd., 448 F.Supp. 1284 (N.D.Ill.1978)(general knowledge of corporation's organization and supporting personalities, quickly learned in any event through normal civil discovery, not disqualifying in otherwise unrelated litigation), affirmed sub nom. Westinghouse Elec. Corp. v. Kerr-McGee Corp., 588 F.2d 221 (7th Cir.), cert.denied 439 U.S. 955, 99 S.Ct. 353, 58 L.Ed.2d 346 (1978). Cf. Emle Indus., Inc. v. Patentex, Inc., 478 F.2d 562, 571–74 (2d Cir.1973)(particularized inquiry demonstrates that facts about former client's corporate relationship with subsidiary, about which lawyer learned in first representation, in fact would be disputed element in succeeding representation). But see Reardon v. Marlayne, 83 N.J. 460, 416 A.2d 852 (1980) (general tactical thinking of former corporate client can always be relevant and useful).

14 General Elec. Co. v. Valeron Corp., 608 F.2d 265, 267 (6th Cir.1979), cert.denied 445 U.S. 930, 100 S.Ct. 1318, 63 L.Ed.2d 763 (1980); American Roller Co. v. Budinger, 513 F.2d 982, 985 (3d Cir.1975).

Rebuttable or Nonrebuttable Nature of the Presumption of Divulgence

A remaining question is whether the substantial-relationship standard should serve as an automatic bar or whether it should be rebuttable. Differing views have been expressed.[15] On the whole, it is better to permit very limited exceptions. Those exceptions should be confined to instances in which a lawyer can demonstrate that, despite appearances, the lawyer in fact was not in a position to gain client confidences in the first representation. For example, suppose that in the prior representation an action against the client was filed in federal court. Wishing to litigate in state court, the client's lawyer retained a second lawyer who was a federal court litigation specialist and whose work for the client was confined solely to arguing, successfully, that the federal court should dismiss on the ground of lack of subject-matter jurisdiction (an issue that would be determined from facts on the face of the pleadings). If such a limited role were demonstrated, the federal litigation specialist should not be barred thereafter from representing a successor client in a matter that—although not the same ongoing matter as was involved in the prior representation [16]—is factually related to it in a substantial way.[17] The factual showing the lawyer would make to defeat the presumptive disqualification produced by the substantial-relationship test would not involve any inquiry into confidential information furnished by the former client and thus would be fully compatible with the spirit of the test.

Aside from similarly exceptional situations, in which confidentiality can be fully protected in the course of listening to a public discussion of whether disqualification is proper, the prophylactic role of the substantial-relationship test can be served only if exceptions are not readily admitted. The wholesale proliferation of exceptions would create serious confusion in application of the former-client conflict rules, particularly in jurisdictions that have adopted the substantial-relationship test as a disciplinary standard, either through the decisional process or by adopting a rule such as Model Rule 1.9. Some sympathetic cases can be adequately handled by limitations on the application of the imputed-disqualification rule (§ 7.6), so that the broadly prophylactic purposes of the substantial-relationship test, without causing overly broad sanctions, limit temptations to profit personally from side switching.

The "Scrivener" and Similar Exceptions

One danger that should be avoided is that of creating categorical exceptions to the substantial-relationship standard. An instance found in some decisions is the scrivener exception: if a lawyer was retained only to draft a

15 Compare, e.g., Government of India v. Cook Indus., Inc., 422 F.Supp. 1057, 1059–60 (S.D.N.Y.1976), affirmed 569 F.2d 737 (2d Cir.1978); Reardon v. Marlayne, Inc., 83 N.J. 460, 416 A.2d 852, 859 (1980), with, e.g., Government of India v. Cook Indus., Inc., 569 F.2d at 741 (Mansfield, J., concurring); Lemelson v. Synergistics Research Corp., 504 F.Supp. 1164, 1167 (S.D.N.Y.1981).

16 It might be argued that the hypothetical in the text could also be analyzed by taking account only of the factual issues involved in the litigation specialist's representation on the subject-matter jurisdiction motion. In that view, there would be no substantial relationship between the prior representation and any other representation in which similar factual issues did not appear. That approach also avoids the need to recognize rebuttable exceptions to the substantial-relationship test. Such a narrow approach to a definition of the factual issues involved in the former representation, however, might permit the specialist to appear later in the same litigation as counsel for the opposing party after it had been refiled in a proper court. Same-suit side switching is not prohibited by the simultaneous-representation rules because, by definition, the lawyer is never involved in simultaneous representation. See § 7.3.2. While confidentiality is not at stake, a reasonable expectation of loyalty on the part of the former client seems to be impaired by permitting the side switching on the facts of the problem.

17 Cf., e.g., Simmon's Inc. v. Pinkerton's, Inc., 555 F.Supp. 300 (N.D.Ind.1983)(factual reconstruction of prior representation, accomplished through use of nonconfidential information, showed no substantial relationship, because lawyer's role was limited to participation at multiparty planning session, at which no confidential information was revealed); City of Cleveland v. Cleveland Elec. Illuminating Co., 440 F.Supp. 193 (N.D.Ohio 1976), affirmed 573 F.2d 1310 (1977), cert.denied 435 U.S. 996, 98 S.Ct. 1648, 56 L.Ed.2d 85 (1978). See also MR 1.9 comment (second paragraph).

document, the lawyer can later represent an adversary of the former client in a substantially related matter.[18] It has also been suggested that some lawyerly roles, such as that of bond counsel,[19] rarely involve significant exposure to client confidential information and thus might be routinely exempted from the substantial-relationship test altogether. Or lawyers who perform only appellate work for a former client might be assumed to have contact with nothing other than public documents from a completed proceeding and thus should enjoy categorical exemption from the substantial-relationship rule.[20]

There is significant danger in proceeding categorically in any of those areas. Lawyers do not invariably perform the same function in the same way in all representations of the same general kind. A mere scrivener of a deed in one case might extensively interview a client in another about tax, title, marital, and other important issues. Appellate work in one instance might be confined to an open record, but in another the appeal could serve as the prelude to an evidentiary hearing that the lawyer anticipates with extensive factual inquiries. In most such instances, it would be highly preferable to purchase confidence in the loyalty and confidentiality of lawyers through predictable and certain application of the substantial-relationship test. In an exceptional case, a lawyer could be permitted to demonstrate that the scope of the representation was indeed entirely devoid of exposure to confidential client information. The showing should, of course, be confined to a demonstration of lack of access to any source of such information without inquiry into the contents of communications. Such an attempted showing should always be subject to defeat by the former client's showing that the lawyer consulted with the client in confidence, that the lawyer examined client files, that the lawyer consulted with another lawyer or financial adviser to the client, or that the lawyer was similarly in a position potentially to gain access to sources of confidential information.

Former Coclients and Coparties

The decisions are divided on the question whether a former coclient is entitled to the protection of the former-client conflict rules. Among coclients, the attorney-client testimonial privilege is narrowed substantially; information confided by any coclient to the common lawyer is not privileged in later litigation between the coclients (§ 6.4.8). Some decisions adopt the view that the former-client conflict of interest rules are therefore irrelevant between former coclients. Thus a lawyer who formerly represented two coclients is permitted to appear as an adversary lawyer for the one former coclient and against the second coclient in the same or a substantially related matter.[21]

But other courts have wisely refused to carve out an exception to the former-client conflict rules for former coclients.[22] They point to the loyalty principle (§ 7.1.3) as an independent and sufficient basis for precluding the lawyer from accepting an adverse subsequent representation. Despite the compromise of confidentiality, a lawyer for coclients is in a particularly delicate position, in which treachery is hardly ever out of the

[18] Phillips v. Phillips, 242 Ga. 577, 250 S.E.2d 418, 419 (1978); Midfelt v. Lair, 221 Kan. 557, 561 P.2d 805, 815 (1977).

[19] City of Cleveland v. Cleveland Elec. Illuminating Co., 440 F.Supp. 193, 207–08 (N.D. Ohio 1976), affirmed 573 F.2d 1310 (1977), cert.denied 435 U.S. 996, 98 S.Ct. 1648, 56 L.Ed.2d 85 (1978).

[20] People v. Jones, 105 Ill.App.3d 1143, 62 Ill.Dec. 25, 435 N.E.2d 823 (1982). Cf. Domed Stadium Hotel, Inc. v. Holiday Inns, Inc., 479 F.Supp. 465, 468 (E.D.La.1979) (where facts indicated that lawyer did not even have attorney-client relationship with objecting party, fact that services involved only appellate work considered as additional factor).

[21] Petty v. Superior Court, 116 Cal.App.2d 20, 253 P.2d 28, 33–34 (1953); Croce v. Superior Court, 21 Cal.App.2d 18, 68 P.2d 369 (1937). Cf. Ex parte Taylor Coal Co., 401 So.2d 1, 8–9 (Ala.1981)(combination of coclient considerations, limited nature of representation, and special need for free choice of lawyer in rural county with sparse lawyer population).

[22] Brennan's, Inc. v. Brennan's Restaurants, Inc., 590 F.2d 168 (5th Cir.1979); Cord v. Smith, 338 F.2d 516 (9th Cir.1964), opinion clarified 370 F.2d 418 (9th Cir.1966); E.F. Hutton & Co. v. Brown, 305 F.Supp. 371 (S.D.Tex. 1969); In re Evans, 113 Ariz. 458, 556 P.2d 792 (1976); Goldstein v. Lees, 46 Cal.App.3d 614, 120 Cal.Rptr. 253 (1975).

question. At the very least, when the coclient relationship is dissolved and disputes arise from precisely the same matter, the lawyer's representation of a former coclient against a former client who is now an adversary, should not be permissible.

Still a third line of authority should also be considered. In those cases a lawyer representing a long-standing client also represents a new client in a temporary coclient relationship. Those decisions have held that if litigation subsequently arises between the long-standing client and the new client, the lawyer can represent the old client against the new one.[23] Those cases are probably based on the notion that the new client has consented in advance to subsequent adverse representation by the common lawyer if litigation between the old and the new client later ensues. Although the decisions are understandable on those terms, the facts of some of the cases do not indicate that adequate disclosure was given to the new client of the full implications of the lawyer's intention to favor the interests of the old client if trouble later arose.[24] The reason for such apparent nonchalance about disclosure—and for a limit on the extent to which those decisions should be applied—is the fact that the new client in each cited instance was a sophisticated business entity represented by separate and independent counsel.[25]

Related issues can arise when two coparties are each represented by separate lawyers, but when, in order to further their mutual interest in the litigation, the coparties share information. It is settled, as a matter of the confidentiality rules, that such pooling of confidential information does not necessarily waive the attorney-client privilege (§ 6.4.9). It has also been held that a former representation of that kind does not disqualify one of the coparties' lawyers from representing the party against the former coparty on a substantially related matter so long as no confidential information in fact was shared.[26] That is consistent with the relaxing of confidentiality between the parties that is accomplished by the pooled-information exception to the privilege. Moreover, in many of those situations each party will be represented by a lawyer at the time the information is shared, thus protecting against indiscriminate revelation of information that would assist the informed party in the future litigation or other disputes.

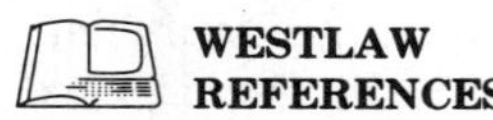

WESTLAW REFERENCES

Adverse Interests

45k20

Real Interests versus Ruse Interests

topic(45 +p interest /3 former)

Benign Conflicts

dr4–101(b)(3) "dr 4–101(b)(3)"

Substantial Relationship

"t.c. theatre" /p substantial** /5 relat!

The Presumption of Divulgence

non-rebuttable rebuttable +1 presumption /p confiden! /4 client attorney lawyer information

Appropriate Comparatives

substantial** /5 relat! /p "cause of action" /p confiden! /4 client attorney lawyer information

The "Scrivener" and Similar Exceptions

scrivener "bond counsel" /p substantial** /5 relat! /p confiden! /s client

---

23 Allegaert v. Perot, 565 F.2d 246, 251 n.7 (2d Cir. 1977); Neiman v. Local 144, 512 F.Supp. 187 (E.D.N.Y. 1981); Domed Stadium Hotel, Inc. v. Holiday Inns, Inc., 479 F.Supp. 465, 468–69 (E.D.La.1979).

24 The problem of consent in advance is considered at § 7.2.4(b).

25 Allegaert v. Perot, 565 F.2d 246, 251 n.7 (2d Cir.1977) (lawyer's failure to clarify potential conflicts of interest was, on facts, irrelevant: "the parties were not only aware of their mutual relationship, but also were as sophisticated, perhaps, as the American corporate community can be.").

26 Wilson P. Abraham Constr. Corp. v. Armco Steel Corp., 559 F.2d 250, 253 (5th Cir.1977); Krebs v. Johns-Manville Corp., 496 F.Supp. 40 (E.D.Pa.1980); Griesemer v. Retail Store Employees Union, 482 F.Supp. 312, 315 (E.D.Pa.1980). The courts refused to presume that confidential information was shared. The party seeking disqualification was required to show that in fact the lawyer gained such information in the former coparty relationship.

§ 7.5 CONFLICTS OF ADVOCATE–WITNESSES

§ 7.5.1 *Difficulties of the Dual Role*

An advocate who attempts to serve as advocate for a client while also testifying in the same case combines roles with diverging demands. Courts have always discouraged it.[27] The possibilities for confusion of the lawyer's proper function have resulted in an advocate-witness rule that generally prohibits a lawyer from attempting the feat.

The advocate-witness rule is applied in three principal areas. First, because the rule is found in the professional regulations, violation can lead to discipline, although this is infrequently imposed and rarely severe.[28] Second, and of greater enforcement value, is the fact that courts accept the rule as the basis for a motion by an opposing party to disqualify the would-be testifying advocate from continuing as advocate. Third, the prohibition against combining the advocate and witness roles finds expression in rules of evidence. A century ago jurisdictions enforced an absolute evidentiary bar against a lawyer testifying for his or her client.[29] That rule has been changed by statute or decision in every American jurisdiction so that the advocate-witness prohibition is no longer an automatic rule of evidence.[30] Those developments have left the motion for disqualification as by far the most important sanction against attempts by a lawyer to combine the advocate and witness roles.

WESTLAW REFERENCES

"advocate-witness rule"

§ 7.5.2 *Developments under the Professional Rules*

Each of the three sets of lawyer regulations drafted in this century—the 1908 Canons, the 1969 Code of Professional Responsibility, and the 1983 Model Rules of Professional Conduct —has prohibited lawyers from combining advocate-witness roles. We will examine each and then, in the context of a critique of the approach of the Model Rules, consider several problems of interpretation and implementation that have arisen.

(a) *1908 Canons*

The Canons prohibited advocates from testifying on behalf of clients, with exceptions for advocate testimony about "purely formal matters" and testimony that was "essential to the ends of justice." [31] The Canons did not explicitly prohibit a lawyer from testifying adverse-

27 Hickman v. Taylor, 329 U.S. 495, 513, 67 S.Ct. 385, 91 L.Ed. 451 (1947); French v. Hall, 119 U.S. 152, 154–55, 7 S.Ct. 170, 30 L.Ed. 375 (1886).

28 Comment, The Lawyer as Witness for His Client, 17 Ala.L.Rev. 308, 311 (1964); Note, Legal Ethics—Enforceability of Canon Prohibiting Attorney's Testimony on Behalf of Client, 33 N.C.L.Rev. 296 (1955). The charge is likely to be found as only a minor element in an array of disciplinary charges. E.g., People v. Spiegel, 193 Colo. 161, 567 P.2d 353 (1977). The sanctioning impact of the rule can also be felt, for example, when courts use it as a ground for denial of a lawyer's motion to represent a client pro hac vice. E.g., In re Rappaport, 558 F.2d 87 (2d Cir.1977).

29 J.Wigmore, Evidence § 1911, at 775 (J.Chadbourn rev.1976). The evidentiary bar was part of the general rule that disqualified interested persons from testifying. Id.

30 Waltzer v. Transidyne Gen. Corp., 697 F.2d 130, 134 (6th Cir.1983), and authorities cited; People v. Burwell, 44 Cal.2d 16, 38, 279 P.2d 744, 756, cert. denied 349 U.S. 936, 75 S.Ct. 788, 99 L.Ed.2d 1265 (1955); People v. Gendron, 41 Ill.2d 351, 243 N.E.2d 208 (1968), cert.denied 396 U.S. 889, 90 S.Ct. 179, 24 L.Ed.2d 164 (1969); Shapiro v. Wendell Packing Co., 366 Mich. 289, 115 N.W.2d 87 (1962); Pittman v. Currie, 414 So.2d 423, 427 (Miss.1982). The removal of the incompetence bar to testimony by a lawyer leaves courts free to enforce the advocate-witness rule more flexibly such as by requiring that an adversary show the strong relevance of a lawyer's testimony before an opposing party's lawyer can be forced to the witness stand. See infra at 382, nn. 67–68. Moreover, a court is empowered to require a lawyer to choose before trial between continuing as an advocate and appearing as a witness and to enforce the lawyer's choice of advocacy by barring the lawyer from the witness stand. E.g., Rushton v. First Nat'l Bank, 244 Ark. 503, 426 S.W.2d 378, 385 (1968); People v. Smith, 13 Cal.App.3d 897, 903–04, 91 Cal.Rptr. 786 (1970); Harris v. State, 78 Wis.2d 357, 254 N.W.2d 291, 298 (1977).

31 ABA Canon 19: "*Appearance of Lawyer as Witness for His Client.* When a lawyer is a witness for his client, except as to merely formal matters, such as the attestation or custody of an instrument and the like, he should leave the trial of the case to other counsel. Except when essential to the ends of justice, a lawyer should avoid testifying in court in behalf of his client."

ly to his or her own client, but in the rare cases where that presented itself, the general prohibition against conflicting interests was held to bar the lawyer from representing the client.[32] Under the Canons, courts occasionally employed the rule as a basis to disqualify a lawyer violating it.[33] On the whole, however, the rule seems to have been one largely commended to the lawyer's good judgment. A multitude of ethics committee opinions attempted to give sure guidance to lawyers about how far the rule in fact was intended to reach.[34]

(b) *1969 Code*

The Code [35] very broadly prohibits the mixture of the roles of advocate and witness by mandatory rules, subject to exceptions dealing with relatively inconsequential testimony or with emergencies in which disqualification of the lawyer would cause serious hardship to the client. A broad imputed-disqualification rule provides that any lawyer associated with the advocate-witness is also disqualified from serving as an advocate in the case.[36]

The Disciplinary Rules draw several distinctions between situations involving testimony in favor of and against one's own client and between the requirements for declining initial representations and withdrawing at a later point.

(1) *Client-Favoring Testimony.* If an advocate or a lawyer associated with the advocate "ought to be" called [37] as a witness in behalf of a client, then the advocate must decline the representation [38] and must withdraw if the need to testify becomes apparent after the representation begins.[39] In either event, the duty to decline or to withdraw is tested by an objective standard. The duty exists when the lawyer "knows or it is obvious" that the lawyer ought to testify.[40] Four exceptions are provided. An advocate need not decline or withdraw if the lawyer's testimony (1) relates to an uncontested matter; (2) (confusingly stated in a different exception) relates to an uncontested matter and concerns a mere formality; (3) relates to the nature and value of legal services rendered in the same case; or (4) is contested and material but disqualification would cause a "substantial hardship" to the advocate's client because of the "distinctive value" of the lawyer or the lawyer's firm in representing the client.[41]

(2) *Client-Harming Testimony.* If a lawyer learns that either he, she, or an associate lawyer may be called as a witness "other than

[32] Cf. ABA Formal Op. 185 (1938)(partner of lawyer who had witnessed murder and who was to testify as chief prosecution witness was precluded from defending the accused).

[33] Erwin M.Jennings Co. v. DiGenova, 107 Conn. 491, 141 A. 866 (1928).

[34] For a collection of opinions, see Wydick, Trial Counsel as Witness: The Code and the Model Rules, 15 U.C. Davis L.Rev. 651, 655–57 (1982).

[35] Recent commentary on the Code's advocate-witness rules has been extensive and largely critical of their breadth, particularly the imputed-disqualification rule. Brown & Brown, Disqualification of the Testifying Advocate—A Firm Rule?, 57 N.C.L.Rev. 597 (1979); Enker, The Rationale of the Rule that Forbids a Lawyer to Be Advocate and Witness in the Same Case, 1977 Am.B. Found. Research J. 455; Lewis, The Ethical Dilemma of the Testifying Advocate: Fact or Fancy?, 19 Hous.L.Rev. 75 (1981); Sutton, The Testifying Advocate, 41 Tex.L.Rev. 477 (1963)(Cannon 19); Wydick, Trial Counsel as Witness: The Code and the Model Rules, 15 U.C. Davis L.Rev. 651 (1982); Comment, The Attorney as Both Advocate and Witness, 4 Creighton L.Rev. 128 (1970); Note, The Advocate-Witness Rule: If Z, Then X. But Why?, 52 NYU L.Rev. 1365 (1977); Note, Professional Ethics—Disciplinary Rule 5–102(A)—Disqualification of Law Firms under the Attorney-Witness Rule, 54 Tul.L.Rev. 521 (1980); Comment, Disqualification of Counsel under the Advocate-Witness Rule: Fair or Futile?, 48 U.Cin.L.Rev. 794 (1979). Comment, The Rule Prohibiting an Attorney from Testifying at a Client's Trial: An Ethical Paradox, 45 U.Cin.L.Rev. 268 (1976).

[36] The imputed-disqualification rule is repeated in each of the two main rules precluding mixture of the advocate and witness roles, DR 5–101(B) and DR 5–102(A) & (B).

[37] The determination of when a lawyer "ought" to testify in aid of a client is considered infra 381–83.

[38] DR 5–101(B).

[39] DR 5–102(A).

[40] MacArthur v. Bank of New York, 524 F.Supp. 1205, 1208–09 (S.D.N.Y.1981). But see J.D. Pflaumer, Inc. v. Dep't of Justice, 465 F.Supp. 746, 747–48 (E.D.Pa.1979) (initial determination of whom client "ought to call" as witness should be left to client).

[41] DR 5–101(B)(1)-(4). The exceptions are also incorporated by reference into the corresponding rule requiring disqualification because of events that occur after the lawyer undertakes representation. See DR 5–102(a). The exceptions are discussed together with the similar exceptions in the Model Rules, infra at 385–388.

in behalf of [the] client," the lawyer must withdraw if it is apparent that the testimony will be "prejudicial" to the client.[42] No exceptions similar to those for client-favoring testimony are provided.

With respect to disqualification for either client-favoring or client-disfavoring testimony, the Code does not permit waiver of the disqualification through consent either by the lawyer's client or by any other person.[43] The Code also provides that the lawyer's disqualification is imputed to all lawyers in his or her firm, again without any provision for consent.[44]

Rationale for the Code's Prohibitions

The Code version of the advocate-witness rule has been defended on several grounds, not all of which are very convincing and not all of which consistently support the breadth of disqualification provided.

(1) *Protecting the Advocate-Witness's Client.* First, various arguments are made for protection of the advocate's own client. A principal concern is that the client's adversary can more easily impeach the client's lawyer as a witness because of the advocate's evident bias as the client's lawyer.[45] The argument is severely limited for several reasons. (i) The problem it identifies is hardly cured by disqualification—the client's adversary can still impeach the former advocate by bringing out the fact of prior representation.[46] (ii) A rule based on concern for the client's interests should be subject to client consent, but the Code creates a nonconsentable conflict. (iii) The difficulty could be cured at least as thoroughly by substituting another lawyer from the same firm, but the Code does not permit same-firm substitutions. A variation on the argument is that combining the roles places the lawyer "in the unseemly and ineffective position of arguing his own credibility."[47] Again, either client consent or substitution from the same firm seems to solve whatever problem might be created—at least as far as the lawyer's client is concerned—but neither is permitted.

(2) *Hobbling the Adversary.* Second, arguments are advanced that the combined roles disadvantage the advocate's adversary be-

42 DR 5-102(B). Surprisingly, the Code says nothing explicitly about declining representation in such circumstances, but presumably the general no-conflict rule (DR 5-101(A)) would apply. That rule, however, contains a client-consent exception which, as will be seen, is generally unavailable in other advocate-witness conflict disqualifications.

43 Despite the absence of a consent provision in the Code, some courts will deny disqualification if the adversary's only objection is based on considerations of the interests of the advocate's own client and if the client has insisted upon the advocate's assistance despite being aware of the practical problems of the dual roles. E.g., General Mill Supply Co. v. SCA Services, Inc., 697 F.2d 704, 715 (6th Cir.1982). Courts also apply procedural waiver rules. For example, a failure to object to an advocate-witness's representation at trial will prevent a litigant from raising the issue on appeal. For an extreme case in the criminal defense context, see United States v. Crockett, 506 F.2d 759 (5th Cir.), cert.denied 423 U.S. 824, 96 S.Ct. 37, 46 L.Ed.2d 40 (1975)(waiver when defense lawyer did not object on this ground when prosecutor subpoenaed defense-lawyer, who only invoked Fifth Amendment about his own involvement in the offense for which defendant was charged and convicted). See also, e.g., United States v. Fiorillo, 376 F.2d 180 (2d Cir.1967).

44 See DR 5-101(B); DR 5-102(A) & (B).

45 See EC 5-9. A variation of the client-protection argument is that the advocate who becomes a witness is disabled from effectively examining himself or herself in order to elicit the most coherent and believable testimony. The objection could readily be met by a much more limited response than full disqualification of the advocate. For example, an associate lawyer pro tempore could be appointed to conduct only the examination of the advocate as a witness. See United States v. Freeman, 519 F.2d 67, 69 (9th Cir.1975). Another adverse result might be that the advocate's testimony would create strategic openings for the other side, such as opening the door to cross-examination of the advocate's client on matters not mentioned in the client's testimony. E.g., Glover v. State, 557 P.2d 922, 925 (Okla.Crim.App.1976), cert.denied 431 U.S. 922, 97 S.Ct. 2193, 53 L.Ed.2d 235 (1977).

The weight of client-protecting concerns increases considerably when the lawyer is called as a witness by an opposing party. That obviously detracts from the lawyer's value to his or her own client and might impair the lawyer's ability to function effectively as an advocate. For such reasons, a defendant in a criminal trial may be deprived of the effective assistance of counsel if the prosecution calls the defense lawyer as a prosecution witness. See infra note 79.

46 Underwater Storage, Inc. v. United States Rubber Co., 314 F.Supp. 546 (D.D.C.1970); People v. Mann, 27 Ill. 2d 135, 188 N.E.2d 665, cert.denied 374 U.S. 855, 83 S.Ct. 1923, 10 L.Ed.2d 1075 (1963).

47 EC 5-9.

cause the adverse party's lawyer will be hobbled in cross-examination.[48] The rationale is sometimes based on a claim that the customarily scathing cross-examination by the opposing lawyer will be seriously constrained due to professional courtesy. The rationale is probably unrealistic, and some forms of it border on the specious. The same assumedly deferential lawyer, it will not be overlooked, is typically moving to disqualify an adversary lawyer and thus to deprive that same professional colleague of a fee. If undue delicacy still precludes effective questioning, the timid lawyer should be the one required to find an able substitute. The same quaking advocate must still cross-examine a lawyer, even if the witness is not also an advocate.

A related rationale is that the advocate-witness will be able to gain additional credibility with the jury because he or she has superior status as a lawyer. That seems inconsistent with the concern about impairing the lawyer's testimony for his or her client and is inconsistent with objections based on a supposedly general public perception that a lawyer will readily lie for clients. Perhaps the argument is that some of those evils will befall the adversary in some cases, and others in others, an empirical proposition that attempts rather unconvincingly to have it both ways. It is also doubtful that undue juror gullibility about the credibility of a lawyer's testimony is lessened by removing the lawyer-witness from the second role of advocate. Finally, to the extent that it is realistic to fear that the jury might give too much weight to the lawyer's testimony, that concern does not support the broad prohibition against substituting a lawyer from the same firm.[49]

(3) *Appearance of Impropriety.* Third, various arguments are made for the proposition that combining the roles will have deleterious effects on public opinion either of trials or of the legal profession. It might be feared that the public will believe, correctly or not, that combining the roles will tempt the lawyer-witness to commit perjury.[50] As has been pointed out in the discussion of other uses of the appearance-of-impropriety argument (§ 7.1.4), a matter as serious as disqualification or discipline cannot confidently rest on anything as amorphous as suspected public misperception of lawyers. On the other hand, if the proposition being advanced is that lawyers are in fact more likely to lie as witnesses if they also are advocates in the same case, then that proposition should be examined free from entanglements with speculative concerns about unknown and unknowable public reactions.

A Better Rationale

In fact, there are perfectly straightforward reasons for concerns that combining the roles can create strong pressure on a lawyer to confuse the distinct roles of advocate and witness. At the outset it is reasonable to assume that the advocate will naturally feel sympathy for his or her client. Moreover, the size of the lawyer's fee in a litigated case often depends on the outcome,[51] whether the fee is explicitly contingent or not. Possibly of greater importance, professional esteem and reputation is reserved mainly for winning lawyers in litigation, not losers. Those strong incentives might cause a lawyer to slant testimony on the witness stand or to recite facts while commenting on the evidence. They are effectively removed by disqualification of a

[48] Id.

[49] A different form of the argument, which begins by noting a kind of harm to the adversary, is sketched below—an argument that does support some form of an advocate-witness rule.

[50] Cf. EC 5–9 (last sentence). Wigmore is reponsible for popularizing and giving respectability to the argument based on the "appearance of impropriety." See J.Wigmore, Evidence § 1911, at 775–88 (J.Chadbourn rev. 1976).

[51] Draganescu v. First Nat'l Bank, 502 F.2d 550 (5th Cir.1974), cert.denied 421 U.S. 929, 95 S.Ct. 1655, 44 L.Ed. 2d 86 (1975)(lawyer for plaintiff, who was to be paid by plaintiff on contingent fee basis, intended to appear as chief trial witness on question of terms of commercial contract that lawyer had negotiated in plaintiff's behalf and defendant was alleged to have breached).

lawyer-witness[52] from the role of advocate. Because false lawyer testimony and overblown oratory would harm the adversary and not the lawyer's client, client consent does not cure the problem. Not all commentators would agree with that assessment, although most of them in recent years have been critical of the advocate-witness disqualification rule. But that assessment seems to be the common-sense notion that underlies much of the strong judicial resistance to the practice—a notion whose dimensions and force are unfortunately obscured by the appearances-of-impropriety locution and other unconvincing arguments to which some courts too uncritically resort.[53]

To say that sound policy supports the rule requiring disqualification of an advocate who will appear as a witness is not, of course, to say that the rule can sensibly be applied in a wooden way. In clumsy judicial hands, the rule has needlessly stripped clients of their trusted lawyers and of the monetary value represented by their fee investment prior to disqualification. In those cases it has served no important interest of the other side, save to give some adversaries a delaying and harassing device. Beyond its impact on individual clients whose lawyers are disqualified, an overly strict advocate-witness rule also threatens the quality of factual investigation and attempts at preventive law by advocates. The rule, and particularly its extension to cause the imputed disqualification of all law-firm lawyers, means that no lawyer in a law firm that a client wished to serve as trial counsel in threatened litigation could safely attend negotiation sessions designed to avert trial or to renegotiate a contractual arrangement that had become unravelled, for fear of becoming a potential witness.[54] Many litigation-avoiding steps that a law firm might take must be avoided, approached with extreme caution, or undertaken at additional expense by other lawyers.[55]

The Rule Run Amok: Comden

The defects in a needlessly severe application of the advocate-witness rule were exposed in the decision of a majority of the California Supreme Court in *Comden v. Superior Court*.[56] Actress Doris Day Comden had signed a contract with a distributing company permitting it to use her name in advertising its pet food. A dispute arose, and she hired a corporate lawyer and his firm to advise her and to negotiate with the company. Her corporate lawyer attended a negotiation meeting at which he assertedly heard a person connected with the company admit facts supporting Day's claim of a breach of the contract. While the defendant later denied that the statement had been made, witnesses other than the corporate lawyer were prepared to testify to the fact. The negotiations failed, and Day retained a partner of the corporate lawyer to file suit against the company. The defendant moved to disqualify the entire firm. Doris Day, as client, consented, indeed was adamant, that her chosen lawyer remain as trial counsel. She requested, at the least, that the court defer passing on the question of disqualification until further discovery could be had to determine whether the lawyer's testimony was necessary. Nonetheless, the court ordered both the corporate lawyer, his

52 For somewhat similar reasons, it is common to find a judge prohibited from serving as both jurist and witness in the same case. Compare, e.g., 28 U.S.C.A. § 455 (recusal rule: "Any justice or judge of the United States shall disqualify himself in any case in which . . . he is or has been a material witness"); with, e.g., Fed.R.Evid. 605 (judge presiding at trial incompetent as witness); West's Ann.Cal.Evid.Code § 703(b)(same); In re Martin, 71 Cal.App.3d 472, 139 Cal.Rptr. 451, 457 (1977). See generally C.McCormick, Evidence § 68 (E.Cleary 3d ed. 1984).

53 Comden v. Superior Court, 20 Cal.3d 906, 912, 145 Cal.Rptr. 9, 11, 576 P.2d 971, 973, cert.denied 439 U.S. 981, 99 S.Ct. 568, 58 L.Ed.2d 652 (1978).

54 MacArthur v. Bank of New York, 524 F.Supp. 1205 (S.D.N.Y.1981).

55 See Brown & Brown, Disqualification of the Testifying Advocate—A Firm Rule?, 57 N.C.L.Rev. 597, 617 (1979).

56 20 Cal.3d 906, 145 Cal.Rptr. 9, 576 P.2d 791, cert.denied 439 U.S. 981, 99 S.Ct. 568, 58 L.Ed.2d 652 (1978). For later reflections on *Comden*, see Maxwell v. Superior Court, 30 Cal.3d 606, 180 Cal.Rptr. 177, 639 P.2d 248 (1982).

partner, and the rest of their firm disqualified.

Following the decision in *Comden*, the California Supreme Court was coerced into changing by rule the strict standard that it had created by decision. The change shifted positions radically. Within a matter of months, a bar-sponsored amendment to the advocate-witness rule was presented to and approved by the court. The new rule provided that the client's written consent would *always* resolve the advocate-witness problem.[57] As in the changing scenes of some mock opera, where only disqualified lawyers once littered the California stage, one would now expect to find only the carcasses of the ignored interests of opposing parties. Purchasing peace for the Doris Days of the world, at the price of refusing ever to heed the interests of a party moving for disqualification, can work different evils as serious as those in *Comden* that called for reform of the California rule. A more discriminating approach would be preferable. It was clearly the intent of the framers of the 1983 Model Rules to provide such an approach.

(c) *1983 Model Rules*

The Model Rules improve upon the 1969 Code in dealing with the advocate-witness problem. Unfortunately the wording of Model Rule 3.7 seriously veils its intended meaning. Model Rule 3.7(a) provides that "a lawyer shall not act as advocate at a trial in which the lawyer is likely to be a necessary witness," subject to exceptions. That cryptic language really couches two rules in one short statement.[58] First, a lawyer generally may not testify at a trial while also appearing as advocate.[59] Second, a lawyer generally may not choose to act as advocate and forego testifying for a client if the lawyer's testimony "is likely to be . . . necessary."

The first rule, against mixing the roles of advocate and witness, is plain enough on the face of MR 3.7(a). The rule's comment rests its rationale squarely on the interests of the client's adversary.[60] The opponent has a legitimate claim to be free of the prejudicial impact on the fact finder that is likely to be caused by the lawyer's testifying to the sworn truth at the same time that the lawyer explains and comments on the weight of the testimony given in the case.[61] The prohibition, therefore, cannot be avoided by the consent of the advocate's own client.

Under one of three exceptions in 3.7(a), a lawyer may continue as advocate, yet testify: (1) if the testimony relates to an uncontested issue; (2) if the testimony relates to the nature and value of legal services in the case; or (3) if disqualification of the lawyer would work "substantial hardship" on the client.[62]

[57] Cal.R.Prof.Cond. Rule 2–111(A)(4)(as amended November 1, 1979). Under Rule 2–111(A)(5), as amended, however, the client's consent is apparently irrelevant if the lawyer's testimony "is or may be prejudicial to his client." The command-response relationship between the California Supreme Court and the State Bar, reflected in the quick demise of the unpopular *Comden* rule, is a perhaps unusually graphic example of bar influence over judicial rule making in the area of bar regulation. See § 2.3.

[58] The confusing conflation of the two rules into one is unfortunate because it does not clearly express either. Moreover, the exceptions provided in MR 3.7(a)(1)-(3) seem clearly more relevant to the first rule (barring testimony) than to the second (electing to forego testifying and proceeding as an advocate), although the exceptions appear to be equally applicable to either part of the rule.

[59] See MR 3.7 comment (first and second paragraphs).

[60] A shaky linguistic argument could be made that MR 3.7(a) excludes the dual role only if the lawyer's testimony is "necessary" and thus that lawyer testimony that is merely cumulative should never disqualify. Such an argument is obviously inconsistent with the rationale for the disqualification rule and with the exception provided for uncontested testimony. Moreover, in many situations in which the argument could be made, the lawyer's testimony is excludable under evidence rules such as Federal Rule of Evidence 403, on the ground that the probative value of the testimony is outweighed by its potential to mislead the jury. Wydick, Trial Counsel as Witness: The Code and the Model Rules, 15 U.C. Davis L.Rev. 651, 685 (1982).

[61] In that light, the advocate-witness rule of both the Model Rules and the Code can be seen to complement the prohibition against a lawyer personally attesting to the truth or falsity of evidence. See DR 7–106(C)(3); MR 3.4(e). See generally § 12.1.2.

[62] The Model Rule exceptions match those provided in the Code's DR 5–101(B)(1)–(4), except that they collapse the Code's uncontested-testimony and formal-testimony exceptions into one and restate the hardship exception to remove a restrictive reading that had caused problems

Those exceptions should be construed as the exclusive bases for permitting an advocate also to appear as a witness in the same case.

When Is a Lawyer's Testimony "Necessary"?

The rule that the lawyer has only one choice—to testify—if his or her testimony is "necessary" for the client appears only murkily from the wording of Model Rule 3.7(a) and hardly at all from its official comment.[63] One who reads the rule might imagine that a lawyer complies with the rule simply by deciding not to testify, regardless of the value of the testimony to the client. Such a decision, of course, would raise serious questions about either the lawyer's competence or about the effect of a conflict of interest. The conflict is between the lawyer's duty of loyalty to the client, which urges the lawyer to give the needed testimony, and the lawyer's economic instincts, which may lead the lawyer to remain in the case as advocate in order to continue earning a fee that otherwise would have to be abandoned.[64]

In order to be consistent with the clear intent of the framers of the Model Rules and the judicial authority that has previously developed, Rule 3.7(a) should be interpreted to require that an objective determination that the lawyer's testimony is necessary always requires the lawyer to step down as advocate. The advocate must assess in advance whether the value of his or her testimony to the client is such that the trial of the case should be left to another lawyer. That prediction can sometimes be made with confidence, but not always. If a motion to disqualify a lawyer is made early in the proceeding and if it is not clear to what extent the lawyer's testimony will be necessary, a suitable resolution is for the court to reserve ruling on the motion until further pretrial discovery and other steps clarify the issue.[65] A lawyer who similarly moves ahead cautiously, subject to later mandatory withdrawal (see § 7.5.2(e)), seems to have responded appropriately to the uncertainty of the situation for disciplinary purposes as well.

Probably no better test of "necessary" can be devised than to inquire whether the absence of the lawyer's testimony would seriously undermine the ability of the client either to survive a motion for a directed verdict by an opposing party or to persuade the fact finder of the greater believability of the client's version of important events.[66] If the client's case would surely fail without the lawyer's testimony, then the lawyer is clearly required to abandon the role of advocate and testify. The lawyer should also testify in any instance in which it is probable, although not certain, that the lawyer's testimony would be considered by a disinterested lawyer to be important to the client's success.

Nothing should turn automatically on the technical classification of the lawyer's possible testimony or the order in which it would be presented. Even if the lawyer would be called only in rebuttal, if the testimony is

under the Code. The exceptions are examined infra at 385–88.

[63] The point was elaborately covered in the suppressed Legal Background note of earlier drafts of the Model Rules. See MR 3.7 legal background note at 152–53 (Proposed Final Draft, May 30, 1981). The note expressed the view that the "ought to be called" language of the Code (which expressed the obligation to testify much more clearly) was objectionable only because it did not sufficiently confine itself to instances in which the lawyer's testimony was "necessary."

[64] The conflict exposed here lies at the root of the lawyer's problem and explains the placement of the advocate-witness rule in the 1969 Code under Canon 5. The Model Rules categorize the problem in the section dealing with the role of "Advocate," the only context in which the problem arises.

[65] See Miller Elec. Constr., Inc. v. Devine Lighting Co., 421 F.Supp. 1020 (W.D.Pa.1976). To be distinguished, of course, is the invited peril of proceeding to a point where withdrawal would work a substantial hardship on the advocate's client, despite a much earlier appearance of the reasonable likelihood of testifying. See infra at 386–88.

[66] The test, in short, is whether absence of the lawyer's testimony would materially impair the client's position on the risk of nonproduction or on either party's risk of nonpersuasion. In relatively unusual situations, a lawyer might also be required to testify by a procedural rule. E.g., International Woodworkers v. Chesapeake Bay Plywood Corp., 659 F.2d 1259 (4th Cir.1981)(designation by client of lawyer as person to respond to discovery under Fed.R.Civ.P. 30(b)(6) indicates that lawyer "ought to" testify on behalf of client).

necessary in the above sense, then the lawyer should appear at the trial only as a witness.[67] But it should not be enough to force an advocate from the case if all that can be said about the lawyer's possible testimony is that it would be relevant and useful.[68]

Cumulative Testimony Is Not Necessary

The most important example of such useful, but not necessary, testimony is a lawyer's testimony that would be merely cumulative of other, credible evidence that is alone sufficient to carry the day.[69] In such a case, the lawyer should be free, with consent of the client, to forego testifying and to proceed as advocate.[70] Decisions under the 1969 Code propound conflicting standards for determining whether a lawyer should testify as a witness for a client. Some of the decisions erroneously require disqualification without regard to the particular value of the lawyer's possible testimony.[71] The better view under the Code, however, is that a lawyer is not disqualified if his testimony is likely to be merely cumulative.[72]

Testimony Involving the Lawyer's Own Conduct

An early draft of the Model Rules contained additional language in the advocate-witness rule that would have extended it beyond occasions when a lawyer actually attempted to testify formally to instances when "the lawyer's own conduct is a material issue." The language was omitted apparently out of concern that it swept too broadly and would create temptations to attempt to manipulate adversaries' lawyers out of a case. It nonetheless captures a useful concept that is well-recognized in the case law.[73] The problem in such situations is that an advocate whose conduct is an important matter of evidence in

[67] J.P. Foley & Co. v. Vanderbilt, 523 F.2d 1357, 1359 (2d Cir.1975); Eurocom, S.A. v. Mahoney, Cohen & Co., 522 F.Supp. 1179, 1181 (S.D.N.Y.1981). See also Hempstead Bank v. Reliance Mortgage Corp., 81 A.D.2d 906, 439 N.Y.S.2d 202, 203 (1981)(lawyer's testimony necessary when unfavorable inference might be drawn from his failure to testify).

[68] Several careful decisions have reached this conclusion under the 1969 Code. E.g., Miller Elec. Constr., Inc. v. Devine Lighting Co., 421 F.Supp. 1020, 1023–24 (W.D. Pa.1976)(merely cumulative lawyer testimony is not necessary); In re Gorfkle, 444 A.2d 934, 940–41 n.6 (D.C. 1982)(lawyer is not disqualified because she uses information from conversation with reluctant witness to cross-examine the witness); Chuck v. St. Paul Fire & Marine Ins., Co., 61 Haw. 552, 606 P.2d 1320 (1980)(lawyer who was participant in negotiating contract or discussing past event that is subject of litigation is not by that reason alone disqualified as advocate); Galarowicz v. Ward, 119 Utah 611, 230 P.2d 576, 580 (1951).

[69] EC 5–10 ("it is not objectionable for a lawyer who is a potential witness to be an advocate if it is unlikely that he will be called as a witness because his testimony would be merely cumulative"). Nothing in MR 3.7 or its comments suggests the same point, although nothing in those places is inconsistent with it. The point was made emphatically in the suppressed Legal Background Note to an earlier comment. See MR 3.3 Legal Background Note at 153 (Proposed Final Draft, May 30, 1981).

[70] As a matter between lawyer and client—and not involving in any way an opposing party—the lawyer's decision to forego testifying in order to serve as advocate involves a potential conflict of interest. See supra at 377. That is particularly true when the lawyer would earn a large fee for acting as advocate and little or no fee if he or she withdrew to testify. The temptation for the lawyer to downplay the importance of his or her testimony should be discussed with the client, and the client should voluntarily consent to the lawyer's recommended choice of the role of advocate.

[71] Compare, e.g., J.P. Foley & Co. v. Vanderbilt, 523 F.2d 1357, 1359 (2d Cir.1975)(examination of transcript of deposition of lawyer compels conclusion that his testimony is necessary to his client's case); Davis v. Stamler, 494 F.Supp. 339, 341–43 (D.N.J.1980), affirmed 650 F.2d 477 (3d Cir.1981)(lawyer must be necessary witness), with, e.g., Supreme Beef Processors, Inc. v. American Consumer Indus., Inc., 441 F.Supp. 1064, 1069 (N.D.Tex.1977) (lawyer "could conceivably" testify); Comden v. Superior Court, 20 Cal.3d 906, 145 Cal.Rptr. 9, 576 P.2d 971, cert.denied 439 U.S. 981, 99 S.Ct. 568, 58 L.Ed.2d 652 (1978)(must appear that lawyer will not be called as a witness).

[72] See authorities cited supra, notes 68, 71.

[73] United States v. Cunningham, 672 F.2d 1064, 1075 (2d Cir.1982)(if advocate who allegedly made statements to his own secretary, about which she could permissibly testify, could cross-examine her and argue that her testimony was not credible, his forensic stance could hardly be taken by the jury as anything but unsworn testimony); United States v. Bates, 600 F.2d 505, 511 (5th Cir.1979); Roby v. State, 587 P.2d 641, 645–46 (Wyo.1978). See also People v. Paperno, 54 N.Y.2d 294, 445 N.Y.S.2d 119, 429 N.E.2d 797 (1981)("unsworn witness" rule can be basis for disqualifying prosecutor who had questioned witness before grand jury and who now prosecuted him for evasive answers, because defendant made substantial and satisfactory showing that prosecutor's conduct before the grand jury would be a relevant and material issue).

a trial can "testify" without ever taking the stand. The advocate's permissible questions in cross-examining witnesses and his or her statements to the jury in arguing issues of credibility and the weight of the evidence supply ample opportunity for the advocate to function as an "unsworn witness" about his or her own out-of-court activities.

Advocate Testimony Adverse to a Client

Suppose that an advocate and the advocate's client agree that the advocate has no testimony to offer in the case but the advocate has been subpoenaed to testify by the party opposing the client. If the lawyer is not a necessary witness for his or her client, then Model Rule 3.7(a) provides, in effect, that the general conflict of interest rules [74] determine whether the fact that the lawyer is likely to be called as a witness by another party requires disqualification.[75] As with the Code's DR 5–102(B), MR 3.7 provides that a lawyer in such a situation should not serve as advocate if the lawyer's truthful testimony will be adverse to his or her own client's interests.

A party generally has freedom to select witnesses to call voluntarily or, if they are unwilling, to force them to testify through subpoena. But the power to call opposing counsel as a witness could be employed in a manipulative way to foist upon that lawyer the role of advocate-witness and thereby drive the lawyer from the case.[76] Courts retain the power to require a party who attempts to force the opposing party's trial lawyer to the witness stand to specify in advance the nature of the testimony sought, so that the court can pass on its relevance in order to further the policy of limiting testimony by advocates.[77] Beyond a minimal showing of relevance, courts will generally require that the opposing party demonstrate that the advocate's testimony will be substantially useful to that party and that the evidence is not available from any other witness in a substantially similar form and with substantially similar weight.

If a party does force an adversary's advocate to the witness stand and the advocate's testimony is helpful to his or her own client, the party eliciting the testimony cannot complain about the lawyer's involuntary mixture of the advocate-witness roles. Pretrial discovery or a few preliminary questions at trial should reveal whether the advocate's testimony will favor or disfavor his or her client. If it favors, the opposing party has invited the adverse reaction, if any, of the fact finder. If the testimony is adverse to the lawyer's client, surely the party who called the lawyer-witness and who receives the benefit of the testimony cannot complain.

Nonetheless, some decisions have intimated that an advocate can be disqualified on motion of an adversary who wants to call the lawyer to give testimony that will, assertedly, be harmful to the disqualified lawyer's own client.[78] The lawyer's client, of course, is aggrieved and can legitimately object in another proceeding that the lawyer's motivation to earn a fee as trial advocate kept the lawyer in the case when a reasonably diligent and loyal advocate would have known that he or she would be called as a hostile witness and thus should withdraw. As will be seen, the advocate who testifies adversely is probably subject to professional discipline if the lawyer failed to withdraw from the case when it first

74 MR 1.7 (simultaneous conflicts); MR 1.9 (former-client conflicts).

75 MR 3.7 comment (last paragraph).

76 Kroungold v. Triester, 521 F.2d 763, 766 (3d Cir. 1975); Ross v. Great Atl. & Pac. Tea Co., 447 F.Supp. 406, 408 (S.D.N.Y.1978); Smith v. Arc-Mation, Inc., 402 Mich. 115, 261 N.W.2d 713, 716 (1978); Galarowicz v. Ward, 119 Utah 611, 230 P.2d 576, 580 (1951).

77 Gajewski v. United States, 321 F.2d 261, 268–69 (8th Cir.1963), cert.denied 375 U.S. 968, 84 S.Ct. 486, 11 L.Ed. 2d 416 (1964); State v. Williams, 656 P.2d 450, 453 (Utah 1982).

78 Freeman v. Kulicke & Soffa Indus., 449 F.Supp. 974, 981 (E.D.Pa.1978)(dictum), affirmed 591 F.2d 1334 (3d Cir. 1979); Ross v. Great Atl. & Pac. Tea Co., 447 F.Supp. 406, 409 (S.D.N.Y.1978)(dictum); Emerald Green Homeowners' Ass'n v. Aaron, 90 A.D.2d 628, 456 N.Y.S.2d 219 (1982).

became apparent that the lawyer would be required to testify.

But none of that should occupy a busy court in which the original litigation is pending. Certainly such a court should not entertain a motion by the unaggrieved opposing party in a civil case. In the special context of criminal trials, the act of the prosecutor unnecessarily calling defense counsel as a witness for the prosecution may amount to a denial of the effective assistance of counsel if it materially interferes with the defendant's access to counsel or denies the defendant a fair trial.[79] In view of the special interest of the prosecution in avoiding subsequent attacks on convictions on the ground of ineffective assistance of counsel, if a defense advocate's testimony will be useful and favorable to the government's case, the trial court has discretion to disqualify the defense lawyer if the testimony will so sharply conflict with the defendant's interests that the conflict is nonconsentable.[80]

Under the general conflict of interest rules, client consent under the Model Rules can remove the adverse-testimony barrier in all but those rare cases in which the lawyer's adverse testimony so sharply conflicts with the client's interests that the client's consent is objectively unreasonable.[81] For example, if a lawyer saw the client shoot another person, the lawyer's testimony would so prejudice the client that no other reasonable lawyer would believe that the lawyer's representation of the client at a subsequent trial for murder would not be adversely affected by the testimony that the lawyer would be required to give.[82] By contrast, under the 1969 Code the test is much more inclusive. The mere fact that the testimony of a lawyer, when called by another party, "is or may be" prejudicial to the client requires disqualification.[83] The Code is open to the interpretation that even slightly adverse testimony would require disqualification. Moreover, under the Code there is no provision for client consent.[84] Thus there is at least some threat under the Code that an adversary could force disqualification of the carefully chosen and fully trusted lawyer for the other side, and that lawyer's entire firm as well, by the strategem of serving a subpoena for testimony by the lawyer about relatively innocuous matters.

Imputed Disqualification

Many of the objections to the scope of the Code's advocate-witness rule have to do with DR 5–105(D), which provides without exception that if a lawyer is disqualified from a representation, then all lawyers affiliated with the lawyer as partner, associate, or in other ways are also automatically disqualified.[85] In response to those criticisms, Model Rule 3.7(b) limits imputed disqualification to those rare situations involving nonconsentable conflicts.[86] For example, suppose a lawyer participates in contract negotiations and could testify about oral statements, made by an adverse party, that materially aid the case of the lawyer's client. Under MR 3.7(a), the lawyer should testify and not appear as trial

79 Kaeser v. State, 96 Nev. 955, 620 P.2d 872 (1980); State v. Thomas, 53 Or.App. 375, 631 P.2d 1387, 1390 (1981), and authorities cited.

80 See United States v. Cortellesso, 663 F.2d 361, 363 (1st Cir.1981).

81 MR 1.7(b)(1) & (2). See generally § 7.2.3.

82 Cf. ABA Formal Op. 185 (1938)(lawyer disqualified as trial counsel when partner will testify for prosecution in murder trial). See also United States v. Cortellesso, 663 F.2d 361 (1st Cir.1981)(defense lawyer's testimony that he had agreed with police in defendant's behalf that stolen goods would not be moved from defendant's basement (from which they subsequently were moved) would produce a "deformity" that not even consent could cure, and thus lawyer must be removed as advocate). Compare, e.g., People v. Baldi, 54 N.Y.2d 137, 444 N.Y.S.2d 893, 899–900, 429 N.E.2d 400 (1981)(defense lawyer permitted to take stand to testify to client's confessions of bizarre crimes in order to bolster defense theory of insanity).

83 DR 5–102(B).

84 The California rule, which was amended for all other purposes to permit written client consent to cure any advocate-witness problem (see supra note 57) goes on to provide an unamended and strict rule, without provision for cure by consent, in any case in which "it is apparent that [the advocate's] testimony is or may be prejudicial to his client." Cal.Rule 2–111(A)(5).

85 The sweep of DR 5–105(D) has been modified by some courts in certain applications. See generally § 7.6.3.

86 See MR 3.7(b); MR 1.7(b); MR 1.10(a) & (c). The California rule (Rule 2–111(A)) has no imputed-disqualification counterpart to its individual disqualification rule.

counsel unless the lawyer's testimony would be merely cumulative. But nothing in the Model Rules prohibits a partner of the lawyer from trying the case, so long as the client consents to the representation after disclosure of the possible hazard that the lawyer-witness will be subject to enhanced impeachment because of interest in the outcome due to association with his or her partner.[87]

The 1969 Code, on its face, is much more restrictive. Every lawyer in the firm of an advocate-witness is vicariously disqualified because of the primary disqualification of the advocate-witness; no exception is made for client consent.[88] Some cases decided under the Code have applied the rule literally.[89] In certain significant areas, however, some courts have balked. A first prominent area involves cases in which a claim is made that an entire governmental law office is disqualified if one of its members testifies. In those cases, typically involving prosecutor offices, judges are unwilling to impose such a drastic remedy.[90]

A second exception involves cases in which a lawyer is a party to litigation. Clearly the lawyer-litigant, even if also a witness, has the right to represent himself or herself. Does the lawyer also have a right to representation by his or her own firm? The Second Circuit, in a line of cases, has held broadly that a federal statute providing a right of litigants to representation "personally or by counsel"[91] entitles a lawyer-litigant to representation by his or her own firm, a right that cannot be impinged upon by the imputed-disqualification corollary to the advocate-witness rule.[92] But if that is a statutory right of lawyer-litigants, it is surely not a right they enjoy solely by dint of being members of the lawyer caste. Logically, if it applies at all to the situation, the statute should apply to all litigants and permit them to choose any law firm they might want, including the firm of an advocate-witness. While the result is pleasing, the headlong plunge from the remote springboard of the federal statute is probably too breathtaking for most courts. Unless a state adopts the Model Rules, then, lawyer-litigants in Code states should have no more prerogatives than litigants who are less privileged by legal learning.

(d) *Exceptions to the Advocate-Witness Rule*

Exception for Uncontested Testimony

Both the Code and the Model Rules except from the advocate-witness ban a lawyer whose only role as witness in the litigation will be to testify to an undisputed matter. The excep-

87 See MR 1.7(b); MR 1.10(c).

88 DR 5–101(B); DR 5–102(A). See, e.g., Comden v. Superior Court, 20 Cal.3d 906, 145 Cal.Rptr. 9, 576 P.2d 971 (1978), cert.denied 439 U.S. 981, 99 S.Ct. 568, 58 L.Ed. 2d 652 (1978).

89 J.P. Foley & Co. v. Vanderbilt, 523 F.2d 1357 (2d Cir. 1975); Hempstead Bank v. Reliance Mortgage Corp., 81 A.D.2d 906, 439 N.Y.S.2d 202, 203 (1981). Other courts, however, have refused to apply the strict and nonconsentable imputed-disqualification rule of the Code. E.g., Field v. Freedman, 527 F.Supp. 935, 942 (D.Kan.1981); Greenebaum-Mountain Mortgage v. Pioneer Nat'l Title Ins. Co., 421 F.Supp. 1348, 1352 (D.Colo.1976).

90 People v. Superior Court of San Luis Obispo County, 84 Cal.App.3d 491, 148 Cal.Rptr. 704, 710 (1978); State ex rel. Goldsmith v. Superior Court, 386 N.E.2d 942, 945 (Ind.1979); State v. Martinez, 89 N.M. 729, 557 P.2d 578, 581 (1976), cert.denied 430 U.S. 973, 97 S.Ct. 1663, 52 L.Ed.2d 367 (1977); State v. Taylor, 301 N.C. 164, 270 S.E.2d 409, 945 (1980). See also Chessman v. Teets, 239 F.2d 205, 214 (9th Cir.1956), vacated on other grounds 354 U.S. 156, 77 S.Ct. 1127, 1 L.Ed.2d 1253 (1956).

91 28 U.S.C.A. § 1654: "In all courts of the United States the parties may plead and conduct their own cases personally or by counsel as, by the rules of such courts, respectively, are permitted to manage and conduct causes therein."

92 Bottaro v. Hatton Associates, 680 F.2d 895, 897 (2d Cir.1982); International Elec. Corp. v. Flanzer, 527 F.2d 1288, 1295 (2d Cir.1975). Accord, Borman v. Borman, 378 Mass. 775, 393 N.E.2d 847, 856–57 (1979); Oppenheim v. Azriliant, 89 A.D.2d 522, 452 N.Y.S.2d 211, 212 (1982). But see, e.g., General Mill Supply Co. v. SCA Services, Inc., 697 F.2d 704, 711 (6th Cir.1982)(in abuse-of-process case against major law firm, in which plaintiff's entire case rested on believability of the advocate-witness's testimony concerning telephone conversation with plaintiff about defendant firm's motive in bringing suit, only disqualification of entire firm would assure that noninterested lawyers would appear who could conduct meaningful settlement discussions); Omni Developments, Inc. v. Porter, 459 F.Supp. 930 (S.D.Fla.1978)(advocate-witness rule prohibits representation of lawyer-litigant by his partner). The *Bottaro* and *Flanzer* decisions presumably do not regard the imputed-disqualification rule of the code as a "rule of such court" under 28 U.S.C.A. § 1654 that can limit a lawyer-litigant's choice of counsel.

tion makes sense because by definition there will be no occasion for the advocate to argue to the fact finder the credibility of uncontested testimony.

Under MR 3.7(a)(1) lawyer testimony that relates to an uncontested matter does not require disqualification. The 1969 Code probably provides much the same thing, but in two subsections that separately cover uncontested matters and formalities in a way that invites possible and unintended distinctions.[93] As examples of formal matters, 1908 Canon 19 mentioned advocate testimony relating to the authentication of a document or its custody. Presumably advocate testimony about such matters would continue to be permissible if it were known to be substantially uncontested.[94] Importantly, under both codes the materiality of the evidence is irrelevant so long as it is uncontested. Even the most devastating testimony can be offered by an advocate without objection if the other side is not prepared to contest the testimony, presumably in good faith.[95] Realistically, of course, it will hardly ever occur that such devastating scenes are acted out at trial without opposition.

Exception for Value of Legal Services

Both the 1969 Code (DR 5–101(B)(3)) and the 1983 Model Rules (MR 3.7(a)(2)) explicitly permit an advocate to testify to the nature and value of legal services rendered in the case.[96] The exception avoids the need for a separate trial or proceeding in cases[97] in which one of the parties is entitled to recover legal fees.[98] In addition, advocates on either side are equally competent to testify on aspects of the same issue, so that either party, if so inclined, may choose to rebut advocate testimony with advocate testimony. Courts have also observed that excluding an advocate from testifying on the witness stand in support of his or her own fee is in conflict with the general right of litigants to appear pro se, a right that the advocate-witness should be entitled to claim because he or she often possesses standing as a party with respect to the fee claim.[99]

Exception for Substantial Hardship

The substantial-hardship exception of Model Rule 3.4(a)(3), although employing some of the same phraseology as the 1969 Code,[1] in fact provides a more flexible standard. The Model Rule comment indicates that the question of hardship is to be resolved by "a balancing . . . between the interests of

93 DR 5–101(B) provides that an advocate may testify

(1) If the testimony will relate solely to an uncontested matter.

(2) If the testimony will relate solely to a matter of formality and there is no reason to believe that substantial evidence will be offered in opposition to the testimony.

The second category is but a species of the genus described by the first. Decisions under the Code rightly draw no distinction between testimony about a formality and any other kind, so long as the testimony is uncontested. E.g., Nakasian v. Incontrade, Inc., 78 F.R.D. 229, 232 (S.D.N.Y.1978).

94 United States v. Trapnell, 638 F.2d 1016, 1025 (7th Cir.1980)(chain of custody of letters).

95 See MR 3.1.

96 DR 5–101(B)(3) of the Code seems to limit the exception to such testimony about legal services rendered "by the lawyer or his firm to the client." The language might be read as if to exclude lawyer testimony about the value (or lack of it) of legal services claimed by the *opposing* party. No reason differentiates the two, and the apparent distinction drawn by the rule has not been drawn by the courts.

97 Ahlers v. C & S Equipment, Inc., 405 So.2d 464 (Fla. App.1981); Biddle v. Chatel, 421 A.2d 3, 5 (D.C.App.1980).

98 MR 3.7 comment (third paragraph). The comment offers as an additional rationale the notion that the judge will have firsthand knowledge about the value of the legal services rendered and thus will be less dependent on the adversary process to test credibility. That is true, of course, only to the extent that the testimony relates to the number of hours of in-court legal services or relates to the novelty or difficulty of the work. Most of the fee in most cases will be earned for out-of-court work, a matter on which the trial judge will presumably lack firsthand information.

99 Theobald v. Botein, Hays, Sklar & Herzberg, 465 F.Supp. 609 (S.D.N.Y.1979); Spilky v. Hirsch, 102 Misc.2d 536, 425 N.Y.S.2d 934 (Sup.Ct.1980). See generally text at note 91.

1 DR 5–101(B)(4) provides an exception "as to any matter, if refusal would work a substantial hardship on the client because of the distinctive value of the lawyer or his firm as counsel in the particular case."

the client and those of the opposing party."[2] Under the 1969 Code, however, several courts had refused to answer any question other than that posed by the words of the Code: whether the lawyer whose disqualification was sought was "of distinctive value . . . as counsel in the particular case."[3] That might mean, as some courts held, that a lawyer must be replaced, even if at great expense, unless the client can demonstrate that no other lawyer could perform as effectively as the client's chosen lawyer.[4]

Under the Model Rules, the sheer expense of replacing a lawyer is sufficient to create an exception, unless the moving party's legitimate interests in removing the lawyer are more substantial. Self-inflicted hardship should trade at only a substantially discounted value. A lawyer should be assumed to be aware of the rule against the mixture of roles. If the lawyer nonetheless continues to expend the client's funds in preparing for trial and thereby becomes uniquely familiar with the facts of the case, the client's more appealing remedy is to look to the lawyer for compensation rather than to presume to be favored by the exception.[5] Similarly, a lawyer who serves as his or her own investigator incurs the unfortunate risk of being required to appear as a witness in behalf of a client to impeach and offer substantive evidence in resistance to a turncoat witness whose trial testimony seriously conflicts with oral statements made in pretrial conversations.[6] On the other hand, if the witness's contrary trial testimony is a surprise, then the substantial-hardship exception permits the lawyer momentarily to testify about prior inconsistent statements by the witness.[7] The fact that trial is to a judge rather than before a jury also permits greater liberality in allowing a lawyer to testify.[8]

In general, the substantial-hardship standard assesses more than the advocate's client's personal wishes and contentment with the lawyer as advocate, as important as those otherwise might be. Mere longevity of the client-lawyer relationship should not be sufficient unless the lawyer has gained important relevant information about the case at hand from prior exposure to the client's affairs.[9] The lawyer's distinction must be shown to be

[2] MR 3.7 comment (last paragraph). A working standard containing some of the same flexibility was urged in ABA Formal Op. 339 (1975), but was not adopted by all courts dealing with disqualification motions.

[3] DR 5–101(B)(4).

[4] MacArthur v. Bank of New York, 524 F.Supp. 1205 (S.D.N.Y.1981); Supreme Beef Processors, Inc. v. American Consumer Indus., Inc., 441 F.Supp. 1064 (N.D.Tex. 1977). But see Universal Athletic Sales Co. v. American Gym. Corp., 546 F.2d 530 (3d Cir.1976), cert. denied 430 U.S. 984, 97 S.Ct. 1681, 52 L.Ed.2d 378 (1977)(no reversible error to permit patent lawyer to serve as advocate and as expert witness in light of great deal of time and resources spent preparing for trial). A similar inflexible position, based on the words "because of the distinctive value of the lawyer," is indicated in In re Lathen, 294 Or. 157, 654 P.2d 1110, 1114 (1982). The *Lathen* court held that although continuing a case because no other lawyer was available to try the case would have caused substantial hardship to the client because of the emotional trauma of waiting for another trial date, the hardship was not recognized in DR 5–101(B)(4).

[5] General Mill Supply Co. v. SCA Services, Inc., 697 F.2d 704, 713–15 (6th Cir.1982).

[6] For that reason the ABA Defense Function Standards § 4–4.3(d) recommends that a defense lawyer should be accompanied to witness interviews by a "third person," who could testify. The correlative rule for prosecutors is ABA Prosecution Function § 3–3.1(f). See United States v. Johnston, 690 F.2d 638, 645 (7th Cir.1982)(en banc); People v. Bonilla, 101 Misc.2d 146, 420 N.Y.S.2d 665 (1979)(prosecutor appearing in videotape of defendant's confession). The third person should not be the accused, in the case of the defense, or the victim, in the case of the prosecutor, because of the danger of creating the impression of an attempt to intimidate the witness. E.g., Parker v. United States, 363 A.2d 975, 978 (D.C.App. 1976). An even more cogent reason for some accused persons not to be necessary interview witnesses is that they would then be required to testify and thus be exposed to prior-conviction impeachment.

[7] In re Ta Chi Navigation Corp., 677 F.2d 225, 230 (2d Cir.1982); Andrea Dumon, Inc. v. Pittway Corp., 110 Ill. App.3d 481, 66 Ill.Dec. 148, 155, 442 N.E.2d 574, 581 (1982); Besette v. Enderlin School Dist. No. 22, 310 N.W.2d 759, 764 (N.D.1981). See also, e.g., Schwartz v. Wenger, 267 Minn. 40, 124 N.W.2d 489, 492 (1963). Cf. United States v. Woodard, 671 F.2d 1097, 1100 (8th Cir. 1982)(no error for trial court to refuse to permit defense lawyer to withdraw near end of long and complicated trial, when intended defense witness refused to testify on grounds of self-incrimination).

[8] Bickford v. John E. Mitchell Co., 595 F.2d 540, 544 (10th Cir.1979); Cartin v. Continental Homes, 134 Vt. 362, 360 A.2d 96, 99 (1976).

[9] Hasnas v. Hasnas, 72 A.D.2d 764, 421 N.Y.S.2d 384, 385 (1979).

relevant to the trial of the particular case in which the question arises. For example, a substantial hardship is not demonstrated by the fact that the advocate-witness speaks the same foreign language as the advocate's client if there is no clear showing of the particular value that the ability might play in the particular case.[10] And the fact that a client's chosen advocate is preeminent in his or her field does not by itself give that lawyer freedom to take cases in which he or she must also take the stand.[11]

(e) *Implementing the Advocate-Witness Rule*

Disqualification Limited to Trials

The advocate-witness disqualification provided in Model Rule 3.7 applies only to the lawyer's role as advocate "at a trial." [12] The obvious intent of the rule is not to disqualify an advocate-witness from performing other legal functions for the client, possibly including court appearances in connection with motions and other preliminary matters that have nothing to do with the lawyer's testimony. Some authority exists under the 1969 Code for leaving to the informed discretion of the trial judge the decision of the question whether the disqualification should operate only with respect to courtroom appearances or apply more extensively to other facets of the representation.[13] A similar discretion seems appropriate under the Model Rules.

If the exception for nontrial appearances is recognized, however, it should not affect the preexisting duty of the advocate-witness to see that the client's trial appearances are left to another competent lawyer. Moreover, as the cases have appreciated, if a pretrial hearing turns on questions of fact, the same advocate-witness constraints may prevent an advocate at the hearing from giving testimony as well.[14] But, in the converse of the first-mentioned situation, if the advocate-witness's only testimony will be confined to pretrial hearings before a judge, that testimony should not disqualify the advocate from serving as advocate at the trial on the merits if the advocate will not testify at trial.[15] Finally, it seems unnecessary to apply the advocate-witness ban if a lawyer who was forced to testify at trial under an exception to the advocate-witness rule wants to argue the appeal and the appeal involves material issues turning on the lawyer's testimony.[16] Appellate judges can be trusted to give the lawyer's arguments only their proper value.

Mandatory Withdrawal

The advocate-witness prohibition does not extend to all employments, but only to those

10 Draganescu v. First Nat'l Bank, 502 F.2d 550, 552 (5th Cir.1974), cert.denied 421 U.S. 929, 95 S.Ct. 1655, 44 L.Ed.2d 86 (1975). See also, e.g., Federated Adjustment Co. v. Sobie, 90 A.D.2d 806, 455 N.Y.S.2d 820, 822 (1982) (relationship of husband (lawyer) and wife (client) is not sufficiently special circumstance in relatively simple litigation).

11 See In re Lathen, 294 Or. 157, 654 P.2d 1110, 1113–14 (1982).

12 MR 3.7(a). The limited imputed-disqualification requirement in MR 3.7(b) refers to acting as an advocate "in" a trial. The "at-in" difference is purely one of word choice.

13 General Mill Supply Co. v. SCA Services, Inc., 697 F.2d 704, 716 (6th Cir.1982)(dictum); Norman Norell, Inc. v. Federated Dep't Stores, Inc., 450 F.Supp. 127, 130–31 (S.D.N.Y.1978); Koger v. Weber, 116 Misc.2d 726, 455 N.Y.S.2d 935 (1982). The practice of an advocate submitting his or her own affidavit on a motion for summary judgment has been permitted, although discouraged. E.g., Inglett & Co. v. Everglades Fertilizer Co., 255 F.2d 342, 349 (5th Cir.1958); Lowell v. Wantz, 85 F.R.D. 290, 291 (E.D.Pa.1980).

14 United States v. Singer, 660 F.2d 1295, 1302–03 (8th Cir.1981), cert.denied 454 U.S. 1156, 102 S.Ct. 1030, 71 L.Ed.2d 314 (1982)(grand jury testimony by prosecutor who was presenting case to grand jury disapproved); People v. Superior Court of San Bernadino County, 86 Cal.App.3d 180, 150 Cal.Rptr. 156, 163 (1978).

15 People v. Superior Court of San Luis Obispo County, 84 Cal.App.3d 491, 148 Cal.Rptr. 704, 711 (1978); People v. Cannon, 25 Ill.App.3d 737, 323 N.E.2d 846, 851–52 (1975). But cf. United States v. Johnston, 690 F.2d 638, 644 (7th Cir.1982)(en banc)(appearance of prosecutor as witness at pretrial suppression hearing would have confronted judge with troublesome prospect of branding prosecutor or defendant as untruthful and thus creating impression of judicial bias; but problem does not require prosecutor's disqualification here, because defendant initiated contact that forced prosecutor to become witness).

16 Cf. Boling v. Gibson, 266 Ark. 310, 584 S.W.2d 14, 21 (1979).

that contemplate litigation.[17] Thus, for example, if a lawyer possesses firsthand knowledge about a neighbor's dispute with a landlord, that does not mean that the lawyer may not represent the neighbor in negotiating an amicable settlement. The fact that sometimes, but seldom, such disputes result in litigation should not be sufficient to require the lawyer to decline the representation. Yet, once employment has been undertaken, the necessity for litigation, and the concomitant necessity that the lawyer testify, may become so apparent that the lawyer must withdraw.[18]

The mandatory-withdrawal rule also applies if the necessity for the lawyer to testify becomes apparent after the litigation is already under way. But, as is required with mandatory withdrawals for other purposes (§ 9.5.4), established judicial rules and procedures must be followed. Those probably will include obtaining court permission to withdraw, particularly in a criminal case. If the court does not permit withdrawal, almost automatic compliance with the undue-hardship exception should permit the lawyer who is forced to stay in the representation also to appear as a witness without violating the professional rules.[19]

Adversary Disqualification Motions

We have thus far considered the 1969 Code and 1983 Model Rules formulations and judicial interpretations of them as interchangeably applicable to both questions of professional discipline and questions of judicial disqualification of a trial lawyer. The motion for disqualification, however, requires closer inspection. It will be recalled that, under the Code, courts will generally disqualify a lawyer from appearing as advocate if he or she will be called to testify by the opposing party and the testimony will be seriously adverse to the lawyer's own client.[20] Much the same system is continued under the Model Rules, although with intimations of a hope that disqualification motions will be less frequently granted.

It is difficult to understand, however, why unconditional disqualification should ever be granted to the opposing party if an adversary's lawyer intends to testify for his or her own client. Why should it not always satisfy any legitimate demand of the opposing party if the court enters a conditional order requiring the potential advocate-witness to select between those roles? [21] If the lawyer chooses to forsake advocacy to testify, the opposing party can have no complaint. If the opposing party's decision is for the lawyer to forego testifying and continue as advocate, there is no confusing mixture of roles and again every legitimate interest of the adversary is protected.[22] A conditional ruling could be entered without any further judicial speculation about whether the lawyer's testimony would be "necessary" to support his or her client's case. That question is also one in which the opposing party can have no legitimate interest and on which the opposing party can seldom be truly illuminating.

One objection to that resolution might be that in some instances a client's agreement that his or her lawyer should forego testifying

[17] DR 5–101(B) refers to "employment in contemplated or pending litigation." Model Rule 3.7 extends its prohibitions only to "act[ing] as advocate at a trial."

[18] In combination, MR 3.7(a)(advocate-witness prohibition) and MR 1.6(a)(1)(mandatory withdrawal) plainly so provide. The Code's DR 5–102(A) requires withdrawal if, after undertaking a representation, "a lawyer learns or it is obvious" that the lawyer ought to be called as a witness for his or her client.

[19] Howell v. State, 293 Md. 232, 443 A.2d 103, 108, n.2 (1982).

[20] See supra at 383–84.

[21] Occasional judicial leanings in that direction can be detected recently. E.g., J.D. Pflaumer, Inc. v. Department of Justice, 465 F.Supp. 746 (E.D.Pa.1979); People v. Smith, 13 Cal.App.3d 897, 903–04, 91 Cal.Rptr. 786 (1970); Borman v. Borman, 378 Mass. 775, 393 N.E.2d 847, 857 (1979); Smith v. Timm, 96 Nev. 197, 606 P.2d 530 (1980) (based, in part, on a complementary rule of court preventing a lawyer who testifies from functioning as an advocate); Besette v. Enderlin School Distr. No. 22, 310 N.W. 2d 759, 764 (N.D.1981); In re Estate of Evans, 238 N.W.2d 677, 680 (S.D.1976).

[22] In that view, the procedure would resemble the discarded common-law evidentiary rule barring lawyers from testifying for their clients on the ground of interest. See supra n.29. The important difference, of course, is that incompetence as a witness could be accepted or rejected by the client as the price for the lawyer's continuation in the case as advocate.

might be a nonconsentable conflict because of the importance to the client of the lawyer's testimony. It is not difficult to imagine such cases. But it does not follow that such lawyer abuses should afford an opposing party the standing to object to the lawyer's role as non-testifying advocate. Such extreme cases, if they exist, should be dealt with in collateral legal-malpractice and lawyer-discipline proceedings, and those responsible for them should vigorously enforce those important client-protecting rules. But violations of the rules should not be a reason for continuing a disqualification procedure that very rarely unearths such outrages and much more commonly seems to be employed for purely tactical reasons of disruption and delay.

An exception should be recognized in criminal cases for prosecution objections to a defense lawyer's decision whether or not to testify if that decision would deprive the accused of the effective assistance of counsel. As with other conflicts of interest of criminal defense counsel, the prosecution has an arguable interest in assuring that such lapses do not result in upset of a resulting conviction on appeal or collateral attack.[23]

Professional Discipline

In an overall view, the Model Rules seem primarily to have been designed as a rule for a trial judge to use in deciding motions to disqualify a party's trial lawyer. The judge is given ample discretion to balance interests of one party against those of the other in determining, for example, whether the substantial-hardship exception of Rule 3.7(a)(3) should be recognized. An important consequence of drafting so large a measure of flexibility and discretion into the rule, however, is that it ill serves the purposes of lawyer discipline. A lawyer charged with violation of the rule will probably be found in violation only in extreme cases. That should probably occur only if the lawyer can make no good faith argument that he or she should be permitted to proceed because of balancing hardships or because of the applicability of some other exception. Another case in which it should be recognized as suitable to find a violation is if a lawyer proceeds to trial only as advocate and thus deprives his or her client of plainly necessary testimony.

WESTLAW REFERENCES

1908 Canons

"canon 19"

1969 Code

imput! /2 disqualif! /5 rule

1983 Model Rules

7–106(c)(3)

When is a Lawyer's Testimony "Necessary?"

45k22 /p necessary /5 testi!

Cumulative Testimony is not Necessary

45k22 /p cumulative

Testimony Involving the Lawyer's Own Conduct

"unsworn witness" /s attorney lawyer counsel**

Imputed Disqualification

5–105(d) /p disqualif!

Exceptions to the Advocate-Witness Rule

Exception for Uncontested Testimony

lawyer attorney counsel** /s testi! /s uncontested (not +1 contested) /p disqualif!

Exception for Value of Legal Services

lawyer attorney counsel** /s testi! /p value nature /3 "legal services"

Exception for Substantial Hardship

"substantial hardship" /p disqualif! /p attorney lawyer counsel** "law firm" client

Implementing the Advocate-Witness Rule

Disqualification Limited to Trials

attorney lawyer counsel** /s testi! /p (pretrial preliminary motion /3 hearing) (court /3 appear!) courtroom litigation /p disqualif!

Mandatory Withdrawal

5–101(b) /p litigat**

23 See § 7.1.7 (standing); id. (prosecutor standing).

§ 7.6 IMPUTED DISQUALIFICATION

§ 7.6.1 General

Lawyers practicing together are in a poor position to give the world assurance that one lawyer is not for many purposes the alter ego of the other. Ties of friendship and finance and ready access to each other's files unite their efforts and interests. Thus a lawyer laboring under a serious conflict of interest cannot usually cure it by simply shifting responsibility for the representation to his or her partner. Even more surely, partners could not represent adverse interests simultaneously.[24] In recognition of such realities, common-law doctrine and professional codes have developed rules that impute to associated lawyers the conflict of interest disabilities of each other. In general, if a lawyer is disabled by a conflict, his or her partners and associates are similarly disabled. Yet, once under way, an "imputed disqualification"[25] rule can gather relentless momentum and be given senseless applications. Courts accordingly have been alert to confine the operation of the imputed-disqualification doctrine to situations that are likely to present substantial risks that the principles of confidentiality and loyalty will be seriously impaired.

WESTLAW REFERENCES

di imputed

§ 7.6.2 Principles and Professional Rules

Imputed Disqualification and the Nature of Firm Practice

The imputed-disqualification doctrine, although sometimes complex in operation, is based on nothing more subtle than common-sense assumptions about the ways that lawyers in firms do their work and the motivations that impel them to share information and support each other's efforts. Perfect confidentiality, if it were required, would be extraordinarily difficult to keep within a typical law firm. Clients come and go throughout the firm's offices and documents are processed by many hands and necessarily pass before many eyes. Files and documents lie on secretaries' desks and are centrally accessible in file rooms and duplicating offices; the notes of associates are spread on library tables; computer systems bring information before many different viewers.[26]

Nor would it serve well the purposes of the partnership form of practice to require that partners keep client matters secret from each other. One of the socially important reasons for law partnerships and similar aggregations of legal talent is to permit lawyers who trust each other's judgment and legal skill to call on each other for help as sounding boards, specialists, and emergency cover.[27] Client authorization to divulge confidential information in obtaining that assistance within the

24 Ross v. Heyne, 638 F.2d 979 (7th Cir.1980)(lawyer did not cross-examine codefendant who testified falsely because he had learned of the falsity of the testimony from law partner who represented codefendant); People v. Lackey, 79 Ill.2d 466, 39 Ill.Dec. 769, 405 N.E.2d 748 (1980)(public defenders from same office cannot represent different clients with conflicting interests).

25 Imputed disqualification is also referred to as "vicarious," "entity," or "intrafirm" disqualification. The "imputed" term is employed in the 1983 Model Rules and will be used here.

26 The suggestion in City of Cleveland v. Cleveland Elec. Illuminating Co., 440 F.Supp. 193, 211 (N.D.Ohio 1976), affirmed 573 F.2d 1310 (6th Cir.1977), cert.denied 435 U.S. 996, 98 S.Ct. 1648, 56 L.Ed.2d 85 (1978), that large-firm imputed disqualification should be confined "to only those lawyers practicing in the attorney's area of concentration" seems to assume a rigidity of physical and personal compartmentalization that exists in probably no firm. Areas of concentration hardly confine documents, secretarial assistance, and, most importantly, a lawyer's occasional or frequent conversational contacts within a firm.

27 "Clients who retain, are billed by, and pay a law firm, can reasonably expect, and often their problems require, that confidences disclosed to one lawyer in the firm will be shared with others in the firm. Indeed, the ability to bring various fields of expertise to bear on the client's problem often serves as a justification for practice as a firm and the very reason for the client's decision to retain the firm. If the reputation and status of the legal profession, and more importantly the freedom and opportunity of the public to obtain adequate legal counseling, are to be preserved, a client must have every reason to expect that disclosures to 'his' law firm will not be used against him by any member or associate lawyer in that firm." Arkansas v. Dean Foods Prods. Co., 605 F.2d 380, 385–86 (8th Cir.1979).

firm is assumed to exist unless the client insists that the lawyer not reveal the information even to other firm lawyers.[28] Sharing client information is done for more than reasons of mutual assistance and colleagueship. The economic structure of firms makes a large fee for one lawyer redound to the benefit of all. The details depend upon the specifics of the partnership agreement, but, at the very least, increasing another lawyer's fees within a firm enhances the firm's ability to afford overhead and, through referrals and sharing of work within the firm, helps to keep all lawyers productive. A similar economic interdependence may to some extent characterize some office-sharing arrangements in which lawyers who are not partners pool their resources to pay for office expenses. In many of those settings, it is appropriate to assume that a secret within the offices of allied lawyers might freely move within them to other associated lawyers.

Firm Economics and Psychology and Client Interests

Beyond confidentiality, a lawyer's sense of loyalty to a client's interests may come under pressure from contrary instincts of other members of the firm. The most obvious source of a threat to loyalty might be economic. Lawyer B represents Client Two, who is involved in litigation with Client One, represented by Lawyer A. Client One is a longstanding firm client whose fees support A and several other firm lawyers. Client Two is a one-shot client who will probably not be able to pay B's normal hourly charge. If A and B practice in separate firms, B of course feels no pressure from A to do anything but seek the best outcome for Client Two. But if they are members of the same firm, Lawyer B has an economic incentive to betray Client Two's interests because the firm's fortunes ride much more on Client One.

Intrafirm pressures can arise from noneconomic causes. Lawyers who are personally involved in litigation as parties or as witnesses might have personal feelings about a matter that, if shared with another firm lawyer actually working on the matter, could affect the latter's ability to function freely.[29] For example, other lawyers in the firm with a different sense of professional detachment might express concern about a colleague's representation of a controversial client. Such pressures should be resisted, but the tension created within the firm creates at least a potential for conflict that, if significant, should be discussed with a client.

Caution in Developing Imputed-Disqualification Rules

If every plausible concern for the confidentiality of all client information or the loyalty of every lawyer within a firm were made a ground for disqualification, confidence in the resulting purity of representations would be purchased at too high a price. The most extreme cases involve a lawyer who moves from one firm to another and, like Typhoid Mary,[30] carries to every lawyer in the second firm all of the disqualifications that afflicted

[28] EC 4–2; MR 1.6(a); MR 1.6 comment (Authorized Disclosure; second paragraph).

[29] For example, in Greene v. Greene, 47 N.Y.2d 447, 418 N.Y.S.2d 379, 391 N.E.2d 1355 (1979), two lawyers left Firm One and joined Firm Two. Firm Two then filed an action in behalf of a plaintiff against third parties and against Firm One itself, alleging breach of fiduciary duties during a time both when the two lawyers were members of Firm One and when they had some involvement in the activities that gave rise to the claim of fiduciary violation. The court ordered disqualification. Cf. Commonwealth v. Leslie, 376 Mass. 647, 382 N.E.2d 1072 (1978), cert.denied 441 U.S. 910, 99 S.Ct. 2006, 60 L.Ed.2d 381 (1979)(lawyer and his wife were close personal friends of victim of assault allegedly perpetrated by client of associated lawyer: no fatal conflict of interest).

[30] The Typhoid Mary sobriquet has frequently been applied to the primarily contaminated lawyer, whose presence in the firm spreads imputed disqualification to all of its members. E.g., LaSalle Nat'l Bank v. County of Lake, 703 F.2d 252, 258 (7th Cir.1983); Kesselhaut v. United States, 555 F.2d 791, 793 (Ct.Cl.1977); Kadish v. Commodity Futures Trading Comm'n, 548 F.Supp. 1031, 1036 (N.D.Ill.1982). Typhoid Mary was an unaffected carrier of typhoid bacteria who used pseudonyms for eight years to avoid detection. Before discovery in 1915, she had caused four outbreaks of typhoid infection, primarily through her work in restaurants. She was detained in isolation in an institution until her death twenty-eight years later. See X Encyclopedia Britannica (Micropaedia) 220 (15th ed.1975). For those so minded, a less innocent slant is suggested by the phrase "fox in the

every lawyer in the first. But even plagues do not spread universally, and precautions can be taken, confidently in some situations, to guard against them. Sober assessment can assure that metaphors from public health history are kept within appropriate bounds in the area of imputed disqualification.

Unrealistic rules on imputed disqualification would exact a heavy price in decreased mobility of lawyers from one firm to another. That would hit hardest at law-student summer clerks and young associates, who move from firm to firm, not always entirely on their own volition. Associations between firms for assistance on distant litigation or in matters that require outside expertise might also be needlessly threatened. The scope and severity of imputed-disqualification rules, more than any other factors, limit the size of firms and compound managerial problems of firms with branch offices in distant cities.[31] Those concerns are not only matters of lawyers, preferences about how they would like to practice law. They also strongly implicate the ability of clients to make a free choice of lawyers. Client choice could become particularly constricted in small communities. And the movement toward greater competence in some areas, through voluntary lawyer specialization in a relatively narrow area of practice, could be unduly retarded by overly strict conflict of interest rules.

Types of Imputed-Disqualification Problems

Clarity can be furthered by preliminary sorting of recurring situations and terminology. While there is no bright line marking off permissible from impermissible contact, it is nonetheless useful to separate imputed-disqualification situations into four types that are commonly encountered and discussed: (1) the possibly disqualifying taint spread from an individual lawyer to another; (2) the taint spread by an individual lawyer to the lawyer's firm; (3) the taint spread by a firm to its individual lawyer members and associates; and (4) the taint spread by one firm to another. It is important to note that there is no reason to think of the fourth category independently of the others as an occasion for disqualification; courts are careful to trace actual relationships between actual lawyers. Firms have disqualification roles only as metaphoric carriers of the taint, contaminating all of their members. In the real world, then, only the first three categories are operational situations in which disqualification might spread. At that, the second and third categories simply note the point of contact at which the carrier firm receives the taint or transmits it.

Primary and Secondary Disqualifications

With respect to individual lawyers, disqualifications can helpfully be further classified as either *primary* or *secondary.* If disqualification results from the lawyer's personal involvement, then it is *primary.* If the disqualification results from the lawyer's membership in a firm in which some other lawyer is primarily disqualified, this can usefully be referred to as *secondary* disqualification. The divide is critical because, as will be seen, the judicial and scholarly sentiment in favor of liberalizing the imputed-disqualification rules relates almost entirely to secondary, and not to primary, disqualifications.

1969 Code

The imputed-disqualification rules have been largely shaped by judicial decisions. The professional rules first addressed the issue in the 1969 Code and again in a 1974 amendment, but in each instance the Code's formulation created significant problems and afforded little guidance in some difficult areas. The Code's general approach, however—to treat imputed disqualifications as an occa-

hen house." E.g., Younger v. Superior Court, 77 Cal.App. 3d 892, 144 Cal.Rptr. 34, 37 (1978).

[31] Lewin, Interest Clash Splits Up Firm, N.Y. Times, Feb. 8, 1983, at D2, col. 1; Ranii, Client Conflict Splits Kirkland & Ellis in D.C., Nat'l L.J., Feb. 14, 1983, at 20, col. 1.

sion for the imposition of sweeping, per se disqualification of all members of an affected law firm—has been followed by the large majority of decisions.

The Code's basic imputed-disqualification rule is stated in DR 5–105(D): if any one lawyer in a firm is disqualified, then all lawyers in the firm are disqualified. No exceptions are provided. Originally the rule stated that it applied only to a lawyer who was required to decline employment or to withdraw "under DR 5–105." [32] The rule was objectionably narrow because it did not extend imputed disqualification to other conflicts, such as those arising because of access to a former client's confidential information (DR 4–101(B)) or due to a former-government-lawyer's conflict (DR 9–101(B)). For example, if a lawyer was required to decline a representation under DR 4–101, on client confidentiality, because of a former-client conflict, a possible reading of the original DR 5–105(D) produced the result that a closely associated lawyer was not disqualified by imputation despite the clear risk that the second lawyer might share secrets with his or her close associate.[33]

To cure that obviously unintended drafting lapse, the ABA amended DR 5–105(D) in 1974 in a series of "housekeeping" amendments.[34] Plainly, the amended rule states a global and unexcepted imputed-disqualification rule that applies to all conflict situations. Yet the 1974 amendment suffers from its own poor draftsmanship. It flatly provides that if any lawyer is required by "a Disciplinary Rule" to decline or withdraw from employment, no other associated or affiliated lawyer may accept the case. That would apply, for example, if a heart attack required a lawyer to withdraw under DR 2–110(B)(3). Read literally, DR 5–105(D) provides that the incapactiated lawyer cannot refer the case with client consent to a trusted and competent partner. Or, under DR 6–101(A), a lawyer who determined that a proposed representation should not be accepted because the prospective client's patent problem was beyond the lawyer's competence would apparently be unable to refer the client to a trusted and extremely able patent-law partner in the lawyer's own firm. Those only illustrate possible, literal applications of the rule; in fact, no such insensible results have been reached by a court or disciplinary agency. The only purpose of the 1974 amendment was to bring all conflict of interest primary disqualifications under the imputed-disqualification rule, including former-government-lawyer conflicts under DR 9–101(B). Courts have consistently read it with that purpose in mind.

A second defect of DR 5–105(D) is that it contains no language allowing waiver of an imputed disqualification by the affected client. The client-consent provisions of DR 5–105(C) refer only to other sections not dealing with imputed disqualification. A close reading of the Code, therefore, might lead one to conclude that imputed disqualifications are absolutely nonwaivable. While analysis of the surface of the language might suggest that conclusion, nothing else supports it. It would be perverse to permit the primarily disqualified lawyer to proceed with client consent under DR 5–105(C), while the remainder of the lawyer's firm would have to be scuttled under DR 5–105(D). The cases sensibly ignore the glitch and recognize that imputed disqualifications are as consentable as are primary disqualifications.[35]

[32] ABA Code of Professional Responsibility, DR 5–105(D) (Final Draft, July 1, 1969).

[33] Such a result is courted in Dodson v. Floyd, 529 F.Supp. 1056 (N.D.Ga.1981), and, at that, is based upon an outdated version of the ABA's Code.

[34] See generally Annotated Code of Professional Responsibility 246 (O.Maru ed.1979). The 1974 amendments also added the words "or any other lawyer affiliated with him or his firm" to the "partner, or associate" lawyers who were originally described as disqualified.

[35] In re Yarn Processing Patent Validity Litigation, 530 F.2d 83, 89–90 (5th Cir.1976); Kagel v. First Commonwealth Co., 534 F.2d 194 (9th Cir.1976); City of Cleveland v. Cleveland Elec. Illuminating Co., 440 F.Supp. 193, 205 (N.D. Ohio 1976), affirmed 573 F.2d 1310 (6th Cir.1977), cert.denied 435 U.S. 996, 98 S.Ct. 1648, 56 L.Ed.2d 85 (1978).

1983 Model Rules—In General

The Model Rules depart significantly from the global and unexcepted sweep of the 1969 Code. The Model Rules attempt to tailor the imputed-disqualification rules to particular conflict of interest situations and to require firm disqualification only if the situation presents a special danger of conflicting representation by other lawyers in the firm. The general rule, Model Rule 1.10, has three major features.

Presently Associated Lawyers. First, MR 1.10(a) provides, in effect, that lawyers presently "associated in a firm" are all subject to imputed disqualification if any one of them practicing alone would be prohibited from representing a client or clients in four situations: (1) if it would involve a present-client conflict of interest prohibited by MR 1.7; (2) if it would involve one lawyer assisting a client to make a gift, to the other lawyer or to a relative of the other lawyer, that is prohibited under MR 1.8(c); (3) if it would offend the former-client conflict rule (MR 1.9); or (4) if it would involve the lawyer representing one client against another that the lawyer had served in intermediation (MR 2.2).

Excluded from the scope of the MR 1.10 imputed-disqualification rule are, for example, such other primary disqualifications as those resulting from business dealings with a client (MR 1.8(a)), from spousal or other family conflicts (MR 1.8(i)), or from conflicts resulting from acquiring an interest in litigated matters (MR 1.8(j)). Thus Partner Two may not draft a will giving a substantial gift from Client A's estate to Partner One or to a close relative of Partner One. But Partner One, without disclosure or client consent, may represent Client B, even though Partner Two would be disqualified by Rule 1.8(i) from representing Client B because his or her lawyer-spouse who practices in another firm represents Client C, whose interests are directly adverse to Client B. And, apparently, Partner One may, if it is otherwise legal, invest in a class action being brought by Partner Two in a way that creates an assignment of part of one of the class member's interest to Partner One.

Also excluded from the automatic imputed-disqualification rule is a conflict arising under MR 3.7 when a lawyer appears as a witness in a case. According to MR 3.7(b), an associated lawyer is disqualified secondarily, in effect, only if the lawyer would be disqualified primarily under the basic conflict of interest rules, MR 1.7 and MR 1.9. That basically means that imputed disqualification is required only if the firm lawyer's testimony will be adverse to the client.

Departing-Lawyer Disqualifications. Second, Model Rule 1.10(b) provides that no lawyer who leaves a firm and no lawyer with whom the departing lawyer becomes associated shall knowingly represent a client "when doing so materially involves a risk" of violating the rules against adverse use of a former client's confidential information (MR 1.6 and MR 1.9(b)). As its comments suggest,[36] MR 1.10(b) creates no per se presumption of disqualification on the part of all lawyers in all future firms with which a disqualified lawyer might become associated. No disqualification will result if the departing lawyer's work in the first firm, or possibly in the second,[37] was sufficiently isolated from a contaminating contact either with the confidential information of the former client or with the later representation of an adversary of the former client.

Cure by Client Consent. Third, unlike DR 5–105(D) of the Model Code, MR 1.10(c) provides in effect that all imputed disqualifications can be dissolved through informed client consent. Taken together with the provisions for client consent in the advocate-witness rule (MR 3.7(b)), that means that only some forms of the conflicts of interest of the former government lawyer may not be cured through former-client consent (MR 1.11).[38]

[36] MR 1.10 comment (Confidentiality).

[37] See § 7.6.4.

[38] For further consideration of the possibilities for cure of former-government-lawyer conflicts through consent, see § 8.10.3(b).

Each of those aspects of MR 1.10 differs sharply from the correlative rules that have been applied by at least some courts under DR 5–105(D). A dominant judicial trend under the Code has been to create per se rules, some of them nonrebuttable, whose net effect has been to spread a very broad imputed-disqualification taint from primarily disqualified lawyers over all associated lawyers. We next turn to a detailed examination of those rules and doctrines.

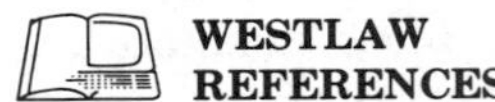

WESTLAW REFERENCES

impute* vicarious** intra-firm /3 disqualif!

"typhoid mary"

---

§ 7.6.3 Workings of Imputed Disqualification Doctrine

Sanctions that might be imposed on lawyers for violating the imputed-disqualification rules, in theory, run the gamut from professional discipline to other judicially enforced remedies, such as the disqualification of lawyers and firms. In practice, discipline is rare,[39] while decisions involving motions to disqualify opposing lawyers and law firms have become increasingly common. As they do with conflicts rules generally,[40] courts sometimes apply a presumption that a lawyer is disqualified even in a case in which the courts would not have upheld a finding that any lawyer had violated mandatory professional rules.

Types of Contaminating Lawyer Contacts

A prominent issue is what types of associations between lawyers will result in imputed disqualification. The formal rank of the particular lawyer who is the connecting link between the lawyers or firms is by itself not critical. "Labels alone—partner, clerk, cocounsel—should [not] control our decisions in so sensitive an area." [41] Nonetheless, judicial tendencies can be detected that are based on the typical features of lawyer relationships. Certainly *partners* are normally assumed to share confidential information about all of a firm's clients, subject to possible rebuttal in a particularly strong case. *Associates* in large firms, on the other hand, are less likely to be exposed to confidential information about clients for whom they perform no work.[42]

If a *cocounsel* relationship between firms is the only connection, courts will insist on some facts beyond the cocounsel status itself before imputing one firm's disqualification to all lawyers in the other.[43] A common illustration would be cocounsel in a litigation associated because of local rule requiring it if the other, managing firm is an out-of-jurisdiction firm admitted only pro hac vice.[44] Imputing disqualifications between the local counsel and the managing firm is entirely unwarranted in the normal course of events. Imputation of a conflict based on the surmise that local counsel knows much of the confidential information about any other than the commonly represented client would be highly unrealistic in most situations. Local counsel may serve as little more than a mail drop and

39 For atypical cases, see, e.g. In re Banks, 283 Or. 459, 584 P.2d 284 (1978); In re Conway, 100 Wis.2d 311, 301 N.W.2d 253 (1981).

40 See § 7.1.7.

41 Fund of Funds, Inc. v. Arthur Andersen & Co., 567 F.2d 225, 235 (2d Cir.1977)(Kaufman, C.J.)(associate in firm recommended by clearly tainted firm worked closely with lawyers in recommending firm).

42 Silver Chrysler Plymouth, Inc. v. Chrysler Motors Corp., 518 F.2d 751 (2d Cir.1975).

43 Akerly v. Red Barn, Inc., 551 F.2d 539 (3d Cir.1977); American Can Co. v. Citrus Feed Co., 436 F.2d 1125 (5th Cir.1971); Consolidated Theatres, Inc. v. Warner Bros. Circuit Management Corp., 216 F.2d 920, 927 (2d Cir. 1954). In Fund of Funds, Ltd. v. Arthur Andersen & Co., 567 F.2d 225, 235 (2d Cir.1977), the court found that cocounsel must be disqualified: "given the extraordinary, sui generis facts underlying this action, the generally stated rule that a 'cocounsel' relationship will not alone warrant disqualification is of little relevance to this case."

44 Realco Services, Inc. v. Holt, 479 F.Supp. 867, 878–80 (E.D.Pa.1979).

have no information about even the client's matter, much less other matters in the managing firm's distant office. Somewhat differently, lawyers and law firms might occasionally serve in an understudy role with respect to major litigation.[45] The tasks of the understudy firm might run all the way from backstopping the first-chair firm in a passive role confined to relatively peripheral matters, such as an adversary's diversionary lawsuits, depositions, discovery requests, and motions, to actually carrying part of the load of research into facts and legal theories, which would bring the second-chair firm much closer to the confidential core of the common client's case. To the extent that the relationship definably involves only ad hoc assignments on minor matters, there is clearly less reason to disqualify than in instances where the two firms work closely on a broad range of the client's problems.

A similar inquiry into the exact nature of the relationship is desirable in the case of such varied relationships as with *legal consultants*, *lawyer expert witnesses*, and some lawyers who are largely retired from practice but who are listed as "*of counsel*" for a firm. On the other hand, the total absence of an existing formal relationship of any kind does not guarantee that no contaminating contacts have occurred. An extreme example of that kind might occur when two law firms begin serious discussions about a future merger of the firms.[46]

Lawyers in solo practice often share offices or expenses under nonpartnership *expense-sharing arrangements.* The language of DR 5–105(D), disqualifying a lawyer's "partner or associate, or any other lawyer affiliated with him or his firm," is ambiguous as to whether it applies to office-sharing arrangements. It has been flatly asserted that lawyers in any such arrangement are to be treated as partners for the purposes of the imputed-disqualification rules.[47] While that course might be the safest for the lawyers involved to follow, it might not be essential if the office arrangements are such that there is no danger of conflicting loyalties or of one lawyer's exposure to confidential information possessed by the other.[48] The corresponding language employed in MR 1.10 is "lawyers associated in a firm." The comment to the rule defines *firm* broadly to include a private firm, the legal department of a corporation or other organization, or a legal services organization.[49] The comment also states that lawyers who merely share office space would not "ordinarily" be regarded as a firm unless they hold themselves out to the public as a firm and in fact conduct their practices as a firm, particularly with respect to access to confidential information.[50] The approach is plainly factual and not categorical or presumptive.

"Double" Imputations

To this point, the linkages examined have been the relatively uncomplicated ones of lawyer and firm. But a secondarily disqualified lawyer may have contacts with another law firm. Does this second firm also become contaminated with all of the lawyer's imputed

45 Fund of Funds, Ltd. v. Arthur Andersen & Co., 567 F.2d 225, 236 (2d Cir.1977)(understudy law firm disqualified because of extensive exposure to client interviews and documents).

46 Pantry Pride, Inc. v. Finley, Kumble, Wagner, Heine, Underberg & Casey, 697 F.2d 524 (3d Cir.1982)(merger of two firms can create imputed disqualifications at time that serious negotiations toward merger begin).

47 In re Opinion No. 415, 81 N.J. 318, 407 A.2d 1197 (1979). But see ABA Informal Op. 1486 (1982)(lawyers with conflicting interests may share office space if reasonable care is taken to protect confidential information and all affected clients consent).

48 United States v. Bell, 506 F.2d 207, 224 (D.C.Cir. 1974); In re Custody of a Minor, 13 Mass.App.Ct. 290, 432 N.E.2d 546, 554 (1982), on rehearing 13 Mass.App.Ct. 1088, 436 N.E.2d 172 (1982), review denied 386 Mass. 1105, 438 N.E.2d 75 (1982)(no imputed disqualification when lawyers share same office suite but with own offices and files and without access to files or clients of each other); cf. In re Smith, 289 Or. 501, 614 P.2d 1136, 1139 (1980)("when two lawyers share office space it may well be that their relationship is such that representing clients with opposing interests, either in actual litigation or in business transactions, would preclude impartial and vigorous representation").

49 MR 1.10 comment (Definition of "Firm"; first paragraph).

50 Id.

disqualifications? For example, suppose that Firm Two is retained by a client as local counsel in an antitrust case at the suggestion of Firm One. The court finds that a lawyer in Firm Two formerly represented an adverse party in a matter substantially related to the present suit. It is clear that all lawyers in Firm Two are secondarily disqualified. Must all lawyers in Firm One also—and automatically—be disqualified?

In general, the courts seem to have handled most such double-imputation problems by refusing to create automatic rules. Instead they have focused on the specific facts to determine whether the confidentiality and loyalty principles would be compromised by permitting the second firm to continue. Particularly if the first firm was itself disqualified on an imputed basis—as when the lawyers actually handling the second matter were not the same lawyers who were involved in the earlier, conflicting representation—disqualification of the second firm has been refused absent a showing by the moving party of some specific factual basis for thinking that confidential information has been communicated to the second firm.[51] On the other hand, if the relationship between the two firms is close, it might be reasonable to assume that confidential information would pass readily between them, thus requiring an imputed disqualification. For example, in a leading Second Circuit case, the same lawyer was an active partner in two different firms in two different cities, causing the court to find that an imputed disqualification was required.[52] Or if a lawyer moves from one small partnership to another, it is natural to assume that the lawyer is extensively acquainted with information about clients of both firms, thus requiring imputed disqualification of the second firm based on every secondary disqualification that the lawyer acquired while a member of the first firm.[53]

Rebuttable Presumption of Secondary Disqualification

Courts have been divided over the extent to which an imputed disqualification should be rebuttable and, if so, what showing suffices to prevent imputed disqualification. The presumption is the legal mechanism by which an imputed disqualification is customarily imposed by courts. Once the moving party makes the necessary showing of primary conflict on the part of a firm lawyer and demonstrates the conditions for the imputed disqualification, it is presumed that all the firm's lawyers are secondarily disqualified.[54] But some presumptions are rebuttable by showing that the state of affairs that is assumed to exist does not exist in fact.

The developed trend of decisions is to regard the imputed-disqualification presumption as rebuttable.[55] Most cases permit the lawyer who is presumptively contaminated to

[51] In re Airport Car Rental Antitrust Litig., 470 F.Supp. 495 (N.D.Cal.1979).

[52] Cinema 5, Ltd. v. Cinerama, Inc., 528 F.2d 1384 (2d Cir.1976).

[53] Bicas v. Superior Court, 116 Ariz. 69, 567 P.2d 1198 (App.1977). But cf. Gilbert v. Knoxville Int'l Energy Exposition, 547 F.Supp. 53 (E.D.Tenn.1982).

[54] The presumption typically works by "presuming" that a lawyer—who is disqualified, for example, because of exposure to confidential information in a former, substantially related representation—is in a position, and is motivated, to share acquired confidential information with other firm lawyers. E.g., Novo Terapeutisk Laboratorium A/S v. Baxter Travenol Lab., Inc., 607 F.2d 186, 197 (7th Cir.1979)(en banc); NCK Org. Ltd. v. Bregman, 542 F.2d 128, 134 (2d Cir.1976); Laskey Bros. v. Warner Bros. Pictures, Inc., 224 F.2d 824, 826 (2d Cir. 1955), cert.denied 350 U.S. 932, 76 S.Ct. 300, 100 L.Ed. 814 (1956); Edelman v. Levy, 42 A.D.2d 758, 346 N.Y.S.2d 347 (1973); Kurbitz v. Kurbitz, 77 Wn.2d 943, 468 P.2d 673 (1970).

[55] Freeman v. Chicago Musical Instrument Co., 689 F.2d 715, 722 (7th Cir.1982)(further evidentiary hearing required to determine whether ex-associate's denial of access to confidential information in former firm sufficed to rebut imputed disqualification; further facts might show size of former firm, area of associate's specialization, lawyer's position in firm, demeanor and creditability of witness); Cheng v. GAF Corp., 631 F.2d 1052, 1056–57 (2d Cir.1980)(primarily and secondarily disqualified lawyer moved to twenty-lawyer office that was held secondarily disqualified for lack of assurance that disqualified lawyer would not inadvertently disclose confidential information), vacated on other grounds, 450 U.S. 903, 101 S.Ct. 1338, 67 L.Ed.2d 327 (1981); Gas-A-Tron of Arizona v. Union Oil Co., 534 F.2d 1322 (9th Cir.), cert.denied 429 U.S. 861, 97 S.Ct. 164, 50 L.Ed.2d 139 (1976)(young associate's limited connection with firm's representation of Shell and Exxon in one and one-half years of work, and

rebut by demonstrating that, in fact, he or she had no access to confidential information. As yet, few courts have permitted rebuttal of the presumption through a demonstration that the contaminated lawyer has been "screened" from contact with otherwise uncontaminated lawyers in a second firm in any cases except those involving the problem of former government lawyers.[56] Screening in the second firm is, however, advocated by the Model Rules in some instances (§ 7.6.6).

The evidentiary showing necessary to defeat the presumption should be faithful to dual aims. First, the court must balance the competing interests of protecting client confidentiality and loyalty, and providing free access to lawyers. And, second, the rebuttal attempt should not force the moving party to divulge confidential information in order to meet the rebuttal. Rebuttal sometimes appears perfunctory and impossible to counter effectively, such as when a court accepts the statement of a litigating lawyer that he or she did not discuss the matter with another firm lawyer who is disqualified.[57] The most satisfactory rebuttal attempts are those made by former firm lawyers, whose recitations about lack of access to confidential information can, if unfounded, be met by affidavits or time records for the old firm showing that there was a significant likelihood of exposure to relevant confidential information. In such a case, the objecting former client is almost invariably represented by the same lawyer or firm to whom the confidential information was originally entrusted. They are the persons in the best position to know whether they in fact shared that information with the departed lawyer. Unless they are prepared to demonstrate that sharing in fact occurred, it should be permissible for the lawyer's new firm to proceed. As an extra precaution, some courts require that all the members of the new firm submit affidavits stating that in fact they have not received any confidential information from the new lawyer.[58]

Silver Chrysler

Such a discrete analysis of facts is exemplified in a leading case refusing to disqualify a lawyer who had worked in a large corporate law firm as a junior associate. In Silver Chrysler Plymouth, Inc. v. Chrysler Motors Corporation,[59] a young associate, while at a large law firm, had worked on several Chrysler matters. He left that firm and became a partner in a smaller firm. One of the clients of the smaller firm sued Chrysler on a claim of the same general kind that other lawyers in the large firm had defended Chrysler against while the young associate was at the firm.

The Second Circuit held that the former associate had made a sufficient showing, through his own affidavit and those of two other associates, who had also left the firm, that his work for the client did not extend to any matter that involved his knowledge of the client's confidential information. The former associate's showing required the client, still represented by the law firm from which he had departed, to come forward with time records or affidavits of other firm lawyers indicating that the associate's account of his exposure to client information was incomplete

his unrebutted denial of receiving any of firm's confidential information substantially related to present case, makes disqualification of associate's new firm unwarranted); Silver Chrysler Plymouth, Inc. v. Chrysler Motors Corp., 518 F.2d 751 (2d Cir.1975)(secondarily disqualified associate in former firm permitted to rebut presumption that he had been in position in former firm to acquire confidential information).

56 The court rejected a claim of sufficient screening in Cheng v. GAF Corp., 631 F.2d 1052 (2d Cir.1980), vacated on other grounds 450 U.S. 903, 101 S.Ct. 1338, 67 L.Ed.2d 327 (1981), but on the ground that the alleged screen was unconvincing in its promise of effectiveness. But see Lemaire v. Texaco, Inc., 496 F.Supp. 1308 (E.D.Tex.1980) (secondarily contaminated law firm not disqualified when primarily disqualified lawyer within it was sufficiently screened and no other law firm in area could be found to handle client's case).

57 Perlstein v. Perlstein, 76 A.D.2d 49, 429 N.Y.S.2d 896 (1980).

58 Novo Terapeutisk Lab. A/S v. Baxter Travenol Labs., Inc., 607 F.2d 186, 197 (7th Cir.1979)(en banc).

59 518 F.2d 751 (2d Cir.1975). The court of appeals relied heavily on the analysis developed in the trial court opinion by Judge Weinstein. See 370 F.Supp. 581 (E.D. N.Y.1973).

or inaccurate. The court was careful to note that it was not convinced that casting the burden back upon the former client in this instance incurred any risk that the client would be compelled to reveal confidential information. Important to the court's analysis was the fact that the original firm was quite large and that the associate's work was largely confined to library research on narrow questions of law. Those facts suggest both that the associate was not regularly exposed to the client's confidential information and that the associate was in no position to deal with the client's affairs treacherously in order to curry favor with a future employer.

The rationale of *Silver Chrysler* is substantially based on the need to prevent imputed-disqualification rules from becoming unduly burdensome restrictions on the ability of young associates to move from or into a firm without causing secondary-disqualification problems.[60] But *Silver Chrysler* does not establish a universal exception of large-firm associates, or even summer clerks, from the imputed-disqualification rules.[61] A different case would have been presented if the original firm had been small or if the departing lawyer had been a partner in the former firm. In either of those instances it would have been more probable that general sharing of information within the firm would have involved that lawyer.[62]

Same-Firm Conflict

It should also be clear from the logic of the *Silver Chrysler* analysis that the presumption of shared confidential information should rarely, if ever, be rebuttable when all the lawyers have remained in the same firm. Quite in contrast to *Silver Chrysler*, here the only lawyers who could recite facts about the operation of the firm and the flow of information within it are the same lawyers whose financial interest is strongly weighted in favor of successful rebuttal of the presumption of disqualification. Only under very exceptional facts should such an attempt succeed.[63]

The Model Rules generally pitch the question of imputed disqualification on the narrow—and necessarily somewhat less determinative—ground of actual risk of a conflict of interest impairment. The drafters of Model Rule 1.10(a) chose, however, to create a per se and nonrebuttable rule for same-firm conflicts. If any lawyer is primarily disqualified because of a conflict of interest of the kind described, then every other lawyer associated

[60] The rationale of *Silver Chrysler*, however, has not gone unchallenged. E.g., Reardon v. Marlayne, Inc., 83 N.J. 460, 416 A.2d 852, 860 (1980)("However, problems of the job market and mobility are not solved by loosening ethical standards required of the profession. The rules of professional behavior are not branches which bend and sway in the winds of the job market and changes in the size and location of law firms. Rather, the rules must be the bedrock of professional conduct.").

[61] Compare Gas-A-Tron of Arizona v. Union Oil Co., 534 F.2d 1322 (9th Cir.), cert.denied 429 U.S. 861, 97 S.Ct. 164, 50 L.Ed.2d 139 (1976)(dictum)(trial court had discretion to disqualify former large-firm associate in present antitrust suit despite his affidavit showing that while he had worked on former client's nonantitrust matters in firm, he had acquired no information relating to present suit). Application of *Silver Chrysler* requires an evidentiary hearing to determine whether the associate can show "clearly and effectively" that he had no contact with confidential information of the objecting firm's client. See Freeman v. Chicago Musical Instrument Co., 689 F.2d 715, 723 (7th Cir.1982).

In *Silver Chrysler* itself, the court did not pass on the ability of the former associate personally to represent the second client, but only on the imputed disqualification of the associate's new firm. A court following *Silver Chrysler* has taken the next step and decided that similarly situated associates are themselves not disqualified. Jackson v. J.C. Penney Co., 521 F.Supp. 1032 (N.D.Ga. 1981).

[62] Bicas v. Superior Court, 116 Ariz. 69, 567 P.2d 1198 (App.1977); Revelstoke Properties, Inc. v. Beaumont Neckwear, Inc., 114 Misc.2d 545, 451 N.Y.S.2d 996 (Civ. Ct.1982)(partner in former firm became associate in new firm; imputed disqualification ordered); Kurbitz v. Kurbitz, 77 Wn.2d 943, 468 P.2d 673 (1970).

[63] A very questionable result was reached in Cossette v. Country Style Donuts, Inc., 647 F.2d 526 (5th Cir.1981)(2–1 decision). The majority held that because the lawyer in the firm who had the contaminating contacts with the firm's present adversary had severed his relationship with the firm and the file left with the firm contained only some general and innocuous memoranda and other papers, the objecting party would be required to show an actual threat of adverse use of confidential information before the firm would be disqualified. The court's apparent assumption that partners in a firm share information only in writing is unsound. *Cossette* was disavowed by Gibbs v. Paluk, 742 F.2d 181 (5th Cir.1984).

with him or her "in a firm" is also disqualified. The drafters realized the difficulty of proving or disproving that a disqualified lawyer's primary conflict has spread to other lawyers in the same firm who are attempting a current representation. On the other hand, under MR 1.10(b), a lawyer's secondary disqualification in an old firm will carry over to the lawyer's new firm only if there is a "material risk" of violating client confidentiality. In either event, the affected client can waive the disqualification.[64]

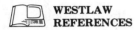

WESTLAW REFERENCES

"silver chrysler" /p 518 +5 751

§ 7.6.4 *Screening as an Alternative to Imputed Disqualification*

Disqualification of a lawyer's present firm—either because of the lawyer's contaminating contact with a previous client or, by force of the imputed-disqualification rules, because of the lawyer's contact with another firm,—has understandably been resisted by lawyers. Such disqualifications impose constraints on law-firm hiring of new personnel, threaten long-standing relationships with clients, and limit the firm's ability to make money and grow. One proposal that has surfaced in recent years is to throw up a "Chinese wall"[65] around the lawyer whose disqualification otherwise threatens to spread to the rest of the firm. The lawyer is purportedly screened from all discussion and exchanges of information about the case (thus protecting confidentiality) and from any share in firm profits relating to the case (thus protecting interests of loyalty to the former client). The concept has enjoyed limited success, finding acceptance primarily in the area of former-government-lawyer conflicts, although its adoption here has been controversial. Outside of that situation, few decisions have approved the screening technique as substitute therapy for the more radical imputed-disqualification quarantine.

The few cases arising out of conflicts other than those of a former government lawyer can quickly be discussed. Success of screening in some former-government-lawyer cases has emboldened some lawyers to attempt to justify continued firm representation in non-governmental conflicts on the basis of an assertedly adequate screen. Those attempts have been notably unsuccessful,[66] although in one case a trial court was persuaded that a screen sufficed when placed, novelly, around an older, retiring lawyer, whose clientele included a minor client who was an adversary of a younger lawyer's more substantial clients.[67] The decision seems to have responded to particularly sympathetic facts; it is inconsistent with cases holding that even the total departure of a disqualified lawyer from a firm does not cure an imputed disqualification.[68] A rather clear possibility still exists that others within the firm possess important confidential information related to them by the departing lawyer.

The tentative judicial applause that has greeted screening has been confined to a small handful of cases dealing with the arguably different conflict of interest problems of

[64] MR 1.10(c).

[65] A person such as this writer, who is occasionally dubious about the efficacy of the "wall" created, hesitates to use a phrase that could be regarded as derisive and thus as having racist overtones. The "Chinese Wall" phrase is used recurringly, presumably with the meaning that the firm's barriers serve the firm as the Great Wall served ancient Chinese emperors, as an elaborate and extraordinary, yet effective and impregnable, barrier against transgression.

[66] Cheng v. GAF Corp., 631 F.2d 1052 (2d Cir.1980), vacated on other grounds 450 U.S. 903, 101 S.Ct. 1338, 67 L.Ed.2d 327 (1981); Westinghouse Elec. Corp. v. Kerr-McGee Corp., 580 F.2d 1311, 1321 (7th Cir.), cert.denied 439 U.S. 955, 99 S.Ct. 353, 58 L.Ed.2d 346 (1978); Fund of Funds, Ltd. v. Arthur Andersen & Co., 567 F.2d 225 (2d Cir.1977); Mallard v. M/V "Germundo," 530 F.Supp. 725 (S.D.Fla.1982), affirmed 746 F.2d 813 (11th Cir.1984); W.E. Basset Co. v. H.C. Cook Co., 201 F.Supp. 821, 824 (D.Conn.1961), affirmed per curiam 302 F.2d 268 (2d Cir. 1962).

[67] Rossworm v. Pittsburgh Corning Corp., 468 F.Supp. 168 (N.D.N.Y.1979). See also Lemaire v. Texaco, Inc., 496 F.Supp. 1308 (E.D.Tex.1980).

[68] Greene v. Greene, 46 N.Y.2d 1072, 416 N.Y.S.2d 795, 390 N.E.2d 302, affirmed as modified 47 N.Y.2d 447, 418 N.Y.S.2d 379, 391 N.E.2d 1355 (1979).

former government lawyers. The cases may not serve as sufficient portents, however, because bar rulings of various kinds have recently been put forward to extend the screening technique generally and sweepingly for former government lawyers. Their chief appeal here is as a palliative to the very broad conflicts disabilities that otherwise would follow a former government lawyer into private practice. Most notably, a private lawyer who formerly dealt with a matter in government service will be disqualified, not only where a private practice client's interests seriously conflict with the position of the government (side switching), but also in cases in which they are in harmony (benign or congruent conflicts).[69] The strictness of those rules is thought to be necessary in order to prevent lawyers still in government service from misusing their discretionary powers to gain advantages for potential private employers.[70] The argument for screening is that cutting off a recent government lawyer from any share in firm profits, and from informational contact of any kind with clients and lawyers in the firm that are dealing with a related matter, will sufficiently serve the interests at stake.[71]

The practicalities of screening arrangements are their most serious weakness. Plainly, even if screening were otherwise acceptable, a screen thrown up late, and only after a motion to disqualify is filed against the firm, evidences a serious lack of resolve and hardly assures properly skeptical courts that contaminating influences and communications have not already occurred.[72] The very few decisions that have recognized screens as exceptions to the imputed-disqualification rule have done so only if the screen surrounded the primarily disqualified lawyer from a very early point in his or her contact with the firm and if the screen contained rather elaborate checks designed to ensure against impermissible contacts between the disqualified lawyer and lawyers in the firm working on the matter.[73]

In the end there is little but the self-serving assurance of the screening-lawyer foxes that they will carefully guard the screened-lawyer chickens. Whether the screen is breached will be virtually impossible to ascertain from outside the firm. On the inside, lawyers whose interests would all be served by creating leaks in the screen and not revealing the leaks would not regularly be chosen as guardians by anyone truly interested in assuring that leaks did not occur. The most porous part of the screen is that which purports to assure courts that the screened lawyer will not share in any fees associated with the disabling client's representation. The opinions accepting screens never recite the size of the lawyer's initial salary relative to comparable lawyers in the firm, nor is any attempt made at later points to determine whether the screened lawyer's fortunes within the firm rose more sharply than otherwise might be expected. Another important and, typically, missing datum is the answer to the question whether the lawyer would have been hired at all except for what the lawyer could bring to the firm or what the lawyer was able to accomplish before joining the firm. Also routinely ignored is the fact that every firm lawyer is keenly interested in the overall financial success of the firm, whether the law-

69 See § 8.10.1.

70 Central Milk Producers Coop. v. Sentry Food Stores, Inc., 573 F.2d 988, 990 (8th Cir.1978)(benign-conflict rule is "based upon sound policy considerations including discouraging government lawyers from handling particular assignments in such a way as to enhance their own future employment and the professional benefit derived from avoiding the appearance of evil.") See generally § 8.10.2.

71 Representative of the recent literature applauding screening is Note, The Chinese Wall Defense to Law-Firm Disqualification, 128 U.Pa.L.Rev. 677 (1980). The view that courts should more readily accept screening seems to ignore the note's own report from the banking industry that screening has been notoriously porous and rests too sanguinely on an assumption that effective law firm measures can regularly be taken to enforce the screen.

72 LaSalle Nat'l Bank v. Lake County, 703 F.2d 252 (7th Cir.1983); Illinois v. Borg, Inc., 553 F.Supp. 178, 183 (N.D. Ill.1982).

73 Armstrong v. McAlpin, 625 F.2d 433 (2d Cir.1980)(en banc), vacated for lack of jurisdiction 449 U.S. 1106, 101 S.Ct. 911, 66 L.Ed.2d 835 (1981); Kesselhaut v. United States, 555 F.2d 791 (Ct.Cl.1977)(per curiam).

yer directly shares in each financial component of that success or not.

Nonetheless, the profession's official stance has recently been strongly, if controversially, in favor of screening for former government lawyers. The opening move was in ABA Formal Opinion 342 (1976), which asserted a possible crisis in the government's ability to attract stardom-destined lawyers, who might fear to lose the option of returning to a more lucrative and professionally rewarding private practice after a stint of government service. The solution of the opinion was to permit screening of the former government lawyer, but only if the screen was approved by the lawyer's former governmental employer. In effect, the opinion merely filled in the lacunae in DR 9–101(B) and DR 5–105(D) of the Code, which do not explicitly provide for waiver of an imputed disqualification by means of client consent.[74]

The next move was by professional rules providing that a described kind of screen is effective without the approval of the former governmental client. Those rules do require notification of some sort to the former government client. One variation is Model Rule 1.11, which requires only that the lawyer be "screened from any participation in the matter and apportioned no part of the fee" and that "written notice" be promptly given to the governmental agency.[75] The rule applicable to District of Columbia lawyers is somewhat more protective in that it requires a signed notification, by the primarily disqualified lawyer, of his or her undertaking to abide by the screen and a similar signed notification, by at least one affiliated lawyer in the firm, describing the firm's compliance with the screen procedures.[76] The least protective arrangement is that approved by a few courts that permit screening to be effective if it is undertaken at the onset of the apparent conflict, despite lack of notice to the government and despite the government's later objection.[77]

The increased availability of screening that has been proposed reflects dubious social policy. Each of the liberalizing steps is taken, among other considerations, in pursuit of the enhancement of lawyers' career mobility. Whether the relaxation of conflict of interest rules represented by a particular kind of screening arrangement is needed to supply that encouragement is highly speculative. At least in the case of a former-government-lawyer conflict, it would seem the wiser course to permit the affected government agency to do the necessary guesswork rather than to foist on the agency unwanted and protested risks of conflicting representations. A waiver of imputed disqualification on the basis of assurances of screening should be effective only if the former governmental client consents. That would seem to be most obviously appropriate if the government claims that the later, private practice representation is of the side-switching variety, in which confidential governmental information could be employed against the interests of the former governmental client if the screen's mesh is too coarse and when the fear of treachery in the handling of the government's affairs before the lawyer leaves for private practice is not an unreasonable concern.

The liberalization in the Model Code seems particularly incongruous because, at the same time that it extends screening without consent to many forms of former-government-lawyer conflicts, it purposefully refuses to permit the government to consent directly to

[74] See also, Ass'n B. City N.Y. Op. 889, 31 Rec.A.B. City N.Y. 552 (1976). Significantly, in Armstrong v. McAlpin, 625 F.2d 433, 443 (2d Cir.1980), vacated on other grounds 449 U.S. 1106, 101 S.Ct. 911, 66 L.Ed.2d 835 (1981), the governmental agency involved and several other governmental agencies filed amicus briefs strongly urging acceptance of screening in that case.

[75] MR 1.11(a)(1), (2) and MR 1.11(b)(1), (2).

[76] D.C. Code of Professional Responsibility DR 9–102 (as amended April 30, 1982). See D.C. Bar Report, June/July 1982, at 4.

[77] Kadish v. Commodity Futures Trading Comm'n, 553 F.Supp. 660 (N.D.Ill.1982); Kesselhaut v. United States, 555 F.2d 791 (Ct.Cl.1977)(per curiam). One decision involving a benign conflict approved a waiver of the disqualification of a former government lawyer's new firm by the opposing party in private litigation without any indication that the former government client itself had approved the screening mechanism. Central Milk Producers Coop. v. Sentry Food Stores, Inc., 573 F.2d 988 (8th Cir.1978).

one of the two major kinds of conflicts covered. Thus a primarily disqualified former government lawyer may not represent in private practice a client whose interests are adverse to a person about whom the lawyer obtained material confidential information in governmental service, and the resulting conflict (even of the benign variety) cannot be cured by the government's consent.[78] On the facts of the leading case, General Motors Corporation v. City of New York,[79] only an explicit statute or regulation [80] would permit a former government antitrust lawyer, with the blessings of the Justice Department, to pursue for a private practice client an alleged antitrust violator whom the lawyer pursued in government service. It is true that permission will be effective if the department goes through the laborious process of putting into place a law that, in effect, overrules the strictures of Model Rule 1.11. But to require such labors of a government agency, under the rationale of protecting its interests, seems gratuitous. The justification for that solicitude might be that the public cannot fully trust current governmental functionaries to give consent, because it might be based on friendship with a former colleague or on their own hopes for similar treatment after they too pass into the private world.[81] If that is the motivating rationale behind Rule 1.11(b), it seems incongruous that those same functionaries should be able to approve screening mechanisms that might prove to be transparent shams.

WESTLAW REFERENCES

"chin*** wall"

§ 7.6.5 *Government and Other Nonprofit Law Offices*

Applicability of the Imputed-Disqualification Rules

Imputed disqualification is based in part on the notion that the bonds of a common profit motive may impel lawyers to share information within the same firm. If a profit motive is absent, one might think to relax the imputed-disqualification rules. The issue has arisen with respect to governmental law offices, public defenders, and civil legal services organizations. One proceeds in each of those areas without guidance from the professional codes, except that interoffice imputed disqualification is not imposed under the Model Rule 1.11 for governmental law offices.[82] The courts have generally applied the same imputed-disqualification rules as are applied to private practice firms, although with greater willingness to treat the presumption of interoffice sharing of confidential information as a rebuttable presumption. In sum, the absence of a profit motivation for impairing client or former-client interests can diminish the relevant risks, but it does not remove all of them.

Arguments can be advanced one way and another about the special features of a governmental or other nonprofit law office that may or may not distinguish it from a private

78 MR 1.11(b). Under the same provision, the lawyer's firm could represent the same client, after appropriate screening of the former government lawyer, even if the former government client vehemently protests. In contrast, the type of conflict covered by MR 1.11(a)(representing a private client in a matter in which the lawyer participated personally and substantially as a public officer or employee) is expressly made subject to waiver by consent of the former government employer. In this setting, screening and notice is not inconsistent in the same way as that pointed out under MR 1.11(b).

79 501 F.2d 639 (2d Cir.1974).

80 MR 1.11(b)("except as law may otherwise expressly permit").

81 See Note, Developments—Conflicts of Interest in the Legal Profession, 94 Harv.L.Rev. 1244, 1432–33 (1981). Nothing in the comments to MR 1.11 throws light on the reason for not providing for consent to the former government lawyer's own representation in MR 1.11(b) situations.

82 Earlier proposed comments to MR 1.10 contained extensive commentary to the effect that imputed-disqualification rules might be different for government agency law offices. Those were deleted in the early 1983 redrafting process. See Proposed Model Rules of Professional Conduct 26–30 (March 11, 1983). In their place, new language was added to the comment to MR 1.11 (last paragraph) to indicate that MR 1.11(c), which prohibits a government lawyer from participating in a matter in which the lawyer participated personally and substantially while in private practice or nongovernmental employment, "does not disqualify other lawyers in the agency with which the lawyer in question has become associated."

practice law firm. In favor of disqualification, it can rightly be pointed out that the will to win cases in any law office can be powerful despite the absence of any profit motive. Public, political, and ideological pressure and sheer professional pride can supply ample incentive. Just as in private firms, lawyers associated in a nonprofit law office rightly support each other and exchange information, and those links can include informal contacts that pay no attention to lines on organization charts. In addition, the existence of organizational lines of authority means that supervisory lawyers can exert influence on subordinate lawyers.

In favor of more flexible imputed-disqualification rules, it can be observed that government lawyers, at least, are under special obligations to do justice in some absolute sense.[83] It may be debated whether that professional ideal is realized often enough to warrant significant alteration of conflicts rules. Also favoring flexibility may be the possibility that there may be much less flexibility in replacing government lawyers or lawyers in other nonprofit offices if all are disqualified. Even if arrangements exist to replace an office of lawyers, they will often be more cumbersome than would be the usual case in private practice, where the entire private bar is readily available as replacements.[84]

Prosecutor Office Conflicts

A common variety of the imputed-disqualification issue in a prosecutor's office occurs when a lawyer who formerly represented an accused person becomes a member of the prosecutor's office. It is clear that the former defense lawyer is disqualified from continuing the prosecution against the former client. Under the imputed-disqualification rules customarily applied to private firms, all other members of the prosecutor's office would also be disqualified. Some decisions have so resolved the problem.[85] A more clinically precise approach is to disqualify only those lawyers in the same governmental office who are subordinate, in the supervisory sense, to the lawyer primarily disqualified.[86] Lastly, some decisions seem to reject entirely the application of imputed disqualification in the government law office context, although they more likely are based on acceptance of particular screening arrangements that are thought to guarantee the absence of contaminating influence.[87] That approach is reflected in Model Rule 1.11(c).[88] If applied without regard to the workability of screening arrangements,

[83] DR 7-103; MR 3.8. See § 13.9.

[84] Some of the most acute conflicts problems occur in situations such as that which led to the institution of the office of special prosecutor in the federal system, following Watergate. A prosecuting attorney appointed by a municipality's chief executive must be disqualified if a question arises concerning possible criminal conduct of the chief executive. E.g., Sapienza v. Hayashi, 57 Haw. 289, 554 P.2d 1131 (1976). But the court cannot secondarily disqualify all members of the prosecutor's office if the result would be that no person remains who is authorized to investigate and make a decision about pressing charges. Id.

[85] Younger v. Superior Court, 77 Cal.App.3d 892, 144 Cal.Rptr. 34 (1978); State v. Chambers, 86 N.M. 383, 524 P.2d 999 (Ct.App.), cert.denied 86 N.M. 372, 524 P.2d 988 (1974); State v. Cooper, 63 Ohio Misc. 1, 409 N.E.2d 1070 (Comm.Pleas 1980).

[86] Arkansas v. Dean Food Prods. Co., 605 F.2d 380, 387 (8th Cir.1979). In particular cases, that approach can result in disqualification of the entire staff of lawyers if the primarily disqualified member has supervisory control over every other staff lawyer. E.g., State v. Tippecanoe County Court, 432 N.E.2d 1377, 1379 (Ind.1982).

[87] United States v. Caggiano, 660 F.2d 184 (6th Cir. 1981), cert.denied 454 U.S. 1149, 102 S.Ct. 1015, 71 L.Ed. 2d 303 (1982)(disqualification of entire United States Attorney's office rejected when defendant's former defense counsel joined office but swore that he had not discussed case with new colleagues); State v. Jones, 180 Conn. 443, 429 A.2d 936 (1980)(3–2 decision)(no imputed disqualification when member of prosecutor's office, who swore he had no conversation with present colleagues about matter, represented accused 12 years previously in somewhat marginally related civil matter); Fox v. Shapiro, 84 Misc. 2d 223, 375 N.Y.S.2d 945 (Sup.Ct.1975). Several of the decisions of that genre have been influenced by the dubious ground taken in ABA Formal Op. 342 (1976). The opinion relied heavily upon the absence of pecuniary motive to assert that imputed disqualification should never apply to a governmental law office. E.g., United States v. Caggiano, 660 F.2d at 190–91.

[88] See MR 1.11(c)(1) and comment (last paragraph). The comment's statement that the primary disqualification of a government lawyer does not disqualify other lawyers seems unfounded until MR 1.11(a) and (b) are contrasted with MR 1.11(c). The former two conflict rules include imputed-disqualification rules; MR 1.11(c) omits any mention of it. Such a categorical treatment of

the approach probably naively assumes that prosecutors can always avoid the temptation to assist new colleagues with helpful inside information or always avoid inadvertent mention of helpful tips. In that light the second approach is also objectionable because its preoccupation with matters of supervisory control ignores the out-of-channels realities of communication and influence within governmental law offices.

Public Defender Offices

Decisions dealing with the question of imputed disqualification within the offices of a public defender similarly stress the absence of financial motivation [89] but, on the whole, are sensitive to the possibilities for conflict of interest that nonetheless might exist. Most decisions prohibit conflicting representations by a public defender office by treating it as a private firm would be treated for conflict purposes.[90] A few jurisdictions appear to go farther and absolutely prohibit joint representations by a public defender office.[91] Protection of client confidentiality will be an important consideration in most public defender cases,[92] but other interests might also be at stake. For a familiar example, if a public defender is confronted with the need to argue that another member of the same office represented an accused in a constitutionally ineffective way in a prior proceeding, the natural instinct to protect the reputation of a colleague, and perhaps of a friend, make the representation thoroughly conflicting.[93] An arguably different case is presented if the public defenders, although employed by the same agency, operate from physically separated offices.[94]

Legal Aid Organizations

The same issues of imputed disqualification have arisen in the context of civil representation by legal aid and other public interest organizations. The general approach is that taken by the leading District of Columbia decision,[95] which rejected the argument that the absence of pecuniary motivations in nonprofit organizations of lawyers and the fact that some of the lawyers practiced in physically separated offices removed all possible threats to confidentiality and loyalty. "Lawyers who practice their profession side by side, literally and figuratively, are subject to subtle influences that may well affect their professional judgment and loyalty to their clients, even though they are not faced with the more easily recognized economic conflict of interest." [96] Here also, it is possible that carefully constructed and policed regulations separating lawyers within the same organiza-

imputed disqualification is uncharacteristic of the general approach of the Model Rules. Moreover, the absence of imputed disqualification in any case is unthinkable without screening, which should be insisted upon with strictness and care. Unfortunately, from all that appears in MR 1.11(c) and its comment, it would be appropriate, for example, for prosecuting lawyers to listen to a former defense lawyer who is now their colleague describe client information about an accused person in a pending investigation.

89 State v. Bell, 90 N.J. 163, 447 A.2d 525, 527–28 (1982).

90 Rodriguez v. State, 129 Ariz. 67, 628 P.2d 950 (1981); Allen v. District Court, 184 Colo. 202, 519 P.2d 351 (1974); People v. Robinson, 79 Ill.2d 147, 37 Ill.Dec. 267, 402 N.E.2d 157 (1979); State v. Bell, 90 N.J. 163, 447 A.2d 525 (1982).

91 Commonwealth v. Westbrook, 484 Pa. 534, 400 A.2d 160 (1979).

92 People v. Wilkins, 28 N.Y.2d 53, 320 N.Y.S.2d 8, 268 N.E.2d 756 (1971)(reversal not required when public-defender office discovered after conviction that witnesses against accused had been represented by same office in unrelated matters because accused was unable to show any possible exchange of information within "largest defense organization in the world").

93 Angarano v. United States, 329 A.2d 453 (D.C.App. 1974); People v. Smith, 37 Ill.2d 622, 230 N.E.2d 169 (1967). See generally Webster, The Public Defender, the Sixth Amendment, and the Code of Professional Responsibility: The Resolution of a Conflict of Interest, 12 Am. Crim.L.Rev. 739 (1975).

94 Babb v. Edwards, 412 So.2d 859 (Fla.1982)(under Florida statute, public defender has discretion to determine whether representation by public defender in another county of same judicial district, with separate office, facilities, and personnel will sufficiently insulate offices to permit another public defender to represent codefendant or whether appointment of private practice lawyer is required).

95 Borden v. Borden, 277 A.2d 89 (D.C.App.1971), noted 6 U.C. Davis L.Rev. 294 (1973), 37 Mo.L.Rev. 346 (1972).

96 277 A.2d at 91.

tion might legitimate what otherwise would be a conflicting representation.[97]

"public defender" (legal +1 aid services) /p impute*
vicarious** intra-firm /3 disqualif!

§ 7.6.6 Spousal and Family Communities of Interest [98]

Spousal Conflicts in a Two-Gender Legal Profession

Historically, it could happen only in the movies that a lawyer-husband would find himself opposing his lawyer-wife in the same litigation.[99] In fact, the history of the American legal profession has until recently been characterized by a largely single-gender bar.[1] But by the year 2000, 30 percent or more of practicing lawyers will be women, the historically underrepresented gender. The growing enrollment of women in law schools in the 1970s and 1980s has raised sharp questions of conflicts of interest between wife and husband who are both lawyers. The problem, to some extent, resembles one that has always existed but has rarely been litigated—conflicts of interest between family members such as father-lawyers and son-lawyers.

Family-Relationship and Spousal-Relationship Conflicts

If family-relationship cases are a suitable analogy, spousal relationship would rarely cause disqualification. The judicial response in the rare cases that discuss the point is not to treat family-member relationship as the same sort of relationship that exists between partners in a law firm, unless a closer financial, business, or similar connection ties their interests together.[2] In the absence of such ties, there seems to be no independent disqualification because of the family relationship alone. Spouses are different, however, in that their arrangements almost invariably include a common-law or consensual pooling of economic resources. Moreover, ties of sentiment typify many spousal relationships in ways that create more strains on the loyalty principle than is the typical case between other adult family members. Spouses also live together, which typically is not true of other adult family members. Sharing of bed, board, and bank account plainly makes spousal conflicts more serious matters. The possibility for inadvertent disclosure of client information is greater here, as is the possibility that one spouse or another will be influenced in the representation of a client because of instincts of common economics or sentiment. For reasons such as those, spousal relationships are sometimes treated as creating imputed disqualifications in other areas of the law.[3]

97 Cf. Flores v. Flores, 598 P.2d 893, 896–97 (Alaska 1979)(right to counsel recognized for defendant in divorce case in which plaintiff is represented by publicly-funded legal aid organization cannot be satisfied by appointment of lawyer for defendant from same organization in absence of regulations relating to record-keeping, access to files, supervision, and physical separation of offices).

98 See generally Kay, Legal and Social Impediments to Dual Career Marriages, 12 U.C. Davis L.Rev. 207 (1979); Note, Legal Ethics—Representation of Differing Interests by Husband and Wife: Appearances of Impropriety and Unavoidable Conflicts of Interests?, 52 Den.L.J. 735 (1975); Note, Ethical Issues Facing Lawyer-Spouse and Their Employers, 34 Vand.L.Rev. 1435 (1981); Comment, Ethical Concerns of Lawyers Who Are Related by Kinship or Marriage, 60 Or.L.Rev. 399 (1981).

99 "Adam's Rib" (MGM 1949).

1 See § 1.4.3 (women in law).

2 Compare Susman v. Lincoln Am. Corp., 561 F.2d 86 (7th Cir.1977); cert. denied 445 U.S. 942, 100 S.Ct. 1336, 63 L.Ed.2d 775 (1980)(class-action status properly denied when one member of plaintiff's lawyer's firm was named as plaintiff in one case and brother of plaintiff's lawyer was named a plaintiff in another); In re W.T. Byrns, Inc., 260 F.Supp. 442 (E.D.Va.1966)(son was lawyer for creditors, father for corporation; father and son were also law partners), affirmed 384 F.2d 471 (4th Cir.1967); Peek v. Harvey, 599 S.W.2d 674 (Tex.Civ.App.1980)(trial court should have disqualified both lawyers when father and son, who were partners in law practice, represented opposing parties).

3 Reece v. Alcoholic Beverage Control Appeals Bd., 64 Cal.App.3d 675, 134 Cal.Rptr. 698 (1976)(regulation disabling spouses of law-enforcement officers to hold liquor license is constitutional); Note, Conflicts of Interest and the Changing Concept of Marriage: The Congressional Compromise, 75 Mich.L.Rev. 1647 (1977)(necessity for le-

While there are reasons, therefore, to apply some kind of imputed-disqualification rule to lawyers who are married to each other, there are weighty reasons to apply only minimal disqualification rules. A chief concern is that inflexible rules would disproportionately burden women lawyers, because currently one-half of all married women lawyers are married to lawyers.[4] It also cannot be ignored that conflict rules that impair the careers or earning capacity of lawyer spouses create pressures for one or the other of them to pursue a separate career or to take unilateral steps in some other way to cure or avoid conflict. It is speculative how those tensions would typically be resolved, but economics would suggest that the spouse earning less would be under greater pressure to yield. According to current earnings statistics, that spouse is more likely to be the wife.[5] An imputed-disqualification rule for spouses would also put constraints on the ability of lawyers or law students to marry one another and thus would interfere with personal choice in a way that is hardly trivial. It would also impose serious constraints on the ability of married lawyers to find legal employment in the same community and, correlatively, the ability of firms to hire a lawyer-spouse without incurring imputed disqualifications.

The Emerging Concept of Limited Imputed Disqualification

The position of courts and bar rules is just emerging but seems clearly pointed toward only limited disqualification. The 1969 Code provided no illumination. The few cases in point generally reject an inflexible rule that a spousal relationship between lawyers creates a per se conflict of interest.[6] The position of the American Bar Association has been less resolute. In Formal Opinion 340 (1975), the ABA ethics committee rejected state ethics opinions that required a strict imputed disqualification for lawyer-spouses and their firms. The opinion correctly stressed that a lawyer-spouse might need to take special precautions to assure that inadvertent disclosure of client confidential information did not occur. But, Opinion 340 worried that even if all precautionary measures were taken, each lawyer's firm should inform its clients of "all circumstances that might cause one to question the undivided loyalty of the law firm," without identifying how extensive that list of worrisome circumstances might be. In every such case client consent was required before the firm could proceed.

A broad imputed-disqualification rule for spouses is rejected in Model Rule 1.8(i). The rule does retain a primary-conflict prohibition against head-to-head adversarial representation by spouses. Thus, in effect, it provides a limited imputed-disqualification rule that treats the spouses for that one purpose as if they were a two-person firm. But it rejects any broader rule[7] of imputed disqualifica-

gal restraints to guard against intergovernmental conflicts of spouses).

4 C.Epstein, Women in Law 340 (1983). To be sure, the disproportionate impact is a direct function of the fact that there are more male than female lawyers. A strict imputed-disqualification rule may therefore be defended as gender-neutral. But the social goal of achieving equal opportunity for women in the legal profession is nonetheless retarded, whatever the source or the motivation of the disparate impact.

5 See § 1.4.3 at 14.

6 Blumenfeld v. Borenstein, 247 Ga. 406, 276 S.E.2d 607 (1981)(improper for trial court to disqualify lawyer and his firm on ground that his wife was member of firm representing opposing party); Batchelor v. Smith, 555 P.2d 871 (Utah 1976)(no denial of effective assistance of counsel when codefendants in criminal case were represented by husband and wife). Cf. In re Paders, 250 App. Div. 418, 294 N.Y.S. 252 (1937)(lawyer who was wife of officer of insurance company suspended because of her practice of representing without consent injured persons referred to her by the company with understanding that she would never vigorously press their claim against insured but would seek a third-party defendant or settle against insured for small sum).

7 MR 1.8(i) contains a curious omission. Its terms are limited to simultaneous representations. Yet many of the same considerations that support a finding of conflict here (danger of purposeful or indavertent disclosure of client information, threat to loyalty because of common sentiment and ecomonic interest) arguably also apply to successive representations. There is no apparent reason to handle spousal former-client conflicts in a way different from simultaneous conflicts.

tion.[8] The primary-conflict rule of MR 1.8(i) is extended to more than spouses and covers any situation in which the two lawyers are "related . . . as parent, child, sibling or spouse." Excluded from the rule are similar but more distant relationships to a lawyer, such as those of grandparents, uncles, and aunts.

Intrafirm Problems of Lawyer-Spouses

Success of a lawyer-spouse in resisting a motion to disqualify or prevailing in an attempted disciplinary action is not, however, a full measure of the problem. Within law firms in which a spouse practices, there may be subtle pressures and barriers because of the fact that the spouse's marriage partner is a member of a rival firm. Some firm member may think that loyalty to the firm might be compromised by the other spouse's rival position. For example, the spouse who is the member of the firm might be thought to be at a disadvantage in attracting new clients from mutual friends or acquaintances. Some spousal lawyers contend with some of those problems by becoming members of the same firm, but that arrangement becomes problematical if the firm includes anyone else. A common resort is for spousal lawyers to arrange their careers so that they specialize in very different areas of the law to minimize conflicts.

[8] MR 1.8 comment (Family Relationship between Lawyers)("The disqualification stated in Rule 1.9(i) is personal and is not imputed to members of firms with whom the lawyers are associated."). The comment also clarifies that lawyers within the noted relationships who practice in the *same* firm are subject to the possibly stricter conflict rules that generally govern same-firm conflicts. Those rules, of course, include imputed disqualification in an appropriate case.

Chapter Eight
SPECIAL CONFLICTS OF INTEREST TOPICS

Table of Sections

---

§ 8.1 GENERAL

Lawyer conflicts of interest have been extensively litigated in recent years. Most of the decisions involve adversary motions to disqualify an opposing lawyer; some involve legal malpractice actions by injured clients. Lawyer discipline also occurs with frequency in some areas of conflicts of interest. The range of special problem areas is impressively broad; this chapter will attempt to canvass the most prominent of them. Separate treatment is essential, for courts have indicated very different levels of impatience or tolerance for incipient lawyer conflicts in different areas, apparently as they perceive more or less need for client protection.

WESTLAW REFERENCES

topic(45) /p conflict*** /3 interest

---

§ 8.2 CONFLICTS OF INTEREST IN CRIMINAL CASES

§ 8.2.1 The Right-to-Counsel Dimension in Criminal Defense Conflicts

The problem of conflicts of interest in representation of an accused in a criminal case could be thought of, mistakenly, as simply a particularized application of the general rules applicable to conflicts of interest in litigation. Those rules, to be sure, are all applicable. What is profoundly different is that an accused in a criminal case can claim special conflict protections afforded by the constitutional right to the effective assistance of counsel. That additional dimension has produced greater sensitivity in identifying conflicts and more stringent rules about waiver of the constitutional protection. Moreover, courts have asserted that special obligations are imposed on a defense lawyer, commensurate to some extent with the constitutional rights of the accused, to avoid conflicts of interest and to report conflicts that do arise in the course of representation.

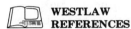

WESTLAW REFERENCES

topic(110) /p conflict*** /3 interest /s effective /5 assistance

§ 8.2.2 *Settings of Criminal Case Conflicts*

Divided Loyalties

Conflicting representations can arise in criminal defense in many ways. The most obvious case, as will be discussed, occurs when the same lawyer represents codefendants whose interests conflict for one or more of many possible reasons. Further, a former client of the lawyer might be seperately represented as a codefendant.[1] A third party might be paying the fee of the lawyer and have interests that are adverse to those of the accused.[2] A former or present client might be the victim of the crime,[3] the prosecutor,[4] or a prosecution witness.[5] Defense counsel might be a potential witness for the accused[6] or might be a prospective codefendant or prosecution witness at the trial.[7]

Conflicts can also arise because of the defense lawyer's legal work for clients that might be involved in various ways in the prosecution. For example, it sometimes occurs in small communities that a lawyer who serves part-time as a government lawyer is appointed to represent an accused in a criminal trial. The incongruous appearance of a lawyer changing hats for the occasion of a court appointment is underscored by the danger that the lawyer's responsibilities and opportunities in public employment will lead to a less than vigorous defense. The most obvious objection is that the ties of an ongoing working relationship and, possibly, of friendship that naturally exist between the government lawyer and law enforcement personnel will preclude forceful cross-examination. Most courts properly refuse to uphold such appointments.[8] As with noncriminal conflict problems in litigation, the conflicts in each such instance can be isolated by careful consideration of the respective interests of the accused and the defense lawyer and by noting the strength and direction of the lawyer's interests.

1 United States v. Young, 644 F.2d 1008 (4th Cir.1981); Yorn v. Superior Court, 90 Cal.App.3d 669, 153 Cal.Rptr. 295 (1979).

2 Wood v. Georgia, 450 U.S. 261, 101 S.Ct. 1097, 67 L.Ed.2d 220 (1981)(employees of "adult" bookstore and theater, who were represented by lawyer hired by their employer in state obscenity prosecution that resulted in their punishment by large fine, now attacked fine as unconstitutionally large).

3 People v. Karas, 81 Ill.App.3d 990, 401 N.E.2d 1026 (1980). See also People v. Blalock, 197 Colo. 320, 592 P.2d 406 (1979)(defense lawyer in sexual assault case previously had sexual liaison with victim but told accused this would not be subject of cross-examination of victim under any circumstances; so blatant a conflict results in ineffective representation requiring new trial).

4 Alabama v. Zuck, 588 F.2d 436 (5th Cir.), cert.denied 444 U.S. 833, 100 S.Ct. 63, 62 L.Ed.2d 42 (1979)(defense lawyer also represented prosecuting attorney in unrelated civil matter).

5 United States v. Shepherd, 675 F.2d 977 (8th Cir. 1982); State v. Rowe, 416 So.2d 87 (La.1982).

6 Commonwealth v. Rondeau, 378 Mass. 408, 392 N.E.2d 1001 (1979). See generally § 7.5.

7 United States v. Panasuk, 693 F.2d 1078 (11th Cir. 1982)(dictum); United States v. De Falco, 644 F.2d 132 (3d Cir.1980); United States v. Scott, 501 F.Supp. 53 (N.D. Ill.1980).

8 People v. Rhodes, 12 Cal.3d 180, 115 Cal.Rptr. 235, 524 P.2d 363 (1974)(city attorney); People v. Fife, 65 Ill. App.3d 805, 22 Ill.Dec. 536, 382 N.E.2d 1234 (1978), affirmed 76 Ill.2d 418, 30 Ill.Dec. 300, 392 N.E.2d 1345 (1979)(lawyer for worker compensation commission). But see State v. Mitchell, 356 So.2d 974 (La.), cert. denied 439 U.S. 926, 99 S.Ct. 310, 58 L.Ed.2d 319 (1978)(assistant city prosecutor); Hudson v. State, 250 Ga. 479, 299 S.E.2d 531 (1983)(probate judge and solicitor of county court).

Representing Codefendants

The most prevelant conflict is a product of what at one time was a relatively common practice in criminal defense practice—the same lawyer represents two or more persons who are accused of related crimes, are often charged in the same indictment or information, and are scheduled for a common trial. Part of the conflict between jointly accused persons arises from the discretionary powers that can be wielded by a prosecutor or judge in criminal cases in the United States.

Through the leverage of plea bargaining (§ 12.10.2), a prosecutor is empowered to treat very differently persons who are equally charged with a common offense. The prosecutor's only reason for favoritism may be that one of the codefendants is willing to plead guilty and testify against the others. In some situations the prosecutor's offer might extend complete immunity to a codefendant in return for needed testimony. Incipient competition for the favor of the prosecutor is present in every criminal case in which there are multiple suspects, whether the codefendants are charged in the same indictment or information or are to be tried separately. The judge possesses similarly vast discretionary powers in most jurisdictions in imposing sentences of radically different severity based on such ephemeral factors as the cooperativeness of one of the codefendants.

Conflicts may also arise because codefendants may testify discrepantly or may wish to employ divergent trial tactics. A person accused as a lookout for a robbery might wish to testify that he or she was oblivious to the criminal intent of colleagues; but a codefendant accused as a principal might wish to deflect responsibility by testifying that the alleged lookout in fact took a major, and more criminally responsible, role.[9] Or, somewhat less dramatically but still with troubling evidentiary inconsistency, one accused might wish to testify to an alibi while the other accused wishes to testify to diminished capacity because both codefendants, while perpetrators, were intoxicated at the time of the offense. Fact finders will feel antagonism when confronted with inconsistent stories from jointly tried defendants. The reaction is a product of the natural, if sometimes erroneous, surmise that inculpatory testimony is probably more believable than self-serving excuses.

Professional Regulations

Nothing in the 1908 Canons or the 1969 Code deals explicitly with conflicts of interest in criminal defense representation.[10] The ABA Defense Function Standards recommend strongly against multiple defendant representations.[11] The comment to MR 1.7 of the 1983 Model Rules contains a similarly worded warning [12] but backs away from flatly prohibiting joint representation, a rule that has been urged by several commentators.[13] Very few disciplinary enforcement proceedings involve alleged violations of the rules in the area of criminal defense, although extremely

[9] If the discrepant testimony of both codefendants is in good faith believed by them to be accurate, perhaps because of differences of interpretation that they place on commonly remembered events, a conflict plainly exists. It becomes exacerbated if one or both of the codefendants intends to offer false exonerating testimony. See § 12.5.4.

[10] The *Glasser* decision (see infra § 8.2.3) is quoted in EC 5–16, n.20, but the Ethical Consideration itself and the relevant Disciplinary Rules deal only with the general topic of disclosures required before obtaining client consent to a multiple representation.

[11] ABA Defense Function Standard 4–3.5(b) (2d ed.1979) ("The potential for conflict of interest in representing multiple defendants is so grave that ordinarily a lawyer should decline to act for more than one of several codefendants except in unusual situations . . . . In some instances, accepting or continuing employment by more than one defendant in the same criminal case is unprofessional conduct.").

[12] MR 1.7 comment (Conflicts in Litigation)("The potential for conflict of interest in representing multiple defendants in a criminal case is so grave that ordinarily a lawyer should decline to represent more than one codefendant. On the other hand, common representation of persons having similar interests is proper if the risk of adverse effect is minimal and the requirements of paragraph (b) [on client consent after consultation] are met.").

[13] Geer, Representation of Multiple Criminal Defendants: Conflicts of Interest and the Professional Responsibilities of the Defense Attorney, 62 Minn.L.Rev. 119 (1978); Lowenthal, Joint Representation in Criminal Cases: A Critical Appraisal, 64 Va.L.Rev. 939 (1978).

aggravated cases can result in discipline of the offending lawyer.[14]

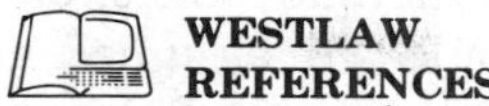

Divided Loyalties

110k641.5 (45k20 /p criminal) /p (former /3 client) witness

Representing Codefendants

(110k641.5 /p (joint dual /3 represent!) (multiple two /4 defendant)) (45k20 /p criminal)

Professional Regulations

(dr d.r. "disciplinary rule" /4 5–101 /p criminal) (m.r. "model rule" /3 1.7) 4–3.5

§ 8.2.3 Constitutional Conflicts Doctrine

Expansive Remedies for Criminal Case Conflicts

The low incidence of professional discipline has not, however, masked the frequency with which criminal defense conflicts arise or the seriousness of the conflicts when a defense lawyer proceeds in spite of their presence. Instead, courts in criminal cases have employed in the criminal law area the common-law remedy of disqualifying a lawyer because of a conflict in representation (§ 7.1.7). Courts in criminal cases have also employed a remedy—reversal of a conviction and a new trial—that is very rarely encountered in civil cases.[15] The courts may permit the accused to move to set aside a conviction even in the absence of a protest during the trial itself.

The enlargement of the client's ability to attack a putatively defective trial result follows from the rise in the importance of the constitutionally protected right to the effective assistance of counsel (§ 14.6.1). Some theories implementing the constitutional protection extended it only when the conflict was sufficiently apparent that the judge or prosecutor should have been aware of it, a discredited doctrinal component thought to be dictated by the "state action" requirement of constitutional protection.[16] Recent right-to-counsel cases, however, recognize the right to reasonably competent representation as an entitlement of the accused that exists as an aspect of due process even if the conflict is not apparent to others (§ 14.6.2).

Conflicts and Effective Assistance

The watershed conflict of interest case was Glasser v. United States,[17] a 1942 decision of a divided Supreme Court. Glasser, a lawyer and former assistant United States attorney, was represented by his retained lawyer, Stewart, at his conspiracy trial with four other codefendants. A codefendant appeared when the trial began with a lawyer who claimed inability to proceed. Over Glasser's objection, Stewart was appointed by the trial court to represent the additional defendant as well. During the course of trial, Stewart failed to object to some testimony damaging to Glasser but favorable to the codefendant.

The Supreme Court reversed Glasser's conviction on two related grounds. The first, and principal, reason was that lawyer Stewart's "struggle to serve two masters" because of the conflict of interest did not fulfill the constitutional requirement for the effective assistance of counsel.[18] Second, regardless of any conflict, the trial court forced Glasser's lawyer to divert his efforts from his original client by jointly representing a codefendant, and thus the state imposed an impermissible burden on Glasser's right to choose to have the benefit of the undivided assistance of counsel.[19]

The next major decision came over thirty-five years later in Holloway v. Arkansas.[20] At two points before a joint trial of codefendants for armed robbery and rapes, the court-appointed lawyer for three codefendants objected to joint representation on the ground that their interests clashed and as a result

[14] Florida Bar v. Vernell, 374 So.2d 473 (Fla.1979).

[15] But cf., e.g., Pennix v. Winton, 61 Cal.App.2d 761, 143 P.2d 940 (1943); Jedwabny v. Philadelphia Transp. Co., 390 Pa. 231, 135 A.2d 252 (1957), cert. denied 355 U.S. 966, 78 S.Ct. 557, 2 L.Ed.2d 541 (1958).

[16] Maxon v. Estelle, 558 F.2d 306, 307 (5th Cir.1977).

[17] 315 U.S. 60, 62 S.Ct. 457, 86 L.Ed. 680 (1942).

[18] 315 U.S. at 70, 75, 62 S.Ct. at 464–65, 467.

[19] 315 U.S. at 75, 62 S.Ct. at 467.

[20] 435 U.S. 475, 98 S.Ct. 1173, 55 L.Ed.2d 426 (1978).

the lawyer could not effectively cross-examine any one of his clients if it was necessary to advance the interests of any other. Without holding a hearing, the trial court overruled the objection and forced the lawyer to proceed. The Supreme Court extended *Glasser* to state court proceedings and reversed the resulting convictions. The Court held that if alerted to the possibility of a conflict,[21] a trial court must conduct a hearing to inquire into the existence of a conflict. If no hearing is conducted after objection, then whenever the trial court has improperly overruled a conflict objection, reversal must follow even if there is no showing of prejudice to the accused because of the conflict.[22] From all that appears from the majority opinion, it is always improper to overrule an objection to joint representation if it is made by a lawyer representing codefendants and thus in a position to assert that a conflict is present, unless the trial court develops by means of a hearing a factual foundation for reaching a different conclusion.[23]

Assumed or Actual Conflict Impact

An important issue left open in *Holloway* was whether, in the absence of an objection, a convicted person was required to make a showing that a claimed conflict of interest resulted in an actual conflict or whether such prejudice would be assumed to exist from likely circumstances.[24] The question was answered, and a showing of actual conflict was required in such a case, in Cuyler v. Sullivan.[25] Three codefendants had been jointly represented in a series of three Pennsylvania murder trials by the same two privately retained lawyers. The Supreme Court held that while it was clear from the facts that the codefendants had been jointly represented,[26] it did not follow that the state trial court was under a duty to initiate an inquiry about the adequacy of representation in the absence of an objection by the accused.[27] Unless the conflict is patent, the trial judge is under no obligation to initiate an inquiry, and on post-conviction attack the defendant is required to demonstrate specifically that an actual conflict adversely affected his or her lawyer's performance.[28] The different, and lesser, showing that obtained reversal in *Holloway* depended on the lawyer's trial objection there. Unfortunately the same lawyer assertedly burdened with the conflict must, under the Court's somewhat improbable view, make the

[21] The Court noted that a lawyer's ability to detail the reasons for his or her perception that a conflict existed was circumscribed by the competing need to avoid disclosing client confidences. See 435 U.S. at 487 n.11, 98 S.Ct. at 1180. A second consideration is that a full disclosure of the lawyer's conflict might impair the privilege against self-incrimination. See Uhl v. Municipal Court, 37 Cal. App.3d 526, 112 Cal.Rptr. 478 (1974).

[22] 435 U.S. at 489, 98 S.Ct. at 1181.

[23] The result in *Holloway* avoided the need to confront a built-in anomaly in the way the case was presented to the court: the same lawyer whose objection to the joint representation had been found defective by the Arkansas courts also argued the case before the Supreme Court. If the Supreme Court had agreed with the argument, embraced by the dissenters, that prejudice-in-fact was required to be shown by each of the codefendants, the lawyer would have been in much the same conflicted position in making the necessary appellate argument in behalf of each of the jointly convicted codefendants.

[24] See 435 U.S. at 487, 98 S.Ct at 1180.

[25] 446 U.S. 335, 100 S.Ct. 1708, 64 L.Ed.2d 333 (1980).

[26] 446 U.S. at 342, 100 S.Ct. at 1714–15. The Court noted that the issue whether the lawyers had jointly represented the codefendants was the kind of issue that was properly open to a federal habeas corpus court to resolve, even if the federal court's resolution was possibly contrary to that of a state court.

[27] In the course of that portion of its decision, the majority explicitly held that the constitutional right to counsel was applicable to a *retained* lawyer who was burdened by a fatally defective conflict of interest. 446 U.S. at 344, 100 S.Ct. at 1716.

[28] 446 U.S. at 346, 100 S.Ct. at 1717. *Cuyler* is difficult to reconcile with Wood v. Georgia, 450 U.S. 261, 101 S.Ct. 1097, 67 L.Ed.2d 220 (1981), in which the same Justice who wrote the majority opinion in *Cuyler* wrote an opinion vacating, on the court's own initiative, a state conviction because the record showed that the convicted codefendants had been represented by a lawyer hired by their employer who had failed to object to the size of fines imposed by the state trial court, thus creating an argument that imprisonment of the employees for nonpayment of the excessive fine was unconstitutional. No objection to joint representation had been made at trial in the state court. The majority did not suggest that it would overlook the requirement of a showing of actual conflict by the convicted employees, however, which may sufficiently reconcile the decisions, at least at the level of holdings.

critical objection to his or her own representation.

Present State of Supreme Court Doctrine

Several common threads run through the Supreme Court decisions. First, the Court has uniformly condemned representations in which the defense lawyer operates under a conflict of interest. Second, if the conflict of interest is blatant and substantial, silence on the part of the accused will not prevent a later attack on a conviction.

Third, suppose that the accused timely objects in the trial court to the joint representation. The Court has held that then the trial court must either (1) appoint separate counsel or (2) conduct a sufficiently searching inquiry to provide a factual basis on which to determine whether the risk of actual conflict is too remote to require separate representation. Theoretically there is also the possibility in the third instance that the prosecution can demonstrate that the objection was so contrived that the action of a trial court in ignoring it and refusing to hold a hearing could not have caused any prejudice. If a reviewing court agrees, that would warrant affirmance, as *Cuyler* suggests. Nothing in *Cuyler*, however, indicates any retreat from the explicit holding of *Holloway* that when a specific objection is made to a joint representation, the defendant need make no showing of prejudice if a joint representation that is burdened with a conflict is permitted to continue without a hearing into the extent of the conflict.

Fourth, if there is no objection at trial, the defendant must show specific prejudice because of an actual conflict; merely hypothetical or conjectural prejudice is insufficient. The only exception is when the conflict is blatant; then prejudice will be assumed. What is unclear from the course of decisions is what constitutes a sufficient showing of actual conflict and to what extent it must appear that prejudice resulted or was threatened. In elaborating on the line of Supreme Court cases, lower courts have employed various approaches in defining the burden that a convicted person must satisfy. A common approach is to require the convicted person to show (1) that the lawyer did not pursue an alternative defense tactic that was available and plausible, but without the need to demonstrate that it certainly would have been more successful than tactics actually employed, and (2) that pursuit of the alternative plausible tactic would have conflicted with other loyalties or interests of the lawyer.[29]

Manipulative Uses of Conflicting Representations

The existence of the *Glasser-Holloway* line of cases might suggest that a defense lawyer so disposed could manipulate the rule for the purpose of planting error in the record. The lawyer could proceed with a conflicting representation with the design that, if convictions resulted, each client would argue—presumably with separate counsel—that the convictions should be set aside because of the conflict.

That possibility is presumably the impetus for the emphatic and restated claim in the Supreme Court's opinions that defense lawyers have an "ethical obligation" not only to avoid conflicting representations but also to "advise the court promptly when a conflict of interest arises during the course of trial." [30] In fact, in an aggravated case a lawyer has been disciplined for similarly lurking in the weeds.[31] The knowing participation of an accused in such a purposely conflict-ridden representation, if proved, might itself be a suffi-

29 Brien v. United States, 695 F.2d 10, 15 (1st Cir.1982), and cases cited.

30 Cuyler v. Sullivan, 446 U.S. 335, 100 S.Ct. 1708, 1717, 64 L.Ed.2d 333 (1980). See also Holloway v. Arkansas, 435 U.S. 475, 98 S.Ct. 1173, 1179, 55 L.Ed.2d 426 (1978); United States v. Dolan, 570 F.2d 1170, 1184 (3d Cir.1978); Mannon v. State, 98 Nev. 224, 645 P.2d 433, 434 (1982). Both Supreme Court opinions cited in support ABA Defense Function Standard § 3.5(b)(1971 ed.). *Cuyler* also cited DR 5–105 and EC 5–15.

31 Florida Bar v. Vernell, 374 So.2d 473 (Fla.1979)(violation of DR 1–102(A)(5) to advise joint defendants in criminal case to plead guilty and, if dissatisfied with sentence, move to set aside plea on ground of lawyer's conflict of interest because of representation of chief prosecution witness).

cient ground for finding that the accused has implicitly waived the right to a conflict-free representation.[32]

Erroneous Rulings on Conflict Objections

A very different problem is presented if a defense lawyer's well-founded objection to proceeding with a conflicting representation is overruled by a trial judge despite the presence of what the lawyer believes to be a disabling conflict of interest. If one of the jointly represented codefendants subsequently testifies at the trial, may the lawyer refuse to cross-examine his or her own witness on the ground of a conflict of interest? To do so rather obviously incurs the risk that the other codefendant's right to the effective assistance of counsel will be jeopardized. But if the lawyer cross-examines his or her own client, confidential information about that client might be exposed and thereby possibly jeopardize *that* party's constitutional right to the effective assistance of counsel.

It is not entirely satisfactory to have a defense lawyer make broad and thus self-proving assertions about the requirements of ethical duties. The lawyer may be overly scrupulous or may be trying to force a continuance to enable a new lawyer to become familiar with the case. Yet if the lawyer is required to supply a sufficiently detailed basis for his or her concern about the need to cross-examine or the need to refuse to do so, that also creates a serious risk of exposing confidential communications of one or both clients.[33] The absence of any clearly correct course of action in such a case suggests the great desirability of separate representation as an automatic response whenever the lawyer objects[34] and plainly underscores the statement in *Holloway* that judges should normally accept at face value a lawyer's assertion that a conflict of interest exists.

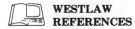

WESTLAW REFERENCES

Expansive Remédies for Criminal Case Conflicts

110k641.5 /p disqualif! (revers** set aside /3 convict***)

Conflicts and Effective Assistance

(glasser /15 62 +4 57) (holloway /15 98 +5 1173) /p effectiv** /3 assist!

Assumed or Actual Conflict Impact

sullivan /15 100 +5 1708

Present State of Supreme Court Doctrine

attorney lawyer counsel** /s conflict*** /4 interest /p test

Manipulative Uses of Conflicting Representations

conflict*** /4 interest /s attorney lawyer counsel** /s duty (ethical** /3 obligat***) /s advise inform /9 court

Erroneous Rulings on Conflict Objections

conflict*** /s interest /p refus*** overrul*** /5 withdraw* /s attorney lawyer counsel**

---

§ 8.2.4 Client Waiver or Consent

Difficulty of the Judicial Role

If no objection to a joint representation is made, to what extent should judges take uninvited steps to assure that the jointly represented codefendants understand their possible peril? A logical and arguably cost-effective method for dealing with conflicts is entirely to prohibit joint representation in criminal defense.[35] That is clearly not constitutionally required and might even raise concerns in some instances about depriving a codefendant of the right to retain counsel free of state interference.[36]

[32] United States v. Alvarez, 580 F.2d 1251 (5th Cir. 1978).

[33] Holloway v. Arkansas, 435 U.S. 475, 98 S.Ct. 1173, 1179, 55 L.Ed.2d 426 (1978).

[34] Jennings v. State, 413 So.2d 24 (Fla.1982)(denial of effective assistance of counsel to client for whom lawyer refused to conduct cross-examination).

[35] Fleming v. State, 246 Ga. 90, 270 S.E.2d 185, cert.denied 449 U.S. 904, 101 S.Ct. 278, 66 L.Ed.2d 136 (1980)(at least in capital cases, every codefendant must have separate counsel). In New Jersey, joint representation of codefendants by the same lawyer or lawyers from the same law office is prohibited unless court approval is obtained. See State v. Bellucci, 81 N.J. 531, 542, 410 A.2d 666 (1980). See also n. 13 supra.

[36] United States v. Curcio, 694 F.2d 14, 22–23 (2d Cir. 1982). See generally § 14.3.7.

Rule 44(c) was added to the Federal Rules of Criminal Procedure in 1980 to place the federal courts under a special preventive rule designed to eliminate the possibility of a serious conflict in a defense representation. The rule obliges a judge to inquire into every joint representation [37] and to advise each codefendant of his or her right to separate representation. Unless there is "good cause to believe" that no conflict is "likely" to arise, the judge is to take measures to protect each defendant's right to counsel.[38] While the goal of pretrial judicial screening to relieve codefendants of unwanted representation by conflict-ridden lawyers is admirable, its workability is doubtful. Defense lawyers and codefendants will rightly be alert to object to any judicial suggestion that an accused might be well advised to place less than full trust in his or her lawyer. Any judge who wishes to inquire under Rule 44(c) into the defendants' understanding of their right to separate representation must choose between exacting responses that remain at a level of uninformative generality or probing for more complete answers in near proximity to matters of trust in the client-lawyer relationship and of confidential client communications.[39]

Defendant Waivers

If confronted with the issue, the Supreme Court might agree with lower courts that an accused who voluntarily relinquishes a known constitutional right to conflict-free representation would be bound by the waiver, no matter how apparently ill-advised.[40] That might be thought to follow from the principle that an accused has the right to refuse to be represented by counsel at all.[41] But an essential finding that would underlie such a holding must be that the accused in fact made a knowing and voluntary waiver of the right to the conflict-free assistance of counsel. Such a finding, in the face of a joint representation with disastrous conflicts, should be quite difficult to reach.

Whatever the outcome of litigation between the accused and the state about the due process rights of the accused, it should be clear that the client's ill-advised waiver of a right to a conflict-free representation has no bearing on whether his or her lawyer has violated professional rules and is thus susceptible to professional discipline for continuing with a representation when there are serious conflicts. As in noncriminal representations, a lawyer should represent codefendants in a criminal case only if no conflict of interest exists or if the clients freely consent after full disclosure in a situation in which the lawyer can adequately protect the interests of all jointly represented codefendants.[42]

Considerations Involved in Consent to Joint Representation

A well-informed and freely consenting codefendant might have sound reasons in relatively unusual cases to consent to joint representation. In retained-lawyer situations, cost saving can be a significant factor to the extent that it is true that the same quality of legal services for two or more codefendants

[37] Rule 44(c) does not explicitly cover the many other types of possible conflicts of interest in criminal defense (see supra § 8.2.2). A judge should certainly be free as well to employ the procedures provided in the rule in order to stanch other kinds of incipient conflicts.

[38] Fed.R.Crim.P. 44(c) had been anticipated by some federal court decisions that required similar warning procedures. E.g., United States v. Atkinson, 565 F.2d 1283 (4th Cir.1977), cert. denied 436 U.S. 944, 98 S.Ct. 2845, 56 L.Ed.2d 785 (1978); United States v. Foster, 469 F.2d 1 (lst Cir.1972). The warning requirements apply only in the judicial setting and do not, for example, require government agencies to warn suspects during pre-indictment investigations that their lawyer is engaged in a conflicting multiclient representation. See United States v. Mierzwicki, 500 F.Supp. 1331 (D.Mo.1980).

[39] United States v. Garafola, 428 F.Supp. 620, 623 (D.N.J.1977)(judicial complaint about then proposed Fed. R.Crim.P. 44(c) as "ineffective charade" and "futile exercise"). Cf. United States v. Zajac, 677 F.2d 61 (11th Cir. 1982)(approval of separate, in camera examinations of defense lawyer in absence of prosecutor and of codefendants in absence of lawyer).

[40] United States v. Curcio, 694 F.2d 14 (2d Cir.1982); United States v. Garcia, 517 F.2d 272 (5th Cir.1975). But cf. United States v. Flanagan, 679 F.2d 1072 (3d Cir.1982), reversed on other grounds 465 U.S. 259, 104 S.Ct. 1051, 79 L.Ed.2d 288 (1984).

[41] See § 14.4.2. See also § 7.2 (client consent).

[42] In re Porter, 283 Or. 517, 584 P.2d 744 (1978).

can be purchased for significantly less than the cost of separate representations.[43] Joint representation can avoid duplication in the gathering of evidence, interviewing witnesses, and retaining experts. In general it can provide a more effective monitoring of developments on both sides of the case. Joint representation can also facilitate access to confidential information of each of the represented parties with a consequent improvement in the ability of the defense lawyer to develop and present a common, consistent defense. Joint representation is not necessary in most jurisdictions in order to achieve sharing of confidential client information without waiver of the attorney-client privilege.[44] But a joint representation more certainly guarantees that the privilege will protect communications of confidential information of one jointly represented party to another.[45]

A single lawyer may also serve joint tactical interests. The lawyer is the only person with whom the prosecutor may deal in an attempt to develop a case through granting favoritism to one of several codefendants.[46] A joint representation can provide better support to individuals who might wish to strike an improvident bargain with the prosecution in order to be released from the perceived greater costs of continued defense.[47]

Nonetheless, it is also true that an accused confronts many potential disadvantages in a joint representation. Most obviously, no single client can obtain the advantage of a better plea bargain in return for testifying for the prosecution—unless the joint lawyer commits a serious breach of loyalty or resigns. Minor characters in a criminal enterprise are more likely to be kept subordinate to the dictates of the major powers. A guilt-by-association reaction may, in fact, occur during trial because of the fact finder's possibly naive assumption that jointly represented codefendants are equally as guilty as the apparently most guilty of them. Complications can readily arise concerning the treatment of evidence or witnesses unless all the codefendants' testimony and the testimony of witnesses appearing for them are perfectly consistent. The fallout from a failed tactic of joint representation will be severe because of the great unlikelihood that a recess would be granted to enable all parties to obtain separate representation.

The extent to which benefits and disadvantages are present in a particular situation, and the cumulative weight of each, must be taken into account by a lawyer in determining whether a conflict of interest in a criminal defense representation is, or is not, a "consentable," or allowable, conflict (§ 7.2.3). Some prosecution offers are too good to turn down, and a per se conflict of interest seems virtually inevitable. A common example is if the prosecution has effectively extended an

43 Whether significant cost savings actually occur may be doubted. See Geer, Representation of Multiple Criminal Defendants, 62 Minn.L.Rev. 119, 160 (1978).

44 The "pooled information" doctrine (§ 6.4.9) in some instances permits sharing of confidential information between separately represented codefendants without waiver of the privilege. E.g., United States v. McPartlin, 595 F.2d 1321 (7th Cir.1979), cert.denied 444 U.S. 833, 100 S.Ct. 65, 62 L.Ed.2d 43 (1979). See generally 2 J.Weinstein & M.Berger, Weinstein's Evidence, at 503–6 to 503–7 (1975).

45 See § 6.4.8.

46 Limited access follows from the *Massiah* doctrine of constitutional law (§ 14.3.2) and, more broadly, from the prohibition in DR 7–104(A)(1) and MR 4.2 against direct contact with a represented party without prior consent of the party's lawyer. Most of the situations discussed in the text will involve serious conflicts of interest, but all parties might be able to consent freely or the case might involve a lawless prosecution in which the prosecutor intends to build a case by forcing false testimony through threats and promises of leniency. But cf., e.g., In re Coordinated Pretrial Proceedings in Petroleum Prods. Antitrust Litig., 502 F.Supp. 1092 (C.D.Cal.1980)(partially disqualifying defense lawyer in civil antitrust case in order to prevent blockading of potential witnesses), vacated 658 F.2d 1355 (9th Cir.1981), cert.denied 455 U.S. 990, 102 S.Ct. 1615, 71 L.Ed.2d 850 (1982). See also § 8.2.5.

47 As with other "advantages" of joint representation, the consideration discussed in the text will be more or less sympathetic depending on whether or not the accused person is "guilty"—a matter which cannot be known with judicial certainty until after trial. The Supreme Court has itself recognized, if not with approval, at least with equanimity, that "certain advantages might accrue from joint representation." It can be " 'a means of insuring against reciprocal recrimination. A common defense often gives strength against common attack.' " Holloway v. Arkansas, 435 U.S. 475, 482–83, 98 S.Ct. 1173, 1177–78, 55 L.Ed.2d 426 (1978), quoting Frankfurter, J., dissenting in Glasser v. United States, 315 U.S. 60, 92, 62 S.Ct. 457, 475, 86 L.Ed. 680 (1942).

offer of immunity to one codefendant in return for truthful testimony. A lawyer who continued to represent that codefendant as well as others who were not extended immunity and whose interests would be harmed by the client's truthful testimony—whether the immunity offer was accepted or rejected—seems to be in a position of impossible conflict.[48] The same sort of nonconsentable conflict would be present if one codefendant wishes to defend by inculpating a jointly represented codefendant.[49]

Informed and Voluntary Consent

Even if the conflict is potentially consentable, of course, a client's consent can authorize the lawyer to proceed only if consent is freely given after full disclosure (§ 7.2.4). The nature of the consultation should depend on the seriousness of the charge, the sophistication and experience of the clients involved, and the likelihood that a seriously conflicting interest, or interests, exists.

The lawyer should discuss with each client at least the following points and the lawyer should be convinced that each is fully understood by each client. The nature and source of all possible conflicts should be carefully reviewed. The lawyer should explain carefully the consequences of a sharing of confidential information and outline any respects, presumably minor, in which sharing of information is not to be mutual and complete. The lawyer's best present thinking on the range of trial strategy options should be reviewed both in the event of separate representation and if joint representation is accepted. Probable and possible theories of defense, witnesses, and likely strategies of the prosecution should be explained. In as much detail as possible, the lawyer should review all material consequences that could result from conflicting client objectives with respect to such matters as plea bargaining, immunity, trial strategy, and client and third-party testimony. The lawyer should review the consequences if one of the codefendants withdraws consent at a later point, as well as the possibility that the trial court might require the lawyer to withdraw from all representations if conflicts develop that are sharper than those presently perceived. The lawyer should discuss fully the constitutional right of each client to an indisputably conflict-free representation and, if relevant, to a court-appointed lawyer. The client should also be urged to consult with an independent lawyer about the conflict and about the wisdom of consenting to it.

After a full-disclosure consultation, the lawyer should accept the joint representation only if personally convinced that each of the affected clients fully understands each of those elements and other relevant information and, nonetheless, unequivocally and freely consents to the joint representation. The course of wisdom strongly suggests that the gist of the conversation and the clients' consent should be in writing and signed by the clients who consent.

Breakdown of a Cooperative Joint Representation

If a joint representation begins cooperatively among codefendants but cooperation breaks down at a later point, the court may disqualify the conflict-ridden lawyer.[50] Disqualification of the individual lawyer will almost always require disqualification of the lawyer's partners or associates as well (§ 7.6). That broad scope of disqualification follows because in the ordinary case in which a lawyer has had access to confidential information of all of the jointly represented defendants, the only acceptable solution is to disqualify the lawyer and the lawyer's firm from representing any defendant once the joint representation has broken down.

48 United States v. RMI Co., 467 F.Supp. 915 (W.D.Pa. 1979)(attempted client waiver of right to conflict-free representation rejected on part of employees who had been extended immunity to testify and who were being represented by corporate defendant's lawyer).

49 United States v. Franzen, 687 F.2d 944 (7th Cir.1982); State v. Ross, 410 So.2d 1388 (La.1982).

50 Davis v. Stamler, 494 F.Supp. 339 (D.N.J.1980), affirmed 650 F.2d 477 (3d Cir.1981).

WESTLAW REFERENCES

Difficulty of the Judicial Role

(federal /3 rule /3 crim! procedur**) fed.r.crim.p*** /s 44(c)

Defendant Waivers

110k641.5 /s waiv**

Considerations Involved in Consent to Joint Representation

advantag! disadvantag! /s joint dual /6 represent!

Informed and Voluntary Consent

consent*** /s joint** dual /6 represent!

Breakdown of a Cooperative Joint Representation

110k641.5 /p disqualif!

§ 8.2.5 Prosecutor Motions to Disqualify Defense Lawyers

The Interest of a Prosecutor in a Conflict-Free Defense

Conflict of interest questions in criminal defense representation are raised in two common ways. In § 8.2.4 we considered the more common of these—attacks on a conviction by the accused who complains about an unduly hobbled representation because of a defense lawyer's conflict of interest. Quite different problems arise if a prosecutor attempts to raise issues about a conflict of interest on the part of defense counsel.

We put to one side cases, which are rare, in which the government clearly has a legitimate axe to grind, such as an allegation that a defense lawyer was previously involved as a prosecutor in the same matter and acquired confidential information about the government's case.[51] If the government's argument is that it seeks to assert the interest of the accused in a conflict-free representation, should courts listen? At present, the state and lower federal courts are divided, with some showing sympathy for rather contrived, or overstated, governmental interests.[52]

The motives of the prosecutor in attempting to drive a wedge between two or more accused persons may or may not be honorable. On the one hand, a conflict of interest may indeed exist under circumstances in which the interests of one accused will be sacrificed by a disloyal defense lawyer in an impermissible attempt to serve the partisan advantage of another client. Plainly the government should be able to take steps to cure an apparently conflicting representation, because an uncured conflict can result in appellate reversal of a conviction.[53]

On the other hand, the situation may be one in which the interests of all defendants, in spite of the appearance of a conflict, may best be served by a joint representation—or so the jointly accused codefendants might believe. The choice should ultimately be left to the accused. So long as the court, on the government's motion, has taken steps to assure that an accused waived the right knowingly and voluntarily, the waiver of the right to a conflict-free representation addresses all legitimate interests of the government.

Some grand jury cases have been decided in favor of a broad disqualification of jointly represented grand jury witnesses on the rationale that separate representation is necessary in order to preserve the secrecy of the grand jury's proceedings.[54] Unless the law provides

[51] United States v. Kitchin, 592 F.2d 900 (5th Cir.1979), cert.denied 444 U.S. 843, 100 S.Ct. 86, 62 L.Ed.2d 56 (1979).

[52] See generally Moore, Disqualification of an Attorney Representing Multiple Witnesses before a Grand Jury: Legal Ethics and the Stonewall Defense, 27 UCLA L.Rev. 1 (1979). See also Note, Dual Representation at the Grand Jury: A Conflict of Interest, 10 Mem.L.Rev. 525 (1980); Note, Supervising Multiple Representation of Grand Jury Witnesses, 57 B.U.L.Rev. 544 (1977). The Supreme Court had the issue before it in Flanagan v. United States, 465 U.S. 259, 104 S.Ct. 1051, 79 L.Ed.2d 288 (1984), but the case was decided on the narrow ground that the disqualification order was not ordinarily appealable.

[53] United States v. Donahue, 560 F.2d 1039 (1st Cir. 1977).

[54] Pirillo v. Takiff, 462 Pa. 511, 341 A.2d 896, reaffirmed 466 Pa. 187, 352 A.2d 11 (1975), cert.denied 423 U.S. 1038, 96 S.Ct. 873, 47 L.Ed.2d 94 (1976). Contra, e.g., In re Investigation Before the April 1975 Grand Jury, 531 F.2d 600, 606 n.11 (D.C.Cir.1976). A decision preceding *Pirillo* had held that a lawyer hired to represent a client who had been subpoenaed to testify in an investigation of the alleged solicitation activities of a second lawyer was properly disqualified because the second lawyer had paid

that a grand jury witness may not repeat to any other person the content of the witness' grand jury testimony, the argument against joint representation collapses.[55] While grand juries might work more effectively if witnesses in fact did not repeat their testimony and while it might be assumed that separately represented grand jury witnesses are less likely to share the contents of their testimony with each other, none of that argues that the right of persons with a common interest in a matter to common representation should be overborne in the name of grand jury efficiency.

WESTLAW REFERENCES

The Interest of a Prosecutor in a Conflict-Free Defense

110k641.5 /p state government** prosecut*** /s motion move* /s disqualif!

§ 8.3 CORPORATE AND OTHER ENTITY CONFLICTS

§ 8.3.1 Cooperation and Discord in Intracorporate Relations

For the most part, at least while prosperity smiles, the interests of a corporation and its constituencies can appear to be in happy agreement. Sometimes agreement is facilitated by the fact that both corporate principals and the corporation itself are represented by a single lawyer or law firm. Joint representation is common, for example, when a cash-short corporate enterprise is just starting up.

But frequently the tranquility that pervades when cooperative wills are bent toward the achievement of common goals is shattered when the corporation or stock in it is sold, when a principal officer leaves the corporation, when a shareholder derivative action is brought against the corporation and its officers and directors, or when a lawyer who has represented the corporation or its officers and directors now appears against the interests of one of them. Those and similar problems of the failed or matured corporate enterprise raise some of the most important conflict issues for corporate lawyers.

WESTLAW REFERENCES

attorney lawyer counsel** /s dual joint /3 represent! /s corporat***

§ 8.3.2 The Entity Representation Doctrine

The General Concept of Loyalty to the Entity

As discussed elsewhere (§ 13.7.2), the basic precept of both the 1969 Code and the 1983 Model Rules is that the lawyer's client is the corporate entity itself[56] rather than any constituent member or group such as directors, officers, shareholders, employees, creditors, or others. That at least is the legal result achieved in resolving conflicts issues for large corporate clients. Recent decisions suggest, however, that a different notion applies to small, closely held corporations. Whatever the size of the corporation, however, certain demands are basic. The loyalty of a corporate lawyer must be directed solely toward the interests of the entity. A corporate lawyer may not assist one group of shareholders to achieve an advantage over others with respect to ownership or control of the enterprise.[57] A corporate lawyer may not aid one

the fee of the disqualified lawyer. Kremer v. Shoyer, 453 Pa. 22, 311 A.2d 600 (1973).

[55] A different, and more substantial, argument is that the lawyer and the grand jury witnesses are part of a criminal conspiracy to defeat the investigation of the grand jury. In such a case, disqualification would be proper. Cf. e.g., In re Investigation before the February 1977 Lynchburg Grand Jury, 563 F.2d 652 (4th Cir.1977).

[56] One case has suggested that for some conflict of interest purposes a corporation's *divisions* may be entities separate from the corporation itself. Federal Trade Comm'n v. Exxon Corp., 636 F.2d 1336 (D.C.Cir.1980)(in view of possibility that "drive group" division of acquired corporation might be required to be divested in antitrust compliance proceeding, and because of parent corporation's alleged competitive stance vis-a-vis drive group, separate counsel was required to represent drive group during divestiture suit to preserve its separate identity).

[57] Egan v. McNamara, 467 A.2d 733 (D.C.App.1983).

group of shareholders, even a majority group, to set up a competing enterprise.[58]

Lawyer-Officer Conflicts in Large Corporations

For large corporations, one form of the conflict of interest question is presented when a former corporate officer or director is engaged in litigation with the corporation. The corporation may be represented by its counsel—a lawyer with whom the former director or officer shared confidential information while with the corporation. The law makes clear that much of that information will be protected by the attorney-client privilege.[59] But it does not necessarily follow that the corporation's lawyer is in a confidential lawyer-client relationship vis-à-vis the individual director or officer who confided the information.[60] Normally a corporate officer or director should assume that confidentiality for communications to the corporation's lawyer is provided for the benefit of the corporation and is not for the officer's personal benefit or protection. Thus the fact that the communication was confidential does not bar the lawyer from appearing in behalf of the corporation against the former official.[61] An alternative method of analysis is to treat the situation as one in which the corporation, and not the officer, controls the question whether to waive confidentiality (§ 6.4.1).

Small Corporations

The position of the Code and the Model Rules, that the lawyer represents only the corporate entity, makes sense primarily in the setting of large, publicly held corporations. As corporate stock ownership is concentrated into fewer and fewer hands, the distinction between corporate entity and shareholders begins to blur. In the case of a sole-owner corporation, they may merge. Often a lawyer for such a partnership corporation will provide personal legal services for corporate principals interchangeably with services for the corporate entity. In recognition of that common reality, one court has held that for conflict of interest purposes a small and closely held corporation and its stockholders are to be treated as virtually identical and inseparable.[62] As a result of such treatment, the lawyer is freer to represent all consenting parties to the corporate venture, as well as the corporation itself, but that also means that the lawyer may not represent any of the parties against any other if the venture sours or if for other reasons disputes arise and consent to continuing joint representation is withdrawn at a later time.[63]

The critical element in the cases seems to be whether the lawyer's performance of legal services for a corporation has been confined to that function or whether the lawyer has also performed personal legal services for corporate principals so as to create the reasonable expectation on the part of one or more principals that the lawyer was representing the

[58] In re Kinsey, 294 Or. 544, 660 P.2d 660 (1983).

[59] See § 6.5. In general the privilege can be asserted only by the corporation and in its interests, not by and for the conflicting interests of an officer.

[60] See MR 1.13 comment (The Entity as the Client; third paragraph).

[61] Fielding v. Brebbia, 479 F.2d 195 (D.C.Cir.1973); Bobbitt v. Victorian House, Inc., 545 F.Supp. 1124, 1126 (N.D. Ill.1982); Wayland v. Shore Lobster & Shrimp Corp., 537 F.Supp. 1220, 1223 (S.D.N.Y.1982); U.S. Indus., Inc. v. Goldman, 421 F.Supp. 7, 11 (S.D.N.Y.1976); Meehan v. Hopps, 144 Cal.App.2d 284, 293, 301 P.2d 10, 14–16 (1956). A similar result was reached on arguably analogous facts in Allegaert v. Perot, 565 F.2d 246 (2d Cir. 1977), where the court held that lawyers for an acquired corporation (which was also represented by independent counsel) were not disqualified from appearing adversely to a receiver of the acquired corporation when its officers knew that the lawyers' primary allegiance was to the acquiring corporation, whose interests they now continued to represent.

[62] In re Brownstein, 288 Or. 83, 602 P.2d 655, 656–57 (1979); In re Banks, 283 Or. 459, 584 P.2d 284, modified 284 Or. 691, 588 P.2d 34, 1 A.L.R.4th 1105 (1978).

[63] Cases cited supra note 62. See also, e.g., Brennan's Inc. v. Brennan's Restaurants, Inc., 590 F.2d 168 (5th Cir. 1979); Teel v. Teel, 400 So.2d 357 (La.App.1981)(lawyer who formerly represented corporation wholly owned by husband cannot represent wife in divorce action in which ownership of stock in corporation is principal issue); In re Nulle, 127 Ariz. 299, 620 P.2d 214, 217 (1980); National Texture Corp. v. Hymes, 282 N.W.2d 890 (Minn.1979); In re Usow, 119 Wis.2d 255, 349 N.W.2d 480 (1984).

principal's personal legal interests. Clear examples of personal legal services are will drafting and estate planning for a principal. Less clear are legal services in connection with loans to the corporation, employment contracts with it, or stock-ownership or stockholding arrangements between groups of shareholders. In those ambiguous instances the lawyer might understand that the services are for the corporation in the interest of furthering its objectives as an entity, while the individuals involved might think that the lawyer's work is intended to confer the maximum legal benefit upon them with respect to such issues as tax advantages and obtaining security and other remedies for the promises of other parties.[64] While such confusions of role and function are most common in small corporations, they can also occur in some large corporations, particularly those with a single controlling shareholder or small group of shareholders.

Clarifying a Corporate Lawyer's Role

It is apparent that the incipient problem of conflicts of lawyers in representing, or appearing to represent, both the corporation and corporate principals is primarily one of assuring clear and complete understanding. All interested parties should be made aware of, and the lawyer should be certain and consistent about, the extent to which the lawyer represents various interests.[65] A lawyer representing a corporation should make his or her limited role particularly clear when dealing with an officer or other agent of the corporation whose interests are adverse to the corporation and who apparently is unaware that the lawyer does not act for the personal interests of that person.

Such an understanding is highly desirable, for example, when a sole lawyer represents more than one principal in the founding of a corporate venture. The founders of the enterprise will typically bring different things of value to the corporation—capital, skills, ideas—and will typically desire different advantages in the corporation's affairs—stock ownership versus salary, security for loans versus liquidity of corporate funds, a voice in policy-making versus operational control. A single lawyer asked to perform the necessary legal work to set up the corporation and see to the legal aspects of its early operations is in the best position to recognize that those differences are patently conflicts of interest. At the very least, the nature of the conflicts and their possible future consequences should be carefully discussed before the lawyer agrees to represent the corporate founders jointly (§ 7.2.4(a)). The lawyer should proceed with a common representation only if all principals fully understand the conflicts involved and agree to a common representation notwithstanding them.[66]

Corporate Former-Client Conflicts

The normal former-client conflict rules (§ 7.4) apply when the corporate lawyer, whether outside or house counsel, ceases to represent the corporation. As the former client, the corporation can object to any representation by its former lawyer that is adverse to the corporation and substantially related to any matter handled by the lawyer during his or her tenure as the corporation's lawyer.[67]

64 Premium Prods. Sales Corp. v. Chipwich, Inc., 539 F.Supp. 427 (S.D.N.Y.1982)(law firm that represented corporation A, whose president was also the president of corporation B did not become the lawyers for corporation B despite the fact that several drafting and other counseling activities were engaged in with respect to the president's interest in corporation B; the principal owner of corporation B never reasonably believed that the law firm was representing the interests of corporation B).

65 See MR 1.13 comment (Clarifying the Lawyer's Role; paragraphs eight and nine); MR 1.2 (e).

66 See generally Legal Ethics Forum, 62 ABA J. 648 (1976). Whether some conflicts are so severe that they may not be consented to is discussed generally in § 7.2.3. In that connection, one expert on minority shareholder issues has opined that most minority shareholders' squeeze-out problems would not have arisen if all parties to partnership corporations had had independent legal representation when the basic corporate rights were being determined. See 63 ABA J. 108 (1977).

67 NCK Org., Ltd. v. Bregman, 542 F.2d 128 (2d Cir. 1976); Chugach Elec. Ass'n v. United States Distr. Court, 370 F.2d 441 (9th Cir.1966), cert.denied 389 U.S. 820, 88 S.Ct. 40, 19 L.Ed.2d 71 (1967); Smith v. New Orleans Fed. Savings & Loan Ass'n, 474 F.Supp. 742 (E.D.La.1979); Federal Savings & Loan Ins. Corp. v. Fielding, 343

Because a lawyer will normally be extensively exposed to corporate business during a tenure as counsel, the scope of disqualification will often be quite broad under the substantial-relationship test for former-client conflicts of interest (§ 7.4.3(b)).

WESTLAW REFERENCES

The General Concept of Loyalty to the Entity

ec e.c. "ethical consideration" /5 5–18

Lawyer-Officer Conflicts in Large Corp

conflict /3 interest /p corporat! entity /p lawyer attorney /p officer director % police

conflict /3 interest /p corporat! /p lawyer attorney /s director officer /p confidential!

45k20 /p corporat! /p confidential!

Small Corporations

conflict! /3 interest /p small (sol** +2 owne! proprietor!) closely-held partnership /s corporat! /p attorney lawyer

Corporate Former Client Conflicts

45k21

topic(45) /p conflict! /3 interest /p former +s client

§ 8.3.3 Lawyer as Director or Investor

Conflicts in Director-Counsel Roles

Confusion and conflict can be created if a corporate lawyer attempts to play roles in addition to that of lawyer for the corporation. A common example is when counsel for a corporation becomes a member of the corporation's board of directors or an officer of the corporation. As discussed elsewhere (§ 13.7.4), critics have recommended that lawyers be prohibited from serving as directors or officers of companies that they advise,[68] and some lawyers wisely attempt to avoid such dual roles.[69] But the economic reality is that outside lawyers often feel that their retainer by the corporation is more secure if they also serve as a member of the corporation's board or management, and attaining that security has tempered judgment. Management may also perceive the relationship as advantageous because the lawyer will gain greater familiarity with the corporation's affairs and because other members of the board will benefit from the presence of a legally trained colleague during their meetings.[70] The lawyer codes do not prohibit the dual role unless the lawyer is unable to exercise independent professional judgment.[71]

Corporate Counsel and Corporate Investor Conflicts

Problems similar to those of a counsel-director can also beset a lawyer who is both corporate counsel and a substantial investor in the corporation. An attempt by outsiders to gain control of the corporation through enlisting the lawyer-shareholder's support can readily create serious conflicts of interest.[72] Even if the corporate lawyer is not a substantial owner of the corporation's stock, the lawyer should not participate in a partisan way if an intracorporate struggle develops for control of the corporation, such as a struggle either to oust or to retain incumbent management.[73]

F.Supp. 537, 545 (D.Nev.1972); Aleut Corp. v. McGarvey, 573 P.2d 473, 475 (Alaska 1978). See also Hull v. Celanese Corp., 513 F.2d 568 (2d Cir.1975)(former member of corporate general counsel staff switched sides to become additional client of plaintiff's lawyer in same litigation).

68 Cary, Professional Responsibility in the Practice of Corporate Law—The Ethics of Bar Associations, 29 Rec. Ass'n.B. City N.Y. 443 (1974). See also authority cited at § 13.7.4 n.13.

69 2 R.Swaine, The Cravath Firm and Its Predecessors 10 (1948).

70 67 ABA J. 1245 (1981)(survey indicates that lawyers, after investment bankers and academicians, are the type of outsider most favored for board membership by present board members.).

71 MR 1.7 comment (Other Conflict Situations). See also State v. Klassen, 207 Kan. 414, 485 P.2d 1295 (1971); ABA Informal Op. 930 (1966); Shipman, Professional Responsibilities of the Corporation's Lawyers, in Professional Responsibility: A Guide for Attorneys 271 (1978).

72 Financial General Bankshares, Inc. v. Metzger, 523 F.Supp 744 (D.D.C.1981)(return of fees and punitive damages awarded to corporation against its former lawyer for breach of fiduciary obligations, including undisclosed attempt to seek control of corporation), vacated for lack of jurisdiction, 680 F.2d 768 (D.D.Cir.1982)(no pendent jurisdiction because of novelty of question under local law).

73 Doe v. A. Corp., 330 F.Supp. 1352, 1355 (S.D.N.Y. 1971), affirmed sub nom. Hall v. A. Corp., 453 F.2d 1375 (2d Cir.1972); ABA Formal Op. 86 (1932). But cf. Federal Savings & Loan Ins. Corp. v. Fielding, 343 F.Supp. 537

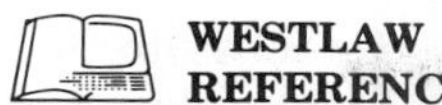

WESTLAW REFERENCES

Conflicts in Director-Counsel Roles

conflict! /3 interest /p corporat! /p lawyer attorney counsel /p dual /s role /p director

topic(45) /p conflict /3 interest /p corporat! /p lawyer attorney counsel /p director

Corporate Counsel and Corporate Investor

conflict /3 interest /p corporat! /p lawyer attorney counselor /p shareholder investor

§ 8.3.4 Shareholder Derivative Actions

The Nature of the Conflict

Shareholder derivative actions are another source of corporate conflicts of interest. The principal issues are two. First, should the same lawyer or law firm represent both the corporation as an entity and one or more officers and directors who, the plaintiff shareholder alleges, are the actual wrongdoers? Second, and aside from the question of joint representation, who in the corporation should hire and direct the lawyer who represents the corporation itself?

Typically a shareholder derivative action is a kind of class action brought by one or more shareholders in behalf of the corporation to recover a judgment in its favor against one or more third parties who are alleged to have wrongfully caused it injury. In effect, the shareholder seeks to compel the defendants to pay damages to the corporation. Often included among the defendants are corporate directors, officers, or other groups of shareholders who are charged with participating in the wrongs. The corporation as an entity is almost invariably named as a nominal defendant because persons controlling it resist the claims of the shareholder plaintiff.

The problem is to find a person who can be trusted to select and direct the efforts of a legal champion for the corporation's interests who does not have conflicting interests of his or her own. But there is often no obvious person connected with the corporation who can clearly be trusted to hire and direct a lawyer to protect the corporation's interests and those interests alone. Despite the fact that the derivative-action plaintiff is asserting the interests of the corporation, it is clearly not a certainty that the corporation's interests will always be foremost in the plaintiff's mind, particularly when matters such as settlement are discussed.[74] The officers who are defendants cannot always be expected to demonstrate single-minded devotion to the corporation's best interests, because those interests may require a sacrifice of their own.

The Rule of Separate Representation

The law here has undergone recent change. On the first question—separate or joint representation—commentators have generally taken the view that separate representation of the corporation should be required in a derivative action, regardless of whether or not the corporation takes an active part in the litigation and whether or not the derivative claim is based on fraud or breach of trust on the part of the individual defendants.[75] Within the past decade the decided weight of authority has swung in that direction, finding that a serious conflict of interest between the corporation and its officers, its directors, and even its majority shareholders precludes their simultaneous representation by the same lawyer or law firm.[76] A similar rule might also apply in litigation by a limited partner against the general partner and the partner-

(D.Nev.1972)(participation by counsel-directors in corporate conflict).

[74] See Messing v. FDI, Inc., 439 F.Supp. 776, 782 n.8 (D.N.J.1977).

[75] 13 W.Fletcher, Corporations § 6025 (rev.ed.1970); H.Henn & J.Alexander, Corporations § 370 (3d ed.1983); Bayne, The Lawyer and Corporate Governance: Conflict of Interest, 26 St.Louis L.Rev. 400 (1982); Riger, Disqualifying Counsel in Corporate Representation, 34 U.Miami L.Rev. 995 (1980); Note, Disqualification of Corporate Counsel in Derivative Actions: Jacuzzi and the Inadequacy of Dual Representation, 31 Hastings L.J. 347 (1979); Note, Independent Representation for Corporate Defendants in Derivative Suits, 74 Yale L.J. 524 (1965).

[76] Cannon v. U.S. Acoustic Corp., 532 F.2d 1118 (7th Cir.1976)(per curiam), affirming in relevant part 398 F.Supp. 209 (N.D.Ill.1975); Murphy v. Washington American League Base Ball Club, Inc., 324 F.2d 394 (D.C.Cir. 1963); Messing v. FDI, Inc., 439 F.Supp. 776, 782 (D.N.J. 1977); Lewis v. Shaffer Stores Co., 218 F.Supp. 238, 240

ship.[77] It has also been held that if joint representation of both the corporation and individual officers is initiated, withdrawal of the corporation's lawyer from representation of the individuals at an early stage of the litigation is sufficient to alleviate the need also to disqualify the lawyer from continuing to represent the corporation.[78]

The requirement of separate representation is produced by a conflict of interests, not by the mere filing of any shareholder derivative action, regardless of the nature of its claims. Claims that are patently spurious, that seek only minor relief, or that do not charge officers or directors with serious wrongdoing may raise no conflict of interest problem that necessitates the additional expense of separate representation.[79] The strictures against joint representation also do not necessarily apply when the theory of the plaintiff-shareholder's action seeks personal or class action recovery that would not rebound directly to the benefit of the corporation. In such nonderivative actions, the interests of the corporation may be less acutely different from those of officers or others accused of wrongdoing.[80] The requirement of separate representation does not necessarily mean that the individual officers and directors must bear the expense of their separate lawyers. It is the law of many states that the corporation may advance litigation expenses to a director or officer.[81] When a corporation directly compensates lawyers who represent individual directors or officers, the normal rules requiring full disclosure and consent apply as in all instances in which a third party pays a lawyer's fee to represent a client.[82]

The second question—who should hire and direct the efforts of the lawyer who represents the corporation as an entity—has been answered primarily in the context of corporate consent to joint representations.

The Dilemma of Cure by Corporate Consent

Many conflicts of interest can be cured by the consent of all affected clients (§ 7.2.2), but a shareholder derivative action that raises substantial conflict of interest problems also raises serious questions about the nature of the consent of the corporation as an entity separate from its codefendant officers and directors. The clearest case would be when the entire board of directors is accused of having injured the corporation, for example, by voting themselves wastefully large directors' fees. It would be mere charade for the same directors to vote the corporation's consent to common representation of themselves and the entity. Even if fewer than a majority of the

(S.D.N.Y.1963); Lower v. Lanark Mut. Fire Ins. Co., 114 Ill.App.3d 462, 70 Ill.Dec. 62, 448 N.E.2d 940 (1983); Haenel v. Epstein, 88 A.D.2d 652, 450 N.Y.S.2d 536, 537–38 (1982); McKay v. Pierce, 86 A.D.2d 655, 446 N.Y.S.2d 403(1982); In re Kinsey, 294 Or. 544, 660 P.2d 660 (1983). Older decisions did not consistently take this view. E.g., Otis & Co. v. Pennsylvania R.R., 57 F.Supp. 680 (E.D.Pa. 1944), affirmed 155 F.2d 552 (3d Cir.1946)(per curiam); Jacuzzi v. Jacuzzi Bros., 243 Cal.App.2d 1, 52 Cal.Rptr. 147 (1946).

77 Schwartz v. Guterman, 109 Misc.2d 1004, 441 N.Y.S.2d 597 (1981), affirmed 86 A.D.2d 804, 448 N.Y.S.2d 650 (1982).

78 Clark v. Lomas & Nettleton Fin. Corp., 79 F.R.D. 641 (N.D.Tex.1978), vacated on other grounds, 625 F.2d 49 (5th Cir.1980), cert.denied 450 U.S. 1029, 101 S.Ct. 1738, 68 L.Ed.2d 224 (1981).

79 Schmidt v. Magnetic Head Corp., 97 A.D.2d 151, 468 N.Y.S.2d 649 (1983); Schwartz v. Guterman, 109 Misc.2d 1004, 441 N.Y.S.2d 597, 598 (1981), affirmed 86 A.D.2d 804, 448 N.Y.S.2d 650(1982); In re Kinsey, 294 Or. 544, 660 P.2d 660 (1983). See also MR 1.13 comment (Derivative Actions). The derivative suit may also be employed as a convenient procedural vehicle for litigation that in fact does not directly involve the corporation in a significant way. E.g., Seifert v. Dumatic Indus. Inc., 413 Pa. 395, 197 A.2d 454 (1964)(50 percent shareholder forced to employ derivative action to force other 50 percent shareholder to honor incorporation agreement where deadlock on four-member board prevented any corporate action; corporation's lawyer not disqualified from representing plaintiff shareholder).

80 McAlinden v. Wiggins, 543 F.Supp. 1004, 1006 (S.D. N.Y.1982)(fraud action seeking damages from corporation and controlling principal); Field v. Freedman, 527 F.Supp. 935 (D.Kan.1981)(direct recovery for fraud sought, plus corporation was defunct).

81 8 Del.Code Ann. § 145(e)(litigation expenses may be advanced on board resolution after benefited director agrees to repay expenditures in event director is adjudged liable for negligence or misconduct). See generally Kaufman, Resolving Conflicts of Interest in Litigation: Insurance, Indemnification and Legal Fees, 31 Bus.Law. 1363 (1976).

82 See generally § 8.8.2. See MR 1.7 comment (Interest of Person Paying for a Lawyer's Service).

directors are named codefendants, the familiar problem of loyalties among board members makes suspect a vote of consent by nondefendant directors.

Devising a solution that is neither charade nor unwarranted intrusion has challenged courts and commentators. The solution resorted to by one court, when the same lawyer undertook to represent both the corporation and its officers and directors despite a serious conflict of interest, was to disqualify the common lawyer from continuing to represent any client and to direct the trial court to appoint new independent counsel for the corporation. The court refused to trust the officers and directors, because of their conflicting interests, to hire a lawyer to defend the separate interests of the corporate entity.[83] Most courts, however, have refused to become entangled in the appointment of substitute lawyers.[84]

Another expedient is to require that the selection of new corporate counsel be made by outside directors not named as defendants in the derivative action. One court that approved a consent to joint representation despite a potential conflict of interest between a corporation and a controlling principal stressed the fact that the board of directors of the corporation approved the joint representation in a meeting not attended by the controlling person.[85] While such ceremonies may give little additional assurance of board independence, they may be the only expedients short of judicial involvement in the selection of independent counsel for the corporation.

§ 8.3.5 Unincorporated Associations

The Modified Entity-Representation Concept

The doctrine of entity representation applies to unincorporated associations as well as to incorporated entities.[86] The doctrine is probably tempered in practice, however, by the realization on the part of courts that the absence of a market for buying and selling shares in the organization deprives members of the association of much alternative means of obtaining relief from unwarranted or corrupt control of the organization by self-serving interests.

Changing of the Guard in an Unincorporated Association

The conflict problem has arisen primarily in connection with dissension within a familiar form of unincorporated association, a labor union. A saga of lawyer conflict of interest decisions was played out in the early 1970s in litigation by a dissident group seeking, ultimately successfully, to remove the leadership of the Mine Workers Union. A lawyer who had represented the incumbent union president in prior litigation charging him with misconduct in office was disqualified by the court from representing the union as an entity in a dissident's derivative action against the union's officers, who were represented by separate counsel.[87] The court found a potential conflict because the union's best interests might be to make a cross claim against the union officers for damages and an accounting because of the misconduct alleged. When the union general counsel and his staff were substituted later as lawyers for the union, the court held that they were also disqualified because they were closely associated with the individual officer-defendants and had represented them as defendants in

[83] Rowen v. LeMars Mut. Ins. Co., 230 N.W.2d 905, 913–16 (Iowa 1975).

[84] See Messing v. FDI, Inc., 439 F.Supp. 776, 778 (D.N.J.1977), and authorities cited.

[85] McAlinden v. Wiggins, 543 F.Supp. 1004, 1006 (S.D. N.Y.1982)(nonderivative action).

[86] MR 1.13 comment (The Entity as the Client; second paragraph). See generally Bartosic & Minda, Union Fiduciaries, Attorneys, and Clients of Interest, 15 U.C. Davis L.Rev. 227 (1981).

[87] Yablonski v. UMW, 448 F.2d 1175 (D.C.Cir.1971) (per curiam), cert.denied 406 U.S. 906, 92 S.Ct. 1609, 31 L.Ed. 2d 816 (1972).

other litigation.[88] The court required that representation of the union be placed in the hands of independent counsel unencumbered by potentially conflicting interests.[89]

Following a union election in which the dissidents turned out the incumbents, the union was realigned as a plaintiff by action of the new leadership of the union. The court now held that it was not impermissible for the successful dissidents' lawyer to become union general counsel and assume representation of the union in the lawsuit.[90] As with shareholder derivative actions, so here the critical factor was the presence or absence of charges that the jointly represented union officers were complicit in acts that were injurious to the union. In the absence of such charges, joint representation was proper.

§ 8.4 INDEMNITY INSURANCE CONFLICTS [91]

§ 8.4.1 Insurance Defense Practice

Large numbers of lawyers are involved in representing insured tort defendants under arrangements with liability insurance companies. The extent of insurance representation is very large in the United States. Very little personal injury litigation is conducted against uninsured defendants.[92] And personal injury litigation comprises a large percentage of the caseload of state courts.

The Insurer-Insured Relationship

Liability insurance policies typically provide that the insurer (the company) will pay any judgment for damages entered against the insured and will bear the cost of providing a defense against a claim for damages, including the cost of hiring a lawyer to represent the interests of the insured. In return for those protections, the company typically retains the right to control the defense of the action and the decision whether to settle any claim.

That superficially straightforward arrangement is fraught with conflict of interest problems for the lawyer whom the company retains to defend a claim against the insured. The principal, although not the only, problem faced by the lawyer is that of accommodating the interest of the company in reducing its costs by limiting the scope of its coverage obligations and the interest of the insured in obtaining the maximum personal advantage from representation by the lawyer supplied by the company. Such an accommodation is required in several areas of commonly recurring problems: cases involving factual questions concerning policy coverage; excess-coverage cases; cases involving apparent noncooperation of the insured or involving collusion between insured and claimant; and subrogation claims by the company in the insured's behalf against the claimant and others.

In each problem area the economic interests of the lawyer might pull in the direction of favoring the insurer client, who will pay the lawyer's fee and serves as an important source of future law business, while general professional ideals impel the lawyer in the direction of protecting the interests of the insured. The accommodation that the law in most jurisdictions seems to require involves compromises with the extreme models suggested by a single-valued pursuit of either of the opposing impulses, although with a decided tilt in favor of the insured.

88 Yablonski v. UMW, 454 F.2d 1036 (D.C.Cir.1971)(per curiam), cert.denied 406 U.S. 906, 92 S.Ct. 1609, 31 L.Ed. 2d 816 (1972). See also Tucker v. Shaw, 378 F.2d 304 (2d Cir.1967); International Bd. of Teamsters v. Hoffa, 242 F.Supp. 246 (D.D.C.1965).

89 Weaver v. UMW, 492 F.2d 580, 583 (D.C.Cir.1973).

90 Id.

91 See generally R.Keeton, Insurance Law 493–99 (1971); Mallen, Insurance Counsel: The Fine Line between Professional Responsibility and Malpractice, 45 Ins.Couns.J. 244 (1978); Morris, Conflicts of Interest in Defending under Liability Insurance Policies: A Proposed Solution, 1981 Utah L.Rev. 457.

92 One study indicated that in Michigan only 1.2 percent of tort liability payments came from uninsured sources. A.Conard, J.Morgan, R.Pratt, C.Voltz & R.Bombaugh, Automobile Accident Costs and Payments, 48, 50 n.54 (1964).

Professional Rules

The lawyer codes recognize the insurance representation problem but afford little specific assistance. The Code's EC 5–17 notes the problem as a typically recurring situation, whose solution requires an analysis of each case to determine the extent to which the lawyer's professional judgement will be affected by differing interests. Rule 1.7 of the 1983 Model Rules provides a general prohibition against conflicting simultaneous representation without client consent and in a comment states only that the arrangement between the company and the lawyer specially retained to represent it must "assure the special counsel's professional independence." [93] Neither set of rules gives more than general guidance, although it is reasonably clear from both that the insurance lawyer's allegiance, if slanted in either direction, must be aligned with the insured.[94]

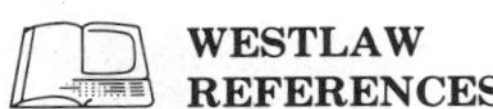
WESTLAW REFERENCES

Indemnity Insurance Conflicts

insur**** /s defense /s attorney lawyer /s conflict! /3 interest

§ 8.4.2 The Dual-Client Doctrine

A Hypothetical Problem

Suppose an insured is sued for damages due to negligence. The claimant's complaint states that the damages arose from a type of occurrence covered by the insurance policy. A lawyer hired by the insurance company, purportedly representing the insured, discovers facts suggesting that the claimant's injuries in fact resulted from a battery committed by the insured—a type of injury for which the policy does not provide coverage. It would plainly be impermissible for the lawyer to press doggedly for additional shreds of evidence relieving the company of liability to the insured under its policy and leaving the insured without insurance protection against the claim.[95] On the other hand, the company has a legitimate interest in limiting its expenditures to those warranted by the policy. It would be asking too much of lawyers to expect them to proceed with attention fixed solely on the interests of the insured without concern for the interests of the company.[96] How, then, is the lawyer to proceed?

The ABA Guiding Principles

Before analyzing the judicial solution to that conflict, it is instructive to assess the accommodations that have been attempted by representatives of the insurance industry and the American Bar Association. Those groups agreed in 1939 that if any diversity of interest between company and policyholder appeared, the policyholder should be fully advised of the situation and invited to retain independent counsel at the policyholder's personal expense.[97] The ABA approved in 1972 a set of "guiding principles" that contained general

93 MR 1.7 comment (Interest of Person Paying for a Lawyer's Service).

94 That appears most clearly in the Model Rules comment, supra, and in footnote 23 to EC 5–17 of the Code.

95 Newcomb v. Meiss, 263 Minn. 315, 116 N.W.2d 593 (1962)(lawyer retained by insurer to represent insured at trial pressed theory that defendant-insured had intentionally struck pedestrian plaintiff with insured automobile, an uninsured tort). See also, e.g., State Farm Mut. Auto Ins. Co. v. Walker, 382 F.2d 548 (7th Cir.1967), cert.denied 389 U.S. 1045, 88 S.Ct. 789, 19 L.Ed.2d 789 (1968); Farm Bureau Mut. Auto Ins. Co. v. Hammer, 177 F.2d 793 (4th Cir.1949), cert.denied 339 U.S. 914, 70 S.Ct. 575, 94 L.Ed. 1339 (1950); Tomerlin v. Canadian Indem. Co., 61 Cal.2d 638, 39 Cal.Rptr. 731, 394 P.2d 571 (1964); Norman v. Insurance Co. of N.America, 218 Va. 718, 239 S.E.2d 902 (1978). See also, e.g., Bartels v. Romano, 171 N.J.Super. 23, 407 A.2d 1248, 1250–51 (1979)(without consent of insured, lawyer retained by company filed third-party action seeking to implead second company (with liability limits of $25,000) in place of first company (with liability limits of $100,000)).

96 United States Fidelity & Guar. Co. v. Louis A. Roser Co., 585 F.2d 932, 938, n.5 (8th Cir.1978): "Even the most optimistic view of human nature requires us to realize that an attorney employed by an insurance company will slant his efforts, perhaps unconsciously, in the interests of his real client—the one who is paying his fee and from whom he hopes to receive future business—the insurance company."

97 See Conference Committee on Adjusters, Statement of Principles, § 4(b)(1939), in 7 Martindale-Hubbell Law Directory 74M-75M (1978). Together with other intergroup treaties, the Statement was repealed in 1980 in the face of threats of antitrust charges. See § 2.4.1.

and elaborate statements of recommended resolutions to various conflict situations.[98] Among other things, the principles provided that the lawyer who was hired by the company to defend under a policy represented the company as primary client and, so long as no conflict of interest existed, the lawyer also represented the insured.[99] If the company's lawyer discovered a question of coverage or other issue creating a conflict of interest, the lawyer was to notify the company and the insured policyholder.[1] Thereafter the lawyer should cease representing the policyholder unless the policyholder agreed, after the lawyer disclosed the nature of the coverage question, that the lawyer should continue the defense (in what posture is not mentioned).[2]

The Cases

Few courts have agreed entirely with the approach of either the ABA guiding principles or the 1939 resolution on coverage questions. What emerges from that body of law is a judicial concept of the company and insured as, in most respects, dual clients of the lawyer retained by the insurance company.[3] Put another way, the lawyer bears the same responsibilities toward the insured as would be the case if the insured had hired the lawyer directly.[4] That dual-representation standard does not, of course, assure that conflicts will not arise. But the standard insists that if conflicts do arise, the lawyer may not proceed with representation of both clients. The lawyer first must obtain the fully informed and voluntary consent of both clients to a continuation of the dual representation despite the conflict, on the assumption that the conflict is consentable,[5] or must withdraw from representation of both clients with respect to any dispute between them if the conflict is nonconsentable or if the clients do not consent. The principal implications of the dual-client doctrine are developed in the following section.

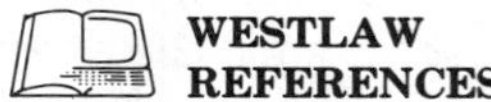
WESTLAW REFERENCES

attorney lawyer /p duty /p client /p insur**** /s conflict! /3 interest

217k514.15

45k20 /p insur****

45k113 /p insur****

§ 8.4.3 Specific Problem Settings

General

Conflicts of interest between the insured and the company can arise in several ways. Analyzed below are several common variations of the conflict problem. In most of the areas courts have indicated rather clearly the way in which a defending lawyer should resolve the conflict.

98 "Guiding Principles" of National Conference of Lawyers and Liability Insurers, in 7 Martindale-Hubbell Law Directory 76M-77M (1978)(repealed); also in 20 Fed.Ins. Couns.J. 95 (1970). At least one court has stated that the Guiding Principles set forth legally binding standards of conduct. Employers Casualty Co. v. Tilley, 496 S.W.2d 552, 559 (Tex.1973).

99 Guiding Principles, § I. Nonetheless, § VI of the Principles stated that information received from the insured indicating a lack of coverage should not be communicated to the insurance company if the information was given under circumstances indicating that the insured believed that the information would be held confidential from the company.

1 Guiding Principles § IV.

2 Guiding Principles § V.

3 Rogers v. Robson, Masters, Ryan, Brumund & Belom, 81 Ill.2d 201, 40 Ill.Dec. 816, 818, 407 N.E.2d 47, 49 (1980) (although defense lawyers were employed by company, the insured was also their client; as such, lawyers owed duty to client independent of insurance policy to obtain client's permission to settle claim); accord Lieberman v. Employers Ins. of Wausau, 84 N.J. 325, 419 A.2d 417, 423–25 (1980), and authorities cited. Some courts take the position that the insured is the "primary" client of the lawyer and the lawyer must act accordingly. E.g., Gibson v. Western Fire Ins. Co., ___ Mont. ___, 682 P.2d 725, 736 (1984).

4 Outboard Marine Corp. v. Liberty Mut. Ins. Co., 536 F.2d 730, 737 (7th Cir.1976); Norman v. Insurance Co. of N.America, 218 Va. 718, 239 S.E.2d 902, 907 (1978); Lysick v. Walson, 258 Cal.App.2d 136, 65 Cal.Rptr. 406, 413 (1968).

5 See § 7.2.2. The conflict may be too bald to be cured by consent in cases, for example, in which the lawyer suspects collusion between the insured and the claimant and intends to cross-examine the insured at trial to expose the fraud and collusion.

Coverage Questions

Courts generally hold that the insurance company's duty to defend the insured exists under the policy if the pleadings or an independent investigation of the facts indicate that the company is potentially liable.[6] Even if most of the opposing party's claims fall outside coverage of the policy, the company is obliged to provide a defense until the company can determine that there is no possibility that the recovery will fall within the coverage of the policy.[7] If the company discovers grounds to suspect that coverage might not exist, it is not free to continue to represent the insured while at the same time preparing a defense against the insured on the question of coverage.[8] The preferred course is for the company to interview the insured about questions of coverage without creating an illusion that the interview is to protect the interests of the insured. Instead, the interview should be preceded by an explicit statement that the question being pursued is whether the policy provides coverage.[9] If the question of coverage cannot be resolved, the company must notify the insured of the coverage question and obtain the permission of the insured to proceed with the defense under a "reservation of rights," which permits it to contest coverage if a judgment is entered against the insured.[10]

Generally, if the company contests coverage or if a conflict of interest otherwise arises, the insured is not required to consent to the reservation-of-rights representation by the lawyer retained by the company but is entitled to hire a separate and independent lawyer at the expense of the company.[11] That solution assures that the insured and the company will each be represented by lawyers who are not burdened with a conflict of interests. If the claimant's case against the insured must be tried, a busy trial court may find that the additional time and complexity of dual representation of the insured at trial is too burdensome and potentially confusing to a jury for invariable deployment at trial. The court has discretion in an unusual case to require the insured to select one counsel to try the case unless an actual conflict of interest appears.[12]

If the lawyer retained by the company obtains an admission from the insured or discovers other evidence that clearly indicates a lack of coverage, the lawyer must withdraw from further representation of the insured.[13] If the insured or the company files a declaratory judgment action for a determination of coverage while the suit for damages is still pending, the lawyer for the insured in the damage action may not represent the company in the declaratory judgment action.[14]

Insured Wishing to Concede Liability

The insured, particularly if related to the claimant, may favor recovery by the claimant because of the absence of personal liability as a result of the insurance coverage. The lawyer may nonetheless proceed in such cases to

[6] United States v. United States Fidelity & Guar. Co., 601 F.2d 1136 (10th Cir.1979); Crum v. Anchor Ins. Co., 264 Minn. 378, 392, 119 N.W.2d 703, 709 (1963).

[7] Bituminous Ins. Cos. v. Pennsylvania Mfrs. Ass'n Ins. Co., 427 F.Supp. 539, 555 (E.D.Pa.1976), and authorities cited; Note, The Insurer's Duty to Defend under a Liability Insurance Policy, 114 U.Pa.L.Rev. 734 (1966).

[8] Employers Casualty Co. v. Tilley, 496 S.W.2d 552 (Tex.1973); Transamerica Ins. Group v. Chubb & Son, Inc., 16 Wn.App. 247, 554 P.2d 1080 (1976); 7A J.Appleman, Insurance Law & Practice § 4693 (1962).

[9] Cf. Saftler v. Government Employees Ins. Co., 95 A.D.2d 54, 465 N.Y.S.2d 20 (1983)(interview between legal malpractice insurer's lawyer and lawyer asserting coverage under malpractice policy).

[10] Richmond v. Georgia Farm Bureau Mut. Ins. Co., 140 Ga.App. 215, 231 S.E.2d 245 (1976).

[11] United States Fidelity & Guar. Co. v. Louis A. Roser Co., 585 F.2d 932, 939 (8th Cir. 1978); Outboard Marine Corp. v. Liberty Mut. Ins. Co., 536 F.2d 730, 737 (7th Cir. 1976); Executive Aviation, Inc. v. National Ins. Underwriters, 16 Cal.App.3d 799, 94 Cal.Rptr. 347, 353–54 (1971); Public Serv. Mut. Ins. Co. v. Goldfarb, 53 N.Y.2d 392, 442 N.Y.S.2d 422, 425 N.E.2d 810 (1981).

[12] Chemprene, Inc. v. X–Tyal Int'l Corp., 55 N.Y.2d 900, 449 N.Y.S.2d 23, 433 N.E.2d 1271 (1982).

[13] State Farm Mut. Auto. Ins. Co. v. Walker, 382 F.2d 548 (7th Cir. 1967), cert. denied 389 U.S. 1045, 88 S.Ct. 789, 19 L.Ed.2d 789 (1968).

[14] See generally § 7.3.2. See also, e.g., Industrial Indem. Co. v. Great American Ins. Co., 73 Cal.App.3d 529, 140 Cal.Rptr. 806 (1977). But see Currington v. Federated Mut. Ins. Co., 145 Ga.App. 350, 243 S.E.2d 713, 714 (1978); Auto-Owners Ins. Co. v. McGaugh, 617 S.W.2d 436, 445 (Mo.App.1981).

vindicate nonliability of the insured.[15] In fact, the insured must proceed carefully, because in some jurisdictions a concession of liability might result in forfeiture of the insurance protection on the notion that conceding liability is inconsistent with the contractual responsibilities of the insured under the cooperation clause of the policy.

Operation of the Confidentiality Rules

No clear authority exists concerning the extent to which the lawyer can share information gained from one client with the other that is consistent with the lawyer's responsibilities to protect confidential client information (§ 6.7). In most situations the question is whether the lawyer can share with the insurance company information gained from the insured that is adverse to the interests of the insured vis-à-vis the insurance company. In view of the general dual-client doctrine (§ 6.4.8), it seems that the lawyer should be able to share with both clients all information learned in the representation unless one client has furnished information only on the understanding that it would not be shared with the other—and the other has been informed of that limitation—or unless a conflict of interest has arisen. Once a substantial risk of a conflict arises, the lawyer should seek no further information from either client until either the conflict is resolved or separate representation is obtained.

Additional Insureds

The clients covered by the duty to defend include persons who are covered under the insurance policy as additional insureds, such as nonowner drivers of insured vehicles. The lawyer owes those insureds the same good faith effort to minimize their personal risk of loss. Thus an insurance company whose lawyer represents both the insured vehicle owner and an additional driver cannot without consent of the driver enter into stipulations (such as admitting that the driver was not operating the vehicle with the permission of the insured) that protect the insured and the company but leave the additional insured exposed to personal liability.[16]

Uninsured Motorist Conflicts

A clear conflict of interest exists under the common policy clause providing coverage to the insured for judgments against an uninsured motorist. If the insured files suit against an uninsured defendant, the insurance company will naturally fear that the defendant will not vigorously defend and that the company may become liable to its insured under the uninsured-motorist coverage in a situation, or in an amount, that is contrary to the outcome that would result if the litigation were vigorously contested. For that reason most jurisdictions permit the insurance company to intervene as a defendant in an insured's suit against an uninsured motorist.[17] The company is not permitted to use against the insured any information gained in the company-insured relationship.[18] And if the uninsured motorist asserts a counterclaim against the insured that creates a duty to defend on the part of the company, the insured can obtain independent representation that must be reimbursed by the company.[19] A variation on the uninsured-motorist conflict is presented when an uninsured plaintiff sues an insured defendant who fails to assert against the plaintiff a counterclaim that

[15] Buchanan v. Buchanan, 99 Cal.App.3d 587, 160 Cal. Rptr. 577 (1979)(in time-barred suit by wife for tort damages against husband, lawyer retained by insurance company properly acted in the "best interests" of husband-insured by moving for dismissal despite husband's contrary wish). But cf. Pennix v. Winton, 61 Cal.App.2d 761, 143 P.2d 940 (1943)(reversal, on appeal by plaintiffs, when judgment for defendant clouded by actions of lawyer for driver-defendant; lawyer, retained by defendant's insurance company, vilified collusive motives of driver-defendant before jury when he testified that, in effect, his own gross negligence had caused injuries to passenger friend).

[16] Ivy v. Pacific Auto. Ins. Co., 156 Cal.App.2d 652, 320 P.2d 140 (1958).

[17] See generally Comment, Insurer Intervention in Uninsured Motorist Cases, 55 Ind.L.J. 717 (1980).

[18] Lima v. Chambers, 657 P.2d 279, 285 (Utah 1982); Barry v. Keith, 474 S.W.2d 876, 878 (Ky.1971).

[19] Lima v. Chambers, 657 P.2d 279 (Utah 1982).

would have to be paid, if successful, by the defendant's own insurance company.[20]

Settlements within and in Excess of Policy Limits

A familiar conflict of interest problem for an insurance lawyer is the differing interests of company and insured with respect to settlement in cases in which the policy coverage is less than the amounts claimed.[21] The clearest case is presented if the company refuses to accept a settlement offer that is within the policy limits but at or near their maximum. For example, suppose a claimant offers to settle a $75,000 claim for $19,500 and the insurance limits are $20,000. The company might calculate that a possible judgment far in excess of the policy limits is costless to it and that the case should be tried so long as there is some probability that the recovery will be less than the settlement offer and the cost of continuing the defense through a trial. The company's sacrifice of the interests of the insured in such cases has led to the development of a body of law providing that such bad faith refusals of the company to settle create liability to the insured in the amount of the liability imposed on the insured in excess of the policy limits. The lawyer may also be liable in damages to the client on a theory of bad faith.[22] The successful claimant can take over that claim of the insured against the company by assignment from the insured and press it against the company.[23] The same duty to proceed in good faith to protect the interests of the insured exists when a settlement offer is made that is in excess of policy limits.[24]

Possible Subrogation Claims against Coinsured Parties

An insurance company that compensates an insured for injuries inflicted by a third party often has a right under the policy to be subrogated to the rights of the insured against the third party. A lawyer hired to file a subrogation claim against the third party sometimes encounters a conflict of interest because other possible defendants are available who can be required to pay additional damages to the insured but recovery against them would be disadvantageous to the company because it also insures them. Suppose, for example, that a lawyer is retained by a worker's compensation insurance company to press a subrogation claim of an injured worker against a nonemployer third party. The worker's claim against the insured employer is typically limited in amount by a statutory schedule, but the worker's claims against a nonemployer third party would not be so limited. A conflict arises if the company has also issued public liability insurance to the third party. Here, as with other conflicts, the lawyer can proceed only with the fully informed consent of the insured—the worker in the example.[25]

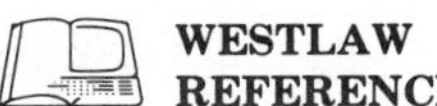

WESTLAW REFERENCES

Coverage

insured /p insurance /p conflict! /3 interest

217.514.7 /p coverage

45.20 /p insur**** /p coverage

[20] Suchta v. Robinett, 596 P.2d 1380, 1385 (Wyo.1979).

[21] See generally Schwartz, Statutory Strict Liability for an Insurer's Failure to Settle, 1975 Duke L.J. 901; Note, Insurer's Liability for Refusal to Settle: Beyond Strict Liability, 50 S.Cal.L.Rev. 751 (1977).

[22] Compare Betts v. Allstate Ins. Co., 154 Cal.App.3d 688, 201 Cal.Rptr. 528 (1984)(damages properly awarded against lawyers for bad faith failure to protect interests of insured), with Purdy v. Pacific Auto. Ins. Co., 157 Cal. App.3d 59, 203 Cal.Rptr. 524 (1984)(no liability when lawyers kept all parties informed of relevant information).

[23] Larraburu Bros., Inc. v. Royal Indem. Co., 604 F.2d 1208 (9th Cir.1979); Riske v. Truck Ins. Ex., 541 F.2d 768 (8th Cir.1976); Communale v. Traders & Gen. Ins. Co., 50 Cal.2d 654, 328 P.2d 198 (1958); Tiger River Pine Co. v. Maryland Cas. Co., 163 S.C. 229, 161 S.E. 491 (1931).

[24] Bell v. Commercial Ins. Co., 280 F.2d 514 (3d Cir. 1960); Hodges v. State Farm Mut. Auto. Ins. Co., 488 F.Supp. 1057, 1063 (D.S.C.1980).

[25] Woodruff v. Tomlin, 616 F.2d 924 (6th Cir.)(en banc), cert. denied 449 U.S. 888, 101 S.Ct. 246, 66 L.Ed.2d 114 (1980)(lawyer hired by insurance company exposed to possible legal malpractice claim by nonconsenting insured for taking steps in subrogation action dictated by interests of company that were potentially disadvantageous to insured).

Liability

conflict! /3 interest /p insured /s insurance insurer /s liability

Confidentiality

conflict! /3 interest /p insur**** /s attorney lawyer /s confiden!

topic(45) /p insur**** /s confiden!

Additional Insured

conflict! /3 interest /s addition! /s insured

Uninsured Motorist

217k467.51 & conflict /3 interest /s insur****

Settlements Within and in Excess of Policy Limits

topic(217) /p conflict /3 interest /p excess! /s policy liability

Possible Subrogation Claims Against Coinsured Parties

conflict! /3 interest /p subrogat! /p coinsured

§ 8.5 BUYER–SELLER CONFLICTS OF INTEREST

The Pervasiveness of Differing Interests

The process by which a buyer and seller of property transact their business is fraught with conflicts of interests. Indeed, a lawyer's simultaneous representation of a buyer and a seller in the same transaction is a paradigm of a conflict of interest. Beginning with such basic elements as determining the price and describing the property to be sold, what one party gets the other must concede. Terms of payment, security for unpaid balances, warranties of quality and of title, date of closing and risk of loss in the interim, tax consequences, and a host of other details should be addressed by each party or the party's adviser in a well-thought-out transaction. When the transaction is a large one—such as the purchase and sale of a residence,[26] commercial property, or a business—the transaction typically becomes further complicated because the additional interests of banks, brokers, tenants, and title insurance companies may intrude.[27]

So long as the parties are separately represented, both may look to their own lawyer for legal advice and assistance in dealing with each of those details. But separate representation is costly, and might be considered unnecessary: negotiating parties may have begun the transaction amicably and ended their discussions readily, agreeing on all that they consider to be the basics. They thus may feel no need to have separate lawyers intervene and may seek out a single lawyer to represent them both. Courts are not of one mind on the question whether the same lawyer can permissibly do so.

General Approach of Lawyer Codes

The 1969 Code does not mention buyer-seller conflicts specifically. But the Code's general rules dealing with conflicts when a lawyer simultaneously represents multiple clients clearly address the problem in part. Under the general rules a lawyer must avoid representing "differing interests" [28] and can represent multiple clients after full disclosure and consent only if the lawyer's professional judgment can still be exercised in behalf of each client during the representation.[29] The 1983 Model Rules are similarly silent on the specific subject, although a comment defines as a nonconsentable conflict a negotiation in which the interests of multiple parties are "fundamentally antagonistic to each other." [30]

The Cases: Dual Representation Following Consent

Judicial attitudes toward simultaneous representation of buyer and seller vary. All agree that simultaneous representation without full disclosure and consent is impermissi-

[26] For an illuminating discussion of the conflict of interest issues in the context of a sale of residential real property, see Moore, Conflicts of Interest in the Simultaneous Representation of Multiple Clients: A Proposed Solution to the Current Confusion and Controversy, 61 Tex.L.Rev. 211, 258–71 (1982).

[27] ABA Special Committee on Residential Real Estate Transactions, Report on the Property Role of the Lawyer in Residential Real Estate Transactions 9–13 (1976)(general descriptions of conflicts of interest between various parties).

[28] DR 5–105(A). See generally § 7.3.4.

[29] DR 5–105(C). See generally § 7.2.2.

[30] MR 1.7 comment (Other Conflict Situations).

ble.[31] Some judges have argued for a complete bar against dual representation.[32] But all American jurisdictions apparently permit such joint representations under at least some circumstances. Some courts give a very limited scope to permitted joint representations and allow a lawyer to represent both buyer and seller, with each party's consent, only in the capacity of "scrivener," after they agree on the basic terms of the transaction.[33] Other courts, some with reluctance,[34] have approved dual representation if an adequate disclosure is given to each client and each client voluntarily consents.[35] Courts also permit a lawyer to prepare all the necessary documents for closing a sales transaction and attend the closing while representing only one party to the transaction so long as the lawyer observes the applicable limitations and avoids giving legal advice to nonclients.[36] Once a lawyer has assumed the dual role, the interests of all clients must be protected. A lawyer who favors one client to the detriment of the interests of others, without their fully informed consent, succumbs to the pressures of one side and fails to exercise independent judgment in behalf of all clients.[37]

WESTLAW REFERENCES

conflict /3 interest /p attorney lawyer buy /p seller

topic(45) /p conflict /3 interest /p buyer transferee obligee mortgagor

topic(45) /p (dual +3 representation) (multiple +3 client)

45k21.10

§ 8.6 CONFLICTS OF INTEREST IN DIVORCE REPRESENTATION [38]

Judicial Control of Marriage Dissolution

In all American jurisdictions, a fully legal marriage can be dissolved only through some type of judicial proceeding. One might imag-

[31] People v. Bollinger, 681 P.2d 950 (Colo.1984); In re Banta, 412 N.E.2d 221 (Ind.1980); State v. Callahan, 232 Kan. 136, 652 P.2d 708 (1982); In re Dolan, 76 N.J. 1, 384 A.2d 1076, 1079–81 (1978)(discipline for representing both sides in real estate transaction); In re Boivin, 271 Or. 419, 533 P.2d 171 (1975); In re Sedor, 73 Wis.2d 629, 245 N.W.2d 895 (1976); Note, Conflicts of Interest in Real Estate Transactions, 6 W.New Eng.L.Rev. 73 (1983). A client whose own lawyer in a sales negotiation secretly represents the other party to the transaction can set aside the transaction on a showing that the other party knew of the lawyer's dual representation. E.g., Holley v. Jackson, 39 Del.Ch. 32, 158 A.2d 803 (1959); City of Hastings v. Jerry Spady Pontiac-Cadillac, Inc., 212 Neb. 137, 322 N.W.2d 369 (1982).

[32] Adams v. Chenowith, 349 So.2d 230 (Fla.App. 1977); In re Dolan, 76 N.J. 1, 384 A.2d 1076, 1082 (1978)(Pashman, J., dissenting). Such an absolute ban on dual representation is currently in force in England and Wales among solicitors, who handle all real estate transactions. See Wickenden, Professional Conduct, Etiquette and Ethics of Solicitors in England, 4 J.Legal Prof. 41, 40–50 (1979)(discussing 1972 amendments to Solicitors Practice Rules).

[33] Blevin v. Mayfield, 189 Cal.App.2d 649, 11 Cal.Rptr. 882 (1961). But cf. In re Barrett, 269 Or. 264, 524 P.2d 1208 (1974)(apparently approving ethics committee opinion disapproving functioning of lawyer as "scrivener" for both parties if this impairs adequate representation of interests of both). Beal v. Mars Larsen Ranch Corp., Inc., 99 Idaho 662, 586 P.2d 1378, 1384 (1978).

[34] In re Dolan, 76 N.J. 1, 384 A.2d 1076, 1081–82 (1978) ("This opinion should serve as notice that henceforth where dual representation is sought to be justified on the basis of the parties' consent, this Court will not tolerate consents which are less than knowing, intelligent and voluntary. Consents must be obtained in such a way as to insure that the client has had adequate time . . . to reflect upon the choice, and must not be forced upon the client by the exigencies of the closing. This applies with equal force to the dual representation of mortgagor and mortgagee."); In re Bauer, 283 Or. 55, 581 P.2d 511, 515 (1978)(in dual representation, lawyer's disclosure to parties should be reduced to writing).

[35] Attorney Grievance Comm'n v. Lockhart, 285 Md. 586, 403 A.2d 1241, 1245 n.6 (1979); In re Boivin, 271 Or. 419, 533 P.2d 171 (1975); Dillard v. Broyles, 633 S.W.2d 636, 642 (Tex.App.1982), cert. denied 463 U.S. 1208, 103 S.Ct. 3539, 77 L.Ed.2d 1389 (1983). Some courts, however, infer consent from very flimsy evidence. See Grundmeyer v. McFadin, 537 S.W.2d 764, 772 (Tex.Civ. App.1976). See also Florida Bar v. Teitelman, 261 So.2d 140 (Fla.1972)(impermissible for seller's lawyer to charge fee to unrepresented buyer, and impermissible for lawyer to represent both without full disclosure and consent).

[36] In re Bauer, 283 Or. 55, 581 P.2d 511 (1978).

[37] Attorney Grievance Comm'n v. Collins, 295 Md. 532, 457 A.2d 1134, 1145 (1983).

[38] See generally Crystal, Ethical Problems in Marital Practice, 30 So.Car.L.Rev. 321, 325–32 (1979); Note, Family Law—Attorney Mediation of Marital Disputes and Conflict of Interest Considerations, 60 N.C.L.Rev. 171 (1981); Note, Simultaneous Representation, 28 Case W.Res.L.Rev. 86, 95–109 (1977). See also § 8.7 (lawyers as mediators).

ine, therefore, that the general principle that prohibits a lawyer from representing opposing parties in litigation (§ 7.3.2) automatically precludes a lawyer from representing both spouses seeking a dissolution. To be sure, that is the definite rule if the dissolution is actively litigated between contending spouses. Some decisions have also extended the rule barring joint representation to any marital dissolution suit without regard to the parties' actual feelings of animosity or contentiousness.[39] But some recent decisions suggest the possibility of a less restrictive approach.

Pros and Cons of Joint Representation

Commentators are divided on whether the informed consent of both spouses should permit a lawyer to represent both parties.[40] Several factors argue against joint representation, and several argue for it. Courts have been concerned with the conflict of interest of the spouses' common lawyer, with the vulnerability of the dissolution or annulment decree to later attack because of the conflict, and with the consequences of that instability for spouses and children in later marriages. For example, a former spouse might later form the belief that an agreement prepared by the common lawyer did not share property equally and may wish to reopen the judgment.[41] The lawyer may also be sued for legal malpractice by one of the commonly represented former spouses on the ground that the lawyer favored the other spouse.[42] Further, joint representation was highly suspect as collusive in an earlier era, in which the state attempted to make divorce an encumbered process in order to assure that marriages were sundered only in narrowly defined situations.

Clients and lawyers, however, were ill served by a conflict of interest rule that always forbade joint representation and required divorcing spouses to undergo the expense of two lawyers. As a result, it was common for a lawyer to represent only one spouse but for the other spouse to be invited to confer with the represented spouse and the lawyer about a settlement agreement or other matters, presumably after appropriate warnings to seek independent counsel.[43] The arrangement was perilous, however, because ethics rules strictly limited the nature of the conversation between the lawyer and the unrepresented spouse[44] because the unrepresented spouse could more readily attack any resulting judgment or settlement on the ground

39 King v. King, 52 Ill.App.3d 749, 10 Ill.Dec. 592, 367 N.E.2d 1358 (1977); Holmes v. Holmes, 145 Ind.App. 52, 248 N.W.2d 564 (1969); Bartlett v. Bartlett, 84 A.D.2d 800, 444 N.Y.S.2d 157, 158 (1981)("This court has repeatedly condemned the practice of one attorney representing both parties in the preparation of a separation agreement."). Cf. MacDonald v. Wagner, 5 Mo.App. 56, 58 (1878)(note to lawyer void when signed by husband to pay for lawyer's legal services in representing wife in divorce and when lawyer then represented both husband and wife in effecting reconciliation). A frequently cited case is Johnson v. Johnson, 141 N.C. 91, 53 S.E. 623 (1906) (same lawyer cannot represent both parties seeking to set aside judgment in annulment action). See generally Restatement (Second) of Agency § 394 comment d (1958)("In divorce proceedings and in other cases in which the public has an interest, it is improper for an attorney to represent even consenting clients who are adversary parties only pro forma.").

40 Compare Moore, Conflicts of Interest in the Simultaneous Representation of Multiple Clients, 61 Tex.L.Rev. 211, 255–56 (1982)(consent should be effective if informed and voluntary), with Silberman, Professional Responsibility Problems of Divorce Mediation, 16 Fam.L.Q. 107 (1982); Kindregan, Conflict of Interest and the Lawyer in Civil Practice, 10 Val.U.L.Rev. 423, 438 (1976).

41 Gardine v. Cottey, 360 Mo. 681, 230 S.W.2d 731, 18 A.L.R.2d 1100 (1950); Bjornstrup v. Cole, 393 P.2d 316 (Wyo.1964). Even jurisdictions that have approved joint representation in some instances will give separation agreements prepared by a jointly-selected lawyer special scrutiny when one of the ex-spouses later attempts to nullify it. Levine v. Levine, 56 N.Y.2d 42, 451 N.Y.S.2d 26, 436 N.E.2d 476, 478–79 (1982).

42 Ishmael v. Millington, 241 Cal.App.2d 520, 50 Cal. Rptr. 592 (1966); Lange v. Marshall, 622 S.W.2d 237 (Mo. App.1981). Among other practical problems, the impropriety of the joint representation could forfeit the lawyer's right to a fee. Cf. Jeffry v. Pounds, 67 Cal.App.3d 6, 136 Cal.Rptr. 373 (1977); MacDonald v. Wagner, 5 Mo. App. 56 (1878).

43 Davidson v. Davidson, 90 Cal.App.2d 809, 819, 204 P.2d 71 (1949); Wilbanks v. Wilbanks, 238 Ga. 660, 234 S.E.2d 915 (1977). See generally Note, Simultaneous Representation: Transaction Resolution in the Adversary System, 28 Case W.Res.L.Rev. 86, 96, 102–103 (1977).

44 The arrangement would be more likely to survive scrutiny under the 1983 Model Rules than under the 1969 Code because of the Rules' relaxation of the Code strictures against giving legal advice to an unrepresented party. See § 11.6.3.

of overreaching,[45] and because some jurisdictions regarded divorces by consent as collusive.[46]

Joint Representation in Uncontested Marriage Dissolutions

Because of almost universal acceptance of no-fault dissolution in recent years,[47] increasing numbers of parting spouses have found it desirable to avoid the additional expense, and often the additional acrimony, that is caused when they hire two lawyers in order to be separately represented.[48]

The states have followed two differing approaches to the problem. One approach continues the traditional rule and prohibits joint representation in a dissolution action as an absolute rule.[49] Another approach, represented by recent decisions in New York and California,[50] discourages joint representation but affords spouses the right to joint representation in a narrow range of cases in which three conditions are met. First, the lawyer must make a full disclosure to both spouses. Second, the spouses must separately consent to the joint representation after the full disclosure.[51] And, third, there must be no contentiousness or serious conflict of interest between the spouses.[52] Importantly, if a lawyer enters into a joint representation of the spouses after those conditions are satisfied and discord or inequity later develops, the lawyer must withdraw from representing *both* parties.[53] Moreover, the lawyer should inform the parties that the normal attorney-client privilege does not apply to jointly represented parties and in later litigation between themselves it might be required that communications to their common lawyer that otherwise would have been confidential be disclosed (see § 6.4.8.)

A lawyer in a state that has not taken an authoritative position on joint representation in amicable dissolutions will find little guidance in the professional rules. The 1969 Code speaks only in general terms on the subject of concurrent representations and does not mention the specific problem of divorce (see

45 Gregory v. Gregory, 92 Cal.App.2d 343, 206 P.2d 1122 (1949); Christian v. Christian, 42 N.Y.2d 63, 396 N.Y.S.2d 817, 365 N.E.2d 849 (1977).

46 In re Reed, 207 La. 1011, 22 So.2d 552 (1945)(lawyer who handled eight consent divorces in three years must have known they were collusive from fact that defendant husband was willing to come to office and sign papers facilitating virtual default divorce).

47 By October 1980 all states but Illinois and South Dakota were counted as no-fault jurisdictions by one commentator. See Note, Family Law—Attorney Mediation of Marital Disputes and Conflict of Interest Considerations, 60 N.C.L.Rev. 171, 171n.1 (1981). Illinois passed a no-fault dissolution statute in 1983, effective July 1, 1984. See Ill.Ann.Stat.—S.H.A. ch. 40, ¶ 401.

48 See generally Silberman, Problems of Divorce Mediation, 16 Fam.L.Q. 107 (1982); Note, supra, 60 N.C.L.Rev. 171 (1981).

49 Ohio Bar Formal Op. 30, in 1 Fam.L.Rep.(BNA) 3109 (1975); N.Y.Cty.Bar Op. 258 (1972), in N.Y. Opinions (1980).

50 Levine v. Levine, 56 N.Y.2d 42, 451 N.Y.S.2d 26, 436 N.E.2d 476 (1982)(if common lawyer makes full disclosure and there is an absence of inequitable conduct, "while the potential conflict of interests inherent in such joint representation suggests that the husband and wife should retain separate counsel, the parties have an absolute right to be represented by the same attorney."); Klemm v. Superior Court, 75 Cal.App.3d 893, 142 Cal.Rptr. 509 (1977). See also, e.g., People v. Meldahl, 200 Colo. 332, 615 P.2d 29 (1980)(discipline for joint representation in absence of full disclosure); Young v. Hecht, 3 Kan.App.2d 510, 597 P.2d 682, 687 (1979); Blum v. Blum, 59 Md.App. 584, 477 A.2d 289, 296–97 (1984)(strongly discouraging joint representation but entertaining possibility if full disclosure and unhesitating consent in unusually amicable dissolution); Halvorsen v. Halvorsen, 3 Wn.App. 827, 479 P.2d 161 (1970)(joint representation permitted).

51 Klemm v. Superior Court, supra, 142 Cal.Rptr. at 514: "Attorneys who undertake to represent parties with divergent interests owe the highest duty to each to make a full disclosure of all facts and circumstances which are necessary to enable the parties to make a fully informed decision regarding the subject matter of the litigation, including the areas of potential conflict and the possibility and desirability of seeking independent legal advice."

52 Levine v. Levine, supra note 50, 436 N.E.2d at 479; Klemm v. Superior Court, supra note 50, 142 Cal.Rptr. at 512.

53 See Klemm v. Superior Court, supra note 50, 142 Cal. Rptr. at 513 (lawyer "would be disqualified from representing either in a contested hearing . . . . There would then exist an actual conflict between them, and an attorney's duty to maintain the confidence of each would preclude such representation."); In re Braun, 49 N.J. 16, 227 A.2d 506 (1967). See also In re Eltzroth, 67 Or.App. 520, 679 P.2d 1369, 1373 n.7 (1984)(when parties' agreement presented obvious inequities on its face and raised issues about equitable disposition of substantial marital asset, lawyer jointly representing spouses was required to withdraw and advise parties to obtain separate counsel).

§ 7.3.1). Despite criticism of early drafts for a similar gap,[54] the 1983 Model Rules do not improve on the uncertainty (see § 8.7.1).

WESTLAW REFERENCES

divorce annulment (dissolution /3 marriage) /p conflict! /3 interest /p attorney lawyer /p joint both dual /s represent!

topic(45) /p divorce annulment (dissolution /3 marriage) /p joint dual both /s represent!

topic(divorce) /p joint both dual /s represent! /p attorney lawyer

§ 8.7 LAWYERS AS MEDIATORS

§ 8.7.1 Lawyers in the Mediation Process

Resolving Disputes Through Mediation

Third-party control over the outcome of a dispute typifies adjudication through the adversary process in courts, administrative agencies, or arbitration. Those forms of the adversary process might be unacceptable to many people because they are expensive, slow, and depersonalized and precisely because the specific outcome is not consented to by participants. Mediation is a set of methods for resolving disputes by which the mediator attempts to induce disputing parties to agree upon a resolution without a third party such as a judge or arbitrator intervening to impose one. Mediation is different from contract negotiation because the mediator is present as a third party who actively participates in the discussions in order to offer suggestions and an impartial perspective and to attempt to persuade the parties to work out arrangements on which both agree.[55] In recent years considerable attention has focused on that model of mediation in areas such as marriage dissolution, other domestic-conflict issues, and labor relations.[56]

Mediation need not always result in a formal "resolution." Sometimes the value of mediation is more subtle. Under some circumstances mediation can lead parties tacitly to adopt an established social model for their relationship but without explicit agreement. For example, mediation might encourage parties with an ongoing relationship to establish regular meetings to air potential grievances. In other settings mediation simply helps parties to understand each other's situation and thus to harmonize their relationship.[57]

The Functions of Lawyers as Mediators

Most importantly for present purposes, some have urged that lawyers take an active role in mediating disputes between clients.[58] Historical support exists for lawyer mediation, although lawyers have infrequently engaged in it. In private practice Louis D. Brandeis sometimes represented dual parties with differing interests in an attempt to urge an accommodation, calling himself "counsel for the situation." [59] In the nature of things, the circumstances in which a lawyer might usefully and properly fulfill such a role must be relatively rare.

54 Schneyer, The Model Rules and Problems of Code Interpretation and Enforcement, 1980 Am.B.Found. Research J. 939, 941. The 1969 Code can be similarly faulted. Prominent voices had called for clarification of the ability of lawyers to represent both spouses at least as early as 1953. See Drinker, Problems of Professional Ethics in Matrimonial Litigation, 66 Harv.L.Rev. 443 (1953). But the Code offered no specific guidance.

55 Fuller, Mediation—Its Forms and Functions, 44 S.Cal.L.Rev. 305 (1971).

56 Friedman, Protection of Confidentiality in the Mediation of Minor Disputes, 11 Cap.U.L.Rev. 181 (1981); Sander, Varieties of Dispute Processing, 70 F.R.D. 79 (1976); Note, Family Law—Attorney Mediation of Marital Disputes and Conflict of Interest Considerations, 60 N.C.L.Rev. 171 (1981); Note, Simultaneous Representation: Transaction Resolution in the Adversary System, 28 Case W.Res.L.Rev. 86 (1977).

57 Fuller, supra, n. 55, at 308.

58 Riskin, Mediation and Lawyers, 43 Ohio St.L.J. 29 (1982); Paul, A New Role for Lawyers in Contract Negotiations, 62 ABA J. 62 (1976)(Paul suggests, however, that the parties retain separate lawyers in addition to the mediator); Nat'l L.J., Aug. 30, 1982, at 1, col. 4; id. Jan. 25, 1982, at 1, col. 1; 68 ABA J. 783 (1982).

59 Frank, The Legal Ethics of Louis D. Brandeis, 17 Stan.L.Rev. 683, 702 (1965). Frank and other comentators agree that the phrase had unfortunate connotations. Id.; Note, Simultaneous Representation: Transaction Resolution in the Adversary System, 28 Case W.Res.L.Rev. 86, 90 (1977). But see G.Hazard, Ethics in the Practice of Law 58–68 (1978). Brandeis's legal ethics were a center of debate in the controversy that surrounded his nomination to the Supreme Court in 1916. See A.Mason, Brandeis: A Free Man's Life 467–78 (1946).

Mediation contemplates a lawyerly role that is in sharp contrast to the traditional advocacy of client interests with blind devotion and single-minded zeal. Lawyers who assume the mediator's role should have special talents of interpersonal relations and perhaps should have special training. The break with the tradition of the lawyer as advocate also creates the potential for confusion in the minds of clients unless the lawyer makes it abundantly clear what role the lawyer contemplates and how that role differs from the traditional role to which one or more of the clients might be accustomed. The mediating lawyer, before the role is assumed, must be certain that all affected clients are fully informed about the radically different nature of the role and fully consent to that type of representation. Moreover, when the lawyer's intended function is to serve as an accommodator or facilitator in behalf of only one client and not as a mediator among commonly represented clients, the lawyer should make it clear to nonclients with whom he or she deals that the role does not involve functioning either as their lawyer or as a mediator.[60]

The Lawyer Regulations

The 1969 Code, in EC 5–20, only obliquely recognizes the conflict-of-interest problems in lawyer mediation between clients. It asserts that lawyers are "often" asked by present or former clients to serve as impartial mediators and states that the role can be undertaken if the lawyer first discloses to each client the nature of the lawyer's relationship with the other client.

A more satisfactorily elaborate regulation is provided in 1983 Model Rule 2.2, on "intermediation." Rule 2.2, in effect, provides separate rules on (1) accepting the role; (2) acting as mediator; and (3) mandatory withdrawal from the role and the consequences of withdrawing. Rule 2.2 states that a lawyer can accept the role of mediator if two basic conditions are met. First, each client must consent after consultation. Second, the lawyer must reasonably believe, employing a workability standard, that mediation has a fair chance of success.

While "mediation" in modern parlance has come to have rather specific and different meanings,[61] Model Rule 2.2 apparently uses the term to cover any simultaneous representation of potentially conflicting interests if the object of the representation is to achieve an accommodation of the interests of the clients.[62] As such MR 2.2 should always be consulted and its more elaborate and specific requirements for client consultation observed before a lawyer undertakes a common representation of clients that will involve attempting to work out differences between them.

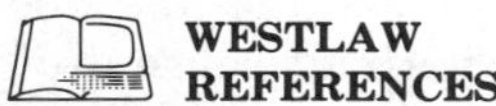
WESTLAW REFERENCES

mediat*** /p attorney lawyer

§ 8.7.2 Client Consultation

General Scope of the Consultation

The Model Rules require client consultation about mediation that is different from, or at least more explicit than, normal conflict of interest consultations in two respects.[63] The lawyer must first discuss with each client the implications of the fact that the lawyer will represent both clients in the mediation, including the advantages and risks involved. Secondly, the lawyer must also consult with each client about the effect of common representation on the lawyer-client privilege.[64]

Risks and Advantages of Mediation

The implications of common representation are several, and the lawyer-mediator should

[60] See MR 2.2 comment (first paragraph).

[61] Professor Silberman, for example, discusses four models of divorce mediation: the single lawyer-mediator; the solo therapist; the lawyer-therapist team; and the advisory-lawyer model. Silberman, Professional Responsibility Problems of Divorce Mediation, 16 Fam.L.Q. 107 (1982).

[62] That is suggested by the range of examples in MR 2.2 comment (third paragraph)(organizing or reorganizing a business; property distribution in settlement of an estate; or "mediating a dispute between clients").

[63] See § 7.2.4 (full disclosure consultation).

[64] MR 2.2(a)(1).

carefully explore all relevant factors with each client. The lawyer represents all parties and cannot sacrifice the interests of one for the advantage of the other. That might mean that a partisan advantage that a party could achieve if separately represented must be foregone. Maximum personal advantage is replaced with maximum mutual accommodation in light of common objectives. The extent to which one or both clients sacrifices other advantages by engaging in mediation depends, among other things, on whether they are mediating against the backdrop of impending litigation (as in marriage dissolution) or whether they seek mutual advantage that can be gained only through agreement (as in the purchase and sale of a business).

Two important implications of mediation are technical and hardly apparent. The first is that if mediation fails, the lawyer is precluded from representing any one of the parties separately without consent of the other.[65] That mandatory withdrawal rule might mean that a failed mediation will result in a substantial increase in legal fees, because each party must retain separate representation as well as compensate the unsuccessful lawyer-mediator.[66] The most important effect on the attorney-client privilege is that in most jurisdictions the lawyer can be called as a witness against either party by the other if litigation subsequently ensues between them (§ 6.4.8).

Consent of the Clients

Once the lawyer has fully informed each client of the important differences between common and separate representation in the matter, the mediation can go forward only if each client consents.[67] Nothing in the Model Rules requires a writing, but a prudent lawyer will reduce to writing, with copies to all clients, both the elements of the consultation that the lawyer has engaged in with both clients and their consent to the lawyer's mediation role.

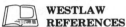

WESTLAW REFERENCES

mediat*** /p attorney lawyer /p client /p disclos! /p consent

§ 8.7.3 Workability Requirement

Reasonable Belief in Suitability and Workability

The second basic requirement of Model Rule 2.2 is that the lawyer must "reasonably believe" [68] that the intended mediation is compatible with the best interests of the clients [69] and can be carried out "impartially and without improper effect on other responsibilities the lawyer has to any of the clients." [70] Determining whether mediation can be effectively carried out requires the lawyer to make a pragmatic, before-the-fact assessment of several factors. Those include the nature of the interests of the parties, the extent to which those interests or the parties' views of them are antagonistic,[71] the nature of any preexist-

[65] MR 2.2(c).

[66] The Model Rules say nothing about a lawyer performing mediation functions under an arrangement in which the lawyer's fee is contingent on successful mediation. The arrangement seems quite dubious, because hinging the lawyer's right to a fee on resolution of the dispute might provide a strong economic incentive for the lawyer-mediator to push a resolution upon one or more unwilling parties.

[67] On the subject of nonconsentable conflicts, see § 7.2.2.

[68] MR 2.2(a)(2) & (3). For the definition of "reasonably believes," see MR Terminology ("denotes that the lawyer believes the matter in question and that the circumstances are such that the belief is reasonable."). "Believes" in id., "denotes that the person involved actually supposed the fact in question to be true. A person's belief may be inferred from circumstances."

[69] MR 2.2(a)(2): "The lawyer reasonably believes that the matter can be resolved on terms compatible with the clients' best interests, that each client will be able to make adequately informed decisions in the matter and that there is little risk of material prejudice to the interests of any of the clients if the contemplated resolution is unsuccessful."

[70] MR 2.2(a)(3).

[71] See MR 2.2 comment: "In some situations the risk of failure is so great that the intermediation is plainly impossible. For example, a lawyer cannot undertake common representation of clients between whom contentious litigation is imminent or who contemplate contentious negotiations. More generally, if the relationship

ing relationships between any of the parties and the lawyer,[72] and the nature of the mediation that is contemplated.

Because the individual clients must assume entire individual responsibility for making their own decisions in the course of the mediation [73] and cannot expect the lawyer's substantial help in making decisions, clients involved in relationships in which one client dominates the other through force of economics, personality, prior relationships, family ties or influence, or other circumstances are not reasonable settings for successful common representation. By its nature, mediation is for parties of equal bargaining strength.

Because mediation has been most frequently employed in domestic relations,[74] it is surprising that the comment to MR 2.2 is silent on whether a lawyer can mediate in such cases.[75] The question deserved comment because of the traditional reluctance of most jurisdictions to permit joint representation in dissolution cases (§ 8.6).[76] Despite the silence of the Model Rules, the clear import of MR 2.2 is to permit mediation in any situation in which the criteria of the rule are satisfied, which would include many dissolution, child-custody, and similar types of cases. The ABA has implicitly confirmed such a reading of the Model Rules by adopting a set of guidelines for lawyer-mediators in domestic relations cases.[77]

WESTLAW REFERENCES

mediat*** /p attorney /p "best interest" compatible work! success! /p client

§ 8.7.4 *Limitations on a Lawyer's Role as Mediator*

Overriding Requirement of Impartiality

If all clients have consented after consultation and the lawyer undertakes a mediation, the lawyer must maintain a relationship with all clients that is as perfectly impartial, as well as mutually helpful, as the circumstances reasonably permit. If the circumstances change, so that impartiality is no longer possible, the representation of both clients must cease. The lawyer must be equally zealous in protecting the interests of both clients.[78] During the mediation the lawyer cannot favor one client with advice or

between the parties has already assumed definite antagonism, the possibility that the clients' interests can be adjusted by intermediation ordinarily is not very good."

[72] For example, impartiality would be difficult to maintain if the lawyer had a long-standing relationship with one client but none with the other. See MR 2.2 comment (Confidentiality and Privilege; second paragraph). A plain illustration of that sort of disabling prior relationship is the lawyer's having a financial or other interest in one of the clients. See In re Holmes, 290 Or. 173, 619 P.2d 1284, 1289–90 (1980).

The Model Rules mention as a factor to be considered the fact that the lawyer had previously represented one of the parties. The ABA Standards of Practice for Family Mediators (1984)(Standard 3), on the other hand, state a flat rule: "In the event the mediator has represented one of the parties beforehand, the mediator shall not undertake the mediation."

[73] MR 2.2(a)(2), 2.2(b), and comment (Consultation; second paragraph).

[74] Cooke, Mediation: A Boon or a Bust?, 28 N.Y.L.Rev. 3, 15 (1983); Silberman, Professional Responsibility Problems of Divorce Mediation, 16 Fam.L.Q. 107 (1982).

[75] An early draft of the Model Rules included a comment mentioning joint representation of spouses in an uncontested dissolution action as an instance in which mediation might be appropriate. See Model Rules 94 (Discussion Draft, Jan. 30, 1980). The deletion of that language without an attempt to resolve the important issue has been criticized. See Schneyer, The Model Rules and Problems of Code Interpretation and Enforcement, 1980 Am.B.Found. Research J. 939–41.

[76] For reasons similar to those that have traditionally been relied upon to prohibit the same lawyer from representing both clients in a dissolution action, a Wisconsin ethics opinion has determined that a lawyer cannot serve as a mediator for clients considering divorce. Wis.B. Ethics Op. E–79–2, 53 Wis.B.Bull. 61 (Jan.1980).

[77] ABA Standards of Practice for Family Mediators (1984), in 22 Fam.L.Q. 457 (1984).

[78] The ABA Standards of Practice for Family Mediators (1984) employ the unfortunate term "participant" rather than "client" to denote the represented parties to the mediation. Nothing else in the document suggests, however, that the lawyer has anything other than a client-lawyer relationship with the "participants," although the relationship is characterized by features that are very different from those in a client-lawyer relationship involving advocacy. The Standards apparently refer to "participants" rather than "clients" because they also deal with mediation by nonlawyers, such as marriage counselors.

MR 2.2 comment (third paragraph) assumes a distinction between at least two kinds of lawyer mediation. In information important to others that the lawyer does not share with them. In fact, the optimal arrangement would be for the lawyer to meet with one client only after giving notice to all clients who are parties to the mediation. The lawyer should take the initiative to inform all clients of significant developments and conversations of which they might be unaware. At a bare minimum, the lawyer must consult with each client about decisions that should be made and the considerations that are relevant in making them, with a view toward each client being able to make adequately informed decisions.[79]

In such consultations the lawyer should be sensitive to the probability that different clients may require more or less information and explanation, depending on their experience and sophistication in the matter under mediation. The lawyer should also consult with each client well in advance of the time when the clients will need to make important decisions, among other things so that they may obtain the advice and assistance of others if any mediating party thinks that desirable. A lawyer-mediator should, of course, do nothing to discourage mediating parties from seeking other advice.

Unfair Outcomes in Mediation

To this point we have discussed the mediator's role entirely in procedural terms. From all that has been said, it would be permissible for a lawyer-mediator to participate in a mediation in which an entirely inequitable agreement resulted, although the procedural protections do much to assure that such an instance will be rare. Most instances that do occur will involve parties who are revealed by facts that are developed in the course of the mediation to be unequal in bargaining strength. The lawyer in such a case is required to withdraw. If the capitulating party indeed does possess equal bargaining strength but also possesses a very different set of values from the lawyer's, the lawyer should be careful to assure that the disadvantaged party has full and appropriate advice about the proposed resolution. If it is clear that a fully informed, capable adult voluntarily agrees to an apparently unfair outcome, only paternalism of an objectionable kind would prevent the lawyer from carrying out the party's wishes, such as by executing in written form what they have agreed to as a result of the mediation. In such a case the "clients' best interests," to which Model Rule 2.2(a)(2) refers, should be defined by the clients involved.

Mandatory Withdrawal

Model Rule 2.2(c) explicitly mandates withdrawal by a mediating lawyer if any one of the clients requests this, if it reasonably appears that the clients' respective "best interests" cannot be achieved amicably, or that the lawyer's impartiality cannot be maintained. A predictably common cause of breakdown is one or more of the clients taking an obdurate bargaining position to which others of the clients will not consent. Personal hostility between the clients can also cause breakdown because it seriously diminishes the likelihood of an amicable settlement of their differences. A clear case of impairment of the lawyer-mediator's impartiality would occur if the lawyer learned information in confidence from one client that was important to the interests of another of the clients and the informing client refused to permit it to be shared. Unless all other affected clients agree to the lawyer's restricted sharing of information, the lawyer would have to end the mediation.

Rule 2.2(c) requires that, if the mediation ends, the lawyer-mediator must withdraw entirely and may not thereafter represent any one of the clients in the matter. For example, if litigation later ensues between the former clients, the lawyer may represent

one the lawyer has a client-lawyer relationship with clients. In the other the lawyer has no such relationship, although the nature of the relationship is not otherwise defined. The latter type of mediation is apparently not covered by MR 2.2.

79 MR 2.2(b).

neither.[80] In view of the mandatory-withdrawal rule, a lawyer is ordinarily well advised to make decisions about breakdown early in the representation in order to save the parties the avoidable expense of separate representations at a later point.

WESTLAW REFERENCES

mediat*** /p attorney lawyer /p impartial!

§ 8.8 CONFLICTS DUE TO THIRD–PARTY CONTROL

§ 8.8.1 General

The pristine professional model has it that a lawyer single-mindedly furthers the interests of one client. But third parties are often intensely interested in the client's legal opportunities or problems. We have already seen the ways in which conflict issues of that kind can arise when a lawyer is retained by an insurance company to represent an insured (§ 8.4). Other settings occur as well in which interests of third parties and their relationship with the client's lawyer can create conflicts.

§ 8.8.2 Third-Party Fee Payment

Division of Economic and Professional Loyalties

The most obvious conflict is created when a person other than the client pays the lawyer's fee. A parent may pay a lawyer to represent a child.[81] One spouse may hire a lawyer to write a will for the other. An employer may retain a lawyer to defend an employee against criminal charges. The danger in all such instances is that the lawyer's loyalty may be influenced by the fee payer's interests and those may conflict with the interests of the lawyer's client. The situation is only apparently different under fee-shifting statutes that provide for the losing party to pay the prevailing party's legal fees. In such circumstances the possibilities for control over the lawyer's discretion in behalf of the prevailing party might be thought to be minimal because of the adversary posture of the parties. In fact, however, the leverage that an opposing party has in settlement negotiations to influence the size of the lawyer's fee in relation to the share of the recovery by the lawyer's client from a settlement fund gives rise to significant and difficult conflict of interest problems.[82] At the very least, in each of the above situations the lawyer's instinct to look with complete fidelity to the client for directions on the course of the representation might be compromised by the third-person source of the fee.

The Professional Rules

Because of the risks involved in such nonclient fee payments, the Code in DR 5–107(A) prohibits a lawyer from accepting compensation or anything else of value from a person other than the client for representing the client unless the client gives informed consent.[83] DR 5–107(B) provides that even if the client consents, the lawyer may not accept from the fee payer any direction or regulation of the lawyer's professional judgment. More broadly, DR 5–105(A) requires a lawyer to decline to represent a client if the exercise of the lawyer's independent judgment might be adversely affected by accepting the representation. And EC 5–21 advises that, among other things, the desires of third persons might impinge on the lawyer's free judgment. Those impingements may find their source in

[80] Green v. Newman, 385 A.2d 171 (D.C.), opinion supplemented 395 A.2d 813 (1978).

[81] People v. White, 127 Mich.App. 65, 338 N.W.2d 556 (1983)(ineffective assistance of counsel because lawyer was more concerned with wishes of client's father, who hired him, than with best interests of client-son concerning desirability of psychiatric examination).

[82] See generally Wolfram, The Second Set of Players: Lawyers, Fee-Shifting, and the Limits of Professional Discipline, 47 L. & Contemp.Probs. 293 (1984). See also Prandini v. National Tea Co., 557 F.2d 1015 (3d Cir. 1977)(bar against negotiating fee portion of class-action settlement until court approval of damage portion of settlement).

[83] Arrington v. National Broadcasting Co., 531 F.Supp. 498, 505–06 (D.D.C.1982)(lawyer adequately explained matter to individual clients and obtained their consent to representation despite his relationship with union).

divergent economic, political, or social interests.

Model Rule 1.8(f) expands to some extent upon the mandatory rule of DR 5–107. It provides that a lawyer must not accept compensation from a third person for a representation of the client unless (1) the client consents after consultation;[84] (2) the fee payer does not interfere with the lawyer's independence of professional judgment or with the client-lawyer relationship; and (3) client information is kept confidential.[85] Model Rule 1.7(b) similarly expands on the concepts alluded to in DR 5–105(A) by prohibiting a lawyer from representing a client if the lawyer's representation will be materially limited by the lawyer's responsibilities to a third person. An exception is provided if (1) the lawyer reasonably believes that representation of the client will not be adversely affected and (2) the client consents after consultation. Finally, MR 5.4(c) copies the language of DR 5–107(B) prohibiting a lawyer from permitting a person who recommends, employs, or pays the lawyer to direct the exercise of the lawyer's professional judgment in representing a client.[86] In summary, under both sets of professional rules third-party fee payments are permissible, but only if the client consents after the lawyer fully informs the client and only if the lawyer's professional judgment is freely excercised in the client's interest.[87]

Cognovit Note Warrants of Attorney

Although apparently never challenged on this ground in a reported case, the typical cognovit note comports with the professional standards only by ignoring them. With local variations the procedure is created by the wording of a common form of promissory note signed by debtors. In it the debtor agrees that judgment on the note when it is due can be obtained at the creditor's discretion through a confession of judgment in any court by any lawyer selected by the creditor. Many states that recognize that "warrant of attorney" procedure for cognovit notes contemplate that the lawyer who confesses judgment against the client-defendant will be selected and paid, at least initially, by the party opposing the defendant-debtor.[88] It is obvious that the work of the lawyer for the debtor in confessing judgment against his or her client clashes directly with the obligations of the professional rules, particularly of MR 1.8(f). The only apparent doctrinal means of rescuing the creditor-hired lawyer from a violation of mandatory rules is to consider that the lawyer represents the creditor and not the debtor, although that description of the relationship fits uncomfortably alongside the fiction that the lawyer represents the debtor in confessing judgment.

Setting the cognovit note to one side, in normal cases a lawyer who represents a client with a third person paying the fee must devote his or her entire loyalty to the pursuit of the client's interests. Pursuing the interests of the fee-paying party adverse to the

[84] "Consultation" is defined in the Terminology section at the beginning of the Model Rules. See § 7.2.4.

[85] See also MR 1.8 comment (Person Paying for Lawyer's Services); MR 1.7 comment (Interest of Person Paying for a Lawyer's Service).

[86] The obvious and confusing overlap between MR 5.4(c) and MR 1.8(f) is the product of amendments to MR 5.4, forced upon the drafting commission at the February 1983 ABA meeting. See Text of Revised Model Rules of Professional Conduct, Legal Times, Feb. 14, 1983, at 23, col. 3.

[87] The direct antecedents of the modern professional rules are Canons 35 and 38 of the 1908 Canons of Ethics. Added in 1928 (see ABA Opinions on Professional Ethics 156 (1967)), Canon 35 prohibited a lawyer from practicing in a way that permitted a lay intermediary to control or exploit the lawyer's services for a client. That restriction gave rise to most of the prohibitions against dual-practice arrangements with nonlawyers such as accountants, banks, trust companies, and collection agencies. See § 16.4 (dual practice). Canon 38, also adopted in 1928, expressly prohibited third-person fee payments without client consent.

[88] See generally D.H. Overmyer Co. v. Frick Co., 405 U.S. 174, 92 S.Ct. 775, 31 L.Ed.2d 124 (1972). In some jurisdictions legislative curtailment of confession-of-judgment provisions in contracts requires that the confession be signed both by the debtor and by a lawyer independently retained by the debtor. See, e.g., West's Ann.Cal. Civ.Proc.Code § 1132; 59 Op.Cal.Atty.Gen. 434 (1976).

interests of the client is plainly impermissible.[89]

Employer-Employee Conflicts

Third-person fee payments become particularly suspicious when coupled with other relationships between the fee payer and the client. One such relationship is that of employer and employee, a relationship that itself threatens the employee-client's freedom of action in the legal matter.[90] The employer's interest may not be to vindicate the employee's interests fully. It might be limited to vindicating them in a way that agrees with or furthers interests of the employer. Because of the law of agency and respondeat superior, conflict inheres in many situations when employee and employer are potentially liable for the same alleged wrong. The employee can attempt to cast full blame on the employer by presenting the defense that the employer required the course of action followed by the employee; the employer can attempt to cast blame on the employee by urging that the employee was acting ultra vires.[91] If the employer pays the lawyer's fee, the employer rather than the employee may influence the lawyer. Suspicions that such may be the situation seem to underlie some of the cases in which courts have disqualified a lawyer hired to represent several witnesses before a grand jury.[92] Such employer-payer arrangements shade by degrees into cases in which a lawyer is retained by an illegal organization to represent its lesser members, who do the dirtier and more exposed work. The lawyer's arrangement with the organization is plainly objectionable both because it creates a conflict of interest and because it furthers the illegal activities of the employer.[93]

Representing Indigent Clients

Despite the obvious dangers involved when lawyers represent clients and third persons pay the fee for the client, in some situations the arrangement serves important social goals and has even earned constitutional protection from the Supreme Court. For some clients it is necessary that a third person pay the lawyer if a lawyer is to be paid at all. Typical is the provision of lawyers for indigent clients in criminal-defender programs funded by the government. So long as the selection of the lawyer-defender and controls over his or her performance, compensation, and promotion are sufficiently insulated from persons and agencies whose interests conflict with the indigent client, the fact that the funds for the lawyer ultimately come from the client's governmental adversary is not fatal.[94] The professional strictures against impairing the professional independence of a

89 People ex rel. Cortez v. Calvert, 617 P.2d 797 (Colo. 1980)(discipline for entering into conflicting representation of woman at request of her live-in companion and filing suit in her name to avoid her marriage to another man); In re Murray, 266 Ind. 221, 362 N.E.2d 128, 132–33 (1977), appeal dismissed 434 U.S. 1029, 98 S.Ct. 758, 54 L.Ed.2d 777 (1978)(violation of DR 5–107(B) when lawyer for two codefendants paid by only one of them permitted paying codefendant to instruct witness for other client).

90 Wood v. Georgia, 450 U.S. 261, 101 S.Ct. 1097, 67 L.Ed.2d 220 (1981); State v. Boone, 154 N.J.Super. 36, 380 A.2d 1158 (1977), certification denied 77 N.J. 493, 391 A.2d 507 (1978). Under the Canons of Ethics it was believed that payment of an employee's legal fees by the employer would constitute unauthorized practice of law and thus was impermissible. See H.Drinker, Legal Ethics 164–65 (1953)(criticism of Canon 35 for outlawry of such arrangements). After the demise of the Canons, unauthorized practice is manifestly no longer an independent concern.

91 See United States v. Bernstein, 533 F.2d 775, 788 (2d Cir.), cert. denied 429 U.S. 998, 97 S.Ct. 523, 50 L.Ed.2d 608 (1976).

92 Pirillo v. Takiff, 462 Pa. 511, 341 A.2d 896, 903–04, opinion reinstated 466 Pa. 187, 352 A.2d 11 (1975), cert. denied 423 U.S. 1083, 96 S.Ct. 873, 47 L.Ed.2d 94 (1976) (fee payment to lawyer for several police officer witnesses before grand jury made by police federation). See § 8.2.5.

93 See In re Abrams, 56 N.J. 271, 266 A.2d 275 (1970) (discipline for representing employee of gambling enterprise). See also United States ex rel. Hart v. Davenport, 478 F.2d 203, 209 (3d Cir.1973)(gambling organization); In re Salus, 321 Pa. 106, 184 A. 70, 71 (1936)(numbers syndicate). See also §§ 13.3.2, 13.3.5.

94 United States v. Robinson, 553 F.2d 429 (5th Cir. 1977), cert. denied 434 U.S. 1016, 98 S.Ct. 735, 54 L.Ed.2d 761 (1978)(arrangement not unconstitutional under which same government that prosecutes defendant also pays fee of his public defender; federal defender system is structured to assure independence of defender-lawyers); cf. ABA Informal Op. 84–1508 (1984)(lawyer employed as nonlawyer by state agency, usually could not, over employer's objection, represent other employees in proceedings against same agency); ABA Informal Op.1474 (1982) (opposing lawyer in military court-martial or related pro-

lawyer for an indigent may be especially buttressed by a constitutional guaranty of at least minimal arrangements to secure that independence.[95] Thus concern with the extent of third-party control may require structuring public-defender organizations in ways that avoid the possibility of impairing the professional independence of lawyer defenders through possible influence from political interests represented on the governing board of the organization.[96]

WESTLAW REFERENCES

conflict! /3 interest /s attorney lawyer /s legal attorney +s fee /s "third party" nonclient

di cognovit note

topic(45) /p cognovit

conflict! /3 interest /p employer /p employee /p attorney legal /s fee /s pay***

conflict /3 interest /p indigent /s client

---

§ 8.8.3 *Legal Advocacy Organizations*

The Nature of Issue-Advocacy Organizations

In recent history, lawyers for clients unable to pay for legal services in noncriminal matters have been supplied by legal aid organizations (§ 16.7.2). The lay intermediary rules were simply, and expressly, made inapplicable to such organizations.[97] As legal aid moved to legal advocacy, however, tensions arose between the advocates of new rights for the poor and underprivileged and those who came to regard issue-advocacy lawyers as intermeddling ideologues forcing political views upon unwitting clients who served merely as convenient means of access to courts.

Constitutional Protection for Third-Party Litigation Sponsorship

The issues of third-party control came to a head in the 1963 Supreme Court decision in NAACP v. Button.[98] A majority of the Court held that Virginia could not constitutionally apply to the NAACP broadly phrased statutes prohibiting solicitation of legal business. In the aftermath of the 1954 Brown v. Board of Education [99] decision striking down state-supported school segregation, Virginia's legislature had in 1956 substantially expanded its antisolicitation statutes to proscribe support for desegregation litigation in many of the forms employed by the NAACP. Among other things, the NAACP actively sought out prospective desegregation plaintiffs, hired and paid staff and private practice lawyers to litigate desegregation cases (but not "separate but equal" cases), and supplied financial assistance in aid of that litigation.

The Supreme Court held that those litigation activities to sponsor litigation were protected by a First Amendment right "to associate for the purpose of assisting persons who seek legal redress for infringements of their constitutionally guaranteed and other rights." [1] The activities of the NAACP, its local affiliates, and its legal staff were held to be "modes of expression and association" protected by the First Amendment "which Vir-

ceeding cannot have command authority over lawyer for soldier client).

[95] Cf. Polk County v. Dodson, 454 U.S. 312, 102 S.Ct. 445, 451, 452, 70 L.Ed.2d 509 (1981)("[I]t is the constitutional obligation of the State to respect the professional independence of the public defenders whom it engages . . . . There can be no fair trial unless the accused receives the services of an effective and independent advocate.").

[96] See the majority and dissenting opinions in In re Amendments to Articles of Incorporation of Defender Ass'n of Philadelphia, 453 Pa. 353, 307 A.2d 906, cert. denied 414 U.S. 1079, 94 S.Ct. 598, 38 L.Ed.2d 486 (1973).

[97] See Canon 35 (adopted 1928)("Charitable societies rendering aid to the indigents are not deemed" lay intermediaries); DR 2–103(D)(1). Cf. MR 6.3.

[98] National Association for the Advancement of Colored People v. Button, 371 U.S. 415, 83 S.Ct. 328, 9 L.Ed.2d 405 (1963). The majority reversed in part the decision of the Virginia Supreme Court in NAACP v. Harrison, 202 Va. 142, 116 S.E.2d 55 (1960). The Virginia court, in an unappealed portion of its decision, had itself held unconstitutional other parts of the Virginia legislation. Those had prohibited advocacy of suits against the state and giving any assistance, financial or otherwise, to such suits.

[99] 347 U.S. 483, 74 S.Ct. 686, 98 L.Ed. 873 (1954), supplemented 349 U.S. 294, 75 S.Ct. 753, 99 L.Ed.2d 1083 (1955).

[1] 371 U.S. at 428, 83 S.Ct. at 335.

ginia may not prohibit under its power to regulate the legal profession."[2] The Court found that the type of litigation engaged in by the NAACP was not merely a technique for resolving private disputes; it was a form of political expression employed to achieve the lawful objective of equality of treatment. Moreover, as an expressive freedom, the right to advocacy is entitled to a "strict" scrutiny standard of review in determining whether the regulation by the state was unconstitutionally vague or overbroad.[3] Correlatively, only a compelling state interest could justify regulation of protected activities; the state's interest in regulating the legal profession, by itself, did not justify the type of encroachment on the rights of advocacy that the state had attempted.[4]

Among other asserted state interests, the majority rejected the state's argument that the intervention of a lay intermediary between an NAACP lawyer and the individual client was a sufficiently compelling interest. The majority thought that the threat of lay-intermediary control arose primarily when the intermediary was motivated by pecuniary gain. Such gain was absent here, and the Court held that the aims and interests of the NAACP had not been shown to be in conflict with persons whom the organization assisted in desegregation litigation.[5] Justice Harlan, in dissent, probably asserts the more realistic view that the absence of pecuniary gain does not assure that a lawyer hired and paid by an organization with strong ideological views will not be influenced by the organization to ignore divergent views and wishes of the lawyer's client.[6] But in subsequent decisions dealing with advocacy activities of labor unions in behalf of the legal interests of individual members, the Supreme Court has continued to resist the claim that preventing all possible lay-intermediary control of the professional judgment of lawyers sufficiently justifies state control of the arrangement.[7]

In sum, it seems rather evident that constitutional protection for legal advocacy organizations in the forms that have been approved by the Supreme Court rests upon a balance struck between concerns over conflict problems and concerns over realizing the ideal of equal access to legal services. The strong ideological interest of an advocacy organization can plainly create a risk that the organization's lawyer will not represent sponsored clients with totally free and independent professional judgment. Nonetheless, if that risk is not incurred, no representation or only inadequate representation would result. The Court apparently deems the latter less acceptable than the former. Moreover, given the Supreme Court's insistence that only a compelling state interest can warrant restrictive regulation, several state court decisions have approved the structure of advocacy organizations only when it is so arranged that nonlawyer control over the organization was limited to matters of general policy, leaving organization lawyers free from nonlawyer control in the exercise of professional judgment in behalf of individual clients.[8]

[2] 371 U.S. at 428–29, 83 S.Ct. at 335–36.

[3] 371 U.S. at 432, 83 S.Ct. at 337.

[4] 371 U.S. at 438–39, 83 S.Ct. at 340–41.

[5] 371 U.S. at 441–43, 83 S.Ct. at 342–43. Justice Harlan's dissenting opinion rests primarily on the ground that the record contained ample evidence to show nonlawyer direction and control of the exercise of professional judgment in the manner in which the NAACP conducted desegregation suits in Virginia.

[6] See 371 U.S. at 462–63, 83 S.Ct. at 353. (Harlan, J., dissenting). See also § 8.14 (class action conflicts).

[7] United Transp. Union v. State Bar of Michigan, 401 U.S. 576, 91 S.Ct. 1076, 28 L.Ed.2d 339 (1971); United Mineworkers v. Illinois State Bar Ass'n, 389 U.S. 217, 88 S.Ct. 353, 19 L.Ed.2d 426 (1967); Brotherhood of Railroad Trainmen v. Virginia State Bar, 377 U.S. 1, 84 S.Ct. 1113, 12 L.Ed.2d 89 (1964). Those decisions are further discussed § 16.5.2 (group legal). See also In re Primus, 436 U.S. 412, 436, 98 S.Ct. 1893, 56 L.Ed.2d 417 (1978)(in view of declared policy of American Civil Liberties Union to avoid interfering with client-lawyer relationship once organization decided to support particular litigation in accordance with organization's policy, mere distant possibility of lay-intermediary interference in client-lawyer relationship does not justify state's proscription of solicitation of case).

[8] In re Education Law Center, Inc., 86 N.J. 124, 429 A.2d 1051 (1981); In re Community Action for Legal Servs., Inc., 26 A.D.2d 354, 274 N.Y.S.2d 779 (1966); Azzarello v. Legal Aid Soc'y of Cleveland, 117 Ohio App. 471, 185 N.E.2d 566 (1962); Touchy v. Houston Legal Found., 432 S.W.2d 690 (Tex.1968).

WESTLAW REFERENCES

topic(45) /p legal /3 aid advoca**

§ 8.8.4 *Lawyer Control by Other Lawyers*

Direction and Management of the Work of Other Lawyers

Lawyer control over other lawyers can also create conflict of interest issues. In many practice settings, two or more lawyers will work on a client's representation but only one of them has ultimate authority. Senior partners or even senior associates in firms typically direct and control the work of junior associates. Lawyers from a distant city typically control litigation in which local rules require that a locally admitted lawyer be associated. And by agreement lawyers not otherwise associated will sometimes arrange that one lawyer will lead the others in the overall direction of a matter of common interest.

It is sometimes said that in such arrangements the subordinate lawyer may safely accede to the final decisions of lead counsel without violating intermediary rules such as DR 5–107(B).[9] While this may be true with respect to legal malpractice or for the purpose of other legal relations among the lawyers involved, it does not necessarily follow that it would also be true with respect to disciplinary liability. Although the 1969 Code was silent on the matter, new provisions in the 1983 Model Rules sensibly place limits on the extent to which a superior lawyer's directions to a subordinate lawyer may safely be followed.[10]

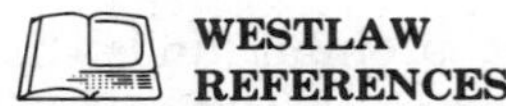

WESTLAW REFERENCES

conflict! /3 interest /p cocounsel lead principal associate /3 lawyer attorney counsel

§ 8.9 GOVERNMENT LAWYERS' CONFLICTS OF INTEREST

§ 8.9.1 *General*

Governmental Interest and Self-Interest

A lawyer in government service is not at all shielded from serious and difficult conflict of interest problems. In fact the conflict problems of government lawyers are in some ways more intractable because of the frequent absence of any single client who can unequivocally direct the lawyer on the substantive position to be taken in a matter and, if necessary, discuss and possibly consent to conflicts in representations. Government lawyers instead are often themselves the custodians of the responsibility to devise public policy in the course of dealing with governmental agencies' legal matters. The resulting conflict of interest issues are many and substantial. Discussed here will be the general nature of the problem, several important ramifications, and the conflicts of a part-time government lawyer. A following section (§ 8.10) discusses the special problems of a former government lawyer.

Coverage of the Professional Rules

Several provisions in the 1969 Code and the 1983 Model Rules deal with the professional responsibilities of current government em-

[9] Ortiz v. Barrett, 222 Va. 118, 278 S.E.2d 833, 840 (1981)(in legal malpractice case, "each lawyer may attempt to persuade the others to his view, but the final decision of lead counsel will not bring those who accede to the decision into violation of DR 5–107(B)."); cf. Pollack v. Lytle, 120 Cal.App.3d 931, 175 Cal.Rptr. 81, (1981) (suit by principal against associate lawyer for breach of fiduciary duty: "an associate lawyer acting as the agent of the principal lawyer . . . acts at the behest of his principal.").

EC 5–12 states that when "cocounsel" are unable to agree on "a matter vital to the representation of their client," that "requires" that the matter be submitted jointly to the client for decision. Unless EC 5–12 describes the rather rare arrangement in which cocounsel are of equal authority in the representation, it is doubtful that most lawyers would think it sound. In most cocounsel arrangements, one lawyer is explicitly or implicitly recognized to be the lead counsel, who makes ultimate decisions in an instance of contrary views or judgments. Rarely will the client be brought in to umpire such disputes. Of course the lead counsel would presumably obtain client consent to important steps in the proceeding that normally would follow only after client approval when a single lawyer is conducting a case. See generally § 4.3.

[10] See MR 5.2; see generally § 16.2.2.

ployees. The Code's DR 8–101(A)(1) forbids a government lawyer from using his or her public position to attempt to obtain a "legislative" advantage for a private practice client where the lawyer "knows or it is obvious that such action is not in the public interest." [11] The Code's general conflict of interest rules prevent a government lawyer from taking action that would be adverse to a former client in a substantially related matter or that would be adverse to a current client in any matter.

Model Rule 1.11(c)(1) provides broadly that a government lawyer must not participate in a governmental matter in which the lawyer participated [12] personally and substantially "while in private practice" or while in nonlegal, nongovernmental employment.[13] Exceptions are provided if "law may otherwise expressly permit" or if under applicable law the government lawyer cannot lawfully delegate authority to act in the matter.

It is critical to an understanding of MR 11.1(c)(1) to observe that it both covers the familiar situation of a lawyer dealing with a matter in government service adversely to a former client and applies to a situtation in which the lawyer deals with the same matter in a way that is congruent with the interests of the former client (§ 8.10.1). It is arguable, as with other parts of MR 1.11, that MR 1.11(c)(1) supplants all other Model Rules dealing with former-client problems. But the more likely interpretation is that MR 1.11(c)(1) is exclusive only on the topic that it uniquely covers—the congruent conflict issue (see § 8.10.2). In other conflict problems, such as former-client problems involving adverse conflicts and imputed disqualification in such conflicts, otherwise applicable rules will apply.[14] Moreover, issues not dealt with even inferentially in MR 1.11(c)(1), such as simultaneous conflicts, are presumably dealt with under otherwise applicable rules (MR 1.7 and MR 1.8).[15]

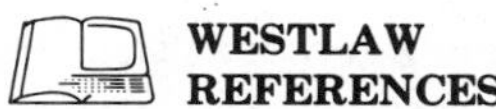
WESTLAW REFERENCES

conflict! /3 interest /p government /3 attorney lawyer

"dr 8–10(a)(1)"

§ 8.9.2 *Government Lawyer Models and Roles*

Models of Governmental Client-Lawyer Relationships

Beyond the professional rules, which themselves are not remarkable for their clarity, conflict problems sometimes arise because of difficulties in conceptualizing the role of a government lawyer. Generalizations about that role [16] give little solace to persons of a practical turn of mind. Whether a government lawyer's client is the "people," the "government," the lawyer's "agency," or the lawyer's "immediate superior" or whether the concept of "client" is rejected altogether in favor of a broader goal of serving "good gov-

[11] MR 1.11(c)(1) goes further and disqualifies the lawyer whether the government action would advance public interest or retard it and whether it is "legislative" or not.

[12] While "participated," in MR 1.11(c)(1), is stated in the past tense, the rule would probably be applied as well in the case of a part-time government lawyer who simultaneously represented a private practice client and dealt with the same matter in his or her governmental role. A similar problem in the use of the past tense in DR 9–101(B)("had" responsibility while a government employee) is also ignored in decisions. E.g., In re Fisher, 400 N.E.2d 1127 (Ind.1980)(simultaneous conflict of part-time government lawyer; violation found under DR 9–101(B)).

[13] MR 1.11(d)(1) provides an expansive definition of "matter." See § 8.10.3(3).

[14] MR 1.11 comment (ninth paragraph) states that MR 1.11(c) "does not disqualify other lawyers in the agency with which the lawyer in question has become associated." That probably is the preferable rule in all instances of government office conflict, although there are arguments to the contrary. See § 7.6.5 (imputed disqualification in government offices); cf. MR 1.11 legal background note 79 (Proposed Final Draft, May 30, 1981)("[Eventual Rule 1.11(c)] does not operate vicariously to disqualify the government lawyer's associates in an agency or department. Rules 1.9 and 1.10, however, operate to protect the government lawyer's former clients from the lawyer's participation in matters adverse to their interests that are substantially related to prior representation.") The comment to the final version of MR 1.11(c) says nothing about imputed disqualifications in a part-time government lawyer's private practice firm.

[15] See MR 1.11 comment (eighth paragraph).

[16] See also § 13.9.

ernment in and of itself,"[17] pursuing any one of those inquiries very far cannot give anything but vague direction.

Variable Nature of the Lawyer's Role

On the street and in the office a government lawyer will more likely appeal to one or the other of those general models, depending upon the type of legal work that the lawyer regularly performs. Government lawyers in some roles deal with real people from the same or other agencies that are allied in interest. A common illustration is the relationship between a prosecutor's office and police. Quite a different role might be played by a state's attorney general who has very wide-ranging authority, deals with many different departments and people in them, and is accustomed to making policy choices. Still a different role is played by a member of a decisional body such as an administrative hearing board. Not all lawyers will fit neatly into one of those or other conceptual packages, and some government lawyers may move between one role and another, often within the same working day. In each such task in each role, a government lawyer's alertness to the lawyer's personal interests; those of external constituencies, such as former or current private-practice clients and law firm members; and those of a wide variety of other governmental employees and officials will often help to identify areas in which interests conflict. The next step is to determine the ways in which the government lawyer with a conflict is to proceed.

An initially helpful clarification is to determine whether the lawyer's role consists more of making policy or of representing clients. If the government lawyer has the authority to make broadly applicable legal decisions within an agency, then there is no point in thinking about a lawyer's conflicts with persons with contrary views in the government, at least not as a matter of lawyer regulation. Those conflicts, if they arise, are policy differences and are appropriately approached as policy issues. On the other hand, if the government lawyer merely serves as the litigational or advice-giving surrogate of another governmental official with decision-making responsibility, then the lawyer's role is more like that of the counselor in private practice. In that setting concerns with confidentiality and devotion to a client's articulated interests, as the client sees them, have more relevance and force. Some government lawyers combine both functions, such as the prosecutor who, at whatever rank, makes policy decisions about the expenditure of prosecutorial resources and similar discretionary decisions yet who may also deal with police officers in ways that for some purposes are close to those of the litigational surrogate in private practice.

Government Lawyers and Policy-Making

States differ concerning the extent to which a government lawyer can make unrestricted policy choices. Those that permit some government lawyers to make final decisions might decline to recognize this power in others. In People ex rel. Deukmejian v. Brown[18] California's attorney general filed suit against the governor, seeking a writ of mandamus against the governor to prevent the enforcement of an allegedly unconstitutional enactment of the state legislature. The California court granted the governor's motion to enjoin the litigation, holding that the attorney general had no ultimate and unrestricted power to sue any other state officer.[19] In effect, the court holds that the

[17] See Note, Developments—Conflicts of Interest in the Legal Profession, 94 Harv.L.Rev. 1244, 1415 (1981).

[18] 29 Cal.3d 150, 172 Cal.Rptr. 478, 624 P.2d 1206 (1981).

[19] Accord Baxley v. Rutland, 409 F.Supp. 1249, 1257 (M.D.Ala.1976); Arizona State Land Dept. v. McFate, 87 Ariz. 139, 348 P.2d 912, 918 (1960); Manchin v. Browning, ___ W.Va. ___, 296 S.E.2d 909 (1982). Contra Connecticut Comm'n on Special Revenue v. Connecticut Freedom of Information Comm'n, 174 Conn. 308, 387 A.2d 533 (1978) (members of attorney general's staff may represent contending state agencies because of office's duty to serve public interest); Feeney v. Commonwealth, 373 Mass. 359, 366 N.E.2d 1262 (1977)(attorney general may prosecute appeal to United States Supreme Court from judgment of federal trial court contrary to the expressed

state's attorney general serves for the purpose of determining the constitutionality of legislation merely as the advice-giving surrogate for the governor. The governor's resolution of that question, based on that advice and possibly on other sources of advice as well, binds the attorney general.

A contrasting model is that of the solicitor general of the United States, an officer who has the ultimate power to decide whether to seek review in the Supreme Court of decisions adverse to most federal government agencies and departments.[20] With such a dispositive power in hand, the solicitor general has no clientlike relationship with individual officers out of which conflicts of interest can arise.

Very different from the role of the solicitor general is that of most prosecutors.[21] The prosecutor-police relationship is typified by unity of purpose, a sense of a real and dangerous common enemy, and an emotional commitment to the full exploitation of legal resources to bring criminals to bay.[22] For those reasons the police-prosecutor relationship can raise conflicts of interest problems. The same prosecutor who investigates a citizen's charge of illegal police surveillance might be called upon to press a criminal charge against the citizen based in part on evidence gathered through the same surveillance. If the investigations are simultaneous, the prosecutor cannot proceed in both.[23] The prosecutor's natural instinct of loyalty to police officers, their shared crime-fighting objectives, and the adversary's natural wish to vindicate the surveillance tactic if its products will be useful in an ongoing prosecution all combine to create too severe a conflict. But a public lawyer's contacts with individual government employees will not invariably lead to a clientlike relationship that creates conflicts. If the lawyer has taken care to assure that the employee does not expect that information will be confidential or that the lawyer is protecting the individual's personal interests, the government lawyer can later even file suit against the individual in the agency's name.[24]

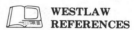

WESTLAW REFERENCES

topic(45) /p government /3 attorney lawyer

45k21.5(2)

synopsis,digest((government /3 lawyer) (attorney solicitor /2 general) prosecutor /s abus! /s power

§ 8.9.3 Simultaneous Conflict Problems

Official versus Official; Agency versus Agency

A simultaneous conflict of interest situation (§ 7.3) can arise when a government lawyer represents two governmental officials who have independent decision-making powers and whose decisions clash on a legal matter.[25] A variation occurs when members of the same agency are involved in official litigation against each other. Suppose, for example, that one member of a three-member commission wishes to challenge the legality of action

objections of state officers he represents)(on remand from Massachusetts v. United States, 429 U.S. 66, 97 S.Ct. 345, 50 L.Ed.2d 224 (1976)); State ex rel. Howard v. Oklahoma Corp. Comm'n, 614 P.2d 45, 52 (Okl.1980)(attorney general may appeal and argue contrary to state-agency staff lawyers who may also appear and argue).

[20] See 28 U.S.C.A. § 518; id. § 519; 28 C.F.R. § 0.20(b); Mendoza v. United States, 672 F.2d 1320, 1326 n.9 (9th Cir.1982), reversed on other grounds 464 U.S. 154, 104 S.Ct. 568, 78 L.Ed.2d 379 (1984); Note, Government Litigation in the Supreme Court: The Roles of the Solicitor General, 78 Yale L.J. 1442 (1969).

[21] See generally Uviller, The Virtuous Prosecutor in Quest of an Ethical Standard: Guidance from the ABA, 71 Mich.L.Rev. 1145, 1164 (1973). See also § 13.10.3 (prosecutorial discretion).

[22] Cf. Perillo v. Advisory Comm. on Professional Ethics, 83 N.J. 366, 416 A.2d 801, 806–08 (1980)(common objectives and frequency of personal contact between municipal lawyer and municipal police precludes lawyer from representing municipality in suit against police officer; propriety of representation of municipality in suit against nonpolice employee turns on nature of actual relationship).

[23] Cf. People v. Superior Court of San Luis Obispo County, 84 Cal.App.3d 491, 148 Cal.Rptr. 704, 712 (1978) (dictum).

[24] Ward v. Superior Court, 70 Cal.App.3d 23, 138 Cal. Rptr. 532 (1977); cf. Perillo v. Advisory Committee on Professional Ethics, supra note 22; Gibson v. Johnson, 35 Or.App. 493, 582 P.2d 452 (1978).

[25] Harceg v. Brown, 512 F.Supp. 788 (N.D.Ill.1981) (state's attorney could not represent both defendant-sheriff, who denied political favoritism charged by plaintiffs, and defendant-chairman of merit commission, who asserted that plaintiffs' charges were correct).

taken by the other two. Sometimes the lawyer's dilemma can be resolved, in rather strong-armed fashion, by treating the conflict itself as a matter of policy and, at least as far as the question of who shall enjoy the taxpayer-paid services of the government's lawyer, by letting the majority vote of the disputing agency members control.[26]

Proceedings against the Lawyer's Agency

A recurring simultaneous conflict question is whether a government lawyer may represent another in an adversary proceeding involving the government lawyer's own agency. A sensible suggestion is made in the Model Rules that government lawyers should be able to represent government employees in proceedings in which the government agency is the opposing party.[27] Presumably that would not permit litigation involving the government lawyer's own responsibilities.[28] But statutory restrictions commonly exist that more broadly bar suits against the governmental employer.[29] For example, lawyers employed by the United States are under a broad statutory prohibition against representing anyone other than the United States before an agency or court.[30]

Dual-Function Conflicts

Problems of conflicts in simultaneous representations can arise from situations in which the same government lawyer has concurrent responsibilities that potentially conflict. A common variation of the problem involves a lawyer from a specialized governmental agency that has responsibility to enforce civil remedies under a statutory scheme who attempts to serve at the same time in the second role of prosecutor of persons for violating the penal version of related laws. The dual-function lawyer is not necessarily disqualified, although a conflict of function can arise.[31]

At the root of the possible conflict is the doctrine that special investigative techniques that can appropriately be employed in the civil area may not be used solely for the purposes of preparing a criminal case. The doctrine requires that the government lawyer act in "good faith." [32] Some decisions finding a conflict of interest between dual roles proceed by imagining that instances might occur in which interests of the occupants of the two

[26] Silver v. Downs, 493 Pa. 50, 425 A.2d 359 (1981)(suit by one government board member to remove two-man majority; plaintiff's motion to disqualify town lawyer from representing defendant members denied in absence of evidence of communication of confidences by plaintiff or other specific grounds for disqualification).

[27] MR 1.7 comment (Conflicts in Litigation). But cf. ABA Informal Ethics Op. 84–1508 (1984)(lawyer employed by state agency in nonlegal role should ordinarily not represent others employed by same agency in administrative hearings against agency).

[28] Bachman v. Pertschuk, 437 F.Supp. 973 (D.D.C.1977) (Federal Trade Commission lawyer could not represent FTC employee in racial discrimination suit against agency).

[29] Triplett v. Azordegan, 421 F.Supp. 998 (N.D.Iowa 1976)(Iowa statute prohibiting person receiving state compensation from representing client in litigation against interests of the state construed to permit state law professors in clinical education program to represent former prisoner in civil rights action against state officer).

[30] 18 U.S.C.A. § 205; United States v. Baer, 575 F.2d 1295, 1298 (10th Cir.1978). An exception is provided in § 205 for representing a person in administrative proceedings without compensation if the client is the subject of a "disciplinary, loyalty or other personnel administration proceeding."

[31] United States v. Birdman, 602 F.2d 547, 561–63 (2d Cir.1979), cert.denied 444 U.S. 1032, 100 S.Ct. 703, 62 L.Ed.2d 668 (1980)(SEC lawyer specially deputized as Justice Department lawyer for participation in grand jury proceedings against SEC target); United States v. Wencke, 604 F.2d 607 (9th Cir.1979); In re Perlin, 589 F.2d 260 (7th Cir.1978); United States v. Dondich, 460 F.Supp. 849 (N.D.Cal.1978). See also In re April 1977 Grand Jury Subpoenas (General Motors Corp.), 573 F.2d 936 (6th Cir.1978)(2–1 decision)(IRS lawyer specially appointed as Justice Department lawyer to assist in grand jury proceeding had conflict requiring termination of grand jury investigation on basis of appearance of impropriety caused by possible unauthorized use of grand jury investigation for civil tax purposes), panel decision reversed and appeal dismissed for lack of jurisdiction, 584 F.2d 1366 (6th Cir.1978)(en banc), cert.denied 440 U.S. 934, 99 S.Ct. 1277, 59 L.Ed.2d 492 (1979).

[32] See United States v. LaSalle Nat'l Bank, 437 U.S. 298, 98 S.Ct. 2357, 2367, 57 L.Ed.2d 221 (1978); Note, Administrative Agency Lawyers' Presence in the Grand Jury Room: Rules to Prevent Abuse, 128 U.Pa.L.Rev. 159 (1979).

roles might, or should, conflict.[33] In effect, those cases reflect the belief that good government requires that courts assure that checks and balances remain in place. That is achieved by having different lawyers occupy the two roles, so that they can independently develop possible second views. Judges writing those decisions are presumably aware of the disadvantages of inefficiency and additional legal expenses that such duplication requires and are prepared to defend their action on the ground that it prevents more costly governmental inefficiency and corruption that might be present if the independent professional view is not provided. It is not inconsistent with that systemic view to approve of a single lawyer representing more than one government agency in a single litigation if their interests in the specific situation are aligned.[34]

Government Lawyers' Personal Interests

Government lawyers have personal interests that might conflict with their official duties. The personal interest with the clearest potential for conflict is financial. One that may be as strong, but more difficult to handle conceptually, is emotional. The financial-interest problem is extensively regulated both in the federal and state governments by legislation.[35] Many laws, like the federal statute,[36] provide only criminal sanctions. Others require public disclosure of financial and business information so that the public can assess the propriety of a government lawyer's involvement in a particular matter.[37] Administrative agency regulations often create or expand upon disclosures required of agency employees. Disclosure requirements raise issues of privacy and of their interrelationship with the attorney-client privilege, but their application to government lawyers has generally been upheld if drawn with reasonably narrow limits.[38]

An emotional interest, in order to be disqualifying, must create a bias or hostility in the government lawyer sufficiently strong to interfere seriously with the lawyer's exercise of public responsibility. Such an interest arises, for example, if a matter extraneous to the lawyer's normal duties interferes, such as if a prosecutor files murder charges against a defendant whose alleged victim is the son of a close friend and fellow prosecutor [39] or if a prosecutor has previously been personally named as a defendant in a civil action, charging him with bad faith in his performance of duties, brought by the person accused in the criminal prosecution.[40] Political interests can also create serious conflicts of interest on the part of a prosecutor, as Watergate made notorious.[41] On the other hand, the remote possibility of inappropriate motives is not itself disabling, such as when a prosecutor files a

33 In re Opinion 452, 87 N.J. 45, 432 A.2d 829 (1981) (two law offices in the same town); In re Opinion No. 415, 81 N.J. 318, 407 A.2d 1197 (1979)(lawyer for municipality and for county in which municipality is located).

34 DeLuca v. Kahr Bros., Inc., 171 N.J.Super. 100, 407 A.2d 1285 (1979).

35 For a catalog of legislation, see Note, Developments—Conflicts of Interest in the Legal Profession, 94 Harv.L.Rev. 1244, 1423 n.36 (1981).

36 18 U.S.C.A. § 208.

37 Hays v. Wood, 25 Cal.3d 772, 160 Cal.Rptr. 102, 603 P.2d 19 (1979)(requirement of political reform act that lawyer officials of state government disclose names of all clients paying fees in excess of $1,000 per year).

38 Compare Hays v. Wood, supra, with American Fed'n of Gov't Employees v. Schlesinger, 443 F.Supp. 431 (D.D.C.1978).

39 People v. Superior Court (Greer), 19 Cal.3d 255, 137 Cal.Rptr. 476, 485, 561 P.2d 1164, 1173 (1977), and authorities cited (prosecutor disqualified). Cf. United States v. Heldt, 668 F.2d 1238, 1275 (D.C.Cir.1981), cert.denied 456 U.S. 926, 102 S.Ct. 1971, 72 L.Ed.2d 440 (1982) (charge that defendants had broken into offices of same United States attorney who pressed ensuing illegal-entry prosection not disabling); United States v. Wright, 588 F.2d 31 (2d Cir.1978), cert.denied 440 U.S. 917, 99 S.Ct. 1236, 59 L.Ed.2d 467 (1979)(claim that wife of U.S. attorney was political opponent of defendant charged with unrelated bribery insufficient to require dismissal of indictment).

40 State v. Cox, 246 La. 748, 167 So.2d 352, 357 (1964).

41 The post-Watergate congressional solution was a "special prosecutor" law that disqualifies the attorney general in a category of cases generally involving high political officers and requires the appointment of a special prosecutor to investigate and make a charging decision. See 28 U.S.C.A. §§ 591–98 (West Supp.1983). The appointment is made by the judges of the United States Court of Appeals for the District of Columbia Circuit. Id. § 49.

criminal charge against a person who has filed a civil action, arising out of the same event, against the prosecutor's employer-municipality.[42]

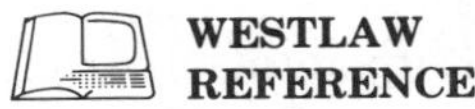

WESTLAW REFERENCES

conflict! /3 interest /s attorney lawyer /p agency government agency /3 lawyer attorney /s conflict! /3 interest /p "grand jury"

topic(45) /p conflict! /3 interest /p government agency /p personal emotional financial

§ 8.9.4 *Former-Client Conflicts*

Former Private or Government Clients

Former-client conflict problems can arise typically, but not invariably, because of a government lawyer's involvement in private practice. A prosecutor may not, of course, press criminal charges against a defendant whom the prosecutor had defended on the same charges while in private practice.[43] Even if the offense is not the same, the prosecutor would also be disqualified if he or she represented the defendant in private practice and obtained confidential information that related to the offense charged.[44]

The former-client bar could even arise within government practice, especially if the lawyer developed a relationship in the former matter that led personnel in the former agency to divulge confidential information. Suppose a government lawyer changed his or her mind about where the path of legality lay and as a result filed suit challenging the legality of action that the lawyer had advised another agency to take. A California decision holds that such naked side switching is impermissible for any lawyer, even the highest-ranking legal officer of the state.[45] The court did not oppose changing one's views about a matter of legal interpretation but based disqualification on a perfunctory application of the irrefutable presumption that the governmental officers who were formerly represented disclosed confidential information to their lawyer.[46] Applying models from private practice to state law officers is questionable because the court does not inquire whether the setting in which the lawyer conferred with the formerly represented state officers was likely to have been one in which confidential information was in fact imparted and personal trust reposed. If such factors had been demonstrated, the result would have been arguably sound on the view that confidential relationships between state officers and other state employees and a state's attorney can be valuable and that former-client rules seek to protect them.[47]

Part-time Government Practice

Part-time lawyering for a governmental body can range from an ad hoc, fee-paying arrangement through a variety of permanent positions for government consulting or advocacy. Because the lawyer concurrently maintains a private practice, possibly in a law firm of several members, the possibilities for conflict are multiplied over those normally confronted by a government lawyer with fewer constituencies. It is still true, for example, that the majority of prosecutors in the United States are not full-time government lawyers

42 People v. Municipal Court (Byars), 77 Cal.App.3d 294, 299, 143 Cal.Rptr. 491 (1978).

43 Chadwick v. Superior Court, 106 Cal.App.3d 108, 164 Cal.Rptr. 864, 867–68 (1980); People v. Curry, 1 Ill.App.3d 87, 272 N.E.2d 669 (1971); Havens v. State, 429 N.E.2d 618, 620 (Ind.1981); Ex parte Spain, 589 S.W.2d 132 (Tex. Crim.App.1979); State ex rel. Moran v. Ziegler, 161 W.Va. 609, 244 S.E.2d 550 (1978)(lawyer who twice consulted with person who told lawyer he had been involved in "a shooting" could not thereafter prosecute even if the defense representation went no further). But cf. People v. Johnson, 105 Cal.App.3d 884, 164 Cal.Rptr. 746, 750–51 (1980)(defendant "impliedly consented" to former public defender's participating in prosecution against him on same charges by failing to raise objection at trial).

44 State v. Jones, 180 Conn. 443, 429 A.2d 936 (1980); People v. Gerold, 265 Ill. 448, 107 N.E. 165 (1914).

45 People ex rel. Deukmejian v. Brown, 29 Cal.3d 150, 172 Cal.Rptr. 478, 624 P.2d 1206 (1981). See also Arkansas v. Dean Foods Prods. Co., 605 F.2d 380, 384 (8th Cir. 1979)(private business corporation represented as member of class by state attorney general in antitrust class action could not be sued during pendency of same suit for unrelated antitrust violation).

46 See § 7.4.3(b)(substantial relationship standard).

47 Jurisdictions that restrictively define the attorney-client privilege for governmental clients might apply the former-client rules in a similarly restrictive way. See generally § 6.5.6.

but are also engaged in private practice.[48] A part-time government lawyer has the same conflict of interest responsibilities as any other lawyer with multiple clients and must avoid representing conflicting interests.[49] In addition, the lawyer may bear special conflict of interest disabilities similar to those borne only by government lawyers.

For example, suppose a private practitioner represents a tort victim in a civil action that seeks to recover damages from an alleged tortfeasor. If the lawyer is also a part-time prosecutor, filing a criminal charge against the defendant based on the same matter would offend no ordinary conflict of interest rule. It is clear in that situation that the prosecutor is acting consistently and not adversely to the interests of any present or past client. But the serious objection remains that the prosecution might be in aid of the part-time prosecutor's private client and not because of an unencumbered exercise of prosecutorial discretion. The prosecutor's duties as a public officer and his or her loyalties as a private practitioner conflict.[50] Similarly, a part-time prosecutor in a small town might be reluctant to cross-examine or criticize police officers, on whose testimony he or she relies in prosecuting cases, and so should be disqualified from defending criminal cases in which they may be witnesses.[51]

Some side-switching decisions, however, impose restrictions of questionable breadth, for example, by categorically disqualifying a part-time government lawyer from engaging in certain types of litigation.[52] Similarly broad prohibitions are sometimes found in state statutes or other special rules.[53] And a lawyer who has previously represented a person who is a judge may find that the judge is required to step down in any case in which the lawyer represents a party.[54] Such strict conflict rules are evidently designed to purchase public contentment with the unquestionable integrity of prosecutions and other governmental work. They may do so, but at a high price.

Courts impose a similar kind of special disqualification rule in some decisions involving the imputed disqualification of the members of a part-time government lawyer's private law firm or of associate lawyers in a governmental law office.[55] Some of the disqualifications are perfectly straightforward, such as that of a lawyer-member of a government board who seeks to review the legal work

48 See U.S. Dep't of Justice (LEAA), State and Local Prosecution and Civil Attorney Systems 4 (1978); Comment, The Part-time State's Attorney in South Dakota: The Conflict between Fealty to Private Client and Service to the Public, 27 S.D.L.Rev. 24, 28 (1981).

49 See § 7.3. See Shaw v. United States, 244 F.2d 930, 938 (9th Cir.1957); In re Gonyo, 73 Wis.2d 624, 245 N.W.2d 893, 894 (1976)(discipline for employing status as district attorney-elect to delay criminal charge against client until lawyer had taken office); EC 8–8.

50 In re Lantz, 420 N.E.2d 1236 (Ind.1981)(discipline of part-time prosecutor who filed bad check charges parallel to civil debt-collection cases); In re Fisher, 400 N.E.2d 1127 (Ind.1980)(discipline of part-time prosecutor for representing mother in civil custody dispute against father who was being prosecuted for criminal confinement by same office of county prosecutor); State v. Tate, 185 La. 1006, 171 So. 108 (1936); Sinclair v. State, 278 Md. 243, 363 A.2d 468 (1976). Threatening to bring criminal charges in such situations has resulted in discipline. E.g., In re Joyce, 182 Minn. 156, 234 N.W. 9 (1930); In re Brunston, 52 Mont. 83, 155 P. 1109 (1916)(disbarment). See also § 13.5.5.

51 See People v. Rhodes, 12 Cal.3d 180, 115 Cal.Rptr. 235, 624 P.2d 363 (1974). A subsequently enacted California statute in effect extends the disability to any city lawyer exercising prosecutorial responsibilities. Cal. Gov't Code § 41805. All city lawyers are disabled from defending charges brought under a city ordinance. Id. § 41805(1).

52 State ex rel. Nebraska State Bar Ass'n v. Hollstein, 202 Neb. 40, 274 N.W.2d 508 (1979)(enforcing, in discipline case, bar ethics opinion that prohibits part-time prosecutor from voluntarily representing anyone charged with crime); Higgins v. Advisory Comm. on Professional Ethics, 73 N.J. 123, 373 A.2d 372 (1977)(lawyer-member of town board may not represent defendant in criminal case filed anywhere in county in which town is located); State v. Hunter, 290 N.C. 556, 227 S.E.2d 535 (1976), cert.denied 429 U.S. 1093, 97 S.Ct. 1106, 51 L.Ed.2d 539 (1977)(refusal to admit pro hac vice prosecutor from another state to defend person accused of murder-robbery).

53 Calif.Gov't Code § 26543 (district attorney prohibited from filing action in which city, district, or political subdivision of state is defendant); Montana Code of Professional Responsibility, DR 2–111(D)(county attorneys and deputies who prosecute may not defend criminal matters anywhere in state).

54 See ABA Judicial Discipline Standards § 4.17 commentary (approved draft 1978).

55 See generally § 7.6.

performed for that body by his or her own partners [56] or that of a prosecutor who obtains an indictment against a person who is being represented by a partner of the prosecutor in a civil suit arising out of the same matter.[57] The risks of economic conflict or of inadvertent divulgence of confidences are too great in such cases. Other decisions, however, go far beyond situations in which an articulatable need for caution exists. For example, one court prohibited a part-time member of the office of the state's attorney general for worker compensation commission matters from representing a person accused of crime.[58] The result can be defended only on the extravagant notion that all information and loyalties of every member of the attorney general's office are imputed to every other, or on the equally extravagant ground of the appearances of impropriety (§ 7.1.4). Other cases, a majority it seems, take a more temperate view.[59]

WESTLAW REFERENCES

conflict! /3 interest /p government agency state /5 attorney lawyer prosecutor /p former /2 client

topic(45) /p conflict! /3 interest /p form /2 client

45k21 /p agency govern!

45k21.5(2)

part-time /s (government agency +s attorney lawyer) prosecutor /p conflict! /3 interest

§ 8.10 CONFLICTS OF FORMER GOVERNMENT LAWYERS

§ 8.10.1 *Special Dimensions of the Conflict*

Public and Professional Perspectives on the "Revolving Door"

The issue of former-government-lawyer conflicts has become a cause cèlébre in recent years and an occasion for both lawyerly and lay opinion by many authors.[60] Public attention is activated by concerns with political evils of the "revolving door"—the process by which lawyers and others temporarily enter government service from private life and then leave it for large fees in private practice, where they can exploit information, contacts, and influence garnered in government service.

The bar's predominant concern has been different. Lawyers are more concerned with restrictions on their ability to mold their careers and to accept lucrative business in law practice. Lawyerly opinion also reflects natural resentment at undeserved lay suspiciousness. Lawyers, but not many nonlawyers, also frequently cite the government's own self-interest. Lawyers worry that government will not be able to attract to its service lawyers of ability and ambition, who would be unwilling to accept a government position if unduly restricted in later private practice opportunities.

56 Howard v. State Comm'n on Ethics, 421 So.2d 37 (Fla.App.1982).

57 State v. Detroit Motors, 62 N.J.Super. 386, 163 A.2d 227 (1960). See also, e.g., West Ann.Cal.Bus. & Prof.Code § 6131(a) (misdemeanor to defend criminal prosecution brought by prosecutor who is partner of defense lawyer).

58 People v. Fife, 65 Ill.App.3d 805, 22 Ill.Dec. 536, 382 N.E.2d 1235 (1978), affirmed 76 Ill.2d 418, 30 Ill.Dec. 300, 392 N.E.2d 1345 (1979). See also Dunn v. Hackworth, 487 F.Supp. 332 (E.D.Mo.), affirmed 628 F.2d 1111 (8th Cir.1980)(noting Missouri rule prohibiting part-time juvenile officer from representing juvenile defendant in any of state's courts).

59 State v. Jones, 180 Conn. 443, 429 A.2d 936 (1980) (disqualification of part-time prosecutor on ground of possession of confidential information from prior related representation did not require disqualification of entire office of state's attorney); People v. Crawford Distrib. Co., 65 Ill.App.3d 790, 22 Ill.Dec. 525, 382 N.E.2d 1223, 1226–28 (1978); State v. Rice, 227 Kan. 416, 607 P.2d 489, 494–95 (1980)(neither part-time judge nor her partners are precluded from representing defendants in criminal cases in other courts in state); State ex rel. Sowa v. Sommerville, 280 S.E.2d 85 (W.Va.1981)(partners and associates of county prosecutor may accept indigent criminal appointments in counties other than that in which prosecutor serves if accused signs written consent).

60 Graceffa, Ethical Considerations of the Federal Lawyer upon Entering Private Practice, 4 W.New Eng.L.Rev. 199 (1981); Lacovara, Restricting the Private Law Practice of Former Government Lawyers, 20 Ariz.L.Rev. 369 (1978); Morgan, Appropriate Limits on Participation by a Former Agency Official in Matters before an Agency, 1980 Duke L.J. 1; Mundheim, Conflict of Interest and the Former Government Employee: Rethinking the Revolving Door, 14 Creighton L.Rev. 707 (1981). For a representative of a somewhat alarmist, nonlawyer view, see P.Stern, Lawyers on Trial 140–46 (1980).

Several attempts have been made to reach a balance between those competing policies and claims. In addition to several landmark judicial decisions, federal and state legislation and agency regulations have played a role, particularly in the aftermath of Watergate, as have ethics committee opinions and proposals to revise the lawyer regulations on the revolving-door problem.

The conflict of interest issues involving a former government lawyer are important in three respects. First, the governmental setting creates special problems in applying otherwise generally familiar theories and standards about former-client conflicts. Second, an entirely novel and additional basis for disqualification of a former government lawyer has been widely recognized, the congruent-interest conflict. Third, the doctrine of imputed disqualification has been diluted, perhaps because of the wide sweep of the congruent-interest conflict doctrine, and has given rise to screening and related procedures in an attempt to ward off disqualification of an entire firm because one former government lawyer is a member (§ 7.6.4).

Adverse-Interest Conflicts

As is the case with conflicts generally (§ 7.4.3), a former government lawyer may not represent a client in private practice if the matter is substantially related to a matter that the lawyer dealt with while employed by the government and if the interests of the current and former clients are adverse. Adverse-interest conflicts involve dangers both of the disclosure of confidential information and of disloyalty to the former client. As an example of a strong case for disqualification, suppose a government lawyer must decide whether to take action on a matter that would be detrimental to a private company. The government lawyer elects not to take the action and then, in private practice, attempts to represent the same private company in defense of eventual governmental action against the client on the same matter.[61] Plainly the traditional rules against adversely representing succeeding clients comfortably include such naked side-switching cases (§ 7.4). Problems that remain, to be explored below, concern the extent to which the lawyer's former work and the later, private practice representation must resemble each other in order to trigger disqualification.

Congruent-Interest Representation Conflicts

The "congruent interest" disqualification is unique to government lawyers and applies primarily in the case of former government lawyers.[62] It arguably does not involve a conflict at all, because it prohibits the lawyer from representing a private practice client even if the interests of the former government client and the new client are entirely parallel. To illustrate the normal rule for non-government lawyers, imagine that the lawyer has represented passenger A and has recovered substantial damages in a suit against a driver. No conflict of interest principle or rule restricts the lawyer from later representing passenger B against the driver with respect to exactly the same accident. B may obtain the benefits of the lawyer's help regardless of the fact that the lawyer might be able to employ to B's advantage information and strategies developed in the representation of A. The

[61] Illinois v. Borg, Inc., 553 F.Supp. 178 (N.D.Ill.1982) (former state lawyer who investigated antitrust implications of bid rigging is disqualified from representing as client alleged bid rigger who defends on ground that failure to bring earlier action against it during time of lawyer's investigation bars present suit by statute of limitations); Traylor v. City of Amarillo, 335 F.Supp. 423 (N.D.Tex.1971)(former city attorney disqualified from attacking constitutionality of ordinance he earlier defended); Osborn v. District Court, 619 P.2d 41 (Colo.1980) (former assistant prosecutor interviewed and counseled alleged rape victim whom she would now cross-examine as private practice defense lawyer for alleged rapist in same case).

[62] In rare cases, congruent-interest conflicts may also involve part-time government lawyers. Cf. Town of Edgartown v. State Ethics Comm'n, 391 Mass. 83, 460 N.E.2d 1283 (1984)(under statute proscribing government employee from acting as agent for anyone other than government agency, lawyer could not represent both town and private parties in common defense of Indian land claims). See generally § 8.9.3.

critical element is that the interests of A and B do not conflict.

The analysis does not change if we move from an area that is entirely private into one that is arguably more connected with the public interest. Suppose that a lawyer in private practice represents Small Soap Company in its suit for damages under the federal antitrust laws against Giant Soap Company. The lawyer would not be disqualified from representing Medium Soap Company against Giant Soap in a succeeding suit for damages based on precisely the same conspiracy. The congruence of interests between Small Soap and Medium Soap would almost certainly mean that the lawyer could represent both clients. In the absence of a conflict—an opposing interest between the two clients—the existence of a substantial relationship between the matters involved in both cases is irrelevant.

Now suppose the lawyer has filed suit in behalf of the government against Giant Soap Company to force divestiture of an acquired company on a theory that, because of the acquisition, Giant Soap has monopolized an industry in conflict with antitrust laws. May the lawyer, after leaving government service and while in private practice, represent Medium Soap Company against Giant Soap in a suit for damages based on the same antitrust conspiracy? Does the absence of opposing interests between Medium Soap and the lawyer's former government client similarly mean that there should be no disqualification?

At this point the rules for the former government lawyer diverge sharply from the normal former-client conflict rules: the lawyer *is* disqualified from representing the successive client in private practice, despite the fact that the interests of the client and the lawyer's former government client are apparently aligned. All that is required for disqualification is the relationship between the former and the succeeding representations.[63]

Rationale for the Congruent-Interest Conflict

Suspicions about a special kind of corruption have produced the doctrine of congruent-interest conflict. Its justification obviously has nothing to do with treacherous use of the government's confidential information against its interests. It is also clear that the lawyer's representation of the successive client itself involves no disloyalty to the former government client. Instead, the rationale for disqualification is rooted in a concern with the impact that any other rule would have upon the decisions and actions taken by the government lawyer during the course of the earlier representation of the government. Both courts and commentators have expressed the fear that permitting a lawyer to take action in behalf of a government client that later could be to the advantage of a private practice client would present grave dangers that a government lawyer's largely discretionary actions would be wrongly influenced by the temptation to secure private practice employment or to favor parties who might later become private practice clients. In the case of Medium Soap, for example, the fear is that the lawyer might have been wrongly influenced to file or to shape the government's action against Giant Soap in the hope of currying favor with future employers.

The fear that government lawyers will misuse government power in that way is not idle. Lawyers who represent the government often exercise enormous discretion unchecked by an actual client who oversees the lawyer's work. For that reason a special rule is needed to remove the incentive for government lawyers to take discretionary decisions with an eye cast toward advantages in future, nongovernmental employment. The broad disqualification rule accomplishes that and, particularly under rubrics that do not invariably require disqualification of the entire firm with which the former government lawyer practices, does

[63] See DR 9–101(B); MR 1.11(a); Canon 36; General Motors Corp. v. City of New York, 501 F.2d 639 (2d Cir. 1974).

it without unnecessarily discouraging lawyers from entering temporary public service.

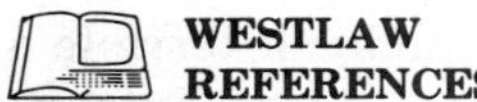
WESTLAW REFERENCES

conflict! /3 interest /p former +s government agency public /s lawyer attorney

former +s government agency /s lawyer attorney /p congruent adverse /s interest

---

§ 8.10.2 *Principles, Professional Rules, and Legislation*

Competing Considerations

Three reasons are advanced for stringent rules disqualifying former government lawyers in matters that were within their official purview during government service.[64] Against them are arrayed three reasons in favor of rules with more toleration for successive representations—reasons that correspond to claimed interests of the government, the lawyer, and private-practice clients. The professional rules and statutes that have emerged reflect different balances of those competing considerations.

Guarding against Corrupt Use of Governmental Power

First, the rule is defended as necessary to prevent corruption in government service. As already discussed, the fear is that a government lawyer otherwise might take action or refuse to take action in order to enhance employability or financial rewards in private practice.[65] The same concern, of course, might also be entertained about a lawyer employed by a corporation, bank, union, or other entity client. Such a lawyer might be similarly tempted to deal with a present employer's legal affairs treacherously in order to curry favor with a prospective private employer. But government, it seems to be concluded, is especially vulnerable and deserves special protections because of the breadth of the public interest in its safe, efficient, and fair operation.

That threat of corruption could range from a lawyer's subverting the government's interests in order to benefit a prospective client or law firm that seeks to elude the government's clutches (producing an adverse-interest conflict)[66] to the other extreme of his or her overzealously prosecuting a target of governmental action for the benefit of a future private practice client or firm whose interests apparently parallel those of the government (producing a congruent-interest conflict).[67]

64 The analysis that follows is mainstream in the legal literature, but parts of it would make many political scientists grimace. The model it assumes is one in which a government with its "own" interests protected by its own lawyers is arrayed against "private" interests protected by private practitioners. The model is simplistic and may be fundamentally unrealistic. An alternative model sees government essentially as the forum for the reallocation of public resources between contending political groups. In that model the government has no substantive interests of its own. Even in that view of politics, conflict of interest rules could perhaps be understood as one of the agreed-upon elements of process that all contending groups wish to see enforced in order to prevent other contenders from gaining undue advantage or entrenchment.

65 Woods v. Covington County Bank, 537 F.2d 804, 814 (5th Cir.1976); Committee for Washington's Riverfront Parks v. Thompson, 451 A.2d 1177, 1186 (D.C.1982); MR 11.1 comment (third paragraph); cf. Armstrong v. McAlpin, 625 F.2d 433, 445 (2d Cir.1980)(en banc), vacated for lack of jurisdiction, 449 U.S. 1106, 101 S.Ct. 911, 66 L.Ed.2d 835 (1981); ABA Formal Op. 37 (1931)("[The purpose underlying the interdiction of former government lawyers in Canon 36 is to avoid] the manifest possibility that his action as a public legal official might be influenced (or be open to the charge that it had been influenced) by the hope of later being employed privately either to uphold or to upset what he had done."); McElwain & Vorenberg, The Federal Conflict of Interest Statutes, 65 Harv.L.Rev. 955, 958 (1952).

66 Woods v. Covington County Bank, 537 F.2d 804, 814 (5th Cir.1976); United States v. Standard Oil Co., 136 F.Supp. 345, 359 (S.D.N.Y.1955).

67 General Motors Corp. v. City of New York, 501 F.2d 639, 640 (2d Cir.1974); Price v. Admiral Ins. Co., 481 F.Supp. 374, 378 (E.D.Pa.1979); Handelman v. Weiss, 368 F.Supp. 258, 264 n.11 (S.D.N.Y.1973)(while in government service the lawyer had "a definite intent . . . to develop a case against the defendants"). The parallel between the government's interests and those of the private practice client might be illusory, of course, if the government's position in the matter was itself distorted by the lawyer's desire to favor the private interest.

Possibly of a different magnitude is the temptation for a government lawyer to take legal action, not because it necessarily serves the best interest of the government, but because it might favorably impress prospective clients and law firms with the lawyer's technical brilliance, without regard to its substantive impact on the government or others.[68]

Inappropriate Use of Government-Derived Information

Second, a former government lawyer should not be able to take unfair advantage of access to confidential government information.[69] Again, arguable abuses cover a range. A government lawyer might simply have access to confidential government information in the normal course of legal work. It has been asserted that employing it in later private practice unfairly advantages the lawyer's private practice client and unfairly disadvantages the client's adversary.[70] The argument is of limited strength because no similar unfairness is found in private-practice, congruent-conflict cases. Perhaps more persuasively, it can also be argued that strict conflict rules enhance the government's ability to offer guarantees of confidentiality to informants. That encourages persons and institutions to release information to the government and facilitates consultation within governmental law offices.[71]

Beyond those general concerns lie more limited, but more powerful, arguments based on some processes by which governments gather information. Government lawyers and law offices have available a terrible array of coercive methods to obtain information—grand jury, police investigation and interrogation, warrants, informers and agents whose activities are immunized, authorized wiretapping, civil investigatory demands, enhanced subpoena power, and the rest. Without broad conflict rules a government lawyer might be tempted to employ those special fact-gathering devices, in ways unintended and otherwise not permitted, in order to obtain an advantage for future private practice purposes.[72] That misuse would unfairly harass citizens, give unfair advantage to the lawyer's private practice clients and law firm, and impair public willingness to accept the legitimate use of those powers.

The Alluring "Appearances" Rationale

The third rationale for disqualifying a former government lawyer is to prevent an "appearance of impropriety"—a vapid concept sometimes employed independently, and thus quite erroneously, to disqualify a former government lawyer [73] and sometimes as a much less direct and meaningful locution that only obscures a sounder reason.[74] The "appearances" rationale has done more to retard

[68] See ABA Formal Op. 342 at 4 n.12 (1975), and authorities cited. Conflict of interest rules, of course, would do little to discourage such mindless legal pyrotechnics unless they prohibited the lawyer altogether from joining a firm or representing a client with a matter pending before the agency. Compare the broad sweep of the federal legislation for one-year and two-year periods, infra 465–67. Compare also MR 1.11(c)(2), prohibiting a government lawyer from negotiating for private employment with a lawyer representing a client for whose matter the government lawyer has personal and substantial responsibility (§ 8.10.3).

[69] See generally MR 1.11 comment (third paragraph).

[70] Armstrong v. McAlpin, 625 F.2d 433, 445 (2d Cir. 1980)(en banc), vacated for lack of jurisdiction 449 U.S. 1106, 101 S.Ct. 911, 66 L.Ed.2d 835 (1981); In re Asbestos Cases, 514 F.Supp. 914 (E.D.Va.1981); Allied Realty, Inc. v. Exchange Nat'l Bank, 283 F.Supp. 464, 467 (D.Minn. 1968), affirmed 408 F.2d 1099 (8th Cir.1969), cert.denied 396 U.S. 823, 90 S.Ct. 64, 24 L.Ed.2d 73 (1969). A weak form of the argument is that a government lawyer should not be paid twice for the same work. See Handelman v. Weiss, 368 F.Supp. 258, 264 (S.D.N.Y.1973).

[71] Kessenich v. Commodity Futures Trading Comm'n, 684 F.2d 88, 98 (D.C.Cir.1982)(avoid apprehension on the part of those to be protected by a government program that the government lawyer who assists them one day will oppose them the next, with consequent loss of candor on part of laymen); United States v. Smith, 653 F.2d 126, 128 (4th Cir.1981).

[72] Woods v. Covington County Bank, 537 F.2d 804, 816–17 (5th Cir.1976); Price v. Admiral Ins. Co., 481 F.Supp. 374, 378 (E.D.Pa.1979); Allied Realty, Inc. v. Exchange Nat'l Bank, 283 F.Supp. 464, 466 (D.Minn.1968), affirmed 408 F.2d 1099 (8th Cir.1969), cert.denied 396 U.S. 823, 90 S.Ct. 64, 24 L.Ed.2d 73 (1969); Hilo Metals Co. v. Learner Co., 258 F.Supp. 23, 28–29 (D.Hawaii 1966); ABA Formal Op. 135 (1951). Corrupt or abusive use of governmental fact-gathering mechanisms also serves as an example of

[73–74] See notes 73 & 74 on page 461.

thinking on problems of conflicts of former government lawyers than any other concept. When that fog is dispelled, the problems are difficult enough, for the rationales for stricter enforcement of strong conflicts rules against a former government lawyer are opposed by other legitimate concerns.

Impairing Governmental Recruitment of Lawyers

Private practice restrictions on former government lawyers might have three arguable negative effects. A first concern is that they will impair the ability of government to attract able lawyers to government service.[75] That results because of an important fact seldom mentioned: the financial rewards for government service are typically far below what financially successful private practitioners earn. It is not likely that government will alter that situation. While it continues, the government apparently hopes to attract able lawyers at low wages primarily for temporary government service. Most of those lawyers will agree to defer income in return for the experience and contacts that can later be exchanged for high incomes back in the private legal job market.

To some extent the "revolving door" that that analysis portrays economically benefits former government lawyers as well as the government, which can attract a supply of good legal talent at lower cost. A secondary payoff for the government might be that the intimacy breeds sympathy. The former government lawyer's familiarity with government policies and laws increases the likelihood of compliance with those same policies and laws on the part of the lawyer's later private practice clients. It is, of course, equally plausible to speculate that the government loses because lawyer-experts know where the soft spots and loopholes are. Other plausible benefits to the government might accrue. Government lawyers who can be assured of ready access to fall-back jobs in the private sector might demonstrate more courage and independence in the exercise of professional judgment while in government service and exercise that courageous judgment more often in the government's interest. The government might also benefit from the mature and informed viewpoints of private practitioners who can be encouraged to take a temporary tour of government service.[76]

But it is difficult to determine whether those benefits accrue to the government in actual practice. It is equally plausible to believe that they are offset by the fact that government lawyers' gazes are distractedly kept on alternative job markets and the fact that the "fresh viewpoint" expressed by the private practice lawyer who enters temporary government service is often a party line for a particular client, industry, or other favored interest. As with other of the policy arguments that can be advanced one way and another, the benefit-to-the-government policy depends upon a speculative assessment of human motivation and behavior that can

an illusory "congruent" conflict of interest. See supra note 67.

73 The "appearance of impropriety" standard is described, and railed against as virtually empty of intellectual content, in § 7.1.4. Nonetheless it has been invoked as the exclusive basis for disqualification of a former government lawyer. See, e.g., ABA Formal Op. 342, at 4 n.13 (1975). Formal Opinion 342 itself offered powerful reasons why the "appearances" rationale was "perhaps the least helpful" of those that could be marshaled. Id. at n.17.

74 Kessenich v. Commodity Futures Trading Comm'n, 684 F.2d 88, 97–98 (D.C.Cir.1982)("appearances" rationale obscures otherwise sound confidentiality analysis).

75 Variations on the recruitment argument are legion in legal literature. E.g., Armstrong v. McAlpin, 625 F.2d 433, 443 (2d Cir.1980)(en banc), vacated for lack of jurisdiction 449 U.S. 1106, 101 S.Ct. 911, 66 L.Ed.2d 835 (1981); Woods v. Covington County Bank, 537 F.2d 804, 812 (5th Cir.1976); United States v. Standard Oil Co., 136 F.Supp. 345, 363 (S.D.N.Y.1955); Reardon v. Marylayne, Inc., 83 N.J. 460, 416 A.2d 852, 861–62 (1980); Formal Op. 342, at 4 (1975); MR 1.11 comment (third paragraph); Association of the Bar of the City of New York, Conflict of Interest and Federal Service 181, 224 (1960); Morgan, Appropriate Limits on Participation by a Former Agency Official in Matters Before an Agency, 1980 Duke L.J. 1, 51–53.

76 Morgan, Appropriate Limits on Participation by a Former Agency Official in Matters before an Agency, 1980 Duke L.J. 1, 53–56; Mundheim, Conflict of Interest and the Former Government Employee: Rethinking the Revolving Door, 14 Creighton L.Rev. 707, 709, 720–21 (1981).

hardly be made with confidence either from the armchair or from the government and private practice law offices. It is also hardly an area of policy that requires a judicial last word. The question of benefit to the government is perhaps a matter best committed for decision to the government agencies whose interests the policies seek to protect. Particularly if a government agency determines that its recruitment efforts would be undeterred by a vigorous anti-conflict standard, a court is hardly in a credible position to disagree.[77]

Providing Freedom of Choice of Counsel

One may also wish to place limits on the sweep of disqualification rules in order to serve a goal that implicitly limits all disqualification rules. It assures that all litigants can obtain competent representation from lawyers of their own choosing, particularly in specialized areas of practice [78] or in cases in which few lawyers are willing to accept the representation.[79] A disqualification of a chosen lawyer therefore should not be based on fanciful or unrealistic suspicions.[80] Yet, while all litigants enjoy the right to be represented by counsel of their choice, that right is not an absolute right to particular counsel regardless of serious and substantial conflicts of interest.[81]

Enhancing Lawyer Career Mobility

As important as other reasons for restraint might be, one comes away from listening to the lawyer's side of the debates over the shape of professional regulations and from reading some judicial decisions with the firm sense that an important result sought is to permit lawyers, in the absence of concrete, demonstrable, and substantial impairment of governmental interests, to mobilize their special skills without hindrance. As a value, that is probably held much higher by affected lawyers than by others.

The 1908 Canons and 1969 Code

Professional rules reflect the policy objectives that compete for supremacy.[82] The 1908 original Canons of Ethics contained no former-government-lawyer provision, but a new Canon was added in 1928. Canon 36 first prohibited a lawyer from accepting legal work "in any matter upon the merits of which he has previously acted in a judicial capacity." Canon 36 went on to provide that a former government lawyer "should not after his retirement accept employment in connection

[77] Compare United States v. Miller, 624 F.2d 1198, 1203 (3d Cir.1980)(testimony of United States Attorney that his office's anticonflict rule, more stringent than DR 9–101(B), had no effect on ability of office to attract and retain lawyers of high quality), with Armstrong v. McAlpin, 625 F.2d 433, 443 (2d Cir.1980)(en banc), vacated for lack of jurisdiction 449 U.S. 1106, 101 S.Ct. 911, 66 L.Ed.2d 835 (1981)(amicus brief of United States asserts that a "decision to reject screening procedures is certain to have serious adverse effect on the ability of government legal offices to recruit and retain well-qualified attorneys"). The issue is not one of sovereign prerogative of coordinate branches of government so much as it is one of access to the facts; on this, an affected agency is obviously in a superior position to a court.

[78] Armstrong v. McAlpin, 625 F.2d 433, 444–45 (2d Cir. 1980)(en banc), vacated for lack of jurisdiction 449 U.S. 1106, 101 S.Ct. 911, 66 L.Ed.2d 835 (1981); Sierra Vista Hospital v. United States, 226 Ct.Cl. 223, 639 F.2d 749, 754 (1981); Chambers v. Superior Court, 121 Cal.App.3d 893, 175 Cal.Rptr. 575, 579 (1981); ABA Formal Op. 342, at 5 (1975).

[79] See Society for Good Will to Retarded Children, Inc. v. Carey, 466 F.Supp. 722, 730 (E.D.N.Y.1979).

[80] United States v. Smith, 653 F.2d 126, 128 (4th Cir. 1981); Woods v. Covington County Bank, 537 F.2d 804, 819 (5th Cir.1976).

[81] United States v. Miller, 624 F.2d 1198, 1203 (3d Cir. 1980); United States v. Ostrer, 597 F.2d 337, 341 (2d Cir. 1979); Silver Chrysler Plymouth Inc. v. Chrysler Motor Corp., 518 F.2d 751, 757 (2d Cir.1975). Cf. Snepp v. United States, 444 U.S. 507, 100 S.Ct. 763, 62 L.Ed.2d 704 (1980)(CIA may reasonably exact promise of employees not to publish information concerning their employment in interest of protecting confidential information despite fact that enforcement of promise impairs former employee's free expression rights).

[82] The California Rules of Professional Conduct contain no rule that directly deals with the former government lawyer, but California courts freely borrow from the ABA Code of Professional Responsibility for the purpose. See Chambers v. Superior Court, 121 Cal.App.3d 893, 175 Cal. Rptr. 575, 578 (1981).

with any matter which he has investigated or passed upon while in such office or employ." [83]

The treatment of the same issues in the 1969 Code is only slightly more complete. In DR 9–101(A) the Code essentially copies the first sentence of Canon 36, prohibiting a former judge from accepting private practice representation in a matter on which the judge passed while acting as judge. And in DR 9–101(B) a former government lawyer is prohibited from accepting "private" employment in a matter in which the lawyer had "substantial responsibility" while a public employee. Other than in those quoted particulars, DR 9–101(B) was copied with few changes from the second sentence of Canon 36.[84]

The 1983 Model Rules

Against that background the drafters of the 1983 Model Rules had the choice of rejecting old learning in order to attempt to write clearer rules at the risk that new language might incur unintended interpretations. Its drafters made both choices in Model Rule 1.11. Two regulations are provided there for the former government lawyer, and each is subject to a screening-and-notice exemption for an imputed disqualification that otherwise is visited in each instance upon the firm of the former government lawyer (§ 7.6.4). First, MR 1.11(a) provides that "a lawyer shall not represent a private client in connection with a matter in which the lawyer participated personally and substantially as a public officer or employee . . . ." An exemption is provided for situations in which "law may otherwise expressly permit." Second, MR 1.11(b) provides that even if the lawyer did not participate in the matter personally and substantially, "a lawyer who has knowledge, acquired as a public officer or employee, of confidential government information [85] about a person may not represent a private client whose interests are adverse to that person in a matter in which the information is material." The Rule again excepts situations in which "law may otherwise expressly permit."

The Model Rule retains the Canon and Code designation of "matter" as the basic focus for comparison of the former government work and the subsequent private practice representation. But MR 1.11(d) specially defines "matter" in a way that very broadly covers many different types of lawyerly or quasi-lawyerly functions. The Code's "substantial responsibility" standard is abandoned for a standard of "participated personally and substantially." [86] On the matter of consent generally, Canon 36 and DR 9–101(B) of the Code provided no exception for the former government client's consent. Model Rule 1.11(a) does explicitly permit waiver of the conflict by consent of the former government client, although MR 1.11(b), on the use of confidential information against a third party, does not.

Rule 1.11: Complementary or Preemptive?

A question about MR 1.11 is whether it is the only former-client conflict rule that operates to disqualify, or not to disqualify, former government lawyers. A suppressed note in an earlier draft suggested that former government lawyers would remain subject to the other conflict of interest rules to the extent that they were stricter.[87] Certain clues remain in the final version of the Model Rules that MR 1.11 is nonexhaustive in a similar

[83] For interpretative ABA ethics committee opinions, see ABA Opinion on Professional Ethics 165–66 (1967).

[84] As will be seen, however, the new allusion in DR 9–101(B) to "private" employment has given rise to an important interpretative question, and the change from Canon 36's "investigated or passed upon" language to the Code's "substantial responsibility" standard has ignited a controversy concerning formal authority.

[85] A definition of "confidential government information" is provided in MR 1.11(e). See infra at § 8.10.3(5).

[86] The "participated personally and substantially" phrase is a quotation from the federal conflict of interest criminal statute. 18 U.S.C.A. § 207. See infra § 8.10.3(2). The definition of "matter" in Rule 1.11(d) also incorporates "any other matter covered by the conflict of interest rules of the appropriate government agency," which would include, for federal agencies, the federal statutory definition and any enlargement on it by agency regulations.

[87] MR 1.9 Legal Background Note, at 67 (Proposed Final Draft, May 30, 1981)(MR 1.9 prohibits former gov-

way.[88] The question is important, because MR 1.11 is not coextensive with other conflict rules. Suppose, for example, that a government lawyer learns confidential governmental information about the pricing practices of an oil company. The lawyer leaves government service and files suit in behalf of an oil purchaser against the same oil company, alleging an illegal pricing scheme and basing his or her knowledge of the scheme in part on the secret government information. If it is legal to do so, can the government consent and thus waive the former government lawyer's conflict? Under MR 1.11(b) the lawyer is disqualified by a rule that does not provide for cure by the government's consent. But MR 1.6(a) provides generally that a client after consultation, may consent to the lawyer's use of the client's confidential information. Does MR 1.6(a) give a warrant to government consent that MR 1.11(b) seems not to allow? [89]

Another significant variation on the question is whether the general imputed-disqualification rule (MR 1.10), with its absence of any provision for screening but its general provision for client consent, also applies to the former government lawyer. If it did, then the special screening-and-notice provisions of MR 1.11(a) and (b), which do not require client consent, would be applicable only in the case of congruent-interest conflicts, the only kind of conflicts not covered by any other conflict of interest rule.[90]

Nothing in the text of the Model Rules answers clearly the question whether MR 1.11 stands alone or merely adds in some way to otherwise applicable rules. Given the overall purposes of MR 1.11 and the other conflict of interest rules, however, the better interpretation is to regard MR 1.11 not as an entirely free-standing enterprise but as a primarily complementary regulation. For the most part it adds protection for former government clients and not additional licenses for former government lawyers. Most importantly, government consent should be required in the case of any future adverse representation, including situations for which MR 1.11 provides screening as a cure for imputed disqualification. It would be incongruous to give governmental clients less protection in that respect than former clients who are not governmental entities. But protection should not be carried to illogical extremes. No reason exists to prevent a former government client from consenting, if it is in compliance with other law, to a former lawyer's use of confidential government information in a subsequent private practice representation, and because client consent would clearly suffice under MR 1.6, it should also suffice under MR 1.11(b).

The District of Columbia Rules

Still another set of regulations on the former-government-lawyer issue requires mention. The District of Columbia bar contains in its membership a large number of former and prospective federal government lawyers. After a long period of debate, the District of Columbia Court of Appeals issued an amended set of Disciplinary Rules under Canon 9 of the District of Columbia Code of Pro-

ernment lawyer from attacking validity of legislative or administrative rule that lawyer participated in drafting).

88 Perhaps the strongest clue is the following sentence from the comment (first paragraph) to MR 1.9, which generally deals with former-client conflicts of interest: "So also a lawyer who has prosecuted an accused person could not properly represent the accused in a subsequent civil action against the government concerning the same transaction." It is a mystery why one would be expected to resort to the general language of MR 1.9 for an answer to a problem that is much more precisely covered, and with the same outcome, in MR 1.11. Cf. also MR 1.11 comment (first and second paragraphs).

89 At the risk of further complicating the example, the problem is even deeper than portrayed. In the given situation it is apparent that either MR 1.11(b) or MR 1.11(a) might apply. In fact, all situations imaginable under MR 1.11(b) seem to fall within the language of MR 1.11(a) as well. And MR 1.11(a) contains a consent clause itself, while MR 1.11(b) does not.

90 The first paragraph of the comment to MR 1.11 in its final form states that MR 1.11 "is a counterpart of Rule 1.10(b), which applies to lawyers moving from one firm to another." In its next most recent incarnation, the same comment had stated that MR 1.11 "goes beyond the prohibition against representing clients with adverse interests stated in Rules 1.9 and 1.10." See MR 1.11 comment, at 44 (Proposed Final Draft, June 30, 1982). Both the Proposed Final Draft language and the eventual comment are distressingly delphic.

fessional Responsibility.[91] The document is more a political démarche than an independent judicial decision. The district's amended DR 9–101(B) employs the standard of "participated personally and substantially" to measure the type of government-service activity covered. The most important part of the new rules is a new DR 9–102. That prescribes an imputed-disqualification rule for the members of the former government lawyer's firm that accepts screening after notice to the government agency but without requiring its consent. At least one affiliated lawyer must also file a document stating that the firm is complying with the screening requirements.[92]

Federal Legislation

Statutory law has grown in importance in regulating former government lawyers and other employees. Until the early 1960s federal conflict of interest legislation was a confusing mélange of scattered statutes.[93] Political scandals involving White House and Pentagon officials led to an overhaul of federal law when Congress enacted a comprehensive conflict of interest statute in 1962.[94] Events during the Watergate era a decade later revealed that the conflict of interest laws remained seriously defective. New and more stringent federal legislation was eventually enacted in the Ethics in Government Act of 1978.[95] Extensive regulations have been issued under authority of the statute by the Office of Government Ethics.[96]

There is no reason to believe that the federal legislation preempts the state or federal professional codes to the extent that the latter contain stricter regulations of former government lawyers. The federal law is a criminal statute and thus is unlikely to regulate effectively all that should be regulated. Nothing in the statute or in its legislative history suggests that it was meant to derogate from the historic function of courts and administrative agencies of adopting and enforcing high professional standards.[97] Courts nonetheless might hesitate to base disqualifications directly on section 207, a criminal statute, because that would be tantamount to finding that the lawyer had committed a crime.[98] In addition, the act contains no language suggesting that it should be extended to the remedy of disqualification in pending litigation.[99] Nonetheless, its use in that way would clearly be compatible with the criminal sanction. Such borrowing would also be comparable to what courts do when they borrow the lawyer code provisions on conflicts in ruling on disqualifi-

[91] See "Revolving Door," 445 A.2d 615 (D.C.1982).

[92] The District of Columbia rule as adopted deleted proposals that would have required (1) that the lawyer's notification to the government agency be by affidavit (a "signed document" now suffices); and (2) that a lawyer in the private practice firm verify under oath the success of the screening effort following completion of the firm's participation in the private practice matter (as stated in the text, the firm need only state in writing that it is imposing appropriate screens but need not certify to their ultimate success).

[93] See generally Association of the Bar of the City of New York, Conflict of Interest and Federal Service (1960).

[94] Pub.L.No. 87–849, § 1(a), 87th Cong., 2d Sess., 76 Stat. 1119 (1962)(effective January 21, 1963). For the background and an early interpretation of the new federal statute, see B.Manning, Federal Conflict of Interest Law (1964).

[95] Pub.L.No. 95–521, 95th Cong., 2d Sess., 92 Stat. 1864, codified in relevant part in 18 U.S.C.A.§ 207, as amended by Pub.L.No. 96–28, §§ 1 & 2, 96th Cong., lst Sess., 93 Stat. 76. An excellent review of the 1978 legislation and its sequel is Morgan, Appropriate Limits on Participation by a Former Agency Official in Matters before an Agency, 1980 Duke L.J. 1, 11–23.

[96] 5 C.F.R. § 737.7.

[97] United States v. Miller, 624 F.2d 1198, 1202 (3d Cir. 1980).

[98] See Kessenich v. Commodity Futures Trading Comm'n, 684 F.2d 88, 95 (D.C.Cir.1982)(in light of disqualification on other grounds, it would be "precipitous" to determine whether § 207 in fact was violated). But cf. United States v. Dorfman, 542 F.Supp. 402, 410 (N.D.Ill. 1982)(while lawyer has not yet violated 18 U.S.C.A. § 207 because representation was interrupted by motion to disqualify, lawyer's appearance is prohibited because continued representation would violate statute and thus offend prohibitions in DR 1–102(A)(3) and (5) against illegal conduct involving moral turpitude and conduct prejudicial to the administration of justice).

[99] The statute does direct that agencies may take disciplinary action against a former employee who, after a hearing, has been found to have violated the statute, including disbarment from the agency for a period not to exceed five years. 18 U.S.C.A. § 207(j).

cation motions.[1] Moreover, the express invocation, in MR 1.11(a) and (b), of otherwise applicable law brings the federal statute directly into play in disqualification cases that rely upon the Model Rules.

The basic arrangement of section 207 is a three-tiered filter of matters with increasingly severe prohibitions. First, in wording that is copied in 1983 Model Rule 1.11, section 207(a) permanently prohibits a former government lawyer from representing any client before a federal agency or court in a matter in which the lawyer while in federal government service "participated personally and substantially." The prohibition applies without regard to the position of the lawyer in the governmental hierarchy so long as the lawyer had the described working relationship to the matter. While that prohibition is narrowest of all those in the statute in the sense that it covers the fewest matters, it is most enduring, because the disqualification is permanent. Second, section 207(c) simply and directly disqualifies certain former government employees from having any contact with their employing agency for a limited period of one year after terminating employment. The restriction applies only to employees of a senior grade.[2] The disqualification is absolute and without regard to any connection between prior matters and current matters. Third, section 207(b) prohibits a former government lawyer, for a period of two years, from acting for a client before the former employing agency or any other federal agency or court in any matter "actually pending under his official responsibility" [3] within a period of one year prior to leaving government service. The prohibition applies to employees of all grades [4] and applies regardless of the lack of any direct contact between the lawyer and the matter.[5]

Section 207 and the regulations under it are technical and detailed and obviously require careful study. Some of the statute's prohibitions plainly are not matched in any of the lawyer codes. As broad as some of the disqualifications are, they are not universal. For example, by its own terms, section 207 generally applies only if the United States "is a party or has a direct and substantial interest" in the private practice matter in which the former government lawyer is proceeding. In any other kind of private practice representation the statute, although not necessarily the professional codes, is inapplicable.[6] The federal statute also exempts any appearance by the lawyer in behalf of the United States, so that a federal lawyer who moves from one federal agency to another is unaffected by the statute. Generally the proscribed activities cover only formal or informal appearances.[7] Office consulting and advising with a client is largely unrestricted.

1 Federal courts are also not prevented by an extravagant "inherent powers" concept from being directed by statute in disqualification matters. See § 2.2.5. Cf., e.g., Wajert v. State Ethics Comm'n, 407 A.2d 125, 47 Pa. Cmwlth. 97 (1979), affirmed 491 Pa. 255, 420 A.2d 439 (1980)(state statute barring former judge from representing clients in judge's court for a period of one year after leaving bench unlawfully infringes "exclusive" authority of state supreme court to supervise the conduct of lawyers).

2 18 U.S.C.A. § 207(d).

3 Section 202(b) defines "official responsibility" in a way that includes coholders of authority and persons in executive positions who might otherwise be thought to be insulated by layers of intermediate supervisors: "the direct administrative or operating authority, whether intermediate or final, and either exercisable alone or with others, and either personally or through subordinates, to approve, disapprove, or otherwise direct government action." At a minimum, for example, the definition effectively precludes a former president of the United States from practicing law for two years with respect to any matter pending within a period of one year from the end of the president's tenure in office.

4 The scope of the activities from which the lawyer is disqualified within the two-year period broadens with responsibility. Under 18 U.S.C.A. § 207(b)(i), all employees are prohibited from representing clients in various forms of appearances. Under § 207(b)(ii), senior-ranking lawyers are also prohibited from some advising or consulting with clients on covered matters while physically present in a hearing room or other agency meeting.

5 United States v. Dorfman, 542 F.Supp. 402 (N.D.Ill. 1982).

6 Woods v. Covington County Bank, 537 F.2d 804, 812 n. 9 (5th Cir.1976).

7 Cf. 18 U.S.C.A. §§ 207(a), (b), (c)(all apply only to "formal or informal appearance," assisting a client in such an appearance, or making written or oral communications for a client).

Some prohibitions apply only to appearances before the employee's own agency, and none extends to appearances before state courts or agencies. Certain kinds of former government lawyers are specifically exempted from the one-year no-contact bar for senior officials; the exempted group includes state and local government employees and certain college academics.[8] By regulation, separate departments or bureaus within a large agency may be designated as separate agencies for purposes of the one-year no-contact ban.[9]

The statutory scheme arguably opens up unintended loopholes. A prominent possible candidate exempts former employees who give in-house assistance to a private client.[10] Another is an implicit exemption for communications with agencies or officials that do not have any "intent to influence." [11] That might permit invocation of one of the most timeworn lobbying canards, the call or letter to a policy maker, not to influence, but solely to discuss "procedural" arrangements and to express only a general concern that the matter is "properly" handled.[12]

Conflict Remedies

The professional regulations and statutes on former-government-lawyer conflicts have been extensively discussed and debated in the legal literature, but the regulations very rarely result in a reported case in which a lawyer is disciplined for a violation.[13] Related criminal statutes concerning conflicts of interest have occasionally been applied in prosecutions of lawyers.[14] The rules are most frequently and vigorously enforced through motions in litigation to disqualify a lawyer claimed to be in violation of them.[15] The volume of disqualification litigation has increased remarkably within the past decade. In part that reflects a general increase in utilization of motions to disqualify opposing lawyers and judicial receptivity to them. Part of the increase might reflect a failure on the part of former government lawyers to acquaint themselves with the applicable conflict of interest rules.[16]

WESTLAW REFERENCES

former +s government agency public /s lawyer attorney /p corrupt! (financial business +s interest)

former +s government agency /s lawyer attorney /p confidential! impropriety

"dr 9–101" "ec 9–3"

former +s government agency /s lawyer attorney /p disqualif!

§ 8.10.3 Application of the Former-Government-Lawyer Rules

General

Implementing the conflict of interest prohibitions imposed on a former government lawyer has involved several discrete problems. Examined here are the following questions: (1) who is a "public employee" for the purpose of the special restrictions on former government lawyers; (2) what constitutes a "substantial responsibility" that disables; (3) how is a "matter" defined; (4) what kinds of

[8] 18 U.S.C.A. § 207(d)(2).

[9] 18 U.S.C.A. § 207(e).

[10] 5 C.F.R. §§ 737.5(b)(6), 737.9(b). See also n. 4 supra. See generally Committee for Washington's Riverfront Parks v. Thompson, 451 A.2d 1177, 1187–90 (D.C.1982).

[11] Cf. 18 U.S.C.A. § 207(a); 5 C.F.R. § 737.9(b).

[12] Cf. Committee for Washington's Riverfront Parks v. Thompson, 451 A.2d 1177, 1190, 1191 (D.C.1982).

[13] For rare cases, see Kentucky Bar Ass'n v. Fitzgerald, 652 S.W.2d 77 (Ky.1983)(reprimand to former judge who violated DR 9–101(A)); In re Biederman, 63 N.J. 396, 307 A.2d 595 (1973)(lawyer representing the state seeking disqualification of contractor from bidding on public projects violated DR 9–101(B) when, in later private practice, he represented the contractor seeking reinstatement).

[14] United States v. Nasser, 476 F.2d 1111 (7th Cir.1973); Shaw v. United States, 244 F.2d 930 (9th Cir.1957).

[15] The Supreme Court, quietly, has apparently affirmed the disqualification remedy for a breach of DR 9–101(B) in a side-switching case. See Mississippi v. United States, 451 U.S. 934, 101 S.Ct. 2012, 68 L.Ed.2d 321 (1981)(per curiam)(for description of case, see 49 U.S.L.Wk. 3799 (1981)).

[16] Wall Street J., Oct. 6, 1981, at 1, col. 5 (General Accounting Office poll of seventy-one ex-officials of Treasury Department finds that sixty were insufficiently aware of postemployment restrictions to avoid conflict of interest problems).

"private employment" are covered; (5) to what extent do concerns about "confidentiality" result in disqualification; (6) what role does "consent" of the former government client play; and (7) how may a government employee negotiate for future employment?

(1) *Public Employee*

Nature of Duties

The paradigm candidate for disqualification is a person who formally functioned as a lawyer for a government client or employer. But neither the Code's DR 9–101(B) nor MR 1.11 confines disqualification to situations in which the former government employee functioned as a lawyer. Both instead refer to service as a "public employee" (DR 9–101(B)) or as a "public officer or employee" (MR 1.11(a), (b), (c)). Thus a lawyer serving in a nonlawyer capacity can be as disqualified as if he or she had functioned as a lawyer.[17]

Governmental Nature of Employer or Client

The cases do not strictly limit the identity of the employer to a body that is governmental in all respects. Generally it is enough that the client-employer exercises some part of the public trust, employing powers usually reserved for public bodies.[18] On the other hand, if the lawyer's duties involved legal work for individual clients, such as in a government legal services office, then the case for describing the lawyer as a public employee for conflicts purposes is weaker.[19] The professional rules are transjurisdictional; the state and federal courts freely disqualify in their own courts lawyers who formerly represented other governments.[20]

Adjudicative Officers

Judges and similar adjudicative officers are also public employees, but with duties and relationships that have called forth separate rules in the 1969 Code and the 1983 Model Rules. The Code's DR 9–101(A) provides that a lawyer must not represent a client in a matter upon whose merits the lawyer acted in a judicial capacity.[21] And EC 5–20 suggests a similar standard for a neutral arbitrator or

[17] American Dredging Co. v. City of Philadelphia, 480 Pa. 177, 389 A.2d 568, 574 (1978)(lawyer who served as officer, executive committee member, and board member of city agency at time challenged action was taken cannot in private practice represent a party suing agency over same matter); ABA Formal Op. 342, at 16 (1975). Similarly, the federal conflict of interest statute, 18 U.S.C.A. § 207, draws no distinctions between serving in one role in government and in another in private practice. See, e.g., Shaw v. United States, 244 F.2d 930 (9th Cir.1957) (lawyer who moonlighted as train dispatcher for federally operated railroad convicted for representing as client persons injured in train collision in which he performed dispatch functions).

[18] It was held in Flego v. Philips, Appel & Walden, Inc., 514 F.Supp. 1178, 1180–82 (D.N.J.1981), that a lawyer's tenure as a compliance attorney with the American Stock Exchange was as a "public employee" on the grounds that the exchange fulfilled a "partnership" role in policing compliance along with the federal Securities Exchange Commission and exercised extraordinary disciplinary powers over exchange members. Handelman v. Weiss, 368 F.Supp. 258, 262–64 (S.D.N.Y.1973), held that a lawyer for the Securities Investor Protection Corporation (SIPC) was a "public employee" for the purposes of DR 9–101(B). The SIPC was created by Congress, and its governing board is appointed by the federal government, although it is not a federal agency.

[19] Woods v. Covington County Bank, 537 F.2d 804 (5th Cir.1976)(reserve officer of the Navy Judge Advocate General Corps was not a former public employee for DR 9–101(B) purposes because his primary duty consisted of representing private individuals with respect to their individual rights, and not the government); Coles, Manter & Watson v. Denver Dist. Court, 177 Colo. 210, 493 P.2d 374, 375 (1972)(lawyer employed in public defender office can represent same client in private practice for fee). But see Mendicino v. Whitchurch, 565 P.2d 460, 475–76 (1977)(lawyer formerly employed in legal aid office could not continue to represent in private practice a legal aid client on same matter); N.Y. St. Ethics Op. 534 (1981), 53 N.Y.St.B.J. 448 (1981)(same).

[20] Traylor v. City of Amarillo, 335 F.Supp. 423 (N.D. Tex.1971)(lawyer disqualified in federal court suit that challenged constitutional validity of ordinance he had defended as city attorney); Homestake Mining Co. v. Board of Environmental Protection, 289 N.W.2d 561, 563 (S.D.1980)(possible disqualification of former federal Environmental Protection Agency lawyer from state court representation).

[21] A judge who retires from the bench to return to private practice is clearly not disqualified from practicing before his or her former colleagues in all cases. See UAW v. National Caucus for Labor Comms., 466 F.Supp. 564, 571 (S.D.N.Y.1979), affirmed 607 F.2d 996 (2d Cir. 1979)(per curiam), cert.denied 444 U.S. 839, 100 S.Ct. 77,

mediator.[22] Model Rule 1.12(a) broadly prohibits any person who acted in a matter in the role of judge or other adjudicative officer,[23] an arbitrator, or law clerk from representing a client in connection with the same matter.[24] The conflict can be cured by consent of all interested parties to the original proceeding after disclosure. An imputed-disqualification rule disqualifies all lawyers in the primarily disqualified lawyer's firm but can be cured by screening the lawyer and giving prompt written notice to the "appropriate tribunal." [25] Stricter rules might be applicable by force of other law. In the case of judicial law clerks, for example, disqualification might extend to any case pending in the court during the clerk's tenure, whether or not the clerk had any personal and substantial participation in the case.[26]

Arbitrators

The reason for the special strictures for adjudicative officers is that the performance of their decison-making function should be entirely neutral.[27] Some arbitrators, however, are appointed with no pretense that they are neutral. Model Rule 1.12(d) accordingly provides that a partisan arbitrator in a multimember arbitration panel who is a lawyer can continue to represent the party whose partisan he or she is. A fortiori, the partisan arbitrator should also be able to represent other clients who were not parties to the arbitration in a matter similar to, or the same as, that involved in the arbitration, so long as their interests do not conflict with those of the originally represented party.[28]

(2) *Substantial Responsibility*

General

The Code and the Model Rules both attempt to differentiate in various ways between matters in which the lawyer played a significant part and those in which the lawyer was not personally concerned. Simply working in the same office building in which a matter is being handled by others clearly does not disqualify. At the other extreme, a situation in which the government lawyer is one of the principal actors is clearly covered.[29] The difficult cases are those in which the lawyer's contact with a case was arguably perfunctory or peripheral or in which the lawyer only theoretically had supervisory responsibility without any personal contact with the matter. Those difficult cases require an elaboration of what DR 9–101(B) means by its reference to a

62 L.Ed.2d 51 (1979). And a former clerk to a judge is not forever barred from practicing as a lawyer before the judge in cases that were not pending during his or her tenure as clerk. Fredonia Broadcasting Corp. v. RCA Corp., 569 F.2d 251, 256 (5th Cir.), cert.denied 439 U.S. 859, 99 S.Ct. 177, 58 L.Ed.2d 167 (1978).

22 See also Fredonia Broadcasting Corp. v. RCA Corp., supra at 255 ("erroneous assumption" for trial judge to think that absence of explicit rule permitted his former law clerk to participate as lawyer in retrial of case originally tried during clerk's term of service; because of clerk's participation as counsel, new trial ordered and trial judge ordered recused).

23 MR 1.12 comment defines "adjudicative officer" to include "judges pro tempore, referees, special masters, hearing officers and other parajudicial officers." The first and last designations clearly include a retired judge recalled to active service.

24 A lawyer who served as a mediator is also disqualified from representing any party to the mediation. See generally § 8.7.

25 On screening generally, see § 7.6.4. In the case of an arbitrator, the "appropriate tribunal" for notice would presumably be an arbitration association, if that was the source of the appointment, or the parties to the arbitration if arbitration was arranged on an ad hoc basis.

26 U.S.Sup.Ct.R. 7 (no judicial law clerk or other former Court employee shall participate "by way of any form of professional consultation or assistance, in any case before this Court until two years have elapsed after such separation" or at any time participate in any way in a case pending before the Court during the employee's tenure); D.C.Cir.R. 4 (no former law clerk or other court employee shall practice as lawyer in any case pending during tenure).

27 MR 1.12 comment, at 81–82 (Proposed Final Draft, May 30, 1981); ABA Code of Judicial Conduct Canon 3.

28 Cf. Society for Good Will to Retarded Children, Inc. v. Carey, 466 F.Supp. 722, 728–29 (E.D.N.Y.1979). Although MR 1.12(a) does not unequivocally provide such an exception for the partisan arbitrator, no apparent policy reason bars such an interpretation.

29 Price v. Admiral Ins. Co., 481 F.Supp. 374, 376 (E.D. Pa.1979)(assistant United States attorney had file, conferred with government investigators, and interrogated persons who were now opposing parties in litigation on same suspicious fire).

matter in which the lawyer "participated personally and substantially." [30]

Formal versus Operational Responsibility

Lawyering for a government agency can be similar to other kinds of work in an organization. Paper is sometimes shuffled with little operational significance. A lawyer in government service might be one of several persons routinely "copied" with correspondence; the lawyer's initials might be required on an insignificant document, or the lawyer's name might be used as one among many or in a very routine fashion. If a government lawyer's involvement with a matter is limited to such perfunctory or peripheral contact, there is obviously less reason for disqualifying the lawyer later in private practice.

The strength of the argument for disqualification might be a function of the proximity or distance between the matters in the public and private employments. A lawyer who had merely an "on the brief" relationship to a matter that was litigated while the lawyer was in government practice stands in rather different situations in later private practice, depending on whether the private practice client is involved in the same litigation or in litigation more tangentially related to the previous government work and on whether the lawyer's position is adverse to or congruent with the lawyer's position in government practice.

Does a government lawyer have "substantial" relationship to a matter if the lawyer's only role in it is supervisory? The use of the word "responsibility" in the Code and the use of the term "personally" in MR 1.11(a) might suggest that the former would include merely supervisory roles but the latter not. In fact, cases under the Code have also rejected a needlessly broad sweep that might ensnare all possible supervisors on the client agency's organization chart.

The question of formal responsibility covers a variety of instances, some of which are arguably distinct from others. At one extreme, consider a government lawyer whose formal, supervisory responsibility includes all matters handled within a large government law office. Such a responsibility might be in the job description of a general counsel of a law department with scores, even hundreds, of lawyers working in it. For some purposes of public policy, it might be fitting to conclude that the lawyer has political "responsibility" of a weighty kind to account for every bit of legal business that transpires within the office. But such a global stretch would be needlessly far-reaching for conflicts purposes. Courts have generally rejected the notion that every contact within a government office should be imputed, either on access-to-information or on supervisory grounds, to other lawyers within the government office.[31]

At the other extreme from purely formal supervision are instances in which a lawyer actively exercises supervisory responsibilities

[30] The "personally and substantially" phrase in MR 1.11(a) is a quotation from the federal conflict of interest statute and its predecessors. 18 U.S.C.A. § 207(a)(3). See the suppressed Legal Background Note to MR 1.11, at 78 (Proposed Final Draft, May 30, 1981). In United States v. Nasser, 476 F.2d 1111, 1115 (7th Cir.1973), the court rejected a lawyer's challenge to the constitutionality of the word "substantially" that is used in the federal conflict of interest law to describe the level of participation. The challenge was rejected because the "statute proscribes perhaps as precisely as possible an unethical practice that can manifest itself in infinite forms."

[31] UAW v. National Caucus of Labor Committees, 466 F.Supp. 564, 570–71 (S.D.N.Y.1979), affirmed 607 F.2d 996 (2d Cir.1979)(per curiam), cert.denied 444 U.S. 839, 100 S.Ct. 77, 62 L.Ed.2d 51 (1979); United States v. Standard Oil Co., 136 F.Supp. 345, 359 (S.D.N.Y.1955); ABA Formal Op. 342, at 9 (1975). Those authorities should be considered to have rejected the "vertical imputation" theory of disqualification, which would reach in ascending hierarchical lines within a government law office. Cf. Kaufman, The Former Government Attorney and the Canons of Professional Ethics, 70 Harv.L.Rev. 657, 666 (1957).

New Jersey courts at one time followed a much more inclusive rule. E.g., State v. Morelli, 152 N.J.Super. 67, 377 A.2d 774 (1977), and authorities cited (automatic disqualification for every member of prosecutor staff regardless of supervisory rank or lack of actual contact with case). The rule has now been narrowed for nonsupervisory lawyers. In re Advisory Opinion No. 361, 77 N.J. 199, 390 A.2d 118, 120–21 (1978)(prosecutor disqualified only if lawyer exercised supervisory responsibility in a broad sense or if nonsupervisory lawyer actually learned information about a matter).

in a particular matter. Those responsibilities can bring the lawyer into direct contact with confidential government information or place the lawyer in a position in which to influence or direct the way in which the legal matter is handled by supervised lawyers. The disqualification rules are clearly applicable in such a case.

Because responsibility is at least in part a matter of arrangements within a governmental law office, it might be possible for a lawyer in the waning months of a government appointment to achieve greater flexibility in private practice by recusing himself or herself from substantial-responsibility participation in new matters that might be the subject of the private practice representation of the lawyer or the lawyer's firm.[32] The arrangement becomes less effective the more powerful the lawyer's official position is, because of the continuing danger of subtle and undetectable influence.[33]

(3) *Matter*

Indeterminacy of "Matter"

Lawyers habitually speak of a client's "matter" when referring to the work being done for a client. The term has the same universal application in law as it does in physics, and with as little precision. A matter that a lawyer is working on is the general collection of facts, issues, blind alleys, options exercised and options that might be considered later, and arguments that are made and those that are held in reserve.[34] It includes things both confidential and public. The thrust of the word is more in the direction of universality than of delimitation. Its comforting vagueness and generality probably explain why "matter" is the term employed in the Canons,[35] the 1969 Code,[36] the 1983 Model Rules,[37] and the federal conflict of interest statute [38] to define the comparative elements in government service and private practice that must not be the same.

Rule Making as a Matter

To what extent is rule making a matter? The federal statute, as well as both MR 1.11(d)(1) and the District of Columbia Code that echo it, contain a special definition of "matter" that, in effect, distinguishes between

[32] Kessenich v. Commodity Futures Trading Comm'n, 684 F.2d 88, 97 (D.C.Cir.1982); Ah Ju Steel Co. v. Armco, Inc., 680 F.2d 751 (C.C.P.A.1982).

[33] Cf. United States v. Dorfman, 542 F.Supp. 402, 408–09 (N.D.Ill.1982)(self-recusal not effective to prevent application of federal statutory two-year restriction on former United States attorney with respect to a matter within his "official responsibility"). But cf. City of Hoquiam v. Public Employment Relations Comm'n, 97 Wn. 2d 481, 646 P.2d 129, 134 (1982)(private practitioner, who was also chairman of public board, who disqualified herself from any participation in matters in which her firm represented party had no "substantial responsibility").

[34] Clearly too fine a line was drawn in United States v. Smith, 653 F.2d 126 (4th Cir.1981). An assistant United States attorney had successfully prosecuted Smith for running a gambling enterprise. The lawyer nogotiated a plea bargain that placed Smith on probation for five years. During probation Smith was again charged with illegal gambling, although the occurrence was unrelated to the earlier charge. He hired the same former United States attorney to defend him on the new charges. The lawyer represented to the court that he would not represent Smith in any probation revocation hearing relating to the earlier charge. On that basis, the court held that there was no violation of DR 9–101(B), in effect permitting the former government lawyer to reshape the matter involved in the second, private practice representation by stipulating an artificially narrow scope for it. It seems extremely doubtful that such line-drawing well serves the policies behind disqualification, particularly the policies concerned with confidentiality.

[35] Canon 36.

[36] DR 9–101(B).

[37] MR 1.11(a). See also MR 1.11(d):

As used in this rule, the term "matter" includes:

(1) Any judicial or other proceeding, application, request for a ruling of other determination, contract, claims, controversy, investigation, charge, accusation, arrest or other particular matter involving a specific party or parties; and

(2) Any other matter covered by the conflict of interest rules of the appropriate government agency.

That language tracks in relevant part the language of the federal conflict of interest statute (18 U.S.C.A. § 207(a)(2)). Exactly the same language is also employed in the 1982 District of Columbia rule. D.C. Code of Professional Responsibility, Definitions ("Matter"), in "Revolving Door," 445 A.2d 615, 618 (D.C.1982).

[38] 18 U.S.C.A. § 207(a)(2): "any judicial or other proceeding, application, request for a ruling or other determination, contract, claim, controversy, investigation, charge, accusation, arrest, or other particular matter involving a specific party or parties."

rule making and adjudication.[39] Adjudication is covered by "matter," while rule making apparently is not. As far as each provision is specifically concerned, then, a government lawyer could be given full responsibility for drafting a regulation and then in private practice could give advice on its proper construction, could file cases based on the rule, and could even attack its validity. Yet at least one case has held that a lawyer who does such government drafting is prohibited from switching sides in private practice and attacking the validity of his or her own work.[40] Nonetheless, the federal statute clearly means to overlook such treachery, at least for the purposes of criminal sanctions.[41]

Whether that is also the ultimate position of the Model Rules depends upon the answer to the question whether a former government lawyer's conflicts of interest are covered only by MR 1.11 or whether other conflict rules also apply.[42] The other Model Rule in point that generally governs former-client conflicts, MR 1.9, seems to be clearly inconsistent with attacking a rule that a lawyer drafted for a former client (§ 7.4.3(b)). It is also true that confidential information is sometimes involved in rulemaking,[43] thus involving the confidentiality principles of both MR 1.9 and, more generally, MR 1.6. In view of the relevance of those policies to some instances of rule making and in view of the settled rule opposing such conflicts under prior law, MR 1.11 should not be read as the only rule bearing on the question.[44]

That analysis does not require that rule making always be considered a "matter" in both government and private practice. For example, a private practitioner who is involved as such in governmental rule making typically will have contact with issues at a high level of generality unaffected by confidential governmental information and would have little opportunity to distort the rule.[45] But a government lawyer's influence on the same rule making process might be a great deal more powerful, particularly if the lawyer plays a major role in drafting or decision making. It would be an unusual case in which confidential government information could permissibly be employed in rule making so that normally the only significant interest is that of guarding against treacherous drafting. A test worth considering is one that prohibits a government lawyer ever from attacking his or her own work, but leaves the lawyer free to advise others about it and to invoke it in litigation, including litigation which seeks to limit it through interpretation.[46]

"Same Facts" Test

A test for "matter" that is favored by some authorities is the "same facts" or "same

[39] That distinction results from inclusion of the limiting phrase "involving a specific party or parties" in each of those regulations at the conclusion of the specification of kinds of matters covered.

[40] Traylor v. City of Amarillo, 335 F.Supp. 423 (N.D. Tex.1971).

[41] At the time the 1979 Ethics in Government Act was considered, a member of Congress objected to the exclusion of rule-making activities. See Separate Views of Congressman Seiberling, H.Rep.No. 115, 96th Cong., 1st Sess. 13, reprinted in 1979 U.S. Code Cong. & Ad. News 328, 337. The narrowing change resulted from persistent criticism of the breadth of the original 1978 enactment.

[42] See supra 463–64.

[43] See Brown v. District of Columbia Bd. of Zoning, 413 A.2d 1276, 1283 (D.C.1980); Note, Business as Usual: The Former Government Attorney and ABA Disciplinary Rule 5–105(D), 28 Hastings L.J. 1537, 1564–65 (1977).

[44] That was the result urged by the Legal Background note of an earlier version of the Model Rules. See MR 1.11, at 78 (Proposed Final Draft, May 30, 1981). But the note has been suppressed (see Model Rules, Scope (last paragraph) and the version of MR 1.11 that the note commented upon contained no definition of "matter."

[45] See Morgan, Appropriate Limits on Participation by a Former Agency Official in Matters Before an Agency, 1980 Duke L.J. 1, 58. Professor Morgan has been apparently miscited for the proposition, which he does not advance, that a *government* lawyer's participation will be similarly limited. See MR 1.11 Legal Background Note, at 78 (Proposed Final Draft, May 30, 1981).

[46] With one important exception, that is essentially the result reached with respect to rulemaking by ABA Formal Op. 342, at 6–7 (1975), quoted in the following note. The definitional approach of the opinion is defectively abstracted from relevant policy, however, and it fails to note the problem of attacking one's own work and the common-law authority disapproving such attacks.

transaction" test.[47] The test is useful for inclusive purposes,[48] but seems to stop short on government work that is transformational. A lawyer who drafts a new regulation for a government employer deals with no discrete "parties," "transactions," and "situations."[49] Nonetheless, as discussed immediately above, a lawyer who does such drafting is rightly prohibited from switching sides in private practice and attacking the validity of the regulation. As is generally the case in law, "tests" are useful but their value is limited. The small vessel of words that they necessarily employ is too fragile and incomplete to contain the full measure of a concept. A richer set of ideas is required if the conflict rules are to hew very closely to their underlying policies. Occasionally, of course, verbal shortcuts are appropriate, even if at the expense of some sensible applications, but only if this gains a marked increase in clarity and predictability. Such an increase certainly is not gained by using the "same facts" approach which is full of quizzical applications.

(4) *Private Employment*

The strict rules for conflicts of former government lawyers apply to a lawyer's move to "private employment" (DR 9–101(B)) in which a "private client" (MR 1.11(a)) is represented. The concepts have generally not been given a restricted interpretation. Employment obviously includes more than employer-employee relationships such as house counsel. It even includes representations in which a lawyer in private practice charges no fee.[50]

To what extent does "private" employment include subsequent legal representation of a governmental client? Courts have applied the strict former-government-lawyer conflicts rules when a lawyer represented another governmental body in a private practice setting.[51] A more difficult question is whether "private" employment should include representing an-

[47] General Motors Corp. v. City of New York, 501 F.2d 639, 651 (2d Cir.1974)(examination of pleadings in case which former government lawyer handled and private practice pleading he later framed shows monopolization by same defendant of same product line in same geographic market); Flego v. Philips, Appel & Walden, Inc., 514 F.Supp. 1178, 1182–83 (D.N.J.1981)(inspection of work done in government investigation of same brokerage firm and pleadings in subsequent suit by former government lawyer against same defendant shows different accounts, account executives, and investors).

ABA Formal Op. 342, at 6 (1975): "Although a precise definition of 'matter' as used in the Disciplinary Rule is difficult to formulate, the term seems to contemplate a discrete and isolatable transaction or set of transactions between identifiable parties. Perhaps the scope of the term 'matter' may be indicated by examples. The same lawsuit or litigation is the same matter. The same issue of fact involving the same parties and the same situation or conduct is the same matter. By contrast, work as a government employee in drafting, enforcing or interpreting government or agency procedures, regulations, or laws, or in briefing abstract principles of law, does not disqualify the lawyer under DR 9–101(B) from subsequent private employment involving the same regulations, procedures, or points of law; the same 'matter' is not involved because there is lacking the discrete, identifiable transactions or conduct involving a particular situation and specific parties." (Footnote omitted.)

[48] The Fifth Circuit in United States v. Trafficante, 328 F.2d 117 (5th Cir.1964), held under Canon 36 and the federal conflict of interest statute that a lawyer in the office of regional counsel of the Internal Revenue Service who negotiated stipulated settlements with Trafficante in the Tax Court could not thereafter represent Trafficante in private practice in connection with the government's attempts to foreclose liens for those claims among others. The court rejected the lawyer's claim that disqualification should be ordered only if precisely the same legal issues were involved in each representation (328 F.2d at 119) or if he acquired knowledge during the government representation that could be used adversely to the government (328 F.2d at 120).

The definition of "matter" can also be influenced by developments in the subsequent litigation in which the question of disqualification arises. For example, in State of Illinois v. Borg, Inc., 553 F.Supp. 178 (N.D.Ill.1982), a government lawyer had investigated bid-rigging activities in downstate Illinois. But in his later private practice representation of a client charged with bid-rigging in the Chicago area, the lawyer argued that the downstate investigation itself had revealed Chicago-area practices and thus that the statute of limitations had then begun to run. Thus, although arguably the "matter" of the government service related only to a distant area of the state, the statute of limitations defense itself made it clear that the same "matter" was involved in both representations. 553 F.Supp. at 181–82.

[49] But cf. ABA Formal Op. 342, supra note 47.

[50] Telos, Inc. v. Hawaiian Tel. Co., 397 F.Supp. 1314, 1317 (D. Hawaii 1975); Flushing Nat'l Bank v. Municipal Assistance Corp., 90 Misc.2d 204, 397 N.Y.S.2d 662, 668 (1977).

[51] General Motors Corp. v. City of New York, 501 F.2d 639 (2d Cir.1974)(former Justice Department lawyer who had participated in filing government's bus monopoly suit against manufacturer is disqualified, after resuming private practice, from representing city in its damage suit based on same monopoly).

other governmental body in a full-time and salaried staff position in another government.

The comment to MR 1.11 asserts that disqualification should result if a lawyer moves from one government to another, such as from city government to a federal agency. Its language might even be read to subject a lawyer moving from one agency to another in the *same* government to the full panoply of conflict rules.[52] Beyond subsequent adverse representations (to which perhaps the comment's language was alone meant to be directed), it is difficult to imagine why a congruent representation in two different governmental bodies or two agencies in the same government should be generally objectionable. Surely the lure of lucre in any government position will corrupt no one.[53] The threat to the former client's confidential information seems fully dealt with by the adverse representation rules. And the objection that a private practice client should not be unfairly advantaged by the superior resources of government in gathering facts will not ordinarily apply to other government agencies or even to other governments within the federal system.

(5) *Confidential Government Information*

The phrase "substantial responsibility" that is used in DR 9–102(B) to describe the government lawyer's role seems to refer to concepts of managerial control, official duty, and the like. Does it also extend to situations in which a government lawyer comes into possession of confidential government information but has no real "responsibility" for the representation? Suppose, for example, that a lawyer simply becomes exposed to confidential information through office gossip or through necessarily overhearing the information in a crowded office. Taken together with application of the confidentiality requirement of MR 1.6 to lawyers who represent governmental clients,[54] MR 1.11 clearly prohibits a subsequent adverse representation in the case of a lawyer's even casual, if substantial, encounter with confidential information in government service.[55]

The question of casually learned information is somewhat more problematical under the Code. While the language of DR 9–102(B) might be ambiguous, cases decided under it generally agree as a policy matter that protecting a governmental client's confidential information can be an important reason for disqualifying a former government lawyer.[56] If a lawyer was in a position in government service to learn confidential information about a matter, he or she may not represent a private practice client in a substantially related matter.[57] As in other former-client situations, so here the purpose of invoking the substantial-relationship standard is to avoid the need for the former client to reveal confidential information in order to protect it. The cases go somewhat further. If a government lawyer's activities and responsibilities result in constant contact with information about most cases of a particular kind in an office, the lawyer is disqualified in all such cases; courts do not require proof that a spe-

52 MR 1.11, comment (fourth paragraph):

> "When the client is an agency of one government, that agency should be treated as a private client for purposes of this Rule if the lawyer thereafter represents an agency of another government, as when a lawyer represents a city and subsequently is employed by a federal agency."

53 Cf. ABA Formal Op. 342, at 6 (1975): "[The danger guarded against by DR 9–101(B)] is that a lawyer may attempt to derive undue financial benefit from fees in connection with subsequent employment, and not that he may change from one salaried government position to another. The balancing consideration . . . is that government agencies should not be unduly hampered in recruiting lawyers employed by other governmental bodies." (Footnote omitted).

54 See § 6.5.6.

55 No similar question arises under MR 1.11(a) because that rule speaks of a lawyer who has "participated" personally and substantially in a matter.

56 Protection of confidential governmental information was articulated as a policy reason for the disqualification rule in DR 9–101(B) in ABA Formal Op. 342, at 3–4 (1975), cited with approval in Kessenich v. Commodity Futures Trading Comm'n, 684 F.2d 88, 97 (D.C.Cir.1982).

57 United States v. Ostrer, 597 F.2d 337 (2d Cir.1979); UAW v. National Caucus of Labor Committees, 466 F.Supp. 564, 568 (S.D.N.Y.1979), affirmed 607 F.2d 996 (2d Cir.1979)(per curiam), cert.denied 444 U.S. 839, 100 S.Ct. 77, 62 L.Ed.2d 51 (1979); Osborn v. District Court, 619 P.2d 41, 45 (Colo.1980).

cific matter pending in the office actually came within the lawyer's purview.[58]

Sensibly, courts have assessed the confidential nature of the government's information at the time that the question is raised in the lawyer's private practice. If the information has been made fully available to the lawyer's private practice adversary and the lawyer is not appearing adversely to a former government client, the lawyer is not disqualified.[59]

Congruent Use of Confidential Information

If a lawyer knows confidential information gained while representing a former government client, may the lawyer use it against an adversary other than the former government employer? In a purely private-practice setting, that would not be objectionable unless the confidential information were used in some way adverse to the former client's interests. But here an additional objection has been made on the ground of fairness. The confidential information that is known to the former government lawyer is not simply unknown to the adversary, it is unknowable—at least in cases in which the information remains confidential. For that reason, among others, courts in such situations have prohibited even congruent-interest representations against private practice adversaries.[60]

Model Rule 1.11(b) devotes an entire subsection to prohibiting such a representation.[61] But Model Rule 1.11(b) only applies if the information is "material"—presumably meaning both relevant and important. It would therefore not apply if no issue likely to be raised in a later representation relates to the confidential information. The cases under the Code generally agree.[62]

Nonevidentiary Information

The definition of confidential information also must not be carried too far in another

[58] Taxpayers, Homeowners & Tenants Protective Ass'n v. Haber, 634 F.2d 182 (5th Cir.1981); United States v. Miller, 624 F.2d 1198 (3d Cir.1980). That "constant access" standard probably goes beyond, although it certainly is at least coterminous with, the old definitions implicit in the reference in Canon 36 to matters that the government lawyer had "investigated" or "passed upon." See Kaufman, The Former Government Attorney and the Canons of Professional Ethics, 70 Harv.L.Rev. 657, 664 (1957). But cf. Woods v. Covington County Bank, 537 F.2d 804, 812, n.10 (5th Cir.1976)(Canon 36 standard of "investigated or passed upon" "has been superseded by the 'substantial responsibility' test of EC 9–3 and DR 9–101(B)"). The statement in Ah Ju Steel Co. v. Armco, Inc., 680 F.2d 751, 754 (C.C.P.A.1982), reversing 520 F.Supp. 1220 (Ct.Int'l Trade 1981), that the acquisition of confidential information is irrelevant to the issue of whether the lawyer had substantial responsibility for a matter, should be rejected. The court rescued itself from serious error by noting that access to confidential information is "indirectly" involved because of the possibility that it might create an appearance of impropriety, a discredited alternative method of analysis in conflicts cases. The court also concluded that any confidential information that the former government lawyer might have possessed was irrelevant to any remaining issue in the representation.

[59] Armstrong v. McAlpin, 625 F.2d 433, 445 (2d Cir. 1980)(en banc), vacated for lack of jurisdiction 449 U.S. 1106, 101 S.Ct. 911, 66 L.Ed.2d 835 (1981)(private practice client is not in position to make unfair use of confidential government information, inter alia, because government employer had turned entire investigation file over to lawyer's present firm and former government lawyer was screened); Flego v. Philips, Appel & Walden, Inc., 514 F.Supp. 1178, 1183 (D.N.J.1981)(full transcripts of all of former government lawyer's interviews available to opposing parties).

[60] General Motors Corp. v. City of New York, 501 F.2d 639 (2d Cir.1974); Allied Realty, Inc. v. Exchange Nat'l Bank, 408 F.2d 1099, 1102 (8th Cir.1969), cert.denied 396 U.S. 823, 90 S.Ct. 64, 24 L.Ed.2d 73 (1969). See generally § 8.10.1.

[61] Rule 1.1(b) is limited to representations in private practice that are adverse to the person about whom the lawyer learned confidential information in government practice. The rule prevents a government lawyer from abusing governmental investigative techniques only to the extent that the information discovered is confidential. It apparently extends to situations in which the lawyer is exploiting confidential information about third parties whose interests are adverse even if they are not litigants.

[62] See Control Data Corp. v. IBM Corp., 318 F.Supp. 145, 147 (D.Minn.1970)(information obtained by former government antitrust lawyer in negotiations against same adversary 15 years earlier no longer of value). Cf. Ah Ju Steel Co. v. Armco, Inc., 680 F.2d 751, 754 (C.C. P.A.1982)(confidential information irrelevant to review of agency action which was based on administrative record); Committee for Washington's Riverfront Parks v. Thompson, 451 A.2d 1177, 1192 (D.C.1982)(equal access to contents of public hearings). Neither *Ah Ju Steel* nor *Riverfront Parks* satisfactorily considers, however, whether all relevant information gained by the lawyer in government employment was equally accessible to the lawyer's present adversary.

important direction. Some things that a former government lawyer will have learned are not readily accessible to anyone outside the agency, but should not be disqualifying. Those involve the advantage of general familiarity with the working of a government agency and expertise in the law applicable to its functions. One of the most valuable things that a former government lawyer might carry away from a government agency is a personal copy of the agency's direct-dial telephone directory. To prevent a former government lawyer from exploiting such advantages in private practice would both effectively disbar the lawyer from too many areas of private practice and unfairly burden former government lawyers as compared to other lawyers who have gained their expertise in nondisabling ways, such as by appearing against the interests of the government agency.

(6) *Government Client Consent*

Consent of a former government client does not cure a former government lawyer's disabilities under Canon 36 and DR 9–101(B). At least no explicit provision for consent appears in either. Under the Model Rules, consent of the former government employer will cure one sort of conflict, but not a second. First, MR 1.11(a) prohibits a lawyer from representing a private client in a matter in which the lawyer "participated personally and substantially" as a government employee, but recognizes an exception if "the appropriate government agency consents after consultation."[63] Neither the text of MR 1.11(a) nor its comment draws any distinction between adverse and congruent representations as far as the effectiveness of a government client's consent is concerned. It should be noted, however, that courts that rely heavily on the "appearance of impropriety" standard for disqualification sometimes assert that the government's consent cannot bind the court.[64]

Second, for reasons that are not apparent, the primary conflict created by MR 1.11(b) because of the possible use of "confidential government information" is not consentable. The reason is not at all apparent and the failure to mention consent might have been inadvertent.[65] The statement in the comment to MR 1.11 that the rule prevents unfair advantage accruing to a private client by reason of the lawyer's former access to confidential information about the adversary suggests no reason why the government agency, or possibly the adversary,[66] should not have the power to consent to such use. Presumably

[63] The comment to Rule 1.11(a) makes it clear that consent will only avail if no statute or regulation circumscribes it. Several federal agencies have promulgated "clearance" regulations that limit the situations in which consent will be given.

The "Terminology" section of the Model Rules defines "consultation" as "communication of information reasonably sufficient to permit the client to appreciate the significance of the matter in question." Because the government will be a former client in the situations under consideration here, and likely will be represented by counsel, the former lawyer's "consultation" would hardly be the sort of confidential and elaborate discussion contemplated in those different situations in which a present client's consent to a conflicting representation is sought. Cf. also MR 4.2 (communicating with another party represented by a lawyer). Indeed, it is unclear why the Model Rule requires any sort of consultation, instead of mere "notice."

[64] In re Asbestos Cases, 514 F.Supp. 914, 920 (E.D.Va. 1981)(en banc), reversed sub nom. Greitzer & Locke v. Johns-Manville Corp., 710 F.2d 127 (4th Cir.1982), cert. denied 459 U.S. 1010, 103 S.Ct. 364, 74 L.Ed.2d 400 (1982); Kesselhaut v. United States, 214 Ct.Cl.124, 555 F.2d 791, 794 (1977)(dictum)(imputed disqualification screening case).

[65] The inadvertence notion is compromised, however, by the fact that the rule goes on at some length to provide for waiver by screening in order to avoid what otherwise would be the imputed disqualification of the former government lawyer's entire firm. Quite anomalously, however, the notice of screening required by MR 1.11(b) is to be sent, not to the former government client, but to the adverse party. To provide in the same rule for waiver of secondary disqualification without even notifying the former client but to reject consent to the primary disqualification (if that was intended) is curious. If the reason for requiring notice only to the adversary is that the former government client is not at all concerned with an MR 1.11(b) conflict, then why is no provision made for consent by the adverse party?

[66] Note that MR 1.11(b) also does not provide for consent to the representation by the opposing party in litigation—the party who presumably would be burdened by the former government lawyer's access to government information. The failure to object, of course, would waive the point for procedural purposes. But MR 1.11(b) is, first of all, a disciplinary rule. At least theoretically, a lawyer would still remain susceptible to discipline even if the opposing party waived the objection or even if the party consented.

the lawyer could proceed even under the present wording of MR 1.11(b) if the government agency reclassified the information as non-confidential. Then the lawyer's client would enjoy no advantage not equally available to every person.

The problem raised by the absence of a provision for consent in MR 1.11(b) raises an important issue of policy. It is not incredible that the government in fact might consent—would even be delighted—if a former government lawyer used information gathered during government service to aid a private practice client. For example, in Woods v. Covington County Bank,[67] returning prisoners of war had invested and lost their considerable back pay in a scheme that had been investigated by federal agencies for fraud. Lawyer Nichols was called from his private practice into a five-day pro bono tour as an active reservist in the Navy Judge Advocate General Corps in order to participate in the investigation. The trial court held that Nichols' tour of duty disqualified him under DR 9–101(B) from continuing to represent in his private practice one Woods, who had contacted Nichols at his firm about filing a fraud recovery suit. The Fifth Circuit reversed. The court concluded that Nichols had not resorted to any governmental investigation technique or source of information that would have been closed to a private practitioner. Furthermore, it was clearly not improper for the government to take the position that justice was on one side in a dispute in which the government had an interest. Thus, any assistance supplied to Nichols' clients through his Navy connections was not unfair to his clients' adversaries.[68] Even if Nichols had employed confidential government information or employed fact-gathering techniques available only to government lawyers, it is difficult to see why the government's consent should not fully authorize those advantages so long as no other legal rule prohibited it.

As with other applications of Rule 1.11, there is one reading of it that would produce a result similar to the court's in the *Woods* case. As previously discussed,[69] the interrelationship between Rule 1.11 and other conflict rules is uncertain. If other rules apply, then the former government client's consent is fully availing under MR 1.6, the general rule on confidential client information, which explicitly allows for consent.

The only reason of policy to resist that conclusion here is the possibility of corruption. The notion underlying much of the former government lawyer rules, it will be recalled, is solicitude for a client—here the government—that is particularly vulnerable to corruption and manipulation against the public interest. It might be objected, in this vein, that the former government lawyer might rely upon cronies still in the agency to grant consent corruptly. Such concerns are fed by occasional reported instances of cronyism.[70] But there seems little reason to carry suspiciousness about present government lawyers to such extremes that they are always imagined vulnerable to the importunings of a former colleague. A somewhat different issue is presented when consent for the purpose of MR 1.11(a) is negotiated while the lawyer is still in government service. Here courts might rightly show special caution.[71]

(7) *Negotiating Employment*

A lawyer's movement from government employment to private practice can be accompanied by transitional conflicts problems if the lawyer's prospective employer is interested in a matter pending before the lawyer's agency. The Canons and the Code did not deal with the problem. The Model Rules in MR 1.11(c)

[67] 537 F.2d 804 (5th Cir.1976).

[68] 537 F.2d at 818.

[69] Supra at 463–64.

[70] CACI, Inc. v. United States, 719 F.2d 1567 (Fed.Cir. 1983)(Justice Department award of contract to company run by former department official who maintained professional and personal relationships with several continuing members of department voided on conflict-of-interest grounds).

[71] Cf. United States v. Dorfman, 542 F.Supp. 402, 405–06 (N.D.Ill.1982). But cf. Greitzer & Locks v. Johns-Manville Corp., 710 F.2d 127 (4th Cir.1982), cert.denied 459 U.S. 1010, 103 S.Ct. 364, 74 L.Ed.2d 400 (1982)(2–1 decision), reversing In re Asbestos Cases, 514 F.Supp. 914, 920 (E.D.Va.1981)(en banc).

(2) deal with it by flatly prohibiting the lawyer from negotiating for future employment with such a person. A similar prohibition against future employment negotiation by judges, arbitrators, and judicial clerks is contained in MR 1.12(b). As with other parts of the former government lawyer area, federal criminal legislation is also germane.[72]

Both the Model Rules and the federal statute use the familiar concepts of "matter"[73] and "participates personally and substantially" to define the scope of the prohibition against negotiating employment. Model Rule 1.11(c)(2) prohibits a government lawyer from negotiating for "private employment" with a party or a party's lawyer but the federal statute prohibits a government lawyer from negotiating for "prospective employment." Construed literally, the federal statute might include employment with another governmental body involved in a covered matter. The same global coverage barring negotiating with interested parties for any "employment" is stated in MR 1.12(b) for a judge or arbitrator.[74] Model Rule 1.11(c)(2) delineates the person with whom negotiations may not be carried on to include "a party or . . . attorney for a party." Read narrowly, that does not proscribe negotiations between the burdened government lawyer and a member of the firm of the described "attorney." But such a narrow reading, particularly in the absence of any "screening" provision, seems to offer too many opportunities for evasion. Here as in other disqualification situations, the entire firm of the blockaded lawyer should be subject to imputed disqualification. No such similarly broad rule affects a judicial law clerk because MR 1.12(b) permits a clerk to negotiate with a party or a party's lawyer after notice to the clerk's judge.

The rule that a government lawyer or a judge cannot "negotiate" prospective employment should not prohibit the lawyer or judge from initially broaching the subject of employment. In a busy court, for example, such breadth would bar all contact about prospective employment between a judge and any of the possible hundreds of lawyers and law firms with matters pending on the judge's calendar. But the bar of the rule should certainly prevent any further official action on the matter pending before the lawyer or judge once tentative mutual interest has been indicated. At that point, even if the lawyer or judge is personally and substantially participating in a matter, it should be sufficient if the lawyer or judge recuses himself or herself from further participation in order to clear the air for further and more serious negotiations about employment. It is important to notice that the bar to negotiation is removed only when the affected lawyer or judge's connection with the matter comes to an end by recusal or other termination. Thus, if recusal is not possible, no alternative suggests itself other than suspending all negotiations about employment until after completion of the matter.

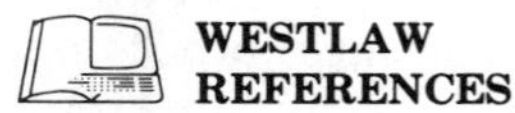
WESTLAW REFERENCES

Public Employee

di public

conflict! /3 interest /p "public employee" /s defin! % definite

conflict! /3 interest /p former** retired judge

conflict! /3 interest /p arbitrator mediator

[72] See 18 U.S.C.A. § 208. Subsection (a) prohibits a government lawyer or other official from "negotiating or [having] any arrangement concerning prospective employment" with any person who has a pending matter in which the government lawyer "participates personally and substantially." Subsection (b) provides for pre-negotiation clearance for inconsequential matters.

[73] MR 1.12 is silent on the point, but presumably the definition of "matter" in MR 1.11(d) would apply in MR 1.12 as well. The comment to MR 1.12 deals with special situations, such as judges of multi-member courts, the definition of "adjudicative officer," and part-time or retired judges.

[74] The breadth of MR 1.12(b) is arguably sufficient to cover the case of a federal judge negotiating with a member of the federal government (a "party") for appointment to another federal judgeship or other office. The word "private" that modifies employment was removed in the final draft of the Model Rules. See MR 1.12(b), at 81 (Proposed Rules of Professional Conduct, March 11, 1983).

conflict /3 interest /p former /s government public agency /s employee lawyer attorney officer

topic(45) /p arbitrator mediator

Substantial Responsibility

disqualif! (conflict! /2 interest) /p former /s government agency public prosecutor /s attorney lawyer /p substantial** personal** formal** /s responsib! participat!

Matter

di matter

former /s government agency public /s attorney lawyer /p matter /s defin! % definite

former /s government agency public /s attorney lawyer /p rulemaking /p matter

former /s government agency public /s attorney lawyer & "same facts test" "same transaction test"

Private Employment

"dr 9-101(b)" & private** /5 employ

former /s government agency /p private** /5 employ****

Confidentiality Government Information

former /5 government agency public /s lawyer attorney /p confidential!

confident! /s government /s information /p former /s attorney lawyer

Government Client Consent

former /5 government /s lawyer attorney /p consent disclos*** /p disqualif! (conflict! /3 interest)

synopsis,digest(former /5 government /s attorney lawyer /p consent disclos****)

§ 8.11 LAWYER BUSINESS DEALINGS WITH CLIENTS

§ 8.11.1 The General Inadvisability of Client-Lawyer Business Deals

Much can be said in favor of an absolute prohibition against a lawyer having nonprofessional business relationships with a client. Such a ban on lawyer-client business dealings has been urged for American lawyers.[75] Business relationships with clients are beset with conflicts of interest and will often involve situations in which the lawyer occupies a dangerously superior bargaining position. The mixture of professional and business relationships can leave the client poorer as a result of the business relationship and the client's legal work neglected.

On the other hand, many lawyers acquire impressive knowledge and a sense of judgment in business matters through their practice, and many clients come to regard their lawyers as both trusted legal advisers and respected business colleagues. American lawyers have traditionally relied upon a mixture of law practice and other business to earn income in small towns and in other situations of marginal demand for legal services. For such reasons, lawyers are not absolutely prohibited from entering into business transactions with clients, but courts regret them and advise strongly against them.[76]

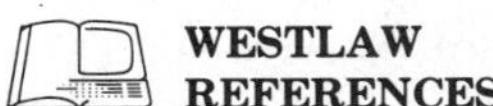
WESTLAW REFERENCES

topic(45) /p client /5 business /5 transaction deal doing

§ 8.11.2 Client-Lawyer Business Deals in the Professional Rules

The 1908 Canons contained no restriction on lawyer-client business dealings other than a prohibition against acquiring an interest in litigation [77] and except for the general prohibition in Canon 11 against any action of a lawyer "whereby for his personal benefit or gain he abuses or takes advantage of the confidence reposed in him by his client." A more straightforward prohibition is contained

[75] Chodos, Lawyer-Client Deals: The End of the Era, 48 L.A. B.Bull. 407, 431–34 (1973).

[76] Committee on Professional Ethics v. Mershon, 316 N.W.2d 895, 899 (Iowa 1982) ("The safest and perhaps best course would have been to refuse to participate personally in the transaction."); In re Lowther, 611 S.W.2d 1, 2 (Mo.1981)("The matter before the Court illustrates the inherent danger of becoming personally involved with the affairs of clients, self-dealing with clients, and of 'taking a piece of the action.' The attorney, with his superior knowledge and education, can pursue this course only at his peril. It is an area wrought with pitfalls and traps and the Court is without choice other than to hold the attorney to the highest of standards under such circumstances."); Greene v. Greene, 56 N.Y.2d 86, 451 N.Y.S.2d 46, 49, 436 N.E.2d 496, 499 (1982); In re Belser, 269 S.C. 682, 239 S.E.2d 492, 494 (1977).

[77] Canon 10. The common-law restrictions on maintenance, champerty, and barratry and their modern remnants are considered at § 8.13.

in the Code's DR 5–104(A), which prohibits a lawyer from entering into a business transaction with a client in which they have differing interests [78] "if the client expects the lawyer to exercise his professional judgment therein for the protection of the client," [79] unless the client consents after full disclosure. That essentially proceduralist approach contents itself with providing lawyer disclosure and client consent as the only protection, with no explicit regard for the underlying fairness of the transaction.[80] The Code does not expressly require a lawyer to advise the client to seek independent legal advice, but courts have insisted that such a duty exists.[81]

Model Rule 1.8(a) [82] is much more concerned with the substantive fairness of the transaction between lawyer and client and requires additional procedural protections. Its coverage is broad: it applies to a direct transaction with a client but extends as well to a lawyer's knowing acquisition of "an ownership, possessory, security or other pecuniary interest adverse to a client." Any such transaction can be entered into only if several conditions are satisfied: (1) the terms must be "fair and reasonable to the client"; (2) the transaction and its terms must be fully disclosed to the client both in writing and "in a manner which can be reasonably understood by the client"; [83] (3) the client must be given a reasonable opportunity to consult independent counsel about the transaction; [84] and (4) the client must consent in writing.[85] Importantly, those conditions are cumulative; the satisfaction of fewer than all four does not amount to compliance. For example, the fact that a transaction is arguably fair and reasonable does not mean that MR 1.8(a) has been complied with if the other requirements of the rule are not satisfied.[86]

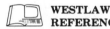

WESTLAW REFERENCES

"dr 5–104(a)"

attorney lawyer /s client /s business /s transaction deal doing /p conflict! differ! adverse /3 interest /p disclos! /p consent

synopsis,digest(client /s business /s transaction deal doing /p independent +2 counsel advice)

---

[78] In the very rare case in which the interests of lawyer and client are entirely congruent in a business transaction, DR 5–104(A) apparently requires no disclosure and consent. For example, a joint investment in the stock of an unrelated company in which the lawyer's and client's bargaining position and risks are equal, falls outside the prohibition. MR 1.8(a), however, covers every "business transaction" with a client and is thus not limited to adverse-interest transactions.

[79] That apparent limitation suggests that the framers of DR 5–104(A) intended it to apply only if a lawyer was performing legal services for the client in the very transaction between lawyer and client. But courts have applied the Code to all business transactions, including situations in which the lawyer does not contemporaneously perform legal work or in which the technical lawyer-client relationship has ended.

[80] Decisions under DR 5–104(A), however, have been heavily influenced by the unfairness of the transaction in holding that a lawyer's participation in the arrangement violated the Code. E.g., Committee on Professional Ethics v. Mershon, 316 N.W.2d 895, 899 (Iowa 1982); In re Wolk, 82 N.J. 326, 413 A.2d 317 (1980).

[81] In re Kali, 124 Ariz. 592, 606 P.2d 808, 811 (1980); State v. Scott, 230 Kan. 564, 639 P.2d 1131, 1135 (1982); Goldman v. Kane, 3 Mass.App.Ct. 336, 329 N.E.2d 770, 773 (1975); In re Wolk, 82 N.J. 326, 413 A.2d 317, 321 (1980). For purposes of a client's suit to rescind, however, the absence of advice to seek independent legal advice is merely one of several factors to be considered in determining the good faith of the lawyer. E.g., Brown v. Commercial Nat'l Bank, 42 Ill.2d 365, 369, 247 N.E.2d 894, 896 (1969), cert.denied 396 U.S. 961, 90 S.Ct. 436, 24 L.Ed.2d 425 (1969).

[82] MR 1.8(a) was inserted by floor amendment at the February 1983 ABA midyear meeting. It borrows, without significant alteration, the language of the California rule on the same subject. See Calif. Rule of Prof. Conduct 5–101.

[83] MR 1.8(a)(1).

[84] MR 1.8(a)(2).

[85] MR 1.8(a)(3).

[86] Pre-Model Rule cases agree. E.g., Ruth v. Crane, 392 F.Supp. 724, 731 (E.D.Pa.1975), affirmed 564 F.2d 90 (3d Cir.1977)(specific performance of lawyer's contract with client decreed on finding that contract was "fair and reasonable" to client, but matter referred to disciplinary agency because of absence of full disclosure to client); In re Weiner, 120 Ariz. 349, 586 P.2d 194, 197 (1978); Committee on Professional Ethics v. Mershon, 316 N.W.2d 895, 900 (Iowa 1982)(violation of DR 5–104(A) is established "even though respondent did not act dishonestly or make a profit on the transaction").

§ 8.11.3 Strict Scrutiny Standard

The Common-Law Standard of Strict Scrutiny

The differences between the Code's DR 5–104(A) and Model Rule 1.8(a) appear large, but they can be overemphasized. While DR 5–104(A) says nothing about the fairness of the underlying transaction, courts and disciplinary agencies have been significantly influenced by the underlying common-law rules governing transactions between fiduciaries and their clients and wards. In general, the established common-law doctrine is that a client who attacks the validity of a transaction with a lawyer can prevail after showing only that the disadvantageous transaction was entered into with a lawyer-fiduciary. In order to uphold the transaction, the lawyer has the burden of showing that he or she took no advantage of the client-lawyer relationship.[87]

Clearly a lawyer cannot deal with a client at arm's length and as if they were strangers. The normal judicial instinct in a market economy—to protect the beneficiaries of hard-driven bargains by sayings such as caveat emptor—gives way to more particularized concerns that client trust in lawyers might be abused and that client trust might be corroded into client wariness about predatory lawyers hunting for bargains. Instead, the law imposes a fiduciary standard that is quite demanding of the lawyer and relatively tolerant and forgiving of the client.[88]

The test that the lawyer must satisfy has been variously stated. Some courts require the lawyer to prove not only that he or she exerted no undue influence but that in every respect the lawyer acted honestly, in good faith, and without exploiting the client's trust.[89] Many courts employ a more emphatic standard and state that the transaction will be regarded as "presumptively fraudulent" and that the lawyer must demonstrate that it is fair in all respects.[90] Some courts assess fairness by a "stranger" test: only if a reasonable lawyer would advise the client to enter into the same transaction with a stranger will a lawyer's contract with a client be deemed fair.[91] Occasionally a court will insist that the lawyer's showing must be by clear and convincing evidence, a burden higher than the normal civil standard of the preponderance of evidence.[92]

Arrangements Covered by the Strict Scrutiny Standard

The strict scrutiny standard applies to all business dealings between lawyer and client after the relationship of lawyer and client has been established. It extends to fee contracts

[87] Dunn v. Record, 63 Me. 17 (1874); Tancre v. Pullman, 35 Minn. 476, 29 N.W. 171, 173 (1886); Shoemaker v. Stiles, 102 Pa. 549 (1883). See generally 1 J.Story, Equity Jurisprudence §§ 310, 311 (W.Lyons 14th ed. 1918) The general view of courts of equity concerning situations in which a lawyer benefits at the client's expense was stated in Stockton v. Ford, 52 U.S. (11 How.) 232, 247, 13 L.Ed. 676 (1850):

> There are few of the business relations of life involving a higher trust and confidence than that of attorney and client, or, generally speaking, one more honorably and faithfully discharged; few more anxiously guarded by the law, or governed by sterner principles of morality and justice, and it is the duty of the court to administer them in a corresponding spirit, and to be watchful and industrious, to see that confidence thus reposed shall not be used to the detriment or prejudice of the rights of the party bestowing it.

[88] Smith v. Bitter, 319 N.W.2d 196, 198 (Iowa 1982) ("harsh and demanding responsibilities of an attorney" who does business with a client); Kribbs v. Jackson, 387 Pa. 611, 621, 129 A.2d 490, 495–96 (1957).

[89] Van Orman v. Nelson, 78 N.M. 11, 427 P.2d 896, 908 (1967); Greene v. Greene, 56 N.Y.2d 86, 451 N.Y.S.2d 46, 49, 436 N.E.2d 496 (1982). Cf. Peaslee v. Pedco, Inc., 388 A.2d 103, 107 (Me.1978)(lawyer with undisclosed interest in business transaction with client has burden "of establishing that the transaction was fair and was entered into with the intelligent consent of the [client], given with accurate knowledge of all the consequences of the transaction.")

[90] Hicks v. Clayton, 67 Cal.App.3d 251, 136 Cal.Rptr. 512, 519 (1977); Kribbs v. Jackson, 387 Pa. 611, 129 A.2d 490, 495–96 (1957)(constructive fraud).

[91] Abstract & Title Corp. v. Cochran, 414 So.2d 284, 285 (Fla.App.1982); Committee on Professional Ethics v. Mershon, 316 N.W.2d 895, 899 (Iowa 1982); McCray v. Weinberg, 4 Mass.App.Ct. 13, 340 N.E.2d 518, 521 (1976); Flanagan v. DeLapp, 533 S.W.2d 592, 595 (Mo.1976); Kirchoff v. Bernstein, 92 Or. 378, 387, 181 P. 746, 749 (1919).

[92] Abstract & Title Corp. v. Cochran, 414 So.2d 284, 285 (Fla.App.1982); In re Bretz, 168 Mont. 23, 542 P.2d 1227, 1245 (1975)(clear and satisfactory evidence).

themselves if they have been entered into or modified after the representation begins.[93] Clients are very vulnerable to lawyer overreaching, because of their trust in their lawyers and because of their lawyers' superior knowledge and skills.[94] Clients may also be susceptible because of their emotional preoccupation with their legal difficulties and, sometimes, because of their relative lack of experience in business matters. Business deals with clients will be subjected to an even stricter scrutiny, therefore, if the client is uneducated or a minor[95] or if the client is burdened with financial difficulties.[96]

The dependency relationship assumed to exist between lawyer and client does not automatically cease when the formal relationship comes to an end. The influence created by the relationship can outlive it and forms a proper basis for imposing continuing fiduciary obligations on a lawyer in a business arrangement with a former client.[97] In fact, in some lawyer dealings with particularly vulnerable and dependent business partners, courts have not hesitated to apply a fiduciary-like standard even if the relationship of lawyer and client technically never existed.[98] A lawyer who deals with a nonlawyer of normal competence who is not a client, however, is not held to a fiduciary standard.[99] The safest course, and perhaps a required one, is for a lawyer to treat any business partner as a client if there is any doubt whether or not the lawyer-client relationship exists with the person.[1]

In limited circumstances, the expertise of a client in a particular transaction might relieve a lawyer of the obligation to take precautionary steps upon which a court might otherwise insist.[2] While both the Code and the Model Rules might seem literally to apply, it would be nonsensical to require a lawyer who seeks to open a checking account with a client bank to conduct the disclosure-and-consent ceremonies with responsible bank officers before doing so.[3] The same limitation on the rule should apply in similar "over the counter" routinized transactions and in those in which the client has at least as much bargaining power as does the lawyer. But in any transaction in which legal knowledge is relevant, the strict rules should apply. Because violation of trust through overreaching in a business transaction with a client strikes at the heart of the client-lawyer relationship, courts have been vigorous in imposing sanc-

93 Lawrence v. Tschirgi, 244 Iowa 386, 57 N.W.2d 46, 48 (1953); Harmon v. Pugh, 38 N.C.App. 438, 248 S.E.2d 421 (1978), cert.denied 296 N.C. 584, 254 S.E.2d 33 (1979)(post representation contingent fee contract). See generally, § 9.1.

94 The concern is not unique to lawyers but extends generally to all situations in which an agent has superior bargaining power because the agent is the object of trust of a bargaining partner or has superior information because of the relationship. E.g., Restatement (Second) of Agency § 387 (1957); Restatement (Second) of Trusts § 2 comment b, § 170 (1959). See generally Kronman, Mistake, Disclosing Information, and the Law of Contracts, 7 J.Legal Stud. 1 (1978).

95 In re Pusser, 273 S.C. 115, 254 S.E.2d 926 (1979); In re Kirven, 267 S.C. 669, 230 S.E.2d 899 (1976).

96 Ames v. State Bar, 8 Cal.3d 910, 106 Cal.Rptr. 489, 506 P.2d 625 (1973); In re May, 96 Idaho 858, 538 P.2d 787 (1975); Goldman v. Kane, 3 Mass.App.Ct. 336, 329 N.E.2d 770 (1975).

97 Alexander v. Russo, 1 Kan.App.2d 546, 571 P.2d 350, 356 (1977); Colstad v. Levine, 243 Minn. 279, 67 N.W.2d 648 (1954); Conner v. Hodgdon, 120 Wn. 426, 207 P. 675 (1922).

98 In re Waleen, 190 Minn. 13, 14, 250 N.W. 798 (1933) (seventy-three-year-old lender to lawyer with very imperfect understanding of business, who was unrepresented by independent lawyer); In re Hurd, 69 N.J. 316, 354 A.2d 78 (1976). Cf. Estreen v. Bluhm, 79 Wis.2d 142, 255 N.W.2d 473, 481 (1977)(lawyer, contracting with nonclient who was not lawyer and unrepresented by counsel, cannot obtain advantage of self-drafted ambiguities in contract). Statutes might impose special restrictions against a fiduciary's use of "insider" information to make a profit at the expense of nonclient persons who lack equal bargaining power because of inferior information. Cf. Chiarella v. United States, 445 U.S. 222, 100 S.Ct. 1108, 63 L.Ed.2d 348 (1980)(printer violated federal securities laws by purchasing securities on basis of insider information obtained in printing plant); In re Bond & Mortgage Guar. Co., 303 N.Y. 423, 103 N.E.2d 721 (1952).

99 Sorenson v. Beers, 614 P.2d 159 (Utah 1980).

1 In re Drake, 292 Or. 704, 642 P.2d 296, 303 (1982).

2 Atlantic Richfield Co. v. Sybert, 51 Md.App. 74, 441 A.2d 1079 (1982), affirmed 295 Md. 347, 456 A.2d 20 (1983); McCray v. Weinberg, 4 Mass.App.Ct. 13, 340 N.E.2d 518 (1976); In re Palmieri, 76 N.J. 51, 385 A.2d 856 (1978).

3 In re Montgomery, 292 Or. 796, 643 P.2d 338, 341 (1982). That sensible exception is explicitly recognized in MR 1.8 comment (Transactions between Client and Lawyer; first paragraph).

tions on lawyers found to have violated the mandatory rules limiting such transactions.[4]

A Lawyer's Financial and Business Interests

The ways in which a lawyer's business interests might directly or indirectly conflict with those of a client are myriad. In the course of representing a client, incidental matters might arise such as the client's need for a surety, an escrow agent, or a title insurance company. A lawyer serving or having an interest in any of those businesses is obviously in a conflict of interest with his or her client.[5] A lawyer may be in need of a loan, and a client may have available funds.[6] Those are specific examples of the general problem of lawyers inviting their clients to invest in or purchase from enterprises in which the lawyer has an interest.[7]

On the other hand, a lawyer might have cash to invest and might learn from representing a client of the possibility of investing or buying an interest in a client's property or business. The Code, but not the Model Rules, discourages lawyers from even inviting themselves into business deals with clients.[8] Whether invited or not, a lawyer who invests in client property or business opportunities is subject to the strict conflict rules. The occasions on which the rules have been applied are numerous. A lawyer might be tempted to purchase a client's property at a foreclosure or other forced sale.[9] Lawyer self-dealing might take the form of a direct purchase from a client whose property is subject to foreclosure because of the client's default on a loan secured by the property.[10] A lawyer who represents a prospering client might learn of a bargain purchase that can be made from a third party and might personally snap up the bargain instead of informing the client of its availability.[11] Bargains might also be readily available to lawyers and their family and friends if lawyers were permitted to self-deal

4 Giovanazzi v. State Bar, 28 Cal.3d 465, 169 Cal.Rptr. 581, 585, 619 P.2d 1005, 1009 (1980)("Because an attorney is a fiduciary to his client, all dealings between them which are beneficial to the attorney must be closely scrutinized for unfairness. Where an attorney's conduct disregards this duty, severe discipline is warranted."). See also, e.g., People v. Razatos, 636 P.2d 666 (Colo.1981), appeal dismissed 455 U.S. 930, 102 S.Ct. 1415, 71 L.Ed.2d 639 (1982); In re Temrowski, 409 Mich. 262, 293 N.W.2d 346 (1980); Stark County Bar Ass'n v. Osborne, 1 Ohio St. 3d 140, 438 N.E.2d 114 (1982); In re Easler, 275 S.C. 269, 269 S.E.2d 765 (1980); In re Sedor, 73 Wis.2d 629, 245 N.W.2d 895 (1976).

5 Caplan v. Harte, 131 Ariz. 357, 641 P.2d 271 (App. 1982)(Arizona statutory prohibition against lawyer or partner serving as client's surety); Roussel & Rosenberg, Lawyer-Controlled Title Insurance Companies: Legal Ethics and the Need for Insurance Department Regulations, 38 Fordham L.Rev. 25 (1979).

6 Instances of ill-advised client loans to lawyers are legion. E.g., In re Kali, 124 Ariz. 592, 606 P.2d 808 (1980) (usurious note with vague terms and extensive powers granted to lawyer-borrower to manage sole security for the loan); Baranowski v. State Bar, 24 Cal.3d 153, 154 Cal.Rptr. 752, 593 P.2d 613 (1979); People v. Cameron, 197 Colo. 330, 595 P.2d 677 (1979)(en banc)(note contained no provision for legal fees in event of suit); In re Leibowitz, 437 N.E.2d 973 (Ind.1982)(loan from client repaid with dishonored checks); State v. Scott, 230 Kan. 564, 639 P.2d 1131, 1135 (1982)(interest-free loan from client not evidenced by note); In re Quinn, 88 N.J. 10, 438 A.2d 321, 322 (1981)(loans from trust funds subject to third party's lien); In re Montgomery, 292 Or. 796, 643 P.2d 338 (1982) (loan at usurious rate); In re Meuer, 108 Wis.2d 434, 321 N.W.2d 301 (1982)(lawyer solicited loan from client's settlement proceeds without supplying financial statement or security, and lawyer subsequently became bankrupt).

7 Miller v. Sears, 636 P.2d 1183 (Alaska 1981); In re Wolk, 82 N.J. 326, 413 A.2d 317 (1980). See generally EC 5–3 (last sentence).

8 EC 5–3 ("A lawyer should not seek to persuade his client to permit him to invest in an undertaking of his client."). See generally H.Drinker, Legal Ethics 109 (1953); In re Nulle, 127 Ariz. 299, 620 P.2d 214, 215 (1980); In re Erlandson, 290 Or. 465, 622 P.2d 727 (1981).

9 The judicial condemnation of lawyer self-dealing by purchase of a client's property at a foreclosure sale is both constant and long-standing. E.g., Stockton v. Ford, 52 U.S. (11 How.) 232, 13 L.Ed. 676 (1850); McArthur v. Goodwin, 173 Cal. 499, 160 P. 679 (1916). See also, e.g., In re Geyler, 114 Ariz. 321, 560 P.2d 1228 (1977); Gaffney v. Harmon, 405 Ill. 273, 90 N.E.2d 785 (1950); Sorenson v. Beers, 585 P.2d 458, 460 (Utah 1978). The prohibition in California is now a formal part of the lawyer rules. See Cal.R.Prof. Conduct R. 5–103 (broadly prohibiting lawyer, in whatever capacity, from directly or indirectly purchasing at probate, foreclosure, or judicial sale).

10 Ames v. State Bar, 8 Cal.3d 910, 106 Cal.Rptr. 389, 506 P.2d 625 (1973); Florida Bar v. Neely, 372 So.2d 89 (Fla.1979). Cf. In re Bond & Mortgage Guar. Co., 303 N.Y. 423, 103 N.E.2d 721 (1952)(liquidation trustee's lawyer, who purchased bonds from bondholders at depressed prices, required to disgorge profits).

11 Golden Nugget, Inc. v. Ham, 95 Nev. 45, 589 P.2d 173, 175 (1979). Some authority suggests that the "client opportunity" rule is limited to situations in which the client is harmed. Cf. Alexander v. Russo, 1 Kan.App.2d

as the legal representative of a decedent's estate or in some similar fiduciary role.[12] Finally, lawyer investment in enterprises or properties that are the subject of litigation can run afoul of special common-law restrictions on champertous and similar purchases that are considered below (§ 8.13).

WESTLAW REFERENCES

attorney lawyer /s client /s business /s transaction deal doing /p fiduciary /p advantage exploit! "arms length"

topic(45) /p business /s transaction deal doing /p fair fairness

conflict! /3 interest /p attorney lawyer /s business financial /3 interest

§ 8.11.4 *Disclosure and Consent in Client-Lawyer Business Dealings*

Disclosure and Consent as Invariants

Disclosure by a lawyer to a client of their differing interests in a business transaction, and the client's consent, can sometimes legitimate the lawyer's actions.[13] If disclosure is not made, courts have been particularly severe with a secretive profiteering at a client's expense.[14] The most obvious reason for requiring disclosure is to permit a client to assess whether to do business and to continue to be represented despite the lawyer's conflicting self-interest. A less obvious, but nonetheless important, function of disclosure is that its absence serves as a strongly negative measure of the good faith of the lawyer. A lawyer who keeps his or her differing interests in a transaction secret from a client demonstrates a lack of candor that rightfully casts a pall of suspicion over the entire transaction.

Full disclosure is an unqualified mandate in both the Code and the Model Rules, and a lawyer's failure to make it cannot be excused on the gound of negligence or ignorance of the requirement.[15] Generally a lawyer cannot rely on suppositions that a client has learned the necessary information from another source or is self-tutored on the important business and legal aspects of the transaction.[16]

The Content of a Full Disclosure

The Code and the Model Rules both require a "full" disclosure.[17] The information disclosed by the lawyer to the client must be complete and intelligible, so that the client can fully understand the following elements: (1) the nature of the transaction and each of its terms;[18] (2) the nature and extent of the lawyer's interest in the transaction; (3) the

546, 571 P.2d 350 (1977)(lawyer advising unwitting client to return stolen property to police with intent of claiming reward offered by insurance company could not recover the reward); MR 1.8 comment (Transactions between Client and Lawyer; first paragraph)("[A] lawyer may not exploit information relating to the representation to the client's disadvantage. For example, a lawyer who has learned that the client is investing in specific real estate may not, without the client's consent, seek to acquire nearby property where doing so would adversely affect the client's plan for investment.").

12 Eschwig v. State Bar, 1 Cal.3d 8, 81 Cal.Rptr. 352, 357, 459 P.2d 904, 909 (1969); Committee on Professional Ethics v. Baker, 269 N.W.2d 463, 466 (Iowa 1978); Bar Ass'n of Baltimore v. Posner, 275 Md. 250, 339 A.2d 657 (1975), cert.denied 423 U.S. 1016, 96 S.Ct. 451, 46 L.Ed.2d 388 (1975); Comment, When Can an Attorney Buy from an Estate or Entity He or His Firm Administered?, 5 J.Legal Prof. 163 (1980).

13 State ex rel. Nebraska Bar Ass'n v. Hollstein, 202 Neb. 40, 274 N.W.2d 508, 516 (1979).

14 Sodikoff v. State Bar, 14 Cal.3d 422, 121 Cal.Rptr. 467, 535 P.2d 331 (1975); In re Capps, 250 Ga. 242, 297 S.E.2d 249 (1982)(lawyer employed full-time by corporation secretly competing in own enterprise and secretly representing second competitor); Committee on Professional Ethics v. Baker, 269 N.W.2d 463 (Iowa 1978) (purchasing farm from client through straw man and reselling at large profit); Lousiana State Bar Ass'n v. Summers, 379 So.2d 1065 (La.1980).

15 In re James, 452 A.2d 163, 167 (D.C.App.1982), cert. denied 460 U.S. 1038, 103 S.Ct. 1429, 75 L.Ed.2d 789 (1983), and authorities cited. The "knowingly" qualification in MR 1.8(a) refers to the acquisition of an adverse property interest and not to the requirement of full disclosure and client consent. The evident purpose of the qualification is to except instances in which unknown purchases are made in behalf of a lawyer, such as by a trustee of a blind trust or by an investment manager with unlimited investment discretion.

16 McCray v. Weinberg, 4 Mass.App.Ct. 13, 340 N.E.2d 518, 521 (1976)(lawyer must use "active diligence" to inform client).

17 DR 5-104(A); EC 5-3; MR 1.8(a)(1)("fully disclosed"). Note again that the disclosure and consent required by MR 1.8(a)(1) and (2) must be in writing. On the content of disclosure in conflicts generally, see § 7.2.4(a).

18 MR 1.8(a)(1).

ways in which the lawyer's participation in the transaction might affect the lawyer's exercise of professional judgment in concurrent legal work for the client, if any;[19] (4) the desirability of the client's seeking independent legal advice if the client is not already independently represented;[20] and (5) the nature of the respective risks and advantages to each of the parties to the transaction.[21]

WESTLAW REFERENCES

attorney lawyer /s client /s business /s transaction deal doing /p disclos! /p consent

§ 8.11.5 Remedies for Improper Business Deals

Lawyer violations of the prohibition against unfair dealing with a client can result in an impressive array of remedies and sanctions against the lawyer. Most of the cases cited in this section involve either decisions imposing discipline on the offending lawyer, which seems to be both customary and strict for detected violations, or decisions granting various forms of equitable relief in order to restore the client to his or her position before the transaction and to require the lawyer to disgorge ill-gotten gains. A lawyer's attempt to cover tracks by arranging transfers to relatives or friends is most often unavailing because of the equitable device of the involuntary or constructive trust.[22]

In a client's suit against the lawyer, defenses that a lawyer might be able to assert if the suit involves nonfiduciary dealings might be precluded by estoppel.[23] The bar of the statute of limitations on a client's suit against a lawyer may be extended until the client-lawyer relationship ends through the "continuous treatment" doctrine.[24] Perhaps the most significant financial risk to a lawyer contemplating a business transaction with a client is that coverage for fraud might be excluded under the lawyer's legal malpractice policy (§ 5.6.8). For prudential reasons such as those, and for reasons of public policy as well, lawyers would always do better to separate entirely their professional representations from their business arrangements.

WESTLAW REFERENCES

lawyer attorney /s client /s business /s transaction deal doing & involuntary constructive +3 trust

lawyer attorney /s client /s business /s transaction deal doing & defense /p estoppel "statute of limitation"

§ 8.12 CLIENT GIFTS AND FIDUCIARY DESIGNATIONS

§ 8.12.1 General

One of the most traditional of lawyerly roles is to oversee the legal aspects of donative transfers of client wealth. Gifts and wills have for centuries involved serious legal issues, and the emergence of income, estate, and gift taxation early in this century has made the legal issues more complex. When arranging donative transfers, clients sometimes may wish to make gifts to lawyers or include lawyers in their future donative plans through designation of the lawyer as trustee, executor, or lawyer for those officers. Both gifts and fiduciary designations involve direct and difficult conflicts of interest.

19 In re Wolk, 82 N.J. 326, 413 A.2d 317, 321 (1980); In re Sedor, 73 Wis.2d 629, 245 N.W.2d 895, 901 (1976).

20 MR 1.8(a)(2). The rationale stated for that rule, in the comment to MR 1.8, is somewhat misleadingly pallid: "In such transactions a review by independent counsel on behalf of the client is often advisable."

21 Miller v. Sears, 636 P.2d 1183, 1188–89 n.7 (Alaska 1981), and authorities cited; In re James, 452 A.2d 163, 167 (D.C.App.1982), cert. denied 460 U.S. 1038, 103 S.Ct. 1429, 75 L.Ed.2d 789 (1983); Committee on Professional Ethics v. Mershon, 316 N.W.2d 895, 899 (Iowa 1982); In re Surgent, 79 N.J. 529, 401 A.2d 522 (1979)(failure to disclose size of profit that lawyer's corporation would make on sale of real estate to client and fact that property's income would probably be insufficient to meet carrying charges).

22 Calzada v. Sinclair, 6 Cal.App.3d 903, 86 Cal.Rptr. 387 (1970). For a review of other remedies available in California, see Clayton v. Hicks, 67 Cal.App.3d 251, 136 Cal.Rptr. 512, 520 (1977).

23 Liebergesell v. Evans, 93 Wn.2d 881, 613 P.2d 1170, 1175 (1980)(estoppel to plead defense of usury in client's suit to recover funds that lawyer borrowed from client).

24 Greene v. Greene, 56 N.Y.2d 86, 451 N.Y.S.2d 46, 50, 436 N.E.2d 496, 500 (1982).

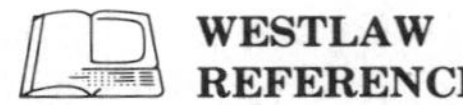

WESTLAW REFERENCES

di fiduciary

di gift

§ 8.12.2 Client Gifts to Lawyers

The Voidability of Client Gifts

Anglo-American law has always been wary of the power that can be exercised over a donor by a close and trusted legal adviser. The possibilities are rife for overreaching, imposition, and undue influence. Thus the rule has always been that client gifts will be set aside without a showing that the lawyer-recipient engaged in actual fraud or that such fraud induced the transfer.[25] All such gifts are potentially tainted, and modern courts in proceedings to set them aside place squarely on the lawyer the burden of proof to establish that the gift is fair, equitable, and not the result of undue influence.[26]

A corresponding professional rule has also been enforced. No provision of the 1908 Canons explicitly addressed the issue. The 1969 Code deals with the problem rather extensively, but only in an Ethical Consideration (EC 5–5). The strong suggestion of the Code is that lawyers should avoid such gifts; should certainly not suggest the idea to a client; and, if pressed by a client, should only accept a gift after urging the client to seek independent advice. Also, a lawyer should prepare an instrument of gift that names him or her as a beneficiary only in extraordinary circumstances. Those strictures of EC 5–5 are given the most forceful effect in cases of gifts in wills, considered below. Decisions under the Code, imposing discipline on lawyers for accepting large gifts from clients, have also cited the general conflict of interest rules of the Code.[27] The decisions insist that a lawyer who contemplates accepting a gift from a client must urge the client to obtain independent advice, must often insist that the transfer be reduced to a writing signed by the client-donor, and must emphasize to the client the desirability of the presence of third parties.[28]

Model Rule 1.8(c) explicitly states that a lawyer may not prepare an instrument of gift that benefits the lawyer, and the rule extends the category of prohibited beneficiaries to include persons who are closely related to the lawyer. The conflict is expressly made subject to the imputed-disqualification rule (§ 7.6) by MR 1.10(a). Surprisingly, nothing in MR 1.8(c) explicitly regulates client gifts *not* made by an instrument, but the comment to Rule 1.8 [29] suggests that the "fair and reasonable" standard of MR 1.8(a), on business transactions and "adverse" property acquisitions, applies to all client gifts. It is sound to apply the MR 1.8 standard, but the matter should be removed from all doubt by amending the ABA version of the rule. Even without an amendment, it would plainly be incongruous if the Rules were interpreted to prohibit the preparation of any instrument of gift to a lawyer, even a perfectly fair one, but to permit all gifts, regardless of fairness, so long as they were not made by a written instrument.

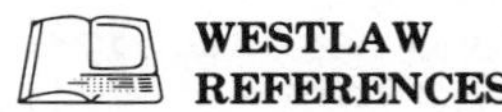

WESTLAW REFERENCES

"ec 5–5"

[25] Welles v. Middleton, 1 Cox 112, 29 Eng.Rep. 1086 (Ch.1784)(lesser showing of incapacity on part of donor required than would be the case to set aside execution of deed to one other than donor's lawyer).

[26] McDonald v. Hewlett, 102 Cal.App.2d 680, 228 P.2d 83 (1951); In re Schuyler, 91 Ill.2d 6, 61 Ill.Dec. 540, 542, 434 N.E.2d 1137, 1139, 1141 (1982); Cuthbert v. Heidsieck, 364 S.W.2d 583, 587 (Mo.1963); Ellenstein v. Herman Body Co., 23 N.J. 348, 129 A.2d 268 (1957); Frost v. Bachman, 283 N.Y. 744, 28 N.E.2d 969 (1940).

[27] Florida Bar v. Jameison, 426 So.2d 16 (Fla.1983)(DR 5–104(A) violated by accepting client's substantial gift to lawyer's foundation, in management of which lawyer was actively engaged); In re Schuyler, 91 Ill.2d 6, 61 Ill.Dec. 540, 544–45, 434 N.E.2d 1137, 1141–42 (1982)(DR 5–104(A) as basis for discipline for accepting large gift from elderly and infirm client); In re Gallop, 85 N.J. 317, 426 A.2d 509, 511–12 (1981)(suspension under DR 5–101(A) for drafting trust for client in which lawyer was both trust beneficiary and trustee).

[28] In re Schuyler, 91 Ill.2d 6, 61 Ill.Dec. 540, 543–44, 434 N.E.2d 1137, 1140–41 (1982); In re Hendricks, 282 Or. 763, 580 P.2d 188, 190 (1978).

[29] MR 1.8 comment (Transactions Between Client and Lawyer; second paragraph).

attorney lawyer /s client /s gift & "undue influence" (conflict! /3 interest) overreach

§ 8.12.3 Lawyers as Beneficiaries of Client Wills

Dangers of Overreaching in Arranging Testamentary Gifts

The question of undue influence by a lawyer who drafts a client's will has become increasingly prominent. The will cases often involve large gifts to the will-drafting lawyer from elderly clients, whom the courts obviously regard as particularly susceptible to overreaching. Suspicious gifts are also more readily detectable because of the possibility of judicial scrutiny during probate. A presumption of fraud similar to that attaching to inter vivos gifts and other property transactions between lawyer and client applies to testamentary gifts made to a lawyer who drafts the instrument.[30] Some judges would go further and disallow all such testamentary gifts, regardless of the circumstances, which might be difficult to prove after the death of the person who was probably the only witness to the client-lawyer consultation on the matter other than the claimant-lawyer.[31] Whether the gift is void or not, many lawyers prefer an untarnished name to riches and refuse to accept testamentary client gifts.[32]

Testamentary Gifts under the Professional Rules

Under the Canons, apparently only Wisconsin strongly discouraged a lawyer from drafting a will in which he or she was named as a substantial beneficiary.[33] And certainly a lawyer's direct request to a client to make a testamentary gift to the lawyer has always been prohibited as a kind of fraud.[34] Under the 1969 Code a growing number of decisions have taken an increasingly prohibitory position, in some jurisdictions amounting to a virtual bar.[35] The decisions emphasize the necessity of having the client's will drafted by another lawyer or at least having an independent lawyer review the will with the client.[36] Some courts, following EC 5–5, have been willing to find exceptions for special circumstances, but only if the facts clearly demon-

30 Haynes v. First Nat'l State Bank, 87 N.J. 163, 432 A.2d 890, 898–99 (1981), and authorities cited; In re Bartel's Will, 33 A.D.2d 987, 307 N.Y.S.2d 260 (1970). See generally Note, Attorney Beware—The Presumption of Undue Influence and the Attorney-Beneficiary, 47 Notre Dame Law. 330 (1971). The presumption applies even if the gift takes the form of giving the lawyer absolute discretion to distribute the estate to charities. E.g., Allen v. Estate of Dutton, 394 So.2d 132, 134–35 (Fla.App.1980), review denied 402 So.2d 609 (1981); Estate of Nelson, 274 N.W.2d 584, 589 (S.D.1978).

31 In re Estate of Smith, 68 Wn.2d 145, 163, 411 P.2d 879, 889 (1966)(dissenting opinion of Rosellini, C.J.). See also In re Karabatian's Estate, 17 Mich.App. 541, 546–47, 170 N.W.2d 166, 169 (1969); Office of Disciplinary Counsel v. Walker, 469 Pa. 432, 366 A.2d 563, 568 (1976) (lawyer named in will, which he drafted, as beneficiary, executor, and attorney to executor required to give full amount of bequest and entire fee collected from estate to other beneficiaries).

32 See the judicial accolade for a lawyer who "timely but gently" turned away an elderly client's twice-offered bequests, in Markell v. Sidney B. Pfeifer Found., Inc., 9 Mass.App.Ct. 412, 402 N.E.2d 76, 91 (1980)("a worthy example of professional probity and skill").

33 State v. Collentine, 39 Wis.2d 325, 159 N.W.2d 50, 53 (1968). See also State ex rel. Nebraska Bar Ass'n v. Richards, 165 Neb. 80, 94–95, 84 N.W.2d 136, 146 (1957) (less stringent warning).

34 In re Glover, 176 Minn. 519, 223 N.W. 921 (1929); Lake County Bar Ass'n v. Patterson, 64 Ohio St.2d 163, 413 N.E.2d 840 (1980). See also In re Theodosen, 303 N.W.2d 104 (S.D.1981)(exerting undue influence on client to leave entire estate to lawyer).

35 The best-known case is Committee on Professional Ethics v. Randall, 285 N.W.2d 161 (Iowa 1979), cert.denied 446 U.S. 946, 100 S.Ct. 2175, 64 L.Ed.2d 802 (1980). In *Randall*, the court disbarred a former president of the ABA, explicitly relying only on EC 5–5. After the decision, the Iowa Supreme Court transferred much of EC 5–5 to a new DR 5–101(B) which absolutely prohibits a lawyer from being named "beneficiary" in a nonrelative's will unless the will is prepared by an unassociated lawyer. See Committee on Professional Ethics v. Behnke, 276 N.W.2d 838 (Iowa), appeal dismissed 444 U.S. 805, 100 S.Ct. 27, 62 L.Ed.2d 19 (1979). For a review of cases in several jurisdictions, see In re Amundson, 297 N.W.2d 433, 438–40 (N.D.1980).

36 People v. Berge, 620 P.2d 23, 27 (Colo.1980)(insufficient for a lawyer to "refer" client, who left lawyer half of estate, to another lawyer who shared office space, did not bill client, kept no client file on matter, and merely served as scrivener); State v. Beaudry, 53 Wis.2d 148, 191 N.W.2d 842 (1971), cert.denied 407 U.S. 912, 92 S.Ct. 2441, 32 L.Ed.2d 686 (1972). See also Magee v. State Bar, 58 Cal.2d 423, 24 Cal.Rptr. 839, 374 P.2d 807 (1962) (private interview with unrelated lawyer negates inference of wrongdoing); In re Estate of Peterson, 283 Minn. 446, 168 N.W.2d 502 (1969).

strate competence in the testator and no lack of care and client loyalty on the part of the lawyer-beneficiary.[37] As in all conflict situations, the lawyer-beneficiary is under a strict obligation to make a full disclosure to the client of the nature of the conflict.[38] A point to stress with the client, particularly if any possible question could be raised about testamentary capacity, is that the lawyer's ability to testify credibly about the testator's state of mind will be impaired by the lawyer's interest in receiving a gift under the will. Indeed, the gift to the lawyer might itself be evidence of lack of testamentary capacity, so that the client's entire testamentary plan could be jeopardized by it.

The absolute prohibition in MR 1.8(c) against a lawyer's preparation of a donative instrument in which the lawyer or a relative of the lawyer is a beneficiary breaks new ground, but it can readily be seen as the logical extension of directions already taken by several courts under the 1969 Code. In view of the substantial risks to a client created by lawyer gifts in wills, the absolute prohibition in the Model Rules is emphatically superior to the facts-and-circumstances approach of the Code.

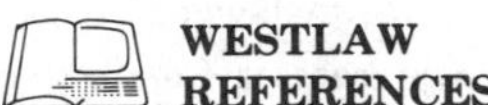
WESTLAW REFERENCES

lawyer attorney /s client /s will /s gift beneficiary "undue influence" overreach! (conflict! /3 interest)

topic(45) /p testator client /s overreach "undue influence" (conflict! /3 interest) /s gift beneficiary

§ 8.12.4 *Lawyer Self-Nomination as Fiduciary*

The Conflict Inherent in Self-Nomination

Will drafting by itself is not particularly remunerative work. What makes a wills practice a lucrative specialty for some lawyers is probating wills. The lawyer's appointment as executor or counsel to the executor to administer an estate can generate handsome fees. That prospect creates serious conflicts of interest: a lawyer drafting a will has a strong economic incentive to secure those lucrative positions for the lawyer or the lawyer's firm. Lawyers can sometimes leave the appointment unmentioned in the instrument, leaving the matter to tacit, reciprocal understandings, such as is a practice of corporate fiduciaries to name as their counsel the lawyer who drafted the trust or will that designated them.[39] The lucrative position is even more certainly secured, however, if the lawyer's nomination to the role is drafted directly into the will or trust as the donor's explicit instruction.

While the self-nominating lawyer might wish to defend the practice of self-nomination on the ground of superior competence to administer the estate, it is readily assailable on conflicts grounds that self-interest is likely to impair the lawyer's best, client-centered judgment in many cases. Most obviously, the lawyer's interest in securing lucrative positions under the instrument creates a disincentive to advise the client about alternative methods of wealth transfer—such as outright

---

37 In re Barrick, 87 Ill.2d 233, 57 Ill.Dec. 725, 429 N.E.2d 842 (1981)(after effective lawyer disclosure, mentally sharp client who was active in managing own financial affairs firmly resisted, for sound reasons, urging of lawyer-beneficiary to consult with another lawyer); In re Tonkon, 292 Or. 660, 642 P.2d 660 (1982)(drafting will with $75,000 gift from elderly and infirm but competent client did not violate DR 5–101(A) when gift, though substantial, was minor part of $6,000,000 estate).

38 In re Vogel, 92 Ill.2d 55, 65 Ill.Dec. 30, 34, 440 N.E.2d 885, 889 (1982).

39 That dubious custom was at one time strongly encouraged by the ABA in a document that has since been repudiated because of evident antitrust problems. See Statement of General Policies sect. (v)(approved by ABA and American Bankers Ass'n, Trust Div'n, (1941), in 7 Martindale-Hubbell 72M, 73M (1978). Courts have recognized the economic self-interest on the part of corporate fiduciaries who, in order to encourage their designation as fiduciary in future wills, appoint the drafting lawyer as their counsel in the administration of the trust or estate, without particular regard to relative qualifications or cost. See In re Estate of Effron, 117 Cal.App.3d 915, 173 Cal.Rptr. 93, 102 (1981), appeal dismissed 454 U.S. 1070, 102 S.Ct. 622, 70 L.Ed.2d 606 (1981). A lawyer who recommends a corporate fiduciary to a client clearly should be required to inform the client, if such is the case, that the fiduciary customarily appoints as counsel to the estate the lawyer who drafted the designating instrument.

gifts—that do not require the additional expenses of executors, trustees, and lawyers.

The Limited Judicial Response

Despite those dangers, only Wisconsin courts have clearly outlawed the practice of a lawyer recommending his or her own designation as executor or lawyer to the executor in a will drafted by the lawyer.[40] None of the lawyer codes comments on the practice, although EC 5–6 states that a lawyer should not "consciously influence" a client in that respect. Under the Model Rules, the intent apparently is to regulate such matters by the "fair and reasonable" standard of MR 1.8(a) and the general conflict provisions of MR 1.7.[41] An appointment obtained by the lawyer's fraud is presumably forbidden on that ground alone,[42] but it is not clear whether any other circumstances are covered by the fair-and-reasonable standard.

Once in a fiduciary position such as that of executor, a lawyer must exercise further caution. The executor's power to designate the lawyer for the estate should rarely be exercised by self-nomination or by designating a member of the executor's own firm. For one thing, obtaining double fees for largely duplicative work is highly objectionable.[43] The executor also places himself or herself in a difficult position from which to scrutinize with objectivity the work of the lawyer for the estate. Further, if the lawyer-executor should appear as a witness in the probate proceeding, the advocate-witness rule (§ 7.5) by its own force might prohibit the appointment in many situations under the Model Rules.

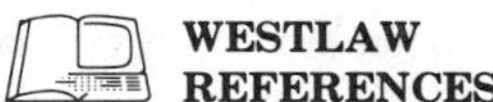

conflict! /3 interest /s attorney lawyer /s fiduciary executor "personal representative" /p will

§ 8.13 MAINTENANCE, CHAMPERTY, AND BARRATRY

The Tradition of Antipathy to Stirring up Litigation

Not so long ago, a considerable area of the law of legal ethics was given over to the mysteries of the Macbethian witches of the common law who stirred the cauldron of despised litigation—maintenance, champerty, and barratry. Those were both common-law crimes that any person, lawyer or nonlawyer, could commit, as well as grounds for severe discipline of lawyers. While their origins are ancient,[44] they exist today only vestigially. Maintenance and champerty continued to be crimes in England until 1967.[45] A few years before they were defanged, Lord Denning defined maintenance as "improperly stirring up litigation and strife by giving aid to one party to bring or defend a claim without just cause or excuse."[46] The most common kinds of

40 State v. Gulbankian, 54 Wis.2d 599, 196 N.W.2d 730 (1972). See also In re Theodosen, 303 N.W.2d 104, 105 (S.D.1981)(dictum). The rationale of *Gulbankian*, unfortunately, is the readily discreditable notion that the lawyer who recommends his or her own appointment as executor to a client violates the DR 2–103(A) prohibition against solicitation. Cf. DR 2–104(A)(1).

41 See the suppressed Legal Background note, MR 1.8(c), at 62 (Proposed Final Draft, May 30, 1981).

42 In re Estate of Weinstock, 40 N.Y.2d 1, 386 N.Y.S.2d 1, 351 N.E.2d 647 (1976)(lawyers who obtained their appointment as coexecutors, entitling each to full fee as executor despite client's emphatic desire to avoid double fees, precluded from serving as executors).

43 In re Theodosen, 303 N.W.2d 104, 106 (S.D.1981). See also ABA Statement of Principles Regarding Probate Practices and Expenses (approved draft 1975), reprinted in Martin, Professional Responsibility and Probate Practices, 1975 Wis.L.Rev. 911, 941.

44 R.Perkins, Criminal Law 523–38 (2d ed.1969); Radin, Maintenance by Champerty, 24 Calif.L.Rev. 48 (1935); Winfield, The History of Maintenance and Champerty, 35 L.Q.Rev. 50 (1919).

45 Criminal Law Act, 1967, ch. 58, §§ 13, 14. The Law Commission study that recommended abolition of champerty and maintenance as criminal offenses and torts urged that "the ancient and unused misdemeanors and the ancient and virtually useless torts . . . be consigned to the museum of legal history." Law Commission, Proposals for Reform of the Law Relating to Maintenance and Champerty 5 (1966).

46 In re Trepca Mines, Ltd., [1962] All E.R. 351, 355 (C.A.). See also Restatement of Contracts § 540(1) (1932). The exception for "just cause" was elaborated upon in id. § 541: "A bargain for maintenance, though the bargain includes an agreement to pay the expense of litigation, is not illegal if entered into from charitable motives and without an intention to make a profit, or in order to determine a question on which a right or duty of the

impermissible maintenance involve financial assistance. Champerty is simply a specialized form of maintenance in which the person assisting another's litigation becomes an interested investor because of a promise by the assisted person to repay the investor with a share of any recovery.[47] Barratry is adjudicative cheerleading—urging others, frequently, to quarrels and suits.[48] All were thought to lead to a corruption of justice because of their tendency to encourage unwanted and unmeritorious litigation, inflated damages, suppressed evidence, and suborned perjury. Those, of course, are the same arguments that have traditionally been made against other aids to impecunious litigants, such as free legal services and the contingent fee.

Contemporary Attitudes Toward Sponsoring Litigation

The common-law strictures against maintenance, champerty, and barratry reflected profound professional and popular distrust of the medieval judicial process, a distrust which is not germane to modern litigation. Ancient court procedures and criminal laws directed at perjury, official corruption, and obstructing justice were seriously defective. But modern penal codes, and modern procedure and evidence law, contain sufficiently articulated devices to pursue those goals.

The old blunderbuss approach of discouraging all assistance to others who attempt to assert their rights through litigation is no longer followed, because it does not predictably produce just results.[49] Social attitudes and political concepts about litigation have also changed, particularly in the United States. American courts have retreated significantly from ancient judicial vigor in enforcing the maintenance, champerty, and barratry defenses to contracts or lawsuits.[50] At a point, the ancient prohibitions, if resurrected, may be so broadly applicable that they bar good faith litigants from a courthouse and thus violate a federal constitutional right of access to adjudication.[51]

Remaining Prohibitions against Litigational Profiteering

Notwithstanding modern attitudes, some suspicions linger about strangers to a dispute who buy their way into it and carry the dispute to court for motives of profit. Lurking here are negative reactions to officious, and profit-motivated, intermeddlers, as well as affirmative instincts that private ordering and nonjudicial resolutions can often serve social interests and litigants' self-interests better than hard-fought and expensive court battles. The former concern is probably more potent, as is suggested by the approach of courts to questions of sanctions. For example, the fact that a lawyer's contract with a client violates prohibitions against champerty or maintenance does not require dismissal of the client's suit,[52] although it may require

maintaining party depends; but if such a bargain is entered into for the purpose of annoying another it is illegal." Put another way, the common-law offenses required a finding of malicious intent. See NAACP v. Button, 371 U.S. 415, 439, 83 S.Ct. 328, 341, 9 L.Ed.2d 405 (1963), and authorities cited. But it is needlessly imprecise to conclude that all lawyer litigation based on personal malice is champertous, as was said in Huene v. Carnes, 121 Cal.App.3d 432, 175 Cal.Rptr. 374, 377 (1981) (lawyer filed medical malpractice action without authorization of client).

47 Brown & Huseby, Inc. v. Chrietzberg, 242 Ga. 232, 248 S.E.2d 631, 633 (1978); Restatement of Contracts § 540(2) (1932).

48 See 4 W.Blackstone, Commentaries *134.

49 Cf. Restatement (Second) of Contracts vol. 2, ch. 8, Introductory Note, at 4 (1981).

50 Martin v. Morgan Drive Away, Inc., 665 F.2d 598, 603 (5th Cir.1982), cert. dismissed 458 U.S. 1122, 103 S.Ct. 5, 73 L.Ed.2d 1394 (1982); Alexander v. Unification Church, 634 F.2d 673, 677 n.6 (2d Cir.1980); Mitchell v. Amerada Hess Corp., 638 P.2d 441, 444–46 (Okl.1981). See generally 14 S.Williston, Contracts § 1715 (3d ed. 1972); 6A A.Corbin, Contracts § 1423 (2d ed.1962).

51 NAACP v. Button, 371 U.S. 415, 83 S.Ct. 328, 9 L.Ed. 2d 405 (1963)(Virginia barratry statute unconstitutional); American Civil Liberties Union v. Tennessee, 496 F.Supp. 218 (M.D.Tenn.1980)(Tennessee barratry statute).

52 Burnes v. Scott, 117 U.S. 582, 589, 6 S.Ct. 865, 869, 29 L.Ed. 991 (1886); Augenti v. Cappellini, 499 F.Supp. 50, 51 (M.D.Pa.1980). See also Lewis v. Black, 74 F.R.D. 1 (E.D.N.Y.1975)(lawyer's purchase of stock for champertous purpose does not disable him from filing suit through other counsel if purchase otherwise valid).

disqualification of the lawyer.[53] Those residual sentiments find expression, in part, in such legal requirements as the contemporaneous-ownership rule, the requirement that the representative shareholder in a derivative action must not have acquired his or her stock interest after the alleged wrong to the corporation,[54] prohibitions against solicitation of clients,[55] and prohibitions against a lawyer's acquisition of an interest in a client's cause of action.

The Prohibition against Lawyers' Acquiring Interests in Litigated Matters

Despite the general demise of the champerty-type prohibitions, decisions and rules still variously prohibit a lawyer's purchase of causes of action on which the lawyer intends to file suit[56] or a lawyer's purchase of a client's interest in property that is the subject of litigation.[57] Obviously the distinction between an impermissible purchase and a legitimate contingent fee may be subtle.[58] Indeed, many of the older cases involving lawyers reflect the law still groping its way toward a grudging acceptance of contingent fees. A permissible avoidance of the antipurchase rule is the arrangement, familiar in many jurisdictions, in which a collection agency buys delinquent accounts and then retains lawyers to file suit on them.[59]

The Canons, Code, and Model Rules very broadly prohibit a lawyer from acquiring an interest in a client's cause of action or the subject of litigation. Canon 10,[60] the Code's DR 5–103(A),[61] and Model Rule 1.8(j)[62] provide blanket prohibitions that contain no exception for client consent.[63] It is critical for a lawyer to be able to identify whether an arrangement with a client is covered by one of those provisions or by one of the rules on business dealings with a client (DR 5–104(A) or MR 1.8(a)), because the latter, but not the former, make an exception for client consent.

Some decisions have read the business-dealing prohibition of Canon 10 and DR 5–103(A) quite broadly to apply to nonlitigation set-

53 People v. Csaban, 103 Misc.2d 1109, 427 N.Y.S.2d 571 (1980).

54 Dimpfel v. Ohio & Miss. Ry., 110 U.S. 209, 3 S.Ct. 573, 28 L.Ed. 121 (1884); Harbrecht, The Contemporaneous Ownership Rule in Shareholder Derivative Suits, 25 UCLA L.Rev. 1041 (1978).

55 See § 14.2.5. The bar perception of a connection between solicitation and "stirring up litigation" was made explicit in 1908 in Canon 28.

56 West.Ann.Cal.Bus. & Prof.Code § 6129. See generally Martin v. Freeman, 216 Cal.App.2d 639, 31 Cal.Rptr. 217 (1963); La.Stat.Ann.—Civ. Code art. 2447. Normally those prohibitions are narrowly confined by a doctrine of "primary purpose," which permits lawyers and others to purchase causes of action if the primary purpose is investment or even speculation, so long as the purpose of suing is "incidental." E.g., Drake v. Northwest Natural Gas Co., 39 Del.Ch. 394, 165 A.2d 452, 455 (1960); Sprung v. Jaffe, 3 N.Y.2d 539, 169 N.Y.S.2d 456, 147 N.E.2d 6 (1957).

57 In re May, 96 Idaho 858, 538 P.2d 787 (1975)(violation of DR 5–103(A) for lawyer to acquire mortgagee interest in house that was subject matter of litigation); West v. Raymond, 21 Ind. 305 (1863)(client's sale of property to lawyer while action pending is void).

58 Reece v. Kyle, 49 Ohio St. 475, 31 N.E. 747 (1892) (lawyer, owed fee for obtaining judgment that client could not afford to collect, permissibly obtained assignment of judgment from client with agreement to divide proceeds if successful in collection).

59 Cohn v. Thompson, 128 Cal.App.Supp. 783, 16 P.2d 364 (1932); Messmer v. Carter, 282 Or. 323, 578 P.2d 788 (1978). Debt-collection agencies are frequently licensed and regulated under state law. See generally Comment, Legal Ethics: Unauthorized Practice of Law by Collection Agencies, 52 Minn.L.Rev. 1300 (1968). Others who attempt to solicit claims for the primary purpose of filing suit may remain subject to the ancient strictures against champertous assignments. E.g., Fairchild Hiller Corp. v. McDonnell Douglas Corp., 28 N.Y.2d 325, 321 N.Y.S.2d 857, 859, 270 N.E.2d 691, 693 (1971).

60 Canon 10: "The lawyer shall not purchase any interest in the subject matter of the litigation which he is conducting."

61 DR 5–103(A): "A lawyer shall not acquire a proprietary interest in the cause of action or subject matter of litigation he is conducting for a client . . . ." The exceptions provided are for attorney liens (DR 5–103(A)(1); see generally § 9.6.3 (attorney liens)), and contingent fees (DR 5–103(A)(2); see generally § 9.4 (contingent fee, generally)).

62 MR 1.8(j) is copied from DR 5–103(A), with only nonsubstantive word changes. It was inserted into the Model Rules by floor amendment at the February 1983 ABA meeting.

63 But cf. In re Ainsworth, 289 Or. 479, 614 P.2d 1127, 1133 (1980)("it may be" that DR 5–103(A) provides no exception for client consent, but court does not decide question whether fully informed client consent would be defense to discipline charge).

tings or to outlaw all lawyer loans to clients.[64] To the extent that acquiring an interest in a client's cause of action involves a conflict-ridden business dealing with a client, the overlap is probably harmless. But some purchases of a client's cause of action are no more objectionable on conflicts grounds than is any other business dealing between lawyer and client, for example, the lawyer's purchasing the entire claim of the client for a fair price. A purchase of a partial interest, of course, does present the possibility that the lawyer will not seek and accept client guidance on major decisions in the lawsuit because of the lawyer's own economic interest in the outcome. That concern lies at the base of the modern prohibition. Nonetheless, if a lawyer's purchase of a client's cause of action is made in a way that avoids the possibility of adverse impact upon a lawyer's exercise of judgment during the course of the representation, no sound reason exists to prevent it, so long as the client consents and the transaction is fair and reasonable.[65]

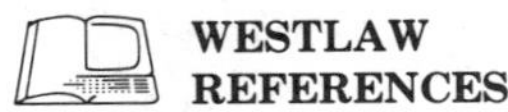
WESTLAW REFERENCES

di champerty

di barratry

74k1

74k3

champerty barratry /p lawyer attorney

attorney lawyer /5 buy*** acquir! acquisition purchas*** /5 interest subject /3 litigation case controversy "cause of action"

"dr 5–103(a)"

§ 8.14 CLASS ACTION CONFLICTS

The Ethical Debate over Class Actions

Class action litigation has become a growth industry since the adoption of the 1965 amendments to the Federal Rules of Civil Procedure, which significantly liberalized the availability of class actions. Those large and amorphous procedural mutants have themselves spawned a number of conflict of interest issues.[66] Conflict is rife within the structure of the class itself. Most obviously, the class representative may have interests and goals that in fact are not shared by represented but absent class members. Occasionally conflict has surfaced in ugly scenes in which class representatives have rejected a fair offer to the class in order to pressure a defendant to make a different offer that would provide greater benefits to the representatives.[67] A lawyer's representation of the members of a class can encounter other simultaneous-representation conflicts.[68] For example, the existence of subclasses and the nature of their separate interests might preclude the designation of one lawyer to represent them all.[69]

[64] State ex rel. Florida Bar v. Oxford, 127 So.2d 107, 109 (Fla.1960)(Canon 10 violated by loaning money to clients to obtain their release from jail in police court representations); In re Witt, 96 Wn.2d 56, 633 P.2d 880, 886 (1981)(acquisition of interest in assets not subject to litigation). Cf. Bar Ass'n of Greater Cleveland v. Nesbitt, 69 Ohio St.2d 108, 431 N.E.2d 323 (1982)(obtaining secret finder's fee on client's loan to third party violation of both DR 5–103(A) and DR 5–104(A)).

[65] Cf. Eikelberger v. Tolotti, 96 Nev. 525, 611 P.2d 1086 (1980)(purchase of client's judgment permissible because representation at an end).

[66] Among the best recent analyses, see Dam, Class Actions: Efficiency, Compensation, Deterrence, and Conflict of Interest, 4 J. Legal Stud. 47 (1975); Garth, Conflict and Dissent in Class Actions: A Suggested Perspective, 77 Nw.U.L.Rev. 492 (1982); Rhode, Class Conflicts in Class Actions, 34 Stan.L.Rev. 1183 (1982); Note, Conflicts in Class Actions and Protection of Absent Class Members, 91 Yale L.J. 590 (1982). The narrower issue examined here, conflict of interest problems of a lawyer representing a class, is discussed in Note, Conflicts of Interest in the Legal Profession, 92 Harv.L.Rev. 1244, 1447–57 (1981). See also Wolfram, The Antibiotics Class Actions, 1976 Am.B.Found. Research J. 251.

[67] See Parker v. Anderson, 667 F.2d 1204, 1211 (5th Cir. 1982), cert.denied 459 U.S. 828, 103 S.Ct. 63, 74 L.Ed.2d 65 (1982)("named plaintiffs should not be able to hold the absentee class hostage" and thus would not be entitled to oppose the settlement "primarily to gain leverage in settling their individual claims . . . at exorbitant figures"). See also Soskel v. Texaco, Inc., 94 F.R.D. 201 (S.D.N.Y.1982)(proposed settlement of uncertified class action rejected because it provided relief only to class representative and none to putative class members).

[68] See generally § 7.3.

[69] See City of Rochester v. Chiarella, 86 A.D.2d 110, 449 N.Y.S.2d 112 (1982)(obvious conflicts between protesting and nonprotesting taxpayers precluded joint representation by single law firm). But cf. Armstrong v. O'Connel, 416 F.Supp. 1325, 1341 (E.D.Wisc.1976), vacated 566 F.2d 1175 (7th Cir.1977)(per curiam); Brandt v. Owens-Illinois, Inc., 62 F.R.D. 160, 171–72 (S.D.N.Y.1973).

As difficult as some lawyer conflicts problems are in class actions, the number and kinds of ethical objections raised by those who oppose class action lawyers give substance to the fear that their objections are merely tactical. Often the objections seem indistinguishable from timeworn criticisms of the class action rules themselves on the ground that the procedures they authorize amount to solicitation [70] or "stirring up litigation".[71]

Class and Lawyer Conflicts

Class action certification issues indicate the ways in which the economic interests of the class lawyer can be pitted against the interests of the class. Most of the federal courts now hold that if a lawyer sues as a plaintiff representing a class, neither the named lawyer nor an associated lawyer may also serve as class counsel.[72] While incipient conflict always exists between a class representative and absent class members, conflict is exacerbated when the lawyer for the class is also the class representative. The lawyer for the class has an economic interest in receiving a fee that is clearly in conflict with the interest of class members in minimizing the fee, an interest that, at least theoretically, an independent class representative can protect against possible overreaching by the class lawyer. That conflict is not abated when the class lawyer will receive compensation from a fund created by settlement or judgment,[73] because the lawyer's reimbursement will leave that much less for distribution to the class.

Despite the prominence of those and similar ethical issues in class actions, nothing in the professional codes addresses them directly. Instead, the matter has been left, correctly, to regulation through the close judicial supervision that ideally attends class actions.[74]

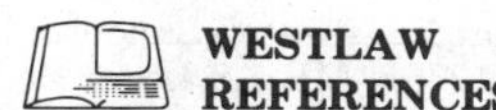

WESTLAW REFERENCES

conflict! /3 interest /s "class action" /s attorney lawyer /p disqualif! % fees

attorney lawyer /s "class action" /p simultaneous multiple /3 representation

synopsis,digest("class action" /s attorney lawyer /p conflict! /3 interest)

§ 8.15 SETTLING RELATED CASES

Both the Code (DR 5–106(A)) and the Model Rules (MR 1.8(g)) prohibit a lawyer from making an aggregate settlement of two or more clients' claims with a single opposing party without fully informing each client and obtaining consent. The problem, of course, is that without client supervision a lawyer might be tempted to sacrifice the interests of one client to gain an advantage for the other. It can arise in both civil[75] and criminal[76] cases and is a specific instance of conflict problems that can arise in simultaneous representa-

[70] Haas, Professional and Ethical Aspects of Antitrust Class Actions, 41 Antitrust L.J. 280 (1971). On the demise of maintenance generally, see § 8.13.

[71] On charges of solicitation in class litigation, see § 8.8.3 (advocacy organizations). See also § 9.2.3 (advancing funds to clients).

[72] A leading case, Kramer v. Scientific Control Corp., 534 F.2d 1085 (3d Cir.), cert.denied 429 U.S. 830, 97 S.Ct. 90, 50 L.Ed.2d 94 (1976), creates a per se rule of automatic disqualification. See also Zylstra v. Safeway Stores, Inc., 578 F.2d 102, 104 (5th Cir.1978). Most courts now seem to prefer a rule of trial court discretion rather than automatic disqualification. See Garonzik v. Shearson, Hayden Stone, Inc., 574 F.2d 1220 (5th Cir.1978), cert.denied 439 U.S. 1072, 99 S.Ct. 844, 59 L.Ed.2d 39 (1979)(overruling *Zylstra*, supra); Brick v. CPC Int'l, Inc., 547 E.2d 185 (2d Cir.1976); Turoff v. May Co., 531 F.2d 1357 (6th Cir.1976). See generally Comment, The Attorney as Plaintiff and Quasi-Plaintiff in Class and Derivative Actions: Ethical and Procedural Considerations, 18 B.C.Indus. & Com.L.Rev. 467 (1977).

[73] See § 16.6.2 (fund theory).

[74] See generally Wolfram, The Second Set of Players: Lawyers, Fee Shifting, and the Limits of Professional Discipline, 47 L. & Contemp. Probs. 293 (1984).

[75] A.Rosenthal, Lawyer and Client: Who's in Charge? 103 (1974)(although prohibited, practice of personal injury lawyers making "package settlements" with insurance companies is not uncommon). See also id. at 59 (ability of personal injury lawyer to get some recovery, even for very marginal claims, as "favor" from insurance adjuster in order to promote goodwill in future, more highly valued negotiations).

[76] Cf. ABA Defense Function Standards § 4–6.2(c)(approved 1979)(unprofessional for defense lawyer to make or seek from prosecutor concessions favorable to one client that are "detrimental to the legitimate interests" of any other client).

tions. The problem also implicates rules providing for client control over settlements and the right to be fully informed about them (§ 4.6.2). The problem, therefore, does not arise when each client has separate representation.[77]

The ban does not outlaw aggregate settlements but does require specifically that each client be fully informed.[78] The professional rules spell out for the occasion two particular matters that must be discussed with each client—the existence and nature of each matter and the extent to which each person will participate in the aggregate settlement.

WESTLAW REFERENCES

"dr 5–106(a)" /p disclos! inform** /p consent

[77] See In re Guardianship of Lauderdale, 15 Wn.App. 321, 549 P.2d 42 (1976); MR 1.8 Legal Background Note, at 64 (Proposed Final Draft, May 30, 1981).

[78] See Continental Coiffures, Ltd. v. Kimble, 270 Pa. Super. 509, 411 A.2d 834, 836 (1979).

Chapter Nine
CLIENT-LAWYER CONTRACTS

Table of Sections

§ 9.1 REGULATION OF CLIENT-LAWYER CONTRACTS

Common-Law, Supervisory, Disciplinary, and Legislative Control

Viewed in one light, an express or implied agreement between a client and lawyer for the latter to perform legal services and the former to pay for them is an agreement that is subject to the ordinary rules of contract. One might therefore expect that under contract law a lawyer who negotiates a very favorable fee could insist that courts enforce the bargain, just as courts will generally enforce bargains. But fee contracts, unlike the generality of contracts, are also subject to special forms of regulation. Many courts would refuse to enforce the lawyer's bargain if they considered the fee to be unreasonable in amount. The special regulation of client-lawyer fee contracts comes about in several different ways. At the outset, the contract is subject to the normal rules of contract law with respect to its formation, consideration, conditions, performance, and remedies.

Quite beyond general common-law rules, however, courts exercise a supervisory power that in one form reshapes the legal rights between client and lawyer. The supervisory power has been exercised both in litigation to which client and lawyers are parties, such as fee suits, and in litigation to which only the client is a party. Courts also exercise disciplinary control over lawyers, which can extend to questions of fee charges. Finally, the legislature also plays a role in regulating fee contracts. While all of the interventions in the client-lawyer relationship have as their objective the protection of the interests of the client, the question needs to be asked whether the limits on lawyer compensation created by some of the regulations do not in the end harm client interests by discouraging lawyers from accepting cases and by driving more competent lawyers into other lines of legal services.[1]

[1] See Special Project, Recent Developments in Attorneys' Fees, 29 Vand.L.Rev. 685, 718 (1976).

Supervisory Power. The basic contractual relationship between client and lawyer is itself subject to an overriding power in courts to affect the terms of the relationship between client and lawyer in ways favorable to the client. That is a power quite different from the common-law power of courts to fashion rules of contract law. The power is derived from the court's special role as protector of vulnerable clients against the depredations of lawyers and as primary regulator of the legal profession. The power has been sparingly used,[2] although, when employed, it has been used robustly. The special judicial power over fee contracts will be referred to here as the *supervisory* power of judges over questions of fee contracts in order to distinguish that judicial power from the more familiar common-law power of judges to decide issues of contract law.

The courts' supervisory power is employed in the otherwise familiar context of lawsuits between lawyers and their clients involving fees. But it is also sometimes employed in otherwise unfamiliar summary and ancillary proceedings, sometimes initiated by the judge without the complaint of any party, which can result in a judicial order directing the lawyer to reduce a fee charge to a client or to refund a fee overcharge. Sometimes the courts' supervisory power is used in rule making, such as when a court promulgates a mandatory maximum fee schedule (§ 9.3.2) or creates a system of mandatory fee arbitration (§ 9.6.2) that directly limits the lawful power of a lawyer to charge the client a fee.

Disciplinary Power. Apart from the power of courts to affect the terms of the contract itself through their supervisory power, courts also exercise a broad regulatory power over lawyers by means of which they can impose regulations and create procedures and remedies especially for fee contracts. Those regulatory powers are different from the courts' supervisory powers because they are enforced outside the context of litigation to which the client is a party. Included are disciplinary rules relating to fee contracts that are enforceable in the established disciplinary process (§ 3.4). Disciplinary controls do not directly enlarge the enforceable legal rights of clients as supervisory powers do. But to a considerable extent disciplinary controls impose practical limits on lawyers that can clearly benefit clients. On occasion, as in the instance of disciplinary agency decisions ordering a lawyer to make restitution to injured clients (§ 3.5.6), the exercise of disciplinary powers can result in direct benefits to clients.

Power of the Legislature. Legislatures have also occasionally imposed limits and controls on client-lawyer contracts or have modified the legal rules affecting fee contracts that courts might impose. Most often that has been done in the context of a larger regulatory scheme, in which the question of fees is an important detail of implementation. For example, a common feature of legislative plans affecting injured workers is a statutory provision that the administrative agency that adjudicates benefits to workers can also set the size of the fee to be paid by an injured worker to his or her lawyer.[3] In many other instances courts have warned the legislature away when it has attempted to regulate the legal profession (§ 2.2.3). Here, however, courts do not ordinarily insist that the matter be left to the exclusive power of the judicial branch. Thus many statutes affecting attorney fees are enforced by the courts. But if the statute, under one interpretation, might have the effect of limiting the court's visitatorial power to inspect the basic client-attorney contract, the tendency of courts is to give the statute an alternative reading that renders it innocuous.[4] The general pattern, then, is

[2] Farmington Dowel Prods. Co. v. Forster Mfg. Co., 421 F.2d 61, 90 (1st Cir.1969) (exercise of court's "supervisory power over the bar" to limit size of contingent fee recovery "is reserved for exceptional circumstances").

[3] 3 A.Larson, Workmens' Compensation § 83.13 (1983); Report of the National Comm'n on State Workmen's Compensation Laws, recommendation 6.15 (1972).

[4] Mack v. Minneapolis, 333 N.W.2d 744, 752–53 (Minn. 1983)(statute conferring power on administrative agency to set fees for lawyer's work there not in violation of exclusive inherent power of court because court can ultimately review all fee awards). That fate has befallen statutes that can be found in several states that declare that the measure of a lawyer's compensation is to be

that fee legislation is generally limited in many states to a role that is essentially ancillary to, and supportive of, the judiciary's own common-law power over lawyers' fees.

The various forms of special control over client-lawyer contracts have clearly not been pervasive or uniform from state to state. Courts seem to exercise their supervisory power over contracts primarily under the pressure of a notable scandal or crisis and otherwise only episodically, rarely, and with no clear pattern or theory of intervention. Bar discipline for unethical fee charges is also rare and seems reserved largely for outrageous cases. Legislative initiatives have been limited, both because lawyers have traditionally dominated state legislatures and possibly because of uncertainties about the limits of legislative power to regulate the legal profession. From the point of view of those clients who consider themselves burdened with unreasonable fee charges, the field appears to be one that is occupied by a judiciary that often neglects to exercise the powers that it has claimed largely for itself.

Supervisory Power of Courts

The doctrine that courts are empowered to scrutinize fee contracts more stringently than commercial contracts generally is one of long standing,[5] although perhaps not all courts subscribe to it.[6] The doctrine is often found applied in cases involving fee agreements exacted by a lawyer after the relationship of trust and confidence between client and lawyer had already been established[7] and when some other basis for the traditional intervention of equity is present. The lawyer in such an instance is treated as a fiduciary because of the presumed vulnerability of the client, and for that reason general fiduciary obligations of fair dealing are imposed.[8] But other decisions do not depend on the vulnerability of the client and announce a broad power to regulate fees simply because they are charged by lawyers.[9] Thus a second rationale for the doctrine is the general principle that lawyers are subject to the supervisory authority of courts before which they practice.[10]

fixed by the client-lawyer agreement. Courts uniformly construe those statutes to refer implicitly to the court's traditional power to supervise the reasonable nature of those agreements. E.g., Gair v. Peck, 6 N.Y.2d 97, 106, 188 N.Y.S.2d 491, 497–98, 160 N.E.2d 43 (1959), cert.denied 361 U.S. 374, 80 S.Ct. 401, 4 L.Ed.2d 380 (1960)(despite statute stating that lawyer's compensation is fixed by agreement with client, "[c]ontingent fees may be disallowed as between attorney and client in spite of contingent fee retainer agreements, where the amount becomes large enough to be out of all proportion to the value of the professional services rendered").

[5] Ridge v. Healy, 251 F. 798, 804 (8th Cir.1918); Thomas v. Turner's Adm'r, 87 Va. 1, 12 S.E. 149 (1890).

[6] Thatcher v. Industrial Comm'n, 115 Utah 568, 207 P.2d 178 (1949)(dictum)("We are not aware of any power in the judiciary to fix or regulate attorney's fees. We do not think it can be inferred from the power to promulgate rules of practice and procedure nor . . . from the auxiliary power to discipline attorneys as officers of the court for unprofessional conduct."). Cf. Shannon v. Cross, 245 Mich. 220, 222 N.W. 168 (1928)(power of courts over practice and procedure does not extend to power to promulgate rule limiting contingent fees so strictly that it prohibits them in large class of cases).

[7] See cases cited n. 6 supra. See also, e.g., Stiers v. Hall, 170 Va. 569, 197 S.E. 450 (1938).

[8] Spilker v. Hankin, 188 F.2d 35 (D.C.Cir.1951)(normal rules of res judicata would not be applied to preclude client's second defense against lawyer's suits to recover on series of notes exacted from client after beginning of relationship); Smitas v. Rickett, 102 A.D.2d 928, 477 N.Y.S.2d 752, 755 (1984)(in view of "established rule that the courts of this State retain authority and implicit control over the supervision of fee arrangements between attorney and client under the court's inherent and statutory power to regulate the practice of law," client was not precluded from raising question of lawyer's fee because of silence on question during prior bankruptcy action). Compare also, e.g., § 8.11 (business dealings with clients), § 8.12 (client gifts to lawyers). Cf., also, § 16.6.2.

[9] Watson v. Cook, 427 So.2d 1312, 1316 (La.App.1983) ("any dispute relative to any attorney client relationship, including the enforcement of the contracts sought to be enforced in the instant proceeding, is subject to the close scrutiny of the courts. . . . [I]t is clear that although parties are permitted to contract and/or agree with respect to attorney's fees, that attorney's fees and all contracts and agreements pertaining to such fees are subject to the review and control of the courts."); Federal Land Bank v. Ambrosano, 89 A.D.2d 730, 453 N.Y.S.2d 857, 859 (1982)(traditional and inherent power of courts to regulate lawyers as basis for disregarding contract measure of fees and awarding only quantum meruit ($6,000) rather than amount of fees billed ($27,441) in contractual fee-shifting case).

[10] Magana v. Platzer Shipyard, Inc., 74 F.R.D. 61, 74 n.9 (S.D.Tex.1977)("Two mutually-exclusive rationales support a judicial review of any contingent fee contract for reasonableness: (1) the special fiduciary nature of the

Supervisory Procedures and Remedies

Courts have exercised their supervisory power over fees in a number of settings. The situations and the courts' approaches have a definite aura of the ad hoc and inventive about them. In one setting, a court will simply place on the judicial agenda in an informal way an order directed to the lawyer to show cause why a fee contract should not be altered, even though the lawyer is not a party to the litigation and despite the fact that no one other than the judge has objected to the size of the fee. In other settings, the court confronts the question of the validity and reasonability of a fee charge in a more traditional way.

Fiduciary Litigation. In suits of a fiduciary nature both state and federal courts have exercised a power of judicial review and have reduced a lawyer's fee charge on the ground that it was excessive. Included are actions involving the estates of minors and incompetents,[11] wrongful death actions,[12] actions involving seamen,[13] and class actions.[14] The courts' power comes directly from their necessary function of approving the settlement or entry of judgment in those suits and supervising distribution of the proceeds in the best interest of the ward. That function, according to the courts, entails the power to determine the reasonability of the fee sought.

To an extent, the cases dealing with settlement of a ward's claim resemble the equity action to approve the account of a trustee. It is well settled that an equity court has jurisdiction to reduce fees paid out of trust assets to lawyers representing the trustee, a beneficiary, or the trust itself.[15] Because the guardian ad litem of a child or the conservator of the estate of an incompetent person is subject to fiduciary duties, a lawyer who contracts with such a party is clearly susceptible to equitable controls.[16] Cases employing a supervisory power over fees may be historically rooted in such equitable concepts, but they have moved far from such origins.

Contingent Fee Contracts. Courts commonly state that contingent fee contracts (§ 9.4) are subject to stricter scrutiny than other types of contracts, including fee contracts based on other methods of computing and paying the fee.[17] While the courts rarely give a reason for asserting a larger measure of power here, the rule probably reflects merely

attorney-client relationship; and (2) the court's disciplinary powers over attorneys practicing before them."), citing Special Project, Recent Developments in Attorneys' Fees, 29 Vand.L.Rev. 685, 710–718 (1976).

[11] Hoffert v. General Motors Corp., 656 F.2d 161 (5th Cir.1981), cert.denied 456 U.S. 961, 102 S.Ct. 2037, 72 L.Ed.2d 485 (1982)(retained lawyer's 40 percent contingent fee, voluntarily reduced to 33 percent after settlement of minor's personal injury claim for $2.5 million within months after suit was initiated, was subject to reduction by trial court to 20 percent as part of process of approving settlement and distributing its proceeds); Rosquist v. Soo Line R.R., 692 F.2d 1107 (7th Cir.1982) (settlement of child's tort action); Friends for All Children, Inc. v. Lockheed Aircraft Corp., 567 F.Supp. 790, 813 (D.D.C.1983).

[12] Krause v. Rhodes, 640 F.2d 214 (6th Cir.1981), cert. denied 454 U.S. 836, 102 S.Ct. 140, 70 L.Ed.2d 117 (1981) (civil rights wrongful death actions); In re Cap'n Rick Corp., 525 F.Supp. 31 (S.D.N.Y.1981), affirmed 685 F.2d 423 (2d Cir.1982)(Death on the High Seas Act and Jones Act claims).

[13] Schlesinger v. Teitelbaum, 475 F.2d 137 (3d Cir.), cert.denied 414 U.S. 1111, 94 S.Ct. 840, 38 L.Ed.2d 738 (1973).

[14] Dunn v. H.K. Porter Co., 602 F.2d 1105, 1109 (3d Cir. 1979).

[15] In re Estate of Gilman, 112 Misc.2d 452, 446 N.Y.S.2d 975 (Sur.Ct.1981)(multimillion-dollar fee payment by trustee to prominent lawyer and to law professor substantially reduced). Under Rule 13–210(d) of the Federal Bankruptcy Rules, "any payment, transfer, or obligation [for legal fees] shall be held valid only to the extent of a reasonable amount as determined by the court." Fee agreements subject to review in that way are those for which the lawyer files a claim in bankruptcy or those payments by the bankrupt to a lawyer made in contemplation of bankruptcy or after bankruptcy commences.

[16] Rosquist v. Soo Line R.R., 692 F.2d 1107, 1110–11 (7th Cir.1982); Hoffert v. General Motors Corp., 656 F.2d 161, 164–65 (5th Cir.1981), cert.denied 456 U.S. 961, 102 S.Ct. 2037, 72 L.Ed.2d 485 (1982).

[17] International Travel Arrangers, Inc. v. Western Airlines, Inc., 623 F.2d 1255, 1257 (8th Cir.1980), cert. denied 449 U.S. 1063, 101 S.Ct. 787, 66 L.Ed.2d 605 (1980); Dunn v. H.K. Porter Co., 602 F.2d 1105, 1108–09 (3d Cir.1979) (court may exercise supervisory power over lawyers to monitor contingent fee contracts and reduce fees if unreasonable); Farmington Dowel Prods. Co. v. Forster, Mfg. Co., 421 F.2d 61, 87 (1st Cir.1969)(courts have "generic power to confine the cost of legal services to a reasonable amount"); In re Cap'n Rick Corp., 525 F.Supp. 31, 37 (S.D.N.Y.1981), affirmed 685 F.2d 423 (2d Cir.1982). In Maine (Me.Bar Rule 8(f)), a contingent fee contract is subject to review, by a judge in the state appointed by the

the ordinary doctrine of supervisory judicial control applied to an area in which the risks of harm to a possibly vulnerable and unsophisticated client may be particularly great.[18] At least in many contingent fee contracts, the clients might well lack bargaining power in dealing with their lawyers or lack the ability to keep track of the lawyer's work.[19] Consistent with that reason for searching supervision, courts have shown insouciance when the client who complained of the terms of an improvident contingent fee contract was a large corporate client that had the benefit of independent legal advice before entering into it.[20]

Summary Proceedings. Courts will occasionally, sometimes on their own motion, entertain the question of the size of a lawyer's fee charge to a client without nice regard to jurisdictional, case or controversy, pleading, or other procedural requirements that normally govern suits.[21] Various theories have been advanced for such extraordinary procedures, including the argument that the court's power is one that is necessary and appropriate for the exercise of courts' inherent control over lawyers as their officers.[22] The federal courts have taken different, and possibly conflicting, positions on the advisability of such interventions,[23] but the basic supervisory power of a federal court to intervene into any fee arrangement that is exorbitant has been conceded even by federal judges who are reluctant to permit interventions of that sort.[24]

Review of Damage Awards. The most obvious area in which courts have claimed a supervisory power to limit the size of attorney fees is in a suit for a fee by a lawyer against a client [25] or in a suit by a client to recover an

chief justice of the state, for a period of one year following the last services rendered. See Nisbet v. Faunce, 432 A.2d 779, 783 (Me.1981). See generally Note, Judicial Power over Contingent Fee Contracts: Reasonableness and Ethics, 30 Case W.Res.L.Rev. 523 (1980).

18 Schlesinger v. Teitelbaum, 475 F.2d 137, 141 (3d Cir. 1973), cert.denied 414 U.S. 1111, 94 S.Ct. 840, 38 L.Ed.2d 738 (1973)("in its supervisory power over the members of its bar, a court has jurisdiction of certain activities of such members, including the charges of contingent fees"): Baumrin v. Cournoyer, 448 F.Supp. 225, 228 (D.Mass. 1978)(federal court has inherent equitable power to pass on reasonableness of contingent fee in any case pending before court). See generally, F.MacKinnon, Contingent Fees for Legal Services 44–45 (1964); Note, Judicial Power over Contingent Fee Contracts: Reasonableness and Ethics, 30 C.Wes.Res.L.Rev. 523, 523–24 (1980).

19 Esser v. A.H. Robins Co., 537 F.Supp. 197, 200 (D.Minn.1982)(in ruling on lawyers' motion to withdraw as attorneys for plaintiffs, court directs that they are not to share in any portion of funds because of unethical relationship, during their representation, with insurance adjuster for defendant).

20 Brobeck, Phleger & Harrison v. Telex Corp., 602 F.2d 866 (9th Cir.1979), cert.denied 444 U.S. 981, 100 S.Ct. 483, 62 L.Ed.2d 407 (1979)(large national corporation liable for $1 million contingency bonus under fee contract negotiated between corporation's chairman, advised by corporation's general counsel, and prominent antitrust lawyer for drafting certiorari petition that was mooted by settlement).

21 In re LiVolsi, 85 N.J. 576, 428 A.2d 1268, 1273–75 (1981)(on client's complaint, court sitting without jury will determine reasonableness of fee in exercise of regulatory power over lawyers as officers of court; trial by jury would undermine court's power to regulate lawyers).

22 In re Innkeepers of New Castle, Inc., 671 F.2d 221, 232 (7th Cir.1982), cert. denied 459 U.S. 908, 103 S.Ct. 212, 74 L.Ed.2d 169 (1982) (concurring opinion).

23 Compare, e.g., United States v. Vague, 697 F.2d 805 (7th Cir.1983)(judge troubled by size of fee to be paid by adult in criminal case should not have pursued question in light of other available remedies), reversing 521 F.Supp. 147 (N.D.Ill.1981), with, e.g., Coffelt v. Shell, 577 F.2d 30 (8th Cir.1978)(trial court could, on own motion, reduce lawyer's fee because of mistrial and because lawyer was unprepared). See also, e.g., Hoffert v. General Motors Corp., 656 F.2d 161 (5th Cir.1981), cert.denied 456 U.S. 961, 102 S.Ct. 2037, 72 L.Ed.2d 485 (1982)(judge had power on own motion to reduce fee charged to minor in personal injury case). While admitting the power to intervene, the majority in *Vague* held that because a judge's holding a hearing on the question of the reasonableness of a fee in the absence of any complaint by the client cast the judge into the role of both prosecutor and judge, the judge should refer the question of the size of the fee to an established ethics committee. *Vague* distinguished cases such as *Hoffert* as involving instances in which a judge was asked to approve an unethical fee in performing the necessary task of approving a settlement and its distribution.

24 United States v. Vague, 697 F.2d 805, 806 (7th Cir. 1983)("[T]he admitted power of a federal judge to take action about an exorbitant fee in the absence of complaint applied to a freely bargained fixed fee . . . may seem paternalistic or worse" but cannot be questioned in light of precedent), citing In re Kutner, 78 Ill.2d 157, 35 Ill.Dec. 674, 399 N.E.2d 963 (1979).

25 Spilker v. Hankin, 188 F.2d 35 (D.C.1951); Wunschel Law Firm, P.C. v. Clabaugh, 291 N.W.2d 331 (Iowa 1980); Kirby v. Liska, 214 Neb. 356, 334 N.W.2d 179, 183 (1983).

assertedly excessive fee.[26] The power has been exercised in other types of fee claims as well. Attorney fees can be awarded as damages against a nonclient in a limited number of cases (§ 16.6.2). In passing on the amount of fees that the jury has awarded as damages in such cases, courts often treat that segment of the damage award as subject to special scrutiny if it is unreasonably large.[27] The same has also been done in suits that involve a claim for attorney fees payable under a contract.[28]

Ancillary Proceedings. Questions of fees may arise in ways connected to a pending matter that permit a court to exercise an ancillary power to investigate a fee question. Thus a court has entertained a claim by the government that a lawyer's exorbitant fee charge in one case impoverished the client to an extent that public funds were necessary to pay for a lawyer in a second proceeding.[29] Some cases have stretched the doctrine of ancillary review of attorney fees quite far.[30]

Future of Supervisory Powers

Courts are positioned to learn occasionally of apparently outrageous fee charges. A natural judicial instinct to do justice and to protect the honor of the legal profession may lead to a hearing on the reasonableness of the fee. But such judicial interventions must in their nature be rare. Courts have no mechanism for the routine reporting of all fees. Some of the highest fees, which are paid by corporate litigants, are unknown except to the parties. Judicial intervention to limit the size of contingent fees paid to plaintiffs' lawyers both creates an appearance of invidious supervision and may lead to the overall diminution of the quality of counsel available to those who must rely on contingent fee representation. The market for legal services is hardly a perfect one, cluttered as it is with restrictions on the availability of information about fees (§ 14.2.4). Because of such imperfections, courts will continue to be tempted to offer protection to clients whom the court suspects to have been overreached by a grasping lawyer. But the courts can hardly assure us that all or even most overreaching that might occur is detected and remedied in that way. To achieve that objective, other methods of reporting and regulation would be necessary.

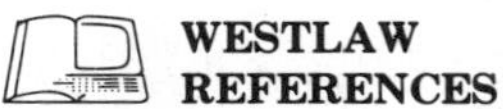
WESTLAW REFERENCES

Supervisory Power

45k143 45k145

attorney lawyer client /s fee contract /p "supervisory power"

Disciplinary Power

attorney lawyer counsel** /s fee contract retainer /s disciplin!

Power of the Legislature

45k131

Contingent Fee Contracts

45k148

---

26 Newman v. Silver, 553 F.Supp. 485, 495 (S.D.N.Y. 1982), affirmed in part, vacated in part on other grounds 713 F.2d 14 (2d Cir.1983).

27 Wuagneux Builders, Inc. v. Candlewood Builders, Inc., 651 S.W.2d 919, 922 (Tex.App.1983).

28 Hebert v. Neyrey, 432 So.2d 396, 401 (La.App.1983), affirmed in part, reversed in part on other grounds 445 So.2d 1165 (1984); Avco Financial Services Trust v. Bentley, 116 Misc.2d 34, 455 N.Y.S.2d 62 (1982).

29 United States v. Strawser, 581 F.Supp. 875 (C.D.Ill. 1984)(on apparent complaint of client and government, lawyer ordered to reduce fee charge by more than half).

30 Coffelt v. Shell, 577 F.2d 30 (8th Cir.1978)(court, in granting motion for mistrial because of lawyer's conflict of interest, permissibly ordered reduction in fee charge from $1,000 to $100 because of termination of trial and because of lawyer's obvious lack of preparation); In re Greenwald, 94 A.D.2d 842, 463 N.Y.S.2d 303 (1983) appeal denied 60 N.Y.2d 551, 467 N.Y.S.2d 1025, 454 N.E.2d 126 (1983)(in granting motion of lawyer to withdraw from criminal defense, court was within discretionary power to order partial refund of prepaid fee).

§ 9.2 FORMATION AND TERMS OF CLIENT–LAWYER CONTRACTS

§ 9.2.1 *Formation of Client-Lawyer Contracts*

Basic Contractual Relationship

As with other contracts, so the client-lawyer contract can be either express or implied. An implied contract can be one that is recognizable from the tacit understanding of the parties as they have gone about the work of a representation for a fee without reaching explicit agreement on the contract of employment.[31] Or an implied contract to pay legal fees can be one "implied in law" rather than in fact in order to avoid unjust enrichment.[32] For example, it is well established that a corporation brought into existence through the efforts of a lawyer employed by its organizers is liable to the lawyer for reasonable attorney fees on a quantum meruit basis.[33] But the fact that a person is benefited because a lawyer performed legal services does not mean that the person would be unjustly enriched unless forced to pay a fee. The benefited person must have been aware of the lawyer's work in behalf of that person and remained silent or in some other way acquiesced in the lawyer's looking to that person for payment of a fee.[34]

Normally, the client whose legal work the lawyer is to perform will be the promisor of the fee, but in many situations another party, such as a parent,[35] relative,[36] spouse,[37] employer,[38] friend, or other party, will undertake to pay the fee and thereafter will be contractually bound to do so. The issue often arises

[31] Spires v. American Bus Lines, 158 Cal.App.3d 211, 204 Cal.Rptr. 531 (1984); Freedman v. Horton, Schwartz & Perse, 383 So.2d 659 (Fla.App.1980); Greenbaum & Browne, Ltd. v. Braun, 88 Ill.App.3d 210, 43 Ill.Dec. 303, 307, 410 N.E.2d 303, 307 (1980); Deutsch, Kerrigan & Stiles v. Rault, 389 So.2d 1373 (La.App.1980), writ refused 396 So.2d 883 (La.1981); Galbreath Mortg. Co. v. Key-Heights-Lowell, Inc., 75 Mich.App. 712, 255 N.W.2d 742 (1977). If the amount of the fee is unspecified, the lawyer is entitled to recover the reasonable value of his or her services. Spires v. American Bus Lines, supra, 204 Cal. Rptr. at 534. Courts have rather uniformly held, however, that there can be no implied agreement to pay a contingent fee. E.g., Warner v. Basten, 118 Ill.App.2d 419, 255 N.E.2d 72 (1969); Wells v. Haynes, 101 Ga. 841, 28 S.E. 968 (1897); Craig v. Jo B. Gardner, Inc., 586 S.W.2d 316, 324 (Mo.1979).

[32] The problem arises frequently in the context of a lawyer for a personal injury plaintiff when the plaintiff has incurred expenses for which physicians, hospitals, and perhaps others have liens against the client's recovery. In one sense, the lawyer's work in recovering a judgment is of direct benefit to the lien holder who should be required to bear some part of the legal expense of recovery. On the other hand, the lien holder has no claim against the tort defendant, and thus the legal services are not for the direct benefit of the lien holder. The cases are not of one view on the matter. Compare, e.g., Aetna Cas. & Surety Co. v. Starkey, 116 Mich.App. 640, 323 N.W.2d 325, 329 (1982)(medical providers subject to claim by injured person's lawyer for payment of portion of fees from amount recovered from insurer under personal insurance protection portion of no-fault coverage); Johnson v. Blue Cross & Blue Shield, 329 N.W.2d 49, 52 (Minn.1983)(lawyer can recover portion of fees against part of recovery subject to lien). One court has held that a lawyer who expressly undertakes to protect the financial interests of a provider of medical services in reimbursement from a client's recovery incurs a client-like obligation to fulfill that undertaking. In re Minor, 681 P.2d 1347 (Alaska 1983).

The quasi-contract issue arises in other areas as well. E.g., Williams v. Williams, 424 So.2d 638 (Ala.App.1982) (mere fact that lawyer for husband recovered proceeds of insurance that redounded to benefit of both spouses in marriage dissolution action furnished no basis for recovery of part of fee from wife).

[33] Arctic Slope Native Ass'n v. Paul, 609 P.2d 32, 35 (Alaska 1980); Ong Hing v. Arizona Harness Raceway, Inc., 10 Ariz.App. 380, 459 P.2d 107 (1969); David v. Southern Import Wine Co., 171 So. 180, 182 (La.App. 1936). But a related corporation, which was benefited by the creation of the first corporation, is not liable for fees in the absence of an undertaking on its behalf to pay them. In re John Rich Enterprises, Inc., 481 F.2d 211 (10th Cir.1973).

[34] Boyce v. Grand Rapids Asphalt Paving Co., 117 Mich. App. 546, 324 N.W.2d 28 (1982); Keene v. Stattman, 256 N.W.2d 295 (Minn.1977).

[35] But even if a parent contacts the lawyer and requests legal services for a child, if the lawyer later signs a contract for fees with the child, the parent is not liable for the lawyer's fee. See Becnel v. Arnouville, 425 So.2d 972 (La.App.1983).

[36] Fagin v. Craig, 611 S.W.2d 488 (Tex.Civ.App.1981), error refused n.r.e. (question of fact whether person who requested lawyer to defend niece's husband had agreed to pay lawyer).

[37] Collins v. Martin, 157 Ga.App. 45, 276 S.E.2d 102 (1981)(question of fact whether husband had authority to bind wife to contract to hire lawyer).

[38] Common situations are those in which a corporation advances legal fees to a director or officer who has been made a party to a shareholder derivative action. E.g., Swenson v. Thibaut, 39 N.C.App. 77, 250 S.E.2d 279, 303

when a lawyer represents a closely held corporation and deals with corporate principals as both principals and individuals. The general rules of agency and contract determine whether the relationship of lawyer and client was between the lawyer and the corporation or between the lawyer and the principal so as to make either liable for legal services rendered for or at the request of the other.[39] The lawyer's relationship of trust and confidence and the obligation to protect confidential information will, however, be with the client—the person or entity whose legal interests the lawyer is retained to protect.[40]

Choice of Lawyer

A person is entitled to contract for legal services with any lawyer willing to perform them. To some extent, a lawyer's ability to accept a client is limited by the rules on mandatory withdrawal (§ 9.5.4). No lawyer is obliged to accept any client or any client's matter (§ 10.2.2), and no client is required to accept the services of a particular lawyer except in court-appointed counsel systems (§ 14.3.4). Occasionally, wills are found with directions that a named lawyer be retained to represent the estate. The prevailing view soundly rejects arguments that such directions are binding on a probate court or on the executor of the estate.[41]

Written Contracts

There is no general requirement that the fee contract be in writing,[42] although a rejected proposal would have inserted such a requirement into the 1983 Model Rules.[43] The surviving language in MR 1.5(b) states that the basis or rate of the fee should "preferably" be communicated to the client in writing.[44] The Model Rules do require, however, that contingent fee contracts be in writing (MR 1.5(c)).[45] Written contracts are required in limited and special circumstances by other law.[46] Courts have urged lawyers not to rely

(1978), appeal dismissed 296 N.C. 740, 254 S.E.2d 182 (1979)(advance permitted by statute).

[39] E.g., Arrow, Edelstein & Gross, P.C. v. Rosco Productions, Inc., 581 F.Supp. 520 (S.D.N.Y.1984)(corporation alone liable for work done for corporation, including work done incorporating it; but individual principals in corporation were liable for work done in their individual interest, such as estate, matrimonial, and criminal defense matters); Verhey v. Cook, 142 Ga.App. 280, 235 S.E. 2d 678 (1977); Gardner v. Rensmeyer, 221 Kan. 23, 557 P.2d 1258 (1976); R.H. Hobson v. Bradley & Drendel, Ltd., 698 Nev. 505, 654 P.2d 1017 (1982)(principal in corporation could not be held jointly liable with corporation for legal work done for corporation in absence of showing that principal was alter ego for corporation or expressly undertook to pay fee); Burk, P.C. v. Burzynski, 672 P.2d 419 (Wyo.1983). See also, e.g., In re John Rich Enterprises, Inc., 481 F.2d 211 (10th Cir.1973)(in absence of evidence that related corporation had made expressed or implied agreement to pay for legal services rendered to another corporation, no basis for holding related corporation liable for lawyer's fee payment).

[40] Cf. § 5.6.2 at 209–210, § 5.6.4 at 223.

[41] Hawaiian Trust Co. v. Hogan, 1 Hawaii App. 560, 623 P.2d 450, 453 (1981); Carton v. Borden, 8 N.J. 352, 85 A.2d 257 (1951). See generally 2 A.Scott, Trusts § 126.3 at 980–82 (3d ed.1967). The sound basis for the rule is the need of the executor or administrator to be able to form a relationship of trust and confidence with the lawyer. That is hardly guaranteed by the fact that the testator at a possibly much earlier time implicitly expressed such confidence. Moreover, given the tendency of will-drafting lawyers to insert their own names or those of lawyers in their firm into wills (§ 8.12.4), it is sound policy to permit another person to second-guess the choice of counsel. Clearly, the mere fact that a lawyer is named in a will as counsel for the estate does not entitle a lawyer to charge the estate a fee if the lawyer rendered no services. In re Succession of Boyenga, 437 So.2d 260 (La.1983).

[42] State by Attorney General v. United States, 64 Hawaii 573, 645 P.2d 311, 313 (1982); Reynolds, Nelson, Theriot & Stahl v. Chatelain, 428 So.2d 829 (La.App. 1983), writ denied 434 So.2d 1098 (1983).

[43] See MR 1.5(b) (Proposed Final Draft, May 30, 1981). The proposal would not have required that the entire contract be in writing, but only the "basis or rate" of the lawyer's fee. That must still be communicated, but possibly orally, to the client under the final version of MR 1.5(b).

[44] See also MR 1.5 comment (Basis or Rate of Fee)("A written statement concerning the fee reduces the possibility of misunderstanding. Furnishing the client with a simple memorandum or a copy of the lawyer's customary fee schedule is sufficient if the basis or rate of the fee is set forth.").

[45] See § 9.4.1.

[46] E.g., Sarja v. Pittsburgh Steel Ore Co., 154 Minn. 217, 191 N.W. 742 (1923), cert.denied 262 U.S. 754, 43 S.Ct. 702, 67 L.Ed. 1216 (1923)(contract for fee with injured worker appearing before worker compensation commission void unless approved in writing by court). On the requirement of a writing in the case of some contingent fees, see § 9.4.1.

on oral fee agreements.[47] Most lawyers prefer to have a written agreement signed very near the beginning of the representation as a matter of sound client relationships, to avoid future misunderstanding, and to gain some additional assurance that the client is committed to the course of action. The desirability of a writing[48] is suggested by occasional statistics from fee arbitration agencies showing that a high percentage of disputes involve unwritten fee agreements.[49] Useful forms abound.[50] Courts quite uniformly resolve ambiguities in a fee contract against the lawyer, who has almost invariably drafted it.[51]

Postinception Contract Changes

The courts are generally in accord that once the initial contract has been formed and the fiduciary relationship of client and lawyer has begun, any change in the contract will be regarded with great suspicion.[52] Courts have in effect treated such alterations as presumptively fraudulent if they have the effect of benefiting the lawyer, such as by raising the amount of the lawyer's compensation.[53] The most suspicious of that kind are "cash on the barrelhead" demands for altered compensation[54] made by lawyers at a critical juncture

47 Briggs v. Clinton Cty. Bank & Trust, 452 N.E.2d 989, 1004 (Ind.App.1983).

48 There are few good reasons not to reduce agreements to writing. In the rare instance in which the jurisdiction accords a "contract" designation to a legal malpractice action, the statute of limitations may be the typically longer period provided for written contracts, if the client-lawyer agreement was in writing, rather than the shorter "tort" period that will be applied when the contract is not written down. E.g., Benard v. Walkup, 272 Cal.App.2d 595, 77 Cal.Rptr. 544 (1969).

49 Marek, Citizens' Advisory Committee: Problems before the Bar's Fee Conciliation Service, 3 District Law. 12, 14 (April/May 1979)(75 percent of cases involve unwritten fee arrangements).

50 One helpful model is found in the Consumer's Union publication, Guide to Consumer Services at 200–01 (rev.ed.1979). Written from a consumer perspective, there is really little there that most lawyers would find objectionable. Its source would offer solace to many clients.

51 Cardenas v. Ramsey County, 322 N.W.2d 191, 193 (Minn.1982); Dublirer v. Lascher, 96 A.D.2d 474, 464 N.Y.S.2d 790, 791 (1983). Disputes about the parties' intentions are much more likely to arise if the contract is unwritten, and courts often give controlling effect to the client's understanding of the unwritten understanding if it is a plausible one. E.g., Kirby v. Liska, 214 Neb. 356, 334 N.W.2d 179, 182 (1983)(ambiguity in oral contract construed against lawyer who is responsible for contract's uncertain nature); Scudder v. Haug, 201 Neb. 107, 266 N.W.2d 232 (1978).

52 With respect to the courts' degrees of caution, there are three sets of fee contracts. (1) The basic contract entered into at the *beginning* of the relationship is not presumptively fraudulent, although it is hardly treated as an arms'-length contract between commercial parties. Special substantive measures of the reasonableness of the bargain and special procedural devices for enhanced judicial scrutiny (§ 9.1.1) commonly apply. (2) A contract entered into *after* the representation begins is viewed with judicial suspicion. Normally, the lawyer must bear the burden of demonstrating that any advantages gained by the alteration are not unreasonable and were not fraudulently obtained. E.g., Spilker v. Hankin, 188 F.2d 35 (D.C.Cir.1951). (3) This category consists of fee contracts that are in fact treated by most courts as *arms'-length* contracts. Those are entered into outside of, and not subject to, the influence of the client-lawyer relationship, such as a contract by an insurance company to pay the legal expenses of an insured. Only the third set of fee contracts are governed by the normal rules of contract.

53 Hamilton v. Ford Motor Co., 636 F.2d 745 (D.C.Cir. 1980); Rader v. Thrasher, 57 Cal.2d 244, 18 Cal.Rptr. 736, 368 P.2d 360 (1962)(postinception change resulting in lawyer's obtaining advantage through the confidential client-lawyer relationship raises presumption of insufficient consideration); In re Vogel, 382 A.2d 275 (D.C.App. 1978)(discipline when lawyer helped himself to additional fee out of client's funds); Attorney Grievance Comm'n v. Kerpelman, 292 Md. 228, 438 A.2d 501, 508 (1981)(discipline for attempting to raise fee after successful result); Jo B. Gardner, Inc. v. Beanland, 611 S.W.2d 317, 320–21 (Mo.App.1980); Baye v. Grindlinger, 78 A.D.2d 690, 432 N.Y.S.2d 624, 625 (1980); Archer v. Griffith, 390 S.W.2d 735, 741 (Tex.1964)(burden on lawyer to show that midstream alteration of method of calculating fee was "fair, honest and equitable"; lawyer's failure to satisfy burden here requires cancellation of deed from client to lawyer).

54 Frank v. Bloom, 634 F.2d 1245, 1251–52 (10th Cir. 1980); Kansas v. Mayes, 216 Kan. 38, 531 P.2d 102 (1975) (patent lawyer disbarred for, among other things, refusing to meet essential patent office deadline unless client paid fee as demanded and for refusing to explain fee charge unless client paid fee for time spent in detailing charge); Griffin v. Rainer, 212 Va. 627, 186 S.E.2d 10 (1972)(change in contract induced by lawyer's threat to withdraw invalid). One court has held that even if the lawyer's demand is not for alteration in the contract, but for a payment of arrears, if the demand is backed by an unreasonable threat to abandon the client, the lawyer forfeits all claim to any compensation, including for work already performed. E.g., Beatty v. LaSonde, 147 Ga.App. 138, 248 S.E.2d 202 (1978)(lawyer refused to proceed with appeal because of client's failure to pay for already accrued legal fees). If the lawyer insists upon increased security for a fee agreed upon previously, courts are less reluctant to enforce the security agreement. E.g., Matthews v. Berryman, 196 Mont. 49, 637 P.2d 822 (1981).

of the representation at which the client's bargaining power is seriously or entirely destroyed because of the lack of time or wherewithal to change lawyers.[55]

WESTLAW REFERENCES

Basic Contractual Relationship

lawyer attorney /s client /s express** implied /s contract agreement

Written Contracts

lawyer attorney /s client /s retainer contract agreement /s writ! "statute of frauds" oral**

Postinception Contract Changes

"fixed fee" contingen! /s renegot! alter! modif! /s "fee agree!" retainer

§ 9.2.2 Methods and Terms of Fee Payment

Basis of Charging

Their are several methods of calculating a lawyer's fee charges and a variety of permissible ways of making payment. Once the basis for charge is agreed to, a lawyer may not unilaterally charge more on the attempted justification that the representation was more onerous or more successful than contemplated.[56] Because methods of calculating fees can vary considerably, the Model Rules wisely require in MR 1.5(b) that a lawyer's "basis or rate of fee shall be communicated to the client, preferably in writing, before or within a reasonable time after commencing the representation." [57]

The commonly employed ways of determining the fee charge are on the basis of a contingent fee (§ 9.4.1), an hourly charge, a fixed fee, or an account stated to the client. Contingent fees are employed most often in personal injury and condemnation claims. Hourly charge is the method used commonly in commercial practices for all but routine legal work. A fixed-fee charge is commonly used in routine and uncomplicated matters such as a simple will, name change, adoption, or a misdemeanor defense—work primarily for middle-income clients. Something like an account-stated arrangment is sometimes, but rarely, found in work for clients able to pay a very large fee. A single-figure fee is sometimes set quarterly or annually or possibly only at the termination of the representation on a particular legal matter, depending on the billing practices of the firm.[58] Under most arrangements, courts have insisted that lawyers make periodic billings, showing accrued charges for times and disbursements, credits for payment, and a statement of balances due from the client.[59]

55 As the California Supreme Court has said, a "contract" to pay a fee made in the courtroom on the lawyer's threat of withdrawal as the trial is about to begin is, of course, not enforceable. Fitzpatrick v. State Bar, 20 Cal. 3d 73, 141 Cal.Rptr. 169, 569 P.2d 763 (1977). See also, e.g., Spilker v. Hankin, 188 F.2d 35 (D.C.Cir.1951).

56 Grossman v. State Bar, 34 Cal.3d 73, 192 Cal.Rptr. 397, 664 P.2d 542 (1983); Attorney Grievance Comm'n v. McIntire, 286 Md. 87, 405 A.2d 273 (1979); Centurian Corp. v. Ryberg, McCoy & Halgren, 588 P.2d 716 (Utah 1978). On the courts' suspiciousness about changes in fee contracts after the fiduciary relationship begins, see supra text at nn. 52–55.

57 MR 1.5 comment (Basis or Rate of Fee) indicates that details of the basis or rate need not be communicated. In a disciplinary rule, the division between essential terms and details is perhaps justified. There is no reason for a lawyer to speculate about whether a matter is one or the other, however, and a competent lawyer would include in the statement all matters that will bear on the fee.

58 In a not-too-distant time, remembered fondly on Wall Street and elsewhere, a typical bill contained no information other than the letterhead and the words "for legal services rendered" with a figure given. Sometimes the understanding was that the figure reflected hourly charges rounded off in some fashion. At other times the figure was simply an unexplained and possibly unexplainable amount that the firm felt its services were worth. Such a method could be practiced, obviously, only with a corporate client whose methods of accounting and validating purchase and service contracts were quite informal. Today the almost universal practice of lawyers is to justify bills with rather elaborate statements that include hours worked. It is very doubtful that in a contested suit a court would allow a lawyer to recover a fee without accounting for its reasonableness. E.g., Epstein, Reiss & Goodman v. Greenfield, 102 A.D.2d 749, 476 N.Y.S.2d 885, 886 (1984).

59 Briggs v. Clinton Cty. Bank & Trust Co., 452 N.E.2d 989, 1004 (Ind.App.1983)(when services are performed for years on end without lawyers' sending bill or statement, natural inference is that services are being rendered gratuitously); In re Koehler, 95 Wn.2d 606, 628 P.2d 461, 462–63 (1981). With respect to "closing statements" in contingent fee cases, see § 9.4.1.

The basis for charging is important for the obvious reason that the total amount of the fee may well depend on it. Less obvious but of great importance in some cases, a lawyer's basis for charging can have profound effects on the lawyer's motivation at critical stages of the representation. The size of the fee and the terms of its payment will create heavy economic pressure on a lawyer's choices with respect to such decisions during the representation as whether to seek a settlement and recommend that a client accept it, whether to invest much or little in pretrial preparation, or whether to pursue an appeal. A lawyer presented with an offer to settle very early in a representation may be under very different economic pressures depending on whether the basis of the fee is contingent on the outcome, is based on the task such as a fixed fee charge, is based on the duration of the service as with the common hourly charge, or is to be paid by a party other than the client (such as the party making the settlement offer in many fee shifting arrangements). How lawyers can be expected to react to the same settlement offer obviously will depend to a significant extent on the differing economic forces at work and on the relative degree of the lawyer's freedom from effective control and supervision by the client.[60]

Disbursements and Similar Separate Charges

A matter that requires clarification in any client-lawyer contract is what the fee charge covers. Firms follow very different practices with respect to individually billing such additional charges as long-distance telephone, telex, travel, copying, printing, and computer use. Some firms include all but extraordinary expenditures of that kind in their office overhead,[61] which is reflected in the lawyer's bill, and thus make no separate charge apart from the fee. Other firms itemize and charge separately for those and possibly other types of "disbursements," as they are often called on bills. Because of professional rules that prohibit advancing funds to clients (§ 9.2.3), some firms have clients make an advance payment of funds that the lawyer will use later to pay some costs of litigation such as filing fees, expert witness fees, and jury fees.[62]

With so many variations in possible practices, the basic contract should describe whether the lawyer's fee includes some or any of such charges and describe which additional charges the lawyer likely will later bill to the client.[63] If the contract does not indicate what the lawyer's fee covers, courts should employ the standard of the client's reasonable expectations in determining whether the client must pay for additional expenses that are separately billed.[64]

Retainer Agreements and Prepayment of Fees

Two arrangements, whose similarities are potentially confusing, begin with a client's paying a fee to the lawyer at the outset of the representation. It would clarify matters somewhat if the former would uniformly be called a *retainer* fee and the latter an *advance fee payment,* but there is no consistent termi-

60 These and related issues are explored in a seminal article. Johnson, Lawyers' Choice: A Theoretical Appraisal of Litigation Investment Decisions, 15 L. & Soc'y Rev. 567 (1981).

61 Office overhead includes the partnership draw and salaries of all lawyers and most other employees, such as secretaries and clerks, rent, heat, utilities, library, depreciation on building and furnishings, and similar expenses. There is some uniformity on separately billing for paralegals on an hourly basis.

62 Unless funds paid for such costs and fees are to be used promptly after receiving them from a client, by far the better practice is to deposit them in a client trust account. Some jurisdictions may require such trust fund treatment. See § 4.8, at 179.

63 Louisiana St. Bar Ass'n v. Edwins, 329 So.2d 437, 445 n.1 (La.1976).

64 Losurdo Bros. v. Arkin Distrib. Co., 125 Ill.App.3d 267, 80 Ill.Dec. 348, 354–55, 465 N.E.2d 139, 145–46 (1984) (in absence of agreement to contrary, copying expense is assumed to be item of office overhead included in fee charge unless expense is extraordinary); Levy v. State, 100 Misc.2d 781, 420 N.Y.S.2d 154, 155–56 (Ct.Cl.1979) (disbursements for which lawyer had primary responsibility not chargeable to client; thus presence of investigator in court to assist in preparation for trial not chargeable).

nology in the area.[65] In one arrangement, the client expects only that the lawyer will be available to handle the client's legal problems during a period of time, often a year, but has no fixed expectation that the fee already paid will cover specific items or that the lawyer's compensation will work out more to the benefit of lawyer or client. The purpose of the agreement is to assure the client that the lawyer will be contractually on call to handle the client's legal matters.[66] It is quite common for the initial payment to be supplemented by an hourly charge that is less than the lawyer's normal hourly charge. In the other arrangement, involving an advance fee payment, the client's understanding is that the lawyer will perform a single legal task, perhaps drawing against the prepayment as it is earned, but charge on a basis that might leave some of the prepayment to be refunded if the lawyer's work is less than expected.[67]

The critical difference between retainers and advance fee payments is that in the case of a retainer fee, the amount paid may be understood by the parties to be both nonrefundable in the event that the lawyer performs less work than contemplated and not to be supplemented in the event that the representation takes more time or effort than the lawyer contemplated.[68] In effect, the lawyer has earned the entire fee just by promising to be available to do future work.[69] But in the case of advance fee payments the lawyer can retain only so much of the fee as the lawyer has earned by actual work.[70] Moreover, until the lawyer has earned an advance fee payment, or possibly until the lawyer has earned incremental parts of it, the funds must be treated as client trust funds subject to the special rules for safeguarding them.[71] The amount paid to a lawyer as a retainer, as defined above, need not be treated as trust funds.[72]

Credit, Interest, and Similar Arrangements

Most states now permit lawyers to make credit arrangements for the payment of fees, such as through client use of credit cards.[73] By the same token, a fee contract can provide

[65] The court in Jacobson v. Sassower, 113 Misc.2d 279, 452 N.Y.S.2d 981, 983–84 (1982), affirmed 122 Misc.2d 863, 474 N.Y.S.2d 167 (1983), affirmed 107 A.D.2d 603, 483 N.Y.S.2d 711 (1985), refers to the two arrangements, respectively, as a general retainer and a special retainer. See also, e.g., 1 S.Speiser, Attorneys' Fees §§ 1:4, 1:8 (1973)(general and special retainer). Further complicating matters is the practice of some lawyers of securing amounts from clients that are more or less understood to be for costs of filing an action or taking other steps. On the characterization of such funds as client trust funds or not, see § 4.8, at 179.

[66] Greenberg v. Remick & Co., 230 N.Y. 70, 129 N.E. 211 (1920). From the lawyer's point of view, the arrangement is desirable because it assures a minimum level of cash flow, assists in planning for staffing, and assures a line of communication to an important client.

[67] Jacobson v. Sassower, 113 Misc.2d 279, 452 N.Y.S.2d 981 (Civ.Ct.1982), affirmed 122 Misc.2d 863, 474 N.Y.S.2d 167 (1983), affirmed 107 A.D.2d 603, 483 N.Y.S.2d 711 (1985).

[68] Cannon v. First Nat'l Bank of East Islip, 98 A.D.2d 704, 469 N.Y.S.2d 101 (1983), affirmed 62 N.Y.2d 1003, 479 N.Y.S.2d 517, 468 N.E.2d 699 (1984).

[69] It is not clear, however, whether a nonrefundable retainer would be valid. A client who has just paid a lawyer $50,000 to perform all occupational health and safety work for a factory that burns down the next day, obviating the need for any legal work, can probably recover the retainer even if it was solemnly called "nonrefundable" in the agreement. Moreover, because the nonrefundable feature chills the client's right to discharge the lawyer (§ 9.5.2), it has been held that such a clause is invalid and the lawyer is only entitled to the reasonable value of his or her services after discharge. See, e.g., Jacobson v. Sassower, 122 Misc.2d 863, 474 N.Y.S.2d 167 (1983), affirmed 107 A.D.2d 603, 483 N.Y.S.2d 711 (1985). But cf., e.g., Alpern v. Hurwitz, 644 F.2d 943, 945 (2d Cir.1981)(dictum)("where the attorney has been employed under a general retainer for a fixed period to perform legal services as the need for them may arise" it would be "error . . . to imply a provision in the contract that it would automatically terminate if the confidential relationship between the parties was 'irretrievably ruptured.' ").

[70] In re Boswell, 242 Ga. 313, 249 S.E.2d 13 (1978); In re Gudmundson, 556 P.2d 212 (Utah 1976).

[71] In re Stern, 92 N.J. 611, 458 A.2d 1279, 1283 (1983) (dictum). On the treatment of trust funds, see § 4.8.

[72] In re Stern, 92 N.J. 611, 458 A.2d 1279, 1284 (1983) (pending further review of proposed adoption of local version of Model Code, court holds "that absent an explicit understanding that the retainer fee be separately maintained, a general retainer fee need not be deposited in an attorney's trust account.").

[73] See Fla.Code DR 2–102(G), DR 2–106(D), DR 3–102(B), DR 4–101(C)(4), DR 5–103(A)(3), DR 5–108, DR 9–102(C); Me.Code DR 2–106(D). See generally ABA Formal Op. 338 (1974)(allowable to take credit cards and, as a necessary aspect, to charge interest on past-due accounts). DR

for a stipulated rate of legal interest on amounts due.[74]

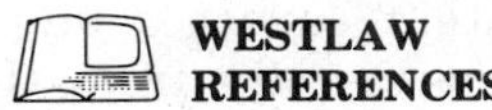

WESTLAW REFERENCES

Retainer Agreements and Prepayment of Fees
45k64 45k137

§ 9.2.3 *Advancing Funds to Clients*

Nature of the General Prohibition

The lawyer codes have struggled with the issue of the extent, if any, to which lawyers should be able to relieve clients of some of the financial burden of enduring litigation.[75] The 1969 Code is somewhat more restrictive than are the 1983 Model Rules. Both prohibit a lawyer from supporting a client's living costs; both permit a lawyer to support a client by loaning the amount of court costs and other expenses of litigation. The basic concern of both is with the conflict of interest created when a lawyer, who is supposed to take direction solely from the client on important decisions in the representation (§ 4.3), has a personal economic interest in the outcome that is created by the hope of repayment of advances for the client's benefit.[76] That is probably what courts have in mind when they refer generally to a policy against a lawyer's acquiring an interest in a litigated matter by advancing costs.[77] Both rules are also transparently concerned with the risk that the promise of money advances would be employed by some lawyers to solicit clients.[78]

Litigation Expenses

Under both the Code's DR 5–103(B)[79] and MR 1.8(e)(1) a lawyer may permissibly advance litigation expenses to a client, but they differ on details. The Code provides that such expenses[80] may be advanced only where the client remains ultimately liable for the expenses regardless of the outcome of the litigation.[81] All advances for that purpose are legitimate, apparently, no matter how impecunious the client, how large the ex-

2–101(B)(18) permits lawyer advertising to contain information about "whether credit cards or other credit arrangements are accepted," which plainly, although implicitly, authorizes credit cards and similar arrangements.

74 ABA Formal Op. 338, supra.

75 Both the Code (DR 5–103(B)("contemplated or pending litigation")) and the Model Rules (MR 1.8(e)("pending or contemplated litigation")) limit their prohibitions against advancing funds to clients for litigation. Presumably, then, a lawyer negotiating a contract for a client is apparently free under the rules to lend money to the client to permit the client to bear through a prolonged process of negotiation. Many of the same concerns on which the rules are based could also extend to situations not involving litigation, although the latter is plainly the situation in which the issue arises most often.

76 EC 5–8. Cf. MR 1.5 comment (Acquisition of Interest in Litigation)(prohibition against impermissible advances is rooted in common-law prohibitions against champerty and maintenance). A related rationale might be to assure that litigation decisions that are made by clients are made with appropriate economic incentives applied. Cf. Baker v. American Broadcasting Co., 585 F.Supp. 291, 294 (E.D.N.Y.1984)(in pro bono civil cases, letter from court to pro bono plaintiffs indicates that litigation expenses would be deducted from recovery "to bring some healthy economic pressure to bear" on plaintiff's litigation decisions).

77 In re Stewart, 121 Ariz. 243, 589 P.2d 886, 888 (1979); Committee on Professional Ethics v. Bitter, 279 N.W.2d 521 (Iowa 1979).

78 In re Carroll, 124 Ariz. 80, 602 P.2d 461, 467 (1979).

79 The Code prohibition is modeled on Canon 42 of the 1908 Canons: "A lawyer may not properly agree with a client that the lawyer shall pay or bear the expenses of litigation; he may in good faith advance expenses as a matter of convenience, but subject to reimbursement." Canon 42, added in 1928, was among the last of the Canons. See ABF Opinions of the Comm. on Prof.Ethics 182 (1967). Cases sometimes also cited Canon 10's prohibition: "A lawyer shall not purchase any interest in the subject matter of the litigation which he is conducting."

80 Eligible expenses are listed in DR 5–103(B) as "court costs, expenses of investigation, expenses of medical examination, and costs of obtaining and presenting evidence." A lawyer could, for example, advance the costs of depositicns. Brown & Huseby, Inc. v. Chrietzberg, 242 Ga. 232, 248 S.E.2d 631 (1978). The reference to medical examination presumably includes only medical examinations for the purpose of preparing testimony or other evidence for trial. MR 1.8(e) refers only to "court costs and expenses of litigation," and neither the rule nor its comment further defines the concept. Presumably it would include at least as much as, but perhaps no more than, is listed in DR 5–203(B).

81 In re Carroll, 124 Ariz. 80, 602 P.2d 461 (1979) (disciplinary violation when lawyer's contingent fee contract explicitly provided that legal expenses would be paid by lawyer and that client would be liable only in event of recovery).

penses, and thus how unlikely that the client would ever repay them out of anything other than a recovery.[82] In fact, bar association opinions have recognized the legitimacy of advancing litigation expenses in pro bono situations. Litigation expenses could be paid without even a client's formal undertaking to pay in several situations in which, because of the client's poverty, it was clear that the client was unable to assume liability for the expenses except as a sheer formality.[83]

The litigation-expense rule of the Model Rules is more permissive than the Code in two ways. First, MR 1.8(e) provides that repayment of the lawyer's advance of litigation expenses "may be contingent on the outcome of the matter." In other words, a lawyer may agree with a client not to charge the client for litigation expenses if the litigation does not turn out successfully.[84] By contrast, under the Code an outright undertaking by a lawyer to pay litigation expenses and not to seek reimbursement directly from the client violates the rule.[85] Second, MR 1.8(e)(2) explicitly recognizes that "a lawyer representing an indigent client may pay court costs and expenses of litigation on behalf of the client." The rule, which obviously builds on the Code authority to the same effect, provides an exception for an area in which, presumably, there will be little unseemly competition among lawyers to outbid each other for the right to represent parties.

Living Expenses

Both the Code[86] and the Model Rules—implicitly but clearly—prohibit a lawyer from making any other financial assistance availa-

[82] Some class action decisions, however, have held that the fact that a lawyer for a class representative was to advance all expenses would be relevant to a determination whether the named representative was an adequate representative of the class. Compare, e.g., National Auto Brokers Corp. v. General Motors Corp., 376 F.Supp. 620 (S.D.N.Y.1974), affirmed 572 F.2d 953 (2d Cir.1978), cert.denied 439 U.S. 1072, 99 S.Ct. 844, 59 L.Ed.2d 38 (1979)(legitimate area of discovery in order to determine whether class representative or class lawyer will be in effective control of suit); Ralston v. Volkswagenwerk A.G., 61 F.R.D. 427 (W.D.Mo.1973), with, e.g., Sanderson v. Winner, 507 F.2d 477 (10th Cir.1974), cert.denied 421 U.S. 914, 95 S.Ct. 1573, 43 L.Ed.2d 780 (1975)(no discovery into financial condition of class representative when class lawyer agrees to advance costs of litigation); Sayre v. Abraham Lincoln Fed. Sav. & Loan Ass'n, 65 F.R.D. 379 (E.D.Pa.1974), amended 69 F.R.D. 117 (E.D.Pa.1975). See also, e.g., In re Mid-Atlantic Toyota Antitrust Litigation, 93 F.R.D. 485 (D.Md.1982)(class lawyer's explicit assurance to class representative that firm had policy of not seeking reimbursement of litigation expenses from clients if lawyers were not successful was violation of Code that precluded class certification).

[83] See generally Baker v. American Broadcasting Co., 585 F.Supp. 291, 294–95 (E.D.N.Y.1984). See ABA Formal Op. 259 (1943); ABA Informal Op. 1361 (1976). The opinions went further. A lawyer was not prohibited from advancing litigation expenses for which the client would not be liable even if the client was not indigent, so long as the lawyer would receive no fee in the case. The absence of fee was thought to remove the conflict of interest or most of it. ABA Formal Op. 259, supra; ABA Informal Op. 889 (1965). Further, litigation expenses could be advanced by an organization of which the lawyer was a member, so long as the organization had no financial interest in the outcome of the litigation other than the recovery of the advanced expenses as court costs. ABA Formal Op. 259, supra; ABA Informal Op. 1361, supra. The practices permitted are those commonly engaged in by advocacy organizations.

[84] Note that MR 1.8(e), in its reference to "contingent on the outcome," does not require that the amount of the expenses be paid out of the recovery. Thus the rule seems to contemplate both the most common case, where a lawyer on contingent fee for a tort claimant advances expenses contingent on recovering a judgment or settlement, as well as all other cases, such as the defense lawyer's agreeing in the same case that the defendant would not be required to reimburse the defense lawyer for litigation expenses unless the ultimate recovery by the plaintiff is below a named figure.

[85] Schlosser v. Jursich, 87 Ill.App.3d 824, 43 Ill.Dec. 257, 410 N.E.2d 257 (1980)(trial court impermissibly directed lawyer to refund amount of court expenses paid by client; theory that ambiguous terms of contingent fee contract might have misled client into reasonably believing that lawyer would bear costs of litigation irrelevant in view of clear legal rule).

[86] The pre-Code authority was clearly divided on the question of living-expense assistance. Compare, e.g., In re Ruffalo, 370 F.2d 447, 461 (6th Cir.1966), reversed on other grounds 390 U.S. 544, 88 S.Ct. 1222, 20 L.Ed.2d 117 (1968)(advances to needy clients for living expenses not unethical); People ex rel. Chicago Bar Ass'n v. McCallum, 341 Ill. 578, 173 N.E. 827, 831 (1930); Committee on Professional Ethics v. Bitter, 279 N.W.2d 521, 523 (Iowa 1979)(advances to clients for living expenses prior to effective date of Code not clearly proscribed by Canons and are thus disregarded), with, e.g., State ex rel. Florida Bar v. Dawson, 111 So.2d 427 (Fla.1959)(lawyer suspended for paying litigation expenses without recourse and advancing personal expense funds); In re Ruffalo, 176 Ohio St. 263, 199 N.E.2d 396, 398 (1964), cert.denied 379 U.S. 931, 85 S.Ct. 328, 13 L.Ed.2d 342 (1964)(advances to needy clients violated Canon 42 because they were not for expenses of litigation, the only permitted expenses). See

ble to a client.[87] The most common instance in which a lawyer might be asked by a client for assistance is an instance in which the prohibition rather clearly applies. That is when personal injury clients, both injured and possibly made impecunious by the defendants' tortious conduct, are unable to survive prolonged litigation without financial assistance. Defendants, aware of the economic pressure burdening unaided plaintiffs, have every economic incentive to prolong the litigation with frivolous motions and discovery. At least on their face, both the Code and the Model Rules prohibit assistance no matter how needful the client. And so have gone most of the decisions under the Code.[88] But several jurisdictions have balked at the strictness of the Code and the economic straits in which it may leave some clients and have provided various measures of limited relief.[89] There is also nothing in any of the codes that prohibits a lawyer from attempting to secure several permitted kinds of assistance for a client, such as by aiding a client to obtain public assistance or unemployment coverage. A lawyer should also be able to help find employment for an impecunious client, including employment in the lawyer's own law office, so long as the terms of employment and pay are in good faith.

WESTLAW REFERENCES

dr5–103(a) "dr 5–103(a)" dr5–103(b) "dr 5103(b)"

§ 9.2.4 Fee Splitting [90]

General Prohibition

Because the ultimate economic incentive for a lawyer in a representation is most often the fee received, the lawyer codes have attempted to assure that no other person will be in a position to receive or share in fees on the general reasoning that fee sharing results in dilution of the lawyer's loyalty and creates conflicts of interest. The codes contain broad prohibitions against fee sharing with nonlawyers for the additional purpose of preventing unauthorized practice. The rules permit some fee sharing among lawyers but with

generally Annot., 8 ALR3d 1155 (1966). The ABA Ethics Committee, however, had taken a strong position against such advances in ABA Formal Op. 288 (1954), which insisted that Canon 42 did prohibit them.

[87] DR 5–103(B) says that a lawyer must not "advance or guarantee financial assistance" while MR 1.8(e) says that a lawyer must not "provide financial assistance." The Model Rule was apparently intended to be as broad as the Code, both covering such things as securing loans for a client from a friendly lending institution on the lawyer's credit.

[88] In re Carroll, 124 Ariz. 80, 602 P.2d 461 (1979); In re Stewart, 121 Ariz. 243, 589 P.2d 886 (1979); Florida Bar v. Wooten, 452 So.2d 547, 548 (Fla.1984), and authorities cited; Attorney Grievance Comm'n v. Engerman, 289 Md. 330, 424 A.2d 362, 367 (1981)(small loans to client); In re Pusser, 273 S.C. 115, 254 S.E.2d 926 (1979)($1,000 loan to client for food and Christmas); Heinzman v. Fine, Fine, Legum & Fine, 217 Va. 958, 234 S.E.2d 282 (1977). The otherwise deaf ears of the courts may, however, be open to the argument that the human suffering of a client would bear on the question of sanctions. See In re Berlant, 458 Pa. 439, 328 A.2d 471, 476 (1974), cert.denied 421 U.S. 964, 95 S.Ct.1953, 44 L.Ed.2d 451 (1975).

[89] The principal case is Louisiana St. Bar Ass'n v. Edwins, 329 So.2d 437 (La.1976)(financial assistance to clients will not violate Code if (1) made to client who has already retained lawyer and without promise of assistance as inducement; (2) expenses limited to minimal living expenses, minor sums necessary to prevent foreclosures, or necessary medical treatment and similar expenses reasonably necessary under the facts; (3) client remained ultimately liable for all advances; and (4) lawyer did nothing to encourage public knowledge of lawyer's practice of making loans to clients).

California's Rules of Professional Conduct, in Rule 5–104(A)(2), depart significantly from the Code by allowing a lawyer to lend money to a client for any purpose. The client must promise in writing to repay the loan (apparently without contingency). And a lawyer must not discuss the availability of a loan with a client before the representation begins—except that the client can be read or shown a copy of Rule 5–104 and the lawyer can explain the rule! (Rule 5–104(C).) See generally Note, Loans to Clients for Living Expenses, 55 Cal.L.Rev. 1419 (1967).

The Minnesota Code was amended in 1981 to add a new DR 5–103(B)(2), providing that "a lawyer may guarantee a loan reasonably needed to enable the client to withstand delay in litigation that would otherwise put substantial pressure on the client to settle a case because of financial hardship rather than on the merits," provided that the client remains ultimately liable for the loan regardless of the outcome and that the lawyer did not promise a loan as inducement to employment. See generally Note, Guaranteeing Loans to Clients under Minnesota's Code of Professional Responsibility, 66 Minn.L.Rev. 1091 (1982).

[90] Both the Code (DR 2–107(A)) and the Model Rules (MR 1.5(e)) refer to fee splitting with the more sonorous phrase *division of fees.* The practice is universally called *fee splitting* by lawyers when speaking to each other.

restrictions in order to avoid brokering in clients.

Fee Splitting with Nonlawyers

The lawyer codes contain numerous restrictions on the ability of a lawyer to share a fee with a nonlawyer.[91] First are the rules that broadly prohibit sharing fees with a nonlawyer—DR 3–102(A) and MR 5.4(a). Their purpose is to prevent the possibility of control of the lawyer by the nonlawyer, who might, in turn, be more interested in his or her own financial return and not at all interested in the client's possibly different interests.[92] They are also designed to prevent situations from arising in which a nonlawyer might be practicing law in violation of the prohibitions against unauthorized practice.[93] Those rules plainly prevent a lawyer from agreeing to pay a nonlawyer for referring clients to the lawyer.[94] In general, a lawyer may, of course, pay employees, suppliers of services, and the like with funds that, if the practice is not losing money, will have been derived from client fees. Those arrangements are examined elsewhere.[95] By convention, they are not covered by the restrictions against fee splitting, which are instead aimed at arrangements under which a nonlawyer is to receive a portion of a fee paid by a particular client or a stated portion of all fees paid.

The second set of restrictions are those designed to assure that a lawyer does not practice in an organization in which a nonlawyer has an ownership interest. Those prohibitions operate to prevent any but lawyers from owning or investing in law firms, whatever the form in which they are established.[96]

Lawyer Fee Splitting

The practice of fee splitting and work division among lawyers, through the routine payment of "forwarding fees," is probably both rife and virtually respectable in many communities.[97] The practice appears wasteful because it compensates the forwarding lawyer for doing little more than passing the client's matter on to another lawyer to handle it.[98]

91 Suppose that because of liens filed against a judgment by others, a plaintiff's judgment has been reduced to a sum that will be entirely consumed by the plaintiff's lawyer's fee if the fee is not reduced. May a court reduce the fee in order to provide some recovery to the plaintiff? For the surprising suggestion that a lawyer in such a case may not be forced to share a fee with a nonlawyer—the lawyer's own client—see Valentino v. Rickners Rhederei, G.M.B.H., 417 F.Supp. 176, 179 (E.D.N.Y.1976) judgment affirmed 52 F.2d 466 (2d Cir.1977). But cf. Scozzari v. Jade Co., 350 F.Supp. 801, 805 (E.D.N.Y.1972). The purpose of the rule—to prevent a nonlawyer from controlling the lawyer in a way detrimental to the interests of the lawyer's client—is plainly inapplicable in such a case.

92 Gassman v. State Bar, 18 Cal.3d 125, 132 Cal.Rptr. 675, 553 P.2d 1147, 1151, (1976); Attorney Grievance Comm'n v. Lebowitz, 290 Md. 499, 431 A.2d 88, 92 (1981) (discipline of lawyer for sharing fees with corrupt insurance adjusters, with whom he negotiated, purportedly at arms' length, for settlements for lawyer's clients).

93 Committee on Professional Ethics v. Lawler, 342 N.W.2d 486, 488 (Iowa 1984).

94 Florida Bar v. Sagrans, 388 So.2d 1040 (Fla.1980) (discipline of lawyer who agreed to compensate chiropractor for medical malpractice cases referred to lawyer); Florida Bar v. Gaer, 380 So.2d 429 (Fla.1980)(fee splitting with forwarding bail bondsman); Columbus Bar Ass'n v. Agee, 175 Ohio St. 443, 196 N.E.2d 98 (1964), cert.denied 379 U.S. 7, 85 S.Ct. 70, 13 L.Ed.2d 22 (1964)(indefinite suspension for splitting fees with "workmen's compensation consultant," who contracted with clients in behalf of self and of defendant lawyer); Utz v. State Bar, 21 Cal.2d 100, 130 P.2d 377 (1942)(suspension for arrangement with "heir hunters"). To an extent, the prohibition against fee splitting with a nonlawyer buttresses the prohibitions in the lawyer codes against compensating any person for recommending employment of the lawyer. See Hansen v. Wightman, 14 Wn.App. 78, 538 P.2d 1238 (1975). But compare Emmons, Williams, Mires & Leech v. State Bar, 6 Cal.App.3d 565, 86 Cal.Rptr. 367 (1970)(one-third forwarding fee exacted by authorized lawyer referral service permissible).

95 See § 16.3 (nonlawyer employees).

96 See § 16.2 (law firms), § 16.4 (dual practice).

97 E.g., Moran v. Harris, 131 Cal.App.3d 913, 182 Cal. Rptr. 519, 523 (1982)("The practice of forwarding fees among lawyers, part of our legal culture . . ., remains with us even though the detrimental effect upon the client appears obvious."); Wall St.J., Feb. 19, 1980, at 1, col.1 (in article about medical malpractice lawyers: "Most states limit the percentage of the award a lawyer can collect to about a third. The lawyer who refers the case to a specialist is entitled to a third of that fee."); D.Rosenthal, Lawyer and Client: Who's in Charge?, at 99–100 (1974)(practice of giving "front-end," one-time referral fees widespread in Manhattan despite ethical rule; lawyer-informants believe bar agencies do not enforce rule strictly unless practice becomes wholesale and thus suggests solicitation of claim by lawyer).

98 See Dunne & Gaston v. Keltner, 50 Cal.App.3d 560, 566–67, 123 Cal.Rptr. 430, 434–35 (1975)(Thompson, J.,

But prohibiting referral would probably have the effect of encouraging marginally competent lawyers to keep cases in an attempt to bumble through. The availability of forwarding fees encourages a lawyer without particular competence in a specialized matter or with a temporary crush of other business in the office to forward a client's matter to a lawyer better equipped to handle it.[99] Yet the lawyer codes regulate fee splitting in ways that the practice of forwarding fees offends in spirit if not literally. Moreover, the regulations do little to protect the interest that clients have in gaining full information about who will handle their matters and how their fees are being divided. Neither the Code nor the Model Rule regulation provides clients with the information that they would desire in order to shop for a better division of fees and responsibilities among other lawyers.

Both the Code (DR 2-107) and the Model Rules (MR 1.5)(e)) permit fee splitting among lawyers only if rather elaborate rituals and restrictions are observed. Violations are disciplinary offenses.[1] In both codes the restrictions apply, however, to fee splitting between lawyers not in the same firm; lawyers in the same firm may share fees in any way they choose.[2] Fee splitting between lawyers not in the same firm is narrowly confined to worker lawyers by the Code, but the Model Rules are more permissive and permit some pure forwarding. As far as they go, the requirements of the lawyer codes are enforced in discipline cases, through denying effect to impermissible fee-splitting agreements,[3] and by denying fee awards to lawyers who participate in impermissible fee splitting arrangements.[4]

DR 2-107. Under DR 2-107(A), lawyers may share a client's fee only if (1) the client

concurring). As pointed out in Moran v. Harris, 131 Cal. App.3d 913, 182 Cal.Rptr. 519, 523 (1982), permitting referral fee splitting is also anomalous in view of the professional rules that require a lawyer who is too busy or unskilled to handle a case not to accept it in the first place.

99 Moran v. Harris, supra, 182 Cal.Rptr. at 523-24. Cf. MR 1.5 comment (Division of Fees). See generally Morgan, The Evolving Concept of Professional Responsibility, 90 Harv.L.Rev. 702, 741-42 (1977). See also, e.g., Hall & Levy, Intra-Attorney Fee-Sharing Arrangements, 11 Val. U.L.Rev. 1 (1976); Note, Attorneys: The Referral Fee: A Split Opinion, 33 Okl.L.Rev. 628 (1980).

1 In re Netchert, 78 N.J. 445, 396 A.2d 1118 (1979) (disbarment for, among other things, fifty-fifty fee splitting with lawyer who forwarded personal injury cases). The court in In re Connaghan, 613 S.W.2d 626 (Mo.1981), held that the prohibition against fee splitting was violated by an attempt to disguise as a forwarding fee a bribe paid in behalf of clients to another lawyer, who was a legislator and who took favorable legislative action in return for the bribes. The description of the bribe as a forwarding fee seemed to follow from the fact that the funds came from clients as purported legal fees. The lawyers involved seem to have richly deserved disbarment; but their offense was hardly fee splitting.

2 See § 16.3.1. The limited circle within which fee splitting can freely be carried on is defined in the Code (DR 2-107(A)) "a partner in or associate of his law firm or law office." The prohibition in MR 1.5(e) is with respect to "lawyers who are not in the same firm." Neither rule clearly states whether fee splitting is permissible between lawyers who share office space or other expenses but are not otherwise in the same partnership or professional corporation. Cf. Koehler v. Wales, 16 Wn.App. 304, 556 P.2d 233, 236 (1976). Both probably prevent an industry from arising within the legal profession similar to temporary-worker agencies for secretarial and many other types of services.

Some agreements that provide for fee splitting after a firm dissolves may be permissible. See generally Corti v. Fleisher, 93 Ill.App.3d 517, 49 Ill.Dec. 74, 417 N.E.2d 764 (1981); In re Silverberg, 75 A.D.2d 817, 427 N.Y.S.2d 480, 482 (1980); Baron v. Mullinax, Wells, Mauzy & Baab, Inc., 623 S.W.2d 457 (Tex.App.1981), error refused n.r.e.

One decision holds that if a client jointly hires two lawyers from separate firms, the rules governing fee splitting do not apply and the fee can be divided as provided in the joint contract. See Fontenot & Mitchell v. Rozas, Manuel, Fontenot & McGee, 425 So.2d 259 (La. App.1982).

3 Altschul v. Sayble, 83 Cal.App.3d 153, 147 Cal.Rptr. 716 (1978); Hofreiter v. Leigh, 124 Ill.App.3d 1052, 80 Ill.Dec. 319, 465 N.E.2d 110 (1984); Palmer v. Breyfogle, 217 Kan. 128, 535 P.2d 955 (1975); Fleming v. Campbell, 537 S.W.2d 118 (Tex.Civ.App.1976), error refused n.r.e.; Belli v. Shaw, 98 Wn.2d 569, 657 P.2d 315, 319 (1983). See generally 28 ALR4th 665 (1984).

4 In re Futuronics Corp., 655 F.2d 463 (2d Cir.1981), cert. denied 455 U.S. 941, 102 S.Ct. 1435, 71 L.Ed.2d 653 (1982)(trial court's denial of over $1 million in fees, to which firms were otherwise entitled, because of impermissible fee splitting agreement was within trial court's discretion); Prandini v. National Tea Co., 557 F.2d 1015, 1019 (3d Cir.1977)(fee splitting agreement between cocounsel, if in violation of Code, disregarded in dividing fees in class action suit); Lewis v. Teleprompter Corp., 88 F.R.D. 11 (S.D.N.Y.1980)(impermissible fee-splitting agreement between lead counsel and other lawyers representing class members denied effect, and lead counsel penalized by reduction in fee); Schroeder v. Schaefer, 258 Or. 444, 477 P.2d 720 (1970)(lawyer who did not inform client of fee-splitting arrangement denied recovery on fee

consents to employment of the other lawyer after a disclosure that the client's fee payment will be split; (2) the fee is divided "in proportion to the services performed and responsibilities assumed" by each lawyer;[5] and (3) the total amount of the fee is not unreasonable for the total amount of legal services rendered.[6] The provision for client disclosure and consent is limited; most obviously it does not require disclosure to the client of the percentage shares of the lawyers involved or of the extent of the responsibility of each lawyer.[7] Cases have rather consistently held that "services performed" requires, at a minimum, that the forwarding lawyer must do more than simply originate the matter and perhaps vaguely consult with the client for client relations purposes thereafter. Each lawyer must work on the matter, and their division of fees must reflect the division of work.[8]

Model Rule 1.5(e). The Model Rules relax the procedures for fee splitting in two respects. First, under MR 1.5(e)(1), either the shares of each lawyer may reflect the respective amounts of services performed, as under DR 2–107(A)(2), or "by written agreement with the client, each lawyer assumes joint responsibility for the representation." [9] In other words, the division of fees can reflect the forwarding lawyer's compensation for forwarding the matter to the second lawyer and need not pretend to be earned through other legal work.[10] Second, the provision for client disclosure and consent is more perfunctory than under DR 2–107(A)(1); all that MR 1.5(e)(2) requires is that the client be advised of "the participation of all the lawyers involved" and "does not object." The rule does not clearly place the responsibility for advising the client on one lawyer or the other, does not require that the client be informed of the fact of fee splitting or its size,[11] and, as in the Code, does not require a disclosure of the extent of work sharing.

Better Regulation of Fee Splitting and Forwarding

Several states have gone further than either the Code or the Model Rules in regulating fee splitting—both by permitting fee splitting under more circumstances than the Code allows and by providing for superior client participation in the process. California's rule, for example, provides for forwarding and fee splitting in any case in which the client consents in writing.[12] The client's written consent can follow only after the client has

contract; possibility recognized of recovery in quantum meruit).

5 So long as the forwarding lawyer has not been substituted out of the representation, that lawyer remains responsible to respond accurately to client requests for information about the progress of the matter. E.g., In re Mims, 280 S.C. 188, 311 S.E.2d 926 (1984). The statement in the Illinois rule that forbids a lawyer to delegate responsibility for representing a client to another lawyer without the client's consent is a useful way to capture the requirement of the continuing responsibilities of the forwarding lawyer. See Ill. Rule 2–109(b).

6 Estate of Vafiades v. Sheppard Bus Service, 192 N.J. Super. 301, 469 A.2d 971, 977 (1983)(special fee to forwarding lawyer made total fee unreasonable).

7 See Carter v. Katz, Shandell, Katz & Erasmous, 120 Misc.2d 1009, 465 N.Y.S.2d 991, 997 (1983)("A client is simply to be made aware that another attorney is jointly or independently representing his or her interests at no additional expense to her therefor. Any further elaboration or specificity regarding the exact arrangement between the collaborating attorneys is not ethically mandated by this Code provision.").

8 Despite the apparent rigidity of DR 2–107(A), courts have not applied it in all possible instances. E.g., Krajewski v. Klawon, 84 Mich.App. 532, 270 N.W.2d 9 (1978) (agreement between lawyer, discharged by client after performing substantial work, and successor lawyer to divide fee in fair way did not offend Code).

9 The assumption of joint responsibility is said by the comment to MR 1.5 (Division of Fees) to "entail the obligations" of MR 5.1 on superior and subordinate lawyers. The phrase "joint responsibility" in the rule is also susceptible to being read as a euphemism for assumption of joint and several liability for legal malpractice purposes, as if the two lawyers were partners.

10 The same result is reached through the Texas version of DR 2–107(A)(2), which provides that fee splitting is permissible if made between lawyers who divide the legal work or if the division "is made with a forwarding lawyer."

11 See MR 1.5 comment (Division of Fee)(the rule "does not require disclosure to the client of the share that each lawyer is to receive").

12 See Calif. Rule 2–108(A)(1). For an experimental seven-year period, California followed a rule that more tightly regulated fee splitting pursuant to the model of the 1969 Code. The present rule was created by an amendment in 1979. See Moran v. Harris, 131 Cal.App.3d 913, 182 Cal.Rptr. 519, 522–23 (1982).

been informed about the fee sharing and its terms.[13] The rule in Illinois goes one step further and requires that the disclosure to the client also include the nature of the responsibilities of each lawyer after the referral.[14] The Illinois rule also spells out the requirement that the forwarding lawyer must agree to assume the same "legal responsibility" for the work as if a partner of the lawyer to whom the case is forwarded.[15]

Forwarding is justifiable on public policy grounds only if it enhances the ability of a client to receive superior legal services. Leaving the client as far in the background as the Code and the Model Rules do is either paternalistic or ignores that policy. The engine that drives both the California and the Illinois forwarding rules is client consent. Their mandated disclosure is much more satisfactory than that required by either the more modest 1969 Code or the even more modest 1983 Model Rules.

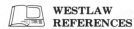

WESTLAW REFERENCES

Fee Splitting with Nonlawyers

dr3–102 "dr 3–102" (fee /2 divi! split!) /s non-lawyer

Lawyer Fee Splitting

dr2–107 "dr 2–107" 45k151 "fee split!"

§ 9.3 PERMISSIBLE FEES

§ 9.3.1 Fair Fee Charges

How Lawyers Set Fees

Are fee charges too high, too low, or about right? Lawyers tend to believe they are about right.[16] Clients think they are too high.[17] Lawyers set fees at figures that will produce as much income as possible yet at the same time not hinder relationships with clients by discouraging clients from retaining the lawyer, bringing back other legal matters, or recommending friends and associates. In keeping with tradition, many lawyers are individually probably conservative about setting fees.[18]

A common way to begin to think about fee charges on an hourly basis is to calculate first the lawyer's office overhead or portion of it if the lawyer practices with others. Add to that the income that the lawyer realistically wants to earn for the year and divide the sum by the probable number of billable hours available in a year. With a fifty-week work year and forty hours per week, one is tempted to think that billing two thousand hours per year would be common. In fact, it is almost unheard of because so many other, nonbillable matters press into the working day—office administration, personal and nonlegal business matters, bar association and civic activities, and general legal reading. Many lawyers find that they can bill no more than twelve to fourteen hundred hours per year. On those assumptions, a lawyer whose office overhead is 40 percent of billings [19] who bills

[13] Calif. R. 2–108(A)(1). The total fee must be reasonable in view of the total services provided. R. 2–108(A)(2).

[14] Ill. Rule 2–107(a)(1).

[15] Ill. Rule 2–107(a)(2)(b).

[16] Law Poll, Fees about Right, Lawyers Say, 68 ABA J. 1562 (1982)(national survey of lawyers indicates 54 percent think fee levels are appropriate; 21 percent, too high; 11 percent, too low).

[17] Davies, Small Business and Legal Services, 65 ABA J. 1806 (1979); Merhige, Delivery of Legal Services, 2 Social Responsibility: Journalism, Law, Medicine 40 (1976); J.Goulden, The Million Dollar Lawyers 160 (1978); Missouri Bar-Prentice Hall Survey: A Motivational Study of Public Attitudes and Law Office Management 118 (1963)(40 percent of public thinks legal fees too high); Time Magazine, July 27, 1981, at 68; Wall St.J., Apr.13, 1978, at 1, col. 1; Green, The High Cost of Lawyers, N.Y. Times Magazine, Aug. 10, 1975, at 8.

[18] Steele & Rothe, Pricing Behavior of Attorneys: An Empirical Study, 14 Forum 1060 (1979)(study indicates that lawyers' price setting corresponds well to ethical requirements but poorly to good management practices). For a general survey of billing practices, see How Firms Bill, Nat'l L.J., Feb. 27, 1984, Spec. Section.

[19] Although one might imagine that overhead could be fixed quite independently of billings, the two are closely linked. The number of clients dictates the amount of secretarial and other clerical assistance, space (rent) needs, office furnishings, copier and stationery expense, and the like. Rent and office furnishings are theoretical-

twelve hundred hours per year would have to charge seventy dollars per hour for an annual income of sixty thousand dollars, the average firm member's salary in a recent year.

Lawyers in fact can employ such theoretical numbers only as loose guides in a competitive market for legal services. The most important limiting factors are the fee levels of other lawyers. Most lawyers beginning a practice—or rechecking moorings—just ask around and attempt to peg their own success at attracting clients into a set of office fees. The fees are nudged up if the client flow through the office is not disproportionately reduced, and lowered if it is necessary to increase net revenue. Because the process essentially involves bidding for clients, a formal bidding for governmental or other clients is now recognized as permissible.[20]

Client Information about Fees

Clients are seriously compromised in their attempts to find out information about their legal rights and about fee charges. Lacking that information, clients are in a poor position to negotiate favorably either for hourly rate, fixed fee, or contingent fee legal services contracts.[21] In addition, the typically long delays experienced by clients in obtaining results from lawyers and the legal system serve to mask actual time-investment decisions by lawyers. Client inability to monitor the time actually spent by lawyers further enhances lawyer control over fees. Although lawyer advertising can permissibly refer to fee charges and contain some information about legal rights, most advertised information deals only with relatively minor matters and contains little helpful information.

The attitude within the legal profession is neutral at best and often hostile toward "fee shoppers" [22]—clients who during an early interview seek complete information about the eventual fee charge for the purpose of comparing it with similar information from another lawyer. Many lawyers structure the initial interview to gain the confidence of the client and create a dependency relationship toward the lawyer. Withholding information about fees can be part of that strategy.

For a long time many clients, although very upset that their lawyers do not settle the question of fees early in the representation,[23] would accept lawyers' initial silence or lawyers' later refusals to account in detail for fee charges. Increasingly, however, clients from the largest corporations to individuals with minor personal problems are realizing the importance of coming to an early understand-

ly the most variable overhead items but are also thought to be the items that are most likely to attract, or repel, clients.

20 Prior to the Supreme Court's decision in National Society of Professional Engineers v. United States, 435 U.S. 679, 98 S.Ct. 1355, 55 L.Ed.2d 637 (1978), the ABA had taken the position that a lawyer could not ethically respond to a request of a city or other client to bid for legal services. ABA Formal Op. 292 (1957). The Court there held, however, that a professional organization's prohibition against competitive bidding was an antitrust violation.

In England in the mid-1930s the Law Society for the first time prohibited one solicitor from undercutting another's fee quotation. The prohibition was occasionally enforced by disciplinary action. See F.Bennion, Professional Ethics 186, 189 (1969). The reported motivation was to correct the "uneconomic" fee cutting resulting from solicitors' desperate search for work during a time of high unemployment.

21 Halpern & Turnbull, An Economic Analysis of Legal Fees Contracts, in Lawyers and the Consumer Interest: Regulating the Market for Legal Services at 178–79 (R.Evans & M.Trebilcock eds.1982).

22 For a view favoring openness, see Grady, J., in Washington v. Pierce, 576 F.Supp. 473, 476 (N.D.Ill.1983) ("Many lawyers speak with contempt of clients who 'fee shop,' and the idea that fees are the result of a free market bargaining process in a competitive market is contrary to experience. We are starting to see a few changes in this picture in the case of large, sophisticated corporate clients. It is high time. But even in these few instances, the emphasis is not on hourly rates—it is on cutting the amount of time spent.").

Possibly more typical is the view, from a practitioner's treatise, that fee shopping is a "vicious practice" that leads to client dissatisfaction and client disloyalty to the lawyer and "only contributes to the down-grading of the standards, as well as the economic status, of the profession." 2 S.Speiser, Attorneys' Fees 513 (1973)(in section entitled "discouragement of fee shoppers").

23 1976 Prentice Hall, Inc., Manual for Managing the Law Office 5361 (Mar.12, 1976)(survey of clients indicates that lawyers do not discuss legal fees in way that clients prefer; many lawyers make clients wait until later in representation before discussing fees despite desire of clients to know at outset what total of fees is estimated to be).

ing with a lawyer that the client will be supplied with detailed and helpful information about fees.[24] Lawyers are urged by the 1969 Code to settle the matter of fees "as soon as feasible" after employment begins.[25] Model Rule 1.5(b) now requires that the lawyer communicate the basis or rate of fee, "preferably in writing, before or within a reasonable time after commencing the representation."

Fee-Setting Practices

Although neither the 1969 Code nor the 1983 Model Rules mention the matter, disciplinary cases resulting in findings of impermissible fees have most often dealt with the process by which the offending lawyer set the fee. Its large size has been an important but secondary factor. Courts have insisted that lawyers be entirely honest in discussing fees with clients [26] or with agencies that will determine fees.[27] Lawyers have been disciplined for misrepresenting to clients that their cases were very difficult in order to justify high fees or a high percentage in contingent fee contracts,[28] for padding bills with exorbitant or unfounded disbursements,[29] or for failing to notify clients promptly when unexpectedly favorable developments made legal services no longer necessary.[30] A lawyer should be forthright in volunteering information if it is reasonably apparent that a client or fee payer is proceeding on a misapprehension of a material fact.[31]

Remedies for Excessive Fee Charges

Clients have an array of remedies available through which to seek vindication of a claim that a lawyer's fee charge was excessive. A complaint can be made to a lawyer disciplinary agency on the ground that an excessive fee violates the applicable lawyer code.[32] Fee arbitration is sometimes available (§ 9.6.2). A client can defend a lawyer's suit to collect a fee on the ground that the fee is excessive and perhaps defeat the lawyer's entire fee claim if the fee charge is exorbitant.[33] Excessive fees may also be a ground for recovering punitive damages in a legal malpractice case.[34]

[24] Nader Offers Business Legal-Fee Tips, N.Y.Times, Apr.13, 1981, at 25, col.3.

[25] EC 2–19. See In re Sawyer, 98 Wn.2d 584, 656 P.2d 503, 505 (1983)("He failed to even discuss his fee with his client and rejected her early efforts to ascertain what she should expect to pay. This failure in itself, while not rising to the level of professional misconduct, falls well short of preferred practice. See . . . EC2–19 (fee arrangement should be clarified '[a]s soon as feasible' after employment and should usually be put in writing.)").

[26] In re O'Bryant, 425 A.2d 1313 (D.C.App.1981)(discipline for misrepresenting to client that client funds retained had been agreed to earlier as lawyer's compensation).

[27] Myers v. Virginia St. Bar ex rel. Second Distr. Committee, 226 Va. 630, 312 S.E.2d 286 (1984)(misrepresentation to probate court).

[28] In re Rappaport, 558 F.2d 87 (2d Cir.1977); Westchester County Bar Ass'n v. St. John, 43 A.D.2d 218, 350 N.Y.S.2d 737 (1974). One lawyer was convicted of a federal offense for an aggravated instance of exaggerating the seriousness of the client's plight in order to extort an exorbitant fee. United States v. Blitstein, 626 F.2d 774 (10th Cir.1980), cert.denied 449 U.S. 1102, 101 S.Ct. 898, 66 L.Ed.2d 828 (1981)(conviction of interstate fraud and violation of travel act by extortion from client of high fee on false representations of seriousness of charges against client).

[29] In re Morris, 72 N.J. 135, 367 A.2d 1172 (1977).

[30] In re Sullivan, 494 S.W.2d 329 (Mo.1973)(lawyer took $1000 retainer from father to defend minor son against charges of manslaughter and illegally transporting dead body but failed to notify promptly when charges were dismissed almost immediately after retainer was paid and without any effort by lawyer).

[31] In re Miller, 287 Or. 621, 601 P.2d 789 (1979)(lawyer disciplined for failure to advise client and fee-paying relatives that court procedure entitled lawyer to look for fee payment to bail funds deposited).

[32] Although it is not predictable, some jurisdictions in some disciplinary cases will order the lawyer to make restitution to affected clients of the amount of an excessive fee. E.g., In re Synder, 276 Or. 897, 559 P.2d 1273, 1275 (1976); In re Burgess, 275 S.C. 315, 270 S.E.2d 436 (1980); In re Hansen, 586 P.2d 413, 417 (Utah 1978) (although no other discipline would be imposed, lawyer was required to make restitution to client of excessive fee within thirty days); In re Noble, 100 Wn.2d 88, 667 P.2d 608, 614 (1983).

[33] See § 9.6.1, at 554–56.

[34] Rodriquez v. Horton, 95 N.M. 356, 622 P.2d 261 (App. 1980)(award of punitive damages in legal malpractice actice action upheld on ground, among others, that lawyer had charged client excessive fee).

Process of Discipline for Excessive Fees

Discipline for excessive fees is rare, although it may have increased somewhat following enactment of the Code in 1969.[35] The lack of enforcement hardly reflects client contentment with high fees, for excessive fees rank high among sources of client dissatisfaction with lawyers. The reason for lax enforcement has to do with the institutional and doctrinal limitations on fee-size enforcement.

The institutional constraints are created by the fact that professional discipline is comfortably in the hands of other lawyers. Lawyers will always be inadequate enforcers of fee limitations because their economic hearts aren't in it. They cannot bring themselves in close cases to judge fee charge as a disciplinary violation. Law practice, as is the rest of commercial life, is imbued with the ethic of free enterprise and its slogans concerning what the market will bear, rugged individualism, and dog-eat-dog. Most lawyers would like to receive handsome fees; to judge another lawyer guilty of having received too much seems like a contradiction in terms. The introduction of nonlawyer viewpoints through fee arbitration committees with some nonlawyer membership holds some promise of bringing about balance, but in a nondisciplinary context.

The second difficulty is doctrinal: the single standard of an excessive fee, as stated in all of the lawyer codes, is necessarily vague because of the greatly varied settings in which fees are charged, and thus uncertain in its application. Disciplinary bodies, already hobbled by economic self-interest, are further stymied by doubts about fairness. As a consequence, none but seriously unreasonable fee charges are found to violate the standard.

Professional Rules on Excessive Fees

There is considerable variation among the lawyer codes in the rules that define permissible fees. Some jurisdictions, following what seems to be the approach of both the 1969 Code and the 1983 Model Rules, have adopted what might be called a mildly regulatory approach. Other jurisdictions, including California, have taken an approach that reserves professional discipline for only the most outrageous and unusual cases.[36] At least, one gathers that such differences exist on the face of the regulations. The wording of regulations may, of course, belie a very different pattern of actual enforcement, perhaps even a common pattern among jurisdictions despite verbal differences in standards.[37]

Charging an excessive fee is a violation under both the Code (DR 2–106(A)) and the Model Rules (MR 1.5(a)). The Code, in DR 2–106(A), proscribes a fee that is "clearly excessive," and DR 2–106(B) defines a test for that concept that is lawyer-centered: "a fee is clearly excessive when, after a review of the facts, a lawyer of ordinary prudence would be left with a definite and firm conviction that the fee is in excess of a reasonable fee." The

35 The 1908 Canons included in Canon 12 an injunction that "lawyers should avoid charges which overestimate their advice and services, as well as those which undervalue them." The number of disciplinary cases for excessive fee charges under the Canons was not large, but cases, particularly those involving contingent fees, were not unknown. E.g., In re Ostensoe, 196 Minn. 102, 103, 264 N.W. 569 (1936)(suspension for, among other things, charging contingent fee of 50 percent in personal injury action); State v. Cannon, 199 Wis. 401, 226 N.W. 385 (1929)(discipline for, among other things, unconscionably charging one-third contingent fee without regard to amount of services performed or needs of client).

36 Calif. Rule 2–107(A): "A member of the State Bar shall not enter into an agreement for, charge or collect an illegal or unconscionable fee." Oklahoma refuses to regard excessive fee charges as a ground for discipline unless the charge is that the amount of the fee is "extortionate or fraudulent." See Rule 1.4(d), as amended June 1980, in Rules Governing Disciplinary Proceedings, 5 Okl. Stat., ch.1, App. 1-A.

It has been claimed that "generally . . . even a finding that a lawyer has charged an excessive fee does not, in itself, warrant disciplinary action. Other elements of wrongdoing (overreaching, appropriation of the client's funds under the guise of charging a fee, and so forth) have to be present." Annotated Code of Professional Responsibility 101 (O.Maru ed.1979), citing 1 S.Speiser, Attorneys' Fees § 1.37 (1973). Speiser cites in support only pre-Code cases and, indiscriminately, decisions from California. The characterization is probably safe only in some jurisdictions.

37 For an extensive collection of cases, see Annot., 11 A.L.R.4th 133 (1982).

test is obviously indeterminate,[38] but it is not subjective. The invocation of the considered judgment of the lawyer of ordinary prudence is not one that varies from lawyer to lawyer. The remainder of DR 2–106(B) then gives a nonexclusive list of eight factors that determine whether a fee meets that test.

In the end, DR 2–106 seems unsettled on whether it means to hold lawyers to a relatively lax standard of "clearly excessive" or whether it propounds a test of "reasonable," although under procedural circumstances in which a relatively high standard of proof (definite and firm conviction) suggests that convictions for violation of a standard of reasonable fees will be relatively uncommon. The reporter's footnotes to DR 2–106 indicate that the wording of the rule might have been influenced by decisions that employed an equitable concept of fraud in measuring the permissible size of fees.[39] On balance, it seems that the reference to "clearly excessive" is simply a way of emphasizing, in jurisdictions that follow a lesser burden of proof, that a fee should be found unreasonable only on definite and firm proof.[40]

The 1983 Model Rules, in the final version of MR 1.5(a), state a test for the permissible limits on the size of fees that is austere and virtually indecipherable but that was intended to be at least as strict as the Code's standard of "clearly excessive." A lawyer's fee under MR 1.5(a) must be "reasonable." Nothing more is said about the topic in the rule or its comment.[41] The same eight factors are copied verbatim from the Code as a nonexhaustive list of criteria.

In contrast to the cryptic final draft, the suppressed "legal background note" to earlier drafts of the Model Rules plainly indicated that the Kutak Commission meant the "reasonable" standard to depart from pre-Code authority and from the California rule, which required that a fee "shock the conscience" or be patently unconscionable before the fee was prohibited.[42] Like the tort standard of the reasonable-person test, the issue here, perhaps even more plainly than was the case with the Code, is to be measured by a legal-community sense of fitness under the circumstances in light of the profession's undertaking of service to clients. Undoubtedly for lawyers the most important datum about the community will be the range of charges among reasonable practitioners. Obviously lawyers will not be disciplined for fees that are in the low or the middle range.[43] The rule does not equate "reasonable" with "aver-

[38] DR 2–106 nonetheless has been upheld against constitutional attacks on the ground of its vagueness. E.g., In re Kennedy, 472 A.2d 1317, 1329–30 (Del.), cert.denied ___ U.S. ___, 104 S.Ct. 2388, 81 L.Ed.2d 346 (1984).

[39] The reporter's footnote 88 cites and quotes from ABA Formal Op. 320 (1968), which refers to a fee "so excessive as to constitute a misappropriation of the client's funds." Several pre-Code decisions had used a test that defined an impermissible fee as one that compelled a finding that the lawyer had overreached the client. E.g., Gray v. Joseph J. Brunetti Constr. Corp., 266 F.2d 809 (3d Cir.), cert. denied 361 U.S. 826, 80 S.Ct. 74, 4 L.Ed.2d 69 (1959).

[40] On the various standards of proof employed in jurisdictions in discipline cases, see § 3.4.4 (burden of proof). The "clearly excessive" standard presumably makes a difference in those few jurisdictions that employ the standard of preponderance of the evidence.

[41] The text of MR 1.5(a) was amended during the August, 1983, floor amendments to the Model Rules by the addition of the eight factors taken from DR 2–106(B). Earlier Kutak Commission versions of the Model Rules had said nothing more about maximum fee size. Earlier drafts had merely required reasonableness in the mandatory rule and then listed factors, with wording somewhat changed from DR 2–106(B), in a comment. See MR 1.6(a) and comment (Reasonableness of Fee; first paragraph)(Discussion Draft, January 30, 1980); MR 1.5(a) and comment (Reasonableness of Fee) (Proposed Final Draft, May 30, 1981). The Commission was obviously at a loss how to deal in a detailed and informative way with excessive fee size as a disciplinary matter.

[42] MR 1.5 legal backgound note, at 35 (Proposed Final Draft, May 30, 1981): "Rule 1.5 eliminates the term 'clearly excessive' and therefore prohibits unreasonable as well as patently unconscionable fees."

[43] A curious controversy was raised concerning whether the requirement in MR 1.5 that a fee be "reasonable" in size precluded unreasonably *low* fees. See 1 ABA/BNA Law.Man.Prof. Conduct 446, 447 (1984)(report of letter from head of Justice Department Antitrust Division to supreme courts in all 40 states known to be considering adoption of Model Rules, raising concern that provision in Model Rules for "reasonable" fees could be construed to require fees that were not "unreasonably" low). It would be perverse, in a rule that is designed to protect the interests of clients, to preclude low fees. The only conceivable argument against low fees is that they are a form of advertising or induce shoddy work. But if it is permissible for a lawyer to advertise low fees (so long, presumably, as the lawyer honors that commitment), it is

age." But if, with an allowance for generosity, a fee is markedly higher than the upper range of fees charged, then it seems to qualify under the Model Rules as unreasonable.[44]

Factors for Assessing Reasonability or Excessiveness [45]

Few of the eight criteria listed in DR 2–106(B) and MR 1.5(a) can be employed definitively in assessing the permissible size of a fee. Some or many might be relevant in a particular case, and the criteria are not assigned specific weights. Moreover, the list excludes some criteria that courts and lawyers commonly employ in testing the reasonableness of a fee. Noninclusion of a factor does not mean that it is inappropriate, because the list in both Code and Model Rules is plainly nonexhaustive.[46] The following will review the eight criteria in the order listed in the lawyer codes and then continue with additional elements that courts and lawyers have also taken into account.

(1) "The time and labor required, the novelty and difficulty of the questions involved, and the skill requisite to perform the legal service properly." Time is a critical element in most fee charges.[47] At the very least, it cannot in most cases be ignored entirely, whatever other factors come into play.[48] Together with the hourly rate, time charges initially determine the fee in most commercial representations.[49] The process is, however, not a mechanical one. Most lawyers using an hourly charge method know that time can be wasted or spent unproductively and thus should not be billed to a client.[50] A lawyer in charge of billing will often "eyeball" a fee

plainly permissible to charge the same fees without advertising. As for shoddy work, clients are much better off being assured of quality work by means other than forcing all lawyers to charge princely sums.

Unfortunately it is true that bar associations in the past have taken the position that a failure to charge a fee is an ethical violation. The ABA's 1908 Canon 12 seemed to treat charging a low fee and charging a high one as equally objectionable: "In fixing fees, lawyers should avoid charges which overestimate their advice and services, as well as those which undervalue them." Ethics opinions advanced a variety of bizarre theories to support the notion that a low fee was unethical. E.g., ABA Informal Op. 1166 (1970)(military assistance lawyer should not provide free legal services to military personnel able to pay fee but should refer such clients to local practitioners, apparently on theory that public funds were involved, although no law or regulation purported to limit this particular fringe benefit of members of armed services); Informal Op. 1236 (1972)(offering legal services at discount impermissible because lawyer would either take a loss or perform services inadequately); Informal Op. 1237 (1972)(problems with group legal services fee schedule because fees might not comport with sentiment of EC 2–17 on desirability of adequate compensation for lawyers); ABA Formal Op. 307 (1962)(fixed-fee annual legal checkup improper because low size of fee might tempt lawyer to perform services in shoddy manner in case requiring substantial work). The above are cited in Annotated Code of Professional Responsibility 104–05 (O.Maru ed.1979). In general, however, the effectively enforced rule was that a lawyer committed no violation of an enforcible norm by charging a low fee or no fee to a client able to pay, provided there was no improper motive for doing so. See, e.g., Brame v. Ray Bills Fin. Corp., 76 F.R.D. 25, 28 (N.D.N.Y.1977); ABA Informal Op. 1339 (1975).

44 The reference here to a "range" of fees is largely theoretical. In practice, the legal community will not have a formal or published range of fees unless it is courting suit under the antitrust laws. In individual cases, there will be little proof of actual community averages. "Expert" witnesses will testify for both sides, with predictably varying reports from the rest of the real world. In the end, the hearing body must determine by its own lights and knowledge of billing practices what a reasonable fee might be.

45 Cf. generally Berger, Court Awarded Attorneys' Fees: What Is Reasonable?, 126 U.Pa.L.Rev. 281 (1977)(extensive review of question of reasonability in context of court-awarded fees).

46 Nolan v. Foreman, 665 F.2d 738, 741 (5th Cir.1982). Both DR 2–106(B) and MR 1.5(a) state that the factors to be considered as guides in determining the reasonableness of a fee "*include*" the eight listed factors.

47 But cf., e.g., Craig v. Jo B. Gardner, Inc., 586 S.W.2d 316 (Mo.1979)(in fee-splitting dispute between plaintiff's lawyers, despite fact that no contemporaneous time records were kept, "it has been held that time taken to perform the services is only one element considered and is ordinarily of minor importance").

48 In re Kutner, 78 Ill.2d 157, 35 Ill.Dec. 674, 677, 399 N.E.2d 963, 966, 11 A.L.R.4th 123 (1979)(regardless of other circumstances, in routine simple battery defense that resulted in guilty plea and involved no unusual issues or exertion, lawyer's fee of $5,000, which worked out to rate of $500 per hour, was excessive).

49 Courts increasingly insist that lawyers who seek court-awarded fees produce reliable contemporaneous time records of the amount of effort expended on a case. E.g., Ortiz v. Safeco Ins. Co., 144 N.J.Super. 506, 366 A.2d 695 (1976), certification denied 73 N.J. 63, 372 A.2d 328 (1977).

50 Cf. Williamson v. John D. Quinn Constr. Co., 537 F.Supp. 613, 617 (S.D.N.Y.1982).

that has been computed on the basis of an hourly charge and reduce it [51] because it simply looks too big in view of the importance of the matter or the client's willingness or ability to pay. By the same token, time spent by a lawyer in needless work—frivolous motions and the like—or work not related to the client's matter [52] is not properly chargeable to a client.[53] The novelty and difficulty of the issues involved in a matter are a rough measure of whether it will take extensive research and other preparation and a long time to unfold. The skill necessary to deal with the matter is a reflection of the lawyer's experience, training, and reputation, which is redundantly listed as the seventh factor.

(2) "The likelihood, if apparent to the client, that the acceptance of the particular employment will preclude other employment by the lawyer." Because of conflict of interest rules, a lawyer who represents a client after an initial consultation is precluded from representing the interests of adverse parties in the same matter. That bears on a fee, presumably, only if other parties with adverse interests would be likely both to have become the lawyer's clients except for the conflict and to have brought in significantly higher fees.[54]

(3) "The fee customarily charged in the locality for similar legal services." Minimum fee schedules, which once flourished,[55] have been suppressed because of the Supreme Court's decision that they are classic violations of the federal antitrust laws.[56] They have been replaced by interfirm exchanges, both outright and surreptitious, of information about fee charges, as lawyers attempt to keep their fees high but not too far out of line.[57] To an extent, lawyers can gain a general idea about fees from national publications.[58]

(4) "The amount involved and the results obtained." Both factors are involved in contingent fee contracts but are also relevant to other fee arrangements. For example, a number of fees have traditionally been fixed as a percentage of the value of property. A lawyer's work for the purchaser of a home is often fixed at one percent of the value of the property. Such fees supposedly indicate the risk a lawyer takes in legal malpractice exposure and roughly reflect the value to the client of the legal service. Results obtained, being usually of economic importance, reflect the increase in the client's wealth and thus the worth of the lawyer's work.

(5) "The time limitations imposed by the client or by the circumstances." That differs from the first factor if the client's demand for legal services involves an emergency or for

51 It goes almost without saying that a fee calculated on an hourly charge basis could never be increased on an impressionistic or any other basis without the client's consent; any other increase is a breach of the fee contract. Lawyers will occasionally concede that other lawyers inflate bills with "phantom hours." See Olson, Truth in Billing, 69 ABA J. 1344 (1983); Nat'l L.J., Jan. 19, 1981, at 2, col.2.

52 A case has held that the cost to a lawyer of researching whether to accept a representation, because of a possibly impermissible conflict of interest, is not properly billable to the client. Heninger & Heninger v. Davenport Bank & Trust Co., 341 N.W.2d 43, 49 (Iowa 1983).

53 State v. Davitt, 234 Kan. 283, 671 P.2d 1123 (1983).

54 The idea was more clearly expressed in 1908 Canon 12(2):

> Whether the acceptance of employment in the particular case will preclude the lawyer's appearance for others in cases likely to arise out of the transaction, and in which there is a reasonable expectation that otherwise he would be employed, or will involve the loss of other employment while employed in the particular case or antagonisms with other clients.

55 Note, A Critical Analysis of Bar Association Minimum Fee Schedules, 85 Harv.L.Rev. 971, 971–72 (1972)(at least thirty-four states and hundreds of local bar associations maintain minimum fee schedules that are used in setting fees by many lawyers). See also, e.g., Mathias, Fee Schedules and Prepaid Legal Services, 4 Balt.L.Rev. 80 (1974).

56 Goldfarb v. Virginia State Bar, 421 U.S. 773, 95 S.Ct. 2004, 44 L.Ed.2d 572 (1975). See § 2.4.1.

57 Cf. Bowles & Phillips, Solicitors' Remuneration: A Critique of Recent Developments in Conveyancing, 40 Mod.L.Rev. 639 (1977)(continuing controversy in England over informal use of "scale charges" after supposed abolition in Solicitor's Remuneration Order 1972 (effective January 1, 1973)).

58 See generally Altman & Weil, Inc., The 1983 Survey of Law Firm Economics (1983)(annual survey of firms showing what firms charge by hour by service categories, information on overhead, earnings of partners and associates, hiring rates, billable hours worked).

other reasons requires a large infusion of staff that creates inefficiencies in a law office because a client's needs bulk so large at times that other matters cannot be handled simultaneously.

(6) "The nature and length of the professional relationship with the client." It is not apparent whether longevity in a client-lawyer relationship is meant to justify a higher or only a lower fee. Gratitude for past fees would suggest a lower fee. At least with a new client there are no ties of sentiment that suggest anything but a market rate.[59]

(7) "The experience, reputation, and ability of the lawyer or lawyers performing the services." In hourly-charge fees, this obviously will be the most important factor. The hourly charge for an experienced lawyer will naturally be higher than for a beginning lawyer. The hourly rate presumably reflects the market value of the accumulated legal skills and technical information, and thus the efficiency, of the lawyer as a legal operative. It perhaps also reflects the market value of the lawyer's prestige and reputation, for what value that might have in negotiations, court appearances, and political lobbying.

(8) "Whether the fee is fixed or contingent." The most important result of the fact that a fee is contingent is that, to the extent that the contingency has an element of risk, a lawyer is justified in charging a higher fee in order to reflect the risk that a lower or perhaps no fee will be received.[60] Limitations on the occasions on which a contingent fee may be employed, the percentage figure that is used, and the base against which the percentage is charged are discussed at a later point (§ 9.4).

The factors mentioned in both DR 2–106(B) and MR 1.5(a) end with the factors listed above. But the list is incomplete because several others are relevant to lawyers, bar disciplinary authorities, and courts in setting fees. They are not specifically listed in the lawyer codes, possibly because lawyer codes are not entirely candid about fee size.

(9) The ABA's list is clearly redolent of the notion, but nowhere states explicitly, that informed consent of the client is a factor, as it clearly is.[61] If the client is a large corporation and is represented in setting the fee by independent counsel who is protecting the corporation's interests, it is doubtful that any fee negotiated and agreed to by the client, no matter how large, would be considered excessive.[62] When courts are confident that market forces impose limits on fee sizes, they are quite content to let those forces work.[63] But if the fee is unconscionably large and involves individuals who may lack effective information and bargaining power, courts are not deterred in finding the fee excessive by the fact that the client has consented.[64]

[59] That seems to be the idea also expressed in 1908 Canon 12(6): "the character of the employment, whether casual or for an established and constant client."

[60] Page v. Schrenker, 439 N.E.2d 694, 697 (Ind.App. 1982).

[61] Calif. Rule 2–107(B) lists several factors that closely resemble the eight factors of DR 2–106(B) and add as a ninth, "(9) The informed consent of the client to the fee agreement."

[62] Cf. Brobeck, Phleger & Harrison v. Telex Corp., 602 F.2d 866 (9th Cir.1979), cert.denied 444 U.S. 981, 100 S.Ct. 483, 62 L.Ed.2d 407 (1979)(court upholds $1 million fee for nationally prominent expert in antitrust law to assist in drafting petition for certiorari to U.S. Supreme Court, agreed to by client under circumstances described in text).

[63] At least to that extent, it is not entirely accurate to state that the law treats fee contracts as contracts between a fiduciary and a protected dependent. G.Hazard, Ethics in the Practice of Law 99 (1979). Only clients requiring the special protection of courts are protected; others are apparently to be treated as sheep to be shorn.

[64] In re Kutner, 78 Ill.2d 157, 35 Ill.Dec. 157, 399 N.E.2d 963, 11 ALR4th 123 (1979)(excessive charge for defense of battery charge). In Florida Bar v. Moriber, 314 So.2d 145, 148 (Fla.1975), the court suggested, in a case involving a lawyer whose contingent fee for "collecting" an estate consumed a third of an inheritance that came to the client by operation of law in any event:

> [The lawyer] relies on the fact that he fully informed the client of the contingency fee arrangement and subsequently discussed all details of the disbursement with him. The client was a night clerk who worked in a New York motel. Presumably, he was not aware of the fees typically charged by attorneys to represent an estate. In any event, even if we presume that the client were an educated and experienced party dealing at arm's length with the respondent, it is our view that an attorney may still be disciplined for overreaching where the fees charged are grossly disproportionate to the services rendered.

(10) Ability of the client to pay is perhaps the most frequent explanation for a lawyer's variations in fee charges.[65] The failure of the lawyer codes to mention client wealth as a factor can be put down to coyness, not reality.[66] Client wealth is also the customary justification cited by lawyers for contingent fee contracts.[67] Courts have occasionally determined that a fee was excessive in part on the basis of the modest resources of the client.[68] Some office fee schedules have a standard lower range of fees (called an eleemosynary charge in some offices) for charitable or other nonprofit institutions.[69]

(11) Related to the ability of the client to pay is the tax treatment of the fee payment by the client. If the fee is deductible, a client will obviously be willing to part with more. The lines that must be drawn are between business and nonbusiness legal fees and noncapital and capital expenditures. Legal fees for noncapital business purposes, such as a hardware store owner's lawsuit against a supplier, can be deducted as ordinary and necessary business expenses. But fee expenditures for personal purposes, such as a divorce or name change, are not deductible. Fees might also not be fully deductible in the year expended because they are capital expenses that can only be capitalized and amortized, if possible, over the useful life of a capital asset.[70]

(12) The nature of the client's business or other pursuit can be important. Within the Code itself, EC 2–18 refers to the "commendable and long-standing" tradition of setting a preferential, lower fee for other lawyers or members of their family.[71] The tradition, unobserved in larger communities, is based on professional solidarity and an instinct to build goodwill.

(13) In almost every case there will be a self-defined upper limit on a permissible fee charge—the amount to which the lawyer and client have agreed. Any charge by a lawyer in excess of that figure is plainly impermissible and thus excessive or unreasonable under the lawyer codes[72] unless the parties have

See also, e.g., Green v. Green, 41 Ill.App.3d 154, 354 N.E.2d 661, 675 (1976).

65 The client's ability to pay is probably the first thing that lawyers actually consider when setting a fee. See Bright, Is It Time to Adjust Your Fees?, 69 ABA J. 1426, 1427 (1983).

66 Occasionally the factor is mentioned as one of many justifying an award in a fee-shifting decision. E.g., Davis v. Myers, 427 So.2d 648, 650 (La.App.1983).

67 In a perverse sense, the only explicitly recognized situation in the Code or Model Rules in which a client's relative wealth may be taken into account is in the case of a contingent fee—based as it is on the client's hoped-for eventual ability to pay. A recovery in behalf of a person who is probably not able to pay a fee otherwise becomes a justification for a high fee that is thus a levy on the situation of poverty followed by sudden wealth.

68 In re Loring, 62 N.J. 336, 301 A.2d 721, 723 (1973). See also, e.g., In re Larson, 121 Ariz. 199, 589 P.2d 442 (1979); Bushman v. State Bar, 11 Cal.3d 558, 113 Cal. Rptr. 904, 522 P.2d 312 (1974). Courts in fee-shifting cases have held that when the party who can afford a larger fee will pay, the fact that the lawyer's original client is poor is not a reason for discounting a fee. E.g., Sassower v. Barone, 85 A.D.2d 81, 447 N.Y.S.2d 966, 971–72 (1982)(wealthy husband could not urge wife's impecuniousness as reason why wife's lawyer's fee should be discounted). Cf., e.g., Kawasaki Motors Corp. v. Finan, 577 F.2d 941, 942 (5th Cir.1978)(in fee-shifting case, relative impecuniousness of client might be relevant in determining fee when lawyer should be on notice that pecuniary value of particular legal services might be limited).

69 When awarding fees, courts have held that a fee to be paid by a charity should be at usual rates in order not to discourage competent lawyers from accepting such cases. See In re Morgan Washington Home, 108 Ill.App. 3d 245, 64 Ill.Dec. 105, 107, 439 N.E.2d 34, 36 (1982).

70 See generally Note, The Deductibility of Legal Expenses, 82 Colum.L.Rev. 392 (1982); Note, Legal Fees Incurred in Litigation Involving Title to Assets—Allocation between Deductible Ordinary Expenses and Nondeductible Capital Expenditures, 126 U.Pa.L.Rev. 1100 (1978); Annot., 29 A.L.R.Fed 221 (1976). The ABA has supported proposals to amend the Internal Revenue Code to provide for the deductibility of all legal fees, a proposal that would redound to the great economic advantage of lawyers. See 51 U.S.L.Wk. 2123 (1982)(resolution of ABA House of Delegates).

71 Arctic Slope Native Ass'n v. Paul, 609 P.2d 32, 38 (Alaska 1980). See 1908 Canon 12: "The reasonable requests of brother lawyers, and of their widows and orphans without ample means, should receive special and kindly consideration."

72 In re Burns, 139 Ariz. 487, 679 P.2d 510, 514 (1984) (overcharging clients by double-charging contingent fee rate on some items of recovery; "DR 2–106 applies not only to excessive fees regardless of agreement, but to situations such as this, when the fee charged is in excess of the fee agreed to by the parties."); Grossman v. State Bar, 34 Cal.3d 73, 192 Cal.Rptr. 397, 399, 664 P.2d 542 (1983)("an attorney may not take compensation over the fixed fee without the client's consent to a renegotiated fee agreement. This is true even if the work becomes more onerous than originally anticipated."); Attorney Griev-

made a proper agreement[73] to modify the amount. Similarly, a lawyer's breach of the fee contract by charging for work not done is an attempt to exact a fee that is by definition excessive and unreasonable.[74] A fee has also been held to be excessive when there was entirely no contractual or other basis for charging it, such as when a lawyer charged a fee to an opposing party[75] or simply (or at least so claimed) made a self-determination of what was due and appropriated a client's property in that amount.[76]

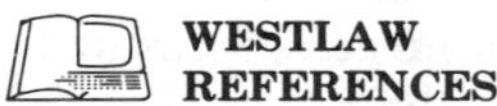

Process of Discipline for Excessive Fees

attorney lawyer counsel** /s client /s fee retainer /10 excessive exorbitant

Professional Rules on Excessive Fees

dr2–106 "dr 2–106"

Factors for Assessing Reasonability or Excessiveness

dr2–106(b) "dr 2–106(b)"

§ 9.3.2 Illegal Fees

Illegal Fees and Their Regulation

A long tradition exists in American law of legislation limiting the amount of legal fees—or prohibiting their payment altogether.[77] The same kinds of regulation survive in several contemporary statutes. The lawyer codes generally require that a lawyer abide by applicable legal limits on fees, whether the limits are imposed by statute, regulation, court rule, or judicial decision. The Code does that clearly in its proscription in DR 2–106(A) of an "illegal" fee. The Model Rules do not specifically cover the point, although presumably the requirement of a "reasonable" fee under MR 1.5(a) would be offended if a fee were illegal.

Kinds of Illegality

Some legislation prohibits charging any fee for some services, probably in order to prevent unscrupulous lawyers from exacting fees for work that is purely ministerial.[78] Some statutes have placed upper limits—some of them absurdly low—on the amount that a lawyer may charge a client.[79] The most notorious is the $10 ceiling imposed by federal

ance Comm'n v. Kerpelman, 292 Md. 228, 438 A.2d 501 (1981)(charging client over ten times more than amount justified by hourly charge agreed to); Attorney Grievance Comm'n v. Leventhal, 279 Md. 350, 369 A.2d 72 (1977) (discipline for cashing retainer check and keeping funds after client, following initial interview, called and discharged lawyer); In re Chasan, 91 N.J. 381, 450 A.2d 1329, 1331 (1982).

[73] On the suspiciousness with which courts approach postrepresentation fee alterations, see § 9.2.1, at 503–04.

[74] Attorney Grievance Comm'n v. Leventhal, 279 Md. 350, 369 A.2d 72 (1977).

[75] People ex rel. Cortez v. Calvert, 200 Colo. 157, 617 P.2d 797, 800 (1980)(discipline for unsuccessful attempt to obtain fee from adverse party for work done in furthering interests of own client).

[76] In re Marine, 82 Wis.2d 602, 264 N.W.2d 285 (1978). Many cases involving misappropriation of a client's funds have the lawyer claiming entitlement to the funds as fees. Courts have rightly been very sceptical of such after-the-fact justifications and noncontemporaneous accountings based on them.

[77] Taft noted phases in Jewish, Roman, English, and American history when lawyers were prohibited from charging fees. See Taft, Ethics in Service 4–7, 15 (1915). The principal objections were that paid lawyers would more likely corrupt justice and that inability to pay a fee created a barrier between litigants and justice. Taft defended fees on two grounds: (1) fees instill greater confidence in the client that the lawyer will be devoted to the client's objectives; and (2) fees "stimulate industry and sincere effort" on the part of lawyers.

Warren cited a Maryland statute of 1725 that regulated fees strictly and allowed planters to pay their legal bills either in tobacco or in currency at a fixed rate. A group of lawyers opposed it, but the statute was extended in 1729 for another three years before being disallowed in an opinion by the Solicitor General of England. See C.Warren, History of the American Bar 113–14 (1911). See also 2 A. Chroust, The Rise of the Legal Profession in America 224–25 (1965); D.Nolan, Readings in the History of the American Legal Profession 103, 105 (1980); Yates & Ayres v. Robertson & Berkeley, 80 Va. 475 (1885).

[78] See Office of Disciplinary Counsel v. Lewis, 493 Pa. 519, 426 A.2d 1138 (1981)(statutory proscription against charging fee for "recovery" of no-fault benefits under client's own policy).

[79] Few decisions have accepted arguments that statutory limitations on fees infringe on the inherent power of courts to regulate the legal profession. E.g., Ingraham v. Dade Cty. School Bd., 450 So.2d 847, 849 (Fla.1984). But see, e.g., Heller v. Frankston, 76 Pa.Cmwlth. 294, 464 A.2d 581 (1983), affirmed 504 Pa. 528, 475 A.2d 1291 (1984).

statute on fees that may be charged for representing a veteran or a veteran's dependent in a matter before the Veteran's Administration, probably as a means of enhancing the value of national veterans organizations that provide free representational assistance to their members.[80] Lawyers assisting black lung claimants are limited by statute and rules in charging clients.[81] Some states have imposed statutory limits on the fees that a medical malpractice plaintiff's lawyer may charge as a fee on the rationale that this will limit the amount of medical malpractice insurance premiums.[82] Many persons who are lawyers practice as public officials under statutes that prohibit them from receiving fees from a private practice.[83] Federal and state statutes often proscribe certain fee arrangements for conflict of interest reasons.[84]

A fee might be illegal because it is paid with tainted funds or is to be put to a purpose that is illegal or against strong public policy. Lawyers have been disciplined for accepting in payment funds that they knew the client to have obtained illegally.[85] Similarly, if the lawyer received a fee that was to be used in part for an illegal purpose, the fee itself has been regarded as illegal.[86]

Excessive Fees in Court-Controlled Fee Situations

In many kinds of litigation a lawyer's fee will be set by judicial order. Included are fee-shifting situations (§ 16.6), probate and similar equity proceedings, bankruptcy,[87] litiga-

80 38 U.S.C.A. §§ 3404, 3405. Violations are punishable by a fine not to exceed $500 and imprisonment not to exceed two years. See also, e.g., 14 U.S.C.A. § 431(c) (limit of $500 in Coast Guard Life Saving Service Claim case). See generally D.Strickland, Limitations on Attorneys' Fees under Federal Law (1961).

For discipline cases, see, e.g., State ex rel. Oklahoma Bar Ass'n v. Fore, 562 P.2d 511, 514 (Okl.1977); In re Morris, 270 S.C. 308, 241 S.E.2d 911, cert.denied 439 U.S. 808, 99 S.Ct. 65, 58 L.Ed.2d 100 (1978).

Attacks on the constitutionality of the Veterans Administration $10 fee limit have not been successful. The issue was put to rest in Walters v. National Ass'n of Radiation Survivors, ___ U.S. ___, 105 S.Ct. 3180, 87 L.Ed.2d 220 (1985), when the Court held that the $10 VA fee limit was not a denial of due process. See also Demarest v. United States, 718 F.2d 964 (9th Cir.1983), cert. denied 466 U.S. 950, 104 S.Ct. 2150, 80 L.Ed.2d 536 (1984); Gendron v. Levi, 423 U.S. 802, 96 S.Ct. 9, 46 L.Ed. 2d 23 affirming per curiam Gendron v. Saxbe, 389 F.Supp. 1303 A(C.D.Cal.1975)(three-judge court).

81 Black Lung Benefits Act, 33 U.S.C.A. § 928(e). For discipline cases, see, e.g., Committee on Professional Ethics v. Christoffers, 348 N.W.2d 227 (Iowa 1984)(suspension for repeatedly entering fee contracts calling for black lung clients to make "gift" to lawyer in excess of statutory maximum).

82 Roa v. Lodi Medical Group, Inc., 129 Cal.App.3d 318, 181 Cal.Rptr. 44 (1982), opinion vacated 37 Cal.3d 920, 211 Cal.Rptr. 77, 695 P.2d 164 (1985). See also, e.g., Ingraham v. Dade Cty. School Bd., 450 So.2d 847 (Fla. 1984)(statute imposing 25 percent limit on contingent fee in suit involving waiver of governmental sovereign immunity).

83 State v. Stakes, 227 Kan. 711, 608 P.2d 997 (1980); In re Synder, 276 Or. 897, 559 P.2d 1273 (1976)(lawyer, after becoming district attorney, continued to work on probate and guardianship matters and received fees from private practice in violation of state statute; restitution of illegal fees ordered to be made to estates).

84 Cf. In re Leasing Consultants Inc., 592 F.2d 103 (2d Cir.1979)(power of trustee in bankruptcy to recover fee paid to law firm in violation of federal conflict of interest statute).

85 In re Prescott, 271 N.W.2d 822, 824 (Minn.1978) (discipline under DR 2–102(A)(4) for lawyer's receiving, as partial payment of fees, funds from loan known by lawyer to have been obtained illegally by client: "The public that is to be protected by professional discipline thus is not limited to the potential clients of unscrupulous lawyers, but includes the general public that ultimately suffers when loans are procured improperly from banks or government agencies.").

A little-studied question is where persons accused of crime get the money to pay legal fees. An invariant practice among private practitioners of criminal defense law is reportedly to require that the fee be paid in advance. See Blumberg, The Practice of Law as a Confidence Game: Organizational Cooptation of a Profession, 1 Law & Soc'y Rev. 15, 27 (1967). If a defendant is unable to pay the lawyer's entire fee in advance, the lawyer might be willing to set a fee, to be prepaid, for each stage of the case, allowing the accused and his or her family to secure funds as the case progresses. See Gilboy, The Social Organization of Legal Services to Indigent Defendants, 1981 Am.B.Found. Research J. 1023, 1028–29. One view is that many legal fees are either the fruit of the crime itself or are paid by further criminal activity carried on in order to meet a lawyer's required fee. Blumberg, supra at 25–26.

86 In re Connaghan, 613 S.W.2d 626 (Mo.1981). Because nineteenth-century courts regarded lobbying as a reprehensible activity, courts would not permit a lawyer to recover a fee for lobbying activities. E.g., Frost v. Belmont, 88 Mass. (6 Allen) 152, 162 (1863).

87 In re Kagan, 93 A.D.2d 238, 461 N.Y.S.2d 323 (1983) (discipline for conviction for violation of 18 U.S.C.A. § 155 for illegal fee agreement in bankruptcy matter involving misrepresentation to bankruptcy court).

tion involving minors and other wards, and the like. A lawyer must, of course, be honest and forthcoming with material information in assisting the court to set the fee, particularly if it is set in an ex parte proceeding.[88] Whether a lawyer may charge and collect a fee from a client in excess of that amount is treated differently by law, depending generally on whether the fee-award system is designed in part to protect the interests of vulnerable clients. In probate, guardianship, and similar proceedings involving vulnerable clients, courts generally prohibit collecting any fee other than that awarded by the court.[89] The same is true in administrative proceedings such as those before worker compensation commissions, where the point of the commission's setting the fee is to protect workers against excessive fee charges.[90] A similar rule, denying a lawyer the right to seek a fee from the client personally, generally applies when a lawyer is appointed by a court to represent an indigent person.[91]

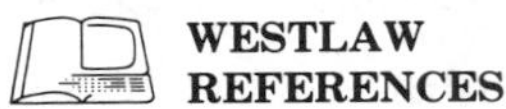

WESTLAW REFERENCES

Kinds of Illegality

attorney lawyer counsel** /s fee retainer /5 "statut! limit!" illegal

§ 9.3.3 Publication-Rights Contracts

Fee Traffic in Clients' Morbid Tales

A problem of endless fascination and extremely little incidence[92] is that presented by fee contracts in which the lawyer's compensation is simply the right to the life story of the client. The device, which is used only in very sensational criminal trials, presents extremely difficult conflict of interest problems. Some lawyers are attracted to the arrangement because even very bad books about sensational murders and similar crimes can sell well to a curious public and can be thrown off quickly with a journalist's help. The difficulty is that the publishers and buyers of such books are not very interested in persons who plead guilty or are found innocent. Publishers are also less interested in accounts that merely track the public record. What sells books is a sensational account of a desperate trial that results in a hanging in which the defense lawyer can recount hitherto unmentionable revelations [93] from the departed client. If that market assessment is accurate, then the defense lawyer's perverted role becomes that of mounting the most sensational, drawn-out, selectively proved, and ultimately unsuccessful defense that can be managed.[94]

---

88 In re Stern, 90 A.D.2d 338, 457 N.Y.S.2d 67 (1982); State ex rel. Oklahoma Bar Ass'n v. Moss, 577 P.2d 1317 (Okl.1978).

89 In re Crane, 96 Ill.2d 40, 70 Ill.Dec. 220, 449 N.E.2d 94 (1983)(obtaining additional legal fees from children clients after being awarded full fees by court); In re James, 267 S.C. 474, 229 S.E.2d 594 (1976)(discipline for failure to inform probate court that lawyer was both executor and lawyer for executor and collecting fees in both capacities). See also, e.g., Myers v. Virginia St. Bar ex rel. Second Distr. Committee, 226 Va. 630, 312 S.E.2d 286 (1984)(charging estate excessive fee through misrepresentation to probate court and to representative of estate). Special legislation has occasionally been enacted to require that lawyers' charges against vulnerable clients be approved by a court. E.g., Jackson v. United States, 485 F.Supp. 1243 (D.Alaska 1980)(reference to federal legislation requiring lawyers for native villages to submit fee claims to Court of Claims).

90 Florida Bar v. Samaha, 407 So.2d 906 (Fla.1981); In re Abrams, 293 Or. 727, 652 P.2d 787, 790–91 (1982) (charging fee in excess of that allowed by worker compensation commission).

91 See generally Annot., 43 A.L.R.3d 1426 (1972). Florida Bar v. W.H.P., 384 So.2d 28 (Fla.1980)(same rule when lawyer was appointed for civil legal aid client).

92 The area is one in which it can be said with complete confidence that the law review articles easily outnumber the decided cases, raising the issue whether the academic profession's morbid interests are similar to those of the general reading public. See, e.g., Lynn, Restricting Attorney Speech about Matters of Recent Employment, 24 Ariz.L.Rev. 531 (1982); Note, Publication Rights Agreements in Sensational Criminal Cases, 68 Cornell L.Rev. 686 (1983); Note, Publication Rights Fee Contracts, 17 U.S.F.L.Rev. 549 (1983); Note, Contracting for Publication Rights in Lieu of Attorney's Fees in Criminal Cases, 31 Buff.L.Rev. 483 (1982); Note, Conflicts of Interests when Attorneys Acquire Rights to the Client's Life Story, 6 J.Leg.Prof. 299 (1981); Note, Conflicting Interests in Lawyer-Client Publication Rights Agreements, 42 U.Pitt. L.Rev. 869 (1981).

93 Fuller v. Israel, 421 F.Supp. 582 (E.D.Ill.1976)(assignment by accused to defense lawyer of one-third royalty interest in all future publications by client accused of multiple murders; assignment objectionable because value of rights would be enhanced by lawyer's keeping some evidence secret).

94 Cf. EC 5–4 ("If, in the course of his representation of a client, a lawyer is permitted to receive from his client a beneficial ownership in publication rights relating to the subject matter of the employment, he may be tempted to

The problems are two—conflict of interests and the revelation of client information that, except for the contract, would be confidential.

Regulating Sensational Client Stories

The property rights of lawyers in a client's sensational life story are regulated in two relevant ways. In probably half of the states, statutes recently enacted now provide that after the allowance of reasonable attorney fees, the proceeds of a sale of the life story of an accused, if found guilty, go first to victims of the crime before the accused can receive anything.[95] The second regulation is a professional rule found in both the 1969 Code (DR 5–104(B)) and, in an expanded form, in the 1983 Model Rules (MR 1.8(d)) that prohibits publication-rights contracts.[96] Both rules prevent a lawyer from negotiating or entering into a publication-rights contract with a client about the matter involved in the representation before the end of the representation. The Code stops at "any arrangement or understanding with a client," which presumably leaves the lawyer free to negotiate contracts for publication rights with publishers and producers,[97] while the Model Rule wisely extends to any agreement with any person if the literary or media rights relate to "a portrayal or account based in substantial part on information relating to the representation."

The decisions have quite uniformly condemned publication-rights contracts for fees, for the reasons already mentioned, although they have typically refused to set aside convictions in the absence of proof that the lawyer's defense in fact was altered because of the potential for conflict created by the publication-rights agreement.[98] In California, whose lawyer code does not specifically outlaw publication-rights contracts,[99] the state's supreme court held in Maxwell v. Superior Court [1] that an indigent accused, who was elaborately advised by a defense lawyer, could waive the protection of the conflict of interest rules and had a right to enter, knowingly and voluntarily, into a publication-rights contract in order to obtain the assistance of retained counsel.[2]

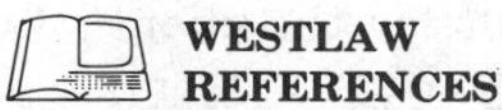
WESTLAW REFERENCES

Regulating Sensational Client Stories

ec5–4 "ec 5–4" dr5–104(b) "dr 5–104(b)"

---

subordinate the interests of his client to his own anticipated pecuniary gain.").

[95] For a listing of statutes, see Note, supra, 68 Cornell L.Rev. at 687–88 n.6.

[96] MR 1.5 comment (Literary Rights) is careful to note that MR 1.5(d) does not prohibit a lawyer in a case that directly involves literary property from taking a contingent fee or an ownership assignment as a fee. Thus a lawyer who represents an impoverished musician in a suit to recover a copyright to a stolen song can agree with the musician-client to a one-third interest in ownership of the copyright if recovered in the litigation.

[97] Cf. United States v. Hearst, 638 F.2d 1190 (9th Cir. 1980), cert. denied 451 U.S. 938, 101 S.Ct. 2018, 68 L.Ed. 2d 325 (1981)(attack on conviction of Patty Hearst on ground that famous defense trial lawyer had obtained $225,000 contract with publisher to write book about case and agreement with client that she would not publish any competing book until eighteen months after lawyer's book appeared).

[98] Fuller v. Israel, 421 F.Supp. 582, 584 (E.D.Ill.1976) (refers to "the repeated disapproval of such contracts by both the bench and bar"). See also, e.g., Wojtowicz v. United States, 550 F.2d 786, 793 (2d Cir.1977), cert.denied 431 U.S. 972, 97 S.Ct. 2938, 53 L.Ed.2d 1071 (1977); Ray v. Rose, 535 F.2d 966, 974 (6th Cir.), cert.denied 429 U.S. 1026, 97 S.Ct. 648, 50 L.Ed.2d 629 (1976); United States v. Hearst, 638 F.2d 1190, 1193 (9th Cir.1980), cert.denied 451 U.S. 938, 101 S.Ct. 2018, 68 L.Ed.2d 325 (1981). Cf. People v. Corona, 80 Cal.App.3d 684, 720, 145 Cal.Rptr. 894 (1978)(conviction of defendant on twenty-five counts of first-degree murder in death of migrant workers reversed because publication-rights contract rendered defense lawyer's defense constitutionally ineffective).

[99] The part of the California Rules of Professional Conduct that is most in point is rule 5–101, on business dealings with a client. See Maxwell v. Superior Court, 30 Cal.3d 606, 180 Cal.Rptr 177, 183, n.6, 639 P.2d 248, 254, n.6 (1982). California courts do, however, often require lawyers to follow the ABA's codes when they go beyond the California Rules. See § 2.6.5, at 64.

[1] Supra.

[2] The basis of the court's holding was that the constitutional right to counsel of the accused, although not absolute, was sufficiently strong in controlling choice of counsel that the trial court abused its discretion in denying the accused the chance to make a knowing and intelligent waiver of a conflict-free representation. The publication-rights contract in the case was nineteen pages long and contained an elaborate, although far from perfect, recitation of the conflict of interest problems that such a contract might create.

§ 9.4 CONTINGENT FEES

§ 9.4.1 *Contingent Fee Contracts*

Nature of Contingent Fees

It is common in representations of injured persons and in other types of litigation [3] in the United States for the lawyer to operate under a contingent fee, a contract that provides that if the plaintiff recovers money from the defendant in litigation or settlement, the lawyer will receive a fee equal to a stated percentage (33 percent is common) of the recovery. To be contingent, a fee need not be measured by a percentage, although that is typical. The critical element is that there be some chance that the lawyer will not receive the fee because the representation ends with an unwanted result for the lawyer's client.[4] For example, a fixed fee could be made contingent by providing that the lawyer would not receive it except upon achieving some described result for the client. Conversely, a percentage fee need not be contingent. House closings are sometimes billed at 1 percent of the sales price, and in many states probate fees are measured by a percentage of the estate's value. In no realistic sense are those fees significantly contingent.[5] The kind of fee that is properly called contingent is one with an element of risk: however its size is measured, it will accrue only on the happening of a future event whose occurrence is not readily predictable.[6]

Status of Contingent Fees

Contingent fees for legal services are well ensconced as a general fixture of client-lawyer contractual relationships in many contemporary areas of the American law. They are commonly used in representing plaintiffs in personal injury and collection cases and property owners in eminent domain condemnation cases. In sharp contrast, lawyers in England,[7] in parts of Canada,[8] and in most of the

[3] Representation under contingent fees is limited almost entirely to plaintiffs. It is used almost universally in personal injury claims—automobile, products liability, medical and other professional malpractice, and similar claims. It is also widely used in tax refund litigation, eminent domain condemnation actions, employment discrimination suits, suits to challenge wills, and collection work. Contingent fees are very prominent in class action litigation for damages, in shareholder derivative actions, and in private actions for antitrust damages. It has been asserted that the key ingredient in vigorous American enforcement of the securities laws is the facilitation that the contingent fee system brings to private enforcement of damage actions. See Pollack, Book Review, 90 Harv.L. Rev. 482, 484 (1976). It was observed some time ago that statutory fee-shifting schemes that require a defendant to pay the attorney fees of the plaintiff create a kind of statutory contingent fee. See Radin, Contingent Fees in California, 28 Calif.L.Rev. 587, 595 (1940).

Whether by accident or not, rarely will lawyers on both sides of litigation be representing their clients on a contingent fee basis. Contingent fee lawyers are almost always opposed by defense lawyers paid on an hourly basis or occasionally on a salaried basis.

[4] When courts attempt to determine whether a fee is contingent, for the purposes of applying a common-law or statutory prohibition against contingent fees, they are rightly concerned with identifying whether the fee is importantly conditioned on favorable future events. E.g., Shanks v. Kilgore, 589 S.W.2d 318, 321–22 (Mo.App.1979) (divorce case). Even if a portion of the fee was paid in advance and was apparently not conditional, other portions of the total fee might be conditional and thus contingent. E.g., Singleton v. Foreman, 435 F.2d 962, 969–70 (5th Cir.1970); McInerney v. Massasoit Greyhound Ass'n, 359 Mass. 339, 269 N.E.2d 211, 218 (1971).

[5] See ABA Spec.Comm. on Residential Real Estate Transactions, The Proper Role of the Lawyer in Residential Real Estate Transactions: His Services and His Compensation 23–24 (1976)(attempted defense of percentage fee based, not on risk that transaction will not occur, but on risk to lawyer of error and consequent malpractice liability, but without attempted empirical demonstration that percentage calibrates with risk).

[6] Cf. Ill. DR 2–106(C)(1): "For purposes of this rule a contingent-fee agreement shall be deemed to be any agreement for the provision of legal services by a lawyer under which the amount of the lawyer's compensation is contingent in whole or part upon the successful accomplishment (by settlement or litigation) of the subject matter of the agreement, regardless of whether the fee is established by formula or in fixed amount."

[7] English courts have steadfastly refused to permit compensation of counsel on a contingent basis. Wellensteiner v. Moer (No.2), [1975] 1 Q.B. 373; In re a Solicitor, [1912] 1 K.B. 302; Darzey v. Metropolitan Bank of England & Wales, 28 T.L.R. 327 (1912). Proposals have been advanced for a modified system under which counsel would be compensated out of a fund that would be replenished by contingent levies on prevailing plaintiffs. Donin, England Looks at a Hybrid Contingent Fee System, 64 ABA J. 773 (1978). That would be done to supplement the resources of national legal aid, which, since the late 1940s, have supplied legal services to the poor in all cases that are deemed meritorious. See § 16.7.2 at n. 30.

[8] See note 8 on page 527.

rest of the world's legal systems are prohibited from charging such a fee. A similar rule obtained for a long time in many states in the United States. Courts lumped the contingent fee in with other champertous practices that were thought to stir up unwanted litigation and involve unscrupulous lawyers in the nefarious business of brokering lawsuits.[9] During the years up to the end of the last century, some jurisdictions outlawed them entirely. Gradually the fee has gained a modicum of general acceptance[10] as courts and legislators have come to realize that the evils that can be associated with contingent fees can be dealt with through more precise means.[11]

The arrival of the contingent fee as a legitimate basis for charging was highlighted by its acceptance into the exclusive club of the ABA in the 1908 Canons of Ethics. Yet careful Victorian lawyers gave it the same reception as they gave to ballroom dancing: that the masses engaged in it and the police did not intervene meant only that it was lawful. It hardly assured its respectability. Acknowledgement of the legitimacy of the contingent fee in the 1908 Canons was similarly guarded and even controversial.[12] But only a few jurisdictions continued to ban it. Given its almost universal use among lawyers who filed personal injury claims in the burgeoning field of automobile injury law, judges and bar associations gradually came around.[13] Formal resistance was eliminated entirely when Maine's legislature repealed its long-standing statutory prohibition in 1965.[14] Despite the now universal acceptance of contingent fees in the United States, however, several important limitations on its use have survived—in criminal defense, domestic relations, and, in some states, lobbying. And the contingent fee

[8] Law Society of Upper Canada, Professional Conduct Handbook 26 (1978); Williston, The Contingent Fee in Canada, 6 Alberta L.Rev. 184 (1967); Arledge, Contingent Fees, 6 Ottawa L.Rev. 374 (1974). Alberta, British Columbia, Manitoba, New Brunswick, Nova Scotia, Quebec, and Saskatchewan permit contingent fees, and only Ontario among the more populous Canadian provinces bans them. Because of differences in the taxing of a portion of legal expenses as costs to the prevailing party, the contingent fee contract is not used as frequently in the parts of Canada where it is permitted. Minish, The Contingent Fee: A Reexamination, 10 Man.L.J. 65 (1979). Actual billing practices together with the practical functioning of two-way fee shifting results in an informal contingency system in Ontario very much like that in the United States. See Kritzer, Fee Arrangements and Fee Shifting: Lessons from the Experience in Ontario, 47 L. & Contemp. Probs. 125, 130–33 (1984).

[9] Scobey v. Ross, 13 Ind. 117 (1859); Lathrop v. Amherst Bank, 50 Mass. 489 (1845); Backus v. Byron, 4 Mich. 535 (1857). See generally Note, Contingent Fee Contracts: Validity, Controls, and Enforceability, 47 Iowa L.Rev. 942 (1962). For the history of the fee in Louisiana, which largely tracked that of the rest of the states, see Coon v. Landry, 408 So.2d 262 (La.1981).

[10] Calls for the end of the ban on contingent fees were heard after the Civil War. See Countryman, The Ethics of Compensation for Professional Service, 16 Am.L.Rev. 240 (1882). Acceptance was fairly general by the end of the nineteenth century. See E.Weeks, A Treatise on Attorneys and Counsellors at Law 717 (2d ed.1892).

[11] McInerney v. Massasoit Greyhound Ass'n, 359 Mass. 339, 269 N.E.2d 211, 217 (1971).

[12] The only issue extensively debated when the ABA adopted the 1908 Canons was a proposed rule on contingent fees. See E.Sunderland, History of the American Bar Association and its Work 111 (1953). The original proposal was for a canon that would have warned that "they lead to abuses and should be under the supervision of the court." 33 ABA Rep. 61 (1908). After heated debate, Canon 13 as actually adopted was only slightly less wary, cautioning that contingent fees "should be under the supervision of the court, in order that clients may be protected from unjust charges." 33 ABA Rep. 80, 579 (1908). An amendment in 1933 removed the language about unjust charges to clients but retained the language urging court supervision. See 58 ABA Rep. 161 (1933).

[13] Markarian v. Bartis, 89 N.H. 370, 199 A. 573, 576 (1938)(contingency of fee "can scarcely be said to offend the public conscience"). One measure of the respectability of the contingent fee is that today most courts would probably permit a court award of a fee of a contingent nature. E.g., Couture v. Mammoth Groceries, Inc., 117 N.H. 294, 371 A.2d 1184 (1977)(one-third award in worker compensation case). Statutes occasionally provide for the award of fees on a contingent basis. E.g., La.Stat.Ann.–Rev.Stat. 47: 1512 (private lawyer representing tax collector to receive fee of 10 percent of taxes found to be due). By no means, however, have all judges lost the traditional sense of disfavor when thinking about contingent fees. E.g., 64 ABA J. 26 (1978)(report of testimony given by Chief Justice Burger to commission in England: "[S]ince it is probably too late . . . to abolish [the institution of contingent fees in the United States] completely, the bar associations themselves ought to take control of it, and, if they do not do it adequately, the courts ought to fix limits").

[14] 1965 Maine Laws, c. 333, amending 17 Me.Rev.Stat. Ann. § 801. The Maine Supreme Court promptly promulgated Rule 88 of the state's civil rules to regulate contingent fee contracts. See generally R.Field, V.McKusick & L.Wroth, Maine Civil Practice § 88.1 (2d ed.1970).

has never entirely shaken off a tawdry reputation gained through assumed association with ambulance chasing, hoodwinking jurors, and concocting spurious claims.[15]

Justifications and Criticisms of Contingent Fees

The justification for contingent fees can be cast entirely on utilitarian grounds: persons who lack any other means should be able to employ the present economic value of possible future recoveries to hire a lawyer.[16] Two other justifications are also often mentioned: the contingent fee permits persons, regardless of their poverty, to spread the risk of defeat in litigation; and the contingent fee puts the lawyer squarely on the side of the client because both will succeed or fail together. If there were a market for buying and selling causes of action, contingent fees would probably not be necessary. Injured parties could sell part of their claims in that market and use the funds to hire lawyers. But such a market is prohibited by laws that ban champertous exchanges and limit the assignability of causes of action (§ 8.13). Banks, lacking assignable security, thus cannot justify lending funds for legal fees on the unsecured hope that a statistical likelihood of recovering will pay off the loan.

Contingent fee lawyers fill the breach. Economically induced by the prospect of sharing in a client's success, a lawyer may be willing to lend the value of legal services and litigation expenses.[17] If and to the extent that the client recovers, the lawyer will get a percentage fee; if the client recovers nothing, the lawyer gets no fee.[18] With a portfolio of clients whose claims bear varying degrees of risk, a lawyer can use a high-percentage recovery in one case to support work on other cases, including those that will turn out to be losers.[19] Another way to understand the typical one-third contingent fee is that it provides lawyers with an expectation of receiving a fee of 16.5 percent in a case in which the chances of prevailing are fifty-fifty. It seems quite defensible to provide an incentive to lawyers to prosecute suits in which the chances of prevailing are about equal.[20] It also seems defensible, in the absence of a better method of cost spreading, to distribute the cost of supplying that legal service among the class of clients who otherwise would find it difficult or impossible to finance legal services on a noncontingent basis.[21]

15 J.O'Connell, The Injury Industry: And the Remedy of No-Fault Insurance 44–48 (1971); Bar Ass'n v. Cassaro, 61 Ohio St.2d 62, 399 N.E.2d 545 (1980); Bar Ass'n v. Zaffiro, 61 Ohio St.2d 69, 399 N.E.2d 549 (1980).

16 Valentino v. Rickners Rhederei, G.M.B.H., 417 F.Supp. 176, 181–82 (S.D.N.Y.1976), affirmed 552 F.2d 466 (2d Cir.1977); Friedman & Ladinsky, Social Change and the Law of Industrial Accidents, 67 Colum.L.Rev. 50, 60 (1967), citing Report of Committee on Contingent Fees, 31 Proceedings of the N.Y.St.B.Ass'n 99, 100–01 (1908). Services other than those of a lawyer can also be purchased by litigants on an unsecured, contingent basis. E.g., Schackow v. Medical-Legal Consulting Service, Inc., 46 Md.App. 179, 416 A.2d 1303, 15 A.L.R.4th 1239 (1980) (validity of contract promising contingent percentage of medical malpractice plaintiff's recovery to legal consulting firm).

17 See generally EC 2–20. The EC offers two rationales. The first is that given in the text. The second is "a successful prosecution of the claim produces a *res* out of which the fee can be paid." That is merely a condition from which the first justification arises and hardly an independent support for the fee. The point is worth noting, for at a later point in EC 2–20 the absence of a res is given as complete justification for forbidding contingent fees in criminal cases. See § 9.4.3.

On the limited extent to which a lawyer may extend a client credit for litigation expenses, see § 9.2.3.

18 Fredric Hayes, Inc. v. Rollins, 435 So.2d 1151 (La. App.1983)(lawyer entitled to no fee under contingent fee contract when client rejected settlement offer).

19 That assumes that lawyers will accept contingent fee cases almost on a random basis as far as their chances of success are concerned. But experienced lawyers can make a prediction about the success of a representation and can refuse to accept cases that are too risky or settle them quickly at any available figure and thus avoid risking much lawyer capital.

20 Leubsdorf, The Contingency Factor in Attorney Fee Awards, 90 Yale L.J. 473, 511 (1981).

21 In fact, injured persons probably don't bear the real economic burden of paying their contingent fees. Defendants, and ultimately premium payers protected by insurance policies, probably bear much of the cost because inflated elements of general damages, such as pain and suffering, are tolerated by courts as a rough measure of the plaintiff's attorney fees. Morris, Liability for Pain and Suffering, 59 Colum.L.Rev. 476, 477 (1959). Pain and suffering and similar nonmonetary damages probably average three times the monetary damages in personal injury claims. See H.Ross, Settled Out of Court 108 (1970); O'Connell, A Proposal to Abolish Defendants'

Contemporary criticisms of the contingent fee are not linked to the fears of champerty of a century ago. Contingent fee contracts can readily be structured to avoid problems posed by prohibitions against acquiring an interest in the client's cause of action.[22] Instead the concern is with the way in which lawyers are able through contingent fees to overreach clients who tend to be both underfunded for litigation and ill equipped to understand the complexities of risk in litigation. The basic problem is that lawyers can use their superior knowledge of the risks and costs involved to set their percentage fee at a high figure that bears little relationship to the time and money that lawyers must put at risk.[23] Many lawyers use contingent fee contracts that have the same percentage fee for all clients regardless of the relative strength of their cases. Pointing to the large number of cases that are settled and never tried, critics argue that in fact contingent fee cases present little risk of actual loss.[24] In any event, some lawyers are able to build portfolios of cases that are all winners, the only question being the magnitude of recovery. Moreover, because the lawyer's incentive is to gain the percentage fee, the lawyer may have a strong economic investment in the client's claim and thus has a strong incentive to settle cases at points that maximize the lawyer's own hourly return rather than the return to clients.[25] Lawyers on contingent fee are said to have an incentive to make a "quick kill" before too many additional hours are spent at possibly only a marginal increase in the lawyer's fee.[26]

Commentators, lawyers, and judges have hotly debated the extent to which those problems harm the interests of clients. Most will agree that even if many of the problems exist, the proper solution is not to abolish the contingent fee unless an adequate substitute is put in its place. As has been said, "the contingent fee 'problem' is a symptom, rather than a cause of a much wider problem—the unequal access to the courts for the poor and near poor." [27]

Permissible Contingent Fees

Some abuses in the use of contingent fees have been dealt with through disclosure and reporting requirements and, in some jurisdictions, through mandatory maximum percentage schedules (§ 9.4.2). For the most part, however, the lawyer codes do not restrict a lawyer in negotiating a contingent fee. The 1969 Code, in DR 5–103(A)(2),[28] permitted contingent fees with few limitations other than that they be reasonable in size. The 1983 Model Rules, in MR 1.5(c),[29] also permit them but require that agreements for such fees be

Payment for Pain and Suffering in Return for Payment of Claimants' Attorneys' Fees, 1981 U.Ill.L.Rev. 333, 334. By the time attorney fees and administrative expenses are paid, recovery by victims under insurance programs may be a low percentage. E.g., N.Y.Times, July 28, 1983 (study by Institute for Civil Justice shows that 37 percent of $600 million spent by defendants and insurers in asbestos cases has gone to plaintiffs, with rest to plaintiffs' lawyers, defense lawyers, and administrative expenses).

22 Swenson v. Thibaut, 39 N.C.App. 77, 250 S.E.2d 279, 301 (1978), appeal dismissed 296 N.C. 740, 254 S.E.2d 183 (1979)(interest in shares of stock recovered by client). See generally § 8.13.

23 Note, Advertising, Solicitation, and the Profession's Duty to Make Legal Counsel Available, 81 Yale L.J. 1181, 1200 (1972)(urging new disciplinary rule that would provide forty-eight-hour cooling-off period, within which client could revoke contingent fee contract).

24 Grady, Some Ethical Questions about Percentage Fees, Litigation 20, 24 (Summer 1976).

25 Morgan, The Evolving Concept of Professional Responsibility, 90 Harv.L.Rev. 702, 732 (1977); Grady, Some Ethical Questions about Percentage Fees, Litigation 20 (Summer 1976); Note, Of Ethics and Economics: Contingent Percentage Fees for Legal Services, 16 Akron L.Rev. 747 (1983).

26 D.Rosenthal, Lawyer and Client: Who's in Charge?, at 96 et seq. (1974)(examples, from estimates of hours worked, how quick-kill settlements are often best strategy for lawyers).

27 Chicago Council of Lawyers, Report on Code of Professional Responsibility 20 (1972).

28 DR 5–103(A)(2)("(A) A lawyer shall not acquire a proprietary interest in the cause of action or subject matter of litigation he is conducting for a client, except that he may . . . (2) Contract with a client for a reasonable contingent fee in a civil case."). See also DR 2–106(B)(8)(permissible factor in determining reasonable fee is whether it is fixed or contingent); DR 2–106(C) (contingent fee in criminal defense forbidden).

29 MR 1.5(c)("A fee may be contingent on the outcome of the matter for which the service is rendered").

in writing and contain certain elements and that a written closing statement be given at the end of the representation.

The Code, in EC 2–20, justifies contingent fees on the ground that they provide a means for the poor to litigate and because they create a *res*, a fund out of which the fee can be paid. But the justification for the fee must be broader, for it is doubtful that courts would limit the use of contingent fees only to circumstances that can be justified in one of those ways. Courts, for example, permit lawyers to charge a contingent fee for representing a *defendant* in a civil case,[30] although neither poverty nor a *res* is a factor. Courts generally seem quite unconcerned that lawyers might agree with wealthy clients to bill on a contingent basis, despite the intimations in the lawyer codes to the contrary.[31] If a client, fully advised about the matter by a lawyer,[32] prefers to have the lawyer share some of the risk of loss in return for a higher fee payment, which will be the usual trade-off, it is difficult to see why the rich should not have what the poor are forced by circumstances to accept.[33]

Writings and Closing Statements

Contingent fee contracts are much too complex and unusual in the experience of nonlawyers to permit a court to infer that a contingent fee contract is implied in fact from the parties' course of dealings.[34] Courts are also rightly hesitant to accept proof of an oral contingent fee contract unless the evidence is clear and convincing.[35] The Model Rules are not content to leave the matter to the common law, but require in MR 1.5(d) that every contingent fee contract be in writing. The requirement was foreshadowed in the Code [36] and follows mandatory-writing rules in several states.[37] Under MR 1.5(d) the written contract must

> state the method by which the fee is to be determined, including the percentage or percentages that shall accrue to the lawyer in the event of settlement, trial or appeal, litigation and other expenses to be deducted from the recovery,

[30] See infra at 533.

[31] Contingent fee contracts have also been upheld with charitable trusts. E.g., In re Morgan Washington Home, 108 Ill.App.3d 245, 64 Ill.Dec. 105, 439 N.E.2d 34 (1982).

The Code, in EC 2–20, states that "although a lawyer generally should decline to accept employment on a contingent fee basis by one who is able to pay a reasonable fixed fee, it is not necessarily improper for a lawyer, where justified by the particular circumstances of a case, to enter into a contingent fee contract in a civil case with any client who, after being fully informed of all relevant factors, desires that arrangement."

The Model Rules are more muted. MR 1.5 comment (Terms of Payment; second paragraph) states only that "when there is doubt whether a contingent fee is consistent with the client's best interest, the lawyer should offer the client alternative bases for the fee and explain their implications."

[32] Full advice to a client in such a situation is, of course, elementary. E.g., In re Reisdorf, 80 N.J. 319, 403 A.2d 873 (1979)(discipline of lawyer who told impecunious client that her only options were contingent fee contract or current payment of hourly charge but failed to inform her of clear right to apply to probate court for periodic payment of legal fees from corpus of estate that was subject of will contest).

[33] See generally Comment, Are Contingent Fees Ethical Where Client Is Able to Pay a Retainer?, 20 Ohio St.L.J. 329 (1959).

[34] Sullivan v. Fawver, 58 Ill.App.2d 37, 42, 206 N.E.2d 492, 494 (1965); Craig v. Jo B. Gardner, Inc., 586 S.W.2d 316, 327, nn.9 & 10 (Mo.1979). But cf. Peebles v. Miley, 439 So.2d 137, 142 (Ala.1983)(maker of note who promises to pay reasonable attorney fee if collection is necessary held to pay holder's lawyer's contingent fee).

[35] Mercy Hospital, Inc. v. Johnson, 390 So.2d 103 (Fla. App.1980); Carmichael v. Iowa State Highway Comm'n, 219 N.W.2d 658 (Iowa 1974); Becnel v. Montz, 384 So.2d 1015 (La.App.1980); Kirby v. Liska, 214 Neb. 356, 334 N.W.2d 179, 182 (1983). Courts have also insisted that the lawyer must prove by clear and convincing evidence that all of the material elements of the contract were explained to the client. E.g., Neville v. Davinroy, 41 Ill. App.3d 706, 355 N.E.2d 86, 88–89 (1976); Kirby v. Liska, supra, 334 N.W.2d at 182–83.

[36] EC 2–19 notes that it is "particularly" important to reduce contingent fee arrangements to a written contract. A lesser policy is enforced by the common-law rule, which generally refuses to find that a contingent fee contract was implied in fact between the parties. E.g., Wells v. Haynes, 101 Ga. 841, 28 S.E. 968 (1897); Warner v. Basten, 118 Ill.App.2d 419, 255 N.E.2d 72 (1969); Craig v. Jo B. Gardner, Inc., 586 S.W.2d 316 (Mo.1979).

[37] Ill. DR 2–106(C)(3)(1980); Me.R.Civ.Proc., Rule 88(d); Mass. DR 23–106(C) & Mass.S.J.C. Rule 3:14, 351 Mass. 795 (1967); Frank v. Peckich, 257 Pa.Super. 561, 391 A.2d 624 (1978)(construing Pa.R.Civ.Proc., Rule 202); Rules Governing Contingent Fees for Members of Wyoming State Bar, Rule 4.

and whether such expenses are to be deducted before or after the contingent fee is calculated.[38]

Omitted from the list in MR 1.5(d) is a matter that should be explicitly covered in any contingent fee contract—the extent of the task that the lawyer undertakes in consideration for the fee. Disputes have frequently arisen over whether a contingent fee contract was meant to cover the lawyer's services after trial, such as defending a client's recovery on appeal. The general rule is that the contract, unless it provides otherwise, impliedly requires the lawyer to defend or prosecute an appeal.[39] That should be treated specifically in the contract.

Model Rule 1.5(d) also requires that the lawyer send the client a closing statement in every case in which the fee is charged on a contingent basis.[40] The purpose of the closing statement is to require the lawyer to show clearly the amount of the recovery, if any, and the method by which the lawyer's share and the client's share of the recovery were calculated. Some states go a step further and require that a copy of the retainer agreement and closing statement be filed with the court.[41]

WESTLAW REFERENCES

Status of Contingent Fees

di champerty

Permissible Contingent Fees

"conting! fee" /s limit! "maximum percentage" dr5–103(a)(2) "dr 5–103(a)(2)"

§ 9.4.2 Calculating Contingent Fees

Rationale for Regulation

Because contingent fees have never been enthusiastically accepted within the legal profession and because of concern with overreaching, courts have imposed limits on the extent to which lawyers may employ them.[42] The limitations are enforced through rule making, through disciplinary controls, and through occasional exercises of supervisory power to revise or set aside fee contracts that meet with judicial disapproval (§ 9.1).

Controlling the Size of Contingent Fees

The size of a typical contingent fee is the product of two factors.[43] One is the percentage figure—a fee, for example, of 33 percent of any recovery by the client. The other is the multiplicand—the base against which the percentage works. A base could be measured in many different ways. In a world of equal bargaining power, clients would reject a uni-

38 See also Ill. DR 2–106(C)(2); Rules Governing Contingent Fees for Members of Wyoming State Bar, Rule 5 (1977).

39 Knight v. DeMarea, 670 S.W.2d 59, 62–63 (Mo.App. 1984). See generally Annot., 13 A.L.R.3d 673, 677–78 (1967).

40 See also Ill. DR 2–106(C)(3); Florida Bar v. Rogowski, 399 So.2d 1390, 1391 (Fla.1981)(required disbursement statement). For the New York rule, see generally Gair v. Peck, 6 N.Y.2d 97, 188 N.Y.S.2d 491, 160 N.E.2d 43, (1959), cert.denied, 361 U.S. 374, 80 S.Ct. 401, 4 L.Ed.2d 380 (1960).

41 Cf. In re Grand Jury Impaneled January 21, 1975, 541 F.2d 373 (3d Cir.1976)(retainer agreement filed with state court clerk under New Jersey rule subject to federal grand jury subpoena despite asserted confidentiality under state rule); United States v. Cortese, 410 F.Supp. 1380, 1381, n.1 (E.D.Pa.1976), affirmed 540 F.2d 640 (3d Cir.1976)(description of filing requirement in Philadelphia).

42 In re Flannery, 150 App.Div. 369, 370, 135 N.Y.S. 612 (1912), affirmed 212 N.Y. 610, 106 N.E. 630 (1914) (contingent fees approved so long as no fraud, concealment, excessive percentages because of unequal knowledge, or purchase of client's cause of action by lawyer).

43 A third relevant factor is the occurrence of the event that entitles the lawyer to the contingent fee. Lawyers have sometimes inartfully described the triggering event, sometimes causing the loss of any fee. E.g., Taggart v. Claxton, 170 Ga.App. 768, 318 S.E.2d 208 (1984)(under written contingent fee contract for percentage of funds recovered, lawyer entitled to no recovery when at trial client elected to pursue remedy of specific performance); Lambert, Roberts, Jaques & Scrivner v. Crabtree, 615 P.2d 1027 (Okl.App.1979)(jury entitled to find lawyer entitled to no fee when contract called for shareholder to give lawyer percentage of value of majority shareholder control of corporation but client settled suit by agreeing to sell all shares at premium). Cf., e.g., Coon v. Landry, 408 So.2d 262 (La.1981)(fee due to lawyer on "proper conclusion" of lawsuit could not be collected when lawyer recovered judgment against defendant but failed to take prompt steps to execute it before defendant left jurisdiction).

form percentage figure and an unvarying multiplicand. One client might agree with a lawyer for a fee of a full third of any recovery in the client's behalf, realizing that there was substantial risk of not recovering anything and that the lawyer would be required to expend considerable effort to achieve success. Another client, who has already negotiated an unsatisfactorily low settlement, offer from an insurance company, might want the base to be only the difference between the insurer's offer and a better figure. A third client, knowing that the case will be relatively easy to settle and involves very high damages, would want a low percentage or a small multiplicand—whatever worked to produce a fair fee. A fourth client, with a difficult case or only a small level of damages, would understand that a lawyer would require a higher percentage of the total recovery as a reasonable fee.

Choice of appropriate percentage figure and multiplicand is more than a matter of the size of the fee, although it is certainly that. The structure of the fee can also make great differences in the economic incentives driving the lawyer at various stages of the representation. A common feature of contingent fee contracts is a scale that has the percentage rising along with the presumed amount of the lawyer's work. For example, the scale might provide a rising scale for settlement before suit, of 20 percent; settlement or recovery after suit is filed but prior to trial, of 25 percent; settlement or recovery after trial begins, of 33 percent; and settlement or recovery after trial or appeal, of 40 percent.[44] From the client's point of view, at least the concept of scaled increases, if not the actual percentage figures, is appropriate because they assure that the lawyer's time investment, to which the stages roughly correspond, does not become disproportionately high and discourage the lawyer from making further time investments that would benefit the client. Yet the scale is hardly perfect. Obviously a lawyer who receives an otherwise attractive settlement offer after completing extensive preliminary investigation and other work except for filing the complaint is under an incentive to advise the client to reject the settlement if the settlement will almost certainly be renewed after the lawyer has filed suit and triggered a higher percentage fee.

Multiplicands: Presence of Risk as Necessary Condition

Measuring the base against which the percentage fee is to be taken can be a matter of routine. The fee contract should carefully detail whether the base is to include or exclude disbursements and setoffs that the client must also pay.[45] In the absence of agreement, courts should construe the contract against its drafter and require that the percentage be taken against the recovery only after reduction for disbursements unless the contract explicitly provides a different multiplicand.[46]

Courts in general have insisted that a contingent fee be truly contingent. The typically elevated fee reflecting the risk to the lawyer of receiving no fee will be permitted only if the representation indeed involves a significant degree of risk.[47] In a leading Iowa deci-

[44] Actual scales vary considerably. A 1966 study by a defense-oriented group surveyed minimum fee schedules and practices in each state. It indicated that percentages ranged from 25–33 percent for settlement before trial, 33–40 percent if trial was necessary, and 50 percent if the case was exceptionally difficult or if an appeal or other posttrial proceeding was necessary. See Spec.Subcomm., A Study of Contingent Fees in the Prosecution of Personal Injury Claims, 33 Ins.Couns.J. 197, 203–13 (1966). Reportedly it is standard practice in the Eastern District of New York to charge a 40 percent percentage in dockworker personal injury cases. See Valentino v. Rickners Rhederei, G.M.B.H., 417 F.Supp. 176, 177 (E.D. N.Y.1976), affirmed 552 F.2d 466 (2d Cir.1977).

[45] Kramer v. Fallert, 628 S.W.2d 671 (Mo.App.1981) (contract calling for percentage of "net" amount recovered required reduction of verdict for client by amount of any counterclaim or offset).

[46] Cf. Dublirer v. Lascher, 96 A.D.2d 474, 464 N.Y.S.2d 790 (1983)(fee of 50 percent of arrears due on installment of purchase price calculated only after reducing amount of installments by amount advanced by plaintiff to bring tax payments on property up-to-date); Miernicki v. Seltzer, 312 Pa.Super. 166, 458 A.2d 566, 569 (1983), affirmed ___ Pa. ___, 479 A.2d 483 (1984), and authorities cited.

[47] Thomton, Sperry & Jensen, Ltd. v. Anderson, 352 N.W.2d 467 (Minn.App.1984)(invalidity of contingent fee

sion, the court refused to enforce a contingent fee agreement, under which a law firm represented a defendant in a defamation action, because the fee was to be measured by a percentage (one-third) of the difference between the amount of unliquidated damages that the plaintiff claimed in the complaint and the amount actually awarded by judgment or settlement.[48] Because plaintiffs routinely request unrealistically high figures for damages in their complaints, the lawyer would very likely earn a very large portion of the fee without risk or much effort.

There is no general prohibition against contingent fee contracts with defendants. Several cases have at least tacitly approved their use.[49] Such fee contracts should be permissible despite the fact that the Code's rationale for contingent fees—providing counsel to the poor and creating a res out of which the fee can be paid—are inapplicable. As in all cases, the mechanism employed to measure the size of the fee must be reasonable.[50]

An absence of real risk, of course, also characterizes representations of some plaintiffs. Some claimants' cases cannot be lost; the only real issue is how high a figure the recovery will be. For a lawyer to charge a supposedly contingent percentage fee against the entire amount recovered represents a fee consisting of very different elements of risk. The clearest case would be one in which a lawyer attempts to charge a supposedly contingent fee with a high percentage figure to collect a client's insurance when there is no indication that the insurer will resist the claim.[51] In the absence of risk a fee that is utterly disproportionate to the amount of work required is unreasonable.[52]

Risk and value measurement has proven troublesome with so-called structured or annuity settlements.[53] In catastrophic accidents, in which a jury might award millions of dollars in damages, defendants have offered settlements in which the plaintiff would receive a relatively small lump sum with annual installments for a period of years, possibly for the rest of the plaintiff's life. The total dollars promised look very high. But the cost to the defendant is relatively low because it can be provided for by purchasing an annuity. Courts, wisely, have generally required that the contingent fee of plaintiffs' lawyers in structured settlements be computed using as the multiplicand the present, discounted value of the payments that the plaintiff will

in partition action in which no question was raised of client's right to retain property); Knight v. DeMarea, 670 S.W.2d 59, 63–64 (Mo.App.1984)(trial court correctly refused to include within amount of multiplicand the value of stock that incontestably belonged to client when only point of litigation was to obtain valuation in excess of that value). Cf. also, e.g., Brown v. Welch, 253 Ga. 118, 317 S.E.2d 520 (1984)(agreement interpreted, by rule of strict construction, to award no fee to lawyer when probate court adjudicated that client took by intestacy; under agreement, client, who was indubitably entitled to intestate share of father's estate, agreed to fee of 25 percent of value of interest that probate court adjudicated in favor of client). See generally Note, The Contingent Fee: Disciplinary Rule, Ethical Consideration, or Free Competition?, 1979 Utah L.Rev. 547, 553–60.

48 Wunschel Law Firm, P.C. v. Clabaugh, 291 N.W.2d 331, 9 A.L.R.4th 181 (Iowa 1980). The plaintiff's complaint sought damages of $17,500. The jury awarded $1,750. Under the fee contract, the defense lawyer's fee, for which they sued, was $5250 (less a $1000 advance fee payment).

49 Cline v. Zappettini, 131 Cal.App.2d 723, 281 P.2d 35 (1955); Dunham v. Bentley, 103 Iowa 136, 72 N.W. 437 (1897); Lipscomb's Administrator v. Castleman, 147 Ky. 741, 145 S.W. 753 (1912); In re Wise, 172 App.Div. 491, 158 N.Y.S. 793 (1916); Board of Education v. Thurman, 121 Okl. 108, 247 P. 996 (1926). Cf. also, e.g., Citizens Bank v. C & H Constr. & Paving Co., 93 N.M. 422, 600 P.2d 1212 (App.1979)(defending, for one-third contingent fee, against opposing party's appeal of judgment in client's favor of $349,998). See generally Comment, Toward a Valid Defense Contingent Fee Contract: A Comparative Analysis, 67 Iowa L.Rev. 350 (1982); Annot., 9 A.L.R.4th 191 (1981).

50 Wunschel Law Firm, P.C. v. Clabaugh, 291 N.W.2d 331, 9 A.L.R.4th 181 (1980).

51 Horton v. Butler, 387 So.2d 1315 (La.App.1980); Hausen v. Davis, 112 Misc.2d 992, 448 N.Y.S.2d 87, 89 (Civ.Ct. 1981)(attempt to collect percentage fee for client's no-fault coverage was "extraordinary" in view of lack of any resistance from insurer); Harmon v. Pugh, 38 N.C.App. 438, 248 S.E.2d 421 (1978), cert.denied 296 N.C. 584, 254 S.E.2d 33 (1979).

52 In re Kennedy, 472 A.2d 1317 (Del.1984), cert.denied ___ U.S. ___, 104 S.Ct. 2388, 81 L.Ed.2d 346 (1984)(discipline of lawyer who charged 50 percent fee to collect temporary total disability payments, to which client had clear entitlement); Harmon v. Pugh, supra.

53 See generally Annot., 31 A.L.R.4th 95 (1984).

receive over the designated period of years.[54] If payment of the fee would consume a disproportionate amount of the initial, lump-sum payment, courts have ordered that the lawyer be paid the contracted-for percentage only as each annual increment is received.[55]

Regulation of Percentage Ranges

Courts have not generally been successful in controlling contingent fees by regulating the size of the percentage charged through the contingent fee. Courts have approached the matter on a case-by-case basis in cases involving lawyer discipline or challenges to the fee by a client or third-party fee payer. They have confronted an array of settings and have attempted to measure, with no tool but a rough concept of fairness, the appropriate level of compensation for presumed risks undertaken. As a result, decisions reducing or failing to reduce the percentage seem largely explicable on the facts before the court and jurisdictional variations in judicial temperament. Courts have generally approved contingent fees of one-third in most personal injury litigation, although sometimes without enthusiasm.[56] Decisions have permitted a charge of 50 percent in cases involving unusual difficulty,[57] which at least leaves the client equally interested in the outcome of the suit. One decision approved a fee of 76 percent,[58] but several decisions have disapproved percentages of 50 percent or lower on facts indicating that the resulting fee was unreasonably large,[59] even though the fee seemed appropriate at the time of the contract.[60]

Some state statutes or rules place mandatory ceilings on contingent fee percentages.[61] Several federal statutes limit the size of contingent fee percentages, such as the Federal Tort Claims Act limitation of 25 percent.[62] The objective of such limitations is to prevent

[54] Pettiford v. Eskwitt, 189 N.J.Super. 485, 460 A.2d 716 (1983); cf. In re Estate of Muccini, 118 Misc.2d 38, 460 N.Y.S.2d 680 (1983)(fee to be calculated on basis of cost to defendant of securing annuity rather than on speculative basis of discounted present value of payments with addition of projected tax saving to client). The statement in Couture v. Mammoth Groceries, Inc., 117 N.H. 294, 371 A.2d 1184, 1185 (1977), that the plaintiff's lawyer in a fee-shifting case was to receive one-third of "any benefits received to date as well as for any future benefits," is ambiguous as to whether the value of the future benefits was discounted.

[55] Sable v. Feinman, 76 Cal.App.3d 509, 142 Cal.Rptr. 895 (1978); In re Chow, 3 Hawaii App. 577, 656 P.2d 105 (1982); Cardenas v. Ramsey County, 322 N.W.2d 191 (Minn.1982). See also, e.g., Godwin v. Schramm, 731 F.2d 153 (3d Cir.1984), cert.denied ___ U.S. ___, 105 S.Ct. 250, 83 L.Ed.2d 187 (1984)(denial of lawyer's claim for percentage of present discounted value of future medical treatment that client would receive free from Veterans' Administration).

[56] Southern Shipbuilding Corp. v. Richardson, 372 So.2d 1188, 1190 (La.1979).

[57] Taylor v. Bemiss, 110 U.S. 42, 3 S.Ct. 441, 28 L.Ed. 64 (1884); In re Innkeepers of New Castle, Inc., 671 F.2d 221 (7th Cir.1982), cert.denied 459 U.S. 908, 103 S.Ct. 212, 74 L.Ed.2d 169 (1982)(50 percent in eminent domain proceeding); Hughes v. Eisner, 14 N.J.Super. 58, 81 A.2d 394 (1951).

[58] Foshee v. Lloyds, New York, 643 F.2d 1162 (5th Cir. 1981). But cf., e.g., Gruskay v. Simenauskas, 107 Conn. 380, 140 A. 724 (1928)(60 percent is excessive and exorbitant).

[59] In re Kennedy, 472 A.2d 1317 (Del.1984), cert.denied ___ U.S. ___, 104 S.Ct. 2388, 81 L.Ed.2d 346 (1984)(discipline for charging 50 percent fee when client clearly entitled to temporary disability payments); Garden Hill Land Corp. v. Succession of Cambre, 306 So.2d 718 (La. 1975) (fee of 50 percent in wrongful death action on its face unreasonable); In re Ostensoe, 196 Minn. 102, 103, 264 N.W. 569 (1936)(50 percent contingent fee in personal injury case unjustifiable); State v. Cannon, 199 Wis. 401, 226 N.W. 385 (1929)(one-third contingent fee unconscionable in amount when fee produced was without regard to amount of services performed or needs of client).

[60] In re Schwartz, 1984 ABA/BNA Lawyers' Man. Prof. Conduct 371 (Ariz.1984)(enforcing fee of 33 percent for claim to which no real defense existed unreasonable, and lawyer suspended for six months, when effect of taking fee payment was to leave client with nothing after medical liens were satisfied).

[61] Gair v. Peck, 6 N.Y.2d 97, 188 N.Y.S.2d 491, 160 N.E.2d 43 (1959), cert.denied 361 U.S. 374, 80 S.Ct. 401, 4 L.Ed.2d 380 (1960). See also, e.g., Mich.Gen.Ct.R.1963, 928 (maximum allowable in any case is one-third); N.J.R. 1:21–7 (originally adopted 1971, effective 1972; as amended (raised) 1976)(schedule of contingent fees, which must be followed in absence of allowance of court, on (1) 50 percent of first $1000 recovered; (2) 40% of next $2000; (3) 33⅓ percent of next $47,000; (4) 25 percent of next $50,000; (5) 20 percent of next $150,000; and (6) 10 percent of any amount over $250,000); American Trial Lawyers Ass'n v. New Jersey Supreme Court, 66 N.J. 258, 330 A.2d 350 (1974). On the validity of statutory limitations in medical malpractice, see generally Annot., 12 A.L.R.4th 1062 (1982). See generally F.MacKinnon, Contingent Fees for Legal Services 183–86 (1964).

[62] 28 U.S.C.A. § 2678. For other federal statutory limitations, see Defense Research Institute, A Study of Contingent Fees in the Prosecution of Personal Injury Claims

overreaching by lawyers of clients who are ignorant of the relative risks and values involved. Unfortunately there is good reason to believe that the schedules are dysfunctional, perhaps seriously so. Courts seem to grant exceptions to the scales routinely on such justifications as the quality of the lawyer or the impressive size of the recovery,[63] as if success in the representation had not already been worked into the formula. Worse, schedules might be utilized by lawyers as a minimum fee schedule, in effect representing them to clients as standard or court ordered.[64] They also might encourage lawyers with contingent fee contracts to underwork.[65]

Suggestions have been made for imaginative contingent fee contracts different from those commonly used. They would combine hourly rates with contingent features in order to assure compatible economic motivations of both lawyer and client.[66] Yet the suggestions are probably limited to very sophisticated clients—possibly only to clients advised by other lawyers—because they depend upon a high level of client information and willingness to act. If clients often cannot make effective decisions about the value of lawyer time and cannot monitor lawyers' time commitments to their cases, lawyers who are corruptly disposed can frustrate more complex contractual arrangements as well as those that are simple.[67]

WESTLAW REFERENCES

45k146 "conting! fee" /s oral verbal unwritten

§ 9.4.3 *Prohibition in Criminal Cases*

History and Rationale of the Prohibition

Some pre-Code authority existed for the proposition that contingent fees in criminal cases were permissible.[68] But the predominant weight of authority then and now is that the use of the contingent fee in criminal defense work is illegal.[69] The customary arguments for illegality revolve vaguely around the character of criminal defense representations. Courts argue that a prohibition is required in criminal cases "because of the dan-

9 (1966). At least one federal court has imposed a fee scale by local rule. Schlesinger v. Teitelbaum, 475 F.2d 137 (3d Cir.1973), cert.denied 414 U.S. 1111, 94 S.Ct. 840, 38 L.Ed.2d 738 (1973)(scale in personal injury actions brought by seamen).

63 Merendino v. FMC Corp., 181 N.J.Super. 503, 438 A.2d 365 (1981).

64 D.Rosenthal, Lawyer and Client: Who's in Charge? 65 (1974)(most lawyers practicing under New York sliding scale of maximum fees told clients that fees were "standard" or "set by the court"); Schwartz & Mitchell, An Economic Analysis of the Contingent Fee in Personal-Injury Litigation, 22 Stan.L.Rev. 1125, 1144 & n.33 (1970); Clermont & Currivan, Improving on the Contingent Fee, 63 Cornell L.Rev. 529, 580–81 (1978); Comment, An Analysis of State Legislative Responses to the Medical Malpractice Crisis, 1975 Duke L.J. 1417, 1444–45. But see F.MacKinnon, Contingent Fees for Legal Services 187–88 (1964)(studies of filed closing statements indicated fees below maximums).

65 Clermont & Currivan, supra at 581 ("[S]uch rate ceilings are largely cosmetic, keeping the final fee at what seems a reasonable level to the outside observer, while still permitting the lawyer covertly to pick and then milk (through underwork) the lucrative cases. Indeed, percentage rate ceilings resemble a speed limit that forbids traveling more than 55 miles in one hour: Lawyers will either stay home or take half-hour trips at 110 miles an hour.").

66 The two important articles in the area are Schwartz & Mitchell, An Economic Analysis of the Contingent Fee in Personal-Injury Litigation, 22 Stan.L.Rev. 1125 (1970); and Clermont & Currivan, Improving on the Contingent Fee, 63 Cornell L.Rev. 529 (1978).

67 Halpern & Turnbull, An Economic Analysis of Legal Fees Contracts, in Lawyers and the Consumer Interest: Regulating the Market for Legal Services at 161 (R.Evans & M.Trebilcock eds.1982). On the general problem of Pareto-optimal principal-agent contracts—the form of contract that cannot be altered to improve the welfare of one party without decreasing the welfare of the other—see Harris & Raviv, Some Results on Incentive Contracts with Imperfect Information, 20 J.Econ. Theory 231 (1979); Shavell, Risk Sharing and Incentives in the Principal and Agent Relationship, 10 Bell J.Econ. 55 (1979).

68 H.Drinker, Legal Ethics 176–77 (1953). Drinker stated that the permission in Canon 13 to charge a contingent fee extended as well to criminal cases. He cited no authority. In his very brief discussion of contingent fees in domestic relations and lobbying, Drinker indicates little familiarity with the judicial decisions.

69 The authority consists largely of secondary authority, chiefly the Restatement of Contracts § 542(2)(1932), which cited no cases in support. See also 6A A. Corbin, Contracts § 1424, at 366–67 (1962), which simply cites dicta in divorce cases. See generally F.MacKinnon, Contingent Fees 52 (1964).

ger of corrupting justice," [70] although it is typically not explained why the criminal defense bench and bar is particularly susceptible to the temptation or why corruption efforts would be any more availing here than in civil cases. The argument is sometimes buttressed by citation of a leading New Mexico decision that involved a contingent fee promised to a private prosecutor to *obtain* a criminal conviction.[71] Given the strictly limited advocacy model under which prosecutors are to exercise a justice-oriented discretion, the dangers of a contingent prosecution fee are far greater and readily distinguishable from a criminal defense contingent fee.[72]

The position advanced by the Code in EC 2–20 is that contingent fees are unacceptable in criminal cases because "legal services in criminal cases do not produce a *res* with which to pay the fee." The argument is curious, because most courts approve contingent fees in types of civil cases in which creation of a res is not the object of the representation.[73] Moreover, the argument makes little economic sense: the accused might be able to continue or resume economically productive work because of an acquittal or because of a sentence that does not include confinement. Such outcomes can be of significant economic value and can produce an ability to pay that would not exist if the accused were incarcerated after a trial.[74] In any event, the economic viability of the arrangement would seem a matter more for client-lawyer discussions than for flat prohibition.

The criminal defense prohibition seems to be largely an historical accident, arising in earlier cases during a time when all contingent fee contracts were generally regarded with great suspicion [75] and surviving by tradition to the present. Economics may play a part in retention of the rule. It has been suggested that the reason for the prohibition is anticompetitive: criminal defense fees for retained lawyers are commonly charged and paid in advance, and that status quo would be threatened by providing a contingent fee option.[76] Most distressingly, the continuation of the prohibition might reflect widespread but largely inarticulate suspicions on the part of bar leaders about the ethics of the small minority of lawyers regularly engaged in criminal defense work.

State of the Law

Whether for sound reasons or weak ones, today virtually every jurisdiction prohibits the use of the contingent fee arrangement when a lawyer represents a defendant in a criminal case.[77] So it is provided in DR 2–106(C): "A lawyer shall not enter into an arrangement for, charge, or collect a contingent fee for representing a defendant in a criminal case." The Model Rules provide a similar explicit prohibition in MR 1.5(a)(8).[78] A lawyer who charges a contingent fee in

70 Peyton v. Margiotti, 398 Pa. 86, 156 A.2d 865, 867 (1959)(cited and quoted at DR 2–106(C) n.90). A stronger case can be made for the prohibition when the contingent fee seems to be in payment for influence peddling, such as when the lawyer's undertaking is to employ corrupt political means to obtain a pardon or a prosecutor's agreement to quash an indictment, situations out of which some earlier cases, and a few modern ones, arise. See, e.g., Price v. Caperton, 62 Ky. (1 Duv.) 207 (1864); Ormerod v. Dearman, 100 Pa.St. 561, 45 Am.Rep. 391 (1882); cf. Peyton v. Margiotti, supra (undertaking to obtain pardon before Christmas).

71 Baca v. Padilla, 26 N.M. 223, 190 P. 730 (1920). The court also noted that there was no basis for a claimed need for the public to obtain prosecutorial services on a contingent fee basis because of inability to finance prosecutorial services in any other way. 190 P. at 731.

72 § 13.10.2.

73 § 9.4.2, at 532–33.

74 In a case involving the appropriate size of a fee to be paid after the fact to a court-appointed lawyer, a court has directed trial courts to take into account "the results achieved" when the defense secures a good result such as probation or an acquittal. See People v. Parks, 109 Ill. App.3d 737, 65 Ill.Dec. 303, 307, 441 N.E.2d 95, 99 (1982).

75 For early cases, see E.Wood, Fee Contracts of Lawyers 35–36 (1936).

76 Morgan, The Evolving Concept of Professional Responsibility, 90 Harv.L.Rev. 702, 734 (1977).

77 DR 2–106(C); MR 1.5(a)(8). The Code of Professional Responsibility by State (1977) lists no significant variations on the criminal defense prohibition in DR 2–106(C).

78 The language was added in the August 1982 debates and made more explicit what earlier drafts would have treated only under a general prohibition against illegal fees, referring to the law of each state. See MR 1.5(c) comment (Terms of Payment; fourth paragraph)(Proposed Final Draft, May 30, 1981).

violation of those restrictions is subject both to professional discipline[79] and to contractual remedies when sued by a client who has paid a fee, possibly under theories that require refund of the entire fee.[80] A representation conducted under a prohibited contingent fee is not, however, for that reason alone rendered constitutionally defective for ineffective assistance of counsel. A showing of actual prejudice is required.[81]

Scope of the Prohibition

Close questions of interpretation can arise over what a prohibited contingent fee is and what defenses are included. Is an arrangement under which a person accused of murdering his or her spouse will pay a criminal defense lawyer out of the proceeds of the decedent's life insurance policy "contingent," when the law would probably prohibit the client from recovering under the policy if convicted of the crime that is charged? [82] What about property received in kind as a fee from a client if the client is accused of a crime, such as drug smuggling, that would make the property seizable contraband if the client were convicted? [83] What is a "criminal case"? Does it include traffic offenses, which for many purposes are treated as administrative or quasi-criminal matters?

What about a client's promise to pay a criminal defense lawyer a "reasonable" amount to be set at the end of the representation? According to a Texas decision, such a contract is consistent with the Code.[84] Under such an arrangement, of course, a lawyer could possibly evade the prohibition against a criminal case contingent fee through the form of the contract. That approach has little to recommend it if the prohibition is to be maintained. If, on the other hand, it should be held, in order to prevent such evasions, that criminal defense lawyers are precluded from contracting to determine fees at the end of the presentation, that would impose an additional restraint upon criminal defense lawyers not imposed on lawyers in other types of work.

Critique of the Criminal Defense Prohibition

Much could be said in favor of permitting contingent fees for criminal defense representations as freely as for any other work. An agreement under which a lawyer would receive a fee—or would receive an additional, incentive fee—only if an accused were not incarcerated might provide a defense lawyer with important added motivation to perform the defense function effectively. The notion that the prospect of losing a contingent fee might impel a desperate defense lawyer to suborn perjury or commit other offenses probably misconceives the costs and risks that would be involved, the extent of existing pressures to engage in those practices, and the manner in which cash flow functions in present private practices in which the contingent fee is commonly used.

The fears raised by the prospect of contingent fees in criminal defense seem unfounded. The criminal justice process is probably no more susceptible to corruption by defense lawyers made overzealous by contingent fees

79 United States ex rel. Simon v. Murphy, 349 F.Supp. 818 (E.D.Pa.1972); Genins v. Geiger, 144 Ga.App. 244, 240 S.E.2d 745 (1977), cert.denied 444 U.S. 991, 100 S.Ct. 521, 62 L.Ed.2d 420 (1979); In re Fasig, 444 N.E.2d 849 (Ind.1983); In re Steere, 217 Kan. 271, 536 P.2d 54 (1975); State v. Hilton, 217 Kan. 694, 538 P.2d 977 (1975).

80 Restatement of Contracts § 545 (1932).

81 Schoonover v. State, 218 Kan. 377, 543 P.2d 881 (1975), cert.denied 424 U.S. 944, 96 S.Ct. 1412, 47 L.Ed.2d 349 (1976). The lawyer in *Schoonover* was later disciplined. See In re Steere, 217 Kan. 271, 536 P.2d 54 (1975).

82 Cf. Commonwealth v. Simon, 446 Pa. 215, 285 A.2d 861 (1971)(convicted person waived argument that lawyer's fee arrangement created conflict of interest because of disincentive to argue for lesser included offenses).

83 Cf. Nat'l L.J., July 9, 1979, at 43, col.1.

84 Mossler v. Foreman, 493 S.W.2d 627 (Tex.Civ.App. 1973), error refused n.r.e. ($250,000 fee reasonable in successful defense in highly publicized murder case). See also Citizens & Nat'l Bank v. Hodnett, 139 Ga.App. 839, 229 S.E.2d 792, 793 (1976)(arrangement under which attorney was to set fee at termination of matter is not a contingent fee). Presumably the test of a reasonable fee, for that limited purpose, would not look to the "results obtained," as otherwise permitted under DR 2–106(B)(4) and MR 1.5(a)(4). Cf. n. 74, infra.

than is the civil system. The private criminal defense bar is probably no more subject to the corrupting temptations of contingent fees than are those—many of whom are, of course, the same lawyers—who are free to accept contingent fees in all of their civil representations. Of perhaps greater weight is a concern that a defense lawyer whose contingent fee would be lost unless there was an acquittal would be tempted to forego plea bargaining for lesser included offenses. But that can readily be remedied through a requirement that the fee arrangement take into account the possible gradations in outcome.

In the end, the cases in which the prohibition makes a major difference are probably those in which an accused with employment, but without assets, is deprived of any choice of private counsel and is relegated to representation by a public defender or other appointed counsel paid at public expense[85] or is induced by circumstances to obtain loans at exhorbitant rates of interest or, possibly, to commit other crimes in order to afford private defense representations.

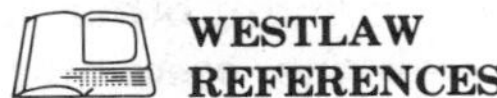
WESTLAW REFERENCES

State of the Law

dr2–106(c) "dr 2–106(c)" 45k146 "conting! fee" /s criminal

§ 9.4.4 *Prohibition in Domestic Relations Cases*

Nature of the Prohibition

The Code contains no explicit prohibition against a contingent fee in a divorce representation, although DR 2–106(A) does forbid charging an "illegal" fee. And EC 2–20 recites that contingent fees "in domestic relations cases are rarely justified."[86] The point is made with quite insufficient force, however, because under the law of most American jurisdictions, it is improper for a lawyer to charge a fee in a divorce case that is either contingent on a favorable judgment or settlement or proportional to the recovery of a certain amount of alimony or property settlement.[87] The Model Rules spell out the prohibition in some detail in Rule 1.5(d):

> A lawyer shall not enter into an arrangement to charge or collect any fee in a domestic relations matter, the payment or amount of which is contingent upon the securing of a divorce or upon the amount of alimony or support, or property settlement in lieu thereof.[88]

The rule is not one of professional regulation alone. The same rule was expressed, for example, in the broad proclamation in the first Restatement of Contracts that a promise by a spouse to pay a lawyer a contingent fee to obtain a divorce or annulment is illegal

---

85 The availability of contingent fee representation in criminal cases would require some adjustment to the present rules of eligibility for publicly-funded defense representation. Under present rules in most jurisdictions, all an indigent accused need assert is middle- or low-income status and, in general terms, inability to obtain representation by private counsel. See § 14.3.3.

86 The statement in EC 2–20 that contingent fees are "rarely" justified in divorce actions has generated confusion. It probably refers to domestic relations cases involving property division after a divorce. See infra at 541. But in Gross v. Lamb, 1 Ohio App.3d 1, 437 N.E.2d 309 (1980), it was interpreted to mean that some divorce representations were themselves, if "rarely," excepted from the prohibition.

87 Barelli v. Levin, 480 F.2d 1207 (7th Cir.1973); McDearmon v. Gordon & Gremillion, 247 Ark. 318, 445 S.W.2d 488 (1969); Newman v. Freitas, 129 Cal. 283, 61 P. 907 (1900); Valparaiso Bank & Trust Co. v. Sims, 343 So. 2d 967 (Fla.App.1977), cert. denied 353 So.2d 678 (1977); In re Wright, 89 Ill.2d 498, 61 Ill.Dec. 140, 434 N.E.2d 293 (1982); Osborne v. Osborne, 384 Mass. 591, 428 N.E.2d 810 (1981); Baskerville v. Baskerville, 246 Minn. 496, 75 N.W.2d 762 (1956); Avant v. Whitten, 253 So.2d 394 (Miss.1971); State v. Jenson, 171 Neb. 1, 105 N.W.2d 459 (1960), cert.denied 365 U.S. 870, 81 S.Ct. 905, 5 L.Ed.2d 860 (1961); Thompson v. Thompson, 70 N.C.App. 147, 319 S.E.2d 315 (1984), reversed ___ N.C. ___, ___ S.E.2d ___ (1985); Longmire v. Hall, 541 P.2d 276 (Okl.App.1975); In re Hill, 261 Or. 573, 495 P.2d 261 (1972); Morfeld v. Andrews, 579 P.2d 426, 434 (Wyo.1978). But see Gross v. Lamb, 1 Ohio App.3d 1, 437 N.E.2d 309 (1980). See generally F.MacKinnon, Contingent Fees for Legal Services 45–49 (1964); 1 S.Speiser, Attorney's Fees § 2.6, at 83 (1973).

The prohibition is sometimes found explicitly in a statute, see Casenote, 108 U.Pa.L.Rev. 1059 n.4 (1960), or in a court rule, see In re Marriage of Wright, 89 Ill. 498, 61 Ill.Dec. 140, 141, 434 N.E.2d 293, 294 (1982); Osborne v. Osborne, 384 Mass. 591, 428 N.E.2d 810, 820 n.12 (1981).

88 Fla. DR 2–106(C) is virtually the same. The language in the last phrases of MR 1.5(d), which refers alternatively to a fee that is proportional to the amount of alimony, support, or property settlement, deals with a practice, also previously prohibited, of a lawyer's contracting to be paid in a domestic relations case by a

and thus void as a matter of contract law.[89] The statement yielded in the Second Restatement to a more general and less clearly condemning notion that "a promise that undermines [the marriage] relationship by tending unreasonably to encourage divorce or separation is unenforceable." [90]

Reconciliation as Justification for the Domestic Relations Exception

The now customary, and quite sound, primary justification for the prohibition against contingent fees [91] in divorce cases is that the arrangement would put strong economic pressure on the lawyer to assure that reconciliation did not occur.[92] While some lawyers might act from altruistic motives, there is hardly any reason to think that such economic heroism would be general.[93] Reconciliation would be just as disastrous to the lawyer's claim for a fee as would be defeat in the divorce action itself. In either event, the lawyer would be deprived of any fee.[94] Despite the clear prohibition, one sometimes encounters in the real world lawyer "ten percenters" who employ a fee proportional to success in obtaining a divorce or favorable property settlement for the client.[95]

stated percentage of property settlement. E.g., In re Brackett, 114 App.Div.257, 99 N.Y.S. 802 (1906), affirmed 189 N.Y. 502, 81 N.E. 1160 (1907); Levine v. Levine, 206 Misc. 884, 135 N.Y.S.2d 304 (1954). Those agreements are void because they induce a lawyer to seek only property for the property settlement and to neglect alimony and child support, which may not be in the best interests of the lawyer's client.

89 Restatement, Contracts § 542(2) (1932). The stricture was enforced in § 545, which provided that the lawyer who charged a contingent fee in a divorce case could recover neither the agreed upon fee nor the value of the legal services actually rendered.

90 Restatement (Second), Contracts § 190, comment c (1979). The prohibition against contingent fees in the first Restatement of Contracts is not mentioned in the second. The second Restatement differs markedly from the first in abandoning the attempt to enumerate most of the important "against public policy" types of bargains. That was done either "because of the myriad of such policies" (Restatement (Second) Contracts Ch. 8, Introductory Note, at vol. 2, p. 3 (1979)) or "because the subjects are so largely governed by legislation" (id., Reporter's Note, at 4) or perhaps for both reasons. It further seems apparent that many of the fusty first Restatement definitions of "illegality" had become anachronisms after almost fifty years of changing laws and social mores.

91 For precisely the same reason, in a retainer agreement with a spouse in a dissolution case, a clause that purports to make a retainer fee nonrefundable should be void. E.g., Volkell v. Volkell, 10 Fam.L.Rptr. 1574 (Sup. Ct.), reversed on other grounds 102 A.D.2d 889, 477 N.Y.S.2d 60 (1984).

92 McDearmon v. Gordon & Gremillion, 247 Ark. 318, 445 S.W.2d 488 (1969); McCarthy v. Santangelo, 137 Conn. 410, 78 A.2d 240 (1951); In re Sylvester, 195 Iowa 1329, 192 N.W. 442 (1923); In re Succession of Butler, 294 So.2d 512 (La. 1974); Youngblood, The Contingent Fee—Reasonable Alternative?, 28 Mod. L.Rev. 330, 333 (1965). The ultimate basis for the mentioned rationale, of course, is a perceived strong public policy in favor of marriage (and against dissolution) and in favor of the permanence of original family homes for children. In view of that rationale, it has been suggested that a suit for divorce charging the defendant with bigamy can be prosecuted by a lawyer under a contingent fee because of the strong public policy against bigamous marriages. See Coviello v. State Bar, 45 Cal.2d 57, 286 P.2d 357 (1955)(refusing to impose discipline for charging a contingent fee on such a rationale). The reasoning goes too far, however, because it cannot be confined to bigamous marriages: there presumably exists an equally strong public policy against marriages that, for example, were illegally contracted or are fraught with cruelty on the part of the defendant. Moreover, there is no reason to think that the pleading of a ground for divorce will inevitably mean that that ground can be established or that capitulation by the defendant amounts to an assurance that the alleged ground for divorce really existed.

Analogously, in Ore.Ethics Op. 429 (1979), it was concluded that a lawyer did not act unethically in becoming sexually involved with a divorce client so long as the divorce didn't involve children and an amicable settlement would not be hindered. That rationale ignores, of course, the lawyer's apparent interest to advise against a reconciliation in light of his or her own sexual interests.

93 Thus the argument that lawyers should be above suspicion and would not attempt to discourage reconciliation for a mere fee is simply unrealistic. See Comment, Professional Responsibility—Contingent Fees in Domestic Relations Actions: Equal Freedom to Contract for the Domestic Relations Bar, 62 N.C.L.Rev. 381, 387 (1984).

94 Yet the policy is not so universal that it should prohibit all contingent fees in divorce litigation. Most obviously, it would be inapplicable to a fee that is contingent on the lawyer's success in *defeating* an opposing spouse's attempt to obtain a divorce and that, for example, provided a fee proportional to the value of property that remained within the marital estate.

95 The disparaging term "ten percenter" is commonly used among lawyers to describe a divorce lawyer who charges clients a fee on this basis, although it rarely appears in the legal literature. The phrase is also known in the world of politics and refers to the charging of fees for obtaining government contracts. See McClelland, The Covenant against Contingent Fees as a Method of Eliminating the "5-Percenter," 41 Corn.L.Q. 399 (1956).

At one time, the California Supreme Court attempted to fashion a facts-and-circumstances application of the proreconciliation rationale. In 1953 the court held that such a contract was valid when the lawyer was retained to represent the defendant spouse in a divorce action that had already been commenced and where, according to the lawyer's later testimony in support of the contingent fee, the client's only expressed intent was to protect his interest in community property.[96] But the prior commencement of the divorce action and the client's status as the defendant are hardly sure measures of the spouse's inability or unwillingness to effect a reconciliation. A recovery of the fee in the California case depended upon the lawyer's testimony about the contents of the client's initial consultation, an ordinarily confidential matter that would be better not exposed in later testimony absent some more compelling justification than permitting the lawyer to recover a contingent fee instead of some other kind.[97] In any event, the California court's approach would require lower courts to engage in suppositious assessments about whether reconciliation would have occurred but for the lawyer's motivation to advise against it because of the contingent fee arrangement.[98] The California courts seem now to have rejected the contingent fee in divorce cases as absolutely as other states.[99]

Economic Necessity and Patterns of Property Distribution

A second rationale for the prohibition stems from the historical fact that contingent fees first gained grudging recognition in situations in which they were necessary to enable an impecunious litigant to obtain counsel. No compelling necessity exists for resort to a contingent fee in order to assure representation to divorce litigants.[1] The spouse in possession of property will typically have no difficulty retaining counsel. And the spouse without immediate control of property—traditionally the wife[2]—is protected in most American jurisdictions by statutory or common-law authority in the courts to compel the spouse with significantly more assets to pay the other spouse's attorney fees.[3]

A further objection to a contingent fee exists when the amount of the promised fee depends on the amounts awarded to a spouse for support or alimony or by way of a property settlement. The lawyer's fee may disrupt the pattern of wealth distribution that the court intended in making the award unless, according to some courts, the fact of the contingent fee is made known to the court in advance.[4] But even if made known to the court, the fact that a lawyer would receive funds proportional, for example, to the amount of property settlement and not pro-

96 Krieger v. Bulpitt, 40 Cal.2d 97, 251 P.2d 673 (1953). The court relied principally on an analogy to a line of cases upholding interspousal agreements to divide property contingent on divorce. Those cases are readily distinguishable, however, because of the absence there of an economically interested third party impelled by the agreement to discourage reconciliation. Read most broadly, *Krieger* could be understood to establish a defendant-spouse exception, permitting a contingent fee whenever the client was the spouse who was sued by the other. Other courts have rejected such a distinction. E.g., State v. Dunker, 160 Neb. 779, 71 N.W.2d 502 (1955); Longmire v. Hall, 541 P.2d 276 (Okl.App.1975).

97 § 6.7.8 on the exception to the confidential client information rule where necessary to collect a fee.

98 Another exception would permit a contingent fee to a lawyer who worked diligently but unsuccessfully to achieve a reconciliation. The court refused to recognize such an exception in McCarthy v. Santangelo, 137 Conn. 410, 78 A.2d 240 (1951). Hinged, as necessarily it would be, on highly subjective elements, the exception would doubtless soon become almost universal.

99 Coons v. Kary, 263 Cal.App.2d 650, 69 Cal.Rptr. 712 (1968)(distinguishing Krieger v. Bulpitt on very narrow reading of its holding).

1 McDearmon v. Gordon & Gremillion, 247 Ark. 318, 445 S.W.2d 488 (1969).

2 Newman v. Freitas, 129 Cal. 283, 61 P. 907, 910 (1900) (apparent assumption that husband would never be awarded fees against wife if he prevailed in his divorce action against her).

3 § 16.6.2 at n. 54 (fees for prevailing party in divorce action). The award of fees at the conclusion of the divorce action is itself subject to criticism on the ground that it may provide the lawyer with an incentive to advise against reconciliation unless the fee award is to be made regardless of reconciliation.

4 Jordan v. Westerman, 62 Mich. 170, 28 N.W. 826 (1886); In re Smith, 42 Wn.2d 188, 254 P.2d 464, 469 (1953).

portional to support or alimony, creates strong economic incentives on the part of the lawyer to lend the greatest weight of advocacy toward a distribution that favors the lawyer and possibly disserves the client and the client's children.[5] Finally, it is customary and desirable that lawyer and client make fee agreements at the beginning of a representation,[6] but at that point a client confronting divorce might well be in an emotional state that does not encourage careful deliberation about the consequences of agreeing to a contingent fee.

Property-Pursuit Exception

A property-pursuit exception is sometimes recognized. When a decree has already been entered that severs the marital relationship but legal work remains to be done to adjudicate interests in property, the rationale of encouraging reconciliation now makes little practical sense, thus relaxing the strongest justification for the prohibition.[7] Therefore, if at that point a lawyer and client enter into a fee agreement[8] that is contingent on success in the property division aspects of the litigation and proportional to their value, this seems relatively unobjectionable. Some few cases have recognized such an exception.[9] It is problematical whether the exception is compatible with the professional regulations,[10] particularly with the sweeping and unexcepting language of MR 1.5(d). The Model Rule, added by floor amendment in August 1982, very broadly prohibits a contingent fee in "a domestic relations matter" that is "contingent"[11] upon "the amount of alimony or support, or property settlement" in the case.

Lawyer Discipline and Remedies

The reach of the domestic relations prohibition and exceptions to it is critical, because professional discipline can be imposed for use of the contingent fee under both the Code and the Model Rules. Moreover, in a proceeding to set a fee, courts have refused to enforce the contract for a contingent fee and have allowed only a smaller amount, based on a quantum meruit measure of the value of the lawyer's actual services to the client.[12] Some authority goes further and denies any fee to the lawyer on the theory that the conflict of interest introduced by the contingent nature of the promised fee makes the entire performance of the lawyer defective.[13]

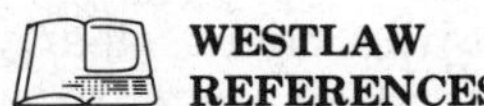

WESTLAW REFERENCES

Nature of the Prohibition

45k146 "conting! fee" /s divorce (dissolution /2 marriage) "domestic relation"

§ 9.4.5 Other Prohibited Contingent Fees

The use of contingent fees has been prohibited by legislation, rule, or judicial decision in a variety of other situations. The federal

[5] See authority cited supra, n. 88.

[6] § 9.2.1 (written contracts).

[7] Olivier v. Doga, 368 So.2d 467 (La.App.), reversed on other grounds 384 So.2d 330 (La.1979).

[8] It is improbable that many situations of the kind described would arise, because typically the same lawyer represents a divorce client from beginning to end. If the same lawyer entered into a new fee agreement with the client after a dissolution decree was entered, but before property division issues were adjudicated, the "midstream" fee agreement would be subject to strict scrutiny under the doctrines controlling compensation arrangements between fiduciary and client. See § 9.2.1 (post-inception contract changes).

[9] Olivier v. Doga, 368 So.2d 467 (La.App.1979), reversed on other grounds 384 So. 2d 330 (La.1979); Salter v. St. Jean, 170 So.2d 94 (Fla.App.1964); Burns v. Stewart, 290 Minn. 289, 188 N.W.2d 760 (1971).

[10] The reference in EC 2–20 and MR 1.5(d) to "domestic relations" is too broad if those rules mean to recognize the exception.

[11] MR 1.5(d) almost certainly means both "contingent" on success in the representation and "proportional" to the amounts recovered or retained by the client.

[12] Morfeld v. Andrews, 579 P.2d 426 (Wyo.1978)(contingent fee in divorce case condemned, but lawyer can still assert common-law retaining lien against client's property to extent of a quantum meruit claim); Ownby v. Prisock, 243 Miss. 203, 138 So.2d 279 (1962); Thompson v. Thompson, 70 N.C.App. 147, 319 S.E.2d 315 (1984) reversed ___ N.C. ___, ___ S.E.2d ___ (1985).

[13] McInerney v. Massasoit Grayhound Ass'n, 359 Mass. 359, 269 N.E.2d 211 (1971); Jordan v. Westerman, 62 Mich. 170, 28 N.W. 826 (1886); Shanks v. Kilgore, 589 S.W.2d 318 (Mo.App.1979).

bankruptcy statutes have been interpreted to preclude some kinds of contingent fees that are charged to bankrupts.[14] A New York rule, commonly found in other states as well, prohibits a lawyer from charging a contingent fee for "recovering" a client's no-fault coverage under the client's own liability policy.[15] A probate code provision in Minnesota prohibits the award of a fee for probating an estate that is proportional to the size of the estate unless the testator agreed in writing to such a basis for charging.[16] A long-standing common-law rule in many jurisdictions prohibits the charging of a contingent fee for lobbying activities before a legislative body, for fear of contributing to the corruption of government.[17] The bulk of the cases date from an era in judicial thinking in which all lobbying was considered a form of corruption. But public attitudes toward both lobbying and contingent fees have changed.[18] It seems clear that concerns over lobbying should no longer prohibit a lawyer-agent from doing for a client what the client clearly is entitled, perhaps constitutionally entitled, to do for himself or herself. Several modern cases are in accord with such a liberalized view so long as the lobbying contract does not contemplate any improper attempt to influence a policymaker.[19] Nothing in the lawyer codes sheds any additional light.[20]

WESTLAW REFERENCES

45k146 "conting! fee" /s prohibit! forbid!

§ 9.5 TERMINATING CLIENT–LAWYER CONTRACTS

§ 9.5.1 Closing Representations

Signaling the Close of a Matter

It should be a standard practice for a lawyer to indicate in some definite way to every client when the lawyer's work is at an end. In cases involving successful outcomes, the closing usually takes the form of a cheerful parting of the ways after the client's final fee payment. But if the outcome is dour or inconclusive or if the representation has no clear point of resolution, it is highly desirable that the lawyer indicate to the client when the lawyer considers that the work that was to be done has been done. The ceremony need take only a short letter, possibly a cover letter to a final billing. Omitting it can lead

[14] Yermakov v. Fitzsimmons, 718 F.2d 1465 (9th Cir. 1983).

[15] Hausen v. Davis, 112 Misc.2d 992, 448 N.Y.S.2d 87, 89 (1981)(citing App.Div., 2d Dep't Rule 691.20(e)(7)).

[16] Minn.Stat.Ann. § 525.515.

[17] Marshall v. Baltimore & O. R.R., 57 U.S. (16 How.) 314, 14 L.Ed. 953 (1853); Noonan v. Gilbert, 68 F.2d 775 (D.C.Cir.1934); Page v. McKinley, 196 Ark. 331, 118 S.W.2d 235 (1938); In re Browning, 23 Ill.2d 483, 179 N.E.2d 14 (1961). See generally E.Wood, Fee Contracts of Lawyers § 89, at 268 (1936)(citing decisions from 1843 to 1926).

[18] The first Restatement of Contracts (1932), which in other respects was quite frumpy, provided evidence of the contemporary outlook on appropriate lobbying in § 559(1). The section provided in effect that a bargain to influence a legislative body or its members "by presenting facts and arguments to show that the desired action is of public advantage" was permissible. That went no further than Canon 26 of the 1908 Canons, which had already provided that a lawyer "may render professional services before legislative or other bodies . . . upon the same principles of ethics which justify his appearance before the Courts." The 1932 Restatement went on in § 563 to state that "the fact that the compensation fixed in a bargain for efforts to secure legislation or official action is contingent on success, is not conclusive evidence that improper means are contemplated in securing the desired results." In a backhanded way, the Restatement obviously takes the position that contingent fees for permissible professional lobbying efforts are not void. The first important decision to recognize the legitimacy of lobbying that properly and publicly seeks to present facts and arguments to persuade was Trist v. Child, 88 U.S. (21 Wall.) 441, 22 L.Ed. 623 (1874). See generally McDowell, The Legality of Lobbying Contracts, 41 Bost.U.L.Rev. 54 (1961).

[19] Hollister v. Ulvi, 199 Minn. 269, 271 N.W. 493 (1937); Herrick v. Barzee, 96 Or. 357, 190 P. 141 (1920); H.Drinker, Legal Ethics 177 (1953). See generally 1 S.Speiser, Attorneys' Fees § 2:4, at 86–88 (1973). Some of the cases distinguish between "favor" legislation, lobbying for which cannot be charged for on a contingent fee basis, and "debt" legislation, which can. E.g., Grover v. Merritt Development Co., 47 F.Supp. 309, 319 (N.D.Minn. 1942)(distinguishing "debt" cases, lobbying here was for a "favor" and thus tended to induce improper solicitation contrary to public policy).

[20] EC 2–20 rather timidly states (the problem of contingent fees for lobbying was well known at the time the Code was drafted) that "in administrative agency proceedings contingent fee contracts should be governed by the same consideration [sic] as in other civil cases."

to misunderstanding and the possibility of confusion in a later legal malpractice suit[21] about the nature of the client's expectations of further steps that the lawyer was to take.

Ideally withdrawal should be a clear-cut decision, and is best if concurred in by the client. But situations might develop in which contact with a client becomes spotty or poor. The client may, for example, have fallen behind in fee payments, or the lawyer may have come to believe that further representation may not be warranted because developments after the initial consultation indicate that the client's legal position is much weaker than first conceived. A lawyer in such cases may be tempted to temporize, doing nothing until the client gets back into contact with a request for information or action. Such a course, however, can find the lawyer defending his or her inaction in a legal malpractice action and, at the least, may produce the kind of communication breakdown that is the source of a great deal of client dissatisfaction.

It is far preferable for the lawyer to precipitate a client decision on whether or not to continue the matter or whether to continue the matter with another lawyer. The lawyer should take some definite step to do so, such as by sending a letter carefully explaining the reason why the representation has slowed and, if appropriate, indicating that the lawyer will consider that the client wishes the lawyer to cease the representation if no further word is received from the client.

Occasionally a representation may, or must, come to an end more abruptly, prior to the completion of the work that the client and lawyer agreed to at the outset. The lawyer codes define several circumstances in which that may occur. Sometimes termination comes about through the client's initiative, through *discharge*; sometimes it comes about through the intiative of the lawyer, through *withdrawal*.[22] The circumstances under which client discharge (§ 9.5.2), mandatory withdrawal (§ 9.5.4), and permissive withdrawal (§ 9.5.3) might occur are discussed at later points. Discussed here are the duties of a lawyer to protect the interests of the client when the representation comes to such a premature end.

Protecting a Client's Interests

However a representation comes to an end, a lawyer is required to take all appropriate steps to protect the client's interests.[23] By definition, all reasonably feasible steps to advance the client's ultimate objectives will have been taken if the representation has taken its full course. If the client's matter is still under way when the lawyer withdraws or is discharged, the lawyer has a responsibility to take reasonable steps in the course of, and consistent with, withdrawal to protect the client's interests. MR 1.16(d) describes the range of steps contemplated:[24]

> (d) Upon termination of representation, a lawyer shall take steps to the extent reasonably practicable to protect a client's interests, such as giving reasonable notice to the client, allowing time for employment of other counsel, surrendering papers and property to which the client is entitled and refunding any advance payment of fee that has not been earned. The lawyer may retain papers relating to the client to the extent permitted by law.

Clearly, withdrawal or discharge in some cases cannot occur as a clean break because of the lawyer's duty to protect client interests.[25] Courts have emphasized particularly the requirement of giving notice to the client in time to permit the client to obtain substitute

[21] For a collection of malpractice cases based on claims of improper lawyer withdrawal, see Annot., 6 A.L.R.4th 342 (1981).

[22] Withdrawal also describes the process that a lawyer must undertake to protect the client's interests as the lawyer disengages from the representation following discharge by the client.

[23] DR 2–110(A)(2); MR 1.16(d); Calif.R. 2–111(A)(2).

[24] DR 2–110(A)(2) is substantially similar, adding gratuitously that the lawyer should also "comply with applicable laws and rules," presumably referring to regulations governing withdrawal after a lawyer has entered an appearance in a hearing.

[25] See also ABA Formal Op. 90 (1932)(even if client agreed in advance that lawyer could withdraw at any time, lawyer could not withdraw under circumstances that client's interests would be prejudiced).

counsel.[26] Subject to the lawyer's right—which a lawyer would be wise almost invariably to ignore—to assert a lien against them (§ 9.6.3), the client's papers and other property [27] must be promptly turned over to the client or to substitute counsel.[28] Courts have disciplined a lawyer who, after withdrawal or discharge, neglected a client's interests to the serious detriment of the client.[29] An extreme form of the problem occurs when a lawyer abandons a law practice and fails to communicate that fact to clients and protect their interests.[30]

Court Permission to Withdraw

Whatever the basis on which a lawyer may wish or be forced to leave a representation, an overriding requirement is that the lawyer first comply with applicable law on withdrawing from pending litigation.[31] Particularly if the matter is on a trial calendar or is scheduled for a hearing, a lawyer may be required to file a motion to obtain court approval to withdraw. The rule is enforced with strictness in criminal cases [32] and usually includes notice to the lawyer's client.[33] Because of the constitutional right of the accused to counsel, a lawyer's absence from any important hearing or the trial itself precludes a criminal case from going forward. Because of demands of speedy trial rules and a social need for prompt disposition of criminal cases, a court will not permit withdrawal if the effect of granting the motion would be to require a continuance that would seriously disrupt the progress of the case or if prior continuances have already been granted.[34] If a lawyer has

[26] Atilus v. United States, 406 F.2d 694, 696 (5th Cir. 1969); Florida Bar v. Dingle, 220 So.2d 9 (Fla.1969); Stafford v. Dickison, 46 Hawaii 52, 374 P.2d 665 (1962); Lamphere v. State, 348 N.W.2d 212, 216 (Iowa 1984); Disciplinary Bd. v. McKennett, 349 N.W.2d 29 (N.D.1984); Sherman v. Heiser, 85 Wis.2d 246, 270 N.W.2d 397 (1978).

[27] With respect to the obligation to refund unearned fees, see § 9.5.2 infra at 546–47.

[28] Cf. EC 2–32; MR 1.16 comment (Assisting the Client Upon Withdrawal; first paragraph). E.g., Nolan v. Foreman, 665 F.2d 738, 742–43 (5th Cir.1982) (client has right under Texas law to return of papers from lawyer on request); In re Kaufman, 93 Nev. 452, 567 P.2d 957 (1977) (discipline of lawyer for refusal to return client's property unless fee contract was altered to increase lawyer's fee); Crawford v. Logan, 656 S.W.2d 360 (Tenn.1983)(lawyer code requires lawyer to deliver to client after discharge lawyer's tape recordings of interviews with woman who had allegedly engaged in adulterous relations with husband of lawyer's client); In re Lindberg, 103 Wis.2d 309, 307 N.W.2d 201 (1981)(discipline for failure to turn over client's papers). See also, e.g., Kallen v. Delug, 157 Cal. App.3d 940, 203 Cal.Rptr. 879 (1984)(contract under which successor counsel agreed to split fee with predecessor counsel, which latter had insisted upon before surrendering client's case files after discharge, void for illegality).

[29] Olguin v. State Bar, 28 Cal.3d 195, 167 Cal.Rptr. 876, 616 P.2d 858 (1980)(failure to promptly provide client with status reports and files on pending case and to promptly respond to inquiries from substitute counsel, with result that substitute counsel did not become counsel of record and client's action was dismissed for lack of prosecution); In re Price, 244 Ga. 532, 261 S.E.2d 349 (1979)(withdrawal without notifying client with result that statute of limitations ran on client's claim); State v. Smith, 228 Kan. 343, 614 P.2d 439 (1980)(failure to proceed with case tantamount to withdrawal without taking steps to protect client's interests); In re Rabb, 83 N.J. 109, 415 A.2d 1168 (1980)(violation of DR 2–110(A)(2) on several occasions when lawyer failed to take any action after initial consultation); Disciplinary Bd. v. McKennett, 349 N.W.2d 29 (N.D.1984)(discipline of lawyer for failure to attend hearing after withdrawal because client rejected settlement that lawyer had negotiated).

[30] People v. Archuleta, 638 P.2d 255 (Colo.1981); Attorney Grievance Comm'n v. Robinson, 287 Md. 690, 415 A.2d 289 (1980); In re Peters, 332 N.W.2d 10 (Minn.1983).

[31] DR 2–110(A)(1); MR 1.16; Calif.R. 2–111(A)(1). There is no corresponding rule in the 1983 Model Rules. Cf. MR 1.16(c)("When ordered to do so by a tribunal, a lawyer shall continue representation notwithstanding good cause for terminating the representation.").

[32] Rules of the U.S.Ct.Apps. for Sixth Circuit, Rule 12(f)(4); Lewis v. State, 279 Ark. 143, 649 S.W.2d 188 (1983); Archie v. State, 95 Nev. 746, 557 P.2d 1153 (1976)(contempt sanction for lawyer's failure to move to obtain permission of court to withdraw); People v. Hall, 46 N.Y.2d 873, 387 N.E.2d 610, 414 N.Y.S.2d 678, cert.denied, 444 U.S. 848, 100 S.Ct. 97, 62 L.Ed.2d 63 (1979).

[33] Turner v. McLain, 459 F.Supp. 898 (E.D.Ark.1978); Womack v. Warden, 95 Nev. 806, 603 P.2d 267 (1979); Miss.Uniform Chanc.Ct.R. 1.08.

[34] In re Cordova Gonzalez, 726 F.2d 16, 20–21 (lst Cir. 1984), cert. denied 466 U.S. 951, 104 S.Ct. 2154, 80 L.Ed. 2d 540 (1984); State v. Bogard, 312 S.E.2d 782 (W.Va.1984). A court may refuse to grant a motion to withdraw even for good cause, such as the client's failure to pay fees as agreed, if substantial burden would be cast on the court by permitting withdrawal. E.g., People v. Woods, 117 Misc.2d 1, 457 N.Y.S.2d 173 (1982). Cf., e.g., Anderson, Calder & Lembke v. District Court, 629 P.2d 603 (Colo.1981)(direction to trial court to permit lawyers for accused in criminal case to withdraw for nonpayment of fees when motion was presented twelve weeks before preliminary hearing and thus in ample time to permit

cause for withdrawal, a court may permit withdrawal despite the objection of the client.[35] If the court denies the right to withdraw, the lawyer's responsibility toward the client and the client's interests should not be diminshed.[36]

In civil cases the same requirements may also be enforced, although with less strictness.[37] In some jurisdictions a motion may not be required, but statutes and rules commonly require at least that a notice of withdrawal or substitution of lawyers be filed.[38] Courts will consider client interests in passing on a motion to withdraw, but they cannot alone dictate the court's action. In a civil suit, a court may permit withdrawal despite the fact that the client will then be unrepresented, even if the client is a corporation and thus unable to proceed pro se.[39]

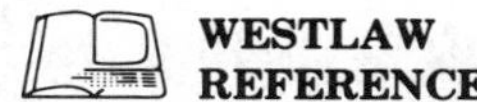
WESTLAW REFERENCES

Court Permission to Withdraw

dr2–110(a)(1) "dr 2–110(a)(1)" dr2–110(a)(2) "dr 2–110(a)(2)"

---

§ 9.5.2 Client Discharge

Right of Client to Discharge Lawyer

It is now uniformly recognized that the client-lawyer contract is terminable at will by the client. For good reasons, poor reasons, or the worst of reasons, a client may fire the lawyer.[40] The lawyer can discuss the matter with the client.[41] But if the client persists, the lawyer's only course is to complete the process of withdrawal.[42] Indeed, one of the four described circumstances mandating with-

substitute counsel to prepare). In some instances, however, a court may be compelled to permit a lawyer to withdraw, whatever the impact on scheduling. Thus, when a lawyer moves to withdraw at a late date because of a prejudicial conflict of interest and the accused has not knowingly and voluntarily waived the conflict, the withdrawal must be permitted. E.g., State v. West, 2 Kan.App.2d 297, 578 P.2d 287 (1978).

35 United States v. Clark, 429 F.Supp. 89 (W.D.Okl. 1976).

36 Pinnell v. Cauthron, 540 F.2d 938, 940 (8th Cir.1976) (reversal of conviction because of ineffective assistance of counsel on part of lawyer who, in irritation after motion to withdraw on ground of nonpayment of fees was denied, refused to conduct effective defense: "The bar's noble tradition of advocacy has here been abandoned for what only can be described as 'money grubbing.' ").

37 Mekdeci v. Merrell Nat'l Labs., 711 F.2d 1510 (11th Cir.1983); Washington v. Sherwin Real Estate, Inc., 694 F.2d 1081 (7th Cir.1982); In re Milovich, 105 Ill.App.3d 596, 61 Ill.Dec. 456, 434 N.E.2d 811 (1982); Catrone v. Catrone, 92 A.D.2d 559, 459 N.Y.S.2d 306 (1983); High Point Bank & Trust Co. v. Morgan-Schultheiss, Inc., 33 N.C.App. 406, 235 S.E.2d 693 (1977), cert.denied 439 U.S. 958, 99 S.Ct. 360, 58 L.Ed.2d 350 (1979); Cardot v. Luff, 262 S.E.2d 889, 892–93 (W.Va.1980). Cf., e.g., Sikes v. Segers, 266 Ark. 654, 587 S.W.2d 554, 557 (1979)(under facts here, abuse of discretion not to grant continuance after attempted discharge of lawyer when mutual mistrust had grown up between them as result of very recent event destroying basis for trust); Atlantic Commercial Dev. Corp. v. Nortek, 403 So.2d 624 (Fla.App.1981)(abuse of discretion to deny subtitution of counsel when case, although complex, was still in pleading stage). Notice of the lawyer's motion to withdraw should be served on the lawyer's client to permit the client to object or obtain substitute counsel. E.g., Sherman v. Heiser, 85 Wis.2d 246, 270 N.W.2d 397 (1978).

38 O'Connell, Goyak & Ball, P.C. v. Silbernagel, 297 Or. 207, 681 P.2d 1159, 1162 (1984). If the overcommitted trial schedule of an opposing lawyer precludes a reasonably prompt trial, a party may be able to move to have opposing counsel removed and the opposing party required to substitute a less-committed lawyer. E.g., Alex N. Sill Co. v. Fazio, 2 Ohio App.3d 65, 440 N.E.2d 807 (1981).

39 Thomas G. Ferruzzo, Inc. v. Superior Court, 104 Cal. App.3d 501, 163 Cal.Rptr. 573 (1980)(nonpayment of fees as agreed and noncooperation are cause for withdrawal).

40 No special formality is required for a client to repudiate a contract of representation. An act of the client indicating an unmistakable purpose to sever relations suffices. E.g., Belli v. Shaw, 98 Wn.2d 569, 657 P.2d 315, 319 (1983)(entering into new contract with new lawyers, with notice to original lawyer of his exclusion from the new agreement, operated as repudiation of old contingent fee contract on which original lawyer sought to recover). See also, e.g., Berry v. Zisman, 70 Mich.App. 376, 245 N.W.2d 758, 760 (1976)(filing action for legal malpractice amounts to discharge); Thomas v. Thomas, 178 Misc. 349, 34 N.Y.S.2d 320 (1942).

41 The Model Rules, in MR 1.16 comment (Discharge; second paragraph), note that a lawyer who is appointed by a court may be under special constraints. For the right of a criminal defendant to proceed pro se and the possibility that a court might reappoint the lawyer as "standby counsel," see § 14.4.2 (standby counsel). The third paragraph of the same comment notes that in some instances there might be a legitimate question of the competence of the client to discharge the lawyer.

42 In re Collins, 246 Ga. 325, 271 S.E.2d 473 (1980) (persistence in representing client after client had discharged lawyer); In re Gudmundson, 556 P.2d 212 (Utah 1976)(refusal to withdraw after discharge); In re Greenlee, 98 Wn.2d 786, 658 P.2d 1 (1983)(discipline of lawyer for refusal to withdraw after discharge by client). In a

drawal under DR 2–110(B) is when "(4) He is discharged by his client."[43] MR 1.16(a)(3) similarly mandates that the lawyer withdraw if "the lawyer is discharged."[44] Client discharge terminates the lawyer's right or responsibility to proceed with the representation. The court and opposing parties cannot continue to recognize the discharged lawyer against the expressed wish of the lawyer's client.[45] Discharge does not necessarily absolve the client of obligations and indeed may trigger obligations on the part of the client.[46]

Consequences of Discharge

The Model Rules wisely counsel a lawyer discharged by a client to put into writing the fact of discharge and the reasons for it.[47] Probably the best practice is to do so in the form of a courteous letter to the client that will also fulfill the purposes of a closing letter. As discussed above, the lawyer must take all necessary steps to protect client interests during the course of withdrawal following discharge. That includes cooperating with successor counsel in protecting the client's interests.[48] If the lawyer has entered an appearance, this should probably be withdrawn and steps taken to notify other parties to the litigation to avoid delay and confusion caused by service of papers on the wrong lawyer. Ordinarily the lawyer's withdrawal should be done in conjunction with substitute counsel's noting his or her appearance so that continuity of representation is assured.

Fee Refund after Discharge or Withdrawal

Any unearned fees, which should probably have been treated as trust funds until that point,[49] should be promptly returned to the client after discharge or withdrawal,[50] preferably with an accounting by way of a final billing statement. The rule, which is now recognized in almost every state that has passed on the question in the last decade, is that a client's discharge of a lawyer ends the lawyer's right to recover on the contract of employment. Thereafter a lawyer can only recover on the basis of quantum meruit—for the reasonable value of the lawyer's services, which in some cases will be less than the contract price.[51]

rare case, a judge may order a lawyer to continue with the representation despite the client's attempted discharge. Whether or not the lawyer agrees with the order, and whether or not the lawyer has independent justification for withdrawing, MR 1.16(c) requires the lawyer to continue with the representation.

43 Inexplicably, the California Rule of Professional Conduct on mandatory withdrawal, Rule 2–111(B), which in every other respect essentially copies the language of the ABA's DR 2–110(B), omits discharge by the client as a reason for mandatory discharge.

44 MR 1.16 comment (Discharge; first paragraph): "A client has a right to discharge a lawyer at any time, with or without cause, subject to liability for payment for the lawyer's services."

45 Tobias v. King, 84 Ill.App.3d 998, 40 Ill.Dec. 400, 402, 406 N.E.2d 101, 103 (1980).

46 Haller v. Wallis, 89 Wn.2d 539, 573 P.2d 1302, 1307 (1978)(construing, West's Rev.Code Wash.Ann. 2.44.040–2.44.050(2) to preclude party from making substitution of counsel without court approval where predecessor counsel's fees have not been paid).

47 MR 1.16 comment (Discharge; first paragraph).

48 For one view of the etiquette of relationships between original and successor lawyers, see generally H.Drinker, Legal Ethics 198–201 (1953).

49 See § 4.8. at 178–79.

50 DR 2–110(A)(3); EC 2–32; MR 1.16(d). E.g., People v. Johnson, 199 Colo. 248, 612 P.2d 1097 (1980)(discipline for retaining unearned advance payment of fees after discharge); Florida Bar v. Fussell, 390 So.2d 68 (Fla.1980) (discipline for delay of several months in returning unearned portion of fee: "Unearned fees do not belong to a lawyer when the attorney-client relationship ends. The lawyer has no further custodial rights to these funds. For the welfare of clients, as well as the image of the individual lawyer and of the organized bar, a prompt refund of unearned fees is dictated."); In re Burr, 267 S.C. 419, 228 S.E.2d 678 (1976)(disbarment for, among other things, withdrawal without permission of tribunal and failure to refund promptly unearned fees paid in advance).

51 State Farm Mut. Ins. Co. v. St. Joseph's Hospital, 107 Ariz. 498, 489 P.2d 837 (1971); Fracasse v. Brent, 6 Cal.3d 784, 100 Cal.Rptr. 385, 494 P.2d 9 (1972); Rosenberg v. Levin, 409 So.2d 1016 (Fla.1982)(on rehearing and reargument); Rhoades v. Norfolk & W.Ry., 78 Ill.2d 217, 35 Ill. Dec. 680, 399 N.E.2d 969 (1979); Martin v. Camp, 219 N.Y. 170, 114 N.E. 46 (1932); Belli v. Shaw, 98 Wn.2d 569, 657 P.2d 315 (1983). But cf., e.g., Anderson v. Gailey, 100 Idaho 796, 606 P.2d 90 (1980)(wrongfully discharged lawyer can recover full contingent fee less amount of expenses lawyer was saved by not being required to complete contract). See generally Annot., 92 ALR3d 690 (1979). See also Demov, Morris, Levin & Shein v. Glantz, 53 N.Y.2d 553, 444 N.Y.S.2d 55, 428

The rule recognizing the right of discharge and relegating a discharged lawyer to a quantum meruit recovery applies to contingent fee contracts, the type of contract involved in most of the reported cases. According to the majority rule, if a client discharges a lawyer without cause under a contingent fee contract, the lawyer has no right to recover a fee, even on a quantum meruit theory, until the happening of the event on which the fee is contingent.[52] Moreover, the amount of quantum meruit recovery should in no case exceed the contract fee. That limitation is necessary to permit the client to exercise the right to discharge with some notion of the ceiling on the additional fee liability that the client must face.[53] If the contract has been substantially performed—for example, a client under a contingent fee contract waits to discharge the lawyer until a favorable settlement offer has been received—courts hold that the lawyer can recover on the contract if the discharge was without cause.[54]

The rationale supporting the rule relegating a discharged lawyer to a quantum meruit recovery is discussed in Fracasse v. Brent,[55] the leading case.[56] The court reasoned that putting the client to the risk of having to pay possibly duplicate fees to two lawyers—the discharged lawyer and substitute counsel—for the same representation would seriously chill the client's right to discharge. The right to discharge, in turn, is vital because without it a client would be forced to proceed with a lawyer whom, for whatever reason, the client no longer trusts. Some pre-*Fracasse* authority, it should be noted, disagreed over the effect of a no-cause discharge on the lawyer's right to retain a client's former payment of a retainer fee if the lawyer's customary hourly charge would not already have used up the amount paid.[57] Given the rationale that strongly discourages chilling the client's right to discharge for any reason, the view is a sound one that no retainer should penalize a client. Thus no retainer should be nonrefundable to the extent that it exceeds a reasonable fee.[58]

N.E.2d 387 (1981)(lawyer may not recover on theory that former client fraudulently induced lawyers to enter into retainer agreement with hidden intent to repudiate it).

52 Fracasse v. Brent, supra; Rosenberg v. Levin, supra; Plaza Shoe Store, Inc. v. Hermel, Inc., 636 S.W.2d 53 (Mo. 1982). Contra, e.g., Becnel v. Arnouville, 425 So.2d 972 (La.App.1983)(after client discharged lawyer without cause, successor counsel lost jury verdict; first lawyer entitled to quantum meruit recovery); Tillman v. Komar, 259 N.Y. 133, 181 N.E. 75 (1932).

53 Rosenberg v. Levin, supra; Chambliss, Bahner & Crawford v. Luther, 531 S.W.2d 108 (Tenn.App.1975). An example of the contrary rule is In re Montgomery, 272 N.Y. 323, 6 N.E.2d 40 (1936)(lawyer, who had completed five-sixths of work for which he was to be paid $5,000, on no-cause discharge by client entitled to award of $13,000 as quantum meruit damages).

54 Kaushiva v. Hutter, 454 A.2d 1373 (D.C.App.1983), cert.denied 464 U.S. 820, 104 S.Ct. 83, 78 L.Ed.2d 93 (1983); Salem Realty Co. v. Matera, 384 Mass. 803, 426 N.E.2d 1160 (1981). If a lawyer is discharged without cause, the lawyer cannot be forced to take his or her quantum meruit recovery out of the fee to be received by substitute counsel, but the client must pay the first lawyer independently of any contractual undertaking that the client might have with substitute counsel. E.g., Adams v. Fisher, 390 So.2d 1248 (Fla.App.1980).

55 6 Cal.3d 784, 100 Cal.Rptr. 385, 494 P.2d 9 (1972).

56 It is a bit mysterious that a case as late as *Fracasse* is treated, as it is, as the leading case. In 1920 a standard treatise on lawyers declared the same rule. See G.Warvelle, Essays in Legal Ethics 183 (2d ed.1920).

57 Compare, e.g., LaRocco v. Bakwin, 108 Ill.App.3d 723, 64 Ill.Dec. 286, 439 N.E.2d 537 (1982)(even under lifetime retainer agreement, client's no-cause discharge converted lawyer's claim to retainer payment into a claim for quantum meruit recovery against it); Richette v. Solomon, 410 Pa. 6, 187 A.2d 910 (1963)(clause in retainer agreement purporting to make it irrevocable by client is invalid), with, e.g., Meagher v. Kavli, 251 Minn. 477, 88 N.W.2d 871 (1958)(lawyer not required to return any portion of retainer fee after no-cause discharge by client).

58 Jacobson v. Sassower, 122 Misc.2d 863, 474 N.Y.S.2d 167 (1983), affirmed 107 A.D.2d 603, 438 N.Y.S.2d 711 (1985). The effect of Calif.R. 2–111(A)(3) is unclear. It provides that on withdrawal a lawyer "shall refund promptly any part of a fee paid in advance that has not been earned," as do the Code and Model Rules. But it continues: "However, this rule shall not be applicable to a true retainer fee which is paid solely for the purpose of insuring the availability of the attorney for the matter." The rule is equally susceptible to two readings. In one, a retainer fee is nonrefundable simply by denominating it a "true retainer" or the like in the fee contract. A second interpretation is more likely in view of other California rules and of the California supreme court's views on the client's right to discharge. That is that a retainer is nonrefundable to the extent that it reasonably compensates a lawyer (subject to California's shock-the-conscience standard of testing fees) for the lawyer's arrangements necessitated by undertaking the retainer.

WESTLAW REFERENCES

Right of Client to Discharge Lawyer

dr2–110(b) "dr 2–110(b)" attorney-client /s terminat! discharge*

Fee Refund After Discharge or Withdrawal

dr2–110(a)(3) "dr 2–110(a)(3)" /s discharge* withdraw! /s refund! return! /3 fee

"conting! fee" /s discharge* withdraw! /s "quantum meruit"

---

§ 9.5.3 Permissive Lawyer Withdrawal

Permissive Withdrawal under the Lawyer Codes

Both the 1969 Code and the 1983 Model Rules list a number of situations in which a lawyer can elect to terminate a representation. The grounds stated are similar in the two sets of rules but are not the same. The California rule, rule 2–111(C), traces the Code language on permissive withdrawal in all material respects.

The Code lists in DR 2–110(C)(1) a number of discretionary grounds, most of which have to do with the client's rejecting the lawyer's sound advice, such as by urging the lawyer to file a groundless action or to take a course of action that is illegal or in violation of a Disciplinary Rule. The lawyer may also withdraw if the spurned advice is based on the lawyer's nonlegal judgment, at least with respect to a matter not pending before a court.[59] A lawyer may also withdraw if continuing the relationship is "likely" to result in a violation of a Disciplinary Rule;[60] an inability to work with cocounsel might impair the client's best interests;[61] the lawyer's physical or mental condition makes it difficult for the lawyer to carry out the representation effectively;[62] the client knowingly and freely consents;[63] or, in a matter before a court, the lawyer believes that the court will find that other good grounds permit withdrawal.[64]

Model Rule 1.16(b) contains a list of permissible withdrawal situations that in most respects matches the Code. A preliminary clarification that emerges only with some difficulty from the language of the rule is that it encompasses two sets of permissive withdrawal situations. The first set is mentioned in an almost offhand way in the main text of MR 1.16(b) itself—withdrawal is always permissible when withdrawal would cause the client no material adverse effect. The second set is the group of numbered situations that follows. It seems clearly intended that a lawyer is permitted to withdraw in those situations even if withdrawal would have a materially prejudicial impact on the client's interests.

According to the specific list in MR 1.16(b), a lawyer may withdraw if the client persists in a course of conduct that the lawyer reasonably believes is criminal or fraudulent (MR 1.16(b)(1)) or the lawyer discovers that in the past the client has used the lawyer's services to perpetrate a crime or fraud (MR 1.16(b)(2)).[65] The reason for withdrawal in such a case is largely reputational. Even if a lawyer does not assist such client conduct, as a lawyer clearly could not, a lawyer is entitled to protect his or her professional and personal reputation and possibly protect a future position as a defendant in a civil or criminal

59 DR 2–110(C)(1)(e).

60 DR 2–110(C)(2). Cf. DR 2–110(B)(2)(mandatory withdrawal if lawyer knows or it is obvious that continuing the representation "will" result in violation of a Disciplinary Rule).

61 DR 2–110(C)(3).

62 DR 2–110(C)(4). Cf. DR 2–110(B)(3)(mandatory withdrawal if lawyer's physical or mental condition makes it "unreasonably" difficult to carry out representation).

63 DR 2–110(C)(5).

64 DR 2–110(C)(6). E.g., Legal Aid Society v. Rothwax, 69 A.D.2d 801, 415 N.Y.S.2d 432 (1979)(lawyer may withdraw if client threatens lawyer with physical violence); Lasser v. Nassau Community College, 91 A.D.2d 973, 457 N.Y.S.2d 343 (1983)(client's requirement that lawyer seek approval of all future actions from another lawyer representing client in related matter was tantamount to lawyer's being superseded by another lawyer and justified withdrawal).

65 The first of those grounds roughly matches DR 2–110(C)(1)(b). But the second ground has no related provision in the Code, which apparently would require a lawyer to continue a representation if the only ground for withdrawal were past misuse of a lawyer's services.

action by refusing to be associated with a perpetrator of the described conduct.[66] Beyond legality, a lawyer may withdraw if the client insists on pursuing a course or an objective that the lawyer considers repugnant or imprudent (MR 1.16(b)(3)), even if the conduct is permissible in every legal sense. As will be discussed below, MR 1.16(b)(4) and (b)(5) apparently expand a lawyer's right to withdraw from unprofitable legal work. And MR 1.16(b)(6) provides a second catchall basis for withdrawal [67] when "other good cause" exists.

Strangely, neither the Code nor the Rules seem to acknowledge several grounds that are common reasons for withdrawal and are so recognized by courts. The most important of the additional reasons are irreparable breakdown of the relationship because of conflict or antagonism between client and lawyer that might have nothing to do with the direction of the legal matter but much to do with personality differences [68] and the unreasonable failure of a client to stay in communication with the lawyer.[69]

Permissive Withdrawal for Client Nonpayment of Fees

Fee problems can lead to withdrawal. A lawyer may come to a point and realize that further work will only create a net loss. That may occur either because the client has failed to make scheduled fee payments or because the lawyer realizes in the light of subsequent developments that the fee initially agreed to was too low.

A lawyer has the right to withdraw in the one but not in the other of the two situations. A client's failure to pay fees or costs as agreed permits withdrawal if the failure is clear and substantial.[70] Occasionally the client's failure is due to the client's general disappearance with neither communication nor fee payment.[71] Nothing, of course, requires the lawyer to insist on a fee payment and often lawyers complete work for clients who have encountered unexpected reversals in their fortunes. If the lawyer intends, however, to insist on payment of past due fees and to withdraw if they are not paid, the lawyer must take definite action. Model Rule 1.16(b)(4) requires the lawyer to give the client a reasonable warning that the lawyer will withdraw unless the client's obligation is fulfilled.[72] As is true of permissive withdrawals generally, the lawyer's action must be clear-cut.[73] The lawyer may not simply fail to take

[66] MR 1.16 comment (Optional Withdrawal; first paragraph).

[67] The first catchall basis for withdrawal is no-adverse-effect withdrawal under the initial language in MR 1.16(b)). See infra at 550–51.

[68] United States v. Mills, 597 F.2d 693, 700 (9th Cir. 1979)(irreconcilable conflict "so great that it resulted in a total lack of communication preventing an adequate defense"); Sikes v. Segers, 266 Ark. 654, 587 S.W.2d 554, 557 (1979)(mutal distrust and antagonism between client and lawyer, destroying basis for trust, required grant of lawyer's motion to withdraw); Landry v. Faulkner, 417 So.2d 1376, 1379 (La.App.1982), writ denied 420 So.2d 985 (1982); Watson v. Black, 161 W.Va. 46, 239 S.E.2d 664 (1977).

[69] Harris v. Wabaunsee, 593 P.2d 86 (Okl.1979).

[70] DR 2–110(C)(1)(f)(lawyer may withdraw if client "deliberately disregards an agreement or obligation to the lawyer as to expenses or fees."); MR 1.16(b)(4)(lawyer may withdraw if "the client fails substantially to fulfill an obligation to the lawyer regarding the lawyer's services and has been given reasonable warning that the lawyer will withdraw unless the obligation is fulfilled."). See also MR 1.16 comment (Optional Withdrawal; second paragraph). E.g., Cullen v. Olins Leasing, Inc., 91 A.D.2d 537, 457 N.Y.S.2d 9 (1982), appeal dismissed 61 N.Y.2d 867, 474 N.Y.S.2d 479, 462 N.E.2d 1197 (1984)(on insolvency of insurer who had hired lawyer to defend insured, lawyer entitled to withdraw for nonpayment of fee despite fact that insured would be left without representation).

[71] Hancock v. Mutual of Omaha Ins. Co., 472 A.2d 867, 869 (D.C.App.1984).

[72] As always, a lawyer must protect a client's interests even if withdrawal is for good cause. A lawyer who had good cause to withdraw because of the client's nonpayment of fees was nonetheless held to have breached an obligation to the client by refusing to take reasonably available steps to avoid serious detriment to the client. See Beatty v. LaSonde, 147 Ga.App. 138, 248 S.E.2d 202 (1978)(lawyer who refused to proceed with client's appeal because of client's failure to pay fees could not recover for work partially completed because of failure to protect against dismissal of client's appeal).

[73] Davis v. State Bar, 33 Cal.3d 231, 188 Cal.Rptr. 441, 444, 655 P.2d 1276, 1279 (1983)(lawyer could not excuse failure to proceed with client's claim on ground of unarticulated and uninvestigated doubts about veracity of

further action in the client's matter[74] but should communicate to the client that the lawyer will withdraw unless the fee payment is made. As with all withdrawals, court permission must be obtained if local rules require it.[75]

When the fee problem is not caused by the client's nonpayment but by the fact that the lawyer's own agreement was improvident, the Code and the Model Rules give apparently conflicting answers. Under the Code, the fact that a lawyer has made an improvident fee contract does not give the lawyer a ground for withdrawal.[76] A lawyer may ask the client to renegotiate the fee contract.[77] But if the client is unwilling to pay more, the lawyer must live with the fee contract as originally agreed.[78] As a matter of contract law, if the lawyer refuses to complete work already undertaken because of the lawyer's dissatisfaction with the client's bargain, the lawyer has breached their contract and possibly may not even recover for partial work already completed. By contrast, under Model Rule 1.16(b)(5) a lawyer apparently may withdraw, even if in breach of a contract,[79] if continuing with the representation "will result in an unreasonable[80] financial burden on the lawyer."

Limits of Permissive Withdrawal

Ordinarily a lawyer who accepts a representation undertakes to see the task through to its completion.[81] A lawyer clearly may not withdraw without a reason if to do so would materially prejudice the client's interests.[82] But if withdrawal would not have that effect, may a lawyer withdraw for no reason or for a not very appealing reason, such as to pursue recreational interests or because the lawyer would prefer to make a higher fee doing extensive work for a new and wealthier client?[83] Model Rule 1.16(b) states, in effect, that an independent circumstance justifying

client; lawyer had to resolve doubts and either withdraw or proceed).

74 Fitzpatrick v. State Bar, 20 Cal.3d 73, 141 Cal.Rptr. 169, 569 P.2d 763 (1977); In re Ambrose, 93 Ill.2d 42, 66 Ill.Dec. 339, 442 N.E.2d 900 (1982)(discipline of lawyer for simply failing to proceed further with client's divorce but without taking definite steps to collect unpaid fee or to withdraw).

75 Courts will not invariably grant withdrawals for nonpayment of legal fees. E.g., Charles Weiner Corp. v. D.Jack Davis Corp., 113 Misc.2d 263, 448 N.Y.S.2d 998 (Civ.Ct.1982).

76 That is implicitly evident from the wording of DR 2–110(C)(1)(f), which recognizes permissive withdrawal only when the client breaches a fee agreement.

77 Midstream fee changes that benefit the lawyer are viewed by courts with great suspicion, and the lawyer will have the burden of justifying the alteration. See § 9.2.1, at 503–04.

78 Lavenson v. Wise, 131 Cal. 369, 63 P. 622 (1901) (lawyer could not ignore contingent fee agreement to collect note, and pursue recovery on quantum meruit basis after suit was unsuccessful); Reynolds v. Sorosis Fruit Co., 133 Cal. 625, 66 P. 21 (1901)(fact that over $4,000 worth of legal services was expended by lawyer in successful prosecution of suit did not warrant award to lawyer in excess of $400 contingent fee agreed to at outset); Burns v. Valene, 298 Minn. 257, 214 N.W.2d 686 (1974)(when client lied to lawyer about prior claims and was compelled to accept token settlement when defense lawyer produced records of twenty-eight previous lawsuits, client's lawyer not entitled to recover on quantum meruit basis because lawyer entered into contingent fee contract and had suspicions, which he did not pursue, that client was not telling truth). See also, e.g., Kansas Bar Ass'n v. Mayes, 216 Kan. 38, 531 P.2d 102 (1975) (disbarment for, among other things, refusal to proceed with undertaken patent applications unless clients paid additional fees).

79 The limitation that a lawyer may withdraw only if that does not cause a materially adverse effect to the interests of the client, mentioned in MR 1.16(b), is an alternative ground for withdrawal and does not seem to limit the six specific grounds listed in the remainder of the rule. Moreover, the client-protecting steps required in MR 1.16(d) are relevant only to the ongoing process of withdrawal; they do not limit the right to withdraw.

80 "Unreasonable," as is notorious, is hardly precise. Its use here appears to refer to the degree of financial hardship under which a lawyer suffers because of the low fee, or possibly because of the absence of a fee as where the lawyer undertook a court-appointed representation. Alternatively, it might be read more expansively to refer as well to contract law, so that withdrawal in breach of contract would not be "reasonable." The discussion in the text, perhaps erroneously, assumes the former reading.

81 MR 1.16 comment (first paragraph).

82 MR 1.16(b). Cf. DR 2–110(A)(2).

83 The example of a possibly f volous reason is illustrative and not exhaustive. Consider a lawyer who has taken on too many clients and finds that, as a result of the large time commitment required, his or her relationship with family members is suffering, although the lawyer is able to continue to represent clients "effectively" within the meaning of DR 2–110(C)(4). To spend more time with his or her family, may a lawyer withdraw from the representation of several clients without preju-

withdrawal is "if withdrawal can be accomplished without material adverse effect on the interests of the client." [84] The Code's DR 2–110(C) is rather clearly opposed. It provides that a lawyer may not request permission to withdraw in a court matter and may not withdraw in other matters unless one of a limited number of grounds applies. Under DR 2–110(C)(5) a lawyer may withdraw if the client knowingly and freely assents, but in other situations good cause is required.[85] Thus the Code does not allow a withdrawal without consent even if withdrawal would not harm an interest of the client. As a disciplinary rule, the approach of the Model Rules is preferable. As a statement about minimal loyalty toward a client and appropriate attitude toward undertakings, the Code speaks on a higher plane. For the purposes of disciplinary enforcement, the two are functionally the same, for it is not likely that a disciplinary body would proceed against a lawyer for a violation of the withdrawal rules in the absence of harm to a client.

WESTLAW REFERENCES

Permissive Withdrawal Under the Lawyer Codes

dr2–110(c) "dr 2–110(C)"

Permissive Withdrawal for Client for Nonpayment of Fees

attorney lawyer counsel** /s withdraw! /s fee /3 unpaid nonpay! (fail*** declin*** +2 pay)

§ 9.5.4 *Mandatory Lawyer Withdrawal*

Mandatory Withdrawal under the Lawyer Codes

The 1969 Code and the 1983 Model Rules also delimit, in roughly parallel fashion, situations in which a lawyer is compelled to withdraw from representing a client. The California rule (rule 2–111(B)) traces the Code, except that it provides no similar rule for mandatory withdrawal after client discharge.[86] No element of the lawyer's discretion is involved, although the general rule of protecting client interests in the process of withdrawal (§ 9.5.1) may affect the timing of withdrawal.

The mandatory withdrawal rules also serve as rules of mandatory nonrepresentation. If a lawyer knows from an initial consultation with a client that circumstances exist that would bring one of the mandatory withdrawal rules into play, the lawyer may not, sensibly enough, even begin the representation.

Both lawyer codes state essentially three [87] situations in which a lawyer must withdraw. They relate to the illegal or unethical nature of work that the representation would require, to the lawyer's physical or mental in-

dicing them further than by necessitating their finding new counsel? The question, of course, might be answered differently as a matter of professional discipline, contract law, and personal morality.

[84] See also MR 1.16 comment (Optional Withdrawal; first paragraph)("A lawyer may withdraw in some circumstances. A lawyer has the option to withdraw if it can be accomplished without material adverse effect on the client's interests. Withdrawal is also justified" on other grounds). Presumably, prejudice to a client would include unusual difficulty in obtaining substitute counsel or an increase in the client's fees because of the need to retain new counsel.

While the right to casually withdraw is thus rather clearly stated in MR 1.16(b), it is internally inconsistent with other parts of the same rule, such as MR 1.16(b)(4), which requires a lawyer first to warn a client before withdrawing for nonpayment of fees. See supra at n. 72. If withdrawal in such a case would not prejudice the client, why is a warning required?

[85] MR 1.16 does not provide an explicitly similar rule. Presumably, however, withdrawal with client consent would be warranted under MR 1.16(b)(6)("other good cause for withdrawal exists"). The 1908 Canons, in Canon 44, seemed to announce a very different rule. A lawyer could withdraw only for "good cause," and purportedly not even the desire or consent of the client would always suffice. Only "reasons of honor or self-respect" warranted withdrawal under Canon 44. That extravagant notion was not carried forward into the 1969 Code or the 1983 Model Rules.

[86] See supra n. 43.

[87] DR 2–110(B) lists four. But the first, relating to harassing litigation, is itself a violation of the Code (DR 7–102(A)(1)) and thus also a mandatory basis for withdrawal under DR 2–110(B)(2). Presumably harassment is independently mentioned for emphasis and because it relates so closely to the use of the rule to limit accepting representations. The omission of a similarly specific mention in MR 1.16(a) is probably merely stylistic.

ability to carry the representation through, and to the client's right to discharge the lawyer.

(1) If continuing in the representation will result in the lawyer's violating the lawyer code, the lawyer must withdraw (DR 2–110(B)(2); MR 1.16(a)(1)). (The Model Rules also require withdrawal if the representation will result in the lawyer's violation of "other law." [88]) Some applications of the rule will be clear, others obscure. If the representation involves an impermissible conflict of interest, for example, the lawyer must either resolve the conflict through client consent or withdraw. The choices are sharply etched. But suppose a client announces to the lawyer an intention to commit a securities fraud using the lawyer's services. In one view of it, it seems that the lawyer may, but need not, withdraw. Because the lawyer presumably will refuse to participate in the securities violation, because law and the professional rules require it, the lawyer will not violate any law or rule. The comment to MR 1.6 [89] is apparently carefully worded to indicate that it is only when the lawyer's conduct will indeed violate a mandatory rule that the lawyer is forced to withdraw. Nonetheless, courts have occasionally stated that when a client insists that a lawyer pursue a course of conduct that, if the lawyer complied, would violate the lawyer code or other applicable law, the lawyer must withdraw even if the lawyer has no intention of following the intentions of the client.[90]

(2) A lawyer must withdraw if the lawyer's physical or mental condition renders it impossible or unreasonably difficult for the lawyer to provide effective representation.[91] The rule is one that reinforces the competence requirements and complements the needs of courts and other legal agencies for expedition.[92]

(3) The clearest instance of mandatory withdrawal is when the client discharges the lawyer, which the client has the right to do at any time (§ 9.5.2). Discharge makes it imperative that the lawyer withdraw and leave the field clear for substitute counsel to take over the client's matter.[93] The client's reasons for discharge may be good, bad,[94] or nonexistent. The client's freedom to discharge the lawyer at any time would be nugatory unless the lawyer were required to withdraw.

[88] There is no other general obligation, under either the Model Rules or the Code, that a lawyer obey the law. Several provisions require obedience to various laws or types of laws. The broadest of those are MR 8.4(b), (c), and (d) in the Model Rules and DR 1–102(A)(3), (4), (5), and (6) in the Code. Suppose that a lawyer is asked by a client who is a foreign country to engage in some emergency legal work. Assume that applicable law requires the lawyer to register as the agent of a foreign country before undertaking any legal work with—we will assume, probably inaccurately—only a fine as the penalty for noncompliance. Undertaking the work without registering first seems to violate the Model Rules (MR 1.16(a)(1)) but not the Code.

[89] MR 1.6 comment (Withdrawal; first paragraph)("If the lawyer's services will be used by the client in materially furthering a course of criminal or fraudulent conduct, the lawyer must withdraw, as stated in Rule 1.16(a)(1).").

[90] People v. Schultheis, 638 P.2d 8, 13 (Colo.1981)(lawyer whose client insists that lawyer present third-party perjured testimony must move to withdraw).

[91] Riccio v. Committee on Professional Standards, 75 A.D.2d 687, 426 N.Y.S.2d 887 (1980)(suspension for, among other things, failure to withdraw from representation of convicted person with pending appeal after lawyer's open-heart surgery required absence from office for several months); In re Gudmundson, 556 P.2d 212 (Utah 1976)(failure to withdraw when physically incapable of continuing work after eye surgery for cataracts).

[92] Green v. Forney Eng'g Co., 589 F.2d 243, 247–48 (5th Cir.1979).

[93] Taylor v. Board of Educ., 187 N.J.Super. 546, 455 A.2d 552, 555 (1983), certification denied 95 N.J. 227, 470 A.2d 441 (1983)(duty of lawyer for school board to withdraw on notice of discharge takes precedence over claim of lawyer to veteran's preference rights under statute); Heinzman v. Fine, Fine, Legum & Fine, 217 Va. 958, 234 S.E.2d 282 (1977); In re Greenlee, 98 Wn.2d 786, 658 P.2d 1 (1983)(discipline for refusal to withdraw after client discharge).

[94] Cf. Note, A Remedy for the Discharge of Professional Employees Who Refuse to Perform Unethical or Illegal Acts: A Proposal in Aid of Professional Ethics, 28 Vand. L.Rev. 805 (1975).

WESTLAW REFERENCES

Mandatory Withdrawal Under the Lawyer Codes

dr2–110(b) "dr 2–110(b)"

§ 9.6 LAWYERS' CLAIMS FOR COMPENSATION

§ 9.6.1 Fee Disputes and Suits

General

Most lawyer bills are eventually paid by clients. In some instances, however, a client will dispute the bill and refuse to pay all or part of it. A conscientious lawyer will then be faced with the prospect of either surrendering what the lawyer considers to be a just claim for compensation or of confronting a client or former client with a demand for payment. Debt collection can be messy business under the relatively anonymous circumstances of ordinary collection practice. When it is pursued against a former ally by a former fiduciary the chances for misunderstanding and bitterness are great, even if the lawyer is careful to avoid abuse and overreaching.[95] Some lawyers under those circumstances do not insist that a client pay a questioned bill, either because of the valued relationship with the client or on a general principle of never becoming involved in fee disputes. As well as providing an occasionally uplifting moment free of the nastiness of commercialism, such a policy may also have the more pragmatic consequences of avoiding emotional upset, loss of goodwill, and possible legal malpractice suits from clients driven to thoughts of retaliation.[96] In addition, lawyers are probably sometimes deterred by the wish not to reveal client confidential information, although the lawyer codes provide that a lawyer is entitled to reveal such information, if necessary, to collect the fee.[97]

Suits for Fees

There is no rule of law or ethics that requires a lawyer inevitably to accept a client's position on a fee dispute.[98] The Code, in EC 2–23, urges lawyers to avoid fee disputes zealously and to attempt to resolve any differences with clients over fees amicably.[99] A

[95] For a rogue's gallery of inappropriate fee collection practices that have led to discipline, see Annot., 91 A.L.R.3d 583 (1979).

[96] According to one study, the percentage of legal malpractice claims arising out of client claims of excessive fee charges was almost as high as claims generated by conflicts of interest and higher than claims arising out of trial malpractice. See Pfennigstorf, Types and Causes of Lawyers' Professional Liability Claims: The Search for Facts, 1980 Am.B.Found. Research J. 255, 272. A specialist in legal malpractice has estimated that from 20 percent to perhaps more than 30 percent of legal malpractice claims and counterclaims arise from fee disputes. Smith, The Pitfalls of Suing Clients for Fees, 69 ABA J. 776, 779 (1983).

[97] See § 6.7.8.

[98] But cf. In re Estate of Wilisch, 384 So.2d 223 (Fla. App.1980)(unsupported statement that lawyer may not ethically file suit against former client for fee until lawyer's motion to withdraw from representation has been granted). Much fuss is sometimes made about the altruism of the English barrister, who is forbidden by professional honor from suing for a fee. E.g., W.Taft, Ethics in Service 8–9 (1915). The picture is somewhat overdrawn. A rule of etiquette, enforced by professional discipline, is that the solicitor who hired the barrister for the client is personally liable to pay the barrister's fee whether or not the solicitor has received funds from the client for that purpose. See F.Bennion, Professional Ethics 174 (1969); T.Lund, A Guide to the Professional Conduct and Etiquette of Solicitors 72 (1960).

[99] A footnote to EC 2–23 cites ABA 1908 Canon 14 ("Controversies concerning compensation are to be avoided by the lawyer so far as shall be compatible with his self-respect and with his right to receive reasonable recompense for his services; and lawsuits with clients should be resorted to only to prevent injustice, imposition or fraud.").

There is no corresponding expression of sentiment in the 1983 Model Rules. An early draft contained a relatively strong statement in a comment concerning fee disputes. See MR 1.6 comment (Dispute over Fees; first paragraph)(Public Discussion Draft, January 30, 1980):

> A lawyer should hesitate to engage in a dispute with a client over a fee. The lawyer should see that the terms of the fee are understood, thus minimizing the possibility of a dispute. A lawyer should not sue for a fee unless the claim is fully justified. If a suit is necessary, the lawyer's superior knowledge of the situation should carry with it the burden of persuasion. If a procedure has been established for resolution of fee disputes, such as an arbitration or mediation procedure established by the bar, the lawyer should abide by it.

While each of those sentiments finds ample support in fee-dispute decisions, commentators were concerned that courts might enforce them as mandatory rules in professional discipline cases. See Schneyer, The Model Rules lawyer who resorts frequently to fee suits, heedless of any restraint, has been disciplined.[1] But suits are not discouraged if "necessary to prevent fraud or gross imposition by the client." [2] Fee suits can be ugly affairs. As mentioned, in filing an answer, a client might feel that a whiff of grapeshot by way of a counterclaim for legal malpractice damages is justified by the facts. The lawyer suing for fees often appears pro se, creating an imbalance of expenditures for legal services that might prove particularly galling to a nonlawyer client. The lawyer's access to the client's deepest confidences, and the realization that these can be spread abroad in the fee suit, may appear treacherously near blackmail.[3]

Judicial Supervision of Fee Suits

Fee suits appear from a distance to be basically suits to recover on a breach of contract or, in some instances, to recover for the reasonable value of personal services. But on closer inspection, the law in virtually every state is clear that lawyers suing clients are not treated as are merchants suing former trading partners.[4] The procedural and remedial landscape is much narrower and more tightly regulated. The burden is on the lawyer to present detailed evidence of services actually rendered.[5] Courts uniformly employ the lawyer codes as limits on the size of a reasonable fee.[6] The use of a confession of judgment note, although countenanced as legitimate in most states, has been condemned when used by a lawyer to collect a fee from a client.[7] If a client defaults in a lawyer's fee suit, courts will go to extra lengths to set the default aside if the value of the judgment greatly exceeds a reasonable fee.[8] Courts are also liberal in employing estoppel and similar

and Problems of Code Interpretation and Enforcement, 1980 Am.B.Found. Research J. 939, 944.

[1] In re Wetzel, 118 Ariz. 33, 574 P.2d 826 (1978). See also, e.g., Office of Disciplinary Counsel v. Kissel, 497 Pa. 467, 442 A.2d 217 (1982)(disbarment for, among other things, use of strong-arm collection tactics to recover claimed fee from client); In re Kauffman, 99 A.D.2d 640, 471 N.Y.S.2d 719 (1984)(discipline for referring affidavit of confessed judgment previously obtained from client as security for fees before completion of all services; fact that lawyer had already earned fees on quantum meruit basis no defense).

[2] Courts generally agree with the view of the Code. E.g., Heninger & Heninger v. Davenport Bank & Trust Co., 341 N.W.2d 43, 51 (Iowa 1983)("Attorneys should endeavor to resolve fee questions amicably, but they should not be left helpless when they render valuable service and confront an alternative of a write-off or a suit. We agree with the trial court that no ethical violation occurred.").

[3] The use of client confidential information in fee disputes must, obviously, be handled discretely. A threat to a client to reveal confidential information unless the client paid a fee has been condemned when the threatened revelation was not necessary for the purpose of collecting the fee aside from its extortionate effect. E.g., Lindenbaum v. State Bar, 26 Cal.2d 565, 160 P.2d 9 (1945) (letter to immigration service office to incite investigation of client's wife after client listed lawyer's fee bill as scheduled debt in bankruptcy); In re Aydelotte, 206 App. Div. 93, 200 N.Y.S. 637 (1923)(letter to client threatening to inform tax officials of alleged tax problem unless client paid lawyer's fee).

The proper treatment of confidential client information in a fee dispute requires only very guarded disclosures and then only when necessary and to persons to whom the lawyer needs to convey the information. The comment to MR 1.6 (Dispute Concerning Lawyer's Conduct; second paragraph) states that "a lawyer entitled to a fee is permitted by [MR 1.6(b)(2)] to prove the services rendered in an action to collect it. This aspect of the rule expresses the principle that the beneficiary of a fiduciary relationship may not exploit it to the detriment of the fiduciary. As stated above, the lawyer must make every effort practicable to avoid unnecessary disclosure of information relating to a representation, to limit disclosure to those having the need to know it, and to obtain protective orders or make other arrangements minimizing the risk of disclosure."

[4] See generally McInerney v. Massasoit Greyhound Ass'n, 359 Mass. 339, 269 N.E.2d 211, 218–19 (1971). Not all features of commercial litigation are rejected by all courts. Some jurisdictions permit a lawyer to recover on the basis of an account stated—a bill sent to the client indicating a balance due for legal services that the client does not dispute within a reasonable time. E.g., Gleason v. Klamer, 103 Cal.App.3d 782, 163 Cal.Rptr. 483 (1980); Reboul, MacMurray, Hewitt, Maynard & Kristol v. Quasha, 90 A.D.2d 466, 455 N.Y.S.2d 86 (1982).

[5] Mercy Hospital, Inc. v. Johnson, 431 So.2d 687, 688 (Fla.App.1983), review denied 441 So.2d 632 (1983); Davis v. Haldi, P.C., 148 Ga.App. 842, 253 S.E.2d 207 (1979); Jacobs v. Holston, 70 Ohio App.2d 55, 434 N.E.2d 738 (1980).

[6] Nolan v. Foreman, 665 F.2d 738, 741 (5th Cir.1982); Johnson v. Tindall, 195 Mont. 165, 635 P.2d 266, 268 (1981); Stanton v. Saks, 311 N.W.2d 584, 585 (S.D.1981).

[7] Hulland v. State Bar, 8 Cal.3d 440, 105 Cal.Rptr. 152, 503 P.2d 608 (1972). See also, e.g., Fall v. State Bar, 25 Cal.2d 149, 153 P.2d 1 (1944)(deceptive and abusive acts by lawyer in collecting fee through note and deed of trust that client had given as security for fees).

[8] Law Offices of Clark v. Altman, 680 P.2d 1125, 1129 (Alaska 1984)("The relationship between Clark and Alt-

doctrines against a lawyer who asserts the statute of limitations as a defense against a client who seeks return of an overpayment of fees.[9]

There are two principal ways in which fee suits differ from other kinds of collection suits between commercial strangers. The fee charged under the fee contract is always subject to reduction by the court in the exercise of a supervisory power over lawyers.[10] And, stemming from the same source, the defenses available to clients are expanded. The chief expansion is through a doctrine, frequently recognized, that a lawyer may forfeit the right to a fee if the lawyer committed a breach of a statute or lawyer code that violated the lawyer's duty toward his or her client during the course of the representation.

The doctrine of fee forfeiture comes in both an expanded and a leaner form. Sometimes the doctrine is applied broadly with the announcement that a lawyer forfeits all claim to compensation on the occurrence of an ethical violation, including fees for services rendered before the violation occurred.[11] Another view is that the windfall of free legal services to the client and the possible disproportion of the penalty of total forfeiture and the violation of the lawyer may be too great.[12] Those courts reserve the sanction of total forfeiture for instances in which the need for its deterrent and retributive impact outweighs the concern with avoiding windfalls and achieving proportionality.[13] Even under that more moderate view, however, the entire fee would be forfeit if the violation of the lawyer's duty to his or her client substantially impaired the

man is that of an attorney attempting to collect a fee from a former client. . . . Clark was thus bound to conduct himself fairly and reasonably toward Altman. In the manner described above these standards were not observed with the exactitude required in a lawyer-client context.").

[9] O'Dowd v. Johnson, 666 S.W.2d 619, 621 (Tex.App. 1984), error refused n.r.e. See also, e.g., Spilker v. Hankin, 188 F.2d 35 (D.C.Cir.1951)(normal rules of res judicata not followed in order to permit client to attack validity of series of notes plaintiff lawyer sought to enforce against her in series of suits).

[10] See generally § 9.1, at 497–500. E.g., MacKenzie v. Belisle, 338 N.W.2d 33, 37 (Minn.1983); Reisch & Klar v. Sadofsky, 78 A.D.2d 517, 431 N.Y.S.2d 591, 592 (1980). A court's reduction of a fee because it is excessive does not establish, for the purposes of the client's defense (discussed next in the text), that the fee should be forfeited because of the lawyer's violation of a fiduciary duty toward the client. The improper act of the lawyer in charging an excessive fee has no causal relationship to the quality of the lawyer's legal services. There is therefore no reason to forfeit the lawyer's entire claim to a fee simply because the lawyer charged too much. Its reduction to a reasonable fee is regarded as forfeit enough. E.g., Heninger & Heninger v. Davenport Bank & Trust Co., 341 N.W.2d 43, 51 (Iowa 1983).

[11] In re New York, N.H. & H. R.R., 567 F.2d 166, 176 (2d Cir.1977), cert.denied 434 U.S. 833, 98 S.Ct. 120, 54 L.Ed.2d 94 (1977); Financial General Bankshares, Inc. v. Metzger, 523 F.Supp. 744, 773 (D.D.C.1981), vacated on other grounds 680 F.2d 768 (D.C.Cir.1982); Kyle v. Kyle, 94 A.D.2d 866, 463 N.Y.S.2d 584, 585, appeal denied 60 N.Y.2d 557, 469 N.Y.S.2d 1025, 457 N.E.2d 808 (1983) ("If the discharge is for cause or misconduct, the attorney has no right to a fee nor to a retaining lien."). The rule may be applied with special strictness where the lawyer has represented two or more parties in violation of conflict of interest rules. E.g., Frank v. Bloom, 634 F.2d 1245, 1257–58 (10th Cir.1980)(dictum); Moses v. McGarvey, 614 P.2d 1363, 1372 (Alaska 1980); American-Canadian Oil & Drilling Corp. v. Aldridge & Stroud, Inc., 237 Ark. 407, 373 S.W.2d 148 (1963)(forfeiture even if no damages shown); Jeffry v. Pounds, 67 Cal.App.3d 6, 136 Cal.Rptr. 373, 375 (1977); Goldstein v. Lees, 46 Cal.App.3d 614, 120 Cal.Rptr. 253 (1975); Rolfstad, Winkjer, Suess, McKennett & Kaiser v. Hanson, 221 N.W.2d 734, 737 (N.D.1974).

[12] Compare, e.g., Spanos v. Skouras Theatres Corp., 364 F.2d 161 (2d Cir.1966), cert. denied 385 U.S. 987, 87 S.Ct. 597, 17 L.Ed.2d 448 (1966)(lawyer, not admitted there, who practiced law in New York by advising client and client's New York lawyers may recover fee despite failure to be admitted pro hac vice), with, e.g., Spivak v. Sachs, 16 N.Y.2d 163, 263 N.Y.S.2d 953, 211 N.E.2d 329 (1965)(strict holding precluding any recovery of fee by unadmitted lawyer practicing law in state, even if temporarily and for out-of-state client). A total-forfeiture doctrine would presumably mean that a lawyer who was suspended or disbarred would lose all right to recover fees from all clients. That is not the general view. See generally Annot., 24 A.L.R.3d 1193 (1969).

[13] Pantry Pride, Inc. v. Finley, Kumble, Wagner, Heine, Underberg & Casey, 697 F.2d 524, 533 (3d Cir.1982); Chicago & W. Towns R.R. v. Friedman, 230 F.2d 364, 369 (7th Cir.1956), cert. denied 351 U.S. 943, 76 S.Ct. 837, 100 L.Ed. 1469 (1956). Compare, e.g., Jackson v. Griffith, 421 So.2d 677 (Fla.App.1982)(no fee recovery on contract or in quantum meruit where lawyer induced client to sign fee contract by coercion, duress, and threats); Feld & Sons, Inc. v. Pechner, Dorfman, Wolfee, Rounick & Cabot, 312 Pa.Super. 125, 458 A.2d 545 (1983)(despite participation in wrong, client can recover amount of fee paid to lawyers who counselled clients to pursue entirely illegal and wrongful course during representation, which resulted in harm to client), with, e.g., Genins v. Geiger, 144 Ga.App. 244, 240 S.E.2d 745 (1977)(lawyer who defended client in criminal case, under contract with void clause providing for contingent bonus, could recover remainder of fee).

value of the legal services rendered for the benefit of the client.[14] Determination of that question requires a careful examination of the individual facts of the case.[15] The lawyer is entitled to compensation for services rendered before or after the ethical violation and whose value was not contaminated by it.[16] And courts have held that a violation of applicable rules may convert the basis of the lawyer's recovery from recovery on the contract to a lesser award based on the value of services actually rendered.[17]

Problems in Performance of Contingent Fee Contracts

A contingent fee contract assumes that the lawyer and client will maintain their relationship through to the end, which, if successful, will result in a fee for the lawyer. Questions have frequently arisen concerning the effect upon the contract if the relationship ends before completion of the work. A lawyer's right to recover the reasonable value of his or her services for partial performance depends generally on whether the reason for termination of the relationship was entirely justifiable on the lawyer's part. A lawyer who withdraws without good cause [18] forfeits any claim to a fee.[19] But, as with other contracts, a contingent fee contract may prove infeasible to perform, as when a lawyer dies before completing work. In such cases it is normally held that the lawyer's death does not forfeit the right of the lawyer's representative to recover the reasonable value of the lawyer's services.[20]

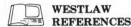

WESTLAW REFERENCES

attorney lawyer counsel** /s sue* suit! /s client /3 fee

§ 9.6.2 Fee Arbitration

Arbitration as an Alternative to Fee Suits or Discipline

A client dissatisfied with the size of a fee or unhappy at the extent or quality of legal services rendered after paying a fee in advance is faced with unpleasant prospects. The idea of hiring a second lawyer to pursue the first through the courts is unattractive because it simply adds additional fees to the original problem. It might be difficult to find a lawyer willing to litigate against another. And the delays of litigation may put economic pressure on the client to forego any relief.

14 Rice v. Perl, 320 N.W.2d 407 (Minn.1982)(lawyer who hired insurance adjuster, with whom he purportedly was negotiating at arm's length in client's behalf, as paid consultant for other alleged work in office forfeits fee because of risk that client's settlement would be void); Holcomb v. Steele, 47 Tenn.App. 704, 342 S.W.2d 236 (1958)(negligence of lawyer in failing to advise client of right to sue coclient in conflict-ridden representation was breach of duty to client and barred right to recover any fee). Some decisions hold that the fee forfeiture may be imposed even if the lawyer acted wrongly but in subjective good faith. E.g., Bryant v. Lewis, 27 S.W.2d 604 (Tex.Civ.App.1930)(conflict of interest representation).

15 Tobias v. King, 84 Ill.App.3d 998, 40 Ill.Dec. 400, 406 N.E.2d 101, 104 (1980); Crawford v. Logan, 656 S.W.2d 360, 365 (Tenn.1983).

16 Pantry Pride, Inc. v. Finley, Kumble, Wagner, Heine, Underberg & Casey, supra n. 13; Jeffry v. Pounds, 67 Cal. App.3d 6, 136 Cal.Rptr. 373, 377 (1977); Beatty v. LaSonde, 147 Ga.App. 138, 248 S.E.2d 202 (1978). See also, e.g., Stein v. Shaw, 6 N.J. 525, 79 A.2d 310 (1951) (lawyer, disbarred during course of representation for ethical violation unrelated to it, entitled to recover reasonable value of services up to limit of agreed fee but with reduction by expense incurred by client in retaining successor counsel to complete legal work necessarily abandoned by plaintiff lawyer after disbarment).

17 Mattioni, Mattioni & Mattioni, Ltd. v. Ecological Shipping Corp., 530 F.Supp. 910, 914 (E.D.Pa.1981)(presence of so-called attorney's consent provision in fee contract, requiring lawyer's consent before suit could be settled, voided entire contingent fee contract and required lawyer to recover on basis of quantum meruit).

18 On the circumstances under which a lawyer may withdraw from a case and still retain a claim for fees for services actually rendered, see generally Annot., 88 A.L.R.3d 246 (1978).

19 Hardison v. Weinshel, 450 F.Supp. 721 (E.D.Wis. 1978)(lawyer who withdrew because he thought incorrectly that client's claim would not succeed at trial forfeited all claim to fee). But see May v. Seibert, 264 S.E.2d 643 (W.Va.1980)(lawyer under contingent fee contract, who negotiated unsuccessful settlement offer but then withdrew without good cause, was nonetheless entitled to share in contingent fee of successor lawyer in proportion to amount of time spent by each when successor lawyer completed settlement at same figure).

20 See generally Annot., 33 A.L.R.3d 1375 (1970).

But the fact that clients unhappy with fees are unable to find effective remedies through litigation hardly means that the problem is not acute. A typical report of bar committees and researchers is that fee disputes are frequent,[21] and a high proportion of client and public complaints about lawyers involve charges of excessive fee charges.[22]

For several reasons bar associations began during the 1970s to institute methods of fee arbitration. Their motives included the perceived injustice of requiring clients to resort to lawsuits to recover unearned fees, the size and magnitude of other disciplinary problems requiring the attention of a limited enforcement staff, the unsuitability of the disciplinary process for many kinds of relatively minor fee overcharges, and the inappropriateness of using disciplinary machinery to coerce a lawyer into making restitution of a disputed portion of a fee.

The design of the fee arbitration systems varies considerably among the many jurisdictions that now provide them.[23] Some fee arbitration systems are merely invitational—providing arbitration services if both client and lawyer agree to accept arbitration.[24] Some plans are mandatory for the lawyer in the sense that a client invocation of arbitration must be accepted by the lawyer.[25] None can be invoked by a lawyer against an unwilling client.[26] Neither the 1969 Code nor the 1983 Model Rules require a lawyer to submit to fee arbitration, although the Model Rules state indeterminately that a lawyer should "conscientiously consider submitting to it." [27]

Various enforcement mechanisms have been provided. California's system provides that the award is binding only if the parties agree beforehand or if an award is not appealed to a court; if the award is appealed, the matter is heard de novo.[28] The award, in effect, can be made advisory by a lawyer who refuses to submit to the award. Minnesota enforces arbitration awards against the lawyer through professional discipline.[29] New Jersey, at the other extreme, makes arbitration results binding on both parties.[30] Some jurisdictions take a middle ground, providing that the arbitration is not binding, but if the award is not honored by the lawyer, the arbitration committee will support the client in a suit to recover the fees or in defense of the lawyer's suit to recover fees by supplying testimony as to the reasonableness of the award and by other possible assistance.[31]

Fee arbitration is probably a positive good. Where available, it is frequently utilized. Its acceptability to a skeptical public is probably proportional to the extent that nonlawyers

21 Wash.St.B. News 5 (Jan.-Feb.1964).

22 Report of Special ABA Committee on Resolution of Fee Disputes 2–4 (1974); ABA Special Committee on Evaluation of Disciplinary Enforcement, Problems and Recommendations in Disciplinary Enforcement 188–89 (1970)(Clark Committee report); Steele & Nimmer, Lawyers, Clients, and Professional Regulation, 1976 Am.B. Found. Research J. 917, 952–54; Comment, Arbitration of Attorney Fee Disputes, 5 UCLA-Alaska L.Rev. 309 (1976).

23 For a review, see Devine, Mandatory Arbitration of Attorney-Client Fee Disputes: A Concept Whose Time Has Come, 14 U.Tol.L.Rev. 1205, 1226–35 (1983).

24 An ABA committee has criticized voluntary fee arbitration systems on the ground that statistics indicate that lawyers frequently refuse to submit to fee arbitration. See Spec. Comm. on Resolution of Fee Disputes of ABA Section of Bar Activities, The Resolution of Fee Disputes: A Report and Model By-Laws 2–3 (1974).

25 Nisbet v. Faunce, 432 A.2d 779 (Me.1981)(client, but not lawyer, may withdraw from arbitration in view of procedure for informal conciliation of filed arbitration requests); Calif.R.Proc. for Hearing of Fee Arbitrations Rule I(1); N.J. Fee Arbitration R. 1:20A–3(a)(lawyer must submit to arbitration if client requests; if lawyer requests, client need not arbitrate). See generally Devine, Mandatory Arbitration of Attorney-Client Fee Disputes: A Concept Whose Time Has Come, 14 U.Tol.L.Rev. 1205 (1983).

26 It might be possible under the arbitration laws of some states, however, to obtain enforcement of an agreement to arbitrate in a client-lawyer contract. Cf., Robinson & Wells, P.C. v. Warren, 669 P.2d 844 (Utah 1983) (arbitration of fee dispute pursuant to clause in client-lawyer contract).

27 MR 1.5 comment (Disputes over Fees).

28 West's Cal. Bus. & Prof. Code §§ 6203(b), 6204(a). See generally Hargarten & Ardisson, Fine Tuning California's Mandatory Attorney Fee Arbitration Statute, 16 U.S.F.L.Rev. 411, 431 (1982).

29 In re Pearson, 352 N.W.2d 415, 417 (Minn.1984).

30 In re LiVolsi, 85 N.J. 576, 428 A.2d 1268 (1981).

31 See generally Spec.Comm. on Resolution of Fee Disputes of ABA Section of Bar Activities, The Resolution of Fee Disputes: A Report and Model By-Laws 1 (1974); In re LiVolsi, 85 N.J. 576, 428 A.2d 1268, 1280 (1981).

are extensively represented as members of fee arbitration panels. It does not seem merely to replace fee suits but provides a method of resolving fee disputes that is superior in several ways to litigation. Many clients probably prefer fee arbitration because of its relatively low cost, informality, and speed.

WESTLAW REFERENCES

attorney lawyer counsel** /s arbitrat! /2 fee

§ 9.6.3 Attorney Liens

Forms of Security for Fee Payment

In many types of representations, a lawyer will not be paid a fee in advance. Payment may come in installments, as the lawyer makes periodic billings, or, as in contingent fee contracts, at the end of the representation. The lawyer in effect extends credit to the client, trusting that the client will indeed pay as undertaken for the lawyer's past services. Should the client not pay, a lawyer could proceed to attempt to collect through a suit and execution on the judgment. But the client may be without assets or may move or hide them, or other creditors might have superior claims to available assets. For such reasons, a judgment for fees may, as any judgment, be uncollectable.

Several methods are available to a lawyer to secure the lawyer's claim for legal fees against the eventuality of nonpayment. The law in most jurisdictions recognizes two basic forms of security; a third possible form of contractual security is controversial. In each case, generalities can be hazarded only on the assumption that law in a particular jurisdiction might vary significantly.[32] First is the retaining lien, a right of the lawyer to hold onto client property or funds that have come into the lawyer's hands until the client pays the lawyer's fee.[33] Second is the charging lien, a right to a portion of the money or other property that is obtained in litigation through the lawyer's efforts.[34] Both the retaining and charging liens operate by force of law and outside any specific contractual arrangement that the parties may have made. Third are a variety of contractual arrangements, such as assignments of interests as security for fee payment, which are of doubtful validity under the lawyer codes.

Lawyers' Security under the Lawyer Codes

The lawyer codes take what is essentially a hands-off attitude toward attorney liens. A properly acquired lien creates an exception both to the rules prohibiting the lawyer from acquiring an interest in a client's cause of action [35] and to the rules requiring the lawyer to handle client funds and property as trust property.[36] If, however, a lawyer asserts a lien interest that the law plainly does not allow, the lawyer can claim no protection against a charge of mishandling the client's property.[37] That becomes critical because of the obscurity under the lawyer codes of con-

32 For example, under a Washington statute, a client may substitute new counsel in a pending court action only after certifying that the fee claims of the discharged lawyer have been paid. See Erickson v. Fargo Van & Storage, Inc., 25 Wn.App. 502, 607 P.2d 894 (1980). In effect, the continuation of the lawsuit is held hostage to satisfying the lawyer's fee claim.

33 See generally Restatement (Second) of Agency § 464(b) (1958)(retaining lien of factor, banker, or attorney-at-law); Restatement of Security § 62(b)(1941)(lawyer's retaining lien).

34 Restatement (Second) of Agency § 464(e)(1958)(lawyer's judgment lien).

35 DR 5–103(A)(1)("A lawyer shall not acquire a proprietary interest in the cause of action or subject matter of litigation he is conducting for a client, except that he may: (1) Acquire a lien granted by law to secure his fee or expenses."); MR 1.8(j) (same). See also EC 5–7 ("[I]t is not improper for a lawyer to protect his right to collect a fee for his services by the assertion of legally permissible liens, even though by doing so he may acquire an interest in the outcome of litigation.").

The notion that a lawyer's lien does not constitute the acquisition of an interest in the client's cause of action has a procedural aspect as well. Despite the lien interest, the lawyer who holds it is not a necessary party to the client's litigation. E.g., Giles v. Russell, 222 Kan. 629, 567 P.2d 845 (1977).

36 Cf. DR 9–102(B)(4); MR 1.15(b) & (c); Calif.R. 8–101(B)(4). See generally § 4.8. E.g., Miller v. Paul, 615 P.2d 615 (Alaska 1980).

37 People ex rel. Goldberg v. Gordon, 199 Colo. 296, 607 P.2d 995 (1980)(at time for which lawyer asserts that lien entitled lawyer to retain client's papers, lawyer was either owed no balance unpaid or lien right had been lost by abuse of the lien); Attorney Grievance Comm'n v.

tractual liens or assignments for security that do not arise by operation of law but only out of the clauses of the contract drafted by the lawyer.[38]

Retaining Liens

The *retaining* lien, or *general* lien as it is also called, was a creature of the common law.[39] Statutes in some states also deal with retaining liens. In some states the statutes have been interpreted as replacing the common-law lien in a restrictive way.[40] In other states, the statutes are regarded as simply restating the common law about the lien or extending the lawyer's rights under them.[41] One state, by statute and order of the lawyer disciplinary agency, has abolished them entirely.[42]

The lien is predicated on the establishment of the client-lawyer relationship.[43] Thus a lawyer acquires no lien on property left with a lawyer following a fifteen-minute initial consultation when the lawyer was merely to examine the papers in order to determine whether to represent the person.[44] The lien applies to the client's property such as papers, books, documents, money, deeds, certificates of stock, and any other valuable property belonging to the client that comes into the lawyer's possession during the representation.[45] A retaining lien does not apply to all funds or other property to which the client may have some sort of ownership or possessory right and that may pass through a lawyer's hands.[46] In general the lien does not apply to funds or property that are delivered to the lawyer for purposes that are inconsistent with the lawyer's asserting a lien.[47] If, for example, client funds were clearly designated to be applied to an escrow account, a lawyer could not assert a lien on the funds as they went through the lawyer's office.[48]

McIntire, 286 Md. 87, 405 A.2d 273, 278 (1979)(retaining lien recognized by law gives lawyer no right to cash check and appropriate proceeds). For personal liability purposes, retention of a client's property under an asserted lien based on a fee claim that exceeds any reasonable fee constitutes the civil wrong of duress of property. E.g., First Nat'l Bank v. Pepper, 547 F.2d 708, 714–15 (2d Cir. 1976).

38 See infra at 562.

39 Ex parte Bush, 7 Vin.Abr. 74, 22 Eng.Rep. 93 (Ch. 1734). See generally 2 E.Thornton, Attorneys at Law §§ 573–77 (1914); Jones, An Attorney's General or Retaining Lien, 20 Am.L.Rev. 727 (1886). A good bit of the common-law expansion of the retaining lien in the United States came about in decisions of the federal courts prior to the decision in Erie v. Tompkins, 304 U.S. 64, 58 S.Ct. 817, 82 L.Ed. 1188 (1938), which put an end to unrestrained common-law adjudication by the federal courts in diversity of citizenship suits. See, e.g., McPherson v. Cox, 96 U.S. (6 Otto) 404, 417, 24 L.Ed. 746 (1877); In re Paschal, 77 U.S. (10 Wall.) 483, 19 L.Ed. 992 (1870). See Note, Attorney's Retaining Lien over Former Client's Papers, 65 Colum.L.Rev. 296, 298 n.24 (1965). Today federal courts do not claim a common-law power independent of state law to recognize attorney liens. E.g., Adams, George, Lee, Schulte & Ward, P.A. v. Westinghouse Elec. Corp., 597 F.2d 570, 573 (5th Cir.1979).

40 Akers v. Akers, 233 Minn. 133, 46 N.W.2d 87 (1951) (reference in statute to "money" and "papers" of client precludes assertion of retaining lien over other kinds of client personal property).

41 See generally Note, Attorney's Retaining Lien over Former Client's Paper, 65 Colum.L.Rev. 296, 300–01 (1965).

42 Op.11 Minn.Prof.Resp.Bd., Minn.Bench & Bar (Feb. 1981), at 55.

43 Thus the client's discharge of the lawyer before the lawyer has perfected the lien, such as by giving required notice to the opposing party, may destroy the basis for asserting the lien. E.g., Rhoades v. Norfolk & W. Ry., 78 Ill.2d 217, 35 Ill.Dec. 680, 399 N.E.2d 969 (1979).

44 Smith v. State, 490 S.W.2d 902 (Tex.Civ.App.1972), motion denied 500 S.W.2d 682 (Tex.1973).

45 See generally Note, Attorneys' Retaining Lien, 6 J.Leg.Prof. 263 (1981). The common-law retaining lien does not apply to real property. E.g., Tuggle v. Williamson, 450 So.2d 93, 95 (Miss.1984).

46 Atlantic & Grt. Lakes S.S. Corp., v. Steelmet, Inc., 431 F.Supp. 327 (S.D.N.Y.1977)(retaining lien does not attach to trial exhibits returned to lawyer's possession pending appeal); McKnight v. Rice, Hoppner, Brown & Brunner, 678 P.2d 1330 (Alaska 1984)(proceeds of client's insurance policy when client was constructive trustee of funds when lawyer's lien attached); Florida Bar v. Bratton, 413 So.2d 754, 755 (Fla.1982)(general rule is that property delivered to lawyer for specific purpose is not subject to retaining lien); Adan v. Abbott, 114 Misc.2d 735, 452 N.Y.S.2d 476 (1982)(fact that lawyer aided client in negotiating contract for book for criminal defendant with future royalty income gives lawyer no lien interest in book or royalties); Micheller v. Oberfrank, 153 N.J. Super. 33, 378 A.2d 1162 (1977)(receipt of trust funds).

47 Restatement of Security § 62, comment on clause (b), at 181 (1941)("The lien does not exist where papers or other chattels are delivered to an attorney for specific purposes inconsistent with the lien.").

48 Mayeri Corp. v. Shea & Gould, 112 Misc.2d 734, 447 N.Y.S.2d 413 (1982); In re Christian, 267 S.C. 410, 228

The lien can only be asserted to the extent of the lawyer's interest; the lien warrants retention of only as much of a client's funds as are claimed in good faith.[49] The lien does not, for example, entitle the lawyer to retain a client's property until the client pays the lawyer for an expense that is properly the lawyer's own, such as the expense of copying a file that the client seeks.[50] Both the retaining and the charging liens are equitable in nature. Thus either can be forfeited if the lawyer abuses it,[51] withdraws without justification,[52] is disbarred,[53] or commits a substantial breach of the client-lawyer contract or of the lawyer's fiduciary obligations.[54] A lawyer who sues a client for a fee may not assert the retaining lien as a basis for refusing to permit the client from obtaining discovery of material in the client's own file.[55]

The retaining lien is enforceable only by possession. Its only use, which can be powerful, is that it gives the lawyer the right to resist efforts by the client to recover the client's property without paying the demanded fee.[56] The lien is lost if the lawyer returns the property to the client.[57] If the client holds out against the pressure exerted by the lawyer's retaining the property, the lawyer cannot sell the property or have a judicial sale conducted to realize its possible intrinsic value. The rule is strictly applied with respect to client funds. The lawyer's retaining lien does not entitle the lawyer to make use of the funds for any purpose; they must be deposited in the lawyer's trust account. The lawyer must seek a prompt resolution of any dispute between lawyer and client over fees.[58]

Except for the fact that the lawyer has a legal right to do so, asserting a retaining lien would be extortionate.[59] As the New Jersey supreme court noted, "it is the inconvenience suffered by the client which determines the

S.E.2d 677 (1976)(discipline for failing to apply excess funds from sale of property to client's escrow account as lawyer has agreed with bank and purchaser).

49 Adams, George, Lee, Schulte & Ward, P.A. v. Westinghouse Elec. Corp., 597 F.2d 570 (5th Cir.1979).

50 In re van Baalen, 123 Ariz. 82, 597 P.2d 985 (1979).

51 People ex rel. Goldberg v. Gordon, 607 P.2d 995 (Colo.1980).

52 Compare, e.g., Marrero v. Christiano, 575 F.Supp. 837, 839 (S.D.N.Y.1983)(withdrawal because client rejected settlement offer not good cause, thus destroying charging lien); Hensel v. Cohen, 155 Cal.App.3d 563, 202 Cal.Rptr. 85 (1984)(same); In re Kaufman, 93 Nev. 452, 567 P.2d 957 (1977)(lawyer who withdrew without cause had no claim to retaining lien), with, e.g., Ambrose v. Detroit Edison Co., 65 Mich.App. 484, 237 N.W.2d 520 (1975)(lawyer discharged without cause could thereafter assert retaining lien in contingent fee case, but only on basis of quantum meruit).

53 In re Woodworth, 85 F.2d 50 (2d Cir.1936); People ex rel. MacFarlane v. Harthun, 195 Colo. 38, 581 P.2d 716, 719 (1978)("[T]he statutory privilege afforded practicing attorneys to assert a 'retaining lien' is . . . waived by conduct that results in suspension or disbarment."); In re Estate of Giddings, 96 Misc.2d 824, 410 N.Y.S.2d 16, 18 (Sur.Ct.1978). Perhaps a preferable rule is that the status of the lawyer at the time of rendering the services, rather than at the time of invoking the lien or the time when the lawyer's claim is challenged, determines the lawyer's right to assert the lien after suspension or disbarment. E.g., Committee on Professional Ethics v. Gartin, 272 N.W.2d 485, 490 (Iowa 1978); Tiringer v. Grafenecker, 38 Misc.2d 29, 239 N.Y.S.2d 567 (1962).

54 Marschke v. Cross, 82 A.D.2d 944, 440 N.Y.S.2d 740 (1981)(lawyer discharged for cause or who engaged in misconduct loses right to claim lien); In re Smith, 292 Or. 84, 636 P.2d 923, 931 (1981)(representing conflicting interests). Compare, e.g., Morfeld v. Andrews, 579 P.2d 426 (Wyo.1978)(lawyer did not lose retaining lien because fee contract in divorce case was contingent; lien can be asserted for quantum meruit).

55 Jenkins v. Eighth Judicial District Court, 676 P.2d 1201 (Colo.1984); Goethel v. First Properties Int'l, Ltd., 363 So.2d 1117 (Fla.App.1978), cert. denied 372 So.2d 468 (Fla.1979).

56 Armstrong v. Zounis, 304 Ill.App. 537, 26 N.E.2d 670 (1940); Petrillo v. Petrillo, 87 A.D.2d 607, 448 N.Y.S.2d 44 (1982).

57 Jones v. Miller, 203 F.2d 131 (3d Cir.1953), cert.denied 346 U.S. 821, 74 S.Ct. 35, 98 L.Ed. 347 (1953).

58 Attorney Grievance Comm'n v. McIntire, 286 Md. 87, 405 A.2d 273, 278 (1979)("[E]ven where such a [retaining] lien may be validly asserted as to client funds in the possession of an attorney, the dictates of DR 9-102 would seem to require that the funds in dispute be deposited in a proper escrow account, and not, as here, appropriated to the lawyer's own use without independent resolution of the underlying fee controversy."); In re Geralds, 402 Mich. 387, 263 N.W.2d 241, 243 (1978)(DR 9-102(A)(2) does not "grant an attorney an alternative means to enforce an attorney lien by helping one's self to funds of a client.").

59 Cf. In re Pitschke, 455 N.E.2d 943 (Ind.1983)(lawyer disciplined for keeping client's child in dispute over funds client allegedly owed lawyer).

value of the lien." [60] The extortionate nature of the retaining lien was more than a California appellate court thought was warranted. In Academy of California Optometrists, Inc. v. Superior Court,[61] the court held that a lawyer would not be permitted to retain client papers that had no intrinsic value to the lawyer and were valuable to the client to the extent that the client's pending litigation would be dismissed if the papers were not produced. New York courts have held that they have the inherent power to require a lawyer to surrender a client's papers if the client posts sufficient security to pay the disputed fee charges, even if surrender of the papers destroys the lien and thus deprives the lawyer of some procedural advantages that retention of the lien might afford.[62]

Charging Lien

The charging lien is the creation of statute in most jurisdictions that recognize it.[63] Because of its statutory origins and its potential for disrupting both ownership interests and the client-lawyer relationship itself, it is narrowly construed,[64] and its statutory requirements closely followed.[65] The lien operates against the interest that the court determines the client has in the property that the lawyer has been retained to protect or acquire for the client. In many jurisdictions the lien does not come into existence until the judgment itself is rendered, and so the lien is also commonly known as a *judgment* lien. The lien does not attach to property not involved in litigation and thus does not attach, for example, to property for which the lawyer has only prepared and filed a deed. By statute the lien has been expanded in some jurisdictions to cover the client's cause of action as well as the judgment.[66] The lien is limited to the fees earned and expenses incurred by the lawyer in the very action that produces the judgment on which the lien is asserted, and cannot relate to other representations.[67] The fees need not be a sum certain. The lien applies even if the amount of the fee is unliquidated. Thus a charging lien can be asserted

60 Brauer v. Hotel Associates, Inc., 40 N.J. 415, 192 A.2d 831 (1963). See also Jenkins v. Weinshienk, 670 F.2d 915, 917 (10th Cir.1982)("a retaining lien's effectiveness depends on the client's inability to gain access to the attorney's papers").

61 51 Cal.App.3d 999, 124 Cal.Rptr. 668 (1975). See also, e.g., Kallen v. Delug, 157 Cal.App.3d 940, 203 Cal. Rptr. 879 (1984)(contract signed by successor counsel, agreeing to split fees with former lawyer in return for latter's turning over client file, void as against public policy; former lawyer had no claim to file and was required to turn it over promptly).

62 Leviten v. Sandbank, 291 N.Y. 352, 52 N.E.2d 898 (1943). See also, e.g., Pomerantz v. Schandler, 704 F.2d 681 (2d Cir.1983); Browy v. Brannon, 527 F.2d 799 (7th Cir.1976)(lawyer validly asserting retaining lien with respect to corporate client's papers could be ordered to turn over papers temporarily to client's trustee in bankruptcy for the purpose of gathering the assets of the estate, but papers to be returned to lawyer for all other purposes until fee is paid); Tri-Ex Enterprises, Inc. v. Morgan Guaranty Trust Co., 583 F.Supp. 1116 (S.D.N.Y.1984) (opposing party can obtain discovery of papers in hands of lawyer when papers are highly relevant to issues to be litigated; lawyer's client cannot inspect papers until fees are paid).

63 In re Hronek, 563 F.2d 296 (6th Cir.1977)(no common-law charging lien in Ohio); Johnson v. Stephens Development Corp., 538 F.2d 664 (5th Cir.1976)(no common-law charging lien in Texas); Diamond v. Diamond, 298 Md. 24, 467 A.2d 510 (1983)(no common-law charging lien in Maryland). In California a charging lien does not arise by operation of law, but such a lien can be created by express language in a fee contract. E.g., In re Estate of McMahon, 68 Cal.App.3d 70, 135 Cal.Rptr. 621, 625 (1977).

The Restatement of Agency (Second) § 464(e)(1958) recognizes, among other agents who have possessory liens, that "an attorney of record who has obtained a judgment has an interest therein, as security for his fees in the case and for proper payments made and liabilities incurred during the course of the proceeding." Some jurisdictions recognize a broader lien that attaches to the client's "cause of action" from the date of filing the complaint.

64 Ross v. Scannell, 97 Wn.2d 598, 647 P.2d 1004 (1982).

65 Reeves v. Frazee, 104 Idaho 463, 660 P.2d 928 (1983) (requirements for perfecting lien and reducing to judgment); Griffin v. New Hampshire Dep't of Employment Security, 117 N.H. 108, 370 A.2d 278, 281 (1977)(statutory exemption makes charging lien inapplicable to award to client from unemployment compensation board).

66 People v. Keeffe, 50 N.Y.2d 149, 428 N.Y.S.2d 446, 405 N.E.2d 1012 (1980).

67 Crolley v. O'Hare International Bank, 346 N.W.2d 156 (Minn.1984). See generally Annot., 23 A.L.R.4th 336 (1983). The same limitation is imposed on retaining liens. E.g., First Nat'l Bank & Trust Co. v. Hyman Novick Realty Co., 72 A.D.2d 858, 421 N.Y.S.2d 733 (1979).

even if the lawyer's basis for a fee claim is only quantum meruit.[68]

The advantages of the charging lien are two. First, the lien prevents distribution of the proceeds of a judgment to a client before payment of the lawyer's fee. Thus, if a defendant pays the proceeds of a judgment or settlement directly to the client in derogation of the lawyer's charging lien, the lawyer has an action against the defendant for the value of the lost lien interest.[69] Second, the lien gives the lawyer priority in distributing the proceeds of the judgment over other creditors of the client who are unsecured or not secured at the time that the lawyer's lien attached.[70]

Contractual Liens as Security for Fees

Contractual agreements between client and lawyer that purport to create[71] liens are of doubtful validity on two scores. First, the permission in the lawyer codes for a lawyer to acquire an interest in a client's cause of action or subject matter of litigation extends to "a lien granted by law to secure his fee or expenses."[72] It does not seem proper to regard a contractual security interest as "a lien granted by law" within the meaning of what was obviously intended as a limited exception to a general rule. Second, to the extent that the contractual security clearly falls outside that rule—for example, because it is a security interest in property such as shares of stock that are in no way related to the "cause of action or subject matter of litigation"[73] to which the prohibition extends—the arrangement may fall afoul of the rules that strictly limit business dealings between lawyer and client (§ 8.11).[74] Nonetheless, authority exists in some states recognizing contractual liens, although on the facts of most of the cases the liens that are thus recognized are not broader than retaining and charging liens generally available.[75] They can thus be understood as permissions to expand a particular jurisdiction's lien to a kind of national norm, but not necessarily beyond.

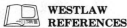

WESTLAW REFERENCES

Retaining Liens

attorney lawyer counsel** /s retaining general /2 lien

Charging Liens

attorney lawyer counsel** /s charging judgment /1 lien

---

[68] Heinzman v. Fine, Fine, Legum & Fine, 217 Va. 958, 234 S.E.2d 282 (1977)(charging lien exists regardless of fact that, after discharge of lawyer by client, lawyer was relegated to claim for reasonable value of fees and could not assert rights under contingent fee contract).

[69] Bryam v. Miner, 47 F.2d 112, 116 (8th Cir.), cert.denied 283 U.S. 854, 51 S.Ct. 648, 75 L.Ed. 1461 (1931); Jarboe v. Hicks, 281 Ark. 21, 660 S.W.2d 930 (1983); Pearlmutter v. Alexander, 97 Cal.App.3d Supp. 16, 158 Cal.Rptr. 762 (1979); Davis v. Great No. Ry., 128 Minn. 354, 151 N.W. 128 (1915); Downs v. Hodge, 413 S.W.2d 519 (Mo.App.1967); Goldstein, Goldman, Kessler & Underberg v. 4000 East River Road Assoc., 64 A.D.2d 484, 409 N.Y.S.2d 886 (1978), affirmed 48 N.Y.2d 890, 424 N.Y.S.2d 896, 400 N.E.2d 1348 (1979); Fary v. Aquino, 218 Va. 889, 241 S.E.2d 799 (1978). Because of the impact upon third parties, a common requirement is for notice to such parties of the nature of the lawyer's lien interest. See generally Annot., 85 A.L.R.2d 859 (1962).

[70] Browy v. Brannon, 527 F.2d 799 (7th Cir.1976)(attorney's lien as provable preference in bankruptcy); In re Continental Vending Mach. Corp., 543 F.2d 986 (2d Cir. 1976); Valentino v. Rickners Rhederei, G.M.B.H., 417 F.Supp. 176 (E.D.N.Y.1976), affirmed 552 F.2d 466 (2d Cir.1977)(priority between lawyer's lien and stevedore's lien for medical and related expenditures); Cetenko v. United California Bank, 30 Cal.3d 528, 179 Cal.Rptr. 902, 906, 638 P.2d 1299, 1303 (1982); Aetna Cas. & Surety Co. v. Atom Foreign Auto Parts, Inc., 116 Misc.2d 250, 455 N.Y.S.2d 531 (1982)(charging lien superior to claim of judgment creditor levying execution and to federal tax lien).

[71] Different are contractual clauses that defeat the lawyer's lien claims. Those are permissible and are strictly construed against the lawyer. E.g., In re Rosenberg, 690 P.2d 1293 (Colo.App.1984)(letter contract, which client returned with lien language struck through, destroyed both retaining and charging lien created by statute).

[72] DR 5-103(A)(1); MR 1.8(j).

[73] DR 5-103(A); MR 1.8(j).

[74] In re May, 90 Idaho 858, 538 P.2d 787 (1975)(under circumstances here, lawyer's acquiring an assignment of client's property as security for fees was impermissible business dealing with client). See generally Note, An Attorney's Acceptance of Assignment of Property as Security for Fee, 4 J.Leg.Prof. 263 (1979).

[75] Eleazer v. Hardaway Concrete Co., 281 S.C. 344, 315 S.E.2d 175 (Ct.App.1984).

Part Three
THE ROLE OF LAWYERS

Chapter Ten
THE ADVERSARY SYSTEM

Table of Sections

§ 10.1 CONCEPT OF THE ADVERSARY SYSTEM

Significance of the Adversary System

In discussions of the character of litigation and other representations by lawyers in the United States, the almost universally accepted term is the *adversary system*. It is often stated that one of the major problems of legal ethics is to determine the proper role for lawyers functioning within that system. A careful speaker would, however, be none too comfortable employing the phrase, because it suggests a kind of ordered arrangement of uniform practices and institutional features that simply does not exist. Lawyers and judges differ sharply over such vital matters as methodology and values. Moreover, the patterns of actual rules and customary litigational practices are themselves quite nonuniform, differing significantly from state to state, from nation to state, from city to town, within the different courts in the same community, and sometimes between one courtroom and another. One has only to spend a few hours observing the summary and uncontested proceedings in a Monday morning drunk court; the later morning observing the pomp, circumstance, and orderly discussion at the Supreme Court; and the afternoon observing a trial involving skillful commercial trial litigators to realize the profoundly different "systems" being employed. A preferable phrase would be "adversary conception," for it is really a generalized ideal to which lawyers and judges most often mean to refer.

A second, and perhaps more important, reservation concerns the extent to which the concept of the adversarial lawyer might be carried beyond the realm of litigation. The core context in which the adversary system is typically discussed is that of the criminal defense lawyer. From there, consideration often moves to civil representation as well, sometimes without noting the profoundly different setting. Once conclusions have been drawn about the proper role of a lawyer in those contexts, they are often generalized into the lawyer's proper function for a client in any other context, including representations that have nothing to do with criminal defense or even with litigation. Possible limitations on a lawyer's permissible resort to adversarial tactics are pursued in the chapter on counselling (Chapter thirteen).

Features of the Adversary System

The adversary system, if it means to refer to the common features of litigation in American civil and criminal courts, seems generally to refer to the following features.

(1) The parties initiate and control the definition of the issues and the presentation of evidence. The initiating party in a criminal prosecution must be the state. In civil proceedings, the decision to sue is made by individuals or entities.

(2) The presentations of the parties' cases are representational. The interested parties do not participate directly, except possibly as witnesses, in their own proceeding. Almost invariably each litigant acts through a hired advocate. The judge deals primarily with the advocates in discussing proceedings in the case, and the system allows the advocates a large amount of discretion to act for and to bind their principals.

(3) The exploration of issues and presentation of evidence is party-centered and contentious from beginning to end.[1] The procedure calls for reciprocating, but largely non-cooperative, statement and counterstatement, proof and counterproof.

(4) Judge and jury are both neutral and passive. They come to the proceeding without demonstrable bias for or against one of the parties. Although the judge rules on motions, objections, and the like, that is almost always in response to a request to act by one of the parties. Neither judge nor jury takes personal initiative in interjecting issues, acquiring or examining evidence, or staking out new directions that the unfolding drama should take.

(5) The proceedings are governed by procedural rules that attempt, for the most part in harmony with the above general features, to regularize the proceedings and make them efficient in terms of expenditures of public resources.

(6) Finally, law and procedures formulate remedial endings to the litigation that are largely either-or in nature (either the plaintiff wins or the defendant, but not both partially) and that must be based only on the issues and evidence that the parties have presented.

Institutionalizing the Adversary System

To some extent, the adversary system as lawyers understand it has been made enduring and unchangeable by decisions of the Supreme Court. Whether they well or ill fit the needs of society, those features are presently part of the Supreme Court's definition of due process that is assured to litigants by the Fifth and Fourteenth Amendments to the Constitution and by the Sixth Amendment guarantee of the right to counsel. In Herring v. New York,[2] the Court held that the Sixth Amendment invalidated a New York statute that gave the trial judge discretion to dispense with final summing up by the defense counsel in bench-tried criminal cases. After reciting a list of due process protections, the Court seemed, in dicta, to announce that the features of the adversarial system were locked into the American judicial system by force of

[1] The adversarial system proceeds on the assumption that every charge might be answered, despite the fact that a large percentage of charges are not and go to judgment by default. Generally, the absence of a party requesting relief will preclude any resulting act of a judge from being judicial in nature, but the absence of a defendant will not, so long as the petitioning party seeks relief from the court under a claim of present right. District of Columbia Ct. of Apps. v. Feldman, 460 U.S. 462, 480, 103 S.Ct. 1303, 1313, 75 L.Ed.2d 206 (1983); In re Summers, 325 U.S. 561, 566–67, 65 S.Ct. 1307, 1310–11, 89 L.Ed. 1795 (1945). The usual result, of course, when a court proceeds with an uncontested petition for relief before it, is for it to grant the relief by default, although the court can exercise a limited inquisitorial function and deny relief if none is legally warranted on the fact of the request. In re Summers, 325 U.S., at 568–69, 65 S.Ct., at 1311–12.

[2] 422 U.S. 853, 95 S.Ct. 2550, 45 L.Ed.2d 593 (1975).

the Constitution.[3] On other occasions, however, the Court has bemoaned the tendency of the adversary system to be characterized by protracted proceedings, formality, and delay and to lack the capacity for reconciliation of differences.[4]

Objectives of the Adversarial System

There is no reason to think that the adversary system sprang fully intellectualized from the brows of a Solon. Many of the rules and practices of the adversarial system are important products of history or culture. The adversary system in the United States is culture-bound beyond an extent that most lawyers would prefer to admit. The same social system that supports professional prizefighting and football, but outlaws chicken fighting, can be seen mirrored in the set of contradictory rules that limit yet then allow aggression and competition in the legal arena. Yet it would be wrong to assume that the adversarial system has not been powerfully shaped by ideas about its proper working.

Several justifying claims for the adversary system are commonly asserted.[5] Most of them can be subsumed under three general claims, which will be examined in turn. Truth, it is claimed, first, is best discovered through the adversarial system. Second, individual legal rights are better protected and vindicated through it. Third, litigants are more likely to be personally satisfied with the results of an adversarial trial. The justifications of the adversary system have not, of course, gone without challenge.[6]

Truth. Most commentators agree that, either as a goal in itself or as an instrumental goal to achieve fair outcomes, the adversarial system should lead to truth. For example, for someone who is primarily interested in the protection of individual rights through the adversarial system, truth about occurrences is an essential ingredient in defining the circumstances so that a correct invocation of rights can be made.[7]

Ascertaining truth is argued to be one of the chief justifications of the adversarial system. It is claimed that it is designed to lead to the truth more surely than competing models for litigation.[8] The lawyers, committed to seeking a partisan victory in the trial by any

[3] 422 U.S. at 857, 95 S.Ct. at 2552–53 ("The decisions of this Court have not given to these constitutional provisions a narrowly literalistic construction. More specificially, the right to the assistance of counsel has been understood to mean that there can be no restriction upon the function of counsel in defending a criminal prosecution in accord with the traditions of the adversary factfinding process that has been constitutionalized in the Sixth and Fourteen Amendments."). See also, e.g., In re Gault, 387 U.S. 1, 87 S.Ct. 1428, 18 L.Ed.2d 527 (1967).

[4] Middendorf v. Henry, 425 U.S. 25, 96 S.Ct. 1281, 1292, 47 L.Ed.2d 556 (1976); Wolff v. McDonnell, 418 U.S. 539, 570, 94 S.Ct. 2963, 2981, 41 L.Ed.2d 935 (1974); Gagnon v. Scarpelli, 411 U.S. 778, 787, 93 S.Ct. 1756, 1762, 36 L.Ed. 2d 656 (1973).

[5] See generally Landsman, The Adversary System: A Description and Defense (1984); G.Hazard, Ethics in the Practice of Law 120–35 (1978); M. Freedman, Lawyers' Ethics in an Adversary System (1975); ABA Standards Relating to the Prosecution and Defense Functions 56–60 (1974); Thibaut, Walker & Lind, Adversary Presentaion and Bias in Legal Decisionmaking, 86 Harv.L.Rev. 386 (1972); Fuller, The Adversary System, in Talks on American Law (H.Berman ed.1971); Professional Responsibility: Report of the Joint Conference, 44 ABA J. 1159 (1958).

[6] M.Frankel, Partisan Justice (1980); J.Frank, Courts on Trial (1949); Frankel, From Private Rights toward Public Justice, 51 NYU L.Rev. 516 (1976); Luban, The Adversary System Excuse, in The Good Lawyer 83 (D.Luban ed.1984); Simon, The Ideology of Advocacy: Procedural Justice and Professional Ethics, 1978 Wisc.L. Rev. 29.

[7] Commentators who are principally associated with a rights-protection justification of the adversarial system would presumably not disagree entirely. See M.Freedman, Lawyers Ethics in an Adversarial System (1975). In criminal trials, for example, it is presumably unjust (and a failure of the adversarial system) if an innocent person is convicted because of false evidence of the prosecution. The reason that is objectionable is that the false evidence casts a seriously erroneous attribution of guilt upon an innocent person.

[8] The way in which that occurs was given its classical expression in Professional Responsibility: Report of the Joint Conference, 44 ABA J. 1159 (1958). The discussion that follows in the text is, it is believed, an argument that follows, but improves upon, the report. The report was the product of a six-year project of a joint committee of the American Bar Association and the Association of American Law Schools. It was first formed in 1952, during the height of the McCarthy era, to attempt to explain the necessity of the adversary system to a skeptical public—and to segments of the bar that were skeptical of the need for the adversary system in some contexts. The joint conference was cochaired by Professor Lon Fuller and lawyer John D. Randall. The report of the conference was authored almost entirely by Fuller.

legal means, are motivated to search diligently for facts and to test the evidence offered by the opposing party through cross-examination and counterevidence. Through the reciprocating process of proof and challenge to proof, the fact finder is best able to determine where the truth lies. The efficiency of the system is also enhanced because the parties, with their trained advocates, are able to reduce the issues to those that truly divide them instead of having the inquisitor canvass all possible issues and differences of fact.

The adversary process is often contrasted with an arbitral system, in which a single inquisitor is to decide a dispute between parties without advocacy from either side. The paradoxical position of the inquisitorial judge is that, as a matter of psychology, one searching for facts and for the limits and nuances of the law is much more likely driven to creative and tireless effort if one is committed to discovering support for a thesis. But once the judge forms and proceeds upon a thesis, the natural human instinct is to resist sloughing off that thesis, and such support as has been gathered for it, in order to investigate conflicting or variant theses.

The inquisitorial system in use in most of the countries of Europe other than Britain is sometimes posed as a model for comparison with the adversarial system.[9] Indeed, some scholars have proposed that some of its features should replace the adversarial system.[10] In the inquisitorial system the process of gathering and sifting facts is performed primarily by judges and not by parties. The judges, however, lack motivation, other than professional esprit, to take a sustained and dispassionate look at the case before forming relatively firm conclusions.[11]

It is often objected that adversarial trials cannot be an effective search for truth because one or perhaps both advocates come to the proceedings prepared to obfuscate, conceal, and distort the truth—to the considerable extent permissible under the rules of perjury, false evidence, and contempt of court. "How the edifice of justice can be supported by the efforts of liars at the bar and ex-liars on the bench is one of the paradoxes of legal logic which the man in the street has never solved." [12] Some have argued that the adversary system nonetheless discovers truth through the same process of discovery that is often employed, when the work is well done, in such fields as science [13] and history. There proposed truth is subjected to the winnowing process of skeptical investigation by other researchers attempting to demonstrate the error of the thesis being tested.[14] The important difference, however, is that scientific and historical investigators do not purposefully use manipulation and half-truths and do not generally argue against known fact as lawyers do. Lawyers are not necessarily attempting to persuade the fact finder to find the truth;

Parts of it are excerpted in the posthumous work Fuller, The Forms and Limits of Adjudication, 92 Harv. 353, 364, 382–85 (1978).

9 Damanska, Evidentiary Barriers to Conviction and Two Models of Criminal Procedure: A Comparative Study, 121 U.Pa.L.Rev. 506 (1975); Damanska, Structures of Authority and Comparative Criminal Procedure, 84 Yale L.J. 480 (1975); Schlesinger, Comparative Criminal Procedure, 26 Buffalo L.Rev. 371 (1977); Rosett, Trial and Discretion in Dutch Criminal Justice, 19 UCLA L.Rev. 353 (1972).

10 G.Tullock, Trials on Trial: The Pure Theory of Legal Procedure 87–104 (1980). Cf. M.Frankel, Partisan Justice (1980).

11 Landes & Posner, Adjudication as a Private Good, 8 J.Leg.Stud. 235 (1979). According to accounts of experience with some forms of the inquisitorial system, the judge in a criminal case may be ill disposed to take any stance but one antagonistic to the accused because, by prior acquaintance with the facts from the dossier prepared in advance by the committing magistrate, the judge has already developed a basis for decision. See Patouris, Book Review, 57 NYU L.Rev. 203, 209–11 (1982).

12 Cohen, Field Theory and Judicial Logic, 59 Yale L.J. 238, 238 (1930).

13 K.Popper, Conjectures and Refutations: The Growth of Scientific Knowledge (1963).

14 Another conventional response is to assert that truth is relative both to the social and historical settings in which events occur and to the value-charged perspective of the observer. Flynn, Professional Ethics and the Lawyer's Duty to Self, 1976 Wash.U.L.Rev. 429, 432; Cohen, Field Theory and Judicial Logic, 59 Yale L.J. 238, 238 (1950). Often cited in this connection is the argument of Kuhn that even scientific truth is relative to its time, with scientific truths yielding to contradictory theses as time unfolds. T.Kuhn, The Structure of Scientific Revolutions (2d ed.1970).

they attempt to persuade the fact finder to find facts favoring their clients.

Rights Vindication. The belief that the adversary system is the system best suited to lead to the vindication of individual rights is founded on two different conceptions of rights. One is the substantive conception of rights as things to be possessed and enjoyed. Here the argument is that the adversarial system is the best way for individuals to secure such rights. A different conception is that the autonomy and privacy of individuals is not sufficiently respected by a state unless deprivations and obligations that are imposed by law are exacted only following a public process in which the person charged with a civil or criminal wrong is given many procedural and forensic advantages. The extreme illustration is the presumption of innocence and all that it procedurally brings with it in the idealized criminal trial.

Particularly when litigation is between individuals or nonpublic institutions, discussions of rights vindication associate the laissez-faire philosophy of economic competition with the adversarial concept of litigational competition.[15] If the economic and litigational institutions share a common historial and theoretical base, then one would expect to find at bottom of each a conception of persons that includes as essential postulates possessive individualism in the substantive realm and a belief in a variety of procedures for regulation that share with Darwin a survival-of-the-fittest sort of resort to procedural governance. The difference between Darwin's world of natural science and the courtroom, however, is important. In the courtroom there are rules designed to assure, to an extent, that the competition is fair. In the adversary system justificatory arguments, belief in fairness constraints results in a strong emphasis upon the process and a corresponding belief in outcomes.

The concept of competitiveness consists of large strains of aggressiveness. For that reason, it is sometimes asserted that the present-day adversarial system "descends in part from trial by battle, in which the government official present at the trial simply refereed the contest." [16] Such statements invoke historical metaphors rather than historical roots or causes. The adversarial system is clearly not a direct, lineal descendant of trial by battle in the sense of sympathetic modeling. The present methods of trial developed specifically as rationalized replacements of battle, test, and oath with their crude and superstitious invocations of divine judgment. It might nonetheless be true that battlelike characteristics that have survived in trials are atavistic emergences of the human qualities that the social arrangement of trials was meant to displace. A similar critique that also looks to the contentious nature of trials is that the adversary system displays a "sporting theory of justice." [17] Others, however, have justified the adversarial system as a kind of acceptable social arrangement in which parties play a fair game with fair rules as a way of working out differences.[18]

Litigant Satisfaction. The third justification for the adversary system is that it affords litigants more satisfaction than competing models of adjudication. That claim also has at least two principal aspects—the intellectual and the emotional.

[15] Kutak, The Adversary System and the Practice of Law, in The Good Lawyer 172, 173–77 (D.Luban ed.1984).

[16] G.Tullock, Trials on Trial: The Pure Theory of Legal Procedure 87 (1980). See also id. 5.

[17] Pound, the Causes of Popular Dissatisfaction with the Administration of Justice, 29 ABA Rep. 395 (1906), reprinted in 57 ABA J. 348 (1971). Pound's speech was received by lawyers with hostility when given. His views did not receive anything like official endorsement until 1976, when the chief justice of the United States embraced them and assisted in sponsoring a National Conference on the Causes of Popular Dissatisfaction with the Administration of Justice. See Erickson, New Directions in the Administration of Justice: Responses to the Pound Conference, 64 ABA J. 48 (1978). For a history of the Pound controversy, see Verkuil, The Emerging Concept of Administrative Procedure, 78 Colum.L.Rev. 258, 265 (1978).

[18] Babcock, Fair Play: Evidence Favorable to an Accused and Effective Assistance of Counsel, 34 Stan.L.Rev. 1133 (1982). The metaphor is hardly powerful, of course, because rules for games almost always assume willing participation.

At the intellectual level, a litigant who has suffered a loss in adversarial litigation at least has the satisfaction of knowing that the result occurred at the end of a process in which the litigant played a major role.[19] The litigant was not forced to sit by as mere observer while governmental officials, over whom the litigant had no hope of control, "lost" the litigant's claim. The participatory justification for the adversary system fits comfortably with related concepts such as citizen participation in governance through voting. But commentators who question the adversary system note that the claims of rights vindication are plausible on their own terms only if one has confidence that the system in fact works as described. The same is true, of course, for claims that the adversary system best finds the truth. But if, as often happens, the parties' lawyers are of significantly different ability or if one party is able to marshal more resources for a sustained fight, the results of litigation can often turn out to frustrate otherwise valid legal claims.

At the emotional level, the aggressiveness of the adversary system may serve for clients the valuable function of permitting them to resolve doubts and qualms about their own aggressive feelings toward an adversary,[20] giving the litigant an occasion for playing out deeply conflicting social conflicts, such as those between order and freedom, or personal conflicts, such as anger and guilt.[21] As a justification for the adversary system, the rationale must assume that the adversarial occasion for harmless aggressive displays replaces and deflects aggressions that would otherwise be acted out in socially harmful ways. It must also assume that the official permission to act aggressively does not dysfunctionally spawn more divisiveness and aggression than would otherwise exist. The literature of alternative dispute resolution argues, or assumes, that the adversarial system does indeed have the socially undesirable effect of creating conflict in society rather than diminishing it.[22]

Comparative Perspectives on Dispute Resolution

It has been observed since at least the time of Tocqueville that a common American instinct is to legalize disputes.[23] Many modern critics have regretted that tendency in American life and have decried a "litigation explosion" that suggests dire social ills and conflicts. Japan is often cited by American commentators as a litigation-free nation whose counterexample the United States should follow. Freedom from strife in Japan is usually documented by comparisons be-

19 See generally Summers, Evaluating and Improving Legal Processes—A Plea for "Process Values," 60 Cornell L.Rev. 1 (1974).

20 Huebner, Scapegoating the Attorney: A Displacement of Marital Anguish, 9 J.Contemp. Psychotherapy 112 (1977). S.Jacoby, Wild Justice: The Evolution of Revenge (1983), argues that the human desire for revenge is successfully domesticated through the mechanisms of law because law provides opportunities for relatively harmless aggression in its procedures.

21 Seidman, Factual Guilt and the Burger Court: An Examination of Continuity and Change in Criminal Procedure, 80 Colum.L.Rev. 436, 442 (1980).

22 J.Lieberman, The Litigious Society (1981); M. Marks, The Suing of America: Why and How We Take Each Other to Court (1981); E.Johnson, V.Kantor, & E.Schwartz, Outside the Courts: A Survey of Diversion Alternatives in Civil Cases (1977); Sander, Varieties of Dispute Processing, 70 F.R.D. 111 (1976); Able, A Comparative Theory of Dispute Institutions in Society, 8 L. & Soc'y J. 217 (1973). See also the "litigation explosion" literature, e.g., Manning, Hyperlexis: Our National Disease, 71 Nw.U.L.Rev. 767 (1977); Barton, Behind the Legal Explosion, 27 Stan.L.Rev. 567 (1975); Glazer, Toward an Imperial Judiciary?, 41 Pub. Interest 104 (1975). But see Galanter, Reading the Landscape of Disputes: What We Know and Don't Know (and Think We Know) about our Allegedly Contentious and Litigious Society, 31 UCLA L.Rev. 4 (1983)(historical and cross-cultural comparisons lend no support to assertions that American courts are in midst of litigation explosion). The explosion, if such is occurring, has been occurring for a long time; at least it has occurred before. E.g., J.Carcopino, Daily Life in Ancient Rome 186–87 (1940)("From the reigns of one emperor to another, litigation was a rising tide which nothing could stem, throwing on the public courts more work than men could muster. To mitigate the congestion of the courts Augustus, as early as the year 2 B.C., was obliged to resign to their use the forum he had built and which bears his name. Seventy-five years later congestion had recurred and Vespasian wondered how to struggle with the flood of suits so numerous that 'the life of the advocates could scare suffice' to deal with them.").

23 A.deTocqueville, Democracy in America 89–93 (J.Mayer & M.Lerner eds.1966).

tween the number of lawsuits and between the number of American lawyers and the number of *bengoshi*, Japan's fully admitted court practitioners.

Here, as always, the danger exists of isolating features of another culture from the surrounding social structure in which the feature is embedded. Assuming *bengoshi* to be the only Japanese equivalent of American lawyers seriously undercounts the many functionaries in Japanese business and government who, although not *bengoshi*, perform tasks that are functionally quite similar to those of the American counsellor. Comparing litigation rates in the two governmental systems ignores the fact that entirely different social pressures work against public disputation in Japan. The absence of litigation in Japan is hardly due to governmental arrangements by which an innate desire of the Japanese people to litigate has somehow been suppressed.[24] The fact may be that Japan is not afflicted by the same amount of litigation as the United States because its homogeneous culture provides methods of deflecting and mediating conflict through close family and friendship groups that are simply irrelevant to the heterogeneous American culture.[25] Some of the difference in litigation rates may also reflect elements that Americans would find unacceptable or irrelevant, such as the absence of protection of certain important human rights.[26]

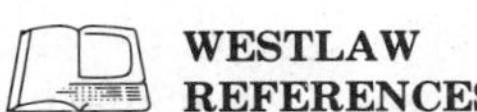

WESTLAW REFERENCES

Features of the Adversary System

default /s den*** /3 relief

Institutionalizing the Adversary System

(95 +5 2550) (422 +5 853) /15 herring

Objectives of the Adversarial System

Truth

adversar*** /2 system /s truth

Rights Vindication

adversar*** /2 system /p right /3 protect*** preserv!

§ 10.2 PRINCIPLE OF PROFESSIONAL DETACHMENT

§ 10.2.1 Lawyers' Professional Isolation from Clients

Principle of Professional Detachment[27]

The accepted view among lawyers is that a lawyer may represent any client—no matter how outrageous, illegal, or immoral the client's past or future conduct might be—so long as the lawyer will not be required in the course of the representation to violate any law or applicable lawyer code. Moreover, once a lawyer has accepted a client the lawyer is bound to use all of the lawyer's professional knowledge and skills to advance the legal interests of the client, regardless of the lawyer's private reservations about the client's course of action based on moral, social, political, or economic reasons (§ 10.3.1). Nonetheless, despite the complete professional commitment, a lawyer is not to be associated with the client's social, moral, political, or economic views or objectives in any way. The general proposition of isolation is often referred to as the principle of professional detachment or nonaccountability.[28]

A large portion of the nonlawyer public rejects the moral and political isolation of lawyers that the principle of professional detachment posits.[29] Many nonlawyers believe that lawyers represent objectionable clients

24 R.Smith, Japanese Society: Tradition, Self, and the Social Order 45 (1983).

25 Smith, Lawyers, Litigiousness, and the Law in Japan, 11 Cornell L.F. 53, 54–55 (Oct.1984).

26 Mayer, Japan: Behind the Myth of Japanese Justice, The American Lawyer (July/Aug.1984), at 13.

27 See generally Schwartz, The Professionalism and Accountability of Lawyers, 66 Calif.L.Rev. 609 (1978); Schwartz. The Zeal of the Civil Advocate, in The Good Lawyer 150 (D.Luban ed.1984).

28 Schwartz, The Professionalism and Accountability of Lawyers, 66 Calif.L.Rev. 669, 673–74 (1978).

29 The issues were examined in a classic debate, carried on in a series of twenty-one letters exchanged between David Dudley Field, a leading New York lawyer who had represented the entrepreneurs Fisk and Gould in their machinations with the Erie Railroad, and Samuel Bowles, a respected and nationally known journalist. Their correspondence was published in a pamphlet, "The Lawyer and His Clients" (1871), and in several periodicals of the times. See Schudson, Public, Private, and Professional

either because they disregard the harm they do, solely to make money, or because they agree with their client's objectives. From that point of view there is no important difference between a lawyer who hides an escaped murderer to prevent his being found by the police and a lawyer who argues in court for suppression of the murderer's confession on a legal technicality.

The professional response is that lawyers, as an aspect of their professional role, occupy a position in which they do not ultimately judge the goodness or badness of their clients as people or the goodness or badness of their clients' objectives,[30] save as they bear on the question whether the client intends to break the law. "[A]n advocate does not vouch for the justness of a client's cause but only for its legal merit."[31] Lawyers have the right to decline most representations on moral grounds, but they are also entitled to accept clients despite personal moral objections to the client's objectives. As functionaries within a system of justice, lawyers say, it is their role to serve as diligent and dedicated facilitators of client objectives. Ordinarily that role calls for the lawyer to maximize to the extent possible the client's partisan position as defined by law. To mix the role of lawyer and the role of law reformer, lawyers claim, is seriously wrong and dangerous and might ultimately prove destructive of important legal rights and dysfunctional socially.

Professional Detachment in the Lawyer Codes

The lawyer codes, of course, agree that the principle of professional detachment is fundamental and supplement it with logically consistent corollaries concerning a lawyer's zeal (§ 10.3.1). At the same time, the lawyer's personal views of morality and similar nonlegal values are not denied. A lawyer may explicitly base advice to a client on such considerations (§ 10.4). A reconciliation of the differences is attempted in the concept that differentiates between public and private morality (§ 10.4.3).

Both the Code and the Model Rules postulate that a lawyer's representation of a client carries no implication that the lawyer agrees with anything other than the sheer legality of the client's position, and even that need be only an arguable legality. Nowhere does the Code state the principle straight out, but hints are abundant, and the principle obviously serves as a logical predicate for several other statements in the Code.[32] The Model Rules do not leave the matter to inference; it clearly proclaims the principle of detachment. Model Rule 1.2(b) states that "a lawyer's representation of a client, including representation by appointment, does not constitute an endorsement of the client's political, economic, social or moral views or activities."[33]

Possible Anomalies in Theories of Detachment

The principle of professional detachment is offered as something desirable in itself and as a defense to charges that lawyers are personally responsible in some sense for immoral acts of their clients. As something desirable, it is explained that through the principle of detachment lawyers are encouraged to accept cases of unpopular clients, and thus access to

Lives: The Correspondence of David Dudley Field and Samuel Bowles, 21 Am.J.Leg.Hist. 191 (1977).

30 Appearing to testify against the nomination of Louis D. Brandeis as a justice of the Supreme Court, Austen Fox, a prominent bar leader, protested Brandeis's arrogating to himself the role of representing clients as "counsel for the situation." Fox insisted "The trouble with Mr. Brandeis is that he never loses his judicial attitude toward his clients. He always acts the part of a judge toward his clients instead of being his clients' lawyer, which is against the practices of the Bar." W.Hurst, The Growth of American Law: The Law Makers 371 (1950), as quoted in Schudson, Public, Private, and Professional Lives: The Correspondence of David Dudley Field and Samuel Bowles, 21 Am.J.Leg.Hist. 191, 210 (1977).

31 Model Rules introduction to section 3, at 59 (Public Discussion Draft, January 30, 1980).

32 For example, the Code's treatment of the question of unpopular causes (§ 10.2.3) and of the relevance of a lawyer's nonlegal views (§§ 4.3 at 157–59, 10.4, 13.3.10, 13.7.5 (nonlegal considerations).

33 See also MR 1.2 comment (Independence from Client's Views or Activities).

legal services is generalized. As a result, no person with a legal entitlement is denied it, because all persons with arguable claims to legal entitlements are assisted. As defense, lawyers explain that when they act in behalf of a client they do only the client's bidding, and they do it in a role that assures that they do not carry personal moral responsibility, a matter that will shortly be discussed.

Note, first, some important assumptions made in establishing the principle of detachment. Most importantly, it rests on an assumption that the lawyer's client directs the lawyer to take steps and to initiate moves in the client's behalf. If an unjust law permits a land speculator to dispossess a poverty-stricken family, it is the speculator who commands the lawyer to act, and not the lawyer who urges or cajoles the speculator to take every advantage that the law allows. If a case can be maneuvered before a lazy or biased judge who will rule unjustly in the client's favor, it is the client that directs the lawyer to take this step, not the other way around. Yet lawyers know that representations often do not work that way. Often lawyers either assume that clients wish to press every possible legal advantage or urge clients to do so. Clients, cowed by what they consider to be superior knowledge, will often follow a lawyer's direction—relying on their own principle of detachment that they are only doing what their wise counsellor has recommended.[34]

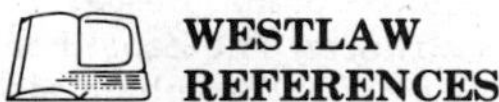

WESTLAW REFERENCES

Professional Detachment in the Lawyer Codes

ec2-27 "ec 2-27" dr2-103(e) "dr 2-103(e)"

§ 10.2.2 Freedom of Professional Employment

Professional Concept of a Duty to Serve

At least in this century, it has never been professional orthodoxy that a lawyer is required to represent any particular client. Yet anciently and now one hears it said that lawyers are obliged to represent every person who wishes to become a client.[35] Typical of such statements is that of John W. Davis defending himself against charges that he acted wrongly in aiding the financial schemes of the financier J. P. Morgan:

> Since the law, however, is a profession and not a trade, I conceive it to be the duty of the lawyer, just as it is the duty of the priest or the surgeon, to serve those who call on him unless, indeed, there is some insuperable obstacle in the way.[36]

The view is either a personal moral view or professional humbug, and might be both. It is suspect when spoken by some lawyers because, confused by self-interest, they may simply be arguing that they were driven by professional duty in acquiring a personal fortune representing rich but odious clients. As a professional matter, it is clear in the United States that no lawyer has a duty to represent any client, except perhaps those who are unable to obtain counsel.

English "Cab Rank" Rule

The ideal that some have urged be adopted by American lawyers is the "cab rank" rule, which is imagined to control acceptance of all cases, including those that are controversial, by English barristers.[37] According to that understanding, a barrister is required to ac-

34 Noonan, Other People's Morals: The Lawyer's Conscience, 48 Tenn.L.Rev. 227, 235–36 (1981).

35 Newman, Representing the Repugnant Client, 86 Case & Comment 22, 24 (1981)(lawyer has both ethical and legal obligation to represent client despite lawyer's personal repugnance); Younger, Professional Responsibility, 43 Brook.L.Rev. 863 (1977)(asserting—without defending except on ground that no lawyer can be certain of the justice of a client's position—that lawyers are obliged to accept all clients, except those who cannot pay the lawyer's fee and those whom the lawyer cannot serve competently).

36 W.Harbaugh, Lawyer's Lawyer: The Life of John W. Davis 199 (1973)(quoting letter from Davis to Julia McDonald, February 15, 1899). Davis was here developing an argument to deflect criticism from himself that he also employed when he ran for president in 1924. See S.Kalish, The Attorney's Role in the Private Organization, 59 Neb.L.Rev. 1, 2–3 (1980).

37 Basten, Control and the Lawyer-Client Relationship, 6 J.Leg.Prof. 7 33–36 (1981); Pollitt, Counsel for the Unpopular Cause: The "Hazard of Being Undone," 43 N.C.L.Rev. 9, 24–25 (1964); Rostow, The Lawyer and His Client, 48 ABA J. 25, 29 (1962); Seasongood, What Em-

cept every client and may not reject an unpopular client's brief because of personal feelings.[38] The actual British system, not surprisingly, runs somewhat less altruistically.[39] Barristers do not talk to prospective clients; in fact they do not talk to solicitors at first. In the English system a client must first find a solicitor who is willing to represent the client.[40] The solicitor in behalf of the client must then approach a barrister's clerk, who has been given discretion by the several barristers in the same chambers over which the clerk presides to accept briefs at fees that the clerk is to negotiate with solicitors. There is little professional control over the clerk's fee quotations. Nor is the clerk required to accept a case in behalf of a barrister who is already fully committed. The cab-rank rule purports to require only that an uncommitted barrister accept any case in which his or her clerk negotiated an appropriate fee with the client's solicitor. Obviously, in setting the fee and in reporting on the state of the barrister's availability, there is adequate room for the clerk to protect barristers against unwanted briefs.

Even if the cab-rank rule operated in England more in the way popularly imagined, the English barrister is hardly the equivalent of the American lawyer. The latter gives advice on a wide range of nonlegal issues of policy, such as business practice, public relations, and psychology. The barrister's role is much more limited to litigation and to giving legal opinions on narrow legal issues.[41] Nonetheless, the cab-rank rule must be a convenience for English barristers, who need not be troubled, as American lawyers are, to explain how, with freedom to select among clients, they sometimes end up with such rotters.

Arguments for a Duty to Choose Clients

An opposite sentiment is less often heard among lawyers[42] but is relatively uniformly held among nonlawyers: that as a moral matter a lawyer should not represent a client if the lawyer does not personally believe that the client's legal position is just, or at least not unjust.[43] Although the view is often denounced by lawyers, it is congenial with cus-

ployments Must a Lawyer Accept?, 2 Prac.Law. 43, 44–45 (May 1956). Some English advocates have claimed that the cab-rank rule is essential in order to preserve access to justice of accused persons in criminal cases. Lord Erskine's flourishing claim is well known: "From the moment that any advocate can be permitted to say that he will or will not stand between the Crown and the subject arraigned in the court where he daily sits to practise, from that moment the liberties of England are at an end." 1 Speeches of Lord Erskine 415 (1847). See also, e.g., Rondel v. Worsley, 1 A.C. 191, 274 (H.L.1969).

[38] Stryker, The Art of Advocacy 274–75 (1954). The supposed corollary of the cab-rank duty-to-serve is that it supports a concept of professional detachment of any lawyer from the justice or injustice of the client's position. The lawyer "may take whomever beckons to whatever destination may be commanded." G.Hazard, Ethics in the Practice of Law 89 (1978).

[39] See generally W.Boulton, Conduct and Etiquette at the Bar 25 (2d ed.1957)(barristers); T.Lund, A Guide to the Professional Conduct and Etiquette of Solicitors 13, 32–33 (1960)(solicitors). For the view that the English cab-rank rule does not assure representation to unpopular causes, see Cooper, Representation of the Unpopular: What Can the Profession Do about this Eternal Problem?, 22 Chitty's L.J. 333 (1974).

[40] H.Drinker, Legal Ethics 139 n.49 (1953), states that a "not very convincing reason for the English rule," which was given in Baldwin, The New American Code of Legal Ethics, 8 Col.L.Rev. 541, 544–45 (1908), is that "barristers are employed only by solicitors, who presumably have satisfied themselves that each case is a proper one." Although hardly a justification, Baldwin's understanding might indicate why the cab-rank rule is accepted by barristers.

On the role of clerks, see Flood, Barristers' Clerks, 4 J.Leg.Prof. 23 (1979).

[41] E.Rostow, The Ideal in Law 155 (1978).

[42] An exception is Schwartz, The Zeal of the Civil Advocate, 1983 Am.B.Found. Research J. 543 (substantially similar to Schwartz, The Zeal of the Civil Advocate, in The Good Lawyer 150 (D.Luban ed.1984)).

[43] J.Auerbach, The Legal Profession after Watergate, 22 Wayne L.Rev. 1287, 1292 (1976); M.Green, The Other Government: The Unseen Power of Washington Lawyers 287 (1975)(a "new lawyer's ethic" should require a lawyer always to justify representations by "his own personal preferences, his own view of 'the public interest' "); P.Stern, Lawyers on Trial 155–59 (1980); Freedman, Personal Responsibility in a Professional System, 27 Cath. U.L.Rev. 191, 199, 204–05 (1978); Lawyers as Hired Guns, Harv.L.Rec., Nov.14, 1969, at 8, col.1 (editorial arguing that lawyers should show "ethical courage" and refuse to advance "interests against the public welfare"). For a discussion from the point of view of moral philosophy, see, e.g., A.Goldman, The Moral Foundations of Professional Ethics 132 (1980)(if prospective client's cause is clearly immoral and "the immorality of the client's purpose outweighs the value of allowing him the autonomy

tomary ways of thinking about morality. Indeed, it is not far from the official stance that the organized bar has itself taken, so long as it is understood to be a statement about moral, and not legal, grounds for objection to a lawyer's representing a particular client. The statement is importantly in error only if it urges that the legal system convert the moral objection into an enforceable legal rule.[44]

Orthodoxy of Professional Freedom to Choose Clients

The lawyer codes in this century[45] have consistently taken the position that, with two exceptions—unpopular clients in need of legal services and court appointments—every lawyer is free to accept or reject any client for reasons personal to the lawyer.[46] Accepting a client is, of course, subject to the applicable rules on such matters as competence and conflict of interest. But a lawyer may refuse to represent a client for any reason at all—because the client cannot pay the lawyer's demanded fee; because the client is not of the lawyer's race or socioeconomic status; because the client is weird or not, tall or short, thin or fat, moral or immoral. For the most part, the lawyer codes, at least in ordinary instances in which access to legal services is not a significant issue, rightly leave matters as personal as the choice of clients for whom to perform personal services to the individual decision of the lawyer.

In the 1969 Code, EC 2–26 states that "a lawyer is under no obligation to act as advisor or advocate for every person who may wish to become his client."[47] Further, EC 2–26 states that the objective of making legal services fully available means that "a lawyer should not lightly decline profferred employment" and "requires acceptance by a lawyer of his share of tendered employment which may be unattractive both to him and the bar generally." The particular context seems to refer to unpopular clients, who might otherwise not be able to retain counsel. The Model Rules are similar. The comment to Model Rule 6.2 speaks of "the lawyer's freedom to select" clients.[48] The sentence preceding it states that "a lawyer ordinarily is not obliged to accept a client whose character or cause the lawyer regards as repugnant."[49] But, similar to the implicit reservation in the Code, the comment to MR 6.2 also notes that the pro bono responsibilities of every lawyer can be fulfilled by "accepting a fair share of unpopular matters or indigent or unpopular clients."

In addition to unpopular clients, court appointments are another exception to the principle of professional freedom to choose clients. A precatory exception for court appointments is contained in EC 2–29, which states a general ethical obligation of lawyers to accept ap-

of pursuing it," then lawyer should refuse representation). The well-known extreme of the position is probably that espoused by William Kunstler in his statement "I only defend those I love." See J.Auerbach, Unequal Justice 290 (1976).

The view is hardly original with moderns. E.g., Cotton Mather, Bonifacius: An Essay to Do Good (Boston, 1710), in Readings in the History of the American Legal Profession 2 (D.Nolan ed.1980)("You will abhor, Sir, to appear in a *Dirty Cause*. If you discern, that your *Client* has an *Unjust Cause*, you will faithfully advise him of it. . . . You will abominate the use of all unfair Arts, to Confound *Evidences*, to Browbeat *Testimonies*, to Suppress what may give Light in the Case.").

[44] German lawyers are reported to operate under a rule that requires them, except perhaps in defense of a person accused of crime, not to accept a case "against the lawyer's personal conviction as to its legal justification and against those rules of law and morals that he ought to take into account." D.Rueschemeyer, Lawyers and Their Society 125 (1973).

[45] See also 1908 Canon of Ethics, Canon 31.

[46] M.Freedman, Lawyer's Ethics in an Adversary System 10 (1975).

[47] Canon 31 of the 1908 Canons of Ethics was even more emphatic:

> No lawyer is obligated to act either as adviser or advocate for every person who may wish to become his client. He has the right to decline employment. Every lawyer upon his own responsibility must decide what employment he will accept as counsel, what causes he will bring into Court for plaintiffs, what cases he will contest in Court for defendants.

[48] MR 6.2 comment (first paragraph).

[49] But cf. Patterson, An Analysis of the Proposed Model Rules of Professional Conduct, 31 Mercer L.Rev. 645, 650 (1980)("by implication [from present MR 1.2(b)], the lawyer has a duty to represent persons even though their cause is an unpopular one").

pointments by a court or bar association to represent a person who is unable, "whether for financial or other reasons," to obtain other counsel. A lawyer should "seek to be excused from such appointments only for 'compelling reasons,'" and these "do not include such factors as the repugnance of the subject matter of the proceeding, the identity or position of a person involved in the case, the belief of the lawyer that the defendant in a criminal proceeding is guilty, or the belief of the lawyer regarding the merits of the civil case." [50]

The 1983 Model Rules go further and convert the precatory approach of the Code into a mandatory rule that lawyers accept court appointments. Model Rule 6.2 states that "a lawyer shall not seek to avoid appointment by a tribunal" [51] but allows an exception for "good cause." Rule 6.2(b) states that good cause includes the fact that "the client or the cause is so repugnant to the lawyer as to be likely to impair the client-lawyer relationship or the lawyer's ability to represent the client." [52]

Criticizing Lawyers for Representing Particular Clients

But to say that a lawyer's choice of clients is a matter of individual discretion is hardly to say that it is beyond moral criticism. Many of the hypothetical reasons listed above for rejecting a client—such as the race or other accidental characteristics of a client—are morally objectionable ones, although they do not violate a mandate of the lawyer codes. One is certainly entitled to say that a lawyer acts immorally if the lawyer *rejects*, on the ground of ethnic origin, a prospective client who is nonetheless readily able to find as competent a lawyer. Is it then right for law students to picket the offices of lawyers who have chosen to *accept* a client and to represent, for example, a large automobile manufacturing client engaged in what the students regard as immoral activities because of the lack of safety of its products? [53] The argument against the act of the students in picketing, aside from possible disagreement with their factual position, is that they are impairing the free availability of lawyers for unpopular clients. But that argument is factually quite unsound in the case of a major automobile manufacturer. Surely a car manufacturer will be able to find many entirely competent lawyers to represent it, given the fees that it is able to pay. It could be argued that a principle of equity is at stake: if manufacturer clients can be the cause of picketing, then other law students could picket a lawyer who represents an abortion clinic, an employment discrimination plaintiff, or other unpopular clients. But that is simply to ignore important factual differences between the two situations in terms of the availability of counsel. A car manufacturer is clearly not unpopular in any sense that impairs ample access to legal counsel; the other clients mentioned might well encounter such difficulties.

There seems no more sensible resolution of the question of the legitimacy of criticism

50 Appointments of the kind alluded to occur very commonly in criminal defense representations in some sections of the nation, in which public defender systems do not exist, but rarely in civil cases. Cf. the "appointment" of Charles Evans Hughes by a bar association, infra at n. 62.

51 Nothing is said in MR 6.2 or its comment about appointments by a bar association. The reference to a "tribunal," a term not defined in the Model Rules, rather plainly points to a court.

52 Other "good cause" exceptions discussed in the comment to MR 6.2 (Appointed Counsel; first paragraph) are "if the lawyer could not handle the matter competently" (which might mean, unfortunately and unfairly, that only criminal defense and possibly other trial lawyers have a clear obligation to accept court appointments in criminal defense cases); "if undertaking the representation would result in an improper conflict of interest, for example, when the client or the cause is so repugnant to the lawyer as to be likely to impair the client-lawyer relationship or the lawyer's ability to represent the client"; and "if acceptance [of the representation] would be unreasonably burdensome, for example, when it would impose a financial sacrifice so great as to be unjust."

53 A confrontation occurred in the late 1960s when a group of law students picketed one of Washington, D.C.'s, largest law firms, protesting the firm's representing large automobile manufacturers, assertedly against the public interest in safer automobiles. The firm's response was that the students were seeking a return to a kind of "McCarthyism." N.Y.Times, Oct.10, 1969, at 30A, cols. 3 & 4. See, e.g., Freedman, Are There Public Interest Limits on Lawyers' Advocacy?, 2 Social Responsibility: Journalism, Law, Medicine 31 (1976).

than a statement similar to the statement assuring professional discretion in lawyers' choice of clients. The question is not entirely the same as that involved in the principle of professional detachment, which concerns itself with the role of a lawyer once it has been assumed.[54] Here the question is whether a lawyer should accept a representation at all. Critics have freedom to criticize a lawyer for a choice of clients, including an arguable legal right to criticize them in public,[55] but the critic should be alert to the need for the freedom of clients to find capable counsel. All of this, of course, says nothing about the moral issue involved in individual lawyer decisions to represent clients in any particular case. Deciding whether lawyers who represent particular manufacturers act morally requires more knowledge of many facts than could be marshaled here.

Last Lawyer in Town: Problem of the Uncounselled Citizen

If it is right that no lawyer need feel it necessary to represent any prospective client and that lawyers may decline to represent a client because of moral objections to the client's intended course of action, it might be that some clients would not be represented at all. The specter of that occurring gives point to the essentially utilitarian argument in support of a rule, such as the English cab-rank rule, that, if adopted, would require American lawyers to accept clients regardless of personal moral objections. The problem is both a social and a personal one.

As a social problem, there is power to the argument that a legal system is unjust if it purports to grant legal rights—to Nazis to give hate-filled speeches, to pornographers to peddle their smut—but provides them with no lawyer, without whose assistance the rights granted cannot be effectively claimed. For that reason, much can be said in support of a claim of social justice that a system should provide some method—court appointments, legal aid, or a voluntary bar mechanism—for providing counsel to all, regardless of their moral stance.[56] In the absence of such a system, an argument has been made that an individual lawyer should feel a moral compulsion to provide legal assistance to a person, to whose objectives in the representation the lawyer has strong moral objections, only when the client seeks an essential human need and it lies within the power of the lawyer, without an undue personal sacrifice, to render the necessary legal assistance.[57] If, under that system of individual moral choice made by individual lawyers, some prospective clients are unable to assert legal rights—in effect because of a unanimous lawyer reaction of moral rejection, a "lawyer's trump" of individual legal right—the solution lies in social and political organization and not in individual obligations of lawyers. To an extent, the solution that has been developed in both the 1969 Code and in the 1983 Model Rules is that lawyers as individuals have a nonmandatory professional obligation to do their fair share of representing unpopular clients. For an individual lawyer, that pits the professional statement of the social ethic of universal legal representation against a lawyer's possible individual moral values.

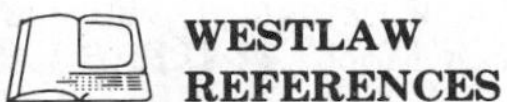

Professional Concept of a Duty to Serve

ec2–26 "ec 2–26" ec2–29 "ec 2–29"

Orthodoxy of Professional Freedom to Choose Clients

attorney lawyer counsel** /p duty free*** /5 accept*** decline* reject*** refuse*** /2 employ!

[54] See § 10.2.1.

[55] The position is also bolstered in an obvious way by arguments concerning the free-expression rights of critics of lawyers.

[56] For such an argument, see Schwartz, The Zeal of the Civil Advocate, in The Good Lawyer 150, 164–69 (D.Luban ed. 1984).

[57] Wolfram, A Lawyer's Duty to Represent Clients, Repugnant and Otherwise, in The Good Lawyer 214 (D.Luban ed.1984).

§ 10.2.3 Unpopular Clients and Causes [58]

Problem of Unpopular Representations

Generations of lawyers have been stirred by stories of great names in Anglo-American law [59] who have undertaken, in the face of popular and professional outcry, the defense of the legal rights of outcasts.[60] John Adams accepted real professional and personal risk when he defended British soldiers accused of murder in the Boston Massacre.[61] Charles Evans Hughes, in behalf of the Association of the Bar of the City of New York, took real professional risks in representing five Socialist legislators who had been denied their seats in the New York Assembly in the heat of anti-Red hysteria after the First World War.[62]

That such golden moments in professional history are treasured by the legal profession as a whole is ironic. When the events that are now celebrated actually occurred, public opinion was strongly opposed to the lawyers' legal assistance to despised persons and professional opinion was divided at best. Professional heroes, like heroes generally, are more easily remembered at a comfortable distance than recognized at moments of crisis and public consternation. The actual role of a lawyer defending an unpopular client is often one of great tension, professional and personal isolation, and humiliation. Often it has been accompanied by a serious decline in the lawyer's clientele and income. Although salutary, the role is also extraordinarily difficult, even personally dangerous.[63] It is simply not the case that heroism of the kind applauded is either typical or sufficient to give counsel to all those who require it.[64] For example, nine years after the 1954 Supreme Court decision that began the process of desegregation, the Court could still refer to "an apparent dearth of lawyers who are willing to undertake" desegregation suits for plaintiffs in some Southern states.[65]

Professional Regulations on Unpopular Representations

The lawyer codes applaud lawyers who represent unpopular clients but stop far short of providing a solution to a lack of representation if that occurs. The Code's EC 2–27 invokes a professional history "replete with instances of distinguished and sacrificial services by lawyers who have represented un-

[58] See generally Schwartz, The Zeal of the Civil Lawyer, in The Good Lawyer 150, 161–69 (D.Luban ed.1984); Wolfram, A Lawyer's Duty to Represent Clients, Repugnant and Otherwise, in id. 214; Ernst & Schwartz, The Right to Counsel and the Unpopular Cause, 20 U.Pitt.L. Rev. 727 (1958).

[59] Some of the names are fictitious, such as Atticus Finch, in *To Kill a Mockingbird*, see Shaffer, The Moral Theology of Atticus Finch, 42 U.Pitts.L.Rev. 181 (1981).

[60] See also D.Mellinkoff, The Conscience of a Lawyer 169–71 (1973)(John Adams and Josiah Quincy); A.Robbins, American Advocacy 274–75 (2d ed.1913)(Erskine's defense of Thomas Paine); Freedman, The President's Advocate and the Public Interest, 27 N.Y.L.J. 1 (1974).

[61] 1 P.Smith, The Life of John Adams 114 et seq. (1962); Reid, A Lawyer Acquitted: John Adams and the Boston Massacre, 18 Am.J.Leg.Hist. 189 (1974).

[62] G.Martin, Causes and Conflicts: The Centennial History of the Association of the Bar of the City of New York 1870–1970, at 206–12 (1970).

[63] See also, e.g., Black, J., dissenting in Cohen v. Hurley, 366 U.S. 117, 138–41, 81 S.Ct. 954, 966–68, 6 L.Ed.2d 156 (1961); In re Anastapalo, 366 U.S. 82, 114–16, 81 S.Ct. 978, 995–96, 6 L.Ed.2d 135 (1961); Goldberger, Would You Defend an Unpopular Cause?, 5 Barrister 46 (Winter 1978); Goldberger, Skokie: The First Amendment under Attack by Its Friends, 29 Mercer L.Rev. 761 (1978); Horowitz & Bramson, Skokie, The ACLU and the Endurance of Democratic Theory, 43 L. & Contemp. Prob. 328 (1979); Nagle & Champagne, The Risks of Defending Unpopular Clients, 2 Student Law. 41 (1973); Symposium, The Right to Counsel and the "Unpopular Cause"—Let Us Admit Impediments, 20 U.Pitts.L.Rev. 749 (1959); Brown, Some Applications of the Rules of Legal Ethics, 6 Minn.L.Rev. 427, 432–34 (1922); Comment, Controlling Lawyers by Bar Association and Courts, 5 Harv.C.R.-C.L.L.Rev. 301 (1970). A good collection of historical incidents is contained in Pollitt, Counsel for the Unpopular Cause: The "Hazard of Being Undone," 43 N.C.L.Rev. 9 (1964).

[64] Clendinen, Rising Death Row Population Burdens Volunteer Lawyers, N.Y.Times, Aug.23, 1982, at Al, col. 5. The scarcity of lawyers in any community who are willing to resist community pressures and defend locally unpopular clients has been given as an argument in favor of an expanded right of all clients to the assistance of out-of-state lawyers. See Spanos v. Skouras Theatres Corp., 364 F.2d 161, 170 (2d Cir.1966), cert.denied 385 U.S. 987, 87 S.Ct. 597, 17 L.Ed.2d 448 (1966). See also Leis v. Flynt, 439 U.S. 438, 99 S.Ct. 698, 58 L.Ed.2d 717 (1979) (Stevens, J., dissenting).

[65] NAACP v. Virginia ex rel. Button, 371 U.S. 415, 443, 83 S.Ct. 328, 343, 9 L.Ed.2d 405 (1963).

popular clients and causes." It continues, "regardless of his personal feelings, a lawyer should not decline representation because a client or cause is unpopular or community reaction is adverse." And EC 2–26 refers broadly to the desirability of lawyers' accepting cases that other lawyers might not: "in furtherance of the objective of the bar to make legal services fully available, a lawyer should not lightly decline proffered employment. The fulfillment of this objective requires acceptance by a lawyer of his share of tendered employment which may be unattractive both to him and the bar generally." Unpopular clients are also mentioned in EC 2–28, which states that a lawyer's desire not to antagonize judges, other lawyers, public officials, or influential members of the community "does not justify his rejection of profferred employment." The implicit notion is that employment can be rejected, but only for good reasons, and that fear of antagonizing powerful adversaries or others is not a good reason. EC 2–19 states that when a lawyer is appointed to defend an unpopular client by a court, a "compelling reason" that might justify the lawyer's asking to be excused from the appointment does "not include such factors as the repugnance of the subject matter of the proceeding,[66] the identity or position of a person involved in the case, the belief of the lawyer that the defendant in a criminal proceeding is guilty, or the belief of the lawyer regarding the merits of the civil case."

The Model Rules essentially follow the Code. As does the Code, the Model Rules state only in nonmandatory comments that a lawyer should feel a professional responsibility to accept the representation of some unpopular clients. That is an aspect of the general nonmandatory duty of every lawyer to perform pro bono services.[67]

Institutional Responsibility for Unpopular Clients

The organized bar has occasionally stated that a "duty" exists on the part of the bar as an entity to provide assistance "even to the most unpopular defendants." [68] Yet the bar has done relatively little to assure that lawyers in fact are made available for unpopular clients or causes,[69] nor has the organized bar been notably active in defending lawyers who have personally undertaken the defense of an unpopular client or who have simply found themselves in such a representation as events unfolded.[70] Similarly, it has been claimed

[66] EC 2–30 cautions that a lawyer should not accept employment "if the intensity of his personal feeling, as distinguished from a community attitude, may impair his effective representation of a prospective client." The distinction drawn is that between repugnance that does not disable the lawyer from proceeding with an effective representation and repugnance that would. The concept basically recognizes the possible conflict of interest between a lawyer's strong personal instincts and the objectives of the client. Conflicts of that kind are recognized in EC 5–2: "A lawyer should not accept proffered employment if his personal interests or desires will, or there is a reasonable probability that they will, affect adversely the advice to be given or services to be rendered the prospective client."

[67] MR 6.2 comment (first paragraph): "The lawyer's freedom to select clients is . . . qualified. All lawyers have a responsibility to assist in providing pro bono publico service. See Rule 6.1. An individual lawyer fulfills this responsibility by accepting a fair share of unpopular matters or indigent or unpopular clients. A lawyer may also be subject to appointment by a court to service unpopular clients or persons unable to afford legal services." On the precatory duty to perform pro bono legal work, see § 16.9. On the question whether the pro bono responsibilities of a lawyer require a lawyer to represent a morally repugnant client in the absence of a need to do so because of the absence of other available counsel, see § 10.2.2, at 574–75.

[68] Proceedings of the House of Delegates, 78 ABA Rep. 118, 133 (1953); Spec. Comm. on Individual Rights as Affected by National Security, Report, 78 ABA Rep. 304 (1953).

[69] But cf. e.g., ABA Formal Op. 334 (1974); ABA Informal Op. 1208 (1972)(governing board of legal services organization may not impose restraints that seek to avoid controversial or unpopular persons or issues). The ABA opinions were a reaction to frequent attempts by governing boards in the late 1960s to impose restrictive criteria on client intake. See Bellow & Kettleson, From Ethics to Politics: Confronting Scarcity and Fairness in Public Interest Practice, 58 Bost.U.L.Rev. 337, 350 (1978).

[70] Goldberger, The "Right to Counsel" in Political Cases: The Bar's Failure, 43 L. & Contemp.Prob. 321 (1979). But cf., e.g., Pollitt, Counsel for the Unpopular Cause: The "Hazard of Being Undone," 43 N.C.L.Rev. 9, 29 (1964)(instances in which bar associations and groups of lawyers have defended lawyers attacked for defense of unpopular causes); J.Stone, Legal Education and Professional Responsibility 1559 (1959)(same). On the same day in 1953 during the height of the McCarthy era, the ABA

that it is improper for a lawyer to attack another lawyer because the latter is representing a particular client, no matter how unpopular or heinous the client may be.[71] Yet there is very little professional impetus to put any disciplinary muscle behind such sentiments. They are certainly widely ignored and may be disputed.[72]

WESTLAW REFERENCES

Professional Regulations of Unpopular Representations

"ec 2-27" ec2-27 "ec 2-28" ec2-28 "ec 2-29" ec2-29

§ 10.3 PRINCIPLE OF ZEALOUS PARTISANSHIP

§ 10.3.1 Nature of the Principle of Zeal

Requirement of Commitment to Client Interests

It is hardly the case in all legal cultures that representing a client entails the lawyer's strong commitment to further the client's position. In other legal cultures, lawyers are expected to further a client's position only if that furthers other interests, such as those of the state apparatus (§ 1.2). In many systems lawyers might have difficulty understanding a concept of client "rights" apart from the interests of the state. Or, carrying to an extreme the saying that lawyers are officers of the court (§ 1.6), one might imagine, contrary to fact, that a lawyer in the United States is expected to function only in a client's behalf when that does not conflict with any other claimed obligation that the lawyer might owe to the judicial system. But no such notions limit the American legal system's ideal of the client-lawyer relationship. Instead, the American lawyer's professional model is that of zeal: a lawyer is expected to devote energy, intelligence, skill, and personal commitment to the single goal of furthering the client's interests as those are ultimately defined by the client. The sentiment was expressed in stirring phrases in the 1908 Canons (Canon 15):

> The lawyer owes "entire devotion to the interest of the client, warm zeal in the maintenance and defense of his rights and the exertion of his utmost learning and ability," [73] to the end that nothing be taken or be withheld from him save by the rules of law, legally applied. No fear of judicial disfavor or public unpopularity should restrain him from the full discharge of his duty. In the judicial forum the client is entitled to the benefit of any and every remedy and defense that is authorized by the law of the land, and he may expect his lawyer to assert every such remedy and defense.

The same concept was first expressed in the United States near the middle of the last century by George Sharswood [74] and has been embraced in both the Code and the Model Rules. The heading of DR 7-101 assumes

(1) authorized its Committee on Communist Tactics, Strategy and Objectives to cooperate with the attorney general to see to the possible disbarment of "communist attorneys" who invoked their right not to incriminate themselves before congressional committees (78 ABA Rep. 132 (1953)); and (2) adopted an amended version of a report of the ABA Committee on Individual Rights as Affected by National Security that:

> *reaffirms the principles* that the right of defendants to the benefit of assistance of counsel and the duty of the bar to provide such aid even to the most unpopular defendants involves public acceptance of the correlative right of a lawyer to represent and defend, in accordance with the standards of the *legal profession*, any client without being penalized by having imputed to him his client's reputation, views or character.
>
> 2. That the Association will support any lawyer against criticism or attack in connection with such representation, when, in its judgment, he has behaved in accordance with the standards of the bar.
>
> 3. That the Association will *continue* to educate the profession and the public on the rights and duties of a lawyer in representing any client, regardless of the unpopularity of either the client or his cause.

78 ABA Rep. 133 (1953)(emphasis in original). For the report of the committee, see id. 304.

71 Gertz v. Robert Welch, Inc., 418 U.S. 323, 353, 94 S.Ct. 2997, 3013, 41 L.Ed.2d 789 (1974)(Burger, C.J., dissenting); Professional Responsibility: Report of the Joint Conference, 44 ABA J. 1159, 1217 (1958).

72 Further on the right to criticize another lawyer for representing a particular client, see § 10.2.2, at 574–75.

73 The quotation indicated in the Canon is not attributed. The source is G.Sharswood, An Essay on Professional Ethics 24 (2d ed.1860).

74 G.Sharswood, supra at 22–33.

that a lawyer will "represent a client zealously," repeating the axiomatic message of Canon 7 of the Code that "a lawyer should represent a client zealously within the bounds of the law." And DR 7–101(A)(1) states negatively that a lawyer "shall not intentionally: (1) Fail to seek the lawful objectives of his client through reasonably available means," while DR 7–101(A)(3) insists that a lawyer not intentionally "prejudice or damage his client during the course of the relationship." [75] Somewhat more positively, EC 7–1 postulates that "the duty of a lawyer, both to his client and to the legal system, is to represent his client zealously within the bounds of the law." The Model Rules state the principle in the comment (first paragraph) to MR 1.3:

> A lawyer should pursue a matter on behalf of a client despite opposition, obstruction or personal inconvenience to the lawyer, and may take whatever lawful and ethical measures are required to vindicate a client's cause or endeavor. A lawyer should act with commitment and dedication to the interests of the client and with zeal in advocacy upon the client's behalf.

The principle of zealous regard for a client's interests is pivotal because it gives direction to definitions of a lawyer's responsibilities concerning relationships with a client (chapter 4), competence (chapter 5), confidentiality (chapter 6), conflicts of interest (chapters 7 and 8), advocacy (chapters 11 and 12), and counselling (chapter 13). In many of the problems discussed there, it will be seen that zeal for a client is not only important but is given primacy, sometimes a startling primacy when client interests come into conflict with the interests of other persons.

Limits on Zeal

Limits on zeal, of course, are acknowledged by all. Indeed, the approach of most discourses on the work of lawyers—as of all of the lawyer codes and treatises such as this—is to postulate a principle of zeal and then move quickly and more voluminously to hedge it about with necessary restrictions and qualifications. The limits on zeal are important because of the interests of third parties and of the legal system itself. A lawyer may not commit a crime in behalf of a client, for example.[76] But it is widely expected that a lawyer will stand ready to perform any service for a client that is appropriate for the advancement of the client's legal rights so long as it violates no law. "Law" in that usage, as is now becoming universally recognized, includes the commands of the lawyer codes when they have been authoritatively adopted and are applicable to a situation. Also relevant are a lawyer's nonlegal views, which a lawyer is free to bring into the client's process of making decisions.[77]

But if the lawyer's client rejects the lawyer's advice—which, of course, the client is free to do[78]—the lawyer may not undercut a client's asserted interest in pursuing a course of legally protected conduct with which the lawyer disagrees (§ 10.4.1). Moreover, the lawyer is under a positive professional obligation to continue the representation with the same zealous regard for furthering the best interests of the client, as the client has now defined them, as if the lawyer had agreed with the client's decision.[79] The lawyer's only op-

[75] State v. Leon, 229 Kan. 178, 621 P.2d 1016 (1981) (lawyer who wrote letter to own client, threatening to seek contempt sanction against client unless she made payment ordered by divorce decree, violated zeal rules of DR 7–101).

[76] 1908 Canon 12 continued, at the point where the quotation in the text ends:

> But it is steadfastly to be borne in mind that the great trust of the lawyer is to be performed within and not without the bounds of the law. The office of lawyer does not permit, much less does it demand of him for any client, violation of law or any manner of fraud or chicane. He must obey his own conscience and not that of his client.

[77] See § 4.3, at 157–59.

[78] See generally § 4.3.

[79] EC 7–9 ("In the exercise of his professional judgment on those decisions which are for his determination in the handling of a legal matter, a lawyer should always act in a manner consistent with the best interests of his client. However, when an action in the best interests of his client seems to him to be unjust, he may ask his client for permission to forego such action.").

The Model Code is ambiguous on the point. MR 1.3 comment (first paragraph), after stating that a lawyer should act zealously in a client's behalf, continues: "However, a lawyer is not bound to press for every advantage tion, which will not always be available, is to withdraw from the representation.[80]

Zealous Advocacy in History

Recent legal history is rich with statements of the ideal of zeal in representing a client. Best known is the stirring defiance of Henry Brougham in his defense as an advocate of Queen Caroline.[81] Appearing in the House of Lords in 1820, he alluded darkly to evidence that might harm the sovereign, King George IV.[82] Brougham argued that no matter the consequences to others or to the kingdom itself, his duty as an advocate compelled him to take every step necessary to advance his client's interests:

> [A]n advocate, in the discharge of his duty, knows but one person in all the world, and that person is his client. To save that client by all means and expedients, and at all hazards and costs to other persons, and, amongst them, to himself, is his first and only duty; and in performing this duty he must not regard the alarm, the torments, the destruction which he may bring upon others. Separating the duty of a patriot from that of an advocate, he must go on reckless of consequences, though it should be his unhappy fate to involve his country in confusion.[83]

It is doubtful that Brougham's words were widely accepted by lawyers of his time as a careful delineation of a lawyer's role, although they were clearly eloquent. Today, however, it seems clear that they reflect the dominant, although hardly universal, professional ethic. The same sentiment of duty to a client, even to the harm of the advocate's own nation, has been repeated more recently.[84]

Lawyers as Hired Guns

Lawyers have ambivalent feelings about the sobriquet "hired gun." For some lawyers, it accuses lawyers of being lackeys who are prepared to perform servile acts of immorality and lawlessness at the beckoning of paying clients.[85] For others, it suggests the macho heroics of the frontier, with the lawyer wearing the white hat and with the proud right to lay about heavily in the client's interests.[86] Interesting as image, the phrase, and others like it, obviously has little bearing on the

that might be realized for a client. A lawyer has professional discretion in determining the means by which a matter should be pursued. See Rule 1.2."

80 See DR 2–110(C)(1)(e)(when client, "in a matter not pending before a tribunal," insists that lawyer pursue a course of conduct "that is contrary to the judgment and advice of the lawyer but not prohibited under the Disciplinary Rules," lawyer has professional discretion to withdraw).

81 Brougham was a cofounder, with Bentham, of the University of London (1828) and the Society for the Diffusion of Useful Knowledge. He later rose to lord chancellor. See R.Webb, Modern England 163, 176, 181–82, 193 (1971); C.New, The Life of Henry Brougham to 1830 (1961).

82 D.Mellinkoff, The Conscience of a Lawyer 188–89 (1973). As Professor Mellinkoff points out, Brougham was alluding to gossip, which was common, that the king himself had engaged in countless indiscretions, and was threatening the king's counsellors, in effect, to introduce the defense of recrimination if they continued to press the suit against Queen Caroline. Less publicly known, but known to Brougham and the king's counsellors, was that the king had himself contracted a marriage with a Roman Catholic, which at that time would cause him automatically to lose his crown. It is the possibility of forcing a secession that Brougham refers to as "involv[ing] his country in confusion."

83 2 Trial of Queen Caroline 8 (1821), cited in D.Mellinkoff, supra at 189 n.10.

84 In re Griffiths, 413 U.S. 717, 724 n.14, 93 S.Ct. 2851, 2856, 37 L.Ed.2d 910 (1973) (in American lawyer's representation of foreign country as a client in litigation or "in other matters . . . the duty of the lawyer, subject to his role as an 'officer of the court,' is to further the interests of his clients by all lawful means, even when those interests are in conflict with the interests of the United States or of a State. But this representation involves no conflict of interest in the invidious sense. Rather, it casts the lawyer in his honored and traditional role as an authorized but independent agent acting to vindicate the legal rights of a client, whoever it may be.").

85 Chief Justice Burger has often fulminated against such accusations. E.g., In re Griffiths, 413 U.S. 717, 731–32, 93 S.Ct. 2851, 2859–60, 37 L.Ed.2d 910 (1973)(Burger, C.J., dissenting).

86 In a system that until very recently was operated almost exclusively by males, the imageries of sports, tavern, and warfare have often been resorted to as metaphors for full-commitment advocacy, sometimes all at once. E.g., Thornton v. Breland, 441 So.2d 1348, 1350 (Miss.1983)("A lawyer is and must be the ultimate advocate. He speaks for and in the interest of his client. He seizes every fair advantage available to his client. And when his client is on the ropes, the lawyer, standing alone if need be, is that one person who, in the interest of his client, skillfully defies the state, the opposing litigant, or whoever threatens. The lawyer is prepared to stand against the forces of hell though others see that as his client's just desert. He assures all adversaries, in the

question of the stance that the role of lawyer justifies and requires.

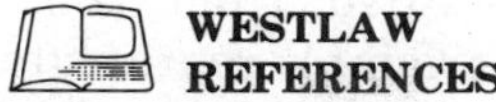
WESTLAW REFERENCES

Requirement of Commitment to Client Interests

attorney lawyer counsel** /s represent! /3 zeal!

Limits on Zeal

attorney lawyer counsel** /s represent! /3 zeal! /50 limit!

§ 10.3.2 Rationale of Zealous Partisanship

Debate over the Lawyer's Role as Advocate

A large gulf divides lawyers and most non-lawyers over the propriety of many controversial aspects of the lawyer's professional role. A much-quoted passage is Macaulay's denunciation of lawyers for their efforts to defeat truth—a passage that speaks the public mind in many eras:

> [Is it] right that a man should, with a wig on his head, and a band around his neck, do for a guinea what, without those appendages, he would think it wicked and infamous to do for an empire; whether it be right that, not merely believing but knowing a statement to be true, he should do all that can be done by sophistry, by rhetoric, by solemn asseveration, by indignant exclamation, by gesture, by play of features, by terrifying one honest witness, by perplexing another, to cause a jury to think that statement false.[87]

The response of lawyers is that the adversary system is capable in the great majority of cases of determining where truth lies and justice is best served. For a lawyer to permit personal doubts to intrude about the truthfulness of client-favoring witnesses and the untruthfulness of those opposed, the lawyer's function would be hobbled by self-doubt and the client's rights wrongly impaired.

In the dominant legal culture in the United States, to ask why it is that a lawyer should be zealous in pursuit of a client's interests is to raise a question the answer to which most lawyers probably feel is intuitively obvious. In a profession noted for its skeptical outlook on general principle, that alone should raise suspicions. Confirming them is the fact that many other legal cultures have no corresponding principle.

The American principle of professsional zeal is entwined with the American conception of legal rights. The concept is shared with some Western European legal systems, but is found in the United States in a form that, for vigor, has no rival anywhere. Basically the principle stems from concepts of individual autonomy. Each individual in a society is the holder of rights, and the legal system provides mechanisms by which individuals can assert and claim the consequences of their rights. Courts and lawyers in that scheme are the facilitators of rights' claimants and the functionaries in processes of resolving disputes over the definition of rights and over the presence or absence of facts supporting a claim of right.

Both the definitional and fact-determining tasks can be difficult and indeterminate, and for that reason dispute resolvers are needed. As the conception of the adversary system has it, the best method of resolving disputes is single-minded representation by client-centered advocates who, in their zeal to assist their clients, are motivated to discover facts and elaborately research and argue the law. The dedication of lawyers to that task is important to correct determinations by courts and possibly other agencies and, thus, to the vindication of rights. In short, lawyers are

vernacular of the streets, "You may get my client but you've got to come through me first.").

A kind of antisocial disposition may be associated with the traditional male domination of the legal profession. Sociologists have noted a tendency to emphasize antisocial behavior in the conventional American notion of masculinity. That masculine ideal is accompanied by a high valuation of authoritarian behavior, a reservoir of repressed aggression, and strong rejection of helping or nurturing behavior. E.g., T.Parsons, Social Structure and Personality ch. 2 (1964); Mindes, Trickster, Hero, Helper: A Report on the Lawyer Image, 1982 Am.B. Found. Research J. 177, 219–26.

[87] G.Macauley, Works of Lord Macaulay 135, 163 (1900).

zealous in protecting the interests of their clients for instrumental reasons: that attitude assures that the system will work well.

§ 10.4 LAWYERS' NONLEGAL VIEWS

§ 10.4.1 Lawyers' Values in Conflict with Clients'

Lawyers' Values in the Counselling Function

A lawyer's obligation of zeal does not require, however, the sacrifice of personal beliefs and instincts. A lawyer's representation of a client does not amount to the lawyer's personal endorsement of the client's political, social, economic, moral, or other views or objectives. But a lawyer is free to express to a client the lawyer's personal views on such matters to the extent that they bear on the representation and the project on which the client has sought the lawyer's help.[88] If the client rejects that advice, the lawyer need not accept the client's viewpoint but may continue the representation with their disagreement now clarified. It is for the client, of course, to determine the course of the representation (§ 4.3). Continuing the representation is not an endorsement of the merits of the client's nonlegal views,[89] no more than such an endorsement resulted from the lawyer's accepting the original representation.[90] The principle of professional detachment is said to immunize the lawyer from contamination by whatever appropriate moral judgments may be made about the lawyer's client (§ 10.2.1).

WESTLAW REFERENCES

"ec 7-5" ec7-5

§ 10.4.2 Lawyers and Law Reform

Law Reform against the Interests of a Client

According to the professional codes, it is desirable for lawyers to engage in reform of the legal system.[91] Indeed lawyers are said to have a special responsibility, because of their position, to take the time to seek reform of unjust laws.[92] Individual lawyers have often been intensely engaged in law reform. But it is certainly not true that lawyers today,[93] any more than a century [94] or a half century ago,[95] are as a group interested in significant change in the existing social and political order. The task of law reform has fallen

[88] EC 7–8; MR 2.1 comment (Scope of Advice; second paragraph). See also § 4.3, at 157–59, § 13.3.10.

[89] EC 7–5 (a lawyer "may continue in the representation of his client even though his client has elected to pursue a course of conduct contrary to the advice of the lawyer so long as he does not thereby knowingly assist the client to engage in illegal conduct or to take a frivolous legal position."

[90] EC 7–17 ("The obligation of loyalty to his client applies only to a lawyer in the discharge of his professional duties and implies no obligation to adopt a personal viewpoint favorable to the interests or desires of his client."

[91] The direction of reform, of course, is carefully not mentioned. E.g., EC 8–9: "The advancement of our legal system is of vital importance in maintaining the rule of law and in facilitating orderly changes; therefore, lawyers should encourage, and should aid in making, needed changes and improvements."

[92] EC 8–1: "By reason of education and experience, lawyers are especially qualified to recognize deficiencies in the legal system and to initiate corrective measures therein. Thus they should participate in proposing and supporting legislation and programs to improve the system, without regard to the general interests or desires of clients or former clients." See also EC 8–2; Model Rules preamble (fifth paragraph)("As a public citizen, a lawyer should seek improvement of the law, the administration of justice and the quality of service rendered by the legal profession. As a member of a learned profession, a lawyer should cultivate knowledge of the law beyond its use for clients, employ that knowledge in reform of the law and work to strengthen legal education."); MR 6.1 (discharge of lawyer's obligation to render public interest legal service might include "service in activities for improving the law, the legal system or the legal profession").

[93] See generally F.Marks, K.Leswing & B.Fortinsky, The Lawyer, the Public, and Professional Responsibility (1978).

[94] Lord Bryce, The American Commonwealth 306–07, 671–76 (1917 ed.)(comments, first published in 1888, that public influence of American bar had generally declined because of inability or unwillingness of bar to deal with social and political issues).

[95] Stone, The Public Influence of the Bar, 48 Harv.L. Rev. 1, 10 (1934). See also, e.g., L.Brandeis, Business—A Profession 318, 321 (1914)(from address in 1912); R.Hofstader, The Age of Reform 163 (1955)(remarks of Henry L. Stimson in 1908).

largely to a small handful of lawyers who work individually or, more commonly, through advocacy and special interest organizations or bar association committees.[96]

To the extent that a lawyer engages in law reform, a lawyer is to do his or her own bidding and not that of a client, unless of course the lawyer is representing a client in a matter involving lobbying or other kinds of legal change.[97] Representational work that involves change in the law is carried on much the same way as are other lawyerly tasks, with the client's interests being the major defining element.[98] Beyond representational lobbying, however, the lawyer codes urge lawyers to seek just laws regardless of positions that might have been previously taken for clients in representations. An instance that many believe illustrates the necessary distinction is a story from the career of an English barrister, Thomas Talfourd.[99] Talfourd found himself representing a client whose cause was immoral but that Talfourd was able to win in court because of an unjust statute. Later, as a member of Parliament, Talfourd helped pass a measure that repealed the objectionable features of the statute.

Paradoxical Value Choices in Law Reform

Talfourd's example and the lawyer codes pose a paradox.[1] One is entitled to ask why Talfourd didn't send the client packing, or retain the case but refuse to urge the applicability of the statute. In a spirit of separation between private practice and public activity, both the Code and the Model Rules urge lawyers to become engaged in law-reform activities regardless of client interests. But both also require lawyers, pursuant to the principle of professional detachment (§ 10.2), to seek every lawful objective for a client regardless of its morality. Is the separation between representational work and personal work valid? The answer lies both in agreeing, or not, with the presuppositions and arguments of the principle of professional detachment, and in a further matter concerning the existence or nonexistence of two realms of moral and psychic relevance for lawyers.

WESTLAW REFERENCES

attorney lawyer counsel** /s "canon 8" "ec 8" ec8

§ 10.4.3 Lawyers and Role Separation

Public, Group, and Private Morality

The nineteenth-century sociologist Emile Durkheim identified ways in which the legal profession and other self-contained professions could develop for themselves a morality that was different from, and clashed with, the public morality of the society within which lawyers functioned. Because the public is not aware of most of what lawyers do or why they do it, lawyers are free within relatively loose bounds to create their own notions of professional right and wrong:

> We might say in this connection that there are as many forms of morals as there are different callings, and since, in theory, each individual carries on only one calling, the result is that

96 Possible conflicts of interest between a lawyer's clients and the objectives of a law reform organization to which the lawyer belongs are dealt with in MR 6.4.

97 When lobbying for a client, a lawyer is to note the separation of advocate and client by indicating that the lawyer appears in a representative role. See § 13.8.2.

98 Some have urged, however, that different and stricter constraints should limit a lawyer's representation of a client when the lawyer functions as a lobbyist. Basically, those critics assert that a lawyer in a lobbying role should espouse only those measures that the lawyer personally believes in:

> Lawyers have no monopoly in legislative hearing rooms, as they have in courtrooms, and so there is less dependence on their services. As legislative witnesses their honest and informed judgment is likely to be of more aid to the lawmakers than their prowess in the adversary process.

Freund, The Moral Education of the Lawyer, 26 Emory L.J. 3, 4 (1977). See also, e.g., Wyzanski, Book Review, 90 Harv.L.Rev. 283, 287 (1976). See also § 13.8.2 (legal and moral limits on lobbying).

99 Professional Responsibility: Report of the Joint Conference, 44 ABA J. 1159, 1162 (1958).

1 Smurl, In the Public Interest: The Precedents and Standards of a Lawyer's Public Responsibility, 11 Ind.L. Rev. 797, 812–13 (1978).

those different forms of morals apply to entirely different groups of individuals.[2]

The process by which lawyers codes of "ethics" are developed fits Durkheim's description closely.[3] Using the assumptions and staying within the professional rules, a lawyer can assert that his or her role-differentiated behavior is justifiable.[4]

The issue of group moralities, individual moralities, and personal moralities is a problem that has concerned moral philosophers[5] and moral psychologists as well as sociologists. The problem is whether it is possible for a lawyer, or a member of any other group that functions with a set of moral values very different from those of the containing society, to function effectively either individually or within and as a member of the containing society.

§ 10.4.4 Personalities and Character of Lawyers

Psychological and Moral Self-Divisions

Is it possible for the same person to march to professional and then to personal drums? Lawyers have developed two reasons for thinking that it is possible to function under a professional morality that is different from private morality without sacrificing personal integrity.

First, it is argued, the commitment that is called for by the duty of zealous representation of a client's interests (§ 10.3) does not call for a personal, emotional commitment. Instead, lawyers are actors who are capable of putting on the transitory character and the moral stance required by their professional work and then readily shedding that role to walk away from it and resume an integral life as a nonprofessional person in family, business, and other personal roles. The professional morality is never accepted or acted upon as a personal morality.

Second, other lawyers disagree and hold that a lawyer can be effective only if the lawyer becomes deeply and emotionally committed to the client's position.[6] Particularly in matters of advocacy, many lawyers think that effective legal work requires the lawyer to share the client's mind and will.[7] Lawyers may also perceive that clients will not believe that a lawyer is performing adequately unless the lawyer is personally committed to the client's point of view.[8] John W. Davis' insistence is typical: "an advocate isn't worth his salt unless he winds up seeing only his own side of the case."[9]

How can such an identification with a client occur if the lawyer knows that the client doesn't morally deserve to prevail? The answer sometimes given is case hardening. Through training and early practice, the truly professional lawyer supposedly acquires an ability to put emotional distance between himself or herself and a client, the client's problem, and others who may be affected by the representation. The lawyer can then function intellectually or skillfully without the hindrance of normal affects or feelings of guilt.

[2] E.Durkheim, Professional Ethics and Civil Morals 5 (1957)(from lectures given in 1897–1900).

[3] §§ 2.3, 2.6.1.

[4] The concept of role differentiation is discussed, among other places, in Wasserstrom, Lawyers as Professionals: Some Moral Issues, 5 Human Rights 1 (1975).

[5] For a brief review of the problem and some of the literature in moral philosophy, see § 2.7.3.

[6] Identification with the client's interests may be necessary for the lawyer in order to present to adversaries a convincing appearance of a dedication to carry out an implicit threat to see the client's case through to any necessary end. See Mindes & Acock, Trickster, Hero, Villain: A Report on the Lawyer Image, 1982 Am.B. Found. Research J. 177, 222.

[7] Profiles: Advocate (Simon Hirsch Rifkind), The New Yorker, May 23, 1983, at 46, 47 (two principal requirements for successful litigation, second of which was: "Litigation is an emotional experience. It calls for identification with the client. I have never seen a great actor who did not identify with the character he impersonated. The same is true of a successful litigator."); 50 U.S.L.Wk. 2085 (1981)(advice by former president of Association of Trial Lawyers of America that presuasiveness in final argument to jury required that lawyer must believe in own case, in client, and in the law).

[8] Thoron, A Course in the Dynamics of Professional Responsibility, in Education in the Professional Responsibilities of the Lawyer 95 (D.Weckstein ed.1970).

[9] H.Harbaugh, Lawyer's Lawyer: The Life of John W. Davis 267 (1973).

There are several problems with such a role definition. Most obviously, it is emotionally schizophrenic.[10] The lawyer's emotions are severed from the lawyer's consciousness. Putting one's emotions out for hire to someone whose objectives the lawyer despises is the sort of personal debasement that may predictably lead to professional burnout and withdrawal and stagnation in law practice. Or, if pressed, it may lead to profound moral skepticism, an utter insensitivity to the human qualities of persons—clients and opponents alike.[11]

Beyond the personal level, it has also been argued that the role model of full-commitment, client-centered advocacy is institutionally schizophrenic. The procedural and legal system are supposedly designed to produce results based on just laws fairly applied on the basis of accurate facts; but a lawyer's objective within that system is to achieve a result favorable to the lawyer's client, possibly despite justice, the law, and the facts.[12] Althought the point can be overstated, by and large it is true that the possible results in litigation are binary—either plaintiff or defendant, but not both, will prevail. The lawyer for each is to strive with full professional commitment to achieve a partisan victory. (Paradoxically, the adversarial system seems to have built into itself advocates whose principal role is, at least half the time, to defeat, if necessary, the intended working of the system.) It must follow either that one or the other of the lawyers is aware that truth and justice should defeat that lawyer's client or that the lawyers are befuddled about the outcome, possibly sympathetically so because of distortion in the facts for reasons beyond the lawyers' control or uncertainty in the applicable legal standard.

§ 10.5 JUSTICE VERSUS MERITS; CRIMINAL DEFENSE

§ 10.5.1 Problem of Legal and Moral Entitlements

No imaginable legal system working in a real world can purport to attain perfect congruence with moral right. Moral claims are occasionally not the sort that can be dealt with in the type of bureaucracy that a legal system in a modern society inevitably must be. It might be thought to be an easy step, then, from that set of social facts to the conclusion that an actor within the legal system, such as a lawyer, is ethically entitled to take steps within the legal system that are consistent with its dictates and expectations.

But while a legal system might permit, or even require, the actor to proceed in that way, it is not clear that the actor's conduct within the legal system is above ethical question. Because there is no necessary congruence between legal entitlement of clients or of lawyers and their moral rights and duties (§ 2.7.3), one might conclude that actions taken by lawyers in behalf of their clients are morally wrong even if legally permissible. The topic is a large and difficult one. It is examined here in the context in which it is most frequently discussed—the defense of persons accused of crime. That context is, obviously, not exhaustive of the problem. Nor does it adequately portray the different ethical problems involved in other settings in which lawyers might represent clients with

[10] For a review of psychological literature relevant to cognitive dissonance in advocating positions contrary to beliefs, see Chemerinsky, Protecting Lawyers from their Profession: Redefining the Lawyer's Role, 5 J.Leg.Prof. 31 (1980). See also Brazil, The Attorney as Victim: Toward More Candor about the Psychological Price Tag of Litigation Practice, 3 J.Leg.Prof. 107 (1978); Greenebaum, Attorneys' Problems in Making Ethical Decisions, 52 Ind.L.J. 627 (1977).

[11] J.Noonan, Persons and Masks of the Law: Cardozo, Holmes, Jefferson, and Wythe as Makers of the Masks (1976); Postema, Moral Responsibility in Professional Ethics, 55 NYU L.Rev. 63 (1980); Elkins, The Legal Persona: An Essay on the Professional Mask, 64 Va.L. Rev. 735 (1978); Wasserstrom, Lawyers as Professionals: Some Moral Issues, 5 Human Rights 1 (1975)("to become and to be a professional, such as a lawyer, is to incorporate within oneself ways of behaving and ways of thinking that shape the whole person. It is especially hard, if not impossible, because of the nature of the professions, for one's professional way of thinking not to dominate one's entire adult life.").

[12] The theme is developed extensively in Simon, The Ideology of Advocacy: Procedural Justice and Professional Ethics, 1978 Wisc.L.Rev. 29.

objectives or traits that a lawyer finds morally objectionable. Those questions are pursued in § 13.3.10; the problem of unpopular clients and causes is examined in § 10.2.3.

§ 10.5.2 *Defense of the Guilty*

Defense of the Innocent and Those Whose Guilt Is Unknown

Probably no lawyer's task is more important, yet beset with more controversy, than that of the criminal defense lawyer. From a historical perspective, the role of the criminal defense lawyer is probably still undergoing a process of rapid and unstable development. A general right to appointed defense counsel in criminal cases is little more than two decades old,[13] and an accused felon has been entitled even to retain counsel for little more than two centuries.[14] Today all probably agree that defense of accused persons known to be innocent is one of the highest callings of a lawyer. Most will also agree that defense of a person whose guilt or innocence is unknown or doubtful is also appropriate. Defense of the known guilty is the center of controversy, as is the general question of the permissible maneuvers that can be employed in criminal defense.

Defense of the Guilty

To start with the most difficult case, the relationship between a lawyer and a client known to be guilty is varied and complex. At its core, the problem involves possible conflicts between morality and law,[15] and the tension between the objectives of the criminal law and those of due process. Consider the following three scaled problems.

First, suppose that a criminal defense lawyer is convinced that his or her client, accused of a crime, is factually innocent but morally guilty. Suppose, for example, that the client is accused of Crime A, which the client did not commit. The client did, however, commit Act B, which is legal but morally objectionable—operated a handgun factory or made exorbitant profits as a slumlord. May the lawyer defend the client against the charge of Crime A?

The answer, of course, must be that the lawyer may defend the client if the lawyer is able.[16] Any other answer would mean that a lawyer's moral judgments about any other aspect of a client's life would disable the lawyer from representing a client. That is required neither by morality nor by law.[17] The problem is a variation of the issue of defense of an unpopular client or cause (§ 10.2.3). A different response is that a lawyer will rarely, if ever, be entitled to conclude from available facts that he or she is so confident of the client's guilt that a full defense should be withheld.[18] If rare, nonetheless there will be instances in which a lawyer will have as much reason to feel confidence in concluding that a client is guilty as charged as to feel confidence about anything else.

13 § 14.3.1 (right to counsel).

14 See generally Langbein, The Criminal Trial before the Lawyers, 45 U.Chi.L.Rev. 263, 308 (1978). The occasional provision of counsel in former times should not be supposed to have provided an accused with the functional equivalent of a modern-day legal champion. E.g., M'Daniel's Case, 19 How.St.Tr. 745, 790 (1755)(argument of Sergeant Davy for the defense: "I must own, that I could not have been prevailed upon to have been counsel for such a set of rogues, had I not been appointed by your lordships.").

15 See generally The Good Lawyer (D.Luban ed.1983); T.Shaffer, On Being a Christian and a Lawyer 45 et seq. (1981); Wasserstrom, Lawyers as Professionals: Some Moral Issues, 5 Human Rights L.Rev. 1, 12 (1975); Mitchell, The Ethics of the Criminal Defense Attorney—New Answers to Old Questions, 32 Stan.L.Rev. 293 (1980).

16 The general view is that no lawyer is *required* to represent any particular client, with a possible exception for court appointments. See § 10.2.2.

17 On the general relationship between a lawyer's moral views and representation of a "repugnant" client, see Wolfram, A Lawyer's Duty to Represent Clients, Repugnant and Otherwise, in The Good Lawyer 214 (D.Luban ed.1983).

18 G.Sharswood, Essay on Profession Ethics 49 (2d ed. 1860)("Men have been known . . . under the influence of some delusion, to confess themselves guilty of crimes which they had not committed: and hence, to decline acting as counsel in such a case, is a dangerous refinement in morals. Nothing seems plainer than the proposition, that a person accused of a crime is to be tried and convicted, if convicted at all, *upon evidence,* and *whether guilty or not guilty,* if the evidence is insufficient to convict him, he has a *legal right* to be acquitted.")(emphasis in original).

Second, suppose that the client is factually guilty of a crime defined by law—but is not convictable. For example, the client is legally entitled to a defense by means of which the lawyer can obtain the suppression of accurate incriminating evidence because the police failed to afford the client a constitutional right during interrogation. May the lawyer, on the basis of his or her moral judgments about the client's criminal acts or about the suppression law itself, refuse to move to suppress the evidence or, even if retained, refuse to provide any defense at all?

Again, the law has spoken. Any lawyer handling the case should move to suppress the evidence despite the fact that that might well result in the acquittal of a factually guilty person. The social costs that result if a guilty person goes free are obviously not inconsequential. At least two social objectives are thwarted. A potentially dangerous person may be turned loose on society, and the efficacy of criminal law for general deterrence is impaired.[19] But the law providing for the exclusion of accurate evidence has itself accepted the obvious risk that the guilty will go free, in order that public officials may be deterred from infringing the rights of all to be free of unlawful interrogations. A lawyer is certainly not legally required to quarrel with the plainly controversial factual and legal grounds that underlie the exclusionary rule.[20]

Third, suppose that the lawyer knows that the client is factually guilty but that a lawyer's eloquence or other lawyerly skills might persuade the factfinder that the prosecution has not satisfied its burden of proof. May the lawyer defend the client? May the lawyer in the course of such a defense attempt to persuade the factfinder that the client is not guilty by such means as the cross-examination of a witness known to be telling the truth? By harming the reputation or invading the privacy of an innocent and truthful witness? Those are the difficult cases probably most often contemplated by persons discussing the issue.

The professional response is that a lawyer is entitled to undertake such tasks, although he or she is not required to do so unless the lawyer is appointed to defend the client by a court.[21] Once the lawyer undertakes the defense, he or she may not refuse to take steps in behalf of the accused because of the lawyer's belief in the guilt of the accused.[22] The lay mind finds the lawyer's conclusion quite problematic.[23] That is due perhaps to different attitudes entertained by lawyers and nonlawyers about two important matters. First, nonlawyers are more likely to be swayed by

19 G.Williams, The Proof of Guilt 258 (1955).

20 A special, and difficult, case is an instance in which the lawyer knows with certainty that a person charged with crime, but who is not convictable if all legal steps are taken, is also highly dangerous. The lawyer in such a case is torn between duties normally required by the lawyer's role and the instinct to prevent harm to innocent third parties. See Mitchell, The Ethics of the Criminal Defense Attorney—New Answers to Old Questions, 32 Stan.L.Rev. 294, 331–32, 334–36 (1980).

21 1908 Canon 5; EC 2–29; MR 3.1; West's Ann.Cal. Bus. & Prof.Code § 6068(c) (lawyer shall support only those proceedings or defenses "as appear to him legal or just, except the defense of a person charged with a public offense"). Occasional, unsupported assertions can be found to the effect that a lawyer is *required* to accept the defense of an accused person despite knowledge of guilt. E.g., Alabama Code of Ethics § 13, 118 Ala. xxiii, xxvii (1898)("attorney cannot reject" defense of one accused of crime because of belief in person's guilt).

22 Bowler v. Warden, 236 F.Supp. 400, 404 (D.Md.1964); Johns v. Smyth, 176 F.Supp. 949, 952 (E.D.Va.1959); United States v. Von der Heide, 169 F.Supp. 560, 567 (D.D.C.1959); People v. Neeley, 90 Ill.App.3d 76, 45 Ill. Dec. 428, 412 N.E.2d 1010 (1980). See generally D.Mellinkoff, The Conscience of a Lawyer (1973)(travails of barrister Phillips, whose client, a butler accused of murdering his master, confessed his guilt to his defense lawyers in the middle of trial). The English and Canadian views remain generally similar to that in the United States. E.g., Orkin, Defence of One Known to Be Guilty, 1 Crim.L.Q. 170 (1958). For the famous and extravagant speech of Lord Brougham to the House of Lords, see D. Mellinkoff, The Conscience of a Lawyer 188–89 (1973).

23 For the lay view that lawyers act immorally or against the law when they defend known guilty persons, see, e.g., 7 The Works of Jeremy Bentham (Rationale of Judicial Evidence) 474–75 (J.Bowring ed.1850)(view of Bentham, a philosopher and nonpracticing lawyer, that lawyer who assisted a guilty client to obtain acquittal was an "accessory after the fact" to the client's felony); Hoffman's Fifty Resolutions in Regard to Professional Deportment, Resolution XV (1836), reprinted in H.Drinker, Legal Ethics 340–41 (appendix E)(1953); Report of the Commissioners on Practice and Pleadings, Code of Civil Procedure 207–208 (1850)(the so-called Field Code); A.Strick, Injustice for All 126 (1977).

the threat to the public welfare posed by acquittals of factually guilty defendants or by tactics such as attacks upon innocent third parties.[24] Lawyers are more likely to think—as they are trained—only of the legal rights of the accused. Second, nonlawyers probably do not share the common lawyerly confidence that the adversarial system systematically convicts the guilty and acquits the innocent. Lawyers believe both that correct results regularly occur and that effective advocacy is important in criminal defenses.[25] Even in view of the high rate of convictions, the two lawyerly beliefs are not inconsistent if we can assume that criminal defense remains necessary in the case of guilty accused persons in order to prevent unjust impositions upon guilty persons, such as excessive charges or sentences.

§ 10.5.3 Role of Defense Counsel

American Conception of the Defense Function

It is clear that the American conception of the criminal defense function is unique. Most other cultures and political systems do not permit the same sweeping powers and opportunities to lawyers for the accused.[26] There is a striking contrast between the presuppositions of those other systems concerning the primacy of societal protection against crime and the romanticized, and often self-congratulatory, accounts of criminal defense lawyers in the United States.[27] English criminal defense lawyers apparently operate under assumptions roughly similar to those common in the United States.[28]

Despite general lawyer acceptance of the American definition of the proper role of defense counsel, however, it seems evident that the actual operation of the defense counsel function is not thought by many lawyers to be professionally or socially desirable. For example, surveys of the prestige and income of lawyers consistently indicate low intraprofessional status and low income for criminal defense lawyers.[29]

Tactics of Defense

Nonetheless, the clearly articulated judicial view is that the American criminal defense

24 This division reflects the broader conflict between the "crime control" and "due process" models of criminal justice. See Packer, Two Models of the Criminal Process, 113 U.Pa.L.Rev. 1 (1964).

25 § 10.1 (justification of the adversary system).

26 On severe restrictions on defense lawyers in nondemocratic political systems, see, e.g., D.Kaminskaya, Final Judgment: My Life as a Soviet Defense Attorney (1982)(USSR); J.Kaplan, Criminal Justice 264–65 (1973) (Bulgaria); N.Y.Times, Sept. 30, 1980, at 3, col.1 (1980) (regulations for defense lawyers in People's Republic of China declare that lawyers should work to "protect the interests of the Government as much as the defendants"); Berman, The Cuban Popular Tribunals, 69 Colum.L.Rev. 1317, 1341 (1969)(quoting description of defense function by law professor at University of Havana: "The first job of a revolutionary lawyer is not to argue that his client is innocent, but rather to determine if his client is guilty and, if so, to seek the sanction that will best rehabilitate him.").

As an extreme example, Ayatollah Sadegh Khalkhali, who sentenced hundreds of persons to execution in the early 1980s in Iran, responded to a rare critic by asking:

> When he says some of the verdicts are not based on principle, did he mean Islamic principles or Western principles? Under Western Principles the criminals have to have lawyers and other matters to escape the law. Yes, it's true, I never paid attention to these principles.

(N.Y.Times, Dec.8, 1980, at 9, col.l.)

27 A.Dershowitz, The Best Defense (1982); A.Kinoy, Rights on Trial (1983); J.Kunen, How Can You Defend Those People? (1983); H.Rothblatt, That Damned Lawyer (1983). For more measured views, see, e.g., L.Weinreb, Denial of Justice: Criminal Process in the United States (1977); Mitchell, The Ethics of the Criminal Defense Attorney—New Answers to Old Questions, 32 Stan.L.Rev. 293 (1980).

28 W.Boulton, Conduct and Etiquette at the Bar 70–72 (6th ed.1975); H.Cecil, Brief to Counsel 151–55 (1972).

29 J.Heinz & E.Laumann, Chicago Lawyers: The Social Structure of the Bar 91 (1982); Ky.B.Ass'n 1977 Economic and Opinion Survey, 41 Ky.Bench & Bar i, viii (1977); Wood, Professional Ethics among Criminal Lawyers, 7 Soc.Prob. 70 (1959). As with much else in criminal defense, spectacular exceptions are probably more widely reported and better known. E.g., Ricks, Drug Lawyer, Wall Street Journal, June 27, 1983, at 1, col.1 (Florida lawyer specializing in defense of drug smugglers grosses $750,000). Other indicators of the low prestige of criminal defense work include the lawyer code prohibitions against the use of contingent fees in criminal defense representations. See § 9.4.3.

The low status of criminal defense lawyers probably reflects suspicions harbored by many judges and lawyers that the punishment of criminals is unduly hindered by defense lawyers. E.g., Hoffman, J., in the "Chicago Seven" trial: "[I]f crime is, in fact, on the increase today, lawyer plays a vital role in the administration of justice.[30] A lawyer functioning in that role owes loyalty to his or her client alone. The defense lawyer may seek, for example, to cast the entire blame upon a codefendant represented by another lawyer, regardless of personal belief in that person's guilt or innocence.[31] A lawyer's refusal to call a witness out of consideration for the witness's reputation is improper.[32] A defense lawyer may not imply to the jury that his or her role as defense counsel is required by court appointment or in other ways imply reluctance to defend an accused whom the evidence strongly shows to have committed a reprehensible crime.[33]

The Zeal of Criminal Defense Counsel

The effective limits on a defense lawyer's loyalty and zeal are quite unclear and can probably be captured only by a vague phrase such as "advocacy in good faith." A lawyer may function as defender only in his or her role as advocate.[34] It would, for example, be both professionally inappropriate and a crime for a lawyer to harbor a fugitive from justice or to aid as an investor the ongoing criminal projects of a client. The formal restraints on a defense lawyer's advocacy are few. The lawyer codes and such compilations as the ABA Defense Function Standards[35] are sometimes cited in judicial opinions as authoritatively limiting the zeal of a defense lawyer. But the reported decisions suggest that few sanctionable limits truly exist other than occasional contempt and similar ad hoc impositions by trial judges (see § 12.1.3). Probably the most effective sanction is a defense lawyer's fear of alienating the judge, which might result in adverse rulings and a heavy sentence for a client of the lawyer, either in the present case or in some future representation.

In general, a defense lawyer must employ his or her best judgment, knowledge, and skill in behalf of an accused client. A lawyer is not required to take a step in behalf of a client that is not based on a good faith belief

it is due in large part to the fact that waiting in the wings are lawyers who are willing to forego their professional responsibilities, professional obligations, professional duty in their defense." See Contempt 207 (D.Wagner & M.Weisman eds.1970).

[30] United States v. Wade, 388 U.S. 218, 256–57, 87 S.Ct. 1926, 1947, 18 L.Ed.2d 1149 (1967)(White, J., concurring and dissenting); Miranda v. Arizona, 384 U.S. 436, 480–81, 86 S.Ct. 1602, 1631, 16 L.Ed.2d 694 (1966)(Warren, C.J., for the Court); id. at 514, 86 S.Ct. at 1648 (Harlan, J., dissenting).

[31] State v. Brown, 644 S.W.2d 418, 421 (Tenn.Crim. App.1982):

> A co-defendant's counsel has no obligation to protect the interests of the co-defendant. His duty and obligation is to his client alone. It is the client who has retained him or for whom he has been appointed to whom his duty of loyalty lies, free of compromising influences and loyalties. . . . His obligation is to represent the interests and only the interests of his client.

See also United States v. Bruner, 657 F.2d 1278, 1288–89 (D.C.Cir.1981). A lawyer's failure to attempt to cast blame on another party because of loyalty to the other party creates an impermissible conflict of interest. E.g., Rodriguez v. State, 129 Ariz. 67, 628 P.2d 950, 953 (1981).

[32] McCann v. State, 446 N.E.2d 1293, 1299 (Ind.1983). But compare ABA Defense Function Standards 272 (approved draft 1979)(praise for defense lawyer who, apparently without agreement of client, foregoes embarrassing cross-examination of known truthful prosecution witness out of deference to his sensibilities).

On a lawyer's refusal to call a witness who will commit perjury, see §§ 12.5.3, 12.5.4.

[33] King v. Strickland, 714 F.2d 1481, 1491 (11th Cir. 1983), reversed on other grounds ___ U.S. ___, 104 S.Ct. 2052, 80 L.Ed.2d 674 (1984). Similarly, a prosecutor arguing to a jury may not describe the extent to which a zealous defense lawyer may go in attempting to persuade or confuse them about the guilt of the accused, even if this is contrary to the advocate's personal belief. E.g., State v. Covington, 290 N.C. 313, 226 S.E.2d 629, 641 (1976); Jones v. State, 580 P.2d 1150, 1153 (Wyo.1978).

[34] For example, a lawyer who knew that a client had committed the criminal acts charged but who, after severing the professional relationship, appeared as a character witness for the accused at the criminal trial was held guilty of professional misconduct. In re Schachne, 5 F.Supp. 680, 682 (E.D.N.Y.1934).

[35] ABA Defense Function Standards (approved 1979). The tone and color of the Standards is patrician and dominated by a crime-control image of defense; it hardly reflects the views of typical defense lawyers in the United States. A few courts have occasionally given the Standards the kind of unquestioned acceptance usually reserved for statutes or other official enactments. E.g., United States v. Radford, 14 M.J. 322, 325 n.5 (U.S.Ct. Mil.App.1982)(cited provisions of Standards are "deemed controlling"). But the dominant judicial view is that they are neither controlling nor an exhaustive statement of the duties of defense counsel. E.g., Strickland v. Washington, ___ U.S. ___, 104 S.Ct. 2052, 2065, 80 L.Ed.2d 674 (1984); Commonwealth v. Tumpson, 242 Pa.Super. 1, 363 A.2d 1129, 1132 (1976).

in the supportability of the move.[36] As far as the right to the effective assistance of counsel is concerned, under the dominant judicial doctrine a lawyer is required to provide the kind of defense expected of competent criminal defense practitioners (§ 14.6.2). Within the resulting large area of professional discretion, a lawyer's own decisions are predominant, at least as a matter of law. Such matters of trial tactics as decisions about which witnesses to call, what objections to make, and what defenses to interpose are normally left to the lawyer's determination.[37] Yet some decisions are ultimately for the client to make. Among them are decisions about what plea to enter,[38] whether to waive a trial by jury,[39] whether the defendant should testify,[40] and whether a convicted person should appeal.[41] And aside from legal requirements concerning decision making, there is good reason to think that a truly effective representation will include extensive consultation with a client about all important decisions in the case, including those over which the lawyer exercises final legal control (see § 4.3).

What means can a defense lawyer employ in defending a client? A defense lawyer's main responsibility is to further the interests of his or her client as defined by the client. Typically the client's interest is to obtain the least costly sanction and an acquittal of all charges if possible.[42] The difficult questions arise when that interest conflicts with the interests of victims, witnesses, prosecutors, judges, or the criminal justice system itself. Whether the means employed can extend to attempts to induce reversible error by the prosecutor or judge has been debated.[43] The lawyer's knowledge that the client is guilty does not substantially affect the kind of defense that should be afforded. The lawyer's knowledge, however, may impose limits, such as those on the use of known perjurious testimony (§ 12.5.4). Decisions are sometimes encountered that suggest that a defense lawyer's role changes from advocacy to cooperation with the court with respect to questions about a proper sentence.[44] They seem inconsistent with the general approach.

§ 10.5.4 Plea Bargaining

Troubling Durability of Plea Bargaining

The institution of plea bargaining gives rise to other difficult problems for defense law-

36 United States v. Metcalfe, 698 F.2d 877, 883 (7th Cir.), cert.denied 461 U.S. 910, 103 S.Ct. 1886, 76 L.Ed.2d 814 (1983)(effective assistance required by Sixth Amendment did not require lawyer to seek psychiatric examination if lawyer believed that claim of mental illness was not made in good faith). See generally § 14.6.3 (the Anders problem).

37 People v. Schultheis, 638 P.2d 8, 12 (Colo.1981); State v. Pratts, 145 N.J.Super. 79, 366 A.2d 1327 (1975), affirmed per curiam 71 N.J. 399, 365 A.2d 928 (1976). See generally ABA Defense Function Standards § 4–5.2(b) (1979 ed.).

38 Brookhart v. Janis, 384 U.S. 1, 86 S.Ct. 1245, 16 L.Ed. 2d 314 (1966); Wiley v. Sowders, 647 F.2d 642 (6th Cir. 1981), cert.denied 454 U.S. 1091, 102 S.Ct. 656, 70 L.Ed.2d 630 (1981)(whether to adopt strategy of accepting full responsibility to protect brother, who was codefendant); State v. Wood, 648 P.2d 71, 91–92 (Utah 1982), cert.denied 459 U.S. 988, 103 S.Ct. 341, 74 L.Ed.2d 383 (1982); State v. Camley, 140 Vt. 483, 438 A.2d 1131, 1134 (1981).

See generally ABA Criminal Defense Function Standards § 4–5.2(a)(1979 ed.). On the problem of whether a trial court should accept any plea but insanity from an evidently insane accused, see Note, The Right and Responsibility of a Court to Impose the Insanity Defense over the Defendant's Objection, 65 Minn.L.Rev. 927 (1981).

39 Sincox v. United States, 571 F.2d 876 (5th Cir.1978) (decision to accept verdict by fewer than all jurors); ABA Defense Function Standards, supra, at § 4–5.2(a)(ii).

40 Hollenbeck v. Estelle, 672 F.2d 451 (5th Cir.1982), cert.denied 459 U.S. 1019, 103 S.Ct. 383, 74 L.Ed.2d 514 (1982). Lawyer control over such decisions may be more absolute in cognate systems, such as that of Canada. E.g., Law Society of Upper Canada, Defending a Criminal Case 282 (1969).

41 Fay v. Noia, 372 U.S. 391, 83 S.Ct. 822, 9 L.Ed.2d 837 (1963).

42 Martin, The Role and Responsibility of the Defense Advocate, 12 Crim.L.Q. 376, 386–87 (1970).

43 For the proposition that such efforts are permissible, e.g., Ratner v. Young, 465 F.Supp. 386 (D.Virgin Islands 1979)(newspaper article accusing lawyers of attempts to induce judge to commit reversible error not libelous because this does not amount to a charge of illegal or unethical behavior). But see, e.g., ABA Defense Function Standards § 4–7.1(c)(1979 ed.).

44 United States v. Unterman, 422 F.Supp. 228, 231 (S.D.N.Y.1976).

yers.[45] Despite significant opposition,[46] plea discussions have become a standard feature of most American criminal courts.[47] Their attractiveness for defendants is that the reward for pleading guilty will almost invariably be the prosecutor's reciprocal undertaking either to reduce the charges (as from robbery to simple assault) or to recommend a light sentence.[48] Some accused persons might also welcome the opportunity to admit guilt publicly in order to make peace with an aroused community or to avoid the delay and anxiety of awaiting an uncertain outcome at trial. But the defendant must gamble that the accepted plea and sentence will be significantly less burdensome than a verdict after a contested trial.[49]

Ethical Issues in Plea Bargaining

Because of the better outcomes that plea bargaining offers, defense lawyers are required as a matter of basic competence to make an effort to plea bargain.[50] A difficult issue raised by the attractiveness of negotiated pleas, as opposed to the hazards of trial, is whether a defense lawyer should participate in such a plea despite knowing that the client either maintains innocence or is indeed innocent.[51] Due process permits a trial judge to accept a guilty plea from a defendant who protests innocence if the defendant admits facts from which a jury could find guilt.[52] The general view of commentators is that a lawyer may participate in such a guilty plea on the notion that guilt or innocence is a matter, in the last analysis, for the client and

45 For discussions of the problems and responsibilities of judges involved in plea bargains, see, e.g., Lefstein, Plea Bargaining and the Trial Judge: The New ABA Standards, and the Need to Control Judicial Discretion, 59 N.C.L.Rev. 477 (1981); Alschuler, The Trial Judge's Role in Plea Bargaining, Part I, 76 Colum.L.Rev. 1059 (1976); Annot., 100 A.L.R.3d 834 (1980); 10 A.L.R.4th 689 (1981); 56 A.L.R.Fed. 529 (1982). On prosecutors, see § 13.10.3. On defense lawyers generally, see Alschuler, The Defense Attorney's Role in Plea Bargaining, 84 Yale L.J. 1179 (1975).

46 See Nat'l Advisory Comm'n on Crim. Justice Standards and Goals, Report on Courts, standard 3.1, at 46 (1973). A vast literature debates the validity of the American institution of plea bargaining. E.g., Alschuler, The Changing Plea-Bargaining Debate, 69 Cal.L.Rev. 652 (1981); Halberstram, Towards Neutral Principles in the Administration of Criminal Justice: A Critique of Supreme Court Decisions Sanctioning the Plea Bargaining Process, 73 J.Crim.L. 1 (1982); Phillips, Voluntariness in the Plea Bargaining Controversy, 16 Law & Soc'y Rev. 207 (1981–1982); Special Double Issue on Plea Bargaining, 13 Law & Soc'y Rev. 189 (1979); Langbein, Torture and Plea Bargaining, 46 U.Chi.L.Rev. 3 (1978).

47 See generally ABA Standards Relating to the Plea of Guilty 1–3 (approved draft 1968); ALI Model Code of Pre-Arraignment Procedure § 350.3, commentary (1975).

Only Alaska has an announced policy against plea bargaining. See M.Rubinstein, Alaska's Ban on Plea Bargaining in Plea Bargaining (W.McDonald & J.Cramer eds.1980). Alaska officials read the statistics to indicate that elimination of plea bargaining has not impaired court efficiency and that sentences increased only for drug offenses and for first-offender property crimes. See Lawscope: Plea Bargaining, 69 ABA J. 26 (1983). But cf. Pike, No-Deal Justice Burns Small Frys, Study Finds, Nat'l L.J., Jan. 12, 1981, p. 3. col. 1. Many prosecutors in other jurisdictions have claimed to have eliminated plea bargaining, but a study has found that few have actually accomplished this. See H.Miller, Plea Bargaining in the United States (1978).

48 Appellate courts generally refuse to permit trial courts to base a harsh sentence explicitly on a defendant's refusal to accept a proferred plea bargain. Annot., 100 A.L.R.3d 834 (1980). But the Supreme Court has held that a pattern of harsher penalties for defendants who stand trial than for defendants who plead guilty does not by itself demonstrate a denial of due process. Corbitt v. New Jersey, 439 U.S. 212, 99 S.Ct. 492, 58 L.Ed.2d 466 (1978). See generally Comment, Plea Bargaining and Trial Penalties: When May the State Legitimately Require Criminal Defendants to Surrender Their Trial Rights, 55 Ind.L.J. 71 (1979).

49 Sometimes the gamble is lost. See, e.g., 69 ABA J. 27 (1983)(accused who had maintained innocence of capital charges of murder and robbery throughout trial accepted sixty-year sentence in plea bargain completed only three minutes before jury returned verdict of innocent on all charges).

50 Martin v. Rose, 717 F.2d 295 (6th Cir.1983)(ineffective assistance of counsel when no effort to plea bargain). The first edition of the ABA Defense Function Standards suggested in the commentary that "plea discussions should be considered as the norm" for defense lawyers in any but the exceptional case. ABA Defense Function Standards 6.1(b), comment (1971 ed.). The 1979 revision omits any such language. See id., 4–6.1(b)(1979 ed.).

51 Damaska, Evidentiary Barriers to Conviction and Two Models of Criminal Procedure: A Comparative Study, 121 U.Pa.L.Rev. 506, 582 (1973)(continental lawyers would never plead innocent client guilty). For a literary treatment, see J. Mills, One Just Man (1974).

52 North Carolina v. Alford, 400 U.S. 25, 91 S.Ct. 160, 27 L.Ed.2d 162 (1970); United States v. Neel, 547 F.2d 95 (9th Cir.1977).

the court to determine and no dissimulation is involved if the facts recited are accurate.[53]

WESTLAW REFERENCES

attorney lawyer counsel** /s duty responsibility /7 represent! /6 criminal

[53] Christie & Pye, Presumptions and Assumptions in the Criminal Law: Another View, 1970 Duke L.J. 927, 931.

Chapter Eleven
LAWYERS AS ADVOCATES

Table of Sections

§ 11.1 ADVOCACY: AN OVERVIEW

The appearance of a lawyer in litigation in behalf of a client is at once the most publicly familiar role for lawyers as well as an uncommon role for the average lawyer. Most lawyers spend little time in courtrooms, and a large percentage spend their entire practice without litigating a case. The dominance of litigation in the public mind reflects history, not present reality. Nonetheless, many lawyers do continue to litigate and the litigating lawyer's role colors much of both the public image and the self-perception of the legal professsion.

The image of the lawyer as litigator also dominates the lawyer codes. A reader of the Canons might be misled to the conclusion that as recently as 1908 most lawyers' work, or at least most legal ethical problems, occurred in the courtroom. The 1969 Code attempted to break out of a preoccupation with the lawyer-litigator, but with only slight success. The 1983 Model Rules attempted to sketch a broader domain, but again with indifferent results. Perhaps the preoccupation with the disciplinary problems of litigator reflects the relative absence of lawyer-litigators from the bodies that draft the rules. Perhaps the drama, contentiousness, moral ambiguity, and public nature of trials draw to litigators more than their share of attention. Perhaps the preoccupation of legal education with litigation bears some responsibility. Whatever the cause, the domination is clear.

This chapter and much of Chapter Twelve will review the major issues confronting litigators. The focus will be upon the courtroom or the moves in litigation that precede courtroom appearances. The basic tension in litigation that must be explored is between a lawyer's duties of loyalty to a client and restraints that are imposed on a lawyer because of the interests of the public, courts, and third parties.

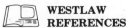

WESTLAW REFERENCES

di advocate

§ 11.2 THE SCREENING FUNCTION

§ 11.2.1 General

The "warm zeal" with which a lawyer is to urge a client's interests is part of the very model of an advocate (§ 10.3.1). But professional rules and substantive law impress limits on a lawyer's zeal. To what extent must a lawyer decline to take steps in litigation for a client that are not warranted by the facts or existing law? May a lawyer, for example, file an action against a defendant solely to gain the advantage of the nuisance value of a settlement for some portion of the defendant's anticipated defense costs? Reciprocally, may a lawyer assert a defense if it is legally insupportable but when the plaintiff's travels on the road to ultimate success will require an extended period of time during which the defendant will have the interest-free use of the money sought? Those and similar questions ask whether, and to what extent, a lawyer should serve as a filter of clients' desires to take aggressive moves in litigation.

WESTLAW REFERENCES

digest,synopsis(zeal! /s attorney lawyer counsel** prosecutor)

§ 11.2.2 Lawyers as Gatekeepers

Lawyer Control and Abuse of Access to Litigation

In many areas, lawyers undoubtedly serve as gatekeepers to the legal process, screening out claims and defenses that they believe should not be pursued.[1] This gatekeeper function is largely the product of, or at least is congruent with, lawyer and client self-interest. An unfounded claim or defense will typically cost its asserter only legal fees, fees that a devastated client will be reluctant to pay and that are unethical to exact.[2] Lawyers have often begun advice to clients to forego litigation with the visibly candid remark that the lawyer would not mind at all earning a fee but that there is little or no chance of success. Such advice, wisely, assumes that the legal outcome will match the law.

But the law and legal process are not perfect. They can be abused by ruthless litigants and their lawyers to harass others, to cause delay, to run up the meter on the other side in order to inflict pain wantonly or to extort a settlement. A lawyer's overzealousness in assisting a client in such nefarious projects may be caused by incompetence, by a lack of professional independence that causes the lawyer to share the client's legally unjustified aggressiveness against an adversary, or by a desire on the part of the lawyer to earn a fee.

Pretrial Discovery Abuses

Pretrial discovery is a current example of abusive litigation tactics. Although they were designed, and can in fact be employed, to simplify and clarify issues, it has become painfully clear that discovery devices can be manipulated to frustrate these ends.[3] Discovery requests can be designed primarily to be burdensome to the other side. Similarly, an opponent's legitimate discovery attempts can be frustrated by groundless objections, incomplete responses, or overdiscovery by inundating the adversary with a "file dump" of largely worthless papers.[4] Plainly, in such areas external controls are needed.

1 Galanter, Reading the Landscape of Disputes, 31 UCLA L.Rev. 4, 19 (1983); Macaulay, Lawyers and Consumer Protection Laws, 14 Law & Soc'y Rev. 115, 116–17 (1979).

2 Baranowski v. State Bar, 24 Cal.3d 153, 154 Cal.Rptr. 752, 593 P.2d 613 (1979)(discipline where large retainer paid after lawyer's overzealous assessment of legal worth of client's case was compounded by lawyer's failure to make any independent legal or factual investigation).

3 National Comm'n for Review of Antitrust Laws and Procedures, Report to the President and the Attorney General, 80 F.R.D. 509, 544–57 (1979); Symposium: Discovery Abuse, 2 Rev.Litigation 1 (1981); J.Ebersole & B.Burke, Discovery Problems in Civil Cases (Fed.Jud. Center 1980).

4 J.Stewart, The Partners 60 (1982).

Minimal Control under Professional Standards and the Common Law

The lawyer codes have consistently reflected the position that not every client wish to litigate should be furthered by a lawyer.[5] Following 1908 Canon 30,[6] the 1969 Code, in DR 7–102(A)(1), provides that a lawyer shall not take action in behalf of a client "when he knows or it is obvious that such action would serve merely to harass or maliciously injure another." Further, under DR 7–102(A)(2) a lawyer is not to assert a claim or defense "unwarranted under existing law" unless it is supported by a good-faith argument for the alteration of existing law. In 1983 Model Rule 3.1 these separate statements are collapsed into a single standard that limits a lawyer to actions or other steps in litigation that are "not frivolous," a standard that explicitly includes actions based on a good-faith argument to alter existing law. Probably in recognition of the attention currently being given to limiting discovery abuses, a separate provision, MR 3.4(d), specifically provides that a lawyer should not make "frivolous" discovery requests or fail to make "reasonably diligent" efforts to comply with proper discovery requests by another party.

Recent Attempts to Control Unwanted Litigation

Those professional standards can very likely do little to restrain advocates from taking steps that, based on other calculations, seem in the best interests of clients. Judicial statements can be found requiring lawyers to question clients closely about doubtful claims, to refuse to assist clients in groundless litigation, and to withdraw if not satisfied that a client's position has merit.[7] But discipline is rarely imposed for violations of the antiharassment rules and then mainly for moves in litigation that sometimes seem more psychopathic than nasty,[8] that involve patently fraudulent schemes,[9] or that arise in limited areas in which courts express a special concern for lawyer forthrightness.[10] Some courts, however, have demonstrated both vigor and care in enforcing the antiharassment professional rules.[11]

The approach of the common law, essentially, was to leave a party oppressed by bad-faith litigation to the costly solace of victory and,

[5] See generally Brazil, Ethical Perspectives on Discovery Reform, 3 Rev.Litigation 51 (1982); Cann, Frivolous Lawsuits—The Lawyer's Duty to Say "No," 52 Colo.L. Rev. 367 (1981); Note, A Lawyer's Duty to Reject Groundless Litigation, 26 Wayne L. Rev. 1561 (1980).

[6] "The lawyer must decline to conduct a civil cause or to make a defense when convinced that it is intended merely to harass or to injure the opposite party or to work oppression or wrong. . . ." Canon 30, in turn, was borrowed from Ala.Code of Ethics § 14, 118 Ala. xxiii, xxvii (1898).

[7] Polk County v. Dodson, 454 U.S. 312, 102 S.Ct. 445, 452, 70 L.Ed.2d 509 (1981); Davis v. State Bar, 33 Cal.3d 231, 188 Cal.Rptr. 441, 444, 655 P.2d 1276, 1279 (1983). Moreover, a suit that would be frivolous if filed in behalf of a client does not become less objectionable when filed in the lawyer's own behalf. E.g., In re Ronwin, 136 Ariz. 566, 667 P.2d 1281 (1983), republished with modifications 139 Ariz. 576, 680 P.2d 107 (1983), cert. denied 464 U.S. 977, 104 S.Ct. 413, 78 L.Ed.2d 351 (1983); Phelps v. Kansas, 226 Kan. 371, 598 P.2d 180 (1979), cert.denied 444 U.S. 1045, 100 S.Ct. 732, 62 L.Ed.2d 731 (1980); In re Hopp, 291 Or. 697, 634 P.2d 238 (1981).

[8] In re Jafree, 93 Ill.2d 450, 67 Ill.Dec. 104, 444 N.E.2d 143 (1982)(disbarment for filing over forty frivolous suits and appeals with papers filled with scurrilous and defamatory statements about judges); In re Crumpacker, 269 Ind. 630, 383 N.E.2d 36 (1978), cert.denied 444 U.S. 979, 100 S.Ct. 481, 62 L.Ed.2d 406 (1979); Office of Disciplinary Counsel v. Kissel, 497 Pa. 467, 442 A.2d 217 (1982).

[9] In re Olkon, 299 N.W.2d 89 (Minn.1980)(filing false insurance claim for presumed client who was undercover police investigator), cert.denied 449 U.S. 1132, 101 S.Ct. 954, 67 L.Ed.2d 119 (1981).

[10] In re Bithoney, 486 F.2d 319 (1st Cir.1973)(suspension for repeated filing of bad faith appeals in immigration cases to delay deportation of clients); In re Wetzel, 118 Ariz. 33, 574 P.2d 826 (1978)(harassing suits against former clients). Some courts seem to apply special strictness to divorce actions. E.g., In re Sullivan, 283 Ala. 514, 219 So.2d 346 (1969), cert.denied 396 U.S. 826, 90 S.Ct. 70, 24 L.Ed.2d 76 (1969); In re Griffith, 283 Ala. 527, 219 So. 2d 357 (1969), cert.denied 396 U.S. 826, 90 S.Ct. 69, 24 L.Ed.2d 76 (1969)(disbarment for falsely pleading that client was resident of state); In re Backes, 16 N.J. 430, 109 A.2d 273 (1954)(suspension for pleading denial, in divorce action, of client's adultery, despite lawyer's knowledge that adultery claim was wellfounded and provable).

[11] In re Rook, 276 Or. 695, 556 P.2d 1351 (1976)(district attorney disciplined for DR 7–102(A)(1) violation for groundless refusal to plea bargain with defendants represented by two unliked lawyers); In re Lauer, 108 Wis.2d 746, 324 N.W.2d 432 (1982).

possibly, to limited tort remedies such as that for malicious abuse of civil process.[12] Asserted fears of chilling litigant access to the courts have thus far prevented much effective relief from such tort-based concepts. Courts also possess a traditional power to enjoin litigation but only in the rare case of extremely vexing and repeated frivolous suits.[13]

The professional standards and the common-law reticence about harassment in litigation have been largely overtaken by recent developments in other arenas, particularly involving fee-shifting for bad-faith litigation. It has become apparent, as complaints about abusive litigation have been heard recently on all sides,[14] that the state of affairs permitted by existing professional and tort regulation is not tolerable. One response has been the judicial development and extension of the doctrine empowering courts to require a party, or the party's lawyer, to pay the legal fees of an adversary oppressed by bad-faith litigation.[15] Another has been the assertion by courts of the power to screen papers and positions of litigants and, on the motion of an aggrieved party or at the court's own behest, to impose sanctions, including fee awards, against a party who engages in harassing or otherwise inappropriate litigation.[16] The sanctions available in those and similar contexts include, in addition, damages,[17] cost sanctions,[18] dismissal or default,[19] and similar preclusion orders against the client.

A prominent example of recent enactments is the relatively strict standard of diligence and good faith exacted in the 1983 amendment to Federal Rule of Civil Procedure 11:[20]

> The signature of an attorney or party constitutes a certificate by him that he has read the pleading; that to the best of his knowledge, information, and belief formed after reasonable inquiry, it is well grounded in fact and is warranted by existing law or a good faith argument for the extension, modification, or reversal of existing law; and that it is not interposed primarily for any improper purpose, such as to harass, to cause delay, or to increase the cost of litigation.

The rule goes on to direct the trial courts that they "shall" impose sanctions on either an offending party or the offending party's lawyer, or both, for violations. Those sanctions may include an award of legal fees. The new federal rules are important both because they underscore offical recognition of the magnitude of the problem of bad-faith litigation and

12 § 5.6.5 (intentional torts). A defending litigant who is induced to settle a claim that, unknown to the promisor, is entirely unfounded can, it is said, avoid the settlement. See Restatement of Contracts § 555 (1932).

13 In re Oliver, 682 F.2d 443 (3d Cir.1982); Clinton v. United States, 297 F.2d 899 (9th Cir.1961), cert.denied 369 U.S. 856, 82 S.Ct. 944, 8 L.Ed.2d 14 (1962); Adams v. American Bar Ass'n, 400 F.Supp. 219 (E.D.Pa.1975). On the possibilities of the use of contempt against an obstructive lawyer, see § 12.1.3.

14 Authorities cited n.43; 52 U.S.L.W. 2471 (1984)(report of speech by Chief Justice Burger at midyear American Bar Association meeting); Kirkham, Complex Litigation—Have Good Intentions Gone Awry?, 70 F.R.D. 199, 202–04 (1976).

15 Roadway Express, Inc. v. Piper, 447 U.S. 752, 100 S.Ct. 2455, 65 L.Ed.2d 488 (1980). See generally § 16.6.2 (traditional exceptions to the anti-fee-shifting rule). Not all courts, however, have been eager to extend the powers of trial judges to sanction bad-faith litigation. E.g., Schnack v. Crumley, 103 Ill.App.3d 1000, 59 Ill.Dec. 607, 431 N.E.2d 1364 (1982)(fee-shifting provision designed to discourage untrue pleadings should be strictly construed).

16 The power has long existed but has rarely been exercised. E.g., Risinger, Honesty in Pleading and Its Enforcement: Some "Striking" Problems with Federal Rule of Civil Procedure 11, 61 Minn.L.Rev. 1 (1976).

17 See generally Annot., 91 A.L.R.3d 661 (1979).

18 United States v. Potamkin Cadillac Corp., 697 F.2d 491 (2d Cir.1983), cert.denied ___ U.S. ___, 103 S.Ct. 3128, 77 L.Ed.2d 1379 (1983)(assessment of double costs plus attorneys' fees to be paid by frivolous appellant's lawyer personally under Fed.R.App.Proc. 38); In re Sutter, 543 F.2d 1030 (2d Cir.1976)(cost sanction not in nature of contempt levied against defense lawyer in criminal case for nonappearance causing continuance); Nesco Design Group, Inc. v. Grace, 577 F.Supp. 414 (W.D.Pa.1983).

19 Sanchez v. Phillips, 46 Ill.App.3d 430, 5 Ill.Dec. 36, 361 N.E.2d 36 (1977).

20 Corresponding language was added to other rules dealing with such matters as motions (Rule 7), pretrial conference (Rule 16(f)), and discovery (Rule 26). The Advisory Committee Notes to the 1983 amendments make it clear that the new rules are to be interpreted expansively and with vigor. Much of the wording of standards in the new rules was taken from the Code and from early drafts of the 1983 Model Rules, but some is plainly stricter than either. The new federal rule finds predicates in such recent legislation as the 1978 California statute requiring that a medical malpractice complaint be accompanied by the plaintiff's lawyer's certificate of consultation with at least one disinterested licensed practitioner. See Cal.Civ.Proc.Code § 411.30 (West Supp.1984).

because they announce both a subjective standard (good faith) and an objective test of diligence (reasonable inquiry) by which to judge the conduct of litigators.[21]

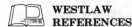

WESTLAW REFERENCES

Lawyer Control and Abuse of Access to Litigation

overzeal! /6 attorney lawyer counsel** prosecutor

Pretrial Discovery Abuses

pretrial /2 discovery /10 abus!

Minimal Control under Professional Standards and the Common Law

"dr 7-102(a)(1)" dr7-102(a)(1) /p harass! injur!

Recent Attempts to Control Unwanted Litigation

313k165

bad-faith /8 litigat!

249k31

§ 11.2.3 Litigational Harassment

Defining Unwanted Litigation

What, after all, is bad faith in litigation? At a minimum, the standard should be one that views the operation of the legal system pragmatically, although not cynically. First, as the lawyer rules state, a claim that is unfounded on existing law, but that straightforwardly seeks a change in existing law that is not utterly implausible, should, in the absence of clear evidence of a different subjective intent, be considered brought in good faith.[22] If no authority exists that is foursquare against the asserted position, it should normally be treated as a matter of first impression that is fit for litigation.[23] No sanction should stand in the way of courageous advocacy of soundly based, even if not yet legally recognized, legitimate claims and rights.

Tactical Litigation

What about litigation stances that are plausible, not for their legal or factual merits, but for sympathetic tactical reasons? Suppose, for example, a lawyer for a tort codefendant is convinced that his or her client will be found liable for substantial damages. But a codefendant, represented by another lawyer, refuses to settle the plaintiff's joint and several claim. As a practical matter, if the lawyer's client concedes liability in a jurisdiction that does not recognize contribution among joint tortfeasors, the result will be that the client will bear the full burden of damages. Thus denial of liability in effect protects the client's ability to spread damages and should violate no ethical or legal norm.[24] Drawing the line between sympathetic and unsympathetic objectives and methods may be difficult. Suppose a lawyer files a suit against persons, over whom the court clearly lacks jurisdiction, in the hope that one or more will fail to object and thus will waive jurisdictional rights. Is that bad faith? [25] Yet there are extreme, and clear, cases of bad-faith litigation, such as a groundless suit brought by an established company against an impecunious competitor in order to drive it from a market.

Easier cases involve patently meritless or frivolous steps—those that have no hope of success on their merits.[26] Two practical reasons exist to explain why courts and other enforcing agencies might be effectively limit-

21 Mens rea is generally required for professional discipline. See § 3.3.1 (mens rea). Thus it would be inappropriate to conclude that every award of legal fees against a lawyer for frivolous litigation necessarily denotes a violation of the antiharassment rules. See In re Lauer, 108 Wis.2d 746, 324 N.W.2d 432, 438–39 (1982).

22 In re Ronwin, 113 Ariz. 357, 555 P.2d 315, 318 (1976), cert.denied 430 U.S. 907, 97 S.Ct. 1178, 51 L.Ed.2d 583 (1977).

23 Christianburg Garment Co. v. EEOC, 434 U.S. 412, 423–24, 98 S.Ct. 694, 701, 54 L.Ed.2d 648 (1978); Overnite Transp. Co. v. Chicago Ind. Tire Co., 697 F.2d 789, 795 (7th Cir.1983); Asai v. Castillo, 593 F.2d 1222, 1225 (D.C. Cir.1978); United States v. Ross, 535 F.2d 346 (6th Cir. 1976).

24 Meagher v. Kavli, 256 Minn. 54, 97 N.W.2d 370 (1959).

25 Textor v. Board of Regents of Northern Illinois University, 87 F.R.D. 751 (N.D.Ill.1980)(Rule 11 violation by lawyers who did not even respond to motions to dismiss by additional parties over whom there was no legal possibility of obtaining personal jurisdiction).

26 Gonzales v. Cassidy, 474 F.2d 67 (5th Cir.1973); Tupling v. Britton, 411 A.2d 349 (D.C.App.1980).

ed to such exotica in imposing sanctions. Unless the matter has already been aired fully in court at a hearing on the merits of the frivolous assertion, important facts supporting the litigant's position will often be protected by the attorney-client privilege.[27] Moreover, imposing sanctions in any but patently frivolous cases involves the risk of imposing sanctions on lawyers, or possibly their clients, for stepping over a line that must necessarily remain in part indistinct and uncertain.

A distinguishable issue concerns not the legality, but the morality, of client litigation. Many lawyers hold it as part of their professional orientation that they are not concerned with the justice or injustice of their client's position in litigation (§ 10.4). Their only responsibility is to assure that any position taken is legally supportable.[28] Thus the fact that a debt clearly is owed has nothing to do with the assertion of the defense of the statute of limitations.[29] But some have urged that lawyers are permitted or indeed are required to take a larger role (§ 10.2.1).

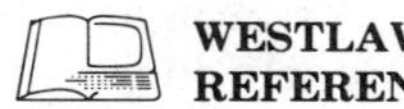
WESTLAW REFERENCES

Defining Unwanted Litigation

good-faith bad-faith /7 litigat!

Tactical Litigation

45k32 /p duty /5 client

§ 11.2.4 Questions of Fact

Factual Foundations

Some problems of bad faith involve the lawyer's lack of a factual foundation for asserted positions. The ideal state of facts is one that permits an objective lawyer confidently to predict a reasonable prospect of success. But less must be acceptable in some circumstances, particularly in those in which the opposing party is in possession of most of the relevant information and resort to discovery is necessary to unearth it. Yet even in such cases, a lawyer should be able to point to more than unsubstantiated rumor and similarly gossamer suspicions.[30] At the very least, a lawyer should be in possession of credible factual information indicating that there is a fair prospect of success on the merits of the claim or defense asserted.[31] And the time to gather and assess the necessary minimal factual foundation is before suit is filed.[32] If a lawyer is in good faith unsure whether his or her client is truthful and believes that a factfinder might credit the story, a sufficient factual basis probably exists.[33] Yet a state of facts, once known, is not static; a lawyer may later learn facts that cast sufficient doubt on the accuracy of previously assumed knowledge that a lawyer cannot proceed in good faith on the now discredited information.[34]

27 Metzger v. Silverman, 62 Cal.App.3d Supp. 30, 133 Cal.Rptr. 355, 362 (Super.1976). See generally § 6.3.

28 The oath for lawyers recommended by the ABA was amended in 1977 to remove language stating an obligation to refuse to represent a client whose case the lawyer thinks is "unjust." Retained was an obligation not to take a case unless the lawyer believes it to be "honestly debatable under the law of the land." See 63 ABA J. 312 (1977).

29 Cf. Zabella v. Pakel, 242 F.2d 452 (7th Cir.1957).

30 Nemeroff v. Abelson, 704 F.2d 652 (2d Cir.1983); Rhinehart v. Stauffer, 638 F.2d 1169 (9th Cir.1979); Miller v. Schweickart, 413 F.Supp. 1059, 1061 (S.D.N.Y.1976).

31 Cf. MR 3.1 comment ("The filing of an action or defense or similar action taken for a client is not frivolous merely because the facts have not first been fully substantiated or because the lawyer expects to develop vital evidence only by discovery.").

32 Cristanelli v. United States Lines, 74 F.R.D. 590 (C.D. Cal.1977).

33 Tool Research & Eng. Corp. v. Henigson, 46 Cal.App. 3d 675, 120 Cal.Rptr. 291, 297–98 (1975).

34 State v. Zeigler, 217 Kan. 748, 538 P.2d 643, 93 A.L.R.3d 869 (1975)(violation of DR 7–101(A)(1) when lawyer sued debtor after being informed that debt had been paid without making any effort to determine accuracy of information).

Irrelevance of the Burden of Proof Placement

It has been argued that a higher standard of candor applies to "affirmative" statements, such as in complaints, and a lesser standard to statements of denial, such as in answers that have the legal effect of calling upon the other party to offer proof of assertions known to be true.[35] Yet it seems equally as objectionable to subject an opponent who is a claimant to the needless expense of proving matters that cannot be controverted as it is to subject a defending opponent to the needless expense of meeting claims that are incontrovertibly unfounded or false. The latter approach seems to be endorsed by the Model Rules.[36]

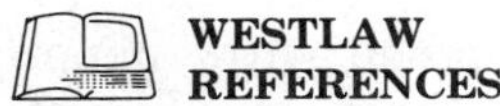

Factual Foundations

"dr 7–101(a)(1)" dr7–101(a)(1) /p inten!

§ 11.2.5 Delay

Delay in Litigation and Its Causes

Prominent among harassment problems is that of delay: instances in which a lawyer takes a step for a client, such as an appeal, that has no chance of success because of its frivolousness but that will have the effect of delaying entry of judgment against the client.[37] Lawyer-caused delay has long troubled thoughtful persons and has been a principal source of lay complaints about lawyers.[38] "The glacial pace of much litigation breeds frustration with the . . . courts and, ultimately, disrespect for the law." [39] Lawyer procrastination in some instances may, of course, also be detrimental to the lawyer's client, a matter discussed elsewhere (§ 5.6—neglect). Whether ultimately injurious to a client's interests or not, lawyer delay can be caused by lawyer self-interest, particularly if the basis on which the lawyer is paid is an hourly charge.[40] Despite the plain injustice of justice delayed, litigation by inaction or obstruction remains a tempting tactic because it can be beneficial to clients.[41]

---

35 Patterson, A Preliminary Rationalization of the Law of Legal Ethics, 57 N.C.L.Rev. 519, 545 (1979)(defensive pleadings are tested by less strict measure of candor).

36 The last sentence of MR 3.1 strongly implies that perfunctory denials are warranted only in proceedings involving incarceration of a client, such as defense of a criminal charge or a civil commitment case. Thus, for example, a general denial in a civil action seeking damages or an injunction could be defended only on the ground, implausible in most cases, that there is a "not frivolous" "basis" for denial of each of the plaintiff's allegations.

37 Muigai v. INS, 682 F.2d 334 (2d Cir.1982)(sanctions against lawyer who filed frivolous appeal in deportation case); People v. Kane, 655 P.2d 390 (Colo.1982)(discipline for frivolous appeal filed solely for delay). Economics plays a large role in frivolous appeals. In the recent era of very high interest rates, many state's laws provided rates of interest on judgments that were strikingly lower than market rates. Judgment debtors thus had strong incentives to appeal simply to forestall the need to pay a judgment. The federal rates of interest were not made comparable to market rates until 1982. See Federal Court Improvement Act of 1982 § 302(a)(2), codified in 28 U.S.C.A. § 1961(a).

38 P.Stern, Lawyers on Trial 151–55 (1980); J.Leiberman, Crisis at the Bar 37–39, 163–66 (1978); C.Dickens, Bleak House (1853); Ethics of the Fathers (Pirke Avoth), ch.5, § 11, Talmud, Judah HaNassi, quoted in Norton, Ethics in Medicine and Law in Lawyers' Ethics (A.Gerson ed.1980) at 259 ("The sword comes upon the world on account of the delay of justice and the perversion of justice."); "Those Lawyers," Time Mag., April 10, 1978, p. 55. See generally H.Zeisel, H.Kalven & B.Buchholz, Delay In the Court (1959); Pound, The Causes of Popular Dissatisfaction with the Administration of Justice, 35 F.R.D. 273, 291 (1964)(originally published in 40 Am.L.Rev. 729 (1906)).

39 Roadway Express, Inc. v. Piper, 447 U.S. 752, 757 n.4, 100 S.Ct. 2455, 2459, 65 L.Ed.2d 488 (1980). See also Nat'l Comm'n for Review of Antitrust Laws, Report to the President and the Attorney General 29 (1978); Edelstein, The Ethics of Dilatory Motion Practice: Time for a Change, 44 Fordham L.Rev. 1069 (1976).

40 Hourly fees are much more typically charged by defense lawyers than plaintiffs' lawyers in many areas. But delay is also found among plaintiffs' lawyers. E.g., Chira v. Lockheed Aircraft Corp., 634 F.2d 664 (2d Cir. 1980); Brown v. Pac. Tel. & Tel. Co., 105 Cal.App.3d 482, 164 Cal.Rptr. 445 (1980); Cucuzzo v. Huntington Hospital, 74 A.D.2d 632, 425 N.Y.S.2d 162 (1980).

41 Some well-known lawyers have made public and apparently shameless boast of their skills in delaying cases. E.g., Bromley, Judicial Control of Antitrust Cases, 23 F.R.D. 417 (1959); Tenth Annual New England Antitrust Conference, 792 Antitrust & Trade Reg.Rptr. A-1, at A-2–A-3 (1976).

Delay in the Lawyer Codes

The 1969 Code contained only an oblique mention of the problem of delay, apparently authorizing it except in cases of undilutedly improper motives.[42] Model Rule 3.2, on the other hand, both faces the issue and squarely imposes on lawyers the affirmative obligation to "make reasonable efforts to expedite litigation consistent with the interests of the client." [43] The test given in the comment to Rule 3.2 for resolving the tension between client interests and expeditious litigation is "whether a lawyer acting in good faith would regard the course of action as having some substantial purpose other than delay. Realizing financial or other benefit from otherwise improper delay in litigation is not a legitimate interest of the client." Plainly, under the Rules delay in litigation can no longer be justified simply by invoking client interest. Enforcement of such a rule, however, will probably require an adjustment to the professional expectations of many lawyers and judges.[44]

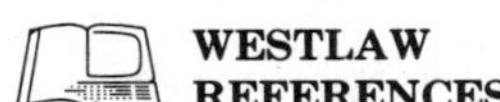
WESTLAW REFERENCES

Delay in Litigation and Its Causes

102k260(4)

Delay in the Lawyer Codes

delay /p "dr 7–102(a)(1)" dr7–102(a)(1)

§ 11.3 ADVOCATES AND JUDGES

§ 11.3.1 The Lawyer-Judge Relationship

The opposing advocates in a trial and the presiding judge comprise the triad on which the adversary system is based. Were the enterprise entirely cooperative, little friction between either advocate and the judge should be expected. But the process is a competitive one and advocates and their clients will naturally be disappointed with setbacks during its course and, most obviously, the losing party and advocate confront the bitterness of ultimate defeat. And it is "a practice familiar in the long history of Anglo-American litigation, whereby unsuccessful litigants and lawyers give vent to their disappointment in tavern or press." [45] Moreover, judges are wielders of power and sometimes must be resisted courageously by lawyers when their power is exercised wrongly.

Yet the position of judges in the adversarial system and the situation of judges as protected yet vulnerable oracles of the law requires that lawyers refrain from needless conflict with judges. By the same token, lawyers should not impinge with inappropriate judicial contact on the neutral position that judges occupy. Those concerns for judicial respect and judicial neutrality are worked out in the professional codes in rules placing limits on lawyer expressions of hostility against judges and limiting an advocate's contacts with judges.

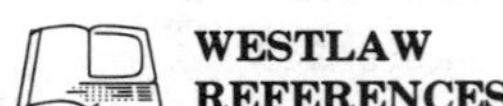
WESTLAW REFERENCES

digest,synopsis(lawyer attorney counsel** /9 judge /9 relationship)

§ 11.3.2 Lawyer Criticism of Judges

Protecting and Exposing Judges

From instincts of both altruism and self-interest most lawyers have exercised admirable restraint and respect in dealing with judg-

[42] DR 7–102(A)(1) states that a lawyer shall not "delay a trial" but only when delay would "merely" serve to harass or maliciously injure another. The wording implies that delay that would also serve the client's interests is permissible. Some decisions have not read the DR that restrictively. E.g., In re Vasser, 75 N.J. 357, 382 A.2d 1114, 1116 (1978)(DR violated by surreptitious contact with scheduling clerk to delay divorce trial until client's criminal trial was over).

[43] See also, e.g., N.Y.Rules Ct. § 1022.8 (McKinney 1983).

[44] People v. Moody, 676 P.2d 691, 695 (Colo.1984)(defense lawyer not ineffective for failure to raise speedy trial defense in view of lawyer's strategy to delay trial "as long as possible so that the prosecution might make a serious error, witnesses' memories might deteriorate, or witnesses may become unavailable.").

[45] United States v. Morgan, 313 U.S. 409, 421, 61 S.Ct. 999, 1004, 85 L.Ed. 1429 (1941).

es who were not, if truth be known, always above fair criticism. Occasionally, however, a lawyer or newspaper editor has unleashed an unfounded and unfair attack on a judge. In order to preserve the appearance of impartiality, judges normally follow the wise tradition of refusing to be drawn into public controversies about their actions. That judicial tradition leaves judges unable to defend themselves against groundless public charges. For such protection judges have traditionally relied upon lawyers, their colleagues for that occasion at least. Lawyers in the main have been willing to defend those unjustly accused.

Yet an occasional judge, no less than an occasional lawyer, is subject to just censure. Lawyers possess special knowledge and legal training that gives them a unique ability to assess the performance of judges. If lawyers were reluctant to call public attention to judicial shortcomings, most incompetent or corrupt judges would probably remain unchastened on the bench.[46] Indeed, some have argued that it is the duty of lawyers to criticize judicial error publicly.[47] Despite feelings of collegiality with most judges, a lawyer may feel that a particular judge deserves no protection. Lawyers are vulnerable to abuses of power by autocratic judges. A lawyer abusively treated by a judge has limited remedies. A complaint to a judicial discipline agency is a possibility—in fact may be required.[48] But reporting is not a remedy likely to bring effective reaction in many jurisdictions. A lawyer's damage suit against a judge will generally run afoul of the judicial immunity doctrine.[49] Thus, lawyers may feel strong motivation to resort to the scourge of publicity to expose perceived judicial corruption, autocracy, or incompetence. At the very least, the Supreme Court has recently said the law gives "[j]udges as persons or courts as institutions . . . no greater immunity from criticism than other persons or institutions." [50]

Public Lawyer Criticism of Judges

The lawyer codes express a special obligation of lawyers not to criticize judges through false accusations,[51] as well as the wish that lawyers might come to the defense of judges unfairly accused.[52] If the lawyer codes were unequivocally limited to prohibition against knowingly false charges by lawyers directed at judges that materially interfere with the administration of justice—to which they assuredly do extend [53]—few problems would be presented. But a current that runs through some judicial opinions is that all lawyer criticism of judges creates public disrespect for the

46 Cf. J.Goulden, The Benchwarmers: The Private World of the Powerful Federal Judges 21–22 (1974)(speculation that prohibition in ethics codes against criticism of judges frightens lawyers from adverse public comments about incompetent or corrupt judges).

47 H.Drinker, Legal Ethics 59–62 (1953).

48 MR 8.3(b); 1908 Canon 29. The 1969 Code contained no correlative provision; the disclosure rule of DR 1–103(B) required only that lawyers respond to inquiries initiated by judicial conduct agencies, not that they volunteer such information.

49 Dean v. Shirer, 547 F.2d 227, 42 A.L.R.Fed. 155 (4th Cir.1976)(mayor-municipal judge immune from suit by lawyer whom judge forced to stand outside courthouse and publicly apologize to judge for prior statement that fair trial could not be obtained in judge's court).

50 Landmark Communications, Inc. v. Virginia, 435 U.S. 829, 839, 98 S.Ct. 1535, 1541, 56 L.Ed.2d 1 (1978), quoting Bridges v. California, 314 U.S. 252, 289, 62 S.Ct. 190, 206, 86 L.Ed. 192 (1941)(Frankfurter, J., dissenting).

51 DR 8–102(B); MR 8.2(a). The sweep of MR 8.2(a) is wider, including statements about "a judge, adjudicatory officer or public legal officer," where DR 8–102 applies only to statements about a "judge or other adjudicatory officer." Presumably the statement in MR 8.2(a) that a lawyer shall not make a statement about such a person "with reckless disregard as to its falsity" assumes, as the text neglects to state, that the statement indeed is false. Reportedly, in many Western European legal systems, rather strict and far-reaching statutes prohibit statements that reflect upon the honor or dignity of judicial officers. See In re Wolfson, 453 F.Supp. 1087, 1090 n.4 (S.D.N.Y.1978).

52 1908 Canon 1; Code EC 8–6; MR 8.2 comment. For an argument that lawyers have a strong obligation to speak in defense of courts, see E.Rostow, The Ideal in Law 163 (1978).

53 In re Jafree, 93 Ill.2d 450, 67 Ill.Dec. 104, 444 N.E.2d 143 (1982)(disbarment for filing over forty frivolous suits and making numerous scurrilous and defamatory statements about state and federal judges); In re Crumpacker, 269 Ind. 630, 383 N.E.2d 36, 45 (1978), cert.denied 444 U.S. 979, 100 S.Ct. 481, 62 L.Ed.2d 406 (1979)(disbarment for intemperate and unfounded attacks upon character and integrity of judge who had ruled against lawyer in emotion-laden litigation).

law or the judiciary and thus should be sanctioned without careful regard for its truth or falsity,[54] possibly because the tone of criticism rather than its factual content is considered objectionable.[55]

Those opinions and their self-solicitude for the respect that lawyers owe judges entirely overlook the fact that there is no provision in the Code prohibiting lawyer disrespect for judges.[56] They also seriously conflict with substantial authority protecting the constitutional right of lawyers to speak freely if accurately.[57] Several Supreme Court decisions have held that citizen criticism of judges outside of the courtroom is constitutionally protected expression.[58]

Any argument that lawyer criticism of judges is entitled to a lesser protection than nonlawyer criticism would have to proceed on the readily rejectable premise that lawyers are not entitled to the normal rights of citizens or on the only slightly stronger argument that there is a substantial and compelling state interest in requiring lawyers to protect judges by never subjecting them to accurate criticism. Certainly when the question before the public is whether a judge should be retained in office in a judicial election, there should not be the slightest doubt that lawyers are constitutionally entitled to debate the merits of a judicial candidacy as vigorously as all other citizens.[59] Nonetheless, lawyers of a flamboyant turn of phrase

54 In re Snyder, 734 F.2d 334 (8th Cir.1984)(lawyer suspended from practice in all federal courts in circuit for six months for private letter sent to district judge's secretary criticizing "extreme gymnastics" required to receive "puny amounts" under court's system of compensating court-appointed lawyers and expressing "extreme disgust" at his handling by court of appeals which twice rejected his undocumented request for additional compensation), reversed ___ U.S. ___, 105 S.Ct. 2874, 86 L.Ed.2d 504 (1985); Justices of Appellate Division, First Dep't v. Erdmann, 39 A.D.2d 223, 333 N.Y.S.2d 863 (1972), reversed 33 N.Y.2d 559, 347 N.Y.S.2d 441, 301 N.E.2d 426 (1973). See also, e.g., In re Sawyer, 360 U.S. 622, 668, 79 S.Ct. 1376, 1399, 3 L.Ed.2d 1473 (1959) (Frankfurter, J., dissenting)(evidently condemning extrajudicial lawyer criticism of judge regardless of truth and lack of impact on proceedings); Louisiana State Bar Ass'n v. Karst, 428 So.2d 406, 409 (La.1983)(violation of DR 8–102(B) when lawyer "intentionally causes accusations to be published which he knows to be false, or which, with the exercise of ordinary care, he should know to be false."). A similar looseness is, unfortunately, carried forward in MR 8.2(a) in its dual standard of (1) false statements by a lawyer about judges and (2) such statements made with "reckless disregard" for their truth or falsity. Although not so limited explicitly, the second ground obviously should extend only to false statements. See note 51, supra.

55 Rinaldi v. Holt, Rinehart & Winston, Inc., 42 N.Y.2d 369, 397 N.Y.S.2d 943, 366 N.E.2d 1299 (1977)(Fuchsberg, J., concurring), cert.denied 434 U.S. 969, 98 S.Ct. 514, 54 L.Ed.2d 456 (1977).

56 The repeal of 1908 Canon 1 removed the only specific reference to disrespect, aside from false charges, as a basis for discipline. See State Bar v. Semaan, 508 S.W.2d 429 (Tex.Civ.App.1974). In California, however, the lawyer's oath continues to require a lawyer to "maintain the respect due to the courts of justice and judicial officers." Cal.Bus. & Prof.Code § 6067 (West 1974). Violation of the oath has led to discipline. See Ramirez v. State Bar, 28 Cal.3d 402, 169 Cal.Rptr. 206, 619 P.2d 399 (1980) (accusations against state court of appeals judges in federal court pleadings).

57 Thatcher v. United States, 212 F. 801, 807 (6th Cir. 1914), appeal dismissed 241 U.S. 644, 36 S.Ct. 450, 60 L.Ed. 1218 (1916). See generally Note, Restrictions on Attorney Criticism of the Judiciary: A Denial of First Amendment Rights, 56 Notre Dame Law. 489 (1981); Note, In re Erdmann: What Lawyers Can Say about Judges, 38 Albany L.Rev. 600 (1974). See generally § 12.2.2 (lawyer free speech).

58 Craig v. Harney, 331 U.S. 367, 67 S.Ct. 1249, 91 L.Ed. 1546 (1947); Pennekamp v. Florida, 328 U.S. 331, 66 S.Ct. 1029, 90 L.Ed. 1295 (1946). Moreover, the general libel standard for statements about public officials is that damage sanctions may be imposed only on proof that the speaker acted with knowledge that the statement was "false or with reckless disregard of whether it is false or not." New York Times Co. v. Sullivan, 376 U.S. 254, 279–80, 84 S.Ct. 710, 725–26, 11 L.Ed.2d 686 (1964); Garrison v. Louisiana, 379 U.S. 64, 85 S.Ct. 209, 13 L.Ed.2d 125 (1964). See generally Rinaldi v. Holt, Rinehart & Winston, Inc., 42 N.Y.2d 369, 397 N.Y.S.2d 943, 366 N.E.2d 1299, cert.denied 434 U.S. 969, 98 S.Ct. 514, 54 L.Ed.2d 456 (1977)(book author's conclusion that judge was incompetent and should be removed from office, because supported with facts, was not libelous even if unreasonable, extreme, or erroneous). Cases like Bradley v. Fisher, 80 U.S. (13 Wall.) 335, 20 L.Ed. 646 (1872) (personal verbal assault by lawyer upon judge after court had recessed but during process of trial), punishing a lawyer for speech connected with an ongoing proceeding, deal not so much with respect for judges as with the necessity to maintain fair proceedings.

59 State Bar v. Semaan, 508 S.W.2d 429 (Tex.Civ.App. 1974)(lawyer's letter to newspaper criticizing judge's qualifications for office not censurable where no issue of falsity raised). But see, e.g., Kentucky Bar Ass'n v. Heleringer, 602 S.W.2d 165 (Ky.1980), cert.denied 449 U.S. 1101, 101 S.Ct. 898, 66 L.Ed.2d 828 (1981)(lawyer disciplined for press conference description of adverse ex parte order in politically sensitive case as "highly unethical and grossly unfair"); State v. Eisenberg, 48 Wis.2d 364, 180 N.W.2d 529 (1970), cert.denied 402 U.S. 987, 91 S.Ct. 1669, 29 L.Ed.2d 153 (1971)(lawyer suspended for

should be aware that a disturbing number of decisions show open judicial hostility toward claims of First Amendment protection for strongly worded lawyer criticism of judges.[60]

Courtroom Conduct

Different issues are presented when a lawyer's criticism of a judge occurs within the context of an ongoing judicial proceeding. Statements in the presence of witnesses, jurors, clients, and others can have a seriously disruptive effect that is normally absent from speech outside the courtroom. The need to assure the efficient dispatch of court business may require that some additional powers of judicial control be recognized (§ 12.1.3).

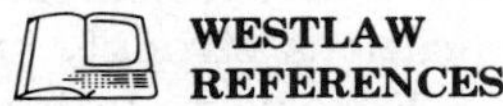

WESTLAW REFERENCES

judicial /3 immunity /s lawyer attorney counsel** /s judge

Public Lawyer Criticism of Judges

"dr 8–102" dr8–102 /p judge

criti! (false /2 statement) /4 judge official /s lawyer attorney counsel**

45k32(8)

§ 11.3.3 Professional Contact with Judges

Because of the importance of preserving the independence and neutrality of judges, lawyers are prohibited from creating situations that would otherwise lead with predictable regularity to corrupting favoritism or to unfair advantage over a litigational adversary. Those rules restrict the extent to which a lawyer may influence a judge by gifts or similar means and the extent to which ex parte communications with a judge can be made.

Unfair Influence

One of the enduring mythologies of public life in many communities—and, doubtless, a reality in some [61]—is that judges can be influenced in their official actions in return for bribes, gifts, political contributions, or other favors. Lawyers can take advantage of that reality or perception either by seeking influence through favors or by representing an ability to do so to gullible clients. Both practices plainly threaten the quality and efficaciousness of judicially administered justice.

The 1908 Canons stated that a lawyer was to do nothing to obtain special favors or consideration from a judge.[62] The 1969 Code contains a narrower prohibition—against a gift or loan to a judge that is not authorized by the Code of Judicial Conduct (DR 7–110(A)).[63] And DR 9–101(C) states that a lawyer may not state or imply an ability to influence improperly any tribunal or public official.[64] Several provisions in the 1983

one year for chacterizing judge's sexual relations with woman lawyer as grounds for felony charges and for newspaper advertisements soliciting support for recall of judge).

[60] In re Frerichs, 238 N.W.2d 764 (Iowa 1976); In re Terry, 271 Ind. 499, 394 N.E.2d 94 (1979), cert.denied 444 U.S. 1077, 100 S.Ct. 1025, 62 L.Ed.2d 759 (1980); In re Lacy, 283 N.W.2d 250 (S.D.1979); In re Raggio, 87 Nev. 369, 487 P.2d 499 (1971). See also, e.g., State ex rel. Inman v. Brock, 622 S.W.2d 36 (Tenn.1981), cert.denied, 454 U.S. 941, 102 S.Ct. 477, 70 L.Ed.2d 249 (1981)(injunction issued by supreme court against further suits by lawyer challenging legality of composition of supreme court because of past filings of papers making scandalous, impertinent, improper, and demeaning allegations about judges).

[61] See J.Noonan, Bribes (1984), for a collection of historical incidents of bribes of judges and other officials.

[62] 1908 Canon 3:

Marked attention and unusual hospitality on the part of a lawyer to a Judge, uncalled for by the personal relations of the parties, subject both the Judge and the lawyer to misconstructions of motive and should be avoided. A lawyer . . . deserves rebuke and denunciation for any device or attempt to gain from a Judge special personal consideration or favor. A self-respecting independence in the discharge of professional duty, without denial or diminution of the courtesy and respect due the Judge's station, is the only proper foundation for cordial personal and official relations between Bench and Bar.

[63] Canon 5C(4) of the Judicial Code narrowly defines the circumstances in which a judge may receive a gift; Judicial Canon 7B(2) describes the restricted arrangements under which a judge may solicit funds to support a judicial election contest. E.g., In re Litman, 272 N.W.2d 264 (Minn.1978)(loans to judge before whom lawyer continued to practice).

[64] In re Fasig, 444 N.E.2d 849 (Ind.1983). The same DR also implies prohibition of actual improper influence of a tribunal. E.g., In re Keiler, 380 A.2d 119, 126 (D.C.App. 1977)(improper influence on labor arbitrator by surreptitious designation of lawyer's own partner as arbitrator).

Model Rules bear more expansively on the problem. Rule 3.5(a) broadly prohibits lawyers from seeking to influence a judge by "means prohibited by law." The comment to this rule suggests that the reference is both to criminal laws prohibiting bribery and similar corruption as well as to the Code of Judicial Conduct with its considerably wider strictures. Model Rule 8.4(f) prohibits a lawyer from assisting a judge to violate the Code of Judicial Conduct. And MR 8.4(e) prohibits a lawyer from stating or implying an ability to exert improper influence on any government agency or official—presumably without regard to the truth or falsity of the claim [65] or to whether an attempted exertion of influence is successful.[66]

The law treats some situations of possible unfair lawyer influence in a categorical fashion. A relationship between lawyer and judge that is such that influence would likely result probably falls under the rules requiring recusal of the judge.[67] But the lawyer's, and not the judge's, disqualification may be required if it appears that the lawyer was retained in the case simply to force the presiding judge's recusal.[68]

Ex Parte Communications

The purpose of the prohibition against ex parte communications is to prevent the communicating side from gaining an unfair advantage in the litigation.[69] The advantage is created, of course, because the communication may influence the judge on an important decision without the absent party being able to rebut or qualify the communication as it is being made and with knowledge of the exact form in which it is made. Such contacts violate the right of every party to a fair hearing, a corollary of which is the right to hear all evidence and argument offered by an adversary.[70] The violation is particularly acute because the calculated secretiveness of such communications strongly suggests their inaccuracy.[71] Moreover, unless the judge promptly reveals or repudiates the communication, the circumstances suggest a receptive and thus prejudicially receptive state of mind in the judge.[72]

For such reasons, ex parte communications by a lawyer with a judge about the merits of a pending matter are prohibited by the 1908 Canons,[73] by DR 7–110(B) of the 1969 Code,[74] and by 1983 Model Rule 3.5(b)[75] The prohibition extends to ex parte contacts by a client or other person acting at the suggestion or direc-

65 Rey v. State, 512 S.W.2d 40 (Tex.Civ.App.1974), appeal dismissed 421 U.S. 926, 95 S.Ct. 1651, 44 L.Ed.2d 83 (1975)(discipline for informing client's father of need for $500 to buy present for presiding judge).

66 Florida Bar v. Saxon, 379 So.2d 1281 (Fla.1980)(violation of DR 7–110(A) prohibition against gifts to judges even if no proof that gift was accepted).

67 Young v. Champion, 142 Ga.App. 687, 236 S.E.2d 783 (1977)(lawyer who is governmental official with power of appointment and removal over judge is disqualified from appearing in a case before that judge).

68 McCuin v. Texas Power & Light Co., 714 F.2d 1255 (5th Cir.1983).

69 EC 7–35. For analogous reasons, federal and state statutes commonly prohibit ex parte communications with administrative agency hearing officers and similar officials. E.g., 5 U.S.C.A. § 557 (d)(1). See generally Government in the Sunshine Act, House Report No. 94–880 (Pt. 1)(1976); Note, Ex Parte Contacts under the Constitution and Administrative Procedure Act, 80 Colum.L.Rev. 379 (1980).

70 Heavey v. State Bar, 17 Cal.3d 553, 131 Cal.Rptr. 406, 551 P.2d 1238 (1976); Herring v. Retail Credit Co., 266 S.C. 455, 224 S.E.2d 663 (1976). Not all ex parte communications, however, amount to a deprivation of due process. E.g., Fotomat Corp. v. Photovest Corp., 606 F.2d 704 (7th Cir. 1979), cert. denied 445 U.S. 917, 100 S.Ct. 1278, 63 L.Ed.2d 601 (1980); Moity v. Louisiana State Bar Ass'n, 414 F.Supp. 180, 183 (E.D.La.1976), affirmed 537 F.2d 1141 (5th Cir.1976).

71 In re Burrows, 291 Or. 135, 629 P.2d 820, 22 A.L.R. 4th 906 (1981).

72 Craven v. United States, 22 F.2d 605, 607 (1st Cir. 1927), cert.denied 276 U.S. 627, 48 S.Ct. 321, 72 L.Ed. 739 (1928).

73 Canon 3: "A lawyer should not communicate or argue privately with the Judge as to the merits of a pending cause."

74 See generally Annot., 22 A.L.R.4th 906 (1983).

75 MR 3.5(b) is broader than the Code or Canons because its reference to "such a person" seems certainly to point to the list of persons in MR 3.5(a), which includes "a judge, juror, prospective juror or other official".

For the California provision, see Calif.R. 7–108(B).

tion of a lawyer.[76] And decisions have expansively applied the prohibition to ex parte contact with judges, hearing officers, court clerks exercising important discretionary functions, and similar officers.[77]

The anticontact obligation is reciprocally applied to judges by their own conduct code.[78] Occasionally, an impermissible ex parte contact may be initiated by a judge, such as by a request to one party to a completed hearing to submit a draft of findings without sending a copy to the other side. Regardless of the good faith of the judge and the contacted lawyer, both the judge and the cooperating lawyer have plainly violated their respective professional obligations.

Permitted ex Parte Contact

Two general exceptions to the ex parte rule have been recognized. A lawyer may contact a judge ex parte when authorized by law,[79] and under the Code, but not under the Model Rules, contact can also be made when the communication is not on "the merits of the cause." Contact authorized by law includes submissions made to obtain ex parte restraining orders,[80] submissions made in camera by order of the judge,[81] or similarly rare occasions.[82] The exception in DR 7–110(B) for ex parte communications that are not about the "merits" of a case invites unfortunate and nice distinctions. One such distinction is the suggestion that it is permissible, because recusal is not addressed to the merits of the parties' claim or defense, to attempt to persuade a judge privately to recuse himself or herself from a case.[83] The distinction is a mischievous one unless it is confined strictly to trivial details of housekeeping in a case, which would certainly not include the designation of the judge for trial or for an important hearing, the setting of the time for trial, or similar matters. The Code's exception for nonmerits communications should be strictly limited to communications that are neither about the factual or legal issues in the case nor about matters that a reasonable lawyer would consider important for tactical or strategic reasons. The nonmerits exception should not be employed in an attempt to differentiate between various phases of the proceeding.[84]

A further exception to the ex parte contact prohibition should be explicitly recognized—

[76] People v. Hertz, 638 P.2d 794 (Colo.1982). DR7–110(B), but not MR 3.5(b), explicitly extends to "caus[ing] another" to make an impermissible ex parte contact.

[77] Noland v. State Bar, 63 Cal.2d 298, 46 Cal.Rptr. 305, 405 P.2d 129 (1965)(court clerk compiling jury list); In re Hancock, 67 Cal.App.3d 943, 136 Cal.Rptr. 901 (1977) (comment to supervising judge after case was assigned to another judge); Florida Bar v. Saphirstein, 376 So.2d 7 (Fla.1979)(hearing officer in lawyer discipline case); Florida Bar v. Mason, 334 So.2d 1 (Fla.1976)(supreme court justices).

[78] Code of Jud. Conduct, Canon 3A(4). The Canon is possibly broader in application than DR 7–110(B) because the latter prohibits ex parte contact in a "pending" matter, while the former's prohibition applies to a "pending *or impending* proceeding" (emphasis supplied).

[79] So provided explicitly in MR 3.5(b) and somewhat elaborately in DR 7–110(B)(1), (3), and (4). The exception in DR 7–110(B)(2) for written ex parte communications if a copy of the writing is promptly delivered to the opposing lawyer or party simply seems not to be an ex parte communication. "Prompt" delivery of a copy of the communication, of course, means in time to enter an effective resistance to it. Cf. In re Bell, 294 Or. 202, 655 P.2d 569 (1982).

[80] Fed.R.Civ.Proc.Rule 65(b); In re Jordan, 293 Or. 788, 652 P.2d 1268 (1982).

[81] ABA Prosecution Function Standards § 2.8 comment (approved draft 1979). Permission to present matters in camera, however, does not provide a license to make supplementary submissions ex parte. See In re Special Sept. 1978 Grand Jury, 640 F.2d 49 (7th Cir.1980). And because in camera submissions, by definition, are not available to the opposing party, they should be reserved for extraordinary circumstances and carefully administered. E.g., Military Audit Project v. Bush, 418 F.Supp. 876, 880 (D.D.C.1976).

[82] See also United States v. Meinster, 488 F.Supp. 1342 (S.D.Fla.1980), affirmed 664 F.2d 971 (5th Cir.1981), cert.denied 457 U.S. 1136, 102 S.Ct. 2965, 73 L.Ed.2d 1354 (1982)(contact by prosecutor to inform judge of information about plot to assassinate him).

[83] Stern Bros., Inc. v. McClure, 236 S.E.2d 222, 224 n.1 (W.Va.1977)(recusal); Cavanagh v. Cavanagh, 118 R.I. 608, 375 A.2d 911, 918 (1977)(meeting to assign case for hearing). But see, e.g., In re Berk, 98 Wis.2d 443, 297 N.W.2d 28 (1980)(impermissible contact to obtain adjournment of criminal prosecution).

[84] In re Burrows, 291 Or. 135, 629 P.2d 820, 22 A.L.R.4th 906 (1981). The strict standard in *Burrows* has since arguably been diluted. See In re Smith, 295 Or. 755, 670 P.2d 1018 (1983).

that for consent by all parties. There is no reason why every trip to a courthouse should be simultaneously duplicated by a lawyer on the other side if the matter is not or no longer in genuine dispute. Efficient dispatch of court business is furthered by recognizing the legitimacy of ex parte contacts so long as they are authorized by all other affected parties and so long as they faithfully conform to what other parties have authorized.[85]

WESTLAW REFERENCES

Unfair Influence

"dr 9–101(c)" dr9–101(c)

judge /5 influenc! /s lawyer attorney counsel**

Ex Parte Communications

di ex parte

"ex parte" /s communicat! discuss! contact! /s "due process"

"dr 7–110(b)" dr7–110(b)

Permitted ex Parte Contact

prompt** /s deliv! /p "dr 7–110(b)"

di recusation

merit /p "dr 7–110(b)" dr7–110(b)

§ 11.4 ADVOCATES AND JURORS

§ 11.4.1 Jury Isolation and Secrecy

Jurors, like judges in nonjury cases, most often hold in their power victory or defeat for an advocate. Unlike judges, jurors are presumptively unsophisticated about law, lawyers, or the legal system and thus would be much more susceptible to prejudicial impressions if advocates were free to contact them outside the trial itself or to influence them improperly during it. Moreover, anciently and today the jury is protected by rules ensuring the secrecy of their deliberations in order to assure their ability to discuss controversial matters among themselves and, occasionally, to blunt the sharp edges of the law.[86] The professional rules, in varying degrees, restrict or prohibit ex parte contact with jurors. Substantive law occasionally carries the restrictions further and imposes separate sanctions. Those restrictions will be reviewed in three phased settings: contact prior to trial, contact during trial, and contact after trial.

WESTLAW REFERENCES

digest,synopsis(jur** /3 secrecy)

193k45

§ 11.4.2 Lawyer Pretrial Contact with Jurors

Lawyers confronted with strangers on a prospective jury panel may wish to learn more about the panel members in order to exercise their challenges to the jury wisely. But, obviously, ex parte pretrial investigations of prospective jurors by a lawyer or a lawyer's agent carry a substantial risk of improper influence. Accordingly, the 1969 Code, in DR 7–108(A), states that lawyers shall not "communicate" directly or indirectly[87] with a person known to be a member of the prospective juror panel,[88] the venire.[89] By DR 7–108(f) the prohibition is extended to contact with any member of the family of a venire member.[90] If a lawyer creates pretrial publicity that might influence prospective ju-

[85] In re Bell, 294 Or. 202, 655 P.2d 569 (1982).

[86] Jury secrecy is assured by various rules modeled on Vaise v. Delaval, 1 Term.Rep. 11, 99 Eng.Rep. 944 (K.B.1785), restricting the extent to which testimony about jury deliberations is admissible in posttrial attacks on verdicts. Statutes in many jurisdictions now make it a crime to eavesdrop on jury deliberations. See n. 96 infra. See generally 8 J.Wigmore, Evidence § 2354 (3d ed.1940); F.James & G.Hazard, Civil Procedure § 7.19 (3d ed.1985); 2 F.Pollock & F.Maitland, The History of English Law 622–630 (2d ed.1923).

[87] DR 7–108(E).

[88] The professional rules apply both to trial juries and to grand juries. E.g., In re Terry, 271 Ind. 499, 394 N.E.2d 94 (1979), cert.denied 444 U.S. 1077, 100 S.Ct. 1025, 62 L.Ed.2d 759 (1980)(grand jury).

[89] The California rule is similar. See Calif.R. 7–106(A). Because the absolute bar against communicating with prospective jurors is continued during the trial by DR 7–108(B), a lawyer's contact with a juror after selection but before trial is also forbidden. See In re Holman, 277 S.C. 293, 286 S.E.2d 148 (1982)(disbarment following contempt conviction for contact with selected juror in criminal case).

[90] In re Two Anonymous Members of the South Carolina Bar, 278 S.C. 477, 298 S.E.2d 450 (1982)(prohibition against contacts with members of "family" of juror ex-

rors, the intricacies of DR 7–107 become relevant (§ 12.2.2).

The 1983 Model Rules, in Rule 3.5(a), prohibit attempts to "influence" a "prospective juror" "by means prohibited by law." [91] A lawyer might mistakenly read this language in isolation to imply that some such attempts at pretrial influence—those not prohibited by law—might be licit. But MR 3.5(b) goes on to state that a lawyer shall not "communicate ex parte" with jurors or prospective jurors,[92] without limitation as to time, place, or the contents of the communication. Thus, under MR 3.5(b), as under DR 7–108, no pretrial juror contact (or, for that matter, contact at any time) is allowed unless explicitly "permitted by law." [93] Finally, MR 3.6, on trial publicity, basically duplicates DR 7–107 with respect to attempts to influence prospective jurors through the media.

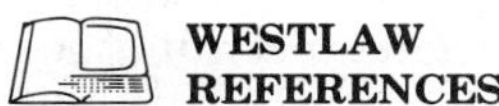
WESTLAW REFERENCES

"dr 7–107" dr7–107 "dr 7–108" dr7–108 /p jur**

§ 11.4.3 *Trial Contact*

Surreptitious contact with a sitting juror during trial in an attempt to influence the juror's verdict is a crime akin to the common-law felony of "embracery." [94] Such contact by a lawyer is plainly in derogation of the operation of the legal system and impermissible.[95] Contact during trial might be defended as necessary in order to gather information about suspected juror misconduct in support of a motion for mistrial or a new trial. But the common-law protection of the secrecy of jury deliberations, and modern legislation,[96] prohibit those contacts as well, or at least make the fruits of such investigations inadmissible in evidence.[97]

Improper influence on jurors can also be attempted in broad daylight, as by an advocate's appearing to be especially solicitous of jurors' interests during a trial. The 1908 Canons scowled at attempts to "curry favor with juries by fawning, flattery or pretended solicitude." [98] Nothing in the 1969 Code or the 1983 Model Rules seems to prohibit the tactic directly, but it is discouraged by the Code [99] and can continue to draw the ire of judges.[1] The most obvious form of impermissible influence on jurors is by improper appeals to their emotions or biases. But little agreement on the limits of propriety can be found in the cases. For example, the ability to shed tears in the jury's presence has been

tends to all persons related by blood or marriage within sixth degree).

91 The framers of the rule intended the term *influence* to include all direct or indirect improper attempts to affect a juror's decision or predisposition. See the suppressed Legal Background Note to MR 3.5 (Proposed Final Draft, May 30, 1981).

92 The conclusion in the text follows from the natural, and obviously intended, reading of "such a person" in MR 3.5(b) to refer to the list of "judge, juror, prospective juror or other official" in MR 3.5(a).

93 DR 7–108(C) states an exception roughly similar to the "permitted by law" phrasing of MR 3.5(b) in its exception for communications "in the course of official proceedings."

94 United States v. Quinn, 543 F.2d 640 (8th Cir.1976); In re Weber, 16 Cal.3d 578, 128 Cal.Rptr. 434, 546 P.2d 1378 (1976)(discipline for solicitation of another to bribe juror); Employers Ins. of Wausau v. Hall, 49 N.C.App. 179, 270 S.E.2d 617 (1980), cert.denied 301 N.C. 720, 276 S.E.2d 283 (1981)(lawyer who attempted to influence juror in another case liable to party for legal fees expended in trial to point at which court was compelled to declare mistrial because of attempt).

95 In re Weishoff, 75 N.J. 326, 382 A.2d 632 (1978).

96 18 U.S.C.A. § 1508. The federal act and many similar state statutes grew out of negative political reactions to reported recordings of jury deliberations during one stage of the Chicago jury project. See H.Kalven & H.Zeisel, The American Jury xiv-xv (1966). An even more stringent statute was passed in England in 1981, primarily to prevent media interviews with jurors in celebrated cases. Contempt of Court Act, 1981, ch. 49, § 8(1)(crime for any person to "obtain, disclose or solicit" information about any matter discussed during jury deliberations).

97 It is presumably on this basis that DR 7–108(B)(2), explicitly, and MR 3.5(a) and (b), apparently, extend their respective anticontact prohibitions to lawyers not connected with the trial of the case.

98 1908 Canon 23.

99 EC 7–36. An argument might be made that MR 3.5(a) indeed outlaws the practice through its prohibition of attempts to "influence" a "juror" "by means prohibited by law". The "law" that prohibits is the common-law tradition opposing fawning upon a jury. See n. 1 infra.

1 Johnson v. Trueblood, 476 F.Supp. 90 (E.D.Pa 1979), vacated on other grounds 629 F.2d 302 (3d Cir.1980), cert.denied 450 U.S. 999, 101 S.Ct. 1704, 68 L.Ed.2d 200 (1981)(pro hac vice appearance of lawyer revoked, among

both accepted [2] and damned [3] by different judges.[4]

In small towns or crowded courthouses and through chance encounter, a lawyer may be thrown together outside the courtroom with a juror in a pending case. The rule of DR 7–108(B)(1) [5] and of MR 3.5(b) is absolute—during a trial a lawyer may not communicate with a juror. The rule has been applied strictly; a lawyer's only permitted comment to a sitting juror who attempts to converse with the lawyer, aside presumably from polite hellos or similar perfunctory greetings, must be politely but firmly to disengage from any conversation.[6]

WESTLAW REFERENCES

di embracery

curry /s favor /s jur**

§ 11.4.4 Posttrial Contact

After a verdict is returned,[7] a losing advocate may wish to interview members of a jury to determine whether juror misconduct existed that might warrant a motion for new trial.[8] The Code accepts that wish as a necessity [9] and allows nonharassing posttrial investigations (DR 7–108(D)).[10] The prevailing advocate will also often be motivated to conduct duplicating or preemptive juror interviews in order to meet a possible later claim of jury misconduct. Finally, either advocate might assert that posttrial interviews with jurors are an important means of self-education on advocacy methods.[11]

But posttrial juror interviews, if conducted ex parte by advocates, can invade the protected secrecy of jury deliberations, subject former jurors to harassment, and create the opportunity for misleading or corrupting jurors with respect to their possible later testimony about juror misconduct. The limited sweep of DR 7–108(D) outlaws only those posttrial interviews that harass or embarrass a juror.[12] But the law in some jurisdictions goes further and prohibits lawyers from conducting posttrial interviews of any kind with jurors.[13] Other jurisdictions permit those interviews unless they violate the professional rules.[14] In a somewhat eliptical fashion, as already discussed, the Model Rules appear to have prohibited most pretrial or posttrial contact with jurors in Rule 3.5(b) unless it is expressly permitted by law. If that interpretation is correct, then posttrial interviews will be per-

other things, for unprofessional solicitude for jurors' welfare).

2 State v. Bailey, 132 Ariz. 472, 647 P.2d 170 (1982) (mistrial not required when prosecutor and case officer cried during testimony of victim's mother on cross-examination; weeping was "spontaneous" and genuine, and jurors did not pay particular attention).

3 People v. Dukes, 12 Ill.2d 334, 146 N.E.2d 14, 67 A.L.R.2d 724 (1957). The suppressed Legal Background Note to MR 3.5 (Proposed Final Draft, May 30, 1981) cited *Dukes* for the proposition that the rule prohibited improper influence on a jury.

4 On the limits of forensics, see generally § 12.1.2.

5 See also Calif.R. 7–106(B).

6 Florida Bar v. Peterson, 418 So.2d 246 (Fla.1982); Omaha Bank for Cooperatives v. Siouxland Cattle Cooperative, 305 N.W.2d 458 (Iowa 1981); In re Delgado, 279 S.C. 293, 306 S.E.2d 591 (1983), cert.denied 464 U.S. 1057, 104 S.Ct. 740, 79 L.Ed.2d 198 (1984). See also In re Bruener, 159 Wash. 504, 294 P. 254 (1930)(disbarment for having affair with juror during trial).

7 Because the anticontact strictures relax significantly under DR 7–108(D) "after discharge of the jury from further consideration of a case," interviews with individual jurors after they are excused from further service but before a verdict is returned should probably be prohibited by the more absolute rule of DR 7–108(B)(1). Cf. Dutton v. State, 452 A.2d 127, 134–35 (Del.1982).

8 EC 7–29.

9 EC 7–29.

10 See also Calif.R. 7–106(D).

11 Elisovsky v. State, 592 P.2d 1221, 1224 n.7, 19 A.L.R.4th 1196 (Alaska 1979); ABA Formal Op. 319 (1967). The self-education claim has met with some judicial skepticism. See United States v. Narciso, 446 F.Supp. 252, 324–25 (E.D.Mich.1977); In re Delgado, 279 S.C. 293, 306 S.E.2d 591, 594 (1983), cert.denied 464 U.S. 1057, 104 S.Ct. 740, 79 L.Ed.2d 198 (1984).

12 Calif.R. 7–106(D) is similar. Brassell v. Brethauer, 305 So.2d 217 (Fla.App.1974), held that DR 7–108(D) is violated by a posttrial juror interview if the lawyer does not have "reasonable grounds" for the interview. Contra State v. Blocker, 211 Kan. 185, 505 P.2d 1099 (1973).

13 N.J.Ct.R. 1:16–1 (no posttrial juror interviews without leave of court for good cause shown); Northern Pac. Ry. v. Mely, 219 F.2d 199, 202 (9th Cir.1954); Olberg v. Minneapolis Gas Co., 291 Minn. 334, 191 N.W.2d 418 (1971). See generally Annot., 19 A.L.R.4th 1209 (1983).

14 Elisovsky v. State, 592 P.2d 1221 (Alaska 1979).

missible only in the few jurisdictions that expressly authorize them.

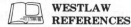

WESTLAW REFERENCES

post-trial post-verdict (conclu! /3 trial) /s jur** /s interview!

§ 11.5 ADVOCATES AND ADVERSARY LAWYERS

The Strivings of Friends

The cherished tradition of lawyering has it, in Shakespeare's words, that adversaries in law "strive mightily, but eat and drink as friends." [15] Proponents of the full advocacy model in the courtroom may countenance sharpness and generally belligerent behavior toward an opposing lawyer, but, we are to believe, lawyers can quickly and regularly shed their mutual belligerence once the official strife is over That probably describes either strife or friendship in a peculiar way; in fact, many lawyers make lasting enemies of colleagues because of representational belligerence.[16] And it is doubtful that the integrity of lawyers' relationships could long survive adversarial brinksmanship in litigation.

Offensive Personalities

Regardless of its effect on the personal relations of lawyers, overblown versions of the full advocacy model can interfere with efficiency of proceedings and cause needless harm. No specific mandatory provision of the 1969 Code [17] or the 1983 Model Rules [18] explicitly forbids excessive spleen towards opposing lawyers, but courts have nonetheless imposed sanctions because of interference with efficient proceedings,[19] because a lawyer's belligerence crossed the line into conduct so plainly improper as to suggest the lawyer's unfitness,[20] because the offending lawyer's conduct was plainly unfair to the opposing lawyer's client,[21] or because the lawyer's conduct was deemed "undignified or discourteous" and "degrading to a tribunal" under DR 7–106(C)(6).[22]

15 W.Shakespeare, The Taming of the Shrew, act I, sc. ii, ln. 281 (1593–94).

16 Lytton, Personal Viewpoint: The Uncivil Practice of Law, 68 ABA J. 388 (1982).

17 Cf. DR 7–106(C)(5)(lawyer shall not fail to comply with known local "customs of courtesy or practice of the bar or a particular tribunal" without first giving notice to opposing counsel); EC 7–37 (avoidance of ill feeling and offensive tactics toward opposing lawyers); EC 7–38 (courtesy and cooperation toward opposing counsel).

18 Cf. MR 4.4 ("respect for the rights of third persons"). That provision was intended to cover relationships with adversary lawyers. See the suppressed Legal Background Note, second-last paragraph (derogatory remarks about opposing counsel) in Model Rules (Proposed Final Draft, May 30, 1981).

19 Independent Investor Protective League & Co. v. Touche Ross & Co., 607 F.2d 530, 534–35 n.5 (2d Cir.), cert.denied 439 U.S. 895, 99 S.Ct. 254, 58 L.Ed.2d 241 (1978)("personal feud" between lawyers wasted time of busy trial and appellate courts on unnecessary discovery and sanction motions); Sanchez v. Sanchez, 435 So.2d 347 (Fla.App.1983)(fees sanction imposed on lawyer who refused to cooperate in correcting plainly erroneous document).

20 In re Crumpacker, 269 Ind. 630, 383 N.E.2d 36, 48–50 (1978), cert.denied 444 U.S. 979, 100 S.Ct. 481, 62 L.Ed.2d 406 (1979)(disbarment for, among other things, repeated and extreme discourtesy and derogatory remarks toward adversary lawyers); Cincinnati Bar Ass'n v. Gebhart, 69 Ohio St.2d 287, 431 N.E.2d 1031 (1982). See also, e.g., Committee on Professional Ethics v. Wilson, 270 N.W.2d 613 (Iowa 1978)(discipline under EC 1–5 and Iowa statutes for assault and battery of another lawyer in courthouse). See generally EC 7–37.

21 Robinson v. Varela, 67 Cal.App.3d 611, 136 Cal.Rptr. 783 (1977)(default judgment vacated because of professional discourtesy in refusing to extend time for filling answer to especially busy adversary lawyer); Williams v. Hertz Corp., 91 A.D.2d 548, 457 N.Y.S.2d 23 (1982), affirmed 59 N.Y.2d 893, 465 N.Y.S.2d 937, 452 N.E.2d 1265 (1983)(default judgment vacated because of professional discourtesy in scheduling hearing despite knowledge of opposing lawyer's physical incapacity). Courts have usually refused, however, to reverse a judgment on the ground that the lawyer for the prevailing party had attacked the lawyer for the losing party. Typically, the refusal to reverse is based on a theory of retaliation. E.g., United States v. Young, ___ U.S. ___, 105 S.Ct. 1038, 84 L.Ed.2d 1 (1985)(while neither defense lawyer nor prosecutor should be permitted to make unfounded and inflammatory attack on opposing advocate, reversal of conviction not required when jury could have understood prosecutor's attack as simply counter to defense lawyer's repeated attacks on prosecutor's integrity). On the doctrine of retaliation, see § 12.1.1 (retaliation).

22 Van Iderstine Co. v. RGJ Contr. Co., 480 F.2d 454 (2d Cir.1973). Oral altercations between lawyers characterized by derogatory personal comments are traditionally euphemized by the legalese "offensive personalities." E.g., Snyder v. State Bar, 18 Cal.3d 286, 133 Cal.Rptr. 864, 866, 555 P.2d 1104, 1106 (1976).

Lawyers' Mutual Undertakings

Mutual respect, candor, and fairness between opposing lawyers can be very helpful in avoiding unnecessary and unproductive disputes about minor or diversionary matters. By professional tradition in many communities, lawyers will accept the word of other lawyers virtually with the same effect as a bond or similarly formal undertaking.[23] If such agreements are breached without justification, and particularly if the circumstances suggest that the breaching lawyer has dealt sharply with his or her adversary, courts have occasionally imposed discipline.[24]

The Lawyer Codes

The modern professional regulations contain little specific regulation of dealings between adversary lawyers. Canon 22 of the 1908 Canons stated that conduct between lawyers "should be characterized by candor and fairness." Very similar language is lacking from the Code and Model Rules.[25] But DR 7-106(C)(5) does require timely notice to an adversary of a lawyer's intent not to comply with "known local customs of courtesy or practice of the bar or a particular tribunal." [26] The Model Rules rejected retention of DR 7-106(C)(5) because it was deemed "too vague to be a rule of conduct enforceable as law." [27] Courts have also sanctioned injurious conduct toward opposing counsel under general provisions of the Code that require a lawyer to avoid conduct that is prejudicial to the administration of justice [28] or that reflects adversely on the lawyer's fitness to practice law.[29] Model Rule 8.4(d) contains a similar prohibition against conduct prejudicial to the administration of justice but it seems doubtful that it should be read to expand the coverage of the Model Rules so as to prohibit conduct prohibited by DR 7-106(C)(5).

WESTLAW REFERENCES

Offensive Personalities

"dr 7-106(c)(6)" dr7-106(c)(6)

The Lawyer Codes

"dr 7-106(c)(5)" dr7-106(c)(5)

§ 11.6 LAWYER DEALINGS WITH NONCLIENTS

§ 11.6.1 General

In the course of representing a client, a lawyer will inevitably come into contact with other persons, some of whom will be represented by another lawyer and others of whom will not. The professional rules provide these third parties with a measure of protection against encroachment and overreaching by their adversary's lawyer. Those protections obviously have the concomitant effect of limiting the extent to which a lawyer can effectuate the interests of clients. The rules apply both in litigation contexts and in all other representations by a lawyer.

23 In England, a somewhat more formalized version is the "solicitor's undertaking," which, when in writing, is absolutely irrevocable and binding. A solicitor who violates such an undertaking is subject to professional discipline. T.Lund, Professional Conduct and Etiquette of Solicitors 73–77 (1960).

24 In re Malloy, 248 N.W.2d 43, 46–47 (N.D.1976).

25 This is criticized in Rubin, A Causerie on Lawyers' Ethics in Negotiation, 35 La.L.Rev. 577, 579 (1975).

26 Collins v. Runsfeld, 44 USLW 2539 (9th Cir.1976); Florida Bar v. Rosenberg, 387 So.2d 935 (Fla.1980). See also, e.g., In re Barrett, 88 N.J. 450, 443 A.2d 678, 681–82 (1982)(violation of DR 1-102(A)(4)(misrepresentation) when lawyer submitted order to court falsely implying approval by adversary lawyer). Cf. Bellm v. Bellia, 150 Cal.App.3d 1036, 198 Cal.Rptr. 389 (1984)(decries lack of professional courtesy in failure to give notice of intent to take default, but failure not per se ground for setting default aside).

27 Model Rules at 136 (Proposed Final Draft, May 30, 1981).

28 In re Zderic, 92 Wn.2d 777, 600 P.2d 1297 (1979) (obtaining continuance on assurance of intent to waive speedy trial requirements but then reneging at client's insistence).

29 Wright v. Roberts, 573 S.W.2d 468 (Tenn.1978). See also, e.g., Monroe v. State Bar, 55 Cal.2d 145, 10 Cal.Rptr. 257, 358 P.2d 529 (1961)(discipline for intentionally deceiving opposing counsel).

§ 11.6.2 Represented Persons

The Prohibition against Direct Communication

A third party represented by another lawyer is given broad protection. In general, a lawyer is entirely barred from any representational contact with a person represented by another lawyer. Contact is permitted only where (1) the contact is authorized by law; or (2) the other lawyer consents to the contact. The prohibition is founded upon the possibility of treachery that might result if lawyers were free to exploit the presumedly vulnerable position of a represented but unadvised party.[30] Moreover, because both DR 7–104(A)(1) and Model Rule 4.2 apply only when the intermeddling lawyer "knows" of the other lawyers's representation, prohibited contact strongly suggests a purposeful attempt to deny the other party the assistance of available counsel.[31]

Although the matter is not entirely clear under the Code,[32] probably DR 7–104(A)(1) and, clearly, MR 4.2 prohibit contact with *any* represented person,[33] including those whose interests are apparently not adverse to the interests of an existing client of the lawyer. Any attempt to distinguish between adverse and nonadverse parties might invite attempts to obtain uncounselled concessions from a represented but uncounselled party at a time before the differing interests of the parties become fully apparent. The breadth of the anticontact rule requires alertness on the part of a lawyer whose social friend or former client is now represented by a different lawyer.[34]

Cases dealing with unauthorized contact with a represented party fall into two groups. In one the offending lawyer apparently contacts the person with an eye to gaining a new client. Naturally, that usually occurs when the lawyer making the contact is not representing another party in the same matter.[35] Prohibition of such contacts is fully supportable for the same reasons that some solicitation of legal business by lawyers is forbidden.[36] The second set of cases involves a lawyer contacting a represented party in the interest of the lawyer's own client. Thus a personal injury defense lawyer might wish to settle a case with a represented claimant without knowledge of the claimant's lawyer.[37]

30 Cf. EC 7–18 ("The legal system in its broadest sense functions best when persons in need of legal advice or assistance are represented by their own counsel").

31 Henson v. State, 97 Okl.Cr. 240, 261 P.2d 916 (1953); Richette v. Solomon, 410 Pa. 6, 187 A.2d 910, 915 (1963). Other objections are that the client's lawyer may be injured through resulting client dissatisfaction and that the client might not receive effective service after the contaminating contact. See Herron v. State Farm Mut. Ins. Co., 56 Cal.2d 202, 14 Cal.Rptr. 294, 297, 363 P.2d 310, 313 (1961).

32 Both DR 7–104(A)(1) and MR 4.2, in the same language prohibit communication with "a party" known to be represented by another lawyer. The title to the DR (but not the Model Rule) speaks of such communication with "one of adverse interest," but this potential limiting reference is not carried forward in the text of the Disciplinary Rule itself.

The text of the cognate California rule is similar to DR 7–104(A)(1). See Calif.R. 7–103 ("Communicating with an Adverse Party Represented by Counsel").

33 Both DR 7–104(A)(1) and MR 4.2 prohibit contact with a represented "party." The lawyerism *party* sometimes refers only to parties in litigation but evidently is here intended to refer broadly to any "person" represented by a lawyer in a matter. Vide "party of the first part" in ancient contracts.

34 Nebraska State Bar Ass'n v. Hollstein, 202 Neb. 40, 274 N.W.2d 508, 517 (1979)(friendship and social contact); In re Sedor, 73 Wis.2d 629, 245 N.W.2d 895, 901 (1976) (recent former client).

35 Ewell v. State Bar, 2 Cal.2d 209, 40 P.2d 264 (1934).

36 § 14.2.5 (solicitation). Some instances of "pirating" clients may be subject to doctrines providing the original lawyer a damage remedy for tortious interference with an advantageous contractual relationship. E.g., Frazier, Dame, Doherty, Parrish & Hanawalt v. Boccardo, Blum, Lull, Niland, Teerlink & Bell, 70 Cal.App.3d 331, 138 Cal. Rptr. 670 (1977); Keels v. Powell, 207 S.C. 97, 34 S.E.2d 482 (1945); compare Ross v. Woyan, 1 Ohio App.3d 39, 439 N.E.2d 428 (1980)(general rule limited by right of client to discharge original lawyer at any time and, thereafter, right of any other lawyer to deal with the client as if unrepresented). Similar relief has been accorded to a lawyer whose client has been induced to breach the lawyer-client contract by an adverse party. See Jackson v. Travelers Ins. Co., 403 F.Supp. 986, 998 (M.D.Tenn.1975), modified on other grounds 563 F.2d 105 (6th Cir.1975), and cases cited.

37 To the extent that such contact results in a loss of a fee to the client's lawyer, the lawyer may be entitled to recover this from the opposing party, e.g., State Farm Mut. Ins. Co. v. St. Joseph's Hospital, 107 Ariz. 498, 489 P.2d 837 (1971)(recovery of fee from insurer of opposing

The dangers here are those of overreaching a momentarily uncounselled client, as well as disrupting the trust and confidence between the claimant and the originally chosen lawyer if the settlement does not end the representation.[38] For those reasons, such contact is universally prohibited.[39] The prohibition extends also to a lawyer's conduct in causing another, such as an investigator or the lawyer's own client, to make the contact.[40]

Second-Lawyer Representations

The breadth of the prohibition against contact with every represented person raises the question whether a lawyer can counsel another lawyer's client about apprehended malpractice, an excessive fee, or other possible client dissatisfactions. Both DR 7-104(A)(1) ("during the course of his representation of a client") and MR 4.2 ("in representing a client") strongly imply that their prohibitions are limited to attempts by the offending lawyer, in representing his or her own client, to drive wedges between other lawyers and clients. The wording of the rules, the inapplicability of the policy of avoiding unwarranted intermeddling with exploitable clients, and the desirability of providing clients with unencumbered access to disinterested advice about important legal matters all strongly support the view that it is permissible for a lawyer to consult with a prospective client currently represented by another lawyer if the client complains of the work being done for the client by the second lawyer.[41] The status of client should not amount to bondage. A client should be able to seek out a professional opinion about the quality of a questioned representation without the necessity of either obtaining prior consent from the other lawyer or requiring the client to end that lawyer's representation.[42]

party), or from the opposing party's lawyer, e.g., Skelly v. Richman, 10 Cal.App.3d 844, 89 Cal.Rptr. 556 (1970).

[38] Carter v. Kamaras, ___ R.I. ___, 430 A.2d 1058 (1981).

[39] See generally Annot., 26 A.L.R.4th 102 (1983); 1 A.L.R.3d 1113 (1965). Solicitors in England are similarly prohibited from contacting the client of another solicitor. See Law Society, Guide to the Professional Conduct of Solicitors 71 (1974). The Supreme Court has commented approvingly upon the anticontact rule in Gulf Oil Co. v. Barnard, 452 U.S. 89, 104, 101 S.Ct. 2193, 2201, 68 L.Ed. 2d 693 (1981).

The anticontact principle finds expression in numerous other contexts. Procedural rules commonly require that pleadings and other papers, other than the initial complaint, are to be served upon the lawyer for a represented party. E.g., Fed.R.Civ.P. Rule 5(b). Papers to be so served include offers of judgment. Id. R.5(a). Before its repeal in 1979, the ABA's treaty with the claims-adjusting industry (Statement of Principles: Claims Adjusting § 5(a-1)(1939, as amplified 1954, 1955, 1964), in 7 Martindale-Hubbell 74M, 75M (1978)) included an undertaking by liability insurers not to permit any employee to contact a claimant represented by a lawyer without the consent of the lawyer.

For lawyer discipline cases, see, e.g., In re Wetzel, 118 Ariz. 33, 574 P.2d 826, 828 (1978); Florida Bar v. Shapiro, 413 So.2d 1184 (Fla.1982); Steere v. State, 445 S.W.2d 253 (Tex.Civ.App.1969). Beyond lawyer discipline, disqualification of the offending lawyer in affected litigation has been approved by some courts. Compare Chronometrics, Inc. v. Sysgen, Inc., 110 Cal.App.3d 597, 168 Cal.Rptr. 196 (1980)(offending lawyer, but not his law firm, properly disqualified), with W.T. Grant Co. v. Haines, 531 F.2d 671 (2d Cir.1976)(refusal to disqualify offending lawyers who violated anti-advice rule for unrepresented persons). Cf. Meat Price Investigators Ass'n v. Spencer Foods, Inc., 572 F.2d 163 (8th Cir.1978)(on facts, no abuse of discretion for trial court to refuse to disqualify lawyers who violated anticontact rule).

In some circumstances, contracts negotiated in the absence of a party's lawyer can be voided by the party. E.g., Mosley v. St. Louis Southwestern Ry., 634 F.2d 942 (5th Cir.), cert.denied 452 U.S. 906, 101 S.Ct. 3032, 69 L.Ed.2d 407 (1981); Mintwood Corp. v. Fonseca, 47 USLW 2019 (D.C.Super.Ct.1978).

[40] DR 7-104(A)(1)("communicate or cause another to communicate"); MR 5.3(c)(1)(ordering or ratifying conduct by nonlawyer assistant that would be violation if engaged in by lawyer); Crane v. State Bar, 30 Cal.3d 117, 177 Cal.Rptr. 670, 672, 635 P.2d 163, 165, (1981); In re Murray, 287 Or. 633, 601 P.2d 780 (1979)(lawyer cannot delegate to own client obligation to obtain consent of lawyer for represented party). But a lawyer is not required to advise a client who intends to contact an opposing party directly not to do so without the opposing lawyer's consent. See ABA Formal Op. 84-350 (1984), withdrawing ABA Formal Op. 75 (1932)(lawyer must attempt to restrain client from contacting opposing party) and ABA Informal Op. 524 (1962)(Formal Op. 75 applies even if opposing parties are husband and wife in nonlitigated matter).

[41] Martini v. Leland, 116 Misc.2d 231, 455 N.Y.S.2d 354, 355 (Civ.Ct.1982). The Code's EC 2-30 apparently refers to a distinguishable problem of the second lawyer assuming to take over the representation on the original matter without clarifying the original lawyer's status, if any, in the continuing representation.

[42] Walsh v. O'Neill, 350 Mass. 586, 215 N.E.2d 915, 26 A.L.R.3d 673 (1966). Canon 7 (third paragraph) provided that it was "the right of any lawyer, without fear or

Corporate Parties

To what extent is a lawyer prohibited from interviewing employees of a corporation or other entity represented by another lawyer? [43] While the Supreme Court, in one way of describing it, has given a broad definition to "client" in the law of attorney-client privilege,[44] its reasoning does not indicate that a similarly broad definition should control application of the anticontact rules. Those rules seek to prevent lawyers from gaining for their clients an unfair advantage over other represented persons and to protect the client against intrusions by an opposing lawyer into the confidential client-lawyer relationship. They are not meant to protect others whose interests might be impaired by factual information willingly shared by the contacted employee. Contact by a lawyer with a corporate employee will typically do little, if anything, to impair the corporate lawyer's own ability to gather information or to advise members of the organization about legal matters. Therefore, attorney-client privilege policies are largely irrelevant. So an employee whose position in a matter is only that of a holder of factual information should be freely accessible to either lawyer.[45]

Application of the anticontact rule to corporate clients should be guided by the policy objective of the rule. The objective of the anticontact rule is to prevent improvident settlements and similarly major capitulations of legal position on the part of a momentarily uncounseled, but represented, party and to enable the corporation's lawyer to maintain an effective lawyer-client relationship with members of management. Thus, in the case of corporate and similar entities, the anticontact rule should prohibit contact with those officials, but only those, who have the legal power to bind the corporation in the matter or who are responsible for implementing the advice of the corporation's lawyer,[46] or any member of the organization whose own interests are directly at stake in a representation.[47] And generally the anticontact rules should apply if an employee or other nonofficial person affiliated with an organization, no matter how powerless within the organization, is independently represented in the matter.[48]

Settlement Bottlenecks

A strict anticontact rule pinches with particular pain when an unreasonable, and possibly disloyal, opposing lawyer refuses to trans-

favor, to give proper advice to those seeking relief against unfaithful or neglectful counsel, generally after communication with the lawyer of whom the complaint is made." Note that prior consultation with the accused lawyer was evidently a matter of individual judgment.

43 At one time the Justice Department took the singularly legalistic position that antitrust division lawyers could interview any of a corporation's officials, when the corporation was represented by a lawyer, on the theory that only the fictive corporate entity was the "client." See Reycraft, Tenth Annual New England Antitrust Conference, BNA Antitrust & Trade Reg.Rep., No. 792, at A-2 (1976).

44 Upjohn Corp. v. United States, 449 U.S. 383, 101 S.Ct. 677, 66 L.Ed.2d 584 (1981). See § 6.5.4.

45 MR 4.2 comment (second paragraph); Vega v. Bloomsburgh, 427 F.Supp. 593, 595 (D.Mass.1977); In re FMC Corp., 430 F.Supp. 1108 (S.D.W.Va.1977). Cf. Ceramco, Inc. v. Lee Pharmaceuticals, Inc., 510 F.2d 268 (2d Cir.1975)(telephone call to corporate employees to obtain factual information relevant to question of venue, although not to be commended, was not kind of misconduct, if misconduct at all, that required disqualification).

46 That is the apparent position taken in MR 4.2 comment (second paragraph). See generally NLRB v. Autotronics, Inc., 596 F.2d 322 (8th Cir.1979)(refusal to enforce cease and desist order negotiated directly by government agency lawyer and president of employer).

47 For example, it has been held that each member of a class is a party for purposes of the anticontact rule. E.g., Kleiner v. First National Bank, 99 F.R.D. 77 (N.D.Ga. 1983)(law firm fined $50,000 for advising client that it was permissible to contact potential members of class); In re Federal Skywalk Cases, 97 F.R.D. 370, 376 (W.D.Mo. 1983); Impervious Paint Indus., Inc. v. Ashland Oil Corp., 508 F.Supp. 720 (W.D.Ky.1981), appeal dismissed 659 F.2d 1081 (6th Cir.1981). The same should also be the result in the case of such directly affected members of entities as partners in a partnership, the principal members of a joint venture, and the beneficiaries of an express trust.

48 This can, however, lead to controversial practices, such as a corporate party blockading an opposing party from interviewing employees by providing them each with independent counsel. See In re Coordinated Pretrial Proceedings in Petroleum Prods. Antitrust Litigation, 658 F.2d 1355 (9th Cir.1981), cert.denied 455 U.S. 990, 102 S.Ct. 1615, 71 L.Ed.2d 850 (1982)(abuse of discretion for trial court to disqualify corporate counsel from representing corporate employees).

mit settlement offers to his or her client.[49] But the ABA ethics committee has refused to recognize an exception here.[50] Instead, the aggrieved party is normally relegated to whatever relief can be gained from a complaint to a court or to a lawyer disciplinary agency because of the opposing lawyer's violation of the obligation to communicate settlement offers to the client. Also, as long as the lawyer does not advise or cause his or her client to do so, there is no general legal rule that prohibits one client from communicating directly with an opposing party.[51]

A possible excepted case involves claims by an injured party against an insured party in which the claimant makes a settlement offer that is within the limits of the opposing party's insurance. Because the opposing party will almost invariably be represented by a lawyer hired by the insurance company, an inherent conflict of interest exists between insurer and insured: it might well be in the interests of the insured to accept the settlement but in the economic interests of the insurer to hazard further litigation.[52] Because of this inherent conflict, some have urged that it should be permissible for the claimant's lawyer to communicate the offer of settlement to both insurer and insured.[53]

Consent Exception

Also problematical is the consent exception. As stated in the lawyer rules, only the opposing lawyer, and, implicitly, not the lawyer's client, may consent to direct contact.[54] To the extent that such a restrictive consent rule is based on fears of harassment of an opposing party, perhaps this could be adequately handled by simply prohibiting harassment and not all contact. Whatever the strength of the objection, however, the professional rules clearly require consent of the opposing lawyer.[55] And consent may even be required when the opposing party is as legally sophisticated as that party's lawyer.[56] The consent requirement may be foregone in isolated instances, however, when it appears that the lawyer's refusal to consent is merely self-protective.[57]

Requiring the consent of an adversary lawyer seems particularly inappropriate when the adversary is a government agency. Constitutional guarantees of access to government [58] and statutory policies encouraging government in the sunshine seem hostile to a rule that prohibits a citizen from access to an adversary governmental party without prior clearance from the governmental party's law-

49 It is no solution to send a letter containing the settlement offer because the anticontact rules apply broadly to any attempt to "communicate." See ABA Informal Op. 1348 (1975).

50 ABA Informal Op. 1348 (1975). On the obligation to transmit settlement offers, see § 4.5 at 165–66. See also MR 1.4 comment (first paragraph).

51 Wilson v. Brand S Corp., 27 Wn.App. 743, 621 P.2d 748, 751 (1980)(no impropriety requiring trial court to refuse to admit lawyer pro hac vice when lawyer said he could not prevent client from making direct contact with represented opposing party); compare In re Marietta, 223 Kan. 11, 569 P.2d 921 (1977)(discipline for having "caused" client-client contact).

52 § 8.4.3.

53 H.Drinker, Legal Ethics 203 (1953). But see ABA Informal Op. 1348 (1975).

54 Leubsdorf, Communicating with Another Lawyer's Client: The Lawyer's Veto and the Client's Interest, 127 U.Pa.L.Rev. 683 (1979)(lawyer should be able to communicate with any other person (1) by letter at any time with a simultaneous copy to the person's lawyer or (2) directly, after informing the person's lawyer of the intended contact).

55 Once consent is given by the opposing lawyer, this might reasonably be construed to consent to a continuing correspondence. See State ex rel. Nebraska State Bar Ass'n v. Hollstein, 202 Neb. 40, 274 N.W.2d 508, 517 (1979).

56 Waller v. Kotzen, 567 F.Supp. 424 (E.D.Pa.1983), appeal dismissed 734 F.2d 9 (3d Cir.1984); Estate of Vafiades v. Sheppard Bus Service, Inc., 192 N.J.Super. 301, 469 A.2d 971, 978 (1983)(negotiations carried on by personal injury plaintiff's lawyer directly with liability insurance company violated DR 7–104(A)(1)).

57 Lewis v. Secretary of HHS, 707 F.2d 246, 250–51 (6th Cir.1983)(lawyer for government can contact lawyer's client despite lawyer's objection in investigation of lawyer's claim for approval of fee to be taken from client's award); cf. Bagwell v. Sportsman Camping Centers, Inc., 144 Ga. App. 486, 241 S.E.2d 602 (1978)(notice required by statute to be given to party sufficiently complied with by notice given to party's lawyer, who refused permission for direct communication with client).

58 U.S.Const., amend. 1 ("Congress shall make no law respecting . . . the right of the people peaceably . . . to petition the Government for a redress of grievances.").

yer. Because of such considerations, the comment to MR 4.2 provides that the rule does not impair the right of a party to speak with governmental officials.[59] A similar exception should be recognized under the Code.[60]

Represented Criminal Suspects

The relative solicitude for undisturbed lawyer-client relationships generally encountered in noncriminal cases might appear to be abandoned in some decisions in which courts deal with represented persons charged with crime.[61] But it would be a mistake to assume that the anticontact rules are inapplicable to prosecutors. The Supreme Court has cautioned against violations of the anticontact rules by prosecutors, although it thus far has refused to create an exclusionary remedy for statements of a represented accused that are obtained in violation of those rules if no constitutional violation has occurred.[62] A possible area of uncertainty has to do with the exception for contact where "authorized by law"—a provision which could overgenerously be construed to permit direct contact in any official investigation.[63]

WESTLAW REFERENCES

The Prohibition against Direct Communication

"ec 7–18"

represent! /p "dr 7–104(a)(1)" dr7–104(a)(1)

45k32(12)

Second Lawyer Representations

topic(45) /p select! chang! /3 attorney lawyer counsel**

Corporate Parties

lawyer attorney counsel** /s interview! communicat! /s employee /s corporat!

Consent Exception

consen! /p dr7–104(a)(1) "dr 7–104(a)(1)"

Represented Criminal Suspects

prosecut! crim! /p consen! /p dr7–104(a)(1) "dr 7–104(a)(1)"

---

[59] MR 4.2 comment (first paragraph)("Communications authorized by law include, for example, the right of a party to a controversy with a government agency to speak with government officials about the matter."). The comment seems to recognize such a right broadly and without regard to the particular content of local law.

The California rule (Calif.R. 7–103) contains the following straightforward exception: "This rule shall not apply to communications with a public officer, board, committee or body."

[60] The Model Rule permission is based on the exception in MR 4.2 for contact "authorized by law." Those words are copied from DR 7–104(A)(1), which should be given a similar interpretation. See generally Note, DR 7–104 of the Code of Professional Responsibility Applied to the Government "Party," 61 Minn.L.Rev. 1007 (1977).

[61] State v. Irving, 231 Kan. 258, 644 P.2d 389, 394 (1982)(semble)(secret taperecording of suspect known to be represented by lawyer not grounds for suppression of incriminating statements). Some of the cases go off on the ground (incongruously so, in view of the strictures of consent generally) that the client-suspect "consented" to waiver of the right to counsel. See Leubsdorf supra n. 54 at 701–702; State v. Norgaard, 201 Mont. 165, 653 P.2d 483 (1982)(valid waiver of constitutional right to counsel despite absence of counsel at time of waiver). But see, e.g., United States v. Howard, 426 F.Supp. 1067, 1071–72 (W.D.N.Y.1977)(even if accused had made knowing waiver, statement should be suppressed if government failed to heed directions of counsel to cease interrogation).

[62] United States v. Henry, 447 U.S. 264, 275 n.14, 100 S.Ct. 2183, 2189, 65 L.Ed.2d 115 (1979)(after finding that Sixth Amendment right to counsel was violated by placing informant in jail cell with represented suspect, Court approvingly notes DR 7–104(A)(1), "although it does not bear on the constitutional question in this case"). The lower federal courts have generally refused to find an equivalence between DR 7–104(A)(1) and the Sixth Amendment right to counsel. See authorities collected in United States v. Fitterer, 710 F.2d 1328, 1333 (8th Cir. 1983), cert.denied 464 U.S. 852, 104 S.Ct. 165, 78 L.Ed.2d 150 (1983). Courts may be stricter, however, with respect to defendant interviews once the right to counsel has attached. E.g., United States v. Morales, 498 F.Supp. 139 (E.D.N.Y.1980). Whatever the standard, an accused must show prejudice in order to obtain judicial relief. See United States v. Morrison, 449 U.S. 361, 101 S.Ct. 665, 66 L.Ed.2d 564 (1981); State v. Yatman, 320 So.2d 401 (Fla. App.1975).

[63] Very broad protection to represented parties is reflected, however, in decisions such as In re Burrows, 291 Or. 135, 629 P.2d 820, 22 A.L.R.4th 906 (1981)(district attorney disciplined for communicating with represented party seeking proposed undercover role regarding unrelated criminal activities). Cf. In re Mauch, 107 Wis.2d 557, 319 N.W.2d 877 (1982)(no violation of rule by district attorney, who made several efforts to have defense lawyer present during defendant-initiated plea bargaining). See also In re Mahoney, 437 N.E.2d 49 (Ind.1982)(lawyer disciplined for contacting represented codefendant of lawyer's own client despite refusal of other lawyer to consent).

§ 11.6.3 *Contact with Unrepresented Persons*

The Prohibition against "Advice"

Necessarily, a lawyer's contact with unrepresented persons is not subject to a broad anticontact rule. Lawyers must deal with a great many unrepresented persons, some of whom have interests adverse to the lawyer's clients. The only general prohibition in the rules is that against misrepresenting the lawyer's representational role, as by giving the unrepresented person legal advice. The prohibition applies certainly if the advice appears to be that of a disinterested legal adviser and perhaps should apply even if the lawyer makes it clear that the advice is not disinterested.

In the 1969 Code, DR 7–104(A)(2) provides that a lawyer "shall not" "give advice to a person who is not represented by a lawyer, other than the advice to secure counsel, if the interests of such person are or have a reasonable possibility of being in conflict with the interests of his client." [64] The advice to obtain separate representation is apparently never mandatory; the force of the prohibition is against giving any *other* kind of advice.[65]

The operation of the rule was explored in the leading case of W.T. Grant Co. v. Haines,[66] where the court was willing to countenance what amounted to interrogation of an adverse party but intimated that obtaining written authorizations from the party to examine otherwise confidential personal papers was impermissible. Important to the court's analysis might have been the fact that the person was an employee of the client, was suspected of engaging in commercial bribery to the disadvantage of his employer, and was being detained for questioning in the employer's office without being told of the facts that suit had already been filed against him for the alleged wrong and that his employer had already decided to fire him. The objectionable "advice," apparently, was the implied advice that the employee's best interests would be served by signing the authorizations.[67]

The apparent effect of 1983 Model Rule 4.3 is different, although its comment suggests that the ultimate scope of the rule is the same as a reasonable reading of DR 7–104(A)(2) would provide. Rule 4.3, on its face, says only that a lawyer must avoid misleading an unrepresented party. Under the rule, misrepresentation can take two forms. First, "a lawyer shall not state or imply that the lawyer is disinterested." Second, if the lawyer reasonably should know that the unrepresented person misunderstands the lawyer's role in the matter, "the lawyer shall make reasonable efforts to correct the misunderstanding."

Rule 4.3 differs from DR 7–104(A)(2) in at least two important respects. First, nothing in Rule 4.3 explicitly limits its prohibitions to unrepresented parties with interests adverse to the client. Thus, misleading an otherwise uninvolved eyewitness by falsely advising that the law requires the person to give a written statement to a lawyer would violate

[64] This tracks fairly closely the last sentence of 1908 Canon 9: "It is incumbent upon the lawyer most particularly to avoid everything that may mislead a party not represented by counsel, and he should not undertake to advise him as to the law."

The existence of a reasonably apparent possibility of a conflict of interests between the lawyer's client and the unrepresented party is a necessary condition to a violation of the DR. See State v. Lemon, 603 S.W.2d 313, 319 (Tex.Civ.App.1980).

[65] Certainly, giving the advice *not* to seek counsel is impermissible. E.g., Vickers v. Gifford-Hill & Co., 534 F.2d 1311 (8th Cir.1976); Office of Disciplinary Counsel v. Walker, 469 Pa. 432, 366 A.2d 563, 568 (1976). See also, e.g., Egan v. Mutual of Omaha, 24 Cal.3d 809, 169 Cal. Rptr. 691, 620 P.2d 141 (1979), cert.denied 445 U.S. 912, 100 S.Ct. 1271, 63 L.Ed.2d 597 (1980)(recovery of compensatory and punitive damages against liability insurer for prohibited act of advising injured person not to retain lawyer).

[66] 531 F.2d 671 (2d Cir.1976).

[67] See also, e.g., Cambron v. Canal Ins. Co., 246 Ga. 147, 269 S.E.2d 426 (1980)(jury could properly find impropriety in lawyer's obtaining waiver from unrepresented party without informing him of pendency of two suits against his interests). While the *Haines* court does not cite them, it might have been influenced by two ABA Informal Opinions that had broadly prohibited lawyers from presenting documents to opposing unrepresented parties for their signature. See ABA Informal Ops. 1140 (1970) and 1255 (1940). Those opinions were "withdrawn" by the ABA ethics committee in ABA Formal Op. 84–350 (1984).

the rule. Second, Rule 4.3 itself imposes no explicit prohibition on giving advice, and accordingly it might be thought permissible to give even legal advice if this is done without misrepresenting the lawyer's role. Nonetheless, and surprisingly, given the text of Rule 4.3, its comment repeats the DR 7–104(A)(2) prohibition against giving advice other than the advice to obtain counsel.[68] Importantly, however, merely presenting a document to an unrepresented party to sign is not in all instances the impermissible giving of advice.[69]

The Scope of Advice

A simple, but unworkable, way to ensure that lawyers would never overreach unrepresented persons would be to prohibit all contact outside of a hearing, deposition, or other formal setting. That solution would incur unacceptable costs. Most obviously, it would prohibit a represented claimant from entering into negotiations with an unrepresented defendant.[70] It is pointless either to require the claimant to pursue the claim only through the expensive and time-consuming formalities of a hearing or to require the unrepresented party to obtain counsel in order to open negotiations of a possible settlement.

Yet when contact is permitted, clear dangers of lawyer overreaching exist because of the lawyer's apparently superior legal knowledge. Situations are readily imaginable in which an unrepresented party might detrimentally repose trust and confidence in the lawyer because of the person's mistaken but reasonable understanding that the lawyer would protect the interests of the unrepresented party.[71]

The lawyer rules attempt to prevent overreaching yet permit some contact through prohibiting the lawyer from giving "advice." But the compromise gives rise to difficult line-drawing problems. The most difficult concerns "implicit advice." A common setting is when a lawyer prepares a settlement document for a client and presents it for signature to an unrepresented adverse party. Is the mere act of presenting the document tantamount to giving the advice that signing it is appropriate? At least when the lawyer makes clear that he or she is representing only the interests of the client, the mere presentation of the document for signing should not constitute implicit advice.[72] Nonetheless, the position of the lawyer is precarious, and a written notice to the unrepresented party, making the lawyer's limited interests quite clear, is advisable.[73]

Prosecutorial Overreaching

Somewhere near the borderlines of entrapment and violation of lawyer regulations are attempts by prosecuting lawyers to obtain evidence against an unrepresented suspect

[68] It is extremely difficult to regard the comment to Rule 4.3 as simply an interpretation of its text. The prohibition against advice must proceed on a theory significantly different from that of avoiding misleading the unrepresented party, at least in cases in which no misleading could reasonably occur. So long as the lawyer does not pretend to be what the comment calls a "disinterested authority on the law," it is readily imaginable that legal advice could be given without any misrepresentation of the lawyer's role. On the dependent status of the comments to Rules, see § 2.6.4 at 63. If indeed the Rules, and not the comments, are the only mandatory standards, then advicegiving alone is not categorically impermissible, although it is plainly frowned upon.

[69] See ABA Formal Op. 84–350 (1984).

[70] The dangers of overreaching in personal injury cases have led several states to enact legislation permitting an injured party to disavow a release obtained shortly after a disabling injury. E.g., West's Ann.Cal.Bus. & Prof.Code § 6152(b); Mitschelen v. State Farm Mut. Auto. Ins. Co., 89 N.M. 586, 555 P.2d 707 (Ct.App.1976).

[71] Fassihi v. Sommers, Schwartz, Silver, Schwartz & Tyler, 107 Mich.App. 509, 309 N.W.2d 645 (1981)(fiduciary relationship can arise between unrepresented party and lawyer of person with unknown adverse interests sufficient to hold lawyer to fiduciary standard of care toward unrepresented party). A lawyer may incur a duty to inform a served defendant that a letter addressed to the lawyer in response to a judicial summons is an answer sufficient to ward off default. E.g., Cooper v. Hall, 489 S.W.2d 409, 416 (Tex.Civ.App.1972); Hansher v. Kaishian, 79 Wis.2d 374, 255 N.W.2d 564, 570 (1977). See also McPartlin v. Fransen, 178 Mont. 178, 582 N.W.2d 1255 (1978)(application of Montana statute requiring adverse party to give notice to party, whose lawyer has died or otherwise been removed, to retain other counsel).

[72] Dolan v. Hickey, 385 Mass. 234, 431 N.W.2d 229 (1982).

[73] In re Bauer, 283 Or. 55, 581 P.2d 511, 515 (1978).

through agents who gain the confidence of the suspect. For the most part, attempts to suppress resulting incriminating statements under constitutional and lawyer regulatory theories have been unsuccessful.[74] Nothing in the 1969 Code bears directly on the problem, but 1983 Model Rule 3.8(c) provides that a prosecutor "shall . . . not seek to obtain from an unrepresented accused a waiver of important pretrial rights, such as the right to a preliminary hearing." Certainly, "important pretrial rights" is broad enough to include the rights to counsel and to silence.[75] Unsought waivers, apparently, are nonetheless acceptable if suspects volunteer them.

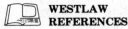

WESTLAW REFERENCES

The Prohibition Against "Advice"

advice advis! /p dr7–104(a)(2) "dr 7–104(a)(2)"

The Scope of Advice

overreach! /p "personal injury" /p releas!

---

[74] United States v. Craig, 573 F.2d 455 (7th Cir.1977), cert.denied 439 U.S. 820, 99 S.Ct. 83, 58 L.Ed.2d 110 (1978). On the advisability of plea bargaining with unrepresented defendants, compare, e.g., ABA Prosecution Function Standards § 3–4.1(b)(1979)(plea discussions without lawyer only if accused refuses to be represented or if court approves; prosecutor nonetheless well advised to make verbatim record), with Fla.R.Crim.P.Rule 3.171 (unlimited permission to conduct plea discussions with unrepresented defendant directly).

[75] The comment to MR 3.8 states that the rule does not apply to an accused representing himself or herself with the approval of the tribunal—a clear reference to the *Faretta* self-representation system. See § 14.4.2. The comment also states that a prosecutor may question a suspect who has knowingly waived his rights to counsel and silence. For the limits on waiver, see § 14.3.1.

Chapter Twelve
LAWYER FORENSICS

Table of Sections

---

§ 12.1 COURTROOM FORENSICS

§ 12.1.1 Nature and Control of Advocacy

Advocacy Skills and Techniques

An assumption that underlies the adversarial system is that the mutually contentious strivings of relatively equal advocates will make truth and justice apparent to the judge and, if different, the fact finder (§ 10.1). In the courtroom, as countless advocacy manuals attest, an advocate's tools of the trade are language, props such as exhibits or a carefully chosen wardrobe, knowledge of procedural and evidentiary rules and of human nature, thorough preparation, and mastery of the skills and techniques of advocacy.[1] Unfortunately, the tools of the trade also, and too often, include dirty tricks, subterfuge, misleading and prejudicial argument, distortion, obfuscation, manipulative efforts to evade the rules of evidence, and an assortment of other forensic outrages that try judges' and adversaries' souls rather than fairly try a contested question of fact or law.

Forensic excesses, although deporable, are probably inevitable in a system of trials that has two limiting characteristics. First, many advocates probably have as their guiding light the objective of client advantage rather than truth or justice (§ 10.3). Only a small step removed from this operational premise is the temptation for a lawyer to suspend during trials a sense of fairness and decency. Second, advocates in trial are mere mortals involved in an intensely dramatic and threatening event in which the stakes for both lawyers and their clients can be very high in terms of outcome, fees, and professional stature. Not every lawyer who confronts the stressful set-

1 Among the best of trial advocacy texts, see R.Keeton, Trial Tactics and Methods (2d ed. 1973); J.Jeans, Trial Advocacy (1975).

ting of a courtroom can be expected to maintain perfect composure, grace, and decency during the entire course of a trial. Unfortunately, such human limitations are sometimes spoken of approvingly by advocates and even by judges in terms of the bravado and aggressiveness desirable for effective advocacy in the courtroom.[2] On the other hand, many experienced advocates, and judges, believe that a frequent cause of inadequacy in trial advocacy is that lawyers overstep ethical bounds.[3]

Control of Advocacy

A lawyer's forensic excesses are subject to formal legal and professional control through several means: (1) indirect judicial control through evidentiary and procedural rulings that may affect advocacy because they threaten to affect the outcome of the litigation; (2) a power of judges to punish lawyers with contempt, fee sanctions, and similar remedies; and (3) professional discipline. By far the most important is the first. Most competent judges go through an entire judicial career without ever imposing a contempt sanction upon a lawyer. And many lawyers whose adapted litigational style is redolent of the barroom brawl are never subjected to professional discipline The reason for judicial restraint in imposing contempt relates to its potential for arbitrariness and its recognized status as a blunderbuss of last resort (see § 12.1.3).

Professional Discipline for Excesses in Advocacy

The reasons for the paucity of professional discipline for abuses in court are less apparent. They do not include an absence of enforceable regulations. As will be seen, professional regulations deal extensively with limits on advocacy. Part of the reason is that most judges and adversary lawyers are reluctant to report violations to disciplinary agencies (see § 12.10). They may feel, for example, that disciplinary agencies are either too busy with more important matters or too ineffectual to warrant the professional affront of a disciplinary complaint. They may also believe that an advocate's extreme tactics are often self-defeating and that defeat is the best and the only needed corrective.

Judicial Control through Trial Rulings

Judicial control through procedural and evidentiary rulings is hardly an ideal method for imposing limits on advocacy. Reliance on such rulings imposes significant constraints on a judge's ability to deal effectively with an erring lawyer. Consider, for example, the quandary facing a trial or appellate court asked to upset a judgment for a party whose lawyer engaged in arguably impermissible trial tactics. To refuse to reverse invites that and other lawyers to resort to the same tactics in future cases. Yet reversal will require an expenditure of additional judicial, party, and witness resources in order to effectuate the sanction. An appellate court will wish to upset a trial court's rulings on questions on excessive forensics only rarely for another important reason. The seriousness of most lawyer violations is best assessed by the judge who is present at the scene and who is in a uniquely favorable position to determine whether and which curative measures are needed. Thus the general approach of appellate courts is to overturn a trial court's ruling on questions of forensic limits only for particularly patent and harmful transgressions.[4] In short, the trial judge's rulings are protected as largely discretionary.[5]

2 People v. Allen, 351 Mich. 535, 544, 88 N.W.2d 433, 437 (1958): "Criminal trials are not basket luncheons, and we seem faintly to recall that in our experience opposing lawyers rarely if ever pelted each other with rose petals . . . ."

3 A. Partridge & G. Bermant, The Quality of Advocacy in the Federal Courts 17 (1978).

4 Draper v. Airco, Inc., 580 F.2d 91 (3d Cir.1978); Fields v. Volkswagen of America, Inc., 555 P.2d 48, 60–61, 84 A.L.R.3d 1199 (Okl.1976).

5 Arizona v. Washington, 434 U.S. 497, 98 S.Ct. 824, 54 L.Ed.2d 717 (1978); Fialkow v. Devoe Motors, Inc., 359 Mass. 569, 270 N.E.2d 798 (1971). See generally Rosenberg, Judicial Discretion of the Trial Court, Viewed from Above, 22 Syr.L.Rev. 635 (1971).

Contemporaneous Objection Rule

For a variety of reasons, trial judges are themselves reluctant to intervene in trials to impose more order than is otherwise requested by an objecting lawyer. One reason has to do with the contemporaneous objection rule and its underpinnings. The rule generally requires that a party request relief before a judge will intervene; at least a party must make such a request and have it denied before a judge's failure to intervene can be a ground for appeal.[6] The rule is founded in part on the deeply imbedded notion of the trial as a largely private quarrel between the parties in which the parties can make up the rules of warfare as they go along.

Retaliation

The concept of private quarrel finds particular exemplification in the judicial doctrine of *retaliation*. That application of the *lex talonis* posits that a party cannot complain of forensic excesses by an opposing advocate if the party's own lawyer engaged in forensic excesses that can be regarded as the provoking cause of the retaliatory response.[7] Another judicial conception might be that the originally prejudicial argument or tactic created an unwarranted jury tilt that is, roughly speaking, corrected by the retaliatory response. Finally, the retaliation doctrine might be based on the pragmatic notion that self-help is preferable to judicial help because of the counterproductive effect of making even a successful objection to many of an opponent's objectionable tactics.

Contemporaneous Objection and the Jury

The limitations of the contemporary objection doctrine become clear if one considers the types of curative judicial responses that an objection might trigger. Suppose, for example, that an opposing lawyer has argued that he or she personally can attest to a fact already testified to by a witness. That is objectionable (§ 12.1.2). But the objection might be overruled, thus seeming to put judicial approval on the lawyer's argument; the only remedy for the incorrect ruling is an expensive and time-consuming appeal. Moreover, frequent objections, even if some are sustained, might be resented by jurors, who feel that they are being deprived of full information.[8]

If the judge, correctly, rules that the argument is impermissible, the usual judicial directive to the jury is a *curative instruction*, telling the jurors that they should disregard the argument.[9] But the supposedly curative instruction may have exactly the reverse effect and "serve only the mnemonic function of giving vividness to the memory trace the jurors are requested to erase".[10] Judges, therefore, are well advised to leave the matter of

[6] See generally McCormick on Evidence § 52 (E.Cleary 3d ed.1984).

[7] United States v. Young, ___ U.S. ___, 105 S.Ct. 1038, 1044–45, 84 L.Ed.2d 1 (1985)(under "invited response" or "invited reply" rule, prosecutor's erroneous arguments, while not encouraged or condoned, may not be ground for reversal unless they deprived accused of fair trial, a question that must be answered in context of defense lawyer's own "opening salvo" that provoked the prosecutor); State v. Brewer, 247 N.W.2d 205, 215–16 (Iowa 1976) (prosecutor's excesses excused because they were provoked by defense counsel's objectionable remarks in closing argument).

[8] Williams v. Beto, 354 F.2d 698, 703 (5th Cir.1965), and cases cited.

[9] Often a litigant must first object to an improper argument and if the objection is sustained, request a curative instruction. E.g., Sabella v. Southern Pac. Co., 70 Cal.2d 311, 74 Cal.Rptr. 534, 449 P.2d 750 (1969), cert.denied 395 U.S. 960, 89 S.Ct. 2100, 23 L.Ed.2d 746 (1969); Rasor v. Retail Credit Co., 87 Wn.2d 516, 554 P.2d 1041, 1051 (1976).

[10] Schofield, Psychology, Law, and the Expert Witness, 11 Am.Psychologist 1, 3 (1956). For that reason it is unfortunate that appellate courts commonly reject arguments about the impermissibility of argument on the ground that the error was waived by failure to request a curative instruction. E.g., Jamshidi v. Bowden, 366 A.2d 522 (Me.1976)(defense counsel in personal injury case should have requested curative instruction after inadvertent mention of insurance coverage by plaintiff). A better rationale in some cases is that the error was not serious enough to require a new trial. In others, the damage done by the impermissible argument is beyond cure and requires a mistrial. E.g., Dunn v. United States, 307 F.2d 883, 886 (5th Cir.1962)("[I]f you throw a skunk into the jury box, you can't instruct the jury not to smell it.").

cautionary instructions to the initiative of the party apparently prejudiced by improper argument.[11] Even if curative instructions were thought efficacious, there would come a point at which the sheer volume of impermissible arguments or other tactics would have to be considered to have so tainted the trial that a fair verdict would be unlikely and a mistrial or a new trial after verdict would be required.[12] A judge has available another curative device that arguably is more efficacious than curative instructions in many situations in jury trials. That is the judge's power to rebuke the offending lawyer in the presence of the jury in order to deter repetitions and, possibly, in order to remove some of the prejudicial effect of the provoking instance.[13] In the last analysis, the first and best line of defense against inappropriate lawyer behavior in the courtroom is firm and fair judicial control.[14]

WESTLAW REFERENCES

Control of Advocacy

attorney lawyer counsel** advoc*** trial /s tactic forensic /p limit! control restrain***

Professional Discipline for Excesses in Advocacy

"dr 7–10(a)" attorney lawyer counsel** trial advoc*** /s tactic forensic /p disciplin***

Judicial Control Through Trial Rulings

attorney lawyer counsel** trial advoc*** /s (remark /7 prejudic***) tactic forensic /p judge judic*** /s rule ruling restrain*** limit! control

Contemporaneous Objection Rule

synopsis,digest("contemporaneous objection rule")

Retaliation

di lex talionis

Contemporaneous Objection & the Jury

rebuke reprimand (cure curative caution*** /4 instruction) /s lawyer counsel** attorney /s judge judic! /p jury

§ 12.1.2 Prohibited Forensic Tactics

A Bestiary of Forensic Excesses

A lawyer blind to any objective but advancing the litigational interests of his or her client could resort to any number of disreputable forensic devices that have been widely practiced. Some of them have gained a kind of near-respectability through successful deployment and because of their much touted rediscovery at countless seminars on trial advocacy. One disapproving catalog of such practices includes the following:[15]

> deliberately rais[ing] an objection simply to interfere with his adversary's flow in opening or summation or to interrupt the witness solely for the sake of interruption. . . . Dropping books and paraphernalia on the floor to distract the jury during opposing counsel's summation, influencing jurors with unsubtle remarks or gestures in the hallway during recess, positioning exhibits not in evidence so that jurors will see them, quoting out of context or purposely misciting cases, and even worse, omitting important authorities from briefs and argument. . . . [T]he intentionally misleading question tendered on cross-examination; the question asked, not in good faith, but merely to have the jury hear the question . . .; and the attempt to coach the witness while he is on the stand.

[11] In some jurisdictions, a sua sponte cautionary instruction on such matters as the right of the accused to remain silent has itself been reversible error. See Hines v. Commonwealth, 217 Va. 905, 234 S.E.2d 262, 264–65 (1977), and authorities cited. Judicial initiative to declare a mistrial for egregiously prejudicial defense argument, however, does not bar a retrial (on double jeopardy grounds) because the defendant will be deemed to have consented to the mistrial. See United States v. Dinitz, 424 U.S. 600, 96 S.Ct. 1075, 47 L.Ed.2d 267 (1976).

[12] Nadeau v. County of Ramsey, 277 N.W.2d 520 (Minn. 1979)(persistent misconduct in examination of witnesses and argument to jury). The difficulties of determining the point at which excludable evidence has a prejudicial impact on jurors are explored in Teitelbaum, Sutton-Barbere & Johnson, Evaluating the Prejudicial Effect of Evidence: Can Judges Identify the Impact of Improper Evidence on Juries?, 1983 Wisc.L.Rev. 1147.

[13] Georgia Mut. Ins. Co. v. Willis, 140 Ga.App. 225, 230 S.E.2d 363, 366 (1976).

[14] See generally N.Dorsen & L.Friedman, Disorder in the Court 192–94 (1973); Simmons v. Southern Pac. Transp. Co., 63 Cal.App.3d 341, 133 Cal.Rptr. 42 (1976); King Pest Control v. Binger, 379 So.2d 660 (Fla.App. 1980), affirmed 401 So.2d 1310 (Fla.1981).

[15] Ordover, The Lawyer as Liar, 2 Am.J.Tr.Advoc. 305, 314 (1979). R.Keeton, Trial Tactics and Methods (2d ed. 1973), extensively analyzes these and similar tactics in light of the Code of Professional Responsibility. See also, e.g., Underwood, Adversary Ethics: More Dirty Tricks, 6 Am.J.Tr.Advoc. 265 (1982).

The professional rules have traditionally taken a great deal of interest in regulating courtroom misbehavior of lawyers, although that interest has waned or at least become more focused in recent codes. The 1908 Canons of Ethics were preoccupied with regulating the conduct of the lawyer as litigator.[16] The 1969 Code deals specifically with the subject in DR 7–106(C), which prohibits a variety of practices, such as intruding irrelevant or inadmissible matters into the case, asserting personal knowledge or belief about contested matters, failure to comply with known customs and rules, and engaging in conduct degrading to a tribunal. The 1983 Model Rules continue most of the Code prohibitions in MR 3.4(c) and (e), 3.5(c), and 4.4. In each instance, the professional rules specifically outlaw only some tactics, leaving others to possible regulation under general prohibitions against disruptive conduct or against disregarding court rules or orders.

Limitations are imposed on forensic practices of lawyers to serve two purposes. One is to avoid improper influence upon the jury as fact finder. While similar limits might be thought appropriate for judges, the normal assumption is that judges are case-hardened to forensic tomfoolery and thus are more able to resist improper argumentation when they sit as fact finders. The second limitation is that a lawyer's forensic pyrotechnics must not be unduly disruptive. They must not impair important interests of judicial administration, of an adversary, of an adversary lawyer, or of witnesses and other participants in the process. The same activity could implicate both interests, as when a lawyer's verbal assault upon an opposing party includes language that amounts to inadmissible evidence. With recognition of such areas of overlap, the two limitations will be separately considered.

Inadmissible Evidence and Impermissible Argument—Backdoor Proof

Lawyers in litigation possess the power to frustrate the rules of evidence by intruding inadmissible matters before an effective objection can be made. A lawyer faced with a too-confining rule of evidence might be tempted to resort to the tactic of asking a witness a question that suggests its own otherwise inadmissible answer, hoping that the jury will draw the intended meaning from the question itself, even if an objection is made and sustained. "How long after the accident was it that you repaired the wheel?" asks for impermissible testimony about postaccident repairs. But whether the question is answered or not, the jury has been alerted by the question to the fact (which the question assumes) that such repairs were made. Such a deliberate use of testimonial questions is misconduct.[17] If the unanswered question has itself fatally infected the trial with irrelevant and prejudicial material, a new trial is required.[18] A familiar application of the rule occurs when a prosecutor knowingly calls a witness who, as the prosecutor has reason to know, will assert a privilege not to testify.[19]

Similarly, a lawyer who has no reason to believe that a matter is subject to proof may not, by pursuing the matter in examining a witness or in arguing to the court, attempt to create the impression that the matter is factual.[20] The same rules govern a lawyer making opening or closing arguments to the jury. In

16 See particularly Canons 15–25.

17 EC 7–25 (last sentence); MR 3.4(c)(lawyer shall not "in trial, allude to any matter that the lawyer does not reasonably believe is relevant"); cf. DR 7–106(C)(2)(impermissible if question is both irrelevant and intended to degrade); Am.Coll. of Tr.Lawyers, Code of Trial Condcut rules 23(e) & (f) (1972). E.g., Hawk v. Superior Court, 42 Cal.App.3d 108, 116 Cal.Rptr. 713 (1974), cert.denied 421 U.S. 1012, 95 S.Ct. 2417, 44 L.Ed.2d 680 (1975); Burdick v. York Oil Co., 364 S.W.2d 766, 770 (Tex.Civ.App.1963). An illustration is an attempt to evade a rule sequestering witnesses by referring to one witness' testimony in the presence of another. See generally, Commonwealth v. Booth, 291 Pa.Super. 278, 435 A.2d 1220, 24 A.L.R.4th 472 (1981). On the ploy of intruding into a trial information that the defendant is insured, see generally Comment, Mention of Defendant's Liability Insurance in the Presence of a Jury, 56 Neb.L.Rev. 153 (1977).

18 People v. DiPaola, 366 Mich. 394, 115 N.W.2d 78 (1962).

19 People v. Giacalone, 399 Mich. 642, 250 N.W.2d 492 (1977), and authorities cited.

20 Kiefel v. Las Vegas Hacienda, Inc., 39 F.R.D. 592 (N.D.Ill.1966), affirmed 404 F.2d 1163, 12 A.L.R.3d 895 (7th Cir.1968), cert.denied 395 U.S. 908, 89 S.Ct. 1750, 23

an opening argument a lawyer may not refer to asserted facts that the lawyer has no reason to believe are fairly supportable by evidence that the lawyer reasonably believes is available, that is at least arguably admissible, and that the lawyer intends to introduce.[21] In a closing argument a lawyer must base argument only on matters already in evidence or fairly inferable from facts in evidence.[22]

Inadmissible Evidence and Impermissible Argument—Lawyer Vouching

A particularly troublesome, and possibly ineradicable, problem is that of lawyers' attesting to the truth or falsity of witnesses' testimony or the justice or injustice of causes. The attestation is objectionable for three reasons: it offends the evidence rule against unsworn testimony because it can be reasonably understood to be based on the lawyer's own knowledge and informed judgments gained when the lawyer investigated the case;[23] it offends the rule against a lawyer playing the roles of both advocate and witness (§ 7.5); and it compromises the principle of professional detachment, by means of which lawyers may represent clients without becoming personally affiliated with an unpopular or antisocial client or position (§ 10.2.1).[24] Such attestations are prohibited by mandatory rules [25] and have been repeatedly condemned by courts.[26]

Yet a lawyer must be allowed to argue to the jury that a witness should not be believed or that it should find in favor of the lawyer's client. "Although a lawyer may suggest, urge, advocate, assert, and contend in his closing speech, he should not give his personal beliefs or state as factual matters not in evidence." [27] Clearly, the area is one of subtlety and some contradiction. Confusing and elusive distinctions abound in the decisions,[28] and courts themselves are not always careful to avoid giving special credit to an advocate's expression of personal belief.[29]

L.Ed.2d 221 (1969)(award of new trial and assessment of costs and legal fees against offending lawyer); Straub v. Reading Co., 220 F.2d 177, 179 (3d Cir.1955)(argumentative objections alluding to a "medical record" not in evidence).

21 DR 7–106(C)(1); EC 7–25 (third sentence); MR 3.4(e). E.g., Frazier v. Cupp, 394 U.S. 731, 736, 89 S.Ct. 1420, 1423, 22 L.Ed.2d 684 (1969).

22 Ayoub v. Spencer, 550 F.2d 164 (3d Cir.1977), cert.denied 432 U.S. 907, 97 S.Ct. 2952, 53 L.Ed.2d 1079 (1977); Warner v. Rossingnol, 538 F.2d 910 (1st Cir.1976); People v. Kyser, 52 A.D.2d 1072, 384 N.Y.S.2d 332 (1976); Rollo v. State, 139 Vt. 26, 421 A.2d 1298 (1980).

23 EC 7–24; United States v. Morris, 568 F.2d 396, 401–02 (5th Cir.1978).

24 EC 7–24; Barnett, Book Review, 90 Harv.L.Rev. 648, 653 (1977).

25 DR 7–106(C)(3), (4); MR 3.4(e). Calif.R. 7–105(1), prohibiting the practice, is the only portion of the California Rules that covers specifically the forensic practices considered here.

26 United States v. Young, ___ U.S. ___, 105 S.Ct. 1038, 84 L.Ed.2d 1 (1985)(both prosecutor and defense counsel have obligation to refrain from interjecting personal beliefs into presentation of case); United States v. Cain, 544 F.2d 1113 (1st Cir.1976)(per Clark, J.); United States v. Phillips, 527 F.2d 1021, 1023–25 (7th Cir.1975). Cf. also, e.g., LaRocca v. Lane, 37 N.Y.2d 575, 376 N.Y.S.2d 93, 338 N.E.2d 606 (1975), cert.denied 424 U.S. 968, 96 S.Ct. 1464, 47 L.Ed.2d 734 (1975)(lawyer who was also ordained priest could constitutionally be ordered not to wear clerical garb while in court, because jurors might ascribe greater measure of veracity and rightness to his advocacy).

27 United States v. Wilkins, 422 F.Supp. 1371, 1377 (E.D.Pa.1976), affirmed 559 F.2d 1210 (3d Cir.1977), vacated on other grounds 441 U.S. 468, 99 S.Ct. 1829, 60 L.Ed. 2d 365 (1979).

28 Compare, e.g., Olenin v. Curtin & Johnson, Inc., 424 F.2d 769, 769 (D.C.Cir.1968)(impermissible to call opposing witnesses "liars"); State v. Smith, 279 N.C. 163, 181 S.E.2d 458 (1971)(reversal for impermissible prosecutorial argument, including characterization of defendant as a "liar"), with, e.g., United States v. Abraham, 541 F.2d 1234 (7th Cir.1976), cert.denied 429 U.S. 1102, 97 S.Ct. 1128, 51 L.Ed.2d 553 (1977)(permissible for prosecutor to argue that "if that wasn't credible evidence, it wouldn't be before you."); State v. Noell, 284 N.C. 670, 202 S.E.2d 750 (1974)(permissible for prosecutor to argue, "I submit to you, that they have lied to you."), modified on other grounds 428 U.S. 902, 96 S.Ct. 3203, 49 L.Ed.2d 1205 (1976). Questionable are opinions permitting a prosecutor to elicit from an immunized prosecution witness testimony that the witness has been told by the prosecutor that he or she would be prosecuted if the prosecutor believed the testimony given was false. E.g., United States v. Araujo, 539 F.2d 287, 290 (2d Cir.1976), cert.denied 429 U.S. 983, 97 S.Ct. 498, 50 L.Ed.2d 593 (1976).

29 Florida Bar v. Weinberger, 397 So.2d 661, 662 (Fla. 1981), appeal dismissed 454 U.S. 934, 102 S.Ct. 67, 70 L.Ed.2d 242 (1981)(majority of court impressed with lawyer's prospects for successful rehabilitation because "his counsel has reported to this Court her disfavor with her client's actions and has so advised her client").

WESTLAW REFERENCES

A Bestiary of Forensic Excesses

dr7-106(c) "dr 7-106(c)"

Inadmissible Evidence & Impermissible Argument–Backdoor Proof

improper inadmissible impermissible /s question evidence testimony argument /s misconduct /s attorney counsel** lawyer

Inadmissible Evidence & Impermissible Argument—Lawyer Vouch

dr7-106(c)(3) "dr 7-106(c)(3)" (personal /4 belief opinion) /s counsel** attorney lawyer /s inadmissible improper impermissible (not /4 admissible proper permissible)

§ 12.1.3 Courtroom Decorum and Contemptuous Advocacy

Control of Disruptive Advocacy

Lawyers have rarely been disciplined or punished for departures from rules of good order and decorum in a courtroom. But that does not necessarily mean that lawyers' conduct in the courtroom has always been exemplary.[30] Instead it may reflect commendable judicial patience with occasional lawyer lapses in the heated atmosphere of trial and wise judicial resort to more flexible and less drastic ways of urging a wayward lawyer back to an orderly course. Restraint also reflects judicial awareness that discipline and, particularly, contempt powers can be abused to punish vigorous advocacy.[31] Similarly, bar disciplinary agencies are well advised not to seek formal sanctions against a lawyer whose only offense has been a single instance of succumbing to the pressures of a hotly contested trial.[32]

The professional rules largely track the law of contempt in this area. Provisions of the Code, however, appear to go beyond contempt law, particularly with respect to conduct that is insulting to a tribunal but not otherwise disruptive. A lawyer is prohibited by DR 7–106(A) from disregarding, or advising a client to disregard, a rule or ruling of a tribunal except in the case of a good-faith and appropriate proceeding to challenge the rule or ruling. And DR 7-106(C)(6) provides that a lawyer shall not engage in "undignified or discourteous conduct which is degrading to a tribunal." [33] The Model Rules are more cryptic. The only relevant rule, MR 3.4(c), prohibits a lawyer from disobeying an obligation under the rules of a tribunal except for an "open refusal based on an assertion that no valid obligation exists."

The Contempt Power [34]

The power of contempt inflicted upon an advocate is an awesome instrument. If due process is necessary "to keep the streams of justice clear and pure," [35] contempt might be necessary in an extreme case to keep them from becoming entirely stopped. Its use against obdurate lawyers is ancient; restraining advocates was the occasion for one of the earliest uses of contempt-like powers in English law.[36] Theoretically, contempt has a levelling sweep: it has been invoked against prosecutors [37] as well as defense lawyers, against government lawyers [38] as well as private practitioners, and even against judges

30 Cf. EC 7-36. The instances of courtroom disruption by lawyers are quite few, according to a national survey taken at a time when much professional and public clamor suggested the contrary. See N.Dorsen & L.Friedman, Disorder in the Court 131–32 (1973).

31 In re Hague, 412 Mich. 532, 315 N.W.2d 524 (1982) (judicial discipline for unjustified and abusive threat of contempt); In re Yengo, 72 N.J. 425, 371 A.2d 41 (1977) (removal of judge from office for abuse of contempt powers, among other offenses).

32 N.Dorsen & L.Friedman, Disorder in the Court 162 (1973).

33 See also EC 7–36; EC 7–37.

34 See generally D. Dobbs, Remedies 2.9 (1973); Dobbs, Contempt of Court: A Survey, 56 Corn.L.Rev. 183 (1971). See also 16.6.2 at 928.

35 A. Denning, The Due Process of Law 1 (1980).

36 3 W. Holdsworth, A History of English Law 391–92 (1923).

37 In re Nam, 65 Haw. 119, 648 P. 2d 1101 (1982).

38 In re Irving, 600 F.2d 1027 (2d Cir.1979), cert.denied 444 U.S. 866, 100 S.Ct. 137, 62 L.Ed.2d 89 (1979)(contempt citation against general counsel of National Labor Relations Board). Cf. In re Kirk, 641 F.2d 684 (9th Cir.1981); People v. Superior Court, 19 Cal.3d 255, 137 Cal.Rptr. 476, 484, 561 P.2d 1164, 1171 (1977)(contempt power is "rarely invoked against a public official").

themselves.[39] But the impact of contempt has fallen on criminal defense lawyers in disproportion to their number among litigators[40] and seems to crop up often in trials that have some controversial political feature or are otherwise closely followed by the media.[41] A few judges seem to have wielded it as a sceptre—a flaunted reminder of power and judicial perogative. Contempt sanctions may be imposed summarily and thus might be a too tempting bludgeon in the hands of a judge with whom a lawyer is embroiled in heated personal controversy. The collateral consequences of a contempt conviction for a lawyer's career and reputation in the legal and general community can be considerable.[42] Contempt is also cumulative, because it may be followed by professional discipline for the same acts.[43]

The primary doctrinal response of courts concerned with the dangers of judicial abuse of contempt is to assure fairness in the procedures employed to impose it. The approach of most judges in both state and federal courts is to resort to contempt only in the most extraordinary circumstances when all other means of persuasion and correction have failed. Intent on the lawyer's part must be shown beyond a reasonable doubt. Intent is present only if the lawyer knows or reasonably should be aware in the heat of controversy that he or she is exceeding the lawyer's proper role and is seriously hindering the proceedings.[44] The propriety of a lawyer's conduct, among other things, may be judged in light of specific directives of codes of professional conduct.[45] In every case, the lawyer's contempt should be shown to have obstructed the administration of justice in a material way.[46]

In order to warrant the summary adjudication of contempt before the proceeding is over, the situation must be one in which this extraordinary remedy[47] is reasonably necessary in order to permit the trial to proceed.[48] This rule should be insisted upon with great care in the case of advocates, because midtrial

39 In re Lemond, 274 Ind. 505, 413 N.E.2d 228 (1980) (lawyers and judges of trial court held in contempt for willful circumvention of foreign child custody decree in contravention of orders of state's intermediate appellate court and supreme court).

40 The apparent discrepancy may be explicable on noninvidious grounds. Mistrials are rarely ordered as a cure for defense counsel misbehavior because of their cost. New trials or appellate reversals following a successful defense cannot be granted to correct for defense excesses because of the double jeopardy clause. Thus only contempt may serve as an effective formal deterrent against defense lawyer excesses. Cf. also, e.g., Ratner v. Young, 465 F.Supp. 386, 391 (D.Virgin Islands 1979) ("scorched earth" method of criminal defense advocacy described).

41 In re Thompson, 454 A.2d 1324 (D.C.App.1982)(defense counsel contempt in criminal trial arising out of farmers' protest march in Washington); Hampton v. Hanrahan, 600 F.2d 600 (7th Cir.1979)(damage action by Black Panthers and mothers of two deceased members for damages arising out of gun battle with police), reversed in part 446 U.S. 754, 100 S.Ct. 1987, 64 L.Ed.2d 670 (1980); Hawk v. Cardoza, 575 F.2d 732 (9th Cir.1978) (defense in 4 and 1/2 month trial of alleged murderer of twenty-five migrant farmworkers); United States v. Dellinger, 461 F.2d 389 (7th Cir.1972)(contempt citations arising out of criminal prosecution against political radicals accused of criminal conspiracy to disrupt 1968 Democratic National Convention). See N.Dorsen & L.Friedman, Disorder in the Court 162 (1973).

42 In re Evans, 450 A.2d 443, 445 (D.C.App.1982).

43 See authorities cited n. 66 infra.

44 Hawk v. Cardoza, 575 F.2d 732, 734–35 (9th Cir. 1978); In re Dellinger, 461 F.2d 389, 400 (7th Cir.1972). On the other hand, civil contempt, because it is remedial, can be sanctioned without a showing of the lawyer's intent. E.g., McComb v. Jacksonville Paper Co., 336 U.S. 187, 69 S.Ct. 497, 93 L.Ed. 599 (1949); Kehm v. Proctor & Gamble Mfg. Co., 580 F.Supp. 913, 916 (N.D.Iowa 1983).

45 United States v. Thoreen, 653 F.2d 1332, 1340 (9th Cir.1981), cert.denied 455 U.S. 938, 102 S.Ct. 1428, 71 L.Ed.2d 648 (1982); State v. Gardner, 91 N.M. 302, 573 P.2d 236, 237 (Ct.App.1977), cert.denied 91 N.M. 249, 572 P.2d 1257 (1977)(failure to cite adverse authority in violation of DR 7–106(B)(1)).

46 In re McConnell, 370 U.S. 230, 234, 82 S.Ct. 1288, 8 L.Ed.2d 434 (1962); In re Kirk, 641 F.2d 684, 687 (9th Cir. 1981).

47 Respectable authority has called for the elimination of midtrial imposition of summary contempt in favor of procedures providing for warnings and posttrial hearings to consider facts and possible sanctions. See N.Dorsen & L.Friedman, Disorder in the Court 232–38 (1973); Kuhns, The Summary Contempt Power: A Critique and a New Perspective, 88 Yale L.J. 39 (1978); Comment, Counsel and Contempt: A Suggestion that the Summary Power Be Eliminated, 18 Duq.L.Rev. 289 (1980).

48 Mayberry v. Pennsylvania, 400 U.S. 455, 91 S.Ct. 499, 27 L.Ed.2d 532 (1971); Offutt v. United States, 348 U.S. 11, 14, 75 S.Ct. 11, 13, 99 L.Ed.2d 11 (1954). The described principle of restaint is part of the general doctrine that courts are limited in contempt cases to "the least possible power adequate to the end proposed." United States v. Wilson, 421 U.S. 309, 319, 95 S.Ct. 1802,

imposition of sanctions can seriously distract the punished advocate from continuing the trial and may necessitate a mistrial or a lengthy adjournment to permit new counsel to resume. When warranted, summary contempt may be adjudged without notice or hearing by a judge in whose presence a contempt has occurred.[49] If contempt other than summary contempt is imposed, such as in the case of a contempt finding deferred until the conclusion of a proceeding or contempt not occurring in the view of the judge, the Supreme Court has said that due process requires an opportunity for notice and a hearing and that the hearing must be before another judge if the alleged contumacious conduct involved embroilment with the sitting judge.[50]

Courthouse Etiquette

Occasionally, local court rules will specify in some detail appropriate court etiquette, such as whether lawyers are to stay at a podium when examining witnesses. Some such rules are designed to speed the proceedings, to avoid harassment of witnesses, or for similarly useful purposes. But others seem concerned with little but matters of taste. The least supportable of judicial decorum regulations are dress codes that specify minutely the appropriate attire for lawyers.[51] A distractingly bizarre form of dress might be a direct affront to a court and warrant sanctions.[52]

The Speech of Advocates

Lawyers should clearly always address judges or other officials with the full measure of respect due their offices.[53] Although a wise judge leaves lawyers' styles of speech and advocacy largely to their own good sense and decent instincts, judges sometimes become involved in a war of words between combative lawyers or, more disturbingly, engage themselves in verbal battle directly with an advocate. In a rare case discipline might be warranted for a lawyer's repeated and apparently habitual excesses[54] or for language that directly challenges or vituperates the judge.[55] But decisions that apparently approve the imposition of contempt merely for discourtesy or disrespect seem to permit the use of an extraordinary remedy for offenses that, although they might be apparent to a subjective

1808, 44 L.Ed.2d 186 (1975), quoting Anderson v. Dunn, 19 U.S. (6 Wheat.) 204, 231, 5 L.Ed. 242 (1821).

49 D.Dobbs, Remedies 94 (1973). A hearing may be required, however, if the contempt citation is based upon contested facts, even if the conduct occurred in the judge's presence. E.g., Nunes v. State, 434 So.2d 366 (Fla. App.1983)(summary contempt precluded when judge and lawyer disagreed whether witness had pointed finger at juror, as lawyer asserted in argument to jury).

50 Taylor v. Hayes, 418 U.S. 488, 94 S.Ct. 2697, 41 L.Ed. 2d 897 (1974); Mayberry v. Pennsylvania, 400 U.S. 455, 91 S.Ct. 499, 27 L.Ed.2d 532 (1971); Suter v. State, 588 P.2d 578 (Okl.Crim.App.1978)(necessity of contempt trial before different judge when magistrate gives press conference about matter). See generally Spruell v. Jarvis, 654 F.2d 1090 (5th Cir.1981)(federal habeas corpus review of state court imposition of contempt sanctions on criminal defense lawyer).

51 Compare, e.g., Sandstrom v. State, 336 So.2d 572 (Fla. 1976)(affirming lawyer's contempt conviction for refusal to wear customary men's tie instead of string tie that lawyer preferred), with, e.g., Jensen v. Superior Court, 154 Cal.App.3d 533, 201 Cal.Rptr. 275 (1984)(trial court could not compel lawyer to remove turban, even if lawyer had no religious, cosmetic, or other reason for wearing it). Different perhaps is a general code that merely specifies, for example, business-style dress. E.g., Friedman v. District Court, 611 P.2d 77 (Alaska 1980)(coat and tie). Historically, the dress of English barristers was regulated in minute detail, down to the cut and length of their beards. See People ex rel. Karlin v. Culkin, 248 N.Y. 465, 162 N.E. 487, 490, 60 A.L.R. 851 (1928). Arguably, violation of a judicially promulgated dress code is sanctionable under the lawyer codes. See DR 7–106(A)("a lawyer shall not disregard . . . a standing rule of a tribunal"); MR 3.4(c)(lawyer shall not "knowingly disobey an obligation under the rules of a tribunal").

52 Florida Bar v. Burns, 392 So.2d 1325 (Fla.1981)(suspension ordered of lawyer who, after his motion for continuance on ground of ill health was denied, appeared for trial in highly publicized case on stretcher in bedclothes the day after he was seen walking about in good health).

53 EC 7–36.

54 Columbus Bar Ass'n v. Riebel, 69 Ohio St.2d 290, 432 N.E.2d 165, 26 A.L.R.4th 99 (1982)(discipline for repeated use of obscene language in contested divorce case, including use of rubber-stamped obscenity in sending correspondence to opposing party and lawyer).

55 In re Dellinger, 502 F.2d 813 (7th Cir.1974), cert.denied 420 U.S. 990, 95 S.Ct. 1425, 43 L.Ed.2d 671 (1975)("vicious personal attack" on judge); In re McAlevy, 94 N.J. 201, 463 A.2d 315 (1983)(discipline for insulting conduct during criminal trial, including use of obscenity after unfavorable judicial ruling).

observer, involve elusive matters of tone, taste, mannerism, culture, or psychology; the particular ethos of isolated courts; and similar important yet evanescent matters that are better left to unofficial counseling, if they are to be dealt with at all.[56]

Moreover, most bars rightly cherish a tradition of vigorous and courageous advocacy that is unmindful of judicial disagreement and that encourages forthright objection to perceived judicial error. Thus a lawyer should be given sufficient latitude to make an objection and to state the ground on which it is based.[57] The Supreme Court spoke for the federal courts and many of the state courts in describing the lengths to which an advocate could permissibly go:

> The arguments of a lawyer in presenting his client's case strenuously and persistently cannot amount to a contempt of court so long as the lawyer does not in some way create an obstruction which blocks the judge in the performance of his judicial duty.[58]

A lawyer's insolence, sarcasm, flippancy, invective, personal comments, disrespect, and other ill-advised lapses from good judgment clearly earn a judge's stern admonishment, a sanction terrible enough to most lawyers. But even such lapses should not be punished by a judge as contempt unless they are repeated to a point at which they become seriously disruptive in a demonstrable way[59] or unless the single lapse is so serious that, by itself and aside from its impact upon the judge's self-esteem, it causes substantial disruption.[60] This is particularly true when the sharp speech occurs out of the presence of the jury or when it is in part attributable to a judge's unreasonable rulings or manner.[61] And language that strongly condemns a judge may be entirely defensible if used in good faith and with reasonable support, such as in a motion to recuse a judge for bias or other wrongdoing.[62]

Lawyer Disobedience to Judicial Orders

The clearest instance of a sanctionable offense is a lawyer's willful refusal to obey a judge's order directed specifically to the lawyer.[63] Whether the lawyer appears in court

[56] Kentucky State Bar Ass'n v. Taylor, 482 S.W.2d 574, 582–83 (Ky.1973).

[57] State v. Boyd, 276 S.E.2d 829 (W.Va.1981).

[58] In re McConnell, 370 U.S. 230, 236, 82 S.Ct. 1288, 1292, 8 L.Ed.2d 434 (1962). The Supreme Court has itself imposed a contempt sanction upon an advocate on only one occasion in recent history. See In re Marshall, 55 S.Ct. 513, 344 (U.S. 1935)(lawyer held in contempt, reprimanded, suspended from practice for six months, and fined $250 for attacking integrity of opposing counsel in certiorari papers).

[59] Sacher v. United States, 343 U.S. 1, 72 S.Ct. 451, 96 L.Ed. 717 (1952); Bar Ass'n of Greater Cleveland v. Carlin, 67 Ohio St.2d 311, 423 N.E.2d 477 (1981); In re Campolongo, 495 Pa. 627, 435 A.2d 581 (1981); State v. Boyd, 276 S.E.2d 829, 833 (W.Va.1981). Courts have, however, approved imposition of contempt sanctions for single instances of offensive language. E.g., Gordon v. United States, 592 F.2d 1215 (1st Cir.), cert.denied 441 U.S. 912, 99 S.Ct. 2011, 60 L.Ed.2d 384 (1979). A pattern of abusive and disruptive behavior in several trials has led to disbarment. E.g., In re Paulsrude, 311 Minn. 303, 248 N.W.2d 747 (1976)(among other things, calling judge who had ruled against lawyer's client a "horse's ass"; after losing in another court, slamming lawbooks on counsel table and saying that court was a "kangaroo court"); In re Vincenti, 92 N.J. 591, 458 A.2d 1268 (1983) (pervasive irrational, intemperate, abusive, and improper conduct, including personal attacks on judges, opposing lawyers, and witnesses).

[60] Gordon v. United States, 592 F.2d 1215 (1st Cir.), cert.denied 441 U.S. 912, 99 S.Ct. 2011, 60 L.Ed.2d 384 (1979); State v. Driscoll, 89 N.M. 541, 555 P.2d 136 (1976) (lawyer, on suffering adverse ruling in opening statement to jury in criminal case, argued with judge, refused to proceed further, and then took off coat and tie and approached bench in threatening manner).

[61] Hampton v. Hanrahan, 600 F.2d 600, 647 (7th Cir. 1979), reversed in part on other grounds 446 U.S. 754, 100 S.Ct. 1987, 64 L.Ed.2d 750 (1980).

[62] Holt v. Virginia, 381 U.S. 131, 85 S.Ct. 1375, 14 L.Ed. 2d 290 (1965)(language used by lawyer in written and oral motion to recuse judge for bias constituted legitimate attempt to raise issue in good faith). Cf. Hogan v. Kunce, 67 Ill.2d 55, 7 Ill.Dec. 63, 364 N.E.2d 50 (1977), cert.denied 434 U.S. 1023, 98 S.Ct. 750, 54 L.Ed.2d 771 (1978)(affirming contempt conviction of lawyer who filed suit against judge, challenging bail practices, while judge was considering appropriate sentence for lawyer's client).

[63] DR 7–106(A); MR 3.4(c). E.g., People v. Haas, 100 Ill. App.3d 1143, 56 Ill.Dec. 521, 427 N.E.2d 853 (1981)(leaving courtroom after being ordered by judge not to leave); In re Maddock, 265 N.W.2d 229 (N.D.1977)(willful disobedience of court order to submit proposed findings and conclusions); In re Ganne, 643 S.W.2d 195 (Tex.Civ.App. 1982)(failure to file amended brief by date ordered by court).

as advocate or as party, willful refusal to conform to an order is sanctionable by discipline[64] or contempt,[65] or both.[66] It is also generally contemptuous for a lawyer to advise a client not to obey a court order.[67] But a lawyer's advice cannot constitutionally be punished as contempt when it is necessary for the good faith purpose of putting into issue the validity of the order[68] or in most instances in which the court lacks jurisdiction to enter the order.[69] Generally, however, it is no defense for the lawyer to argue that the order disobeyed was erroneous in a nonjurisdictional sense.[70] It is also a defense that the lawyer was physically or mentally unable to comply with the order.[71]

A troublesome situation ensues when a judge's order to a lawyer has the direct effect of stifling advocacy. A familiar illustration is a trial judge's order for a lawyer not to make further objections or not to argue the legal basis for an objection. Such orders may be of questionable wisdom, because they cut off discourse between advocate and judge and prevent an advocate from performing his or her traditional and proper role. Yet, at some point, discourse may no longer be useful and a judge must have the power to compel a lawyer to be silent so that the proceeding can proceed. After a lawyer has been given sufficient opportunity to state a basis for his or her legal position, the lawyer's continued argumentation, despite a judge's direct order to proceed or to cease a line of argument, is contemptuous.[72] Similarly, an order to cease examining a witness or not to continue a line of questioning must be obeyed.[73] The lawyer must accept the frustration and disappointment even of a clearly erroneous ruling and rely on appellate reversal.[74] If an advocate is in doubt whether a judge has entered an order or, instead, has merely sustained an

64 People ex rel. Aisenberg v. Young, 198 Colo. 26, 599 P.2d 257 (1979)(lawyer who disobeyed order of federal court to produce records of assets in judgment-enforcement proceeding punished by state court as violation of DR 7-106(A)); In re Clostermann, 276 Or. 261, 554 P.2d 467 (1976)(discipline case; order of trial court, whether right or wrong, must be obeyed by advocate).

65 Maness v. Meyers, 419 U.S. 449, 458–60, 95 S.Ct. 584, 590–92, 42 L.Ed.2d 574 (1975); United States v. Dinitz, 538 F.2d 1214 (5th Cir.1976), cert.denied 429 U.S. 1104, 97 S.Ct. 1133, 51 L.Ed.2d 556 (1977)(disobedience of court order for lawyer to leave courtroom).

66 In re Yengo, 92 N.J. 9, 455 A.2d 457 (1983); In re Leeds, 87 A.D.2d 96, 450 N.Y.S.2d 506 (1982).

67 Davis v. Goodson, 276 Ark. 337, 635 S.W.2d 226 (1982), cert.denied 459 U.S. 1154, 103 S.Ct. 798, 74 L.Ed. 2d 1002 (1983). See also Maness v. Meyers, supra n. 65, 419 U.S. at 459–60, 95 S.Ct. at 591–92.

68 A limited exception is sometimes recognized for orders that cannot be reviewed except by collateral attack on a citation for contempt. See § 12.3.2(f). If the order of the trial court, challenged in good faith under the exception, is affirmed, the practice is to afford the lawyer a reasonable additional period of time within which to comply. E.g., In re Murphy, 560 F.2d 326, 41 A.L.R.Fed. 102 (8th Cir.1977).

69 State ex rel. Askin v. Dostgert, 295 S.E.2d 271 (W.Va. 1982)(lawyer's refusal to comply with order of judge to give security for his good behavior not punishable as contempt when lawyer successfully demonstrated that court lacked jurisdiction to issue order); Mellor v. Cook, 597 P.2d 882 (Utah 1979)(lawyer not in contempt for advising clients to ignore restraining order issued by court without power to do so). The well-known subtleties of United States v. United Mine Workers Union, 330 U.S. 258, 67 S.Ct. 677, 91 L.Ed. 884 (1947), also require consideration. The Court there held that even a court without jurisdiction could issue an enforceable injunctive order, if necessary, to preserve the status quo pending the court's determination of the question of its own jurisdiction.

70 Maness v. Meyers, 419 U.S. 449, 458–59, 95 S.Ct. 584, 590–91, 42 L.Ed.2d 574 (1975); Chapman v. Pacific Tel. & Tel. Co., 613 F.2d 193, 197 (9th Cir.1979). But cf., e.g., Chaleff v. Superior Court, 69 Cal.App.3d 721, 138 Cal. Rptr. 735 (1977)(public defender had right to refuse to serve as advisory counsel to indigent accused because accused insisted on nonmeritorious defense and representation would have been unreasonably difficult for lawyer).

71 Hughes v. Superior Court, 106 Cal.App.3d 1, 164 Cal. Rptr. 721 (1980)(reasonably prepared lawyer whose case was surprisingly called for trial early unable to proceed); In re Brookins, 153 Ga.App. 82, 264 S.E.2d 560, 564 (1980) (same). Cf. In re Seely, 427 N.E.2d 879 (Ind.1981)(contempt for appearing for trial too intoxicated to proceed).

72 Pennsylvania v. Local 542 Union of Operating Engineers, 552 F.2d 498 (3d Cir.1977), cert.denied 434 U.S. 822, 98 S.Ct. 67, 54 L.Ed.2d 79 (1977); In re Dellinger, 461 F.2d 389, 398–99 (7th Cir.1972); In re Dellinger, 502 F.2d 813, 816 (7th Cir.1974), cert.denied 420 U.S. 990, 95 S.Ct. 1425, 43 L.Ed.2d 671 (1975).

73 Sandstrom v. State, 402 So.2d 461 (Fla.App.1981), review denied 412 So.2d 470 (1982), cert. denied ___ U.S. ___, 105 S.Ct. 787, 83 L.Ed.2d 781 (1985).

74 Reversal might also be necessary because the judge's erroneous ruling restricting the lawyer was impressed upon the lawyer by a threat of contempt that caused the lawyer reasonably to refrain from other proper lines of inquiry or argument. E.g., United States v. Kastenbaum, 613 F.2d 86 (5th Cir.1980).

objection on distinguishable grounds or has taken only a tentative position on a question, the lawyer is well advised to seek clarification before risking contempt. But a lawyer should not be held in contempt unless the judge's order is reasonably clear and unambiguous.[75] And a lawyer plainly should not be held in contempt for attempting in good faith to obtain clarification of the court's order when it is necessary to permit the advocate to proceed with the trial.[76]

From a judge's perspective, among the most important orders for lawyers to obey are those setting trial and other courtroom schedules. The decisions differ on the question whether a lawyer who fails to appear or is substantially tardy at a scheduled court hearing is subject to summary contempt sanctions.[77] All agree that a lawyer's willful disregard of a scheduled court appointment can be punished as contempt after full notice and hearing.[78] Under modern procedural rules an increasing number of jurisdictions subject offending lawyers to monetary sanctions in noncontempt proceedings for courtroom tardiness or truancy.[79]

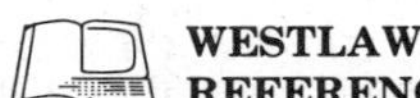

WESTLAW REFERENCES

Control of Disruptive Advocacy

dr7–106(c)(6) "dr 7–106(c)(6)" (conduct behavior action /3 counsel** attorney lawyer /4 improper discourteous undignified)

The Contempt Power

attorney counsel** lawyer /s contempt /s conduct behav*** act! /s improper** impermissible

The Speech of Advocates

45k10 93k10 % jurisdiction**

Lawyer Disobedience to Judicial Orders

attorney counsel** lawyer advocate /s sanction /9 refus** violat** disobey /s order command /s court judic*** judge

§ 12.2 LAWYERS' EXTRAJUDICIAL FREEDOMS

§ 12.2.1 Freedoms in the Controlled Courtroom Environment

To what extent, if any, does a person lose the freedoms to speak, write, and associate with others outside the courtroom when the person becomes, or attempts to become, a member of the legal profession? As has been seen, a lawyer in the courtroom loses a measure of the freedom of expression that persons in uncontrolled environments enjoy (§ 12.1.3). The justification for courtroom control of free expression is the necessity to maintain order so that the judicial process may function effectively. This section asks whether a lawyer's expression and associations outside the courtroom are subject to that or a similarly justified constraint.

75 International Longshoreman's Ass'n v. Philadelphia Marine Trade Ass'n, 389 U.S. 64, 76, 88 S.Ct. 201, 208, 19 L.Ed.2d 236 (1967); Hudson v. Jenkins, 288 N.W.2d 566 (Iowa 1980).

76 Ramsey County Public Defender's Office v. Fleming, 294 N.W.2d 275 (Minn.1980).

77 Compare, e.g., Thyssen, Inc. v. S/S Chuen On, 693 F.2d 1171 (5th Cir.1982)(lawyer may not be punished summarily for contempt for failure to appear); United States v. Willett, 432 F.2d 202 (4th Cir.1970)(same); State v. Stout, 100 N.M. 472, 672 P.2d 645 (1983)(same), with, e.g., In re Hunt, 367 A.2d 155 (D.C.1976), cert.denied 434 U.S. 817, 98 S.Ct. 54, 54 L.Ed.2d 72 (1977)(tardiness as summary contempt); Murphy v. State, 46 Md.App. 138, 416 A.2d 748 (1980)(failure to appear as direct contempt punishable summarily).

78 United States v. Marx, 553 F.2d 874 (4th Cir.1977) (contempt conviction for willful failure to appear at scheduled trial because client had not paid fee); Kidd v. Caldwell, 371 So.2d 247 (La.1979); In re Halsey, 646 S.W.2d 306 (Tex.Ct.App.1983). A single instance of oversleeping is not willful, e.g., In re James, 307 Pa.Super. 570, 453 A.2d 1033 (1982), but absence because of the press of office matters is not a sufficient excuse, e.g., Commonwealth v. Marcone, 487 Pa. 572, 410 A.2d 759 (1980), nor is it justifiable that the lawyer's trial schedule has become unmanageable, e.g., In re Gratehouse, 415 A.2d 1388 (D.C.App.1980). Continued repetition of failure to appear has led to indefinite suspension of a lawyer. See In re Baldwin, 278 S.C. 292, 294 S.E.2d 790 (1982).

79 Miranda v. Southern Pac. Transp. Co., 710 F.2d 516 (9th Cir.1983)(monetary sanction); In re Hunter, 673 F.2d 211 (8th Cir.1982)(appellant's lawyer, who had moved for oral argument but then did not appear, ordered to pay expenses of attendance of appellee's lawyers); Beit v. Probate & Family Court Dep't, 385 Mass. 854, 434 N.E.2d 642, 29 A.L.R.4th 151 (1982)(assessment of costs, quoting Franz Kafka); House v. Circuit Court, 112 Wis.2d 14, 331 N.W.2d 859 (App.1983)(assessment of jury costs).

Fair Trial versus Free Expression

Most of the difficult problems center on the free speech rights of advocates, which, in turn, are part of the general problem of fair trials versus free expression. The seemingly unresolvable debate over fair-trial-free-expression involves the extent, if any, to which the interest of litigants, lawyers, the press, and the public in sharing information about ongoing civil and criminal cases should be compromised, if necessary, by suppressing or muting publicity or even knowledge about the case in order to assure a fair trial. The competition between the values of free expression and fair trial involves an array of issues that might be resolved differently for different actors. That follows from the fact that judges, lawyers, litigants, witnesses, court functionaries, the press, and the general public all have different roles and interests in trials that might be affected in different ways by more or less freedom of expression about trials. The rights and responsibilities of lawyers are not necessarily the same as those of all other participants in a proceeding, but an understanding of surrounding law is a necessary foundation for considering claims that have been made for special limitations on lawyers' free expression.

Fair Trial, Free Press

Recent decisions of the Supreme Court have emphasized the importance of fair trials but have taken decided steps favoring free expression and requiring that corresponding risks to the orderliness of judicial proceedings be borne. The Supreme Court has held that an accused is constitutionally entitled to a trial in a proceeding conducted with decorum and without prejudicial media distractions.[80] And the accused is entitled to trial by jury members who have not been so exposed to media or other publicity about the facts before or during trial that a fair trial is precluded.[81] But the Supreme Court has held that because of the sixth amendment guarantee of a public trial in criminal prosecutions,[82] the media must be admitted in all except the most extraordinary circumstances. Lower federal courts have held that a similar right of access to civil litigation is protected by the First Amendment.[83]

Access to Court and Disclosure of Proceedings

The form of access by the public, however, is subject to regulation. A constantly debated topic is the extent, if any, to which the photographic and electronic media should be permitted to photograph, tape, or record ongoing trials.[84] But once information about litiga-

[80] Sheppard v. Maxwell, 384 U.S. 333, 86 S.Ct. 1507, 16 L.Ed.2d 600 (1966); Estes v. Texas, 381 U.S. 532, 85 S.Ct. 1628, 14 L.Ed.2d 543 (1965).

[81] Sheppard v. Maxwell, supra 384 U.S., at 362, 86 S.Ct., at 1522; KPNX Broadcasting Co. v. Arizona Superior Court, 459 U.S. 1302, 103 S.Ct. 584, 586, 74 L.Ed.2d 498 (Rhenquist, Circuit Justice, 1982); In re Russell, 726 F.2d 1007, 1009 (4th Cir.1984), cert.denied ___ U.S. ___, 105 S.Ct. 134, 83 L.Ed.2d 74 (1984).

[82] Waller v. Georgia, 467 U.S. 39, 104 S.Ct. 2210, 81 L.Ed.2d 31 (1984)(closure of suppression hearing over objection of accused must meet tests of overriding interest likely to be prejudiced by open hearing, closure no broader than necessary to protect that interest and no reasonable alternative to closure, and trial court must make findings adequate to support closure); Press-Enterprise Co. v. Superior Court, 464 U.S. 501, 104 S.Ct. 819, 78 L.Ed.2d 629 (1984)(under similar standard, state may not close voir dire of jurors in criminal proceeding); Globe Newspaper Co. v. Superior Court, 457 U.S. 596, 102 S.Ct. 2613, 73 L.Ed.2d 248 (1982); Richmond Newspapers, Inc. v. Virginia, 448 U.S. 555, 100 S.Ct. 2814, 65 L.Ed.2d 973 (1980). See also, e.g., Frank Lyon Co. v. United States, 435 U.S. 561, 98 S.Ct. 1291, 55 L.Ed.2d 550 (1978)(recognizing common-law right of access to judicial records, here supplanted by provisions of legislation on access to presidential materials); National Broadcasting Co. v. Meyers, 635 F.2d 945 (2d Cir.1980)(television station may broadcast videotapes of congressman's alleged participation in criminal transactions staged as part of ABSCAM undercover investigation).

[83] Publicker Ind., Inc. v. Cohen, 733 F.2d 1059 (3d Cir. 1984)(press and public can be excluded from civil proceeding only for articulated and overriding interest that can be served in no less restrictive way).

[84] The Supreme Court has approved a Florida rule permitting, over defense objections, radio, television, and still photographic coverage and broadcast of a criminal trial. See Chandler v. Florida, 449 U.S. 560, 101 S.Ct. 802, 66 L.Ed.2d 740 (1981). Experiments in more than a dozen states with various broadcast schemes have apparently left lawyers more negative than other groups of

tion has been gathered without violation of valid law, its dissemination can be suppressed by court order or statute only in exceptional cases. A court may issue a "gag order" with respect to the product of an opposing party's compelled discovery in order to assure parties that the discovery process will not be abused when discovery is sought of confidential and sensitive information.[85] But generally a court may not impose a gag order on litigants and others with respect to information already lawfully in their possession.[86]

WESTLAW REFERENCES

Fair Trial, Free Press

media press /s access expos*** /s (fair /4 trial) "sixth amendment"

Access to Court and Disclosure to Proceedings

media press /s photo! tape record /s trial (court /4 proceeding process)

§ 12.2.2 Extrajudicial Expressive Rights of Lawyers

Lawyers' Freedoms: In General

The extremes of clearly protected and clearly regulatable lawyer expression can be briefly sketched. In general, a lawyer enjoys the same rights as other citizens to speak or write on any matter, assuming that he or she plays no lawyerly role in the matter under comment.[87] Particularly in matters of political concern, the courts have generally refused to relegate lawyers to a second-class citizenship with respect to expressive rights.[88] Even within lawyer roles, lawyers have recently won from the Supreme Court a qualified constitutional right to free expression in lawyer advertising (§ 14.2.3). Beyond that, as the following section and the section on lawyer criticism of judges (§ 11.3.2) will suggest, clarity is lost.

It can also be said with certainty that lawyers are subject to regulation for some forms of plainly harmful speech, again as with all citizens. For example, false advertising is subject to regulation by the state, whether expressed by a lawyer or by a nonlawyer

observers. See Lawpoll: Cameras in the Courtroom?, 68 ABA J. 416 (1982); Cameras in the Courtroom, 47 U.S.L.Wk. 2347 (1978)(Florida experiment).

85 Seattle Times Co. v. Rhinehart, 467 U.S. 20, 104 S.Ct. 2199, 81 L.Ed.2d 17 (1984).

86 Smith v. Daily Mail Pub. Co., 443 U.S. 97, 99 S.Ct. 2667, 61 L.Ed.2d 399 (1979)(state statute proscribing publication of name of child subject to juvenile court proceedings unconstitutional as applied to newspapers' report of truthful information lawfully obtained); Landmark Communications, Inc. v. Virginia, 435 U.S. 829, 98 S.Ct. 1535, 56 L.Ed.2d 1 (1978)(newspaper cannot be proceeded against criminally for publication of information lawfully obtained about confidential judicial discipline proceeding). See also, e.g., United States v. Kilpatrick, 52 U.S. L.W. 2434 (10th Cir.1984)(withdrawal of order prohibiting West Publishing Company from printing federal district court opinion highly critical of government lawyers), on writ of mandamus from 570 F.Supp. 505 (D.Colo.1983). Cf. Gulf Oil Co. v. Bernard, 452 U.S. 89, 101 S.Ct. 2193, 68 L.Ed.2d 693 (1981)(no authority in federal rules for broad order prohibiting communication by class counsel with members of class in class action).

87 Polk v. State Bar, 374 F.Supp. 784 (N.D.Tex.1974) (lawyer protected by first amendment when, in capacity of private citizen, criticized "dishonest and unethical district attorney and a perverse judge"); Eisenberg v. Boardman, 302 F.Supp. 1360 (W.D.Wis.1969)(statutorily required lawyer's oath to respect judges is constitutional only if interpreted to apply to in-court statements); State Bar v. Semaan, 508 S.W.2d 429 (Tex.Civ.App.1974)(lawyer who called identified judge "midget among giants" outside of court was constitutionally protected under false and reckless standard of *New York Times v. Sullivan*).

88 All of the opinions in In re Sawyer, 360 U.S. 622, 79 S.Ct. 1376, 3 L.Ed.2d 1473 (1959), for example, seem to concur that speech by a lawyer abstractly attacking rules of law or the administration of justice could not constitutionally be used to discipline a lawyer. But cf., e.g., State v. Russell, 227 Kan. 897, 610 P.2d 1122 (1980), cert.denied 449 U.S. 983, 101 S.Ct. 400, 66 L.Ed.2d 245 (1980)(public censure for negligently untruthful political advertising despite concession by disciplinary administrator that speech was constitutionally privileged); State ex rel. Angel v.Woodahl, 555 P.2d 501 (Mont.1976)(state attorney general convicted for contempt, without discussion of constitutional issues, for Kiwanis Club speech criticizing judges for delay in series of corruption prosecution cases; judges had been appointed by governor against whom attorney general was then engaged in election race). See generally Annot., 26 A.L.R.4th 170 (1983).

(§ 14.2.4).[89] And speech or writing advising a client to commit a criminal act can itself be punished as a crime.[90] The areas of difficulty are those in which a lawyer's speech is not clearly and validly made criminal but in which the state nonetheless claims that the speech intrudes upon an important state interest. A principal area of conflict involves lawyer speech about pending cases.

Extrajudicial Comment on Pending Cases

The professional rules on lawyer comment on pending proceedings are generally rules of restriction. They stand in sharp contrast to the background, just discussed, of broadly protected freedom of expression enjoyed by nonlawyers concerning matters in litigation. Canon 20 of the original 1908 Canons of Ethics, in the asserted interest of preserving an aura conducive to a fair trial, "generally" condemned lawyer comments to the media about pending or anticipated litigation. The canons served to add sanctions to a professional wish that lawsuits be tried in the courts and not in the press. Between 1936 and 1941 a press-bar committee wrestled with the question of public comments by lawyers, among other issues, but could reach no agreement.[91] Fair-trial-free-expression matters came to a head following the Supreme Court's 1966 decision in Sheppard v. Maxwell,[92] which condemned as a violation of due process a criminal trial made a travesty by media commentary and intrusions aided and abetted by participating lawyers. The *Sheppard* decision led to further professional study and the ABA's adoption in 1968 of fair-trial-free-press standards limiting lawyer publicity that posed a substantial likelihood of preventing a fair trial.[93]

1969 Code on Trial Comments

The ABA's 1969 Code incorporates the 1968 standards as DR 7–107.[94] The essential directive of the Code for all lawyers is "no comment." Basically, DR 7–107 proscribes any "extrajudicial comment that a reasonable person would expect to be disseminated by means of public communication" with respect to two types of information. For the stages of criminal proceedings beginning with the investigation until the beginning of jury selection, a lawyer can make such statements only if they are limited to cryptic information of the most rudimentary kind. The permitted information is contained in lists of factual matters that vary with the stage of the criminal proceeding. The general test of DR 7–107 is a "reasonable likelihood" of prejudicial impact on the proceeding. During jury selection and later stages, and during all stages of professional disciplinary proceedings,[95] juvenile pro-

[89] In re Friedland, 275 Ind. 214, 416 N.E.2d 433 (1981), cert.denied 454 U.S. 857, 102 S.Ct. 308, 70 L.Ed.2d 153 (1981)(lawyer disbarred for threatening suit against staff and members of disciplinary commission and witnesses before commission unless charges were dropped and witnesses changed testimony).

[90] United States v. Perlstein, 126 F.2d 789, 792 (3d Cir. 1942), cert.denied 316 U.S. 678, 62 S.Ct. 1106, 86 L.Ed. 1752 (1942). See also, e.g., In re Colson, 412 A.2d 1160, 1165 (D.C.App.1979)(conviction on guilty plea of obstruction of justice for fomenting adverse publicity to prejudice ongoing criminal trial of object of presidential disfavor (Daniel Ellsberg) warrants disbarment); In re Ojala, 289 N.W.2d 108 (Minn.1979)(suspension for publishing materials known to have been stolen from files of another lawyer).

[91] E.Sunderland, History of the American Bar Association and Its Work 198–99 (1953).

[92] 384 U.S. 333, 86 S.Ct. 1507, 16 L.Ed.2d 600 (1966).

[93] 93 ABA Rep. 116–122 (1968)(vote of ABA House of Delegates adopting ABA Advisory Committee on Fair Trial and Free Press, Standards Relating to Fair Trial and Free Press (1966)). The "substantial likelihood" standard was taken from language in Sheppard v. Maxwell, 384 U.S. 333, 362–63, 86 S.Ct. 1507, 1522, 16 L.Ed.2d 600 (1966).

[94] DR 7–107 n.85. As there indicated, the 1968 Fair Trial Standards, which dealt only with criminal cases, were incorporated into DR 7–107(A) through (D). The remainder of DR 7–107, (E) through (J), created a similar pattern for juvenile proceedings, professional discipline proceedings, civil trials, and administrative proceedings and created a limitation to it for lawyer self-defense and for lawyer participation in public proceedings (DR 7–107(I)).

[95] Pre-Code, see, e.g., In re Woodward, 300 S.W.2d 385 (Mo.1957)(mailing to public 25,000 to 35,000 postcards flamboyantly critical of disciplinary investigation for courthouse solicitation). But cf. State v. Nelson, 210 Kan. 637, 504 P.2d 211 (1972)(comments critical of past disciplinary proceeding when sought out by press not violative of DR 7–107).

ceedings, civil actions,[96] and administrative proceedings,[97] a lawyer is basically precluded from any comment for public dissemination that is "reasonably likely to interfere with a fair" proceeding. The clearest instance of potential for such inteference is prosecutorial comment on a pending case, and occasional decisions can be found in which a court has applied DR 7–107 to a prosecuting lawyer for such public comment.[98] In all cases the proscriptions are limited to a lawyer who is participating in or is associated with the proceeding and to members of the lawyer's firm.[99] Other lawyers, presumably, remain free to make comments for the media about pending matters.

The Model Rules

The 1983 Model Rules track the methodology but differ significantly from the 1969 Code in the sweep of regulation. The Model Rules also rely upon an ABA-drafted set of fair-trial-free-press standards, these drafted in 1978.[1] But the 1978 standards were significantly narrower than their predecessors of a decade earlier in order to take account of intervening decisions finding constitutional infirmities in DR 7–107. The resulting Model Rule 3.6 proscribes an extrajudicial statement by a lawyer [2] only if a relatively strict test is met by the state. Under MR 3.6(a) the state must show that "the lawyer knows or reasonably should know that [the extrajudicial statement] will have a substantial likelihood of materially prejudicing an adjudicative proceeding."

The "substantial likelihood" test of the Model Rules plainly permits more extrajudicial commentary by lawyers than does the "reasonable likelihood" test of DR 7–107. Rule 3.6(b) provides an apparently nonexhaustive list of particulars that "ordinarily" would be likely to be prejudicial if revealed in an extrajudicial statement. It is unclear whether the MR 3.6(b) list of statements that are there said to be "likely" to be materially prejudicial shifts to the lawyer making such a comment the burden of demonstrating that the statement in fact did not have the effect presumed. Rule 3.6(a) states that a violation occurs only if there is a "substantial" likelihood of such impact. Moreover, showing that likelihood is part of the constitutionally required minimum standard. Given the text of MR 3.6 and the constitutional background against which it was written, a disciplinary enforcement agency should bear that burden regardless of the type of comment.

[96] In re Porter, 268 Or. 417, 521 P.2d 345 (1974), cert.denied 419 U.S. 1056, 95 S.Ct. 639, 42 L.Ed.2d 653 (1974). The federal courts have to some extent narrowed the reach of DR 7–107 in civil cases as a result of action taken by the 1980 Judicial Conference of the United States. The Conference adopted a resolution abandoning general restrictions on lawyer comment in civil litigation in favor of recommended special orders when needed in individual cases. See Revised Report of the Judicial Conf. Comm. on the Operation of the Jury System on the "Free Press-Fair Trial" Issue, 87 F.R.D. 519 (adopted Sept. 25, 1980).

[97] In re Richmond, 285 Or. 469, 591 P.2d 728 (1979); Widoff v. Disciplinary Bhd., 54 Pa.Cmwlth. 124, 420 A.2d 41 (1980), cert.denied 455 U.S. 914, 102 S.Ct. 1266, 71 L.Ed.2d 454 (1982).

[98] United States v. Coast of Maine Lobster Co., 538 F.2d 899 (lst Cir.1976)(newspaper comment by supervising prosecutor during pendency of prominent white-collar criminal trial urging stern punishment of such crime requires new trial); Hughes v. State, 437 A.2d 559 (Del. 1981)(interview published, while jury was separated over weekend, in which prosecutor referred to lie detector test); In re Hansen, 584 P.2d 805 (Utah 1978)(deputy attorney general—since elected to office of state attorney general—censured, among other things, for television comments in violation of DR 7–107(B)(6)).

[99] Companion cases in New Jersey have interpreted this aspect of DR 7–107 in an expansive way. See In re Hinds, 90 N.J. 604, 449 A.2d 483, 495–96 (1982)(lawyer who "holds himself out to be a member of the defense team" is subject to DR 7–107(D)); In re Rachmiel, 90 N.J. 646, 449 A.2d 505, 512–13 (1982)(DR 7–107(B)(6) applies to lawyer who was previously prosecutor but who was in private practice and not participating in case at time of comments).

[1] MR 3.6 comment (second paragraph); Model Rules at 144 (Proposed Final Draft, May 30, 1981). See generally ABA Standards Relating to Fair Trial and Free Press § 8–1.1 (amended 1978).

[2] Possibly through oversight, MR 3.6 is not limited to a lawyer connected with a case in any way and thus might be thought to extend to any lawyer, including, for example, a lawyer in public office. The policy and constitutional infirmities of such a wide application are patent. Possibly the rule assumes that only a lawyer intimately connected with the case would be in a position to satisfy the requirement that a lawyer know that the statement will have a substantial likelihood of material prejudice to the proceeding.

Most, but not all, of the statements on the MR 3.6(b) list relate to criminal cases. One particularly important effect of the list is to eliminate the permission for comment on physical evidence at the time of its seizure.[3] Although the rule applies to any "adjudicative proceeding," the list is clearly applicable primarily to jury trials.[4] Moreover, because of the fact that prosecutor statements are typically much more likely to influence prospective jurors, Rule 3.6, like DR 7-107, can be violated more readily by prosecutors in criminal cases than by defense lawyers or by lawyers in any other setting.[5] The Model Rules recognize that difference in a special rule (MR 3.8(e)) requiring prosecutors to exercise reasonable care to assure that law enforcement personnel do not make extrajudicial comments prohibited to the prosecutor by MR 3.6. No similar responsibility is imposed on nonprosecution lawyers.[6]

Lawyer Commentary in the Courts

The broad provisions of DR 7-107 have been enforced by some courts with a vigor that is difficult to reconcile with recent Supreme Court decisions on free expression. Arguing that lawyers are officers of the court (cf. § 1.6) charged with a special responsibility to assure the fairness of trials, those decisions have upheld DR 7-107 against free speech, vagueness, and overbreadth attacks.[7] Lawyers who had previously not complied with DR 7-107 have been refused admission pro hac vice.[8] One case has even condemned a lawyer's suggestion to a juror in a completed case to talk to the media about the case.[9]

Other courts have refused to countenance the striking generality of the standards of DR 7-107. Those courts find a variety of possible constitutional defects in DR 7-107 but disagree on the precise scope of constitutional inquiry. Two standards have been embraced. Under the stricter, a lawyer may not be punished for speech about a pending matter unless the statements "pose a serious and eminent threat of interference with the fair administration of justice."[10] That is essentially the standard adopted by the framers of the 1983 Model Rules and the 1978 ABA Fair

3 See Model Rules Code Comparison, at 143 (Proposed Final Draft, May 30, 1981); id. Legal Background Note, at 148-49.

4 The suppressed legal background note to an earlier draft of the Model Rules stated that "only in rare circumstances" would the strict standard of material prejudice permit application of Rule 3.6 to a bench trial. See Model Rules at 146 (Proposed Final Draft, May 30, 1981). The note also indicated that the rule might also be applicable to grand jury and similar pretrial proceedings, to defense lawyers as well as prosecutors, civil actions, disciplinary proceedings, and administrative hearings. Id. 147-48.

5 Some commentators have argued that the anticomment rule should apply *only* to prosecutors and not to criminal defense lawyers because the defense requires access to pretrial publicity in order to counter adverse nonlawyer publicity about the accused, that is fomented by actions and statements of the police at the time of the report of the crime and the arrest of the accused and because the fair-trial right implicated by the anticomment rules should be waivable by the accused. E.g., Freedman & Starwood, Prior Restraints on Freedom of Expression by Defendants and Defense Attorneys, 29 Stan.L.Rev. 607 (1977); Hirst, Silence Orders—Preserving Political Expression by Defendants and Their Lawyers, 6 Harv.Civ.Rts.—Civ.Lib.L.Rev. 595, 604, 606-08 (1976). That position was rejected by the Model Rules framers on the ground that the public interest in fair trials protected by anticomment rules is broader than the interest assertable by any particular accused person. See Model Rules legal background note, at 148 (Proposed Final Draft, May 30, 1981).

6 Such a restriction, however, may be inferrable from MR 5.3. See § 16.3.1.

7 In re Hinds, 90 N.J. 604, 449 A.2d 483 (1982)("reasonable likelihood" standard of DR 7-107 can constitutionally be applied to lawyer's extrajudicial harsh criticism of judge in political criminal trial). Opinions have often relied on a statement in Sheppard v. Maxwell, 384 U.S. 333, 361-63, 86 S.Ct. 1507, 1522, 16 L.Ed.2d 600 (1966), referring to the "conceded" power of courts to control extrajudicial statements by counsel. Aside from being dicta, the statement is sharply limited by the facts. *Sheppard* upheld an argument, by an accused, that the atmosphere of pretrial and trial publicity generated primarily by a prosecutor and permitted by the trial judge had denied him a fair trial.

8 State v. Ross, 36 Ohio App.2d 183, 304 N.E.2d 396 (1973), appeal dismissed 415 U.S. 904, 94 S.Ct. 1397, 39 L.Ed.2d 461 (1974). But cf. Eisenberg v. Boardman, 302 F.Supp. 1360, 1362-63 (W.D.Wis.1969)(state statute requiring oath of lawyers to respect courts is constitutional because interpreted to apply only in court with usual free speech rights existing outside).

9 State v. Young, 181 N.J.Super. 463, 438 A.2d 344 (App.Div.1981).

10 Chicago Council of Lawyers v. Bauer, 522 F.2d 242, 249 (7th Cir.1975), cert.denied 427 U.S. 912, 96 S.Ct. 3201, 49 L.Ed.2d 1204 (1975). See also, e.g., Ruggieri v. Johns-Manville Prods. Co., 503 F.Supp. 1036 (D.R.I.1980)(deny-

Trial Free Press Standards.[11] The other standard, permitting greater state restriction, requires only a "reasonable likelihood" of interference with a fair trial—the standard articulated in DR 7–107 itself and in the 1966 *Sheppard v. Maxwell* decision.[12] While the Supreme Court has not recently passed on the specific question of a lawyer's free speech rights, its general approach to speech restrictions in recent terms has been cautious and overtly protective of speech. Justice Holmes's famous aphorism about "clear and present danger" [13] has been refined by the Court in the context of publicity about trials and, particularly, in the context of decisions limiting the power of the state to proscribe criticism of judges or the judiciary. The Supreme Court has recently said that "the operations of the courts and the judicial conduct of judges are matters of utmost public concern." [14] The Court has also said that injury to the reputation of judges or of judicial institutions is an insufficient basis for state suppression of free expression.[15] To be sure, in 1959 five members of the Court, in In re Sawyer,[16] refused to extend the clear-and-present-danger test to extrajudicial comments by lawyers. And, from a narrow point of view, a system of adjudication would undoubtedly operate more smoothly if all persons, including lawyers, were prohibited from making any public comment. But the recent decisions of the Court dealing with free speech commentary on trials and with lawyer free speech in the area of lawyer advertising (§ 14.2.3) make it doubtful that the Court would resist the logic of extending significant constitutional protection to the extrajudicial comments of lawyers. The right should be limited only after a particularized showing of an inescapable need to impose a gag order or impose retrospective sanctions in order to further a compelling state interest other than the suppression of free speech or press.

Class Actions

Another area raising lawyer free speech issues concerns the ability of a lawyer for a class in a class action to communicate with members of the class who did not hire the lawyer initially. For several years a standing recommendation for federal judges in class actions was to enter a broad order at the outset of the action prohibiting lawyers in the case, among others, from contacting nonclient members of the class.[17] But in Gulf Oil Co. v. Bernard [18] the Supreme Court held that the federal courts lacked the power, under the federal rules, to enter a broad class action gag

ing defendant asbestos manufacturers' motion to disqualify plaintiff's lawyer for comments on nationally televised program reflecting adversely on character of manufacturers); Markfield v. Ass'n of the Bar of City of N.Y., 49 A.D.2d 516, 370 N.Y.S.2d 82, 85 (1975), appeal dismissed 37 N.Y.2d 794, 375 N.Y.S.2d 106, 337 N.E.2d 612 (1975) (discipline under DR 7–107 can be imposed only when extrajudicial comment poses "clear and present danger" to administration of justice). See also In re Lasswell, 296 Or. 121, 673 P.2d 855 (1983)(prosecutor cannot be found in violation of DR 7–107 without showing that he subjectively intended to prejudice fair trial rather than to give a public account for his performance in office in a matter of public importance).

11 Model Rules at 145 (Proposed Final Draft, May 30, 1981); 2 ABA Standards for Criminal Justice § 8–1.1(a) and comment (2d ed.1978).

12 Hirschkop v. Snead, 594 F.2d 356, 370 (4th Cir.1979) (en banc). For the view, however, that there is no constitutionally significant difference between the "reasonable likelihood" and "clear and present danger" standards, see Note, A Constitutional Assessment of Court Rules Restricting Lawyer Comment on Pending Litigation, 65 Cornell L.Rev. 1106 (1980).

13 Schenck v. United States, 249 U.S. 47, 52, 39 S.Ct. 247, 249, 63 L.Ed. 470 (1919).

14 Landmark Communications, Inc. v. Virginia, 435 U.S. 829, 840, 98 S.Ct. 1535, 1542, 56 L.Ed.2d 1 (1978).

15 435 U.S. at 841–42, 98 S.Ct. at 1542–43.

16 360 U.S. 622, 79 S.Ct. 1376, 3 L.Ed.2d 1473 (1959).

17 Manual on Complex Litigation, part II, ¶ 1.41 (1973 ed.)(suggested local rule number 7). Some decisions actively encouraged class communication, however, so long as it had not been proscribed by a specific order. E.g., Pettway v. American Cast Iron Pipe Co., 576 F.2d 1157, 1178 (5th Cir.1978), cert.denied 439 U.S. 1115, 99 S.Ct. 1020, 59 L.Ed.2d 74(1979)(class representative provided "excellent representation" in scheduling periodic meetings and circulating newsletter to class members during pendency of suit); Allen v. Isaac, 100 F.R.D. 373, 375 (N.D.Ill.1983).

18 452 U.S. 89, 101 S.Ct. 2193, 68 L.Ed.2d 693 (1981).

order, leaving unanswered the broader question of the constitutionality of such an order.[19]

Moral Considerations

The constitutional and other legal protections accorded to a lawyer's freedom of expression remain exceedingly murky and the lower court decisions widely variant.[20] As a matter of personal morality there is no more reason for a lawyer of discretion and sound judgment to exercise all possible constitutional freedoms in this area than there is in most others. Conscientious lawyers will presumably continue to respect the importance of support for courts, judges, and the integrity of ongoing proceedings so long as there is the slightest possibility that extrajudicial comment might impede these interests, and in the absence of a compelling reason to risk impairment of these interests in order to further a greater good, such as the exposure of corruption or the protection of a client.

WESTLAW REFERENCES

Lawyers' Freedoms In General

attorney lawyer counsel** /s sanction control restrain* regul*** /s individual citizen /s "first amendment" (free*** /3 speech speak express! write)

1969 Code on Trial Comments

dr7-107 (d.r. "disciplinary rule" /5 7-107)

Lawyer Commentary in the Courts

dr7-107 (d.r. "disciplinary rule" /5 7-107) /p (free*** /s speech speak express!) vague! overbr!

Class Actions

452 +5 89 /10 bernard

§ 12.2.3 Other Freedom Restrictions: The Oath Cases

In a variety of other ways, lawyers' constitutional freedoms have been subjected to special restraints. Restrictions are most supportable when they are imposed in the course of a lawyer's work and thus can possibly be defended because of the need to restrain lawyers from corrupting or distorting the legal system.[21] Occasionally, however, a jurisdiction has attempted to impose requirements on lawyers that relate to nonlawyer activities that normally would be beyond regulation.

A particularly restive problem is the periodic attempt in some jurisdictions to impose tests upon the beliefs and political sentiments of bar applicants.[22] The avowed interest of the state in imposing the tests is to assure that applicants possess the character and fitness necessary to function effectively as lawyers. But a committee's notion of requisite character and fitness has often required scrutiny of applicants' beliefs and associations. In the aftermath of the McCarthy and Cold War eras of the 1950s, applicants made constitutional attacks upon bar admission requirements that they reveal prior political associations and that they swear oaths of various kinds. The constitutional validity of those procedures was tested most recently in 1971 in a trilogy of Supreme Court decisions. The cases were decided by a sharply divided Court

19 For differing views, compare, e.g., Bernard v. Gulf Oil Co., 619 F.2d 459 (5th Cir.1980) (en banc), affirmed on other grounds 452 U.S. 89, 101 S.Ct. 2193, 68 L.Ed.2d 693 (1981)(class action gag order unconstitutional prior restraint), with, e.g., Johnston v. Beneficial Management Corp., 26 Wn.App. 671, 614 P.2d 661 (1980), reversed 96 Wn.2d 708, 638 P.2d 1201(1982).

20 See particularly § 11.3.2 on lawyer criticism of judges.

21 Humphreys, Hutcheson & Moseley v. Donovan, 568 F.Supp. 161 (M.D.Tenn.1983), affirmed 755 F.2d 1211 (6th Cir.1985)(federal labor statute permissibly infringed on lawyers' first amendment rights of speech, privacy, and association when it required lawyers to register and make disclosures as a "labor persuader" for clients). See generally § 12.1.3 (contempt limits on forensics).

22 In re Levine, 97 Ariz. 88, 397 P.2d 205 (1964)(reversing admission committee's denial of bar admission on ground of applicant's public criticism of FBI and its director). Compare In re Ronwin, 136 Ariz. 566, 667 P.2d 1281(1983), republished with editorial modifications 139 Ariz. 576, 680 P.2d 107 (1983), cert.denied 464 U.S. 977, 104 S.Ct. 413, 79 L.Ed.2d 247 (1984)(bar applicant's assumed good-faith belief that he was object of conspiracy by state supreme court, most of the federal bench, the organized bar, the bar admission committee, and lawyers who had appeared against him could constitutionally be taken into account for purpose of assessing mental fitness of applicant to practice law).

and against the background of decisions that had suggested that inquiries by character and fitness committees into applicants' associations and beliefs were relatively unhindered by free speech and association claims.[23]

The first of the 1971 cases, Baird v. State Bar of Arizona,[24] held that a question on a bar application asking whether the applicant was or ever had been a member of the Communist party or any organization advocating the violent overthrow of the United States offended the first and fourteenth amendments. A four-member plurality opinion by Justice Black emphasized a broad freedom of association that was inconsistent with such inquiries. Justice Stewart's concurring opinion focused on the narrow ground that the first and fourteenth amendments permitted inquiry only into knowing membership in organizations advocating violent overthrow. The same arrangement of opinions and justices decided in the second case, In re Stolar,[25] that three questions on the Ohio bar application also offended the Constitution. The first question inquired about membership in organizations advocating violent overthrow and was struck down, as in *Baird*. Two other questions, asking for lists of the names and addresses of all organizations of which the applicant was or had been a member, were also struck down. The plurality opinion of Justice Black rested on an applicant's right, secured by the freedom of association provided for in the first amendment, not to be pressured into avoiding organizations that might displease bar admission committee members. Justice Stewart concurred by force of a precedent[26] that had upheld the constitutional right of public school teachers not to answer similar questions.

The third 1971 case, Law Students Civil Rights Research Council, Inc. v. Wadmond,[27] is the limiting decision. In it Justice Stewart wrote the majority decision, now joined by the dissenters in the other two decisions for a new five-to-four majority that approved a New York character and fitness questionnaire and oath. The Court first upheld a query whether the applicant was a *knowing* member of an organization advocating violent overthrow and, if so, whether the applicant had the specific intent to further that aim. Second, the Court approved a required oath that stated that the applicant, without any reservations, was loyal to, and ready to support, the Constitution of the United States. On the whole, *Wadmond* has become the template against which states have since measured the constitutional validity of various questionnaires and oaths required of applicants. Now, as then, most applicants probably think little of such ceremonies. For some few, they smack much more of officiousness about political and personal beliefs than of anything relevant to law practice and they continue to raise concerns about needless and ineffectual state intrusions into matters of individual freedom.

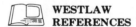

WESTLAW REFERENCES

free*** /s speech speak express! /p #bar /5 admission admit! application applicant member

§ 12.3 ADVOCATES AND EVIDENCE

§ 12.3.1 Truth in the Service of Client Interests

No logically defensible theory of the adversary system can ignore the importance, if not

[23] Konigsberg v. State Bar, 366 U.S. 36, 81 S.Ct. 997, 6 L.Ed.2d 105 (1961) (California could refuse to admit to practice an applicant who advocated violent overthrow of the government and, to that end, could reject a person who refused to answer a question about present or past membership in the Communist party); In re Anastaplo, 366 U.S. 82, 81 S.Ct. 978, 6 L.Ed.2d 135 (1961) (Illinois could refuse to admit applicant who refused to answer question of character and fitness committee whether he was member of Communist party). See also In re Anastaplo, 3 Ill.2d 471, 121 N.E.2d 826 (1954), cert.denied 348 U.S. 946, 75 S.Ct. 439, 99 L.Ed. 740 (1955).

[24] 401 U.S. 1, 91 S.Ct. 702, 27 L.Ed.2d 639 (1971).

[25] 401 U.S. 23, 91 S.Ct. 713, 27 L.Ed.2d 657 (1971).

[26] Shelton v. Tucker, 364 U.S. 479, 81 S.Ct. 247, 5 L.Ed. 2d 231 (1960).

[27] 401 U.S. 154, 91 S.Ct. 720, 27 L.Ed.2d 749 (1971).

the centrality, of truth in litigation (§ 10.1). Yet some observers of the American judicial system have wondered whether truth is a regularly achieved product of litigation, whether the discovery of truth in litigation to the extent that it occurs is not more the result of serendipity than design, and whether advocates are capable of discriminating between truth and falsity in a careful and systematic way. Those doubts are not weak, nor are they necessarily an adverse reflection upon the morals of lawyers. The search for truth is not the only business about which lawyers must concern themselves. They are also charged by their office with duties of zealously furthering the interests of their clients and of maintaining confidentiality in protecting client information. Those three objectives—truth, zeal, and confidentiality—can pull in different directions. The resulting gravitational phenomena will be explored here in the context of advocates and their dealings with evidence, with witnesses, and with special witnesses—their own clients.

WESTLAW REFERENCES

synopsis,digest(attorney lawyer counsel** advocate /s duty duti! /s zeal! truth! confiden!)

§ 12.3.2 *Withholding and Disclosing Evidence*

Litigator Initiative and Control

The dealings of advocates with evidence involve issues of candor, of falsification, and of suppression or the extent to which evidence must be shared with other adversaries. Those issues arise because of two central premises of the American adversarial concept. The first is that lawyers as advocates are almost entirely responsible for gathering and selecting the evidence that will be considered by the factfinder. The second is that, by and large, there is no general obligation to share the results of pretrial knowledge with either adversaries or the court except to the extent that an advocate believes that revelation will advance the litigational interests of his or her client. Judges and jurors have no responsibility to gather evidence and indeed commit grave error if they attempt to do so on their own.[28] That restraint on the presiding officer contrasts sharply with the responsibility of judges in many European systems. These judicial magistrates have the chief responsibility for ferreting out facts and lawyers are strictly limited in the extent to which they may legally conduct independent investigations or interviews.[29]

Nonrevelation of Relevant and Material Evidence

A general operating principle for American litigators is that evidence known to them is private and proprietary. A party or lawyer who learns of evidence has no general professional or legal obligation to reveal it either to an adversary or to the fact finder.[30] Such information is considered to be the product of the effort, or the plain luck, of the knowing party and, at least in a prima facie sense, "belongs" to the party whose luck, effort, and resources unearthed it. The evidence can, of course, be revealed when deployed in a hearing or trial for the benefit of the lawyer's client. But neither lawyer nor client is under any obligation to come forward unbidden with information that is unknown to the other side, even if the other side will surely lose its case in the absence of knowledge of that evi-

[28] United States v. Grinnell Corp., 384 U.S. 563, 583, 86 S.Ct. 1698, 1710, 16 L.Ed.2d 778 (1966); E.I.DuPont & Co. v. Collins, 432 U.S. 46, 97 S.Ct. 2229, 2235, 53 L.Ed.2d 100 (1977); Rinehart v. Brewer, 421 F.Supp. 508, 518–19 (S.D. Iowa 1976), affirmed 561 F.2d 126 (8th Cir. 1977); In re Turner, 421 So.2d 1077 (Fla.1982).

[29] Damaska, Evidentiary Barriers to Conviction and Two Models of Criminal Procedure: A Comparative Study, 121 U.Pa.L.Rev. 506, 550, 559 (1972); Lind, Thibault & Walker, A Cross Cultural Comparison of the Effect of Adversary and Inquisitorial Processes on Bias in Legal Decisionmaking, 62 Va.L.Rev. 271. 275–76 (1976).

[30] Former federal judge Marvin E. Frankel has lead an effort to change the professional rules to require a lawyer in a civil case to disclose all material evidence favorable to the other side. See, e.g., Frankel, The Search for Truth Continued: More Disclosure, Less Privilege, 54 U.Colo.L.Rev. 51 (1982).

dence.[31] The other side must find its own admissible evidence and cannot in any way rely on a duty of the opposing party to volunteer favorable evidence.[32]

That traditional view has been seriously eroded by the institution of pretrial discovery in civil cases—the judicially enforced machinery available for the compulsory pretrial revelation of information in the possession of other parties. "Modern instruments of discovery serve a useful purpose . . . . They together with pretrial procedures make a trial less of a game of blindman's buff and more a fair contest with the basic issues and facts disclosed to the fullest practicable extent".[33] But discovery rules impose no blanket disclosure obligation. Most discovery rules provide that a party seeking the benefits of discovery must make specific triggering requests in order to impose disclosure obligations.[34] Once a proper inquiry is made, modern discovery systems impose a legal duty to respond.[35] In some circumstances, they also impose a supplementation duty—an obligation to supplement past discovery responses that were false or misleading when made or have become so by virtue of new circumstances.[36] Discovery in criminal cases is significantly more limited, although at least in theory the prosecutor is under a constitutional duty to disclose important helpful evidence to the accused (§ 13.10.5).

Voluntary Disclosure of Evidence

A separate question is the extent to which advocates can decide to go beyond their legal duties and to reveal information to adversaries or to others voluntarily. If the information is covered by the broad protection of the rules of confidentiality, disclosure of information damaging to the client's interests without the client's permission is not permitted (§ 6.7.5). With that exception a lawyer is free to disclose information that is not confidential or otherwise restricted. For example, if the information has been obtained from an opposing party and is damaging to that party, a lawyer, unless restricted by a court order or other law,[37] nonetheless can ordinarily reveal the information freely to third persons.

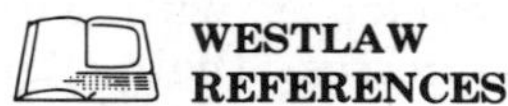

WESTLAW REFERENCES

Nonrevelation of Relevant & Material Evidence

attorney lawyer counsel** advocate /s information evidence fact /p duty oblig! /s disclose reveal revelat! "come forward"

31 Miranda v. Arizona, 384 U.S. 436, 86 S.Ct. 1602, 16 L.Ed.2d 694 (1966) (Harlan, J., dissenting); N.Y. County Bar Ethics Op. 309 (1933); C.Curtis, It's Your Law 17 (1954); S.Williston, Life and Law 271 (1941). In criminal cases, compare, e.g., EC 7-13 (duty of prosecutor to reveal evidence favorable to defense states "responsibilities different from those of a lawyer in private practice"), with, e.g., People v. White, 57 N.Y.2d 129, 454 N.Y.S.2d 964, 440 N.E.2d 1310 (1982)(defense lawyer under no duty to come forward with alibi witness discovered during pretrial investigation despite trial judge's belief that earlier revelation would have saved prosecutor and court system time and expense in unfounded prosecution).

32 Kerwit Med. Prods., Inc. v. N. & H. Instruments, Inc., 616 F.2d 833, 837 (5th Cir.1980)(neither plaintiff nor plaintiff's lawyer was under obligation to disclose to defendant or to court facts from which defense could have been fashioned); People v. White, 57 N.Y.2d 129, 454 N.Y.S.2d 964, 440 N.E.2d 1310 (1982). But cf., e.g., Toledo Bar Ass'n v. Fell, 51 Ohio St.2d 33, 364 N.E.2d 872 (1977)(violation of DR 7-102(A)(3) for lawyer not to disclose death of client when he knew established practice of worker compensation agency to deny claim for permanent total disability upon notice of death).

33 United States v. Proctor & Gamble Co., 356 U.S. 677, 682, 78 S.Ct. 983, 986, 2 L.Ed.2d 1077 (1958).

34 For an argument that discovery rules should be rewritten to require a party making a claim to disclose, without inquiry, all information on which it is based, see Glaser, A New Law of "Supply and Demand" in Discovery, 69 ABA J. 320 (1983).

35 Litton Systems, Inc. v. ATT, 700 F.2d 785 (2d Cir. 1983), cert. denied 464 U.S. 1073, 104 S.Ct. 984, 79 L.Ed. 2d 220 (1984)(pattern of concealment of evidence frustrating discovery efforts warrants trial court's denial of all costs and fees to prevailing party otherwise entitled to recover these expenses); Rozier v. Ford Motor Co., 573 F.2d 1332 (5th Cir.1978)(judgment set aside and new trial ordered for defendant's failure to produce document requested in discovery even in absence of showing of substantial prejudice).

36 Fed.R.Civ.Proc. Rule 26(e).

37 The question has arisen frequently in products liability and similar cases in which a manufacturer has unsuccessfully attempted to prevent one plaintiff's lawyer from sharing discovered information with other plaintiffs' lawyers in suits involving the same product. E.g., Farnum v. G.D. Searle & Co., 339 N.W.2d 384 (Iowa 1983), and cases cited. Selling valuable documents by one not under a duty to deliver them to the vendee is generally not unlawful. See Restatement of Contracts § 553(2) (1932).

Voluntary Disclosure of Evidence

attorney lawyer counsel** advocate /s information evidence fact /p volunt! volition /s disclose reveal revelat! "come forward"

§ 12.3.3 Falsifying Facts

Advocates' Responsibilities for Accuracy

A lawyer's failure to reveal evidence that is helpful, but unknown, to an adversary is quite different from presenting, either in discovery or at a trial, evidence that an advocate knows to be false. The shift from a lawyer who passively countenances an opponent's defeat in the absence of critical evidence to a lawyer who actively offers distorted facts in evidence generally defines the line between permissible and impermissible advocacy.

Lawyers vouch for evidence they present as advocates in two general, limited ways. First, when, as is the usual case, a lawyer presents documents, testimony, or other evidence during the course of an adversarial hearing, the lawyer in effect warrants that he or she does not know that the evidence is false.[38] Even if a lawyer innocently presents false evidence without knowledge of its falsity, later discovery of its falsity may require corrective measures, including disclosure of the falsity of the evidence to the court (§ 12.6.4). Second, when a lawyer offers evidence or states facts to the fact finder directly, the lawyer is warranting that the testimony or document is what it purports to be and is accurate to the best of the lawyer's knowledge.[39] A lawyer states facts directly when the lawyer testifies as a witness or in other ways makes statements that are meant to be taken as factual. A clearly impermissible instance is the misstatement of facts in an appellate brief.[40] Another example is a lawyer's reciting facts that purport to be known personally to the lawyer, such as facts that justify a favorable ruling on a procedural matter. Making a false statement of supporting facts to a judge in order to obtain a continuance, for example, clearly violates mandatory standards.[41]

Presenting Documents as Evidence

Documents prepared by lawyers provide the grease facilitating the business of courts and a great deal of commerce. If the written work produced or offered in evidence by lawyers could not be accepted at face value as valid and fairly reflective of the facts and matters that they purported to state, then the practice of law and the operation of courts would become wastefully more cumbersome, expensive, and contentious. Lawyers who knowingly [42] prepare or offer false documents [43]—

[38] DR 7–102(A)(4); MR 3.3(a)(4). See also § 12.5.3 (perjury).

[39] DR 7–102(A)(5)(lawyer shall not "knowingly make a false statement of law or fact"); MR 3.3(a)(1)("lawyer shall not knowingly . . . (1) make a false statement of material fact or law to a tribunal"). E.g., In re Walton, 676 P.2d 1078, 1088 (Alaska 1983), appeal dismissed ___ U.S. ___, 105 S.Ct. 54, 83 L.Ed.2d 6 (1984)(serving and filing pleadings with fabricated exhibit attached); In re Darby, 273 Ind. 309, 403 N.E.2d 1074 (1980)(misrepresentation to judge of state of court date conflicts); Cornell v. Albuquerque Chem. Co., 92 N.M. 121, 584 P.2d 168, 171 (App.1978)(false statement in brief); In re Goodman, 158 App.Div. 465, 143 N.Y.S. 577 (1912)(deceiving judge in bench-tried bastardy proceeding by representation that absent witness would testify favorably to client). See also, e.g., In re Kleindienst, 132 Ariz. 95, 644 P.2d 249 (1982)(perjury in depositions and before state bar; one year's suspension); Office of Disciplinary Counsel v. Grigsby, 493 Pa. 194, 425 A.2d 730 (1981)(disbarment for false swearing in driver's license application and in answer to garnishment proceeding brought by creditor of lawyer).

[40] United States v. Jefferson, 714 F.2d 689, 697 (7th Cir. 1983)(factual statements in brief unsupported by trial transcript); United States v. Wycoff, 545 F.2d 679, 682 n. 2 (9th Cir.1976), cert.denied 429 U.S. 1105, 97 S.Ct. 1135, 51 L.Ed.2d 556 (1977)(failure to refer to parts of trial record necessary to be considered in interests of completeness); Ashbaugh v. State, 272 Ind. 557, 400 N.E.2d 767, 772 (1980)(same).

[41] Florida Bar v. Oxner, 431 So.2d 983 (Fla.1983).

[42] DR 7–102(A)(5); MR 3.3(a)(1), (4). But see, e.g., In re Bybee, 629 P.2d 423, 425 (Utah 1981)(discipline for making represntions to court and opposing counsel that lawyer "either knew or should have known" were false); Rooney v. Whitechurch, 585 P.2d 1202, 1204 (Wyo.1978) (lawyer who prepared false affidavit either assisted client in conduct tantamount to perjury or, if he ineptly failed to investigate facts as he claimed, demonstrated total incompetence to engage in law practice). See generally §§ 12.4.3, 12.5.3.

[43] J.Stewart, The Partners 94 (1983).

falsely worded,[44] falsely copied,[45] falsely signed,[46] falsely dated,[47] or falsely notarized [48]—and present them in litigation as something other than what they are, are typically dealt with quite harshly by courts.[49] Similar rules apply to physical evidence: altering or tampering with physical evidence in a way that changes its appearance or import in important ways is unlawful.[50]

 **WESTLAW REFERENCES**

Advocate's Responsibilities for Accuracy

prof.code code /5 6068 6103 6128 /p inten!

Presenting Documents as Evidence

attorney lawyer counsel** advocate /s kn*w! intend intention! cognit! /s prepar! offer! present! /p (false /7 evidence document!) perjur!

§ 12.3.4 Distorting Facts

Beyond the prohibition against presenting blatantly false evidence, what restraints are placed on lawyers to prevent their taking steps in litigation to create impressions in the mind of the fact finder that a lawyer knows to be false? For example, may a lawyer introduce into evidence a copy of a contract signed by only one party, knowing that another copy of the same contract exists that was later, and bindingly, signed by both parties? [51] May a lawyer defending in a criminal case involving contested eyewitness testimony arrange to have a person who is not in fact the accused sit at counsel table without informing the court or the prosecutor in order to "test" the in-court identification of prosecution witnesses? [52] An early draft of the Model Rules would have created an explicit obligation for lawyers to avoid creating misleading impressions through advocacy.[53] Failure to enact an explicit rule, however, may not be decisive. The Model Rules contain vague and possibly broad provisions whose cognate provisions in the Code have created a similar obligation.[54] In addition, some situations will be covered by MR 3.3(a)(2), which imposes a duty on a lawyer to "disclose a material fact to a tribunal

44 In re Stump, 621 P.2d 263 (Alaska 1980)(fabricated letter); In re Pray, 64 Nev. 402, 183 P.2d 627 (1947) (lawyer falsely verified complaint containing known false statement about duration of divorce client's residence in state); In re Brooks, 274 S.C. 601, 267 S.E.2d 74 (1980), cert.denied 449 U.S. 984, 101 S.Ct. 401, 66 L.Ed.2d 246 (1980)(preparation of false affidavit that misrepresented facts of alleged criminal offense); In re Judd, 629 P.2d 435 (Utah 1981)(motion containing factual statements known to be false); In re Krueger, 103 Wis.2d 192, 307 N.W.2d 184 (1981)(divorce petition containing allegation of residence known to be false). See also In re Simpson, 645 P.2d 1223 (Alaska 1982)(misrepresentation in response to discovery request that was result of gross negligence not violation of antideceit rules but was violation of competence rule (DR 6–101(A)).

45 People v. Klein, 179 Colo. 408, 500 P.2d 1181 (1972) (indefinite suspension for presenting false carbon copy in disciplinary hearing); Kentucky Bar Ass'n v. Hammond, 619 S.W.2d 696 (Ky.1981)(forging physician's name to fraudulent medical report).

46 Committee on Professional Ethics v. Roberts, 312 N.W.2d 556 (Iowa 1981)(discipline for knowingly presenting document containing factually true statements but with forged signature of client); In re Barrett, 88 N.J. 450, 443 A.2d 678 (1982).

47 Howard v. Gulf, C. & S.F. Ry., 135 S.W. 707 (Tex.Civ. App.1911).

48 In re Coughlin, 91 N.J. 374, 450 A.2d 1326 (1982) (false jurat); In re Kraus, 289 Or. 661, 616 P.2d 1173, 1176–77 (1980)(false notarial acknowledgement on purported client affidavit).

49 See generally Annot., 40 A.L.R.3d 169 (1971).

50 MR 3.4(a); cf. DR 7–102(A)(3), (6). E.g., In re Barrow, 278 S.C. 276, 294 S.E.2d 785 (1982)(removing warning label from antenna that plaintiff client was holding at time of electrical accident on which suit was brought; both tampering lawyer and his associate who later learned of tampering were required to reveal the tampering to the opposing side); In re Nunn, 73 Minn. 292 (1898) (altering public land records in office of court clerk).

51 Nat'l L.J., Jan. 5, 1981, at 3, col. 1; In re A, 276 Or. 225, 554 P.2d 479 (1976)(lawyer's duty to inform fact finder of misimpression created by client's testimony). This may be one of the relatively rare instances in which MR 3.3(a)(2)—which prohibits a lawyer's knowing failure "to disclose a material fact to a tribunal when disclosure is necessary to avoid assisting a criminal or fraudulent act by the client"—would create obligations arguably beyond those of MR 3.3(a)(4).

52 United States v. Thoreen, 653 F.2d 1332 (9th Cir. 1981), cert.denied 455 U.S. 938, 102 S.Ct. 1428, 71 L.Ed.2d 648 (1982)(affirming contempt conviction of lawyer); Miskovsky v. State ex rel. Jones, 586 P.2d 1104 (Okl.Crim. App.1978)(same); ABA Informal Op. 914 (1966)(conduct unethical under Canons). See also, e.g., In re Metzger, 31 Hawaii 929 (1931)(lawyer disciplined for substituting forged exhibit for stated purpose of testing expert witness in murder trial); In re Friedman, 76 Ill.2d 392, 30 Ill.Dec. 288, 392 N.E.2d 1333 (1979).

53 MR 3.1(a)(3)(Discussion Draft, January 30, 1980).

54 See authorities cited nn. 44–49.

when disclosure is necessary to avoid assisting a criminal or fraudulent act by the client."

Yet it is certainly not a standard requirement that an American advocate always avoid distorting facts. American law and professional regulations are not entirely consistent on related matters but, as will be seen in connection with testimony of witnesses, a lawyer on occasion is permitted to create distortion in order to aid a client's cause (§ 12.4.5).

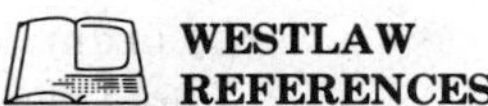

WESTLAW REFERENCES

Lawyer counsel** attorney advocate / argu! prepar! offer! present /s mislead*** misimpress*** distort! /s evidence document!

§ 12.3.5 Document Destruction and Other Suppression of Evidence

The Lawyer Codes on Evidence Alteration or Suppression

Altering evidence is a species of the general problem of suppressing evidence. The motivation for an adversary to suppress evidence in litigation is strong. But rules exist that, in ways that are not always clear, restrict the extent to which suppression can be accomplished. The approach of the 1969 Code was not to create independent rules requiring preservation of evidence, but simply to proscribe suppression of evidence by means that were proscribed by other provisions of the law.[55] The final version of the 1983 Model Rules rejected earlier drafts that would have created a more stringent obligation.[56] As a result, MR 3.4(a), as does the Code, provides merely that a lawyer must not "unlawfully" alter, destroy, or conceal "a document or other material having potential evidentiary value." Rule 3.4(a), moreover, is complemented by Rule 3.3(a)(2), which requires a lawyer to disclose material facts (here, the former existence of documents) if this is necessary to avoid assisting a criminal or fraudulent act by a client.

Criminal and Other Sanctions for Offenses Against Existence and Integrity of Evidence

The laws that prohibit evidence destruction, to which the professional rules presumably refer, are found chiefly in criminal statutes dealing with offenses commonly called obstruction of justice[57] and with criminal contempt[58] but can also be found in noncriminal law. A lawyer who knowingly advises a client to destroy documents in violation of such a law can also be found guilty of conspiracy to commit the substantive offense of obstruction.[59] The federal courts have generally limited the scope of such criminal statutes to destruction during an already pending proceeding.[60] But the law of many states goes further and covers destruction on the eve of filing or even extends to reasonably foresee-

[55] DR 7–102(A)(3)(lawyer shall not conceal or knowingly fail to disclose that which "he is required by law to reveal"). No similar provision appeared in the 1908 Canons.

[56] For the history of earlier versions, see Oesterle, A Private Litigant's Remedies for an Opponent's Inappropriate Destruction of Relevant Documents, 61 Tex.L.Rev. 1185, 1217, 1218 (1983).

[57] 18 U.S.C.A. § 1503.

[58] 18 U.S.C.A. § 401(3)(contempt for "disobedience or resistance to [court's] lawful writ, process, order, rule, decree, or command.").

[59] United States v. Perlstein, 126 F.2d 789, 792 (3d Cir.), cert.denied 316 U.S. 678, 62 S.Ct. 1106, 86 L.Ed. 1752 (1942)(affirming conviction of conspiracy to obstruct future judicial proceeding by advising client to destroy documents if proceeding brought); Clark v. State, 159 Tex.Cr.R. 187, 261 S.W.2d 339, cert.denied 346 U.S. 855, 74 S.Ct. 69, 98 L.Ed.2d 369 (1953)(lawyer who advised client over telephone to throw away murder weapon guilty of accessory offense).

[60] Pettibone v. United States, 148 U.S. 197, 207, 13 S.Ct. 542, 546, 37 L.Ed. 419 (1893). But a lawyer's advice to a client, given before proceedings begin, to destroy documents when proceedings do begin, can be punished as a conspiracy to obstruct justice. See United States v. Perlstein, 126 F.2d 789, 796 (3d Cir.1942), cert.denied 316 U.S. 678, 62 S.Ct. 1106, 86 L.Ed. 1752 (1942). Moreover, an official investigation is a proceeding susceptible to criminal obstruction by document destruction. E.g., United States v. Fruchtman, 421 F.2d 1019 (6th Cir.1970), cert.denied 400 U.S. 849, 91 S.Ct. 39, 27 L.Ed.2d 86 (1970). Cf. United States v. Rodgers, ___ U.S. ___, 104 S.Ct. 1942, 80 L.Ed.2d 492 (1984)(18 U.S.C.A. § 1001 on making false statement "in any matter within the jurisdiction of any department or agency of the United States" applies to criminal investigations).

able proceedings.[61] One noncriminal source of a legal obligation not to destroy documents can be found in the developing law of civil discovery. Destruction or concealment of documents after they have been requested in civil discovery, in addition to raising issues of obstruction and criminal contempt, is a straightforward violation of a party's obligation under procedural rules to turn over such material.[62] A lawyer's assistance in such an enterprise should similarly be regarded as unlawful [63] and thus a violation of the professional duty to make disclosures required by law.

Whether or not a law violation occurs, document destruction or similar evidence suppression may also be unsound because, if discovered, evidence of the destruction may be admissible in evidence at the trial itself as a circumstance showing consciousness of guilt or liability.[64] Suppression also might lead to one or more of a variety of sanctions against a party or the party's lawyer, such as a penalty default, the imposition of an obligation to pay legal fees to an adversary because of bad faith, or an obligation on the part of lawyers to pay a fine.[65] Destruction of potentially favorable evidence by a prosecutor may lead to dismissal of a prosecution if the destruction deprives the accused of the possibility of proving a defense.[66] A California court has also held that evidence destruction can give rise to a damage action by a person deprived of an opportunity to win a lawsuit.[67]

"Document Retention"

Yet the law cannot require every person or business to retain all documents and other evidence that might conceivably be involved in future litigation. Storage and indexing costs can be high.[68] Accordingly, cases have recognized that it might be legitimate to destroy or discard routinely material that later is claimed to have evidentiary value if destruction is motivated by the need to preserve filing space or to preserve the material in a more durable or usable form.[69] From that

[61] Oesterle, supra n. 56, 1208–1209. See also, e.g., State v. Johnson, 122 Ariz. 260, 594 P.2d 514 (1979); In re Williams, 221 Minn. 554, 23 N.W.2d 4, 9 (1946)(disbarment, inter alia, for destruction of client's holographic instructions for distribution of estate); State v. Cassatly, 93 N.J.Super. 111, 225 A.2d 141 (1966)(offense of obstructing justice for destruction of tape recording known to be wanted in criminal proceeding).

[62] In re Air Crash Disaster Near Chicago, Illinois, 90 F.R.D. 613 (N.D.Ill.1981). A notorious instance involved a lawyer from a major law firm who concealed a document requested by the opposing side in an antitrust case and lied about its existence. See J.Stewart, The Partners 327–365 (1983); Kiechel, The Strange Case of Kodak's Lawyers, Fortune, May 8, 1978, at 188; Wessel, Institutional Responsibility: Professionalism and Ethics, 60 Neb.L.Rev. 504 (1981). The lawyer served a sentence for contempt, see 885 A.T.R.R. A-12 (Oct. 19, 1978); the firm was discharged by the client and eventually paid $675,000 to the client in settlement of a malpractice claim. See Wall Street Journal, Oct. 11, 1983 at 1, col. 1.

[63] In re Air Crash Disaster Near Chicago, Illinois, 90 F.R.D. 613 (N.D.Ill.1981)(imposition of sanctions on corporate plaintiff for lawyer's gross negligence and intentionally misleading responses to discovery requests and court orders to provide discovery).

[64] United States v. Brashier, 548 F.2d 1315, 1325 (9th Cir.1976), cert.denied 429 U.S. 1111, 97 S.Ct. 1149, 51 L.Ed.2d 565 (1977); United States v. Cirillo, 468 F.2d 1233, 1240 (2d Cir.1972), cert.denied 410 U.S. 989, 93 S.Ct. 1501, 36 L.Ed.2d 188 (1973); Bradley v. State, 561 P.2d 548 (Okl.Crim.App.1977).

[65] Roadway Express, Inc. v. Piper, 447 U.S. 752, 761–64, 100 S.Ct. 2455, 2461–63, 65 L.Ed.2d 488 (1980)(fee sanctions of discovery rules and judicial doctrine providing for fee shifting when opposing party has acted in bad faith reaffirmed); Litton Systems, Inc. v. American Tel. & Tel. Co., 700 F.2d 785 (2d Cir.1983), cert.denied 464 U.S. 1073, 104 S.Ct. 984, 79 L.Ed.2d 220 (1984)(pattern of intentional concealment of evidence by plaintiff's lawyers warrants trial court's ruling refusing to award prevailing party usual statutory award of legal fees).

[66] See generally Comment, Judicial Response to Governmental Loss or Destruction of Evidence, 39 U.Chi.L. Rev. 542 (1972). Dismissal of a prosecution is more likely if the loss or destruction was intentional. E.g., Brady v. Maryland, 373 U.S. 83, 83 S.Ct. 1194, 10 L.Ed.2d 215 (1963); People v. Poole, 192 Colo. 56, 555 P.2d 980 (1976) (undercover agent purposefully shaved off beard before testifying). Dismissal may also be ordered when the loss was merely negligent. E.g., Garcia v. District Court, 197 Colo. 38, 589 P.2d 924 (1979).

[67] Smith v. Superior Court, 151 Cal.App.3d 491, 198 Cal.Rptr. 829 (1984).

[68] In one extraordinarily complex antitrust case, billions of pages of documents were retained and stored at a reported cost of several millions of dollars each year. See In re IBM Corp., 687 F.2d 591, 594 (2d Cir.1982).

[69] United States v. McCallie, 554 F.2d 770 (6th Cir. 1977); United States v. Dupree, 553 F.2d 1189 (8th Cir. 1977), cert.denied 434 U.S. 986, 98 S.Ct. 613, 54 L.Ed.2d 480 (1977). But see United States v. Harrison, 173 U.S. App.D.C. 260, 524 F.2d 421 (1975); United States v. Harris, 543 F.2d 1247 (9th Cir.1976).

recognition of the legitimacy of document destruction under some circumstances has grown the practice of "document retention" systems. Those are euphemistically named and lawyer-designed programs intended to remove from business files both relatively valueless documents as well as all potentially adverse evidence.[70] Some of those systems—designed, if truth be known, to destroy evidence—play dangerously near the edges of legality and rely only on difficulties of proving motivation to escape sanctions.

Physical Evidence of Client Crimes

Are the obligations of a criminal defense lawyer any different with respect to preserving physical evidence? Surprisingly, a defense lawyer may be under special obligations to preserve physical evidence that is adverse to a client's interests and possibly to turn the evidence over to the prosecutor. A leading case is the decision of the Alaska court in Morrell v. State.[71] A lawyer's client drew a "kidnapping plan" that he left in his car where it was later found by a friend who gave it to the lawyer. The court held that the lawyer was required to turn the document over to prosecutors. The duty was founded on precedent and on the court's interpretation of a criminal statute prohibiting concealment of evidence. The approach of the *Morrell* decision has been generally followed.[72] Thus, a defense lawyer who comes into possession of either the products of apparent crime, such as stolen money or goods,[73] or instrumentalities of crime, such as weapons,[74] is required to turn these over to the prosecutor. Some courts have gone further and have required defense lawyers to turn over evidence that is neither contraband nor instrumentality.[75]

But courts have drawn the line at the turnover obligation just described and have generally protected under the attorney-client privilege the lawyer's information about the source of the incriminating evidence if that source is the lawyer's client.[76] The privilege is waived, however, if the lawyer came into possession of the evidence unlawfully, for example, as the result of the lawyer's participation in a conspiracy to conceal it,[77] or if the lawyer has altered the location or changed the appearance of the evidence.[78] The line

[70] See generally Oesterle, A Private Litigant's Remedies for an Opponent's Inappropriate Destruction of Relevant Documents, 61 Tex.L.Rev. 1185 (1983); Fedders & Guttenplan, Document Retention and Destruction: Practice, Legal and Ethical Considerations, 56 Notre Dame Law. 5 (1980); Note, Legal Ethics and the Destruction of Evidence, 88 Yale L.J. 1665 (1979).

[71] 575 P.2d 1200 (Alaska 1978).

[72] People v. Meredith, 29 Cal.3d 682, 175 Cal.Rptr. 612, 631 P.2d 46 (1981)(lawyer who, on information supplied by client, directed office investigator to find victim's partially burned wallet in trash can and remove it for inspection was required to turn wallet over to prosecutor). See generally Note, People v. Meredith: The Attorney-Client Privilege and the Criminal Defendant's Constitutional Rights, 70 Cal.L.Rev. 1048 (1982); Note, Disclosure of Incriminating Physical Evidence Received from a Client: The Defense Attorney's Dilemma, 52 Colo. L.Rev. 419 (1981); Note, The Right of a Criminal Defense Attorney to Withhold Physical Evidence Received from His Client, 38 U.Chi.L.Rev. 211 (1970).

[73] In re January 1976 Grand Jury, 534 F.2d 719 (7th Cir.1976)(money received by clients, bank robbery suspects); In re Ryder, 263 F.Supp. 360 (E.D.Va.1967), affirmed 381 F.2d 713 (4th Cir.1967)(stolen money and sawed-off shotgun); State v. Dillon, 93 Idaho 698, 471 P.2d 553 (1970), cert.denied 401 U.S. 942, 91 S.Ct. 947, 28 L.Ed.2d 223 (1971)(property burglarized from home of murder victim).

[74] People v. Investigation into a Certain Weapon, 113 Misc.2d 348, 448 N.Y.S.2d 950 (1982)(ammunition and ammunition clip); State ex rel. Sowers v. Olwell, 64 Wn. 2d 828, 394 P.2d 681 (1964)(lawyer required to turn over knife obtained from client and possibly used as murder weapon).

[75] Morrell v. State, 575 P.2d 1200 (Alaska 1978)(client-drawn "kidnapping plan" not indicated to have been directly employed in offense); State v. Carlin, 7 Kan.App. 2d 219, 640 P.2d 324 (1982)(client's tape recordings of threatening conversations).

[76] People v. Nash, 110 Mich.App. 428, 313 N.W.2d 307 (1981), affirmed 418 Mich. 196, 341 N.W.2d 439 (1983); State ex rel. Sowers v. Olwell, 64 Wn.2d 828, 394 P.2d 681 (1964). See also West Virgina v. Douglass, 20 W.Va. 770, 783 (1882), cited in People v. Meredith, 29 Cal.3d 682, 175 Cal.Rptr. 612, 617, 631 P.2d 46, 51 (1981).

[77] State ex rel. Oklahoma Bar Ass'n v. Harlton, 669 P.2d 774 (Okl.1983)(suspension following conviction of crime of accessory for concealing gun); In re Abuza, 178 App.Div. 757, 166 N.Y.S. 105 (1917)(disbarment when lawyer concealed client's jewelry and sat silent while client lied about its location).

[78] People v. Meredith, 29 Cal.3d 682, 175 Cal.Rptr. 612, 631 P.2d 46 (1981).

drawn here is obviously a fine one. It reflects the effort of courts to protect the confidentiality of the client-lawyer relationship and to avoid impairing the lawyer's instincts of client loyalty except in instances in which recognition of the privilege would result in lawyers becoming the secret repository of the fruits and instrumentalities of client crimes.

WESTLAW REFERENCES

Lawyer Code on Evidence Alteration Suppression

dr7–107(a) (d.r. "disciplinary rule" /5 7–106(a)) ("model rule" m.r. /5 3.4)

Criminal & Other Sanctions for Offenses Against Existence & Integrity of Evidence

attorney lawyer counsel** advocate /s destr! abscond "deep-six" /7 evidence document!

Physical Evidence of Client Crimes

attorney lawyer counsel** advocate /s "physical evidence" /s preserv! turn-over disclos! destr! hid! conceal*** alter change

§ 12.4 ADVOCATES AND WITNESSES

§ 12.4.1 Dealing with Witnesses

Persons who are potential witnesses in a proceeding present many of the same ethical problems as do lawyer dealings with documents. But witnesses both are ambulatory and have utility as sources of evidence that is dependent on their willingness to testify truthfully. Lawyers, accordingly, may not induce witnesses either to flee or hide to prevent others from obtaining their testimony, or to falsify their testimony. American lawyers are free to interview both friendly and adverse potential witnesses. But both in undergoing interviews and in trial testimony, witnesses have interests of privacy, reputation, and self-respect that are given a measure of protection.

A problem that may be encountered when a lawyer interviews any potential witness is the avoidance of the necessity for the lawyer-interviewer to appear later as a witness in order to impeach the witness if the witness changes stories in trial testimony. The major complication is the rule that a lawyer may not conduct a trial if the lawyer should be called as a witness (§ 7.5). In order to avoid the problem, a sound practice is to conduct interviews (at least with hostile or evasive witnesses) through an investigator or with a third person present who can be called as an impeachment witness at trial.[79]

§ 12.4.2 Discouraging or Suppressing Testimony

Limits on Discouraging Testimony

An instinct of an advocate who discovers a witness whose recollection of events is unfavorable to a client's position might be to discourage the witness from testifying. Doing so, however, is fraught with legal risks. At one extreme, a lawyer may not attempt to persuade a witness to avoid a lawful subpoena [80] or try to persuade a witness not to testify for reasons such as friendship or fear.[81] A

79 ABA Prosecution Function § 3–3.1(f)(1980 ed.); id. Defense Function § 4–4.3(d) and commentary (Interviews by the Lawyer Personally). Cf. Parker v. United States, 363 A.2d 975 (D.C.App.1976)(inadvisability of accused accompanying defense lawyer to witness interview).

80 DR 7–109(A); Calif.Rule 7–107(B); cf. MR 3.4(a)(limited to "unlawful" obstruction of another party's access to evidence). See also, e.g., Williamson v. Superior Court, 21 Cal.3d 829, 148 Cal.Rptr. 39, 582 P.2d 126 (1978) (settlement unlawful because of promise to withdraw expert witness); People v. Kenelly, 648 P.2d 1065 (Colo. 1982)(lawyer suspended for assisting client to negotiate settlement of civil case in return for client's promise to evade subpoena in opposing party's criminal trial); In re Lutz, 101 Idaho 24, 607 P.2d 1078 (1980)(lawyer suspended for drafting release including promise of tort claimant not to testify against client in criminal case); Restatement of Contracts § 554 (1932). Dissuading a person from attending a proceeding to give testimony is commonly made a crime. E.g., Model Penal Code § 241.6(1)(c)(1980); West's Ann.Cal.Penal Code § 136.1(a). See also In re Holmes, 145 Cal.App.3d 934, 193 Cal.Rptr. 790 (1983)(lawyer in contempt for advising prospective witness in civil case to evade subpoena); State Board v. Lane, 93 Minn. 425, 101 N.W. 613 (1904)(discipline for advising witness in criminal case to remain in hiding).

81 North Carolina State Bar v. Graves, 50 N.C.App. 450, 274 S.E.2d 396 (1981)(attempt to persuade witness to invoke testimonial privilege in return for assurance that lawyer's client would protect witness in same way); State v. Howe, 247 N.W.2d 647 (N.D.1976)(threatening to sue witness under subpoena as offense of witness tampering). See also, e.g., L'Orange v. Medical Protective Co., 394 F.2d 57, 62 (6th Cir.1968)(medical malpractice insurer

more difficult question is whether a lawyer may accurately advise a witness of his or her right to refuse to testify on the ground of self-incrimination. Under a vague "corrupt motives" test, courts have suggested that a lawyer may be convicted for giving a nonclient witness such advice, despite its aptness, if the advice was given with the intent of protecting the lawyer's client rather than the interests of the prospective witness.[82] In the absence of such corrupt motives, however, a defense lawyer can advise a potential prosecution witness of the witness' right against self-incrimination.[83]

Blockading Witnesses

A lawyer should generally not attempt to blockade a witness from an adversary by limiting access to the witness. Witnesses do not "belong" to either party and generally should be as available for interviews to one side as to the other.[84] Thus a prosecutor may not advise witnesses against speaking to a defense lawyer.[85] The cases do not agree whether a defense lawyer may permissibly advise a witness against talking to the prosecutor or of a right not to come to court if not subpoenaed.[86] The Defense Function Standards state that, aside from advising a witness about the right not to self-incriminate, a defense lawyer should do nothing to discourage the witness from cooperating with the prosecutor.[87] But rules that preclude an advocate from taking steps to deny an opposing lawyer access to witnesses do not control a court. For example, a court concerned about the veracity of a nonclient [88] witness' trial testimony may condition midtrial interviews on the presence of opposing counsel.[89]

WESTLAW REFERENCES

Limits on Discouraging

dr7–109(b) (d.r. "disciplinary rule" /5 7–109(b))

Blockading Witnesses

attorney lawyer counsel** /p encourag! urge* advise* pursua! influence! /s not decline* refus*** /9 testi! cooperat*** communicat*** & not /5 client

§ 12.4.3 *Coaching and Falsifying Testimony*

Lawyer interviews with witnesses in preparation for testimony have become an accepted

may not threaten to cancel malpractice policy of dentist planning to testify for plaintiff in malpractice lawsuit); McInnis v. State, 618 S.W.2d 389 (Tex.Civ.App.1981), cert.denied 456 U.S. 976, 102 S.Ct. 2242, 72 L.Ed.2d 851 (1982)(disbarment for arranging death of prospective witness).

82 United States v. Fayer, 523 F.2d 661 (2d Cir.1975). See also United States v. Baker, 611 F.2d 964 (4th Cir. 1979), and cases cited.

83 ABA Defense Function Standards § 4–4.3(b)(1980 ed.) (citing ABA Informal Ethics Op. 575 (1962)).

84 IBM Corp. v. Edelstein, 526 F.2d 37 (2d Cir.1975) (right of all parties to interview any witness in private without consent or presence of opposing lawyer); Woodruff v. Tomlin, 593 F.2d 33, 42 (6th Cir.1979), on rehearing 616 F.2d 924, cert.denied 449 U.S. 888, 101 S.Ct. 246, 66 L.Ed.2d 114 (1980); Lundy v. State, 521 S.W.2d 591 (Tenn.Crim.App.1976).

85 The leading case is Gregory v. United States, 369 F.2d 185 (D.C.Cir.1966). See also, e.g., State v. Covington, 290 N.C. 313, 226 S.E.2d 629 (1976); State v. York, 291 Or. 535, 632 P.2d 1261 (1981); ABA Prosecution Function Standards § 3–3.1(c)(1980); Annot., 90 A.L.R.3d 1231 (1979). It may be permissible, however, for the prosecutor to advise witnesses to take precautions during interviews or to insist upon being interviewed by the prosecutor before a defense interview. Cf., e.g., United States v. Nardi, 633 F.2d 972 (1st Cir.1980); United States v. Parker, 549 F.2d 1217 (9th Cir.1977), cert.denied 430 U.S. 971, 97 S.Ct. 1659, 52 L.Ed.2d 365 (1977). Cf. also United States v. Valenzuela-Bernal, 458 U.S. 858, 102 S.Ct. 3440, 73 L.Ed.2d 1193 (1982)(government deportation of prospective defense witnesses not violation of due process).

86 Compare, e.g., Hannon v. Superior Court, 19 Cal.3d 588, 138 Cal.Rptr. 885, 564 P.2d 1203 (1977)(defense lawyer who urged defense witness to remain silent prior to trial not guilty of suppression), with, e.g., State v. Martindale, 215 Kan. 667, 527 P.2d 703 (1974)(lawyer disciplined for truthfully answering prosecution witnesses questions whether they were required to wait in courthouse if not under subpoena and for failing to inform trial judge thereafter why they were absent).

87 ABA Defense Function Standards § 4–4.3(c)(1980 ed.).

88 For the limitation that a lawyer in a criminal case may not be prevented from consulting with a client-accused, see § 14.6.4.

89 State v. Lenarchick, 74 Wis.2d 425, 247 N.W.2d 80, 99 A.L.R.3d 906 (1976); Commonwealth v. Ballino, 349 Mass. 505, 516, 209 N.E.2d 308, 316 (1965). But see, e.g., David v. State, 269 Ark. 498, 601 S.W.2d 864 (1980) (impermissible for trial court to permit sheriff to listen to defense lawyer's interview of own witness).

and standard practice in the United States.[90] By contrast, continental jurisdictions are quite severe in their prohibition against lawyer preparation of witnesses for hearings.[91] The English practice requires a barrister to speak to his or her client only with the solicitor present, but as in the United States, it is accepted that a lawyer may prepare a witness both for direct and cross-examination.[92]

Preparation of a witness is known by a variety of sobriquets—coaching, rehearsing, horseshedding, prepping, sandpapering.[93] Its dangers are obvious: a lawyer in possession of the stories of all friendly witnesses is in a position to orchestrate a common tale that can better "avoid the pitfalls of contradiction and refutation by judicious fabrication." [94] The extent to which the practice is thus abused is unknowable, and conjecture is divided.[95] The line between legitimate and disreputable preparation is largely one of the lawyer's intentions. A lawyer may legitimately attempt to refresh a witness' memory, to assist the witness to testify in a straightforward and effective way, and to help the witness be prepared to meet improper or suggestive lines of hostile examination. On the other hand, a lawyer may not assist or school a witness in twisting or distorting the witness' subjective memory and, thus, the truth as far as the witness knows it.

Overall, the lawyer's objective in preparing a witness for future testimony should be to assist the witness to testify truthfully and effectively. A witness is required to testify in his or her own words once on the witness stand and not simply to parrot words and phrases supplied by a lawyer.[96] The limitations on lawyer coaching of witnesses are corollaries of a broader prohibition against a lawyer's knowing use of false testimony in presenting a case, which is discussed below (§ 12.5.3). A lawyer who advises a witness about the law or about desired testimony before seeking the witness' own version of events comes dangerously near subornation of perjury; whether a violation is in fact committed is a question of the lawyer's intention and of his or her knowledge about the client's foreseeable reaction to the lawyer's information.[97] Because of the perceived acute dangers of tampering, some courts assert a power to prohibit a lawyer from speaking with a nonclient witness during a recess in testimo-

[90] ALI-ABA, Civil Trial Manual, ch. 7 (1981); 3 J.Wigmore, Evidence § 788 (J.Chadbourne rev.1970); State v. McCormick, 298 N.C. 788, 259 S.E.2d 880, 882 (1979)("It is not improper for an attorney to prepare his witness for trial, to explain the applicable law in any given situation and to go over before trial the attorney's questions and the witness' answers so that the witness will be ready for his appearance in court, will be more at ease because he knows what to expect, and will give his testimony in the most effective manner that he can. Such preparation is the mark of a good trial lawyer . . . and is to be commended because it promotes a more efficient administration of justice and saves court time."). A lawyer probably may consult with a witness about answers that the witness will give to a deposition on written questions that have already been propounded. E.g., 4A J.Moore, Federal Practice ¶ 31.02 (1983).

[91] Damaska, Presentation of Evidence and Factfinding Precision, 123 U.Pa.L.Rev. 1083, 1089 n.12 (1975); Rosett, Trial and Discretion in Dutch Criminal Justice, 19 UCLA L.Rev. 353, 365–67 (1972).

[92] H.Cecil, Brief to Counsel 102 (2d ed.1972). Normally a barrister would not interview any witness other than the client and an expert witness; fact witnesses are interviewed by the solicitor. Id. at 134. In the solicitor's interview it is accepted practice to review potentially difficult questions that the witness might be asked on cross-examination. Id. at 154.

[93] Geders v. United States, 425 U.S. 80, 89–91, 96 S.Ct. 1330, 1335–36 47 L.Ed.2d 592 (1976)(coaching).

[94] In re Stroh, 97 Wn.2d 289, 644 P.2d 1161, 1165 (1982), cert.denied 459 U.S. 1202, 103 S.Ct. 1187, 75 L.Ed. 2d 434 (1983).

[95] Compare, e.g., 3 J.Wigmore, Evidence § 788 (J.Chadbourne rev.1970)(right to interview witnesses before trial is often abused), with, e.g., United States v. Allen, 542 F.2d 630, 633 (4th Cir.1976)(Craven, J.)(apprehension of untrue or tailored distortions is "greatly exaggerated"), cert.denied 430 U.S. 908, 97 S.Ct. 1179, 51 L.Ed.2d 584 (1977).

[96] In re Mitchell, 244 Ga. 766, 262 S.E.2d 89 (1979) (disbarment for encouraging six witnesses for client to testify to same fictitious name when asked in trial testimony); In re Eldridge, 82 N.Y. 1961 (1880)(lawyer suspended for writing out answers for witness).

[97] The scenario of a lawyer stimulating "recollection" by reciting a favorable, if provable, rule of law is played out in J.Voelker, Anatomy of a Murder (1958)(play written pseudonymously by Judge Richard Traver). See also, e.g., In re Bear, 578 S.W.2d 928 (Mo.1979)(evidence insufficient to show that lawyer's "schedule of events" shown to witness was intended to influence witnesses to testify falsely); Shawcross, The Functions and Responsibilities of an Advocate, 13 Rec.A.B.C.N.Y. 483, 491–92 (1958).

ny.[98] Prosecutors, because of the power of their office, must be particularly alert to the dangers of improper influence on prosecution witnesses [99] and of improper intimidation of defense witnesses.[1]

WESTLAW REFERENCES

attorney lawyer counsel** /s school*** coach*** rehears*** /s witness

§ 12.4.4 Harassing Witnesses

The Autonomy of Persons Who Are Witnesses

While competent representation might require lawyers to interview witnesses, a lawyer must take account of the right of witnesses to be free from overreaching, misrepresentation, invasion of privacy, and similar improper investigative techniques.[2] An area of continuing controversy is that of secret recording of witnesses. The matter is regulated to some extent by federal and state law, but an ABA ethics committee opinion has announced a much more sweeping prohibition.[3]

Privacy of Witnesses

The federal Omnibus Crime Control Act generally proscribes the use of interstate facilities, such as telephone lines, to record communications without the permission of at least one of the participants to the conversation.[4] Statutes in several states extend beyond the prohibitions of the federal statute and prohibit surreptitious use of eavesdropping or recording devices in additional circumstances.[5] A lawyer's violation of such a prohibition in investigating a case is plainly impermissible.[6]

The ABA ethics committee, in Formal Opinion 337 (1974), went much further than the

98 On the general matter of "sequestering" witnesses, see 6 J.Wigmore, Evidence § 1837 (J.Chadbourne rev. 1970). The Supreme Court in Geders v. United States, 425 U.S. 80, 96 S.Ct. 1330, 47 L.Ed.2d 592 (1976), held that a lawyer could not be prevented from consulting with his criminal defendant client during a recess in the client's testimony. See § 14.6.4.

99 Carsey v. United States, 129 U.S.App.D.C. 205, 392 F.2d 810 (1967); United States v. Jones, 542 F.2d 186, 211 (4th Cir.)(dictum), cert.denied 426 U.S. 922, 96 S.Ct. 2629, 49 L.Ed.2d 375 (1976); Buchanan v. State, 554 P. 2d 1153 (Alaska 1976); People v. Pendleton, 75 Ill.App.3d 580, 31 Ill.Dec. 294, 394 N.E.2d 496 (1979).

1 United States v. MacCloskey, 682 F.2d 468 (4th Cir. 1982)(prosecutor's warning to defense witness' lawyer destroyed her right to choose to testify freely); Reese v. United States, 467 A.2d 152 (D.C.App.1983)(no intimidation sufficient to warrant reversal where prosecutor comment to defense witness' lawyer was informational).

2 Florida Bar v. Snow, 436 So.2d 48 (Fla.1983)(misrepresentation to witness); In re Harrington, 128 Vt. 445, 266 A.2d 433 (1970); In re Knight, 129 Vt. 428, 281 A.2d 46 (1971)(discipline of lawyers for arranging to have opposing party seduced to motel for purpose of gathering incriminating evidence in divorce case). See generally Annot., 13 A.L.R.3d 1010 (1967)(lawyer discipline for creation of false evidence and invasions of privacy to secure evidence in divorce cases).

3 ABA Formal Op. 337 (1974).

4 18 U.S.C.A. §§ 2510–2520. The consent of one participant permits recording the communication without the knowledge of other participants. §§ 2511(2)(c), (d); United States v. White, 401 U.S. 745, 91 S.Ct. 1122, 28 L.Ed.2d 453 (1971). Beyond the secret recording of communication transmissions such as telephone calls, the Omnibus Crime Control Act also comprehensively prohibits many other forms of surreptitious evidence gathering with electronic surveillance devices, makes sale or possession of such devices illegal, prohibits the use of communications gathered in violation of the Act in any federal or state court, and provides civil and criminal penalties for violations. See 18 U.S.C.A. §§ 2511–2513, 2515, 2520.

5 West's Ann.Calif.Penal Code § 632; Ill.Rev.Stat. 1977, ch. 38, §§ 14–1 et seq. (prohibition of use of any eavesdropping device to hear or record any private conversation unless with consent of all parties to conversation); People v. Wyrick, 77 Cal.App.3d 903, 144 Cal.Rptr. 38 (1978)(prosecution of lawyer who, without consent, recorded his telephone conversation with physician during attempt to settle personal injury case).

6 People v. Wallin, 621 P.2d 330 (Colo.1981); People v. Selby, 198 Colo. 386, 606 P.2d 45 (1979). See generally Abramousky, Surreptitious Recording of Witnesses in Criminal Cases, 57 Tul.L.Rev. 1 (1982). Cf. DR 7–102(A)(8)(lawyer shall not "knowingly engage in other illegal conduct"); MR 4.4 (lawyer shall not "use methods of obtaining evidence that violate the legal rights" of a third person). But cf. Netterville v. Mississippi State Bar, 397 So.2d 878 (Miss.1981)(no violation when lawyer had secretary take transcript of conversation on extension telephone because nature of information requested of other party—list of names and addresses—reasonably imported to other party probability if not certainty of recording for future use). In addition to professional discipline, an aggrieved party may be entitled to recover damages from a lawyer who participates in a secret recording or eavesdropping scheme in violation of law. E.g., Remington v. Remington, 393 F.Supp. 898 (E.D.Pa.1975)(private damage action against spouse and private detective for violation of federal statute).

law in most jurisdictions and asserted that a lawyer was virtually never authorized to make secret and unconsented recordings of any conversation, regardless of the legality of this action under applicable law.[7] The opinion stressed avoidance of the appearance of impropriety as a rationale,[8] although it also rested, somewhat shakily, on provisions of the 1969 Code proscribing deception.[9] The limitation of the prohibition in 1983 Model Rule 4.4 against methods of obtaining evidence that violate legal rights of third persons is inconsistent with the approach of Opinion 337 and should serve to overrule it.

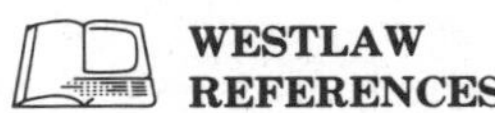

WESTLAW REFERENCES

Privacy of Witnesses

attorney lawyer counsel** /s record! tape /s conversation conference /s surreptitious** secret** stealth***

§ 12.4.5 Cross-Examination

Cross-Examination and Witness Discomfort

To nonlawyers, perhaps the most troublesome form of lawyer harassment of witnesses occurs on the witness stand. A lawyer enjoys enormous advantages over an adverse witness because of the lawyer's forensic training and ability to employ leading or suggestive questions, because of evidence rulings confining the power of witnesses to give complete answers, and because of the unfamiliarity of most witnesses with the trial setting.[10] Harassment of witnesses threatens to distort the fact-finding process in the particular trial, is offensive to witnesses, and seriously discourages potential witnesses from coming forward or from agreeing to testify.[11] Modern evidence rules place an affirmative obligation on trial judges to protect witnesses against harassment or undue embarrassment.[12] But relevant and material questions must be answered by a witness regardless of the extent to which a truthful answer might disgrace a witness.[13] An instance in point is a witness' right to invoke the privilege against self-incrimination. A lawyer is under no obligation to warn a witness that such a right exists or that the witness' testimony is potentially hazardous.[14]

Cross-Examining about Truthful Testimony

General agreement exists among commentators that defense counsel in a criminal case may permissibly cross-examine a witness known to be telling the truth in an effort to

[7] Opinion 337 noted that several state ethics committees had previously reached the same conclusion. See generally Abramovsky, supra n. 6, at 18–25. Opinion 337 provided only a limited exception for law enforcement officers operating under "strict statutory limitations conforming to constitutional requirements."

[8] For a critique of the "appearances" rationale, see § 7.1.4.

[9] DR 1–102(A)(4).

[10] See generally J.Atkinson & P.Drew, Order in Court: The Organisation of Verbal Interaction in Judicial Settings (1979).

[11] In re Crumpacker, 269 Ind. 630, 383 N.E.2d 36, 49 (1978), cert.denied 444 U.S. 979, 100 S.Ct. 481, 62 L.Ed.2d 406 (1979); State v. Phelps, 226 Kan. 371, 598 P.2d 180 (1979), cert.denied 444 U.S. 1045, 100 S.Ct. 732, 62 L.Ed. 2d 731 (1980)(described as classic case of badgering witness, in which lawyer then objected to judge that witness was crying). Lawyer harassment of witnesses has also been condemned because it constitutes "offensive personalities"—as if the offense were merely one of lack of proper etiquette. E.g., Bull v. McCuskey, 96 Nev. 706, 615 P.2d 957 (1980).

[12] Fed.Rules Evid.R. 611(a)(3): "the court shall exercise reasonable control over the mode and order of interrogating witnesses and presenting evidence so as to . . . (3) protect witnesses from harassment or undue embarrassment." See also, e.g., Pool v. Superior Court, 139 Ariz. 98, 677 P.2d 261, 266–67 (1984)(witness has right to be treated fairly by counsel and judge has power and duty to compel fair and reasonable treatment of witnesses); Commonwealth v. Rooney, 365 Mass. 484, 495–96, 313 N.E.2d 105 (1974)(same).

[13] See generally Brown v. Walker, 161 U.S. 591, 598, 16 S.Ct. 644, 647, 40 L.Ed. 819 (1896); 3A J.Wigmore, Evidence § 986 (J.Chadbourne rev.1970); Annot., 88 A.L.R.3d 304 (1978).

[14] See generally De Luca v. Whatley, 42 Cal.App.3d 574, 117 Cal.Rptr. 63 (1974)(lawyer cannot be held liable to witness for calling witness to testify in course of defending client, knowing that witness would probably incriminate himself); ABA Defense Function Standard § 4–4.3(b)(1980 ed.)("not necessary" for lawyer to caution interviewed witness of self-incrimination or right to counsel protections); Gold, Split Loyalty: An Ethical Problem for the Criminal Defense Lawyer, 14 Cleve.-Mar.L.Rev. 65, 72 (1966).

persuade the jury not to believe the witness.[15] Justice White's description of the role of defense counsel has often been quoted:

> If [defense counsel] can confuse a witness, even a truthful one, or make him appear at a disadvantage, unsure or indecisive, that will be his normal course. Our interest in not convicting the innocent permits counsel to put the State to its proof, to put the State's case in the worst possible light, regardless of what he thinks or what he knows to be the truth. Undoubtedly there are some limits which defense counsel must observe but more often than not, defense counsel will cross-examine a prosecution witness, and impeach him if he can, even if he thinks the witness is telling the truth, just as he will attempt to destroy a witness he thinks is lying.[16]

The justifiability of a system of searching for "weaknesses" in a witness' testimony with no regard to its accuracy is most supportable, if supportable at all, in the context of the criminal justice system (§ 10.5.3). It seems extremely doubtful that it should be extended to civil cases and, it is entirely clear, should form no part of a prosecutor's arsenal [17] (see § 13.10.4).

WESTLAW REFERENCES

synopsis,digest(harass! embarass! disgrace* /10 witness**)

§ 12.4.6 Compensating Witnesses

Payments to Nonexpert Witnesses

Lawyers are generally prohibited from paying or offering to pay money or other rewards to witnesses in return for their testimony.[18] It is permissible, however, to pay reasonable amounts to witnesses to compensate for lost wages incurred in testifying, and for travel and similar expenses, and to pay a customary witness fee.[19] Prosecutors who make "protection programs" available to prosecution witnesses, who offer "street money" to informants in return for information leading to convictions, or who arrange to defer sentencing of a government witness until after he or she gives testimony against another defendant are doubtless engaged in enterprises that would be unlawful for nongovernment lawyers and that are troublesome because they plainly risk influencing testimony in return for rewards.[20]

15 A.Amsterdam, Trial Manual for the Defense of Criminal Cases § 370 at 2–327 (2d ed.1972); Bress, Professional Ethics in Criminal Trials: A View of Defense Counsel's Responsibility, 64 Mich.L.Rev. 1493, 1494 (1966)(on rationale that defense is entitled to put prosecution to its proof); Burger, Standards of Conduct for Prosecution and Defense Personnel: A Judge's Viewpoint, 5 Am.Crim.L.Q. 11, 14–15 (1966)(on rationale that this is merely to "test the truth of the prosecution's case"); M.Freedman, Lawyers' Ethics in an Adversary System 79–80 (1975). Compare ABA Defense Function Standards § 7.6(b) at 272–73 (1974)(semble)(truthful, respectable witness should not be subjected to embarrassing cross-examination), with id. 4–7.6(b)(1980 ed.)(lawyer's knowledge that witness is telling truth does not preclude cross-examination but should "if possible" be taken into account).

16 United States v. Wade, 388 U.S. 218, 257–58, 87 S.Ct. 1926, 1947–48, 18 L.Ed.2d 1149 (1967)(White, J., dissenting and concurring in part). Justice White was hardly praising such a system; his recitation of the ordinary workings of the defense lawyer was prelude to an argument that such a system should not be extended to pretrial lineups because the presence of counsel would do nothing to increase their reliability.

17 ABA Prosecution Standards § 3–5.7 (1980 ed.)("A prosecutor should not use the power of cross-examination to discredit or undermine a witness if the prosecutor knows the witness is testifying truthfully.").

18 DR 7–109(C)(lawyer may not offer "payment of compensation to a witness contingent upon the content of his testimony"); Calif.R. 7–107(C)(same); cf. MR 3.4(b)(lawyer shall not "offer an inducement to a witness that is prohibited by law"). E.g., In re Howard, 69 Ill.2d 343, 14 Ill.Dec. 360, 372 N.E.2d 371 (1977)(lawyer suspended for twice paying arresting officer, assertedly to testify truthfully); Committee on Professional Ethics v. Halleck, 325 N.W.2d 117 (Iowa 1982)(offering restitution in return for favorable testimony by potential witness against client on theft charge); In re Dondi, 95 A.D.2d 349, 466 N.Y.S.2d 708 (1983)(suspension of lawyer for paying police officer to influence his testimony in civil action), reversed 63 N.Y.2d 331, 482 N.Y.S.2d 431, 472 N.E.2d 281 (1984).

19 DR 7–109(C)(1), (2); EC 7–28; MR 3.4, comment (third paragraph); Calif.R. 7–107(C)(1), (2).

20 Cf., e.g., United States v. Ricco, 549 F.2d 264 (2d Cir. 1977), cert.denied 431 U.S. 905, 97 S.Ct. 1697, 52 L.Ed.2d 389 (1977)(federal "witness protection program"); United States v. Gray, 626 F.2d 494 (5th Cir.1980), cert.denied 449 U.S. 1091, 101 S.Ct. 887, 66 L.Ed.2d 820 (1981)(payments of $37,000 and $25,000 in informant fees made informant's testimony suspect but not inadmissible). For criticism of deferred sentencing, see M.Freedman, Lawyers' Ethics in an Adversary System 89–90 (1975).

Compensating Expert Witnesses

The situation of expert witnesses is different in one respect—a lawyer may pay an expert a fee for testifying whose amount is in effect an inducement to testify. The amount of the payment must be "reasonable" but need not reflect the expert's lost wages or similar expenses.[21] The rules provide, however, that a payment to an expert—or to any witness [22]—may not be contingent on the outcome of the case because of the improper inducement this might pose to an expert to testify falsely in order to earn a higher fee or any fee at all.[23] Impermissible contingent arrangements would include bonuses, payments to be made only out of a reward, and the like.[24]

Arguments have been made that the same necessity that justifies the contingent fee for lawyers also warrants a contingent fee for expert witnesses. But the special need to assure the reasonable accuracy of a witness' testimony and the greater difficulty for a juror to determine the falsity of perjured expert testimony justifies the prohibition.[25] Nonetheless, an air of unreality overhangs the prohibition in many instances because the rules specifically provide that a lawyer may "advance" or "guarantee" the payment of a witness fee.[26] Particularly when the lawyer represents an impecunious client, the economic reality of the situation strongly suggests that the client will not pay either the lawyer who has advanced fees to an expert or an expert whose compensation, although fixed, is to be paid at the conclusion of the litigation.[27] Alternatively, it might be permissible for the expert to be promised a contingent fee for consultation services with only a small fee for actual testimony fixed.[28]

The tarnished ideal of expert testimony is testimony based entirely on the witness' honest scientific data and opinion.[29] In truth, however, many expert witnesses are as much hired-gun advocates as are the lawyers for whom they work. Lawyers are expected to seek out experts whose testimony will favor their side, secure in the knowledge that their opponents will probably find an opposing expert view.[30] The relationship is not entirely mercantile and proprietary, however, as is reflected, for example, in the general view that it is permissible for an advocate to con-

[21] DR 7–109(C)(3); MR 3.4, comment (third paragraph); Calif.R. 7–107(C)(3). Like legal fees (see § 16.6.1), expert witness fees are not generally recoverable as costs of suit. See authorities collected in Quy v. Air America, Inc., 667 F.2d 1059 (D.C.Cir.1981).

[22] Cf. Aetna Cas. & Sur. Co. v. Broadway Arms Corp., 281 Ark. 128, 664 S.W.2d 463 (1984)(issue whether lawyer on contingent fee may appear as witness in same case).

[23] DR 7–109(C); MR 3.4, comment (third paragraph); Calif.R. 7–107(C). The statement in the Model Rule comment that the "common law" of "most jurisdictions" prohibits contingent expert witness fees is curiously tentative in view of explicit prohibition of the practice in the lawyer codes. The common law, to be sure, also enforces the prohibition. E.g., Restatement of Contracts § 552(2) (1932); Belfonte v. Miller, 212 Pa.Super. 508, 243 A.2d 150 (1968)(contingent expert witness fee agreement is void).

[24] But cf. Pappalardo v. Parklane Hosiery Co., 67 A.D.2d 526, 415 N.Y.S.2d 878 (1979), appeal dismissed 48 N.Y.2d 634, 421 N.Y.S.2d 196, 396 N.E.2d 479 (1979) (permissible to agree with expert witnesses that they would look for their compensation only to a court award in the event that representation was successful).

[25] Person v. Association of the Bar of the City of New York, 554 F.2d 534 (2d Cir.1977), reversing 414 F.Supp. 144 (E.D.N.Y.1976), cert.denied 434 U.S. 934, 98 S.Ct. 403, 54 L.Ed.2d 282 (1977). The holding of the district court in *Person* that DR 7–109(C) lacked sufficient rational basis to withstand constitutional attack under a right-of-access argument was widely approved by student commentators. E.g., 81 Dick.L.Rev. 655 (1978); 52 Ind.L.J. 671 (1977); 55 N.C.L.Rev. 709 (1978); 39 U.Pitt.L.Rev. 511 (1978); 80 W.Va.L.Rev. 328 (1978); 1977 Wis.L.Rev. 603; 86 Yale L.J. 1680 (1977). For a defense of the conventional rationale, see, e.g., In re Schapiro, 144 App.Div. 1, 128 N.Y.S. 852 (1911).

[26] DR 7–109(C); Calif.R. 7–107(C). See generally § 9.2.3 (advancing funds to clients).

[27] Seigal v. Merrick, 619 F.2d 160, 166–67 (2d Cir.1980) (Friendly, J.).

[28] Schackow v. Medical-Legal Consulting Service, Inc., 46 Md.App. 179, 416 A.2d 1303, 15 A.L.R.4th 1239 (Spec. App.1980); ABA Informal Op. 1375 (1976).

[29] Wessel, Institutional Responsibility: Professionalism and Ethics, 60 Neb.L.Rev. 504, 516 (1981).

[30] In re Goldman, 179 Mont. 526, 588 P.2d 964, 979 (1978). But cf. State v. Wahlberg, 296 N.W.2d 408 (Minn. 1980)(improper for prosecutor to argue to jury that defendant's psychiatrists were paid to give favorable diagnosis).

tact without consent an expert witness retained by an adversary.[31]

WESTLAW REFERENCES

synopsis,digest(expert /4 witness /s compensat*** expense fee /s reasonable contingen**)

§ 12.5 ADVOCATES AND PERJURY [32]

§ 12.5.1 The Problem of Perjury

Possible Divergence between Client and Social Interest

A lawyer faced with perjurious testimony by a client or friendly witness confronts the choice between client interest and social interest in a most poignant form. One instinct might be to remain silent in order to protect the interests of the lawyer's client in the litigation. Possibly the lawyer's silence would also protect the client against disclosure as the source of the lawyer's knowledge or even as a perjurer.[33] A powerfully conflicting instinct will be to resist the perjury because it is false and in order to preserve the truth-finding function of the trial and thereby the workability and validity of the law itself.[34]

The perjury problem has troubled lawyers for a long time [35] and has occasioned considerable scholarly interest.[36] Despite the centrality and difficulty of the perjury problem, the professional regulations spoke in barely detectable whispers about it until the adoption of the 1983 Model Rules, which took a strong position against a lawyer's participation, even if unwillingly, in the presentation of perjury. The Model Rules comport with the great weight of decided cases but conflict with some recent lower court decisions on constitutional issues in criminal cases. The Model Rules also rejected a prior ABA "compromise" solution that has attracted some judicial attention.

The Extent of Perjury

The extent to which trials in the United States are infected with perjury is, by the nature of the problem, unknown and probably unknowable in any systematic way. Anecdotal evidence is mixed.[37] Even for a witness disposed to attempt it, perjury is not a risk-

31 1908 Canon 39 ("a lawyer may properly interview any witness or prospective witness for the opposing side in any civil or criminal action without the consent of opposing counsel or party."); ABA Formal Op. 14 (1929). But see Miles v. Farrell, 549 F.Supp. 82, 84–85 (N.D.Ill. 1982). See generally § 11.6.2.

32 For extended treatment by the author, see Wolfram, Client Perjury, 50 So.Cal.L.Rev. 809 (1977); Wolfram, Client Perjury, the Kutak Commission and the Association of Trial Lawyers on Lawyers, Lying Clients, and the Adversary System, 1980 Am.B.Found. Research J. 964.

33 Participation in perjury may be defended on other utilitarian grounds, such as gathering proof against corruption. E.g., In re Friedman, 76 Ill.2d 392, 30 Ill.Dec. 288, 392 N.E.2d 1333 (1979)(state's attorney who instructed police officer to testify falsely in order to gather evidence against lawyer who had offered to bribe officer violated Code, regardless of intent to arrest corrupt lawyer; fatal error was in not obtaining prior consent of judge).

34 Robert Bolt in A Man for All Seasons (Vintage ed. 1962, at xi-xiv) refers to Oliver Cromwell's "contemptuous shattering of the forms of the law by an unconcealed act of perjury [which] showed how fragile for any individual is that shelter" beneath the forms of the law.

35 G.Sharswood, An Essay on Professional Ethics 46–50 (2d ed.1860)(lectures originally given in 1854); G.Warvelle, Essays in Legal Ethics 103–106, 109–110 (1902). See generally D.Mellinkoff, The Conscience of a Lawyer 134–40 (1973).

36 Brazil, Unanticipated Client Perjury and the Collision of Rules of Ethics, Evidence, and Constitutional Law, 44 Mo.L.Rev. 601 (1979); Curtis, The Ethics of Advocacy, 4 Stan.L.Rev. 3 (1951); Drinker, Some Remarks on Mr. Curtis' "The Ethics of Advocacy," 4 Stan.L.Rev. 349 (1952); Frankel, The Search for Truth: An Umpireal View, 123 U.Pa.L.Rev. 1031 (1975); Freedman, Professional Responsibility of the Criminal Defense Lawyer: The Three Hardest Questions, 64 Mich.L.Rev. 1469 (1966); M.Freedman, Lawyers' Ethics in an Adversary System (1975); Lawry, Lying, Confidentiality, and the Adversary System of Justice, 1977 Utah L.Rev. 653; Lefstein, The Criminal Defendant Who Proposes Perjury: Rethinking the Defense Lawyer's Dilemma, 6 Hofstra L.Rev. 665 (1978); Noonan, The Purpose of Advocacy and the Limits of Confidentiality, 64 Mich.L.Rev. 1485 (1966); Polster, The Dilemma of the Perjurious Defendant: Resolution, Not Avoidance, 28 Case West.Res.L.Rev. 3 (1977); Pye, The Role of Counsel in the Suppression of Truth, 1978 Duke L.J. 921; Uviller, The Advocate, the Truth, and Judicial Hackles: A Reaction to Judge Frankel's Idea, 123 U.Pa.L.Rev. 1067 (1975).

37 For the view that perjury is pervasive in trials and rarely results in the imposition of criminal sanctions, see, e.g., U.S. President's Commission on Law Enforcement and Administration of Criminal Justice, The Challenge of Crime in a Free Society 141 (1967); Arkin & Bogatin,

less enterprise. It will usually be detected by an adversary and, to the extent that this is effective, can be probed by cross-examination [38] and by impeachment evidence. Theoretically, perjury can result in a criminal prosecution, although the charge is very rarely brought.[39] Revealed perjury may humiliate the perjurer and result in the grant of a new trial.[40] An adverse party can argue to a jury that if it detects perjury, it should take this into account in judging the credibility of all other testimony offered by the perjurious party.[41] A judge, in imposing sentence, may explicitly rely on a convicted defendant's perjury in trial testimony.[42] And a doctrine akin to collateral estoppel precludes a litigant from taking a testimonial position in later litigation that would render perjurious any testimony given by that person in a prior proceeding.[43]

Disincentives against Lawyer Use of Perjury

Most lawyers are probably deterred by several factors from resorting to perjury to aid a client's cause.[44] Most prominent for many lawyers will be a personal sense of principle or honor. Others will be deterred at least by a fear of outraging peers or community.[45] Pragmatically, many lawyers probably believe that perjury is readily detected by the fact finder and is thus tactically unsound. Even if a jury could be hoodwinked, a judge might detect the falsity and order a new trial or treat the lawyer harshly as a sharp and unworthy practitioner.[46] In an extreme case the lawyer may be prosecuted for suborning perjury.[47]

Perjury in Civil Litigation—The Unpunished Crime, New York L.J., May 25, 1984, p. 1, col. 3; Fair & Moskowitz, The Lawyer's Role: Watergate as Regularity Rather than Aberration, 2 J.Contemp.L. 75, 79 (1975); McClintock, What Happens to Perjurers, 24 Minn.L.Rev. 727 (1940); Comment, Perjury: The Forgotten Offense, 65 J.Crim.L. & Criminology 361 (1974).

38 Bronston v. United States, 409 U.S. 352, 358–59, 93 S.Ct. 595, 599–600, 34 L.Ed.2d 568 (1973); 5 J.Wigmore, Evidence § 1367, at 32 (J.Chadbourne rev.1974)(cross-examination is "beyond any doubt the greatest legal engine ever invented for the discovery of truth"); L.Nizer, My Life in Court 327 (1961)("If an opponent permits his client to lie, . . . if I am prepared and persistent, such a witness cannot survive"). For a contrasting view, see, e.g., McCormick, The Scope and Art of Cross-Examination, 47 Nw.U.L.Rev. 177, 196 (1952).

39 Comment, Perjury: The Forgotten Offense, 65 J.Crim.L. & Criminology 361 (1974).

40 The adoption of Fed.R.Civ.P. Rule 60(b)(3) in 1938 changed the rule of United States v. Throckmorton, 98 U.S. (8 Otto) 61, 25 L.Ed. 93 (1878), that a judgment could not successfully be attacked on the ground that it was obtained by the use of perjured testimony. See generally 11 C.Wright & A.Miller, Federal Practice & Procedure § 2861, at 194–96 (1973). Most states now follow a similar rule. See generally Annot., 38 A.L.R.3d 812 (1971).

41 See generally 3A J.Wigmore, Evidence § 1010, at 983 (J. Chadbourne rev.1970).

42 United States v. Grayson, 438 U.S. 41, 98 S.Ct. 2610, 57 L.Ed.2d 582 (1978).

43 Evans v. United States, 408 F.2d 369 (7th Cir.1969); Crawford v. United States, 519 F.2d 347, 350 (4th Cir. 1975), cert.denied 423 U.S. 1057, 96 S.Ct. 791, 46 L.Ed.2d 647 (1976). And see Myers v. Butler, 556 F.2d 398 (8th Cir.1977), cert. denied 434 U.S. 956, 98 S.Ct. 483, 54 L.Ed. 2d 314 (1977)(lawyer-accused who testified at guilty plea hearing that he had received no promises with respect to term of imprisonment was precluded later from suing his defense lawyer for breach of now alleged warranty that accused would not go to jail).

44 Troubling indications exist, however, that at least in some legal communities, lawyers are not unwilling to participate in perjury and even to suborn it. See Berentson, Integrity Test: Five of Thirteen Lawyers Fail, American Lawyer (May 1980), at 15.

45 See generally S.Bok, Lying: Moral Choice in Public and Private Life (1978).

46 An interesting, and controversial, application of this reaction is State v. Miller, 128 Ariz. 112, 624 P.2d 309 (Ct. App.1981). The court held that it was proper to admit as rebuttal evidence, in a perjury prosecution against a lawyer for false testimony in a civil proceeding, the testimony of the judge who had presided in the civil case. The judge testified that his opinion of the defendant's untruthfulness was based on his duties as fact finder in the civil case.

47 United States v. Root, 366 F.2d 377 (9th Cir.1966), cert.denied 386 U.S. 912, 86 S.Ct. 861, 17 L.Ed.2d 784 (1966); In re Allen, 52 Cal.2d 762, 344 P.2d 609 (1959); Burns v. Clayton, 237 S.C. 316, 117 S.E.2d 300 (1960). Normally, however, no damage action is available to a party injured through the perjury of a witness in a judicial proceeding because of a doctrine of absolute immunity. See generally Briscoe v. Lahue, 460 U.S. 325, 103 S.Ct. 1108, 75 L.Ed.2d 96 (1983). A client who commits perjury on a lawyer's advice and suffers damage as a result is not entitled to recover damages against the lawyer because of the doctrine of in pari delicto. E.g., Feld & Sons, Inc. v. Pechner, Dorfman, Wolffe, Rounick & Cabot, 312 Pa.Super. 125, 458 A.2d 545 (1983), appeal dismissed 504 Pa. 177, 470 A.2d 525 (1984). But any fees paid to the lawyer for the representation are recoverable in order to prevent the lawyer from acquiring gain from a

Professional discipline has usually been visited on a lawyer for participation in perjured testimony after the lawyer's conviction of the crime of perjury or subornation.[48] Those hard-core perjury cases form at least a starting point, for they illuminate the rule that a lawyer confronted with perjury must remonstrate with the perjurer—attempt to persuade the perjurious witness, even if a client in a criminal case, to testify truthfully. The chief area of controversy lies beyond this and concerns perjury that a client or friendly witness insists upon against the lawyer's advice and in which, therefore, the lawyer will, if anything, be an unwilling participant.

WESTLAW REFERENCES

Possible Divergence Between Client & Social Interest

synopsis,digest(attorney counsel** lawyer advocate /s kn*w! inten! belie** possib! /25 perjur!)

Disincentive Against Lawyer Use of Perjury

dr7–102(a)(4) (d.r. "disciplinary rule" /5 7–102(a)(4)) (e.c. ethical consideration /5 7–26) "defense function 4–5.2(b)"

§ 12.5.2 What Lawyers Know

Before inquiring into a lawyer's duty when confronted with perjury, it is well to attempt to define those circumstances that trigger an obligation on the part of a lawyer to react to perjury. Are reasonable suspicions sufficient, or, at the other extreme, is the standard that of knowledge beyond doubt?

Both of the ABA lawyer codes require certain knowledge.[49] The 1969 Code, in DR 7–102(A)(4), states that a lawyer shall not "knowingly" use perjury.[50] The 1983 Model Rules contain a similar standard, and a similar rule, in Rule 3.3(a)(4).[51] The terminology section of the Rules states that such a level of knowledge "denotes actual knowledge of the fact in question. A person's knowledge may be inferred from circumstances." The latter sentiment makes it clear that a lawyer's denial of knowledge is not conclusive on the question. And, as in the criminal law, a lawyer's conscious avoidance of knowledge of the falsity of evidence should not prevent a finding of actual knowledge.[52] For instances in which a lawyer's knowledge of the falsity of evidence does not rise to this level, Model Rule 3.3(c) states that a lawyer has professional discretion, but not a duty, to refuse to offer evidence that the lawyer "reasonably believes"

wrongful representation. See Berman v. Coakley, 243 Mass. 348, 137 N.E. 667 (1923); Feld & Sons, Inc., supra.

48 In re Kristovich, 18 Cal.3d 468, 134 Cal.Rptr. 409, 556 P.2d 771 (1976)(discipline after conviction for lawyer's own perjury); In re Allen, 52 Cal.2d 762, 344 P.2d 609 (1959)(discipline after conviction of subornation conspiracy); People ex rel. Attorney General v. Beattie, 137 Ill. 553, 27 N.E. 1096 (1891); Attorney Grievance Commission v. Green, 278 Md. 412, 365 A.2d 39 (1976); In re Stroh, 97 Wn.2d 289, 644 P.2d 1161 (1982), cert.denied 459 U.S. 1202, 103 S.Ct. 1187, 75 L.Ed.2d 434 (1983).

Instances of discipline for suborning perjury not preceded by a conviction do, however, occur. E.g., Garlow v. State Bar, 30 Cal.3d 912, 180 Cal.Rptr. 831, 640 P.2d 1106 (1982); North Carolina State Bar v. DuMont, 52 N.C.App. 1, 277 S.E.2d 827 (1981), affirmed in relevant part 304 N.C. 627, 286 S.E.2d 89 (1982)(suborning false deposition testimony by defendant's lawyer in medical malpractice case).

49 The California rule most nearly in point, Rule 7–105(1), states that "in presenting a matter to a tribunal" a lawyer shall "employ, for the purpose of maintaining the causes confided to him such means only as are consistent with truth, and shall not seek to mislead the judge, judicial officer or jury by an artifice or false statement of fact or law." The language of the rule leaves open many questions, including that of the knowledge standard.

50 See generally People v. Schultheis, 638 P.2d 8, 11 (Colo.1981). A lawyer cannot elude responsibility for known future perjury by procuring an uninformed lawyer to make the court appearance during which the first lawyer's client will testify falsely. See Medoff v. State Bar, 71 Cal.2d 535, 78 Cal.Rptr. 696, 455 P.2d 800 (1969).

EC 7–26 confusingly seems to allude to a standard different from that of DR 7–102(A)(4) when it states that a lawyer should not use false evidence when the lawyer "knows, or from facts within his knowledge, should know, that such testimony or evidence is false, fraudulent, or perjured." Perhaps the reference in EC 7–26 is to instances in which a lawyer consciously avoids knowledge of the falsity of testimony. Cf. n. 52 infra.

51 A lawyer shall not "knowingly" offer evidence that the lawyer "knows" to be false.

52 United States v. Hanlon, 548 F.2d 1096 (2d Cir.1977) ("conscious avoidance" doctrine sustains conviction of making false statements).

to be false.[53] If the lawyer's disquietude about a client's intended testimony is the result of mere conjecture or an unsubstantiated opinion, however, the lawyer should present the testimony.[54] Importantly, even if the lawyer's suspicion permits formation of a reasonable belief that the evidence is false—and thus permits its nonintroduction under Rule 3.3(c)—this does not entitle, or require, the lawyer to make disclosure or take other remedial action under Rule 3.3(a)(4), because the lawyer does not "know" the evidence to be false. Disclosure of false evidence that results in revelation of confidential client information in these circumstances would violate Rule 1.6(a), just as it would violate DR 4-101(B).[55]

WESTLAW REFERENCES

dr7-102(a)(4) (d.r. "disciplinary rule" /5 7-102(a)(4)) (e.c. ethical consideration /5 7-26) "defense function 4-5.2(b)"

§ 12.5.3 Dealing with False Testimony

Variability of Requirements

What, specifically, must a lawyer do when unwillingly confronted with testimony that is favorable to a client's position but that the lawyer knows to be false? The answer depends largely upon the context and in some particulars varies with the jurisdiction. It is rather clearly settled law that civil cases are governed by strict rules prohibiting lawyer participation in perjury and requiring lawyer correction, including disclosure, if necessary, of surprise perjury or perjury discovered after the fact. The responsibility of a criminal defense lawyer may be similar but at present is unsettled.

Perjury in Civil Cases

The duties of a lawyer confronted with a client or friendly witness intent on perjury can be analyzed in terms of remonstration, withdrawal, calling witnesses, eliciting testimony, arguing to the factfinder, and disclosure. A lawyer's obligations in these respects flow from the provisions of DR 7-102(A)(4) of the 1969 Code, providing that a lawyer shall not "knowingly use perjured testimony or false evidence," and from 1983 Model Rule 3.3(a)(4), which provides that: "a lawyer shall not knowingly . . . offer evidence that the lawyer knows to be false. If a lawyer has offered material evidence and comes to know of its falsity, the lawyer shall take reasonable remedial measures."

Remonstration is clearly required: a lawyer must attempt to persuade a client not to present or, if it is presented, to correct, false testimony.[56] Remonstration in most cases should cover the fact that perjury is a criminal offense, the risks of its detection, the importance of truthful testimony, the lawyer's duty to withdraw,[57] and the extent of the lawyer's duty to disclose perjury. Cases very broadly agree that a lawyer whose client

53 The Model Rules' terminology section merely states that this denotes that the lawyer believes the matter in question and that the belief is reasonable in the circumstances. Other terminological entries define *believes* and *reasonably*, the latter specifically denoting "the conduct of a reasonably prudent and competent lawyer." For an arguable example of an unreasonable belief, see United States ex rel. Wilcox v. Johnson, 555 F.2d 115 (3d Cir. 1977)(ineffective assistance of counsel when defense lawyer reported his "mere unsubstantiated opinion" to judge that defendant would testify perjuriously about an alibi).

54 United States ex rel. Wilcox v. Johnson, 555 F.2d 115, 122 (3d Cir.1977).

55 State v. Regier, 228 Kan. 746, 621 P.2d 431 (1980) (revealing unconfirmed suspicions about client perjury to two district judges in order to have court investigate suspicions violates DR 4-101).

56 The Model Rules state the remonstration requirement three times. See MR 3.3, comment (False Evidence, Perjury by a Criminal Defendant, and Remedial Measures). The Code's remonstration requirement is inferable from DR 7-102(B)(1) (lawyer "shall promptly call upon his client to rectify" fraud). Note, however, that DR 7-102(B)(2), on nonclient fraud, does not contain similar language. Courts have uniformly applied a remonstration requirement in instances of client perjury. E.g., Committee on Professional Ethics v. Crary, 245 N.W.2d 298 (Iowa 1976); Attorney Grievance Comm'n v. Sperling, 296 Md. 558, 463 A.2d 868 (1983); In re Malloy, 248 N.W.2d 43 (N.D.1976); In re A, 276 Or. 225, 554 P.2d 479 (1976). See also, e.g., In re Robinson, 151 App.Div. 589, 136 N.Y.S. 548 (1912). On the extent of scholarly agreement and on the contents of a remonstration, see Wolfram, Client Perjury, 50 So.Cal.L.Rev. 809, 846-47 (1977).

57 See infra at n. 58.

nonetheless insists on presenting false testimony is required to *withdraw* from the representation, if necessary, to avoid engaging in the presentation of the testimony.[58] The rule is also clear with respect to a lawyer who *calls a witness* whose testimony the lawyer knows will be false. The lawyer controls access to the witness stand and may not call a witness if the lawyer knows that perjurious testimony will result.[59] In the instance of a witness who will testify truthfully to some questions but falsely to others, a lawyer may not *put a question* to a witness knowing that the witness will respond with false testimony. That follows from the obligation not to call a perjurious witness to the stand.[60] It also operates independently in the case of surprise perjury—when a friendly witness or client surprises a lawyer by beginning to testify falsely on the witness stand. By similar extension, a lawyer may not argue in *summation* that the fact finder should accept, as credible, evidence that the lawyer knows is false.

If a lawyer complies with those rules, and the client refuses to correct perjury already given, is the lawyer under a duty of *disclosure?* The answer is the only significant area of disagreement among the decisions with respect to perjury in civil cases. Canon 29 of the 1908 Canons of Ethics stated that a lawyer in a trial "in which perjury has been committed" should report the matter to a prosecutor.[61] But the ABA ethics committee, in Formal Opinion 287 (1953), held that, despite the disclosure canons, a lawyer should not reveal a client's perjury in a divorce case because the lawyer's disclosure would violate a client confidence. The enactment of the prohibition against perjury in DR 7–102(A)(4) and the requirement to disclose a client's fraud in DR 7–102(B)(1) of the 1969 Code possibly override Formal Opinion 287.[62] Several states indeed have required that a lawyer disclose perjury, even if that of a client and even if the lawyer obtained information about the perjury as the result of a client communication.[63] Decisions in other jurisdictions disagree and refuse to impose a disclosure obligation.[64]

58 In re A, 276 Or. 225, 554 P.2d 479 (1976); In re Malloy, 248 N.W.2d 43 (N.D.1976). Little authority exists on whether a lawyer bears any further obligation after withdrawal. For example, if a lawyer knows that a client who intends to commit perjury has obtained the assistance of a second lawyer, may or must the first lawyer reveal the client's perjurious intentions to the second lawyer? Compare, e.g., ABA Formal Opinion 268 (1945)(duty not to reveal client's intended perjury to second lawyer in these circumstances), with, e.g., Law Society, A Guide to the Professional Conduct of Solicitors § 9.3(3), at 51 (1974)(first solicitor ought to reveal to second his knowledge that client requested suppression of evidence).

59 In re Zanger, 266 N.Y. 165, 172, 174, 194 N.E. 72, 74–75 (1935); In re Schapiro, 144 App.Div. 1, 128 N.Y.S. 852, 858 (1911).

60 DR 7–102(A)(4)("use" false evidence); MR 3.3(a)(4) ("offer" false evidence).

61 Canon 41 required a lawyer to report to "the injured person or his counsel" the fraud or deception of the lawyer's own client.

62 The obscurity of the 1969 Code on client perjury problems has been a frequent subject of complaint. See, e.g., Hazard, The Legal and Ethical Position of the Code of Professional Ethics, in 5 Social Responsibility: Journalism, Law, Medicine 5, 9 (L.Hodges ed.1979):

"The world will not go to hell if lawyers were permitted in criminal cases to put clients on the stand who, to the lawyer's knowledge, have every intention of committing perjury. The world will not go to hell—and certainly it will not become heaven—if lawyers are prohibited from doing that. What does seem insupportable, however, is that there be no established rule on such a question."

63 Committee on Professional Ethics v. Crary, 245 N.W.2d 298 (Iowa 1976). See also, e.g., In re Hoover, 46 Ariz. 24, 46 P.2d 647 (1935); Hinds v. State Bar, 19 Cal.2d 87, 119 P.2d 134 (1941); Florida Bar v. Agar, 394 So.2d 405 (Fla.1980); In re Nadler, 91 Ill.2d 326, 63 Ill.Dec. 460, 438 N.E.2d 198 (1982); State v. Hoover, 223 Kan. 385, 574 P.2d 1377, 1381 (1978); In re Carroll, 244 S.W.2d 474 (Ky. 1951); In re Mendelsohn, 150 App.Div. 445, 135 N.Y.S. 438 (1912); In re King, 7 Utah 2d 258, 322 P.2d 1095 (1958). For statements of a disclosure obligation in criminal cases, see infra n. 80. The Iowa rule resulting from the *Crary* decision, supra, has been narrowed by an amendment to the Iowa Code of Professional Responsibility. Iowa DR 7–102(B)(1) now provides that if disclosure is prevented by the attorney-client privilege, the lawyer must "immediately withdraw from representation of the client unless the client fully discloses the fraud to the person or tribunal." See Iowa Code Ann. § 622.10.

64 In re Malloy, 248 N.W.2d 43, 45–46 (N.D.1976); In re A, 276 Or. 225, 554 P.2d 479, 486 (1976); cf. In re Hardenbrook, 135 App.Div. 634, 643, 121 N.Y.S. 250 (1909), affirmed per curiam 199 N.Y. 539, 92 N.E. 1086 (1910)(dictum)(arguendo assumption that professional ob-

Disclosure of Perjury under the 1969 Code

In 1974 the ABA amended DR 7–102(B)(1) by adding an exception, not adopted in most states, that prohibits disclosure of a client's fraud if the lawyer knows of the fraud through a "privileged communication." The ABA ethics committee, in Formal Opinion 341 (1975), interpreted "privileged communication" to include both a confidence (matters covered by the testimonial attorney-client privilege) and a secret (matters beyond the privilege, protected by DR 4–101(A)). Although the concept of fraud in DR 7–102(B)(1) is clearly broad enough to include perjury, it is not certain that a lawyer is always precluded by Opinion 341 from disclosing a client's intention to commit perjury. While it has been maintained that Opinion 341 prohibits disclosure of client perjury in almost all instances,[65] an astute observer has pointed out that the force of DR 4–101(C)(3), exempting from the scope of a privileged communication "the intention of his client to commit a crime and the information necessary to prevent it," is sufficient to leave information about future perjury within the duty to disclose that is posited by the amended version of DR 7–102(B)(1).[66] In any event, no similar amendment was made to DR 7–102(B)(2) which requires disclosure when "a person other than [the lawyer's] client has perpetrated a fraud upon a tribunal." Apparently, therefore, despite the 1974 amendment, disclosure continues to be required in all states that have adopted DR 7–102(B)(2) for perjury by nonclient friendly witnesses.

Disclosure of Perjury under the 1983 Model Rules

The meandering and unsteady course of regulation by the ABA took another turn with the adoption of the 1983 Model Rules—this time in the form of a strict, and clearly stated, disclosure requirement.[67] Rule 3.3(a)(4) requires that "if a lawyer has offered material evidence and comes to know of its falsity, the lawyer shall take reasonable remedial measures." [68] The Comment states that "if necessary to rectify the situation, an advocate must disclose the existence of the client's deception to the court or to the other party." [69] The comment recognizes, as it must, that "such a disclosure can result in grave consequences to the [lawyer's] client, including not only a sense of betrayal but also loss of the case and perhaps a prosecution for perjury. But the alternative is that the lawyer cooperate in deceiving the court, thereby subverting the truth-finding process which

ligation to client would preclude lawyer from revealing client perjury to court).

65 Wolfram, Client Perjury, 50 So.Cal.L.Rev. 809, 837 n. 106 (1977).

66 Rotunda, When the Client Lies: Unhelpful Guides from the ABA, 1 Corp.L.Rev. 34, 39 (1978). See also, e.g., People v. Salquerro, 107 Misc.2d 155, 433 N.Y.S.2d 711, 713 (Cty.Ct.1980); Burger, Counsel for The Prosecution and Defense—Their Roles under the Minimum Standards, 8 Am.Crim.L.Q. 2, 7 (1969). The holding in State v. Hinojos, 95 N.M. 659, 625 P.2d 588, 589 (Ct.App.1980), that a client's admission to his lawyer of an intent to suborn perjury in another proceeding is not excepted from the attorney-client privilege seems unfounded. Professor Rotunda's analysis, however, creates the arguably anomalous result that DR 7–102(B)(1) as amended in 1974 requires disclosure only of perjury known in advance and not of surprise perjury or of perjury already committed, on the reasoning that the lawyer in these cases did not know in advance of the client's intent to commit a crime.

67 For general reviews of the Model Rules proposals on perjury, see Hodes, The Code of Professional Responsibility, the Kutak Rules, and the Trial Lawyer's Code: Surprisingly, Three Peas in a Pod, 35 U.Miami L.Rev. 739 (1981); Wolfram, Client Perjury: The Kutak Commission and the Association of Trial Lawyers on Lawyers, Lying Clients, and the Adversary System, 1980 Am.B.Found. Research J. 964.

68 The perjury-disclosure rule of MR 3.3(a)(4) stands in contrast to the antidisclosure position of MR 1.6 with respect to nonlitigation client fraud. See § 12.6.4. Both matters were intensely debated and passed by divided votes during the February 1983 meeting of the ABA. It is difficult to distinguish between the situations in any principled way.

69 MR 3.3, comment (False Evidence; third paragraph). A following comment (MR 3.3, comment (Remedial Measures))—dealing apparently only with client perjury in a criminal case—states that disclosure should be made to "the court," which is then to decide what further remedial steps, if any, are to be taken. In civil cases the lawyer has the choice of making disclosure either to the court or to the opposing party.

the adversary system is designed to implement."

In the stark choice of values between the interests of a perjurious client and those of the adversarial system, the Model Rules take the conservative course of preserving the values of the system in the search for truth and avoiding a rule that would "in effect coerce the lawyer into being a party to fraud on the court." [70] They do so, moreover, without leaving any discretion to the lawyer: depending on the circumstances, either the lawyer is required to take remedial measures, including disclosure, to correct the perjury (MR 3.3(a)(4)) or the lawyer is required not to reveal confidential client information (MR 1.6(a)). A similarly nondiscretionary path was indicated in the 1969 Code prior to the 1974 amendment to DR 7–102(B)(1).

Several important features of the Model Rule require emphasis. First, disclosure is plainly required even if the perjury is that of the lawyer's own client and even if the lawyer knows of the client's perjury because of what otherwise would be a confidential communication.[71]

Second, under MR 3.3(a)(4) the lawyer's duty apparently exists only when "the lawyer has offered" false evidence. That language raises several points. Apparently there is no remedial duty for a lawyer who is not functioning as trial counsel or not functioning as trial counsel at the time of the false testimony.[72] It appears that no disclosure obligation exists until false material evidence has actually been offered. A lawyer is under no requirement, specifically, to disclose a client's intention to commit perjury in the future, no matter how certain the lawyer may be that the intention will be carried out. In civil cases, of course, the lawyer would be required to keep the client off the witness stand. But in criminal cases, in which the accused controls access to the witness stand, a lawyer will be confronted with a client on the stand prepared, if asked, to commit perjury. In short, prior to the commission of perjury the lawyer's lips are sealed; as soon as perjury is committed, the lawyer must take remedial steps. There is also no limitation of the disclosure rule to instances in which, in presumed violation of MR 3.3(a)(4), the lawyer knew of the falsity of the testimony when it was given. Later discovery of false testimony triggers the obligation to remedy the perjury.

Finally, it is not entirely clear whether the lawyer's duties under MR 3.3(a)(4) extend to all witness' testimony, whether elicited by the lawyer or by other advocates. The "offer evidence" language is susceptible of being limited to testimony (or documents and the like) elicited only by the lawyer. But in view of the broad rationale of the rule—to ensure truthful testimony and to implement lawyers' duty of candor to the courts [73]—it should be read to extend as well to situations in which most perjurious testimony is probably given, such as in response to cross-examination of the lawyer's own client by an opposing lawyer.

Third, the MR 3.3(a)(4) obligation is to "take reasonable remedial measures" and then only with respect to false evidence that is "material." That obligation arguably is narrower than that stated in DR 7–102(B)(1), which explicitly mandates disclosure and extends to any "fraud." Thus a plaintiff's lawyer who discovers after a verdict that his or her client has committed perjury in a case in which the defendant prevailed on all issues would have no duty under the Model Rules to disclose because there is nothing to remedy. Arguably, a duty exists in that instance under the Code. An interesting question under MR 3.3(a)(4) is whether a lawyer who suspects

[70] MR 3.3 comment (False Evidence; third paragraph).

[71] See, explicitly, MR 3.3(b)(disclosure duty applies "even if compliance requires disclosure of information otherwise protected by rule 1.6").

[72] But when a lawyer, although not actively asking the questions that result in client perjury, nonetheless is functioning as cocounsel at the trial or other hearing, the disclosure obligation should exist. The important point is that the lawyer knows of the perjury and is in a position to do something about it. Cf. Committee on Professional Ethics v. Crary, 245 N.W.2d 298 (Iowa 1976) (disclosure obligation under similar facts under Code).

[73] MR 3.3 comment (False Evidence; paragraph two).

that a verdict will go against his or her client despite, or perhaps because of, the client's perjury, can wait to take remedial measures until after learning the outcome of the verdict in order to determine if remedial measures are indeed necessary.

Fourth, MR 3.3(b) provides a time limitation. A lawyer's duty to disclose operates only with respect to client testimony that the lawyer learns is false before the "conclusion of the proceeding." [74] Although arguably ambiguous as a literal matter ("the duties stated . . . continue to the conclusion of the proceedings"), the clear meaning of MR 3.3(b) is that disclosure duties *arise* only during proceedings and not thereafter. It should not be read as if the disclosure duty only *exists* during the proceeding and is in some way extinguished thereafter if the lawyer defaults on the disclosure duty without detection before a decree is entered.

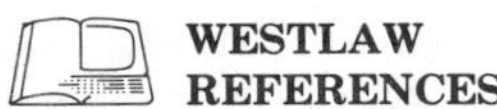
WESTLAW REFERENCES

Perjury in Civil Cases

45k32 45k42 & tribunal court /s fraud

Disclosure of Perjury Under the 1983 Model Rules

attorney lawyer counsel** /s perjur! /p betray** confidence privilege*

§ 12.5.4 Perjury by Persons Accused of Crime

Traditional Equivalence with Civil Cases

Until relatively recently, the general professional understanding was that the same obligations that operated in civil cases also controlled a defense lawyer in a criminal prosecution. (Prosecuting lawyers are under even more stringent obligations.[75]) Thus cases held that a defense lawyer was required to remonstrate [76] with a criminal defendant who had announced an intention to commit perjury and seek to withdraw [77] if the remonstration was unsuccessful; was required not to call a witness who would commit perjury or to elicit perjured testimony from a witness already on the stand even if the witness was the accused;[78] was not permitted to argue the believability of testimony known to be false;[79] and was required to disclose client or other perjury to the court.[80] A trial court has dis-

[74] MR 3.3, comment (Duration of Obligation): "A practical time limit on the obligation to rectify the presentation of false evidence has to be established. The conclusion of the proceeding is a reasonably definite point for the termination of the obligation." While this rationale, as stated, extends only to false testimony, the same time limit also operates with respect to other MR 3.3(a) disclosure obligations, such as that for adverse legal authority. See § 12.8 (disclosure of legal authority). Interestingly, because of the MR 3.3(b) time limitation, the Model Rules would also prohibit disclosure in the factual situation that was the basis for the ABA ethics committee's antidisclosure ruling in Formal Opinion 287 (1953). There the lawyer had learned of the client's perjury three months after entry of the decree.

[75] § 13.10.5 (prosecutor—disclosure obligations).

[76] Board of Overseers of the Bar v. Dineen, 1 BNA/ABA Lawyers' Manual on Professional Conduct 45 (Maine, Dec.29, 1982)(lawyer disbarred for failure to remonstrate with client-accused who intended to, and did, commit perjury in defense testimony); People v. Collier, 105 Mich.App. 46, 306 N.W.2d 387 (1981).

[77] In re Palmer, 296 N.C. 638, 252 S.E.2d 784 (1979). Courts will rarely permit criminal defense counsel to withdraw if trial is imminent and will do so only in extraordinarily rare situations during trial. See generally § 9.5.3. Generally, a defense lawyer should not reveal the specific reason for the motion to withdraw if doing so would infringe upon client confidential information. E.g., People v. Schultheis, 638 P.2d 8 (Colo.1981). For a proposal to create an Advisory Council of experienced trial lawyers who would hold closed hearings on motions to withdraw in such cases, see Erickson, The Perjurious Defendant: A Proposed Solution to the Defense Lawyer's Conflicting Ethical Obligations to the Court and to His Client, 59 Denv.L.J. 1 (1981).

[78] United States ex rel. Von der Hyde, 169 F.Supp. 560, 567 (D.D.C.1959)(dictum); State v. Whiteside, 272 N.W.2d 468 (Iowa 1978); Askew v. State, 617 S.W.2d 642 (Mo. App.1981); State v. Robinson, 290 N.C. 56, 224 S.E.2d 174, 179–80 (1976); American College of Trial Lawyers, Code of Trial Conduct rule 4(a)(rev.ed.1972). Barristers are bound by similar rules in criminal cases in England. See Shawcross, The Functions and Responsibilities of an Advocate, 13 Rec.A.B.C.N.Y. 483, 504 (1958).

[79] Commonwealth v. Alderman, 292 Pa.Super. 263, 437 A.2d 36, 40 (1981).

[80] United States ex rel. Wilcox v. Johnson, 555 F.2d 115, 122 n.13 (3d Cir.1977)(DR 4–101(C)(3) read to require disclosure); McKissick v. United States, 379 F.2d 754, 761–62 (5th Cir.1967); Thornton v. United States, 357 A.2d 429, 437–38 (D.C.), cert. denied 429 U.S.1024, 97 S.Ct. 644, 50 L.Ed.2d 626 (1976); State v. Henderson, 205 Kan. 231, 468 P.2d 136, 140 (1970); People v. Salquerro,

cretion to grant a defense lawyer's motion to withdraw and substitute new counsel after disclosure of a client's intended perjury but is not required to do so and is unlikely to grant the motion, because it would almost invariably require a new trial.[81] If an accused insists that defense counsel present perjured testimony through non-client third persons, the lawyer may not do so.[82]

Essentially those same antiperjury obligations are legislated by the Model Rules by virtue of the fact that Rule 3.3 applies regardless of the nature of the case.[83]

Inventive Procedures: The Defense Function Standards

Perjury by a person accused of crime, however, presents two special doctrinal complications. Unlike a litigant in a civil case, a criminal defendant is protected by the constitutional right to the effective assistance of counsel [84] and almost certainly is constitutionally entitled to take the witness stand and to give testimony regardless of defense counsel's advice or objections.[85] The Model Rules accept the right of the accused to testify as basic.[86] Because of considerations such as those, the ABA at one time took the position, in Defense Function Standard 7.7(c),[87] that a defense lawyer whose attempt to remonstrate and withdraw was unsuccessful should put the accused on the witness stand. But after eliciting bare identification of the client-witness, defense counsel could only invite the client to make a (perjurious) statement under "open narrative"—a rarely employed, and then often objected to, form of testimony in which the accused would make a factual statement without further guidance from defense counsel.[88] Thereafter, defense counsel was not to refer to perjurious testimony in

107 Misc.2d 155, 433 N.Y.S.2d 711, 713 (Cty.Ct.1980); State v. Robinson, 290 N.C. 56, 224 S.E.2d 174, 179–80 (1976). Contra, e.g., In re Goodwin, 279 S.C. 274, 305 S.E.2d 578 (1983).

81 Coleman v. State, 621 P.2d 869, 882 (Alaska 1980), cert.denied 454 U.S. 1090, 102 S.Ct. 653, 70 L.Ed.2d 628 (1981); State v. Henderson, 205 Kan. 231, 468 P.2d 136 (1970); People v. Salquerro, 107 Misc.2d 155, 433 N.Y.S.2d 711, 713–14 (Cty.Ct.1980); State v. Robinson, 290 N.C. 56, 224 S.E.2d 174 (1976); Carter v. Bordenkircher, 159 W.Va. 717, 226 S.E.2d 711 (1976). If the lawyer is not permitted to withdraw, he or she should participate fully in all aspects of the trial other than the presentation of perjurious testimony. See People v. Schultheis, 638 P.2d 8 (Colo.1981); cf. Coleman v. State, supra (notes, without approval, that trial judge required defense lawyer to continue with defense and to elicit suspected perjury as if it were credible).

82 The leading case is People v. Schultheis 638 P.2d 8 (Colo.1981). See also, e.g., State v. Tyus, 232 Kan. 325, 654 P.2d 947 (1982).

83 See generally MR 3.3 comment (Perjury by a Criminal Defendant); id. (Constitutional Requirements)("The general rule—that an advocate must disclose the existence of perjury with respect to a material fact, even that of a client—applies to defense counsel in criminal cases, as well as in other instances.").

84 See generally § 14.6.1.

85 Although the point has never been authoritatively resolved by the Supreme Court, most modern authority agrees that the Court would so hold. E.g., ABA Prosecution and Defense Function Standards § 5.2(a)(iii)(1980 ed.); United States v. Bifield, 702 F.2d 342 (2d Cir.1983), cert.denied ___ U.S. ___, 103 S.Ct. 2095, 77 L.Ed.2d 304 (1983); United States ex rel. Wilcox v. Johnson, 555 F.2d 115, 120 (3d Cir.1977); McClendon v. People, 174 Colo. 7, 481 P.2d 715, 719 (1971); State v. Rosillo, 281 N.W.2d 877 (Minn.1979); Gallup v. State, 559 P.2d 1024, 1026–27 (Wyo.1977). On the Supreme Court's views, compare, e.g., Jones v. Barnes, 463 U.S. 745, 103 S.Ct. 3308, 3312, 77 L.Ed.2d 987 (1983)("It is . . . recognized that the accused has the ultimate authority to make certain fundamental decisions regarding the case, as to whether to plead guilty, waive a jury, testify in his or her own behalf, or take an appeal."); Faretta v. California, 422 U.S. 806, 819 n.15, 95 S.Ct. 2525, 2533, 45 L.Ed.2d 562 (1975)("it is now accepted . . . that an accused has a right . . . to testify on his own behalf."), with United States v. Grayson, 438 U.S. 41, 54, 98 S.Ct. 2610, 2617, 57 L.Ed.2d 582 (1978)("perhaps" accused has constitutional right to testify in own behalf).

86 MR 1.2(a)("In a criminal case, the lawyer shall abide by the client's decision, after consultation with the lawyer, as to . . . whether the client will testify."). See generally § 4.3.

87 ABA Standards for Criminal Justice Defense Function, standard 7.7(c)(1971 ed.). In view of continuing work on revisions of the Code of Professional Responsibility, 7.7(c) was deleted from the recommended revisions of the Standards approved by the ABA in 1979. See ABA Standards for Criminal Justice, Editorial Note to Standard 4–7.7, at 4.95 (1980 ed.). The 7.7(c) approach was ultimately rejected by the ABA House of Delegates when MR 3.3 was adopted in 1983.

88 A variant gambit might be for defense counsel to conduct only a perfunctory direct examination in the hope that the prosecution would bring out the perjurious "story" of the defendant on cross-examination. The gambit, obviously, will almost certainly founder on the prosecution's predictable refusal to ask any questions. Such a result met what may have been such a plan in Marino v. United States, 600 F.2d 462 (5th Cir.1979)(no ineffective

summation but was under a duty not to disclose it. Although 7.7(c) has received some judicial and scholarly acceptance,[89] its incoherent attempt to have it both ways on client perjury caused its rejection as a model for regulation in the Model Rules.[90]

Freedman-ATLA Full-Advocacy Solution

Another possible solution is to reject the normally applicable antiperjury rules and require instead that a defense lawyer whose remonstration and withdrawal efforts are unsuccessful [91] participate in the presentation of known client perjury as if it were not false. That position, first made prominent by Professor Monroe Freedman,[92] gives primacy to the client-protection policies of confidentiality and adversarial zeal,[93] but at the expense of truth. Such a position might also be defended on the ground of the special loyalty owed by defense lawyers to clients.[94] Some cases and commentators [95] come close to accepting that position because of constitutional considerations. The case most often pointed to, Lowery v. Cardwell,[96] for example, held that due process was violated by a defense lawyer convinced that his client was committing surprise perjury on the witness stand. The particular conduct of the lawyer to which the court pointed was his motion to withdraw after his client testified. The Ninth Circuit believed that, under the circumstances, the trial judge, who was trying the case without a jury, must have understood that the motion was based on the client's perjury. Plainly, the decision holds that disclosure of client perjury, at least in a bench trial, violates due

assistance of counsel when prosecutor refused to cross-examine in such circumstances).

89 United States ex rel. Smith v. Fogel, 403 F.Supp. 104, 106 (N.D.Ill.1975); United States v. Radford, 14 M.J. 322 (Mil.App.1982); Thornton v. United States, 357 A.2d 429, 437, n.14 (D.C.App.1976), cert.denied 429 U.S. 1024, 97 S.Ct. 644, 50 L.Ed.2d 626 (1976); In re Goodwin, 279 S.C. 274, 305 S.E.2d 578 (1983); Erickson, The Perjurious Defendant: A Proposed Solution to the Defense Lawyer's Conflicting Ethical Obligations to the Court and to His Client, 59 Den.L.J. 75 (1981); Lefstein, The Criminal Defendant Who Proposes Perjury: Rethinking the Defense Lawyer's Dilemma, 6 Hofstra L.Rev. 665 (1978). For critiques of the 7.7(c) resolution, see, e.g., Pino, Attempting to Regulate Perjurious Testimony: Massachusetts Experience, in Lawyers' Ethics: Contemporary Dilemmas 183, 185 (A.Gerson ed.1980); Wolfram, Client Perjury, 50 So.Cal.L.Rev. 809, 849–53 (1977).

90 MR 3.3 comment (Perjury by a Criminal Defendant; third paragraph).

91 It is sometimes overlooked that Professor Freedman's ultimate position was that a defense lawyer was required to attempt to withdraw in the face of a client's announced intention to commit perjury in self-defense so long as this could be done without revealing a client confidence. See Freedman-ATLA Lawyer's Code, infra n. 92, rule 6.6 and comment.

92 Freedman, Professional Responsibility of the Criminal Defense Lawyer: The Three Hardest Questions, 64 Mich.L.Rev. 1469 (1966). The argument is restated, and expanded to an array of civil representations, in M.Freedman, Lawyers Ethics in an Adversary System (1975), and in proposed professional rules authored by Professor Freedman under the sponsorship of the Association of Trial Lawyers of America. See Commission on Professional Responsibility of the Roscoe Pound-American Trial Lawyers Foundation, The American Lawyer's Code of Conduct, rule 1.2 (Public Discussion Draft, June 1980). For a critique of the Freedman-ATLA position, see Wolfram, Client Perjury: The Kutak Commission and the Association of Trial Lawyers on Lawyers, Lying Clients, and the Adversary System, 1980 Am.B.Found. Research J. 964.

93 Professor Freedman's analysis stems from an illustration in which an innocent person is accused of a serious crime and wishes to commit perjury by removing himself from apparently guilty circumstances. See Freedman, Three Hardest Questions, supra n. 92 at 1474. The illustration may be distorting because some would regard it as an extreme instance in which a lie can be defended morally because of the great disproportionality between the lie and the bad consequences of the truth. Cf., e.g., Munzer, Book Review, 77 Mich.L.Rev. 421, 431–32 (1979).

94 See generally Fried, The Lawyer as Friend, 85 Yale L.J. 1060 (1976). But cf. In re Easton, 289 Or. 99, 610 P.2d 270 (1980), cert.denied 449 U.S. 862, 101 S.Ct. 166, 66 L.Ed.2d 79 (1980)(bar applicant who testified falsely in his dissolution action to protect friends from harassment lacked good moral character requisite to admission to practice; avowed belief in a higher personal ethic than the law permits shows lack of ability to represent and advise clients).

95 Bowman, Standards of Conduct for Prosecution and Defense Personnel: An Attorney's Viewpoint, 5 Am. Crim.L.Q. 28, 30 (Fall 1966); Exum, The Perjurious Criminal Defendant: A Solution to His Lawyer's Dilemma, 6 Social Responsibilty: Journalism, Law, Medicine 16 (L.Hodges ed.1980).

96 575 F.2d 727 (9th Cir.1978).

process.[97] But both in *Lowery* and in a subsequent decision, the Ninth Circuit pointed out that a defense lawyer was not required to participate in a client's perjury. Instead the court endorsed the passive approach of the ABA's Standard 7.7(c).[98]

Only the Supreme Court can finally resolve the controversy over the extent to which, if any, the various antiperjury rules offend due process rights or the right to counsel of an accused. In apparently analogous areas, the Supreme Court has not espoused principles that would protect perjurious testimony and in dicta has suggested views fundamentally at odds with such an approach.[99]

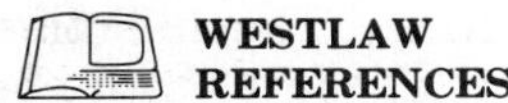

WESTLAW REFERENCES

Inventive Procedures: The Defense Function Standard

mr1.2 (m.r. "model rule" /5 1.2) ("defense function" /5 7.7)

Freeman – ATLA Full Advocacy Solution

575 +10 727 & cardwell

§ 12.6 DISCLOSING CLIENT WRONGDOING

§ 12.6.1 Lawyer Disclosure Adverse to a Client

Forensic and Counseling Disclosure Obligations

A lawyer's obligation to disclose a client's perjury (§ 12.5.3) is only one instance of several disclosure obligations imposed upon lawyers. The general purposes of those obligations are to arrest the most excessive forms of advocacy, to avoid predictably serious miscarriages of justice, and to prevent a client's use of a lawyer's services for the purpose of inflicting serious harm on others. The disclosure obligations impinge upon the lawyer's instinct of single-minded loyalty and devotion to the client's partisan interests. Some, such as the perjury disclosure obligation, require that client confidential information be revealed, if necessary, in order to prevent or correct the revealed wrong. Because of their interrelationships, this section will consider several disclosure issues, including some that transcend advocacy and carry into the lawyerly roles of counsellor and advisor. In addition to perjury and the specific problems treated

97 See also, e.g., Arizona v. Jefferson, 126 Ariz. 341, 615 P.2d 638 (1980); Butler v. United States, 414 A.2d 844 (D.C.App.1980). A concurring opinion in *Lowery*, by Judge Hufstedler, would have based decision on the broader ground that even passive refusal by a lawyer to participate in the presentation of client perjury in a criminal case deprives the accused of the effective assistance of counsel. See 575 F.2d at 732. For a sympathetic reading of this position, see generally Brazil, Unanticipated Client Perjury and the Collision of Rules of Ethics, Evidence, and Constitutional Law, 44 Mo.L.Rev. 601 (1979).

98 575 F.2d at 731; United States v. Campbell, 616 F.2d 1151, 1152–53 (9th Cir.1980), cert.denied 447 U.S. 910, 100 S.Ct. 2998, 64 L.Ed.2d 861 (1980).

99 Jenkins v. Anderson, 447 U.S. 231, 100 S.Ct. 2124, 65 L.Ed.2d 86 (1980)(once defendant takes the stand, normal due process prohibition against use of prearrest silence as evidence of guilt does not prevent its use to impeach); Fletcher v. Weir, 455 U.S. 603, 102 S.Ct. 1309, 71 L.Ed.2d 490 (1982)(same with respect to postarrest silence); United States v. Havens, 446 U.S. 620, 100 S.Ct. 1912, 1916, 64 L.Ed.2d 559 (1980)("We have repeatedly insisted that when defendants testify, they must testify truthfully or suffer the consequences. This is true even though a defendant is compelled to testify against his will."); Holloway v. Arkansas, 435 U.S. 475, 480 n.4, 98 S.Ct. 1173, 1176, 55 L.Ed.2d 426 (1978)("the record reveals that both the trial court and defense counsel were alert to defense counsel's obligation to avoid assisting in the presentation of what counsel had reason to believe was false testimony, or, at least, testimony contrary to the version of facts given to him earlier and in confidence. Cf. ABA, Standards . . . The Defense Function § 7.7(c), at 133 (1974)."); United States v. Wong, 431 U.S. 174, 97 S.Ct. 1823, 52 L.Ed.2d 231 (1977)(no right to commit perjury even if constitutional privilege against self-incrimination at stake). See also Polster, The Dilemma of the Perjurious Defendant: Resolution, Not Avoidance, 28 Case W.Res.L.Rev. 3, 6–22 (1977)(Supreme Court would not hold that perjurious accused is denied any constitutional right if defense counsel refused to participate in known client perjury).

here, other disclosure obligations and issues are discussed elsewhere.[1]

The Lake Pleasant Bodies Case

A case that captures—and perhaps overdramatizes—the issues involved in disclosure of client wrongdoing is the much-discussed Lake Pleasant Bodies case.[2] Robert Garrow had been arrested in Lake Pleasant, a town in the Adirondack Mountains of New York, and charged with a murder. Although Garrow was suspected of other murders of persons who had mysteriously disappeared, no additional charges had been filed. Two lawyers from Syracuse, Frank Armani and Francis Belge, defended Garrow. During confidential conversations with Garrow, the lawyers learned that he had indeed committed other murders. Garrow gave them directions and drew a map that they used to locate the bodies of two of Garrow's victims. They took photographs of the remains, in one case moving a skull several feet to locate it near the rest of the corpse.

Armani and Belge, after consultation with another lawyer, decided to keep the information secret. The father of one of the victims, hearing in Chicago that Garrow was a suspect in other murders, came to one of the lawyers' offices and pleaded for information; the lawyer gave him none. Later the lawyers attempted to plea bargain with the prosecutor in Garrow's behalf, offering to provide information on two unsolved murders in exchange for leniency. Their offer was rejected. At Garrow's subsequent trial his lawyers relied primarily upon a defense of insanity. As part of this defense, Garrow testified to the two previously mentioned uncharged murders and one other.[3] That same afternoon his lawyers defended their actions in a press conference. The resulting public and media furor included many calls by other lawyers for their disbarment.[4]

The only formal legal action ultimately taken against the lawyers was the indictment of lawyer Belge for violation of a state statute requiring anyone knowing of the death of a person unattended by a physician to report this to authorities. The indictment was dismissed by the trial court on the broad ground that the actions of the lawyer were compelled by the attorney-client privilege.[5] Although affirming, the intermediate appellate court took pains to base its decision on the narrow ground that the lawyer's actions, which otherwise would have violated the law, were shielded by the attorney-client privilege "insofar as the communications were to advance a client's interests." [6] The court rejected the argument of an absolute attorney-client privilege:

> [W]e note that the privilege is not all-encompassing and that in a given case there may be conflicting considerations. We believe that an at-

[1] § 12.3.3 (nonrevelation of evidence); §§ 13.5.7, 13.5.8 (negotiation); § 13.10.5 (prosecutorial disclosure).

[2] An account of the representation has been written by one of the defense lawyers involved and a journalist. See T.Alibrandi & F.Armani, Privileged Information (1984).

[3] People v. Garrow, 51 A.D.2d 814, 379 N.Y.S.2d 185 (1976)(although strategy of putting Garrow on stand might be questioned by some, it was not ineffective assistance of counsel, because it provided evidence of insanity through testimony to past crimes and bizarre behavior).

[4] For a later debate see Hobin & Jensen, The Impropriety of the Attorneys' Actions in the Lake Pleasant Case, in Lawyers' Ethics: Contemporary Dilemmas 145 (A.Gerson ed.1980); Callahan & Pitkow, The Propriety of the Attorneys' Actions in the Lake Pleasant Case, in id. 156. See also, e.g., Debate: The Garrow Case and Professional Responsibility in the Adversary System, in Teaching Professional Responsibility (P.Keenan ed.1979), at 315 ff.; Comment, Legal Ethics: Confidentiality and the Case of Robert Garrow's Lawyers, 25 Buff.L.Rev. 211 (1975). Lawyer Belge was later censured (see In re Belge, 59 A.D.2d 497, 400 N.Y.S.2d 407 (1977)) and then suspended for three years (Belge v. Office of Grievance Committees, 75 A.D.2d 408, 429 N.Y.S.2d 808 (1980)), on unrelated disciplinary charges.

[5] People v. Belge, 83 Misc.2d 186, 372 N.Y.S.2d 798 (Co. Ct.1975), affirmed 50 A.D.2d 1088, 376 N.Y.S.2d 771 (1975), affirmed 41 N.Y.2d 60, 359 N.E.2d 377, 390 N.Y.S.2d 867 (1976). The trial court noted, however, that the lawyer's failure to report the whereabouts of the body "was in a sense, obstruction of justice" and intimated that if this had been the charge "the work of this Court would have been much more difficult than it is." 372 N.Y.S.2d at 803.

[6] People v. Belge, 50 A.D.2d 1088, 376 N.Y.S.2d 771 (1975), affirmed 41 N.Y.2d 60, 390 N.Y.S.2d 867, 359 N.E.2d 377 (1976).

> torney must protect his client's interests, but also must observe basic human standards of decency, having due regard to the need that the legal system accord justice to the interests of society and its individual members.
>
> We write to emphasize our serious concern regarding the consequences which emanate from a claim of an absolute attorney-client privilege. Because the only question presented, briefed and argued on this appeal was a legal one with respect to the sufficiency of the indictments, we limit our determination to that issue and do not reach the ethical questions underlying this case.[7]

Despite the court's misgivings, the state bar's ethics committee ultimately wrote an opinion that concluded that, not only had the lawyers acted permissibly, but disclosure would have violated DR 4–101(B).[8] The lawyers could not disclose either the murders or the location of the bodies because this information was the result of a confidential client communication.

Values at Stake in Disclosure Problems [9]

Most lawyers are spared the sort of wrenching decisions that faced the defense lawyers in the Lake Pleasant case. But aside from the ghastly tasks undertaken by Armani and Belge and the repugnance of their client's deeds, their quandary is of the same general kind frequently encountered in law practice. The confidentiality principle and a lawyer's acquired instinct to protect client interests can clash with the interests of others whom a client's acts have harmed or can foreseeably harm in the future. It has also been argued, dubiously, that a stringent requirement of disclosure of client wrongdoing would provide beneficial therapy. In that view, disclosure would in fact enhance rather than impede the client-lawyer relationship because both client and lawyer would be forced to admit and to confront openly the existence of distrust that, it is argued, afflicts many client-lawyer relationships.[10]

Three broad approaches to the choice of values between client confidentiality and third-party and other social interests are discernible. First, confidentiality could be raised from doctrine to overriding principle, such that a lawyer would always be required to protect a client's interests regardless of impacts on third parties. That would treat the values of confidentiality and the adversary system as absolutes and would require defense of the implied proposition that their social or other values are uniformly superior to those of competing interests and proposed resolutions.[11] Second, and conversely, third-party and other social interests could be made predominant, so that interests of client confidentiality and loyalty would have to yield uniformly in instances of client wrongdoing.[12] A third, much more complex approach would be to develop criteria or categories that at-

[7] 50 A.D.2d 1088, 376 N.Y.S.2d 771, 772 (1975).

[8] N.Y.St.Bar.Ethics Op. 479 (1978). See also In re Armani, 83 Misc.2d 252, 371 N.Y.S.2d 563 (Co.Ct.1975) (approval of fees for appointed counsel beyond normal limits because of extraordinary circumstances).

[9] See generally Kramer, Clients' Frauds and Their Lawyers' Obligations: A Study in Professional Irresponsibility, 67 Geo.L.J. 991 (1979); Greenbaum, Clients' Frauds and Their Lawyers' Obligations: A Response to Professor Kramer, 68 Geo.L.J. 191 (1979); Hoffman, On Learning of a Corporate Client's Crime or Fraud—The Lawyer's Dilemma, 33 Bus.Law. 1389 (1978); Note, Client Fraud and the Lawyer: An Ethical Analysis, 62 Minn.L. Rev. 89 (1977). For a discussion of the problem in the context of a public-interest lawyer dealing with a welfare client's "fraud" in underreporting income, see Bellow & Kittleson, From Ethics to Politics: Confronting Ethics and Scarcity in Public Interest Practice, 58 Bost.U.L.Rev. 337, 363–72 (1978).

[10] Burt, Conflict and Trust between Attorney and Client, 69 Geo.L.J. 1015 (1981).

[11] The failure to appreciate and to attempt to defend this choice is a chief shortcoming in the approach of M.Freedman, Lawyers' Ethics in an Adversary System (1975). See Noonan, The Purposes of Advocacy and the Limits of Confidentiality, 64 Mich.L.Rev. 1485, 1489 (1966).

[12] Primarily because of consequentialist considerations such as those in the text, a moral philosopher has argued that a moral duty exists to reveal client confidences in order to prevent serious harm that is likely to occur and even to reveal past crimes because of the interest in social justice and restitution. S.Bok, Secrets 127–131 (1982). As a matter of professional regulation, of course, there is no general "law enforcement" exception to confidentiality rules. For example, when a lawyer knows of a client's desperate financial condition and her previous intent to divorce her recently slain husband, because of confidential communications, to reveal this information in a nontestimonial setting to prosecuting authorities investigating the slaying violates DR 4–101(B). Cf. In re Rhame, ___ Ind. ___, 416 N.E.2d 823 (1981).

tempt to differentiate instances in which either client interests or public interests are to be given preference. To a large extent, the variegated treatment of disclosure problems in the 1969 Code and the 1983 Model Rules reflects such a sophisticated approach. To some extent, however, it may also reflect less reasoned and more political responses.

WESTLAW REFERENCES

Lake Pleasant Bodies Case

51 +10 814 & garrow

§ 12.6.2 *Active Involvement versus Passive Knowledge*

Active lawyer involvement in client wrongdoing is largely foreclosed. As is developed elsewhere,[13] a lawyer may not knowingly assist a client to accomplish illegal or fraudulent ends. If a client insists on a course of conduct that would be illegal or fraudulent, a lawyer is required to withdraw instead of assisting in the scheme (§ 9.5.4). If other law requires a lawyer actively involved in a client's wrongdoing to disclose information, despite its otherwise confidential nature, then professional rules adopt these disclosure requirements.[14]

Apart from actively participating in client wrongdoing, a lawyer may have information about a client's past or intended wrongdoing and thus may be in a position to prevent or to correct it. What other action must or may be taken by a lawyer in the passive situation of knowing of but not participating in a client's wrongdoing? One model, already considered, is that of client perjury (§ 12.5.3). There it was seen that courts generally agree that a lawyer must resort, if necessary, to disclosure to prevent or correct client perjury. Is the same true of other client wrongdoing?

WESTLAW REFERENCES

attorney lawyer counsel** /s disclos! reveal*** /s wrong-doing illegal***

§ 12.6.3 *Whistle-Blowing*

Sociology of Disclosure

Disclosure of the wrongs of another is an issue freighted with much emotional, cultural, and moral baggage. A lawyer who remains silent about a client's wrongdoing conjures up for some the image of the immoral bystander who does nothing to help a victim of crime.[15] For others, however, disclosure to the detriment of another person with whom one has a prior relationship of trust is reprehensible. The pervasiveness of that attitude in popular and legal culture is attested by the widespread reference to lawyer disclosure by terms such as *snitch, rat, squeal*, and similar phrases from the argot of the underworld [16] or *tattle* and similar words from the playground. The commonly employed phrase *whistle-blowing* often carries the connotation of an officious pretender. And the experience of persons who have blown whistles is a kind of ostracism within one's former group, apparently because of a pervasive group feeling that the whistle-blower cannot be trusted.[17] That instinct might be particularly acute in the case of lawyer whistle-blowers. The client who is "betrayed" has often paid a fee to the lawyer to perform the work in the course of which the client's asserted wrongdoing was discovered. And disclosure is diametrically at odds with the customary lawyerly attitude of full devotion to the client's welfare. Lawyer disclosure of client wrongdoing, without

[13] § 12.5.3 (client perjury); § 13.3.2 (advice on legal limits).

[14] DR 7-102(A)(3); cf. MR 4.1. See, e.g., In re Labendz, 95 N.J. 273, 471 A.2d 21 (1984)(mandatory disclosure violation under DR 7-102(A)(3) when lawyer participated with client in perpetrating fraud on lending institution).

[15] See generally A.Goldman, The Moral Foundations of Professional Ethics 105–106 (1980).

[16] Note, "Stool Pigeon" Canons: A Comment on Certain Sections of Canons 28 and 29 of the ABA Code of Ethics, 41 Conn.B.J. 339 (1967).

[17] Wall St.J., Nov. 9, 1977, p.1, col.4 (unemployment and harassment experienced by corporate lawyer who revealed questionable political contributions to federal authorities).

doubt, is an act both socially wrenching and occupationally hazardous in the present milieu.

Moral Judgment and Moral Action

On closer inspection, however, it is not clear that whistle-blowing is either categorically right or wrong.[18] Much depends on motivation. There are three major reasons for condemning a whistle-blower. First, the grandstanding that sometimes accompanies publicized instances creates doubt about the integrity of the revealer's motives. One may also tend to balk at what sometimes appears to be a claim of moral superiority or at least an overdisplay of moral heroism. Second, whistle-blowers are often self-authorized and have jumped lines of authority. They thus subject the rest of us to the vagaries of their consciences. Third, whistle-blowing often takes the form of a betrayal of trust. Whistle-blowers had access to the information that is publicly spilled only because they shared in the trust and confidence of colleagues, coworkers, clients, or others whose regard the whistle-blowers have spurned.

Yet, while those reasons seem strong ones for disapproving of the acts of some whistle-blowers, they say nothing about whistle-blowing in general. They require us only to ascertain the motives of the apparent altruist. If the whistle-blower's motives are in order, then further objection to disclosure can proceed only on the extreme position that being the subject of media attention, jumping normal lines of authority, and betraying trust are never permissible. But that position is hardly sustainable, and the first is often not a matter of choice in any event.

Reacting to Disclosure Problems

As will be apparent, the course of action that a lawyer should follow in attempting to prevent client wrongdoing is not always clear. Possibly compounding those uncertainties might be a reluctance of local ethics committees to render a prompt, or any, advisory opinion on the lawyer's responsibilities. At least in the most troublesome case, in which the lawyer's information comes from a client communication, a substantial difficulty often is determining the scope of the attorney-client privilege. Yet some ethics committees refuse to give advice on the scope of the privilege on the ground that this is a question of "law" beyond the province of an "ethics" committee.[19]

Two courses of action seem well-advised in any confrontation with client wrongdoing, although they will not assure a satisfactory outcome. First, a lawyer should consult with neutral and available sources of expert guidance, such as the chair of an ethics committee, a bar disciplinary counsel, or a judge or other knowledgeable expert. The discussions should reveal as much of the facts underlying the problem as is consistent with confidentiality obligations. Second, it is always sound to reduce to a file memorandum both the contents of the client confidential information and the considerations that have led the lawyer to a decision.[20]

In practice it is probably true that most future acts of client wrongdoing are prevented by effective client counseling. The client's lawyer often assists the client to realize that the act is both against the law and ill-advised on ethical, economic, public relations, and other grounds (see § 4.3). Even if the client's course of conduct has reached a point at which its consequences cannot be remedied without disclosure, a lawyer might well advise that extreme step. No jurisdiction prohibits a lawyer from advising a client to disclose information, even if no legal obligation exists compelling disclosure on the part of either lawyer

[18] See generally Luban, Corporate Counsel and Confidentiality, in Ethics in the Legal Profession (F.Elliston ed. forthcoming).

[19] ABA Formal Op. 247 (1942).

[20] Callan & David, Professional Responsibility and the Duty of Confidentiality: Disclosure of Client Misconduct in an Adversary System, 29 Rutgers L.Rev. 332, 393 n.250 (1976); ABA Defense Function Standards § 7.7(c)(1974).

or client.[21] Lawyers should not always assume that a client would refuse to make disclosures that seem desirable on moral or other grounds simply because the law does not compel disclosure. To assume that clients always wish only to assert all possible legal rights regardless of moral or other nonlegal considerations may often be factually inaccurate and, in any event, is disrespectful of clients with more altruistic instincts.[22] If, after a full and complete discussion of the problem, a client agrees to disclosure, this effectively waives the confidentiality principle (see § 6.7.7).

WESTLAW REFERENCES

45k32(13) 45k32(14)

§ 12.6.4 Disclosure under the Lawyer Codes

1908 Canons

The provision of the 1908 Canons dealing with client confidential information, Canon 37, specifically provided that "the announced intention of a client to commit a crime is not included within the confidences which [the lawyer] is bound to keep. He may make such disclosures as may be necessary to prevent the act or protect those against whom it is threatened." Canon 41 went on to provide a mandatory disclosure rule. If a lawyer discovered that "some fraud or deception has been practiced, which has unjustly imposed upon the court or a party, he should endeavor to rectify it; at first by advising his client, and if his client refuses to forego the advantage thus unjustly gained, he should promptly inform the injured person or his counsel, so that they make take appropriate steps." Apparently, however, only client acts characterizable as fraud, deception, or crime were to be disclosed. Even in the case of a client's clear intention to take a life, from all that is said, a lawyer is not required to take remedial steps.[23] And despite the apparent bias of the Canons in favor of harm prevention, a confused series of ethics committee opinions often ignored or distinguished away the disclosure canons and enjoined silence upon lawyers in a variety of client wrongdoing situations.[24]

1969 Code: The Basic Provisions

The 1969 Code traces the 1908 Canons. It requires both confidentiality and disclosure and ignores the collision course on which these inconsistent professional obligations have been put. The principle of confidentiality is broadly sketched in DR 4–101(A) (see § 6.7.3), but DR 4–101(C) provides that "a lawyer may reveal . . . (3) the intention of his client to commit a crime and the information necessary to prevent the crime." Thus it appears that a lawyer who learns in the course of a confidential client interview that the client intends to commit murder or some other crime "may" take steps to prevent the

[21] State v. Harper, 214 Neb. 911, 336 N.W.2d 597 (1983), cert.denied 465 U.S. 1013, 104 S.Ct. 1016, 79 L.Ed.2d 246 (1984)(failure to prevent accused from revealing to court type of carcinogenic agent used to poison victims, including three victims who could not adequately be treated unless information about agent was quickly made known, not ineffective assistance of counsel).

[22] Fried, The Lawyer as Friend: The Moral Foundations of the Lawyer-Client Relation, 85 Yale L.J. 1060, 1088 (1976); Lehman, The Pursuit of a Client's Interest, 77 Mich.L.Rev. 1078, 1087 (1979); Alschuler, The Search for Truth Continued, the Privilege Retained: A Response to Judge Frankel, 54 U.Colo.L.Rev. 67, 74 (1982).

[23] Compare Spaulding v. Zimmerman, 263 Minn. 346, 116 N.W.2d 704, 710 (1962)(when defense lawyer knew of defense physician's report of unknown life-threatening and easily correctable condition of opposing party, "no canon of ethics or legal obligation may have required [defense lawyers] to inform" that party; nonetheless, trial court had discretion to reopen judgment after settlement by uninformed party).

[24] For reviews of the bewildering series of opinions of the ABA ethics committee dealing with disclosure of client wrongdoing, see, e.g., the samplings of opinions collected in A.Kaufman, Problems in Professional Responsibility 111–118 (1976); Wolfram, Client Perjury, 50 So.Cal.L.Rev. 809, 837 n.105 (1977); Callan & David, Professional Responsibility and the Duty of Confidentiality: Disclosure of Client Misconduct in an Adversary System, 29 Rutgers L.Rev. 332, 358 n.114, 362–65 (1976). Part of the confusion has recently been relieved by ABA Formal Op. 84–349 (1984), that "withdraws" ABA Formal Ops. 155 (1936) and 156 (1936).

crime. Disclosure is discretionary [25] and no other provision of the Code generally requires disclosure to frustrate future criminal acts by the client.[26] The quoted permission to disclose applies only to a client "crime" and not to an injurious client act that violates no criminal law, although it also appears to apply to all crimes without regard to their seriousness.

Fraud Disclosure under DR 7–102(B)(1)

Some noncriminal acts, however, as well as some that are also crimes, are covered by the retrospective disclosure requirement of DR 7–102(B)(1). That provision, perhaps the most controversial and confusing of all those found in the Code, provides a mandatory disclosure rule much like that of Canon 41:

> A lawyer who receives information clearly establishing that: (1) His client has, in the course of the representation, perpetrated a fraud upon a person or tribunal shall promptly call upon his client to rectify the same, and if his client refuses or is unable to do so, he shall reveal the fraud to the affected person or tribunal.[27]

Several features of the 1969 Code's approach to lawyer disclosure of fraud bear emphasis. Under DR 7–102(B)(1) the lawyer's reaction to client fraud is to come in two stages. First, the lawyer must remonstrate with the client in an attempt to persuade the client to rectify the fraud.[28] Second, if remonstration does not obtain results, then disclosure is required. The disclosure rule is limited to frauds perpetrated by a lawyer's client. A companion rule, DR 7–102(B)(2), does require lawyer revelation of fraud by a person other than the lawyer's client, but this is limited to fraud "upon a tribunal"; unlike DR 7–102(B)(1), no mention is made of nonclient fraud "upon a person." Thus DR 7–102(B)(2) is limited essentially to perjury by friendly witnesses who are not clients.

The rationale thought to support DR 7–102(B)(1) is not entirely clear. If prevention or frustration of fraud were alone its rationale, it would be difficult to defend the limitation of the rule to client frauds that occur "in the course of the representation" and not to those about which the lawyer has definite information but that occur before or after the representation begins or ends.[29] That limitation suggests that the remonstration and disclosure obligation might have as much to do with assuring that lawyers play no role in client's frauds in order to protect the legal profession against criticism and suspicion.

25 The ABA Defense Function Standards provided in standard 3.7(d)(approved draft 1971) that a lawyer "must" reveal information necessary to prevent a client crime "which would seriously endanger the life or safety of any person" if "the lawyer believes such action on his part is necessary to prevent it." A similar gloss can be found in the nonauthoritative footnote 16 to DR 4–101(C)(3), quoting ABA Formal Op. 314 (1965). The obligation seems to have been spontaneously generated and finds no support in the Code.

When the Supreme Court of Florida adopted the Code, it modified DR 4–101(C)(3) to provide that "a lawyer *shall* reveal . . . the intention of his client to commit a crime and the information necessary to prevent the crime." (Emphasis supplied.) See Fla. Code of Professional Responsibility DR 4–101(D)(2). It is doubtful that the Florida drafters meant these words literally. On their face they would absurdly require a lawyer to report client double-parking and similar minor infractions of criminal law. Similarly, it seems doubtful that DR 4–101(C)(3) itself was intended to permit lawyer disclosure of even petty offenses, yet no qualification for significant offenses is provided there.

26 DR 4–101(C)(4) does provide that a lawyer "*may*" reveal client confidential information "when *permitted* under Disciplinary Rules or *required* by law or court order." That insensible, if not chaotic, verbiage appears to suggest that a lawyer confronted with the positive commands of law or a judge can elect not to obey. Nonetheless, there is no general obligation in the law, at least in the criminal law, to report even a crime threatened as serious as murder. Most American jurisdictions refuse to impose anything like the misprision of felony rule of the common law. See W.LaFave & A.Scott, Criminal Law 502–505 (1972).

27 An ABA amendment in 1974 suggested that states add an explicit exception for confidential information. See infra text at nn. 30–35.

28 It does not appear that the remonstration requirement was intended to be diluted by the 1974 amendment to DR 7–102(B)(1) that excepted instances in which "the information" (presumably the information necessary to accomplish revelation) was protected as a privileged communication.

29 Such a limitation might be defensible on the pragmatic ground that any greater obligation would be unduly onerous. Cf. MR 3.3 comment (Duration of Obligation).

The chief difficulty with the original version of DR 7–102(B)(1) in the 1969 Code is that it is entirely silent about problems that will almost certainly arise because lawyer revelations will compromise confidential client information. Is revelation required in all instances? Or just in those exotic instances in which a lawyer would know of a client's fraud through other than confidential information? Or is only a partial compromise of the broad protection of confidential client information intended—and, if so, to what extent? Is it important to know whether the lawyer's services were involved, innocently on the lawyer's part, in perpetrating the client's fraud, or is revelation required regardless of the extent of the lawyer's involvement?

1974 ABA Amendment Removing Disclosure Obligation

In 1974 the ABA acted to resolve these ambiguities by amending DR 7–102(B)(1).[30] The amendment would add to the end of the rule the words "except when the information is protected as a privileged communication." [31] Although the reference to "privilege" in the amendment suggests a basis for a narrower meaning, the ABA ethics committee, in Formal Opinion 341 (1975), interpreted the exception to apply to both confidences and secrets normally protected against disclosure by DR 4–101(B).[32] That interpretation of the 1974 amendment effectively vitiates the disclosure requirement [33] of DR 7–102(B)(1). The result seems surprising for an amendment and one hardly required by its language.[34] At the time of the adoption of the 1983 Model Rules fewer than twenty states had adopted the amendment.[35]

1983 Model Rules

The 1983 Model Rules eventually adopted a fraud-disclosure position at least as limited as that achieved by the 1974 ABA amendment after it was broadly interpreted by the ABA ethics committee in 1975. But the Model Rules position differs sharply from recommendations of the Kutak Commission, which had drafted the Rules, and from the law that today applies in most of the states whose courts have discussed the issue. The clash between those positions has produced, by any measure, the most heated professional and public controversy concerning the Model Rules.[36]

[30] See generally Annotated Code of Professional Responsibility 321–26 (A.Maru ed.1979).

[31] The timing of the 1974 amendment might suggest a relationship to Watergate. In fact, however, the immediate stimulus for the amendment to DR 7–102(B)(1) was the threat of widespread lawyer damage liability to persons injured because of the lawyer's failure to reveal client fraud in the course of dealings in regulated securities. Most of the concern arose out of the *National Student Marketing* case, which was filed against two prestigious law firms, among other defendants, by the SEC in 1972. See SEC v. National Student Marketing Corp., [1971–1972 Transfer Binder] Fed.Sec.L.Rpt. (CCH) ¶ 93,360 (D.D.C.Feb. 3, 1972)(text of complaint); 360 F.Supp. 284, 59 F.R.D. 305 (D.D.C.1973). See § 12.6.6.

[32] "The balancing of the lawyer's duty to preserve confidences and to reveal frauds is best made by interpreting the phrase 'privileged communication' in the 1974 amendment to DR 7–102(B) as referring to those confidences *and secrets* that are required to be preserved by DR 4–101."

(ABA Formal Opinion 341 (1975)(emphasis supplied).)

[33] ABA Formal Opinion 341 (1975) and the 1974 amendment itself, however, do not affect that portion of DR 7–102(B)(1) requiring remonstration. See supra n.28.

[34] Wolfram, Client Perjury, 50 So.Cal.L.Rev. 809, 836–37 (1977).

[35] Iowa has adopted a narrower variation on the 1974 amendment, which provides an exception to the disclosure rule only when the lawyer is barred from doing so by the state's attorney-client privilege statute. See Ia. Code of Prof. Resp. DR 7–102(B)(1), as amended January 21, 1980.

[36] Redlich, Disclosure Provisions of the Model Rules of Professional Conduct, 1980 Am.B.Found.Research J. 981 ("[W]ere it not for the disclosure provisions, which many critics decry as fundamentally altering the lawyer-client relationship, the proposed Model Rules might have generated widespread support, or perhaps indifference, from most segments of the bar."); Abramovsky, Confidentiality: The Future Crime—Contraband Dilemmas, 85 W.Va. L.Rev. 929 (1983); Subin, War over Client Confidentiality: In Defense of the Kutak Approach, Nat'l L.J., Jan. 19, 1981, at 22, col. 1. Much, but hardly all, of the disclosure/confidentiality controversy was generated by the Association of Trial Lawyers of America, a group predominantly comprised of plaintiff personal injury lawyers, who proposed a competing set of model lawyer rules that would have drastically restricted lawyer disclosure. See Roscoe Pound-American Trial Lawyers Foundation Commission on Professional Responsibility, The American Lawyer's

The Kutak Commission's Drafts

Consistent with its policy of affording broad protection to the public, the Kutak Commission promulgated proposed rules at an early stage that mandated disclosure in some situations and provided significant areas of discretionary disclosure, as did the 1908 Canons.[37] Those proposals were substantially retracted in later drafts, until ultimately the Kutak Commission would have provided only for nonmandatory disclosure, and then only in two situations. First, revelation would be permitted if the lawyer believed that it was necessary to prevent the client from committing a criminal or fraudulent act that the lawyer believed was likely to result in death, substantial bodily harm, or substantial injury to the financial interests or property interests of another.[38] Second, revelation was also permitted "to rectify the consequences of a client's criminal or fraudulent act in the commission of which the lawyer's services had been used." [39] Unlike DR 7–102(B)(1), the proposed Model Rule would not have required a lawyer to disclose a client's fraud in either situation. Even those relaxations of the 1969 Code, however, were insufficient to obtain lawyer approval in the ABA House of Delegates.

Model Rule 1.6(b)(1)

The ultimately adopted Model Rule on client wrongdoing—Rule 1.6(b)(1)—does not *require* disclosure in any situation of client fraud or wrongdoing, no matter how wrongful the act or ghastly the consequences. (In sharp and arguably inconsistent contrast, disclosure of client perjury or other wrongdoing before a tribunal is required by Rules 3.3(a)(2) and (4).) [40] And Rule 1.6(b)(1) *permits* disclosure only in a single instance, that in which earlier recommendations of the Kutak Commission would have made disclosure mandatory: when reasonably necessary to prevent the client from committing a criminal act likely to result in "imminent death or substantial bodily harm." [41] If Rule 1.6(b)(1) were adopted by local jurisdictions, that would for the first time in American law require a lawyer by formal rule to keep silent about all client wrongdoing that was protected against disclosure by no law other than the law of professional regulations. Unlike DR 7–102(B)(1), the Model Rule does not require remonstration with a client who intends to commit, or has already committed, an illegal or fraudu-

Code of Conduct (public discussion draft, June 1980). Contrary to that document's position, its chief reporter, Professor Monroe Freedman, had argued at one time that lawyers should be required to reveal confidential information necessary to prevent a life-threatening crime from occurring. See Freedman, Are There Public Interest Limits on Lawyers' Advocacy?, 2 Social Responsibility: Journalism, Law, Medicine, at 31, 36 (L.Hodges ed. 1976).

37 MR 1.7, 1.13(c), 3.1, 4.2 (Discussion Draft, Jan. 30, 1980). This first officially published draft of suggested rules (1) mandated disclosure (MR 1.7(b)), when necessary, to prevent the client from committing an act that would result in death or serious bodily injury to another person, and to the extent required by law and other professional rules; (2) permitted disclosure (MR 1.7(c)(2)), when apparently necessary, to prevent or rectify the consequences of a deliberately wrongful act by the client unless the lawyer had been retained after the act to represent the client concerning it; (3) permitted disclosure of some kinds of illegality of an agent of a client corporation or similar entity (MR 1.13(c)); (4) mandated disclosure, when necessary, to correct various misapprehensions of fact and law during trials (MR 3.1); and (5) mandated disclosure of facts during negotiations in a variety of circumstances (4.2).

38 MR 1.6(b)(2)(Proposed Final Draft, May 30, 1981). Disclosure in such a case was reluctantly supported by Professor Monroe Freedman. See M.Freedman, Lawyers' Ethics in an Adversary System 6 (1975); Freedman, Panel Discussion, 35 U.Miami L.Rev. 639, 646–47 (1981).

39 Id. MR 1.6(b)(3).

40 § 11.5.3.

41 MR 1.6 comment (Withdrawal; first paragraph) does, however, state that a lawyer is required to withdraw from a representation if the lawyer's services would be used by a client to further a criminal or fraudulent course of conduct. After withdrawal, a lawyer could (but apparently is not required to) "withdraw or disaffirm any opinion, document, affirmation, or the like." Id. (Withdrawal; second paragraph).

Following adoption of the amendment, in February 1983, a bill was introduced and hearings had in the Senate on proposed legislation to make lawyer nondisclosure of a client's fraud a federal crime in certain situations. See Hearing on S. 485 before the Subcommittee on Criminal Law of the Senate Committee on the Judiciary, April 28, 1983. No further action was taken on the bill.

lent act.[42] Finally, because of the great breadth of definition of confidential client information in MR 1.6(a)("information relating to representation of a client") and the absence of any exception for future crime or fraud, it is uncertain whether the confidentiality obligation is offset by force of other law in these instances.[43] The eventually adopted MR 1.6 is thus a substantially weaker rule on client disclosure than provided for in the original version of DR 7–102(B)(1), the version in effect in most states when the Model Rules were approved by the ABA.

Model Rule 4.1(b)

In light of those effects of Rule 1.6, it is important to note the apparent utter irrelevance of Rule 4.1(b).[44] That rule, much like DR 7–102(B)(1) after its 1974 and 1975 reworking by the ABA, first requires broadly that a lawyer shall disclose material facts when "necessary to avoid assisting a criminal or fraudulent act by a client." But an exception then strips away all but trivial applications of the requirement by going on to say that the requirement does not exist when "disclosure is prohibited by rule 1.6." Again, because of the all-inclusive nature of the definition of confidential client information in Rule 1.6, no substantial duties are created by Rule 4.1(b) unless, which is not clear, disclosure permissions or requirements posited by other law—such as the law of fraud or securities law—override Rule 1.6. Even in that instance, obviously, the obligation is created despite, and not because of, Rule 4.1(b). Possibly through inadvertence, neither MR 1.6 nor any other Model Rule explicitly permits a lawyer to make a disclosure of confidential client information when required to do so by other law.[45] It would, of course, be absurd to put a lawyer into the position of having to choose between violating a professional obligation or a duty imposed by other valid law.

WESTLAW REFERENCES

1908 Canons

canon /4 37 41 /s confiden! disclos!

1969 Code: The Basic Provisions

dr4–101 (d.r. "disciplinary rule" /5 4–101)

Fraud Disclosure Under DR 7–107.(B)(1)

dr7–102(b) (d.r. "disciplinary rule" /5 7–102(b))

1974 ABA Amendment Removing Disclosure Obligation

dr7–102(b) (d.r. "disciplinary rule" /5 7–102(b)) /p privilege*

The Kutak Commission's Drafts

"model rule" /50 kutak

§ 12.6.5 Judicial Doctrines on Disclosure

Client Fraud in the Courts

Relatively few judicial decisions have dealt with the question of a lawyer's duty to disclose client fraud or similar wrongdoing. Those that have, however, suggest an approach that is much less protective of client interests regardless of the cost and much more receptive to a disclosure obligation than is reflected in the adopted version of the 1983 Model Rules. Several jurisdictions have disciplined lawyers for failure to disclose client fraud under DR 7–102(B)(1) of the 1969 Code, even though it was evident that disclosure

42 The comment to MR 1.6 (Disclosure Adverse to Client; last paragraph) does mention that "where practical, the lawyer should seek to persuade the client to take suitable action" but this is stated only in the context of the limited disclosure permitted by the rule. Moreover, the comment to MR 1.2(d) on criminal, fraudulent, and prohibited transactions does not mention remonstration beyond stating that a lawyer "is required to give an honest opinion about the actual consequences that appear likely to result from a client's conduct."

43 MR 1.6 comment (Disclosures Otherwise Required or Authorized; second paragraph): ". . . [A] lawyer may be obligated or permitted by other provisions of law to give information about a client. Whether another provision of law supersedes Rule 1.6 is a matter of interpretation beyond the scope of these Rules, but a presumption should exist against such a supersession."

44 MR 4.1(b) originally appeared in earlier drafts of the Model Rules that created significant disclosure obligations not covered by any confidentiality requirement. Its appearance in the finally adopted version may be largely of archeological interest.

45 A provision permitting lawyer disclosure when "otherwise permitted by law" (MR 1.7(c)(4)(Public Discussion Draft, Jan. 30, 1980)) was deleted when the controverted other portions of the same rule were drastically reduced in scope.

would require revelation of confidential client information.[46] And decisions have permitted a lawyer to invoke DR 7–102(B)(1) as justification for revealing confidential information about wrongful client acts.[47] The circumstances, as required by DR 7–102(B), must indicate "clearly" that fraud has been committed.[48] The courts in those cases both disregarded and acted contrary to the apparent weight of professional opinion as reflected in bar ethics committee opinions.[49]

The Scope of "Fraud"

The disclosure obligations in DR 7–102(B) apply to instances of "fraud" and are apparently limited to such acts. Particularly in view of the fact that most required disclosures are at the expense of the principle of client confidentiality, fraud should not be defined as expansively as has been done in some other areas of the law.[50] The knowingly false misrepresentation standard discussed elsewhere (§§ 13.5.7, 13.5.8) should also be employed here. Rather clearly, not all client wrongdoing, even if criminal, is fraudulent. Thus a client's wrongful act in violating a court order is not inherently fraudulent and therefore may not need to be disclosed.[51] It also follows that there should be no requirement under the rules to make disclosure in the much mooted situation of the lawyer whose client confidentially reveals that he or she committed a crime for which an innocent person is about to be punished.[52] Finally, as discussed elsewhere, the authorities disagree on the question whether "fraud" includes client perjury or other false evidence in trials.[53]

Fraud on "Tribunals" and Similar Bodies

The disclosure requirement in DR 7–102(B)(2) and part of the disclosure obligation of DR 7–102(B)(1) apply to frauds "on a tribunal." The "Definitions" at the conclusion of the Code define "tribunal" to include "all courts and all other adjudicatory bodies." While the double use of "all" obviously stretches for wide inclusion, many administrative agencies can be regarded as "adjudicatory bodies" only if the concept of adjudication is taken very far from its judicial roots. And legislative bodies are certainly not included.[54] Despite the rela-

46 In re Price, 429 N.E.2d 961 (Ind.1982)(failure to inform welfare office of client's receipt of funds making client ineligible for continuing Medicaid benefits); In re Drexler, 290 Minn. 542, 546 n.7, 188 N.W.2d 436 (1971) (elaborate scheme to conceal client's assets from client's wife in violation of court order); Bar Ass'n of Greater Cleveland v. Cassaro, 61 Ohio St.2d 62, 399 N.E.2d 545 (1980)(fraudulent scheme to obtain worker compensation benefits).

47 Meyerhoffer v. Empire Fire & Marine Ins. Co., 497 F.2d 1190 (2d Cir.1974), cert.denied 419 U.S. 998, 95 S.Ct. 314, 42 L.Ed.2d 272 (1974). See generally § 6.7.8 (lawyer self-defense).

48 Florida Bar v. Brennan, 377 So.2d 1181 (Fla.1979) (defense counsel impermissibly reported to court that he thought client was not being candid with lawyer in denying use of firearm in robbery). The few cases that have discussed the matter agree that the scienter required is similar to that required in criminal cases. E.g., In re Price, 429 N.E.2d 961, 964 (Ind.1982). Scienter should include instances of "studied ignorance" on the part of the lawyer—proceeding, for example, with a representation through deliberate avoidance of positive knowledge of facts that the lawyer had every reason to believe. See United States v. Maniego, 710 F.2d 24, 28 (2d Cir.1983), and cases cited.

49 See n. 46, supra.

50 Calan & David, Professional Responsibility and the Duty of Confidentiality: Disclosure of Client Misconduct in an Adversary System, 29 Rutgers L.Rev. 322, 359 (1976). Contra Note, Client Fraud and the Lawyer—An Ethical Analysis, 62 Minn.L.Rev. 89, 106 (1977).

51 In re Callan, 66 N.J. 401, 331 A.2d 612 (1975).

52 A.Powell, I Can Go Home Again 287–92 (1943); Powell, Privilege of Counsel and Confidential Communications, 6 Geo.B.J. 333 (1944)(lawyer knew from client that client had committed murder for which another person had been wrongly convicted and sentenced to death).

53 § 12.5.3 (client perjury). The Commentary to section 7.7(c) in the 1971 ABA Standards Relating to the Defense Function (see § 12.5.4 at 661–62) stated that: "It should be noted that DR 7–102(B), which requires a lawyer to reveal a 'fraud' perpetrated by his client on a tribunal, is construed as not embracing the giving of false testimony in a criminal case." A more awesome feat of "construing" does not readily come to mind. Such an inelegant, if easy, way out of the perjury problem in criminal cases has not been adopted by any court.

54 EC 8–5 contains the curious and apparently mandatory statement that a lawyer-lobbyist who possesses unprivileged information of "fraudulent, deceptive, or otherwise illegal conduct" by a participant in a proceeding "before a tribunal or legislative body" should reveal this to "appropriate authorities." The reference to legislative bodies is duplicated in no DR.

tive clarity of meaning, it is difficult to understand why the Code limits reportable fraud to "tribunal" fraud. Indeed, the more one departs from the adjudicatory model, with its adversarial presentation of two points of view, arguably the greater is the need for candor in order to protect the process. Thus, in a substantially nonadjudicatory proceeding, such as an application to the Patent Office for a patent, there is an arguably greater need for assistance from lawyers to curb or, if unsuccessful, to expose fraudulent practices.[55]

The force of considerations such as the above led to the enactment in the Model Rules of a provision to deal with the one instance in which disclosure is mandatory under the Rules, false testimony. Rule 3.9 explicitly extends most of the candor and fairness duties imposed on litigators in judicial proceedings onto "a lawyer representing a client before a legislative or administrative tribunal in a nonadjudicative proceeding." Rule 3.9 incorporates by reference all of the candor and fairness duties of Model Rules 3.3, 3.4, and 3.5 *except* the rule on candor in ex parte proceedings (MR 3.3(d)), and some of Rule 3.4 requiring good faith in discovery (MR 3.4(d)), prohibiting the statement of a personal belief in litigated matters (MR 3.4(e)), and prohibiting blockading of potential witnesses (MR 3.4(f)). Those strictures were apparently considered inappropriate limitations on lawyers in administrative or legislative representations.

Importantly, however, the candor and fairness requirements that are not excepted from MR 3.9 apply only to a lawyer representing a client before a legislative or administrative "tribunal." According to the comment to MR 3.9, they do not apply to a lawyer engaged in "a negotiation or other bilateral transaction" with a governmental body in behalf of a client.[56] That leaves some matters clear, others quite murky. The missing key is any definition in the Model Rules of "tribunal" that is similar to or different from that in the Code. Unless "tribunal" in MR 3.9 means *entities* (which seems grotesque), then it must refer to trial-type proceedings in which witnesses are examined, evidence is presented, the parties are entitled to participate fully, and the decision will be made by a fact finder on the basis of evidence and argument developed at the proceeding.[57] Those proceedings occur in legislative bodies only in such rare events as impeachment proceedings. They occur more commonly in proceedings of administrative agencies, such as hearings on license applications, proceedings to decertify a particular person or company, and agency action to impose fines or other sanctions. But such common legislative and administrative events as testimony before an inquiry commission or testimony before a committee or board holding hearings on proposed legislation or regulations would not constitute a "tribunal."

At least in legislative and administrative trial-type situations, in governmental representations a lawyer's duties to make full disclosure under the Model Rules may be quite broad. As a result, there is a great disparity between a lawyer's obligation to disclose client perjury and other evidentiary falsifications before a broad range of "tribunals" under rules 3.3 and 3.9 as compared with rule 1.6, which by force of MR 3.3(b), does not permit any disclosures other than in life-threatening situations.

Continuing Offenses

Even in the several jurisdictions that have gone beyond the lawyer codes and have mandated disclosure for future wrongs of a client, the law is in an unsatisfactorily unsettled state with respect to the obligations of a lawyer to disclose or keep confidential information about a client's continuing criminal of-

[55] Henry, Ethics in United States Patent Practice, 62 ABA J. 465, 467–68 (1976). Fraud on the patent office by a lawyer's client might be covered by DR 7–102(B)(1) which, more broadly than DR 7–102(B)(2), includes frauds against "a person" as well as upon a "tribunal."

[56] MR 3.9 comment (third paragraph).

[57] In which case, the qualification in MR 3.9 that the lawyer's representation be in a "nonadjudicative proceeding" is itself grotesquely contradictory, unless it is simply redundant because it then refers to the already described fact that the forum is not a court.

fenses.[58] By a process of what sometimes seems to be legislative whimsy, some criminal acts that have occurred in the past are given an indefinitely contemporaneous aspect by the criminal law. Theft, for example, becomes possession of stolen property, or escape becomes the offense of remaining a fugitive.

Generally courts have held that the "crime or fraud" exception to the attorney-client privilege applies to continuing offenses (§ 6.4.10). Deciding whether a lawyer should be required to reveal information about a client's continuing offenses involves a particularly difficult weighing of the policies of confidentiality and crime prevention. At least where the offense is factually indistinguishable—aside from its temporal continuation—from a past offense about which the client has consulted a lawyer, it seems much the better result to extend the primacy of the confidentiality principle here as much as in the case of any past occurrence.

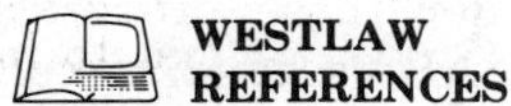
WESTLAW REFERENCES

Client Fraud in the Courts

dr7-102(b) (d.r. "disciplinary rule" /5 7-102(b) /p confiden!

The Scope of "Fraud"

dr7-102(b) (d.r. "disciplinary rule" /5 7-102(b)) /p fraud

Fraud on "Tribunals" and Similar Bodies

define definition /4 tribunal

Continuing Offenses

attorney-client /s privilege /s continu! ongoing /s offense wrong-doing

§ 12.6.6 Disclosure in Securities and Corporate Practice

Much of the controversy within the legal profession over the scope of disclosure obligations has been stimulated by the insistence of the Securities Exchange Commission in several recent administrations that lawyers sometimes must act to prevent or to disclose client violations of national securities laws.[59] That controversy holds both great interest for securities lawyers and has afforded a battleground for the conflict between proponents of confidentiality and those who place a higher value on protecting innocent parties against a client's wrongdoing.[60]

National Student Marketing

The first event which riveted the attention of the legal profession was the National Student Marketing litigation, filed by the SEC in 1972. The suit charged that partners in two major New York and Chicago law firms had violated federal securities laws by permitting a public offering of stock to occur in the closing of a merger transaction despite their knowledge[61] at the time of the closing that the offering documents contained material omissions. A federal court eventually held that the lawyers indeed had violated federal securities laws.[62] Their liability as aiders and

[58] For example, the gyrating course of opinions of the ABA ethics committee mapped in A.Kaufman, Problems in Professional Responsibility 116–18 (1976).

[59] See generally Johnson, The Expanding Responsibility of Attorneys in Practice before the SEC: Disciplinary Proceedings under Rule 2(e) of the Commission's Rules of Practice, 25 Mercer L.Rev. 637 (1974); Lipman, The SEC's Reluctant Police Force: A New Role for Lawyers, 49 NYU L.Rev. 437 (1974); Hoffman, On Learning of a Corporate Client's Crime or Fraud—The Lawyer's Dilemma, 33 Bus.Law. 1389 (1978); Kramer, Clients' Frauds and Their Lawyers' Obligations: A Study in Professional Irresponsibility, 67 Geo.L.J. 991 (1979).

[60] Small, Attorney's Responsibilities under Federal and State Securities Laws: Private Counsellor or Public Servant?, 61 Cal.L.Rev. 1189 (1973); Lipman, supra n.59; Redlich, Lawyers, the Temple, and the Market Place, 30 Bus.Law. 65 (1975); Lorne, The Corporate and Securities Adviser, The Public Interest, and Professional Ethics, 76 Mich.L.Rev. 425 (1978); Williams, Corporate Accountability and the Lawyer's Role, 34 Bus.Law. 7 (1978).

[61] Lawyer liability would not, however, exist in the absence either of actual knowledge of the fraudulent matters or, possibly, of reckless disregard of facts that indicated fraud. E.g., Franke v. Midwestern Okla. Dev. Auth., 428 F.Supp. 719 (W.D.Okl.1976), vacated on other grounds 619 F.2d 856 (10th Cir.1980).

[62] SEC v. National Student Marketing Corp., 457 F.Supp. 682 (D.D.C.1978). The court refused to grant the SEC its requested injunction against future securities violations because the court found no basis to believe that the law firms involved posed a threat of future violations.

Among the post mortem examinations of the court's opinion, see Gruenbaum, Corporate/Securities Lawyers: Disclosure, Responsibility, Liability to Investors, and *Na-*

abettors followed from their breach of a duty to their client company's shareholders that required them to attempt at least to delay the closing after they came into possession of knowledge of the fraud.[63]

The court refused to hold that the securities laws also required them to disclose their clients' securities violation if the mandated attempts to delay the closing were unavailing. Refusal to adopt a disclosure duty, however, depended on the facts of the case and on the court's narrow reading of the charge against the lawyers as limited to their acts involving the merger. They found that nothing the lawyers could have done would have affected the merger itself once it was completed.[64] Importantly, the decision thus found it unnecessary to take a position on the question whether disclosure would be required in other situations, such as when lawyers were explicitly charged with a securities violation for postmerger action or inaction. Nonetheless, because of the aider and abettor finding on the basis of failure to stop the closing, the law firms already stood exposed to potential liability for enormous sums in damages to injured parties.[65]

SEC Rule 2(e)

While *National Student Marketing* was pending in the courts, the SEC was considering somewhat related proposals to amend rule 2(e) of its rules admitting lawyers to practice before the agency.[66] A rule amendment proposed by a public interest group would have required lawyers to disclose client fraud committed upon the SEC or upon a third party. The proposal would have required disclosure to the agency or to the defrauded party even if confidential client information (but not information specifically protected by the attorney-client privilege) was involved.[67] The SEC refused to order this proposal published for comments but did order published for comments a revised proposal that required inside and outside counsel to report an extensive array of employee law violations to a company's board of directors and to certify to the SEC the company's and its lawyers' compliance with investigative and internal reporting requirements. The Commission's order indicated that it took no position on the proposal.[68] The bar's reaction to the proposals was strongly negative.[69] The SEC decided in 1980 not to consider those proposals further because of the ABA's pending consideration of the Kutak Commission proposals.[70]

The Carter-Johnson Case

But the SEC also had pending before it a second administrative matter with loud echoes of the *National Student Marketing* case. An SEC administrative law judge recommend-

tional Student Marketing Corp., 54 N.Dame Law. 795 (1979); Patterson, The Limits of the Lawyer's Discretion and the Law of Legal Ethics: *National Student Marketing* Revisited, 1979 Duke L.J. 1251. Among the legal journalistic accounts, see J.Goulden, The Million Dollar Lawyers 126–71 (1978).

63 457 F.Supp. at 712–713.

64 457 F.Supp. at 714–15.

65 Several damage actions, including a class action, had been filed against the law firms. Attempts to have the damage actions dismissed were unsuccessful. See Wachovia Bank & Trust Co. v. National Student Marketing Corp., 650 F.2d 342 (D.C.Cir.1980), cert.denied 452 U.S. 954, 101 S.Ct. 3098, 69 L.Ed.2d 965 (1981). Eventually the actions were settled by all defendants, involving reported payments of $1.95 million and $1.3 million by the two law firms. Nat'l L.J., Sept. 20, 1982, at 4, col. 2–3.

66 The importance of disciplinary power for the SEC is that this could be employed to expand the regulatory reach of the agency. Aside from such regulatory extensions, the securities laws themselves probably do not require a lawyer to do more than comply with generally accepted professional standards in order to avoid a finding of even negligent failure to comply with aider and abettor standards. Cf. SEC v. Arthur Young & Co., 590 F.2d 785 (9th Cir.1979)(auditor firm not in violation of securities-law aider and abettor standards when it complied with generally accepted professional standards).

67 Petition of the Institute for Public Interest Representation (May 25, 1978), reprinted in Curzan & Pelesh, The Changing Role of Outside Counsel: A Proposal for a Legal "Audit," 56 Notre Dame Law. 838, 840 n.15 (1981).

68 SEC Release No. 34–16,045, 44 Fed.Reg. 44,881 (1979).

69 Wheat, The Impact of SEC Professional Responsibility Standards, 34 Bus.Law. 969 (1979); Gross, Attorneys and Their Corporate Clients: SEC Rule 2(e) and the Georgetown "Whistle Blowing" Proposal, 3 Corp.L.Rev. 197 (1980).

70 SEC Release No. 34–16,769, 45 Fed.Reg. 30,454 (1980).

ed that the agency take disciplinary action, under its existing rule 2(e),[71] against two lawyers for their failure to take action despite their knowledge of a client's noncompliance with SEC reporting and disclosure regulations. Eventually a majority of the commission refused to approve a finding of a violation, but only because of previous unclear interpretations of rule 2(e).[72] The commission indicated that in the future it would discipline a lawyer who continued to represent a client but failed to take steps to end a client's noncompliance with the SEC's disclosure rules.[73]

Auditor Inquiries

Both the *National Student Marketing* case and the SEC rule 2(e) matters centered attention on what can be termed the "passive" duties of a securities lawyer: what affirmative steps may or must be taken by the lawyer to prevent client violation of the securities laws? Another problem related to securities law practice deals with the impingement upon the confidentiality principle of a lawyer's possible disclosure obligations when the lawyer is taking the active step of responding to auditors' requests for information.[74] A lawyer's full and accurate response to such requests may call for public revelation of either client wrongdoing or other facts that could supply the basis for legal action against a client. For example, such a revelation might lead to a lawsuit by injured consumers, competitors, or disgruntled minority shareholders. Information in the lawyer's possession about such matters is plainly treated as confidential under both the 1969 Code (DR 4-101(A)) and the 1983 Model Rules (MR 1.6).

Generally the command of securities law and of professional regulations here is the same. A lawyer may not knowingly make a material misstatement in the response and should take steps such as refusing to respond or withdrawing, if necessary, to avoid misstatement while maintaining confidential client information. But refusal to respond or withdrawal are themselves tantamount to revelation, because an auditor may then refuse to give the required certification of the completeness of the client's records. The most acute form of the problem occurs if a corporate client's auditors seek information from the company's lawyer about pending or threatened litigation that might affect its financial situation.[75] While client consent clearly could authorize a lawyer's full response, this obviously exposes the client to the risk of litigation that otherwise would not occur and might result in waiver of the attorney-client privilege for the purpose of testimony about the same transaction in future litigation (§ 6.4.6). As a result, a corporation would be under an incentive to keep information from a lawyer in order not to incur the risks of disclosure. Despite those difficulties, auditors insisted upon some form of disclosure sufficient to comply with their own professional requirements of a complete audit and in order to protect themselves against the risk of liability to persons who might claim that they were misled by a certified but incomplete financial statement.

71 17 C.F.R. § 201.2(e)(SEC may discipline lawyer found not to possess requisite qualifications to represent others, to lack character or integrity, to have engaged in unethical or improper professional conduct, or to have willfully violated any securities law or regulation).

72 In re Carter and Johnson, SEC Release No. 34–17,597 in CCH Fed.Sec.L.Rep. ¶ 82,847 (Feb. 28, 1981). The response of lawyers to the prospect of agency discipline was predictably quite adverse. E.g., Block & Ferris, SEC 2(e)—A New Standard of Ethical Conduct or an Unauthorized Web of Ambiguity?, 11 Cap.U.L.Rev. 501 (1982).

73 In re Carter & Johnson, supra at 84,145.

74 The public-interest group proposal rejected by the SEC in 1980 would also have required a full report to a company's auditors of all "violations or probable violations" of described kinds discovered by the company's lawyers. See SEC Release No. 34–16,045, 44 Fed.Reg. 44,881 (1979). See supra n.67

75 The auditors' position insisting on full disclosure was in part motivated by an interest in protecting themselves against possible liability to defrauded purchasers of securities. See generally Note, Attorney Responses to Audit Letters: The Problem of Disclosing Loss Contingencies Arising from Litigation and Unasserted Claims, 51 NYU L.Rev. 838 (1976); Comment, Securities Lawyers' Responsibility and Accountants' Liability: Disclosure of Contingent Liabilities, 53 Tex.L.Rev. 1483 (1975).

The ultimate resolution of the problem was a joint communique, called a Statement of Policy, officially approved by the ABA in 1975 and the American Institute of Certified Public Accountants in 1976.[76] Essentially the Statement of Policy gives full protection to the confidentiality principle at the obvious expense of a full audit of the company's actual financial condition. The statement requires a responding lawyer to mention only (1) litigation already pending, or to refer the auditor to lawyers handling the litigation; and (2) claims not yet in litigation but already asserted by another party. The lawyer is under no obligation to comment on unasserted contingent liabilities unless directed by the client.

Disclosure and Entity Clients

Mention should also be made of a defeated proposal of the Kutak Commission that the Model Rules authorize a lawyer to disclose that an employee of an entity client, such as a corporation or government agency, intended to commit an illegal act threatening serious harm to the entity.[77] The proposal was supported both on the now familiar argument that the rights of intended victims of illegality might require protection through disclosure [78] and on the much broader ground that a lawyer for an entity should be free to resort even to public disclosure if the lawyer in his or her considered judgment believed that disclosure was necessary in order to protect the interests of the entity itself.[79] It was opposed on the grounds that its mere existence would seriously impair the corporate client-lawyer relationship principally in making the flow of information more restricted and that, being discretionary, it would hardly ever be availed of by corporate lawyers.[80]

The provision for discretionary disclosure was removed through a floor amendment in February 1983, leaving a broad and general injunction to lawyers to protect client information in all such instances (MR 1.13(b)) and referring a lawyer to the possibility of withdrawal (MR 1.13(c)). Whether the proposed permission would very frequently have been invoked is debatable. The vulnerability of any corporate lawyer whistle-blower makes it exceedingly doubtful that much self-destructive and discretionary behavior of the described type would have occurred.[81]

WESTLAW REFERENCES

National Student Marketing

457 +10 682 & "national student marketing"

SEC Rule 2(e)

"securities regulation" & "rule2(e)"

Auditor Inquiries

lawyer counsel** attorney /p securities /7 violat! /25 disclos! privilege** confiden!

§ 12.7 DISCLOSURE IN EX PARTE AND SIMILAR PROCEEDINGS

The professional rules and judicial decisions assert that lawyers have occasional duties to compromise client interests or even to disclose confidential client information in presenting cases. Decisions requiring disclosure of perjury are a prominent example (§ 12.5.3). An assortment of other disclosure obligations are occasionally insisted upon. Some of the instances involve face-to-face communications between judge and lawyer. They seem to be particularizations of a general duty imposed on lawyers not to mislead judges and are thus concerned with the trustworthiness of the affected lawyer. In other situations disclosure

76 Statement of Policy Regarding Lawyers' Responses to Auditors' Requests for Information, 31 Bus.Law. 565 (1975). See generally Benson, Lawyers' Responses to Audit Inquiries—A Continuing Controversy, 144 J.Accountancy 72 (July, 1977).

77 MR 1.13(c) (Proposed Final Draft, May 30, 1981). See also § 13.7.5.

78 Ferrara & Steinberg, The Role of Inside Counsel in the Corporate Accountability Process, 4 Corp.L.Rev. 3 (1981)(unofficial views of general counsel of SEC).

79 MR 1.13 legal background note, at 92–93 (Proposed Final Draft, May 30, 1981).

80 Higginbotham, "See No Evil, Hear No Evil, Speak No Evil"— Developing a Policy for Disclosure by Counsel to Public Corporations, 7 J.Corp.L. 285 (1982).

81 Slovak, The Ethics of Corporate Lawyers: A Sociological Approach, 1981 Am.B.Found. Research J. 753.

is required to correct deficiencies of the adversary system. These latter professional obligations seem less concerned with the character and fitness of lawyers and more preoccupied with assuring that injustices do not occur in the adversary system.[82]

Ex Parte Representation

Significant case authority supports the proposition that a lawyer representing a client before a judge in an ex parte hearing is held to a significantly higher standard of candor than he or she would have been if the hearing had been contested. Thus lawyers have been disciplined for inducing a judge to sign an order without revealing that another judge had previously refused to grant the same requested relief[83] or that another judge had scheduled a contested hearing to consider whether to grant the requested relifef.[84] Candor is particularly insisted upon when the proceeding is conducted ex parte at the request of the party or lawyer who then made an incomplete disclosure.[85] Complete candor is also required, in retrospect, when the failure to correct a judge's misunderstanding of the facts is attributable to the lawyer's motivation to protect a dubious fee arrangement or a similar proprietary interest of the lawyer.[86]

Fiducial Proceedings

Courts are also more likely to insist on an exceptional level of candor, and thus require disclosure of material facts, when the interests of a vulnerable person are at stake, such as in a probate, adoption, guardianship, conservatorship, or similar proceeding.[87] Occasionally courts insist that lawyers accord their own jurisdiction a ward-like solicitude, requiring full disclosure from all lawyers of facts that might deprive the court of jurisdiction.[88] Both situations are apparently instances in which the social policies favoring

[82] In re Selser, 15 N.J. 393, 105 A.2d 395, 401–402 (1954)(strict disclosure duties are enforced against lawyers so that the truth will be revealed and justice will triumph).

[83] Snyder v. State Bar, 18 Cal.3d 286, 133 Cal.Rptr. 864, 555 P.2d 1104 (1976); Di Sabatino v. State Bar, 27 Cal.3d 159, 162 Cal.Rptr. 458, 606 P.2d 765 (1980); In re Opacak, 257 Minn. 600, 101 N.W.2d 606 (1960).

[84] In re Barnes, 281 Or. 375, 574 P.2d 657 (1978)(prosecutor reprimanded for obtaining search warrant for blood sample from alleged rapist without revealing setting of same request for later hearing before another judge). See also Harkin v. Brundage, 276 U.S. 36, 56, 48 S.Ct. 268, 275, 72 L.Ed. 457 (1928)(lawyer, who purposefully caused delay in appointment of state court receiver until a more favorable federal court receiver could be appointed without disclosing to federal court that state action was pending, caused "a fraud not only upon the state court but upon the federal court itself").

[85] Addison v. Brown, 413 So.2d 1240 (Fla.App.1982), affirmed 428 So.2d 663 (Fla.1983).

[86] In re Arlan's Dept. Stores, Inc., 615 F.2d 925 (2d Cir. 1979)(nondisclosure by firm acting as special counsel for debtor of forwarding and fee arrangements); Lewis v. TelePrompter Corp., 88 F.R.D. 11 (S.D.N.Y.1980)(failure to disclose fee-splitting arrangement among law firms in application for fees in class-action case); In re Turner, 83 N.J. 536, 416 A.2d 894 (1980)(failure to disclose to receivership court lawyer's receipt of check from insolvent corporation in payment of fee claim); In re Rensch, 333 N.W.2d 713 (S.D.1983)(failure to disclose fee arrangement with purportedly indigent client); In re Witt, 96 Wn.2d 56, 633 P.2d 880, 886 (1981)(failure to disclose to judge at time of client's sentencing that client's ability to pay fine was seriously impaired by terms of lawyer's prior business arrangement with client). See also, e.g., Hennigan v. Harris County, 593 S.W.2d 380 (Tex.Civ.App.1979) (judgment against lawyer for fraud affirmed where lawyer failed to inform court of receipt of legal fees prior to obtaining execution for judgment for fees).

[87] Potter v. Moran, 239 Cal.App.2d 873, 49 Cal.Rptr. 229 (1966)(failure of trustees and their lawyer to disclose conflicting simultaneous representation of life beneficiaries as extrinsic fraud); In re Estate of Gullett, 92 Ill. App.2d 405, 234 N.E.2d 551, 554 (1968)(lawyer-coexecutor's duty to report waste of estate by coexecutor to court); State ex rel. Nebraska State Bar Ass'n v. McArthur, 212 Neb. 815, 326 N.W.2d 173 (1982)(less-than-complete disclosure in probate proceeding); In re Walker, 87 A.D.2d 555, 448 N.Y.S.2d 474 (1982)(adoption proceeding); In re Greene, 290 Or. 291, 620 P.2d 1379 (1980) (suspension for failure to reveal in ex parte application for approval of purchase of property for guardianship estate that guardian owned interest being sold). See also, e.g., Ramey v. Thomas, 382 So.2d 78 (Fla.App.), review denied 389 So.2d 116 (1980)(lawyer impermissibly obtained adoption without revealing that previous proceeding seeking adoption had failed and that public agency advised against adoption); In re Rudie, 290 Or. 471, 622 P.2d 1098 (1981)(ex parte application for guardianship of alleged cult member).

[88] Douglas v. Donovan, 704 F.2d 1276 (D.C.Cir.1983) (facts affecting possible mootness); Amherst & Clarence Ins. Co. v. Cazenovia Tavern, Inc., 59 N.Y.2d 983, 466 N.Y.S.2d 660, 453 N.E.2d 1077 (1983)(mootness); R.Stern & E.Gressman, Supreme Court Practice 896 (5th ed.1976). For expansive expressions of a duty of lawyers to inform the court of matters not related to jurisdiction, see, e.g.,

results based on all known material facts are so strongly preferred that the normal client-protecting instincts of lawyers are overridden.

The basis for requiring disclosure in such cases is unclear in the 1969 Code but clear and wide sweeping in the 1983 Model Rules. The Code's requirements are insecurely set in vague or question-begging provisions, such as those broadly prohibiting lawyer dishonesty [89] or conduct impeding the administration of justice,[90] or provisions prohibiting failing to disclose matters required by law to be disclosed.[91] The 1983 Model Rules, in MR 3.3(d), enunciate a broad disclosure rule in ex parte proceedings that is rather clearly based on a policy of full ventilation of all relevant fact issues:

> (d) In an ex parte proceeding, a lawyer shall inform the tribunal [92] of all facts known to the lawyer which will enable the tribunal to make an informed decision, whether or not the facts are adverse.

A comment adds the perhaps important qualification that this duty extends to disclosures that the lawyer "reasonably believes" [93] are necessary to enable the judge to reach an informed decision.[94] And a comment to MR 3.8 adds the important note that a prosecutor's presentation to a grand jury is subject to the full disclosure rule of MR 3.3(d).[95]

Client Identity

While the relevant information would almost certainly be a matter of record in any event, lawyers are generally not entitled to keep secret the identity of their clients when litigating in behalf of a client. Under the Code a lawyer is required to identify both the client and, if different, the person who employed the lawyer unless this information is privileged or irrelevant (DR 7–106(B)(2)). Because the client's identity is not normally privileged against disclosure (see § 6.3.5), the exception will not often apply. Under the Model Rules the similar obligation apparently applies only in nonadjudicative proceedings in legislatures or administrative agencies.[96]

WESTLAW REFERENCES

Ex Parte Representation

lawyer counsel** attorney /p ex-parte /s candor honest*

Fiduciary Proceedings

lawyer counsel** attorney /s fiducia*** /s candor honest* disclos! reveal revelation /5 tribunal court

Client Identity

lawyer counsel** attorney /s disclos! reveal*** revelation secret** /s client /5 identity

---

Fusari v. Steinberg, 419 U.S. 379, 390–91, 95 S.Ct. 533, 540, 42 L.Ed.2d 521 (1975)(Burger, C.J., concurring)(lawyers required to advise court "of any development which may conceivably affect an outcome"); State v. White, 94 Wn.2d 498, 617 P.2d 998 (1980)(defense counsel's duty to inform court of trial setting beyond mandatory speedy-trial time limitation). Cf. § 12.8 (legal authority).

89 In re Nigohosian, 88 N.J. 308, 442 A.2d 1007, 1010 (1982)(nondisclosure as conduct involving dishonesty, fraud, deceit, or misrepresentation under DR 1–102(A)(4) and as conduct prejudicial to the administration of justice under DR 1–102(A)(5)).

90 State ex rel. Nebraska State Bar Ass'n v. McArthur, 212 Neb. 815, 326 N.W.2d 173, 175 (1982)(failure to disclose facts and submitting incomplete report to probate court "served to demean that court of justice and its judicial officer, impeded and obstructed the administration of justice, and brought discredit to respondent, the profession, and the courts").

91 United States v. Crawford, 707 F.2d 447 (10th Cir. 1983). Occasionally, however, explicit legal rules will require a lawyer to make disclosure. E.g., In re Arlan's Dept. Stores, Inc., 615 F.2d 925 (2d Cir.1979)(disclosure requirements of rules of bankruptcy procedure).

92 Note that by clear implication the obligation does not extend to a "legislative or administrative tribunal" by force of MR 3.9.

93 See the "Terminology" section at the beginning of the Model Rules.

94 MR 3.3 comment (Ex Parte Proceedings).

95 MR 3.8 comment (first paragraph).

96 MR 3.9 (lawyer in a nonadjudicative proceeding before a legislative or administrative tribunal "shall disclose that the appearance is in a representative capacity"). The same affirmative disclosure obligation is not imposed on lawyers representing clients in courtroom litigation or in adjudicative proceedings before legislatures or administrative agencies, perhaps because it was thought that this is commonly required by procedural rules in courts in any event.

§ 12.8 DISCLOSING ADVERSE LEGAL AUTHORITY

Scope of the Disclosure Duty

Both the 1969 Code, in DR 7-106(B)(1), and the 1983 Model Rules, in Rule 3.3(a)(3), require a lawyer to disclose known adverse legal authority if it is not disclosed by other lawyers in the case. The Model Rule is copied from the Code.[97] The rule is subject to either technical, and narrow, readings or to broader constructions. It is open to the interpretation, for example, that only those rare authorities need be disclosed that, if known, would destroy the client's position. Rarely will a lawyer attempt to assert a position in the face of such contrary authority, but instances do occur.[98] The rule has been supported[99] and attacked[1] in the legal literature, although it has very rarely been invoked against a noncompliant lawyer in a reported case.

Rationale of the Law-Disclosure Requirement

The arguments of principle against a law-disclosure obligation are some of the same arguments generally offered against other disclosure rules—such a rule is unnecessary in the context of the adversarial system and places the advocate in the needlessly compromised position of doing injury to the client's interests. One of the principal arguments against disclosure rules—the protection of client confidentiality—is, of course, almost certainly irrelevant in most imaginable instances because the lawyer's knowledge of legal authority will almost always come from nonconfidential sources. Thus the disclosure rule does not have the effect of impairing the openness of client-lawyer communications, as is claimed for some other disclosure requirements.

The arguments in favor of the mandatory disclosure rule are problematical on two related scores. The justifications are that legal argument should be addressed to the legal premises properly applicable to the case[2] and that the complexity of the law requires disclosure so that the court can fairly and accurately resolve the matter.[3] But, first, it is not clear that the costs of the mandatory rule (compromise of a lawyer's loyalty) can regularly achieve a worthwhile end. Moreover, to the extent that the opposing party loses an important *legal position or argument* because of ignorance of the law, the loss closely resembles waivers of legal positions by incompetent or poorly prepared litigators. In those other waiver situations, courts have been unwilling to compromise the knowledgeable lawyer's full-advocacy role.[4] Second, the rule is arguably inconsistent with the refusal to create a

[97] No equivalent rule existed in the 1908 Canons, although ABA Formal Opinion 146 (1935) asserted that such a duty was embodied in Canon 22 ("The conduct of the lawyer before the Court and with other lawyers should be characterized by candor and fairness."). An early draft of the Model Rules would have gone further and required disclosure of any authority "that would probably have a substantial effect on the determination of a material issue." MR 3.1(c) (Discussion Draft, Jan. 30, 1980).

[98] Southern Pac. Transp. Co. v. Public Utilities Comm'n, 716 F.2d 1285, 1291 (9th Cir.1983), cert.denied ___ U.S. ___, 104 S.Ct. 1908, 80 L.Ed.2d 457 (1984); Cicio v. City of New York, 98 A.D.2d 38, 469 N.Y.S.2d 467 (1983)(city's lawyers failed to cite authorities directly adverse to position in present appeal although city was unsuccessful party to two of these precedents).

[99] Hazard, Arguing the Law: The Advocate's Duty and Opportunity, 16 Ga.L.Rev. 821 (1982); Smith & Metzloff, The Attorney as Advocate: "Arguing the Law," 16 Ga.L. Rev. 841 (1982)(criticizing an earlier, and rejected, version of Model Rule 3.3(a)(3) but agreeing with the approach of DR 7-106(B)(1)); Uviller, Zeal and Frivolity: The Ethical Duty of the Appellate Advocate to Tell the Truth about the Law, 6 Hofstra L.Rev. 729 (1977); Pye, The Role of Counsel in the Suppression of Truth, 1978 Duke L.J. 921, 938; Thode, The Ethical Standard for the Advocate, 39 Texas L.Rev. 575, 585–86 (1961).

[1] Freedman, Arguing the Law in an Adversary System, 16 Ga.L.Rev. 833 (1982). See also G.Warvelle, Essays in Legal Ethics 196 (1920)(a lawyer "is under no obligation to present, or comment upon, those phases of the law that may seem to militate against his client's cause, and he may combat the application of such adverse law, whether advanced by the court or opposing counsel. These rights are clear and of universal recognition in all courts of justice.").

[2] MR 3.3 comment (Misleading Legal Argument).

[3] EC 7-23.

[4] § 4.6.1 (procedural forfeiture). Nonetheless, the court in Minority Police Officers Ass'n v. City of South Bend, 721 F.2d 197, 199 (7th Cir.1983), asserted extravagantly that a lawyer could not decide to ignore doubts about subject-matter jurisdiction in order to obtain a ruling on the merits.

general obligation to reveal *facts* that are directly adverse to the client's position (see § 12.3.2). Indeed, fact revelation is probably more necessary to a fair result because information about facts is accessible only to the parties, while the law is almost always equally accessible to both lawyers and, for that matter, to a judge or the judge's clerk.[5] It is only a partial response to note that a decision on a legal issue will have wide public impact because of the doctrine of stare decisis. In most probable instances in which the obligation would arise—in evidentiary and similar rulings in trial courts—the ruling will have no or little stare decisis effect.

Both the Code and the Model Rule provisions bristle with interpretative issues. Among others, what is a "controlling jurisdiction" whose adverse legal authorities must be cited? Does this include, for example, rulings of a federal district court in a federal habeas corpus proceeding with respect to a state court criminal proceeding? What is the last point in a proceeding at which a lawyer may satisfy the disclosure obligation? Or must disclosure always be made in the first instance? Must disclosure be made of the overturning or other nullification of an authority that was on point and apparently valid when cited?[6] Is a legal authority "directly adverse" if a nonfrivolous argument can be made distinguishing it?

The mandatory reach of the rule is effectively neutralized in many real-life settings because it merely parallels what prudence dictates independently. Effective advocacy of a client's legal position will most often involve full revelation of adverse authorities, together with arguments distinguishing or criticizing them. Candor here both takes the wind from an opponent's sails and instills judicial trust in the quality and completeness of presentation. If nothing else, a court's late discovery that an advocate has failed to confront an adverse authority is likely to produce the impression that the awakened precedent, because suppressed, should be regarded as particularly vicious.

WESTLAW REFERENCES

Scope of the Disclosure Duty

dr7–106(b) (d.r. "disciplinary rule" /5 7–106(b))

§ 12.9 DISCLOSING JURY TAMPERING

The Code, in DR 7–108(G), requires a lawyer to report promptly[7] to the court any improper[8] conduct by a juror or venireman, or by anyone toward such a person, "of which the lawyer has knowledge.[9] The Code's disclosure rule has been frequently invoked by courts, normally under circumstances raising no significant confidentiality issue.[10] If the

[5] The English barrister is under an unquestioned obligation to cite all relevant law to the judge, whether favorable or unfavorable. Whether as result or cause, it is not customary for an English judge to perform private legal research about the law in a case, although the judge may reserve judgment in order to study the record or cited cases more fully. See Pugsley, The Advocate's Duty to the Court, in Fundamental Duties (D.Lasok et al. eds. 1980), at 114, 119.

In the American tradition of advocacy, it is perhaps not whimsical to suggest that the rationale of the law-disclosure obligation is to prevent embarrassment to judges, who are supposed to know the law but not the facts or the legal positions that parties may wish to assert or waive. Under such a theory, of course, the rule is far too broad because it includes many instances in which a judge would not be expected to know the law, or should not be embarrassed by ignorance.

[6] Croy v. Skinner, 410 F.Supp. 117, 125 n.7 (N.D.Ga. 1976)(when principal case relied on in a brief is reversed after submission, good practice dictates submission of supplementary brief drawing court's attention to reversal).

[7] A lawyer's failure to report promptly may constitute a waiver of that party's ability to object to the juror misconduct. E.g., Omaha Bank v. Siouxland Cattle Cooperative, 305 N.W.2d 458 (Iowa 1981). On the due diligence required with respect to juror misconduct discovered after trial, see Elisovsky v. State, 592 P.2d 1221, 1228 (Alaska 1979).

[8] In re R, 276 Or. 365, 554 P.2d 522 (1976)(if court later determines that conduct was improper, despite lawyer's reasonable belief to contrary, ethical violation has occurred).

[9] See also Calif.R. 7-106(G). The asserted basis for the disclosure rule is the duty of a lawyer to aid in protecting the integrity of the jury system. See EC 7–32.

[10] State v. Young, 181 N.J.Super. 463, 438 A.2d 344 (App.Div.1981). Cf. Smith v. Phillips, 455 U.S. 209, 220, 102 S.Ct. 940, 947, 71 L.Ed.2d 78 (1982)(conduct of prosecutor in not disclosing to defense or to trial court that one

lawyer knows that a client intends to bribe a juror or engage in similar wrongful conduct, the "future crime" notion strips the lawyer's information of its otherwise confidential nature and leaves the disclosure obligation intact.[11] It has also been held that even if a client who is the source of the lawyer's information is not involved in or a beneficiary of the wrongful conduct, still the lawyer must disclose the information, although the lawyer may not be required to divulge the client's identity unless no other means are available to investigate the incident satisfactorily.[12]

The 1983 Model Rules contain no provision similar to DR 7–108(G) of the Code. Rule 3.5(a) does prohibit a lawyer from illegally seeking to influence a juror or potential juror, and rule 3.5(b) prohibits ex parte communications with such a person. A lawyer who has knowledge of such a violation on the part of another lawyer is required by rule 8.3(a), in certain circumstances, (see § 12.10) to inform the appropriate professional authority but not, apparently, the court adjudicating the matter in which the possibly contaminated juror presently sits. In that respect the rule seems unduly limited; if disclosure is required at all, it should run both to the disciplinary authorities and to the affected tribunal.

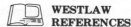

WESTLAW REFERENCES

dr7–108(g) (d.r. "disciplinary rule" /5 7–108(g))

§ 12.10 DISCLOSING LAWYERS' MISCONDUCT

§ 12.10.1 Reporting Lawyer Wrongdoing [13]

The Lawyer Code Reporting Requirements

Both the 1969 Code, in DR 1–103(A),[14] and the 1983 Model Rules, in Rule 8.3(a), impose a mandatory reporting obligation on every lawyer with respect to other lawyers' [15] violations of the professional rules.[16] Probably no other professional requirement is as widely ignored by lawyers subject to it.[17] Lawyer complaints form a relatively small percentage of the complaints received by lawyer discipline agencies.[18] And some of those probably are moti-

of jurors in pending murder trial had applied for job with prosecutor's office not condoned but not violation of due process here).

[11] In re Doe, 551 F.2d 899, 901 (2d Cir.1977)(duty to report involvement of client, accused in criminal case, in ongoing attempt to bribe juror).

[12] In re Kozlov, 79 N.J. 232, 398 A.2d 882 (1979)(attorney-client privilege protects identity of client who told lawyer of juror misconduct in unrelated case).

[13] See generally Thode, The Duty of Lawyers and Judges to Report Other Lawyers' Breaches of the Standards of the Legal Profession, 1976 Utah L.Rev. 95; Note, The Lawyer's Duty to Report Professional Misconduct, 20 Ariz.L.Rev. 509 (1978).

[14] Some jurisdictions omitted DR 1–102(A) entirely (District of Columbia, Massachusetts, Washington) or removed its mandatory force by use of the precatory auxiliary verb *should* (Arizona, Florida, New Jersey, North Carolina). See ABA Code of Professional Responsibility by State 5–6 (1977).

[15] ABA Informal Opinion 1279 (1973) asserted that a lawyer who fails to report his or her *own* violation of another Disciplinary Rule violated DR 1–103(A), but no case seems to support this rather strained and clearly redundant reading.

[16] The 1908 Canons of Ethics provided in Canon 29 ("Upholding the Honor of the Profession") that "lawyers should expose without fear or favor before the proper tribunals corrupt or dishonest conduct in the profession . . ." and specifically enjoined lawyers to report the condemned practice of "stirring up litigation directly or through agents" "to the end that the offender may be disbarred."

[17] J.Carlin, Lawyers' Ethics 153 (1966). Carlin cites fear of retaliation, lack of concern, and a belief in the greater effectiveness of other enforcement measures, such as cutting off referrals, as reasons for lawyers' failure to report. Strong emotional or philosophical reaction against disclosure may play a part for some. E.g., Arkin, Self-Regulation and Approaches to Maintaining Standards of Professional Integrity, 30 U.Miami L.Rev. 803, 815 (1976)(Code's reporting obligation is abandonment of "discretion and judgment and basic human decency"); Brown, ABA Code of Professional Responsibility: In Defense of Mediocrity, 6 Trial 29, 30 (Aug.-Sept. 1970)(Code criticized as creating "a true 'Gestapo' informer system, with each attorney legally bound to police his brother attorney").

[18] Schneyer, The Model Rules and Problems of Code Interpretation and Enforcement, 1980 Am.B.Found. Research J. 939, 950 (lawyers file only 10–15% of grievances). See also ABA Spec. Comm. on Evaluation of Disciplinary Enforcement, Problems and Recommendations in Disciplinary Enforcement (Clark Report) 167 (1970):

vated by self-interest or self-protection of the complaining lawyer or of a client.[19]

Yet the general absence of professional peer complaints should not automatically be attributed solely to sullen indifference, craven cowardliness, or clubbish protectionism among lawyers. Filing a disciplinary complaint can incur substantial personal risk for a lawyer if the subject of the complaint is a lawyer in a position of power in the profession or in the legal system.[20] Particularly in small communities or when the lawyers for other reasons have close practice relationships, friendships and future clientele and fees might be seriously at risk. Retaliation might also take the form of a defamation suit, although generally complaining parties are afforded absolute immunity.[21] It is doubtless desirable that lawyers often incur such risks and report other lawyers' violations in order to protect the public against lawyer depredations that would otherwise be largely undetectable and in order to enhance the image and thus the accessibility of the legal profession.[22] But it is more than trifling to make it obligatory to report, as both the Code and the Model Rules do. Those obligations, however, seem to result in discipline only in rare cases, and then as one charge among many.[23]

Scope of the Reporting Requirement

At least at the verbal level, the Code and the Model Rules differ with respect to the kind of lawyer misdeeds that trigger the reporting obligation. Much has been made of the fact that the Code, in DR 1–103(A), becomes operative without apparent limitation when an observing lawyer has knowledge of a "violation" even if it is of a trivial nature.[24] The fact, of course, is that no recorded instance exists of a lawyer disciplined under the Code for failure to report a trivial violation. Nonetheless, the addition in MR 8.3(a) of language indicating that the observed violation must be one "that raises a substantial question as to that lawyer's honesty, trustworthiness or fitness as a lawyer in other respects" is a correct and welcome beginning on clarification. As a standard for imposing a mandatory obligation, however, it is unfortunately vague and indefinite. Both DR 1–103(A) and MR 8.3(a) require only that a lawyer "possess" or "have" knowledge of another lawyer's violation. In each instance, the standard requires less than absolute certainty.[25]

Although lawyers and judges have the necessary background to evaluate the conduct of attorneys and are far better equipped than laymen to recognize violations of professional standards, relatively few complaints are submitted to disciplinary agencies by members of the profession. This fact has been cited as a major problem by nearly every disciplinary agency in the United States surveyed by this Committee. . . .

[19] Committee of Professional Ethics v. Hanson, 244 N.W.2d 822 (Iowa 1976)(law partners searched office of respondent lawyer after he announced intention to leave partnership, and found quantities of marijuana, other drugs, and records indicating use of client funds for personal purposes; their subsequent complaint resulted in respondent's disbarment); In re Montgomery, 292 Or. 796, 643 P.2d 338 (1982)(new lawyers representing principals in attempt to recover usurious loan from former counsel). Lawyers representing plaintiffs in legal malpractice suits have an incentive to report the matter sued on to the appropriate lawyer discipline agency as well, in order to avoid a retaliatory charge of a violation of the reporting requirement.

[20] In re Gonyo, 73 Wis.2d 624, 245 N.W.2d 893 (1976) (two lawyers who filed complaint about conduct of prosecutor were subsequently charged with serious criminal offenses by prosecutor).

[21] United States v. Hurt, 177 U.S.App.D.C. 15, 543 F.2d 162, 167 (1976); Kerpelman v. Bricker, 23 Md.App. 628, 329 A.2d 423 (1974). See § 3.4.2.

[22] It is either nominalistic or question-begging to assert, as does MR 8.3 comment (first paragraph), that the concept of professional self-regulation by itself dictates a reporting obligation. See Schneyer, The Model Rules and Problems of Code Interpretation and Enforcement, 1980 Am.B.Found. Research J. 939, 950–51 ("If the courts determined that the Rules should be enforced solely through a combination of voluntary grievances or tips and agency-initiated investigations, and if the reporting requirement was dropped as a result, 'self-regulation' would hardly have been transformed into something else.").

[23] Attorney Grievance Comm'n v. Kahn, 290 Md. 654 431 A.2d 1336, 1342 (1981)(failure to report as one of many charges in ambulance-chasing scheme).

[24] MR 8.3 comment (third paragraph).

[25] Cf. Williams v. Council of the North Carolina Bar, 46 N.C.App. 824, 266 S.E.2d 391 (1980)(North Carolina DR 1–103(A) requires that lawyer have knowledge of "clear" violation).

Neither the Code nor the Model Rules requirement applies if reporting would require disclosure of confidential client information.[26] The effect of that exception substantially narrows the requirement but does not eliminate it. The clearest example of application of the exception would be when a lawyer is professionally consulted by another lawyer with respect to a past violation of professional rules. Reporting would not be required because of the exception for confidential client information.[27] But confidentiality extends much farther. For illustration, suppose that an opposing lawyer in litigation commits a disciplinary violation. If the violation causes disadvantage to the observing lawyer's client, no confidentiality rule excepts the violation from mandatory reporting.[28] That is also a situation, of course, in which zeal in the client's interests might independently suggest the desirability of a complaint. On the other hand, assume that the opposing lawyer's violation works to the advantage of the observing lawyer's client, for example, because the other lawyer's blatantly incompetent representation of the opposing party gave a substantial litigation advantage to the observing lawyer's client. Disclosure might alert the opposing litigant and occasion an attack on the client's advantage. To that extent disclosure would impinge upon the "secret" of a client under the 1969 Code and is excepted— indeed, disclosure is prohibited.[29]

The reporting obligation of MR 8.3(a) is narrower than the Code's DR 1–103(A) in one material way. The confidentiality rule extends to all "information relating to representation of a client," the only relevant exception being that for "disclosures impliedly authorized to carry out the representation." [30] Thus, reporting is foreclosed if it would entail revelation of any client information, whether or not revelation would prejudice the client's interests. Reporting under rule 8.3(a), therefore, is required only (1) when to do so would affirmatively advance a client's interests; or (2) when reporting would not involve revelation of any information relating to the representation of a client.

Violations within a lawyer's own firm are subject to a much narrower reporting requirement, if any, than violations known about nonfirm lawyers. Because of the reach of the confidentiality rules under both the Code and the Model Rules, only disciplinary violations harmful to a firm's client (embezzlement from client trust funds or representation of conflicting interests, for example) are generally subject to the reporting requirement. That follows because an affected client would generally be benefitted by revealing only those kinds of violations. Also included within the reporting requirement would be most instances of illicit advertising and solicitation and similar offenses by any firm lawyer, because reporting these offenses would generally not involve client information. In the nature of things, reporting the violations of nonfirm lawyers that are observed other than when representing a client will rarely involve client information and thus will rarely be excepted from the reporting requirement.

Reporting Judicial Misconduct

The Code's DR 1–103(A) apparently does not require a lawyer to report conduct of a judge that is a violation of the Code of Judicial Conduct but that does not violate the Code of Professional Responsibility.[31] The converse is not true, however. Judges are

26 DR 1–103(A)("a lawyer possessing unprivileged knowledge"); MR 8.3(c)("This rule does not require disclosure of information otherwise protected by rule 1.6.").

27 See also MR 8.3 comment (fourth paragraph).

28 Under MR 1.6(a) that would be true so long as reporting the violation pursuant to MR 8.3(a) advances an interest of the reporting lawyer's client.

29 DR 4–101(A)("secret" includes information gained in the professional relationship disclosure of which "would be likely to be detrimental to the client").

30 § 6.7.2. The comment to MR 8.3 (second paragraph) suggests in precatory language that a lawyer "should" encourage a client to consent to the disclosure of Rule 1.6 information in order to file a complaint if this would not substantially prejudice the client.

31 A lawyer-judge's violation of the Code of Professional Responsibility would fall under the proscription of DR 1–102(A)(1), and thus an observing lawyer would be under the reporting requirement of DR 1–103(A).

under an obligation to report unprofessional conduct of lawyers. That is required by redundant provisions of both the Code of Judicial Conduct (Canon 3B(3)) [32] and, if the judge is also a lawyer, of the Code of Professional Responsibility (DR 1–103(A)). Model Rule 8.3(b) extends beyond the Code by requiring a lawyer who knows of a judge's violation of a rule of judicial conduct to inform the appropriate authority.[33] Under the Model Rules all judges would presumably remain subject to the requirement of Canon 3B(3) to report lawyer violations of applicable professional rules.

WESTLAW REFERENCES

dr1–103(a) (d.r. "disciplinary rule" /5 1–103(a))

Scope of the Reporting Requirement

dr1–103(a) (d.r. "disciplinary rule" /5 1–103(a)) /p unprivileged privileged

Reporting Judicial Misconduct

topic(227) & misconduct (violat! /7 code) unprofessional /p report***

§ 12.10.2 Cooperating with Disciplinary Agencies

Both the Code (DR 1–103(B)) and the Model Rules (Rule 8.1(b)), in substantially similar language, require a lawyer to respond to proper requests for the lawyer to supply information to a disciplinary agency. The requirement is not limited to giving testimony when compelled to do so by coercive process and thus clearly includes furnishing information when it is requested at an investigatory stage. Unlike the reporting requirement, the rule of cooperation applies to investigations and proceedings involving both other lawyers [34] and the very lawyer from whom the information is sought.[35] The failure to cooperate is an entirely separate offense from the matter being investigated. Both the Code and Model Rule regulations also explicitly apply to requests for information from judicial disciplinary agencies. Model Rule 8.1(b) applies to requests by bar admission authority; the Code, apparently through oversight, does not.[36]

WESTLAW REFERENCES

topic(45) /p cooperat! inform! /5 investigat! disciplin!

[32] "A judge should take or initiate appropriate disciplinary measures against a judge or lawyer for unprofessional conduct of which the judge may become aware." Unlike the Code of Professional Responsibility, the ABA Code of Judicial Conduct generally employs "should" as an indication of a mandatory rule.

[33] As with the correlative rule requiring lawyer reporting of other lawyers' violations (MR 8.3(a)), the rule requiring reports of judicial code violations is subject to the limitation that the violation must raise "a substantial question as to the judge's fitness for office" and the exception of MR 8.3(c) for revelations that would require disclosure of confidential client information.

[34] In re Ojala, 289 N.W.2d 108 (Minn.1979)(ignoring telephone calls and letters requesting information about public charges respondent made against other lawyer and judge).

[35] See also § 3.4.3.

[36] Cf. DR 1–101(B) (lawyer shall not further the admission of applicant known to be unqualified).

Chapter Thirteen
LAWYERS AS COUNSELORS

Table of Sections

---

§ 13.1 OVERVIEW OF A LAWYER'S WORK

The Predominance of Office Work

In the course of a working day the average general practitioner will engage in a number of legal tasks, each involving different legal doctrines, legal skills, legal processes, legal institutions, clients, and other interested parties. Even the increasing numbers of lawyers in specialized practice will usually perform at least some legal services outside their specialty. And even within a narrow specialty such as tax practice, a lawyer will shift from one legal task or role such as advice-giving to an importantly different one such as representing a client before an administrative agency. By no means will most of this work involve litigation, unless the lawyer is one of the relatively rare types—a litigator who specializes in this work to the exclusion of much else. Instead, the work will require the lawyer to have mastered the full range of traditional lawyer skills of client counseling, advice-giving, document drafting, and negotiation. And increasingly lawyers find that the new skills of evaluation and mediation are both effective for many clients and a source of employment.

Most lawyers will engage in nonlitigation legal work or in litigation work that is constrained in very important ways, at least theoretically, so as to remove from it some of the salient features of adversarial litigation. Of these special roles, the most prominent is that of prosecutor (§ 13.10). In some lawyers' work the constraints are imposed both by the nature of the client and by the way in which the lawyer is organized into a social unit to perform that work. The most common of these roles are those of corporate practice and government legal service.

Each of these roles and settings for legal practice presents its unique challenges of ethics and professional regulation. In many of them those challenges are just beginning to be understood and studied. In some of them, such as corporate practice, the development of the role and its regulation has provoked much controversy. In others, such as that of the prosecutor, the role is more traditional but is the continuing subject of questioning and scrutiny from courts in the form of common-law and constitutional developments.

WESTLAW REFERENCES

di mediation

§ 13.2 OFFICE COUNSELING [1]

§ 13.2.1 Counseling Function

Counseling and the Client-Lawyer Relationship

Neither courtroom, boardroom, or even the law library is the place in which many lawyers do most of their work. Its typical architectural setting is the place in which most lawyers spend the great bulk of their time, their law offices.[2] A good part of a lawyer's day will be spent discussing legal matters with clients, probing for facts and client attitudes, and giving advice, drafting documents, or taking other legal steps in response to identified legal issues. The entire realm of the communicative relationship between lawyer and client is here generically and broadly referred to as counseling.

What can sometimes be lost in a lawyer's conception of his or her counseling work is that there is more in the office than a "legal problem." It is much more important for the lawyer to understand that legal issues come attached to autonomous persons who typically have lived with their problems and will continue to live with their solutions or failures to solve them. Client problems are not only—and perhaps not even primarily—legal. They must be seen in all their dimensions, including moral, psychological, and economic dimensions beyond the strictly legal. Also important is the lawyer's self-awareness—an understanding of the lawyer's own humanity and its important involvement in every representation. The failure of lawyers to appreciate that they deal here with emotions, human values, beliefs, secret hopes and fears, prejudices, all of the aspects of humanity, is probably the single most important reason for client dissatisfaction with legal services.[3]

The general nature of the client-lawyer relationship is examined elsewhere (chapter 4). What we examine here is the nature of the practice setting in which a lawyer can best fulfill the social and personal objectives of lawyering—performing effective service for a client with a legal problem that does not involve litigation. For reasons developed earlier (chapter 4), our assumption will be that the lawyer's self-perception is that of the non-preemptive counsellor. The lawyer neither attempts to preempt important areas of client autonomy nor is willing to accede to unreasonable client demands for sacrifices of the lawyer's personal or professional autonomy in performing legal services.

Lawyer Counselors: Officers of the Law?

If lawyers are "officers of the court" (cf. § 1.6), are they also rightly considered "officers of the law," with responsibilities beyond that of maximizing the interests of their cli-

[1] The writings of four prolific scholars predominate in this and allied fields—Brown, Redmount, Shaffer, and Watson. See generally L.Brown & E.Dauer, Planning by Lawyers: Materials on a Nonadversarial Legal Process, pt. I, ch. 3; pt. II (1978); L. Brown, Preventive Law (1950); R.Redmount & T.Shaffer, Legal Interviewing and Counseling (1980); T.Shaffer, Legal Interviewing and Counseling (1976); A.Watson, The Lawyer in the Interviewing and Counseling Process (1976); A.Watson, Psychiatry for Lawyers (1968). Also very influential are G.Bellow & B.Moulton, The Lawyering Process (1978); D.Binder & S.Price, Legal Interviewing and Counseling (1977). The pioneering work is H.Freeman, Legal Interviewing and Counseling (1963). See also H.Freeman & H.Weihofen, Clinical Law Training (1972).

[2] Brown, The Law Office—A Preventive Law Laboratory, 104 U.Pa.L.Rev. 940 (1956).

[3] Lawyers probably greatly underestimate the extent to which clients are concerned with the friendliness and effort of the lawyer rather than with the result produced. See Missouri Bar Prentice-Hall Survey: A Motivational Study of Public Attitudes and Law Office Management (1963).

ents in counseling and related tasks? Two principal arguments can be made that lawyers in nonlitigation roles have a greater duty to protect third-party and other public interests than is true of lawyers functioning as litigators.[4]

First, counseling often concerns the future, and the client's impacts upon others can often be arranged to minimize or to maximize imposition upon others.[5] Litigation normally concerns the past and operates on the relatively more confined universe described in the litigated issues.

Second, to the extent that counseling involves their interests, third parties may not be represented by counsel, may be unaware that the lawyer and client are considering affecting their interests, and are not protected by a court or any similar official buffer. Litigation, on the other hand, takes place with at least the prospect of equal advocacy on both sides and is conducted according to due process constraints, and its outcome is controlled by a neutral arbiter. Different counseling settings will make those asserted differences more or less apt. For example, in some negotiations both parties are equally represented by competent lawyers and they can achieve, or at least seek, even better protection for their own interests than court rules might provide. Thus a negotiating party may be able to insist upon a contractual term providing for liquidated damages if a fact asserted in negotiations by the other side is not accurate and thereby achieve a measure of interest-protection that is superior to the results of litigation.

Three central questions can be raised throughout any discussion of counseling. First, to what extent is the nature of the counseling function importantly different from the function of the lawyer as an advocate in litigation? Second, to what extent does the function permit the lawyer and client to maximize their expectations—the client for a solution to the problem that impelled the client to the lawyer's office, the lawyer for professionally satisfying and monetarily rewarding work? Third, to what extent does society, the legal system, or the legal profession have a legitimate reason for altering the relationship and roles that the client and lawyer would define for themselves? Those questions will be pursued in this section, which concentrates upon the general phenomenon of counseling, as well as in succeeding sections that examine special types of counseling settings and special problems of representation.

Counseling in the Lawyer Codes

Counseling functions have only recently received much attention in the lawyer codes. The 1908 Canons of Ethics and the 1969 Code of Professional Responsibility gave little attention to nonlitigation functions of lawyers.[6] One finds there no comprehensive treatment of the unique ethical problems that arise in advising, lobbying, negotiating, and other lawyer roles. Even as to problems that are common to both litigation and nonlitigation the Canons and Code do not recognize that ethical problems might differ in the two realms.[7]

The treatment of nonlitigation lawyer roles in the 1983 Model Rules is more extensive, but the Model Rules have been faulted for an unwillingness to put more distance between litigation ethics and counseling ethics.[8] An example is the Code's treatment of conflicts of interest. From all that can be gathered from

[4] E.Cheatham, Cases on the Legal Profession 181 (2d ed.1955); Schwartz, The Professionalism and Accountability of Lawyers, 66 Calif.L.Rev. 669, 671 (1978); Thode, The Ethical Standard for the Advocate, 39 Texas L.Rev. 575, 579 (1961).

[5] Cf. EC 7–3.

[6] Blackmun, Some Thoughts on Ethics, 24 Emory L.J. 1, 12 (1975)("[B]oth the old Canons and the new Code primarily concern the lawyer only as a party in the adversary process.").

[7] Brown & Brown, What Counsels the Counselor? The Code of Professional Responsibility's Ethical Considerations—A Preventive Law Analysis, 10 Valp.L.Rev. 453 (1976); Redmount, Client Counseling and the Regulation of Professional Conduct, 26 St.L.L.Rev. 829 (1982).

[8] Brown & Dauer, Professional Responsibility in Nonadversarial Lawyering: A Review of the Model Rules, 1982 Am.B.Found. Research J. 519.

the Model Rules, the same strictures are to be applied to conflict of interest issues whether they arise in the course of representing multiple clients in litigation or in an office counseling setting. But it should be plain that quite different considerations should govern the legitimacy of multiple representation in drafting a partnership agreement than in representing partners in litigation over a partnership agreement.[9]

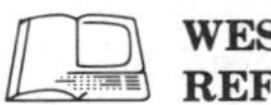

WESTLAW REFERENCES

attorney lawyer /6 counseling /6 client

§ 13.2.2 Stages of Counseling

Diagnosis, Legal Operation, Resolution

The client-lawyer counseling relationship will run through a course of interactions that ideally, and probably typically, consists of three identifiable stages. During each of the stages a lawyer will also carry on independent legal functions such as analysis, investigation, research, drafting, negotiation, and planning. First, at the beginning of the relationship, lawyer and client will conduct one or more *diagnostic interviews*. That stage will involve fact investigation, an inquiry into the client's objectives, a discussion of the nature of the client-lawyer relationship that is contemplated, and the lawyer's explanation of his or her role in the matter.

Second will be a stage of *legal operation*, during which the lawyer will make a legal evaluation of the client's matter, recommend and discuss with the client a course of action, and undertake to perform the legal tasks that the client and lawyer have selected as the most appropriate. During the course of his or her work the lawyer will continue to consult with the client about possible adjustments in expectations or tasks and in order to keep the client informed about the progress of the matter.

Third, the representation will reach some more or less satisfactory *resolution*. That will consist of closure on the legal matter, a confirmation between lawyer and client that the lawyer's services are at an end, a settlement of the lawyer's fee, and, optimally, an educative and retrospective self-evaluation by the lawyer.

Obviously, not all legal representations require that the client-lawyer relationship last beyond the initial interview. An unresolvable conflict of interest, an unremediable legal situation, an inability to reach agreement on a fee or on an appropriate role for lawyer and client may all terminate the relationship at its outset. More seriously, the relationship may proceed in a less-than-ideal fashion with, for example, the lawyer controlling one or more aspects of the representation with little actual client participation, or the client may refuse to participate extensively in any aspect of the case but leave its management entirely to the lawyer. As with all client wishes, such a client instruction should be accepted by the lawyer only after both lawyer and client understand the important reasons supporting, and consequences flowing from, such a representation.

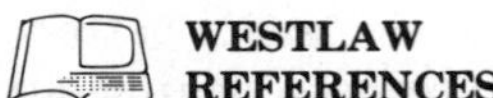

WESTLAW REFERENCES

attorney lawyer /5 client /5 interview!

§ 13.2.3 Counseling Techniques

Confrontational and Preventive Approaches

Two basic approaches are available to a lawyer and client in their choice of a specific legal operation—litigation or preventive[10] law. Litigation involves a confrontational resort to a third-party dispute resolver, typically a judicial system, in order to gain a coercive legal advantage over another. Litigation is largely retrospective, looking mainly to-

[9] Compare, e.g., § 7.3.2 (simultaneous representation in litigation) with, e.g., § 8.7 (lawyer as mediator).

[10] The concept and phraseology of "preventive law" is at least half a century old. E.g., Cavers, Ante-Mortem Probate: An Essay in Preventive Law, 1 U.Chi.L.Rev. 440 (1934). The concept and its practice have been extensively developed by Professor Louis M. Brown. See L.Brown, Preventive Law (1950).

ward the past and attempting to achieve a legally compelled realignment of interests based on past conduct.

Preventive law is prospective. It aims to avoid litigation if possible, through resort to planning and accommodation strategies. Those include such familiar strategies as contracts, wills, partnership and similar types of entity organizations, estate and business planning, as well as such relatively unfamiliar and emerging techniques as legal audits.[11] Adoption of preventive-law approaches expresses a preference for litigation avoidance because of its high monetary, emotional, and time-commitment costs and the parties' relative loss of the freedom to shape the process and its outcomes to meet the changing desires of participants.[12]

Preventive-law approaches do not necessarily exclude the possibility of litigation. Litigation can be forced upon a client by an obdurate opposite party who regards filing a suit as a measure to be taken early in a relationship. Moreover, it would be naive to assume that a client's reasonable expectations will always be met with a cooperative and accommodating response by other parties whose involvement is necessary. Thus a client may occasionally be forced to resort to filing a suit on his or her own behalf in order to prevent or remedy fraud or a similar imposition.

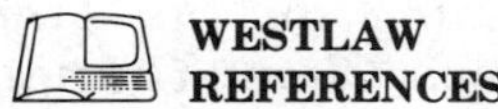
WESTLAW REFERENCES

di litigation

---

§ 13.2.4 *Objectives of Counseling*

Power, Compassion, and Social Control

Counseling can serve one or more of three objectives. First, counseling can seek to maximize the acquisitive or dynastic instincts of a client by lending the client legal assistance in acquiring, conveying, or protecting property interests or in acquiring or protecting power. Second, counseling can provide psychological support to a client under what can be intense emotional pressure. Third, a lawyer's counseling can serve as a mechanism of social control by performing the socially desirable function of encouraging law compliance on the part of clients.

The lawyer's function of counseling a client with respect to property and power acquisition is by far the most familiar. It is the objective toward which much statutory, administrative, and case law is explicitly addressed. It is the aspect of office practice with which lawyers are, if anything, too preoccupied.[13] If certain steps are taken or not taken, a fine or damages must be paid. If certain facts are proven, a legally compelled kind of property disposition will be made in a marriage dissolution, probate, or corporate takeover. If certain documents are filed on time, a client can become a candidate for elective office or collect a pension or avoid the draft. This is the mileu of legal rights, of gross social adjustment, of the positivist view of legal ordering.

Psychology of Counseling

The psychological function of counseling is less well understood by lawyers.[14] Legal education probably pays too little attention to its centrality in client-lawyer relationships. Yet in all professional relationships with clients or customers, the psychological needs of the person being provided the service may be the most compelling reason why the professional's services were sought.[15]

11 Brown, Legal Audit, 38 So.Calif.L.Rev. 431 (1965).

12 See § 10.1 at 565–69.

13 Redmount, Attorney Personalities and Some Psychological Aspects of Legal Consultation, 109 U.Pa.L.Rev. 972 (1961).

14 Fey & Goldberg, Legal Interviewing from a Psychological Perspective: An Attorney's Handbook, 14 Willa.L. Rev. 217 (1978); Lehman, The Pursuit of a Client's Interests, 77 Mich.L.Rev. 1078 (1979); Shaffer, A Lesson from Trollope for Counselors at Law, 35 W.&L.L.Rev. 727 (1978); Elkins, A Counseling Model for Lawyering in Divorce Cases, 53 Notre Dame Law. 229 (1977).

15 T.Parsons, Essays in Sociological Theory 382 (1954); Goffman, On Cooling the Mark Out: Some Aspects of

Law Compliance

Law compliance is achieved in client counseling, assuming that it is the lawyer's own objective for the client, in two ways. Most obviously, law compliance is achieved by arranging the client's affairs in a fashion that complies with all applicable legal rules. Also important, however, is the lawyer's potential role in explaining to a client the operation of the legal system relevant to the client's legal matter. In that way the client can understand success or failure in the system against the possibilities and limits of the system.[16]

There is empirical support for believing that lawyers often fail to inform clients adequately about the workings of the legal system, so that clients often believe that routine and legitimate procedures are irregular and corrupt.[17] Too often lawyers explain to their clients that failure in the legal system resulted from the corruption or incompetence of legal administrators, rather than because of the unpredictable or problematic nature of the client's own legal claims or the facts supporting them or because of limitations of the lawyer's own skill or time commitment.

§ 13.3 ADVISING CLIENTS

§ 13.3.1 Client Objectives and Legal Uncertainty

A vital counseling function of lawyers is to give legal advice to clients. Often a client is more interested in complete legal safety than in testing the limits of legality. For a host of reasons—morality, economics, public and interpersonal relations, and similar long-term and short-term considerations—a client may seek advice that stays well away from grey areas. And a lawyer will often wisely discuss such nonlegal considerations with a client (§ 4.3). But a client may be impelled by circumstances or attitude to seek to aggressively push legality to its limits, and possibly beyond. It would be improbable that a lawyer could perform the lawyerly function of advice-giving in such a situation in the same way in which a lawyer advises on legally and morally unquestionable transactions.

In areas of legal ambiguity, or of plainly illegal conduct, to what extent is a lawyer responsible for advice given to a client? Certainly a lawyer may not advise a client how best to avoid detection for a future criminal act. But may a lawyer advise a client who contemplates a crime about the extradition laws of various countries? Or advise a client where the knife's-edge limits of the law lie with respect to liability for the manufacture of a dangerous product? Does it matter whether the lawyer has reason to know that the client's interest in the advice is for the purposes of good faith law compliance or for bad faith reasons such as breaking the law but avoiding detection or effective sanctions? Are all of those questions to be answered in the same way regardless of the nature of the legal rule—criminal law, regulatory requirement, common-law rule of tort—that is involved? What about a lawyer's advice to a client concerning conscientious client opposition to a legal rule? Those and similar issues are addressed in the materials that follow.

§ 13.3.2 Advising on the Limits of the Law: Client Crimes

Lawyers as Accomplices

Client illegality and lawyer complicity in it can range over a spectrum. At one extreme is direct and knowing lawyer participation in a client enterprise that violates a valid criminal law. Because the role of lawyer gives no occupant of it any criminal law immunity, such participation subjects the lawyer to the criminal sanctions provided for violation of

Adaptation to Failure, in Human Behavior and Social Processes 482 (A.Rose ed.1962).

[16] Bahr, Client Counseling for Frustration of Expectations: We Can Learn from the Dying, 49 Tenn.L.Rev. 511 (1982).

[17] Fisher & Humphreys, Costly Misconceptions of Law and Legal Services: The Small Business Owner versus the Chicago Personal Property Tax, 1978 Am.B.Found. Research J. 545.

the law.[18] The fact that the lawyer's part in the criminal enterprise was an otherwise traditional lawyerly function, such as advice-giving [19] or legal drafting,[20] also does not immunize the lawyer from criminal responsibility.

Thus a lawyer who advises a client, correctly, that a planned transaction is contrary to criminal law, but who then proceeds to prepare documents or in other ways assists the client in the illegal enterprise, is liable as a conspirator.[21] A lawyer's conduct that facilitates a client's commission of a crime comes comfortably within the definitions of accomplice in modern criminal law or, in the common-law terminology, the definition of principal in the second degree or accessory before the fact.[22]

Lawyers who give facilitating advice to a client who is about to commit a crime have only two possibly differentiating features to their conduct. One, which is common to accomplices generally, concerns the issue whether the lawyer knows of the client-principal's criminal designs.[23] The second, and related element, is that the client-lawyer relationship itself is such that a lawyer in appropriate circumstances is entitled to give a client the benefit of reasonable doubts with respect to the client's possible noncriminal implementation of the lawyer's advice.[24] Also related to both points is the fact that a lawyer's customary relationship of trust and confidence with a client may understandably make the lawyer less suspicious than a stranger would be about what the client intends. Whatever the factual strength of those claims, they are merely evidentiary complications. They do not disturb the underlying doctrine that lawyers can indeed be accomplices in crimes by giving their clients legal advice for the purpose of aiding or assisting the client in a project known to consist of acts constituting a criminal offense.

Regulation of Advice on Illegal Client Acts

The lawyer codes take regulatory positions that are not clearly congruent with the criminal law of conspiracy and accomplice liability. The 1969 Code appears to go much further than the criminal law. One provision of the 1983 Model Rules may fall short of prohibiting lawyer conduct that is criminal and in

18 United States v. Haimowitz, 725 F.2d 1561, 1571 (11th Cir.1984), cert.denied ___ U.S. ___, 105 S.Ct. 563, 83 L.Ed.2d 504 (1984)(conspiracy to commit mail fraud and to obstruct interstate commerce by extortion); United States v. Clovis Retail Liquor Dealers Trade Ass'n, 540 F.2d 1389 (10th Cir.1976)(conviction of lawyer for participation in criminal conspiracy to fix prices); State v. Romano, ___ R.I. ___, 456 A.2d 746, 759–60 (1983)(conspiracy to commit illegal entry into manufacturing plant by providing to coconspirators safe haven at lawyer's home near plant); Cogdill v. First Dist. Comm., 221 Va. 376, 269 S.E.2d 391 (1980)(procuring client for purpose of prostitution).

19 United States v. Perlstein, 126 F.2d 789 (3d Cir.1942), cert.denied 316 U.S. 678, 62 S.Ct. 1106, 86 L.Ed. 1752 (1942)(affirming conviction for conspiracy to obstruct future judicial proceeding by advising client to destroy documents if proceeding brought); United States v. Loften, 518 F.Supp. 839 (S.D.N.Y.1981).

20 United States v. Arrington, 719 F.2d 701 (4th Cir. 1983), cert.denied 465 U.S. 1028, 104 S.Ct. 1289, 79 L.Ed. 2d 691 (1984)(lawyer who acquired bogus titles to construction equipment guilty of aiding and abetting if he knew equipment was stolen). In Rex v. Delaval, 3 Burr. 1434, 97 All E.Rep. 913 (King's Bench 1763), a lawyer was convicted of participation in an unlawful conspiracy to remove a young woman from the control of Bates, a musician, and place her in the hands of Sir Francis Delaval for the purpose of prostitution. Judge Mansfield upheld the charge against Bates, the musician, and Sir Francis, but also against Fraine, the lawyer who drafted the indenture of apprenticeship. Fraine, said Mansfield, must have known that Sir Francis had no facilities for teaching music to apprentices and thus it was impossible for him to have been ignorant of the real intent of the transaction. A distinguishable case is one in which the lawyer has insufficient information about the client's project to be chargeable with knowledge. E.g., Johnson v. Youden [1950] 1 K.B. 544 (solicitor who facilitated conveyance at price in excess of regulations not criminally liable in absence of proof of lawyer's knowledge of how price was calculated).

21 SEC v. Universal Major Industries Corp., 546 F.2d 1044 (2d Cir.1976), cert.denied 434 U.S. 834, 98 S.Ct. 120, 54 L.Ed.2d 95 (1977). See Redlich, Lawyers, The Temple, and the Marketplace, 30 Bus.Law. 65, 70 (Spec.Issue 1975).

22 See generally W.LaFave, Modern Criminal Law 617 (1978). An accessory before the fact differs from a principal in the second degree only in not being actually or constructively present at the commission of the offense.

23 § 13.3.3 at 695–96.

24 On the problems of the state of a lawyer's knowledge and ambiguity in law, see § 13.3.3 at 696–97.

other respects seems merely congruent with the criminal law that would apply to all lawyers in any event.

1969 Code. In the Code, DR 7–102(A)(7) broadly provides that a lawyer representing a client shall not "counsel or assist his client in conduct that the lawyer knows to be illegal or fraudulent." [25] The California rule is similar.[26] Nowhere does the Code suggest that "illegal" is limited to criminal violations alone,[27] although the few disciplinary decisions under DR 7–102(A)(7) involve lawyers who assisted a client in criminal conduct.[28] And EC 7–5 makes it clear that a lawyer should not counsel a client on how to avoid punishment for violations of the law. No authority, apparently, has interpreted "counsel or assist" in DR 7–102(A)(7), particularly with respect to the question whether it requires something more than a lawyer's passive participation in illegality.[29]

1983 Model Rules. Rule 1.2(d) of the 1983 Model Rules provides a rule similar to DR 7–102(A)(7), but the rule is limited to "criminal and fraudulent" client conduct and introduces a potentially confusing exception. Rule 1.2(d) states that

> (d) A lawyer shall not counsel a client to engage, or assist a client, in conduct that the lawyer knows is criminal or fraudulent, but a lawyer may discuss the legal consequences of any proposed course of conduct with a client and may counsel or assist a client to make a good faith effort to determine the validity, scope, meaning or application of the law.

As will be discussed at a later point,[30] MR 1.2(d) clearly is a narrower rule than DR 7–102(A)(7).

The narrowness of MR 1.2(d) is evident in one situation that was clearly intended and in a second, possible, situation that is shocking and might well be inadvertent. First, the rule is limited to advice about "criminal or fraudulent" client conduct, whereas DR 7–102(A)(7) extends to "illegal" conduct.[31] Second, and shockingly, if so, the exception in MR 1.2(d) stating that a lawyer may "discuss" legal consequences of "any proposed course of conduct" on its face is open to the interpretation that a lawyer may give legal advice to a client about various methods of operating a proposed drug-smuggling ring, murdering a political rival or disgruntled spouse, or cheating a trusting business partner. The essential condition would be that the lawyer's advice remain at the personally uncommitted level of "discuss" and not heat up to the level of "counsel" or "assist." That reading of the rule is supported by a comment to Rule 1.2(d) that states that "[t]here is a critical distinction between presenting an analysis of legal aspects of questionable conduct and recommending the means by which a crime or fraud might be committed with impunity," [32] al-

25 An ambiguity lurks in DR 7–102(A)(7) that has potential for strange results. In In re Connaghan, 613 S.W.2d 626 (Mo.1981), a lawyer accepted $20,000 from a client as a fee and, without the client's knowledge, used part to bribe a legislator. The court held that because the client did no wrong, the lawyer did not violate DR 7–102(A)(7). But the court found that several other, more general disciplinary rules were violated.

26 Calif.R. 7–101:

> A member of the State Bar shall not advise the violation of any law, rule or ruling of a tribunal unless he believes in good faith that such law, rule or ruling is invalid. A member of the State Bar may take appropriate steps in good faith to test the validity of any law, rule or ruling of a tribunal.

27 The California rule, supra, which refers globally to "law, rule or ruling of a tribunal" is also clearly not limited to criminal law violations.

28 In re Nulle, 127 Ariz. 299, 620 P.2d 214 (1980)(advising client to file false application for liquor license); In re Schneider, 98 Ill.2d 215, 74 Ill.Dec. 500, 456 N.E.2d 2 (1983)(counseling clients to provide false information to prosecutor); In re Agnew, 311 N.W.2d 869 (Minn.1981) (advising client facing several misdemeanor charges that he had "49 options" (to flee the state)); Toledo Bar Ass'n v. Kitchen, 69 Ohio St.2d 338, 432 N.E.2d 195 (1982) (persistence in negotiating sale of machine after forming accurate belief that machine was stolen).

29 Cf. In re Prescott, 271 N.W.2d 822, 823–24 (Minn. 1978)(DR 1–102(A)(4) on dishonesty, fraud, deceit, and misrepresentation prohibits both active as well as passive participation in process of obtaining loans by false pretenses). But cf. M.Freedman, Lawyers Ethics in an Adversary System 60 (1975)("counsel or assist" in Code refers to "an active kind of participation in the client's illegal act, going beyond merely giving advice about the law").

30 § 13.3.9.

31 Id.

32 MR 1.2 comment (Criminal, Fraudulent and Prohibited Transactions; first paragraph). A further comment indicates that suggesting how a client's wrongdoing can

though the nature of that critical distinction is not made clear.[33]

Such a profoundly disturbing reading of Rule 1.2(d) would obviously be resisted by any body presented with the issue. More likely, the "but" clause at the end of MR 1.2(d) is an inartful attempt to draw attention to the possible ambiguity of a client's intentions and the common ambiguity of law ("questionable conduct").[34] The problem of legal ambiguity hardly requires a laissez-faire approach to discussing crimes.[35] Possibly the language was also intended to permit a lawyer to attempt to persuade a client intending wrongdoing not to engage in it. Other language in the comment suggests such a limiting reading.[36]

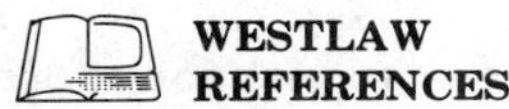

WESTLAW REFERENCES

410k201(2)

attorney lawyer /s client /s advice advis! /s criminal unlawful** illegal** fraudulent** /s act** action activity behavior

"dr 7-102(a)(7)" dr7-102(a)(7) "ec 7-5" "model rule 1.2(d)"

§ 13.3.3 *Knowledge Issues* [37]

Both DR 7-102(A)(7) and MR 1.2(d) limit their proscriptions to lawyer advice or assistance in client conduct that the lawyer "knows" to be of the defined kind. Two problems of knowledge are harbored in those words. First is the problem of the lawyer's factual knowledge: when does a lawyer possess facts from which knowledge of the illegal nature of the client's enterprise must be drawn? Second is the problem of knowledge of law: given ambiguity in the law, under what circumstances is a lawyer held to know that the law condemns known client activity?

Knowing Facts

In some philosophically exotic uses of "knowledge," it can be asserted that humans know nothing. But the concept of knowledge in the codes should instead track the cognate concept in the criminal law and the law of torts. Knowledge as used in those fields is an experiential concept of broad application, and its use in the disciplinary codes should be interpreted in the same practical way.[38] If, in the practical world, one assuredly is aware of an object or phenomenon, then the person "knows" it.

The knowability of things will, of course, depend upon the accessibility of facts, tempered by the lawyer's presumed greater knowledge of legal matters. Future events, for example, cannot always be known with the same degree of certainty as past events. That also tends to be true of subjective phe-

be concealed would be an instance of a lawyer's furthering of the client's illegal purpose.

33 The drafter of the Model Rules has suggested a distinction between "unsuggestive advice" (the lawyer as legal oracle) and advice or other assistance that is "pure instrumentalism." Hazard, How Far May a Lawyer Go in Assisting a Client in Legally Wrongful Conduct?, 35 U.Miami L.Rev. 669, 671 (1981). That distinction, carried to the extent of attempting to validate a lawyer's serving as a "mere scrivener" for a client's criminal projects, was rejected centuries ago. See Rex v. Delaval, supra n.20. The distinction seems to suppose, erroneously, that a lawyer must "encourage" wrongful conduct before the lawyer is complicit in it, even for the purposes of criminal law. Willing participation suffices. See United States v. Loften, 518 F.Supp. 839 (S.D.N.Y.1981). Cf. also, In re Rosenthal, 73 Ill.2d 46, 21 Ill.Dec. 893, 382 N.E.2d 257 (1978), cert.denied 440 U.S. 961, 99 S.Ct. 1505, 59 L.Ed.2d 775 (1979)(disbarment for participating in and facilitating extortion scheme perpetrated against client even if lawyer's participation was unwilling and solely to protect client).

34 § 13.3.3 at 696–97.

35 Specifically, the wording of MR 1.2(d) was the result of a retreat from the broader rule, stated in the original version of the Rules, that "a lawyer shall not give advice which the lawyer can reasonably foresee will: (1) be used by the client to further an illegal course of conduct." (MR 2.3(a)(Discussion Draft, Jan.30, 1980)).

36 MR 1.2 comment (Criminal, Fraudulent and Prohibited Transactions; second paragraph): "A lawyer may not continue assisting a client in conduct that the lawyer originally supposes is legally proper but then discovers is criminal or fraudulent. Withdrawal from the representation, therefore, may be required."

37 See also § 12.5.2 (what lawyers know in the context of perjured testimony).

38 Hodes, The Code of Professional Responsibility, The Kutak Rules, and the Trial Lawyer's Code: Surprisingly, Three Peas in a Pod, 35 U.Miami L.Rev. 739, 802–810 (1981).

nomena, such as states of mind [39] or phenomena that can only be known through the exercise of largely subjective or intuitive cognition, such as many human qualities (a generally truthful or untruthful client, a reputation for fair dealing). But certainly one can have reasonable certainty about future events (leaving your money on the sidewalk on Times Square will result in its loss) or about evaluative or subjective elements (driving an automobile through a school zone at 100 miles per hour, as children crowd a crosswalk, is dangerous).

Studied Ignorance

For the most part, a lawyer is not under an obligation to seek out information. But, as in the criminal law, a lawyer's studied ignorance of a readily accessible fact by consciously avoiding it is the functional equivalent of knowledge of the fact.[40] A lawyer is not under an obligation to undertake arduous investigations at the slightest reason for suspicion. But some situations or known facts will be sufficiently suspicious that a reasonable lawyer would want to know more. As a lawyer, one may not avoid the bright light of a clear fact simply by averting one's eyes or turning one's back.[41] Knowledge is also a dynamic concept. A lawyer, on the basis of then known facts, might legitimately begin a representation in furtherance of a client enterprise thought to be lawful. If the lawyer later discovers facts indicating that the enterprise is unlawful, the latter state of knowledge generates a new duty and the lawyer may no longer assist the client.[42]

Ambiguity in the Law

Under some circumstances the limits of the law can be difficult to state with certainty. Law can be even more ambiguous than nonpredictive factual propositions because advice about law is often a guess about what a legal decision maker will say the law is at a future time. (Other, distinguishable, forms of legal ambiguity inhere in some theories of civil disobedience or in theories of legal desuetude. See § 13.3.8.) Legal ambiguity can be a function of choice-of-law difficulties. In such a case a lawyer's good faith assessment of which state's law will apply should suffice.[43] It is also preferable to employ a good faith standard to assess the validity of a lawyer's advice about the law of a particular jurisdiction rather than a standard that permits a

[39] EC 7-5 ("In many cases a lawyer may not be certain as to the state of mind of his client, and in those situations he should resolve reasonable doubts in favor of his client.").

[40] Wyle v. R.J.Reynolds Indus., Inc., 709 F.2d 585, 590 (9th Cir.1983)(law firm's deliberate ignorance of client's practices constituted equivalent of knowledge of the truth); Hazard, How Far May a Lawyer Go in Assisting a Client in Legally Wrongful Conduct?, 35 U.Miami L.Rev. 669, 672, 678, 682 (1981). In the criminal law area, see, e.g., United States v. Nicholson, 677 F.2d 706, 710–11 (9th Cir.1982); United States v. Hanlon, 548 F.2d 1096 (2d Cir. 1977). In the securities area, see, e.g., SEC v. Universal Major Indus. Corp., 546 F.2d 1044 (2d Cir.1976), cert.denied 434 U.S. 834, 98 S.Ct. 120, 54 L.Ed.2d 95 (1977)(lawyer is liable as aider and abettor of client's violation of federal securities laws if lawyer issues an opinion letter that opines that a transaction is legal if it is unlawful on the basis of facts then available to the lawyer). See generally M.Freedman, Lawyers Ethics in an Adversary System, ch.5 (1975); Roscoe Pound-American Trial Lawyers Foundation, The American Lawyer's Code of Conduct 8–10 (Discussion Draft 1980).

Decisions disagree over the critical issue whether negligence alone is sufficient to support a finding that a lawyer has violated the securities laws, but in most of the cases the point becomes moot on the court's finding that the lawyer's conduct was at least reckless if not willful. Compare, e.g., SEC v. Universal Major Indus. Corp., supra (violation can be predicated on negligence alone), with, e.g., SEC v. Coffey, 493 F.2d 1304 (6th Cir.1974), cert.denied 420 U.S. 908, 95 S.Ct. 826, 42 L.Ed.2d 837 (1975)(negligence alone insufficient).

[41] MR 1.3. Legal Background Note, at 22 (Proposed Final Draft, May 30, 1981), and authorities cited. E.g., United States v. Benjamin, 328 F.2d 854, 863 (2d Cir.), cert.denied 377 U.S. 953, 84 S.Ct. 1631, 12 L.Ed.2d 497 (1964)(lawyers cannot "escape criminal liability on a plea of ignorance when they have shut their eyes to what was plainly to be seen"); Wright v. Roberts, 573 S.W.2d 468, 474 (Tenn.1978)(lawyer could not claim ignorance of contents of restraining order served on him when he advised client to ignore it).

[42] MR 1.2 comment (Criminal, Fraudulent and Prohibited Transactions; second paragraph).

[43] Demarest v. Superior Court, 103 Cal.App.3d 791, 165 Cal.Rptr. 641 (1980)(Louisiana lawyer did not act improperly by advising client to file Louisiana child custody action to defeat ex-spouse's California judgment of temporary custody).

lawyer to resolve all questions about legal ambiguity in favor of assisting all of a client's legally questionable enterprises.[44] Here, as with facts, a lawyer must avoid replacing a sound professional judgment about the limits of the law with a wished-for ambiguity in legal proscriptions in a one-sided search for justification for a client's dubious projects.[45]

WESTLAW REFERENCES

attorney lawyer /s client /s criminal** illegal** fraud! unlawful** /3 act** action activity /p know! ignoran!

§ 13.3.4 White-Collar Crime

There is analytically very little, if any, difference between giving advice on how to obtain a gun permit to a client who intends to commit a murder and giving advice to officers of a client corporation that is about to commit a fraud on how to structure the transaction to best avoid detection, to launder money, or to stash receipts in offshore bank accounts. Our revulsion at the former, however, is for some reason more instinctive. The difference that we sometimes intuitively draw is that between familiar offenses and "white-collar crime." Lawyers are probably more likely to be engaged as advisers in the latter than in the former. Indeed, because of the transactional complexity of some white-collar criminal schemes, it is unlikely that they would be ventured without the active complicity of a lawyer.[46]

The concept of white-collar crime is not simply a matter of applying existing criminal law sanctions to persons who have plainly been violating criminal laws all along but who eluded prosecution because of laxness in enforcement.[47] At least part of the white-collar crime phenomenon of recent years is comprised of greatly expanded federal and state statutory definitions. Those have redefined as criminal a number of business, financial, political, and similar practices that were traditionally regarded as more or less accepted, or at least were endured, by large segments of the American public.[48] Recently, highly publicized prosecutions of Watergate defendants, public figures implicated in staged bribery by bogus oil sheiks, and a variety of business figures,[49] are sharp reminders that activities on the murky edge of traditional hardball politics and business practices can be indictable offenses. That reality must obviously be taken into account by any lawyer advising a client about the limits of the law.

WESTLAW REFERENCES

"white-collar crime"

§ 13.3.5 Ongoing Illegal Enterprises

White-collar crime typifies a kind of client illegality that does not always occur in one violent episode with a clear beginning and end. Some persons are engaged in continuing criminal activities as a business or repeatedly engage in criminal episodes. To what extent

44 Westlake v. Abrams, 565 F.Supp. 1330, 1350 (N.D.Ga. 1983)("While serving as an advocate, an attorney should resolve in favor of his client doubts as to the bounds of the law. In serving as an advisor, an attorney should give his professional opinion as to what the ultimate decisions of the courts would likely be as to the applicable law.").

45 One of the least supportable excesses of M.Freedman, Lawyers' Ethics in an Adversary System (1975), is the extension of arguments for client-oriented lawyer action from the area of advocacy to the entirely different field of client counseling. As a glaring example, arguments for a lawyer's exclusive focus on the interests of his or her client that Professor Freedman develops, in the context of the criminal defense function, he then applies without qualification to lawyers who advise clients about non-criminal law matters when issuing securities. Id., at 20–24.

46 Stone, The Public Influence of the Bar, 48 Harv.L. Rev. 1, 8–9 (1934). In commenting on the financial manipulations that led to the Great Depression, Justice Stone stated that "such departures from the fiduciary principle do not usually occur without the active assistance of some member of our profession."

47 Silbert, Defense Counsel in the Grand Jury—The Answer to the White Collar Criminal's Prayers, 15 Am. Crim.L.Rev. 293, 294 (1978).

48 Hannay, Introduction to Symposium on White Collar Crime, 11 Am.J.Crim.L.Rev. 817 (1973); Seymour, Social and Ethical Considerations in Assessing White-Collar Crime, 11 Am.Crim.L.Rev. 821 (1973).

49 Ross, How Lawless Are Big Companies?, Fortune (Dec. 1, 1980), at 56 (11.2% rate of conviction of corporate criminality among over 1,000 of nation's largest corporations during 1970–1980).

may a lawyer agree to represent such a client or give advice to a client engaged in such an ongoing enterprise?

Continuing Offenses

If the client's conduct constitutes a continuing offense, a lawyer may not assist the client in successfully prolonging or profiting from the offense. Thus negotiating in behalf of a client to receive payment for the return of stolen property to its owner is unethical and can be criminal.[50] If an enterprise is entirely illegal, for example, an illegal gambling business, a lawyer's agreement to represent members of the organization when arrested impermissibly contributes to the success of the illegal operation.[51] The lawyer's obligations are to urge the client to cease the criminal activity, to withdraw if the client does not, and possibly to disclose the wrongdoing.[52] If, however, the enterprise is lawful but its operation occasionally results in criminal charges for isolated acts, a lawyer can be retained to provide criminal defense services.[53]

Crime-Supported Enterprises

An emerging problem for law enforcement is the criminal enterprise whose profits are invested in otherwise lawful activities.[54] The federal Racketeer Influenced and Corrupt Organizations Act (RICO) has been interpreted to make criminal a lawyer's counseling racketeers on the investment of proceeds from illegal operations.[55] At least when a lawyer knows that an enterprise is built upon criminal activity, advising participants on means of investing profits of the activity supports the activity just as much as does a lawyer's advice about the illegal aspects of the enterprise.

WESTLAW REFERENCES

attorney lawyer /5 client /p continu! ongoing +5 crim**** fraudulent** illegal** +s conduct act** activity behavior enterprise offense

---

§ 13.3.6 Fraudulent and Sham Transactions

Fraud

Both DR 7-102(A)(7) and MR 1.2(d) prohibit lawyer assistance in client conduct that is "fraudulent." The term is undefined in the Code but is defined in the terminology section of the Model Rules as "conduct having a purpose to deceive and not merely negligent misrepresentation or failure to apprise another of relevant information." Approximately the same definition should apply to the usage in DR 7-102(A)(7) and other instances in the Code in which "fraud" is used.[56] It is a narrower definition of fraud than has developed

[50] People v. Pic'l, 31 Cal.App.3d 731, 183 Cal.Rptr. 685, 646 P.2d 847 (1982)(negotiating return of stolen racing car to owner in return for agreement not to prosecute is offense of bribing a witness and offense of compounding felony).

[51] ABA Formal Op. 281 (1952); In re Disbarment Proceedings, 321 Pa. 81, 184 A. 59 (1936); In re Abrams, 56 N.J. 271, 266 A.2d 275 (1970); In re Garber, 95 N.J. 597, 472 A.2d 566 (1984)(suspension for representing eyewitness to murder at same time social and professional relationship was maintained with murder defendant; aggravating factor was lawyer's relationship with "reputed" organized-crime figure). See generally Schwartz, The Lawyer's Professional Responsibility and Interstate Organized Crime, 38 Notre Dame Law. 711 (1961).

[52] § 12.6.5.

[53] MR 1.2 comment (Criminal, Fraudulent and Prohibited Transactions; fourth paragraph) (MR 1.2(d) "does not preclude undertaking a criminal defense incident to a general retainer for legal services to a lawful enterprise."); Amusement Devices Ass'n v. Ohio, 443 F.Supp. 1040 (S.D.Ohio 1977)(statute prohibiting lawyer from representing any criminal syndicate is unconstitutionally broad because it applies to after-the-fact representation and to representation with respect to lawful as well as criminal activities).

[54] Guralnick, Someone Has to Defend the Drug Dealers, Stud.Law. at 12 (Feb.1984); Taylor, Laundry Service—More Professionals Like Lawyers, Bankers Said to Hide Drug Loot, Wall St.J., July 25, 1983, p.1, col.1.

[55] United States v. Loften, 518 F.Supp. 839 (S.D.N.Y. 1981).

[56] Note, however, that DR 1-102(A)(4) proscribes lawyer "dishonesty, fraud, deceit, or misrepresentation." That expression, obviously, includes more than fraud alone. With respect to the element of intention, cf., e.g., In re McGrath, 96 A.D.2d 267, 468 N.Y.S.2d 349 (1983)(merely negligent misrepresentation of limits of insurance coverage during settlement negotiation in personal injury case is violation of DR 1-102(A)(6) because lawyer's negligence reflected adversely on fitness to practice law).

in some other areas of the law, such as in the federal law of securities regulation.[57]

Fraud is an unfortunately broad, elastic, and inexact term,[58] perhaps necessarily so in view of the endlessly creative flimflam invented by its practitioners to frustrate the rights of others. "The law does not define fraud; it needs no definition; it is as old as falsehood and as versable as human ingenuity." [59]

Fraud in the context of a lawyer's advise to a client includes a client's knowingly false statements, acts, documents, or similar communications that intentionally induce another person to act or to fail to act in reasonable reliance on the misrepresentation, and it usually involves an element of personal gain of a financial or similar kind or a litigational advantage.[60] Fraud should be limited to a conscious course of dealing and should not be extended to instances of unintentional or merely negligent acts.[61] An intentional misrepresentation or a misrepresentation made recklessly without regard to its truth or falsity, however, should be regarded as fraudulent if the other elements of fraud are also present.[62] Under numerous circumstances, silence can be a misrepresentation if it has the effect of inducing another person justifiably to infer that the silence is communicative.[63]

Sham Transactions

Not all sham transactions are fraudulent. For example, in a California case a lawyer was disciplined for assisting his client to construct a sale and resale arrangement through a straw person in order to disguise a usurious loan as a profit on the resale.[64] But if all parties to the transaction were equally aware of the sham, it was not a fraud—although it might have been illegal under a theory other than fraud. That distinction is relevant today only under the Model Rules and not under the Code, because only the Code (DR 7–102(A)(7)), and not the Model Rules (MR 1.2(d)), extends to other "illegal" acts. The same should also be true of such shams as migratory divorces, so long as they involve no false pleading or testimony.[65] Even under the stricter view of the Code, avoiding otherwise applicable law through such conduct, so long

57 L.Loss, "Fraud" and Civil Liability under the Federal Securities Laws (1983).

58 Cf., e.g., W. Prosser & W. Keeton, Torts § 105, at 727 (5th ed.1984)("fraud" is both a confusing term and one "so vague that it requires definition in nearly every case").

59 Weiss v. United States, 122 F.2d 675, 681 (5th Cir. 1941)(Holmes, J.), cert.denied 314 U.S. 687, 62 S.Ct. 300, 86 L.Ed. 550 (1941).

60 People v. Yoakum, 191 Colo. 269, 552 P.2d 291, 297 (1976)(giving false financial statement to bank to obtain personal loan); In re Grand Jury Subpoena Duces Tecum, 165 N.J.Super. 211, 397 A.2d 1132 (1978), affirmed 171 N.J.Super. 475, 410 A.2d 63 (App.Div.1979)(procurement by alleged indigent of services of public defender by knowing misrepresentation of assets); In re Cauthen, 267 S.C. 448, 229 S.E.2d 340 (1976)(client's check-kiting scheme). See also, e.g., Beeck v. Kapalis, 302 N.W.2d 90 (Iowa 1981)(fraudulent misrepresentation that plaintiff had filed suit against correct defendant with mistake not revealed until expiration of statute of limitations).

61 The New York version of the 1969 Code contains a special definition of "fraud" in its "Definitions" that seems consistent with the purposes behind rules such as DR 7–102(B) and thus probably accurately restates its limits:

"(9) 'Fraud' does not include conduct, although characterized as fraudulent by statute or administrative rule, which lacks an element of scienter, deceit, intent to mislead, or knowing failure to correct misrepresentations which can be reasonably expected to induce detrimental reliance by another."

62 ABA Formal Op. 346 (revised), at 3 (1982). On the question of the lawyer's state of mind, see § 13.3.3.

63 § 13.5.7 (concealment and nondisclosure).

64 Bryant v. State Bar, 21 Cal.2d 285, 131 P.2d 523 (1942).

65 See generally J.Pike, Beyond the Law 48–50 (1963); Drinker, Problems of Professional Ethics in Matrimonial Litigation, 66 Harv.L.Rev. 443 (1953); Adams & Adams, Ethical Problems in Advising Migratory Divorce, 16 Hastings L.J. 60 (1964). Courts have been particularly severe with lawyers who have filed false pleadings or documents or introduced known perjury in migratory divorces. E.g., Weir v. State Bar, 23 Cal.3d 564, 152 Cal.Rptr. 921, 591 P.2d 19 (1979)(disbarment, among other things, for knowingly submitting false information to immigration office in connection with client's sham divorce and remarriage to American citizen); In re Javits, 35 A.D.2d 442, 316 N.Y.S.2d 943 (1971), appeal denied 29 N.Y.2d 488, 278 N.E.2d 654, 328 N.Y.S.2d 1025, cert.denied 409 U.S. 980, 93 S.Ct. 311, 34 L.Ed.2d 243 (1972)(discipline for bribery and false statements in obtaining migratory divorces); In re Krueger, 103 Wis.2d 192, 307 N.W.2d 184 (1981)(reprimand for counselling client, who lived in Illinois, to rent room in Wisconsin in order to create false evidence of residency).

as it is not otherwise fraudulent or illegal, is not impermissible.

Advising on Tax Questions

Not all tax returns are fraudulent, but some are, and many of those involve lawyer complicity that raises serious issues under both the Code and the Model Rules.[66] In addition, specific obligations for tax lawyers are also stated in the Internal Revenue Code[67] and in regulations of the federal Treasury Department.[68]

The attitude is sometimes encountered among tax practitioners that anything that one can get away with in behalf of a client is legitimate. That attitude assumes that lawyers owe no duty to use restraint in giving tax advice because the only loser is the government or because the tax laws are irrational and arbitrary or are interpreted by the government in such ways. A lawyer may also erroneously assume that a full-advocacy stance that might be legitimate in litigating a tax question is also appropriate in preparing tax returns or making other submissions to the tax authorities.[69] Similar attitudes are found in other areas of legal practice involving government agencies and suffer from the fallacy of diminished responsibility in dealing with large organizations and from a failure to recognize the importance of law compliance in those areas. The argument for a broader responsibility in the area of tax practice, however, is uniquely supportable because the national and most state and local taxation systems rely upon citizen self-assessment and thus call forth at least a measure of nonadversarial cooperativeness.[70]

The range of ethical issues in tax practice runs from the blatant to the subtle. Some lawyer practices, such as back-dating deeds in order to change tax consequences, are classic instances of fraud and are plainly both illegal and in violation of the lawyer codes. A recent variation is found in some abusive tax shelters that often involve a lawyer's opinion based on hypothetical facts that the lawyer knows do not exist.[71]

Many areas of ethical difficulty in tax practice involve problems of proof, such as the state of mind of a taxpayer or other subjective elements. The words of EC 7–6 have often been quoted: "In many cases a lawyer may not be certain as to the state of mind of his client, and in those situations he should resolve reasonable doubts in favor of his client." The sentence that immediately precedes that one draws a distinction between a client's "existing" state of mind and the "creation" of false evidence.[72] A client's statement that "I am dying and want to reduce my estate by making some gifts" involves little room for "reasonable doubts." A lawyer's assistance in making the gifts and then constructing a paper record from which to argue with tax officials that the property transferred is not part of the client's estate because the gifts were not made in contemplation of death receives no warrant from EC 7–6. To be sure, if the reasons for doubt are grounded in uncertain facts rather than in a desire to reach a strate-

[66] Practitioners and scholars in the tax area are unique in the extent to which they attend to ethical issues. See generally ABA Section on Taxation Guidelines to Tax Practice, 31 Tax Law. 551 (1978); B.Wolfman & J.Holden, Ethical Problems in Federal Tax Practice (1981); Cooper, The Avoidance Dynamic: A Tale of Tax Planning, Tax Ethics, and Tax Reform, 80 Colum.L.Rev. 1553 (1980); Marson, Tax Shelter Opinions: Ethical Responsibilities of the Tax Attorney, 9 Ohio N.U.L.Rev. 237 (1982); Paul, The Lawyer as a Tax Advisor, 25 Rocky Mt. L.Rev. 412 (1953); Paul, The Responsibilities of the Tax Adviser, 63 Harv.L.Rev. 377 (1950); Walters, Ethical and Professional Responsibilities of Tax Practitioners, 17 Gonz.L.Rev. 23 (1981).

[67] 26 U.S.C.A. §§ 6694–95.

[68] Treas.Dept.Circular No.230, 31 C.F.R. § 10 (1981).

[69] Some of this confusion is reflected in ABA Formal Op. 314 (1965), which defines a stance for all tax-lawyering issues that seems to derive primarily from a litigator-like position of representing a client "before" the tax department. Preparing and filing a return, of course, is quite different from negotiating with tax officials or litigating in a tax court.

[70] Caplin, Responsibilities of the Tax Advisor—A Perspective, 40 Taxes 1030 (1962); Tarleau, Ethical Problems in Dealing with Treasury Representatives, 8 Tax L.Rev. 10, 11–13 (1952); Schenk, Book Review, 95 Harv.L.Rev. 1995, 2005 (1982).

[71] The matter of tax shelter advice is reviewed extensively in ABA Formal Op. 346 (revised)(1982).

[72] Corneel, Ethical Guidelines for Tax Practice, 28 Tax. L.Rev. 1, 26 (1972).

gically advantageous legal position, these can be resolved in favor of the client.

On matters of the interpretation of the tax laws, considerable support exists for the view that a lawyer may assist any dubious tax scheme or position for a client so long as there is a good faith argument for the proposition that it is legal.[73] A more appropriate stance is that a lawyer's assistance should conform to what the lawyer in good faith believes a court would hold if the tax question were litigated.[74]

No better general standard can be stated than that a lawyer can take client-favoring positions so long as there is a "reasonable basis" in good faith for doing so.[75] It is not a reasonable basis to be aware that tax officials rarely audit returns for questionable transactions of a particular kind.[76] Here, as elsewhere, it is unlikely that any sure guide to appropriate practice can be given that is itself not subjective, or at least personal. An honest lawyer of good legal skills who, in Edmond Cahn's words, takes care to "exercise intelligence and wisdom and judgment" [77] will have fewer problems (and these will largely be factual ones) than other lawyers.

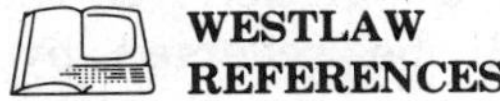

WESTLAW REFERENCES

di fraud

attorney lawyer /s assist! aid*** /s client /s fraud! sham transaction act action activity conduct** behavior /p disciplin! disbar! disqualif!

"dr 7–102(a)(7)" dr7–102(a)(7)

§ 13.3.7 *Defying Court Orders*

Advising Defiance

A lawyer may understandably regret an adverse judicial ruling but may not advise a client to disobey a direct court order or participate with a client in such disobedience.[78] A lawyer who does so is punishable for contempt [79] and violates specific provisions of the 1969 Code (DR 7–106(A)), the California Rules ((Rule 7–101), and at least when the client's contempt would be criminal contempt, the 1983 Model Rules (MR 1.2(d)). A lawyer commits no violation, of course, by giving the client good-faith advice about the limits of the court order.[80]

The Maness v. Meyer Exception

A narrow exception must also be noted for the types of challenges to rulings involved in the Supreme Court's decision in Maness v. Meyers.[81] The Court there held that a state court violated the federal Constitution when it punished a lawyer for contempt for advising a client to refuse to answer a question after the lawyer's objection on self-incrimination

[73] ABA Formal Op. 314 (1965); B.Bitker, Professional Responsibility in Federal Tax Practice, 270 (1970); Johnson, Does the Tax Practitioner Owe a Dual Responsibility to His Client and to the Government?—The Theory, 15 S.Cal.Tax Inst. 25, 31–32 (1963); Rowen, When May a Lawyer Advise a Client that He May Take a Position on His Tax Return?, 29 Tax.Law. 237, 256–57 (1976).

[74] EC 7–3. A variation on this position is to take more extreme tax positions in behalf of a client but to disclose sufficient fact on the return to alert the tax authorities to the existence of the issue whenever the lawyer does not in good faith believe that the client has the better of the legal argument. See Panel Discussion on "Questionable Positions," 32 Tax.Law. 13, 27–28 (1978). Such a position apparently relies on governmental transaction costs such as the "audit lottery"—the great unlikelihood that an agency with limited enforcement budget will detect the problem on the client's return. E.g., Nolan, Audit Coverage and Private Tax Planning, 27 Nat'l Tax J. 425 (1974).

[75] ABA Formal Op. 314 (1965).

[76] See generally Nolan, Audit Coverage and Private Tax Planning, 27 Nat'l Tax J. 425 (1974).

[77] E.Cahn, The Moral Decision 247 (1955); Cahn, Ethical Problems of Tax Practitioners, in Confronting Injustice 255 (L.Cahn ed.1966).

[78] Committee on Professional Ethics v. Crary, 245 N.W.2d 298 (Iowa 1976)(participating in, and counseling evasion of, custody decree, among other things, by removing child from state); Attorney Grievance Comm'n v. Kerpelman, 288 Md. 341, 420 A.2d 940 (1980), cert.denied 450 U.S. 970, 101 S.Ct. 1492, 67 L.Ed.2d 621 (1981); In re Daly, 291 Minn. 488, 189 N.W.2d 176 (1971); Territory v. Clancy, 7 N.M. 580, 37 P. 1108 (1894); In re Apfel, 202 A.D. 76, 195 N.Y.S. 325 (1922); Wright v. Roberts, 573 S.W.2d 468 (Tenn.1978).

[79] Davis v. Goodson, 276 Ark. 337, 635 S.W.2d 226 (1982), cert.denied 459 U.S. 1154, 103 S.Ct. 798, 74 L.Ed. 2d 1002 (1983)(lawyer guilty for advising client in open court not to obey direct order of court).

[80] In re Watts, 190 U.S. 1, 23 S.Ct. 718, 47 L.Ed. 933 (1903)(lawyer who, in good faith but ultimately erroneously, advises client on invalidity of federal court order cannot be held in contempt).

[81] 419 U.S. 449, 95 S.Ct. 584, 42 L.Ed.2d 574 (1975).

grounds was overruled. *Maness* has sometimes been read broadly to warrant a lawyer's advice to defy a court order whenever the lawyer has a good faith reason for thinking the court's order may be erroneous. But the case plainly stands for a much narrower proposition.

The *Maness* Court took pains to point out that the case involved an unusual circumstance: if the lawyer's client had answered the question that was objected to, it would have been impossible to "unring the bell" and recapture the now public and possibly incriminatory information, because state law provided no other means of protecting the self-incrimination interest of the client.[82] *Maness* thus rests on the narrow ground, applicable only to similar questions of privilege or immunity, that a lawyer may advise defiance, when absolutely necessary, in order to obtain appellate review of a trial court order thought in good faith to be erroneous. If other means of obtaining review or of protecting the client's interests are available or if compliance with the erroneous order would not have the same destructive effects as in *Maness* that case provides no protection for defiant advice.[83]

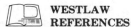

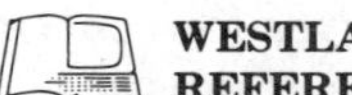
WESTLAW REFERENCES

attorney lawyer /p def*** defiance disregard*** disobe! contempt /p 7-101 7-106(a)

maness +5 meyer /12 95 +5 584 /p contempt defian*** def***

§ 13.3.8 *Test Cases, Desuetude, and Civil Disobedience*

Test Cases

The lawyer codes all recognize that a lawyer may advise and assist a client to defy a law, rule, or ruling that is thought to be invalid.[84] The phenomenon alluded to is the well-recognized American institution of the *test case*—a willful violation of a law for the good faith purpose of putting its validity into issue in litigation.[85] But limitations must be observed on the form of defiance. The allusions to "good faith" and "appropriate steps" in the lawyer codes suggest, for example, that surreptitious defiance of a court ruling or a defiance that does not contemplate further, particularly appellate, review of any legal issue is not appropriate.[86]

Certainly there is no constitutional right to pick and choose which laws or rulings to advise a client to obey.[87] The lawyer must have a good faith basis for believing that the law or ruling challenged can be argued to be invalid on constitutional or other legal grounds.[88] It may not even be enough that a known individual judge will invalidate the law, if the lawyer believes that that judge's rulings will be reversed by an appellate court.[89] Moreover, a lawyer must be aware when advising about civil disobedience that the client may bear serious consequences if the lawyer's analysis of the law's invalidity is wrong.

[82] 419 U.S. at 460, 95 S.Ct. at 592.

[83] State ex rel. Angel v. Woodahl, 171 Mont. 13, 555 P.2d 501 (1976).

[84] DR 7-106(A)(a lawyer "may take appropriate steps in good faith to test the validity of such rule or ruling"); Calif.R. 7-101 (similar); MR 1.2(d)(lawyer "may counsel or assist a client to make a good faith effort to determine the validity, scope, meaning or application of the law").

[85] The American doctrine that denies legal effect to invalid legal prescriptions is at least as old as Marbury v. Madison, 5 U.S. (1 Cranch) 137, 2 L.Ed. 60 (1803)("[A] legislative act, contrary to the constitution, is not law."). See generally M.Kadish & S.Kadish, Discretion to Disobey: A Study of Lawful Departures from Legal Rules, ch. 3 (1973).

[86] Wright v. Roberts, 573 S.W.2d 468, 473 (Tenn.1978).

[87] Attorney Grievance Comm'n v. Kerpelman, 288 Md. 341, 420 A.2d 940, 957-58 (1980), cert.denied 450 U.S. 970, 101 S.Ct. 1492, 67 L.Ed.2d 621 (1981).

[88] Maness v. Meyers, 419 U.S. 449, 458-60, 95 S.Ct. 584, 590-92, 42 L.Ed.2d 574 (1975). See generally Cowen, The Lawyer's Role in Civil Disobedience, 47 N.C.L.Rev. 587 (1969); DiSalvo, The Fracture of Good Order: An Argument for Allowing Lawyers to Counsel the Civilly Disobedient, 17 Ga.L.Rev. 109 (1982); Greenblatt, Defense of the Civilly Disobedient, 13 N.C.Cent.L.Rev. 158 (1981).

[89] In re Daly, 291 Minn. 488, 189 N.W.2d 176 (1971) (justice of peace prepared to hold Federal Reserve system unconstitutional).

Desuetude

More problematical are laws that are widely ignored and seldom or never enforced because they were made for another day or in defiance of widespread and strongly felt citizen resistance. May a lawyer advise a client that a particular course of conduct, although unlawful, almost certainly will not be challenged? May a lawyer go further and assist a client in a course of conduct that all or most other persons would pursue, even if the conduct is illegal in the sense of contravening an unenforced law? Generally, American courts have refused to recognize a defense of desuetude to criminal offenses.[90] And, on the whole, lawyers serve the interests of society better if they urge upon clients the desirability of complying with all valid laws, no matter how widely violated by others they may be. Lawyers must also beware that apparent desuetude does not reflect only a temporary era of lax enforcement or a momentary outbreak of defiance to particular laws. Nonetheless, a course of conduct that, although contrary to law or regulation, is widely and openly practiced and tolerated by officials responsible for enforcement is hardly one that seems important to suppress, unless the legal system itself is corrupt. A lawyer's assistance in such a course of conduct should at least be subject to a mild sanction if it is found impermissible.[91]

Civil Disobedience

A critical legal and moral issue is whether a lawyer may assist a client to violate a law that will plainly be enforced and upheld against attacks on its validity but that the client regards as morally unjust. The problem starts in the realm of test case and may move to that of civil disobedience or, indeed, of revolution. If all avenues of legal attack on the assertedly unjust law have been exhausted, only compliance or forms of extralegal defiance remain. Any course of action other than advising compliance plainly violates the lawyer codes and, possibly, other law. Whether the occasion is sufficiently extraordinary and the prospects of legal reform sufficiently unlikely to warrant law violation as an ethical matter is obviously a question of conscience of the most dire sort.[92]

WESTLAW REFERENCES

di desuetude

di "civil disobedience"

attorney lawyer /s client advice advis! /p obsolete desuetude (civil +3 disobedien!)

---

§ 13.3.9 *Unconscionable, Tortious, and Other Unlawful Acts*

To this point, the focus has been upon client conduct that is criminal, fraudulent, or contrary to a direct ruling of a court. Are the considerations different if the client's conduct is not of this description but violates other law? For example, what if the client wishes to pursue a course of conduct that is unconscionable under applicable law but is not criminal, fraudulent, or in violation of a court order? What of client conduct that violates the law of torts, contracts, property, or some other noncriminal law that does not deal with fraud? The answer to those questions is ambiguous under the Code. Under the Model Rules a lawyer who assists the conduct described definitely commits no professional offense.

Other Illegality under the Code.

The conduct forbidden in the Code's DR 7–102(A)(7) extends to a lawyer's assistance of client activity that is either "illegal" or fraudulent. There is little case authority firmly establishing the definitional limits of the

[90] Commonwealth v. Stowell, 389 Mass. 171, 449 N.E.2d 357 (1983)(desuetude is not defense to crime of adultery). See also, e.g., Schlachet v. Schlachet, 84 Misc.2d 782, 378 N.Y.S.2d 308 (1976)(separation agreement cannot give right of predivorce sexual freedom while state law makes adultery crime).

[91] Louisiana State Bar Ass'n v. Weinstein, 416 So.2d 62 (La.1982)(widespread practice, tolerated by government-agency head, of using false statements in application for federal assistance warrants only public reprimand).

[92] Symposium, 67 Va.L.Rev. 1–248 (1981)(inspired by A.Woozley, Law and Obedience (1979)).

quoted term. Some older cases have disciplined lawyers for advising clients to commit intentional torts or to breach contracts.[93] A Delaware decision holds that advising a client concerning conduct that amounted to the intentional tort of malicious prosecution violates the rule of the DR.[94]

Important commentators support the proposition that the limitations on lawyers should extend beyond client criminal acts to include at least a lawyer's act of assisting a client in unconscionable conduct.[95] The objection that the law of unconscionability, breach of contract, tort, or the like is often unsettled [96] does not distinguish the area under consideration from that of criminal law. There, as has been seen (§ 13.3.3), the ambiguity of law is dealt with through the doctrine that a lawyer with a reasonable and good faith basis for concluding that the conduct is legal may so advise a client without risk of incurring a disciplinary sanction for ultimately being proved wrong. A similar doctrine for other illegal client acts should suffice here as well.

The matter is relevant to a lawyer-adviser in at least two situations. One involves a lawyer who drafts for a client a document that contains known illegal or unenforceable terms when the lawyer's tactical motivation is to provide the client with an arguing point against a person who is unaware of the legal defect in the client's position. For example, a lawyer may consider inserting an "adults only" clause in a lease in a jurisdiction whose law has recently been changed to invalidate such clauses. The lawyer may know that many tenants are unaware of the new law and would comply with the unenforceable term. The moral dimensions of such chicanery seem clear; its legal consequences are not.[97]

Another strategem is a lawyer's drafting a contractual term that is apparently in favor of an unadvised or ill-advised third party but that, unknown to the third party, contains legal booby traps that the client can later spring to trump the third party's apparent advantage and to obtain gain for the client. For example, some states treat harshly lenders of money at usurious rates of interest by making the loan uncollectable or worse.[98] Some authority holds that a lawyer who drafts such a note is subject to discipline when his or her client is the favored borrower and the unwitting lender is an unrepresented party.[99] At least some of those situations can also be analyzed as fraud.

Nonfraudulent Illegality under the Model Rules

The 1983 Model Rules are much narrower. The Rules do not limit a lawyer's advice, even encouragement, to a client about unlawful acts so long as the acts are not criminal or fraudulent. The limitation of MR 1.2(d) to

93 Model Rules Legal Background Note, at 20–22 (Proposed Final Draft, May 30, 1981). On the right of a third party to recover damages from a lawyer for such conduct, see, e.g., Silver v. George, 1 Haw.App. 331, 618 P.2d 1157 (1980), affirmed 64 Haw. 503, 644 P.2d 955 (1982)(innocent third-party payee of note can recover against lawyer for note makers who knowingly drafted unenforceable usurious note); compare Howes v. Curtis, 104 Idaho 563, 661 P.2d 729 (1983)(third party cannot recover against lawyer for other party who drafted usurious loan when plaintiff was aware that interest exceeded lawful rate). See generally §§ 5.6.4, 5.6.5.

94 In re Mekler, 406 A.2d 20, 23 (Del.1979).

95 See especially Rubin, A Causerie on Lawyers' Ethics in Negotiation, 35 La.L.Rev. 577 (1975). Professor Schwartz draws a distinction between assisting a client in unconscionable and similar projects and giving "advice to a client that a particular course of action is not unlawful." Schwartz, The Professionalism and Accountability of Lawyers, 66 Cal.L.Rev. 669, 686 (1978).

96 Model Rules Legal Background Note, at 20 (Proposed Final Draft, May 30, 1981)(making argument such as referred to in text in the context of a client's intentional tort that is noncriminal).

97 Compare, e.g., Ass'n B. City N.Y. Op. 722 (1948) (lawyer may not insert in contract provisions that are known to be void as against public policy under decision of court of last resort), with, e.g., In re Thompson, 416 F.Supp. 991, 996 (S.D.Tex.1976)(although "inexcusable and in obvious disregard of the purposes" of bankruptcy act, unfounded threats by unsecured creditor and its lawyer against discharged bankrupt, to coerce bankrupt to pay discharged debt, do not constitute contempt of order of discharge).

98 Perhaps the extreme is Texas, where interest in excess of double the amount permitted results in forfeiture of the principal to the borrower and entitles the borrower to double the amount of interest and a lawyer's fee. See Tex.Rev.Civ.Stat. art. 5069–1.06 (Vernon 1971).

99 In re Young, 177 Minn. 203, 225 N.W. 97 (1929).

"criminal or fraudulent" conduct of a client was intended by the framers of the rule to be substantially narrower than the proscription in DR 7–102(A)(7) against advising a client on "illegal or fraudulent" conduct.[1]

A recommendation of the drafting Kutak Commission, that a lawyer be prohibited from counseling or assisting a client "in the preparation of a written instrument containing terms the lawyer knows are expressly prohibited by law,"[2] was deleted in February 1983. That prohibition was itself a substantial retreat from the Commission's original position favoring a bar against a lawyer's assisting a client to conclude an agreement "that the lawyer knows or reasonably should know is illegal, contains legally prohibited terms, would work a fraud, or would be held to be unconscionable as a matter of law."[3]

The apparent narrowness of Model Rule 1.2(d), however, may be deceptive in at least one area. A client act that violates no specific criminal law prohibition and is not fraudulent may nonetheless constitute criminal contempt.[4] Presumably Rule 1.2(d) prohibits advice about such acts as well as about acts specifically defined as crimes.

WESTLAW REFERENCES

lawyer attorney /5 client /s unconscionable tortious fraud! (unlawful** illegal** +s act action conduct behavior) /p disciplin! disbar! disqualif! % topic(110)

"dr 7–102(a)(7)" dr7–102(a)(7) /p illegal*** unlawful** unconscionable breach** fraud!

§ 13.3.10 Repugnant or Imprudent Client Projects

Repugnant Conduct

A client, after consulting with a lawyer, may resist a lawyer's advice and decide to embark on a course of conduct that is reasonably supportable as a matter of law but against which the lawyer has advised on moral or similar nonlegal grounds. The client, of course, retains the power to decide to act against the lawyer's advice, and the lawyer should be certain that the client is aware of this.[5] Yet a lawyer is not required to abide by the client's decision, at least in the sense of being required thereafter to assist the client in a repugnant project. Both the Code, in DR 2–110(C)(1)(e) and EC 7–8, and the Model Rules, in MR 1.16(b)(3), recognize that a lawyer may withdraw from the representation in such a situation.[6]

Imprudent Projects

What of intended client conduct for which some legal support can be found but that the lawyer nonetheless believes will be held to be unlawful? As was developed earlier (§ 13.3.3), reasonable legal ambiguities may be resolved in favor of a client. But there is

[1] Model Rules Legal Background Note, at 20 (Proposed Final Draft, May 30, 1981).

[2] MR 1.2(d)(Final Draft, Nov.1982); MR 1.2(d)(Proposed Final Draft, May 30, 1981).

[3] MR 4.3 (Discussion Draft, Jan.30, 1980). The provision on unconscionability was patterned on section 2–302 of the Uniform Commercial Code, authorizing a court to refuse to enforce a promise if "the court as a matter of law finds the contract or any clause of the contract to have been unconscionable at the time it was made." The use of the unconscionability standard for a rule of professional regulation was criticized on the ground that the rule was unfairly indeterminate because of the looseness of the "totality of circumstances" approach that courts employ to assess unconscionability and the significant variation in the doctrine among jurisdictions. Lowenthal, A General Theory of Negotiation Process, Strategy, and Behavior, 31 U.Kan.L.Rev. 69, 103–105 (1982).

[4] Cf., e.g., Fidelity Mortgage Investors v. Camelia Builders, Inc., 550 F.2d 47 (2d Cir.1976), cert.denied 429 U.S. 1093, 97 S.Ct. 1107, 51 L.Ed.2d 540 (1977)(lawyer guilty of contempt for advising creditor client to file state court action against debtor despite bankruptcy rule provision that filing of bankruptcy petition automatically stays all state court actions).

[5] EC 7–8. See §§ 4.3, 4.5.

[6] In rare situations no other lawyer may be available to assist the client in a repugnant project. A lawyer's withdrawal would then leave the client without legal assistance to obtain an advantage that the law allows. A narrow duty to continue the representation is examined in Wolfram, A Lawyer's Duty to Represent Clients, Repugnant and Otherwise, in The Good Lawyer, at 214 (D.Luban ed.1983). An argument for a broader duty to represent a repugnant client in litigation is made in Schwartz, The Zeal of the Civil Advocate, in id. at 150, 161–69. See generally §§ 10.2.2, 10.4.1.

no requirement that they need be. Withdrawal, as just stated, is available if the lawyer's concern with the unlawfulness or imprudence of the conduct is strong. But may a lawyer both refuse to participate in the conduct yet fail to withdraw? A curious rule in the 1969 Code, DR 7–101(B)(2),[7] suggests such a muddled resolution, but it should not permit a lawyer to continue a representation and thus dictate a course of legal conduct to a client who is unaware of the client's right to discharge the lawyer. Instead, DR 7–101(B)(2) should be read as simply an illustrative situation in which withdrawal is available.[8] Although the text of DR 2–110(B), on mandatory withdrawal, seems not to cover the situation, it appears evident that a lawyer would be required to withdraw under the circumstances described in DR 7–101(B)(2) if the point of disagreement between lawyer and client is at all substantial. A similar impasse cannot develop under the Model Rules. Rule 1.2(a) requires a lawyer to abide by a client's decisions concerning the objectives of the representation, and Rule 1.16(a)(1) mandates withdrawal if the lawyer's continuance in the representation would violate another Model Rule.

WESTLAW REFERENCES

lawyer attorney /s client /s improper illegal*** unlawful** unconscionable /s act behavior conduct action activity /p withdraw! "professional responsibility" disciplin! disbar!

dr2–110(c)(1) "dr 2–110(c)(1)" dr7–101(b)(2) "dr 7–101(b)(2)" "ec 7–8"

§ 13.4 EVALUATION[9]

§ 13.4.1 A Lawyer's Role as Evaluator

The Nature of Evaluation

Clients may request their lawyers to serve as legal evaluators—to give a legal opinion on a matter for the eyes of third parties. The role, although a familiar one, has only recently received attention. A client wishes to sell or obtain financing on property, and the buyer or lender requires a legal opinion on the state of the client's title. A client wishes to sell investments in an enterprise, and purchasers or underwriters want an opinion about the legality of the transaction or about the tax or other consequences of their purchase. A legislative body has pending before it legislation of questionable legal effect or validity, and a lawyer for a government agency is requested to report on the issues raised. In such settings the lawyer's role is significantly different from that of either advocate for a client or confidential adviser to a client. The lawyer's opinion will be made public to nonclients, at least to a degree, and normally the lawyer knows that it will influence their important decisions. Thus the interests of third parties will be directly affected by the lawyer's evaluation. The difficult issue is the extent to which the client-retained legal evaluator should serve as disinterested legal appraiser instead of as a sophisticated and possibly only partially revealed advocate of positions and conclusions favorable to the lawyer's client.[10]

Evaluators in the Lawyer Codes

The lawyer's role as evaluator was not specifically mentioned in either the Canons or the Code. The 1983 Model Rules deal with

[7] "In his representation of a client, a lawyer may . . . refuse to aid or participate in conduct that he believes to be unlawful, even though there is some support for an argument that the conduct is legal."

[8] Cf. EC 7–8, EC 7–9.

[9] See generally Report, Legal Opinions to Third Parties: An Easier Path (Report of three bar association committees), 34 Bus.Law. 1891 (1979); Block & Barton, Internal Corporate Investigations: Maintaining the Confidentiality of Corporate Client's Communications with Investigative Counsel, 35 Bus.Law. 5 (1979); Fuld, Lawyers' Standards and Responsibilities in Rendering Opinions, 33 Bus. Law. 1295 (1978).

[10] The issue can be confronted in detailed instructions to the lawyer-evaluator or in legislation or regulations outlining the evaluator's functions. See, e.g., Curzan & Pelesh, The Changing Role of Outside Counsel: A Proposal for a Legal "Audit," 56 Notre Dame Law. 838, 847 (1981).

the role in a special Rule 2.3, but the rule does not deal with the vital question of the nature of the lawyer-evaluator's duties, if any, to third parties.

Model Rule 2.3, as finally promulgated by the ABA, deals explicitly with a lawyer's role as evaluator but has little independently significant content. It states that a lawyer "may" undertake an evaluation in behalf of a client [11] for the use of a third person if the lawyer reasonably believes that the task is compatible with the lawyer's other responsibilities to the client (MR 2.3(a)(1)) and if the client consents after consultation (MR 2.3(a)(2)). Information gained by the lawyer in the course of making the evaluation remains confidential except to the extent that disclosure is necessary in making an evaluation report (MR 2.3(b)).[12] To a large extent those descriptive statements and rules would doubtless obtain in the absence of specific language such as that in MR 3.2.

Three significant legal issues arise in the course of an evaluation. First is the delineation of the circumstances in which a lawyer may serve as evaluator. Second is an issue of confidential client information. The third issue is the extent of the lawyer's duties toward third persons who, by definition, the lawyer knows will use the report.

§ 13.4.2 Eligible Evaluators

Compatibility with Other Assignments

Model Rule 2.3(a)(1) requires that a lawyer contemplating serving as an evaluator must believe in the reasonable compatibility of the assignment with the lawyer's other responsibilities. The requirement seems to be that the evaluator must be able to exercise relative independence in performing the role of evaluator. The comment to MR 3.2 (duty to third person) illustrates a "normally" incompatible evaluation situation. A lawyer defending a client in litigation against charges of fraud is asked by the client to perform an evaluation of the same or related transactions for third parties. The situation that the drafters of the comment undoubtedly had in mind was the role of "special counsel" to the corporation in shareholder derivative litigation.[13] The special counsel advises the "litigation committee" of a corporation in deciding whether to support the plaintiff's position or to recommend that the litigation be discontinued. The comment follows the decisions holding that the special counsel must be a law firm not previously engaged by the corporation, or at least not regularly engaged.[14]

Yet it is not apparent why the Model Rule should limit the role of evaluator to "compatible" situations. The requirements of substantive law in a specific context might preclude a lawyer from accepting the role, or a third party might be entitled to insist upon an independent lawyer without entanglements with a client whose affairs are to be evaluated. But if neither law nor contract limits a lawyer's capacity to fulfill the role, it is not apparent why the professional rules should attempt to do so.

Model Rule 2.3 does not state explicitly that a lawyer must invariably refuse to serve as evaluator if the report will be regarded as unreliable because of the advocate-evaluator's apparent bias. Normally, competence alone requires disclosure of such a limitation to the client. A lawyer hired to perform an evaluation in a context, such as of a special litigation committee, in which the evaluation

11 MR 2.3 comment (Definition; third paragraph), suggests that it is essential that the client be the person whose affairs are being evaluated in order that the lawyer's role be truly that of evaluator rather than investigator or the like. Nothing seems to turn on the terminological nicety whether the lawyer's role is properly called that of "evaluator."

12 Presumably the extent of disclosure of otherwise confidential information is one of the matters that must be discussed during the client consultation required by MR 2.3(a)(2). See generally § 6.7.7.

13 See generally DeMott, Defending the Quiet Life: The Role of Special Counsel in Director Termination of Derivative Suits, 56 Notre Dame Law. 850 (1981).

14 Abbey v. Control Data Corp., 603 F.2d 724, 727 (8th Cir.1979), cert.denied 444 U.S. 1017, 100 S.Ct. 670, 62 L.Ed.2d 647 (1980); Lewis v. Anderson, 615 F.2d 778, 780 (9th Cir.1979), cert.denied 449 U.S. 869, 101 S.Ct. 206, 66 L.Ed.2d 89 (1980).

would be of limited or no value should advise the client corporation about the severe limits on the lawyer's utility. But if, for reasons sufficient to the client, the competently advised corporation wishes to proceed, there is no reason to prevent the lawyer from preparing an evaluation. If the client consents after consultation, the client's interests are presumably protected.

Third parties will naturally be very reluctant to rely on a report of an evaluator who simultaneously functions as an advocate or as a legal adviser to a client in the same matter.[15] Third parties may insist upon the appointment by the client of a disinterested lawyer of the kind contemplated by MR 2.3(a)(1).[16] The lawyer's dual role should, of course, be revealed to the third party if the third party is not fully aware of it. If that role is not revealed sufficiently, a substantial issue of fraud on both the client's and the lawyer's parts could arise.

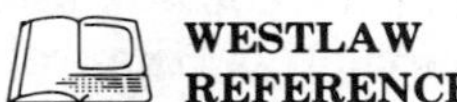

WESTLAW REFERENCES

doe /12 675 +5 482 /p attorney lawyer /10 client

§ 13.4.3 Confidentiality in Evaluation

The extent to which client information may be revealed in making an evaluation is primarily governed by the normal rules of confidentiality. A lawyer may disclose such information only with the express or implied consent of the client.[17] The Supreme Court, in effect, has encouraged internal corporate investigations through an expansive corporate attorney-client privilege,[18] but revelation of privileged matters to nonclients in an evaluation report would probably be held to waive the privilege.[19]

Confidentiality in evaluation is a matter of careful planning and execution of the evaluation and, most importantly, of the development of the terms of the undertaking in consultation with the client before it begins.[20] A well-advised client would likely require that the lawyer submit a draft evaluation report to the client for review prior to its release to third parties. An issue of the need to reveal confidential client information that was not foreseen at the outset will arise only in special circumstances. The terms of the third party's demand for an evaluation might require that the lawyer report without client preview of the evaluation report. Or the lawyer's inability to give a full report because of protection of client information may in "passkey" situations mean that wary third parties will refuse to consummate the transaction with the lawyer's client. In either case, removal of the protection for any confidential client information is largely an issue of knowing and intelligent waiver of the privilege by the client (§ 6.4.2). In one area—that of lawyer responses to requests for information by auditors—a jointly worked-out approach has been approved by the American Bar Association and the national organization of certified public accountants.[21]

15 In re Doe Corp., 675 F.2d 482, 491 (2d Cir.1982) (lawyers closely related to a corporate client may be "torn between a desire to see the firm prosper and their professional and legal obligations"; when an investigation of possible wrongdoing is required, "the wiser course may be to hire counsel with no other connection to the corporation to conduct investigations").

16 In settlements with the Securities Exchange Commission involving improper political payments in the 1970s, the SEC was most willing to accept reports of internal corporate investigations when the internal investigating committee was advised by special outside counsel. See Sommer, The Impact of the SEC on Corporate Governance, 41 Law & Contemp.Probs. 115, 127–34 (1977).

17 § 6.7.7.

18 Upjohn Co. v. United States, 449 U.S. 383, 101 S.Ct. 677, 66 L.Ed.2d 584 (1981).

19 Osterneck v. E.T. Barwick Ind., Inc., 82 F.R.D. 81 (N.D.Ga.1979)(evaluation report prepared for submission to special review commission formed by corporation pursuant to settlement of litigation with regulatory agency not privileged). See generally § 6.4.6.

20 An earlier version of MR 2.3(a) would have required that the terms on which the evaluation was to be made be stated in writing. See MR 2.3(a)(2)(Proposed Final Draft, May 30, 1981). Despite the deletion of the writing requirement, a full, written delineation of the arrangement is highly desirable. See Smith, Preventing Errors in Securities Transactions, 30 S.C.L.Rev. 243, 269–74 (1979).

21 § 11.8.2(i)(3). The Statement of Policy Regarding Lawyers' Responses to Auditors' Requests for Information (1975) is referred to approvingly in MR 2.3 comment (Financial Auditors' Requests for Information).

WESTLAW REFERENCES

upjohn /12 101 +5 677 /p attorney lawyer counsel** /10 client /p confiden!

osterneck +5 barwick /12 82 +5 81 /p disclos! waiv*** privileg**

§ 13.4.4 Duties to Third Parties

Interests of Third Parties

In some financial transactions a favorable opinion letter from a lawyer is indispensable to complete a vital stage. The power wielded by evaluating lawyers in those settings is significant. The often-repeated metaphorical comparison of the Second Circuit is that "In our complex society the accountant's certificate and the lawyer's opinion can be instruments for inflicting pecuniary loss more potent than the chisel or the crowbar." [22]

Model Rule 2.3 does not purport to define the nature of the evaluator's duties toward third parties for whose benefit the evaluation is conducted.[23] Legal malpractice decisions have differed over the lawyer's liability to nonclients for damages under circumstances similar to an evaluation, with the present majority of decisions opposed to liability (§ 5.6.4). Developments in the area of federal securities indicate that the law there may move in the direction of civil damages liability, at least when the evaluating lawyer's failure to disclose information itself violates securities law.[24] The only specific requirement of the Model Rules is that the evaluation report to third parties must detail all material limitations on the scope of the evaluator's review of factual or legal matters.[25]

From the point of view of third parties, the most valuable role for the evaluator is that approaching an auditor, with full power and responsibility to ferret out facts and legal issues and to exercise independent professional judgment in assessing their legal import. A responsible lawyer with a valued reputation to protect will often insist on performing evaluations in much that way.[26] The antithesis of a useful evaluation report is the whitewash, or cover-up.[27] If the lawyer's client imposes significant limitations or refuses to comply with conditions of the evaluation once it is undertaken, the Model Rules leave the lawyer's further obligations to "law." [28]

Tax and Securities Opinion Letters

Law other than that of the lawyer codes is beginning to supply answers to several nettling questions left open under both prior law and the lawyer codes. Two significant areas are those of tax shelter opinion letters and opinion letters in securities regulation. In general their thrust is to require fuller disclosure in opinion letters and to deny their use for cover-up or deception.

An opinion letter must disclose that it is based in material part on hypothetical facts.[29] The evaluating lawyer is required to deter-

[22] United States v. Benjamin, 328 F.2d 854, 863 (2d Cir.), cert.denied 377 U.S. 953, 84 S.Ct. 1631, 12 L.Ed.2d 497 (1964).

[23] MR 2.3 comment (Duty to Third Persons).

[24] § 12.6.6.

[25] MR 2.3 comment (Access to and Disclosure of Information):

> Under some circumstances . . . the terms of the evaluation may be limited. For example, certain issues or sources may be categorically excluded, or the scope of search may be limited by time constraints or the noncooperation of persons having relevant information. Any such limitations which are material to the evaluation should be described in the report.

[26] In Diversified Industries, Inc. v. Meredith, 572 F.2d 596 (8th Cir.1977)(en banc), the court stated that lawyers conducting an investigation of charges that their corporate client's employees had created an illegal slush fund were under an obligation, based on the 1969 Code, "to conduct the inquiry in an independent and ethical manner." 572 F.2d at 610. The court did not identify in the Code the source of the obligation. In any event, the type of investigaton conducted in *Meredith*, with a confidential report submitted only to the corporate client's board of directors, is not an evaluation in the contemplation of the Model Rules because the report was not distributed to nonclients.

[27] Cf., e.g., Carley, Close Encounters—Was Law Firm's Study of Citibank's Dealings Abroad a Whitewash?, Wall St.J., Sept. 14, 1982, p.1, col.6.

[28] MR 2.3 comment (Access to and Disclosure of Information).

[29] Generally, a material part of an opinion letter can be based on hypothetical facts only if it is reasonable to do so and if this is disclosed. See ABA Formal Op. 346 at 6 (1982)(tax shelter opinions); ABA Formal Op. 335, at 5

mine the accuracy of facts stated by the client if the lawyer has reason to suspect that they are inaccurate or incomplete.[30] It is impermissible for an opinion without prominent disclosure to deal with fewer than all material legal issues.[31] It is also impermissible for a lawyer to issue a negative opinion if the lawyer knows that it will be included in offering materials of the client without prominent notation and thus create the risk that purchasers or investors will misunderstand the import of the opinion.[32] And a lawyer may issue a partial opinion (opining only on the tax and not the securities aspects of an offering of a tax shelter, for example) only if this is revealed and does not mislead.[33]

Those generalizations follow the basic philosophy that an evaluator should act candidly and give due regard to the interests of persons who can reasonably be expected to rely on the evaluator's opinion. Although they are based largely on guidelines applicable to opinion letters in relatively narrow areas, their basic thrust seems relevant to all evaluation reports, such as opinion letters that are known by the lawyer to be intended for other interested readers.

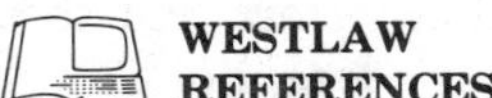

WESTLAW REFERENCES

opinion +2 letter /p disciplin! disbar! disqualif! malpractice deception deceiv*** /p lawyer attorney counsel**

§ 13.5 NEGOTIATION

§ 13.5.1 Nature of the Negotiation Function

Negotiation by a lawyer occurs whenever a lawyer, in behalf of a client, communicates with another person in an attempt to obtain things of value through concession or agreement. The most common object of value that a lawyer seeks in behalf of a client is the third person's binding contractual promise, but it might include an outright conveyance, gift, forbearance, grant, or anything else of value. In all negotiations the client's interests are obviously in conflict, at least formally, with those of other parties to the transaction. The setting in which the negotiation is carried on may range from a fully adversarial relationship, typified by opposing lawyers negotiating the possible settlement of a lawsuit, to cooperative discussions between prospective business associates settling in an apparently amicable spirit the terms of an ongoing business partnership. Central to all settings, whether they are overtly antagonistic or not, are issues of truth in negotiation and the limits on the use of force, threats, puffery, and similar persuasive devices.

§ 13.5.2 Negotiation Settings

Freedom and Constraint in Negotiating

Negotiations take place in quite different settings. One important variable is the presence or absence of litigation as a backdrop.[34]

(1974); Treas.Circ. 230, 31 C.F.R. §§ 10.33, 10.51(j), 10.52(b)(1984). See also Croy v. Campbell, 624 F.2d 709 (5th Cir.1980); SEC v. Frank, 388 F.2d 486 (2d Cir.1968); Ass'n B.City N.Y. Comm. on Taxation, Proposed Amendments with Respect to Tax Shelter Opinions, 36 Rec.Ass'n B.City N.Y. 133, 138 (1981). ABA Formal Op. 346, supra, states that a lawyer should not issue a tax shelter opinion letter if it "discusses *purely* hypothetical facts." (Emphasis supplied.)

30 ABA Formal Op. 335 (1974); ABA Formal Op. 346, at 5–6 (1982).

31 Treas.Circs. 230, 31 C.F.R. § 1033(a)(2)(1984). An original version of ABA Formal Opinion 346 held that a lawyer should not issue a tax shelter opinion letter in the absence of a "reasonable likelihood" that the investing taxpayer would obtain the sought-after tax benefit of the shelter. See 67 ABA J. 1057 (1981). The revised Opinion 346, 68 ABA J. 471 (1982), abandoned this absolute rule in favor of a more general prohibition against "a false opinion which ignores or minimizes serious legal risks." ABA Formal Op. 346 (revised), at 2 (1982).

32 Treas. Circ. 230, 31 C.F.R. § 10.33(a)(5)(iii)(1984); ABA Formal Op. 346, at 8 (1982).

33 ABA Formal Op. 346, at 6–7 (1982); cf. Treas. Circ. 230, 31 C.F.R. § 10.33(a)(1)(iii)(1984). But a lawyer may not, in a tax shelter opinion letter, deal only with selected tax issues. Instead the letter must give an "overall evaluation" whether the material tax benefits sought will more likely than not be realized. See Treas. Circ. 230, supra, § 10.33(a)(5).

34 The typology in these sentences follows Schwartz, The Professionalism and Accountability of Lawyers, 66 Cal.L.Rev. 669, 675–76 (1978).

Another variable is whether the parties negotiate under a requirement that a judge independently approve any agreement reached, such as in the proposed settlement of class action litigation, in suits by minors or incompetent persons, or in plea bargains in criminal cases. Whether more or less candor is required in those settings may depend on judgments concerning the relative vulnerability of the process to corruption, the presence or absence of alternative means of assuring accuracy of facts, and greater or lesser duties of candor imposed by the private or public nature of the surroundings.

Negotiating the End to Lawsuits

The general process of negotiating settlements to lawsuits is vital to the operation of the adversary system as it is practiced in the United States. In a recent year (1982), some 94.2 percent of all civil cases disposed of in the federal courts were terminated without trial and some high percentage of these were by settlement.[35] In the same year, only 14.8 percent of federal criminal cases disposed of during the year were tried.[36] The great majority of the rest were undoubtedly disposed of by negotiated plea bargains. Good statistics are not kept for state courts, but comparable rates for both civil and criminal cases probably obtain there as well.[37] Indeed, study of litigated cases and their outcomes might in many areas distort the "average" resolution of disputes in those areas through negotiated settlements. In divorce, for example, it has been observed that the private ordering achieved by lawyers in divorce representation may only roughly approximate the results that the legal system reaches in adjudicated cases.[38]

Litigation-Free Negotiating

Many other kinds of negotiation take place in an environment free of impending litigation. That is true, for example, when lawyers representing the prospective seller and buyer of a business meet to deal about price and other terms of the sale. To be sure, a careful negotiator keeps an eye on the possibility that the negotiated agreement may be the subject of later litigation. But, unlike settlement discussions in litigation, a failure to reach agreement here may not have significant consequences for the parties, assuming that other buyers and sellers are active in the market. Even if collapse of the negotiations would bitterly disappoint one or both parties, there will not automatically be a resort to court for an imposed resolution of their privately unbridgeable differences.

Other types of negotiations, however, are more deadend, in the sense that neither party wishes to end the negotiations. While a failure to reach agreement does not permit resort to a third-party decision maker, the pressure to avoid a mutually destructive alternative to agreement may pressure the parties to continue to seek a negotiated compromise of their differences. A union and employer in the midst of a strike can each be under great economic pressure to negotiate an agreement. Nations whose armaments threaten the existence of each other and the rest of the world will, hopefully, feel irresistible pressures of politics and morality to negotiate toward peaceful settlements of differences.

Lawyers' Roles in Negotiations

Lawyers can be found in all such negotiations. In many of them, no professional negotiator but a lawyer or the lawyer's client can lawfully carry on discussions because of the rules of unauthorized practice (§ 15.1). That

[35] Admin. Off. of U.S. Courts, Federal Jud. Workload Statistics (Calendar Year 1982), at A20 (1983).

[36] Admin. Off. of U.S. Courts, Federal Offenders in the U.S. Distr. Cts. (1982), at 13 (1983).

[37] H.Ross, Settled Out of Court: The Social Process of Insurance Claims Adjustment 136 (1970)(90–95 percent of all civil damage cases are settled without trial); J.Bond, Plea Bargaining and Guilty Pleas 13–15 (1975)(various sources cited for estimates of plea bargained dispositions ranging up to 95 percent of criminal cases).

[38] Mnookin & Kornhauser, Bargaining in the Shadow of the Law: The Case of Divorce, 88 Yale L.J. 950 (1979).

characterizes negotiated settlements and plea bargains in pending cases. Negotiators in those arenas must know law and legal institutions in order to function effectively. Lawyers are also found negotiating business deals and even in international peace and disarmament negotiations. A negotiating lawyer's role as legal consultant might be secondary in some of those settings. A lawyer's chief value as negotiator might be in a capacity to deal creatively with the challenge of ordering a future course of interactions between the negotiating parties that maximizes the protections and benefits for each.

A lawyer-negotiator's freedom of maneuveur will also vary considerably from one type of representation to another. A lawyer who represents an injured, unsophisticated, and possibly impoverished claimant in a personal injury claim has great freedom of action.[39] That power can be so great that significant ethical issues arise concerning the client's autonomous power to share in controlling the representation (§§ 4.3, 4.6). At the other extreme, a client's extensive experience and sophistication may place the client on a relatively equal footing with a lawyer. A corporate or other entity client may have a complex organizational arrangement that encumbers with bureaucratic constraints the lawyer's ability to affect negotiation strategies. Similar constraints may be imposed by the nature of the client's relationships with others, such as coparties.

Negotiations are also constrained by quite different rules of social convention and etiquette. Good breeding and high formality may characterize discourse at international economic conferences but are irrelevant or even disfunctional in some back-alley brawls that pass for negotiation in, for example, some lower criminal courts. Tactics that are accepted in bargaining on the courthouse steps may be unheard of in the corporate boardroom. A lawyer's success as a negotiator may depend as much on his or her ability to work within, or against, such conventions and constraints as on knowledge of law and psychology, verbal skills, and meticulous knowledge of the facts.

Fair Outcome of Negotiation

In a perfect world's legal system, one would be hard-pressed to think of any good reason to uphold negotiated transfers or agreements that were not fair and based on a full understanding of the relevant facts and legal obligations by all parties to them. But in the aggressive and imperfect world of twentieth-century business, the operating assumption is that both parties will, and should, attempt to obtain bargains that are not fair but "good." There are two ways of gaining such bargains short of luck or outright theft. One method is coercion—forcing the other party with a threat to expose embarrassing information, for example, to sign an agreement or threatening to sell to someone else an article desired by a prospective purchaser. The other method is deception—painting an old horse to make it appear much younger and more valuable or falsely stating that an automobile offered for sale has never been in a wreck. In general the law prohibits some methods of exerting force and deception as means of achieving agreements and provides a system of remedies to compensate victims of agreements obtained through those means.[40] But a fair measure of coercion and deception remains lawful.

Bargaining in Imperfect Markets

Three general features make the legal world of bargaining a different one from an imaginable utopia. First, the definitions of both force and fraud are limited so as to exclude many otherwise sympathetic instances. For example, a person may agree to sell valuable property at a very low price or on other unfavorable terms because of economic coercion, perhaps a desperate need to pay for emergency medical care. A party

39 A description of the negotiation process in personal injury insurance claims is given by a sociologist in H.Ross, Settled out of Court 136–75 (2d ed.1980).

40 See generally D.Dobbs, Remedies ch.9 (fraud and deceit) and § 10.2 (coercion)(1973).

who knowingly obtains a bargain from such a hard-pressed seller can keep it. Fraud is also limited. As will be seen, conventions in the business world and judicial assumptions about relatively equal information between bargainers converts many outright lies into legally harmless wind. Second, negotiations are conducted for the most part aggressively, in a fluid factual situation, and not in writing. As a result, problems of proving force or fraud are common. Third, negotiating parties are often not equal in their access to information, in their bargaining skills, and in their willingness to accept risk. Some negotiating sets are far apart in one or more of those features. Yet a system of commercial transactions must protect the stability of agreements and cannot permit them to be undone except for weighty reasons.

Considerations such as those, plus an abiding and dominant judicial faith in a relatively unregulated marketplace, mean that many areas of business negotiating are dominated by the mindsets of caveat emptor and survival of the economically strongest. Those attitudes have sometimes emerged in other fields in which their assumptions are irrelevant, whatever their strength in the business world. There is much less reason, for example, to treat divorcing spouses and their lawyers as involved in a "business" struggle calling for judicial deference to the product of their negotiations.

Taking the above description as roughly accurate and as a given, what role should lawyers play in negotiation if not the same role that the law allows principal participants in the economic war of all against all? Is a lawyer as free as a client to muck about in the nether reaches of unfair overreaching, abusive tactics, and unconscionable results so long as no specific rule of law is offended? Or should lawyers, differently from their clients, be required to abide by a higher standard? Prominent voices have called for a higher standard.[41] But, as we will see, the lawyer codes in most respects leave negotiating lawyers on the same legal and regulatory plane as their clients.

§ 13.5.3 Negotiation Tactics in General[42]

Lawyer-Negotiators as Client Agents

Under agency law a lawyer conducting negotiations in behalf of a client acts as the agent of the client[43] and thus cannot use force or fraud in negotiations if the client legally may not do so. A lawyer's use of unlawful force or fraud in negotiations under many circumstances will subject the client to all of the other party's legal remedies for force or fraud in the same manner as if the client had personally engaged in the force or fraud. Moreover, the lawyer may be personally subject to professional discipline[44] and possibly to a damage action by the coerced or defrauded party.

Is the situation one of perfect legal and moral congruence between lawyer and client? From a moral or professional point of view, may a lawyer do everything that is legally permissible for a client to do? The answer, as a matter of morality, must be negative. Some things that are legal to do are immoral.[45] Is the same thing true as a matter of professional regulation? Or do the lawyer codes merely track otherwise applicable law with respect to limits on a lawyer's use of lawful force and fraud in negotiation?

[41] Rubin, A Causerie on Lawyers' Ethics in Negotiation, 35 La.L.Rev. 577 (1975); Schwartz, The Professionalism and Accountability of Lawyers, 66 Cal.L.Rev. 669 (1978). Judge Rubin would amend the lawyer codes to require two additional, general rules: (1) "[t]he lawyer must act honestly and in good faith;" and (2) "[t]he lawyer may not accept a result that is unconscionably unfair to the other party." Neither standard seems to be rigidly tied to legal concepts. 35 La.L.Rev. at 589, 591. Professor Schwartz's standard is more detailed but generally would not impose additional constraints on the means a lawyer employs in negotiations. His recommended standard limits the permissible results of negotiations to those that are nonfraudulent, legal, and comply with all other constraints of law dealing with voidable contracts and, to an extent, torts. 66 Cal.L.Rev. at 685–86.

[42] For an overall analysis of the negotiation process, see Lowenthal, A General Theory of Negotiation Process, Strategy, and Behavior, 31 U.Kan.L.Rev. 69 (1982).

[43] § 4.2.

[44] § 13.3.6.

[45] § 2.7.

If professional rules hobble a lawyer in negotiating in ways that clients are not, then a well-advised client would dispense with a negotiator's services, if possible, or would hire negotiators who are not lawyers. A client who wished to obtain the benefit of a lawyer for legal assistance in a transaction would have to accept the handicap of a hobbled negotiator. Moreover, bargaining inequalities would be produced. A party to a negotiation who was not represented by a lawyer would have a substantial advantage over another party who was represented, at least if the lawyer abided by the professional rules and if the opposite party did not suffer a net detriment because of the absence of legal assistance. Because of considerations such as those, the effective professional restraints on lawyers as negotiators have tended toward the minimal.

Competitive and Accommodative Approaches to Negotiation

The subject of negotiating by lawyers is beginning to receive some systematic attention.[46] In general, two stereotypes of negotiating strategies can be compared.[47] One is competitive. The negotiator employs deception and force, and the negotiation is characterized by hostility, emotional unrestraint, and manipulative behavior. The other strategy is accommodative or cooperative. The negotiator seeks to build trust, improve communication, search for mutual advantage, and remain flexible and receptive to possibilities for agreement rather than discord. In fact, of course, many negotiators borrow characteristics of both strategies. Both approaches are consistent with at least the minimal requirements of the lawyer codes. As a matter of decency and long-range societal interest, the cooperative approach obviously has much more to recommend itself as a general matter.[48] Social science research also indicates that it is significantly more successul in advancing a client's interests.[49]

§ 13.5.4 Force—Lawyer Extortion [50]

Criminal Law and Lawyer Code Limits on Coercion

Some few lawyers, possessed of overly authoritarian personalities, might be tempted to resort to coercion in negotiations as a method of choice. Many of those lawyers would probably be surprised in researching the law of extortion, a potential quagmire for overly aggressive negotiators. Lawyer use of coercion is limited by external law and possibly, to an extent, by professional rules on threats of criminal prosecution.

Some threats are plainly legitimate, and others plainly are not. A lawyer representing a client with a legitimate claim enforceable against another may state to the other person that suit for collection will be brought unless the debt is paid. Just as obviously, a lawyer may not employ coercive or extortion-

[46] G.Bellow & B.Moulton, The Lawyering Process (1978); H.Edwards & J.White, The Lawyer as a Negotiator (1978); H.Freeman & H.Weihofen, Clinical Law Training: Interviewing and Counseling (1972); M.Meltsner & P.Schrag, Public Interest Advocacy: Materials for Clinical Legal Education (1974); G.Nierenberg, Fundamentals of Negotiating (1973); G.Williams, Legal Negotiation and Settlement (1983).

[47] A large-scale study of the negotiating patterns of lawyers (largely male) determined that 65 percent of lawyers employ the "cooperative" style of negotiating and 24 percent employ a "competitive" style, and that lawyers who employ the former style are significantly more effective negotiators. See G.Williams, Legal Negotiation and Settlement 19 (1983). See also, e.g., Lowenthal, A General Theory of Negotiation Process, Strategy, and Behavior, 31 U.Kan.L.Rev. 69 (1982).

[48] Some have speculated, however, that a lawyer's negotiating behavior is heavily determined by personality and that lawyer codes should not "gratuitous[ly]" direct lawyers how to behave in negotiations. See White, Machiavelli and the Bar: Ethical Limitations on Lying in Negotiation, 1980 Am.B.Found. Research J. 926 n.2. The observation ignores the extent to which other law regulates lawyer (and nonlawyer) behavior in negotiation. It may also overlook the substantial reasons for insisting that lawyers not resort to socially harmful forms of negotiating behavior.

[49] G.Williams, Legal Negotiating and Settlement (1983).

[50] For a discussion, see Livermore, Lawyer Extortion, 20 Ariz.L.Rev. 403 (1978). For a discussion of the problem in an exotic setting, see Schornhorst, The Lawyer and the Terrorist: Another Ethical Dilemma, 53 Ind.L.J. 679 (1978).

ate tactics that violate the criminal law.[51] An underworld threat conveyed by a lawyer that the client would break a debtor's thumbs in the absence of prompt payment is clearly forbidden, regardless of the legitimacy of the debt. But application of the law of extortion to lawyers cannot be neatly captured except in extreme situations. There are numerous gray areas here, as well as in the decisions disciplining lawyers for aggressive negotiation tactics.

Threats of Extraneous Harm

Threats to cause harm unrelated to the client's demand tread near or over the borderline of criminal extortion.[52] A lawyer's threat to publicize embarrassing photographs of a defendant's marital infelicities unless the defendant settled an unrelated personal injury action would be a classic instance of criminal extortion.[53] It would be no defense for the lawyer that the client's claim for personal injury damages was well founded and reasonable in amount.[54] But may a lawyer employ the same threat if it is delivered in the course of negotiating a proposed settlement in a divorce action and if adultery is an available ground for divorce? According to a Vermont decision, a lawyer conveying such a threat is guilty of the offense of attempted extortion.[55] Distinguishable, except possibly for close questions of a wrongful intent, would be a letter from the negotiator in such a case conveying to a defendant a description of evidence (presumably properly obtained) of adultery. The statements, however, apparently must carefully avoid mention of publicity; otherwise the threat in the offer can fairly be read as one to publicize instead of one to file suit. The latter is generally a permissible threat; the former is not.

Threats to Harass

Next, consider conduct that may not be criminally extortionate. Assuming arguendo that it is not criminally extortionate, may a lawyer threaten to file a groundless lawsuit in order to coerce concessions in favor of a client from an opposing party in negotiations? Federal law on collection practices prohibits any "threat to take any action that cannot legally be taken or that is not intended to be taken," [56] but the statute does not apply to lawyers.[57] The lawyer codes, of course, prohibit filing a groundless suit (§ 11.2), but anamolously they say nothing about threats to perform acts that would violate that or any other portion of the lawyer codes. Nonetheless, courts have relied upon general standards in the Canons and Code to discipline lawyers for abusively threatening to file suits [58] or threat-

[51] DR 7-102(A)(8); DR 1-102(A)(3); cf. MR 8.4(b).

[52] Also, a lawyer who employs threats to obtain legal business may be guilty of extortion, even if the threatened conduct relates to the legal business sought. See Carricarte v. State, 384 So.2d 1261 (Fla.), cert.denied 449 U.S. 874, 101 S.Ct. 215, 66 L.Ed.2d 95 (1980)(lawyer's threat to inspire adverse newspaper publicity and to organize residents of a development unless developer agreed to lawyer's demands to represent the developer, made "maliciously" and "with the intent to acquire pecuniary gain," constituted felony extortion).

[53] ALI Model Penal Code § 223.4(c)(Proposed Official Draft 1962).

[54] United States v. Spears, 568 F.2d 799 (10th Cir.1978), cert.denied 439 U.S. 839, 99 S.Ct. 127, 58 L.Ed.2d 137 (1978).

[55] State v. Harrington, 128 Vt. 242, 260 A.2d 692 (1969).

[56] 15 U.S.C.A.§ 1692e(5)(Federal Fair Debt Collection Practices Act). The act also prohibits "the use of any false representation or deceptive means to collect or attempt to collect any debt" (§ 1692e(10)) and "any conduct the natural consequence of which is to harass, oppress, or abuse any person" (§ 1692d).

[57] 15 U.S.C.A. § 1692a(6)(f).

[58] Committee on Professional Ethics v. Michelson, 345 N.W.2d 112, 117 (Iowa1984)(letter to debtor's employer indicating bad publicity that would flow from employee's arrest for theft for nonpayment of debt and suggesting that employer initiate disciplinary action against debtor to force payment was action taken merely to harass or maliciously injure another in violation of DR 7-102(A)(1)); State v. Zeigler, 217 Kan. 748, 538 P.2d 643, 93 A.L.R.3d 869 (1975)(DR 1-102(A)(6) as basis for suspending lawyer for sending debt-collection letter intoning "Oh! The Joy of Being Sued!!"); In re Dows, 168 Minn. 6, 209 N.W. 627, 47 A.L.R. 265 (1926). See also Kentucky State Bar Ass'n v. Taylor, 482 S.W.2d 574 (Ky.1972)(improper to threaten newspaper reporter, a potential witness against client, with libel suit for prior story about lawyer).

ening to subject the other party to embarrassing publicity.[59]

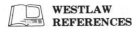

WESTLAW REFERENCES

di extortion

"dr 7–102(a)" dr7–102(a) "dr 1–102(a)" dr1–102(a) /p threat! coerc! extort! harass!

dr1–102(a) "dr 1–102(a)" dr1–102(a) "dr 1–102(a)" /p threat! coerc! extort! harass!

§ 13.5.5 Threat of Criminal Prosecution

Tactical Value of Threats to Invoke the Criminal Process

Much of what causes a person to be potentially civilly liable may also trench upon criminal law. An automobile accident can spawn both lawsuits for damages against the driver and, at least theoretically, a prosecution for careless driving. The bankruptcy of a company can bring against its managers both civil collection suits as well as possible criminal prosecutions for fraud. But the prosecutor may have a different agenda, or less incriminating information, than does a civil litigant. May a lawyer for such a civil litigant employ, or threaten to employ, a report to the prosecutor in order to gain negotiating leverage in the civil suit?

Legal Limitations on Criminal Threats

Threats to report crimes in such circumstances are condemned under several bodies of law, both because they constitute potentially oppressive uses of the criminal law to defeat just claims or defenses in civil litigation and because, if the threat is successful, crimes will not be reported because the threatening party will pay with silence for the advantage sought through the threat.[60] In many jurisdictions an attempt to obtain money under a threat to report the alleged debtor to the police is a form of criminal extortion.[61] Correspondingly, the law of contract makes the promisor's contract voidable because of duress.[62] The threat may also be actionable by the threatened party as a tort, such as abuse of process.[63]

Criminal Threats under the Lawyer Codes

Some, but not all, of the professional rules prohibit such threats. The 1969 Code, in DR 7–105(A), broadly proscribes such tactics: "A lawyer shall not present, participate in presenting, or threaten to present criminal charges solely to obtain an advantage in a civil matter." The 1908 Canons contained no similar prohibition.[64] The California rule is

59 People ex rel. Brundage v. Blakemore, 309 Ill. 311, 141 N.E. 138 (1923)(lawyer disbarred for publicizing claim against corporation in newspaper); In re Chadsey, 141 A.D. 458, 156 N.Y.S. 456 (1910), affirmed 201 N.Y. 592, 95 N.E. 1124 (1911)(suspension for noncriminal threat (because of absence of attempt to extort money) to reveal sexual misconduct if letters incriminating lawyer's client were not returned).

60 Cf. EC 7–21 (subversion of criminal process; frustration of civil process by undue discouragement of resort to courts with civil suits and defenses; and undermines public confidence in legal system).

61 Libarian v. State Bar, 38 Cal.2d 328, 239 P.2d 865 (1952). On the other hand, some state statutes provide for dismissal of misdemeanor criminal charges on the recommendation of the injured party after compromise is reached with the accused-tortfeasor. E.g., Idaho Code §§ 19–3401, 19–3402. And the Model Penal Code provision on extortion was amended during discussions in the ALI to permit threats of criminal charges to be made during negotiation of a civil claim relating to those same charges. See ALI Proceedings 171 (1954). That was done in order "not to intrude into what many regard as legitimate negotiating tactics." Model Penal Code § 223.4 comment (f), at 213 (1980). But the exception to the extortion provision applies only if the civil claim is asserted "honestly." Id. § 223.4 (last sentence). Cf. also, e.g., New York—McKinney's Penal Law § 135.75 (affirmative defense to charge of extortion by threat of criminal charges if "defendant reasonably believed the threatened charge to be true and . . . his sole purpose was to compel or induce the victim to take reasonable action to make good the wrong which was the subject of such threatened charge."); Or.R.S. § 164.035 (same).

62 Restatement (Second) of Contracts § 176(1)(b)(1979).

63 Kinnamon v. Staitman & Snyder, 66 Cal.App.3d 893, 136 Cal.Rptr. 321 (1977); Robinson v. Fimbel Door Co., 113 N.H. 348, 306 A.2d 768 (1973)(dicta); Annot., 27 A.L.R.3d 1113 (1969).

64 However, in In re Gelman, 230 A.D. 524, 527, 245 N.Y.S. 416 (1930), the court censured a lawyer for using criminal prosecution threats to advance a client's position in a meritorious civil suit because it amounted to "unprofessional conduct." *Gelman* cited in support a case involving baseless charges, In re Abrahams, 158 A.D. 595, 143 N.Y.S. 927 (1913). See also, e.g., In re Young, 177 Minn. 203, 225 N.W. 97 (1929)(discipline for advising and

even broader than the Code, extending to threats to present administrative or disciplinary charges as well.[65]

The Code proscription is itself broadly worded. A lawyer may not take any part in "presenting" a criminal charge so long as the lawyer's motivation is the one described. Courts applying the rule commonly draw no distinction between well-founded or ill-founded charges[66] or between serious crimes and minor infractions. The decisions have also not accepted lawyer arguments that a veiled allusion to the criminal nature of a person's conduct or the like does not constitute a "threat"[67] or that the lawyer was motivated by concerns in addition to "solely" obtaining an advantage in civil litigation.[68] The courts apply the Code rule as a pure attempt prohibition; a violation is made out by proof of a threat, regardless of the fact that no criminal charges are in fact brought or any settlement achieved.[69] It has also been held that DR 7-105(A) is violated when a lawyer *delays* a criminal matter in order to obtain an advantage in a civil suit.[70]

Although it is susceptible of such a reading, DR 7-105(A) should not be construed to prohibit a lawyer from merely reporting facts of a possible law violation to the appropriate authorities.[71] Indeed, in view of the arduous obligations that a lawyer is burdened with, under DR 7-101(B), to report even a client's fraud, it would be anamolous if a report of a nonclient had exactly the opposite effect. The report should be discrete, without putting pressure on the prosecutor to take action; should not be conveyed to the person charged; and should not by its timing suggest a punitive or extortionate intent.

Threats by Public Officers

The extortionate force of a threat to invoke the criminal law, and its opprobriousness, are increased when the lawyer who delivers the threat holds an official position in which he or she can more readily carry it out.[72] Should this mean that a lawyer for a public body that is being sued for asserted civil rights violations by its employees is prohibited from linking settlement of that suit with a criminal prosecution of the plaintiffs?[73] While there is

procuring settlement with promise that underage client would not press carnal-knowledge charge).

[65] Calif.R.7-104. On the limited applicability of the Code to threats other than criminal threats, see 13.5.6.

[66] In re Vollintine, 673 P.2d 755 (Alaska 1983); cf. In re Thompson, 416 F.Supp. 991 (S.D.Tex.1976)(threat of criminal suit to force payment of debt discharged in bankruptcy). Some cases hold, however, that a threat to file a well-founded criminal charge is not made "solely" for the purpose of obtaining an advantage in a civil suit but is also for the laudable purpose of reporting crime and is thus permissible. E.g., In re Decato, 117 N.H. 885, 379 A.2d 825 (1977). That reasoning anomalously permits lawyers to do what contracting parties are forbidden. See Restatement (Second) of Contracts § 176(1)(b) and comment (c)(1981).

[67] In re Vollintine, 673 P.2d 755 (Alaska 1983)(emphasis in letter that conduct complained of constituted a crime); Crane v. State Bar, 30 Cal.3d 117, 177 Cal.Rptr. 670, 635 P.2d 163 (1981)(statement that conduct was offense together with notations on letter that copies were being sent to official agency); In re Barrett, 88 N.J. 450, 443 A.2d 678 (1982)(statement that "we are also pursuing the possibility of criminal action" against employees of corporate debtor).

[68] People ex rel. Gallagher v. Hertz, 198 Colo. 522, 608 P.2d 335 (1979).

[69] In re Charles, 290 Or. 127, 618 P.2d 1281 (1980).

[70] In re Vasser, 75 N.J. 357, 382 A.2d 1114 (1978) (conversation with clerk to suppress criminal charge against client in order to protect client's interests in pending divorce action). The holding makes sense on the policy basis of DR 7-105(A) of avoiding impairments of the criminal process, although it is clear that no individual accused was abusively threatened. See also, e.g., In re Lutz, 101 Idaho 24, 607 P.2d 1078 (1980)(discipline for attempting to enforce covenant of witness not to testify against lawyer's client in criminal case in return for favorable settlement of witness' civil claim against client).

[71] People ex rel. Gallagher v. Hertz, 198 Colo. 522, 608 P.2d 335 (1979)(dicta)("respondent went far beyond the acceptable limits of simply informing the responsible official of a suspected crime and allowing that official to conduct his own investigation and reach his own conclusion").

[72] In re Littell, 260 Ind. 187, 294 N.E.2d 126 (1973) (judge severely sentenced person who had breached contract with business associates of judge); In re Joyce, 182 Minn. 156, 234 N.W. 9 (1930)(suspension of lawyer who used position as county attorney to obtain indictments against two defendants in claims asserted by his clients).

[73] Cf., e.g., Hoines v. Barney's Club, Inc., 28 Cal.3d 603, 170 Cal Rptr. 42, 620 P.2d 628, 26 A.L.R.4th 229 (1980)(6-3 decision)(state's dismissal of disturbing the peace charge in explicit return for release signed by accused of

no impingement here on the policy of encouraging citizen reports of crimes to the police, there is clearly a potential for oppressive invocation of the criminal law to gain leverage in a civil matter. The prosecutor's actions seem indistinguishable from, indeed more objectionable than, a mere threat by a civilian lawyer and should be prohibited.[74]

Threats and the Model Rules

The 1983 Model Rules do not contain a prohibition similar to DR 7–105(A). But the absence of a specific provision in the Model Rules may mislead an unwary lawyer reader. Much suit-threatening conduct may be proscribed under the general Model Rule against criminal conduct adversely reflecting on fitness (MR 8.4(b)). The position of the drafters of the Model Rules was that extortionate, fraudulent, or otherwise abusive threats were covered by other, more general prohibitions in the Model Rules and thus that there was no need to outlaw such threats specifically.[75] The final version of the Model Rules is narrower than earlier drafts, however, and it is difficult to see that any threats are proscribed by the final version of the Model Rules beyond those kinds of threats that fall afoul of the jurisdictions' criminal law definition of extortion. Thus, abusively harassing another with threats of a well-founded criminal complaint may be permissible under the Model Rules—a clear, and unfortunate, diminution of the protections afforded by the Code. The behavior permitted by the Model Rules, if engaged in by a client legally in some states, is sufficiently close to the edge of legality and so unappealing a tactic in general that it would better have been prohibited outright in the Model Rules.

WESTLAW REFERENCES

attorney lawyer /5 threat! /11 criminal crime

45k58 /p threat! /p crim****

§ 13.5.6 *Threat of Noncriminal Proceedings*

The lawyer codes of California[76] and Maine[77] go farther than the ABA Code and prohibit a lawyer from presenting or threatening to present "administrative or disciplinary" charges in addition to criminal charges. The distinction drawn in the Code between threats of criminal charges and threats of other types of proceedings parallels the law of contracts. There, a good faith threat to commence a civil proceeding is not generally regarded as duress, even if the threat is without foundation. The Restatement rationalizes that result on the basis that duress exists only if there is no reasonable alternative but to yield to the threat and that defense of the civil action would "usually" be a reasonable alternative.[78] But such a threat is improper as a matter of contract law if made in bad faith,[79] or if the threat is accompanied by property seizure, abusive tactics, emotional consequences, or similar compounding factors.[80]

all civil claims against persons involved in arrest does not invalidate release).

[74] McDonald v. Musick, 425 F.2d 373 (9th Cir.), cert. denied 400 U.S. 852, 91 S.Ct. 54, 27 L.Ed.2d 90 (1970) (denial of due process for prosecutor to move to amend indictment to add other offense when defendant refused to dismiss civil rights action against police). See also, e.g. In re Doe, 546 F.2d 498, 502 (2d Cir.1976); People ex rel. Gallagher v. Hertz, 198 Colo. 522, 608 P.2d 335 (1979)(six-month suspension for failure to separate functions of special fraud prosecutor in securities area and duties of lawyer for receiver in major securities matter); State ex rel. Nebraska State Bar Ass'n v. Gobel, 201 Neb. 586, 271 N.W. 2d 41 (1978)(county prosecutor); M. Freedman, Lawyers Ethics in an Adversary System 92 (1975).

[75] Model Rule 8.4, legal background note (Proposed Final Draft, May 30, 1981)(last paragraph).

[76] Calif.R. 7–104. See Lindenbaum v. State Bar, 26 Cal. 2d 565, 160 P.2d 9 (1945)(reporting ex-client's wife to immigration officials as punitive measure after client who owed lawyer legal fees filed bankruptcy).

[77] Me. Bar Rule 3.6(d).

[78] Restatement (Second) of Contracts § 175 comment b, at 476 (1981). Unadorned threats are countenanced, not because they are not coercive, but, it is said, in order to further the policy of permitting free access to the courts. See Adams v. Crater Well Drilling, Inc., 276 Or. 789, 556 P.2d 679, 681 n.5 (1976), citing Dawson, Duress through Civil Litigation, 45 Mich.L.Rev. 571 (1947).

[79] Restatement (Second) of Contracts § 176(1)(c)(1979).

[80] Restatement (Second) of Contracts § 175 comment b, at 476 (1981).

Although all jurisdictions appear generally to permit most threats of a civil suit,[81] at least three distinguishable situations must be noted. (1) A lawyer's threat to file a noncriminal proceeding, if in violation of a broad criminal extortion statute, violates the general lawyer code prohibitions against criminal conduct. (2) A lawyer's threat to file a civil suit might violate other criminal laws, such as those dealing with witness tampering or obstruction of justice.[82] (3) A lawyer's threat to resort to some kinds of noncriminal relief may fall afoul of the prohibition in DR 9-101(C)[83] against stating or implying an ability to "influence improperly or upon irrelevant grounds any tribunal, legislative body, or public official.[84]

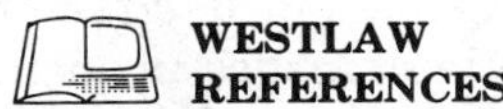

"dr 9-101(c)" dr9-101(c) /p threat! coerc! influenc!

---

§ 13.5.7 Deception in Tort and Contract Law

Uncertain Limits of the Law Prohibiting Deception

The question of the extent to which a negotiating lawyer may rely upon misrepresentations or play upon the ignorance of the other party to obtain a client advantage is one to which no easy answer exists. The law of misrepresentation is more complex and variable than many negotiators may imagine. The professional regulations, here as with other aspects of negotiation, incorporate that law with all of its convolutions but do little else to regulate lawyer behavior other than to provide an additional sanction, lawyer discipline, for the same offense.

Misrepresentation in Tort and Contract[85]

The law concerning deception is found principally in the criminal law,[86] in the law of misrepresentation and mistake in torts, and in the law of mistake and fraud in contract law.[87] The variations in the state of the law are great among jurisdictions and can be confusingly varied among decisions within the same jurisdiction. Although treatise generalities about state-by-state variations are at least as suspect here as elsewhere, an attempt will be made to portray the flavor of the law primarily through paraphrase of the relevant Restatements, a manner that will illustrate the potential risks from false statements or nondisclosures in negotiating.

[81] Even California and Maine prohibit only threats of "administrative and disciplinary" action and not the threat of civil suits, even those as dire as civil commitment or receivership. In some circumstances it may also be permissible in all jurisdictions to threaten in good faith to file a civil suit, even if the threat has the specific intended effect of preventing the filing of criminal charges against the lawyer's client. See In re Gonyo, 73 Wis.2d 624, 245 N.W.2d 893 (1976)(lawyer of client accused of crime permissibly threatened prosecutor with civil action contesting authority of prosecutor to proceed with the criminal action).

[82] State v. Howe, 247 N.W.2d 647 (N.D.1976)(lawyer's telephone call to complaining witness, prefaced with remark that lawyer was not making a threat, that stated that pressing charges might lead lawyer to sue witness "for everything you've got and charge you with neglect" could constitute crime of witness tampering).

[83] The Model Rules contain essentially the same rule in MR 8.4(e).

[84] In re Mollozzi, 73 N.J. 76, 372 A.2d 611 (1977)(violation of DR 9-101(C) for lawyer to threaten client's debtor to "file a formal complaint" through office of state senator unless debt was paid).

[85] See generally Restatement (Second) of Contracts §§ 159-173 (1981); Restatement (Second) of Torts §§ 525-557A (1977); D.Dobbs, Remedies ch.9 (1973); A.Farnsworth, Contracts ch.4 (1980); W.Prosser, Torts ch.18 (4th ed.1971); James & Gray, Misrepresentation—Pt. I, 37 Md.L.Rev. 286 (1977); id.— Pt. II, 37 Md.L.Rev. 488 (1978).

[86] There is no common-law criminal offense called *fraud*. The principal common-law cognate was the offense of obtaining property by false pretenses. W.LaFave & A.Scott, Criminal Law § 90 (1972). Modern criminal codes attempt to avoid pointless distinctions between closely related statutes by combining the offenses of false pretenses, larceny, and embezzlement into one offense of "theft" with several elaborations such as "theft by deception." Id. at 677-78.

[87] An increasing number of statutory remedies for deception also exist, such as the federal securities laws, provisions of the Uniform Commercial Code, and full-disclosure laws regulating such consumer industries as automobile sales. Some of those are obviously of more relevance to lawyers than others because of greater lawyer involvement in the regulated transactions.

In general, legal liability for misrepresentations rests on false statements made either intentionally or negligently. Contract law goes further and permits avoidance or reformation of a contract for innocent misrepresentations that are material to formation of the contract. The law of warranties and special statutory arrangements regulating such things as securities trading may impose additional legal liability for misstatement without fault. All of those bodies of law recognize limited duties to make disclosures in bargaining.

Intentionally False Statements

Tort Law. In the law of torts, pecuniary injury caused by intentionally false statements entitles the injured party to recover damages or to receive the benefit of other affirmative relief such as an injunction, constructive trust, or equitable lien. Under somewhat less stringent rules,[88] the law of contracts permits the injured party to void or reform the contract. The Restatement (Second) of Torts defines an actionable fraudulent misrepresentation as "a misrepresentation of fact, opinion, intention or law [made] for the purpose of inducing another to act or to refrain from action in reliance upon it." [89] Fraudulent misrepresentations include

(1) statements known or believed to be materially different from existing fact;[90]

(2) statements made without the degree of confidence in their accuracy that the speaker states;[91]

(3) statements lacking the supporting basis asserted for them;[92]

(4) ambiguous statements with a false meaning made without regard for how they will be understood;[93] and

(5) partially true statements that materially mislead because of the speaker's failure to state needed additional or qualifying information.[94]

Whether the statement results in tort liability depends on additional factors, including the speaker's intent to induce reliance, reasonable reliance on the part of the auditor, and pecuniary loss.[95]

Contract Law. Contract law, with its milder remedies of contract avoidance and reformation, goes further. Most importantly, avoidance or reformation may be obtained if the misrepresentation is *either* fraudulent or material, while damages in tort are generally recoverable only if *both* elements are present.[96] Thus contract law will give relief for unintentional misrepresentations if they materially affect the bargain.

Puffing and Other Excepted Misrepresentations

Some deals are too good to be true, and some representations are too preposterous, jocular, suspicious, or trite [97] to induce reasonable reliance. A measure of salt is required particularly if the person making the representation is one of adverse interest,[98] as will ordinarily be the case in negotiating. "The habit of vendors to exaggerate and of purchasers to depreciate the value of the article which they are selling or buying is well known." [99] Both contract and tort law recognize loose but not terribly broad categories of these conventionalized lies upon which no one

[88] Restatement (Second) of Contracts ch.7, Topic 1, at 425 (1981).

[89] Restatement (Second) of Torts § 525 (1977).

[90] Rest.2d Torts § 526(a)(1977).

[91] Rest.2d Torts § 526(b)(1977).

[92] Rest.2d Torts § 526(c)(1977).

[93] Rest.2d Torts § 527(1977).

[94] Rest.2d Torts § 529 (1977); see also Rest.2d Contracts § 159 comment (b)(1981).

[95] See generally Rest.2d Torts § 525 (1977).

[96] Rest.2d Contracts, ch. 7, Topic 1, at 425 (1981), inviting comparison between id. § 164 comment a and Rest.2d Torts § 538 (1977).

[97] Learned Hand, J., in Vulcan Metals Co. v. Simmons Mfg. Co., 248 F.2d 853, 856 (2d Cir.1918): "Such statements, like the claims of campaign managers before election, are rather designed to allay the suspicion which would attend their absence than to be understood as having any relation to objective truth."

[98] Rest.2d Torts § 542 (1977).

[99] Rest.2d Torts § 543 comment f (1977).

may reasonably rely in determining to enter into a contract. The categories relate to some, but by no means all, statements of future facts,[1] opinions—particularly opinions about matters of quality, value, and authenticity,[2]—and intentions.[3]

Such misstatements excepted from creation of liability are known as *puffing* or *chaffering*. The exceptions are based on assumptions about human behavior in business dealings and on "reasonable standards of fair dealing." For both purposes judges draw meaning in part from what they believe to be prevailing market practices.[4] Those practices do not always insist on the truth. It may be permissible under them, for example, to lie about one's intended use of a piece of property in order to prevent the intending seller from asking a higher price.[5]

The puffing exception is not based on belief in legal magic that turns some lies into truth. It is based on the reasonability of the reaction of specific listeners to specific misstatements. Importantly, that means that contract negotiators must accept gullible persons for the naifs they are: a gullible person's greater readiness to rely may be held reasonable under some circumstances.[6] Generally, the puffery privilege to lie one's head off[7] has not been favored, and in many instances its legality comes down to a jury question of the materiality of the statement and the justifiability of the auditor in relying on it.[8]

Unintentional Misrepresentation

The law of torts recognizes damage liability for certain negligent misrepresentations. Generally, the duty to exercise due care arises only when, in a business setting, the negligent misrepresenter intends the information to influence the recipient and the recipient is a member of a small group intended to be guided by the information.[9] Moreover, the Restatement of Torts also supports liability for innocent (nonnegligent) misrepresentations in a sale, rental, or exchange bargain but with damages limited to the difference in values between the misrepresented and the actual states of facts.[10] In the law of contracts a bargain is voidable or subject to reformation if an entirely innocent misrepresentation is made, so long as the misrepresentation is material and induces the other party's assent, and the other party's reliance on its accuracy is reasonable.[11]

[1] Rest.2d Contracts § 159, comment c (1981)(misrepresentation about future facts actionable only as contractual promises, if at all; but unenforceable promise or prediction of future events may imply present facts relating to capability or the like that are subject to misrepresentation).

[2] Rest.2d Contracts § 168 (1981). The Uniform Commercial Code in § 2–313(2) specifically provides that "an affirmation merely of the value of the goods or a statement purporting to be merely the seller's opinion or commendation . . . does not create a warranty." For circumstances in which reliance on another's opinion is justifiable, see Rest.2d Contracts § 169. One may reasonably rely on a statement about law in many circumstances. See id. § 170. See also Rest.2d Torts §§ 538A, 545 (1977).

[3] Rest.2d Contracts § 171 (1981); cf. Rest.2d Torts § 544 (1977) (circumstances in which statement of intention may be material, as in statement of intended purposes to which officers of corporation selling bonds intend to put the proceeds).

[4] Rest.2d Contracts § 172 (1981). On the extent of a shift in business community ethical standards and its effect upon the law of fraud, see James & Gray, Misrepresentation—Pt. II, 37 Md.L.Rev. 488, 511 (1978).

[5] Rest.2d Contracts § 171, comment a, illustration 2 (1981).

[6] Rest.2d Torts § 538(2)(b)(1977); W.Prosser, Torts 716–17 (4th ed.1971).

[7] W.Prosser & W.Keeton, Torts 757 (5th ed.1984).

[8] Id.

[9] Rest.2d Torts § 552 (1977). The House of Lords decision in Hedley Byrne & Co. v. Heller & Partners, Limited, [1964] A.C. 465, has proved widely influential in the United States. The case goes beyond the Restatement and holds that a negligent, though honest, misrepresentation might create liability for damages apart from any contract or fiduciary relationship. The duty of care would be found when (1) the injured party sought information from a person possessed of special skills and (2) the party whose information was sought knew or should have known that reliance was being placed on the accuracy of the information furnished. E.g., Rozny v. Marnul, 43 Ill.2d 54, 250 N.E.2d 656, 35 A.L.R.3d 487 (1969).

[10] Rest.2d Torts § 552C (1977).

[11] Rest.2d Contracts § 164 (1981).

Concealment and Nondisclosure [12]

In two situations, a negotiating party may be liable to the other bargainer for failure to communicate information. First is the civil wrong of concealment. If a party intentionally conceals a material fact or takes action that prevents the other party from acquiring the uncommunicated information, the concealing party is as liable, and to the same extent, as if he or she had actively represented the nonexistence of the concealed fact.[13]

Second, in some circumstances a party is under a duty to disclose facts. We will refer to this hereafter as passive misrepresentation. Liability for passive misrepresentation will exist if the other bargaining party is induced to believe in the nonexistence of undisclosed facts by the first party's failure to make a statement about these facts. In business transactions an affirmative duty of disclosure exists in any of the following circumstances:

(1) if the other party is entitled to know the fact because of a fiduciary or similar relationship between the bargainers;[14]

(2) if the first party states a half-truth—a materially misleading partial representation;[15]

(3) if subsequently acquired information indicates the falsity of a previous representation that was true when made;[16]

(4) if the first party learns that a previous false representation, which, when made, was reasonably thought not to induce action or inaction, in fact is about to induce the other party to action;[17]

(5) if the relationship between the parties, business custom, or other objective factors create a known reasonable expectation of disclosure of facts basic to the transaction;[18]

(6) if the party knows that disclosure would correct a mistake of the other party as to the contents or effects of a writing that evidences part or all of their agreement;[19] or

(7) if the party knows that the other party labors under a mistake of fact as to a basic assumption and if nondisclosure amounts to bad faith or a failure to act in accordance with reasonable standards of fair dealing.[20]

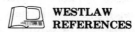

WESTLAW REFERENCES

di deception

di puffing

"dr 7-102(a)(5)" dr7-102(a)(5) /p fals!

§ 13.5.8 Deception under the Professional Regulations

Uncertain Scope of the Lawyer Codes

The law of professional regulation of lawyer deception in negotiations is thin rags against the rich tapestry of tort, contract, and other law that surrounds it. The lawyer codes have mainly contented themselves with incorporation of at least the main part of other substantive law rules as limitations on the negotiating activity of lawyers. As with other problems of this kind, the extent of a lawyer's obligation is seriously complicated by the requirement to protect client information. Few reported decisions deal with issues of any difficulty. As a result, one can say with confi-

[12] For circumstances in which misrepresentation by silence may constitute a crime, see R. Perkins, Criminal Law 380–81 (3d ed.1982).

[13] Rest. 2d Torts § 550 (1977); Rest. 2d Contracts § 160 (1981). In Stare v. Tate, 21 Cal.App.3d 432, 98 Cal.Rptr. 264 (1971), a lawyer prepared a counteroffer in a manner that concealed a mistaken figure supplied by the other side. The court held that the known mistake of fact by the opposing party was a basis for reforming the eventual agreement to reflect the true state of facts. Such a case could also be analyzed on the basis of fraudulent concealment.

[14] Rest. 2d Contracts § 161(d)(1981); Rest. 2d Torts § 551(2)(a)(1977).

[15] Rest. 2d Contracts § 159, comment (b)(1981); Rest. 2d Torts §§ 529, 551(2)(b)(1977).

[16] Rest.2d Contracts § 161(a)(1981); Rest.2d Torts § 551(2)(c) (1977).

[17] Rest.2d Contracts § 161(a)(1981); Rest.2d Torts § 551(2)(d) (1977).

[18] Rest.2d Torts § 551(2)(e)(1977); cf. Rest.2d Contracts § 161(b) (1981).

[19] Rest.2d Contracts § 161(c)(1981).

[20] Rest.2d Contracts § 161(b)(1981).

dence, in general, only that active misrepresentation is prohibited, while passive misrepresentation is problematical.

1908 Canons and 1969 Code

The authors of the 1908 Canons were content to fulminate in a broad way against a lawyer's "violation of law or any manner of fraud or chicane," [21] and to urge honesty as well as patriotism upon all lawyers.[22] The 1969 Code adopts a more legalistic, if still quite general, approach. Under DR 7–102(A)(5) a lawyer shall not "knowingly make a false statement of law or fact." And, as discussed elsewhere,[23] DR 7–102(A)(7) provides that a lawyer shall not "counsel or assist his client in conduct that the lawyer knows to be illegal or fraudulent." The DR 7–102(A)(5) obligation seems to cover much, if not all, of the same ground as the law of torts and contracts on intentional [24] misrepresentation and clearly covers misstatements employed to commit crimes involving deceit. But, as discussed elsewhere,[25] it is not clear whether or not the reference in DR 7–102(A)(7) to "illegal" conduct of a client refers to any body of law other than criminal law and to the possibly more limited law of "fraud." If "illegal" is construed more broadly, it well might include some of the substantive law of misrepresentation, including intentional passive misrepresentation. Thus DR 7–102(A)(7) would expand beyond DR 7–102(A)(5) to include certain affirmative disclosure obligations of tort and contract law. If, for example, business custom requires a disclosure to prevent the opposite party from continuing the negotiations under a misapprehension of basic fact,[26] a negotiating lawyer would be required by that law to make disclosure and, under a broad interpretation of DR 7–102(A)(7), would also be required to disclose by force of a professional rule as well.

1983 Model Rules

The Model Rules are unfortunately confusing. Early drafts of what became the 1983 Model Rules would have imposed significantly greater, or at least more explicit, obligations of candor on lawyers who negotiate. That would have been true particularly with regard to disclosures mandated by the law of passive misrepresentation.[27] The final version of the Model Rules consists of a confusing set of rigid but contradictory commands, not all of the literal terms of which the same lawyer could possibly obey. The tangled skein was produced by the process of extensive floor amendment that significantly reshaped important parts of the Model Rules in the February 1983 meeting of the ABA House of Delegates. It takes elaboration to reveal.

Rule 4.1. Under MR 4.1(a) a lawyer shall not "make a false statement of material fact

[21] ABA Canon 15.

[22] ABA Canon 32.

[23] § 13.3.2.

[24] In In re McGrath, 96 A.D.2d 267, 468 N.Y.S.2d 349 (1983), however, the court disciplined a lawyer for a material negligent misrepresentation in negotiating a settlement in a personal injury case under DR 1–102(A)(6) because his conduct reflected adversely on his fitness to practice law. The lawyer, whose own files contained accurate information about the existence of another insurance policy providing $1 million in excess coverage, maintained to his opponent that insurance coverage was limited to a single policy providing only $200,000. In addition to discipline, the lawyer, his client, and others were found liable for substantial damages for the misrepresentations. See Slotkin v. Citizens Cas. Co., 614 F.2d 301 (2d Cir.1979), cert.denied 449 U.S. 981, 101 S.Ct. 395, 66 L.Ed.2d 243 (1980).

[25] § 13.3.2.

[26] See supra at nn.14–20 (disclosure obligation in such an instance); Rest.2d Torts § 551(2)(e)(1977); Rest.2d Contracts § 161(b)(1981). E.g., Virzi v. Grand Trunk Warehouse & Cold Storage Co., 571 F.Supp. 507 (E.D. Mich.1983)(lawyer representing plaintiff who would have been an excellent witness in his own behalf but who died while settlement negotiations were pending had professional duty to court and to defense counsel to reveal fact of death before concluding settlement); Price v. Superior Court, 139 Cal.App.3d 518, 188 Cal.Rptr. 832 (1983)(duty to disclose to overworked prosecutor that his colleague responsible for case file had refused plea bargain now again proposed by defense counsel).

[27] MR 4.1(b)(Proposed Final Draft, May 30, 1981) would have required a lawyer to make disclosure if the lawyer knew that "(1) in the circumstances failure to make the disclosure is equivalent to making a material misrepresentation; (2) disclosure is necessary to prevent assisting a criminal or fraudulent act, as required by rule 1.2(d); or (3) disclosure is necessary to comply with other law."

or law to a third person." [28] As with DR 7-102(A)(5), this appears to incorporate at least all substantive law on positive misrepresentation. But, because of MR 1.6, the final version of MR 4.1, dealing with "truthfulness in statements to others," might confine a lawyer's duty to that of avoiding positive false statements. Recall that the ABA's MR 1.6 imposes virtually absolute strictures against disclosure of client information and that the definition of nondisclosable information is global regardless of the source of the information (§ 6.7.2). Thus it may be that the client-disfavoring information that the law of passive misrepresentation requires the client to reveal may not be revealed by the client's lawyer because of the confidentiality rule.

Rule 4.1(b), at first glance, seems to go on to state an affirmative disclosure duty corresponding to passive misrepresentation law. But it may be a closed loop: a lawyer shall not "knowingly" "fail to disclose a material fact to a third person when disclosure is necessary to avoid assisting a criminal or fraudulent act by a client, unless disclosure is prohibited by rule 1.6." Because MR 1.6 prohibits most if not all imaginable disclosures in the circumstance stated by the first part of MR 4.1(b), the "unless" clause entirely stops the lawyer's mouth from uttering the disclosures that the rule otherwise requires. Rule 4.1(b) becomes a meaningless semantic puzzle lacking even linguistic interest. Interest, and confusion, is gained by enlarging the puzzle to take account of other parts of the Model Rules.

Other Law. Before proceeding, we should note that the February 1983 amendments to MR 4.1 produced a strange, but not entirely anamolous, result concerning the operation of other law. The amendments dropped language of earlier proposed versions of the Rules requiring a lawyer to make disclosure, when necessary, to comply with other law.[29] The amendment was unfortunate. The notion might have been that adoption of the Model Rules would implicitly repeal other legal compulsion on lawyers to make disclosures under the circumstances described in MR 4.1(b). That would be true at least with respect to state law [30] in jurisdictions whose courts claim the overriding power to enact rules of lawyer regulation (§ 2.2.3) or in which the Model Rules were enacted as legislation. The Model Rules themselves, however, indicate that no such supersession of other law by the Rules was intended and, in fact, that other law might supersede Rule 1.6, although the Rules urge a presumption against such supersession.[31]

Rule 8.4(c). The complicating factor on passive misrepresentation is that the same series of February 1983 floor amendments that produced the broad confidentiality rule (MR 1.6) also wrote into the Model Rules, over the protest of its drafters, general provisions in MR 8.4 describing certain kinds of misconduct in very vague phrases imported from DR 1-102(A) of the Code. Among those is MR 8.4(c), defining professional misconduct to include "engag[ing] in conduct involving dishonesty, fraud, deceit or misrepresentation." Rule 8.4(c) does not mention any possible excuse on the ground of a need to protect client information under Rule 1.6. Thus, in jurisdictions in which lawyer nondisclosure in negotiations would amount to "dishonesty, fraud, deceit or misrepresentation" under ap-

28 This language survived without significant change from the earliest public version of the Kutak Commission's drafts. See MR 4.2(b)(Discussion Draft, Jan.30, 1980)("a lawyer shall not make a knowing misrepresentation of fact or law").

29 The requirement in the 1981 version of MR 4.1(b)(3), supra, of making disclosure when "necessary to comply with other law" was not carried forward into the final version. Other limited disclosure rules survived, but all make reference to the general limitation of MR 1.6 on client information. See MR 8.1(b) (affirmative duty to correct misapprehension known to have arisen in bar application or discipline proceeding); MR 8.3 (reporting misconduct of lawyers and judges).

30 A state's promulgation of the Model Rules as law could not, of course, displace the legal obligations of that state's lawyers under federal law. See § 2.2.5. It would be incoherent to assert that a lawyer violates a state's disciplinary rules, in this instance MR 1.6, when a lawyer obeys the compulsion of federal law.

31 MR 1.6, comment (Disclosures Otherwise Required or Authorized). See also § 12.6.4 (fraud disclosure).

plicable law, it could be argued that disclosure is required under Rule 8.4(c), notwithstanding that compromise of some kinds of client information is necessary. An alternative, here as elsewhere, is that a lawyer could avoid the problem of disclosure by refusing to continue the negotiations in behalf of the client and withdrawing from the representation (§ 9.5.3).

Rule 4.1 versus Rule 8.4. While such a reading of MR 8.4(c) would bring the Model Rules into agreement with the substantive law of passive misrepresentation, it would ignore the apparently overriding import of the exception in MR 4.1(b). Surely, if the public policies in favor of exposing most [32] client crime are displaced by the need to protect all client information, as the finally adopted versions of MR 4.1(b) and MR 1.6 seem to imagine, then it is difficult to understand why the presumably no more important policies of preventing dishonesty, deceit, and misrepresentation displace client information interests. Linguistically critical here is the fact that "fraud" is mentioned in both MR 4.1(b) and MR 8.4(c). A less bizarre reading of those two rules is that MR 4.1(b), with its self-swallowing exception, trumps MR 8.4(c). The problem is obviously one that cries out for clarification before a jurisdiction adopts the Model Rules.

The Ideal Extent of a Disclosure Obligation

In what way should the Model Rules be clarified? Should lawyers labor under the same obligation to make disclosure as other negotiators because of the law of passive misrepresentation? In view of the fact that passive misrepresentation is unlawful (to the extent that it is), in view of the fact that a client is legally disabled from failing to fulfill these disclosure obligations, and in view of the fact that a lawyer's immunized nondisclosure under the Model Rules would nonetheless create legal liability on the part of his or her principal, the client, it is difficult to argue that client interests truly require the kind of sweeping protection imparted by MR 4.1(b).

Commentators have advanced several arguments to deflect disclosure obligations away from negotiating lawyers. Their general import is that a disclosure obligation creates serious dilemmas for lawyer negotiators. First, a lawyer often would not be certain whether the opposing party was not feigning ignorance precisely in order to induce a forced disclosure containing other information as well. Second, a failure to make disclosure might subject the transaction to possible future attack, and this would most disadvantage the clients of skilled and diligent negotiators. Third, use of the lawyer's skills in behalf of an opposing party would put the lawyer in the unaccustomed position of responsibility for both sides of the transaction.[33] A fourth reason, more persuasive than any mentioned so far, is limited to information difficult to obtain: a lawyer will have no or less incentive to incur expense to gather information if it must be shared with other bargaining parties.[34] Thus a lawmaker might decide to protect information against the disclosure if knowledge of it was costly and, for example, it was not simply a casual byproduct of holding property. Fifth, it has also been argued that strict rules on truthfulness in negotiation are undesirable because they could be violated

[32] Recall that under MR 1.6(b)(1), the only exception from the antidisclosure rule is for permission to reveal information necessary "to prevent the client from committing a criminal act that the lawyer believes is likely to result in imminent death or substantial bodily harm." Economic crimes, and crimes against the person that are not sufficiently threatening, may not be disclosed.

[33] Hazard, The Lawyer's Obligation to Be Trustworthy when Dealing with Opposing Parties, 33 S.C.L.Rev. 181, 194 n.46 (1981), lists those three arguments, particularly the second, as the reasons why the Kutak Commission withdrew an earlier proposal that would have required a lawyer to "be fair" in negotiations. For the earlier version, see MR 4.2(a)(Discussion Draft, Jan.30, 1980). To the extent that "fair" agreements are not a required objective of the law of misrepresentation, the arguments have some merit. To the extent that that law does seek to achieve fairness, they are weak.

[34] Kronman, Mistake, Disclosure, Information, and the Law of Contracts, 7 J.Leg.Stud. 1 (1978).

with impunity because of nonpublic setting of most negotiations.[35]

Even if the problematical factual and policy premises of the arguments for nondisclosure were accepted, the striking fact about them is that individually and as a group they could as well be addressed to the developing substantive law of passive misrepresentation. Yet, in that area, the movement has been in the direction of more disclosure rather than less. If all other negotiating parties and their agents are required to accept the costs of disclosure rules, it is not imaginable that lawyers should form a separate class of privileged passive liars. Regardless of the merits of the debate over passive misrepresentation, the point not to be lost sight of is that both the Code, in DR 7–102(A)(5), and the Model Rules, in MR 4.1(a), prohibit active misrepresentation in nearly identical language.[36]

Puffing and Chaffering

The law of active misrepresentation in effect provides that both lawyers and their clients are free to indulge in the ritualistic and presumably harmless lying that is legally permissible under the concepts of puffing or chaffering. The category of permissibly false statements varies among the states. Local law, in turn, is undoubtedly influenced by locally prevailing business practices. Clearly, however, there is no general doctrine under which all lies in negotiation are transmuted into legally harmless puffing. If not otherwise deterred, a competent lawyer, of course, would carefully research local law before resorting to lies in negotiations.

No exhaustive review of the limited universe of puffing will be attempted here. In general, caution is indicated. Some commentators claim that false statements of a client's intentions or instructions to a lawyer-negotiator are permissible puffing.[37] The comment to MR 4.1, for example, states that

> under generally accepted conventions in negotiation, certain types of statements ordinarily are not taken as statements of material fact. Estimates of price or value placed on the subject of a transaction and a party's intentions as to an acceptable settlement of a claim are in this category, and so is the existence of an undisclosed principal except where nondisclosure of the principal would constitute fraud.[38]

A lawyer who understands those general statements as a green light for aggressively untruthful negotiation strategies could incur disaster for a client. The adverb "ordinarily" in the comment must be heavily emphasized. Decisions have held, for example, that mis-

[35] White, Machiavelli and the Bar: Ethical Limitations on Lying in Negotiation, 1980 Am.B.Found. Research J. 926. Professor White's house-of-cards argument is that lawyers will frequently violate rules if detection is difficult and that frequent violations of one rule will create lawyer cynicism about all rules.

[36] The only difference in language is the addition of the adjective "material" to "fact" in MR 4.1(a). That was part of a general effort by the Model Rules framers to confine what otherwise might be senselessly extreme applications of the Rules. No instances were cited, however, in which the potentially more universal sweep of DR 7–102(A)(5) had been applied to discipline a lawyer for a nonmaterial false statement.

[37] Hazard, The Lawyer's Obligation to Be Trustworthy When Dealing with Opposing Parties, 33 S.C.L.Rev. 181, 183 (1981), citing only White, Machiavelli and the Bar: Ethical Limitations on Lying in Negotiation, 1980 Am.B. Found.Research J. 926, 927. Professor White's article deals with a decidedly different topic (disguising one's true minimum position) and, in any event, cites as *his* authority only two popular manuals on negotiating written by the same person. That authority purports to tell everyman, and not specifically lawyers, how to win at negotiations. The manuals, of course, cite nothing. See L.Karrass, Give and Take: The Complete Guide to Negotiating Strategies and Tactics 23, 107 (1974); L.Karrass, The Negotiating Game: How to Get What You Want 187 (1970). In fact, Professor White's article does delimit the ways in which the law of misrepresentation sometimes makes a statement of value a promise, although at a point not cited by Professor Hazard. See id. 1980 Am.B. Found. Research J. at 932.

[38] MR 4.1, comment (Statements of Fact). The suppressed "legal background" note to predecessor versions of the comment, which remained essentially unchanged from that draft, did not reveal any discussion or cite any authority for this statement. See Model Rules at 162, 163–65 (Proposed Final Draft, May 30, 1981). The earliest public version of the Rules contained a much more temporate statement respecting puffing. See Model Rules at 89–91 (Discussion Draft, Jan.30, 1981).

The reference in the quoted MR 4.1 comment to a "material" fact may be more sweeping than appears. A fact can be material either because a reasonable person would attach importance to it in deciding on a course of action in the transaction or because the person making the representation has reason to know that the auditor in fact attaches such importance to it, although a reasonable person would not. See Rest.2d Torts § 538(2)(1977).

statements about value can indeed create liability.[39]

Also included as permissible puffing are some statements about the strengths and weaknesses of a client's legal position. That is supportable in part by the doctrine that a lawyer's appraisal of such matters is hard-core work product protected from discovery in litigation in all circumstances.[40] Yet that rationale applies only to revelations someone attempts to force from a lawyer and not at all to volunteered statements that are false. Here, as in other examples of puffing, a careful lawyer, intent on negotiating a legally protectable bargain, would be very circumspect in making or implying false and misleading statements about intention.

Obtaining Accurate Information

A lawyer alert to possible misstatements of fact by an opposite negotiator can do more than simply attempt to guess at the truth. It has been said that there are two ways of obtaining information in negotiations—either undertake an independent investigation with its attendant costs or accept assurances about the information from the other negotiating party.[41] A third method, at least a variation on the second, ought to be added: the accuracy of information can itself be made a contractual condition. It is common practice in the purchase of a business, for example, to include as appendices to the contract the financial records supplied by the seller, accompanied by contractual warranties of their accuracy under stated penalties. Contracting for the guaranteed accuracy of information is itself not without cost but can lessen the risks of untrustworthy statements.

Fair Deals

Most of the lawyer code provisions that restrict a lawyer in negotiating are strategic limitations. None says that a lawyer who proceeds in a fair way may not accept in behalf of a client a result that is substantively unfair. A question of morality may arise, however, when a lawyer is confronted with an entirely incompetent or unwise opposing party in negotiations who is willing to settle for an arrangement that favors the lawyer's client more than it should.[42] *Should*, obviously, is a loaded word and assumes that a lawyer has both acted fairly in making representations to the other side and has fully consulted with his or her client about the lawyer's restive feelings about the outcome. At the end of the day, the choice is a personal one for the lawyer. So long as the client is legally entitled to insist on concluding the unfair deal, a lawyer is not free to sabotage the arrangement, but if it can be done without harming the client's interests, the lawyer remains free to withdraw (§ 9.5.3).

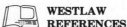

WESTLAW REFERENCES

"dr 7–102(a)" dr7–102(a) /p attorney counsel** lawyer /s illegal*** fraud!

45k58 /p misrepresent! /p "professional responsibility"

§ 13.6 MEDIATION

The Value of Mediation

The role a lawyer assumes in mediating a conflict between clients is one of the most useful and satisfying yet one of the most professionally delicate roles that a lawyer might assume. The problem, the conflicting interests between the clients, is obvious and

[39] See authorities cited, e.g., in W. Prosser & W. Keeton, Torts 758 (5th ed.1984). An illustration of an impermissible misstatement of value would be a false statement by a lawyer negotiating a private-placement sale of a security that it is trading at a stated price. See Rest.2d Torts § 538A comment g (1977).

[40] Southern Ry. v. Lanham, 403 F.2d 119, 131–32, 33 A.L.R.3d 427 (5th Cir.1968); Clermont, Surveying Work Product, 68 Corn.L.Rev. 755 (1983); Cooper, Work Product of the Rulesmakers, 53 Minn.L.Rev. 1269, 1283 (1969). See § 6.6.

[41] Hazard, The Lawyer's Obligation to Be Trustworthy When Dealing with Opposing Parties, 33 S.C.L.Rev. 181, 184 (1981).

[42] Bellow & Kettleson, From Ethics to Politics: Confronting Scarcity and Fairness in Public Interest Practice, 58 Bost.U.L.Rev. 337, 372–78 (1978).

involved.[43] The benefits, which may not be obvious, are substantial. In many situations outside of actual litigation between parties, it will be possible for a lawyer and two or more clients who are interested in mediation to satisfy the requirements for voluntary consent to the lawyer's role in the mediation. If that is possible, mediation can provide the opportunity for significant savings of legal fees, take far less time, exact much less of an emotional toll, and provide opportunities for flexible structuring of a solution tailored to the parties' wishes. This section considers the nature of the role that the lawyer then undertakes.

Professional Regulation of Mediation

The role of mediator was alluded to in the 1969 Code in an offhand way that suggested that lawyers routinely handled mediation as a matter of course.[44] That almost certainly was not the case, and it is clear that the role of mediator is one not to be approached with only perfunctory attention to the risks involved. Model Rule 2.2, on a lawyer as "intermediary," for the first time attempts to put the role in perspective. A reading of the rule reveals that mediation is not so much an entirely separate lawyerly role as it is the performance of one of several roles—advising, drafting, counseling—under a potential conflict of interests. The three parts of the rule deal with deciding whether to initiate the relationship, the nature of consultation during the mediation, and the need for withdrawal if it is requested or if the conditions for mediation no longer are satisfied.

Deciding whether to Undertake Mediation

The mediator's role is to be initiated only after extensive client consultation, after the lawyer concludes that the conditions for effective mediation are present, and after each client freely consents. The consultation prior to entry into mediation that is mandated by MR 2.2(a)(1) must cover discussion of the nature and implications of the common representation, "including the advantages and risks involved." Particularly if any party has had prior experience with the lawyer, the clients should be informed that the mediating lawyer will not function as the partisan of any one of the parties to the exclusion of others.[45] The lawyer must also discuss the negative impact of the joint representation on the attorney-client privilege.[46] Finally, after the completion of the consultation process, each client must freely consent.[47]

The lawyer's own assessment under MR 2.2(a)(2) and (a)(3) should review whether mediation can serve the best interests of each client; whether each client will be able to make adequately informed decisions during the course of the mediation, whether the risk of material prejudice to any party, if mediation fails, is disproportionate to the benefits to be derived in light of the probabilities of success and failure; and whether the lawyer can conduct the mediation impartially and without adverse impact on any other responsibility that the lawyer has to any of the clients.[48]

Consulting during Mediation

MR 2.2(b) directs the mediating lawyer, during the course of mediation, to consult with each client about decisions to be made

43 §§ 7.3, 8.5.

44 EC 5–20: "A lawyer is often asked to serve as an impartial arbitrator or mediator in matters that involve present or former clients. He may serve in either capacity if he first discloses such present or former relationships."

45 MR 2.2 comment (Consultation).

46 See § 6.4.8. The diminution of the privilege in mediations is mentioned in MR 2.2 comment (Confidentiality and Privilege).

47 See also § 7.2.4 (consultation and consent in conflicts of interest generally).

48 The last criterion unfortunately suggests that a lawyer might, for example, decide to mediate in a situation involving a long-standing client and a client previously unknown to the lawyer. The prospects for lawyer impartiality are low in such a case.

and factors bearing on them. That is a particularized version of the general duty, under MR 1.4, of periodic communication with all clients (§ 4.5). The objective is that each client should be fully informed in order to be able to make effective decisions. Although client confidential information will be exchanged between the parties, the mediating lawyer must otherwise protect it.[49] Although the rule is silent on the matter, it should be permissible for the lawyer and all clients to undertake the representation on the explicit understanding that some client's information will not be shared with one or more other client's involved so long as withholding the information does not operate unfairly to disadvantage or mislead any other party to the mediation.

Withdrawal from Mediation

A special mandatory withdrawal rule is supplied by MR 2.2(c). The mediating lawyer must withdraw if any of the clients requests this[50] or if any of the necessary preconditions to mediation no longer obtains. Thereafter the lawyer may not represent any of the parties in the intermediation.[51]

The Mediator's Role

Mediation might be appropriate in a variety of settings.[52] The situations are as diverse as the kinds of interclient difficulties that a lawyer confronts. The mediation might be the only service a lawyer performs or one among many. It might last for mere minutes or continue indefinitely over years. It has been proposed as an alternative dispute device for resolution of such conflicts as divorce and partnership dissolutions.[53] It might also be appropriate for constructing new relationships, such as organizing or restructuring a business or other organization, merging existing businesses, creating joint ventures or similar undertakings, and forming other relationships in which two or more clients wish to participate in a common transaction.

It is plain that "[p]rinciples of conduct applicable to appearance in open court do not . . . resolve the issues confronting the lawyer who must assume the delicate task of mediating among opposing interests."[54] Mediation is a process in which differences are not sharpened for the purpose of permitting a neutral fact finder to choose between them. The lawyer is not an arbitrator—a role that assumes no confidential relationship with the parties but instead involves only the receipt of information from them and rendition of a decision. The lawyer's role as mediator is to advise the several clients fully about their respective rights (including, if relevant, their rights against each other), their legal opportunities, the facts, and the positions of each party in order to work out a satisfactory resolution of existing or potential conflicts. One such resolution might entail the lawyer's personally serving as arbitrator, but the decision to follow such a resolution would come only after a full examination by all parties of the facts, the law, and other options.

A salient characteristic of mediation is that the lawyer has a lawyer-client relationship with each client—and, hence, lawyer-client responsibilities toward each client. A confusingly similar, but importantly different, relationship might be entered into by a lawyer in attempting to reconcile differences between a client and, for example, a creditor who is not the lawyer's client. While the nonclient party to the conversation might trust the lawyer, the lawyer should be careful not to mislead that person about the lawyer's ultimate loyalty to the client. In a true mediation, each client should be able to rely on the mediator's fairness, openness, trustworthiness, and legal expertise. As in other joint representations, the rules of client confidentiality are inevitably different (see § 6.4.8). Unless the affected

[49] MR 2.2 comment (Confidentiality and Privilege).

[50] See also MR 1.16(a)(3); § 9.5.4.

[51] The withdrawal rule is a particularization of the former-client conflict of interest rules. See MR 2.2 comment (Withdrawal); § 7.2.4(b) at 348–49.

[52] G.Hazard, Ethics in the Practice of Law 61–62 (1978).

[53] Rich, The Role of Lawyers: Beyond Advocacy, 1980 Brig.Y.L.Rev. 767.

[54] Professional Responsibility, Report of the Joint Conference, 44 ABA J. 1159, 1160 (1958).

client explicitly agrees otherwise after consultation, each client must be fully apprised of all relevant facts, legal matters, and, especially, options and alternatives. It is for each client, and not for the lawyer, to make ultimate choices between options and alternatives.

Middle Counsel

A variation on the mediation concept is Randolph Paul's suggestion for a "middle counsel." [55] The middle counsel meets with the parties to resolve differences, drafts documents, and discusses the proposed arrangement with the parties. But the parties retain their own lawyers, who perform the customary client-oriented examination of the mediated transaction, although their role in negotiation of language and terms is limited. With independent representation, the interests of the parties are fully protected in a partisan manner that is impossible and impermissible for a single-lawyer mediator. The arrangement is obviously suitable only for substantial transactions, such as negotiation of business mergers, in which both parties contemplate significant expenditures for lawyers.

Divorce Mediation

Mediation has received particular attention recently in divorce.[56] For some time, observers have complained that the presence of adversary lawyers in a divorce can exacerbate rather than solve problems, principally because some lawyers, habituated to the milieu of litigation, act as provocateurs rather than conciliators.[57] Whether a mediator who is a stranger to the parties, and possibly to their cultural, economic, and social backgrounds, can often serve effectively as mediator has been doubted.[58] Situations involving a dominant spouse, a previous representation of one of the spouses, a great disparity of sophistication or business experience, large differences in personal wealth, or any significant dispute over property division or child custody clearly bode ill for mediation.

Advisability of Mediation

Mediation will always remain a somewhat delicate and controversial role for lawyers. By definition it thrusts a lawyer into a conflict of interest situation in which the lawyer can merely hope, but cannot accurately predict in most instances, that the parties' differences can be fairly and amicably resolved. The role of "lawyer for the situation," advocated by Louis Brandeis,[59] has been judged by an admirer of his as a role never to be assumed by a wise lawyer.[60] That is too extreme a view. Certainly, however, mediation is a role that should be approached, and proceeded through, with great circumspection and with willingness to abandon the representation if failure to achieve a fair reconciliation looms as a probability.

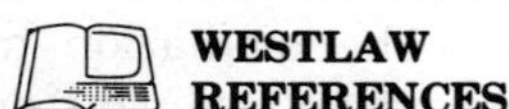

WESTLAW REFERENCES

di mediation

lawyer attorney counsel** /6 mediat! arbitrat! /p "professional responsibility" "model rule"

---

[55] Paul, A New Role for Lawyers in Contract Negotiations, 62 ABA J. 93 (1976).

[56] Mnookin, Child-Custody Adjudication: Judicial Functions in the Face of Indeterminacy, 39 L.& Contemp.Prob. 226 (1975); Mnookin & Kornhauser, Bargaining in the Shadow of the Law: The Case of Divorce, 88 Yale L.J. 950, 990–96 (1979); Silberman, Professional Responsibility Problems in Divorce Mediation, 7 BNA Fam.L.Rptr. 4001 (1975); Spencer & Zammit, Mediation-Arbitration: A Proposal for Private Resolution of Disputes between Divorced or Separated Parents, 1976 Duke L.J. 911.

[57] R.Eisler, Dissolution 40 (1977); M.Vanton, Marriage—Grounds for Divorce 99–100 (1977).

[58] Felstiner, Influences of Social Organization on Dispute Processing, 9 L.& Soc'y Rev. 63 (1974).

[59] One of the charges raised at the confirmation hearings of Justice Louis D. Brandeis, in 1916, was that he had unethically represented conflicting interests while in private practice. At least some of the charges were doubtless motivated by the fact that Brandeis was regarded as a political radical and would be the first Jew confirmed as a justice. See A.Mason, Brandeis: A Free Man's Life (1946); A.Todd, Justice on Trial (1964).

[60] Frank, The Legal Ethics of Louis D. Brandeis, 17 Stan.L.Rev. 683, 708 (1965).

§ 13.7 CORPORATE PRACTICE

§ 13.7.1 Lawyers and Corporations [61]

The corporate form of enterprise dominates American business. It also predominates in much of the sphere of activity of charities and other human-services enterprises, social clubs, advocacy and other special-interest groups, colleges and universities, and a host of similar nonprofit organizations. Because much urban law practice involves service to business, questions relating to corporate practice are critical for many lawyers. The precise extent to which lawyers are wholly or partly engaged in corporate practice is not known, but studies indicate that approximately half of the effort of all urban lawyers is devoted to corporate clients.[62] Despite the centrality of corporate practice, the lawyer codes have only recently given attention to its discrete issues of professional responsibility.[63]

From political and social points of view, it seems clear that the service of lawyers to corporations has been indispensable in assisting owners and managers of corporations to maintain their prerogatives [64] and in providing a legal framework for the existing economic order.[65] Whether corporate lawyers serve merely as the "obsequious servants of business" [66] or exercise significant independent influence is debatable and might not be a question susceptible of a unitary answer regardless of time, place, and circumstances. The question has been posed by lawyers themselves. Justice Harlan F. Stone wondered aloud during the depths of the Depression whether financial institutions would have run so completely amok if corporate lawyers had attempted to exert greater restraint in advising their corporate clients.[67]

Lawyers who perform corporate work are readily divisible into two groups that are separately considered here only for the purpose of general exposition. Normally, however, a reference to corporate counsel will encompass both. *In-house,* or inside, counsel function as corporate employees devoting all of their professional time to the service of a single client. *Outside* counsel are in private law practice and typically advise several corporate clients but sometimes devote all their practice to a single client. The differences between an in-house lawyer and an outside lawyer with a single corporate client begin most obviously with the fact that the former receives a salary and the latter negotiates a fee, but the contrasts are more extensive.

Finally, this section also considers the controversial question of a lawyer's responsibilities when attempting to give legal advice within a corporate structure. Included is discussion of the ultimate question of a lawyer's whistle-blowing within, and possibly outside, the corporation in furtherance of law compliance.

61 For a general bibliography, see Selected Bibliography, 56 Notre Dame Law. 947 (1981).

62 J.Heinz & E.Laumann, Chicago Lawyers—The Social Structure of the Bar 40–42 (1982)(53 percent of total legal effort of broad cross-section of urban lawyers devoted to corporate client matters, 40 percent to personal clients, and 8 percent unspecified): Pashigian, The Number and Earnings of Lawyers: Some Recent Findings, 1978 Am.B. Found. Research J. 51, 77–81 (approximately half of total receipts of legal services industry comes from business and government). For the speculation that no more than 10 percent of lawyers are engaged in legal services directly for large corporations and government agencies, see G.Hazard, Ethics in the Practice of Law xii-xiii (1978).

63 Kaplan, Some Ruminations on the Role of Counsel for a Corporation, 56 Notre Dame Law. 873, 877 (1981). A volume devoted largely to the professional responsibility issues of advisers to large corporations is G.Hazard, Ethics in the Practice of Law (1978). For empirical studies of the extent to which lawyers in corporate practice adhere to formal ethical standards and how that adherence compares to lawyers in other forms of practice, see J.Carlin, Lawyers' Ethics (1966); E.Smigel, The Wall Street Lawyer (1964); Slovak, The Ethics of Corporate Lawyers: A Sociological Approach, 1981 Am.B.Found. Research J. 753.

64 A.Berle & G.Means, The Modern Corporation and Private Property 69–75 (2d ed.1968); C.Mills, The Power Elite 289 (1956); B.Russell, A History of Western Philosophy 74 (1972 reprint of 1945 ed.).

65 Berle, Legal Profession and Legal Education: Modern Legal Profession, in 9 Ency.Soc.Sci. 341 (1933).

66 Stone, The Public Influence of the Bar, 48 Harv.L. Rev. 1, 9 (1934).

67 Id.

WESTLAW REFERENCES

digest,synopsis(counsel** lawyer attorney) /2 corporate! /p ethic! (professional +1 conduct responsibility)

§ 13.7.2 Corporate Client-Lawyer Relationship

Who Is the Client?

Despite the fact that the corporation has become commonplace in business and a much litigated feature of American law at least since the early nineteenth century,[68] it is only in recent years that questions have been raised about the legal and professional relationship that a lawyer for a corporate client bears to the corporation as a legal entity, as opposed to the lawyer's relationships with corporate shareholders, officers, directors, employees, creditors, and other possible constituencies. The answers to the question of relationship given in the lawyer codes tend to be pat and satisfyingly high-minded but insufficient in dealing with the complex texture of real corporate life.[69]

Corporation-as-Entity

The Code's answer[70] to the conundrum of the corporate client's identity is given in EC 5–18:

> A lawyer employed or retained by a corporation or similar entity owes his allegiance to the entity and not to a stockholder, director, officer, employee, representative, or other person connected with the entity. In advising the entity, a lawyer should keep paramount its interest and his professional judgment should not be influenced by the personal desires of any person or organization.

The corporation-as-entity concept stated in EC 5–18 reflects the general decisional approach.[71] It is primarily a product of the legal imagination and carries forward the general legal fiction of the corporation as a separate person. The concept has been significant mainly in the area of lawyer conflicts of interest, where it is general doctrine that a lawyer representing a corporation normally does not also represent persons connected with the corporation, such as officers and directors (§ 8.3.2). But even in its most obvious area of application, EC 5–18 is not a helpful guide to specific issues.[72]

Moreover, to the extent that EC 5–18 expresses not identification of the corporate client, but a corporate lawyer's exclusive focus of loyalty—in, note, an Ethical Consideration—the rule may be inappropriately hostile to more public dimensions of a corporate lawyer's responsibilities.[73] Courts have accordingly refused to apply the concept as an iron law of corporate structure. For example, in the leading case of Garner v. Wolfinbarger,[74] the court rejected the entity concept as a reason to bar plaintiff shareholders from access to legal advice previously given to the

68 J.Hurst, The Legitimacy of the Business Corporation in the Law of the United States, 1780–1970 (1970).

69 For a review of some of the complexities of the problem, see G.Hazard, Ethics in the Practice of Law 43–57 (1978).

70 Nothing in the 1908 Canons of Ethics bore on the question. Taylor, The Role of Corporate Counsel, 32 Rutgers L.Rev. 237, 241 (1979), reads ABA Formal Op. 202 (1940) to stand for the proposition that the corporate lawyer owes "ultimate responsibility to the board of directors." But the opinion simply asserted that a lawyer who was aware of a trust company officer's wrongdoing could make disclosure to the board because "such a disclosure would be to the client itself and not to a third person." The remainder of the opinion speaks of "the trust company" as the client.

71 Lane v. Chowning, 610 F.2d 1385 (8th Cir.1979)(lawyer who represented bank for 40 years owed no fiduciary obligation to chairman of bank and thus could participate in effort to remove him for participation in illegal bank loan); United States Industries, Inc. v. Goldman, 421 F.Supp. 7, 11 (S.D.N.Y.1976); ABC Trans Nat'l Transp., Inc. v. Aeronautics Forwarders, Inc., 90 Ill.App.3d 817, 46 Ill.Dec. 186, 413 N.E.2d 1299, 1301 (1980); Fassihi v. Sommers, Schwartz, Silver, Schwartz & Tyler, 107 Mich. App. 509, 309 N.W.2d 645, 648 (1981). See also, e.g., Pollack, The SEC Lawyer: Who Is His Client and What Are His Responsibilities, 49 Geo.Wash.L.Rev. 453 (1981); Fanchon & Marco, Inc. v. Leahy, 351 Mo. 428, 173 S.W.2d 417, 433 (1943).

72 Accord Forrow, The Corporate Law Department Lawyer: Counsel to the Entity, 34 Bus.Law. 1797, 1799 n. 6 (1979).

73 Frank, A Higher Duty: A New Look at the Ethics of the Corporate Lawyer, 26 Cleve.St.L.Rev. 337 (1977).

74 430 F.2d 1093, 1101 (5th Cir.1970), cert.denied 401 U.S. 974, 91 S.Ct. 1191, 28 L.Ed.2d 323 (1971). See generally § 6.5.5.

corporation's board of directors by corporate counsel.

In everyday life a corporation's planning, buying and selling, producing and consuming, advice giving and advice seeking, record keeping, and similar dealings are all carried out not by fictive corporate personalities, but by individual persons. A corporation's lawyer necessarily maintains relationships with individuals within a corporation in ways that lead them to confide information to the lawyer and that encourage them to act on the lawyer's advice. Their normal expectation, doubtless, is that the lawyer's conception of corporate objectives largely agrees with their own. A principal might even come to think of the corporation's lawyer as "my" lawyer as well. That will occur particularly, as is common, when their relationship is long-standing and develops social as well as professional dimensions.[75] To the extent that the objectives of principal and corporation are in agreement, that relationship is both natural and useful, or at least benign. But if those objectives diverge, the principal's natural trust and friendship with the corporation lawyer must, in effect, be repudiated for the good of the corporation—or so EC 5–18 of the Code directs.

At such points, another complication intrudes—the nature of the corporate structure. The pristine model of a corporation consists of only a board of directors, officers, and employees. Yet ranging away from that model are quite different kinds of organizations. At one extreme is the very large and complex multidivision, multinational corporation. At another extreme is the sole-shareholder corporation, which is often quite small in scope and personnel. Many such small corporations are little more than incorporated sole proprietorships or partnerships. It would be remarkable if the Code's corporation-as-entity conceptualization fit equally well in all those contexts.

Even if the kind of corporation is held constant, within any corporate structure are actors with very different powers and relationships among themselves. The approach of EC 5–18 is no help in dealing with difficult issues of conflict within the corporate structure.[76] If, for example, the chief executive officer of a corporation proposes to violate a law, can or must a corporation's lawyer report this to the corporation's board of directors? Is the answer to that question dependent on whether the lawyer was hired by the president or by the board of directors? On whether the lawyer's source of information about the president's proposal was received from the president, from some other principal, or accidentally? "Corporation-as-entity" supplies no food for thinking about such problems.

An ultimately absurd extension of the corporation-as-entity approach would be to argue that a corporate lawyer indeed has no living principal in the lawyer's principal-agent relationship with the corporation. Accordingly, a lawyer representing a corporation could refuse to be bound, directed, or supervised by any single person or collection of persons within the corporation. Surprising support for such a view can be found in general language in DR 5–107(B). The rule states that a lawyer employed by a "person" to render legal services to "another" should not permit the person to "direct or regulate his professional judgment in rendering such legal services." And EC 5–24 specifically refers to the corporate setting, with its "non-lawyers serving as directors or officers," when it provides that "a lawyer must decline to accept direction of his professional judgment from any layman." So a lawyer directed to accept settlement of corporate litigation by the president of a corporation, who is otherwise properly exercising a function under the articles and bylaws of the corporation, seemingly may refuse to do so.

75 Lane v. Chowning, 610 F.2d 1385 (8th Cir.1979)(forty years' service by lawyers to banking corporation gave rise to no fiduciary obligation to bank chairman in absence of proof that lawyers had performed personal legal services for chairman).

76 Pierce, The Code of Professional Responsibility in the Corporate World: An Abdication of Professional Self-Regulation, 6 Mich.J.L.Ref. 350, 361 (1973).

Acceptance of such an interpretation of the rule would leave a lawyer not with just a vaguely defined client, but with no client at all. While it seems strained to reject the straightforward reading of the Code outlined above, it clearly should be rejected and has not been urged by any court or commentator. Taken together with other law, DR 5–107(B) and EC 5–24 probably mean nothing more than that a lawyer must accept direction only from persons in the corporation who are lawfully given the power to give such direction. Who that person or group might be is primarily a matter of the particular internal structure arranged for each corporate client.

A Functional Model in the Model Rules

Despite the limitations that are apparent in the EC 5–18 approach, early versions of the Model Rules embraced essentially the same notion.[77] The final version of Model Rule 1.13 on corporate representation, however, was extensively revised, in February 1983, in the floor amendment process in the ABA House of Delegates.[78] The resulting delineation in MR 1.13(a) is more realistic:

> (a) A lawyer employed or retained by an organization represents the organization acting through its duly authorized constituents.

The change does not mean that the Model Rule now contemplates that a lawyer represents both the entity and any of its constituents as joint clients.[79] The Rule at least states the operational generality that a lawyer must normally look to individuals and not to mouthless legal fictions for direction in the representation. But, as is also true of EC 5–18, the general approach of MR 1.13(a) begs more questions than it effectively answers if, unwisely, it is read in isolation from the remainder of Rule 1.13. Among other things, one might gather from it that a lawyer's independence in pursuing the interests of the corporation could always be circumscribed by mandate of any employee authorized to direct the lawyer's work. But, as will be seen (§ 13.7.5), that is not the view reflected in the remainder of MR 1.13.

In one respect, MR 1.13 expands significantly the coverage of EC 5–18 because it applies to any client "organization" and not only to corporations. The comments state that MR 1.13 applies to "unincorporated associations"[80] and to "governmental organizations."[81] To the extent that it might be critical for a lawyer to know whether MR 1.13 or a different Model Rule applies, the vagueness of those phrases might be confusing. Fortunately, the looseness of reference is inoffensive. Model Rule 1.13 only elucidates, in the particular context of organizational representations, certain obligations that could also be traced from more generally applicable rules.

In the end, pursuit of a definitive answer to the question of the identity of a corporate client may be of secondary importance and perhaps even a misleading diversion. The pivotal matters are the consequences and legitimacy of following one model or another in

[77] MR 1.13(a)(Revised Final Draft, June 30, 1982): "[A corporate lawyer] represents the organization as distinct from its directors, officers, employees, members, shareholders or other constituents."

[78] ABA House Comm. on Drafting, Synopsis of Amendments to Proposed Model Rules of Professional Conduct 42 (Dec.30, 1982).

[79] An amendment offered by the American College of Trial Lawyers that would have provided that a lawyer jointly represents the entity as well as its directors, employees, and shareholders did not pass. See id. at 42. MR 1.13, comment (The Entity as Client; third paragraph) states that the fact that interviews with a corporate employee or officer are protected by the attorney-client privilege "does not mean, however, that constituents of an organizational client are the clients of the lawyer."

[80] MR 1.13, comment (The Entity as Client; second paragraph). At a time when predecessor versions of MR 1.13 stated rules that were quite different for lawyers representing organizational clients, the "legal background" note, now suppressed, defined its scope even more expansively. Organizational clients would have included "an unincorporated association, limited partnership, joint venture or similar organization." The note also intimated that the question whether an organizational client was to be considered an entity depended on other substantive law and that the answer might vary with particular circumstances. See Model Rules at 90 (Proposed Final Draft, May 30, 1981).

[81] MR 1.13, comment (Government Agency).

a discrete context. The issues out of which the question most frequently arises are two. (1) In case a divergence of interests arises between the entity and one of its constituents, how should a corporate lawyer handle the attendant conflict of interests problems? That problem is discussed primarily at another point (§ 8.3). (2) Who within the corporate structure ultimately defines client objectives and gives client responses to corporate counsel's suggested moves in a representation? That question is pursued here.

Corporate Lawyers as Fiduciaries

The entity-as-client concept of corporate representation can be understood as an attempt to fit corporate clients into molds originally cast for individual clients. The same conceptual conflation may also attend thinking about the nature of the responsibilities of corporate counsel toward a corporate client. The general judicial approach has been to assert that a lawyer for a corporation owes the same duties to that client as to a client who is an individual.[82] The relationship is a fiduciary one.[83] But a corporate lawyer does not owe similar fiduciary responsibilities to any individual officer or director of the corporation.[84]

Relationship with Corporate Principals

Yet those generalities can readily be taken too far. It is simply not true that a corporate lawyer can safely feel free of any fiduciary constraint when dealing with, or against, an officer or other member of a corporate client. First, loyalty to the corporation and zealous representation of its interests will require a corporate lawyer to maintain the trust and confidence of all persons in the corporation in order to assure access to important facts and in order to maintain effective lines of communication for the lawyer's advice. Second, legal duties owed to the corporation, such as the lawyer's duties to protect client information (§ 6.7), almost automatically entail protecting the communicative interests of individuals within the organization. To the extent that the business affairs of officers and members of the corporation are indistinguishable from the business affairs of the corporation, protecting client communications and other information protects both entity and its constituents. Third, the doctrine that a lawyer owes no fiduciary obligation to a corporate officer is no warrant for attacks on corporate employees.[85] Instead, the doctrine is a corollary to the requirement that when the interests of the corporation as a whole and any of its officers or members materially diverge, corporate counsel is required to pursue the interests of the whole and not the divergent interests of any of its parts. In short, a corporate lawyer may attack the interests of an officer only because of the lawyer's overriding duty to pursue the interests of the corporation.[86]

[82] In re Capps, 250 Ga. 242, 297 S.E.2d 249 (1982)(house counsel).

[83] Lane v. Chowning, 610 F.2d 1385 (8th Cir.1979); Bryan v. Bartlett, 435 F.2d 28, 37 (8th Cir.1970), cert.denied, 402 U.S. 915, 91 S.Ct. 1373, 28 L.Ed.2d 658 (1971)(corporate lawyers owe corporation same fiduciary obligations as directors do); Illinois Tool Works, Inc. v. Kovac, 43 Ill.App.3d 789, 2 Ill.Dec. 472, 357 N.E.2d 639 (1976). Several courts have also held that a lawyer who files a shareholder derivative action owes a fiduciary obligation to the shareholders of the corporation in whose behalf the suit is brought. E.g., Certain-Teed Prod. Corp. v. Topping, 171 F.2d 241 (2d Cir.1948); Lewis v. Teleprompter Corp., 88 F.R.D. 11 (S.D.N.Y.1980); Clarke v. Greenberg, 296 N.Y. 146, 71 N.E.2d 443, 169 A.L.R. 944 (1947).

[84] Lane v. Chowning, 610 F.2d 1385 (8th Cir.1979)(chief executive officer and chairman of corporation); Stratton Group, Ltd. v. Sprayregen, 466 F.Supp. 1180 (S.D.N.Y. 1979)(directors and officers).

[85] Financial Gen. Bankshares, Inc. v. Metzger, 523 F.Supp. 744 (D.D.C.1981)(impermissibly disloyal for corporate counsel to assist hostile effort to take over management of corporation), vacated for lack of jurisdiction, 680 F.2d 768 (D.C.Cir.1982).

[86] For example, Lane v. Chowning, 610 F.2d 1385 (8th Cir.1979), held that a corporate lawyer rightfully worked for the dismissal of the corporation's chairman and chief executive officer because of his violations of law. The holding followed, not so much from the absence of any fiduciary duty to the officer (which would have permitted, presumably, an attack on the officer regardless of its justification), but from the fact that the attack was necessary in order to protect the interests of the corporation.

Clarifying Corporate Counsel's Role

It is usually harmless if a corporate officer or employee comes to regard corporate counsel as a personal representative, so long as there is no divergence between personal and corporate interests. But when divergence occurs, fairness requires the lawyer to inform such a person that the lawyer's first loyalties lie elsewhere. Even a nonlawyer with some sophistication in legal matters might assume, erroneously, that all of that person's confidential communications to the organization's lawyer are protected by the attorney-client privilege from being used adversely against his or her personal interests.

Model Rule 1.13(d) wisely requires that a lawyer for an organization carefully explain the focus of the lawyer's loyalties in such a case. The requirement is limited to factual circumstances in which it is "apparent"[87] that a divergence of interests exists. It is advisable for a lawyer for an organization to go beyond the mandatory rule, however, and explain the limits on the lawyer's role to all persons in the organization whose interests might in the future come into conflict with those of the organization. Moreover, while the rule is silent on the matter, it also seems advisable for the lawyer to inform the person whose interests are actually in conflict that communications are not confidential with respect to the organization itself. Under the Code, a corporate lawyer has no guidance on such matters other than whatever guidance is supplied by the rules on dealing with unrepresented persons (see § 11.6.3).

WESTLAW REFERENCES

"ec 5–18"

wolfinbarger /12 430 +5 1093 /p corporat!

topic(corporations) /p fiduciary /3 duty obligation responsibility /9 lawyer counsel** attorney

corporat! /2 lawyer counsel** attorney /9 fiduciary /3 duty responsibility obligation /3 breach!

§ 13.7.3 House Counsel

The Modern Status of House Counsel

Recent decades have witnessed a dramatic increase in the importance of house counsel for corporations. In the late 1960s more than half of all United States business corporations employed one or more house counsel.[88] The number of house counsel positions has continued to rise.[89] At one time, studies indicated that the position was one of lower prestige within the legal profession than the position of outside counsel.[90] To an extent, the house counsel position might suffer in prestige from a history of staffing such positions with large-firm associates passed over for partnership.[91] Lesser prestige might also reflect an historical tendency for house lawyers to engage in less specialized and less dramatic legal work than outside counsel.[92]

87 "Apparent" is not defined in the Terminology section of the Rules. "Reasonably should know" is the apparently cognate phrase that is defined. As MR 1.13, comment (Clarifying the Lawyer's Role; second paragraph) points out, the factual circumstances of each case determine the extent of the lawyer's duty to warn.

88 Brakel & Loh, Regulating the Multistate Practice of Law, 50 Wash.L.Rev. 669, 730 n.100 (1975)(National Industrial Conference Board surveys of all corporations show 47 percent in 1959, and 61 percent in 1967, with in-house counsel, with most employment in corporations with more than 1,000 employees). See also Q.Johnstone & D.Hopson, Lawyers and Their Work ch.6 (1967).

89 Nat'l L.J., Feb.23, 1981, p.1, col.2 (survey shows 50,000 lawyers on corporate payrolls, a doubling in number in 15 years). In 1982 a national professional organization called the American Corporate Counsel Association was formed with membership open to house counsel. See 50 U.S.L.Wk. 2575 (1982).

90 Slovak, Giving and Getting Respect: Prestige and Stratification in a Legal Elite, 1980 Am.B.Found. Research J. 31 (survey-findings report relatively strongly felt "house counsel stigma" resulting from relegation of house counsel to kind of second-class citizenship by elite partners in private law firms). Professor Slovak found, however, that whatever stratification existed did not seem to interfere with effective house counsel-outside counsel relationships in the interest of the corporate client.

91 P.Hoffman, Lions in the Street 7 (1973)("Cravath" system of providing alternative careers for passed-over associates relegated them to counsel offices of client corporations or to other, smaller firms).

92 Slovak, Working for Corporate Actors: Social Change and Elite Attorneys in Chicago, 1979 Am.B. Found. Research J. 465, 488.

But as fees and legal work of outside counsel have increased, corporate clients have become increasingly resistant to high fees and loss of control over legal matters associated with outside counsel.[93] Improvements in both the compensation[94] and the work environment of house counsel have resulted in the increased attractiveness of the position as a career of first preference for many lawyers, including graduates of elite law schools, who at one time shunned it.

Several features of the practice of house counsel are appealing. Salaries are comparable to those of medium-sized law firms.[95] Benefits, such as health, maternity and paternity, and disability plans, matching savings and investment plans, cafeteria and company-store discounts, gratis services, and group life insurance, are often superior to those in law firms.[96] Vacation benefits may include comparable vacation periods, but house lawyers probably find it easier to schedule them. Work hours tend to be shorter and certainly are more regular. Perhaps the most significant difference is job security. Associates in large law firms must suffer the anxiety of "making partner" at the risk of being forced from the firm. But a house lawyer will not typically face the need to ascend to certain exclusive supervisory positions in order to avoid losing his or her job.[97] Another important change is that in-house lawyers are doing an increased amount of interesting legal work traditionally assumed by outside counsel, such as litigation and work in specialty areas of counseling like antitrust and products liability law.[98]

Legal Status

Despite the sole-client nature of their work, house counsel are for most purposes treated in the law of professional regulation in precisely the same fashion as lawyers in private practice. House counsel, when functioning as a lawyer,[99] can and must invoke the attorney-client privilege and observe the other rules designed to protect client information.[1] House counsel are fully subject to the disciplinary powers of the state in which they practice and the state, if different, in which they are licensed.[2] Client corporations are owed the same duties of zeal and loyalty by house counsel.[3] On the affirmative side, when house counsel appear in court as advocates

[93] Lynch, Moving the Law Inside at Mass Mutual, 70 ABA J. 44 (1984); Stewart, Major Banks Loosen Links to Law Firms, Use In-House Counsel, Wall St.J., Apr.26, 1984, at 1, col.6; Gottlieb, U.D.C. Moving to Limit Costs of Consultants, N.Y.Times, Apr.1, 1983, at B1, col.6 (public corporation); Reynolds, Is In-House "In"?, 6 D.C. District Law. at 31 (May/June 1982); Lancaster, Companies Expanding Legal Staffs as the Cost of Outside Work Soars, Wall St.J., Mar.1, 1982, at 25, col.4; Robinson & Confer, Soaring Fees Spur Dramatic In-House Growth, Nat'l L.J., Mar.30, 1981, at 1, col.3.

[94] For 1983 figures, see 70 ABA J. 48 (1984).

[95] Weil, Insurance Companies and Their Lawyers: The Cost Squeeze, 55 N.Y.St.B.J. Jan.1983, at 42, 44 (1981 salary figures). Compare also, e.g., 69 ABA J. 152 (1983) (report of Altman & Weil survey for 1982), with, e.g., Nat'l L.J., Dec.20, 1982, p.2, col.2 (report of Abbott Langer survey showing higher compensation figures). "Compensation compression"—caused by increasing senior attorney salaries at slower rates than beginning rates—may afflict house counsel more than private practitioners. See Bodine, Corporate Lawyers Improving but Their Salaries Aren't, Nat'l L.J., Dec.24, 1979, at 6, col.1.

[96] Weil, supra, 55 N.Y.St.B.J., at 44.

[97] A factor that may be equally true in private practice is that corporate counsel employers may tend to cut staff sizes during periods of business recession. E.g., Wall St. J., Apr.5, 1983, at 1, col.5 (half of 50 largest company legal staffs either cut or frozen during recession in 1982).

[98] Wall St.J., Aug.1, 1978, at 1, col.5 (report of survey of corporate legal officers).

[99] For sometimes difficult questions regarding whether house counsel is functioning as a lawyer or as a business person, see Simon, The Attorney Client Privilege as Applied to Corporations, 65 Yale L.J. 953, 970–73 (1956).

[1] Paper Converting Mach. Co. v. FMC Corp., 215 F.Supp. 249 (E.D.Wisc.1963); Georgia-Pac. Plywood Co. v. United States Plywood Corp., 18 F.R.D. 463 (S.D.N.Y. 1956).

[2] In re Capps, 250 Ga. 242, 297 S.E.2d 249 (1982)(discipline of in-house counsel who without permission engaged in commercial venture competing with corporate client-employer and represented another competitor in applying for competing truck-line permit).

[3] For example, corporations have recovered damages against house counsel for legal malpractice during their tenure. E.g., Instrument Systems Corp. v. Whitman, Ransom & Coulson, 77 Misc.2d 719, 354 N.Y.S.2d 514 (1974); Fowler v. American Fed. of Tobacco Growers, Inc., 195 Va. 770, 80 S.E.2d 554 (1954).

they are entitled to receive the same consideration as are private practitioners.[4]

Courts and bar committees have shown some inclination, sensibly, to be less restrictive with unauthorized-practice rules in the case of house counsel and, in recognition of the needs of modern business corporations and the uniform custom of house counsel, have permitted in-house practitioners to give occasional office advice wherever the corporation's interests require.[5] Some states go further and expressly except house counsel from the requirement of membership in the local bar, even if the lawyer is permanently located in the jurisdiction, so long as the house counsel's work is confined to out-of-court counseling of the corporate employer.[6]

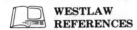

WESTLAW REFERENCES

di house counsel

§ 13.7.4 Outside Counsel

Role of Outside Counsel

Of all the nonemployee assistants on which a large modern corporation relies, no person fulfills a function potentially more vital than outside counsel. Accountants, management recruiters, advertising executives, bankers, public relations consultants, and similar fee-earning adjuncts each perform an important role. But outside lawyers often serve as the critical link between corporations and their regulators, corporations and courts, and corporations and allies and competitors. On the whole, that appraisal is one that is shared by corporation executives.[7]

The nature of the legal tasks performed by outside counsel for a corporate client is hardly uniform. Those tasks range from an isolated memorandum on a hypothetical question of law to an intensive and ongoing relationship in the role of general counsel considering all of the company's important legal problems and consulting widely within the corporation. Recent cost-consciousness on the part of many corporations has caused greater client reliance on in-house legal staff and more client insistence on both supervision of the work of outside counsel and accountability on the part of outside counsel for charges for legal services and related expenditures.[8]

Counsel-Director

A perennial question among corporate lawyers is the extent to which a corporate lawyer should give nonlegal business advice to a corporate executive.[9] The argument against such a role is that outside counsel can best maintain professional detachment and credibility by not appearing to mix business and legal advice. On the other hand, a blending of the roles can give outside counsel better access to facts and thus can give the client the benefit of intimate knowledge obtained in extensive corporate experience. To some extent the same choices confront house counsel as well.

[4] U.S.Steel Corp. v. United States, 730 F.2d 1465 (Fed. Cir.1984)(in absence of showing of greater chance of inadvertent or accidental disclosure of confidential hearing material because they worked in environment of single company, lower court impermissibly denied house counsel same access rights as were extended to private practice cocounsel).

[5] Zenith Radio Corp. v. Radio Corp. of America, 121 F.Supp. 792, 794 (D.Del.1954).

[6] Zenith Radio Corp. v. RCA, 121 F.Supp. 792, 794 (D.Del.1954); Comm. on Unauth. Pract. of Law Op. 14, 96 N.J.L.J. 398 (1973); ABA Informal Op. 657 (1963).

[7] Allen, How Executives Rate Accountants, Lawyers, PR Specialists and Others, Wall St.J., Dec.2, 1980, p.25, col.4 (report of Wall Street Journal/Gallup survey indicates majority of corporate executives satisfied with work of lawyers).

[8] M.Wessel, The Rule of Reason: A New Approach to Corporate Litigation (1976); Chayes, Greenwald & Winig, Managing Your Lawyer, 83 Harv.Bus.Rev. 84 (Jan./Feb. 1983)(advice to corporations on how to deal with outside legal expenses that in 1977 amounted nationally to $18.6 billion); Ruder, A Suggestion for Increased Use of Corporate Law Departments in Modern Corporations, 23 Bus. Law. 341 (1968); Lewin, Putting Litigation on a Budget—Some Major Corporations Stress Trims, N.Y.Times, Apr. 2, 1982, at D1, col. 3; Lavine, Outside Counsel Are Feeling the Corporate Whip, Nat'l L.J., Jan.26, 1981, at 1, col.3.

[9] Urging a broad view, see, e.g., Gossett, The Corporation Lawyer's Social Responsibilities, 60 ABA J. 1517 (1974); see generally Legal Ethics Forum—Matters of Business versus Legal Matters, 64 ABA J. 1597 (1978).

The ultimate variation of the question, although other factors are also involved, is whether a lawyer should agree to serve as an officer[10] or a member of the board of directors of a client corporation.[11] The 1969 Code says nothing on the subject, and the 1983 Model Rules apparently permit it.[12] At least the practice of serving as both counsel and director for a large corporate client is unsound and should be prohibited by law.[13] The practice has recently decreased somewhat among major national corporations,[14] as corporations attempt to obtain outside directors who are more like-minded to management in response to changes in corporate governance requirements.[15] Nonetheless, roughly half of the nation's largest corporations have outside counsel sitting on their boards and the firms of those lawyers earn large sums in legal fees from their corporations.[16]

The burdens assumed by a lawyer who becomes a client's director are substantial. The relationship is a decided threat to the professional independence of counsel. The lawyer puts his or her own legal advice to the vote of the rest of the board under circumstances in which the pressures are inevitably great to conform to the board's preferred, business-dictated conception of legal obligations. The board's probable preference for collegiality and deference to management prerogatives and the will of the board's majority clashes with the lawyer's duty to act on occasion as the corporate nag, or conscience. What is good for business and what the law requires may be very different things, but the need to draw this distinction is particularly great for a person who purports to draw upon both kinds of expertise and make both kinds of judgments.[17]

Other, possibly secondary reasons exist to prohibit the practice. A counsel-director and his or her firm is disqualified from representing the corporation in any suit in which the lawyer is named as a defendant-director.[18] The lawyer's conversations with corporate personnel may later be held to have been in the role of director rather than of counsel, thus invalidating attorney-client privilege claims that the corporation may attempt to

10 Cf. Cottonwood Estates, Inc. v. Paradise Builders, Inc., 128 Ariz. 99, 624 P.2d 296, 303 (1981)("Here, the lawyer is being called into court to answer for his acts as an officer where his corporate ministerial duties conflicted with his professional duty to exercise independent judgment on behalf of his client.").

11 The issue is reviewed in SEC Staff Report on Corporate Accountability 452–57 (1980).

12 MR 1.7 comment (Other Conflicts Situations; fourth paragraph). The concluding sentence of that comment to MR 1.7, the general rule on conflicts of interest, states: "If there is material risk that the dual role [of director-counsel] will compromise the lawyer's independence of professional judgment, the lawyer should not serve as a director." Many would contend that the risk always exists, see infra n. 13, but presumably the comment does not impose such a preclusive rule.

13 Lorne, The Corporate and Securities Adviser, the Public Interest, and Professional Ethics, 76 Mich.L.Rev. 423, 490–95 (1978); Cary, Professional Responsibility in the Practice of Corporate Law—The Ethics of Bar Associations, 29 Rec.Ass'n B. City N.Y. 443, 446 (1974); Ruder, The Case Against the Lawyer-Director, 30 Bus. Law. 41 (1975); Swaine, Impact of Big Business on the Profession: An Answer to Critics of the Modern Bar, 35 ABA J. 89, 170 (1949). The practice is prohibited, for example, to accountants in the United States by their profession. See Am. Ass'n of Certified Pub. Accountants, Code of Ethics, Rule 101 (1980). In England a barrister is prohibited from representing any corporation on whose board he or she sits, see W.Boulton, Conduct and Etiquette at the Bar 34 (6th ed.1975), but a solicitor may serve in both capacities, see T.Lund, A Guide to the Professional Conduct and Etiquette of Solicitors 13, 32–33 (1960).

14 Nat'l L.J., Feb.23, 1981, p.1, col.2 (SEC review of 1,000 companies' proxy statements shows that 49 percent have outside counsel sitting on board in 1980, compared with 57.6 percent in 1979); Lewin, Business and the Law—When Rules Differ for Some, N.Y.Times, Aug.24, 1982, at D2, col.1, at 2 (SEC report of 25 percent decline in number of sitting outside counsel since 1979). See generally Outside Counsel, Inside Director: Lawyers on the Boards of American Industry (1974).

15 Nat'l L.J., Dec.3, 1979, at 8, col. 1.

16 Nat'l L.J., Jan.25, 1982, at 1, col. 3. See generally Outside Counsel, Inside Director: Lawyers on the Boards of American Industry (1974).

17 Cottonwood Estates, Inc. v. Paradise Builders, Inc., 128 Ariz. 99, 624 P.2d 296, 303 (1981)(". . . Here, the lawyer is being called into court to answer for his acts as an officer where his corporate ministerial duties conflicted with his professional duty to exercise independent judgment on behalf of his client.").

18 Harrison v. Keystone Coca-Cola Bottling Co., 428 F.Supp. 149 (M.D.Pa.1977). Under entity disqualification rules in the conflict of interest area, the lawyer-director's entire firm is also disqualified. See § 7.6.2.

make.[19] The dual role may also increase the potential for damage liability of the director-lawyer who may assume a higher standard of care as director.[20] Those risks seem hardly worth the incremental increase, if any, in the lawyer's gain in knowledge about corporate affairs that is typically cited in defense of the practice.[21] In any event, a comparable increase in knowledge can be gained through attendance at board meetings without the lawyer's becoming a full legal member of the group.[22]

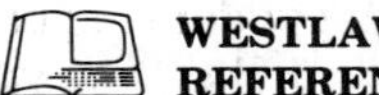

WESTLAW REFERENCES

corporat! /s independent outside /2 counsel** lawyer attorney /p disciplin! (conflict /3 interest)

§ 13.7.5 Corporate Advising

Advising in a Bureaucracy

A corporation with more than a few officers and employees takes on characteristics of a bureaucracy. The positive goals sought through constructing large business organizations are to separate and specialize functions and to concentrate resources to obtain economies of scale. Attaining those goals requires measures such as imposing standardized procedures and hierarchical controls. But standardization and hierarchy can tend toward dispersing and avoiding individual responsibility. While thoughtful persons pursue more responsive and integrated operation within a corporate bureaucracy, a lawyer advising the corporation as either inside or outside counsel must contend with existing deflections and ambiguities of responsibility, as well as with corporate actors who arrogate powers to themselves that are unintended or illegitimate.

Corporate Governance and Organization

In part, the corporate bureacracy is formed pursuant to law, but law only partially and imperfectly delineates the offices and persons who hold responsibility.[23] The law that bears on questions of corporate structure includes such potentially disparate sources as state corporation and agency law and growing areas of federal regulation such as securities law. In general legal theory, the shareholders are the ultimate legal owners of the corporation, for whose benefit the corporation is to be managed. But shareholders in a large corporation may have no effective means of control over its actual operation against the will of management except through sale of their shares or, very occasionally, through the cumbersome process of removing directors or making rough structural changes in the corporation's articles or bylaws.

For most matters, the board of directors is legally recognized as the authority of highest and often last resort.[24] The board's role is generally to direct policy and review corporate operations. But even an active board meets only monthly, and then according to an agenda prepared by management. The powers and responsibilities of boards of major corporations have recently been expanding, particularly in the case of committees of outside directors. Yet it is unlikely that management by board committees will prove a lasting or significant feature of corporate gov-

19 See generally § 6.3.2; see SEC v. Gulf & Western Indus., Inc., 518 F.Supp. 675, 683 (D.D.C.1981); Marco v. Dulles, 169 F.Supp. 622, 631 (S.D.N.Y.1959), appeal dismissed 268 F.2d 192 (2d Cir.1959)(lawyer who served as outside counsel "as a director cannot be separated from his acts as a member of the firm").

20 Cf. Escott v. BarChris Constr. Co., 283 F.Supp. 643, 687, 2 A.L.R.Fed. 86 (S.D.N.Y.1968). It has been argued, however, that precisely because a lawyer-director will also be personally liable, his or her advice is likely to be regarded by other directors as more credible, because offered by a true insider. Note, Corporate Counsel on the Board of Directors: An Overview, 10 Cumb.L.Rev. 791, 793–94 (1980).

21 Forrow, The Corporate Law Department Lawyer: Counsel to the Entity, 34 Bus.Law. 1797, 1817 (1979) (argument applied to house counsel-director); Harris, The Case for the Lawyer-Director, 30 Bus.Law. 58, 59 (1975).

22 Comment, Corporate Counsel on the Board of Directors: An Overview, 10 Cumb.L.Rev. 791 (1980).

23 See generally M. Eisenberg, The Structure of the Corporation: A Legal Analysis (1976); C.Stone, Where the Law Ends: The Social Control of Corporate Behavior (1975); Eisenberg, Legal Models of Management Structure in the Modern Corporation, 63 Calif.L.Rev. 375 (1975); Note, Decisionmaking Models and the Control of Corporate Crime, 85 Yale L.J. 1091 (1976).

24 Model Business Corporation Act § 35 (1977).

ernance beyond a few particularly troublesome situations.

The principal officers of a typical coporation manage it. Implementing and generating policy on a day-to-day basis is in the hands of the chief executive officer of the corporation, who almost invariably is also chairman of the board or president. The usual practice is for the board of directors to delegate to the chief executive officer, sometimes only implicitly, its power to appoint and to direct other principal officers. The task of specifying the duties of those other officers, including inside counsel and often outside counsel, and the nature of their relationships among themselves is also typically left to the chief executive officer. Occasionally, both duties and relationships may be formalized as company policy in large corporations.

Other critical constituencies of a corporation include its nonmanagement employees, who, particularly if represented by a union, can take formal action to affect corporate labor policy, and its creditors, to whom corporations often surrender at least some limiting control over the magnitude of debt and related operating questions of a financial nature.

Lawyer Communication and Access

For both inside and outside counsel the critical bureaucratic necessity is to communicate information and obtain access to influence within the corporation. Satisfactory communication and access are necessary to perform effectively the professional functions of fact gathering and advice giving. But communication and access can also serve a lawyer's personal interests in gaining remuneration, responsibility, and advancement. Also involved are such subsidiary questions as budgeting, supervision, communication channels and their relative rigidity, staffing decisions, and follow-through on legal advice or other services.

Several features of corporate bureaucracy affect inside and outside counsel differently.[25] The role of inside counsel may be more circumscribed by bureaucratic rigidity and blockage within a corporation because inside counsel functions physically within the other parts of that structure, and economically is almost entirely dependent upon a single client.[26] The nature of the "client"-lawyer relationship between house counsel and corporate personnel differs from the typical outside client-counsel relationship in several respects. (1) The relationship with house counsel is likely to be ongoing and indefinite and may not be confined to a single kind of legal matter. (2) The relationship with house counsel typically is organizationally mandated and is less likely to be the result of a freely contracted client-lawyer relationship. (3) The relationship between house counsel and corporate personnel is part of a larger organizational scheme of things that can impose constraints and influences on the relationship that do not exist in most private-practice representations.

But outside counsel to a corporation almost invariably work within a structured bureaucracy as well, a large law firm.[27] Lawyers in the firm operate under the powerful incentive of maximizing legal fees through pleasing an important client. Moreover, outside counsel must contend with an existing corporate bureaucracy when gathering information and giving legal advice.[28] Thus outside counsel, in a sense, may be doubly constrained. While each bureaucracy is different, we can expect

[25] See generally Szabad & Gersen, Inside vs. Outside Counsel, 28 Bus.Law. 235 (1972).

[26] For reflections on the role of house counsel within a corporation's organization, see generally Davis, Reflections of a Kept Lawyer, 53 ABA J. 349 (1967); Ferrara & Steinberg, The Role of Inside Counsel in the Corporate Accountability Process, 4 Corp.L.Rev. 3 (1980); Corporate Law Department Forum, 34 Bus.Law. 819; Rust, What the Chief Executive Looks for in His Corporate Law Department, 33 Bus.Law. 811 (1978). For a sociological examination, see Slovak, The Ethics of Corporate Lawyers: A Sociological Approach, 1981 Am.B.Found. Research J. 753.

[27] E.Smigel, The Wall Street Lawyer 277–86 (1964).

[28] Cf. MR 1.4 comment (second paragraph)("When the client is an organization or group, it is often impossible or inappropriate to inform every one of its members about its legal affairs; ordinarily, the lawyer should address communications to the appropriate officials of the organization.").

each to exert strong influences. For outside counsel the overridingly important question is the point of entry into the client's corporate structure.

A perennial problem is whether outside counsel report to house counsel or to some other officer.[29] Probably without exception, outside counsel prefer to remain free to communicate at any level, including the highest, within a corporation. But corporate clients seem increasingly to prefer outside counsel to be accountable to house counsel at least for routine communications and advice. The arrangement probably enhances communication and supervision and may reflect the increasingly important role and organizational power of house counsel.

Advising on Law Compliance

A lawyer hired by a corporation, as either employee or independent contractor, serves as the helping counsellor and adviser to the corporation. The lawyer's effectiveness serves the ends of the entity by avoiding unnecessary legal complications. It may also serve society's goals to the extent that the lawyer's advice advances the policy objectives of statutes, regulations, and the common law.

So long as the corporate lawyer's considered view is that a proposed course of action (or inaction) is fully in accord with the law and otherwise unobjectionable, the lawyer's advice to proceed will be a welcome, if normally expected, clearance. But when the lawyer's advice must be that the client's course of action is ill-advised and should not proceed, several issues can arise. First, should a lawyer's advice be strictly limited to "legal" matters, or should the lawyer also raise nonlegal considerations? Second, if the client's intended course of action is legally faulty, but the corporate official whom the lawyer advises rejects the lawyer's advice, what further action should or may the lawyer take?

Nonlegal Considerations

Beyond giving nonlegal business advice, should a lawyer attempt to influence corporate behavior with moral, political, or economic views? The answer of the lawyer codes, as explored elsewhere,[30] is that such views can indeed be validly offered, although there certainly is no professional requirement that they be discussed.[31]

Because of the business environment in which he or she works, however, a corporate lawyer may feel that nonlegal views will be perceived as particularly irrelevant in the corporate milieu. At least, it might be thought, corporate managers will not welcome such views unless they can be convincingly portrayed as an important element of legal interpretation and thus narrowly utilitarian for the client's purposes.[32] A corporate lawyer may believe that the business environment is pervaded by the ultimate bureaucratic deflection of moral responsibility: the assigned and only role of corporate managers is to maximize profits for shareholders through corporate growth.

Surely an emphasis on corporate profit and growth is unobjectionable in a capitalistic system. Controversy develops when it is asserted that that narrow role provides all the guidance that is legitimately relevant to the role.[33] It is becoming accepted, however, that pursuit of the goal of profit maximization by corporate managers does not exclude relevant ethical and similar considerations. Those matters can be germane in corporate decision

[29] McKinney, Relationship with Outside Counsel, 34 Bus.Law. 921 (1979)(advocating relationship through house counsel); Taylor, The Role of Corporate Counsel, 32 Rutgers L.Rev. 237 (1979)(advocating direct relationship with board of directors).

[30] §§ 4.3, 10.2, 13.3.10.

[31] EC 7–8; MR 2.1, comment (Scope of Advice; second paragraph).

[32] The MR 2.1 comment offers that utilitarian rationale in support of a lawyer's advising on "moral and ethical considerations." Id. (Scope of Advice; second paragraph) ("Although a lawyer is not a moral advisor as such, moral and ethical considerations impinge upon most legal questions and may decisively influence how the law will be applied."). That approach leaves nonutilitarian moral advice without a stated rationale.

[33] Dodge v. Ford Motor Co., 204 Mich. 459, 170 N.W. 668, 684, 3 A.L.R. 413 (1919); Friedman, The Social Responsibility of Business Is to Increase Its Profits, N.Y. Times Mag., Sept.13, 1978, p. 32.

making for reasons relating to profit maximization, for example, to increase public and community acceptance of the corporation. An outside lawyer with many clients in an industry and with partners and associates expert in related areas of the law can often detect incipient areas of negative public opinion before solutions less desirable than those suggested by the lawyer are mandated by external regulation.[34] Quite beyond having such instrumental justifications, the ethical, social, and political impacts of corporate decisions are appropriate and desirable criteria for guiding corporate conduct for the overriding reason that corporations exist and act in a world in which these impacts in fact occur. Thus lawyers advise in a situation in which human actors in a corporation must accept responsibility for the consequences of their acts.[35]

But the relevance of non-profit-maximizing considerations to corporate decision making hardly demonstrates that it is a lawyer's proper work to purvey views on these matters to clients. It might be thought improbable that the market for legal services, corporate or otherwise, would value a "legal" service, unless it were free, that promised mainly guilt, if rejected, or noneconomic good feelings, if accepted. Yet a corporate lawyer who never mentioned what the lawyer perceived to be important ethical or other human dimensions of corporate decision making would be chargeable with the ultimate form of immorality—treating persons, corporate managers in this instance, as less than the autonomous and thoughtful people they are or may be. Many corporate managers, because they are not corporate drones, as vulgarly and unkindly imagined, might be willing if not delighted to discuss non-profit-maximizing considerations that should influence management's choice of options. That conversation, if held with a sympathetic and knowledgeable corporate lawyer, might be particularly valuable because of the moral roots of much law. In such a conversation, a lawyer should inform a client competently about the law, not confuse advice about law with ideas about extralegal considerations, and not assume a tone of magisterial superiority or reflect an assumption that lawyers are uniquely qualified to pass on nonlegal matters.

Rejected Advice

As discussed above, a corporate lawyer's advice may have many possible audiences, from a low-ranking employee to the chairman of the board of directors or, possibly, even to the shareholders. If the lawyer's advice is that contemplated action or inaction is illegal but the advice is rejected or action is taken inconsistent with it, what further action may or must a lawyer take? In the final analysis, if the situation is serious, may or must a lawyer disclose intended corporate wrongdoing to a corporation's board of directors or even to its shareholders? May or must a corporate lawyer withdraw? The Model Rules, but not the 1969 Code, state an obligation to take action and attempt to provide guidance to such a lawyer.

In general terms, MR 1.13(b) and (c) offer advice on how a lawyer should proceed in certain instances of corporate illegality.[36] Floor amendments to MR 1.13, in February 1983, removed its most controversial provision, which would have authorized corporate

34 Taylor, The Role of Corporate Counsel, 32 Rutgers L.Rev. 237, 247–48 (1979).

35 See generally ALI Principles of Corporate Governance: Analysis and Recommendations § 2.01 (tent. draft no.2, 1984). For strongly stated versions of the point, with programs for reform, see J.Deutsch, Selling the People's Cadillac: The Edsel and Corporate Responsibility (1976); R.Nader, M.Green & J.Seligman, Taming the Giant Corporation (1976).

36 The final version of MR 1.13 enacted by the ABA clearly creates no obligation or permission unique to lawyers representing organizational clients. See MR 1.13, comment (Relation to Other Rules). Previous versions of the same comment confusingly intimated that, although the lawyer's authority and responsibilities were "concurrent" with other rules, MR 1.13 might "independently" create new rules. See MR 1.13, comment (Relation to Other Rules) at 84 (Proposed Final Draft, May 30, 1981). The language referring to independent rules was eliminated from the final version of the comment.

lawyers to take "further remedial action" that the lawyer reasonably believed to be "in the best interest of the organization" in instances of clear law violations that portended substantial injury to the organization.[37] The rule as finally adopted thus leaves intact the general approach, ultimately adopted in the Model Rules, of strictly limiting lawyer disclosure of client wrongdoing (see § 12.6).

What remains in MR 1.13 is a road map to guide a lawyer's search, within the organizational geography of a corporate client, for a person or body willing and able to countermand a subordinate's illegal action. The February 1983 amendment changed the rule from one that would have created an important exception to the rules on confidential client information to a relatively limited rule that aims to assist a lawyer to fulfill a mandate to provide reasonably competent legal service to an organizational client by protecting its important interests (§ 5.1). It does so, first, by defining the occasions on which competence calls for a lawyer's further action beyond advising about law compliance and, second, by suggesting means by which a competent lawyer might obtain compliance.

Occasions for Mandatory Action

Rule 1.13(b) states that a lawyer who "knows" (see § 13.3.3) of ongoing or planned organizational illegality must take reasonable steps to protect the organization's interests. That aspect of Rule 1.13(b) should not be understated: it creates for the first time a clear and relatively broad obligation on the part of corporate counsel to take action within the organization to reverse corporate decisions that threaten a violation of "legal obligation." The scope of "legal obligation" appears to include all kinds of legal duties, whether they arise from criminal law, statutory law, administrative regulations, or any other legal source. But MR 1.13(b) describes and limits a corporate lawyer's duty in four important ways, some of which are not obvious:

(1) The action must be that of an "officer, employee or other person associated with the organization." A lawyer's knowledge of actions by others that would harm an organizational client, however, might also require a lawyer's response, at least as a matter of competence, even if this situation is not specifically covered by MR 1.13(b).

(2) The illegality must relate to the lawyer's representation. That definitional aspect is designed apparently to discourage (although not to prohibit) lawyers from officiously interfering in corporate affairs, even if serious and client-threatening illegality is afoot, so long as the illegality is outside any matter on which the lawyer's assistance was sought.

(3) Only illegality "likely to result in substantial injury to the organization" requires action. Again, the apparent objective is not to encourage lawyers to disrupt the ways in which corporate responsibilities are normally structured in order to respond to insubstantial law violations.[38] Note, particularly, that the rule is not limited to illegalities that violate legal rights of the corporation. A law violation, such as the illegal manufacture of a defective product, that threatens injury to nonclient third parties could still result in injury to the organization because of the threat of suits.[39]

(4) The illegality is limited to one that is "a violation of a legal obligation to the organization, or a violation of law which reasonably might be imputed to the organization." Clearly covered are all injuries to the corpora-

[37] MR 1.13(c)(Proposed Final Draft, May 30, 1981).

[38] MR 1.13, comment (The Entity as Client; fourth paragraph)(urging caution in going "over the head" of an organizational person normally responsible for acting on the lawyer's advice). The same objective, apparently, explains the language in MR 1.13(b)(third sentence) requiring a lawyer to "minimize disruption of the organization" when designing measures to obtain countermanding law compliance.

[39] The client-centered definition seems, however, to exclude instances of injuries to third persons caused by illegal client conduct if it appears unlikely that the third parties in fact would be aware of the injury, able to identify the lawyer's client as its perpetrator, and bring suit to recover damages. The only protection for third parties in such instances would be the minimal ones implicit in Rules 1.6, 1.2(d), and similar rules.

tion, such as a serious instance of waste of corporate assets, as well as all acts of an officer or employee that would create liability for the corporation under the doctrine of respondeat superior. But an officer's illegality that is not within that doctrine—such as a corporate officer's criminal plan to smuggle drugs for personal gain—would not be covered by MR 1.13.[40] Note that the functional effect of that limitation is largely, if not precisely, coterminous with the second limitation. It is unlikely that an illegality that does not violate a corporate client's right or that is not imputable to a client would nonetheless be a matter on which the lawyer represents the organization as a client, as opposed to representing an officer as a client at the request or while in the pay of the corporation.

Available Options

A lawyer confronted with a corporate client's officer or employee who intends to commit a law violation of the described kind is required by MR 1.13(b) to take some appropriate action to stop or prevent the ongoing or planned illegal activity: "the lawyer shall proceed as is reasonably necessary in the best interest of the organization." What, precisely, a lawyer might do is left largely to the lawyer's good judgment under the press of circumstances. The rule directs the lawyer's attention particularly to the seriousness of the violation, its probable consequences, the "scope and nature" of the lawyer's representation,[41] the position and motivation of the intending law violator, and any applicable policies of the organization.

The specific options mentioned in the rule are asking reconsideration by the advice-rejecting officer; urging that a second legal opinion be sought; and going over the head of the officer who has both rejected the lawyer's initial legal advice and spurned other attempts to achieve law compliance. None of the listed options is mandatory;[42] indeed, a lawyer could fail to select any one of them and, by designing still another option such as sending a senior colleague to counsel with the recalcitrant corporate agent, fully comply with the rule. The most drastic option mentioned (MR 1.13(b)(3)) is referring the matter to the "highest authority that can act in behalf of the organization as determined by applicable law." The comment apparently limits that authority to the board of directors or possibly to the independent directors on the board.[43] Although under applicable law the shareholders could overrule the board on most matters, obtaining shareholder action in most instances would require revealing confidential client information in violation of Rule 1.6. In the case of a closely held corporation, however, resort to a shareholder meeting might both be efficacious and result in no impingement on Rule 1.6. The explicit requirement of Rule 1.13(b), that the measures taken must not result in impairing the corporate client's information under Rule 1.6, means that corrective action cannot include notifying public agencies or persons who have already been victimized by the illegality.[44]

[40] Query whether MR 1.13 would apply to an officer's resort to illegal activities in order to obtain financing for a failing corporation. The thrust of the rule is to leave the answer to such questions to the doctrine of respondeat superior. Note also that MR 1.6(b)(1) permits even public disclosure if the client's act threatens "substantial bodily harm," as drug smuggling well might.

[41] A lawyer with general responsibility for all of a client's legal affairs would naturally be able to deal more effectively and with more persons within the organization than in the case of a lawyer hired only to give a narrow legal opinion on a specific matter.

[42] Even when earlier versions of MR 1.13 contained a permissive disclosure provision, the general counsel of the SEC urged the ABA to make the option of informing the board of directors mandatory in all cases and not to permit the lawyer to weigh the seriousness of the violation. See 49 U.S.L.Wk. 2127 (Aug.19, 1980).

[43] MR 1.13 comment (The Entity as Client; fifth paragraph).

[44] But under MR 1.6 comment (Withdrawal; second paragraph), if a lawyer's services have been used by a client in a course of criminal or fraudulent conduct, the lawyer may "withdraw or disaffirm any opinion, document, affirmation, or the like"—apparently without regard to whether such action would expose the client's course of conduct.

Withdrawal

Model Rule 1.13(c) states that if a corporate lawyer's efforts to obtain corrective action are unavailing, the lawyer "may" resign under Rule 1.16 if the action "clearly" violates the law and will result in substantial injury to the client. The provision, which was added by floor amendment, seems merely to invoke the general permissive withdrawal rules (§ 9.5.3). It does not incorporate an independent rule of mandatory resignation for corporate lawyers, as some critics had urged. Part of the reason for rejecting such an approach was undoubtedly the drastic impact such a rule would have on house counsel. Note, however, that even house counsel is required to withdraw under Rule 1.16(a)(1) if further representation will result in the lawyer's violation of the Model Rules or other law.

Rule 1.13 in Perspective

Rule 1.13 calls forth neither heroism nor much action on the part of a lawyer for an organization. The rule and the comments are filled with cautions about not upsetting apple-carts and not going over heads. Parts of it seem to have been drafted by a young firm associate overawed by visions of the intimidating boardroom of a multinational corporate client. If anything, the rule is too solicitous of organization charts and customary corporate etiquette, at least in some situations that it defines as occasions for action. A lawyer confronted with an officer about to plunge a publicly held corporation into certain ruin by a clearly illegal waste of its assets is hardly owed the tender regard suggested by some language in the rule.

A lawyer with more grit than portrayed in the rule can proceed more resolutely without fear of violating the rather minimal dictates of the rule. Even if a lawyer proceeds rashly and smashes corporate traditions of silence and reserve to the discomfort of all concerned, it seems farfetched and pointless to imply, as the Rule does, that such a loud shout in the library is enough to subject the lawyer to professional discipline if no other harm is done. That assumes, of course, that the lawyer's inappropriate uproar causes no injuries beyond those inflicted on sensitivities. A more substantial injury, such as compromising protected client information, on the other hand, is prohibited by the rule.[45]

§ 13.8 LAWYERS AND THE POLITICAL PROCESS

§ 13.8.1 Lawyers in American Politics

The relationship between lawyers and the political process is a study in dualism. In the positive dimension, lawyers have rightly been called the "high priests of politics," [46] playing a predominant role in molding legislation and public policy throughout the nation's history.[47] Of fifty-two signers of the Declaration of Independence in 1776, twenty-five were lawyers.[48] When the Constitution was drafted in Philadelphia in the summer of 1787, thirty-one of the fifty-six members to the convention were lawyers. Of American presidents, vice presidents, and cabinets members between 1877 and 1934, 70 percent were lawyers.[49] Of the thirty-nine persons who have served as president (through Reagan), twenty-two have been lawyers. More than half of the state and national legislators have been lawyers over the course of the nation's history. Generalizing from his American impressions of

45 MR 1.13(b) wisely warns a lawyer to attend to that risk when designing responsive measures.

46 H.Eulau & J.Sprague, Lawyers in Politics 11 (1964).

47 See generally 2 J.Bryce, The American Commonwealth 306–307 (rev.ed.1911); Weber, Politics as a Vocation, in From Max Weber: Essays in Sociology 94–95 (H.Gerth & C.Mills eds.1946).

48 D.Mathews, The Social Background of Political Decision-Makers 30 (1954). The motion to secede from Britain was made by Virginia lawyer Richard Henry Lee, seconded by Massachusetts lawyer John Adams (later the second president of the United States), and referred to a committee of four lawyers, headed by lawyer (at least law-trained) Thomas Jefferson, that drafted the actual Declaration of Independence.

49 H.Eulau & J.Sprague, Lawyers in Politics 11 (1964).

over a century ago, Alexis de Tocqueville believed that "in all free governments, of whatsoever form they may be, members of the legal profession will be found at the head of all parties." [50]

Yet many lawyers remain uncertain, even distrustful, of the political process as a method for serving client interests, let alone as a possible part of their legal careers.[51] Their attitude reflects myths, shared with the public, about the inescapable corruption and byzantine workings of the political process. For many, *lobbyist* remains a term of opprobrium.[52] Many lawyers also believe that the judicial process is a preferable forum for attempting to vindicate client interests because of its smaller scale, greater manageability, and greater predictability. For some lawyers, the preference is probably a reflex or fixation left over from a legal education dominated more by appellate case reports than by statutory or administrative materials. Surprisingly, that attitude is found even among public-interest lawyers.[53] That may be particularly ironic if it is true, as theorists have asserted, that legal change becomes truly effective only when it is reinforced by political action.[54]

While relatively few lawyers engage directly in the political process either as legislator, policymaker, or legislative lobbyist, the powerful role that these representatives play raises important issues of professional ethics.

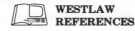

WESTLAW REFERENCES

di lobbyist

§ 13.8.2 *Lawyer-Lobbyists*

The Work of Lawyer-Lobbyists

Lawyers who are lobbyists, or "representatives," as they sometimes prefer to be called, serve as informal lawmakers and policy implementers.[55] The paradigm is the "Washington lawyer," a lawyer and sometimes a former governmental official who expertly protects a client against governmental regulations or guides a client through the legislative or bureaucratic maze.[56] Law firms specializing in lobbying are found in most major governmental centers.[57] The range of lawyer-lobbyists' political activities includes those that are nakedly partisan and forthrightly political. For example, lawyers may be more

[50] A.de Tocqueville, Democracy in America 279 (15 World's Great Classics 1900), quoted in Kampelman, The Washington Lawyer: Some Musings, in Lawyers' Ethics: Contemporary Dilemmas at 239 (A.Gerson ed.1980). More recent comparativists, however, have concluded that the extent of lawyer influence in political affairs in other democracies is much less than in the United States. See Heinz, The Power of Lawyers, 17 Ga.L.Rev. 891 (1983).

[51] White, The State of the Law: The Bar's Responsibility, 17 Gonz.L.Rev. 849, 856 (1982).

[52] The begrudging acceptance of the legitimacy of lobbying activities can be traced, for example in the First Restatement of Contracts (1932). It provided (§ 559(1)) that a bargain to influence a legislative body or its members "otherwise than by presenting facts and arguments to show that the desired action is of public advantage, is illegal." And a bargain "to conceal the identity of a person on whose behalf arguments to influence legislation are made, is illegal" (id. § 559(2)). Cf. Restatement (Second) of Contracts § 198 illustration 3 (1982).

[53] J.Handler, E.Hollingsworth & H.Erlanger, Lawyers and the Pursuit of Legal Rights 76–81 (1978); Rabin, Lawyers for Social Change: Perspectives on Public Interest Law, 28 Stan.L.Rev. 207 (1976).

[54] S.Scheingold, The Politics of Rights: Lawyers, Public Policy, and Political Change (1974). See also, e.g., Fetner, Public Power and Professional Responsibility: Julius Henry Cohen and the Origins of the Public Authority, 21 Am.J.Leg.Hist. 15, 17–18 (1977).

[55] See generally Clune, A Political Model of Implementation and Implications of the Model for Public Policy, Research, and the Changing Roles of Law and Lawyers, 69 Iowa L.Rev. 47 (1983). One of the most powerful lobbying organizations is the American Bar Association, which, because of its elite status and its posture as an oracle of "neutral" law, has great influence in lobbying. See A.Melone, Lawyers, Public Policy and Interest Group Politics (1977).

[56] C.Horsky, The Washington Lawyer (1952); Cohen, The Washington Lawyer—A Contrived Legend, 38 Geo. Wash.L.Rev. 767 (part of Symposium, Inside Washington Law: The Roles and Responsibilities of the Washington Lawyer, id. 527–787 (1970)). The Washington lawyer and his or her influence over policy-making is currently being studied through a project funded by the American Bar Foundation. See 68 ABA J. 833 (1982).

[57] 70 ABA J. 31 (1984)(merger of law firm and public relations and lobbying firm in state capitol). Existing law firms have obtained skilled assistance in lobbying by hiring nonlawyer professional lobbyists as employees. See 69 ABA J. 1207 (1983).

generous contributors of funds to political campaigns than any other occupational group.[58] Lobbying also includes substantial contributions to policy-making through direct involvement as private lawyers in the processes of government. And, at their most innocuous, lawyer-lobbyists function as the lay historians and political scientists of government as they attempt to advise clients by divining the probable future course of an agency's policy development on the basis of internal history and external political constraints.[59]

Criticisms of Lawyer-Lobbyists

Not all applaud the efforts of lawyer-lobbyists, of course. Many governmental functionaries have a low regard for the value of lawyer participation in public policy-making. Some nonlawyer policymakers, for example, prefer to see lawyers confined only to technically "legal" subjects.[60] Such disdain may be based on the fact that lawyers upstage some policymakers or impose unwanted restrictions on their freedom of action.

Criticism may, however, be directed toward the methods by which lawyer "fixers" obtain political favors, not on the merits of their proposals for political action, but because of their client's political power—if indeed that criticism is truer of lawyer-lobbyists than of others. The notorious instances of such political fixing that come to public view probably distort the extent to which lawyer-lobbyists are able to gain results for clients through sheer political influence. In any event, DR 9–101(C) of the Code states that a lawyer should not state or imply an ability to influence a tribunal, legislative body, or public official "improperly or upon irrelevant grounds."[61] And most lawyer-lobyists are probably accurate when they claim only the knowledge and ability to obtain access to the offices of policymakers, where they attempt to influence policy by the persuasiveness of the ideas they present.

Some critics have asserted that lawyer-lobbyists have gained too much political power for clients whose interests assertedly conflict with the public interest.[62] The objection raises difficult questions. One is to define the public interest (§ 16.8). Another is to arrive at a rationale for limiting the assistance of lawyer-lobbyists to some client projects but not others, although both are legal.

Legal and Moral Limits on Lobbying

One broad issue for lawyer-lobbyists is whether the lawyer's appropriate role is similar to that of advocacy in court or whether, instead, a lawyer must bear some personal professional responsibility for the results of lobbying. If the latter is the standard, then a lawyer must exercise special restraint in achieving goals and employing methods that the lawyer could not personally endorse. Probably most lawyer-lobbyists believe that the full-advocacy model is appropriate.[63] Going to a legislative session is the same, for that purpose, as going to court.

[58] Fialka, Making Friends: Legal Professional Tops All Others in Financing Candidates for Congress, Wall St.J., Aug.16, 1983, p.1, col.1 (survey based on analysis of Federal Election Commission contribution records).

[59] C.Horsky, The Washington Lawyer 71–73 (1952).

[60] Kissinger, Domestic Structure and Foreign Policy, 95 Daedelus 503 (1966); Hayes & Abernathy, Managing Our Way to Economic Decline, 58 Harv.Bus.Rev. July/Aug. 1980, at 67.

[61] In re Sears, 71 N.J. 175, 364 A.2d 777 (1976)(suspension for unsuccessful attempt to influence federal agency officials improperly, creating impression of ability to do so, and false testimony about efforts).

MR 8.4(e) copies DR 9–101(C) except that it does not proscribe a stated ability to influence "upon irrelevant grounds" in addition to influence by "improper" means. Lawyers who are public officials are prohibited by DR 8–101(A)(3) from accepting anything of value when the lawyer knows or it is obvious that the transaction is "for the purpose of influencing his action as a public official." No specific provision of the Code other than DR 9–101(C) explicitly prohibits a lawyer from making the gift (unless, perhaps, the bribing lawyer is also a public official; see DR 8–101(A)(1)). See In re Connaghan, 613 S.W.2d 626 (Mo.1981). But particularly if the offense of bribery is committed, the transaction likely falls under general provisions of DR 1–102(A). In re Connaghan, supra. See also MR 3.5(a)(lawyer shall not seek to influence an "official by means prohibited by law").

[62] M.Green, The Other Government: The Unseen Power of Washington Lawyers (1978).

[63] McDonald, Book Review, Trial Magazine at 38, 39 (Nov./Dec.1975).

Others have argued, however, that the difference in environment between courtroom and legislative hallway requires greater limitations on lobbying.[64] A lobbyist often does not work in the face of adversarial opposition, under generalized principles of advocacy enforced by routinely observed rules of evidence and procedure and with a public record by which to assess the lawyer's presentation of facts and argument.[65] Opposing points of view may not receive the fair hearing that would be accorded in court. And the decision maker is not systematically protected from influences that might produce a biased result, or required always to base decision only on matters properly brought before him or her.[66] For those reasons it may be argued that a lawyer-lobbyist should be required to urge as policy only those measures that the lawyer personally regards as in conformance with the public interest. To put it another way, the lawyer should be required to assert, if pressed, that he or she agrees in good faith with the policy objectives espoused in behalf of a client in lobbying activity.[67]

An insistence on congruence between a client's views and those of a lawyer-lobbyist, however, would clearly conflict with the principle of professional detachment applied in most other lawyer representations. Under the principle it is not presumed that a lawyer necessarily agrees with a client's political, social, economic, or other views (§ 10.2.1). The approach of the Code on lobbying accords with the principle. It states that a lawyer may advocate positions as a lobbyist in behalf of a client with which the lawyer does not personally agree (EC 8–4) and that a lawyer representing a client before an administrative agency should advance the client's interests within the bounds of the law (EC 7–15).[68] Model Rule 3.9 and its comment are less explicit, but evidently conform to the Code's "advocacy" model for lobbyists.

As with similar problems, the defect (if one exists) by which lawyers can gain advantages for clients through political influence is in the lobbying process itself. It does not inhere in the kind of work that lawyers, as such, do when they lobby. All lobbyists, including those many who are not lawyers, operate without special professional constraints, and it is difficult to support the position that lawyers should be uniquely disqualified by professional rules to take legally permissible steps in lobbying in behalf of a client.

All of the preceding relates to the realms of general law and the law of professional regulation. An entirely different objection is that a lawyer who, for example, lobbies to loosen regulations on flammable fabrics for children's use is morally, rather than legally, accountable for his or her lawyerly work, even if it is entirely legal and violates no professional rule. As in other situations in

[64] Such a differentiation is implicit in the contrast, for example, between EC 8–5 of the Code and DR 7–102(B). The former states a very broad obligation to disclose, with respect to a lawyer-lobbyist's nonprivileged knowledge, "fraudulent, deceptive, or otherwise illegal conduct" by any participant in the legislative process. The latter is much narrower in scope. The mandatory disclosure statement in EC 8–5 is, of course, merely advisory (see § 2.6.3). It was added in the final drafting of the Code and appears to have been demoted from a DR by concerns over separation-of-powers limitations on the power of a court to mandate conduct in the legislative process. See Annotated Code of Professional Responsibility 382–83 (O.Maru ed.1979).

[65] Barnett, Book Review, 90 Harv.L.Rev. 648, 650 (1977).

[66] C.Horsky, The Washington Lawyer 35–36 (1952); Mikva, Interest Representation in Congress: The Social Responsibilities of the Washington Lawyer, 38 Geo.Wash. L.Rev. 651, 653, 668 (1970); Cutler, Book Review, 62 Yale L.J. 853, 855–56 (1953); Cutler, Book Review, 83 Harv.L. Rev. 1746, 1751 (1970).

[67] EC 7–16 notes that a lawyer's role in representing a client before a legislative body is "quite diferent" from representing a client in court but makes nothing more of the distinction. It merely urges innocuously that the identity of the lawyer's client should be revealed if not privileged and that the lawyer should abide by all applicable laws and rules. Cf. also, Grant v. Reader's Digest Ass'n, 151 F.2d 733 (2d Cir.1945)(per Hand, J.), cert.denied 326 U.S. 797, 66 S.Ct. 492, 90 L.Ed.2d 485 (1946)(published statement that lawyer had been a legislative representative for the Communist party was tantamount to saying he believed in its aims and purposes and thus could be found libelous per se).

[68] Cf. also 1908 Canon 26: "A lawyer openly . . . may render professional services . . . in advocacy of claims before departments of government, upon the same principles of ethics which justify his appearance before the Courts."

which similar questions arise,[69] it cannot be maintained that the role of lawyer (or, certainly, lobbyist) morally warrants a lawyer to advance any client cause whatever. A lawyer-lobbyist's attempt to guide through the legislative process a constitutional amendment to reinstitute slavery is, all can presumably agree, immoral. Similar and more difficult moral judgments must be made by lawyers who are requested by clients to use their legal and political abilities to achieve morally questionable but less patently objectionable goals. Relevant to the moral judgment are considerations, such as those mentioned, of the weaknesses of the political process.[70] But also relevant, and probably of greater importance, is the ultimate impact of the goal sought by the client and the nature of a lawyer's moral responsibility to persons, if any, whose lives would be diminished by the political action that the lawyer is requested to effectuate.

Lawyers and the Administrative Process

A related arena in which questions arise concerning the appropriate level of zeal in behalf of a client is that of agency practice. In fact, a lawyer's activities in representing a client before an administrative agency will often bear many of the hallmarks of lobbying. Here also, for similar reasons, critics have contended that the full-advocacy model is inappropriate for agency practice by lawyers.[71]

Agency practice is assertedly different either because of structural differences or because of the greater importance of fair results. In respect to structure it is argued that agency proceedings are often not adversarial in nature and thus that no opposing advocate is present to assure the accuracy and fairness of the action requested. In terms of fairness, various arguments, depending on context, are made for a greater need to protect members of the public, comparable taxpayers, or other vulnerable populations.

The lawyer codes, however, do not require abandonment of the full-advocacy model of representation in practice before administrative agencies. The Code's EC 7–15 recognizes possible differences between types of proceedings, adversarial and nonadversarial, but does not elaborate different standards. The 1983 Model Rules similarly suggest no different standard for practice before an adminstrative agency.

To an extent, special vulnerabilities of some administrative agencies or the public have been recognized in other law. But instead of placing candor obligations on lawyers, the remedy chosen has been that of penalizing the lawyer's client for overzealous representation by the agent. A prominent example is a decision of the Supreme Court in 1945 holding that the special needs of the Patent Office for candor in passing upon an unchallenged application for a patent required a high standard of disclosure to the patent examiner.[72] The remedy for failure to make disclosure is not to punish the patentee's lawyer but to leave the client's patent vulnerable to attack on the ground of nondisclosure.[73]

Required Disclosures in Lobbying

The lawyer codes do impose on lawyers' lobbying activities special strictures concerning revelations of the lawyer's representative role and, possibly, the lawyer's knowledge of political corruption. There is an important limitation, however, in the general scope of some of the rules in both the 1969 Code and the 1983 Model Rules. Both DR 7–106(B)(2) and MR 3.9 apply only to representations before a "tribunal." While both rules employ definitions of "tribunal" broad enough to include some nonjudicial proceedings, their

69 See generally § 10.2.2.

70 See supra at 749.

71 Marquis, An Appraisal of Attorneys' Responsibilities before Administrative Agencies, 26 Case West.L.Rev. 295 (1976); Schwartz, The Missing Rule of Professional Conduct, 52 LA B.J. 10 (1976).

72 Precision Instrument Mfg. Co. v. Automotive Maint. Mach. Co., 324 U.S. 806, 818, 65 S.Ct. 993, 999, 89 L.Ed. 1381 (1945).

73 Precision Instrument Mfg. Co. v. Automotive Maint. Co., supra. See Henry, Ethics in United States Patent Practice, 62 ABA J. 465 (1976), and authorities cited.

scope may be limited to trial-type proceedings in legislative or administrative bodies.[74]

To the extent they apply to some but not other types of nonjudicial proceedings, DR 7–106(B)(2)[75] and MR 3.9 require that a lawyer who participates in the proceeding in a representative capacity disclose this fact.[76] The requirement prevents lawyer-lobbyists from masquerading in the role of concerned citizen in supporting or opposing legislation or other policy. But it is not clear why the game is of professional concern if it is countenanced by the body before which appear actors who, if unmasked, would not be lawyers.[77] Surely a sober legislator or administrator must be aware that a roomful of lawyers at a hearing is not a set containing only public-spirited citizens taking time off from their busy law practice.[78] The hearing officer or others might be interested in knowing the identity of the lawyer's lobbying client, but MR 3.9 does not require revelation and DR 7–106(B)(2) is ambiguous on the subject.[79]

Finally, mention should be made of EC 8–5, which contains the curious statement, in mandatory form, that a lawyer-lobbyist "should reveal to appropriate authorities" unprivileged information of "fraudulent, deceptive, or otherwise illegal conduct" by a participant in a proceeding "before a tribunal or legislative body."[80]

WESTLAW REFERENCES

"dr 9–101(c)" dr9–101(c) /p influen!

lobby! /s attorney lawyer counsel** /p disclos! (conflict /3 interest)

§ 13.8.3 *Lawyer-Legislators*

Lawyers in State and National Legislatures

The Code, in EC 8–8, encourages lawyers to serve as legislators, asserting that lawyers are uniquely qualified to make contributions to the legislative process. Historically, little encouragement was needed, for lawyers have been heavily represented in legislative bodies. The percentage has declined in recent years,[81] probably because of more stringent conflict of interest laws and perhaps because the increasing demands of legislative service preclude simultaneous law practice as a practical matter. Even when the numbers were quite large, however, studies indicate that the fact

74 Code definitions; MR 3.9. See § 12.6.5.

75 The statement assumes, perhaps too readily, that DR 7–106(B)(2) is to be read together with EC 8–4. Footnote 5 to EC 8–4 notes that it was founded upon a California Rule (Rule 11), the relevant portions of which were not carried forward in the 1975 recasting of the California Rules.

76 MR 3.9 does so specifically. DR 7–106(B)(1) so provides by requiring a lawyer to disclose the "identity" of the lawyer's clients "unless privileged or irrelevant." The Code gives no hint of what the test of relevance might be.

77 Many public bodies, of course, require registration of lobbyists or provide some other method of identification. In that and other relevant respects, EC 7–16 (with respect to legislative lobbying) and MR 3.9 comment (first paragraph)(more globally) require a lawyer to comply with those and other applicable rules.

78 The rationale offered in MR 3.9 comment (second paragraph), that legislators and administrators have a "right" to expect that lawyers will deal with them as they deal with courts, rather strongly begs the question and is empirically dubious if it means to imply, as a matter of fact, that political officers tend to expect that lawyers will perform in legislative lobbies as they are to behave in court. More seriously objectionable are instances in which a lawyer appears in a legislative hearing to oppose legislation in one guise (as spokesperson for a bar committee, for example) without disclosing that clients of the lawyer also wish to defeat the legislation. See 64 ABA J. 1645 (1978).

79 The exception in DR 7–106(B)(2) for instances in which a client's identity is "privileged" raises all of the problems of determining whether this is to be given a broad or narrow meaning. See § 12.6.4. The DR is further obscured by the exception for "irrelevant" client identity, a concept that is nowhere defined. Moreover, EC 7–15 creates a further exception for instances in which a lawyer simply seeks information from an agency that is available to the general public. See also EC 8–4.

80 The disclosure "obligation" of EC 8–5 is not duplicated in any DR other than, in part, in DR 7–102(B)(1). See generally § 12.6 (disclosure—client wrongdoing). Its only regulatory impact would be in jurisdictions that enforce the ECs as compulsory rules. See § 2.6.3.

81 Insurance Information Institute, Occupational Profile of State Legislatures (1979)(survey shows decline of percentage of lawyers in state legislatures from 26 percent to 20 percent between 1966 and 1979 and that less than majority of members of House of Representatives were lawyers for first time in 30 years). The Senate, however, remained over half lawyers (65 percent) in 1979. See Congress.Quarterly, Jan.30, 1979, at 81.

that a legislator is a lawyer has no quantifiable effect on the person's voting record.[82] The promise of EC 8–8 for unique lawyer contributions to legislation, therefore, may be unrealized in practice.

Conflicts of Interest [83]

It is well known, occasionally a matter of notoriety, that legislators can become involved in conflict of interest situations because their decisions on legislative matters affect personal or business interests of the legislator or the interests of clients or customers of the legislator.[84] Lawyers in most legislative bodies are drawn into the problem because they generally are allowed to practice law despite their official position. Their right to practice may be justified on the ground of sustaining the concept of a citizen legislature by permitting less wealthy candidates to serve and on the ground that a single legislator's possible influence on an opposing governmental officer or agency in litigation is typically not great.[85] Lawyer-legislators thus often continue a simultaneous part-time law practice. Statutes and legislative rules sometimes regulate the extent of the practice [86] or the amount of income that it can generate or require public disclosure of income. But few regulatory schemes are so stringent as to remove all conflict of interest problems.

The Code attempts to regulate the conflict problem—but leaves large areas of uncertainty and discretion. The rules in DR 8–101(A) apply generally to a lawyer who serves as a "public official." They (1) prohibit a lawyer-official from obtaining a "special advantage" in "legislative matters" for himself, herself, or a client—but only if the action sought is not "in the public interest";[87] (2) prohibit the use of the lawyer's public position to influence a "tribunal" [88] to act in favor of the official or a client of the official; and (3) prohibit the lawyer-public official from accepting bribes. The first prohibition, in DR 8–101(A)(1), does not even clearly prohibit a lawyer-legislator

[82] H.Eulau & J.Sprague, Laywers in Politics: A Study in Professional Convergence (1964); Derge, The Lawyer in the Indiana General Assembly, 6 Midwest J.Pol.Sci. 19, 21 (1962).

[83] See generally Rep. of Ass'n B.City N.Y.Spec.Comm. on Congr.Ethics, Congress and the Public Trust (1970); Pillans, Legislation, Conflicts of Interest: A New Approach, 18 U.Fla.L.Rev. 675 (1965).

[84] To choose examples sufficiently distant in time, compare, e.g., 12 Memoirs of John Quincy Adams ch.XIII, at 235 (C.Adams ed. 1877), quoted in Comment, Legislators as Private Attorneys: The Need for Legislative Reform, 30 UCLA L.Rev. 1052 (1983)("It occurs to me that this double capacity of a counsellor in courts of law and a member of a legislative body affords opportunity and temptation for contingent fees of a very questionable moral purity.")(letter of John Quincy Adams rejecting legal business), with, e.g., J.Kennedy, Profiles in Courage 53 (1960)(quoting letter from Senator Daniel Webster to president of Bank of the United States at same time that Senate was debating bank's charter: "my retainer has not been received or refreshed as usual.").

[85] Perkins, The New Federal Conflict-of-Interest Law, 76 Harv.L.Rev. 1209, 1210 (1963).

[86] 18 U.S.C.A. § 203 (members of Congress and other officers and employees of United States prohibited from receiving compensation for services rendered before any federal agency, but no similar restriction on federal court actions); Admin.Proc.Act, 5 U.S.C.A. § 501 (firm practicing before any agency of United States may not use name of member of Congress or other government employee in advertising); Georgia Dep't of Human Resources v. Sistrunk, 249 Ga. 543, 291 S.E.2d 524 (1982)(Georgia constitution, but not Code of Professional Responsibility, interpreted to prohibit part-time state legislator from representing for a fee any client in any civil proceeding in which state or one of its agencies is an opposing party); Office of Disciplinary Counsel v. Eilberg, 497 Pa. 388, 441 A.2d 1193 (1982)(member of Congress suspended for five years for violation of 18 U.S.C.A. § 203, supra); Reilly v. Ozzard, 33 N.J. 529, 166 A.2d 360, 89 A.L.R.2d 612 (1960) (lawyer-legislator who is also lawyer for municipality cannot engage in lobbying in behalf of the municipality because of the "dual offices" doctrine of state constitutional law); Or.Const. Art. 15, § 7 (lawyer-legislator may not represent individual in suit against state).

[87] ABA Informal Op. 1182 (1972) broadly interpreted the rule to allow a lawyer-legislator to accept a retainer from an electric utility that was the subject of legislation. If the lobbying is conducted before the very body of which the lawyer is a member, however, the potential for conflict is too acute to be tolerable. E.g., In re Shear, 72 N.J. 474, 371 A.2d 282 (1977).

[88] Cf., e.g., People v. Municipal Court (Wolfe), 69 Cal. App.3d 714, 138 Cal.Rptr. 235 (1977)(member of city council, which directly controlled salaries of individual police officers, should not represent defendants in criminal actions in which those employees appear as witnesses); People ex rel. Gallagher v. Hertz, 608 P.2d 335 (Colo. 1979)(office of district attorney is not "tribunal," and thus lawyer's use of public position to influence that office improperly did not violate DR 8–101(A)(2)).

from lobbying for a private client, apparently, so long as it is not "obvious that such action is not in the public interest." [89] The rule, obviously, would be difficult to violate.[90] To the extent that a lawyer-legislator is prohibited by the Code from representing a client, however, it is important for the lawyer to examine further the possible ramifications of DR 5–105(D) on entity disqualification of other members of the lawyer's firm, a topic examined at another point (§ 7.6).[91]

The approach of the Model Rules to lawyer-legislator conflicts, in MR 1.11(c), is uncharacteristically more general than that of the Code. The rule simply folds every lawyer, including a lawyer-legislator, who is a "public officer or employee" into a group of specific subrules on conflicts of interest that are examined elsewhere (§ 8.9).

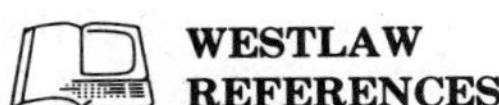

lawyer attorney /s legislator "public official" /p influen! (conflict /3 interest) % alcohol** chemical**

"ec 8–8" "dr 8–101(a)" dr8–101(a)

§ 13.9 GOVERNMENT LAWYERS

§ 13.9.1 *Legal Advisers and Policy Makers*

Ambiguity of the Role of Government Lawyer

As is true of corporate lawyers (§ 13.7), government lawyers sometimes occupy important yet highly ambiguous positions. Their role combines responsibility both for making and implementing policy choices and for taking legal steps such as filing or defending litigation. The ranks of government lawyers include full-time employees of governmental units and departments; elected or appointed officials with legal functions, such as an attorney general or a solicitor general; and private practitioners who are retained for consultation or litigation by a governmental body.

Nature of Employment [92]

The tenure of a government lawyer is a matter of statute, of regulation, and, if valid, of contract.[93] A limited kind of tenure is provided to government lawyers and other government employees under Supreme Court decisions protecting against dismissal of non-confidential employees for reasons of party affiliation.[94] An entirely different problem in many agencies is to retain able government lawyers against the lure of higher pay and

89 The pre-Code decision in In re Becker, 16 Ill.2d 488, 158 N.E.2d 753, 756–57 (1959), held that a member of the state legislature could appear as a lawyer in behalf of a client before an agency that was created and funded by the legislature so long as the agency's action in the individual matter was not subject to direct legislative review.

90 Cady, Canons to the Code of Professional Responsibility, 2 Conn.L.Rev. 222, 243–44 (1969).

91 See also ABA Formal Op. 306 (1962)(members of lawyer-legislator's law firm can represent clients before legislature to extent permitted by law), modifying ABA Formal Op. 296 (1959)(members of lawyer-legislator's firm may not represent client before legislative hearing committee while lawyer remains member of legislature).

92 See generally D.Horowitz, The Jurocracy: Government Lawyers, Agency Programs, and Judicial Decisions (1977).

93 Fiorentino v. United States, 221 Ct.Cl. 545, 607 F.2d 963 (1979), cert.denied 444 U.S. 1083, 100 S.Ct. 1039, 62 L.Ed.2d 768 (1980). Contra Paige v. Harris, 584 F.2d 178 (7th Cir.1978)(tenure by estoppel is constitutionally protected property right).

94 Branti v. Finkel, 445 U.S. 507, 100 S.Ct. 1287, 63 L.Ed.2d 574 (1980)(county assistant public defenders protected against firings for not belonging to political party in power); Elrod v. Burns, 427 U.S. 347, 96 S.Ct. 2673, 49 L.Ed.2d 547 (1976)(process servers, juvenile court bailiff, and security guard). The immunity against discharge does not apply, however, if the position is one of a policy-making and confidential nature, in which political affiliation is an appropriate requirement for the effective performance of the public office involved. Branti v. Finkel, supra, 445 U.S. at 517. But cf. Connick v. Myers, 461 U.S. 138, 103 S.Ct. 1684, 75 L.Ed.2d 708 (1983)(5–4 decision) (government lawyer's discharge constitutional if in interest of preventing disruption of office, undermining authority of superior, or destroying close working relationships).

greater prestige often associated with private practice, in which the lawyer's government experience can be an attractive asset.[95]

Statutes commonly prohibit full-time government lawyers from maintaining a private practice.[96] To the extent that a government lawyer is permitted to maintain a private practice, the lawyer must comply with restrictions against representations adverse to the governmental client[97] and with the lawyer code strictures against use of official power to assist a private practice client[98] and against impermissible conflicts of interest (§ 8.9.3).

Regulation of Government Lawyers

Government lawyers are subject in their professional work to statutes, regulations, and the lawyer codes. Also, uniquely among lawyers, they are government actors directly subject to state and federal constitutional limitations. The lawyer codes apply through one of several methods. Some government departments have adopted a lawyer code through agency action. Other agencies require that agency lawyers be admitted to practice in a state, which makes the lawyer code of the state applicable. Additional regulation or guidance on professional issues might be attempted by a bar association of government lawyers.[99]

Government lawyers who are admitted to practice by a state may be disciplined by the state's lawyer disciplinary agency.[1] A federal government lawyer may be disciplined by an agency of a state in which he or she was admitted.[2] Although rarely disciplined relative to their number, government lawyers who are convicted of a disciplinary violation can be visited with stern sanctions because of their asserted special duty to avoid transgressions.[3]

Lines of Authority

Who is the client of a government lawyer? The question, which seems straightforward, in fact disguises complexities that arise in very different settings, in many of which it should be given different answers. The question is most difficult to answer satisfactorily in the case of a policy-making position such as attorney general; it is relatively easily answered, and can be localized to a specific person who is the "client," in the case of a government lawyer whose responsibilities are either focused upon a single governmental agency or consist of representation of a specific individual, such as individual military personnel in military legal assistance programs.[4] The problem becomes most nettlesome when two governmental agencies come into conflict, perhaps in litigation, and each claims that the same government lawyer must represent its point of view or when two different government lawyers purport to be the higher or more legitimate representative of a single governmental agency.

95 Meredith Associates, Inc., Rep. to the FTC: Attorney and Attorney Manager Recruitment, Selection and Retention (1976); Solomon, Practice of Law in the Federal Government—Career or Training Ground?, 38 Geo.Wash. L.Rev. 753 (1970). On the conflict of interest problems of former government lawyers who have passed through the "revolving door" into private practice, see § 8.10.

96 Madera v. Gendron, 59 Cal.2d 798, 31 Cal.Rptr. 302, 382 P.2d 342, 6 A.L.R.3d 555 (1963).

97 18 U.S.C.A. § 205 (lawyer employed by federal government may not appear adversely to United States or the District of Columbia or to any of their agencies).

98 DR 8–101(A)(2).

99 Poirier, The Federal Government Lawyer and Professional Responsibility, 60 ABA J. 1541 (1974)(reprinting text of "Federal Ethical Considerations," adopted as adjuncts to 1969 Code by National Council of Federal Bar Association in 1973).

1 The question of separation of powers raised by the use of judicial power to discipline employees of other branches of government has not been raised. Cf. § 2.2.3—inherent powers—negative.

2 In re Lotito, 250 Ga. 537, 299 S.E.2d 559 (1983)(federal lawyer suspended for federal court conviction of cocaine possession); Robinson v. Grievance Committee, 70 A.D.2d 209, 420 N.Y.S.2d 430 (1979), cert.denied 449 U.S. 830, 101 S.Ct. 97, 66 L.Ed.2d 34 (1980)(former assistant United States attorney in District of Columbia disbarred in New York for selling confidential information about pending criminal investigations to persons thought to be members of organized crime).

3 In re Lotito, 250 Ga. 537, 299 S.E.2d 559 (1983)(Justice Department lawyer convicted of cocaine possession given enhanced sanction because he occupied "public office" and discharged "public responsibility").

4 ABA Formal Op. 343 (1977).

Statutes sometimes attempt to provide a chain-of-command structure for legal representation within a government. Thus state law may provide that the state's attorney general is the highest-ranking legal officer, in whose name all legal proceedings are to be taken with ultimate control over those proceedings, even if the state in fact is represented by specially retained private counsel in a particular case.[5] Similarly, a lower-ranking government lawyer may be required to proceed in handling a legal matter as directed by a supervising lawyer. That direction is legitimate, so far as the lawyer codes are concerned, unless the direction is to proceed in a way that violates the lawyer code itself.[6]

Interagency Conflict

Interagency conflict can arise when two agencies cannot agree on the disposition of a legal issue and, consequently, cannot agree on how to direct a lawyer performing legal services for both agencies.[7] Variations on the issue involve such perennial difficulties as whether a state's attorney general can challenge the constitutionality of enactments of the state legislature or, relatedly, whether a state officer can require a state's attorney general to provide representation despite the opinion of the attorney general that the position of the officer is not legally tenable.[8] The situations tend to proliferate when an election changes the political party of an administration, leaving some entrenched lawyers of the former administration in protected offices, or when an elected lawyer-politician is of a different party from an elected executive officer. On nonconstitutional issues some states require that an attorney general conduct litigation to which an agency is a party as directed by the responsible officers of the agency.[9] If an agency wishes, and is authorized to do so, it may appear in litigation represented by its own in-house lawyer rather than rely upon the services of an attorney general who is unsympathetic to its position.[10] In the federal government, however, the power to initiate and settle lawsuits and to decide whether to appeal adverse decisions is vested generally and exclusively in the attorney general.[11]

Legal Authority of Government Legal Offices

Related to the issues raised in interagency conflicts are questions of the authority of a government lawyer. Traditional offices, such as that of attorney general or solicitor general, can derive scope and limits of authority from tradition, such as the common law.[12] But in some states the duties and powers of

[5] Beedenbender v. State, 100 Miss.2d 482, 419 N.Y.S.2d 838 (N.Y.Ct.Cl.1979).

[6] MR 5.2. Similarly, the supervisory lawyer has responsibility to see that a subordinate lawyer complies with the lawyer code. MR 5.1 comment (first paragraph). Cf. EC 7–14 (implicit assumption that government lawyer without discretionary powers should "advise his superiors and recommend the avoidance of unfair litigation" but abide by their decision if they determine to press ahead).

[7] President Carter established a Federal Legal Council under which it was encouraged to submit legal disputes between agencies to the Attorney General for resolution. Exec.Order No. 12146, 3 C.F.R. 4090 (1980)(Exec. Order No. 12,146; July 18, 1979).

[8] Manchin v. Browning, 296 S.E.2d 909 (W.Va.1982) (secretary of state can compel attorney general to take position, in litigation against the secretary by a private citizen, that reapportionment statute is unconstitutional).

[9] Motor Club of Iowa v. Dept. of Transp., 251 N.W.2d 510 (Iowa 1977); Fitzgerald v. Baxter State Park Authority, 385 A.2d 189 (Me.1978).

[10] State ex rel. Howard v. Oklahoma Corp. Comm'n, 614 P.2d 45 (Okla.1980).

[11] 28 U.S.C.A. §§ 516–519; Confiscation Cases, 74 U.S. (7 Wall.) 454, 458, 19 L.Ed. 196 (1868); Interstate Commerce Comm'n v. Southern Ry., 543 F.2d 534 (5th Cir. 1976). Federal regulations provide for the solicitation of the views of affected agencies. 28 C.F.R. § 0.168(a)(1984). The relationships between the Justice Department, the United States attorneys, and federal agencies are examined in J.Eisenstein, Counsel for the United States: U.S. Attorneys in the Political and Legal Systems (1978). Occasionally Congress has conferred upon an agency or its lawyers the power to control litigation in which it has an interest and over which the attorney general accordingly has no authority. E.g., S&E Contractors, Inc. v. United States, 406 U.S. 1, 92 S.Ct. 1411, 31 L.Ed.2d 658 (1972).

[12] Island-Gentry Joint Venture v. State, 57 Haw. 259, 554 P.2d 761 (1976)(control of settlement of eminent domain action against state); Nat'l Ass'n Attys.Gen. Comm. on Off. of Atty.Gen., Common Law Powers of State Attorneys General (1975). A familiar example is the common-law power of a state's attorney general to inquire into the operation of public charities under the doctrine of cy pres. E.g., Oleksy v. Sisters of Mercy, 74 Mich.App. 374, 253 N.W.2d 772 (1977); Israel v. National

legal officers such as the attorney general are defined by statutory law and cannot be expanded by resort to common law.[13] In general a single government lawyer of inferior rank has no power to bind the government or a governmental agency.[14] That authority resides either in the highest-ranking legal officer responsible for the matter or in the head of the agency.[15]

WESTLAW REFERENCES

branti /12 100 +4 1287 /p political!

§ 13.9.2 *Discretion of Government Lawyers*

Regulation of Government Lawyers by Professional Codes

Both professional regulations and other law speak of the discretion exercised by government lawyers, although with different emphases. The law provides generally that a government lawyer entrusted with responsibility to take legal action, such as deciding whether to file or defend lawsuits, has a power that is discretionary.[16] An exercise of that discretion, as illustrated by the awesome power of a prosecutor to decide whether or not to file charges against a suspect (§ 13.10), is reviewable at the instance of a person allegedly aggrieved by the officer's action or inaction only for clear abuse. A government lawyer appointed or elected through a political party apparatus will obviously have in mind political considerations in determining how to order budgetary and personnel priorities.[17] But to what extent is a government lawyer properly held to account, under the law of professional regulation, for an arguably questionable exercise of discretion, either in addition to or quite beyond whatever remedies are provided by other law?

At this point in some discussions of the exercise of discretion by government lawyers, one common approach is to attempt to analogize a government lawyer's work to that of a lawyer in private practice and to attempt to identify the lawyer's governmental "client."[18] Various candidates are offered, such as the "government;"[19] the lawyer's "agency;"[20] the "head" of the agency;[21] the lawyer's "immediate superior," whoever has the power to

Board of YMCA, 117 R.I. 614, 369 A.2d 646 (1977); 4 A.Scott, Trusts § 391 (3d ed.1967). Doctrinally, the question of the extent of the powers and discretion of an attorney general is said to turn on the question whether the particular office carries the extensive common-law powers conferred on that office in England (as in the federal government) or whether state law circumscribes those powers and provides other, more limited responsibilities and powers. E.g., Manchin v. Browning, supra n.8.

13 Gillies v. Schmidt, 38 Colo.App. 233, 556 P.2d 82, 87 (1976).

14 United States v. Beebe, 180 U.S. 343, 21 S.Ct. 371, 45 L.Ed. 563 (1901)(United States not bound by unauthorized compromise of civil suit by assistant United States attorney); United States v. Schine, 260 F.2d 552, 557 (2d Cir. 1958), cert.denied 358 U.S. 934, 79 S.Ct. 318, 3 L.Ed.2d 306 (1959); United States v. Kates, 419 F.Supp. 846, 858 (E.D.Pa.1976).

15 The attorney general, for example, controls the institution of criminal litigation for the United States. E.g., United States v. Jackson, 433 F.Supp. 239 (W.D.N.Y. 1977), affirmed 586 F.2d 832 (2d Cir.1978), cert.denied 440 U.S. 913, 99 S.Ct. 1227, 59 L.Ed.2d 462 (1979). But the power to control litigation does not extend as far as warranting the attorney general or his or her subordinate lawyers to pass without further question upon all legal questions that might arise in the litigation. E.g., Investment Co. Institute v. Camp, 401 U.S. 617, 626–27, 91 S.Ct. 1091, 1097, 28 L.Ed.2d 367 (1971)(administrative officials and not appellate counsel are responsible for exercising expertise to elaborate and enforce statutory commands).

16 United States v. City of Chicago, 411 F.Supp. 218, 246 (N.D.Ill.1976), affirmed and reversed in part on other grounds 549 F.2d 415 (7th Cir.1977), cert.denied 436 U.S. 932, 98 S.Ct. 2832, 56 L.Ed.2d 777 (1978); Berge v. Gorton, 88 Wn.2d 756, 567 P.2d 187, 191 (1977).

17 Weinstein, Some Ethical and Political Problems of a Government Attorney, 18 Me.L.Rev. 155, 158–66 (1966).

18 See generally Lawry, Who Is the Client of the Federal Government Lawyer? An Analysis of the Wrong Question, 37 Fed.B.J. (Fall 1978), at 61.

19 MR 1.13 comment (Government Agency).

20 Professional Ethics Committee, Federal Bar Ass'n, Op. 73–1, 32 Fed.B.J. 71, 72 (1973)(government lawyer is to serve the "public interest sought to be served by the governmental organization of which he is a part"). Critiquing that view, e.g., Schnapper, Legal Ethics and the Government Lawyer, 32 Rec. Ass'n B. City N.Y. 649 (1977).

21 Carlock, The Lawyer in Government, in Listen to the Leaders in Law 255, 268–69 (1963).

hire and fire;[22] or the "people."[23] Another, related approach is to abandon the "who is the client" inquiry and to posit that the role of the government lawyer is to serve "good government in and of itself,"[24] the "public interest,"[25] "justice,"[26] or a similar abstraction that is not tied to a particular entity.

An able government lawyer so disposed can undoubtedly do much that is praiseworthy and beneficial to the public weal by offering advice to public administrators on matters of public policy.[27] But which of the entities and abstractions listed above are to serve as the working guide by which a government lawyer should exercise judgment, and by which of those guides should a lawyer be led if the lawyer believes that advice rejected by an administrator should have been accepted? The answer, it is submitted, is that it depends. Distinctions must be drawn between the ordinary and the extraordinary, between some kinds of reasons for balking and others, and between levels of responsibility and authority within government.

The Heightened Obligation of Fairness

Decisions abound in which an action by a government lawyer has been criticized because, although it would have been acceptable for a lawyer for a private-practice client to take the step in question, a government lawyer is said to owe a higher standard of discretionary fairness than do private lawyers.[28] Sometimes that is put on the ground that a government is a powerful litigant and is in a position to employ the sheer force of superior resources to gain a legal advantage against an adversary.[29] The rationale is questionable in some instances because of what in fact may be severe restrictions on government legal budgets and, to the extent it is true, because it has not served as a limitation on advocates for very wealthy litigants in private practice. A sounder rationale is that a lesser standard erodes citizen confidence in the fairness of government and that all citizens are entitled to fairness in dealing with a government whose measures they are asked to support and obey. As such, that is a rationale for limits on all exercises of governmental discretion and not just of lawyerly discretion, although it certainly includes that as well.

What "fairness" requires of a government lawyer that is different from what is required of a lawyer representing a nongovernmental client is, of course, a large and, in part, debatable question. Fairness certainly requires considerable restraint in the use of strategies in litigation that a government lawyer de-

[22] Ass'n B. City N.Y., Professional Responsibility of the Lawyer: The Murky Divide between Right and Wrong 111 (1976); Comment, The Litigation Function of the Iowa Attorney General, 63 Iowa L.Rev. 1264 (1978).

[23] Support for selection of one of those abstractions, but no guidance as to which specifically, is given in EC 5–18 which provides that a lawyer representing a corporation "or similar entity" represents the entity and not any constituency in the entity. See § 13.7.2.

[24] Note, Conflicts of Interest in the Legal Profession, 94 Harv.L.Rev. 1244, 1415 (1981).

[25] Lawry, Confidences and the Government Lawyer, 57 N.C.L.Rev. 625, 637 (1979). Cf. Model Rules, Scope (fourth paragraph).

[26] Cf. Professional Responsibility: Report of the Joint Conference, 44 ABA J. 1159, 1218 (1958)(government lawyer is "possessed of important governmental powers that are pledged to the accomplishment of one objective only, that of impartial justice"); but cf., e.g., A.C.L.U. Official Clashes with Prison Lawyers, 63 ABA J. 1365 (1977) (lawyer-director of law enforcement group, after noting that criminal defense lawyers do not adhere to standard of "do justice": "Is it because you are employed by a public agency that you're supposed to do justice?").

[27] Lasswell & McDougal, Legal Education and Public Policy: Professional Training in the Public Interest, 52 Yale L.J. 203, 208–211 (1943).

[28] May Dep't Stores Co. v. Williamson, 549 F.2d 1147, 1150 (8th Cir.1977)(Lay, J., concurring)(duty of Department of Justice not to engage in relitigation and forum shopping that is permissible for private litigants); Caleshu v. United States, 570 F.2d 711 (8th Cir.1978) (Ross, J., concurring)(criticism of tax authority lawyers for legal, but unreasonable, choice of forum); Zimmerman v. Schweiker, 575 F.Supp. 1436, 1440 (E.D.N.Y.1983) (if lawyer in private practice would have advised client not to defend claim, then "a fortiori" a government defense lawyer should do same); City of Los Angeles v. Decker, 18 Cal.3d 860, 135 Cal.Rptr. 647, 558 P.2d 545 (1977)(improper argument to jury based on facts of record but contrary to nonrecord facts known to government lawyer).

[29] EC 7–14; Christiansburg Garment Co. v. EEOC, 434 U.S. 412, 422–23 n.20, 98 S.Ct. 694, 700–01 n. 20, 54 L.Ed. 2d 648 (1978); EEOC v. Datapoint Corp., 457 F.Supp. 62, 65, n.10 (W.D.Tex.1978).

ploys simply to harass or delay, the use of questionable tactics when negotiating, and generally the resort to the hollow forms of the law rather than to their legitimating spirit. Also implicated, and imposing outer limits on fairness, are the principles of client loyalty and confidentiality. Those principles, as exemplified in the doctrines involving conflict of interest (§ 8.9) and confidential client information (§ 6.5.6), are discussed at other points.

Levels of authority and kinds of legal matters are implicated in various ways. For example, if a lawyer employed by a governmental agency files an answer to a complaint seeking damages for a claim that the lawyer knows is factually well founded and legally supportable (aside from its timeliness), the answer should include a legally available defense of statute of limitations, even if the lawyer's perception is that the defense in a particular instance would be unjust in a broader sense. The lawyer certainly should seek appropriate permission not to plead the defense but clearly should be bound by the direction of agency superiors. Different issues are involved when an attorney general, authorized to do so, must devise a policy to plead the statute of limitations in all suits in which the government is defending. Here the justice of applying the statute is one of the critical issues that must be confronted.

Whistle-Blowing

Some questions of the use of discretionary power by a government lawyer may be problematical. Others may be less difficult as matters of law, but personally highly charged. Suppose a subordinate lawyer in a government agency is participating in a confidential matter that the lawyer discovers involves a plot to commit an illegal break-in to the office of a psychiatrist for a politically disfavored citizen.[30] Most obviously, it is clear that the lawyer may not participate in the illegal act; government lawyers, certainly no less than lawyers in private practice, may not engage in illegal acts (§ 13.3.2). Certainly the lawyer may also attempt to persuade others who are in on the plot to desist. But may the lawyer report the intended crime to the attorney general, if he or she is also not a coconspirator, to members of Congress, or to the press in order to prevent it or, once the illegal act has occurred, to expose the perpetrators to public justice?

At least in dramatic terms, the most chilling question of personal responsibility is whether a government lawyer is ever entitled to divulge secret information in order to alert other government officials or the public to the known fact of illegal acts on the part of other government officers. The question, much debated in the wake of Watergate, raises fundamental questions about the nature of the relationship between government workers and their governmental and political superiors and about the immediate working milieu of which government lawyers are a part.

It is clear that the lawyer code rules on confidentiality apply to government lawyers, although the extent of the protection and its application to government clients is still quite undeveloped.[31] Generally, under the 1969 Code, the scope of confidentiality for government lawyers is much less than that under the 1983 Model Rules. The general exception of information about client illegality under the Code permits, and in some jurisdictions may require, that a government lawyer disclose wrongdoing by others in the government in a wide array of instances in which disclosure is prohibited under the Model Rules (§ 12.6.4). The comment to MR 1.13 indicates some liberality on the matter, but it probably

[30] The allusion, transparently, is to the break-in to the office of Dr. Lewis J. Fielding, the psychiatrist for Daniel Ellsberg, who had leaked the "Pentagon papers." The break-in was conducted by operatives of the Nixon administration in 1971. See generally United States v. Liddy, 542 F.2d 76 (D.C.Cir.1976).

[31] § 6.5.6. MR 1.6 comment (sixth paragraph)(added by amendment, Aug.1983): "The requirement of maintaining confidentiality of information relating to representation applies to government lawyers who may disagree with the policy goals that their representation is designed to advance." Much of the information volunteered by John Dean to congressional Watergate investigators prior to his testimony, for example, seems to fall afoul of the comment. Cf. MR 1.13 comment (Government Agency).

only applies to confidential discussions within the agency itself in a lawyer's attempt to obtain compliance with the law.[32]

WESTLAW REFERENCES

government** /3 lawyer attorney counsel** /s profession** /2 code

§ 13.10 PROSECUTORS

§ 13.10.1 Constituencies of Prosecutors

The duties of prosecutors span much more than half the theoretical realms of lawyerly responsibility within criminal law practice. They are the only governmental officers responsible for obtaining convictions of the guilty in litigated criminal cases; but they also bear alone the state's considerable responsibility to see that no innocent person is prosecuted, convicted, or punished. The dual role called for is in marked contrast to the nature of the defense function (§ 10.5.2).[33] The prosecutor's dual role leaves the office much nearer that of a judicial officer than that of partisan advocate.[34] Maintaining the "justice"-oriented stance that the dual role implies is one of the most psychologically difficult tasks that lawyers are asked to perform but, it is rigorously insisted upon both by the lawyer codes and by the courts (§ 13.10.3). As a corollary, prosecutors are under special duties to employ restraint in selecting cases and crime perpetrators for prosecution, in making the many other discretionary decisions about charges and recommended sentence, in employing tactics to advance the prosecution during trials, and in assuring that essential information useful to the defense is made available in a timely fashion.

Prosecutors' Constituencies

The office of prosecutor can best be conceptualized as a lawyer with no client but with several important constituencies.[35] The police are an important constituency,[36] although for most purposes individual police officers with whom a prosecutor holds confidential meetings are not the lawyer's client.[37] Victims of crime are also clearly not clients, although the demands of some victims for revenge or removal of an alleged offender from the streets, supported by public pressure inflamed by periodic media attention, may present strong pressure to prosecute. A trial

32 § 13.7.5.

33 Professional Responsibility: Report of the Joint Conference, 44 ABA J. 1159, 1218 (1958). The Joint Conference Report alludes to three rationales: (1) as an institutional matter, the prosecutor's power can be abused because of the absence of a client who can restrain the prosecutor; (2) abuse of prosecutorial powers erodes public confidence in the criminal law and raises questions about the legitimacy of all law; and (3) government has an ethical and political responsibility not to oppress citizens.

34 On the "quasi-judicial" label applied to prosecutors, see, e.g., State v. Chambers, 86 N.M. 383, 524 P.2d 999, 1002–1003, cert.denied 86 N.M. 372, 524 P.2d 988 (1974), and authorities cited. The phrase is not merely rhetorical. Courts have held that the quasi-judicial nature of a prosecutor's role may make the issuance of the writ of prohibition appropriate. E.g., McGinley v. Hynes, 51 N.Y.2d 116, 432 N.Y.S.2d 689, 412 N.E.2d 376, 16 A.L.R. 4th 102 (1980), cert.denied 450 U.S. 918, 101 S.Ct. 1364, 67 L.Ed.2d 344 (1981)(prosecutor's investigative role more that of police officer than quasi-judicial role assumed in prosecuting accused).

35 A barbaric exception is found in those few jurisdictions that continue to recognize the common-law institution of the private prosecutor, a lawyer in private practice hired by an alleged victim to bring or assist a criminal prosecution. E.g., State v. Atkins, 163 W.Va. 502, 261 S.E.2d 55 (1979), cert.denied 445 U.S. 904, 100 S.Ct. 1081, 63 L.Ed.2d 320 (1980). See also State v. Riser, 294 S.E.2d 461 (W.Va.1982)(in absence of contemporaneous objection, no error for private prosecutor hired by alleged victim to participate in criminal trial despite fact that he had also filed damage action against accused, apparently on contingent fee basis).

36 See generally J.Jacoby, The American Prosecutor 109–129 (1980). On relationships between U.S. attorneys and investigative agencies see generally J.Eisenstein, Counsel for the United States: U.S. Attorneys in the Political and Legal Systems ch. 8 (1978).

37 For example, a prosecutor cannot claim that police information supplied in confidence is protected by the privilege if the information is otherwise discoverable. Cf., e.g., Smith v. State, 465 N.E.2d 1105 (Ind.1984). But in suits not directly involving the interests of accused persons, a prosecutor who seeks the confidences of police when representing the state in a prosecution in which the defense asserts police misconduct, may not thereafter represent the city in seeking contribution against the police officers involved after a tort action based on the same misconduct is lost. E.g., ABA Inf.Op.1282 (1973); § 8.9.3 and authorities cited at nn. 22 & 23.

prosecutor's office often must rely upon another office for appellate services, such as the office of the state's attorney general, with whom good relations must be maintained and whose unwillingness to argue positions on appeal may constrain the way in which the trial office can function.

The prosecutor's office is also under more or less political pressure that varies with such factors as whether and by whom the chief prosecutor and deputies are appointed or elected, their tenure in office, and the source of the office's funding.[38] As an institution, almost every prosecutor's office is under constant pressure from the judiciary to reduce caseload and to arrange case schedules to expedite and lighten the judges' work. Often that must be accomplished within a severely limited budget, which sometimes means that prosecutors are only marginally prepared, at best, for the trial of routine cases.

Neither police, victims, judges, nor other government functionaries, however, can properly be regarded as the clients of a prosecutor. Government lawyers, as has previously been discussed (§ 13.9), are best regarded as having one client or another depending upon their particular role. The emotionally satisfying statement is that the client of every prosecutor is the public. A less emotive but more realistic conceptualization is that prosecutors in a position to make policy decisions should regard the public as their client, while prosecutors in subordinate roles should regard their superiors in the office as the effective client for matters on which office policy has been set or specific directions given, unless a superior directs a subordinate lawyer to violate the law or the professional rules.

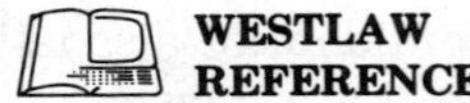
WESTLAW REFERENCES

di prosecutor
topic(110) /p "private prosecutor"
topic(45) /p prosecutor

§ 13.10.2 *Responsibilites of Prosecutors*

The general notion that a prosecutor has a duty to do justice and not to win cases is a truism often repeated but quite difficult to abide by as an emotional and professional matter. The locus classicus for discussion of the extraordinary duties of a prosecutor is Berger v. United States:[39]

> The United States Attorney is the representative not of an ordinary party to a controversy, but of a sovereignty whose obligation to govern impartially is as compelling as its obligation to govern at all; and whose interest, therefore, in a criminal prosecution is not that it shall win a case, but that justice shall be done. As such, he is in a peculiar and very definite sense the servant of the law, the twofold aim of which is that guilt shall not escape or innocence suffer. He may prosecute with earnestness and vigor—indeed, he should do so. But, while he may strike hard blows, he is not at liberty to strike foul ones. It is as much his duty to refrain from improper methods calculated to produce a wrongful conviction as it is to use every legitimate means to bring about a just one.

The duty of fairness applies even if the prosecutor strongly believes in good faith that the accused is guilty.[40] The duty is emphasized in the lawyer codes with respect to both charging decisions and evidence disclosure,[41] matters that will be discussed below.

Regulation of Prosecutors

Prosecutors are almost invariably lawyers[42] and, as such, are fully subject to the lawyer

[38] SEC v. Wheeling-Pittsburgh Steel Corp., 648 F.2d 118 (3d Cir.1981)(on facts, insufficient showing that U.S. senator had exerted impermissible pressure to initiate investigation of possible securities law violation).

[39] 295 U.S. 78, 88, 55 S.Ct. 629, 633, 79 L.Ed. 1314 (1935).

[40] State v. Sha, 292 Minn. 182, 193 N.W.2d 829 (1972).

[41] DR 7–103; EC 7–13; MR 3.8; Calif.R. 7–102. The title to DR 7–103 suggests that its rules apply to any lawyer "performing the duty of public prosecutor or other government lawyer." But the only duties mentioned have to do with criminal prosecution. A similarly broad title adorns Calif.R. 7–102, which is derived from DR 7–102.

[42] Phagan v. State ex rel. Eyssen, 510 S.W.2d 655 (Tex. Civ.App.1974)(judgment of disbarment against district attorney requires him to relinquish office). A distinctly minority view is that a public prosecutor is immune from

codes[43] and other law applicable in the jurisdiction. That includes the courts' power of contempt,[44] professional discipline,[45] and whatever other supervisory power the court possesses over all lawyers.[46] One finds, however, that prosecutors are relatively rarely subjected to professional discipline.[47] That probably does not reflect uniformly superior conduct as compared with defense counsel or lawyers in other roles. Instead, disciplinary agencies are probably reluctant to pursue complaints against prosecutors that may be motivated by resentment at convictions or that might be politically motivated by a desire to compromise the political power of the prosecutor's office.

Control of Prosecutors through Judicial Rulings

Lawyer disciplinary agencies may also note that much of the area of the lawyer codes applicable to a prosecutor's behavior is enforceable in the criminal proceeding itself as constitutional or statutory limitations on a prosecutor's permissible advocacy. For example, contact between a lawyer-prosecutor and an accused represented by counsel is not merely a violation of the lawyer codes (see § 11.6.2); it may also be a violation of the Constitution or other law for which sanctions can be imposed in the criminal proceeding itself.[48] Thus bar regulators might believe that prosecutorial breaches of the lawyer codes that do occur are sufficiently policed by reversals and new trials. The continuing appearance of judicial findings of prosecutor impropriety, however, suggests a lack of will on the part of disciplinary agencies. Little additional regulation is supplied by private actions for money damages, primarily because of a broad immunity from suit that prosecutors enjoy.[49] The prosecutor's office, therefore, may be one that is restrained only by ethical and moral considerations, by anticipation of failure in prosecutions,[50] and by a possible fear of engendering the outrage of a

disciplinary proceedings during his or her term of office. E.g., Simpson v. Alabama St. Bar, 294 Ala. 52, 311 So.2d 307 (1975)(bar association had no authority to discipline prosecutor during term of office for either official or nonofficial acts that violated the Code of Professional Responsiblity).

43 People v. Guerrero, 47 Cal.App.3d 441, 120 Cal.Rptr. 732 (1975); State v. Locklear, 294 N.C. 210, 241 S.E.2d 65 (1978). But see Burgett v. State, 646 S.W.2d 615 (Tex.Ct. App.1983)(Code's disciplinary rules apply in civil cases but not in criminal prosecutions if in conflict with statute). The ABA Prosecution Function Standards are not authoritative but merely advisory. E.g., State v. Annis, 114 Ariz. 464, 561 P.2d 1236 (App.1976).

44 Weiss v. Burr, 484 F.2d 973 (9th Cir.1973), cert.denied 414 U.S. 1161, 94 S.Ct. 924, 39 L.Ed.2d 115 (1974); Owen v. City Court, 123 Ariz. 267, 599 P.2d 223 (1979); State ex rel. Angel v. Woodahl, 171 Mont. 13, 555 P.2d 501 (1976); In re Levine, 372 Pa. 612, 95 A.2d 222 (1953), cert.denied, 346 U.S. 858, 74 S.Ct. 72, 98 L.Ed. 371 (1953).

45 Price v. State Bar, 30 Cal.3d 537, 179 Cal.Rptr. 914, 638 P.2d 1311 (1982)(discipline for altering trial evidence and negotiating directly with accused for favored treatment after conviction in return for promise of accused not to reveal alteration); In re Friedman, 76 Ill.2d 392, 30 Ill.Dec. 288, 392 N.E.2d 1333, 10 A.L.R.4th 589 (1979); In re Barnes, 281 Or. 375, 574 P.2d 657 (1978)(discipline for failure to make full disclosure to judge in ex parte application for search warrant); In re Shafir, 92 N.J. 138, 455 A.2d 1114 (1983)(discipline for falsifying office records in order to justify proposed plea bargain to superior); In re Weishoff, 75 N.J. 326, 382 A.2d 632 (1978)(suspension of former prosecutor for ticket fixing); In re Wolfson, 82 A.D.2d 587, 442 N.Y.S.2d 548 (1981)(conviction of selling marijuana).

46 United States v. Baskes, 442 F.Supp. 322 (N.D.Ill. 1977); In re FMC Corp., 430 F.Supp. 1108, 1110 (S.D.W. Va.1977); People v. Superior Court, 19 Cal.3d 255, 137 Cal.Rptr. 476, 561 P.2d 1164 (1977).

47 N.Dorsen & L.Friedman, Disorder in Court 187 (1973); Alschuler, Courtroom Misconduct by Prosecutors and Trial Judges, 50 Texas L.Rev. 629, 670–75 (1972).

48 Massiah v. United States, 377 U.S. 201, 84 S.Ct. 1199, 12 L.Ed.2d 246 (1964). As another example, a prosecutor's failure to use due diligence to produce a witness for trial not only violates EC 7–13 but may violate the confrontation clause of the Fifth Amendment. E.g., People v. Payne, 30 Ill.App.3d 624, 332 N.E.2d 745 (1975); State v. Keairns, 9 Ohio St.3d 228, 460 N.E.2d 245 (1984).

49 Imbler v. Pachtman, 424 U.S. 409, 96 S.Ct. 984, 47 L.Ed.2d 128 (1976). *Imbler* was based, in part, on the rationale that professional discipline supplied an effective remedy for a prosecutor's wrongful and injurious conduct toward an accused person. See 424 U.S. at 428–29. But discipline is rarely visited on prosecutors. See supra n.47.

50 The jury may serve a function of protecting against prosecutorial arbitrariness. E.g., Ludwig v. Massachusetts, 427 U.S. 618, 96 S.Ct. 2781, 49 L.Ed.2d 732 (1976). While the theoretical power of judges to review exercises of prosecutorial discretion are limited (see infra n. 59), individual judges can temper prosecutorial overzealousness through their own discretionary rulings and findings.

community for egregious offenses against the sense of public decency.

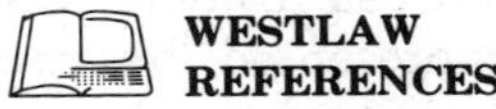

WESTLAW REFERENCES

berger /12 55 +4 629 /p prosecutor*** /s duty responsibility

---

§ 13.10.3 *Prosecutorial Discretion* [51]

Prosecutors and the Shaping of Criminal Law Enforcement

The operational definition of citizen conduct that is criminal depends on decisions, whether wise ones or not, made by a prosecutor.[52] The prosecutor's discretion in some jurisdictions includes the ultimate power of life or death, because of the prosecutor's power to select cases in which to request the death penalty.[53] Through discretionary plea bargaining [54] and grants of immunity from prosecution in exchange for testimony,[55] a prosecutor can bestow extraordinarily important benefits on persons who are thereby coerced into cooperation with the prosecutor. "There is no doubt that the breadth of discretion that our country's legal system vests in prosecuting attorneys carries with it the potential for both individual and institutional abuse." [56] Because of those awesome powers, most jurisdictions limit the initiation of prosecutions to lawyers specifically authorized to proceed as prosecutors [57] and incapacitate private citizens from bringing a criminal prosecution.[58] Courts generally take the position that they can play only a strictly limited role in reviewing a prosecutor's exercise of discretion because of the constitutionally required separation of powers of the executive and the judiciary.[59]

51 See generally F.Miller, Prosecution (1970); Friedman, The Prosecutor: A Model for Role and Function, 1978 Wash.U.L.Rev. 109; Cox, Prosecutorial Discretion: An Overview, 13 Am.Crim.L.Rev. 383 (1975).

52 "The prosecutor has more control over life, liberty, and reputation than any other person in America." Robert H. Jackson, The Federal Prosecutor, 24 J.Am.Jud. Soc'y 18, 18 (1940). See also Confiscation Cases, 74 U.S. (7 Wall.) 454, 19 L.Ed. 196 (1868); United States v. Nixon, 418 U.S. 683, 94 S.Ct. 3090, 41 L.Ed.2d 1039 (1974); United States v. Cox, 342 F.2d 167, 171 (5th Cir.), cert.denied, 381 U.S. 935, 85 S.Ct. 1767, 14 L.Ed.2d 700 (1965).

53 C.Black, Capital Punishment: The Inevitability of Caprice and Mistake 15, 37–44 (1974); Bedau, Witness to a Prosecution: The Death Penalty and the Dawson Five, 8 Black L.J. 7, 25–28 (1983). Surely a prosecutor possesses no more awesome power than that of plea bargaining in death penalty cases. See the several opinions in Jurek v. Texas, 428 U.S. 262, 96 S.Ct. 2950, 49 L.Ed.2d 929 (1976).

54 § 13.10.6.

55 18 U.S.C.A. § 6003 (United States attorney may determine whether immunity should be granted because immunized testimony is "necessary to the public interest").

56 Bordenkircher v. Hayes, 434 U.S. 357, 365, 98 S.Ct. 663, 54 L.Ed.2d 604 (1978) (footnote omitted).

57 28 U.S.C.A. § 547(1)(authority of United States attorneys to prosecute); F.R.Crim.Proc. 6(d)(only "attorneys for the government" may be present at sessions of grand jury); United States v. Prueitt, 540 F.2d 995 (9th Cir. 1976), cert.denied 429 U.S. 1063, 97 S.Ct. 790, 50 L.Ed.2d 780 (1977)(scope of powers of lawyer specially appointed to prosecute under 28 U.S.C.A. § 515(a); People v. Municipal Court, 27 Cal.App.3d 193, 103 Cal.Rptr. 645, 66 A.L.R.3d 717 (1972) (vacating lower court order authorizing private lawyer to act as special prosecutor when district attorney's office refused to file complaint). In England decisions to prosecute are made by the police. E.g., A.Wilcox, The Decision to Prosecute (1972).

58 Prosecution Function Standards § 3–2.1 (approved 1979); Comment, Private Prosecution: A Remedy for District Attorneys' Unwarranted Action, 65 Yale L.J. 209, 218–22 (1955).

59 The Supreme Court has recently reaffirmed the doctrine that the executive branch, and not the courts, is responsible for initiating criminal prosecutions and, subject to constitutional constraints, determining which offenses shall be prosecuted and charges filed, Garrett v. United States, ___ U.S. ___, 105 S.Ct. 2407, 85 L.Ed.2d 764 (1985), and which offenders shall be prosecuted, Wayte v. United States, ___ U.S. ___, 105 S.Ct. 1524, 84 L.Ed.2d 547 (1985)(government's policy of "passive enforcement" of draft registration law that resulted in prosecutions only of self-proclaimed nonregistrants or of nonregistrants reported by others did not violate First Amendment free speech or Fifth Amendment due process rights of accused persons). See also, e.g., Newman v. United States, 127 U.S.App.D.C. 263, 382 F.2d 479, 480 (1967); United States v. Cox, 342 F.2d 167, 171 (5th Cir. 1965), cert.denied 381 U.S. 935, 85 S.Ct. 1767, 14 L.Ed.2d 700 (1965); State ex rel. Hamstead v. Dostert, 313 S.E.2d 409 (W.Va.1984). That view has been challenged, most notably in 2 K.Davis, Administrative Law Treatise 278–80 (2d ed.1978); K.Davis, Discretionary Justice: A Preliminary Inquiry (1969); Gifford, Equal Protection and the Prosecutor's Charging Decision: Enforcing an Ideal, 49 Geo.Wash.L.Rev. 659 (1981); Frase, The Decision to File Federal Criminal Charges: A Quantitative Study of Prosecutorial Discretion, 47 U.Chi.L.Rev. 246, 299–301 (1980).

Charging Decisions

Theoretically it is possible to imagine that a prosecutor's discretion might be unlimited, nonexistent, or some intermediate third state of partial limitation. With unlimited discretion, the prosecutor could bring any charge for any reason, regardless of the presence or absence of facts and law supporting prosecution or regardless of the prosecutor's subjective reasons for selecting a particular defendant for prosecution. That, of course, defines a realm of official lawlessness envisioned by Kafka's imagination[60] and suffered by subjects of dictatorships. But the second, and diametrically opposite regime, a legal system that attempted to withhold all discretion from prosecutors, would be unworkable. It would be naive and impossible to require a prosecutor to prosecute every person who fits within statutory definitions of criminal conduct. The statutes defining crime are necessarily too general, the public resources devoted to prosecution too limited, and the need for wise discretion and mercy in the application of the criminal law too great.

Probable Cause

The problem, then, has been to delineate what a prosecutor may legitimately take into account about society, about an individual, and about the individual's acts in deciding whether or not to prosecute. A standard describing the legitimate exercise of discretion must generally require a prosecutor to charge an accused with crime only when the prosecutor can support the charge with a valid statute and with facts available in the form of apparently admissible evidence.[61]

The lawyer codes all express a similar requirement in their restriction that a prosecutor may not prosecute if he or she "knows" that "probable cause" does not support a prosecution.[62] The requirement should be enforced as a continuing one; if at any point the prosecutor becomes aware of the fact that evidence is no longer available to support a prima facie case, the now unsupported offenses should be dropped.[63] The Code, in DR 7–103(A), but not MR 3.8(a) or Prosecution Function Standard 3–3.9(a), goes on to provide that a prosecutor's initiation of charges is also impermissible when "it is obvious" that probable cause is lacking. In other words, the Code apparently requires that good cause be measured by both subjective and objective standards. For example, a prosecutor who subjectively believes that probable cause exists only because he or she is too busy to realize that a prosecution is not thus supported violates the rule. Presumably, however, the Code requires no more than a reasonable investigation of all available information and legal material normally consulted. Further important refinements of standard are necessary, such as on the questions of the prosecutor's subjective motivation for bringing charges and on the question of the relevance of the prosecutor's subjective beliefs about guilt or innocence.

Improper Motives

Should it matter that a prosecutor selects a particular offender for prosecution for improper reasons such as race, religion, or political beliefs or because of public clamor, if in fact there is ample evidence to sustain a charge that the offender violated a valid criminal statute? The cautious answer of the

60 Franz Kafka, The Trial (W. & E. Muir trans.1969).

61 DR 7–103(A); MR 3.8(a); Calif.R. 7–102; Prosecution Function Standards § 3–3.9 (approved 1979).

62 Only in rare instances has a prosecutor been publicly disciplined for breach of the obligation to prosecute only on probable cause. E.g., In re Gonyo, 73 Wis.2d 624, 245 N.W.2d 893 (1976). Some would require that the prosecutor be personally convinced that the accused is guilty beyond a reasonable doubt. E.g., M.Freedman, Lawyers' Ethics in an Adversary System 85–88 (1975). See also Kaplan, The Prosecutorial Discretion—A Comment, 60 Nw.L.Rev. 174, 178–79 (1965); Nadjari, Panel Discussion: Professional Responsibility in the Practice of Criminal Law, in Professional Responsibility of the Lawyer: The Murky Divide between Right and Wrong 62 (1976).

63 Roehl v. State, 77 Wis.2d 398, 253 N.W.2d 210 (1977) (misconduct for prosecutor to read indictment to jury containing three charges that could only be sustained on testimony of witnesses prosecutor knew were unavailable for trial).

courts has been that such selective prosecution, if proven, can lead to dismissal of the charges.[64] The leading case is Yick Wo v. Hopkins,[65] an 1886 decision in which the Supreme Court reversed the conviction of a Chinese person for operating a laundry without a license because the record showed that almost all Chinese who applied for a license were refused, while almost all non-Chinese applicants were granted licenses. As was true in *Yick Wo*, the fact that the accused is guilty of the substantive offense is irrelevant; discriminatorily selective prosecution is a complete defense.[66] A related and also impermissible form of arbitrariness is filing charges vindictively, for example, because the accused has exercised a constitutional[67] or statutory[68] right.[69] But rarely will arbitrary enforcement of the law be so clearly evident. Most forms of discrimination or vindictiveness are far more subtle and insidious[70] and most practitioners of discrimination too crafty to leave clear evidence.

Appropriate Factors in Exercising Discretion

Notwithstanding the rightful indignation of courts at arbitrary prosecution decisions, a prosecutor may and must rely on individuating factors in making a wise decision whether to charge.[71] A prosecutor's perception that an offender is particularly dangerous or that a kind of criminal activity or actor is particularly susceptible to deterrence should be an acceptable basis for selecting defendants and charges. It is generally agreed that those and similar factors can legitimately be taken into account in both plea bargaining and in deciding whether and what offenses to charge in the first place.[72] A variation on the problem is encountered when a prosecutor decides to charge with tax evasion a suspected profes-

[64] A concern with selective prosecution confined to a particular prosecutor may more approppropriately lead to recusal of the prosecutor who suffers the disabling bias. E.g., People v. Superior Court, 19 Cal.3d 255, 137 Cal. Rptr. 476, 561 P.2d 1164 (1977)(recusal of district attorney in murder case involving victim who was child of employee of office). Recusal of the prosecutor would be proper in any case in which the accused was a former client and the prosecution involved a substantially related matter or in which the defendant and the prosecutor were embroiled in simultaneous civil litigation. See §§ 8.9.4, 8.9.5; Ganger v. Peyton, 379 F.2d 709 (4th Cir. 1967). A court may prevent prosecutorial harassment in the form of filing charges without bringing them to trial by denying a motion by the prosecutor to nolle prosequi filed charges. Cf. Rinaldi v. United States, 434 U.S. 22, 98 S.Ct. 81, 54 L.Ed.2d 207 (1977)(dicta); United States v. Hamm, 659 F.2d 624 (5th Cir.1981)(en banc)(dicta). In one case in which the court found that a prosecutor had brought charges in bad faith and probably for publicity, the court enjoined the prosecution. Shaw v. Garrison, 467 F.2d 113 (5th Cir.1972), cert.denied 409 U.S. 1024, 93 S.Ct. 467, 34 L.Ed.2d 317 (1972)(federal injunction against state court prosecution for perjury of accused who had successfully defended himself against former prosecution for involvement in attempt to assassinate President Kennedy).

[65] 118 U.S. 356, 6 S.Ct. 1064, 31 L.Ed. 220 (1886). Leading modern cases include United States v. Berrios, 501 F.2d 1207 (2d Cir.1974); United States v. Falk, 479 F.2d 616 (7th Cir. 1973).

[66] Oyler v. Boles, 368 U.S. 448, 456, 82 S.Ct. 501, 505, 7 L.Ed.2d 446 (1962); Two Guys from Harrison-Allentown, Inc. v. McGinley, 366 U.S. 582, 588, 81 S.Ct. 1135, 6 L.Ed. 2d 551 (1961). See generally Annot., 95 A.L.R.3d 280 (1979); Annot., 45 A.L.R.Fed. 732 (1979). Another form of impermissible criteria for prosecuting is encapsulated in the concept of *vindictiveness* in prosecution, as in adding charges to an indictment to punish a defendant who elects a constitutional right to jury trial. See generally Schwartz, The Limits of Prosecutorial Vindictiveness, 69 Iowa L.Rev. 127 (1983).

[67] Blackledge v. Perry, 417 U.S. 21, 94 S.Ct. 2098, 40 L.Ed.2d 628 (1974); North Carolina v. Pearce, 395 U.S. 711, 89 S.Ct. 2072, 23 L.Ed.2d 656 (1969). Cf., Bordenkircher v. Hayes, 434 U.S. 357, 98 S.Ct. 663, 54 L.Ed.2d 604 (1978); United States v. Goodwin, 457 U.S. 368, 102 S.Ct. 2485, 73 L.Ed.2d 74 (1982).

[68] United States v. DeMarco, 550 F.2d 1224 (9th Cir. 1977)(appearance of vindictiveness for exercise of statutory venue rights requires dismissal of charges).

[69] Impermissible prosecutorial vindictiveness would also require dismissal if it could be demonstrated clearly that a lawyer extensively engaged in criminal defense work was charged with an offense in retaliation for prior successful defenses. Cf. United States v. Blitstein, 626 F.2d 774 (10th Cir.1980), cert.denied 449 U.S. 1102, 101 S.Ct. 898, 66 L.Ed.2d 828 (1981)(charge of vindictive prosecution not sustained).

[70] Some sources of improper motivation may be institutional. A few jurisdictions, for example, retain statutory authorization for the compensation of public prosecutors on a case-by-case basis, which creates economic incentives to overprosecute. See ABA Prosecution Function Standards § 2.3(e) commentary at 62 (1971).

[71] See generally F.Miller, Prosecution: The Decision to Charge a Suspect with a Crime 173–280 (1974).

[72] Uviller, The Virtuous Prosecutor in Quest of an Ethical Standard: Guidance from the ABA, 71 Mich.L. Rev. 1145, 1148 (1973).

sional criminal whose membership in the crime business is not itself provable. The hypothetical instance really is merely an illustration of the general truth that a prosecutor's discretion often and necessarily will be based on factors that themselves are not demonstrably true with the same certainty as is guilt of the offense charged. Scholars generally agree that the prosecutor's decision to prosecute vigorously is legitimate here.[73]

The Role of Personal Knowledge

A different question is whether a prosecutor may permissibly charge a suspect so long as there is sufficient evidence to support a probable-cause finding, with a crime that the prosecutor personally believes was not committed. There is a distinction between the objective state of the evidence and a prosecutor's personal evaluation of it—for example, a prosecutor's personal belief that a favorable witness is lying or mistaken. As a matter of DR 7–103(A), it has been held that only an objective test should be applied.[74] But if the evidence is clear that a prosecutor has pursued charges despite personal knowledge that the accused was innocent,[75] it seems intolerable to permit the appearance of probable cause merely on paper to affirm the validity of the exercise of discretion. Empirically it probably is true that the great majority of prosecutors file charges only if personally convinced through operation of the screening process of the police and the prosecutor that the accused is guilty of the offense charged.[76]

WESTLAW REFERENCES

bordenkircher /12 98 +4 663 /p prosecutor*** /s discretion***

"probable cause" /s prosecutor*** /s discretion***

"dr 7–103(a)" dr7–103(a) /p prosecut!

§ 13.10.4 Prosecutors and Advocacy

Litigation Tactics[77]

The most striking difference between a prosecutor and a defense lawyer or any nongovernmental lawyer is that a prosecutor is much more constrained as an advocate. The assigned objective of a partisan advocate is to obtain litigational success for his or her client, to "win." The prosecutor's required objective is emphatically different. It is to secure the result, whether conviction or acquittal, indicated by a good faith inspection of the facts and the law.[78] That is not necessarily "winning" in the conventional sense of litigation, obtaining convictions to add to a lifetime total of victories and defeats.[79] Justice Douglas put the matter more forcefully:[80]

> The function of the prosecutor under the Federal Constitution is not to tack as many skins of victims as possible to the wall. His function is to vindicate the right of people as expressed in the laws and give those accused of crime a fair trial.

[73] Uviller, supra; M.Freedman, Lawyers' Ethics in an Adversary System 85 (1975). Cf. Prosecution Function Standards § 3.9 commentary (b), at 94 (1971 ed.).

[74] In re Burrows, 291 Or. 135, 629 P.2d 820, 22 A.L.R.4th 96 (1981)(action of judge at preliminary hearing binding accused over for trial necessarily establishes "probable cause" under DR 7–103(A)).

[75] J.Goulden, The Benchwarmers 382 (1974)(allegation that prosecutor of Charles Chaplin for paternity crime pressed charges, despite knowledge that Chaplin was innocent, in order to rebut false public charges that prosecutor had been bribed to discontinue case).

[76] Kaplan, The Prosecutorial Discretion—A Comment, 60 Nw.U.L.Rev. 174, 178 (1965). Another approach is theoretically possible, so long as the prosecutor is candid. As envisioned by the 1898 Alabama Code of Ethics, if a prosecutor is doubtful about guilt but is not confident about the need for a nolle prosequi, the prosecutor could be directed to "submit the case, with such comments as are pertinent, accompanied by a candid statement of his own doubts." Ala.Code Ethics § 12, 118 Ala. xxiii, xxvii (1898). The approach seems not to have been widely employed.

[77] See generally ABA Prosecution Function Standards §§ 3–5.2—3–5.9 (2d ed.1979); Alschuler, Courtroom Misconduct by Prosecutors and Trial Judges, 50 Texas L.Rev. 629 (1972).

[78] United States v. Wade, 388 U.S. 218, 87 S.Ct. 1926, 1947, 18 L.Ed.2d 1149 (1967)(Clark, J., concurring). The prosecutor's role is similarly defined in both England and Canada. E.g., Rex v. Banks, [1916] 2 K.B. 621 (England); Savage, The Duties and Conduct of Crown and Defence Counsel in a Criminal Trial, 1 Crim.L.Q. 164 (1958).

[79] People v. Speaks, 156 Cal.App.2d 25, 319 P.2d 709 (1957).

[80] Donnelly v. DeChristoforo, 416 U.S. 637, 648–49, 94 S.Ct. 1868, 1873–79, 40 L.Ed.2d 431 (1974).

Yet the more conscientious a prosecutor is in reaching a decision that charges against a suspect are well deserved, the more difficult it may be for a prosecutor to proceed through pretrial and trial with the ability to resuspend judgment about whether convicting the accused is fair.[81] Nonetheless, the legal system uniformly insists upon prosecutorial restraint despite the prosecutor's presumed personal conviction of the guilt of the accused.

Forensic Fairness

An important corollary of the fairness requirement is that the prosecutor not employ forensic gambits whose use by other lawyers may be tolerated. While probably no definitive rules or exhaustive list can be formulated, it is clear that a prosecutor can more readily infect a trial with reversible error than can litigators in noncriminal cases. Prosecutorial misconduct can occur through such gambits as interrupting defense counsel's examination of witnesses;[82] acting with unfair belligerence toward opposing counsel,[83] the accused,[84] or defense witnesses; pursuing plainly impermissible lines of questioning[85] or argument;[86] and similar tactics.

A prosecutor bears special responsibilities to deal fairly in presenting a case ex parte to a grand jury.[87] The prosecutor must do nothing, aside from presenting evidence, that would cause the grand jury to be biased against a suspect or that would induce the grand jury not to reach a decision independently of the prosecutor.[88]

False Evidence

A prosecutor must also assure that full and undistorted facts are presented at trial. Clearly a prosecutor is subject to at least the same level of restraint that is imposed on all lawyers in their dealings with evidence, witnesses, and forensic techniques.[89] A prosecutor should present no evidence that he or she knows to be false;[90] violation of this duty offends due process and requires reversal.[91]

[81] Whether prosecutors typically possess the unusual psychological equipment necessary to carry out their postulated dual role should be doubted. See Felkenes, The Prosecutor: A Look at Reality, 7 Sw.U.L.Rev. 98 (1975). A system such as the British, in which the decision to charge and the prosecution are activities of entirely separate offices and persons (police and prosecuting attorneys), may permit the dual role to be fulfilled more effectively.

[82] State v. Boyd, 160 W.Va. 234, 233 S.E.2d 710 (1977) (laughing and talking to others at counsel table, among other incidents).

[83] United States v. Bourg, 598 F.2d 445 (5th Cir.1979) (ridiculing defense lawyer's objections and implying that defense was frivolous); People v. Podwys, 6 Cal.App.2d 71, 44 P.2d 377 (1935). But cf., e.g., United States v. Young, ___ U.S. ___, 105 S.Ct. 1038, 1044–45, 84 L.Ed.2d 1 (1985)(under "invited response" or "invited reply" rule, prosecutor's erroneous personal attack on defense lawyer, while not encouraged or condoned, may not be ground for reversal unless it deprived accused of fair trial, a question that must be answered in context of defense lawyer's own "opening salvo" that provoked the prosecutor).

[84] Pool v. Superior Court, 139 Ariz. 98, 677 P.2d 261 (1984)(unfairly berating accused on cross-examination); People v. Fosselman, 33 Cal.3d 572, 189 Cal.Rptr. 855, 659 P.2d 1144 (1983)(inflammatory cross-examination).

[85] McGuire v. State, ___ Nev. ___, 677 P.2d 1060 (1984) (reversing and imposing personal sanction for prosecutor's repeated impermissible questions and argument).

[86] Berger v. United States, 295 U.S. 78, 55 S.Ct. 629, 79 L.Ed.2d 1314 (1935); Tucker v. Zant, 724 F.2d 882 (11th Cir.1984)(several instances of inadmissible final argument to jury in death sentence case made conviction fundamentally unfair and required reversal on federal habeas corpus); United States v. Modica, 663 F.2d 1173 (2d Cir. 1981), cert.denied 456 U.S. 989, 102 S.Ct. 2269, 73 L.Ed.2d 1284 (1982); State v. Reilly, 446 A.2d 1125 (Me.1982) (argument to jury that defense lawyer knew police testified truthfully and that accused had testified falsely).

[87] For the purpose of presenting a case to a grand jury, the prosecutor is subject to the special disclosure rules applicable to ex parte proceedings. See MR 3.8 comment (first paragraph); § 12.7.

[88] United States v. Hogan, 712 F.2d 757 (2d Cir.1983) (indictment dismissed because prosecutor's misconduct before grand jury was fundamentally unfair); United States v. Serubo, 604 F.2d 807 (3d Cir.1979); United States v. Chanen, 549 F.2d 1306 (9th Cir.1977), cert.denied 434 U.S. 825, 98 S.Ct. 72, 54 L.Ed.2d 83 (1977).

[89] See generally §§ 12.1, 12.3, 12.4, 12.5.

[90] The extent of police and informer perjury at criminal trials is unknowable, but impressionistic reports indicate that it is common in some communities. E.g., P.Chevigny, Police Power: Police Abuses in New York City 141–43 (1969); Younger, The Perjury Routine, 3 Crim.L.Bull. 551 (1967).

[91] Miller v. Pate, 386 U.S. 1, 87 S.Ct. 785, 17 L.Ed.2d 690 (1967); Alcorta v. Texas, 355 U.S. 28, 78 S.Ct. 103, 2 L.Ed.2d 9 (1957); Mooney v. Holohan, 294 U.S. 103, 55 S.Ct. 340, 79 L.Ed. 791 (1935). On the use of false affidavits to obtain a search warrant, see Franks v. Delaware, 438 U.S. 154, 98 S.Ct. 2674, 57 L.Ed.2d 667 (1978). Courts have occasionally granted new trials when the

A "knowing" use of false evidence is probably necessary to constitute a violation of the lawyer codes,[92] but for the purposes of a new trial motion, unwitting use of false evidence may form the basis for setting a conviction aside. The prosecutor must take reasonable steps to assess the truth or falsity, and not just the plausibility, of evidence that will be offered.[93] More is required than nonparticipation in solicitation of false testimony. Clearly a prosecutor cannot argue to the jurors that they should credit testimony that the prosecutor knows is false.[94] Beyond that, a prosecutor must make reasonable efforts to verify the accuracy of testimony if it later becomes apparent that the testimony is false in part [95] or if the prosecutor has another reasonable basis for suspecting the accuracy of the evidence.[96] As soon as the falsity of testimony is discovered, the prosecutor must see that it is corrected.[97]

131k10

prosecutor*** /7 fals! +5 testimony evidence affidavit

§ 13.10.5 Mandatory Disclosure to the Accused

The Brady Disclosure Requirement

The obligation to correct perjured prosecution testimony is usually accomplished by disclosing the correct information to the defense.[98] Such prosecution disclosures are generally required by due process under the standards developed following the approach of the Supreme Court in Brady v. Maryland.[99]

prosecutor was unaware of the falsity of the evidence. E.g., Barbee v. Warden, 331 F.2d 842 (4th Cir.1964); but see Rosner v. United States, 516 F.2d 269 (2d Cir.1975), cert.denied 427 U.S. 911, 96 S.Ct. 3198, 49 L.Ed.2d 1203 (1976); The prosecutor's duty to assure the accuracy of evidence is enhanced, rather than denigrated, by the decision in Briscoe v. Lahue, 460 U.S. 325, 103 S.Ct. 1108, 75 L.Ed.2d 96 (1983), holding that a police officer who testified perjuriously for the prosecution was not liable for damages under the civil rights statutes. On the showing necessary for posttrial relief from a conviction on the ground of false evidence, see generally Annot., 69 A.L.R.Fed. 657 (1984).

92 ABA Prosecution Function Standards § 3–5.6(a) (1980); but cf. id. § 5.6 commentary (approved 1979) (discipline should be "limited to those cases where the falsity of the evidence was known to, or reasonably should have been discovered by, the prosecutor"). Knowing use is sufficient without a further showing of a particular malicious design by the prosecutor to harm the accused. See In re Friedman, 76 Ill.2d 392, 30 Ill.Dec. 288, 392 N.E.2d 1333, 10 A.L.R.4th 589 (1979)(prosecutor use of false testimony in undercover operation to obtain evidence against corrupt judges violates lawyer code when no prior permission was obtained from nonsuspect judge); Price, Remarks, Proceedings at the National Judicial Conference on Standards for the Administration of Criminal Justice, 57 F.R.D. 229, 443 (1972).

93 United States v. Kelly, 543 F.Supp. 1303, 1309–1310 (D.Mass.1982), citing U.S. Dep't. of Justice, Proving Federal Crimes, at 8–3 to 8–4 (J.Cissell ed.1980)(prosecutor may not present evidence that "he actually knows, or should know, to be false"). See also United States v. Kelly, supra, 550 F.Supp. 901 (D.Mass.1982)(accepting bar committee findings, giving benefit of doubt to lawyer, by not recommending disciplinary proceedings).

94 In re Drieband, 273 A.D. 413, 77 N.Y.S.2d 585 (1948) (prosecutor censured for knowing use of false evidence in summation to jury).

95 United States v. Banks, 383 F.Supp. 389 (D.S.D.1974), appeal dismissed 513 F.2d 1329 (8th Cir.1975).

96 United States v. Samango, 450 F.Supp. 1097 (D.Haw. 1978), affirmed 607 F.2d 877 (9th Cir.1979).

97 United States v. Agurs, 427 U.S. 97, 103–04, 96 S.Ct. 2392, 2397, 49 L.Ed.2d 342 (1976); Giglio v. United States, 405 U.S. 150, 92 S.Ct. 763, 31 L.Ed.2d 104 (1972); Napue v. Illinois, 360 U.S. 264, 79 S.Ct. 1173, 3 L.Ed.2d 1217 (1959). In the case of perjured testimony before a grand jury, the defect can be cured by reindictment without the tainted testimony. E.g., United States v. Udziela, 671 F.2d 995 (7th Cir.1982), cert.denied 457 U.S. 1135, 102 S.Ct. 2964, 73 L.Ed.2d 1353 (1982).

98 A reciprocal obligation of disclosure by the accused of course, does not exist. The accused carries the special protections afforded by the privilege against self-incrimination, the presumption of innocence, the attorney-client privilege, and the attorney work-product doctrine. While those protections may not warrant a general prohibition against all prosecution discovery of defense information prior to trial, see United States v. Nobles, 422 U.S. 225, 95 S.Ct. 2160, 45 L.Ed.2d 141 (1975), they do create a mine field of constitutional and other restrictions that must be negotiated before defense disclosure can be required. See generally People v. Collie, 30 Cal.3d 43, 177 Cal.Rptr. 458, 634 P.2d 534, 23 A.L.R.4th 776 (1981).

99 373 U.S. 83, 83 S.Ct. 1194, 10 L.Ed.2d 215 (1963) (postsentencing discovery that prosecution had withheld statement by accomplice confessing to actual homicide for which defendant was convicted). See also United States v. Bagley, ___ U.S. ___, 105 S.Ct. 3375, 87 L.Ed.2d 481 (1985)(*Brady* rule requires that prosecutor produce evidence useful to impeach government witnesses, as well as exculpatory evidence); Smith v. Phillips, 455 U.S. 209, 102 S.Ct. 940, 71 L.Ed.2d 78 (1982)(nondisclosure of fact that juror had applied for employment with district attorney's office not prejudicial under facts of case); United States v. Agurs, 427 U.S. 97, 96 S.Ct. 2392, 49 L.Ed.2d 342

The due process duty to disclose is based on the elemental notion that a conviction should rest only on accurate evidence and on a record that is as complete on the question of innocence as is permitted by the state of information available to the prosecution at trial. Occasional decisions have also declared in noncriminal litigation that a government lawyer must disclose important facts unknown to the lawyer's adversary.[1]

In general the scope of the constitutional disclosure duty varies, depending on whether or not the defense has made a request for undisclosed information and on the "material" nature of the information.[2] Three different situations can arise. First, if the prosecutor's use of false evidence was knowing, the nondisclosed information will be considered material if "there is any reasonable likelihood that the false testimony could have affected the judgment of the jury." [3] Second, the Supreme Court has employed a very similar standard when the defense specifically requested information and the prosecution failed to reveal it. Then the evidence will be deemed material if "the suppressed evidence might have affected the outcome of the trial." [4] Third, when no defense request has been made or, which is the same thing, the defense has only made a general request, the prosecution is under an independent duty to disclose if "the omitted evidence creates a reasonable doubt that did not otherwise exist." [5] That standard includes evidence that goes to the heart of the factual questions of guilt or innocence, as well as evidence that well might have altered the jury's belief in the credibility of a crucial government witness.[6] In other words, the prospects for finding a *Brady* violation are greater in the first and second situations; in the third situation, involving no defense request or only a general request for information, the defendant has the more difficult task of showing that the judge or jury probably would have acquitted if the information had been disclosed.

Mandatory Disclosure under the Professional Regulations

The prosecutor's disclosure obligation is restated in the lawyer codes in language that parallels, but is not coextensive with, the obligations independently required by due process.[7] Discipline, of course, may be imposed for a prosecutor's knowing violation of the *Brady* requirements, because any such due process violation seems well within the nondisclosure violation defined in DR 7-103(B) and MR 3.8(d).[8] Decisions following *Brady* have also required reversal of a conviction, however, if exculpatory information was personally known not to the prosecutor but only

(1976)(nondisclosure of victim's criminal record not prejudicial under facts of case); Giglio v. United States, 405 U.S. 150, 92 S.Ct. 763, 31 L.Ed.2d 104 (1972)(nondisclosure of promise of leniency to key prosecution witness); Giles v. Maryland, 386 U.S. 66, 87 S.Ct. 793, 17 L.Ed.2d 737 (1967).

[1] City of Los Angeles v. Decker, 18 Cal.3d 860, 135 Cal. Rptr. 647, 558 P.2d 545 (1977)(new trial due to government lawyer's argument to jury that there was no need for airport parking, which was best use for which condemnee sought compensation, when lawyer knew that airport commission had determined additional need for such parking); cf. EC 7-14 ("a government lawyer in a civil action . . . has the responsibility to seek justice and to develop a full and fair record").

[2] On the difficulties of reconciling the decisions on materiality and differentiating between specific and general requests for information, see Babcock, Fair Play: Evidence Favorable to an Accused and Effective Assistance of Counsel, 34 Stan.L.Rev. 1133 (1982). See also Adlerstein, Ethics, Federal Prosecutors, and Federal Courts: Some Recent Problems, 6 Hofstra L.Rev. 755 (1978).

[3] United States v. Agurs, 427 U.S. 97, 103–04, 96 S.Ct. 2392, 2397, 49 L.Ed.2d 342 (1976).

[4] United States v. Agurs, supra, 427 U.S. at 104, 96 S.Ct. at 2397. See also United States v. Bagley, ___ U.S. ___, 105 S.Ct. 3375, 87 L.Ed.2d 481 (1985).

[5] United States v. Agurs, supra, 427 U.S. at 112, 96 S.Ct. at 2401.

[6] Giglio v. United States, 405 U.S. 150, 154, 92 S.Ct. 763, 766, 31 L.Ed.2d 104 (1972).

[7] DR 7-103(B); MR 3.8(d); ABA Prosecution Function Standards § 3-3.11 (1980). Calif.R. 7-102, which otherwise copies DR 7-103, does not contain language parallel to DR 7-103(B).

[8] In re Brophy, 83 A.D.2d 975, 442 N.Y.S.2d 818 (1981) (discipline following conviction in federal court of willfully depriving citizen of individual right to *Brady* disclosure).

to the police.[9] A prosecutor should not be considered to have violated the professional rules in such an instance unless the prosecutor's ignorance was contrived.

The nondisclosure rules of due process and the lawyer codes are the same with respect to nondisclosure when no request or a general request has been made, again with the qualification that police nondisclosure unknown to a prosecutor suffices for a due process but not a disciplinary violation. But a false statement by a prosecutor or the knowing use of false evidence that does not seriously infect the trial, and thus that does not require relief from the conviction under *Brady*, should nonetheless expose the prosecutor to professional discipline.[10] By the same token, disclosure of *Brady* material long after a court order requires it, but not so late as to infect the trial with reversible error, should subject the offending prosecutor to professional discipline.[11]

Following the *Brady* decision, in 1963, the Federal Rules of Criminal Procedure were revised in 1966 to enhance the ability of the accused to prepare for trial.[12] In addition, federal law specifically entitles the accused to obtain access to substantially verbatim recorded statements of prosecution witnesses.[13] Similar extensions of the discovery rights of accused persons in state prosecutions have occurred in many states. It is not clear whether the provisions of DR 7–103(B) and MR 3.8(d) cover prosecutor violations of such nonconstitutional rules. But the general requirement of DR 7–102(A)(3) to comply with disclosure obligations imposed by law clearly covers such situations. As is noted elsewhere (§ 12.6.4), no parallel to DR 7–102(A)(3) survives in the Model Rules.

WESTLAW REFERENCES

brady +4 maryland /12 83 +4 1194 /p prosecut! /s disclos!

digest,synopsis(duty obligat! /3 disclos! reveal**** nondisclos! /9 prosecut!)

§ 13.10.6 Plea Bargaining

Problematical Power to Plea Bargain

An illustration of the reach and limits of prosecutorial discretion is supplied by plea bargaining.[14] While the Supreme Court has accepted the legitimacy of plea bargaining,[15]

[9] Fulford v. Maggio, 692 F.2d 354 (5th Cir.1982), reversed on other grounds, 462 U.S. 111, 103 S.Ct. 2261, 76 L.Ed.2d 794 (1983); United States v. Jensen, 608 F.2d 1349 (10th Cir.1979).

[10] United States v. Perez-Gomez, 638 F.2d 215 (10th Cir. 1981). For a reported example of a false prosecutor statement of the nonexistence of exculpatory evidence that was then produced and led to an acquittal, see Sellers v. United States, 574 F.Supp. 767, 770 (W.D.N.C. 1983).

[11] Both DR 7–103(B) and MR 3.8(d) require "timely" disclosure. For disciplinary purposes, that should not be interpreted to mean "at the last possible moment when disclosure is necessary in order to avoid reversible error." The rules should be read to require disclosure either at the time when ordered to do so or, in the absence of an order, at a time when the duty to disclose is known and no reasonable basis for nondisclosure remains. Depriving defense counsel of an opportunity to study and investigate the new evidence further is not, of course, a reasonable basis. See generally United States v. Starusko, 729 F.2d 256, 264–65 (3d Cir.1984); Johnson v. State, 577 P.2d 230, 234 (Alaska 1978). A trial court can delay the time of disclosure for compelling reasons, such as to protect prosecution witnesses against harm after a showing of specific and corroborated evidence of threats. See United States v. Higgs, 713 F.2d 39 (3d Cir.1983), cert.denied 464 U.S. 1048, 104 S.Ct. 725, 79 L.Ed.2d 185 (1984).

[12] F.R.Crim.P. 16.

[13] See generally Jencks v. United States, 353 U.S. 657, 77 S.Ct. 1007, 1 L.Ed.2d 1103 (1957); 18 U.S.C.A. § 3500 (the so-called Jencks Act, which codified and to some extent extended the *Jencks* decision). Discovery under the Jencks Act is not subject to limitation by a lawyer work-product exception when the statement is obtained by a government lawyer. See Goldberg v. United States, 425 U.S. 94, 96 S.Ct. 1338, 47 L.Ed.2d 603 (1976).

[14] See generally A.Goldstein, The Passive Judiciary: Prosecutorial Discretion and the Guilty Plea (1981); Alschuler, The Prosecutor's Role in Plea Bargaining, 36 U.Chi.L.Rev. 50 (1968); Special Issue on Plea Bargaining, 13 Law & Soc'y Rev. 189 (1979). Professor Goldstein urges that judges begin to develop a common-law set of limits on plea bargaining and that hearings on plea bargains be made potentially more adversarial by giving crime victims a formal role in them. Id. at 72–73. For similar proposals for crime victims, see, e.g., Nat'l Advisory Council on Criminal Justice Standards and Goals, Courts, Standard 1.2, at 24 (1973).

[15] Santobello v. New York, 404 U.S. 257, 92 S.Ct. 495, 30 L.Ed.2d 427 (1971); Blackledge v. Allison, 431 U.S. 63, 97 S.Ct. 1621, 52 L.Ed.2d 136 (1977).

the practice gives the prosecutor great powers that are attended by equally large responsibilities. A plea bargain is essentially a contract, although one made under circumstances that in the commercial world would normally call for the special protections of the doctrine of unconscionability. While a prosecutor is under no obligation to offer a plea bargain or to agree to any offer by a defendant,[16] once an agreement has been reached, the prosecutor's side of the bargain must be fulfilled.[17]

A prosecutor has broad discretion in selecting the number and kind of charges to be pressed and the type and length of sentence to be recommended on conviction. For that reason prosecutor overreaching of an accused is impermissible.[18] "The most meticulous standards of promise and performance must be met by prosecutors engaged in negotiating such agreements." [19] Clearly a prosecutor may not resort to an unjustifiable standard such as race or religion in determining whether to negotiate and what types of pleas to offer [20] nor resort to actual or threatened physical harm or mental coercion in order to induce an accused to accept a proferred plea.[21] But a prosecutor's threat to increase charges if an accused refuses an offered plea is not unconstitutional according to a divided Supreme Court.[22] And it may be permissible for a prosecutor to offer a "package deal" that is conditional on its acceptance by several jointly charged defendants, despite the potential that such offers have to create conflicts of interest between the persons jointly charged.[23]

WESTLAW REFERENCES

di plea bargaining

prosecut! /s plea-bargain! /s threat! coerc!

---

[16] Weatherford v. Bursey, 429 U.S. 545, 97 S.Ct. 837, 51 L.Ed.2d 30 (1977); People v. Smith, 53 Cal.App.3d 655, 126 Cal.Rptr. 195 (1975)(trial court has no power to permit accused to plead guilty to included lesser offense over objection of prosecutor). A prosecutor may not, however, refuse to plea bargain on an arbitrary basis. See In re Rook, 276 Or. 695, 556 P.2d 1351 (1976)(district attorney disciplined for refusal to plea bargain with any defendant represented by two lawyers groundlessly suspected of involvement in organized crime).

[17] Santobello v. New York, 404 U.S. 257, 92 S.Ct. 495, 30 L.Ed.2d 427 (1971); Blackledge v. Allison, 431 U.S. 63, 97 S.Ct. 1621, 52 L.Ed.2d 136 (1977). See generally Westen & Westin, A Constitutional Law of Remedies for Broken Plea Bargains, 66 Cal.L.Rev. 471 (1978). Courts have differed over the question whether the "offer and acceptance" law of contracts is to apply unaltered to plea bargains. Compare, e.g., United States v. Cooper, 594 F.2d 12 (4th Cir.1979)(regardless of reliance, a prosecutor's plea offer must ordinarily remain open for a reasonable period of time) with, e.g., Virgin Islands v. Scotland, 614 F.2d 360 (3d Cir. 1980). See Annot., 16 A.L.R.4th 810 (1982).

[18] Machibroda v. United States, 368 U.S. 487, 82 S.Ct. 510, 7 L.Ed.2d 473 (1962)(plea allegedly induced by prosecutor's promises to accused accompanied by threat to bring other charges if accused told his lawyer about plea bargain). Some courts have relied on strict contract-like doctrines, such as analogies to the statute of frauds, to prevent attacks on broken plea promises by a prosecutor. E.g., Siegel v. New York, 691 F.2d 620 (2d Cir.1982), cert.denied 459 U.S. 1209, 103 S.Ct. 1201, 75 L.Ed.2d 443 (1983) (no denial of due process when prosecutor refused to abide by oral portion of plea bargain in view of state's policy requiring writing). But the ethics of the prosecutor's conduct, of course, are not limited to due process considerations.

[19] United States v. Phillips Petroleum Co., 435 F.Supp. 622, 640 (N.D.Okla.1977). Cf., United States v. Benchimol, ___ U.S. ___, 105 S.Ct. 2103, 85 L.Ed.2d 462 (1985)(prosecutor, who agreed to recommend sentence, was under no obligation to explain reasons to judge or to make recommendation "enthusiastically").

[20] Oyler v. Boles, 368 U.S. 448, 456, 82 S.Ct. 501, 505, 7 L.Ed.2d 446 (1962).

[21] Brady v. United States, 397 U.S. 742, 750, 90 S.Ct. 1463, 1469, 25 L.Ed.2d 747 (1970).

[22] Bordenkircher v. Hayes, 434 U.S. 357, 98 S.Ct. 663, 54 L.Ed.2d 604 (1978). See generally Pizzi, Prosecutorial Discretion, Plea Bargaining and the Supreme Court's Opinion in Bordenkircher v. Hayes, 6 Hast.Con.L.Q. 269 (1978). A variation on the *Bordenkircher v. Hayes* gambit is to overcharge an accused with more offenses than the prosecutor actually intends to present evidence on at trial or with a severity of offense that the evidence probably does not warrant. It is one of the prosecutorial abuses that are most heavily criticized by defense counsel. See Prosecution Function Standards § 3.9 commentary (e), at 98 (1971 ed.).

[23] In re Ibarra, 34 Cal.3d 277, 193 Cal.Rptr. 538, 666 P.2d 980 (1983). On the problems for lawyers engaged in simultaneous negotiation of settlements in behalf of several clients, see § 8.15 (settling related cases).

Part Four
DELIVERY OF LEGAL SERVICES

Chapter Fourteen
THE NEED FOR A LAWYER

Table of Sections

---

§ 14.1 CLIENT NEEDS FOR LEGAL SERVICES

Defining and Measuring the Need for Legal Services

The existence in a society of a large number of professionally trained legal advisers who earn considerable livelihoods providing legal services suggests that the general population has frequent and widespread legal needs. The need for legal services on the part of nonlawyers has generally been assumed rather than studied. Yet it is by no means clear to what extent nonlawyers require legal services or, differently, to what extent the present methods of satisfying client demands for legal services leave significant client demands unmet.

The variety of client needs is as diverse as the kinds of work that lawyers perform—ranging from legal advice given to large enterprises and governmental organizations on massive and complex operations to five-minute conversations with low-income individuals about financially trivial matters. Client resort to another person to satisfy a client need for legal services in each of those situations is obviously not an automatic reflex. In each case the importance of the matter to the person or persons that are affected by the operation of the legal system might be great, yet the economic aspects of the contrasting situations strongly suggest that much effort will be spent on a financially significant matter and nothing or little on those of little economic importance. For good or for ill, "we live in a society where the distribution of legal assistance, like the distribution of most other goods and services, is generally regulated by the dynamics of private enterprise." [1]

[1] Fuller v. Oregon, 417 U.S. 40, 53, 94 S.Ct. 2116, 2124, 40 L.Ed.2d 642 (1974).

One potential barrier to client satisfaction of a perceived need for legal services is thus economic in nature—the client's inability to afford legal services.

A second barrier, and perhaps an equally fundamental one, is that a nonlawyer may be unaware that the problem is a legal one or that a lawyer's assistance might be valuable. For example, a person about to be evicted from an apartment might imagine that the landlord, being the owner of the building, is entitled to evict without prior notice. Yet the tenant's lease or state law might entitle the tenant to procedural and substantive protections. A lawyer is in the best position both to give advice about the tenant's rights and to invoke the complex and mysterious mechanisms of the legal system to protect those rights. If the nonlawyer is unaware that the problem is one for which the legal system provides a possible solution and is unaware or distrustful of the value of the services of a lawyer, the nonlawyer's legal problem and a possible solution to it will go unrecognized. The extent to which such ignorance or distrust prevents nonlawyers from resorting to lawyers is relatively high.[2] And the official position of the organized bar is that the public requires education in order to be able to recognize the need for legal services.[3]

Third, alternatives to lawyers as suppliers of legal services are often severely limited. A lawyer will typically be the only person able to perform advice-giving and representational services because of rules forbidding the unauthorized practice of law and heavily penalizing a nonlawyer who otherwise would be willing to serve the client's need for legal services (§ 15.1). But nonlawyers might be able to resolve some, and perhaps many, kinds of legal problems satisfactorily without resort to lawyers or to the legal system and perhaps without even identifying the problem as a legal one.

Nonlawyer Recognition of Legal Problems

The extent to which members of the general public and demographic subgroups within it recognize legal problems, and as a consequence resort to lawyers for solutions to them, was the subject of an extensive empirical study conducted by a group of researchers supported by the American Bar Foundation. The study results[4] suggest that the pattern of legal problem incidence and lawyer use is complex and to some extent counterintuitive. The general conclusions of the study were that (1) there are large differences in the rate of incidence of legal problems; (2) there are also large differences in the extent to which a lawyer's services will be invoked, depending on the kind of legal problem, ranging from 80 percent resort to lawyers for will preparation to less than 1 percent for job discrimination problems; (3) differences in lawyer-use rates among demographic subgroups might often be explainable by differences in the incidence of legal problems experienced by different subgroups; and (4) a person's willingness to accept the need to resort to a lawyer for help on a legal problem generally correlated with legal experience—the number of times that a person had consulted a lawyer.[5]

The ABF study was designedly limited. For example, its description of quintiles to measure economic demographics of respondents had the highest family income group (in

[2] See generally B.Curran, The Legal Needs of the Public 261–64 (1977).

[3] EC 8–3: "Members of the public should be educated to recognize the existence of legal problems and the resultant need for legal services, and should be provided methods for intelligent selection of counsel."

[4] B.Curran, The Legal Needs of the Public (1977).

[5] B. Curran, supra 259–65. The further conclusions drawn from the Curran study and its underlying statistics are that bar association public relations campaigns that attempt to improve the public image of the bar are unlikely to encourage large numbers of nonlawyers to seek legal services and that public awareness of the existence of legal problems may be much less important than age and experience in determining whether a lawyer's services are sought. See Note, An Assessment of Alternative Strategies for Increasing Access to Legal Services, 90 Yale L.J. 122 (1980). See also Avichai, Trends in the Incidence of Legal Problems and in the Use of Laywers, 1978 Am.B.Found. Research J. 289 (mathematical analysis of ABF statistics suggests that increase in legal problems and in demand for legal services will continue to grow, at least in near future).

1973 dollars) at $15,594 or above. Many lawyers in 1973 probably never or rarely saw a client with an income as low as that of the study's highest group. Secondly, the study focused primarily upon nonbusiness problems, again leaving unstudied a vast area of intensive legal work.

Nonlegal Ways of Meeting Perceived Legal Needs

The definition of *legal need* also involves a more slippery concept than at first appears. Even if, problematically, we assume that all laws should remain unaltered and all systems for administering laws in place, the extent to which nonlawyers must resort to law and legal institutions is still relatively unmeasured. Instead of consulting a lawyer about job discrimination, for example, a worker may simply attempt to live with the situation, change jobs, or go to a union steward to invoke a grievance procedure provided under a collective bargaining agreement. Instead of suing to recover damages for breach of contract, a business person might resort to intragroup controls, such as an informal boycott to pressure the nonconforming promisor to adhere to a promise.[6] The extent to which persons with real legal problems solve them in those alternative ways is unknown. And the resort to nonlegal solutions might also have colored the extent to which respondents to the ABF study indentified their problems as legal ones in the first place. Whatever its unanswered questions, however, the ABF study unequivocally demonstrates that many legal problems exist that are either not recognized as legal or not taken to lawyers for solutions.

Social Solutions to the Problem of Unmet Legal Service Needs

Recognition of an unmet need for legal services traditionally had led to one of two approaches. First, as represented by the legal aid movement (§ 16.7.2) and the system of court-appointed counsel in criminal cases (§ 14.3.1), one response is to attempt to equalize access to legal services for those unable to afford them.[7] Some reformers have proposed a national legal services program that would universally subsidize legal services in the marketplace.[8] The second approach is to get to the root of the problem by redesigning parts of the legal system so as to remove the need for anyone affected by some laws to have a lawyer. The original small-claims court movement, for example, stressed a remove-the-lawyer objective very strongly.[9]

The former approach (access to legal services) assumes that the system should, or will, remain essentially entrepreneurial, with civil litigants self-selecting themselves to resort to court or to other legal processes for aggressive pursuit of consciously recognized legal rights under the indispensable guidance of a professional lawyer. One unfortunate result of that approach may be that persons whose needs are newly met in that way may become heavily dependent on their lawyers to vindicate their legal rights.[10] The approach may also be misguided to the extent that it assumes that the reason for nonuse of the legal system is because of the lack of a lawyer rather than ignorance about important legal rights and ignorance about the value of having a lawyer.[11]

The problem of educating the public about the availability of legal services and of educating lawyers to handle them is currently met

[6] Comment, The Statute of Frauds and the Business Community: A Re-Appraisal in Light of Prevailing Practices, 66 Yale L.J. 1038 (1957).

[7] F. Marks, The Legal Needs of the Poor: A Critical Analysis 10 (1971); Carlin & Howard, Legal Representation and Class Justice, 12 UCLA L.Rev. 381 (1965); M.Cappelletti, Access to Justice (1978–1979).

[8] M.Frankel, Justice: Commodity or Public Service 7–8 (1978).

[9] Steele, The Historical Context of the Small Claims Courts, 1981 Am.B.Found. Research J. 293, 295.

[10] Cahn & Cahn, The War on Poverty: A Civilian Perspective, 73 Yale L.J. 1317 (1964); Cahn & Cahn, Power to the People or the Profession?—The Public Interest in Public Interest Law, 79 Yale L.J. 1005 (1970). See generally I.Illich, Disabling Professions (1977).

[11] Mayhew, Institutions of Representation: Civil Justice and the Public, 9 Law & Soc'y Rev. 401 (1975).

primarily by lawyer referral programs and by advertising and solicitation of clients by lawyers. The extent to which those activities have met either with success or with bar and court approval, of course, is another matter.

WESTLAW REFERENCES

need** demand*** /3 legal +3 service aid assistance /p lawyer attorney counsel** /s duty obligat!

§ 14.2 INFORMATION ABOUT LEGAL SERVICES

§ 14.2.1 Lawyer Referral and Law Lists

Lawyer Referral Services

One method of conveying information about the availability of legal services to a broad segment of the public is through lawyer referral services.[12] The traditional lawyer referral service has been conducted under the direct auspices of a bar association. Advertising in such places as telephone directories has provided one of the few means of informing the public of the existence of the service. Once aware, a prospective client calls or visits the service and is given, not legal advice or services, but the names of several attorneys who have agreed to cooperate with the service. Sometimes, but not invariably, the bar organization sponsoring the referral service imposes limitations on the participating lawyers that must be complied with—for example, charging referred clients according to a maximum fee schedule. While the point is somewhat controverted, it seems likely that traditional lawyer referral services have not had a major impact on public awareness of the availability of legal services.

Non-Bar Association Referral Services

With the general liberalization of lawyer advertising rules in the late 1970s, however, the possibility developed of joint-advertising arrangements under which several lawyers not otherwise associated in a law practice would combine to provide advertising with a single telephone number. Callers would be referred to the participating attorneys by specialty or in rotation or in other fashion.

The difficulty with such an arrangement in many jurisdictions is the narrowness of DR 2–103(C)(1), which permits a lawyer to participate only in lawyer referral services "operated, sponsored or approved by a bar association".[13] Most bar associations probably have no arrangements for "approving" such joint-advertising arrangements, and they remain of doubtful validity. The 1983 Model Rules contain no limiting reference to referral services such as that in DR 2–103(C)(1). Instead, the reference to lawyer referral in the comment to MR 7.2 is broadly permissive, although it is limited to nonprofit referral plans: "a lawyer may participate in not-for-profit lawyer referral programs and pay the usual fees charged by such programs." [14]

Limitations of Traditional Referral Services

Lawyer referral systems characteristically aim to provide information to a prospective client about individual lawyers in order to facilitate the client's search for legal assistance. The information supplied consists of little more than the lawyer's name and telephone number, with no indication of the lawyer's competence or fees. In fact, most bar association referral services are open to all lawyers admitted to practice, and the typical lawyer member is newly admitted or other-

[12] See generally B. Christenson, The Lawyer Referral Service (tent. draft 1967); Carlin, The Advancing State of the Art of Lawyer Referral, 30 Baylor L.Rev. 543 (1978) (describing the 1978 ABA "Statement of Standards and Practices for a Lawyer Referral Service"); ABA Informal Opinion 1139 (1970).

[13] "Bar association" is defined in the "Definitions" section of the Code to extend to specialized bar associations. It is uncertain under the Code exactly how small, informal, or otherwise ad hoc a group can be and still constitute a "bar association."

[14] The limitation to "not-for-profit" referral services seems simply to limit the open-ended permission to these services. Services that are run for profit, such as individual lawyers and law firms, are presumably subject only to the general rules on advertising (MR 7.1 and 7.2).

wise not terribly busy with other legal work. Whether that group is likely to be more or less competent than nonreferral lawyers is debatable.[15]

Bar Institutional Advertising

A different emphasis is provided in bar association institutional advertising about legal rights and problems. In recent years, several bar associations have experimented with telephone services (themselves advertised in telephone directories) that permit a caller to listen to a brief tape-recorded message describing common legal issues. The service does not, however, provide any information about the availability of individual lawyers who can assist a prospective client.

Law Lists

Law Lists are collections of the names of lawyers and other information about them gathered into book form for the use of subscribers. The most famous is the Martindale-Hubbell multivolume collection, which attempts to include the names and some minimal other information about all admitted lawyers in the United States and, for a minority of selected lawyers, indicates a particularly high "rating". Other law lists are keyed to particular areas of legal service, such as personal injury or collection work. All are published by private concerns that make their money by charging selected lawyers a sizable fee for the privilege of advertising information, such as the lawyer's credentials, representative clients, special abilities, and honors. The size of the fee that the listing company can charge depends upon the amount of business that is generated for listed lawyers by circulation of the publication. In some types of practice, lawyers may receive substantial referral business through advertising in a law list.[16]

Deregulation of Law Lists

Following the approach of the 1908 Canons, the 1969 Code originally regulated lawyer advertising in law lists by limiting its approval to "reputable" lists and then "conclusively" establishing that status for lists approved by a special committee of the ABA.[17] The involvement of the American Bar Association in regulating law lists ended abruptly in 1977. Under the threat of antitrust suits (§ 2.4.1), [18] the ABA in that year dropped any reference to law lists in the Code as part of the process of amending the provisions on advertising. The 1983 Model Rules similarly contain no regulatory mention of law lists. Those publications, like telephone directories and other publications, are treated today simply as other accepted kinds of lawyer advertising.

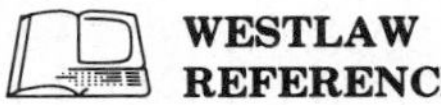

lawyer attorney /2 referral +2 service system program /p "bar association"

di law list

§ 14.2.2 The Economics and History of Lawyer Advertising

Overview of the Advertising Controversy

For a time within recent memory, lawyer advertising was strictly and broadly forbidden by official rules. During the 1970s and early 1980s, however, radical changes in the rules have been produced by the pressure of anti-

[15] EC 2–15 asserts that lawyer referral systems make it possible for nonlawyers to employ "competent" lawyers. The sentiment is either factual or wishful, and apparently the latter.

[16] M.Altman & R.Weil, How to Manage Your Law Office § 3.08 (1976)(importance of law directories as method by which corporate counsel find outside counsel and obtain impression of quality).

[17] See the original DR 2–102(A)(6)(1969), which is drawn largely from 1908 Canon 27. The restrictive list of items of information that a lawyer's entry in a reputable law list might contain was the inspiration for later "laundry list" enumerations of permissible content of public advertising by lawyers.

[18] One of the suits was filed directly against the ABA and resulted in a judgment that dismissed the ABA as a defendant but held that a state's attempted restriction of a consumer group's nonapproved law list offended the Constitution. See Consumers Union, Inc. v. American Bar Ass'n, 427 F. Supp. 506 (E.D.Va.1976), vacated 433 U.S. 917, 97 S.Ct. 2993, 53 L.Ed.2d 1104 (1977), on remand 470 F.Supp. 1055 (E.D.Va.1979).

trust lawsuits and, more directly, by decisions of the United States Supreme Court, declaring that many forms of lawyer advertising were constitutionally immune from governmental regulation. Those developments have expanded the types and amount of formal advertising messages that lawyers attempt to send to prospective clients, but hardly to the degree feared by many lawyers when they were first unfolding.

Despite initial impressions of euphoria or gloom, lawyer advertising remains an activity rarely engaged in by the great majority of lawyers. It is apparently of economic utility only to lawyers engaging in relatively mass-client forms of practice.[19] The attractiveness of advertising depends upon the extent to which the unit cost of advertising can be efficiently allocated to new clientele that it generates. If the firm's business is devoted to typically "one-shot" litigants[20]—divorce, bankruptcy, misdemeanor offenses, personal injury and worker compensation claimants, title examination for residential purchases, and the like—then the volume of new clientele or the fee value of individual cases must be quite high to generate an acceptable cost-per-client of advertising expenditures. If a law firm's business is characterized by long-standing and continuing relationships between the firm and "repeat-player" clients—antitrust defense work, business litigation and corporate advice generally—then advertising may be pointless, because those clients do not shop frequently for new counsel and, when they do, they do not permit anything so insubstantial as advertising to influence their choice.[21]

History of Lawyer Advertising

Lawyer advertising does not really have a history of its own; instead, most of the major moves and shifts in the area parallel closely those in other professional fields such as medicine, dentistry, and accounting. Traces of lawyer advertising have been found as early as 1802, when a lawyer published a "card" in a Tennessee newspaper.[22] Similar advertising appeared regularly until well after the Civil War, although it began to decrease in many areas as it acquired the "stigma of vulgarity."[23] Victorian snobbery denigrating any calling that besmirched itself by taking on the trappings of a "trade" led the socially ambitious elements of the organized bar to oppose lawyer advertising. Virtue was to be its own display, and the young lawyer of pluck, competence, and trustworthiness would soon gain a substantial client following through a deserved good reputation.[24] The desire of some lawyers to control competition by eliminating advertising probably also played a part.

Yet the bar's sentiments about advertising were still sufficiently ambiguous at the beginning of this century that the 1908 Canons did not completely prohibit advertising. Canon 27 acknowledged that "the publication or circulation of ordinary simple business cards, being a matter of personal taste or local custom, and sometimes of convenience, is not *per se* improper.[25] But Canon 27 prohibited any other sort of advertising—whether done directly through "circulars, advertisements, through touters or by personal communications" or done indirectly by a lawyer, "such as

19 Hazard, Pearce & Stempel, Why Lawyers Should Be Allowed to Advertise: A Market Analysis of Legal Services, 58 NYU L.Rev. 1084 (1983).

20 The "one-shot" and "repeat-player" terminology is developed in a different context in Galanter, Why the "Haves" Come Out Ahead: Speculations on the Limits of Legal Change, 9 Law & Soc'y Rev. 95 (1974). See also Galanter, Afterward: Explaining Litigation, 9 Law & Soc'y Rev. 347 (1975).

21 See M.Altman & R.Weil, How to Manage Your Law Office § 3.08 (1976), for a general discussion of the way in which corporate counsel go about finding outside counsel and determining their quality. The most important sources of selection listed are Martindale-Hubbell, inertia (continue to use the same firm as the predecessor general counsel), and recommendations of other lawyers.

22 See D.Calhoun, Professional Lives in America 82–83 (1965).

23 Id. at 82.

24 See the original wording of 1908 Canon 27, in ABA Opinions on Professional Ethics 75 (1967).

25 Id. Somewhat altered language survived several amendments of Canon 27 throughout its life, permitting the "customary use of simple professional cards."

furnishing or inspiring newspaper comments, or procuring his photograph to be published . . . and all other like self-laudation."

Despite the breadth of the prohibition against advertising, economic reality continued to tempt some lawyers to stretch the limits of the exception to the prohibition or to ignore it entirely. The bar fought back with extraordinary vigor, and the antiadvertising ethic became quite general, at least as applied to overt public advertising. Bar campaigns were periodically mounted to snuff out lawyer advertising, and enormous quantities of lawyer time and energy were expended on ethics committee opinions dealing with the line between permissible and impermissible self-publicization.[26] The bar resisted attempted inroads by related service industries that did not prohibit advertising through vigorously enforcing the bar's position on unauthorized practice issues.[27]

The bar's success in enforcing the antiadvertising rules[28] did not mean that lawyers abandoned efforts to attract the business of prospective clients. Lawyers were forced to employ less efficient and possibly more time-consuming and costly methods of making their availability known. Some prospective clients were probably deterred from seeking legal advice because of ignorance about basic legal rights or about the availability of particular lawyers. The absence of information also affected clients who were dissatisfied with their lawyers. Without information about other lawyers, a disgruntled client might be forced by lack of information into continuing an unwanted representation.[29]

During the 1970s, an increasing number of lawyers and the Justice Department raised issues about the legality of the antiadvertising rules on antitrust and free expression grounds.[30] Many other lawyers were concerned that legalized lawyer advertising would seriously impair their professional image, create costly and indecorous competition for clients, lower the quality of legal services to clients, and generally degrade the legal profession.[31] Several courts had refused to heed these concerns, however, and had refused to enforce broad antiadvertising rules.[32] In 1975 the Supreme Court, in Goldfarb v. Virginia State Bar,[33] applied the federal antitrust laws to minimum fee schedules promulgated and enforced by bar associations. The logic of *Goldfarb* arguably applied to other bar restraints such as prohibitions against advertising. The response of the ABA was to liberalize the advertising rules of the Code

[26] The commonly accepted estimate is that half of the ABA's ethics opinions through the late 1960s dealt with advertising and related issues. See § 2.6.6.

[27] For example, advertising by banks at one point appeared to threaten lawyers by suggesting that bank trust officers could perform, more cheaply, services that bank customers were unnecessarily taking to lawyers. The response of lawyers was to confront banks with the threat of unauthorized practice litigation, resulting in a treaty under which banks agreed not to disparage lawyers in their advertising. (See "Statement of General Policies", Clause iv of the National Conference Group (of ABA and American Bankers Association, Trust Division) (1941), in Martindale-Hubbell 72M, 73M (1978)). In the same year (1941), a similar approach was employed and resolution was achieved with publishers of materials that might be used by prospective clients in lieu of lawyers' services and with title insurance companies ("Declaration of Principles", section 2 (1969), 7 id. 82M.). (See Initial Statement (1941) and Supplement Statement (1946) of agreement between the ABA and various publishers in 7 Martindale-Hubbell 80M-82M (1978)). See generally § 15.1.

[28] Much different was the experience with lawyer solicitation. See § 14.2.5.

[29] D.Rosenthal, Lawyer and Client: Who's in Charge? 55 (1974).

[30] See generally ABA, Annual Report of the President, 1975–1976, at 2–5 (1976)(review of Code of Professional Responsibility provisions on advertising in light of antitrust and First Amendment developments, including commencement of Justice Department antitrust suit against ABA).

[31] A reading of the pages of the American Bar Association Journal in the years 1976–78 confirms that the established bar took an alarmist view of advertising developments. In November 1977 an ABA-commissioned opinion poll of members indicated that an overwhelming majority of lawyers regarded lawyer advertising and the public image of the legal profession as the most vital issue confronting the profession. See Lawpoll, 63 ABA J. 1541 (1977).

[32] The most prominent decision was that of the California Supreme Court, in Jacoby v. California St. Bar, 19 Cal.3d 359, 138 Cal.Rptr. 77, 562 P.2d 1326 (1977).

[33] 421 U.S. 773, 95 S.Ct. 2004, 44 L.Ed.2d 572 (1975). See § 2.4.

slightly in August 1976. The amendments permitted the advertising of additional information in approved law lists but retained most of the advertising prohibitions.[34] It was upon this restless scene that the Supreme Court in 1977 intruded with Bates v. Arizona State Bar,[35] holding that broad prohibitions against lawyer advertising constituted unconstitutional restraints on a lawyer's freedom of expression.

WESTLAW REFERENCES

lawyer attorney /s advertis! /s "professional responsibility"

45k32(9)

lawyer attorney /s advertis! /s prohibit! restrict! & date(before 1978)

§ 14.2.3 Lawyer Advertising and the Constitution

Bates and Its Aftermath

When recent law graduates John R. Bates and Van O. Steen decided to expand the clientele of their new legal clinic through advertising, they confronted a 1969 Code that essentially forbade it. The barrier was enforced with a vigor not matched for many other forms of lawyer misconduct, and state courts generally supported the position of the bar. The Arizona bar attacked their modest 1976 newspaper advertisement of "legal services at very reasonable rates" together with a list of specific fees which their legal clinic was prepared to charge for five common legal services.[36] The rejection by the United States Supreme Court of the state court's imposition of discipline in Bates v. Arizona State Bar[37] launched the Court and lower courts into an extensive reworking of the constitutionally permissible limits on state regulation of lawyer advertising.

Doctrinally the Court had already laid the groundwork for the 1977 *Bates* outcome in earlier decisions holding that "commercial speech" was subject to a measure of constitutional protection, even if a less-inclusive protection than that extended to noncommercial speech.[38] What remained in the majority opinion in the *Bates* decision was to reject arguments that the new commercial speech doctrine should not apply to protect lawyer advertising because of asserted differences between law practice and other commercial activities. The Court rejected six arguments offered by the bar to immunize lawyer advertising from the new commercial speech doctrine. The Court's rationale was important as the limits of lawyer advertising were explored in subsequent cases.

(1) The Court rejected an argument based on bar fears of adverse effects on professionalism. The Court refused to believe that either lawyers or clients labored under the illusion that a fee-earning lawyer was engaged in other than a commercial activity. The Court also thought it improbable that the public reputation of lawyers was attributable to the absence of advertising.

(2) The Court was also unconvinced that all lawyer advertising was inherently misleading. It believed that some legal services could rightly be regarded as routine and thus advertised for a set price.[39] Not all prospective clients were incapable of preliminary self-diagnosis of their need for legal representation.

[34] The August 1976 amendments are commented on critically in the opinion of Justice Powell in In re R.M.J., 455 U.S. 191, 194 n.4, 102 S.Ct. 929, 195, 71 L.Ed.2d 64 (1982).

[35] 433 U.S. 350, 97 S.Ct. 2691, 53 L.Ed.2d 810 (1977).

[36] Uncontested divorce with and without representation, uncontested adoption, uncontested and nonbusiness bankruptcy, and change of name.

[37] 433 U.S. 350, 97 S.Ct. 2691, 53 L.Ed.2d 810 (1977).

[38] The watershed cases extending a measure of First Amendment protection to commercial speech were Bigelow v. Virginia, 421 U.S. 809, 95 S.Ct. 2222, 44 L.Ed.2d 600 (1975); and Virginia Pharmacy Bd. v. Virginia Consumer Council, 425 U.S. 748, 96 S.Ct. 1817, 48 L.Ed.2d 346 (1976). Those cases overturned a doctrine of long standing that commercial speech was not entitled to any constitutional protection. See Valentine v. Chrestensen, 316 U.S. 52, 62 S.Ct. 920, 86 L.Ed.2d 1262 (1942).

[39] In Zauderer v. Office of Disciplinary Counsel, ___ U.S. ___, 105 S.Ct. 2265, 85 L.Ed.2d 652 (1985), the Court held that advising prospective clients in advertising about their legal rights to pursue a defective-product claim against a manufacturer of an intrauterine device and using an accurate illustration of the device were constitutionally protected.

Moreover, the cure for client ignorance was more information rather than less.

(3) Nor was the Court persuaded that lawyer advertising would have an adverse impact on the administration of justice because it would stir up unwanted litigation. The Court refused to accept the premise that most litigation brought as a result of advertising would categorically be unworthy of judicial attention. Instead, the Court stressed the desirability of informing prospective clients about lawyers and legal rights.

(4) The Court regarded arguments about deleterious economic effects of lawyer advertising as both mainly irrelevant to First Amendment considerations and probably unfounded. The bar expressed fears that average fees would increase and entry barriers would harm young lawyers because of high advertising costs.[40] The Court found it as plausible to suspect that it was the absence of advertising that prevented effective price competition and thus maintained fees at artificially high levels. The entry-barrier argument assumed that there were more cost-effective ways for a new lawyer to attract clients, but the bar had also prohibited other likely methods of directly attracting clients.

(5) The Court rejected the contention that lawyer advertising would lead to lower quality legal services. The bar argued that lawyers would cut corners in order to deliver a standard package of advertised services regardless of individual client needs. But the Court noted that incentives to cut corners by doing shoddy work existed regardless of advertising, that several bar-sponsored lawyer referral programs prescribed maximum fees, and that standardizing legal services might reduce error in any event.[41]

(6) The Court also rejected the bar's argument that qualified protection of lawyer advertising would lead to enforcement difficulties and wholesale lawyer violations of more particularized restrictions. Instead, the Court believed that most lawyers would behave as they always had—upholding the integrity and honor of their profession and the legal system.

On the specific facts of the *Bates* case, the Court held that the challenged newspaper advertisement contained no statement that permitted discipline. The reference to a "legal clinic" would readily be understood by consumers to refer to standardized and multiple services such as those provided by these lawyers. The reference to "very reasonable rates" appeared well-founded in view of the bar's own evidence of prevailing charges for similar services in the community. And the assertion by the bar that the advertisement was misleading because it failed to indicate that a name change could be accomplished without a lawyer's services in some instances failed both for lack of proof that local name change procedures were sufficiently simple and because the lawyers had made a practice of advising name-change clients to make the change themselves when the case was uncomplicated.

Although *Bates* plainly marked the end of broad prohibitions against lawyer advertising, the Court stated that carefully limited regulation might be consistent with the commercial speech doctrine in several areas.[42] First, "[a]dvertising that is false, deceptive, or misleading of course is subject to restraint." [43] In that connection, the requirements for accuracy might be made stricter than would be tolerable in non-commercial speech areas. As an example, the Court first alluded vaguely to "quality of services" claims in lawyer advertising, intimating that they might be sufficiently insusceptible of measurement to war-

40 See generally Coase, Advertising and Free Speech, 6 J.Leg.Stud. 1 (1977); Craswell, Beales & Salop, The Efficient Regulation of Consumer Information, 24 J.L. & Econ. 491 (1981); Martyn, Lawyer Advertising: The Unique Relationship between First Amendment and Antitrust Protections, 23 Wayne St.L.Rev. 167 (1976).

41 A study of the operation of a multi-office clinic structured around advertising suggests that the Court's assessment was accurate, indeed was understated because of its finding that the quality of legal service for routinized matters was actually improved. See McChesney & Muris, The Effect of Advertising on the Quality of Legal Services, 65 ABA J. 1503 (1979).

42 See 433 U.S. at 383–84, 97 S.Ct. at 2708–09.

43 433 U.S. at 383, 97 S.Ct. at 2708.

rant restriction.[44] Second, advertising of illegal services could be restrained. Third, in-person solicitation might not be protected by the First Amendment. Fourth, possibly some limited supplementation by way of disclaimer or the like might be warranted, even in otherwise permissible advertising. Fifth, the Court intimated that advertising on the electronic media might present special problems warranting special limitations. In short, "reasonable restrictions on the time, place, and manner of advertising" would be constitutional.[45]

Effects of the Bates Decision

Bates created a furor in many parts of the bar but has proved to have had remarkably little effect on the way that most lawyers conduct the business end of their practices. Despite dire forecasts of rampant, and objectionable, lawyer advertising, most lawyers have not advertised;[46] some that have advertised discovered that it was not cost-effective and have discontinued it;[47] and the advertising that has appeared does not seem, on the whole, to have borne out the fears that it would be deceptive and misleading. If not a non-event, *Bates* and its progeny may rightly be regarded as a mini-event.

Nonetheless, some states continued to read *Bates* very narrowly, and the ABA's proposed amendments to the Code of Professional Responsibility to "conform" the Code to *Bates* offered only a minimally constitutional set of rules.[48] But in In re R.M.J.[49] the Court reversed a Missouri decision that had disciplined a lawyer for newspaper advertising that exceeded the Missouri "laundry list" of permitted statements by including a statement about his membership in the bars of the Illinois and United States Supreme Courts and by listing areas of practice other than those on the approved list and for mailing his announcement card to persons with whom he had no prior relationship.

WESTLAW REFERENCES

digest,synopsis(lawyer attorney /s advertis! /p constitution! unconstitutional % "attorney general")

lawyer attorney /5 advertis! /p "first amendment" /p bates /12 97 +4 2691

§ 14.2.4 Scope of Regulatory Power

Current Limits on State Power

The constitutional protection of the commercial-speech doctrine still leaves lawyer ad-

[44] The category of "quality" claims is obviously a loose one. One court, for example, refused to find that advertising that a lawyer would charge no fee if an advertised service were not performed within five days was a quality claim, describing it as merely a promise of prompt service, a matter fully within the lawyer's powers. See State ex rel. Oklahoma Bar Ass'n v. Schaffer, 648 P.2d 355, 359 (Okl.1982).

[45] 433 U.S. at 384, 97 S.Ct. at 2709.

[46] Lawpoll: Lawyer Advertising Levels Off; P.R. Use Growing, 70 ABA J. 48 (1984)(same percentage (13 percent) of polled lawyers advertised in 1984 and 1983, compared with 3 percent in 1978). The percentage of advertising lawyers rises sharply as the lawyer's income and the size of law firm decreases. Lawpoll: Advertising Attracting neither Participants nor Supporters, 67 ABA J. 1618–19 (1981).

[47] Most lawyers (more than eight of ten) who advertise continue to do so, however. Lawpoll, supra.

[48] In the immediate post-*Bates* era some states issued temporary advertising rules that only prohibited false or misleading advertising, in those words. E.g., In re Administrative Order 1978–4, 402 Mich. lxxxvi, (1978); In re Amendment to Code, 81 Wis.2d xii (1977). Many states, however, gave way only grudgingly. E.g., Florida Bar v. Kaiser, 397 So.2d 1132, 1134 (Fla.1981)(lawyer who attempted to advertise to full extent permitted by law "would be well advised to skate on thicker ice"); In re R.M.J., 609 S.W.2d 411, 412 (Mo.1980)("We respectfully decline to enter the thicket of attempting to anticipate and to satisfy the subjective *ad hoc* judgments of a majority of the justices of the United States Supreme Court."), reversed 455 U.S. 191, 102 S.Ct. 929, 71 L.Ed.2d 64 (1982); In re Petition for Rule of Court Governing Lawyer Advertising, 564 S.W.2d 638 (Tenn.1978)(although reluctant to abandon the "time-honored" tradition of prohibiting advertising, court must bow to *Bates* decision).

[49] 455 U.S. 191, 102 S.Ct. 929, 71 L.Ed.2d 64 (1982). *R.M.J.* joins the wax museum of Supreme Court cases whose curious names reflect the need to provide some measure of privacy to litigants in an otherwise mercilessly public proceeding. E.g., Roe v. Wade, 410 U.S. 113, 93 S.Ct. 705, 35 L.Ed 147 (1973); Bivens v. Six Unknown Named Agents, 403 U.S. 388, 91 S.Ct. 1999, 29 L.Ed.2d 619 (1971). In *R.M.J.* anonymity was dictated by the sanction imposed by the Missouri Supreme Court—an assertedly "private" reprimand.

vertising subject to more regulation than would be applied to expression fully protected by the First Amendment.[50] The Court, for example, has stated that the new commercial speech doctrine does not permit a commercial advertiser to invoke the "overbreadth" doctrine. That doctrine in other areas has permitted a regulated party to attack an overbroad regulation without a demonstration that his or her own communication was specifically protected by the First Amendment. But the Court has insisted that commercial advertisers are not in need of the same protection against "chilling" of their speech, because they know their goods and services and thus are in a superior position to evaluate the accuracy of their messages and because their economic motivation assures that they will vigorously press their communication rights.[51] The factual assumptions underlying those assertions are hardly self-evident, particularly as applied to lawyer advertisers.[52] At the least, however, the approach of the Supreme Court in both *Bates* and *R.M.J.* indicates that the burden of proving that a lawyer's advertising is subject to regulation falls upon the state.[53]

Despite areas of uncertainty, the Supreme Court's current analysis of the extent of the states' remaining regulatory power over lawyer advertising seems to trace the following steps. First, the state has the burden of demonstrating that a lawyer's advertising is in conflict with either a substantial state interest or an arguable state interest. If the interest is substantial—for example, preventing consumer fraud through false or misleading advertising—then regulation is warranted without a further showing. If the interest is merely arguable—for example, preventing consumers from being misled by use of the word "clinic" in a firm name—then the state has the further burden of demonstrating (a) that the lawyer's communication violates a specific rule; (b) that the violation in fact implicates a substantial state interest that can be demonstrated on the facts of the particular case; and (c) that application of the regulation is no broader than necessary to vindicate the state's particularized interest.[54] Many areas of litigated lawyer advertising and the First Amendment can be explained by resort to such a formulation.

Specific Types of Lawyer Advertising

Against the developing constitutional background, some questions of lawyer advertising have received recurring attention in the courts.[55]

(1) *Stimulating Publicity.* The traditional prohibition against a lawyer's "stimulating" media publicity should no longer be valid.[56] Fawning on the media is objectionable on character grounds perhaps, but the First Amendment rights of the lawyer, the lawyer's derivative claim of a need to publicize a client's version of publicly debated events by commenting on pending cases (§ 12.2.2), and the right of the media to gather and broadcast information clearly overrides any such merely plausible state interest. Paying a publicist to obtain publicity is as unobjectionable as is advertising itself. Thus there can be no objection to a lawyer's hiring a public relations or advertising consultant.[57] The prohibition

[50] See generally Symposium on Commercial Speech, 46 Brooklyn L.Rev. 389 (1980). Several specific kinds of state restraints on lawyer advertising are analyzed in Andrews, Lawyer Advertising and the First Amendment, 1981 Am.B.Found. Research J. 967.

[51] Bates v. Arizona State Bar, 433 U.S. 350, 381, 97 S.Ct. 2691, 2707–08, 53 L.Ed.2d 810 (1977). See also Central Hudson Gas & Elec. Corp. v. Public Serv. Comm'n, 447 U.S. 557, 564 n.6, 100 S.Ct. 2343, 2350, 65 L.Ed.2d 341 (1980); Virginia State Bd. of Pharmacy v. Virginia Citizens Consumer Council, Inc., 425 U.S. 748, 772 n.24, 96 S.Ct. 1817, 1831, 48 L.Ed.2d 346 (1976).

[52] Farber, Commercial Speech and First Amendment Theory, 74 Nw.U.L.Rev. 372, 385–392 (1979).

[53] See the discussion in In re Marcus, 107 Wis.2d 560, 320 N.W.2d 806, 814–815 (1982).

[54] In re R.M.J., 455 U.S. 191, 203–04 n.15, 102 S.Ct. 929, 937–38, 71 L.Ed.2d 64 (1982); Central Hudson Gas & Elec. Corp. v. Public Service Comm'n, 447 U.S. 557, 563–64, 100 S.Ct. 2343, 2350, 65 L.Ed.2d 341 (1980).

[55] For a general review, see Annot., 30 A.L.R.4th 742 (1984).

[56] Jacoby v. State Bar, 19 Cal.3d 359, 138 Cal.Rptr. 77, 562 P.2d 1326, 4 A.L.R.4th 273 (1977).

[57] But cf. DR 2–103(B) and (C).

in DR 2–101(I) against paying a representative of the media for "professional publicity in a news item" might be sustainable on the ground that the compensation creates a substantial likelihood that the news item would be misleading.[58]

(2) *False Claims.* Clearly subject to state regulation is lawyer advertising that is false or misleading.[59] A state may regulate advertising that is potentially misleading by requiring a disclaimer or further explanation.[60] Both the Code (DR 2–101(A)) and the Model Rules (MR 7.1) begin with prohibitions against false or misleading advertising but then diverge. The Code goes into elaborate detail in describing advertising material that is not proscribed (DR 2–101(B)). But MR 7.1 contents itself with defining *false and misleading* to include material misrepresentations (including passive misrepresentation by nondisclosure of important explanatory detail), a message that creates an unreasonable expectation of results or implies that the lawyer can achieve results in a manner prohibited by other Model Rules, or that draws comparisons with other lawyers' services unless the comparison can be substantiated.

(3) *Self-Laudation.* Controversy surrounds the question whether a state may permissibly enforce a rule such as DR 2–101(B), which prohibits "self-laudatory" advertising statements by a lawyer. The only apparently permissible basis of regulation is that mentioned in *Bates*—that such claims are not susceptible of proof.[61] That rationale would cover such claims as "most successful litigator" or the like. It would perhaps also cover "member of Million Dollar Verdict Club," because, even if the club existed and the lawyer were a member, mention of the fact might create unjustified expectations in prospective clients. But advertising "thirty years of law practice," if this is true, should probably be protected. While such a statement is plainly susceptible to a self-laudatory meaning, as is the case with most effective advertising, the implication that experience tends to bring higher quality services is unassailable as a general proposition.

(4) *Specialization/Concentration.* The Court in *R.M.J.*. held that a lawyer's listing of areas of practice was constitutionally protected even if some of them differed from the areas that the state rules permitted mentioning and others on the lawyer's advertised list used descriptive phrases different from those required by the court's rules to be used for similar areas. The case may stand for the narrow proposition that once a state permits "area" advertising, it must proceed very carefully and probably cannot regulate strictly. But whether *Bates* and *R.M.J.* require the states to accept specialization advertising at all remains unsettled.[62] Both the Code (DR 2–105(A)) and the Model Rules (MR 7.4) proscribe specialty advertising.

(5) *Disclaimers and Qualifications.* The favorable mention of required disclaimers in the *Bates* decision has led several jurisdictions to rely upon mandatory disclaimers and quali-

[58] The prohibition in MR 7.2(c) is broader in that it prohibits giving anything of value to a person for recommending the lawyer's services except for advertising and lawyer referral plans. Its comment, however, suggests that it is limited to traditional touting arrangements (§ 14.2.5).

[59] People v. Roehl, 655 P.2d 1381 (Colo.1983)(advertising set price for divorce but then merely supplying responding clients with inadequate form and instruction sheet); Florida Bar v. Budish, 421 So.2d 501 (Fla.1982) (advertising name change for $75 but charging client $100 fee plus $44 for costs); Kentucky Bar Ass'n v. Gangwish, 630 S.W.2d 66 (Ky.1982)(advertising "20 percent" discount).

[60] Bates v. Arizona State Bar, 433 U.S. 350, 384, 97 S.Ct. 2691, 2709, 53 L.Ed.2d 810 (1977); In re R.M.J., 455 U.S. 191, 201, 102 S.Ct. 929, 936, 71 L.Ed.2d 64 (1982); Zauderer v. Office of Disciplinary Counsel, ___ U.S. ___, 105 S.Ct. 2265, 2281–83, 85 L.Ed.2d 652 (1985). See also, e.g., Mezrano v. Alabama St. Bar, 434 So.2d 732 (Ala. 1983)(constitutional for state rule to require all lawyer advertising to contain disclaimer of quality or expertise claims).

[61] Bates v. Arizona State Bar, 433 U.S. 350, 366, 97 S.Ct. 2691, 2700, 53 L.Ed.2d 810 (1977).

[62] Compare, e.g., In re Johnson, 341 N.W.2d 282 (Minn. 1983)(DR 2–105(B) unconstitutional on its face and as applied), with, e.g., Spencer v. Justices of Supreme Court of Pennsylvania, 579 F.Supp. 880 (E.D.Pa.1984)(permissible to prohibit use of words such as "experienced," "expert," "highly qualified," and "competent," as subjective claims difficult for nonlawyer to measure or verify).

fying language quite substantially.[63] Alabama, for example, requires that any mention of a fee in advertising must include qualifying language giving an accurate estimate of court costs and a disclaimer stating that no representation is made about quality or expertise.[64] But the mention of disclaimers in *Bates* should not be read in isolation from the rest of the opinion, particularly apart from its language concerning the required narrowness of regulations. The rationale of *Bates* is hardly consistent with mandatory disclaimers that are only arguably relevant to an advertised message.[65]

(6) *Advertising Screening.* *Bates* itself intimated that a state could require lawyer advertisers to submit copies of advertisements to a screening agency after publication or to retain copies of advertisements for a prescribed period.[66] The Model Rules (MR 7.2(b)) require retention of a record and copy of all advertising for two years. It is problematical whether requiring a lawyer to submit advertising copy for prepublication "clearance" by a court or bar is constitutional.[67] It seems extremely unlikely that the Supreme Court would permit a state to require a lawyer to litigate the constitutionality of an antiadvertising rule before advertising.[68]

(7) *Electronic Media.* Several jurisdictions have continued to prohibit all electronic media advertising, in reliance on the Supreme Court's statement in *Bates* that this area may be particularly susceptible to regulation.[69] The basis for that excepted treatment is mysterious.[70] Surely the potential breadth of broadcast of the statement argues as much for protecting it as for its special regulation. And copying and preserving records of broadcasts is surely no insurmountable problem and presumably could be required. Other jurisdictions have permitted television or radio advertising but under substantial restrictions that limit the information that can be provided visually and orally so as to eliminate any dramatic value or attractiveness.[71] The barrier is particularly critical to multioffice legal clinics that require mass-response advertising on television in order to prosper.[72] Both the final version of the Code (DR 2–101(B)) and the Model Rules (MR 7.2(a)) permit advertising on television and radio although several states have refused to permit it under local rules.

(8) *Direct Mail.* The form of advertising that is nearest to solicitation in its possible person-to-person impact is direct mailing. It is prohibited under DR 2–101(B), but permitted to an extent by MR 7.2(a) and MR 7.3. Apparently inconsistent decisions concerning direct mail communications to strangers can probably be substantially reconciled by the differing susceptibility of the recipients of the communications to undue influence or over-

63 See also, e.g., DR 2–101(B)(25)(necessary qualifying language concerning fixed-fee advertising); MR 7.2(d)(any advertising must include name of at least one lawyer responsible for contents).

64 Lyon v. Alabama St. Bar, 451 So.2d 1367 (Ala.1984), cert. denied ___ U.S. ___, 105 S.Ct. 385, 83 L.Ed.2d 320 (1984).

65 Spencer v. Justices of the Supreme Court of Pennsylvania, 579 F.Supp. 880 (E.D.Pa.1984).

66 Bates v. Arizona State Bar, 433 U.S. 350, 381, 97 S.Ct. 2691, 2707–08, 53 L.Ed.2d 810 (1977).

67 Cf. Virginia Bd. of Pharmacy v. Virginia Citizens Consumer Council, Inc., 425 U.S. 748, 765, 96 S.Ct. 1817, 1827, 48 L.Ed.2d 346 (1976)(commercial speech doctrine "may also make inapplicable the prohibition against prior restraints").

68 But see In re Felmeister, 95 N.J. 431, 471 A.2d 775 (1984).

69 In re Professional Ethics Advisory Comm. Op. 475, 89 N.J. 74, 444 A.2d 1092 (1982), appeal dismissed sub nom. Jacoby & Meyers v. Supreme Court of New Jersey, 459 U.S. 962, 103 S.Ct. 285, 74 L.Ed.2d 272 (1982). Contra, e.g., Grievance Committee v. Trantolo, 192 Conn. 15, 470 A.2d 228 (1984); In re Petition for Rule of Court, 564 S.W.2d 638 (Tenn.1978). For criticism of the "electronic media" exception from the commercial speech doctrine, see Rotunda, The Commercial Speech Doctrine in the Supreme Court, 1976 U.Ill.L.F. 1080, 1098–1100.

70 Grievance Committee v. Trantolo, 192 Conn. 27, 470 A.2d 235 (1984)(because prohibition against electronic media advertising would be of doubtful constitutionality, DR 2–101 should be read to prohibit such only if false or misleading).

71 Committee on Professional Ethics v. Humphrey, 355 N.W.2d 565 (Iowa 1984).

72 Cf. Nat'l L.J., Apr.16, 1984, at 2, col.2 (one national clinic spent 17 percent of total of $17,803,300 spent by all nations' lawyers on television advertising in 1983).

reaching.[73] A blanket prohibition, such as that in the Code, against direct mail advertising regardless of the recipient or message is constitutionally suspect.[74]

The approach of the Model Rules is slightly more yielding: a lawyer may engage in direct-mail advertising under MR 7.3 if the recipients are not known by the lawyer to currently need legal services of the kind advertised by the lawyer but might find such services "in general . . . useful." The apparent rationale is to direct mail away from persons whose emotional or physical condition makes them susceptible to overreaching, but the criterion chosen in MR 7.3 is almost perverse from a communications point of view because it permits mailings only to less-interested recipients.

(9) *Intra-Lawyer Communications.* The Code, in DR 2–102(A)(2) prohibits a lawyer from including anything but rather rudimentary information in communications from one lawyer to another, such as a solicitation by the communicating lawyer for the other to recommend the first lawyer's services. In view of *R.M.J.*, the ABA ethics committee has conceded that the rule is almost certainly unconstitutional.[75] The sophistication of the audience makes it highly unlikely that anything other than false or misleading statements would have much potential for harm.

(10) *Firm Names.* Much ado has been made about firm names, probably because of their goodwill value. The Code prohibits "trade names" in DR 2–102(B). The *R.M.J.* decision protected the use of "clinic" in a firm name, but apparently on the Court's understanding that the firm was conducted as a high-volume, routine-services enterprise and because the state had not offered any defensible reason for thinking that the term was misleading or otherwise objectionable.[76] Most jurisdictions permit "professional corporation" or a similar addition to the end of a firm's name (DR 2–102(B)). Acceptance of firm names with the name of one or more deceased lawyers is also

[73] Compare, e.g., Grievance Comm. v. Trantolo, 192 Conn. 27, 470 A.2d 235 (1984)(direct mailing to realtors permissible); In re Appert, 315 N.W.2d 204 (Minn.1981) (letters and brochures advertising lawyers' availability to handle complex litigation against drug-device manufacturer on contingent fee basis constitutionally protected); Koffler v. Joint Bar Ass'n, 51 N.Y.2d 140, 432 N.Y.S.2d 872, 412 N.E.2d 927 (1980), cert.denied 450 U.S. 1026, 101 S.Ct. 1733, 68 L.Ed.2d 221 (1981)(mass mailings to realtors and property owners); Kentucky Bar Ass'n v. Stuart, 568 S.W.2d 933 (Ky.1978)(letters to realtors soliciting legal services in closings), with, e.g., State v. Moses, 231 Kan. 243, 642 P.2d 1004 (1982)(discipline for direct mailing to home sellers); In re Alessi, 60 N.Y.2d 229, 469 N.Y.S.2d 577, 457 N.E.2d 682 (1983), cert.denied 465 U.S. 1102, 104 S.Ct. 599, 80 L.Ed.2d 130 (1984)(prohibition against direct mailings to realtors constitutional because of conflict of interest problems); In re Rule of Court, 564 S.W.2d 638 (Tenn.1978)(insurmountable problems of enforcement permit prohibition of distribution of circulars or handbills).

Even courts that generally permit direct mail solicitation continue to exert "time, place, and manner" regulation. E.g., In re Appert, supra, 315 N.W.2d at 215 (permissible to regulate "self-laudatory" phrase in permitted brochure); In re Greene, 54 N.Y.2d 118, 444 N.Y.S.2d 883, 429 N.E.2d 390 (1981), cert.denied 455 U.S. 1035, 102 S.Ct. 1738, 72 L.Ed.2d 153 (1982)(letters to realtors requesting that they recommend lawyer to customers regulatable because they created danger of conflict of interest).

[74] Spencer v. Justices of Supreme Court of Pennsylvania, 579 F.Supp. 880 (E.D.Pa.1984); Kentucky Bar Ass'n v. Stuart, 568 S.W.2d 933 (Ky.1978); Koffler v. Joint Bar Ass'n, 51 N.Y.2d 140, 432 N.Y.S.2d 872, 412 N.E.2d 927 (1980), cert.denied 450 U.S. 1026, 101 S.Ct. 1733, 68 L.Ed.2d 221 (1981).

[75] ABA Informal Op. 84–1504 (1984).

[76] The Court seems implicitly to have required that the "clinic" in fact have at least those operating characteristics. Some subsequent decisions have been restrictive in permitting the use of the word "clinic" to describe a law practice. E.g., Bishop v. Committee on Professional Ethics, 521 F.Supp. 1219 (S.D.Iowa 1981), vacated 686 F.2d 1278 (8th Cir.1982)(validity of Iowa rule prohibiting use of "clinic" in firm name unless office was limited to routine services); Mezrano v. Alabama St. Bar, 434 So.2d 732 (Ala.1983)(use of "clinic" for law practice geographically proximate to, but not connected with, state university potentially misleading). The Supreme Court, in a very problematical commercial speech decision, has gone as far as permitting a state to prohibit the use of trade names altogether. Friedman v. Rogers, 440 U.S. 1, 99 S.Ct. 887, 59 L.Ed.2d 100 (1979). *Friedman* has been relied upon as authority for prohibiting any use of a trade name by a lawyer. In re Sekerez, 458 N.E.2d 229, 242 (Ind.1984), cert.denied ___ U.S. ___, 105 S.Ct. 182, 83 L.Ed.2d 116 (1984); In re Oldtowne Legal Clinic, 285 Md. 132, 400 A.2d 1111 (1979). But cf. Florida Bar v. Fetterman, 439 So.2d 835 (Fla.1983)("The Law Team" not false or misleading); In re Shannon, 292 Or. 339, 638 P.2d 482 (1982)(prohibition against use of trade names interpreted to apply only to false and misleading trade names). See generally Annot., 26 A.L.R.4th 1083 (1983).

widely permitted (DR 2–102(B)), but that hardly seems constitutionally required, because it is potentially misleading to some prospective clients.

A relatively common, and restrictive, requirement is that all lawyers mentioned in a firm name must be admitted to practice in the jurisdiction.[77] That has meant that multistate law firms that have lawyer names in their own name are unable to advertise in some jurisdictions even if all lawyers who would perform advertised services within the jurisdiction have been admitted there.[78] The Model Rules, in MR 7.5(a), limit firm names only by a false-and-misleading standard and only require that multijurisdictional firms indicate jurisdictional limitations on lawyers' abilities to practice when a full listing of the lawyers' names is given, as on a traditional letterhead.

(11) *Firm Signs.* As have letterheads, so firm signs—or *shingles*, as they have traditionally been called—have been the subject of exacting regulation. It is doubtful how much of that regulation survives the First Amendment, even if the firm sign is taken far from its traditional unobtrusive place and instead is mounted on a billboard. The reference to "outdoor" advertising in MR 7.2(a) seems clearly to authorize billboard advertising.

(12) *Letterheads.* Meticulous rules governing the contents of letterheads have been traditional. In view of recent decisions, however, much of the regulation is questionable.[79] Most lawyers will probably continue to comply without challenging the regulations, however, because letterheads are hardly a very effective form of advertising.

Under the 1969 Code, as amended, letterheads and their contents are apparently regarded as involving a solicitation issue and not one of advertising. For example, consider whether a lawyer who is also a certified public accountant may state, truthfully, on a law office letterhead that he or she is a CPA. If the publication is advertising, then DR 2–101(B)(12) applies and permits advertising of this "technical and professional license." But the letterhead rule—DR 2–102(A)(4)—plainly does not permit the CPA designation. The difference, if there is one, presumably relates not to the type of information but to the presumed uses to which the informational format might be put. The Code apparently reflects a belief that letterheads can be used in situations that the Code would treat as solicitation as opposed to the more widely dispersed and, if false or misleading, more readily detectable forms of communication involved in advertising. The approach of the Model Rules is quite different: the basic rule of MR 7.5(a) is that letterheads are restricted only by the false-and-misleading limitations of the general advertising rule.

WESTLAW REFERENCES

attorney lawyer /5 advertis! /p "commercial speech"

attorney lawyer /5 advertis! /p interest rule regulation /s violat! conflict!

attorney lawyer /5 advertis! /s false misleading self-laudatory

topic(45) /p advertis! /s television radio electronic!

attorney lawyer /5 advertis! /s mail!

---

§ 14.2.5 Solicitation

History and Methods of Solicitation

As with a lawyer who advertises, a lawyer who actively seeks out prospective clients is engaged in a practice that has a long, if disreputable, history and in this century has been flatly prohibited by professional rules. Abraham Lincoln solicited clients unabashed-

---

77 But see, e.g., New York Crimin. & Civ. Cts. Bar Ass'n v. Jacoby, 61 N.Y.2d 130, 472 N.Y.S.2d 890, 460 N.E.2d 1325 (1984).

78 Attorney Grievance Comm'n v. Hyatt, 52 U.S.L.Wk. 2605 (Md.Cir.Ct.1984); In re Professional Ethics Advisory Comm. Op. 475, 89 N.J. 74, 444 A.2d 1092 (1982), appeal dismissed sub nom. Jacoby & Meyers v. Supreme Court of New Jersey, 459 U.S. 962, 103 S.Ct.285, 74 L.Ed.2d 272 (1982).

79 But cf. In re Advisory Committee Opinion No. 447, 86 N.J. 473, 432 A.2d 59 (1981)(validity of rule prohibiting lawyer from including truthful CPA designation on letterhead).

ly.[80] In several notable instances in the nation's legal history—including the Peter Zenger case, the Aaron Burr case, the Dred Scott case, and others—prominent lawyers, without the prior invitation of the client, approached a person in legal trouble and offered their services.[81] Despite very stern measures taken for decades by bar associations, the practice continues, perhaps thrives.

The methods of solicitation are as various as are the possible routes to the source of persons with legal troubles.[82] Lawyers—either directly or through their runners, cappers, or touts—have paid money to taxi drivers in "divorce haven" states who brought prospective divorce clients from the airport to the lawyer's office;[83] have accepted referrals from a nonlawyer who solicited prospective clients of a mass accident for the lawyer in the hope of becoming his investigator;[84] have paid gratuities to police officers, ambulance drivers, doctors and other medical workers in emergency rooms, or professional runners who might be first aware of a personal injury,[85] or to bail bond writers or others involved in the criminal process;[86] or have had nonlawyer employees find and sign up prospective clients.[87]

Attempts to Suppress Solicitation

Courts and bar associations have resorted to several methods and remedies to eradicate in-person solicitation. It is prohibited everywhere today by professional rules except in a few jurisdictions such as the District of Columbia and Illinois, where it is regulated. Solicitation is a crime in many states[88] and has been the target of injunctions in some.[89] Some courts will disqualify a lawyer from continuing to represent a solicited client in litigation, although probably the majority of courts refuse to impose that remedy.[90] Con-

80 Boden, Five Years after Bates: Lawyer Advertising in Legal and Ethical Perspective, 65 Marq.L.Rev. 547, 547–48 (1982)(mail solicitation by Lincoln of both county and railroad in litigation brewing between them), citing J.Duff, A.Lincoln, Prairie Lawyer 31 (1960).

81 In re Ades, 6 F.Supp. 467, 475–76 (D.Md.1934)(Soper, J.)(lawyer acting in behalf of political organization is entitled to volunteer his services to a minority person accused of multiple murders).

82 See generally Annot., 5 A.L.R.4th 866 (1981).

83 State Bar v. Raffetto, 64 Nev. 390, 183 P.2d 621 (1947).

84 In re Carroll, 124 Ariz. 80, 602 P.2d 461 (1979).

85 Louisiana St. Bar Ass'n v. Beard, 374 So.2d 1179 (La. 1979); Attorney Grievance Comm'n v. Engerman, 289 Md. 330, 424 A.2d 362 (1981); In re Maran, 80 N.J. 160, 402 A.2d 924 (1979)(paying doctor to refer patients to law firm). Cf. 1908 ABA Canon 28:

> It is disreputable to hunt up defects in titles or other causes of action and inform thereof in order to be employed to bring suit or collect judgment, or to breed litigation by seeking out those with claims for personal injuries or those having any other grounds of action in order to secure them as clients, or to employ agents or runners for like purposes, or to pay or reward, directly or indirectly, those who bring or influence the bringing of such cases to his office, or to remunerate policemen, court or prison officials, physicians, hospital *attachés* or others who may succeed, under the guise of giving disinterested friendly advice, in influencing the criminal, the sick and the injured, the ignorant or others, to seek his professional services.

86 Jackson v. State, 140 Ga.App. 288, 231 S.E.2d 805 (1976); In re Siegel, 80 A.D.2d 145, 438 N.Y.S.2d 119 (1981), appeal denied 54 N.Y.2d 602, 443 N.Y.S.2d 1025, 426 N.E.2d 754 (1981); ABA Defense Function Standards § 4–2.3(a) (1982).

87 Kitsis v. State Bar, 23 Cal.3d 857, 153 Cal.Rptr. 836, 592 P.2d 323 (1979)(elaborate scheme of radio-equipped cars, visits to auto repair shops for tips, visits to hospitals and sites of accidents); In re Schlossman, 85 A.D.2d 702, 445 N.Y.S.2d 765 (1981); In re Oxman, 496 Pa. 534, 437 A.2d 1169 (1981), cert.denied 456 U.S. 975, 102 S.Ct. 2240, 72 L.Ed.2d 849 (1982).

88 33 U.S.C.A. § 928(e); In re Arnoff, 22 Cal.3d 740, 150 Cal.Rptr. 479, 586 P.2d 960 (1978); Florida Bar v. Pace, 426 So.2d 553 (Fla.1983)(resignation following conviction for soliciting); Woll v. Kelley, 409 Mich. 500, 297 N.W.2d 578 (1980).

89 State ex rel. Beck v. Lush, 170 Neb. 376, 103 N.W.2d 136 (1960). Cf. Great Western Cities, Inc. v. Binstein, 476 F.Supp. 827 (N.D.Ill.1979), affirmed 614 F.2d 775 (7th Cir. 1979)(injunction against soliciting claims against land developer denied on ground, among others, that developer had unclean hands on basis of failure to deny defrauding lot owners).

90 Fisher Studio, Inc. v. Loew's, Inc., 232 F.2d 199 (2d Cir.1956), cert.denied 352 U.S. 836, 77 S.Ct. 56, 1 L.Ed.2d 55 (1956). See also Magida v. Continental Can Co., 231 F.2d 843 (2d Cir.1956), cert.denied 351 U.S. 972, 76 S.Ct. 1031, 100 L.Ed. 1490 (1956)(court-awarded fee permitted despite solicitation of plaintiff-client in successful shareholder derivative action in violation of Canons); Hahn v. Boeing Co., 95 Wash.2d 28, 621 P.2d 1263 (1980)(on motion to appear pro hac vice, inquiry into solicitation of plaintiff-client improper because it was irrelevant to ability of lawyer or capacity to serve client effectively).

tracts to perform solicitation services are unenforceable,[91] and in some states a solicited client-lawyer contract to pay fees is itself unenforceable.[92] Bar associations in many states have launched periodic campaigns against solicitation and assertedly attendant evils, such as falsifying claims.[93] Radical solutions have been proposed, such as making a lawyer unnecessary in a legal problem by providing nonlegal or nonlitigated means of redress.[94] Nonetheless, solicitation is probably quite widespread, and judicial hostility to enforcement of the antisolicitation rules is not unknown.[95]

Reasons for the Survival of Solicitation

There are two sides to solicitation—two motivations that might lead a lawyer to seek out clients and advise them to retain him or her as a lawyer. One situation involves prospective clients who will probably be represented by *some* lawyer—for example, persons aware of their legal rights who are seriously injured and in a hospital or arrested for a serious crime. A lawyer's motivation in soliciting such clients is probably competitive: to gain legal business that otherwise would go to other lawyers. That is probably the dominant reason for solicitation and is primarily a problem of economic competition among lawyers. For that reason antitrust officials have expressed concern that overly broad solicitation rules are anticompetitive.[96] Solicitation can also involve problems of the invasion of the privacy of prospective clients[97] and of consumer fraud because of possible overreaching and misrepresentation by lawyers competing with each other for legal business. Those are the reasons most often given by courts and bar associations for broad antisolicitation rules.

The second situation involves persons ignorant of the law who, except for the advice to employ a lawyer, would lose valuable legal rights. Such persons also might have been seriously injured and might now be about to sign entirely inadequate releases offered by insurance adjusters.[98] Or such persons might have been arrested and are about to talk to the police in ignorance of the advantages of a lawyer.[99]

Solicitation in the former case strikes us as neutral at best, regrettable if it involves fraud

91 Marvin N. Benn & Assoc., Ltd. v. Nelsen Steel & Wire, Inc., 107 Ill.App.3d 442, 63 Ill.Dec. 251, 437 N.E.2d 900 (1982); Holland v. Sheehan, 108 Minn. 362, 122 N.W. 1 (1909).

92 Rhoades v. Norfolk & W. Ry., 78 Ill.2d 217, 35 Ill.Dec. 680, 399 N.E.2d 969 (1979).

93 Cohen v. Hurley, 366 U.S. 117, 81 S.Ct. 954, 6 L.Ed. 156 (1961). See also, e.g., Tybor, Media Hoax Hits Lawyers in Chicago, Nat'l L.J., Feb.25, 1980, at 1, col.4 ("sting" investigation by newspaper assertedly revealed extensive ring of lawyers involved in filing fraudulent insurance claims through solicited clients).

94 H.Drinker, Legal Ethics 64 (1953)(removing temptation to chase ambulances by making recovery by injured persons automatic and nonlitigatable); O'Connell, A Proposal to Abolish Defendants' Payment for Pain and Suffering in Return for Payment of Claimants' Attorneys' Fees, 1981 U.Ill.L.Rev. 333.

95 Cohen v. Hurley, 366 U.S. 117, 148 n.37, 81 S.Ct. 954, 972, 6 L.Ed.2d 156 (1961)(dissenting opinion of Black, J.) (in case involving judicial inquiry into ambulance-chasing: "[T]he true nature of the underlying controversy in this case [is] a controversy between economically competing groups of lawyers"); In re Schwartz, 231 N.Y. 642, 132 N.E. 921, 923 (1921)(dissenting opinion joined by Pound and Cardozo, JJ., and Hiscock, Ch.J.)(judgment of disbarment unfounded because solicitation is merely offense "against good taste rather than good morals."); Pirsig, A Traditional Course in Professional Responsibility, in Education in the Professional Responsibilities of the Lawyer 75, 83–85 (D.Weckstein ed.1970).

96 E.g., 53 U.S.L.Wk. 2114 (Aug.8, 1984)(remarks of chief of Justice Department's Special Litigation Section).

97 In re Beattie, 275 S.C. 305, 270 S.E.2d 624 (1980) (lawyer who was also ordained minister solicited persons in their hospital rooms).

98 An alternative to solicitation in such a case is to make illegal the solicitation of settlements by insurance adjusters from persons who are not in a situation in which they can exercise their normal judgment. E.g., Calif. Laws, 1976, ch. 1016 (release solicited from person in medical facility within fifteen days of admission presumptively fraudulent); N.Y.—McKinney's Jud.Law § 480 (unlawful for any person to enter hospital to secure release from injured person within fifteen days after injuries sustained).

99 The *Miranda* warning has largely vitiated the need for solicitation in criminal cases—if the procedure is followed—because arrested persons will be informed of their basic legal rights and of their right to the assistance of a lawyer. See infra at 794.

or invasion of privacy.[1] Solicitation in the latter case strikes us as an important means of assuring that persons are aware of their legal rights.[2] Unfortunately, it is very difficult to distinguish the situations from each other because they are precisely the same except for the subjective knowledge of the prospective client about legal rights.

Professional Regulations

The 1908 Canons as originally enacted condemned solicitation in the strongest terms[3] and imposed an obligation on every member of the bar who had knowledge of such activities "immediately to inform thereof, to the end that the offender may be disbarred."[4] The matter was more meticulously regulated in the 1969 Code in DR 2–103 and 2–104.[5] Those forbid a lawyer to recommend employment of himself, herself, or an associated lawyer to a person who has not sought the lawyer's advice (DR 2–103) and forbid a lawyer who has given a person unrequested advice to take legal action to accept that person as a client (DR 2–104(A)).[6] Earlier drafts of the 1983 Model Rules would have permitted solicitation in certain circumstances,[7] but the final version of MR 7.3 broadly prohibits in-person solicitation and many forms of solicitation through the mail.

A few jurisdictions have permitted solicitation in many more circumstances than the ABA would allow. Illinois' 1980 Code contains a provision on solicitation as liberal as any.[8] The rule prohibits solicitation only when the condition of the person solicited is such that the lawyer reasonably should know that the person cannot exercise reasonable judgment,[9] when the person has informed the lawyer not to communicate, or when the solicitation involves duress or harassment.[10] The District of Columbia rule is similar to solicitation rules that various federal agencies have adopted,[11] since it was significantly amended in 1978 following the *Bates* decision.[12] The rule bars in-person solicitation only if it involves false or misleading claims or undue influence, if the prospective client's mental or physical condition makes it unlikely that the client can exercise considered judgment, or if the client has expressed a wish not to be solicited.[13]

Permissible Soliciting

The professional rules have always permitted types of activity that, aside from arbitrary

1 A third possible situation exists when a lawyer solicits a prospective client who, as the lawyer knows, has no legal claim but the lawyer falsely suggests the contrary in order to charge a fee. See Morgan, The Emerging Concept of Professional Responsibility, 90 Harv.L.Rev. 702, 721–22 (1977). Such cases are unusual in actual practice because most solicited cases involve personal injury claims that are handled on a contingent fee basis. Some personal injury cases, however, may be solicited in that way in order to perpetrate fraud upon defendants or insurance companies even though the "plaintiff" is not injured or is not injured by any fault of the defendant but can be made to appear so by false evidence.

2 M.Freedman, Lawyers' Ethics in an Adversary System, ch.10 (1975); Comment, Solicitation by the Second Oldest Profession: Attorneys and Advertising, 8 Harv. Civ.Rts.-Civ.Lib.L.Rev. 77 (1973); Comment, A Critical Analysis of Rules against Solicitation by Lawyers, 25 U.Chi.L.Rev. 674 (1958). Cf. EC 2-2: "The legal profession should assist laymen to recognize legal problems because such problems may not be self-revealing and often are not timely noticed."

3 1908 Canons 27, 28.

4 1908 Canon 28.

5 See also Calif.Prof.Cond.R. 2–101(B).

6 Strictly, the Code does not prohibit solicitation of a client so long as the person solicited has initiated the contact with the lawyer. Rhoades v. Norfolk & W. Ry., 78 Ill.2d 217, 35 Ill.Dec. 680, 399 N.E.2d 969 (1979).

7 See MR 9.3 (Discussion Draft, Jan.30, 1980).

8 Ill. Code Rule 2–103(c).

9 Such a limited restriction on solicitation was recommended in Note, Advertising, Solicitation and the Professional Duty to Make Legal Counsel Available, 81 Yale L.J. 1181, 1199–1200 (1972).

10 The Illinois rule (Rule 2–103(d)) also prohibits giving or promising "anything of value" to "another person" to initiate contact with a prospective client. The rule precludes the use of runners or cappers, and apparently even nonlawyer assistants in a lawyer's own office.

11 ICC Rules and Regulations, 49 C.F.R. § 1000 (1983).

12 The D.C. Code was again amended in 1981, however, to prohibit soliciting clients in and around the courthouse because of an uproar created by a group of aggressively competing lawyers. See Ranii, Judges Ban Courthouse Solicitation, Nat'l L.J., June 29, 1981, at 2, col.1.

13 D.C.Code DR 2–103, as amended 1978.

conventions of terminology, would themselves be called solicitation. They involve situations in which the potential problems of invasion of privacy and overreaching arguably do not so clearly exist.

A lawyer may generally recommend that he be employed by a former *client, relative, or close friend*,[14] persons who presumably know the lawyer well enough not to be easily misled and whose friendship the lawyer would be more loath to offend by invading their privacy. That exception has led newly admitted lawyers to join social clubs without number in order to put themselves into friendly contact with the maximum number of prospective clients.

The Code and the Model Rules permit solicitation of legal business from *other lawyers*.[15] That departs from pre-Code authority that tended to prohibit all forms of solicitation that "stirred up litigation." [16] It is fully supportable by the other, and modern, rationale for suppressing solicitation because of the absence of significant risks of overreaching, misrepresentation, or invasion of privacy.

Under the 1969 Code a lawyer may also solicit prospective clients when employed by a *qualified legal services organization*,[17] although some courts have frowned on the practice for reasons of taste and respectability.[18] The exception is required because of the broad constitutional protection that the Supreme Court has given to legal advocacy groups (§ 16.5.2). Solicitation through a lawyer referral service is also permissible.[19]

The extent to which a lawyer may solicit as clients persons who have already been designated as *members of a certified class action* in which the lawyer represents the class has been debated. There seems little reason, other than partisan advantage, to resist a rule that would leave the class' lawyer free to contact members of the class for any purpose, but should regard with suspicion any individual contracts to pay the lawyer an amount in addition to the award made out of the class recovery.[20]

Constitutional Issues in Solicitation

Two lines of cases in the Supreme Court suggested at one time that solicitation might enjoy a large measure of constitutional protection. Several decisions had held that lawyer solicitation in behalf of a legal advocacy group was constitutionally immune from state regulation. Those cases rested, not on the expressive rights of lawyers, but on the rights of the prospective clients to obtain access to the courts and to vindicate their legal rights through litigation.[21] After the Court's deci-

14 DR 2–104(A)(1). The 1983 Model Rules may be narrower because, while MR 7.3 excludes "a prospective client with whom the lawyer has . . . family or prior professional relationship," there is no mention of friendships. E.g., Goldthwaite v. Disciplinary Bd., 408 So.2d 504 (Ala.1982)(permissible for lawyer to recommend his employment to chairman of bank, friend and former client, to represent estate of dying cousin).

15 DR 2–103(A)(only soliciting "layperson" prohibited); MR 7.3 (solicitation from "a prospective client" prohibited).

16 In re Hubbard, 267 S.W.2d 743 (Ky.1954).

17 DR 2–103(D); cf. MR 7.2 comment (Paying Others to Recommend a Lawyer)(mention of advertising, but not of solicitation, by "legal aid agency or prepaid legal services plan"). None of the Model Rules alludes to legal services solicitation. At least solicitation that is protected by the federal Constitution plainly must be allowed. Among other things, the failure to deal with the matter in the Model Rules leaves uncertain the application of 42 U.S.C.A. § 2996f(a)(5)(A) which prohibits a legal services lawyer for an organization funded by the National Legal Services Corporation from soliciting a client "in violation of professional responsibilities" for the purpose of making a lobbying representation (an activity that is prohibited except in behalf of a specific client).

18 Kentucky Bar Ass'n v. Wilkey, 609 S.W.2d 370 (Ky. 1980)(provision of DR 2–103(D)(1), permitting solicitation of lawyer employed by legal aid office, enforced because of clarity of the permission afforded by the rule, despite court's misgivings because such activity is "not in keeping with what we regard as respectable professionalism"), quoted in Gaetke, Solicitation and the Uncertain Status of the Code of Professional Responsibility in Kentucky, 70 Ky.L.J. 707, 723 n.91 (1982).

19 DR 2–103(C)(1); MR 7.2 comment (Paying Others to Recommend a Lawyer).

20 See § 12.2.2 (class actions).

21 NAACP v. Button, 371 U.S. 415, 83 S.Ct. 328, 9 L.Ed. 2d 405 (1963); Brotherhood of R.R. Trainmen v. Virginia, 377 U.S. 1, 84 S.Ct. 1113, 12 L.Ed.2d 89 (1964); United Transp. Union v. Michigan Bar, 401 U.S. 576, 91 S.Ct. 1076, 28 L.Ed.2d 339 (1971); United Mine Workers v. Illinois St. Bar Ass'n, 389 U.S. 217, 88 S.Ct. 353, 19 L.Ed. 2d 426 (1967). See § 16.5.2.

sion in Bates v. Arizona State Bar,[22] it could also be argued that solicitation involved a personal constitutional right of a lawyer to free expression.[23] In two 1978 decisions, the Court made it clear that the latter direction was not one the Court wished to pursue in the instance of "pecuniary gain" solicitation, but that the former line of cases supported a First Amendment privilege to solicit in behalf of ideological litigation.

The first case, Ohralik v. Ohio State Bar Association,[24] involved classical ambulance-chasing, and held that the states could outlaw it entirely. In the second decision, In re Primus,[25] the Court held that a state could not constitutionally punish a lawyer who sought to further political and ideological goals through associational activity that consisted of in-person and mail solicitation of a prospective client. The *Ohralik* client was a minor injured eleven days earlier in an automobile accident whom the lawyer, armed with an employment contract, had visited uninvited while she was in traction in a hospital room. Thus, the Court found that the state could act to avoid the evils to which anti-solicitation rules were directed—the dangers of overreaching because face-to-face contact provided the opportunity for the lawyer to create pressure without the opportunity for the prospective client to reflect and to gather other points of view, the danger of invasion of the prospective client's privacy, and the difficulty of monitoring the lawyer's representations to the solicited person. *Ohralik* has thus been understood as a decision that permits states to outlaw all in-person solicitation of clients for pecuniary gain.[26]

In contrast, the client in *Primus* was a poor person who had been sterilized as part of a community's campaign to sterilize welfare mothers. The lawyer, Primus, had given a speech to sterilized women telling them that her organization, the American Civil Liberties Union, would represent them in a suit challenging the legality of the sterilization program and seeking damages for them. Although the Court in *Primus* might have thought otherwise, it seems plain that the same evils that the state could legitimately guard against in classical ambulance-chasing settings could also arise there. But broader First Amendment protection [27] was warranted both because those evils were less plausibly involved and because of the non-pecuniary and ideological nature of the lawyer's reasons for soliciting. But *Primus* clearly does not stand for the proposition that a lawyer wrapped in ideological garments and advocating non-commercial ideas is free to represent any client regardless of professional constraints if those can be based on a compelling state interest.[28]

Situations have arisen that partake of both the *Ohralik* pecuniary motivation and the *Primus* solicitation by mail or through neutral third parties. Courts have generally held that when such solicitations do not involve the same kinds of dangers of overreaching, fraud, and undue pressure as were involved in *Ohralik*, the lawyer's activities may be constitutionally protected.[29]

22 433 U.S. 350, 97 S.Ct. 2691, 53 L.Ed.2d 810 (1977).

23 The Court had intimated a broad protection for solicitation earlier in Bigelow v. Virginia, 421 U.S. 809, 826, 95 S.Ct. 2222, 2234–35, 44 L.Ed.2d 600 (1975): "Regardless of the particular label asserted by the state—whether it calls speech 'commercial' or 'commercial advertising' or 'solicitation'—a court may not escape the task of assessing the First Amendment interest at stake and weighing it against the public interest allegedly served by the regulation."

24 436 U.S. 447, 98 S.Ct. 1912, 56 L.Ed.2d 444 (1978).

25 436 U.S. 412, 98 S.Ct. 1893, 56 L.Ed.2d 417 (1978).

26 Woll v. Kelley, 116 Mich.App. 791, 323 N.W.2d 560, 566 (1982).

27 It is unclear whether *Primus* extends full First Amendment protection, including the overbreadth doctrine, to non-pecuniary and ideological solicitation. E.g., Pulaski, In-Person Solicitation and the First Amendment, 1979 Ariz.St.L.J. 23, 48.

28 Board of Educ. v. Nyquist, 590 F.2d 1241, 1245 (2d Cir.1979)(state may legitimately restrict representations by appropriately narrow conflict of interest rules).

29 Grievance Comm. v. Trantolo, 192 Conn. 27, 470 A.2d 235 (1984)(mailing brochure and invitation to firm open house to realtors); Kentucky Bar Ass'n v. Stuart, 568 S.W.2d 933 (Ky.1978)(law firm's letter to real estate agencies giving information about credentials and availability to perform real estate services not improper in-person solicitation); In re Jaques, 407 Mich. 26, 281 N.W.2d 469

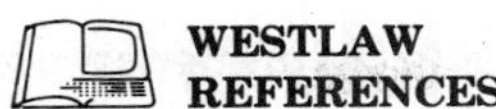

WESTLAW REFERENCES

attorney lawyer /9 in-person /3 solicit!

topic(45) /p solicit! /p "professional responsibility" "dr 2-103" dr2-103 "dr 2-104" dr2-104

ambulance +1 chas! /p lawyer attorney

digest,synopsis(attorney lawyer /s solicit! /s constitution! unconstitutional)

§ 14.3 RIGHT TO COUNSEL IN CRIMINAL CASES

§ 14.3.1 *Constitutional Bases*

Background of the Sixth Amendment

The Sixth Amendment to the United States Constitution provides that "the accused" in "all criminal prosecutions" shall enjoy the right "to have the assistance of counsel for his defense." In recent decades the Supreme Court has greatly expanded the occasions on which persons accused of crime, whether in state or federal courts, are entitled to the assistance of counsel under the Sixth Amendment and under other provisions of the Constitution. The Sixth Amendment, as is notorious, ran quite against the attitude that for centuries prevailed in English criminal law. English judges steadfastly refused to permit prisoners in felony cases to obtain the assistance of counsel, retained counsel certainly included.[30] The reason seems to have been general hostility against defendants and, perhaps, some concern that pettifoggery of lawyers would needlessly confound matters. Unfortunately for those entoiled in its meshes, English criminal justice employed procedures whose informality and sheer unreliability shock us today.

The Emergence of a Guarantee of Counsel

The constitutional right to counsel reflects a belief embodied in other parts of the Constitution as well that a charge of criminal conduct should not be taken as equivalent to an official determination of guilt. But during most of its existence, the Sixth Amendment remained a pious hope rather than a realized practice. State and federal legislation also declared a right to appointed counsel if an accused was unable to afford a lawyer (§ 14.3.5), but the statutory rights were also widely ignored. The basic problem was indigence: because many persons accused of crime were unable to afford lawyers, they went to their trials and to their almost inevitable punishment without any legal assistance.

The constitutional right to counsel of an indigent accused was not insisted upon by the Supreme Court until its 1931 decision in Powell v. Alabama.[31] The Court there required Alabama to appoint counsel for the Scottsboro defendants, an alleged case of interracial rape in which capital punishment had been imposed and that had caused an international furor. The Court stressed the gravity of the charge, the complexity of the law and court proceedings, and the conflicting nature of pivotal parts of the evidence. But in Betts v. Brady[32] the Court limited the applicability of *Powell* in state courts only to extraordinary cases in which the denial of appointed counsel denied fundamental fairness. In contrast, in Johnson v. Zerbst[33] the Supreme Court placed the federal courts under a constitutional obligation to appoint counsel routinely in felony cases. While an increasing number of states appointed counsel as a matter of course

(1979)(lawyer who asked union business agent who was not his runner or agent to recommend him to injured union members engaged in permissible solicitation because of lack of in-person contact with prospective clients and because of lack of evidence that business agent would fail to make independent and informed evaluation about lawyer's qualifications).

30 Betts v. Brady, 316 U.S. 455, 466, 62 S.Ct. 1252, 1258, 86 L.Ed. 1595 (1942); Powell v. Alabama, 287 U.S. 45, 60, 53 S.Ct. 55, 58, 77 L.Ed. 158 (1932); 9 W.Holdsworth, A History of English Law 232–33 (1926).

31 287 U.S. 45, 53 S.Ct. 55, 77 L.Ed 158 (1932).

32 316 U.S. 455, 62 S.Ct. 1252, 86 L.Ed. 1595 (1942).

33 304 U.S. 458, 58 S.Ct. 1019, 82 L.Ed. 1461 (1938).

in indigence cases involving serious charges, the practice was not universal.

Gideon and Argersinger

Finally, in the landmark 1963 decision of Gideon v. Wainwright,[34] the Court reversed *Betts* and held that a right to appointed counsel existed in every case in which the defendant could not afford counsel if a felony was charged. *Gideon* was extended in 1972 by Argersinger v. Hamlin,[35] holding that the right to counsel attached to any criminal charge, including a misdemeanor, if imprisonment was one of the sanctions imposed. The Supreme Court later limited *Argersinger* by holding that an uncounselled conviction was not unconstitutional if imprisonment was not part of the sentence actually imposed.[36] One difference between the right recognized in *Argersinger* and that in *Gideon* is that significantly fewer misdemeanor defendants are unable to afford counsel because of the lower legal fees typically charged for such cases.[37]

On the whole, the Supreme Court has been expansive in defining the "criminal prosecutions" to which the right to counsel extends. The right to counsel extends to both felonies (*Gideon*) and misdemeanors (*Argersinger*) if the accused is incarcerated. The right also extends to juvenile delinquency proceedings.[38] By contrast, a summary court-martial of a member of the military is not a criminal proceeding, despite the possibility that confinement can be imposed.[39]

The Theory of the Right to Counsel: Fairness versus Efficiency

The Supreme Court has vacillated over the underlying theory of a constitutional right to counsel. Early cases emphasized the mysteriousness and complexity of the law and legal proceedings and the consequent inability of even a highly educated nonlawyer to understand them without the "guiding hand of counsel at every step in the proceedings." [40] But some early cases also balanced the value of a lawyer against its cost and attempted to assess the nature and relative value of the freedom deprivation that conviction without counsel would entail.[41] Later cases such as *Gideon* and *Argersinger* emphasized the desirability of assuring fair trials. Fairness considerations indicated that a lawyer's expert legal services were critical.[42] More recently the court has reintroduced considerations of the cost of providing legal services and the possibly minimal nature of the freedom deprivation involved in particular areas. As a

34 372 U.S. 335, 83 S.Ct. 792, 9 L.Ed.2d 799 (1963). The history of the case has been described by a law-trained journalist. A.Lewis, Gideon's Trumpet (1964).

35 407 U.S. 25, 92 S.Ct. 2006, 32 L.Ed.2d 530 (1972). See also Baldasar v. Illinois, 446 U.S. 222, 100 S.Ct. 1585, 64 L.Ed.2d 169 (1980)(uncounseled misdemeanor conviction cannot be employed under enhancement statute to convert subsequent misdemeanor conviction into felony).

36 Scott v. Illinois, 440 U.S. 367, 99 S.Ct. 1158, 59 L.Ed. 2d 383 (1979). Nonetheless, statutes in several states extend a right to counsel if imprisonment is authorized under a charge, regardless of whether it is in fact imposed. See Scott v. Illinois, supra, 440 U.S. at 386 nn. 18–22, 99 S.Ct. at 1168–69 (dissenting opinion of Brennan, J.). See also 1 ABA Standards for Criminal Justice, Providing Defense Services § 5–4.1 (1980)("Counsel should be provided in all criminal proceedings for offenses punishable by imprisonment, regardless of their denomination as felonies, misdemeanors, or otherwise.").

37 See Nat'l Legal Aid & Defender Ass'n, The Other Face of Justice 82–83 (1973).

38 In re Gault, 387 U.S. 1, 87 S.Ct. 1428, 18 L.Ed.2d 527 (1967). A right to counsel also exists in a proceeding to determine whether a juvenile will be tried in a juvenile or a regular criminal court. Kent v. United States, 383 U.S. 541, 86 S.Ct. 1045, 16 L.Ed.2d 84 (1966).

39 Middendorf v. Henry, 425 U.S. 25, 96 S.Ct. 1281, 47 L.Ed.2d 556 (1976).

40 Powell v. Alabama, 287 U.S. 45, 68–69, 53 S.Ct. 55, 63–64, 77 L.Ed. 158 (1932). See also Johnson v. Zerbst, 304 U.S. 458, 462–63, 58 S.Ct. 1019, 1022, 82 L.Ed. 1461 (1938). Although the Sixth Amendment was designed in part to protect those unfamiliar with the mysterious operations of the legal system, the right to counsel in a criminal case extends to lawyers as well as to others accused of crime. Glasser v. United States, 315 U.S. 60, 70, 62 S.Ct. 457, 464–65, 86 L.Ed. 680 (1942); State v. Stein, 70 N.J. 369, 360 A.2d 347, 358 (1976). More is at stake than familiarity with law. A person accused by the prosecution and beset by opposing witnesses requires the objective and emotionally less involved assistance of a champion who is not personally accused of crime.

41 Betts v. Brady, 316 U.S. 455, 62 S.Ct. 1252, 86 L.Ed. 1595 (1942).

42 Gideon v. Wainwright, 372 U.S. 335, 342, 83 S.Ct. 792, 795, 9 L.Ed.2d 799 (1963); Argersinger v. Hamlin, 407 U.S. 25, 28, 92 S.Ct. 2006, 2008, 32 L.Ed.2d 530 (1972).

result, the Court once again has ignored fair-trial considerations [43] or stressed the unfortunate alterations in the proceedings that would inevitably be introduced if lawyers regularly appeared in them.[44]

Waiver of Counsel

The Court has similarly vacillated in the line of cases that have attempted to define the circumstances in which an accused is held to have waived the right to counsel.[45] The course of waiver decisions has been particularly irregular in the *Miranda* jurisprudence. A Court resolutely wishing to remove uncertainty from lower court applications of the *Miranda* rule (which requires interrogation to stop once the accused has requested counsel) [46] has thrown out confessions obtained from an apparently compliant accused who two days earlier had invoked his *Miranda* right to obtain the assistance of a lawyer [47] and from a barely conscious patient in an intensive care ward who had just engaged in a shoot-out with police during a narcotics raid.[48] But a weeping sixteen-year-old who wished to speak to his probation officer before talking to his interrogators has been held to have waived effectively his right to counsel,[49] as has an accused who invoked a right to remain silent (although apparently not to have a lawyer appointed) but two hours later agreed to discuss an unrelated crime without a lawyer after another *Miranda* warning was given.[50] Once a lawyer has in fact been appointed or retained, however, the rules of waiver may be more strict. In Brewer v. Williams [51] the Court held that after a prisoner was represented by counsel, the police could not attempt to induce a waiver of counsel or an incriminating statement.

Equal Protection and Indigence

At their core the right-to-counsel cases are cases of equal protection regardless of economic status. Each starts with a claim by a poor person that poverty prevented him or her from hiring a lawyer. To some extent, the Court has acknowledged the right of a person involuntarily brought into the criminal justice system not to be discriminated against on the basis of poverty. The probable high-water mark was reached in the cases holding that an indigent convicted person was constitutionally entitled to a trial transcript at state expense to assist in appealing the conviction.[52]

But subsequent cases have refused to extend the logic of those cases very far and have turned the inquiry away from a concern with equality toward a concern with minimal process entitlements.[53] Cases under the latter

[43] Scott v. Illinois, 440 U.S. 367, 99 S.Ct. 1158, 59 L.Ed. 2d 383 (1979).

[44] Middendorf v. Henry, 425 U.S. 25, 96 S.Ct. 1281, 1292, 47 L.Ed.2d 556 (1976)(lawyers would convert brief, informal hearings into attenuated proceedings that would consume resources); Gagnon v. Scarpelli, 411 U.S. 778, 787, 93 S.Ct. 1756, 1762, 36 L.Ed.2d 656 (1973).

[45] As with other constitutional rights, the right to counsel may be waived only if the accused does so knowingly and intelligently. See generally, Note, Proposed Requirements for Waiver of the Sixth Amendment Right to Counsel, 82 Colum.L.Rev. 363 (1982). If the right is so waived, an accused can proceed without the protection of a lawyer—including that most drastic of steps, proceeding to a full trial alone. Faretta v. California, 422 U.S. 806, 95 S.Ct. 2525, 45 L.Ed.2d 562 (1975). See § 14.4.2.

[46] Miranda v. Arizona, 384 U.S. 436, 473–74, 86 S.Ct. 1602, 1627–28, 16 L.Ed.2d 694 (1966).

[47] Edwards v. Arizona, 451 U.S. 477, 101 S.Ct. 1880, 68 L.Ed.2d 378 (1981).

[48] Mincey v. Arizona, 437 U.S. 385, 98 S.Ct. 2408, 57 L.Ed.2d 290 (1978).

[49] Fare v. Michael C., 442 U.S. 707, 99 S.Ct. 2560, 61 L.Ed.2d 197 (1979).

[50] Michigan v. Mosley, 423 U.S. 96, 96 S.Ct. 321, 46 L.Ed.2d 313 (1975). Cf., Smith v. Illinois, ___ U.S. ___, 105 S.Ct. 490, 83 L.Ed.2d 488 (1984)(once accused has made unambiguous request for counsel, interrogation must cease; responses of accused to postrequest interrogation cannot be used to cast doubt on clarity of original request and its legal effects).

[51] 430 U.S. 387, 97 S.Ct. 1232, 51 L.Ed.2d 424 (1977).

[52] Draper v. Washington, 372 U.S. 487, 83 S.Ct. 774, 9 L.Ed.2d 899 (1963); Lane v. Brown, 372 U.S. 477, 83 S.Ct. 768, 9 L.Ed.2d 892 (1963); Griffin v. Illinois, 351 U.S. 12, 19, 76 S.Ct. 585, 590–91, 100 L.Ed. 891 (1956)("[d]estitute defendants must be afforded as adequate appellate review as defendants who have money enough to buy transcripts").

[53] Compare Ross v. Moffitt, 417 U.S. 600, 616, 94 S.Ct. 2437, 2446–47, 41 L.Ed.2d 341 (1974), with Douglas v. California, 372 U.S. 353, 83 S.Ct. 814, 9 L.Ed.2d 811 (1963) ("There is lacking that equality demanded by the Fourteenth Amendment where the rich man, who appeals as

doctrine argue that the equal protection clause of the Fourteenth Amendment "does not require absolute equality or precisely equal advantages" [54] and does not require a state to "equalize economic conditions." [55] What the Fourteenth Amendment does prohibit in the area of legal representation is only "unreasonable" distinctions.[56] The resulting inquiry seeks to rationalize refusals to allocate state resources to legal services on the ground that other, substituted proceedings (for example, a direct appeal of right) or substituted services (for example, amateur "jailhouse lawyers") can provide a minimally adequate substitute for counsel.[57]

The Right to Counsel in Practice and in Theory

Predictions to the contrary notwithstanding, *Argersinger* and *Gideon* have not produced a significant burden for state courts or state budgets.[58] Efficiency might be suspected, but studies suggest a more somber reality. While the Supreme Court has broadly declared a right to counsel in any case in which imprisonment results, studies disturbingly suggest that the right is widely ignored or evaded and that successful challenges are not mounted because of the expense and time required to obtain postconviction review.[59] Other studies suggest that the sentences of defendants in criminal cases who do not have appointed or retained counsel are significantly less severe than for those with counsel.[60] If accurate, those findings raise serious questions about the willingness of courts in fact to support the right of accused persons to enjoy representation by counsel.

Official doctrine is quite different and requires that trial judges both inform a person accused of crime of the right to counsel and give the accused the information necessary to permit a knowing and informed exercise of it.[61] If an accused person appears at any critical stage of the proceedings without counsel, the trial court is obliged to inquire whether the accused is aware of his right to counsel.[62] If a convicted person was not represented or informed of the right to counsel, the conviction must be reversed without regard to possible arguments about harmless error, because the harmless error doctrine here would require too much speculation about possible outcomes if unrepresented de-

of right, enjoys the benefits of counsel's examination into the record, research of the law, and marshalling of arguments on his behalf, while the indigent, already burdened by a preliminary determination that his case is without merit, is forced to shift for himself."). See also Evitts v. Lucey, ___ U.S. ___, 105 S.Ct. 830, 83 L.Ed.2d 821 (1985) (denial of effective assistance of counsel at critical stage of proceedings (appeal of right) can be attacked on due process grounds despite waiver of attack on ground of denial of equal protection).

54 Ross v. Moffitt, supra, 417 U.S. at 612, 94 S.Ct. at 2444, quoting San Antonio Independent School District v. Rodriguez, 411 U.S. 1, 24, 93 S.Ct. 1278, 1291–92, 36 L.Ed. 2d 16 (1973).

55 Ross v. Moffitt, supra, 417 U.S. at 612, 94 S.Ct. at 2444, quoting Griffin v. Illinois, 351 U.S. 12, 23, 76 S.Ct. 585, 592–93, 100 L.Ed. 891 (1956).

56 Ross v. Moffitt, supra, 417 U.S. at 612, 94 S.Ct. at 2444–45, quoting Rinaldi v. Yaeger, 384 U.S. 305, 310, 86 S.Ct. 1497, 1500, 16 L.Ed.2d 577 (1966).

57 A similar kind of watered-down, minimalist egalitarianism in providing legal service will also be seen in the area of the effective assistance of counsel (§ 14.6).

58 See Ingraham, The Impact of Argersinger—One Year Later, 8 L. & Soc'y Rev. 614 (1974).

59 See generally Allison, Problems in the Delivery of Legal Services, 63 ABA J. 518, 520 (1977).

60 See Alschuler, The Defense Attorney's Role in Plea Bargaining, 84 Yale L.J. 1179, 1271 n.252 (1975), and authorities cited.

61 United States v. Harlan, 696 F.2d 5 (1st Cir.1982) (defendant who dismissed his retained lawyer because of size of his fee charge should not have been permitted to proceed pro se without being informed of his right to court-appointed counsel); United States v. Martin-Trigona, 684 F.2d 485 (7th Cir.1982).

62 Brewer v. Williams, 430 U.S. 387, 404, 97 S.Ct. 1232, 1242, 51 L.Ed.2d 424 (1977); Carnley v. Cochran, 369 U.S. 506, 513–16, 82 S.Ct. 884, 888–90, 8 L.Ed.2d 70 (1962). The court held in Baylor v. United States, 360 A.2d 42 (D.C.App.1976), cert.denied, 429 U.S. 1024, 97 S.Ct. 643, 50 L.Ed.2d 626 (1976), that the duty of a judge to assure that the accused is properly represented was properly exercised by a judge's recommendation to an accused that he accept new appointed counsel instead of his formerly appointed lawyer because of his present lawyer's doubtful competence. The court approved the intervention only on finding that there was ample basis on which the trial judge based his doubts about the experience and ability of the lawyer in a felony case.

fendants had instead been assisted by counsel.[63]

WESTLAW REFERENCES

di sixth amendment

topic(110) /p right /2 counsel** lawyer attorney /s indigen** poor

argersinger /12 92 +4 2006 /p right /2 counsel** lawyer attorney

digest(waiv! /5 right /2 counsel** lawyer attorney /s knowingly /2 intelligently)

92k250.2(2)

right /2 counsel** lawyer attorney /s indigen** poor /s "equal protection"

§ 14.3.2 *Critical Stages in Criminal Proceedings*

General

The Supreme Court has confined the constitutional right to counsel in criminal cases to so-called critical stages of the proceedings. Their demarcation is still in process. The problem has been to determine which interactions between a suspect and the state, within an acknowledged "criminal proceeding," constitute events whose potential outcome might substantially prejudice the accused in ways that legal insight and skillful advocacy can either lessen or eliminate altogether. The time at which the encounter occurs and the nature of the encounter are obviously central features of inquiry.

A Catalog of Critical Stages

Examples illustrate the illusiveness of the Court's line-drawing process when defining critical stages. The Supreme Court has held that a person has the right to counsel at a *preliminary hearing* if the purpose of the hearing is to determine probable cause,[64] or if action taken at the preliminary hearing will later be determinative in other ways of a substantial right of the accused.[65] The right to counsel attaches to a *postarrest lineup*[66] but not to a photographic "showup," at which a victim is shown photographs of persons including an indicted person,[67] or to a lineup conducted before charges have been brought.[68]

The right continues through all of the important stages of *trial* until judgment is entered. Thereafter a convicted person is entitled to the assistance of counsel for a *sentencing hearing*[69] and for a first *appeal* provided by the state as of right.[70] Beyond the initial appeal, however, the Court's shifting majority has tended to be less generous in recognizing the right to such "collateral" proceedings as "discretionary" appeals.[71] A fortiori there is no right to counsel in a federal habeas corpus or other *postconviction attacks* on a state court judgment in a criminal case.[72] There is no right to counsel in a state-initiat-

[63] United States v. Welty, 674 F.2d 185, 194 n.6 (3d Cir. 1982). Contra United States v. Gipson, 693 F.2d 109, 112 (10th Cir.1982), cert.denied 459 U.S. 1216, 103 S.Ct. 1218, 75 L.Ed.2d 455 (1983).

[64] Coleman v. Alabama, 399 U.S. 1, 90 S.Ct. 1999, 26 L.Ed.2d 387 (1970).

[65] Compare Hamilton v. Alabama, 368 U.S. 52, 82 S.Ct. 157, 7 L.Ed.2d 114 (1961)(counsel required at preliminary hearing because failure to plead certain affirmative defenses would result in waiver under state law), with Pointer v. Texas, 380 U.S. 400, 85 S.Ct. 1065, 13 L.Ed.2d 923 (1965)(counsel not necessary at preliminary hearing at which accused is not required to plead).

[66] United States v. Wade, 388 U.S. 218, 87 S.Ct. 1926, 18 L.Ed.2d 1149 (1967). See also Moore v. Illinois, 434 U.S. 220, 98 S.Ct. 458, 54 L.Ed.2d 424 (1977)(Sixth Amendment violated by victim identification of accused in absence of counsel after initiation of adversary criminal proceedings).

[67] United States v. Ash, 413 U.S. 300, 93 S.Ct. 2568, 37 L.Ed.2d 619 (1973).

[68] Kirby v. Illinois, 406 U.S. 682, 92 S.Ct. 1877, 32 L.Ed. 2d 411 (1972).

[69] Mempa v. Rhay, 389 U.S. 128, 88 S.Ct. 254, 19 L.Ed. 2d 336 (1967); Gardner v. Florida, 430 U.S. 349, 97 S.Ct. 1197, 51 L.Ed.2d 393 (1977).

[70] Evitts v. Lucey, ___ U.S. ___, 105 S.Ct. 830, 83 L.Ed.2d 821 (1985); Douglas v. California, 372 U.S. 353, 83 S.Ct. 814, 9 L.Ed.2d 811 (1963); Swenson v. Bosler, 386 U.S. 258, 87 S.Ct. 996, 18 L.Ed.2d 33 (1967).

[71] Ross v. Moffitt, 417 U.S. 600, 94 S.Ct. 2437, 41 L.Ed. 2d 341 (1974).

[72] Williams v. Missouri, 640 F.2d 140, 144 (8th Cir. 1981), cert.denied 451 U.S. 990, 101 S.Ct. 2328, 68 L.Ed.2d 849 (1982)(habeas corpus); United States v. Degand, 614 F.2d 176, 179 (8th Cir.1980)(federal postconviction attack). In addition to failing the "critical stage" test, habeas corpus is also claimed to be "civil" and not criminal litigation. E.g., United States v. Somers, 552 F.2d 108, 110 n.6 (3d Cir.1977).

ed proceeding seeking *probation or parole revocation*, at least if the state is not represented by a law-trained prosecutor [73] or in *prison disciplinary hearings*.[74] A refusal to extend the right to counsel to those and similar proceedings is sometimes justified on the ground that the presence of a lawyer would undesirably strip the proceedings of efficiency or informality.[75]

The interrogation cases might also be viewed as right-to-counsel cases concerned with defining critical stages, but the Court's analysis in Miranda v. Arizona [76] emphasized more the fact that the coercive atmosphere of custodial questioning made it necessary to provide counsel in order to preserve the Fifth Amendment privilege against self-incrimination. In Massiah v. United States [77] the Court also employed a similarly combined Fifth and Sixth Amendment analysis to extend the right to counsel to a case in which a secret informer cooperating with the prosecution elicited incriminating statements from an indicted person.

WESTLAW REFERENCES

"critical stage" /s right /5 attorney counsel** lawyer /s constitution**

"probable cause" /p "preliminary hearing" /s right /5 attorney counsel** lawyer

§ 14.3.3 *Implementing the Right to Counsel—Indigence*

Determining Entitlement to Court-Appointed Counsel

The federal constitutional requirement to provide free legal assistance to a person accused of crime rests, in the final analysis, upon the indigence of the accused.[78] Practices differ concerning the extent to which a meticulous showing of indigence is required. Typically, the person asserting indigence must file a sworn statement giving some detail about financial circumstances.[79] The criteria for poverty also vary.[80] A commonly employed standard inquires whether the person presently has assets and income sufficient to pay prevailing fees for lawyers in private practice for matters of the kind involved in the case without prejudicing the person's ability to provide other necessities for himself or herself and for dependents.[81] A common requirement is that the applicant liquidate or encumber any available property.[82]

It is impermissible to refuse to find poverty because persons liable for the support of the litigant are able to supply funds. A failure of those persons to provide funds for legal services would leave the accused unrepresent-

---

[73] Gagnon v. Scarpelli, 411 U.S. 778, 93 S.Ct. 1756, 36 L.Ed.2d 656 (1973).

[74] Baxter v. Palmigiano, 425 U.S. 308, 96 S.Ct. 1551, 47 L.Ed.2d 810 (1976).

[75] Gagnon v. Scarpelli, supra, 411 U.S. at 790, 93 S.Ct. at 1763 ("the presence and participation of counsel will probably be both undesirable and constitutionally unnecessary in most [probation] revocation proceedings"); United States v. Mandujano, 425 U.S. 564, 581, 96 S.Ct. 1768, 1778, 48 L.Ed.2d 212 (1976)(presence of counsel would undesirably destroy secrecy and investigative purposes of grand jury proceedings).

[76] 384 U.S. 436, 469–70, 86 S.Ct. 1602, 1625, 16 L.Ed.2d 694 (1966).

[77] 377 U.S. 201, 84 S.Ct. 1199, 12 L.Ed.2d 246 (1964).

[78] A person who is not indigent may, according to some cases, be tried without a lawyer if the person is given a reasonable opportunity to obtain counsel and fails to do so for no reason or an inadequate one. United States v. Weninger, 624 F.2d 163 (10th Cir.1980), cert.denied 449 U.S. 1012, 101 S.Ct. 568, 66 L.Ed.2d 470 (1980); United States v. Fowler, 605 F.2d 181 (5th Cir.1979), cert.denied 445 U.S. 950, 100 S.Ct. 1599, 63 L.Ed.2d 785 (1980).

[79] United States v. McQuade, 647 F.2d 938 (9th Cir. 1981), cert.denied 455 U.S. 958, 102 S.Ct. 1470, 71 L.Ed.2d 677 (1982); State v. Pina, 90 N.M. 181, 561 P.2d 43 (1977).

[80] For example, client eligibility standards for a legal services organization might differ from those insisted upon by courts in determining whether a litigant should be permitted to proceed in forma pauperis. E.g., In re Southern Tier Legal Services, 100 Misc.2d 1068, 420 N.Y.S.2d 591 (1979).

[81] United States v. Deutsch, 599 F.2d 46 (5th Cir.), cert.denied 444 U.S. 935, 100 S.Ct. 283, 62 L.Ed.2d 194 (1979); Stapp v. State, 249 Ga. 289, 290 S.E.2d 439 (1982); State v. Thompson, 253 N.W.2d 608 (Iowa 1977). See generally People v. Chism, 17 Mich.App. 196, 169 N.W.2d 192, 51 A.L.R.3d 1104 (1969).

[82] Morger v. Superior Court, 637 P.2d 310 (Ariz.App. 1981).

ed.[83] For similar reasons, the fact that others have provided bail money or other defense expenses for an accused does not necessarily mean that they will provide funds for legal fees as well.[84]

A common feature of the federal and some state court-appointed-counsel systems is a reimbursement obligation in the event that the person is convicted and later becomes able to repay[85] the government for the cost of a court-appointed lawyer. Although such a scheme might make an indigent person reluctant to accept court-appointed counsel, it does not place an unconstitutional burden on the exercise of the right to counsel.[86] States occasionally employ such conditional reimbursement obligations as a part of probation,[87] but some federal courts will not.[88] Parents or other guardians under a legal obligation to provide necessaries to a minor may also be held liable to reimburse a state, if financially able, for an expenditure for legal fees as necessaries.[89]

WESTLAW REFERENCES

fuller +4 oregon /12 94 +4 2116 /p right /5 attorney counsel** lawyer

recoup! reimburs! repay! /5 state county government court /p right /5 counsel** attorney lawyer

§ 14.3.4 *Staffing the Right to Counsel*

General

Two models have been followed in providing legal assistance to indigent defendants in cases in which the Constitution or a statute provides a right to counsel. The oldest and still the most common method is the *appointment system*, in which a court or, occasionally, a bar association undertakes to appoint lawyers from private practice to defend indigent persons on a case-by-case basis. Those systems differ among themselves on such important details as whether or not the appointed lawyer is compensated. The other model is the *public defender system*, in which a permanent staff of defense lawyers provides legal assistance to all persons unable to afford representation. Under either model, the accused is typically given no voice in the selection of counsel and has no right to the assistance of more than one lawyer.

Limits on Right to Select Counsel-of-Choice

The lack of any right of the accused to select a particular lawyer has repeatedly been stated.[90] The matter is more complex, however, than that truism might suggest. The

83 People v. Gustavson, 131 Ill.App.2d 887, 269 N.E.2d 517 (1971); Opinion of the Justices, 121 N.H. 531, 431 A.2d 144 (1981).

84 People v. Wood, 91 Ill.App.3d 414, 46 Ill.Dec. 706, 414 N.E.2d 759 (1980), cert.denied 454 U.S. 847, 102 S.Ct. 166, 70 L.Ed.2d 135 (1981); State v. Morgenstein, 147 N.J. Super. 234, 371 A.2d 96 (1977).

85 Reimbursement is provided, for example, under the Federal Criminal Justice Act. 18 U.S.C.A. § 3006A(f). E.g., United States v. Bracewell, 569 F.2d 1194 (2d Cir. 1978); United States v. Wetzel, 488 F.2d 153 (8th Cir. 1973). An Iowa statutory procedure permits a litigant with encumbered assets to obtain governmental payment of legal expenses subject to later governmental encumberancing of the assets. See State v. Gilroy, 313 N.W.2d 513 (Iowa 1981).

86 Fuller v. Oregon, 417 U.S. 40, 94 S.Ct. 2116, 40 L.Ed. 2d 642 (1974). The fees-reimbursement statute may not differ in significant degree from other debtor legislation, such as in stripping the fee-debtor of generally available state law exemptions. See James v. Strange, 407 U.S. 128, 92 S.Ct. 2027, 32 L.Ed.2d 600 (1972). A requirement that a person who has been *acquitted* nonetheless repay the state for the cost of legal services furnished at state expense denies due process. See Olson v. James, 603 F.2d 150 (10th Cir.1979).

87 People v. Romero, 192 Colo. 106, 559 P.2d 1101 (1976); Haynes v. State, 26 Md.App. 43, 337 A.2d 130, 79 A.L.R.3d 1016 (1975); State v. Barklind, 87 Wash.2d 814, 557 P.2d 314 (1976).

88 United States v. Turner, 628 F.2d 461 (5th Cir.1980), cert.denied 451 U.S. 988, 101 S.Ct. 2325, 68 L.Ed.2d 847 (1981). But see, e.g., United States v. Allen, 596 F.2d 227 (7th Cir.1979), cert.denied 444 U.S. 871, 100 S.Ct. 149, 62 L.Ed.2d 97 (1979).

89 York v. Johnson, 206 Neb. 200, 292 N.W.2d 31 (1980), and cases cited. A lawyer hired and paid by a parent of an accused to assist a court-appointed lawyer in defense work is under no obligation to share those funds with the state. See United States v. Crosby, 602 F.2d 24 (2d Cir. 1979).

90 Morris v. Slappy, 461 U.S. 1, 103 S.Ct. 1610, 75 L.Ed. 2d 610 (1983); Drumgo v. Superior Court, 8 Cal.3d 930, 106 Cal.Rptr. 631, 506 P.2d 1007, 66 A.L.R.3d 984 (1973), cert.denied 414 U.S. 979, 94 S.Ct. 272, 38 L.Ed.2d 223 (1973). Cf. Harris v. Superior Court, 19 Cal.3d 786, 140 Cal.Rptr. 318, 567 P.2d 750 (1977)(abuse of discretion to refuse to appoint willing lawyer who had developed ex-

question often arises in the context of a request by the defendant for a continuance in order to retain other counsel. Such requests are addressed to the discretion of the trial court, and discretion should be exercised in light of the costs, if any, that would be imposed by the continuance that is necessary to permit a new lawyer to prepare a defense.[91] The dissatisfaction of the accused with appointed counsel, if it does not affect the lawyer's ability to proceed with a competent defense, does not require substitution of counsel.[92] On the other hand, if no continuance or other disruption of the trial will result, a request by an accused to replace one lawyer with another available lawyer must be granted in the absence of any substantial reason for denying it.[93]

Conversely, if a trial court orders withdrawal of a lawyer over the objection of the defendant and without the request of the replaced lawyer, a constitutional deprivation of counsel may result,[94] unless the state can demonstrate a compelling interest of its own in assuring a particular kind of representation that is sufficiently strong to overcome the defendant's right to choose an advocate (§ 8.2.5). Because an accused has the constitutional right to proceed with no legal assistance whatever (§ 14.4.2), a trial court should not be empowered to remove, over the knowing and intelligent objection of the accused, a court-appointed lawyer on the ground of the lawyer's incompetence.[95]

On the question of the number of court-appointed lawyers, federal courts have recognized a statutory right to the appointment of two lawyers in capital cases.[96] The states generally recognize a discretion in a trial court to appoint additional counsel if the complexity of the case requires it.[97]

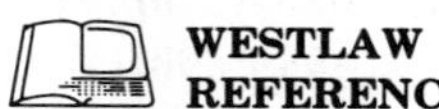

WESTLAW REFERENCES

110k641.6(3) /p appoint! /5 counsel** attorney lawyer

§ 14.3.5 Appointment Systems

Historical Reliance on Court Appointments

The power of a court to "appoint" a member of the bar to provide legal services to a person accused of crime [98] is one of ancient lineage. An English statute of 1495 provided that a pauper could proceed without the cus-

tensive acquaintanceship with facts in sensational trial and enjoyed trust and confidence of accused persons in view of fact that trial court had no substantial reason to refuse appointment).

In England, by contrast, the indigent accused is provided an advocate at state expense but the accused is free to select an advocate of his or her own choosing. See Friesen, Judicial Administration Lessons from England, 71 F.R.D. 469, 470 (1976). Moreover, the lawyer is paid at rates that are substantially the same as those paid to privately retained lawyers. Id.

[91] Morris v. Slappy, supra; Ungar v. Sarafite, 376 U.S. 575, 84 S.Ct. 841, 11 L.Ed.2d 921 (1964).

[92] E.g., United States v. Young, 482 F.2d 993 (5th Cir. 1973); People v. Walker, 18 Cal.3d 232, 133 Cal.Rptr. 520, 555 P.2d 306 (1976); State v. Fallis, 205 Neb. 465, 288 N.W.2d 281 (1980).

[93] E.g., Milkovich v. State, 73 Wis.2d 464, 243 N.W.2d 198 (1976).

[94] E.g., United States v. Laura, 607 F.2d 52 (3d Cir. 1979)(retained local counsel); Harling v. United States, 387 A.2d 1101, 3 A.L.R.4th 1218 (D.C.1978)(appointed counsel). But cf. People v. Stroble, 36 Cal.2d 615, 226 P.2d 330 (1951), affirmed 343 U.S. 181, 72 S.Ct. 599, 96 L.Ed. 872 (1952)(trial judge empowered to remove one public defender on ground of judge's objection to lawyer's tactics in case, when replacement public defender competently represented accused at trial).

[95] See Smith v. Superior Court, 68 Cal.2d 547, 68 Cal. Rptr. 1, 440 P.2d 65 (1968).

[96] 18 U.S.C.A. § 3005 (person "indicted for treason or other capital crime" upon request shall be assigned "such counsel, not exceeding two, as he may desire"); United States v. Watson, 496 F.2d 1125 (4th Cir.1973). But the right to two lawyers is not of constitutional dimension and requires a specific request by the accused for additional counsel. United States v. Blankenship, 548 F.2d 1118 (4th Cir.1976), cert.denied 425 U.S. 978, 96 S.Ct. 2182, 48 L.Ed.2d 803 (1976).

[97] Compare, e.g., State v. Barfield, 298 N.C. 306, 259 S.E.2d 510 (1979), cert.denied 448 U.S. 907, 100 S.Ct. 3050, 65 L.Ed.2d 1137 (1980)(no abuse of discretion in first-degree murder-by-poison case), with, e.g., Keenan v. Superior Court, 31 Cal.3d 424 180 Cal.Rptr. 489, 640 P.2d 108 (1982), appeal dismissed 459 U.S. 937, 103 S.Ct. 246, 74 L.Ed.2d 194 (1982)(abuse of discretion to refuse to appoint second defense lawyer in defense involving 120 witnesses, extensive scientific evidence, complex prosecution case, and only eight weeks to prepare for trial).

[98] On the extent of the obligation of lawyers to accept appointments, see § 16.9 (pro bono). Court appointments may also occur for special purposes, as in the case of

tomary payment of court fees and judges were urged to appoint attorneys and counsel to assist the pauper without fee.[99] Prior to the decisions of the Supreme Court extending the right to counsel, federal courts and most state courts relied exclusively upon no-fee appointments of counsel in criminal cases when the court found that counsel was particularly necessary. Even after the right to counsel became general, most federal courts continued to rely upon an appointment system.

In 1964 Congress enacted the Criminal Justice Act,[1] which both provides for methods of appointing lawyers and authorizes the expenditure of federal funds for their minimal compensation.[2] The federal system operates through plans adopted by the federal districts. Typically they provide for judicial appointment of a lawyer from a group of private practitioners who voluntarily list themselves as available for appointments. Many state systems are similar, although some state courts have "drafted" lawyers involuntarily to serve as defense counsel.[3] In some federal districts the Criminal Justice Act plans provide for the appointment of lawyers from an established legal aid or defender program or create a special staff of federal public defenders.

Once appointed, the court-appointed lawyer's duties and his or her relationship with the client are in most respects similar to those of a privately retained lawyer. Failure to carry out the responsibilities of the appointment can result in discipline.[4] The lawyer's expenditure of time and effort in the client's behalf and the instincts of loyalty felt for the client's rights should not be diminished because the representation began with an appointment[5] or because of the fact that the lawyer is paid poorly or nothing at all for his or her work.

Financing and Compensation

Financing of court-appointed systems has created periodic crises in several jurisdictions.[6] Legislative bodies on the whole have not supplied adequate funds for defense fees. Occasionally courts have held that particularly time-consuming representations mandated fees in excess of legislative limits,[7] and a

appointment of a special prosecutor from the private bar because of a conflict of interest. E.g., In re Morse, 157 N.J.Super. 104, 384 A.2d 562 (1978).

99 4 W.Holdsworth, A History of English Law 538 (1924).

1 See 18 U.S.C.A. § 3006A. See generally Bonsal, the Criminal Justice Act—1964 to 1976, 52 Ind.L.J. 135 (1976). The court in United States v. Bowe, 698 F.2d 560 (2d Cir.1983), suggested that the federal courts retain an inherent power to appoint counsel in cases not provided for by the Criminal Justice Act, in that case for a witness in a criminal case who wished to assert a privilege against self-incrimination.

The federal act also provides for the appointment and compensation of experts, investigators, and similar assistance. See 18 U.S.C.A. § 3006A(a) & (e); United States v. Durant, 545 F.2d 823 (2d Cir.1976)(appointment of fingerprint expert mandatory if critical to defense); United States v. Fessel, 531 F.2d 1275 (5th Cir.1976)(private psychiatric services if necessary for preparation of insanity defense).

2 The federal statute was amended in 1984 to increase the rate of compensation for the first time in twenty years. The new allowances are for fees, not to exceed sixty dollars per hour for work out of court. See Criminal Justice Act Revision of 1984, § 1901, Pub.L.No. 98–473, 1984, U.S. Cong. and Admin. News (98 Stat.) 2185.

3 The typical problem is the unattractiveness of appointments because of the lack of adequate or even minimal compensation for appointed lawyers. Forced appointments have thus far withstood constitutional challenge on involuntary servitude and similar grounds. E.g., Sontag v. State, 629 P.2d 1269 (Okl.Cr.App.1981), cert.denied 454 U.S. 1142, 102 S.Ct. 1001, 71 L.Ed.2d 294 (1982); In re Frankel, 119 N.J.Super. 579, 293 A.2d 196 (N.J.App.Div.1972), appeal denied 62 N.J. 75, 299 A.2d 73 (1972), cert.denied 409 U.S. 1125, 93 S.Ct. 939, 35 L.Ed.2d 257 (1973). See also § 16.9.

4 Archie v. State, 92 Nev. 746, 557 P.2d 1153 (1976); In re Hunoval, 294 N.C. 740, 247 S.E.2d 230 (1977).

5 In re Gibson, 444 N.E.2d 852 (Ind.1983). Brusque talk in Morris v. Slappy, 461 U.S. 1, 13, 103 S.Ct. 1610, 1621, 75 L.Ed.2d 610 (1983), rejects the argument that the Constitution requires a "meaningful attorney-client relationship" between an indigent and his or her court-appointed lawyer. The decision seems committed to rejecting the constitutional, rather than the professional, need for such a relationship.

6 State ex rel. Wolff v. Ruddy, 617 S.W.2d 64 (Mo.1981), cert.denied 454 U.S. 1142, 102 S.Ct. 1000, 71 L.Ed.2d 293 (1982).

7 People ex rel. Conn v. Randolph, 35 Ill.2d 24, 219 N.E.2d 337, 18 A.L.R.3d 1065 (1966)(statutory fee limitation could not constitutionally be applied to extraordinarily lengthy and complex multiple representations); Bias v. State, 568 P.2d 1269 (Okl.1977). See also Williamson v. Vardeman, 674 F.2d 1211 (8th Cir.1982)(unconstitutional

notable New Hampshire decision held unconstitutional in its entirety a statute that provided less than what the court judged to be reasonable fees.[8]

The general judicial attitude, however, is insouciant. Most courts insist that court-appointed lawyers should expect no fees [9] or fees significantly less than those earned by privately retained lawyers.[10] Nor are court-appointed lawyers permitted to seek other sources of payment. A common feature of court-appointment systems is that the appointed lawyer may not attempt to collect an additional fee from the indigent accused or the family or friends of the accused.[11]

WESTLAW REFERENCES

digest,synopsis("criminal justice act" (18 +4 3006a) /p appoint! /5 counsel** attorney lawyer)

---

§ 14.3.6 Public Defender Systems

General

The second major model for providing defense services is the public defender office, a publicly or privately funded office of lawyers who perform defense services on a regular and continuing basis. The earliest public defender system was established in Oklahoma in 1922.[12] The 1964 federal Criminal Justice Act empowers the creation of federal public defender programs in each of the federal districts.[13] In both federal and state courts, public defender programs are most common in metropolitan areas with high criminal caseloads. Some public defender offices have responsibilities that extend beyond felony and misdemeanor defense representation and might include certain civil legal aid cases.[14]

Staffing, Structure, and Politics

The staffing and structure of public defender offices varies widely. California employs a civil service approach that hires lawyers on the basis of competitive merit examinations.[15] New York, at the other extreme, employed a political appointment system, part of which the Supreme Court held violated the First and Fourteenth Amendments because it resulted in dismissal of public defenders following an election solely because of their membership in the losing political party.[16] Defender programs have been structured in very different ways. In some states the public defender is an appointed governmental official who operates the program with public funds.[17] In other states, management of the program is vested in a board of directors that must contain both public and private representation, in-

for state to require court-appointed lawyer to make out-of-pocket expenditures in behalf of indigent accused).

8 Smith v. State, 118 N.H. 764, 394 A.2d 834, 3 A.L.R.4th 568 (1978). See also State ex rel. Partain v. Oakley, 159 W.Va. 805, 227 S.E.2d 314 (1976); Johnson v. City Comm'n, 272 N.W.2d 97 (S.D.1978).

9 United States v. Dillon, 346 F.2d 633 (9th Cir.1965), cert.denied 382 U.S. 978, 86 S.Ct. 550, 15 L.Ed.2d 469 (1966); Vise v. County of Hamilton, 19 Ill. 78, 79 (1857); State v. Monaghan, 184 N.J.Super. 340, 446 A.2d 185 (1982).

10 Metropolitan Dade County v. Bridges, 402 So.2d 411 (Fla.1981); State v. Rush, 46 N.J. 399, 217 A.2d 441, 21 A.L.R.3d 804 (1966); Tappe v. Circuit Court, 326 N.W.2d 892 (S.D.1982); State v. Sidney, 66 Wis.2d 602, 225 N.W.2d 438 (1975). Some quite remarkably low fee awards have been upheld, but none of correspondingly high magnitude has come to light. E.g., Dickens v. State, 153 Ga.App. 834, 267 S.E.2d 269 (1980)(award of less than $7 per hour for 175-hour defense of person accused of three crimes, two of which were punishable by death, did not abuse trial court's discretion under standard allowing additional award if there is "protracted representation due to extraordinary circumstances"; death penalty cases are not extraordinary in Georgia).

11 E.g., Willcher v. United States, 408 A.2d 67 (D.C.Ct. Apps.1979)(affirming conviction for soliciting fee for representation of indigent); Kentucky Bar Ass'n v. Dungan, 586 S.W.2d 15 (Ky.1979)(disbarment for charging fee to mother of indigent and testifying falsely about fee), cert.denied 444 U.S. 1033, 100 S.Ct. 704, 62 L.Ed.2d 669 (1980).

12 Cuff, Public Defender System: The Los Angeles Story, 45 Minn.L.Rev. 715, 726 (1961). See also M.Goldman, The Public Defender (1971).

13 18 U.S.C.A. § 3006A(h)(2)(A).

14 West's Ann. Cal.Gov.Code § 27706 (public defender responsible for providing counsel for workers in certain wage claims and for indigents in certain welfare claims).

15 West's Ann.Cal.Gov. Code § 27703.

16 Branti v. Finkel, 445 U.S. 507, 100 S.Ct. 1287, 63 L.Ed.2d 574 (1980).

17 E.g., Conn. Gen.Stat.Ann. §§ 54–80, 54–81a; Minn. Stat.Ann. § 611.12.

cluding representation from political power sources such as the office of the mayor.

The relationship between defender programs and the political process is a troubled one. As the Supreme Court has stated, implicit in the right to counsel guaranteed by the federal Constitution is the notion that an accused will have counsel free of state control:

> "There can be no fair trial unless the accused receives the services of an effective and independent advocate. . . . [I]t is the constitutional obligation of the State to respect the professional independence of the public defenders whom it engages. . . ."[18]

Tension between that ideal and reality is caused by two main factors. Public defender positions are jobs, and, in the wrong hands, they can be regarded sheerly as matter to be dealt with as political patronage. Criminal conviction statistics are also a matter of political concern, and that can lead to political pressure to limit the vigor or adequacy of a defender program. Those political concerns raise serious and difficult issues about the extent to which rightful oversight of public funds can be effectuated through political involvement in the governance of a public defender system.[19]

Some judges can also exert influence that stifles professional independence. Those judges may wrongly regard public defenders as part of the court bureaucracy much as are bailiffs and judicial clerks—available to perform their functions in ways compatible with the judicial-administration objectives of judges. Courts have asserted from time to time that public defenders are not to be so regarded or treated; courts should allow public defenders at least as much independence of the courts as is allowed privately retained lawyers.[20]

Public Defender Systems and their Clientele

One of the serious anomalies in public defender representation is that the inmate culture carries an image of the public defender as ineffectual when compared to court-appointed or privately retained private practitioners.[21] In part, that image might be traceable to an inmate belief that public defenders follow professional goals when they come into conflict with goals of client service.[22] A bureaucratic practice that can contribute to the impression of "assembly-line justice" is that of assigning a specific public defender indefinitely to a particular courtroom where only one function (initial charge, trial, or sentencing) is performed. As a result, an accused person experiencing the other functions in different courtrooms will see a different public defender at each stop.[23] In all systems, high caseload and the public defender's sameness of work assignment can lead to stagnation.[24] Despite client perceptions and plausible reasons to suspect that they are well-founded, however, the public defender pro-

18 Polk County v. Dodson, 454 U.S. 312, 102 S.Ct. 445, 451, 452, 70 L.Ed.3d 509 (1981).

19 See the majority and dissenting opinions in In re Amendments to Articles of Incorporation of Defender Ass'n of Philadelphia, 453 Pa. 353, 307 A.2d 906 (1973). cert.denied 414 U.S. 1079, 94 S.Ct. 598, 38 L.Ed.2d 486 (1973). See Mounts, Public Defender Programs: Professional Responsibility and Competent Representation, 1982 Wisc.L.Rev. 473.

20 Hough v. State, 24 Cal.2d 522, 150 P.2d 448 (1944). See generally David, Institutional or Private Counsel: A Judge's View of the Public Defender System, 45 Minn.L. Rev. 753 (1961).

21 Wilkerson, Public Defenders as Their Clients See Them, 1 Am.J.Crim.L. 141 (1972); Casper, Did You Have A Lawyer When You Went to Court? No, I Had a Public Defender, 1 Yale Rev.L. & Soc.Act. 4 (1971).

22 Etheridge, Lawyers Versus Indigents: Conflict of Interest in Professional-Client Relations in the Legal Profession, in The Professions and Their Prospects 245 et seq. (E.Freidson ed.1973).

23 R. Hermann, Counsel for the Poor 33 (1977). The ABA has taken a position against such "stage" or "horizontal" public defender systems. The chief difficulties are that an accused will be represented by several members of the staff during a proceeding, no member will probably become very familiar with the case, and overall planning, coordination, and client communication suffer. See ABA Standards for Criminal Justice § 5.54 commentary (1974). See generally Gilroy, The Social Organization of Legal Services to Indigent Defendants, 1981 Am.B. Found. Research J. 1023.

24 Wise, Current Realities of Public Defender Programs: A National Survey and Analysis, 10 Crim.L.Bull. 161, 166 (1974).

grams probably provide legal services that are at least as protective of the interests of accused persons as does court-appointed or privately retained representation.[25]

WESTLAW REFERENCES

di public defender

§ 14.3.7 *Right to Retained Counsel*

Recognition of the Right

Prior to the right-to-counsel revolution in the Supreme Court, the traditional method of obtaining legal assistance in criminal cases was to retain a lawyer in private practice. Retained defense lawyers remain, of course, an important source of legal assistance, although the great majority of criminal defense work in imprisonment cases is conducted through court-appointed lawyers or public defenders. The relative underutilization of private practitioners does not, of course, indicate their lesser qualifications or abilities but, instead, reflects the harsh reality that money must be paid to purchase the sometimes higher-quality assistance of a private practitioner.[26] If money is paid, or a lawyer otherwise agrees to accept a private-practice representation of a person, the Constitution nonetheless remains relevant in defining and protecting the client-lawyer relationship.

It seems clear on principle that an accused has a constitutional right of significant dimensions to be represented by retained counsel. That has not been seriously doubted since the Supreme Court's often-quoted statement in Powell v. Alabama[27] that when the right to counsel exists, "a defendant should be afforded a fair opportunity to secure counsel of his own choice." [28] The Supreme Court in 1980, in Cuyler v. Sullivan,[29] held that the same standard of effective assistance of counsel applied in retained-counsel cases as in court-appointed cases.[30]

Just as often as the right has been affirmed, however, it has also been said that it is not absolute. An accused is not entitled to impose on legitimate interests of the prosecution and the judicial system in order to obtain last-minute continuances to accommodate the schedule of private counsel or to permit a dilatory accused to obtain private assistance for the first time.[31] A legitimate state inter-

25 See R. Hermann, E.Single & J.Boston, Counsel for the Poor (1977)(study shows case outcomes similar with public defender or retained counsel; some marginally greater chance of good case outcome with institutional public defender as opposed to court-appointed system; nonetheless, defendants had marked antipathy toward public defenders because of suspicions about both loyalties and abilities).

26 Morris v. Slappy, 461 U.S. 1, 103 S.Ct. 1610, 1622, 75 L.Ed.2d 610 (1983)(Brennan, J., concurring).

27 287 U.S. 45, 53, 53 S.Ct. 55, 77 L.Ed. 158 (1932). See also, e.g., Chandler v. Fretag, 348 U.S. 3, 10, 75 S.Ct. 1, 99 L.Ed. 4 (1954)("a necessary corollary [to the right to be heard by counsel] is that a defendant must be given a reasonable opportunity to employ and consult with counsel; otherwise the right to be heard by counsel would be of little worth. . ."); Crooker v. California, 357 U.S. 433, 439, 78 S.Ct. 1287, 1291, 2 L.Ed.2d 1448 (1958); House v. Mayo, 324 U.S. 42, 65 S.Ct. 517, 89 L.Ed. 739 (1945).

28 The Court, in *Powell*, found a constitutional violation both because no opportunity to secure counsel was given the defendants and because such appointment of counsel as the trial court made was "so close upon the trial as to amount to a denial of effective and substantial aid." 287 U.S. at 53.

29 446 U.S. 335, 100 S.Ct. 1708, 64 L.Ed.2d 333 (1980). Older cases had drawn distinctions between the incompetence of retained and court-appointed counsel. For example, in Fitzgerald v. Estelle, 505 F.2d 1334, 1336–37 (5th Cir.1974)(en banc), cert.denied 422 U.S. 1011, 95 S.Ct. 2636, 45 L.Ed.2d 675 (1975), a majority of the Fifth Circuit held that ineffective assistance of a retained lawyer (other than ineffectiveness that rendered the trial fundamentally unfair) would not offend the Sixth Amendment. After *Cuyler*, however, "any distinction between retained and assigned counsel for purposes of the Sixth Amendment seems to have been swept from the boards." Solina v. United States, 709 F.2d 160, 165 (2d Cir.1983) (Friendly, J.).

30 It seems consistent with *Cuyler* to hold that an accused may waive the effective assistance of retained counsel, and insist upon representation by a lawyer whose abilities are seriously doubted by the trial judge, in the absence of any strong state interest in disqualifying the lawyer. E.g., Smith v. Superior Court, 68 Cal.2d 547, 68 Cal.Rptr. 1, 440 P.2d 65 (1968).

31 United States ex rel. Spurlark v. Wolff, 683 F.2d 216 (7th Cir.1982); United States v. Bragan, 499 F.2d 1376 (4th Cir.1974); United States v. Burton, 584 F.2d 485 (D.C.Cir.1978), cert.denied 439 U.S. 1069, 99 S.Ct. 837, 59 L.Ed.2d 34 (1979); People v. Gzikowski, 32 Cal.3d 580, 186 Cal.Rptr. 339, 651 P.2d 1145 (1982); State v. McFadden, 292 N.C. 609, 234 S.E.2d 742 (1977).

est in assuring that the accused is afforded a conflict-free representation may authorize disqualification of a retained lawyer in an extreme case.[32] In the absence of a compelling state interest, however, the accused should be accorded continuances in order to obtain the assistance of retained counsel,[33] should not be deprived of assets with which to hire a lawyer,[34] and should not be prevented from having reasonable access to a retained lawyer.[35]

§ 14.4 RIGHT TO SELF-REPRESENTATION

§ 14.4.1 Pro Se Litigation

General

Litigants and courts existed long before lawyers, and the concept that a litigant should be entitled to press or defend a case without a trained lawyer is deeply entrenched in American law. The right of a litigant to proceed in the federal courts without a lawyer has been protected by statute since the original 1789 legislation establishing the federal courts.[36] The same right is apparently recognized in all the states. The basis of pro se[37] appearance is historical and remains largely unexplored.

Courts frequently caution litigants about the dangers of appearing against a represented adversary in view of the highly technical and arcane nature of law. Judges are also concerned that untrained litigants will waste the time and resources of courts and opposing parties. But it is not clear that conerns about risks to self-interest and burdens on courts are either invariably well-founded[38] or sufficiently forceful to preclude the exercise of individual autonomy implicit in a claim of the right to self-representation. The latter sentiment—control over one's own juridical destiny—persuaded the Supreme Court to recognize a constitutional right to self-representation in criminal cases.

Limitation to Natural Persons

The category of litigants who may invoke the pro se right is curiously limited in one respect. Individuals are, of course, entitled so to proceed. And a lawyer-litigant has the same right to proceed pro se as any other individual litigant.[39] But following the common-law approach, modern courts generally refuse to permit corporations, partnerships, and similar artificial entities to appear pro se

32 United States v. Cunningham, 672 F.2d 1064 (2d Cir. 1982); cf. Maxwell v. Superior Court, 30 Ca.3d 606, 180 Cal.Rptr. 177, 639 P.2d 248 (1982). See generally § 8.2.5.

33 Chandler v. Fretag, 348 U.S. 3, 75 S.Ct. 1, 99 L.Ed. 4 (1954).

34 People v. Holland, 23 Cal.3d 77, 151 Cal.Rptr. 625, 588 P.2d 765 (1978)(funds of defendant, not proven to be contraband, could not be withheld if effect was to force him to accept court-appointed lawyer); Jacobson v. Jacobson, 151 N.J.Super. 62, 376 A.2d 558 (1977).

35 State v. Welch, 135 Vt. 316, 376 A.2d 351 (1977). See generally § 14.6.4. Courts occasionally refuse to hold that a constitutional right to counsel was infringed, for example by pre-indictment prosecutorial overreaching of a lawyer, on the ground that the right to counsel only attaches after a criminal proceeding is formally instituted. E.g., Ostrer v. Aronwald, 434 F.Supp. 379, 395 (S.D. N.Y.1977), affirmed 567 F.2d 551 (2d Cir.1977). That approach confuses issues concerning the outermost limits on state power to withhold appointed counsel with the analytically different question of barriers against governmental interference with voluntary client-lawyer relationships already formed.

36 Faretta v. California, 422 U.S. 806, 812, 95 S.Ct. 2525, 2529–30, 45 L.Ed.2d 562 (1975); Osborn v. Bank, 22 U.S. (9 Wheat.) 738, 829, 6 L.Ed. 204 (1824). The statute is now 28 U.S.C.A. § 1654.

37 Pro se appearances are sometimes referred to as appearances "in propria persona", particularly in older cases. E.g., United States v. Plattner, 330 F.2d 271, 274 (2d Cir.1964).

38 Pro se appearances have been urged as particularly appropriate in small-claims and similar alternative tribunals with informal and flexible procedures. See R.Spurrie, Inexpensive Justice: Self-Representation in the Small Claims Court (1980). A federal judge has pointed out that as a practical matter a pro se litigant will more likely be able to argue to the jury that it should not follow the law contained in the judge's instructions. See Kaufman, The Right of Self-Representation and the Power of Jury Nullification, 28 Case West.L.Rev. 269 (1978).

39 Theobald v. Botein, Hays, Sklar & Hertzberg, 465 F.Supp. 609 (S.D.N.Y.1979); Hickman v. Frerking, 4 Kan. App.2d 590, 609 P.2d 682 (1980)(lawyer admitted only in another jurisdiction may appear pro se); Koger v. Weber, 116 Misc.2d 726, 455 N.Y.S.2d 935 (Sup.Ct.1982)(lawyer not disqualified from appearing pro se on the argument that this would violate the rule against an advocate also appearing as a witness).

through an officer, director, or member.[40] The reasons commonly given for the broad prohibition— that a corporation is not a "person" and can only act through agents, that courts would be burdened with confusing litigation, and that sharp practices would result—seem either logically circular or empirically debatable.[41] The ban against pro se appearances by nonlawyer officers of a corporate party is not universal. Occasionally a jurisdiction will recognize exceptions—for example, in the case of small claims courts, where the necessity of obtaining counsel is said to be inconsistent with the purposes for creating a tribunal for small claims.[42]

The "No Special Treatment" Rule

Courts reflect differing attitudes toward pro se litigants, with the prevailing judicial attitude one of begrudging acceptance. The traditional view is that no special consideration will be given to a person proceeding pro se.[43] Instead, they are held to the same procedural and substantive standards as litigants with lawyers.[44] Active judicial involvement in the trial to tip the scales in favor of the pro se litigant, such as by suggesting possible theories of recovery or defense that have been overlooked, has been both discouraged[45] and defended.[46] Correlatively, a pro se litigant is entitled to at least the same latitude as a lawyer would enjoy with respect to the bounds of permissible advocacy.[47] In a somewhat contrasting tone, the Supreme Court, in *Faretta v. California*, assured lower courts that recognizing a constitutional pro se right would not cause serious burdens: the right, according to the Court, was not an exemption from the duty "to comply with relevant rules of procedural and substantive law."[48] If a pro se litigant engages in a course of conduct that is both contrary to rules and disrupts the court's proceedings, the court can revoke the

[40] In re Victor Publishers, Inc., 545 F.2d 285 (lst Cir. 1976); Move Organization v. United States Dep't of Justice, 555 F.Supp. 684, 693 (E.D.Pa.1983); Merco Constr. Engineers, Inc. v. Municipal Court, 21 Cal.3d 724, 147 Cal.Rptr. 637, 581 P.2d 636 (1978); Oahu Plumbing & Sheet Metal, Ltd. v. Kona Constr., Inc., 60 Hawaii 372, 590 P.2d 570 (1979); In re DePew, 98 Idaho 215, 560 P.2d 886 (1977)(disbarred lawyer could not sue pro se to recover legal fees that were owed to his professional corporation); Land Management, Inc. v. Dept. of Environmental Protection, 368 A.2d 602 (Me.1977). See generally, Cotner, May a Corporation Act as Its Own Attorney?, 16 Cleve.Mar.L.Rev. 173 (1967). An extension of the rule prohibits the maintenance of a shareholder derivative action or similar representative litigation by a nonlawyer appearing pro se. See Phillips v. Tobin, 548 F.2d 408 (2d Cir.1976); Martin v. Middendorf, 420 F.Supp. 779 (D.D.C.1976).

[41] See In re Holliday's Tax Services, Inc., 417 F.Supp. 182 (E.D.N.Y.1976) (Weinstein, J.), affirmed 614 F.2d 1287 (2d Cir.1979).

[42] Prudential Ins. Co. v. Small Claims Court, 76 Cal. App.2d 379, 173 P.2d 38 (1946). Relatedly, a corporation has been permitted to apply for registration of a sister-state judgment under the uniform enforcement of foreign judgments act on the theory that registration calls upon the court clerk to perform merely a ministerial and not a judicial act. See Tom Thumb Glove Co. v. Han, 78 Cal. App.3d 1, 144 Cal.Rptr. 30 (1978).

[43] Nelson v. Gaunt, 125 Cal.App.3d 623, 178 Cal.Rptr. 167, 175 (1981)(physician in medical malpractice suit appeared for trial with no lawyer); Stein v. Lewisville Ind. School Dist., 481 S.W.2d 436, 439 (Tex.Civ.App.1972), appeal dismissed 414 U.S. 948, 94 S.Ct. 272, 38 L.Ed.2d 203 (1973).

[44] International Fidelity Ins. Co. v. Wilson, 387 Mass. 841, 443 N.E.2d 1308, 1312 (1983); In re Brewster, 115 N.H. 636, 351 A.2d 889 (1975)(per curiam); Meyers v. First Nat'l Bank, 3 Ohio App.3d 209, 444 N.E.2d 412, 413 (1981).

[45] Swenson v. Dittner, 183 Conn. 289, 439 A.2d 334, 338–39 (1981). See generally ABA Standards of Judicial Administration, Trial Courts § 2.23 at 45–47 (1976).

[46] United Artists Corp. v. Freeman, 605 F.2d 854, 857 (5th Cir.1979)(trial judge should have advised pro se party deponent about limits of his claim of privilege not to answer deposition questions on ground of self-incrimination). The Supreme Court in Haines v. Kerner, 404 U.S. 519, 520, 92 S.Ct. 594, 595, 30 L.Ed.2d 652 (1972), directed the federal courts to apply less stringent standards to technical defects in complaints filed by pro se litigants. See also Hughes v. Rowe, 449 U.S. 5, 101 S.Ct. 173, 66 L.Ed.2d 163 (1980)(per curiam)(federal statutes providing for award of fees to prevailing party in civil rights actions should rarely, if ever, be applied against pro se prisoner litigant).

[47] A pro se litigant is "clearly entitled to as much latitude in conducting his defense as we have held is enjoyed by counsel vigorously espousing a client's cause." In re Little, 404 U.S. 553, 555, 92 S.Ct. 659, 660, 30 L.Ed. 2d 708 (1972). See also Mayberry v. Pennsylvania, 400 U.S. 455, 91 S.Ct. 499, 27 L.Ed.2d 532 (1972); Cersosimo v. Cersosimo, 188 Conn. 385, 449 A.2d 1026, 1031 (1982) (error to deny pro se litigant normal discovery).

[48] Faretta v. California, 422 U.S. 806, 834–35 n.46, 95 S.Ct. 2525, 2541, 45 L.Ed.2d 562 (1975).

permission to appear pro se and require the litigant to retain a lawyer [49] or be represented by a court-appointed lawyer.

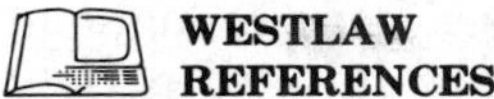

di pro se

topic(45) /p "pro se"

§ 14.4.2 *The Pro Se Right in Criminal Cases*

The Faretta Doctrine

Although the right to appear pro se is very widely recognized, courts at one time took the position that the right to counsel guaranteed by the Sixth Amendment required them to appoint counsel to represent an accused despite the expressed preference of the accused to dispense with appointed counsel and conduct his or her own defense. In Faretta v. California,[50] however, the Supreme Court held that an accused who made a "knowing and intelligent" waiver [51] of the constitutional right to the assistance of counsel could invoke a right to self-representation that all courts are bound to honor.

The basis of the right to self-representation was found to be implied by the structure and history of the Sixth Amendment, which guarantees the right to counsel in criminal cases.[52] The assistance of counsel is a personal right of the accused and cannot be forced upon an unwilling recipient. Even if self-representation clearly disadvantages the accused, a knowing and free choice to proceed without a lawyer's assistance must be honored "out of 'that respect for the individual which is the lifeblood of the law.' " [53]

Faretta implicates two rights—the right to counsel as well as that of self-representation. An accused who appears in court without counsel and insists upon proceeding without a lawyer must be informed about two distinct matters. First, the accused should be informed of his or her right to counsel, including the right to court-appointed counsel if he or she is unable to retain private counsel.[54] Second, only after the accused understands the right to counsel should the judge's inquiry turn to the question whether the accused wishes to proceed with counsel or to forego counsel with all that that entails.[55]

The preferred right, or at least the judicially presumed normal wish of an accused, is to appear with counsel. That preference is seen in the rule that, unlike in the right-to-counsel situation, a person who appears at trial with counsel is not entitled to a judicial recitation of the right to appear pro se.[56] Moreover,

[49] Faretta v. California, supra, 422 U.S. at 834 n.46, 95 S.Ct. at 2540; In re Estate of Rappaport, 109 Misc.2d 640, 440 N.Y.S.2d 532 (Surr.Ct.1981). If a pro se litigant abuses the judicial process through repeated frivolous lawsuits, courts may enjoin future similar suits unless the litigant is represented by a lawyer. E.g., Pavilonis v. King, 626 F.2d 1075 (1st Cir.1980), cert.denied 449 U.S. 829, 101 S.Ct. 96, 66 L.Ed.2d 34 (1980); Board of County Commissioners v. Howard, 640 P.2d 1128 (Colo.1982), appeal dismissed 456 U.S. 968, 102 S.Ct. 2228, 72 L.Ed.2d 841 (1982)(frivolous suits by disbarred lawyer). Egregious misconduct by pro se litigant may be sanctioned by punishment for contempt. E.g., People v. Robinson, 100 Ill. App.3d 660, 56 Ill.Dec. 208, 427 N.E.2d 288 (1981).

[50] 422 U.S. 806, 95 S.Ct. 2525, 45 L.Ed.2d 562 (1975).

[51] Faretta v. California, supra, 422 U.S. at 835, 95 S.Ct. at 2541. "Knowing" is a better word than "intelligent," for it is clear that the defendant's lack of wisdom or prescience in rejecting a lawyer's assistance is irrelevant to an effective waiver of counsel and invocation of the *Faretta* right. E.g., United States v. Curcio, 680 F.2d 881, 888 (2d Cir.1982).

[52] 422 U.S. at 819, 95 S.Ct. at 2533.

[53] 422 U.S. at 834, 95 S.Ct. at 2540 (quoting Illinois v. Allen, 397 U.S. 337, 350–51, 90 S.Ct. 1057, 1064–65, 25 L.Ed.2d 353 (1970)(Brennan, J., concurring)).

[54] Piankhy v. Cuyler, 703 F.2d 728 (3d Cir.1983)(denial of right to counsel where trial court conducted *Faretta* inquiry without informing accused of right to appointed counsel).

[55] A model for a thoroughgoing inquiry by a trial judge when an accused refuses counsel is contained in People v. Lopez, 71 Cal.App.3d 568, 138 Cal.Rptr. 36 (1977). The general approach of the federal courts is not to insist upon a particular set of questions and responses, but to leave the content of the inquiry to the trial judge's discretion. See United States v. Bailey, 675 F.2d 1292, 1301 n.13 (D.C.Cir.1982), cert.denied 459 U.S. 853, 103 S.Ct. 119, 74 L.Ed.2d 104 (1982), and authorities cited. In *Faretta* itself the Court stated that the defendant must be "made aware of the dangers and disadvantages of self-representation." 422 U.S. at 835, 95 S.Ct. at 2541.

[56] Tuckson v. United States, 364 A.2d 138 (D.C.App. 1976).

once the right to counsel has been waived through invocation of the *Faretta* right to self-representation, a defendant who is convicted may not, of course, argue ineffective assistance of counsel.[57]

Standby Counsel

Proper judicial grant of a request for self-representation does not always end the question of right to counsel. An accused may request, or may be provided over protest, the services of *standby* or advisory counsel.[58] Or an accused may request a *hybrid*, or mixed, representation, with a lawyer conducting much of the trial and the accused conducting only some parts, such as the final summation to the jury.[59] The general judicial view is that *Faretta* does not require judicial acceptance of hybrid representations but that they are consistent with that decision.[60] Those cases present complex and difficult issues of the required and desirable relationship between defendants and their lawyers.[61]

Nonlawyer Assistance

The "tax protest" and kindred movements in recent years have brought into courts litigants who have invoked a right to the assistance of nonlawyers in conducting court proceedings. Courts have rejected arguments that the federal or state constitutions confer such a right, pointing out that recognzing it would require acceptance of unauthorized practice of the law.[62] Those results are compatible with the self-representation right acknowledged in Faretta v. California[63] on the view that the right to personal autonomy recognized there is still protected by the right of the litigant to appear pro se.

The Supreme Court has, however, recognized the special problems that incarcerated persons almost inevitably encounter in gaining access to the courts in instances, such as postconviction relief proceedings, in which no right to counsel exists. The Court has accordingly recognized a limited Fifth Amendment due process right to the assistance of jailhouse lawyers in preparing legal papers.[64]

[57] Faretta v. California, supra, 422 U.S. at 835 n.46, 95 S.Ct. at 2541; United States ex rel. Smith v. Pavich, 568 F.2d 33 (7th Cir.1978). The same result obtains a fortiori in civil cases. E.g., Connecticut Light & Power Co. v. Kluczinsky, 171 Conn. 516, 370 A.2d 1306, 1310 (1976).

[58] That possibility was acknowledged in *Faretta*. See 422 U.S. at 835 n.46, 95 S.Ct. at 2541. In McKaskle v. Wiggins, 465 U.S. 168, 104 S.Ct. 944, 79 L.Ed.2d 122 (1984), the Court held that, once appointed, standby counsel could participate in a trial before a judge, even over the objection of his or her "client," so long as all disputes between lawyer and client were resolved in favor of the client whenever the matter was one that normally would be left to the discretion of a lawyer.

[59] Bontempo v. Fenton, 692 F.2d 954 (3d Cir.1982), cert.denied 460 U.S. 1055, 103 S.Ct. 1506, 75 L.Ed.2d 935 (1983). Courts in civil cases, however, have generally not permitted hybrid appearances. E.g., Move Organization v. City of Philadelphia, 530 F.Supp. 764 (E.D.Pa.1982); Thomas v. National State Bank, 628 P.2d 188 (Colo.App. 1981).

[60] United States v. Williams, 534 F.2d 119 (8th Cir. 1976), cert.denied 429 U.S. 894, 97 S.Ct. 255, 50 L.Ed.2d 177 (1976); Hooks v. State, 416 A.2d 189 (Del.1980); Moore v. State, 83 Wis.2d 285, 265 N.W.2d 540 (1978), cert.denied 439 U.S. 956, 99 S.Ct. 356, 58 L.Ed.2d 348 (1978).

[61] See the majority and dissenting opinions in McKaskle v. Wiggins, 465 U.S. 168, 104 S.Ct. 944, 79 L.Ed.2d 122 (1984). See generally Chused, Faretta and the Personal Defense: The Role of a Represented Defendant in Trial Tactics, 65 Cal.L.Rev. 636 (1977).

[62] A leading set of cases is Turner v. American Bar Ass'n, 407 F.Supp. 451 (N.D.Tex. 1975), affirmed sub nom. Taylor v. Montgomery, 539 F.2d 715 (7th Cir.1976), and Pilla v. American Bar Ass'n, 542 F.2d 56 (8th Cir.1976). On the arguments against nonlawyer representation in unauthorized practice cases, see § 15.1.2.

[63] 422 U.S. 806, 95 S.Ct. 2525, 45 L.Ed.2d 562 (1975), discussed in preceding section.

[64] See Johnson v. Avery, 393 U.S. 483, 490, 89 S.Ct. 747, 751, 21 L.Ed.2d 718 (1969); Wolff v. McDonnell, 418 U.S. 539, 577–80, 94 S.Ct. 2963, 2985, 41 L.Ed.2d 935 (1974). The right of access to the courts can be satisfied by prison officials in alternative ways, such as by providing the resources of an adequate law library or providing prisoners with a lawyer-staffed legal assistance program. See Bounds v. Smith, 430 U.S. 817, 828, 97 S.Ct. 1491, 1498, 52 L.Ed.2d 72 (1977). If counsel is provided, a state is not obliged to supply a law library or other alternative legal resources to aid a prisoner in a pro se representation. E.g., United States v. Wilson, 690 F.2d 1267 (9th Cir. 1982), cert.denied 464 U.S. 867, 104 S.Ct. 205, 78 L.Ed.2d 178 (1983); Spates v. Manson, 644 F.2d 80 (2d Cir.1981). See also infra, at 809–810.

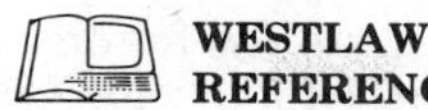
WESTLAW REFERENCES

110k641.4(5)

faretta /12 95 +4 2525 /p "pro se" self-represent! /p waiv!

§ 14.5 RIGHT TO COUNSEL IN CIVIL CASES

General

Courts have been generally unreceptive to the claims of unrepresented litigants that they should enjoy a right to appointed counsel in a proceeding that the court is not prepared to denominate as criminal. Litigants are normally entitled to retain a lawyer to represent their interests [65] in both civil court actions and administrative proceedings, but government has no general obligation to supply counsel.[66] Courts may be empowered by statute to appoint counsel in civil cases, but normally that does not create an absolute right to counsel.[67] The Supreme Court has similarly denied that a general right to counsel exists in civil cases, although it has recognized such a right in limited circumstances. Some states, by legislation or judicial decision, have carved out discrete, excepted areas of noncriminal litigation in which counsel must be appointed.

On one level, the Supreme Court's restrictive approach to the right to counsel in civil cases plausibly arrays doctrinal objections to deployment of a more generous right because of what the Court itself has characterized as the minimal fiscal impact that such a right would impose upon the states. Yet the outcome leaves largely in place a litigational system in which the quality of justice rendered in individual cases depends in important part upon the ability of a litigant to buy justice.[68] To some extent, the resulting maladministration of justice has been corrected in individual cases through programs of legal assistance to the poor.[69] But to the extent that those partial and incomplete solutions are ineffective, the spectre of the pans of justice misaligned by the weight of dollars continues to haunt American judicial and administrative systems.

The absence of a constitutional right to appointed counsel does not mean that the state is free to interfere with a litigant's access to retained counsel in civil matters. In the many circumstances in which due process entitles a party to a fair hearing in a court or before an administrative agency, a party who may be directly affected by the proceeding is entitled by the due process clause to retain private counsel and to have the lawyer present to protect the party's interests in the proceeding.[70]

Reach of the Constitution

Because a civil litigant most often is not in risk of imprisonment as a direct result of civil proceedings, the Sixth Amendment right to counsel "in all criminal prosecutions" is inap-

[65] Goldberg v. Kelly, 397 U.S. 254, 270–71, 90 S.Ct. 1011, 1021–22, 25 L.Ed.2d 287 (1970); Rivera v. Marcus, 696 F.2d 1016 (2d Cir.1982)(attempt to remove foster children from home of custodial half-sister required due process procedures, including opportunity to retain counsel).

[66] Ramirez v. INS, 550 F.2d 560, 563 (9th Cir.1977) (deportation proceeding); Nees v. SEC, 414 F.2d 211, 221 (9th Cir.1969); Williams v. Capitol County Mut. Fire Ins. Co., 594 S.W.2d 558 (Tex.Civ.App.1980). For arguments in favor of a broader right to counsel in civil cases, see, e.g., Swygert, Should Indigent Civil Litigants in the Federal Courts Have a Right to Appointed Counsel?, 39 Wash. & Lee L.Rev. 1267 (1982); Weinstein, The Poor's Right to Equal Access to the Courts, 13 Conn.L.Rev. 651 (1981); Johnson & Schwartz, Beyond Payne: The Case for a Legally Enforceable Right to Representation in Civil Cases for Indigent California Litigants, 11 Loy.L.A.L.Rev. 249 (1978).

[67] Moss v. ITT Continental Baking Co., 83 F.R.D. 624 (E.D.Va.1979). There is, however, a right to call upon a judge to exercise his or her discretion whether to appoint counsel. E.g., United States v. McQuade, 579 F.2d 1180 (9th Cir.1978); Caston v. Sears, Roebuck & Co., 556 F.2d 1305 (5th Cir.1977). See also Hilliard v. Volcker, 659 F.2d 1125 (D.C.Cir.1981)(administrative agency must inform unsuccessful pro se complainant that, in event of suit to challenge agency's adverse ruling, court has discretion to appoint counsel).

[68] See generally Hermann & Donahue, Fathers Behind Bars: The Right to Counsel in Civil Contempt Proceedings, 14 N.M.L.Rev. 275 (1984).

[69] See generally § 16.7.2 (legal aid); § 16.9 (pro bono).

[70] Goldberg v. Kelly, 397 U.S. 254, 270–71, 90 S.Ct. 1101, 1021–22, 25 L.Ed.2d 287 (1970); Sartain v. SEC, 601 F.2d 1366, 1375 (9th Cir.1979).

plicable.[71] Instead, the approach of the Supreme Court and lower courts is to determine whether a right to counsel exists as the result of a case-by-case, *due process* analysis under the Fifth and Fourteenth Amendments.

The principal due process case is Lassiter v. Department of Social Services.[72] A state court held that a mother serving a lengthy prison sentence for murder of her husband was an unfit parent and terminated her parental rights to the custody of her minor child. The Supreme Court held that the failure of the state to appoint counsel for the admittedly indigent mother did not offend due process. The decision follows previous cases in employing for right-to-civil-counsel questions a three-part balancing formula that had been developed to determine whether due process requires particular procedural protections. The approach requires an examination of (1) the private interests at stake, (2) the government's interests, and (3) the extent of the risk that the absence of the procedural protection—here, counsel—will lead to erroneous results in the litigation.

The Court in *Lassiter* found that parental termination proceedings did affect a commanding interest of the parent,[73] and that the state's only distinctive interest—in avoiding the cost of appointed counsel—was minimal. The critical factor in the case was the lack of a significant, incremental advantage to the defending parent of a lawyer's assistance. The Court held that the procedures employed in the state court were sufficient to avoid significant risk of error because the facts in the trial were relatively uncomplicated and no expert testimony was presented.[74]

Lassiter's case-by-case approach incurs a heavy price of uncertainty. In every case, a court must determine whether the particular facts, legal issues, and procedural devices involved require the assistance of counsel. For example, the decision has done little to resolve the sharp division of authority over whether counsel must be appointed to represent a putative father in a paternity action brought by the state.[75]

[71] The rule is becoming fairly well settled that due process requires the appointment of counsel for an indigent accused of contempt involving imprisonment, whether denominated criminal or civil. United States v. Bobart Travel Agency, 699 F.2d 618 (2d Cir.1983); United States v. Anderson, 553 F.2d 1154 (8th Cir.1977); Henkel v. Bradshaw, 483 F.2d 1386 (9th Cir.1973); McNabb v. Osmundson, 315 N.W.2d 9 (Iowa 1982); Ferris v. State ex rel. Maass, 75 Wis.2d 542, 249 N.W.2d 789 (1977). But see, e.g., Sword v. Sword, 399 Mich. 367, 249 N.W.2d 88 (1976); State v. Rael, 97 N.M. 640, 642 P.2d 1099 (1982). Imprisonment is a possible sanction for either type of contempt, and the resulting threat to the liberty interests of the alleged contemner makes the right-to-counsel cases in the criminal area readily applicable. See generally Note, Due Process in the Civil Nonsupport Proceeding: The Right to Counsel and Alternatives to Incarceration, 61 Tex.L.Rev. 291 (1982); Note, The Indigent Defendant's Right to Court-Appointed Counsel in Civil Contempt Proceedings for Nonpayment of Child Support, 50 U.Chi.L. Rev. 326 (1983).

[72] 452 U.S. 18, 101 S.Ct. 2153, 68 L.Ed.2d 640 (1981).

[73] A later, different majority of the Court called the "freedom of personal choice in matters of family life" such as that involved in *Lassiter* a "fundamental liberty interest" protected by the Fourteenth Amendment. Santosky v. Kramer, 455 U.S. 745, 102 S.Ct. 1388, 71 L.Ed.2d 599 (1982)(in parental rights termination case, due process requires that state prove facts by "clear and convincing" evidence standard and not lesser preponderance-of-evidence standard).

[74] The five-person majority of the Court also extended the comforting reassurance that all previous decisions had held that a right to counsel existed in parental rights termination cases, 452 U.S. at 30–31, 101 S.Ct. at 2161, and that "informed public opinion" and the statutes of 33 states and the District of Columbia required the appointment of counsel in most parental termination cases. 452 U.S. at 33–34, 101 S.Ct at 2162–63. In Walters v. National Ass'n of Radiation Survivors, ___ U.S. ___, 105 S.Ct. 3180, 87 L.Ed.2d 220, (1985), the Court held that a statutory fee limit of $10, that effectively precluded participation of lawyers in Veterans Administration claims hearings, did not deny due process because it had not been shown that the absence of lawyers in the generality of VA claims cases would substantially impair the accuracy of these nonadversarial proceedings.

[75] Compare, e.g., Reynolds v. Kimmons, 569 P.2d 799 (Alaska 1977)(due process-based right to counsel); Salas v. Cortez, 24 Cal.3d 22, 154 Cal.Rptr. 529, 593 P.2d 226, cert.denied 444 U.S. 900, 100 S.Ct. 209, 62 L.Ed.2d 136 (1979); Hepfel v. Bashaw, 279 N.W.2d 342, 4 A.L.R.4th 352 (Minn.1979), with, e.g., Nordgren v. Mitchell, 524 F.Supp. 242 (D.Utah 1981), affirmed 716 F.2d 1335 (10th Cir.1983)(no due process violation to deny request for counsel); Iowa ex rel. Hamilton v. Snodgrass, 325 N.W.2d 740 (Iowa 1982). See also S. v. S., 595 S.W.2d 357 (Mo.Ct. App.1980)(where paternity of child is in dispute in custody case, guardian ad litem must be appointed to represent interests of child).

Limits of the Boddie "Access to Court" Doctrine

Litigants seeking a broader right to counsel in civil cases occasionally have relied on the "access to court" argument that prevailed in the 1971 Supreme Court decision in Boddie v. Connecticut.[76] *Boddie* struck down a state statute requiring the prepayment of a filing fee for divorce plaintiffs on the ground that the statute violated due process because it denied indigent plaintiff access to the court. Subsequent decisions, however, have narrowed the possible reach of *Boddie*.[77] The prevailing view is that a due-process-based right to counsel exists only when the absence of counsel forms a direct barrier to a litigant's participation in litigation that affects a vital interest of the litigant.

The narrowed *Boddie* test and the *Lassiter* approach probably converge. Presumably, if the indigent litigant can show the required denial of access due to the absence of counsel, the balancing process of *Lassiter* also requires counsel. *Lassiter*, however, does at least emphasize that access to a civil judicial proceeding through sheer bodily presence at it may not suffice. Even when the litigant is physically present at the hearing, if the litigant is unable to function effectively there—for example because of an inability to understand the proceedings—the right to a fair hearing may be violated if a lawyer is not provided.[78]

Nonlawyer Assistance

Depending on the nature of the interest asserted by the litigant and the nature of the hearing, the legal assistance minimally required by the Constitution need not invariably be supplied by a lawyer. The Supreme Court's flexible "due process" right to counsel on occasion has only entitled the aggrieved party to the help of a person sufficiently skilled in the subject of the hearing to provide "qualified and independent" assistance.[79] That variable approach has been followed most prominently in civil litigation by or against an incarcerated person. Such litigation presents special difficulties because obvious security interests are implicated if a prisoner were permitted to appear pro se and because declaring a broad right to counsel would cause fiscal and other burdens.[80]

The response of judges has been a doctrine that requires that prisoners be allowed access to courts with some legal assistance, but that stops short of requiring that aid be in the form of an individual lawyer. The leading case, Bounds v. Smith,[81] held that the adequate, effective, and meaningful access to the courts guaranteed by due process to inmates required that the state provide prisoners with adequate law libraries or the adequate assistance of persons with some legal training or experience. The prisoner-access right covers more than habeas corpus and similar litiga-

[76] 401 U.S. 371, 91 S.Ct. 780, 28 L.Ed.2d 113 (1971).

[77] Kras v. United States, 409 U.S. 434, 93 S.Ct. 631, 34 L.Ed.2d 626 (1973)(no constitutional infirmity in statute requiring prepayment of filing fee in bankruptcy); Ortwein v. Schwab, 410 U.S. 656, 93 S.Ct. 1172, 35 L.Ed.2d 572 (1973)(filing fee of $25.00 to obtain state court appellate review of state welfare agency reduction of welfare benefits not unconstitutional). The progeny of *Boddie*, restrictively limiting its apparent reach, is criticized in L.Tribe, American Constitutional Law 1008–10 (1978).

[78] Sims v. Harris, 631 F.2d 26 (4th Cir.1980).

[79] Vitek v. Jones, 445 U.S. 480, 500, 100 S.Ct. 1254, 1267, 63 L.Ed.2d 552 (1980)(concurring opinion of Powell, J.)(hearing on involuntary transfer of incarcerated felon from state prison to mental hospital requires "qualified and independent" assistance but not necessarily that of lawyer if, for example, trained medical or paramedical advisor could provide adequate assistance); Downing v. LeBritton, 550 F.2d 689 (1st Cir.1977)(state university may constitutionally limit pool of representatives for mentally retarded terminated employee to fellow employees for post-termination proceedings). By contrast, in Gabrilowitz v. Newman, 582 F.2d 100 (1st Cir.1978), the court held that it was a denial of due process to exclude a student's lawyer from a university disciplinary hearing arising from the same facts as a pending criminal charge.

[80] Similar problems confront litigation by or against persons involuntarily committed to mental institutions. See generally Brewster v. Dukakis, 675 F.2d 1 (1st Cir. 1982)(discussion of extent to which state can be required to fund "legal advocacy" program for persons institutionalized in state mental hospital).

[81] 430 U.S. 817, 97 S.Ct. 1491, 52 L.Ed.2d 72 (1977). The *Bounds* decision extended the holding in Johnson v. Avery, 393 U.S. 483, 89 S.Ct. 747, 21 L.Ed.2d 718 (1969), that illiterate state prisoners had a due process right to the assistance of "jailhouse lawyers" in the preparation of legal documents.

tion relating to the prisoner's conviction. It extends as well to civil rights litigation attacking conditions of confinement and similar matters.[82]

WESTLAW REFERENCES

right /5 counsel** lawyer attorney /s civil /s indigen! poor

lassiter /12 101 +4 2153 /p right /5 counsel** attorney lawyer

§ 14.6 EFFECTIVE ASSISTANCE OF COUNSEL

§ 14.6.1 The Right to Effective Assistance

Attacks on Judgments Due to Defective Assistance

The right to counsel would be hollow if holders of the right regularly received only incompetent representation by their appointed lawyers. Incompetence can stem from many factors. In chronic forms it can result from inexperience, defective training, or inappropriate professional attitudes toward standards of quality or toward clients. Incompetence might befall a normally competent lawyer because of momentary inattention or the pressure of other parts of the lawyer's caseload. The traditional reaction of the courts has been to foist the errors of counsel, whatever their source or nature, upon the client. That posture persists today in civil representations, although cracks in the otherwise massed judicial ranks are detectable.[83] The client is left mainly to the uncertain relief of a legal malpractice recovery or is relegated to the uncertain status of complainant before a lawyer discipline agency.[84]

In criminal cases the law has been similar in practical outcome. The "farce and mockery" constitutional standard that was traditionally applied to measure the effectiveness of a defense lawyer's work produced, obviously, few reversals. But a recent trend of decisions heralds a more meaningful constitutional requirement of competence in criminal defense. The new standard is at least nominally keyed to the ordinary, and not the minimal, standard of competent practice. Whether liberalization of the standard will produce a corresponding increase in the number of convictions set aside, or an overall enhancement in the competence of counsel, remains to be seen.

The doctrine that a defense lawyer's incompetence requires setting aside the conviction stems primarily from the Sixth Amendment right to counsel and the Fifth Amendment right to due process in criminal proceedings. Those constitutional rights have been made applicable to the states through the Fourteenth Amendment due process clause (§ 14.3.1). The Supreme Court has indicated that a lawyer's defective services will not be a ground for reversal unless they had an impact upon a "critical stage" of the criminal proceeding (§ 14.3.2). Thus a lawyer's failure to file a discretionary appeal is not constitutionally ineffective assistance because of the rule that there is no right to counsel for such appeals.[85]

82 See Wolff v. McDonnell, 418 U.S. 539, 94 S.Ct. 2963, 41 L.Ed.2d 935 (1974). Some states have gone farther than the Supreme Court. California's highest court, for example, has held that an indigent prisoner seeking to defend a civil suit has an absolute right to the appointment of counsel at state expense. See Payne v. Superior Court, 17 Cal.3d 908, 132 Cal.Rptr. 405, 553 P.2d 565 (1976)(en banc).

83 Link v. Wabash R.R., 370 U.S. 626, 633–34, 82 S.Ct. 1386, 1390, 8 L.Ed.2d 734 (1962); United States v. Rogers, 534 F.2d 1134 (5th Cir.1976), cert.denied 429 U.S. 940, 97 S.Ct. 355, 50 L.Ed.2d 309 (1976); Everett v. Everett, 319 Mich. 475, 29 N.W.2d 919 (1947); cf. Sartain v. Securities and Exchange Comm'n, 601 F.2d 1366, 1375 (9th Cir. 1979)(conflict of interest among codefendants in lifetime expulsion proceeding not shown to have offended due process on facts here). But cf. In re Marriage of Park, 27 Cal.3d 337, 165 Cal.Rptr. 792, 612 P.2d 882 (1980)(California rule permitting setting aside judgment if litigant was denied "fair adversary hearing" satisfied when absent party at dissolution proceeding was inadequately represented by lawyer); Thelen v. Thelen, 3 N.C.App. 684, 281 S.E.2d 737 (1981)(out-of-state plaintiff incompetently represented by district attorney under Uniform Reciprocal Enforcement of Support Act entitled to new trial for "excusable neglect" of lawyer). See generally § 4.6.1 (procedural forfeitures).

84 Watson v. Moss, 619 F.2d 775 (8th Cir.1980); Cruz v. Montoya, 660 P.2d 723, 728 (Utah 1983).

85 Wainwright v. Torna, 455 U.S. 586, 587–88, 102 S.Ct. 1300, 1301, 71 L.Ed.2d 475 (1982)(per curiam)("Since re-

The charge of ineffective assistance has become a very common ground of attack following conviction during the past two decades. A decision to make the argument can hardly be based realistically on the probability that it will be accepted, for rarely will a court find constitutionally defective assistance. It is even rarer to find a disciplinary proceeding brought against a defense lawyer for incompetent representation.[86] The scarcity of reversals or discipline, however, cannot be taken as an accurate measure of satisfaction with the work done. There is substantial discontent with the quality of criminal defense work. But the statistics do stand as mute testimony to the failure of the disciplinary process as a means of assuaging that discontent over the quality of defense services.[87]

Tactical Uses of Incompetence

The existence of a standard that permits an accused to obtain reversal of a conviction on the ground of ineffective assistance raises the possibility that a lawyer might purposefully provide an insufficient defense in order to obtain reversal of any ensuing conviction. Courts have frowned on such practices.[88] When the tactic has been obvious, some courts have tended to focus more upon the need to frustrate it than upon the need to assure that the accused has received a fair trial.[89] So long as the lawyer's actions at trial can be explained on other grounds, regardless of the implausibility of those grounds given the evident motives of the lawyer, the courts who concentrate upon defense motives will not reverse the conviction.[90]

From the point of view of the individual lawyer, the temptation to plant error in the record through purposefully careless representation is objectionable on at least two heads. First, if the client's case is not already hopeless, the tactic may increase the risk that the lawyer's client will be convicted and thus may offend the principles of client loyalty and of competence itself. Second, even if the strategem could redound in some way to the advantage of the client, it abuses the judicial process.

A different problem is created on appeal or in postconviction proceedings if there is some arguable basis for a claim of a lawyer's ineffective assistance. Should the same lawyer who conducted the allegedly defective trial representation also argue his or her own ineptitude in order to set the conviction aside?[91]

spondent had no constitutional right to counsel, he could not be deprived of the effective assistance of counsel by his retained counsel's failure to file the application timely."). See also, e.g., Brown v. United States, 551 F.2d 619 (5th Cir.1977)(retained lawyer's allegedly incompetent representation of suspect early in police investigation could not be ineffective because no "critical stage" of proceedings against suspect had yet been reached); State v. Claudio, 59 N.Y.2d 556, 466 N.Y.S.2d 271, 453 N.E.2d 500 (1983)(same).

86 Isolated examples involve total failures to represent, such as failure to file an appellate brief. E.g., In re Withey, 537 F.2d 324 (9th Cir.1976); In re Margolin, 518 F.2d 551 (9th Cir.1975); United States v. Rivera, 473 F.2d 1372 (9th Cir.1972); Attorney Grievance Commission v. Sherman, 295 Md. 229, 454 A.2d 359 (1983); Murphy v. Committee on Professional Standards, 82 A.D.2d 957, 439 N.Y.S.2d 782 (1981).

87 Bazelon, The Defective Assistance of Counsel, 42 U.Cinn.L.Rev. 1, 17 (1973).

88 In an analogous situation, the Supreme Court has asserted that "defense counsel have an ethical obligation to avoid conflicting representations and to advise the court promptly when a conflict of interest arises during the course of trial." Cuyler v. Sullivan, 446 U.S. 335, 346, 100 S.Ct. 1708, 1717, 64 L.Ed.2d 333 (1980). In a footnote, the Court cited as authority DR 5–105, EC 5–15, and the ABA Defense Function Standards (§ 3.5(b)(1971 draft). Neither Code provision states such a duty in any but the most indirect way. The Defense Function Standards (Standard 4–3.5(b)(iii) in the 1979 edition) are somewhat less equivocal, requiring that in most instances the consent of the defendant to a conflicted representation be "made a matter of judicial record".

89 United States v. Altamirono, 633 F.2d 147, 150–51 (9th Cir.1980), cert.denied 454 U.S. 839, 102 S.Ct. 145, 70 L.Ed.2d 120 (1981); Washington v. Jones, 33 Wn.App. 865, 658 P.2d 1262, 1266 (1983).

90 For example, the court in Washington v. Jones, supra, 658 P.2d at 1267, stated that the conduct of a lawyer was "inappropriate and unprofessional." The lawyer's motion to suppress certain evidence had been denied by the trial court, and thereafter he refused to cross-examine any subsequent witness or introduce any evidence in defense. The court might have been suggesting that discipline of the lawyer rather than reversal of the conviction was the appropriate remedy.

91 See generally Webster, The Public Defender, the Sixth Amendment, and the Code of Professional Responsibility: The Resolution of a Conflict of Interest, 12 Am. Crim.L.Rev. 739 (1975); Note, Ineffective Counsel's Last Act—Appeal?, 1979 Ariz.St.L.J. 595.

The problem is basically one of the lawyer's conflict of interest between making the most persuasive argument for overturning the conviction and protecting the lawyer's own reputation both generally and before the particular court in which the argument must be made.[92] In addition, the court might regard the lawyer's attack as either condescending or, as above, contrived—in neither event giving it a hospitable hearing.

Retained Lawyer

Because of the doctrinal requirements that a prisoner show "state action" in order to make out a consitutional violation (§ 14.6.2), some courts have held that a retained lawyer—as opposed to a court-appointed lawyer—could not commit a blunder that was constitutionally objectionable.[93] But in a 1980 decision the Supreme Court repudiated that view.[94] The Court reasoned that the state was sufficiently implicated by the very fact that the conviction itself was tainted by the retained lawyer's incompetence.[95] The sufficiency of representation by a retained lawyer, therefore, must be tested by the same standard applied to court-appointed counsel.[96]

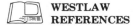

WESTLAW REFERENCES

digest,synopsis(ineffectiv! incompeten! defect! /s assistance /5 counsel** attorney lawyer /p sixth /3 amendment)

cuyler +4 sullivan /12 100 +4 1708 /p inadequat! ineffectiv! incompeten! defect! /s counsel** attorney lawyer

§ 14.6.2 Standards of Effective Assistance

General

Debate over the effective assistance standard has concerned which articulated "test" is generally to be applied. In answering the question, courts began with uniform acceptance of a farce-and-mockery standard under which it was very difficult to demonstrate error by the lawyer that sank to the level of a constitutional violation. Within the past decades, however, the great majority of courts migrated to, or towards, a "reasonable level of competence" standard that roughly equated the constitutonal standard with the standard commonly employed to test competence in legal malpractice cases. The Supreme Court was remarkably delphic about the competing standards, until the 1984 decision in Strickland v. Washington,[97] when the Court itself adopted the "reasonable competence" standard.[98]

Farce and Mockery

The older standard requiring truly outlandish lawyer incompetence can be traced in part

[92] The problem can also be one of incompetence of a lawyer in failing to raise the question of his or her own, or another lawyer's, ineffective representation. E.g., Gagliardi v. Flint, 564 F.2d 112 (3d Cir.1977), cert.denied 438 U.S. 904, 98 S.Ct. 3122, 57 L.Ed.2d 1147 (1978)(conviction attacked on ground that postconviction lawyer failed to argue that original lawyer had rendered ineffective assistance).

[93] United States v. Bubar, 567 F.2d 192, 202 (2d Cir. 1977), cert.denied 434 U.S. 872, 98 S.Ct. 217, 54 L.Ed.2d 151 (1977); Spencer v. State, 385 So.2d (Advance Sheet) 119 (Fla.App.), on rehearing 389 So.2d 652 (Fla.App.1980).

[94] Cuyler v. Sullivan, 446 U.S. 335, 100 S.Ct. 1708, 64 L.Ed.2d 333 (1980).

[95] 446 U.S. at 343–45. The Court's result had been anticipated by recent lower court decisions. E.g., Fitzgerald v. Estelle, 505 F.2d 1334 (5th Cir.1974)(en banc), cert.denied 422 U.S. 1011, 95 S.Ct. 2636 45 L.Ed.2d 675 (1975); United States ex rel. Hart v. Davenport, 478 F.2d 203 (3d Cir.1973); State v. Kellogg, 263 N.W.2d 539 (Iowa 1978).

[96] Strickland v. Washington, 466 U.S. 668, 104 S.Ct. 2052, 2063, 80 L.Ed.2d 674 (1984); Cuyler v. Sullivan, 446 U.S. 335, 100 S.Ct. 1708, 64 L.Ed.2d 333 (1980); Ex parte Duffy, 607 S.W.2d 507 (Tex.Crim.App.1980)(en banc).

[97] 466 U.S. 668, 104 S.Ct. 2052, 80 L.Ed.2d 674 (1984).

[98] See also Cuyler v. Sullivan, 446 U.S. 335, 344, 100 S.Ct. 1708, 1716, 64 L.Ed.2d 333 (1980)("A guilty plea is open to attack on the ground that counsel did not provide the defendant with 'reasonably competent advice.' "), quoting McMann v. Richardson, 397 U.S. 759, 770–71, 90 S.Ct. 141, 1448–49, 25 L.Ed.2d 763 (1970)(guilty plea is not open to attack if based on "reasonably competent advice"; trial courts must determine whether trial counsel's "advice was within the range of competence demanded of attorneys in criminal cases" because "defendants facing felony charges are entitled to the effective assistance of competent counsel"); Tollett v. Henderson, 411 U.S. 258, 260, 93 S.Ct. 1602, 1604, 36 L.Ed.2d 235 (1973)(*McMann* range-of-competence standard quoted).

to the doctrinal problem of "state action." [99] Under a now discarded view,[1] a prisoner wishing to demonstrate that the "state" had caused a deprivation of due process had to show that the lawyer's incompetence was sufficiently visible to either of the two persons in the courtroom who indisputably did act for the state—the judge or the prosecutor—so as to charge their master, the state, with responsibility for failing to correct the lawyer's incompetence.[2] Any conviction resulting from less obvious incompetence was to be remedied through a legal malpractice action against the faithless lawyer.[3] The most questionable application of that rationale was in the case of public defenders or other court-appointed defenders who were, in many senses, state functionaries.[4] In several states the move from a farce-and-mockery standard began in cases dealing with a public defender's competence.[5]

Farce-and-mockery received several variant formulations, some differing from others in subtle ways. Some courts insisted that a convicted person must demonstrate very clearly both that the conviction was unfair and that the lawyer's error was of a particularly outrageous kind.[6] Other courts identified their version of the test as less strict, asserting that the phrase farce-and-mockery was merely symbolic of the heavy burden necessary to show unfairness.[7] Because the standards insisted upon a minimal level of competence, few new trials were ordered under it and those tended to be instances of truly execrable representation.[8] Under steady attack, the farce and mockery standard and its variants

[99] U.S. Const., amend. XIV, § 1 ("nor shall any state deprive any person of life, liberty, or property, without due process of law").

[1] The clearest rejection of this limited view of state action is Cuyler v. Sullivan, supra (conflict of interest of privately retained lawyer can create due process objection). See supra n.65.

[2] Perez v. Wainwright, 640 F.2d 596 (5th Cir.1981), cert. denied 456 U.S. 910, 102 S.Ct. 1759, 72 L.Ed.2d 168 (1982) (false assertion by defense lawyer in open court that he had filed appeal in client's behalf not state action when neither judge nor prosecutor was aware of falsity of statement); In re Hodge, 262 F.2d 778, 780 (9th Cir.1958); United States ex rel. Darcy v. Handy, 203 F.2d 407, 427 (3d Cir.1953), cert. denied 346 U.S. 865, 74 S.Ct. 103, 98 L.Ed.2d 375 (1953). More broadly, state procedural due process violations of all kinds were at one time conceptualized by the Supreme Court in minimalist terms such as "sham or pretense". See Palko v. Connecticut, 302 U.S. 319, 327, 58 S.Ct. 149, 152–53, 82 L.Ed. 288 (1937). Such a limited view of state action first found expression in the Civil Rights Cases, 109 U.S. 3, 11, 3 S.Ct. 18, 21, 27 L.Ed. 835 (1883). Moreover, federal habeas corpus review of state court convictions was originally extremely limited to only the most egregious of errors. See generally, Note, Developments—Federal Habeas Corpus, 83 Harv.L.Rev. 1038, 1042–62 (1970).

Those and similar special barriers may continue to play a role in defining the reach of the effective counsel guarantee. In Engle v. Isaac, 456 U.S. 107, 134, 102 S.Ct. 1558, 1575, 71 L.Ed.2d 783 (1982), in the particular context of federal habeas corpus, the Court stated that "We have long recognized . . . that the Constitution guarantees criminal defendants only a fair trial and a competent attorney. It does not insure that defense counsel will recognize and raise every conceivable constitutional claim."

[3] Courts employed similar logic in arguing that even court-appointed lawyers were the "agents" only of their clients and "bound" their clients by their acts, even if these were performed incompetently. State v. Dreher, 137 Mo. 11, 38 S.W. 567 (1897)(gross incompetence of trial lawyer for person sentenced to death cannot be basis for reversal but only of negligence suit), cited in Strazzella, Ineffective Assistance of Counsel Claims: New Uses, New Problems, 19 Ariz.L.Rev. 443 (1977).

[4] Polk County v. Dodson, 454 U.S. 312, 102 S.Ct. 445, 70 L.Ed.2d 509 (1981), held that a public defender was not liable for damages under 42 U.S.C.A. § 1983 for an alleged failure to prosecute an appeal from a criminal conviction. The opinion was careful to point out, however, that the statutory construction question before it was not identical to the constitutional "state action" issue, which it expressly refused to consider. See 454 U.S. at 322 n.12, 102 S.Ct. at 451–52.

[5] People v. Pope, 23 Cal.3d 412, 152 Cal.Rptr. 732, 590 P.2d 859 (1979)(farce and sham standard abandoned for public defender; standard for privately retained defense counsel left open); People v. Frierson, 25 Cal.3d 142, 158 Cal.Rptr. 281, 599 P.2d 587 (1979)(privately retained lawyers subject to same standard as established months earlier in *Pope*).

[6] Brown v. State, 443 N.E.2d 316, 319 (Ind.1983)(presumption of lawyer's full discharge of duty can be overcome only by showing that proceedings became a "mockery and shocking to the conscience of the court"); People v. Dean, 31 Ill.2d 214, 201 N.E.2d 405 (1964)(new trial required only if trial counsel's conduct was so defective as to make defense sham or farce); State v. Sneed, 284 N.C. 606, 201 S.E.2d 867 (1974).

[7] McQueen v. Swenson, 498 F.2d 207, 214 (8th Cir.1974); Schoonover v. State, 2 Kan.App.2d 481, 582 P.2d 292, 296–97 (1978).

[8] In re Smith, 3 Cal.3d 192, 90 Cal.Rptr. 1, 474 P.2d 969 (1970)(lawyer for appellant convicted of rape filed appellate brief of twenty pages of facts and one page of legal argument urging that state failed to carry burden of proving that rape victim was not married to accused; such brief in case where record bristled with plainly

were followed in a dwindling minority of jurisdictions,[9] and numbers of former adherents continued to announce watered-down versions of the older doctrine that moved closer to a standard of reasonable competence.[10]

Reasonable Competence

The Supreme Court was among the first of the courts to suggest a break with the farce-and-mockery standard but among the last to do so explicitly. The most renowned, but not the earliest, case to announce a definite break with farce and mockery and to require reasonably competent assistance was the 1973 decision of the District of Columbia federal court of appeals in United States v. DeCoster.[11] The *DeCoster* decision was influenced by the decision of the Supreme Court in 1970 in McMann v. Richardson.[12] While refusing to adopt any particular formulation, or to disavow explicitly the farce-and-mockery standard, the *McMann* opinion had stated that the quality of advocacy must be "within the range of competence demanded of attorneys in criminal cases." [13] The similarity of the range-of-competence notion to the established conceptualizations of the ordinarily competent lawyer standard in the law of torts strongly suggested more than a toothless test.[14] The doctrinal break with the farce-and-mockery cases is accomplished by holding that due process does not invariably require that the lawyer's errors be obvious to the judge or prosecutor. Instead due process is offended by the absence of a fair trial, regardless of the source or contemporaneous visibility of the fatal defect.[15] The great majority of American jurisdictions had abandoned the

arguable legal issues was "ludicrous" and required new appeal).

9 Wilson v. State, 99 Nev. 362, 664 P.2d 328 (1983). A 1980 tabulation of state decisions showed a clear trend in state decisions away from the farce and mockery standard. Annot., 2 A.L.R.4th 27, 46 (1980). Subsequent decisions continued the trend. State v. Watson, 134 Ariz. 3, 653 P.2d 351 (1982); Henderson v. Commonwealth, 636 S.W.2d 648, 650 (Ky. 1982). Among the federal circuits, only the Second Circuit continued to assert that the farce-and-mockery standard remained viable. See Romero v. United States, 459 U.S. 926, 926, 103 S.Ct. 236, 237, 74 L.Ed.2d 187 (1982)(opinion of White, J., dissenting from denial of certiorari). Eventually, the Second Circuit rejected the test. See Trapnell v. United States, 725 F.2d 149 (2d Cir.1983).

10 Metcalf v. State, 451 N.E.2d 321, 323 (Ind.1983)("The review standard is a mockery of justice test, modified by the adequate representation standard."). Occasionally the change has occurred by means of a gradual dilution of the strictures of the farce and mockery standard in its application rather than in its expression. E.g., Schoonover v. State, 2 Kan.App.2d 481, 582 P.2d 292 (1978) ("complete absence of counsel" test of Kansas supreme court is functionally same as "range of normal competency" and similar standards because those restate malpractice standard and court would not adopt any lesser standard); White v. State, 309 Minn. 476, 248 N.W.2d 281, 285 (1976)("reasonableness" standard announced by Eighth Circuit is in fact test that had recently been applied in state courts under farce-and-mockery label).

11 487 F.2d 1197 (D.C.Cir.1973). The same court later held that the new standard was to be applied retroactively, United States v. Butler, 504 F.2d 220 (D.C.Cir.1974), a result that is commonly reached. Hellard v. State, 629 S.W.2d 4, 7–8 (Tenn.1982), and cases cited.

12 397 U.S. 759, 90 S.Ct. 1441, 25 L.Ed.2d 763 (1970).

13 397 U.S. at 771, 90 S.Ct. at 1449. See also, e.g., Moore v. United States, 432 F.2d 730, 736 (3d Cir.1970) ("customary skill and knowledge which normally prevails at the time and place").

14 United States v. Easter, 539 F.2d 663, 666 (8th Cir. 1976), cert. denied 434 U.S. 844, 98 S.Ct. 145, 54 L.Ed.2d 109 (1977)("trial counsel fails to render effective assistance when he does not exercise the customary skills and diligence that a reasonably competent attorney would perform under similar circumstances"); Marzullo v. Maryland, 561 F.2d 540, 545 (4th Cir.1977)(resemblance noted between "normal competency" measure and test for tort liability set out in Restatement (Second), Torts § 299A (1965)), cert.denied 435 U.S. 1011, 98 S.Ct. 1885, 56 L.Ed.2d 394 (1978); State v. Harper, 57 Wis.2d 543, 557, 205 N.W.2d 1 (1973)("the representation must be equal to that which the ordinarily prudent lawyer, skilled and versed in criminal law, would give to clients who had privately retained his services").

15 Cuyler v. Sullivan, 446 U.S. 335, 344–45, 100 S.Ct. 1708, 1716, 64 L.Ed.2d 333 (1980)(without articulating any particular "test" of effectiveness of counsel, Court finds that conflict of interest of retained counsel constituted violation of due process because defective representation implicates state in a trial that is unfair). The emphasis upon the fairness of the trial process, rather than upon visibility of its various components, is also apparent in decisions dealing with kinds of assistance other than legal. Compare, e.g., Caldwell v. Mississippi, ___ U.S. ___, 105 S.Ct. 2633, 86 L.Ed.2d 231 (1985)(no due process denial on facts of particular case in state's refusing to provide assistance of criminal investigator, fingerprint expert, and ballistics expert), with, e.g., Ake v. Oklahoma, ___ U.S. ___, 105 S.Ct. 1087, 84 L.Ed.2d 53 (1985)(denial of due process to deny accused court-appointed psychiatrist on facts, including facts that insanity was only defense and nonexpert evidence strongly suggested insanity).

farce and mockery standard and its variants by 1984.

The break became complete by the Court's 1984 holding in Strickland v. Washington [16] that the standard by which federal courts were to review state convictions on habeas corpus was that of reasonable competence. Tying the question of competence securely to a due process rationale of fairness in criminal trial process and outcomes,[17] the Court announced a formulation of competence under which "the proper measure of attorney performance remains simply reasonableness under prevailing professional norms." [18] Eschewing any attempt to be definitive, the Court perceived at least the following "basic duties," which were to measure performance: loyalty, advocacy, consultation, communication, and "such skill and knowledge as will render the trial a reliable adversarial testing process." [19] The standard requires a showing of actual incompetence,[20] strongly presumes competence, and is to be applied without the distorting benefit of hindsight.[21] Moreover, a convicted person is required to demonstrate that there is a "reasonable probability" that the lawyer's actual incompetence caused a difference in the outcome of the criminal trial.[22]

The shift from farce and mockery to a reasonable-competence standard may represent only a change in terminology, despite the obvious implication that courts should scrutinize the effectiveness of counsel with greater care. An impression gained from the reported decisions is that the shift does indeed betoken an increased judicial willingness to undertake a more searching inquiry and to accept the increased costs of overturned convictions and new trials that the new standard implies.

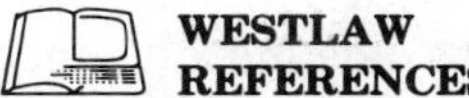

WESTLAW REFERENCES

farce /3 mockery /s inadequat! ineffectiv! incompeten! defect! effective /4 assistance /4 counsel** attorney lawyer

strickland /12 104 +4 2052 reasonab! /3 competen!

§ 14.6.3 *Application of the Effectiveness Standard*

Defining the Elements of Effective Assistance

Courts have generally been unwilling to catalog in advance precisely what defaults by a defense lawyer will result in a finding that the representation lies beyond the range of required competence. Some have attempted to offer guidance by pointing to general collections of guidelines such as the ABA Code of Professional Responsibility [23] or the ABA Defense Function Standards.[24] But the trial in a criminal case is too fluid, complex, and dynamic to permit much precise rule making on the question of lawyer competence. A part of the definitional problem is that appellate and postconviction review courts are in a relatively poor position to assess the quality of advocacy. Incompetence, as well perhaps as some otherwise hidden competence, may elude detection when only the cold record can be examined. Transcripts convey nothing of tone of voice, facial expression, juror inattention or other reactions, and other nuances of

16 466 U.S. 668, 104 S.Ct. 2052, 80 L.Ed.2d 674 (1984).

17 ___ U.S. at ___-___, 104 S.Ct. at 2063–64 ("An accused is entitled to be assisted by an attorney, whether retained or appointed, who plays the role necessary to ensure that the trial is fair. . . . The benchmark for judging any claim of ineffectiveness must be whether counsel's conduct so undermined the proper functioning of the adversarial process that the trial cannot be relied on as having produced a just result.").

18 ___ U.S. at ___, 104 S.Ct. at 2065.

19 ___ U.S. at ___, 104 S.Ct. at 2065.

20 See also United States v. Cronic, 466 U.S. 648, 104 S.Ct. 2039, 80 L.Ed.2d 657 (1984).

21 ___ U.S. at ___, 104 S.Ct. at 2066.

22 ___ U.S. at ___, 104 S.Ct. at 2068.

23 Marzullo v. Maryland, 561 F.2d 540, 544 (4th Cir. 1977), cert.denied 435 U.S. 1011, 98 S.Ct. 1885, 56 L.Ed.2d 394 (1978).

24 Strickland v. Washington, 466 U.S. 668, 104 S.Ct. 2052, 2065, 80 L.Ed.2d 674 (1984); United States v. DeCoster, 487 F.2d 1197, 1203 (D.C.Cir.1973); Baxter v. Rose, 523 S.W.2d 930, 936 (Tenn.1975); State v. Felton, 110 Wis.2d 485, 329 N.W.2d 161, 170–71 (1983).

the behavior of judge, lawyers, jurors, and witnesses.

Some generalities, however, can be ventured. First, clearly the concept of reversible error does not adequately encompass all of the instances of incompetent counsel. For example, most errors by a judge in instructing the jury can in effect be waived by the procedural forfeiture doctrine that typically requires that the defense lawyer make a timely objection to the instruction. Yet the lawyer's failure to make an objection, while it might technically immunize the instruction, nonetheless can itself upset the resulting conviction because of the lawyer's incompetence in incurring the forfeiture.[25] Second, as the law of ineffective assistance matures, some categories of responsibility are emerging with sufficient clarity to permit more careful definition. By the same token, it is also true that some areas of alleged incompetence—such as in the choice between available, but mutually inconsistent, trial strategies—will only rarely be subject to judicial second-guessing. Third, reviewing courts have generally appreciated that contemporaneity rather than hindsight is the only legitimate vantage point from which to measure the work of trial counsel.[26] Moreover, what the Constitution requires is competent representation, not necesssarily an acquittal. Fourth, the defense lawyer's good faith (or lack of it) is irrelevant in most instances; the inquiry is an objective one that examines only the behavior of the lawyer and its impact on the trial, not the lawyer's bona fides or other mental states.

Basic Lawyer Credentials

The threshold credentials required for constitutionally effective representation are strikingly low. The cases hold that, allowing for identifiable gaffes in the course of trial, a total neophyte must be considered equipped to handle any criminal case.[27] In fact, in some settings the "lawyer" who provides assistance need not be trained as a lawyer or admitted to the bar. Several states, for example, have approved programs in which law students can represent accused persons under the supervision of an admitted lawyer, and such representations have generally been approved.[28] Lawyer imposter cases usually result in reversal without requiring the convicted person to show specific instances of incompetence or to demonstrate that a law-trained advocate would have obtained a more favorable result.[29]

[25] Arthur v. Bordenkircher, 715 F.2d 118 (4th Cir.1983) (ineffective assistance when lawyer cooperated with trial judge in framing jury instructions explaining prior procedural history of case, including fact that another jury, whose verdict had been set aside on appeal, had convicted accused on same charge).

[26] Strickland v. Washington, 466 U.S. 668, 104 S.Ct. 2052, 2065–66, 80 L.Ed.2d 674 (1984).

[27] United States v. Cronic, 466 U.S. 648, 104 S.Ct. 2039, 80 L.Ed.2d 657 (1984)(lawyer's youth and inexperience in case that involved complex issues, serious charges, inaccessible witnesses, and short time for trial preparation do not avoid necessity of showing actual ineffectiveness); United States ex rel. Williams v. Twomey, 510 F.2d 634, 639 (7th Cir.1975), cert.denied 423 U.S. 876, 96 S.Ct. 148, 46 L.Ed.2d 109 (1975); State v. Felton, 110 Wis.2d 485, 329 N.W.2d 161, 168 (1983)(public defender new to practice in jurisdiction who had never tried felony case and few criminal cases did not per se render ineffective assistance in complex murder case). But cf., e.g., State v. Williams, 93 Ill.2d 309, 67 Ill.Dec. 97, 444 N.E.2d 136 (1982)(lawyer's eventual disbarment due to serious misconduct in unrelated probate case that took place at same time as questionable tactics in criminal trial requires finding of incompetence), cert.denied, ___ U.S. ___, 104 S.Ct. 2666, 81 L.Ed.2d 371 (1983).

[28] The leading case is People v. Perez, 24 Cal.3d 133, 155 Cal.Rptr. 176, 594 P.2d 1, 3 A.L.R.4th 339 (1979). Commentators have divided over the wisdom of student representation of defendants. E.g., Galperin, Law Students as Defense Counsel in Felony Trials: The "Guiding Hand" out of Hand, 46 Albany L.Rev. 400 (1982); Monaghan, Gideon's Army: Student Soldiers, 45 Bost. U.L.Rev. 445 (1965); Brown, The Trumpet Sounds: Gideon—A First Call to the Law School, 43 Tex.L.Rev. 312 (1964).

[29] Solina v. United States, 709 F.2d 160 (2d Cir.1983) (Friendly, J.); Cheatham v. State, 364 So.2d 83 (Fla.App. 1978), cert.denied 372 So.2d 471 (1979); People v. Felder, 47 N.Y.2d 287, 418 N.Y.S.2d 295, 391 N.E.2d 1274 (1979). Cf. People v. Cox, 12 Ill.2d 265, 146 N.E.2d 19, 68 A.L.R. 2d 1134 (1967)(conviction resulting from imposter's representation of fourteen-year-old in murder case reversed on circumstances of case). If the "lawyer" was law-trained but lacked a normally required credential, such as a local license, because of reasons not related to ability, courts are more likely to require a showing of prejudice. E.g., People v. Wilson, 626 P.2d 709 (Colo.App.1980), affirmed 652 P.2d 595 (1982), cert.denied 459 U.S. 1218, 103 S.Ct. 1221 75 L.Ed.2d 457 (1983)(lawyer fully trained and qualified but who had not taken local oath); People v. Brewer, 88 Mich.App. 756, 279 N.W.2d 307 (1979)(retained lawyer

The initial appointment of a properly credentialed lawyer will not invariably satisfy all of the demands that an accused thereafter might make for effective assistance. A lawyer's assistance might later become defective because of serious and irreconcilable conflict between lawyer and client, events such as succumbing to alcoholism or other incapacities that render the lawyer incompetent, or a conflict of interest. In such situations the trial court is required to appoint substitute counsel.[30]

The Anders Problem

In a representation for a fee, lawyer and client will make many decisions about whether particular moves that could be made in the case are worth the lawyer's effort. For example, they might decide that, given a small chance of success on appeal, the fees necessary to prepare an appellate brief and present oral argument are better not spent. The same economic constraints do not operate, of course, when counsel is appointed for an indigent accused. With no economic hindrance, an indigent client may wish that a great many steps be taken that would not be taken, for economic or other reasons, if fees were being charged. If it is the court-appointed lawyer's judgment that the step is unlikely to succeed, can the client nonetheless compel the court-appointed lawyer to proceed?

In Anders v. California,[31] the Supreme Court held that the due process and right to counsel guarantees of the Constitution required that a court-appointed lawyer press forward with an appeal even if the lawyer was certain that it would not succeed. The constitutional requirement is that the state furnish a lawyer who "acts in the role of an active advocate." [32] The lawyer must proceed unless he or she conscientiously believes that the appeal is wholly frivolous. In that event the lawyer should move to withdraw and is required to file what has come to be called an "*Anders brief*"—a brief that discusses anything in the record that "arguably supports" an appeal.[33] A copy of the brief must be sent to the appellant to permit him or her to raise any additional issues. The appellate court must then fully examine the record to determine whether the appeal indeed is frivolous. The appeal may be dismissed if the court agrees. If, however, the court discovers any legal points "arguable on their merits (and therefore not frivolous)," [34] it must appoint new counsel and order regular appellate review.[35]

The *Anders* directives are confusing if not contradictory. The case requires, first, that the lawyer list any nonfrivolous issue that "arguably supports" an appeal in a brief that is to accompany a motion to withdraw on the ground that the appeal is wholly frivolous. The appellate court must then examine the brief and the record and assess whether the lawyer has correctly characterized the appeal. If the appellate court finds that any of the cited issues, or any others, are "arguable on their merits," then a new lawyer must be appointed to brief and argue the case in the regular way. Apparently, the Court in *Anders* intended to describe the originally briefed points as nonfrivolous but nonarguable, for only then would the cermony it describes be coherent. In effect, then, the Court

suspended for nonpayment of bar dues). But cf. Solina v. United States, supra, 709 F.2d at 164 (defective assistance of unadmitted person may arise, not only from lack of competence, but from fear that vigorous defense might lead judge or prosecutor to inquire about lawyer's defective credentials).

30 United States v. Williams, 597 F.2d 667 (9th Cir. 1979), cert.denied 444 U.S. 885, 100 S.Ct. 179, 62 L.Ed.2d 116 (1979)(irreconcilable conflict) People v. Manson, 61 Cal.App.3d 102, 132 Cal.Rptr. 265, 326–27 (1976), cert.denied 430 U.S. 986, 97 S.Ct. 1686, 52 L.Ed.2d 382 (1977)(death of lawyer in midtrial); Commonwealth v. McLaughlin, 469 Pa. 407, 366 A.2d 238 (1976)(total lack of cooperation, communication, and trust).

31 386 U.S. 738, 87 S.Ct. 1396, 18 L.Ed.2d 493 (1967).

32 386 U.S. at 744, 87 S.Ct. at 1400.

33 386 U.S. at 744, 87 S.Ct. at 1400. See also Polk County v. Dodson, 454 U.S. 312, 102 S.Ct. 445, 70 L.Ed.2d 509 (1981).

34 386 U.S. at 744, 87 S.Ct. at 1400.

35 Exceedingly rarely, but occasionally, a lawyer has incorrectly assayed the *Anders* value of the appeal and, much less than granting the lawyer's request to withdraw because of lack of merit, the appellate court has reversed the conviction. E.g., United States v. Lawson, 598 F.2d 879 (4th Cir.1979).

must assume three categories of issues: (1) issues that are wholly frivolous and that do not have to be considered further by either counsel or court; (2) issues that are not substantial enough to warrant concluding that the appeal is anything but wholly frivolous but that nonetheless for, presumably, some other reason warrant discussion in an *Anders* brief accompanying a motion to withdraw; and (3) issues that arguably support a nonfrivolous appeal and whose presence in the record triggers an obligation on the part of the appellate court to appoint new counsel to argue those points fully.

Such hair-splitting among possible arguments hardly describes an operable test. As a result the practice of many court-appointed lawyers is to prepare and file a brief that discusses both arguable points as well as points that are not arguable in order to comply clearly with the *Anders* directive of active advocacy.[36] Perhaps a sensible solution is to require appellate lawyers always to file a brief without a motion to withdraw on the grounds of frivolousness, even if the lawyer believes that there is no arguable basis for appellate relief, thus avoiding the nice line drawing that *Anders* requires.[37]

If neither an *Anders* brief or a full-advocacy brief is filed, is the appointed lawyer required to assert only those grounds that the lawyer conscientiously feels are arguable or must the appeal include all arguable grounds that the client insists be asserted? In Jones v. Barnes,[38] a court-appointed lawyer and his incarcerated client corresponded about the client's appeal. The client wished several arguments to be pressed in the appeal. His lawyer agreed that two of those, and an additional argument that he suggested, were the strongest and unsuccessfully argued only those three on appeal. His client filed a pro se brief arguing the omitted points. The Court held that *Anders* does not require argument of all nonfrivolous points urged by the client if the lawyer's professional judgment is that sound tactics dictate that the lawyer limit the issues to be pressed on the court.[39] If that is true on appeal, when typically a more deliberative and consultative approach to tactics can be enjoyed, it must be even more so at trial.

The *Jones v. Barnes* decision may stand for a much broader constitutional principle that most [40] reasonable tactical choices by a court-appointed lawyer, even if made against the strong insistence of the client, do not offend the Constitution. Such a principle, of course, does violence to the parallelism that the effective assistance doctrine seeks to maintain between representations by retained and appointed lawyers. It appears to do so in order to replace the economic constraints of the

36 One court has insisted that court-appointed counsel in an appeal by a parent from a deprivation of parental rights adjudication never seek to withdraw even if the lawyer conscientiously believes that no nonfrivolous argument can be made. See In re Hall, 99 Wn.2d 842, 664 P.2d 1245 (1983). The court's implicit assumption must have been either that all possible appeals contain at least one arguable point for reversal or that some appointed appellate lawyers should argue frivolous points in order to fulfil their function. A similar assumption apparently underlies *Anders* itself with respect to the obligation to list and discuss discussable issues in a wholly frivolous case.

37 Such a procedure has been insisted upon in Massachusetts. See Commonwealth v. Moffitt, 383 Mass. 201, 418 N.E.2d 585 (1981). Asserting that a lawyer has a professional responsibility not to advance groundless contentions on appeal, the court suggested that a lawyer could present his or her personal views in a separate section of the brief, so long as a copy was sent to appellant, as *Anders* requires in every case. See 418 N.E.2d at 589–90.

38 463 U.S. 745, 103 S.Ct. 3308, 77 L.Ed.2d 987 (1983).

39 The *Jones* opinion noted the common advice given appellate lawyers to confine argument to a limited number of the strongest arguments available. See 463 U.S. at 751–53, 103 S.Ct. at 3312–13. The Court acknowledged that the ABA Standards for Criminal Appeals required a lawyer to accede to a client's insistence that a particular contention be raised. (See ABA Standards for Criminal Justice, Criminal Appeals § 21–3.2, at 21–42 (2d ed.1980). But the Court refused to find that the practice was required by the Constitution. See 463 U.S. at 753 n.6, 103 S.Ct at 3313. Both the concurring opinion of Blackmun, J., and the dissenting opinion joined by Brennan and Marshall, JJ., expressed the view that as an ethical matter, a lawyer should argue on appeal all nonfrivolous issues that the client wishes to press. See 463 U.S. at 754, 760, 103 S.Ct. 3314, 3317. Nothing in the majority opinion contradicts that view. See further § 4.3.

40 Excepted, presumably, would be such nonwaivable rights as the right to jury trial, to plead, to take the witness stand, and to file an appeal. See § 4.6.3.

private practice setting with the professional judgment constraints of an appointed lawyer.

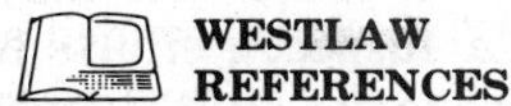

WESTLAW REFERENCES

"anders brief" /p appeal! /p arguab**

anders +4 california /12 87 +4 1396 /p right /5 counsel** attorney lawyer

§ 14.6.4 *State Interference with the Right to Counsel*

General

Representation by an otherwise competent lawyer can be rendered ineffective because of snares and traps set in the lawyer's way. If the state plays a part in creating such obstacles, the right to counsel may be violated. Several types of possible state interference will be considered here in this nonexhaustive survey: (1) interference with the client's access to a lawyer for consultation; (2) surreptitious infiltration into the defense camp; and (3) law office searches.

Hindering Access to Counsel

The state may seek to deprive a client of the assistance of counsel through segregating the lawyer and client. One kind of deprivation is a judicial order that interdicts against client-lawyer consultation during a recess while the client is being cross-examined by an adversary. In Geders v. United States,[41] the Supreme Court held that a trial court order prohibiting communication between lawyer and client in a seventeen-hour overnight recess between direct and cross-examination deprived the accused of effective assistance.[42] Lower courts have extended the *Geders* rule to cover all recesses in the trial regardless of length.[43] The *Geders* rule or a common-law cognate has also been extended to civil cases.[44] While authority is sparse, *Geders* should not be recognized as a per se rule applicable regardless of the need for a selective embargo of the client. In an extreme case, for example, involving national defense secrets, a narrowly drawn prohibition against client-lawyer consultation might be permissible.[45] Probably no more satisfactory approach can be devised than balancing the need for secrecy against the clear need of a client to consult with his or her lawyer and of a lawyer to obtain direction and information from the client. Employing that approach, courts have refused to permit prison officials to interdict mail between lawyers and prison inmates.[46]

41 425 U.S. 80, 96 S.Ct. 1330, 47 L.Ed.2d 592 (1976).

42 The Court stated that the trial court's concern that the client-witness' lawyer would improperly coach the client could be dealt with by adroit cross-examination by the prosecutor, by refusing to grant a recess and continuing with cross-examination immediately, or through similar means. If all measures fail, the mere risk of perjured testimony cannot override the right and need of an accused to consult with his or her lawyer. See 425 U.S. at 91, 96 S.Ct. at 1336–37.

43 United States v. Conway, 632 F.2d 641 (5th Cir.1980) (lunch recess); United States v. Allen, 542 F.2d 630 (4th Cir.1976)(two midtrial recesses, one of twenty minutes and the other for one minute), cert.denied 430 U.S. 908, 97 S.Ct. 1179, 51 L.Ed.2d 584 (1977). Some courts have applied a stricter ruling, assuming a constitutional violation regardless of the length of the recess but then finding that the violation was harmless because of the brevity of the recess. E.g., DiLapi v. United States, 651 F.2d 140 (2d Cir.1981), cert.denied 455 U.S. 938, 102 S.Ct. 1428, 71 L.Ed.2d 648 (1982); Stubbs v. Bordenkircher, 689 F.2d 1205 (4th Cir.1982), cert.denied 461 U.S. 907, 103 S.Ct. 1879, 76 L.Ed.2d 810 (1983); Bova v. State, 410 So.2d 1343 (Fla.1982).

44 Potashnick v. Port City Constr. Co., 609 F.2d 1101, 1117–19 (5th Cir.1980)(trial court prohibition against client-lawyer consultation during seven-day civil trial violates due process), cert.denied 449 U.S. 820, 101 S.Ct. 788, 66 L.Ed.2d 22 (1980). Montgomery Elev. Co. v. Superior Court, 135 Ariz. 432, 661 P.2d 1133 (1983)(en banc)(abuse of discretion for trial judge to exclude lawyer for party from attending deposition); Cartin v. Continental Homes, 134 Vt. 362, 360 A.2d 96 (1976)(abuse of discretion for judge to require lawyer to remain in chambers during recess to prevent consultation with client during recess in her testimony). Cf. Mohr v. Montana Distr. Court, 660 P.2d 88 (Mont.1983)(recognizing authority to contrary, Montana rule is that judge may not bar plaintiff's lawyer from session at which defendant's physician takes medical history; lawyer can, however, be barred from physical examination itself).

45 Compare United States v. Hung, 667 F.2d 1105 (4th Cir.1981)(protective order prohibiting defense counsel from disclosing to clients contents of national security secret documents in espionage trial permissible), cert.denied 454 U.S. 1144, 102 S.Ct. 1004, 71 L.Ed.2d 296 (1982).

46 Taylor v. Sterrett, 532 F.2d 462, 473–75 (5th Cir.1976) (prisoner's mail to lawyer may not be inspected, and mail from lawyer to inmate may only be inspected for contraband in presence of inmate). See generally Wolff v. McDonnell, 418 U.S. 539, 94 S.Ct. 2963, 41 L.Ed.2d 935

The states may not unreasonably restrict or penalize efforts of a lawyer to contact a client or of a client to contact a lawyer.[47] An explicit request by a detained person to contact his lawyer by telephone must normally be honored.[48] A request by a lawyer to consult with a client in jail must similarly be honored and cannot be denied arbitrarily [49] or foiled in order to gain an investigative advantage.[50] So long as communication is possible, however, creating inconvenience inadvertently, such as by moving a prisoner to a distant location for other good reasons, would normally not deprive a client of a right of access to counsel.[51]

Once lawyer and client have consulted, the state may not penalize the client's exercise of the right. Thus a prosecutor may not argue to a jury that a suspect's efforts to contact a lawyer are evidence of guilt,[52] and an accused who invokes the right to remain silent until a lawyer has been consulted may not be impeached at a subsequent trial on the ground of silence in the face of accusation.[53]

Infiltration of the Defense Camp

"[T]he essence of the Sixth Amendment right is privacy of communication with coun-

(1974)(permissible for state to inspect lawyer mail to inmate for contraband in presence of inmate).

[47] The right of access by lawyer to client is uniformly recognized in such texts as the ABA Defense Function Standards (Standard 4–2.1, 4–2.2 (1979 ed.)), the ABA Standards for Providing Defense Services (Standards 5–5.1, 5–7.1 (1979 ed.)), and the Uniform Rules of Criminal Procedure (Rule 242(a) & (b) (1974)).

[48] For example, a person arrested for drunk driving must be permitted to telephone a lawyer to consult about whether to submit to a sobriety test. Heles v. South Dakota, 530 F.Supp. 646 (D.S.D.1982), vacated as moot 682 F.2d 201 (8th Cir.1982); McNutt v. Superior Court, 133 Ariz. 7, 648 P.2d 122 (1982); Prideaux v. State, 310 Minn. 405, 247 N.W.2d 385 (1976); People v. Gursey, 22 N.Y.2d 224, 292 N.Y.S.2d 416, 239 N.E.2d 351 (1968). See also, e.g., Gholson v. Estelle, 675 F.2d 734 (5th Cir.1982) (Sixth Amendment violation to deny murder suspect opportunity to consult with lawyer prior to state-initiated psychiatric examination); United States v. Hinckley, 672 F.2d 115 (D.C.Cir.1982)(statement of accused who had allegedly attempted presidential assassination suppressed when taken following lawyer's unsuccessful attempt to contact accused and when officers had failed to contact local lawyer recommended by lawyer whom accused had reached by long-distance telephone); Beltram v. Appellate Department, 66 Cal.App.2d 711, 136 Cal.Rptr. 211 (1977)(statutory cause of action for damages for denial of jailed client's request to contact lawyer).

Governmental denial of a client's request to consult a lawyer about a civil matter may also have consequences in civil litigation. See Mosley v. St. Louis S.W. Ry., 634 F.2d 942 (5th Cir.1981), cert.denied 452 U.S. 906, 101 S.Ct. 3032, 69 L.Ed.2d 407 (1981)(governmental officer's refusal to honor employees' request to consult with lawyer before signing settlement voided settlement of employment discrimination claim); Swope v. Bratton, 541 F.Supp. 99, 109 (W.D.Ark.1982)(denial of time off so governmental employee could consult lawyer about pending disciplinary action denied due process).

[49] See generally Procunier v. Martinez, 416 U.S. 396, 94 S.Ct. 1800, 40 L.Ed.2d 224 (1974)(prison regulations and practices that unreasonably and arbitrarily restrict ability of inmates to consult with lawyers and paralegals unconstitutionally deprives inmates of access to courts).

[50] Darwin v. Connecticut, 391 U.S. 346, 88 S.Ct. 1488, 20 L.Ed.2d 630 (1968); People v. Smith, 93 Ill.2d 179, 66 Ill.Dec. 412, 442 N.E.2d 1325 (1982), cert.denied 461 U.S. 937, 103 S.Ct. 2107, 77 L.Ed.2d 312 (1983)(denial of Fifth Amendment right against self-incrimination for police to interrogate accused without first permitting lawyer, who had so requested, to consult with him); People v. Garofolo, 46 N.Y.2d 592, 415 N.Y.S.2d 810, 389 N.E.2d 123, 18 A.L.R.4th 658 (1979)(deprivation of Sixth Amendment right to counsel when, for lack of adequate procedures, lawyer's attempt to reach incarcerated client by telephone were not successful until after client had waived rights and given confession). Cf. Phillips v. Bureau of Prisons, 591 F.2d 966 (D.C.Cir.1979)(permissible to deny entrance by paralegal into federal prison to interview prisoners because of paralegal's history of seriously disruptive conduct while formerly incarcerated there).

[51] United States v. Kirk, 534 F.2d 1262 (8th Cir.1976), cert.denied 430 U.S. 906, 97 S.Ct. 1174 51 L.Ed.2d 581 (1977)(thirty-mile trip one-way to consult with client not unduly burdensome). Compare State v. Haynes, 288 Or. 59, 602 P.2d 272 (1979)(unconstitutional to take confession from accused after he waived right to counsel when accused had been removed from one jail to another in order to foil efforts of lawyer to contact him), cert.denied 446 U.S. 945, 100 S.Ct. 2175, 64 L.Ed.2d 802 (1980).

[52] United States v. McDonald, 620 F.2d 559 (5th Cir. 1980); Zemina v. Solem, 573 F.2d 1027 (8th Cir.1978); United States v. Liddy, 509 F.2d 428, 443–45 (D.C.Cir. 1974), cert.denied 420 U.S. 911, 95 S.Ct. 833, 42 L.Ed.2d 842 (1975). See also State v. Larmond, 244 N.W.2d 233 (Iowa 1976)(reversal where trial judge excoriated accused for whispering instructions to his lawyer during closing argument of prosecutor). But cf. Sulie v. Duckworth, 689 F.2d 128 (7th Cir.1982), cert.denied 460 U.S. 1043, 103 S.Ct. 1439, 75 L.Ed.2d 796 (1983)(request of accused at post-arrest interrogation to see lawyer before speaking to police can be introduced as evidence of sanity at time of offense).

[53] Doyle v. Ohio, 426 U.S. 610, 96 S.Ct. 2240, 49 L.Ed.2d 91 (1976).

sel." [54] Consistent with the requirement of the attorney-client privilege that protected communications take place in a confidential setting (§ 6.3.7), the effective assistance of counsel presupposes that unreasonable state intrusions into the privacy of client-lawyer communication will not be made. That requires that reasonable efforts be made to permit consultation between a jailed client and his or her lawyer in privacy.[55] But requiring the client to make a nontestimonial disclosure of the fact that he or she contacted a lawyer does not impermissibly impinge on the right to counsel.[56]

In a distressingly large number of decisions in recent years, courts have been confronted with claims of constitutional or other violations of the right to counsel due to police intrusion into the client-lawyer relationship. Rather clearly, if a convicted person could establish that a government agent had surreptitiously overheard a conversation between lawyer and client and the information had been employed as a significant aid in obtaining the conviction, the client's rights would be violated.[57] Suppose the agent, more boldly, masquerades as a confederate of the client and becomes privy to client-lawyer communications openly but under false pretenses. Here, again, use of the information should be suppressed.[58]

Dismissal of the prosecution is not a customary remedy even if a government agent was privy to defense secrets. Before significant relief can be obtained, the accused must show that the informant gave information to the police and that the information was employed to the substantial detriment of the accused.[59] Other decisions have required that the conversation into which the informant intruded must have been held in an aura of confidentiality at least approaching that necessary for invoking the attorney-client privilege. If the informant was not an intimate who might reasonably be expected to sit in on such conversations, courts hold that the client had no reasonable expectation of privacy in the conversation.[60]

54 United States v. Rosner, 485 F.2d 1213, 1224 (2d Cir. 1973), cert.denied 417 U.S. 950, 94 S.Ct. 3080, 41 L.Ed.2d 672 (1974).

55 Ahrens v. Thomas, 434 F.Supp. 873 (W.D.Mo.1977), affirmed in part, modified in part on other grounds 570 F.2d 286 (8th Cir.1978); Moore v. Janning, 427 F.Supp. 567 (D.Neb.1976); Keker v. Procunier, 398 F.Supp. 756 (E.D.Cal.1975). An alternative rule providing a kind of privacy is to prohibit any testimony by jailer eavesdroppers on the contents of client-lawyer conversations. See State Dep't of Public Safety v. Kneisl, 312 Minn. 281, 251 N.W.2d 645 (1977). In People v. Harfmann, 38 Colo.App. 19, 555 P.2d 187 (1976), the court held that police observation through a one-way mirror of a lawyer passing narcotics to his inmate client in an enclosed interview room required suppression of the testimony of the police in a subsequent prosecution of the lawyer for narcotics offenses.

56 United States v. Mountain States Tel. & Tel. Co., 516 F.Supp. 225 (D.Wyo.1981)(subpoena of telephone records of client that include record of calls to lawyer's office not breach of attorney-client privilege or of right to counsel).

57 O'Brien v. United States, 386 U.S. 345, 87 S.Ct. 1158, 18 L.Ed.2d 94 (1967); Black v. United States, 385 U.S. 26, 87 S.Ct. 190, 17 L.Ed.2d 26 (1966). Both cases rested on the illegality of the search under the Fourth Amendment search and seizure clause. Courts have rested the same rule on the Sixth Amendment right to counsel. E.g., Briggs v. Goodwin, 698 F.2d 486 (D.C.Cir.1983), on rehearing 712 F.2d 1444 (D.C.Cir.1983), cert.denied 464 U.S. 1040, 104 S.Ct. 704, 79 L.Ed.2d 169 (1984); Barber v. Municipal Court, 24 Cal.3d 742, 157 Cal.Rptr. 658, 598 P.2d 818 (1979); In re Kozak, 256 N.W.2d 717 (S.D.1977).

58 As much was conceded by the government in Weatherford v. Bursey, 429 U.S. 545, 97 S.Ct. 837, 51 L.Ed.2d 30 (1977); and Hoffa v. United States, 385 U.S. 293, 87 S.Ct. 408, 17 L.Ed.2d 374 (1966). See also Caldwell v. United States, 205 F.2d 879 (D.C.Cir.1953), cert.denied 349 U.S. 930, 75 S.Ct. 773, 99 L.Ed. 1260 (1955); Coplon v. United States, 191 F.2d 749 (D.C.Cir.1951), cert.denied 342 U.S. 926, 72 S.Ct. 363, 96 L.Ed. 690 (1952).

59 Weatherford v. Bursey, 429 U.S. 545, 558, 97 S.Ct. 837, 845, 51 L.Ed.2d 30 (1977); United States v. Morrison, 449 U.S. 361, 101 S.Ct. 665, 66 L.Ed.2d 564 (1981); Bishop v. Rose, 701 F.2d 1150, 1156 (6th Cir.1983); United States v. Ryan, 548 F.2d 782 (5th Cir.1976), cert.denied 429 U.S. 939, 97 S.Ct. 354, 50 L.Ed.2d 308 (1976).

The task of demonstrating prejudice, though formidable, can be facilitated by permitting broad discovery into wiretap logs, records, and similar products and records of the secret investigation. E.g., United States v. Alter, 482 F.2d 1016 (9th Cir.1973); United States v. Fannon, 435 F.2d 364 (7th Cir.1970), cert.denied 401 U.S. 1012, 91 S.Ct. 1265, 28 L.Ed.2d 549 (1971). An in camera examination of the government's informant file may also be required. See United States v. Tramunti, 425 F.Supp. 342 (S.D.N.Y. 1976).

60 United States v. Melvin, 650 F.2d 641 (5th Cir.1981); United States v. Gartner, 518 F.2d 633 (2d Cir.1975), cert.denied 423 U.S. 915, 96 S.Ct. 222, 46 L.Ed.2d 144 (1975); United States v. King, 536 F.Supp. 253 (C.D.Cal. 1982).

No violation of the client's constitutional rights may occur if the client's own lawyer is the informant to the government. If the government acts simply as auditor and takes no affirmative steps to intrude into the relationship between lawyer and client, a constitutional violation might not occur.[61] Aside from constitutional issues, of course, the lawyer's voluntary disclosure may violate professional requirements (§ 6.7.5).

A similar showing of violation plus prejudice is generally required if a client complains that governmental barriers have been thrown in the way of effective lawyer representation. In United States v. Morrison,[62] for example, the Court was willing to assume that a Sixth Amendment violation was shown when government agents bypassed a suspect's lawyer and attempted both to induce her to cooperate with their investigation and to disparage the abilities of her retained lawyer. But the Court refused to dismiss the indictment in the absence of any showing that the government's conduct had actually impaired the ability of the accused to maintain her defense.[63]

Law Office Searches

Law office searches have occurred with greater frequency in recent years.[64] The attempt to obtain evidence against the lawyer's clients, or possibly against the lawyer, can take the form of search warrants, subpoenas, telephone wiretapes, or other electronic surveillance.[65] The law has refused to give categorical primacy to either law enforcement interests or confidentiality interests in this area. Instead, the approach that is beginning to prevail is to attempt to accomodate both sets of interests through procedural requirements that provide for effective judicial scrutiny of seriously threatening police intrusions while requiring lawyer disclosure of matter that in fact enjoys no privileged status.

The first case to reach the issue, surprisingly, was decided only a few years ago. The case held that a warrant to search a law office could not issue unless the police made a sufficient showing that the lawyer was personally involved in the client's criminal activity or that there was some threat that the matter searched for would be destroyed if prior warning were given through a subpoena or similar

61 SEC v. Gulf & Western Ind., Inc., 518 F.Supp. 675 (D.D.C.1981)(affirmative defense of agency misconduct because of tampering with defendant-company's general counsel sufficiently refuted by findings that agency neither solicited nor received confidential information); State v. Sandini, 395 So.2d 1178 (Fla.App.1981), review denied 408 So.2d 1095 (Fla.1981), cert.denied 456 U.S. 926, 102 S.Ct. 1971, 72 L.Ed.2d 440 (1982)(lawyer's unauthorized disclosure to police of confidential client information not denial of Sixth Amendment right because it preceded any other step in prosecution and thus no right to counsel had attached). Decisions such as United States v. Henry, 447 U.S. 264, 100 S.Ct. 2183, 65 L.Ed.2d 115 (1980)(Sixth Amendment violated by undercover informer's conversations with cell mate awaiting trial despite fact that client initiated conversation), are distinguishable because in our assumed instance the government auditor is not misrepresenting his or her role.

62 449 U.S. 361, 101 S.Ct. 665, 66 L.Ed. 2d 564 (1981).

63 449 U.S. at 365, 101 S.Ct. at 668. See also, e.g., United States v. Ryan, 548 F.2d 782 (5th Cir.1976), cert.denied 429 U.S. 939, 97 S.Ct. 354, 50 L.Ed.2d 308 (1978)(no due process violation when government informer, acting on own initiative, warned lawyer not to represent accused further).

64 See generally Bloom, The Law Office Search: An Emerging Problem and Some Suggested Solutions, 69 Geo.L.J. 1 (1980); Comment, Search of the Lawyer's Office—Court Sanctioned Threat to Confidential Communications, 32 Ala.L.Rev. 92 (1980); Note, The Assault on the Citadel of Privilege Proceeds Apace: The Unreasonableness of Law Office Searches, 49 Fordham L.Rev. 708 (1981); Note, Search and Seizure of Attorney's Office as Violative of Attorney-Client Privilege, 3 Crim.Just.J. 359 (1980).

Law office searches flourished following the decision in Zurcher v. Stanford Daily, 436 U.S. 547, 98 S.Ct. 1970, 56 L.Ed.2d 525 (1978), upholding the constitutionality of searches of the premises of nonsuspect third parties—in *Zurcher*, a student newspaper office. See generally 1 W.Ringel, Searches and Seizures, Arrests and Confessions § 2.5, at 2–15 to 2–16 (2d ed.1980).

65 Zwerling, Federal Grand Juries v. Attorney Independence and the Attorney-Client Privilege, 27 Hast.L.J. 1263 (1976). The ABA House of Delegates passed a resolution at its February 1981 meeting condemning lawyer subpoenas. See 49 U.S.L.Wk. 2523 (1981). Courts seem to insist that the grand jury's need to question the lawyer or examine his or her documents be shown with specificity in order to prevent abusive intrusions into client confidences. E.g., In re Special Grand Jury (Harvey), 676 F.2d 1005 (4th Cir.1982), opinion withdrawn 697 F.2d 112 (4th Cir.1982).

process.[66] The decision was based on the detrimental impact of a search warrant upon the attorney-client privilege, client confidentiality, the work product doctrine, and the constitutional right to counsel. Particularly troubling was the fact that the police, in executing the warrant, would necessarily be exposed to files of innocent clients and to nonseizable parts of the suspect client's own files.[67] To protect against those risks the court created a subpoena-preference rule. A lawyer should be given an opportunity, if so advised, to resist issuance of the subpoena in court before matters asserted to be confidential were exposed to the possible view of searchers. Other courts, however, have shown no similar chariness about permitting police searches.[68]

California has developed a different process by statute. It provides procedures under which searches are conducted by neutral, law-trained persons who presumably will attend to the need for client confidentiality.[69] A distinction recognized both in the cases and in the California legislation is that a search warrant is proper if the lawyer is shown to be personally implicated in the crime [70] or if the search or subpoena issues arise as part of a disciplinary investigation of the lawyer.[71]

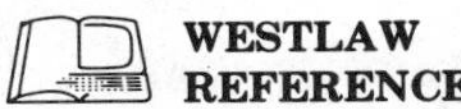

WESTLAW REFERENCES

geders /12 96 +4 1330 /p recess*** consult!

morrison /12 101 +4 665 /p "sixth amendment"

"law office" /3 search!

---

66 See O'Connor v. Johnson, 287 N.W.2d 400 (Minn. 1979).

67 287 N.W.2d at 405.

68 National City Trading Corp. v. United States, 487 F.Supp. 1332 (S.D.N.Y.), affirmed 635 F.2d 1020 (2d Cir. 1980).

69 See generally Deukmejian v. Superior Court, 103 Cal. App.3d 253, 162 Cal.Rptr. 857 (1980)(remanding for continuation of law office search pursuant to new California statute). Compare the regulations on law office searches issued by the Justice Department in 1981. 46 Fed.Reg. 1302.

70 West's Ann. Calif.Pen. Code § 1524(c)(procedure specially regulating law office searches not applicable if lawyer is "reasonably suspected of engaging or having engaged in criminal activity related to the documentary evidence for which a warrant is requested"); United States v. Loften, 507 F.Supp. 108 (S.D.N.Y.1981), 518 F.Supp. 839 (S.D.N.Y.1981)(telephone wiretap); Law Offices of Morley v. MacFarlane, 647 P.2d 1215 (Colo.1982) (otherwise proper search warrant issued in connection with charge that lawyer and client were engaged in crime not violative of attorney-client privilege). See also In re September 1978 Grand Jury, 640 F.2d 49 (7th Cir.1980)(if government, in course of in camera hearing, can show that lawyer was engaged in crime, court will enforce subpoena dueces tecum despite claims of attorney-client privilege and work product). Cf. Andresen v. Maryland, 427 U.S. 463, 96 S.Ct. 2737, 49 L.Ed.2d 627 (1976); Burrows v. Superior Court, 13 Cal.3d 238, 118 Cal.Rptr. 166, 529 P.2d 590 (1974).

71 In re Kennedy, 442 A.2d 79 (Del.1982)(required audit of lawyer's trust records, necessarily maintained under DR 9-102, does not violate lawyer's privacy).

Chapter Fifteen
THE RIGHT TO PRACTICE LAW

Table of Sections

---

§ 15.1 AUTHORIZED AND UNAUTHORIZED PRACTICE

§ 15.1.1 Nature and Background of Unauthorized Practice Regulation

Bar Admission and Unauthorized Practice

In the United States many tasks of a more or less legal nature may be undertaken only by a lawyer. The only general exception is that persons who are directly affected may undertake to handle their own legal problems by arguing their own cases, writing their own wills, or copying out their own deeds.[1] But no one else may engage in the practice of law—a concept that courts and bar associations have given a very broad meaning.

Bar admission is the court- and lawyer-controlled process of certification by which a person becomes entitled to engage in what otherwise would be unauthorized practice. Without a limited admission process, obviously, there could be no meaningful unauthorized practice system. Similarly, without a meaningful unauthorized practice doctrine, there could be no meaningful restrictions on admission. The two together have been employed within the past half century to formalize a lawyer monopoly over a vast area of regulation and activity that extends far beyond courtroom litigation.

History of Unauthorized Practice[2]

Nonlawyers have not always been excluded from practicing law, even from practicing as advocates in courtrooms. For almost a century the constitution of Indiana provided that any person could practice law in that state's courts, whether admitted by the courts or not.[3] During the same period similar laws in

[1] See § 14.4 (right to self representation).

[2] See generally J.Hurst, Growth of American Law 319–25 (1950); Rhode, Policing the Professional Monopoly: A Constitutional and Empirical Analysis of Unauthorized Practice Prohibitions, 34 Stan.L.Rev. 1, 6–10 (1981); Christensen, The Unauthorized Practice of Law: Do Good Fences Really Make Good Neighbors—or Even Good Sense?, 1980 Am.B.Found. Research J. 159, 161–201.

[3] Ind.Const. art. VII, § 21 (1851, repealed 1933). See Stevens, Two Cheers for 1870: The American Law School, in Law in American History at 500 (D.Fleming & B. Bailyn eds.1971). Dean Roscoe Pound sneered at this legislative excess in what he called the "era of decadence" in the history of the United States bar. See R.Pound, The Lawyer from Antiquity to Modern Times 231 (1953).

several other states also permitted nonlawyers to represent parties in litigation.[4] During the colonial period, several colonies not only permitted nonlawyers to appear as advocates but prohibited a professional caste of lawyers from arising by outlawing the charging of fees.

Scattered remnants of civilian law practice survive. In Oregon a nonlawyer may still represent another person in civil or criminal actions in a justice court.[5] Such permissiveness is and was exceptional, however, for the dominant doctrine for at least the last several centuries in both American and English courts has been that a nonlawyer may not appear in court to represent another person. But by and large the traditional doctrine of unauthorized practice stopped at the bar of the courtroom. Courts enforced the doctrine mainly by regulating who could enter an appearance in litigation.

Outside the courthouse, nonlawyers in earlier periods of American history freely performed tasks that today would be called the unauthorized practice of law. Beginning in the 1880s, various enterprises turned to activities that involved legal work and performed them as part of their services.[6] Title guaranty companies and debt collection agencies arose as freestanding enterprises. Existing institutions expanded their operations to include legal matters, such as trust departments of banks drafting wills and certified public accountants giving tax advice. That general pattern still obtains in England and other countries in Europe, where there has never been a prohibition against nonlawyers performing such legal functions as giving legal advice[7] or preparing some kinds of legal documents.[8]

A vigorous and expansive doctrine of unauthorized practice did not appear upon the American scene until sometime after the First World War.[9] Particularly after the beginning of the Depression bar associations and then for a period of almost half a century, bar associations and allied lawyers waged a campaign to eradicate unauthorized practice. The ABA's committee on unauthorized practice was founded in 1930,[10] and the first issue of the *Unauthorized Practice News* appeared four years later.[11] An explicit campaign began to encourage state and local bar associations to form their own unauthorized practice committees. Within a matter of years, those committees were hounding alleged unauthorized practitioners with a zeal and sense of purpose that was not often matched by bar disciplinary committees in their attempts to control wayward lawyers.

About the same time, courts began to announce sweeping common-law doctrines of exclusive lawyer competence in suits brought by bar associations against persons and institu-

4 Drinker lists Michigan, New Hampshire, Maine, and Wisconsin as having either statutes or constitutional provisions during the latter part of the nineteenth century that provided for essentially universal legal practice. See H.Drinker, Legal Ethics 19 (1953). Dean Griswold recalled a similar statutory enactment in Massachusetts, in force from 1790 to 1930, under which any persons—including, reportedly, a disbarred lawyer—could appear in Massachusetts courts as counsel for another if armed with a written power of attorney. See E.Griswold, Law and Lawyers in the United States 15–16 (1965).

5 Oregon St. Bar v. Wright, 280 Or. 693, 573 P.2d 283, 289 (1977).

6 J.Hurst, The Growth of American Law 319 (1950).

7 M.Zander, Legal Services for the Community 329 (1978); M.Zander, Lawyers and the Public Interest 174 (1968); Q.Johnstone & D.Hopson, Lawyers and Their Work 486–89 (1967).

8 Rhode, Policing the Professional Monopoly: A Constitutional and Empirical Analysis of Unauthorized Practice Prohibitions, 34 Stan.L.Rev. 1, 89–90 (1981).

9 Professor Hurst has traced the beginnings of modern unauthorized practice campaigns to an unauthorized practice committee of the New York County Lawyers Association that was first appointed in 1914 to deal with competition from title and trust companies. J.Hurst, The Growth of American Law 323 (1950). And see Rhode, Policing the Professional Monopoly: A Constitutional and Empirical Analysis of Unauthorized Practice Prohibitions, 34 Stan.L.Rev. 1, 7 (1981).

10 55 ABA Rep. 94 (1930).

11 The organization and politics of national and local bar association committees on unauthorized practice are discussed in Q.Johnstone & D.Hopson, Lawyers and Their Work 187–96 (1967). A measure of the growing strength of the unauthorized practice movement was that the 1908 Canons of Ethics, which had said nothing about unauthorized practice, were amended in 1937 to add Canon 47, the last of the Canons, which strongly condemned it.

tions that were claimed to be unauthorized practitioners of law. The fact that widespread enforcement, and expansion, of an unauthorized practice doctrine did not occur before the onset of the Great Depression, which greatly reduced the earnings of lawyers as well as others, suggests that the bar's newly kindled concern with protecting potential clients against incompetent and unscrupulous charlatans may also have been mixed with hopes of enlarging the exclusive market for legal services.[12]

Interprofessional Treaties

Once bar associations had developed bodies of judicial doctrine indicating that courts would be cooperative in expanding and assuring the lawyer monopoly, bar associations could approach organized groups of potential competitors and dictate terms of cooperation between them and lawyers.[13] Beginning in the mid-1930s, committees formed by the American Bar Association negotiated treaties with many groups, including accountants (1951),[14] architects (1968), banks with trust functions (1941), claims adjusters (1939), collection agencies (1937), liability insurance companies (1969), life insurance companies (1946), professional engineers (1969), lawbook publishers (1941), real estate title companies (1969), realtors (1942), and social workers (1964).[15] The treaties, which were customarily called statements of principles, were typically one-sided and called on bar associations and lawyers to do little that was inconvenient, while aggressively describing broad areas of prohibition for the affected group of would-be competitors.[16]

In 1975 in the *Goldfarb* decision[17] the Supreme Court in effect made many provisions of the interprofessional treaties untenable under the federal antitrust laws. Many of them were soon rescinded.[18] Some of the treaties have been replaced with innocuous and much less ambitious statements of interprofessional relations. The documents are carefully reviewed by antitrust counsel before final approval. Their wording is circumspect, carefully pointing out that they are advisory and voluntary only.[19] They now studiously avoid efforts, common in the older treaties, to define areas of unauthorized practice.

Relevance of Antitrust Laws

The era of vigorous bar campaigns against unauthorized practice came to an end in 1975. Until the *Goldfarb* decision, the activities of the unauthorized practice committees of the ABA and state and local bar associations were studies in anticompetitive behavior. The committees aggressively pursued unauthorized practitioners, threatened disciplinary action against cooperating lawyers, published bromides and warnings, and prepared and sponsored rallying publications and resolutions at bar meetings. The ABA's committee was particularly active and published a periodical—*The Unauthorized Practice News*—that is a rich source of information about

12 W.Hurst, The Growth of American Law 323 (1950).

13 See generally Q.Johnstone & D.Hopson, Lawyers and Their Work 184–87 (1967).

14 The date given is the date of the first approval of a treaty. Most of the treaties were negotiated pursuant to a campaign to secure unauthorized practice agreements with affected nonlawyer organizations pursuant to an ABA House of Delegates resolution adopted in 1940.

15 8 Martindale-Hubbell Law Directory 71M et seq. (1978) for text of these treaties.

16 The treaties' limitations also had incidental benefits for affected nonlawyer professionals. They defined, in effect, areas in which a nonlawyer should not be held negligent for failure to act if the area was defined in a relevant treaty as one reserved to lawyers. E.g., Wilkinson v. Rives, 116 Cal.App.3d 641, 172 Cal.Rptr. 254 (1981) (title examiner who failed to give legal advice to customer would have violated unauthorized practice treaty by doing so and thus was exonerated from claim of professional malpractice).

17 Goldfarb v. Virginia State Bar, 421 U.S. 773, 95 S.Ct. 2004, 44 L.Ed.2d 572 (1975). See generally § 2.4.1.

18 Rescission was either by the ABA House of Delegates or, on occasion, by the ABA's board of governors and took place beginning with the August 1979 ABA meeting, when the board of governors warned that all treaties should be rescinded. See 66 ABA J. 129 (1980). That action followed close on the heels of a Justice Department suit against a local bar association for violation of the antitrust laws through enforcement of an interprofessional treaty. See Nat'l L.J., Mar.26, 1979, at 29, col.1.

19 Nat'l Conf. of Lawyers and CPAs, Lawyers and Certified Public Accountants: A Study of Interprofessional Relations 3, 13 (1981).

attitudes and objectives of lawyers engaged in unauthorized practice work.

But the Supreme Court's holding in *Goldfarb* that bar association anticompetitive activity was subject to the federal antitrust laws, meant the end of unauthorized practice committees as freewheeling organizations of interested lawyers. A federal trial court decision in 1977 held that a bar association's issuance of opinions that purported to define areas of unauthorized practice also offended the antitrust laws.[20] Federal officials threatened further antitrust responses because of unauthorized practice activities of bar associations [21] and filed at least one suit.[22] The activities of both national and local bar committees were severely cut back. Most remaining unauthorized practice regulation was channeled through state supreme courts, which will probably slow and retard enforcement.[23] The unauthorized practice committees in several states were disbanded.[24] The ABA's committee on unauthorized practice was itself finally terminated by the ABA House of Delegates in 1984.[25]

The significant, if partial, retreat of bar associations from the field of unauthorized practice, however, does nothing to alter the common-law and statutory prohibitions against unauthorized practice that are enforced by state courts. As the arguable product of state action, those measures—even if anticompetitive in their purpose and effect—may be effectively immune from scrutiny under the federal antitrust laws.[26] While bar association involvement in bringing unauthorized practice suits remains an untested matter under federal antitrust laws, in most states bar associations have continued to enforce, if much more circumspectly, anticompetitive unauthorized practice rules.

Constitutional Issues in Unauthorized Practice

At least four kinds of federal constitutional issues are raised by unauthorized practice rules under state law. Those issues relate to concerns about free expression, about access to courts, about fair notice of proscribed conduct, and about fairness in the tribunals that determine questions of unauthorized practice.

Because of concerns about free expression, courts have generally been unwilling to impose unauthorized practice limitations on publications that contain legal advice.[27] Access to courts has been a constitutional doctrine of some persisting vigor in the Supreme Court. In one set of cases, the court held that a state may not proscribe activities of an organization that seeks to advance its members' interests through the legal process.[28] In another, the Court held that there is a constitutional right of access to courts without, in those cases, economic restrictions.[29] It re-

[20] Surety Title Ins. Agency, Inc. v. Virginia State Bar, 431 F.Supp. 298 (E.D.Va.1977). The Fourth Circuit ordered the district court decision vacated and the case held in abeyance pending proceedings that were pending before the Virginia Supreme Court to alter the method for issuing unauthorized practice opinions. See 571 F.2d 205 (4th Cir.1978), cert.denied 436 U.S. 941, 98 S.Ct. 2838, 56 L.Ed.2d 781 (1978). The method eventually adopted was clearly designed to give the Virginia Supreme Court sufficient involvement in the issuance of opinions to support an argument that the activity was now exempt from the federal antitrust laws under the state action doctrine. See § 2.4.2. The ABA House of Delegates, in one of the last acts involving the now disbanded unauthorized practice committee, approved a model rule for unauthorized practice advisory opinions that was modeled on the Virginia system. See ABA/BNA Lawyers' Manual on Prof. Conduct 93, 95 (1984).

[21] Editorial, 63 ABA J. 455 (1977); Trustbusters Eye ABA UPL Opinion, 63 ABA J. 1702 (1977); 841 Antitrust & Trade Reg. Rep. D-2, at D-4 (Dec.1, 1977).

[22] Nat'l L.J., Mar.26, 1979, at 29, col.1 (Justice Department suit against county bar association for conspiracy to monopolize and restrain trade through statement of principles).

[23] Bars Reforming Their UPL Processes, 64 ABA J. 1215 (1978).

[24] Rhode, Policing the Professional Monopoly, 34 Stan. L.Rev. 1, 14–15 (1981)(as of 1980–81, seven states had abolished committees out of antitrust apprehensions).

[25] ABA/BNA Lawyers' Manual on Professional Conduct at 381 (1984).

[26] On the operation of the so-called state action defense in federal antitrust law, see § 2.4.2.

[27] See infra at 838–39.

[28] Those cases are discussed in § 16.5.2.

[29] See § 14.5.

mains to be seen whether those cases will be extended to override similar barriers, such as unauthorized practice barriers that, for example, prohibit nonlawyers from representing persons in court who otherwise would lack representation.

The concern about fair notice relates to the notoriously open-ended nature of the tests for determining whether conduct constitutes unauthorized practice. For the most part, state courts have avoided the issue by first restraining specifically described conduct and then punishing further conduct as a violation of the injunction.[30] The issue concerning the fairness of hearing bodies refers to the fact that lawyers, the group that has a direct pecuniary interest in preventing competition from alleged unauthorized practitioners, is the same group that has a dominant hand in enforcing the rules. The fair-hearing issue is raised by Gibson v. Berryhill,[31] which is probably irrelevant to most states' unauthorized practice procedures but which at least serves to demarcate the limits of self-interested regulation. The Court there held that a state licensing board composed entirely of optometrists who practiced alone lacked the impartiality required by due process to determine whether to terminate the licenses of other optometrists who accepted employment with a large corporate employer that dispensed a large volume of eyeglasses. The Court's obvious concern with the direct and substantial economic interest of the optometrists arguably applies to lawyers involved in unauthorized practice.[32] But subsequent decisions suggest that *Gibson* applies only to situations in which the members of the biased board actually adjudicate an occupational entitlement and possess an economic interest that is substantially and directly involved.[33]

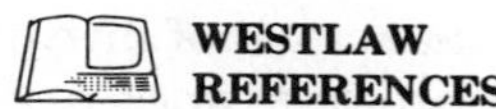

WESTLAW REFERENCES

di practice

unauthorized +1 practice /2 law legal /s committee /7 american state local +1 "bar association"

american state local +1 "bar association" /p treaty (statement +2 principle) /p accountant architect bank** "claim adjust*r"

"collection agency" ((liability life +1 insurance) title +1 company) realtor engineer publisher "social worker"

"unauthorized practice news"

department /2 justice /p "bar association" /p antitrust

unauthorized +1 practice /2 law legal /p constitution** (free*** +2 speech expression assembl*)

---

§ 15.1.2 Rationale of Unauthorized Practice Law

Making the Case for Special Protection

Unauthorized practice law means that most of what lawyers do every day can be done by no one else. The bar's largely successful campaign against unauthorized practice has left a large field free from nonlawyer competition, thus securing a lawyer monopoly over most of the areas of operation of the legal process, a monopoly that one is tempted to conclude is primarily for the benefit of lawyers.[34] At the margins, unauthorized practitioners continue to be motivated to attempt to make inroads. In part that results from an anomaly in the present state of unauthorized practice protection. The major inroads by nonlawyers have come in those areas in which the special skills and training of lawyers are least needed and thus in which it has been easiest for nonlawyers to duplicate the competence of lawyers without great expense and with high consumer acceptance. The commercial success of divorce kits and similar nonlawyer intrusions

[30] See infra at 845.

[31] 411 U.S. 564, 93 S.Ct. 1689, 36 L.Ed.2d 488 (1973).

[32] The argument is made in Rhode, Policing the Professional Monopoly, 34 Stan.L.Rev. 1, 52–53 (1981).

[33] Friedman v. Rogers, 440 U.S. 1, 99 S.Ct. 887, 59 L.Ed. 2d 100 (1979)(presence on disciplinary body of persons who might profit indirectly from decision does not violate due process).

[34] Morgan, The Emerging Concept of Professional Responsibility, 90 Harv.L.Rev. 702, 712 (1977). See also, e.g., Friedman, Freedom of Contract and Occupational Licensing 1890–1910: A Legal and Social Study, 53 Calif. L.Rev. 487 (1965)(bar admission standards and procedures administered to restrict entry of potential competitors).

suggests that clients both find lawyer charges in the area unjustifiably high and believe that having two highly trained and qualified lawyers on each side of a dissolution proceeding is a serious squandering of educational, legal, and economic resources.

Lawyers have offered four justifications to explain the bar's fervor for pursuing unauthorized practitioners: protecting clients against harmful incompetence; protecting the legal system against the consequences of incompetence or lack of integrity by nonlawyers; providing the necessary framework for regulating lawyers; and, although rarely admitted, enhancing the economic position of lawyers. Taken separately or together, the arguments are strikingly problematical as justification for the wide sweep of current unauthorized practice law. They also closely resemble arguments that arborists, architects, cosmetologists, dentists, plumbers, and a host of other occupational groups have made for costly monolopies in their areas of business.[35]

(1) Client Harm at the Hands of Nonlawyers

The justification for unauthorized practice that lawyers proclaim first and most frequently is that practice by "unqualified" persons would seriously harm clients. The harms that must be guarded against are said to be many. The evils most frequently mentioned are incompetence, impairment of professional independence, and excessive fees. To be persuasive, the argument would have to demonstrate two core propositions. First, it would be necessary to demonstrate that lawyers under an unauthorized practice system are on average significantly more protective of client interests than nonlawyer practitioners would be in the absence of unauthorized practice rules. Second, it is necessary to demonstrate that in fact potential clients would be worse off without unauthorized practice protection.[36] In other words, even if one can safely assume that a purchaser of residential real estate is more competently represented by a graduate of a prestigious law school with years of experience and fee rates to match, one is still entitled to inquire whether the purchaser would be worse off if form documents used for a purchase agreement were filled out in the purchaser's behalf by a real estate agent with a high-school diploma who specializes in purchases of residential real estate and whose employer charges nothing extra for the document work. The proposition that the client is better off paying the lawyer than the agent is hardly obvious at an intuitive level.

Superior Lawyer Performance. Detected instances of unauthorized practice cover a wide landscape, ranging from instances in which established institutions such as banks and

35 Georgia Ass'n of American Institute of Architects v. Gwinnett County, 238 Ga. 277, 233 S.E.2d 142 (1977)(suit by local association of architects to prevent professional engineer from designing and supervising construction of fire station on ground that engineer's acts constituted unauthorized practice of architecture). Reading works that analyze the arguments of other occupational groups will rapidly uncover most of the major themes, and many of the minor patterns, of the unauthorized practice debate in law. E.g., Comment, Legalized Denturism: Demand, Public Health, and the Legislative Response, 74 Nw.U.L.Rev. 97 (1979). See generally Kennedy, The Lawyer as Professional: Examination, Licensing, and the Problem of Deceptive Packaging, 7 Fla.St.L.J. 601 (1979); Moore, The Purpose of Licensing, 4 J.L. & Econ. 93, 93 n. 1 (1961)(quoting chairman of state tree surgeon examining board: "The intent of the tree expert law was primarily to protect the public against tree quacks, shysters and inexperienced persons.").

Many economists and legal scholars hold the view that professional self-regulation is often anti-competitive in both motivation and effect. E.g., M.Friedman, Capitalism and Freedom 140 (1962); W.Gellhorn, Individual Freedom and Governmental Restraints 105–51 (1956); Gellhorn, The Abuse of Occupational Licensing, 44 U.Chi. L.Rev. 6 (1976). It is not entirely clear to some whether, in fact, lawyers have taken advantage of the opportunities for cartelization that is implied by their monopoly power through control of licensure. Several studies have detected significant anti-competitive effects. E.g., Holen, Effects of Professional Licensing Arrangements on Interstate Labor Mobility and Resource Allocation, 73 J.Pol. Econ. 492 (1965); Marizi, Occupational Licensing and the Public Interest, 82 J.Pol.Econ. 399 (1974). But others have restudied the same data and found no significant evidence of anti-competitive lawyer licensing control. Getz, Siegfried & Calvani, Competition at the Bar: The Correlation between the Bar Examination Pass Rate and the Profitability of Practice, 67 Va.L.Rev. 863 (1981)(no significant evidence of anti-competitive licensure practice on national basis but study not designed to detect anti-competitive practices in any particular jurisdiction).

36 Morgan, The Evolving Concept of Professional Responsibility, 90 Harv.L.Rev. 702, 708 (1977).

real estate offices assist customers with forms such as mortgages, deeds, and promissory notes that have legal effect to instances in which sharp operators attempt legal tasks that are entirely beyond their abilities. In the first set of cases, it is probably not true that the average lawyer is more competent than the average bank or real estate clerk who has become a specialist at performing certain tasks.[37]

In the second set of cases, involving sharp operators, the argument of superior lawyer performance is, in a superficial way, doubtless accurate in many instances. It is probably true that lawyers today are on average more competent and trustworthy than the average unauthorized practitioners that operate in some shady areas. But that state of affairs is not at all necessarily inherent in the fact that the unauthorized practitioner is not a lawyer. It is almost certainly due to the more obvious fact that some kinds of unauthorized practice are plainly against the law. The relevant comparison of competence and integrity would be between lawyers, with their expensive and prolonged process of training and certification, and nonlawyers, with whatever training and certification they would devise in a legal system in which it would make economic sense to incur the financial cost of preparation for a stable and lawful career. There are as many reasons to think that nonlawyers would want to develop competence and integrity standards at least equal to those of lawyers in order to avoid malpractice liability and to compete effectively with lawyers by maintaining client goodwill.

The argument based on lawyer superiority also asserts that lawyers are more competent and trustworthy than nonlawyers because lawyers are subject to special regulations. Thus EC 3–1, in explaining why public policy justifies confining the practice of law to lawyers, asserts that "the public can better be assured of the requisite responsibility and competence [of those who undertake to render legal services] if the practice of law is confined to those who are subject to the requirements and regulations imposed upon members of the legal profession." And, according to EC 3–3, "a non-lawyer who undertakes to handle legal matters is not governed as to integrity or legal competence by the same rules that govern the conduct of a lawyer." But those assertions are either debatable or represent limitations that are self-incurred. For one matter, it is simply not true that nonlawyers who commit legal malpractice are subject to different liability rules. The view uniformly taken by courts is that a nonlawyer who, for example, writes a will is subject to the same high standard of care of a legal specialist that would be applied to a lawyer performing the same legal task.[38]

Arguments like those found in EC 3–1 and EC 3–3 imply that lawyer regulations are much more stringent than what the law imposes on nonlawyers and that the lawyer regulations are uniformly enforced, but neither proposition is widely accepted by others than lawyers. The argument might be that lawyers are held to stricter standards because of the thoroughness of screens for integrity that are imposed at the admission stage or because of the supplementary deterrent of professional discipline for incompetence or untrustwor-

[37] "[R]eal estate brokers may know more property law, trust officers more estate law, architects more construction law, and accountants more tax law than lawyers who do not specialize in these areas." Weckstein, Limitations on the Right to Counsel: The Unauthorized Practice of Law, 1978 Utah L.Rev. 649, 650.

[38] The leading case is Biakanja v. Irving, 49 Cal.2d 647, 320 P.2d 16 (1958). See also, e.g., Williams v. Jackson Co., 359 So.2d 798 (Ala.Civ.App.1978),writ denied 359 So. 2d 801 (1978); Wright v. Langdon, 274 Ark. 258, 623 S.W. 2d 823 (1981); Torres v. Fiol, 110 Ill.App.3d 9, 65 Ill.Dec. 786, 441 N.E.2d 1300 (1982); Latson v. Eaton, 341 P.2d 247 (Okl.1959); Mattieligh v. Poe, 57 Wn.2d 203, 356 P.2d 328 (1960). On unauthorized practice assumptions, the rule holds nonlawyers to a standard of care that is presumably so high that they cannot perform according to its dictates. In that view, its enforcement is designed to deter unauthorized practice because of the high risk of liaiblity that an unauthorized practitioner presumably incurs. See Biakanja v. Irving, supra 320 P.2d at 19. Courts have not been willing, however, to hold that violation of an unauthorized practice statute constitutes negligence per se in the absence of a demonstrated injury to the plaintiff because of the defendant's unauthorized practice. E.g., Kronzer v. First Nat'l Bank, 305 Minn. 415, 235 N.W.2d 187 (1975).

thiness. But neither of those propositions is true. Integrity screens at the admission stage probably do not work (§ 15.3). And lawyers are rarely disciplined for incompetence, excessive fee charges, or lack of professional independence.[39] The law of malpractice, contract and fiduciary limits on fee charges, and agency rules requiring loyalty to a principal would probably protect clients almost as well. Thus it is far from clear that clients and third parties would be exposed to a significantly greater risk of unethical nonlawyer practice if there were no law of unauthorized practice.

Protection of consumers against unethical nonlawyer practitioners, if needed, does not have to take the form of unauthorized practice rules. While some nonlawyers[40] are not presently subject to regulatory discipline for incompetence or unethical behavior,[41] the same courts who have developed the law of unauthorized practice can change that situation. The courts in most jurisdictions claim a lawmaking competence under the inherent powers doctrine[42] that seems sufficiently broad to require that nonlawyers be regulated in ways that impose competence sanctions as stringent as those provided for lawyers.[43] If the courts lack the power, then adequate protection could be obtained through legislation.[44]

Proponents of unauthorized practice regulation argue that there is one competence-based skill that the average lawyer possesses that is not possessed by the average nonlawyer—the ability to identify unusual legal problems or those that lie outside the area directly involved. This, the "seamless web" argument,[45] is both dubious and paternalistic. It dubiously assumes that such problems are so unusual that nonlawyers will be unaware of them and yet that they will arise with sufficient frequency that the protection that can be afforded by a more expensive generalist is often required. The argument also assumes that clients cannot be trusted to choose for themselves whether they want to pay for the extra protection of a generalist instead of the narrower protection of a nonlawyer specialist.

Client Need for Protection. Even if it were assumed that nonlawyers were not as competent or trustworthy as the average lawyer, it would remain to be demonstrated that they should therefore be prevented from performing legal services. It is perfectly compatible with assumptions of lesser nonlawyer competence and trustworthiness to conclude that clients nonetheless do not need or want the protection of unauthorized practice laws. Clients might still have sound reasons to prefer the services of nonlawyers. Most obviously, clients who are aware of the limitations on the abilities and ethics of nonlawyers might rationally want to hire them despite their shortcomings because, in a free competitive market for legal services, those shortcomings will bring lower prices. There are many tasks that lawyers now perform—such as preparing simple wills, handling residential real estate transfers, walking clients through uncontested divorces or obtaining a name change, and representing clients in small claims courts and in many administrative matters—that require little legal ability and that many trained nonlawyers could doubtless

[39] See § 5.1, at 190–91, (competence); § 9.3, at 516 (excessive fee charges); and § 8.8 (conflicts of interest due to third-party control).

[40] Other nonlawyers, such as real estate agents, stockbrokers, and accountants, are subject to stringent competence and character tests and examinations and are certified by local and national certification boards.

[41] Many are, such as realtors and accountants.

[42] § 2.2.2.

[43] In 1982, for example, the Washington State Bar Association recommended to the state's supreme court adoption of a rule that would create a limited lay license that would permit certified closing officers in residential real estate transactions to transact what the court had previously determined to be the practice of law. See State Ponders Limited Lay License, 68 ABA J. 662 (1982).

[44] In fact, however, courts have sometimes frustrated legislative attempts to deal precisely with unauthorized practice problems by claiming that the legislation was unconstitutional under the negative aspect of the inherent powers doctrine (see § 2.2.3). E.g., Professional Adjusters, Inc. v. Tandon, 433 N.E.2d 779, 29 A.L.R.4th 1144 (Ind.1982)(statute authorizing certified public adjusters to negotiate settlements between insurers and persons protected by liability insurance policies unconstitutional).

[45] Q.Johnstone & D.Hopson, Lawyers and Their Work 174 (1967); Weckstein, Limitations on the Right to Counsel: The Unauthorized Practice of Law, 1978 Utah L.Rev. 649, 651.

perform as competently as many lawyers. Moreover, they are sufficiently common and uncomplex that opportunities for consumer fraud would be minimal.

Nonlawyers are hardly ever consulted about the wisdom of particular unauthorized practice rules.[46] Beyond being uninvited, the protection is probably unwanted and thus paternalistic in a most objectionable way. On rare occasions when the public has been able to voice an opinion, the results have been discouraging for those who believe that unauthorized practice law aids consumers.[47] Because of the absence of alternatives, many litigants take the route of self-representation, an entitlement which is itself very much opposed to paternalistic attempts to force unwanted advocates upon clients.[48] Nonlawyers make few complaints about unauthorized practice matters; proceedings against alleged unauthorized practitioners are almost always the result of lawyer or bar committee initiatives.[49] Several groups of nonlawyers have been organized in recent years, one of whose principal aims is to eliminate the lawyer monopoly on some kinds of legal services.[50] Indications are that the great majority of nonlawyers believe that they are ill-served by the present broad protection of unauthorized practice law.[51]

Supporters of broad unauthorized practice rules at this point are forced to argue that in fact clients are in a poor position to judge whether their problem is one for which a nonlawyer can provide adequate services because clients lack the necessary information on which to make such judgments.[52] In part, the absence of client information about legal services stems from bar-imposed or bar-inspired limitations on advertising about legal services (§ 14.2.4). Moreover, if an industry of nonlawyer practitioners were permitted to form, there is as much reason to think that informed guides to competent and trustworthy practitioners would exist in that field as in other technical fields or with similarly technical products.

(2) Preventing Harm to the Legal System

Proponents of broad unauthorized practice rules also argue that, in the absence of such rules, courts and other legal institutions would be seriously impaired because of the incompetence and lack of integrity of nonlawyer practitioners. As is the argument about harm to clients, so this argument is also both empirically dubious and, even if factually well-founded, hardly supports the breadth of rules that presently are in force. The claim that is usually made is based on assumptions

[46] Very few states have nonlawyers on unauthorized practice committees. The few that do include nonlawyers never include nonlawyers in sufficient number or who are appointed by an authority such that it warrants a hope that the nonlawyer members will take significantly different policy positions from those of lawyer members. See Rhode, Policing the Professional Monopoly, 34 Stan.L.Rev. 1, 58–60 (1981); Wolfram, Barriers to Effective Public Participation in Regulation of the Legal Profession, 62 Minn.L.Rev. 619, 642–43 (1978).

[47] See the popular ballot vote taken in connection with the Arizona real estate controversy, infra at 842.

[48] Morgan, The Evolving Concept of Professional Responsibility, 90 Harv.L.Rev. 702, 708–09 (1977).

[49] Rhode, Policing the Professional Monopoly, 34 Stan. L.Rev. 1, 33–36 (1981).

[50] Rhode, supra, 34 Stan.L.Rev. at 4 n.6, 72; Sylvester, The People vs. Lawyers: More Groups Cash in on Hatred of Lawyers, Nat'l L.J., Jan.9, 1984, at 1, col.1.

[51] B.Curran & F.Spaulding, The Legal Needs of the Public 231 (1977)(82 percent of nonlawyers responding to 1974 survey agreed with statement that "many things that lawyers handle—for example, tax matters or estate planning—can be done as well and less expensively by nonlawyers—like tax accountants, trust officers of banks and insurance agents"). The commercial success of do-it-yourself kits and form books is a market measure of the same judgment. Rhode, supra, 34 Stan.L.Rev. at 3–4.

[52] Presumably that is the basis for the "holding out" cases that find unauthorized practice in the mere act of a nonlawyers' representing himself or herself to be a lawyer or being available to provide legal services. E.g., In re Amalgamated Dev. Co., 375 A.2d 494 (D.C.1977), cert.denied 434 U.S. 924, 98 S.Ct. 403, 54 L.Ed.2d 282 (1977); Florida Bar v. Martin, 432 So.2d 54 (Fla.1983). Most such cases seem to be rather blatant instances of consumer fraud and probably could be handled as such without resort to the law of unauthorized practice. That may characterize unauthorized practice by some notaries public, particularly among clients who are familiar with legal practice customs only in Spanish-speaking cultures, in which a *notario publico* is a licensed lawyer. See 68 ABA J. 1357 (1982).

of incompetence. It is thought that nonlawyers, because they are ignorant of law and unskilled in legal matters, would clog the courts with unfounded claims and defenses; slow trials with bumbling attempts to seek the admission of inadmissible evidence; encumber administrative hearings with legally irrelevant arguments and presentations; create litigation and confusion with ineffective deeds, wills, and other legal instruments; and generally throw the legal system into chaos. Clients, presumably, would hire such incompetent nonlawyers only out of ignorance, which is dubious to assume.

If the argument is that nonlawyers would resort to such tactics out of guile rather than ignorance (and thus that clients would prefer to hire them because of their ruthlessness), it is sufficient to note that courts have the power to enforce adequate sanctions against their clients through rules of procedural (and substantive) forfeiture (§ 4.6.1) and, as mentioned above, through enlarging the disciplinary scope of rules and procedures that now bind only lawyers.

(3) Assuring a Basis for Professional Discipline

A third rationale is that unauthorized practice restrictions are necessary to provide a basis for imposing lawyer discipline and other regulation. There are several supposed illustrations. For one thing, without a doctrine of unauthorized practice, most of the sting would be removed from disbarment or suspension of lawyers who violate the lawyer codes or other norms of the legal profession.[53] Yet that is, of course, only an argument for applying unauthorized practice rules to unfrocked lawyers, but hardly to every nonlawyer.

Another arguable regulatory need can be seen from considering the poor competitive position in which lawyers would be placed if they were forced to compete for clients with practitioners who were not, for example, constrained by antisolicitation or antiadvertising rules. If a bank established a department of nonlawyer "estate specialists," prepared to write wills and probate estates, lawyers would be competitively disadvantaged because of the bank's possibly superior ability to advertise and to solicit clients from bank customers.[54] But that concern is also of limited weight in justifying any particular unauthorized practice rule. It might be as much an argument that lawyer codes should not competitively constrain lawyers unless the net social value of such constraints more than offsets the costs imposed by the resulting lawyers' monopoly. The bar has never attempted to demonstrate that such a net gain is achieved by unathorized practice rules.

(4) Protecting Lawyers against Competition

A final rationale—although one not often uttered outside of meetings and publications of lawyers—is that unauthorized practice rules protect a valuable lawyers' monopoly. Unauthorized practice rules warn nonlawyers off the field so that lawyers have more work and more freedom to charge higher fees. Because lawyers hired by banks can neither write wills nor probate estates, there is that much more economic gain for the limited number of lawyers who are alone authorized to do the work. It is obviously difficult to put much policy clothing on such nakedly self-regarding claims. The argument that law should be practiced in the absence of competition because competition for clients would encourage lawyers to engage in unethical methods of businessgetting and shoddy means of costcutting has been explicitly rejected by the Supreme Court in holding that lawyers are to be subjected to much the same antitrust

53 Such a result would seriously impair the deterrent impact of lawyer discipline. It is not wholly satisfactory to respond, cf. R.Posner, Economic Analysis of Law 346 (1973), that the solution is to extend the reach of lawyer codes and lawyer disciplinary sanctions to all, including nonlawyers, who engage in law-like practices. The additional cost of such an extension would, of course, be substantial but arguably would be more than offset by the elimination of the monopoly "tax" that present unauthorized practice rules impose on clients.

54 Lawyers could not similarly compete because of self-incurred limitations on dual practice (§ 16.4) and solicitation (§ 14.2.5). Those, obviously, would also be changed.

rules[55] and are to be allowed much the same freedom to advertise[56] as other people in businesses. The appeal, then, must remain simply a rallying cry for lawyers to shout to each other but to keep close in their hearts as unauthorized practice rules are argued for in public forums on other grounds that purport to pay more attention to the public interest.

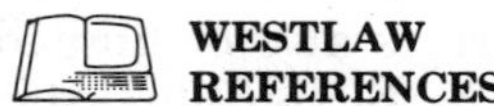
WESTLAW REFERENCES

rationale (client consumer public /5 harm injur*** protect*** interest) incompeten*** competen*** expert*** skill /10 unauthorized +1 practice /2 law legal

---

§ 15.1.3 *Workings of Unauthorized Practice Doctrine*

Regulating Unauthorized Practice

Courts in many jurisdictions have claimed that the courts possess the inherent power to define and regulate the unauthorized practice of law. Federal courts have also claimed an inherent power to regulate unauthorized practice, but only to the extent of unauthorized practice before the federal courts themselves.[57] Some state courts have gone further, however, and have held that the courts have an exclusive power to deal with unauthorized practice under the negative aspect of the inherent powers doctrine (§ 2.2.3). Accordingly, they have struck down as unconstitutional usurpations of judicial power any attempt by a legislative or administrative body to modify the rules of unauthorized practice.[58] Some courts, however, will accept modest legislative initiatives on the notion that such regulation should be respected out of comity for a coordinate branch.[59] Some few courts have gone beyond even that approach and have refused to assert the questionable doctrine that the judiciary has a greater interest than the legislature in affecting the shape of law practice outside of court activities.[60]

It is difficult to defend as even sensible any position but the last. If a statute disagrees with a judicial view and permits nonlawyer practice outside of court, no legitimate judicial interest is at stake. To be blunt, it is simply not the business of courts to see to the general good order of society by declaring void statutes that have been enacted in the exercise of the police powers of an elected legislature. Judges might, perhaps with reason, consider themselves unbiased experts on appropriate measures for unauthorized practice outside of court. By the same token, they could be considered experts on the law of torts, contracts, and much else of common-law provenance that comes before them. It is thus legitimate for courts to develop doctrines of unauthorized practice as an exercise of common-law powers in the absence of legislation. But self-described expertise is clearly no basis for declaring acts of a legislature unconstitutional. As courts remind us interminably in other contexts, it is only the constitutionality and not the wisdom of statutes that should be in issue. Courts should leave

55 Goldfarb v. Virginia State Bar, 421 U.S. 773, 95 S.Ct. 2004, 44 L.Ed.2d 572 (1975). See § 2.4.1.

56 Bates v. Arizona State Bar, 433 U.S. 350, 97 S.Ct. 2691, 53 L.Ed.2d 810 (1978). See § 14.2.3.

57 United States v. Peterson, 550 F.2d 379, 384–85 (7th Cir.1977).

58 Merco Constr. Eng'rs, Inc. v. Municipal Court, 21 Cal.3d 724, 147 Cal.Rptr. 631, 581 P.2d 636 (1978); Idaho St. Bar Ass'n v. Idaho Pub. Utilities Comm'n, 102 Idaho 672, 637 P.2d 1168 (1981); Professional Adjusters, Inc. v. Tandon, 433 N.E.2d 779, 29 A.L.R.4th 1144 (Ind.1982); Cowern v. Nelson, 207 Minn. 642, 290 N.W. 795 (1940); Hagan & Van Camp v. Kasler Escrow, Inc., 96 Wn.2d 443, 635 P.2d 730 (1981).

59 State ex rel. Frieson v. Isner, 285 S.E.2d 641, 654 (W.Va.1981); State ex rel. Reynolds v. Dinger, 14 Wis.2d 193, 109 N.W.2d 685 (1961).

60 Florida Bar v. Moses, 380 So.2d 412, 417–18 (Fla. 1980); State Bar of Michigan v. Galloway, 124 Mich.App. 271, 335 N.W.2d 475, 479–80 (1983); Detroit Bar Ass'n v. Union Guardian Trust Co., 282 Mich. 216, 276 N.W. 365 (1937); In re Cannon, 206 Wis. 374, 395, 240 N.W. 441 (1932)("[C]ourts have no concern with the qualifications of lawyers except in so far as they are permitted to participate in the administration of the law in actions and proceedings in courts of law and equity. . . . The legislature may establish such qualifications as it chooses for those who are permitted to act as conveyancers, examiners of title, organizers of corporations, or any other type of legal services which [do] not give them power to influence the course of justice as administered by courts.").

legislatures to their own wisdom or folly in defining unauthorized practice in all areas that do not directly involve appearances by advocates in judicial proceedings themselves.[61]

Definitions of Unauthorized Practice

Aside from the limited applicability of federal antitrust and constitutional law, the shape and reach of unauthorized practice law is a matter of state regulation.[62] On the whole, state law has been characterized by its broad sweep and imprecise definition.[63] The courts have often reached conclusions that a particular activity is unauthorized practice only after the most superficial examination of the activity, of precedent, and of the rationale for the doctrine. Some decisions take the position that a comprehensible definition is not possible but are nonetheless not induced to reexamine underlying premises and assumptions.[64] Other judges have more thoughtfully observed that many definitions of unauthorized practice are obviously inadequate because they would proscribe almost all areas of commercial and governmental activity.[65] A vital consideration, too often overlooked, is "the natural tendency of all professions to act in their own self interest," which requires that courts "closely scutinize all regulations tending to limit competition in the delivery of legal services to the public." [66]

The position of both the 1969 Code and the 1983 Model Rules is that no uniform definition of unauthorized practice is desirable or necessary because the question is one of local law.[67] Each document, nonetheless, attempts to offer a rationale for the restriction. The Code stresses in EC 3–5 a lawyer's "professional judgment" and "educated ability to relate the general body and philosophy of law to a specific legal problem of a client." Where that special judgment about individual applications is not required, EC 3–5 allows that nonlawyers should be able to engage in certain occupations even if they require "a special knowledge of law in certain areas." [68] The comment to Model Rule 5.5 endorses an apparently similar definition when it states that unauthorized practice restrictions do not prevent a lawyer from providing advice and instruction to nonlawyers who presumably will not work under the lawyer's supervision or direction even if their employment requires knowledge of law. Examples given in the comment are claims adjusters, employees of financial or commercial institutions, social workers, accountants, and persons employed in government agencies.

61 See Comment, Control of Unauthorized Practice of Law: Scope of Inherent Judicial Power, 28 U.Chi.L.Rev. 162 (1960).

62 Attempts by national banks to claim a special position by reason of federal preemption of state law have been rejected by state courts. E.g., State Bar Ass'n v. Connecticut Bank & Trust Co., 145 Conn. 222, 140 A.2d 863 (1959); Green v. Huntington Nat'l Bank, 4 Ohio St.2d 78, 212 N.E.2d 585 (1965)("estate analysis" for bank customers).

63 Numerous scholarly examinations of areas of unauthorized practice have concluded that the reach of doctrine is often unsupported by persuasive reasons. E.g., Christensen, The Unauthorized Practice of Law: Do Good Fences Really Make Good Neighbors—or Even Good Sense?, 1980 Am.B.Found. Research J. 159, 203–12 (analysis of legitimacy of unauthorized practice restrictions indicates that most reasons for restrictions are irrelevant to areas protected); Martin, Professional Responsibility and Probate Practice, 1975 Wisc.L.Rev. 911 (broad definition of practice of law in probate area has discouraged development of narrow lay specialties that could accomplish better and cheaper probate administration).

64 See generally State Bar of Arizona v. Arizona Land Title & Trust Co., 90 Ariz. 76, 366 P.2d 1, 8–9 (1961), modified 91 Ariz. 293, 371 P.2d 1020 (1962).

65 Baron v. City of Los Angeles, 2 Cal.3d 535, 86 Cal. Rptr. 673, 469 P.2d 353, (1970)(lobbying is practice of law in sense that it is one of activities engaged in by lawyers in a representative capacity, but more precise definition required to delineate services that only lawyers may perform); State Bar v. Cramer, 399 Mich. 116, 249 N.W.2d 1, 7 (1976).

66 Florida Bar v. Brumbaugh, 355 So.2d 1186, 1189 (Fla. 1978).

67 ABA Formal Op. 198 (1939), quoted at EC 3–5 n.2; MR 5.5 comment ("The definition of the practice of law is established by law and varies from one jurisdiction to another.").

68 The occupations listed in EC 3–5 are said to ones in which "legal judgment" is not exercised but in which the nonlawyer requires a special knowledge of law. Included are "court clerks, police officers, abstracters, and many governmental employees."

The decisions of courts have employed several definitional starting points,[69] not all of them consistent with one another or with the apparent position of the lawyer codes. Among the most frequently encountered are the professional judgment test, the traditional areas of law practice test, and the incidental legal services test.

The professional judgment test attempts to determine the scope of unauthorized practice functionally, by testing to determine whether the activity in question is one in which a lawyer's presumed special training and skills are relevant.[70] The test can then be applied either on a case-by-case basis or according to categories of activities. Because a case-by-case approach would leave nonlawyers to speculate about whether a particular instance involved unauthorized practice, courts generally create categories of activity that are thought to involve frequent instances of the need for specialized legal training and skill. The test is seriously deficient, however, because many activities of commercial life require the exercise of legal judgment yet are far too numerous and commonly engaged in to warrant treatment as instances of proscribed unauthorized practice. An additional fact, often overlooked by courts, is that some legal skill and knowledge can readily be attained and deployed effectively by nonlawyers. The correct form of the test should inquire whether the matter handled was of such complexity that only a person trained as a lawyer should be permitted to deal with it. Applied without preconceptions, very few functions would fall under the test.

The test that defines law practice by looking to traditional areas of law practice is essentially tautologous, unhelpfully defining the practice of law as that which lawyers do.[71] Because lawyers perform almost every function known in the commercial and governmental realm, such a definition would obviously be too global to be workable. It would also impose costs on the public that would be intolerable.

The incidental legal services test asks whether the activity claimed by a bar association to constitute unauthorized practice is simply an adjunct to a routine in the business or commercial world that is not itself law practice. For example, courts have held that a real estate agent who fills in forms in closing a real estate transaction is not engaged in law practice so long as the form work is a mere incident to the practice of real estate brokering. Courts also insist that no separate fee be charged for the form work. The test is the converse of the test that looks to traditional legal practice. It, too, fits with the underlying theories of unauthorized practice only to the extent that it examines whether the routine of filling out forms involves a serious threat of incompetence to consumers.

Typology of Unauthorized Practice

The proliferation of unauthorized practice situations seems bounded only by limits on the imaginative powers of bar association unauthorized practice committees in creating legal theories and of those who wish to share in the pie of potential legal fees in distinguishing precedent. Sampled here will be only the more important and recurring areas.[72]

Court Appearances. Courts have uniformly held that the clearest affront to the unauthorized practice concept is given by a nonlawyer who appears in a court hearing purporting to

[69] See generally Q.Johnstone & D.Hopson, Lawyers and Their Work 163–79 (1967).

[70] Agran v. Shapiro, 127 Cal.App.2d Supp. 807, 273 P.2d 619 (1954); Gardner v. Conway, 234 Minn. 468, 48 N.W.2d 788, 795–96 (1951)(difficult question of law criterion).

[71] State Bar Ass'n v. Connecticut Bank & Trust Co., 145 Conn. 222, 140 A.2d 863, 870 (1958)(quoting Grievance Comm. v. Payne, 128 Conn. 325, 22 A.2d 623, 626 (1941)): the practice of law is the performance "of any acts . . . in or out of court, commonly understood to be the practice of law."

[72] Several occupations in which unauthorized practice conflicts have arisen are not explicitly treated below. On architects, see, e.g., Q.Johnstone & D.Hopson, Lawyers and Their Work 315–54 (1967). Social workers, accountants, bank officers, trust companies, insurance agents, business and professional consultants of all kinds, professional engineers, ministers, librarians, and others are all affected.

represent another.[73] Courts have uniformly rejected assertions of litigants that their right to self-representation carries with it a corollary right to lay assistance in court (§ 14.4.2). The presence or absence of an undertaking to pay a fee is irrelevant.[74] The rule is not, however, everywhere ironclad. Some few jurisdictions have created exceptions for nonlawyer representation before justice of the peace and similar courts, presumably as a convenience to the poor and to those in rural areas.[75] In all such proceedings, of course, there generally is an appeal de novo to a higher court. Different is the exception that has been followed in some New England states. There a nonlawyer may represent others in litigation in the courts of general jurisdiction but only occasionally and not commonly.[76] The rule is apparently based on the notion of letting litigants make their own choice of advocates but without allowing a professional class of nonlawyer litigators to arise.[77]

It is clearly worth considering whether the judicial world would be very much altered if the rule were that a litigant might be represented by anyone in a proceeding, but that the requirements of procedure, evidence, and other judicial regulations would be applied uniformly. Control over ethical conduct and, if needed, enforcement of educational and skills training requirements could take the form of nonlawyer licensing. The desirability of such a limited license to practice seems particularly compelling in small claims, marriage dissolution, name change, misdemeanor defense, and similar types of low-visibility litigation that often involves persons unable to afford lawyers or in which the amounts at stake do not warrant expenditure for the fees of lawyers. In form it would closely resemble systems that are found in most states that permit law students to represent clients in court under student practice rules.[78] In practice the representation might even become superior to the much-denigrated levels of competence among advocates who currently appear in minor cases as the licensed practitioners acquired experience and expertise in the narrow subject matters that would probably make up their caseloads.

Practice before Administrative Agencies. The apparent orthodoxy among state courts is that a nonlawyer who represents another before an administrative agency is engaged in unauthorized practice of law if the representation involves legal knowledge and skills of

[73] Weber v. Garza, 570 F.2d 511 (5th Cir.1978)(rejecting argument for nonlawyer's appearance as "next friend" of party); United States v. Taylor, 569 F.2d 448 (7th Cir. 1977), cert.denied 435 U.S. 952, 98 S.Ct. 1581, 55 L.Ed.2d 803 (1978)(disbarred lawyer); United States v. Grismore, 546 F.2d 844, 847 (10th Cir.1976)(same disbarred lawyer as in *Taylor*, supra); Vaid v. State, 165 Ga.App. 823, 302 S.E.2d 631 (1983)(criminal conviction for filing petition in bankruptcy court); Bilodeau v. Antal, 123 N.H. 39, 455 A.2d 1037 (1983)(nonlawyer-expert in field of medical malpractice not entitled to appear either as counsel or cocounsel); Stokes v. Village of Wurtsboro, 123 Misc.2d 694, 474 N.Y.S.2d 660 (Sup.Ct.1984)(execution of power of attorney by client does not enlarge powers of nonlawyer to represent in litigation). Some decisions have suggested that a judge can permit representation by a nonlawyer in the judge's discretion. E.g., United States v. Whitesel, 543 F.2d 1176 (6th Cir.1976)(dicta), cert.denied 431 U.S. 967, 97 S.Ct. 2924, 53 L.Ed.2d 1062 (1977).

[74] Ginn v. Farley, 43 Md.App. 229, 403 A.2d 858, 861 (1979); Bilodeau v. Antal, supra; Oregon St. Bar v. Wright, 280 Or. 693, 573 P.2d 283, 292–93 (1977), and authorities cited.

[75] Oregon St. Bar v. Wright, supra, 573 P.2d at 288–89 (Oregon statute construed to permit any person to represent a party in civil or criminal proceeding in justice of peace court); States ex rel. Frieson v. Isner, 285 S.E.2d 641, 654 (W.Va.1981)(statute permits nonlawyers to represent others in magistrate courts casually and not for pay). Some jurisdictions also permit nonlawyer law enforcement officers to prosecute minor offenses in justice courts. E.g., State v. Aberizk, 115 N.H. 535, 345 A.2d 407, 408 (1975); State ex rel. McLeod v. Seaborn, 270 S.C. 696, 244 S.E.2d 317 (1978).

[76] Graustein v. Barry, 315 Mass. 518, 53 N.E.2d 568, 569–70 (1944); In re Unification of New Hampshire Bar, 109 N.H. 260, 248 A.2d 709, 713 (1968). Similar in apparent motivation is a California statute that permits one spouse to represent the other if both are joined as defendants and both appear pro se. West's Ann. Cal.Code Civ.Proc. § 371; cf. Abar v. Rogers, 124 Cal.App.3d 862, 177 Cal.Rptr. 655 (1981)(§ 371 inapplicable to husband and wife who are coplaintiffs).

[77] Cf. Bump v. Barnett, 235 Iowa 308, 16 N.W.2d 579, 582–83 (1944)(statute permitting nonlawyer appearances in small claims court should not be construed to encourage growth of "justice court lawyers" who might pervert purpose of creating a "poor men's court"); State ex rel. Frieson v. Isner, 285 S.E.2d 641, 655 (W.Va.1981).

[78] See § 14.3.4.

advocacy.[79] Some decisions let bar associations play dog in the manger with impecunious litigants who are unlikely to be able to hire lawyers if nonlawyers cannot represent them in administrative proceedings.[80] Statutes or agency rules that have attempted to broaden the power of nonlawyers to represent others in agency proceedings have sometimes been struck down as a violation of the exclusive inherent power of courts to regulate the practice of law.[81] Some courts, however, have given way in part so long as the permission extends to relatively minor matters.[82]

Several state courts have taken the high road of constitutional statesmanship and, refusing to find that the legislature's dealings with proceedings in administrative agencies relates to judicial functions in an important way, have upheld legislation authorizing nonlawyer representation in administrative proceedings.[83] The federal courts have taken the highest road of all and have simply refused to interfere in the way that administrative agencies choose to conduct their proceedings. As a result, many federal administrative proceedings are characterized by nonlawyer representation.[84]

Giving Advice. Courts have sometimes characterized a nonlawyer's practice as unauthorized if it involved giving legal advice.[85] The obvious, and now familiar, difficulty with such a definition is its breadth. For that reason, courts have searched for narrower tests. One factor often accompanying such decisions is the preparation of legal documents in addition to giving advice.[86] Such a

[79] White v. Idaho Forest Industries, 98 Idaho 784, 572 P.2d 887, 891 (1977); People ex rel. Chicago Bar Ass'n v. Goodman, 366 Ill. 346, 8 N.E.2d 941, 111 A.L.R. 1 (1937), cert.denied 302 U.S. 728, 58 S.Ct. 49, 82 L.Ed. 562 (1937); Public Serv. Comm'n v. Hahn Transp., Inc., 253 Md. 571, 253 A.2d 845, 850 (1969); Michigan Hospital Ass'n v. Michigan Employment Security Comm'n, 123 Mich.App. 667, 333 N.W.2d 319, 321 (1983); Clark v. Austin, 340 Mo. 467, 101 S.W.2d 977 (1937); State ex rel. Johnson v. Childe, 147 Neb. 527, 23 N.W.2d 720 (1946); State ex rel. State Bar v. Keller, 16 Wis.2d 377, 114 N.W.2d 796 (1962), modified 21 Wis.2d 100, 123 N.W.2d 905 (1963), cert.denied 377 U.S. 964, 84 S.Ct. 1643, 12 L.Ed.2d 734 (1964). See generally 2 K.Davis, Administrative Law § 12.3, 412–15 (2d ed.1978); Annot., 13 A.L.R.3d 812 (1967). Compare, e.g., Rathburn v. Industrial Comm'n, 39 Colo. 433, 566 P.2d 372, 373–74 (1977)(asking one question of witness in administrative proceeding does not constitute unauthorized practice of law). Courts generally permit nonlawyers to assist others in filling out forms for claims before administrative agencies so long as no actual representation at a contested hearing is involved. E.g., Lukas v. Bar Ass'n of Montgomery Cty., 35 Md.App. 442, 371 A.2d 669 (1977); Goodman v. Beall, 130 Ohio St. 427, 200 N.E. 470 (1936).

[80] For example, the court in West Virginia St. Bar v. Earley, 144 W.Va. 504, 109 S.E.2d 420 (1959), refused to permit a nonlawyer to represent a claimant before the worker compensation commission, despite the fact that most cases before the commission involved claims for temporary disability, in which it would be uneconomic for a claimant to hire a lawyer. The representative whose activities were enjoined in *Earley* was a union agent. It is not clear that the Supreme Court decisions holding that unions and similar advocacy organizations and their members have a constitutional right to form legal services organizations would extend to unauthorized practice. See generally § 16.5.2. Other decisions have refused to find that representation before a worker compensation commission is unauthorized practice. E.g., Eagle Indemnity Co. v. Industrial Accident Comm'n, 217 Cal. 244, 18 P.2d 341 (1933); Goodman v. Beall, 130 Ohio St. 427, 200 N.E. 470 (1936).

[81] Idaho St. Bar Ass'n v. Idaho Pub. Utilities Comm'n, 102 Idaho 672, 637 P.2d 1168 (1981). For a criticism of the rationale and result, see § 2.2.3.

[82] Hunt v. Maricopa Cty. Employees Merit System Comm'n, 127 Ariz. 259, 619 P.2d 1036 (1980); Denver Bar Ass'n v. Public Utilities Comm'n, 154 Colo. 273, 391 P.2d 467, 13 A.L.R.3d 799 (1964); State ex rel. Pearson v. Gould, 437 N.E.2d 41 (Ind.1982)(no unauthorized practice in employee grievance hearing in which nonlawyer commission members conducted proceeding, employee was represented by nonlawyer representative from employees' union, hearings were held during working hours and in offices of employer, and decision of commission was reviewable).

[83] Eagle Indemnity Co. v. Industrial Accident Comm'n, 217 Cal. 244, 18 P.2d 341 (1933); State Bar of Michigan v. Galloway, 124 Mich.App. 271, 335 N.W.2d 475 (1983).

[84] vom Baur, Administrative Agencies and Unauthorized Practice of Law, 48 ABA J. 715, 716–17 (1962); Note, Representation of Clients before Administrative Agencies: Authorized or Unauthorized Practice of Law?, 15 Val.U.L.Rev. 567, 572–73 (1981).

[85] In re Amalgamated Dev. Co., 375 A.2d 494, 499 (D.C. App.1977), cert.denied 434 U.S. 924, 98 S.Ct. 403, 54 L.Ed. 2d 282 (1977)(advising inventors on patentability under federal patent law); Florida Bar v. Mills, 410 So.2d 498 (Fla.1982)(advising prisoners on case law affecting prisoners' rights and appellate procedures); Florida Bar v. Larkin, 298 So.2d 371 (Fla.1974)(retired lawyer, member of bar of Illinois but not of Florida, giving advice and assistance on wills to friends for compensation); People v. Life Science Church, 113 Misc.2d 952, 450 N.Y.S.2d 664 (1982), appeal dismissed 93 A.D.2d 774, 461 N.Y.S.2d 803 (1983).

[86] In re Turner, 355 So.2d 766 (Fla.1978)(advising on and drafting corporate charters, bylaws, pension plans, employment agreements, health plans, and trust agree-

line seems to be drawn in the "kit" cases [87] and to characterize many of the decisions involving estate planning.[88] Yet courts have stopped short of outlawing all document preparation, yielding to common sense and public need by permitting will preparation by a nonlawyer in an emergency, for example.[89]

Courts are more willing to find that advice constituted unauthorized practice if a fee was charged for it.[90] Of course, the advice is equally dangerous, if it is dangerous at all,[91] whether given freely or for a fee. Yet those decisions nonetheless draw a convenient line between commercialized advice giving, which is an activity that predictably would be repeated in order to gain revenue, and, on the other hand, advising that may be the natural product of friendship or other affinities that courts should be loath to restrict. The presence or absence of pecuniary gain is a dividing line that the Supreme Court has also employed in differentiating between protected and unprotected free speech.[92] Clearly, to treat every utterance of legal advice as unauthorized practice would run afoul of expressive and associational rights recognized by the Supreme Court.[93]

Do-It-Yourself Kits and Forms. The persistence of a popular belief that in many situations every person can be his or her own lawyer has led to the recent rise of an industry of publishing and consulting that sells to mass markets do-it-yourself approaches for common legal matters.[94] Unauthorized practice committees have fought the development with typical spirit but seem to be losing the battle. Courts have responded with line-drawing tests that probably do little to stem the sale of those products but effectively prevent the service from being as useful to consumers as it might be. In the process, certifiable folk heroes have been created.[95] The do-it-yourself mechanisms are many: books that contain both forms and informational material that a purchaser-reader might use to fill out the forms; kits of forms, for example, for an uncontested marriage dissolution, that the purchaser might personally fill out after obtaining information about how to fill them out; and various scrivener services in which a nonlawyer fills out forms pursuant to dictation from a customer.

Nonlawyer entrepreneurs have a particularly useful argument in those areas—the First Amendment. As a general proposition, the state may not suppress publications on the ground that they may include legal advice or, if put to use, may create legal consequences. Thus courts have traditionally permitted printers to print forms (often prepared

ments); Committee on Professional Ethics v. Gartin, 272 N.W.2d 485, 487 (Iowa 1978)(preparing income tax returns); In re Estate of Margow, 77 N.J. 316, 390 A.2d 591, 595 (1978)(legal counselling on nuances of amending and drafting a will plus preparation of will).

[87] See infra text at notes 94–98.

[88] See generally Hyrne, Unauthorized Practice in Estate Planning and Administration: A Mild and Temperate Dissent, 24 U.Fla.L.Rev. 647 (1977).

[89] In re Estate of Peterson, 230 Minn. 478, 42 N.W.2d 59 (1950).

[90] Fitchette v. Taylor, 191 Minn. 582, 254 N.W. 910, 94 A.L.R. 356 (1934).

[91] For reasons that have been repeated in this section, it is often simply untrue that a nonlawyer's legal advice is less sound than a lawyer's. Most lawyers would themselves probably admit that a tax accountant's legal advice on a tax matter is better than the advice of the average person admitted to a state's bar. New York, apparently alone among the states, has sensibly by legislation provided for a special and limited license for "legal consultants." See N.Y.Ct.Apps.R., part 521 (McKinney 1981). The practice is limited to persons who have been admitted to practice law in a foreign country and who are available to serve as consultants on questions of the law of the foreign country.

[92] See generally § 14.2.3. See also Rhode, Policing the Professional Monopoly, 34 Stan.L.Rev. 1, 62–70 (1981).

[93] Hopper v. City of Madison, 79 Wis.2d 120, 256 N.W.2d 139, 145 (1977)(activities of nonlawyer employees of tenants union in advising tenants on simple legal matters are protected by First Amendment). See generally § 16.5.2 (associational freedom); § 14.2.3 (commercial speech doctrine); § 14.2.5 (constitutional issues in solicitation).

[94] The do-it-yourself divorce kit movement is extensively analyzed in light of social goals of marriage dissolution law and on the basis of empirical study of actual practices in marriage dissolution in Project, The Unauthorized Practice of Law and Pro Se Divorce: An Empirical Analysis, 86 Yale L.J. 104 (1976). See also, e.g., Note, Divorce Kit Dilemma: Finding the Public Interest, 19 J.Fam.L. 729 (1981).

[95] Newsweek, Aug. 22, 1983, at 69 (Furman); Wall St. J., Sept.3, 1976, at 1, col.1.

by lawyer entrepreneurs) and sell them to both lawyers and the public.[96] The line that many courts have drawn uses the absence of personal advice to demark permissible practices: selling forms or kits is not unauthorized practice so long as they are not accompanied by advice, either in writing or in person, that is personalized in the sense of being directed to the specific problem of a designated or readily identifiable person.[97] The Florida courts have permitted nonlawyers to operate "secretarial services" to fill out forms for no-fault divorces but only if the nonlawyer prepares the forms from written instruction received in advance from the customer and does not give any legal advice or select forms for the customer's use.[98]

Corporate House Counsel Practice. Prohibitions against the practice of law by corporations can be found in the statute books of most states.[99] One thinks of them as miscataloged with materials on unauthorized practice; the prohibition appears to relate instead to a conflict of interest problem.[1] Yet, historically and economically speaking, the catalog is correct. Prohibitions against corporate law practice are a clumsy, but possibly effective, way of eliminating a potential source of competition against lawyers. By force of the prohibition lawyers can forestall attempts to form the capital structures necessary to make law practice a true consumer product for a mass market. It also prevents competition from banks, insurance companies, title insurance companies, and other potential competitors. The prohibition presented a momentary embarrassment when, for tax reasons, it made economic sense for lawyers to practice in the corporate form. That was gotten around by obtaining state legislation permitting lawyers to form "professional corporations" (§ 16.2.4).

The most obvious bite of the prohibition against practice of law by a corporation is that a corporation cannot appear pro se in litigation but must always appear represented by a lawyer who is properly admitted to practice.[2] A similar rule has been applied to

96 Courts have, however, differed over whether the forms can be accompanied by written instructions for their use. Compare, e.g., Florida Bar v. American Legal & Bus. Forms, Inc., 274 So.2d 225 (Fla.1973)(sale of form permissible if not accompanied by instructions for use) (partially overruled in Florida Bar v. Brumbaugh, 355 So. 2d 1186, 1194 (Fla.1978)); Palmer v. Unauthorized Practice Comm., 438 S.W.2d 374 (Tex.Civ.App.1969), with, e.g., State Bar v. Cramer, 399 Mich. 116, 249 N.W.2d 1 (1976) (sale of legal forms with instructions for use not unauthorized practice); Oregon St. Bar v. Gilchrist, 272 Or. 552, 538 P.2d 913 (1975). See generally Annot., 71 A.L.R.3d 1000 (1976).

97 Grievance Committee v. Dacey, 154 Conn. 129, 222 A.2d 339, 22 A.L.R.3d 1092 (1966), appeal dismissed 386 U.S. 683, 87 S.Ct. 1325, 18 L.Ed.2d 404 (1967)(dealer in mutual funds engaged in unauthorized practice by giving to clients booklet that contained forms and instructions for trust arrangement when dealer prepared and supervised execution of trusts by clients); State Bar v. Cramer, 399 Mich. 116, 249 N.W.2d 1, 8–9 (1976)(dicta); New York Cty. Lawyers Ass'n v. Dacey, 21 N.Y.2d 694, 287 N.Y.S.2d 422, 234 N.E.2d 459, (1967), adopting dissenting opinion 28 A.D.2d 161, 171, 283 N.Y.S.2d 984, 998 (1967)(selling "How to Avoid Probate" book with forms and instructions not unauthorized practice); State v. Winder, 42 A.D.2d 1039, 348 N.Y.S.2d 270 (1973)("Divorce Yourself Kit"); People v. Divorce Assoc. & Pub. Ltd., 95 Misc.2d 340, 407 N.Y.S.2d 142 (1978). See also, e.g., Delaware St. Bar Ass'n v. Alexander, 386 A.2d 652, 12 A.L.R.4th 637 (Del.1978), cert.denied 439 U.S. 808, 99 S.Ct. 65, 58 L.Ed. 2d 100 (1978)(action of nonlawyer members of divorce reform group in giving specific legal advice to, and appearing as "next friend" in court hearings for, divorce action parties was unauthorized practice); State ex rel. Schneider v. Hill, 223 Kan. 425, 573 P.2d 1078 (1978) (affirming trial court by equally divided court); In re Thompson, 574 S.W.2d 365 (Mo.1978).

98 Florida Bar v. Furman, 451 So.2d 808 (Fla.1984), appeal dismissed ___ U.S. ___, 105 S.Ct. 316, 83 L.Ed.2d 254 (1984)(sentence to thirty days actual imprisonment for violation of previous order); Florida Bar v. Furman, 376 So.2d 378 (Fla.1979), appeal dismissed 444 U.S. 1061, 100 S.Ct. 1001, 62 L.Ed.2d 744 (1980)(entry of original order enjoining legal advice or form selection for customers of secretarial service); Florida Bar v. Brumbaugh, 355 So.2d 1186 (Fla.1978). See also, e.g., Colorado Bar Ass'n v. Miles, 192 Colo. 294, 557 P.2d 1202 (1976)(not unauthorized practice for public stenographer or scrivener who is nonlawyer to prepare for other persons pleadings and other written instruments). Florida is currently considering a simplified dissolution procedure, proposed by the Florida bar, that would allow parties to obtain a divorce without representation by counsel. See 10 Fam.L.Rptr. 1148 (1984). For later developments in the *Furman* litigation, see infra at n.41.

99 Statutes collected in Unauthorized Practice Handbook 64–71 (J.Fisher & D.Lachmann eds.1972).

1 The conflict of interest origins of the prohibition against the practice of law by a "lay intermediary" are examined in § 8.8.

2 Commercial & R.R. Bank v. Slocomb, 39 U.S. (14 Pet.) 60, 65, 6 L.Ed. 204 (1840); Osborn v. Bank, 22 U.S. (9 Wheat.) 738, 830, 6 L.Ed. 204 (1824)(per Marshall, C.J.)("a corporation . . . can appear only by attorney"); In re

partnerships [3] and to unincorporated associations.[4] Exceptions do exist, although they hardly abound.[5] Some cases support an exception that a corporation in liquidation or bankruptcy may be represented by a nonlawyer principal if requiring representation by a lawyer would effectively bar a hard-pressed corporation from bankruptcy or similar relief.[6]

There is little reason to think that courts will depart from the traditional and rigid rule against corporate pro se litigation, but its support seems surprisingly weak.[7] The common objection that any other result would burden courts with clumsy and time-consuming litigation does not distinguish corporations from individuals, who, of course, can appear pro se regardless of their incompetence in trying cases (§ 14.4.1). Surely there is no basis for thinking that frivolous or paranoiac litigators are any more likely to appear in the corporate form. The objection that nonlawyers are not subject to the disciplinary control that courts can exert over lawyers is similarly beside the point. The objection also neglects to observe that in any court appearance a nonlawyer is subject to control through the contempt power and other measures to prevent abuse (§ 12.1.1). The argument that a corporation can act only through agents is also beside the point unless the nonlawyer who appears is a stranger to the corporation.

Outside the courtroom the practice of law by corporations is also generally proscribed. The general rule permitting natural persons to do their own legal work is again inapplicable to corporations.[8] On occasion, however, some types of nonprofit corporate law practice may be privileged because of constitutional rights. The New Jersey supreme court held, for example, that a nonprofit corporation organized to provide legal services to the poor was entitled to hire lawyers to engage in public interest functions through giving advice and litigating issues relating to state education policy.[9] More broadly, the Supreme Court has held in a series of cases that advocacy organizations and their members have a constitutional right to gather together for the purpose of furthering legal interests (§ 16.5.2).

Real Estate Transactions. Many third parties other than lawyers are involved in real estate transactions—employees of real estate brokers, title insurance companies, and lending institutions also are frequently involved. The prospects for overlapping functions, and thus for competitive and unauthorized practice conflicts, has been richly realized in the field.[10] A century ago, land-transfer systems

Victor Publishers, Inc., 545 F.2d 285, 286 (1st Cir.1976); Mercu-Ray Ind., Inc. v. Bristol-Meyers Co., 392 F.Supp. 16 (S.D.N.Y.1974), affirmed 508 F.2d 837 (2d Cir.1974); Merco Constr. Eng'rs, Inc. v. Municipal Court, 21 Cal.3d 724, 147 Cal.Rptr. 631, 581 P.2d 636 (1978); Oahu Plumbing & Sheet Metal, Ltd. v. Lona Constr., Inc., 60 Hawaii 372, 590 P.2d 570, 572–73 (1979), and authorities cited; Midwest Home Sav. & Loan Ass'n v. Ridgewood Inc., 123 Ill.App.3d 1001, 79 Ill.Dec. 355, 463 N.E.2d 909 (1984); Wicker Enterprises, Inc. v. Dahler, 347 N.W.2d 543 (Minn.1984); Lefkowitz v. Napatco, Inc., 51 N.Y.2d 434, 434 N.Y.S.2d 925, 415 N.E.2d 916 (1980).

3 First Amendment Found. v. Village of Brookfield, 575 F.Supp. 1207 (N.D.Ill.1983).

4 MOVE Organization v. United States Dep't of Justice, 555 F.Supp. 684, 692–93 (E.D.Pa.1983).

5 In New York, for example, a society for the prevention of cruelty to children may appear by a nonlawyer representative when the society is appointed to serve as guardian of a child in a custody dispute. See Rapp v. Rapp, 101 Misc.2d 375, 438 N.Y.S.2d 154 (Fam.Ct.1979).

6 In re Holliday's Tax Services, Inc., 417 F.Supp. 182 (E.D.N.Y.1976), affirmed 614 F.2d 1287 (2d Cir.1979) (bankruptcy); In re Ellis, 53 Hawaii 23, 487 P.2d 286 (1971), cert.denied 405 U.S. 1075, 92 S.Ct. 1500, 31 L.Ed. 2d 809 (1972)(nonlawyer officer of dissolved corporation as trustee for creditors and stockholders).

7 For attempts to justify the rule, see, e.g., Merco Constr. Eng'rs, Inc. v. Municipal Court, 21 Cal.3d 724, 147 Cal.Rptr. 631, 637, 581 P.2d 636, 641 (1978); Oahu Plumbing & Sheet Metal, Ltd. v. Kona Constr., Inc., 60 Hawaii 372, 590 P.2d 570, 573–74 (1979); Austrian, Lance & Stewart, P.C. v. Hastings Properties, Inc., 87 Misc.2d 25, 385 N.Y.S.2d 466 (1976).

8 Kentucky St. Bar Ass'n v. Tussey, 476 S.W.2d 177 (Ky.1972).

9 In re Education Law Center, Inc., 86 N.J. 124, 429 A.2d 1051 (1981).

10 Sometimes the shoe will be on the other foot, such as when a lawyer who is not a licensed real estate broker attempts to collect a realtor's commission for assertedly bringing buyer and seller together. See generally Annot., 23 A.L.R.4th 230 (1983).

were much more primitive than today. Probably most real estate transactions were handled entirely by the parties involved or with a lawyer's help. In recent decades, the lawyer's role in such transactions has been increasingly eroded.[11]

One area of conflict involves the preparation of the documents involved in a real estate transfer—purchase agreements, deeds, mortgages, notes, property descriptions, and the like. Two lines of cases have evolved—the first, formalistic and the second, functional. The first holds that a nonlawyer who prepares any such documents is engaged in unauthorized practice, because filling out a form that has legal consequences involves, in even the most routine case, the exercise of legal knowledge and judgment.[12] Another group of jurisdictions holds that realtors and others may fill out purchase contracts, deeds, and other forms as a routine part of their business so long as there is no separate charge for the service or legal advice given.[13] Those jurisdictions are apparently the majority, although tabulation is complicated by significant differences between jurisdictions.

One of the most remarkable flaps in unauthorized practice history involved land transactions. Trouble began when the Arizona supreme court issued a very restrictive decision that barred real estate agents and title insurance companies from preparing legal documents necessary for residential real estate transactions.[14] Realtors formed an association that obtained over 100,000 signatures, placing on the general election ballot a proposed constitutional amendment to reverse the court's decision. It carried by a margin of over four to one, giving the only plebescite results to date on unauthorized practice.

Controversy also surrounds title insurance companies.[15] Some states permit title insur-

[11] Raushenbush, Who Helps the Home Buyer?, 1979 Ariz.St.L.J. 203. See also the ABA's defense to congressional inquiries into the cost of home closings and the lawyer's role in them. ABA Spec. Comm. on Residential Real Estate Transactions, Report: The Proper Role of the Lawyer in Residential Real Estate Transactions—His Services and His Compensation (approved by ABA House of Delegates, February 17, 1976).

[12] Coffee Cty. Abstract & Title Co. v. State ex rel. Norwood, 445 So.2d 852 (Ala.1983); State Bar of Arizona v. Arizona Land & Title Co., 90 Ariz. 76, 366 P.2d 1 (1961) (title insurance companies and realtors); Illinois St. Bar v. Schafer, 404 Ill. 45, 87 N.E.2d 773 (1949)(realtors); Federal Intermediate Credit Bank v. Kentucky Bar Ass'n, 540 S.W.2d 14 (Ky.1976)(bank employee); Hagan & Van Camp v. Kasler Escrow, Inc., 96 Wn.2d 443, 635 P.2d 730 (1981). The Illinois court later explained that in *Schafer* it had not intended to preclude a realtor from filling in the blanks on a form for a purchase money agreement. See Chicago Bar Ass'n v. Quinlan & Tyson, Inc., 34 Ill.2d 116, 214 N.E.2d 771 (1966).

[13] Pope Cty. Bar Ass'n, Inc. v. Suggs, 274 Ark. 250, 624 S.W.2d 828 (1981); Chicago Bar Ass'n v. Quinlan & Tyson, Inc., 34 Ill.2d 116, 214 N.E.2d 771 (1966); New Jersey St. Bar Ass'n v. New Jersey Ass'n of Realtor Bds., 186 N.J.Super. 391, 452 A.2d 1323 (1982), approved as modified 93 N.J. 470, 461 A.2d 1112, order supplemented 94 N.J. 449, 467 A.2d 577 (1983); Gustafson v. V.C. Taylor & Sons, Inc., 138 Ohio St. 392, 35 N.E.2d 435 (1941); State ex rel. Reynolds v. Dinger, 14 Wis.2d 193, 109 N.W.2d 685 (1961)(after hundred-year history of practice by realtors, bar could point to no harm caused to sellers or purchasers). See also, e.g., Miller v. Vance, 463 N.E.2d 250 (Ind. 1984)(bank employees); Washington St. Bar Ass'n v. Great Western Union Fed. Sav. & Loan Ass'n, 91 Wn.2d 48, 586 P.2d 870 (1978)(same).

Instructive here is the experience in California, where realtors have always filled out documents in connection with residential real estate transactions. Fewer than one purchase in five involve lawyers, yet a vigorous effort to unearth unauthorized practice harms in that state has failed to reveal harm from realtor form-filling. See Comment, The Unauthorized Practice of Law by Laymen and Lay Associations, 54 Calif.L.Rev. 1331, 1343 (1966). See also Weckstein, Limitations on the Right to Counsel: The Unauthorized Practice of Law, 1978 Utah L.Rev. 649, 655; Rhode, Policing the Professional Monopoly, 34 Stan. L.Rev. 1, 82, 88 (1981). Louisiana courts permit "land men" to negotiate transactions in percentage interests in mineral property and prepare the necessary documents. See Crawford v. Deshotels, 351 So.2d 295 (La.App.1977), affirmed 359 So.2d 118 (La.1978). On surveyors, see, e.g., Batchelder v. Mantak, 136 Vt. 456, 392 A.2d 945 (1978) (permissible to do land-record research and prepare set of maps based on research).

[14] Arizona St. Bar v. Arizona Land Title & Trust Co., 90 Ariz. 76, 366 P.2d 1 (1961). See Adler, Are Real Estate Agents Entitled to Practice a Little Law?, 4 Ariz.L.Rev. 188 (1963); Hamner, Title Insurance Companies and the Practice of Law, 14 Baylor L.Rev. 384 (1962); Marks, The Lawyers and the Realtors: Arizona's Experience, 49 ABA J. 139 (1963); Bernstein, The Arizona Realtors and the 1962 Arizona Constitutional Amendment, 29 Unauth. Pract. News 169 (1963).

[15] See generally Q.Johnstone & D.Hopson, Lawyers and Their Work 273–314 (1967)(examination of operation of title insurance companies); Payne, Title Insurance and the Unauthorized Practice of Law Controversy, 53 Minn. L.Rev. 423 (1969). Part of the problem has to do with a vestigial legal doctrine about corporations that practice law. See supra at 840–41 (unauthorized practice by corporations). Many lawyer complaints about title insur-

ance companies to conduct title searches with nonlawyers. Others permit the companies to conduct searches and give title opinions but require that lawyers conduct the searches. And Iowa prohibits them altogether.[16] Commentators agree that in most instances title searching is a routine that does not require a lawyer's skills and training.[17] Title insurance companies are also often found in the midst of transactions preparing documents that are often forms prepared by lawyers with blanks to be filled in. In general, courts have drawn lines here similar to those drawn for realtors.[18]

Insurance Adjusters. Several states have statutes that regulate the function of "public adjusters"—nonlawyers who are empowered, after passing an examination administered by the state's insurance commission, to negotiate claims against insurance companies.[19] The statutes seem to have been intended primarily to permit small insurance companies, or companies with only a few policyholders in an area, to retain independent adjusters to investigate and evaluate claims asserted against insurance companies. But several of the statutes are broad enough to permit an adjuster to represent an insured in presenting a claim against an insurance company.

The question is whether an adjuster in either capacity is engaging in unauthorized practice. On the whole, courts have been relatively unconcerned about unauthorized practice with respect to an adjuster's work for an insurance company if it consists of investigating the facts of a loss, evaluating the value of claims, recommending a value to the insurance company for settlement of a claim (at least if liability is not contested), and filling out forms for releases and the like.[20] Obviously, paternalism would be carried to ludicrous extremes if insurance companies were denied the power to make their own decisions about whether they wished to be served by lawyers or nonlawyers in carrying out their own functions and furthering their own interests. With respect to possible unethical conduct that harms third parties, that, again, can be more precisely regulated. Courts have generally refused to permit insurance adjusters to represent the public in filing insurance claims against insurers, either on the ground that a statute permitting such practice is unconstitutional [21] or that the statute should be interpreted as restricted by the traditional concept of unauthorized practice,[22] or have

ance have to do with alleged deceptions practiced when the companies exclude from coverage the most likely causes of title defects. See Balbach, Title Assurance: A New Approach to Unauthorized Practice, 41 Notre Dame Law. 192 (1965). As with similar unauthorized practice complaints, the matter could be handled straightforwardly as consumer fraud or a matter of insurance regulation instead of outlawing all title insurance.

16 Chicago Title Ins. Co. v. Huff, 256 N.W.2d 17 (Iowa 1977).

17 Whitman, Home Transfer Costs: An Economic and Legal Analysis, 62 Geo.L.J. 1311, 1334 (1974)("the use of legally trained professionals to perform . . . routine tasks constitutes an enormous waste of skill and causes increased overall costs to parties."). See also, e.g., Brossman & Rosenberg, Title Companies and the Unauthorized Practice Rules: The Exclusive Domain Reexamined, 83 Dick.L.Rev. 437, 468 (1978); Payne, Title Insurance and the Unauthorized Practice of Law Controversy, 53 Minn. L.Rev. 423 (1969).

18 State Bar v. Guardian Abstract & Title Co., 91 N.M. 434, 575 P.2d 943 (1978)(may not give legal advice or use legal skills to fill in forms but may fill in blanks if ordinary citizen in exercise of common sense could provide largely factual detail).

19 See generally Annot., 29 A.L.R.4th 1156 (1984). For a list of jurisdictions, see Professional Adjusters, Inc. v. Tandon, 433 N.E.2d 779, 787, 29 A.L.R.4th 1144 (Ind. 1982)(dissenting opinion).

20 Wilkey v. State, 244 Ala. 568, 14 So.2d 536, 151 A.L.R. 765 (1943), cert.denied 320 U.S. 787, 64 S.Ct. 195, 88 L.Ed. 473 (1943); Willhite v. Marlow Adjustment, Inc., 623 S.W.2d 254, 261 (Mo.App.1981); State ex rel. Junior Ass'n of Milwaukee Bar v. Rice, 236 Wis. 38, 294 N.W. 550 (1940). Courts have drawn the line at giving legal advice to the company, such as advice about a claim that the company might have or about the value of contested claims. E.g., Wilkey v. State, supra (legal advice to insurance company and drafting document regarding subrogation claims as unauthorized practice); State ex rel. Junior Ass'n of Milwaukee Bar v. Rice, supra (same, but with respect to claims directly against company).

21 Professional Adjusters, Inc. v. Tandon, 433 N.E.2d 779, 29 A.L.R.4th 1144 (Ind.1982)(statute permitting public adjusters to represent public, and thus engage in unauthorized practice, unconstitutional under doctrine of inherent powers). For a critique of the use of the inherent powers doctrine in this area, see supra at 834–35.

22 Dauphin Cty. Bar Ass'n v. Mazzacaro, 465 Pa. 545, 351 A.2d 229 (1976), and authorities cited; Finchette v.

been restrictive in their interpretation of adjuster statutes.[23]

Collection Agencies. A good bit of the business of collecting accounts receivable and debts has generally been gathered into the arms of collection agencies. They are often required to be licensed by state law and are regulated by state and federal law with respect to abusive collection practices.[24] The ultimate power to collect debts is through suit and execution. In some states, collection agencies are denied the legal right to buy debts for collection under real party in interest laws that restrict such assignments.[25] But in other states suits by assignees for collection can be brought by them in their own name with lawyers retained by them.[26]

In general, collection agencies are like any other business enterprise with respect to unauthorized practice.[27] In most states they may not file suits through nonlawyer employees.[28] The states generally agree, however, that contacting debtors directly to collect debts and negotiating with debtors to adjust a bill or schedule its payment is not unauthorized practice.[29] What other steps short of filing suit might constitute law practice vary by state.[30] Some states hold that a threat to file suit made by a nonlawyer collection agency employee constitutes unlawful law practice because a determination whether to file suit requires a determination of the elements of a cause of action.[31] The states are divided on the question whether a collection agency may forward an uncollected claim to a lawyer of its own choice in order to have a suit filed on it if the creditor-customer has agreed to this in advance.[32] It is also unauthorized practice for a collection agency to hire lawyers as its own employees for the purpose of taking legal action.[33]

Taylor, 191 Minn. 582, 254 N.W. 910, 94 A.L.R. 356 (1934). For a critical examination of the *Mazzacaro* result and a broad critique of traditional unauthorized practice rules, see Hunter & Klonoff, A Dialogue on the Unauthorized Practice of Law, 25 Vill.L.Rev. 6 (1979).

[23] In New York, for example, the statute has been interpreted to permit public adjusting only of fire insurance losses, and not those relating to flood, burglary, or other losses. See Gross v. Reliance Ins. Co., 119 Misc.2d 270, 462 N.Y.S.2d 776 (Sup.Ct.1983).

[24] See generally Fair Debt Collection Practices Act, P.L. 95–109, 95th Cong., 1st Sess. (1977), amending Consumer Credit Protection Act, 15 U.S.C.A. §§ 1601 et seq. Lawyers have also been restricted in the use of such tactics as mass mailings of collection letters on the lawyers' letterheads. See ABA Informal Op. 1368 (1976).

[25] Nelson v. Smith, 107 Utah 382, 154 P.2d 634, 157 A.L.R. 512 (1944); State ex rel. St. Bar v. Bonded Collections, Inc., 36 Wis.2d 643, 154 N.W.2d 250 (1967). Some states that have such real party in interest laws treat their violation by collection agencies as unauthorized practice. E.g., State ex rel. Norvell v. Credit Bureau of Albuquerque, 85 N.M. 521, 514 P.2d 40 (1973).

[26] Cruz v. Lusk Collection Agency, 119 Ariz. 356, 580 P.2d 1210 (App.1978); Le Doux v. Credit Research Corp., 52 Cal.App.3d 451, 125 Cal.Rptr. 166 (1975); Thibodeaux v. Creditors Serv., Inc., 191 Colo. 215, 551 P.2d 714 (1976). The court in Messmer v. Carter, 282 Or. 323, 578 P.2d 788 (1978), raised but did not pass upon the question whether the inherent powers doctrine voided a state statute that permitted collection agencies to sue in their own name.

[27] See generally Note, Collection Agencies and the Unauthorized Practice of Law, 1 J.Leg.Prof. 155 (1976).

[28] J.H. Marshall & Assoc., Inc. v. Burleson, 313 A.2d 587 (D.C.App.1973); Bump v. Barnett, 235 Iowa 308, 16 N.W.2d 579 (1944); State ex rel. Frieson v. Isner, 285 S.E. 2d 641 (W.Va.1981). But see United Securities Corp. v. Pantex Pressing Mach., 98 Colo. 79, 53 P.2d 653 (1935) (nonlawyer collection agent could file suit in justice court).

[29] State ex rel. Porter v. Alabama Ass'n of Credit Executives, 338 So.2d 812, 814 (Ala.1976). See generally Annot., 27 A.L.R.3d 1152 (1969).

[30] Compare Patterson v. Professional Adjustment Serv., Inc., 544 S.W.2d 617 (Tenn.App.1976)(permissible for nonlawyer agents to fill out blanks supplied by court clerk's office to obtain execution by sheriff).

[31] State ex rel. Porter v. Alabama Ass'n of Credit Executives, 338 So.2d 812, 814 (Ala.1976); In re Lyon, 301 Mass. 30, 16 N.E.2d 74, 76 (1938).

[32] Compare, e.g., State ex rel. Porter v. Dun & Bradstreet, Inc., 352 F.Supp. 1226 (N.D.Ala.1972), aff'd mem. 472 F.2d 1049 (5th Cir.1973)(not unauthorized practice); State ex rel. Porter v. Alabama Ass'n of Credit Executives, supra, 338 So.2d at 815 (quoting from ABA "statement of principles" treaty with committee of debt collection agencies, which also deals with such matters as forwarding claims for suit to lawyers who own interests in the collection agency), with, e.g., State ex rel. State Bar v. Bonded Collections, Inc., 36 Wis. 643, 154 N.W.2d 250, 27 A.L.R.3d 1138 (1967)(collection agency that, with consent of creditor, hired lawyer and directed lawyer's activities in collection suit was engaged in unauthorized practice by serving in place of client).

[33] State ex rel. Freebourn v. Merchants' Credit Service, 104 Mont. 76, 66 P.2d 337 (1937); State v. James Snaford Agency, 167 Tenn. 339, 69 S.W.2d 895 (1934).

Remedies for Unauthorized Practice

Most jurisdictions make available an array of remedies to combat unauthorized practice, although most of them are enforced only by bar association unauthorized practice committees.[34] Most jurisdictions have enacted statutes that make unauthorized practice a minor criminal offense, but they have produced few actual criminal prosecutions.[35] Unauthorized practice committees in most states are empowered to issue warnings and opinions. Bar associations are commonly recognized as having standing as an aggrieved party [36] to bring civil actions against alleged violators, although in practice unauthorized practice committees determine whether to bring suit. Suits in fact are few.[37] Bar groups prefer to rely upon negotiated settlements, and most targets of investigations are quick to recede in the face of bar pressure.

When litigation is resorted to, the remedy most often sought is an injunction, although several others are also available.[38] Those have three significant advantages for enforcement purposes. First, in almost all states juries do not sit in injunction actions; thus the probable sympathy of nonlawyers for some unauthorized practitioners is made irrelevant. Second, the injunction decree can itself specify the conduct that the respondent is required to avoid, thus mooting possible constitutional objections to unauthorized practice statutes and rules because of their vagueness.[39] Third, the sanction of contempt [40] can threaten both civil and criminal

[34] For a thorough examination of the actual enforcement practices in each state, see Rhode, Policing the Professional Monopoly, 34 Stan.L.Rev. 1, 11–44 (1981).

[35] See misdemeanor statutes of thirty-seven jurisdictions listed in Rhode, Policing the Professional Monopoly, 34 Stan.L.Rev. 1, 11 n.39 (1981). See also Unauthorized Practice Handbook 312 et seq. (J.Fisher & D.Lachmann eds.1972). Because unauthorized practice is a crime in most states, a defendant in most bar association unauthorized practice suits may be able to assert a privilege against self-incrimination in the civil suit. E.g., Minnesota St. Bar Ass'n v. Divorce Assistance Ass'n, 311 Minn. 276, 248 N.W.2d 733, 739 (1976).

[36] A person defending against a claim of another who, although now represented by competent counsel, was earlier represented by an assertedly unauthorized practitioner should not be able to defend on that ground unless it can be shown that the asserted unauthorized practice violation caused injury to the complaining party. E.g., Reliable Collection Agency, Inc. v. Cole, 59 Hawaii 503, 584 P.2d 107, 7 A.L.R.4th 1136 (1978). The cases are divided on the question whether the fact that a party is represented in the litigation itself by an unauthorized practitioner should lead to dismissal of the action or other relief beyond simply striking the pleadings and other documents submitted by the unauthorized representative. Compare, e.g., Guajardo v. Luna, 432 F.2d 1324 (5th Cir.1970)(dismissal of civil suit brought by state prisoner in behalf of his father); Davis v. University of Arkansas Medical Center & Collection Agency, Inc., 262 Ark. 587, 559 S.W.2d 159 (1977), with, e.g., Owens v. Bank of Brewton, 53 Ala.App. 529, 302 So.2d 114 (1974)(motion denied to dismiss appeal on ground that appealing party's lawyer was not duly admitted).

[37] Rhode, supra, 34 Stan.L.Rev. at 56.

[38] Other remedies against unauthorized practitioners include declaratory relief, e.g., Blodinger v. Broker's Title, Inc., 224 Va. 201, 294 S.E.2d 876 (1982)(declaratory judgment action by lawyers against title insurance company that employed nonlawyers in title searches, on ground that title insurance company had claimed that lawyer's refusal to deal was antitrust violation); denial of attorney fees under arrangements that otherwise call for fee shifting, e.g., O'Neil Lumber Co. v. Nickelodean Cos., ___ Mont. ___, 617 P.2d 1291 (1980); a requirement that fees already collected be refunded, e.g., State v. Midland Equities, Inc., 117 Misc.2d 203, 458 N.Y.S.2d 126 (1982); and precluding from serving as executor under a will a person who had engaged in unauthorized practice in drafting it, e.g., In re Estate of Margow, 77 N.J. 316, 390 A.2d 591 (1978). Administrative remedies include suspending the license of a real estate agent or other licensed professional because of unauthorized law practice in that profession. E.g., Duncan & Hill Realty, Inc. v. Department of State, 62 A.D.2d 690, 405 N.Y.S.2d 339 (1978), appeal denied 45 N.Y.2d 709, 409 N.Y.S.2d 1027, 381 N.E.2d 615 (1978). See generally Note, Remedies Available to Combat the Unauthorized Practice of Law, 62 Col.L.Rev. 501 (1962).

[39] Dauphin Cty. Bar Ass'n v. Mazzacaro, 465 Pa. 545, 351 A.2d 229 (1976). The Supreme Court has dismissed an appeal for want of a substantial federal question in a case that raised the question whether a state's unauthorized practice statute was unconstitutional. See Hackin v. Arizona, 389 U.S. 143, 88 S.Ct. 325, 19 L.Ed.2d 347 (1967)(summary order), dismissing appeal from 102 Ariz. 218, 427 P.2d 910 (1967). See also, e.g., Wright v. Lane Cty. Dist. Court, 647 F.2d 940 (9th Cir.1981).

[40] In modern cases, punishment for contempt most often is preceded by a proceeding in which an injunction is issued; the contempt citation is for alleged violation of the injunctive order. But courts have also held that unauthorized practice may be punished directly by contempt sanctions without the necessity of an intervening injunctive order. E.g., United States v. Marthaler, 571 F.2d 1104 (9th Cir.1978); Unauthorized Practice of Law Committee v. Grimes, 654 P.2d 822 (Colo.1982); Florida Bar v. Walzak, 380 So.2d 428 (Fla.1980)(nonlawyer who falsely held himself out to be lawyer and collected legal fees from several persons permanently enjoined and sen-

retribution and thus presents a powerful incentive for an unauthorized practitioner to capitulate.[41]

WESTLAW REFERENCES

unauthorized +1 practice /2 law legal /s defin! mean***

unauthorized +1 practice /2 law legal /p "professional judgment" train*** skill knowledge

secretar! (divorce /4 form kit) scrivener draftsmen draftsperson /s non-lawyer /p practice /5 law legal

---

§ 15.1.4 Lawyers and Unauthorized Practice

Unauthorized Practice by Lawyers

Admission to the bar does not immunize a lawyer from a charge of unauthorized practice. Lawyers are under two sets of obligations that enlist them as allies in the campaign against unauthorized practice. First, they are not to assist nonlawyers in activities that are unauthorized practice. Second, lawyers themselves are not to engage in the several kinds of unauthorized practice in which lawyers, acting alone, can engage.

Assisting Unauthorized Practitioners

The lawyer codes prohibit a lawyer from aiding a nonlawyer in unauthorized practice.[42] For example, lawyers have been disciplined for assisting unauthorized practice by suspended or disbarred lawyers,[43] by judges who were disqualified from practicing law,[44] by debt collectors by lending them the lawyer's name,[45] by entrepreneurs who were selling purported tax-saving trusts,[46] and by banks that were engaged in unauthorized legal services to bank customers.[47] The specific conduct that is forbidden varies with the law of each jurisdiction. Neither the Code nor the Model Rules attempt to define unauthorized practice except by reference to the law of the states.[48] Because of the marked lack of precision in the definition of unauthorized practice, it would be intolerable to hold a lawyer to a prophet's standard of clairvoyance about unclear areas of practice in a jurisdiction.[49] While ordinarily a violation of the prohibition against aiding unauthorized practice would be handled as a lawyer disciplinary matter within the exclusive jurisdiction of the state's lawyer disciplinary agency, authority also exists for permitting lower courts to entertain suits by bar associations to enjoin the unauthorized practice of law by a lawyer.[50]

tenced to five months' imprisonment); In re Kading, 74 Wis.2d 405, 246 N.W.2d 903, 906 (1976)(dicta).

41 In one of the few cases in recent decades in which an unauthorized practitioner was imprisoned for violation of a court order, the governor signed a pardon order long before the sentence was served. For the adjudication of contempt, see Florida Bar v. Furman, 451 So.2d 808 (Fla. 1984), appeal dismissed ___ U.S. ___, 105 S.Ct. 316, 83 L.Ed.2d 254 (1984).

42 DR 3–101(A)("A lawyer shall not aid a non-lawyer in the unauthorized practice of law."); MR 5.5(b)("A lawyer shall not . . . (b) assist a person who is not a member of the bar in the performance of activity that constitutes the unauthorized practice of law.").

43 In re Schelly, 94 Ill.2d 234, 68 Ill.Dec. 502, 446 N.E.2d 236 (1983); In re Bailey, 97 N.M. 88, 637 P.2d 38 (1981); In re Riely, 101 A.D.2d 351, 475 N.Y.S.2d 473 (1984). See also, e.g., Crawford v. State Bar, 54 Cal.2d 659, 7 Cal.Rptr. 746, 355 P.2d 490 (1960); In re Lacy, 234 Mo.App. 71, 112 S.W.2d 594 (1937); In re Lerner, 270 App.Div. 602, 61 N.Y.S.2d 661 (1946).

44 In re Bonafield, 75 N.J. 490, 383 A.2d 1143, 1144–45 (1978).

45 Kentucky Bar Ass'n v. Tiller, 641 S.W.2d 421 (Ky. 1982); In re DeVinny, 255 N.W.2d 832 (Minn.1977).

46 People ex rel. MacFarlane v. Boyls, 197 Colo. 242, 591 P.2d 1315 (1979).

47 Thompson v. Chemical Bank, 84 Misc.2d 721, 375 N.Y.S.2d 729, 736 (N.Y.Cty.Civ.Ct.1975).

48 EC 3–5; MR 5.5 comment.

49 In re Depew, 98 Idaho 215, 560 P.2d 886, 890 (1977) (when evidence left some doubt whether conduct constituted unauthorized practice, hearing committee properly found no disciplinary action was warranted). Somewhat less obviously wrong is the statement in Kentucky Bar Ass'n v. Tiller, 641 S.W.2d 421, 422 (Ky.1982), that a lawyer can violate DR 3–101(A) by negligent conduct and thus that lack of specific knowledge that the lawyer's nonlawyer associates were engaged in unauthorized practice was no defense.

50 Cuyahoga Cty. Bar Ass'n v. Gold Shield, Inc., 52 Ohio Misc. 105, 369 N.E.2d 1232 (Comm.Pleas 1975)(operation of nonqualifying group legal services corporation for profit).

An area of interest is the scope of a lawyer's responsibility for unauthorized practice by paralegals, clerks, secretaries, investigators, or other employees of the lawyer.[51] In general, a lawyer must exercise close supervisory control over nonlawyer employees to assure that they do not engage in unauthorized practice.[52] The obscurity of many unauthorized practice rules can make the practice of paraprofessionals and other nonlawyer employees hazardous and needlessly prevent a useful and economical service from being performed.[53] Particularly in the case of highly trained and competent paralegals, the arguments in favor of more permissive rules on unauthorized practice and less strict rules on lawyer supervision are compelling.[54]

Multijurisdictional Practice

According to the lawyer codes, a lawyer admitted in one jurisdiction violates the lawyer code of that jurisdiction by practicing law in another jurisdiction in which the lawyer is not admitted.[55] That rule probably extends as far as to permit a state to discipline a lawyer for unauthorized practice before a federal court or agency, at least if there is no pretense that the lawyer was authorized by federal law to practice there.[56] Apparently the theory of regulating such extraterritorial conduct at all is that it says something troubling about the lawyer's attitudes toward legality. It is difficult to imagine any other ground on which the original jurisdiction should be concerned about practice elsewhere if the only negative aspect of it is failure to comply with another jurisdiction's registration or admission rules.[57]

Neither lawyer code says anything about the reverse situation—whether a lawyer admitted only in a distant jurisdiction may be disciplined by a jurisdiction in which the lawyer is not admitted but in which the lawyer nonetheless practices law. The lawyer cannot be disciplined, a result that is anamolous only on its surface. The reason has to do with the structure of discipline: only lawyers admitted to practice in a jurisdiction are subject to discipline there. Thus, by description, the lawyer here is beyond the disciplinary reach of the offended jurisdiction.[58] But courts have held that a lawyer who practices within a jurisdiction without admission is subject to other sanctions, such as injunctive or declaratory relief[59] or forfeiture of any fee for services unlawfully rendered there.[60]

[51] See generally People v. Alexander, 53 Ill.App.2d 299, 202 N.E.2d 841, 13 A.L.R.3d 1132 (1964)(lawyer's clerk who, in response to trial judge's request, prepared order showing mistrial, and who then appeared before court to inform court of employer-lawyer's inability to attend hearing not engaged in unauthorized practice).

[52] § 16.3.1 at 895.

[53] Comment, Legal Paraprofessionals and Unauthorized Practice, 8 Harv.C.R.-C.L.L.Rev. 104, 117–18 (1973).

[54] 69 ABA J. 1812 (1983)(local bar association policy permitting paralegals to handle real estate closings with lawyer-drafted checklist but without lawyer supervision).

[55] In one of the few discipline cases, the charge was apparently not contested. In re Larson, 324 N.W.2d 656 (Minn.1982)(representing client in neighboring state in which lawyer was not admitted).

[56] Florida Bar v. Penn, 421 So.2d 497, 501 (Fla.1982). A state has no power, however, to declare that practice before a federal agency is unauthorized if it is warranted by federal law or regulations, even if in conflict with state unauthorized practice rules. See § 15.2.5. Occasionally, however. local lawyers have plainly interfered with federal programs of providing legal services to military personnel and their dependents through the invocation of unauthorized practice rules for reasons of economic self-interest. See Marks, Military Lawyers, Civilian Courts, and the Organized Bar: A Case Study of the Unauthorized Practice Dilemma, 56 Mil.L.Rev. 1 (1972).

[57] Practice elsewhere involving conduct that violates another specific provision of the lawyer code has been held to be a basis for discipline in the lawyer's home jurisdiction. See § 3.3.4 at 97.

[58] A court has held that it doubted whether a lawyer suspended in jurisdiction A, but not in jurisdiction B, had committed unauthorized practice by giving advice, in his office in A, to a client about a matter that would be filed in the courts of jurisdiction B. At the time, the lawyer was in the legitimate process of closing his office in jurisdiction A because of the suspension there. Attorney Grievance Comm'n v. Willcher, 287 Md. 74, 411 A.2d 83 (1980)(under DR 3–101). But cf. Ark.Stat. § 25–201 (unlawful for lawyer to practice law if suspended in any state).

[59] See supra at 845–46; infra at 867–68.

[60] Lozoff v. Shore Heights, Ltd., 66 Ill.2d 398, 6 Ill.Dec. 225, 362 N.E.2d 1047 (1977)(Wisconsin-admitted lawyer who practiced law in Illinois in behalf of Illinois-based client by negotiating in behalf of client for real estate transaction in Illinois).

A lawyer admitted in one state can often obtain permission to practice in another state (§ 15.4.3). Often the permitted practice requires association with local counsel. Presumably local counsel violates the rule against aiding unauthorized practice if, to that lawyer's knowledge, the requirements for in-state practice have not been satisfied by the out-of-state lawyer.

Suspended or Disbarred Lawyers

Practice of law by a suspended lawyer is unauthorized practice and can be dealt with in all of the procedural ways available to deal with nonlawyer unauthorized practice.[61] In addition, unauthorized practice may be grounds for imposing additional discipline,[62] rejecting a petition for reinstatement,[63] or holding the lawyer in contempt of the order of suspension or disbarment.[64] In general, a suspended lawyer has no greater power to practice law than a nonlawyer, and the same conduct constitutes unlawful practice for both.[65] Thus, as is true for nonlawyers as well, the right to litigate pro se does not include the right of a suspended lawyer to litigate in behalf of anyone else, even the lawyer's spouse, as a coparty.[66] As is also true in unauthorized practice law, so here a suspended lawyer who merely holds himself or herself out as a lawyer[67] or gives legal advice without charging a fee[68] engages in unauthorized practice.

Some decisions have intimated that the practice of law from which a suspended lawyer is barred may include some activities and services that are legitimately performed by nonlawyers if they are also customarily performed by lawyers.[69] But suspension or disbarment does not by itself preclude a lawyer from continuing to practice in another jurisdiction in which the lawyer as yet remains licensed to practice.[70]

[61] People ex rel. MacFarlane v. Howard, 612 P.2d 1081 (Colo.1977)(disbarred lawyer enjoined from appearing before courts or administrative agencies in purported appearance *in propria persona* in behalf of land trust or any similar trust of which disbarred lawyer may claim to be trustee); Florida Bar v. Kaiser, 397 So.2d 1132 (Fla.1981) (injunction against New York-admitted lawyer holding self out as lawyer in Florida); State v. Bucci, ___ R.I. ___, 430 A.2d 746 (1981)(criminal conviction for unauthorized practice while under suspension), ___ R.I. ___, 442 A.2d 865 (1982)(disbarment for conviction).

[62] People v. Belfor, 200 Colo. 44, 611 P.2d 979 (1980) (practice of law while under suspension violates DR 3–101(B); In re Depew, 98 Idaho 215, 560 P.2d 886 (1977) (along with other violations, practice of law by filing complaint for client while under suspension violated DR 1–102(A)(4), (5) and warranted disbarment); State v. Schumacher, 214 Kan. 1, 519 P.2d 1116 (1974)(suspended lawyer held in contempt and suspended indefinitely); In re Allper, 94 Wn.2d 456, 617 P.2d 982, 991–92 (1980) (disbarment for, among other offenses, continuing to practice following suspension).

[63] In re Robeson, 575 P.2d 771 (Alaska 1978); In re Christianson, 215 N.W.2d 920 (N.D.1974).

[64] In re Boswell, 148 Ga.App. 519, 251 S.E.2d 596 (1978); In re Spar, 100 A.D.2d 71, 473 N.Y.S.2d 192 (1984).

[65] Farnham v. State Bar, 17 Cal.3d 605, 131 Cal.Rptr. 661, 665, 552 P.2d 445, 449 (1976)(legal advice and drafting legal documents); In re Eisenberg, 96 Wis.2d 342, 291 N.W.2d 565 (1980)(unauthorized practice by appearing before administrative agency for corporation of which suspended lawyer was president and sole shareholder). See generally § 3.5.4, at 130–31.

[66] Tardiff v. State Bar, 27 Cal.3d 395, 165 Cal.Rptr. 829, 612 P.2d 919 (1980).

[67] In re Caldwell, 15 Cal.3d 762, 125 Cal.Rptr. 889, 543 P.2d 257 (1975); Florida Bar v. Kaiser, 397 So.2d 1132 (Fla.1981); In re Peterson, 274 N.W.2d 922, 926 (Minn. 1979); In re Teplin, 82 A.2d 296, 441 N.Y.S.2d 463 (1981).

[68] State v. Bucci, ___ R.I. ___, 430 A.2d 746, 748–49 (1981).

[69] In re Robson, 575 P.2d 771, 781 (Alaska 1978)(because of prior recognition as lawyer, suspended lawyer must be particularly prudent in avoiding appearance of holding self out as lawyer); State v. Butterfield, 172 Neb. 645, 111 N.W.2d 543 (1961); In re Esler, 275 S.C. 400, 272 S.E.2d 32 (1980)(preparing, executing, and filing deed when not under direct supervision of lawyer and final work product was not subject to approval of licensed lawyer); Ia. S.Ct.R., Rule 123.5(a), as amended 1977 ("Any attorney suspended pursuant to this rule shall refrain, during such suspension, from all facets of the ordinary law practice including but not limited to the examination of abstracts, consummation of real estate transactions, preparation of legal briefs, deeds, buy and sell agreements, contracts, wills and tax returns."). See generally Annot., 87 A.L.R.3d 279 (1978).

[70] Kentucky Bar Ass'n v. Signer, 533 S.W.2d 534, 536 (Ky.1976), appeal after remand 558 S.W.2d 582 (Ky.1977) (per curiam); In re Weiner, 530 S.W.2d 222, 224, 81 A.L.R.3d 1272 (Mo.1975). See also Employees' Retirement System v. Waldron, 285 Md. 175, 401 A.2d 172, 177 (1979)(retired judge who, by Maryland statute, was disqualified from practicing law while continuing to receive retirement benefits not thereby disabled from practicing law in another jurisdiction where authorized to practice

Occupationally Disqualified Lawyers

Every jurisdiction disqualifies from the practice of law some lawyers whose present employment is thought to be inconsistent with representing private-practice clients. Thus it is commonly required that judges, court clerks, law enforcement agents, prosecutors, and government lawyers not engage in private law practice.[71] The lawyer codes prohibit a lawyer from practicing law in a jurisdiction in violation of the "regulations" of the legal profession in that jurisdiction.[72] The quoted language refers to statutes and the common law of the jurisdiction. Thus a judge [73] or government lawyer [74] who practices law in violation of a statute violates the lawyer code.

WESTLAW REFERENCES

d.r. +1 3–101(a)

"unauthorized practice" /s paralegal "law clerk"

§ 15.2 BAR ADMISSION REQUIREMENTS

§ 15.2.1 Bar Admission: General

Interconnection with Unauthorized Practice

The general pattern in the United States is that tasks that are held to constitute the practice of law may, under the law of unauthorized practice (§ 15.1), be undertaken only by a licensed lawyer. Licensure through admission to the bar is thus the process by which a person today becomes entitled to engage in what otherwise would be unauthorized practice. The law was not always that way,[75] but since the beginning of this century the barriers to admission to practice have been raised along with the barriers against unauthorized practice.

As with other occupational certification processes, bar admission consists of a long series of high hurdles that purport to assure that successful applicants have the ability and character necessary for competent and effective law practice. The major hurdles that have traditionally existed define minimum standards for the bar applicant's education (both undergraduate and law schooling), age (twenty-one or older), citizenship,[76] and local residence. Beyond those hurdles, an applicant must successfully deal with a bar examination [77] and character review (§ 15.3) and take a prescribed oath.[78]

A state's decision whether or not to admit an applicant to law practice has obvious importance to the applicant. A refusal to admit typically means that three or more years of educational costs and potential income foregone during law school have been largely lost. An unsuccessful applicant is denied the potential earning power available to licensed law-

there by that jurisdiction's laws). On reciprocal discipline, see § 3.4.6.

71 See generally Unauthorized Practice Handbook 36–58 (J.Fisher & D.Lachmann eds.1972). In the case of judges of courts of limited jurisdiction, court clerks, registers of deeds, coroners, and the like, the prohibition often only covers the geographical subdivision of the state in which the person is an official.

72 DR 3–101(B)("A lawyer shall not practice law in a jurisdiction where to do so would be in violation of regulations of the profession in that jurisdiction."); MR 5.5(a)("A lawyer shall not . . . (a) practice law in a jurisdiction where doing so violates the regulation of the legal profession in that jurisdiction."). The plural *regulations* in the Code and the singular *regulation* in the Model Rules seem to have the same meaning.

73 In re Bonafield, 75 N.J. 490, 383 A.2d 1143 (1978) (lawyer who practiced law while serving as judge of compensation commission, in violation of statute, disciplined for violation of DR 3–101(B)).

74 Louisiana St. Bar Ass'n v. Mitchell, 375 So.2d 1350 (La.1979)(assistant district attorney).

75 On the law in Indiana and several other states that permitted any person to practice law, see § 15.1.1, at 824–25.

76 But see In re Griffiths, 413 U.S. 717, 93 S.Ct. 2851, 37 L.Ed.2d 910 (1973)(state bar admission requirement of U.S. citizenship unconstitutional).

77 See § 5.3.

78 On the constitutional problems of lawyer admission oaths that require expressions of political or other beliefs, see § 12.2.3. Some state examining committees continue to press the matter of assuring that applicants foreswear false ideologies. E.g., Pushinsky v. West Virginia Bd. of Bar Examiners, 266 S.E.2d 444 (W.Va.1980)(striking down oath on advocacy of overthrow and knowing membership in overthrow-advocacy organization).

yers, which is higher than that of many other occupational groups. Bar admission for many applicants is also the gateway to enhancement of social prestige. Law has often served as an instrument of social mobility—an accessible avenue to preferment in politics, public service, business, marriage, and social groups. Those benefits of bar admission might also be denied.

Admission of new lawyers is of interest not only to those who apply. The public has an interest in being assured that admission standards are not unreasonably high, thus reducing artificially the number of lawyer-competitors and maintaining high levels of fees. The public is also concerned that admission standards and procedures not be applied in ways that arbitrarily discriminate against otherwise qualified applicants on the grounds of race, ethnicity, or economic status. Some lawyers claim that the public is just as clearly concerned that persons who practice law not harm their clients' interests because of their incompetence or lack of integrity. The bar has argued that the only way of assuring the necessary minimum levels of competence and character is through a rigorous system of bar admission standards. Nonetheless, serious questions have been raised about many aspects of the mandatory process by which a person becomes a lawyer.

Regulatory Authority

The courts are recognized in most states as possessing the exclusive power to set standards for admission to the bar. Under the inherent powers doctrine (§ 2.2), the state's supreme court is empowered to make bar admission rules even in the absence of statute or explicit constitutional delegation. The court can, moreover, preclude the other branches of government from affecting those standards except in a complementary way.[79]

Bar admission standards are restrictive, not welcoming. Their effect, and possibly the motive of many in the bar establishment, has been to exclude to some degree the *Unter mensch* of American life.[80] The rules, although nominally made by courts, are in fact almost everywhere generated by committees of lawyers operating in close alignment with bar associations.[81] They have withstood a variety of constitutional and other legal attacks.[82]

Effect of Bar Admission

Bar admission is an all-or-nothing proposition in most situations. A person not admitted to practice can perform for clients very few of the services that a lawyer may (§ 15.1.3). But once admitted to practice, a lawyer may handle any matter for any client regardless of its complexity or magnitude. Once in a lawyer's possession, a license to practice can be taken away only through the bar disciplinary procedure prescribed for that jurisdiction (§ 3.2).[83] Smaller periodic hurdles may remain. Almost all states now en-

79 In re LiVolsi, 85 N.J. 576, 428 A.2d 1268, 1278 (1981). See generally Degnan, Admission to the Bar and the Separation of Powers, 7 Utah L.Rev. 82 (1960). See also, e.g., Jeffers, Government of the Legal Professional: An Inherent Judicial Power Approach, 9 St.Mary's L.J. 385 (1978); Robertson, Separation of Powers and the Regulation of the Practice of Law in Oregon, 13 Willamette L.J. 273 (1977); Currie & Resh, Separation of Powers: Control of Courts and Lawyers, 47 Wis.B.Bull. 7 (1974).

80 J.Auerbach, Unequal Justice (1976); Bell, Do Bar Examinations Serve a Useful Purpose?, 57 ABA J. 1215 (1971); Symposium, The Minority Candidate and the Bar Examination, 5 Black L.J. 120 (1976); Plotkin, Coal Handling, Steamfitting, Psychology, and Law, 27 Am.Psychologist 202 (1972).

81 Huber, Entry to the Bar: Who Is in Charge?, 14 Houst.L.Rev. 25 (1977).

82 Younger v. Colorado St. Bd. of Law Examiners, 625 F.2d 372 (10th Cir.1980)(constitutionality of state rule denying right to sit for bar examination for fourth time); Davidson v. Georgia, 622 F.2d 895 (5th Cir.1980); Bowens v. Board of Law Examiners, 57 N.C.App. 78, 291 S.E.2d 170 (1982)(no unlawful delegation of legislative authority to bar examiners; subjective grading of bar examination not unconstitutional); In re Chamley, 349 N.W.2d 56 (S.D.1984)(requirement of membership in bar as condition of right to practice not in violation of right-to-work provision of state constitution). See generally Special Project, Admission to the Bar: A Constitutional Analysis, 34 Vand.L.Rev. 655 (1981).

83 Misconduct in the admission process itself can lead to discipline in the form of voiding the admission. E.g., People v. Culpepper, 645 P.2d 5 (Colo.1982)(materially false statement in application by use of fraudulent under-

force an annual registration requirement.[84] As part of the process, lawyers pay a fee that is used to support such things as the system of lawyer discipline in the state.

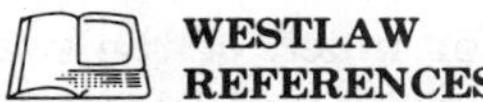

WESTLAW REFERENCES

synopsis (attorney lawyer /s bar practice /s admission admit!)

admission admit! /s bar /p requir! restrict! /p "unauthorized practice"

constitution! unconstitutional /s bar /3 admission admit!

§ 15.2.2. Educational Requirements

Mandatory Legal and Undergraduate Education

Explicit educational requirements are a very recent occurrence in the American bar. As late as 1900 not a single American jurisdiction required that an applicant have either a college or a law school degree.[85] Mandatory education has been imposed mainly in the present century and largely through the device of a state requirement that a bar applicant must have graduated from a law school accredited by the American Bar Association. Those rules, in turn, have imposed increasingly rigorous requirements on law schools that wish to receive ABA accreditation.[86] The requirement of ABA accreditation of a law school in satisfaction of a state's educational requirement has been upheld against repeated constitutional attack.[87]

The main educational requirements are two. First, in over 90 percent of American jurisdictions a bar applicant must have graduated from a law school that was accredited by the ABA.[88] The ABA accreditation standards currently insist upon a minimum of three years of residence and satisfactory completion of the work in a prescribed number of courses. Some few jurisdictions still permit the alternative and traditional method of "reading law" in a lawyer's office.[89] Second, the ABA accreditation standards themselves require in most cases that a student admitted to law school have earned a four-year college degree before receiving a law degree. Proposals are sometimes made to go further and require that an applicant satisfy an apprenticeship requirement before admission.[90]

graduate degree that had also been employed to gain admission to law school).

84 Overseers of Bar v. Lee, 422 A.2d 998 (Me.1980), appeal dismissed 450 U.S. 1036, 101 S.Ct. 1751, 68 L.Ed. 2d 233 (1981); Berberian v. Kane, ___ R.I. ___, 425 A.2d 527 (1981); In re Petition of Tennessee Bar Ass'n, 532 S.W.2d 224, 229 (Tenn.1975)(Tennessee becomes fortieth state to require annual registration).

85 L.Friedman, A History of American Law 525 (1973).

86 See generally Note, ABA Approval of Law Schools: Standards, Procedures, and the Future of Legal Education, 72 Mich.L.Rev. 1134 (1974); ABA Section of Legal Education and Admission to the Bar, A Review of Legal Education in the United States: Law Schools and Bar Admission Requirements (1977). With respect to the impact of ABA accreditation standards upon the shape and direction of American legal education, see § 5.2.

87 See generally Note, Conclusive Presumptions and the Right to Take the Bar Examination: Is ABA Imprimatur Necessary?, 46 U.Colo.L.Rev. 79 (1974).

88 But see, e.g., In re Proposed Amendments to Practice of Law Rules, 187 Mont. 159, 609 P.2d 263 (1980)(refusing to limit law schools to those approved by ABA).

89 In New York, in addition to education through four years of college and three of law school, a bar applicant may be able to satisfy the educational requirement either by law office study for four years after a year of law school or by proof of an equivalent legal education in a foreign law school. See Rules for the Admission of Attorneys, 22 N.Y.C.R.R. [pt. 520] §§ 520.4 (law office study), 520.5 (study of law in foreign country). Clerking in a law office was a standard method of becoming a lawyer until into this century. Clerking would be done even by law school graduates in order to gain a sponsor and to prepare for the oral bar examination in the local court. See Huber & Meyer, Admission to the Practice of Law in Texas: An Analytical History, 15 Houst.L.Rev. 485, 503–05 (1978).

90 Pennsylvania had such an apprenticeship requirement in the 1950s and 1960s. It is remembered by some as a system for providing a source of cheap compulsory labor for lawyers already admitted to practice. See Nat'l L.J., Apr.14, 1980, at 4, col.1 (comment by drafter of proposed California apprenticeship legislation). A South Carolina apprenticeship rule, adopted in 1979 and applying only to trial practice, avoids the forced-labor problem by providing that the apprenticeship can be satisfied by sitting in court and watching trials. See Nat'l L.J., July 9, 1979, at 8, col.1. An internship requirement is part of the experimental federal court trial-bar rule in effect in some few districts. See § 5.4 at 201–02.

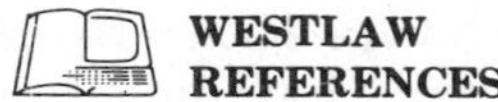
WESTLAW REFERENCES

admission admit! /3 practice bar /s education! /s requir!

§ 15.2.3 Residence Requirements

Residence Requirements and Privileges and Immunities

A common requirement in many states' bar admission rules is that the applicant be a state resident.[91] In a case now pending before the Supreme Court, an attack on New Hampshire's requirement of residence at the time of taking the oath of attorney is being heard.[92] The First Circuit, in a split decision by its entire membership, held that the state requirement violated the privileges and immunities clause of the federal Constitution.[93] The decision had been anticipated by other courts that have struck down residency requirements for either admission on examination or admission on motion.[94]

Citizenship

Apparently for much of the nation's history, aliens were not barred from admission to practice in the states.[95] The first prohibitions against noncitizens becoming lawyers seem to have coincided with the sorry era of late nineteenth-century American history when anti-alien sentiment began to shape legislation.[96] The Supreme Court held in 1973[97] that a requirement in a state's admission rule that an applicant be a citizen was unconstitutional on the ground that the status of resident alien was a "suspect classification" that required the state to bear a heavy burden of justification under a strict scrutiny standard. The Court was unconvinced that either justification that the state offered—assuring adequate qualifications to practice law or the nature of

[91] The residence requirement can, of course, vary considerably in terms of the time at which the applicant must satisfy the residence requirement and in the durational feature of the test for residence. Among other possibilities, a state could require residence at the time of applying to take a bar examination, at the time of sitting for the examination, or at the time of taking the oath of attorney.

[92] Supreme Court of New Hampshire v. Piper, 723 F.2d 110 (1st Cir.1983)(en banc), affirmed ___ U.S. ___, 105 S.Ct. 1272, 84 L.Ed.2d 205 (1985).

[93] The doctrinal difficulties are considerable. The Slaughterhouse Cases, 83 U.S. (16 Wall.) 36, 21 L.Ed. 394 (1873), had very narrowly interpreted the privileges and immunities clause, leaving them a virtual dead letter. Two 1978 decisions had, however, revitalized them. Baldwin v. Fish & Game Comm'n, 436 U.S. 371, 98 S.Ct. 1852, 56 L.Ed.2d 354 (1978); Hicklin v. Orbeck, 437 U.S. 518, 98 S.Ct. 2482, 57 L.Ed.2d 397 (1978)("Alaska hire" statute requiring that employers give preference in hiring to Alaska residents unconstitutional). Under those decisions, the state must demonstrate that nonresident lawyers are a "peculiar source of the evil" at which regulation can permissibly be addressed. See Hicklin, supra, 437 U.S. at 526–27. Just a year before the *Baldwin* and *Hicklin* decisions, however, the Supreme Court had summarily affirmed a lower court's holding that a state residence requirement was constitutional. Wilson v. Wilson, 416 F.Supp. 984 (D.Or.1976), affirmed 430 U.S. 925, 97 S.Ct. 1540, 51 L.Ed.2d 768 (1977)(per curiam).

[94] Stalland v. South Dakota Bd. of Law Examiners, 530 F.Supp. 155 (D.S.D.1982); Strauss v. Alabama St.Bar, 520 F.Supp. 173 (N.D.Ala.1981); Noll v. Alaska Bar Ass'n, 649 P.2d 241 (Alaska 1982); In re Jadd, 391 Mass. 227, 461 N.E.2d 760 (1984)(abolishing rule requiring residence for lawyer seeking admission on motion); Gordon v. Committee on Character and Fitness, 48 N.Y.2d 266, 422 N.Y.S. 2d 641, 397 N.E.2d 1309 (1979); Sargus v. West Virginia Bd. of Law Examiners, 294 S.E.2d 440 (W.Va.1982). Those courts have rejected the two principal arguments made in support of a residence requirement. The argument that a nonresident is not amenable to service of process if questions arise about the lawyer's work ignores the fact that less restrictive alternatives are available, such as a requirement that a lawyer designate an in-state agent-for-service. The argument that nonresidents are, for that reason, less familiar with local law fails because of the possibility of testing for knowledge of local law on the state's bar examination. The alleged additional administrative workload of investigating character ignores the availability of the National Conference of Bar Examiners and its nationwide investigatory services.

[95] Bradwell v. Illinois, 83 U.S. (16 Wall.) 130, 139, 21 L.Ed. 442 (1872): "This right [to be admitted to practice] in no sense depends on citizenship of the United States. It has not, as far as we know, ever been made in any State, or in any case, to depend on citizenship at all. Certainly many prominent and distinguished lawyers have been admitted to practice, both in the State and Federal courts, who were not citizens of the United States or of any State."

[96] J.Highan, Strangers in the Land 46, 161, 183 (1963); M.Konvitz, The Alien and the Asiatic in American Law 190–211 (1946); Note, Constitutionality of the Restrictions on Aliens' Right to Work, 50 Colum.L.Rev. 1012 (1957).

[97] In re Griffiths, 413 U.S. 717, 93 S.Ct. 2851, 37 L.Ed. 2d 910 (1973).

the quasi-official status of lawyers as officers of the court—sufficed.

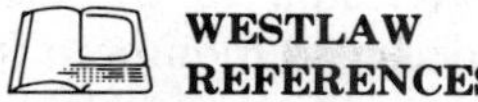
WESTLAW REFERENCES

admission admit! /s practice bar /s residen! /s requir! /p constitution! unconstitutional (privilege /2 immunity)

§ 15.2.4 Admission in Federal Courts

General Pattern of Court-by-Court Admission

To an observer, membership in the bars of the federal courts looks like the work of petty fiefdoms of medieval Europe. Each federal district court, each of the federal court of appeals,[98] each of the specialized federal courts, and the Supreme Court have their own bar. To be able to practice in any of those separate courts, a lawyer must obtain a separate admission to its bar. An attempt to practice without being admitted is unauthorized practice.[99] But like citizenship in a minor kingdom, admission to most of the federal courts is mainly a matter of a bit of expense and some paperwork—and membership in the bar of some other court.

Variations exist. Some judges, who are restless unless they are marching the troops about, insist on attempting experiments and imposing restrictions in order to upgrade the quality of new recruits. On the whole, however, one can slip into a new federal bar membership at one's relative ease.[1] Someday, sensibly, admission to the federal courts will be federal in nature: admission will be to a single bar for the trial and intermediate appellate courts.[2] Membership in the Supreme Court[3] will probably remain a separate matter so that thousands of lawyers, who will never file another motion there, can obtain admission and receive in return an impressive certificate for their office walls.[4]

Federal District Courts

The federal district courts provide by local rule for admission.[5] At one time it was not uncommon for each district to have its own examinations, typically oral, that a lawyer was required to pass.[6] Today most of the actual work of character and competence testing is left to the states,[7] although the ultimate question of admission remains one that is theoretically controlled by federal law and

[98] See generally F.R.App.Proc. 46.

[99] City of Princeton v. Francisco, 454 F.Supp. 33 (S.D. Iowa 1978).

[1] Several federal districts are experimenting with an admission standard that requires special training and experience before being eligible for the federal court's trial bar. See § 5.4, at 201–02.

[2] The concept of a national bar, but with special requirements and preconditions, was discussed but not recommended in the report of the Devitt Committee. See Report to Jud.Conf. of U.S., Standards for Admission, 79 F.R.D. 187 (1978). Common bar membership is now provided for in the federal courts of appeal, which provide under F.R.App.Proc.Rule 46(a) that admission to a court of appeal can be premised on admission to the Supreme Court, any state court, or any federal district court. But, frustratingly, one must still obtain admission to each separate circuit despite the common standard.

[3] U.S.S.Ct.R. 5.

[4] Some justices have protested the cheapening of the coin by automatic admission of applicants to the Supreme Court. E.g., In re Rose, 71 L.Ed.2d 862 (1982)(Burger, C.J., and O'Connor, J., dissenting). It seems unlikely that a court with the pressing caseload of the Supreme Court would find it useful to provide the fair hearings that due process would seem to require in order to provide a finer screen of applicants. On the requirement of a hearing, see, e.g., In re Berkan, 648 F.2d 1386, 1389–90 (1st Cir.1981).

[5] The Judiciary Act of 1789 provided that the rules of the federal courts should determine which persons were admissible as lawyers to practice there. Judiciary Act of 1789, ch.20, § 35, 1 Stat. 92, now codified as 28 U.S.C.A. § 1654. For a time after the 1948 revision of the Judicial Code, that provision was omitted, but it was restored by Act of May 24, 1949, ch. 139, § 91, 63 Stat. 103. Federal courts may also derive authority from the Rules Enabling Act, 28 U.S.C.A. § 2071, and F.R.Civ.Proc.Rule 83, empowering the local federal courts to make rules of "practice" not inconsistent with the Federal Rules. See In re Abrams, 521 F.2d 1094, 1099 (3d Cir.1975)(en banc), cert.denied 423 U.S. 1038, 96 S.Ct. 574, 46 L.Ed.2d 413 (1975).

[6] Reportedly two districts recently required applicants to pass written bar examinations that were imposed in addition to any state examination requirements. See Frankel, Curing Lawyers' Incompetence: Primum Non Nocere, 10 Creighton L.Rev. 613, 616 n.50 (1977).

[7] "[A] lawyer is admitted into a federal court by way of a state court." Theard v. United States, 354 U.S. 278, 281, 77 S.Ct. 1274, 1276, 1 L.Ed.2d 1342 (1957)(Frankfurter, J.).

general federal standards.[8] A typical arrangement is to require that a lawyer applying for membership be a member in good standing of the bar of the state in which the federal court sits or, possibly, of some other court.[9] Lawyers appearing for the United States, on the other hand, need only be admitted to the bar of any jurisdiction.

Restricted federal court bar membership is defended on the ground of limiting the number of cases filed for purposes of docket control, avoiding a temptation for a lawyer to choose a federal over a state tribunal despite a more advantageous (but inaccessible) state forum, assuring that the lawyer will have a local office and location for service of papers and to make scheduling of hearings more flexible, and assuring ethical conduct by a known local standard.[10] As with all localizing rules, one must also assess the possibility that the rule is motivated by an interest in protecting the local market for legal services.[11] For lawyers who do not intend to practice frequently in a particular federal district court, a ready alternative for occasional appearances is admission pro hac vice, which is usually accorded as a matter of course.[12]

Effect of Federal Bar Membership

Once a lawyer has been admitted to the bar of a federal court, only that court may suspend or take away the lawyer's membership.[13] The result is a system of federal court discipline, which, however, is very closely patterned on action taken in the state court in which lawyers are also members (§ 3.6.1). So long as a lawyer continues as a member of a federal court bar, the lawyer may continue to practice law relating to that membership despite discipline imposed by other courts with respect to other bar memberships.[14]

WESTLAW REFERENCES

admission admit! /3 federal /3 bar practice % evidence

§ 15.2.5 Practice before Administrative Agencies

Variations in Regulation

Two regulatory patterns can be seen governing appearances before administrative agencies. Probably the majority of state courts take the position that only the courts themselves may regulate practice before an administrative agency. As a result, customary unauthorized practice rules apply, and only lawyers may provide representation before administrative agencies in such states.[15] The second pattern is represented by the federal system and is also followed in some states. Those courts have been content to permit the legislature and the administrative

[8] United States v. Peterson, 550 F.2d 379 (7th Cir.1977); Elder v. Metropolitan Freight Carriers, Inc., 543 F.2d 513 (3d Cir.1976)(state law to the contrary notwithstanding, federal courts are empowered to devise and apply own rules of maximum attorney fees and apply these in diversity as well as other kinds of cases); Triplett v. Azordegan, 421 F.Supp. 998 (N.D.Iowa 1976)(state statute purporting to limit ability of state employees (law professors) to act as advocates inapplicable with respect to federal court civil rights litigation).

[9] There are several variations. One (D.Mass. R. 5(a)) requires only that the lawyer be admitted to the bar of the state in which the federal court sits, Massachusetts, or to the bar of any other federal district court. At the other extreme is a requirement in the District of New Jersey that a lawyer be a member in good standing of the the sitting-state bar. See In re Roberts, 682 F.2d 105 (3d Cir.1982)(limitation to New Jersey bar members constitutional). See also, e.g., Galahad v. Weinshienk, 555 F.Supp. 1201 (D.Colo.1983)(upholding similar rule in D.Colo.).

[10] In re Roberts, 682 F.2d 105, 108 (3d Cir.1982).

[11] Cf. Galahad v. Weinshienk, 555 F.Supp. 1201 (D.Colo. 1983)(federal court rule not susceptible to attack on basis of federal antitrust statutes because statute conferring rule-making power trumps antitrust statutes as matter of statutory interpretation).

[12] In re Evans, 524 F.2d 1004 (5th Cir.1975). On pro hac vice admission, see § 15.3.

[13] Selling v. Radford, 243 U.S. 46, 48, 37 S.Ct. 377, 378–79, 61 L.Ed. 585 (1917).

[14] Id.

[15] See § 15.1.3, at 837–38. Some courts, however, have accepted as a matter of "comity" some legislative expansion of the right of nonlawyers to appear before administrative agencies. E.g., Idaho St. Bar Ass'n v. Idaho Pub. Utilities Comm'n, 102 Idaho 672, 637 P.2d 1168 (1981).

agencies to define for themselves what, if any, restrictions should be imposed on agency appearances and representations.[16] In one case in the federal system, in the Patent Office, that power includes the power to exclude a lawyer from practice before the agency, despite the fact that the lawyer is fully licensed by the highest court of a state, unless the lawyer passes a special examination in the specific lore of the agency.[17]

One of the significant features of the federal arrangement is that several agencies admit nonlawyers to practice before them.[18] An unpublished study of thirty-five federal administrative agencies showed that fourteen permitted only lawyer representation,[19] sixteen allowed anyone to serve as a representative,[20] and five admitted lawyers automatically and admitted nonlawyer representatives if they could satisfy stated eligibility requirements.[21] Examples of the last category include the Internal Revenue Service [22] and the Interstate Commerce Commission.[23]

Federal Preemption of Questions of Federal Practice

Once a person, whether a lawyer or a nonlawyer, has been admitted to practice before a federal agency, a state court loses the power to regulate that practice in ways that are inconsistent with the form of regulation provided by federal law.[24] Thus, in Sperry v. Florida,[25] the Court held that Florida could not preclude a nonlawyer who had been admitted to practice as a patent agent before the federal Patent Office from advising clients in Florida about Patent Office matters despite the fact that such advice by a nonlawyer

[16] Goldsmith v. United States Bd. of Tax Appeals, 270 U.S. 117, 122, 46 S.Ct. 215, 220, 70 L.Ed. 494 (1926)(while many federal agencies are expressly empowered by statute to prescribe qualifications for who may practice before them, even in the absence of specific empowerment, "so necessary is the power and so usual is it that the general words by which the Board is vested with the authority to prescribe the procedure in accordance with which its business shall be conducted include as part of the procedure rules of practice for the admission of attorneys."); Koden v. United States Dep't of Justice, 564 F.2d 228 (7th Cir.1977)(Immigration and Naturalization Service and Board of Immigration Appeals); Charlton v. F.T.C., 543 F.2d 903 (D.C.Cir.1976)(Federal Trade Commission); Herman v. Dulles, 205 F.2d 715 (D.C.Cir.1953) (International Claims Commission); Schwebel v. Orrick, 153 F.Supp. 701, 704 (D.D.C.1957), affirmed on other grounds 251 F.2d 919 (D.C.Cir.1958) cert.denied 356 U.S. 927, 78 S.Ct. 716, 2 L.Ed.2d 759 (1958)(Securities and Exchange Commission); Brown v. District of Columbia Bd. of Zoning. 413 A.2d 1276, 1279 (D.C.1980). See generally vom Baur, Standards of Admission to Practice before Federal Administrative Agencies (Survey of the Legal Profession 1953); Gellhorn, Qualifications for Practice before Boards and Commissions, in Symposium, Law and Lawyers in the Modern World, 15 U.Cinn.L.Rev. 123, 196–99 (1941).

[17] 5 U.S.C.A. § 500(e). With the exception of the Patent Office, every other federal agency is required by the Agency Practice Act of 1965, 5 U.S.C.A. § 500, to admit lawyers to practice before them without further examination or certification.

[18] Todd Shipyards v. Director, Office of Workers' Compensation Programs, 545 F.2d 1176 (9th Cir.1976)(authorization under 20 C.F.R. § 702.334 for "lay representative" to represent claimant under federal longshoremen's act); 48 Fed.Reg. 44,765 (1984)(amendment to regulations of Federal Trade Commission to permit designated nonlawyer expert to conduct cross-examination of opposing party's expert witness in agency hearings). A significant difference between lawyer and nonlawyer practitioners remains. A nonlawyer's professional relationship with a represented party is not that of lawyer and client for the purposes of applying the attorney-client privilege. See generally Petersen, Attorney-Client Privilege in Internal Revenue Service Investigations, 54 Minn.L.Rev. 67 (1969).

[19] 14 C.F.R. § 302.11 (Federal Communications Commission).

[20] 29 C.F.R. § 100 (National Labor Relations Board).

[21] Weckstein, Limitations on the Right to Counsel: The Unauthorized Practice of Law, 1978 Utah L.Rev. 649, 658 n.50.

[22] 26 C.F.R. § 601.502 (practice before Treasury Department open to lawyers admitted to practice elsewhere, certified public accountants, and "enrolled agents" who pass test or demonstrate experience in tax matters).

[23] 49 C.F.R.§ 1100.8(a)(c)(appearance by lawyer admitted elsewhere or by "class B" practitioners, who pass examination on transportation law and practice).

[24] A significant area of conflict that has never resulted in definitive litigation involves attempts by state bar unauthorized practice committees to prevent federal lawyers from affording representation to federal employees. See Marks, Military Lawyers, Civilian Courts, and the Organized Bar: A Case Study of the Unauthorized Practice Dilemma, 56 Mil.L.Rev. 1 (1972).

[25] 373 U.S. 379, 83 S.Ct. 1322, 10 L.Ed.2d 428 (1963). Decisions such as Grace v. Allen, 407 S.W.2d 321 (Tex. Civ.App.1966), holding that the federal entitlement applies only to appearing before the federal agency and not to office activities such as legal research, seem inconsistent with *Sperry*. There is no indication in the Treasury Department regulations that an enrolled accountant or other nonlawyer agent is limited to appearing before the agency without research, preparation of witnesses, or client consultation.

otherwise constituted the unauthorized practice of law in the eyes of the Florida court.

The *Sperry* doctrine generally applies to the aspects of practice of both lawyer and nonlawyer practitioners that are regulated by the federal agency.[26] But *Sperry* announces a relatively specific doctrine—not one that immunizes all possible aspirants to federal protection. Simply practicing patent law, for example, affords no immunity against state regulation if the practitioner is not admitted to the bar of the Patent Office.[27] Admission to practice before a federal agency also does not by force of federal law require a state to permit a nonlawyer to practice before a state agency that deals with similar matters.[28] The *Sperry* rule is also not a shield against all state professional discipline. A lawyer who commits what is defined as a disciplinary offense under state law may be disbarred or suspended from practice in the state courts despite the lawyer's membership in the bar of the federal agency and even if the offensive conduct occurred in the course of a federal agency representation.[29]

WESTLAW REFERENCES

admission admit! /4 practice /s federal** administrative /4 agency department commission

sperry +4 florida /12 373 +4 379 /p admit! admission /s practice

§ 15.3 COMPETENCE AND CHARACTER

§ 15.3.1 Choosing Suitable Practitioners

Objectives of Restrictions on Admission

It is easy enough to formulate the reasons that might motivate an unauthorized practice committee to seek out, quite in good faith, unlicensed practitioners of law and a bar examining committee to restrict entry to local practice. The ideals are that anyone who practices law should be competent to do so and should be possessed of character traits that will assure that the powerful position of lawyer will not be put to unlawful or unethical ends. Those goals, if they could be achieved, would be laudable indeed.

That many individuals have strong traits of moral or immoral behavior or that some individuals are more competent than others is incontestable. At some level of generality, most would probably also agree that certain traits of character and competence are likely to lead to good or bad lawyering. What is quite controversial is whether or not those traits can be sufficiently described and individually identified to assure that a bar admissions process that attends to them seriously can be both productive and noninvidious. Views will differ, but there is important empirical and analytical support for the proposition that the goals cannot be regularly achieved and that the attempts to achieve them have often led to exclusion of potential lawyers on socially and morally indefensible grounds.[30]

[26] Silverman v. State Bar of Texas, 405 F.2d 410 (5th Cir.1968)(state anti-advertising rule could not be applied to preclude telephone directory advertising permitted by regulation of Patent Office, to which lawyer was admitted).

[27] Amalgamated Dev. Co. v. Committee on Unauthorized Practice, 375 A.2d 494 (D.C.App.1977), cert.denied 434 U.S. 924, 98 S.Ct. 403, 54 L.Ed.2d 282 (1977); In re Lawrence Peska Assoc., Inc., 90 Misc.2d 59, 393 N.Y.S.2d 650 (1977).

[28] State ex rel. State Bar v. Keller, 21 Wis.2d 100, 123 N.W.2d 905 (1963), cert.denied 377 U.S. 964, 84 S.Ct. 1643, 12 L.Ed.2d 734 (1964)(not inconsistent with Interstate Commerce Commission admission system to bar nonlawyer "class B" ICC practitioner from representing clients before state administrative agency that deals with transportation issues of same general kinds as those dealt with in ICC cases).

[29] In re Davis, 264 N.W.2d 371, 373 (Minn.1978). One could hypothesize a case in which the state's imposition of discipline would not be permissible because it was inconsistent with the point of the federal administrative admission—for example, disbarring a lawyer in state court because the lawyer challenged the constitutionality of a state statute in a federal administrative hearing.

[30] See generally Rhode, Moral Character as a Professional Credential, 94 Yale L.J. 491 (1984). Professor Rhode argues that history shows that the character test for bar admission has been capriciously administered, and psychology teaches that this must inherently be so.

A second ground on which to question testing and exclusion for competence and character is that even if the exclusion could be demonstrated to be fairly and accurately conducted, it still needs to be shown that barring incompetent or unethical practitioners through the admissions process is the best method of assuring that legal services are rendered efficiently. Perhaps one should believe that well-informed consumers of legal services are able to assess those traits for themselves and that one can be assured that the market is a preferable way of driving out incompetents or rascals. One difficulty with the bar's attempting to preassess competence and character is that the public might be misled into thinking that admission is a certification that every lawyer still in practice is worthy of patronage and confidence.[31] Lawyers do not in fact think that of all of their brethren and sisters.

Assuring Competence in Lawyers

Competence in bar applicants is assured primarily through educational requirements (§ 15.2.2) and, in most states, a bar examination (§ 5.3). As the discussion elsewhere indicates, there is room for substantial doubt that a person who has successfully passed a bar examination is qualified to conduct the entire range of legal tasks that bar admission permits. That is, nonetheless, the legal effect of every state's bar certification.

Lawyers' Responsibilities for the Admissions Process

Both the 1969 Code and the 1983 Model Rules place on lawyers certain minimum[32] responsibilities to see to the successful operation of the bar admission process. Applicants, once they become lawyers, are subject to discipline under DR 1–101(A) for making a materially false statement or deliberately failing to disclose a material fact on a bar application.[33] The Model Rules contain a similar, although somewhat broader, rule in MR 8.1.[34] A person already a lawyer is required by DR 1–101(B) not to further the application of a person known by the lawyer to be unqualified. A lawyer who is aware that a bar applicant has violated DR 1–101(A) is presumably obliged by DR 1–103(A) to disclose that fact.[35] By a similar process, MR 8.1 and MR 8.3 require certain disclosures by lawyers about false statements or failures to disclose by a bar applicant and, in MR 8.1, require a lawyer to respond to lawful demands for information from an admission agency. The rules are among the least enforced in the lawyer codes. Lawyers are very rarely called upon to play any role in the bar admission process, and then they act mainly as volunteers.

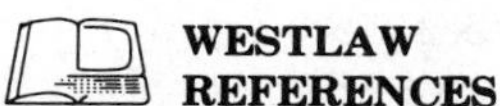

WESTLAW REFERENCES

digest,synopsis(admit! admission /5 bar (law /3 practice) /p competen** character)

admit! admission /5 bar practice /p "professional responsibility"

45k7

45k4 /p (moral /3 character) competen**

The chief difficulties are the absence of agreement on the meaning of good character, the unavailability of tests that can effectively assess character, and the intrusive and invidious nature of criteria that are often applied.

[31] Courts have claimed that admission does constitute such a holding out, but they must mean it figuratively. E.g., Pennobscot Bar v. Kimball, 64 Me. 140, 146 (1875).

[32] EC 8–7 states the loftier aim that lawyers actively assist in ensuring that applicants are qualified. See also EC 1–1, 1–2, 1–3, and 1–6.

[33] People v. Culpepper, 645 P.2d 5 (Colo.1982); In re Farrar, 242 Ga. 312, 249 S.E.2d 12 (1978).

[34] The disclosure obligation in MR 8.1(b), with respect to failure to disclose, is broader than the corresponding rule in DR 1–101(A), which is limited to failures to disclose material facts that are "requested." The requirement in MR 8.1(b) also extends to disclosures "necessary to correct a misapprehension known by the person to have arisen in the matter."

[35] The applicant's violation of DR 1–101(A) is a violation of DR 1–102(A)(1). Thus a lawyer is obliged by DR 1–103(A) to disclose that violation of DR 1–102.

§ 15.3.2 *Assessing Character*

How Character Is Assessed in Bar Admissions

The process of character assessment for admission to practice in many states is primarily a process of self-reporting that is carried on on paper. Only in a very few states does it take a very active form. A candidate must typically submit answers to a questionnaire that might ask about arrests, convictions, bankruptcy, civil judgments, and similar scrapes. An applicant must sometimes submit letters of reference, and sometimes one or more of these must be from lawyers.[36] Law schools are often required by states to certify something about the character of their graduates, although rarely will a law school ever certify anything but acceptable character ratings, probably because it feels incapable of anything else.[37]

The examining committees themselves are almost invariably committees of volunteers, almost all of them lawyers. Many bar examining committees now employ the services of the National Conference on Bar Examiners to conduct computer investigations that are like credit checks and might detect such recorded matters as unreported convictions or judgments. Some states require that applicants submit themselves to personal inverviews with members of a character committee. Only California and Florida have paid staff directly involved in admissions. In Florida, by report, the large staff of full-time investigators conducts extensive screening examinations.[38] When all has been said and done, only about fifty persons a year in the United States are denied admission to practice on character grounds.[39]

Despite the effort sometimes expended by examining committees, most persons who are now lawyers will candidly admit that they have little idea how the bar committee that declared them to be of good character established a reliable basis for that impression. The likely explanation is that bar committees are not looking for good people who will be good lawyers. They are only looking for very bad people—the problem cases. They do so, not so much because the standard of desirable character is a low one,[40] but because of time and staff limitations and the difficulty of dealing confidently with any but clear cases. The recorded instances in which bar committees have rejected candidates involve, almost without exception, a person whose prior misdeeds were a matter of a public and accessible rec-

[36] The process, at least on paper, in some states is quite formal. Delaware, apparently alone among the states, requires that a lawyer "preceptor," who is personally acquainted with or has interviewed the applicant, investigate the applicant's background (if lacking personal knowledge of it), interview the applicant, and be able to certify that the application is accurate and complete. See In re Green, 464 A.2d 881 (Del.1983). Nine states still retain a process, much ballyhooed by the ABA in the 1930s, that requires a student to register and submit to a bar screening on beginning law studies. See Rhode, Moral Character as a Professional Credential, 94 Yale L.J. 491, 519 (1984). The intent of the process was to give advance warning to high-risk applicants and to begin to socialize students to the ethos of the legal profession.

[37] That does not mean that law schools are not significant "morals" barriers to law practice. Particularly in a time of surplus applications, law schools probably relied on assumptions about moral character in making marginal decisions. Whether that would continue in a falling market seems dubious.

[38] Moore, Lawyer Screening: Fact or Fiction?, 15 Syllabus (Sept.1984), at 1 (description of Florida process by its executive director: program with staff of twenty-four full-time members and annual budget of $1.3 million supported entirely by applicant fees).

[39] Rhode, Moral Character as a Professional Credential, 94 Yale L.J. 491, 516 (1984).

[40] To the contrary, an often-cited opinion insists that:

> " 'upright character' . . . is something more than an absence of bad character. . . . It means that [an applicant for admission] must have conducted himself as a man of upright character ordinarily would, should, or does. Such character expresses itself not in negatives nor in following the line of least resistance, but quite often in the will to do the unpleasant thing if it is right, and the resolve not to do the pleasant thing if it is wrong."

In re Farmer, 191 N.C. 235, 131 S.E. 661, 663 (1926). See also, e.g., In re G.W.L., 364 So.2d 454, 459 (Fla.1978)(lack of good moral character can be proved by conduct other than that which constitutes moral turpitude). But cf., e.g., Konigsberg v. State Bar of California, 353 U.S. 252, 263, 77 S.Ct. 722, 728, 1 L.Ed.2d 810 (1957)(construing California law, "these cases appear to define 'good moral character' in terms of an absence of proven conduct or acts which have been historically considered as manifestations of 'moral turpitude.' "); Reese v. Board of Comm'rs of State Bar, 379 So.2d 564, 569 (Ala.1980).

ord—such as a conviction, disbarment, or civil judgment. Without such previously established and clearly documented records, most bar committees apparently do not feel that they can assess from background, interviews, or the opinions of others that a person lacks the minimally appropriate character.

In unusual cases in which an issue about moral character has been raised, due process guarantees apply. An applicant rejected by a bar committee on the grounds of character must be given the reasons for that determination and an opportunity for a hearing on them before a neutral body.[41] Courts often say that the burden of proof is on the applicant to demonstrate good character, although in practice that means little more than fulfilling the application requirements and responding to an interview.[42] When a general showing of good character has been made, then the burden of proving that the applicant lacks the claimed good character shifts to those who oppose the admission.[43] A different approach is followed by some courts in an instance in which the character committee has rested a decision to reject an application on a fact, such as a conviction for a crime, that plausibly supports their decision. Those courts say that the applicant then has the burden of proving rehabilitation from the crime.[44]

What Is "Good Moral Character"

Bar admissions standards now and traditionally,[45] and in every jurisdiction,[46] have called for something along the lines of "good moral character" in applicants. Only its antiquity and traditional use could possibly defend it against claims of unconstitutional vagueness.[47] "Moral" can be determined by a person using the test in either of two general ways. The reference may be to private moral beliefs that individuals employ to guide their own conduct. Or, much more broadly, it may be able to derive a public morality—a set of moral beliefs about proper behavior are so insistently felt that the society as a whole commands that all persons comply with them.

If the test refers to private instincts, then the task of a bar admission committee becomes the implausible one of admitting hardly anyone. The test would require the committee to exclude all persons whose actions or beliefs would be viewed as "immoral" by any person's moral instincts or, more narrowly, by the instincts of any significant group of persons. Thus, for example, men or women who used cosmetics, tobacco, pork, alcohol, marijuana, or cola drinks would be excluded along

41 Willner v. Committee on Character, 373 U.S. 96, 83 S.Ct. 1175, 10 L.Ed.2d 224 (1963); In re Childs, 101 Wis.2d 159, 303 N.W.2d 663 (1981).

42 Konigsberg v. State Bar, 366 U.S. 36, 41–42, 81 S.Ct. 997, 1001–02, 6 L.Ed.2d 105 (1961); Greene v. Committee of Bar Examiners, 4 Cal.3d 189, 93 Cal.Rptr. 24, 480 P.2d 976 (1971); In re Evinger, 629 P.2d 363, 367 (Okl.1981).

43 In re Rogers, 297 N.C. 48, 253 S.E.2d 912 (1979).

44 Several courts say that rehabilitation in that context must be proved by clear and convincing evidence. E.g., In re Cason, 249 Ga. 806, 294 S.E.2d 520, 522 (1982); In re David H., 283 Md. 632, 392 A.2d 83, 97 (1978); In re Davis, 380 Ohio St.2d 273, 313 N.E.2d 262, 264–65 (1974).

45 On the history of the character requirement, see Rhode, Moral Character as a Professional Credential, 94 Yale L.J. 491, 494–503 (1984). As in unauthorized practice, so in the case of bar character requirements, the era of attempted enforcement through bar committees began around the time of the First World War, seemed to peak during the Depression, and is now carried on in what seems to be a largely perfunctory way in many states.

46 Konigsberg v. State Bar, 366 U.S. 36, 40–41, 81 S.Ct. 997, 1001–02, 6 L.Ed.2d 105 (1961). The requirement is found in both Roman law and early common law. See Comment, Good Moral Character and Admission to the Bar: A Constitutionally Invalid Standard?, 48 U.Cinn.L. Rev. 876, 876 (1979).

47 Courts have uniformly upheld "good moral character" and similar tests against due process attacks because of their vagueness. Typically the reason given is that the test has been in use for a long time. E.g., In re Willis, 288 N.C. 1, 215 S.E.2d 771, 777, cert.denied 423 U.S. 976, 96 S.Ct. 389, 46 L.Ed.2d 300 (1975). The Supreme Court has itself justified the standard on much the same lines. See Konigsberg v. State Bar, 353 U.S. 252, 262–63, 77 S.Ct. 722, 727–28, 1 L.Ed.2d 810 (1957)(footnotes omitted):

> "The term 'good moral character' has long been used as a qualification for membership in the Bar and has served a useful purpose in this respect. However the term, by itself, is unusually ambiguous. It can be defined in an almost unlimited number of ways for any definition will necessarily reflect the attitudes, experiences, and prejudices of the definer. Such a vague qualification, which is easily adapted to fit personal views and predilections, can be a dangerous instrument for arbitrary and discriminatory denial of the right to practice law."

with applicants who had practiced birth control, had abortions or premarital sex, or didn't believe in God, because significant groups of people in society have personal moral beliefs that condemn those acts.

The concept of public morality might attempt to resolve the problem of nearly chaotic moral opinion by stipulating that only those moral beliefs held by a majority of people should be imposed. There are apparently insurmountable problems, however, in attempting to validate one's estimate of majority views on moral issues (even if one assumes the validity of imposing majoritarian views on moral issues); in keeping the moral tables current as views change and, in some way, dealing with persons excluded or included previously; and in assaying whether a local or a wider area of population should define the appropriate group for testing.

A method of avoiding the necessity to obtain agreement on moral beliefs would be to have a small group impose their own moral views on bar applicants, perhaps through a bar character committee that is given only the charge of assessing "good moral character" without reference to anything except their own moral beliefs.[48] But there is absolutely no legitimizing moral or social principle that would permit such an ad hoc imposing of moral views. That must be the case particularly where, as in the case of bar character committees, there is no public and little professional control over their membership.

A final method of assaying good moral character is the reverse of the first—instead of excluding all who offend the moral beliefs of a group, the bar committee should admit all persons whose conduct, if questioned, would be regarded as moral by any significant group of people.[49] That sort of lowest-common-denominator standard would admit to law practice anyone who could defend behavior by indicating any segment of our pluralistic society that countenances the behavior. The likely effect, of course, is to remove good moral character as a relevant focus of inquiry in most bar applications. In fact, that seems to be the dominant practice and philosophy of most bar admission committees.

Good Lawyerly Character

It could be objected, however, that a concept of good moral character becomes aimless as a social norm only if one fails to keep foremost the purpose for which the inquiry is being posed. The point of asking questions about moral character in bar applications is presumably not a general concern with the good moral life or to reward or punish certain behaviors. The effort instead is to ascertain whether the applicant is suited to the practice of law. Indeed, the Supreme Court has insisted that a state may not exclude a person from the bar for reasons that have no rational relationship to an applicant's fitness to practice law.[50] The chief inquiry should thus be whether the applicant has those aspects of

[48] Cf. In re Anastapalo, 366 U.S. 82, 102, 81 S.Ct. 978, 989–90, 6 L.Ed.2d 135 (1961)(dissenting opinion)(statement of member of character committee that applicant's "belief in the Deity . . . has a substantial bearing upon his fitness to practice law"). Professor Rhode's empirical survey of the operation of character committees has revealed a fascinating array of ideosyncratic determinations. In Michigan, for example, one candidate was initially denied admission by the committee (he was later admitted by the court) because of violating a fishing license statute ten years earlier, but other candidates were admitted who had been convicted of child molesting and conspiring to bomb a public building. See Rhode, Moral Character as a Professional Credential, 94 Yale. L.J. 491, 538 (1984).

[49] Cf., e.g., In re Brodie, 394 F.Supp. 1208, 1211 (D.Or. 1975)(homosexual behavior does not involve conduct inconsistent with "good moral character" requirement of Immigration and Nationality Act because several government groups no longer prohibit public employment to homosexuals and American Psychiatric Association no longer regards homosexuality as mental illness).

[50] Schware v. Board of Bar Examiners, 353 U.S. 232, 239, 77 S.Ct. 752, 756, 1 L.Ed.2d 796 (1957):

> A State can require high standards of qualification, such as good moral character or proficiency in its law, before it admits an applicant to the bar, but any qualification must have a rational connection with the applicant's fitness or capacity to practice law. . . . Obviously an applicant could not be excluded merely because he was a Republican or a Negro or a member of a particular church. Even in applying permissible standards, officers of a State cannot exclude an applicant when there is no basis for their finding that he fails to meet these standards, or when their action is invidiously discriminatory. . . .

personality and attitudes that will minimally guarantee good lawyering.

Moral character in a sense directly applicable to bar applicants might include such items as the frequently quoted catalog listed by Justice Frankfurter: "qualities of truth-speaking, of a high sense of honor, of granite discretion, of the strictest observance of fiduciary responsibility."[51] But to apply such a test to a candidate who has done little in life than live at home and at schools is totally unrealistic if it asks for repeated instances of such good character, particularly of the latter two.

Areas of Detected Character Deficit

Whether the task can be carried off or not, what traits do character committees and courts claim show significant indication of the presence or absence of good character? An inventory of traits that emerge from reported cases in which committees or courts have balked at admitting a candidate might include the following: a disposition to be law-abiding; a sense of fairness and honor in financial dealings; an attitude of responsibility that leads the person to fulfill commitments and obligations that have been undertaken or imposed; and a regard for truth and honesty. What follows is a sampling of the decisions that have denied or permitted admission to the bar on explicit grounds.[52]

Financial Dealings. If truly predictive, a lawyer's course of conduct when entrusted with funds of others in business dealings may suggest how the applicants might handle funds of clients. Courts have relied on as evidence of defective character, among other things, reckless business dealings resulting in the loss of funds of persons who trusted in the applicant.[53] The fact that a candidate has, perhaps legally, placed personal assets beyond the reach of creditors who are morally owed debts has been influential in denying admission.[54] A few decisions have held that taking advantage of a period of great leniency in personal bankruptcy laws to shake off just debts that the applicant could readily have repaid indicates an unacceptable character.[55]

Criminal Conviction.[56] Criminal conviction[57] is by far the most commonly reported

[51] Schware v. Board of Bar Examiners, 353 U.S. 232, 247, 77 S.Ct. 752, 760, 1 L.Ed.2d 796, 64 A.L.R.2d 288 (1957)(Frankfurter, J., concurring).

[52] Included is an occasional decision involving reinstatement of a disbarred or suspended lawyer. On reinstatement generally, see § 3.5.5. Various courts may treat such cases differently from original admission cases, either by being more lenient (perhaps because the lawyer is too old to change careers readily or has family obligations) or stricter (because of a belief that a lawyer with a prior history of certified professional misconduct is for that reason presumptively of a suspicious character).

[53] In re Lubonovic, 248 Ga. 243, 282 S.E.2d 298, 300 (1981); In re Appell, 116 N.H. 400, 359 A.2d 634 (1976). But cf., e.g., Hall v. Committee of Bar Examiners, 25 Cal. 3d 730, 159 Cal.Rptr. 848, 602 P.2d 768 (1979)(failure to express remorse for conduct, as manager of employment agency, that had resulted in twenty-day suspension of license as employment agent did not demonstrate absence of good character).

[54] In re Loker, 285 Md. 645, 403 A.2d 1269 (1979) (reinstatement case).

[55] In re Gahan, 279 N.W.2d 826 (Minn.1979)(lawyer anticipating lucrative career who took opportunity presented by amendment of bankruptcy law to obtain exoneration from sizable student loan obligations, although not faced with economic necessity, demonstrated disregard of right of others). See also Board of Bar Examiners v. G.W.L., 364 So.2d 454 (Fla.1978); In re Taylor, 293 Or. 285, 647 P.2d 462 (1982). But compare Board of Bar Examiners v. Groot, 365 So.2d 164 (Fla.1978)(applicant admitted after personal bankruptcy to liquidate past debts because of other heavy obligations for alimony and child support). There are two difficulties in the bankruptcy cases. First, does a state court's apparent negative reliance on the fact of a bankruptcy discharge lawfully obtained in federal court violate the supremacy clause? Second, when does the fact of voluntary bankruptcy suggest character traits inappropriate in a lawyer? Some decisions dealing with discipline of lawyers have taken a much more lighthearted view of the lawyer's voluntary bankruptcy, even if the lawyer's evident intent was to defeat the just claim of a client who sought the return of client funds. Prantil v. State Bar, 23 Cal.3d 243, 152 Cal. Rptr. 351, 589 P.2d 859 (1979).

[56] See generally Annot., 88 A.L.R.3d 192 (1978)(conviction of crime); Annot., 88 A.L.R.3d 1052 (1978)(draft law offenses); Comment, Past Crimes and Admission to the Bar, 5 J. Legal Prof. 179 (1980). Convictions can be taken as conclusive evidence of commission of the crimes of which the accused was found guilty, but proof of charges or of arrests is not competent evidence of the conduct that might or might not underlie them. See Schware v. Board of Bar Examiners, 353 U.S. 232, 241, 77 S.Ct. 752, 757, 1 L.Ed.2d 796 (1957).

[57] The general rule in discipline cases is that an acquittal of a crime does not bar a lawyer disciplinary agency from relying on proof of the same alleged criminal con-

reason for denying admission, but very few, if any, offenses are so disabling that a person will be excluded from the bar in every state because of the offense. In very general terms, courts seem to be influenced by the nature of the original offense,[58] the length of imprisonment or size of fine, whether the applicant has received or sought a pardon or expungement,[59] the age and circumstances of the applicant at the time of the offense,[60] whether the crime was isolated or repeated,[61] whether the offense occurred during or after law school,[62] the number of years ensuing between the offense and application, whether the applicant expresses understanding and remorse, and whether the applicant was candid about the offense.[63]

Are there crimes so serious that a court should never thereafter be satisfed that the applicant is worthy of trust? Courts have admitted applicants who, a number of years earlier, had been convicted of serious crimes such as armed robbery.[64] Probably any court would reject the application of a person who showed no remorse for a particularly serious offense or who indicated an inability to distinguish other clear instances of correct behavior. But it would be highly unusual that such persons, even if they survived law school, would still be out of prison. And very few authorities can be cited for the proposition that some crimes are disabling for life.[65]

Sex.[66] The law will probably always have an absorbing interest in sex—probably an interest that in some manifestations cannot be considered healthy. At the same time, much of what the most publicly prudish members of society disapprove of is found to be illegal in some states. Thus disqualifying from bar membership persons whose sexual practices or orientations are unpopular can in those states be defended vigorously, not as an insistence upon a narrow sexual morality as such, but as an objection to an attitude of indiffer-

duct to impose professional discipline (§ 3.3.2). The same rule is followed in bar admission cases. E.g., Martin B. v. Committee of Bar Examiners, 33 Cal.3d 717, 190 Cal. Rptr. 610, 661 P.2d 160 (1983)(dicta)(while acquittal did not preclude reexamination, when alleged ten-year-old offense could not fairly be retried it was error to admit partial and potentially distorted evidence of it). An applicant can validly be required to disclose offenses that have been expunged. See Wilson v. Wilson, 416 F.Supp. 984 (D.Or.1976), affirmed 430 U.S. 925, 97 S.Ct. 1540, 51 L.Ed.2d 768 (1977).

58 In re Kesselman, 100 A.D.2d 606, 473 N.Y.S.2d 826 (1984)(conviction, seven years prior to court's ruling, of criminal sale of controlled substance not itself disqualifying).

59 In re G.L.S., 586 F.Supp. 375 (D.Md.1984), order affirmed 745 F.2d 856 (4th Cir.1984)(en banc)(because felon, admitted to practice by state's highest court on close vote, would be ineligible to serve on federal jury and would be disenfranchised in many states, application to federal bar would be held in abeyance until applicant exhausted pardon procedures, which would also provide court with investigative mechanism it otherwise lacked); Maryland St. Bar Ass'n v. Boone, 255 Md. 420, 258 A.2d 438, 444–45 (1969); In re Davis, 61 Ohio St.2d 371, 403 N.E.2d 189 (1980); In re Estes, 580 P.2d 977, 980 (Okl. 1978)(expungement of conviction for conspiracy to import marijuana).

60 "[W]e have considered participation in unlawful incidents at an early age to be youthful indiscretions, which should not bar admittance to our bar after several years of law-abiding conduct." Martin B. v. Committee of Bar Examiners, 33 Cal.3d 717, 190 Cal.Rptr. 610, 661 P.2d 160 (1983).

61 In re Cason, 249 Ga. 806, 294 S.E.2d 520 (1982) (failure to prove rehabilitation following convictions on various misdemeanor offenses, mainly involving shoplifting, over ten-year period).

62 In re G.S., 291 Md. 182, 433 A.2d 1159 (1981)(repeated petty theft by twenty-six-year-old college graduate while in law school precludes admission); In re Taylor, 293 Or. 285, 647 P.2d 462, 467 (1982)(perjury at criminal trial for shoplifting that occurred during applicant's first year of law school, with other defects in record, results in denial of admission).

63 In re Willis, 288 N.C. 1, 215 S.E.2d 771, appeal dismissed 423 U.S. 976, 96 S.Ct. 389, 46 L.Ed.2d 300 (1975).

64 In re Application of G.L.S., 292 Md. 378, 439 A.2d 1107, 30 A.L.R.4th 1000 (1982)(fourteen years earlier, at age nineteen, applicant had driven getaway car in armed bank robbery; served six years in various high-security prisons; and given incomplete information about conviction and incarceration on application); In re David H., 294 Md. 546, 451 A.2d 657 (1982)(admission approved despite repeated thefts over period of time). But cf., e.g., In re Moore, 308 N.C. 771, 303 S.E.2d 810 (1983)(murder conviction twelve years prior to examination by board, together with testimony of subsequent threats to kill, sufficient to demonstrate lack of rehabilitation).

65 But cf. In re Application of G.L.S., 292 Md. 378, 439 A.2d 1107, 1119–20, 30 A.L.R.4th 1000 (1982)(dissenting opinion); In re Keenan, 314 Mass. 544, 50 N.E.2d 785, 788 (1943); In re Roger MM, 96 A.D.2d 1133, 466 N.Y.S.2d 873 (1983)(past criminal conduct, which consisted of convictions for bank robbery and first-degree murder, operates to bar admission to practice in state).

66 See generally Annot., 21 A.L.R.4th 1109 (1983).

ence to legal obligations. Yet in times of changing social mores, most judges have appreciated that even unwelcome changes in sexual practices, and certainly those that break no law, are matters of intense personal integrity and privacy and thus should not ordinarily affect a decision whether to admit an applicant.[67] A leading Florida decision has held that private, noncommercial homosexual acts between consenting adults, even if illegal, are not relevant to proving unfitness to practice law and thus may not be investigated or inquired into by a bar examining investigation.[68]

Veracity.[69] Many courts have insisted that no moral trait is more important to a lawyer than honesty.[70] Courts have been particularly harsh with applicants who have concealed information sought on an application questionnaire or have given misleading or incomplete responses.[71] Perjury offenses are also treated as quite inconsistent with a lawyer's obligations.[72] Lack of candor may also concern courts, which have refused to admit an applicant who has failed to file tax returns.[73]

Psychological Problems. Courts occasionally have relied upon evidence of psychological difficulties as indicating a personality that would not function effectively as a lawyer.[74] The obvious difficulties in relying on such evidence are that inquiries into an applicant's psychological background are intrusive;[75] a judge's perception of psychological difficulties might be objectionably influenced by political, life-style, or similar factors; and the psychological assessment and prognosis might be inaccurate.[76]

Politics and Ideology. Supreme Court decisions have apparently settled it that bar examiners may ask questions about knowing membership in the Communist party [77] and administer oaths that exclude honest appli-

67 Cord v. Gibb, 219 Va. 1019, 254 S.E.2d 71 (1979) (unorthodox living arrangement (unmarried and unrelated man living with woman applicant), which is unacceptable to some segments of society, bears no rational relationship to fitness to practice law).

68 In re N.R.S., 403 So.2d 1315 (Fla.1981). In an earlier decision, the Florida court had held that an applicant who had admitted homosexual preferences to a bar examining board could not be denied admission on a record containing no allegations of actual criminal acts. In re Florida Bd. of Bar Examiners, 358 So.2d 7 (Fla.1978). See generally Comment, Good Moral Character and Homosexuality, 5 J. Legal Prof. 139 (1980).

69 See generally Annot., 30 A.L.R.4th 1020 (1984).

70 Kosseff v. Board of Bar Examiners, 475 A.2d 349, 353 (Del.1984).

71 In re Walker, 112 Ariz. 134, 539 P.2d 891 (1975), cert.denied 424 U.S. 956, 96 S.Ct. 1433, 47 L.Ed.2d 363 (1976); In re Green, 464 A.2d 881 (Del.1983)(lawyer applying for admission on motion failed to disclose nonpublic ethics sanctions and pending proceedings in state of original admission); In re Beasley, 243 Ga. 134, 252 S.E.2d 615 (1979); In re Ascher, 81 Ill.2d 485, 44 Ill.Dec. 95, 411 N.E.2d 1 (1980), cert.denied 450 U.S. 919, 101 S.Ct. 1365, 67 L.Ed.2d 345 (1981); In re Jenkins, 94 N.J. 458, 467 A.2d 1084 (1983); In re Willis, 288 N.C. 1, 215 S.E.2d 771, 781 (1975), appeal dismissed 423 U.S. 976, 96 S.Ct. 389, 46 L.Ed.2d 300 (1975).

72 Gardner v. Gwinnett Circuit Bar Ass'n, 241 Ga. 614, 247 S.E.2d 64 (1978)(offer to lawyer to give testimony favorable to lawyer's client in return for money).

73 In re H.H.S., 373 So.2d 890 (Fla.1979).

74 In re Ronwin, 136 Ariz. 566, 667 P.2d 1281 (1983), republished with editorial modifications 139 Ariz. 576, 680 P.2d 107 (1983), cert.denied ___ U.S. ___, 104 S.Ct. 413, 78 L.Ed.2d 351 (1983).

75 Robertson v. Board of Bar Examiners, 443 So.2d 77 (Fla.1983), cert.denied ___ U.S. ___, 105 S.Ct. 96, 83 L.Ed. 2d 42 (1984)(no violation of constitutional privacy rights to require all applicants to disclose histories of all psychological and medical treatments and authorize release of all records by doctors and others); In re Applicant, 443 So.2d 71 (Fla.1983).

76 The Arizona court, in the *Ronwin* case, supra, clearly appreciated the first point, see 667 P.2d at 1288, but possibly not the second.

77 The Supreme Court has held that a state bar examining committee may require an applicant to answer a question about membership in the Communist party. Konigsberg v. State Bar, 366 U.S. 36, 81 S.Ct. 997, 6 L.Ed. 2d 105 (1961); In re Anastaplo, 366 U.S. 82, 81 S.Ct. 978, 6 L.Ed.2d 135 (1961). The same result would probably be reached even following the Court's 1971 decisions see § 12.2.3, none of which directly condemned mere inquiry into membership in a specific organization, although they did condemn broad inquiries into association and beliefs. See, e.g., Carfagno v. Harris, 470 F.Supp. 219, 222 (E.D. Ark.1979)(permissible under *Konigsberg* for bar questionnaire to require answer to question: "Are you now, or have you at any time been, a member of the Communist Party?"). Yet the Court held in Schware v. Board of Bar Examiners, 353 U.S. 232, 245–46, 77 S.Ct. 752, 759–60, 1 L.Ed.2d 796 (1957), and Konigsberg v. State Bar, 353 U.S. 252, 267, 77 S.Ct. 722, 730, 1 L.Ed.2d 810 (1957), that the mere fact of past membership in the Communist party would not support an inference that a bar applicant did not have good moral character in the absence of evidence of aiding or abetting of illegal acts or knowledge or support of such acts. Presumably, the only valid point of

cants who believe in the violent overthrow of the government and have a specific intent to bring that about (§ 12.2.3). Several states continue to enforce such requirements,[78] presumably on the belief that the tests effectively bar from law practice persons who would act destructively toward the law.[79] They probably do nothing to exclude truly subversive people, or to assist in identifying persons who would perform inadequately as lawyers,[80] and exclude only those of unorthodox political views, whose honesty by itself might be thought to commend them to positions of trust.[81]

Validity of Character Tests

Confidence in the innateness, stability, and testability of character traits led an ABA committee to propose at one time that all applicants to law schools should be tested for character in order to exclude those with defective characters, who would predictably engage in future serious professional misconduct.[82] Lawyering is hardly the only aspect of life for which we wish we had predictive tests that would assess with reasonable accuracy the likelihood of future conduct of a socially inappropriate kind. But the history of predicting behavior of individuals supplies little confidence that such a state has been achieved in any field, including those of professional discipline, preventive detention, or sentencing.[83]

As a generality, the objective of assuring the good moral character of lawyers is unshakably appropriate. In elaboration and application to bar applicants, the phrase quickly becomes meaningless, conceptual, and highly individualized. Its continued use permits, if it does not invite, errant or impermissible criteria such as discriminatory or oppressive viewpoints. While awaiting the development of a more appropriate standard or future breakthroughs in a science of predicting behavior, courts and bar committees should not pretend that they are more clairvoyant than the rest of humanity when employing a murky phrase such as "good moral character."

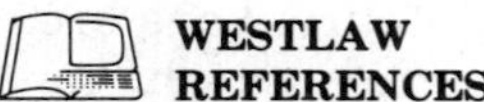
WESTLAW REFERENCES

digest,synopsis(character /3 moral /s admit! admission /s bar (law /3 practice) /p requir!)

attorney lawyer /s admission admit! /s character /s "due process"

What is "Good Moral Character"

di moral

"good moral character" /s standard test definit! requir! admission /s practice bar

konigsberg /12 366 +4 36 /p "good moral character"

45k7 /p convict! parole* expunge! "criminal record" guilty crime

admit! admission /4 practice bar /p sex homosexual! premarital extramarital /p character

asking the permitted question about past or present membership is as a prelude to other inquiries into knowing advocacy to incite illegal acts.

78 Carfagno v. Harris, 470 F.Supp. 219 (E.D.Ark.1979).

79 No such justification can explain the oath that denied admission to the Illinois bar of the applicant in In re Summers, 325 U.S. 561, 65 S.Ct. 1307, 89 L.Ed. 1795 (1945). The Court there held that it was constitutionally permissible for a state to require every applicant—including those whose religious beliefs prohibited them from taking the oath—to swear that they would join the state militia in time of war. The decision seems at odds with later decisions of the Court which have insisted upon a rational relationship between the state qualification and the practice of law.

80 Pushinsky v. Board of Law Examiners, 266 S.E.2d 444, 450 (W.Va.1980).

81 Despite all the turmoil of the times about draft offenses, only one reported decision has been found involving denial of admission to a draft offender from the Vietnam era. In In re Walker, 112 Ariz. 134, 539 P.2d 891, 88 A.L.R.3d 1045, cert.denied 424 U.S. 956, 96 S.Ct. 1433, 47 L.Ed.2d 363 (1975), the court denied admission to a person who had failed to register for the draft for eight years because of claimed psychological problems and not out of resistance to the Vietnam war.

82 ABA Section of Leg. Educ. and Admissions to the Bar, Report of the Spec. Comm. on the Feasibility of Establishing a Procedure for Reviewing the Character and Fitness of Candidates for Law School Admission Prior to Their Acceptance as Students (January 28, 1972). See Jaworski, President's Page, 58 ABA J. 667 (1972). But see, Dershowitz, Preventive Disbarment: The Numbers Are Against It, 58 ABA J. 815 (1972).

83 For a review of the psychological literature, indicating no scientific basis for predictions about future behavior, see Rhode, Moral Character as a Professional Credential, 94 Yale L.J. 491, 556–61 (1984).

§ 15.4 MULTIJURISDICTIONAL PRACTICE

§ 15.4.1 *Practicing Law in a Federal Nation*

Local Licensure and National Practice

One of the salient features of the American legal profession is that it is balkanized by the geographical limits of state lines. A lawyer's license is good for one state only; every other state will treat the lawyer as virtually an unauthorized practitioner if the lawyer practices outside his or her state of admission.[84] The justifications are two: assuring competence in local law, necessary because, it is said, local law differs so much from state to state; and assuring that courts of the state will be able to exercise disciplinary control over a lawyer for professional misconduct. Even the national federal courts pay at least lip service to state lines by generally limiting admission to local lawyers (§ 15.2.4).

Within its own borders, each state enjoys a large measure of freedom to admit or exclude persons from law practice as dictated by the powers in the state—typically the state supreme court and local bar associations. The federal Constitution and federal antitrust laws have put some limits on zenophobia and protectionism, but by and large local lawyers have been able to take advantage of the opportunity presented by federalism to place high walls around their own preserve.[85] The restrictions on out-of-state lawyers are a recent invention. Admission to the bar of other states was historically all the warrant a judge needed in order to admit a lawyer from another state without further examination. Particularly since the Second World War and the development of modern transportation and communications,[86] the restrictions on interstate law practice have actually increased almost in direct but inverse proportion to the need for interstate law practice.

Submerged in the process have been sentiments such as those in EC 8–3 that "clients and lawyers should not be penalized by undue geographical restraints upon representation in legal matters, and the bar should address itself to improvements in licensing, reciprocity, and admission procedures consistent with the needs of modern commerce." [87] As with other licensure restrictions, so here one must consider the distinct possibility that the rules are motivated by the local bar's desire to be protected against out-of-state competition.[88] Because the restrictions involve nonresident lawyers and interstate law practice, they naturally seem susceptible to challenge under the spirit, if not the actual reach, of the privileges and immunities clause,[89] the com-

84 The obligation of a local license does not apply to an out-of-state lawyer appearing pro se any more than a local license is required for a nonlawyer litigant who appears pro se. E.g., Hickman v. Frerking, 4 Kan.App.2d 590, 609 P.2d 682 (1980). See also § 14.4.

85 See generally Brakel & Loh, Regulating the Interstate Practice of Law, 50 Wash.L.Rev. 699, 700 (1975) ("Resistance to the phenomenon of increased interstate practice of law is prevalent today. A network of legal rules and regulations is aimed at restricting the practice of out-of-state ('foreign') lawyers."). For a bibliography, see id. at 700 n.3.

86 Q.Johnstone & D.Hopson, Lawyers and Their Work 21 (1967).

87 See also EC 3–9 ("[T]he demands of business and the mobility of our society pose distinct problems in the regulation of the practice of law by the states. In furtherance of the public interest, the legal profession should discourage regulation that imposes territorial limits that unreasonably imposes upon the right of a lawyer to handle the legal affairs of his client or upon the opportunity of a client to obtain the services of a lawyer of his choice in all matters including the presentation of a contested matter in a tribunal before which the lawyer is not permanently admitted to practice.").

88 In Sanders v. Russell, 401 F.2d 241, 246 (5th Cir. 1968), the court considered three justifications for Mississippi's restrictions on admissions pro hac vice, including "the financial or economic interests of the members of the Mississippi bar."

89 See generally Note, A Constitutional Analysis of State Bar Residency Requirements under the Interstate Privileges and Immunities Clause of Article IV, 92 Harv. L.Rev. 1461 (1979). For one context in which privileges and immunities arguments have prevailed, see § 15.2.3.

Constitutional protections against state restrictions on the right to travel, which were first established in Shapiro v. Thompson, 394 U.S. 618, 89 S.Ct. 1322, 22 L.Ed.2d 600 (1969), have been held not to apply to interstate travel for the purpose of law practice because law practice is not a "vital benefit," "fundamental right," or "basic necessity of life" that the *Shapiro* holding protects. E.g., Salibra v. Supreme Court of Ohio, 730 F.2d 1059, 1065 (6th Cir.1984), cert. denied ___ U.S. ___, 105 S.Ct. 295, 83 L.Ed.2d 230 (1984); Lowrie v. Goldenhersh, 716 F.2d 401, 412–13 (7th Cir.1983); Hawkins v. Moss, 503 merce clause,[90] the equal protection clause, and the federal antitrust laws.[91]

As a result of restrictive state rules, the movements of a national economy, which has generally ignored state lines in its expansion and present operations, have been followed only at a timid distance by the practice of law. The demands of national business have nonetheless been met by an extensive national system of informal lawyer referral operating between firms, by branch offices recently created by multistate law firms, and by some lawyers' accommodating to the apparent stricture of state localism.[92] The limitations have also assured the sales of national lawyer directories that are necessary for lawyers and business people who are forced by state restrictions to deal with strangers in protecting their vital legal interests. The other options for a lawyer who wishes to engage in a fully licensed practice in more than one state are sitting for another state's bar examination and fulfilling its other requirements for local licensure, undergoing the process of permanent licensure available in some states that is known as admission on motion, or, for litigation only, obtaining admission pro hac vice.

State-Line Lawyering

A problem much nearer to home burdens lawyers who live near a state line and who could readily practice law in more than one state. They have often been bedeviled by cartel-like regulations that have attempted to confine them to one jurisdiction or another.[93] The Supreme Court, in a notable decision that sharply limited the Fourteenth Amendment protections available to interstate lawyers, held that it was constitutional for a state to require that a lawyer maintain only one office, and that in the state, in order to retain a local license to practice.[94] New York, typical of other states, provides that a nonresident lawyer, even if otherwise a member in good standing of the New York bar, may not practice law in the state unless he or she maintains a bona fide office in the state.[95]

F.2d 1171, 1179 (4th Cir.1974), cert.denied 420 U.S. 928, 95 S.Ct. 1127, 43 L.Ed.2d 400 (1975).

90 See generally Note, Commerce Clause Challenge to State Restrictions on Practice by Out-of-State Attorneys, 72 Nw.U.L.Rev. 737 (1978).

91 See generally § 2.4.1; Pashigian, Occupational Licensing and the Interstate Mobility of Professionals, 22 J.L. & Econ. 1 (1979). Because of the state action doctrine (§ 2.4.2), however, and the fact that most restrictions are in the form of rules adopted and enforced by courts, it is unlikely that the rules themselves can be successfully challenged under the federal antitrust laws. Bar association participation in shaping anticompetitive restrictions may, however, violate antitrust laws.

92 Multistate law firms can operate in the large majority of states that permit the formation of a law partnership or professional corporation with one or more lawyers who are not locally admitted. At least in theory, membership in a multistate law firm does not enlarge the ability of an out-of-state lawyer to practice locally, even within the branch office of the firm. Service to clients that involves local practice is supposed to be relegated only to locally admitted members of the firm. Failure of out-of-state firm members to respect those restrictions has, in one case, led to a very broad injunction against unauthorized practice. See Florida Bar v. Savitt, 363 So. 2d 559, 560 (Fla.1978).

93 Fairfield Bar Committee v. Esterman, 174 Conn. 548, 392 A.2d 452 (1978)(Connecticut rule requiring that lawyer, here from neighboring state, moving for admission on motion must satisfy bar committee of intent to practice primarily in state). Courts occasionally recognize the incongruity of discrimination against out-of-state lawyers and change their rules. E.g., In re Sackman, 90 N.J. 521, 448 A.2d 1014 (1982)(changing former rule that required that (a) lawyers who resided in New Jersey maintain "bona fide" office there but (b) lawyers who resided elsewhere maintain "principal" office there). Some courts, with uncommon use of their powers, refuse to impose geographical tethers on locally admitted lawyers. See Archer v. Ogden, 600 P.2d 1223 (Okl.1979) (statute requiring locally admitted lawyers to maintain office in state as condition of practicing in local courts unconstitutionally infringed on court's exclusive power to regulate law practice).

94 Martin v. Walton, 368 U.S. 25, 82 S.Ct. 1, 7 L.Ed.2d 5 (1961)(per curiam). The Kansas rule upheld there required that a duly licensed Kansas lawyer associate "local" Kansas counsel for any Kansas appearance if the lawyer regularly practiced in the courts of another jurisdiction (Missouri) as well.

95 N.Y.—McKinney's Jud.Law § 470; Cheshire Academy v. Lee, 112 Misc.2d 1076, 448 N.Y.S.2d 112 (Civ.Ct. 1982). A lawyer so encumbered must, like the lawyer in *Walton*, associate local counsel in order to practice in the courts of the lawyer's own jurisdiction. Generally, bar rules do not require lawyers to maintain offices at all in order to retain a license, although often the lawyer registration system in a state will require a registered mailing address. Some states have explicitly forbidden local courts to insist on local mailing addresses for a lawyer admitted to practice in the state. E.g., Ill.S.Ct.R. Rule 701(b), as amended 1980.

Interstate Lawyering with a Local License

The restrictions of states against out-of-state practice have not, in the few decisions dealing with the question, been given a uniformly wooden application. The matter has come up in a few cases that have concerned the right of an out-of-state lawyer to recover legal fees for work for a forum client or to obtain other forum relief.[96] While the cases are as yet few, the portent is plain for quite difficult and complex questions of choice of law.[97]

Several generalizations about interstate law practice might be hazarded with some confidence. First, consider practice settings in which the lawyer in question functions solely within a jurisdiction in which the lawyer is fully licensed. It seems clear that no distant state has the power to prohibit the lawyer from advising a client, in the lawyer's own state, about the distant state's law. That should be the case even if the client is a citizen of the distant state and the legal matter relates to factors that are physically present there, such as land that is being sold.[98] If the lawyer's work involves the preparation of a document that is intended to be given legal effect in the distant state—such as a deed, mortgage, or will—the distant state still has no power to discipline the lawyer but would seem to have the naked power to refuse to acknowledge the effect of the documents. So long as the lawyer's work is allowable under the law of the place where the lawyer is admitted and practicing, however, no reason of logic or policy suggests why the other state would in fact deny the document effect (if it is otherwise unobjectionable) for the sole reason that it was prepared elsewhere.

Second, it seems clear that if the lawyer travels to the distant state and is physically present there when rendering legal services, the distant state has the power to treat this as unauthorized practice. In fact, however, several states have tolerated in-state law practice if the client is a regular client for whom the lawyer typically performs work in the lawyer's own licensed state and either (1) the lawyer's presence is an isolated occurrence and the work is not extensive in duration[99] or (2) the in-state practice is more extensive but is "incidental" to advising a client on a multi-

[96] By statute and court decision, several states have ruled that a lawyer may not recover fees for legal services performed within the state by an unadmitted lawyer. E.g., Emery v. Hovey, 84 N.H. 499, 153 A. 322 (1931). For other contexts in which the legitimacy of interstate practice has arisen, see, e.g., State ex rel. Ayamo v. State Bd. of Governors, 24 Wn.2d 706, 167 P.2d 674, 676 (1946)(lawyer, admitted in Indiana, who had practiced for several years in one-person office in Washington denied permission to be admitted to practice in Washington because violation of Washington unauthorized practice rule was "unethical per se").

[97] Moskowitz, Can D.C. Lawyers Cut the Ties that Bind?, Juris Doctor, Sept. 1976, at 34 (question whether differences in imputed-disqualification rules between District of Columbia and states following approach of ABA would mean that stricter D.C. rules would apply to any lawyer practicing law there regardless of where lawyer served former client). See generally § 2.6.1, at 50-51 (choice of law issues).

[98] Thus an unadmitted lawyer who performs otherwise lawful legal services with a lawyer admitted in another state is not an unauthorized practitioner for the purposes of the prohibitions of the other state against splitting fees with a nonlawyer. See Dietrich Corp. v. King Resources Co., 596 F.2d 422 (10th Cir.1979).

[99] In re Opinion of the Justices, 289 Mass. 607, 194 N.E. 313, 317 (1935)("[T]he occasional drafting of simple deeds, and other legal instruments when not conducted as an occupation or yielding substantial income may fall outside the practice of the law."); Lindsey v. Ogden, 10 Mass.App.Ct. 142, 406 N.E.2d 701, 708 (1980)(New York lawyer overseeing execution in Massachusetts of will of longtime client who was Massachusetts resident); Bennet ex rel. Federal Bar Ass'n v. Goldsmith, 280 N.Y. 529, 19 N.E.2d 927 (1939). Cf. Reisman v. Martori, Meyer, Hendricks & Victor, 155 Ga.App. 551, 271 S.E.2d 685 (1980) (Arizona firm, requested by Georgia physician to come to Georgia on emergency basis and defend attempt by employing hospital to decertify physician, was not required to comply with statute requiring foreign corporations to register to do business in state because representation was not extended on continuous basis). Compare, e.g., Florida Bar v. Jackson, 398 So.2d 817 (Fla.1981)(legal employment with city in state); Spivak v. Sachs, 16 N.Y.2d 163, 263 N.Y.S.2d 953, 211 N.E.2d 329 (1965) (unauthorized practice when California lawyer remained in New York for fourteen days to advise New York client on divorce and property settlement matters). But not all decisions have embraced an exception for isolated and short-term lawyering. See People v. Ring, 26 Cal.App.2d Supp. 768, 70 P.2d 281 (1937).

state problem.[1] But courts will find that unauthorized practice has occurred if the unadmitted lawyer practices persistently in the state, so that the practice takes on the character of a regular course of business.

Third, extensive and persisting law practice within a jurisdiction by a lawyer not licensed locally will almost certainly be proscribed by a state if it has taken on the character of a regular course of business or consists of appearances before courts or administrative agencies there.[2] That is clear, at least, if the practice consists of state law matters. Whether the federal Constitution prevents a state from excluding an out-of-state lawyer from representing a client with a federal claim has been mooted, but some important variations on the question remain undecided.[3] If the lawyer's representation, for example, before a federal court or administrative agency, was permissible under federal law, the supremacy clause prohibits a state from treating that activity as unauthorized practice.[4] If the lawyer's work consists of state court litigation, even of cases that are based entirely on federal law, apparently a state may regulate admission on the same basis as for state-law based litigation.[5] The undecided questions relate primarily to out-of-court advice, document preparation, and similar office work for clients.[6]

Multistate Law Firms

One solution for a law firm troubled by state insularity is to serve a client with a national business and nationwide legal problems through branch offices in several states. A quite different motivation for multistate practice is to expand a legal-clinic practice that relies heavily on advertising through me-

[1] Appell v. Reiner, 43 N.J. 313, 204 A.2d 146 (1964). The "incidental practice" approach has been recognized by other courts. E.g., Lozoff v. Shore Heights, Ltd., 66 Ill. 2d 398, 6 Ill.Dec. 225, 227, 362 N.E.2d 1047, 1049 (1977); Spivak v. Sachs, 16 N.Y.2d 163, 263 N.Y.S.2d 953, 955, 211 N.E.2d 329, 331 (1965). See also, e.g., In re Waring's Estate, 47 N.J. 367, 221 A.2d 193 (1966)(New York lawyer who had extensively represented decedent could, after his death and employment of New Jersey lawyers for most local work, serve as lawyer for the estate at request of executor when New Jersey work was limited to consultation with New Jersey lawyer and remainder involved multistate work).

[2] Bluestein v. State Bar, 13 Cal.3d 162, 118 Cal.Rptr. 175, 529 P.2d 599 (1974)(California lawyer aided unauthorized practice by sending client to unadmitted person who held himself out as expert in European law); In re Roel, 3 N.Y.2d 224, 165 N.Y.S.2d 31, 33, 144 N.E.2d 24, 26 (1957), appeal dismissed 355 U.S. 604, 78 S.Ct. 535, 2 L.Ed.2d 524 (1958)(Mexican lawyer not licensed in New York regularly advised New York residents on Mexican divorce law); Florida Bar v. Neadel, 297 So.2d 305 (Fla.1974).

[3] The Second Circuit stated in an extensive dictum in Spanos v. Skouras Theatres Corp., 364 F.2d 161, 169–71 (2d Cir.)(en banc)(Friendly, J.), cert.denied 385 U.S. 987, 87 S.Ct. 597, 17 L.Ed.2d 448 (1966), that the federal privileges and immunities clause would prohibit a state from excluding a lawyer, admitted only in another state, who, while physically present for an extended period in the state, advised a client on federal legal matters. The specific issue in the suit was whether a client could defend the lawyer's suit for legal fees on the basis of a statute voiding the fee claim of an out-of-state lawyer for unauthorized practice. The court held that the client was estopped to rely on the statute because the client's local counsel had neglected to move to have the plaintiff admitted pro hac vice. In dictum in a footnote in a per curiam decision, the Supreme Court in Leis v. Flynt, 439 U.S. 438, 442, n.4, 99 S.Ct. 698, 701, 58 L.Ed.2d 717 (1979), stated that the discussion in *Spanos* of the privileges and immunities point "must be considered to be limited, if not rejected entirely" by Norfolk & W. Ry. v. Beatty, 423 U.S. 1009, 96 S.Ct. 439, 46 L.Ed.2d 381 (1975). *Beatty* held that a state was not required to admit pro hac vice a lawyer who wished to represent a client in a Federal Employers Liability Act case. *Leis* stated that it was not deciding the analytically different question whether a client of the excluded lawyer could assert a constitutional right to the lawyer's services and hence to the lawyer's admission. See 439 U.S. at 442 n.4, 99 S.Ct. at 701.

[4] Sperry v. Florida ex rel. Florida St. Bar, 373 U.S. 379, 83 S.Ct. 1322, 10 L.Ed.2d 428 (1963). See § 15.2.5, at 855–56.

[5] Norfolk & Western Ry. v. Beatty, 400 F.Supp. 234 (S.D.Ill.1975)(three-judge court), affirmed per curiam 423 U.S. 1009, 96 S.Ct. 439, 46 L.Ed.2d 381 (1975)(state could constitutionally restrict out-of-state lawyer from appearing pro hac vice to represent defendant-railroad client in "numerous" Federal Employee Liability Act cases pending in state's courts).

[6] The few extant state decisions are generally hostile to claims of a "federal office practice" exception. E.g., In re Kearney, 63 So.2d 630 (Fla.1953)(admission to bar of U.S. Supreme Court, Tax Court, and Treasury Department, but not to Florida bar, did not authorize opening Florida office to practice as "federal tax counsel"); Ginsburg v. Kovrak, 392 Pa. 143, 139 A.2d 889 (1958), appeal dismissed 358 U.S. 52, 79 S.Ct. 95, 3 L.Ed.2d 46 (1958) (upholding injunction against maintaining office for law practice in Pennsylvania despite admission to bars of District of Columbia and federal court in Pennsylvania and lawyer's claim of exclusive federal law practice); In re Page, 257 S.W.2d 679 (Mo.1953).

dia that is interstate in nature.[7] The legal and professional complications in carrying off such a plan arise because of rules in some states that prohibit the use of a lawyer's name in a firm name if the lawyer is not locally admitted.[8] Also relevant are restrictive state rules on fee splitting with nonlawyers and limitations on nonlawyer ownership of an interest in a law firm.[9] Some of the states have rules that are sufficiently strict that no workable method of opening a branch office there is feasible. If it is possible to establish a branch office, that theoretically does not expand the right to practice of firm lawyers who are not locally admitted. But at least to the extent that a nonlawyer employee could engage in similar activities, an out-of-state lawyer can, while under the supervision and control of a locally admitted lawyer, conduct research, investigate facts, and, perhaps only with a locally admitted lawyer present, advise clients.[10]

International Law Practice

Frustrations similar to those that restrict interstate law practice have confronted American lawyers who have attempted to render legal services to multinational clients because of restrictions of other countries on local law practice. Some American lawyers have been admitted to the bars of foreign countries and can practice freely there,[11] but the barriers in some countries [12] are as restrictive as some of those thrown up here.[13]

WESTLAW REFERENCES

interstate nonresident /s law /s practice /s restrict! requir! /p constitution! unconstitutional

45k10

92k230.3(9) & nonresident foreign /s attorney lawyer

§ 15.4.2 Admission on Motion

Admission Derived from Sister-State Admission

As the United States expanded westward in the last century, probably the most common method of becoming admitted to the bar of new states was through *admission on motion*—admission simply on submitting a motion for admission accompanied by an affidavit that described the lawyer's training and the fact of admission to the bar of another court, typically one further east.[14] That method of admission has been retained in the majority of states, except for a dozen or so states that generally tend to be states with warmer climates, where many lawyers from northern states retire.[15] A state's refusal to

[7] Compare New York Crim. & Civ. Cts. Bar Ass'n v. Jacoby, 61 N.Y.2d 130, 472 N.Y.S.2d 890, 460 N.E.2d 1325 (1984)(permissible for legal-clinic firm, with names of lawyers admitted only in California, to open branches in New York so long as firm had one New York partner and practice in New York was conducted entirely by locally admitted lawyer-employees), with In re Advisory Comm. Opinion 475, 89 N.J. 74, 444 A.2d 1092 (1982), appeal dismissed 459 U.S. 962, 103 S.Ct. 285, 74 L.Ed.2d 272 (1982)(disciplinary rule requiring that all names in firm name be members of local bar constitutional).

[8] See generally Singer, Hunter, Levine, Seeman & Stuart v. Louisiana St. Bar Ass'n, 378 So.2d 423, 6 A.L.R.4th 1244 (La.1979)(right of interstate firm to be formed as partnership with one or more locally licensed lawyers with appropriate notations on firm letterhead of limitations of practice; state statute, purporting to make such practice criminal, void under inherent powers doctrine); Note, Regulating Multistate Law Firms, 32 Stan.L.Rev. 1211 (1979).

[9] See §§ 9.2.4, at 510; § 16.2.1, at 879.

[10] Cf. Spanos v. Skouras Theatres Corp., 364 F.2d 161, 168 n.1 (2d Cir.1966), cert.denied 385 U.S. 987, 87 S.Ct. 597, 17 L.Ed.2d 448 (1966).

[11] In re Griffiths, 413 U.S. 717, 730, 93 S.Ct. 2851, 2859 37 L.Ed.2d 910 (1973)(Burger, C.J., dissenting).

[12] See generally Note, Providing Legal Services in Foreign Countries: Making Room for the American Attorney, 83 Colum.L.Rev. 1767 (1983); "Lawyer, Go Home," 64 ABA J. 34 (1978)(report of expulsion campaign by lawyers in Japan against firms from New York and Hong Kong).

[13] New York, apparently unique among the states, offers a limited license under which a foreign lawyer may advise clients on foreign law. A large number of foreign firms have branch offices in New York as a result. See Nat'l L.J., Oct. 29, 1984, at 1, col.4. New York also permits foreign lawyers to appear pro hac vice. See N.Y. Ct.Apps. Rules for Admission of Attorneys and Counsellors at Law, 22 N.Y.C.R.R. § 520.7(e)(McKinney 1981), as amended 1980.

[14] Huber & Myers, Admission to the Practice of Law in Texas: An Analytical History, 15 Houst.L.Rev. 485, 496–98 (1978).

[15] Ariz.S.Ct. R.28(c)(1); Fla.S.Ct.R. Relating to Admissions to the Bar, art. I, § 1. According to Munnecke, Gaining Bar Admission in Another Jurisdiction, 89 Case

extend admission on motion is probably constitutional.[16] California and a few other states take a middle course, admitting on motion, but only after the newly arrived lawyer passes a special lawyer's bar examination that covers fewer subjects.[17]

Admission on motion, which is also called *reciprocity admission*, is invariably conditioned and limited. A condition imposed by some states, and hence the name, is that a lawyer who wishes to transfer a bar membership must be from a state that would afford reciprocity to the admitting state's lawyers.[18] Apparently all states that admit on motion require that the lawyer must have been practicing in the state of original admission for a period of years.[19] The requirement is defended on the ground that it affords the admitting state a basis on which to judge character and competence.[20] It also prevents the bar admission equivalent of Gretna Green marriages—admission of lawyers who, having failed the local bar examination, find another state whose examination they can pass and then promptly return to the first state for admission on motion. Nonetheless, apparently only a few states require that the standards for admitting a lawyer in the original jurisdiction were substantially the same as those in the motion state.[21] And despite the normal requirement that the practice have been in another state, most states have until recently required that the moving lawyer already be a resident of the admitting state at the time of the motion.[22]

Admission on motion on more generous terms is sometimes extended only to a favored few—who, in addition to their small number, seem by the nature of their practices to be unlikely competitors against the state's general practitioners. Such generosity is commonly extended to professors in a law school within the state,[23] legal services lawyers,[24] in-house corporate counsel,[25] or law students

& Comment 16 (March/April 1984), thirty states and the District of Columbia admit on motion, seven states provide a special lawyer's examination for lawyers already admitted in another jurisdiction, and the remaining thirteen states require a full bar examination procedure for all admissions.

16 So a majority of the Supreme Court said, in dictum in a footnote in a per curiam opinion. Leis v. Flynt, 439 U.S. 438, 445 n.5, 99 S.Ct. 698, 701, 58 L.Ed.2d 717 (1979) (per curiam).

17 West's Ann.Cal.Bus. & Prof. Code § 6062(d); In re Nenno, 472 A.2d 815, 819 (Del.1983)(Delaware admission on limited examination requires test only on Delaware procedure and legal ethics).

18 Hawkins v. Moss, 503 F.2d 1171, 1179 (4th Cir.1974), cert.denied 420 U.S. 928, 95 S.Ct. 1127, 43 L.Ed.2d 400 (1975)(reciprocity requirement constitutional). See generally Annot., 14 A.L.R.4th 7 (1982). Reportedly, ten states enforce reciprocity. See Munnecke, supra n.15 at 18.

19 Salibra v. Supreme Court of Ohio, 730 F.2d 1059 (6th Cir.1984), cert.denied ___ U.S. ___, 105 S.Ct. 295, 83 L.Ed. 2d 230 (1984)(constitutionality of prior-practice rule); Lowrie v. Goldenhersh, 716 F.2d 401, 412–13 (7th Cir. 1983)(same); In re Nenno, 472 A.2d 815 (Del.1983)(requirement of five years' practice in original state "next preceding" motion interpreted to permit reasonable interval to become established in motion state). Definitions of the practice of law can be strict. E.g., Undem v. State Bd. of Law Examiners, 266 Ark. 683, 587 S.W.2d 563 (1979)(service as bank president not law practice); In re Sasseville, 336 N.W.2d 624 (N.D.1983)(period of work as state's public utilities commissioner does not qualify for inclusion in required five years' practice in state of original admission).

20 Shapiro v. Cooke, 552 F.Supp. 581, 586–87 (N.D.N.Y. 1982), affirmed 702 F.2d 46 (2d Cir.1983)(per curiam).

21 In re Ferriman, 487 Pa. 45, 408 A.2d 844 (1979) (requirement of graduation from law school approved by ABA); In re Schatz, 80 Wn.2d 604, 497 P.2d 153 (1972) (same). The inquiry into the other state's standards sometimes appears to be pointlessly academic. E.g., Lane v. Board of Law Examiners, 295 S.E.2d 670 (W.Va.1982) (fact that California has lesser standards for undergraduate and law school education disqualifies all California bar memberships for purposes of admission on motion in West Virginia, even in case of applicant whose own credentials (college degree, graduation from ABA-approved law school, and passing bar examination with one of highest failure rates in nation) met standards of both states).

22 On the constitutionality of state residence restrictions, see § 15.2.3. It has been held constitutional for a state to require that a lawyer applying for admission on motion be a resident of the state and intend to practice full-time as a member of the state's bar even if there is no requirement that lawyers admitted following a bar examination continue to practice full-time in the state. Brown v. Supreme Court of Virginia, 359 F.Supp. 549 (E.D.Va.1973)(three-judge court), affirmed per curiam 414 U.S. 1034, 94 S.Ct. 534, 38 L.Ed.2d 327 (1973).

23 Wyo.S.Ct. R. 26, as amended 1977 (law professors with at least two years' teaching; provided that license is lost when licensee discontinues full-time teaching).

24 Minn.Rs. for Adm'n R.xiv, as amended 1979; W.Va. Code of Rules for Admission to Practice of Law, Rule 7.000.

25 Ohio S.Ct.R.VI(5)("Every attorney admitted to the practice of law in another state, but not in Ohio who

working in approved clinical programs that almost invariably serve indigent clients.[26]

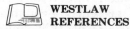

WESTLAW REFERENCES

attorney lawyer /p (admission admit! /3 motion)
reciprocity /p practice /s law

§ 15.4.3 Appearance Pro Hac Vice

One-Suit Lawyering in a Foreign Jurisdiction

With variations in matters of detail,[27] every court from the United States Supreme Court[28] to state trial courts[29] permits unadmitted lawyers to appear in litigation. The details relate to such matters as whether the admitting state requires reciprocity (the lawyer's home state would also admit the admitting state's lawyers pro hac vice on the same terms), requirements that the lawyer not appear in pro hac vice cases frequently,[30] and the need to associate local counsel. In most instances the matter is of no moment and permission is extended as a matter of course as a professional courtesy.[31] But there is no right to such an admission, and denials have occurred.

Association of Local Counsel

State and federal court rules commonly require that local counsel be associated with the out-of-state lawyer.[32] The degree of association ranges from the practice of merely supplying a local name that can be used as a mail drop for notices of scheduling and serving papers to a requirement that local counsel cosign all documents and be personally present during all court appearances.[33] The debatable rationales for the local counsel rule

performs legal services in this state solely for his employer as a full-time employee shall also file a Certificate of Registration and pay the fee as required by the foregoing sections of this Rule. Said registration shall continue in force only so long as such attorney is so employed."); Mich.R. for Bd. Law Examiners, R.5D. Cf. Skahan v. Powell, 8 Kan.App.2d 204, 653 P.2d 1192, 1197 (1982) (lawyer employed as house counsel not engaged in professional representative capacity that required license). Admission under a special license may become a trap, however, if the lawyer later wishes to apply for admission on motion. See Salibra v. Supreme Court of Ohio, 730 F.2d 1059 (6th Cir.1984), cert.denied ___ U.S. ___, 105 S.Ct. 295, 83L.Ed.2d 230 (1984)(Ohio rule constitutional that requires that lawyer seeking admission on motion have practiced at least five years but credits only out-of-state practice and does not credit in-state practice under corporate counsel license), disapproving Stein v. Coleman, 214 U.S.P.Q. 118 (W.D.Mich.1982).

26 Ninth Cir. R. 27, as amended 1980; N.J.S.Ct. R. 1.21–3, as amended 1979; App.Div., Third Dep't Rule 805.5, 22 N.Y.—McKinney's Civ.Prac.R. at 1894.3, as amended 1979; Wisc.S.Ct.R. III E, as amended 1978. See generally Walker, A Model Rule for Student Practice in the United States Courts, 37 Wash. & Lee L.Rev. 1101 (1980).

27 See generally A.Katz, Admission of Nonresident Attorneys Pro Hac Vice (1968); Note, Retaining Out-of-State Counsel: The Evolution of a Federal Right, 67 Colum.L.Rev. 731 (1967); Note, Attorneys: Interstate and Federal Practice, 80 Harv.L.Rev. 1711 (1967); Note, The Practice of Law by Out-of-State Attorneys, 20 Vand.L. Rev. 1276 (1967).

28 Dennis v. United States, 340 U.S. 887, 71 S.Ct. 133, 95 L.Ed. 644 (1950).

29 Brakel & Loh, Regulating the Multistate Practice of Law, 50 Wash.L.Rev. 699, 702 (1975)("Admission *pro hac vice* is evidently a routine matter in all states"). The statement in Leis v. Flynt, 439 U.S. 438, 444, n.5, 99 S.Ct. 698, 701, 58 L.Ed.2d 717 (1979), that pro hac appearances are not permitted in California, is simply wrong and was so at the time of the court's opinion. See Magee v. Superior Court, 8 Cal.3d 949, 106 Cal.Rptr. 647, 506 P.2d 1023 (1973). For a list of the jurisdictions' rules, see Nat'l L.J., Jan.12, 1981, at 29, col.1. The annual Martindale-Hubbell's Law Directory also lists pro hac vice rules. See also generally Annot., 20 A.L.R.4th 855 (1983).

30 See Norfolk & Western Ry. v. Beatty, 400 F.Supp. 234 (S.D.Ill.1975)(three-judge court), affirmed per curiam 423 U.S. 1009, 96 S.Ct. 439, 46 L.Ed.2d 381 (1975)(constitutionality of application of Illinois pro hac vice rule to prohibit out-of-state lawyers from appearing in "numerous" Federal Employers Liability Act cases pending in state courts).

31 But cf., e.g., Silverman v. Browning, 414 F.Supp. 80 (D.Conn. 1976)(three-judge court)(constitutionality of Connecticut's newly enacted rule permitting pro hac vice appearance only on showing of "good cause").

32 MacNeil v. Hearst Corp., 160 F.Supp. 157 (D.Del. 1958); Oswald v. State, 214 Kan. 162, 519 P.2d 624 (1974); Begg v. Roman Catholic Archdiocese of New Orleans, 380 So.2d 666 (La.App.1980), writ denied 381 So.2d 1236 (La.1980)(requirement of associating local counsel not satisfied by "association" with lay litigant who otherwise appeared pro se); State ex rel. Douglas v. Bigelow, 214 Neb. 464, 334 N.W.2d 444, 446 (1983); In re Smith, 301 N.C. 621, 272 S.E.2d 834 (1981)(requirement of local counsel is nonwaivable). See generally Annot., 45 A.L.R.2d 1065 (1956). At least one federal court requires the association of local counsel when a party's lawyer, even if a lawyer of the sitting state, does not have an office in the district or one (of two) of the districts adjoining it. See Ostrer v. Aronwald, 425 F.Supp. 962, 966 (S.D.N.Y.1976).

33 Kan.S.Ct.R. 116 (out-of-state lawyer must have local lawyer "associated and personally appearing with him in

have to do with protecting the lawyer's own client and protecting the power of the local courts to proceed in the absence of the out-of-state lawyer. It also supplies a measure of employment to local lawyers and serves as a deterrent to out-of-state lawyers who wish to practice locally to avoid the additional expense to their clients.[34] Almost all courts will permit an out-of-state lawyer to appear to move for a continuance without associating local counsel if it is necessary to protect the rights of a client who is distant from the place of litigation and when the client has not yet had an opportunity to make a knowledgeable choice of local counsel.

Limitations on Pro Hac Vice Practice

A very important line in pro hac vice practice must currently be drawn between litigation and office work. No state has yet provided a similar this-trip-only license to practice for client counseling, mediation, document preparation, or any other law office task not relating to local litigation.[35] As a result, there is no presently available method to practice outside of court in another jurisdiction without incurring some risk of violating the other jurisdiction's rules on unauthorized practice.[36]

Standards for Determining Pro Hac Vice Motions

Pro hac vice admission is often said to be discretionary with the judge before whom the lawyer will appear.[37] Decisions differ on the breadth and extent of permissible inquiry and the array of factors that the admitting judge may take into account in deciding whether to grant or deny a motion for admission [38] or to rescind an order that previously granted the motion.[39] Some cases should probably be understood as rules for particularly obstreperous

the action, hearing or proceeding"); State v. Woodward, 383 A.2d 661 (Me.1978)(notice of appeal was nullity when signed only by lawyer admitted pro hac vice and not by either party or local counsel); In re Palafox, 100 N.M. 563, 673 P.2d 1296 (1983)(contempt findings against both out-of-state and local counsel for violation of rule requiring, among other things, that local counsel cosign all papers and be personally present in court during all proceedings); Dorador v. State, 573 P.2d 839, 841 (Wyo. 1978)(local counsel is expected to take active part in representation and be available to share responsibility).

34 The rationales are critiqued in Misner, Local Associated Counsel in the Federal District Courts; A Call for Change, 67 Cornell L.Rev. 345 (1982). Despite the additional expense, a court has held that a requirement of associating local counsel does not violate the constitutional guarantee of the right to counsel, even if an accused person could not afford both out-of-state counsel of his choice and local counsel. Ford v. Israel, 534 F.Supp. 1128 (W.D.Wisc.1982), affirmed 701 F.2d 689 (7th Cir.1983), cert.denied 464 U.S. 832, 104 S.Ct. 114, 78 L.Ed.2d 114 (1983).

35 No extant authority seems to deal with the question of the need for pro hac vice admission to conduct a deposition in another state.

36 Lozoff v. Shore Heights, Ltd., 66 Ill.2d 398, 6 Ill.Dec. 225, 362 N.E.2d 1047 (1977)(out-of-state lawyer denied fee for extensive in-state legal work in negotiating contract for client and preparing documents).

37 In re Rappaport, 558 F.2d 87, 90 (2d Cir.1977); Skahan v. Powell, 8 Kan.App.2d 204, 653 P.2d 1192, 1195–96 (1982)(order disqualifying lawyer previously admitted pro hac vice within sound discretion of trial judge); Leonard v. Johns-Manville Corp., 57 N.C.App. 553, 291 S.E.2d 828, 829 (1982), review denied 306 N.C. 558, 294 S.E.2d 371 (1982).

38 Compare, e.g., Thoma v. A.H.Robins Co., 100 F.R.D. 344 (D.N.J.1983)(under broad discretion given to federal trial courts, motion late in pretrial for admission of house counsel denied on finding that house counsel had contributed to course of obstruction of discovery); Ross v. Reda, 510 F.2d 1172 (6th Cir.1975), cert.denied 423 U.S. 892, 96 S.Ct. 190, 46 L.Ed.2d 124 (1975)(no violation of right to counsel for state court to deny admission pro hac vice because of refusal of activist lawyer (William Kunstler) to limit extrajudicial comments during coming trial), with, e.g., In re Evans, 524 F.2d 1004 (5th Cir.1975)(admission pro hac vice may be denied only for reason that would warrant disbarment of lawyer); Hahn v. Boeing Co., 95 Wn.2d 28, 621 P.2d 1263 (1980)(trial judge improperly looked into question of whether representation resulted from impermissible solicitation of client).

39 Koller v. Richardson-Merrell, Inc., 737 F.2d 1038 (D.C.Cir.1984)(sharp practices of lawyers admitted pro hac vice that did not amount to violations of Code of Professional Responsibility cannot be basis for disqualification of lawyers), vacated for want of jurisdiction ___ U.S. ___, 105 S.Ct. 2757, 86 L.Ed.2d 340 (1985); Skahan v. Powell, 8 Kan.App.2d 204, 653 P.2d 1192 (1982)(disqualification of out-of-state lawyer, previously admitted pro hac vice, for engaging in other local practice); State v. Kavanaugh, 52 N.J. 7, 243 A.2d 225 (1968), cert.denied 393 U.S. 924, 89 S.Ct. 254, 21 L.Ed.2d 259 (1968). The Supreme Court's decision in Leis v. Flynt, 439 U.S. 438, 99 S.Ct. 698, 58 L.Ed.2d 717 (1979)(per curiam), holding that there was no due process right of a lawyer to a hearing on a motion for admission pro hac vice, is not at all inconsistent with the holding in Cooper v. Hutchinson, 184 F.2d 119 (3d Cir.1950), that, once so admitted, the

judges rather than for general consumption.[40] The problem is hardly trivial. At times and for some causes, the bar's boast that lawyers will spring to the defense of unpopular clients and causes [41] would have been a false, if pious, wish, had it not been for the work of out-of-state lawyers.[42] Restrictions on appearances emerged during the 1960s as an apparent tactic by which unsympathetic Southern judges attempted to hobble civil rights litigants [43] and can be used in other contexts by judges who are unsympathetic to a client or cause.

Nonetheless, the validity of unexplained state restrictions on pro hac vice admissions was upheld by the Supreme Court in Leis v. Flynt [44] against a limited constitutional attack. The Court held that an out-of-state lawyer did not have a right protected by due process to be admitted pro hac vice. But *Leis* acknowledged that it was not reaching the issue whether such a denial infringed constitutionally protected interests of the lawyer's client.[45] Apparently, however, it does not violate the federal Constitution for the state to deny a pro hac vice motion for no reason or for an arbitrary reason as far as the interests of the lawyer are concerned.[46] And apparently it would violate neither the lawyer's nor

lawyer was admitted for the "entire cause" and could not constitutionally be terminated without good reason. Cf. Johnson v. Trueblood, 629 F.2d 302 (3d Cir.1980)(in exercise of inherent supervisory power over district courts, hearing required prior to revocation of grant of motion to appear pro hac vice).

40 In re Evans, 524 F.2d 1004 (5th Cir.1975)(although not specifically noting notorious history of arbitrariness of trial judge in question, court announces general rule that lawyers are not to be denied pro hac vice admission except for reasons that would warrant their disbarment).

41 See § 10.2.3.

42 Indeed, in a great many of the frequently cited instances in which famous lawyers have courageously defended unpopular causes or clients, they have done so under a pro hac vice appearance. See Leis v. Flynt, 574 F.2d 874, 878–79 (6th Cir.1978)(Merrit, J.), reversed 439 U.S. 438, 99 S.Ct. 698, 58 L.Ed.2d 717 (1979): "Nonresident lawyers have appeared in many of our most celebrated cases. For example, Andrew Hamilton, a leader of the Philadelphia bar, defended John Peter Zenger in New York in 1735 in colonial America's most famous freedom-of-speech case. Clarence Darrow appeared in many states to plead the cause of an unpopular client, including the famous *Scopes* trial in Tennessee where he opposed another well-known, out-of-state lawyer, William Jennings Bryan. Great lawyers from Alexander Hamilton and Daniel Webster to Charles Evans Hughes and John W. Davis were specially admitted for the trial of important cases in other states. A small group of lawyers appearing *pro hac vice* inspired and initiated the civil rights movement in its early stages. In a series of cases brought in courts throughout the South, out-of-state lawyers Thurgood Marshall, Constance Mottley and Spottswood Robinson, before their appointments to the federal bench, developed the legal principles which gave rise to the civil rights movement."

43 Sherman, The Right to Representation by Out-of-State Attorneys in Civil Rights Cases, 4 Harv.C.R.-C.L.L. Rev. 65 (1968); Comment, "Yankee Go Home"—Civil Rights Volunteer Attorneys and the Unauthorized Practice of Law, 53 Cornell L.Rev. 117 (1967); Note, Constitutional Right to Engage an Out-of-State Attorney, 19 Stan. L.Rev. 856 (1967). Included among the restrictive rules were prohibitions against more than one pro hac vice appearance per year. Sanders v. Russell, 401 F.2d 241 (5th Cir.1968)(federal trial judge's rule with that restriction struck down). Civil rights lawyers were also prosecuted for unauthorized practice. Sobel v. Perez, 289 F.Supp. 392 (E.D.La.1968)(enjoining such a prosecution). See also, e.g., Lefton v. City of Hattiesburg, 333 F.2d 280 (5th Cir.1965).

44 439 U.S. 438, 99 S.Ct. 698, 58 L.Ed.2d 717 (1979)(per curiam).

45 439 U.S. at 442 n.4, 99 S.Ct. at 701. The clients were Flynt and his magazine, *Hustler*, who had been indicted for violations of Ohio's pornography laws. Because the indictments were pending, they could not resort to federal court to challenge the denial of admission of their lawyers. Their lawyers did not argue, and perhaps did not have standing to argue, the rights of their clients. Cf., e.g., Solomon v. Emanuelson, 586 F.Supp. 280 (D.Conn.1984)(client can raise constitutional right of client's lawyer to be free of residence restriction on admission on motion).

46 The lawyers in *Flynt* argued only a due process right to a hearing on the denial of their motion to appear pro hac vice. Finding no protected property interest in such an appearance, the Supreme Court majority refused to find that there was a due process right to a hearing. See 439 U.S. at 441–44, 99 S.Ct. at 700–701. (The Court's analysis suggests that it would have reached a different conclusion if the lawyers had been denied admission on motion, which is well articulated as a right in those states that permit it.) From the facts in the Court's opinion, there are at least two reasons why the state court might have denied the application. The lawyers had originally simply entered an appearance as if they were entitled to practice without permission, and the trial court might have taken this to suggest lack of knowledge of local procedures or, perhaps, an attitude of disdain toward local rules. The defendants were probably ill regarded by many in the community, and it is not unimaginable that some trial judges in the country would for that reason place obstacles in the lawyers' way. The Court apparently means to intimate that even such a plainly anti-First Amendment basis for denial pro hac vice admission does not violate the lawyer's due process rights. Whether it would deny the client's constitutional rights is, again, another matter.

the client's constitutional rights if the state were to refuse to admit any lawyer pro hac vice.[47]

For many observers, the existing pattern of artificial barriers to interstate law practice are indefensible. The demands of national businesses that their trusted and experienced counsel be able to conduct their legal business on a national basis create inevitable pressures for national legislation that lowers or eliminates many of the existing state-line barriers.[48]

WESTLAW REFERENCES

di pro hac vice

topic(92) /p "pro hac vice"

"pro hac vice" /s restrict! limit!

45k10 & "pro hac vice"

---

[47] Cf. 439 U.S. at 442 nn.4 & 5, 99 S.Ct. at 701–702.

[48] See the proposals offered in Comisky & Patterson, The Case for a Federally Created National Bar by Rule or Legislation, 55 Temple L.Q. 945 (1982).

Chapter Sixteen
FORMS AND FUNDING OF LAW PRACTICE

Table of Sections

§ 16.1 THEORIES ABOUT PAYING FOR LEGAL SERVICES

Scope of Chapter

This chapter considers the means by which legal services are made available to clients and the ways in which lawyers are paid for their work. The two are, of course, directly connected. Lawyers in a work-for-pay economy do not work for free; in fact, most lawyers, as do most other persons in a trade or profession in America, aspire to handsome livelihoods and attempt to calibrate the income from their practices accordingly. If law is not a trade, as lawyers of another generation insisted, it is clearly affected by economics, just as a trade is. And today lawyers no longer quibble with the description of law practice as a money-getting business as well as a profession that aspires to lofty accomplishments unaffected by economics.

If it is simple to understand why lawyers insist on being paid for their work, it is not as easy to understand why their clients should be the ones to pay them. Part of the economic issues concern fee charges to clients (chapter nine), but that assumes that the law requiring clients to contract to pay their lawyers is sound. Underlying that assumption are large social issues. This chapter considers some of those issues, including such basic questions as how and why clients must pay for what the law purports to allow them as legal entitlements; how clients are enabled to meet the costs of legal services by transfers from other potential fee-payers through group legal service programs, from opposing parties in fee-shifting arrangements, or from the state or charitable organizations in the provision of legal services to the poor; and the extent to which lawyers individually and through bar associations have worked to provide free legal services pro bono.

The chapter begins here with a general consideration of the payment-for-justice issue. It continues with a consideration of the internal ownership, financing, operation, and management of law firms. The chapter concludes with sections considering the economic impact of legal services upon clients.

Paying for Justice Services

One of the most bitter complaints lodged against King John by his barons in their confrontation in 1235 was that they and their retinue were required to purchase justice from the king's judges. One of the glories of Englishmen, embodied in the Magna Carta, was to have been that the king's justice need not be bought and was not to be for sale. Yet then and now it is the plain fact that a person who does not purchase the services of a lawyer is in a seriously—perhaps hopelessly—disadvantaged situation in the quest for justice from the state. Justice clearly is rationed, and often on economic grounds.[1] Other than a serious theoretical lapse, what might explain and justify the fact that persons who seek the law's justice are required to buy assistance? The answers involve a redefinition of justice that departs in some important ways from the conception made popular by the phraseology of the Magna Carta, and an understanding of some mythologies about the law.

The Magna Carta conception of justice was that it was the due of Englishmen; being a subject of the sovereign bestowed an entitlement to the king's justice. To be required to pay money to obtain one's birthright struck the barons at Runnymede as a perversion of status and thus of justice. Some emotional appeal still attaches to the conception of justice as one's entitlement, either in the sense of birthright or in the sense of something that we have earned by paying taxes, fighting in wars, or simply being good citizens and observing the obligations of the law on our own part.

But both lawyers and citizens also think of public justice in a different sense. We sometimes think of the law as the system of boundary lines that gives us ownership of property and rights. In that latter sense, it is comfortable to think of hiring a legal caretaker, just as it is comfortable to pay for a caretaker for our valuable personal possessions. That conception of justice is not so much attached to status, and thus is not so static, as it is attached to the importance of exchanges and transactions with others in which we give and take and earn entitlements through agreements and understandings that we are free to make or not as we choose. The conditions under which agreements and understandings should be enforced might be difficult to determine, requiring the expenditure of funds to hold trials or administrative proceedings to adjudicate entitlements. Because the dispensing of justice requires the expenditure of the funds of others of the public to hire judges and administrators, one who seeks justice should bear part of the cost of obtaining it. Moreover, the contract concept would be offended if one were supplied with legal assistance from a state agent. That, too, should be a matter of private choice and agreement.

Part of the common-law mythology, also connected to the pre-industrial revolution notice of justice, is that the law both should be and is accessible to everyman. Particularly in the colonies and the early years of the United States, a very strong popular sentiment was that the common law was simple enough that no one required a lawyer. If persons chose to hire lawyers, that was for their own convenience and the charge should be borne by them alone. A person accused of crime, for example, had nothing to fear if innocent. The law was plain, a good judge would see to its correct application, and a jury of sympathetic peers would pierce sophistry and fabrication to find the true facts. A lawyer was largely superfluous to this simple scene, and certainly a lawyer's charge, because it was a luxury, was one's own lookout.

1 Hazard, Rationing Justice, 8 J. Law & Econ. 1 (1965).

The law-for-everyman concept was probably factually erroneous even in its eighteenth- and nineteenth-century heyday. It is clearly unsupportable today. Law and legal institutions have become—whether necessarily or not—far too complex to permit the easy assumption that expert legal assistance is a luxury in working one's way through the system of justice. That throws one back upon contract notions alone as justifications for being required to expend one's own resources to hire lawyers in order to obtain what the law allows. As the materials on fee shifting indicate (§ 16.6), those notions do not invariably dictate that a person personally bear the expense of a lawyer. And, as many have agreed, in the case of the poor (§ 16.7) it is unfair to force those who cannot afford legal services to face the demands of the legal system without assistance paid for by others who are able to do so.

WESTLAW REFERENCES

[no queries]

§ 16.2 LAW FIRMS

§ 16.2.1 Nature of Law Firms and Firm Practice

Solo Practice

The traditional American lawyer is a lawyer who practices alone. The number of solo practitioners has declined over the past century, until now a minority of lawyers practice alone. But the solo practice will surely endure as an attractive form of law practice. Its great advantage is that a solo practitioner is free of entangling relationships that constrain and limit. The instinct to be captain of one's own ship is, to be sure, often acted out on a small deck. Solo practitioners earn markedly less than lawyers in firms. Solo practice has other inescapable disadvantages. With only the time, experience, learning, ability, and clientele of one lawyer to go around, solo practice creates periods of enormous demand. Consequently, solo practitioners often swing from period of serious overwork to times of little work, perform too little research, and sometimes lose or upset clients because of inability to perform specialized or multilawyer tasks. A solo practitioner cannot afford to surrender large blocks of time and as a result is unable to provide representation in prolonged litigation or to deal well with personal illness, disability, or even vacations. The satisfactions, instead, are those that come from the knowledge that one's accomplishments are personal and from having the unencumbered ability to make decisions that affect both clients and the lawyer's personal and professional life.

The Rise of Multilawyer Law Practice

If law is a profession (§ 1.5), it is also clearly a business with all of the small and mean details that the word *business* would bring to the Victorian mind. In addition to being a life worth living, the practice of law, as Holmes put it, is also "the laborious study of a dry and technical system, the greedy watch for clients and practice of shopkeepers' arts, the mannerless conflicts over often sordid interests." [1] One of the shopkeepers' arts that the large majority of modern lawyers must master is that of functioning with other lawyers in highly organized law firms. Firms must also confront the sordid reality that as they grow larger, their public responsibilities increase and, along with their public responsibilities, their susceptibility to public scrutiny.[2]

The growth of firms of more than one or two persons can be traced to the latter years of the nineteenth century, when larger firms developed in order to handle the increasingly

[1] Holmes, The Profession of the Law (February 17, 1886), in The Holmes Reader 99 (J.Marke ed.1955).

[2] Thus, in recent years, large law firms have had to learn to live with the reality of seeing their revered founders' names attached to litigation that draws into question the conformity of the firm's hiring practices to the minimal requirements of the federal civil rights statutes. E.g., Hishon v. King & Spalding, 467 U.S. 69, 104 S.Ct. 2229, 81 L.Ed.2d 59 (1984); Kohn v. Royall, Koegel & Wells, 496 F.2d 1094 (2d Cir.1974); Lucido v. Cravath, Swaine & Moore, 425 F.Supp. 123 (S.D.N.Y.1977); Blank v. Sullivan & Cromwell, 418 F.Supp. 1 (S.D.N.Y.1975).

complex litigation that growing economic units were engaged in and the increasing growth of governmental regulation. As firms began to grow in size, thoughtful lawyers complained that the nature of legal work was changing from one in which individual relationships of direct responsibility to clients were the rule to one in which law firms took on all the impersonality and bustle of business concerns.[3]

Remarkably, the image projected by both the 1969 Code and, more understandably, the 1908 Canons of Ethics is that the typical lawyer is a solo practitioner. There are some references in the Code to lawyers practicing in firms, although very few to other forms of practice, such as lawyers in corporate general counsel offices (§ 13.7.3) and in government legal offices (§ 13.9). But the Code apparently does not recognize the truisms that firms are different from a collection of solo practitioners who share the rent and that the division of function and responsibility within a firm can create both different and greater problems of professional responsibility than those that confront a solo practitioner.

The Nature of Firm Practice

On the surface, it might seem that questions of the internal structure and operation of a law firm are remote from considerations of the professional responsibilities of lawyers functioning within the firm. But those questions are often directly relevant to the principles of the 1969 Code and the 1983 Model Rules for several reasons. Several provisions of both lawyer codes, as will be seen below, relate directly to questions of structure. Moreover, to the extent that exposure to liability for damages is an important incentive for lawyers to abide by standards of professional conduct and competence, it is important to understand the ways in which lawyers may be responsible for the faults of other lawyers with whom they are allied in practice. As will be seen, the degree of vicarious liability may vary with the kind of legal structure employed to operate the law practice. In a broader sense, many issues of professionalism, such as fee setting, contracts with clients, and conflicts of interest, can best be examined against a background of understanding the forms in which law practice is carried on.

Organization of lawyers into firms means an increase in size, which brings problems inevitably associated with size. With size, and because of other changes in the relationships between lawyers and clients in large firms, the role of large-firm lawyers is tending increasingly toward technically narrow and specialized work.[4] Many large law firms have been built, and are sustained, by a relationship with a single large client such as a bank or major multinational corporation. That single client both supplies the firm with a predictable and large number of legal matters and annual billings and results in referrals of significant additional clients to the firm. But such a large client also threatens the professional independence of the firm and places great pressure on other lawyers within the firm to defer to the professional judgment of the lawyer who customarily serves as the sole secure link between firm and client.[5]

Limitations on Law Firm Growth, Capitalization, and Management

The extent to which law practice is still carried on exclusively in organizations that nowhere exceed one thousand members suggests either something necessarily very fragmented in the market for legal services or something very restrictive about structural limitations on the size of firms. The truth is that the size of firms is confined by limitations on two aspects of structure—client in-

[3] J.Dos Pasos, The American Lawyer 25 (1907); J.Cohen, The Law: Business or Profession 31 (rev.ed. 1924).

[4] Nelson, Practice and Privilege: Social Change and the Structure of Large Law Firms, 1981 Am.B.Found. Research J. 95.

[5] For reasons such as those, some firms have imposed strict limits (such as 15 percent) on the percentage of work done in the firm for a single client. See J.Stewart, The Partners 218 (1982).

take and capitalization. The chief intake limitation is the necessity of avoiding conflicts of interest. Because of conflicts rules, particularly the rule that imputes to all firm members the conflicts of each member, there is a size beyond which a firm encounters an uneconomical number of disabling conflicts.[6]

The chief capitalization restraint on the growth of law firms is that both the 1969 Code and the 1983 Model Rules prohibit a lawyer from practicing law in a firm in which a nonlawyer owns an interest or is in a position to manage or direct the lawyer.[7] Through much of their drafting history, the Model Rules contained a remarkable provision that was little debated but that, if adopted, would have loosened those restrictions radically.[8] That proposal was deleted to bring MR 5.4 back into general conformity with the 1969 Code except, possibly, with respect to group legal services (§ 16.5). The limitations are defended in the Model Rules as "traditional" and as designed to protect the lawyer's professional independence of judgment.[9] The prohibition against nonlawyer ownership of law firms has been examined by economists with an eye toward assessing whether the resulting phenomenon of exclusively worker-owned enterprises is economically efficient. The general, and not surprising, conclusion is that it is not.[10]

Sale or Assignment of Interest in Law Practice

In the rest of the commercial world, when a person has spent a career building up good will among customers, one of the nest eggs for retirement is the economic value in the going business. That can be sold to a younger practitioner, who is quite prepared to pay for an easier entree into an established business with an existing flow of clientele. Not so in law practice. The uniform position of courts and bar associations is that there is no legally or ethically recognized good will in a law practice that a lawyer can sell,[11] pledge, assign, divide as an asset on marriage dissolution,[12] pay taxes on, or give away. But there are probably legitimate ways of capturing some of the economic value of an established practice with careful planning.

A client's files are not subject to sale or other voluntary or involuntary transfer be-

[6] Conflict of interest problems are examined in chapters seven and eight. On imputed disqualification, see § 7.6.

[7] DR 2–103(C), (D)(limitations on group legal services); DR 3–102(A)(lawyer must not share legal fees with nonlawyer); DR 3–103(A)(lawyer must not enter into partnership with nonlawyer if any of business of partnership is practice of law); DR 5–107(C)(lawyer must not practice in law professional corporation in which nonlawyer owns interest or has position of director or officer or has power to direct lawyers); MR 5.4 (a)(no fee sharing with nonlawyer); MR 5.4(b)(no law partnership with nonlawyer); MR 5.4(d)(no membership in professional corporation in which nonlawyer owns interest or has power to direct).

[8] The high-water mark was MR 5.4 (Proposed Final Draft 1981). That version of MR 5.4 would have permitted a lawyer to "be employed by an organization in which a financial interest is held or managerial authority is exercised by a nonlawyer, or by a lawyer acting in a capacity other than that of representing clients, such as a business corporation, insurance company, legal services organization or government agency," so long as the organization provided written guarantees of compliance with the rules on professional independence, client confidentiality, advertising and solicitation, and fees.

[9] MR 5.4 comment.

[10] See generally Evans, Professionals and the Production Function: Can Competition Policy Improve Efficiency in the Licensed Professions? in Occupational Licensure and Regulation at 233 (S.Rottenberg ed.1980); Prichard, Incorporation by Lawyers, in Lawyers and the Consumer Interest: Regulating the Market for Legal Services at 321 (R.Evans & M.Trebilcock eds.1982).

[11] EC 4–6 ("The obligation of a lawyer to preserve the confidences and secrets of his client continues after the termination of his employment. Thus a lawyer should not attempt to sell a law practice as a going business because, among other reasons, to do so would involve the disclosure of confidences and secrets."); Geffen v. Moss, 53 Cal.App.3d 215, 125 Cal.Rptr. 687 (1975); Dwyer v. Jung, 133 N.J.Super. 343, 336 A.2d 498, 499 (1975), appeal granted and matter remanded 68 N.J. 177, 343 A.2d 464(1975), affirmed 137 N.J.Super. 135, 348 A.2d 208(1975)("A lawyer's clients are neither chattels nor merchandise, and as practice and goodwill may not be offered for sale."); Siddall v. Keating, 8 A.D.2d 44, 185 N.Y.S.2d 630 (1959).

[12] A court may, however, take into account the earning potential of a lawyer because of his or her membership in a law firm or other measures of the economic worth of membership in a firm as an economic value to be considered in dissolving a marriage. See Stolowitz v. Stolowitz, 106 Misc.2d 853, 435 N.Y.S.2d 882, 886 (1980); Dugan v. Dugan, 92 N.J. 423, 457 A.2d 1 (1983); In re Lukens, 16 Wn.App. 481, 558 P.2d 279 (1976). See generally Annot., 74 A.L.R.3d 621 (1976).

cause they belong to the client and not to the lawyer. Moreover, a transfer of client files to a lawyer not in the same firm, without prior client consent, would violate the confidentiality rules (§ 6.7.5). It has also been held that an agreement to sell a law practice in which the selling lawyer agrees to encourage existing clients to patronize the purchasing lawyer is void because it is contrary to public policy.[13]

An older lawyer can, however, enter into some kinds of agreements with younger lawyers that secure some of the same economic results as a sale. For example, it appears to be permissible for a lawyer who is contemplating retirement to enter into a partnership with a younger lawyer under which, after a period of initial practice together, the younger lawyer agrees to fund a retirement and survivor program that is based on future firm income. The prohibition in the lawyer codes against fee splitting with nonfirm lawyers does not apply to retirement plans.[14] In any such arrangement, of course, the retiring lawyer should obtain the fully informed and voluntary consent of clients to the new lawyer's assuming responsibility for their legal matters. That and similar arrangements do not substitute for free saleability. Among other things, because of the nonassignability of goodwill, it is difficult to extract the present economic value of a going law practice in any secured arrangement with a lending institution or other source of a large amount of capital or in the case of the sudden death or disability of a lawyer.

WESTLAW REFERENCES

lawyer attorney /s fee partnership interest /7 nonlawyer

dr2–103 "dr 2–103" "model rule 5.4"

transfer*** sell*** sale assign! /7 law /2 practice firm /p "professional responsibility"

attorney lawyer /s transfer sell*** sale assign! /s law /2 practice firm /s retir!

§ 16.2.2 Subordinate and Supervising Lawyers

The Responsibility of Senior Firm Lawyers

Lawyers in every multiple-lawyer setting interact with each other in senior-junior ways that are similar, whether in private-practice law firms, government law offices, or corporate general counsel offices. Those interactions will be discussed here using the generic term *firm* to cover them all.

From one point of view, perhaps the best way to train young firm lawyers is to do as law schools do—push the junior into deep water as a test and a lesson in swimming. The difference, of course, is that there are no clients in the first year of law school. In a law firm, professional pride, the threat of liability, fear of censure or dismissal by clients, and concern for high-quality legal services for clients dictate that junior lawyers be supervised in their work. It also dictates that they be admonished for improper conduct and, if necessary, terminated for major infractions or to protect client interests.[15] As debatable as some issues of professional ethics may be, work must proceed and responsibility

13 Geffen v. Moss, 53 Cal.App.3d 215, 125 Cal.Rptr. 687, 694 (1975).

14 DR 2–107(B). The same rule can be extracted, with some difficulty, from MR 5.4(a)(3). The Model Rule provisions apply to the right to include *nonlawyer* employees of a firm in profit-sharing compensation or retirement plans. A fortiori, former *lawyers* in a firm should be able to receive the same treatment. The lack in the Model Rules of a precisely correlative provision to DR 2–107(B) is confusing and regrettable but appears to have been inadvertent.

DR 2–107(B) is probably broader than even a generous reading of MR 5.4(a), however, with respect to the types of separation agreements that are not for the purpose of retirement. The Code specifically permits fee-splitting separation agreements, but the Model Rule provision on nonlawyer employees does not provide for profit-sharing separation agreements.

15 In Harman v. La Crosse Tribune, 117 Wis.2d 448, 344 N.W.2d 536, 540 (1984), cert.denied ___ U.S. ___, 105 S.Ct. 58, 83 L.Ed.2d 9 (1984), the court held that a law firm justifiably terminated a lawyer who as a politician had made public statements attacking the integrity of a newspaper that was a major client of the firm, although the lawyer had not actually worked on any client matter.

for calling close questions must rest with the lawyer ultimately responsible for assuring that the client is competently represented.

Quite apart from the issue of control of the individual work by individual senior lawyers with whom a junior lawyer may be working, every responsible member of the firm shares in the firm's collective responsibility for the firm's work. In part the question is one of morality, as well as a legal and organizational issue.[16] While division of labor is a desirable and necessary aspect of organizational structure, no firm member should rest content that the organizational lines of authority and communication that have been established will inevitably and always work satisfactorily or are themselves above criticism and improvement. At the very least, as many commentators have observed, a law firm that assumes some collaborative responsibility for the moral climate of the firm's practice can improve morale, the quality of work, and, perhaps, the moral standards of the firm's lawyers and other employees.[17] Some firms have institutionalized the effort through a firm ethics committee.[18]

Junior Lawyers and Law Firm Ethics

Young lawyers new to law practice may feel uneasy making ethical decisions in a multi-lawyer organization. Particularly in larger firms, associates at the beginning of their careers may have very little information about the work habits and personalities of individual partners and little control over their initial assignment to partners and senior associates with whom they must work. Many associates come technically prepared but quite unaccustomed to the ways of law firms and of working with clients. They are likely, sometimes with cause, to be awed by the professional prowess of partners and intimidated by the magnitude and importance of client matters. Associates very quickly develop strong loyalties to a supporting partner, who may be the passkey to discretionary salary increases, favorable work assignments, greater professional responsibility and more interesting work, and advancement in the firm. The relationship and the work environment, in short, leave associates with little ethical room to maneuver and readily susceptible to direction and even to hints and more subtle directive cues from senior lawyers.

Responsibilities of Senior and Supervising Lawyers

The 1969 Code does not specifically require senior lawyers to supervise junior lawyers.[19] It does contain the charge, in DR 1–102(A)(2), that a lawyer should not "circumvent a Disciplinary Rule through actions of others," [20] but that does not cover instances in which the senior lawyer does not initiate the violation. Nonetheless, decisions under the Code have insisted that senior lawyers labor under a responsibility to supervise junior lawyers.[21] "[N]ewly admitted attorneys in a law firm should be given guidance and supervision by their senior colleagues." [22] Concomitantly, decisions have intimated that supervised lawyers are justified in deferring to the well-

[16] See generally, e.g., Flores & Johnson, Collective Responsibility and Professional Roles, 93 Ethics 537 (1983).

[17] Wessel, Institutional Responsibility: Professionalism and Ethics, 60 Neb.L.Rev. 504, 512–13 (1981); Schneyer, The Model Rules and Problems of Code Interpretation and Enforcement, 1980 Am.B.Found. Research J. 939, 947.

[18] Cf. MR 5.1 comment (second paragraph)(reference to a "special committee" to deal with ethical problems in firms).

[19] The closest that the Code comes to a general statement is in the Preliminary Statement, which states that a lawyer "should ultimately be responsible for the conduct of his employees and associates in the course of the professional representation of the client."

[20] MR 8.4(a) is broader. It provides that a lawyer should not "violate or attempt to violate the rules of professional conduct, knowingly assist or induce another to do so, or do so through the acts of another."

[21] In re Crane, 400 Mich. 484, 255 N.W.2d 624, 628 (1977)(dicta); In re Berlant, 458 Pa. 439, 328 A.2d 471, 474 (1974), cert.denied 421 U.S. 964, 95 S.Ct. 1953, 44 L.Ed.2d 451 (1975)(senior lawyer is not relieved of culpability because preparation of false contingent fee statements was delegated to associate and senior thus may not have "dirtied his hands with the manual task"). Cf., e.g., Office of Disciplinary Counsel v. Eilberg, 497 Pa. 388, 441 A.2d 1193, 1196 (1982)(lawyer cannot foist full responsibility for receipt of illegal fee onto partner).

[22] In re Barry, 90 N.J. 286, 447 A.2d 923, 925 (1982).

considered judgments of their employing superiors on doubtful questions. No such thing as an absolute Nuremberg, or superior-orders, defense is recognized for acts that are plainly illegal or in violation of the lawyer codes.[23] Courts have, however, taken into account as a mitigating factor the relative youth and inexperience of a junior lawyer involved in a dishonest or otherwise wrongful scheme with a trusted senior lawyer.[24]

The regrettable absence from the Code of a specific provision dealing with supervision is remedied in the 1983 Model Rules. As does MR 5.3 on nonlawyer employees (§ 16.3.1), MR 5.1 bases supervisory responsibility on a concept of reasonable care and does not make supervising lawyers the insurers of junior-lawyer compliance with professional obligations.

The responsibilities of firm lawyers under MR 5.1 can be considered from three perspectives. First, every partner [25] in a law firm is responsible under MR 5.1(a) to make "reasonable efforts" to see that the firm has in place and operating the appropriate measures [26] necessary to give "reasonable assurance" that all lawyers in the firm conform to the rules of professional conduct. Apparently, every lawyer who fails to fulfill that responsibility has committed a disciplinary violation even if it has had no causal effect, that is, even if no other lawyer in the firm has committed an ethical violation that occurred or was undetected because of the absence of appropriate measures.[27]

Second, every lawyer who has "direct supervisory authority" over another lawyer has special responsibilities to make "reasonable efforts" to assure that that lawyer conforms to the rules of professional conduct. That provision places squarely on a senior lawyer working with a junior lawyer the duty to take active steps to check the actual working habits of the junior lawyer and, when necessary, to admonish the junior lawyer or take other steps necessary to bring the lawyer's conduct into conformity with the rules. Ignoring the work of a junior lawyer for whom the senior has supervisory responsibility is a violation of the rule.[28]

Third, a rule of limited vicarious responsibility for the ethical violations of other lawyers applies differentially to all lawyers and to partners and supervising lawyers. All lawyers are liable to discipline under MR 5.1(c)(1) if the lawyer "orders, or with knowledge of

[23] In re Callahan, 442 N.E.2d 1092, 1094–95 (Ind.1982) (young associate who acquiesced in, and benefited from, extortion scheme concocted by successful senior lawyer cannot be excused because of subordinate relationship); Attorney Grievance Comm'n v. Kahn, 290 Md. 654, 431 A.2d 1336, 1351 (1981)(associate could not excuse engaging in fraudulent, illegal, and unethical practices by need to retain job as associate with employer or by pervasiveness of similar practices among lawyers in same locality). Cf. ABA Informal Op. 1203 (1972). A lawyer's degree of culpability in wrongful acts may depend on whether the lawyer reasonably relied on a trusted legal colleague for information about the state of facts. Cf. In re Gross, 91 A.D.2d 1145, 458 N.Y.S.2d 366, 367(1983), appeal denied 58 N.Y.2d 608, 462 N.Y.S.2d 1025, 448 N.E.2d 1358 (1983) (lawyer disciplined less severely than his brother, a lawyer in another city, for falsely endorsing checks made out to their deceased father on strength of brother's assurance that governmental office issuing checks had authorized the practice).

[24] In re Moore, 280 S.C. 178, 312 S.E.2d 1, 3 (1984).

[25] The Terminology section of the Model Rules defines a partner as "a member of a partnership and a shareholder in a law firm organized as a professional corporation." Unfortunately for present purposes, the definition excludes senior lawyers in corporate general counsel offices or government legal offices. Yet MR 5.1 comment (first paragraph) asserts that MR 5.1(a) "refer[s] to lawyers who have supervisory authority over the professional work of a firm or legal department of a government agency. This includes members of a partnership and the shareholders in a law firm organized as a professional corporation; lawyers having supervisory authority in the law department of an enterprise or government agency; and lawyers who have intermediate managerial responsibilities in a firm." The rough-hewn drafting effort here seems to have been to control the meaning of "partner" in MR 5.1 by a definition whose sweep is much more global than that in the Terminology section.

[26] MR 5.1 comment (second paragraph) notes that the measures will vary considerably, depending on the size and nature of work of a firm, and suggests that firms of all sizes engage in continuing education concerning professional ethics.

[27] See generally Schneyer, The Model Rules and Problems of Code Interpretation and Enforcement, 1980 Am. B.Found. Research J. 939, 948.

[28] MR 5.1 comment (paragraph five); id. (paragraph two).

the specific conduct, ratifies" [29] the other lawyer's violation. A lawyer who is a partner or a supervising lawyer has a further responsibility: under MR 5.1(c)(2), such a lawyer must also take "reasonable remedial action" to avoid or mitigate the effects of conduct of another lawyer. The duty extends, in the case of partners, to the conduct of any other lawyer in the firm and, in the case of a supervising nonpartner, to the conduct of a lawyer whom the first lawyer supervises.

Responsibilities of Junior Lawyers

The Model Rules, in MR 5.2, also improve upon the Code in their explication of the duties of "subordinate" lawyers. The general rule of MR 5.2(a) is that a subordinate lawyer cannot excuse what otherwise would be a violation of the ethical rules with an argument that the subordinate lawyer acted at the direction of a lawyer, including a lawyer who had hire-or-fire or similar organizational power over the subordinate lawyer. But under MR 5.2(b), if the matter is reasonably arguable and the subordinate lawyer acts pursuant to a supervisory lawyer's "reasonable resolution of an arguable question [30] of professional duty," the junior lawyer has not violated the Model Rules.

The Model Rules, for sufficient reasons, go only as far as resolving the disciplinary-organizational quandary that a junior lawyer faces when confronted with a debatable question. A decision within the firm must be made one way or another and it is certainly appropriate to have the lawyer-in-charge call the shots on debatable questions. The Model Rules also seem to assume, although they do not require, that a discussion will occur between senior and junior lawyers that, one hopes, will lead to better ethical decisions. Suppose, however, that the junior lawyer remains unpersuaded, although adequately overruled. Should the junior lawyer proceed with a step that he or she, with deference, remains convinced is unethical? The question is not one charged with disciplinary implications, but it does speak to the general moral climate of the firm. In all instances but those in which the junior lawyer's services are truly indispensable to the particular client matter and the matter is one of substantial importance, the better practice would be for the firm to provide as a matter of course that a junior associate can withdraw from a particular representation and be assigned to other matters. In the long run, the protection of autonomous ethical decision making can only redound to the benefit of the firm and its lawyers. In some cases, perhaps, the junior lawyer's only ethically appropriate reaction might be to take the extreme step of resigning from the firm.

WESTLAW REFERENCES

senior supervis! /s attorney lawyer /s responsib! culpab! liab! /s junior associate subordinate

junior associate subordinate /s attorney lawyer partner /s senior supervis! /p disciplin!

---

§ 16.2.3 Lawyer Partnerships

Applicability of General Partnership Law and Lawyer Codes

The law relating to partnerships, including the provisions of the Uniform Partnership Act in force in a jurisdiction,[31] is generally applicable to partnerships of lawyers engaged

[29] "Ratifies" is apparently used in its customary legal sense of taking affirmative steps to approve of the violation. A lawyer who simply knows of another lawyer's ethical violation but does nothing about it is subject, apparently, only to the limited obligations of MR 8.3(a) on reporting serious ethical violations to a lawyer disciplinary agency. It is not clear why a lawyer should not be required also, or perhaps first, to attempt to correct the situation within the firm.

[30] MR 5.2 comment (second paragraph) indicates that the question itself, in addition to its resolution, must be one that is "reasonably arguable." It gives the concrete example of a question whether, under MR 1.7, a conflict of interest between two clients exists. Presumably the reference is to a question of conflict that can only be resolved under the open-ended provisions of MR 1.7.

[31] See generally Uniform Partnership Act § 2 ("business" of partnership includes "every trade, occupation, or profession"). E.g., Jewel v. Boxer, 156 Cal.App.3d 171, 203 Cal.Rptr. 13, 17 (1984); Resnick v. Kaplan, 49 Md. App. 499, 434 A.2d 582, 588 (1981). The provisions of the Uniform Partnership Act have been adopted with local alterations in almost all American jurisdictions.

in the practice of law.[32] With respect to the internal operation of a law practice, that means that the provisions of partnership law apply to such questions as the creation of a partnership,[33] its name,[34] the identification and treatment of partnership property,[35] the termination of the partnership at the death or departure of a partner, the degree of control and participation in firm profits and losses, and the extent to which partners can practice and derive income from clients and other sources outside the partnership. In addition, of course, the lawyer-partners all remain fully subject to the provisions of the lawyer codes. The lawyer codes should specifically apply to lawyer-partners' dealings among themselves, at least in the sense that those dealings can be indicative of a lawyer's general competence, attitude toward legal obligations, and ability to assume fiduciary responsibilities.[36]

Partners as Agents of Partnership and Each Other

As a member of a partnership, each partner possesses the power to affect profoundly the fortunes of each other member of the partnership. The general law of partnership liability is that if the activities of any partner relate to the course of the partnership business, those activities may create contractual [37] and tort [38] liability that binds the entire membership of the partnership. The liability extends to the seizure and execution sale of partnership assets, such as a law library, furniture, and the like. More importantly, the liability extends to the personal assets of each member of the partnership. The rule of joint and several liability does not, however, mean that law partners are the alter ego of each other for all legal purposes.[39]

Partnerships—Express, Implied, and Apparent

Law partnerships are based on contractual undertakings, although the contract may be either express or implied and need not be in writing.[40] Moreover, even if lawyers practicing together in fact have no partnership relationship, their activities may present the appearance of a partnership to the outside world and specifically to clients. Under general partnership law, lawyers who are in fact not

32 See generally Annot., 175 A.L.R. 1310 (1948).

33 For tax reasons (e.g., Keller v. Commissioner, 77 T.C. 1014 (1981), affirmed 723 F.2d 58 (10th Cir. 1983)), it may be economically useful for lawyers to incorporate themselves as professional corporations and then have the professional corporation join a law partnership as an entity. In Informal Op. 1471 (1981) it was held that nothing in the Code prohibited the arrangement. See also, e.g., N.C.Code; DR 2–102(C) (as amended 1980) (words added to indicate approval of professional corporations' becoming members of law partnership). See generally Note, Law Firms: Selected Partnership Tax Problems of Formation and Admission of New Partners, 59 Neb.L.Rev. 679 (1980).

34 The lawyer code advertising provisions on firm names, of course, apply. See § 14.2.4, at 785–86. A partnership name may consist of the name of only one lawyer. EC 2–11 ("a lawyer in private practice should practice only under a designation containing . . . the name of one or more of the lawyers practicing in a partnership").

35 United States v. Mandel, 437 F.Supp. 258, 261 (D.Md. 1977)(lawyer's time records as partnership property).

36 People v. Pittam, 194 Colo. 104, 572 P.2d 135 (1977) (en banc); Levi v. Mississippi St. Bar, 436 So.2d 781, 785–86 (Miss.1983); In re O'Grady, 92 N.J. 623, 458 A.2d 1285 (1983); In re Berkeley, 174 App.Div. 205, 160 N.Y.S. 1093 (1916), affirmed 243 N.Y. 597, 154 N.E. 621 (1926). The court in In re Lowther, 611 S.W.2d 1, 2 (Mo.1981), expressed reservations about applying the 1969 Code to dealings between partners on the erroneous ground that the purpose of the Code is to protect only the public and not lawyers from each other. In private litigation between former partners, however, it is appropriate for the court to honor a stipulation that matters of professional impropriety will not be an issue in an accounting proceeding. See Nishman v. DeMarco, 76 A.D.2d 360, 430 N.Y.S.2d 339 (1980), appeal dismissed 53 N.Y.2d 642, 438 N.Y.S.2d 787, 420 N.E.2d 979(1981).

37 Blue Print Co., Inc. v. Ford Marrin Esposito Witmeyer & Bergman, 102 Misc.2d 1090, 424 N.Y.S.2d 970 (Civ.Ct.1980), affirmed on opinion below 107 Misc.2d 239, 438 N.Y.S.2d 170 (App.Term 1981)(one law partner may bind all others with respect to undertaking to third-party service supplier).

38 On the vicarious, joint and several liability of the members of a law partnership for tortious conduct of partners, see § 5.6.6.

39 Grayson v. Wofsey, Rosen, Kweskin & Kuriansky, 40 Conn.Sup. 1, 478 A.2d 629 (Sup.Ct.1984)(partners are not agents of each other for purposes of receipt of process in legal malpractice action).

40 The desirability of a writing is typically appreciated by lawyers much more for their clients than for themselves. The need is often forcefully driven home by the death of a managing partner or other cataclysmic event. E.g., In re Lester, 87 Misc.2d 717, 386 N.Y.S.2d 509 (Sup. Ct.1976).

partners may be liable as if they were partners to clients and others who have relied on the appearance of a partnership.[41] Beyond the law of apparent partnership, or as it is also sometimes called, the law of partnership by estoppel, the lawyer codes also provide that lawyers who are not members of a partnership should not hold themselves out as such when that is not a fact.[42] The law of apparent partnership accomplishes much the same purpose through joint and several liability sanctions. But the codes usefully prevent ambiguous situations from arising in which the protection of clients through joint and several liability would be subject to doubt because of possible difficulties in proving such factual elements as an individual client's reliance. The codes also prevent possible misrepresentation to clients of the extent of the liability of associated lawyers.[43]

Terms of Partnership Agreement

The lawyer codes impose few limitations on the ability of lawyers to make whatever provisions they wish in forming a partnership.[44] One limitation is that the agreement may not contain a restrictive covenant limiting the right of any partner to practice law after termination of the partnership except as a condition to payment of retirement benefits.[45] Another restriction is that no member of a partnership to practice law may be a nonlawyer.[46] A partnership may consist, at least theoretically, of any number of lawyers greater than one. And the same lawyer may be a member of more than one law partnership.[47]

Associates

Most partnerships of more than a few members have nonpartner lawyers practicing with the firm, who are universally called associates.[48] Their legal status is that of employees

[41] Blackmon v. Hale, 1 Cal.3d 548, 558, 83 Cal.Rptr. 194, 199, 463 P.2d 418, 423 (1970); In re Estate of Pinckard, 94 Ill.App.3d 34, 49 Ill.Dec. 346, 417 N.E.2d 1360 (1980). Because the liability is based on estoppel, the lawyer must have acted or failed to act in a way that created a reasonable appearance of a partnership. An act by another lawyer, of which the lawyer alleged to be liable was unaware, does not suffice. See Brown v. Gerstein, 17 Mass.App.Ct. 558, 460 N.E.2d 1043, 1052, review denied 391 Mass. 1105, 464 N.E.2d 73 (1984). Moreover, the plaintiff must in fact have been misled by the appearance of a partnership. Collins v. Levine, 156 Ga.App. 502, 274 S.E.2d 841 (1980).

[42] DR 2–102(C); EC 2–13; MR 7.5 (d). E.g., Florida Bar v. Heller, 409 So.2d 1030 (Fla.1982); Attorney Grievance Comm'n v. Crowther, 295 Md. 23, 453 A.2d 140 (1982); In re Laubenheimer, 113 Wis.2d 680, 335 N.W.2d 624 (1983).

[43] ABA Formal Op. 115 (1934)(holding out as partners when that is not factual is misrepresentation that person is under "consequent joint and several responsibility" to all clients). See also ABA Formal Op. 277 (1948); ABA Formal Op. 126 (1935); ABA Formal Op. 106 (1934).

[44] Altman and Weil recommend that a written partnership agreement cover at least the following elements: definition of income (fees for such matters as guardianships, directorships, part-time salaries); death and disability (voluntary and involuntary retirement); funding of firm interests with insurance; continuity and firm dissolution; definition and division of firm capital (valuation of work in progress, capital accounts, when and in what form capital is paid in); how new partners are admitted and employment of associates; ownership of files and other firm papers and allocation of responsibilty for clients; rights of partners to manage and vote; arbitration of disputes; limitations on nonpartnership activities; leaves of absence; expenses of partners to be paid by partnership; methods of accounting and fiscal year; and financial policies. See Nat'l L.J., Oct. 23, 1979, at 1, col.4.

[45] DR 2–108(A); MR 5.6(a); ABA Formal Op. 300 (1961). Attorney Grievance Comm'n v. Hyatt, 52 U.S.L. Wk. 2605 (Md.Cty.Ct.1984)(clauses in legal clinic's employment contracts with staff lawyers prohibiting employees from establishing other clinics after departing and from contacting former clients in any way violates DR 2–108). The rationale for the rule is to protect the autonomy of lawyers and the ability of clients to freely choose counsel. See MR 5.6 comment (first paragraph); Dwyer v. Jung, 133 N.J.Super. 343, 336 A.2d 498 (1975), appeal granted and matter remanded 68 N.J. 177, 343 A.2d 464 (1975), affirmed 137 N.J. Super. 135, 348 A.2d 208 (1975) (lawyers may not enter into partnership agreement prohibiting themselves from representing former clients upon termination of partnership). An agreement in violation of the rule is unenforceable. E.g., Dwyer v. Jung, supra; In re Silverberg, 75 A.D.2d 817, 427 N.Y.S.2d 480 (1980); Gray v. Martin, 63 Or.App. 173, 663 P.2d 1285 (1983), review denied 295 Or. 541, 668 P.2d 384 (1983); Hagen v. O'Connell, Goyak & Ball, 68 Or.App. 700, 683 P.2d 563 (1984)(provision in buy-sell agreement for stock of professional corporation).

[46] Calif.R. 3–103.

[47] ABA Formal Op. 330 (1970).

[48] See generally Nelson, The Changing Structure of Opportunity: Recruitment and Careers in Large Law Firms, 1983 Am.B.Found. Research J. 109 (sociological

and agents of the partnership.[49] Associates normally practice with a firm for a number of years, sometimes as many as ten, before being considered for partnership.[50] Many associates join large firms with no intention of staying the long course until a partnership decision, but use employment as a firm associate as training for a future career with a smaller firm, in corporate or government practice, or in solo practice. Although employed rarely or never in some large firms, lateral hires of partners or senior associates from other firms has become somewhat more common.[51]

Partners jealously guard election to the partnership both because of the reputation of the firm and because partners derive economic benefit from the fact that associate billings average a higher figure than associates' salaries and other benefits. As a result, many associates that are quite capable of practicing law as competently as many partners are not elected to partner status. The resulting selectivity stimulates competition within the firm among associates in ways that can blunt ethical instincts. Associates who are passed over at the time of a partnership decision suffer probably the most excruciating depression that a lawyer can encounter professionally,[52] but most find rewarding careers, sometimes in quite comparable firms.[53] A very few at some firms may become permanent associates. The criteria for election to partner are inherently subjective to a high degree,[54] but a firm should obviously not employ abritrary criteria that do not relate to ability to contribute to the firm.[55]

Despite their nonownership status in a law firm, associates bear much the same responsibilities for devotion to client service and protection as do partners. Associates are fully responsible for compliance with the applicable lawyer codes and other law, subject to an exception for doubtful ethical questions under some circumstances (§ 16.2.2). As employees and agents of the partnership, associates have a fiduciary obligation to protect the interests of the firm when that does not conflict with dictates of client loyalty.[56]

Of Counsel Relationships

Many larger firms have on their letterhead the name of one or more lawyers with the indication that their status in the firm is "of counsel." The designation is one purely of art and has no independent legal significance. The lawyer is either a partner, a retired partner, an employee such as an associate, or a shareholder or employee of a professional corporation. The only disciplinary significance of the term is a restrictive one. According to the lawyer codes, a lawyer who does not have an actual relationship with a firm should not be listed as "of counsel." [57] Indeed, an opinion of the ABA stated in 1972 that the of-counsel lawyer must have a "close, continuing, personal" relationship with the firm. The point is that of false advertising. The concern is that a firm might pay a famous

study of early years of practice of firm associates in increasingly specialized large firms).

[49] A share in profits does not mean that a lawyer is a partner in the firm. See Farrow v. Cahill, 663 F.2d 201, 205 (D.C.Cir.1980).

[50] For a description of the process, see Hishon v. King & Spalding, 467 U.S. 69, 104 S.Ct. 2229, 2236, 81 L.Ed.2d 59 (1984)(Powell, J., concurring). Practices vary considerably from one region, and even one firm, to another. See Nat'l L.J., Apr. 12, 1982, at 1, col.3.

[51] Nat'l L.J., Oct.31, 1983, at 1, col.1.

[52] Nat'l L.J., Oct.24, 1983, at 28, col.1; Wall St.J., Jan.3, 1982, at 1, col.1.

[53] Dunnan, When You Don't Make Partner, 70 ABA J. 68 (1984).

[54] Lynch, How Law Firms Select Partners, 70 ABA J. 65 (1984).

[55] Hishon v. King & Spalding, 467 U.S. 69, 104 S.Ct. 2229, 81 L.Ed.2d 59 (1984)(law partnership liable for damages for alleged gender-discriminatory refusal to elect woman associate to partner). See generally How the Hishon Decision Will Affect Your Firm, 70 ABA J. 58 (1984).

[56] Cf. In re Hendricks, 282 Or. 763, 580 P.2d 188 (1978) (discipline of associate for failure to advise law firm that he had borrowed money from client who then owed firm for legal services and whose account receivable was later assigned to collection agency by law firm).

[57] DR 2–102(A)(4); Calif.Rule 2–103(A)(4). Cf. MR 7.5(a) (lawyer shall not use a firm name or letterhead that violates rule of MR 7.1 against false and misleading statements about lawyer's services).

politician or practitioner simply to have the lawyer's name dress up its letterhead and its power and glory reflect on the firm to induce clients to think that the lawyer could provide services or benefits to them, although the lawyer had no actual relationship with the firm.

Partnership Dissolution

Law partnerships are, on the whole, at-will agreements from which any partner is free to withdraw, although not without proper financial consequences. Unless the partnership agreement provides otherwise, the partnership is dissolved by force of law when a lawyer leaves or is expelled,[58] enters bankruptcy,[59] dies,[60] or ascends to the bench.[61] Remaining members of the former partnership can agree to continue to carry on in a new partnership after the withdrawal of one or more members.[62] Dissolution does not automatically end the partnership's existence or the power of partners to act in behalf of the dissolving partnership, for winding up partnership affairs must intervene before the partnership is terminated.[63] The breakup of a partnership should be provided for in the partnership agreement. Sometimes it is not, and the absence of provisions for disposition of firm assets on dissolution can, when added to the occasionally bitter emotions attending breakups, lead to remarkably unprofessional disputes and litigation. The litigation normally takes the form of a request for an accounting by the excluded partner.[64] Whatever the emotions involved, the law and the lawyer codes require that partners deal with each other fairly and as fiduciaries in the course of breakup and in winding up partnership affairs after dissolution.[65]

Client Relationships after Firm Dissolution

Often the thorniest issue in a partnership breakup is the economic benefit of retainers with clients. Lawyers interested in the question will rarely find local authority of help in judicial decisions or ethics committee opinions. The matter relates to two kinds of legal work—that done for client business that was already undertaken at the time the partnership dissolves and those separate matters un-

58 In re Vann, 78 A.D.2d 255, 434 N.Y.S.2d 365 (1980), affirmed 54 N.Y.2d 936, 445 N.Y.S.2d 139, 429 N.E.2d 817 (1981); Uniform Partnership Act § 31(1)(b), (d) & (2).

59 Uniform Partnership Act § 31(5).

60 Howe v. Horton, Davis & McCaleb, 85 Ill.App.3d 970, 41 Ill.Dec. 268, 407 N.E.2d 766 (1980); Uniform Partnership Act § 31(4).

61 Justice v. Laing, 19 Ind.App. 272, 49 N.E. 459 (1898).

62 In re Vann, 54 N.Y.2d 936, 445 N.Y.S.2d 139, 429 N.E.2d 817 (1981). Such an arrangement leaves at least two partnerships in existence: the new partnership and the old partnership for the purpose of winding up. A departing partner may, of course, enter or begin a new partnership as well.

63 Saltzberg v. Fishman, 123 Ill.App.3d 447, 462 N.E.2d 901, 905 (1984); Howe v. Horton, Davis & McCaleb, 85 Ill. App.3d 970, 41 Ill.Dec. 268, 269, 407 N.E.2d 766, 767 (1980). During dissolution, each partner has the implied power to bind all members of the partnership by acts in the course of winding up. E.g., Pettigrew & Bailey v. Pickle, 429 So.2d 340 (Fla.App.1983)(postdissolution act of partner, in releasing claim for malicious prosecution that arose prior to dissolution, bound all partnership members).

64 Consaul v. Cummings, 222 U.S. 262, 32 S.Ct. 83, 56 L.Ed. 192 (1911); Munyan v. Curtis, Mallet-Prevost, Colt & Mosle, 99 A.D.2d 716, 472 N.Y.S.2d 321 (1984); Levin v. Barish, 314 Pa.Super. 347, 460 A.2d 1174 (1983), order affirmed in part, reversed in part on other grounds 505 Pa. 514, 481 A.2d 1183 (1984).

65 Consaul v. Cummings, 222 U.S. 262, 32 S.Ct. 83, 56 L.Ed. 192 (1911); Jewel v. Boxer, 156 Cal.App.3d 171, 203 Cal.Rptr. 13 (1984)(in absence of agreement to divide postdissolution fees from predissolution retainers, neither remaining nor departed partner entitled to extra compensation for concluding former partnership's business because they owed that duty to each other as former partners); Sheradsky v. Moore, 389 So.2d 1206 (Fla.App. 1980), review denied 399 So.2d 1145 (Fla.1981)(same); Resnick v. Kaplan, 49 Md.App. 499, 434 A.2d 582 (1981) (same); Folsom v. Woodburn, Wedge, Blakey & Jeppson, ___ Nev. ___, 683 P.2d 9 (1984)(same); Platt v. Henderson, 227 Or. 212, 361 P.2d 73 (1961)(same); Seale v. Sledge, 430 So.2d 1028 (La.App.1983), writ denied 437 So.2d 1155 (La.1983) (same, as to client that departing partner had begun to represent prior to joining partnership that he later left). Contra Cofer v. Hearne, 459 S.W.2d 877, 879 (Tex.Civ.App.1970). See also, e.g., Rosenfeld, Meyer & Susman v. Cohen, 146 Cal.App.3d 200, 194 Cal.Rptr. 180, 188–89 (1983)(legal duty of partner not to dissolve law partnership with withdrawal in bad faith); Levi v. Mississippi St. Bar, 436 So.2d 781, 785–86 (Miss.1983)(discipline for deception in accounting in dissolution). On the requirement of fair dealing when one law partner purchases the partnership interest of another, see, e.g., Baker v. Cummings, 4 App.D.C. 230 (1894); Kelly v. Delaney, 136 App.Div. 604, 121 N.Y.S. 241 (1910).

dertaken for former partnership clients by one or more of the former partners after dissolution. The well-settled rule for the unfinished business of existing clients is that the partnership agreement controls the right of the partners to share in fees, regardless of when the fees are billed, how much or how little effort is required to complete the unfinished business, which lawyer performs the actual services, and when the services are performed.[66] No former partner may shirk his or her fair share of uncompleted work; each partner remains jointly responsible to see to the completion of the work undertaken, which normally entails each lawyer's completing work that he or she has begun.[67] Steering, as it is called,[68] former firm client's to oneself thus has no effect upon the right of other former partners to recover their partnership share of all fee income from predissolution client matters.[69]

Clients may, however, have additional and different legal matters that require legal services and that are not legally the unfinished business of the dissolved partnership. The difficult question must then be faced of which lawyer—a departing or a remaining partner—is entitled to deal with former-firm clients. Attempting to resolve the issue by referring to clients as "files" and debating which client each lawyer "owns," or to which lawyer a client "belongs," [70] obscures and distorts the client-lawyer relationship. The compelling fact is that the client-lawyer relationship is personal; clients should accordingly have a free choice of counsel.[71] The best way to accommodate interests that pull in sometimes conflicting directions is to permit clients to make their own choice [72] but to penalize lawyers who employ methods of gaining clients that overreach the clients, breach fiduciary obligations to other partners during the existence of the partnership,[73] or falsely and unfairly disparage former colleagues. In the case of an associate who is not a partner, the preferable view is that the associate breaches a fiduciary obligation of loyalty to the firm by attempting to persuade existing- or former-firm clients to retain the former associate after his or her withdrawal.[74] But the associ-

66 See authorities cited supra n.65. By contrast, when an associate or other nonpartner lawyer leaves a firm with a client whose work the associate completes, the respective shares of the old firm and the associate have been divided on the basis of the reasonable value of the services that each contributed. See McLean v. Michaelowsky, 117 Misc.2d 699, 458 N.Y.S.2d 1005 (1983).

67 Jewel v. Boxer, 156 Cal.App.3d 171, 203 Cal.Rptr. 13 (1984)(neither dissolution nor executing new, postdissolution retainer agreements affects division of fees or responsibilty of each partner to complete work undertaken).

68 Nishman v. DeMarco, 76 A.D.2d 360, 430 N.Y.S.2d 339, 343 (1980), appeal dismissed 53 N.Y.2d 642, 438 N.Y.S.2d 787, 420 N.E.2d 979 (1981).

69 Rosenfeld, Meyer & Susman v. Cohen, 146 Cal.App. 3d 200, 194 Cal.Rptr. 180 (1983).

70 Saltzberg v. Fishman, 123 Ill.App.3d 447, 78 Ill.Dec. 782, 788, 462 N.E.2d 901, 907 (1984).

71 Missan v. Schoenfeld, 111 Misc.2d 1022, 445 N.Y.S.2d 856, 859 (1981)(partners "cannot and do not control the clients involved, who may at any time discharge their counsel. The plaintiff did not have a property right to any of these clients and may not seek legal redress because the clients voluntarily chose new counsel after the partnership dissolution.").

72 In re Silverberg, 81 A.D.2d 640, 438 N.Y.S.2d 143, 144 (1981)("After dissolution, each former partner is free to practice law individually, and has the right to accept retainers from persons who had been clients of the firm"); Koehler v. Wales, 16 Wn.App. 304, 556 P.2d 233, 236 (1976)("Clients are not merchandise. They cannot be bought, sold, or traded. The attorney-client relationship is personal and confidential, and the client's choice of attorneys in civil cases is near absolute."). Cf., e.g., Dwyer v. Jung, 133 N.J.Super. 343, 336 A.2d 498, 499, appeal granted and matter remanded 68 N.J. 177, 343 A.2d 464, affirmed 137 N.J.Super. 135, 348 A.2d 208 (1975)(restrictive covenant in partnership agreement against representing firm clients after dissolution unenforceable); In re Silverberg, 75 A.D.2d 817, 427 N.Y.S.2d 480 (1980)(same).

Cf. ABA Informal Op. 1417 (1979)(law firm may not require departing firm members to agree not to hire away present firm associates).

73 In re Silverberg, 81 A.D.2d 640, 438 N.Y.S.2d 143, 144 (1981)(solicitation of partnership clients for personal benefit of partner who secretly plans to dissolve partnership and set up separate law practice breaches fiduciary duty to other partners and to partnership and breaches partnership agreement). Cf. Attorney Grievance Comm'n v. Kahn, 290 Md. 654, 431 A.2d 1336, 1349 (1981) (discipline for misappropriation of information from partner's file to facilitate plan to represent former partner's clients).

74 Saltzberg v. Fishman, 123 Ill.App.3d 447, 78 Ill.Dec. 782, 788, 462 N.E.2d 901, 907 (1984); Adler, Barish, Daniels, Levin & Creskoff v. Epstein, 482 Pa. 416, 393 A.2d 1175 (1978), cert.denied 442 U.S. 907, 99 S.Ct. 2817, 61 L.Ed.2d 272 (1979)(associates enjoined from contacting former clients of firm where associates, while still at

ate should be entitled to send notice of the withdrawal to clients for whom the associate formerly and personally performed legal services.[75]

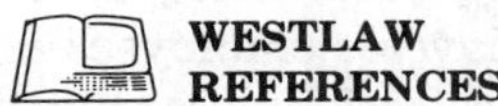

WESTLAW REFERENCES

Applicability of General Partnership Law and Lawyer Codes

attorney lawyer /s law legal profession! /s partnership /p "uniform partnership act" "professional responsibility"

45k30

Partners as Agents of Partnership and Each Other

digest,synopsis (law +1 firm partner! /s agent partner! /s bind bound liab!)

45k30 /p liab!

Partnerships—Express, Implied and Apparent

"dr 2–102(c)" dr 2–102(c) "ec 2–13"

Terms of Partnership Agreement

"dr 2–108(a)" dr 2–108(a) (law legal +1 partner! /p "restrictive covenant")

Associates

45k30 45k115 /p associate

Of Counsel Relationships

[no queries]

Partnership Dissolution

law +1 partnership /s dissol! % marriage

topic(45) /p law +1 partnership /s dissol! breakup

§ 16.2.4 *Lawyer Professional Corporations*

History of Lawyer Professional Corporations [76]

The traditional stance of the organized bar was that to incorporate a law practice was to treat law practice as a business rather than a profession, and thus it was prohibited. But the other available forms of law practice entities received much less favorable tax treatment under the federal income tax laws than did professional corporations formed by members of other professions, such as physicians and accountants. The disparate tax treatment of corporations and partnerships or sole proprietorships led to lawyer pressure on bar associations and courts to permit incorporation. In 1961 the ABA ethics committee ruled that the practice of law in the corporate form did not itself constitute an ethical violation.[77]

From the beginning, the 1969 Code permitted lawyers to form joint professional corporations with the condition that directors, officers, and stockholders were lawyers.[78] The 1983 Model Rules, in MR 5.4(d), provide for the same conditional permission, with the additional requirement that no nonlawyer employee could have the power to direct or control the professional judgment of a lawyer. All states [79] have now enacted either explicit statutory permission for incorporation of a law practice or broad professional corporation codes [80] that deal with many professions, including law. Incorporation under such a stat-

firm, had developed line of credit at bank for new firm based on claims of stable of clients, all of whom were existing firm clients; had violated antisolicitation rules by personally soliciting firm clients to switch to prospective new firm; and, after leaving old firm, had mailed former-firm clients forms to use to discharge former firm and retain new firm).

[75] Cf. ABA Informal Op. 1466 (1981)(associate resigning from firm may send personal letter to clients for whose matters he or she was directly responsible, informing them of change to another firm). But cf. ABA Informal Op. 787 (1964)(associate may send notice only to personal clients, and not "firm's" client on whose matters associate worked); id. Op. 910 (1966).

[76] See generally H.Henn & J.Alexander, Laws of Corporations 138–43 (3d ed.1983).

[77] ABA Formal Op. 303 (1961).

[78] EC 5–24.

[79] See generally CCH Professional Corporations Handbook ¶5001, at 4001–02 (1973). The Colorado permission to incorporate is contained in a court rule. Colo.R.Civ. Proc.Rule 265. See also CCH Professional Corporations Handbook ¶4002 for special court rules in several states limiting or otherwise regulating law professional corporations.

[80] The American Law Institute has developed a Professional Corporation Act supplement to the Model Business Corporation Act. See Professional Corporations Supplement to the Model Business Corporation Act, 32 Bus.Law. 289 (1976), 33 Bus.Law. 929 (1977).

ute gains the tax advantages available to other businesses that are similarly incorporated, although these are subject to legislative retraction, as has recently occurred.

Beyond the purpose of gaining tax advantages, lawyers practicing together may seek to form a professional corporation in order to immunize each other as shareholders from the kind of joint and several liability that is the lot of partners (see §§ 5.6.6, 16.2.3). A single-lawyer professional corporation, of course, creates little effective limitation on liability because the lawyer, as negligent agent, is personally liable for harm in any event.[81] In multilawyer practices the protection of the corporate form is potentially substantial. A lease signed in the name of a law professional corporation by one of its members in his or her role as corporate officer, for example, does not create personal liability for rent payments on the part of any individual shareholder-member.[82] In a partnership both the signing lawyer and all other partners would be personally responsible for the liabilities incurred in behalf of the partnership. If the same rules were applied in a legal malpractice action, only the negligent lawyer and the professional corporate employer would be liable to the injured client. The liability of other members of the professional corporation would be limited to the extent of their investment in the corporation. The corporate form, however, does not bring only beneficial legal consequences. For example, a lawyer member of even a single-member professional corporation may not claim personal constitutional protections with respect to papers and records belonging to the corporation.[83]

The limitation of liability with respect to client suits for malpractice or other wrongs committed by lawyer employees or shareholders in a law professional corporation is problematical. The lawyer codes explicitly prohibit a lawyer from entering into an agreement with a client to exonerate the lawyer from malpractice liability to the client.[84] It seems inconsistent for the lawyer to be able to limit the malpractice liability of partners in a transaction that is secret and of which the client need be given no notice. Moreover, the limitation of liability is inconsistent with the rationale for prohibiting nonpartner lawyers from holding themselves out as partners (§ 16.2.3). For such reasons, several courts have refused to attach the limited liability protection to lawyer professional corporations, at least with respect to client suits for malpractice.[85]

In other ways as well, courts have indicated that the creation of law professional corporations is generally limited to the purpose of obtaining whatever tax advantages legislative bodies leave in place. Altering the form of the business entity does not, however, alter the fact that all of the lawyers practicing in it remain fully subject to the lawyer codes.[86] No nonlawyer may become an officer or member of a law professional corporation,[87] just as no nonlawyer may have an interest or control in any other form of law practice entity. And

[81] See generally Restatement (Second) of Agency § 343 (1958).

[82] We're Assoc. Co. v. Cohen, Stracher & Bloom, P.C., 103 A.D.2d 130, 478 N.Y.S.2d 670 (1984), appeal granted ___ N.Y.2d ___, 472 N.E.2d 49 (1984). See generally Restatement (Second) of Agency § 320 (1958).

[83] Reamer v. Beall, 506 F.2d 1345 (4th Cir.1974), cert.denied 420 U.S. 955, 95 S.Ct. 1338, 43 L.Ed.2d 431 (1975); In re Zisook, 88 Ill.2d 321, 58 Ill.Dec. 786, 793–94, 430 N.E.2d 1037, 1044–45 (1981), cert.denied 457 U.S. 1134, 102 S.Ct. 2962, 73 L.Ed.2d 1352 (1982). See generally Bellis v. United States, 417 U.S. 85, 89–90, 94 S.Ct. 2179, 2183–84, 40 L.Ed.2d 678 (1974). Cf. also, e.g., In re DePew, 98 Idaho 215, 560 P.2d 886 (1977)(lawyer who brought action for legal fees in behalf of his single-lawyer professional corporation after suspension from practice engaged in unauthorized practice of law).

[84] DR 6–102(A); MR 1.8(h).

[85] See generally First Bank & Trust Co. v. Zagoria, 250 Ga. 844, 302 S.E.2d 674 (1983)(limitation of liability of shareholders of law professional corporation extends only to obligations of a purely business and nonprofessinal nature). Ohio provides joint and several responsibility for obligations to clients by explicit rule of the state's supreme court. See Reiner v. Kelley, 8 Ohio App.3d 390, 457 N.E.2d 946, 951–52 (1983). See also § 5.6.6.

[86] In re Florida Bar, 133 So.2d 554, 4 A.L.R.3d 375 (Fla. 1961); In re New Hampshire Bar, 110 N.H. 356, 266 A.2d 853 (1970); In re Education Law Center, Inc., 86 N.J. 124, 429 A.2d 1051, 1057 n.6 (1981).

[87] Florida Bar v. Hunt, 429 So.2d 1201 (Fla.1983); In re Rhode Island Bar Ass'n, 106 R.I. 752, 263 A.2d 692, 696 (1970). Cf. Street v. Sugarman, 202 So.2d 749 (Fla.1967).

a law professional corporation may not engage directly in an activity that is not the practice of law.[88]

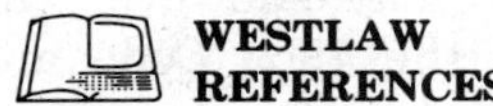

"dr 6–102(a)" dr6–102(a) "ec 2–24"

"florida bar" /12 133 +4 554 /p corporat! entity

§ 16.2.5 *Associated Lawyers*

Forms and Significance of Associated Practices

Lawyers who do not intend to enter into a partnership or a professional corporation arrangement might still wish to form a loose relationship for temporary or long-term sharing of expenses or for joint work on the matter of a single client. The relationships can take many forms. A lawyer with an unusual and short-term increase in work may hire another lawyer on a temporary basis, either as an employee or as an independent contractor. The working arrangement might contemplate that the additional lawyer would work in the original lawyer's office or in his or her own. A lawyer may hire another lawyer as a consultant on a particular matter or as an expert witness. The relationship may contemplate a more indefinite duration. An older lawyer may enlarge his or her office space slightly in order to provide free or reduced rental accommodations for a younger lawyer in return for the latter's agreement to devote a certain number of hours per month to clients of the landlord-lawyer. A common arrangement is for two or more solo practitioners to agree to share one or more of the expenses associated with the practice of the participating lawyers, but not to share otherwise in profits or losses. The arrangement might run from sharing the expense of a law library, rent for a suite of offices, hiring a secretary or other employee, office equipment, or the like. Typically each lawyer in an office-sharing or similar arrangement maintains complete autonomy in dealing with clients and with subordinate lawyers.

Protecting Client Confidential Information

In all such arrangements, the paramount concern must be with the confidentiality of client matters. The professional rules permit a lawyer to share client information only with lawyers in the same firm.[89] Thus disclosure of client information to lawyers in a shared-office arrangement is permissible only with prior permission of the affected client. For that reason, without prior client consent a lawyer may not retain or speak to a lawyer from outside the firm for consultation about client confidential matters. Whether lawyers are a firm for this purpose does not depend on their formal legal status. Lawyers may practice together as contracting parties without forming a partnership.[90] The important question is whether a client would understand that the lawyer consulted was a regular and trusted colleague of the client's chosen lawyer. Normally, a close relationship between associated lawyers may not be indicated by an office sign, building directory sign, telephone listing, or the like that contains a listing such as "Jones and Smith, attorneys" because that

[88] Network Affiliates, Inc. v. Schack, 682 P.2d 1244 (Colo.App.1984)(law firm incorporated as professional corporation could not conduct business of selling television advertising material to other lawyers).

[89] EC 2–22 ("Without the consent of his client, a lawyer should not associate in a particular matter another lawyer outside his firm."); EC 4–2 ("Unless the client otherwise directs, a lawyer may disclose the affairs of his client to partners or associates of his firm. . . . [I]n the absence of consent of his client after full disclosure, a lawyer should not associate another lawyer in the handling of a matter; nor should he, in the absence of consent, seek counsel from another lawyer if there is a reasonable possibility that the identity of the client or his confidences or secrets would be revealed to such lawyer."); cf. MR 1.6 comment (Authorized Disclosure; second paragraph). For ABA ethics committee opinions, see Annotated Code of Professional Responsibility 173 (O.Maru ed.1979).

[90] Levine v. Goldberg, 2 A.D.2d 409, 156 N.Y.S.2d 587 (1956); Willis v. Crawford, 38 Or. 522, 63 P. 985 (1901); Fitzsimmons v. Robb, 193 Pa. 518, 44 A. 558 (1899). The definitions of "firm" in the Model Rules (Terminology; MR 1.10 comment (Definition of "Firm")) are directed to other questions but do not exclude a nontechnical conception of "firm" for the present purpose.

impermissibly suggests that they are a partnership.[91]

WESTLAW REFERENCES

"ec 2–22" "ec 4–2" "model rule 1.6"

§ 16.3 NONLAWYER EMPLOYEES OF LAWYERS

§ 16.3.1 Scope of Lawyer Responsibility

Importance of Nonlawyer Employees

The nature of practice in many firms requires that nonlawyer assistants be hired to staff the office; indeed, it is inconceivable that firms of much size could operate without many such nonlawyer employees. Nonlawyer employees do work of all kinds, except that they are not to engage in the unsupervised practice of law or take public steps, such as signing pleadings, that constitute the practice of law. Despite the broad scope of the work of such employees, it remains largely true that they function as the alter ego of every lawyer in the firm [92] and every lawyer in the firm remains responsible for their supervision. That is true as a matter of the law of professional discipline and under general agency principles. The theory of supervisory responsibility may, however, differ significantly under the 1969 Code and under the 1983 Model Rules.

Supervisory Responsibility under the 1969 Code and the 1983 Model Rules

As the Code recognizes in EC 3–6, it is both efficient and proper for lawyers to delegate many tasks, although not all responsibility for them, to nonlawyers.[93] Nonlawyer employees are not themselves subject to the lawyer codes, at least in the sense that no lawyer disciplinary agency has claimed jurisdiction over them.[94] But courts have held that lawyers have full supervisory responsibility to see that the work of all employees is compatible with the requirements of the lawyer codes and with other law.[95] A lawyer has responsibility for the work of his or her employees that is performed at the lawyer's direction and under the lawyer's control.[96] A lawyer's responsibilities are not simply to avoid participating in the wrongdoing of nonlawyer em-

91 On the prohibition against associated lawyers holding themselves out as partners when they in fact lack that legal relationship, see supra 885. On the specific example, see MR 7.5 comment (second paragraph) ("[L]awyers sharing office facilities, but who are not in fact partners, may not denominate themselves as, for example, 'Smith and Jones,' for that title suggests partnership in the practice of law."). While partnership law will often require a finding that lawyers who practice together without an express or implied partnership agreement are nonetheless liable to a client as if they were partners (see § 16.2.3 at 884–85), it is not inevitable that a joint office sign will lead all courts to conclude that the lawyers are liable as apparent partners. See Joseph v. Greater New Guide Baptist Church, Inc., 194 So.2d 127, 130 (La.App.1966), writ refused 250 La. 379, 195 So. 2d 647 (1967)(fact that lawyers shared office space and operated under name of "Avery & Dickens" does not automatically lead to conclusion that they were partners).

92 For many agency purposes, employees of a lawyer are treated as the lawyer's alter ego. For example, notice to an employee is notice to the lawyer. E.g., In re Estate of Caha, 195 Neb. 333, 237 N.W.2d 870, 875 (1976).

93 Cf. also MR 5.3 comment (first and second sentences).

94 Cf. Code Preamble (Code "cannot apply to nonlawyers," but Code's provisions "do define the type of ethical conduct that the public has a right to expect not only of lawyers but also of their non-professional employees and associates in all matters pertaining to professional employment.").

95 Code Preamble ("A lawyer should ultimately be responsible for the conduct of his employees and associates in the course of the professional representation of the client."); EC 3–6 (delegation of work to nonlawyer employees "is proper if the lawyer maintains a direct relationship with his client, supervises the delegated work, and has complete professional responsibility for the work product."); DR 7–107(J)("A lawyer shall exercise reasonable care to prevent his employees and associates from making an extra-judicial statement that he would be prohibited from making"); EC 7–28 (lawyer should see that client and nonlawyer employees observe restrictions on contact with witnesses and payments to them). See also, e.g., In re Schroeter, 80 Wn.2d 1, 489 P.2d 917 (1971) (general obligation to supervise under 1908 Canons). Florida has made the point explicit in a new DR 3–104(C): "A lawyer or law firm that employs non-lawyer personnel shall exercise a high standard of care to assure compliance by the non-lawyer personnel with the applicable provisions of the Code of Professional Responsibility. The initial and the continuing relationship with the client must be the responsibility of the employing attorney." See also Iowa Code DR 3–104.

96 Crane v. State Bar, 30 Cal.3d 117, 177 Cal.Rptr. 670, 672, 635 P.2d 163, 165 (1981).

ployees and to correct known deficiencies, although they certainly include those and similar duties.[97] A lawyer must exercise a high degree of care in the hiring and training of employees.[98] A lawyer also has responsibility to be aware at least of the major areas of responsibility and the actual work habits of employees and to exercise effective supervision.[99]

Cases decided under the Code have been particularly strict in insisting that lawyers exercise effective control over employees dealing with client funds. Lawyers are responsible for seeing that such employees are acting in full compliance with the special fiduciary rules that apply to a lawyer's responsibilty for client funds and other property (§ 4.8).[1] If deficiencies occur, they are attributable to the lawyer either on the theory that trust accounts are the full responsibility of the lawyer [2] or that the lawyer failed to properly supervise the employee.[3] Courts applying the 1969 Code provisions on client funds have stated that the requirement of adequate supervision is one of strict liability [4] and is not excused by a reasonable belief in the competence of the employee.[5]

On the other hand, Model Rule 5.3 adopts the arguably less stringent standard of a reasonably efficient bureaucracy. The rule seems to have been drafted with a large departmentalized firm rather than a small law office in mind. First, the rule states that it is the responsibility of every lawyer in a firm, apparently regardless of the firm's size and the lawyer's place in the hierarchy, to make "reasonable efforts" to assure that the firm has in effect "measures that give reasonable

[97] In re Shaw, 88 N.J. 433, 443 A.2d 670, 674 (1982) (knowing participation with employee in "confidence game" to defraud client); In re Robinson, 151 App.Div. 589, 136 N.Y.S. 548 (1912), affirmed 209 N.Y. 354, 103 N.E. 160 (1913)(no defense that lawyer did not actually participate in offending conduct of employees so long as lawyer knew of it and took no steps to correct it). See DR 1–102(A)(2)("a lawyer should not circumvent a Disciplinary Rule through actions of others").

[98] In re Shaw, 88 N.J. 433, 443 A.2d 670, 674 (1982). In *Shaw*, the court noted that although it lacked any disciplinary jurisdiction over the nonlawyer employee that had acted with the lawyer to defraud a client, "we would tend to look askance . . . at any lawyer's establishing an office relationship with one who had been implicated previously in an unscrupulous scheme like the one presented here."

[99] Spindell v. State Bar, 13 Cal.3d 253, 118 Cal.Rptr. 480, 530 P.2d 168 (1975). Because of assumptions that the lawyer-employer exercises a high degree of professional supervision over the work of nonlawyer employees, it is often held that special licensure, or other restrictions that otherwise would encumber such employees, do not apply. E.g., Grossman v. Vaupel, 13 Cal.App.3d 706, 710, 91 Cal.Rptr. 876 (1970)(secretary of lawyer exempt from registration under statute regulating debt-collection work); Calif. Atty. Gen. Op. No. CV 73–311, CCH Prof. Corp. Handbook ¶9348 (1976)(employee of law firm exempt from tax-preparer-registration statute).

[1] State v. Caenen, 235 Kan. 451, 681 P.2d 639, 642 (1984)(failure to notify client of receipt of funds cannot be excused by failure of responsible employee to keep proper records); In re Olkon, 324 N.W.2d 192 (Minn.1982)(failure to keep client funds in trust account could not be excused on ground that lawyer had delegated responsibility to employees); Attorney Grievance Comm'n v. Goldberg, 292 Md. 650, 441 A.2d 338 (1982)(lawyer responsible for acts of employee in drawing checks on client funds for improper purposes); In re Rabb, 73 N.J. 272, 374 A.2d 461, 464 (1977)(lawyer cannot effectively place blame for commingling on associate lawyer or on defects in bookkeeping system set up by outside accountants); In re Rude, 88 S.D. 416, 221 N.W.2d 43, 48 (1974)("Nor can the attorney escape censure by pleading ignorance of his financial affairs or by pointing the finger of guilt at his employees. He is bound to conduct the affairs of his office in such a manner that his client's funds are safeguarded").

[2] Giovanazzi v. State Bar, 28 Cal.3d 465, 169 Cal.Rptr. 581, 586, 619 P.2d 1005, 1010 (1980); Vaughn v. State Bar, 6 Cal.3d 847, 857, 100 Cal.Rptr. 713, 494 P.2d 1257 (1972).

[3] Fitzpatrick v. State Bar, 20 Cal.3d 73, 569 P.2d 763, 768, 141 Cal.Rptr. 169 (1977); In re Privette, 92 N.M. 32, 582 P.2d 804 (1978)(failure to supervise employees with result that funds were embezzled by employee).

[4] In re Holman, 297 Or. 36, 682 P.2d 243, 256 n.8 (1984). It was asserted in MR 5.4 legal background note at 174–75 (Proposed Final Draft, May 30, 1981) that "an interpretation of EC 3–6 as imposing liability in disiciplinary proceedings similar to that imposed in civil litigation under the doctrine of *respondeat superior* would be inconsistent with existing judicial precedent." The cited precedent does not bear out the statement. Indeed, one substantially refutes it. Vaughn v. State Bar, 6 Cal.3d 847, 100 Cal.Rptr. 713, 719, 494 P.2d 1257, 1263 (1972) (ignorance of lawyer of receipt of funds does not exonerate "because the Board's conclusion that he engaged in a course of conduct involving gross negligence and carelessness, tantamount to moral turpitude, rests ultimately upon petitioner's responsibility to supervise the work of his associate attorney and his clerical staff. . . [E]ven though an attorney cannot be held responsible for every detail of office procedure, he must accept responsibility to supervise the work of his staff.").

[5] In re Weston, 92 Ill.2d 431, 65 Ill.Dec. 925, 928, 442 N.E.2d 236, 239 (1982).

assurance" that the conduct of nonlawyer employees is compatible with the lawyer's own professional obligations (MR 5.3(a)). From all that appears, a lawyer with such assurances can proceed in ignorance of actual practices, although it seems doubtful that courts in fact will so interpret the rule. Second, the "lawyer having direct supervisory authority" over a nonlawyer employee[6] must make "reasonable efforts" to ensure that the employee functions in ways that are compatible with the lawyer's (and presumably other lawyers') professional obligations (MR 5.3(b)). Third, a lawyer bears personal professional responsibility for a nonlawyer's conduct that would constitute a violation of the Model Rules if the person were functioning as a lawyer if the lawyer ordered or knowingly ratified the conduct (MR 5.3(c)(1)) or failed to take reasonable remedial action at a time when that would have been effective—but that obligation applies only to partners and the particular lawyer who has direct supervisory authority over the offending employee (MR 5.3(c)(2)).[7] While the provisions of MR 5.3 are susceptible of a reading that would make the responsibilities of lawyers considerably less than under the 1969 Code, that is not their apparent intended thrust.

Nonlawyer Employees and Client Confidential Information

Employees necessarily and permissibly come into contact with client confidential information in the course of their work, and therefore a lawyer must assume responsibility to assure that it is not disclosed or used in a way that the lawyer could not disclose or use it.[8] A lawyer should take care to select employees suitable to being trusted with confidential client information and to assure that employees understand their responsibilities and stand by them.[9] Because of the exposure of employees to confidential information, their movement between law firms may create some of the same conflict of interest problems that movements of lawyers create.[10] The same regard for careful treatment of confidential client information should also be taken when a lawyer employs nonlawyer independent contractors or other services outside the lawyer's firm.[11]

6 The rather clear, if unstated, assumption of MR 5.3 is that *some* lawyer in the firm will have such "direct supervisory authority" over nonlawyer employees as a product of the "measures giving reasonable assurance" in MR 5.3(a). Presumably that lawyer could be a lawyer-office manager or a lawyer who functions part-time as a supervisor of one or more employees.

7 If one only reads the words, MR 5.3(c)(2) seems to say that a nonpartner lawyer in a firm who has full knowledge that a partner's secretary was systematically draining client funds from a trust account has no responsibility to do anything about it. An obligation might be derived from a rather strained interpretation of MR 5.3(a) so that it applies to more than simply the training manuals and organization charts of supervision and responsibility.

8 DR 4–101(D)("A lawyer shall exercise reasonable care to prevent his employees, associates, and others whose services are utilized by him from disclosing or using confidences or secrets of a client, except that a lawyer may reveal the information allowed by DR 4–101(C) through an employee."); EC 4–2; MR 5.3(b); MR 5.3 comment. Computerization of modern law offices, and the presence, in computer and other files, of commercially valuable client information, has created security problems of large magnitude for firms. See Sealing the Computer Leak, 70 ABA J. 25 (1984)(employees' unauthorized use of information by cracking law firm's computer code and using information to conduct insider trading on stock market).

9 EC 4–2 (lawyer should exercise care in selecting and training nonlawyer employees in order to preserve confidentiality of client information); EC 4–5 (lawyer should be diligent in efforts to prevent misuse of client information by employees and associates); MR 5.3 comment. See also ABA 1908 Canon 37 (lawyer should not use confidences of client for private advantage of lawyer's employees).

10 Herron v. Jones, 276 Ark. 493, 637 S.W.2d 569 (1982) (secretary with access to client information who left one law firm and went to another created no disqualifying conflict because of precautions taken by secretary and by second firm to avoid disclosure). In one way of looking at it, the lawyer's conflict of interest that the Ohio courts found in In re Ruffalo, 390 U.S. 544, 88 S.Ct. 1222, 20 L.Ed.2d 117 (1968), inhered in the fact that the lawyer hired a nonlawyer employee whose own work created a conflict of interest. See also, e.g., Rice v. Perl, 320 N.W.2d 407 (Minn.1982)(denial of fees, because of conflict of interest, to lawyer who hired claims adjuster for insurance carrier that lawyer opposed).

11 ABA Informal Op. 1364 (1976) withdrew ABA Informal Op. 1267 (1973), which had purported to prohibit the transmittal of client information to outside data processing service firms without prior disclosure and consent of the client. See also EC 4–3.

Lawyer and Nonlawyer Employee Contact with Clients

Despite the fact that nonlawyer employees may be privy to the direst client secrets, a lawyer must maintain ultimate responsibility for dealing with clients. A lawyer must maintain a direct relationship with every client [12] and exercise direct professional supervision over all work done for a client.[13] A nonlawyer should not be put into a position in which the lawyer's contact with clients is seriously encumbered by an employee.[14] And a nonlawyer employee or assistant should not be allowed to engage in activities that are the unauthorized practice of law.[15]

Prohibition against Fee Sharing with Nonlawyer Employees

For reasons that assertedly have to do with assuring professional control over the representation of clients,[16] the lawyer codes prohibit a lawyer from splitting fees with a nonlawyer, including nonlawyer employees.[17] Nothing prohibits lawyer employees in a firm from sharing in fees in any way that the lawyers in the firm may agree upon among themselves. Thus a lawyer cannot pay a nonlawyer employee a salary contingent on the amount of earnings of the law office.[18] Prior to 1980, the 1969 Code, in DR 3–102(A)(3), permitted an exception so that a lawyer could include a nonlawyer employee in a retirement plan even though the plan was based in whole or part on a profit-sharing system of computation. Then, by a 1980 amendment, the exception was expanded to include "compensation" plans that were similarly based wholly or in part on profit sharing. Both permissions were continued in Rule 5.4 of the 1983 Model Rules. The cognate rule in California, Rule 3–102(A)(3), however, extends the permission only to retirement plans.

WESTLAW REFERENCES

Supervisory Responsibility Under the 1969 Code and the 1983 Model Rules

(disciplin! /p 3–104(c)) "ec 3–6" "ec 7–28"

45k29

topic(45) /p client /3 funds /s secretary clerk agent employee personnel

Non-lawyer Employees and Client Confidential Information

client /s confiden! /p employee personnel clerk secretary agent /p "dr 4–101" "ec 4–2" "ec 4–5" "professional responsibility"

Prohibition Against Fee Sharing with Non-lawyer Employee

*disciplin! /p shar** sharing split! /s fee /s non-lawyer secretary clerk 3–102(a)*

---

[12] In addition to actively supervising each stage of a representation, a lawyer should have in place sufficient employees and office procedures that permit clients to get in touch with a lawyer without undue trouble or delay, In re Palmieri, 75 N.J. 488, 383 A.2d 1142 (1978), and that assure that important dates and other obligations can be met in a timely fashion, In re Famularo, 67 N.J. 20, 334 A.2d 331 (1975).

[13] State ex rel. Okl. Bar Ass'n v. Braswell, 663 P.2d 1228, 1231–32 (Okl.1983).

[14] In Attorney Grievance Comm'n v. Goldberg, 292 Md. 650, 441 A.2d 338 (1982), the court found the lawyer guilty of competence and zealousness violations for permitting a recalcitrant office manager to block mail and phone calls and, ultimately, a letter from the disciplinary agency.

[15] A nonlawyer employee is not engaged in unauthorized practice by doing preparatory work in a case; investigating; interviewing clients preliminary to a lawyer's conference; and performing similar functions that permit the employing lawyer to carry the representation forward on the lawyer's own examination, approval, or additional work. But a nonlawyer may not handle matters on his or her own, such as by handling uncontested probate matters, or preparing wills, leases, mortgages, and the like for clients' signatures. E.g., Crawford v. State Bar, 54 Cal.2d 659, 7 Cal.Rptr. 746, 355 P.2d 490 (1960)(disbarred lawyer hired as "clerk" by own son-lawyer and, in effect, carrying on prior practice); Ferris v. Snively, 172 Wash. 167, 19 P.2d 942 (1933). Cf., e.g., Sanchez v. State Bar, 18 Cal.3d 280, 133 Cal.Rptr. 768, 769, 555 P.2d 889, 890 (1976)(gross neglect by having nonlawyer employee sign pleading); In re Berkos, 93 Ill.2d 408, 67 Ill.Dec. 111, 444 N.E.2d 150 (1982)(suspension for neglect for failing to supervise secretary who corresponded directly with client and falsely explained why appeal had been dismissed). See generally Annot., 13 A.L.R.3d 1137 (1967).

[16] Cf. EC 3–8 (prohibition against fee splitting with nonlawyer apparently rationalized on ground of avoiding aid to, or encouragement of, nonlawyer in practicing law).

[17] DR 3–102(A). See also 1908 Canon 34 ("No division of fees for legal services is proper, except with another lawyer").

[18] In re Shapiro, 90 A.D.2d 22, 455 N.Y.S.2d 604 (1982).

§ 16.3.2 Paralegals

By far the most striking development in the staffing of modern law offices within the past twenty years has been the emergence of paralegals—nonlawyer employees who have special education or training to deal with some legal problems within a law office environment.[19] To an extent, the modern paralegal resembles the office apprentice in postcolonial New England.[20] The lawyer's motivation for hiring a relatively skilled assistant is economic: the assistant's greater skill permits more efficient work, but the restrictions on law practice give the legal assistant no other outlet for competitive sale of the service.[21] Because paralegals are nonlawyers, the general observations about the scope and limits of the work of nonlawyer employees (§ 16.3.1), the responsibility of lawyer-employers to provide adequate supervision, and possible legal malpractice by nonlawyer employees [22] are also, of course, relevant.

The most difficult legal question involved in paralegalism is defining the permissible practice of law by paralegals. Concern over unauthorized practice and the maintenance of high competence and ethical standards have been traditional arguments used by the American Bar Association in its assertion of a proper role in regulating the education and credentials of paralegals.[23] Most of what paralegals do in a law office would be the unauthorized practice of the law if performed by a paralegal serving a client when not under a lawyer's supervision. The broad concept of unauthorized practice would clearly cover routine paralegal activities such as legal research and the preparation of legal documents. The privotal concern is that a lawyer who is a full member of the bar be responsible for close supervision of the work of a paralegal and that certain activities, such as client counseling,[24] signing legal documents,[25] and appearing in contested court matters,[26] not be delegated.[27] The safe, if not the required, course is for all of the work of a paralegal to be channeled to a client or a public agency through a supervising lawyer.[28]

[19] See generally Endacott, Systemization and the Legal Assistant in the Law Office, 54 Neb.L.Rev. 46 (1975); Brown, The Paralegal Profession, 19 How.L.Rev. 117 (1976); Brickman, Expansion of the Lawyering Process through a New Delivery System: The Emergence and State of Legal Paraprofessionals, 71 Colum.L.Rev. 1153 (1971); Sproul, Use of Lay Personnel in the Practice of Law: Mid-1969, 25 Bus.Law. 11 (1969); Note, The Revitalization of the Legal Profession through Paralegalism, 30 Baylor L.Rev. 841 (1980).

[20] Q.Johnstone & D.Hopson, Lawyers and Their Work 574–75 (1967); R.Pound, Lawyers from Antiquity to Modern Times 191–92 (1953).

[21] Cf. Lawpoll: Use of Paralegals Makes Good Business Sense, 69 ABA J. 1626 (1983)(54 percent of polled ABA members use paralegals because of increased client billings; paralegal income started at average of $14,700, and top salaries averaged $21,000); Ulrich, Legal Assistants Can Increase Your Profits, 69 ABA J. 1634 (1983).

[22] Moon, Lashinger & Redic, Paralegal Malpractice: New Profession, New Responsibility, 18 Trial 40 (Jan. 1982).

[23] Haskell, Issues in Paralegalism: Education, Certification, Licensing, Unauthorized Practice, 15 Ga.L.Rev. 631 (1981). An antitrust attack on the role of the ABA in accrediting paralegal training institutes was rejected in Paralegal Institute, Inc. v. American Bar Association, 475 F.Supp. 1123 (E.D.N.Y.1979), affirmed 622 F.2d 575 (2d Cir.1980).

[24] Bluestein v. State Bar, 13 Cal.3d 170, 118 Cal.Rptr. 175, 529 P.2d 599 (1975)(advising clients on foreign law); Florida Bar v. Pascual, 424 So.2d 757 (Fla.1982)(representing client at closing, giving legal advice, and corresponding "for the firm" on lawyer's stationery). New York, apparently alone among the states, provides for a limited license for foreign-law consultants, who may do restricted advising of clients on matters of the law of a foreign country. See N.Y.—McKinney's Jud. Law § 53(c).

[25] Sanchez v. State Bar, 18 Cal.3d 280, 133 Cal.Rptr. 768, 555 P.2d 889 (1976)(gross negligence of lawyer in permitting circumstances to exist in which secretary and law clerk signed lawyer's name to legal documents); In re Easler, 275 S.C. 400, 272 S.E.2d 32 (1980)(work of disbarred lawyer in preparing, executing, and filing deed for client as unauthorized practice).

[26] State v. Pacific Concrete & Rock Co., 57 Hawaii 574, 560 P.2d 1309 (1977).

[27] In re Sekerez, 458 N.E.2d 229, 238–39 (Ind.1984), cert.denied ___ U.S. ___, 105 S.Ct. 182, 83 L.Ed.2d 116 (1984)(aiding unauthorized practice by permitting law students employed in "legal clinic" office to answer client inquiries over telephone). Iowa is one of the few states to have attempted to describe in detail the responsibilities of supervising lawyers for the work of paralegals. See Iowa Code of Professional Responsibility DR 3–104(A)-(E)(as amended 1976). See also Ia. EC 3–6 (as amended 1980) (limited definition of "legal assistant" permitted to carry and use business card of firm).

[28] Ulrich & Clarke, Working with Legal Assistants: Professional Responsibility, 67 ABA J. 992 (1981).

WESTLAW REFERENCES

paralegal /p "unauthorized practice"
paralegal /p disciplin!

§ 16.4 DUAL PRACTICE

General

Lawyers sometimes have some of the specialized abilities of nonlawyers, such as the ability to do accounting work, and may wish to seek out clients for an accounting practice as well as a law practice. Or a lawyer may wish to form a partnership with an accountant in order to do tax work more effectively. In either case, the combination of legal and nonlegal work is sensible and of probable benefit to clients. In their different ways, however, the two types of dual practice—alone with two hats or together with a nonlawyer expert—are fenced in with restrictions under the lawyer codes.

Dual Practice by a Lawyer

The bar's traditional concern about a lawyer with another profession was that the lawyer would employ the other profession as a "feeder" for the lawyer's law practice in violation of the rules against solicitation. Thus lawyers who were accountants, real estate agents, or bankers, or who even operated a dry goods store, could be suspected of meeting potential law clients in those other businesses and inducing them to hire the lawyer for legal services. It was also objected, not very consistently, that, first, a lawyer who was held out as a dual practitioner would be recognized as a specialist, contrary to the bar's traditional reluctance to permit specialist recognition and, second, that a dual practitioner would be spread too thin and would not be able to keep up in both fields. The resistance found expression in elaborate rules prohibiting practicing the second business or profession from the same office out of which the lawyer practiced law [29] and restricting advertising of the second profession.[30]

The restrictions were imbedded into the 1969 Code in DR 2–102(E), which provided that:

> A lawyer who is engaged both in the practice of law and another profession or business shall not so indicate on his letterhead, office sign, or professional card, nor shall he identify himself as a lawyer in any publication in connection with his other profession or business.

The ABA relented a trifle in its Formal Opinion 328 (1972), which at least permitted a lawyer-accountant to practice both professions in the same office. But that was valid only if all of the prohibitions of the 1969 Code were observed, including those in DR 2–102(E) relating to advertising and letterheads.[31] Despite its obvious First Amendment problems, the rule remained in the Code until it was deleted by an amendment in February 1980, four years after the Supreme Court had held that the First Amendment protected truthful lawyer advertising (§ 14.2.3). Nonetheless, some jurisdictions have remained unswayed and are quite restrictive about lawyer advertising of other professional degrees or competence.[32]

The repeal of DR 2–102(E) does not mean that a dual-practice lawyer now operates without constraint. A lawyer continues to remain fully subject to the lawyer codes, even if the lawyer holds another certificate and even if the lawyer's work with clients involves fields and professions other than law.[33] The issue under the Model Rules, to the extent it remains one, will be handled under the rele-

[29] ABA Informal Op. 1032 (1968)(lawyer-accountant employed by accounting firm should not represent accounting clients before Internal Revenue Service despite fact that IRS admitted accountants to practice before it).

[30] These are reviewed, and the dual practice of law and accounting condemned, in Levy & Sprague, Accounting and Law: Is Dual Practice in the Public Interest? 52 ABA J. 1110 (1966). See also Wilson, The Attorney-CPA and the Dual Practice Problem, 36 U.Det.L.J. 457 (1959).

[31] The issues are examined in Comment, The Dual Practitioner—DR 2–102(E), 5 J.Leg.Prof. 191 (1980).

[32] In re Advisory Committee Opinion 447, 86 N.J. 473, 432 A.2d 59 (1981)(restrictions on truthful advertising of "CPA" designation on law firm letterhead upheld).

[33] In re Dwight, 117 Ariz. 407, 573 P.2d 481 (1977). In Dinis v. Hanrahan, 12 Mass.App.Ct. 884, 421 N.E.2d 1250 (1981), the court held that it was proper for a lawyer, who was both attorney for the administratrix of an estate and

vant rules on advertising and lawyer publicity and under other rules for particular issues.

Dual Practice by Lawyer and Nonlawyer

A lawyer who sets up a practice with an accountant or other allied professional, however, confronts another problem—the problem of aiding unauthorized practice by a nonlawyer. Unlike an accountant who is not a lawyer, a lawyer who is also an accountant and who practices alone normally need not be concerned with the unauthorized practice of either profession.[34] But a lawyer who practices in the same office with a nonlawyer-accountant or other professional must contend with the restrictions against aiding unauthorized practice (§ 15.1.4)[35] and against nonlawyer ownership or management of a law practice (§ 16.3.1).[36] In general those restrictions mean that the nonlawyer must be directly supervised by the lawyer and may not engage in acts that constitute the practice of law, such as making court appearances. Moreover, the nonlawyer may not be given an ownership or managerial role in the enterprise if any part of its work involves the practice of law. Other issues may also arise, such as the spread of a possible imputed or other kind of conflict of interest disqualification because of activities of the nonlawyer professional.[37]

WESTLAW REFERENCES

"dr 2-102(e)" dr2-102(e)
"dr 3-101" dr3-101

§ 16.5 GROUP LEGAL SERVICES

§ 16.5.1 Meeting the Legal Service Needs of the Middle Class

Legal Services for the Middle Class

To a certain extent, the middle class is the segment of society for which the problem of providing legal services has been most intractable.[38] For the economic upper classes, legal services are a matter of a little more or a little less, depending on consumer choice and competition of legal service providers with other service providers for attractive quality and prices. Wealth is often accompanied by sophistication in business, or with good advice on such dealings, and matters such as fees and competence of a lawyer are typically not large issues. At the other end of the economic scale, persons with no or little funds are not in the market for legal services and, to an extent, both public (§ 16.7.3; § 14.3.4) and

a registered real estate broker, to submit a claim for a real estate broker's commission for sale of land from the estate, as well as a claim for attorney fees. Yet the court also held that the amount of the broker's fee was not the prevailing market rates of real estate brokers, but only the reasonable value of the lawyer's work in making the sale.

34 But cf., e.g., In re Menack, 92 A.D.2d 336, 460 N.Y.S.2d 54, 56 (1983)(lawyer-accountant notified clients only that he could no longer represent them in legal matters and continued to provide for their accounting needs without notifying them by certified mail of suspension from practice as bar rules required).

35 For example, a lawyer in In re Smith, 5 Bankr.Rptr. 92 (D.D.C.1980), was denied a fee in a bankruptcy case on the court's finding that the lawyer had violated the prohibitions of DR 3–101, on aiding the unauthorized practice of law, by operating a dual law practice-debt consolidation business from his law office, in which nonlawyer personnel participated.

36 The Federal Trade Commission for some time has opposed the ABA's position restricting dual professional practices. See Wall St.J., Dec. 22, 1977, at 4, col.2 (nationwide investigation by FTC's Boston office of bar association restrictions, including those on legal clinics and specialty enterprises in which lawyers work with accountants or psychologists).

37 Cf. Naxon Telesign Corp. v. GTE Information Systems, Inc., 89 F.R.D. 333 (N.D.Ill.1980)(refusing to disqualify lawyer in patent litigation despite fact that nonlawyer "technical expert" in patent matters shared office space with lawyer and would appear as expert witness).

38 N.Y.St.B.Found., A Lawyer at a Price People Can Afford (J.Brickman & D.Eakeley eds.1974); B.Christensen, Lawyers for People of Moderate Means (1970); Meserve, Our Forgotten Client: The Average American, 57 ABA J. 1092 (1971)(20 percent of American population is poor and eligible for legal aid; 10 percent is rich and thus can afford legal services; 70 percent are middle-income and are underserved by lawyers); Cheatham, A Lawyer When Needed: Legal Services for the Middle Class, 63 Colum.L.Rev. 973 (1963); Note, Legalizing Nonlawyer Proprietorship in the Legal Clinic Industry: Reform in the Public Interest, 9 Hofstra L.Rev. 625, 625 n.2 (1981). See generally ABA Spec. Comm. to Survey Legal Needs, Final Report (1978); B.Curran, The Legal Needs of the Public (1977).

private (§ 16.7.2) legal assistance is sometimes available. Those whose incomes are in the middle range, however, are not poor enough to be eligible for public or private legal aid, yet they have neither the funds nor the knowledge to permit them to resort readily to lawyers for the solution of legal problems.

The size of a potential middle-class market for legal services has also grown greatly in the 1970s and 1980s. Maturation of the "baby boom," increased education, and the tendency of women to seek employment have increased family assets. Lower birth rates and increased divorce have raised the number of households. Increased urbanization of the population has also probably increased both interpersonal problems and the involvement of people with large, impersonal governmental organizations. Government itself has greatly increased legal entitlements in some areas. Those factors have combined to produce a younger, more educated, more affluent, and more rights-conscious client group, whose needs for legal services have increased and whose demands for legal services have risen to match their demands for other kinds of personal services.

It has become something of an article of faith among observers of the legal profession that middle-income individuals have needs for legal services that are not adequately met.[39] Significant elements of the bar have developed a good deal of enthusiasm for developing new methods of delivering legal services to the middle class, both to meet those needs and to provide additional employment for the burgeoning ranks of lawyers. Specifically, "group legal services" has been touted as a means by which middle-income clients can be educated about legal services and directed to lawyers who are competent to meet those needs at affordable prices. The organized bar was initially quite hostile to group legal services in the original version of the 1969 Code of Professional Responsibility. Succeeding years have brought amendments that have softened the opposition, often in reaction to strong regulatory pressure from national antitrust enforcers.

This section considers a variety of forms of law practice that have been attempted to broaden the availability of legal services. It begins with consideration of decisions of the Supreme Court holding that a constitutional right exists under which the states are required to give an indeterminate amount of flexibility to organizations and their members to design their own forms of legal service programs. The types of legal service plans that have evolved are then considered and assessed. The section concludes with an examination of the lawyer codes and other forms of regulation to which group legal plans have been subjected.

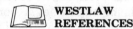

WESTLAW REFERENCES

[no queries]

§ 16.5.2 *Constitutional Freedom to Deal with Legal Needs*

In a series of four decisions,[40] the Supreme Court has held that civil rights groups and unions have the right to urge their members to litigate issues of interest to the group and to refer those members who wish to do so to lawyers named by the organization or retained by it. The first case, NAACP v. Button,[41] held, in 1963, that the first amendment prohibited Virginia from attempting to outlaw the NAACP's program of selecting and paying lawyers to bring school desegregation cases and of recommending that potential desegregation plaintiffs permit their names to be used in such suits. In Brotherhood of Railroad Trainmen v. Virginia ex rel. Virgin-

[39] On the extent to which an unmet need for legal services exists, see § 14.1 (client needs).

[40] NAACP v. Button, 371 U.S. 415, 83 S.Ct. 328, 9 L.Ed. 2d 405 (1963); Brotherhood of Railroad Trainmen v. Virginia ex rel. Virginia State Bar, 377 U.S. 1, 84 S.Ct. 1113, 12 L.Ed.2d 89 (1964); United Mine Workers v. Illinois State Bar Ass'n, 389 U.S. 217, 88 S.Ct. 353, 19 L.Ed.2d 426 (1967); United Transp. Union v. State Bar of Michigan, 401 U.S. 576, 91 S.Ct. 1076, 28 L.Ed.2d 339 (1971).

[41] Supra n. 40.

ia State Bar,[42] decided the next year, the court held that the states could not treat as unlawful solicitation and unauthorized practice a program under which a union advised injured member-workers and their families to obtain legal assistance before settling claims and recommending specific lawyers to handle the claims of members and their families if they wished.[43] United Mine Workers v. Illinois State Bar Association[44] held, in 1967, that a union plan under which a private-practice lawyer salaried by the union handled worker compensation claims of union members and their families was constitutionally protected. Finally, in 1971, in United Transportation Union v. State Bar of Michigan,[45] the Court reaffirmed the constitutional invulnerability of the trainmen's union regional counsel plan, and in the process rejected several attempts by the state bar to distinguish and limit the Court's prior decisions. The Court's opinion promised a broad protection for the kinds of union legal services plans involved and perhaps for others.[46]

The Court in the four decisions—all involving majority opinions written by Justice Black—based the right to engage in group legal services activities on two grounds. First, the first amendment right to freedom of assembly[47] entitles individuals to associate together for the purpose of securing adequate legal counsel and to communicate with each other on this subject. In order to effectuate the right of assembly, states must permit lawyers to cooperate with groups who wish to exercise the right. Second, the first amendment right to petition for the redress of grievances[48] also supports the right of individuals to group together to seek the most effective and most affordable counsel to gain their legal rights in courts and administrative agencies.

The four decisions reach rather far, but perhaps not as far as some have wished to read them. The Court has made clear that the rights asserted by organization members need not be constitutional civil rights or even federal rights. The claims involved need not relate to the collective interests of the group as opposed to individual members' interests. Thus the Court has held that the right existed not only in the context of referral of federal civil rights cases by the NAACP,[49] but also in the context of closed-panel referral of worker compensation claims by a mineworkers' union.[50] Nothing in the language of the majority opinion in any of the cases suggests that the right that the Court recognized is relevant only to legal claims that are of even general interest to the referring organization, although on their facts each case did deal with such claims. Nor is anything in the majority opinions necessarily inconsistent with extending the right to membership organizations that are established specifically for the purpose of asserting legal claims or rights.

42 Supra n. 40.

43 The railroad union's "regional counsel" plan is described in Railroad Trainmen, supra n. 40, 377 U.S. at 4, 84 S.Ct. at 115.

44 Supra n. 40.

45 Supra n. 40.

46 See 401 U.S. at 585–86, 91 S.Ct. at 1082:

> [T]he principle here involved cannot be limited to the facts of this case. At issue is the basic right to group legal action . . . . The common thread running through our decisions . . . is that collective activity undertaken to obtain meaningful access to the courts is a fundamental right within the protection of the First Amendment. However, that right would be a hollow promise if courts could deny associations of workers or others the means of enabling their members to meet the costs of legal representation. . . ."

47 U.S.Const. amend. 1 ("Congress shall make no law . . . abridging . . . the right of the people peaceably to assemble"). See NAACP v. Button, supra, 371 U.S. at 437, 83 S.Ct. at 340; Brotherhood of Railroad Trainmen v. Virginia ex rel. Virginia State Bar, supra, 377 U.S. at 5, 84 S.Ct. at 1116; United Mine Workers v. Illinois State Bar, supra, 389 U.S. at 221–23, 225, 88 S.Ct. at 355–56, 357; United Transportation Union v. State Bar of Michigan, supra, 401 U.S. at 580, 91 S.Ct. at 1079.

48 U.S.Const. amend. 1 ("Congress shall make no law . . . abridging . . . the right of the people . . . to petition the Government for a redress of grievances."). See Brotherhood of Railroad Trainmen v. Virginia ex rel. Virginia State Bar, supra, 377 U.S. at 5, 7, 84 S.Ct. at 1116, 1117; United Mine Workers v. Illinois State Bar, supra, 389 U.S. at 221–23, 88 S.Ct. at 355–57.

49 NAACP v. Button, supra, 371 U.S. at 444–45, 83 S.Ct. at 343, 344 (dicta).

50 United Mine Workers v. Illinois Bar Ass'n, supra (state worker compensation claims).

But again, the facts of each case are consistent with such a limiting reading. And some lower courts have taken descriptive language in the Supreme Court's opinions to suggest that the constitutional right that the Court intended to recognize should be confined to "collective activity undertaken to obtain meaningful access to the courts."[51] According to one such decision, when the beneficiaries of the plan are not substantially united in interest, are not in particular need of information concerning their legal rights, and are not in need of practical and economical access to courts, then the constitutional protections do not apply.[52]

The Court itself has not actively extended the associational rights that it recognized in the four legal services decisions. The Court has indicated that those decisions may rest more on litigational (petition of grievances) rights than on associational freedoms.[53] And, aside from federal antitrust considerations, there seems to be no other federal basis for a claim of right to practice in a for-profit law organization controlled or owned by nonlawyers. In a 1973 decision the Court upheld against a due process attack a state law that required that licensed pharmacists own a majority of the stock of any corporation that operated a pharmacy.[54] In sum, the constitutional protection for group legal services recognized by the Supreme Court applies with certainty only to nonprofit advocacy organizations. Its future extension, or contraction, in the context of other group legal service arrangements must await further decisions by the Court.

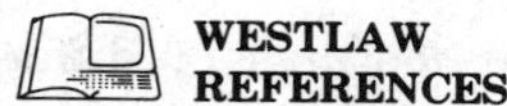
WESTLAW REFERENCES

naacp +4 button /12 83 +4 328 /p right +5 (legal /3 service represent!) attorney lawyer counsel**

naacp union organization group /p legal /2 redress service represent! /p "first amendment" constitution! unconstitutional

§ 16.5.3 Types of Group Legal Service Plans

Varieties of Group Legal Services

It is misleading to speak of group legal service plans as a unitary phenomenon, for there currently exist many types of organizations delivering services of varying kinds to different types of client groups. The plan that apparently was the earliest in this country was the Physicians' Defense Company, which was established in Indiana in 1889 to defend then uninsured physicians against medical malpractice suits.[55] Several thousand group legal service plans currently operate, although many of these consist only of a discount arrangement between individual law firms and a group, with no prepayment or guarantee of services. A recent informal estimate is that 10 million persons are covered by some form of group legal service plan.[56] Many of the plans have been developed through collective bargaining agreements between unions and employers in heavily unionized industries. Their growth has apparently stagnated in recent years as union and union member attention has been drawn to more central economic issues. The most salient differences between the plans will be examined here; the following section assesses

[51] United Transp. Union v. Michigan State Bar, 401 U.S. 576, 585, 91 S.Ct. 1076, 1082, 28 L.Ed.2d 339 (1971).

[52] Board of Education of New York City v. Nyquist, 590 F.2d 1241, 1244–45 (2d Cir.1979).

[53] See Garcia v. Texas State Bd. of Medical Examiners, 421 U.S. 995, 95 S.Ct. 2391, 44 L.Ed.2d 663 (1975), affirming memorandum 384 F.Supp. 434 (W.D.Tex.1974)(no associational right to form alternative, health maintenance organization for low-income persons in contravention to state law). See generally L.Tribe, American Constitutional Law § 16–52 (1978).

[54] North Dakota St. Bd. of Pharmacy v. Snyder's Drug Stores, Inc., 414 U.S. 156, 94 S.Ct. 407, 38 L.Ed.2d 379 (1973). The majority stressed the rationality of avoiding majority ownership by "people who do not know anything about" the licensed activity (there pharmacy) that "calls for knowledge in a high degree." 414 U.S. at 166, quoting Liggett Co. v. Baldridge, 278 U.S. 105, 114, 49 S.Ct. 57, 59, 73 L.Ed. 204 (1928)(Holmes, J., dissenting).

[55] Pfennigstorf & Pfaff, Legal Defense Programs for the Medical Profession: A Historical and Comparative Account, in Legal Service Plans: Approaches to Regulation at 395 (W.Pfennigstorf & S.Kimball eds.1977).

[56] Nat'l L.J., Sept. 5, 1983, at 12, col. 3 (estimate of executive director of National Resource Center for Consumers of Legal Services).

the principal features of different kinds of group legal services plans.

Basic Features of Plans

The common element of all plans is that they involve a contract or agreement between a group and a lawyer or lawyers to provide some form of representation to the group's members. The agreement may or may not include discounted fees or prepayment of benefits in their behalf either by the members to be represented or by a third party such as an employer or union. The plan may be managed by a professional administrator; by the lawyers who provide the services; by a third-party payer such as an insurance company; or by the beneficiaries themselves. The legal services covered under the plan may be either extensive or minimal. And the services may be provided by preselected lawyers or, under other plans, by any lawyer in private practice that the beneficiary wants to consult.

Open- and Closed-Panel Plans

The last-mentioned feature involves the difference between *closed-panel* and *open-panel* plans—by far the most publicly controverted aspect of group legal services. Under a *closed-panel* arrangement, the benefits of the plan are extended only to members who use the services of a selected group of lawyers. Depending on the terms of the plan, those may be either lawyers on the permanent staff of the plan's administration—such as in a legal aid clinic or a student legal services office—or lawyers in a community who have been selected to participate in the plan because of their experience, training, and competence. Under *open-panel* arrangements, which bar associations have strongly favored,[57] any lawyer in a locality is eligible to provide legal services to plan members and receive compensation from the plan. The only credential required is a license to practice law that has not been suspended.

Three Types of Plans

The varieties of group legal plans have been extensively cataloged by Pfennigstorf and Kimball.[58] They describe three basic types of plans: legal clinics; group consultation or referral plans; and risk-spreading, or insurance, plans. Some plans share features of two or possibly combine features of all three categories, but, in any event, they provide convenient and understandable paradigms in a sometimes confusing field.

Legal Clinics. Group plans of this kind are organized to serve low- and middle-income clients at maximum efficiency and minimum cost but without elements of strong group organization or prepayment. They usually accomplish those objectives by providing a staffed office to give low-cost, high-efficiency, mass-practice legal services. A law firm providing legal services to middle-income clients may fit the definition, as would less traditional arrangements, such as single-office or multistate and multioffice "clinics" that provided highly routinized legal services to a large number of clients on a relatively narrow range of legal problems. A variant that has been allowed in California and a few other states, are "law store" desks or areas in department stores that sell legal services just as insurance or other services are sold at other counters in the same store.[59] As a terminological nicety, it is probably inaccurate to term many such arrangements group legal services in the absence of some sort of arrangement with a group to service its members.

Consultation-or-Referral Plans. Such a plan involves a group contract with lawyers to provide, at reduced fees, initial consulta-

57 The contentious movement of the lawyer codes away from strictly required open-panel plans toward broader acceptance of closed-panel arrangements is discussed in § 16.5.5.

58 Pfennigstorf & Kimball, Legal Service Plans: A Typology, 1976 Am.B.Found. Research J. 411, 456–99. For other helpful reviews of types of plans, see, e.g., S.Mackenzie, Group Legal Services (1975); B.Christensen, Group Legal Services 8–36 (1967).

59 Nat'l L.J., June 28, 1982, at 30, col. 1; Nat'l L.J., May 14, 1979, at 7, col. 1 (opening of first "law store" legal services center in Montgomery Ward department store chain).

tion and, possibly, subsequent services.[60] Many of the existing plans have been organized in California, where the lawyer code has for a decade permitted them. In fact since 1979 California has broadly permitted and encouraged lawyers to engage in group legal services.[61] Similar arrangements have been worked out in other states, often in the form of "umbrella" law firms established in close conformance to ABA Informal Opinion 1388 (1977), which, in careful language, sees nothing wrong with at least an intrastate firm that was formed for the purpose of providing legal services to employees or members of bona fide membership associations and that operated through referrals to "associate" law firms specializing in various areas.

The bargaining element distinguishes consultation-or-referral plans from clinics; the lack of any significant prepayment [62] distinguishes them from insurance plans. There are several thousand such plans, and they are by far the most common form of group legal service plan. They typically provide some screening of participating lawyers and offer such features as free initial consultation, consultation by telephone, and twenty-four-hour emergency service. Clients are also often given the benefit of a guaranteed lower fee for some routine legal services.

Those and similar services probably serve in many plans as "loss leaders" for the lawyers involved. In some of the plans the fees charged for services that are not covered by the schedule of benefits may be higher than community averages for comparable services. Clients still receive the benefit of a presumably reliable referral and, if provided, reduced costs for scheduled services. Participating lawyers benefit because a heavier and more predictable flow of clients permits office efficiencies, economic and market planning, and possible follow-up representations for possibly lucrative and unscheduled legal services. Benefitted groups under existing plans include employee groups, especially teachers' associations, and church and consumer groups.

Insurance Plans.[63] In risk-spreading, or insurance, plans, the dominant feature is prepayment of legal expenses so that the client's contingent needs for legal services can be met without payment, or through significantly reduced payment, of legal fees. Instead the fees are paid by an insurer who derives revenue from assessments on members of the plan in the form of legal insurance premiums. Many, but not all, of the insurance plans also serve a brokerage function, bringing clients together with lawyers selected and designated by the plan administrator. Most plans cover both unplanned as well as predictable legal expenses, so that the plans' usage depends more on contingencies related to client-members' ignorance of benefits or reluctance to use lawyers.

Another kind of risk-spreading plan is found in some employee legal services plan,

[60] At least it seems clear that reduced fees are one of the incentives for members to follow the group's lead to a particular law office. Pfennigstorf and Kimball note, however, that some such plans may actually charge higher fees than prevail in the community, suggesting that the contracting group has seriously underplayed its bargaining power and that the plan in fact gives no economic benefit to members. Pfennigstorf & Kimball, Legal Service Plans: A Typology, 1976 Am.B.Found.Research J. 411, 458–59.

[61] The present rule is Calif.R.Prof.Conduct 2–102, as amended 1979. The former Rule 2–104 and its predecessor, Rule 20, broadly permitted consultation-and-referral plans, but they and other rules were more restrictive of other forms of group legal services.

[62] Some consultation-or-referral plans do include an element of prepayment to cover a "free" initial consultation, but this charge will be small compared to the fees that participating lawyers normally charge. In other plans, staff lawyers provide initial consultations on a prepaid basis, then refer cases out to other participating lawyers in small "boutique" firms of specialists who charge a standard fee. Still others use a prepaid element to provide an annual preventive "family legal checkup" of perhaps four hours.

[63] An early but still quite timely analysis of the concept and, in theory, its workability is Stolz, Insurance for Legal Services: A Preliminary Study of Feasibility, 35 U.Chi.L.Rev. 417 (1968). In W.Pfennigstorf, Legal Expense Insurance: The European Experience in Financing Legal Services (1975), a leading authority examines several European systems and notes their general irrelevance to the legal and lawyering situations in the United States.

subsidized by employers or unions or both.[64] It is formed with an eye less to insuring against contingent legal needs than to simply funding employee use of lawyers, whether electively or not.[65] Employee benefit plans can themselves bear the risk that claims will exceed allotted benefits, or they can buy protection against excess exposure from a commercial insurance company.

Several states have recently enacted statutes permitting insurance companies to offer legal expenses insurance.[66] In addition to employee plans, insurance plans for some time have been offered for other groups as well, including military personnel,[67] students, automobile club members,[68] cooperative members, and credit union members. In some instances, and particularly in the instance of automobile club plans, legal service benefits may be limited to services related to the nature of the group, such as those associated with automobile accidents or traffic violations. Still other plans are offered by insurance companies to individuals who are not members of any organized group. Yet others operate on much the same basis but are offered, not by commercial insurance companies, but by nonprofit corporations that are analogous in their form and in the way they are regulated to Blue Cross-Blue Shield in the health area. Frequently those organizations provide only administration of the plan and assign the risk-carrying function to commercial insurers. Many such nonprofit corporations have been formed jointly by bar associations and groups such as teachers' associations and unions.

WESTLAW REFERENCES

digest(group plan prepaid /3 "legal service")

"legal service" /p open** close* /2 panel

topic(insurance) /p plan group prepaid corporation program /s "legal service"

§ 16.5.4 Strengths and Weaknesses of Group Legal Service Plans

General Goals of Group Legal Services

The composite goals of legal service plans can be fairly simply stated, although not all plans aim to accomplish all the goals listed. Plans seek to educate beneficiaries to the possible existence of legal problems and to the availability of lawyers. They then seek to make legal services of good quality accessible to members of the plan at a reasonable price. The plans sometimes strive to make the prices (fees) lower than those prevailing in the community. Some plans also seek to provide a risk-spreading, or insurance, factor by prepaying benefits and providing greater potential benefits for contingent legal needs than the amount of fees assessed against members. Some plans constitute a method of subsidizing legal services by third parties, such as employers or the government. Others are supported by assessments against beneficiaries or against both beneficiaries and the employer, as in some union-sponsored plans. Finally,

64 For a description of one such plan, see F.Marks, R.Hallauer & R.Clifton, The Shreveport Plan: An Experiment in the Delivery of Legal Services (1974). Some employee plans are regulated by federal law. See § 16.5.5.

65 Because of their feature of providing reimbursement for expenditures for legal services that are nonfortuitous (such as having a will drafted), many such plans are probably not subject to state insurance law regulation. E.g., Feinstein v. Attorney General, 36 N.Y.2d 199, 366 N.Y.S.2d 613, 326 N.E.2d 288 (1975).

66 See generally R.Billings, Prepaid Legal Services § 8.34 (1981 & cum.supp.1984)(listing well over half the states with legislation authorizing some form of legal expense insurance). The legislative movement has been supported in many states by the insurance industry. While the theoretical grounds exist on which courts could strike down the legislation in many states under the inherent powers doctrine (see § 2.2.3), lawyers and bar associations in most states would probably be unwilling to lock political horns with the insurance industry. The insurance industry is both an important client for many lawyers and very powerful politically in many state legislatures.

67 Group legal services in the context of the military services has had a fascinating history all its own. It is traced in Marks, Military Lawyers, Civilian Courts, and the Organized Bar: A Case Study of the Unauthorized Practice Dilemma, 56 Mil.L.Rev. 1 (1972). See also, e.g., Woods v. Covington Cty. Bank, 537 F.2d 804, 808 n.4 (5th Cir.1976).

68 See generally Pfennigstorf, Automobile Clubs as Carriers of Legal Expense Insurance, in Legal Service Plans: Approaches to Regulation at 349 (W.Pfennigstorf & S.Kimball eds.1977).

some plans seek to advance particular interests common to the group through litigation, lobbying, and negotiation. But others provide benefits for an array of legal services that have little or nothing to do with the group's corporate reason for being.

Whether reasonably coherent sets of those goals are compatible or can be achieved in practice is, however, debatable. The following material discusses both the objections to the goals of legal service plans and the way in which plans can be structured to minimize problems and maximize benefits.

Member Education in Legal Rights

The degree to which plans can and should undertake client education about the use of legal services is subject to dispute. Traditionally, the organized legal profession has discouraged "stirring up" litigation, not only through its codes but also through criminal laws that forbid champerty and similar offenses (§ 8.13). At present, however, it seems clear that the first amendment guarantees both groups and lawyers the right to inform potential clients accurately of their legal rights and of the accessibility of group-service lawyers.[69] But is such education effectively advanced by the availability of group legal services? Studies of existing legal service plans indicate that they have not radically changed the tendency of consumers to understate legal needs and underuse legal services and to concentrate usage in traditional areas such as property, domestic, and tort law areas with only a moderate increase in the use of legal services.[70]

A traditional objection to greater access to lawyers is that greater access will result in greater social costs, because lawyers and plan members will spawn litigation, resulting in increased burdens on courts and increased legal costs necessarily incurred by other parties to their litigation. But it seems unlikely that most lawyers will be interested in trivial suits under a moderately well-regulated plan. Experience with present plans suggests that nuisance litigation has not been a problem.[71] Nonfrivolous suits, of course, should not be discouraged by placing barriers in the way of access to legal services. Theoretically, increased prepayment of fees or their subsidization could diminish the cost of frivolous suits to clients and to lawyers hired by a plan on a salaried basis or paid by a plan on an hourly charge basis. There is no existing yardstick by which plans can measure the amount of lawyer and court time that a small-dollar case is "worth." It is likely that legal service plans that do not include relatively low ceilings on total legal fee expenditures or a cost-sharing feature will encounter overutilization by some clients. But overutilization may not be a sufficiently large problem either to warrant expensive detection and prevention mechanisms in plans or, certainly, to justify opposition to all forms of group legal services.

Increased Accessibility of Lawyers

Sponsors of group legal service plans often aim at a principal goal of increasing the ability of plan members to find lawyers who will render services of good quality at affordable prices. That aspires essentially to a brokering function of matching clients with lawyers possessing skills appropriate to the clients' needs. There are sound reasons to think that that goal of legal service plans may be their most salient contribution to providing legal services to middle-income clients. There are also reasons to think that the goal can best be achieved through closed-panel arrangements and readily available neighborhood legal clinics.[72]

[69] See generally § 16.5.2 (associational freedom); § 14.2 (lawyer advertising).

[70] L.Deitch & D.Weinstein, Prepaid Legal Services: Socioeconomic Impacts 5–6, 85–90 (1976). A study of the Shreveport, Louisiana, experiment with a "judicare" feature, which relies upon an open-panel resort to community lawyers with voucher reimbursement, reported some higher use of lawyers in a studied population, although several factors suggested that the rise in use was temporary. See F.Marks, R.Hallauer & R.Clifton, The Shreveport Plan 61–67 (1974).

[71] L.Deitch & D.Weinstein, supra at 90–91.

[72] See Project, An Assessment of Alternative Strategies for Increasing Access to Legal Services, 90 Yale L.J. 122 (1980)(re-analyzing data collected in the 1973–74 ABA

Whatever ability an average citizen once might have had to make an informed and wise choice of a lawyer based on community reputation, clients in a modern, transient, urbanized community clearly lack any reliable reputational basis for choosing a lawyer. Therefore, to the extent that a legal services plan retains or recommends only generally competent and skillful lawyers, clients can take advantage of a corporate knowledgeability about lawyers' reputations and credentials that the individual clients could never hope to acquire personally. Moreover, to the extent that the plan either facilitates legal services of only a relatively specialized and routinized sort, such as real estate closings, or identifies lawyers by their expertise in relevant specialties, such as immigration law, clients can find lawyers who can provide services in the most efficient form.

One might object to either the desirability or the possibility of that sort of lawyer brokerage on a number of grounds. It can be argued that increased lawyer advertising will obviate the need for other measures of assuring sound information about lawyer quality and that a client is better able than a third party to evaluate both the appropriate qualities of lawyers and the client's subjective predilections about the kind of lawyer to choose. But quality claims are precisely the matter that the states are most reluctant to permit lawyers to advertise (§ 14.2.4). Local bars have been extremely reluctant to permit specialization advertising (§ 5.5). Moreover, it is doubtful that consumers in a society saturated with advertising will either be given or retain enough relevant information to be able to make effective and discriminating choices based on quality when a need for legal services arises. Most clients will also be unwilling to spend enough time to become knowledgeable about lawyer credentials and their significance. Indeed, it can be argued that legal talent and skill are sufficiently unmeasurable that most clients might prefer to rely on the subjective judgment of an informed third party than on facts about legal education and years of practice.

The extent to which plans can perform a useful brokerage and referral function varies considerably with the type of plan. Many open-panel plans, including nearly all those sponsored by bar associations, provide reduced fees for consultation and specified services, but they are, by definition, open to all members of the bar who wish to participate. Consequently, the plans do not indicate the relative quality of participating lawyers or their degree of specialization, except perhaps by indicating the areas in which the lawyer is willing to accept cases. Such self-designations, obviously, provide little assurance of true specialization. The same features characterize open-panel plans offered by insurance companies, employers, and other sponsors.

Only closed-panel plans, or those open-panel plans whose administration includes some referral service of a fairly selective kind or which limits lawyer participation to specially selected firms, can hope to regularly associate clients with specially qualified lawyers. Closed panels also offer the potential advantage that the staff will develop expertise in problems that characterize a given client group—landlord-tenant law for students; worker compensation claims for union members; and the like. Closed panels also are more likely to be able to deal with typical group concerns through efficient and discriminating use of methods such as test cases, class actions, and lobbying. Those techniques have been widely publicized as a feature of legal services for the poor under the Legal Services Corporation (§ 16.7.3), and they are at least theoretically transferrable to group legal services for middle-income constituencies as well.

A standard objection to such arguments concerning enhanced quality of closed-panel plans is that conflicts of interest will inevitably arise between the plan as employer and

Survey of Legal Needs, note concludes that prepaid plans with closed panels are best calculated to encourage lawyer use for those with membership in groups that could provide such plans and that, for others, legal clinics were much more likely than bar association lawyer referral plans to enhance access).

the individual client.[73] The presence and extent of conflict will doubtless vary with the type of sponsoring organization and the nature of the group represented. Conflict may be less likely, for example, in union plans because of the close identity of the union with its members' interests, and more likely in a commercial insurance plan because of the profit motive that would induce a plan lawyer to render minimal services in order to enhance the profits of the sponsoring insurance company that selects or designates the lawyer.[74]

Law Reform and Group Power

Concerted representation of middle-income groups, particularly by closed-panel lawyers who take the interests of the group into account, may in fact have a significant impact upon substantive law and on the operation of government. To that extent, group-interest advocacy can redound to the benefit of all or most plan members through enhancing their individual and group legal rights. Representation of consumer and environmental group interests, for prominent examples, have placed before courts and administrative agencies group points of view that otherwise would have been advocated only by individuals or not at all. Other middle-income interests, such as the interests of tenants, may also be advocated more powerfully when well organized into a group legal arrangement.

The extent of the net increase in the political clout of middle-income persons that could be effected through group legal services is debatable. Middle-income persons already possess a modicum of political power through traditional advocacy organizations, and it is speculative whether a great increase in membership in group legal service organizations would produce a corresponding impact on the legal-economic balance of power. It is equally imaginable that an emerging power bloc of middle-income persons would be countered by another—a tenants union met by a newly organized association of landlords. Thus the law-reform effects of group legal services may be minimal or even disfunctional to the long-range goals of organizers.

Decreasing the Cost of Legal Services

Group legal services are frequently advocated as a means of securing reduced costs of quality legal services for middle-income clients. The ways that cost reduction is thought to occur are several. First, the sheer bargaining ability of a group may bring about lower individual fees because the contracting lawyers perceive an economic advantage through a continual relationship and many clients. Because a group can use expertise in hiring lawyers, members of the group need not bear the high search costs[75] for lawyers that are otherwise necessary. Even under open-panel arrangements, lawyers may be willing to agree to reduced charges simply in order to have access to fees that will pay overhead if necessary and because they will be compensated (as most plans provide) for initial consultations that are often not billed or billed at lower rates. When lawyers organize a plan, as opposed to a well-organized client-interest group, such cost-saving features may be reduced or nonexistent.

Prices may also be reduced because group legal service allows more efficient use of resources. Specialization by salaried lawyers can achieve higher quality without a price increase. Routinization through repetitive handling of common problems of group members can lead to lower prices, not only because it reduces lawyers' research time, but also because routinization facilitates the use of forms, computers, and paralegal staff for tasks that do not require legal judgment. Such cost savings are obviously gained most predictably in closed-panel arrangements or if

73 For an assessment of the conflict of interest problems, see § 8.8.

74 Cf. § 8.4 (insurance practice conflicts).

75 Search costs might be represented either in the cost of time off from employment spent in an attempt to shop for the best lawyer at a given price or in the form of a premium paid by a client who takes a legal problem to a prestigious law firm that charges high prices.

the plan uses a modified open-panel system in which clients are referred to open-panel lawyers who already specialize.

Finally, efficiencies of a relatively unmeasurable and speculative kind may be achieved through test-case litigation, lobbying, or negotiation with regard to legal problems common to many group members. Beneficial law reform or other legal results are then achieved without large numbers of individual legal actions and lawyer fees.

Claims that group legal services will reduce client costs have not gone unchallenged. The degree of cost saving that results from bargaining between the group and the lawyers who provide services depends on the expertise and dedication of the staff of the group. Plans sponsored by bar associations, or that are offered by insurance companies to a diffuse client group without organized bargaining power, may produce relatively few or no economic concessions. Moreover, if health insurance provides a comparable experience, the presence of a third-party financer, who attempts to spread costs to other subscribers, may actually encourage unnecessary use by subscribers and a failure of cost-containment features that private, marketplace bargaining for legal services does provide to an extent. Diffusion of risk of expense may result in a corresponding diffusion of motivation in keeping low the price charged by a lawyer to a participating plan. The plan as cost spreader may be insufficiently motivated to contain costs if higher costs (and a correspondingly high profit margin) can be passed along in the form of higher assessments on group members.

Another expressed fear of the bar with respect to economic competition of any sort is that fees will be lowered only as the result of cost cutting that comes at the expense of quality legal services. Empirical studies indicate that in fact legal service operations can provide as high a quality of lawyering as is generally available in the community.[76] Problems may arise particularly in prepaid plans in which services are contracted for with cooperating lawyers depending on the type of legal problem and without regard to its complexity or difficulty. Lawyers may thus be tempted to minimize services to any given client in order to service as many clients as possible. It may be difficult to develop realistic and fair guidelines to measure the amount of time that should be devoted to a given case. Particularly because actuarial experience with claims may be scarce with new plans, prepaid plans may generate more claims for benefits than the plan can adequately fund. The reverse situation may also develop: a plan may overestimate the number and size of claims for plan benefits, plan assessments may be set too high, and lawyers may spend an unwarranted amount of time on individual cases in order to justify their salaries or the continuation of the plan.

Risk Spreading through Group Legal Services

Some plans, but by no means all of them, serve the goal of spreading the risk of the cost of legal services by prepaying specified services and spreading their cost among all members of the plan, just as health insurance spreads risk and cost among subscribers. Either open-panel or closed-panel plans may provide that feature.

A difficulty, or an anomaly, in risk spreading through group legal service arrangements is that many legal service costs are considerably more predictable and marginally affordable than are health costs.[77] It would be senseless, for example, to provide a group legal service plan if its only benefit were that members, in return for their assessment, could have their wills written. Will writing is not catastrophically expensive; insuring against its cost, which will necessarily incur the administrative and profit costs of the plan's sponsoring risk spreader, is as unnecessary for middle-income persons as is insuring

[76] Muris & McChesney, Advertising and the Price and Quality of Legal Services: The Case for Legal Clinics, 1979 Am.B.Found. Research J. 179.

[77] See generally W.Pfennigstorf, Legal Expense Insurance: The European Experience in Financing Legal Services (1975).

against the cost of a new automobile. Moreover, the timing of having a will written is almost entirely elective (except for deathbed wills), and a will is hardly an absolute need for most middle-class persons in any event. Similarly, most middle-income persons can frequently foresee decisions and exert some control over costs for matters such as drafting a will, obtaining a divorce or name change, defending against a misdemeanor charge (instead of paying the fine), or buying property. Some kinds of unforeseeable and possibly high legal expenses are already provided for through risk spreading inherent in contingent fee representation of plaintiffs and representation of defendants under conventional public liability insurance on automobiles, homes, and small businesses.

To the extent that potential clients see their legal service costs as largely noncontingent, the prepayment feature offers few advantages over paying for services after they are rendered. Indeed, a plan subscriber incurs the risk of paying, through plan assessments, for legal services for others without reaping commensurate benefits. Moreover, depending on the method of making assessments, a plan may find itself in a conflict of interest situation in that expanded client education might create greater claims on the plan and reduce its profitability or increase its cost.

For those reasons, plans with large prepayment features may offer relatively restricted services, such as criminal defense representation, defense of civil cases not covered by public liability insurance, and plaintiff's litigation not covered by contingent fee representation. In other areas, in which claims for services are not so contingent, it seems reasonable to expect that prepayment will in fact represent a form of third-party payment, for example by employers or unions that seek to educate their employees or members and provide them with a fringe benefit while establishing the amount of the contribution as a flat figure in advance.

Impact on the Legal Profession

The benefits and disadvantages of group legal services for the members of the legal profession are problematical and depend greatly upon the kind of plan involved and upon the varying segments of the legal profession being considered. Lawyers who might potentially be affected by group legal services have feared them perhaps as much out of ignorance of their probable competitive effects as from well-founded facts. Some lawyers clearly are not susceptible to competitive pressures. Large-firm practice of corporate law, of course, is not affected in any important way.[78]

Group legal services, to the extent that they stimulate demand for legal services, would help to provide new jobs for recent graduates. Quality control of legal services might also be enhanced, perhaps leading to increased pressures for quality control for lawyers not participating in plans. A substantial increase in group legal service plans would doubtless accelerate the trend away from solo practice into salaried legal positions. That would occur because closed panels theoretically offer efficiencies and expertise through specialization and mass production that makes efficient use of expensive equipment such as computers, that are priced out of the reach of solo practitioners. Lower prices charged by some group legal plans may make solo practice uneconomical and drive solo practitioners into their own group practices. Lower prices and competition for middle-income clients are also a reason why many solo practitioners and small-firm lawyers oppose group legal services.[79] Their persistent opposition has been

[78] Although the point might stretch terminology, large firms engage in an activity analogous to group legal services in their representation (and sometimes in their prior creation) of trade associations and other lobbying and litigation groups to advance the interests of member companies. The costs of the legal services are underwritten by member assessments to the association, which then hires a law firm to provide legal and lobbying services.

[79] P.Stern, Lawyers on Trial 108–09 (1980); J.Lieberman, Crisis at the Bar ch. 4 (1978); Nat'l L.J., May 5, 1982, at 3, col. 1; id., Nov. 19, 1979, at 3, col. 1; Colvin & Kramer, Group Legal Service Plans in Wisconsin, 48 Wisc.B.Bull. 47, 53–54 (Feb.1975); Riedmueller,

one of the reasons that the attention of national antitrust authorities has been attracted to the group legal services controversy.

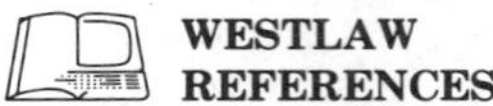
WESTLAW REFERENCES

prepaid plan group corporation program /s "legal service" /p access!

prepaid plan group corporation program /3 "legal service" /p conflict! /3 interest

§ 16.5.5 Regulation of Legal Service Plans

Variety of Regulation

Legal service plans are subject to regulation by a variety of agencies and methods, including state law on insurance and lawyers and federal laws governing employee benefits, antitrust, and taxes. The extent and possible impact of regulation from each source varies with the type of plan involved. So, too, do the problems that are thought to necessitate regulation and the public policies that have been developed to deal with the problems.

Insurance Regulation

Many of the legal service plans that possess a risk-spreading feature present dangers common to insurance generally. There is first the obvious problem of guaranteeing that the premiums paid in fact adequately cover the claims made. Second, the plan should succeed in providing the kind and quality of services paid for and promised to clients. Insurance regulation is well suited to the first task, but not the second. Even as to the first task, an insurance regulatory agency accustomed to the kind of financial stability desirable in massive companies insuring catastrophic risks may miss the point of the possible marginal benefit of smaller, newer, entrepreneurial insurers, whose small financial base may be matched by the limited exposure to risk involved in legal expense insurance. Coverage of various types of group legal plans under state insurance laws is often quite unclear.

Federal Regulation

Several federal statutes relating to labor relations, antitrust, and federal income taxation bear directly or indirectly upon group legal services.[80] The federal Employees Retirement Income Security Act of 1974 (ERISA)[81] generally regulates employee pension and benefit plans, including certain group legal service plans offered by employers or by employee associations such as unions. Those plans falling under the federal act are preempted from state regulation, although the extent of preemption is quite uncertain.[82] Such preemption may include such matters as the barriers to lawyer participation in closed-

Group Legal Services and the Organized Bar, 10 Colum. J.L. & Soc.Prob. 228 (1974); Fendler, Are We Hearing the Death Knell of the General Practice of Law, 33 Unauth. Pract. News 18–30 (Spring-Summer 1967).

80 In addition to the matters discussed in the text, a 1973 amendment to the Taft-Hartley Act gives the right to include legal expense insurance in the benefits that can be paid into jointly administered employer-union trusts, with the significant limitation that beneficiaries be given free choice of the counsel or plan they wish to choose. See Taft-Hartley Act (Labor Management Relations Act of 1947) § 302(c)(as amended), in 29 U.S.C.A. § 186(c)(8).

A tax amendment in 1976 provided that, in the case of contributions by an employer to a qualified plan providing employee group legal services, the gross income of employees need include neither the amount of the employer's contribution nor the value of legal services provided under the plan. Further, certain trusts and other nonprofit organizations established to administer legal service plans can be nontaxable. See generally Johnson, Group Legal Services Plans and Section 2134 of the Tax Reform Act of 1976, 52 L.A.B.J. 474 (Mar.1977). The 1976 amendment was effective for five years and has been periodically renewed, in amended forms, thereafter. See Internal Revenue Code §§ 201, 501(c)(20).

81 Employee Retirement Income Security Act of 1974, Pub.L. No. 93–406, 88 Stat. 829 (codified in various sections of 5, 18, 29, 31, 42 U.S.C.A.). For a preenactment review of the issues, see Bartosic & Bernstein, Group Legal Services as a Fringe Benefit: Lawyers for Forgotten Clients through Collective Bargaining, 59 Va.L.Rev. 410 (1973). For a discussion of ERISA issues, see R.Billings, Prepaid Legal Services ch.6 (1981).

82 R.Billings, Prepaid Legal Services §§ 8.12-.17, § 8.29, at 440 n.1 (1981); W.Bolger, S.DeMent & J.Pozzo, Group Legal Service Plans 170–76 (1981); Pfenningstorf & Kimball, Employee Legal Services Plans: Conflicts between Federal and State Regulation, 1976 Am.B.Found. Research J. 787. See generally Kilberg & Heron, The Preemption of State Law under ERISA, 1979 Duke L.J. 383.

panel group legal plans that the 1969 Code attempted to throw up. Generally, ERISA applies only to "prepaid" legal service plans[83] and thus does not apply to plans that do not spread risk, but merely secure lower fees for members or that provide consultation and referral. Those plans do not pose a risk of great member loss in the event that the plan becomes financially unstable, is maladministered, is promoted in a misleading way, or is unfairly discriminatory in its benefits. Thus, federal regulation is markedly less needed than for such things as retirement and survivor pension funds. Other exemptions may exist for group legal plans of local governmental units, churches, and third-party carriers (Blue Cross-Blue Shield type plans).

Group legal service plans themselves, because they are combinations that arguably restrain trade in commerce, are susceptible to federal antitrust scrutiny.[84] Those plans that extend a guaranteed set of legal fees to members of an organization set prices, but arguably not impermissibly because the plans can serve competitive purposes. The plans also do not rigidly set prices because nothing prevents clients from seeking other legal service providers outside the plan at competitive prices. Those few group legal service plans that are regulated as insurance under state law are exempt from federal antitrust law under the McCarron-Ferguson Act.[85]

Probably the more significant antitrust question is whether the kinds of ethical rules that stifled the formation of legal services plans, as found in the 1969 Code, and the activities of some of the persons and organizations that have sponsored and enforced them, are not themselves in violation of the antitrust laws.[86] For example, by preventing the entry into the legal services market of commercial insurance companies and other profit-making enterprises, the ethical rules stifle capital formation that may be important to developing competitive price structures under classical open-enterprise antitrust analysis. As will next be seen, the dominant bar position has been one of hostility toward most forms of group legal service plans.

State Lawyer Code Regulation

(a) *1969 Code*

Original Version of the Code

In general, a lawyer's participation in group legal services confronts two kinds of roadblocks under the lawyer codes in force in many of the states.[87] The codes, which differ drastically from one state to another with respect to group legal services, thus create two barriers to effective and widespread availability of a variety of forms of group legal service programs. First, the codes have strictly limited the extent to which a lawyer may practice law under arrangements in which nonlawyers play a role as plan administrator, fee payer, or lawyer selector.[88] Second, the codes also contain antiadvertising

83 ERISA § 3 (1).

84 See generally Meeks, Antitrust Aspects of Prepaid Legal Services Plans, 1976 Am.B.Found. Research J. 855.

85 See 15 U.S.C.A. §§ 1101–1115; R.Billings, Prepaid Legal Services § 8.31 (1981).

86 Meekes, Antitrust Aspects of Prepaid Legal Services Plans, 1976 Am.B.Found. Research J. 855; Francis & Johnson, The Emperor's Old Clothes: Piercing the Bar's Ethical Veil, 13 Willamette L.J. 221 (1977); Sims, Competition at the Bar, 61 ABA J. 1069 (1975)(excerpt from address by special assistant to assistant attorney general in charge of antitrust); 809 Antitrust & Tr.Reg.Rptr. A-11 (Apr.14, 1977)(report of clearance of bar association plan after elimination of lawyer-board to set standard fees); 677 Antitrust & Tr.Reg.Rptr. A-1 (Aug. 20, 1974) (speech by assistant attorney general in charge of antitrust). State supreme courts that promulgate and enforce anticompetitive ethical rules enjoy immunity from antitrust damages under the "state action" exception to the antitrust laws. See § 2.4.2. But questions still remain concerning the application of the state action doctrine to injunctive actions against state supreme court justices acting in their capacity as promulgators and enforcers of anticompetitive lawyer code rules and with respect to suits against bar associations and lawyers that participate in and actively sponsor such anticompetitive regulation.

87 See generally B.Christensen, Lawyers for People of Moderate Means 225–91 (1970); Schwartz, Changing Patterns of Legal Service, in Law in a Changing America 109–24 (1968). See also Collins, Automobile Club Activities—The Problem from the Standpoint of the Clubs, 5 L. & Contemp.Probs. 3 (1938); Llewellyn, The Bar's Troubles, and Poultices—and Cures, id. at 104.

88 See generally B.Christensen, Group Legal Services 45 (1967)("The . . . objective of present restrictions on the

and antisolicitation rules that somewhat limit the extent to which a lawyer can advertise to a group or negotiate with its leadership in order to work out a group legal services arrangement.[89] The drafting technique by which regulation has been achieved over group legal service plans in all versions of the Code has been indirect. The Code has not attempted to regulate the plans directly, but has specified in various restrictive ways those kinds of organizations with which a lawyer can cooperate.

The ABA Code, as originally approved in August 1969, was strikingly restrictive of group legal services. The Code's drafting committee had first been much more receptive and recommended a rule that would have permitted lawyers to cooperate with any "bona fide, non-profit" organization that provided group legal services to its members "as an incident to its primary activities." [90] The proposal generalized and broadened the apparent reach of the Supreme Court's decisions on advocacy organizations and unions by extending permissible lawyer involvement to plans operated by any nonprofit organization, apparently, other than one created for the purpose of evading the rule. Conceivably it would have permitted automobile clubs to offer legal services for automobile torts along with towing and trip arrangements. But because of intense lawyer opposition,[91] the adopted version of the Code replaced that provision with one that permitted lawyers to cooperate with most types [92] of group legal services organizations "only in those instances and to the extent that controlling constitutional interpretation at the time of the rendition of the services requires the allowance of such legal service activities." [93]

1974 Houston [94]Amendments

Under pressure from antitrust officials and from lawyers concerned about the strongly restrictive approach taken in the 1969 Code, the ABA amended the group legal service provisions of the Code in 1974. The 1974 amendment dropped the embarrassing language [95] on constitutionally mandated plans. But the new version not only retained the requirement that legal services be provided only as an incidental purpose of the organiza-

obtaining of lawyers' services through group arrangements—preservation of the lawyer's independence in the exercise of his professional judgment and in the discharge of his professional responsibilities to his clients—is at the heart of the group legal services question."); Weihofen, Practice of Law by Motor Clubs—Useful but Forbidden, 3 U.Chi.L.Rev. 296 (1936); Weihofen, "Practice of Law" by Non-Pecuniary Corporations: A Social Utility, 2 U.Chi.L. Rev. 119 (1934); Note, Legalizing Nonlawyer Proprietorship in the Legal Clinic Industry: Reform in the Public Interest, 9 Hofstra L.Rev. 625 (1981); Note, Unauthorized Practice of Law by Lay Organizations Providing the Services of Attorneys, 72 Harv.L.Rev. 1334 (1959).

89 See generally Allison v. Louisiana State Bar Ass'n, 362 So.2d 489, 5 A.L.R.4th 852 (1978).

90 DR 2–101(D)(3)(Preliminary Draft, January 15, 1969).

91 The tenor of the opposition can be gathered from, e.g., Pitts, Group Legal Services: A Plan to Huckster Professional Services, 65 ABA J. 633 (1969), replying to Cady, The Future of Group Legal Services, 55 ABA J. 420 (1969).

92 All versions of the Code have also authorized lawyer participation in legal aid or public defender offices of an approved kind (§§ 16.7.2, 16.7.3, 14.6.3), military legal assistance office programs (DR 2–103(D)(2)), and approved lawyer referral services (§ 14.2.1).

93 DR 2–103(D)(5)(Final Draft, July 1, 1969). The reporter for the 1969 Code has stated that its provisions on group legal services were not innovative because of considerable bar opposition. The ultimate version was thus "more in the nature of a lateral pass of the problem to the United States Supreme Court than an attempt to find solid grounds upon which to regulate group legal services." Sutton, The American Bar Association Code of Professional Responsibility: An Introduction, 48 Tex.L. Rev. 255, 262 (1970). Those who ponder the football analogy might wish to argue with the type of offensive maneuver involved. Even as drafted, DR 2–103(D)(5) bristled with interpretative and constitutional problems—most obviously the attempt to limit federal constitutional rights to prospective-only application by bar association and state law rule making.

94 In the group legal services literature, the 1974 and 1975 amendments are commonly referred to by the names of the cities in which the ABA met when they were adopted. See Annotated Code of Professional Responsibility 73, 75 (O.Maru ed.1979)("Houston" amendments in 1974; "Chicago" amendments in 1975).

95 In addition to the incongruity of disbarring a lawyer for performing activities very closely related to those that the Supreme Court had said were constitutionally protected, the 1969 version of the Code in effect called upon ethics committees to interpret the Constitution in order to determine whether a lawyer had violated the Code. Ethics committees are uniformly prohibited by their constitutive regulations from passing on any question of "law." See § 2.6.6.

tion, but also required that—except for civil rights organizations—the plan members be entitled to select counsel of their own choosing as opposed to the plan's own lawyers. The plan was also required to pay the fees of the counsel so selected at a rate equivalent to the cost of lawyers provided by the plan's own lawyers. In effect, the 1974 amendments outlawed effective closed-panel plans other than in the instance of civil rights organizations.

The insistence on open-panel plans seemed to place the ABA Code at odds with the Supreme Court's earlier decision, in 1967, in United Mine Workers v. Illinois State Bar,[96] in which the Court had held that states were required to permit unions to offer closed-panel representation to members who wished to litigate worker compensation claims. Although the Court did not address the constitutionality of requiring the union to permit members to opt at union expense for counsel other than the lawyer supplied by the union, such an option would fairly clearly impair the plan's objective of providing members with the most effective counsel.

1975 Chicago Amendments

The ABA came under strong pressure to retreat from its 1974 amendment. Opposition was widespread among consumer groups, particularly because of the ABA's attempted elimination of closed-panel plans. Unions, which had recently been empowered by federal legislation to work legal service programs into fringe benefit packages,[97] were instrumental in having hearings held before a congressional subcommittee at which a federal antitrust official hinted darkly that the 1974 Code amendments raised significant antitrust issues.[98] A national organization of group legal service plans filed a federal antitrust suit against the ABA within months after the 1974 amendments were adopted.[99]

In 1975 the ABA bowed to political and legal pressure and again modified its group legal services rule. This time the rule required that members who wished to select counsel other than that selected by the plan had to be permitted to do so, but the rule omitted any reference to reimbursement. Instead, DR 2–103(D)(4)(e) substituted a requirement that the plan provide "appropriate relief" and "an appropriate procedure" (presumably a grievance mechanism of some kind) for any member who asserted that representation by a lawyer selected by the plan would be inadequate or unethical. Although the point is debatable,[100] it seems most reasonable to conclude that, in view of the Supreme Court precedent and the deletion of the mandatory-compensation language of the 1974 amendment, closed-panel plans need not pay for outside representation, at least if the plan's lawyers can adequately represent the complaining member.

The 1975 amendments also eliminated the requirement that the rendition of legal services be only an incidental purpose of the

96 389 U.S. 217, 88 S.Ct. 353, 19 L.Ed.2d 426 (1967).

97 See infra at 910–11 (1974 ERISA amendments).

98 See Testimony of Bruce B. Wilson, Deputy Assistant Attorney General, Antitrust Division, in Hearings on The Organized Bar: Self-Serving or Serving the Public? Before the Subcomm. on Representation of Citizen Interests of the Senate Comm. on the Judiciary, 93 Cong., 2d Sess. (1974), reprinted at 60 ABA J. 791 (1974). Even after the ABA restrictions on group legal services were loosened, federal regulatory agencies have expressed concern about anti-competitive restrictions by state and local bar associations. E.g., 64 ABA J. 33 (1978)(news report of announcement of FTC nationwide probe).

99 See 2 Group Leg.Rev., No.2, Feb.1975, at 1 (report of suit filed by National Consumer Center for Legal Services and several members against ABA, Tennessee State Bar Association, and several bar officials, for declaratory judgment that Houston group legal services amendments violated the first and fourteenth amendments, the Sherman antitrust act, and federal pension legislation).

100 Arguments opposed to, and in favor of, mandatory reimbursement built in part on a piece of legislative history. The 1975 amendments were accompanied by "comments" from the drafting committee that included the statement that DR 2–103(D)(4)(e) would "enable a member or beneficiary in either an open or closed panel plan to use counsel other than that furnished or paid for by the organization, and to assure plan provisions which, where reasonable to do so, will provide relief such as reimbursement in whole or in part, alternative legal services or in some other way." The language referring disjunctively to relief "such as reimbursement" and concerning relief "in some other way" rather plainly assumes that reimbursement is not required. For the text of the comments, see Annotated Code of Professional Responsibility 76 (O.Maru ed.1979).

sponsoring organization. Instead, the Code imposed the following requirements, some of which were new in 1975, but others of which were carried over from previous versions of the Code.

First, where the 1974 version of the Code had banned all profit-making organizations from offering legal service plans, the 1975 amendments provided somewhat more narrowly, in DR 2–103(D)(4)(a), that the organization could derive no profit from the rendition of legal services.[1] An employer could therefore offer group legal service plans to employees, so long as the employer derived no profit from the plan. Moreover, the same provision requires that any profit-making sponsor of a plan must not "employ, direct, supervise or select" the plan lawyers. That may be complied with, for example, by establishing a trust or other nonprofit organization to administer the plan. The only exception to the prohibition against direct employment is for liability insurance carriers who have traditionally chosen counsel to represent insured persons (§ 8.4.1).

That language effectively prevents commercial insurance companies from offering (for a profit, which is the point of their business) any legal service plan in which the insurer selects the plan lawyers. It also purports to prohibit employers (although presumably not unions, which are not profit making) from offering closed panel plans. The constitutionality and wisdom of the prohibitions are doubtful, although they are readily complied with in the case of employers through trustee forms of plan administrators.

Second, the 1975 amendments also prohibited lawyers from initiating or promoting legal service plans for the primary purpose of promoting the employment of the lawyer or his or her own firm (DR 2–103(D)(4)(b)). The plan's sponsor could also not be operated for the purpose of benefiting lawyers in their capacity as private practitioners outside the plan's area of operation (DR 2–103(D)(4)(c)).[2] Apparently some second representations of that kind are permissible so long as that is not "the purpose" of the plan. Whether a legal services plan that provided for referrals to a closed panel of lawyers for initial consultations only would comply with that provision seems doubtful.

Third, the 1975 amendments required a cooperating lawyer to recognize that the member-beneficiary is the lawyer's client, and not the sponsoring organization (DR 2–103(D)(4)(d)). The obligation was made somewhat more specific in DR 2–103(C)(2)(b), which provided that a lawyer could cooperate with a group legal services organization only if "the lawyer remains free to exercise his professional judgment on behalf of his client," and by the introductory language in DR 2–103(D), which stated that there must be "no interference with the exercise of independent professional judgment in behalf of his client." Those provisions are consonant with the broad and traditional requirement that the served person be recognized as client regardless of who pays the lawyer (§ 8.8.2).

Fourth, in addition to the provision in DR 2–103(D)(4)(e), already discussed, concerning grievance procedures, a cooperating lawyer could not have reason to know that the orga-

[1] The continuing bar opposition to the entry of commercial insurance companies into the legal expense insurance market led to authorizing legislation in some states. In Florida, the state supreme court elected to treat the question as one for cooperative regulation by the legislature and the supreme court. See In re Amendment to Integration Rule, Art. XIX (Group Legal Services), 409 So.2d 480 (Fla.1982). Apparently under the stimulus of the legislation, and at least contemporaneous with its passage, the Florida court also adopted an amendment sponsored by the state bar that changed the Florida lawyer code provision on group legal services to one modeled on the California rule (see infra n. 8) and on the then pending, but later rejected, proposals of the committee drafting what became the 1983 Model Rules. See In re Petition to Amend DR 2–103(D)(5), 409 So.2d 481 (Fla. 1982).

[2] This replaces a more stringent provision in the 1974 amendments that prohibited lawyers who cooperated with a legal service plan from accepting any private employment not covered by the plan from any person who had been the lawyer's client under the plan. The intent, obviously, is to prevent lawyers from using legal service plans as "feeders" of clients for nonservice business. The 1974 version had accomplished this in draconian fashion by prohibiting all second-matter representations that were not covered by the plan.

nization was in violation of law or rules of court.[3] Moreover, the organization had to file[4] an annual report of the operation of the plan. The report had to show the terms of the plan, its "schedule of benefits" for members or beneficiaries, its charges, its agreements with cooperating lawyers, and its financial results.

Reprise on the 1969 Code

A perceptive commentator on the 1969 Code has stated that "no amendments to the Code have attracted more attention or created more controversy than the amendments to subsection (D)(4), which concerns group legal services."[5] General hostility to group legal service plans bristles through the technical language of the amended Code.[6] Such hostility is difficult to comprehend except as arising from parochial economic interests of lawyers who might be put at a competitive disadvantage by group legal service plans. Clearly, adequate restrictions can be built into many kinds of legal service plans not permitted under the Code's 1975 amendments that would arrest most of the objections that have been made to group legal plans and that are not simply based on objections to competition as such. Complaints have, to be sure, been made by general practitioners in solo practice and small firms that their bar association should protect them from competition, which customarily is termed "cutthroat" or inked with similar dark phrases when competition is mentioned in such contexts. But such anticompetitive protection by a bar association, at the expense of clients, places lawyers and their bar associations in direct conflict with the economic interests of clients—a conflict that can be resolved in only one way on the profession's own pretentions. Federal and state antitrust law also seems to require a similar resolution. A state of regulation nearer to that competition-neutral point may have been reached under the 1983 Model Rules.

(b) *1983 Model Rules*

Kutak Commission Recommendations

The recommendations of the drafting Kutak Commission for a provision on group legal services created little of the loud controversy that many other proposals produced. But in its quieter way it would have produced a much more profound effect on the shape of law practice. Through several drafts, a predecessor to what became MR 5.4 provided that so long as four relatively mild conditions were satisfied, a lawyer could be employed by any kind of organization.[7] Specifically included were organizations owned or managed by a nonlawyer or by a lawyer acting in a nonlawyer capacity, "such as a business corporation, insurance company, legal services organization or government agency." The four conditions required that there be no interference with the lawyer's exercise of independent professional judgment or with the lawyer-client relationship, that confidential client information be protected, that the arrangement not involve impermissible advertising or solicitation, and that the fee be reasonable in amount. A rather similar rule had been in effect in California since 1979.[8]

[3] DR 2–103(D)(4)(f). The reference to applicable legal requirements is presumably to state insurance law and national labor law. It could not be a reference to the Code itself, because no part of the Code applies directly to group legal service organizations.

[4] Again, the requirement is not imposed directly on the organization. DR 2–103(D)(4)(g) instead states that a cooperating lawyer must not know or have reason to know that the organization has failed to file such a report.

[5] Annotated Code of Professional Responsibility 70 (O.Maru ed.1979).

[6] Only some of the hostile tone and nothing substantive was altered by a 1977 amendment to the Code that, among other things, changed the previous wording of DR 2–103(D) from a statement that a general prohibition against solicitation "does not prohibit" recommendation or employment by a group legal service plan to an expression that a lawyer may be recommended or employed or "may cooperate with" such a described organization.

[7] MR 5.4 (Proposed Final Draft, May 30, 1981).

[8] Calif.R.Prof. Conduct rule 2–102(A):

> The participation of a member or a member's firm in a bona fide program, activity or organization that furnishes, recommends, or pays for legal services, including but not limited to group, prepaid and voluntary legal service organizations, programs or activities is encouraged, and is not, of itself, a violation of

Final Version of Model Rule 5.4

In the final process of debating the Model Rules, the original proposal was dropped and other language replaced it in MR 5.4 that does not mention group legal services. One might be tempted to conclude that the removal of the proposed MR 5.4 had removed the permission for lawyer participation in a broad number of group legal service systems. But that conclusion is not at all warranted by the language that in fact appears in the final version. The new MR 5.4(a) and (b) provide that a lawyer may not share legal fees or form a law-practice partnership with a nonlawyer (§ 16.2.1). MR 5.4(c) provides that a lawyer should not permit the lawyer's professional judgment in rendering legal services to be directed by another person who recommends, employs, or pays the lawyer to render legal services for another (§ 8.8.2). Finally, MR 5.4(d) prohibits a lawyer from practicing for a "professional corporation or association authorized to practice law for a profit" if a nonlawyer owns an interest, is a director or officer, or has the right to direct or control the professional judgment of the lawyer. (The language of MR 5.4(d) rather plainly indicates that its proscription is limited to joint ownership of professional corporations (§ 16.2.4).)

The Future of Group Legal Services under the Model Rules

If group legal services are permitted at all under the Model Rules, it appears that all of the forms of group legal services organizations discussed above [9] are permissible under them, and many that the Code outlawed are now not proscribed. Clearly there is nothing in the Model Rules that requires open-panel arrangements, and that issue can at last be interred if states adopt MR 5.4 intact. The administrative filing of annual reports, schedules of benefits, and financial statements from group legal services required by the Code is no more required of group legal service organizations than it is of any other kind of law-practice firm. The requirement that lawyers exercise independent professional judgment (MR 5.4 (c)) requires only—although the point is independently important—that a lawyer exercise professional judgment only in the interests of the lawyer's client and not in the interests or at the direction of a third party. But that rule has become traditional in group legal service arrangements and hardly proscribes participation in them.

But within the echoing emptiness of the Model Rules, is there nothing to proscribe, or perhaps even to limit, group legal services? All that stand in the way of a confident negative answer—no, the Model Rules have left group legal services to the marketplace—are the provisions of MR 5.4(a) prohibiting fee sharing. It could be argued that any lawyer who is paid by funds generated from a group legal service organization is engaged in "fee splitting" with a nonlawyer employer in violation of the rule. That would be to suggest that the Model Rules, by that provision alone, have outlawed any employment of a lawyer by a group legal service plan if payment comes from the plan to the lawyer or if the lawyer makes payments to the plan as a condition of participation in it—both being arrangements that were permissible under the Code. More fundamentally, such a reading is directly at odds with Model Rule 6.3 and its comment. MR 6.3 broadly permits lawyers to serve as "director, officer or member of a legal services organization, apart from the law firm in which the lawyer practices." [10] And its comment asserts that "lawyers should

these rules. A program or activity is not bona fide if its organization or operation allows any third person, organization or group to interfere with or control the performance of the member's duties to his or her clients; or allows unlicensed persons to practice law; or allows any third person, organization or group to receive directly or indirectly any part of the consideration paid to the member of the State Bar except as permitted by these rules; or would violate rule 2–101 [on advertising].

[9] See § 16.5.3.

[10] MR 6.3 is principally directed at conflicts of interest between the lawyer's private-practice clients and clients of other lawyers in the lawyer's firm. It simply provides, in MR 6.3(a), that the lawyer should not participate in

be encouraged to support and participate in legal service organizations." [11] The provisions of MR 6.3 grew out of conflict of interest difficulties encountered by lawyers from private practice firms who served on the boards of legal services organizations for the poor. But there is nothing in its language or history that strongly suggests that it should be limited to poverty programs.[12]

What, then, does MR 5.4(a) mean by its prohibition that "a lawyer or law firm shall not share legal fees with a nonlawyer"? The answer is not entirely clear, but the best reading is to consider that the rule is addressed to those forms of third-party payments, outside the context of bona fide legal service organizations, to persons who perform impermissible solicitation of clients. In this reading, MR 5.4(a) becomes a counterpart of the prohibition of MR 7.3 prohibiting solicitation in person "or otherwise" and operates to prohibit explicitly the common unlawful practice of fee splitting with touts, runners, and cappers (§ 14.2.5). The rule also serves, as MR 5.4(a)(3) implies, as a barrier against nonlawyer employee ownership in traditional law firms.

Beyond those provisions, the Model Code can be seen to be very permissive with respect to group legal service plans so long as the plan and its administrators do not attempt to direct a lawyer's professional judgment or interfere in the client-lawyer relationship. A for-profit insurance company apparently may directly hire and pay a lawyer to represent a client under a legal insurance plan. An employer can directly hire lawyers to provide legal services to employees as part of a fringe-benefit legal service program. A college or any other organization could hire a lawyer to provide legal services to members or constituents. Any of those, and similar arrangements, could be operated with closed panels, including in-house staffs of lawyers directly retained by the group legal services plan or its administrator, or any variety of open panel. A lawyer or law firm could operate under an umbrella arrangement of consultation and referral with other law firms or engage in other forms of consultation and referral. Finally, a lawyer could directly promote a legal services organization for the purpose of securing employment of the lawyer or the lawyer's firm, an activity prohibited by the Code's DR 2–103(D)(4)(b).

WESTLAW REFERENCES

prepaid plan group corporation program /3 "legal service" /p regulat!

insurance insured /p regulat! coverage /p prepaid group plan corporation program /3 "legal service"

prepaid plan group corporation program /3 "legal service" /p "professional responsibility" ethic! disciplin!

"united mine worker" +6 illinois /18 88 +4 353 /p "legal service"

---

any decision or action of the legal services organization that would be incompatible with the lawyer's obligation to a client as tested by the general conflict of interest rule (MR 1.7) and, in MR 6.3(b), that the lawyer should similarly not participate in such action or decision if the effect of the conflict would be felt in the opposite direction—upon the legal services organization's client (MR 6.3(b)). But MR 6.3 is premised on the permissibility of a lawyer's serving as "director, officer or member of a legal services organization."

[11] Nowhere in the Model Rules is *legal services organization* defined. The "Terminology" provisions allude to such organizations as "firms." Its reference to MR 1.10 leads to a comment there (Definition of "Firm"; (third paragraph) that assumes that "lawyers in legal aid" may be "employed in the same unit of a legal service organization." But the juxtaposition of usage is hardly convincing evidence that the concept of legal services is exhausted by legal aid. Finally, in common professional parlance, "legal services" is more often used in connection with poverty law programs, particularly those sponsored or funded by the National Legal Services Corporation (see § 16.7.3). But, again, usage is hardly rigid or uniform, and it is simply implausible to argue that "legal service organization" has a commonly understood, unitary meaning. It probably means what it says on its face—an organization providing legal services.

[12] An illuminating bit of legislative history is that an attempt was made by the ABA's Special Committee on Prepaid Legal Services to amend MR 5.4, before its final approval, to make it clear that nothing in it made it unethical for a lawyer to cooperate with a group legal services program. The amendment was voted down after a counterargument that it was unnecessary because the rule, in the form in which it was eventually passed, did not bar such participation. See 52 U.S.L.Wk. 2078 (Aug. 9, 1983).

§ 16.6 FEE SHIFTING

§ 16.6.1 American Rule

Origins of the American Rule

In the courts of the United States, both in the federal system and in all states except Alaska,[13] the general rule is that each litigant must bear his or her own expenses of litigation, including attorney fees. The only general exception is to award the prevailing party "costs," which consist of sums that are typically trivial in comparison with the amount of attorney fees that both victor and vanquished must pay to their lawyers. The result sometimes forcefully reminds prevailing litigants of Pyrrhus's lament—one more such victory and we will be undone. It is common knowledge that the British [14] and Canadian [15] practices differs radically from that followed in America. Those legal systems employ two-way fee shifting: the prevailing party, whether plaintiff or defendant, is entitled to tax against the losing party a part of his or her legal fees along with other costs of the action. What is somewhat less widely known is that, in addition to the British commonwealth, the great majority of industrial democracies also reject the position of the United States.[16] The rule could be as fittingly called the "only-in-America rule."

The origins of the American rule are quite recent and quite specific to indigenous legal culture. By contrast, the European fee-shifting system is ancient [17] and can readily be traced to Roman law in the fifth century, before the Code of Justinian.[18] The peculiar American position that eventually denied taxing attorney fees did not begin in that form. Statutes in the colonies from the beginning had regulated the costs that a losing party must pay. Allowable costs included a measure of legal fees along with the other charges that the litigation had imposed on the prevailing party. But antilawyer sentiment caused legislatures to incorporate in the cost rules strict limits on the fees that lawyers could charge, and thus that the losing party was forced to reimburse.[19] A scholar has argued that the American rule arose from attempts by American lawyers to free themselves from legislative fee limitations; they were able to do so by disengaging fee shifting from the question of costs. That left losing parties liable only for costs and prevailing parties

[13] Alaska Stat. 09.60.010; Alaska Rules.Civ.Proc., Rule 82(a). The Alaska practice dates to an act of Congress in 1900 that established civil government in Alaska. The purpose of the rule is to compensate a prevailing party, partially, for attorney fees justifiably incurred. E.g., Davis v. Hallett, 587 P.2d 1170, 1171 (Alaska 1978). Under the rule, a prevailing litigant is entitled to recover fees according to a schedule. The fact that a client was not obliged to pay a lawyer anything (e.g., Gregory v. Sauser, 574 P.2d 445 (Alaska 1978)), or was obliged to pay the lawyer only a small charge because of the lawyer's generosity (e.g., Arctic Slope Native Ass'n v. Paul, 609 P.2d 32 (Alaska 1980)), does not preclude awarding a reasonable sum. Under the Alaska rule, its courts have felt impelled to create exceptions in order not to stifle some favored forms of suits. E.g., Southeast Alaska Conservation Council, Inc. v. State, 665 P.2d 544, 552–54 (Alaska 1983)(under "public interest" exception, trial court erred in awarding fees against nonprevailing public interest plaintiff that raised important issue of interest to wide group of public under circumstances where no public agency was likely to litigate issue).

[14] R.Jackson, The Machinery of Justice in England 518 (7th ed.1977).

[15] M.Orkin, The Law of Costs (1968); Watson, Bringing Fairness to the Costs System—An Indemnity Scheme for the Costs of Successful Appeals and Other Proceedings, 19 Osgoode Hall L.J. 448 (1981).

[16] Pfennigstorf, The European Experience with Attorney Fee Shifting, 47 L. & Contemp.Probs. 37 (1984); Rowe, The Legal Theory of Attorney Fee Shifting: A Critical Overview, 1982 Duke L.J. 651; Cappelletti & Garth, Access to Justice: The Newest Wave in the Worldwide Movement to Make Rights Effective, 27 Buff.L.Rev. 181, 187 (1978). A residue of the fading American influence on the Japanese legal system following the Second World War is that Japan also follows the American rule except for the routine award of legal fees to a prevailing personal injury plaintiff. See Jokima & Taniguchi, Access to Justice in Japan, in 1 Access to Justice 689, 705 (1978).

[17] 4 W.Holdsworth, A History of English Law 536–38 (1924).

[18] L.Wenger, Institutes of the Roman Law of Civil Procedure 334 (rev.ed.1940), cited in Pfennigstorf, The European Experience with Attorney Fee Shifting, 47 L. & Contemp.Probs. 37, 42 (1984).

[19] The statement in Restatement (Second) of Torts § 914 comment a (1979), that the American rule "goes back to a time when the small amounts awarded for 'costs' were in fact adequate, or nearly so, to reimburse [a prevailing party] for the expenses for litigation," seems historically inaccurate unless it is taken to mean that the legislators who enacted the minuscule cost statutes wanted to force lawyers to accept very small fees.

liable for their own fees without any claim for fee reimbursement against the losing party.[20]

Attacks on the American Rule

Even without its disreputable history, in which lawyers seem to have played a self-serving and ignoble role, the American rule strikes many thoughtful persons as unjust on an intuitive level. The notion that a possessor of legal rights should swallow most of the enormous expense that was necessarily incurred in order to vindicate them seems wrong on its face. The rule has been virulently and often attacked by legal scholars.[21] Nonlawyer citizens are widely assumed to be aware of the rule and to be opposed to it. Jurors, for example, are probably aware of the rule in some kinds of litigation and may increase an award of general damages in order to compensate a successful plaintiff.[22]

The American rule has been defended by courts on the basis of arguments that often blend faulty history and defective economics with poor logic.[23] A commonly encountered makeweight is that fee shifting would deter the poor who have meritorious claims.[24] The argument ignores the fact that a truly poor person can be informed by his or her lawyer that the realistic chances of being pursued by a prevailing opponent for a fee award are quite small and that personal bankruptcy may be a relatively painless solution if pursuit does occur. The argument also ignores the fact that because of the absence of fee shifting, a poor person with a relatively modest claim can be seriously outmatched by a well-capitalized defendant willing to spend enough to make victory unprofitable for the plaintiff. The defendant can accomplish that by forcing on the plaintiff a large expenditure for attorney fees, such as by overindulging in expensive discovery. If those with little funds are deterred from pressing their claims, the solution is not to continue the American rule but to provide for one-way fee shifting in favor of claimants.

Another makeweight thought to support the American rule is that the independence of advocates would be seriously impaired by fee shifting because an advocate's earnings would "flow from the pen of the judge before whom he argues." [25] That ignores the readily available alternative procedure of referring the question of the size of the fee award to a master (as in England) or to another judge [26] or awarding fees according to a schedule of presumptive fee charges (as in Alaska). A third argument is that fee shifting would uniformly encourage more lawyering, and thus more litigation because both parties would be encouraged to think that they would recover their legal fees.[27] But, even assuming two-way fee shifting, as in England, that would

[20] Leubsdorf, Toward a History of the American Rule on Attorney Fee Recovery, 47 L. & Contemp.Probs. 9 (1984).

[21] The most vigorous attacks were launched by Professor Ehrenzweig. See Shall Counsel Fees Be Allowed?, 26 Cal.St.B.J. 107 (1951); Reimbursement of Counsel Fees and the Great Society, 54 Cal.L.Rev. 792 (1966). See also McLaughlin, The Recovery of Attorney's Fees; A New Method of Financing Legal Services, 40 Fordham L.Rev. 761 (1972); Stoebuck, Counsel Fees Included in Costs: A Logical Development, 38 U.Colo.Rev. 202 (1966); Kuenzel, The Attorney's Fee: Why Not a Cost in Litigation?, 49 Iowa L.Rev. 75 (1963); McCormick, Counsel Fees and Other Expenses as an Element of Damages, 15 Minn.L. Rev. 619 (1931); Note, Court Awarded Attorneys' Fees and Equal Access to the Courts, 122 U.Pa.L.Rev. 636 (1974).

[22] An express agreement among jurors to make such an extralegal award is ground for a new trial. E.g., Dunn v. White, 206 Kan. 278, 479 P.2d 215, 47 A.L.R.3d 1289 (1970); White Cabs v. Moore, 146 Tex. 101, 203 S.W.2d 200 (1947). But mere juror discussion of fee shifting without an agreement probably will not result in a new trial. Krouse v. Graham, 19 Cal.3d 59, 137 Cal.Rptr. 863, 562 P.2d 1022 (1977); Comment, Impeachment of Jury Verdicts, 25 U.Chi.L.Rev. 360, 368 (1958).

[23] Law students have had fun taking apart decisions such as Ritter v. Ritter, 381 Ill. 549, 46 N.E.2d 41 (1943) (inter alia, fact that statute to allow recovery of attorney fees as costs (in real actions) was not enacted until sixth year of reign of Edward I (1275) means that fee recovery was not part of the "common law").

[24] Summit Valley Indus. v. Local 112, United Bd. of Carpenters, 456 U.S. 717, 102 S.Ct. 2112, 2117, 72 L.Ed.2d 511 (1982), citing F.D. Rich Co. v. United States ex rel. Industrial Lumber Co., 417 U.S. 116, 129, 94 S.Ct. 2157, 2165, 40 L.Ed.2d 703 (1974).

[25] Summit Valley Indus. v. Local 112, supra.

[26] Rowe, The Legal Theory of Attorney Fee-Shifting: A Critical Overview, 1982 Duke L.J. 651, 657 n.27.

[27] Goodhart, Current Judicial Reform in England, 27 NYU L.Rev. 395, 405–06 (1952)(rehearsing arguments

only be true to the extent that the parties acted uneconomically by ignoring the fact that by expending fees they would also be reciprocally incurring a risk of higher fees of the other side or to the extent that the parties rationally thought that an additional expenditure of fees would enhance their overall chance of prevailing.

Economics of Fee Shifting

More recently scholars have paid careful attention to the economics of fee shifting and have concluded that the questions that must be confronted in determining the best way of altering the American rule are by no means simply answered.[28] Effective fee-shifting reform requires that attention be paid to the fee-shifting policy or practice itself as well as to the particular context in which the shift would occur. While some instances of fee shifting would doubtless encourage appropriate results (on the assumption that policies favoring those results had been carefully defined in advance), more than one counterintuitive misfortune might be incurred if American courts were to reject the American rule and wholeheartedly embrace a general rule, such as that in England, calling for two-way fee shifting in all types of cases.

An example of possible counterintuitive consequences can be seen from analyzing the assertion, which has often been made, that requiring the loser to pay the winner's attorney fees would generally encourage a higher rate of settlements because the party with the weaker case now would then confront the risk of losing even more money by rejecting a settlement opportunity and persisting with litigation.[29] But an enhanced willingness to settle would only occur when both parties realized that one of them had the "weaker" case.[30] If the parties began with a great disparity in their views of the respective merits of their positions, adding fee shifting to the calculus would merely give them more dollars over which to differ.[31] In fact, it can just as plausibly be imagined that English-style fee shifting in this situation could perversely serve, in some instances, to prolong the litigation and make it more costly as the parties, driven by their conflicting dreams of sure success, piled up needless lawyer fees on the assumption that they would be paid by the other party.

The effects of fee shifting would also differ depending on the degree of involvement of lawyers in the litigation. An example is complex antitrust litigation, an activity which is lawyer-intensive. The handling of those kinds of cases would be much more likely to be affected by fee shifting than would be litigation that is relatively less lawyer-intensive, such as personal injury actions arising out of intersection collisions. Differences in lawyer involvement can be significant in other ways. If fee-shift payments were to be made by a party who was not effectively in control of important decisions about investment of lawyer effort in the litigation, fee shifting might lead to unintended consequences, such as prolonged litigation and consequently higher fees. Most obviously, if lawyers controlled important decisions in litigation, their economic motivation might be to run up the size of fees because their clients,

that have been offered against the English indemnity principle).

28 Symposium, 47 L. & Contemp.Probs. 1 (1984), especially Rowe, Predicting the Effects of Attorney Fee Shifting, id. at 139 (analysis of economics of fee shifting in nontechnical language). See also, e.g., Braeutigam, Owen & Panzar, An Economic Analysis of Alternative Fee Shifting Systems, 47 L. & Contemp.Probs. 173 (1984); Shavell, Suit, Settlement, and Trial: A Theoretical Analysis under Alternative Methods for the Allocation of Legal Costs, 11 J.Leg.Stud. 55 (1982); Mause, Winner Takes All: A Re-Examination of the Indemnity System, 55 Iowa L.Rev. 26 (1969).

29 Sands, Attorneys' Fees as Recoverable Costs, 63 ABA J. 510, 515 (1977)(so assumed, although calling for further study before reforms enacted).

30 Indeed, when an actor realizes that there is a significant risk of liability and a further risk of having to pay the injured party's fees, the fee shift can have the desired effect of providing additional incentive to the calculating actor not to violate the law. See R.Posner, Economic Analysis of Law 143 (2d ed.1977). In that way fee shifting, in those instances, has the potential to contribute to substantive policies as well as procedural ones.

31 Shavell, Suit, Settlement, and Trial: A Theoretical Analysis under Alternative Methods for the Allocation of Legal Costs, 11 J.Leg.Stud. 55, 65–68 (1982).

and not they, would have to bear the risk of paying for them.[32] The point here is that fee-shifting reform must attempt to take account of the differing extents to which parties, on the one hand, and their lawyers, on the other, might be affected by the additional risks imposed by adverse fee shifting.[33] Interests of others who would possibly exert control, such as insurers, must also be calculated.

In addition to differences in the extent to which they in fact control their own litigational fates and are affected by the outcomes, different kinds of litigants would experience different abilities to stay the course in the face of risk. As economists say, they may have different degrees of risk aversion. Two major factors contribute to risk aversion in litigation. First, the parties facing each other in litigation may have quite different levels of involvement in such matters. Some parties are "one-shotters," engaged in the only litigation that they will ever face.[34] A "repeat player" opponent, who is often engaged in litigation—an insurance company, a business corporation, or a governmental agency—can more knowledgabply calculate the risks of litigation and has the additional reassurance that the risk of guessing wrong in a lawsuit can be spread over a number of cases in a litigation "portfolio." Adding a fee-shifting risk would affect those parties quite differently.[35] Second, different attitudes toward risk can be produced by gross wealth differences. A party with little in the way of discretionary wealth would naturally calculate $10,000 in possible fee-shifting liability quite differently from a person whose range of choice was less circumscribed because he or she possessed a greater stock of wealth.

The Future of Fee-Shifting Reform

The only safe across-the-board conclusion that can be drawn about alterations of the American rule on fee shifting seems to be that across-the-board generalizations should be viewed with great caution. There is doubtless much force to the intuitive feeling that the American rule often produces injustice. In moving away from it, however, effective reform will much more likely take the form of situation-specific modifications of the risk of fee payment. In fact, just that process has been occurring in the recent history of common-law and legislative reshaping of the American rule. On the whole, courts have continued to insist that they will not modify the American rule without legislative direction. But, at the same time, courts have hewn off small, discrete parts of it through exceptions, which will be examined next. The cautious degree of incremental change in the common law contrasts sharply with the significant amount of federal and state legislation that has made inroads on the effective reach of the American rule (§ 16.6.3). Of great importance is the fact that the emerging American "rule" is that of one-way fee shifting in favor of claimants seeking remedies for the enforcement of legal rights.[36]

[32] The lawyer might be motivated in some instances to be more "economical" than the client because the lawyer bears more of the risk of misfortune. A classic illustration of that kind of differential in client and lawyer incentives, from outside the field of fee shifting, occurs in the typical personal injury case being handled by a plaintiff's lawyer on a contingent fee basis. The contingent feature can provide powerful incentive to the plaintiff's lawyer to obtain an early settlement, even if at a significantly lower figure than could be obtained after trial, because of the steeply increasing marginal production of each additional hour of lawyer time that would have to be invested in the case. See Schwartz & Mitchell, An Economic Analysis of the Contingent Fee in Personal-Injury Litigation, 22 Stan.L.Rev. 1125 (1970).

[33] See generally Wolfram, The Second Set of Players: Lawyers, Fee Shifting, and the Limits of Professional Discipline, 47 L. & Contemp.Probs. 293 (1984).

[34] Galanter, Why the "Haves" Come Out Ahead: Speculation on the Limits of Legal Change, 9 L. & Soc'y Rev. 95 (1974).

[35] It has been recognized, for example, that the English fee-shift system means that plaintiff class actions are severely restricted. See Wallersteiner v. Moir (No. 2), [1975] 1 All E.R. 849 (C.A.), cited in Dewees, Prichard & Trebilcock, An Economic Analysis of Cost and Fee Rules for Class Actions, 10 J.Leg.Stud. 155, 156 n.15 (1981).

[36] See generally R.Larson, Federal Court Awards of Attorney's Fees (1981)(nearly one hundred federal statutes providing for fee shifting); Note, State Attorney Fee Shifting Statutes: Are We Quietly Repealing the American Rule?, 47 L. & Contemp.Probs. 321 (1984)(survey of all fee-shifting legislation in all fifty states and District of Columbia (over two thousand statutes) indicates very strong tendency to enact plaintiff-favoring, one-way fee-shift legislation in discrete areas).

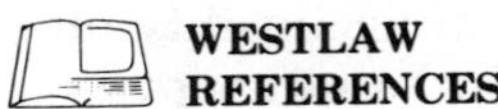
WESTLAW REFERENCES

"fee shift!"

attorney lawyer counsel** /s (fee /8 award! reimburs!) fee-shift! /p "american rule"

§ 16.6.2 Common-Law Exceptions

Traditional and Recent Common-Law Exceptions

The customary statement of the American rule consists of the generalization that both parties must bear their own litigation expenses but almost invariably mentions three exceptions—instances in which the parties have provided for fee shifting by *contract*, a *statute* permits fee shifting, or the losing party has litigated or otherwise acted in *bad faith*.[37] Those are by far the most important and commonly applied exceptions. But there are several others, including exceptions for litigation in which a fund is created, for fees as recoverable damages, and for litigation in which the prevailing party has served as a private attorney general. Not all exceptions are recognized, or recognized as generously, by all courts. Some of the exceptions, such as the contract and statutory exceptions, fit comfortably within traditional common-law assumptions denying fee shifting as a general matter. Others, however, such as the bad faith and damages exceptions, rest on the acceptance of concepts that, if generalized, would undermine the American rule.

Contract Exception

The general rule of contract law is that persons are free to set limits for themselves on the remedies that will be awarded in the case of breach and to enlarge the description of permissible damages and remedies so long as the values fixed are not so large that they offend public policy.[38] Despite the fact that legal fees are not normally awarded to the prevailing party, a promise to pay fees in a contract will be enforced, at least up to a reasonable amount. Most obviously, if a liability insurance company breaches a contract to supply a defense to an insured and thereby causes the insured to incur personal legal expenses, the insured can recover the legal expenses as damages for breach of contract.[39] Recovery from a grantor of the cost of a quiet title action that was reasonably necessary to defend the grantee's title is probably best thought of as based on an implied promise to indemnify the grantee for necessary legal expenses.[40]

Because the matter is one of contract law and does not depend on the exercise of a court's extraordinary power to employ equitable principles to award fees, a trial court has no discretionary common-law power to refuse to enforce such a contract.[41] But a court may refuse to enforce a fee-shift promise, as it may with similar kinds of promises, if its amount or other terms make it an unreasonable penalty.[42] Statutes also frequently alter the ex-

[37] See generally Alyeska Pipeline Serv. Co. v. Wilderness Society, 421 U.S. 240, 260–64, 95 S.Ct. 1612, 1623–25 44 L.Ed.2d 141 (1975).

[38] Restatement (Second) of Contracts § 356 (1979). Courts in Nebraska, however, will apparently refuse to enforce any contractual agreement to pay attorney fees. E.g., Quinn v. Godfather's Investments, Inc., 217 Neb. 441, 348 N.W.2d 893 (1984).

[39] See generally Annot., 49 A.L.R.2d 694 (1956).

[40] Glass v. Gulf Oil Corp., 12 Cal.App.3d 412, 96 Cal. Rptr. 902 (1970); Summa Corp. v. Greenspun, 607 P.2d 569 (Nev.1980).

[41] Brickell Bay Club Condominium Ass'n v. Forte, 397 So.2d 959 (Fla.App.1981), review denied 408 So.2d 1092 (1981).

[42] Restatement (Second) of Contracts § 356 comment d (1979). See also, e.g., Cable Marine, Inc. v. M/V Trust Me II, 632 F.2d 1344, 56 A.L.R.Fed. 867 (5th Cir.1980) (trial court within discretion in refusing to enforce contract to pay fees when promisee unreasonably rejected settlement offer only slightly less than sum eventually recovered); Jenkins v. Wise, 58 Haw. 592, 574 P.2d 1337, 1345 (1978)(amount must be reasonable and fee must have been reasonably and necessarily incurred by party seeking award); Equitable Lumber Corp. v. IPA Land Devel. Corp., 38 N.Y.2d 516, 381 N.Y.S.2d 459, 344 N.E.2d 391 (1976); National Bank v. Myers, 75 Wn.2d 287, 450 P.2d 477 (1969). A court will also refuse to enforce a contractual *limitation* on attorney fee awards if it would conflict with the public policy behind a fee-shifting statute. E.g., P & C Thompson Bros. Constr. Co. v. Rowe, 433 So.2d 1388, 1389 (Fla.App.1983); cf. Quill Co. v. A.T. Cross Co., ___ R.I. ___, 477 A.2d 939 (1984)(promisor of covenant not to sue in contract not required to pay opposing party's legal fees in defense of promisor's suit in absence of evidence of promisor's bad faith in filing action).

tent to which fee-shifting clauses are enforceable when circumstances suggest that the contract was one of adhesion,[43] or a statute may prohibit fee shifting altogether in such cases.[44] A California statute, which has been followed elsewhere, provides automatic reciprocity to a clause in a contract that purports to allow only one party (almost invariably the party who supplies the form for the contract) to recover fees in the event of suit.[45]

Upholding a contractual promise to pay legal fees is unexceptional and does not impugn the general rule forbidding judicial fee shifting. The plain fact is that the fee shift occurs because the courts enforce the parties' agreement to do so and not because of any common-law power of courts to order a fee to be paid.

Fund Exception

Unrelated doctrinally to the contract exception is the commonly accepted doctrine, founded in the murky law of "quasi contract," that a litigant who expends attorney fees in creating a common fund from which others may also benefit is entitled to compensation for a share of those fees from the benefited persons. The compensation is extracted directly from the common fund itself. Under a closely related theory, the expenses, including attorney fees, of litigation by a trustee that was undertaken to benefit or protect trust property can be charged against assets in the trust.[46]

In the 1939 decision in Sprague v. Ticonic National Bank,[47] a scholarly opinion by Justice Frankfurter purported to find in equity jurisprudence a general power in the chancellor to make an award in a common-fund situation. The plaintiff had sued and established the liability of a number of solvent institutions who had provided bonded protection for the plaintiff's trust deposit with a bank that had failed. The sum of the established liabilities far exceeded the amount necessary to reimburse the plaintiff, and, according to the Court, under the doctrine of stare decisis the funds were thus available to provide the same protection to several other trust beneficiaries. The Court held that the plaintiff could recover her attorney fees from the fund in a way that, in effect, allocated a fair portion of their charge to other benefited parties. Justice Frankfurter purported to find the power to award fees in federal equity jurisprudence, which was based, in turn, on English equity practice.[48] His reading of English equity practice was, of course, correct. But it would have been equally correct to say that English *law* courts in the seventeenth and eighteenth centuries also awarded fees. What he was examining was not equity or law so much as an entirely different way of thinking about fee shifting.

Sprague might have been understood by subsequent cases to have opened the door to

[43] The same result is sometimes reached by decision. E.g., Weidman v. Tomaselli, 81 Misc.2d 328, 365 N.Y.S.2d 681 (1975), affirmed 84 Misc.2d 782, 386 N.Y.S.2d 276 (1975).

[44] Federal Deposit Ins. Corp. v. Timbalier Towing Co., 497 F.Supp. 912, 929 (N.D.Ohio 1980)(Ohio statute prohibiting enforcement of any clause in promissory note or contract to pay attorney fees in event of suit for breach).

[45] West's Ann.Cal.Civ.Code § 1717. See generally Reynolds Metals Co. v. Alperson, 25 Cal.3d 124, 158 Cal.Rptr.1, 599 P.2d 83 (1979); Berge v. International Harvester Co., 142 Cal.App.3d 152, 190 Cal.Rptr. 815, 823–24 (1983) (consumer could recover under one-way fee clause in sales contract in vendor's favor, despite fact that contract was declared unenforceable against consumer); Comment, Attorney's Fees and Civil Code 1717, 13 Pac.L.J. 233 (1981). Courts have refused to create reciprocity by decision. E.g., Gulf Homes, Inc. v. Goubeaux, 136 Ariz. 33, 664 P.2d 183, 188 (1983); White v. Fox, 665 P.2d 1297, 1300 (Utah 1983). On the other hand, some states provide by statute for the right to recover attorney fees in all suits on oral or written contracts, whether fee shifting is provided for by explicit agreement or not. Ariz.Rev.Stat. § 12–341.01; Vernon's Ann. Texas Civ. St. art. 2226.

[46] See generally Annot., 24 A.L.R.4th 624 (1983).

[47] 307 U.S. 161, 59 S.Ct. 777, 83 L.Ed. 1184 (1939).

[48] See 307 U.S. at 164–69, 59 S.Ct. at 778–81. Inexplicably, and without returning to examine the English equity law on the point, the opinion at a later point added the apparently gratuitous restriction that the allowance of fees in federal equity was "appropriate only in exceptional cases and for dominating reasons of justice." Id. at 167. For a later critique of portions of Justice Frankfurter's reading of the nineteenth-century federal equity practice, see Alyeska Pipeline Co. v. Wilderness Society, 421 U.S. 240, 257–58, 95 S.Ct. 1612, 1621–22, 44 L.Ed.2d 141 (1975).

the award of attorney fees in any federal case that could be described as equitable. In fact, it has not generally been read so broadly. Decisions have instead applied *Sprague* to the situations suggested by its facts and thus as recognizing only a traditional common-fund exception, but it has been applied in law as well as in equity actions.[49] Courts claim that the theory supporting the doctrine is that of unjust enrichment,[50] rather than any general power to make a fee award in actions that a court is prepared to call "equitable" in nature.[51] Some states employ a somewhat broader fee-shifting power that is directly based on supposed equitable traditions. Some, for example, permit fee shifting when a partner is forced to bring a suit to dissolve the partnership and for an equitable accounting.[52] A disinterested stakeholder who resorts to equity for protection in an interpleader action can be awarded attorney fees.[53] Divorce actions, with their roots in equity and canon law, are uniformly treated as instances in which one party, typically the husband, can be required to pay the legal expenses of the other.[54]

Common-Benefit Exception

In some jurisdictions, the fund theory has been expanded into a common-benefit doctrine that permits an award of fees to a party who has prevailed in an action in a way that benefits many other litigants. The difference between common-benefit and common-fund cases is that in the former there is no identifiable pot of money from which the fees can be paid. The benefited persons are often not parties to the litigation and therefore could not constitutionally be ordered, without a separate proceeding, to pay the fees expended in their supposed behalf. The solution in common-benefit cases is to order the hapless defendant to pay the fees. Thus, unlike the common-fund doctrine, the common-benefit rule is a true kind of fee shift that requires indemnification of the prevailing party by the loser. The Supreme Court has rejected common-benefit fee shifts for the federal courts as a general proposition,[55] although it has approved the award of fees in some arguably similar settings, including shareholder deriva-

49 Trustees v. Greenough, 105 U.S. (15 Otto) 527, 26 L.Ed. 1157 (1881). See also Boeing Co. v. van Gemert, 444 U.S. 472, 100 S.Ct. 745, 62 L.Ed.2d 676 (1980); Mills v. Electric Auto-Lite Co., 396 U.S. 375, 90 S.Ct. 616, 24 L.Ed.2d 593 (1970); Sprague v. Ticonic Nat'l Bank, 307 U.S. 161, 59 S.Ct. 777, 83 L.Ed. 1184 (1939); Central R.R. & Banking Co. v. Pettus, 113 U.S. 116, 5 S.Ct. 387, 28 L.Ed. 915 (1885). See generally Dawson, Lawyers and Involuntary Clients: Attorney Fees from Funds, 87 Harv. L.Rev. 1597 (1974). On the problems of allocating attorney fees among multiple claimants who have expended different amounts of effort in benefiting multiple claimants, see generally Annot., 42 A.L.R. Fed.134 (1979).

50 The doctrinal underpinnings of the common-fund theory are not as strong as its proponents might suppose. The doctrine of unjust enrichment has not generally permitted volunteers to confer unsought advantages on strangers and then claim a portion of the gain as compensation for their efforts. Professor Dawson has made the point in a series of articles: Lawyers and Involuntary Clients in Public Interest Litigation, 88 Harv.L.Rev. 849 (1975); Lawyers and Involuntary Clients: Attorney Fees from Funds, 87 Harv.L.Rev. 1597 (1974); The Self-Serving Intermeddler, 87 Harv.L.Rev. 1409 (1974).

51 Boeing Co. v. van Gemert, 444 U.S. 472, 100 S.Ct. 745, 749, 62 L.Ed.2d 676 (1980); Mills v. Electric Auto-Lite Co., 396 U.S. 375, 392, 90 S.Ct. 616, 24 L.Ed.2d 593 (1970).

52 A.J. Richey Corp. v. Garvey, 132 Fla. 602, 182 So. 216, 219 (1938).

53 Phillips Petroleum Co. v. Hazlewood, 534 F.2d 61, 63 (5th Cir.1976); Minnesota Mut. Life Ins. Co. v. Gustafson, 415 F.Supp. 615, 619 n.4 (N.D.Ill.1976); Aetna Life Ins. Co. v. Outlaw, 411 F.Supp. 824, 825 (D.Md.1976); Brentwood Bank v. Rudman, 538 S.W.2d 744, 746 (Mo.App. 1976).

54 Aside from the powers of a court of equity, the practice of awarding legal fees to the wife has also been defended by invoking the common-law duty of a husband to provide "necessaries" for his wife, which included legal fees to defend her interests. E.g., In re Knuppenburg, 422 F.Supp. 274 (E.D.Mich.1976)(fee award to wife nondischargeable in federal bankruptcy because it is for support of wife); Sassower v. Barone, 85 A.D.2d 81, 447 N.Y.S.2d 966, 970 (1982). Cf. Poesy v. Bunney, 98 Idaho 258, 561 P.2d 400, 406 (1977)(common-law power to require ex-husband to pay legal expenses involved in appeal of question of postdivorce child custody). Most jurisdictions now have statutes that specifically cover the matter of attorney fee awards in divorce. E.g., Gove v. Gove, 71 Mich.App. 431, 248 N.W.2d 573 (1976); Annot., 22 A.L.R.4th 407 (1983)(award of prospective fees).

55 Boeing Co. v. van Gemert, 444 U.S. 472, 100 S.Ct. 745, 749–50, 62 L.Ed.2d 676 (1980); Alyeska Pipeline Co. v. Wilderness Society, 421 U.S. 240, 263–67, 95 S.Ct. 1612, 44 L.Ed.2d 141 (1975); Junker v. Crory, 650 F.2d 1349, 1363 (5th Cir.1981).

tive actions,[56] even if the litigation produces no fund from which an award of fees could be made.[57]

Private Attorney General Exception

Several states, most notably California,[58] have approved a fee shift in the case of (1) a litigant who vindicates an important [59] public policy (2) in a suit [60] in which the plaintiff has undertaken litigation expenses that are disproportionate to the personal financial benefit that the plaintiff might expect from the litigation and (3) in which the result of the litigation broadly benefits other members of the public. The basic thrust of the exception is to encourage litigation that will benefit the public and that would not otherwise be brought because the personal stake of any individual litigant would not otherwise warrant the expenditure of funds necessary for legal fees.[61] The concept, which has obvious roots in the common-benefit doctrine,[62] was rejected by the Supreme Court in the much-discussed Alyeska Pipeline Company v. Wilderness Society [63] decision and by several state courts.[64]

[56] Mills v. Electric Auto-Lite Co., 396 U.S. 375, 392–96, 90 S.Ct. 616, 24 L.Ed.2d 593 (1970)(fees awardable to successful plaintiff in shareholder derivative action, even though only relief afforded was to require making disclosure to investors). The arguable irreconcilability between *Mills* and *Alyeska Pipeline*, supra n. 55, has not always been appreciated. E.g., Loring v. City of Scottsdale, 721 F.2d 274 (9th Cir.1983)(common-benefit notion invoked to uphold award of fees in nondamage class action to establish that city had unlawfully taken right-of-way).

The essentially one-way fee shift that occurs in shareholder derivative actions because of the common-fund theory is of critical importance to that kind of litigation. In England, under a two-way fee-shift regime, the virtual absence of shareholder actions can be explained, not on the greater honesty of English business practices, but on the absence of the one-sided American inducements to suit. See L.Gower, Company Law 591 n.63 (3d ed.1969), cited in Kaplan, An American Lawyer in the Queen's Courts: Impressions of English Civil Procedure, 69 Mich. L.Rev. 821, 839, n.39 (1971).

[57] In Hall v. Cole, 412 U.S. 1, 93 S.Ct. 1943, 36 L.Ed.2d 702 (1973), the Court held that a lawyer for a small group of trade union members, who had prevailed in a suit against the union to correct conditions within the union, were to be compensated by the union directly on the notion that in this way the union members themselves, who were claimed to have benefited from the suit, could be forced to compensate the lawyers. See 412 U.S. at 8–9. The case is located somewhere between the common-fund cases and the private attorney general concept, which the Court later disapproved in *Alyeska Pipeline* supra n.55.

[58] Seranno v. Priest, 20 Cal.3d 25, 141 Cal.Rptr. 315, 569 P.2d 1303 (1977). See also, e.g., Hellar v. Cenarrusa, 106 Idaho 571, 682 P.2d 524, 530–31 (1984)(legislative reapportionment); Silva v. Botsch, 121 N.H. 1041, 437 A.2d 313 (1981)(litigation by town selectman to retain his elected seat). The *Seranno v. Priest* doctrine was subsequently codified in West's Ann.Calif.Civ.Code § 1021.5. The statute is broader, providing, for example, for a private attorney general fee shift to the plaintiff even if a fund is created out of which the fees could be paid under the fund theory. See § 1021.5 subd. (c). California courts have held that a fee award is appropriate, even if the litigation results in a dismissal of the plaintiff's action, so long as there has been some causal connection between the maintenance of the action and action favorable to the public taken by the defendant. See Westside Community for Independent Living, Inc. v. Obledo, 33 Cal.3d 348, 188 Cal.Rptr. 873, 883, 657 P.2d 365, 367–68 (1983).

In Alaska, where fee-shifting is routinely done according to a schedule that provides partial indemnity for fees of the prevailing party by the losing party, a trial court has discretion to award full attorney fees, even if in excess of the fee schedule, to a public interest plaintiff. See Anchorage v. McCabe, 568 P.2d 986, 994 (Alaska 1977). Attorney fees are not rewarded against a public interest plaintiff who has failed to prevail, on the ground that such awards would deter citizens from litigating issues of public importance. Whitson v. Anchorage, 632 P.2d 232 (Alaska 1981).

[59] The case need not be a landmark decision; it suffices if it merely applies existing rights. Press v. Lucky Stores, Inc., 34 Cal.3d 311, 193 Cal.Rptr. 900, 904, 667 P.2d 704, 708 (1983).

[60] The California court has drawn the line at quasi-legislative proceedings before administrative agencies, in which the private attorney general fee shift will not occur. Consumers Lobby against Monopolies v. Public Utilities Comm'n, 25 Cal.3d 891, 160 Cal.Rptr. 124, 603 P.2d 41 (1979).

[61] Seranno v. Priest, 20 Cal.3d 25, 45–46, 141 Cal.Rptr. 315, 325–26, 569 P.2d 1303 (1975); Woodland Hills Resident Ass'n v. City Council, 23 Cal.3d 917, 941–42, 154 Cal. Rptr. 503, 516, 593 P.2d 200 (1979). Cf., Baggett v. Gates, 32 Cal.3d 128, 185 Cal.Rptr. 232, 649 P.2d 874 (1982).

[62] That is most evident in the limitation that the litigation must itself, and not merely because of stare decisis ripple effects, result in discernible benefit to a large segment of the public. E.g., Pacific Legal Foundation v. California Coastal Comm'n, 33 Cal.3d 158, 188 Cal.Rptr. 104, 109, 655 P.2d 306, 311 (1982)(litigation that benefited only single owner of parcel of land not subject to private attorney general fee shifting).

[63] 421 U.S. 240, 95 S.Ct. 1612, 44 L.Ed.2d 141 (1975).

[64] Hamer v. Kirk, 64 Ill.2d 434, 442, 1 Ill.Dec. 336, 356 N.E.2d 524, 528 (1976); Providence Journal Co. v. Mason, 116 R.I. 614, 359 A.2d 682, 90 A.L.R.3d 383 (1976). In Washington an initial outright rejection of the private

The majority in *Alyeska* believed that recognizing the exception would force the federal courts either to make drastic new inroads into the American rule in the absence of legislative guidance or to make difficult and possibly invidious distinctions between types of plaintiffs and the particular kinds of public policies under which they sued.[65]

The legislative response was prompt. Congress, in 1976, passed the Civil Rights Attorney's Fees Awards Act that gave federal courts discretion to allow fees to prevailing parties in all actions brought under the federal civil rights statutes.[66] Because most federal court litigation involving issues of the kind found in private attorney general suits can be framed as a civil rights action,[67] the legislation has had the effect of answering the Court's concern about differentiating among plaintiffs by indicating that all plaintiffs are to be treated equally with respect to fee shifting.[68] In addition, because the defendants, in order to be subject to the civil rights statutes, must be public bodies, the civil rights fee award approach assures that the defendants who must pay fees have a way, through taxation, of spreading the cost of the benefit.

A theoretical case can be made for the proposition that litigation is a public good and thus that the state should always pay the legal fees of both winner and loser, at least as long as each had a good faith reason for resorting to a court for the settlement of their controversy.[69] Among other things, the case could build on the fact that the state already bears a significant percentage of the costs of litigation in every case (judicial salaries, capital and upkeep expenditures for courthouses, etc.) and does not seek compensation for those costs from either party except through the relatively minor exactions of "costs" assessed against the loser. Such a general public-funding notion would doubtless be rejected in the present-day American legal culture as quite implausible.[70] A more modest version of the argument is that in some types of fee-shifting situations, such as the private attorney general area, the specific rationale for awarding fees to the prevailing party supplies no reason to impose the disincentive and cost of a fee shift on the losing party, and some reason to provide for payment of fees for publicly useful litigation out of public funds.[71]

Bad Faith and Harassment

In harmony with the American rule, American courts insist that there is no general cause of action to recover from a plaintiff in a prior suit legal fees that were reasonably and necessarily expended in that suit to defend against a groundless claim.[72] While expenditures for legal fees are recoverable as an

attorney general exception has more recently been partially retracted. Compare Swift v. Island County, 87 Wn. 2d 348, 552 P.2d 175, 184 (1976), with Miotke v. City of Spokane, 101 Wn.2d 307, 678 P.2d 803, 821–22 (1984) (private attorney general exception applied in litigation successfully challenging patently unconstitutional state action).

65 421 U.S. at 269, 95 S.Ct. 1627.

66 Pub.L. 94–559, 94th Cong., 2d Sess. (1976), codified in 42 U.S.C.A. § 1988.

67 That became clear following the Court's decision in Maine v. Thiboutot, 448 U.S. 1, 100 S.Ct. 2502, 65 L.Ed.2d 555 (1980), to the effect that a federal statutory claim asserted under the broad § 1983 of the civil rights laws could form the basis for a fee award under the 1976 fee statute.

68 As will be seen, however, defendants are to be treated less preferentially. See infra at 929-30. On the Civil Rights Fee Award statute, see generally, e.g., Malson, In Response to Alyeska—The Civil Rights Attorney's Fees Awards Act of 1976, 21 St.Louis L.J. 430 (1976); Comment, Attorney's Fees in Damage Actions under the Civil Rights Attorney's Fees Awards Act of 1976, 47 U.Chi.L. Rev. 332 (1980); Note, Promoting the Vindication of Civil Rights through the Attorney's Fees Awards Act, 80 Colum.L.Rev. 34 (1980).

69 Gold, Controlling Procedural Abuses: The Role of Costs and Inherent Judicial Authority, 9 Ottawa L.Rev. 44, 61 (1977).

70 Relatively minor versions of the same concept can, however, be found in legislation that provides, for example, that a workers' compensation commission must bear the expense of defending in court an award by the commission to a worker against a compensation insurer or employer. 3 A.Larson, Law of Workmen's Compensation § 83.10 (1976).

71 Walker, Court Awarded Attorney's Fees under the Private Attorney General Concept: A Defense Perspective, 23 U.Kan.L.Rev. 653, 678 (1975); Awarding of Attorneys' Fees in Federal Courts: Hearings before the Subcomm. on Courts, Civil Liberties, and the Administration of Justice of the House Comm. on the Judiciary, 95th Cong., 1st & 2d Sess. 67 (1977–1978).

72 Ritter v. Ritter, 381 Ill. 549, 46 N.E.2d 41 (1943).

element of damages in a successful tort action for malicious prosecution or abuse of civil process,[73] the plaintiff will be successful on that ground only if the restrictive requirements of those torts can be met (§ 5.6.5). Several states and the federal system for a long time had statutes and rules on the books that empowered courts to award attorney fees for bad faith litigation,[74] but the statutes were rarely invoked until recently. Judges were notoriously reluctant to exercise available sanctions. They were traditionally more willing to admonish and cajole than to impose real sanctions as a deterrent; were more likely to slap wrists than impose significant sanctions; and were not likely to insist that an imposed sanction be actually paid if eventual compliance ensued.[75]

Recently, however, courts have markedly increased the use of fee shifting as a sanction for bad faith litigation under both statutes and rules and under common-law powers. The Supreme Court, in a number of decisions, has declared that a federal common-law power allows federal courts to require a litigant to pay the attorney fees of an opposing party if the litigant acted in bad faith or oppressively.[76] Statutes and rules have broadened the scope of allowable relief.[77] Many state courts follow a similar general rule allowing a fee award in instances of bad faith litigation.[78] An action is brought in bad faith when it is entirely without colorable merit and has been asserted wantonly, for the purpose of harassment or delay, or for other improper motives.[79] Some courts are willing to find the necessary bad faith in the action of the defendant that leads to the lawsuit,[80] but other courts require that the bad faith be found in the conduct of the litigation itself.[81] The pow-

[73] See generally Restatement (Second) of Torts § 671(b) & comment c (1976)(attorney fees as special damages in action for malicious prosecution); id. § 681(c) & comment d (damages in action for "wrongful civil proceedings").

[74] See generally Annot., 68 A.L.R.3d 209 (1976)(state statutes on attorney fee awards to party harassed by untrue allegations or denials); Annot., 12 A.L.R. Fed. 910 (1972)(28 U.S.C.A. § 1927).

[75] See authorities collected in Brazil, Improving Judicial Controls over the Pretrial Development of Civil Actions, 1981 Am.B.Found. Research J. 875, 922.

[76] Roadway Express, Inc. v. Piper, 447 U.S. 752, 765–67, 100 S.Ct. 2455, 2463–64, 65 L.Ed.2d 488 (1980); Alyeska Pipeline Co. v. Wilderness Society, 421 U.S. 240, 258–59, 95 S.Ct. 1612, 1622, 44 L.Ed.2d 141 (1975); F.D. Rich Co. v. United States ex rel. Industrial Lumber Co., 417 U.S. 116, 129, 94 S.Ct. 2157, 2165, 40 L.Ed.2d 703 (1974); Vaughan v. Atkinson, 369 U.S. 527, 82 S.Ct. 997, 8 L.Ed. 2d 88 (1962). See also, e.g., Perichak v. Electrical Workers, Local 601, 715 F.2d 78 (3d Cir.1983)(claim plainly based on perjured testimony persistently asserted). Fee awards against governmental litigants for bad faith litigation are rare but not unknown. E.g., EEOC v. New Enterprise Stone & Lime Co., 74 F.R.D. 628 (W.D.Pa. 1977).

[77] 28 U.S.C.A. § 1927; U.S.S.Ct.R. 49.2 (amended 1980); West's Fla.S.A. § 57.105 ("The court shall award a reasonable attorney's fee to the prevailing party in any civil action in which the court finds that there was a complete absence of a justiciable issue of either fact or law raised by the losing party."); Idaho R.Civ.Proc., Rule 54(e)(1)(as amended effective 1979); Wis. Laws of 1977, ch. 209 (frivolous claims and counterclaims), in W.S.A. § 814.025(3)(b). See generally Annot., 67 A.L.R. Fed. 319 (1984)(under Fed.R.App.Proc. 38). Appellate courts, while not hostile, have exhorted lower courts to use care in applying such punitive measures. E.g., Knorr Brake Corp. v. Harbil, Inc., 738 F.2d 223, 226–27 (7th Cir.1984); Mission Denver Co. v. Pierson, 674 P.2d 363, 365–66 (Colo. 1984).

[78] Appliances, Inc. v. Yost, 186 Conn. 673, 443 A.2d 486 (1982)(under Connecticut statute for fee award against defendant for asserting defense without cause or for purpose of delay); Whitten v. Progressive Cas. Ins. Co., 410 So.2d 501, 505 (Fla.1982)(under Florida statute on virtually frivolous claims); Third Establishment, Inc. v. 1931 North Park Apartments, 93 Ill.App.3d 234, 48 Ill. Dec. 765, 417 N.E.2d 167 (1981)(Illinois statute permitting award of fees when allegations made without reasonable cause are found to be untrue); Shanks v. Williams, 53 Md.App. 670, 455 A.2d 450 (1983)(Maryland rule on proceeding in bad faith, without substantial justification, or for purpose of delay); Harkeem v. Adams, 117 N.H. 687, 377 A.2d 617 (1977)("bad faith, vexatiously, wantonly, or for oppressive reasons"); State ex rel. Crockett v. Robinson, 67 Ohio St.2d 363, 369, 423 N.E.2d 1099 (1981)(bad faith).

[79] McCandless v. Great Atl. & Pac. Tea Co., 697 F.2d 198 (7th Cir.1983); Browning Debenture Holders' Committee v. DASA Corp., 560 F.2d 1078, 1088 (2d Cir.1977).

[80] Hall v. Cole, 412 U.S. 1, 15, 93 S.Ct. 1943, 1951, 36 L.Ed.2d 702 (1973)(dicta)(bad faith may be found, not only in the actions that lead to the lawsuit, but also in the conduct of the litigation); Roadway Express, Inc. v. Piper, 447 U.S. 752, 766, 100 S.Ct. 2455, 2464, 65 L.Ed.2d 488 (1980); Richardson v. Communication Workers, 530 F.2d 126 (8th Cir.1976), cert.denied 429 U.S. 824, 97 S.Ct. 77, 50 L.Ed.2d 86 (1976); County of Inyo v. City of Los Angeles, 78 Cal.App.3d 82, 144 Cal.Rptr. 71 (1978). See also, e.g., General Refractories Co. v. Rogers, 240 Ga. 228, 239 S.E.2d 795, 800 (1977).

[81] Shimman v. Union of Operating Engineers, 744 F.2d 1226 (6th Cir.1984)(en banc), cert.denied ___ U.S. ___, 105 S.Ct. 1191, 84 L.Ed.2d 337 (1985).

er of courts extends beyond an award against the losing litigant. The Supreme Court held, in Roadway Express, Inc. v. Piper,[82] that a federal court has the inherent power to require a *lawyer* for a litigant to pay the attorney fees of an opposing party if the lawyer knowingly acted in bad faith.[83]

The common-law version of the rule apparently originated in contempt actions,[84] at least in cases involving willful contempt,[85] although the courts sometimes also invoke an equity power that might go beyond contempt cases. The exception is probably also based on a damage theory borrowed from the law of unjust litigation. The bad faith exception works to generalize that doctrine, expanding it to fit instances in which all of the elements of the malicious prosecution and abuse of process torts cannot be made out. Recent expansions and strong judicial endorsements of the bad faith litigation justification for fee shifting suggest that judicial impatience with burgeoning dockets has led to a judicial reassessment of free access to courts that in part underlies the American rule.

Exception for Fees as Recoverable Damages

Courts in many jurisdictions have invoked an ill-defined doctrine permitting a prevailing party to recover attorney fees as damages. Common are recoveries as damages of fees expended in successful defense of an action that forms the basis for a later claim of malicious prosecution or abuse of process.[86] Courts have occasionally permitted a former client in a legal malpractice action to recover as damages legal fees expended in a reasonable attempt through another lawyer to repair the consequences of the defendant-lawyer's negligence.[87] According to at least one decision, recovery can be obtained even if the corrective action was unsuccessful.[88] A federal court has permitted an antitrust plaintiff to recover as damages the amount of legal fees that the plaintiff incurred when challenging unlawful conduct of the defendant before an administrative agency.[89] Those decisions seem consistent with the "tort of another" provision of section 914(2) of the Second Re-

82 447 U.S. 752, 764–67, 100 S.Ct. 2455, 2463–64, 65 L.Ed.2d 488 (1980).

83 See also, e.g., Potamkin Cadillac Corp. v. United States, 697 F.2d 491 (2d Cir.), cert.denied 462 U.S. 1144, 103 S.Ct. 3128, 77 L.Ed.2d 1379 (1983); Nemeroff v. Abelson, 704 F.2d 652 (2d Cir.1983); Stanziale v. First Nat'l Bank, 74 F.R.D. 557 (S.D.N.Y.1977); Bauguess v. Paine, 75 Cal.App.3d 21, 142 Cal.Rptr. 29 (1977); Tuttle v. Palmer, 118 N.H. 553, 392 A.2d 574, 575 (1978); Brown v. Brown, 4 Ind. 627 (1853); Goussous v. Modern Food Market, Inc., 93 A.D.2d 417, 463 N.Y.S.2d 550 (1983). Fee shifting can also be ordered against a lawyer in federal court under 28 U.S.C.A. § 1927 (unreasonably and vexatiously multiplying proceedings). The holding of the Supreme Court to the contrary in Roadway Express, Inc. v. Piper, 447 U.S. 752, 100 S.Ct. 2455, 65 L.Ed.2d 488 (1980), was changed shortly thereafter by legislation. Pub.L. 96–349, § 3, 94 Stat. 1156 (1980). For applications of § 1927, see, e.g., Gordon v. Heimann, 715 F.2d 531 (11th Cir.1983); Acevedo v. Immigration and Naturalization Service, 538 F.2d 918, 921 (2d Cir.1976); In re Bithoney, 486 F.2d 319 (1st Cir.1973).

84 Toledo Scale Co. v. Computing Scale Co., 261 U.S. 399, 426–28, 43 S.Ct. 458, 67 L.Ed. 719 (1923)(award of attorney fees for opposing party's willful disobedience of court order as part of fine for contempt); Fleischmann Distilling Corp. v. Maier Brewing Co., 386 U.S. 714, 718, 87 S.Ct. 1404, 1407, 18 L.Ed.2d 475 (1967).

85 Lichtenstein v. Lichtenstein, 425 F.2d 1111 (3d Cir. 1970). See generally Annot., 43 A.L.R.3d 793 (1972). See also, e.g., Cook v. Ochsner, Foundation Hospital, 559 F.2d 270, 272 (5th Cir.1977)(willfulness of violation of court's order need not be shown).

86 See generally Prosser and Keeton on Torts 888, 895 (W.Keeton ed.1984); D.Dobbs, Remedies 196 (1973). See also, e.g., Annot., 30 A.L.R.3d 1443 (1970)(recoverability of attorney fees as element of punitive damages).

87 United Fidelity Life Ins. Co. v. Law Firm of Best, Sharp, Thomas & Glass, 624 F.2d 145 (10th Cir.1980); Hinman, Straub, Pigors & Manning v. Broder, 89 A.D.2d 278, 456 N.Y.S.2d 834, 836 (1982).

88 Sorenson v. Fio Rito, 90 Ill.App.3d 368, 45 Ill.Dec. 714, 413 N.E.2d 47 (1980)(attorney fees incurred in unsuccessful effort to mitigate damages flowing from defendant-lawyer's negligent failure to file estate and inheritance tax returns on time).

89 City of Mishawaka v. American Elec. Power Co., 616 F.2d 976 (7th Cir.1980), cert.denied 449 U.S. 1096, 101 S.Ct. 892, 66 L.Ed.2d 824 (1981). Cf. also, e.g., Associated General Contractors v. Construction & General Laborers Local No. 563, 612 F.2d 1060 (8th Cir.1979)(recovery under federal labor law of attorney fees incurred in proceeding seeking to remedy illegal work stoppage). But cf. Summit Valley Industries v. Local 112, United Bd. of Carpenters, 456 U.S. 717, 102 S.Ct. 2112, 72 L.Ed.2d 511 (1982)(attorney fees expended before national labor board as result of unlawful labor practice of union not recoverable as damages under statutory cause of action for unfair labor practice).

statement of Torts.[90] The theory of that cause of action is that a party who has been thrust into litigation because of the wrongful act of another should not be required to bear the attorney fees associated with that action.[91]

What unifies those decisions is the apparent doctrine that if a wrongful act of the defendant has involved the plaintiff in litigation or other legal straits and the plaintiff as a practical consequence has been required to expend legal fees to protect the plaintiff's legal interests, the plaintiff can recover the amount of the legal fees as damages.[92] The striking fact about that doctrine and the recoverable-damage cases themselves, however, is that courts have difficulty justifying and distinguishing the allowance of fee awards in light of the American rule. The usual judicial explanation is to treat situations in which they will be allowed as "exceptional" and the like. The fact, relied upon by some courts, that the attorney fees were incurred in a separate proceeding [93] may limit the reach of the recoverable-damage exception, but it does so on a ground that seems entirely artificial. On the other hand, if courts were to recognize a general doctrine that a party who was forced to litigate a claim or defense, because of action or inaction by the opposing party in violation or derogation of the first party's legal obligations, could recover as damages the amount of fees necessarily incurred, there would be little left of the American rule. It seems, then, that the recoverable-damages exceptions are simply bits and pieces of that doctrine, snipped out of the broader fabric to cover some particularly compelling facts in an individual case. It remains as a troubling and unsteady doctrinal reminder of the disquieting and unfair nature of many applications of the American rule.

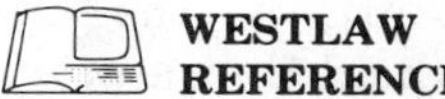

attorney lawyer counsel** /s (fee /8 award! reimburs!) fee-shift! /p "american rule" /s exception

topic(cost) /p "american rule"

digest(fee /p "american rule" /s exception)

alyeska +6 "wilderness society" /12 95 +4 1612 /p "private attorney general"

digest,synopsis("bad faith" harass! /7 attorney lawyer counsel** /3 fee)

"roadway express" +5 piper /12 100 +4 2455 /p fee /3 lawyer attorney counsel**

102k171

---

§ 16.6.3 Legislative Exceptions

Magnitude and Types of Legislative Inroads

A large number of statutes have been enacted in recent years modifying the American rule in particular kinds of cases.[94] The general approach of courts is to construe the statutory inroads broadly, particularly when the award of fees will have the effect of furthering a specific legislative policy.[95] The overall approach of legislatures and courts is to be

[90] Restatement (Second) of Torts § 914(2)(1979): "One who through the tort of another has been required to act in the protection of his interests by bringing or defending an action against a third person is entitled to recover reasonable compensation for loss of time, attorney fees and other expenditures thereby suffered or incurred in the earlier action." See, e.g., Gray v. Don Miller & Assoc., Inc., 35 Cal.3d 498, 198 Cal.Rptr. 551, 674 P.2d 253 (1984).

[91] Langeland v. Farmers State Bank, 319 N.W.2d 26, 33 (Minn.1982); Central Trust Co. v. Goldman, 70 A.D.2d 767, 417 N.Y.S.2d 359, 361 (1979), appeal dismissed 47 N.Y.2d 1008, 420 N.Y.S.2d 221, 394 N.E.2d 290 (1979).

[92] The text is a paraphrase of the reasoning in decisions such as Shoemaker v. Takai, 57 Hawaii 599, 561 P.2d 1286, 1290 (1977); Hill v. Okay Constr. Co., 312 Minn. 324, 252 N.W.2d 107, 121 (1977); and Dorofee v. Planning Bd. of Township of Pennsauken, 187 N.J.Super. 141, 453 A.2d 1341, 1343–44 (1982).

[93] Hill v. Okay Constr. Co., 312 Minn. 324, 252 N.W.2d 107, 121 (1977); Hinman, Straub, Pigors & Manning v. Broder, 89 A.D.2d 278, 456 N.Y.S.2d 834, 836 (1982).

[94] By one count, Congress passed over one hundred fee-award statutes in the ten years after 1974. 70 ABA J. 16 (1984). See also, e.g., R.Aronson, Attorney-Client Fee Arrangements: Regulation and Review 156–62 (1980); Nat'l L.J., May 25, 1981, at 30, col.3 (citation to thirty-six federal statutes providing for fee awards against United States). See generally R.Larson, Federal Court Awards of Attorneys' Fees (1981).

[95] Blum v. Stenson, 465 U.S. 886, 104 S.Ct. 1541, 79 L.Ed.2d 891 (1984)(fees under Civil Rights fee-shift statute are to be awarded at prevailing rates and not at cost to publicly funded or pro bono lawyers); New York Gaslight Club, Inc. v. Carey, 447 U.S. 54, 100 S.Ct. 2024, 64 L.Ed.2d 723 (1980)(Civil Rights Act fee-award statute extended to state administrative agency proceedings); Bradley v. School Bd., 416 U.S. 696, 94 S.Ct. 2006, 40

more reluctant to award fees against an unsuccessful plaintiff than against an unsuccessful defendant.[96] The different treatment can usually be traced to a concern that restrictions on plaintiffs might frustrate statutory policies aimed at encouraging suits by alleged victims of unlawful conduct.[97] For example, the Supreme Court, in the *Christiansburg Garment* case,[98] held that a prevalling defendant in a Title VII action should not ordinarily be awarded fees unless the court found that the plaintiff's case was frivolous, unreasonable, or without foundation. The Court restricted the defendant's right to recover fees despite acknowledging the fact that successful plaintiffs in such cases are awarded fees as a matter of course and regardless of the good faith of the losing defendant.[99] One-way fee shifting does not invariably favor plaintiffs. Defendants may also occasionally be the specific objects of legislative concern. A Washington statute, for example, provides for one-way fee shifting to a nonresident defendant if the defendant is brought into the state's courts by a long-arm statute and prevails.[1]

Policy Objectives of Legislative Fee Shifting

The objectives of fee shifting are many and various. The significant number of statutory modifications of the American rule in the past decade do not necessarily reflect total dissatisfaction with the American rule and certainly do not indicate wholehearted acceptance of the English system of automatic two-way fee shifting. Most fee-shift statutes, which shift fees only to prevailing parties who are plaintiffs or favor plaintiffs more than defendants, thus seem based on concepts that litigation of the kind covered by the legislation should be encouraged.[2] Some statutes in effect regard some litigation as particularly worthy of being broadly subsidized by the public through public payment for successful litigation.[3] Some provide equally for two-way fee shifting, apparently accepting the British rationale that a fee shift is required, at least in the covered cases, in order to make the prevailing party whole.

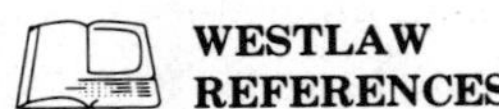
WESTLAW REFERENCES

"american rule" /s legislat! statut! /s fee /3 shift! award!

L.Ed.2d 476 (1974)(fee-award statute construed to allow fees earned prior to passage of statute); Mourning v. Family Publications Service, Inc., 411 U.S. 356, 93 S.Ct. 1652, 36 L.Ed.2d 318 (1973); Newman v. Piggie Park Enterprises, Inc., 390 U.S. 400, 88 S.Ct. 964, 19 L.Ed.2d 1263 (1968)(per curiam)(fee awards should be made to successful civil rights plaintiff as matter of course and not only in cases in which defendant's conduct warranted punitive award).

Some courts have approached fee-shift statutes with the clumsy and thoughtless tools of statutory canons and "strictly construed" them for reasons that seem to further no articulatable legislative or judicial goal. E.g., Model Indus., Inc. v. Walsh Press & Die Co., 111 Ill.App. 3d 572, 67 Ill.Dec. 403, 444 N.E.2d 639, 641 (1982)(strict construction because penal in nature); Texas Indus., Inc. v. Roach, 426 So.2d 315, 317 (La.App.1983); Ryan v. Mo-Mac Properties, 644 S.W.2d 791, 794 (Tex.Civ.App.1982) (penal in nature and in derogation of common law). See also, e.g., 111 East 88th Partners v. Simon, 106 Misc. 693, 434 N.Y.S.2d 886, 890 (1980)(dicta)(court looks with disfavor on fee-award statute because it puts price on exercise of right to day in court).

96 Postow v. OBA Federal Sav. & Loan Ass'n, 627 F.2d 1370, 1386–88 (D.C.Cir.1980); Boksa v. Keystone Chevrolet Co., 553 F.Supp. 958, 962 (N.D.Ill.1982); Ravenwood Church v. Starbright, Inc., 168 Ga.App. 870, 310 S.E.2d 582, 584 (1982).

97 See Roadway Express, Inc. v. Piper, 447 U.S. 752, 762, 100 S.Ct. 2455, 2462, 65 L.Ed.2d 488 (1980); Watkins v. Labor & Industry Review Comm'n, 117 Wis.2d 753, 345 N.W.2d 482 (1984)(legislative intent, under fair employment act, to make victim of discrimination whole entails power to award attorney fees).

98 Christiansburg Garment Co. v. Equal Employment Opportunity Comm'n, 434 U.S. 412, 98 S.Ct. 694, 54 L.Ed. 2d 648 (1978).

99 Newman v. Piggie Park Enterprises, 390 U.S. 400, 402, 88 S.Ct. 964, 966, 19 L.Ed.2d 1263 (1968).

1 S.S. Kresge Co. v. Port of Longview, 18 Wn.App. 805, 573 P.2d 1336 (1977).

2 See generally Zemans, Fee Shifting and the Implementation of Public Policy, 47 L. & Contemp.Probs. 187 (1984); Percival & Miller, The Role of Attorney Fee Shifting in Public Interest Litigation, 47 L. & Contemp. Probs. 233 (1984).

3 That may be the basis for fee shifting in successful Freedom of Information Act suits. See 5 U.S.C.A. § 552(a)(4)(E); Conf.Rep.No. 1200, 93d Cong., 2d Sess. 4–5, reprinted in [1974] U.S. Code Cong. & Admin. News 6285, 6288.

§ 16.6.4 Ethical Issues in Fee Shifting

Lawyers as the Second Set of Players

Analysis of the effects of fee shifting is complex enough when analysis is confined, as it often is, to the motivations of the litigants. An important further complication is that lawyers might have different incentives as the result of fee shifting than do their clients. Thus some significant problems concerning the professional responsibilities of lawyers in fee-shifting cases have arisen.[4]

The basic problem is that lawyers can often exert control over decisions that are critical to the success or failure of litigation. The professional ideal is that a lawyer will fully inform a client about important questions in a case and abide by the client's determinations of them (§ 4.3). In reality, however, lawyers who are so disposed have at least two means of evading the responsibility to follow a client's directions. First, a lawyer may simply ignore the professional ideal and conduct the case as if the lawyer were the principal player, controlling the client and making pivotal decisions without even the pretense of abiding by the client's wishes. Or, second, a lawyer may manipulate the client's decision by the kind of advice given.

Most clients are unable independently to assess the soundness of a lawyer's advice to press ahead or to settle, to engage in extensive or limited discovery, to file many motions or none at all, to offer copious expert testimony or little, to appeal or to accept a disappointingly small recovery or unfavorable outcome, and in similar matters. The client is in the unenviable position of being required to trust that the lawyer's advice is in the best interests of the client. But often a lawyer's economic interests are not aligned with those of the client. And occasionally an opposing party may drive a wedge between lawyer and client by force of the fee-shifting provisions relevant to the case.

Dealing with Inflated or Deflated Fee Awards

An example of the latter difficulty is portrayed in cases such as Prandini v. National Tea Co.[5] The court imposed a rule that lawyers in a class action suit, in which a statute provided for fee shifting, could not negotiate the amount of the fee until after the court had approved any negotiated settlement of the merits of the case. *Prandini* involved facts that suggested to the court that the lawyer for the class might have been willing to accept an award for the class that was too low in return for the defendant's willingness to agree to a fee award that was very generous. Other cases involve the reverse situation: the defendant offers a handsome settlement amount for the client in return for the lawyer's agreement to claim a small fee or none at all despite a right to do so under a fee-shifting statute.[6]

Both situations work to frustrate the objectives of victim compensation and deterrence of unlawful conduct that often underlie fee-shifting statutes. The *Prandini* solution could be applied to both situations, although it has the effect of leaving the offering defendant unsure of the precise total of fee claims that might be involved in a settlement.[7] A more extreme, although perhaps a more effec-

[4] Those issues have recently been scrutinized in the legal literature. E.g., Calhoun, Attorney-Client Conflicts of Interest and the Concept of Non-Negotiable Fee Awards under 42 U.S.C. § 1988, 55 U.Colo.L.Rev. 341 (1984); Wolfram, The Second Set of Players: Lawyers, Fee Shifting, and the Limits of Professional Discipline, 47 L. & Contemp.Probs. 293 (1984).

[5] 557 F.2d 1015 (3d Cir.1977).

[6] Reportedly, such offers are quite common in some types of litigation. E.g., Levin, Practice, Ethical and Legal Considerations Involved in the Settlement of Cases in which Statutory Attorney's Fees Are Authorized, 14 Clearinghouse Rev. 515, 515 n.7 (1980); 68 ABA J. 23 (1982). Cf. Krause v. Rhodes, 640 F.2d 214 (6th Cir.1981), cert.denied 454 U.S. 836, 102 S.Ct. 140, 70 L.Ed.2d 117 (1981)(approval, over objection of lawyer, of settlement that was conditioned on very low attorney fee award). In Opinion 80–94, the New York City Bar Association Ethics Committee held that a defendant's lawyer who made such an extortionate offer in a case involving civil rights or civil liberties committed an ethical violation by attempting to exploit a conflict of interest between the plaintiff and the plaintiff's lawyer. See 36 Rec. A.B. City N.Y. 507, 510 (1981).

[7] The Supreme Court noted the desirability of that knowledge for a defendant, although the Court did not

tive, step would be for courts to adopt the general position that fee awards are not negotiable between the parties and must always be submitted to the court for determination of an appropriate award.[8] It has also been argued that a lawyer's agreement to forego a claim for fees that has been extorted as a condition to obtaining a favorable settlement for the lawyer's client should not bind the lawyer. Instead, the lawyer should later be able to claim the fee that the fee-shifting statute or rule provides, and the offering party's defense based on the agreement to an inadequate award should be disregarded because of the public policy behind the fee-shift regulation.[9]

WESTLAW REFERENCES

fee-shift! /p "professional responsibility" ethic! disciplin! duty

prandini /12 557 +4 1015 /p fee award

§ 16.7 LEGAL SERVICES FOR THE POOR

§ 16.7.1 Legal Needs of the Poor

Legal Needs of the Poor in a Market for Legal Services

No one believes that the poor lack funds because they lack legal services. But many lawyers and others believe that the conditions of poverty could be significantly relieved if the poor had lawyers to assist them in dealing with the landlords and merchants with whom they must deal in the market and the functionaries with whom they must deal in the governmental bureaucracy.[10] The poor have had access to legal services in the market economy only through lawyers in private practice who have been willing to represent an impoverished client for free. While pro bono publico service is one of the bar's proudest boasts [11] and supposedly one of the hallmarks of a profession,[12] it is not clear whether many lawyers have performed much pro bono work of that kind.[13]

Social Strategies for Legal Services for the Poor

Traditionally, legal services to the poor have been provided not through the market but by a small group of lawyers who have been directly or indirectly involved in private or semi-private legal aid organizations. Supported primarily from private charity, legal aid offices were for decades the only effective recourse for the poor. Beginning with the War on Poverty in the early 1960s, the federal government began a program of subsidized legal services for low-income persons. The program evolved into the National Legal Services Corporation, which has led a tumultuous political existence. The differences between traditional legal aid and present-day poverty lawyers involve much more than differences in sources of funding. Profoundly varying approaches to client service have led to several difficult questions of professional ethics.

WESTLAW REFERENCES

di pro bono

"ec 2-24" "ec 2-25" /p "pro bono" indigen! poor (legal public /2 service assistance aid)

---

assert that it was indispensable for settlements, in White v. New Hampshire Dep't of Empl. Security, 455 U.S. 445, 453 n.15, 102 S.Ct. 1162, 1167, 71 L.Ed.2d 325 (1982).

8 Calhoun, Attorney-Client Conflicts of Interest and the Concept of Non-Negotiable Fee Awards under 42 U.S.C. § 1988, 55 U.Colo., L.Rev. 341 (1984).

9 Wolfram, supra note 4, at 314–19. The court so held in Shadis v. Beal, 685 F.2d 824 (3d Cir.), cert.denied 459 U.S. 970, 103 S.Ct. 300, 74 L.Ed.2d 282 (1982).

10 The extent to which the poor have legal problems and resort to lawyers to solve them is analyzed in B.Curran, The Legal Needs of the Public 127–28, 152–57 (1977).

11 See EC 2–24, EC 2–25.

12 Wade, Public Responsibilities of the Learned Professions, 21 La.L.Rev. 130, 131 (1960).

13 Compare Handler, Hollingsworth, Erlanger & Ladinsky, The Public Interest Activities of Private Practice Lawyers, 61 ABA J. 1388 (1975)(level of pro bono work for poor on part of private practitioners is quite low), with D.Maddi, The Private Practicing Bar and Legal Services for Low-Income People (1971)(sample of lawyers responding to survey indicates that 47 percent performed some legal services for every person who consulted them within recent year regardless of ability to pay).

§ 16.7.2 Legal Aid [14]

History of the Legal Aid Movement

The first [15] legal aid society was a private organization established in New York City in 1876 by the German Society to protect newly arrived immigrants from exploitation.[16] Ten years later, in Chicago, a second organization was founded by the Protective Agency for Women and Children.[17] And in 1888 a legal aid group open to the poor of all nationalities and genders was founded by the Chicago Ethical Culture Society. Similar organizations gradually proliferated, until Reginald Heber Smith reported in his Justice and the Poor that, in 1917, forty-one cities had some kind of legal aid group, handling 117,201 cases.[18] Smith also reported, however, that the level of legal aid for the poor was totally inadequate.[19] His critique extended not only to the lack of counsel, although this was serious, but, more fundamentally, asserted that the entire justice system was frequently used to disadvantage the poor.

A temporary increase in legal aid activity during the 1920s resulted from Smith's prodding.[20] But progress was arrested and then reversed in the later years of the Depression. At the onset of economic difficulties, which were harshest for the poor, the work load of legal aid agencies increased dramatically, without any increase in resources, to the point where their ability to meet demand decreased seriously.[21] The demonstrated inability of legal aid societies to relieve the lives of the poor led to a decrease in caseload.[22] Following the Depression and the Second World War, legal aid continued a slow, steady growth that appeared to reflect a commitment to only minimal legal services to the poor. Legal aid offices were burdened with high caseloads, their lawyers were either volunteers from private practice or underpaid lawyers, who often worked alone and tended to avoid litigation, and more so appeals, because they lacked time or resources to handle the caseload.

Financing of Legal Aid

The forms in which legal aid societies obtained their funding varied. The volunteer time of private lawyers was and remains a valuable contribution not reflected in their budgets. Private religious and ethnic groups were early donors. Traditionally, charitable funds, such as the Community Fund, and bar associations have contributed a significant percentage to legal aid budgets.[23] Beginning early in the movement, public funding from local governments played a part, although over time this source of funding decreased, in large part because of governmental budgetary constraints imposed by the Depression. Moreover, some lawyers opposed governmen-

[14] A useful bibliography is contained in Huber, Thou Shalt Not Ration Justice: A History and Bibliography of Legal Aid in America, 44 Geo.Wash.L.Rev. 754 (1976).

[15] Earlier, between 1865 and 1868, when it was abolished, the Freedman's Bureau had attempted to provide free legal services to poor freed slaves. See Westwood, Getting Justice for the Freedman, 16 How.L.J. 492 (1971).

[16] See generally J. McGuire, The Lance of Justice (1928)(history of the New York Legal Aid Society); J.Bradway, Legal Aid Work and the Organized Bar (1939); J.Bradway, The Work of the Legal Aid Committees of Bar Associations (1938); E.Brownell, Legal Aid in the United States (1951); E.Johnson, Justice and Reform 3–19 (1974).

[17] R.Smith, Justice and the Poor 135–36 (1919).

[18] R.Smith, supra at 147, 152, 192.

[19] See E.Johnson, supra n. 16, at 11, 12.

[20] The ABA formed a Special Committee on Legal Aid in 1920 under the chairmanship of Charles Evans Hughes and made the committee a standing committee the next year. The National Legal Aid and Defender Association was founded in 1923 with ABA support. See Huber, Thou Shalt Not Ration Justice: A History and Bibliography of Legal Aid in America, 44 Geo.Wash.L.Rev. 754, 755–56 (1976).

[21] The history of the caseload in legal aid societies during the early Depression and later years is revealed in a table in E.Brownell, Legal Aid in the United States 167–68 (1951). During the Depression the attitude of the ABA ethics committee toward legal aid underwent a discernible shift. The position intimated in ABA Formal Op. 166 (1936) was that legal aid was justified by the "present economic structure" (presumably the Depression), but by 1939 the tone in ABA Formal Op. 191 was more supportive ("free legal clinics carried on by the organized bar . . . serve a very worthwhile purpose and should be encouraged").

[22] Caseload, which had peaked in 1933 at 331,970, decreased to a low of 185,488 in 1943 and rose to only 344,616 in 1948.

[23] E.Johnson, Justice and Reform 16–18 (1974).

tal funding because of feared evils of governmental control of the bar. That antipathy was greatedly increased during the 1950s, partly because of the mood created by the anticommunist crusades of that decade and the threatening example of government-financed legal services that were established in Great Britain in 1949.[24]

Equal-Justice Purposes of Traditional Legal Aid

The organizational motivation of legal aid agencies into the 1960s was generally based on a concept of equal justice for the rich and poor rather than on a concept of eradicating poverty or causing social change. The poor were to be given the same right to access to legal services that the rich enjoyed to assert their legal rights in courts, legislatures, and administrative agencies. At least when poor persons are defendants in suits brought against them by persons able to hire lawyers, a strong equity argument exists for supplying free lawyers to persons who are otherwise defenseless against a governmentally imposed legal burden.[25] More broadly, it has been argued that when effective implementation of legal rights requires the assistance of a lawyer in order to obtain meaningful access to what the law allows, all clients should be recognized as having a right of access that entails the moral and political right to free legal services if that is necessary because of poverty.[26] Also playing a part in defining the task of legal aid may have been the less altruistic desire of some lawyers to avoid the need to handle nonremunerative cases themselves and to facilitate child-support recoveries that would reduce the costs of public welfare for legal aid clients. The kind of client service that the equal-justice philosophy espoused resulted in legal aid representation that occurred primarily in the lower state and local courts and that seldom focused on issues of substantive or procedural changes in definitions of the rights of poor persons.

Legal Services and Social Change

In the 1960s an entirely different concept of legal aid was conceived, first by theorists and then by politicians and activists, who ultimately transformed the funding and direction of legal services for the poor. Instead of seeking equal justice for the poor, the new theorists sought to bring about social change by changing the laws that affected the poor.[27] There was obviously no sharp line between client service for the poor and social change, but the different philosophies led to significant differences in emphasis, tactics, and priorities. Indeed, the new theorists could plausibly claim that legal services for the rich had always included lobbying and administrative agency action seeking legal change.

Several different theories of social change emerged in the new movement of legal services for the poor. One theory has been described as "social rescue"—freeing an individual from criminal charges, bad housing, or civil court judgments that served to keep the person from taking a productive place in society. A second theory views legal services as part of community economic development. Once a community gets onto its collective economic feet through government grants, the local economy will itself support legal services appropriate to the new circumstances of the

24 Id. at 17–18. E.g., Smith, Introduction to E.Brownell, Legal Aid in the United States at xvi-xvii (1951); Storey, The Legal Profession versus Regimentation: A Program to Counter Socialization, 37 ABA J. 100 (1951).

25 J.Katz, Poor People's Lawyers in Transition 2–3 (1982).

26 Breger, Legal Aid for the Poor: A Conceptual Analysis, 60 N.C.L.Rev. 282 (1982).

27 See generally Cahn & Cahn, The War on Poverty: A Civilian Perspective, 73 Yale L.J. 1317 (1964); Carlin & Howard, Legal Representation and Class Justice, 12 UCLA L.Rev. 381 (1965). The shift in emphasis can be traced in such period literature as Conference Proceedings: The Extension of Legal Services to the Poor (J.Stats ed.1964)(conference sponsored by Department of Health, Education, and Welfare); and Law and Poverty: 1965 (P.Wald ed.1965)(working paper for National Conference on Law and Poverty). The notion that the federal government might fund programs that could possibly compete with private practitioners for clients even some of whom might be able to afford a fee was viewed with alarm by some lawyers. E.g., Bethel & Walker, Et Tu, Brute!, 1 Tenn.B.J. 11 (August 1965).

community. That theory has receded in importance with the demise early in the 1960s of community development corporations as a federal program. A third theory is that legal services should be employed for the kind of community organization that will permit the poor to exercise collective political and legal power. That theory raises problems of solicitation and incitement of litigation that have slowly subsided in importance. Its most effective tactics have also been prohibited in all nationally funded legal service programs. A fourth theory is that legal services should be employed in ways that efficiently achieve law reform within the existing social and legal order. That, it is argued, can be achieved through appeals and class actions in test cases that raise issues of broad importance to the poor and through legislative and administrative lobbying. The issues raised may seek to alter the formal structure of the law or to force state agencies and dominant economic interests to conform to existing legal norms.

The social-change philosophy was first put into practical operation when the Ford Foundation decided to spend several million dollars to fund experiments in the rendition of various social services, including legal services, through neighborhood centers rather than from centralized offices in urban areas.[28] Included among the legal services projects that were funded were proposals that sought to use lawyers to change laws and practices that were discriminatory against the poor and therefore were thought to cause poverty. In effect, lawyers' services through legal aid were suggested as a method of attacking legal structures that themselves contributed to the status of poverty.[29]

Legal Aid and the Legal Needs of the Poor

Almost certainly, the legal aid resources traditionally made available to the poor were inadequate even on the equal-justice assumptions that underlay traditional legal aid. In 1949, 43 percent of the country's large cities had no legal aid agency at all,[30] and those that did have agencies lacked sufficient lawyers to handle the caseload of the low-income population.[31] In 1962 the combined budgets of over two hundred legal aid organizations had grown to only $3.5 million dollars, compared with national budgets of $.7 million in 1938 and $1.5 million in 1948. The 1962 figure meant that less than .2 percent of the nation's legal resources were being used for the approximately 25 percent of the population who were unable to afford a lawyer.[32] Clearly the initiatives suggested by the Ford Foundation experiments called for greatly increased funding levels if these approaches were to be generalized in all communities. The source for funding of both traditional legal aid and of more wide-sweeping social change through law reform was, many persons thought, to be found in the federal government. Federal welfare agencies had already begun to fund legal service programs,

[28] See generally E.Johnson, Justice and Reform 21–35 (1974).

[29] See generally Cahn & Cahn, The War on Poverty: A Civilian Perspective, 73 Yale L.J. 1317 (1964). A critical element of the Cahns' suggested future for legal aid was that neighborhood law offices be controlled by the poor clientele rather than by the dominant political or bureaucratic communities, which were often themselves either causes of poverty or barriers to its alleviation and who could not safely be offended by legal aid lawyers if those communities controlled the agency.

[30] E.Brownell, Legal Aid in the United States (1961 supp.) at 68 n.17. In the same year, 1949, England inaugurated a comprehensive system of free legal aid to the poor throughout the country. See generally M.Zander, Legal Services for the Community (1978); S.Pollock, Legal Aid—The First Twenty-Five Years (1975); Pollock, Legal Aid: A Tale of Two Nations, 62 ABA J. 1429 (1976). With the exception of England, the United States, and some socialist countries, the provision of legal aid to those unable to afford legal services is still at a frontier stage of development. See generally Perspectives on Legal Aid (F.Zemans ed.1979).

[31] T.Goodman & M.Walker, The Legal Services Program: Resource Distribution and the Low Income Population (1975).

[32] Put another way, the expenditures for legal aid and public defender services (thus including legal services for criminal defense) expended by 224 legal aid and public defender organizations in 1963 should have been sixty times greater if the same level of expenditures for legal services for rich and poor were to be achieved. See H.Stumpf, Community Politics and Legal Services 124–25 (1975).

but without any well-developed national policy on expenditures for legal services.

WESTLAW REFERENCES

"legal aid" /s poor disadvantag** indigen!
"legal aid" /s funding funded financing budget!

§ 16.7.3 *Government-Funded Legal Services for the Poor*

Legal Services in the War on Poverty

Beginning in 1963, shortly after the announcement of President Lyndon Johnson's War on Poverty, serious consideration began to be given to creating the organization to fund legal services for the poor that became the Legal Services Program within the newly formed Office of Economic Opportunity (OEO).[33] The American Bar Association, perceiving the likelihood of federal funding and desiring to influence its shape, unanimously endorsed federal funding in 1965 but called for maximum utilization of existing legal aid societies and for continued control by lawyers rather than OEO's own Community Action Programs.[34] The first director of OEO's legal services program thus confronted three groups that wanted federal funding to be controlled in different ways: the Community Action Program wanted to have legal services controlled by its own segment of the social services bureaucracy; the neighborhood centers group wanted to separate legal services from the social services bureaucracy and to work on law reform; and the organized bar and existing legal aid organizations wanted federal funding to go to traditional models of service-oriented legal aid. The legislation that officially created the Office of Legal Services in 1966 did nothing to sort out the contending groups.[35]

The early grants under the Legal Services Program reflected the respective strengths of the three groups. Existing legal aid organizations and state and local bar associations were given a significant voice in grant approval procedures and as sponsors of several grants. The Office of Legal Services was given an independent status within OEO,[36] but grantees were sometimes sponsored at the local level by Community Action Program agencies, and the support of such agencies was often sought by independent grant applicants. Neighborhood poverty groups were often ignored in grant applications, but OEO imposed grant conditions that attempted to ensure that law-reform goals and representation of poverty interests were considered. Lawyer-dominated judicare programs were not funded at first, although some were eventually given funds.[37]

During the first complete year of the Office of Legal Services (July 1966 to July 1967), grants increased from 155 to 300 grantee agencies and from $25 million to over $40 million in amount. The programs varied from small local operations to large statewide organizations. Over 40 percent of the new grants were to existing old-line legal aid societies.[38] Because of pressure from bar associations, OEO's rules required that lawyers constitute a majority of the members of the governing boards of both traditional legal aid

[33] See generally E.Johnson, Justice and Reform 39–70 (1974); Pye, The Role of Legal Services in the Antipoverty Program, 31 Law & Contemp.Probs. 211 (1966).

[34] The national bar organizations have traditionally supported national funding for legal services with impressive shows of strength. On the other hand, some—but by no means all—local bar associations have often been obstructive and antagonistic to actual legal service programs.

[35] Economic Opportunity Amendments of 1966, Pub.L. No. 89–794, 80 Stat. 1462 (repealed by Act of July 25, 1974, Pub.L. No. 93–355, 88 Stat. 390).

[36] For a review of the bureaucratic infighting involved, see E.Johnson, Justice and Reform 135–62 (1974). The semi-independence of the Office of Legal Services within OEO resulted in its sharing power to approve grants with national officials in the Community Action Program. But the Office successfully resisted becoming subordinate to regional and local CAP officials. In 1969, after the election of President Nixon, the CAP program was dismantled and legal services became a totally independent entity with only a formal relationship to OEO. See Note, Legal Services—Past and Present, 59 Corn.L.Rev. 960 (1974).

[37] E.Johnson, supra at 117–21.

[38] Id. at 99–101.

organizations and newer legal services organizations.[39] As a result, established members of the community and the organized bar were frequently in control of the programs. That strategy put programs into operation quickly and gained political support for them, but resulted in boards dominated by members who sometimes opposed the law-reform goals of OEO.[40] The influence of law-reform proponents was advanced primarily through several community groups, through grant conditions imposed by the national office, through national publications such as the *Clearinghouse Review* and the *Poverty Law Reporter*, through the institution of training programs and backup centers for legal services lawyers, and through the establishment of a Reginald Heber Smith fellowship program to recruit and train promising legal services lawyers. The backup centers not only provided scholarly analysis in support of programs but also undertook to coordinate a national litigation strategy and to serve as cocounsel on cases, where necessary, in order to attempt to bring about law reform.[41] Of critical importance was the fact that OEO announced in 1967 that law reform through test case litigation was to be a primary objective of the Office of Legal Services.[42]

National Legal Services Corporation

A new phase in legal services for the poor emerged in 1971 with the proposal by the Nixon administration, backed by the organized bar, to establish a new public legal services corporation to administer federal funding for legal services.[43] The proposal resulted from problems of political interference with OEO by members of Congress in behalf of constituents troubled by Office of Legal Services litigation [44] and from the Nixon administration's own discomfort with OEO and many of its policies. That discomfort had led the president to abolish OEO by executive order in 1973, leaving the Office of Legal Services as its sole survivor. Many governors and mayors had complained to the president about the law-reform activities of legal services programs. An independent corporation would both insulate the president from such complaints and permit long-term reshaping of its policies through appointments to its board of directors. The legal services branch of the now defunct OEO continued an increasingly demoralized existence with annual funding at a frozen level while political forces thrashed out pivotal questions of control and function of the proposed corporation.

At last, in 1974, a bill became law that created the Legal Services Corporation, over whose board the president had only partial appointment power, and that imposed numerous restrictions on the law-reform activities of funded agencies. The corporation is prohibited from interfering with the client-lawyer relationship between grantee lawyers and their clients.[45] And the corporation is not to usurp the power of the states to regulate professional responsibility and bar admissions.[46] Also prohibited are such activities as picketing and civil disturbances [47] and most political activi-

[39] Id. at 121–26.

[40] Id. at 102, 164. For a detailed examination of one bar-dominated board and the initial hostility of a local bar, see Stumpf, Schroerluke & Dill, The Legal Profession and Legal Services: Explorations in Local Bar Politics, 6 L. & Soc'y Rev. 47 (1971).

[41] E.Johnson, supra at 176–82.

[42] Harvard Conference on Law and Poverty, Proceedings, March 17–19 (1967).

[43] See generally George, Development of the Legal Services Corporation, 61 Corn.L.Rev. 681 (1976); Note, Legal Services—Past and Present, 59 Corn.L.Rev. 960, 982–88 (1974); Note, To Protect the Rights of the Poor: The Legal Services Corporation Act of 1971, 19 Kan.L.Rev. 641 (1971); Note, Legal Services Corporation: Curtailing Political Interference, 81 Yale L.J. 231 (1971).

[44] One of the most famous political controversies involving an OEO-funded legal services organization and local political powers occurred in California, where the California Rural Legal Assistance program was accused of unethical behavior by the administration of then-governor Reagan. See generally Falk & Pollak, Political Interference with Publicly Funded Lawyers: The CRLA Controversy and the Future of Legal Services, 24 Hast. L.J. 599 (1973); Note, The Legal Services Corporation: Curtailing Political Interference, 81 Yale L.J. 231 (1971).

[45] 42 U.S.C.A. § 2996e(b)(3).

[46] Id.

[47] § 2996c(b)(5).

ties.[48] Class actions are restricted but not prohibited;[49] representation is barred in school desegregation litigation, most abortion cases, and selective service or military desertion cases;[50] and courts are empowered to order that the corporation pay legal fees of an opposing party in cases brought maliciously or for harassment.[51] Because of complaints about out-of-state poverty lawyers stirring up trouble in other states, a restriction requires that all program lawyers be admitted to practice in the jurisdiction in which assistance is initiated.[52]

Funding for the new Legal Services Corporation was increased from the $71.5 million level that had obtained during the four-year freeze on Office of Legal Services funding to $88 million in fiscal year 1976. That level was still far below the ABA's own estimates of the need for minimally adequate legal services.[53] In 1975 a report indicated that only 59.5 percent of the almost twenty-nine million poor persons eligible for legal services lived in geographic areas in which legal services were theoretically available.[54] Funding for the National Legal Services Corporation increased from $70 million in 1975 to $321 million in 1981.[55] At its height, it had funded 323 independent programs with combined staff of approximately 6,000 lawyers, 2,800 paralegals, plus secretaries and clerks.[56] In 1980 it handled about 1.5 million legal matters for about a million poor persons, only one-fifth of whom were employed. Despite the rhetoric of its detractors and defenders, the corporation has primarily served to expand the client-service approach of traditional legal aid.[57] At that, it has been estimated that the corporation was handling only one-eighth of the needs of the poor.[58]

The National Legal Services Corporation has continued to exist in an atmosphere of political controversy, organizational instability, and general hostility from many powerful political figures. President Reagan announced in early 1982 that he intended to abolish the corporation.[59] The announcement came a year after the corporation's budget was cut from $321 million to $241 million.[60] Resisted by the American Bar Association and powerful interests in Congress, the president has nonetheless appointed a new board

48 The corporation is not to attempt to influence legislation, except legislation affecting itself or when invited to testify by a legislative body (§ 2996e(c)). The corporation may not make political contributions (§ 1996c(d)(3)) or seek directly to influence ballot measures except through good faith legal services to clients that call for such advice (§ 1996c(d)(4)). Neither the corporation nor a recipient is to be "identified" with a political party or candidate (§ 1996c(e)(1)). Grantees are prohibited from using funds to influence legislation or executive or agency action (§ 2996c(a)(5)). Clients who seek to influence such rules may be represented in lobbying efforts, but grantee lawyers may not solicit such cases (§ 2996c(a)(5)(A)). Among other restrictions, grantees' lawyers are prohibited from engaging in political activities and voter registration except in connection with client representation (§ 2996c(a)(6)).

49 Any class action must be approved by a grantee's project director, according to guidelines. § 1996c(d)(5)(as amended 1983).

50 § 2996c(b)(7)-(9).

51 § 2996c(f).

52 42 U.S.C.A. § 2996e(b)(4).

53 One widely quoted estimate was that the expenditure of more than $250 million was necessary in the 1960s to fund a minimally adequate legal services program. See Breger, The Legal Services Corporation: A Report to the Bar, 39 Tex.B.J. 423, 424 (May 1976). Writing somewhat earlier, a noted comparativist described the American expenditures, state and federal, for legal services programs as "trivial." See Cappelletti & Gordley, Legal Aid: Modern Themes and Variations, 24 Stan.L.Rev. 347, 379 (1972).

54 L.Goodman & M.Walker, The Legal Services program: Resource Distribution and the Low Income Population 13–16 (1975). On the improbable assumption that an average legal services lawyer could handle five hundred cases per year, the study estimated that the nation's then 2,000 legal services lawyers could handle only one-fourth of the estimated four million legal problems experienced by the 17.2 million poor persons living in areas theoretically served by programs. Id.

55 Legal Services Corporation, Annual Report 7–8 (1979); id. (1981).

56 Cramton, Crisis in Legal Services for the Poor, 26 Vill.L.Rev. 521, 529 (1981).

57 Bellow, Turning Solutions into Problems: The Legal Aid Experience, 34 NLADA Briefcase 106 (1977).

58 Cramton, supra at 530–31.

59 Cramton, supra.

60 Legal Services Corporation, Annual Report 7 (1981). The funding cutback caused the extraordinary issuance of ABA Formal Op. 347 (1981), which gave advice on the duties of legal service program lawyers and board members to protect client interests despite the need to withdraw when a program lost its funding.

for the corporation, employing interim appointments not subject to senatorial approval, which is not sympathetic to the original intent of the corporation and of most of its supported programs.[61]

WESTLAW REFERENCES

legal +1 aid assist! service /s funding funded financing budget! /s government** federal**
federal national +1 "legal services corporation"
legal +1 aid service assist! /p (office +2 economic +1 opportunity) oeo
legal +1 aid service assist! /p federal** government! /2 fund*** /p restrict! barred prohibit!

---

§ 16.7.4 *Legal Services Lawyering and Client-Lawyer Relationships*

Central Issues of Client Loyalty and Service

Several arguments, objections really, have been advanced concerning the nature of the work of law reform that legal services lawyers have been engaged in since the founding of the OEO Office of Legal Services over twenty years ago.[62] Some of the same concerns have been raised about the representation of clients by lawyers for advocacy organizations that are not funded publicly.[63] To describe them as public interest concerns overstates the case somewhat, because lawyers who are not publicly funded are not bound to serve a particular constituency of clients as legal services lawyers are. With that necessary qualification, we will consider those concerns as collectively applicable to lawyers who attempt to serve a clientele broader than an individual client or clients who have retained the lawyer. Those concerns, which are hardly trivial, are with the accountability of legal services lawyers, the deforming effect of law reform upon their relationship with their clients, and the impact of law reform upon client service.

Accountability and the Deformed Client-Lawyer Relationship

To an extent, law-reform representation can change the traditional client-lawyer relationship because a legal services lawyer may pursue a case that was originally necessary or beneficial to an individual client beyond the point where the client's interests are being advanced. The lawyer's motivation is to benefit a larger clientele, the poor. The lawyer may actually harm the individual client's interests, such as by failing to seek a settlement that would benefit only the client in order to preserve the client's standing to litigate an issue of broad importance. Or a lawyer's advocacy may protect the interests of the client and a segment of the poor population but harm various poor persons or groups of the poor. For example, an attempt to prevent loan companies from seizing household goods of the poor as collateral for loans may have the unintended effect of restricting credit for the less creditworthy of the poor, raising interest rates, or both. A suit to mandate welfare grants to persons newly residing in a state may have the unintended, but foreseeable, effect of reducing welfare grants generally. Traditional clients, of course, sometimes bring test cases and sometimes accept short-term disadvantages in pursuit of long-term goals. The difference in the legal services context is that the decision to seek broader objectives is, realistically speaking, made by the legal services lawyer and not by any client or group of clients.

The problem is not merely that of who makes decisions, which can be a merely for-

[61] Legal Services: LSC May Get a Senate-Confirmed Board Yet, 70 ABA J. 42 (1984); LSC Suffers a New Setback in Attempt to Limit Funds, Nat'l L.J., Sept.10, 1984, at 10, col.1; N.Y.Times, Oct. 22, 1984, at A-17, col.1 (congressional questions concerning LSC grants to conservative organizations); Wise, Is There Life after LSC?, Nat'l L.J., Apr.11, 1983, at 1, col.2 (effects of 24 percent budget cut, resulting in loss of 1,267 lawyers of staff of 5,678 two years earlier); Drew, A Reporter at Large: Legal Services, The New Yorker, Mar. 1, 1982, at 97.

[62] See generally Agnew, What's Wrong with the Legal Services Program, 58 ABA J. 930 (1972).

[63] Similar problems afflict lawyers for the American Civil Liberties Union, the National Association for the Advancement of Colored People, the Wilderness Society, and similar advocacy organizations that engage in client representation as part of their activities.

mal problem if both lawyer and client would make the same decision. If the primary objective of a legal services lawyer is law reform rather than client service, the lawyer may be motivated to substitute the objectives and interests of a larger group for the objectives and interests of the individual client that the traditional model of the client-lawyer relationship assumes will govern critical decisions in the representation (§ 4.3). Moreover, to the extent that a larger group's wants are the claimed justification for ignoring the individual client's interests, a legal services lawyer must often admit that he or she only assumes that these wants have a certain content, for the lawyer has almost certainly done nothing material to determine what in fact those desires might be.

Yet the solution to the divergence of interest between individual and group cannot be to insist that a lawyer always be guided by the individual's interest. Among other things, such an insistence would mean that group representation is never permissible unless it can be undertaken with formal regard for the individual interests of all group members. The well-known complexities and imponderables of obtaining meaningful and unanimous consent of individuals to group action make such an insistence quite dubious if it is attempted to be defended on the grounds of either individual autonomy or economy. Moreover, to make individual client interest the supreme value denies the possibility of public interest representation. That is objectionable because it denies the possibility of achieving legal advantages for groups except in the extraordinary case in which there is perfect congruence between individual and group preferences. If it is correct to believe, as some legal services adherents argue, that effective law reform can be achieved only through test cases and class actions, then denial of a power of decision to legal services lawyers also denies that such law reform can be attempted.

Where should decision-making authority reside in such circumstances? It has often been argued by opponents of legal services lawyers that their handling of test cases serves, not the enlightened self-interest of the poor, but the political theories of the lawyers themselves, who have no other personal stake in the representation. Thus, it is argued, legal services lawyers should be accountable, if not to clients, at least to groups of poor persons or to local elected officials or to a national strategy shaped by officials who, because they are elected or appointed, are more accountable than are legal services lawyers.

The issues raised by those arguments are both speculative and complex. In general, if a lawyer consults either individual or group, the lawyer's advice will often carry the day. But that will often occur because of defective abilities of group members to make their own decisions and to question those of others. In any event, any group that can be assembled for meaningful consultation will be representative of the larger group—the poor who will be affected by a decision—only to some unknowable and imperfect degree. Consultation may provide merely a pretextual legitimacy to a decision that may harm one segment of the poor and benefit another. Consultation with some groups or individuals, such as politicians whose own constituencies would be affected by a decision, is the least likely way of gaining real legitimacy for a lawyer's decision unless the constituencies' interests are perfectly consistent with those of the lawyer's client. Only in the latter case does the fact, if it is a fact, that the politician is elected by an effectively working democratic process have any material bearing on the legitimacy or weight of the politician's views. A politician's most powerful constituencies are often the segments of the general public who are likely to be in conflict with the poor on law-reform issues—landlords, banks, merchants, and employers. Indeed, if the politician's interests were aligned more with the interests of the poor, presumably the structural change in the law sought by a legal services lawyer would have already been accomplished by legislation. In the nature of things, there is probably no better way of achieving effective law reform, if indeed that can be achieved through the legal process, than by permitting legal service and other public interest lawyers to make critical decisions themselves. They should do that by honestly consulting their own best conception of what the public interest dictates. In reality that is the way in which public interest lawyers have generally functioned when possible.

Nonetheless, attention to the normal sensitivities of persons and the traditions of the legal profession are probably warrant enough for strongly urging a legal services or other public interest lawyer to consult with any client whose case the lawyer intends to handle as a test case. Except in the most extraordinary circumstances, unless the client is willing to consent to a representation in which the lawyer may reject a client's advice about tactically important matters in the interest of a larger group, the lawyer should decline to represent the client.[64] The client's consent, of course, is hardly unconstrained. The client's choices are probably effectively limited to a representation with unwanted conditions or no representation at all. But unless one can argue that the lawyer involved is duty bound to provide an unconditioned representation, the client's lack of freedom of choice cannot be of overriding importance.

Law Reform versus Client Service

One argument that law reform should not be funded at all by the federal government is that law reform detracts from the service of individual clients' needs for legal services. While legal services lawyers are litigating in one test case the duty of landlords to provide habitable premises as defined by a building code, they are not obtaining divorces for several other possible legal services clients. The extent to which such displacement actually occurs is unclear. It has been estimated that service cases actually occupy the vast majority of the man-hours of legal services organizations, sometimes to the chagrin of national directors.[65] In one of the most aggressive and controversial programs, for example, California Rural Legal Assistance, it was estimated that routine service matters comprised more than 95 percent of the number of matters handled and 80 percent of lawyer time.[66] Whatever the magnitude, however, it is clear that law reform must have the effect of denying lawyers who are involved the time to attend to some client service matters.[67]

The argument that law reform should accede to needs for client service, if logically extended under the circumstances that have always characterized legal service programs, is an argument that law reform should never be attempted. That is true because federal and other funding for legal services for the poor has never begun to approach the levels required to satisfy client service needs. A judgment that client service is always more important for the needs of the poor than law reform would be extremely dubious and, in any event, is the sort of open-textured decision that can be made only as a matter of general policy. Congress has never decreed that law reform is impermissible in the absence of complete satisfaction of client service needs.

A related problem of law-reform activities is that they are relatively ineffective.[68] Law reform is generally limited to litigation under Legal Services Corporation grants because of restrictions on political organizing activities. The advantages of litigation are that it is readily available and relatively inexpensive.

[64] See generally Note, The New Public Interest Lawyers, 79 Yale L.J. 1069, 1131–32 (1970).

[65] S.Brakel, Judicare 80 n.9 (1974).

[66] Falk & Pollak, What's Wrong with Attacks on the Legal Services Program, 58 ABA J. 1287, 1289 (1972).

[67] Law reform can nonetheless be defended for its indirect beneficial effects on client service. Legal services lawyers are much more apt to suffer occupational burnout if confined only to routine, client service cases. See generally J.Katz, Poor People's Lawyers in Transition (1982). Law-reform work can thus serve to improve morale, extend the effective tenure of legal services lawyers, and attract young and idealistic lawyers.

[68] For disparate approaches to the same conclusion, see generally Hazard, Law Reforming in the Anti-Poverty Effort, 37 U.Chi.L.Rev. 242 (1970), and Abel, Socializing the Legal Profession: Can Redistributing Lawyers' Services Achieve Social Justice?, 1 Law & Policy Quar. 5 (1979).

Litigation to obtain law reform assumes that judicial decisions are unrestrained by political considerations and are based only on principle regardless of social outcome. But it is clear that there are severe limits on judicial law reform. Judges may themselves not be as eager as are legal services lawyers to upset the existing balance of economic forces.[69] If judge-made law gets too far out of line with social perceptions, it will be reversed or frustrated legislatively or administratively. Judicial lawmaking does not include any effective power to create new programs from whole cloth and to raise funds or even to order legislatures effectively to do so. Thus the results of law reform through litigation are likely to be incremental, reversible or otherwise avoidable, and necessarily of limited value to any constituency. Yet it is not obvious that relieving the plight of the poor is any more efficiently accomplished through client service work. In the absence of sweeping political change, a case can be made for the relative efficaciousness of both tactics.[70]

A final objection to some forms of legal service concerns meritorious but uneconomical disputes that involve, in effect, a possibly unintended law-reform effect of some legal service representations. Some cases that are otherwise eligible for legal service program benefits involve claims or defenses that, if a middle-income client were involved, would not be brought to a lawyer or would be quickly disposed of because the amounts of money involved are small. If a legal service lawyer, employed on a salaried basis by the program, provides the legal services necessary to give the client with a small claim or defense full representation without regard to the amount at stake, the low-income client receives better legal services than would a person paying for a lawyer. Some representations of that kind can be defended on the ground that small amounts of money mean more to the poor. But legal services lawyers can win such cases simply by forcing them to trial, because that requires the opposing party, if represented by a lawyer, to incur legal fees that are disproportionate to the amounts at stake.

No simple solution appears to such problems, which could clearly be substantial. That the poor are themselves often victimized by the legal system is hardly a compelling reason for winking at the possible injustice of free legal services for the poor to those who happen to oppose the client. As one expedient, some programs have declined to undertake plaintiffs' cases against private parties where the case could be handled on a contingent fee basis by a private lawyer if the amount involved were economically worthwhile. Yet nearly all programs are willing to defend small claims against eligible clients.

Control of Legal Services Lawyers

The model client-lawyer relationship has it that the lawyer is subject to control only by the client (§ 4.1, § 8.8). In the past some courts have objected to the control of legal services organizations by boards of nonlawyers.[71] Such objections have been rendered moot for two reasons. First, the Legal Services Corporation Act now requires lawyer control of all boards of grantee legal service organizations.[72] Second, the Code and the Model Rules both recognize that nonprofit lay groups have the right to hire and supply counsel to beneficiaries in accord with Su-

69 For an early study of the generally cautious and sometimes hostile reception that judges and lawyers gave to law-reform efforts of legal services lawyers, see Stumpf & Janowitz, Judges and the Poor: Bench Responses to Federally Financed Legal Services, 21 Stan.L.Rev. 1058 (1969).

70 A further objection is that lawyer-dictated solutions to poverty problems are dysfunctional because that approach undermines any effort to develop competence in poor people to solve their own problems. See F.Marks, The Legal Needs of the Poor: A Critical Analysis 14–17 (1971); Cahn & Cahn, What Price Justice: The Civilian Perspective Revisited, 41 Notre Dame Law. 927 (1966).

71 In re Community Action for Legal Services, 26 A.D.2d 354, 274 N.Y.S.2d 779 (1966)(refusal to approve applications by organizations controlled by nonlawyer boards to operate legal services programs because, among other reasons, lawyers' activities would be subject to lay control, which would affect lawyers' exercise of judgment in behalf of clients).

72 42 U.S.C.A. § 2996c(f)(nine-member council, majority of whom must be lawyers locally admitted to practice).

preme Court decisions establishing a constitutional right of advocacy.[73]

Remaining, however, are issues of the extent to which legal service program boards, or the corporation itself, or even Congress, should be able to control the policies and litigation strategies of legal service lawyers. In general, the line that has been drawn divides general policies, which may be controlled by boards or regulations, and the implementation of particular tactics in individual cases, which is subject to control only by the lawyers involved. The legal services legislation contains several restrictions on handling certain kinds of cases—school desegregation, criminal cases, abortion cases, and selective service cases. In Formal Opinion 324 (1970), the ABA ethics committee ruled that a governing board had the "right and obligation" to establish and enforce general policy, including financial eligibility criteria for clients, selection of services to be offered clients, setting priorities for allocating resources and available lawyer time, and determining the types of cases in which representation could be offered.[74]

Permissible board policies are to take the form of broad guidelines rather than case-by-case review.[75] The board may, however, require lawyers to divulge information about clients to determine whether board policies are being followed and a staff lawyer would not violate the prohibitions against disclosure of client information by complying. But the board should not interfere with a lawyer's handling of a particular case. General policy might prohibit a lawyer from expanding a client's case into a class action if law reform is not a priority of the program and such a tactic is not necessary to protect the client's interests. Case-by-case review of class actions is impermissible, both because it interferes too specifically with a lawyer's exercise of independent professional judgment in behalf of a client and because a board's determinations might be too susceptible to community and political influence. A lawyer's decision to initiate a class action may be reviewed by an all-lawyer committee, but only in an advisory capacity. Lobbying can similarly be restricted only as a general policy matter, and a lawyer must be free to employ lobbying in effectively representing a program client. Essentially those same lines have been drawn in the Legal Service Corporation Act itself.[76]

Legal Services Conflicts of Interest

As do other lawyers and other kinds of law firms, legal service program lawyers may confront conflict of interest problems.[77] The problem is more acute, however, because some legal matters may involve two or more persons who are eligible for assistance. A common example is a divorce between poor persons. Many programs have worked out arrangements with local bar associations under which the bar will provide pro bono representation to a person eligible for legal services but whose representation by legal service program lawyers would cause a conflict.

The predominance of lawyers on legal service program boards that is required by the legal services legislation has produced significant conflict of interest problems for lawyer-board members, as well as for the service, when the interests of a program client and those of a private practitioner or his or her firm conflict. Originally, the ABA ethics committee took the position that if a service lawyer already represented a client, a lawyer-board member and his or her firm were pre-

[73] See generally § 16.5.2.

[74] Governing boards were exhorted by the ABA committee, however, to avoid yielding to pressures to deny representation to unpopular clients or to importunings of local governmental officials. ABA Formal Op. 324, at 5.

[75] The line suggested may be difficult to distinguish in practice. A lawyer's motivation to employ lobbying in behalf of an individual client in a program that gives priority to client service rather than law reform, for example, would be difficult to second-guess but nonetheless might be suspect.

[76] 42 U.S.C.A. § 2996e(d)(5)(class actions must be approved by project directors but not by any group outside program); § 2996f(a)(5)(restrictions on lobbying in act do not preclude lobbying on behalf of eligible client).

[77] With respect to the possibly different application of imputed disqualification rules to legal service program staffs of lawyers, see § 7.6.5 (nonprofit law offices).

cluded from representing an adverse party.[78] In the face of strong bar opposition, however, the committee issued Formal Opinion 345 (1979), which retreated from the apparent position that board members were in a client-lawyer relationship with all program clients. Instead, the opinion provided that board lawyers and their firms could represent clients with interests adverse to a program client so long as steps were taken to assure the independence of advice and judgment of the lawyers on both sides and so long as both clients and the membership of the board were informed of the relationship. Model Rule 6.3 takes a more permissive stance in order to avoid discouraging lawyers from serving on the boards of legal service programs.[79] The rule recognizes, realistically, that the only significant conflict threat is that the board lawyer might attempt to influence a program lawyer or program policy. Accordingly the lawyer is disqualified from participating in a decision or action of the board if either the lawyer's client [80] or a program client would be adversely affected by the board action. Thus, if a matter is pending before the board on the use of class actions and a client of the lawyer is threatened with a suit by a program client that might be turned into a class action, the lawyer should abstain from the board's deliberations and decision.

Judicare versus Staffed-Office Programs

Judicare is the popular name for a variety of legal services programs that reimburse private lawyers with government funds for representing indigent clients.[81] OEO funded seven judicare experiments. In each the clients were certified as eligible for the program by a local welfare office. Clients were given a card that would be honored for legal services performed by any lawyer in the client's county or an adjoining one. Any lawyer could refuse any client or refuse to participate in the program at all, although most lawyers participated. The program covered only civil matters and excluded fee-generating cases, income tax matters, and patent and copyright problems. A lawyer who agreed to represent an eligible client notified the program's central office of the identity of the client and the type of case handled. On completion the lawyer billed the central office, which reimbursed the lawyer at a figure set as a percentage of the then prevailing minimum fee schedule. A maximum fee per case and a maximum aggregate amount of fees that a single lawyer could receive annually were also set. Judicare programs have not been traditionally supported by the Legal Service Corporation [82] but are strongly favored by bar associations. [83]

Most legal services programs, however, are operated from offices staffed with lawyers who are employed to devote all of their time to poor clients. The program board sets general policy that a program director is responsible for implementing. Staff lawyers accept clients who meet program eligibility guidelines and provide legal services required by the client's legal problem. They have available to them the services of backup centers and an esprit that often leads to common efforts with other poverty law centers and programs.

[78] ABA Informal Op. 1395 (1977).

[79] MR 6.3 comment (first paragraph).

[80] Neither MR 6.3 nor its comment indicates whether the imputed disqualification rules of MR 1.10 extend the prohibitions of MR 6.3 to instances in which a client represented by another lawyer in the firm of the board lawyer has interests in conflict with a program client. Obviously a lawyer aware of such a potential conflict would be best advised not to participate in the board decision or action. In the absence of language suggesting a more permissive rule, that result should be assumed to be mandated by MR 1.10 itself.

[81] Government compensation of private practitioners for legal services to low-income persons are common in European legal systems. See M.Cappelletti, J.Gordley & E.Johnson, Toward Equal Justice: A Comparative Study of Legal Aid in Modern Societies 27–58, 85–108 (1975).

[82] In 1983, however, a new board of the corporation altered that policy and required that at least 12.5 percent of grant funds be used in ways that provide opportunities for involvement of lawyers in private practice in providing services to eligible clients. See Leg. Serv. Corp. Instruction 83–6, 48 Fed.Reg. 53763 (Nov. 23, 1983).

[83] 52 U.S.L.Wk. 2473 (1984)(resolution of ABA House of Delegates urging increase in judicare programs by Legal Services Corporation); 49 U.S.L.Wk. 2126 (1980)(resolution urging amendment of LSC statutes to mandate judicare).

The literature of legal services abounds with disputes among researchers concerning the merits of the judicare as opposed to the staffed-office approach.[84] Statistical data is often resorted to in the debate, although it is sketchy and of dubious comparability from one program to another. The principal issue seems to be the extent to which law-reform work can be accomplished effectively in judicare programs.[85] The much greater familiarity of staffed-office lawyers with many matters that relate only to the poor probably permits such lawyers to begin with a superior ability to spot important and developing law reform issues and to call upon available resources more efficiently for assistance in law reform litigation or lobbying. It seems evident that, because of the multiple-lawyer staffing and the availability of backup centers, the staffed-office program will be much more readily able to litigate complex issues of constitutional and administrative law in either state or federal courts than a solo or small-firm practitioner in private practice could hope to be. On the other hand, staffed offices have a history of rapid turnover of lawyers,[86] and not all legal services lawyers are gifted litigators or dedicated to law-reform goals. Staffed offices, with their heavy reliance on paralegal assistants and low-budget appearance, probably strike most clients as second-rate justice and highly impersonal. The youth of staff lawyers, and their often evident eschewing of business-like dress and manners, may lead clients to believe that they could not get "regular" law jobs. Studies to date have not convincingly demonstrated whether one model or another, or a hybridized variation on them, is superior.

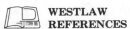

WESTLAW REFERENCES

Central Issues of Client Loyalty and Service

topic(45) /p legal +1 aid service assistance +1 organization corporation society

legal +1 aid service assist! /3 corporation organization society /p client /p account! (conflict! /3 interest) "professional responsibility"

Law Reform versus Client Service

law legal +2 reform /s poor indigen! disadvantag!

Judicare versus Staffed Office Programs

judicare /s program concept

---

84 See generally Goodman & Feuillan, The Trouble With Judicare, 58 ABA J. 476 (1972); Brakel, The Trouble with Judicare Evaluations, 58 ABA J. 704 (1972); S.Brakel, Judicare: Public Funds, Private Lawyers, and Poor People (1974); S.Brakel, Wisconsin Judicare: A Preliminary Appraisal (1972); Brakel, Judicare in West Virginia, 65 ABA J. 1346 (1979); Brakel, Free Legal Services for the Poor—Staffed Office versus Judicare: The Client's Evaluation, 1973 Wisc.L.Rev. 532; Zander, Judicare or Staff? A British View, 64 ABA J. 1436 (1978); Masotti & Corsi, Legal Assistance for the Poor: An Analysis and Evaluation of Two Programs, 44 J.Urb.L. 483 (1967); Marsh, Neighborhood Law Office or Judicare?, 25 Legal Aid Briefcase 12 (1966). See also Saltzman, Private Bar Delivery of Civil Legal Services to the Poor, 34 Hast.L.J. 1165 (1983)(supporting hybrid system combining elements of both staffed office and judicare). The Legal Service Corporation's own evaluation of several forms of legal services delivery gave pure judicare (that is, judicare without a staff backup component) low marks on desirable impact on the poverty community served. See The Delivery Systems Study—A Policy Report to the Congress and the President of the United States (1980). The study was not without its critics. See Nat'l L.J., Apr.12, 1980, at 12, col.3.

85 Subsidiary issues include the extent to which costs could be controlled under judicare. See Johnson, Lawyers' Choice: A Theoretical Appraisal of Litigation Investment Decisions, 15 Law & Soc'y Rev. 567, 596–97 n.26 (1981). The English legal aid system attempts to handle the problem of case selection and levels of lawyer charges by providing that public payment of legal fees will be made only in those cases identified in advance as eligible for payment. See 1 Royal Comm'n on Legal Services, Final Report ¶¶13.1-.72 (1979).

86 Rapid turnover and burnout among poverty lawyers is not constant. One study found a much lower turnover rate among lawyers who participated in reform litigation with substantial responsibility for its outcome and who practiced in an office with allied lawyers who shared a sense of the significance of the work being done. See Katz, Lawyers for the Poor in Transition: Involvement, Reform, and the Turnover Problem in the Legal Services Program, 12 Law & Soc'y Rev. 275 (1978); J.Katz, Poor People's Lawyers in Transition 108–22 (1982). Another study has suggested that the restlessness of legal services lawyers does not generally involve a loss of commitment to legal services, but often merely reflects career changes common to young lawyers. See J.Handler, E.Hollingsworth & H.Erlanger, Lawyers and the Pursuit of Legal Rights 8–9, 11–12 (1978).

§ 16.8 PUBLIC INTEREST PRACTICE

Nature of Public Interest Practice

The general concept of policy-oriented advocacy has come to be known as public interest practice. Most lawyers accept as clients any person willing to pay the lawyer's customary fee charge, regardless of the nature of the legal matters involved. And, at least in a loose sense, many lawyers would claim with Louis Brandeis that they are doing good while doing well in a lucrative private law practice because their advice and other legal services for clients lead to compliance with accepted public policy.[87] But some lawyers reject the lawyer-as-technician model that the traditional role suggests and instead select clients primarily on the basis of the lawyer's belief that advancing the particular client's interests would advance socially desirable goals that the lawyer also espouses.[88] Implicit in the notion is a belief that not all that the law permits or protects is in the public interest. Thus it becomes the responsibility of a public interest lawyer to pick and choose among possible clients to select only those whose legal claims will advance social or moral good. Historically such lawyers represented indigent clients in cases with important civil liberties or civil rights issues at stake. More recently representation has extended to such other areas as employment discrimination, environmental defense, and rights for the elderly or mentally ill.

Funding Public Interest Practice

One of the hallmarks of public interest practice is that lawyers attempt to provide representation to clients and causes that would otherwise not be represented.[89] As a natural result, public interest lawyers have quite often found it necessary to attempt to find funds to support a public interest practice because of the failure of the market to bring forward clients willing to expend personal assets to advocate public interest causes.[90]

Public interest practice acquired its present familiar name during the mid-1960s and received momentum from a series of annual grants from the Ford Foundation to public interest law firms that began in 1973[91] and

[87] Brandeis, The Opportunity in the Law, 39 Am.L.Rev. 555 (1905). See also Professional Responsibility: Report of the Joint Conference, 44 ABA J. 1159, 1160 (1958); Krash, Professional Responsibility to Clients and the Public Interest: Is There a Conflict?, 55 Chi.B.Rec. 31 (1975); Auerbach, Some Comments on Mr. Nader's Views, 54 Minn.L.Rev. 503 (1970); Fortas, Thurman Arnold and the Theater of the Law, 79 Yale L.J. 988, 996 (1970). Brandeis, however, criticized corporate lawyers of his day for not doing a better job of advising their corporate clients. For Brandeis their failing was in their neglect to advise corporations to recognize labor unions.

[88] Bellow & Kettleson, From Ethics to Politics: Confronting Scarcity and Fairness in Public Interest Practice, 58 Bost.U.L.Rev. 337, 337 (1978); Rabin, Lawyers for Social Change: Perspectives on Public Interest Law, 28 Stan.L.Rev. 207, 209 n.8 (1976).

[89] Concentration upon the interests of those unable to afford legal representation is a common element of those who bestow the term *public interest* upon a practice. E.g., G.Harrison, The Public Interest Law Firm—New Voices for New Constituencies 9 (1973); Cooke, Public Interest Law and Lawyers for the Public Interest, 34 Rec. A.B. City N.Y. 6, 7 (1979); Council for Public Interest Law, Balancing the Scales of Justice 3 (1976); Note, In Defense of an Embattled Mode of Advocacy: An Analysis and Justification of Public Interest Practice, 90 Yale L.J. 1436 (1981).

[90] For a review of funding sources for public interest law firms, see Council for Public Interest Law, Balancing the Scales of Justice: Financing Public Interest Law in America (1976). The failure of the market to create a demand for legal services in public interest areas is caused mainly by two quite different elements. First, and most obviously, some clients and their causes are poor and cannot afford legal services. That cause explains the traditional absence of much advocacy in such areas as welfare rights and race discrimination, which are of interest primarily, if not exclusively, to low-income persons. Second, some problems—such as a clean environment—cannot be litigated without overcoming substantial "free rider" problems. Most persons do not have a sufficient economic interest in a clean environment, safe products, or good government to be motivated to spend the enormous sums necessary to oppose heavily capitalized industries and their large law firms and governmental organizations and their legal staffs. Public interest organizations are able to aggregate the individual interests of many persons and support advocacy in such areas. Those persons may be relatively well-off, as is true generally of members of such advocacy organizations as the Sierra Club, Consumers Union, and the League of Women Voters.

[91] Ford Foundation, The Public Interest Law Firm: New Voices for New Constituencies (1973). The grants were designed to fund firms who were dedicated to pursuing legal claims in areas other than the traditional ones

ended in 1980.[92] Public interest firms and organizations now employ between five hundred and one thousand lawyers in over one hundred organizations.[93] It is primarily carried on in law offices supported by interest group foundations, as is the case of the National Association for the Advancement of Colored People Legal Defense Fund and the American Civil Liberties Union, two of the oldest public interest law organizations. Some lawyers also attempt to sustain a full- or part-time public interest practice with fee-generating cases in private law firms.[94] The increase in fee-shifting arrangements (§ 16.6) has given modest economic support to the concept.[95] Because of the insistence of some law school graduates that their careers offer such possibilities, some law firms have institutionalized public interest departments so that interested young associates and presumably other lawyers in the firm can participate in part-time public interest practice.[96] Calls for the organized bar to finance public interest firms [97] have gone largely unheeded. Efforts to create a greater supply of lawyers for public interest practice by imposing a requirement that lawyers donate time to such practice have also failed (§ 16.9).

Problematical Nature of the Claim to a Public Interest Practice

The implicit claim by public interest lawyers that *public interest* is a describable unitary concept carries important assumptions of a philosophical kind that are often unstated. There is in traditional political philosophy a conception of the "public good" as a legitimating end of political life. The presupposition of the modern welfare state as exemplified by most Western democracies is that the state reflects the communal concerns of all for the minimal welfare of all. But that theory of the state is under significant attack from theorists who portray the state as composed of interest groups, each of which strives with all others for a larger share of advantage.[98] It is only in the former sense that it is comprehensible to assert a claim to public interest law practice as opposed to special interest law

of civil rights and civil liberties, such as the environment and the rights of disabled persons, in order to provide legal assistance to interests that had not previously received legal representation.

[92] N.Y. Times, Jan.5, 1980, at 8, col.3.

[93] Lewin, Public Interest Bar Grows, Nat'l L.J., Jan.28, 1980, at 3, col.2 (survey by Council for Public Interest Law shows 117 public interest law centers employing 711 lawyers). The asserted unwillingness of lawyers to pursue careers in public interest law is probably due much more to the absence of employment than to a lack of commitment on the part of young lawyers. See Erlanger, Young Lawyers and Work in the Public Interest, 1978 Am.B.Found. Research J. 83.

[94] See generally F.Marks, K.Leswing & B.Fortinsky, The Lawyer, the Public, and Professional Responsibility ch. 6 (1972); Berlin, Roisman & Kessler, Public Interest Law, 38 Geo.Wash.L.Rev. 675 (1970). A distinct advantage of private-practice law firms is that they can be undeterred by limitations on lobbying activity that restrain public interest firms that are attempting to maintain a tax-exempt nonprofit status under 26 U.S.C.A. § 501(c)(3). See id. § 501(h)(lobbying expenditure ceiling). Procedures by which a public interest law firm could obtain tax-exempt status are contained in Rev.Proc. 71–39, 1971–1 C.B. 575, as amplified by Rev.Proc. 75–13, 1975–1 C.B. 662. The basic ruling, providing for tax-exempt status of public interest firms that provide representation in cases in which representation by traditional firms would not be economically feasible, is Rev.Rul. 75–74, 1975–1 C.B. 152. Receipt of court-awarded fee awards does not affect tax-exempt status. Rev.Rul. 75–76, 1975–1 C.B. 154.

[95] Fee shifting has been urged as an important way of funding public interest lawyers who wish to represent persons who are otherwise without funds to afford effective representation. See Hermann & Hoffman, Financing Public Interest Litigation in State Court: A Proposal for Legislative Action, 63 Corn.L.Rev. 173 (1978).

[96] Law firm arrangements are reviewed in F.Marks, The Lawyer, The Public, and Professional Responsibility 65–116 (1972). Very few firms have a long tradition of public interest work, id. at 78, and most that have inaugurated the practice did so because of pressure from law students, who expected to find such opportunities in firms that recruited them. Id. at 77. New Jersey created the office of public advocate to serve as a kind of state-funded public interest practice. See Comment, The Department of the Public Advocate—Public Interest Representation and Administrative Oversight, 30 Rut.L.Rev. 386 (1977); Mount Laurel Township v. Public Advocate, 83 N.J. 522, 416 A.2d 886 (1980).

[97] Marshall, Financing Public Interest Law Practice: The Role of the Organized Bar, 61 ABA J. 1487 (1975) (speech of Supreme Court Justice to committee of ABA); Rogovin, Public Interest Law: The Next Horizon, 63 ABA J. 334 (1977).

[98] In the political-economic realm, for example, see R.Posner, The Economics of Justice 103 (1981); Stigler, The Theory of Economic Regulation, 2 Bell J.Econ. & Mgmt. Sci. 3 (1971).

practice. And even if the public good is agreed upon as the focal point for definitional purposes, it is notorious that there is little possibility of consensus about exactly what is in the public interest or how that interest should be determined.[99] To all except those who ardently agree with a public interest lawyer's position, claiming the crown of public interest for one's advocacy is probably regarded most often as an attempt to wrap ideology in socially compelling rhetoric.

For a time, almost all organizations that called themselves public interest organizations were described by most persons as left-wing.[1] In the last decade, however, a number of right-wing public interest legal organizations have been funded, whose stated objective is to counteract existing public interest advocacy organizations.[2] In practice, one now confronts an array of organizations claiming to advocate the public interest in law that are splayed widely across the spectrum of possible social and political interest groups.

Designation as a public interest lawyer is more than a matter of possibly arrogating social good will or moral superiority. It is also connected to matters of independent legal significance. Organizations of public interest lawyers enjoy special legal advantages, such as the constitutionally protected right to solicit clients[3] and to be free of other governmental restraints that may be imposed upon non-advocacy organizations or persons.[4] Typically, however, the courts employ tests of eligibility for such special legal treatment that do not require a determination of whether the public interest is in fact served by the position advocated.

Public Interest Practice and the Principle of Professional Detachment

For many lawyers, the concept of public interest law practice, if in fact it is not used to describe all law practice,[5] is too narrow and unacceptably unprofessional.[6] If a claim by a lawyer that his or her client represents the public interest is taken seriously, one might imagine that a lawyer who opposes that lawyer in litigation in behalf of an adversary client is taking a position opposed to the public interest. While the second lawyer's work can still be legitimated under the concept of professional detachment (§ 10.2), the second lawyer's client is cast in the unfavorable political and moral light of being opposed to the

[99] See generally V.Held, The Public Interest and Individual Interests (1970); Nomos V: The Public Interest (C.Friedrich ed.1962); Cahn & Cahn, Power to the People or the Profession?—The Public Interest in Public Interest Law, 79 Yale L.J. 1005 (1970); Hegland, Beyond Enthusiasm and Commitment, 13 Ariz.L.Rev. 805 (1971).

[1] The temporary dominance of left-wing public interest groups provided artificial support for descriptions of public interest practice that characterized many early analyses. E.g., B.Weisbrod, J.Handler & N.Komesar, Public Interest Law 76–79 (1978).

[2] Blodgett, The Ralph Naders of the Right, 70 ABA J. 71 (1984); Nat'l L.J., May 23, 1983, at 1, col.2 (report on growth of extensively financed conservative public interest law firms); N.Y. Times, Apr.22, 1982, at B 10, col.3 (same); Nat'l L.J., Dec.24, 1979, at 1, col.1 (same).

[3] NAACP v. Button, 371 U.S. 415, 83 S.Ct. 328, 9 L.Ed. 2d 405 (1963); In re Primus, 436 U.S. 412, 98 S.Ct. 1893, 56 L.Ed.2d 417 (1978); Developmental Disabilities Advocacy Center, Inc. v. Melton, 689 F.2d 281, 287–88 (1st Cir. 1982). See generally § 16.5.2.

[4] United Automobile Workers v. National Right to Work Legal Defense Foundation, Inc., 590 F.2d 1139 (D.C. Cir. 1978).

[5] A resolution proposed to the ABA House of Delegates by the ABA Special Committee on Public Interest Practice in August 1975 defined public interest law as:

> Legal service provided without fee or at a substantially reduced fee, which falls into one or more of the following areas:
>
> 1. Poverty Law
> 2. Civil Rights Law
> 3. Public Rights Law
> 4. Charitable Organization Representation
> 5. Administration of Justice.

See S.Jaffe, Public Interest Law: Five Years Later 45 (1976).

Aside from the characteristic of free or reduced fee charges, there is little in the definition that defines.

[6] For reasons such as those mentioned in the text, efforts to obtain broad bar support for public interest practice have usually foundered at the definitional stage. E.g., Public Interest Practice Obligation, 62 ABA J. 1289 (1976)(report of amended resolution of ABA House of Delegates on implementation of 1975 ABA resolution concerning professional responsibility of all lawyers to provide public interest legal services).

public interest.[7] Of equal concern to some is the fact that wide acceptance of the concept of public interest representation would impair the operation of the principle of professional detachment itself because, unless lawyers were hopelessly at odds about the nature of the public interest, some clients with claims recognized by the legal system would receive no representation (§ 10.2.2).

WESTLAW REFERENCES

Nature of Public Interest Practice

di public interest

digest("public interest" /3 attorney lawyer (law /2 firm practice))

Funding Public Interest Practice

"public interest" /3 firm practice /s funding funded financing

Problematical Nature of the Claim to a Public Interest Practice

"public good" /5 means meaning defin!

§ 16.9 PRO BONO LEGAL SERVICES

Nature and Extent of Pro Bono Practice

Pro bono[8] service typically refers to legal work that lawyers do for free and that may have some public-spirited or charitable motivation behind it.[9] It might range from a lawyer's spending years of uncompensated effort to obtain the release of a person that the lawyer is convinced was convicted wrongfully to five minutes of free legal advice to a poor person unable to afford counsel.[10] The unique value in pro bono work that a lawyer might do is to provide legal services that would otherwise not be provided. Historically that has been the most important way in which legal services have been made available to persons not able to afford legal fees. Legal aid (§ 16.7.2) and government-funded legal service programs (§ 16.7.3) are quite recent. Court appointments of lawyers, which are themselves a form of mandated pro bono, have been rare in civil cases.

Pro bono is hardly a precise term. If asked to describe their pro bono work, lawyers often employ the phrase expansively to cover any useful work of a charitable or good-citizenship nature that is done without compensation.[11] But that work, while doubtless worthwhile, is not work unique to lawyers and might involve self-interested motivations, such as when a lawyer seeks to curry favor with judges, prospective clients, or other lawyers. Time spent on bar committee work or in government legal service, while specifically legal, often does not supply services that would otherwise be unavailable and often reflects a self-interested effort to shape public policy to the lawyer's liking. Pro bono work is performed out of a spirit of service and fulfills needs that would otherwise go unmet. Lawyer time that is

7 One of the few bar-funded public interest firms, the Beverly Hills Bar Association Law Foundation, was dissolved after several stormy years of conflict between its staff and lawyers and bar officials whose funds supported it, primarily over issues affecting clients of private practice lawyers who were members of the bar association. See J.Handler, E.Hollingsworth & H.Erlanger, Lawyers and the Pursuit of Legal Rights 111–12 (1978).

8 The full Latin phrase is pro bono publico—"for the good of the public"—but the *publico* is hardly ever mentioned. Without that adjective, the phrase loses whatever substantive content it otherwise possesses. It attributes to lawyers perhaps too much familiarity with Latin to conclude that the omission is a Freudian slip. But cf. Smurl, In the Public Interest: The Precedents and Standards of a Lawyer's Public Responsibility, 11 Ind.L.Rev. 797, 801 (1978).

9 Work for free or at reduced fees may also reflect the workings of a complex set of relationships in which lawyers feel obliged to perform the work because they are requested to do so by friends, relatives, other clients, or persons who are the source of clients or other benefits. The importance of such "intermediaries" in pro bono practice is investigated in Lochner, The No Fee and Low Fee Legal Practice of Private Attorneys, 9 Law & Soc'y Rev. 431 (1975).

10 Methods and suggested structures for arranging pro bono services within law firms, general counsel offices in corporations, and government legal offices are suggested in ABA Spec. Comm. on Public Interest Practice, Implementing the Lawyer's Public Interest Practice Obligation (1977); and ABA Young Lawyers Section, Opening the Door for Pro Bono (1980).

11 F.Marks, K.Leswing, B.Fortinsky, The Lawyer, the Public, and Professional Responsibility 8 (1972)(in survey, lawyers listed as pro bono work such activities as serving on boards of symphony orchestras, opera associations, hospitals, and school districts and umpiring in Little League baseball games).

otherwise spent in uncompensated pursuits, while doubtless valuable in many cases, is the sort of labor that many lawyers would willingly accept in order to gain the personal benefits, other than moral satisfaction, that accompany them.

Lawyers have regarded pro bono work with professional pride. It is supposedly one of the distinguishing features that marks off a profession from a self-interested business pursuit.[12] It can also be a burden if it imposes too much on a lawyer's time or if a lawyer is not convinced that the object of benevolence is unable to pay.[13] The line between eager volunteerism, reluctant compliance, and rejection is obviously dependent on the lawyer's own sense of professional and personal values. Studies have reached conflicting conclusions about the extent to which lawyers in fact engage in pro bono work. Bar leaders tend to assert that lawyers engage in a great deal of pro bono work, although they stop short of asserting that the pro bono work actually done is sufficient to fulfill the needs for legal services of those unable to pay. Probably many lawyers, perhaps a majority, engage in no pro bono work and the bulk of the work is performed by the few.[14] Some few lawyers, such as judges in jurisdictions that prohibit judges from practicing law, may be legally precluded from pro bono practice.[15] Lawyers in large firms are often assumed to be extensively engaged in pro bono services, as a function of noblesse oblige and their greater opportunity to do so without great financial sacrifice.[16] But solo practitioners probably perform more pro bono work in the precise sense [17] because they more frequently come into contact with people who need legal services and are unable to pay a fee.

Whatever the precise level of actual pro bono work by lawyers, it is clear that the extent of pro bono work has never begun to match the need for legal services of poor people. Traditionally the ethical rules have contained only general exhortations to lawyers to be generous in order to make legal services available to those unable to afford them, but no specific statement that any individual lawyer is required to perform pro bono services. The Code's EC 2–25, noting that the need of the poor for legal services has been met "in part" by lawyers who volunteer their services, exhorts lawyers to "find time to participate in serving the disadvantaged" and states that rendition of such services "continues to be an obligation of each lawyer" despite the availability of legal aid and legal services programs.[18] Because the statements, however strong, are not duplicated in a Disci-

[12] R.Pound, The Lawyer from Antiquity to Modern Times 5 (1953).

[13] The ABA has occasionally chided charitable organizations for assuming that they should comfortably rely on free legal services by volunteer lawyers. See Nat'l Conf. of Lawyers and Social Workers, Statement on Legal Counsel for Voluntary Social Agencies (approved by ABA, 1965), in 7 Martindale-Hubbell 84M, 85M (1978)(lawyers who are board members of social agencies "ought not to be expected" to contribute free legal services in addition to time spent on board, for they are usually very busy; their board term may be limited, resulting in periodic change in source of advice; and "legal advice is a valuable commodity," which "ought to be paid for like" other professional and trade services).

[14] Lawpoll: Public Interest Legal Services, 68 ABA J. 912 (1982)(68 percent of polled lawyers engage in some public interest practice, but most heavily served clients are charitable organizations); Handler, Hollingsworth, Erlanger & Ladinsky, The Public Interest Activities of Private Practice Lawyers, 61 ABA J. 1388 (1975)(substantially reproduced in J.Handler, E.Hollingsworth & H.Erlanger, Lawyers and the Pursuit of Legal Rights 92–101 (1978)(60 percent of lawyers report spending less than 5 percent of billable hours on pro bono work; lawyers who did most of the pro bono work during billable hours were also more likely to do after-hours pro bono work; most work was for relatives or friends or for organizations to which lawyer belonged and concerned routine legal services not involving social change). See also § 16.7.1, at n.13.

[15] Lawyers employed by a government may also be barred from certain kinds of pro bono work by restrictions on representing a client against the governmental employer. E.g., 18 U.S.C.A. § 205 (1982)(federal employee may not represent client in action against either federal government or government of District of Columbia).

[16] Large firms have been urged to encourage pro bono work and structure the work assignments of lawyers in ways that facilitate that involvement. Note, Structuring the Public Service Efforts of Private Law Firms, 84 Harv. L.Rev. 410, 411 (1970).

[17] Handler, Hollingsworth, Erlanger & Ladinsky, supra n.14 at 1392–93.

[18] Cf. also EC 8–3 ("Those persons unable to pay for legal services should be provided needed services.").

plinary Rule (§ 2.6.3), it is clear that in most states the obligation referred to is not enforceable through professional discipline.

Calls for more lawyer participation in pro bono legal services intensified during the 1970s as efforts expanded to provide legal services to the poor (§ 16.7.3). In 1975 the ABA House of Delegates adopted a resolution stating that it is "the basic professional responsibility of each lawyer engaged in the practice of law to provide public interest legal services."[19] Model Rule 6.1, as originally proposed in early 1980, would have imposed an enforceable mandatory duty on every lawyer to perform pro bono services.[20] Loud and sustained opposition from the bar[21] led to a retreat to a rule that, although it states that a lawyer "should" perform pro bono services, is plainly only precatory.[22] The only institutional responsibility, then, that the organized legal profession in the United States has ever accepted for providing legal services to the poor is to employ the admittedly limited and inefficacious powers of bar association and regulatory exhortation.

Court Appointments

Most judicial systems have historically relied on appointment systems to provide counsel to persons who were not represented and have insisted that lawyers be required to serve without compensation if the appointment system provides none.[23] The appointment systems are predominantly concerned with criminal defense, although some apply to civil litigants who wish to proceed with a court-appointed lawyer or, as it is sometimes called, in forma pauperis.[24] Appointment systems almost invariably operate with panels of volunteer lawyers.[25] In the occasional case in

19 ABA Ann.Rep. 11–12 (1975).

20 MR 8.1 (Discussion Draft, January 30, 1980). A draft that was not officially circulated would have required forty hours of free legal services per year. See Nat'l L.J., Oct.29, 1979, at 2., col.2. That, as well as all mandatory pro bono proposals, suffer to an extent because they require only self-reporting and thus could easily be evaded in bad faith without any fear of detection. The unpublished draft proposal was similar to a proposal, which appeared almost simultaneously, adopted by a majority of the Special Committee on the Lawyer's Pro Bono Obligations of the Association of the Bar of the City of New York, Recommendation and Report: Toward a Mandatory Contribution of Public Service Practice by Every Lawyer (1979). The committee proposal would have provided for a minimum of thirty hours of pro bono work annually, increasing to a range of between forty and seventy hours. Eligible pro bono work was rather broadly defined but excluded general bar association and continuing legal education work and community services of a nonlegal kind. The proposal was rejected by the association's executive committee. See 36 Rec. Ass'n B. City N.Y. 9 (1981).

21 Humbach, Serving the Public Interest: An Overstated Objective, 65 ABA J. 564 (1979).

22 MR 6.1 comment (first paragraph)(MR 6.1 expresses "policy" adopted by ABA in 1975 resolution on pro bono services, "but is not intended to be enforced through disciplinary process"). The nonenforceable nature of the MR 6.1 "should" was clearly stated in the suppressed legal background note that accompanied interim drafts. See MR 6.1 legal background note (Proposed Final Draft, May 30, 1981)("Rule 6.1 continues the nonobligatory professional standard set forth in the current Code"). In 1983 the Florida Supreme Court rejected an amendment to the state's bar rules, which was proposed by a group of lawyers and opposed by the state bar, that would have mandated either twenty-five hours of free legal services to the poor, a payment of $500 to a bar foundation providing free legal services, or participation in the bar's interest-on-trust-accounts program, whose funds also went to the foundation. See In re Emergency Delivery of Legal Services to the Poor, 432 So.2d 39 (Fla.1983).

23 On the operation of appointment systems generally, see § 14.3.5. For a history of the very occasional appointment of counsel in both civil and, to a somewhat greater extent, criminal cases, see Shapiro, The Enigma of the Lawyer's Duty to Serve, 55 NYU L.Rev. 735, 739–62 (1980).

24 See generally, e.g., 28 U.S.C.A. § 1915(a)(general in forma pauperis statute); Whisenant v. Yuam, 739 F.2d 160 (4th Cir.1984)(because of exceptional circumstances, district court abused discretion by failing to appoint counsel for plaintiff in civil rights action seeking recovery of damages); Merritt v. Faulkner, 697 F.2d 761 (7th Cir.), cert.denied 464 U.S. 986, 104 S.Ct. 434, 78 L.Ed.2d 366 (1983) (same). See generally Catz & Guyer, Federal in Forma Pauperis Litigation: In Search of Judicial Standards, 31 Rutg.L.Rev. 655 (1978). The federal statute authorizes a court merely to permit a litigant to proceed without prepayment of costs and to appoint counsel by requesting a lawyer to serve; it does not provide any mechanism for paying a lawyer. Lewis v. Precision Optics, Inc., 612 F.2d 1074 (8th Cir.1980).

25 Nelson v. Redfield Lithograph Printing, 728 F.2d 1003 (8th Cir.1984)(incumbent on chief judge of each federal district to seek cooperation of bar associations and federal practice committees to develop list of volunteer lawyers for civil pro bono cases). The fact that a lawyer is appointed by a court under a plan that provides for no compensation for the lawyer does not preclude a court from ordering that the lawyer be paid a fee at prevailing market rates under an otherwise available fee-shifting statute or rule. Blum v. Stenson, ___ U.S. ___, 104 S.Ct.

which the issue has arisen, courts have insisted that a lawyer's compliance with a court appointment is a matter of professional obligation even if the lawyer is ordered to serve without compensation.[26] At least one case has resulted in a lawyer's discipline for refusing to comply with a court-appointment order.[27] The burdens of court appointments that are imposed on lawyers have probably come to be increasingly uneven and inequitable. Courts and appointment systems tend to draft lawyers who practice in the areas in which the appointment is needed (criminal defense and welfare law) or who frequently appear in court. Those tend to be lawyers who already serve the poor and who may be among the least well paid in the legal profession.[28] Appointments are rare among senior lawyers who practice the much more lucrative trade of corporate practice.

Mandatory Pro Bono

The failure of voluntary pro bono efforts and court-appointment systems to provide adequate service to the poor in an equitable way has inspired proposals, such as that of the commission that drafted the 1983 Model Rules, to require lawyers to perform free legal services. Lawyers in general have strongly opposed them.[29] Few jurisdictions have seriously considered them. Proponents of mandatory pro bono have advanced several supporting arguments, including arguments based on assumed characteristics of a profession [30] or on lawyers' burdens as officers of the court,[31] the uniqueness of the services performed by lawyers,[32] and the fact that lawyers have created a monopoly on legal services by precluding others from practicing law through strict unauthorized practice limitations.[33]

To date, the argument against mandatory pro bono have carried the day. The chief arguments against such a duty are that making pro bono mandatory demeans the charita-

1541, 79 L.Ed.2d 891 (1984); Watkins v. Mobile Housing Bd., 632 F.2d 565, 567 (5th Cir.1980)(per curiam): Folsom v. Butte Cty. Ass'n of Governments, 32 Cal.3d 668, 186 Cal.Rptr. 589, 652 P.2d 437 (1982).

26 Bradshaw v. United States District Court, 742 F.2d 515 (9th Cir.1984)(dicta)(in some situations, district courts may have power to order lawyer to represent in forma pauperis plaintiff in civil case); United States v. Dillon, 346 F.2d 633 (9th Cir.1965), cert.denied 382 U.S. 978, 86 S.Ct. 550, 15 L.Ed.2d 469 (1966); Yarbrough v. Superior Court, 150 Cal.App.3d 388, 197 Cal.Rptr. 737 (1983); State v. Keener, 224 Kan. 100, 577 P.2d 1182, 1184–85 (1978), cert.denied 439 U.S. 953, 99 S.Ct. 350, 58 L.Ed.2d 344 (1978); State v. Rush, 46 N.J. 399, 411–12, 217 A.2d 441 (1966); Sontag v. State, 629 P.2d 1269 (Okl.Crim.App. 1981), cert.denied 454 U.S. 1142, 102 S.Ct. 1001, 71 L.Ed. 2d 294 (1982); State ex rel. Acocella v. Allen, 288 Or. 175, 604 P.2d 391, 394 (1979); In re Hamaas, 279 S.C 592, 310 S.E.2d 440 (App.Ct.1983). See also, e.g., Nat'l L.J., Oct. 11, 1982, at 2, col.3 (order of judges in El Paso, Texas, that each lawyer in county take two divorce cases without compensation each year because of backlog threatened by cutback in funding of Legal Services Corporation).

27 In re Hunoval, 294 N.C. 740, 247 S.E.2d 230 (1977) (lawyer's refusal to file petition for certiorari because of his belief that he would not be paid warrants twelve-month suspension under aggravated circumstances). See also In re Spann, 183 N.J.Super. 62, 443 A.2d 239 (1982) (contempt sanction upheld).

28 Cheatham, Availability of Legal Services: The Responsibility of the Individual Lawyer and of the Organized Bar, 12 UCLA L.Rev. 438, 444 (1965)(neither lawyer, grocer, nor house builder should be required to provide free stock in trade to needy, particularly because burden would fall disproportionately upon solo practitioners, who tend to be much closer to poor clients); Note, The Uncompensated Appointed Counsel System: A Constitutional and Social Transgression, 60 Ky.L.Rev. 710 (1972).

29 Lawpoll: Public Interest Legal Services, 68 ABA J. 912 (1982)(81 percent of lawyers polled currently opposed mandatory pro bono, against 88 percent who opposed in 1978; but 49 percent of law students polled favored mandatory pro bono).

30 F.Marks, K.Leswing & B.Fortinsky, The Lawyer, the Public, and Professional Responsibility 280–81 (1972); Christensen, The Lawyer's Pro Bono Publico Responsibility, 1981 Am.B.Found. Research J. 1, 7–14; Smith, A Mandatory Pro Bono Service Standard—Its Time Has Come, 35 Emory L.J. 727 (1981).

31 Rosenfeld, Mandatory Pro Bono: Historical and Constitutional Perspectives, 2 Cardozo L.Rev. 255, 279–82 (1981), and authorities cited.

32 Spec. Comm. on Lawyer's Pro Bono Obligations, Ass'n of Bar City N.Y., Recommendation and Report: Toward a Mandatory Contribution of Public Service Practice by Every Lawyer 9 (1979).

33 C.Fried, Right and Wrong 188 n. (1978); Christensen, The Lawyer's Pro Bono Publico Responsibility, 1981 Am. B.Found. Research J. 1, 14–18; Spencer, Mandatory Public Service for Attorneys: A Proposal for the Future, 12 S.W.U.L.Rev. 493, 500–01 (1981); F.Marks, K.Leswing & B.Fortinsky, The Lawyer, The Public, and Professional Responsibility 288–93 (1972).

ble instinct that should characterize it [34] and that lawyers should not be singled out by the state to donate their valuable services unless similar burdens are imposed on doctors, dentists, and other similarly situated professionals.[35] A pro bono requirement does have the inevitable effect of mandating a transfer of wealth, either from the lawyer personally or, if the lawyer is able to transfer its burdens to other clients through higher fees, from paying clients.[36] Constitutionally based forms of the argument include characterizations of the requirement as involuntary servitude, a denial of equal protection because of the invidious treatment of lawyers compared to other professionals, and an uncompensated taking of lawyers' property.[37] A broader form of the argument is that the duty to provide counsel to indigent persons is a duty of society, and not of lawyers.[38]

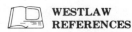

WESTLAW REFERENCES

Nature and Extent of Pro Bono

di pro bono

digest("pro bono")

78k13.17(21)

"pro bono" /p "bar association" "professional responsibility"

Court Appointments

"pro bono" /p court /3 appoint!

di in forma pauperis

Mandatory Pro Bono

"pro bono" /s mandatory requir! obligat!

---

34 Sundberg, Professional Duty and Pro Bono, 55 Fla. B.J. 502, 503 (1981).

35 Shapiro, The Enigma of the Lawyer's Duty to Serve, 55 NYU L.Rev. 735, 775 (1980); Sellinger, Equality in the Relief of Destitution Abroad: A Test Case in Distinguishing Duties from Charity, in 2 Windsor Yearbook of Access to Justice 53, 72–73 (1982).

36 G.Hazard, Ethics in the Practice of Law 87–88 (1978).

37 The constitutional arguments are reviewed and, rightly, rejected in Rosenfeld, Mandatory Pro Bono: Historical and Constitutional Perspective, 2 Cardozo L.Rev. 255 (1981); Torres & Stansky, In Support of a Mandatory Public Service Obligation, 29 Emory L.J. 997, 1015–20 (1980); and Note, Court Appointment of Attorneys in Civil Cases: The Constitutionality of Uncompensated Legal Assistance, 81 Colum.L.Rev. 366 (1981). For other considerations of the constitutional arguments, see, e.g., Shapiro, The Enigma of the Lawyer's Duty to Serve, 55 NYU L.Rev. 735, 762–77 (1980); Hunter, Slave Labor in the Courts—A Suggested Solution, 74 Case & Comm. 3 (1969); Ervin, Uncompensated Counsel: They Do Not Meet the Constitutional Mandate, 49 ABA J. 435 (1963). If a jurisdiction's mandatory plan requires the lawyer to make out-of-pocket payments, such as for filing fees of a court-appointed client, the system is more susceptible to constitutional attack as an uncompensated taking. See Williamson v. Vardeman, 674 F.2d 1211 (8th Cir.1982).

38 Fried, The Lawyer as Friend: The Moral Foundations of the Lawyer-Client Relation, 85 Yale L.J. 1060, 1079 (1976).

*

Appendix A
WESTLAW REFERENCES

I. INTRODUCTION

This informational appendix is designed to aid the reader in the general use of the WESTLAW system and more specifically to demonstrate how WESTLAW can be used in conjunction with this text to help make research in the area of professional responsibility law swift and complete.

II. THE WESTLAW SYSTEM

WESTLAW is a computer-assisted legal research service of West Publishing Company. It is accessible through a number of different types of computer terminals. The materials available through WESTLAW are contained in databases stored at the central computer in St. Paul, Minnesota.

To use the WESTLAW service a "query" or search request, is typed into the terminal and sent to the central computer. There it is processed and all of the documents that satisfy the search request are identified. The text of each of these documents is then stored on magnetic disks and transmitted to the user via a telecommunication network. This data then appears on the user's terminal, where it may be reviewed and evaluated. The user must then decide if the displayed documents are pertinent or if further research is desired. If further research is necessary, the query may be recalled for editing, or an entirely new query may be sent. Documents displayed on the terminal may be printed or, on some terminals, the text may be stored on its own magnetic disks.

III. IMPROVING LEGAL RESEARCH WITH WESTLAW

The WESTLAW system is designed for use in conjunction with the more traditional tools of legal research. In principle, WESTLAW works as an index to primary and secondary legal materials. Yet it differs from traditional digests and indices in that more terms can be researched, and more documents retrieved.

Through WESTLAW it is possible to index, or search for any significant term or combination of terms in an almost infinite variety of grammatical relationships by formulating a query composed of those terms. Unlike manual systems of secondary legal sources that reference only a few key terms in each document, WESTLAW is capable of indexing every key word. This enables documents to be located using terms not even listed in manual reference systems.

In addition to its expanded search term capabilities, WESTLAW, through its numerous databases, enables the user to research issues in any and every jurisdiction quickly and efficiently. The queries found in this text are primarily designed to access WESTLAW's federal and state case law databases. However, WESTLAW provides access to many specialized libraries as well. For example, WESTLAW contains separate topical databases for areas of federal and state law such as tax, securities, energy, and government contracts.

WESTLAW also includes the text of the United States Code and the Code of Federal

Regulations, the Federal Register, West's INSTA-CITE™, Shepard's® Citations, *Black's Law Dictionary* and many other legal sources. Furthermore, because new cases are continuously being added to the WESTLAW databases as they are decided by the courts, the documents retrieved will include the most current law available on any given issue.

In addition, WESTLAW queries augment the customary role of footnotes to the hornbook text by directing the user to a wider range of supporting authorities. Readers may use the preformulated queries supplied in this edition "as is" or formulate their own queries in order to retrieve cases relevant to the points of law discussed in the text.

IV. QUERY FORMULATION

a. General Principles

The art of query formulation is the heart of WESTLAW research. Although the researcher can gain technical skills by using the terminal, there is no strictly mechanical procedure for formulating queries. One must first comprehend the meaning of the legal issue to be researched before beginning a search on WESTLAW. Then the user will need to supply imagination, insight, and legal comprehension with knowledge of the capabilities of WESTLAW to formulate a useful query. Effective query formulation requires an alternative way of thinking about the legal research process.

Using WESTLAW is a constant balancing between generating too many documents and missing important documents. In general, it is better to look through a reasonable number of irrelevant documents than it is to be too restrictive and miss important material. The researcher should take into consideration at the initial query formulation stage what he or she will do if too many, or not enough documents are retrieved. Thought should be given as to how the query might be narrowed or the search broadened, and what can be done if the initial search retrieves zero documents.

Some issues by their very nature will require more lengthy queries than others; however, it is best to strive for efficiency in structuring the query. Look for unique search terms that will eliminate the need for a lengthy query. Keep in mind that WESTLAW is literal. Consider all possible alternative terms. Especially consider inherent limitations of the computer. It doesn't think, create, or make analogies. The researcher must do that for the computer. The computer is designed to look for the terms in the documents in relationships specified by the query. The researcher should know what he or she is looking for, at least to the extent of knowing how the terms are likely to show up in relevant documents. Always keep in mind the parameters of the system as to date and database content.

The WESTLAW Reference Manual should be consulted for more information on query formulation and WESTLAW commands. The Reference Manual is updated periodically to reflect new enhancements of WESTLAW. It provides detailed and comprehensive instructions on all aspects of the WESTLAW system and offers numerous illustrative examples on the proper format for various types of queries. Material contained in the Reference Manual enables the user to benefit from all of the system's capabilities in an effective and efficient manner.

b. The WESTLAW Query Defined

The query is a message to WESTLAW. It instructs the computer to retrieve documents containing terms in the grammatical relationships specified by the query. The terms in a query are made up of words and/or numbers that pinpoint the legal issue to be researched.

An example of the kind of preformulated queries that appear in this publication is reproduced below. The queries corresponding to each section of the text appear at the end of the section.

The query appearing below is taken from Chapter 8, Section 8.2.3, and appears at the end of this section of the text.

```
conflict*** /4 interest /s attorney lawyer
counsel** /s duty (ethical** /3 obligat***)
/s advise inform /9 court
```

This query instructs WESTLAW to retrieve documents containing a form of the root CONFLICT within four words of INTEREST within the same sentence as ATTORNEY, LAWYER, or a form of the root COUNSEL, all within the same sentence as DUTY, or a form of the root ETHICAL, within three words of a form of the root OBLIGAT, all within the same sentence as ADVISE or INFORM, all within nine words of COURT.

This query illustrates what a standard request to WESTLAW looks like—words or numbers describing an issue, tied together by connectors. These connectors tell WESTLAW in what relationships the terms must appear. WESTLAW will retrieve all documents from the database that contain the terms appearing in those relationships.

The material that follows explains the methods by which WESTLAW queries are formulated, and shows how users of *Modern Legal Ethics* can employ the preformulated queries in this publication in their research of professional responsibility law. In addition, there are instructions that will enable readers to modify their queries to fit the particular needs of their research.

c. *Selection of Terms*

After determining the legal issue that is to be researched, the first step in query formulation is to select the key terms from the issue that will be used as search terms in the query. Words, numbers, and various other symbols may be used as search terms.

The goal in choosing search terms is to select the most unique terms for the issue. In selecting such terms it is frequently helpful to imagine how the terms might appear in the language of the documents that will be searched by the query. Moreover, it is necessary to consider the grammatical and editorial structure of the document. This involves a consideration of how the writer of the document (i.e., judge or headnote and synopsis writer) has worded both the factual and legal components of the issue involved in the case.

Although traditional book research generally starts with a consideration of the general legal concepts under which particular problems are subsumed, WESTLAW research starts with a consideration of specific terms that are likely to appear in documents that have addressed those problems. This is so because documents are retrieved from WESTLAW on the basis of the terms they contain. The more precise the terms, the more relevant the search results will be. For example, in researching obscenity and the Twenty-First Amendment, inclusion of the unique terms "Twenty-First Amendment" or "equal protection" rather than say the common term "constitution" would retrieve more specific, and hopefully more pertinent documents.

Once the initial search terms have been selected for a query, it is important to consider synonyms, antonyms, and other alternatives for the search terms. A space left between each of these alternative terms will be read as an "or" in WESTLAW. (See section d: Query Formulation: Proximity Connectors.) The nature of the legal issue will determine which alternative terms are desirable.

d. *The Format of Search Terms*

Once the key search terms have been selected, it is necessary to consider the proper form in which the term should appear in the query. As WESTLAW is literal in its search for terms, and as a term may appear in a variety of ways, derivative forms of each search term must be considered. There are two devices available on WESTLAW for automatically generating alternative forms of search terms in a query. The first of these is the Unlimited Root Expander, the symbol (!). Placement of the ! symbol at the end of the root term generates other forms containing the same root. For example, adding the ! symbol to the root REINSTAT in the following query:

reinstat! /p attorney

instructs the computer to generate the words REINSTATE, REINSTATES, REINSTATED, REINSTATING, and REINSTATEMENT as search terms for the query. Yet time and space are saved by not having to include each of these alternatives in the query.

The second device used to automatically generate alternative forms of search terms is the Universal Character, the symbol (*). This symbol permits the generation of all possible characters by placing one or more asterisks at the location in the term where the universal character is desired. For example, placing three asterisks on the root DISCIPLIN in the following query:

disciplin*** /s lawyer

instructs the computer to generate all forms of the root term with up to three additional characters. Thus, the terms DISCIPLINE, DISCIPLINES, DISCIPLINED, DISCIPLINING, and DISCIPLINARY would be generated by this query. The symbol * may also be embedded inside of a term as in the following query:

int**state /s practice

This will generate the alternative terms INTERSTATE and INTRASTATE without the need to enter both terms. As WESTLAW automatically generates plural forms for search terms (e.g., the endings -s -es and -ies) it is generally unnecessary to use the root expansion devices to obtain plural forms of search terms.

e. Proximity Connectors

Once the search terms and alternate search terms have been selected the next consideration is how these terms may be ordered so as to retrieve the most relevant documents. The connectors and their meanings appear below.

1. *Space (or).* A space between search terms is read as an "or" by WESTLAW. For example, leaving a space between the query terms ATTORNEY and LAWYER:

attorney lawyer

instructs the computer to retrieve documents that contain either the word ATTORNEY or the word LAWYER or both.

2. *(&) Ampersand.* The symbol & means "and." Placing it between two terms instructs the computer to retrieve documents that contain both of the terms without regard to word order. For example, inserting the & between the terms ATTORNEY and DISCIPLINARY:

attorney & disciplinary

commands the computer to retrieve documents that contain both the term ATTORNEY and the term DISCIPLINARY anywhere in the text. The ampersand may also be placed between groups of alternative terms. By placing an & between ATTORNEY or LAWYER and DISCIPLINARY or DISBARMENT:

attorney lawyer & disciplinary disbarment

documents containing the terms ATTORNEY and/or LAWYER and the terms DISCIPLINARY and/or DISBARMENT may be retrieved.

3. */p (same paragraph).* The /p symbol means "within the same paragraph." It requests that the terms to the left of the /p appear within the same paragraph as the terms to the right of the connector. For example, placing the /p between MALPRACTICE and MISREPRESENT:

malpractice /p misrepresent

instructs the computer to retrieve documents in which both the terms MALPRACTICE and MISREPRESENT appear in the same paragraph. The terms on each side of the /p connector may appear in the document in any order within the paragraph. As with the & connector the /p may be placed between groups of alternative terms. Thus, the query

malpractice negligence /p misrepresent fraud

will succeed in retrieving all documents in which the terms MALPRACTICE and/or NEGLIGENCE appear in the same paragraph as MISREPRESENT and/or FRAUD.

4. */s (same sentence).* The /s symbol requires that the search terms so connected

occur within the same sentence. A /s placed between LAWYER and CONFIDENTIAL

lawyer /s confidential

will retrieve documents that contain the words LAWYER and CONFIDENTIAL in the same sentence, without regard to which of these terms occur first in the sentence. As with the previous connectors, the /s may be placed between groups of alternative terms. Inserting the /s between the terms LAWYER or COUNSEL and CONFIDENTIAL or SECRET

lawyer counsel /s confidential secret

instructs the computer to retrieve documents with the terms LAWYER and/or COUNSEL and the terms CONFIDENTIAL and/or SECRET regardless of which terms appear first.

5. *+s (precedes within sentence).* The +s symbol requires that the term to the left of the +s connector precede the terms to the right of the connector within the same sentence. The query

former +s government

instructs the computer to retrieve all documents in which the word FORMER precedes the word GOVERNMENT where both words appear in the same sentence. This connector may also be used between groups of alternative terms. Thus, the query

former previous +s government agency

commands the computer to retrieve all documents in which the terms FORMER and/or PREVIOUS precedes the terms GOVERNMENT and/or AGENCY in the same sentence.

6. */n (numerical proximity—within n words).* The /n symbol means "within n words." Where n represents any whole number between 1 and 255, inclusive. It requests that the term to the left of the /n appear within the designated number of words as terms to the right of the connector. For example, in the following query:

conflict /3 interest

the computer is instructed to retrieve all documents in which the term CONFLICT appears within 3 words of the term INTEREST, without regard to word order. In addition, the + symbol may be used to require that the terms to the left of the numerical proximity connector precede the terms to the right of the connector. Thus, the query above could be altered to require that CONFLICT precede INTEREST by no more than 3 words by replacing the /3 connector with the +3 connector.

conflict +3 interest

Both the /n and the +n connectors may also be used between groups of alternative search terms. For example:

joint dual +3 representation

instructs the computer to retrieve all documents in which the words JOINT or DUAL occur within the three words preceding the words REPRESENTATION.

7. *" " (quotation marks).* The " " (quotation marks) symbol is the most restrictive grammatical connector. When used to enclose search terms it requires that the computer retrieve only those documents in which enclosed terms appear exactly as they do within the quotation marks. For example, placing the following words within quotation marks

"professional responsibility"

commands the computer to retrieve all documents in which the terms PROFESSIONAL and RESPONSIBILITY occur in precisely the same order as they do within the quotation marks.

The quotation marks symbol is especially effective when searching for legal terms of art, legal concepts, or legal entities that occur together as multiple terms. Some examples are:

"disciplinary rule" "ethical consideration" "moral turpitude"

8. *% (exclusion/but not).* The % symbol may be translated as "but not." It instructs the computer to exclude documents that contain terms appearing after the percentage symbol. For example, to retrieve documents containing the term RIGHT within the three words of COUNSEL but not the term CRIMINAL, the following query would be used:

right /3 counsel % criminal

Any document containing the word CRIMINAL would automatically be excluded in the document search.

The connectors described above may be used in a variety of combinations, enabling the user to fine-tune a query to meet his or her specific research needs.

V. ADVANCED SEARCH TECHNIQUES

a. The Field Search

Within any given database a more specialized search may be conducted. Rather than searching the entire text of a case for a designated query term, the search may be limited to specific portions of the case by conducting a "field search." A search may be restricted to a particular field (or portion) of a document by incorporating the field name into the query, followed by the field search terms enclosed in parenthesis.

The fields available for WESTLAW case law databases are described below.

1. *Title Field:* The title field may be used to retrieve a particular case on WESTLAW. The ampersand, rather than the v. is used between the names of the parties. Thus, to retrieve the case entitled *Maryland State Bar Association, Inc. v. Spiro T. Agnew* the following query would be used:

```
title(maryland & agnew)
```

2. *Citation Field:* The citation field may be used for any document for which a citation exists in the WESTLAW databases. The proper database must first be selected. A numerical proximity connector is then used instead of the publication name to separate volume and page number. For example, to retrieve the case appearing at 318 A.2d 811, the Atlantic database must be selected. The following query may then be used:

```
citation(318 +7 811)
```

3. *Court Field:* The court field permits searches for case law to be restricted to particular states, districts, or courts. The correct database in which to conduct the search must be chosen. For example, to restrict a search to cases appearing in the Atlantic Reporter from the District of Columbia and Maryland, the following query could be used in the "atl" database:

```
court(dc md) & 45k38
```

4. *Judge Field:* A search may be limited to the individual or majority opinion of a particular judge. To retrieve all cases in which Justice Powell has authored an opinion the following query would be used:

```
judge(powell)
```

5. *Synopsis Field:* The synopsis field consists of the editorially prepared summary of the case found immediately after the title. By reading the synopsis it may be determined if the decision generally encompasses the legal issue being researched without reading the entire decision.

The synopsis field search can be especially useful in focusing broad queries which might retrieve too many cases if the entire case was searched. For example, the following query would limit retrieval to cases in which the American Rule in fee shifting was a key element:

```
synopsis("american rule")
```

6. *Topic Field:* The topic field contains the West topics and Key Numbers assigned to the headnotes in a case. A search in this field may be conducted by using either the West topic name or by using the West topic number designated for that topic. For example, the West digest topic of Attorney and Client has been given the number 45. Thus, in order to retrieve cases classified under the digest topic Attorney and Client either of these two queries could be used:

```
topic("attorney and client") /p represent! /4 child! juvenile minor incompetent
```

or

```
topic(45) /p represent! /4 child! juvenile minor incompetent
```

7. *Digest Field:* The digest field contains digest paragraphs prepared by West editors. It includes headnotes, corresponding digest topics and Key Numbers, the title and citation of the case, courts, and year of decision. The digest field can be used to search for terms which are not among the West topic headings. For example, the following query

may be used to research conflict of interest cases even though this is not one of the West topic headings.

digest((conflict! /3 interest) /s attorney lawyer counsel**)

8. *Headnote Field:* A headnote search limits the search to the language of the headnote, exclusive of the digest topic and Key Number lines and case identification information. Thus, the headnote field is useful in conducting a search where exclusion of the topic name, the key number or the title of the case is necessary to retrieve only the most pertinent cases. For example, if the query includes statute or rule numbers the digest field can be helpful to exclude unwanted citation and key numbers. The query found below is an illustration of this function. The search, run in the United States District Court database will retrieve cases discussing attorney's fees under the Civil Rights Attorney's Fees Awards Act of 1976.

headnote(42 +5 1988 /s fee /p "professional responsibility")

9. *Opinion Field:* The opinion field contains the text of the case, court and docket numbers, and the names of the attorneys and judges participating. The opinion field search is useful in retrieving cases in which a particular attorney, judge or witness has been involved. The following format can be used to retrieve this information:

opinion(melvin /s belli)

Note: Terms may be searched for in clusters of fields by joining any number of field names by commas. This technique is illustrated below:

synopsis,digest("class action" /s attorney lawyer /p conflict! /3 interest)

With this query documents containing the terms CLASS ACTION, ATTORNEY, LAWYER, CONFLICT!, and INTEREST in either the synopsis or digest portions of the case will be retrieved.

b. *Field Browsing*

The WESTLAW fields listed above may be used in yet another way. This second method, known as field browsing, may be used with any query. Once a search has been completed, the documents retrieved may be scanned by entering the "f" command. A list of fields available for browsing is then displayed. Once a field has been selected, WESTLAW will display only the specified field(s).

The WESTLAW Reference Manual should be consulted for further instruction on using WESTLAW fields for searching or browsing.

c. *Date Restrictions*

WESTLAW may be instructed to retrieve documents appearing before, after or on a specified date, as well as within a range of dates. To use the date restricter the term DATE, followed in parentheses by the words BEFORE and/or AFTER, or the abbreviations BEF and/or AFT, or the symbols < and > must be included in the query. Note that the month, day and year may be included to further restrict the search. Date restrictions should be placed at the beginning or end of the query and connected to the query by an ampersand. The following are examples of how the date restriction may be used within a query:

date(after 1965) & adversar*** /2 system /s truth

date(aft 1965) & adversar*** /2 system /s truth

adversar*** /2 system /s truth & date(bef 1982)

adversar*** /2 system /s truth & date(aft may 10, 1965 and bef feb 28, 1981)

d. *Key Number Searching*

Searches may be performed using West Digest Topic and Key Numbers as search terms. When using this search technique, the query consists of the West Digest Topic Number followed by the letter k (or the ? symbol available on WALT keyboards) and then the Key Number classified as a subheading under the Digest Topic and Key Number. For example, to retrieve cases under the Digest Topic classification of Attorney and Client (Digest Topic number 45), and under its subsection or Key Number for Attorney's Clerks and

Agents, (Key Number 29), the following queries would be used.

```
45k29 or 45 29
```

A complete list of Digest Topic and their numerical equivalents appears in the WESTLAW Reference Manual and is also available on-line in the WESTLAW database directory.

e. *The Find Command*

The FIND command may be used at any point in a search to retrieve a particular case from WESTLAW. No matter what the database, a case may be displayed by typing FIND followed by the case citation. For example:

```
find 97 sct 2691
```

will retrieve the case of *Bates v. State Bar of Arizona* no matter what the database. To return to the original screen, the GOBACK command is then entered.

f. *The Locate Command*

The LOCATE command may be used when viewing documents retrieved by a search query, to find documents within the search results which contain certain words or word. To locate a term LOCATE or LOC is typed followed by the ENTER key. On the screen which follows the LOCATE terms are then typed. The terms may or may not be words contained in the query. WESTLAW will then search the documents retrieved by the query to find the LOCATE terms. For example, to search the documents retrieved by the query:

```
conflict! /3 interest /p former +s government
agency public /s lawyer attorney
```

for those documents containing the term "agency," type LOCATE, followed by the terms "ENVIRONMENTAL PROTECTION". Those documents containing the terms "ENVIRONMENTAL PROTECTION" will then be displayed.

VI. CITATION RESEARCH WITH WESTLAW

a. *Shepard's® Citations on WESTLAW*

From any point in WESTLAW, case citations may be entered to retrieve Shepard's listings for those citations. To enter a citation to be Shepardized, the following format is used:

```
sh 97 sct 2691
```

or

```
sh 97 s.ct. 2691
```

or

```
sh 97sct2691
```

When the citation is entered, Shepard's listings for the citation will be displayed. To shepardize a citation it is not necessary to be in the same database as that of the citation. For example, a Supreme Court citation may be entered from the Pacific Reporter database.

b. *WESTLAW as a Citator*

It is possible to retrieve new cases citing previous decisions by using WESTLAW itself as a citator. Using WESTLAW as a citator complements Shepard's Citations by retrieving very recent decisions not yet included in Shepard's. Because citation styles are not always uniform, special care must be taken to identify variant forms of citations.

Retrieving Cases that Cite Other Court Decisions

WESTLAW can be used as a citator of other court decisions if the title of the decision, its citation, or both, are known. When only the title of the case is known, use the following format:

```
bates /7 arizona
```

This query instructs the computer to retrieve all documents citating the case of *Bates v. State Bar of Arizona.* The /7 numerical connector requires that the term BATES occur within seven words of the term ARIZONA.

If the citation of the case is known, it may be added to the query to retrieve only those documents citing the correct case name and case citation. For example, to retrieve cases that have referred to the *Bates* decision by its citation, 433 sct 350 the following format may be used:

433 +7 350

If both the citation & the case title are known, one or both of the case name terms may be used to retrieve all documents citing this case. The queries below illustrate this format.

bates /7 arizona /15 433 +7 350

or

bates /15 433 +7 35

or

arizona /15 433 +7 350

West's INSTA–CITE™

INSTA–CITE, West Publishing Company's case history system, allows users to quickly verify the accuracy of case citations and the validity of decisions. It contains prior and subsequent case histories in sequential listings, parallel citations and precedential treatment.

Some examples of the kind of direct case history provided by INSTA–CITE are: "affirmed," "certiorari denied," "decision reversed and remanded," and "judgment vacated." A complete list of INSTA–CITE case history and precedential treatment notations appears in the WESTLAW Reference Manual.

The format for entering a case citation into Insta-Cite consists of the letters IC followed by the citation, with or without spaces and periods:

ic 433 u.s. 350

or

ic 433 us 350

or

ic 433us350

VII. SPECIAL FEATURES

a. *Black's Law Dictionary*

WESTLAW contains an on-line version of Black's Law Dictionary. The dictionary incorporates definitions of terms and phrases of English and American law.

The dictionary may be accessed at any point while using WESTLAW by typing DI followed by the term to be defined:

di

To obtain definitions of a phrase, enter the command DI followed by the phrase without quotation marks:

di judge pro tempore

If the precise spelling of a term to be defined is not known, or a list of dictionary terms is desired, a truncated form of the words may be entered with the root expansion symbol (!) attached to it:

di bar!

This example will produce a list of dictionary terms beginning with the root BAR. From the list of terms a number corresponding to the desired term can be entered to obtain the appropriate definition of BARRISTER.

VIII. WESTLAW HORNBOOK QUERIES

a. *Query Format*

The queries that appear in this publication are intended to be illustrative. They are approximately as general as the material in the Hornbook text to which they correspond.

Although all of the queries in this publication reflect proper format for use with WESTLAW, there is seldom only one "correct" way to formulate a query for a particular problem. The queries reflect a wide range of alternative ways that queries may be structured for effective research. Such variance in query style reflects the great flexibility that the WESTLAW system affords its users in formulating search strategies.

For some research problems, it may be necessary to make a series of refinements to the queries such as the addition of search terms or the substitution of different grammatical connectors, to adequately fit the particular needs of the individual researcher's problem. The responsibility remains with the researcher to "fine-tune" the WESTLAW queries in accordance with his or her own research requirements. The primary usefulness of the preformulated queries in this hornbook is in providing users with a foundation upon which further query construction can be built.

Individual queries in this hornbook may retrieve from one to over a hundred cases, depending on the database to which they are addressed. If a query does not retrieve any cases in a given database, it is because there are no documents in that database which satisfy the proximity requirements of the query. In this situation, to search another database with the same query, enter the letter S followed by the initials DB, followed by the new database identifier. Thus, if a query was initially addressed to the District Courts (dct) database, but retrieved no documents, the user could then search the Courts of Appeals (cta) database with the same query by entering the following command:

```
s db cta
```

The maximum number of cases retrieved by a query in any given database will vary, depending on a variety of factors, including the relative generality of the search terms and proximity connectors, the frequency of litigation or discussion of the issue in the courts and administrative bodies, and the number of documents comprising the database.

b. *Textual Illustrations*

Examples from the text of this edition have been selected to illustrate how the queries provided in this treatise may be expanded, restricted, or altered to meet the specific needs of the reader's research in the area of professional responsibility law. A portion of Chapter 6 section 6.6.2 of this text appears below. The footnotes have been omitted for purposes of brevity.

> *Scope of Work Product*
>
> The [work product] doctrine operates as an exception to the normal broad sweep of the pretrial discovery rules: a party in litigation may not use the discovery devices to obtain from any other party materials prepared by the other party's lawyer or the lawyer's agent in anticipation of litigation. The privilege is qualified, however, in much the same way that *Hickman* was qualified: the inquiring party can gain access to some of those materials by demonstrating a substantial need for them and that their substantial equivalent cannot be obtained without undue hardship. The federal rules also recognize an unqualified right of any person to obtain a copy of the person's own substantially verbatim witness statement taken by a lawyer. While comprehensive, the procedural rule both raises interpretative issues and has not precluded application of the *Hickman v. Taylor* doctrine to areas of civil discovery that are not covered by the literal language of the work product rule and to areas outside pretrial discovery in civil litigation.
>
> Several important problems are not directly resolved by the rule. A question raised by adapting new technology to law practice is the extent to which the work product privilege extends to materials in a computer system maintained by a law firm.

This excerpt discusses the work product doctrine and exceptions to it. In order to retrieve documents discussing this point of law, the following preformulated query is given as a suggested search strategy on WESTLAW:

```
attorney counsel** lawyer /s "work product"
/s computer! hardship "mental impression" need
verbatim
```

In the text of a case retrieved by the query, the paragraph below appears.

```
R 2 OF 16    P 27 OF 30 NE    T
445 N.E.2d 894
counsel vehemently maintained throughout the course
of defendant's trial that the state's attorney was not
complying with the court's pre-trial discovery order.
The state's attorney was equally insistent that all
discoverable materials were turned over to defense
counsel as they became available to the State.
```

In fact, interview notes taken of forty-one potential witnesses were not turned over to defense counsel until after the trial was in progress. When the existence of these notes was disclosed, the trial court ordered the state's **attorney** to submit them to him for an in camera examination to determine whether they constituted privileged **work product** material or substantially **verbatim** reports of oral statements discoverable under authority of Brady v. Maryland (1963), 373 U.S. 83, 83 S.Ct. 1194, 10 L.Ed.2d 215. The trial court determined that twelve of the forty-one notes contained some discoverable material. These were tendered to defense counsel accordingly. The remaining twenty-nine witness interview notes were likewise submitted to defense counsel for examination following defendant's conviction for purposes of perfecting his arguments on appeal.

The query can be altered in a number of ways to tailor it to the needs of the individual researcher. For example, to research the waiver of the work product doctrine, the following query could be used:

attorney counsel** lawyer /s "work product" /s waiv**

By adding WAIV** and deleting the terms COMPUTER!, HARDSHIP, "MENTAL IMPRESSION", NEED and VERBATIM, the query retrieves documents involving the waiver of the work doctrine. One such document retrieved from the Pacific (pac) database is shown below.

R 1 OF 7 P 35 OF 37 PAC T
702 P.2d 360
opinion work product immunity extends to documents prepared in anticipation of previous, terminated litigation or threatened litigation, we cannot sustain the broad assertions of work product immunity to prevent discovery of the documents here sought. Whether styled as a showing of a sufficiently compelling need or as a **waiver** of the **work product** immunity, we find that the respondent's reliance, in this litigation upon the advice of **counsel** as a major justification for their actions, renders the advice and actions of counsel a central issue, and deimmunizes the **attorney's** opinion **work product.** (FN20)

Just how a query is altered will depend upon the research objectives of the individual.

IX. RANKING DOCUMENTS RETRIEVED ON WESTLAW: AGE AND TERM OPTIONS

Documents retrieved by a query can be ordered in either of two ways. One way is to order documents by their dates, with the most recent documents displayed first. This is ranking by AGE. Using the AGE option is suggested when the user's highest priority is to retrieve the most recent decisions from a search.

Alternatively, documents can be ranked by the frequency of appearance of query terms. This is ranking by TERMS. When a search is performed with the TERMS option, the cases containing the greater number of different search terms will be displayed first.

When a database is accessed by entering a database identifier, WESTLAW responds with a screen requesting that the query be entered. At this point the user may select which type of ranking, AGE or TERMS, is desired.

The queries offered in this hornbook were formulated and tested for relevancy with use of the TERMS option. Accordingly, in certain instances use of the AGE option with the preformulated queries may display less relevant, yet more recent cases, first.

X. CONCLUSION

This appendix has demonstrated methods that can be used to obtain the most effective research results in the area of professional responsibility. The addition of WESTLAW references at the end of each section of the text opens the door to a powerful and easily accessed computerized law library.

The queries may be used as provided or they may be tailored to meet the needs of researcher's specific problems. The power and flexibility of WESTLAW affords users of this publication a unique opportunity to greatly enhance their access to and understanding of professional responsibility.

*

Table of Cases

References are to section and note.

A, In re, 276 Or. 225, 554 P.2d 479 (1976)—§ **12.3.4 n. 51; § 12.5.3 n. 56, 58, 64.**

A. and B., In re, 44 N.J. 331, 209 A.2d 101 (1965)—§ **7.2.4 n. 2.**

A., Barbara v. John G., 145 Cal.App.3d 369, 193 Cal.Rptr. 422 (1983)—§ **5.6.1 n. 30.**

ABA Trans Nat'l Transp., Inc. v. Aeronautics Forwarders, Inc., 90 Ill.App.3d 817, 46 Ill.Dec. 186, 413 N.E.2d 1299 (1980)—§ **13.7.2 n. 71.**

Abagis, In re, 386 Mass. 1001, 435 N.E.2d 1042 (1982)—§ **3.4.2 n. 74.**

Abar v. Rogers, 124 Cal.App.3d 862, 177 Cal.Rptr. 655 (1981)—§ **15.1.3 n. 76.**

Abbey v. Control Data Corp., 603 F.2d 724 (8th Cir.1979)—§ **13.4.2 n. 14.**

Abbott, State v., 273 S.C. 170, 255 S.E.2d 673 (1979)—§ **4.2 n. 17.**

Abbott Laboratories v. Centaur Chemical Company, 497 F.Supp. 269 (N.D.Ill.1980)—§ **7.4.1 n. 55.**

Abeles v. State Bar, 9 Cal.3d 603, 108 Cal.Rptr. 359, 510 P.2d 719 (1973)—§ **3.3.1 n. 63.**

Aberizk, State v., 115 N.H. 535, 345 A.2d 407 (1975)—§ **15.1.3 n. 75.**

Abood v. Detroit Bd. of Educ., 431 U.S. 209, 97 S.Ct. 1782, 52 L.Ed.2d 261 (1977)—§ **2.4.1 n. 19.**

Abraham, United States v., 541 F.2d 1234 (7th Cir.1976)—§ **12.1.2 n. 28.**

Abraham Const. Corp., Wilson P. v. Armco Steel Corp., 559 F.2d 250 (5th Cir.1977)—§ **6.4.9 n. 41; § 7.1.6 n. 74; § 7.4.3 n. 26.**

Abrahams, In re, 158 A.D. 595, 143 N.Y.S. 927 (1913)—§ **13.5.5 n. 64.**

Abrams, In re, 293 Or. 727, 652 P.2d 787 (1982)—§ **9.3.2 n. 90.**

Abrams, In re, 521 F.2d 1094 (3d Cir.1975)—§ **3.4.5 n. 95; § 3.6.1 n. 10, 12, 14, 16; § 15.2.4 n. 5.**

Abrams, In re, 56 N.J. 271, 266 A.2d 275 (1970)—§ **8.8.2 n. 93; § 13.3.5 n. 51.**

Abstract & Title Corp. v. Cochran, 414 So.2d 284 (Fla.App. 1982)—§ **8.11.3 n. 91, 92.**

Abuza, In re, 178 App.Div. 757, 166 N.Y.S. 105 (1917)—§ **12.3.5 n. 77.**

Academy of California Optometrists, Inc. v. Superior Court, 51 Cal.App.3d 999, 124 Cal.Rptr. 668 (1975)—§ **9.6.3; § 9.6.3 n. 61.**

Acevedo v. Immigration and Naturalization Service, 538 F.2d 918 (2d Cir.1976)—§ **16.6.2 n. 83.**

Ackerman, In re, 95 N.J. 147, 469 A.2d 924 (1984)—§ **4.5 n. 20.**

Ackerman, In re, 263 Ind. 309, 330 N.E.2d 322 (1975)—§ **3.5.6 n. 76.**

Ackermann, In re, 99 Ill.2d 56, 75 Ill.Dec. 415, 457 N.E.2d 409 (1983)—§ **3.3.3 n. 26.**

Acocella, State ex rel. v. Allen, 288 Or. 175, 604 P.2d 391 (1979)—§ **16.9 n. 26.**

Acorn Printing Co. v. Brown, 385 S.W.2d 812 (Mo.Ct.App. 1964)—§ **1.6 n. 21.**

Adams v. American Bar Ass'n, 400 F.Supp. 219 (E.D.Pa. 1975)—§ **11.2.2 n. 13.**

Adams v. Chenowith, 349 So.2d 230 (Fla.App.1977)—§ **8.5 n. 31.**

Adams v. Crater Well Drilling, Inc., 276 Or. 789, 556 P.2d 679 (1976)—§ **13.5.6 n. 78.**

Adams v. Fisher, 390 So.2d 1248 (Fla.App.1980)—§ **9.5.2 n. 54.**

Adams v. Peck, 43 Md.App. 168, 403 A.2d 840 (1979)—§ **5.6.5 n. 16.**

Adams, George, Lee, Schulte & Ward, P.A. v. Westinghouse Elec. Corp., 597 F.2d 570 (5th Cir.1979)—§ **9.6.3 n. 39, 49.**

Adams, State v., 277 S.C. 115, 283 S.E.2d 582 (1981)—§ **6.3.5 n. 11.**

Adan v. Abbott, 114 Misc.2d 735, 452 N.Y.S.2d 476 (1982)—§ **9.6.3 n. 46.**

Addington v. Texas, 441 U.S. 418, 99 S.Ct. 1804, 60 L.Ed. 2d 323 (1979)—§ **3.4.4 n. 39, 41.**

Addison v. Brown, 413 So.2d 1240 (Fla.App.1982)—§ **12.7 n. 85.**

Adelman v. Rosenbaum, 133 Pa.Super. 386, 3 A.2d 15 (1938)—§ **5.6 n. 28.**

Ades, In re, 6 F.Supp. 467 (D.Md.1934)—§ **14.2.5 n. 81.**

Adger v. State, 584 P.2d 1056 (Wyo.1978)—§ **4.1 n. 7.**

Adler v. Robson, Miller & Osserman, 121 Misc.2d 411, 467 N.Y.S.2d 810 (1983)—§ **4.2 n. 55.**

Adler, Barish, Daniels, Levin & Creskoff v. Epstein, 482 Pa. 416, 393 A.2d 1175 (1978)—§ **16.2.3 n. 74.**

Administrative Order, In re, 1978-4, 402 Mich. lxxxvi (1978)—§ **14.2.3 n. 48.**

Advisory Committee Opinion No. 447, In re, 86 N.J. 473, 432 A.2d 59 (1981)—§ **14.2.4 n. 79; § 16.4 n. 32.**

Advisory Comm. Opinion No. 475, In re, 89 N.J. 74, 444 A.2d 1092 (1982)—§ **15.4.1 n. 7.**

Advisory Opinion No. 361, In re, 77 N.J. 199, 390 A.2d 118 (1978)—§ **8.10.3 n. 31.**

Brent v. Board of Trustees of Davis & Elkins College, ___ W.Va. ___, 311 S.E.2d 153 (1983)—§ **5.1 n. 17.**
Brentwood Bank v. Rudman, 538 S.W.2d 744 (Mo.App. 1976)—§ **16.6.2 n. 53.**
Bretz, In re, 168 Mont. 23, 542 P.2d 1227 (1975)—§ **8.11.3 n. 92.**
Brewer v. Wegmann, 691 F.2d 216 (5th Cir.1982)—§ **5.3 n. 83.**
Brewer v. Williams, 430 U.S. 387, 97 S.Ct. 1232, 51 L.Ed. 2d 424 (1977)—§ **14.3.1;** § **14.3.1 n. 51, 62.**
Brewer, People v., 88 Mich.App. 756, 279 N.W.2d 307 (1979)—§ **14.6.3 n. 29.**
Brewer, State v., 247 N.W. 2d 205 (Iowa 1976)—§ **12.1.1 n. 7.**
Brewster, In re, 115 N.H. 636, 351 A.2d 889 (1975)—§ **14.4.1 n. 44.**
Brewster v. Dukakis, 675 F.2d 1 (1st Cir.1982)—§ **14.5 n. 80.**
Brewster, United States v., 165 U.S.App.D.C. 1, 506 F.2d 62 (1974)—§ **17.5.2 n. 94.**
Brick v. CPC Int'l, Inc., 547 F.2d 185 (2d Cir.1976)—§ **8.14 n. 72.**
Brickell Bay Club Condominium Ass'n v. Forte, 397 So.2d 959 (Fla.App.1981)—§ **16.6.2 n. 41.**
Bricker, In re, 90 N.J. 6, 446 A.2d 1195 (1982)—§ **1.6 n. 20.**
Bridges v. California, 314 U.S. 252, 62 S.Ct. 190, 86 L.Ed. 192 (1941)—§ **11.3.2 n. 50.**
Briedman, In re, 102 A.D.2d 427, 477 N.Y.S.2d 144 (1984)—§ **3.3.4 n. 34.**
Brien v. United States, 695 F.2d 10, 15 (1st Cir.1982)—§ **8.2.3 n. 29.**
Briggs v. Clinton Cty. Bank & Trust, ___ Ind.App. ___, 452 N.E.2d 989 (1983)—§ **9.2.1 n. 47;** § **9.2.2 n. 59.**
Briggs v. Goodwin, 698 F.2d 486 (D.C.Cir.1983)—§ **14.6.4 n. 57.**
Brink v. DaLesio, 82 F.R.D. 664, 674 (D.Md.1979)—§ **6.3.2 n. 55.**
Brink's, Inc. v. City of New York, 717 F.2d 700 (2d Cir. 1983)—§ **3.4.3 n. 96.**
Briscoe v. Lahue, 460 U.S. 325, 103 S.Ct. 1108, 75 L.Ed.2d 96 (1983)—§ **12.5.1 n. 47;** § **13.10.4 n. 91.**
Brobeck, Phleger & Harrison v. Telex Corp., 602 F.2d 866 (9th Cir.1979)—§ **9.1 n. 20;** § **9.3.1 n. 62.**
Brock, State ex rel. Inman v., 622 S.W.2d 36 (Tenn.1981)—§ **11.3.2 n. 60.**
Brockway Glass Co. v. Hartford-Empire Co., 36 F.Supp. 470 (W.D.N.Y.1941)—§ **6.6.1 n. 30.**
Brode v. Brode, 278 S.C. 457, 298 S.E.2d 443 (1982)—§ **4.4 n. 89.**
Brodie, In re, 394 F.Supp. 1208 (D.Or.1975)—§ **15.3.2 n. 49.**
Brodson, State v., 11 Wis.2d 124, 103 N.W.2d 912 (1960)—§ **3.5.5 n. 49.**
Brody v. Montalbano, 87 Cal.App.3d 725, 151 Cal.Rptr. 206 (1978)—§ **5.6 n. 27.**
Brody v. Ruby, 267 N.W.2d 902 (Iowa 1978)—§ **5.6 n. 29;** § **5.6.4 n. 54.**
Bronson, In re, 246 Ga. 136, 269 S.E.2d 27 (1980)—§ **3.5.3 n. 73.**
Bronston, United States v., 658 F.2d 920 (2d Cir.1981)—§ **7.1.1 n. 6;** § **7.1.7 n. 77.**
Bronston v. United States, 409 U.S. 352, 93 S.Ct. 595, 34 L.Ed.2d 568 (1973)—§ **12.5.1 n. 38.**
Brookhart v. Janis, 384 U.S. 1, 86 S.Ct. 1245, 16 L.Ed.2d 314 (1966)—§ **10.5.3 n. 38.**
Brookhaven Landscape & Grading Co. v. J.F. Barton Contracting Co., 681 F.2d 734 (11th Cir.1982)—§ **3.5.3 n. 76.**
Brookins, In re, 153 Ga.App. 82, 264 S.E.2d 560 (1980)—§ **12.1.3 n. 71.**
Brooks, In re, 274 S.C. 601, 267 S.E.2d 74 (1980)—§ **12.3.3 n. 44.**
Brophy, In re, 83 A.D.2d 975, 442 N.Y.S.2d 818 (1981)—§ **13.10.5 n. 8.**
Brotherhood of Maintenance Employees v. Hash, 294 S.E.2d 96 (W.Va.1982)—§ **4.2 n. 35.**
Brotherhood of Railroad Trainmen v. Virginia ex rel. Virginia State Bar, 377 U.S. 1, 84 S.Ct. 1113, 12 L.Ed.2d 89 (1964)—§ **8.8.3 n. 7;** § **14.2.5 n. 21;** § **16.5.2;** § **16.5.2 n. 40, 47, 48.**
Brown, In re, 97 Wn.2d 273, 644 P.2d 669 (1982)—§ **3.5.2 n. 37.**
Brown, In re, 94 Wn.2d 750, 620 P.2d 101 (1980)—§ **3.5.7 n. 1.**
Brown, In re, 49 N.J. 16, 227 A.2d 506 (1976)—§ **7.1.6 n. 70.**
Brown, In re, 104 Ariz. 387, 453 P.2d 958 (1969)—§ **4.6.2 n. 73.**
Brown v. Board of Bar Examiners, 623 F.2d 605 (9th Cir.)—§ **2.5 n. 76;** § **3.4.5 n. 67.**
Brown v. Board of Education, 347 U.S. 483, 74 S.Ct. 686, 98 L.Ed. 873 (1954)—§ **8.8.3;** § **8.8.3 n. 99.**
Brown v. Brown, 4 Ind. 627 (1853)—§ **16.6.2 n. 83.**
Brown v. Commercial Nat'l Bank, 42 Ill.2d 365, 247 N.E.2d 894 (1969)—§ **8.11.2 n. 81.**
Brown v. District of Columbia Bd. of Zoning, 413 A.2d 1276 (D.C.1980)—§ **8.10.3 n. 43;** § **15.2.5 n. 16.**
Brown v. E.W. Bliss Co., 72 F.R.D. 198 (D.Md.1976)—§ **4.6.1 n. 32;** § **5.6.1 n. 4.**
Brown v. Gerstein, 17 Mass.App.Ct. 558, 460 N.E.2d 1043 (1984)—§ **16.2.3 n. 41.**
Brown v. McGarr, 583 F.Supp. 734 (N.D.Ill.1984)—§ **5.4 n. 3.**
Brown v. Oregon State Bar, 293 Or. 446, 648 P.2d 1289—§ **2.2.4 n. 71.**
Brown v. Pac. Tel. & Tel. Co., 105 Cal.App.3d 482, 164 Cal. Rptr. 445 (1980)—§ **11.2.5 n. 40.**
Brown v. State, 443 N.E.2d 316 (Ind.1983)—§ **14.6.2 n. 6.**
Brown v. Supreme Court of Virginia, 359 F.Supp. 549 (E.D.Va.1973)—§ **15.4.2 n. 22.**
Brown v. United States, 551 F.2d 619 (5th Cir.1977)—§ **14.6.1 n. 85.**
Brown v. Walker, 161 U.S. 591, 16 S.Ct. 644, 40 L.Ed. 819 (1906)—§ **12.4.5 n. 13.**
Brown v. Welch, 253 Ga. 118, 317 S.E.2d 520 (1984)—§ **9.4.2 n. 47.**
Brown v. Wheeler, 437 So.2d 521 (Ala.1983)—§ **4.2 n. 30.**
Brown, People v., 111 Cal.App.3d 523, 168 Cal.Rptr. 806 (1980)—§ **4.4 n. 99.**

Brown, People ex rel. Deukmejian v., 29 Cal.3d 150, 172 Cal.Rptr. 478, 624 P.2d 1206 (1981)—§ **8.9.4 n. 45.**

Brown, State v., 644 S.W.2d 418 (Tenn.Crim.App.1982)—§ **10.5.3 n. 31.**

Brown, United States v., 587 F.Supp. 1005 (E.D.Pa.1984)—§ **3.5.6 n. 78.**

Brown, United States v., 478 F.2d 1038 (7th Cir.1973)—§ **6.3.6 n. 48.**

Brown & Huseby, Inc. v. Chrietzberg, 242 Ga. 232, 248 S.E.2d 631 (1978)—§ **8.13 n. 47;** § **9.2.3 n. 80.**

Brown & Williamson Tobacco Corp. v. Daniel Int'l Corp., 563 F.2d 671 (5th Cir.1977)—§ **7.3.2 n. 15.**

Browning, In re, 23 Ill.2d 483, 179 N.E.2d 14 (1961)—§ **9.4.5 n. 17.**

Browning Debenture Holders' Committee v. DASA Corp., 560 F.2d 1078 (2d Cir.1977)—§ **16.6.2 n. 79.**

Brownstein, In re, 288 Or. 83, 602 P.2d 655 (1979)—§ **8.3.2 n. 62.**

Browy v. Brannon, 527 F.2d 799 (7th Cir.1976)—§ **9.6.3 n. 62, 70.**

Broyles v. Brown Engineering Co., 275 Ala. 35, 151 So.2d 767 (1963)—§ **5.6.2 n. 69.**

Broyles v. Califano, 495 F.Supp. 4 (E.D.Tenn.1980)—§ **4.2 n. 32.**

Bruener, In re, 159 Wash. 504, 294 P. 254 (1930)—§ **11.4.3 n. 6.**

Brumberg v. Chunghai Chan, 25 Misc.2d 312, 204 N.Y.S.2d 315 (1959)—§ **4.6.2 n. 53.**

Brundage, People ex rel. v. Blakemore, 309 Ill. 311, 141 N.E. 138 (1923)—§ **13.5.4 n. 59.**

Bruner, United States v., 657 F.2d 1278 (D.C.Cir.1981)—§ **10.5.3 n. 31.**

Brunston, In re, 52 Mont. 83, 155 P. 1109 (1916)—§ **8.9.4 n. 50.**

Bryam v. Miner, 47 F.2d 112 (8th Cir.1931)—§ **9.6.3 n. 69.**

Bryan v. Bartlett, 435 F.2d 28 (8th Cir.1970)—§ **13.7.2 n. 83.**

Bryant v. Lewis, 27 S.W.2d 604 (Tex.Civ.App.1930)—§ **7.2.4 n. 93;** § **9.6.1 n. 14.**

Bryant v. State Bar, 21 Cal.2d 285, 131 P.2d 523 (1942)—§ **13.3.6 n. 64.**

Brydonjack v. State Bar, 208 Cal. 439, 281 P. 1018, 66 A.L.R. 1507—§ **2.2.2 n. 31.**

Bubar, United States v., 567 F.2d 192 (2d Cir.1977)—§ **14.6.1 n. 93.**

Bucci, State v., ___ R.I. ___, 430 A.2d 746 (1981)—§ **3.5.4 n. 4;** § **15.1.4 n. 61, 68.**

Buchanan v. Buchanan, 99 Cal.App.3d 587, 160 Cal.Rptr. 577 (1979)—§ **8.4.3 n. 15.**

Buchanan v. State, 554 P.2d 1153 (Alaska 1976)—§ **12.4.3 n. 99.**

Bucher & Willis Consulting Engineers v. Smith, 7 Kan. App.2d 467, 643 P.2d 1156 (1982)—§ **4.2 n. 50.**

Buckley v. Gray, 110 Cal. 339, 42 P. 900 (1895)—§ **5.6.4 n. 49.**

Buckley, United States v., 586 F.2d 498 (5th Cir.1978)—§ **6.3.4 n. 75.**

Bull v. McCuskey, 96 Nev. 706, 615 P.2d 957 (1980)—§ **5.6 n. 28, 32;** § **12.4.5 n. 11.**

Bump v. Barnett, 235 Iowa 308, 16 N.W.2d 579 (1944)—§ **15.1.3 n. 28, 77.**

Bunch, United States v., 730 F.2d 517 (7th Cir.1984)—§ **17.5.5 n. 74.**

Buntrock v. Buntrock, 419 So.2d 402 (Fla.App.1982)—§ **7.1.6 n. 72;** § **7.4.2 n. 65, 79.**

Burden v. Church of Scientology, 526 F.Supp. 44 (M.D.Fla. 1981)—§ **6.3.5 n. 25.**

Burdick v. York Oil Co., 364 S.W.2d 766 (Tex.Civ.App. 1963)—§ **12.1.2 n. 17.**

Burgess, In re, 275 S.C. 315, 270 S.E.2d 436 (1980)—§ **9.3.1 n. 32.**

Burgess, In re, 177 Mont. 493, 582 P.2d 356 (1978)—§ **3.5.3 n. 75.**

Burgett v. State, 646 S.W.2d 615 (Tex.Ct.App.1983)—§ **13.10.2 n. 43.**

Burgin v. Mississippi State Bar, 453 So.2d 689 (Miss. 1984)—§ **3.5.6 n. 62.**

Burk, P.C. v. Burzynski, 672 P.2d 419 (Wyo.1983)—§ **9.2.1 n. 39.**

Burlington Indus. v. Exxon Corp., 65 F.R.D. 26 (D.Md. 1974)—§ **6.5.4 n. 90.**

Burnes v. Scott, 117 U.S. 582, 6 S.Ct. 865, 29 L.Ed. 991 (1886)—§ **8.13 n. 52.**

Burns, In re, 139 Ariz. 487, 679 P.2d 510 (1984)—§ **5.1 n. 26;** § **9.3.1 n. 72.**

Burns v. Clayton, 237 S.C. 316, 117 S.E.2d 300 (1960)—§ **3.4.5 n. 53;** § **12.5.1 n. 47.**

Burns v. Huffstetler, 433 So.2d 964 (Fla.1983)—§ **2.2.4 n. 71.**

Burns v. Stewart, 290 Minn. 289, 188 N.W.2d 760 (1971)—§ **9.4.4 n. 9.**

Burns v. Valene, 298 Minn. 257, 214 N.W.2d 686 (1974)—§ **9.5.3 n. 78.**

Burnside v. McCrary, 384 So.2d 1292 (Fla.App.1980)—§ **5.6.6 n. 45, 46.**

Burr, Ex parte, 22 U.S. (9 Wheat.) 529, 6 L.Ed. 152—§ **2.2.2 n. 18, 42;** § **2.2.5 n. 77;** § **3.1 n. 18;** § **3.6.1 n. 9.**

Burr, In re, 267 S.C. 419, 228 S.E.2d 678 (1976)—§ **9.5.2 n. 50.**

Burrows, In re, 291 Or. 135, 629 P.2d 820 (1981)—§ **3.4.5 n. 79;** § **11.3.3 n. 71, 84;** § **11.6.2 n. 63;** § **13.10.3 n. 74.**

Burrows v. Superior Court, 13 Cal.3d 238, 118 Cal.Rptr. 166, 529 P.2d 590 (1974)—§ **14.6.4 n. 70.**

Bursten v. Green, 172 So.2d 472 (Fla.App.1965)—§ **4.6.2 n. 53.**

Burt v. Gahan, 351 Mass. 340, 220 N.E.2d 817 (1966)—§ **4.2 n. 58.**

Burton, In re, 472 A.2d 831 (D.C.App.1984)—§ **4.8 n. 7.**

Burton, State v., 163 W.Va. 40, 254 S.E.2d 129 (1979)—§ **6.3.7 n. 50.**

Burton, United States v., 584 F.2d 485 (D.C.Cir.1978)—§ **14.3.7 n. 31.**

Burwell, People v., 44 Cal.2d 16, 279 P.2d 744 (1955)—§ **7.5.1 n. 30.**

Bush, Ex parte, 7 Vin.Abr. 74, 22 Eng.Rep. 93 (Ch.1734)—§ **9.6.3 n. 39.**

Bushman v. State Bar, 11 Cal.3d 558, 113 Cal.Rptr. 904, 522 P.2d 312 (1974)—§ **9.3.1 n. 68.**

Carlin, State v., 7 Kan.App.2d 219, 640 P.2d 324 (1982)—§ **6.3.7 n. 59;** § **12.3.5 n. 75.**

Carlson, Collins, Gordon & Bold v. Banducci, 257 Cal.App. 2d 212, 64 Cal.Rptr. 915 (1967)—§ **6.7.8 n. 7.**

Carmichael v. Iowa State Highway Comm'n, 219 N.W.2d 658 (Iowa 1974)—§ **9.4.1 n. 35.**

Carnley v. Cochran, 369 U.S. 506, 82 S.Ct. 884, 8 L.Ed.2d 70 (1962)—§ **14.3.1 n. 62.**

Carpenter Co., E.R., v. ABC Carpet Co., 98 Misc.2d 1091, 415 N.Y.S.2d 351 (Civ.Ct.1979)—§ **6.4.7 n. 20.**

Carricarte v. State, 384 So.2d 1261 (Fla.1980)—§ **5.6.5 n. 70;** § **13.5.4 n. 52.**

Carroll, Commonwealth ex rel. v. Tate, 442 Pa. 45, 274 A.2d 193—§ **2.2.1 n. 12.**

Carroll, In re, 124 Ariz. 80, 602 P.2d 461 (1979)—§ **3.4.2 n. 80;** § **3.5.2 n. 51;** § **9.2.3 n. 78, 81, 88;** § **14.2.5 n. 84.**

Carroll, In re, 244 S.W.2d 474 (Ky.1951)—§ **12.5.3 n. 63.**

Carroll v. Rountree, 34 N.C.App. 167, 237 S.E.2d 566 (1977)—§ **5.6.2 n. 70.**

Carsey v. United States, 129 U.S.App.D.C. 205, 392 F.2d 810 (1967)—§ **12.4.3 n. 99.**

Carter v. Bordenkircher, 159 W.Va. 717, 226 S.E.2d 711 (1976)—§ **12.5.4 n. 81.**

Carter v. Folcarelli, 121 R.I. 667, 402 A.2d 1175 (1979)—§ **3.4.1, n. 57;** § **3.4.4 n. 33.**

Carter v. Kamaras, 430 A.2d 1058 (R.I.1981)—§ **11.6.2 n. 38.**

Carter v. Katz, Shandell, Katz & Erasmous, 120 Misc.2d 1009, 465 N.Y.S.2d 991 (1983)—§ **9.2.4 n. 7.**

Carter v. Romano, ___ R.I. ___, 426 A.2d 255 (1981)—§ **3.5.4 n. 98.**

Carter v. Ross, 461 A.2d 675 (R.I. 1983)—§ **4.8 n. 98.**

Carter v. Walsh, 122 R.I. 349, 406 A.2d 263 (1979)—§ **3.5.2 n. 34, 48;** § **3.5.4 n. 16;** § **5.1 n. 24.**

Carter, State v., 641 S.W.2d 54 (Mo.1982)—§ **6.3.8 n. 79.**

Carter, State v., 578 P.2d 1275 (Utah 1978)—§ **6.3.2 n. 61.**

Cartin v. Continental Homes, 134 Vt. 362, 360 A.2d 96—§ **2.6.3 n. 55;** § **7.5.2 n. 8;** § **14.6.4 n. 44.**

Carton v. Borden, 8 N.J. 352, 85 A.2d 257 (1951)—§ **9.2.1 n. 41.**

Cartwright, In re, 282 N.W.2d 548 (Minn.1979)—§ **3.4.3 n. 98.**

Cartwright, State ex rel. v. Oklahoma Indus. Authority, 629 P.2d 1244 (Okl.1981)—§ **6.5.6 n. 23.**

Caruso, United States ex rel. v. Zelinsky, 689 F.2d 435 (3d Cir.1982)—§ **4.5 n. 25.**

Cary, In re, 90 Wn.2d 762, 585 P.2d 1161 (1978)—§ **3.5.2 n. 8;** § **3.5.6 n. 55;** § **4.8 n. 4, 7.**

Case, In re, 262 Ind. 118, 311 N.E.2d 797 (1974)—§ **3.5.6 n. 76.**

Cason, In re, 249 Ga. 806, 294 S.E.2d 520 (1982)—§ **15.3.2 n. 44, 61.**

Cass v. State, 58 N.Y.2d 460, 461 N.Y.S.2d 1001, 448 N.E.2d 786 (1983)—§ **17.2.3 n. 62.**

Cassatly, State v., 93 N.J.Super. 111, 225 A.2d 141 (1966)—§ **12.3.5 n. 61.**

Cassidy, In re, 89 Ill.2d 145, 432 N.E.2d 274 (1982)—§ **4.5 n. 20;** § **5.1 n. 46.**

Castello, In re, 273 Ind. 136, 402 N.E.2d 970 (1980)—§ **3.5.2 n. 26, 54.**

Caston v. Sears, Roebuck & Co., 556 F.2d 1305 (5th Cir. 1977)—§ **14.5 n. 67.**

Catrone v. Catrone, 92 A.D.2d 559, 459 N.Y.S.2d 306 (1983)—§ **9.5.1 n. 37.**

Cauthen, In re, 267 S.C. 448, 229 S.E.2d 340 (1976)—§ **13.3.6 n. 60.**

Cavanaugh v. Cavanaugh, 118 R.I. 608, 375 A.2d 911 (1977)—§ **11.3.3 n. 83.**

Central Fla. Legal Services, Inc. v. Eastmoore, 517 F.Supp. 497 (M.D.Fla.)—§ **2.2.5 n. 89.**

Central Hudson Gas & Elec. Corp. v. Public Service Comm'n, 447 U.S. 557, 100 S.Ct. 2343, 65 L.Ed.2d 341 (1980)—§ **14.2.4 n. 54;** § **14.2.5 n. 51.**

Central Milk Producers Co-op v. Sentry Food Stores, Inc., 573 F.2d 988 (8th Cir.1978)—§ **7.1.7 n. 25;** § **7.2.1 n. 41;** § **7.6.4 n. 70, 77.**

Central R.R. & Banking Co. v. Pettus, 113 U.S. 116, 5 S.Ct. 387, 28 L.Ed. 915 (1885)—§ **16.6.2 n. 49.**

Central Trust Co. v. Goldman, 70 A.D.2d 767, 417 N.Y.S.2d 359 (1979)—§ **16.6.2 n. 91.**

Centurian Corp. v. Ryberg, McCoy & Halgren, 588 P.2d 716 (Utah 1978)—§ **9.2.2 n. 56.**

Ceramco, Inc. v. Lee Parmaceuticals, Inc., 510 F.2d 268 (2d Cir.1975)—§ **11.6.2 n. 45.**

Cersosimo v. Cersosimo, 188 Conn. 385, 449 A.2d 1026 (1982)—§ **14.4.1 n. 47.**

Certain-Teed Prod. Corp. v. Topping, 171 F.2d 241 (2d Cir. 1948)—§ **13.7.2 n. 83.**

Cetenko v. United California Bank, 30 Cal.3d 528, 179 Cal. Rptr. 902, 638 P.2d 1299 (1982)—§ **9.6.3 n. 70.**

Chacharis v. Fadell, 438 N.E.2d 1032 (Ind.App.1982)—§ **5.6.5 n. 97.**

Chadha v. Immigration & Naturalization Serv., 462 U.S. 919, 103 S.Ct. 2764, 77 L.Ed.2d 317—§ **2.2.3 n. 44.**

Chadsey, In re, 141 A.D. 458, 156 N.Y.S. 456 (1910)—§ **13.5.4 n. 59.**

Chadwick v. Superior Court, 106 Cal.App.3d 108, 164 Cal. Rptr. 864 (1980)—§ **8.9.4 n. 43.**

Chahoon v. Commonwealth, 62 Val (21 Gratt.) 822 (1871)—§ **6.4.9 n. 30.**

Chaleff v. Superior Court, 69 Cal.App.3d 721, 138 Cal. Rptr. 735 (1977)—§ **12.1.3 n. 70.**

Chalpin v. Brennan, 114 Ariz. 124, 559 P.2d 680 (Ct.App. 1976)—§ **5.6.4 n. 45;** § **5.6.5 n. 87.**

Chambers, In re, 292 Or. 670, 642 P.2d 286 (1982)—§ **5.1 n. 18, 37.**

Chambers v. Oklahoma Bar Ass'n, 203 Okl. 583, 224 P.2d 583 (1950)—§ **17.4.2 n. 64.**

Chambers v. Superior Court, 121 Cal.App.3d 893, 175 Cal. Rptr. 575 (1981)—§ **8.10.2 n. 78, 82.**

Chambers, State v., 86 N.M. 383, 524 P.2d 999 (App. 1974)—§ **7.6.5 n. 85;** § **13.10.1 n. 34.**

Chambliss, Bahner & Crawford v. Luther, 531 S.W.2d 108 (Tenn.App.1975)—§ **9.5.2 n. 53.**

Chamley, In re, 349 N.W.2d 56 (S.D.1984)—§ **15.2.1 n. 82.**

Champion Int'l Corp. v. International Paper Co., 486 F.Supp. 1328 (N.D.Ga.1980)—§ **6.4.6 n. 9.**

Chandler v. Florida, 449 U.S. 560, 101 S.Ct. 802, 66 L.Ed. 2d 740 (1981)—§ **12.2.1 n. 84.**

Dodson v. Floyd, 529 F.Supp. 1056 (N.D.Ga.)—§ **2.6.3 n. 53;** § **7.6.2 n. 33.**

Doe, In re, 117 Misc.2d 197, 456 N.Y.S.2d 312 (Cty.Ct. 1982)—§ **6.3.5 n. 25.**

Doe, In re, 662 F.2d 1073 (4th Cir.1981)—§ **6.4.10 n. 59.**

Doe, In re, 551 F.2d 899 (2d Cir.1977)—§ **12.9 n. 11.**

Doe, In re, 546 F.2d 498, 502 (2d Cir.1976)—§ **13.5.5. n. 74.**

Doe v. A Corp., 330 F.Supp. 1352 (S.D.N.Y.1971)—§ **6.3.4 n. 2;** § **6.3.4 n. 4;** § **7.1.6. n. 67;** § **7.1.7 n. 90;** § **8.3.3 n. 73.**

Doe v. Board on Professional Responsibility, 717 F.2d 1424 (D.C.Cir.)—§ **2.2.5 n. 75.**

Doe v. Pringle, 550 F.2d 596 (10th Cir.)—§ **2.5 n. 73;** § **3.4.5 n. 65, 71.**

Doe, People v., 99 Misc.2d 411, 416 N.Y.S.2d 466 (1979)—§ **6.3.6 n. 46.**

Doe Corp., In re, 675 F.2d 482 (2d Cir.1982)—§ **13.4.2 n. 15.**

Doerr, State ex rel. Nebraska St. B. Ass'n v., 216 Neb. 504, 344 N.W.2d 464 (1984)—§ **5.1 n. 50.**

Dolan, In re, 76 N.J. 1, 384 A.2d 1076 (1978)—§ **8.5 n. 31, 32, 34.**

Dolan v. Hickey, 385 Mass. 234, 431 N.W.2d 229 (1982)—§ **11.6.3 n. 72.**

Dolan, United States v., 570 F.2d 1170 (3d Cir.1978)—§ **7.2.3 n. 30, 63.**

Domed Stadium Hotel, Inc. v. Holiday Inns, Inc., 479 F.Supp. 465 (E.D.La.1979)—§ **7.4.3 n. 20, 23.**

Donahue, United States v., 560 F.2d 1039 (1st Cir.1977)—§ **8.2.4 n. 53.**

Donaldson v. Haldave, 7 Cl. & F. 762, 7 Eng.Rep. 1258 (H.L.1840)—§ **5.6.2 n. 58.**

Dondi, In re, 95 A.D.2d 349, 466 N.Y.S.2d 708 (1983)—§ **12.4.6 n. 18.**

Dondich, United States v., 460 F.Supp. 849 (N.D.Cal. 1978)—§ **8.9.3 n. 31.**

Donnelly v. DeChristoforo, 416 U.S. 637, 94 S.Ct. 1868, 40 L.Ed.2d 431 (1974)—§ **13.10.4 n. 80.**

Donnersbach v. State, 444 N.E.2d 1184 (Ind.1983)—§ **6.3.5 n. 21, 27.**

Donohoe, In re, 90 Wn.2d 173, 580 P.2d 1093 (1978)—§ **7.1.7 n. 77.**

Donovan v. Fitzsimmons, 90 F.R.D. 583 (N.D.Ill.1981)—§ **6.5.5 n. 6, 7.**

Donovan, People ex rel. Dep't of Public Works v., 57 Cal. 2d 346, 19 Cal.Rptr. 473, 369 P.2d 1 (1962)—§ **6.1.4 n. 9.**

Dorador v. State, 573 P.2d 839 (Wyo.1978)—§ **15.4.3 n. 33.**

Dorfman, United States v., 542 F.Supp. 402 (N.D.Ill. 1982)—§ **7.1.4 n. 37;** § **8.10.2 n. 5, 98;** § **8.10.3 n. 33, 71.**

Dorofee v. Planning Bd. of Township of Pennsauken, 187 N.J.Super. 141, 453 A.2d 1341 (1982)—§ **16.6.2 n. 92.**

Doster, State v., 276 S.C. 647, 284 S.E.2d 218 (1981)—§ **6.3.4 n. 97.**

Dostert, State ex rel. Askin v., 295 S.E.2d 271 (W.Va. 1982)—§ **2.2.4 n. 71;** § **12.1.3 n. 70.**

Dostert, State ex rel. Hamstead v., 313 S.E.2d 409 (W.Va. 1984)—§ **13.10.3 n. 59.**

Douglas, Estate of (Surr.Ct.N.Y.Cty.1980) 104 Misc.2d 430, 428 N.Y.S.2d 558—§ **1.6 n. 24.**

Douglas v. California, 372 U.S. 353, 83 S.Ct. 814, 9 L.Ed.2d 811 (1963)—§ **14.3.1 n. 53;** § **14.3.2 n. 70.**

Douglas v. Donovan, 704 F.2d 1276 (D.C.Cir.1983)—§ **12.7 n. 88.**

Douglas v. Parks, 68 N.C.App. 496, 315 S.E.2d 84 (1984)—§ **5.6.3 n. 19.**

Douglas v. State Bar, 183 Mont. 155, 598 P.2d 1080—§ **2.3 n. 17.**

Douglas, State v., 217 Neb. 199, 349 N.W.2d 870—§ **2.6.1 n. 15.**

Douglas, State ex rel. v. Bigelow, 214 Neb. 464, 334 N.W.2d 444 (1983)—§ **15.4.3 n. 32.**

Dowdy, In re, 247 Ga. 488, 277 S.E.2d 36 (1981)—§ **4.8 n. 37.**

Downing v. LeBritton, 550 F.2d 689 (1st Cir.1977)—§ **14.5 n. 79.**

Downs v. Hodge, 413 S.W.2d 519 (Mo.App.1967)—§ **9.6.3 n. 69.**

Dows, In re, 168 Minn. 6, 209 N.W. 627 (1926)—§ **13.5.4 n. 58.**

Doyle v. Ohio, 426 U.S. 610, 96 S.Ct. 2240, 49 L.Ed.2d 91 (1976)—§ **14.6.4 n. 53.**

Doyle v. Schlensky, 120 Ill.App.3d 807, 76 Ill.Dec. 466, 458 N.E.2d 1120 (1983)—§ **5.6.4 n. 57.**

Doyle v. State Bar, 32 Cal.3d 12, 184 Cal.Rptr. 720, 648 P.2d 942 (1982)—§ **3.4.3 n. 8;** § **3.5.2 n. 48;** § **4.8. n. 26, 31;** § **5.1 n. 44.**

Draganescu v. First Nat'l Bank, 502 F.2d 550 (5th Cir. 1974)—§ **7.5.2 n. 10, 51.**

Drago v. Bounagurio, 46 N.Y.2d 778, 413 N.Y.S.2d 910, 386 N.E.2d 821 (1978)—§ **5.6. n. 34.**

Drake, In re, 292 Or. 704, 642 P.2d 296 (1982)—§ **8.11.3 n. 1.**

Drake v. Northwest Natural Gas Co., 39 Del.Ch. 394, 165 A.2d 452 (1960)—§ **8.13 n. 56.**

Draper, In re, 317 A.2d 106 (Del.1974)—§ **4.8 n. 11.**

Draper v. Airco, Inc., 580 F.2d 91 (3d Cir.1978)—§ **12.1.1 n. 4.**

Draper v. Washington, 372 U.S. 487, 83 S.Ct. 774, 9 L.Ed. 2d 899 (1963)—§ **14.3.1 n. 52.**

Dreher, State v., 137 Mo. 11, 38 S.W. 567 (1897)—§ **14.6.2 n. 3.**

Dresden v. Willock, 518 F.2d 281 (3d Cir.1975)—§ **4.8 n. 10.**

Drexler, In re, 290 Minn. 542, 188 N.W.2d 436 (1971)—§ **12.6.5 n. 46.**

Dreyer v. Illinois, 187 U.S. 71, 23 S.Ct. 28, 47 L.Ed. 79—§ **2.2.5 n. 88.**

Drieband, In re, 273 A.D. 413, 77 N.Y.S.2d 585 (1948)—§ **13.10.4 n. 94.**

Driscoll, State v., 116 R.I. 749, 360 A.2d 857 (1976)—§ **6.3.7 n. 58.**

Driscoll, State v., 89 N.M. 541, 555 P.2d 136 (1976)—§ **12.1.3 n. 60.**

Drumgo v. Superior Court, 8 Cal.3d 930, 106 Cal.Rptr. 631, 506 P.2d 1007 (1973)—§ **14.3.4 n. 90.**

Drummond v. Stahl, 127 Ariz. 122, 618 P.2d 616 (App. 1980)—§ **7.1.7 n. 4.**

Duarte, People v., 79 Ill.App.3d 110, 34 Ill.Dec. 657, 398 N.E.2d 332 (1979)—§ **6.3.7 n. 56.**

Eikelberger v. Tolotti, 96 Nev. 525, 611 P.2d 1086 (1980)—§ **5.6.5 n. 3;** § **8.13 n. 65.**

Eisenberg, In re, 81 Wis.2d 175, 259 N.W.2d 745, 747 (1977)—§ **3.3.1 n. 63; 3.3.2 n. 78;** § **4.8 n. 94;** § **15.1.4 n. 65.**

Eisenberg v. Boardman, 302 F.Supp. 1360 (W.D.Wis. 1969)—§ **12.2.2 n. 8;** § **12.2.2 n. 87.**

Eisenberg, State v., 48 Wis.2d 364, 180 N.W.2d 529 (1970)—§ **11.3.2 n. 59.**

Eisenstein, United States v., 731 F.2d 1540 (11th Cir. 1984)—§ **4.7 n. 88.**

El Paso Co., United States v., 682 F.2d 530 (5th Cir.1982)—§ **6.3.2 n. 54;** § **6.4.3 n. 85.**

Elder v. Metropolitan Freight Carriers, Inc., 543 F.2d 513 (3d Cir.)—§ **2.6.1 n. 91;** § **15.2.4 n. 8.**

Eldridge, In re, 82 N.Y. 1961 (1880)—§ **12.4.3 n. 96.**

Eleazer v. Hardaway Concrete Co., 281 S.C. 344, 315 S.E.2d 175 (Ct.App.1984)—§ **9.6.3 n. 75.**

Elisovsky v. State, 592 P.2d 1221 (Alaska 1979)—§ **11.4.4 n. 11, 14;** § **12.9 n. 7.**

Ellen v. Rhodes, 507 F.Supp. 734 (S.D.Ohio 1981)—§ **7.1.6 n. 60.**

Ellenstein v. Herman Body Co., 23 N.J. 348, 129 A.2d 268 (1957)—§ **8.12.2 n. 26.**

Elliott, In re, 268 S.C. 522, 235 S.E.2d 111 (1977)—§ **3.3.4 n. 41.**

Ellis, In re, 53 Hawaii 23, 487 P.2d 286 (1971)—§ **15.1.3 n. 6.**

Ellis v. Brotherhood of Railway Clerks, ___ U.S. ___, 104 S.Ct. 1883, 80 L.Ed.2d 428—§ **2.3 n. 20.**

Ellis v. Frawley, 165 Wis. 381, 161 N.W. 364 (1917)—§ **1.5 n. 3.**

Elrod v. Burns, 427 U.S. 347, 96 S.Ct. 2673, 49 L.Ed.2d 547 (1976)—§ **13.9.1 n. 94.**

Eltzroth, In re, 67 Or.App. 520, 679 P.2d 1369 (1984)—§ **8.6 n. 53.**

Emerald Green Homeowners' Ass'n v. Aaron, 90 A.D.2d 628, 456 N.Y.S.2d 219 (1982)—§ **7.5.2 n. 78.**

Emergency Delivery of Legal Services to the Poor, In re, 432 So.2d 39 (Fla.1983)—§ **16.9 n. 22.**

Emery v. Hovey, 84 N.H. 499, 153 A. 322 (1931)—§ **15.4.1 n. 96.**

Emeson, People v., 638 P.2d 293 (Colo.1981)—§ **3.4.2 n. 87.**

Emle Industries, Inc. v. Patentex, Inc., 478 F.2d 562 (2d Cir.1973)—§ **7.1.3 n. 21;** § **7.1.7 n. 15, 24;** § **7.2.1 n. 41;** § **7.4.2 n. 63;** § **7.4.3 n. 3, 13.**

Emmanuel, State v., 42 Wn.2d 799, 259 P.2d 845 (1953)—§ **6.4.9 n. 30.**

Emmons, Williams, Mires & Leech v. State Bar, 6 Cal. App.3d 565, 86 Cal.Rptr. 367 (1970)—§ **9.2.4 n. 94.**

Empire Linotype School, Inc. v. United States, 143 F.Supp. 627 (S.D.N.Y.1956)—§ **7.2.1 n. 42.**

Employees' Retirement System v. Waldron, 285 Md. 175, 401 A.2d 172 (1979)—§ **15.1.4 n. 70.**

Employers Casualty Co. v. Tilley, 496 S.W.2d 552 (Tex. 1973)—§ **8.4.2 n. 98;** § **8.4.3 n. 8.**

Employers Ins. of Wausau v. Hall, 49 N.C.App. 179, 270 S.E.2d 617 (1980)—§ **11.4.3 n. 94.**

Emslie v. State Bar, 11 Cal.3d 210, 113 Cal.Rptr. 175, 520 P.2d 991 (1974)—§ **3.4.4 n. 27.**

Engle v. Isaac, 456 U.S. 107, 102 S.Ct. 1558, 71 L.Ed.2d 783 (1982)—§ **14.6.2 n. 2.**

Englishtown Sportswear, Ltd. v. Tuttle, 547 F.Supp. 700 (S.D.N.Y.1982)—§ **7.1.6 n. 76.**

Ennis v. Ennis, 88 Wis.2d 82, 276 N.W.2d 341 (1979)—§ **7.1.7 n. 5.**

EPA v. Mink, 410 U.S. 73, 93 S.Ct. 827, 35 L.Ed.2d 119 (1973)—§ **6.5.6 n. 12, 14.**

Epstein, Reiss & Goodman v. Greenfield, 102 A.D.2d 749, 476 N.Y.S.2d 885 (1984)—§ **9.2.2 n. 58.**

Equitable Lumber Corp. v. IPA Land Devel. Corp., 38 N.Y.2d 516, 381 N.Y.S.2d 459, 344 N.E.2d 391 (1976)—§ **16.6.2 n. 42.**

Erickson v. Fargo Van & Storage, Inc., 25 Wn.App. 502, 607 P.2d 894 (1980)—§ **9.6.3 n. 32.**

Erickson, State ex rel. Nebraska St. Bar Ass'n v., 204 Neb. 692, 285 N.W.2d 105 (1979)—§ **3.3.3 n. 21;** § **3.5.2 n. 8, 45, 53;** § **5.1 n. 51.**

Erie v. Tompkins, 304 U.S. 64, 58 S.Ct. 817, 82 L.Ed. 1188 (1938)—§ **9.6.3 n. 39.**

Erie County Water Authority v. Western N.Y. Water Co., 304 N.Y. 342, 107 N.E.2d 479 (1952)—§ **3.2 n. 35.**

Erlandson, In re, 290 Or. 465, 622 P.2d 727 (1981)—§ **8.11.3 n. 8.**

Esch v. Superior Court, 577 P.2d 1039 (Alaska 1978)—§ **2.2.4 n. 71.**

Eschwig v. State Bar, 1 Cal.3d 8, 81 Cal.Rptr. 352, 459 P.2d 904 (1969)—§ **8.11.3 n. 12.**

Escott v. BarChris Constr. Co., 283 F.Supp. 643 (S.D.N.Y. 1968)—§ **5.6.5 n. 84;** § **13.7.4 n. 20.**

Esler, In re, 275 S.C. 400, 272 S.E.2d 32 (1980)—§ **15.1.4 n. 69.**

Esser v. A.H. Robins Co., 537 F.Supp. 197 (D.Minn.)—§ **2.2.5 n. 78;** § **9.1 n. 19.**

Estate of (see name of party)

Estates Theatres, Inc. v. Columbia Pictures Ind., Inc., 345 F.Supp. 93 (S.D.N.Y.1972)—§ **7.1.7 n. 19;** § **7.3.3;** § **7.3.3 n. 40.**

Estelle v. Smith, 451 U.S. 454, 101 S.Ct. 1866, 68 L.Ed.2d 359 (1981)—§ **6.2.3 n. 46.**

Estes, In re, 580 P.2d 977 (Okl.1978)—§ **15.3.2 n. 59.**

Estes, In re, 390 Mich. 585, 212 N.W.2d 903, 92 A.L.R.3d 275 (1973)—§ **4.6.2 n. 71.**

Estes v. Texas, 381 U.S. 532, 85 S.Ct. 1628, 14 L.Ed.2d 543 (1965)—§ **12.2.1 n. 80.**

Esteva v. House of Segram, Inc., 314 F.2d 827 (7th Cir. 1963)—§ **5.1 n. 42.**

Estreen v. Bluhm, 79 Wis.2d 142, 255 N.W.2d 473 (1977)—§ **8.11.3 n. 98.**

Eurocom, S.A. v. Mahoney, Cohen & Co., 522 F.Supp. 1179 (S.D.N.Y.1981)—§ **7.5.2 n. 67.**

Evans, In re, 661 P.2d 171 (Alaska 1983)—§ **3.4.3 n. 89.**

Evans, In re, 450 A.2d 443 (D.C.App.1982)—§ **12.1.3 n. 42.**

Evans, In re, 229 Kan. 182, 621 P.2d 991 (1981)—§ **3.5.4 n. 98.**

Evans, In re, 113 Ariz. 458, 556 P.2d 792 (1976)—§ **3.5.2 n. 16;** § **7.4.2 n. 72;** § **7.4.3 n. 22.**

Evans, In re, 524 F.2d 1004 (5th Cir.1975)—§ **15.2.4 n. 12;** § **15.4.3 n. 38, 40.**

Feldshuh, In re, 84 A.D.2d 284, 445 N.Y.S.2d 974 (1982)—§ **3.5.4 n. 92.**

Felmeister, In re, 95 N.J. 431, 471 A.2d 775 (1984)—§ **14.2.4 n. 68.**

Felton, State v., 110 Wis.2d 485, 329 N.W.2d 161 (1983)—§ **14.6.3 n. 24, 27.**

Fenaille & Despeaux v. Coudert, 44 N.J.L. 286 (1882)—§ **5.6.2 n. 88.**

Fentress, People v., 103 Misc.2d 179, 425 N.Y.S.2d 485 (Cty.Ct.1980)—§ **6.3.7 n. 58;** § **6.4.4 n. 96.**

Ferrer v. State, 434 So.2d 15 (Fla.App.1983)—§ **3.5.3 n. 74.**

Ferri v. Ackerman, 444 U.S. 193, 100 S.Ct. 402, 62 L.Ed.2d 355 (1979)—§ **5.6.3 n. 23.**

Ferri v. Rossetti, 483 Pa. 327, 396 A.2d 1193 (1979)—§ **5.6.3 n. 23.**

Ferrichs, In re, 238 N.W.2d 764 (Iowa 1976)—§ **11.3.2 n. 60.**

Ferriman, In re, 487 Pa. 45, 408 A.2d 844 (1979)—§ **15.4.2 n. 21.**

Ferris v. Snively, 172 Wash. 167, 19 P.2d 942 (1933)—§ **16.3.1 n. 15.**

Ferris v. State ex rel. Maass, 75 Wis.2d 542, 249 N.W.2d 789 (1977)—§ **14.5 n. 71.**

Ferruzzo, Inc., Thomas G., v. Superior Court, 104 Cal.App. 3d 501, 163 Cal.Rptr. 573 (1980)—§ **9.5.1 n. 39.**

Fessel, United States v., 531 F.2d 1275 (5th Cir.1976)—§ **14.3.5 n. 1.**

Feuerstein, In re, 93 N.J. 441, 461 A.2d 750 (1983)—§ **4.8 n. 9.**

Failkow v. Devoe Motors, Inc., 359 Mass. 569, 270 N.E.2d 798 (1971)—§ **12.1.1 n. 5.**

Fickett v. Superior Court, 27 Ariz.App. 793, 558 P.2d 988 (1976)—§ **5.6.4 n. 53, 54.**

Fidelity Mortgage Investors v. Camelia Builders, Inc., 550 F.2d 47 (2d Cir.1976)—§ **13.3.9 n. 4.**

Field v. Freedman, 527 F.Supp. 935 (D.Kan.1981)—§ **8.3.4 n. 80, 89.**

Fielding v. Brebbia, 479 F.2d 195 (D.C.Cir.1973)—§ **7.1.6 n. 70;** § **8.3.2 n. 61.**

Fields v. Volkswagen of America, Inc., 555 P.2d 48 (Okl. 1976)—§ **12.1.1 n. 4.**

Fife, People v., 65 Ill.App.3d 805, 22 Ill.Dec. 536, 382 N.E.2d 1234 (1978)—§ **8.2.2 n. 8;** § **8.9.4 n. 58.**

Fife, People v., 65 Ill.App.3d 805, 22 Ill.Dec. 536, 382 N.E.2d 1235 (1978)—§ **8.9.5 n. 58.**

Filing, In re, 316 N.W.2d 556 (Minn.1982)—§ **3.5.7 n. 90.**

Fillion v. Troy, 656 S.W.2d 912 (Tex.Civ.App.1983)—§ **5.6.3 n. 33.**

Financial Bankshares, Inc. v. Metzger, 680 F.2d 768 (D.C. Cir.)—§ **2.2.2 n. 37.**

Financial General Bankshares, Inc. v. Metzger, 523 F.Supp. 744 (D.D.C.1981)—§ **7.1.7 n. 87;** § **7.2 n. 75;** § **8.3.3 n. 72;** § **9.6.1 n. 11;** § **13.7.2 n. 85.**

Finch v. State Bar, 28 Cal.3d 659, 170 Cal.Rptr. 629, 621 P.2d 253 (1981)—§ **3.3.3 n. 21;** § **3.5.1 n. 99;** § **3.5.2 n. 39;** § **3.5.6 n. 57.**

Finch v. Wallberg Dredging Co., 79 Idaho 521, 322 P.2d 701 (1958)—§ **7.4.1 n. 54.**

Finchette v. Taylor, 191 Minn. 582, 254 N.W. 910 (1934)—§ **15.1.3 n. 22.**

Fingers, State v., 564 S.W.2d 579 (Mo.App.1978)—§ **6.3.7 n. 52.**

Fiorentino v. United States, 221 Ct.Cl. 545, 607 F.2d 963 (1979)—§ **13.9.1 n. 93.**

Fiorillo, United States v., 376 F.2d 180 (2d Cir.1967)—§ **7.5.2 n. 43.**

Firestone Tire & Rubber Co. v. Risjord, 449 U.S. 368, 101 S.Ct. 669, 66 L.Ed.2d 571 (1981)—§ **7.1.7 n. 35.**

First Amendment Found. v. Village of Brookfield, 575 F.Supp. 1207 (N.D.Ill.1983)—§ **15.1.3 n. 3.**

First Bank & Trust Co. v. Zagoria, 250 Ga. 844, 302 S.E.2d 674 (1983)—§ **2.6.1 n. 16;** § **5.6.6 n. 48, 49, 50;** § **16.2.4 n. 85.**

First Municipal Leasing Corp. v. Blankenship, Potts, Aikman, Hagin & Stewart, 648 S.W.2d 410 (Tex.Civ.App. 1983)—§ **5.6.4 n. 41.**

First Nat'l Bank v. Pepper, 547 F.2d 708 (2d Cir.1976)—§ **9.6.3 n. 37.**

First Nat'l Bank v. Rapides Bank & Trust Co., 145 Ga. App. 517, 244 S.E.2d 51 (1978)—§ **7.1.5 n. 50.**

First Nat'l Bank & Trust Co. v. Hyman Novick Realty Co., 72 A.D.2d 858, 421 N.Y.S.2d 733 (1979)—§ **9.6.3 n. 67.**

First Nat'l Bank of East Islip v. Brower, 42 N.Y.2d 471, 398 N.Y.S.2d 875, 368 N.E.2d 1240—§ **2.2.2 n. 31.**

First Wisconsin Mortgage Trust v. First Wisconsin Corp., 86 F.R.D. 160 (E.D.Wis.1980)—§ **6.4.6 n. 13;** § **7.1.7 n. 2.**

Fischel, In re, 557 F.2d 209 (9th Cir.1977)—§ **6.3.6 n. 45.**

Fisher, In re, ___ Ind. ___, 400 N.E.2d 1127 (1980)—§ **8.9.1 n. 12;** § **8.9.4 n. 50.**

Fisher v. United States, 425 U.S. 391, 96 S.Ct. 1569, 48 L.Ed.2d 39 (1976)—§ **6.1.3 n. 6;** § **6.1.4 n. 36;** § **6.2.3;** § **6.2.3 n. 43;** § **6.3.2 n. 66;** § **6.3.4 n. 77;** § **6.3.5;** § **6.3.5 n. 34, 36;** § **6.6.1 n. 28.**

Fisher Studio, Inc. v. Loew's, Inc., 232 F.2d 199 (2d Cir. 1956)—§ **14.2.5 n. 90.**

Fiske v. Buder, 125 F.2d 841 (8th Cir.1942)—§ **7.1.7 n. 91.**

Fitchette v. Taylor, 191 Minn. 582, 254 N.W. 910 (1934)—§ **15.1.3 n. 90.**

Fitterer, United States v., 710 F.2d 1328 (8th Cir.1983)—§ **11.6.2 n. 62.**

Fitzgerald v. Baxter State Park Authority, 385 A.2d 189 (Me.1978)—§ **13.9.1 n. 9.**

Fitzgerald v. Estelle, 505 F.2d 1334 (5th Cir.1974)—§ **14.3.7 n. 29;** § **14.6.1 n. 95.**

Fitzpatrick v. State Bar, 20 Cal.3d 73, 141 Cal.Rptr. 169, 569 P.2d 763 (1977)—§ **9.2.1 n. 55;** § **9.5.3 n. 74;** § **16.3.1 n. 3.**

Fitzsimmons v. Robb, 193 Pa. 518, 44 A. 558 (1899)—§ **16.2.5 n. 90.**

Fitzsimmons v. State Bar, 34 Cal.3d 327, 193 Cal.Rptr. 896, 667 P.2d 700 (1983)—§ **4.8 n. 6, 33, 36.**

Flanagan v. DeLapp, 533 S.W.2d 592 (Mo.1976)—§ **8.11.3 n. 91.**

Flanagan v. United States, 459 U.S. 1101, 103 S.Ct. 721, 74 L.Ed.2d 948 (1983)—§ **8.2.4 n. 52.**

Flanagan, United States v., 679 F.2d 1072 (3d Cir.1982)—§ **7.2.3 n. 63;** § **8.2.4 n. 40.**

Flannery, In re, 150 App.Div. 369, 135 N.Y.S. 612 (1912)—§ **9.4.2 n. 42.**

Flego v. Phillips, Appel & Waldin, Inc., 514 F.Supp. 1178 (D.N.J.1981)—§ **8.10.3 n. 18, 47, 59.**

Fleischmann Distilling Corp. v. Major Brewing Co., 386 U.S. 714, 87 S.Ct. 1404, 18 L.Ed.2d 475 (1967)—§ **16.6.2 n. 84.**

Fleming v. Campbell, 537 S.W.2d 118 (Tex.Civ.App.)—§ **2.6.1 n. 4;** § **9.2.4 n. 3.**

Fleming v. State, 246 Ga. 90, 270 S.E.2d 185 (1980)—§ **8.2.4 n. 35.**

Fleming, State v., 230 Kan. 260, 634 P.2d 444 (1981)—§ **5.1 n. 46.**

Fletcher v. Krise, 120 F.2d 809 (D.C.Cir.1941)—§ **3.5.4 n. 11.**

Fletcher v. Weir, 455 U.S. 603, 102 S.Ct. 1309, 71 L.Ed.2d 490 (1982)—§ **12.5.4 n. 99.**

Fling, In re, 316 N.W.2d 556 (Minn.1982)—§ **4.8 n. 37, 50, 95.**

Flinn, In re, 243 Ga. 342, 253 S.E.2d 692 (1979)—§ **5.1 n. 44.**

Flood v. Commissioner, 468 F.2d 904 (9th Cir.1972)—§ **6.7.8 n. 6.**

Flores v. Flores, 598 P.2d 893 (Alaska 1979)—§ **7.6.5 n. 97.**

Flores, People v., 71 Cal.App.3d 559, 139 Cal.Rptr. 546 (1977)—§ **6.3.4 n. 77, 81.**

Flores, United States v., 628 F.2d 521 (9th Cir.1980)—§ **6.3.5 n. 21.**

Florida Bar, In re, 133 So.2d 554 (Fla.1961)—§ **1.6 n.8;** § **5.6.6 n. 48;** § **16.2.4 n. 86;** § **17.3.2 n. 87.**

Florida Bar v. Abrams, 402 So.2d 1150 (Fla.1981)—§ **3.4.5 n. 83, 89.**

Florida Bar v. Agar, 394 So.2d 405 (Fla.1980)—§ **12.5.3 n. 63.**

Florida Bar v. American Legal & Bus. Forms, Inc., 274 So. 2d 225 (Fla.1973)—§ **15.1.3 n. 96.**

Florida Bar v. Ball, 406 So.2d 459 (Fla.1981)—§ **6.7.8 n. 11.**

Florida Bar v. Bern, 425 So.2d 526 (Fla.1982)—§ **3.5.2 n. 42.**

Florida Bar v. Blalock, 325 So.2d 401 (Fla.1976)—§ **4.8 n. 98.**

Florida Bar v. Borns, 428 So.2d 648 (Fla.1983)—§ **4.8 n. 25.**

Florida Bar v. Bratton, 413 So.2d 754 (Fla.1982)—§ **3.5.4 n. 3;** § **9.6.3 n. 46.**

Florida Bar v. Breed, 378 So.2d 783 (Fla.1979)—§ **4.8 n. 98.**

Florida Bar v. Brennan, 377 So.2d 1181 (Fla.1979)—§ **6.3.4 n. 6;** § **12.6.5 n. 48.**

Florida Bar v. Brumbaugh, 355 So.2d 1186 (Fla.1978)—§ **15.1.3 n. 66, 96, 98.**

Florida Bar v. Budish, 421 So.2d 501 (Fla.1982)—§ **3.5.6 n. 71;** § **14.2.4 n. 59.**

Florida Bar v. Burns, 392 So.2d 1325 (Fla.1981)—§ **12.1.3 n. 52.**

Florida Bar v. Byron, 424 So.2d 748 (Fla.1982)—§ **3.5.7 n. 95.**

Florida Bar v. Carter, 429 So.2d 3 (Fla.1983)—§ **3.5.2 n. 41.**

Florida Bar v. Clark, 359 So.2d 863 (Fla.1978)—§ **3.5.5 n. 37.**

Florida Bar v. Cooper, 429 So.2d 1 (Fla.1983)—§ **3.5.5 n. 29.**

Florida Bar v. Davis, 419 So.2d 325 (Fla.1982)—§ **3.5.7 n. 99.**

Florida Bar v. Dingle, 220 So.2d 9 (Fla.1969)—§ **9.5.1 n. 26.**

Florida Bar v. Doe, 384 So.2d 30 (Fla.1980)—§ **3.4.3 n. 97.**

Florida Bar v. Drizin, 435 So.2d 796 (Fla.1983)—§ **3.5.5 n. 29.**

Florida Bar v. Fassett, 384 So.2d 1288 (Fla.1980)—§ **3.5.7 n. 96.**

Florida Bar v. Fetterman, 439 So.2d 835 (Fla.1983)—§ **14.2.4 n. 76.**

Florida Bar v. Furman, 451 So.2d 808 (Fla.1984)—§ **15.1.3 n. 41, 98.**

Florida Bar v. Furman, 376 So.2d 378 (Fla.1979)—§ **15.1.3 n. 98.**

Florida Bar v. Fussell, 390 So.2d 68 (Fla.1980)—§ **9.5.2 n. 50.**

Florida Bar v. G.B.T., 399 So.2d 357 (Fla.1981)—§ **3.4.2 n. 72.**

Florida Bar v. Gaer, 380 So.2d 429 (Fla.1980)—§ **9.2.4 n. 94.**

Florida Bar v. Gaskin, 403 So.2d 425 (Fla.1981)—§ **5.1. n. 48.**

Florida Bar v. Gentry, 447 So.2d 1342 (Fla.1984)—§ **3.4.5 n. 76.**

Florida Bar v. Glick, 397 So.2d 1140 (Fla.1981)—§ **3.5.7 n. 94.**

Florida Bar v. Greenspahn, 396 So.2d 182 (Fla.1981)—§ **3.5.2 n. 44.**

Florida Bar v. Hartnett, 398 So.2d 1352 (Fla.1981)—§ **3.5.4 n. 4.**

Florida Bar v. Hawkins, 444 So.2d 961 (Fla.1984)—§ **3.5.7 n. 91.**

Florida Bar v. Heller, 409 So.2d 1030 (Fla.1982)—§ **16.2.3 n. 42.**

Florida Bar v. Hunt, 441 So.2d 1201 (Fla.1983)—§ **16.2.4 n. 87.**

Florida Bar v. Jackson, 398 So.2d 817 (Fla.1981)—§ **15.4.1 n. 99.**

Florida Bar v. Jaffe, 428 So.2d 252 (Fla.1983)—§ **3.5.4 n. 17.**

Florida Bar v. Jameison, 426 So.2d 16 (Fla.1983)—§ **8.12.2 n. 27.**

Florida Bar v. Kaiser, 397 So.2d 1132 (Fla.1981)—§ **14.2.3 n. 48;** § **15.1.4 n. 61, 67.**

Florida Bar v. Lancaster, 448 So.2d 1019 (Fla.1984)—§ **3.4.4 n. 27.**

Florida Bar v. Larkin, 420 So.2d 1080 (Fla.1982)—§ **3.3.3 n. 27.**

Florida Bar v. Larkin, 370 So.2d 371 (Fla.1979)—§ **3.5.7 n. 87.**

Florida Bar v. Larkin, 298 So.2d 371 (Fla.1974)—§ **2.2.2 n 24;** § **15.1.3 n. 85.**

Florida Bar v. Leopold, 399 So.2d 978 (Fla.1981)—§ **3.5.3 n. 70.**

Florida Bar v. Lund, 410 So.2d 922 (Fla.1982)—§ **3.5.4 n. 92.**

Florida Bar v. McCain, 330 So.2d 712 (Fla.1976)—§ **17.4.2 n. 60.**

Florida Bar v. Martin, 432 So.2d 54 (Fla.1983)—§ **15.1.2 n. 52.**

Florida Bar v. Mason, 334 So.2d 1 (Fla.1976)—§ **11.3.3 n. 77.**

Florida Bar v. Mills, 410 So.2d 498 (Fla.1982)—§ **15.1.3 n. 85.**

Florida Bar v. Moriber, 314 So.2d 145 (Fla.1975)—§ **9.3.1 n. 64.**

Florida Bar v. Moses, 380 So.2d 412 (Fla.1980)—§ **2.2.3 n. 52, 59;** § **15.1.3 n. 60.**

Florida Bar v. Nagel, 440 So.2d 1287 (Fla.1983)—§ **3.5.4 n. 86.**

Florida Bar v. Neadel, 297 So.2d 305 (Fla.1974)—§ **15.4.1 n. 2.**

Florida Bar v. Neale, 384 So.2d 1264 (Fla.1980)—§ **5.1 n. 36.**

Florida Bar v. Neely, 372 So.2d 89 (Fla.1979)—§ **8.11.3 n. 10.**

Florida Bar v. Nemec, 390 So.2d 1190 (Fla.1980)—§ **5.6.7 n. 59.**

Florida Bar v. Oxner, 431 So.2d 983 (Fla.1983)—§ **12.3.3 n. 41.**

Florida Bar v. Pace, 426 So.2d 553 (Fla.1983)—§ **14.2.5 n. 88.**

Florida Bar v. Page, 419 So.2d 332 (Fla.1982)—§ **3.5.4 n. 95.**

Florida Bar v. Pascual, 424 So.2d 757 (Fla.1982)—§ **16.3.2 n. 24.**

Florida Bar v. Penn, 421 So.2d 497 (Fla.1982)—§ **3.5.4 n. 7;** § **15.1.4 n. 56.**

Florida Bar v. Perri, 435 So.2d 827 (Fla.1983)—§ **3.5.4 n. 82.**

Florida Bar v. Peterson, 418 So.2d 246 (Fla.1982)—§ **11.4.3 n. 6.**

Florida Bar v. Pettie, 424 So.2d 734 (Fla.1982)—§ **3.3.1 n. 56;** § **3.5.2 n. 37, 57.**

Florida Bar v. Prior, 330 So.2d 697 (Fla.1976)—§ **3.3.2 n. 80;** § **3.5.2 n. 28;** § **3.5.4 n. 98;** § **17.5.2 n. 31.**

Florida Bar v. Ragano, 403 So.2d 401 (Fla.1981)—§ **4.8 n. 24.**

Florida Bar v. Randolph, 238 So.2d 635 (Fla.1970)—§ **3.4.2 n. 79.**

Florida Bar v. Reese, 421 So.2d 495 (Fla.1982)—§ **3.5.2 n. 54.**

Florida Bar v. Rhodes, 355 So.2d 774 (Fla.1978)—§ **3.3.4 n. 44.**

Florida Bar v. Rogowski, 399 So.2d 1390 (Fla.1981)—§ **3.5.6 n. 75;** § **3.5.7 n. 87;** § **9.4.1 n. 40.**

Florida Bar v. Rosenberg, 387 So.2d 935 (Fla.1980)—§ **11.5 n. 26.**

Florida Bar v. Routh, 414 So.2d 1023 (Fla.1982)—§ **3.5.4 n. 92.**

Florida Bar v. Sagrans, 388 So.2d 1040 (Fla.1980)—§ **9.2.4 n. 94.**

Florida Bar v. Samaha, 407 So.2d 906 (Fla.1981)—§ **9.3.2 n. 90.**

Florida Bar v. Saphirstein, 376 So.2d 7 (Fla.1979)—§ **11.3.3 n. 77.**

Florida Bar v. Savitt, 363 So.2d 559 (Fla.1978)—§ **15.4.1 n. 92.**

Florida Bar v. Saxon, 379 So.2d 1281 (Fla.1980)—§ **11.3.3 n. 66.**

Florida Bar v. Seidler, 375 So.2d 849 (Fla.1979)—§ **3.5.4 n. 92.**

Florida Bar v. Shapiro, 413 So.2d 1184 (Fla.1982)—§ **11.6.2 n. 39.**

Florida Bar v. Simon, 171 So.2d 372 (Fla.1964)—§ **3.4.4 n. 16.**

Florida Bar v. Snow, 436 So.2d 48 (Fla.1983)—§ **12.4.4 n. 2.**

Florida Bar v. Steinbach, 427 So.2d 733 (Fla.1983)—§ **3.5.5 n. 26.**

Florida Bar v. Stockman, 370 So.2d 1146 (Fla.1979)—§ **5.1 n. 35.**

Florida Bar v. Teitelman, 261 So.2d 140 (Fla.1972)—§ **8.5 n. 35.**

Florida Bar v. Thompson, 310 So.2d 300 (Fla.1975)—§ **3.5.4 n. 9.**

Florida Bar v. Tifford, 373 So.2d 919 (Fla.1979)—§ **3.3.2 n. 82.**

Florida Bar v. Turner, 369 So.2d 581 (Fla.1979)—§ **3.3.4 n. 47.**

Florida Bar v. Ullensvang, 400 So.2d 969 (Fla.1981)—§ **3.3.3 n. 31.**

Florida Bar v. Vernell, 374 So.2d 473 (Fla.1979)—§ **8.2.2 n. 14;** § **8.2.3 n. 31.**

Florida Bar v. W.H.P., 384 So.2d 28 (Fla.1980)—§ **9.3.2 n. 91.**

Florida Bar v. Walzak, 380 So.2d 428 (Fla.1980)—§ **15.1.3 n. 40.**

Florida Bar v. Weinberger, 397 So.2d 661 (Fla.1981)—§ **12.1.2 n. 29.**

Florida Bar v. Welty, 382 So.2d 1220 (Fla.1980)—§ **3.5.3 n. 71.**

Florida Bar v. White, 384 So.2d 1266 (Fla.1980)—§ **3.4.3 n. 7;** § **4.8 n. 31.**

Florida Bar v. Wilson, 425 So.2d 2 (Fla.1983)—§ **3.5.2 n. 39.**

Florida Bar v. Winn, 208 So.2d 809 (Fla.1968)—§ **3.5.6 n. 82.**

Florida Bar v. Wooten, 452 So.2d 547 (Fla.1984)—§ **9.2.3 n. 88.**

Florida Bar, State ex rel. v. Dawson, 111 So.2d 427 (Fla. 1959)—§ **9.2.3 n. 86.**

Florida Bar, State ex rel. v. Oxford, 127 So.2d 107 (Fla. 1960)—§ **8.13 n. 64.**

Florida Bd. of Bar Examiners, In re, 443 So.2d 71 (Fla. 1983)—§ **15.3.2 n. 75.**

Florida Bd. of Bar Examiners, In re, 358 So.2d 7 (Fla. 1978)—§ **15.3.2 n. 68.**

Florida Bd. of Bar Examiners, In re (1977) 350 So.2d 1072—§ **1.5 n. 15.**

Florida Bd. of Bar Examiners re L.K.D., In re, 397 So.2d 673, 676 (Fla.1981)—§ **3.3.2 n. 85.**

Florida St. Bar Ass'n, Petition of, 40 So.2d 902 (Fla. 1949)—§ **2.2.2 n. 41;** § **2.3 n. 10.**

Floro v. Lawton, 187 Cal.App.2d 657, 10 Cal.Rptr. 98 (1960)—§ **5.6.3 n. 11.**

Florsheim, In re, 77 A.D.2d 9, 432 N.Y.S.2d 9 (1980)—§ **3.5.2 n. 42.**

Flushing Nat'l Bank v. Municipal Assistance Corp., 90 Misc.2d 204, 397 N.Y.S.2d 662 (1977)—§ **8.10.3 n. 50.**

Geurts, In re, 290 Or. 241, 620 P.2d 1373 (1980)—§ **3.4.3 n. 99;** § **5.1 n. 46.**

Geyler, In re, 114 Ariz. 321, 560 P.2d 1228 (1977)—§ **8.11.3 n. 9.**

Gholson v. Estelle, 675 F.2d 734 (5th Cir.1982)—§ **14.6.4 n. 48.**

Giacalone, People v., 399 Mich. 642, 250 N.W.2d 492 (1977)—§ **12.1.2 n. 19.**

Gibbs v. Paluk, 742 F.2d 181 (5th Cir.1984)—§ **7.1.4 n. 26;** § **7.6.3 n. 63.**

Gibson, In re, 444 N.E.2d 852 (Ind.1983)—§ **14.3.5 n. 5.**

Gibson v. Berryhill, 411 U.S. 564, 93 S.Ct. 1689, 36 L.Ed.2d 488 (1973)—§ **3.2 n. 25;** § **15.1.1;** § **15.1.1 n. 31.**

Gibson v. Johnson, 35 Or.App. 493, 582 P.2d 452 (1978)—§ **8.9.3 n. 24.**

Gibson v. Talley, 156 Ga.App. 593, 275 S.E.2d 154 (1980)—§ **5.6.6 n. 45.**

Gibson v. Western Fire Ins. Co., ___ Mont. ___, 682 P.2d 725 (1984)—§ **8.4.2 n. 3.**

Gibson, Dunn & Crutcher v. Superior Court, 94 Cal.App.3d 347, 156 Cal.Rptr. 326 (1979)—§ **5.6.3 n. 21;** § **5.6.6. n. 54.**

Giddens v. State Bar, 28 Cal.3d 730, 170 Cal.Rptr. 812, 621 P.2d 851 (1981)—§ **3.4.1 n. 56;** § **3.4.2 n. 82.**

Giddings, In re Estate of, 96 Misc.2d 824, 410 N.Y.S.2d 16 (N.Y.Sur.Ct.1978)—§ **3.5.4 n. 11, 12;** § **9.6.3 n. 53.**

Gideon v. Wainwright, 372 U.S. 335, 83 S.Ct. 792, 9 L.Ed. 2d 799 (1963)—§ **14.3.1;** § **14.3.1 n. 34, 42.**

Giglio v. United States, 405 U.S. 150, 92 S.Ct. 763, 31 L.Ed. 2d 104 (1972)—§ **13.10.4 n. 97;** § **13.10.5 n. 6, 99.**

Gilbert v. Knoxville Int'l Energy Exposition, 547 F.Supp. 53 (E.D.Tenn.1982)—§ **7.6.3 n. 53.**

Giles v. Maryland, 386 U.S. 66, 87 S.Ct. 793, 17 L.Ed.2d 737 (1967)—§ **13.10.5 n. 99.**

Giles v. Russell, 222 Kan. 629, 567 P.2d 845 (1977)—§ **4.6.2 n. 58;** § **9.6.3 n. 35.**

Gillett v. Gillett, 269 Mich. 364, 257 N.W. 719 (1934)—§ **7.4.3 n. 99.**

Gillies v. Schmidt, 38 Colo.App. 233, 556 P.2d 82 (1976)—§ **13.9.1 n. 13.**

Gillis, In re, 402 Mich. 286, 262 N.W.2d 646 (1978)—§ **3.3.2 n. 92.**

Gillock v. Board of Professional Responsibility, 656 S.W.2d 365 (Tenn.1983)—§ **3.3.1 n. 58.**

Gilman, In re Estate of, 112 Misc.2d 452, 446 N.Y.S.2d 975 (Sur.Ct.1981)—§ **9.1 n. 15.**

Gilroy, State v., 313 N.W.2d 513 (Iowa 1981)—§ **14.3.3 n. 85.**

Ginn v. Farley, 43 Md.App. 229, 403 A.2d 858 (1979)—§ **15.1.3 n. 74.**

Ginsberg, In re, 1 N.Y.2d 144, 151 N.Y.S.2d 361, 134 N.E.2d 193 (1956)—§ **3.3.2 n. 82.**

Ginsburg v. Kovrak, 392 Pa. 143, 139 A.2d 889 (1958)—§ **15.4.1 n. 6.**

Giovanazzi v. State Bar, 28 Cal.3d 465, 169 Cal.Rptr. 581, 619 P.2d 1005 (1980)—§ **3.5.1 n. 99;** § **4.8 n. 4;** § **8.11.3 n. 4;** § **16.3.1 n. 2.**

Gipson, United States v., 693 F.2d 109 (10th Cir.1982)—§ **14.3.1. n. 63.**

Gittleman, In re, 101 A.D.2d 88, 474 N.Y.S.2d 796 (1984)—§ **3.5.4 n. 3.**

Giulisni v. Chuck, 1 Hawaii App. 379, 620 P.2d 733 (1980)—§ **5.6.3 n. 70.**

Glacier Gen. Assurance Co. v. Superior Court, 95 Cal.App. 3d 836, 157 Cal.Rptr. 435 (1979)—§ **6.4.8 n. 23.**

Glade v. Superior Court, 76 Cal.App.3d 738, 143 Cal.Rptr. 119 (1978)—§ **6.4.8 n. 26;** § **6.4.10 n. 47.**

Glanton, State v., 231 N.W.2d 31 (Iowa 1975)—§ **17.6.2. n. 72.**

Glass v. Gulf Oil Corp., 12 Cal.App.3d 412, 96 Cal.Rptr. 902 (1970)—§ **16.6.2 n. 40.**

Glasschroeder, In re, 113 Wis.2d 672, 335 N.W.2d 621 (1983)—§ **3.3.3 n. 30.**

Glasser v. United States, 315 U.S. 60, 62 S.Ct. 457, 86 L.Ed. 680 (1942)—§ **8.2.3;** § **8.2.3 n. 17;** § **8.2.4 n. 47;** § **14.3.1 n. 40.**

Gleason v. Klamer, 103 Cal.App.3d 782, 163 Cal.Rptr. 483 (1980)—§ **9.6.1 n. 4.**

Glen Arms Estate, People v., 230 Cal.App.2d 841, 41 Cal. Rptr. 303 (1965)—§ **6.3.5 n. 7;** § **6.5.6 n. 16.**

Glenn v. Haynes, 192 Va. 574, 66 S.E.2d 509 (1951)—§ **5.6.2 n. 58.**

Glenn v. State Bar, 14 Cal.2d 318, 94 P.2d 43 (1939)—§ **4.6.2 n. 73.**

Glenn, People v., 68 A.D.2d 626, 417 N.Y.S.2d 934 (1979)—§ **6.3.5 n. 17.**

Glenna v. Sullivan, 310 Minn. 162, 245 N.W.2d 869 (1976)—§ **5.6.2 n. 75.**

Glidden v. Terranova, 12 Mass.App.Ct. 597, 427 N.E.2d 1169 (1981)—§ **5.6.3 n. 24.**

Globe Newspaper Co. v. Superior Court, 457 U.S. 596, 102 S.Ct. 2613, 73 L.Ed.2d 248 (1982)—§ **12.2.1 n. 82.**

Glover, In re, 176 Minn. 519, 223 N.W. 921 (1929)—§ **8.12.3 n. 34.**

Glover v. State, 557 P.2d 922 (Okla.Crim.App.1976)—§ **7.5.2 n. 45.**

Glueck v. Jonathan Logan, Inc., 653 F.2d 746 (2d Cir. 1981)—§ **7.1.6 n. 62;** § **7.3.2 n. 22.**

Gobel, State ex rel. Nebraska State Bar v., 201 Neb. 586, 271 N.W.2d 41 (1978)—§ **13.5.5 n. 74.**

Godefroy v. Jay, 7 Bing. 413, 131 Eng.Rep. 159 (1831)—§ **5.6.3 n. 24.**

Godfrey Pontiac, Inc., Bob v. Roloff, 291 Or. 318, 630 P.2d 840 (1981)—§ **2.6. n. 14;** § **5.6 n. 35.**

Godwin v. Schramm, 731 F.2d 153 (3d Cir.1984)—§ **9.4.2 n. 55.**

Goethel v. First Properties Int'l, Ltd., 363 So.2d 1117 (Fla. App.1978)—§ **9.6.3 n. 55.**

Gold, In re, 77 Ill.2d 224, 32 Ill.Dec. 912, 914, 396 N.E.2d 25, 27 (1979)—§ **3.2 n. 21.**

Gold Coast Raceway, Inc. v. Ehrenfeld, 392 So.2d 1002 (Fla.App.1981)—§ **6.3.2 n. 57.**

Goldberg, In re, 460 A.2d 982 (D.C.App.1983)—§ **3.4.5 n. 88.**

Goldberg v. Kelly, 397 U.S. 254, 90 S.Ct. 1101, 25 L.Ed.2d 287 (1970)—§ **14.5 n. 65, 70.**

Goldberg v. United States, 425 U.S. 94, 96 S.Ct. 1338, 47 L.Ed.2d 603 (1976)—§ **6.6.2 n. 54;** § **13.10.5 n. 13.**

Goldberg, People ex rel. v. Gordon, 199 Colo. 296, 607 P.2d 995 (Colo.1980)—§ **5.1 n. 34;** § **9.6.3 n. 37, 51.**

Goldchip Funding Co., In re, No. 75–1674 (3d Cir.1975)—§ **3.5.4 n. 78.**

Hampton v. Hanrahan, 600 F.2d 600 (7th Cir.1979)—§ **12.1.3 n. 41, 61.**

Hamstead, State ex rel. v. Dostert, 313 S.E.2d 409 (W.Va. 1984)—§ **13.10.3 n. 59.**

Hancock, In re, 67 Cal.App.3d 943, 136 Cal.Rptr. 901 (1977)—§ **11.3.3 n. 77.**

Hancock v. Mutual of Omaha Ins. Co., 472 A.2d 867 (D.C. 1984)—§ **9.5.3 n. 71.**

Handelman v. Hustler Magazine, Inc., 469 F.Supp. 1048 (S.D.N.Y.)—§ **2.6.1 n. 7.**

Handelman v. Weiss, 368 F.Supp. 258 (S.D.N.Y.1973)—§ **7.1.7 n. 85;** § **8.10.2 n. 67, 70;** § **8.10.3 n. 18.**

Handgards, Inc. v. Johnson & Johnson, 413 F.Supp. 926 (N.D.Cal.1976)—§ **6.4.7 n. 17.**

Handy, United States ex rel. Darcy v., 203 F.2d 407 (3d Cir.1953)—§ **14.6.2 n. 2.**

Hankamer v. Templin, 143 Tex. 572, 187 S.W.2d 549 (1945)—§ **3.3.2 n. 89.**

Hankins, United States v., 424 F.Supp. 606 (N.D.Miss. 1976)—§ **6.3.7 n. 61.**

Hanley, In re, 13 Cal.3d 448, 119 Cal.Rptr. 5, 530 P.2d 1381 (1975)—§ **3.5.2 n. 31.**

Hanlon, United States v., 548 F.2d 1096 (2d Cir.1977)—§ **12.5.2 n. 52;** § **13.3.3 n. 40.**

Hannon v. Superior Court, 19 Cal.3d 588, 138 Cal.Rptr. 885, 564 P.2d 1203 (1977)—§ **12.4.2 n. 86.**

Hanratty, In re, 277 N.W.2d 373 (Minn.1979)—§ **3.3.2 n. 86;** § **3.4.1 n. 54;** § **3.5.7 n. 5.**

Hansen, In re, 318 N.W.2d 856 (Minn.1982)—§ **3.3.3 n. 25.**

Hansen, In re, 586 P.2d 413 (Utah 1978)—§ **7.2.4 n. 94;** § **7.3.2 n. 19;** § **9.3.1 n. 32.**

Hansen, In re, 584 P.2d 805 (Utah 1978)—§ **3.5.2 n. 21, 63;** § **3.5.6 n. 71;** § **3.6.1 n. 22;** § **12.2.2 n. 98.**

Hansen v. State Bar, 23 Cal.3d 68, 151 Cal.Rptr. 343, 587 P.2d 1156 (1978)—§ **5.1 n. 35.**

Hansen v. Wightman, 14 Wn.App. 78, 538 P.2d 1238, 1244 (1975)—§ **3.3.2 n. 74;** § **9.2.4 n. 94.**

Hansher v. Kaishian, 79 Wis.2d 374, 255 N.W.2d 564 (1977)—§ **11.6.3 n. 71.**

Hanson, In re, 532 P.2d 303 (Alaska 1975)—§ **17.4.3 n. 68.**

Harceg v. Brown, 512 F.Supp. 788 (N.D.Ill.1981)—§ **8.9.3 n. 25.**

Hardenbrook, In re, 135 App.Div. 634, 121 N.Y.S. 250 (1909)—§ **12.5.3 n. 64.**

Hardison v. Weinshel, 450 F.Supp. 721 (E.D.Wis.1978)—§ **9.6.1 n. 19.**

Harfmann, People v., 638 P.2d 745 (Colo.1981)—§ **3.4.4 n. 27.**

Harfmann, People v., 38 Colo.App. 19, 555 P.2d 187 (1976)—§ **14.6.4 n. 55.**

Harkeem v. Adams, 117 N.H. 687, 377 A.2d 617 (1977)—§ **16.6.2 n. 78.**

Harkin v. Brundage, 276 U.S. 36, 48 S.Ct. 268, 72 L.Ed. 457 (1928)—§ **12.7 n. 84.**

Harlan, United States v., 696 F.2d 5 (1st Cir.1982)—§ **14.3.1 n. 61.**

Harlen v. City of Helena, ___ Mont. ___, 676 P.2d 191—§ **2.2.3 n. 54.**

Harling v. United States, 387 A.2d 1101 (D.C.Ct.App. 1978)—§ **14.3.4 n. 94.**

Harlow v. Fitzgerald, 457 U.S. 800, 102 S.Ct. 2727, 73 L.Ed.2d 396 (1982)—§ **17.3.3 n. 21.**

Harlton, State ex rel. Oklahoma Bar Ass'n v., 669 P.2d 774 (Okl.1983)—§ **12.3.5 n. 77.**

Harman v. La Crosse Tribune, 117 Wis.2d 448, 344 N.W.2d 536 (1984)—§ **16.2.2 n. 15.**

Harmon v. Pugh, 38 N.C.App. 438, 248 S.E.2d 421 (1978)—§ **8.11.3 n. 93;** § **9.4.2 n. 51, 52.**

Harper, In re, 69 A.D.2d 236, 418 N.Y.S.2d 470 (1979)—§ **3.5.2 n. 54.**

Harper v. Burgess, 701 F.2d 29, 31 BNA Fair Empl. Act Cas. 450 (4th Cir.1983)—§ **4.2 n. 15.**

Harper v. District of Columbia Comm. on Admissions, 375 A.2d 25 (D.C.App.1977)—§ **5.3 n. 87.**

Harper & Row Publishers, Inc. v. Decker, 423 F.2d 487 (7th Cir.1970)—§ **6.5.4 n. 75.**

Harper, State v., 214 Neb. 911, 336 N.W.2d 597 (1983)—§ **12.6.3 n. 21.**

Harper, State v., 57 Wis.2d 543, 205 N.W.2d 1 (1973)—§ **14.6.2 n. 14.**

Harrington, In re, 134 Vt. 549, 367 A.2d 161 (1976)—§ **3.5.5 n. 35.**

Harrington, In re, 128 Vt. 445, 266 A.2d 433 (1970)—§ **12.4.4 n. 2.**

Harrington, State v., 128 Vt. 242, 260 A.2d 692 (1969)—§ **13.5.4 n. 55.**

Harris, In re, 88 N.J.L. 18, 95 A. 761 (1915)—§ **3.5.2 n. 31;** § **3.5.6 n. 82.**

Harris v. Harvey, 419 F.Supp. 30 (E.D.Wis.1976)—§ **17.3.3 n. 16.**

Harris v. New York, 401 U.S. 222, 91 S.Ct. 643, 28 L.Ed.2d 1 (1971)—§ **6.2.4 n. 50.**

Harris v. State, 437 N.E.2d 44 (Ind.1982)—§ **4.5 n. 25.**

Harris v. State, 78 Wis.2d 357, 254 N.W.2d 291 (1977)—§ **7.5.1 n. 30.**

Harris v. Superior Court, 19 Cal.3d 786, 140 Cal.Rptr. 318, 567 P.2d 750 (1977)—§ **14.3.4 n. 90.**

Harris v. Wabaunsee, 593 P.2d 86 (Okl.1979)—§ **9.5.3 n. 69.**

Harris, People v., 57 N.Y.2d 335, 456 N.Y.S.2d 694, 442 N.E.2d 1205 (1982)—§ **6.3.7 n. 56.**

Harris, United States v., 543 F.2d 1247 (9th Cir.1976)—§ **12.3.5 n. 69.**

Harrison, In re, 461 A.2d 1034 (D.C.App.1983)—§ **4.8 n. 94.**

Harrison v. Keystone Coca-Cola Bottling Co., 428 F.Supp. 149 (M.D.Pa.1977)—§ **13.7.4 n. 18.**

Harrison, United States v., 173 U.S.App.D.C. 260, 524 F.2d 421 (1975)—§ **12.3.5 n. 69.**

Harrop v. Western Airlines, Inc., 550 F.2d 1143 (9th Cir. 1977)—§ **4.6.2 n. 54.**

Hart, United States ex rel. v. Davenport, 478 F.2d 203 (3d Cir.1973)—§ **8.8.2 n. 93;** § **14.6.1 n. 95.**

Harthun, People ex rel. MacFarlane v., 195 Colo. 38, 581 P.2d 716 (1978)—§ **9.6.3 n. 53.**

Harthun, People v., 197 Colo. 1, 593 P.2d 324 (1979)—§ **3.5.6 n. 62.**

Harvey v. Connor, 85 Ill.App.3d 1061, 41 Ill.Dec. 381, 407 N.E.2d 879 (1980)—§ **5.6.1 n. 38.**

Henry, United States v., 447 U.S. 264, 100 S.Ct. 2183, 65 L.Ed.2d 115 (1980)—§ **11.6.2 n. 62;** § **14.6.4 n. 61.**

Hensel v. Cohen, 155 Cal.App.3d 563, 202 Cal.Rptr. 85 (1984)—§ **9.6.3 n. 52.**

Henson v. State, 97 Okl.Cr. 240, 261 P.2d 916 (1953)— § **11.6.2 n. 31.**

Hepfel v. Bashaw, 279 N.W.2d 342 (Minn.1979)—§ **14.5 n. 75.**

Herbert v. Lando, 73 F.R.D. 387 (S.D.N.Y.1977)—§ **6.4.4 n. 91;** § **6.4.6 n. 13.**

Hercules, Inc. v. Exxon Corp., 434 F.Supp. 136 (D.Del. 1977)—§ **6.3.2 n. 66;** § **6.6.2 n. 47.**

Herman v. Dulles, 205 F.2d 715 (D.C.Cir.1953)—§ **3.6.2 n. 27;** § **15.2.5 n. 16.**

Herrick v. Barzee, 96 Or. 357, 190 P. 141 (1920)—§ **9.4.5 n. 19.**

Herring v. New York, 422 U.S. 853, 95 S.Ct. 2550, 45 L.Ed. 2d 593 (1975)—§ **10.1;** § **10.1 n. 2.**

Herring v. Retail Credit Co., 266 S.C. 455, 224 S.E.2d 663 (1976)—§ **11.3.3 n. 70.**

Herron v. Jones, 276 Ark. 493, 637 S.W.2d 569 (1982)— § **16.3.1 n. 10.**

Herron v. State Farm Mut. Ins. Co., 56 Cal.2d 202, 14 Cal. Rptr. 294, 363 P.2d 310 (1961)—§ **11.6.2 n. 31.**

Hersch, In re, 108 Wis.2d 450, 321 N.W.2d 927 (1982)— § **3.5.4 n. 84.**

Hershberger, In re, 288 Or. 559, 606 P.2d 623 (1980)— § **3.5.6 n. 71.**

Herston v. Shitesell, 348 So.2d 1054 (Ala.1977)—§ **5.6.2 n. 86.**

Hertz, People v., 638 P.2d 794 (Colo.1982)—§ **11.3.3 n. 76.**

Hertz, People ex rel. Gallagher v., 198 Colo. 522, 608 P.2d 335 (1979)—§ **13.5.5 n. 68, 71, 74;** § **13.8.3 n. 88.**

Heslin v. Connecticut Law Clinic of Trantolo & Trantolo, 190 Conn. 510, 461 A.2d 938—§ **2.2.3 n. 46.**

Hester v. Martindale-Hubbell, Inc., 659 F.2d 433 (4th Cir. 1981)—§ **2.4.1 n. 38.**

Hetland, In re, 275 N.W.2d 582 (Minn.1978)—§ **3.5.4 n. 16.**

Hetzel, In re, 118 Wis.2d 257, 346 N.W.2d 782 (1984)— § **3.5.7 n. 99.**

Hicklin v. Orbeck, 437 U.S. 518, 98 S.Ct. 2482, 57 L.Ed.2d 397 (1978)—§ **15.2.3 n. 93.**

Hickman v. Frerking, 4 Kan.App.2d 590, 609 P.2d 682 (1980)—§ **14.4.1 n. 39;** § **15.4.1 n. 84.**

Hickman v. Taylor, 329 U.S. 495, 67 S.Ct. 385, 91 L.Ed. 451 (1947)—§ **6.3.6 n. 44;** § **6.5.4 n. 81;** § **6.6.1;** § **6.6.1 n. 25, 31;** § **6.6.3;** § **7.5.1 n. 27.**

Hicks v. Clayton, 67 Cal.App.3d 251, 136 Cal.Rptr. 512 (1977)—§ **8.11.3 n. 90.**

Hicks v. State, 422 S.W.2d 539 (Tex.Civ.App.1967)—§ **3.3.1 n. 70.**

Higbie, In re, 6 Cal.3d 562, 99 Cal.Rptr. 865, 493 P.2d 97 (1972)—§ **3.3.2 n. 6.**

Higgins v. Advisory Comm. on Professional Ethics, 73 N.J. 123, 373 A.2d 372 (1977)—§ **8.9.4 n. 52.**

Higgins v. Committee on Professional Ethics, 73 N.J. 123, 373 A.2d 372 (1977)—§ **7.1.4 n. 46.**

Higgs, United States v., 713 F.2d 39 (3d Cir.1983)— § **13.10.5 n. 11.**

High Point Bank & Trust Co. v. Morgan-Schultheiss, Inc., 33 N.C.App. 406, 235 S.E.2d 693 (1977)—§ **9.5.1 n. 37.**

Hilgers, People v., 200 Colo. 211, 612 P.2d 1134 (1980)— § **3.4.2 n. 86;** § **3.5.4 n. 95, 96.**

Hill, In re, 261 Or. 573, 495 P.2d 261 (1972)—§ **9.4.4 n. 87.**

Hill v. Mynatt, 59 S.W. 163 (Tenn.Ch.App.1900)—§ **5.6.2 n. 86.**

Hill v. Okay Constr. Co., 312 Minn. 324, 252 N.W.2d 107 (1977)—§ **5.6.2 n. 65;** § **5.6.3 n. 27;** § **7.1.7 n. 96;** § **7.2.1 n. 38;** § **16.6.2 n. 92, 93.**

Hill v. State, 114 Ga.App. 527, 151 S.E.2d 818 (1966)— § **4.8 n. 21.**

Hill v. United States, 50 U.S. (9 How.) 386, 13 L.Ed. 185 (1850)—§ **17.3.3 n. 3.**

Hill v. Willmott, 561 S.W.2d 331 (Ky.App.1978)—§ **5.6 n. 34.**

Hill, State ex rel. Schneider v., 223 Kan. 425, 573 P.2d 1078 (1978)—§ **15.1.3 n. 97.**

Hilliard v. Volcker, 659 F.2d 1125 (D.C.Cir.1981)—§ **14.5 n. 67.**

Hillman v. Commissioner, 687 F.2d 164 (6th Cir.1982)— § **6.4.3 n. 82.**

Hilo Metals Co. v. Learner Co., 258 F.Supp. 23 (D.Hawaii 1966)—§ **8.10.2 n. 72.**

Hilton, State v., 217 Kan. 694, 538 P.2d 977 (1975)—§ **4.8 n. 17, 19;** § **9.4.3 n. 79.**

Himmel v. State Bar, 4 Cal.3d 786, 94 Cal.Rptr. 825, 484 P.2d 993 (1971)—§ **3.4.5 n. 57.**

Hinckley, United States v., 672 F.2d 115 (D.C.Cir.1982)— § **14.6.4 n. 48.**

Hinds, In re, 90 N.J. 604, 449 A.2d 483 (1982)—§ **12.2.2 n. 7, 99.**

Hinds v. State Bar, 19 Cal.2d 87, 119 P.2d 134 (1941)— § **12.5.3 n. 63.**

Hines, In re, 275 S.C. 411, 272 S.E.2d 169 (1980)—§ **3.5.4 n. 4.**

Hines v. Commonwealth, 217 Va. 905, 234 S.E.2d 262 (1977)—§ **12.1.1 n. 11.**

Hinman, Straub, Pigors & Manning v. Broder, 89 A.D.2d 278, 456 N.Y.S.2d 834 (1982)—§ **16.6.2 n. 87, 93.**

Hinojos, State v., 95 N.M. 659, 625 P.2d 588 (Ct.App. 1980)—§ **12.5.3 n. 66.**

Hirschkop v. Snead, 594 F.2d 356 (4th Cir.1979)—§ **12.2.2 n. 12.**

Hishon v. King & Spalding, ___ U.S. ___, 104 S.Ct. 2229, 81 L.Ed.2d 59 (1984)—§ **1.4.3;** § **1.4.3 n. 99;** § **16.2.1 n. 2;** § **16.2.3 n. 50, 55.**

Hiss, In re, 368 Mass. 447, 333 N.E.2d 429 (1975)—§ **3.5.2 n. 38;** § **3.5.5 n. 23, 41.**

Hladek v. John A. Dalsin & Son, 310 Minn. 178, 245 N.W.2d 593 (1976)—§ **4.6.2 n. 69.**

Hobson, R.H., v. Bradley & Drendel, Ltd., 698 Nev. 505, 654 P.2d 1017 (1982)—§ **9.2.1 n. 39.**

Hodge, In re, 262 F.2d 778 (9th Cir.1958)—§ **14.6.2 n. 2.**

Hodge & Zweig, United States v., 548 F.2d 1347 (9th Cir. 1977)—§ **6.3.5 n. 28, 31;** § **6.4.10 n. 54.**

Hodges v. Carter, 239 N.C. 517, 80 S.E.2d 144 (1954)— § **5.6.2;** § **5.6.2 n. 66.**

Hodges v. Doctors Hospital, 150 Ga.App. 77, 256 S.E.2d 625 (1979)—§ **4.2 n. 28.**

Hodges v. State Farm Mut. Auto. Ins. Co., 488 F.Supp. 1057 (D.S.C.1980)—§ **8.4.3 n. 24.**

Hodgson, United States v., 492 F.2d 1175 (10th Cir.1974)—§ **6.3.4 n. 77.**

Hoffa v. United States, 385 U.S. 293, 87 S.Ct. 408, 17 L.Ed. 2d 374 (1966)—§ **14.6.4 n. 58.**

Hoffert v. General Motors Corp., 656 F.2d 161 (5th Cir.)—§ **2.2.1 n. 14;** § **9.1 n. 11, 16, 23.**

Hoffman v. Franklin Cty. Mercantile Bank, 666 S.W.2d 446 (Mo.App.1984)—§ **5.6.4 n. 45.**

Hofreiter v. Leigh, 124 Ill.App.3d 1052, 80 Ill.Dec. 319, 465 N.E.2d 110—§ **2.6.1 n. 4;** § **9.2.4 n. 3.**

Hogan v. Kunce, 67 Ill.2d 55, 7 Ill.Dec. 63, 364 N.E.2d 50 (1977)—§ **12.1.3 n. 62.**

Hogan, United States v., 712 F.2d 757 (2d Cir.1983)—§ **13.10.4 n. 88.**

Hohman, State v., 233 Kan. 183, 660 P.2d 567 (1983)—§ **3.5.2 n. 54.**

Hoidale v. Cooley, 143 Minn. 430, 174 N.W. 413 (1919)—§ **7.1.7 n. 14.**

Hoines v. Barney's Club, Inc., 28 Cal.3d 603, 70 Cal.Rptr. 42, 620 P.2d 628 (1980)—§ **13.5.5 n. 73.**

Holcomb v. Steele, 47 Tenn.App. 704, 342 S.W.2d 236 (1958)—§ **7.3.3 n. 32;** § **9.6.1 n. 14.**

Holland v. Lawless, 95 N.M. 490, 623 P.2d 1004 (Ct.App. 1981)—§ **5.6.5 n. 87.**

Holland v. Sheehan, 108 Minn. 362, 122 N.W. 1 (1909)—§ **14.2.5 n. 91.**

Holland, People v., 23 Cal.3d 77, 151 Cal.Rptr. 625, 588 P.2d 765 (1978)—§ **14.3.7 n. 34.**

Hollenbeck v. Estelle, 672 F.2d 451 (5th Cir.1982)—§ **10.5.3 n. 40.**

Holley v. Jackson, 39 Del.Ch. 32, 158 A.2d 803 (1959)—§ **8.5 n. 31.**

Holliday's Tax Services, Inc., In re, 417 F.Supp. 182 (E.D. N.Y.1976)—§ **14.4.1 n. 41;** § **15.1.3 n. 6.**

Hollingsworth, State ex rel. Oregon St. Bar v., 286 Or. 477, 595 P.2d 484 (1979)—§ **3.5.7 n. 93.**

Hollis, In re, 95 N.J. 253, 471 A.2d 10 (1984)—§ **5.1 n. 52.**

Hollister v. Ulvi, 199 Minn. 269, 271 N.W. 493 (1937)—§ **9.4.5 n. 19.**

Holloway v. Arkansas, 435 U.S. 475, 98 S.Ct. 1173, 55 L.Ed.2d 426 (1978)—§ **1.6 n. 26;** § **8.2.3;** § **8.2.3 n. 20, 23, 30, 33;** § **8.2.4 n. 47;** § **12.5.4 n. 99.**

Hollstein, State ex rel. Nebraska St. Bar Ass'n v., 202 Neb. 40, 274 N.W.2d 508 (1979)—§ **1.6 n. 24;** § **3.4.4 n. 33;** § **8.9.4 n. 52;** § **8.11.4 n. 13;** § **11.6.2 n. 55.**

Holman, In re, 297 Or. 36, 682 P.2d 243 (1984)—§ **3.4.4 n. 29;** § **4.8 n. 13;** § **16.3.1 n. 4.**

Holman, In re, 277 S.C. 293, 286 S.E.2d 148 (1982)—§ **11.4.2 n. 89.**

Holmes, In re, 145 Cal.App.3d 934, 193 Cal.Rptr. 790 (1983)—§ **12.4.2 n. 80.**

Holmes, In re, 290 Or. 173, 619 P.2d 1284 (1980)—§ **7.1.5 n. 50;** § **7.2.3 n. 62;** § **8.7.3 n. 72.**

Holmes, In re, 226 Kan. 579, 612 P.2d 148 (1979)—§ **3.3.3 n. 25.**

Holmes v. Holmes, 145 Ind.App. 52, 248 N.W.2d 564 (1969)—§ **8.6 n. 39.**

Holmes, People v., 90 Ill.App.3d 606, 46 Ill.Dec. 106, 413 N.E.2d 546 (1980)—§ **5.6.5 n. 94.**

Holt v. Virginia, 381 U.S. 131, 85 S.Ct. 1375, 14 L.Ed.2d 290 (1965)—§ **1.5 n. 14;** § **12.1.3 n. 62.**

Homestake Mining Co. v. Board of Environmental Protection, 289 N.W.2d 561 (S.D.1980)—§ **8.10.3 n. 20.**

Honeywell, Inc. v. Piper Aircraft Corp., 50 F.R.D. 117 (M.D.Pa.1970)—§ **6.6.2 n. 41.**

Hooks v. State, 416 A.2d 189 (Del.1980)—§ **14.4.2 n. 60.**

Hoopes, United States v., 545 F.2d 721 (10th Cir.1976)—§ **4.7 n. 88.**

Hoover, In re, 46 Ariz. 24, 46 P.2d 647 (1935)—§ **12.5.3 n. 63.**

Hoover v. Ronwin, ___ U.S. ___, 104 S.Ct. 1989, 80 L.Ed.2d 590 (1984)—§ **5.3 n. 86.**

Hoover, State v., 223 Kan. 385, 574 P.2d 1377 (1978)—§ **12.5.3 n. 63.**

Hopfl, In re, 48 N.Y.2d 859, 424 N.Y.S.2d 350, 400 N.E.2d 292 (1979)—§ **3.3.2 n. 76.**

Hopkinson v. State, 632 P.2d 79 (Wyo.1981)—§ **6.3.3 n. 73.**

Hopp, In re, 291 Or. 697, 634 P.2d 238 (1981)—§ **3.5.2 n. 23;** § **11.2.2 n. 7.**

Hoppe v. Klapperich, 224 Minn. 224, 28 N.W.2d 780 (1947)—§ **5.6 n. 28;** § **17.3.3 n. 12.**

Hoppe v. Ranzini, 158 N.J.Super. 158, 385 A.2d 913 (1978)—§ **5.6.3 n. 11.**

Hopper v. City of Madison, 79 Wis.2d 120, 256 N.W.2d 139 (1977)—§ **15.1.3 n. 93.**

Hoquiam, City of v. Public Employment Relations Comm'n, 97 Wn.2d 481, 646 P.2d 129 (1982)—§ **8.10.3 n. 33.**

Horne v. Peckham, 97 Cal.App.3d 404, 158 Cal.Rptr. 714 (1979)—§ **5.5 n. 16;** § **5.6.2 n. 5, 86, 95.**

Horowitz, In re, 482 F.2d 72 (2d Cir.1973)—§ **6.1.4 n. 9;** § **6.4.4 n. 96, 97.**

Horowitz v. Alaska Bar Association, 609 P.2d 39 (Alaska 1980)—§ **2.3 n. 15.**

Horto, In re, 100 N.M. 13, 665 P.2d 275—§ **3.4.4 n. 46.**

Horton v. Butler, 387 So.2d 1315 (La.App.1980)—§ **9.4.2 n. 51.**

Hospital Bldg. Co. v. Trustees of Rex Hospital, 691 F.2d 678 (4th Cir.)—§ **2.4.2 n. 55.**

Houchin, In re, 290 Or. 433, 622 P.2d 723 (1981)—§ **3.5.2 n. 67.**

Hough v. State, 24 Cal.2d 522, 150 P.2d 448 (1944)—§ **14.3.6 n. 20.**

House v. Circuit Court, 112 Wis.2d 14, 331 N.W.2d 859 (App.1983)—§ **12.1.3 n. 79.**

House v. Mayo, 324 U.S. 886, 65 S.Ct. 689, 89 L.Ed. 1435 (1945)—§ **14.3.7 n. 27.**

Housler v. First Nat'l Bank of East Islip, 484 F.Supp. 1321 (E.D.N.Y.1980)—§ **6.7.8 n. 19.**

Houston Gen. Ins. Co. v. Superior Court, 108 Cal.App.3d 958, 166 Cal.Rptr. 904 (1980)—§ **6.4.8 n. 23, 24.**

Hovel v. Minneapolis & St. L.R.R., 165 Minn. 449, 206 N.W. 710 (1926)—§ **7.1.6 n. 59.**

Howard, In re, 297 Or. 174, 681 P.2d 775 (1984)—§ **3.3.2 n. 5.**

Howard, In re, 75 A.D.2d 933, 427 N.Y.S.2d 540 (1980)—§ **3.3.2 n. 77.**

Jenkins v. Wheeler, 69 N.C.App. 140, 316 S.E.2d 354 (1984)—§ **5.6.4 n. 53.**

Jenkins v. Wise, 58 Haw. 592, 574 P.2d 1337 (1978)—§ **16.6.2 n. 42.**

Jennings v. Lake, 267 S.C. 677, 230 S.E.2d 903 (1976)—§ **5.6.3 n. 30.**

Jennings v. State, 413 So.2d 24 (Fla.1982)—§ **8.2.3 n. 34.**

Jennings, United States v., 724 F.2d 436 (5th Cir.1984)—§ **3.3.2 n. 80.**

Jennings Co., Erwin M. v. DiGenova, 107 Conn. 491, 141 A. 866 (1928)—§ **7.5.2 n. 33.**

Jensen v. Superior Court, 154 Cal.App.3d 533, 201 Cal. Rptr. 275 (1984)—§ **12.1.3 n. 51.**

Jensen, United States v., 608 F.2d 1349 (10th Cir.1979)—§ **13.10.5 n. 9.**

Jenson, State v., 171 Neb. 1, 105 N.W.2d 459 (1960)—§ **9.4.4 n. 87.**

Jerome, In re, 31 Ill.2d 284, 201 N.E.2d 440 (1964)—§ **3.4.2 n. 65.**

Jewel v. Boxer, 156 Cal.App.3d 171, 203 Cal.Rptr. 13 (1984)—§ **16.2.3 n. 31, 65, 67.**

Jimenez v. Aristeguieta, 311 F.2d 547 (5th Cir.1962)—§ **17.6.3 n. 79.**

John Doe Corp., In re, 675 F.2d 482 (2d Cir.1982)—§ **6.4.4 n. 99;** § **6.4.10 n. 56, 59, 61, 66.**

Johns v. Smyth, 176 F.Supp. 949 (E.D.Va.1959)—§ **10.5.2 n. 22.**

Johnson, In re, 93 Ill.2d 441, 67 Ill.Dec. 114, 444 N.E.2d 153 (1983)—§ **3.5.2 n. 58.**

Johnson, In re, 341 N.W.2d 282 (Minn.1983)—§ **14.2.4 n. 62.**

Johnson, In re, 322 N.W.2d 616 (Minn.1982)—§ **3.3.3 n. 30.**

Johnson, In re, 244 Ga. 109, 259 S.E.2d 57 (1979)—§ **3.5.5 n. 34.**

Johnson, In re, 92 Wn.2d 349, 597 P.2d 113, 114 (1979)—§ **3.5.5 n. 47.**

Johnson, In re, 106 Ariz. 73, 471 P.2d 269 (1970)—§ **3.3.2 n. 9.**

Johnson v. Avery, 393 U.S. 483, 89 S.Ct. 747, 21 L.Ed.2d 718 (1969)—§ **14.4.2 n. 64;** § **14.5 n. 81.**

Johnson v. Blue Cross & Blue Shield, 329 N.W.2d 49 (Minn.1983)—§ **9.2.1 n. 32.**

Johnson v. City Comm'n, 272 N.W.2d 97 (S.D.1978)—§ **14.3.5 n. 8.**

Johnson v. Director of Professional Responsibility, 341 N.W.2d 282 (Minn.1983)—§ **5.5 n. 22, 28.**

Johnson v. Frontier Ford, Inc., 68 Ill.App.3d 315, 24 Ill. Dec. 908, 386 N.E.2d 112 (1979)—§ **6.3.4 n. 75.**

Johnson v. Johnson, 141 N.C. 91, 53 S.E. 623 (1906)—§ **8.6 n. 39.**

Johnson v. Jones, 103 Idaho 702, 652 P.2d 650 (1982)—§ **5.6.3 n. 7.**

Johnson v. MacCoy, 278 F.2d 37 (9th Cir.1960)—§ **17.3.3 n. 13.**

Johnson v. State, 577 P.2d 230 (Alaska 1978)—§ **13.10.5 n. 11.**

Johnson v. Stephens Development Corp., 538 F.2d 664 (5th Cir.1976)—§ **9.6.3 n. 63.**

Johnson v. Tesky, 57 Or.App. 133, 643 P.2d 1344 (1982)—§ **4.6.2 n. 56, 59.**

Johnson v. Tindall, ___ Mont. ___, 635 P.2d 266 (1981)—§ **9.6.1 n. 6.**

Johnson v. Trueblood, 476 F.Supp. 90 (E.D.Pa.1979)—§ **11.4.3 n. 1;** § **15.4.3 n. 39.**

Johnson v. Youden, (1950), 1 K.B. 544—§ **13.3.2 n. 20.**

Johnson v. Zerbst, 304 U.S. 458, 58 S.Ct. 1019, 82 L.Ed. 1461 (1938)—§ **14.3.1;** § **14.3.1 n. 33, 40.**

Johnson, People v., 26 Cal.3d 557, 162 Cal.Rptr. 431, 606 P.2d 738 (1980)—§ **7.3.3 n. 42.**

Johnson, People v., 105 Cal.App.3d 884, 164 Cal.Rptr. 746 (1980)—§ **8.9.4 n. 43.**

Johnson, People v., 199 Colo. 248, 612 P.2d 1097 (1980)—§ **9.5.2 n. 50.**

Johnson, State v., 122 Ariz. 260, 594 P.2d 514 (1979)—§ **12.3.5 n. 61.**

Johnson, State ex rel. v. Childe, 147 Neb. 527, 23 N.W.2d 720 (1946)—§ **15.1.3 n. 79.**

Johnson, United States ex rel. Wilcox v., 555 F.2d 115 (3d Cir.1977)—§ **12.5.2 n. 53, 54, 85.**

Johnston v. Beneficial Management Corp., 26 Wn.App. 671, 614 P.2d 661 (1980)—§ **12.2.2 n. 19.**

Johnston, United States v., 690 F.2d 638 (7th Cir.1982)—§ **7.5.2 n. 6, 15.**

Johnstone v. State Bar, 64 Cal.2d 153, 49 Cal.Rptr. 97, 410 P.2d 617 (1966)—§ **4.8 n. 12.**

Jones, In re, 119 Wis.2d 891, 350 N.W.2d 139 (1984)—§ **3.4.4 n. 15.**

Jones, In re, 294 N.W.2d 651 (S.D.1980)—§ **3.3.1 n. 58.**

Jones, In re, 506 F.2d 527 (8th Cir.1974)—§ **4.3.1 n. 60.**

Jones v. Barnes, 463 U.S. 745, 103 S.Ct. 3308, 77 L.Ed.2d 987 (1983)—§ **12.5.4 n. 85;** § **14.6.3;** § **14.6.3 n. 38, 39.**

Jones v. Board of Comm'rs of Alabama St. Bar, 737 F.2d 996 (11th Cir.1984)—§ **5.3 n. 83.**

Jones v. District Court, 617 P.2d 803 (Colo.1980)—§ **4.4 n. 97.**

Jones v. Jones, ___ Mont. ___, 620 P.2d 850 (1980)—§ **6.3.5 n. 10.**

Jones v. Miller, 203 F.2d 131 (3d Cir.1953)—§ **9.6.3 n. 57.**

Jones v. RCA Music Service, 530 F.Supp. 767 (E.D.Pa. 1982)—§ **5.6.5 n. 11.**

Jones v. Schlender, 102 Idaho 776, 640 P.2d 1177 (1982)—§ **4.2 n. 58.**

Jones v. State, 580 P.2d 1150 (Wyo.1978)—§ **10.5.3 n. 33.**

Jones, People v., 105 Ill.App.3d 1143, 62 Ill.Dec. 25, 435 N.E.2d 823 (1982)—§ **7.4.3 n. 20.**

Jones, State v., 99 Wn.2d 735, 664 P.2d 1216 (1983)—§ **4.4 n. 99.**

Jones, State v., 180 Conn. 443, 429 A.2d 936 (1980)—§ **7.1.7 n. 5;** § **7.4.3 n. 97;** § **7.6.5 n. 87;** § **8.9.4 n. 44, 59.**

Jones, State ex rel. Oklahoma Bar Ass'n v., 566 P.2d 130, 132 (Okl.1977)—§ **3.3.2 n. 78.**

Jones, United States v., 542 F.2d 186, (4th Cir.1976)—§ **12.4.3 n. 99.**

Joos v. Auto Owners Insur. Co., 94 Mich.App. 419, 288 N.W.2d 433 (1979)—§ **4.5 n. 27;** § **5.6.2 n. 65.**

Joos v. Drillock, 127 Mich.App. 99, 338 N.W.2d 736 (1983)—§ **4.6.2 n. 63, 76.**

Kosseff v. Board of Bar Examiners, 475 A.2d 349 (Del. 1984)—§ **15.3.2 n. 70.**
Kovel, United States v., 296 F.2d 918 (2d Cir.1961)— § **6.3.4 n. 81;** § **6.3.6 n. 46, 48;** § **6.3.8 n. 79.**
Kozak, In re, 256 N.W.2d 717 (S.D.1977)—§ **14.6.4 n. 57.**
Kozlov, In re, 79 N.J. 232, 393 A.2d 882 (1979)—§ **6.3.5 n. 30, 31;** § **12.9 n. 12.**
KPNX Broadcasting Co. v. Arizona Superior Court, 459 U.S. 1302, 103 S.Ct. 584, 74 L.Ed.2d 498—§ **12.2.1 n. 81.**
Kraft v. United States, 238 F.2d 794 (8th Cir.1956)— § **17.6.5 n. 1.**
Krainz v. Attorney Grievance Comm'n, 413 Mich. 1106, 320 N.W.2d 54 (1982)—§ **3.4.2 n. 70.**
Krajewski v. Klawon, 84 Mich.App. 532, 270 N.W.2d 9 (1978)—§ **9.2.4 n. 8.**
Kramer, In re, 92 Ill.2d 305, 65 Ill.Dec. 860, 442 N.E.2d 171 (1982)—§ **4.8 n. 46.**
Kramer v. Fallert, 628 S.W.2d 671 (Mo.App.1981)—§ **9.4.2 n. 45.**
Kramer v. Scientific Control Corp., 534 F.2d 1085 (3d Cir. 1976)—§ **8.14 n. 72.**
Kras v. United States, 409 U.S. 434, 93 S.Ct. 631, 34 L.Ed. 2d 626 (1973)—§ **14.5 n. 77.**
Kratzer v. Kratzer, 595 S.W.2d 453 (Mo.App.1980)—§ **6.3.7 n. 53.**
Kraus, In re, 295 Or. 743, 670 P.2d 1012 (1983)—§ **3.5.4 n. 2, 3.**
Kraus, In re, 289 Or. 661, 616 P.2d 1173 (1980)—§ **12.3.3 n. 48.**
Kraus v. Davis, 6 Cal.App.3d 484, 85 Cal.Rptr. 846 (1970)—§ **7.2.1 n. 41.**
Krause v. Rhodes, 640 F.2d 214 (6th Cir.1981)—§ **9.1 n. 12;** § **16.6.4 n. 6.**
Krebs v. Johns-Manville Corp., 496 F.Supp. 40 (E.D.Pa. 1980)—§ **7.1.4 n. 34;** § **7.1.6 n. 74;** § **7.4.3 n. 26.**
Kreda v. Rush, 550 F.2d 888 (3d Cir.1977)—§ **7.1.7 n. 29.**
Kremer v. Shoyer, 453 Pa. 22, 311 A.2d 600 (1973)—§ **8.2.4 n. 54.**
Kresge Co., S.S. v. Port of Longview, 18 Wn.App. 805, 573 P.2d 1336 (1977)—§ **16.6.3 n. 1.**
Kribbs v. Jackson, 387 Pa. 611, 129 A.2d 490 (1957)— § **8.11.3 n. 88, 90.**
Krieger v. Bulpitt, 40 Cal.2d 97, 251 P.2d 673 (1953)— § **9.4.4 n. 96, 99.**
Kristovich, In re, 18 Cal.3d 468, 134 Cal.Rptr. 409, 411, 556 P.2d 771 (1976)—§ **3.3.2 n. 88;** § **12.5.1 n. 48.**
Kronzer v. First Nat'l Bank, 305 Minn. 415, 235 N.W.2d 187 (1975)—§ **15.1.2 n. 38.**
Krough, In re, 85 Wn.2d 462, 536 P.2d 578 (1975)—§ **3.3.2 n. 13.**
Kroungold v. Triester, 521 F.2d 763 (3d Cir.1975)—§ **7.5.2 n. 76.**
Krouse v. Graham, 19 Cal.3d 59, 137 Cal.Rptr. 863, 562 P.2d 1022 (1977)—§ **16.6.1 n. 22.**
Krueger, In re, 103 Wis.2d 192, 307 N.W.2d 184 (1981)— § **12.3.3 n. 44;** § **13.3.6 n. 65.**
Ktsanes v. Underwood, 525 F.2d 740 (7th Cir.)—§ **2.6.1 n. 77;** § **3.4.5 n. 68, 69.**
Kuehn v. Garcia, 608 F.2d 1143 (8th Cir.1979)—§ **5.6.2 n. 63.**
Kuiper v. District Court, ___ Mont. ___, 632 P.2d 694 (1981)—§ **6.3.2 n. 53;** § **6.5.4 n. 90.**
Kunin, In re, 252 Ga. 310, 313 S.E.2d 697 (1984)—§ **3.5.6 n. 79.**
Kurbitz v. Kurbitz, 77 Wn.2d 943, 468 P.2d 673 (1970)— § **7.6.3 n. 54, 62.**
Kurtenbach v. TeKippe, 260 N.W.2d 53 (Iowa 1977)— § **5.6.2 n. 48, 52, 55.**
Kury v. Commonwealth, 62 Pa.Cmwlth. 174, 435 A.2d 940—§ **2.2.3 n. 61.**
Kuska v. Folkes, 73 Ill.App.3d 540, 391 N.E.2d 1082 (1979)—§ **4.2 n. 38.**
Kuta, In re, 86 Ill.2d 154, 56 Ill.Dec. 56, 427 N.E.2d 136 (1981)—§ **3.5.4 n. 10;** § **3.5.5 n. 24;** § **3.5.6 n. 69.**
Kutner, In re, 78 Ill.2d 157, 35 Ill.Dec. 674, 399 N.E.2d 963 (1979)—§ **9.1 n. 24;** § **9.3.1 n. 48, 64.**
Kuvara, In re, 97 Wn.2d 743, 649 P.2d 834 (1982)—§ **3.3.2 n. 9;** § **3.3.4 n. 42.**
Kuzman, In re, 335 N.E.2d 210 (Ind.)—§ **2.6.2 n. 34, 36.**
Kyle v. Kyle, 94 A.D.2d 866, 463 N.Y.S.2d 584 (1983)— § **9.6.1 n. 11.**
Kyser, People v., 52 A.D.2d 1072, 384 N.Y.S.2d 332 (1976)—§ **12.1.2 n. 22.**

L.J. v. J.B., 150 N.J.Super. 373, 375 A.2d 1202 (1977)— § **6.3.3 n. 68.**
Labadot v. Labadot, 328 So.2d 747 (La.App.1976)—§ **17.6.2 n. 72.**
Labendz, In re, 95 N.J. 273, 471 A.2d 21 (1984)—§ **12.6.2 n. 14.**
Lacey, In re, 283 N.W.2d 250 (S.D.1979)—§ **3.5.2 n. 61.**
Lackey, People v., 79 Ill.2d 466, 39 Ill.Dec. 769, 405 N.E.2d 748 (1980)—§ **7.6.1 n. 24.**
Lacy, In re, 234 Mo.App. 71, 112 S.W.2d 594 (1937)— § **3.5.4 n. 10;** § **15.1.4 n. 43.**
Lacy, In re, 283 N.W.2d 250 (S.D.1979)—§ **11.3.2 n. 60.**
Lafayette, City of v. Louisiana Power & Light Co., 435 U.S. 389, 98 S.Ct. 1123, 53 L.Ed.2d 364—§ **2.4.2 n. 49.**
Laffey v. Court of Common Pleas, 503 Pa. 103, 468 A.2d 1084—§ **2.2.4 n. 71.**
Lake County Bar Ass'n v. Gargiulo, 62 Ohio St.2d 239, 404 N.E.2d 1343 (1980)—§ **7.3.2 n. 13;** § **7.3.3 n. 26.**
Lake County Bar Ass'n v. Needham, 66 Ohio St.2d 116, 419 N.E.2d 1104—§ **2.6.3 n. 60**
Lake County Bar Ass'n v. Patterson, 64 Ohio St.2d 163, 413 N.E.2d 840 (1980)—§ **8.12.3 n. 34.**
Lalli Enterprises, Inc., Victor v. Skippy Candle Corp., 578 F.Supp. 1384 (S.D.N.Y.1984)—§ **4.6.2 n. 69.**
Lamar v. American Finance System, Inc., 577 F.2d 953 (5th Cir.1978)—§ **5.1 n. 18.**
Lamar v. McCord, 245 Ark. 401, 432 S.W.2d 753 (1968)— § **6.5.6 n. 15.**
Lamb v. Barbour, 188 N.J.Super. 6, 455 A.2d 1122 (1982)— § **5.6.3 n. 6.**
Lamb v. Schmidt, 285 U.S. 222, 52 S.Ct. 317, 76 L.Ed. 720 (1932)—§ **5.6.5 n. 94.**
Lamberis, In re, 93 Ill.2d 222, 66 Ill.Dec. 623, 443 N.E.2d 549 (1982)—§ **3.3.4 n. 41.**
Lambert, In re, 79 N.J. 74, 397 A.2d 1086 (1979)—§ **3.3.4 n. 33.**

Lee v. Todd, 555 F.Supp. 628 (W.D.Tenn.1982)—§ **7.1.7 n. 26.**
Lee, United States v., 107 F. 702 (C.C.E.D.N.Y.1901)—§ **6.3.5 n. 20.**
Leeds, In re, 87 A.D.2d 96, 450 N.Y.S.2d 506 (1982)—§ **12.1.3 n. 66.**
Leer v. Chicago, M. St. P. & P. Ry., 308 N.W.2d 305 (Minn. 1981)—§ **6.5.4 n. 85;** § **6.6.3 n. 56.**
Lefkowitz v. Napatco, Inc., 51 N.Y.2d 434, 434 N.Y.S.2d 925, 415 N.E.2d 916 (1980)—§ **15.1.3 n. 2.**
Lefrak v. Arabian American Oil Co., 527 F.2d 1136 (2d Cir. 1975)—§ **7.1.7 n. 13.**
Lefton v. City of Hattiesburg, 333 F.2d 280 (5th Cir. 1965)—§ **15.4.3 n. 43.**
Legal Aid Society v. Rothwax, 69 A.D.2d 801, 415 N.Y.S.2d 432 (1979)—§ **9.5.3 n. 64.**
Lehet, In re, 95 N.J. 466, 472 A.2d 127 (1984)—§ **3.5.2 n. 19.**
Leibowitz, In re, 437 N.E.2d 973 (Ind.1982)—§ **8.11.3 n. 6.**
Leibowitz, In re, 88 A.D.2d 646, 442 N.Y.S.2d 802 (1981)—§ **3.4.2 n. 65.**
Leis v. Flynt, 439 U.S. 438, 99 S.Ct. 698, 58 L.Ed.2d 717 (1979)—§ **3.4.5 n. 60;** § **10.2.3 n. 64;** § **15.4.1 n. 3;** § **15.4.2 n. 15, 16;** § **15.4.3;** § **15.4.3 n. 29, 39, 42, 44, 46.**
Lemaire v. Texaco, Inc., 496 F.Supp. 1308 (E.D.Tex.1980)—§ **7.6.3 n. 56;** § **7.6.4 n. 67.**
LeMaster, In re, ___ Ind. ___, 433 N.E.2d 787 (1982)—§ **3.3.1 n. 55.**
Lemelson v. Synergistics Research Corp., 504 F.Supp. 1164 (S.D.N.Y.1981)—§ **7.4.3 n. 15.**
Lemon, State v., 603 S.W.2d 313 (Tex.Civ.App.1980)—§ **11.6.3 n. 64.**
Lemond, In re, 274 Ind. 505, 413 N.E.2d 228 (1980)—§ **12.1.3 n. 39.**
Lenarchick, State v., 74 Wis.2d 425, 247 N.W.2d 80 (1976)—§ **12.4.2 n. 89.**
Lenske, State ex rel. Oregon St. Bar v., 284 Or. 23, 584 P.2d 759 (1978)—§ **3.5.4 n. 9.**
Leon, State v., 229 Kan. 178, 621 P.2d 1016 (1981)—§ **10.3.1 n. 75.**
Leonard, In re, 12 Or. 93, 6 P. 426—§ **1.4.3 n. 76.**
Leonard v. Johns-Manville Corp., 57 N.C.App. 553, 291 S.E.2d 828 (1982)—§ **15.4.3 n. 37.**
Leonard, State ex rel. Nebraska St. Bar Ass'n v., 212 Neb. 379, 322 N.W.2d 794 (1982)—§ **3.3.4, n. 34.**
Leonardis, State v., 73 N.J. 360, 375 A.2d 607—§ **2.2.1 n. 11.**
Leopold, In re, 469 Pa. 384, 366 A.2d 227, 230–231 (1976)—§ **3.1, n. 12.**
Lerner, In re, 270 App.Div. 602, 61 N.Y.S.2d 661 (1946)—§ **15.1.4 n. 43.**
Leslie, Commonwealth v., 376 U.S. 647, 382 N.E.2d 1072 (1978)—§ **7.6.2 n. 29.**
Lespier, United States v., 558 F.2d 624 (1st Cir.1977)—§ **3.5.3 n. 76.**
Lesser, In re, 101 A.D.2d 349, 475 N.Y.S.2d 402 (1984)—§ **3.3.3 n. 24.**
Lester, In re, 87 Misc.2d 717, 386 N.Y.S.2d 509 (Sup.Ct. 1976)—§ **16.2.3 n. 40.**
Levanti v. Tippen, 585 F.Supp. 499 (S.D.Cal.)—§ **2.5 n. 68.**
Leverson, In re, 195 Minn. 42, 260 N.W. 480 (1935)—§ **3.4.5 n. 84.**
Levi v. Mississippi St. Bar, 436 So.2d 781 (Miss.1983)—§ **3.4.5 n. 53, 79;** § **16.2.3 n. 36, 65.**
Levin, In re, 101 Ill.2d 535, 79 Ill.Dec. 161, 463 N.E.2d 715 (1984)—§ **5.1 n. 35.**
Levin v. Barish, 314 Pa.Super. 347, 460 A.2d 1174 (1983)—§ **16.2.3 n. 64.**
Levine, In re, 97 Ariz. 88, 397 P.2d 205 (1964)—§ **12.2.3 n. 22.**
Levine, In re, 372 Pa. 612, 95 A.2d 222 (1953)—§ **13.10.2 n. 44.**
Levine v. Goldberg, 2 A.D.2d 409, 156 N.Y.S.2d 587 (1956)—§ **16.2.5 n. 90.**
Levine v. Levine, 56 N.Y.2d 42, 451 N.Y.S.2d 26, 436 N.E.2d 476 (1982)—§ **8.6 n. 41, 50, 52;** § **9.4.4 n. 88.**
Leviten v. Sandback, 291 N.Y. 352, 52 N.E.2d 898 (1943)—§ **9.6.3 n. 62.**
Levitsky v. Prince George's Cty., 50 Md.App. 484, 439 A.2d 600 (1982)—§ **6.3.5 n. 7;** § **6.3.8 n. 79.**
Levitt v. Levitt, 9 Mass.App.Ct. 894, 403 N.E.2d 143 (1980)—§ **7.1.7 n. 9.**
Levy, In re, 37 N.Y.2d 279, 372 N.Y.S.2d 41, 333 N.E.2d 350 (1975)—§ **3.3.2 n. 78.**
Levy v. State, 100 Misc.2d 781, 420 N.Y.S.2d 154 (Ct.Cl. 1979)—§ **9.2.2 n. 64.**
Lewis v. Anderson, 615 F.2d 778 (9th Cir.1979)—§ **13.4.2 n. 14.**
Lewis v. Black, 74 F.R.D. 1 (E.D.N.Y.1975)—§ **8.13 n. 52.**
Lewis v. Precision Optics, Inc., 612 F.2d 1074 (8th Cir. 1980)—§ **16.9 n. 24.**
Lewis v. S.S. Baune, 534 F.2d 1115 (5th Cir.1976)—§ **4.6.2 n. 78.**
Lewis v. Secretary of HHS, 707 F.2d 246 (6th Cir.1983)—§ **11.6.2 n. 57.**
Lewis v. Shaffer Stores Co., 218 F.Supp. 238 (S.D.N.Y. 1963)—§ **8.3.4 n. 76.**
Lewis v. State, 279 Ark. 143, 649 S.W.2d 188 (1983)—§ **9.5.1 n. 32.**
Lewis v. State Bar, 28 Cal.3d 683, 170 Cal.Rptr. 634, 621 P.2d 258 (1981)—§ **5.1 n. 27;** § **5.5 n. 16.**
Lewis v. State Bar, 9 Cal.3d 704, 108 Cal.Rptr. 821, 511 P.2d 1173 (1973)—§ **3.3.4 n. 45.**
Lewis v. Teleprompter Corp., 88 F.R.D. 11 (S.D.N.Y. 1980)—§ **9.2.4 n. 4;** § **12.7 n. 86;** § **13.7.2 n. 83.**
Lewis v. Unigard Mut. Ins. Co., 83 A.D.2d 919, 442 N.Y.S.2d 522 (1981)—§ **7.1.7 n. 9.**
Librarian v. State Bar, 38 Cal.2d 328, 239 P.2d 865 (1952)—§ **13.5.5 n. 61.**
Licata v. Spector, 26 Conn.Sup. 378, 225 A.2d 28 (1966)—§ **5.6.4 n. 54.**
Lichtenstein v. Lichtenstein, 425 F.2d 1111 (3d Cir.1970)—§ **16.6.2 n. 85.**
Liddy, United States v., 542 F.2d 76 (D.C.Cir.1976)—§ **13.9.2 n. 30.**
Liddy, United States v., 509 F.2d 428 (D.C.Cir.1974)—§ **14.6.4 n. 23.**
Lieber, In re, 442 A.2d 153 (D.C.App.1982)—§ **5.1 n. 7.**
Liebergesell v. Evans, 93 Wn.2d 881, 613 P.2d 1170 (1980)—§ **8.11.5 n. 23.**

McKenna, In re, 16 Cal.2d 610, 107 P.2d 258 (1940)—§ **5.6.1 n. 43.**

McKeon, In re, ___ Mont. ___, 656 P.2d 179 (1982)—§ **3.5.5 n. 21, 46;** § **3.5.6 n. 59, 77.**

McKinnon v. Disciplinary Bd., 264 N.W.2d 448 (N.D.1978)—§ **3.5.7 n. 90.**

McKinnon v. Tibbetts, 440 A.2d 1028 (Me.1982)—§ **5.6.5 n. 67.**

McKissick v. United States, 379 F.2d 754 (5th Cir.1967)—§ **12.5.4 n. 80**

McKnight v. Rice, Hoppner, Brown & Brunner, 678 P.2d 1330 (Alaska 1984)—§ **9.6.3 n. 46.**

McLaughlin v. Philadelphia Newspapers, Inc., 465 Pa. 104, 348 A.2d 376 (1975)—§ **3.4.4 n. 16, 17.**

McLaughlin, Commonwealth v., 469 Pa. 407, 366 A.2d 238 (1976)—§ **14.6.3 n. 30.**

McLean v. Michaelowsky, 117 Misc.2d 699, 458 N.Y.S.2d 1005 (1983)—§ **16.2.3 n. 66.**

McLeod, State ex rel. v. Seaborn, 270 S.C. 696, 244 S.E.2d 317 (1978)—§ **15.1.3 n. 75.**

McMahon, In re Estate of, 68 Cal.App.3d 70, 135 Cal.Rptr. 621 (1977)—§ **9.6.3 n. 63.**

McMann v. Richardson, 397 U.S. 759, 90 S.Ct. 1441, 25 L.Ed.2d 763 (1970)—§ **14.6.2;** § **14.6.2 n. 11, 82, 98.**

McManus, In re, 75 N.J. 238, 381 A.2d 352 (1978)—§ **3.3.3, n. 31.**

McMorris v. State Bar, 35 Cal.3d 77, 196 Cal.Rptr. 841, 672 P.2d 431 (1983)—§ **4.5 n. 20.**

McMorris v. State Bar, 29 Cal.3d 96, 171 Cal.Rptr. 829, 623 P.2d 781 (1981)—§ **5.1 n. 12.**

McNabb v. Osmundson, 315 N.W.2d 9 (Iowa 1982)—§ **14.5 n. 71.**

McNally v. Stonehenge, Inc., 242 Ga. 258, 248 S.E.2d 653 (1978)—§ **4.2 n. 39.**

McNeal v. Allen, 95 Wn.2d 265, 621 P.2d 1285 (1980)—§ **5.6.5 n. 1.**

McNulty v. McNulty, 81 A.D.2d 5S1, 437 N.Y.S.2d 438 (1981)—§ **6.3.4 n. 76.**

McNutt v. Superior Court, 133 Ariz. 7, 648 P.2d 122 (1982)—§ **14.6.4 n. 48.**

McPartlin v. Fransen, 178 Mont. 178, 582 N.W.2d 1255 (1978)—§ **11.6.3 n. 71.**

McPartlin, United States v., 595 F.2d 1321 (7th Cir. 1979)—§ **6.4.9 n. 30, 32, 36;** § **8.2.4 n. 44.**

McPherson v. Cox, 96 U.S. (6 Otto) 404, 24 L.Ed. 746 (1877)—§ **9.6.3 n. 39.**

McQuade, United States v., 647 F.2d 938 (9th Cir.1981)—§ **14.3.3 n. 79.**

McQuade, United States v., 579 F.2d 1180 (9th Cir.1978)—§ **14.5 n. 67.**

McQueen v. State, 272 Ind. 229, 396 N.E.2d 903 (1979)—§ **3.2 n. 23.**

McQueen v. Swenson, 498 F.2d 207 (8th Cir.1974)—§ **14.6.2 n. 7.**

McWhorter, In re, 405 Mich. 563, 284 N.W.2d 472 (1979)—§ **4.8 n. 29.**

McWhorter, In re, 407 Mich. 278, 284 N.W.2d 472 (1979)—§ **3.4.2 n. 66.**

McWhorter, Ltd. v. Irvin, 154 Ga.App. 89, 267 S.E.2d 630 (1980)—§ **5.6.2 n. 70.**

M.S. v. Wermers, 557 F.2d 170 (8th Cir.)—§ **2.2.1 n. 14.**

Machibroda v. United States, 368 U.S. 487, 82 S.Ct. 510, 7 L.Ed.2d 473 (1962)—§ **13.10.6 n. 18.**

Mack v. Minneapolis, 333 N.W.2d 744 (Minn.1983)—§ **9.1 n. 4.**

Mackey, United States v., 405 F.Supp. 854 (E.D.N.Y. 1975)—§ **6.3.1 n. 52.**

Macumber, State v., 112 Ariz. 569, 544 P.2d 1084 (1976)—§ **6.4.1 n. 10.**

Maddock, In re, 265 N.W.2d 229 (N.D.1977)—§ **12.1.3 n. 63.**

Madera, In re, 39 A.D.2d 202, 333 N.Y.S.2d 329 (1972)—§ **3.5.6 n. 77.**

Madera v. Gendron, 59 Cal.2d 798, 31 Cal.Rptr. 302, 382 P.2d 342 (1963)—§ **13.9.1 n. 96.**

Magana v. Platzer Shipyard, Inc., 74 F.R.D. 61 (S.D.Tex. 1977)—§ **9.1 n. 10.**

Magar, In re, 296 Or. 799, 681 P.2d 93 (1984)—§ **5.1 n. 25.**

Magee v. State Bar, 58 Cal.2d 423, 24 Cal.Rptr. 839, 374 P.2d 807 (1962)—§ **8.12.3 n. 36.**

Magee v. Superior Court, 8 Cal.3d 949, 106 Cal.Rptr. 647, 506 P.2d 1023 (1973)—§ **15.4.3 n. 29.**

Magida v. Continental Can Co., 231 F.2d 843 (2d Cir. 1956)—§ **14.2.5 n. 90.**

Mahaney, United States v., 27 F.Supp. 463 (N.D.Cal. 1939)—§ **6.3.4 n. 2, 3.**

Mahoney, In re, 437 N.E.2d 49 (Ind.1982)—§ **11.6.2 n. 63.**

Mahoning County Bar Ass'n v. Franko, 168 Ohio St. 17, 151 N.E.2d 17 (1958)—§ **17.3.2 n. 74.**

Mahr, In re, 276 Or. 939, 556 P.2d 1359 (1976)—§ **3.3.2 n. 2, 93.**

Maine v. Thiboutot, 448 U.S. 1, 100 S.Ct. 2502, 65 L.Ed.2d 555 (1980)—§ **16.6.2 n. 67.**

Malinauskas v. United States, 505 F.2d 649 (5th Cir. 1974)—§ **6.3.5 n. 11.**

Mallard v. M/V "Germundo," 530 F.Supp. 725 (S.D.Fla. 1982)—§ **7.6.3 n. 66.**

Malloy, In re, 248 N.W.2d 43, 47 (N.D.1976)—§ **3.3.1 n. 45;** § **5.6.3 n. 23;** § **6.4.3 n. 86;** § **11.5 n. 24;** § **12.5.3 n. 56, 58, 64.**

Malloy v. Sullivan, 387 So.2d 169 (Ala.1980)—§ **5.6.3 n. 23.**

Maloney, In re, 620 S.W.2d 362, 365 (Mo.1981)—§ **5.1 n. 47, 56.**

Malvin, In re, 466 A.2d 1220 (D.C.App.1983)—§ **3.3.2 n. 80.**

Manchin v. Browning, 296 S.E.2d 909 (W.Va.1982)—§ **8.9.2 n. 19;** § **13.9.1 n. 8, 12.**

Mandel, In re, 94 A.D.2d 278, 464 N.Y.S.2d 168 (1983)—§ **3.5.4 n. 99.**

Mandel, United States v., 437 F.Supp. 258 (D.Md.1977)—§ **16.2.3 n. 35.**

Mandell, In re, 89 Ill.2d 14, 59 Ill.Dec. 97, 431 N.E.2d 382 (1982)—§ **3.5.5 n. 42, 44.**

Mandujano, United States v., 425 U.S. 564, 96 S.Ct. 1768, 48 L.Ed.2d 212 (1976)—§ **14.3.2 n. 75.**

Maness v. Meyers, 419 U.S. 449, 95 S.Ct. 584, 42 L.Ed.2d 574 (1975)—§ **6.3.4 n. 80;** § **12.1.3 n. 65, 67, 70;** § **13.3.7;** § **13.3.7 n. 81;** § **13.3.8 n. 88.**

Maniego, United States v., 710 F.2d 24 (2d Cir.1983)—§ **12.6.5 n. 48.**

Mann, People v., 27 Ill.2d 135, 188 N.E.2d 665 (1963)— § **7.5.2 n. 46.**

Mannis, In re, 295 Or. 594, 668 P.2d 1224 (1983)—§ **4.8 n. 96.**

Mannon v. State, 98 Nev. 224, 645 P.2d 433 (1982)—§ **8.2.3 n. 30.**

Manson, People v., 61 Cal.App.3d 102, 132 Cal.Rptr. 265 (1976)—§ **14.6.3 n. 30.**

Maples, In re, 249 Ga. 502, 291 S.E.2d 708 (1982)—§ **5.1 n. 59.**

Maragos, In re, 285 N.W.2d 541 (N.D.1979)—§ **3.3.3 n. 26;** § **3.4.4 n. 33.**

Maran, In re, 80 N.J. 160, 402 A.2d 924 (1979)—§ **4.8 n. 99;** § **14.2.5 n. 85.**

Marbury v. Madison, 5 U.S. (1 Cranch) 137, 2 L.Ed. 60 (1803)—§ **3.4.3 n. 91;** § **13.3.8 n. 85.**

Marco v. Dulles, 169 F.Supp. 622 (S.D.N.Y.)—§ **7.2.1 n. 42;** § **13.7.4 n. 19.**

Marcone, Commonwealth v., 487 Pa. 572, 410 A.2d 759 (1980)—§ **12.1.3 n. 78.**

Marcus, In re, 107 Wis.2d 560, 320 N.W.2d 806 (1982)— § **3.4.4 n. 30;** § **3.5.7 n. 3;** § **14.2.5 n. 53.**

Marcus v. State (1982) 290 S.E.2d 470—§ **1.6 n. 20.**

Marcy, People v., 91 Mich.App. 399, 283 N.W.2d 754 (1979)—§ **6.3.8 n. 79.**

Mardirosian v. American Institute of Architects, 474 F.Supp. 628 (D.D.C.)—§ **2.4.1 n. 31.**

Margolin, In re, 518 F.2d 551 (9th Cir.1975)—§ **3.6.1 n. 22;** § **14.6.1 n. 86.**

Margow, In re Estate of, 77 N.J. 316, 390 A.2d 591— § **2.2.2 n. 30;** § **15.1 n. 38;** § **15.1.3 n. 86.**

Marietta, In re, 223 Kan. 11, 569 P.2d 921 (1977)—§ **11.6.2 n. 51.**

Marine, In re, 82 Wis.2d 612, 264 N.W.2d 290 (1979)— § **3.4.3 n. 89;** § **4.8 n. 31, 45;** § **7.1.7 n. 14;** § **9.3.1 n. 76.**

Marino v. United States, 600 F.2d 462 (5th Cir.1979)— § **12.5.4 n. 88.**

Markarian v. Bartis, 89 N.H. 370, 199 A. 573 (1938)— § **9.4.1 n. 13.**

Markell v. Sidney B. Pfeifer Found., Inc., 9 Mass.App.Ct. 412, 402 N.E.2d 76 (1980)—§ **8.12.3 n. 32.**

Markfield v. Ass'n of the Bar of Cty.N.Y., 49 A.D.2d 516, 370 N.Y.S.2d 82 (1975)—§ **12.2.2 n. 10.**

Marker v. Greenberg, 313 N.W.2d 4 (Minn.1981)—§ **5.6.4 n. 54, 58.**

Marks, In re, 72 A.D.2d 399, 424 N.Y.S.2d 229 (1980)— § **4.8 n. 98.**

Marquardt v. Fein, 25 Wn.App. 651, 612 P.2d 378 (1980)— § **5.1 n. 43.**

Marrero v. Christiano, 575 F.Supp. 837 (S.D.N.Y.1983)— § **9.6.3 n. 52.**

Marriage of (see name of party)

Marschke v. Cross, 82 A.D.2d 944, 440 N.Y.S.2d 740 (1981)—§ **9.6.3 n. 54.**

Marshall, In re, 55 S.Ct. 513 (U.S.1935)—§ **12.1.3 n. 58.**

Marshall v. Baltimore & O.R.R., 57 U.S. (16 How.) 314, 14 L.Ed. 953 (1853)—§ **9.4.5 n. 17.**

Marshall v. Marshall, 140 Cal.App.2d 475, 295 P.2d 131 (1956)—§ **6.3.7 n. 53.**

Marshall & Assoc., Inc., J.H. v. Burleson, 313 A.2d 587 (D.C.App.1973)—§ **15.1.3 n. 28.**

Mart v. Schlumberger, Ltd., 422 So.2d 1205 (La.App. 1982)—§ **4.6.2 n. 78.**

Marthaler, United States v., 571 F.2d 1104 (9th Cir. 1978)—§ **15.1.3 n. 40.**

Martin, In re, 71 Cal.App.3d 472, 139 Cal.Rptr. 451 (1977)—§ **7.5.2 n. 52;** § **17.6.2 n. 63.**

Martin v. Burns, 102 Ariz. 341, 429 P.2d 660 (1967)— § **5.6.2 n. 83.**

Martin v. Camp, 219 N.Y. 170, 114 N.E. 46 (1932)—§ **9.5.2 n. 51.**

Martin v. Freeman, 216 Cal.App.2d 639, 31 Cal.Rptr. 217 (1963)—§ **8.13 n. 56.**

Martin v. Hall, 20 Cal.App.3d 414, 97 Cal.Rptr. 730 (1971)—§ **5.6.3 n. 23.**

Martin v. Middendorf, 420 F.Supp. 779 (D.D.C.1976)— § **14.4.1 n. 40.**

Martin v. Morgan Drive Away, Inc., 665 F.2d 598 (5th Cir. 1982)—§ **8.13 n. 50.**

Martin v. Rose, 717 F.2d 295 (6th Cir.1983)—§ **10.5.4 n. 50.**

Martin v. State Bar, 20 Cal.3d 717, 144 Cal.Rptr. 214, 575 P.2d 757 (1978)—§ **3.5.2 n. 365.**

Martin v. Walton, 368 U.S. 25, 82 S.Ct. 1, 7 L.Ed.2d 5 (1961)—§ **15.4.1 n. 94.**

Martin, State v., 231 Kan. 481, 646 P.2d 459 (1982)—§ **5.1 n. 45.**

Martin, State v., 274 N.W.2d 893 (S.D.1979)—§ **6.3.7 n. 58.**

Martin-Trigona, United States v., 684 F.2d 485 (7th Cir. 1982)—§ **14.3.1 n. 61.**

Martindale, State v., 215 Kan. 667, 527 P.2d 703 (1974)— § **3.3.1 n. 46;** § **12.4.2 n. 86.**

Martinez, State v., 89 N.M. 729, 557 P.2d 578 (1976)— § **7.5.2 n. 90.**

Martinez Rivera v. Trias Monge, 587 F.2d 539 (1st Cir. 1978)—§ **3.4.5 n. 64.**

Martini v. Leland, 116 Misc.2d 231, 455 N.Y.S.2d 354 (Civ. Ct.1982)—§ **11.6.2 n. 41.**

Marx, United States v., 553 F.2d 874 (4th Cir.1977)— § **12.1.3 n. 78.**

Maryland Am. Gen. Ins. Co. v. Blackmon, 639 S.W.2d 455 (Tex.1982)—§ **6.3.4 n. 94;** § **6.4.10 n. 62.**

Maryland St. Bar Ass'n v. Agnew, 271 Md. 543, 318 A.2d 811, 814 (1974)—§ **3.1 n. 11;** § **3.3.2 n. 2.**

Maryland State Bar Ass'n v. Boone, 255 Md. 420, 258 A.2d 438 (1969)—§ **15.3.2 n. 59.**

Maryland St. Bar Ass'n v. Frank, 272 Md. 528, 325 A.2d 718 (1974)—§ **3.3.2 n. 87.**

Marzullo v. Maryland, 561 F.2d 540 (4th Cir.1977)— § **14.6.2 n. 14;** § **14.6.3 n. 23.**

Mason v. Village of Ravena, 114 Misc.2d 487, 451 N.Y.S.2d 994 (1982)—§ **6.4.8 n. 37.**

Massachusetts v. United States, 429 U.S. 66, 97 S.Ct. 245, 50 L.Ed.2d 224 (1976)—§ **8.9.2 n. 19.**

Massiah v. United States, 377 U.S. 201, 84 S.Ct. 1199, 12 L.Ed.2d 246 (1964)—§ **13.10.2 n. 48;** § **14.3.2;** § **14.3.2 n. 77.**

Masters, In re, 91 Ill.2d 413, 63 Ill.Dec. 449, 455, 438 N.E.2d 187, 193 (1982)—§ **3.3.1 n. 56;** § **5.6.2 n. 62.**

Miotke v. City of Spokane, 101 Wn.2d 307, 678 P.2d 803 (1984)—§ **16.6.2 n. 64.**
Mirabelli, In re, 79 N.J. 597, 401 A.2d 1090 (1979)—§ **3.3.2 n. 78.**
Miranda v. Arizona, 384 U.S. 436, 86 S.Ct. 1602, 16 L.Ed. 2d 694 (1966)—§ **10.5.3 n. 30;** § **12.3.2 n. 31;** § **14.3.1 n. 46;** § **14.3.2;** § **14.3.2 n. 76.**
Miranda v. Southern Pac. Transp. Co., 710 F.2d 516 (9th Cir.1983)—§ **12.1.3 n. 79.**
Mishawaka, City of v. American Elec. Power Co., 616 F.2d 976 (7th Cir.1980)—§ **16.6.2 n. 89.**
Miskovsky v. State ex rel. Jones, 586 P.2d 1104 (Okl.Crim. App.1978)—§ **12.3.4 n. 52.**
Missan v. Schoenfeld, 111 Misc.2d 1022, 445 N.Y.S.2d 856 (1981)—§ **16.2.3 n. 71.**
Mission Denver Co. v. Pierson, 674 P.2d 363 (Colo.1984)—§ **16.6.2 n. 77.**
Mississippi v. United States, 451 U.S. 934, 101 S.Ct. 2012, 68 L.Ed.2d 321 (1981)—§ **8.10.2 n. 15.**
Mississippi St. Bar v. Attorney-Respondent, 367 So.2d 179 (Miss.1979)—§ **3.4.3 n. 93.**
Mississippi St. Bar v. Phillips, 385 So.2d 943, 945 (Miss. 1980)—§ **3.3.2 n. 77.**
Mitchell, In re, 249 Ga. 280, 290 S.E.2d 426 (1982)—§ **3.5.5 n. 42.**
Mitchell, In re, 244 Ga. 766, 362 S.E.2d 89 (1979)—§ **12.4.3 n. 96.**
Mitchell v. Amerada Hess Corp., 638 P.2d 441 (Okl.1981)—§ **8.13 n. 50.**
Mitchell v. Ass'n of Bar of City of N.Y., 40 N.Y.2d 153, 386 N.Y.S.2d 95, 351 N.E.2d 743 (1976)—§ **3.3.2 n. 80;** § **3.5.4 n. 87, 98.**
Mitchell v. Bromberger, 2 Nev. 345 (1866)—§ **6.7.8 n. 7.**
Mitchell v. School Bd. of Leon County, 335 So.2d 354 (Fla. Ct. App.1976)—§ **6.5.6 n. 15.**
Mitchell, People v., 86 A.D.2d 976, 448 N.Y.S.2d 332 (1982)—§ **6.3.7 n. 65.**
Mitchell, State v., 356 So.2d 974 (La.1978)—§ **8.2.2 n. 8.**
Mitchell, United States v., 372 F.Supp. 1239 (S.D.N.Y. 1973)—§ **6.6.2 n. 48.**
Mitschelen v. State Farm Mut. Auto. Ins. Co., 89 N.M. 586, 555 P.2d 707 (Ct.App.1976)—§ **11.6.3 n. 70.**
MM., In re Roger, 96 A.D.2d 1133, 466 N.Y.S.2d 873 (1983)—§ **15.3.2 n. 65.**
Mobley v. State, 409 So.2d 1031 (Fla.1982)—§ **6.3.7 n. 50.**
Model Indus., Inc. v. Walsh Press & Die Co., 111 Ill.App.3d 572, 67 Ill.Dec. 403, 444 N.E.2d 639 (1982)—§ **16.6.3 n. 95.**
Modica, United States v., 663 F.2d 1173 (2d Cir.1981)—§ **13.10.4 n. 86.**
Moffitt, Commonwealth v., 383 Mass. 201, 418 N.E.2d 585 (1981)—§ **14.6.3 n. 37.**
Mohawk Data Sciences Corp. v. Industrial Comm'n, 671 P.2d 1335 (Colo.App.1983)—§ **4.2 n. 47.**
Mohr v. Montana Distr. Court, 660 P.2d 88 (Mont.1983)—§ **14.6.4 n. 44.**
Moiel v. Sandlin, 571 S.W.2d 567 (Tex.Civ.App.1978)—§ **5.6 n. 29.**
Moity v. Louisiana State Bar Ass'n, 414 F.Supp. 180 (E.D. La.1976)—§ **11.3.3 n. 70.**
Molezzo Reporters v. Patt, 94 Nev. 540, 579 P.2d 1243 (1978)—§ **4.2 n. 58.**
Mollozzi, In re, 73 N.J. 76, 372 A.2d 611 (1977)—§ **13.5.6 n. 84.**
Monaghan, State v., 184 N.J.Super. 340, 446 A.2d 185 (1982)—§ **14.3.5 n. 9.**
Monroe v. State Bar, 55 Cal.2d 145, 10 Cal.Rptr. 257, 358 P.2d 529 (1961)—§ **11.5 n. 29.**
Montag v. State Bar, 32 Cal.3d 721, 186 Cal.Rptr. 894, 652 P.2d 1370 (1982)—§ **3.3.1 n. 61.**
Monteiro, In re, ___ Nev. ___, 684 P.2d 506 (1984)—§ **3.3.2 n. 82.**
Montgomery, In re, 292 Or. 796, 643 P.2d 338 (1982)—§ **8.11.3 n. 3, 6;** § **12.10.1 n. 19.**
Montgomery, In re, 272 N.Y. 323, 6 N.E.2d 40 (1936)—§ **9.5.2 n. 53.**
Montgomery Elev. Co. v. Superior Court, 135 Ariz. 432, 661 P.2d 1133 (1983)—§ **14.6.4 n. 44.**
Monti v. Tangora, 99 Ill.App.3d 575, 425 N.E.2d 597 (1981)—§ **4.2 n. 52.**
Montriou v. Jeffreys, 2 Car. & P. 113, 172 Eng.Rep. 51 (Nisi Prius 1825)—§ **5.6.2 n. 78.**
Moody v. IRS, 654 F.2d 795 (D.C.Cir.1981)—§ **6.4.10 n. 53.**
Moody, People v., 676 P.2d 691 (Colo.1984)—§ **11.2.5 n. 44.**
Mooney v. Holohan, 294 U.S. 103, 55 S.Ct. 340, 79 L.Ed. 791 (1935)—§ **13.10.4 n. 91.**
Moore, In re, 280 S.C. 178, 312 S.W.2d 1 (1984)—§ **16.2.2 n. 24.**
Moore, In re, ___ Ind. ___, 453 N.E.2d 971 (1983)—§ **3.4.4 n. 40;** § **3.5.2 n. 65.**
Moore, In re, 308 N.C. 771, 303 S.E.2d 810 (1983)—§ **15.3.2 n. 64.**
Moore v. Illinois, 434 U.S. 220, 98 S.Ct. 458, 54 L.Ed.2d 424 (1977)—§ **14.3.2 n. 66.**
Moore v. Janning, 427 F.Supp. 567 (D.Neb.1976)—§ **14.6.4 n. 55.**
Moore v. State, 83 Wis.2d 285, 265 N.W.2d 540 (1978)—§ **14.4.2 n. 60.**
Moore v. State Bar, 62 Cal.2d 74, 41 Cal.Rptr. 161, 396 P.2d 577 (1964)—§ **5.6.6 n. 42.**
Moore v. United States, 432 F.2d 730 (3d Cir.1970)—§ **14.6.2 n. 13.**
Morales v. Field, DeGoff, Huppert & MacGowan, 99 Cal. App.3d 307, 160 Cal.Rptr. 239 (1979)—§ **5.6.5 n. 72.**
Morales, United States v., 498 F.Supp. 139 (E.D.N.Y. 1980)—§ **11.6.2 n. 62.**
Moran v. Harris, 131 Cal.App.3d 913, 182 Cal.Rptr. 519 (1982)—§ **9.2.4 n. 12, 97, 98, 99.**
Moran, State ex rel. v. Ziegler, ___ W.Va. ___, 244 S.E.2d 550 (1978)—§ **8.9.4 n. 43.**
Morelli, State v., 152 N.J.Super, 67, 377 A.2d 774 (1977)—§ **8.10.3 n. 31.**
Moreno, State v., 128 Ariz. 257, 625 P.2d 320 (1981)—§ **6.4.7 n. 14.**
Morfeld v. Andrews, 579 P.2d 426 (Wyo.1978)—§ **9.4.4 n. 12, 87;** § **9.6.3 n. 54.**
Morford, In re, 46 Del. 144, 80 A.2d 429 (1951)—§ **3.4.4 n. 33.**
Morgan, In re, 95 N.M. 653, 625 P.2d 582 (1981)—§ **3.5.7 n. 90.**

Morgan, United States v., 313 U.S. 409, 61 S.Ct. 999, 85 L.Ed. 1429 (1941)—§ **6.5.6 n. 19;** § **11.3.1 n. 45.**

Morgan Washington Home, In re, 108 Ill.App.3d 245, 64 Ill.Dec. 105, 439 N.E.2d 34 (1982)—§ **9.3.1 n. 69;** § **9.4.1 n. 30.**

Morgenstein, State v., 147 N.J.Super. 234, 371 A.2d 96 (1977)—§ **14.3.3 n. 84.**

Morger v. Superior Court, 637 P.2d 310 (Ariz.App.1981)—§ **14.3.3 n. 82.**

Moritz v. Medical Protective Co., 428 F.Supp. 865 (W.D. Wis.1977)—§ **6.4.8 n. 23;** § **7.4.2 n. 65.**

Morowitz v. Marvel, 423 A.2d 196 (D.C.1980)—§ **5.6 n. 25, 34.**

Morrell v. State, 575 P.2d 1200 (Alaska 1978)—§ **12.3.5;** § **12.3.5 n. 71, 75.**

Morris, In re, 270 S.C. 308, 241 S.E.2d 911 (1978)—§ **7.3.4 n. 45;** § **9.3.2 n. 80.**

Morris, In re, 72 N.J. 135, 367 A.2d 1172 (1977)—§ **7.3.3 n. 32;** § **9.3.1 n. 29.**

Morris v. Slappy, 461 U.S. 1, 103 S.Ct. 1610, 75 L.Ed.2d 610 (1983)—§ **4.5 n. 22;** § **14.3.4 n. 90, 91;** § **14.3.5 n. 5;** § **14.3.7 n. 26.**

Morris, State v., 101 Idaho 120, 609 P.2d 652 (1980)—§ **6.4.7 n. 15.**

Morris, United States v., 568 F.2d 396 (5th Cir.1978)—§ **12.1.2 n. 23.**

Morrison, United States v., 449 U.S. 361, 101 S.Ct. 665, 66 L.Ed.2d 564 (1981)—§ **11.6.2 n. 62;** § **14.6.4;** § **14.6.4 n. 59, 62.**

Morse, In re, 157 N.J.Super. 104, 384 A.2d 562 (1978)—§ **14.3.5 n. 98.**

Mortgage Trust v. First Wis. Corp., 422 F.Supp. 493 (E.D. Wis.1976)—§ **7.1.7 n. 96.**

Moses v. McGarvey, 614 P.2d 1363 (Alaska 1980)—§ **9.6.1 n. 11.**

Moses, State v., 231 Kan. 243, 642 P.2d 1004 (1982)—§ **14.2.4 n. 73.**

Mosk v. Superior Court, 25 Cal.3d 474, 159 Cal.Rptr. 494, 601 P.2d 1030 (1979)—§ **2.2.1 n. 10.**

Mosley v. St. Louis Southwestern Ry., 634 F.2d 942 (5th Cir.1981)—§ **11.6.2 n. 39;** § **14.6.4 n. 48.**

Mosness, In re, 39 Wis. 509, 20 Am.Rep. 55 (1876)—§ **2.2.3 n. 45.**

Moss v. ITT Continental Baking Co., 83 F.R.D. 624 (E.D. Va.1979)—§ **14.5 n. 67.**

Moss, State ex rel. Oklahoma Bar Ass'n v., 577 P.2d 1317 (Okl.1978)—§ **3.5.7 n. 99;** § **9.3.2 n. 58.**

Mossler v. Foreman, 493 S.W.2d 627 (Tex.Civ.App.1973)—§ **9.4.3 n. 84.**

Motor Club of Iowa v. Dept. of Transp., 251 N.W.2d 510 (Iowa 1977)—§ **13.9.1 n. 9.**

Mount Laurel Township v. Public Advocate, 83 N.J. 522, 416 A.2d 886 (1980)—§ **16.8 n. 96.**

Mountain States Tel. & Tel. Co., United States v., 516 F.Supp. 225 (D.Wyo.1981)—§ **14.6.4 n. 56.**

Mourning v. Family Publications Service, Inc., 411 U.S. 356, 93 S.Ct. 1652, 36 L.Ed.2d 318 (1973)—§ **16.6.3 n. 95.**

Move Organization v. United States Dep't of Justice, 555 F.Supp. 684 (E.D.Pa.1983)—§ **14.4.1 n. 40;** § **14.4.2 n. 59;** § **15.1.3 n. 4.**

Muccini, In re Estate of, 118 Misc.2d 38, 460 N.Y.S.2d 680 (1983)—§ **9.4.2 n. 54.**

Muigai v. INS, 682 F.2d 334 (2d Cir.1982)—§ **11.2.5 n. 37.**

Mullane v. Central Hanover Bank & Trust Co., 339 U.S. 306, 70 S.Ct. 652, 94 L.Ed. 865 (1950)—§ **4.2 n. 20.**

Mullins, State v., 26 Ohio App.2d 13, 268 N.E.2d 603 (1971)—§ **6.4.10 n. 44.**

Munday v. Brown, 617 S.W.3d 897 (Tenn.App.1981)—§ **4.2 n. 41.**

Mundy, State ex rel. Memmel v., 75 Wis.2d 276, 249 N.W.2d 573 (1977)—§ **4.4 n. 15.**

Municipal Court, People v., 27 Cal.App.3d 193, 103 Cal. Rptr. 645 (1972)—§ **13.10.3 n. 37.**

Municipal Court (Byars), People v., 77 Cal.App.3d 294, 143 Cal.Rptr. 491 (1978)—§ **8.9.3 n. 42.**

Municipal Court (Wolfe), People v., 69 Cal.App.3d 714, 138 Cal.Rptr. 235 (1977)—§ **13.8.3 n. 88.**

Muniz v. State, 575 S.W.2d 408 (Tex.Civ.App.1978)—§ **3.3.2 n. 6.**

Munyan v. Curtis, Mallet-Prevost, Colt & Mosle, 99 A.D.2d 716, 472 N.Y.S.2d 321 (1984)—§ **16.2.3 n. 64.**

Murphy, In re, 560 F.2d 326 (8th Cir.1977)—§ **6.4.10 n. 58;** § **6.6.2 n. 42;** § **12.1.3 n. 68.**

Murphy v. Committee on Professional Standards, 82 A.D.2d 957, 439 N.Y.S.2d 782 (1981)—§ **14.6.1 n. 86.**

Murphy v. Riggs, 238 Mich. 151, 213 Mich. 110 (1927)—§ **6.3.4 n. 2.**

Murphy v. State, 46 Md.App. 138, 416 A.2d 748 (1980)—§ **12.1.3 n. 77.**

Murphy v. Washington American League Base Ball Club, Inc., 324 F.2d 394 (D.C.Cir.1963)—§ **8.3.4 n. 76.**

Murphy, United States ex rel. Simon v., 349 F.Supp. 818 (E.D.Pa.1972)—§ **9.4.3 n. 79.**

Murray, In re, 266 Ind. 221, 362 N.E.2d 128 (1977)—§ **3.4.4 n. 10;** § **8.8.2 n. 89.**

Murray, In re, 287 Or. 633, 601 P.2d 780 (1979)—§ **11.6.2 n. 40.**

Murvin, State v., 304 N.C. 523, 284 S.E.2d 289 (1981)—§ **6.3.7 n. 53.**

Myerberg, Sawyer & Rue v. Agee, 51 Md.App. 711, 446 A.2d 69 (1982)—§ **5.6.3 n. 30.**

Myers v. Aragona, 21 Md.App. 45, 318 A.2d 263 (1974)—§ **5.6.6 n. 43.**

Myers v. Butler, 556 F.2d 398 (8th Cir.1977)—§ **5.6.3 n. 23;** § **12.5.1 n. 43.**

Myers v. Virginia St. Bar ex rel. Second Distr. Committee, 226 Va. 630, 312 S.E.2d 286 (1984)—§ **9.3.1 n. 27;** § **9.3.2 n. 89.**

Mylar v. Wilkinson, 435 So.2d 1237 (Ala.1983)—§ **5.6.3 n. 7.**

Myrtle Beach Lumber Co. v. Globe Int'l Corp., 281 S.C. 290, 315 S.E.2d 142 (1984)—§ **4.2 n. 27.**

N.H.B. Ass'n, In re Petition of, 122 N.H. 971, 453 A.2d 1258 (1982)—§ **4.8 n. 55.**

N.R.S., In re, 403 So.2d 1315 (Fla.1981)—§ **15.3.2 n. 68.**

NAACP v. Virginia ex rel. Button, 371 U.S. 415, 83 S.Ct. 328, 9 L.Ed.2d 405 (1963)—§ **8.8.3;** § **8.8.3 n. 98;** § **8.13 n. 46, 51;** § **10.2.3 n. 65;** § **14.2.5 n. 21;** § **16.4 n. 40;** § **16.5.2;** § **16.5.2 n. 47, 49;** § **16.8 n. 3.**

111 East 88th Partners v. Simon, 106 Misc. 693, 434 N.Y.S.2d 886 (1980)—§ **16.6.3 n. 95.**

O'Neil v. Bergan, 452 A.2d 337 (D.C.App.1982)—§ **5.6.2 n. 62.**

O'Neil v. Cunningham, 118 Cal.App.3d 466, 173 Cal.Rptr. 422 (1981)—§ **5.6.5 n. 4, 5.**

O'Neil Lumber Co. v. Nickelodean Cos., ___ Mont. ___, 617 P.2d 1291 (1980)—§ **15.1.3 n. 38.**

O'Neill v. Gray, 30 F.2d 776 (2d Cir.1929)—§ **5.6.2 n. 94.**

Ong Hing v. Arizona Harness Raceway, Inc., 10 Ariz.App. 380, 459 P.2d 107 (1969)—§ **9.2.1 n. 33.**

Opacak, In re, 257 Minn. 600, 101 N.W.2d 606 (1960)—§ **12.7 n. 83.**

OpDyke v. Kent Liquor Market, Inc., 40 Del.Ch. 316, 79 F.R.D. 658 (N.D.Tex.1978)—§ **7.1.7 n. 96;** § **7.2.4 n. 6;** § **7.3.4 n. 53.**

Opinion No. 415, In re, 81 N.J. 318, 407 A.2d 1197 (1979)—§ **7.6.3 n. 47;** § **8.9.3 n. 33.**

Opinion 452, In re, 87 N.J. 45, 432 A.2d 829 (1981)—§ **8.9.3 n. 33.**

Opinion of the Justices, 121 N.H. 531, 431 A.2d 144 (1981)—§ **14.3.3 n. 83.**

Opinion of the Justices, In re, 289 Mass. 607, 194 N.E. 313 (1935)—§ **15.4.1 n. 99.**

Opinion of the Justices, In re, 279 Mass. 607, 180 N.E. 725 (1932)—§ **2.2.3 n. 55.**

Oppenheim v. Azriliant, 89 A.D.2d 522, 452 N.Y.S.2d 211 (1982)—§ **7.5.2 n. 92.**

Orcutt Co. v. Green, 204 U.S. 96, 27 S.Ct. 195, 51 L.Ed. 390—§ **12.5;** § **12.5 n. 32.**

Oregon State Bar v. Gilchrist, 272 Or. 552, 538 P.2d 913 (1975)—§ **15.1.3 n. 96.**

Oregon State Bar v. Wright, 280 Or. 693, 573 P.2d 283 (1977)—§ **15.1.1 n. 5;** § **15.1.3 n. 74, 75.**

Oregon St. Bar, State ex rel. v. Hollingsworth, 286 Or. 477, 595 P.2d 484 (1979)—§ **3.5.7 n. 93.**

Oregon St. Bar, State ex rel. v. Lenske, 284 Or. 23, 584 P.2d 759 (1978)—§ **3.5.4 n. 9.**

Oregon State Bar, State ex rel. v. Robeson, 291 Or. 505, 632 P.2d 1255—§ **2.2.3 n. 46, 55;** § **4.8 n. 53.**

Oregon St. Bar, United States v., 405 F.Supp. 1102 (D.Or. 1975)—§ **2.4.1 n. 24.**

Oregon St. Bar, United States v., 385 F.Supp. 507 (D.Or. 1974)—§ **2.4.1 n. 24;** § **2.4.2 n. 52.**

Ormerod v. Dearman, 100 Pa.St. 561, 45 Am.Rep. 391 (1882)—§ **9.4.3 n. 70.**

Oroshnik v. Schweiker, 569 F.Supp. 399 (D.N.J.1983)—§ **4.2 n. 31.**

Orr v. Waldorf-Astoria Hotel Co., 291 F. 343 (8th Cir. 1923)—§ **5.6.3 n. 16.**

Ortiz v. Barrett, 222 Va. 118, 278 S.E.2d 883 (1981)—§ **5.6.6. n. 52, 53;** § **8.8.4 n. 9.**

Ortiz v. Safeco Ins. Co., 144 N.J.Super. 506, 366 A.2d 695 (1976)—§ **9.3.1 n. 49.**

Orton, In re, 97 Wn.2d 243, 643 P.2d 448 (1982)—§ **5.1 n. 35.**

Ortwein v. Schwab, 410 U.S. 656, 93 S.Ct. 1172, 35 L.Ed.2d 572 (1973)—§ **14.5 n. 77.**

Osborn v. Bank, 22 U.S. (9 Wheat.) 738, 6 L.Ed. 204 (1824)—§ **4.2 n. 32;** § **14.4.1 n. 36;** § **15.1.3 n. 2.**

Osborn v. District Court, 619 P.2d 41 (Colo.1980)—§ **6.7.5 n. 80;** § **8.10.1 n. 61;** § **8.10.3 n. 57.**

Osborn, United States v., 561 F.2d 1334 (9th Cir.1977)—§ **6.3.4 n. 81, 98;** § **6.3.5 n. 39.**

Osborn, United States v., 409 F.Supp. 406 (D.Or.1975)—§ **6.3.5 n. 19.**

Osborne v. Osborne, 384 Mass. 591, 428 N.E.2d 810 (1981)—§ **9.4.4 n. 87, 88.**

Ostensoe, In re, 196 Minn. 102, 264 N.W. 569 (1936)—§ **9.3.1 n. 35;** § **9.4.2 n. 59.**

Osterneck v. E.T. Barwidk Ind., Inc., 82 F.R.D. 81 (N.D.Ga. 1979)—§ **13.4.3 n. 19.**

Ostrer v. Aronwald, 434 F.Supp. 379 (S.D.N.Y.1977)—§ **14.3.7 n. 35.**

Ostrer v. Aronwald, 425 F.Supp. 962 (S.D.N.Y.1976)—§ **15.4.3 n. 32.**

Ostrer, United States v., 597 F.2d 337 (2d Cir.1979)—§ **8.10.2 n. 81;** § **8.10.3 n. 57.**

Ostrer, United States v., 422 F.Supp. 93 (S.D.N.Y.1976)—§ **6.3.3 n. 71.**

Oswald v. State, 214 Kan. 162, 519 P.2d 624 (1974)—§ **15.4.3 n. 32.**

Otis & Co. v. Pennsylvania R.R., 57 F.Supp. 680 (E.D.Pa. 1944)—§ **8.3.4 n. 76.**

O'Toole v. Franklin, 279 Or. 513, 569 P.2d 561 (1977)—§ **5.6 n. 25, 29, 34;** § **5.6.4 n. 43.**

Ott v. Smith, 413 So.2d 1129 (Ala.1982)—§ **5.6.3 n. 20.**

Otter Tail Power Co. v. United States, 410 U.S. 366, 93 S.Ct. 1022, 35 L.Ed.2d 359—§ **2.4.2 n. 53.**

Outboard Marine Corp. v. Liberty Mut. Ins. Co., 536 F.2d 730 (7th Cir.1976)—§ **5.6.3 n. 22;** § **8.4.2 n. 4;** § **8.4.3 n. 11.**

Overmyer Co., D.H. v. Frick Co., 405 U.S. 174, 92 S.Ct. 775, 31 L.Ed.2d 124 (1972)—§ **8.8.2 n. 88.**

Overnite Transp. Co. v. Chicago Ind. Tire Co., 697 F.2d 789 (7th Cir.1983)—§ **11.2.3 n. 23.**

Overseers of Bar v. Lee, 422 A.2d 998 (Me.1980)—§ **15.2.1 n. 84.**

Owen v. City Court of Tucson, 123 Ariz. 267, 599 P.2d 223—§ **2.2.1 n. 10;** § **13.10.2 n. 44.**

Owens v. Bank of Brewton, 53 Ala.App. 529, 302 So.2d 114 (1974)—§ **15.1.3 n. 36.**

Ownby v. Prisock, 243 Miss. 203, 138 So.2d 279 (1962)—§ **9.4.4 n. 12.**

Oxford, State ex rel. Florida Bar v., 127 So.2d 107 (Fla. 1960)—§ **8.13 n. 64.**

Oxman, In re, 496 Pa. 534, 437 A.2d 1169 (1981)—§ **14.2.5 n. 87.**

Oyler v. Boles, 368 U.S. 448, 82 S.Ct. 501, 7 L.Ed.2d 446 (1962)—§ **13.10.3 n. 66;** § **13.10.6 n. 20.**

Ozer, In re, 93 A.D.2d 129, 461 N.Y.S.2d 40 (1983)—§ **5.1 n. 34.**

P & C Thompson Bros. Constr. Co. v. Rowe, 433 So.2d 1388 (Fla.App.1983)—§ **16.6.2 n. 42.**

Paauwe, In re, 294 Or. 171, 654 P.2d 1117 (1982)—§ **4.6.2 n. 74.**

Pacheco, People v., 199 Colo. 470, 618 P.2d 1102 (1980)—§ **3.4.4 n. 16.**

Philadelphia, City of v. Westinghouse Elec. Corp., 205 F.Supp. 830 (E.D.Pa.1962)—§ **6.3.5 n. 8.**

Philadelphia Newspapers, Inc. v. Disciplinary Board, 468 Pa. 382, 363 A.2d 779 (1976)—§ **3.4.4 n. 17.**

Phillips, In re, 510 F.2d 126 (2d Cir.1975)—§ **3.4.2 n. 69, 78.**

Phillips v. Bureau of Prisons, 591 F.2d 966 (D.C.Cir. 1979)—§ **14.6.4 n. 50.**

Phillips v. Mississippi St. Bar, 427 So.2d 1380 (Miss. 1983)—§ **3.5.5 n. 29.**

Phillips v. Phillips, 242 Ga. 577, 250 S.E.2d 418 (1978)—§ **7.4.3 n. 8, 18.**

Phillips v. State Bar, 14 Cal.3d 492, 121 Cal.Rptr. 605, 535 P.2d 733 (1975)—§ **4.8 n. 38.**

Phillips v. Tobin, 548 F.2d 408 (2d Cir.1976)—§ **14.4.1 n. 40.**

Phillips, United States v., 699 F.2d 798 (6th Cir.1983)—§ **7.1.7 n. 36.**

Phillips, United States v., 527 F.2d 1021 (7th Cir.1975)—§ **12.1.2 n. 26.**

Phillips Petroleum Co. v. Hazlewood, 534 F.2d 61 (5th Cir. 1976)—§ **16.6.2 n. 53.**

Phillips Petroleum Co., United States v., 435 F.Supp. 622 (N.D.Okla.1977)—§ **13.10.6 n. 19.**

Phoenix Properties, Inc. v. Umstead, 245 Ga. 172, 264 S.E.2d 8 (1980)—§ **4.6.2 n. 50.**

Piankhy v. Cuyler, 703 F.2d 728 (3d Cir.1983)—§ **14.4.2 n. 54.**

Picciano, In re, 81 A.D.2d 1000, 439 N.Y.S.2d 221 (1981)—§ **3.4.3 n. 98.**

Piccini, United States v., 412 F.2d 591 (2d Cir.1969)—§ **6.5.4 n. 91.**

Pickens, Barns & Abernathy v. Heasley, 328 N.W.2d 524 (Iowa 1983)—§ **5.6.3 n. 11.**

Pic'l, People v., 31 Cal.App.3d 731, 183 Cal.Rptr. 685, 646 P.2d 847 (1982)—§ **13.3.4 n. 50.**

Pic'l, People v., 114 Cal.App.3d 824, 171 Cal.Rptr. 106 (1981)—§ **6.4.10 n. 54.**

Pierce, In re, 71 A.D.2d 1036, 420 N.Y.S.2d 49 (1979)—§ **3.5.4 n. 89.**

Pierson, In re, 280 Or. 513, 571 P.2d 907 (1977)—§ **4.8 n. 98.**

Pierson v. Ray, 386 U.S. 547, 87 S.Ct. 1213, 18 L.Ed.2d 288 (1967)—§ **2.5 n. 69.**

Pilla v. American Bar Ass'n, 542 F.2d 56 (8th Cir.1976)—§ **14.4.2 n. 62.**

Pillsbury Co. v. Conboy, 459 U.S. 248, 103 S.Ct. 608, 74 L.Ed.2d 430 (1983)—§ **3.4.3 n. 4.**

Pina, State v., 90 N.M. 181, 561 P.2d 43 (1977)—§ **14.3.3 n. 79.**

Pinckard, In re Estate of, 94 Ill.App.3d 34, 49 Ill.Dec. 346, 417 N.E.2d 1360 (1980)—§ **16.2.3 n. 41.**

Pinello, In re, 100 A.D.2d 64, 473 N.Y.S.2d 7 (1984)—§ **3.3.3 n. 31.**

Pinnell v. Cauthron, 540 F.2d 938 (8th Cir.1976)—§ **9.5.1 n. 36.**

Pirillo v. Takiff, 462 Pa. 511, 341 A.2d 896 (1975)—§ **7.1.7 n. 20, 21;** § **8.2.4 n. 54;** § **8.8.2 n. 92.**

Pitschke, In re, 455 N.E.2d 943 (Ind.1983)—§ **9.6.3 n. 59.**

Pitt v. Yalden, 4 Burr, 2060, 98 Eng.Rep. 74 (K.B.1767)—§ **5.6.2 n. 76, 77.**

Pittam, People v., 194 Colo. 104, 572 P.2d 135 (1977)—§ **16.2.3 n. 36.**

Pittman v. Currie, 414 So.2d 423 (Miss.1982)—§ **7.5.1 n. 30.**

Plant v. Trust Co., 168 Ga.App. 909, 310 S.E.2d 745 (1983)—§ **4.2 n. 48.**

Platt v. Henderson, 227 Or. 212, 361 P.2d 73 (1961)—§ **16.2.3 n. 65.**

Plattner, United States v., 330 F.2d 271 (2d Cir.1964)—§ **14.4.1 n. 37.**

Plaza Shoe Store, Inc. v. Hermel, Inc., 636 S.W.2d 53 (Mo. 1982)—§ **9.5.2 n. 52.**

Pledger v. Burnup & Sims, Inc., 432 So.2d 1323 (Fla.App. 1983)—§ **5.6 n. 18.**

Podwys, People v., 6 Cal.App.2d 71, 44 P.2d 377 (1935)—§ **13.10.4 n. 83.**

Poesy v. Bunney, 98 Idaho 258, 561 P.2d 400 (1977)—§ **16.6.2 n. 54.**

Pohlman, In re, 248 N.W.2d 833 (N.D.1976)—§ **3.5.7 n. 1, 83.**

Pointer v. Texas, 380 U.S. 400, 85 S.Ct. 1065, 13 L.Ed.2d 923 (1965)—§ **14.3.2 n. 65.**

Polk v. State Bar, 374 F.Supp. 784 (N.D.Tex.1974)—§ **12.2.2 n. 87.**

Polk County v. Dodson, 454 U.S. 312, 102 S.Ct. 445, 70 L.Ed.2d 509 (1981)—§ **1.5 n. 15;** § **5.6.3 n. 23;** § **8.8.2 n. 95;** § **11.2.2 n. 7;** § **14.3.6 n. 18;** § **14.6.2 n. 4;** § **14.6.3 n. 33.**

Pollack v. Lytle, 120 Cal.App.3d 931, 175 Cal.Rptr. 81 (1981)—§ **5.6.6 n. 54;** § **8.8.4 n. 9.**

Pomerantz v. Schandler, 704 F.2d 681 (2d Cir.1983)—§ **9.6.3 n. 62.**

Pontarelli, In re, 393 Ill. 310, 66 N.E.2d 83 (1946)—§ **3.3.2 n. 98.**

Pontchartrain State Bank v. Poulson, 684 F.2d 704 (10th Cir.1982)—§ **4.2 n. 52.**

Pool v. Superior Court, 139 Ariz. 98, 677 P.2d 261 (1984)—§ **12.4.5 n. 12;** § **13.10.4 n. 84.**

Poole, People v., 192 Colo. 56, 555 P.2d 980 (1976)—§ **12.2.5 n. 66.**

Pope Cty. Bar Ass'n, Inc. v. Suggs, 274 Ark. 250, 624 S.W.2d 828 (1981)—§ **15.1.3 n. 13.**

Pope, People v., 23 Cal.3d 412, 152 Cal.Rptr. 732, 590 P.2d 859 (1979)—§ **14.6.2 n. 5.**

Popelka, Allard, McCowan & Jones v. Superior Court, 107 Cal.App.3d 496, 165 Cal.Rptr. 748 (1980)—§ **6.4.7 n. 19.**

Porcelli, In re, 77 Ill.2d 473, 34 Ill.Dec. 158, 160, 397 N.E.2d 830, 832 (1979)—§ **3.3.1 n. 68.**

Port of Seattle v. Rio, 16 Wn.App. 718, 559 P.2d 18 (1977)—§ **6.5.6 n. 15.**

Porter, In re, 283 Or. 517, 584 P.2d 744 (1978)—§ **7.2.3 n. 59;** § **7.2.4 n. 85;** § **8.2.4 n. 42.**

Porter, In re, 268 Or. 417, 521 P.2d 345 (1974)—§ **12.2.2 n. 96.**

Porter v. Doe (Mass.1983)—§ **3.4.4 n. 23.**

Porter v. Wilson, Walch, Fortner, Robinson & Beese, 384 So.2d 190 (Fla.App.1980)—§ **4.7 n. 87.**

Porter, State ex rel. v. Alabama Ass'n of Credit Executives, 338 So.2d 812 (Ala.1976)—§ **15.1.3 n. 29, 31, 32.**

Porter, State ex rel. v. Dun & Bradstreet, Inc., 352 F.Supp. 1226 (N.D.Ala.1972)—§ **15.1.3 n. 32.**

Portman v. George McDonald Law Corp., 99 Cal.App.3d 988, 160 Cal.Rptr. 505 (1979)—§ **5.6.5 n. 6, 87.**

Portnow v. Berg, 593 S.W.2d 843 (Tex.Civ.App.1980)—§ **4.2 n. 58.**

Posler, In re, 393 Mich. 38, 222 N.W.2d 511 (1974)—§ **3.4.2 n. 76.**

Postow v. OBA Federal Sav. & Loan Ass'n, 627 F.2d 1370 (D.C.Cir.1980)—§ **16.6.3 n. 96.**

Potamkin Cadillac Corp. v. Karmgard, 100 Misc.2d 627, 420 N.Y.S.2d 104 (Civ.Ct.1979)—§ **6.3.5 n. 25.**

Potamkin Cadillac Corp. v. United States, 697 F.2d 491 (2d Cir.1983)—§ **11.2.2 n. 18;** § **16.6.2 n. 83.**

Potashnick v. Port City Constr. Co., 609 F.2d 1101 (5th Cir. 1980)—§ **14.6.4 n. 44;** § **17.5.5 n. 4, 10.**

Potter v. Moran, 239 Cal.App.2d 873, 49 Cal.Rptr. 229 (1966)—§ **12.7 n. 87.**

Powell v. Alabama, 287 U.S. 45, 53 S.Ct. 55, 77 L.Ed. 158 (1932)—§ **1.5 n. 15;** § **14.3.1;** § **14.3.1 n. 30, 31, 40;** § **14.3.7;** § **14.3.7 n. 27, 28.**

Powers v. Board of Public Works, 216 Cal. 546, 15 P.2d 156 (1932)—§ **7.1.7 n. 85.**

Prandini v. National Tea Co., 557 F.2d 1015 (3d Cir. 1977)—§ **8.8.2 n. 82;** § **9.2.4 n. 4;** § **16.6.4;** § **16.6.4 n. 5.**

Prantil v. State Bar, 23 Cal.3d 243, 152 Cal.Rptr. 351, 589 P.2d 859 (1979)—§ **15.3.2 n. 55.**

Prater v. Game Time, Inc., 134 Mich.App. 669, 351 N.W.2d 882 (1984)—§ **4.2 n. 38.**

Pratt, In re, 99 Wn.2d 905, 665 P.2d 400 (1983)—§ **4.2 n. 29.**

Pratt v. State, 39 Md.App. 442, 387 A.2d 779 (1978)—§ **6.3.6 n. 47;** § **6.3.8 n. 79.**

Pratts, State v., 145 N.J.Super. 79, 366 A.2d 1327 (1975)—§ **10.5.3 n. 37.**

Pravda, In re, 101 A.D.2d 80, 474 N.Y.S.2d 509 (1984)—§ **3.5.3 n. 69.**

Pray, In re, 64 Nev. 402, 183 P.2d 627 (1947)—§ **12.3.3 n. 44.**

Precision Instrument Mfg. Co. v. Automotive Maint. Mach. Co., 324 U.S. 806, 65 S.Ct. 993, 89 L.Ed. 1381 (1945)—§ **13.8.2 n. 72;** § **13.8 n. 73.**

Preiser v. Rodriguez, 411 U.S. 475, 93 S.Ct. 1827, 36 L.Ed. 2d 439 (1973)—§ **3.4.5 n. 75.**

Premium Prods. Sales Corp. v. Chipwich, Inc., 539 F.Supp. 427 (S.D.N.Y.1982)—§ **8.3.2 n. 64.**

Prescott, In re, 271 N.W.2d 822 (Minn.1978)—§ **9.3.2 n. 85;** § **13.3.2 n. 29.**

Presnell v. Board of Cty. Rd. Commissioners, 105 Mich. App. 362, 306 N.W.2d 516 (1981)—§ **4.6.2 n. 68.**

Press v. Lucky Stores, Inc., 34 Cal.3d 311, 193 Cal.Rptr. 900, 667 P.2d 704 (1983)—§ **16.6.2 n. 59.**

Press-Enterprise Co. v. Superior Court, ___ U.S. ___, 104 S.Ct. 819, 78 L.Ed.2d 629 (1984)—§ **12.2.1 n. 82.**

Preston, State v., 38 Wis.2d 582, 159 N.W.2d 684 (1968)—§ **3.4.4 n. 33.**

Price, In re, 244 Ga. 532, 261 S.E.2d 349 (1979)—§ **9.5.1 n. 29.**

Price, In re, 429 N.E.2d 961 (Ind.1982)—§ **12.6.5 n. 46, 48.**

Price v. Admiral Ins. Co., 481 F.Supp. 374 (E.D.Pa.1979)—§ **8.10.2 n. 67, 72;** § **8.10.3 n. 29.**

Price v. Caperton, 62 Ky. (1 Duv.) 207 (1864)—§ **9.4.3 n. 70.**

Price v. State Bar, 30 Cal.3d 537, 179 Cal.Rptr. 914, 638 P.2d 1311 (1982)—§ **13.10.2 n. 45.**

Price v. Superior Court, 139 Cal.App.3d 518, 188 Cal.Rptr. 832 (1983)—§ **13.5.8 n. 26.**

Prichard v. United States, 181 F.2d 326 (6th Cir.1950)—§ **6.3.2 n. 56;** § **6.3.3 n. 71.**

Prideaux v. State, 310 Minn. 405, 247 N.W.2d 385 (1976)—§ **14.6.4 n. 48.**

Priest v. Hennessy, 51 N.Y.2d 62, 431 N.Y.S.2d 511, 409 N.E.2d 983 (1980)—§ **6.3.2 n. 62;** § **8.8.3 n. 7.**

Primus, In re, 283 N.W.2d 519 (Minn.1979)—§ **3.5.6 n. 58.**

Primus, In re, 436 U.S. 412, 98 S.Ct. 1893, 56 L.Ed.2d 417 (1978)—§ **8.8.3 n. 7;** § **14.2.5;** § **14.2.5 n. 25;** § **16.8 n. 3.**

Princeton, City of v. Francisco, 454 F.Supp. 33 (S.D.Iowa 1978)—§ **15.2.4 n. 99.**

Pringle, State v., 233 Kan. 726, 667 P.2d 283 (1983)—§ **4.8 n. 2, 23, 40.**

Privette, In re, 92 N.M. 32, 582 P.2d 804 (1978)—§ **16.3.1 n. 3.**

Proctor & Gamble Co., United States v., 356 U.S. 677, 78 S.Ct. 983, 2 L.Ed.2d 1077 (1958)—§ **12.3.2 n. 33.**

Procunier v. Martinez, 416 U.S. 396, 94 S.Ct. 1800, 40 L.Ed.2d 224 (1974)—§ **14.6.4 n. 49.**

Professional Adjusters, Inc. v. Tandon, 443 N.E.2d 779 (Ind.1982)—§ **15.1.2 n. 44;** § **15.1.3 n. 19, 21, 58.**

Professional Ethics Advisory Comm. Op. 475, In re, 89 N.J. 74, 444 A.2d 1092 (1982)—§ **14.2.4 n. 69, 78.**

Promovoyage v. Bosco, 557 F.Supp. 1366 (S.D.N.Y.1983)—§ **5.6.5 n. 72.**

Proposed Amendments to Practice of Law Rules, In re, 187 Mont. 159, 609 P.2d 263 (1980)—§ **15.2.2 n. 88.**

Proposed Rules Relating to Grievance Procedures, In re, 115 N.H. 310, 341 A.2d 272 (1975)—§ **3.4.2 n. 63.**

Provencal v. Provencal, 122 N.H. 793, 451 A.2d 374 (1982)—§ **4.4 n. 2;** § **6.3.2 n. 63.**

Providence Journal Co. v. Mason, 116 R.I. 614, 359 A.2d 682 (1976)—§ **16.6.2 n. 64.**

Prudential Ins. Co. v. Small Claims Court, 76 Cal.App.2d 379, 173 P.2d 38 (1946)—§ **14.4.1 n. 42.**

Public Serv. Comm'n v. Hahn Transp., Inc., 253 Md. 571, 253 A.2d 845 (1969)—§ **15.1.3 n. 79.**

Public Serv. Mut. Ins. Co. v. Goldfarb, 53 N.Y.2d 392, 442 N.Y.S.2d 422, 425 N.E.2d 810 (1981)—§ **8.4.3 n. 11.**

Public Taxi Serv., Inc. v. Barrett, 44 Ill.App.3d 452, 2 Ill. Dec. 789, 357 N.E.2d 1232 (1976)—§ **5.6.3 n. 22.**

Publicker Ind., Inc. v. Cohen, 733 F.2d 1059 (3d Cir.1984)—§ **12.2.1 n. 83.**

Puckett, United States v., 692 F.2d 663 (10th Cir.1982)—§ **6.3.5 n. 35.**

Purdy v. Pacific Auto. Ins. Co., 157 Cal.App.3d 59, 203 Cal. Rptr. 524 (1984)—§ **8.4.3 n. 22.**

Robinson, People v., 79 Ill.2d 147, 37 Ill.Dec. 267, 402 N.E.2d 157 (1979)—§ **7.6.5 n. 90.**
Robinson, People v., 100 Ill.App.3d 660, 56 Ill.Dec. 208, 427 N.E.2d 288 (1981)—§ **14.4.1 n. 49.**
Robinson, State v., 290 N.C. 56, 224 S.E.2d 174 (1976)—§ **12.5.4 n. 78, 80, 81.**
Robinson, State ex rel. Crockett v., 67 Ohio St.2d 363, 423 N.E.2d 1099 (1981)—§ **16.6.2 n. 78.**
Robinson, United States v., 553 F.2d 429 (5th Cir.1977)—§ **8.8.2 n. 94.**
Robinson & Wells, P.C. v. Warren, 669 P.2d 844 (Utah 1983)—§ **9.6.2 n. 26.**
Robson, In re, 575 P.2d 771 (Alaska 1978)—§ **15.1.4 n. 69.**
Roby v. State, 587 P.2d 641 (Wyo.1978)—§ **7.5.2 n. 73.**
Rochat, In re, 295 Or. 533, 668 P.2d 376 (1983)—§ **3.3.1 n. 56.**
Rochester, City of v. Chiarella, 86 A.D.2d 110, 449 N.Y.S.2d 112 (1982)—§ **8.14 n. 69.**
Rochester City Bank v. Suydam, 5 How.Pr. 254 (N.Y.Sup. Ct.1951)—§ **6.7.8 n. 5.**
Rochlin, In re, 100 A.D.2d 263, 474 N.Y.S.2d 14 (1984)—§ **3.3.3 n. 27.**
Rodgers, United States v., ___ U.S. ___, 104 S.Ct. 1942, 80 L.Ed.2d 492 (1984)—§ **12.3.5 n. 60;** § **14.6 n. 83.**
Rodriguez v. Horton, 95 N.M. 356, 622 P.2d 261 (App. 1980)—§ **5.6.2 n. 5;** § **5.6.3 n. 33;** § **9.3.1 n. 34.**
Rodriguez v. State, 129 Ariz. 67, 628 P.2d 950 (1981)—§ **7.1.4 n. 35;** § **7.6.5 n. 90;** § **10.5.3 n. 31.**
Roe v. Wade, 410 U.S. 113, 93 S.Ct. 705, 35 L.Ed. 147 (1973)—§ **14.2.3 n. 49.**
Roehl v. State, 77 Wis.2d 398, 253 N.W.2d 210 (1977)—§ **13.10.3 n. 63.**
Roehl, People v., 655 P.2d 1381 (Colo.1983)—§ **5.1 n. 14;** § **14.2.4 n. 59.**
Roel, In re, 3 N.Y.2d 224, 165 N.Y.S.2d 31, 144 N.E.2d 24 (1957)—§ **5.6.2 n. 88;** § **15.4.1 n. 2.**
Rogers, In re, 297 N.C. 48, 253 S.E.2d 912 (1979)—§ **15.3.2 n. 43.**
Rogers v. Concrete Sciences, Inc., 394 So.2d 212 (Fla.App. 1981)—§ **4.2 n. 29.**
Rogers v. Robson, Masters, Ryan, Brumund & Belom, 81 Ill.2d 201, 40 Ill.Dec. 816, 407 N.E.2d 47—§ **2.6.1 n. 5;** § **4.6.2 n. 57, 63, 76;** § **8.4.2 n. 3.**
Rogers, United States v., 534 F.2d 1134 (5th Cir.1976)—§ **14.6.1 n. 54.**
Roggensack, State v., 19 Wis.2d 38, 119 N.W.2d 412 (1963)—§ **3.3.4, n. 32.**
Rohan, In re, 21 Cal.3d 195, 145 Cal.Rptr. 855, 578 P.2d 102, 106 (1978)—§ **3.1 n. 17.**
Rolfstad, Winkjer, Suess, McKennett & Kaiser v. Hanson, 221 N.W.2d 734 (N.D.1974)—§ **7.1.7 n. 87;** § **9.6.1 n. 11.**
Rolle v. Nolan, 119 Misc.2d 1050, 464 N.Y.S.2d 930 (N.Y. Civ.Ct.1983)—§ **3.4.2 n. 63.**
Rollins, In re, 281 S.C. 467, 316 S.E.2d 670 (1984)—§ **4.8 n. 3.**
Rollo v. State, 139 Vt. 26, 421 A.2d 1298 (1980)—§ **12.1.2 n. 22.**
Romanian American Interests, Inc. v. Scher, 94 A.D.2d 549, 464 N.Y.S.2d 821 (1983)—§ **5.6.3 n. 11.**
Romero v. United States, 459 U.S. 926, 103 S.Ct. 236, 74 L.Ed.2d 187 (1982)—§ **14.6.2 n. 9.**
Romero, People v., 192 Colo. 106, 559 P.2d 1101 (1976)—§ **14.3.3 n. 87.**
Romano, State v., ___ R.I. ___, 456 A.2d 746 (1983)—§ **13.3.2 n. 18.**
Romo v. Southern Pac. Transp. Co., 71 Cal.App.3d 909, 139 Cal.Rptr. 787 (1977)—§ **6.3.4 n. 82.**
Rondeau, Commonwealth v., 378 Mass. 408, 392 N.E.2d 1001 (1979)—§ **8.2.2 n. 6.**
Rondel v. Worsley, 1 A.C. 191 (H.L.1969)—§ **10.2.2 n. 37.**
Rondel v. Worsley, 1967, 1 All E.Rep. 467 (C.A.), [1967] 3 All E.Rep. 657 (H.L.)—§ **5.6.2 n. 97.**
Ronningen v. Hertogs, 294 Minn. 7, 199 N.W.2d 420 (1972)—§ **5.6.2 n. 51.**
Ronwin, In re, 113 Ariz. 357, 555 P.2d 315 (1976)—§ **11.2.3 n. 22.**
Ronwin, In re, 136 Ariz. 566, 667 P.2d 1281 (1983)—§ **11.2.2 n. 7;** § **12.2.3 n. 22;** § **15.3.2 n. 74, 76.**
Ronwin v. Hoover, 466 U.S. 558, 104 S.Ct. 1989, 80 L.Ed.2d 590—§ **2.4.2;** § **2.4.2 n. 44, 48.**
Rook, In re, 276 Or. 695, 556 P.2d 1351, 1357 (1976)—§ **3.3.1 n. 48, 59;** § **11.2.2 n. 11;** § **13.10.6 n. 16.**
Rooney v. Whitechurch, 585 P.2d 1202 (Wyo.1978)—§ **12.3.3 n. 42.**
Rooney, Commonwealth v., 365 Mass. 484, 313 N.E.2d 105 (1974)—§ **12.4.5 n. 12.**
Root, United States v., 366 F.2d 377 (9th Cir.1966)—§ **12.5.1 n. 47.**
Rose, In re, 71 L.Ed.2d 862 (1982)—§ **15.2.4 n. 4.**
Rosenbaum, In re, 72 A.D.2d 251, 424 N.Y.S.2d 435 (1980)—§ **3.3.2 n. 12.**
Rosenberg, In re, 690 P.2d 1293 (Colo.App.1984)—§ **9.6.3 n. 71.**
Rosenberg v. Levin, 409 So.2d 1016 (Fla.1982)—§ **9.5.2 n. 51, 52, 53.**
Rosenfeld, Meyer & Susman v. Cohen, 146 Cal.App.3d 200, 194 Cal.Rptr. 180 (1983)—§ **16.2.3 n. 65, 69.**
Rosenthal, In re, 90 N.J. 12, 446 A.2d 1198 (1982)—§ **5.1 n. 46.**
Rosenthal, In re, 73 Ill.2d 46, 21 Ill.Dec. 893, 382 N.E.2d 257 (1978)—§ **13.3.2 n. 33.**
Rosenzweig, In re, 259 N.W.2d 252 (Minn.1977)—§ **4.2 n. 14.**
Rosillo, State v., 281 N.W.2d 877 (Minn.1979)—§ **12.5.4 n. 85.**
Rosner v. United States, 516 F.2d 269 (2d Cir.1975)—§ **13.10.4 n. 91.**
Rosner, United States v., 485 F.2d 1213 (2d Cir.1973)—§ **14.6.4 n. 54.**
Rosquist v. Soo Line R.R., 692 F.2d 1107 (7th Cir.1982)—§ **9.1 n. 11, 16.**
Ross, In re, 99 Nev. 657, 668 P.2d 1089 (1983)—§ **3.4.4 n. 17.**
Ross, In re, ___ Nev. ___, 656 P.2d 832 (1983)—§ **3.2 n. 25.**
Ross v. Caunters, 3 W.L.R. 605 (Chancery 1979)—§ **5.6.4 n. 52.**
Ross v. Great Atl. & Pac. Tea Co., 447 F.Supp. 406 (S.D. N.Y.1978)—§ **7.5.2 n. 76, 78.**
Ross v. Heyne, 638 F.2d 979 (7th Cir.1980)—§ **7.6.1 n. 24.**

Swetz, In re, 103 Wis.2d 301, 307 N.W.2d 654 (1981)— § **3.5.7 n. 1.**
Swift v. Island County, 87 Wn.2d 348, 552 P.2d 175 (1976)—§ **16.6.2 n. 64.**
Swope v. Bratton, 541 F.Supp. 99 (W.D.Ark.1982)— § **14.6.4 n. 48.**
Sword v. Sword, 399 Mich. 367, 249 N.W.2d 88 (1976)— § **14.5 n. 71.**
Swoyer, State v., 228 Kan. 799, 619 P.2d 1166 (1980)— § **7.3.2 n. 12.**
Sylvester, In re, 195 Iowa 1329, 192 N.W. 442 (1923)— § **9.4.4 n. 92.**
Szymanski, In re, 400 Mich. 469, 255 N.W.2d 601 (1977)— § **3.5.3 n. 75.**
Szymkowski v. Szymkowski, 104 Ill.App.3d 630, 60 Ill.Dec. 310, 432 N.E.2d 1209 (1982)—§ **4.6.2 n. 54.**

T.C. Theatres Corp. v. Warner Bros. Pictures, Inc., 113 F.Supp. 265 (S.D.N.Y.)—§ **2.6.2 n. 36;** § **7.4.2 n. 64;** § **7.4.3;** § **7.4.3 n. 8, 98.**
T.C. Theatres, Inc. v. Warner Bros. Circuit Management Corp., 216 F.2d 920 (2d Cir.1954)—§ **7.4.1 n. 54.**
T.D.S., In re, 289 N.W.2d 137 (Minn.1980)—§ **6.3.3 n. 68.**
Ta Chi Navigation Corp., In re, 677 F.2d 225 (2d Cir. 1982)—§ **7.5.2 n. 7.**
Tadier v. American Photocopy Equipment Co., 531 F.Supp. 35 (S.D.N.Y.1981)—§ **7.1.7 n. 14;** § **7.2.4 n. 72.**
Taff's Estate, In re, 63 Cal.App.3d 319, 133 Cal.Rptr. 737 (1976)—§ **4.2 n. 40.**
Taggart v. Claxton, 170 Ga.App. 768, 318 S.E.2d 208 (1984)—§ **9.4.2 n. 43.**
Taglione, United States v., 546 F.2d 194 (5th Cir.1977)— § **4.7 n. 88.**
Tancre v. Pullman, 35 Minn. 476, 29 N.W. 171 (1886)— § **8.11.3 n. 87.**
Tanner v. Farmer, 243 Or. 431, 414 P.2d 340 (1966)— § **6.3.4 n. 98.**
Tappe v. Circuit Court, 326 N.W.2d 892 (S.D.1982)— § **14.3.5 n. 10.**
Tapper, In re, 102 A.D. 332, 447 N.Y.S.2d 16 (1984)— § **3.5.2 n. 62.**
Tarasoff v. Regents of University of California, 17 Cal.3d 425, 131 Cal.Rptr. 14, 551 P.2d 334 (1976)—§ **5.6.4 n. 61.**
Tardiff v. State Bar, 27 Cal.3d 395, 165 Cal.Rptr. 829, 612 P.2d 919 (1980)—§ **3.5.5 n. 31;** § **15.1.4 n. 66.**
Tarkowski, People v., 106 Ill.App.3d 597, 62 Ill.Dec. 367, 435 N.E.2d 1339 (1982)—§ **4.2 n. 39.**
Tasby v. United States, 504 F.2d 332 (8th Cir.1974)— § **6.4.7 n. 14.**
Tate, Commonwealth ex rel. Carroll v., 442 Pa. 45, 274 A.2d 193 (1971)—§ **2.2.1 n. 12.**
Tate, State v., 185 La. 1006, 171 So. 108 (1936)—§ **8.9.4 n. 50.**
Taxpayers, Homeowners & Tenants Protective Ass'n v. Haber, 634 F.2d 182 (5th Cir.1981)—§ **8.10.3 n. 58.**
Tayloe v. Sandiford, 20 U.S. 13, 7 Wheat. 13, 5 L.Ed. 384 (1822)—§ **12.32 n. 55.**
Taylor, In re, 293 Or. 285, 647 P.2d 462 (1982)—§ **15.3.2 n. 62.**
Taylor, In re, 567 F.2d 1183 (2d Cir.1977)—§ **7.1.7 n. 22.**
Taylor v. Bemiss, 110 U.S. 42, 3 S.Ct. 441, 28 L.Ed. 64 (1884)—§ **9.4.2 n. 57.**
Taylor v. Board of Educ., 187 N.J.Super. 546, 455 A.2d 552 (1983)—§ **9.5.4 n. 93.**
Taylor v. City of Amarillo, 335 F.Supp. 423 (N.D.Tex. 1971)—§ **8.10.3 n. 40.**
Taylor v. Hayes, 418 U.S. 488, 94 S.Ct. 2697, 41 L.Ed.2d 897 (1974)—§ **12.1.3 n. 50.**
Taylor v. Montgomery, 539 F.2d 715 (7th Cir.1976)— § **14.4.2 n. 62.**
Taylor v. Sheldon, 172 Ohio St. 118, 173 N.E.2d 892 (1961)—§ **6.3.2 n. 64.**
Taylor v. Sterrett, 532 F.2d 462 (5th Cir.1976)—§ **14.6.4 n. 46.**
Taylor, State v., 301 N.C. 164, 270 S.E.2d 409 (1980)— § **7.5.2 n. 90.**
Taylor, United States v., 569 F.2d 448 (7th Cir.1977)— § **15.1.2 n. 73.**
Taylor Coal Co., Ex parte, 401 So.2d 1 (Ala.1981)—§ **6.4.8 n. 21;** § **7.1.4 n. 41;** § **7.4.3 n. 21, 97.**
Tedesco, State v., 175 Conn. 279, 397 A.2d 1352—§ **2.2.4 n. 69;** § **3.2 n. 23.**
Teel v. Teel, 400 So.2d 357 (La.App.1981)—§ **7.3.2 n. 16;** § **8.3.2 n. 63.**
Telos, Inc. v. Hawaiian Tel. Co., 397 F.Supp. 1314 (D.Hawaii 1975)—§ **8.10.3 n. 50.**
Temrowski, In re, 409 Mich. 262, 293 N.W.2d 346 (1980)— § **8.11.3 n. 4.**
Tenner v. State Bar, 28 Cal.3d 202, 168 Cal.Rptr. 333, 617 P.2d 486 (1980)—§ **3.3.3 n. 20.**
Tennessee Bar Ass'n, In re Petition of, 532 S.W.2d 224 (Tenn.1975)—§ **15.2.1 n. 84.**
Tensley, State v., 249 N.W.2d 659 (Iowa 1977)—§ **6.1.4 n. 9;** § **6.4.4 n. 89.**
Teplin, In re, 82 A.2d 296, 441 N.Y.S.2d 463 (1981)— § **15.1.4 n. 67.**
Terkeltoub, In re, 256 F.Supp. 683 (S.D.N.Y.1966)—§ **6.6.2 n. 50.**
Territory v. Clancy, 7 N.M. 580, 37 P. 1108 (1894)— § **13.3.7 n. 78.**
Terry, In re, 271 Ind. 499, 394 N.E.2d 94 (1979)—§ **11.3.2 n. 60;** § **11.4.2 n. 88.**
Terry v. Kemper Ins. Co., 390 Mass. 450, 456 N.E.2d 465 (1983)—§ **4.2 n. 22;** § **4.8 n. 21.**
Tew, In re, 249 Ga. 587, 292 S.E.2d 721 (1982)—§ **3.5.4 n. 17.**
Texas Indus., Inc. v. Roach, 426 So.2d 315 (La.App.1983)— § **16.6.3 n. 95.**
Textor v. Board of Regents of Northern Illinois University, 87 F.R.D. 751 (N.D.Ill.1980)—§ **11.2.3 n. 25.**
Thatcher v. Industrial Comm'n, 115 Utah 568, 207 P.2d 178 (1949)—§ **9.1 n. 6;** § **11.3.2 n. 57.**
Theard v. United States, 354 U.S. 278, 77 S.Ct. 1274, 1 L.Ed.2d 1342 (1957)—§ **3.4.5 n. 63, 92;** § **3.6.1 n. 21;** § **15.2.4 n. 7.**
Thelen v. Thelen, 3 N.C.App. 684, 281 S.E.2d 737 (1981)— § **14.6.1 n. 83.**
Theobald v. Botein, Hays, Sklar & Herzberg, 465 F.Supp. 609 (S.D.N.Y.1979)—§ **7.5.2 n. 99;** § **14.4.1 n. 39.**

Waller v. Georgia, ___ U.S. ___, 104 S.Ct. 2210, 81 L.Ed.2d 31 (1984)—§ **12.2.1 n. 82.**

Waller v. Kotzen, 567 F.Supp. 424 (E.D.Pa.1983)—§ **11.6.2 n. 56.**

Wallersteiner v. Moir (No. 2) (1975) 1 All E.R. 849 (C.A.)—§ **16.6.1 n. 35.**

Wallin, People v., 621 P.2d 330 (Colo.1981)—§ **12.4.4 n. 6.**

Walls v. Mississippi State Bar, 437 So.2d 30, 33 (Miss. 1983)—§ **3.3.2 n. 74.**

Walsh, In re, 623 F.2d 489 (7th Cir.1980)—§ **6.3.4 n. 76;** § **6.3.5 n. 25.**

Walsh v. O'Neill, 350 Mass. 586, 215 N.E.2d 915 (1966)—§ **11.6.2 n. 42.**

Walters v. National Ass'n of Radiation Survivors, ___ U.S. ___, 105 S.Ct. 3180, ___ L.Ed.2d ___ (1985)—§ **9.3.2 n. 80;** § **14.5 n. 74.**

Walton, In re, 676 P.2d 1078 (Alaska 1983)—§ **3.4.4 n. 35, 40, 42;** § **12.3.3 n. 39;** § **15.4.1 n. 95.**

Walton, In re, 251 N.W.2d 762, 764 (N.D.1977)—§ **3.1 n. 17;** § **4.8 n. 98.**

Waltzer v. Transidyne Gen. Corp., 697 F.2d 130 (6th Cir. 1983)—§ **7.5.1 n. 30.**

Ward v. Arnold, 52 Wn.2d 581, 328 P.2d 164 (1958)—§ **5.6.3 n. 6;** § **5.6.4 n. 35.**

Ward v. Superior Court, 70 Cal.App.3d 23, 138 Cal.Rptr. 532 (1977)—§ **6.5.6 n. 22;** § **8.9.3 n. 24.**

Ward v. Village of Monroeville, 409 U.S. 57, 93 S.Ct. 80, 34 L.Ed.2d 267 (1972)—§ **3.2 n. 25;** § **17.5.5 n. 56.**

Warden v. Hayden, 387 U.S. 294, 87 S.Ct. 1642, 18 L.Ed.2d 782 (1967)—§ **6.6.1 n. 27.**

Warden, People ex rel. Vogelstein v., 150 Misc. 714, 270 N.Y.S. 362 (1934)—§ **6.3.5 n. 27.**

Waring's Estate, In re, 47 N.J. 367, 221 A.2d 193 (1966)—§ **15.4.1 n. 1.**

Warnaco, Inc. v. Freund, 94 F.R.D. 237 (E.D.N.Y.1980)—§ **6.3.4 n. 77.**

Warner v. Basten, 118 Ill.App.2d 419, 255 N.E.2d 72 (1969)—§ **9.2.1 n. 31;** § **9.4.1 n. 36.**

Warner v. Rossingnol, 538 F.2d 910 (1st Cir.1976)—§ **12.1.2 n. 22.**

Warren v. Bureau of Land Management, 724 F.2d 776 (9th Cir.1984)—§ **4.2 n. 31.**

Wartzman v. Hightower Prods., Ltd., 53 Md.App. 656, 456 A.2d 82 (1983)—§ **5.6.3 n. 31.**

Warzyn, State ex rel. Oklahoma Bar Ass'n v., 624 P.2d 1068 (Okl.1981)—§ **3.4.2 n. 77.**

Washington v. Jones, 33 Wn.App. 865, 658 P.2d 1262 (1983)—§ **14.6.1 n. 89, 90.**

Washington v. Pierce, 576 F.Supp. 473 (N.D.Ill.1983)—§ **9.3.1 n. 22.**

Washington v. Sherwin Real Estate, Inc., 694 F.2d 1081 (7th Cir.1982)—§ **9.5.1 n. 37.**

Washington v. State, 441 N.E.2d 1355 (Ind.1982)—§ **6.7.4 n. 72.**

Washington-Baltimore Newspaper Guild v. Washington Star Co., 543 F.Supp. 906 (D.D.C.1982)—§ **6.5.5 n. 7.**

Washington State Bar Ass'n v. Great Western Union Fed. Sav. & Loan Ass'n, 91 Wn.2d 48, 586 P.2d 870 (1978)—§ **15.1.3 n. 13.**

Watkins v. Labor & Industry Review Comm'n, 117 Wis.2d 753, 345 N.W.2d 482 (1984)—§ **16.6.3 n. 97.**

Watkins v. Mobile Housing Bd., 632 F.2d 565 (5th Cir. 1980)—§ **16.9 n. 25.**

Watson v. Black, 161 W.Va. 46, 239 S.E.2d 664 (1977)—§ **9.5.3 n. 68.**

Watson v. Cook, 427 So.2d 1312 (La.App.1983)—§ **9.1 n. 9.**

Watson v. District Court, 199 Colo. 76, 604 P.2d 1165 (1980)—§ **7.1.7 n. 96.**

Watson v. Moss, 619 F.2d 775 (8th Cir.1980)—§ **14.6.1 n. 84.**

Watson, People v., 46 Cal.2d 818, 299 P.2d 243 (1956)—§ **6.3.4 n. 84.**

Watson, State v., 134 Ariz. 3, 653 P.2d 351 (1982)—§ **14.6.2 n. 9.**

Watson, United States v., 496 F.2d 1125 (4th Cir.1973)—§ **14.3.4 n. 96.**

Wattigny v. Lambert, 408 So.2d 1126 (La.App.1981)—§ **5.6.5 n. 97.**

Watts, In re, 190 U.S. 1, 23 S.Ct. 718, 47 L.Ed. 933 (1903)—§ **13.3.7 n. 80.**

Waugh v. British Railways Bd., (1979) 3 W.L.R. 150 (House of Lords 1979)—§ **6.6.3 n. 56.**

Wayland v. Shore Lobster & Shrimp Corp., 537 F.Supp. 1220 (S.D.N.Y.1982)—§ **8.3.2 n. 61.**

Wayte v. United States, ___ U.S. ___, 105 S.Ct. 1524, 84 L.Ed.2d 547 (1985)—§ **13.10.3 n. 59.**

Wearly v. FTC, 462 F.Supp. 589 (D.N.J.1978)—§ **6.3.4 n. 90.**

Weatherford v. Bursey, 429 U.S. 545, 97 S.Ct. 837, 51 L.Ed. 2d 30 (1977)—§ **13.10.6 n. 16;** § **14.6.4 n. 58, 59.**

Weaver, In re, 272 Ind. 491, 399 N.E.2d 748 (1980)—§ **3.4.5 n. 85.**

Weaver v. Devendorf, 3 Denio (N.Y.) 117 (1846)—§ **17.3.3 n. 37.**

Weaver v. Superior Court, 572 P.2d 425 (Alaska 1977)—§ **3.2 n. 23.**

Weaver v. UMW, 492 F.2d 580 (D.C.Cir.1973)—§ **8.3.5 n. 89, 90.**

Webb v. Pomeroy, 8 Kan.App.2d 246, 655 P.2d 465 (1982)—§ **5.6.3 n. 8.**

Webb v. State, 580 P.2d 295 (Alaska 1978)—§ **1.6 n. 20;** § **3.5.2 n. 63.**

Weber, In re, 16 Cal.3d 578, 128 Cal.Rptr. 434, 546 P.2d 1378 (1976)—§ **11.4.3 n. 94.**

Weber v. Garza, 570 F.2d 511 (5th Cir.1978)—§ **15.1.3 n. 73.**

Weber, Inc., Fred v. Shell Oil Co., 566 F.2d 602 (8th Cir. 1977)—§ **7.1.4 n. 33, 46;** § **7.1.6 n. 74.**

Weeden Eng. Corp. v. Hale, 435 So.2d 1158 (La.App. 1983)—§ **4.2 n. 58.**

Weidekind v. Tuolumne County Water Co., 74 Cal. 386, 19 P. 173 (1887)—§ **7.4.2 n. 61.**

Weidman v. Tomaselli, 81 Misc.2d 328, 365 N.Y.S.2d 681 (1975)—§ **16.6.2 n. 43.**

Weil v. Investment/Indicators, Research & Mgmt., Inc., 647 F.2d 18 (9th Cir.1981)—§ **6.4.4 n. 96;** § **6.4.5 n. 5;** § **6.4.6 n. 13;** § **6.5.5 n. 10.**

Weiner, In re, 547 S.W.2d 459 (Mo.1977)—§ **3.4.4 n. 35.**

Table of Model Code of Professional Responsibility

Canons

Ethical Considerations

Disciplinary Rules

Table of Model Rules of Professional Conduct

Rule	Sec.	Note
1.1	4.1	1
	5.1	
	5.1	31
	5.1	32
	5.1	33
1.1(b)	8.10.3	61
1.2	4.3	72
	4.3	73
	4.3	74
	4.3	75
	4.6.2	72
	7.2.1	39
	7.4.2	85
1.2(a)	4.3	72
	4.5	25
	4.6.2	
	4.6.2	70
	12.5.4	86
	13.3.10	
1.2(b)	10.2.1	
	10.2.2	49
1.2(c)	5.6.7	
1.2(d)	4.4	90
	12.6.4	42
	13.3.2	
	13.3.2	35
	13.3.3	
	13.3.5	53
	13.3.6	
	13.3.7	
	13.3.8	84
	13.3.9	
	13.3.9	2
	13.5.8	27
	13.7.5	39
1.2(e)	4.5	
	8.3.2	65
1.2 comment	10.2.1	33
	13.3.2	32
	13.3.2	36
	13.3.3	42
	13.3.5	53
1.3	7.2.1	39
	10.3.1	
	10.3.1	79
	13.3.3	41
1.4	4.5	
	4.5	23
	4.5	25
	4.5	26
	4.6.2	75
	13.6	
1.4(a)	4.5	
	4.6.2	75
1.4(b)	4.5	
	4.6.2	75
1.4(d)	9.3.1	36
1.4 comment	11.6.2	50
	13.7.5	28
1.5	9.2.4	9
	9.3.1	42
	9.3.1	43
1.5(a)	9.3.1	
	9.3.2	
	9.3.1	41
	9.3.1	46
1.5(a)(4)	9.4.3	84
1.5(a)(8)	9.4.3	
	9.4.3	77
1.5(b)	9.2.1	
	9.2.1	43
	9.2.2	
	9.3.1	
1.5(c)	9.2.1	
	9.4.1	
	9.4.1	29
	9.4.3	78
1.5(d)	9.3.3	96
	9.4.1	
	9.4.4	
	9.4.4	10
	9.4.4	11
1.5(e)	9.2.4	
	9.2.4	2
	9.2.4	90
1.5(e)(1)	9.2.4	
1.5(e)(2)	9.2.4	
1.5 comment	9.2.1	44
	9.2.2	57
	9.2.3	76
	9.2.4	11
	9.2.4	99
	9.3.3	96
	9.4.1	31
	9.6.2	27
1.6	6.3.4	79
	6.3.8	75
	6.7.2	
	6.7.2	61
	6.7.2	62
	6.7.2	65
	6.7.3	
	6.7.3	68
	6.7.4	70
	6.7.6	91
	6.7.7	
	6.7.8	3
	7.4.2	
	7.4.2	85
	7.4.2	87
	7.6.2	
	8.10.2	
	8.10.3	

	Sec.	Note
5.3(a)	16.3.1	
	16.3.1	6
	16.3.1	7
5.3(b)	16.3.1	
	16.3.1	8
5.3(c)(1)	11.6.2	40
	16.3.1	
5.3(c)(2)	6.3.1	
	16.3.1	7
5.3 comment	6.7.5	78
	16.3.1	8
	16.3.1	9
	16.3.1	93
5.4	8.8.2	86
	16.2.1	
	16.2.1	8
	16.3.1	
	16.3.1	4
	16.5.5	
	16.5.5	7
	16.5.5	12
5.4(a)	9.2.4	
	16.2.1	7
	16.2.1	14
	16.5.5	
5.4(a)(3)	16.2.1	14
	16.5.5	
5.4(b)	16.2.1	7
	16.5.5	
5.4(c)	8.8.2	
	8.8.2	86
	16.5.5	
5.4(d)	16.2.1	7
	16.2.4	
	16.5.5	
5.4 comment	16.2.1	9
5.5	15.1.3	
5.5(a)	15.1.4	72
5.5(b)	15.1.4	42
5.5 comment	15.1.3	67
	15.1.4	48
5.6(a)	16.2.3	45
5.6 comment	16.2.3	45
6.1	10.2.3	67
	10.4.2	92
	16.9	
6.1 comment	16.9	22
6.2	10.2.2	
	10.2.2	51
	10.2.2	52
6.2(b)	10.2.2	
6.2 comment	10.2.2	48
	10.2.3	67
6.3	8.8.3	97
	16.5.5	
	16.5.5	10
	16.7.4	80
6.3(a)	16.5.5	10
6.3(b)	16.5.5	10
6.3 comment	16.7.4	79
6.4	10.4.2	96
6.6	12.5.4	91
7.1	5.5	27
	11.2.2	20
	14.2.1	14
7.1 (Cont'd)	14.2.4	
	16.2.3	57
7.2	14.2.1	
	14.2.1	14
7.2(a)	14.2.4	
7.2(b)	12.2.4	
7.2(c)	14.2.4	58
7.2(d)	14.2.4	63
7.2 comment	14.2.5	17
	14.2.5	19
7.3	14.2.4	
	14.2.5	
	14.2.5	15
	16.5.5	
7.4	5.5	26
	5.5	27
	14.2.4	
7.4(a)	5.5	26
	14.2.4	
	16.2.3	57
7.4(c)	5.5	27
7.5(d)	16.2.3	42
7.5 comment	16.2.5	91
7.7(c)	12.5.4	87
8.1	15.3.1	
	16.9	20
8.1(b)	12.10.2	
	13.5.8	29
	15.3.1	34
8.2(a)	11.3.2	51
	11.3.2	54
8.2 comment	11.3.2	52
8.3	12.10.1	30
	13.5.8	29
	15.3.1	
8.3(a)	12.9	
	12.10.1	
	12.10.1	28
	12.10.1	33
	16.2.2	29
8.3(b)	11.3.2	48
	12.10.1	
8.3(c)	12.10.1	26
	12.10.1	33
8.3 comment	12.10.1	22
	12.10.1	24
8.4	3.3.2	
	3.3.2	14
	3.3.2	15
	3.3.2	16
	13.5.5	75
	13.5.8	
8.4(a)	3.3.3	
	3.3.3	17
	16.2.2	20
8.4(b)	3.3.2	
	3.3.3	
	9.5.4	88
	13.5.4	51
	13.5.5	
8.4(c)	3.3.3	18
	9.5.4	88
	13.5.8	
8.4(d)	3.3.3	19
	9.5.4	88

Table of Canons of Professional Ethics

Canons

	Sec.	Note
Canon 1	11.3.2	52
	11.3.2	56
Canon 3	11.3.3	62
	11.3.3	73
Canon 5	10.5.2	21
Canon 6	7.1.2	
	7.3.1	
	7.3.3	
	7.4.2	
	7.4.3	90
Canon 7	11.6.2	42
Canon 9	11.6.3	64
Canon 10	8.11.2	77
	8.13	
	8.13	60
	8.13	64
Canon 11	8.11.2	
Canon 12	1.5	
	9.3.1	35
	9.3.1	43
	9.3.1	71
	10.3.1	76
Canon 12(2)	9.3.1	54
Canon 12(6)	9.3.1	59
Canon 13	9.4.3	68
Canon 14	9.6.1	99
Canon 15	10.3.1	
	13.5.8	21
Canon 15–25	12.1.2	16
Canon 19	7.5.2	31
Canon 20	12.2.2	
Canon 22	11.5	
	12.8	97
Canon 23	11.4.3	98
Canon 24	17.5.2	8
Canon 26	9.4.5	18
	13.8.2	68
Canon 27	14.2.1	17
	14.2.2	
	14.2.2	24
Canon 27 (Cont'd)	14.2.2	25
	14.2.5	3
Canon 28	8.13	56
	12.6.3	16
	14.2.5	3
	14.2.5	4
	14.2.5	85
Canon 29	11.3.2	48
	12.5.3	
	12.6.3	16
	12.10.1	16
Canon 30	11.2.2	
	11.2.2	6
Canon 31	10.2.2	45
	10.2.2	47
	17.5.3	
Canon 32	1.6	
	13.5.8	22
Canon 34	16.3.1	17
Canon 35	8.8.2	87
	8.8.2	90
	8.8.3	97
Canon 36	8.10.1	63
	8.10.2	
	8.10.2	84
	8.10.3	
	8.10.3	35
	8.10.3	48
	8.10.3	58
Canon 37	12.6.4	
	16.3.1	9
Canon 38	8.8.2	87
Canon 39	12.4.6	31
Canon 41	12.5.3	61
	12.6.4	
Canon 42	9.2.3	79
	9.2.3	86
Canon 44	9.5.3	85
Canon 47	15.1.1	11

*

Table of A.B.A. Standards

*

Table of A.B.A. Ethics Committee Opinions

A.B.A. FORMAL OPINIONS

A.B.A. FORMAL OPINIONS

A.B.A. INFORMAL OPINIONS

A.B.A. INFORMAL OPINIONS

A.B.A. INFORMAL OPINIONS

Index

References are to Pages

References are to Pages

References are to Pages

References are to Pages

†